**Ralf Sube
Günther Eisenreich
Wörterbuch
Physik
Dictionary of
Physics**

Dipl.-Math. Ralf Sube
Prof. Dr. rer. nat. habil. Günther Eisenreich

Dictionary of Physics

English
German

containing approximately 75 000 terms
bilingual students edition

1987

Verlag Harri Deutsch · Thun und Frankfurt am Main

Dipl.-Math. Ralf Sube
Prof. Dr. rer. nat. habil. Günther Eisenreich

Wörterbuch Physik

Englisch
Deutsch

mit etwa 75 000 Wortstellen
zweisprachige Studentenausgabe

1987

Verlag Harri Deutsch · Thun und Frankfurt am Main

CIP-Kurztitelaufnahme der Deutschen Bibliothek

Sube, Ralf:
Wörterbuch Physik: engl., dt.; mit etwa 75 000 Wortstellen / Ralf Sube; Günther Eisenreich. — Zweisprachige Studentenausg. — Thun; Frankfurt am Main: Deutsch, 1987.
  Parallelsacht.: Dictionary of physics
  ISBN 3-87144-940-7
NE: Eisenreich, Günther:; HST

ISBN 3 87144 940 7

Copyright by VEB Verlag Technik, Berlin, 1987
Lizenzausgabe für den Verlag Harri Deutsch, Thun
Gesamtherstellung: Fuldaer Verlagsanstalt GmbH

DIRECTIONS FOR THE USER OF THE DICTIONARY

1. Samples of alphabetical arrangement

air wing
Airy['s[disk
Airy['s[free wave
Airy functions
Airy['s[integral

drop counter
drop fall
droplet model
droplet spectrum
drop method

grobe Dichtematrix
Grobeinstellung
grobe Spektralphotometrie
Grob-Fein-Trieb
Grobkornbild

Spur
Spurbegrenzung
Spurbildung
Spurbreite
Spur der Fläche

2. Signs and abbreviations

( ) bispiral condenser (cooler) = bispiral condenser *or* bispiral cooler

[ ] circuit-breaking transient [phenomenon] = circuit-breaking transient *or* circuit-breaking transient phenomenon

/ axial symmetry / in = in axial symmetry
Kerns / innerhalb des = innerhalb des Kerns

< > these brackets contain explanations

s. see

s. a. see also

USED ABBREVIATIONS

⟨ac.⟩ acoustics
⟨acc.⟩ particle accelerators

⟨aero.⟩ mechanics of gases, gas dynamics; aeromechanics, aerodynamics

⟨astr.⟩ astrophysics; astronomy
⟨bio.⟩ biophysics; biochemistry; biology
⟨chem.⟩ chemistry; chemical engineering

⟨cryst.⟩ crystallography, physics of crystals; solid state physics

⟨el.⟩ electricity; electronics; electrical engineering

⟨elast.⟩ elasticity

⟨el.chem.⟩ electrochemistry
⟨el.opt.⟩ corpuscular optics; electronic optics

⟨gen.⟩ general term

⟨geo.⟩ geophysics; geology

⟨hydr.⟩ mechanics of liquids, hydromechanics; hydrodynamics; hydrology; hydrometry

⟨magn.⟩ magnetism
⟨math.⟩ mathematics
⟨meas.⟩ metrology

⟨Ak.⟩ Akustik
⟨Beschl.⟩ Teilchenbeschleuniger
⟨Aero.⟩ Mechanik der Gase, Gasdynamik; Aeromechanik, Aerodynamik

⟨Astr.⟩ Astrophysik; Astronomie
⟨Bio.⟩ Biophysik; Biochemie; Biologie
⟨Chem.⟩ Chemie; chemische Verfahrenstechnik
⟨Krist.⟩ Kristallographie, Kristallphysik; Festkörperphysik

⟨El.⟩ Elektrizität; Elektronik; Elektrotechnik

⟨Elast.⟩ Elastizität

⟨El.chem.⟩ Elektrochemie
⟨El.opt.⟩ Korpuskularoptik; Elektronenoptik

⟨allg.⟩ allgemeiner Begriff
⟨Geo.⟩ Geophysik; Geologie
⟨Hydr.⟩ Mechanik der Flüssigkeiten, Hydromechanik; Hydrodynamik; Hydrologie; Hydrometrie
⟨Magn.⟩ Magnetismus
⟨Math.⟩ Mathematik
⟨Meß.⟩ Metrologie

⟨mech.⟩ classical mechanics

⟨met.⟩ physical metallurgy

⟨meteo.⟩ meteorology
⟨micr.⟩ microscopy
⟨mol.⟩ molecular physics

⟨nucl.⟩ nuclear physics
⟨num.math.⟩ numerical mathematics; data processing
⟨opt.⟩ optics
⟨phot.⟩ photography; photochemistry
⟨phys.⟩ physics
⟨phys.chem.⟩ physical chemistry
⟨qu.⟩ quantum theory; quantum mechanics; quantum electrodynamics

⟨rad.⟩ radio engineering; radar
⟨rel.⟩ relativity

⟨semi.⟩ semiconductor physics
⟨spectr.⟩ spectroscopy, spectrometry
⟨stat.⟩ statistics (mathematical, physical, or biological)
⟨techn.⟩ engineering; technology
⟨therm.⟩ thermodynamics; heat engineering

⟨tv.⟩ television
⟨vac.⟩ vacuum physics

⟨Mech.⟩ klassische Mechanik
⟨Met.⟩ Metallkunde

⟨Meteo.⟩ Meteorologie
⟨Mikr.⟩ Mikroskopie
⟨Mol.⟩ Molekularphysik

⟨Kern.⟩ Kernphysik
⟨num. Math.⟩ numerische Mathematik; Datenverarbeitung
⟨Opt.⟩ Optik
⟨Phot.⟩ Photographie; Photochemie
⟨Phys.⟩ Physik
⟨phys. Chem.⟩ physikalische Chemie
⟨Qu.⟩ Quantentheorie; Quantenmechanik; Quantenelektrodynamik

⟨Funk.⟩ Funktechnik; Radartechnik
⟨Rel.⟩ Relativitätstheorie

⟨Halb.⟩ Halbleiterphysik

⟨Spektr.⟩ Spektroskopie, Spektrometrie
⟨Stat.⟩ Statistik (mathematische, physikalische und biologische)
⟨Techn.⟩ Technik

⟨Therm.⟩ Thermodynamik; Wärmetechnik

⟨Fs.⟩ Fernsehen
⟨Vak.⟩ Vakuumphysik

Vorwort zur zweisprachigen Ausgabe

Diese zweisprachige Ausgabe (Englisch-Deutsch) ist ein Auszug der viersprachigen Originalausgabe (Englisch-Deutsch-Französisch-Russisch). Während die Originalausgabe — bestehend aus drei Bänden — ein umfangreiches und entsprechend teures Werk vorwiegend für Bibliotheken und Institute ist, konnte unter Verzicht auf die weniger benutzten Sprachen Französisch und Russisch eine sehr preiswerte einbändige Broschur herausgegeben werden. Damit steht insbesondere Studenten ein ausführliches Wörterbuch zum zumutbaren Preis zur Verfügung.

Bei einem so vielseitigen und umfassenden Gebiet wie der Physik, das zudem noch in einer stürmischen Entwicklung begriffen ist, ist die Abgrenzung zu benachbarten Fachrichtungen oft schwierig; außerdem kann ein so umfassendes Grundlagenwörterbuch — mit 75 000 Wortstellen — nicht der teilweise sprunghaften Entwicklung einzelner Teilgebiete wie, z. B. Hochenergiephysik, Kernphysik u. a., gerecht werden. Inzwischen liegen von einem der Autoren, Herrn Ralf Sube, verschiedene Spezialwörterbücher vor bzw. sind in Vorbereitung, und zwar zu den Gebieten *Kerntechnik*, *Strahlenschutz* und *Hochenergiephysik*, in denen auch die modernen Entwicklungen berücksichtigt sind.

Wir hoffen, daß die vorliegende zweisprachige Ausgabe sich vielen Interessenten nützlich erweist.

Frankfurt am Main, Januar 1987   Verlag Harri Deutsch

A

A band, anisotropic band, A segment, Q-disk	Q-Streifen *m*, anisotrope Querscheibe (Schicht) *f* <Muskel>
A band <157—187 Mc/s>	A-Band *n* <157...187 MHz>
Abashian-Booth-Crowe anomaly	s. ABC-anomaly
abat-voix	s. acoustic baffle
abaxial	s. off-axis
Abbe['s] coefficient	s. constringence
Abbe['s] comparator principle, comparator principle [of E. Abbe]	Komparatorprinzip *n* [von E. Abbe], Abbesches Komparatorprinzip, meßtechnischer Grundsatz *m*
Abbe condenser, Abbe microscope condenser	[einfacher] Hellfeld-Durchlichtkondensor *m*, Abbescher Mikroskopkondensor (Kondensor) *m*, Mikroskopkondensor nach Abbe; Abbe-Beleuchtungsapparat *m*
Abbe hemisphere, glass hemisphere of crystal spectrometer	Halbkugel *f* von Abbe, Abbesche Halbkugel *f*
Abbe invariant, invariant of refraction	Abbesche Invariante *f*, Invariante der Brechung
Abbe microscope condenser	s. Abbe condenser
Abbe number	s. constringence
Abbe prism, Pellin-Broca prism	Abbe-Prisma *n*, Pellin-Broca-Prisma *n*
Abbe['s] refractometer	Abbe-Refraktometer *n*, Abbesches Refraktometer *n*
Abbe['s] sine condition, sine condition	Abbesche Sinusbedingung *f*, Sinusbedingung
Abbe test plate	Abbesche Testplatte *f*; Abbesche Figur *f*
Abbot silver-disk pyrheliometer	s. silver-disk pyrheliometer
abbreviated Doolittle method, Gauss-Doolittle method	Gauß-Doolittle-Methode *f*, verkürzte Doolittle-Methode *f*
ABC-anomaly, Abashian-Booth-Crowe anomaly, ABC	ABC-Anomalie *f*, Abashian-Booth-Crowe-Anomalie *f*, ABC
abduction of heat	s. heat removal
Abegg['s] rule	Abeggsche Regel *f*
Abel equation, Abel['s] integral equation	Abelsche Integralgleichung *f*
Abelian differential <of the first, second, third kind>	Abelsches Differential *n* <erster, zweiter, dritter Gattung>
Abelian function	abelsche Funktion *f*
Abelian group, commutative group	abelsche Gruppe *f*, kommutative Gruppe
Abelian integral <of the first, second, third kind>	Abelsches Integral *n* <erster, zweiter, dritter Art>
Abelian theorem	Abelscher Satz *m* <Laplace-Transformation>
Abel['s] identity, Abel['s] partial summation formula, summation by parts	Abelsche partielle Summation *f*, Abelsche Umformung *f*
Abel['s] integral equation, Abel equation	Abelsche Integralgleichung *f*
Abel['s] partial summation formula, Abel['s] identity	Abelsche partielle Summation *f*, Abelsche Umformung *f*
Abel['s] test for convergence	Abelsches Konvergenzkriterium *n*
Abel['s] theorem	Abelscher Grenzwertsatz (Stetigkeitssatz, Konvergenzsatz) *m*; Abelsches Theorem *n* <für Abelsche Integrale>
aberration, image defect, defect <e.g. of lens, eye>	Aberration *f*, Abbildungsfehler *m* <z. B. Linse, Auge>; Linsenfehler *m*, Linsenaberration *f*
aberrational ellipse	Aberrationsellipse *f*
aberration angle (constant)	s. angle of aberration
aberration from linearity; linearity error; deflection linearity error	Linearitätsabweichung *f*; Linearitätsfehler *m*
aberration of light, light aberration	Aberration *f* des Fixsternlichts (Lichtes), Lichtaberration *f*, Fixsternaberration *f*
aberration of the magnetic field from periodicity	Feldfehler *m*, Periodizitätsstörung *f*
aberration time	Aberrationszeit *f*
abeyance	= latent state
abherent, release (parting) agent	Antikleber *m*
ability of adsorption	s. adsorption ability
ability of oxidizing	s. oxidability
ability to be magnetized, magnetizability	Magnetisierbarkeit *f*
abioseston	Abioseston *n*
ablation	Oberflächenabschmelzung *f*, Ablation *f*
Abney grating mounting	s. Abney mounting
Abney law	Abneysches Gesetz *n*
Abney mounting [of diffraction grating], Abney grating mounting	Abneysche Gitteraufstellung *f*
Abney phenomenon	Abneysches Phänomen *n*
abnormal audibility zone	s. zone of abnormal audibility
abnormal crystallization	anomale Kristallisation *f*
abnormal discharge	s. abnormal glow discharge
abnormal dispersion	s. anomalous dispersion
abnormal glow discharge, abnormal discharge	anomale Glimmentladung (Entladung) *f*
abnormal glow regime	Gebiet *n* der anomalen Glimmentladung (Entladung)
abnormal hyperfine splitting	anomale Hyperfeinaufspaltung *f*
abnormal recrystallization	anormale Rekristallisation *f*
above[-]threshold	oberschwellig
Abragam-Jeffries effect	s. solid state effect
Abraham['s] excitator	Abrahamscher Erreger *m*
abrasion, marine erosion <geo.>	Abrasion *f*, marine Erosion *f* <Geo.>
abrasion	s. a. abrasive wear
abrasion border	Schliffgrenze *f*; Schliffbord *m*
abrasion hardness	s. abrasive hardness
abrasion resistance, abrasion strength, abrasive strength	Abriebfestigkeit *f*, Abschleiffestigkeit *f*; Verschleißfestigkeit *f* [bei Abrieb]
abrasive hardness, abrasion hardness	Schleifhärte *f*
abrasive hardness	s. a. scratch hardness
abrasive platform	s. shore terrace
abrasive strength	s. abrasion resistance
abrasive wear, abrasion	abrasiver Verschleiß *m*, Abrieb *m*; Gleitverschleiß *m*; Korngleitverschleiß *m*
abrasivity	Schleifschärfe *f*, Schleißschärfe *f*
abridged spectrophotometry	grobe Spektralphotometrie *f*
abruption	s. rupture <mech.>
abrupt junction <semi.>	abrupter (schroffer, scharfer) Übergang *m* <Halb.>
abscissa of convergence	Konvergenzabszisse *f*
abscission, segmentation, constriction	Abschnürung *f*
abscission layer <bio.>; separating layer; separating film	Trennschicht *f*, Trennungsschicht *f*
absence of collisions, absence of shocks	Stoßfreiheit *f*
absence of correlation	Unkorreliertheit *f*, Nullkorrelation *f*
absence of eddies	s. absence of vortices
absence of gravity, weightlessness, zero gravity, null[-] gravity; imponderability, imponderableness	Schwerelosigkeit *f*
absence of heredity	Nachwirkungsfreiheit *f*
absence of hysteresis	Hysteresefreiheit *f*
absence of inertia	s. non-inertia
absence of orientation, non-orientation	Unorientiertheit *f*
absence of shocks, absence of collisions	Stoßfreiheit *f*

absence of strain	Verspannungsfreiheit *f*	absolute temperature, Kelvin temperature, temperature on the Kelvin scale	absolute Temperatur *f*, Kelvin-Temperatur *f*
absence of vortices, absence of eddies, eddy freedom, irrotationality	Wirbelfreiheit *f*, Wirbellosigkeit *f*	absolute temperature scale [of Kelvin], Kelvin temperature scale, Kelvin scale, Kelvin['s] absolute temperature scale	absolute Temperaturskala (Temperaturskale) *f* [von Kelvin], Kelvin-Skala *f*, Kelvin-Skale *f*, Kelvins absolute Temperaturskala, absolute thermodynamische Temperaturskala
absolute age determination, absolute dating	absolute Altersbestimmung *f*
absolute atomic weight	absolute Atommasse *f*, absolutes Atomgewicht *n*
absolute black body	s. black body
absolute brightness	s. absolute stellar magnitude	absolute term, constant term	Absolutglied *n*
absolute ceiling, theoretic[al] ceiling	theoretische Gipfelhöhe (Deckenhöhe) *f*	absolute theory in electrodynamics	Absoluttheorie *f* in der Elektrodynamik
absolute convergence	unbedingte Konvergenz *f*, absolute Konvergenz	absolute thermal e.m.f.	absolute Thermo-EMK *f*, absolute Thermospannung (Thermokraft) *f*
absolute dating	s. absolute age determination
absolute differential calculus	s. Ricci calculus	absolute threshold of luminance <opt.>	absolute Empfindlichkeitsschwelle *f*, Absolutschwelle *f*, absolute Reizschwelle *f*, generelle Schwelle *f*, Grundschwelle *f*, Minimum *n* perceptibile; absolute Unterschiedsschwelle (Wahrnehmungsschwelle) *f* <bezogen auf Helligkeit>
absolute discontinuity	absolute Unstetigkeit *f*
absolute electrometer	s. Kelvin absolute electrometer
absolute elongation	s. elongation
absolute extremum, global extremum, extremum in the large	absolutes Extremum *n*, Extremum im Großen
absolute future of the event	absolute Zukunft *f* des Ereignisses
absolute growth rate, absolute rate of growth, rate of increase (gain)	absolute Wachstumsrate *f*, Zuwachsrate *f* <Stat.>	absolute time, Newtonian absolute time	absolute Zeit *f*, Newtonsche absolute Zeit
absolute height	s. true height	absolute time scale	absolute Zeitskala *f*
absolute H-magnetometer, absolute horizontal magnetometer	absolutes *H*-Magnetometer (Horizontalmagnetometer) *n*
absolute humidity, vapour concentration	absolute Feuchtigkeit *f*	absolute unit, rationalized unit, c.g.s. unit	absolute Einheit *f*, CGS-Einheit *f*
		absolute vacuum	s. free space
absolute index of refraction	s. refractive index	absolute value <of a real or complex number>; modulus <of a complex number>	Betrag *m*, Absolutbetrag *m*, absoluter Betrag, Absolutwert *m* <einer reellen oder komplexen Zahl>; Modul *m* <einer komplexen Zahl>
absolute joule	s. joule
absolutely additive	s. countably additive
absolutely continuous	absolut stetig
absolutely convergent	absolut konvergent, unbedingt konvergent
		absolute value	s. a. actual value <meas.>
		absolute value	s. a. magnitude <of a vector>
absolutely integrable	absolut integrierbar
absolutely / taken	dem Betrage nach	absolute value indication	s. indication of absolute value
absolute magnetometer	Absolutmagnetometer *n*, absolutes Magnetometer *n*	absolute vertical magnetometer	s. absolute *Z*-magnetometer
absolute magnitude	s. absolute stellar magnitude	absolute viscosity	s. coefficient of viscosity
absolute parallelism	s. teleparallelism	absolute zero, absolute zero of temperature	absoluter Nullpunkt *m*, absoluter Temperaturnullpunkt *m*
absolute past of the event	absolute Vergangenheit *f* des Ereignisses
absolute permeability <of a medium>, permeability; normal permeability <of a ferromagnetic>	absolute Permeabilität *f*, Permeabilität <Medium>; Normalpermeabilität *f*, normale Permeabilität <bei Ferromagnetika>	absolute Z-magnetometer, absolute vertical magnetometer	absolutes *Z*-Magnetometer (Vertikalmagnetometer) *n*
		absorbability	Absorbierbarkeit *f*, Absorptionsfähigkeit *f*; Saugfähigkeit *f*
absolute permeability of free space	s. permeability of free space
absolute permeability of vacuum	s. permeability of free space
absolute permittivity	s. permittivity
absolute pitch	s. sence of absolute pitch	absorbance	s. optical extinction
absolute pyrheliometer	Absolutpyrheliometer *n*, absolutes Pyrheliometer *n*	absorbance index <opt.>	s. decimal extinction coefficient <opt.>
absolute pyrheliometry	Absolutpyrheliometrie *f*	absorbancy	s. optical extinction
absolute rate of growth	s. absolute growth rate	absorbancy index <opt.>; absorption index <therm.>	Absorptionsindex *m* <Therm., Opt.>
absolute refractive index	s. refractive index
absolute refractory period	absolute Refraktärzeit *f*
absolute refractory phase	absolutes Refraktärstadium *n*	absorbed dose, absorbed radiation dose	Energiedosis *f*, absorbierte Dosis (Strahlungsdosis) *f*
absolute roughness size	äquivalente Sandrauhigkeit *f*	absorbed dose rate	Energiedosisleistung *f*
absolute specific mass	s. specific gravity	absorbed matter, absorbed substance	absorbierter Stoff *m*, Absorptiv *n*
absolute stability margin	absoluter Stabilitätsrand *m* [der Wurzeln]	absorbed quantity, surface excess	Oberflächenüberschuß *m*
absolute stellar brightness	s. absolute stellar magnitude	absorbed radiation dose	s. absorbed dose
absolute stellar magnitude, absolute magnitude, absolute [stellar] brightness	absolute Helligkeit *f*, absolute Größenklasse *f* <Gestirn>	absorbed radiation energy <opt.>	absorbierte Energie *f* <Opt.>
		absorbed substance	s. absorbed matter
absolute strength	s. modulus of rupture	absorbent, absorbing agent, absorbing material <chem.>	Absorptionsmittel *n*, Absorbens *n* <pl.: Absorbenzien>, Absorber *m* <Chem.>
absolute system of units	s. c.g.s. system
absolute technical atmosphere, ata	absolute technische Atmosphäre *f*, Atmosphäre Absolutdruck, at Absolutdruck <früher: ata>
		absorber <of reactor>	Absorber *m* <Reaktor>

absorber <of refrigerator>	Absorber m <Kältemaschine>	absorption dynamometer	Bremsdynamometer n
absorber <of wave guide>	Absorber m, Absorberwiderstand m <Hohlleiter>	absorption edge	s. absorption discontinuity <spectr.>
absorber/1/v	s. 1/v absorber	absorption energy, energy of absorption	Absorptionsenergie f
absorber material	s. absorbing material	absorption equivalent	Absorptionsäquivalent n
absorbing agent	s. absorbent <chem.>	absorption extraction	absorptive Extraktion f
absorbing circuit	s. absorption circuit <el.>	absorption factor	s. absorptance
absorbing material, absorber material <of reactor>	Absorbermaterial n <Reaktor>	absorption factor	s. acoustical absorption factor
absorbing material	s. a. sound absorber	absorption filter <el., opt.>	Absorptionsfilter n <El., Opt.>
absorbing material	s. a. absorbent <chem.>		
absorbing resistance, absorption resistance	Schluckwiderstand m		
absorbing rod	Absorberstab m	absorption frequency	Absorptionsfrequenz f
absorbing wedge, absorption wedge	Absorptionskeil m		
absorptance, absorption factor, absorptivity, absorptive power	Absorptionsvermögen n, Absorptionsgrad m, Absorptionszahl f	absorption frequency meter	Absorptionsfrequenzmesser m
		absorption half-value layer	s. absorption half-value thickness
		absorption half-value thickness, absorption half-value layer	Halbwertsdicke (Halbwertschicht) f für Absorption, Absorptionshalbwertsdicke f
absorptiometer	Absorptiometer n		
absorptiometry, absorption measurement	Absorptiometrie f, Absorptionsmessung f	absorption hardening [of the neutron spectrum], neutron hardening by absorption	Absorptionshärtung f [des Neutronenspektrums]
absorption, sucking [up], suction, imbibition	Aufsaugen n, Aufnahme f; Einsaugung f; Absorption f		
		absorption heat, heat of absorption	Absorptionswärme f
absorption <e.g. of energy, humidity>	Aufnahme f, Absorption f, Schluckung f <z. B. Energie, Feuchtigkeit>	absorption hygrometer	Absorptionshygrometer n
absorption <of an impact>	Auffangen n <Stoß>	absorption index <therm.>; absorbancy index <opt.>	Absorptionsindex m <Therm., Opt.>
absorption <of radiation; chem.>	Absorption f; Schluckung f <Strahlung; Chem.>		
absorption <of a vacancy>	Anlagerung f <Leerstelle>		
absorption analysis, spectral absorption analysis	Absorptionsspektralanalyse f, Absorptionsanalyse f	absorption in the matrix lattice, fundamental absorption, lattice absorption	Grundgitterabsorption f
absorption axis	Absorptionshauptachse f, Absorptionsachse f		
		absorption isotherm	Absorptionsisotherme f
absorption band	Absorptionsbande f	absorption limit	s. absorption discontinuity <spectr.>
absorption band of ozone	s. ozone band	absorption line	Absorptionslinie f
absorption branch	Saugzweig m		
absorption by impurities, tail absorption <absorption confined to emission centres or raising electrons from emission centres into the conduction band>	Ausläuferabsorption f, Störstellenabsorption f, Absorption f in der Ausläuferbande	absorption loss	Schluckverlust m, Absorptionsverlust m, Schluck m
		absorption machine	s. absorption refrigerator
		absorption mean free path, mean free path for absorption	[mittlere freie] Absorptionsweglänge f, mittlere freie Weglänge f für Absorption
absorption capacity <of turbine>	Schluckfähigkeit f, Schluckvermögen n <Turbine>		
absorption circuit, absorbing circuit, suction circuit, wave trap, absorption trap, trap <el.>	Saugkreis m, Absorptionskreis m, Wellenfalle f, Wellensaugkreis m, Sperrkreis m <El.>	absorption measurement	s. absorptiometry
		absorption modulation	Absorptionsmodulation f
		absorption of heat	s. heat absorption
		absorption of moisture	s. moisture absorption
		absorption of radiation [energy]	s. radiation absorption
absorption coefficient <el.>	Absorptionskoeffizient m <El.>	absorption of sound, sound absorption, acoustic[al] absorption	Schallabsorption f, Schallschluckung f
absorption coefficient, energy absorption coefficient <nucl.>	Absorptionskoeffizient m (in cm⁻¹), Energieabsorptionskoeffizient m <Kern.>	absorption of water	s. water intake
		absorption operator	s. annihilation operator
		absorption photometer	Absorptionsphotometer n
absorption coefficient	s. a. linear absorption coefficient <in Lambert's law>	absorption power meter	s. absorption wattmeter
		absorption probability, absorption rate	Absorptionswahrscheinlichkeit f
absorption coefficient [for sound]	s. acoustical absorption factor <ac.>	absorption pump	Absorptionspumpe f
absorption coefficient multiplied by the factor λ/4π	s. extinction coefficient multiplied by the factor λ/4π	absorption rate; uptake rate	Aufnahmegeschwindigkeit f
		absorption rate	s. a. absorption probability
absorption continuum, continuous absorption spectrum	Absorptionskontinuum n, kontinuierliches Absorptionsspektrum n	absorption refrigerator, absorption machine, vapour-absorption refrigerator	Absorptionskältemaschine f, Sorptionskältemaschine f, Absorptionskühlmaschine f
absorption cross-section, cross-section for absorption	Absorptions[wirkungs]querschnitt m, Wirkungsquerschnitt m für (der) Absorption		
absorption cross-section [of antenna]	s. beam area	absorption resistance	s. absorbing resistance
		absorption shift	Absorptionsverschiebung f
absorption discontinuity, absorption edge, absorption limit <spectr.>	Absorptionskante f	absorption spectrochemical analysis using X-rays, X-ray absorption [spectrochemical] analysis, X-ray absorptiometry	Röntgenabsorptionsspektralanalyse f, Röntgenabsorptionsanalyse f, chemische Analyse f durch Röntgenstrahlenabsorption
absorption discontinuity	Absorptionssprung m		

absorption 12

absorption spectrophotometry	Absorptionsspektralphotometrie *f*	accelerating gap, accelerating slit	Beschleunigungsstrecke *f*, Beschleunigungsspalt *m*
absorption spectroscopy	Absorptionsspektroskopie *f*	accelerating grid; accelerator grid	Beschleunigungsgitter *n*
absorption spectrum, dark-line spectrum	Absorptionsspektrum *n*	accelerating impact	Beschleunigungsstoß *m*
absorption tail	s. long wavelength tail	accelerating period	Beschleunigungsperiode *f*
absorption trap	s. absorption circuit <el.>	accelerating slit	s. accelerating gap
absorption wattmeter, absorption power meter	Absorptionswattmeter *n*, Absorptionsleistungsmesser *m*	accelerating tube	Beschleunigungsrohr *n*
		accelerating unit, accelerator	Beschleunigungsanlage *f*, Beschleuniger *m*
		accelerating voltage	Beschleunigungsspannung *f*
		accelerating wave <el.>	Beschleunigungswelle *f*, beschleunigende Welle *f*
absorption wave meter	Absorptionswellenmesser *m*	acceleration; rate of speed	Beschleunigung *f*
		acceleration, acceleration vector	Beschleunigungsvektor *m*, Beschleunigung *f*
absorption wedge, absorbing wedge	Absorptionskeil *m*	acceleration <astr.>	Akzeleration *f* <Astr.>
absorption with excitation of lattice vibrations	Absorption *f* mit Anregung von Gitterschwingungen (Schwingungen der schweren Gitterbausteine)	acceleration along the path	Bahnbeschleunigung *f*
		acceleration due to gravity	s. acceleration of gravity
absorptive power	s. absorptance	acceleration due to lunar gravity, Moon's gravity acceleration	Mondbeschleunigung *f*, Fallbeschleunigung (Schwerebeschleunigung) *f* auf dem Mond
absorptivity, internal absorption factor of unit length	Reinabsorptionsmodul *m*; Reinabsorptionsgrad *m*, bezogen auf die Längeneinheit; Reinabsorptionsgrad für die Schichtdicke Eins, bezogener spektraler Absorptionskoeffizient *m*, Extinktionskoeffizient *m*	acceleration due to rotation	s. rotational acceleration
		acceleration energy	Energie *f* der Beschleunigung, Beschleunigungsenergie *f*, Appell-Funktion *f*, Appellsche Funktion *f*
absorptivity	s. a. absorptance	acceleration field <mech.>	Beschleunigungsfeld *n* <Mech.>
abstraction of heat	s. heat removal		
abstract number	s. relative quantity	accelerationless, non-accelerated, unaccelerated	beschleunigungslos, unbeschleunigt
abundance of isotopes, isotopic abundance, fractional isotopic abundance, relative abundance [of the isotope]	Isotopenhäufigkeit [der Elemente] *f*, Häufigkeit *f* der Isotope, relative Häufigkeit [des Isotops], relative Isotopenhäufigkeit, Häufigkeit des Isotops; prozentualer Anteil *m* [des Isotops]	acceleration meter	s. accelerometer
		acceleration of Coriolis	s. Coriolis acceleration
		acceleration of creep	Erhöhung *f* der Kriechgeschwindigkeit
		acceleration of gravity, gravity (gravitational) acceleration, acceleration due to gravity, value of gravity, gravity constant	Erdbeschleunigung *f*; Gravitationsbeschleunigung *f*, Schwerebeschleunigung *f*; [absolute] Fallbeschleunigung *f*
abundance of the element, relative abundance [of the element]	Elementenhäufigkeit *f*, Elementhäufigkeit *f*, relative Häufigkeit *f* des Elements, Häufigkeit (prozentualer Anteil *m*) des Elements		
		acceleration of higher order	Beschleunigung *f* höherer Ordnung (Art)
		acceleration of transport[ation], acceleration of translation	Führungsbeschleunigung *f*
abundance ratio	Häufigkeitsverhältnis *n*		
abundance ratio [of isotopes]	s. relative isotopic abundance	acceleration potential	Beschleunigungspotential *n*
		acceleration radiation	s. synchrotron radiation
abundant year, perfect year, annus abundans	überzähliges Gemeinjahr *n* <im jüdischen Kalender>	acceleration regime	Beschleunigungsbetrieb *m*
		acceleration vector, acceleration	Beschleunigungsvektor *m*, Beschleunigung *f*
abundant year, leap year	Schaltjahr *n* <Gregorianischer Kalender>	acceleration wave <mech.>	Beschleunigungswelle *f* <Mech.>
abyssal	s. deep-ocean		
abyssal region, abyssal zone	Abyssalregion *f*, Abyssalbereich *m*, Abyssal *n*, abyssale Zone *f*, Tiefseetafel *f*	acceleration work	Beschleunigungsarbeit *f*
		accelerator, accelerator of reaction, accelerant [of reaction], reaction accelerator, accelerating agent, [positive] catalyst	Reaktionsbeschleuniger *m*, Beschleuniger *m* [der Reaktion], Akzelerator *m*, positiver Katalysator *m*, Katalysator <Chem.>
abyssal rock	s. intrusive rock		
abyssal zone	s. abyssal region		
accelerant [of reaction]	s. accelerator <chem.>		
accelerated cathode excitation, A.C.E., ACE	beschleunigte Katodenerregung *f*	accelerator	s. a. accelerating unit
accelerated commutation	s. overcommutation	accelerator	s. a. atomic particle accelerator
accelerated corrosion test, quick (rapid) corrosion test	Schnellkorrosionsversuch *m*	accelerator grid; accelerating grid	Beschleunigungsgitter *n*
		accelerator of polymerization	s. initiator
accelerated creep	s. accelerating flow	accelerator of reaction	s. accelerator <chem.>
accelerated [particle] current, particle current, current of accelerated particles <acc.>	Teilchenstrom *m* <Beschl.>	accelerometer, acceleration meter	Beschleunigungsmesser *m*, Beschleunigungsmeßgerät *n*
		accent	s. prime <sign of operation>
accelerated test, quick test, rapid test	Schnellversuch *m*, Kurz[zeit]versuch *m*, kurzzeitiger Versuch *m*	accented quantity, primed quantity	gestrichene Größe *f*
		accentuation	s. pre[-]emphasis
accelerating agent	s. accelerator <chem.>	accentuator, selective amplifier	Selektivverstärker *m*, selektiver Verstärker *m*
accelerating anode	Beschleunigungsanode *f*; Voranode *f*		
		acceptance, accepting <stat.>	Annahme *f*, Nichtverwerfung *f* <Stat.>
accelerating cycle	Beschleunigungszyklus *m*		
accelerating field <el.>	Beschleunigungsfeld *n*, beschleunigendes Feld *n*	acceptor, acceptor impurity, p-type impurity	Akzeptor *m*, p-Typ-Verunreinigung *f*
		acceptor	s. a. series resonant circuit
accelerating flow, tertiary creep, accelerated creep	Beschleunigungskriechen *n*, beschleunigtes (tertiäres) Kriechen *n*, drittes Kriechstadium *n*	acceptor bond	Akzeptorbindung *f*
		acceptor centre	Akzeptorzentrum *n*
		acceptor circuit	s. series resonant circuit
		acceptor impurity	s. acceptor

acceptor level	Akzeptorniveau n, Akzeptorterm m	achromatized Ramsden eyepiece	s. Kellner['s] eyepiece
access <num. math.>	Zugriff m, Zugang m <num. Math.>	achromatopsia	Achromatopsie f, totale Farbenblindheit f
accessible boundary point	erreichbarer Randpunkt m	acicular galaxy, acicular nebula	nadelförmige Galaxis f, nadelförmiger Nebel m
access of air / without	unter Luftabschluß, bei Luftabschluß	acid [according to Brønsted]	s. proton donor
accessory attachment	s. supplementary apparatus	acid amide-imide tautomerism	Säureamid-Imid-Tautomerie f
accident, average <of reactor>	Havarie f <Reaktor>	acid-base equilibrium	Säure-Base[n]-Gleichgewicht n
accidental, random, chance	zufällig, Zufalls-, zufallsbedingt		
accidental coincidence	s. spurious coincidence	acid-base indicator, pH indicator, colour indicator, indicator	pH-Indikator m, Säure-Basen-Indikator m, Neutralisationsindikator m, Farbindikator m, Indikator m
accidental count	Zufallszählung f, Zufallsimpulse mpl		
accidental earth	s. earth fault		
accidental error	s. sampling error		
accidental fluctuation	s. random fluctuation	acid-base theory	Säure-Base-Theorie f
accidental ground	s. short-circuit to earth		
accidental resonance, random resonance	zufällige Resonanz f	acid cleavage	Säurespaltung f
		acid concentration, acid density	Säuredichte f, Säurekonzentration f
accolade	Accolade f, Hindernis n von Klammerform	acid content	Säuregehalt m
accommodation	s. amplitude of accommodation	acid density, acid concentration	Säuredichte f, Säurekonzentration f
accommodation coefficient, thermal leakage modulus	Akkommodationskoeffizient m	acid determination	s. acidimetry
		acid fume, acid gas, acid vapour	Säuredampf m
accommodation kink, accommodation kinking	plastische Verformung f durch Abgleiten <mechanische Zwillingsbildung>	acidimetry, acid determination	Acidimetrie f, Säurebestimmung f, Säuremessung f
		acidity, degree of acidity	Acidität f, Säuregrad m
accommodation width	s. amplitude of accommodation	acid number, acid value	Säurezahl f, SZ
accommodometer	Akkommodometer n	acid radical, acid residue	Säurerest m, Säureradikal n
accommodometry	Akkommodationsmessung f, Akkommodometrie f	acid strength	Säurestärke f
accompanying element	begleitendes Element n, Begleitelement n	acid value, acid number	Säurezahl f, SZ
		acid vapour, acid fume, acid gas	Säuredampf m
accomplishment	s. carrying out		
accretion	s. increase		
accretion of interstellar matter	Zusammenschluß (Einfang) m interstellarer Materie, Materieeinfang m	acline, aclinic line	Akline f, Nullisokline f
accumulated dose	s. cumulative dose		
accumulated error, indexing error <of division or pitch>	Summenteilfehler m	acoustic admittance, admittance <ac.>	[akustischer] Wellenleitwert m, akustische Admittanz f, akustischer Leitwert m <Ak.>
accumulation, congestion, aggregation; storing; stocking	Häufung f, Anhäufung f; Anreicherung f; Akkumulation f; Ansammlung f; Speicherung f; Aufspeicherung f	acoustical absorption	s. absorption of sound
		acoustical absorption coefficient (factor), acoustical absorptivity, sound absorption factor, sound absorption coefficient, absorption coefficient [for sound], sound absorptivity, damping factor (coefficient), degree of absorption, absorption factor	Schallabsorptionsgrad m, Schallschluckgrad m, Schluckgrad m, Schallschluckzahl f, Schluckzahl f, Schallabsorptionskoeffizient m, Schallabsorptionsfaktor m, Absorptionskoeffizient m, Dämpfungskonstante f, Absorptionsgrad m <Ak.>
accumulation factor	Akkumulationsfaktor m, Anreicherungsfaktor m		
accumulation of heat	s. heat storage		
accumulation point, limiting point, limit point, cluster point, point of accumulation; limit element <math.>	Häufungspunkt m, Grenzpunkt m; Häufungsstelle f; Häufungswert m <Math.>		
		acoustical branch of lattice vibration	s. acoustical lattice vibration
accumulative crystallization	Sammelkristallisation f, Korngrößerung f	acoustical feedback; howling, howl, fringe howl	akustische Rückkopplung (Rückwirkung) f; Rückkopplungspfeifen n, Pfeifen n
accumulative dosimetry	speichernde Dosimetrie f		
accuracy / having n-figure	s. significant digits / having n		
accuracy in measurement	s. accuracy of measurement	acoustical image, sound image	Schallbild n, akustisches Bild n, akustische Abbildung f
accuracy of measurement, accuracy in measurement, measurement accuracy, precision of measurement, measurement precision	Meßgenauigkeit f	acoustical insulation	s. sound insulation
		acoustical lattice vibration, acoustical branch of lattice vibration	akustische Gitterschwingung f, akustischer Zweig m der Gitterschwingungen
		acoustically hard (rigid)	s. sound-hard
accuracy of movement	Ganggenauigkeit f	acoustically rigid boundary [surface]	s. sound-hard boundary
acentric, non-centric	azentrisch, nichtzentrisch, nichtzentriert	acoustically soft, sound-soft, yielding	schallweich
achromatic, antispectroscopic	achromatisch; unbunt; farbfehlerfrei	acoustically soft boundary [surface]	s. sound-soft boundary
achromatic colour, hueless colour	achromatische (unbunte) Farbe f	acoustical material	s. sound absorber
achromatic line	s. isogyre	acoustical particle velocity	s. particle velocity <ac.>
achromatic locus, Planckian locus	Unbuntgebiet n, Unbuntbereich m, Ortskurve f des schwarzen Strahlers	acoustical pressure, sound (sonic) pressure	Schall[wechsel]druck m, akustischer Druck m
		acoustical pyrometer	Schallpyrometer n
		acoustical quantity	s. quantity of sound field
achromatic vision	s. achromatism <of eye>	acoustical radiator, sound emitter	Schallstrahler m, Schallgeber m
achromatism	Achromasie f, Farbfehlerfreiheit f		
achromatism, achromatic vision <of eye>	Achromatismus m, Achromasie f, Zapfenblindheit f <des Auges>		

acoustical radiometer, sound radiometer	Schallradiometer n [nach Altberg], akustisches Radiometer n, Schall[strahlungs]druckwaage f, Schallwaage f, Schallstrahlungsdruckmesser m	acoustic figures	s. Chladni['s] figures
		acoustic frequency	s. audio[-]frequency
		acoustic frequency branch [of the elastic spectrum]	s. acoustic branch
		acoustic generator	s. sound generator
acoustical reduction coefficient, acoustical reduction factor, sound reduction factor	Schalldämmzahl f, Dämmzahl f, Reduktionsmaß n; Schallisolationsmaß n	acoustic grating	akustisches Gitter (Beugungsgitter) n
		acoustic heating	akustische Aufheizung f
		acoustic holography	akustische Holographie f
acoustical reflection coefficient	s. reflection coefficient <ac.>	acoustic horn, [sound] horn, sound funnel <ac.>	Schalltrichter m, Trichter m <Ak.>
acoustical reflection factor	s. reflection coefficient <ac.>	acoustic impedance, impedance <ac.>	akustische Impedanz f, Schallimpedanz f, akustischer Widerstand m
acoustical reflectivity	s. reflection coefficient <ac.>		
acoustical resonance	s. sound resonance	acoustic inductance (inductive reactance, inertance, inertia)	s. acoustic mass
acoustical spectrograph, sound spectrograph	Schallspektrograph m		
acoustical spectrography	s. sound spectrography	acoustic interferometer, sound interferometer	Schallinterferometer n
acoustical spectrometer	Schallspektrometer n	acoustic interval	s. musical interval
acoustical spectroscopy, sound spectroscopy	Schallspektroskopie f	acoustic irradiation	Beschallung f
		acoustic leak[age]	Tonstreuung f
acoustical spectrum	s. sound spectrum	acoustic lens, sound lens	akustische Linse f Schallinse
acoustical transmission coefficient	s. acoustical transmission factor	acoustic line, sound conductor; sound line	Schalleiter m Schalleitung f
acoustical transmission factor, sound transmission factor, transmission factor [for sound], acoustic[al] transmission coefficient, sound transmission coefficient, transmission coefficient [for sound], acoustic[al] transmittivity, sound transmittivity <ac.>	Schalltransmissionsgrad m, Schalldurchlaßgrad m, Schalltransmissionskoeffizient m, Schalltransmissionsfaktor m, Durchlaßgrad m, Durchlässigkeitsgrad m <Ak.>	acoustic mass, acoustic inertance, acoustic inertia, acoustic inductance, acoustic inductive reactance	akustische Masse (Trägheit) f, induktiver akustischer Blindwiderstand m, akustisch induktiver Blindwiderstand; akustische Induktivität (Selbstinduktivität) f
		acoustic-mechanical efficiency	akustisch-mechanischer Wirkungsgrad m
		acoustic model of particle scattering	akustisches Modell n der Streuung
acoustical transmittivity	s. acoustical transmission factor	acoustic pattern	s. Chladni['s] figures
acoustical velocity	s. particle velocity <ac.>	acoustic perception, sound perception	Schallwahrnehmung f
acoustical velocity	s. velocity of sound <ac.>		
acoustical volume velocity	s. volume velocity <ac.>	acoustic phonon	akustisches Phonon n
		acoustic power	s. sound energy flux
acoustical wave, sound (sonic) wave	Schallwelle f	acoustic power level	s. sound power level <ac.>
		acoustic power meter, sound power meter	Schalleistungsmesser m
acoustic analysis	s. sound analysis		
acoustic approximation	akustische Näherung f	acoustic pressure receiver, sound pressure receiver	Schalldruckempfänger m
acoustic baffle, baffle; abat-voix <ac.>	Schallwand f, Schallschirm m		
		acoustic radiation	s. radiation of sound
acoustic beam	s. beam of sound	acoustic radiation pressure, sound radiation pressure, radiation pressure in sound (acoustics), pressure of sound radiation	Schallstrahlungsdruck m
acoustic birefringence	s. acoustic double refraction		
acoustic branch [of the elastic spectrum], acoustic frequency branch [of the elastic spectrum]	akustischer Zweig m [des elastischen Spektrums]		
		acoustic radiation resistance	s. characteristic acoustic impedance
acoustic capacitance	s. acoustic compliance		
acoustic capacitive reactance	s. acoustic compliance	acoustic ray	s. ray of sound
		acoustic reactance	akustische Reaktanz f, akustischer Blindwiderstand
acoustic cavitation	s. cavitation induced by ultrasonics		
		acoustic resistance	akustischer Widerstand m, Schall[wellen]widerstand m, Schallwellenstandwert m, Standwert m, akustische Resistanz f, akustischer Wirkwiderstand m
acoustic coagulation	s. supersonic coagulation		
acoustic compliance, acoustic capacitance, acoustic capacitive reactance	kapazitiver akustischer Blindwiderstand m, akustisch kapazitiver Blindwiderstand, akustische Federung f; akustische Kapazität f		
		acoustic shadow, sound shadow	Schallschatten m
acoustic concentration	s. focusing of sound	acoustics of buildings	s. room acoustics
acoustic concentrator	s. sound concentrator	acoustic sounder	s. sonic echo sounder
acoustic delay line	s. ultrasonic delay line	acoustic source	s. source of sound
acoustic density	akustische Dichte f	acoustic spark chamber, sonic spark chamber	akustische Funkenkammer f, Funkenkammer mit akustischer Lokalisierung
acoustic dipole	akustischer Dipol m		
acoustic direction finder	akustischer Peiler m	acoustic state equation	s. acoustic equation of state
		acoustic stiffness, sound hardness	Schallhärte f, Schallhemmung f, Hemmung f, akustische Steife f
acoustic dispersion	s. sound dispersion		
acoustic dissipation factor	s. dissipation factor <ac.>		
		acoustic temperature	akustische Temperatur f
acoustic double refraction, acoustic birefringence	akustische Doppelbrechung f	acoustic thermometer	akustisches Thermometer n
		acoustic transmittivity	s. acoustical transmission factor <ac.>
acoustic duct, auditory passage	Gehörgang m		
		acoustic wavelength	Schallwellenlänge f
acoustic efficiency	akustischer Wirkungsgrad m	acoustimeter, phonometer	Schallstärkemesser m, Akustimeter n
acoustic energy, sound (sonic) energy	Schallenergie f		
		acoustochemistry	Akustochemie f
acoustic equation of state, acoustic state equation	akustische Zustandsgleichung f	acoustoelectric effect	akustoelektrischer Effekt m
		acoustomagnetoelectric effect, AME effect	akustomagnetoelektrischer Effekt m, AME-Effekt m

acronycal, acronychal — akronychisch
act — s. event <nucl.>
acting force, active (impressed) force — eingeprägte Kraft f
actinic light, actinic radiation — aktinische Strahlung f
actinic screen — s. luminescent screen
actinide elements (group), actinides, actinide series — Aktiniden npl, Actiniden npl, Gruppe f der Aktiniden
actinism, actinity — Aktinität f, lichtchemische (photochemische) Wirksamkeit f
actinium, $_{89}$Ac — Aktinium n, Actinium n, $_{89}$Ac
actinium emanation — s. actinon
actinium family, actinium radioactive family (series) — s. actinium series
actinium series, actinium radioactive series, $4n+3$ series, uranium-actinium [radioactive] series; actinium [radioactive] family, radioactive family of actinium, $4n+3$ family, uranium-actinium [radioactive] family, radioactive family of uranium-actinium — Aktiniumzerfallsreihe f, Aktiniumreihe f, $(4n+3)$-Zerfallsreihe f, Zerfallsreihe f des Aktiniums, Uran-Aktinium-Zerfallsreihe f, Uran-Aktinium-Reihe f, Zerfallsreihe des Aktinourans; radioaktive Familie f des Urans, Aktiniumfamilie f, radioaktive Familie des Aktinourans, Uran-Aktinium-Familie f
actino-electric effect, actinoelectricity, Stoletov effect — Stoletow-Effekt m, aktinoelektrischer Effekt m
actinometer filter — Aktinometerfilter n, Strahlungsfilter n
actinometry — Aktinometrie f
actinometry — s. a. pyranometry
actinometry — s. a. pyrheliometry
actinon, $^{219}_{86}$Ru, An — Aktinon n, Actinon n, An, $^{219}_{86}$Ru
action; actuation <control> — Eingriff m, Einwirkung f; Wirkungseingriff m
action <quantity> — Wirkung f <Größe>; Aktion f, Aktionskraft f, „actio" f
action — s. a. effect <on>
action and reaction — Wirkung f und Gegenwirkung f, actio f et reactio f
action at a distance, action at distance, distant (long-range, remote) action, long-range effect — Fernwirkung f, langreichweitige Wirkung f
action-at-a-distance theory — s. theory of action at a distance
action at distance — s. action at a distance
action control — s. manipulated variable
action current — Aktionsstrom m
action current due to the heart, heart action current — Herzaktionsstrom m
action integral — s. principal function
action magnitude — s. quantity of action
action of force — s. application of force
action of heat, heat (thermal) action, effect of heat, heat (heating, thermal) effect — Wärmewirkung f; Wärmeeinwirkung f; Wärmeangriff m
action of inertia relative to [the variable] q — Trägheitswirkung f bezüglich der Variablen q
action of no forces / under the — s. no forces / under
action of pinhole camera, pinhole action — Lochkamerawirkung f, Lochkammerwirkung f
action of radiation — s. radiation effect
action of the walls, wall action, influence of the walls, wall influence — Wandeinfluß m, Wandwirkung f
action potential — Aktionspotential n, Aktionsspannung f
action potential of the heart — Herzaktionsspannung f
action principle, principle of action — Wirkungsprinzip n
action principle — s. a. Hamilton['s] principle
action quantity — s. quantity of action
action quantum — s. Planck['s] constant
action spectrum — Wirkungsspektrum n, [spektrale] Wirkungskurve f

action turbine — s. impulse turbine
action variable — Wirkungsvariable f
action water turbine, impulse water turbine — Freistrahlturbine f, Strahlturbine f, hydraulische Aktionsturbine f
action wave, wave of action — Wirkungswelle f
activate — Aktivierungsprodukt n, aktivierte Substanz f
activated adsorption — s. chemisorption
activated carbon, activated charcoal, activated coal — Aktivkohle f, A-Kohle f, Adsorptionskohle f /
activated complex, active complex — aktivierter Komplex m, aktiver Komplex
activated mechanism — s. interchange mechanism of diffusion
activated valency — betätigte Valenz f
activation <of luminescence>, luminescence activation — Aktivierung f [der Lumineszenz], Lumineszenzaktivierung f
activation <of the glide system> — Betätigung f <Gleitsystem>
activation, radioactivation <nucl.> — Aktivierung f <Kern.>
activation — s. a. excitation
activation analysis — Aktivierungsanalyse f
activation analysis / by — aktivierungsanalytisch
activation cross-section, cross-section for activation — Aktivierungsquerschnitt m, Wirkungsquerschnitt m für (der) Aktivierung, Aktivierungswirkungsquerschnitt m
activation energy, heat of activation, activation heat, energy of activation <therm., chem.> — Aktivierungsenergie f, Aktivierungswärme f <Therm., Chem.>
activation energy of formation — Bildungsaktivierungsenergie f
activation enthalpy — s. enthalpy of activation
activation entropy — s. entropy of activation
activation heat — s. activation energy
activation integral — Aktivierungsintegral n
activation of valence — Valenzbetätigung f
activation overpotential, activation overvoltage; activation polarization — Aktivierungsüberspannung f; Aktivierungspolarisation f
activation potential — Aktivierungspotential n, Aktivierungsspannung f
activation yield — Aktivierungsausbeute f
activator <of luminescence>, luminescence (luminescent) activator, luminogen, phosphorogen — Aktivator m [der Lumineszenz], Lumineszenzaktivator m, Luminogen n, Phosphorogen n
activator <of flotation> — Beleber m <der Flotation>

active complex — s. activated complex
active component, resistive (ohmic) component — Wirkstromkomponente f, ohmsche Komponente f
active component — s. a. real component
active constituents of the atmosphere, weathering factors — Atmosphärilien pl
active core — s. core <of reactor>
active current, real (wattful) current — Wirkstrom m, Wattstrom m
active day — s. disturbed day
active dipole, driven dipole, radiating dipole — Strahlungsdipol m, strahlender Dipol m, Dipolstrahler m
active electrode, exploring electrode — Reizelektrode f, differente Elektrode f
active element, in-phase (real) element — Wirkelement n
active emanation — s. emanation
active energy — Wirkarbeit f, Wirkenergie f; Wirkverbrauch m
active-energy meter, energy meter, watt-hour meter — Wattstundenzähler m, Wirkverbrauchszähler m, WV-Zähler m
active flight, powered flight, rocket flight — Antriebsflug m, Treibflug m
active force — s. acting force
active lattice — s. core <of reactor>
active load, actual (resistive, ohmic) load — Wirklast f; ohmsche Belastung f

active | | | | **16**

active load reaction, resistive load reaction	Wirklastrückwirkung f, Wirklaststoß m	acuity of the spot, spot acuity	Punktschärfe f
active mass <of rocket>	aktive Masse f <Rakete>	acuity of vision	s. visual acuity
active movement <bio.>	Eigenbewegung f <Bio.>	acute bisectrix	spitze (erste) Bisektrix f, spitze (erste) Mittellinie f
active power, real power, actual power, power, wattage <el.>	Wirkleistung f, Wattleistung f, Wattstärke f, Wirkanteil m der Leistung, Wirkleistungskomponente f <El.>	acuteness <ac.>	Schärfe f <Ak.>
		acyclic <of flow>	s. circulation-free
		acyclic irrotational motion, acyclic potential motion	Potentialströmung f ohne Zirkulation
active region, active solar region	Aktivitätsgebiet n		
active resistance	s. resistance <el.>	acyclic potential motion	s. acyclic irrotational motion
active slip system	betätigtes Gleitsystem n	adamantine	diamantartig, mit Diamantstruktur
active solar region, active region	Aktivitätsgebiet n		
active sonar	s. ultrasonic echo-sounding device	Adams-Bashforth method (process)	Adamssches Interpolationsverfahren n
active spot	s. corona point	Adams extrapolation [method]	Adams Extrapolation f, Adamssches Extrapolationsverfahren (Verfahren) n
active Sun, disturbed Sun	gestörte Sonne f, aktive Sonne		
active sunspot prominence	aktive Fleckenprotuberanz f	Adams['] formula of interpolation, Adams['] interpolation formula	Adamssche Interpolationsformel f
active voltage, real voltage	Wirkspannung f, Wattspannung f, Wirkkomponente f (Wirkanteil m) der Spannung, Wirkspannungskomponente f	Adams-Störmer method, Störmer['s] method	Störmersches Extrapolationsverfahren n
		adaptation brightness, adaptation luminance, field luminance	Adaptationshelligkeit f, Adaptationsintensität f, Adaptationsleuchtdichte f, Gesichtsfeldleuchtdichte f
activity <chem.>	Aktivität f <Chem.>		
activity; intensity of radioactivity; radioactivity <nucl.>	Aktivität f <Größe, in Ci>; Anzahl f der zerfallenden Atome pro Zeiteinheit <Zerf./Zeiteinheit>; Radioaktivität f	adaptation of the cones	s. instantaneous adaptation
		adaptation of the rods	Daueradaptation f; Stäbchenanpassung f
activity coefficient	Aktivitätskoeffizient m	adaptation process, course of adaptation	Adaptationsvorgang m, Adaptationsprozeß m, Adaptationsverlauf m
activity curve	s. decay curve <nucl.>		
activity cycle	s. solar cycle	adaptation to light	s. light adaptation
activity decay, decay of radioactivity	Aktivitätsabfall m	adapting	s. fitting <math.>
		adapting filter	Angleichfilter n
activity density relative to surface, surface density of activity	Flächenaktivität f, spezifische Flächenaktivität, Flächendichte f der Aktivität, Aktivitätsdichte f je Flächeneinheit	adaptive control	adaptive Regelung f
		adaptive control; self-adjustment	Selbsteinstellung f
		adaptometer	Adaptometer n, Lichtsinnprüfer m
		added carrier concentration	s. excess carrier concentration
activity meter, radioactivity meter	Aktivitätsmesser m	added facility	s. supplementary apparatus
		added ion	s. impurity ion
activity of the waves	Wellentätigkeit f	adding day, intercalary day, leap day	Schalttag m
actual current, useful current	Nutzstrom m		
actual efficiency	s. actual power	addition <process> <chem.; techn.>	Zusetzung f, Zusatz m, Zugeben n, Zugabe f, Zufügung f <Vorgang>
actual energy	s. kinetic energy		
actual load	s. active load	addition, composition <process> <mech.>	Zusammensetzung f <Vorgang> <Mech.>
actual output, [useful] output, effective (power) output; useful power; power delivery	Nutzleistung f, Leistung f; Leistungsabgabe f		
		addition	s. a. attachment
actual output	s. a. actual power	additional band, sideband <spectr.>	Nebenbande f <Spektr.>
actual power, actual efficiency, actual output, real power	tatsächliche (effektive, wirkliche) Leistung f, Effektivleistung f	additional circuit	s. booster circuit
		additional condition	Zusatzbedingung f
		additional drag	s. trailing-edge drag
		additional equipment	s. supplementary apparatus
actual power	s. a. active power <el.>	additional inductance	s. incremental inductance
actual pressure	s. static pressure	additional measurement	Nachmessung f
actual value <control>	Istwert m [der Regelgröße]	additional noise	s. undesired noise
		additional optical system	s. additional system <opt.>
		additional point <geodesy>	Neupunkt m
		additional resistance	s. series resistance
		additional resistance	s. trailing-edge drag
		additional short-circuit current, supplementary short-circuit current	Zusatzkurzschlußstrom m
actual value, true value, absolute value, real value <meas.>	Istwert m, wahrer (tatsächlicher) Wert m, Absolutwert m <Meß.>		
		additional system, additional optical system <opt.>	optisches Zusatzsystem n, Zusatzsystem, Zusatzeinrichtung f <Opt.>
		additional treatment	s. subsequent treatment
		additional unit	s. supplementary apparatus
actuation, response	Ansprechen n	addition compound, additive compound	Additionsverbindung f, Anlagerungsverbindung f
actuation	s. a. action <control>	addition crystal	Additionskristall m, Additionsgitter n
actuation time	s. response time		
actuator <ac.>	Aktuator m <Ak.>		
actuator	s. a. final control element		
actuator disk	Impulsscheibe f	addition of velocities, addition theorem of velocity (velocities)	Additionstheorem n der Geschwindigkeiten
acuity of focusing, focusing acuity	Bündelungsschärfe f		
		addition polymerization, addition reaction, polyaddition, additive reaction	Polyaddition f, Polyadditionsreaktion f, Additionsreaktion f
acuity of hearing, hearing (auditory) acuity	Gehörschärfe f, Schärfe f des Gehörs, Hörschärfe f		

adjoint

addition position	Additionsstellung f
addition product, polyaddition product	Polyaddukt n, Polyadditionsprodukt n
addition reaction	s. addition polymerization
addition theorem of velocities (velocity)	s. addition of velocities
additive compound	s. addition compound
additive mixing <el.>	additive Mischung f <El.>
additive mixture [of colours], additive synthesis	additive Farbmischung f, additive Mischung f
additive process, stochastic process with independent increments, differential process	stochastischer Prozeß m mit unabhängigen Zuwächsen, additiver [stochastischer] Prozeß, Differentialprozeß m, räumlich homogener Markoffscher Prozeß
additive reaction	s. addition polymerization
additive synthesis	s. additive mixture
additive term	additives Glied n, additiver Term m, Zusatzglied n, Zusatzterm m
add-on unit	s. supplementary apparatus
adduct	s. EDA complex
adherence	s. adhesion
adherence number	Adhäsionszahl f, Adhäsionsbeiwert m
adherent point, point of closure <of the set>	Berührungspunkt m, adhärenter Punkt m, Limespunkt m <der Menge>
adherent vortex, bound vortex, bound vorticy	gebundener Wirbel m
adhering	s. adhesion
adherometer	Adhäsiometer n
adherometry	Adhäsionsmessung f, Adhäsiometrie f
adhesion, adherence, adhering; sticking	Adhäsion f; Haften n, Haftung f; Anhaften n
adhesion coefficient	Haftwert m
adhesion heat, heat of adhesion	Adhäsionswärme f
adhesion pressure	Adhäsionsdruck m
adhesion tension	s. adhesive tension
adhesive force	s. adhesiver power
adhesiveness	s. adhesive power
adhesive power, adhesive force, adhesivity, tackiness	Adhäsionskraft f, Haftkraft f, Haftfestigkeit f, Haftvermögen n, Haftfähigkeit f, Haftigkeit f, Klebkraft f, Bindekraft f, Zusammenhangskraft f
adhesive stress	s. adhesive tension
adhesive tension, adhesion tension, adhesive stress	Haftspannung f
adhesive water, pellicular water	Haftwasser n, Grundfeuchtigkeit f
adhesivity	s. adhesive power
adiabat	s. adiabatic curve
adiabatic	s. adiabatic curve
adiabatically closed	adiabatisch abgeschlossen
adiabatically unattainable	adiabatisch unerreichbar
adiabatic approximation	adiabatische Näherung f
adiabatic calorimeter	adiabatisches Kalorimeter n, Kalorimeter mit veränderlicher Temperatur
adiabatic change of state	adiabatische Zustandsänderung f, adiabatische Umwandlung f
adiabatic chart, adiabatic diagram	Adiabatendiagramm n
adiabatic coefficient of bulk compressibility	s. isentropic compressibility
adiabatic compressibility	s. isentropic compressibility
adiabatic condition, condition of adiabaticity	Adiabasiebedingung f, Adiabatenbedingung f
adiabatic curve, adiabatic [line], adiabat	Adiabate f
adiabatic curve of condensation, condensation adiabat, Hugoniot curve for condensation shock	Kondensationsadiabate f, Hugoniotsche Kurve f für Kondensationsstoß
adiabatic demagnetization	adiabatische Entmagnetisierung f
adiabatic diagram, adiabatic chart	Adiabatendiagramm n
adiabatic ellipse	s. velocity ellipse
adiabatic equation	s. Poisson['s] relation
adiabatic exponent	s. ratio of the specific heats
adiabatic factor	Adiabasiefaktor m
adiabatic gradient	s. adiabatic temperature gradient
adiabatic hypothesis	Adiabatenhypothese f
adiabatic index	s. ratio of the specific heats
adiabatic invariance, parameter invariance	adiabatische Invarianz f, Parameterinvarianz f
adiabatic invariant of eddy (vortex)	adiabatische Wirbelinvariante f
adiabatic ionization potential, true (spectroscopic value of) ionization potential	adiabatische Ionisierungsspannung f, wahre Ionisierungsspannung
adiabaticity, adiabatism	Adiabasie f
adiabatic-jacket microcalorimeter	s. adiabatic microcalorimeter
adiabatic law for quantized states [of Ehrenfest]	s. Ehrenfest['s] adiabatic law
adiabatic line	s. adiabatic curve
adiabatic microcalorimeter; adiabatic-jacket (adiabatic-shell) microcalorimeter	adiabatisches Mikrokalorimeter n
adiabatic model [of the nucleus], adiabatic nuclear model	adiabatisches Modell n [des Kerns], adiabatisches Kernmodell n
adiabatic modulus	adiabatischer Modul m
adiabatic nuclear model	s. adiabatic model
adiabatic partition	adiabatische Zwischenwand f
adiabatic principle, adiabatic theorem	Adiabatenprinzip n, Adiabatensatz m
adiabatic saturation temperature	adiabatische Sättigungstemperatur f
adiabatic screen	adiabatischer Schirm m
adiabatic-shell microcalorimeter	s. adiabatic microcalorimeter
adiabatic temperature gradient, adiabatic gradient	adiabatischer Temperaturgradient (Gradient) m, adiabatisches Gefälle n
adiabatic theorem	s. adiabatic principle
adiabatic trap	s. mirror machine
adiabatic wall	s. insulated wall
adiabatism	s. adiabaticity
adiactinic	adiaktinisch, nicht durchlässig für aktinische Strahlung
adiaphanous, non-translucent	adiaphan, nicht durchscheinend
adiathermic	s. athermanous
adion, adsorbed ion	Adion n, Haftion n
adjacency effect	s. neighbourhood effect
adjacent, infinitely adjacent	unendlich benachbart
adjacent bond	Nachbarbindung f
adjacent-channel interference; monkey chatter, monkey-chatter interference; splatter	Nachbarkanalstörung f; Splatter m
adjacent channel selectivity	Nahselektion f, Selektivität f gegenüber dem Nachbarkanal
adjacent event	benachbartes Ereignis n
adjacent wave	Nebenwelle f
adjoint <of the matrix>, adjoint matrix	Adjunktenmatrix f, adjungierte Matrix f
adjoint <of the matrix>	s. a. adjoint matrix
adjoint differential equation, adjoint of the differential equation	adjungierte Differentialgleichung f
adjoint matrix, adjoint, Hermitian (Hermitean) conjugate matrix, associate (conjugate, transposed and conjugate) matrix, Hermitian (Hermetean) conjugate <of the matrix>	adjungierte (begleitende, hermitsch konjugierte, konjugiert[-] transponierte, transponiert-konjugierte, transjungierte) Matrix f

adjoint

adjoint matrix	*s. a.* adjoint <of the matrix>
adjoint of the differential equation	*s.* adjoint differential equation
adjoint operator, adjoint transformation	adjungierter Operator *m*, adjungierte Transformation *f*
adjoint space, conjugate [space], dual (polar) space	adjungierter (dualer) Raum *m*, Dual *m*, konjugierter (polarer) Raum
adjoint transformation	*s.* adjoint operator
adjugate matrix	*s.* inverse <of the matrix>
adjunction	Adjunktion *f*
adjustable capacitor, variable capacitor	veränderbarer (veränderlicher, variabler) Kondensator *m*, Stellkondensator *m*, stellbarer (verstellbarer, regelbarer) Kondensator *m*, Regelkondensator *m*
adjustable gain amplifier	*s.* variable-gain amplifier
adjustable inductor	*s.* variometer
adjustable in steps	in Stufen verstellbar (einstellbar, regelbar), stufenweise regelbar
adjustable range thermometer	*s.* Beckmann thermometer
adjustable resistor	*s.* variable resistor
adjustable transformer	*s.* variable ratio transformer
adjusting potentiometer	*s.* balancing potentiometer
adjustment	Justierung *f*; Justage *f* <nur El.>
adjustment <of discriminator>	Einstellung *f* <Diskriminator>
adjustment, balancing [out], zero balance <el.>	Abgleich *m*, Nullabgleich *m* <El.>
adjustment <math.>	Ausgleichung *f* <Math.>
adjustment <to>; setting; setting-up; regulation	Stellen *n*; Einstellung *f*; Verstellung *f*; Richten *n* <auf>; Regulierung *f*, Einregulierung *f* <auf>, Einregeln *n* <auf>, Regeln *n*; Einstimmen *n*
adjustment button	*s.* focus control button
adjustment mark; framing index, index mark	Einstellmarke *f*
adjustment of errors	Fehlerausgleichung *f*, Fehlerausgleich *m*
adjustment performance <of molecular process>	Einstelldauer *f* <Molekularprozeß>
Adler tube	*s.* transverse field amplifier
admissible error	zulässiger Fehler *m*, Unsicherheit *f*
admissible error <control>	zulässige Regelabweichung *f* <Regelung>
admission of fluid to turbine blades, discharge of turbine	Beaufschlagung *f* der Turbine
admission velocity	*s.* entrance velocity
admittance <el.>	Admittanz *f*, Scheinleitwert *m*, Wechselstromleitwert *m*, Gesamtleitwert *m* <El.>
admittance	*s. a.* acoustic admittance <ac.>
admittance coefficient, admittance matrix coefficient, *Y* coefficient [of four-terminal network]	*Y*-Koeffizient *m* [des Vierpols]
admittance matrix	*Y*-Matrix *f*; Leitwertmatrix *f* <Vierpol>; Wellenleitwertmatrix *f* <Wellenleiter>
admittance matrix coefficient	*s.* admittance coefficient
admittance of driving point	*s.* input admittance
admittance operator	*s.* symbolic admittance
admittance per unit length	Leitwertbelag *m*; Wellenleitwertbelag *m*, Wellenleitwert *m* pro Längeneinheit
admittance tensor	Admittanztensor *m*
admittance-type partial-fraction network	Leitwert-Partialbruchschaltung *f*
admixture	*s.* impurity
adsorbability	Adsorbierbarkeit *f*
adsorbate, adsorbed matter	Adsorptiv *n*, adsorbierter Stoff *m*, Adsorbat *n*
adsorbate <adsorbing + adsorbed substance>	Adsorbat *n* <Adsorbens mit adsorbiertem Stoff>
adsorbed film, adsorption layer	Adsorptionsschicht *f*
adsorbed ion	*s.* adion
adsorbed matter, adsorbate	Adsorptiv *n*, adsorbierter Stoff *m*, Adsorbat *n*
adsorbed solid solution, anomalous solid solution, anomalous mixed crystals	Adsorptionsmischkristalle *mpl*, anomale Mischkristalle *mpl*
adsorbent	*s.* adsorbing substance
adsorber	*s.* adsorbing substance
adsorbing energy, energy of adsorption	Adsorptionsenergie *f*
adsorbing power	*s.* adsorption power
adsorbing substance, adsorbent, adsorber	Adsorbens *n* <*pl.*: -enzien>, Adsorptionsmittel *n*, Adsorber *m*
adsorptiometry	*s.* adsorption measurement
adsorption <on>	Adsorption *f* <an>
adsorption ability, ability of adsorption	Adsorptionsfähigkeit *f*
adsorption-active	adsorptionsaktiv
adsorption analysis	Adsorptionsanalyse *f*
adsorption balance	Adsorptionswaage *f*
adsorption capacity	*s.* adsorption power
adsorption catalysis	Adsorptionskatalyse *f*
adsorption chromatography, liquid-solid chromatography, chromatographic adsorption	Adsorptionschromatographie *f*
adsorption coefficient	Adsorptionskoeffizient *m*
adsorption-desorption	*s.* two-site sorption
adsorption double-electric layer, adsorption double layer	Adsorptionsanteil *m* der elektrochemischen Doppelschicht
adsorption entropy	*s.* entropy of adsorption
adsorption equation of Gibbs	*s.* Gibbs' adsorption equation
adsorption equilibrium	Adsorptionsgleichgewicht *n*
adsorption exponent	Adsorptionsexponent *m*
adsorption force	Adsorptionskraft *f*
adsorption formula of Gibbs	*s.* Gibbs' adsorption equation
adsorption formula of Langmuir	*s.* Langmuir['s] adsorption equation
adsorption formula of Volmer	*s.* Volmer['s] equation
adsorption heat, heat of adsorption	Adsorptionswärme *f*
adsorption hysteresis	Sorptionshysterese *f*, Adsorptionshysterese *f*
adsorption isobar	Adsorptionsisobare *f*
adsorption isostere	Adsorptionsisostere *f*
adsorption isotherm	Adsorptionsisotherme *f*
adsorption isotherm of Freundlich	*s.* Volmer['s] equation
adsorption isotherm of Gibbs	*s.* Gibbs' adsorption equation
adsorption isotherm of Langmuir	*s.* Langmuir['s] adsorption equation
adsorption isotherm of Volmer	*s.* Volmer['s] equation
adsorption layer, adsorbed film	Adsorptionsschicht *f*
adsorption limit	Adsorptionsgrenze *f*
adsorption measurement, adsorptiometry	Adsorptionsmessung *f*, Adsorptiometrie *f*
adsorption of impurities	*s.* impurity adsorption
adsorption potential	Adsorptionspotential *n*
adsorption power, adsorptivity, adsorption capacity, adsorbing power	Adsorptionsvermögen *n*, Adsorptionskapazität *f*, Bindungsvermögen *n*
adsorption pump, adsorption vacuum pump	Adsorptionspumpe *f*
adsorption rule of Hahn	Adsorptionsregel *f* von Hahn
adsorption series	Adsorptionsreihe *f*

adsorption space	Adsorptionsraum m	aerial switching, antenna switching, lobe switching	Antennenumschaltung f, Antennenumtastung f
adsorption spectrometer	Adsorptionsspektrometer n	aerial triangulation	Lufttriangulation f, Luftbildtriangulation f
adsorption strength, strength of adsorption	Adsorptionsstärke f, Stärke f der Adsorption	aero-acoustics	Luftschalltechnik f
adsorption structure	Adsorptionsstruktur f	aerocartograph; photogrammetric plotting instrument, machine plotting photogrammetric photographs, instrument capable of plotting from aerial photographs, restitution apparatus	Luftbildkartiergerät n, Bildkartiergerät n; Luftbildauswertegerät n
adsorption thermostat	Adsorptionsthermostat m, Desorptionsthermostat m		
adsorption trap	Adsorptionsfalle f		
adsorption vacuum pump	s. adsorption pump		
adsorptivity	s. adsorption power		
adulterant	s. impurity		
advance, advancing; leading, lead; speed-up	Voreilung f	aerocolloid	Aerokolloid n
		aerodynamic angle of attack	s. geometrical incidence
advance	s. a. forward movement	aerodynamic angle of incidence	s. geometrical incidence
advance angle	s. lead angle ⟨control⟩		
advance coefficient, coefficient of advance	Voreilungskoeffizient m	aerodynamic balance, wind tunnel balance	Windkanalwaage f, aerodynamische Waage f
advanced energy conversion	höhere Energieumwandlung f	aerodynamic balance	aerodynamischer Ausgleich m
advanced potential	avanciertes Potential n		
advanced reactor	fortgeschrittener Reaktor m		
advanced wave	avancierte Welle f	aerodynamic centre, focus, centre of pressure ⟨of profile⟩	aerodynamischer Mittelpunkt m, Neutralpunkt m, Druck[mittel]punkt m, Druckzentrum n ⟨Profil⟩
advance of perihelion, perihelion motion	Periheldrehung f, Perihelbewegung f, Perihelpräzession f, Perihelverschiebung f		
		aerodynamic coefficient	aerodynamischer Beiwert m
advance of phase	s. phase leading	aerodynamic derivative, resistance derivative, partial air force	partielle Ableitung f von aerodynamischen Kräften ⟨oder Momenten⟩
advancer	s. phase advancer		
advancing	s. advance		
advancing	s. forward movement	aerodynamic drag, drag, aerodynamic (air) resistance, resistance of air; windage	Luftwiderstand m
advancing motion	s. translational motion		
advancing rate, rate of advance	Voreilgeschwindigkeit f		
advancing wave	s. travelling wave	aerodynamic force, air force	Luftkraft f, aerodynamische Kraft f
advantage factor	optimales Bestrahlungsverhältnis n, Advantagefaktor m, Vorteilfaktor m, Überhöhungsfaktor m, Flußfaktor m		
		aerodynamic heating	aerodynamische Erwärmung f, Erhitzung f durch die Reibungswärme
advection fog	Advektionsnebel m	aerodynamic lift	s. dynamic lift ⟨aero., hydr.⟩
advective frost	Windfrost m, Advektivfrost m	aerodynamic lift	s. lift ⟨aero., hydr.⟩
		aerodynamic noise	aerodynamisches Rauschen n
advective layer	Advektionsschicht f	aerodynamic resistance	s. aerodynamic drag
aeolian erosion	s. deflation		
Aeolian harp	Äolsharfe f	aerodynamics	Aerodynamik f, Lehre f vom Flug
aeolian tone	Anblaston m		
aeolight	modulierbare Glimmlampe f; Glimmlichtoszillographenlampe f, Glimmlichtoszillograph m; Punktglimmlampe f	aerodynamic spectrum	aerodynamisches Strömungsbild n
		aerodynamic time	aerodynamische Zeit[einheit] f
		aerodynamic tunnel	s. wind tunnel
aeolotropic, eolotropic	äolotrop, anisotrop	aerodynamic volume displacement	Luftverdrängung f, verdrängtes Luftvolumen n
aeolotropy	Äolotropie f		
aerial booster, antenna booster, antenna amplifier	Antennenverstärker m	aeroelasticity	Aeroelastizität f, Aeroelastik f
aerial camera	s. air camera	aeroelastic triangle of forces, Collar triangle	Collarsches Dreieck n
aerial coupling, antenna coupling	Antennenkopplung f, Antennenankopplung f	aerofoil border of attack, aerofoil profile nose	s. profile nose
aerial dust filter, dust filter	Staubfilter n	aerogel	Aerogel n
		aerogradiometer	Luftgradiometer n, Aerogradiometer n
aerial effect, antenna effect	Antenneneffekt m	aerohydrodynamic	strömungsdynamisch
aerial efficiency, antenna efficiency	Antennenwirkungsgrad m	aerohydrodynamics, fluid dynamics	Strömungsdynamik f, Aerohydrodynamik f
		aerolite, stony meteorite, meteoritic stone, meteorolite	Steinmeteorit m, Aerolith m, Meteorstein m, Asiderit m
aerial fog, fog caused by developers exposed to air	Luftschleier m		
aerial gain, gain of antenna, power gain, directive gain, aerial power gain ⟨of antenna⟩	Antennengewinn m, Gewinn m der Antenne; Antennenrichtfaktor m, Leistungsgewinn m; Strahlbündelungsfaktor m; Richt[strahl]schärfe f, Strahlschärfe f, Bündelungsschärfe f, Strahlgüte f, Bündelungsgüte f, Güte f der Bündelung	aerological map, altitude chart, upper-air chart	Höhenkarte f, aerologische Karte f; Höhenströmungskarte f
		aerology	Aerologie f, Physik f der freien Atmosphäre
		aeromagnetic survey-[ing]	aeromagnetische Vermessung f
		aeromagnetometer airborne magnetometer	Aeromagnetometer n
aerial photograph, aerophotogram	Luftmeßbild n, Luftaufnahme f, Luftbild n, Aeroaufnahme f	aerometer	Aerometer n, Luftdichtemesser m
		aeronomy	Aeronomie f
		aerophily	Aerophilie f
aerial power gain	s. aerial gain	aerophotogram	s. aerial photograph
aerial spacing; interferometer base	Antennenabstand m; Interferometerbasislänge f, Interferometerbasis f, Basislänge f	aerophotogrammetric map	s. photogrammetric map
		aerophotogrammetry	s. air photogrammetry
		aerosol, sogasoid	Aerosol n, Luftkolloid n

aerosol 20

aerosol filter	Aerosolfilter n, Schwebstoffilter n; absolutes Filter n
aerosol particle, aerosol particulate, particulate [of aerosol]	Aerosolteilchen n, Schwebeteilchen n, Schwebstoffteilchen n, schwebendes Teilchen n, Schweb[e]stoff m, Schwebekörper m
aerosol particulates present in the air	Luftplankton n, Aeroplankton n
aerosol spectrometer	Aerosolspektrometer n
aerosol transport	s. silt transport
aerotaxis	Aerotaxis f
aerothermochemistry	Aerothermochemie f
aerothermodynamics	Aerothermodynamik f
aerothermoelasticity	Aerothermoelastizität f
aerotopographic map	s. photogrammetric map
aerotriangulation	Aerotriangulation f [im Raum]; Aeropolygonierung f; Aeronivellement n
aerotropism	Aerotropismus m
aether	s. ether <opt.>
aethrioscope	s. differential thermometer
afferent	afferent <Bio.>
affine connected space, affinely connected space	affin-zusammenhängender Raum m
affine connection, affine transfer	affiner Zusammenhang m, affine Übertragung f
affine group	affine Gruppe f
affinely connected space, affine connected space	affin-zusammenhängender Raum m
affine transfer	s. affine connection
affine transformation, affinity <math.>	affine Transformation f, affine Abbildung f, Affinität f <Math.>
affinity <chem., el.chem., therm.>; [generalized] force <irreversible therm.>	Affinität f <Chem., El.chem., Therm.>
affinity	s. a. affine transformation <math.>
affinor	Affinor m
affinor	s. a. tensor
affluent of cold air, afflux of cold air	Kaltluftzufuhr f, Kaltluftzufluß m
afflux	s. water-surface ascent
afocal image, telescopic image	brennpunktlose (afokale, teleskopische) Abbildung f
after-accelerating tube, after-accelerator tube	Nachbeschleunigungsrohr n
after-acceleration <acc.>	Nachbeschleunigung f
after-accelerator tube	s. after-accelerating tube
after bay	s. lower pool
aftercooler	Nachkühler m
after count, after discharge, re[-]ignition	Nachentladung f, Nachimpuls m, Wiederzündung f; Nachzündung f; Rückzündung f
aftercurrent <el.>	Nachstrom m <El.>
after discharge	s. after count
after-discharge spark	Nachentladungsfunke m
after-effect, remanence; memory effect	Nachwirkung f, Nachwirkungseffekt m, Nachwirkungserscheinung f
after-effect function, elastic after-effect function	Nachwirkungsfunktion f
afteremission	s. exoelectronic emission
after[]flow	s. plastic after flow
afterglow; persistence <of screen>	Nachleuchten n <Lumineszenz>; Nachglimmen n; Nachglühen n <Dämmerungserscheinung>
afterglow duration	s. persistence
afterglow screen	s. persistence screen
after-heat, shut-down heat <of reactor>	Nachwärme f, Restwärme f, Abschaltwärme f <Reaktor>
after-heat <therm.>, residual heat capacity	Restwärme f <Therm.>
afterimage, residual image	Nachbild n
after-potential	Nachpotential n
after-power <of reactor>	Restleistung f <Reaktor>
after pulse	Nach[lauf]impuls m; Nachläufer m; Spätimpuls m
after[-]shock <geo.>	Nachläufer m, Nachläuferstoß m, Nachschock m
aftershock wave <geo.>	Nachläuferwelle f, Nachläufer m
after-treatment	s. subsequent treatment
aftertrial	s. testing
age	s. Fermi age <nucl.>
age determination	s. dating
age distribution	Altersverteilung f, altersmäßige Verteilung f
age equation	Fermi-Alter-Gleichung f, Altersgleichung f
age estimation	s. dating
age-hardening, precipitation hardening, dispersion hardening; maraging	Aushärtung f, Ausscheidungshärtung f, Aushärtung f; Martensitaushärtung f
age hardening at elevated temperature[s]	s. hot work hardening <of metals>
age hardening at room temperature	s. room-temperature ageing <of metals>
age hardening by cold work[ing]	s. room-temperature ageing <of metals>
ageing, aging, seasoning <of material>	Alterung f <natürliche, der Werkstoffe>
ageing	s. a. aging <of neutrons>
ageing at room temperature	s. room-temperature ageing <of metals>
ageing fog	Alterungsschleier m
ageing with increased temperatures	s. hot work hardening
age measurement	s. dating
ageostrophic	ageostrophisch
ageotropic	ageotrop
ageotropism	Ageotropismus m
age theory	[Fermische] Alterstheorie f, Fermi-Alterstheorie f, Fermische Theorie f der Neutronenbremsung (Bremsung), Fermische Theorie des Neutronenalters
agglomeration	Agglomeration f
agglomeration	s. a. sintering
agglutinability	Agglutinationsvermögen n
agglutinant	s. binder
agglutination	Agglutination f, Verklumpung f, Verklebung f, Zusammenballung f
aggregate	s. set <math.>
aggregate of eight hydrols	Achteraggregat n [von Wasser]
aggregate of four hydrols	Viereraggregat n <von Wasser>
aggregate of points	s. scatter diagram
aggregate recoil	Molekülrückstoß m, Aggregatrückstoß m
aggregate strength, composite strength	zusammengesetzte Festigkeit f
aggregation	Aggregation f, Zusammenballung f <durch Kohäsion>
aggregation	s. a. accumulation
aggregation state	s. state of aggregation
aggregative polarization	Aggregatpolarisation f
aging, ageing <of neutrons>	Alterung f, kontinuierliche Abbremsung f
aging	s. a. ageing <of material>
agitation, excitation; excitement <bio.>	Erregung f <Bio.>
agitation <techn.>	Bewegung f, [turbulente] Durchmischung f, Mischung f, Verwirblung f
agitation	s. a. excitation
agitation	s. a. shaking

agonic line, isogonic [zero] line	Agone *f*, Nullisogone *f*	**aircraft sextant,** bubble sextant	Libellensextant *m*
		air cushion, cushion of air	Luftkissen *n*; Luftpolster *n*
agravic, weightless, imponderable	schwerelos	**air-cushion craft (vehicle)**	s. hovercraft
agricultural physics, agrophysics	Agrophysik *f*	**air damping,** air friction damping	Luftdämpfung *f*, Luftkammerdämpfung *f*
agrophysics, agricultural physics	Agrophysik *f*		
AG synchrotron	s. alternating gradient synchrotron	**air dielectric**	Luftdielektrikum *n*
Aharonov-Bohm effect	Aharonov-Bohm-Effekt *m*	**air-dielectric capacitor**	s. air capacitor
Ahren['s] triple prism	Ahrens-Prisma *n*, Polarisationsprisma *n* nach Ahrens, Ahrenssches Prisma *n*	**air dose**	s. free air dose
		air-dried, air-dry	lufttrocken, luftgetrocknet
		air-earth current, vertical current	luftelektrischer Vertikalstrom *m* [bei Schönwetterlage], Vertikalstrom, vertikaler elektrischer Strom *m*, vertikaler Leitungsstrom *m*, Luft-Erde-Strom *m*, Schönwettervertikalstrom *m*
aiming, taking the aim; sighting <opt.>	Visieren *n*, Visur *f*; Zielen *n*; Visierkunst *f*; Richten *n* <Opt.>		
aiming axis	s. collimation axis		
aiming error	s. collimation error		
aiming line	s. collimation axis		
aiming-off, allowance <opt.>	Vorhalten *n* <Opt.>	**air-earth current density**	Dichte *f* des luftelektrischen Vertikalstroms, Vertikalstromdichte *f*
air arc, arc burning in air	Luftbogen *m*		
air avalanche	Luftlawine *f*	**air ejector,** ejector, air jet pump	Luftstrahlpumpe *f*, Saugstrahlpumpe *f*, Strahlpumpe *f*, Strahlsauger *m*
airborne	durch die Luft verschleppt, mit der Luft mitgeführt, in der Luft schwebend, freischwebend, lufttransportiert, luftverfrachtet		
		air entrainment, entrainment of air	Luftmitführung *f*
		air equivalent	Luftäquivalent *n*
airborne contamination	Kontamination *f* der Luft, Luftkontamination *f*, Luftverseuchung *f*, [radioaktive] Verseuchung *f* der Luft	**air equivalent ionization chamber**	s. air-wall ionization chamber
		air equivalent material	s. air-wall material
		air excess [number]; air factor, air ratio	Luftverhältnis *n*, Luftfaktor *m*; Luftüberschußzahl *f*
airborne magnetometer, aeromagnetometer	Aeromagnetometer *n*	**air-filled ionization chamber**	s. free[-]air ionization chamber
airborne oil fog, oil mist, oil fog	Ölnebel *m*	**air flash**	s. cloud lightning discharge
airborne radioactivity, atmospheric radioactivity, radioactivity of air	Radioaktivität *f* der Luft, Luftradioaktivität *f*, in der Luft vorhandene Radioaktivität	**air-flow meter,** air meter	Luftmengenmesser *m*
		airfoil of delta shape	s. delta wing
		airfoil of infinite span	Tragflügel (Flügel) *m* unendlich großer Spannweite
airborne sound, sound transmitted in air, sound in air	Luftschall *m*		
		airfoil profile, airfoil section, wing profile, airfoil flap	Tragflügelprofil *n*, Flügelprofil *n*, Profil *n* des Tragflügels
airborne sound insulation	Luftschalldämmung *f*		
air-bubble viscometer	Luftblasenviskosimeter *n*	**airfoil theory**	Tragflügeltheorie *f*
air burst	Explosion *f* in der Atmosphäre, Hochexplosion *f*		
air camera, aerial camera	Luftbildaufnahmegerät *n*, Luftbildmeßkammer *f*	**air force**	s. aerodynamic force
		air friction, windage	Luftreibung *f*
		air friction damper	Luftdämpfer *m*
		air friction damping	s. air damping
air cap, compression cap	Verdichtungszone *f* <z. B. vor dem Meteorkörper>	**air gap;** magnet gap, pole gap, magnet space, gap <magn.>	Luftspalt *m*; Interferrikum *n* <Magn.>
air capacitor, air-dielectric capacitor, air-spaced capacitor	Luftkondensator *m*		
air chamber model, air vessel model	Windkesselmodell *n*	**air gap**	s. a. spark gap
		air-gap width	s. width of air gap
air circulation	Luftumwälzung *f*; Luftzirkulation *f*, Luftumlauf *m*	**airglow,** air glow, self-luminescence of upper atmosphere	Eigenleuchten *n* der Erdatmosphäre, atmosphärisches Eigenleuchten, Wiederleuchten *n*, Himmelsleuchten *n*, Luftleuchten *n*, Luftglühen *n*
air circulation	s. a. atmospheric circulation		
air close to the soil surface	s. near-ground air		
air column, column of air	Luftsäule *f*	**airglow layer,** emitting (emission) layer, glow-emitting layer	Emissionsschicht *f*, Schicht *f* des Nachthimmelsleuchtens
air conditioning, conditioning of air	Luftkonditionierung *f*, Luftaufbereitung *f*, Luftbehandlung *f*, Klimatisierung *f*, Konditionierung *f* der Luft		
		air inrush	Lufteinbruch *m*; Luftdurchbruch *m*, Luftdurchtritt *m*; Luftdurchgang *m*
air conduction <ac.>	Luftleitung *f* <Ak.>	**air ionization**	s. ionization of air
air-cooled tube, dry tube, metal-cooled tube	luftgekühlte Röhre *f*, Luftkühlröhre *f*, Trockenröhre *f*, Metallkühlröhre *f*	**air ionization chamber**	s.free[-]air ionization chamber
		air jet pump	s. air ejector
air core <el.>	Luftkern *m* <El.>	**air jet pump**	s. jet pump
air-core betatron	s. iron-free betatron	**air lens**	Luftlinse *f*
air-core coil, air-cored solenoid	Luftspule *f*	**air lift; air lift pump**	Druckluftheber *m*, Druckheber *m*, Lufteberanlage *f*; Druckluftwasserheber *m*, Wasserluftpumpe *f*; Mammutpumpe *f*
		air light	Luftlicht *n*; Albedo *f* des Luftplanktons <Weber>
air-core magnet	eisenloser Magnet *m*		

air line <spectr.>	Luftlinie f, Luftspektrallinie f <Spektr.>	Airy-Heiskanen isostatic system, Airy-Heiskanen system	Isostasie f nach Airy[-Heiskanen]; isostatisches System n nach Airy[-Heiskanen]
air liquefaction	Luftverflüssigung f		
air liquefier	Luftverflüssigungsmaschine f	Airy['s] integral	s. rainbow integral of Airy
airlock	Luftschleuse f	Airy['s] points	Airysche Punkte mpl
airlock <of electron microscope>	Schleuse f <Elektronenmikroskop>	Airy['s] rainbow integral	s. rainbow integral of Airy
air-magnetic cross-section, cross-section of magnetic path in air	luftmagnetischer Querschnitt m	Airy['s] rainbow theory, rainbow theory of Airy	Regenbogentheorie f von Airy, Airysche Theorie f des Regenbogens
air-mass boundary	s. boundary of the air mass	Airy['s] relation	Airysche Tangentenbedingung f
air meter	s. air-flow meter		
air moisture	s. atmospheric moisture	Airy spirals	Airysche Spiralen fpl
air moisture measurement	s. hygrometry	Airy['s] stress function, potential function of Airy	Airysche Spannungsfunktion f, Potentialfunktion f von Airy, Airy-Spannungsfunktion f
air particle, particle of air	Luftpartikel f, Luftteilchen n		
air photogrammetry, aerophotogrammetry	Luftbildmessung f, Aerophotogrammetrie f; Luftphotogrammetrie f	Aitken counter	Aitkenscher Kernzähler m, Aitken-Zähler m
		Aitken['s] criterion [for double stars]	Aitkensches Kriterium n [für Doppelsterne]
"air photo mosaic"	s. mosaic <photogrammetry>	alabamine	s. astatine
air plasma	Luftplasma n	alabamium	s. astatine
air plug	Luftpfropfen m	Alaskian-type glacier	s. piedmont glacier
air pollution	s. atmospheric pollution	albany grease	s. grease
air pressure	s. barometric pressure	albedo, reflecting ability	Albedo f, Rückstrahl[ungs]vermögen n
air pressure head, atmospheric pressure head, barometric height	atmosphärische Druckhöhe f, Luftdruckhöhe f, Atmosphärendruckhöhe f	albedo	s. a. reflection coefficient <for particles, e.g. neutrons>
air ratio	s. air excess		
air recirculation	Luftrücklauf m, Luftrückführung f; Rückluft f	albedo	s. a. Bond['s] albedo <opt.>
		albedo of the clouds, cloud albedo	Wolkenalbedo f
air resistance	s. aerodynamic drag	Albert effect <phot.>	Albert-Effekt m <Phot.>
air scatter	Luftstreustrahlung f	albumen process <phot.>	Eiweißverfahren n, Taupenot-Verfahren n <Phot.>
airscrew	s. propeller		
airscrew blade	s. blade	alcohol thermometer, spirit thermometer	Alkoholthermometer n
air seal	Luftabschluß m	Alembert['s] auxiliary force / d'	s. force of inertia
		Alembert['s] differential equation / d'	s. differential equation of d'Alembert-Lagrange
air seismology	s. seismology of atmosphere	Alembert equation / d', d'Alembert system, linear system with constant coefficients	d'Alembertsches System n [von gewöhnlichen Differentialgleichungen], homogenes lineares Differentialgleichungssystem n mit konstanten Koeffizienten, lineares System mit konstanten Koeffizienten
air separation	Luftzerlegung f		
air separation	Windsichtung f, Sichtung f		
air separator, pneumatic sizer	Windsichter m		
air shower	Luftschauer m	Alembert equation / d' <el.>	d'Alembertsche Gleichung f <El.>
air shrinkage, dry shrinkage	Trockenschwindung f	Alembert-Euler formula / d'	d'Alembert-Eulersche Formel f, Formel von d'Alembert-Euler <für die Beschleunigung>
air-sonde	s. test balloon		
air-spaced capacitor	s. air capacitor	Alembert formula / d'	d'Alembertsche Formel f
airspeed <aero.>	Fluggeschwindigkeit f, Relativgeschwindigkeit f [gegenüber Luft] <Aero.>	Alembert['s] general integral / d'	d'Alembertsches allgemeines Integral n, d'Alembertsche Lösung f <der Wellengleichung>
air streak, atmospheric streak, air (atmospheric) stria	Luftschliere f		
		Alembertian / d', d'Alembertian operator, Dalembertian, □	d'Alembertscher Operator m, D'Alembert-Operator m, Viereckoperator m, □
air streamline, streamline <meteo.>	Stromlinie f, Strombahn f, Strömungslinie f, Luftstromlinie f, Luftstrombahn f, Luftströmungslinie f <Meteo.>	Alembertian operator / d'	s. Alembertian / d'
		Alembert-Lagrange variational principle/d'	s. Lagrange-d'Alembert principle
air stria	s. air streak	Alembert['s] paradox/ d'	s. hydrodynamic paradox of d'Alembert
air telescope	Luftfernrohr n		
air temperature	s. shade temperature	Alembert['s] principle/d'	d'Alembertsches Prinzip n, Lagrangesches Prinzip, D'Alembert-Prinzip n, Prinzip n von d'Alembert
air thermometer, atmospherical thermometer	Luftthermometer n		
air trajectory, trajectory of air [particle]; trajectory of air mass	Luftbahn f, Lufttrajektorie f, Trajektorie f der Luftteilchen	Alembert['s] ratio test / d'	s. Cauchy['s] ratio test
		Alembert solution / d	d'Alembertsche Lösung f, Bernoullische Lösung
air vessel model, air chamber model	Windkesselmodell n	Alembert system / d	s. Alembert equation / d'
air-wall ionization chamber	Luftwändekammer f, luftäquivalente Ionisationskammer f	Alembert['s] test [for convergence] / d'	s. Cauchy's ratio test
		Alfvén flow	Alfvén-Strömung f, Alfvénsche Strömung f
air-wall material, air equivalent material	Luftwändematerial n, luftäquivalentes Material n	Alfvén number	Alfvén-Zahl f, Alfvénsche Zahl f, magnetische Mach-Zahl f
air wave, atmospheric wave	Luftwoge f, Luftwelle f		
air wedge	s. lame étalon	Alfvén['s] phase velocity	s. Alfvén['s] velocity
air wing	s. wind turbine	Alfvén['s] velocity, Alfvén['s] phase velocity	Alfvénsche Phasengeschwindigkeit (Geschwindigkeit) f, Alfvén-Geschwindigkeit f
Airy['s] disk	Airy-Scheibchen n, Airysches Beugungsscheibchen		
Airy['s] free wave	s. swell	Alfvén wave	Alfvén-Welle f, Alfvénsche Welle f
Airy functions	Airysche Funktionen fpl		

algebra; hypercomplex system	Algebra f; hyperkomplexes System n, assoziative K-Algebra (R-Algebra) f	allobar	Allobar n
algebraic adjoint	s. cofactor <math.>	allocatalysis	Allokatalyse f
algebraic branch point	s. algebraic singularity	allocation, allotment	Zuteilung f, Zuordnung f, Verteilung f
algebraic multiplicity o the eigenvalue	Rang m (algebraische Vielfachheit f) des Eigenwertes	allochromatic	allochromatisch, fremdfarbig, gefärbt
algebraic operation	s. composition <math.>	allochromatic colouration, allochromatism	allochromatische Färbung f, Fremdfärbung f
algebraic singularity, algebraic branch point	algebraische Singularität f, algebraischer Verzweigungspunkt m, algebraische singuläre Stelle f	allogyric double refraction, circular double refraction, circular birefringence	zirkulare Doppelbrechung f
algebra of currents	s. current algebra	alloisomerism	s. geometrical isomerism
algebra of logic	s. Boolean algebra	allomerism	Allomerie f
algebroid function	algebroide Funktion f	all-or-none law, all-or-none-principle	Alles-oder-Nichts-Gesetz n, Alles-oder-Nichts-Prinzip n
Algol-type eclipsing binary, Algol variable	Algol-Veränderlicher m, Algol-Stern m, Bedeckungsveränderlicher m vom Algol-Typ	allotment, allocation	Zuteilung f, Zuordnung f, Verteilung f
alhidade, alidade, sight-rule, sighting arm	Alhidade f	allotment, dosage	Dosierung f, Zumessung f
		allotriomorphic, xenomorphic, anhedral	allotriomorph, xenomorph, fremdgestaltig
alidade circle	Alhidadekreis m	allotrope	s. allotropic modification
alighting [on water]	s. landing on water	allotropic change	s. allotropic transformation
alignment <geo.>	Fluchtung f; Ausfluchtung f, Richten n <Geo.>	allotropic modification, allotropic phase, allotrope	allotrope Modifikation f
alignment <phys., chem.>, orientation	Orientierung f, Ausrichtung f <Phys., Chem.>	allotropic transformation, allotropic change	allotrope Umwandlung f
alignment	s. a. alignment nomogram	allowable limits	s. tolerance
alignment chart	s. alignment nomogram	allowable working stress	s. permissible stress
alignment nomogram, alignment chart, alignment, self-computing chart	Fluchtliniennomogramm n, Fluchtlinientafel f, Fluchtentafel f, kollineare Rechentafel f	allowance <opt.>, aiming-off	Vorhalten n <Opt.>
		allowance	s. a. tolerance
		allowance	s. a. gap <techn.>
alignment of tuned circuit, subsequent adjustment	Nachstimmung f	allowed l-forbidden transition	s. unfavoured transition
		allowedness, permissibility, permission	Erlaubtheit f
aliquot, aliquot part	aliquoter Teil m, Aliquot n	allowed transition	erlaubter Übergang m
aliquot string	Aliquotsaite f	alloyage	s. alloying <met.>
alkali earth	s. alkaline earth	alloy-diffused transistor, alloy diffusion transistor	legierungsdiffundierter (diffusionslegierter) Transistor m, Legierungsdiffusionstransistor m
alkali earth metal, alkaline earth metal	Erdalkalimetall n		
alkali metal	Alkalimetall n		
alkali-metal vapour lamp	Alkalidampflampe f, Alkalimetallampe f	alloyed junction, alloy junction	legierter (einlegierter) Übergang m, Legierungsübergang m
alkalimeter	Alkalimeter n, Laugenmesser m	alloyed zone, alloy zone	Legierungsschicht f, Legierungsschichtzone f
alkaline earth, alkali earth	alkalische Erde f, Erdalkali n	alloying, alloyage, melting together, fusion <met.>	Legieren n, Zusammenschmelzung f, Verschmelzung f, Zuschmelzung f <Met.>
alkaline earth group	Erdalkaligruppe f		
alkaline earth metal	s. alkali earth metal		
alkaline earth metal spectrum	s. alkaline earth spectrum		
alkaline earth spectrum, alkaline earth metal spectrum	Erdalkalispektrum n, Zweielektronenspektrum n	alloying constituent; alloying element	Legierungsbestandteil m; Legierungskomponente f; Legierungselement n
		alloy junction	s. alloyed junction
alkaline number, alkalinity number	Alkalitätszahl f, AZ	alloy zone, alloyed zone	Legierungsschicht f, Legierungsschichtzone f
alkaline reserve	Alkalireserve f	all-pass element	Allpaßelement n, reiner Phasenschieber m
alkalinity	Alkalität f		
alkalinity number	s. alkaline number	all-pass filter, all-pass network, universal filter (network)	Allpaß m
alkali spectrum	Alkalispektrum n		
allactinic radiation	allaktine Strahlung f		
Allard['s] relation	Tragweitenformel f [von Allard], Allardsche Tragweitenformel	all-purpose lens	Universalobjektiv n, Standardobjektiv n
		all-round looking radar	s. panoramic radar
all-band antenna	Allbereichantenne f, Allwellenantenne f	alluvial cone	s. debris cone
		alluvial soil	s. drift soil
all-dielectric filter	s. multilayer dielectric interference filter	almost certain convergence <stat.>	fast sichere Konvergenz f, starke Konvergenz <Stat.>
all-dry high-vacuum pump	s. sorption pump	almost everywhere, a. e.	fast überall
allelotropy	Allelotropie f	almost free-molecule flow	fast freie Molekularströmung f
Allen belt / Van	s. Allen radiation belt / Van		
Allen layer / Van	s. Allen radiation belt / Van	almost-periodic <e.g. of a function>	fastperiodisch <z. B. Funktion>
Allen radiation belt / Van, radiation (Van Allen) belt, extraterrestrial zone of radiation, [Van Allen] radiation zone, Van Allen zone (layer), trapped-radiation region	Strahlungsgürtel m [der Erde], Van-Allen-Gürtel m, van Allenscher Strahlungsgürtel, Van-Allen-Strahlungsgürtel m, Strahlengürtel m [der Erde]	almucantar[at]; parallel of altitude	Almukantar m; Azimutalkreis m
		aloft wind	s. high-altitude wind
		alpen-glow, alp-glow	s. Alps glow
		alpha active	s. alpha radioactive
		alpha activity, alpha radioactivity	Alpha-Aktivität f; Alpha-Radioaktivität f
Allen radiation zone / Van	s. Allen radiation belt / Van	alpha branch	Alpha-Zweig m, Alpha-Verzweigung f
Allen zone / Van	s. Allen radiation belt / Van		
alligation, rule of alligation	Mischungsrechnen n	alpha counter, alpha meter <including electronic equipment>	Alpha-Zähler m, Alpha-Zählgerät n

alpha

alpha counter	s. a. alpha counter tube
alpha counter tube, alpha counter	Alpha-Zählrohr n
alpha cut-off frequency	Alpha-Grenzfrequenz f, Alpha-Abschneidefrequenz f
alpha decay	s. alpha disintegration
alpha-deuteron model	Alpha-Deuteron-Modell n
alpha disintegration, alpha decay	Alpha-Zerfall m, Alpha-Umwandlung f
alpha disintegration constant, alpha decay constant	Alpha-Zerfallskonstante f
alpha disintegration energy, alpha decay energy	Alpha-Zerfallsenergie f, Alpha-Umwandlungsenergie f
alpha disintegration scheme, alpha decay scheme	Alpha-Zerfallsschema n
alpha dosimetry	s. alpha-particle dosimetry
alpha emitter, alpha-ray emitter	Alpha-Strahler m
alpha emitting	s. alpha radioactive
alpha-iron	s. ferrite
alpha meter	s. alpha counter <including electronic equipment>
alpha-neutron reaction, <α, n>-reaction	Alpha-Neutron-Reaktion f, <α, n>-Reaktion f
alpha particle, alpha ray; helion, helium nucleus <⁴He>	Alpha-Teilchen n; Helion n, Heliumkern m <⁴He>
alpha-particle binding energy	Alpha-Bindungsenergie f, Bindungsenergie f des Alpha-Teilchens
alpha-particle detector	Alpha-Detektor m, Detektor m für Alpha-Strahlung
alpha-particle dosimetry, alpha[-ray] dosimetry	Alpha-Strahldosimetrie f, Alpha-Dosimetrie f
alpha-particle model [of nucleus]	Alpha-Teilchenmodell n [des Atomkerns], Alpha-Teilchen-Kernmodell n
alpha-particle radiation	s. alpha radiation
alpha-particle radioautography	Alpha-Autoradiographie f
alpha-particle source, source of alpha-particles	Alpha-Strahlungsquelle f, Alpha-Quelle f
alpha particle spectrometer	s. alpha spectrometer
alpha particle spectrometry	s. alpha spectrometry
alpha-particle spectrum, alpha spectrum	Alpha-Spektrum n, Alpha-Teilchenspektrum n
alpha-particle thickness gauge (meter)	Alpha-Dickenmesser m
alpha-particle track, alpha track	Alpha-Spur f, Alpha-Teilchen-Spur f
alpha process	s. triple-alpha process
alpha-proton reaction, <α, p>-reaction	Alpha-Proton-Reaktion f, <α, p>-Reaktion f
alpha radiation, alpha rays, alpha-particle radiation	Alpha-Strahlung f, Alpha-Strahlen mpl, radioaktive Alpha-Strahlung f
alpha radiator	s. alpha emitter
alpha radioactive, alpha active, alpha emitting	alpha-aktiv, alpha-strahlend
alpha radioactivity	s. alpha activity
alpha ray	s. alpha particle
alpha rays	s. alpha radiation
alpha spectrometer, alpha particle (ray) spectrometer	Alpha-Spektrometer n, Alpha-Strahlspektrometer n
alpha spectrometry, alpha particle (ray) spectrometry	Alpha-Spektrometrie f, Alpha-Strahlspektrometrie f
alpha spectrum	s. alpha-particle spectrum
alphatopic	alphatop
alpha track, alpha-particle track	Alpha-Spur f, Alpha-Teilchen-Spur f
alpha transformation	s. alpha disintegration
alpha transition <nucl.>	Alpha-Übergang m <Kern.>
alphatron, alphatron gauge	Alphatron n
Alphen effect / Van alphina particle, ³He nucleus, tau, τ	Van-Alphen-Effekt m Alphina-Teilchen n, ³He-Kern m
Alpine glacier, Alpine-type glacier	Firnfeldgletscher m, alpiner Gletschertyp m
Alps glow, alp-glow, alpen-glow	Alpenglühen n
altazimuth	Altazimut n (m)
altazimuth mounting	altazimutale Fernrohrmontierung f
alteration, falsification <of the results>	Verfälschung f [der Meßergebnisse]
alteration	s. a. change <gen.>
alteration	s. a. weathering <geo.>
alteration theory	Alterationstheorie f
alternant	s. Vandermonde determinant
alternate bending strength	s. alternating bending strength
alternated derivative	alternierende Ableitung f
alternate-immersion test, alternating-immersion test	Wechseltauchversuch m, Wechseltauchprüfung f
alternate load (strain)	s. alternating load
alternating, alternation	Alternieren n; Abwechseln n, [periodischer] Wechsel m
alternating, skew-symmetric[al], antisymmetric[al] <math.>	schiefsymmetrisch, alternierend, antisymmetrisch <Math.>
alternating bending	Biegeschwingungsbeanspruchung f; Biegewechselbeanspruchung f, Biegewechsel m, Wechselbiegebeanspruchung f, Wechselbiegung f
alternating bending machine, alternating bending test machine	Wechselbiegemaschine f
alternating bending strength, alternate bending strength	Wechselbiegefestigkeit f, Dauerbiegefestigkeit f
alternating bending stress	Wechselbiegespannung f
alternating bending test, reversed bending fatigue test	Wechselbiegeversuch m, Wechselbiegeprüfung f, Wechselbiegedauerversuch f
alternating bending test machine, alternating bending machine	Wechselbiegemaschine f
alternating component	s. alternating-current component
alternating-current alternation	s. alternation <of current>
alternating-current arc, a. c. arc	Wechselstrombogen m; Wechselstromlichtbogen m
alternating-current arc lamp, a. c. arc lamp	Wechselstrombogenlampe f
alternating-current behaviour, a. c. behaviour	Wechselstromverhalten n
alternating-current bridge, a. c. bridge, alternating-current (a. c.) measuring bridge	Wechselstrombrücke f, Wechselstrommeßbrücke f
alternating-current bridge thermostat, a. c. bridge thermostat	Wechselstrombrückenthermostat m, Wechselstrombrücken-Temperaturwächter m
alternating-current component, alternating component <of pulsating current>, a. c. component of current; alternating part of direct current	Wechselstromkomponente f, Wechselstromanteil m, Wechselkomponente f, Wechselstromglied n
alternating-current conductivity, a. c. conductivity	Wechselstromleitfähigkeit f
alternating-current converter voltmeter, a. c. converter voltmeter	Wechselstromwandler-Voltmeter n
alternating-current coupling, a. c. coupling	Wechselstromkopplung f
alternating-current cycle, a. c. cycle	Wechselstromperiode f

alternating-current - direct-current instrument (meter), a. c.s-d. c. instrument, a. c. -d. c. meter, universal instrument — Allstromgerät n, Allstrommeßgerät n

alternating-current electronic voltmeter, a. c. electronic voltmeter, alternating-current (a. c.) thermionic voltmeter — Wechselstrom-Röhrenvoltmeter n, Wechselspannungs-Röhrenvoltmeter n

alternating-current energy, a. c. energy — Wechselenergie f, Wechselstromenergie f

alternating-current excitation, a. c. excitation, excitation by alternating current — Wechselerregung f, Wechselstromerregung f

alternating-current field — s. alternating electric field

alternating-current field strength, a. c. field strength — Wechselfeldstärke f, Wechselstromfeldstärke f

alternating-current flame lamp — s. flame lamp

alternating-current gain, a. c. gain — Wechselstromverstärkung f

alternating-current half-wave — s. alternation ‹of current›

alternating-current hum — s. hum

alternating-current Josephson effect, a. c. Josephson effect — Wechselstrom-Josephson-Effekt m, Josephson-Effekt m 2. Art

alternating-current magnetic field — s. alternating magnetic field

alternating-current magnetization curve, a. c. magnetization curve — Wechselstrom-Magnetisierungskurve f

alternating-current measuring bridge — s. alternating-current bridge

alternating-current microvoltmeter, a.c. microvoltmeter; microvolter — Mikrovoltmeter n für Wechselspannung, Mikrowechselspannungsmesser m

alternating-current output [power] — s. alternating-current power

alternating-current potentiometer, alternating (a. c.) potentiometer, Drysdale compensator — Wechselstromkompensator m, Wechselstrompotentiometer n, Wechselspannungspotentiometer n

alternating-current power, a. c. power, alternating-current output [power], a. c. output [power] — Wechselstromleistung f, Wechselleistung f

alternating-current rectification, a. c. rectification, single-phase rectification — Wechselstromgleichrichtung f

alternating-current resistance — s. impedance ‹el.›

alternating-current standard, a. c. standard — Wechselstromnormal n

alternating-current theory, a. c. theory — Wechselstromlehre f, Wechselstromtheorie f

alternating-current thermionic voltmeter — s. alternating-current electronic voltmeter

alternating-current to direct-current converter, a. c.-d. c. converter — Wechselstrom-Gleichstrom-Umformer m, Wechselstrom-Gleichstrom-Wandler m, Wechsel-Gleichstromwandler m, Wechselstrom-Gleichstrom-Konverter m

alternating-current voltage, alternating voltage (potential), a. c. voltage — Wechselspannung f, Wechselstromspannung f

alternating-current voltage standard — s. alternating-voltage standard

alternating-current voltmeter, a. c. voltmeter — Wechselspannungsmesser m, Wechselstromvoltmeter n

alternating electric field, alternating-current (a. c.) field — elektrisches Wechselfeld n, Wechselstromfeld n

alternating electromotive force, alternating e.m.f. — Wechsel-Urspannung f; Wechsel-EMK f

alternating field, alternative field — Wechselfeld n

alternating flow, alternating flux — Wechselfluß m, Wechselkraftfluß m

alternating-gradient accelerator, strong-focusing accelerator, AG accelerator, AG-focused accelerator — AG-Maschine f, AG-Beschleuniger m, Teilchenbeschleuniger m mit starker Fokussierung, Beschleuniger m mit starker Fokussierung

alternating-gradient focusing, AG focusing, strong focusing — AG-Fokussierung f, starke Fokussierung f, Fokussierung mit alternierendem Gradienten, Courant-Fokussierung f

alternating gradient synchrotron, strong-focusing synchrotron, AG synchrotron, AGS — AG-Synchrotron n, AG-Maschine f, Synchrotron n mit starker Fokussierung, AGS

alternating hysteresis, dynamic hysteresis — Wechselfeldhysteresis f, dynamische Hysteresis f

alternating-immersion test — s. alternate-immersion test

alternating impact bending test — Wechselschlagbiegeversuch m, Schlagbiegeversuch m bei Wechselbelastung

alternating impact test — Wechselschlag[dauer]versuch m, Dauerwechselschlagversuch m

alternating kernel, antisymmetric kernel, skew-symmetrical kernel — schiefsymmetrischer (alternierender, antisymmetrischer) Kern m

alternating light — Wechsellicht n; Wechselbelichtung f

alternating light diaphragm — Wechsellichtblende f

alternating light method — s. alternating light technique

alternating light photometer — Wechsellichtphotometer n

alternating light technique, alternating light method — Wechsellichtmethode f; Wechsellichtverfahren n

alternating load, alternating loading (stress, strain), alternate strain, alternate load — Wechsellast f; Wechselbeanspruchung f, Wechselbelastung f, wechselnde Belastung f

alternating load deformation, alternating strain — Wechselverformung f

alternating loading — s. alternating load

alternating magnetic field, alternating-current (a.c.) magnetic field — magnetisches Wechselfeld n

alternating magnetization — s. variable magnetization

alternating magnetization — s. remagnetization

alternating method, Schwarz['s] alternating method, "alternierendes Verfahren" — alternierendes Verfahren n [von H. A. Schwarz], Schwarzsches alternierendes Verfahren

alternating part, alternating share — alternierender (schiefsymmetrischer) Anteil m

alternating part of direct current — s. alternating-current component

alternating-phase focusing — Fokussierung f mit alternierender Phase

alternating polarity — Wechselpolarität f, wechselnde Polarität f

alternating potential — s. alternating-current voltage

alternating potentiometer — s. alternating-current potentiometer

alternating pressure; alternating shock load — Wechseldruck m

alternating quantity, oscillating quantity ‹el.› — Wechselgröße f, Schwingung f ‹El.›

alternating series — alternierende Reihe f, Wechselreihe f

alternating share, alternating part — alternierender (schiefsymmetrischer) Anteil m

alternating

alternating shock load, alternating pressure	Wechseldruck *m*
alternating strain, alternating load deformation	Wechselverformung *f*
alternating strain	s. a. alternating load
alternating stress <mech.>	Wechselspannung *f*, wechselnde Spannung *f*
alternating stress	s. a. alternating load
alternating stress amplitude	s. range of alternating stresses
alternating sum	alternierende Summe *f*, Wechselsumme *f*
alternating tension and compression stress fatigue strength	s. fatigue strength
alternating tensor, antisymmetrical tensor, skewsymmetrical tensor, antisymmetric tensor <math.>	schiefsymmetrischer (alternierender, antisymmetrischer, antimetrischer) Tensor *m*, Antitensor *m*
alternating tensor	s. a. multivector <math.>
alternating tensor density, skew-symmetric tensor density	alternierende (schiefsymmetrische) Tensordichte *f*
alternating torque	Wechselmoment *n*
alternating voltage	s. alternating-current voltage
alternating-voltage standard, alternating-current (a. c.) voltage standard	Wechselspannungsnormal *n*
alternation, alternating	Alternieren *n*; Abwechseln *n*, [periodischer] Wechsel *m*
alternation <of tensor>	Alternation *f*, Schiefsymmetrischmachen *n*, Schiefsymmetrisieren *n*
alternation <bio.>	Alternans *m*; Alternanz *f*, Alternation *f* <Bio.>
alternation <of current>, alternating-current alternation (half-wave), a. c. half-wave <el.>	Wechselstromhalbperiode *f*, Wechselstromhalbwelle *f*, Halbperiode *f* der Wechselgröße <El.>
alternation law of multiplicities	spektroskopischer Wechselsatz *m*, Multiplizitätenwechselsatz *m*, Rydbergscher Wechselsatz, Wechselsatz der Multiplizitäten, Wechselsatz [von Rydberg]
alternation of intensity	s. intensity alternation
alternation of load, alternation of stress	Lastwechsel *m*
alternation of polarity, polarity alternation (reversal), reversal of polarity, pole change (changing, reversal), poling; turnover	Polwechsel *m*; Umpolung *f*, Umkehrung *f* der Polarität, Polaritätsumkehrung *f*
alternation of stress, alternation of load	Lastwechsel *m*
alternative field	s. alternating field
alternative normal form, disjunctive normal form	disjunktive Normalform *f*, alternative Normalform
alternative of Fredholm	Fredholmsche Alternative *f*, Fredholmscher Alternativsatz *m*
alternative variability, dichotomy, discontinuous (qualitative) variability <stat.>	alternative (diskontinuierliche, qualitative) Variabilität *f*, Alternativvariabilität *f*, Dichotomie *f* <Stat.>
alternative wave, seismic alternative wave	Wechselwelle *f*, seismische Wechselwelle
alternator, permutation symbol, e-system	Levi-Cività-Dichte *f*, Tensordichte *f* von Levi-Cività, Levi-Civitàsche Tensordichte *f*
"alternierendes Verfahren"	s. alternating method
altigraph, recording altimeter	Höhenschreiber *m*, registrierender Höhenmesser *m*, Altigraph *m*
altimeter, altitude meter (measuring instrument); height indicator (finder)	Altimeter *n*, Höhenmesser *m*; Höhenfinder *m*, Höhensucher *m*
altimetrical chart, altimetric map	s. hypsometric map
altimetric survey	s. contour survey
altimetry	s. hypsometry
altitude, elevation <of star> <astr.>	Höhe *f*, Gestirnshöhe *f*, Sternhöhe *f* <Astr.>
altitude	s. a. flying altitude
altitude chamber	s. low-pressure chamber
altitude chart, aerological map, upper-air chart	Höhenkarte *f*, aerologische Karte *f*; Höhenströmungskarte *f*
altitude circle	s. vertical circle
altitude curve	s. isohypse
altitude difference	s. difference of level
altitude effect <of cosmic rays>	Höheneffekt *m* <kosmische Strahlung>
altitude error	s. level error
altitude flow	s. high-altitude stream
altitude front, upper front	Höhenfront *f*
altitude line	s. isohypse
altitude measurement	s. hypsometry
altitude measuring instrument, altitude meter	s. altimeter
altitude of stage separation, staging altitude	Stufentrennungshöhe *f* <Höhe, bei der sich die Raketenstufe abtrennt>
altitude of the pole	Polhöhe *f*
altitude research, research of high atmosphere	Höhenforschung *f*
altitude rocket, high-altitude rocket, high-altitude-research rocket, upper-air sounding rocket	Höhenrakete *f*, Höhenforschungsrakete *f*
altitude stream	s. high-altitude stream
altitude temperature, temperature aloft, hypsometric temperature	Höhentemperatur *f*
altitude weather map	Höhenwetterkarte *f*
alto-cumulus <*pl.*: -li>, fleece cloud, Ac	Altocumulus *m*, Altokumulus *m* <*pl.*: -li>, grobe Schäfchenwolke *f*, mittelhohe Haufenwolke *f*; Moazagotl-Wolke *f* <in Gebirgen mit Föhn>
alto[-]cumulus castellatus, castellatus, Ac. cast.	Altocumulus *m* castellatus, turmartige Schäfchenwolke *f*, Castellatuswolke *f*, Ac. cast.
alto-cumulus lenticularis	s. lenticular cloud
alto-stratus <*pl.*: -ti>, As	Altostratus *m* <*pl.*: -ti>, mittelhohe Schichtwolke *f*
altostratus lenticularis	Altostratus *m* lenticularis, lineare Wolke *f*
aluminium backing	s. metal backing
aluminium-leaf electroscope	Aluminiumblättchenelektroskop *n*
alum structure	Alaunstruktur *f*
Alvarez structure	Alvarez-Struktur *f* [zur Beschleunigung]
alveolar structure	Alveolarstruktur *f*
always safe geometry, infinitely safe geometry	absolut sichere Geometrie *f*
alychn, zero isolychn, locus of stimuli with zero luminosity, plane of zero luminosity	Alychne *f*, Nullisolychne *f*, Ebene *f* der Helligkeit Null
Amagat	s. Amagat unit
Amagat['s] law, law of additive volumes <of partial volumes>	Amagatsches Gesetz *n*
Amagat law	s. a. Amagat-Leduc law
Amagat-Leduc law (rule), Amagat (Leduc) law	Amagat-Leducsche Regel *f*
Amagat unit, Amagat	Amagatsche Einheit *f*, Amagat-Einheit *f*, Amagat *n*
amaurosis	s. blindness
ambient humidity	Umgebungsfeuchtigkeit *f*
ambient illumination, ambient lighting, environmental lighting	Umgebungsbeleuchtung *f*

ambient light	Umgebungslicht n; Raumlicht n	Ampère['s] circuital law	s. Ampère['s] law
ambient lighting	s. ambient illumination	ampere conductor	s. ampere turn
ambient medium	Umgebung f, umgebendes Medium n	Ampère['s] formula	Ampèresches Gesetz n, Ampèresche Formel f <Kraftwirkung auf ein stromdurchflossenes Leiterelement im magnetischen Feld; Kraftwirkung zweier stromdurchflossener Leiterelemente aufeinander>
ambient temperature, temperature of the surrounding air, environmental temperature	Umgebungstemperatur f		
ambiguous representation	zweideutige Darstellung f		
ambiplasma	Ambiplasma n	Ampère['s] law, Ampère['s] circuital law	Durchflutungsgesetz n, AmpèreschesVerkettungsgesetz n, erster Maxwellscher Hauptsatz f
ambipolar diffusion	ambipolare Diffusion f		
ambipolar diffusion coefficient	Koeffizient m der ambipolaren Diffusion, ambipolarer Diffusionskoeffizient		
		Ampère['s] law	s. a. Laplace theorem
Ambronn['s] imbibition method	s. imbibition method	Ampère['s] law in the differential form	s. first equation of Maxwell
Ambursen dam	s. flat-slab buttress dam	Ampère['s] molecular current	s. molecular current
AME effect	s. acoustomagnetoelectric effect	Ampère['s] rule	s. corkscrew rule
amendment	s. correction	ampere-second, As, coulomb, C	Coulomb n, C, Coul, Cb, Amperesekunde f, As
American meson	s. muon		
American Standard pitch	s. philharmonic pitch	ampere turn, ampere winding (conductor, bar)	Amperewindung f, Aw
americium, $_{95}$Am	Amerizium n, Americium n, $_{95}$Am		
		ampere turns	s. number of turns <el.>
ametropia, ametropy, deficiency of vision, defective vision, sight deficiency	Ametropie f, Fehlsichtigkeit f	ampere-turns per unit length	s. current coverage
		ampere winding	s. ampere turn
		Amperian float rule	s. corkscrew rule
Amici-Bertrand lens	Amici-Bertrand-Linse f, Bertrand-Linse f	amperometry, amperometric titration	Amperometrie f, amperometrische Titration f
Amici lens	Amici-Linse f	amphidromic <math.>	amphidrom <Math.>
Amici prism	Amici-Prisma n, Browning-Prisma n	amphidromic points	Punkte mpl gleichen Fluteintritts, Amphidromiepunkte mpl
Amici prism	s. a. ridge prism		
amicron	Amikron n	amphion	s. amphoteric ion
		amphiprotic solvent, amphoteric solvent	amphoteres (amphiprotisches) Lösungsmittel n
amoeboid movement	amöboide Bewegung f		
Amontons['] law	s. Charles law	ampholyte, amphoteric electrolyte	Ampholyt m, amphoterer Elektrolyt m
amorphism, amorphousness, structurelessness	Amorphie f, Strukturlosigkeit f, Gestaltlosigkeit f	ampholytoid	amphoteres Kolloid n, Ampholytoid n
amorphousness	s. amorphism		
amorphous plasticity	amorphe Plastizität f, banale Plastizität	amphoteric electrolyte	s. ampholyte
		amphoteric ion, hybrid ion, zwitterion, dipolar ion, dual ion, amphion, inner salt	Zwitterion n, amphoteres Ion n, Ampho-Ion n
amount	s. amount of substance		
amount of adsorption, amount of the substance adsorbed	adsorbierte Menge f		
		amphotericity	s. amphoteric property
amount of calculation, volume of computation	Rechenaufwand m	amphoteric property, amphotericity	amphotere Eigenschaft f, amphoterer Charakter m
amount of clouds	s. cloudiness <in eights or octas>	amphoteric solvent, amphiprotic solvent	amphoteres Lösungsmittel n
amount of energy	Energiemenge f	amplification; intensification; enhancement; boost, boosting	Verstärkung f; Intensivierung f
amount of energy contained	s. energy content		
amount of evaporation in mm	s. evaporation height	amplification, continuous excitation <of boundary layer>	Anfachung f
amount of heat, quantity of heat, heat quantity	Wärmemenge f, Wärme f		
amount of infiltration	Versickerungsmenge f	amplification by R-C coupling	Widerstandsverstärkung f
amount of information	s. information content		
amount of material (matter)	s. amount of substance	amplification factor	s. gain
amount of rainfall	s. height of precipitation	amplification factor of the valve, valve gain	Röhrenverstärkungsfaktor m, Verstärkungsfaktor m der Elektronenröhre
amount of rotation	Drehwert m		
amount of rotation [in Faraday effect], angle of rotation [in Faraday effect]	Drehungswinkel m [beim Faraday-Effekt], magnet[opt]ische Drehung [der Polarisationsrichtung]	amplification of light	s. light amplification
		amplification stage	s. amplifier stage
		amplifier cascade, amplifier chain, chain of amplifiers	Verstärkerkette f
amount of substance, amount of matter (material), amount	Stoffmenge f, Menge f		
		amplifier characteristic, gain characteristic	Verstärkerkennlinie f, Verstärkercharakteristik f, Verstärkerkurve f, Verstärkungsverlauf m
amount of the substance adsorbed, amount of adsorption	adsorbierte Menge f		
		amplifier coupling	Verstärkerstufenkopplung f
amount of torsion (twist)	s. twist per unit length	amplifier element	Verstärkerglied n, Verstärkungsglied n
amount of twist	s. angle of torsion	amplifier gain <in Np>	Verstärkungsgrad m <in Np>
amount of wear	Verschleißbetrag m		
		amplifier gain	s. gain <el.>
amount weighed, quantity (initial) weighed, weighed amount (quantity)	Einwaage f, eingewogene Menge f	amplifier noise; set noise	Verstärkerrauschen n; Verstärkergeräusch n
		amplifier plug-in	s. plug-in amplifier
amperage	s. current <el.>	amplifier stage, amplifying (amplification) stage, stage of amplification	Verstärkerstufe f, Verstärkungsstufe f
ampere, A, a, amp.	Ampere n, A, Amp.		
ampere balance, Ampère balance, current balance, electrodynamic balance	Stromwaage f		
		amplifier subassembly	s. plug-in amplifier
		amplifier tube	s. amplifying tube
ampere bar	s. ampere turn	amplifier unit	s. plug-in amplifier

amplifier valve	s. amplifying tube	amplitude tangent, t am, tan am, tg am	Tangens amplitudinis m, tan am, tg am
amplifying klystron	Verstärkerklystron n	amplitude-[to-]time conversion	Amplitude-Zeit-Transformation f
amplifying stage	s. amplifier stage	amplitude unbalance	Amplitudenungleichgewicht n
amplifying tube, amplifying valve, amplifier tube (valve)	Verstärkerröhre	Amsler vibrophore ‹for fatigue testing›	Amsler-Pulsator m; Amslersche (hochfrequente) Drehschwingmaschine f
amplifying vibrograph	schreibender Schwingungsmesser m mit Verstärker, Vibrograph m mit Verstärker	amyriotic field	amyriotisches Feld n
ampliscaler, scale of one hundred circuit	Hundertfachuntersetzer m, Hundertfachzähler m	anabatic clouds	Aufgleitbewölkung f
amplitude ‹of vibration, oscillation›, vibration amplitude, oscillation amplitude	Amplitude f, [maximale] Schwingungsweite f, Schwingweite f, Schwing[ungs]amplitude f, Schwingungsausschlag m, Höchstausschlag m, Oszillationsamplitude f, Scheitelwert m ‹Schwingung›	anabatic front	s. anafront
		anabatic wind; ascending (upward) wind, upwind, upwash; updraft, updraught; upward current	Aufwind m, anabatischer Wind m
		anabolism, assimilation ‹bio.›	Anabolismus m, Assimilation f; Baustoffwechsel m
		anacamptic	s. catoptric
amplitude, polar angle, argument, arg ‹of a complex number›	Argument n, arg, arc ‹komplexe Zahl›	anacamptics	s. catoptrics
		anaclastics, dioptrics	Dioptrik f, Lehre f von der Brechung des Lichtes
amplitude-amplitude response	s. amplitude response	anafront, anabatic front	Anafront f, Aufgleitfront f
amplitude analyzer, pulse-amplitude analyzer, pulse height analyzer, kicksorter	Impulshöhenanalysator m, Impulsamplitudenanalysator m, Amplitudenanalysator m, Impulsanalysator m		
		anagalactic, extragalactic	extragalaktisch, außergalaktisch, anagalaktisch
amplitude characteristic	s. amplitude response	anaglyphic method	Anaglyphenverfahren n
amplitude clipping	s. pulse-height clipping	anaglyph images	s. anaglyphs
amplitude contrast	Amplitudenkontrast m	anaglyphs, anaglyph images	Anaglyphen mpl, Anaglyphenbilder npl
amplitude contrast method	Amplitudenkontrastverfahren n		
amplitude discriminator	s. discriminator	anaglyph viewer	Anaglyphenbrille f
amplitude factor	s. crest factor	anallactic point	anallaktischer Punkt m
amplitude-frequency curve	s. amplitude-response	anallactic telescope	anallaktisches Fernrohr n
		analog-digital computer	s. hybrid computer
amplitude function ‹qu.›	Amplitudenfunktion f, zeitunabhängige Wellenfunktion f ‹Qu.›	analog for heat flow	Wärmeströmungsanalogie f
		analog method	Analogieverfahren n, Ähnlichkeitsmethode f
amplitude grating	Amplitudengitter n		
amplitude hologram	Amplitudenhologramm n	analogous polymeric compound	s. polymer-analogue
amplitude limiter (lopper)	s. peak limiter	analog state	s. isobaric analog state
		analog state	s. a. isobaric analog state
amplitude margin, gain margin	Amplitudenrand m, Amplitudenabstand m	analogy of membrane	s. soap film analogy
		analysis	s. evaluation ‹of dates›
amplitude of accommodation, extent of accommodation, accommodation width, accommodation ‹in dioptres›	Akkommodationsbreite f, Akkommodationsvermögen n, Akkommodationsvorrat m, Akkommodationsfähigkeit f des Auges	analysis of covariance, covariance analysis	Kovarianzanalyse f, Mitstreuungszerlegung f
		analysis of crystal structure	s. crystal-structure determination
		analysis of energy levels	s. term analysis
		analysis of regression	Regressionsanalyse f
amplitude of fluctuation of the luminous intensity	Welligkeit f ‹Wechselstromlichtquelle›	analysis of the oscillation	Zerlegung (Analyse) f der Schwingung
amplitude of stress, stress amplitude, stress range ‹mech.›	Spannungsamplitude f; Schwingbreite f der Spannung ‹Mech.›	analysis of variance, variance analysis, ANOVA	Varianzanalyse f, Streuungszerlegung f, F-Verfahren n
		analysis situs	s. topology
amplitude of the fault	s. fault height ‹geo.›	analytical balance, assay balance	Analysenwaage f, Feinwaage f
amplitude of tide	s. tidal range		
amplitude-phase grating	Amplitudenphasengitter n		
amplitude resolution	Amplitudenauflösung f, Amplitudenauflösungsvermögen n	analytical gap	s. electrode separation
		analytical line, [important] identifying line ‹spectr.›	Analysenlinie f, Haupt[nachweis]linie f ‹Spektr.›
amplitude resonance, displacement resonance	Amplitudenresonanz f		
amplitude response, amplitude characteristic	Amplitudengang m	analyzer; evaluation equipment	Analysator m; Auswertegerät n
		analyzing magnet, magnetic analyzer	magnetischer Analysator m, Magnetanalysator m, Analysiermagnet m
amplitude response, amplitude-amplitude response	Amplitude-Amplitude-Charakteristik f, Amplitudenkurve f, Amplitudenverlauf m, Amplitudengang m	anamorphoscope	Spiegelanamorphot m
		anamorphoser, anamorphosing lens	s. anamorphotic lens
		anamorphosis ‹opt.›	Anamorphose f, Verstreckung f, Verzerrung f, Rückformung f ‹Opt.›
amplitude response, amplitude-response curve, amplitude-frequency curve	Amplitude-Frequenz-Gang m, Amplitudenfrequenzgang m, Amplitude-Frequenz-Kennlinie f, Amplitudencharakteristik f, Amplitudengang m	anamorphote [lens]	s. anamorphotic lens
		anamorphotic attachment	anamorphotischer Objektivvorsatz (Vorsatz) m, Anamorphotvorsatz m
amplitude specimen	Amplitudenobjekt n	anamorphotic lens, anamorphote lens, anamorphote, anamorphosing lens, anamorphoser, distorting lens	Zerrlinse f, Verzerrungslinse f, anamorphotische Linse f, Anamorphotlinse f; Anamorphot m (n)
amplitude spectrum	Amplitudenspektrum n		
amplitude structure	Amplitudenstruktur f		
amplitude swing, variation of amplitude	Amplitudenhub m	anamorphotic mirror	Zerrspiegel m, anamorphotischer Spiegel m, Anamorphotspiegel m

anamorphotic optical system, anamorphotic optics	Zerroptik f, anamorphotische Optik f, Anamorphotoptik f, Verzerrungsoptik f
anaphoresis	Anaphorese f
anastigmat, anastigmatic objective	Anastigmat m (n)
anastigmatism	Anastigmatismus m, Anastigmasie f
anatexis <geo.>	Anatexis f, Anatexe f, Wiederaufschmelzen n <Geo.>
anchor ice	s. ground ice
anchoring	s. locking <of dislocations>
anchor ring	s. torus <math.>
anchor-ring method	Bügelmethode f, Abreißmethode f, Lamellenmethode f
ancillary unit	s. supplementary apparatus
Anderson a.c. bridge, Anderson bridge	Anderson-Brücke f
Andes glow	Andenleuchten n
Andrade['s] approximate formula	s. Andrade['s] formula
Andrade['s] creep law	Andradesches Gesetz n
Andrade effect	Andrade-Effekt m
Andrade['s] formula, Andrade['s] approximate formula	Näherungsformel f von Andrade, Andradesche Näherungsformel (Gleichung f)
Andrews diagram	s. pressure-volume diagram of fluids
Andrews isotherm	Andrews-Isotherme f
anechoic chamber, anechoic sound chamber, non-echo chamber, anechoic (unechoic, dead, deadened) room <ac.>	schalltoter Raum m, reflexionsfreier Raum <Ak.>
anechoic chamber, anechoic room <lined by cotton wool>	Watteraum m
anechoic room (sound chamber)	s. anechoic chamber <ac.>
anelasticity	Anelastizität f, anelastische Erscheinung f
anelastic material	s. Poynting-Thomson body
anelectric, non-electrolysable	nichtelektrolysierbar, anelektrisch
anelectrolyte, non-electrolyte	Nichtelektrolyt m, Anelektrolyt m
anemogram	Anemogramm n, Windregistrierstreifen m, Windregistrierung f
anemograph, recording anemometer	Anemograph m, Wind[geschwindigkeits]schreiber m, Windregistrierapparat m
anemometer, wind gauge	Anemometer n, Windgeschwindigkeitsmesser m, Windmeßgerät n, Windmesser m
anemometer detector	Anemometerbrücke f
anemometer of windmill type	s. vane anemometer
anemometry, wind[-velocity] measurement	Anemometrie f, Wind[geschwindigkeits]messung f
aneroid, aneroid barometer, metal barometer, bellows gauge	Aneroidbarometer n, Federbarometer n, Federdruckmesser m, Dosenbarometer n, Vidi-Dose f, Metallbarometer n, Kapselbarometer n, Holosterikbarometer n
aneroidograph	Aneroidbarograph m
Anger function	Angersche Funktion f, Anger-Funktion f
angle, angle space	Winkelraum m
angle brace	s. diagonal member
angle characteristic function, angle characteristic T	s. angle eikonal
angle correlation	s. angular correlation
angle correlation coefficient, angular correlation coefficient	Winkelkorrelationskoeffizient m, Koeffizient m für die Winkelkorrelation
angled	s. oblique
angled lever	s. bent lever
angled reflector	s. corner reflector <el.>
angle eikonal; angle characteristic T, angle characteristic function, Hamilton['s] angle characteristic [function]	Winkeleikonal n; Hamiltons charakteristische Funktion f T, charakteristische Funktion T [von Hamilton]
angle from ascending node to perihelion	s. argument of perihelion
angle lever	s. bent lever
angle measuring instrument	s. goniometer
angle measuring microscope	Winkelmeßmikroskop n
angle modulation	Winkelmodulation f
angle modulation, phase-angle modulation	Phasenwinkelmodulation f, Pendelmodulation f
angle of aberration, aberration constant (angle)	Aberrationswinkel m, Aberrationskonstante f
angle of arrival <of wave>	Einstrahlwinkel m <Welle>
angle of attack, angle of incidence	Anstellwinkel m, Anströmwinkel m
angle of backscattering, backscattering angle, backscatter angle	Rückstreuwinkel m, Rückwärtswinkel m
angle of break, breaking angle	Reißwinkel m
angle of capillarity	s. angle of contact
angle of cast, angle of throw	Wurfwinkel m
angle of contact, contact (wetting) angle, angle of capillarity, boundary (rim) angle	Kontaktwinkel m, Randwinkel m, Grenzwinkel m, Benetzungswinkel m
angle of contact	s. a. angle of embrace
angle of creation	Erzeugungswinkel m
angle of declination	s. declination
angle of departure [of the electrons]	Startwinkel m [der Elektronen]
angle of departure	s. a. angle of elevation
angle of depression	s. depression angle
angle of distortion <theory of elasticity>	Scherungswinkel m <Elastizitätstheorie>
angle of divergence, divergence angle	Divergenzwinkel m, Divergenz f; Streuungswinkel m; Spreiz[ungs]winkel m
angle of downwash	Abwindwinkel m
angle of elevation, elevation, angle of departure	Elevationswinkel m, Elevation f, Höhenwinkel m, Erhebungswinkel m, Erhebung f
angle of elevation measurement	s. measurement of elevation
angle of embrace, angle of contact (wrap), wrapping angle; span angle	Umfassungswinkel m; Umschlingungswinkel m
angle of emergence	Austrittswinkel m; Beobachtungsrichtung f <Echelle>; Ausfallswinkel m <z. B. Linse>
angle of emission, angle of radiation	Emissionswinkel m, Strahlungswinkel m, Ausstrahlungswinkel m, Abstrahl[ungs]winkel m, Austrittswinkel m
angle of entry	s. angle of incidence
angle of fault, fault angle	Sprungwinkel m, Verwerfungswinkel m
angle of flap deflection, deflection of flap	Klappenausschlag m
angle of flow	Strömungswinkel m, Stromwinkel m
angle of friction, limiting angle [of friction], angle of repose	Reibungswinkel m, Gleitwinkel m, Grenzwinkel m [der Reibung]
angle of friction	s. a. slope of repose
angle of glare	Blendungswinkel m
angle of impact, shock angle	Stoßwinkel m
angle of incidence, incidence angle, angle of entry	Einfallwinkel m, Inzidenzwinkel m; Eintrittswinkel m; Auftreffwinkel m
angle of inclination <mech.>, tilt[ing] angle	Kippwinkel m, Kippungswinkel m <Mech.>
angle of inclination	s. a. inclination
angle of inclination	s. a. magnetic dip
angle of interlinking, interlinking angle	Verkettungswinkel m
angle of internal friction	Winkel m der inneren Reibung
angle of intersection, intersection angle	Schnittwinkel m
angle of lag, lag angle; retardation angle	Nacheil[ungs]winkel m; Verzögerungswinkel m
angle of lead, lead angle	Voreilwinkel m, Voreilungswinkel m

angle of lead, lead angle <opt.	Vorhaltwinkel m, Vorhaltewinkel m <Opt.>	angular aperture, angular field <opt.>	Öffnungswinkel m, Aperturwinkel m <Opt.>
angle of lead	s. a. lead angle <control>	angular attenuation	Winkeldämpfung f
angle of magnetic inclination	s. magnetic dip	angular coefficient, slope, ascent, gradient <of the curve>	Anstieg m, Richtungskoeffizient m, Steigung f, Neigung f <Kurve>
angle of natural slip (slope)	s. slope of repose	angular condition, condition for the angles	Winkelbedingung f
angle of overlap, overlap angle	Überlappungswinkel m	angular correlation, directional (angle) correlation	Winkelkorrelation f, Richtungskorrelation f
angle of polarization	s. Brewster angle		
angle of radiation	s. angle of emission	angular correlation coefficient, angle correlation coefficient	Winkelkorrelationskoeffizient m, Koeffizient m für die Winkelkorrelation
angle of refraction	s. retraction angle		
angle of repose	s. angle of friction		
angle of repose (rest)	s. a. slope of repose	angular cut-off frequency, cut-off angular frequency	Winkelgrenzfrequenz f
angle of rotation [in Faraday effect]	s. amount of rotation		
angle of second curvature	s. angle of torsion <math.>	angular defect	Winkeldefekt m
angle of separation	s. angle under which the liquid is separated from a spherical surface	angular deformation	s. angle of shear
		angular degree	s. degree of angle
		angular derivative	Winkelableitung f, Winkelderivierte f
angle of shear, angle of slide, angular deformation, angular dilatation, shear angle, shear strain	Schiebung f, Schubwinkel m, Schubverformung f, Winkeländerung f, Gleitwinkel m, Winkel m der Scherung, Gleitung f, Scherung f	angular deviation loss	Winkelabweichungsverlust m
		angular diameter, apparent diameter <of star>	scheinbarer Durchmesser m; Winkeldurchmesser m <Gestirn>
angle of sideslip	Schiebewinkel m	angular dilatation	s. angle of shear
angle of sight	Zielwinkel m	angular discordance	Winkeldiskordanz f
angle of situation	s. parallactic angle		
angle of slide	s. angle of shear	angular dispersion	Winkeldispersion f
angle of slope slope angle	Böschungswinkel m, Hangneigung f, Neigungswinkel m, Gefälle n; Steigung f; Böschungsverhältnis n	angular distance, angular separation	Winkelabstand m, Winkeldistanz f
		angular distribution, directional distribution	Winkelverteilung f, Richtungsverteilung f
angle of slope	s. a. inclination		
angle of stall, critical angle of attack	kritischer Anstellwinkel m	angular distribution	s. a. phase space distribution
		angular divergence, angular spread	Richtungsdivergenz f, Winkeldivergenz f
angle of sweep, sweep angle	Pfeilwinkel m <Flügel>	angular division	Winkelteilung f
angle of throw, angle of cast	Wurfwinkel m	angular division measuring apparatus (device, instrument)	Winkelteilungsmeßgerät n
angle of tilt	Kippfehler m, Kippungsfehler m	angular excess	Winkelexzeß m
angle of tilt	s. a. tilt angle	angular field, angle of view <opt.>	Bildwinkel m, Bildfeldwinkel m <Opt.>
angle of torsion, angle of second curvature <math.>	Windungswinkel m, Schmiegungswinkel m, Torsionswinkel m <Math.>	angular field	s. a. angular aperture <opt.>
		angular focusing	s. direction focusing
angle of torsion, angle of twist, torsional angle [of twist], torsion angle, amount of twist	Torsionswinkel m, Verdreh[ungs]winkel m, Drill[ungs]winkel m	angular frequency, radian frequency; pulsatance, pulsation <especially el.>	Kreisfrequenz f, Winkelfrequenz f
		angular frequency of Larmor precession	s. Larmor angular frequency
angle of twist per unit length	spezifischer Verdrehwinkel m	angular impulse, impulsive moment, moment of plane area	Flächenträgheitsmoment n, geometrisches Trägheitsmoment n, Trägheitsmoment n des Querschnitts, Moment n zweiter Ordnung
angle of valence	s. valence angle		
angle of view	s. angular field <opt.>		
angle of vision	Gesichtsfeldwinkel m, Dingwinkel m		
angle of wrap	s. angle of embrace		
angle-preserving	s. equiangular	angular kinetic energy	s. rotational energy
angle-preserving mapping	s. conformal mapping	angular magnification, apparent magnification, magnifying power, convergence ratio	Winkelverhältnis n, Winkelvergrößerung f, Angularvergrößerung f, Konvergenzverhältnis n, Tangensverhältnis n
angle protractor	s. goniometer		
angle protractor	s. contact goniometer		
angle space, angle	Winkelraum m		
angle straggling	Winkelstreuung f, Richtungsstreuung f	angular mechanical impedance	s. mechanical rotational impedance
angle thermometer	Winkelthermometer n	angular mechanical reactance	s. mechanical rotational reactance
angle under which the liquid is separated from a spherical surface, angle of separation	Abreißwinkel m	angular mechanical resistance	s. mechanical rotational resistance
		angular minute	s. minute <of angle>
		angular mode	Transversalschwingung[smode] f
angle variable, angular variable	Winkelvariable f		
angry sea	s. rough sea	angular momentum, moment of momentum, twist; angular momentum vector	Drehimpuls m, Impulsmoment n; Drehimpulsvektor m, Drall m, Schwung m
ångström	s. ångström unit		
Ångström band	Ångström-Bande f		
Ångström['s] pyrheliometer	s. compensation pyrheliometer		
Ångström pyrheliometric scale, Ångström scale, Uppsala scale	Ångström-Skala f, Upsala-Skala f	angular momentum conservation law, law of conservation of angular momentum, law of conservation of moment of momentum, principle of conservation of angular (moment of) momentum, principle of conservation of areas	Drehimpulssatz m, Drehimpulserhaltungssatz m, Erhaltungssatz m des Drehimpulses, Satz m von der Erhaltung des Drehimpulses (Schwunges), zweiter Impulssatz m der Mechanik
Ångström['s] turbidity coefficient (parameter)	s. turbidity coefficient		
ångström unit, ångström, Å, AU	Ångström-Einheit f, Ångström n, Å, Å. E.		
angular acceleration, rotational acceleration	Winkelbeschleunigung f, Drehbeschleunigung f		

angular momentum due to the intrinsic rotation	s. spin angular momentum	anisotropic distortion	anisotrope Verzeichnung f
angular momentum matrix element	Drehimpulsmatrixelement n	anisotropic distortion	s. a. spiral distortion
		anisotropic energy	s. energy of magnetic anisotropy
angular momentum operator	Operator m des Drehimpulses, Drehimpulsoperator m	anisotropy coefficient (constant)	s. magnetocrystalline anisotropy constant
angular momentum quantum number	s. secondary quantum number	anisotropy energy	s. energy of magnetic anisotropy
angular momentum tensor	Drehimpulstensor m	anisotropy energy density	s. magnetocrystalline anisotropy energy density
angular momentum vector	s. angular momentum	anisotropy factor, dissymmetry factor	Anisotropiefaktor m
angular moment vector <of gyroscope>	Kreiselimpuls m, Impulsmoment n, Drehimpuls m, Schwung m, Drall m	anisotropy of form, form anisotropy, form effect	Formanisotropie f, Gestaltanisotropie f, magnetische Scherung f, Scherung
angular radius	s. apparent semi-diameter	anisotropy relaxation	Anisotropierelaxation f, anisotrope Relaxation f
angular resolution, angular resolving power	Winkelauflösung f, Winkelauflösungsvermögen n		
angular second	s. second <of angle>	anisotropy relaxation constant	Anisotropierelaxationskonstante f, Konstante f der anisotropen Relaxation, Konstante der Anisotropierelaxation
angular semi-diameter	s. apparent semi-diameter		
angular sensitivity	s. directional sensitivity		
angular separation, angular distance	Winkelabstand m, Winkeldistanz f		
angular separation	Winkel m zwischen zwei Richtungen, eingeschlossener Winkel	Anissovitch-Dachno-Valuyev effect	Anissowitsch-Dachno-Walujew-Effekt m
		annealing <of radiation damage>, defect annealing	Ausheilung f [durch Temperaturerhöhung], Ausglühen n <Strahlenschäden durch Erhitzung>
angular spectrum	Winkelspektrum n		
angular speed, rotational speed, magnitude of angular velocity, rate of angular motion	Winkelgeschwindigkeit f, Betrag m der Winkelgeschwindigkeit, Betrag des Winkelgeschwindigkeitsvektors, Drehgeschwindigkeit f	annealing colour	s. tempering colour
		annealing in vacuo	s. vacuum annealing
		annealing point, upper annealing point <of glass>	oberer Kühlpunkt m, Entspannungspunkt m, Entspannungstemperatur f
angular spread, angular divergence	Richtungsdivergenz f, Winkeldivergenz f	annealing to demagnetizing temperature, annealing to the critical temperature of demagnetization	Entmagnetisierungsglühen n
angular thickness	Winkeldicke f		
angular variable, angle variable	Winkelvariable f		
angular velocity, angular velocity vector	Winkelgeschwindigkeitsvektor m, [Vektor m der] Winkelgeschwindigkeit f	annealing twin, recrystallization twin	Rekristallisationszwilling m
		annihilation <of dislocation>	Versetzungsannihilation f, Auflösung f (Annihilation f, Annihilieren n, Vernichtung f) von Versetzungen
angular velocity of Larmor precession	s. Larmor angular frequency		
angular velocity vector	s. angular velocity		
angular width [of the beam]	s. beam divergence	annihilation <nucl.>	Annihilation f, Zerstrahlung f, Vernichtung f <Kern.>
anharmonicity constant, constant of anharmonicity	Anharmonizitätskonstante f	annihilation cross-section, cross-section for annihilation	Vernichtungsquerschnitt m, Wirkungsquerschnitt m für (der) Vernichtung, Vernichtungswirkungsquerschnitt m
anharmonic oscillator, non-linear oscillator	anharmonischer (nichtharmonischer, nichtlinearer) Oszillator m		
anharmonic ratio, cross ratio, double ratio	Doppelverhältnis n		
anhedral	s. allotriomorphic	annihilation gamma quantum, annihilation gamma-ray	s. annihilation photon
anholonomic constraint	s. non-holonomic constraint		
anhysteretic magnetization curve	s. ideal magnetization curve		
animated picture	s. moving picture	annihilation of electron-positron pairs associated with neutrino-antineutrino pair production	Elektron-Positron-Paarvernichtung f mit Bildung eines Neutrino-Antineutrino-Paares
anion acid, anionic acid	Anionsäure f		
anion base, anionic base	Anionbase f		
anion exchange	Anionenaustausch m; Anionenumtausch m <im Boden>		
		annihilation of particles [with antiparticles]	Teilchenvernichtung f [durch Antiteilchen]
anionic	s. anionic detergent		
anionic acid	s. anion acid	annihilation operator, destruction operator, absorption operator	Vernichtungsoperator m
anionic agent, anionic detergent	anionaktiver Stoff m		
anionic base, anion base	Anionbase f	annihilation photon, annihilation quantum, annihilation gamma-ray, annihilation gamma quantum	Zerstrahlungsphoton n, Zerstrahlungsquant n, Zerstrahlungs-Gamma-Quant n, Vernichtungsphoton n, Vernichtungsquant n, Vernichtungs-Gamma-Quant n, Annihilationsphoton n, Annihilationsquant n, Annihilations-Gamma-Quant n
anionic conduction	Anionenleitung f		
anionic conductivity	Anionenleitfähigkeit f		
anionic conductor	Anionenleiter m		
anionic defect conduction	Anionenmangelleitung f, Anionendefektleitung f		
anionic detergent, anionic agent, anionic	anionaktiver Stoff m		
anionic excess conduction, anionic surplus conduction	Anionenüberschußleitung f		
		annihilation radiation	Vernichtungsstrahlung f, Annihilationsstrahlung f
anion mobility	Anionenbeweglichkeit f		
anionotropy	Anionotropie f, Tautomerie f mit Platzwechsel des Anions	annihilation rate, destruction rate	Vernichtungsrate f
		annihilation spectrum	Zerstrahlungsspektrum n, Annihilationsspektrum n, Vernichtungsspektrum n
anion transference number, anion transport number, transport number of the anion	Anionenüberführungszahl f		
		annihilation star	Zerstrahlungsstern m
anion vacancy	s. negative[-]ion vacancy	annual aberration	jährliche Aberration f
aniophile	s. Lewis acid		
anisentropic flow	s. non-isentropic flow	annual amount <e.g. of atmospheric precipitations>	Jahresmenge f <z. B. Niederschläge>
anisotopic element	s. pure element		
anisotropic band, A band, A segment, Q-disk	Q-Streifen m, anisotrope Querscheibe (Schicht) f <Muskel>		
		annual average	s. yearly average

annual equation <of the Moon>	jährliche Gleichung f, jährliche Ungleichheit f <Mond>	anomalous dispersion, abnormal dispersion	anomale Dispersion f
annual mean	s. yearly average	anomalous E-layer	s. sporadic E-layer
annual parallax, heliocentric parallax; parallax	jährliche (heliozentrische) Parallaxe f; Parallaxe	anomalous mixed crystals	s. adsorbed solid solution
		anomalous propagation	s. non-standard propagation
annual variation	Jahresgang m, jährliche Variation (Änderung) f	anomalous series	anomale Spektralserie f, anomale Serie f
annular Bloch line	s. circular Bloch line	anomalous solid solution	s. adsorbed solid solution
annular coil	s. toroid <el.>	anomalous water	s. polywater
annular diaphragm, annular stop, annulus <opt.>	Ringblende f <Opt.>	anomalous Zeeman effect	anomaler (zusammengesetzter) Zeeman-Effekt m, Zeeman-Effekt der Multiplettsysteme
annular eclipse, ring-like eclipse	ringförmige Finsternis f	anomaly in refraction, refraction anomaly	Refraktionsanomalie f
annular gap	s. annulus <techn.>	anoptral contrast	Anoptralkontrast m
annular lens	Kreisringlinse f <magnetisch>; Ringlinse f <elektrisch>	anorthic [crystal] system	s. triclinic crystal system
		anorthoscopic illusion	s. Zöllner phenomenon
annular lens condenser	Ringlinsenkondensor m, Ringlinse f <Opt.>	ANOVA	s. analysis of variance
annular stop	s. annular diaphragm	ansatz	s. statement <math.>
annular structure <e.g. of proton>	Ringstruktur f <z. B. des Protons>	Anschütz compass, Anshutz compass	Anschützscher Einkreiselkompaß m, Anschützscher Kreiselkompaß m
annular-total eclipse	ringförmig-totale Finsternis f	antagonism (antagonistic action) of ions	Ionenantagonismus m
annular wave	Ringwelle f		
annular wire loop	Drahtring m	antagonistic pairs <colour vision>	Gegenfarben fpl [nach Hering]
annulus, circular ring	Kreisring m		
		antapex of the Sun	s. polar antapex
annulus, annular gap, ring slot <techn.>	Ringspalt m, ringförmiger Spalt m <Techn.>	Antarctic axis pole	s. austral pole
		antecedent	s. inverse image
annulus	s. a. annular diaphragm	antenna amplifier, antenna booster, aerial booster	Antennenverstärker m
annulus	s. a. toroid <el.>		
annus abundans, abundant year, perfect year	überzähliges Gemeinjahr n <im jüdischen Kalender>	antenna array	s. directional antenna array
		antenna booster, aerial booster, antenna amplifier	Antennenverstärker m
annus deficiens, deficient (imperfect) year	mangelhaftes Gemeinjahr n		
		antenna coupling, aerial coupling	Antennenkopplung f, Antennenankopplung f
anode compartment, anode space	Anodenraum m		
		antenna damping	Antennendämpfung f
anode current distortion, transconductance distortion	Steilheitsverzerrung f, Anodenstromverzerrung f	antenna effect, aerial effect	Antenneneffekt m
		antenna effective height	s. effective height of the antenna
anode dark space	Anodendunkelraum m		
anode detector, plate detector, grid-bias detector, power detector	Anodengleichrichter m, Richtverstärker m	antenna effective temperature	s. antenna temperature
		antenna efficiency, aerial efficiency	Antennenwirkungsgrad m
anode differential resistance	s. internal resistance <of thermionic valve, triode>		
		antenna major lobe	s. main lobe
anode disintegration	s. anode sputtering	antenna null, null of directivity pattern	Nullstelle f der Richtcharakteristik
anode dissipation, plate dissipation	Anodenverlustleistung f, Anodengleichstromleistung f		
		antennas uniformly spaced around the circumference of a circle	Kreisgruppenantenne f, Kreisgruppe f von Antennen
anode drop (fall)	Anoden[spannungsab]fall m, Spannungsabfall m an der Anode		
		antenna switching, aerial (lobe) switching	Antennenumschaltung f, Antennenumtastung f
anode glow, positive glow, anode sheath	positives (anodisches) Glimmlicht n, positive Glimmschicht f, Anoden[glimm]licht n, Anodenglimmhaut f, Anodenbüschellicht n; positives Büschel n	antenna switching	s. a. beam switching
		antenna temperature, antenna effective temperature, effective temperature of the antenna, effective antenna temperature	Antennen[wirk]temperatur f, wirksame (effektive) Antennentemperatur, Wirktemperatur f (Effektivtemperatur f, wirksame Temperatur f, effektive Temperatur) der Antenne
anode modulation, plate modulation	Anodenmodulation f, Anodenspannungsmodulation f		
		anterior defect	vorderer Defekt m [des Integralkerns]
anode plasma	Anodenplasma n		
anode rays	Anodenstrahlen mpl	anterior-posterior view	s. AP view
anode sheath	s. anode glow	anterior projection	s. PA view
anode space, anode compartment	Anodenraum m	anterior shutter	s. front diaphragm <phot.>
		anthelic arc	schiefer Bogen m der Gegensonne, Arctowskischer Bogen
anode sputtering, anode disintegration	Anodenzerstäubung f		
		anthelion, countersun	Gegensonne f
anode voltage distortion	Durchgriffsverzerrung f, Anodenspannungsverzerrung f	anti-automorphism	Antiautomorphismus m
		antibaryon resonance	Antibaryonenresonanz f
anodic flame	s. positive flame	antibase-base system of Bjerrum	Bjerrumsches Antibase-Base-System n
anodoluminescence	Anodolumineszenz f		
		antibonding orbital, nonbonding orbital	Antivalenzbahn f, lockerndes Orbital n, lockernder (bindungslockernder) Zustand m, bindungslockerndes (nichtbindendes) Orbital, nichtbindender Zustand m, spinabgesättigte Bahn f, spinabgesättigtes Orbital
anomalistic month, anomalistic revolution	anomalistischer Monat m, anomalistischer Umlauf m		
anomalous diffusion [of plasma], Bohm diffusion	anomale Diffusion f [des Plasmas], Bohm-Diffusion f		
		anticatalysis	s. inhibition <chem.>
		anticatalyst	s. inhibitor <chem.>

anticatalyzer	s. inhibitor <chem.>	antiferromagnetism	Antiferromagnetismus m
anticathode mirror, anticathode target	Antikatodenspiegel m	antiferromagnon	Antiferromagnon n, Spinwelle f im Antiferromagnetikum
anticaustic, secondary caustic	Antikaustik f, sekundäre Kaustik f	anti-flare coating	s. anti-reflection coating
anticentre, anti-epicentre	Antizentrum n, Antiepizentrum n	antifluorite lattice	Antiflußspatgitter n, Antifluoritgitter n
anticlastic surface, surface of negative total curvature	antiklastische Fläche f	anti-focal point	Antifokus m
		antifoggant, fog inhibitor, fog prevention agent	schleierverhindernder Zusatz m, schleierverhinderndes Mittel n, Schleierschutzmittel n, Schleierverhütungsmittel n, schleierwidriges Mittel
anticlinal [fold], anticline, saddle, upfold <geo.>	Antiklinale f, Sattel m, Gewölbe n, Einsattlung f, Antikline f <Geo.>		
anticlinal ridge	Sattelrücken m; Sattellinie f [der Falte]	anti-Frenkel defect	Anti-Frenkel-Fehlordnung f, Anti-Frenkel-Defekt m
		antigravity filtration	s. vacuum filtration
		anti[-]halation backing; light-screening photographic layer, anti[-]halation layer	Hinterguß m; Antihaloschicht f, Antilichthofschicht f; Lichthofschutzschicht f; lichthoffreie Schicht f
anticline	s. anticlinal fold <geo.>		
anti-clockwise direction	s. counterclockwise direction		
anticlockwise process	s. left-handed cycle		
anticoincidence	Antikoinzidenz f	anti[-]halation layer	s. anti[-]halation backing
anticoincidence circuit; anticoincidence stage	Antikoinzidenzschaltung f; Antikoinzidenzstufe f	anti[-]halation undercoat	Zwischenguß m
		anti-Hermitian, antihermitian	s. skew-Hermitian
anticoincidence counter	Antikoinzidenzzähler m	antihermitian part	antihermitescher Anteil m
		anti-hole	Antiloch n
		anti-homomorphism	Antihomomorphismus m
anticoincidence stage	s. anticoincidence circuit		
anti-colour centre	Antifarbzentrum n	anti-hunt circuit	Dämpfungskreis m
anticommutation relations (rules), Fermi-Dirac commutation relations	Fermi-Diracsche Vertauschungsrelationen fpl	antihyperbolic cosine	s. inverse hyperbolic cosine
		antihyperbolic cotangent	s. inverse hyperbolic cotangent
		antihyperbolic function, inverse hyperbolic function, area-hyperbolic function, ar-function	Areafunktion f, ar-Funktion f
anticommutator	Antikommutator m		
anticommute	antikommutieren		
anticosine, inverse (arc) cosine, arc cos, cos⁻¹	Arkuskosinus m, arc cos		
anticotangent, inverse (arc) cotangent, arc cot, arc ctg, cot⁻¹, ctg⁻¹	Arkuskotangens m, arc cot	antihyperbolic sine	s. inverse hyperbolic sine
		antihyperbolic tangent	s. inverse hyperbolic tangent
		anti-isomorphism	Antiisomorphie f
		anti-isomorphism <math.>	Antiisomorphismus m, antiisomorphe Abbildung f <Math.>
anti-creep device	Leerlaufhemmung f		
anticyclone	s. High		
anticyclone	s. mobile anticyclone	antijamming ability, noise stability, noise immunity	Störstabilität f, Störfestigkeit f, Störsicherheit f; Störspannungsfestigkeit f
anticyclonic activity	Hochdrucktätigkeit f, Antizyklonentätigkeit f		
anticyclonic branch	s. high-pressure branch		
anticyclonic centre, high-pressure centre, centre of high pressure [area]	Hochdruckkern m, Kern m des Hoch[druckgebiete]s, Hochdruckschwerpunkt m	anti-linear	antilinear
		antilog, antilogarithm	Numerus m, Antilogarithmus m
		antimatter	Antimaterie f
anticyclonic situation	Hochdruckwetterlage f, Hochdrucklage f	antimer	s. enantiomer
		antimerical	s. enantiomorphous <chem.>
		antimetal	s. non-metal
		antimetric four-pole, antimetric four-terminal network	antimetrischer Vierpol m
anticyclonic vorticity	antizyklonale Vorticity f, antizyklonaler Wirbel m		
		antimony point	s. freezing point of antimony
anti-damping	s. continuous excitation	antineutrino operator, operator of antineutrino	Antineutrinooperator m, Operator m des Antineutrinos
antiderivative, primitive, indefinite integral	Stammfunktion f, primitive Funktion f, [unbestimmtes] Newtonsches Integral n		
		antinodal point, negative nodal point	negativer Knotenpunkt m
antidiffusing grid	s. moving grid		
antidiffusing grid (screen)	s. anti[-]diffusion grid	antinodal point, antinode, loop <of oscillation, standing wave>	Schwingungsbauch m; Wellenbauch m, Bauch m [der stehenden Welle]
antidiffusing screen	s. moving grid		
anti[-]diffusion grid, antidiffusion screen, antidiffusing grid (screen)	Streustrahlenblende f, Sekundärstrahlenblende f	antinode of potential, potential loop	Spannungsbauch m
		antinode of the longitudinal wave	Druckbauch m
antidiffusion grid	s. a. moving grid	anti-operation	s. complementary operation
antidiffusion screen	s. moving grid	antioxidant, antioxygen oxidation inhibitor, oxidation preventive, oxidation retarder	Oxydationsinhibitor m, Oxydationsverhinderer m, Antioxydans n <pl.: Antioxydanzien>, Antioxygen n
antidromic	antidromisch		
anti-electron	s. positron		
anti-epicentre	s. anticentre		
antiferroelectric	Antiferroelektrikum n, antiferroelektrischer Stoff m		
antiferroelectricity	Antiferroelektrizität f		
		anti-parallax mirror	Ablesespiegel m
antiferromagnet, antiferromagnetic material	Antiferromagnetikum n, antiferromagnetischer Stoff m	antiparallel, opposite [in direction], oppositely directed, of opposite direction	antiparallel; entgegengesetzt gerichtet, entgegengerichtet
antiferromagnetic Curie point (temperature)	s. Néel point		
antiferromagnetic material	s. antiferromagnet	antiparallel circuit	s. antiparallel connection
		antiparallel connection, antiparallel circuit, back-to-back connection	Antiparallelschaltung f
antiferromagnetic resonance	antiferromagnetische Resonanz f		
		antiparalysis pulse	s. gating pulse

antiparticle	Antiteilchen n, Antipartikel f	anvil ‹of the micrometer›	Meßamboß m [des Mikrometers], Amboß m [des Mikrometers]
antiparticle of electron	s. positron	anvil cloud	amboßähnliche Wolke f, Incusform f
antiphase, in phase opposition, in opposition	gegenphasig, [um] 180° phasenverschoben		
		AO method	s. method of atomic orbitals
		apastron	Apastron n, Sternferne f
antiphase	s. a. opposite phase	aperiodical; dead-beat [aperiodical]; non-oscillating, non-periodic; strongly damped	aperiodisch; nichtperiodisch; nichtschwingend; eigenschwingungsfrei; aperiodisch gedämpft
anti[-]phase boundary	Antiphasengrenzfläche f		
anti[-]phase domain, out-of-step domain	Antiphasenbereich m, antiphasiger Bereich m, Antiphasendomäne f, Antidomäne f	aperiodic antenna, untuned aerial	aperiodische Antenne f
antiplane strain	„antiplane strain" n	aperiodograph	Aperiodograph m, Umwandler m von Coradi
antipodal space, spherical space	sphärischer Raum m	apertometer, aperture meter	Apertometer n
antipolar	Antipolare f	aperture ‹of aerial›	Apertur f ‹Antenne›
antipole	Antipol m	aperture, aperture width ‹of radiator›	Öffnungsweite f ‹Strahler›
anti-position	anti-Stellung f		
antiprincipal point, negative principal point	negativer Hauptpunkt m	aperture	s. a. effective aperture
		aperture aberration	s. spherical aberration
		aperture antenna	Aperturantenne f
antiquark	Antiquark n	aperture correction	Aperturkorrektion f, Aperturblendenkorrektion f
anti-reflection coating, anti-reflex coating, anti-flare coating	reflexvermindernde (reflexmindernde) Schicht f, reflexvermindernder Belag m, T-Belag m, Antireflexbelag m, Antireflexschicht f, Reflexschutzschicht f	apertured diaphragm, pinhole diaphragm, diaphragm; perforated screen ‹opt.›	Lochblende f ‹Opt.›
		apertured disk, aperture (perforated) disk	Lochscheibe f; Lochblendenscheibe f
antiresonance	s. parallel resonance	apertured disk	s. a. Nipkow disk
anti-Schottky defect	Anti-Schottky-Fehlordnung f, Anti-Schottky-Defekt m	aperture diaphragm, aperture stop	Öffnungsblende f, Aperturblende f
antiselena	Gegenmond m		
anti-selfadjoint	antiselbstadjungiert		
antisensitization	Antisensibilisierung f	aperture disk	s. apertured disk
		apertured shadow mask	s. shadow mask ‹tv.›
anti-shielding factor	„anti-shielding"-Faktor m, Antiabschirmungsfaktor m	aperture effect, Stiles-Crawford effect	Apertureffekt m; Stiles-Crawford-Effekt m
antisine, inverse (arc) sine, arc sin, sin⁻¹	Arkussinus m, arc sin	aperture effect	s. a. disk of aberration
		aperture mask	s. shadow mask ‹tv.›
antisolar point	Gegenpunkt m der Sonne, Gegensonnenpunkt m	aperture meter, apertometer	Apertometer n
antisotypic	anti[i]sotyp	aperture of the illuminator's aperture stop; condenser aperture	Beleuchtungsapertur f
antisotypism	Anti[i]sotypie f		
antispectroscopic	s. achromatic		
anti-Stokes line	Anti-Stokes-Linie f, antistokessche (anti-Stokessche) Linie f	aperture ratio, relative aperture, ratio of the lens aperture ‹of objective›	Öffnungsverhältnis n, relative Öffnung f, [geometrisch-optische] Lichtstärke f ‹Objektiv›
anti-Stokes phosphorescence	anti-Stokessche Phosphoreszenz f, Anti-Stokes-Phosphoreszenz f	aperture stop	s. aperture diaphragm
		aperture width ‹of the radiator›, aperture	Öffnungsweite f ‹Strahler›
antisymmetrical	s. alternating ‹math.›	apex ‹astr.›	Apex m ‹Astr.›
antisymmetrical neutral [meson] theory	antisymmetrische neutrale Mesonentheorie (Theorie) f	apex ‹opt.›, vertex	Scheitel m ‹Opt.›
		apex	s. a. peak ‹gen.›
antisymmetrical tensor	s. alternating tensor	apex	s. a. vertex ‹geometry; cryst.›
antisymmetric in time, time-antisymmetric	zeitantisymmetrisch	apex angle [of cone]	Öffnungswinkel m [des Kegels]
antisymmetric kernel	s. alternating kernel	apex drive, centre feed	Mittelpunktspeisung f, Mittenspeisung f
antisymmetric molecular orbital configuration-interaction method	s. configuration-interaction method		
		apex of the Sun	s. solar apex
		aphelic velocity	Aphelgeschwindigkeit f
antisymmetric tensor	s. alternating tensor	aphotic zone	aphotische Zone f, lichtlose Zone
antisymmetrization	Antisymmetrierung f, Antisymmetrisierung f	aphylactic projection ‹US›	vermittelnde Abbildung f
antisymmetry, skew symmetry	Antisymmetrie f, Schiefsymmetrie f	aplanat, aplanatic objective	Aplanat m (n)
antitangent, inverse (arc) tangent, arc tg, arc tan, tg⁻¹, tan⁻¹	Arkustangens m, arc tan, arc tg	aplanatic mirror	s. coma-free mirror
		aplanatic objective	s. aplanat
		aplanatic points	aplanatische Punkte mpl, aplanatisches Punktepaar n
anti-thixotropy	Antithixotropie f		
antitrades, antitrade winds, countertrades	Antipassat m	aplanatic reflecting telescope	aplanatisches Spiegelsystem n, komafreies Spiegelteleskop (Spiegelfernrohr) n
antitrigonometrical function, inverse circular (trigonometrical) function, cyclometric (arc-trigonometric) function	Arkusfunktion f, zyklometrische Funktion f, inverse trigonometrische Funktion, Kreisbogenfunktion f, arc-Funktion f	aplanatic surface, Cartesian surface	kartesische Fläche f, aplanatische Fläche
		aplanatism	Aplanasie f
		apocentre ‹astr.›	Apogalaktikum n ‹Astr.›
		apocentre ‹mech.›	Apozentrum n ‹Mech.›
antitwilight	Gegendämmerung f	apochromat, apochromatic objective	Apochromat m (n)
antiunitary	antiunitär		
Antoine['s] equation	Antoinesche Gleichung f		
Antonoff['s] rule	Antonowsche Regel f	apochromatism	Apochromasie f

apocynthion	s. apolune	apparent power consumption	Scheinverbrauch m
apogean velocity	Apogäumsgeschwindigkeit f		
apolar	s. non-polar	apparent radiant	scheinbarer Radiant m
apolar adsorption	apolare Adsorption f	apparent radius	s. apparent semi-diameter
apolune, apocynthion	Apolunium n, Mondferne f	apparent remanence	s. retentivity
		apparent resistance	s. impedance
apomictic	apomiktisch	apparent semi-diameter, apparent radius, angular semi-diameter (radius)	scheinbarer Radius m, Winkelradius m, Winkelwert m des Radius
A position	s. A site		
a posteriori probability	s. inverse probability		
apostilb, asb	= $1/\pi$ cd/m²	apparent sidereal day, true sidereal day	wahrer Sterntag m
apothecaries' system	„apothecary"-System n <Masseeinheiten für Drogen>	apparent sidereal time, true sidereal time	wahre Sternzeit f
apparatus for remote measurements	s. telemeter	apparent solar day, true solar day	wahrer Sonnentag m
apparent acronycal rising	scheinbarer akronychischer Aufgang m	apparent solar time, true solar time; sundial time	wahre Sonnenzeit f; wahre Ortszeit f
apparent additional mass	s. virtual mass	apparent solubility	Scheinlöslichkeit f
apparent brightness [of a star]	s. apparent stellar brightness	apparent specific gravity	s. apparent density
		apparent speed of wind, apparent velocity of wind	scheinbare Windgeschwindigkeit f
apparent conduction [of heat]	s. eddy conduction	apparent stellar brightness, apparent stellar magnitude, apparent brightness [of a star]	scheinbare Helligkeit f <Gestirn>
apparent conductivity	s. eddy conductivity		
apparent cosmic setting	scheinbarer kosmischer Untergang m		
apparent current	Scheinstrom m		
apparent density [of powders], bulk (packed, powder) density; apparent specific gravity, apparent weight, bulk specific gravity, bulk weight	Rohdichte f <in kg/m³>; Schüttdichte f, Schüttmasse f, scheinbare Dichte f <kg/m³>; Schüttgewicht n, Scheingewicht n, Schüttwichte f, Rohwichte f <in kp/m³>	apparent Sun, true Sun	wahre Sonne f
		apparent surface area	scheinbare Oberfläche f
		apparent symmetry	Scheinsymmetrie f
		apparent target luminance	[scheinbare] Zielleuchtdichte f, Zielhelligkeit f, wahrgenommene Leuchtdichte f des schwarzen Ziels
apparent diameter, angular diameter <of star>	scheinbarer Durchmesser m; Winkeldurchmesser m <Gestirn>		
apparent diffusion	s. eddy diffusion	apparent temperature	s. effective temperature
apparent diffusivity	s. eddy diffusivity	apparent terminal impedance	scheinbarer Wellenwiderstand m des Leitungsabschlusses, scheinbarer Abschlußwiderstand m
apparent elastic limit	technische Elastizitätsgrenze f		
apparent energy; apparent work	Scheinenergie f, scheinbare Energie f; Scheinarbeit f, scheinbare Arbeit f	apparent thermal conductivity	s. eddy conductivity
apparent-energy meter, volt-ampere-hour[ ] meter	Scheinverbrauchszähler m, Voltamperestundenzähler m	apparent turbulent kinematic viscosity	s. eddy viscosity
		apparent value	Scheinwert m [der Wechselgröße]
apparent equilibrium, false equilibrium	scheinbares Gleichgewicht n	apparent velocity of wind	s. apparent speed of wind
apparent error, seeming error	scheinbarer (plausibelster) Fehler m	apparent viscosity	s. eddy viscosity
apparent force	s. fictitious force	apparent volume, bulk volume	Schüttvolumen n, scheinbares Volumen n
apparent friction	s. turbulent friction		
apparent front, false front, pseudofront	Scheinfront f	apparent weight	s. apparent density
		apparent work	s. apparent energy
apparent half-life	scheinbare Halbwertzeit f	apparent yield point, apparent yield strength	technische Streckgrenze f
apparent heat conduction	s. eddy conduction		
apparent height [of reflection], equivalent height [of reflection], virtual height [of reflection]	scheinbare Reflexionshöhe f, scheinbare Höhe f	appearance of fading, occurrence of fading	Schwundeinbruch m
		appearance of fatigue, fatigue effect	Ermüdungserscheinung f
		appearance of a meteor	Auftauchen (Aufleuchten) n eines Meteors
apparent horizon, visible horizon, terrestrial horizon, sensible horizon, local horizon, sea horizon	scheinbarer Horizont m; Kimm f, natürlicher (sichtbarer) Horizont, Meereshorizont m, Sichthorizont m	appearance potential	Erscheinungspotential n, Appearancepotential n
		Appell['s] equations of motion	Appellsche (Gibbs-Appellsche) Bewegungsgleichungen fpl, Gibbs-Appellsche Gleichungen fpl
apparent inertia, virtual inertia	virtuelle Trägheit f, scheinbare Trägheit	Appell['s] polynomial	Appellsches Polynom n
apparent magnification	s. angular magnification	Appell['s] theorem	Appellscher Satz m
apparent magnitude	s. apparent stellar brightness	Appelrot['s] condition	Appelrotsche Bedingung f
apparent molar quantity	scheinbare molare Größe f	Applegate diagram	Applegate-Diagramm n
apparent molar volume	scheinbares Molvolumen n		
apparent noon, true noon	wahrer Mittag m	Appleton layer <el.>, F-layer	F-Schicht f, Appleton-Schicht f <El.>
apparent permeability	Scheinpermeabilität f	application of force, action of force	Kraftangriff m, Angreifen n (Angriff m) der Kraft
apparent phase angle	Scheinphasenwinkel m	applied climatology, microclimatology	angewandte Klimatologie f, Mikroklimatologie f, Kleinklimatologie f
		applied current	eingeprägter Strom m
apparent place [of star], apparent position [of star]	scheinbarer Ort m [des Gestirns], scheinbarer Sternort m	appraisal <US>	s. evaluation
		appreciation of distance, judgment of distance, distance appreciation (judgment)	Entfernungsschätzung f
apparent pole, true pole	wahrer Pol m		
apparent position [of star]	s. apparent place		
		approach, approximation	Näherung f, Approximation f; Annäherung f
apparent power	Scheinleistung f, scheinbare Leistung f	approach	s. a. encounter <e. g. of stars>

AP projection	s. AP view	arch	s. inverse hyperbolic cosine
approximate measurement	Grobmessung f	arch dam, arched dam	Bogenstaumauer f, Gewölbesperre f
approximate value	s. approximative value	arched gravity dam, arch-gravity dam	Bogenschwergewichtsmauer f, Bogengewichtsmauer f, Bogengewichtssperre f
approximating function	s. approximation function		
approximation, approach	Näherung f, Approximation f; Annäherung f	Archimedean screw, spiral pump	Archimedische Schnecke f
approximation function, approximating function	Näherungsfunktion f, approximierende Funktion f	Archimedean screw, Archimedean spiral, Archimedes['] spiral, spiral of Archimedes	Archimedische Spirale f
approximation method of M. J. Lighthill	s. Poincaré-Lighthill-Kuo method		
approximation of quasi-saturated state	Näherung f des quasigesättigten Zustandes	Archimedes['] law	s. Archimedes principle
approximation theory	Approximationstheorie f	Archimedes number, Ar	Archimedische Zahl f, Archimed-Zahl f, Ar
approximative value, approximate value	Näherungswert m	Archimedes['] principle, Archimedes['] law	Archimedisches Prinzip (Gesetz) n, Prinzip von (des) Archimedes
appulse <astr.>	Berührung f <Astr.>		
a priori bound	a-priori-Schranke f, Apriorischranke f	Archimedes['] spiral	s. Archimedean screw
a priori estimation	Aprioriabschätzung f, a priori-Abschätzung f	architectural acoustics	s. room acoustics
		arc hum, arc noise, singing of the arc	Summen n des Lichtbogens
a priori probability, prior probability, probability a priori	apriori-Wahrscheinlichkeit f, Anfangswahrscheinlichkeit f, Wahrscheinlichkeit f a priori	arc-hyperbolic cosine	s. hyperbolic cosine
		arc-hyperbolic cotangent	s. hyperbolic cotangent
uprotic acid	aprotische Säure f	arc-hyperbolic sine	s. hyperbolic sine
apse, apsis <pl.: apsides>	Apside f, Apsidenpunkt m <pl.: Apsiden>	arc-hyperbolic tangent	s. hyperbolic tangent
		arcing	Lichtbogenbildung f, Ausbildung f des Lichtbogens
apse line, line of apsides	Apsidenlinie f		
apsis	s. apse	arcing-over, arc-over	Bogendurchbruch m; Bogenüberschlag m; Lichtbogenüberschlag m
AP view, AP projection, anterior-posterior view, posterior (dorsal) projection	Projektion f von vorn nach hinten	arcing voltage, arc potential (voltage)	Lichtbogenspannung f; Bogenspannung f
		arc lamp of the projector	s. projector arc lamp
APW method	s. augmented plane wave method	arc length, length of arc gap	Lichtbogenlänge f; Bogenlänge f
aquarium reactor	s. swimming pool reactor	arc length	s. a. curve length <math.>
aqueous homogeneous reactor, aqueous reactor	wäßrig-homogener Reaktor m, homogener wäßriger Reaktor, Wasserlösungsreaktor m	arc line	Bogenlinie f
		arc migration	Lichtbogenwanderung f
aqueous rock	s. sedimentary rock	arc noise, arc hum, singing of the arc	Summen n des Lichtbogens
aquifer	s. water-bearing stratum	arc of curve	Kurvenbogen m
aquifuge, impermeable stratum	wasserundurchlässige Schicht f, Wassertrennungsschicht f	arc of discharge	Entladungsfaden m, Entladungsbogen m
aquo-ion, hydrated ion	Hydration n, Ionenhydrat n	arc of Lowitz, lateral tangential arc to 22°-halo	seitlicher Berührungsbogen m des kleinen Ringes, Lowitzscher [schiefer] Bogen m
aquoluminescence	Aquolumineszenz f		
aquolysis, hydrolysis, hydrolyzation	Hydrolyse f, Aquatisierung		
		arc of the circle	s. circular arc
Arago disk	Arago-Scheibe f, Aragosch Scheibe f	arc of traverse	Schwenkungswinkel m
Arago point	Arago-Punkt m, Aragoscher Punkt m	arc oscillation	Lichtbogenschwingung f, Poulsen-Schwingung f
Arago['s] spot	s. bright spot of Poisson	arc-over	s. arcing-over
arbitrary unit	willkürliche Einheit f	arc-over gap, arc gap	Lichtbogenstrecke f, Bogenstrecke f
arbitrational analysis	Schiedsanalyse f	arc physics	Lichtbogenphysik f
arborescent crystal	s. dendrite		
arbor Saturni, lead tree	Bleibaum m	arc plasma	Bogenplasma n; Lichtbogenplasma n
		arc plot	s. arc characteristic
arc, electric arc, voltaic arc <el.>	[elektrischer] Bogen m; [elektrischer] Lichtbogen m	arc potential, arc[ing] voltage	Lichtbogenspannung f, Bogenspannung f
		arc resistance, resistance to arc	Lichtbogenfestigkeit f, Lichtbogensicherheit f
arc at break	s. break arc		
arc at make	s. closing arc	arcronograph	s. oscillograph
arc[-]back	s. backfire <of rectifier>	arc shooting	Bogenschießen n
arc burning in air, air arc	Luftbogen m		
arc characteristic, characteristic of the arc discharge, arc plot	Bogencharakteristik f; Lichtbogencharakteristik f, Lichtbogenkennlinie f; Bogendiagramm n	arc sine	s. antisine
		arc source of ions	s. arc discharge ion source
		arc space	Lichtbogenraum m
		arc spark	Bogenfunke m
arc column	s. column of gas in arc discharge	arc spectrum	Bogenspektrum n
		arc tangent	s. antitangent
arc co-ordinate	s. curve length <math.>	Arctic axis pole	s. boreal pole
arc cotangent	s. anticotangent	arc-to-glow transition	Übergang m Lichtbogen – Glimmstrom, Umschlagen n der Bogenentladung in die Glimmentladung, Übergang von der Bogenentladung zur Glimmentladung
arc current	Lichtbogenstrom m; Bogenstrom m		
arc discharge, electric arc [in gas]	Bogenentladung f		
arc discharge ion source, arc source of ions	Bogen[entladungs]ionenquelle f	arc transmitter, Poulsen transmitter	Poulsen-Sender m, Lichtbogensender m
arc-drop voltage	s. burning voltage		
arc flame	Bogenflamme f	arc-trigonometric function	s. antitrigonometric[al] function
arc gap, arc-over gap	Lichtbogenstrecke f; Bogenstrecke f		

Arcus	s. curve length <math.>	aridity <meteo.>	Aridität f, Trockenheit f, Dürre f <Meteo.>
arc voltage	s. arc potential		
Ardenne [ion] source / Von	s. duoplasmatron ion source	aridity index	Ariditätsindex m, Trockenheitsindex m
area, area of surface, surface area	Flächeninhalt m, Inhalt m <Fläche>, Fläche f; Oberfläche f, Oberflächeninhalt m	aristostigmat, aristostigmatic lens	Aristostigmat m (n)
		arithmetic average (mean)	arithmetischer Mittelwert m, arithmetisches Mittel n, Durchschnitt m
area constant	Flächenkonstante f		
area contact, large-area contact	Flächenkontakt m	Arkadyev['s] experiment	Versuch m von Arkadjew, Arkadjewscher Versuch
area-equivalent	s. area-preserving	Arkel-De Boer technique, Van Arkel process, de Boer process, hot[-]wire process (technique), iodide process, filament-growth method	Aufwachsverfahren (Heißdrahtverfahren) n [nach van Arkel und de Boer], Van-Arkel-de-Boer-Methode f
area-hyperbolic function	s. antihyperbolic function		
areal acceleration, surface (sector) acceleration	Flächenbeschleunigung f		
areal curl, surface curl, Curl	Flächenrotation f, Flächenwirbel m, Flächenrotor m, Sprungrotor m, Rot		
		armature <of magnet or relay>	Anker m <Magnet, Relais>
areal derivative, surface derivative	Flächenableitung f	armature reaction	Ankerrückwirkung f, Rotorrückwirkung f, Rotorreaktion f, Ankerreaktion f
areal divergence	s. surface divergence		
areal element	s. element of area		
areal eruption	Arealeruption f, Flächeneruption f	armature stroke	Ankerhub m
		armed lever	s. bent lever
areal gradient	s. surface gradient	armillary sphere	Armillarsphäre f, Armille f
areal metric, surface metric	Flächenmetrik f	arm of couple	s. arm of the couple
area load	Flächenbelastung f	arm of the bridge, branch of the bridge, bridge arm (branch)	Brückenzweig m, Zweig m der Brücke, Schenkel m der Brücke
areal velocity, surface (area, superficial) velocity	Flächengeschwindigkeit f		
area measurement	s. planimetering	arm of [the] couple, arm of the force, moment (force) arm	Kraftarm m, Arm m des Kräftepaares; Hebelarm m
area method <astr., geo., nucl.>	Flächenmethode f <Astr., Geo., Kern.>		
area moment circle, Mohr['s] area moment circle	Trägheitskreis m, Mohrscher Trägheitskreis	arm of the microscope, microscope arm	Tubusträger m
		arm of the spiral nebula	s. spiral arm
		Armstrong modulation	s. zero-phase modulation
area monitor	Raumüberwachungsgerät n, Lokalmonitor m, Flächenmonitor m	Aron circuit	Aron-Schaltung f, Zweiwattmeterschaltung f, Zweileistungsmesserschaltung f
		Ar point	s. recalescence point
area monitoring	Bereichsüberwachung f; Flächenüberwachung f; Raumüberwachung f	arranged in line	s. mounted in line
		arrangement <of n things k at a time> <combinatorial analysis>	Variation f <von n Elementen zur k-ten Klasse>, Kombination f mit Berücksichtigung der Reihenfolge <Kombinatorik>
area of crystal	s. crystal domain <cryst.>		
area of hysteresis loop	s. enclosed area of hysteresis loop		
area of moments, moment area	Momentenfläche f	arrangement	s. a. configuration
		arrangement for measuring	s. measuring arrangement
area of single vision	s. Panum['s] area		
area of sunspot, spot area	Fleckenfläche f	arrangement without repetitions	Variation f ohne Wiederholung
area of surface	s. area		
area-preserving, area-equivalent, equi-areal, of equal area	flächentreu, inhaltstreu	arrangement with repetitions	Variation f mit Wiederholung
		array for measuring	s. measuring arrangement
area-preserving mapping, equi-areal (equivalent) mapping	flächentreue (äquivalente, inhaltstreue) Abbildung f	arrest <of dislocations>	Hemmung f <Versetzungen>
		arrester	s. discharge gap <el.>
		arrester	s. spark gap
area rule	Querschnittsregel f, „area rule" f, Flächenregel f	arrest line	s. cyster shell marking
		arrest lines	s. clam shell markings
area sketch	s. location sketch	arrest point	s. critical point
area velocity	s. areal velocity	Arrhenius['] equation	Arrheniussche Gleichung (Formel) f
areometer, densimeter, hydrometer	Aräometer n, Senkwaage f, Spindelsenkwaage f, Senkspindel f, Schwimmwaage f, Spindel f, Densimeter n	Arrhenius equation, Arrhenius-Guzman equation	Arrhenius-Guzmansche Gleichung f, Arrhenius-Guzman-Gleichung f
		arrival	s. incidence <e.g. of wave>
areopyknometer	Aräopyknometer n, Weithalspyknometer n	Arsonval galvanometer / D'	s. moving-coil galvanometer
		arsonvalization	Arsonvalisation f, d'Arsonvalisation f
ar-function	s. antihyperbolic function		
arg	s. amplitude <of a complex number>	artefact, artifact, artifice	Artefakt m
		artesian head	artesische Druckhöhe f
Argand diagram (plane)	s. complex plane		
argon age	Argonalter n	artesian pressure	artesischer Druck m
		artesian water	artesisches Wasser n, gespanntes Wasser (Grundwasser n)
argon method, potassium-argon method (dating), K-Ar (^{40}K-^{40}Ar) method	Argonmethode f, Kalium-Argon-Methode f, Argon-Kalium-Methode f	artesian well	artesischer Brunnen m, Steigbrunnen m, Rohrbrunnen m
argument	s. amplitude <of a complex number>	articulated bracket	Gelenkarm m
		articulated quadrangle	s. linked quadrilateral
argument	s. independent variable	articulated quadrilateral	s. linked quadrilateral
argument of latitude	Argument n der Breite	articulation	s. intelligibility
argument of perihelion, angle from ascending node to perihelion	Perihelabstand m vom Knoten, Abstand m des Perihels vom aufsteigenden Knoten	articulation equivalent	Verständlichkeitsäquivalent n
		articulation for logatomes (syllables)	s. logatom articulation
		artifact, artifice	s. artefact
argument principle	Argument[en]prinzip n, Prinzip n vom Argument, Satz m vom logarithmischen Residuum	artifice, trick, wrinkle	Kunstgriff m, Kniff m

artificial ag[e]ing	s. preaging	aspherical mirror	asphärischer Spiegel m
artificial double refraction	erzwungene (künstliche) Doppelbrechung f	aspherical surface	asphärische (deformierte, nichtkuglige) Fläche f
artificial Earth's satellite, [man-made] Earth's satellite, Earth-circling (terrestrial) satellite, spoutnik, sputnik	künstlicher Erdsatellit m, Erdsatellit, Sputnik m	aspherical top [molecule]	asymmetrisches Kreiselmolekül n, Molekül n vom Typ asymmetrischer Kreisel, asymmetrischer Kreisel m
artificial horizon, gyroscopic horizon, gyrohorizon	künstlicher Horizont m, Kreiselhorizont m, Fliegerhorizont m, Horizont[al]kreisel m	asphericity, aspherizing	Deformation f, Abweichung f von der Kugelfläche
		aspherizing	s. asphericity
		aspiration	s. suction
artificial line, artificial transmission line, line simulator, extension line (lead, pad), continuation lead	künstliche Leitung f, künstliche Übertragungsleitung f, Leitungsnachbildung f, Verlängerungsleitung f	aspiration psychrometer, ventilated psychrometer; Assmann psychrometer	Aspirationspsychrometer n; Aßmann-Aspirationspsychrometer n, Aßmann-Psychrometer n, Aßmann n
artificially radioactive, artificial radioactive	künstlich radioaktiv	aspiring pump, suction pump	Saugpumpe f, Absaugpumpe f
artificial satellite, man-made satellite	künstlicher Satellit m, Satellit	assay balance	Probierwaage f, Justierwaage f
artificial transmission line	s. artificial line	assay balance	s. a. analytical balance
artificial transmutation of elements	künstliche Umwandlung f von Elementen	assay weight	Probiergewicht[sstück] n, Richtgewicht[sstück] n, Probegewicht[sstück] n
artificial year	s. civil year	assemblage	Menge f <Math.>
ascending	s. ascent	assembly <of reactor>	Anordnung f; Kassette f
ascending branch, rising branch (portion) <of a curve>	aufsteigender (ansteigender) Ast m	assertion, proposition <math.>	Behauptung f <Math.>
ascending branch of the decay curve	Anklingkurve f, ansteigender Ast m der Zerfallskurve	assigned force, force density	Kraftdichte f
		assignment, determining, determination	Bestimmung f
ascending current <bio.>	aufsteigender Strom (Reizstrom) m <Bio.>	assignment <to>, ascribing <to>, attribution <to>	Zuschreiben n, Zuordnung f
ascending motion, ascension, lifting <meteo.>	Aufwärtsbewegung f; Steigbewegung f, aufsteigende Bewegung f; Hebung f <Meteo.>		
		assignment problem	Zuordnungsproblem n
ascending node	aufsteigender Knoten m	assimilation, photochemical assimilation	[photochemische] Assimilation f
ascending part of the trajectory	Aufstiegsbahn f	assimilation	s. a. anabolism <bio.>
		assimilation number	Assimilationszahl f
ascending prominence, rising prominence	aufsteigende Protuberanz f	assimilation product	Assimilat n
		assimilation quotient	Assimilationsquotient m
ascending source, ascending spring	aufsteigende Quelle f	assimilation rate	Assimilationsrate f
ascending velocity	s. climbing speed	assistor	Assistor m
ascending wind	s. anabatic wind	Assmann psychrometer	s. aspiration psychrometer
ascension, ascent <astr.>	Aszension f, Aufstieg m	associate, association	Assoziat f
ascension	s. a. ascending motion	associate [Bertrand] curves	s. Bertrand curves
ascensional difference	Aszensionsdifferenz f	associated <with>	zugeordnet, assoziiert
ascent <astr.>, ascension	Aszension f, Aufstieg m <Astr.>	associated corpuscular emission	sekundäre Korpuskularemission f, korpuskulare Sekundärstrahlung f
ascent, ascending <geo.; meteo.>	Aufstieg m; Aufgleiten n <Geo.; Meteo.>		
ascent	s. a. increase	associated function [of the eigenfunction]	zugeordnete Funktion f [zur Eigenfunktion]
ascent	s. a. slope <of the curve>		
ascent	s. a. water-surface ascent	associated ion complexes	assoziierte Ionenkomplexe mpl
ascribing	s. assignment <to>		
A segment	s. A band	associated ion pair	s. ion pair
aseismic region, non seismic region	aseismischer Raum m	associated Laguerre function	verallgemeinerte Laguerresche Funktion f
aser, amplifier based on stimulated emission of radiation	Aser m, Quantenverstärker m	associated Laguerre polynomial	verallgemeinertes Laguerresches Polynom n
		associated Legendre function [of the first kind], Legendre['s] associated function [of the first kind]	zugeordnete Legendresche Funktion f, zugeordnete Kugelfunktion f erster Art, Legendresche zugeordnete Funktion [erster Art]
ash breeze	s. calm		
ash cloud	Aschenwolke f		
ashen light, earth-shine	aschgraues Mondlicht (Licht) n; Erdlicht n, Erdschein m		
ashing	Veraschung f, Verbrennung f zu Asche	associated Legendre function of the second kind, Legendre['s] associated function of the second kind	zugeordnete Legendresche Funktion f zweiter Art, zugeordnete Kugelfunktion f zweiter Art, Legendresche zugeordnete Funktion zweiter Art
A site, A position, tetrahedral site	Tetraederplatz m, tetraedrischer Lückenplatz m, Tetraederlücke f, A-Lage f, Tetraederzentrum n	associated Legendre polynomial	zugeordnetes Legendresches Polynom n, Legendresches zugeordnetes Polynom
ASMO Cl method	s. configuration-interaction method	associated liquid	Assoziationsflüssigkeit f, angelagerte Flüssigkeit f, „associated liquid" f
aspect [-]ratio <or its reciprocal> <of aerofoil>	Seitenverhältnis n <Flügel>, Flügelstreckung f, Streckung f <Tragflügel>		
asperity	s. roughness	associated molecule, association complex	Übermolekel f, Übermolekül n, Assoziationskomplex m
aspherical, non-spherical	nichtsphärisch, nichtkugelförmig, nichtkuglig, asphärisch	associated particles method, method of associated particles	Methode f der assoziierten Teilchen

associated production	assoziierte (zugeordnet-gemeinsame) Erzeugung f, Assoziation f, „associated production" f	Aston['s] dark space, primary dark space	Astonscher Dunkelraum m, erster Dunkelraum
associated spherical harmonic	zugeordnete Kugelfunktion f		
associated wave	Begleitwelle f	Aston['s] isotope rule, Aston['s] rule, Aston['s] whole number rule, isotope rule	Astonsche Isotopenregel f, Isotopenregel [von Aston], Astonsche Regel f <für stabile Kerne>
associate matrix	s. adjoint matrix		
association, associate	Assoziat n		
association <geo.>	Vergesellschaftung f <Geo.>	astral ray <bio.>	Polstrahl m <Bio.>
association	s. a. association of molecules	astrionics	Astrionik f; Raumschiffelektronik f
association by hydrogen bonds	s. hydrogen bond association		
association colloid, micellar colloid	Assoziationskolloid n, Mizellkolloid n	astrocamera	s. astrograph
		astrochemistry	s. space chemistry
association complex	s. associated molecule	astrogeology, planetology	Astrogeologie f, Planetologie f
association energy	s. energy of association		
association factor	s. degree of association	astrogeophysics	Astrogeophysik f
association of molecules, chemical (molecular) association, association	Assoziation (Zusammenlagerung) f von Molekülen, Übermolekülbildung f	astrograph, astrographic camera, astrographic refractor, astrographic telescope, photographic telescope, astrocamera	Astrograph m, photographischer Refraktor m, photographisch benutztes Linsenfernrohr n, photographisches Fernrohr n, Astrokamera f
association polymorphism	Assoziationspolymorphie f		
associative groupoid (system)	s. semi-group	astrographic chart	s. star map
		astrographic plate, astrophotographic plate, astroplate	Astroplatte f
associative law, associativity law	Assoziativgesetz n, assoziatives Gesetz n, Anreihungsregel f		
		astrographic refractor (telescope)	s. astrograph
assumption	s. supposition		
assumption that a cross section remains plane after bending	s. Bernoulli's hypothesis	astroid, four-cusped hypocycloid, tetracuspid	Astroide f, Sternkurve f, vierspitzige Hypozykloide f
assurance coefficient	s. safety factor	astrolabe	Astrolabium n, Analemma n
astable circuit, unstable circuit	instabiler Kreis m	astrometer	s. star photometer
		astrometry, spherical astronomy, uranometry	Astrometrie f, sphärische Astronomie f, Positionsastronomie f, Uranometrie f
astable multivibrator	astabiler Multivibrator m		
astatic control	s. integral control		
astatic controller	s. integral controller	astron	s. siriometer
astatic equilibrium	astatisches Gleichgewicht n	astronomical azimuth	s. azimuth <astr.>
astatic gravimeter	s. astatized gravimeter	astronomical eyepiece	astronomisches Okular n, Okular ohne Bildumkehr
astatic instrument	astatisches Instrument (Gerät, Meßgerät) n		
astatic magnetometer	Astatomagnetometer n, astatisches Magnetometer	astronomical photography	s. astrophotography
astatic microphone	s. non-directional microphone	astronomical photometer	s. star photometer
astatic needles, astatic pair of needles	astatisches Nadelpaar n	astronomical photometry, astrophotometry, stellar photometry	Astrophotometrie f, astronomische Photometrie f, Photometrie der Gestirne, Sternphotometrie f
astatic system	s. system with zero position error		
astatine, $_{85}$At	Astat n, $_{85}$At	astronomical refraction	astronomische Refraktion (Strahlenbrechung) f
astatism of first order <control>	I-Verhalten n		
		astronomical spectroscopy	s. astrospectrometry
		astronomical telescope, Kepler telescope	astronomisches (Keplersches) Fernrohr n, Kepler-Fernrohr n
astatization, astatizing, rendering astatic	Astasierung f		
		astronomical triangle	s. polar triangle
astatized gravimeter, astatic gravimeter	astatisches Gravimeter n	astronomical unit, AU, au	astronomische Einheit f, AE, A. E., astr. Einh.
astatizing	s. astatization	astronucleonics	Astronukleonik f
astenosphere, tectosphere	Astenosphäre f, Tektosphäre f	astrophotographic plate	s. astrographic plate
		astrophotography, astronomical photography	Astrophotographie f, Himmelsphotographie f
aster, astrosphere <of mitosis>	Astrosphäre f, Strahlenzone f, Sphäre f <Mitose>	astrophotometer	s. star photometer
		astrophotometry	s. astronomical photometry
asterisk <math. symbol>	Stern m, Sternchen n <math. Symbol>	astroplate	s. astrographic plate
		astrospectrograph, stellar spectrograph	Sternspektrograph m, Astrospektrograph m
asterism	Asterismus m		
asteroid, planetoid, minor planet, small planet	Planetoid m, Asteroid m, Kleiner Planet m, Zwergplanet m	astrospectrometry, astrospectroscopy, astronomical spectroscopy, stellar spectroscopy (spectrometry)	Astrospektrometrie f, Astrospektroskopie f, Sternspektrometrie f, Sternspektroskopie f
astigmatic difference	astigmatische Differenz f		
astigmatic mounting	astigmatische Gitteraufstellung f		
		astrosphere <of mitosis>, aster	Astrosphäre f, Strahlenzone f, Sphäre f <Mitose>
astigmatic pencil [of rays]	astigmatisches (schneidenförmiges) Bündel n	astrotaxis	Astrotaxis f
		A subgroup <in the periodic table>	Hauptgruppe f <im Periodensystem>
astigmatism, spot-shape distortion	Astigmatismus m, Punktlosigkeit f, Entpunktung f; Zweischalenfehler m, Astigmatismus schiefer Bündel		
		asymmetric[al], unsymmetric[al], dissymmetric[al], nonsymmetric[al]	asymmetrisch, unsymmetrisch, nichtsymmetrisch
astigmatism against the rule, inverse astigmatism	Astigmatismus m gegen die Regel, Astigmatismus inversus	asymmetrical dispersion	asymmetrische Dispersion f
		asymmetrical distribution	s. skew distribution
astigmatism with the rule	gerader Astigmatismus m, Astigmatismus nach der Regel, Astigmatismus rectus	asymmetrical heterostatic circuit [of Kelvin]	Doppelschaltung f, asymmetrisch-heterostatische Schaltung f [nach Kelvin]

asymmetrical

asymmetrical load	s. unbalanced load	atmospheric absorption	Luftabsorption f, atmosphärische Absorption f, Absorption in der Atmosphäre
asymmetrical multivibrator	unsymmetrischer Multivibrator m		
asymmetric class	s. hemihedry of the triclinic system	atmospherical extinction; extinction of light in the air	atmosphärische (astronomische) Extinktion f, Extinktion in der Atmosphäre, Strahlenschwächung f in der Erdatmosphäre, Strahlungsvernichtung f (Extinktion des Lichtes) in der Atmosphäre, Luftextinktion f
asymmetric crystal system	s. triclinic crystal system		
asymmetric fold, oblique fold	schiefe Falte f		
asymmetric gyroscope	s. unsymmetrical top		
asymmetric sideband transmission	s. vestigial-sideband transmission		
asymmetric system	s. triclinic crystal system		
asymmetry, unsymmetry, dissymmetry, nonsymmetry	Asymmetrie f, Unsymmetrie f, Nichtsymmetrie f, Dissymmetrie f	atmospherical thermometer	s. air thermometer
		atmospheric charge	s. charge of air
		atmospheric circulation, air circulation	atmosphärische Zirkulation f, Kreislauf m der Luft, Luftkreislauf m
asymmetry coefficient, coefficient of asymmetry	Asymmetriebeiwert m, Asymmetriekoeffizient m		
asymmetry parameter	Asymmetrieparameter m		
asymmetry potential	Asymmetriepotential n	atmospheric conditions	s. weather
asymptote, asymptotic curve	Asymptote f, asymptotische Kurve f, Schmiegtangente f	atmospheric convergence, convergence ‹meteo.›	Konvergenz f, Massenkonvergenz f ‹Meteo.›
		atmospheric counterradiation	s. sky back radiation
asymptotically efficient, efficient ‹stat.›	effizient ‹Stat.›	atmospheric depth	Atmosphärentiefe f, Tiefe f der Atmosphäre
asymptotically equal ‹to›, ≅	asymptotisch gleich, ≅		
asymptotic behaviour	asymptotisches (infinitäres) Verhalten n, Asymptotik f	atmospheric dispersion	Dispersion f der Atmosphäre, atmosphärische Dispersion
asymptotic cone	Asymptotenkegel m		
asymptotic curve, asymptotic line	Asymptotenlinie f, Haupttangentenlinie f, Haupttangentenkurve f, Inflexionskurve f, Wendelinie f, Schmiegtangentenkurve f	atmospheric divergence, divergence ‹meteo.›	Divergenz f, Massendivergenz f ‹Meteo.›
		atmospheric duct, tropospheric duct, wave duct in the atmosphere, duct	Troposphärenkanal m, atmosphärischer Wellenleiter m, Wellenleiter [in der Atmosphäre], „duct" m, Dukt m
asymptotic curve	s. a. asymptote		
asymptotic direction	Asymptotenrichtung f		
asymptotic equivalence	asymptotische Gleichheit f, asymptotische Äquivalenz f bezüglich Division	atmospheric electricity	Luftelektrizität f
		atmospheric excess pressure	s. atmosphere above atmospheric pressure
asymptotic expansion	s. asymptotic power series		
asymptotic line	s. asymptotic curve	atmospheric fog, distance fog	Entfernungsschleier m
asymptotic model	s. asymptotic universe		
asymptotic normality	asymptotische Normalität f	atmospheric haze, haze	Dunst m, atmosphärischer Dunst
asymptotic path ‹in function theory›	Zielweg m, asymptotischer Weg m, Bestimmtheitsweg m, Konvergenzweg m ‹Funktionentheorie›	atmospheric humidity	s. atmospheric moisture
		atmospheric ionization	s. ionization of air
		atmospheric layer	Atmosphärenschicht f
asymptotic power series [expansion], asymptotic representation, asymptotic series, asymptotic expansion, semi-convergent series	asymptotische Reihe (Entwicklung) f, semikonvergente Reihe, halbkonvergente Reihe; asymptotische Darstellung f	atmospheric microvariation	s. barometric microvariation
		atmospheric moisture, air moisture, atmospheric humidity	Luftfeuchtigkeit f, Luftfeuchte f, atmosphärische Feuchtigkeit f
		atmospheric nitrogen	Luftstickstoff m
		atmospheric optics, meteorological optics	atmosphärische (meteorologische) Optik f, Optik der Atmosphäre
asymptotic universe, asymptotic model ‹of the first or second kind›	asymptotische Welt f, Modell n einer asymptotischen Welt ‹erster oder zweiter Art›		
		atmospheric overvoltage	luftelektrische Überspannung f, atmosphärische Überspannung, äußere Überspannung
asymptotic value ‹in function theory›	Zielwert m, asymptotischer Wert m, Konvergenzwert m ‹Funktionentheorie›		
		atmospheric pollution, pollution of the atmosphere, air pollution, pollution (infection) of air	Verunreinigung f der Luft, Luftverunreinigung f, Verunreinigung der Atmosphäre, Luftverschmutzung f
asynchronism	Asynchronie f		
athermal solution	s. athermic solution		
athermanous, adiathermic, non-diathermic, heatproof, heat-tight, impermeable to heat	atherman, adiatherman, wärmeundurchlässig, wärmedicht, undurchlässig für Wärmestrahlung		
		atmospheric precipitation	s. precipitation ‹meteo.›
		atmospheric pressure	s. barometric pressure
		atmospheric pressure	s. standard pressure
athermic solution, athermal solution	athermische Lösung f	atmospheric pressure chart, atmospheric pressure map	Luftdruckkarte f
Atkinson cycle	Atkinsonscher Kreisprozeß m, Atkinson-Prozeß m		
atmograph, evaporigraph	Atmograph m, Evaporigraph m	atmospheric-pressure counter	Normaldruckzählrohr n
atmometer	s. evaporimeter	atmospheric pressure head	s. air pressure head
atmosphere	Atmosphäre f, Lufthülle f; Luftkreis m		
atmosphere, new atmosphere, at atmosphere	technische Atmosphäre f, at	atmospheric pressure map	s. atmospheric pressure chart
		atmospheric pressure wave, baric wave, barometric variation	Luftdruckwelle f
	s. a. medium ‹chem.›		
atmosphere ‹of dislocations›	s. a. Cottrell atmosphere		
atmosphere above atmospheric pressure, atmospheric excess pressure	Atmosphäre f Überdruck, at Überdruck ‹früher: atü›	atmospheric radioactive radiation, radioactive radiation in the lower atmosphere	Luftstrahlung f, radioaktive Strahlung f der unteren Luftschichten
		atmospheric radioactivity	s. airborne radioactivity
atmosphere of hydrogen	s. hydrogen atmosphere		

atmospheric radio noise, atmospherics, spherics, sturbs, statics, sferics	atmosphärische (luft-elektrische, statische) Störungen *fpl*, Atmospherics *pl*, Spherics *pl*	atomic burst atomic charge, atomic number, ordinal number, proton number, number, Z, at. No. <nucl.>	atomic*s*. blast Ordnungszahl *f*, Kernladungszahl *f*, Kernladung *f*, Ladungszahl *f*, Atomnummer *f*, Protonenzahl *f*, Z, OZ <Kern.>
atmospheric refraction	[atmosphärische] Refraktion *f*, atmosphärische Strahlenbrechung *f*	atomic clock, atomic timing device	Atomuhr *f*
atmospherics	*s*. atmospheric radio noise	atomic compound, homopolar compound, covalent compound	Atomverbindung *f*, kovalente (homöopolare, unpolare) Verbindung *f*
atmospheric seismology	*s*. seismology of atmosphere	atomic configuration	*s*. atomic arrangement
atmospheric streak (stria)	*s*. air streak	atomic constant, constant of atomic physics	Konstante *f* der Atomphysik, atomphysikalische (atomare) Konstante, Atomkonstante *f*
atmospheric subsidence, subsidence	atmosphärisches Absinken *n*, Absinken *n* der Luftmasse		
atmospheric tides, tides in the atmosphere, barometric tides	Atmosphärengezeiten *pl*, Gezeiten *pl* der Atmosphäre	atomic core atomic crystal, valence crystal, homopolar crystal, atomic-lattice crystal	*s*. atomic trunk Atomkristall *m*, Atomgitterkristall *m*, Valenzkristall *m*, homöopolarer Kristall *m*, Kristall vom Atomgittertyp
atmospheric turbidity	Lufttrübung *f*		
atmospheric wave, air wave	Luftwoge *f*; Luftwelle *f*		
atmospheric wave	*s. a.* space wave <el.>		
atmospheric window, window in Earth's atmosphere	Fenster *n* der Atmosphäre	atomic decay atomic defect [in the lattice], atomic imperfection	*s*. decay atomarer Gitterbaufehler (Gitterfehler) *m*, atomare Störstelle *f*, atomarer Gitterdefekt *m*
atom-bound electron	*s*. atomic electron		
atom form amplitude, atomic scattering amplitude	Atomstreuamplitude *f*, Atomformamplitude *f*		
atom form factor, atomic form factor, [atomic] scattering factor	Atomformfaktor *m*, Atom[streu]faktor *m*, [atomarer] Streufaktor *m*	atomic description atomic dimensions, atomic order	atomistische Beschreibung *f* atomare Dimensionen *fpl* (Größenordnung *f*)
		atomic disintegration	*s*. decay
		atomic dispersion	Atomdispersion *f*
		atomic displacement	*s*. discomposition
atomic, atom-physical	atomphysikalisch	atomic electron, atom-bound electron	Atomelektron *n*, atomgebundenes Elektron *n*
atomic absorption coefficient, atomic energy absorption coefficient	atomarer Absorptionskoeffizient *m*, atomarer Energieabsorptionskoeffizient *m*	atomic electron shell, atomic (electronic, electron) shell, atomic envelope, shell of electrons	Elektronenhülle *f* [des Atoms], Atomhülle *f*
atomic absorption spectroscopic analysis	Atom-Absorptionsspektralanalyse *f*	atomic emission spectroscopy	Emissions-Atomspektroskopie *f*
atomic absorption spectroscopy	Absorptions-Atomspektroskopie *f*	atomic energy	*s*. nuclear energy
atomic accelerator	*s*. atomic particle accelerator	atomic energy absorption coefficient	*s*. atomic absorption coefficient
atomical	atomar <aus einem Atom bestehend>; atomartig	atomic energy level, atomic level	Energieniveau *n* des Atoms Atomniveau *n*
atomically dispersed	atomdispers		
atomic arrangement, atomic configuration	[räumliche] Anordnung *f* der Atome	atomic energy storage battery	*s*. atomic battery
atomic attenuation coefficient	atomarer Schwächungskoeffizient *m*	atomic envelope atomic evaporation heat	*s*. atomic electron shell atomare Verdampfungswärme *f*
atomic battery, atomic energy storage battery, nuclear battery, radioactive (radioisotope) battery, isotopic power generator	Radionuklidbatterie *f*, Isotopenbatterie *f*, Kernbatterie *f*, radioaktive Batterie *f*, radioaktive Spannungsquelle *f*, Atombatterie *f*	atomic explosion atomic explosion atomic explosion test (trial)	*s*. atomic blast *s*. fragmentation *s*. atomic blast
		atomic form factor	*s*. atom form factor
		atomic fraction	Atombruch *m*
atomic beam	Atomstrahl *m*	atomic fragmentation	*s*. fragmentation
atomic-beam maser	Atomstrahlmaser *m*	atomic frequency	Atomfrequenz *f*
		atomic g factor	*s*. Landé['s] *g*-factor
atomic-beam maser oscillator	Atomstrahlgenerator *m*	atomic heat	Atomwärme *f*
atomic-beam method, atomic-beam technique	Atomstrahlmethode *f*	atomic-hydrogen maser	Maser *m* mit atomarem Wasserstoff
atomic-beam resonance technique	Atomstrahl-Resonanzmethode *f*	atomic imperfection atomic interspace	*s*. atomic defect Raum *m* zwischen den Atomen
atomic-beam source	Atomstrahllichtquelle *f*, Atomstrahlquelle *f*	atomic ion atomicity	Atomion *n* Atomigkeit *f* <Anzahl der Atome im Molekül>; Atomistik *f*
atomic-beam technique	*s*. atomic-beam method		
atomic binding	*s*. atomic bond	atomicity	*s. a.* valency
atomic blast; atomic burst (explosion), nuclear blast (burst, explosion); atomic bomb burst (explosion); atomic [explosion] test, nuclear [explosion] test, atomic [explosion] trial, nuclear [explosion] trial	nukleare Explosion (Sprengung) *f*, Atomexplosion *f*, Kernexplosion *f*; Kernbombenexplosion *f*, Atombombenexplosion *f*, Kernwaffentest *m*, Kernwaffenversuchsexplosion *f*, Kernwaffenexplosion *f*	atomic lattice, atomic space lattice <of crystal>	Atomgitter *n* <Kristall>
		atomic-lattice crystal	*s*. atomic crystal
		atomic level	*s*. atomic energy level
		atomic link[age]	*s*. atomic bond
		atomic magnetic moment, magnetic moment of the atom; atomic paramagnetic moment, paramagnetic moment of the atom	magnetisches Moment *n* des Atoms; paramagnetisches Moment des Atoms
atomic bomb burst (explosion)	*s*. atomic blast		
atomic bond, covalent bond, covalent link[age], electron-pair bond, electron coupling, homopolar bond, atomic link[age], atomic (homopolar) binding, homopolar link[age], exchange coupling	Atombindung *f*, Elektronen[paar]bindung *f*, kovalente Bindung *f*, homöopolare Bindung, Kovalenz *f*, Kovalenzbindung *f*, unitarische Bindung, Austauschbindung *f*		
		atomic mass, isotope (isotopic) weight	Massenwert *m*, Atommasse *f*, Isotopenmasse *f*, Isotopengewicht *n*
		atomic mass	*s. a.* mass of the atom

atomic

atomic mass conversion factor, mass conversion factor	Smythe-Faktor m, Smythescher Faktor m $<=$ 1,000275, Umrechnungsfaktor zwischen Atomgewicht und ME>	atomic species	s. nuclide
		atomic spectroscopy	Atomspektroskopie f
		atomic spectrum	Atomspektrum n
		atomic state	Atomzustand m, Energiezustand m des Atoms
atomic mass unit, amu, physical mass unit	atomare Masseneinheit f, Atommasseneinheit f, [atomphysikalische] Masseneinheit, Kernmasseneinheit f, kernphysikalische Masseneinheit, ME; amu	atomic stopping power	atomares Bremsvermögen n
		atomic structure, atom structure	Atombau m, Atomaufbau m, Atomstruktur f
		atomic surface	Atomrand m, Atomoberfläche f
atomic millimass unit	s. unified atomic millimass unit	atomic susceptibility	atomare Suszeptibilität f, Atomsuszeptibilität f
atomic model, atom model	Atommodell n	atomic system of units	s. system of atomic units
		atomic test	s. atomic blast
atomic molecule, covalent molecule, homopolar molecule	Atommolekül n, kovalentes (homöopolares, unpolares) Molekül n	atomic timing device	s. atomic clock
		atomic torso	s. atomic trunk
		atomic transformation (transmutation)	s. nuclear transformation <nucl.>
atomic nucleus, nucleus [of atom]	Atomkern m, Kern m [des Atoms]	atomic trial	s. atomic blast
atomic number	s. atomic charge <nucl.>	atomic trunk, atomic core (torso, residue), core	Atomrumpf m
atomic orbital, AO, a.o.	Atomorbital n, Atom[bahn]funktion f, „atomic orbital", Bahnfunktion f der Elektronen im Atom, AO	atomic unit, natural unit, Hartree unit	Hartree-Einheit f, atomare (natürliche) Einheit f
		atomic vibration, atomic oscillation	Atomschwingung f
atomic orbital method	s. method of atomic orbitals	atomic volume	Atomvolumen n
atomic order	s. atomic dimensions	atomic waste, radioactive waste, rad waste	radioaktiver Abfall m, Atomabfall m, Atommüll m
atomic oscillation	s. atomic vibration		
atomic paramagnetic moment	s. atomic magnetic moment		
atomic particle accelerator, particle (atomic) accelerator, accelerator, charged-particle accelerator, machine	Teilchenbeschleuniger m, Beschleuniger m [für geladene Teilchen], Beschleunigungsanlage f, Beschleunigungsmaschine f, Maschine f	atomic wave function	Atomwellenfunktion f
		atomic weight, relative atomic weight	Atomgewicht n, relative Atommasse f, Atomverhältniszahl f
		atomic weight scale	s. scale of atomic weights
atomic percent	s. atom percent	atomic weight unit, awu	Atomgewichtseinheit f, Einheit f der relativen Atommasse, chemische Masseneinheit f, chemisches Atomgewicht n
atomic photoelectric effect	s. photoionization		
atomic physics, atom physics	Atomphysik f <Kern- und Hüllenphysik>		
atomic physics in its proper sense, physics of the orbital electrons	Atomphysik f im engeren Sinne, Hüllenphysik f, Physik f der Atomhülle	atomistic	atomistisch <aus Atomen bestehend>
		atomistic structure	atomistische Struktur f
		atomization; spraying; sputtering	Zerstäubung f, Verdüsung f; Vernebelung f, Verstäubung f; Sprühen n; Versprühen n
atomic plane, lattice plane, net plane, net <cryst.>	Netzebene f, Gitterebene f <Krist.>		
atomic polarizability	Atompolarisierbarkeit f, atomare Polarisierbarkeit f, Kernverschiebungspolarisierbarkeit f		
atomic polarization, infra-red polarization	Atompolarisation f, atomare Polarisation f, Kernverschiebungspolarisation f, Atomverschiebungspolarisation f	atomization jet	s. spray nozzle
		atomization pressure	Zerstäubungsdruck m
		atomizer, blowgun; pulverizer; spray[er]	Zerstäuber m; Vernebler m
atomic power	s. nuclear energy	atom jump	Atomsprung m
atomic radiation	Atomstrahlung f	atom model, atomic model	Atommodell n
atomic radius	s. covalent radius	atom percent, atomic percent, gramme-atomic percentage, atom%, at.%	Atomprozent n, Atom-%, At.-%
atomic ratio	Atomverhältnis n		
atomic refraction	Atomrefraktion f	atom-physical	s. atomic
atomic residue	s. atomic trunk	atom physics, atomic physics	Atomphysik f <Kern- und Hüllenphysik>
atomic rocket	Atomrakete f <gerichtete Abstrahlung von Kernzerfallsprodukten als Treibstoff>	atom site, lattice site, site [in the lattice], atomic site, lattice position	Gitterplatz m, Gitterstelle f
atomic rotation	Atomrotation f, Atomdrehung f	atom structure	s. atomic structure
atomics	Atomphysik f und angrenzende Wissenschaftszweige mpl, Atomwissenschaft f	atom-transfer reaction	s. isotopic exchange reaction
		atrio-ventricular node	Atrioventrikularknoten m [von Aschoff-Tawara], Aschoff-Tawarascher Knoten m
atomic scattering coefficient <nucl.>	atomarer Streukoeffizient m <Kern.>	attachment, capture, trapping, addition	Anlagerung f
		attachment coefficient, coefficient of attachment	Anlagerungskoeffizient m
atomic scattering factor	s. scattering factor		
atomic scattering factor	s. a. atom form factor	attachment energy, energy of attachment	Anlagerungsenergie f, Anlagerungsarbeit f
atomic second, physical second	Atomsekunde f, physikalische Sekunde f	attachment frequency	Anlagerungsfrequenz f, Einfangfrequenz f
atomic shell	s. atomic electron shell	attachment lens	s. supplementary lens
atomic site	s. atom site	attachment prism, supplementary prism	Vorsatzprisma n
atomic space lattice, atomic lattice <of crystal>	Atomgitter n <Kristall>		
		attain <a value>	annehmen <Wert>; erreichen; erzielen
atomic spacing	s. interatomic distance		

attemperation	s. temperature control	attenuation per unit length <el.>	s. attenuation constant <of the line>
attemperator	s. thermoregulator	attenuation tenth-value thickness	s. tenth-value layer
attempt frequency	Gamow-Frequenz f	attenuator, vibration absorber	Schwingungsdämpfer m, Wellendämpfer m; Schwingungstilger m
attenuated total reflexion, ATR	verminderte Totalreflexion f		
attenuating material	s. attenuator <nucl.; opt.>	attenuator, attenuation network <el.>	Dämpfungsnetzwerk n <El.>
attenuating material	s. sound insulator <ac.>	attenuator, damping resistance; damping resistor <el.>	Dämpfungswiderstand m <El.>
attenuation, attenuation of radiation, radiation attenuation	Schwächung f [der Strahlung], Strahlenschwächung f, Strahlungsschwächung f	attenuator, attenuating material <nucl.; opt.>	Schwächer m, schwächendes Material n, Schwächungsmaterial n, Schwächungsstoff m, Schwächungskörper m <Kern.; Opt.>
attenuation	s. a. fading		
attenuation along the line, damping along the line	Leitungsdämpfung f		
attenuation band	s. stop band		
attenuation coefficient, attenuation constant (factor) <nucl.>	[totaler] Schwächungskoeffizient m <Kern.>	atto..., a <10⁻¹⁸>	Atto..., a <10⁻¹⁸>
		attracted disk electrometer	s. Kelvin absolute electrometer
attenuation coefficient <in theory of visibility>	Schwächungskoeffizient m, Schwächungsexponent m [im Lambertschen Absorptionsgesetz] <für terrestrische Extinktion>; Schwächungsexponent	attracting centre	s. attractive centre
		attracting mass	anziehende Masse f
		attraction	Anziehung f, Attraktion f
		attraction force	s. attractive force
		attraction of the Earth	s. earth['s] attraction
attenuation coefficient	s. a. damping exponent	attraction plate, pole plate <bio.>	Polkappe f <Bio.>
attenuation compensation, attenuation equalization	Dämpfungsausgleich m, Dämpfungsentzerrung f	attraction potential	Anziehungspotential n
		attraction power	s. attractive force
attenuation constant <of the line>, attenuation per unit length <el.>	Dämpfungskonstante f [der Leitung], Dämpfungsbelag m; kilometrische Dämpfung f, Dämpfungsmaß n, Leitungsdämpfung f je Kilometer <für Leitungen> <El.>	attractive centre, centre of attraction, attracting centre	anziehendes Zentrum n, Anziehungszentrum n
		attractive force, force of attraction, attraction force (power), attractive power	Anziehungskraft f, anziehende Kraft f; Attraktion f
attenuation constant	s. a. damping exponent	attractive force of magnet	s. magnetic attraction
attenuation constant	s. a. attenuation coefficient <nucl.>	attractive power	s. attractive force
attenuation cross-section, cross-section for attenuation	Schwächungsquerschnitt m, Wirkungsquerschnitt m für (der) Schwächung, Schwächungswirkungsquerschnitt m	attribute of colour	Farbattribut n, Farbmerkmal n
		attribution <to>	s. assignment <to>
		Atwood['s] free-fall apparatus, Atwood['s] machine	Atwoodsche Fallmaschine f
attenuation due to losses [by reflection and interaction]	Verlustdämpfung f	Aubert phenomenon	Aubert-Phänomen n
		audibility range	s. frequency range of hearing
attenuation equalization	s. attenuation compensation	audibility zone, region of audibility	Hörbarkeitsgebiet n, Hörbarkeitszone f
attenuation factor <of the attenuator>	Schwächungsfaktor m <schwächendes Material>	audible frequency	s. audio[-]frequency
attenuation factor	s. a. attenuation coefficient <nucl.>	audible range	s. hearing distance
		audible sound, audio sound	Hörschall m
attenuation factor	s. a. damping exponent	audible spectrum	s. frequency range of hearing
attenuation half-value layer, attenuation half-value thickness	Halbwertsdicke (Halbwertschicht) f für Schwächung, Schwächungshalbwertsdicke f	audible spectrum	s. sound spectrum
		audio amplifier, audio[-]frequency amplifier, note amplifier; low-frequency amplifier, l.f. amplifier	Niederfrequenzverstärker m, NF-Verstärker m; Tonfrequenzverstärker m
attenuation in forward direction	s. attenuation in the passband	audio-band	s. audio frequency band
attenuation in the opposite direction	Rückendämpfung f, Rückdämpfung f	audio[-]frequency, audible (acoustic, tone, musical) frequency, low frequency, AF, A.F., a.f., af, LF, L.F., l.f., lf <16–20000 c/s>; voice (speech) frequency, VF, V.F., v.f.	Tonfrequenz f, Hörfrequenz f, Niederfrequenz f, NF <16...20000 Hz); Sprechfrequenz f, Sprachfrequenz f
attenuation in the passband, attenuation in forward direction	Durchlaßdämpfung f		
attenuation in the suppressed band	Sperrdämpfung f		
attenuation length	Dämpfungslänge f, reziproke Dämpfungskonstante f	audio[-]frequency amplifier	s. audio amplifier
		audio frequency analyzer	s. sound analyzer
attenuation length <nucl.>	Schwächungslänge f <Kern.>	audio frequency band, audio-band, a.f. band	Tonfrequenzband n, Hörfrequenzband n, Niederfrequenzband n, NF-Band n
attenuation mean free path, mean free path for attenuation	[mittlere freie] Schwächungsweglänge f, mittlere freie Weglänge f für Schwächung, Schwächungslänge f	audio-frequency filter, a.f. filter; low-frequency filter, l.f. filter; low-frequency rejection, l.f. rejection	Niederfrequenzfilter n, NF-Filter n; Niederfrequenzsiebkette f, NF-Siebkette f; Niederfrequenzsperre f, NF-Sperre f
attenuation network <el.>, attenuator	Dämpfungsnetzwerk n <El.>		
attenuation of radiation	s. attenuation	audio frequency oscillator	s. audio generator
attenuation of sound, sound attenuation; damping of sound, sound damping	Schalldämmung f; Schalldämpfung f; Schallhemmung f	audio-frequency output (power, power output)	s. speech power
		audio frequency range, audio range, range of audiofrequency, A.F. range, A.F.	Tonfrequenzbereich m, Tonfrequenzgebiet n, Hörfrequenzbereich m, Niederfrequenzbereich m, NF-Bereich m, NF
attenuation of the material	s. mechanical hysteresis		

audio frequency signal generator	s. audio generator	"ausstrahlungsbedingung"	s. radiation condition
audio frequency standard	Tonfrequenznormal n	austausch <meteo.>	Luftmassenaustausch m <Meteo.>
audio generator, audio frequency [signal] generator, tone generator, audio [frequency] oscillator, tone oscillator (source)	Tonfrequenzgenerator m, Tongenerator m, Tonsender m, Tonquelle f; Tonfrequenzsummer m	"austausch" coefficient	s. effective turbulent diffusivity
		austausch region, exchange layer <meteo.>	Austauschschicht f <Meteo.>
		austempering	austenitische Härtung f, Zwischenstufenvergütung f
audiogram, threshold audiogram	Audiogramm n	austral axis pole, austral pole, Antarctic axis pole	geomagnetischer Südpol m, australer Pol m, australer Hauptpol m, antarktischer Magnetpol m [der Erde], nordmagnetischer Hauptpol
audio level, sound level	Tonpegel m		
audiometry	Audiometrie f, Hörschärfemessung f		
		Autler-Townes effect	Autler-Townes-Effekt m
audio oscillator	s. audio generator	autoadhesion	s. autohesion
audio power	s. speech power	autoagglutination	Autoagglutination f
audio range	s. audio frequency range	autobarotropy	Autobarotropie f
audio sound, audible sound	Hörschall m	autocapacity coupling	Kopplung f durch gemeinsame Kapazität
audio spectrum	s. sound spectrum		
auditory acuity	s. acuity of hearing		
auditory localization	s. binaural location		
auditory ossicle	Gehörknöchelchen n	autocatalytic, self-catalyzed	autokatalytisch
auditory passage, acoustic duct	Gehörgang m	autochemogram	Autochemogramm n, Autoradiogramm n als Resultat einer chemischen Reaktion
auditory sensation, sensation of hearing	Hörempfindung f		
auditory sensation area	s. frequency range of hearing	autocoagulation	Autokoagulation f
auditory sensitivity	s. hearing sensitivity	autocollimating spectrograph, autocollimation spectrograph	Autokollimationsspektrograph m
auditory stimulation	Schallreizung f		
auditory stimulus	Schallreiz m, akustischer Reiz m	autocollimating spectroscope [of Pulfrich]	Autokollimationsspektroskop n [nach Pulfrich], Pulfrichsches Autokollimationsspektroskop
aufbauprinciple, "Aufbau" principle, aufbauprinzip, building-up principle, Bohr['s] aufbauprinzip, principle of the successive building up of atoms	Aufbauprinzip n, Permanenz f der Quantenzahlen		
		autocollimating telescope	s. autocollimator
		autocollimation prism	Autokollimationsprisma n
Auger coefficient	Auger-Koeffizient m	autocollimation spectrograph	s. autocollimating spectrograph
Auger effect	Auger-Effekt m		
Auger electron	Auger-Elektron n	autocollimator, autocollimating telescope	Autokollimationsfernrohr n
Auger shower	s. extensive shower		
Auger transition	s. radiationless transition	autocomplex coacervate	Autokomplexkoazervat n
augmentation	s. increase	autocondensation	Selbstkondensation f, Autokondensation f
augmentation distance	s. extrapolation distance		
augmentation of the valence angle	Valenzwinkelaufweitung f	autocorrelation, serial correlation	Autokorrelation f, Autoregression f, Eigenkorrelation f, Eigenregression f, Reihenkorrelation f, Reihenregression f
augmented interval	übermäßiges Intervall n		
augmented plane wave method, APW method	erweiterte Methode f der ebenen Wellen		
aural masking, aural masking effect, masking effect, masking [of sound] <ac.>	Verdeckungseffekt m, Verdeckung f [des Schalls], Schallmaskierung f, Maskierung f [des Schalls], Verschleierung f [des Schalls], Tonmaskierung f <Ak.>	autocorrelation coefficient	Autokorrelationskoeffizient m
		autocorrelation function, [serial] correlation function <statistics>; self-correlation function <scattering>	Autokorrelationsfunktion f, Korrelationsfunktion f
		autocorrelogram	Autokorrelogramm n
aural microphonic	s. cochlear microphonic	autodyne detector	Autodyn[e]detektor m
aureola	s. halo	autodyne spectrometer	Autodyn[e]spektrometer n
aureola	s. aureole <opt., meteo.>	autoelectronic current	s. field emission current
aureole, aureola <opt., meteo.>	Aureole f, Hof m kleiner Art, einfacher Kranz m	autoelectronic emission	s. field emission of electrons
aureole, aureola, corona <opt., meteo.>	Kranz m, Kranzerscheinung f, Korona f, Strahlenkranz m <Opt., Meteo.>	autoexcitation, self-excitation	Selbsterregung f, Eigenerregung f
		autoformer	s. autotransformer
aureole <of arc>	Aureole f <Lichtbogen>	autofrettage	Autofrettage f; Kaltrecken n
auricular fibrillation	Vorhofflimmern n	autogeneous ignition	s. self[-]ignition
auricular frequency	Vorhofsfrequenz f	auto-guidance	s. homing guidance
		autogyration	s. autorotation
aurora <pl.: aurorae>, polar lights, polar aurora	Polarlicht n, polare Aurora f	autohesion, autoadhesion, self-adhesion	Autohäsion f
aurora australis	s. southern lights	autoignition	s. self[-]ignition
aurora borealis	s. northern lights	autoinductive coupling	induktive Querkopplung f, Spartransformatorkopplung f, Autotransformatorkopplung f, induktive T-Kopplung f
auroral belt	s. auroral zone		
auroral fading, fading due to polar aurora	Polarlichtschwund m; Nordlichtschwund m		
auroral form	Polarlichtform f		
auroral frequency	Polarlichthäufigkeit f	autoionization, preionization	Autoionisation f, Autoionisierung f, Präionisation f, Präionisierung f, Selbstionisation f, Selbstionisierung f
auroral line	grüne Nordlichtlinie f, Auroralinie f		
auroral spectrum	Polarlichtspektrum n; Nordlichtspektrum n		
		autoluminescence	Autolumineszenz f
auroral zone, auroral belt	Polarlichtzone f, Zone f der Polarlichter (Polarlichterscheinungen)	autolysate, autolyzate	Autolysat n
		autolysis	Autolyse f, Selbstauflösung f
		autolyte	Autolyt m

autolyzate s. autolysate
automatic control, automatische (selbsttätige)
self-control Steuerung f, Steuerung;
Selbststeuerung f, Selbstlenkung f; automatische
(selbsttätige) Regelung f,
Regelung
automatic control s. a. closed-loop control
automatic control Regelungstheorie f,
theory, control theory, Regelungsmathematik f
theory of automatic control, theory of control
systems
automatic correction s. self-correction
automatic dividing Schraubenteilmaschine f
engine with calibrated
worm
automatic following s. servo control
automatic interlock s. squagging
automatic potentiom- selbstabgleichendes (selbst-
eter, self-balancing kompensierendes) Poten-
potentiometer tiometer n, selbstabgleichender (selbsttätiger)
Kompensator m
automatic potentiom- s. electronic potentiometer
eter with electronic
circuit
automatic potentiom- s. mechanical potentiometer with servo eter
[-mechanism]
automatic sealing, Selbstdichtung f
self-sealing, self-tightening
automatic stabilization, Festwertregelung f
constant value control
automatic zero balance s. motor for automatic zero
motor, automatic balance
zeroing motor
automorphic s. idiomorphic <cryst.>
automorphic potential automorphes Potential n
automorphism Automorphismus m, automorphe Abbildung f
automorphous s. idiomorphic <cryst.>
autonomous inverter selbstgeführter Wechselrichter m
autonomous system [of autonomes (stationäres)
differential equations] Differentialgleichungssystem n, autonomes (stationäres, dynamisches)
System n [von Differentialgleichungen]
autoparametric autoparametrische Resonanz
resonance f
autopressuregram Autoradiogramm n als
Resultat einer Druckreaktion
autoprotective tube Strahlenschutzröhre f
autoprotolysis Autoprotolyse f, Säure-Base-
Disproportionierung f
autoradiochromatog- Autoradiochromatographie
raphy f
autoradiogram, auto- s. radioautograph
radiograph <US>
autoradiography <US> s. radioautography
autoreduplication, Auto[re]duplikation f,
self-duplication; Autoreproduktion f,
self-reproduction <bio.> identische Reduplikation
f, Replikation f, Selbstverdopplung f; Selbstreproduktion f <Bio.>
autoregressive autoregressive Transformation
transformation formation f
autorotation, autogyration Autorotation f
autosensitization Autosensibilisierung f
autotransformer, Autotransformator m,
autoformer Spartransformator m,
Einspulentransformator m
autotropic autotropisch
autotropism Autotropismus m
aut[o]oxidation, Autoxydation f, stille
self-oxidation Verbrennung f

autumnal equinox, Herbstäquinoktium n,
northern autumnal Herbst-Tagundnacht-
equinox gleiche f
autumnal equinox Herbstpunkt m, Waage-
[point], autumnal punkt m, Herbstäqui-
point, autumn equi- noktialpunkt m
nox, first point of Libra,
northern autumnal
equinox

auxanogram Auxanogramm n
auxanograph Auxanograph m
auxiliary apparatus s. supplementary apparatus
auxiliary equation s. characteristic equation
auxiliary gap s. electrode separation
auxiliary lens s. supplementary lens
auxiliary mirror s. secondary mirror
auxiliary point, satellite exzentrischer Standpunkt m
station <geo.> <Geo.>
auxiliary quantity s. subsidiary quantity
auxiliary valence s. secondary valence
auxiliary variable, Hilfsvariable f, Hilfs-
subsidiary variable veränderliche f
auxochrome s. auxochrome group
auxochrome group, auxochrome Gruppe f,
auxochrome Auxochrom n, Farbbildungshelfer m
auxoflorence Auxoflorenz f, Fluoreszenzverstärkung f
auxograph Auxograph m
availability, degree of Verfügbarkeit f, Ver-
availability fügbarkeitsgrad m
available gain s. gain <el.>
available noise power verfügbare Rauschleistung f
avalanche breakdown Lawinendurchbruch m,
Lawinendurchschlag m
avalanche diode Lawinendiode f
avalanche discharge Lawinenentladung f
avalanche multiplication lawinenartige Ladungs-
[of charge carriers], trägervervielfachung f
avalanche-type multi- (Vervielfachung f der
plication Ladungsträger)
avalanche noise Lawinenrauschen n
avalanche transistor, Lawinentransistor m
avalanche-type transistor
avalanche-type multi- s. avalanche multiplication
plication
avalanche-type s. avalanche transistor
transistor
avalanche wind Lawinenwind m
aventurization, puncti- Aventurisieren n
form flashing
average <of reactor>, Havarie f <Reaktor>
accident
average s. a. mean
average binding energy s. binding fraction
per nucleon
average charge density s. mean density of charge
averaged beam current mittlerer Strahlstrom m
average decrement of s. mean energy decrement
energy
average density of s. mean density of charge
charge
average determination s. averaging
average distance from s. jump distance
interstice to interstice
average element of orbit s. mean element of orbit
average energy decre- s. mean energy decrement
ment
average energy [expend- mittlerer Energieaufwand m
ed in the gas] per ion zur Bildung eines Ionen-
pair formed, average paares im Gas, [mittlerer]
energy to make (pro- Ionisierungsaufwand m,
duce) an ion pair in im Mittel zur Bildung
gas eines Ionenpaares benötigte Energie f
average error, mean durchschnittlicher (ein-
error facher mittlerer) Fehler m
average information mittlerer Informations-
content, entropy [of in- gehalt m, Informations-
formation source], entropie f, Entropie f
negentropy, negative [der Informationsquelle],
entropy Negentropie f, negative
Entropie
average information s. entropy per symbol
content per symbol
average ionization s. mean ionization energy
energy
average life[time] s. mean life
average logarithmic mittleres logarithmisches
energy decrement, Energiedekrement n,
mean logarithmic energy mittlerer logarithmischer
decrement (loss) Energieverlust m
average molecular mittleres Molekulargewicht
weight, average relative n, Durchschnittsmole-
molecular mass kulargewicht n, durchschnittliches Molekulargewicht, mittlere relative
Molekularmasse f

average orbital element	s. mean element of orbit	axial moment of resistance	s. equatorial moment of resistance
average output of the pulse, average pulse output	s. mean power of the pulse	axial multipole	axialer Multipol m
		axial object point	Achsendingpunkt m
average relative molecular mass	s. average molecular weight	axial plane	s. optic axial plane
		axial point	Achsenpunkt m
average sensitivity / of, of normal sensitivity	normalempfindlich	axial pole	Achsenpol m
		axial pressure, axial thrust	Axialdruck m
		axial pressure load	axiale Druckbeanspruchung f
average sidereal day, mean sidereal day	mittlerer Sterntag m		
		axial quantum number	s. magnetic quantum number
average solar day, mean solar day	mittlerer Sonnentag m		
		axial radius of gyration, axial radius of inertia	axialer Trägheitsradius m, axialer Trägheitsarm m
average value	s. mean		
average variability, mean variability	mittlere Veränderlichkeit f	axial ratio	Achsenverhältnis n
averaging, average determination, determination of average	Mittelung f, Mitteln n, Mittelwertbildung f, Mittelbildung f; Mittelungsprozeß m	axial ratio	s. a. crystallographic axial ratio
		axial ray, central ray <opt.>	Zentralstrahl m, Achsenstrahl m
averaging operator	Mittelungsoperator m, Operator m der Mittelwertbildung	axial refraction	s. effective power <of spectacle lens>
		axial resisting moment	s. equatorial moment of resistance
avertence	Verschwenkung f		
Avery test	s. Erichsen cupping test	axial response	s. axial sensitivity
AVF cyclotron, azimuthally varying [magnetic] field cyclotron, [relativistic] isochronous cyclotron	AVF-Zyklotron n, Zyklotron n mit azimutal variierendem Feld, [relativistisches] Isochronzyklotron n	axial section method	s. technique of axial section
		axial sensitivity, axial response	axialer Übertragungsfaktor m, axiale Empfindlichkeit f
		axial symmetry	Axialsymmetrie f, Achsensymmetrie f
Avogadro['s] constant	s. Avogadro['s] number		
Avogadro['s] hypothesis, Avogadro['s] law	Avogadrosches Gesetz n, Avogadrosche Regel (Hypothese) f, Satz m des Avogadro	axial symmetry / in, axially symmetric, axisymmetric, symmetric about an axis	axialsymmetrisch, achsensymmetrisch
Avogadro['s] number, Avogadro['s] constant, N, N_A <in mole^{-1}>	Loschmidtsche Zahl (Konstante) f, Loschmidt-Konstante f, Avogadro-Konstante f, N_L, L <in mol^{-1}>	axial tension, axial traction	zentrischer (mittiger, axialer) Zug m
		axial tensor	axialer Tensor m
avoirdupois system, avdp	„avoirdupois"-System n	axial thrust	s. axial pressure
avometer	s. volt-ohm-ammeter	axial vector, pseudovector	axialer Vektor m, Pseudovektor m, Drehvektor m, rotatorischer Vektor, Achsenvektor m
axial aberration of the ray	axiale Strahlaberration f		
axial ametropy	Achsenametropie f		
axial angle <photogrammetry>	Achsenwinkel m <Photogrammetrie>	axial vector coupling	s. pseudovector coupling
		axial vector interaction	s. pseudovectorial interaction
axial angle	s. a. optic axial angle		
axial application of force	zentrischer (mittiger) Kraftangriff m	axifugal	s. centrifugal
		axiomatic field theory	axiomatische Feldtheorie f
axial colour	Achsenfarbe f	axiomatics	Axiomatik f
axial compression	zentrischer (mittiger) Druck m, axiale Kompression f	axiom of choice, multiplicative axiom (principle), choice axiom, principle of choice	Auswahlaxiom n, Auswahlprinzip n, Axiom m der Auswahl
axial compression	s. a. crippling load		
axial coupling	s. pseudovector coupling		
axial elongation; longitudinal extension per unit length	axiale Verlängerung f; Streckung f, relative Streckung f (Dehnung f)	axiom of continuity	Stetigkeitsaxiom n, Axiom n der Kontinuität
		axiotron	Axiotron f
axial flow	s. axisymmetric flow	axipetal	s. centripetal
axial force, longitudinal force	Axialkraft f, Längskraft f, Normalkraft f <im Stab>	axis of collimation	s. collimation axis
		axis of contraction, axis of shortening	Schrumpfungsachse f
axial image point	Achsenbildpunkt m		
axial impact	s. longitudinal impact	axis of crystal, crystal (crystallographic) axis	Kristallachse f, kristallographische Achse f
axial interaction	s. pseudovectorial interaction		
axial line wave, wave along the wire, wave along the line	Drahtwelle f	axis of drag, drag axis	Widerstandsachse f
		axis of easy magnetization	s. easy direction of magnetization
axially symmetric	s. axial symmetry / in	axis of equilibrium	Achse f des Gleichgewichts, Gleichgewichtsachse f
axially symmetric flow	s. axisymmetric flow		
axially symmetric stress [distribution]	s. rotationally symmetric stress	axis of floatation	Schwimmachse f
		axis of gravity	s. centroid axis
axial magnification, longitudinal magnification	Tiefenverhältnis n, Tiefenmaßstab m, Tiefenvergrößerung f, Axialvergrößerung f, Längsvergrößerung f, longitudinale Vergrößerung f	axis of homology	Homologieachse f
		axis of imaginaries, imaginary axis	imaginäre Achse f
		axis of incidence, perpendicular [of incidence], normal to the reflecting surface	Einfallslot n, Einfallsnormale f
axial mode, longitudinal mode	Axialschwingungsmode f, Longitudinalschwingungsmode f		
		axis of inertia	Trägheitsachse f
axial moment	axiales Moment n, axial wirkendes Moment	axis of intersection of waterplanes	Achse f der Schwimmfläche, Schwimmflächenachse f
axial moment of inertia	s. moment of inertia about a line	axis of order n	s. symmetry axis of order n
		axis of oscillation, axis of vibration	Schwingungsachse f
axial moment of inertia of the line, equatorial moment of inertia of the line	axiales Linienträgheitsmoment n, äquatoriales Linienträgheitsmoment	axis of perspectivity	Perspektivitätsachse f
		axis of precession	Präzessionsachse f
		axis of revolution	s. axis of rotation

axis of rotary inversion	s. rotation-reflection axis	azimuthal angle	s. a. direction angle
axis of rotation, rotation[al] axis, axis of revolution	Drehachse f, Drehungsachse f, Umdrehungsachse f; Rotationsachse f, Achse f <Rotationskörper>	azimuthal effect	Azimuteffekt m
		azimuthally varying field accelerator, AVF accelerator	AVF-Beschleuniger m, Beschleuniger m mit azimutal veränderlichem Magnetfeld
axis of rotation	s. a. axis of symmetry <cryst.>		
axis of shear	Achse f der Scherung, Scherungsachse f	azimuthally varying [magnetic] field cyclotron	s. AVF cyclotron
axis of shortening, axis of contraction	Schrumpfungsachse f	azimuthal mode	Azimutalwelle f, Azimutal- schwingung f
axis of single wave velocity	s. primary optic axis	azimuthal mounting	azimutale Fernrohr- montierung f
axis of stereophoto- grammetric survey	Aufnahmeachse f	azimuthal pinch	s. theta-pinch
axis of suspension	Pendelachse f	azimuthal projection, azimuth projection, zenithal projection	Azimutalprojektion f, azimutale (zenitale) Projektion f, Zenital- projektion f, Azimutal- entwurf m, azimutaler (zenitaler) Entwurf m, Zenitalentwurf m
axis of symmetry	Symmetrieachse f		
axis of symmetry, symmetry[-]axis, rotation[-]axis, axis of rotation <cryst.>	Symmetrieachse f [erster Art], Drehsymmetrie- achse f, Drehungsachse f, Drehachse f, Rotations- achse f, Gyre f <Krist.>		
axis of symmetry [of the figure]	Figurenachse f	azimuthal quadrant	Azimutalquadrant m
		azimuthal quantum number	s. secondary quantum number
axis of tension, axis of traction	Zugachse f	azimuthal refraction	Azimut[al]refraktion f
axis of the bar (beam)	s. centre line of the bar	azimuthal resolution, azimuthal resolving power	azimutales Auflösungsver- mögen n, Tangentialauf- lösungsvermögen n, Tangentialauflösung f
axis of the celestial sphere	Himmelsachse f, Weltachse f		
axis of the centre of vortex	s. vortex axis	azimuthal rotation	Azimutalrotation f
		azimuth and elevation scope, azel scope	Azimut-Höhe-Bildschirm m, Azimut-Höhe-Schirm m
axis of the column	s. centre line of the bar		
axis of the lens	s. optical axis of the lens		
axis of the rod	s. centre line of the bar	azimuth angle	s. direction angle
axis of the second sort	s. rotation-reflection axis	azimuth gyro	s. azimuth gyroscope
axis of the second sort of order n	s. n-al axis of the second sort	azimuth gyroscope, azimuth gyro, directional gyroscope	Azimutkreisel m, Kurs- kreisel m
axis of the shower	Schauerachse f		
axis of the top	s. gyroaxis		
axis of the vortex	s. vortex axis	azimuth mark	s. mark
axis of three-fold symmetry	s. triad axis	azimuth projection	s. azimuthal projection
		azimuth quantum number	s. secondary quantum number
axis of thrust [action]	Schubachse f	azimuth radiation pattern	s. horizontal-plane directional pattern
axis of tilt, tilting axis	Verkantungsachse f	azimuth scope	Azimutschirm m, Azimut- anzeigeschirm m
axis of torsion	s. torsional axis		
axis of traction, axis of tension	Zugachse f	azimuth star	Azimutstern m
		azimuth station	s. Laplace azimuth station
axis of twist	s. screw axis <cryst.>		
axis of twist	s. torsional axis		
axis of vibration, axis of oscillation	Schwingungsachse f		
axis of yaw, yaw axis	Gierachse f	**B**	
axis of zero lift	s. zero lift line		
axisymmetric	s. axial symmetry / in rotationssymmetrische (axialsymmetrische) Strömung f		
axisymmetric flow, axially symmetric flow, axial flow		Baader['s] déformation test	s. defo test
		Babcock['s] star	Babcockscher Stern m
axode, axoid	Achsenfläche f, Axoid n	Babinet absorption rule	Babinetsche Regel (Absorp- tionsregel) f
axon, neurite	Axon n, Neurit m, Achsenzylinder m	Babinet compensator, Jamin compensator	Babinet-Kompensator m, Babinetscher Kompen- sator m
axonometer	Axonometer n		
axonometric, clinographic	axonometrisch	Babinet point	Babinet-Punkt m, Babinet- scher Punkt m
axonometric chart	axonometrisches Diagramm n	Babinet['s] principle, Babinet['s] theorem	Babinetsches Prinzip (Theorem) n, Theorem von Babinet
axonometry	Axonometrie f		
axoplast	Axoplasma n		
Ayrton equation	Ayrtonsche Gleichung f	Bach['s] theory [for plates]	Bachsche Näherungstheorie f [für Platten]
Ayrton resistor	Ayrton-Widerstand m	bacillary structure	s. fibre structure
Ayrton shunt	s. universal shunt	back-and-forth motion	s. reciprocating motion
Azbel-Kaner resonance	Azbel-Kaner-Resonanz f	back conductance	Sperrleitwert m
azel scope	s. azimuth and elevation scope		
azeotrope, azeotropic mixture, constant boiling[-point] mixture	azeotropes Gemisch n, Azeotrop n, azeotrope Mischung f	back co-ordination bond	s. back donation
		back coupling	s. feedback
		back-coupling window	Rückkopplungsloch n, Rückkopplungsfenster n
azeotrope, azeotropic curve	Azeotrope f		
azeotropic	azeotrop	back current	s. reverse current <semi.>
azeotropic curve	s. azeotrope	back current relay	s. directional relay
azeotropic mixture	s. azeotrope	back diaphragm, rear diaphragm	Hinterblende f
azeotropic point	azeotroper Punkt m		
azeotropy	Azeotropie f	back diffusion	Rückdiffusion f
azimuth, astronomical (geoidal) azimuth <astr.>	Azimut n, astronomisches Azimut n <Astr.>	back diffusion loss	Rückdiffusionsverlust m
azimuth	s. a. direction angle	back direction	s. reverse direction <semi.>
azimuthal angle <in microscope illumination>	Beleuchtungsazimut n, Azimutalwinkel m	back donation, back co- ordination bond, dative bond	Rückbindung f

back 48

back echo	Rückenecho n
back edge <of the pulse>	s. trailing edge
back effect, back-layer effect	Hinterwandeffekt m
back electromotive force	s. counter electromotive force
back electron	Rückelektron n, Rückkehrelektron n, Umkehrelektron n
back-emf, back e.m.f.	s. counter electromotive force
back e.m.f. cell, stabilizing cell	Gegenzelle f
backfire, arc[-]back, backkick, inverse ignition <of rectifier>	Rückzündung f <Gleichrichter>
back fire (firing, flash)	s. light-back
back focal length	s. image focal length
back focus	s. image focus
Back-Goudsmit effect	Back-Goudsmit-Effekt m
background <nucl.>	Untergrund m; Nulleffekt m <Kern.>
background	s. a. natural background radiation
background activity	Untergrundaktivität f
background brightness	Grundhelligkeit f
background collimating mark; background collimating point	Hintergrundmarke f, Bildhintergrundmarke f; Rahmen-Hintergrundmarke f
background count	s. background pulse
background counting rate	Nulleffektzählrate f, Untergrundzählrate f
background electrolyte	s. supporting electrolyte
background eradication	s. fog elimination <phot.>
background gamma radiation	s. gamma-ray background
background level	s. noise level
background meteor activity	Meteortätigkeit f außerhalb der großen Meteorströme
background monitor	Untergrundmonitor m, Untergrundüberwachungsgerät n
background pulse; background count	Nulleffektimpuls m, Untergrundimpuls m; Untergrundzählimpuls m, Untergrundzählstoß m
background radiation	s natural background radiation
background scattering	Untergrundstreuung f
background star	s. field star
backheating <of magnetron cathode>	Überheizung f <Magnetronkatode>
back heating [effect]	Rückheizung f, Rückheizungseffekt m
backing <of film>	s. film base <phot.>
backing material	s. base material
backing plate	s. supporting plate
backing pump	s. forepump
backkick	s. backfire <of rectifier>
backlash	s. gap <techn.>
backlash	s. pulling effect <el.>
backlash	s. reverse grid current
back-lash potential	s. reverse grid voltage
back-layer effect, back effect	Hinterwandeffekt m
back-layer photocell	s. back-wall photovoltaic cell
back lens, rear lens	Hinterlinse f
back lobe	Hinterkeule f, Hinterlappen m, Hinterzipfel m
Bäcklund transformation	Bäcklund-Transformation f
back nodal point	s. image nodal point
back-off voltage	s. inverse voltage <el.>
back pointer	Zentralstrahlindex m
back potential backpressure, back pressure, counterpressure, reaction pressure	s. inverse voltage <el.> Gegendruck m
back principal plane	s. image principal plane
back pulse front	s. trailing edge
back reaction, reverse reaction	Rückreaktion f; Rekombinationsreaktion f; Rückbildungsprozeß m, Rückbildung f <Raketentechnik>
back-reflection Laue pattern, back-reflection pattern, back-reflection photograph, back-reflection Laue photograph, back-reflection photogram, back-reflection Laue photogram, Laue back-reflection photograph, Laue back-reflection photogram	Rückstrahlaufnahme f [nach Laue], Laue-Rückstrahlaufnahme f, Rückstrahldiagramm n [nach Laue], Laue-Rückstrahldiagramm n, Rückstrahl-Laue-Aufnahme f, Rückstrahl-Laue-Diagramm n
back-reflection method [in X-ray diffraction], back-reflection Laue method, back-reflection Laue photography, back-reflection photography, Laue back-reflection method, Laue back-reflection photography	Rückstrahlverfahren n, Rückstrahlungsverfahren n, Rückstrahlaufnahmeverfahren n, Rückstrahlaufnahme f, Röntgen-Rückstrahlverfahren n, Röntgen-Rückstrahlungsverfahren n, Laue-Rückstrahlverfahren n, Laue-Rückstrahlungsverfahren n, Rückstrahl-Laue-Methode f, Rückstrahl-Laue-Verfahren n, Rückstrahlungs-Laue-Methode f, Rückstrahlungs-Laue-Verfahren n
back resistance, reverse resistance	Sperrwiderstand m, Widerstand m in Sperrichtung; Rückwiderstand m
backscatter	s. backscattering
backscatter angle	s. angle of backscattering
backscatter cross-section, backscattering cross-section, cross-section for backscattering	Rückstreuquerschnitt m, Wirkungsquerschnitt m für (der) Rückstreuung
backscattered <of radiation>	[zu]rückgestreut, rückwärts gestreut, rückdiffundiert <Strahlung>
backscatter effect, backscatter phenomenon	Rückstreueffekt m
backscatterer	Rückstreumaterial n, Rückstreukörper m, Rückstrever m
backscatter factor	Rückstreufaktor m
backscatter gauge, backscattering gauge	Rückstreumeßgerät n, Reflexionsmeßgerät n, Rückstrahlungsmeßgerät n, Rückdiffusionsmeßgerät n
backscatter gauging, backscattering gauging, thickness measurement by backscatter[ing]	Rückstreudickenmessung f, Reflexionsdickenmessung f
backscattering, backscatter, reflection; rediffusion <of electrons>	Rückstreuung f, Reflexion f, Rückdiffusion f
backscattering, backward scattering <opt.>	Rückwärtsstreuung f, Rückstreuung f <Opt.>
backscattering angle	s. angle of backscattering
backscattering cross-section	s. backscatter cross-section
backscattering error	Unterlagefehler m, Rückstreufehler m
backscattering gauge	s. backscatter gauge
backscattering gauging	s. backscatter gauging
backscattering loss	s. backscatter loss
backscattering method	s. backscatter technique
backscattering peak, backscatter peak	Rückstreupeak m, Rückstreumaximum n
backscattering technique	s. backscatter technique
backscattering thickness, backscatter thickness	Rückstreudicke f, Rückdiffusionsdicke f

backscattering thickness gauge (meter)	s. backscatter thickness gauge	backward wave, backward-fading wave <el.>	Rückwärtswelle f, rückläufige (rücklaufende) Welle f <El.>
backscatter intensity, intensity of backscattered radiation	Rückstreuintensität f, Rückstrahlintensität f	backward wave	s. a. backward travelling wave <el.>
backscatter loss, backscattering loss, spill	Rückstreuverlust m	backward-wave oscillator	Rückwärtswellenoszillator m
backscatter method	s. backscatter technique	backward-wave tube	s. carcinotron
backscatter peak, backscattering peak	Rückstreupeak m, Rückstreumaximum n	backwash	s. backstreaming
backscatter phenomenon, backscatter effect	Rückstreueffekt m	back wash[ing]	s. reextraction
backscatter technique, backscattering technique, backscatter method, backscattering method	Rückstreuverfahren n, Reflexionsverfahren n, Rückstrahlungsverfahren n, Rückdiffusionsverfahren n, Rückstreumethode f	backwater	Rückstau m
		backwater curve, backwater profile, stagnation curve	Staukurve f, Staulinie f
		backwater function	Staufunktion f
		backwater profile	s. backwater curve
backscatter thickness, backscattering thickness	Rückstreudicke f, Rückdiffusionsdicke f	backwater surface	Staufläche f, Stauhaltung f
backscatter thickness gauge (meter), backscattering thickness meter (gauge)	Rückstreudickenmesser m, Reflexionsdickenmesser m		
		backwater surge, backwater wave	Stauschwall m
		back wave	s. reflected wave
back side of the cyclone, rear side of the cyclone	Zyklonenrückseite f, Zyklonenrücken m	Bacon hydrox cell	Bacon-Element n
		bacterial strain	Bakterienstamm m
back sight, plus sight	Rückwärtsvisur f, Rückwärtsvisieren n	bad conductor	s. poor conductor
		Bader['s] approximation	Badersche Näherung (Näherungsdarstellung) f
back stream, backstreaming; return flow, receding, flowing back; reverse flow; backwash; down flow	Rückstrom m, rücklaufende (zurücklaufende, auslaufende, rückkehrende) Strömung f, Rückströmung f, rücklaufender Strom m, Rückwärtsstrom m; Rücklauf m, Zurückfließen n, Zurückströmen n	Badger rule	Badgersche Regel f
		Baer['s] law [/von]	von Baersches Gesetz n
		Baeyer['s] strain theory, strain theory	Baeyersche Spannungstheorie f
		baffle <ac.>, acoustic baffle, abat-voix	Schallwand f, Schallschirm m
		baffle	s. a. partition <chem.>
back stream of electrons	s. reverse current <el.>	baffle	s. a. paddle <hydr.>
"back stress" <of dislocations>	Gegenspannung f <Versetzungen>	baffle column, baffle-plate column; baffle spray tower	Rieselblechkolonne f; Rieselfilmkolonne f
Bäckström filter	Bäckström-Filter n		
back-to-back connection	s. antiparallel connection	baffle-plate column; baffle spray tower	s. baffle column
back-to-back ionization chamber, double ionization chamber	Doppelionisationskammer f [nach Rutherford], Rutherfordsche Doppelionisationskammer (Ionisationskammer f), Doppelkammer f	baffling wind	s. variable wind
		bag filter	Beutelfilter n, Taschenfilter n
		Baily['s] beads	Perlschnurphänomen n
		Bainbridge mass spectrograph	Bainbridgescher Massenspektrograph m, Massenspektrograph nach Bainbridge
back-up material	s. base material		
back vergence, image (rear) vergence	bildseitige Vergenz f, Bildvergenz f	bainitic hardening	Isothermhärtung f, Thermalhärtung f, Bainithärtung f
back vertex image distance	s. image distance from the vertex	Baker-Nathan effect, hyperconjugation	Hyperkonjugation f, Baker-Nathan-Effekt m
back-wall cell, back-wall photovoltaic cell, back-layer photocell	Hinterwandzelle f, Hinterwandphotoelement n	Baker-Schmidt camera, Baker-Schmidt telescope	Baker-Schmidt-System n, Schmidt-Baker-System n, Baker-Schmidt-Spiegel m, Schmidt-Baker-Spiegel m
backward-acting control	s. closed-loop control		
backward cone	Nachkegel m		
backward depth of field	s. rear depth of field	Bakker equation	Bakker-Gleichung f
backward difference	absteigende Differenz f, vorwärts genommene Differenz	balance, equilibrium; stability	Gleichgewicht n; Stabilität f
		balance, equilibrium	Bilanz f; Balance f; Gleichgewicht n
backward difference quotient	rückwärtiger Differenzenquotient m	balance; pair of scales, scales <US also sing.>	Waage f
backward diffused, retrodiffused	zurückdiffundiert, rückdiffundiert	balance, equilibrium	Gleichgewicht n
backward direction	s. reverse direction <semi.>		
backward-fading wave	s. backward wave <el.>		
backward mirror-coated	s. mirror-lined	balance, balance wheel <of clock>	Unruhe f, Unruh f <Uhr>
backward propagation	Rückwärtsausbreitung f	balance <el.>; symmetry	Symmetrie f <El.>
backward scattering	s. backscattering <opt.>		
backward short-circuit current, reverse short-circuit current	Rückwärts-Kurzschlußstrom m	balance, balancing circuit, balancing network <el.>	Nachbildung f, Netznachbildung f, Leitungsnachbildung f, Nachbildungsnetzwerk n <El.>
backward thrust	Bremsschub m	balance	s. a. budget
		balance	s. a. equilibrium / be in
backward transfer admittance	Rückwärtsscheinleitwert m	balance	s. a. equal-arm lever
backward transfer impedance, reverse transfer impedance	Leerlaufkernwiderstand m rückwärts; Übertragungswiderstand m rückwärts	balance attenuation, return loss	Fehlerdämpfung f, Nachbilddämpfung f, Fehlerdämpfungskoeffizient m
		balance barometer	Waagebarometer n
backward travelling wave, backward wave <el.>	rücklaufende (rückläufige, gegenläufige) Wanderwelle f, Rückwärts-Wanderwelle f, Rückwärts[wander]welle f	balance condition, condition for balance <of the bridge>	Abgleichbedingung f <Brücke>

balanced

balanced amplifier	s. push-pull amplifier
balanced chemical equation, balanced equation	stöchiometrische Reaktionsgleichung f
balanced circuit, balanced wire circuit <el.>	symmetrischer Kreis m <El.>
balanced equation, balanced chemical equation, rate equation	stöchiometrische Reaktionsgleichung f
balanced feeder	Parallelspeiseleitung f
balanced ionization chamber	symmetrische Ionisationskammer f
balanced load	symmetrische Belastung (Last) f
balanced mixture	balancierte (äquilibrierte) Mischung f
balanced modulation, push-pull modulation	Gegentaktmodulation f
balanced modulator, bridge modulator, modulation bridge	Ringmodulator m, Ringmodulatorschaltung f, Doppel-Gegentaktmodulator m, Gegentaktmodulator m, Modulationsbrücke f
balanced multivibrator, symmetrical multivibrator	symmetrischer Multivibrator m
balanced output, symmetric (push-pull) output	symmetrischer Ausgang m, Gegentaktausgang m
balanced-to-unbalanced transformer	s. balun
balanced valve amplifier	s. push-pull amplifier
balanced wire circuit	s. balanced circuit <el.>
balance each other	s. equilibrium / be in
balance equation, rate (kinetic) equation <el.>	Bilanzgleichung f, kinetische Gleichung f <El.>
balance error	Nachbildfehler m, Nachbildungsfehler m
balance for three-component force measurements, three-component balance	mechanische Dreikomponentenwaage f
balance meter	s. null detector
balance method, balancing method	Abgleichverfahren n
balance of bridge	Brückengleichgewicht n, Gleichgewicht n der Brücke
balance of energy	s. energy balance
balance of phases	s. phase coincidence
balance of Westphal	s. direct-reading balance of Westphal
balance out <hand>	einspielen <Zeiger>
balance radiometer	Waagebalkenradiometer n
balance-type potentiometer	s. potentiometer <el.>
balance wheel <of clock>, balance	Unruhe f, Unruh f <Uhr>
balance wheel clock; balance wheel watch	Unruhuhr f
balancing, balancing motion	Wippbewegung f
balancing <el.>, symmetrization	Symmetrierung f, Symmetrisierung f
balancing	s. a. adjustment <el.>
balancing	s. a. compensation
balancing	s. a. equilibration <mech.>
balancing calculation	s. calculus of observations
balancing circuit	s. balance <ei.>
balancing force	Kompensationskraft f
balancing instrument	s. null detector
balancing line	Symmetrier- und Transformationsleitung f, ST-Leitung f
balancing loop	Symmetrierungsschleife f
balancing method, balance method	Abgleichverfahren n
balancing method	s. a. null method
balancing motion, balancing	Wippbewegung f
balancing network	s. balance <el.>
balancing out	s. adjustment <el.>
balancing potentiometer, adjusting (compensating) potentiometer	Abgleichpotentiometer n, Ausgleichspotentiometer n
balancing weight, weight	Gewichtsstück n, Massenstück n, Gewicht n
Balashov coefficient, generalized Talmi coefficient	Balaschow-Koeffizient m, verallgemeinerter Talmi-Koeffizient m
Balescu-Lenard-Quernsey equation	Gleichung f von Balescu-Lenard-Quernsey, Balescu-Lenard-Quernsey-Gleichung f
B-algebra	s. Banach algebra
B*-algebra	s. C*-algebra
ball and line float	s. composite float
ball antenna	s. spherical antenna
ballast, control gear, stabilizer, ballast unit <of discharge lamp>	Vorschaltgerät n <Entladungslampe>
ballast lamp	s. barretter
ballast resistance	s. barretter
ballast resistance	s. load resistance
ballast resistor	[selbstregelnder] Vor-[schalt]widerstand m, vorgeschalteter Widerstand m
ballast resistor	s. a. load resistance
ballast resistor	s. barretter
ballast tube	s. barretter
ballast unit	s. control gear
ball condenser, ball cooler	Kugelkühler m
ball governor	s. centrifugal governor
ball indentation test, ball test	Kugeldruck-Härteprüfung f, Kugeldruckversuch m
ballistical galvanometer	ballistisches Galvanometer (Drehspulgalvanometer) n, Stoßgalvanometer n, Stromstoßgalvanometer n
ballistic coefficient <or its reciprocal>	ballistischer Koeffizient m
ballistic constant, [ballistic] galvanometer constant	ballistische Konstante f, [ballistic] Galvanometerkonstante f, ballistischer Reduktionsfaktor m
ballistic curve	ballistische Kurve f
ballistic deflection	ballistischer Ausschlag m, Stoßausschlag m
ballistic demagnetization (demagnetizing) factor	ballistischer Entmagnetisierungsfaktor m
ballistic factor, damping factor <US>; overshoot [-ing], overswing <of a measuring instrument>	Überschwingung f, <Meßgerät>
ballistic missile; ballistic rocket	ballistische Rakete f
ballistic pendulum	ballistisches Pendel n, Stoßpendel n, Stoßwaage f
ballistic rocket; ballistic missile	ballistische Rakete f
ballistics	Ballistik f
ballistic wave	s. head wave
ballistocardiography	Ballistokardiographie f
ball lightning, globe lightning, fireball	Kugelblitz m
ball manipulator, ball-socket manipulator	Kugel[gelenk]manipulator m
balloelectric effect	s. Lenard effect
ball of fire, fireball <nucl.>	Feuerball m <Kern.>
balloon-borne rocket, balloon-launched rocket	ballongestartete Rakete f
balloon-borne telescope	Ballonteleskop n
balloon-launched rocket	s. balloon-borne rocket
balloon satellite	Ballonsatellit m
ball-socket manipulator, ball manipulator	Kugelmanipulator m
ball test	s. ball indentation test
ball variometer, spherical-coil variometer	Kugelvariometer n
Balmer continuum	Balmer-Kontinuum n
Balmer decrement	Balmer-Dekrement n
Balmer discontinuity	Balmer-Sprung m
Balmer formula	Balmer-Formel f, Balmer-Serienformel f, Balmersche Serienformel f

Balmer limit, limit of the Balmer series — Balmer-Grenze *f*
Balmer line — Balmer-Linie *f*
Balmer series — Balmer-Serie *f*

Balmer term — Balmer-Term *m*
balun, balanced-to-unbalanced transformer; bazooka — Symmetriertopf *m*, Symmetrier[ungs]transformator *m*, Symmetrietransformator *m*, Sperrtopf *m*, 2 × λ/4-Symmetriertransformator *m*; λ/4-Symmetriertransformator *m*

Baly cell, Baly tube — Baly-Rohr *n*, Balysches Absorptionsgefäß *n*

Banach-adjoint transformation — Banach-adjungierte Transformation *f*
Banach algebra, B-algebra, complete normed algebra — Banach-Algebra *f*, B-Algebra *f*, vollständige normierte Algebra *f*
Banachiewicz['s] scheme — Banachiewicz-Schema *n*
Banach space, complete normed space — Banach-Raum *m*, vollständiger normierter Raum *m*

Banach-Steinhaus theorem, uniform-boundedness principle — Banach-Steinhausscher Satz *m*, Satz von Banach und Steinhaus
band — s. energy band
band — s. a. spectral band
band-band recombination — s. band-to-band recombination
band-band scattering, band-to-band scattering, interband scattering — Band-Band-Streuung *f*, Zwischenbandstreuung *f*
band-band transition — s. band-to-band transition
band cloud — bandartige Wolke *f*, bänderartige Wolke

band contour, band envelope — Bandenkontur *f*, Bandenenveloppe *f*
band edge <cryst.> — Bandkante *f* <Krist.>

band edge — s. a. band head <opt.>
band edge energy — Bandkantenenergie *f*

banded muscle, striated muscle — quergestreifter Muskel *m*
banded spectrum — s. channelled spectrum
banded structure — Zeilenstruktur *f*

banded structure, ghost structure — Bänderstruktur *f*, Streifenstruktur *f*
band-elimination filter — s. band-stop filter
band envelope, band contour — Bandenkontur *f*, Bandenenveloppe *f*
band filter, band-pass filter <opt.> — Bandfilter *n* <Opt.>
band gap — s. gap <in band model>
band group, band system — Bandensystem *n*
band head, head (edge) of the band, band edge — Bandenkante *f*, Bandkante *f*, Bandenkopf *m* <Opt.>
band-impurity transition, band-to-impurity transition — Band-Störstelle-Übergang *m*
banding — s. striation
band loudspeaker — s. ribbon loudspeaker
band model, energy band model, model of energy bands — Bändermodell *n*, Energiebändermodell *n*, Energiebänderschema *n*
band of clouds, cloud band — Wolkenband *n*
band of moving phase, moving phase band, solvent front — Laufmittelfront *f*, Front *f* des Laufmittels, Fließmittelfront *f*
band of secondary slip — s. stria <cryst.>
band of totality, zone of totality, total zone of obscuration — Totalitätszone *f*
band origin <opt.> — s. origin of the band
band-pass filter <opt.>, band filter — Bandfilter *n* <Opt.>
band pressure level — Schalldruckpegel *m* in einem vorgegebenen Frequenzband
band progression — s. progression of bands
band-rejection filter — s. band-stop filter
band sequence, sequence (series, set) of bands — Bandengruppe *f*

band-spectroscopical — bandenspektroskopisch, molekülspektroskopisch

band spectrum — Bandenspektrum *n*

band spread, spreading of the band — Bandspreizung *f*, Spreizung *f* des Bandes
band-stop filter, band-elimination filter, band-rejection filter — Bandsperre *f*, Bandsperrfilter *n*

band strength — Bandenstärke *f*
band structure <cryst.> — Bänderstruktur *f* <Krist.>
band suspension — Bandaufhängung *f*
band switching — s. range switching
band system, band group — Bandensystem *n*
band theory [of metals], theory of the energy bands — Bändertheorie *f* [der Metalle], Bandtheorie *f*

band-to-band recombination, band-band (interband, direct) recombination — Band-Band-Rekombination *f*, Zwischenbandrekombination *f*, direkte Rekombination *f*
band-to-band scattering, band-band (interband) scattering — Band-Band-Streuung *f*, Zwischenbandstreuung *f*
band-to-band transition, band-band (interband, interzone) transition — Band-Band-Übergang *m*, Zwischenbandübergang *m*

band-to-impurity transition, band-impurity transition — Band-Störstelle-Übergang *m*
band-type field (magnetic) balance, thread-type magnetic (field) balance — Bandwaage *f*, magnetische Bandwaage, Fadenwaage *f*, magnetische Fadenwaage
bandwidth compression, bandwidth narrowing; frequency compression — Frequenzbandkompression *f*; Frequenzbandverschmälerung *f*

band with ray structure, RB — Band *n* mit Strahlenstruktur
bang — s. supersonic bang
bang-bang servo — s. on-off control
bank, roll, rolling <aero.> — Querlage *f*; Querneigung *f*, Querkippung *f*, Krängung *f*; Rollen *n*, Rollbewegung *f*; Rollflug *m*

bank <math.>, border — Schnittufer *n*, Ufer *n* <Math.>
banked winding — s. series winding
bank erosion — s. erosion of the bank
bank of clouds, cloud bank — Wolkenbank *f*; Wolkenwand *f*
bank of contacts — s. contact panel
bantam tube (valve) — s. miniature tube
bar; column <mech.>, rod — Stab *m* <Mech.>
bar <of test pattern> — Balken *m* <Testbild>

bar, b <unit of pressure> — Bar *n*, b
Barba['s] law — Barbasches Gesetz *n*
Barbier degree, °B — Barbier-Grad *m*, °B
bar chart — s. histogram
Bardeen-Cooper-Schrieffer theory [of superconductivity], theory of Bardeen-Cooper-Schrieffer, B.C.S. (BCS) theory — Bardeen-Cooper-Schrieffer-Theorie *f*, Bardeen-Cooper-Schrieffersche Theorie *f* [der Supraleitung], BCS-Theorie *f*
Bardeen-Herring source — Bardeen-Herringsche Versetzungsquelle *f*, Bardeen-Herring-Quelle *f*

bar diagram — s. histogram
bar drawing, mandrel drawing — Stangenzug *m*, Ziehen *n* über einen Dorn
bare mass — s. mechanical mass
bare nucleon — s. nucleor
bare particle — nacktes Teilchen *n*
bare pile — s. bare reactor
bare reactor, naked reactor, naked pile, bare pile — unreflektierter (nackter) Reaktor *m*, Reaktor ohne Reflektor
baric gradient — s. barometric gradient
baric system — Luftdrucksystem *n*, Luftdruckgebilde *n*
baric wave — s. atmospheric pressure wave
bar in tension — s. tie rod
barion, baryon — Baryon *n*
barium crown, baryta crown — Barytkron *m*
barium flint, baryta flint — Barytflint *m*
barium white, blanc fixe — Barytweiß *n*

Barker [crystallographic] index — Barker-Index *m*, Barkerscher Index *m*
Barkhausen criterion for oscillators — Barkhausensche Selbsterregungsbedingung *f*

Barkhausen discontinuity	Barkhausen-Sprung m, Magnetisierungssprung m	barometric gravimeter barometric height, barometric altitude	Gravimeter-Höhenmesser m barometrische Höhe f
Barkhausen effect	Barkhausen-Effekt m	barometric height	s. a. barometer reading
Barkhausen-effect noise, Barkhausen noise	Barkhausen-Rauschen n, Barkhausen-Geräusch n	barometric height barometric leg, barometric pipe	s. a. air pressure head Fallrohr n
Barkhausen formula	Barkhausensche Röhrenformel f	barometric levelling	s. barometric measurement of altitude
Barkhausen-Kurz oscillations, retarding-field oscillations	Barkhausen-Kurz-Schwingungen fpl, Bremsfeldschwingungen fpl, Elektronentanzschwingungen fpl	barometric maximum barometric measurement of altitude (height[s]), barometric levelling (altimetry), pressure measurement of height	s. High barometrische Höhenmessung f
Barkhausen-Kurz oscillator [circuit]	s. retarding-field oscillator	barometric microvariation, atmospheric microvariation	barometrische Unruhe f, atmosphärische Unruhe
Barkhausen noise, Barkhausen-effect noise	Barkhausen-Rauschen n, Barkhausen-Geräusch n		
Barkhausen oscillator	s. retarding-field oscillator	barometric minimum	s. cyclone <meteo.>
Barkhausen['s] sound comparison method	Hörvergleichsverfahren n	barometric pipe, barometric leg	Fallrohr n
Barkla['s] experiment	Barklascher Versuch m, Versuch von Barkla	barometric pressure, atmospheric pressure, level gauge, air pressure	atmosphärischer Druck m, barometrischer Druck, Luftdruck m
Barlow disk	Barlowsches Rad n, Barlow-Rad n	barometric pressure gradient	s. barometric gradient
Barlow lens	Barlow-Linse f	barometric tendency, pressure tendency	barometrische (barische) Tendenz f, Drucktendenz f, Tendenz des Luftdrucks, Barometertendenz f
Barlow['s] rule	Barlowsche Regel f		
bar magnet	Stabmagnet m		
		barometric tides	s. atmospheric tides
barn, b	Barn n <Kurzzeichen: barn, b>	barometric trough, trough [of low pressure] <meteo.>	Tiefdruckrinne f, Druckrinne f, Tiefdruckfurche f; Drucktrog m, Tiefdrucktrog m, Trog m
Barnard['s] star, runaway star	Barnard-Stern m, Barnardscher Stern m, Pfeilstern m		
barn doors, limitation diaphragm, snoot	Strahlenbegrenzungsblende f	barometric variation	s. atmospheric pressure wave
Barnett effect, magnetization by rotation	Barnett-Effekt m, Magnetisierung f durch Rotation, mechano-magnetischer Effekt m	barometry, measurement of atmospheric pressure	Luftdruckmessung f, Barometrie f
		barophoresis	Barophorese f
		baroscope, open end barometer	Baroskop n
baroclincity, baroclinity	barokline Massenverteilung f, Baroklinie f	barosphere	Barosphäre f <Atmosphäre oberhalb 8 km>
barocline	Baroklinie f		
baroclinic equilibrium	baroklines Gleichgewicht n	barotropic effect	barotrop[isch]es Phänomen n
baroclinity	s. baroclincity		
bar of circular section, rod	Rundstab m; Stange f	barotropic equation	barotrope Zustandsgleichung f
		barotropic equilibrium	barotropes Gleichgewicht n
bar of the variometer, variometer bar	Variometerstab m, Stab m des Variometers	barotropic field	barotropes Feld n, Barotropiefeld n
barogyroscope	Barygyroskop n	barotropic flow	barotrope Strömung f
baroluminescence	Barolumineszenz f		
		barotropy	Barotropie f, barotrope Massenverteilung f
barometer correction	Barometerkorrektion f		
barometer effect, barometric effect	Barometereffekt m	barrage cell (photocell) barrage with stop planks against logs, stoplog dam	s. photovoltaic cell Dammbalkenwehr n
barometer error of clock, pressure coefficient of clock	druckbedingter Gang m der Uhr, barometrischer Fehler m der Uhr	barred galaxy, barred nebula, barred spiral	Balkenspirale f
barometer reading, barometric height, reading of the barometer	Barometerstand m		
barometric altimeter, pressure altimeter, height measuring barometer	barometrischer Höhenmesser m, Höhenbarometer n	barrel distortion, negative distortion	tonnenförmige (negative) Verzeichnung f, Tonnenverzeichnung f <Opt.>; Tonnenverzerrung f <Fs.>
barometric altimetry	s. barometric measurement of altitude	barretter; ballast resistance (resistor)	Bolometerwiderstand m, Bolometerdraht m, Bolometer n <El.>, Bar[r]etter m
barometric altitude, barometric height	barometrische Höhe f		
barometric chamber	s. Torricelli vacuum		
barometric column	Barometersäule f		
barometric condenser	Fallrohrkondensator m, barometrischer Kondensator	barretter, current regulator [tube], current stabilizer, ballast tube, ballast (resistance) lamp	Stromregelwiderstand m, Stromregelröhre f, Stromregulator m, Stromstabilisatorröhre f, Stabilisatorröhre f, Stromregler m, Ballaströhre f, Widerstandslampe f
barometric distribution law	s. barometric equation		
barometric effect, barometer effect	Barometereffekt m		
barometric equation (formula), barometric (gravitational) distribution law	barometrische Höhenformel f, Barometerformel f	barretter, iron-hydrogen barretter	Eisenwasserstoffwiderstand m, Eisenwiderstand m
		barretter-type wattmeter	s. bolometer power meter
barometric gradient, barometric pressure gradient, baric gradient; height equivalent to 1 Torr of pressure drop	barometrischer Gradient m, barischer Gradient; barometrische Höhenstufe f, Höhenstufe	barrier	Schranke f; Barriere f; Sperre f; Wall m; Berg m
		barrier	s. a. potential barrier
		barrier	s. internal barrier layer
		barrier	s. surface barrier layer

barrier capacitance   s. barrier-layer capacitance
barrier diffusion   Trennwanddiffusion f, Diffusion f durch eine poröse Wand
barrier diffusion method, partition method   Trennwanddiffusionsverfahren n, Isotopentrennung f durch Diffusion durch eine poröse Wand
barrier electrode   s. blocking electrode
barrier factor, [barrier] penetration factor, barrier permeability (penetrability), permeability (penetrability) of the barrier, transparency of the potential barrier, barrier transparency   Durchlässigkeit f des Potentialwalls, Durchlässigkeit der Potentialschwelle, Durchdringungsfaktor m, Durchdringungskoeffizient m; Gamow-Faktor m
barrier-film rectifier   s. barrier-layer rectifier
barrier grid   Sperrgitter n
barrier-grid storage tube   s. radechon
barrier height   s. height of potential barrier
barrier height for internal rotation, barrier height for rotation in molecules   Höhe f des Potentialwalls bei Molekülrotation
barrier layer <at semiconductor surface>, surface barrier [layer], barrier, blocking layer, boundary surface (layer), boundary, transient region <at the semiconductor-metal contact> <semi.>   Randschicht f, Grenzschicht f, Oberflächensperrschicht f, Oberflächenbarriereschicht f, Oberflächenrandschicht f, Oberflächenbarriere f, Oberflächengrenzschicht f <Halb.>
barrier layer   s. a. internal barrier layer
barrier-layer capacitance, barrier (depletion-layer) capacitance, capacitance of the p-n junction, junction (transition region, transition, space charge) capacitance   Sperrschichtkapazität f, Übergangskapazität f; Randschichtkapazität f, Grenzschichtkapazität f
barrier-layer cell (detector)   s. photovoltaic cell
barrier-layer effect; depletion layer effect   Sperrschichteffekt m; Randschichteffekt m
barrier layer equation   Randschichtgleichung f
barrier layer model   s. barrier model
barrier layer noise   Randschichtrauschen n, Grenzschichtrauschen n; Sperrschichtrauschen n
barrier-layer photocell   s. photovoltaic cell
barrier-layer photoeffect   s. photovoltaic effect
barrier-layer photoelectric cell   s. photovoltaic cell
barrier-layer photoelectric effect   s. photovoltaic effect
barrier-layer photovoltaic cell   s. photovoltaic cell
barrier layer photovoltaic effect   s. photovoltaic effect
barrier layer potential, barrier potential, boundary potential   Randschichtpotential n, Grenzschichtpotential n; Sperrschichtpotential n
barrier-layer rectification, rectification by barrier layer   Randschichtgleichrichtung f, Grenzschichtgleichrichtung f; Sperrschichtgleichrichtung f
barrier-layer rectifier, barrier-film rectifier, metal rectifier, metallic rectifier, p-n junction rectifier, junction rectifier, contact rectifier <semi.>   Randschichtgleichrichter m, Grenzschichtgleichrichter m, Sperrschichtgleichrichter m, Metall-Halbleiter-Gleichrichter m <Halb.>
barrier layer resistance, barrier resistance, junction resistance   Randschichtwiderstand m, Grenzschichtwiderstand m, Übergangswiderstand m; Sperrschichtwiderstand m
barrier layer temperature, temperature of the barrier layer, junction temperature <semi.>   Randschichttemperatur f, Grenzschichttemperatur f; Sperrschichttemperatur f <Halb.>
barrier layer thickness   s. barrier width
barrier model, potential barrier model   Potentialwallmodell n
barrier model, barrier layer model   Sperrschichtmodell n
barrier of energy   s. energy threshold
barrier penetrability (penetration factor, permeability)   s. barrier factor
barrier photo-e.m.f.   Sperrschicht-Photo-EMK f
barrier potential, barrier layer potential, boundary potential   Randschichtpotential n, Grenzschichtpotential n; Sperrschichtpotential n
barrier resistance   s. barrier layer resistance
barrier thickness   s. barrier width
barrier to dislocations   Versetzungshindernis n
barrier transparency   s. barrier factor
barrier width, width of potential barrier   Potentialbreite f, Breite f des Potentialwalls
barrier width, barrier [layer] thickness, width (thickness) of the barrier layer; junction width (thickness); depletion layer width   Randschichtdicke f, Randschichtbreite f, Grenzschichtdicke f, Grenzschichtbreite f; Sperrschichtdicke f, Sperrschichtbreite f
Barrow generator   s. multitone
bar suspension, yoke suspension   Wiegeaufhängung f, Jochaufhängung f, Schwerpunktaufhängung f
Bartels number   Bartels-Zahl f
Bartlett force, spin-exchange force   Bartlett-Kraft f, Spinaustauschkraft f
Bartlett operator, spin-exchange operator   Bartlett-Operator m, Spinaustauschoperator m
Bartlett potential, spin-exchange potential   Bartlett-Potential n, Potential n der Bartlett-Kräfte, Spinaustauschpotential n
Bartlett['s] theorem   Bartlettscher Satz m, Satz von Bartlett
bar to be tested   s. test bar
bar vibration, vibration of the bar   Stabschwingung f; Stäbeschwingung f
barycentre   s. centre of mass
barycentric co-ordinates, barycentric system, centre-of-mass system [of co-ordinates], centre-of-mass frame <mech., astr.>   baryzentrische Koordinaten fpl, baryzentrisches System n, Schwerpunktsystem n, Massenmittelpunktsystem n <Mech., Astr.>
barycentric velocity, mean mass velocity, centre-of-mass velocity   baryzentrische Geschwindigkeit f, mittlere Massenschwindigkeit f, Schwerpunkt[s]geschwindigkeit f
barye, microbar, dyne per square centimetre, ba, μbar, μb <especially ac.>   Mikrobar n, μbar, μb <besonders Ak.>
barygyroscope   s. gravity controlled gyroscope
baryon, barion   Baryon n
baryon charge, baryon number   Baryonenladung f, Baryon[en]zahl f
baryon decuplet   Baryondekuplett n
baryon family   Baryonenfamilie f
baryon field   Baryonenfeld n
baryon number   s. baryon charge
baryon number conservation law, law of conservation of baryon number   Satz m von der Erhaltung der Baryonenzahl, Baryonenzahlerhaltungssatz m, Erhaltungssatz m der Baryonenzahl
baryon physics   Baryonphysik f, Baryonenphysik f
baryon resonance   Baryonenresonanz f
baryotropism   Baryotropismus m
barysphere, siderosphere   Barysphäre f, Siderosphäre f
baryta cathode   Bariumoxidkatode f, Bariumoxidglühkatode f
baryta crown, barium crown   Barytkron m
baryta flint, barium flint   Barytflint m
basal glide   Basistranslation f
basal metabolic rate, basal metabolism   s. basic metabolism
basal plane <US>, epipolar plane   Kernebene f
bascule   s. equal-arm lever

base <math., e.g. of power, logarithm, group>; radix <of number system>	Basis f <Math., z. B. Potenz, Logarithmus, Gruppe, Zahlensystem>	basic colour	s. primary colour
		basic component <of radio-frequency radiation of the Sun>, base level	Grundstrahlung f, Grundkomponente f
base <semi.>; base electrode	Basiselektrode f; Basis f <Halb.>	basic diagram	s. schematic circuit diagram <el.>
base	s. a. base line <of the rangefinder>	basic equation	s. fundamental equation
		basic frequency	s. fundamental frequency
base	s. a. film base <phot.>	basic hydrostatic equation	s. equation of hydrostatics
base [according to Brønsted]	s. proton acceptor	basicity, basic capacity	Basizität f
base bulk resistance	s. bulk resistance of base	basic metabolism, basic turnover, basal metabolism, basal metabolic rate	Grundumsatz m, Grundstoffwechsel m, Ruheumsatz m, Erhaltungsumsatz m, GU
base-centred	basiszentriert, seitenflächenzentriert, basisflächenzentriert, [einfach] flächenzentriert		
base-collector conductance	Basis-Kollektor-Leitwert m	basic point, fundamental point <math.>	Grundpunkt m
base-collector diode	Basis-Kollektor-Diode f	basic quantity	s. fundamental quantity
		basic radiance	reduzierte Strahldichte f
base contact, base terminal	Basisanschluß m, Basiskontakt m	basic research	s. fundamental research
		basic stimulus	Mittelpunktsvalenz f
base electrode; base <semi.>	Basiselektrode f; Basis f <Halb.>	basic transit angle	Grundlaufwinkel m
		basic turnover	s. basic metabolism
base electrolyte	s. supporting electrolyte	basic unit	s. fundamental unit
base exchange	s. cation exchange	basilar membrane	Basilarmembran f, Membrana f basialis
base flow	s. seepage flow		
base-ground transistor	Transistor m in Basisschaltung, basisgeerdeter Transistor	basin	s. flask
		basin	s. river basin <geo.>
		Basset['s] function	s. Macdonald['s] function
		Basson detector	Basson-Detektor m
		batch	s. preparation <chem.>
		batch distillation	diskontinuierliche (unstetige) Destillation f, Chargendestillation f, Postendestillation f
base impedance [of antenna]	Fußpunktwiderstand m; Anschlußwiderstand m		
		Batchelor['s] criterion	Batchelor-Kriterium n, Batchelorsches Kriterium
base level, basic component <of radio-frequency radiation of the Sun>	Grundstrahlung f, Grundkomponente f	Batchelor number, Ba	Batchelor-Zahl f, Batchelorsche Kennzahl (Zahl) f, Ba
base line, base <of the rangefinder>	Standlinie f, Basis f, Basislinie f, Stehlinie f <Entfernungsmesser>	batch of metal	s. melt
		batch process	diskontinuierliches (unstetiges) Verfahren n, Chargenprozeß m, Postenverfahren n
base material, backing (back-up, support, supporting, carrier) material	Trägermaterial n; Trägerwerkstoff m		
base material	s. a. film base <phot.>	Bateman-Dirichlet principle	Bateman-Dirichletsches Prinzip n
basement <geo.>	Grundgebirge n, Basement n, Sockel m <Geo.>	Bateman-Kelvin principle, Bateman principle, Bateman['s] variational principle	Bateman-Kelvinsches Prinzip n
base metal	Nichtedelmetall n, unedles Metall n		
base of erosion	Erosionsbasis f	bath	s. heating bath
base of microscope	s. microscope base	bathmometry	Wendepunktmethode f, Bathmometrie f
base of the cloud	s. cloud base		
base of the notch	s. groove of the notch	bathochrome, bathochromic	bathochrom; farbvertiefend
base of the pulse, pulse base	Impulsbasis f, Impulsfuß m, Basis f <Impuls>	bathochromic effect, bathochromism	Farbvertiefung f, Bathochromie f
base of the wave, wave base	Wellenbasis f, Wellenfuß m	batholite, batholith	Batholith m
base of the whirlwind, foot of the whirlwind	Trombenfuß m	bathometer	s. bathymeter
		bathyal region	bathyaler Bereich m, bathyale Zone f, Kontinentalabhang m
base plate	s. supporting plate		
base point	Basispunkt m		
base point <series of points>; centre, vertex <of pencil>	Trägerpunkt m	bathymeter, bathometer	Bathometer n, Bathymeter n, Meerestiefenmesser m, Wassertiefenmesser m, Tiefenmesser m
base ratio; base-to-distance ratio; base-to-height ratio	Basisverhältnis n <Photogrammetrie>		
		bathymetric chart, bathymetric map	Tiefenkarte f, Isobathenkarte f, bathymetrische Karte f
base region	Basiszone f; Basisschicht f		
base resistance	Basiswiderstand m	bathymetric curve	bathygraphische Kurve f, Tiefenkurve f, hypsographische Kurve des Seebebens
base spreading resistance	Basisausbreitungswiderstand m		
base strength	Basenstärke f		
base support	s. supporting plate	bathymetric map	s. bathymetric chart
base surge	Basiswolke f	bathymetry	s. deep-sea sounding
base terminal	s. base contact	Batschinski-McLeod relation	Batschinski-McLeodsche Relation f
base thickness	s. base width		
base thickness modulation, Early effect, base width modulation	Early-Effekt m, Basisbreitenmodulation f	Batschinski relation	Batschinskische Beziehung f, Batschinski-Beziehung f
		battery capacity	s. charging capacity
base-to-distance ratio; base-to-height ratio	s. base ratio <photogrammetry>	battery of capacitors	s. capacitor battery
		baud, Bd	Baud n, Bd
base veil	Grundschleier m, Untergrundschleier m	baumé, degree Baumé, °Bé	Baumé-Grad m, Baumé n, °Bé
		Baumé['s] hydrometer	Baumé-Aräometer n
base width, base thickness	Basisbreite f, Basiszonendicke f, Breite f der Basiszone	Baumé [hydrometer] scale, lunge scale	Baumé-Skala f, Baumé-Skale f
base width modulation	s. Early effect	Baumhauer experiment	Baumhauer-Versuch m, Versuch m von M. Baumhauer
basic capacity, basicity	Basizität f		
basic cell	s. unit cell <cryst.>		
basic circuit diagram	s. schematic circuit diagram	Bauschinger['s] effect, prestressing	Bauschinger-Effekt m
basic cleavage	s. flow cleavage		

Baveno twin	Bavenoer Zwilling m	beam divergence, beam spread, radiation beam divergence (angular width), angular width [of the beam]	Strahldivergenz f, Strahlstreuung f
Bayard-Alpert [ionization] gauge, Bayard and Alpert ionization gauge	Bayard-Alpertsches Ionisationsmanometer n, Ionisationsmanometer nach Bayard-Alpert		
bay disturbance, magnetic bay	Baystörung f, Baistörung f, Buchtstörung f	beam divider	Reiterlineal n, Reiterskale f, gekerbte Skale f der Balkenoberkante
Bayes['] theorem, inverse probability theorem	Bayesscher Satz m, Bayes Theorem n, Theorem von Bayes	beam extractor, extractor, ejector <acc.>	Ausschleusvorrichtung f, Strahlauslenkvorrichtung f, Ejektionssystem n, Ejektor m, Extraktionssystem n <Beschl.>
bazooka	s. balun		
B-body	s. Bingham body		
B.C.S. (BCS) theory	s. Bardeen-Cooper-Schrieffer theory	beam factor	Strahlenfaktor m
beach, sea[-]shore, shore, strand	Strand m	beam focusing	s. focusing <opt.>
		beam geometry	Strahlgeometrie f
beach	s. a. triangulation signal	beam guidance, guiding of the beam	Strahlführung f
beach migration, shore migration	Küstenversetzung f, Strandversetzung f, Strandvertriftung f	beam hole, beam tube <of reactor>	Strahlenkanal m, Strahlrohr n <zur Herausführung des Strahls für Bestrahlungen außerhalb des Reaktors>
beach ridge, chenier	Strandwall m		
beacon	s. radiobeacon <el.>		
bead	Siedesteinchen n	beam intensity	s. instantaneous intensity
		beam limiter	s. beam-limiting device
		beam limiting, limitation of the beam; radiation stop	Strahlbegrenzung f; Strahlenbegrenzung f; Bündelbegrenzung f
beaded screen; crystal beaded screen	Perlwand f, Kristallperlwand f; Glasperl[en]wand f		
		beam-limiting device, beam limiter (stop)	Strahlbegrenzer m, Bündelbegrenzer m
bead lightning, chain lightning, pearl necklace	Perlschnurblitz m	beam load, beam loading, beam power	Strahlleistung f
bead thermistor	Perlthermistor m, Perlenthermistor m	beam modulation factor	Strahlmodulationsfaktor m
bead transistor	Perltransistor m	beam of light, light beam; pencil of light, light[-ray] pencil	Lichtbündel n; Lichtbüschel n
beaking drop effect	s. Lenard effect		
beam, rocking beam, scale beam	Waagebalken m	beam of light	s. a. ray of light
		beam of rays	s. beam <of radiation>
beam <of radiation>, beam (bundle) of rays; pencil <of rays>, fan of rays	Strahlenbündel n, Bündel n, Strahl m; Strahlenbüschel n <in der Ebene>	beam of sound, sound (acoustic, sonic) beam	Schallstrahlenbündel n, Schall[wellen]bündel n
		beam plate	Strahlblech n, Strahlplatte f
beam <of vernier caliper>	Schiene f <des Meßschiebers>	beam position sensor	Strahlfühler m
		beam potential	s. beam voltage
beam <acc.>, particle beam	Teilchenstrahl m, Strahl m <Beschl.>	beam power, beam load, beam loading	Strahlleistung f
beam; girder <mech.>	Balken m; Träger m, Tragbalken m; Fachwerkträger m <Mech.>	beam power valve, beam tube <US>	„beam-power"-Röhre f, Beamtetrode f, Strahlröhre f
beam alignment, beam centring	Strahlzentrierung f, Strahleinrichtung f, Strahlausrichtung f, Strahleinstellung f		
		beam reactor	Reaktor m mit herausgeführten Neutronenbündeln
beam angle	s. beam aperture		
beam aperture, beam width, beam angle, spread angle	Bündelöffnung f, Bündelapertur f; Bündelbreite f; Strahlöffnung f; Strahlapertur f, Strahlquerschnitt m; Öffnungswinkel m des Bündels; Strahlbreite f	beam-rider guidance	Leitstrahllenkung f, Leitstrahlführung f
		beam ripple	Strahlwelligkeit f
		beam scale, beam balance	Balkenwaage f
		beam shaping	Strahlformung f
beam area, effective aerial area, effective area of the antenna, effective absorbing area, absorption cross-section [of antenna]	wirksame (effektive) Antennenfläche f, Antennen[wirk]fläche f, Wirkfläche (Absorptionsfläche, wirksame Fläche, effektive Fläche) f der Antenne	beam source	Strahlquelle f
		beam splitter	Strahlteiler m
		beam splitter, beam splitter plate, beam splitting plate, splitting plate	Strahlungsteilerplatte f, Teilerplatte f, Strahlenteilungsplatte f, Teilungsplatte f, Trennplatte f
beam balance, beam scale	Balkenwaage f	beam splitting prism, Kösters biprism, Kösters['] interference double prism	Strahlenteilungsprisma n, Interferenz-Doppelprisma (Doppelprisma) n nach Kösters, Interferenzdoppelprisma [nach Kösters], Köstersches Doppelprisma
beam catcher, beam trap	Strahl[en]fänger m, Strahl[en]auffänger m, Strahl[en]abfänger m		
beam centring	s. beam alignment		
beam chamber	Strahlemissionskammer f, Bündelemissionskammer f		
beam convergence, convergence of the beam, corradiation	Bündelkonvergenz f, Konvergenz f des Strahlenbündels	beam splitting system	Strahlspaltungssystem n, Strahlteilungssystem n
beam coupling	s. electronic coupling	beam spread	s. beam divergence
beam coupling coefficient, beam coupling factor	Strahlkopplungskoeffizient m	beam stacking	Strahlspeicherung f, „beam stacking" n, Aufstapelung f der Teilchenpakete
beam cross-section	Strahlquerschnitt m		
beam current, intensity of the beam current	Strahlstrom m, Strahlstromstärke f	beam stop	s. beam-limiting device
		Beams['] ultracentrifuge	Ultrazentrifuge f nach Beams, Beamssche Ultrazentrifuge
beam current density	Strahlstromdichte f		
beam deflection tube	s. cathode-ray tube		
beam defocusing	Strahlentbündelung f, Strahldefokussierung f	beam suppression	Strahlunterdrückung f
beam density <acc.>	Strahldichte f <Beschl.>		

beam   56

beam switching	Strahlschwenkung f	Bechstein tube photometer	Tubusphotometer n nach Bechstein, Bechsteinsches Tubusphotometer
beam switching, antenna switching, lobe switching, lobing	Leitstrahldrehung f, Schwenkung f des Richtdiagramms; Keulenumtastung f, Keulenumtastverfahren n	Beck arc	Beck-Bogen m, Beck-Lichtbogen m
		Beck arc flame	s. positive flame
		Beck effect	Beck-Effekt m
beam transport system	Strahlauslegung f, strahloptisches Transportsystem n, Strahltransportsystem n	Becke['s] law	Beckesches Gesetz n
		Becke line	Beckesche Linie f
		Becker gas	Becker-Gas n
beam trap	s. beam catcher	Beck flame	s. positive flame
beam tube, beam valve	Bündel[ungs]röhre f, Röhre f mit Elektronenbündelung	Beckmann rearrangement, Beckmann transformation	Beckmannsche Umlagerung f, Beckmann-Umlagerung f
beam tube	s. a. beam hole	Beckmann thermometer, adjustable range thermometer	Beckmann-Thermometer n
beam tube <US>	s. a. beam power valve		
beam valve	s. beam tube		
beam voltage, beam potential	Strahlspannung f		
beam width	s. beam aperture	Beckmann transformation	s. Beckmann rearrangement
beam width	s. lobe width <for antennas>	Beck['s] vertical illuminator	Vertikalilluminator m nach Beck, Planglasilluminator m [nach Beck], [geneigtes] Planglas n
bearing, radiobearing	Peilwert m, Funkazimut n		
bearing, direction finding; radiobearing, radio bearing, radiogoniometry, radio direction finding	Peilung f; Funkpeilung f, Radiogoniometrie f		
		Becquerel effect, Becquerel photoeffect, photovoltaic effect	Becquerel-Photoeffekt m, Becquerel-Effekt m, photogalvanischer Effekt m
bearing	s. a. support <mech.>		
bearing area	s. seat		
bearing capacity	s. carrying capacity	Becquerel effect <phot.>	Becquerel-Effekt m <Phot.>
bearing contact area ratio	s. ratio of bearing contact area	Becquerel phosphoroscope	s. phosphoroscope
bearing finder	s. direction finder	Becquerel photoeffect	s. Becquerel effect
bearing friction, pivot friction	Lagerreibung f	Becquerel photovoltaic cell	Elektrolytzelle f
bearing index, bearing number	Lagerzahl f	Becquerel rays	Becquerel-Strahlen mpl
		bed	s. stratum <geo.>
bearing indicator scope	s. display of direction finder	bedded volcano, stratovolcano	Schichtvulkan m, Stratovulkan m
bearing line	Peillinie f, Peilstrahl m		
bearing number, bearing index	Lagerzahl f	bedding, stratification <geo.>	Lagerung f; Schichtung f <Geo.>
bearing plane, blade bearing recess <of the balance>	Pfanne f <Waage>	bedding cleavage	s. primary cleavage
		bedding force diagram	s. shearing force diagram
		bed load	s. boulder <geo.>
bearing reaction	Lagerreaktion f	bed load sampler, sediment sampler, sediment catcher	Geschiebefänger m; Geschiebefangkasten m; Geschiebefangbeutel m
bearing strength	s. carrying capacity		
bearing surface, supporting surface <mech.>	tragende Fläche f, Tragfläche f <Mech.>	Beer['s] formula	Beersche Formel f
		Beer['s] law, Lambert-Beer law	Lambert-Beersches (Beersches) Gesetz n
bearing zone width, width of bearing zone	Peilbreite f	beginning of plasmolysis	Plasmolyseeintritt m
beat, beat vibration, beating	Schwebung f, Überlagerung f <von Wellen>	beginning of the ebb tide	Vorebbe f
beat amplitude	Schwebungsamplitude f, größter Schwebungsausschlag m	beginning of the flood tide	Vorflut f
		begin of boiling	Siedebeginn m
beat cycle, beat period, period of beat	Schwebungsperiode f, Schwebungsdauer f		
beat frequency, beat rate, note frequency	Schwebungsfrequenz f, Schwebungszahl f	begin of combustion	Verbrennungsbeginn m, Verbrennungseinsatz m
		behavior <US>	s. behaviour
beat frequency oscillator	s. heterodyne	behaviour, behavior <US>; response; performance; properties; characteristics; parameters	Verhalten n; Eigenschaften fpl; Charakteristika npl, Charakteristiken fpl; Parameter mpl
beating, dashing (wash) of the waves	Wellenschlag m		
beating	s. a. beat		
beat method	s. heterodyne beat method	behaviour	s. a. shape
beat note	s. heterodyne note	bei[-function], Kelvin function of the first kind	Kelvinsche (Thomsonsche) Funktion f erster Art, bei-Funktion f, bei
beat of beat	Schwebschwebung f, Schwebung f der Schwebungen		
beat period, period of beat, beat cycle	Schwebungsperiode f, Schwebungsdauer f	Beilby layer	Beilby-Schicht f
		Békésy-type audiometer	Békésy-Audiometer n, Hörschärfemesser m nach von Békésy
beat rate, beat frequency, note frequency	Schwebungsfrequenz f, Schwebungszahl f	bel, B	Bel n, B
Beattie and Bridgman equation [of state], Beattie-Bridgman equation [of state]	Beattie-Bridgmansche Zustandsgleichung f, Beattie-Bridgman-Gleichung f, Beattie- und Bridgmansche Gleichung f	Bellamy pastagram, pastagram	Bellamy-Diagramm n, Pastagramm n
		Bellani pyranometer	Kugelpyranometer n [von Bellani], Bellani-Pyranometer n
beat tone	s. heterodyne note	bell counter	s. end-window counter
beat vibration	s. beat	bell-crank lever	s. bent lever
Beaufort number, wind of Beaufort force	Beaufort-Zahl f, Beaufort-Windstärke f, Beaufort-Stärke f, Windstärke f nach Beaufort	bell manometer, floating bell manometer	Tauchglockendruckwaage f, Tauchglockenmanometer n, Glockenmanometer n
		bellow gauge	s. bellows-type pressure gauge
Beaufort scale [of wind force], Beaufort wind scale	Beaufort-Skala f [der Windstärke]		
		bellows	s. sylphon bellows
		bellows	s. expansion bellows
Beaumé scale	s. Baumé scale	bellows-and-strap arrangement, sylphon bellows, bellows	Faltenbalg m, Balg m; Balgmembran f
Bechstein['s] photometer	Photometeraufsatz m nach Bechstein, Bechstein-Photometer n, Taschenphotometer n von Bechstein; Photometerkopf m nach Bechstein		

bellows gauge s. aneroid barometer
bellows [pressure] Dosenmanometer n, Feder-
  gauge, bellows-type   balgmanometer n
  pressure gauge
bell pressure gauge, Glockenmanometer n
  bell-type manometer
bell-shaped curve s. error curve
bell-shaped pulse, Glockenimpuls m
  Gaussian pulse

bell-type manometer, Glockenmanometer n
  bell pressure gauge
Below['s] law <of current Belowsche Stromvertei-
  distribution>   lungsgleichung f,
   Belowsches Stromver-
   teilungsgesetz n
Below['s] region Belowsches Stromüber-
   nahmegebiet (Gebiet) n
Belson diagram, Belson Belson-Diagramm n,
  pattern   Belson-Bild n
belt s. phase belt <el.>
Bel['s] tensor Belscher Tensor m
belt of west winds, west Westwindgürtel m,
  wind belt   Westwindzone f
Beltrami['s] differential Beltramische Differential-
  equation   gleichung f
Beltrami['s] diffusion Beltramische Diffusions-
  equation, diffusion   gleichung f, Diffusions-
  equation of Beltrami   gleichung von Beltrami
Beltrami flow Beltrami-Strömung f
belt scanner s. mirror drum scanner
belt-type generator s. Graaff generator / Van de
Bemporad function Bemporad-Funktion f
Bénard [convection] Bénardsche Zelle (Konvek-
  cell, convection cell   tionszelle) f, Bénard-
   Zelle f
bench mark, survey ma k; Nivellementszeichen n,
  witness mark <US>   Nivellements[fest]punkt
   m, Nivellementsfestlegung
   f; Höhenmarke f; Fest-
   punkt m, Fixpunkt m
bend <mech.> Faltung f <Mech.>
bend, bending; warping, Krümmung f; Biegung f;
  warp; curvature; buckling   Wölbung f

bend s. a. bowing under load
   <mech.>
bending, flexure, folding Biegung f <Mech.>
  <mech.>

bending s. a. bowing under load
bending s. a. warping
bending couple, bending Biegemoment n, Biegungs-
  moment, flexural torque   moment n
  (couple, moment),
  moment of flexure
bending force Biegungskraft f, Biegekraft f
bending force s. a. shear force <mech.>
bending force constant Kraftkonstante f der Knickschwingung (Spreiz-
   schwingung; Deforma-
   tionsschwingung)
bending frequency Knickschwingungsfrequenz
   f, Spreizschwingungs-
   frequenz f; Deformations-
   schwingungsfrequenz f
bending in flexure s. cross bending
bending line, deflection Biegelinie f, Biegungslinie
  curve, curve of deflection
bending line plane, Biegungsebene f
  flexural plane, plane of
  flexure
bending moment s. bending couple
bending moment density Biegemomentdichte f

bending moment dia- s. moment diagram
  gram
bending of light [rays] s. light-ray bending
bending of rays Strahlenkrümmung f,
   Strahlkrümmung f
bending rigidity, bending Biegesteifigkeit f, Biegungs-
  stiffness (strength),   steifigkeit f, Biegesteif-
  flexural stiffness (rigidity)   heit f
bending strength, flexural Biegefestigkeit f, Biegungs-
  strength, flexural trans-   festigkeit
  verse strength

bending stress, flexural Biegebeanspruchung f
  load

bending stress, transverse Biegespannung f, Biegenor-
  stress, flexural stress   malspannung f
bending stress fatigue Dauerbiegefestigkeit f
  limit

bending test for shaped Winkelbiegeversuch m
  steel, bend test for shaped   <Ausbreit- oder Zusam-
  steel   menschlagversuch>
bending vibration, b; Knickschwingung f, Spreiz-
  deformation vibration   schwingung f; Biegungs-
   schwingung f, Bindungs-
   Biegungs-Schwingung f;
   Deformationsschwingung
   f
bending wave, flexural Biegungswelle f, Biege-
  wave   welle f
bending with rotating Umlaufbiegebeanspruchung
  bar, rotating bending   f, Umlaufbiegung f
bend test for shaped Winkelbiegeversuch m
  steel, bending test for   <Ausbreit- oder Zusam-
  shaped steel   menschlagversuch>
Benedicks effect, inverse [1.] Benedicks-Effekt m
  Thomson effect
Benham colour, Fechner Benham-Farbe f, Fechner-
  colour   Benhamsche Farbe f,
   Flimmerfarbe f, poly-
   phäne Farbe
Benham top Benham-Scheibe f
Benioff sum Benioff-Summe f
Bennett equation Bennett-Gleichung f
Bennett temperature Bennett-Temperatur f
bent crystal, curved gebogener (gewölbter)
  crystal   Kristall m
bent dislocation gekrümmte Versetzung f
bent electron gun, geknicktes Strahl-
  bent gun   erzeugungssystem n,
   geknicktes Elektronen-
   strahl-Erzeugungssystem n

benthos Benthos n
bent lever, angle[d] lever, Winkelhebel m
  armed lever, crank[ed]
  lever, bell-crank (knee)
  lever, [knee-]toggle lever
bent-lever balance, Zeigerwaage f
  dial balance
bent light ray, bent ray krummer (gekrümmter)
   Lichtstrahl m
bent mirror, curved gewölbter Spiegel m, ge-
  mirror   krümmter Spiegel
bent ray, bent light ray krummer (gekrümmter)
   Lichtstrahl m
benz, Bz Benz n, Bz
ber s. ber-function
Berek['s] coincidence Koinzidenzkriterium n
  criterion, coincidence   [von Berek]
  criterion [of Berek]
Berek compensator Kalkspatkompensator m
   (Kompensator m, Kom-
   pensationsprisma n) nach
   Berek, Berek-Kompen-
   sator m, Berekscher
   Kompensator, Berek-
   Prisma n, Bereksches
   Prisma n
ber-function, Kelvin Kelvinsche (Thomsonsche)
  function of the second   Funktion f zweiter Art,
  kind, ber   ber-Funktion f, ber
Bergeron-Findeisen Bergeron-Prozeß m,
  process, Bergeron   Bergeron-Findeisen-
  process   Prozeß m

Bergmann series, Bergmann-Serie f,
  fundamental series   Fundamentalserie f
  <spectr.>   <Spektr.>
Berkefeld filter Berkefeld-Kerze f
Berkeley-Hartley Osmometer n nach Berke-
  osmometer, osmometer   ley und Hartley,
  due to Berkeley and   Berkeley-Hartley-
  Hartley   Osmometer n
berkelium, $_{97}$Bk Berkelium n, $_{97}$Bk
Berlin phenomenon Berliner Phänomen n

Bernoullian polynomial, Bernoullisches Polynom n
  Bernoulli['s] polynomial
Bernoulli['s] binomial s. binomial distribution
  distribution
Bernoulli constant Bernoullische Konstante f
Bernoulli-De s. Hospital['s] rule / [De] l'
  l'Hospital['s] rule

Bernoulli 58

Bernoulli['s] differential equation s. Bernoulli['s] equation

Bernoulli distribution s. binomial distribution

Bernoulli['s] equation, Bernoulli['s] differential equation — Bernoullische Differentialgleichung f

Bernoulli['s] equation, Bernoulli['s] pressure equation, Bernoulli['s] theorem [in hydrodynamics] — Bernoullische Gleichung (Energiegleichung) f, Bernoulli-Gleichung f, hydrodynamische Druckgleichung f, Bernoullischer Satz m, Bernoullisches Theorem n <Hydr.>

Bernoulli-Euler law — Bernoulli-Eulersches Biegungstheorem n

Bernoulli['s] hypothesis, hypothesis of plane cross-sections, assumption that a cross section remains plane after bending — Bernoullische Annahme f, Bernoullische Hypothese f

Bernoulli['s] inequality — Bernoullische Ungleichung f

Bernoulli['s] law of large numbers s. Bernoulli['s] theorem

Bernoulli-l'Hospital['s] rule s. Hospital['s] rule / [De] l'

Bernoulli['s] number — Bernoullische Zahl f, Bernoulli-Zahl f

Bernoulli['s] polynomial, Bernoullian polynomial — Bernoullisches Polynom n

Bernoulli['s] pressure equation s. Bernoulli['s] equation

Bernoulli['s] theorem, Bernoulli['s] law of large numbers — Bernoullischer Grenzwertsatz (Satz) m, Bernoullisches Theorem n (Gesetz n der großen Zahlen), Satz m von Bernoulli

Bernoulli['s] theorem [in hydrodynamics] s. Bernoulli['s] equation

Berthelot['s] calorimeter, bomb calorimeter, calorimetric bomb — kalorimetrische Bombe f [nach Berthelot], Bombenkalorimeter n, Berthelot-Bombe f, Berthelotsche Bombe

Berthelot['s] equation [of state] s. Berthelot['s] state equation

Berthelot['s] principle, Berthelot-Thomsen principle — Berthelot[-Thomsen]sches Prinzip n, Berthelot-Prinzip n

Berthelot['s] rule — Berthelotsche Regel f, Regel von Berthelot

Berthelot['s] state equation, Berthelot['s] equation [of state] — Berthelotsche Zustandsgleichung (Gleichung) f, Berthelot-Gleichung f

Berthelot-Thomsen principle s. Berthelot principle

berthollide, berthollide compound, non-daltonide, non-Daltonian compound — Berthollid n, berthollide (nichtdaltonide) Verbindung f, Nichtdaltonid n

Bertin surface — Fläche f gleichen Gangunterschieds, Gangunterschiedsfläche f, Bertinsche Fläche f, Bertin-Fläche f

Bertrand curves, associate [Bertrand] curves, conjugate [Bertrand] curves — Bertrandsche Kurven fpl; Bertrandsches Kurvenpaar n

Bessel['s] [differential] equation — Besselsche Differentialgleichung (Gleichung) f

Bessel['s] formula [of interpolation], Bessel['s] interpolation formula — Besselsche Formel f, Besselsche Interpolationsformel f

Bessel function, cylinder (cylindrical, Fourier-Bessel) function, cylindrical harmonic — Zylinderfunktion f, Bessel-Funktion f, [Fourier-]Besselsche Funktion f

Bessel function, Bessel function of the first kind — Bessel-Funktion f [erster Art], Besselsche Funktion f, Zylinderfunktion f erster Art

Bessel function of the second kind, Neumann['s] [Bessel] function, Weber['s] function, Weber['s] (Neumann['s]) Bessel function of the second kind — Neumann-Funktion f, Neumannsche Funktion f, Zylinderfunktion (Bessel-Funktion) f zweiter Art, Webersche Funktion f, Weber-Funktion f

Bessel function of the third kind, Hankel function — Hankelsche Funktion (Zylinderfunktion) f, Hankel-Funktion f, Zylinderfunktion (Bessel-Funktion) f dritter Art

Besselian [fictitious] year, fictitious year — Besselsches Jahr n, annus fictus m

Bessel['s] identity — Besselsche Identität f

Bessel['s] inequality — Besselsche Ungleichung f, Bessel-Ungleichung f <Hilbert-Raum>; Dreiecksungleichung f <für Vektoren>

Bessel['s] integral [equation] — Besselsche Integraldarstellung f [der Zylinderfunktionen]

Bessel['s] interpolation formula s. Bessel['s] formula

Bessel['s] method <of determining the focal length> — Brennpunktverfahren n von Bessel

best estimator — beste Schätzung (Schätzfunktion) f

beta absorption gauge — Beta-Absorptionsdickenmesser m

beta-activity, beta-radioactivity — Beta-Aktivität f

beta-backscattering; beta reflection — Beta-Rückstreuung f; Beta-Reflexion f

beta bifurcation, beta branch — Beta-Zweig m, Beta-Verzweigung f

Beta Canis Majoris star, Beta Cephei-type star — Beta Cephei-Stern m, Beta Canis Majoris-Stern m

beta decay s. beta disintegration

beta disintegration, beta decay, beta process, beta transformation — Beta-Zerfall m, Beta-Umwandlung f, Beta-Prozeß m

beta disintegration electron, beta-decay electron — Beta-Zerfallselektron n

beta disintegration energy — Beta-Zerfallsenergie f

beta disintegration scheme, beta decay scheme — Beta-Zerfallsschema n

beta disintegration series, beta decay series — Beta-Zerfallsreihe f

beta emission s. beta-particle emission

beta-emitter, beta-radiator — Beta-Strahler m

beta emitter only s. pure beta emitter

beta flow s. transient creep

beta[-]function, Eulerian integral of the first kind, B-function — Betafunktion f, Eulersches Integral n erster Art, B-Funktion f

beta-gamma coincidence — Beta-Gamma-Koinzidenz f, β-γ-Koinzidenz f

beta gauge, beta thickness gauge (meter) — Beta-Dickenmesser m

beta instability — Beta-Instabilität f, Instabilität f gegen Beta-Zerfall

Beta Lyrae-type star — Beta Lyrae-Stern m

beta particle, beta ray — Beta-Teilchen n

beta-particle autoradiography <US>, beta-particle radioautography — Beta-Autoradiographie f

beta-particle backscattering gauge, beta backscatter thickness meter — Beta-Reflexionsdickenmesser m, Beta-Rückstreudickenmesser m

beta-particle detector — Beta-Detektor m, Detektor m für Beta-Strahlung

beta-particle dosimeter — Beta-Dosimeter n, Beta-Strahldosimeter n

beta-particle emission, beta emission (radiation) — Beta-Emission f; Beta-Strahlung f

beta-particle radiation s. beta radiation

beta-particle radioautography, beta-particle autoradiography — Beta-Autoradiographie f

beta-particle recoil, beta recoil — Beta-Rückstoß m

beta-particle scintillation spectrometer, scintillation beta-particle spectrometer	Szintillations-Beta-Spektrometer *n*	**Betti number**	Bettische Zahl *f*
beta-particle source, beta source	Beta-Quelle *f*, Beta-Strahlungsquelle *f*	**Betti['s] reciprocal (reciprocity) theorem, Betti['s] theorem**, reciprocity theorem of Maxwell and Betti, reciprocal theorem in classical elasticity theory, Maxwell and Betti reciprocity theorem, theorem of reciprocity	Bettischer Reziprozitätssatz (Satz) *m*, Bettisches Reziprozitätstheorem *n*, Satz von Betti (der Gegenseitigkeit der elastischen Verschiebungen)
beta-particle spectrograph	Beta-Spektrograph *m*		
beta-particle spectrometer	Beta-Spektrometer *n*, Beta-Strahlspektrometer *n*		
beta-particle spectrum	Beta-Spektrum *n*, Beta-Energiespektrum *n*, Beta-Strahlenspektrum *n*	**between-class correlation**	s. interclass correlation
beta process	s. beta disintegration	**between-class (between-group) variance**	s. interclass variance
beta radiation, beta rays, beta-particle radiation	Beta-Strahlung *f*, radioaktive Beta-Strahlung	**Betz-Keune profile**	Betz-Keune-Profil *n*
beta radiation	s. a. beta-particle emission	**Be variable [star]**	Be-Veränderlicher *m*, Be-Stern *m*
beta-radiator, beta-emitter	Beta-Strahler *m*	**bevel protractor**	s. clinometer
beta-radioactive standard	Beta-Standard *m*	**Beverage antenna**; wave antenna	Beverage-Antenne *f*, Langdrahtantenne *f*; Wellenantenne *f*
beta-radioactivity, beta-activity	Beta-Aktivität *f*	**Bezold-Abney phenomenon**	Bezold-Abneysches Phänomen *n*
beta ray	s. beta particle	**Bezold-Brücke phenomenon**, Brücke-Bezold phenomenon	Bezold-Brückesches (Brücke-Bezoldsches) Phänomen *n*
beta rays	s. beta radiation		
BET area, B.E.T. area, Brunauer-Emmett-Teller area	BET-Fläche *f*, Brunauer-Emmett-Teller-Fläche *f*	**BF₃ counter, BF₃ neutron counter**	BF₃-Neutronenzählrohr *n*, BF₃-Zählrohr *n*, Bortrifluoridzählrohr *n*
beta recoil, beta-particle recoil	Beta-Rückstoß *m*	**Bhabha exchange force**, Bhabha force	Bhabha-Kraft *f*
beta reflection	s. beta-backscattering	**Bhabha scattering**, electron-positron scattering	Elektron-Positron-Streuung *f*, Bhabha-Streuung *f*
beta-reflection coefficient	Beta-Reflexionskoeffizient *m*, Beta-Rückstreukoeffizient *m*		
beta source	s. beta-particle source	**B-H curve, B/H curve**	s. magnetization curve
beta-spectrometer	s. beta-particle spectrometer	**B-H loop, B/H loop**	s. hysteresis loop <el.>
beta-stable	beta-stabil	**B horizon**	s. illuvial soil <geo.>
beta thickness gauge (meter)	s. beta gauge	**biamperometric titration**	s. dead-stop titration
betatopic	betatop	**Bianchi identity**	[Padova-]Bianchische Identität *f*
beta transformation	s. beta disintegration		
beta-transition	Beta-Übergang *m*	**bias**	s. bias voltage <el.>
betatron, induction accelerator <acc.>	Betatron *n*, Elektronenschleuder *f*, Schleuder *f*, induktiver Beschleuniger *m*, Induktionsbeschleuniger *m* [von Kerst]	**bias**	s. systematic error
		bias	s. grid-bias voltage
		biased field	Verschiebungsfeld *n*
		bias effect	Vorspannungseffekt *m*
		biasing voltage <el.>	Verlagerungsspannung *f*
betatron acceleration	Betatronbeschleunigung *f*		
betatron effect	Betatroneffekt *m*		
betatron oscillation, Kerst oscillation	Betatronschwingung *f*, Kerst-Schwingung *f*	**biasing voltage**	s. a. bias voltage <el.>
		bias magnetization	s. magnetic biasing
betatron particle capture	Betatroneinfang *m*, Einfang *m* in den Betatronbetrieb	**bias resistor**	s. grid leak
		bias voltage, biasing (polarization) voltage, bias, priming <el.>	Vorspannung *f* <El.>
betatron radiation	Betatronstrahlung *f*		
betatron regime	Betatron[beschleunigungs]betrieb *m*	**bias voltage**	s. a. grid-bias voltage
		biaxiality, diaxiality	Zweiachsigkeit *f*
betatron start	Betatronstart *m*	**biaxial spherical harmonic [function]**	zweiachsige Kugelfunktion *f*
BET equation <of adsorption>	BET-Gleichung *f* <Adsorption>		
Bethe['s] approximation	Bethesche Näherung *f*	**biaxial stress**	s. plane stress
Bethe['s] approximation method, Bethe['s] method	Näherungsmethode *f* von Bethe, Bethesche Methode (Annahme) *f*, Bethe-Methode *f*	**bicentral dark-ground condenser [with two reflecting surfaces]**	Zweispiegelkondensor *m*, Zweiflächen-Spiegelkondensor *m*, bizentrischer Dunkelfeldkondensor *m*
Bethe-Bloch relation	Bethe-Blochsche Beziehung *f*, Bethe-Bloch-Gleichung *f*	**bi-characteristic** <math.>	Bicharakteristik *f*, Strahl *m* <Math.>
Bethe cycle	s. carbon-nitrogen cycle	**bichromate cell**, chromic acid cell	Chromsäureelement *n*
Bethe effect	Bethe-Effekt *m*	**bichromatic**	s. dichroic
Bethe hole coupler, single-hole directional coupler	Bethe-Koppler *m*, Einloch-Richtungskoppler *m* [nach Bethe], Richtungskoppler *m* mit einem Loch	**bicolour, bicoloured**	s. dichroic
		bicoloured group	s. double-colour group
		bicommutant	Bikommutant *m*
Bethe['s] method	s. Bethe['s] approximation method	**biconcave lens**	Bikonkavlinse *f*, bikonkave Linse *f*
Bethe-Salpeter [wave] equation	s. Salpeter-Bethe equation	**biconical antenna**, double-cone[-shaped] antenna	Doppelkegelantenne *f*
Bethe-Weizsäcker cycle	s. carbon-nitrogen cycle		
B.E.T. isotherm, Brunauer-Emmett-Teller isotherm	BET-Isotherme *f*	**biconical seal**	Doppelkonusdichtung *f*
B.E.T. method, Brunauer-Emmett-Teller method	BET-Methode *f*, BET-Verfahren *n*, Methode *f* von Brunauer-Emmett-Teller	**bi-continuous mapping**, topological mapping, topological transformation, homeomorphism <math.>	topologische (beiderseits stetige) Abbildung *f*, Homöomorphismus *m*, Homöomorphie *f*, topologischer Isomorphismus *m* <Math.>
B.E.T. theory, BET theory; theory of adsorption isotherms of Brunauer, Emmett and Teller	BET-Theorie *f*, Brunauer-Emmett-Tellersche Theorie *f*		
		biconvex lens	Bikonvexlinse *f*, bikonvexe Linse *f*

bicrystal	s. twin <cryst.>	bimetallic pyrometer, metallic pyrometer, expansion pyrometer	Bimetallpyrometer n, Metallpyrometer n, Ausdehnungspyrometer n
bicyclic system	s. two-loop system		
bidentate ligand	zweizähniger (zweizähliger) Ligand m		
bidirectional counter, reversible (forward / reverse, forward-backward, up-down) counter	Vor-Rückwärts-Zähler m, Vorwärts-Rückwärts-Zähler m	bimetallic rectifier	s. semiconductor rectifier
		bimetallic strip; bimetal	Bimetallstreifen m, Bimetallfeder f; Bimetall n
bidual	s. second adjoint space	bimetallic thermometer	s. metallic thermometer
Biela['s] comet	Bielascher Komet m	bimirror	s. Fresnel['s] mirror
Bienaymé-Chebyshev inequality	s. Chebyshev['s] inequality	bimodal	s. double-humped
		bimodal distribution, double-peaked distribution	zweigipflige Verteilung f, bimodale Verteilung
Bierbaum hardness [number]	Bierbaum-Härte f		
bifilar electrometer	s. Wulf electrometer	bimoment	Bimoment n
bifilar gravimeter	Zweifadengravimeter n	binary, binary star, double star	Doppelstern m; Doppelsternsystem n
bifilar oscillograph	s. loop oscillograph		
bifilar suspension, double suspension	bifilare Aufhängung f, Doppelfadenaufhängung f, Bifilaraufhängung f, Zweifadenaufhängung f, Zweidrahtaufhängung f	binary	s. a. physical double star
		binary collision, two-body collision [process], two-particle collision	Zweierstoß m, Zweifachstoß m, Zweiteilchenstoß m Zweikörperstoß [-prozeß] m
bifocal lens	Zweistärkenglas n, Doppelfokusglas n, Bifokalglas n		
bifocal surface	Zweistärkenfläche f, Doppel[stärken]fläche f, bifokale Fläche f	binary combination band	Zweifachkombinationsbande f
		binary cycle	Zweistoff-Kreisprozeß m
bifocal tube, double-focus tube	Doppelfokusröhre f	binary engine	Wärmekraftmaschine f mit zwei Arbeitsstoffen
bifolium	Zweiblatt n, Bifolium n	binary fission	s. bipartition <nucl.>
bifurcated shock [wave], lambda shock [wave], lambda-type shock wave, λ-shock	Gabelstoß m, gegabelter Stoß m, gegabelter Verdichtungsstoß m, Lambda-Stoß m, λ-Stoß m	binary kernel	Zweikörperkern m
		binary lens; twin lens	Zwillingslinse f; Doppellinse f, Bilinse f
bifurcation	s. branching	binary mixture, two-component mixture	Zweistoffgemisch n, Zweikomponentengemisch n, binäres Gemisch n, binäre Mischung f
bifurcation point, branching point <hydr., aero.>	Spaltungspunkt m, Bifurkationspunkt m, Verzweigungspunkt m <Hydr., Aero.>		
		binary scale <math.>	Paarleiter m, binäre Skala f, Verbindungsskala f
big bang	[großer] Urknall m	binary star, binary, double star	Doppelstern m; Doppelsternsystem n
Bigeleisen series	Bigeleisensche Reihe f		
bigrid	s. tetrode	binary star	s. a. physical double star
big tide	s. spring tide	binary system, two-component system	binäres (zweikomponentiges) System n, Zweistoffsystem n, Zweikomponentensystem n
biharmonic function	biharmonische Funktion f, Bipotentialfunktion f		
bihole	Doppeldefektelektron n, Doppelloch n, Biloch f	binaural difference	binaurale Parallaxe f
bijection, bijective mapping	s. one-to-one mapping	binaural effect, Hornbostel-Wertheimer effect	Binauraleffekt m, Hornbostel-Wertheimer-Effekt m
bilateral antenna	zweiseitig gerichtete Antenne f; Zweirichtungsstrahler m, Zweiseitenstrahler m		
		binaural localization [of sound], binaural location (sound locating, sound location), auditory localization	binaurale Ortung f, Zweiohrortung f, zweiohrige Schallortung f; Richtungshören n
bilateral area track, bilateral track	Doppelzackenschrift f, Zweizackenschrift f		
bilateral constraint	zweiseitige Bedingung (Bindung, Zwangsbedingung) f		
		binder, binding agent, agglutinant	Bindemittel n, Binder m
bilateral Laplace transform[ation], two-sided Laplace transformation	zweiseitige (bilaterale) Laplace-Transformation f	binding electron	s. bonding electron
		binding energy <of the particle>	Bindungsenergie f <Teilchen>
bilaterally symmetric	zweiseitig symmetrisch	binding energy <cryst.>, cohesive energy	Bindungsenergie f <Krist.>
bilateral network	Zweirichtungsnetzwerk n		
		binding energy as a function of atomic and neutron number, binding energy surface	Bindungsenergiefläche f
bilateral slit	symmetrischer (bilateraler) Spalt m		
bilateral slit of Krüss	s. Krüss bilateral slit		
bilateral track	s. bilateral area track	binding force, linkage (bonding, chemical binding) force	Bindungskraft f, chemische Bindungskraft
bilens; double lens	Bilinse f; Biglas n; Doppellinse f		
bilinear covariant <theory of invariants>	bilineare Kovariante f, Überschiebung f	binding fraction, average binding energy per nucleon, mean binding energy per nucleon	mittlere Bindungsenergie f [pro Nukleon], mittlere Bindungsenergie pro Kernbaustein, Bindungsenergie pro Nukleon
bilinear form	Bilinearform f		
bilinear invariant	bilineare Invariante f		
bilinear mapping (transformation)	s. homographic transformation	binding moment	s. bond moment
		binding state, state of binding	Bindungszustand m
Billet half (split) lens	Billetsche Halblinsen fpl		
billiard ball	s. hard sphere	Binet['s] ellipsoid	Binet-Ellipsoid n, Binetsches Ellipsoid (Trägheitsellipsoid) n, Trägheitsellipsoid von Binet
billiard-ball collision	s. elastic collision		
"billiard ball" model	s. hard-sphere model		
billow, first-order wave, wave [of the first order]	Woge f, Welle f erster Ordnung	Binet['s] formula	Binetsche Formel f
		bineutron, dineutron	Dineutron n, Doppelneutron
billow cloud	s. undulated cloud	bing-bang	
Bilt number / De Bilt	De-Bilt-Zahl f		
bimetal	s. bimetallic strip	Bingham body, Bingham plastic (fluid, material, model), B-body	Binghamscher Körper m, Körper mit Fließfestigkeit, B-Körper m
bimetallic actinometer	s. Robitzsch bimetallic actinometer		
		Bingham equation	Binghamsche Gleichung f, Bingham-Gleichung f
bimetallic pyranograph	s. Robitzsch bimetallic pyranograph		

Bingham fluid	s. Bingham body	bioluminescence	Biolumineszenz f
Bingham formula	Binghamscher Reibungsansatz m, Bingham-Ansatz m	biometry; biostatistics	Biometrie f; Biostatistik f
		biopotential, bioelectrical potential	bioelektrisches Potential n, Biopotential n
Bingham material (model, plastic)	s. Bingham body	biorthonormal system	Biorthonormalsystem n
binistor	Binistor m	bioseston	Bioseston n
binocular, binocular (doublet) telescope, binoculars	Doppelfernrohr n, binokulares Fernrohr n, Binokel n	biostatistics	s. biometry
		biot, Bi	= 10 A
		Biot biplate, Biot plate	Biotsche Doppelplatte f
binocular; by two eyes	binokular, beidäugig; zweiäugig	Biot-Fourier equation	s. heat equation
		Biot['s] law, Biot['s] relation	Biotsches Gesetz n
binocular contrast	binokularer Kontrast m		
		Biot modulus (number)	s. Nusselt number
binocular field of view, binocular visual field	binokulares (gemeinsames) Gesichtsfeld n, Deckfeld n	Biot plate, Biot biplate	Biotsche Doppelplatte f
		Biot['s] relation	s. Biot['s] law
		biotron	Biotron n
binocular mat	Schlüssellochmaske f	Biot-Savart['s] law	s. Laplace['s] theorem <el.>
		Biot-Savart['s] law of vortex	Biot-Savartsches Wirbelgesetz n
binocular parallax, stereoscopic parallax, parallactic difference	stereoskopische (parallaktische) Differenz f, Querdisparation f, stereoskopische Parallaxe f, Stereoparallaxe f, Netzhautbildparallaxe f	Biot-Savart relation	s. Laplace['s] theorem
		bipartition, division in two; halving, bisection	Zweiteilung f; Halbierung f
		bipartition, binary fission <nucl.>	binäre Spaltung f <Kern.>
binoculars	s. binocular	biphase half-wave rectifier	Zweiphasen-Einweg-Gleichrichter m
binocular single vision	s. Panum['s] vision		
binocular telescope	s. binocular	biphase inverter	s. two-phase inverter
binocular vision	Binokularsehen n, beidäugiges (zweiäugiges) Sehen n	biplate rectifier	s. two-anode rectifier
		bipolar centre, BP centre, bipolar region	bipolares Gebiet n, BM-Gebiet n, Bereich m mit bipolarem Magnetfeld
binocular visual field	s. binocular field of view		
binodal [curve]	s. solubility curve		
binodal seiche	zweiknotige Seiche f	bipolar co-ordinates	Bipolarkoordinaten fpl, bipolare Koordinaten fpl
binomial [antenna] array	Binomialantennenanordnung f	bipolar derivation	bipolare Ableitung f
binomial coefficient	Binomialkoeffizient m, Binomialzahl f	bipolar field emission	bipolare Feldemission f
		bipolar region	s. bipolar centre
binomial distribution [of Bernoulli], binomial frequency distribution, Bernoulli['s binomial] distribution	[Bernoullische] Binomialverteilung f, Bernoullische (binomiale) Verteilung f, Bernoulli-Verteilung f	bipolar transistor, injection transistor	bipolarer Transistor m, Injektionstransistor m
binomial expansion	Entwicklung f in eine binomische Reihe, Binomialentwicklung f, binomische Entwicklung	bipolar X-ray tube	Zweipol-Röntgenröhre f
		biprism; double prism	Biprisma n, Doppelprisma n
binomial formula, binomial theorem	binomische Formel f, binomischer Satz (Lehrsatz) m, Binomialformel f	bi[-]propellant	Zweikomponententreibstoff m, Zweikomponentensystem n, Zweistoffsystem n <Raketentreibstoff>
binomial frequency distribution	s. binomial distribution		
binomial series	Binomialreihe f, binomische Reihe f	bi-propellant liquid rocket [system]	Zweistoffrakete f, Zweistoffsystem n <Rakete>
binomial theorem	s. binomial formula		
binormal; unit binormal, unit second normal	Binormale f, Binormalenvektor m	bipyramid <cryst.>	Bipyramide f, Dipyramide f
bioacoustics	Bioakustik f	bipyramidal class	s. orthorhombic holohedry
biocatalyst, biochemical catalyst	Biokatalysator m, Wirkstoff m, Ergin n	bipyramidal class	s. paramorphic hemihedry of the tetragonal system
		biquadratic equation, quartic equation, equation of the fourth degree	biquadratische Gleichung f, Gleichung vierten Grades
biocolloid	Biokolloid n		
biocrystal	Biokristall m		
bioelectrical potential, biopotential	bioelektrisches Potential n, Biopotential n	bi[-]quartz [of Soleil]	s. Soleil
		biquaternion	Biquaternion f
bioelectric current	bioelektrischer Strom m, Biostrom m	bird flight	Vogelflug m, Schwingenflug m
bioelectricity, bioelectric phenomena	bioelektrische Erscheinungen fpl, Bioelektrizität f	birdie <el.>	Zwitschern n <El.>
		bireflectance, bi-reflection	Bireflexion f, Reflexionspleochroismus m
biofilter	s. biological filter		
biological damage	biologischer Schaden m, biologische Strahlenschädigung f	birefringence, double refraction	Doppelbrechung f
		birefringence due to deformation	Deformationsdoppelbrechung f
biological effect, biological effect of radiation	biologische Wirkung f [der Strahlung], biologische Strahlenwirkung f, biologischer Strahlungseffekt m		
		birefringent, doubly refracting, double-refracting	doppelbrechend
biological effect of radiation	s. biological effect	Birge-Mecke rule	Birge-Meckesche Regel f
biological filter, trickling filter, biofilter	Filterglocke f, Bakterienfilter n, Biofilter n, Tropfkörper m	Birge-Sponer extrapolation, Birge-Sponer method	Birge-Sponer-Verfahren n, Birge-Sponer-Methode f
biological half-life	biologische Halbwertzeit f	Birkhoff ergodic theorem	s. individual ergodic theorem
		Birkhoff-von Neumann lemmas	Birkhoff-von Neumannsche Sätze mpl
		Birnbaum series	Birnbaumsche Reihe f
		birotation	s. mutarotation
biological shield	biologische Abschirmung f, biologischer Schild m	birth-and-death process	s. Feller-Arley process

birth of a star	Sterngeburt f	"black body" constant	s. Stefan-Boltzmann['s] constant
birth process	Yule-Furry-Prozeß m, Geburtsprozeß n, Zugangsprozeß n	black-body furnace	s. hollow space
		black-body furnace of Lummer-Pringsheim	s. Lummer-Pringsheim black-body furnace
birth-rate	s. production rate ‹nucl.›	black-body radiation, black-body thermal radiation, temperature radiation, cavity radiation	schwarze Strahlung f, Hohlraumstrahlung f, Schwarzkörperstrahlung f, Strahlung des schwarzen Körpers, schwarze Hohlraumstrahlung
biscuit, metal biscuit, metallic sponge	Metallschwamm m, Bisquit m, reduziertes Metall n		
bisecting line, bisector, bisectrix	Halbierende f, Halbierungslinie f		
bisecting plane	winkelhalbierende Ebene f		
bisection	s. bipartition		
bisector, bisectrix, bisecting line	Halbierende f, Halbierungslinie f	black-body radiator	s. black body
bisector, bisectrix ‹of the angle›	Winkelhalbierende f	black-body temperature, luminance (radiance, brightness) temperature	schwarze Temperatur f, Schwarzkörpertemperatur f, Plancksche Temperatur f
bisector, bisectrix ‹pl.: -ices›, mean line ‹crystal optics›	Bisektrix f, Mittellinie f ‹Kristalloptik›	black-body thermal radiation	s. black-body radiation
bisectrix interference figure, interference figure ‹of crystals in the polarizing microscope›	Achsenbild n ‹von Kristallen›	black-bulb thermometer, blackened bulb thermometer, "in vacuo" thermometer, radiation thermometer, solar thermometer	Schwarzkugelthermometer n, Strahlungsthermometer n, Insolationsthermometer n, Solarthermometer n
Bishop['s] ring	Bishops[scher] Ring m		
bi-signal zone	s. equisignal zone		
bismuth spiral	Wismutspirale f, Lenardsche Wismutspirale		
bisphenoid, disphenoid ‹cryst.›	Bisphenoid n, Disphenoid n, Doppelkeil m ‹Krist.›	Black characteristic	Black-Diagramm n, Blacksche Charakteristik f
bisphenoidal class	s. enantiomorphous hemihedry of the orthorhombic system	black cold, black frost	trockene Kälte f
		black content	Schwarzanteil m, Schwarzgehalt m
bisphenoidal class	s. tetartohedry of the second sort of the tetragonal system	blackened bulb thermometer	s. black-bulb thermometer
bispherical co-ordinates	räumliche Bipolarkoordinaten fpl	blackening, blacking	Schwärzung f
		blackening	s. a. optical density ‹phot.›
bispinor	Bispinor m	blackening bath	Schwärzungsbad n
bispinor distribution	Bispinordistribution f		
		Blackett relation	Blackett-Gleichung f
bispiral condenser (cooler)	Doppelspiralkühler m	Blackett['s] theory [of geomagnetism]	Blackettsche Theorie f, Theorie von Blackett
bistable multivibrator	s. flip-flop	black filter	s. Wood filter
Bitter coil, coil of Bitter type, spiral-staircase coil	Bitter-Spule f, Bittersche Spule f	black frost, black cold	trockene Kälte f
		black hole	schwarzes Loch n
Bitter figure, Bitter [powder] pattern, powder pattern	Bitterscher Streifen m, Pulverfigur f	blacking, blackening	Schwärzung f
		blacking	s. a. optical density
		blacking-out	s. black[-]out ‹opt.›
bi-unique mapping	s. one-to-one mapping	black light, dark light, near ultraviolet	Schwarzlicht n, nahes Ultraviolett n
bivariant system	s. divariant system		
bivariate cumulative distribution; bivariate cumulative distribution function; bivariate distribution; bivariate distribution function	zweidimensionale Verteilung f; zweidimensionale Verteilungsfunktion f		
		black-light lamp, Wood['s] lamp	Analysenlampe f, Schwarzlichtlampe f, Schwarzglaslampe f
bivariate normal distribution	zweidimensionale Normalverteilung f		
		black-light region, near ultra-violet [region] ‹320—400 nm›	Schwarzlichtbereich m, Bl-Bereich m ‹320 ··· 400 nm›
bivariate point distribution	s. scatter diagram		
bivector	Bivektor m; Plangröße f, Ausdehnungsgröße f zweiter Stufe, Ebenengröße f ‹im dreidimensionalen Raum›	Blackmann-Putter['s] principle, principle of Blackmann and Putter	Prinzip n von Blackmann-Putter, Blackmann-Puttersches Prinzip
		Blackman reaction	s. dark reaction
		black masking	s. veiling by black
Bjerknes['] circulation theorem	Bjerknessche Zirkulationssatz m, Bjerknessches Zirkulationstheorem n, Zirkulationssatz nach Bjerknes, Zirkulationstheorem nach Bjerknes	blackness	s. opacity
		blackness	s. impermeability to light
		blackout, blackout effect	Totalschwund m
		blackout, long-time fading	Langzeitschwund m
Bjerknes['] theorem, Bjerknes['] vorticity theorem	Bjerknesscher Wirbelsatz m, Bjerknessches Wirbeltheorem n, Wirbelsatz (Wirbeltheorem) von Bjerknes	black[-]out, blacking-out; darkening; deepening ‹of colour›; dimming, subduing ‹of light›; damping ‹of light› ‹opt.›	Verdunklung f; Abdunkeln n; Lichtdämpfung f ‹Opt.›
Bjerrum doublet	Bjerrumsche Doppelbande f	blackout	s. a. blocking ‹el.›
Bjerrum['s] theory of conductivity	Bjerrumsche Leitfähigkeitstheorie f	blackout effect	s. blackout
		blackout interval	Verdunklungsintervall n
black-and-white-group	s. magnetic space group	black-out pulse	s. blanking pulse
black-and-white-group	s. colour group	black point	s. location of black
black-and-white pyranometer	Schwarz-Weiß-Pyranometer n	black prong	s. heavy branch
		black saturation	Schwarzsättigung f
black-and-white space group	s. magnetic space group		
		black screen	schwarzer Schirm m
		black shaded	schwarzschattiert
black body, blackbody ‹US›, full radiator, complete radiator, blackbody radiator, Planckian radiator, absolute black body; ideal black body	schwarzer Körper (Strahler) m, Planckscher Strahler m, absolut schwarzer Körper, Schwarzkörper m, Schwarzstrahler m, ideal (vollkommen) schwarzer Körper, idealer Temperaturstrahler m, Idealstrahler	black shaded ‹of chromatic colour›	s. a. non-zero black content / having
		black shading	s. veiling by black
		black shortness	Schwarzbruch m
		black track	s. heavy branch

black veiling	s. veiling by black	bleeding	s. colour fringe
black-white group	s. magnetic space group	blemish, storage blemish	Speicherfehler m
black-white group	s. colour group	blend <of stellar spectral lines>	Überschneidung (Überlappung) f von stellaren Absorptionslinien, „blend" m
blade <of current meter or vane>, screw, wheel	Schaufel f, Flügelschaufel f		
blade <e.g. of propeller>, propeller blade, airscrew blade	Flügel m <z. B. Propeller>, Propellerflügel m, Propellerblatt n, Schraubenblatt n, Schraubenflügel m, Flügelblatt n, Luftschraubenblatt n	blended lamp	s. mixed ligth lamp
		blending <of sounds> <ac.>	Verschmelzung f [von Klängen] <Ak.>
		blending <of plastics>	s. a. mixing <mech.>
		blending	s. a. fusion
blade bearing	s. knife-edge bearing	blending of the colours, shading[-off] of the colours; running of the colours	Verlaufen n der Farben
blade bearing recess, bearing plane <of the balance>	Pfanne f <Waage>		
		blind	s. diaphragm <opt.>
blade grid, vane grid, grid <hydr., aero.>	Schaufelgitter n, Flügelgitter n, Gitter n <Hydr., Aero.>	blinding glare	Absolutblendung f, blindmachende Blendung f
blades	s. blading	blindness, amaurosis	Blindheit f, Schwarzblindheit f, Vollblindheit f, Caecitas f; Amaurose f, „schwarzer Star" m
blade stirrer	Schaufelrührer m		
blade vibration	Schaufelschwingung f		
blading; blades	Schaufelanordnung f; Beschaufelung f	blind power	s. reactive power
		blind spot	blinder Fleck m, Mariottescher Fleck
Blagden['s] law	Blagdensches Gesetz n	blink comparator, blink microscope	Blinkkomparator m
blanc fixe	s. barium white		
blank	s. crystal blank	blink method	s. blink technique
blanket, breeding blanket	Brutmantel m, Brutzone f, Blanket n	blink microscope, blink comparator	Blinkkomparator m
		blink of ice	s. ice blink
		blink technique, blink method	Blinkverfahren n
		blip	s. overshoot <of pulse>
		blister	s. shrinkage cavity
		blizzard	Blizzard m
blanket conversion ratio	äußeres Konversionsverhältnis n, Blanket-Konversionsverhältnis n, Konversionsverhältnis für das Blanket	blob	Blob n, Traube f <in der Kernemulsion>
		blob density	Blobdichte f
blanketing effect	„blanketing"-Effekt m, Blanketingeffekt m	Bloch band	s. energy band
		Bloch['s] constant	Blochsche Konstante f
blanking, retrace blanking <of cathode-ray tube>	Dunkelsteuerung f, Dunkeltastung f, Strahlunterdrückung f	Bloch equation	Blochsche Gleichung (Integralgleichung) f, Bloch-Gleichung f
blanking, marking, separation <of pulse>	Austastung f, Ausblendung f	Bloch['s] function	Blochsche Wellenfunktion (Eigenfunktion) f
blanking interval	Austastlücke f		
		Bloch-Grüneisen equation, Grüneisen formula	Bloch-Grüneisen-Gleichung f, Grüneisen-Blochsche Widerstandsformel f
blanking pulse, black-out pulse	Ausblendimpuls m, Austastimpuls m		
		Bloch interaction	Blochsche Wechselwirkung f, Bloch-Wechselwirkung f
blank run; blank test	Kontrollversuch m; Blindversuch m		
Blasius law of skin friction	Blasiussches Gesetz n	Bloch['s] law	s. magnetic $T^{3/2}$ law
		Bloch line	Bloch-Linie f
Blasius profile	Blasius-Profil n	Bloch-Nordsieck transformation	Bloch-Nordsiecksche Transformation f, Bloch-Nordsieck-Transformation f
Blasius solution	Blasiussche Funktion (Grenzschichtgleichung) f		
Blasius['] theorem, formula (theorem) of Blasius	Blasiusscher Satz m, Blasiussche Formel f, Blasius-Formel f		
		Bloch orbital	Bloch-Orbital n
		Bloch susceptibility, dynamic susceptibility	Blochsche (dynamische) Suszeptibilität f
Blasius['] variable, variable of Blasius	Blasiussche Variable f		
		Bloch['s] theorem	Blochsches Theorem n
blast	s. shock wave	Bloch['s] $T^{3/2}$ law for magnetization	s. magnetic $T^{3/2}$ law
blast diffraction	Beugung f von Verdichtungsstößen		
		Bloch wall	s. domain boundary
blasting	s. overdriving <el.>	Bloch wall displacement	s. boundary movement
blast line, explosion line	Sprenglinie f	Bloch wall friction	s. domain boundary friction
blast of wind; gust <of wind>	Windstoß m	Bloch wall parameter, exchange stiffness parameter	Bloch-Wand-Parameter m
blast wave	s. expansive wave		
blaze	Bereich m maximaler Intensität des Echelettegitters, „blaze" n	Bloch·wave	Blochsche Welle f
		block <geo.>	Block m; Scholle f <Geo.>
		block	s. a. rectangular parallelepiped <math.>
blaze	s. a. mirage		
Blazhko effect	Blashko-Effekt m	block	s. a. pulley block <mech.>
bleaching <of colour centres>	Ausbleichen n, Entfärbung f <Farbzentren>	blockage	s. blocking
		blockage effect, stopband effect <of filter>; blocking action	Sperrwirkung f, Sperreffekt m
bleaching out, fading <phot.>	Fading n, Abblassen n, Verblassen n, Ausbleichen n, Abklingen n <Phot.>		
		block and tackle	s. pulley block <mech.>
Bleakney['s] mass spectrometer	Bleakney-Massenspektrometer n, Massenspektrometer n nach Bleakney	block boundary	Blockgrenze f
		blocked impedance	s. open-circuit impedance
		block fault	Schollenüberschiebung f
Blears effect	Blears-Effekt m	block gate	Block-Gateelektrode f, Substratelektrode f
bleeder resistor	Vorbelastungswiderstand m		
		block gauge	s. slip gauge
		blocking; interlocking, locking; cut-off; rejection; paralysis; blackout; bottoming <el.>	Sperrung f <El.>
bleeding, syneresis	Synärese f, Sinaerese f, Synäresis f		

blocking	s. a. interlock	bluff ‹hydr.›, bluff body	Phantom n, Körper m mit hohem Strömungswiderstand, Körper mit quer überströmten scharfen Kanten ‹Hydr.›
blocking	s. a. locking ‹ot disiocations›		
blocking action	s. stop-band effect		
blocking bias, blocking voltage ‹e.g. of a valve›	Sperrspannung f ‹z. B. Röhre›	blunder	s. mistake ‹math.›
		blunt body, blunt-nosed body	stumpfer Körper m, Widerstandskörper m
blocking capability	Sperrfähigkeit	blur	s. diffuseness ‹opt.›
		blur circle	s. disk of aberration
		blurred	s. smeared
		blurring ‹opt.›	Verschwimmen n ‹Opt.›
		blurring	s. a. smearing-out ‹gen.›
		blurring	s. a. unsharpness ‹opt.›
blocking characteristic	s. reverse characteristic	Board of Trade ohm	s. international ohm
blocking condition	s. off state	boat form	Wannenform f
blocking diode, inverse diode	Sperrdiode f, Sperrschichtdiode f	bob	s. plumb
		bob of the pendulum, pendulum bob, pendulous body	Pendelkörper m; Pendellinse f; Pendelscheibe f
blocking effect	Blockierungseffekt m; Blockeffekt m		
		bob-weight	s. counterweight
blocking electrode, barrier (unidirectional, rectifying) electrode	sperrende Elektrode f, Sperrelektrode f	Bode['s] diagram, Bode['s] plot	Bode-Diagramm n
		Bode['s] law	s. law of planetary distances
blocking generator	s. blocking oscillator		
blocking junction	s. rectifying junction	Bode['s] method	s. frequency method
blocking layer ‹semi.›	s. internal barrier layer	Bodenstein number, Bo	Bodenstein-Zahl f, Bo
blocking layer cell (photocell)	s. photovoltaic cell	Bode['s] plot	s. Bode['s] diagram
		bodily seismic wave, bodily (subsurface, internal) wave ‹geo.›	Raumwelle f ‹Geo.›
blocking oscillator, self-quenching (squegging, blocking) generator	Sperrschwinger m, Blockingoszillator m		
		bodily tides	s. earth tides
		bodily wave	s. bodily seismic wave
blocking period, ungated period ‹el.›	Sperrperiode f ‹El.›	body; mass, ground ‹el.›	Masse f, Körper m; Erde f
		body-borne sound	s. sound conducted through solids
blocking period	s. a. firing time	body burden	s. whole body dose
blocking ratio	Sperrverhältnis n	body capacitance, capacitance of the human body	Körperkapazität f
blocking state	s. off state		
blocking-up ‹with›, choking ‹with›	Anwehung f, Zuwehung f ‹mit›		
		body-centered ‹US›	s. body centred
blocking voltage	s. blocking bias	body-centred, space-centred, body-centered ‹US›, space-centered ‹US›, b. c.	raumzentriert, innenzentriert, r. z.
block-relaxation, group relaxation	Blockrelaxation f		
block structure	s. mosaic structure		
Bloembergen-Purcell-Pound theory, BPP theory	Bloembergen-Purcell-Pound-Theorie f, BPP-Theorie f	body-centred cubic, cubic space-centred, cubic body centred, b. c. c., BCC, B. C. C.	kubisch raumzentriert, kubisch innenzentriert, k. r. z., krz
blondel	= 1 lx		
Blondel-Rey law	Blondel-Reysches Gesetz n	body-centred cubic lattice, b. c. c. lattice, BCC lattice	kubisch raumzentriertes Gitter n, k. r. z.-Gitter n, krz-Gitter n
blood-brain barrier	Blut-Gehirn-Schranke f		
blood rain	Blutregen m, roter Regen m	body colour, opaque colour (pigment)	Deckfarbe f
bloom, gleam; glimmer; glint	Schimmern n; Schimmer m		
		body conductivity, conductivity of the human body	Körperleitfähigkeit f
blooming, coating ‹opt.›	Oberflächenvergütung f, Objektivvergütung f, Vergütung f, T-Schutz m		
		body contact	s. earth fault
		body fineness ratio, fineness ratio ‹of body›	Schlankheitsgrad m ‹Körper›
blooming of the lens, lens blooming (coating)	Linsenvergütung f, Blauung f der Linse		
		body-fixed system	s. body system
blow ‹of flute pipe›	Anblasen n ‹Lippenpfeife›	body force, volume force, volumetric force	Volum[en]kraft f
blow	s. a. impact		
blowgun	s. atomizer	bodying	s. inspissation ‹chem.›
blowhole segregation	Gasblasenseigerung f	body of good streamline shape	s. streamlined body
blowing off the boundary layer, boundary layer blowing	Wegblasen n der Grenzschicht		
		body of microscope, microscope body	Mikroskopstativ n, Stativ n des Mikroskops
blowing of the arc	Beblasung f des Bogens		
blown flap	Ausblasspalt m	body of revolution (rotation), solid of revolution (rotation), revolution solid	Rotationskörper m, Drehkörper m, Umdrehungskörper m
blow-out coil	Blasspule f; Funkenlöschspule f		
		body of the wave, wave	Wellenkörper m
		body of water, water mass	Wasserkörper m, Wassermasse f
blow pipe, flue pipe, labial pipe	Lippenpfeife f, Labialpfeife f	body section device	s. laminograph
blowpipe assay (proof, test)	Lötrohranalyse f, Lötrohrprobe f	body section radiography, body section roentgenography, stratigraphy, tomography, laminography; X-ray scanning analysis	Schichtaufnahmeverfahren n, Körperschichtaufnahmeverfahren n, Röntgenschicht[aufnahme]verfahren n, Schichtaufnahme[methode] f, Körperschichtaufnahme f, Röntgenschichtaufnahme f, Schichtbildaufnahme f, Schichtbildaufnahmeverfahren n, Schnittbildverfahren n, Tomographie f, Stratigraphie f
blue brittleness	Blaubrüchigkeit f, Blausprödigkeit f		
blue flame, non-luminous (dark, roaring) flame	blaue Flamme f, entleuchtete Flamme, Bunsen-Flamme f, nichtleuchtende (brausende) Flamme		
blue glow	s. cathode glow		
blue stellar object	s. quasage	body system [of co-ordinates], body-fixed system [of co-ordinates]	körperfestes Koordinatensystem n, fest mit dem Körper verbundenes Koordinatensystem
blue straggler	„blue straggler" m, „blauer Vagabund" m		

Boer process / de	s. Arkel-De Boer technique	boiling point raising (rising)	s. elevation of the boiling point
Boff diode	s. step recovery diode	boiling-point thermometer	s. hypsometer
Bogoliubov['s] integral equation	Bogoljubowsche Integralgleichung f	boiling range, boiling interval, boiling point interval	Siedebereich m, Siedepunktsintervall n
Bogoliubov-Valatin transformation	Bogoljubow-Walatinsche Transformation f, Bogoljubow-Walatin-Transformation f		
Bohm diffusion	s. anomalous diffusion	boiling reactor	s. boiling water reactor
Bohnenberger eyepiece	Bohnenbergersches Okular n, Okular nach Bohnenberger	boiling temperature	s. boiling point
		boiling temperature of water	s. boiling point of water
Bohr atom, Bohr atom model, Bohr model	Bohrsches Atommodell n, Atommodell von Bohr, Bohrsches Modell n [des Wasserstoffatoms]	boiling water reactor; boiling reactor	Siedewasserreaktor m; Siedereaktor m
Bohr['s] aufbauprinzip	s. aufbauprinciple		
Bohr['s] correspondence principle, correspondence principle	Korrespondenzprinzip n [von Bohr], Bohrsches Korrespondenzprinzip	Bois balance (magnetometer) / Du	Du-Bois-Magnetometer n, Du-Boissches Magnetometer n, Permeabilitätswaage f
Bohr['s] equation	s. Bohr['s] frequency condition	bolide <astr.>, fireball	Feuerkugel f, Bolid m <Astr.>
Bohr['s] formula, Bohr['s] quantum condition	Bohrsche Quantenbedingung f	bologram	Bologramm n, Bolometerdiagramm n, Bolometerschreibstreifen m
Bohr['s] frequency condition, Bohr['s] equation; Einstein['s] formula of radiation theory	Bohrsche Frequenzbedingung f, Frequenzbedingung f, Frequenzpostulat n	bolometer; bolometric instrument	Bolometer n, Bolometerbrücke f, bolometrisches Meßgerät n
bohrium	s. hahnium		
Bohr-Kramers-Slater statistical theory	Bohr-Kramers-Slatersche Theorie f; statistische Theorie von Bohr, Kramers und Slater	bolometer power meter, bolometer wattmeter, barretter-type wattmeter	Bolometer-Leistungsmesser m, Bolometer-Wattmeter n, bolometrischer Leistungsmesser m
Bohr magneton, electronic Bohr magneton, Bohr unit	Bohrsches Magneton n	bolometric correction	bolometrische Korrektion f
		bolometric instrument	s. bolometer
Bohr magneton number	magnetisches Moment n je Atom, ausgedrückt in Bohrschen Magnetons	bolometric magnitude	s. bolometric stellar magnitude
		bolometric radiation temperature	s. effective temperature <astr.>
Bohr orbit	Bohrsche Bahn (Wasserstoffbahn, Quantenbahn) f, Bohrscher Kreis m	bolometric radiation temperature	s. total radiation temperature <opt.>
Bohr['s] postulates	Bohrsche Postulate npl	bolometric stellar magnitude, bolometric magnitude <of star>	bolometrische Helligkeit f <Gestirn>
Bohr['s] quantum condition	s. Bohr['s] formula		
Bohr radius	Bohrscher Radius (Wasserstoffradius, Atomradius) m, erster Bohrscher Radius m, Radius der ersten Bohrschen Bahn	Boltzmann atomic constant, Boltzmann['s] constant, k, k	Boltzmann-Konstante f, [Planck-]Boltzmannsche Konstante f, Planck-Boltzmann-Konstante f, Plancksche Konstante
Bohr['s] selection principle	[Bohrsches] Auswahlprinzip n	Boltzmann distribution	s. Boltzmann['s] factor
Bohr-Sommerfeld['s] theory	Bohr-Sommerfeldsche Theorie f	Boltzmann distribution; Boltzmann['s] distribution law, Maxwell-Boltzmann distribution law	Boltzmann-Verteilung f, Boltzmannsche Verteilung f, Boltzmann-Verteilungsfunktion f; Boltzmannsches Verteilungsgesetz n
Bohr theory, Bohr['s] theory of the [hydrogen] atom	Bohrsche Theorie f [des Wasserstoffatoms], Bohrsche Atomtheorie (Quantentheorie) f		
Bohr unit	s. Bohr magneton		
Bohr-Wheeler theory [of fission]	Bohr-Wheelersche Theorie f	Boltzmann-Drude constant	Boltzmann-Drudesche Konstante $f < = (^3/_2)k >$
boiling cooling	s. evaporative cooling	Boltzmann['s] entropy law, Boltzmann equation	s. Boltzmann principle
boiling down, evaporation to dryness	Eindampfung f zur Trockne		
boiling heat transfer	Wärmeübertragung f (Wärmeübergang m, Wärmeaustausch m) bei Verdampfung	Boltzmann['s] equation, Maxwell-Boltzmann equation	Boltzmannsche Stoßgleichung f, Stoßgleichung [von Boltzmann], kinetische Boltzmann-Gleichung f (Gleichung f von Boltzmann), Maxwell-Boltzmannsche Stoßgleichung (Gleichung), Boltzmann-Gleichung f, Maxwell-Boltzmann-Gleichung f
boiling interval	s. boiling range		
boiling point, boiling temperature, b.p.	Siedepunkt m, Siedetemperatur f, Kochpunkt m, Verdampfungspunkt m, Verdampfungstemperatur f, Sp., Kp.		
boiling-point curve	s. liquidus <in condensation of mixed vapours>		
boiling point depression	s. lowering of the boiling point	Boltzmann['s] ergodic hypothesis, ergodic hypothesis, principle of continuity of path	Ergodenhypothese f, Boltzmannsche Ergodenhypothese
boiling point diagram	Siedediagramm n	Boltzmann['s] factor, Boltzmann distribution	Boltzmann-Faktor m, Boltzmannscher Faktor m, Boltzmann-Koeffizient m
boiling point elevation	s. elevation of the boiling point		
boiling point interval	s. boiling range	Boltzmann['s] factor	s. a. Stefan-Boltzmann['s] constant
boiling-point method [of vapour-pressure measurement]	Siedepunktmethode f, ebullioskopische Methode f <der Dampfdruckbestimmung>	Boltzmann['s] fluctuation hypothesis	Boltzmannsche Fluktuationshypothese f
		Boltzmann['s] function	s. H-function
boiling point of sulphur	s. sulphur point	Boltzmann gas	Boltzmann-Gas n
boiling point of water, boiling temperature of water, steam point	Dampfpunkt m, Wasserdampfpunkt m, Siedepunkt (Verdampfungspunkt) m des Wassers, Wassersiedepunkt m	Boltzmann['s] H-function	s. H-function
		Boltzmann['s] H-theorem, H-theorem [of Boltzmann and Lorentz]	[Boltzmannsches] H-Theorem n, Boltzmannscher H-Satz m

Boltzmann['s] law	Boltzmannsches Gesetz n	bond length, bond distance	Bindungslänge f, Bindungsabstand m, Valenzabstand
Boltzmann law of radiation	s. Stefan-Boltzmann law	bond line	s. valence line
Boltzmann principle, Boltzmann['s] entropy law, entropy law of Boltzmann, Boltzmann equation	Boltzmann-Prinzip n, Boltzmannsches Prinzip (Entropiegesetz) n, Entropiegesetz von Boltzmann, Boltzmannsche Beziehung f	bond moment, binding moment	Bindungsmoment n
		bond orbital	s. bonding orbital
		bond order, order of the bond	Bindungsordnung f, Ordnung f der Bindung
		bond polymorphism	Bindungspolymorphie f
Boltzmann['s] ratio	Boltzmann-Verhältnis n	bond strength, strength of bond	Bindungsstärke f; Festigkeit f der Bindung, Bindungsfestigkeit f
Boltzmann['s] relativistic equation	relativistische Boltzmann-Gleichung f		
Boltzmann statistics	s. Maxwell-Boltzmann statistics	bond structure, bonding structure	Bindungsstruktur f
Boltzmann tail	Boltzmann-Schwanz m	Bond['s] system of notation	Bondsche Bezeichnung f
Boltzmann['s] transport equation, Maxwell-Boltzmann transport equation	Boltzmannsche Transportgleichung f	bond tautomerism	Bindungstautomerie f
		bond type	Bindungsart f, Bindungstyp m
		bone conduction	Knochenleitung f, ossale Leitung f
Boltzmann['s] triple integral function of H (t)	s. H-function	bone glass	s. opal glass
Boltzmann-Vlasov equation	s. Vlasov equation	bone seeker; bone-seeking element	Knochensucher m
bolus	Bolus m		
bolus	s. a. bolus material <bio.>	Boolean algebra; Boolean lattice; algebra of logic; circuit (switch) algebra	Boolesche Algebra f, Algebra von Boole; Boole-Verband m, Boolescher Verband m; Algebra der Logik; Schalt[ungs]algebra f
bolus material; bolus <bio.>	Bolusmaterial n, Streumaterial n [für den Bolus] <Bio.>		
Bolzano-Weierstrass theorem	Satz m von Bolzano-Weierstraß		
bomb	s. spark <opt.>	boom, giraffe <in the emulsion>	Giraffe f <in der Emulsion>
bombarded particle, struck (target) particle	beschossenes (getroffenes) Teilchen n, Targetteilchen	boominess	Hohlraumresonanz f, Mittönen n, Mitschwingen n des Hohlraums; Dröhnen n
bombarding particle, incident particle, projectile	Beschußteilchen n, Geschoßteilchen n, einfallendes (einlaufendes) Teilchen n		
bombardment <by, with particles>	Beschuß m, Beschießung f, Bestrahlung f	booming	s. drone <ac.>
bomb calorimeter	s. Berthelot's calorimeter	boost, compensation <el.>	Anheben n <El.>
bomb furnace	Bombenofen m	boost	s. a. amplification
bomb tube	Bombenrohr n, Einschmelzrohr n, Schießrohr n, Einschlußrohr n	boost	s. a. stimulation
		boost charge, boosting charge	Teilladung f
		booster	Treibdampfpumpe f, Treibmittelpumpe f, Booster m
bomb tube	s. a. sealing tube	booster circuit, additional circuit	Hilfsstromkreis m, Zusatzstromkreis m; Zusatzschaltung f
bond, bonding material <o fuel element>	Verbindungsmaterial n, Verbindungsschicht f <Brennelement>		
		booster diode	s. efficiency diode
		booster light	s. fill-in light
bond	s. a. chemical bond	boosting	s. amplification
Bond['s] albedo, spherical albedo, albedo, reflection coefficient <opt.>	sphärische Albedo f [nach Bond], Albedo <Opt.>	boosting charge, boost charge	Teilladung f
		Boot magnetron	s. "long anode" cavity magnetron
bond angle	s. valence angle	bootstrap, nuclear democracy	Bootstrap m, „bootstrap" m
bond[-]breaking	s. breakage		
bond chain, valence chain, chain of valencies	Valenzkette f, Bindungskette f	bootstrap approximation	„bootstrap"-Näherung f, „self-consistent"-Modell n von Zachariasen
bond direction	Valenzrichtung f		
		bootstrap dynamics	„bootstrap"-Dynamik f
bond distance	s. bond length	Borchers class, equivalence class of local fields	Borchers-Klasse f
bond eigenfunction	Eigenfunktion f des gebundenen Zustandes		
bond energy <chem.>	Bindungsenergie f <Chem.>	borda	s. kilogram[me]
bonderizing	Bondern n, Bonder-Verfahren n	Borda-Carnot theorem	Borda-Carnotscher Satz m, Satz über den Stoßverlust
bond fixation, Mills-Nixon effect	Mills-Nixon-Effekt m	Borda['s] method	s. substitution method
		Borda mouthpiece	Bordasches Mundstück n, Borda-Mündung f
bonding electron, binding electron, outer shell electron, peripheral electron, valence electron <chem., nucl.>	Valenzelektron n, bindendes Elektron n, Bindungselektron n, Außenelektron n, äußeres (kernfernes) Elektron, Elektron der Außenschale	Borda phenomenon	Bordasche Erscheinung f
		border, bank <math.>	Schnittufer n, Ufer n <Math.>
		border curve, limiting curve	Grenzkurve f
bonding force	s. binding force	border effect	s. Eberhard effect <phot.>
bonding material	s. bond <of fuel element>	bordering	Umbördeln n, Aufbördeln n
bonding orbital, bond orbital	Bindungsorbital n, bindendes Orbital n, Bindungsbahn f, gemeinsame Elektronenbahn f		
		bordering <math.>	Rändern n <Math.>
		border-line case, limiting case; extreme case	Grenzfall m; Extremfall m
bonding structure, bond structure	Bindungsstruktur f	border of the nucleus; nuclear surface	Kernoberfläche f; Kernrand m
		border zone	s. peripheral region

Bordini effect	Bordini-Effekt m	boson spectrum	s. meson spectrum
bore ⟨hydr.⟩	Sprungwelle f, Stürmer m ⟨Hydr.⟩	bottle; flask; jar	Flasche f; Fläschchen n
		bottle sample	s. silt sample
bore	s. a. high tide raised by a storm	bottle silt sampler	Schöpfflasche f für Schwebstoffe, Schwebstoffschöpfflasche f
boreal axis pole, boreal pole, Arctic axis pole	geomagnetischer Nordpol m, borealer Pol [(Hauptpol) m, arktischer Magnetpol m [der Erde], südmagnetischer Hauptpol	bottom current	Bodenströmung f, Bodenstrom m; Sohlenströmung f, Grundströmung f
		bottom fusion	s. precipitating fusion
borehole logging, well logging	Bohrlochuntersuchung f, Karottage f	bottoming	s. blocking ⟨el.⟩
		bottoming voltage	s. knee voltage
Borel field	Borel-Körper m, Borelsches System n	bottom-layer	s. near-soil ⟨meteo.⟩
		bottom of the conduction band	Unterkante f (untere Kante f, unterer Rand m) des Leitungsbandes
Borel field of events	Borelsches Ereignisfeld n		
Borel-Lebesgue covering theorem	Borel-Lebesguescher Überdeckungssatz m, Überdeckungssatz von Borel-Lebesgue	bottoms	s. still bottom heel
		bottom stage ⟨of separating unit⟩	Anfangsstufe f, erste Stufe f ⟨Trennkaskade⟩
Borel set	Borel-Menge f, Borelsche Menge f	bottom standing wave, eddy motion of the water particles near the bottom	Grundwalze f
Born['s] approximation	Bornsche Näherung f		
Born-Green-Yvon equation	Born-Green-Yvon-Gleichung f	bottom velocity	Sohlengeschwindigkeit f
		bottom water	s. deep water ⟨geo.⟩
Born-Haber cycle, Haber-Born cycle	Born-Haberscher (Haber-Bornscher, Bornscher) Kreisprozeß m	Bouguer-Beer law, Bouguer['s] law [of absorption], Lambert['s] law [of absorption]	[Bouguer-]Lambertsches Absorptionsgesetz n, Lambertsches Gesetz n
Born-Infeld theory	Born-Infeldsche Theorie f		
Born-Kármán['s] periodic boundary condition	s. Born-von Kármán boundary condition	Bouguer['s] halo, Ullsa['s] ring	Halo m von Bouguer, Bouguers Halo
Born-Mayer force	Born-Mayer-Kraft f	Bouguer['s] law [of absorption]	s. Bouguer-Beer law
Born-Oppenheimer approximation	Born-Oppenheimersche Näherung f	Bouguer['s] reduction	Bouguer-Reduktion f
Born-Oppenheimer theorem	Born-Oppenheimer-Theorem n, Satz n von Born-Oppenheimer	Bouguer wave number	Bouguersche Wellenzahl f, Bouguer-Wellenzahl f
		boulder, boulder stone, rubble; bed load ⟨of river⟩ ⟨geo.⟩	Geröll n; fluviatiles Geröll, Flußgeröll n, Schotter m; marines Geröll, Brandungsgeröll n; Geschiebe n ⟨Gletscher⟩, Glazialgeschiebe n ⟨Geo.⟩
Born-von Kármán boundary condition, Born-Kármán['s] periodic boundary condition, periodic boundary condition, cyclic boundary condition	Born-von Kármánsche Randbedingung f, Born-Kármánsche Randbedingung, Bornsche Randbedingung, periodische Randbedingung, Randbedingung der Periodizität		
		bounce, bound, shock, impact, knock-on, impingement, impinging	Aufschlag m, Aufprall m, Anprall m, Prall m
		bound ⟨math.⟩	Schranke f ⟨Math.⟩
		bound ⟨of operator⟩; norm ⟨math.⟩	Norm f ⟨Math.⟩
boron counter [tube], boron-filled counter [tube]	Borzählrohr n, Zählrohr n mit Borfüllung	bound; boundary, limit, limitation; margin; rim	Grenze f; Begrenzung f; Rand m; Berandung f
boron equivalent	Boräquivalent n	boundary ⟨math.⟩	Rand m ⟨Math⟩
boron-filled counter [tube], boron counter [tube]	Borzählrohr n, Zählrohr n mit Borfüllung	boundary	s. a. boundary layer
		boundary	s. a. interface
		boundary	s. a. surface
boron-lined counter [tube]	mit Bor ausgekleidetes Zählrohr n, Zählrohr mit Borauskleidung	boundary angle	s. angle of contact
		boundary between air masses	s. boundary of the air mass
Borrmann effect, Campbell-Borrmann effect	Borrmann-Effekt m	boundary collocation	Randkollokation f
Bosanquet['s] law	Bosanquetsches (magnetisches Ohmsches) Gesetz n	boundary concentration, boundary density	Randkonzentration f, Randdichte f
Bose-Einstein commutation relation	Bose-Einsteinsche Vertauschungsrelation f		
		boundary condition ⟨math.⟩	Grenzbedingung f; Randbedingung f; Randwertbedingung f ⟨Math.⟩
Bose-Einstein condensation, Einstein condensation	Bose-Einstein-Kondensation f, Einstein-Kondensation f	boundary condition	s. a. boundary layer condition
		boundary condition of the first kind	s. Dirichlet['s] boundary condition
Bose-Einstein distribution; Bose-Einstein distribution function (law)	Bose-Einstein-Verteilung f; Bose-Einstein-Verteilungsfunktion f, Bose-Einsteinsche Verteilungsfunktion	boundary condition of the second kind	s. Neumann['s] boundary condition
		boundary condition of the third kind, third boundary condition	Randbedingung f dritter Art, dritte Randbedingung
Bose-Einstein gas, Bose-Einstein perfect gas, Bose gas	Bose-[Einstein-]Gas n, Bose-Einsteinsches ideales Gas n, Bosonengas n		
		boundary contrast, edge contrast	Grenzkontrast m, Randkontrast m
Bose-Einstein liquid, Bose-liquid	Bose-Flüssigkeit f	boundary curve	Randkurve f
		boundary density	s. boundary concentration
Bose-Einstein particle	s. bose particle	boundary displacement [of the injection]	Randverdrängung f [der Injektion]
Bose-Einstein perfect gas	s. Bose-Einstein gas	boundary effect	s. edge effect
Bose-Einstein statistics	Bose-[Einstein-]Statistik f, Bose-Einsteinsche Statistik f, BE-Statistik f	boundary emission, edge emission	Kantenemission f
		boundary fault, peripheric (circumferential) fault	Randverwerfung f, Randstörung f
Bose gas	s. Bose-Einstein gas		
Bose-liquid, Bose-Einstein liquid	Bose-Flüssigkeit f		
		boundary film lubrication, boundary lubrication	Grenzschmierung f
Bose operator	Bose-Operator m		
Bose particle, boson, Bose-Einstein particle	Boson n, Bose-Teilchen n	boundary layer, friction layer, shear layer ⟨hydr.⟩	Grenzschicht f, Reibungsschicht f, Scher[ungs]schicht f ⟨Hydr.⟩
boson field	Bose-Feld n, Bosonenfeld n		

boundary layer blowing, blowing off the boundary layer	Wegblasen n der Grenzschicht	bound cross-section, bound scattering cross-section, cross-section for bound scattering	Streuquerschnitt m von gebundenen Atomen, Wirkungsquerschnitt m für (der) Streuung an gebundenen Atomen
boundary-layer condition, boundary condition	Grenzflächenbedingung f, Grenzbedingung f	boundedness <math.>	Beschränktheit f <Math.>
boundary-layer control	Grenzschichtbeeinflussung f, Grenzschichtsteuerung f	bounded operator	beschränkter Operator m
boundary layer displacement thickness, displacement thickness [of boundary layer]	Verdrängungsdicke f [der Grenzschicht], Grenzschicht-Verdrängungsdicke f	bounded variation	s. limited variation
		bound energy	gebundene Energie f, Helmholtz-Wärme f, Entropieglied n der Gibbs-Helmholtzschen Gleichung
boundary layer equations	Grenzschichtgleichungen fpl, Grenzschicht-Differentialgleichungen fpl	bound-free transition	gebunden-freier Übergang m, Gebunden-frei-Übergang m
boundary layer excitation	s. excitation of boundary layer	bounding surface	s. interface
boundary layer flow	Grenzschichtströmung f	bounding surface	s. surface
boundary-layer friction	Grenzflächenreibung f	bound magnetism	gebundener Magnetismus m
boundary layer region, interface region	Grenzschichtgebiet n, Grenzschichtbereich m	bound scattering cross-section	s. bound cross-section
boundary layer separation	Grenzschichtablösung f	bound vector, fixed vector, localized vector, field vector	gebundener Vektor m
boundary layer suction	s. sucking away of boundary layer	bound vortex (vorticity), adherent vortex	gebundener Wirbel m, tragender Wirbel
boundary layer theory	Grenzschichttheorie f		
boundary layer thickness	Grenzschichtdicke f	bound water	gebundenes Wasser n
boundary-layer transition, transition to turbulence in boundary layer	Umschlag m laminar-turbulent in der Grenzschicht, Grenzschichtumschlag m	Bourdon gauge, Bourdon pressure gauge, Bourdon spiral (tube), Bourdon type gauge, Bourdon type pressure gauge, spring pressure gauge	Bourdon-Manometer n, Bourdon-Rohr n, Bourdon-Röhre f, Bourdonsche Röhre f, Bourdon-Feder f, Bourdonsches Manometer (Federrohrmanometer) n, Feder[rohr]manometer n, Druckfeder f, Federdruckmesser m
boundary-layer velocity profile	Grenzschicht[-Geschwindigkeits]profil n		
boundary lubrication, boundary film lubrication	Grenzschmierung f, Grenzschichtschmierung f	Boussinesq number, Boussinesq similarity number	Boussinesq-Zahl f, Boussinesqsche Kennzahl f, Boussinesq-Ähnlichkeitskennzahl f, B
boundary movement, [Bloch] wall displacement, displacement of Bloch wall	Bloch-Wand-Verschiebung f, Wandverschiebung f, Verschiebung f der Bloch-Wand	Boussinesq-Papkovich solution, Papkovich solution	[Boussinesq-]Papkowitsch-Lösung f
boundary of shadow	s. shadow border	Boussinesq['s] problem, problem of Boussinesq [and Cerruti], problem of the plane (half-space), half-space problem	Boussinesqsches Problem n, Problem von Boussinesq
boundary of the air mass, air-mass boundary, boundary between air masses	Luftmassengrenze f		
boundary part, marginal part	Randpartie f	Boussinesq similarity number	s. Boussinesq number
boundary point, frontier point	Randpunkt m	Bow condition	Bowsche Bedingung f
boundary potential	s. barrier potential	bowing under load; bend, bending; deflection; flexure <mech.>	Durchbiegung f <Mech.>
boundary problem, boundary value problem	Randwertaufgabe f, Randwertproblem n		
boundary resistance	s. critical resistance	bow shock	s. head wave
boundary stress <mech.>	Randspannung f, Randlast f	bow wave	Bugwelle f
		box	s. housing
boundary surface	s. interface	box argument	s. Dirichlet['s] principle
boundary surface	s. surface	box compass	s. compass
boundary value	Randwert m	box development	s. tank development
		boxed magnet	s. shell-type magnet
boundary value problem, boundary problem	Randwertaufgabe f, Randwertproblem n	box fold, flat-topped fold	Kofferfalte f
		box level	s. circular level
boundary value problem of the first kind	s. Dirichlet['s] problem	box principle	s. Dirichlet['s] principle
boundary value problem of the second kind	s. Neumann['s] problem	Boyle and Mariotte['s] law	s. Boyle['s] law
boundary value problem of the third kind	s. third boundary value problem	Boyle-Charles law, Boyle equation, Boyle-Gay-Lussac law, ideal gas law, perfect gas law, perfect gas equation [of state], gas law, law for ideal gas	Boyle-[Mariotte-]Gay-Lussacsches Gesetz n, Boyle-Charlessches Gesetz, Zustandsgleichung f der idealen Gase, Gasgleichung f, [ideales] Gasgesetz n, Clapeyronsche Zustandsgleichung
boundary wave; interfacial wave, wave at interface	Grenzschichtwelle f; Grenzflächenwelle f, Trennungsflächenwelle f		
bound-bound transition	gebunden-gebundener Übergang m, Gebunden-gebunden-Übergang m		
		Boyle equation	s. Boyle-Charles law
		Boyle-Gay-Lussac law	s. Boyle-Charles law
bound charge, polarization charge	Polarisationsladung f	Boyle['s] law, [Boyle and] Mariotte['s] law	Boyle-Mariottesches (Boylesches) Gesetz n
bound charge density	s. density of polarization charge	Boyle['s] point; Boyle['s] temperature	Boyle-Punkt m, Boylescher Punkt m; Boyle-Temperatur f
bound coherent cross-section	kohärenter Streuquerschnitt m von gebundenen Atomen, Wirkungsquerschnitt m für kohärente Streuung an gebundenen Atomen	Bozorth curve	Bozorth-Kurve f
		BP centre	s. bipolar centre
		B position	s. B site
		BPP theory, Bloembergen-Purcell-Pound theory	Bloembergen-Purcell-Pound-Theorie f, BPP-Theorie f
		bra, bra vector	bra-Vektor m, „bra" n
		brace, curly bracket	geschweifte Klammer f

Brace compensator, Brace instrument	Bracescher Kompensator m	Bragg-Williams approximation	Bragg-Williamssche Näherung f
Brace polarizer	Bracescher Polarisator m	Braginsky limiting current	Braginskischer Grenzstrom m
brachistochrone, curve of shortest descent	Brachistochrone, Brachystochrone f	brain wave	Gehirnwelle f
		brake-field tube	s. retarding field tube
brachistochronic motion	brachistochrone Bewegung f	brake horse power, effective horse power	Bremspferdestärke f; Bremsleistung f <in PS>
brachyanticlinal <geo.>, brachyanticlyne	Brachyantiklinale f, Brachyantikline f <Geo.>	brake rocket [engine]	s. decelerating rocket
brachyaxis	Brachyachse f	brake thermal efficiency	s. overall efficiency
brachymedial	Brachymedial n	brake torque, braking moment, retarding torque	Bremsmoment n
brachysynclinal, brachysynclinal fold, brachysyncline <geo.>	Brachysynklinale f, Brachysynkline f, Schüssel f; Pfanne f <Geo.>	braking, checking, retardation <mech.>	Bremsung f, Bremsen n, Hemmung f, Abbremsung f <Mech.>
brachytelescope	Brachyteleskop n [nach Foster und Fritsch], Brachyt n	braking curve	Bremskurve f
		braking moment, brake (retarding) torque	Bremsmoment n
Brackett series	Brackett-Serie f	braking radiation	s. bremsstrahlung
Bradbury layer	Bradbury-Schicht f	braking rocket	s. decelerating rocket
Bradley['s] determination of the velocity of light, Bradley['s] method of measuring the velocity of light	Bradleysche Methode f zur Bestimmung der Lichtgeschwindigkeit	braking torque <of a meter>	Bremsmoment n <Zähler>
		branch <of lightning>	Abzweigung f, Verästelung f, Gabelung f, Zweig m, Ast m <Blitz>
bradyseism	Bradyseisme f, bradyseismische Schwingung f [der Erdkruste], langsame Schwingung der Erdkruste	branch, branching, branching-off, tapping <el.>	Abzweigung f, Abzweig m, Ableitung f <El.>
		branch	s. a. jump <num. math.>
		branch [circuit]	s. shunt <el.>
Bragg angle	s. glancing angle	branch circuit	s. subcircuit
Bragg case, reflection case	Bragg-Fall m	branch current, branch stream	Teilstrom m, Zweigstrom m
Bragg['s] condition	s. Bragg['s] equation		
Bragg['s] cone	Braggscher Kegel m	branch current, current in the branch, shunt current <el.>	Zweigstrom m, Teilstrom m, Nebenschlußstrom m <El.>
Bragg curve [of specific ionization]	Braggsche Kurve (Ionisationskurve) f, Bragg-Kurve f		
		branch cut, branch line <of Riemann surface> <math.>	Verzweigungsschnitt m, Schnitt m <Riemannsche Fläche> <Math.>
Bragg['s] diffraction spectrograph	Gitterspektrograph m von Bragg, Braggscher Gitterspektrograph	branched chain reaction	s. branching-chain reaction
Bragg diffractometer	Beugungsgerät n nach Bragg, Bragg-Diffraktometer n	branched molecule	verzweigtes Molekül n
		branched solution	verzweigte Lösung f
Bragg['s] equation, Bragg['s] condition, Bragg['s] reflection condition, Bragg['s] law, Bragg['s] relationship	Braggsche Gleichung (Formel, Bedingung, Reflexionsbedingung, Beziehung) f, Reflexionsbedingung von Bragg, Wulff-Braggsche Gleichung (Bedingung)	branching, ramification; bifurcation; furcation, forking	Verzweigung f, Verästelung f, Aufspaltung f, Aufzweigung f; Gabelung f; Gabelteilung f
		branching	s. a. multiple disintegration
		branching	s. a. branch <el.>
Bragg['s] focusing condition	Braggsche Fokussierungsbedingung f	branching-chain reaction, branched chain reaction	duale (verzweigte) Kettenreaktion f, gleichzeitiges Ablaufen n beider Kettenreaktionsarten
Bragg-Gray principle	Bragg-Grayches Prinzip n, Bragg-Gray-Prinzip n		
Bragg-Gray relation	Bragg-Graysche Beziehung f	branching decay	s. multiple disintegration
Bragg interference	Bragg-Interferenz f, Röntgenstrahlinterferenz f nach Bragg	branching ellipsoid	Verzweigungsellipsoid n
		branching factor	Verzweigungsfaktor m
		branching fraction	Verzweigungsanteil m
Bragg['s] law	Braggsches Gesetz n	branching index	Verzweigungsindex m; Verzweigtheitsindex m
Bragg['s] law	s. a. Bragg['s] equation		
Bragg method	s. Bragg['s] rotating crystal method	branching of chain, chain branching	Kettenverzweigung f
Bragg reflection	Braggsche Reflexion f, Bragg-Reflexion f; Bragg-Reflex m, Braggscher Reflex m	branching-off	s. branch <el.>
		branching point <el.>	Stromverzweigungspunkt m, Stromverzweigung f
Bragg reflection angle	s. glancing angle	branching point	s. a. bifurcation point
Bragg['s] reflection condition	s. Bragg['s] equation	branching point	s. a. branch point <math.>
Bragg['s] relationship	s. Bragg['s] equation	branching process, branching stochastic process	Verzweigungsprozeß m, Vervielfachungsprozeß m, verzweigter stochastischer Prozeß m
Bragg['s] rotating crystal method, rotating crystal method, Bragg method, rotation method, technique of rotation photograph	Drehkristallmethode f [von Bragg], Braggsche Drehkristallmethode (Methode) f, Drehkristallverfahren n, Braggsches Verfahren n, Methode von Bragg		
		branching ratio, percentage probability <nucl.>	Verzweigungsverhältnis n, Abzweigverhältnis n <Kern.>
		branching rule [in spectra]	Verzweigungsregel f [für Spektren]
Bragg rule	Braggsche Regel f	branching stochastic process	s. branching process
Bragg scattering	Braggsche Streuung f		
Bragg['s] soap bubble model	s. soap bubble model	branch line	Verzweigungslinie f
Bragg spectrograph	s. Bragg spectrometer	branch line	s. a. branch cut <math.>
Bragg spectrometer, crystal spectrometer, deflection spectrometer; Bragg spectrograph, crystal spectrograph	Kristallspektrometer n, Braggsches Spektrometer (Röntgenspektrometer) n, Bragg-Spektrometer n; Braggscher Spektrograph (Röntgenspektrograph, Drehkristallspektrograph) m, Bragg-Spektrograph m, Ablenkungsspektrograph m	branch of disintegration	s. branch of the radioactive family <nucl.>
		branch of the band	Bandenzweig m, Zweig m der Bande
		branch of the bridge	s. arm of the bridge
		branch of the circuit <el.>	Zweig m des Stromkreises, Stromzweig m <El.>

branch of the curve	Kurvenzug *m*, Zug *m* der Kurve, Kurvenast *m*, Kurvenzweig *m*, Ast (Zweig) *m* der Kurve	breakdown filament; breakdown streamer	Durchschlagkanal *m*; Durchschlagstreamer *m*
branch of the radioactive family, branch of disintegration, disintegration (decay) branch <nucl.>	Zweig *m* der radioaktiven Zerfallsreihe, Zerfallszweig *m*, Unterfamilie *f* <Kern.>	breakdown in air, electrical breakdown in air	Luftdurchschlag *m*, elektrischer Durchschlag *m* in Luft
		breakdown of symmetry	s. symmetry breaking
branch of the shower (stream)	s. stream branch <astr.>	breakdown of the arc	s. striking of the arc
		breakdown overvoltage, ignition overvoltage	Zündüberspannung *f*
branch point, branching point <of Riemann surface or graph>; branchtype singularity; cross point <of graph> <math.>	Verzweigungspunkt *m*, Windungspunkt *m* <Riemannsche Fläche *oder* Graph>; Verzweigung *f*; Kreuzungspunkt *m*, eigentlicher Knotenpunkt *m* <Graph> <Math.>	breakdown potential	s. breakdown voltage
		breakdown streamer; breakdown filament	Durchschlagkanal *m*; Durchschlagstreamer *m*
		breakdown strength of turn	Windungsfestigkeit *f*
		breakdown time	Durchbruchzeit *f*, Durchschlagszeit *f*
branch point	s. a. node <el.>	breakdown voltage, breakdown potential, puncture voltage, sparking voltage, disruptive voltage	Durchschlagspannung *f*, Durchschlagpotential *n*, Durchbruch[s]spannung *f*
branch stream	s. branch current		
branch transmission [of sound]	verzweigte Schallübertragung *f*		
branch-type singularity	s. branch point <math.>		
Branley-Lenard effect	s. volume ionization	breakdown voltage <of discharge>, striking voltage (potential), firing voltage, starting voltage (potential), ignition voltage (potential, threshold) <of discharge *or* tube>; energizing voltage <of discharge lamp>; glow potential	Zündspannung *f*, Durchbruch[s]spannung *f*, Zündpotential *n*
Braun tube	s. cathode-ray tube		
Bravais biplate	Bravaissche Doppelplatte *f*		
Bravais correlation coefficient, productmoment correlation coefficient, Pearson['s] coefficient [of correlation]	Maßkorrelationskoeffizient *m*, Produkt-Moment-Korrelationskoeffizient *m*, gewöhnlicher (Pearsonscher, Bravaisscher) Korrelationskoeffizient *m*		
Bravais lattice, translation lattice	Bravais-Gitter *n*, Bravais-Netz *n*, Translationsgitter *n*, einfaches (Bravaissches) Translationsgitter, Raumgittertyp *m*	breaker <hydr.>	Brecher *m* <Hydr.>
		breaker	s. a. circuit breaker <el.>
		breakers	Brandung *f*
		break excitation, excitation at break	Öffnungsreiz *m*
Bravais['] law	Bravaissches Gesetz *n*	break impulse, break pulse, pulse at break	Öffnungsimpuls *m*, Abreißimpuls *m*
Bravais-Miller index	s. Miller-Bravais index		
bra vector, bra	bra-Vektor *m*, „bra" *n*	breaking <of wave>	Brechen *n* <Welle>
Brayton cycle	s. Joule cycle	breaking	s. a. breakage <of the bond>
Brazilian twin	Brasilianer Zwilling *m*	breaking	s. a. demulsification
		breaking	s. a. disconnection <el.>
Brazil law	Brasilianer Gesetz *n*	breaking	s. a. switching <el.>
breadth of the spectral line	s. line width	breaking angle, angle of break	Reißwinkel *m*
break, break distance, length of break	Schaltstrecke *f*, Gesamtschaltstrecke *f*	breaking arc	s. break arc
		breaking current	Anfangswert *m* des Ausschaltstromes, Ausschaltstrom *m*, Ausschaltstromstärke *f*
break, fraction, salient point; kink, knee <of the curve>	Knick *m*; Knie *n*; Abknicken *n* <Kurve>		
		breaking elongation, fracture (failing) strain, total extension; ultimate elongation in percent, increase in gauge length after rupture in percent, elongation at break	Bruchdehnung *f*
break	s. a. rest contact		
break	s. a. break-through		
break	s. a. opening		
breakability; crackiness; fragility; brittleness; friability; shortness; rottenness <of steel>	Zerbrechlichkeit *f*, Brüchigkeit *f*; Sprödigkeit *f*		
		breaking frequency	s. switching frequency
		breaking length	Reißlänge *f*
breakage, breaking <of the bond>, bond[-]breaking	Auftrennung *f*, Bruch *m*, Lösung *f*, Aufspaltung *f* <Bindung>, Bindungsbruch *m*	breaking load, fracture (fracturing) load, load at rupture <mech.>	Bruchlast *f*; Höchstlast *f*; Reißlast *f*, Zerreißlast *f*
		breaking moment, moment of rupture	Bruchmoment *n*
break arc, arc at break, breaking arc	Abreißbogen *m*, Öffnungs[licht]bogen *m*; Unterbrechungslichtbogen *m*	breaking off, rupture <el.>	Abreißen *n* <El.>
		breaking of viscosity, viscosity breaking	Viskositätsabnahme *f*, Zähigkeitsabnahme *f*
break[-]away, breakdown <of fluid flow>	Abreißen *n* <Strömung>	breaking period	s. switching time
		breaking point	s. break-through
break[-]away <of dislocation>	Ablösung *f* <Versetzung>	breaking point	s. modulus of rupture
		breaking radiation	s. bremsstrahlung
break[-]away velocity	Abreißgeschwindigkeit *f*	breaking spark	s. break spark
		breaking strength (stress)	s. tensile strength
break contact	Trennkontakt *m*		
break contact	s. a. rest contact	breaking stress	s. fracture stress
break current, current [induced] at break; opening current	Abreißstrom *m*, Öffnungsstrom *m*; Unterbrechungsstrom *m*	breaking up	s loosening
		breaking-up of the equilibrium orbit, stable-orbit break-up	Sollkreissprengung *f*
break distance	s. break	breaking-up of the rocket stage	Abwerfen *n* (Abtrennung *f*) der Raketenstufe, Trennung *f* der Raketenstufen
breakdown, dielectric (disruptive) breakdown; disruptive discharge; puncture; punch-through	[dielektrischer] Durchschlag *m*, [eigentlicher] elektrischer Durchschlag, Durchbruch *m*; Felddurchschlag		
breakdown, collapse, caving-in, sinking <geo.>	Zusammenbruch *m*, Zusammenfallen *n*, Einsturz *m*, Einbruch *m* <Geo.>	break jack, disconnect jack, transfer jack	Trennklinke *f*
breakdown	s. a. break[-]away <of fluid flow>	break-off diagram	Reißdiagramm *n*
breakdown	s. a. failure		
breakdown field [strength]	s. dielectric strength		

break-off method	Reißverfahren n
break-off of oscillations	Abreißen n der Schwingungen
break-off viscosity <of lubricants>	Abbruchviskosität f <Schmiermittel>
breakover current	s. deflecting current
breakover voltage	s. sweep voltage
break point	Klarpunkt m <Titration; kristalline Flüssigkeit>
break point <of curve>	Knickpunkt m
break point <of emulsion>	Entmischungspunkt m <Emulsion>
break point	s. a. branch point
break point	s. a. break-through
break pulse	s. break impulse
break spark, spark at break, breaking spark; touch spark; opening spark; switching spark	Abreißfunke[n] m; Unterbrechungsfunke[n] m; Unterbrecherfunke[n] m; Öffnungsfunke[n] m; Schaltfunke[n] m
break strain	s. fracture stress
break-through, break[ing] point, break <through the adsorbent>	Adsorptionsschwelle f, Durchbruch m <durch den Adsorbenten>
break-through of glide	Durchbruch m der Gleitung, Gleitungsdurchbruch m
break-through resistance, differential Zener resistance	Durchbruchwiderstand m, differentieller Zener-Widerstand m
break time	s. opening time <el.>
break-up	s. loosening
break-up in the weather	s. rapid change of weather
break voltage, voltage at break, voltage induced at break	Abreißspannung f, Öffnungsspannung f
breakwater <hydr.>	Wellenbrecher m, Wellenfalle f <Hydr.>
breathing vibration	Pulsationsschwingung f, pulsierende Schwingung f
breeder, breeder reactor	Brutreaktor m, Brüter m, Brüterreaktor m, Brütreaktor m
breeding; converting, conversion <of fertile material>	Brüten n, Brutvorgang m; Konvertieren n, Konversion f <Kernbrennstoff>
breeding blanket	s. blanket
breeding cycle	Brutzyklus m, Brutkreislauf m
breeding doubling time	s. doubling time
breeding gain; conversion gain	Brutgewinn m
breeding material	s. fertile material
breeding ratio	s. conversion ratio
breeze	Brise f, gleichmäßiger Seewind m
breeze	s. a. light breeze
B region	s. upper mantle
Breit['s] [classical] formula	Breitsche Formel f
Breit interaction	Breit-Wechselwirkung f, Breitsche Wechselwirkung f
Breit-Rabi formula	Breit-Rabi-Formel f
Breit-Wigner formula	Breit-Wigner-Formel f, Dispersionsformel f für isoliertes Resonanzniveau
Breit-Wigner resonance	Breit-Wigner-Resonanz f
Breit-Wigner theory of resonance scattering	Breit-Wignersche Theorie f der Neutronenresonanzstreuung
bremsspectrum, retardation spectrum, bremsstrahlung spectrum	Bremsspektrum n, Bremsstrahlungsspektrum n, Bremskontinuum n
bremsstrahlung, bremsstrahlung (collision) radiation, continuous X-rays (X-radiation, X-ray radiation), braking (breaking, slowing-down, deceleration) radiation	Brems[röntgen]strahlung f, Röntgenbremsstrahlung f, Röntgenbremskontinuum n, kontinuierliche (weiße) Röntgenstrahlung f, weißes Röntgenlicht n, Elektronenbremsstrahlung f
bremsstrahlung photon, bremsstrahlung quantum	Bremsstrahlungsquant n, Bremsstrahlungsphoton n
bremsstrahlung radiation	s. bremsstrahlung
bremsstrahlung spectrum	s. bremsspectrum
brewster $<= 10^{-7}$ cm²/kg>	Brewster $n <= 10^{-7}$ cm²/kg>
Brewster angle, polarizing angle, angle of polarization	Brewsterscher Winkel (Reflexionswinkel) m, Polarisationswinkel m, Reflexionswinkel von Brewster
Brewster['s] bands, Brewster['s] fringes	Brewstersche Streifen (Interferenzstreifen) mpl, Brewsterstreifen mpl
Brewster incidence	Brewster-Einfall m, Einfall m unter dem Brewsterschen Winkel
Brewster['s] law	Brewstersches Gesetz n
Brewster point	Brewster-Punkt m, Brewsterscher Punkt m
Brewster stereoscope, prismatic stereoscope	Prismenstereoskop n [nach Brewster], Brewstersches Prismenstereoskop, Brewsters Stereoskop n
Brezina biplate	Brezinasche Doppelplatte f
bridge anemometer	Brückenanemometer n
bridge arm	s. arm of the bridge
bridge beam	s. transverse beam <mech.>
bridge branch	s. arm of the bridge
bridge circuit (connection), lattice network	Brückenschaltung f
bridge diagonal	Brückendiagonale f
bridged-T network, bridged T-section	überbrücktes T-Glied n, Brücken-T-Vierpol m, Brücken-T-Schaltung f, überbrückte T-Schaltung f, Brückensternschaltung f
bridge for coupling measurements	Kopplungsmeßbrücke f
bridge ligand	s. bridging ligand
bridge modulator	s. balanced modulator
bridge rectifier	s. Graetz rectifier
bridge rectifier circuit	s. Graetz rectifier
bridge scale	s. weighing bridge
bridging; connection across	Überbrückung f
bridging circuit	Überbrückungsschaltung f
bridging gain	Überbrückungsgewinn m
bridging ligand, bridge ligand	Brückenligand m
bridging loss	Überbrückungsverlust m
bridging resistance	s. shunt resistance
Bridgman effect	Bridgman-Effekt m, innerer Peltier-Effekt m
Bridgman heat	Bridgman-Wärme f
Bridgman['s] method, Bridgman-Stockbarger method (technique), Bridgman['s] technique	Bridgman-Methode f, Bridgman-Verfahren n, Bridgman-Stockbarger-Verfahren n, Absenkmethode f von Bridgman, Bridgman-Stockbarger-Methode f, Kristallzüchtung f aus der Schmelze nach der Methode von Bridgman
Brigg['s] (Briggsian) logarithm, common (decimal, vulgar) logarithm, logarithm to base 10, lg, log₁₀	Briggscher (gemeiner, dekadischer) Logarithmus m, Logarithmus zur Basis 10, Zehnerlogarithmus m, lg, $\log_{10}$
bright adaptation	s. light adaptation
bright-dark field condenser	Wechselkondensor m, Durchlicht-Hellfeld-Dunkelfeld-Kondensor m, Hellfeld-Dunkelfeld-Kondensor m
brightener, optical brightener	optischer Aufheller m, optisches Bleichmittel n, Weißtöner m, „brightener" m

brightening

brightening, bright-up, bright intensification <of cathode-ray tube>	Hell[igkeits]steuerung *f*, Helltastung *f* <Elektronenstrahlröhre>	Brinell['s] hardness test, brinelling, Brinell test	Kugeldruck-Härteprüfung *f* [nach Brinell], Kugeldruckversuch *m* [nach Brinell], Härteprüfung *f* nach Brinell, Brinell-Härteprüfung *f*, Brinellscher Kugeldruckversuch *m*, Brinellsche Kugeldruckprobe *f*
brightening, brightening up; clearing, clearing up <opt.>	Aufhellung *f* <Opt.>		
brightening towards the limb, limb brightening	Randaufhellung *f*	brinelling, wear by impacts, impact wear	Stoßverschleiß *m*
brightening up	*s.* brightening	Brinell number	*s.* Brinell hardness
bright field, bright ground	Hellfeld *n*	Brinell test	*s.* Brinell hardness test
bright-field condenser	Hellfeldkondensor *m*	brine thermostat	Solethermostat *m*
bright-field illumination	Hellfeldbeleuchtung *f*	brisant explosion	*s.* explosive
		British Association ohm	*s.* British Association Unit <= 0.988 Ω>
bright-field image	Hellfeldabbildung *f*; Hellfeldbild *n*	British Association Unit, British Association ohm, B.A.U., ohmad <= 0.988 Ω>	Ohmad *n*, British Association Unit *f*, B. A. U. <= 0.988 Ω>
bright-field microscopy, bright-field observation	Hellfeldmikroskopie *f*, Hellfeldbeobachtung *f*		
		British meson	*s.* pi meson
		British mile	*s.* statute mile
bright-field microscopy in transmitted light	*s.* transmitted-light bright-field microscopy	brittle crack	Sprödriß *m*
bright-field observation	*s.* bright-field microscopy	brittle-ductile transition	Umwandlung *f* (Übergang *m*) spröde-duktil
bright-field vertical illumination	Auflicht-Hellfeldbeleuchtung *f*, Innenbeleuchtung *f*	brittle fracture	Sprödbruch *m*, spröder Bruch *m*
		brittle in tension	spannungsspröde
bright-field vertical-illumination condenser; bright-field vertical illuminator	Auflicht-Hellfeldkondensor *m*; Auflicht-Hellfeldilluminator *m*	brittleness	*s.* breakability
		brittle point, brittle temperature, freezing temperature	Sprödigkeitspunkt *m*, Sprödigkeitstemperatur *f*, Brittlepunkt *m*
bright fireball, great fireball	heller Bolid *m*, großer Bolid		
bright giant, bright giant star	heller Riese *m*, heller Riesenstern *m*	brittle strength	Sprödfestigkeit *f*, Festigkeit *f* gegenüber Sprödbruch
bright ground	*s.* bright field	brittle temperature	*s.* brittle point
bright intensification	*s.* brightening <of cathode-ray tube>	Brix degree	Brix-Grad *m*
		brize	*s.* kilogram[me]
bright nebula, bright nebulosity	heller Nebel *m*	broad beam	breites Bündel *n*, Großfeld *n*
brightness	*s.* luminosity		
brightness	*s.* lightness	broad-beam measurement	Messung *f* mit breitem Bündel, Messung bei breitem Bündel, Großfeldmessung *f*
brightness	*s.* stellar brightness <astr.>		
brightness contrast	*s.* luminance contrast	broad-crested weir; flat-crested (long-crested) weir	Überfall *m* mit flacher Kante, flachkantiger Überfall; flachkantiges Wehr *n*, Wehr mit flacher Kante
brightness difference	*s.* difference in luminance		
brightness discrimination	Helligkeitsunterscheidung *f*; Helligkeitsunterscheidungsvermögen *n*; Farbhelligkeits-Unterscheidungsvermögen *n*		
		broadening; widening	Verbreiterung *f*
		broadening, widening, expansion <mech.>	Erweiterung *f* <Mech.>
brightness distribution	Helligkeitsverteilung *f*	broadening by damping	*s.* natural broadening
		broadening of lines by exchange interaction, exchange broadening	Austauschverbreiterung *f*
brightness distribution curve	Helligkeitskurve *f*, Helligkeitsverlauf *m*		
brightness flicker	Helligkeitsflimmern *n*	broadening of the spectral lines	*s.* line broadening
brightness fluctuation, luminance fluctuation	Helligkeitsschwankung *f*	broadside	*s.* fill-in light
brightness of the image, image brightness	Bildhelligkeit *f*; Bildleuchtdichte *f*	broadside antenna array, broadside array	Querstrahler *m*; Quergruppe *f*; Dipolgruppe *f* mit phasengleich geschalteten Elementen
brightness range	*s.* luminance range		
brightness temperature	*s.* radiation temperature		
brightness temperature	*s. a.* black-body temperature		
bright segment	klarer Schein *m*, helles Segment *n*		
bright spot of Poisson, Poisson['s] spot, Arago['s] spot	Poissonscher Fleck *m*, Aragoscher Fleck		
bright-up	*s.* brightening <of cathode-ray tube>		
brilliance, brilliancy	*s.* luminosity		
Brillouin doublet	Brillouinsches Dublett *n*, Brillouin-Dublett *n*		
Brillouin effect	Brillouin-Effekt *m*, Brillouinsches Phänomen *n*	Brocken bow (spectre), spectre of the Brocken	Brockengespenst *n*
Brillouin['s] function	Brillouinsche Funktion *f*, Brillouin-Funktion *f*	Brodhun['s] mirror apparatus	Spiegelapparat *m* [nach Brodhun]
Brillouin['s] paradox	Brillouinsches Paradoxon *n*	Brodhun photometer	Brodhunsches Sektorenphotometer (Photometer) *n*, Sektorphotometer *n* nach Brodhun
Brillouin scattering	Brillouin-Streuung *f*		
Brillouin zone	Brillouinsche Zone *f*, Brillouin-Zone *f*	Broglie['s] equation / de	*s.* Broglie relation / de
Brillouin zone boundary, zone boundary	Begrenzung *f* der Brillouinschen Zone	Broglie formula / de	*s.* Broglie relation / de
		Broglie frequency / de	De-Broglie-Frequenz *f*, de Brogliesche Frequenz
Brinell hardness, Brinell [hardness] number, BHN	Brinell-Härte *f*, Brinellsche Härte *f*, Härtezahl *f* nach Brinell, Kugeldruckhärte *f*, HB, H_B	Broglie pilot principle / de	de Brogliesches Pilotprinzip *n*, Prinzip *n* der Führungswelle

Broglie relation / de, de Broglie's equation (formula)	De-Broglie-Beziehung f	**bubble formation**	s. bubbling
Broglie wave / de	s. matter wave	**bubble gage <US>**	s. bubble gauge
Broglie wavelength / de, wavelength of the de Broglie wave[s]	De-Broglie-Wellenlänge f, de Brogliesche Wellenlänge f, Materiewellenlänge f	**bubble gauge, bubble gage <US>, bubble counter**	Gasblasen-Strömungsmesser m, Bläschengasometer n
broken line <math.>	Streckenzug m, Polygonzug m <Math.>	**bubble level**	s. level
broken line	s. a. dotted curve	**bubble model [of crystal]**	s. soap bubble model
broken symmetry	gebrochene Symmetrie f	**bubble nucleation**	s. bubbling
broken transit instrument, mirror transit instrument	Durchgangsinstrument n mit geknicktem Fernrohr	**bubble nucleus**, bubble centre	Blasenkeim m
brontograph	Brontograph m, Gewitterschreiber m	**bubble of turbulence**	s. element of turbulence
bronzing	s. toning	**bubble overvoltage**	Überspannung f durch Gasblasenbildung, Gasblasen-Überspannung f
Brouwer['s] fixed point theorem	Brouwerscher Fixpunktsatz m	**bubble plate**, bubble-cap plate	Glockenboden m
Brownian fluctuations	Brownsche Schwankungen fpl	**bubble-plate column, bubble-plate tower**, bubble-cap column, bubble-cap tower	Glockenbodenkolonne f
Brownian motion, Brownian movement, transient motion	Brownsche Bewegung f, Brownsche Molekularbewegung f	**bubble point**	„bubble point" m, Blasenbildungspunkt m
Brownian particle, brownon	Brownsches Teilchen n, Brownon n	**bubble pressure**	Blasendruck m
Brownian process, Wiener['s] process <math.>	Wienerscher Prozeß m, Wiener-Prozeß m <Math.>	**bubble quadrant**	Libellenquadrant m
		bubble raft	s. soap bubble model
Brownian rotation	Brownsche Drehschwingung (Rotationsbewegung) f	**bubble sextant**, aircraft sextant	Libellensextant m
		bubbling, bubble nucleation, bubble formation	Blasenbildung f, Bläschenbildung f
Browning spectrograph	Browningscher Spektralapparat m, Prismenspektrograph m nach Browning	**bubbling**, bubbling through	Durchperlen n, Sprudeln n
brownon	s. Brownian particle		
Bruce antenna	s. rhombic antenna	**bubbling**, sparging	Durchsprudeln n; Druckluftmischen n; pneumatisches Rühren n; Barbotage f
Brückner period	Brückner-Periode f		
Brueckner approximation	Brueckner-Näherung f		
bruising	s. crushing	**bubbling through**	s. bubbling
Brunauer, Emmett, and Teller adsorption equation	s. Brunauer-Emmett-Teller isotherm	**Buchmann-and-Meyer pattern**, Christmas-tree pattern	Buchmann-Meyer-Diagramm n
Brunauer-Emmett-Teller area	s. BET area	**Büchner filter, Büchner funnel**	Büchner-Trichter m, Schlitzsiebnutsche f
Brunauer-Emmett-Teller isotherm, B.E.T. isotherm, Brunauer, Emmett, and Teller adsorption equation	BET-Isotherme f	**bucket**, phase-stable bucket, phase stability region	stabiler Phasenbereich m, phasenstabiler Bereich m, Phasenstabilitätsbereich m, „bucket" n
		bucket wheel rotor	Schalenkreuz n
		bucking	s. compensation
Brunauer-Emmett-Teller method	s. B.E.T. method	**Buckingham-Corner potential**	Buckingham-Corner-Potential n
Bruns eikonal	Brunssches Eikonal n	**Buckingham model**	Buckingham-Modell n, Buckinghamsches Modell
brush	s. contact brush		
brush	s. isogyre	**Buckingham['s] pi theorem**	s. pi theorem
brush discharge, brushing discharge, bunch discharge, spray discharge, tree discharge	Büschelentladung f, Spritzentladung f; Spritzfeuer n	**Buckingham (exp-6) potential**	Buckingham(exp-6)-Potential n, Buckinghamsches (exp-6)-Potential n
brushing	s. corona	**bucking voltage**	s. compensating voltage
brushing discharge	s. brush discharge	**bucking voltage**	s. inverse voltage <el.>
brushing electrode, spraying electrode	Sprühelektrode f	**buckling**; flexural buckling; lateral buckling; kinking	Knickung f; Ausknickung f, seitliches Ausweichen n, seitliche Ausknickung f
brush light	Büschellicht n		
brush light arc	Büschellichtbogen m	**buckling** <of reactor>	Buckling n, Flußwölbung f <Reaktor>
Br value	s. magnetic rigidity	**buckling**	s. a. bending
B site, B position, octahedral site	Oktaederplatz m, oktaedrischer Lückenplatz m, Oktaederlücke f, B-Lage f, Oktaederzentrum n	**buckling**	s. a. warping
		buckling load	s. critical load of Euler
		buckling strength	s. cross breaking strength
B subgroup <in the periodic table>	Nebengruppe f <im Periodensystem>	**buckling stress**	Beulspannung f
		buckling test, crippling test	Knickversuch m
bubble cap	Bodenglocke f	**buckling vector**	Bucklingvektor m, Flußwölbungsvektor m
bubble-cap column	s. bubble-plate column		
bubble-cap plate	s. bubble plate	**Bucky, Bucky grid (screen)**	s. moving grid
bubble-cap tower	s. bubble-plate column	**Bucky rays**	s. grenz rays
bubble centre, bubble nucleus	Blasenkeim m	**Budde effect**	Budde-Effekt m
bubble chamber	Blasenkammer f, Glaser-Kammer f	**budget**, balance	Haushalt m
		buffer action, buffering	Puffer[wirk]ung f, Abpufferung f
bubble counter	s. bubble gauge	**buffer capacity**	Pufferkraft f
bubble density	Blasendichte f		
bubble domain, magnetic bubble cylindrical domain <magn.>	Magnetblase f, „Blasen"bereich m, zylinderförmiger Weissscher Bezirk m, Zylinderbereich m	**buffer circuit**, separation circuit	Pufferschaltung f, Trenn[ungs]kreis m, Pufferkreis m
		buffering	s. buffer action

buffer stage	s. intermediate stage	bulk moisture, volume moisture	Volum[en]feuchtigkeit f
buffet[ing] <aero.>	Schütteln n, Schüttelbewegung f	bulk phase	Volum[en]phase f
build-in arch	-hingeless arch	bulk photoconductivity	Volum[en]photoleitfähigkeit f
building an isomer	s. raising and lowering		
building-up principle	s. aufbauprinciple	bulk photo-electromotive force, bulk photo e.m.f.	Volum[en]-Photo-EMK f
building-up time	s. rise time <e.g. of pulse>		
build-up: transient oscillation	Einschwingen n	bulk photoemissive effect	s. volume photoemissive effect
build-up; synthesis <chem., nucl.>	Synthese f; Aufbau m <Chem., Kern.>	bulk photovoltaic effect, volume photovoltaic effect	Volum[en]sperrschichtphotoeffekt m
build up, build-up <radiobiology>	Zuwachs m, Aufbau m <Strahlenbiologie>	bulk potential, volume potential	Volum[en]potential n
build-up	s. a. increase		
build-up effect	Aufbaueffekt m	bulk radiator, volume radiator	Volum[en]strahler m
build-up factor	Zuwachsfaktor m, Aufbaufaktor m, Fano-Faktor m	bulk resistance, path resistance	Bahnwiderstand m
		bulk resistance of base, base bulk resistance	Basis-Bahnwiderstand m, Bahnwiderstand m der Basis
build-up time, transient time, transient period, transition time, rise time <of oscillation>	Einschwingzeit f, Einschwingdauer f, Einschwingungszeit f; Einstellzeit f; Anstiegszeit f; Aufbauzeit f; Beruhigungszeit f <Schwingung>	bulk resistance of collector, collector path resistance	Kollektor-Bahnwiderstand m, Bahnwiderstand m des Kollektors
		bulk resonance, volume resonance	Volum[en]resonanz f
		bulk scattering	Volum[en]streuung f
build-up time	s. a. rise time	bulk strain	s. volume strain
build-up time	s. a. rise time <e.g. of pulse>	bulk temperature, temperature of the bulk	Volum[en]temperatur f, Temperatur f im Innern (Volumen); mittlere Temperatur <bezogen auf Wärmemassenstrom>
built-in edge	eingespannter Rand m		
built-in microscope	Einbaumikroskop n		
built-in mounting	s. rigid fixing		
built-in reactivity, excess reactivity	Reaktivitätsreserve f; Überschußreaktivität f, eingebaute Reaktivität f		
bulb; swelling; bulge	Wulst m	bulk viscosity, volume viscosity, compressional viscosity, pressure viscosity, second viscosity	Volum[en]viskosität f, zweite Viskosität f, Kompressionsviskosität f, Kompressionszähigkeit f, Druckviskosität f, Kompressionsreibung f, Volum[en]reibung f, Volum[en]zähigkeit f
bulb barometer	s. cistern barometer		
bulge; swelling; bulb	Wulst m		
bulging, protrusion, convexity	Ausbauchung f; Ausbuchtung f; Ausbeulung f, Konvexität f		
		bulk volume	s. apparent volume
		bulk weight	s. apparent density
		bulk weight	s. weight per unit volume
		Bulygin number	Bulygin-Zahl f
bulging factor	Ausbauchungsfaktor m	bump <geo.>	Rundhöcker m, Rundbuckel m <Geo.>
bulk, bulk material	Schüttgut n, Schüttmasse f		
		bumpy air	s. choppy wind
bulk / in	s. loose	bunch, packet, pack[age] <e.g. of waves, particles>	Paket n, Verdichtung f, „bunch" m <z. B. von Wellen, Teilchen>
bulk absorption, volume absorption	Volum[en]absorption f		
bulk activity	Volum[en]aktivität f		
bulk boiling, nucleate boiling, nucleate bubbling	Blasenverdampfung f, Blasensieden n, Bläschensieden n	bunch discharge	s. brush discharge
		buncher <acc.>	Phasenbündelungsröhre f, Bündelungsröhre f, Buncher m; Bündelungsteilröhre f <Beschl.>
bulk coefficient of friction	s. second viscosity coefficient		
bulk concentration	s. concentration by volume		
bulk conductivity	Volum[en]leitfähigkeit f, elektrische Volumenleitfähigkeit f, Massenleitfähigkeit f	buncher, buncher space, input resonator <of the klystron>	Eingangs[hohl]resonator m, Eingangshohlraum m, Steuerraum m, Steuerkreis m, Steuerresonator m <Klystron>
bulk cross-section	s. total cross-section		
bulk crystallization, volume crystallization	Volum[en]kristallisation f	bunching, grouping [of electrons] <in the klystron>	Paketbildung f, Paket[is]ierung f, Phasenfokussierung f, Zusammenballung f, Ballung f, Bündelung f <der Elektronen im Klystron>
bulk current, volume current <el.>	Volum[en]strom m <El.>		
bulk density	s. apparent density		
bulk density	s. volume density		
bulk elasticity	s. compressibility <therm.>	bunching	s. a. phase grouping
bulk fluorescence, volume fluorescence	Volum[en]fluoreszenz f	bunching angle, transit angle; transit phase angle	Laufwinkel m, Laufzeitwinkel m
bulking	s. increase of volume	bunching region	s. drift space
bulk junction[-gate] field effect transistor	s. junction-gate field-effect transistor	bundle of inclined tubes	Schrägrohrbündel n
		bundle of optical fibres, fibre bundle	Fiberoptik f, Faseroptik f
bulk lifetime, volume lifetime	Volum[en]lebensdauer f	bundle of pipes	s. nest of pipes
		bundle of rays	s. beam of radiation
bulk magnetostriction	s. volume magnetostriction	bundle of rays parallel to each other	s. parallel beam
bulk material	s. bulk	bundle of rods	Stabbündel n
bulk modulus [of elasticity], volumetric modulus [of elasticity], compressibility (compression) modulus, modulus of compression (cubic compressibility, volume elasticity expansion, dilatation), volume elasticity <quantity>	Volum[en]elastizitätsmodul m, Volum[en]elastizität f, Kompressionsmodul m, Volum[en]kompressibilität f, Volum[en]dehnungsmodul m, Raumdehnungsmodul m, Raummodul m, Modul m der kubischen Ausdehnung <Größe>	bundle of tubes	s. nest of pipes
		bundle of water tubes, festoon	Siederohrbündel n
		Buniakowsky-Schwarz inequality	s. Schwarz['s] inequality
		Bunsen absorption coefficient	Bunsenscher Absorptionskoeffizient m

Bunsen burner	Bunsen-Brenner m, Blaubrenner m
Bunsen effusiometer	s. effusiometer
Bunsen ice calorimeter, ice calorimeter, cold calorimeter	Eiskalorimeter n [nach Bunsen], Bunsensches Eiskalorimeter, Bunsen-Kalorimeter n
Bunsen['s] law of effusion, effusion law of Bunsen	Bunsensches Ausströmungsgesetz n, Ausströmungsgesetz von Bunsen
Bunsen photometer, grease spot photometer	Fettfleckphotometer n [von Bunsen], Bunsen-Photometer n
Bunsen-Roscoe reciprocity law, law of reciprocity, reciprocity law	Bunsen-Roscoesches Gesetz (Reziprozitätsgesetz) n, Reziprozitätsgesetz [von Bunsen und Roscoe], Lichtmengengesetz n, Gesetz n von Bunsen und Roscoe
Bunsen-Schilling effusiometer	s. effusiometer
Bunsen screen	Bunsen-Photometerschirm m, Bunsen-Schirm m
Bunten barometer	Luftfalle f [nach Bunten]
buoyancy	s. hydrostatic buoyancy
buoyancy	s. a. lift <aero., hydr.>
buoyancy correction <in weighing>	Auftriebskorrektion f <beim Wägen>
buoyant (buoyant) force	s. lift <aero., hydr.>
buoyant lift	s. hydrostatic buoyancy <hydr.>
buoyant stability	s. isostatic equilibrium
buran	s. snow storm
burbling	s. stall <aero.>
burden <of organ or organism>	Strahlenbelastung f, Belastung f <Organ oder Körper>
Burger-Dorgelo-Ornstein [sum] rule <for atomic spectra>	Burger-Dorgeloscher Summensatz m, Burger-Dorgelo-Ornsteinsche Summenregel f
Burgers body	s. Burgers solid
Burgers circuit	Burgers-Umlauf m
Burgers dislocation	s. screw dislocation
Burgers material (solid), Burgers body, viscoelastic solid, viscoelastic material	Burgersscher Körper m, viskoelastischer Körper, viskoelastisches Material n, viskoelastische Substanz f
Burgers vector, characteristic (slip) vector	Burgers-Vektor m
burial ground, grave yard, dumping ground	[radioaktiver] Friedhof m, Vergrabungsstelle f, Abfallager n
burn, consumption, burning-up <e.g. of electrodes>	Abbrand m, Abbrennen n <z. B. von Elektroden>
burnable poison	[ab]brennbarer Absorber m
burner-type lamp	Verbrennungslampe f
burn-in <of screen>	Einbrennen n <Leuchtschirm>
burning of carbon [electrode], burn-up of carbon [electrode]	Kohleabbrand m, Abbrand m der Kohleelektrode
burning out, burn-out <of rocket stage>	Ausbrennen n <Raketenstufe>
burning point, burning temperature	Brennpunkt m, Brenntemperatur f
burning time	s. firing duration
burning up, burn-up	Ausbrennen n
burning-up	s. a. burn
burning velocity	s. velocity of combustion
burning velocity <US>	s. rate of flame propagation
burning voltage, running (operating, maintaining, working) voltage; arc-drop voltage; service voltage <of discharge, arc>	Brennspannung f, Betriebsspannung f; Arbeitsspannung f, Gebrauchsspannung f <Entladung, Bogen>
burn-out, cut-off <of the rocket>	Brennschluß m <infolge Treibstoffmangels> <Rakete>
burn-out	Durchbrennen n; Durchschmelzen n; Ausbrennen n
burn-out	s. a. burning out
burn-out altitude	Brennschlußhöhe f
burn-out point	Durchbrenntemperatur f, Durchbrennpunkt m
burn-out ratio	Sicherheitsfaktor m gegen Durchbrennen
burn-up <of fuel>	Abbrand m, Ausbrand m <Reaktor; in % oder MWd/t>
burn-up	s. a. burning up
burn-up fraction <in %>	relativer Abbrand m, Abbrandtiefe f <in %>
burn-up of carbon [electrode]	s. burning of carbon
burn-up time <nucl.>	Abbrandzeit f <Kern.>
burst, bursting <e.g. of canning>	Aufreißen n, Aufplatzen n, Platzen n <z. B. Hülle>
burst <of cosmic rays>	Ionisationsstoß m, Explosionsschauer m, Hoffmannscher Stoß m <kosmische Strahlung>
burst	s. a. radio burst
burst effect	„burst"-Effekt m, Bursteffekt m
Burstin effect	Burstin-Effekt m
bursting	s. burst <e.g. of canning>
bursting	s. rupture <mech.>
burst pulse corona [discharge], impulse corona	intermittierende Koronaentladung f, Stoß[impuls]korona f, Koronaentladung mit intermittierendem Charakter; einmaliger Koronadurchschlag m
Busemann biplane	Busemannscher Doppeldecker m
bushing; leading through, lead-through; lead-in; feed-through <el.>	Durchführung f <El.>
bushing transformer	Durchführungsstromwandler m, Durchführungswandler m
bushing transformer	Durchsteck[strom]wandler m
butterfly diagram	Schmetterlingsdiagramm n
butterfly diaphragm	Schmetterlingsblende f
butterfly phenomenon	Schmetterlingsphänomen n
buttress dam, hollow dam	Pfeilerstaumauer f, aufgelöste Staumauer f
Buys-Ballot['s] law, Buys Ballot['s] law of storms	Buys-Ballotsches Gesetz (Windgesetz) n, barisches Windgesetz, Windgesetz nach Buys-Ballot
buzz[ing] <of gyroscope>	Surren n <Kreisel>
by-pass <therm., el.>; subsidiary line <el.>	Nebenleitung f, Umgehungsleitung f, Um[führungs]leitung f, Umgehungsstrang m, Bypass m, Bypassleitung f
by-pass	s. a. shunt <el.>
by-pass capacitor	s. parallel capacitor
by-pass connection	Umgehungsschaltung f
by-pass filter	Umgehungsfilter n
by-reaction, side reaction	Nebenreaktion f

C

Cabannes-Daure effect	Cabannes-Daure-Effekt m
Cabannes factor	Cabannes-Faktor m
Cabibbo angle	Cabibbo-Winkel m
cabinet resonance	Gehäuseresonanz f
cable capacitance	Kabelkapazität f, Ladekapazität f des Kabels
cable reduction factor, cable-sheath protection factor	Kabelreduktionsfaktor m, Kabelmantelschutzfaktor m
cable-sheath loss, sheath loss	Mantelverlust m

cable-sheath

cable-sheath protection factor	s. cable reduction factor	calculated, cal.; theoretical, theor.	theoretisch, theor.; berechnet, ber.
cable-suspended current meter	Schwimmflügel m	calculated value	s. theoretical value
		calculation	s. evaluation <of dates>
cable theory [of excitation]	Kabeltheorie f [der Nervenleitung]	calculation for adjust for errors	s. calculus of observations
		calculation for the [mechanical] strength, strength calculation	Festigkeitsberechnung f
cable transit time	Kabellaufzeit f		
cabling	s. circuit wiring	calculation of ephemerides	Ephemeridenrechnung f
cadmium cell	s. cadmium photocell		
cadmium cell	s. cadmium normal cell	calculation of most probable values	s. calculus of observations
cadmium cell	s. Weston normal standard cell		
		calculator	s. desk calculating machine
cadmium cut-off, cadmium cut-off energy	Kadmiumgrenze f, Einfanggrenze f im Kadmium, Kadmium-Abschneideenergie f	calculus	s. infinitesimal calculus
		calculus of approximations, approximation calculus	Näherungsrechnung f
cadmium difference	Kadmiumdifferenz f	calculus of differences, calculus of finite differences	Differenzenrechnung f
cadmium neutron	Kadmiumneutron n, kadmisches Neutron n		
cadmium normal cell, cadmium cell	Kadmium-Normalelement n, Kadmiumelement n	calculus of observations, calculation for adjust for errors, computation of adjustment, compensation computation, calculation of most probable values, balancing calculation	Ausgleichungsrechnung f, Ausgleichsrechnung f
cadmium photocell, cadmium cell <opt.>	Kadmium-Photozelle f, Kadmiumzelle f <Opt.>		
cadmium ratio	Kadmiumverhältnis n		
		calculus of probabilities (probability)	s. probability theory
cadmium-selenide photoresistance cell, CdSe photoresistance cell	Kadmiumselenid-Widerstandszelle f, Kadmiumselenidzelle f, CdSe-Widerstandszelle f	calculus of residues	Residuenrechnung f, Residuenkalkül m, Residuenmethode f
cadmium standard cell	s. Weston normal standard cell	calculus of variations, variational calculus	Variationsrechnung f
cadmium-sulphide photoresistance cell, CdS photoresistance cell	Kadmiumsulfid-Widerstandszelle f, Kadmiumsulfidzelle f, CdS-Widerstandszelle f	Calderon['s] doubly refracting biplate, Calderon plate, calcite biplate [of Calderon]	Calderonsche Doppelplatte f, Calderonsche Halbschattenplatte f, Calcit-Doppelplatte f
		Caldonazzo flow	Caldonazzosche Strömung f
Cady['s] [absorption] method	Cadysche Absorptionsmethode f	calefaction	s. Leidenfrost['s] phenomenon
Cady['s] rule	Cadysche Regel f, Regel von Cady	calendar year	s. civil year
		calender effect	Kalandereffekt m
caesium-antimony photocell, Cs-Sb photocell	Zäsium-Antimon-Photozelle f, Zäsium-Antimon-Zelle f, Zäsium-Antimon-Vakuumzelle f, Cs-Sb-Photozelle f	C*-algebra, B*-algebra, completely regular Banach algebra	C*-Algebra f
		calibrated focal length, focal distance of photogrammetric lens, camera constant	Kammerkonstante f, Kamerakonstante f <Photogrammetrie>
caesium-chloride structure	Zäsiumchloridstruktur f		
caesium-oxygen photocell	Zäsiumoxid[photo]zelle f, Zäsiumoxidvakuumzelle f, Zäsium-Sauerstoff-Photozelle f, Zäsium-Sauerstoff-Zelle f	calibrating plot	s. calibration curve
		calibrating pulse generator	Eichimpulsgenerator m
		calibrating radiation source, calibrating source [of radiation]	s. standard source
cage dipole	Käfigdipol m		
cage effect	s. Frank-Rabinowitsch [cage] effect	calibration, gauging, graduation	Eichung f, Kalibrierung f; Einmessen n
cage rotor	s. squirrel-cage rotor		
Cailletet-Mathias law, [rectilinear diameter] law of Cailletet and Mathias, law of the rectilinear diameter	Cailletet-Mathiassche Regel f, Gesetz n der [geraden] Mittellinie, Regel vom geradlinigen Durchmesser, Cailletet-Mathiassches Gesetz	calibration apparatus	s. standard instrument
		calibration by comparison, comparison calibration	Vergleichseichung f
		calibration capacitor	s. standard capacitance
cake ice, pancake ice	Tellereis n, Pfannkucheneis n	calibration curve, calibration plot, calibrating plot	Eichkurve f
caking	s. sintering <of ceramics>		
cal	s. calorie	calibration factor, gauge factor	Eichfaktor m
Cal	s. kilo[-] calorie		
calandria, cooling coil	Schlangenkühler m	calibration frequency	s. standard frequency
		calibration instrument	s. standard instrument
calcareous spar	s. Iceland spar	calibration line, standard line; standard transmission line	Eichleitung f
calciothermic process, calciothermics; calciothermy	Calciothermie f, Kalziothermie f; kalziothermisches Verfahren n		
		calibration plot, diagram of reference	Eichdiagramm n, Bezugsdiagramm n
calcite biplate [of Calderon]	s. Calderon doubly refracting biplate	calibration plot	s. a. calibration curve
calcite CaCO₃	s. Iceland spar	calibration source	s. standard source
calcite interferometer	Kalkspatinterferometer n	californium, ₉₈Cf	Kalifornium n, Californium n, ₉₈Cf
calcium age	Kalziumalter n, geologisches Alter n nach der Kalziummethode	caliper[s]	s. vernier caliper
		call-counting meter	s. message register
calcium flocculi	Kalziumflocculi mpl	Callendar['s] equation	Callendarsche Gleichung f, Callendar-Gleichung f
calcium K line spectroheliogram	s. K spectroheliogram		
calcium method	Kalziummethode f, Kalium-Kalzium-Methode f	Callendar-Mollier equation [of state]	Callendar-Molliersche Zustandsgleichung f, Zustandsgleichung nach Callendar und Mollier
calcium parallax	Kalziumparallaxe f		

Callendar radio balance	*s.* radiation balance
Callier coefficient	Callier-Quotient *m*
Callier effect	Callier-Effekt *m*
calliper [gauge]	*s.* vernier caliper
call meter	*s.* message register
calm, ash breeze	Windstille *f*, Stille *f*, Kalme *f*, Flaute *f*
calm	*s. a.* magnetically quiet
calm arc, quiet arc	ruhig leuchtender Bogen *m*, ruhiger Bogen
calm belt	Kalmengürtel *m*
calm polar light, quiet polar light	ruhiges Polarlicht *n*, ruhige Polarlichtform *f*
calomel electrode, mercury-mercurous chloride electrode	Kalomelelektrode *f*
calorelectric effect [in flame plasma]	kalorelektrischer Effekt *m* [im Flammenplasma]
caloric	Kalorikum *n*, Wärmestoff *m*
caloric coefficient	kalorischer Koeffizient *m*
caloric equation of state, caloric state equation	kalorische Zustandsgleichung *f*
caloric power	*s.* heat output
caloric power	*s.* net calorific value
caloric quantity	kalorische Größe *f*
caloric radiation	*s.* heat radiation
caloric state equation	*s.* caloric equation of state
caloric theory	Wärmestofftheorie *f*
caloric unit	kalorische Einheit *f*
caloric unit	*s. a.* unit of heat
caloric value	*s.* net calorific value
calorie, cal <e.g. 4 °C calorie, 20 °C calorie>	Kalorie *f*, cal <z. B. 4-°C-Kalorie, 20-°C-Kalorie>
calorie unit	*s.* calorie
calorific capacity	*s.* heat capacity
calorific energy, thermal (heat) energy, thermal work, heat work, heat	Wärmeenergie *f*, thermische Energie (Arbeit) *f*, Wärmearbeit *f*, Wärme *f*
calorific power	*s.* heat output, net calorific value
calorific radiation	*s.* heat radiation
calorific value	*s.* net calorific value
calorimeter, calorimetric apparatus	Kalorimeter *n*, Wärme[mengen]messer *m*
calorimeter	*s. a.* sample container
calorimetering	*s.* calorimetry
calorimeter jacket, jacket of the calorimeter	Kalorimeterisolierung *f*, Isolierung *f* des Kalorimeters
calorimeter liquid	Kalorimeterflüssigkeit *f*
calorimetric apparatus, calorimeter	Kalorimeter *n*, Wärme[mengen]messer *m*
calorimetric bomb	*s.* Berthelot['s] calorimeter
calorimetric dosimetry	kalorimetrische Dosimetrie *f*
calorimetric measurement	kalorimetrische Messung *f*, Kalorimetermessung *f*
calorimetric power meter, calorimetric wattmeter	Kalorimeterleistungsmesser *m*, kalorimetrischer Leistungsmesser *m*, Kalorimeterwattmeter *n*, Leistungsmesser mit Wasserkalorimeter
calorimetry, heat measurement; calorimetering	Kalorimetrie *f*, Wärme[mengen]messung *f*; Kalorimetrieren *n*
calory	*s.* calorie
calutron separation	*s.* separation of isotopes by electromagnetic method
Calvet['s] calorimeter	Calvetsches Kalorimeter *n*
calving <of glacier>	Kalben *n* <Gletscher>
Calzecchi-Onesti effect	*s.* coherer effect
cam, cam disk	Kurvenscheibe *f*
cam <math.>	Kurvenkörper *m* <Math.>
camber	*s.* mean camber
camber	*s.* sag
camber changing flap, trailing-edge flap, flap <of airfoil>	Wölbungsklappe *f*, Klappe *f* <Tragflügel>
cam disk	Nockenscheibe *f*, Nocken *m*

cam disk, cam	Kurvenscheibe *f*
camera clara	*s.* camera lucida
camera constant	*s.* calibrated focal length
camera for electron diffraction, electron diffraction camera	Elektronenbeugungskamera *f*, Kamera *f* für Elektronenbeugungsaufnahmen
camera for X-rays	*s.* X-ray camera
camera lucida, camera clara	Camera *f* lucida, Camera *f* clara
camera microscope, microscope with built-in photomicrographic camera	Kameramikroskop *n*
camera obscura, pinhole camera	Lochkamera *f*, Portasche Kamera *f*, Camera *f* obscura
Cameron band	Cameron-Bande *f*
Campbell-Borrmann effect	*s.* Borrmann effect
Campbell-Freeth circuit	Campbell-Freeth-Schaltung *f*
Campbell-Stokes sunshine recorder	Sonnenscheinautograph *m* nach Campbell und Stokes
Campbell['s] theorem	Campbellsches Theorem *n*, Satz *m* von Campbell
can	*s.* fuel element can
Canada balsam	Kanadabalsam *m*
Canadian inch	*s.* inch
canal of Mars	Marskanal *m*
canal ray, positive ray	positiver Strahl *m*, Kanalstrahl *m*
canal-ray analysis	Kanalstrahlanalyse *f*
canal-ray discharge	Kanalstrahlentladung *f*
canal-ray-discharge ion source	Kanalstrahlionenquelle *f*
canal-ray-discharge tube, canal-ray tube	Kanalstrahlrohr *n*
canal-ray method, positive-ray method	Kanalstrahlmethode *f*
canal-ray particle	Kanalstrahlteilchen *n*, Kanalstrahl *m*
canal-ray tube	*s.* canal-ray-discharge tube
canal theory	Kanaltheorie *f*
canal vortex	Kanalwirbel *m*
canal wave	Kanalwelle *f*
cancellation, extinction, extinguishing <of radiation> <gen.>	Auslöschung *f*, Löschung *f*, Extinktion *f* <Strahlung>, Strahlungsvernichtung *f*, Strahlungsschwächung *f*, Strahlungsextinktion *f*, Strahlenschwächung *f*, Strahlenvernichtung *f*, Strahlenextinktion *f*
cancellation <math.>	Kürzen *n*, Kürzung *f*; Wegheben *n*, Wegkürzen *n* <Math.>
cancellation	*s. a.* compensation
candela, cd	Candela *f*, cd
candela per square meter, cd/m², nit, nt <opt.>	Candela *f* je Quadratmeter, cd/m², Nit *n*, nt <Opt.>
candle ice	*s.* needle ice
candle power	*s.* international candle power
candle power	*s.* luminous intensity
candoluminescence	Kandolumineszenz *f*
can material, canning material, canning	Hüllenwerkstoff *m*, Hüllenmaterial *n*
canned rotor	gekapselter Rotor *m*, gekapselter Läufer *m*
canning, cladding, jacketing <fuel elements>	Umhüllung *f*, Einhülsung *f*, Einhüllung *f*, Kapselung *f* <Brennelemente>
canning	*s. a.* encapsulating
canning	*s. a.* fuel element can
canning [material]	*s.* can material
canonical assembly, [macro]canonical ensemble	[makro]kanonische Gesamtheit *f*
canonical average	*s.* canonical mean
canonical co-ordinate	*s.* canonical variable
canonical correlation coefficient	kanonischer Korrelationskoeffizient *m*
canonical dissection	kanonische Zerschneidung *f*
canonical distribution	*s.* Gibbs['] distribution
canonical element	kanonisches Bahnelement *n*
canonical ensemble	*s.* canonical assembly
canonical equation of state	kanonische Zustandsgleichung *f*

canonical

canonical equations [of motion]	s. Hamilton['s] canonical equations	capacitance diode	s. varactor
canonical field theory	kanonische Feldtheorie f	capacitance-inductance bridge	Kapazitäts-Induktivitäts-Meßbrücke f
canonical form, Hamiltonian form	kanonische Gestalt (Form) f, Hamiltonsche Form (Gestalt)	capacitance meter, farad meter	Kapazitätsmesser m
canonically conjugate co-ordinate	s. canonically conjugate quantity	capacitance of interconnecting wires	Verbindungskapazität f
canonically conjugate momentum	kanonisch konjugierter Impuls m	capacitance of the human body, body capacitance	Körperkapazität f
		capacitance of the p-n junction	s. barrier-layer capacitance
		capacitance per unit length	Kapazitätsbelag m; kapazitiver Belag m
		capacitance standard	s. standard capacitance
canonically conjugate quantity; canonically conjugate variable; canonically conjugate co-ordinate	kanonisch konjugierte Variable f, konjugierte Variable; kanonisch konjugierte Koordinate f; kanonisch konjugierte Größe f, konjugierte Größe	capacitance strain gauge, capacity strain gauge	kapazitiver Dehnungsmeßstreifen (Dehnungsmesser) m
		capacitance transducer, capacitor transformer	kapazitiver Wandler (Spannungswandler) m, Kapazitätswandler m
		capacitance tube, capacitance valve	Kapazitanzröhre f
canonical mean, canonical average	kanonisches Mittel n	capacitance unbalance, capacity unbalance	Kapazitätsunsymmetrie f
canonical momentum	kanonischer Impuls m	capacitance valve, capacitance tube	Kapazitanzröhre f
canonical momentum density	kanonische Impulsdichte f	capacitance-voltage characteristic	Kapazitäts-Spannungs-Charakteristik f, Kapazitäts-Spannungs-Kennlinie f
canonical normal system	kanonisches Normalsystem n		
canonical transformation	kanonische Transformation (Abbildung) f	capacitive coupling, capacity (electric, electrostatic, condenser) coupling	kapazitive (elektrische, elektrostatische) Kopplung f; kapazitive Ankopplung f
canonical transformation group	kanonische Transformationsgruppe f		
canonical transformation of Mathieu	s. Mathieu transformation	capacitive current, capacitance (capacity) current	kapazitiver Strom m, Kapazitätsstrom m
canonical variable, canonical co-ordinate	kanonische Variable (Veränderliche, Koordinate) f, allgemeine Koordinate	capacitive divider	s. capacitive voltage divider
		capacitive drop <of voltage, in potential>	kapazitiver Spannungsabfall m
cantilever; cantilever beam; semi-beam, semi-girder, overhang, overhanging beam (end)	einseitig eingespannter Balken (Träger) m, freitragender Balken, Kragbalken m, Konsolbalken m, Freiträger m, Kragträger m, Konsolträger m; Ausleger m	capacitive electrostatic generator	s. capacitive generator
		capacitive gauge	s. capacitive transducer
		capacitive generator, capacitive electrostatic generator	kapazitiver [elektrostatischer] Generator m, Kapazitätsgenerator m
		capacitively loaded	kapazitiv belastet
canting, tilting over, overturn, upturning <geo.>	Überkippung f, Kippung f <Geo.>	capacitive manometer, capacitive pressure gauge	kapazitives Membranmanometer n
Cantor['s] diagonal process, diagonal process	Diagonalverfahren n, Cantorsches Diagonalverfahren n	capacitive potential divider	s. capacitive voltage divider
caoutchouc[-like] elasticity, entropy elasticity	Kautschukelastizität f, Entropieelastizität f	capacitive pressure gauge, capacitive manometer	kapazitives Membranmanometer n
cap	s. hood <techn.>	capacitive reactance, condensance, negative reactance	kapazitiver Blindwiderstand m, kapazitiver [elektrischer] Widerstand m, Kondensanz f, Kapazitanz f
cap	s. spherical cap <math.>		
capability of swelling	Quellbarkeit f, Quellfähigkeit f		
capable of luminescence	lumineszenzfähig	capacitive sender	s. capacitive transducer
		capacitive susceptance	s. condensive susceptance
		capacitive transducer; capacitive gauge; capacitive sender	kapazitiver Meßgeber m
capacitance, electric[al] capacitance, electric capacity, capacity; value of the capacitance <el.>	Kapazität f, elektrische Kapazität; Kapazitätswert m <El.>		
		capacitive voltage divider, capacitive [potential] divider, capacitor [voltage] divider	kapazitiver Spannungsteiler m
capacitance	s. a. condensive susceptance <el.>		
capacitance box	Kapazitätskasten m [für Meßzwecke]	capacitor, condenser <el.>	Kondensator m; Kapazität f <El.>
capacitance box with plugs, plug capacitance box	Stöpselkondensator m	capacitor bank	s. capacitor battery
		capacitor battery, battery of capacitors, cascade battery, capacitor bank	Kaskadenbatterie f, Kondensatorenbatterie f, Kondensatorbatterie f
capacitance bridge, farad bridge	Kapazitätsmeßbrücke f, Kapazitätsbrücke f		
		capacitor chain, capacitor line, condenser chain	Kondensatorkette f, Kondensatorleitung f
capacitance circuit	Stromkreis m mit Kapazität, Kapazitätskreis m	capacitor divider	s. capacitive voltage divider
		capacitor dosimeter, capacitor-type dosimeter	Kondensatordosismesser m, Kondensatordosimeter n
capacitance coefficient	s. coefficient of capacitance		
capacitance connected in series for pulling the resonance frequency of a crystal oscillator, pulling capacitance	Ziehkapazität f	capacitor electrometer, condenser meter	Kondensatorelektrometer n
		capacitor electrometer with Faraday cage	Becherelektrometer n, Kondensatorelektrometer n mit Faraday-Becher
capacitance current	s. capacitive current	capacitor field method, method of capacitor field	Kondensatorfeldmethode f
capacitance current	s. residual current		
capacitance decade [box]	s. decade capacitance box	capacitor for comparison	s. reference capacitor
		capacitor ignition	s. capacitor-type ignition

78

capacitor ionization chamber, capacitor-type ionization chamber	Kondensator[ionisations]- kammer f	capillary electrometer, Lippmann['s] capillary electrometer, Lippmann electrometer	[Lippmannsches] Kapillar- elektrometer n, Lipp- mannscher Spannungs- messer m, Spannungs- messer nach Lippmann
capacitor line	s. capacitor chain		
capacitor phase shifter	s. static phase advancer	capillary elevation	s. capillary rise
capacitor transformer	s. capacitance transducer	capillary energy	Kapillarenergie f
capacitor-type band accelerator, capacitor- type belt accelerator	Kondensatorbandgenerator m	capillary equilibrium	Kapillargleichgewicht n
		capillary flaw	s. hair-line
capacitor-type dosimeter	s. capacitor dosimeter	capillary force, capillaric force	Kapillarkraft f, Haar- [röhrchen]kraft f
capacitor-type ignition, capacitor-type start, capacitor ignition	Kippzündung f, Konden- satorzündung f	capillary-gravity wave	Kapillar-Schwerewelle f, Kapillarschwerewelle f
capacitor-type ioniza- tion chamber, capacitor ionization chamber	Kondensator[ionisations]- kammer f	capillary height [of ascent]	s. capillary rise
capacitor-type start	s. capacitor-type ignition	capillary-inactive, surface-inactive	oberflächeninaktiv, kapillarinaktiv
capacitor voltage divider	s. capacitive voltage divider		
capacitron	Kapazitron n	capillary layer	Kapillarschicht f
capacity, holding (cubic, volumetric, volume) capacity	Fassungsvermögen n, Aufnahmevermögen n, Aufnahmefähigkeit f	capillary-level oscilla- tion, level oscillation	Kapillarniveauschwingung f
		capillary method	Kapillarmethode f
capacity, power	Leistungsvermögen n, Kapazität f, Leistung f	capillary microscope, capillaroscope	Kapillarmikroskop n
capacity <e.g. of accumu- lator, in Ah> <el.chem.>	Kapazität f <z. B. Akkumu- lator, in Ah> <El.Chem.>	capillary microscopy, capillaroscopy	Kapillarmikroskopie f
capacity <of ion exchanger>	Kapazität f <Ionenaus- tauscher>	capillary osmosis	Kapillarosmose f
		capillary phenomenon	Kapillarerscheinung f, Kapillarphänomen n
capacity <num.math.>, word length	Wortlänge f <num. Math.>	capillary potential	kapillares Potential n
		capillary pressure	Kapillardruck m, Krüm- mungsdruck m, Normal- druck m der Oberflächen- spannung
capacity	s. a. capacitance <el.>		
capacity	s. a. volume		
capacity coupling	s. capacitive coupling		
capacity current	s. capacitive current	capillary rise, capillary height [of ascent], height of [capillary] rise, height of ascent, capillary eleva- tion, elevation	kapillare Steighöhe f, Steig- höhe [in der Kapillare], Kapillaranstieg m, Kapil- laraszension f, kapillare Hebung f, kapillare Erhebung f
capacity for heat	s. heat capacity		
capacity measure, measure of capacity; dry measure	Hohlmaß n; Raummaß n		
capacity of heat	s. heat capacity		
capacity of saturation	Sättigungsvermögen n	capillary rise method	Steighöhenmethode f
capacity strain gauge	s. capacitance strain gauge	capillary space	Kapillarraum m
capacity unbalance	s. capacitance unbalance	capillary stem correc- tion	s. thermometric correction
cap formation	Kappenbildung f		
capillaric force	s. capillary force	capillary structure	Kapillarstruktur f, adrige Struktur f
capillarity	Kapillarität f		
		capillary suction	kapillares Ansaugen n
capillarity correction, capillary correction	Kapillaritätskorrektion f, Kapillarkorrektion f	capillary supercon- ductivity	Kapillarsupraleitfähigkeit f
capillaroscope, capillary microscope	Kapillarmikroskop n	capillary tension	s. capillary constant
		capillary theory	Kapillaritätstheorie f
capillaroscopy, capillary microscopy	Kapillarmikroskopie f	capillary theory [of separation]	Kapillaritätstheorie f [der Gastrennung]
capillary, capillary tube	Kapillare f, Kapillarröhrchen n, Kapillarröhre f, Kapillarrohr n, Haar- röhrchen n, Haarröhre f	capillary tube	s. capillary
		capillary vessel	s. capillary <bio.>
		capillary viscometer, caplastometer	Kapillarviskosimeter n
capillary, capillary vessel <bio.>	Kapillare f, Kapillargefäß n, Haargefäß n <Bio.>	capillary water, interstitial water	Kapillarwasser n, Poren- wasser n
capillary action, capillary effect	Kapillarwirkung f	capillary waves, ripples; rippling, ripple, ruffle	Kapillarwellen fpl, Kräusel- wellen fpl, Rippel[wel- le]n fpl, Krauswellen fpl, Riffeln fpl; Kräuselung f
capillary-active	s. surface active		
capillary activity	s. surface activity		
capillary analysis	Kapillaranalyse f	capillary wire	s. Wollaston wire
capillary arc	Kapillarbogen m	capillator	Kapillator m
capillary-arc ion source, ion capillary-arc source, ion capillary-type source	Kapillarbogen-Ionenquelle f	caplastometer	s. capillary viscometer
		cap plasmolysis	Kappenplasmolyse f
		cap prominence	Kappenprotuberanz f
capillary attraction	Kapillarattraktion f, Kapil- laranziehung f, kapillare Hebung (Erhebung) f	cap rock	s. cover rock
		capture; trapping <of electrons>	Einfang m, Einfangen n
capillary condensation	Kapillarkondensation f	capture	s. a. attachment
capillary constant, spe- cific cohesion, Laplace['s] constant, capillary tension	Kapillarkonstante f, Kapillaritätskonstante f, Kapillarspannung f	capture channel	Einfangkanal m
		capture coefficient	Einfangfaktor m, Einfang- koeffizient m
capillary correction, capillarity correction	Kapillaritätskorrektion f, Kapillarkorrektion f	capture cross-section, cross-section for capture	Einfang[wirkungs]quer- schnitt m, Wirkungsquer- schnitt m für Einfang, Wirkungsquerschnitt m des Einfangs
capillary crack	s. hair-line		
capillary depression, meniscus depression	Kapillardepression f; kapillare Senkung f		
capillary effect, capillary action	Kapillarwirkung f	capture cross-section /1/v	$1/v$-Einfangquerschnitt m
		capture cross-section for thermal neutrons	s. thermal capture cross- section
capillary electrode	Kapillarelektrode f		

capture gamma radiation, capture gamma-rays, capture gammas, neutron capture gamma-rays	Einfang-Gamma-Quanten npl, Einfang-Gamma-Strahlung f, Gamma-Strahlung f beim (n,γ)-Prozeß	carbon-to-carbon bond (linkage)	Kohlenstoff-Kohlenstoff-Bindung f, C—C-Bindung f
capture mean free path, mean free path for capture	Einfangweglänge f, mittlere freie Einfangweglänge, mittlere freie Weglänge f für Einfang	carburation, carburetting, carburization	Karburieren n
		carburization, carburizing; cementation, carbonization <of steel>	Aufkohlung f, Einsetzen n; Zementierung f <Stahl>
		Carcel lamp	Carcel-Lampe f
capture of neutrons on a fast time scale	s. r process <astr.>	carcinotron, backward-wave tube	Carcinotron n, Rückwärtswellenröhre f, Karzinotron n
capture of neutrons on a slow time scale	s. s process	cardan	s. universal joint
		cardanic suspension	s. gimbal
capture probability	Einfangwahrscheinlichkeit f	cardan joint	s. universal joint
capture radiation	Einfangstrahlung f	Cardano['s] formula, Cardan['s] solution [of the cubic]	Cardanische Formel f, Cardanosche Formel
capture region, phase capture region	Phaseneinfangbereich m	Cardan['s] suspension	s. gimbal
capture resonance	Einfangresonanz f	cardiac output	s. minute volume
capture sphere, trapping sphere	Einfangkugel f	cardiac pacemaker	s. pacemaker
		cardiac work	Herzarbeit f
capture theory <of comets>	Einfangtheorie f <Kometenherkunft>	cardinal	s. power <math.>
		cardinal distance <opt.>	Kardinalstrecke f, Grundstrecke f <Opt.>
capture theory <of multiple stars ><astr.>	Theorie f des gegenseitigen Einfangens der Komponenten eines Mehrfachsternsystems, Einfangtheorie f <Astr.>	cardinal element <opt.>	Kardinalelement n, Grundelement n <Opt.>
		cardinality	s. power <math.>
		cardinal number	s. power <math.>
		cardinal point	Himmelsrichtung f, Himmelsgegend f, Weltgegend f; Haupthimmelsrichtung f
capture width, width for capture	Einfangbreite f		
carat, metric carat, carat metric, k, kk, c, karat	metrisches Karat n, Karat, k <= 200 mg>		
Carathéodory['s] axiom of inaccessibility, Carathéodory['s] principle	s. principle of inaccessibility	cardinal point <opt.>	Kardinalpunkt m, Grundpunkt m <Opt.>
		cardinal stimulus	Definitionsvalenz f
carat metric	s. metric carat	cardinal surface <opt.>	Kardinalfläche f, Grundfläche f <Opt.>
carbohydrate metabolism	Kohlenhydratstoffwechsel m	cardioid, cardioid curve, heart contour (shape, line)	Kardioide f, Herzkurve f, Herzlinie f
carbon arc	Kohlebogen m, Kohlelichtbogen m, Kohlenbogen m	cardioid characteristic	s. cardioid diagram
carbon arc lamp	s. lamp with solid carbons	cardioid condenser	Kardioidkondensor m
carbon chain	Kohlenstoffkette f	cardioid curve	s. cardioid
carbon cycle <bio.>	Kohlenstoffkreislauf m, Kohlenstoffzyklus m	cardioid diagram, cardioid characteristic	Nierencharakteristik f, Kardioidcharakteristik f, Kardioiddiagramm n, Kardioidkennlinie f
carbon cycle	s. a. carbon-nitrogen cycle		
carbon-dioxide ice	s. dry ice	cardioid method, cardioid technique	Herzkurvenmethode f
carbon fibre	Kohlenstoffaser f	card of the compass	s. compass card
carbon filament lamp	Kohlefadenlampe f	Carey-Foster bridge	Carey-[Foster-]Brücke f
		Carius tube	s. sealing tube
carbon-film resistor	Kohleschichtwiderstand m, Folienwiderstand m	Carlsbad law	Karlsbader Gesetz n
		Carlsbad twin	Karlsbader Zwilling m
		Carlson['s] [S_n] method	s. S_n method
		Carman equation	Carmansche Gleichung f
		Carnot['s] cycle, Carnot working cycle	Carnotscher Kreisprozeß (Prozeß) m, Carnot-Prozeß m
carbonification	Inkohlung f	Carnot engine, Carnot heat engine	Carnot-Maschine f
carbonization	Karbonisation f; Durchkohlung f; Kohlung f; Verkohlung f	Carnot['s] function of temperature	Carnotsche Temperaturfunktion f
		Carnot heat engine, Carnot engine	Carnot-Maschine f
carbonization	s. a. carburization		
carbon method	s radiocarbon dating	carnotization, carnotizing	Carnotisierung f
carbon-nitrogen cycle, nitrogen-carbon cycle, carbon cycle, Bethe cycle, Bethe-Weizsäcker cycle <nucl.>	Bethe-Weizsäcker-Zyklus m, Kohlenstoff-Stickstoff-Zyklus m, C-N-Zyklus m, Kohlenstoffzyklus m, Stickstoff-Kohlenstoff-Zyklus m, Kohlenstoff-Stickstoff-Kreislauf m, Stickstoff-Kohlenstoff-Kreislauf m <Kern.>	Carnot law, Carnot['s] theorem <therm.>	Carnotsches Prinzip (Theorem) n
		Carnot refrigerator	Carnotsche Kältemaschine f
		Carnot['s] theorem	Carnotsches Theorem n
		Carnot['s] theorem	s. a. Carnot law <therm.>
		Carnot transition	Carnotscher Stoß m
		Carnot working cycle	s. Carnot cycle
carbon-platinum shadow casting	Platin-Kohle-Simultanbedampfung f, Kohle-Platin-Schrägbedampfung f, Platin-Kohle-Schrägbeschattung f	Carpenter effect	Carpenter-Effekt m
		Carré['s] freezer	Carrésche Eismaschine f
		carrier, transfer agent	Träger m, Übertrager m, Überträger m
carbon replica	Kohleabdruck m	carrier, support <math.>	Träger m <Math.>
carbon resistance thermometer	Kohlewiderstandsthermometer n	carrier <radiochemistry>	Träger m <Radiochemie>
carbon resistor, cracked-carbon resistor	Kohlewiderstand m	carrier	s. a. charge carrier
		carrier	s. a. support
		carrier	s. a. carrier-wave frequency
		carrier addition	Trägerzusatz m
carbon sol; soot colloid[al solution]	Rußkolloid n	carrier analysis	Trägeranalyse f
carbon star, C star	Kohlenstoffstern m, C-Stern m	carrier avalanche, charge carrier avalanche	Trägerlawine f, Ladungsträgerlawine f

carrier break-through, charge carrier breakthrough — Trägerdurchbruch m, Ladungsträgerdurchbruch m
carrier compound — Trägerverbindung f
carrier concentration — s. charge carrier density
carrier current — Träger[frequenz]strom m, trägerfrequenter Strom m
carrier current — s. a. carrier flow
carrier density — s. charge carrier density
carrier depletion, charge carrier depletion — Trägerverarmung f, Ladungsträgerverarmung f; Trägerabreicherung f, Ladungsträgerabreicherung f
carrier deviation — Trägerversatz m

carrier distillation; carrier distillation method — Trägerdampfdestillation f; „carrier-distillation"-Methode f
carrier exchange diffusion — Trägeraustauschdiffusion f
carrier extraction, charge carrier extraction — Ladungsträgerextraktion f, Trägerextraktion f
carrier fading — Trägerschwund m
carrier flow, charge carrier flow, flow (stream) of charge carriers, [charge] carrier stream; [charge] carrier current — Trägerfluß m, Ladungsträgerfluß m, Trägerströmung f, Ladungsträgerströmung f; Trägerstrom m, Ladungsträgerstrom m
carrier fluid — s. carrier liquid
carrier-free — trägerfrei
carrier frequency — s. carrier-wave frequency
carrier frequency range, carrier range — Trägerfrequenzbereich m, Trägerbereich m
carrier gas — Schleppgas n, Trägergas n

carrier generation — s. charge carrier generation
carrier injection, charge carrier injection — Ladungsträgerinjektion f, Trägerinjektion f, Ladungsträgereinbau m, Trägereinbau m

carrier interval, carrier separation — Trägerabstand m, Trägerfrequenzabstand m

carrier jump, charge carrier jump — Trägersprung m, Ladungsträgersprung m
carrier liquid, liquid carrier; carrier fluid, fluid carrier — Trägerflüssigkeit f
carrier material — s. base material
carrier migration — s. charge carrier migration
carrier mobility, charge carrier mobility — Trägerbeweglichkeit f, Ladungsträgerbeweglichkeit f
carrier multiplication, charge carrier multiplication — Trägervervielfachung f, Ladungsträgervervielfachung f
carrier noise — Trägerrauschen n

carrier occupancy — s. carrier population
carrier oscillation — Trägerschwingung f
carrier pair generation — s. electron-hole pair generation
carrier phase — Trägerphase f
carrier population; carrier occupancy — Trägerbesetzung f, Ladungsträgerbesetzung f

carrier precipitation — Trägerfällung f

carrier production — s. charge carrier generation
carrier range, charge carrier range — Trägerreichweite f, Ladungsträgerreichweite f
carrier range, carrier frequency range — Trägerfrequenzbereich m, Trägerbereich m
carrier reinsertion, reinsertion of carrier — Trägerwellenzusatz m, Trägerzusatz m <El.>
carrier replenishment, charge carrier replenishment, replenishment of charge carriers, carrier supply, charge carrier supply, supply of charge carriers — Trägernachlieferung f, Ladungsträgernachlieferung f, Nachlieferung f von Ladungsträgern, Trägernachschub m, Ladungsträgernachschub m. Nachschub m von Ladungsträgern; Trägerauffüllung f, Ladungsträgerauffüllung f, Auffüllung f von Ladungsträgern

carrier residue — Trägerrest m
carrier rocket, carrier vehicle; launching booster (vehicle, rocket); satellite launcher — Trägerrakete f
carrier separation — s. carrier interval
carrier solution — Trägerlösung f

carrier spectrum, charge carrier spectrum — Trägerspektrum n, Ladungsträgerspektrum n
carrier stream — s. carrier flow
carrier supply — s. carrier replenishment
carrier-to-noise ratio — Träger-Rausch-Verhältnis n, Träger/Rausch-Verhältnis n

carrier transfer, carrier transport — Trägertransport m, Ladungsträgertransport m
carrier transmission — Trägerfrequenzübertragung f, trägerfrequente Übertragung f

carrier transport, carrier transfer — Trägertransport m, Ladungsträgertransport m
carrier trap, charge carrier trap — Trägerfalle f, Ladungsträgerfalle f
carrier trapping, charge carrier trapping — Trägerhaftung f, Ladungsträgerhaftung f; Trägereinfang m, Ladungsträgereinfang m

carrier vehicle — s. carrier rocket
carrier velocity, charge carrier velocity — Trägergeschwindigkeit f, Ladungsträgergeschwindigkeit f
carrier voltage — Trägerspannung f

carrier wave — Trägerwelle f
carrier-wave frequency, carrier frequency, carrier <el.> — Trägerfrequenz f, Träger m, Grundfrequenz f, TF <El.>
Carrington length — Carrington-Länge f
carrying a current — s. current-carrying
carrying-away, carrying off; dragging, drag; entrainment — Wegtransportieren n, Wegtragen n, Forttragen n; Mitführung f, Mitbewegung f, Mitnahme f; Mitschleppen n, Mitreißen n; Mitgehen n

carrying capacity, bearing capacity, bearing strength — Tragfähigkeit f, Tragkraft f

carrying off — s. carrying-away
carrying out, carrying through, making, accomplishment, execution, performance, implementation <e.g. of an experiment> — Durchführung f, Ausführung f <z. B. Experiment>, Versuchsausführung f, Versuchsdurchführung f
carrying[-]over — s. transfer
carrying through — s. carrying out
Carson['s] transformation — Carson-Transformation f
Cartan form — Cartansche Form f
Carte du Ciel, star map; astrographic chart — Sternkarte f, Himmelskarte f
Carter loop (stub) — Carter-Schleife f
Cartesian co-ordinates, Cartesian co-ordinate system, parallel co-ordinates; Cartesian system [of co-ordinates] — kartesische (cartesische) Koordinaten fpl, Parallelkoordinaten fpl; kartesisches (cartesisches) Koordinatensystem n
Cartesian devil, Cartesian diver, Cartesian imp — kartesischer (Cartesischer, Cartesianischer) Taucher m
Cartesian folium — s. Descartes['s] folium
Cartesian imp — s. Cartesian devil
Cartesian oval — Cartesisches Oval n

Cartesian surface, aplanatic surface — kartesische Fläche f, aplanatische Fläche
Cartesian system [of co-ordinates] — s. Cartesian co-ordinates
Cartesian vector — kartesischer Vektor m, Vektor im kartesischen Koordinatensystem

cartogram — Kartogramm n
cartographic projection — s. map projection
caryoplasm — Karyoplasma n
cascade, cascade shower, multiplication shower <nucl.> — Kaskadenschauer m, Kaskade f, Multiplikationsschauer m <Kern.>

cascade

cascade — *s. a.* gaseous diffusion cascade
cascade [/ in] — *s.* series connected
cascade accelerator — *s.* cascade generator
cascade action, cascade control (combination) — Kaskadenregelung *f*, Reihensteuerung *f*
cascade activation — Kaskadenaktivierung *f*
cascade amplifier — Kaskadenverstärker *m*, Stufenverstärker *m*
cascade battery — *s.* capacitor battery
cascade circuit — *s.* cascade connection <el.>
cascade combination, cascade action (control) — Kaskadenregelung *f*, Reihensteuerung *f*
cascade connected — *s.* series connected
cascade connection, connection in cascade <el., chem.>; cascade circuit <el.>; tandem connection <el.>; concatenation <chem.> — Kaskadenschaltung *f*, Schaltung *f* in Kaskade <El., Chem.>
cascade connexion — *s. a.* series connection
cascade control — *s.* cascade action
cascade decay — Kaskadenzerfall *m*
cascade demagnetization — Kaskadenentmagnetisierung *f*
cascade diffusion equation — Kaskaden[diffusions]gleichung *f*
cascade electron — Kaskadenelektron *n*
cascade emission — *s.* cascade radiation
cascade excitation — Kaskadenerregung *f*
cascade flow, flow past (through) cascade — Gitterströmung *f*, Gitte durchströmung *f*
cascade gamma-rays, successive gamma-rays — Kaskaden-Gamma-Strahlung *f*, Gamma-Quantenemission *f* in einer Kaskade
cascade generator, cascade accelerator, multiplier circuit electrostatic accelerator, voltage-multiplication-type generator, Cockcroft-Walton generator (apparatus, accelerator), Cockcroft and Walton generator, Cockcroft apparatus (generator, accelerator), Greinacher-Cockcroft-Walton generator; Greinacher-Cockcroft generator, Greinacher accelerator — Kaskadengenerator *m*, Kaskaden-Hochspannungsgenerator *m*, Kaskadenbeschleuniger *m*; Cockcroft-Walton-Generator *m*, Cockcroft-Walton-Kreis *m*, Kaskadengenerator nach Greinacher, Spannungsvervielfacher *m* nach Greinacher
cascade hyperon — *s.* Xi-hyperon
cascade image converter — Kaskadenbildwandler *m*
cascade luminescence — Kaskadenlumineszenz *f*
cascade method [of heterochromatic comparison], step-by-step method [of heterochromatic comparison] — Kleinstufenverfahren *n*
cascade model — Kaskadenmodell *n*
cascade of decimal counting units — Dekadenkette *f*
cascade of separating units — *s.* gaseous diffusion cascade
cascade particle — *s.* Xi-hyperon
cascade phosphor screen — *s.* cascade screen
cascade principle — Vervielfachungsprinzip *n*, Kaskadenprinzip *n*
cascade radiation, cascade emission — Kaskadenstrahlung *f*, Kaskadenemission *f*, Emission *f* in einer Kaskade
cascade screen, cascade phosphor screen — Kaskadenschirm *m*, Lumineszenzschirm *m* mit Kaskadenanregung, Leuchtstoffschichtenschirm *m*, Mehrschichten-Leuchtschirm *m*
cascade shower — *s.* cascade <nucl.>
cascade transformer — Kaskadenwandler *m*
cascade transition — Kaskadenübergang *m*, kaskadenartiger (sukzessiver) Übergang *m*
cascade tube, cascade X-ray tube — Kaskadenröntgenröhre *f*, Kaskadenröhre *f*
cascade unit, radiation length, radiation unit, Heitler unit — e-Wertstrecke *f*, Strahlungslänge *f*, Strahlungseinheit *f*, Kaskadeneinheit *f*, Heitlersche Einheit *f*, Heitler-Einheit *f*
cascade X-ray tube, cascade tube — Kaskadenröntgenröhre *f*, Kaskadenröhre *f*
cascading — Kaskadierung *f*
cascode, cascode amplifier — Kaskodenverstärker *m*, Kaskodeverstärker *m*
cascode stage — Kaskodestufe *f*, Kaskodenstufe *f*
case — *s.* housing
cased opal [glass] — *s.* flashed opal glass
case hardening — Einsatzhärtung *f*
Case['s] method — Casesche Methode *f*
Caserati-Weierstrass theorem — Satz *m* von Caserati-Weierstraß, Weierstraßscher Näherungssatz *m*
Casimir coefficient — Casimirscher Koeffizient *m*, Casimir-Koeffizient *m*
Casimir operator — Casimir-Operator *m*
casing — *s.* housing
cask <US>, casket — *s.* flask
Cassegrain antenna — Cassegrain-Antenne *f*
Cassegrain coudé system, Cassegrain coudé telescope — Cassegrain-Coudésystem *n*, Cassegrain-Coudé-teleskop *n*
Cassegrain focus — Cassegrain-Fokus *m*
Cassegrain reflecting telescope, Cassegrain reflector, Cassegrain telescope — Cassegrainsches Spiegelteleskop *n*, Spiegelteleskop nach Cassegrain, Cassegrain-Reflektor *m*
Cassinian curve (oval) — *s.* oval of Cassini
Cassini['s] division — Cassinische Teilung *f*, Cassini-Teilung *f*
cassinoid — *s.* oval of Cassini
cast, projection, throw <mech.> — Wurf *m*; Werfen *n* <Mech.>
cast — *s. a.* range of the projection
castellatus, towering, cas <meteo.> — castellatus, zinnenförmig, türmchenförmig, zinnenartig, cas <Meteo.>
castellatus — *s. a.* alto-cumulus castellatus
Castigliano['s] [first] theorem, theorem of Castigliano — Satz *m* von Castigliano, Castiglianoscher Satz
Castigliano['s] [second] theorem, theorem of Castigliano, theorem of minimum strain energy, theorem of least work — Castiglianosches Prinzip *n*, Minimalprinzip *n* für die Spannungen
casting crack — *s.* contraction crack
Castner-Kellner cell — *s.* rocking cell
cast-off vortex, starting (initial) vortex — Anfahrwirbel *m*
cast shadow — *s.* shadow
cast texture, texture of cast metal, texture resulting from casting — Gußtextur *f*
catabatic front — *s.* catafront
catabatic surface — *s.* surface of subsidence
catabolism, katabolism, dissimilation, disassimilation — Katabolismus *m*, Dissimilation *f*; Betriebsstoffwechsel *m*
catacaustic [line] — Katakaustik *f*, katoptrische Kaustik *f*, katakaustische Linie *f*
cataclase — Kataklase *f*, Gesteinszertrümmerung *f*
cataclastic structure — Kataklasgefüge *n*, kataklastische Struktur *f*
cataclysmic variable [star] — Eruptionsveränderlicher *m*
catacoustics — Echolehre *f*, Lehre *f* vom Echo, Katakustik *f*
catadioptric element — katadioptrisches [optisches] Element *n*
catadioptric lens, mirror-lens objective — katadioptrisches Objektiv *n*, Spiegellinsenobjektiv *n*

catadioptrics, science of reflection and refraction of light — Katadioptrik *f*, Lehre *f* von der Reflexion und Brechung des Lichtes
catadioptric system, lens-mirror system — Spiegellinsensystem *n*, Spiegellinse *f*, katadioptrisches System *n*
catadioptric telescope — katadioptrisches Fernrohr *n*, Spiegellinsenfernrohr *n*

catafactor — Kataindex *m*

catafront, catabatic front, katafront — Katafront *f*

catalator, ferment model — Katalator *m*, Fermentmodell *n*
catalogue of star brightness — Helligkeitskatalog *m*
catalogue of stellar parallaxes — Parallaxenkatalog *m*
catalogue of stellar spectra — Spektralkatalog *m*
catalogue of variable stars — Veränderlichenkatalog *m*
catalyst, catalyzer, catalytic agent — Katalysator *m*
catalyst — *s. a.* accelerator <chem.>
catalyst bed — Katalysatorbett *n*
catalyst deterioration — *s.* catalyst poisoning
catalyst poison — *s.* catalytic poison
catalyst poisoning, catalyst deterioration, poisoning (deterioration) of catalyst — Vergiftung *f* des Katalysators, Katalysatorvergiftung *f*
catalytic agent — *s.* catalyst
catalytic combustion, surface combustion, flameless combustion — katalytische Verbrennung *f*

catalytic exchange reaction — katalytische Austauschreaktion *f*
catalytic poison, catalyst (catalyzer) poison — Katalysatorgift *n*, Kontaktgift *n*
catalyzer — *s.* catalyst
catalyzer poison — *s.* catalytic poison
cataphoretic mobility — kataphoretische Beweglichkeit *f*
catapoint — Katapunkt *m*, katakaustischer Punkt *m*
catarometer — *s.* catharometer
catarometry — *s.* catharometry
catastrophic absorption [of cosmic rays] — Absorption *f* der kosmischen Strahlung unter Bildung von Mesonenschauern
catastrophic degradation — Alterung *f* mittels übergroßer Stromstöße

catastrophic theory, doctrine of catastrophe[s] <geo.> — Kataklysmentheorie *f*, Katastrophentheorie *f*
catastrophic transition — Katastrophenübergang *m*, direkter Photomesonenübergang *m*

catathermometer, katathermometer, Kata-thermometer — Katathermometer *n* [nach Hill]
catatonosis — Katatonose *f*
catavothre — *s.* ponor
catcher <of klystron> — Auskoppelraum *m* <Klystron>

catchment [area] — *s.* drainage area
catelectrotonus — Katelektrotonus *m*
catenary, catenary curve, funicular curve (line) — Kettenlinie *f*, Seilkurve *f*, Katenoide *f*; Segelkurve *f*
catenoid — Katenoid *n*, Kettenfläche *f*

catenoidal horn — Kettenlinienhorn *n*, kettenlinienförmiges Horn *n*, Kettenflächenhorn *n*, Katenoidhorn *n*, Katenoidtrichter *m*

cathamplifier — *s.* cathode follower
catharometer, catarometer, katharometer — Kat[h]arometer *n*, Wärmeleitfähigkeitsmesser *m*, Wärmeleitfähigkeits[meß]gerät *n*

catharometric cell, katharometric cell — Wärmeleitfähigkeitsmeßzelle *f*
catharometry, catarometry, katharometry — Kat[h]arometrie *f*, Wärmeleitfähigkeitsmessung *f*
cathetometer, comparator — Kathetometer *n*
cathode amplifier — *s.* cathode follower
cathode beam — *s.* electron beam
cathode bias — Katodenvorspannung *f*

cathode border, cathode edge — Katodensaum *m*
cathode compartment, cathode region — Katodenraum *m*, Katodengebiet *n*

cathode contamination, cathode poisoning, poisoning of cathode — Katodenvergiftung *f*, Vergiftung *f* der Katode
cathode-coupled circuit — *s.* cathode follower
cathode-coupled multivibrator — katodengekoppelter Multivibrator *m*, Multivibrator mit Katodenkopplung
cathode current density — Katodenstromdichte *f*
cathode cylinder — *s.* cylindrical cathode
cathode dark space — Katodendunkelraum *m*

cathode deposit — Katodenniederschlag *m*
cathode disintegration — *s.* cathode sputtering
cathode drop — *s.* cathode fall
cathode edge — *s.* cathode border
cathode edge of the negative glow, glowing seam — Glimmsaum *m*

cathode emissivity — *s.* emissivity of cathode
cathode fall, cathode drop <US> — Katodenfall *m*, Katodenspannungsabfall *m*
cathode fall region, cathode fall zone, region of cathode fall, zone of cathode fall — Katodenfallraum *m*, Katodenfallgebiet *n*

cathode feedback — Katodenrückkopplung *f*

cathode follower, cathode follower circuit, cathode-coupled circuit, grounded anode amplifier — Katodenverstärker *m*, Katodenfolger *m*, Katodenfolgeschaltung *f*, Anodenbasisschaltung *f*, Anodenbasisverstärker *m*, Anodenbasisstufe *f*, Katodenkopplung *f*, Katodynschaltung *f*

cathode glow, cathode light, blue glow — Katodenglimmlicht *n*, Katodenlicht *n*, Katodenglühen *n*

cathode grid, space-charge grid, control grid — Raumladegitter *n*, Raumladungs[zerstreuungs]gitter *n*
cathode hum — Katodenrauschen *n*

cathode layer — Katodenschicht *f*
cathode layer effect — Katodenschichteffekt *m*, Katodenschichtwirkung *f*
cathode light — *s.* cathode glow
cathode liquor, catholyte — Katolyt *m*, Katholyt *m*, Katodenflüssigkeit *f*
cathode luminescence — *s.* cathodoluminescence
cathode of the rieseliconoscope — Rieselkatode *f*
cathode poisoning — *s.* cathode contamination
cathode ray — *s.* electron beam
cathode ray accelerator — *s.* electron accelerator
cathode-ray display of direction finder — *s.* display of direction finder
cathode-ray oscillograph (oscilloscope), electron oscillograph (oscilloscope) — Elektronenstrahloszillograph *m*, Katodenstrahloszillograph *m*
cathode ray pencil — *s.* electron beam

cathode-ray tube, electron-beam tube, thermionic tube (valve), beam deflection tube, Braun tube, electron-ray tube	Elektronenstrahlröhre f, Katodenstrahlröhre f, Katodenstrahlrohr n, Braunsche Röhre f, Braunsches Rohr n	cat's eye diaphragm	Katzenaugenblende f, Aubert-Blende f
		cat's eye photometer	Katzenaugenphotometer n, Danjon-Photometer n
cathode-ray tube display, electronic image; electronique picture	Elektronenbild n	Cauchy['s] boundary condition	Cauchysche Randbedingung f
cathode-ray tube for flying-spot scanner, pick-up tube	Abtaströhre f [für Lichtpunktabtaster]	Cauchy condition, Cauchy['s] condition for convergence, Cauchy['s] [convergence] theorem, Cauchy['s] test for convergence	Cauchysche Bedingung f, Cauchy-Bedingung f, [allgemeines] Cauchysches Konvergenzkriterium n, Cauchysches (allgemeines) Konvergenzprinzip n
cathode region	s. cathode compartment		
cathode saturation current, saturation current of cathode	Katodensättigungsstrom m, Katodenergiebigkeit f		
cathode sputtering, cathodic sputtering (evaporation), cathodic (cathode) disintegration	Katodenzerstäubung f	Cauchy['s] convergence criterion (test)	s. Cauchy['s] nth root test
		Cauchy['s] convergence test of the second kind	s. Cauchy['s] ratio test
cathodic chronaxy	katodische Chronaxie f	Cauchy['s] convergence theorem	s. Cauchy condition
cathodic disintegration	s. cathode sputtering	Cauchy-convergent sequence	s. Cauchy sequence
cathodic etching	katodische Ätzung f	Cauchy data	s. initial data
cathodic evaporation	s. cathode sputtering	Cauchy['s] deformation tensor	Cauchyscher Deformationstensor m
cathodic excitation	katodische Reizung f <Bio.>		
cathodic flame	s. negative flame	Cauchy['s] dispersion formula	Cauchysche Dispersionsformel f
cathodic jump of potential	Katodensprung m		
cathodic reduction, electrolytic reduction	elektrolytische (kathodische) Reduktion f	Cauchy distribution, Cauchy frequency distribution	Cauchysche Verteilung f, Cauchy-Verteilung f
cathodic sputtering	s. cathode sputtering		
cathodoluminescence	Katodolumineszenz f	Cauchy['s] ellipsoid of polarization	Cauchysches Polarisationsellipsoid n
cathodophosphorescence	Katodophosphoreszenz f		
		Cauchy-Euler equation	s. Cauchy-Lagrange equation
		Cauchy frequency distribution	s. Cauchy distribution
catholyte, cathode liquor, catolyte	Kat[h]olyt m, Katodenflüssigkeit f	Cauchy-Hadamard formula (theorem)	Satz m von Cauchy-Hadamard, Cauchy-Hadamardsche Formel f <für den Konvergenzradius>
cation electrode	Kationenelektrode f		
cation exchange, base exchange	Kationenaustausch m, Basenaustausch m; Kationenumtausch m <im Boden>	Cauchy integral	Cauchysches Integral n
		Cauchy['s] integral convergence test	s. Cauchy['s] integral test
cation exchange capacity, CEC, sorption capacity	T-Wert m, Austauschkapazität f, Kationenaustauschkapazität f, Sorptionskapazität f	Cauchy['s] integral formula	Cauchysche Integralformel f, Integralformel von Cauchy
		Cauchy['s] integral test [for convergence], Maclaurin-Cauchy test, Cauchy['s] integral convergence test <math.>	Integralkriterium n [für Konvergenz] <Math.>
cation exchanger, cationite	Kationenaustauscher m, Kationit m		
cationic acid	Kationsäure f		
cationic agent, cationic detergent	kationaktiver Stoff m	Cauchy['s] integral theorem	s. Cauchy['s] theorem
cationic base	Kationbase f	Cauchy kernel	Cauchyscher Kern m
cationic conduction	Kationenleitung f	Cauchy law of similarity	Cauchysches Ähnlichkeitsgesetz n
cationic conductivity	Kationenleitfähigkeit f		
cationic conductor	Kationenleiter m	Cauchy['s] mean value formula	s. second mean value theorem of the differential calculus
cationic defect conduction	Kationenmangelleitung f, Kationendefektleitung f		
cationic detergent, cationic agent	kationaktiver Stoff m	Cauchy['s] nth root test, root test, Cauchy['s] convergence test, Cauchy['s] radical test for convergence, Cauchy['s] convergence criterion	Wurzelkriterium n, Cauchysches Konvergenzkriterium, zweites Cauchysches Konvergenzkriterium n
cationic excess (surplus) conduction	Kationenüberschußleitung f		
cationite	s. cation exchanger		
cation mobility	Kationenbeweglichkeit f		
cationoid	s. electrophilic	Cauchy['s] number, Cauchy similarity number, C	Cauchy-Zahl f, Cauchysche Zahl (Kennzahl, Ähnlichkeitskennzahl) f, C
cationoid addition	elektrophile (kationoide) Addition f		
cationoid rearrangement	s. electrophilic rearrangement		
cationoid substitution, electrophilic substitution	elektrophile (kationoide) Substitution f	Cauchy['s] principal value, principal value of the integral	Cauchyscher Hauptwert m, Hauptwert [des Integrals]
cationoid transposition	s. electrophilic rearrangement	Cauchy problem	s. initial-value problem
		Cauchy product	Cauchy-Produkt n <von Reihen>, Cauchysches Produkt n, Cauchysche Produktreihe f
cationotropic	kationotrop		
cationotropy	Kationotropie f, Tautomerie f mit Platzwechsel des Kations		
		Cauchy['s] radical test for convergence	s. Cauchy['s] nth root test
cation site	Kationenplatz m, Kationenstelle f	Cauchy['s] ratio test, ratio test, generalized ratio test, d'Alembert['s] ratio test, d'Alembert['s] test [for convergence], Cauchy['s] convergence test of the second kind	[Cauchysches] Quotientenkriterium n, erstes Cauchysches Konvergenzkriterium n, d'Alembertsches Konvergenzkriterium (Kriterium) n
cation transference (transport) number	s. transport number of the cation		
cation vacancy	s. positive ion vacancy		
catiophile	s. Lewis base		
catisallobar, katisallobar	Katisallobare f		
catolyte	s. catholyte		
catopter	s. reflecting surface	Cauchy['s] residue theorem, theorem of residues, residue theorem	Residuensatz m
catoptric, anacamptic	katoptrisch, Reflexions-		
catoptric lens	s. catoptric objective		
catoptric objective, catoptric lens, mirror objective, mirror lens	Spiegelobjektiv n, katoptrisches Objektiv (Mikroskopobjektiv) n, Reflexionsobjektiv n	Cauchy-Riemann conditions, Cauchy-Riemann [differential] equations, Riemann relations	Cauchy-Riemannsche Differentialgleichungen (Gleichungen, partielle Differentialgleichungen) fpl
catoptrics, anacamptics, science of light reflection	Katoptrik f, Lehre f von der Reflexion des Lichtes		

Cauchy-Schwarz inequality	s. Schwarz['s] inequality
Cauchy sequence, Cauchy-convergent sequence, fundamental sequence	Cauchy-Folge *f*, Fundamentalfolge *f*
Cauchy similarity number	s. Cauchy['s] number
Cauchy['s] stress tensor	Cauchyscher Spannungstensor *m*
Cauchy['s] test for convergence	s. Cauchy condition
Cauchy['s] theorem, Cauchy['s] integral theorem	Cauchyscher Integralsatz *m*, Integralsatz von Cauchy, Hauptsatz *m* der Funktionentheorie
Cauchy['s] theorem	s. a. Cauchy condition
caudad acceleration	Beschleunigung *f* in Richtung Kopf-Beine
Cauer filter	Cauer-Filter *n*
Cauer['s] reactance theorem	[Cauersches] Vierpolreaktanztheorem *n*, Cauersches Reaktanztheorem *n* [für Vierpole], Reaktanztheorem von Cauer [für Vierpole]
cauliflower	s. congestus
causal connection, causal nexus	Kausalbeziehung *f*, kausaler Zusammenhang *m*, Kausalzusammenhang *m*, Kausalnexus *m*
causal Green's function	kausale Ausbreitungsfunktion (Greensche Funktion)
causality condition	Kausalitätsbedingung *f*
causality principle	s. principle of causality
causality violation, violation of causality	Kausalitätsverletzung *f*, Verletzung *f* der Kausalität
causal nexus	s. causal connection
causal principle	s. principle of causality
cause and effect	Ursache *f* und Wirkung *f*
cause-and-effect relationship	Ursache-Wirkung[s]-Beziehung *f*
cause variable	s. regressor
causing; effecting; inducing, induction; production	Verursachen *n*, Bewirken *n*, Bedingen *n*, Hervorrufen *n*; Auslösung *f*; Erzeugung *f*
caustic, caustic line	Kaustik[linie] *f*, kaustische Linie *f*
caustic	s. caustic surface
caustic embrittlement	Laugensprödigkeit *f*, Laugenbrüchigkeit *f*
causticity	Kaustizität *f*
caustic line	s. caustic
caustic surface, caustic	Kaustik[fläche] *f*, kaustische Fläche *f*
Cavalieri['s] theorem	Cavalieri-Prinzip *n*, Cavalierisches Prinzip *n*
cavalier perspective	Kavalierperspektive *f*, frei-isometrische Perspektive (Parallelperspektive) *f*
cave, solution cavity <geo.>	Karsthöhle *f* <Geo.>
Cavendish['s] torsion balance	Cavendishsche Drehwaage *f*, Drehwaage von Cavendish
cave water	Höhlenwasser *n*
cave water	Karstwasser *n*
caving	s. cavitation
caving bank	Prallhang *m*
caving-in	s. breakdown <geo.>
cavitating flow, cavity flow	Kavitationsströmung
cavitation, cavity formation; caving	Kavitation[sbildung] *f*, Hohlraumbildung *f*, Hohlsog *m*, Kavitieren *n*
cavitation bubble; cavity	Kavitationsblase *f*; Kavitationshohlraum *m*
cavitation centre, cavitation nucleus	Kavitationskeim *m*
cavitation damage	Kavitationsschaden *m*, Kavitationszerstörung *f*
cavitation effect	s. cavitation phenomenon
cavitation erosion, erosion due to cavitation	Kavitationserosion *f*, Kavitationsangriff *m*
cavitation induced by ultrasonics, cavitation produced by ultrasonics, acoustic (supersonic) cavitation	Kavitation *f* durch Schallwellen, Ultraschallkavitation *f*
cavitation nucleus	s. cavitation centre
cavitation number, cavitation parameter	Kavitationszahl *f*, Kavitationsparameter *m*
cavitation phenomenon, effect of cavitation, cavitation effect	Kavitationserscheinung *f*
cavitation produced by ultrasonics	s. cavitation induced by ultrasonics
cavitation shock	Kavitationsstoß *m*
cavitation shock wave	Kavitationsstoßwelle *f*
cavitation threshold	Kavitationsschwelle *f*
cavitation tunnel, water tunnel	Kavitationsprüfstand *m*
cavity, hollow	Hohlraum *m*, Höhlung *f*, Kavität *f*; Hohlstelle *f*
cavity; cavitation bubble	Kavitationsblase *f*; Kavitationshohlraum *m*
cavity <as a material defect>, flaw	Hohlraum *m*, Kaverne *f*
cavity, druse cavity <geo.>	Drusenraum *m* <Geo.>
cavity	s. a. resonant cavity
cavity absorbent	Hohlraumabsorber *m*, Hohlraum-Schallabsorber
cavity band-pass filter	Hohlraumbandpaß *m*
cavity cathode, concave cathode	Hohlraumkatode *f*, Hohlspiegelkatode *f*, konkave Katode *f*
cavity chamber	s. cavity ionization chamber
cavity coefficient	s. void coefficient
cavity collapse	Blasenimplosion *f*, Blaseneinsturz *m*, Einsturz *m* der Flüssigkeitshohlräume
cavity drag	Kavitätswiderstand *m*
cavity field <introduced by Onsager>	Hohlraumfeld *n* <von Onsager>
cavity flow, cavitating flow	Kavitationsströmung *f*
cavity formation	s. cavitation
cavity frequency meter	s. cavity wavemeter
cavity ionization	Hohlraumionisation *f*
cavity ionization chamber, cavity chamber	Hohlraumionisationskammer *f*, Hohlraumkammer *f*
cavity magnetron	s. magnetron
cavity maser	s. resonant-cavity maser
cavity pressure	Hohlraumdruck *m*
cavity radiation	s. black-body radiation
cavity resonance	Hohlraumresonanz *f*
cavity resonator, resonator, resonance chamber	Hohl[raum]resonator *m*, Resonator *m*; Hohlraumkreis *m*, Hohl[rohr]kreis *m*
cavity resonator	s. a. resonant cavity
cavity resonator wavemeter	s. cavity wavemeter
cavity-type parametric amplifier, resonant-cavity parametric amplifier	parametrischer Verstärker *m* mit Hohlraumresonator
cavity vibration	Hohlraumschwingung *f*
cavity wavemeter, resonant cavity wavemeter (frequency meter), cavity resonator wavemeter, cavity frequency meter	Hohlraumfrequenzmesser *m*, Hohlraumwellenmesser *m*
Cayley-Hamilton theorem, Hamilton-Cayley theorem	Cayley-Hamiltonscher Satz *m*, Satz von Cayley-Hamilton
Cayley-Klein parameters	Cayley-Kleinsche Parameter *mpl*
Cayley number, Cayley['s] octave <math.>	Cayley-Zahl *f*, [Cayleysche] Oktave *f* <Math.>
Cayley parameter	Cayleyscher Parameter *m*, Parameter von Cayley-Euler-Gauß
Cayley['s] table	s. multiplication table
Cayley transformation	Cayley-Transformation *f*

C band <4.0 – 5.6 or 4.9 – 7.05 Gc/s>	C-Band n <4,0 ··· 5,6 oder 4,9 ··· 7,05 GHz>
C-bias	s. grid-bias voltage
cee [electrode], C-shaped electrode <in the Berkeley proton synchrotron>	C-Elektrode f, Cee n, C-förmig gebogenes Rohr n
ceiling	Gipfelhöhe f, Deckenhöhe f
ceiling	s. a. cloud height
ceiling light projector	s. cloud ceilometer
ceiling of the atmosphere, top of the atmosphere	Atmosphärengipfel m, Grenze f der Erdatmosphäre, Atmosphärengrenze f
ceiling shower	Deckenschauer m
ceilometer	s. cloud ceilometer
cel = 1 cm/s	Cel n, cel = 1 cm/s
celestial body	Himmelskörper m
celestial equator	Himmelsäquator m
celestial guidance, stellar guidance	Astrolenkung f
celestial horizon, true (geocentric) horizon	wahrer Horizont m, geozentrischer Horizont
celestial latitude	s. ecliptic[al] latitude <astr.>
celestial latitude and longitude	s. ecliptic[al] co-ordinates
celestial longitude	s. ecliptic[al] longitude
celestial-mechanical	himmelsmechanisch
celestial mechanics	Himmelsmechanik f
celestial meridian	Himmelsmeridian m, Deklinationskreis m
celestial north pole	nördlicher Himmelspol m, Nordpol m des Himmels, Himmelsnordpol m
celestial south pole	südlicher Himmelspol m, Südpol m des Himmels, Himmelssüdpol m
celestial sphere, sphere <astr.>	Himmelskugel f, Himmelssphäre f, Sphäre f <Astr.>
cell <for isotope separation>	Trenngruppe f <Isotopentrennung>
cell; cubicle; element; cellule <of wing>	Zelle f
cell	s. a. voltaic cell
cell cavity, cell space <bio.>	Zell[en]hohlraum m, Zellraum m <Bio.>
cell colloid	Zellkolloid n
cell constant	Zellkonstante f, Widerstandskapazität f
cell division, division; fission [of cell] <bio.>	Zellteilung f, Teilung f [der Zelle] <Bio.>
cell division rate	s. division rate
cell dose	Zell[en]dosis f
cell electromotive force	s. electromotive force of the cell
cell elongation <bio.>	Zellstreckung f <Bio.>
cell frequency, subclass number	Klassenbesetzung f
cell membrane, membrane of the cell	Zellmembran f; Plasmamembran f
cell metabolism	Zellstoffwechsel m, Zellmetabolismus m
cell model	s. lattice-cell theory
cell nucleus	s. nucleus <bio.>
cell of high-pressure area, cell of the High	Hochdruckzelle f
cell permeability	Zellpermeabilität f
cell physiology, cellular physiology	Zellphysiologie f
cell polarity <bio.>	Zellpolarität f <Bio.>
cell population	Zellpopulation f
cell reaction	Zellenreaktion f
cell respiration	Zellatmung f
cell sap, vacuolar sap	Zellsaft m
cell size <in nuclear emulsion>	Zellenlänge f, Zellengröße f <Kernspuremulsion>
cell space	s. cell cavity <bio.>
cell structure	s. cellular structure
cell theory	s. lattice-cell theory
cellular circulation	zelluläre Zirkulation f, Zellularzirkulation f
cellular convection	zelluläre Konvektion f
cellular filter	Zellenfilter n
cellular grid	Wabenblende f
cellular method	Methode f der Elementarzellen, Zellenmethode f
cellular method	s. a. Wigner-Seitz method
cellular mirror [of Ritchey]	Zellenspiegel m [nach Ritchey], Ritchey-Spiegel m
cellular network, grid (reticular) structure, gridwork	Netzstruktur f, Netzverband m, Netzwerk n
cellular physiology, cell physiology	Zellphysiologie f
cellular radiobiology	zelluläre Radiobiologie f
cellular rotary filter	Zellendrehfilter n
cellular structure, cell structure	Zellenstruktur f, zellulare (zelluläre) Struktur f, Zellen[auf]bau m
cellular theory	Zellulartheorie f
cellular tissue	Zell[en]gewebe n
cellular vortex	zellularer Wirbel m
cellule	s. cell <of wing>
cell voltage	s. electromotive force of the cell
cell wall	Zellwand f, Zellenwand f
cell with a coil outside the vessel <of high-frequency titrator>	Induktionszelle f, Meßzelle f im Spulenkern
cell with metallic plates <of high-frequency titrator>	Kapazitätszelle f, Meßzelle zwischen Kondensatorbelegungen
Celsius scale, centigrade scale, centesimal temperature scale	Celsius-Skala f, Celsius-Skale f, Zentigradskala f, zentesimale Temperaturskala f
cementation	s. carburization
cementing of lenses	Verkittung f von Linsen
censored distribution	zensierte Verteilung f
cent <unit of reactivity or in phonometry>	Cent n, cent <Einheit der Reaktivität und in der Phonometrie>
centennial precession, secular precession	säkulare Präzession f, Säkularpräzession f
centesimal angular minute	s. centesimal minute
centesimal angular second	s. centesimal second
centesimal balance, centesimal weighing machine	Zentesimalwaage f
centesimal circle graduation, centesimal division (graduation)	s. centesimal system
centesimal minute [of angle], centesimal angular minute, c, min	Neuminute f, Zentigon n, c
centesimal second [of angle], centesimal angular second, cc, sec	Neusekunde f, cc
centesimal system, centesimal division [of angle], centesimal [circle] graduation	Neugradteilung f, neue Teilung f, Zentesimalteilung f
centesimal temperature scale	s. Celsius scale
centesimal weighing machine, centesimal balance	Zentesimalwaage f
centi..., c	Zenti..., c
centigrade, degree centigrade, degree Celsius, °C	Grad m Celsius, Celsius-Grad m, Zentigrad m, °C
centigrade scale	s. Celsius scale
centigrade temperature	Celsius-Temperatur f
centigrade thermometer	Celsius-Thermometer n
centile	s. percentile
centimetre-gramme-second-biot system	s. c.g.s.b. system
centimetre-gramme-second-franklin system	s. c.g.s.f. system
centimetre-gramme-second system	s. c.g.s. system
centimetre wave, superhigh frequency wave, S.H.F. wave <1–10 cm>	Zentimeterwelle f <1 ··· 10 cm>
centimetre wavelength [range]	s. superhigh frequency range

centinormal, hundredth-normal, 0.01 N, N/100 — hundertstelnormal, zentinormal, 0,01 n, n/100

centinormal solution, hundredth-normal solution, 0.01 N solution — Hundertstelnormallösung f, 0,01 n Lösung f

central; centric[al] — zentral; zentrisch, Mittelpunkts-, mit Mittelpunkt <Math.>

central anticyclone — Zentralhoch n, zentrales Hochdruckgebiet n

central anticyclonic situation — Zentralhochlage f

central axis [of inertia] — zentrale Trägheitsachse f

central body <mech., astr.> — Zentralkörper m <Mech., Astr.>

central collision — s. central impact
central conic — Mittelpunktskegelschnitt m

central curve — Mittelpunktskurve f, zentrische Kurve f

central definition — Zentralschärfe f

central density [of stellar interior] — Zentraldichte f, Mittelpunktsdichte f, zentrale Dichte f

central depression — zentrale Depression f, Stammbecken n

central difference quotient — zentraler Differenzenquotient m

central distance, central separation — Zentraldistanz f

central ellipse — Zentralellipse f
central ellipsoid [of inertia] — Zentralellipsoid n, Trägheitsellipsoid n für den Massenmittelpunkt

central ellipsoid — s. a. ellipsoid of gyration
central eruption, Strombolian eruption — Zentraleruption f, Schloteruption f

Central[-] European time, Middle[-] European time, C.E.T., CET — Mitteleuropäische Zeit f, MEZ

central eye, middle-eye, Cyclopean eye — imaginäres Deckauge n, Mittelauge n, Zyklopenauge n, sensorisches Doppelauge n

central field approximation — Zentralfeldnäherung f

central force — Zentralkraft f
central force field — Zentralkraftfeld n, Zentralkräftefeld n

central gap — zentrale Lücke f, Zentrallücke f

central gas stream — Kerngas n
central impact, central (head-on) collision — zentraler (gerader) Stoß m, Zentralstoß m

centralizer; commutant — Zentralisator m; Kommutant m

central limit theorem — zentraler Grenzwertsatz m

central line <of the spectrum> — Zentrallinie f [des Spektrums]
central line — s. a. elastic axis <elasticity>
central mirror — s. corner cube
central moment, moment about the mean — zentrales Moment n, Zentralmoment n
central moment of inertia — zentrales Trägheitsmoment n

central peak — Zentralberg m
central perspective — s. perspective
central perspective / in — s. perspective
central-point triangulation — Zentralpunkttriangulation f
central potential, potential of central forces — Zentralpotential n, zentrales Potential n, Potential der Zentralkräfte

central principal axis [of inertia] — zentrale Haupttrageheitsachse f
central principal moment of inertia — zentrales Haupttrageheitsmoment n

central projection — s. perspective
central projection / in — s. perspective
central quadric — Mittelpunktsquadrik f

central ray, axial ray <opt.> — Zentralstrahl m, Achsenstrahl m
central ray — Mittel[punkts]strahl m
central separation — s. central distance
central spot <cryst.> — Primärstrahlfleck m <Krist.>
central star, nucleus of the planetary nebula — Zentralstern m [des planetarischen Nebels]
central surface — Mittelpunktsfläche f, zentrische Fläche f
central surface — s. a. evolute surface
central symmetry — Zentralsymmetrie f, Punktsymmetrie f

central zero instrument, centre-zero instrument, zero centre meter — Gerät n mit zentralem Nullpunkt, Instrument n mit zentralem Nullpunkt

centre, vortex point <of differential equation> — Wirbelpunkt m <Differentialgleichung>
centre, centre of force (the field) — Kraftzentrum n, Zentrum n [der Kraft]
centre — s. a. focus
centre — s. a. focus <geo., meteo.>
centre — s. a. luminescence centre
centre — s. a. base point <series of points>

centre condition — Mittelpunktsbedingung f <Sternmodell>
centred affine group — zentroaffine (zentrierte affine) Gruppe f
centred collinear transformation — s. centred homographic transformation
centred compressional wave — zentrierte Verdichtungswelle f
centred expansion fan — s. Prandtl-Meyer flow
centred homographic transformation, centred collinear transformation, centred transformation — zentrierte kollineare Abbildung (Transformation) f, zentrierte Abbildung (Transformation)

centred rarefactional wave — zentrierte Verdünnungswelle f
centred structure, centric structure — zentrische Struktur f
centred transformation — s. centred homographic transformation

centre feed — s. apex drive
centre frequency, midfrequency <for frequency modulation> — Mittelfrequenz f, Mittenfrequenz f <Frequenzmodulation>
centre head, [self-]centring head — Zentrierkopf m
centre-limb variation — s. centre-to-limb variation
centre line, line of centres <of the force system> — Zentrallinie f [des Kräftesystems]

centre line <math.>, line of centres — Zentrale f <Math.>

centre line — s. a. median
centre line average height, CLA — Mittenrauhigkeit f, Mittenrauhwert m
centre line of the bar (beam; column; rod), axis of the bar (rod; column; beam) — Stabachse f, Stabmittellinie f; Balkenachse f, Balkenmittellinie f
centre of activity, solar centre of activity — Aktivitätszentrum n
centre of aerophotogram — Bildmittelpunkt m, Mittelpunkt m <Luftmeßbild>
centre of area — s. centroid
centre of attraction — s. attractive centre
centre of buoyancy, centre of the displaced fluid, centre of gravity of liquid displaced by a floating body — Auftriebszentrum n, Auftriebsmittelpunkt m, Auftriebsschwerpunkt m, Schwerpunkt m des verdrängten Flüssigkeitsvolumens, Schwerpunkt der verdrängten Flüssigkeitsmenge, Verdrängungsschwerpunkt m, Formschwerpunkt m

centre of compression and twist, centre of twist, neutral point, centre of twist and elastic compression — Zentrum n der Kompression und Drehung, Zentrum der Torsion und elastischen Kompression, Drillmittelpunkt m, Torsionsmittelpunkt m

centre of crystallization — s. nucleus of crystal
centre of curvature — Krümmungsmittelpunkt m <Kurve, Fläche>; Hauptkrümmungsmittelpunkt m <Fläche>

centre of curvature surface	s. evolute surface	centre of the displaced fluid	s. centre of buoyancy
centre of cyclonic pressure	s. cyclonic centre	centre of the field, centre [of force]	Kraftzentrum n, Zentrum n [der Kraft]
centre of dilatation	Dilatationszentrum n	centre of the stream cross-section	s. stream cross-section centre
centre of dislocation	s. a. dislocation kernel		
centre of dispersion, virtual focus	Zerstreuungspunkt m, virtueller Brennpunkt m	centre of the wave, wave centre, origin of the wave	Wellenzentrum n
centre of emission	s. emission centre	centre of thrust	s. thrust centre
centre of explosion	s. explosion centre	centre of twist [and elastic compression]	s. centre of compression and twist
centre of force	s. centre		
centre of gravity	Gravitationszentrum n, Schwerezentrum n, Schwerkraftzentrum n	centre of vision	s. centre of perspectivity
		centre of volume, centre of mass of a volume	Volum[en]schwerpunkt m, Volum[en]mittelpunkt m
centre of gravity	s. a. centre of mass	centre of vorticity	Wirbeltopf m
centre of gravity of an area	s. centroid		
centre of gravity of liquid displaced by a floating body	s. centre of buoyancy	centre of water-line section	s. water-line centre
		centre point	s. neutral point
centre-of-gravity system <nucl.>, centre-of-mass [co-ordinate] system, centre-of-inertia system	Massenmittelpunktssystem n, Schwerpunkt[s]system n, S-System n, Massenzentrumsystem n <Kern.>	centre tap [connection]	s. centre tapping
		centre-tapped coil	Stromteiler m
		centre tapping, centre tap [connection]	Mittelanzapfung f, Mittelabgriff m
centre of gyration	s. centre of rotation		
centre of high pressure [area]	s. anticyclonic centre	centre-to-centre distance (spacing)	Mittenabstand m, Mittelpunktsabstand m
centre of inertia	s. centre of mass	centre-to-limb variation, centre-limb variation	Mitte-Rand-Variation f
centre-of-inertia system	s. centre-of-mass system		
centre of inflexions <mech.>	Wendepol m <Mech.>	centre triangulation	Mittelpunkttriangulation f, Bildmittelpunkttriangulation f
centre of instantaneous accelerations	s. instantaneous centre of accelerations		
centre of instantaneous velocities	s. instantaneous centre of velocities	centre-zero instrument	s. central zero instrument
		centric[al]	s. central
centre of inversion	Inversionszentrum n	centric structure, centred structure	zentrische Struktur f
centre of low-pressure [area]	s. cyclonic centre	centrifugal; axifugal	zentrifugal
centre of mass, mass (inertia) centre, centre of inertia, centre of gravity, barycentre	Massenmittelpunkt m, Schwerpunkt m, Trägheitsmittelpunkt m	centrifugal acceleration	Zentrifugalbeschleunigung f
		centrifugal action	s. centrifuging operation
		centrifugal barrier	Zentrifugalbarriere f, Zentrifugalschwelle f
centre-of-mass co-ordinate system	s. centre-of-mass system	centrifugal distortion	Zentrifugalverzerrung f, Zentrifugalabplattung f
centre-of-mass frame	s. barycentric co-ordinates	centrifugal fault	s. overfault <geo.>
centre-of-mass integral	s. mass centre integral	centrifugal field	Zentrifugalkraftfeld n
centre-of-mass law	s. centre-of-mass theorem		
centre of mass of a volume	s. centre of volume	centrifugal flyball	s. centrifugal governor
		centrifugal force, force of transport	Zentrifugalkraft f, Fliehkraft f, Schleuderkraft f
centre-of-mass system, centre-of-mass co-ordinate system, centre-of-inertia system, centre-of-gravity system <nucl.>	Massenmittelpunktsystem n, Schwerpunkt[s]system n, S-System n, Massenzentrumsystem n <Kern.>	centrifugal friction governor	Zentrifugalreibungsregulator m
		centrifugal governor, centrifugal flyball, ball governor, centrifugal regulator	Fliehkraftregler m, Zentrifugalregler m, Zentrifugalregulator m, Schwungkugelregler m
centre-of-mass system [of co-ordinates]	s. barycentric co-ordinates	centrifugal moment	s. product of inertia
centre-of-mass theorem, centre-of-mass law, theorem of centre of mass, fundamental theorem <rel.>	Schwerpunktsatz m, Satz m vom Massenmittelpunkt, Impulssatz m <Rel.>	centrifugal pendulum	Zentrifugalpendel n, Fliehpendel n
		centrifugal potential	Zentrifugalpotential n, Fliehpotential n
		centrifugal pump	s. rotodynamic pump
		centrifugal regulator	s. centrifugal governor
		centrifugal stretching	Zentrifugalaufweitung f, Zentrifugaldehnung f
		centrifugation	s. centrifuging operation
centre-of-mass velocity	s. barycentric velocity	centrifuge, centrifuge separator	Zentrifuge f, Zentrifugiergerät n, Schleuder f, Trennschleuder f, Trennzentrifuge f
centre of oscillation	Schwingungsmittelpunkt m		
centre of percussion <mech.>	Stoßzentrum n, Perkussionszentrum n <Mech.>		
centre of perspectivity, eye position, centre of projection, centre of vision	Perspektivitätszentrum n, Auge n, Augenpunkt m, Blickzentrum n, Projektionszentrum n	centrifuge microscope	Zentrifugenmikroskop n
		centrifuge separator	s. centrifuge
		centrifuging	s. centrifuging operation
		centrifuging operation, centrifuging, centrifugal action, centrifugation	Zentrifugierung f, Trennung f mit der Zentrifuge, Schleuderarbeit f, Ausschleuderung f, Separierung f
centre of pressure, metacentre	Metazentrum n		
centre of pressure <elast.>	Druck[mittel]punkt m, Druckzentrum n <Elast.>		
centre of pressure	s. a. aerodynamic centre	centring diaphragm	Zentrierblende f
centre of projection	s. centre of perspectivity	centring head, centre head, self-centring head	Zentrierkopf m
centre of repulsion, repulsive centre	abstoßendes Zentrum n, Abstoßungszentrum n	centring lathe	s. centring machine <opt.>
centre of ripening	s. sensitivity speck	centring lens with ruled cross	Zentrierglas n, Objektträger m mit Strichkreuz
centre of rotation, rotation centre, centre of gyration, gyration centre, pivot [point], swivel point	Drehpol m, Drehpunkt m, Drehzentrum n, Rotationspol m, Rotationszentrum n, Pol m, Gyrationszentrum n	centring machine	Zentrierapparat m
		centring machine, centring lathe <opt.>	Zentriermaschine f <Opt.>
centre of suspension	Aufhängemittelpunkt m		
centre of symmetry, symmetry[-]centre, symmetry of inversion	Symmetriezentrum n	centring microscope	Zentriermikroskop n

centring rod	Stablot n, starres Lot n, Lotstab m, Zentrierstab m, Zentrierstock m	certain event, certainty	sicheres Ereignis n
centring telescope	Zentrierfernrohr n [nach Fraunhofer]	certainty cessation cestral tube	s. certain event s. chain stopping <chem.> Kestralröhre f, Kegelstrahlröhre f
centring thread	Schnurlot n	c.g.s.b. system [of units], centimetre-grammesecond-biot system	CGSBi-System n, Zentimeter-Gramm-Sekunde-Biot-System n
centriole	Zentralkörperchen n, Zentriol n	c.g.s.e.m.u. system	s. electromagnetic system of units
centripetal, axipetal	zentripetal	c.g.s.e.s.u. system	s. electrostatic system of units
centripetal [component of] acceleration centripetal fault centripetal force centrobaric rule centroclinal	s. normal acceleration s. tension fault <geo.> Zentripetalkraft f s. Guldin's rule zentroklinal	c.g.s.f. system [of units], centimetre-grammesecond-franklin system c.g.s. system [of units], C.G.S. system [of units], CGS-system [of units], centimetre-gramme-second system, absolute system of units, physical system of units	CGSFr-System n, Zentimeter-Gramm-Sekunde-Franklin-System n CGS-System n, cgs-System n, CGS-Maßsystem n, Zentimeter-Gramm-Sekunde-System n, absolutes [wissenschaftliches] Einheitensystem n, physikalisches Einheitensystem
centrode, poid	Momentanzentrenkurve f, Wälzbahn f, Zentrode f, Mittelpunktsbahn f		
centroid <of an area>, centre of [gravity of an] area	Flächenmittelpunkt m, Flächenschwerpunkt m		
centroid axis, axis of gravity, gravity axis	Schwerlinie f, Schwerpunkt[s]achse f, Schwerachse f, [raumfeste] Impulsachse f	c.g.s. unit chad <= 1 neutron/cm² or = 10¹² neutrons/cm² s>	s. absolute unit Chad n, chad <= 1 Neutr./cm² oder = 10¹² Neutr./cm² s>
centroid method <stat.> centroid ray	Schwerpunktmethode f Schwerstrahl m	Chadwick-Goldhaber effect chafing chain chain balance	Chadwick-Goldhaber-Effekt m s. fretting corrosion s. collision chain Kettenwaage f
centrosurface centrosymmetric	s. evolute of surface zentralsymmetrisch, punktsymmetrisch		
centrosymmetric class	s. holohedry of the triclinic system	chain branching, branching of chain chain carrier, chain propagator chain combustion	Kettenverzweigung f Kettenträger m, kettentragendes Radikal n s. chain-reaction-propagating combustion
centurial year cepheid cepheid parallax <parallax determined from period-luminosity relation of variable star>	Säkularjahr n s. Delta Cepheid-type star Veränderlichenparallaxe f		
		chain decay chain determinant chain disintegration, chain decay, series decay (disintegration)	s. chain disintegration s. iterative determinant Kettenzerfall m, Kettenumwandlung f
cepheid variable [star] ceramet ceramic capacitor, ceramicon	s. Delta Cepheid-type star s. cermet keramischer Kondensator m, Keramikkondensator m		
		chain-dotted line chain element chain ending chain explosion chain fissions chain fission yield	s. dot-and-dash curve s. chain segment s. chain stopping Kettenexplosion f s. fission chain reaction Gesamtspaltproduktausbeute f, Gesamtspaltausbeute f
ceramic fuel, ceramic fuel material ceramic-metal tube, metal-ceramic tube ceramicon ceramic-to-metal seal ceraunograph	keramischer Brennstoff m, Keramikbrennstoff m Metall-Keramik-Röhre f s. ceramic capacitor s. metal-ceramic seal Ceraunograph m		
		chain growth, chain propagation, chain propagation reaction, propagation reaction	Kettenwachstum n, Kettenwachstumsreaktion f, Wachstumsreaktion f, Kettenfortpflanzung[s-reaktion] f, Fortpflanzungsreaktion f
Čerenkov chamber Čerenkov counter, Čerenkov detector Čerenkov effect, Vavilov-Čerenkov (Cherenkov, Tcherenkov) effect Čerenkov electron	Čerenkov-Kammer f Čerenkov-Zähler m, Čerenkov-Detektor m Čerenkov-Effekt m, [Wawilow-]Tscherenkow-Effekt m Čerenkov-Elektron n		
		chain initiation, initiation [of chain], initiating the chain; chain starting, starting of the chain <chem.> chain interruption chain isomerism	Ketteninitiierung f, Initiierung f, Ketteninduzierung f; Kettenstart m, Kettenstartreaktion f s. chain stopping <chem.> Kettenisomerie f
Čerenkov light	Čerenkov-Licht n		
Čerenkov loss	Čerenkov-Verlust m	chain lightning, bead lightning chain matrix chain molecule chain of acting elements	Perlschnurblitz m s. iterative matrix Kettenmolekül n Wirkungskette f
Čerenkov radiation, Čerenkov rays	Čerenkov-Strahlung f, Wawilow-Tscherenkow-Strahlung f		
cerimetric analysis, cerimetry cerium[-activated] glass	Zerimetrie f, Cerimetrie f Ce-aktiviertes (zeraktiviertes) Glas n	chain of amplifiers chain of auditory ossicles chain of collisions chain of primary valencies, primary valence chain chain of valencies, bond (valence) chain chain process, chain reaction	s. amplifier cascade Gehörknöchelchenkette f, Gehörknöchelchenreihe f s. collision chain Hauptvalenzkette f Valenzkette f, Bindungskette f Kettenreaktion f, Kettenprozeß m
cermet, ceramet, metal-ceramic mixture	Cermet n, metallkeramischer (keramometallischer) Werkstoff m, Metall-Nichtmetall-Sinterwerkstoff m, Keramik-Metall-Gemisch n, Keramometall n, Metallkeramik f; Sinterwerkstoff m		
		chain propagation [reaction] chain propagator	s. chain growth s. chain carrier

chain

chain pulley	Kettenrolle f	change of phase <astr.>	Phasenwechsel m <Astr.>
chain-reacting amount (mass)	s. crit <nucl.>	change of second order	s. second order transition
chain-reacting pile, critical reactor <nucl.>	kritischer Reaktor m <Kern.>	change of shape	s. non-dilatational strain
		change of sign	s. reversal of sign
chain-reacting pile	s. a. reactor <nucl.>	change of state, change in state (phase); change of (in) aggregation state	Zustandsänderung f; Änderung f des Aggregatzustandes
chain-reacting sphere, critical sphere	kritische Kugel f		
chain reaction, chain process	Kettenreaktion f, Kettenprozeß m	change of stratification	Umschichtung f
chain reaction	s. a. nuclear chain reaction		
chain-reaction-propagating combustion, chain combustion	Kettenverbrennung f, Diffusionsverbrennung f	change of the variable, substitution of the variable	Substitution f der Variablen, Einführung f einer neuen Veränderlichen, Variablensubstitution f, Variablentransformation f
chain rule	s. conjoined rule of three		
chain segment	s. link of chain		
chain starting	s. chain initiation	change of the wind, wind shift	Winddrehung f; Änderung f der Windrichtung, Wind[richtungs]änderung f
chain stopper, [chain] terminator	Kettenbrecher m		
chain stopping, chain termination, termination [of the chain], chain ending (interruption), interruption of chain, cessation <chem.>	Kettenabbruch m, Kettenabbruchreaktion f, Kettenbruch m <Chem.>	change of tide	s. turn of tide
		change of variables, transformation of variables, variable transformation <bio., stat.>	Variablentransformation f <Bio., Stat.>
chain stopping (termination) factor	Kettenabbruchfaktor m	changeover contact	s. two-way contact
		changeover frequency	s. switching frequency
chain terminator, chain stopper	Kettenbrecher m	changeover rate	s. switching rate
		changeover switch	s. double-throw switch
chair form	Sesselform f	changeover switching, changing-over, switching[-over], [inter]change <el.>	Umschaltung f; Umstellung f <El.>
chamber, compartment	Kammer f, Raum m, Teilraum m		
chambered level tube	Kammerlibelle f	changing load[ing], changing stress	veränderliche Beanspruchung (Belastung) f
chamber gas, filling gas of the chamber	Kammergas n, Füllgas n der Kammer	changing-over	s. changeover switching
		changing stress	s. changing load
Chamberlain-Wiegand counter	Chamberlain-Wiegand-Zähler m, Zähler m nach Chamberlain und Wiegand	changing tube	Wechseltubus m
		channel, flume <hydr.>	Gerinne n, Wasserrinne f <Hydr.>
chance, random, accidental	zufällig, Zufalls-, zufallsbedingt	channel <hydr.>	Kanal m <Hydr.>
		channel	s. a. counting channel
chance coincidence	s. spurious coincidence	channel	s. communication channel
chance decision	Zufallsentscheidung f, zufällige Entscheidung f	channel capacity	Kapazität f des Kanals, Kanalkapazität f, Übertragungsfähigkeit f des Kanals, Informationskapazität f
chance event, event <stat.>	zufälliges Ereignis n, Ereignis n <Stat.>		
chance rate	Zufallszählrate f, Zählrate f der Zufallsimpulse		
		channel diaphragm	Kanalblende f
chance variable	s. random variable	channel diffusion	Kanaldiffusion f
Chandlerian period	s. Chandler's period	channel-edge adjustment	Kanalbreiteneinstellung f
Chandler['s] motion of the pole, free nutation	Chandlersche Polbewegung (Nutation) f, freie Nutation		
		channel flow	Kanalströmung f
		channeling [effect]	s. radiation streaming
		channelled spectrum, banded (fluted) spectrum	kanneliertes (kannelierten, kanneliertes) Spektrum n, Platteninterferenzspektrum n
Chandler['s] period, Chandlerian period	Chandlersche Periode f, Chandler-Periode f, Periode der Chandlerschen Nutation		
		channel line	Stromstrich m
		channelling, swallow holes <geo.>	Karren pl, Schratten pl, Karrenfurche f; Rillenkarren pl, Kannellierung f; Kluftkarren pl; Karrenfeld n
Chandrasekhar approximation	Chandrasekhar-Näherung f		
Chandrasekhar['s] mean	Mittelwert m nach Chandrasekhar, Chandrasekharsches Mittel n		
		channelling [effect]	s. radiation streaming
		channelling effect factor, streaming factor	Kanal[effekt]faktor m, Kanalverlustfaktor m
Chandrasekhar['s] method, Wick['s] method	Wicksche Methode f, Verfahren n von Chandrasekhar, Methode der diskreten Ordinaten	channel number, channel No.	Kanalnummer f, Kanal-Nr. f
		channelography	Kanalographie f
change; alteration; varying; variation <gen.>	Änderung f; Veränderung f; Variation f; Schwankung f; Abänderung f <gen.>	channelon	Kanalon n, Kanalquant n
		channel position	Kanallage f
		channel pulse	Kanalimpuls m
change <met.>, transition, transformation, phase change	Umwandlung f, Übergang m. Phasenumwandlung f, Phasenübergang m <Met.>	channel pulse-height analyzer	s. multichannel pulse-height analyzer
		channel radius, radius of nuclear reaction channel	Kanalradius m, Radius m des Reaktionskanals
change	s. a. inversion <gen.>		
change	s. a. changeover switching	channel separation, channel spacing	Kanalabstand m
change in aggregation state, change in phase (state), change of aggregation state	s. change of state		
		channel spin	Kanalspin m
		channels ratio method	Kanalverhältnismethode f
change of co-ordinates, transformation of coordinates, co-ordinate transformation	Koordinatentransformation f, Koordinatenwechsel m	channel through the shielding	s. shield opening
		channel wave	s. guided wave <geo.>
change of form	s. deformation <mech.>	channel width, partial reaction width <nucl.>	Kanalbreite f, Partialbreite f des Kanals <Kern.>
change of permittivity in excited state	DK-Effekt m		

chaotic box	Chaoskasten *m*
chaotic motion	*s.* disordered motion
chaotic motion of the molecules	*s.* molecular motion
Chaoul tube	Chaoul-Röhre *f*
Chaplygin['s] approximation	Tschaplyginsche Näherung *f*
Chaplygin['s] condition	Tschaplyginsche Bedingung *f*, Tschaplygin-Bedingung *f*
Chaplygin['s] correspondence principle	Tschaplyginsches Korrespondenzprinzip *n*
Chaplygin['s] equation	Tschaplygin-Gleichung *f*, Tschaplyginsche Gleichung *f*, Stromfunktionsgleichung *f* [nach Tschaplygin]
Chaplygin['s] fluid	Tschaplygin-Flüssigkeit *f*, Tschaplyginsche Flüssigkeit *f*
Chaplygin['s] [hypergeometric] function	Tschaplyginsche Funktion *f*
Chaplygin-Molenbroek transformation	*s.* Molenbroek-Chaplygin transformation
Chapman-Enskog method	Chapman-Enskogsche Methode *f*
Chapman['s] equation	Chapmansche Gleichung *f*, Gleichung von Chapman, Chapman-Gleichung *f*
Chapman function	Chapman-Funktion *f*
Chapman-Jouguet condition, Chapman-Jouguet state	Chapman-Jouguetsche Bedingung *f*
Chapman-Jouguet detonation	Chapman-Jouguetsche Detonation *f*
Chapman-Jouguet state	*s.* Chapman-Jouguet condition
Chapman-Kolmogoroff equation	Chapman-Kolmogoroffsche Gleichung *f*
Chapman layer	Chapman-Schicht *f*
Chapman-Störmer current ring	*s.* Störmer current ring
Chappius band	Chappius-Bande *f*
character	*s.* behaviour
character	*s.* sign
character	*s.* character of the representation
character	*s.* group character
character display tube	*s.* viewing storage tube
character figure [for the day]	*s.* magnetic character figure
character group	Charaktergruppe *f*, duale Gruppe *f*
characteristic; characteristic curve, characteristic line	Charakteristik *f*, charakteristische Kurve *f* <*auch* Math.>; Kennlinie *f*
characteristic, number characteristic	Charakterzahl *f*
characteristic <of beacon>	Kennung *f*
characteristic <of logarithm>	Kennziffer *f*, Charakteristik *f* <Logarithmus>
characteristic <num. math.>	Charakteristik *f* <Maschinendarstellung des Exponenten> <num. Math.>
characteristic	*s. a.* similarity parameter
characteristic	*s.* dynamic characteristic
characteristic	*s.* parameter <gen.>
characteristic	*s.* slip line
characteristic acoustic impedance, characteristic acoustic resistance, characteristic impedance, [acoustic] radiation resistance <ac.>	Schallwellenwiderstand *m*, Schallwiderstand *m*, Schallkennimpedanz *f*, Wellenwiderstand *m* <Ak.>
characteristic admittance, surge (natural) admittance <of transmission line>	Wellenleitwert *m* <Leitung>
characteristic admittance, image admittance <of four-terminal network>	Wellenleitwert *m* <Vierpol>
characteristic admittance, [characteristic] wave admittance <of waveguide>	Wellenleitwert *m*, charakteristischer Wellenleitwert <Wellenleiter>
characteristic admittance of free space, characteristic admittance of vacuum, surge admittance of vacuum (free space)	Wellenleitwert *m* des freien Raumes, Wellenleitwert des Vakuums
characteristic angular frequency	*s.* natural angular frequency
characteristic band	Schlüsselbande *f*
characteristic boundary value problem	charakteristisches Randwertproblem *n*, charakteristische Randwertaufgabe *f*, Charakteristiken-Randwertproblem
characteristic curve, Hurter and Driffield curve, Hurter-Driffield (H-D, H. and D., *D* log *E*) curve, exposure–density relationship <phot.>	[photographische] Schwärzungskurve *f*, charakteristische Kurve *f*, Gradationskurve *f*; Hurter-Driffield-Kurve *f* <Phot.>
characteristic curve	*s. a.* characteristic
characteristic curve family	*s.* family of characteristic[s]
characteristic curve family of the rectifier	Richtkennlinienfeld *n* [des elektrischen Ventils]
characteristic curve of oscillation	Schwing[ungs]kennlinie *f*
characteristic curve of the thermionic valve	*s.* current-voltage characteristic
characteristic curve tracer	*s.* characteristic recorder
characteristic datum	*s.* parameter <gen.>
characteristic Debye temperature	*s.* Debye temperature
characteristic determinant	*s.* secular determinant
characteristic determinant of the four-terminal network, quadripole determinant	Vierpoldeterminante *f*
characteristic diagram [of Prandtl and Busemann], characteristic line diagram, Prandtl-Busemann characteristic line diagram	charakteristisches Diagramm *n* von Prandtl und Busemann, Charakteristikendiagramm *n* nach Prandtl-Busemann, Prandtl-Busemannsches Charakteristikendiagramm
characteristic diagram of the thermionic valve	*s.* current-voltage characteristic
characteristic Einstein temperature, Einstein [characteristic] temperature	charakteristische Einsteinsche Temperatur *f*, Einsteinsche charakteristische Temperatur, Einstein-Temperatur *f*
characteristic energy, intrinsic energy	Eigenenergie *f*, innere Energie *f*
characteristic equation, secular equation, frequency equation, auxiliary equation	charakteristische (säkulare) Gleichung *f*, Säkulargleichung *f*, Frequenzgleichung *f*
characteristic equation	*s. a.* equation of state
characteristic equations of the two-terminal-pair network	*s.* characteristic relations of the two-terminal-pair network
characteristic exponent	charakteristischer Exponent *m*
characteristic feature	*s.* distinguishing feature
characteristic frequency <spectr.>	charakteristische Frequenz *f* <Spektr.>
characteristic frequency	*s. a.* natural frequency
characteristic function <of a set>	charakteristische Funktion *f*, Indikatorfunktion *f* <Menge>
characteristic function <therm., math.>	charakteristische Funktion *f* <Therm., Math.>
characteristic function	*s. a.* eigenfunction
characteristic function [of Hamilton]	*s.* Hamilton's characteristic function
characteristic hydraulic number, hydraulic discriminant	hydraulische Kennzahl *f*
characteristic impedance, image impedance <of four-terminal network>	Kennwiderstand *m*, Kennimpedanz *f*, Wellenwiderstand *m*, Spiegel[bild]impedanz *f* <Vierpol>
characteristic impedance, surge (natural) impedance <of the transmission line>	Wellenwiderstand *m* <Leitung>, Leitungswellenwiderstand *m*

characteristic impedance, [characteristic] wave impedance <of waveguide>	[charakteristischer] Wellenwiderstand m, Feld[wellen]widerstand m <Wellenleiter>	characteristic X-ray line spectrum	s. characteristic X-ray spectrum
characteristic impedance	s. a. characteristic acoustic impedance <ac.>	characteristic X-rays, characteristic X radiation, characteristic radiation; fluorescent radiation, X-ray fluorescence radiation	charakteristische Röntgenstrahlung (Strahlung) f, Eigen[röntgen]strahlung f, Röntgeneigenstrahlung f; Fluoreszenzstrahlung f, Röntgenfluoreszenzstrahlung f, Barkla-Strahlung f, Fluoreszenzröntgenstrahlung f
characteristic impedance of vacuum (free space), surge impedance of vacuum (free space)	Wellenwiderstand m des freien Raumes, Wellenwiderstand des Vakuums		
characteristic in the hodograph plane	s. hodograph characteristic	characteristic X-ray spectrum, [characteristic] X-ray line spectrum	charakteristisches Röntgenspektrum n, Röntgenlinienspektrum n
characteristic line	s. characteristic	character of radiation	s. type of radiation
characteristic line diagram	s. characteristic diagram	character of the representation, character	Charakter m der Darstellung
characteristic matrix	charakteristische Matrix f	character storage (writing) tube	s. viewing storage tube
characteristic matrix of the two-terminal-pair network, quadripole (four-pole) matrix	Vierpolmatrix f	charge, electric charge, quantity of electricity <quantity> <el.>	[elektrische] Ladung f, Ladungsmenge f, Elektrizitätsmenge f, Elektrizitätsladung f, Strommenge f <Größe> <El.>
characteristic motion	s. proper motion		
characteristic number	s. eigenvalue <of a matrix>		
characteristic number of energy	s. eigenvalue of energy	charge	s. a. fuel charge
characteristic of the arc discharge	s. arc characteristic	charge	s. preparation <chem.>
		charge	s. strain <mech.>
characteristic of the hodograph equation	s. hodograph characteristic	charge / without, neutral, electrically neutral; uncharged, of zero charge <el.>	neutral, elektrisch neutral; ungeladen, ladungsfrei, ohne Ladung <El.>
characteristic of the thermionic valve	s. current-voltage characteristic		
characteristic period	s. natural period		
characteristic plane, exceptional plane	charakteristische Ebene f	charge balance	Ladungswaage f
characteristic plotter	s. characteristic recorder	charge carrier, carrier; charged particle carrier <semi., el.>	Ladungsträger m, Träger m <Halb., El.>
characteristic polynomial	s. secular determinant <of matrix>	charge carrier avalanche, carrier avalanche	Trägerlawine f, Ladungsträgerlawine f
characteristic radiation	s. characteristic X-rays	charge carrier breakthrough	s. carrier break-through
characteristic recorder, characteristic curve tracer, [characteristic] plotter, co-ordinate plotter	Kennlinienleser m, Kennlinienschreiber m, Koordinatenschreiber m; Ortskurvenschreiber m	charge carrier concentration	s. charge carrier density
		charge carrier current	s. carrier flow
characteristic relations of the two-terminal-pair network, characteristic equations of the two-terminal-pair network, quadripole (four-pole) relations, quadripole (four-pole) equations	Vierpolgleichungen fpl	charge carrier density, carrier density, density of [charge] carriers, charge carrier concentration, carrier concentration, concentration of [charge] carriers	Ladungsträgerdichte f, Trägerdichte f, Ladungsträgerkonzentration f, Trägerkonzentration f
		charge carrier depletion	s. carrier depletion
characteristic root	s. eigenvalue <of a matrix>	charge carrier extraction, carrier extraction	Ladungsträgerextraktion f, Trägerextraktion f
characteristics	s. behaviour	charge carrier flow	s. carrier flow
characteristics family	s. family of characteristics	charge carrier generation, carrier generation, charge carrier production, carrier production	Ladungsträgergeneration f, Ladungsträgererzeugung f, Ladungsträgerbildung f, Trägergeneration f, Trägererzeugung f, Trägerbildung f
characteristic state, eigenstate, proper state	Eigenzustand m		
characteristic strip	charakteristischer Streifen m		
characteristic surface <opt.>	Kennfläche f <Opt.>	charge carrier injection	s. carrier injection
characteristic system	charakteristisches Gleichungssystem (System) n	charge carrier jump, carrier jump	Trägersprung m, Ladungsträgersprung m
characteristic temperature	charakteristische Temperatur f	charge carrier migration, carrier migration	Ladungsträgerbewegung f, Bewegung f der Ladungsträger, Trägerbewegung f, Ladungsträgerwanderung f, Trägerwanderung f
characteristic temperature	s. a. Debye temperature		
characteristic temperature [of Weiss]	s. Weiss temperature		
characteristic time	s. time constant <el.>	charge carrier mobility, carrier mobility	Trägerbeweglichkeit f, Ladungsträgerbeweglichkeit f
characteristic time delay	charakteristische Verzögerung f		
characteristic value <of construction element>	Kennwert m, charakteristischer Wert m <Bauteil, Baugerät>	charge carrier multiplication	s. carrier multiplication
		charge carrier production	s. charge carrier generation
characteristic value	s. a. eigenvalue <of a matrix>	charge carrier range, carrier range	Trägerreichweite f, Ladungsträgerreichweite f
characteristic value	s. a. parameter <gen.>		
characteristic value of energy	s. eigenvalue of energy	charge carrier replenishment	s. carrier replenishment
characteristic vector, Burgers vector	Burgers-Vektor m	charge carrier spectrum, carrier spectrum	Trägerspektrum n, Ladungsträgerspektrum n
characteristic vector	s. a. eigenvector	charge carrier stream	s. carrier flow
characteristic vibration	s. vibrational mode	charge carrier supply	s. carrier replenishment
characteristic wave admittance	s. characteristic admittance <of waveguide>	charge carrier trap, carrier trap	Trägerfalle f, Ladungsträgerfalle f
characteristic wave impedance	s. characteristic impedance <of waveguide>	charge carrier trapping	s. carrier trapping
		charge carrier velocity	s. carrier velocity
characteristic wavelength	charakteristische Wellenlänge f	charge cloud, charged cloud	Ladungswolke f
characteristic X radiation	s. characteristic X-rays	charge-conjugate	ladungskonjugiert

charge conjugation [operation]	Ladungskonjugation f
charge conjugation	s. a. charge invariance
charge conservation	s. conservation of charge
charge conservation law	s. law of conservation of charge
charge-controlled	ladungsgesteuert
charge co-ordinate	s. isobaric spin co-ordinate
charge-current density [four vectors]	s. four-vector of electric current
charge-current potential	s. four potential
charged cloud, charge cloud	Ladungswolke f
charge density, electric charge density, density of charge	[elektrische] Ladungsdichte f, elektrische Dichte f
charge density operator, operator of charge density	Ladungsdichteoperator m
charge displacement	Ladungsverschiebung f
charge dissipation	Ladungsableitung f
charge distribution	Ladungsverteilung f; Ladungsaufbau m <Meteo.>
charged nuclear particle track	s. nuclear track
charge doublet	s. isobaric spin doublet
charged particle	geladenes Teilchen n, geladene Partikel f, Ladungsteilchen n
charged-particle accelerator	s. atomic particle accelerator
charged particle carrier	s. charge carrier
charged particle equilibrium, CPE, C.P.E.	Gleichgewicht n geladener Teilchen
charged particle equilibrium phase, equilibrium (synchronous) phase	Sollphase f, Synchronphase f, Gleichgewichtsphase f
charged particle principle of coherent acceleration	s. principle of charged particle coherent acceleration
charged potential	geladenes Potential n
charged pseudoscalar [meson] theory	geladene pseudoskalare Mesonentheorie (Mesonenfeldtheorie, Theorie) f
charged scalar meson theory, charged scalar theory	geladene skalare Mesonentheorie (Mesonenfeldtheorie, Theorie) f
charge exchange, umladung, recharging, recharge, reversal of charge	Umladung f, Trägerumladung f, Trägerumwandlung f; Ladungsaustausch m
charge exchange cross-section, cross-section for charge exchange	Umladungs[wirkungs]querschnitt m, Wirkungsquerschnitt m für (der) Umladung
charge exchange current	Ladungsaustauschstrom m
charge exchange density	Umladungsdichte f
charge exchange energy, energy of charge exchange	Umladungsenergie f
charge exchange force	s. Heisenberg force
charge-exchange injection	Injektion f mit Ladungsaustausch (Umladung), Einschuß m mit Ladungsaustausch (Umladung)
charge exchange operator	s. Heisenberg['s] operator
charge exchange potential	s. Heisenberg potential
charge-exchange scattering	Ladungsaustauschstreuung f, Austauschstreuung f, Streuung f mit Umladung, Umladungsstreuung f
charge-exchange splitting, line splitting by charge exchange	Austauschaufspaltung f, Ladungsaustauschaufspaltung f
charge exchange term, recharge term	Umladungsterm m
charge feedback amplifier	ladungsgegengekoppelter Verstärker m
charge fluctuation of the vacuum, charge vacuum fluctuation	Nullpunktschwankung (Vakuumschwankung) f der Ladung, Nulladungsschwankung f, Nullpunktschwankung des Elektronenfeldes (Elektron-Positron-Feldes), Vakuumschwankung des Elektronenfeldes (Elektron-Positron-Feldes)
charge independence of nuclear forces	Ladungsunabhängigkeit f der Kernkräfte
charge invariance, charge conjugation, C-invariance	Ladungsinvarianz f, C-Invarianz f
charge-mass ratio	s. charge-to-mass ratio
charge multiplet	s. isobaric spin multiplet
charge number of the ion, oxidation number (state), electrovalency	[elektrochemische] Wertigkeit f des Ions, Oxydationszahl f, Oxydationsstufe f, Ladungswert m
charge of air, atmospheric charge	Luftladung f
charge of the Earth	Erdladung f, Ladung f des Erdkörpers
charge of the electron	s. electronic charge
charge operator	Ladungsoperator m, Operator m der Ladung
charge parity	Ladungsparität f, Parität f der Ladung
charge passage	s. charge transition
charge product	Ladungsprodukt n
charge pulse; charging pulse	Ladeimpuls m, Ladestoß m; Ladungsstoß m
charge quantum number	s. nuclear charge quantum number
charge renormalization, renormalization of charge	Ladungsrenormierung f
charge-retention interaction	Wechselwirkung f mit Beibehaltung (Erhaltung) der Ladung
charge reversal, reversal of charge	Ladungsumkehr f, Ladungsumkehrung f
charge separation	Ladungstrennung f
charge singlet	s. isobaric spin singlet
charge space	s. isobaric space
charge state	Ladungszustand m
charge-storage diode	s. step recovery diode
charge storage tube	Ladungsspeicherröhre f
charge symmetry	Ladungssymmetrie f
charge time constant, charging time constant	Ladezeitkonstante f; Aufladezeitkonstante f
charge-to-mass ratio, charge-mass ratio, specific charge	spezifische Ladung f, Ladung-Masse-Verhältnis n
charge-to-mass ratio of the electron, electronic charge-to-mass ratio, electron specific charge, specific electronic charge	spezifische Ladung f des Elektrons, spezifische Elektronenladung f
charge transfer, charge transport	Ladungsüberführung f, Ladungstransfer m, Ladungsübertragung f, Ladungsübergang m, Ladungstransport m
charge transfer reaction, transfer reaction	Ladungstransferreaktion f, Ladungsüberführungsreaktion f, Transferreaktion f, Überführungsreaktion f
charge-transfer spectrum	Ladungsüberführungsspektrum n, Ladungstransferspektrum n, Ladungsaustauschspektrum n
charge transition, charge passage	Ladungsdurchtritt m, Ladungsdurchgang m
charge transport	s. charge transfer
charge triplet	s. isobaric spin triplet
charge vacuum fluctuation	s. charge fluctuation of the vacuum
charge variable	Ladungsvariable f
charging belt	Ladungstransportband n, Band n <Bandgenerator>
charging capacitance	Ladekapazität f
charging capacitor	Ladekondensator m
charging capacity, battery capacity	Ladefähigkeit f, Ladevermögen n, Ladekapazität f
charging current	Ladestrom m, Ladestromstärke f
charging factor	Ladefaktor m

charging

charging pulse; charge pulse	Ladeimpuls m, Ladestoß m; Ladungsstoß m	check point	s. control point <geo.>
charging resistance	s. resistance during charge	check room	s. test room
charging resistor	s. resistance during charge	cheese antenna, cheese-type antenna	Käseantenne f, Käseschachtelantenne f
charging time constant, charge time constant	Ladezeitkonstante f; Aufladezeitkonstante f		
charging voltage	Ladespannung f	chelant, chelating (sequestering) agent	Chelatbildner m
chargistor	Chargistor m		
Charles['] law, Amontons['] law	Amontonssches (Charlessches) Gesetz n	chelate, chelate compound	Chelat n, Chelatverbindung f; Metallchelat n
Charles['] law	s. a. Gay-Lussac law		
charm	Charme m, Charm[e]zahl f		
Charpak[-type] chamber	Charpak-Funkenkammer f, Charpak-Kammer f		
Charpy impact test, Charpy test	Charpysche Pendelschlagprobe f	chelate effect	Chelateffekt m
chart of isohyets, map of isohyets	Regenkarte f, Isohyetenkarte f	chelating action, chalation, sequestration	Chelatbildung f, Chelation f, Chelierung f
chart of isohypses	s. hypsometric map		
chart of nuclides	s. isotope chart	chelating agent	s. chelant
chart of temperature variations, temperature variation chart (map)	Temperaturkarte f	chelation	s. chelating action
		chelatometry; complexometry; compleximetry	Komplexometrie f, Komplexmetrie f, Chelatometrie f
chart recorder (recording instrument), strip chart recorder, strip chart [recording] instrument, standard recorder, printing reader	Registrierstreifenschreiber m, Streifenschreiber m, Streifenblattschreiber m, Streifendiagrammschreiber m, Registrierschreiber m	chemical adsorption	s. chemisorption
		chemical age	chemisches Alter n
chart scale, scale of the chart	Kartenmaßstab m, Maßstab m der Karte	chemical alteration	s. chemical weathering
		chemical association	s. association of molecules
Chasles['] theorem	Chaslesscher Satz m	chemical atomic weight scale	s. chemical mass scale
chatter	s. chattering		
chatter	s. shaking	chemical binding effect	Einfluß m der chemischen Bindung
chatter amplitude	Prellamplitude f, Prellschwingungsamplitude f	chemical binding force	s. binding force
		chemical bond, bond	[chemische] Bindung f
chattering, chatter; chatter vibration	Prellung f; Prellschwingung f	chemical cell	s. voltaic cell
		chemical colour	s. pigment
		chemical decomposition, decomposition <chem.>	Zersetzung f, chemische Zersetzung, Zerfall m, chemischer Zerfall <Chem.>
chatter mark	Rattermarke f, Ratternarbe f		
chatter vibration	s. chattering		
Chattock gauge	s. two-fluid manometer	chemical defect [in crystals]	chemische Fehlordnung f [in Kristallen]
Chebyshev['] alternant (alternation)	Tschebyscheffsche Alternante (Abwechslung) f		
Chebyshev amplifier, Chebyshev chain amplifier	Tschebyscheff-Verstärker m, Tschebyscheffscher Kettenverstärker m	chemical diffusion coefficient, interdiffusion coefficient	Interdiffusionskoeffizient m
		chemical displacement, chemical shift	chemische Verschiebung f, „chemical shift" m
Chebyshev['s] approach (approximation)	Tschebyscheffsche Annäherung (Approximation) f	chemical dosemeter	chemisches Dosimeter n
		chemical exchange	chemischer Austausch m
Chebyshev array	s. Dolph-Chebyshev array	chemical hydration, primary hydration	primäre (physikalische) Hydratation f
Chebyshev chain amplifier	s. Chebyshev amplifier	chemical impurity	s. impurity <cryst., semi.>
Chebyshev['s] equation	Tschebyscheffsche Differentialgleichung f	chemical-kinetic isotope effect, kinetic isotope effect	chemisch-kinetischer Isotopieeffekt m, kinetischer Isotopieeffekt
Chebyshev filter	Tschebyscheff-Filter n		
Chebyshev fluctuation	Tschebyscheff-Schwankung f, Tschebyscheffsche Schwankung f	chemical kinetics	s. reaction kinetics
		chemical labelling	spezifische (chemische) Markierung f
Chebyshev['s] formula	Tschebyscheffsche Formel f, Tschebyscheff-Formel f	chemical mass	s. mass on chemical scale
Chebyshev['s] function <of the first or second kind>	Tschebyscheffsche Funktion f, Tschebyscheff-Funktion f <erster (I.) oder zweiter (II.) Art>	chemical mass scale, chemical atomic weight scale, chemical scale of atomic masses	chemische Atomgewichtsskala f, chemische Massenskala f
		chemical physics	chemische Physik f
		chemical pigment	s. pigment
Chebyshev['s] inequality, Bienaymé-Chebyshev inequality	Tschebyscheffsche Ungleichung f, Ungleichung von Tschebyscheff[-Bienaymé] f	chemical potential, partial molal free energy, partial specific Gibbs function	chemisches (thermodynamisches) Potential n, [partielle] molare freie Enthalpie f, [partielle] molare freie Gibbssche Energie f
Chebyshev['s] interpolation	Tschebyscheffsche Interpolation f		
Chebyshev['s] polynomial <of the first or second kind>	Tschebyscheffsches Polynom n, Tschebyscheff-Polynom n <erster (I.) oder zweiter (II.) Art>	chemical protection against radiation, radiation-chemical protection	chemischer Strahlenschutz m
check	s. testing		
check-back	s. control check	chemical protector, radiation protector, radiation blocker	Strahlenschutzstoff m, chemischer Strahlenschutz[stoff] m, Strahlenblocker m
check-back frequency	s. repetition rate		
check circuit	s. test circuit		
checkered	s. staggered		
checking	s. braking <mech.>	chemical purity <chem.>, purity	Reinheit f, chemische Reinheit <Chem.>
checking	s. testing	chemical reaction zone	Zone f der chemischen Reaktion
checking circuit	s. test circuit		
checking for gas leaks	s. leak hunting	chemical reactor, reactor, reaction apparatus <chem.>	chemischer Reaktor m, Reaktor, Reaktionsapparat m <Chem.>
check[ing] instrument; test[ing] instrument, tester; inspection instrument	Prüfinstrument n, Prüfgerät n		

chemical reduction <chem.>, reduction, electronation <el. chem.>	Reduktion f, chemische Reduktion <Chem.>	Child-Langmuir [-Schottky] law	Child[-Langmuir]sches Gesetz n, Gesetz von Child und Langmuir, Emissionsgesetz n, Entladungsgesetz n, Drei-Halbe-Gesetz n, $U^{3/2}$-Gesetz n, Langmuir-Childsches Raumladungsgesetz n (Gesetz), Langmuir-Childsche Formel f, Gesetz von Langmuir und Child
chemical resistance, chemical stability	chemische Beständigkeit (Stabilität, Widerstandsfähigkeit) f		
chemical ripening	chemische Reifung f		
chemical rocket	chemische Rakete f		
chemical scale of atomic masses	s. chemical mass scale	chilling	s. quenching <of metals>
chemical separation of isotopes	chemische Isotopentrennung f	chimney effect	Kaminwirkung f
chemical shift	s. chemical displacement	chip	s. nuclear fragment <nucl.>
chemical source of current	s. voltaic cell	chirality	Chiralität f, „chirality" f, Rechts- oder Linkshändigkeit f
chemical stability	s. chemical resistance		
chemical-thermodynamic isotope effect	chemisch-thermodynamischer Isotopieeffekt m	chiral symmetry	chirale Symmetrie f
chemical thermodynamics, thermo[-]chemistry	Thermochemie f, chemische Thermodynamik f	chi-squared distribution, χ^2 distribution	Chi-Quadrat-Verteilung f [nach Helmert-Pearson], χ^2-Verteilung f
chemical topology	chemische Topologie f		
chemical tracer	spezifischer (chemischer) Tracer m	chi-squared test, chi-square test, χ^2 test	Chi-Quadrat-Test m, χ^2-Test m
chemical weathering, chemical alteration, decomposition <geo.>	chemische Verwitterung f, Gesteinszersetzung f <Geo.>	Chladni['s] acoustic figures, Chladni['s] figures, Chladni['s] sound figures, acoustic figures, sound (acoustic) pattern, vibration patterns, sand figures	Chladnische Klangfiguren fpl, Schwingungsfiguren fpl
chemiluminescence, cold emission [of light]	Chemilumineszenz f, Reaktionsleuchten n, kaltes Licht (Leuchten) n		
chemisorption, chemical adsorption, activated (irreversible) adsorption	Chemisorption f, Chemosorption f, chemische (irreversible, aktivierte; gehemmte) Adsorption f	choice	s. selection
		choice axiom	s. axiom of choice
chemisorption bond	Chemisorptionsbindung f	choice of parameters	s. proportioning
chemisorption hysteresis	Chemisorptionshysterese f	choke, choking coil, reactive coil, inductor	Drossel f, Drosselspule f
chemoautotrophic metabolism, chemoautotrophism	Chemoautotrophie f		
chemodinese	Chemodinese f	choke coupling, impedance (reactor) coupling	Drosselkopplung f
chemokinesis	Chemokinesis f		
chemolysis	Chemolyse f	choke coupling	s. a. inductance-capacitance coupling
chemomagnetization	Chemomagnetisierung f	choked flange	Sperrflansch m
chemonastic	chemonastisch		
chemonasty	Chemonastie f		
chemonuclear fuel element	chemonukleares Brennelement n	choked nozzle	Düse f zur Beschleunigung auf Schallgeschwindigkeit
chemonuclear reactor	Chemiereaktor m		
chemosphere	Chemosphäre f		
chemostat	Chemostat m	choked tunnel, choked wind tunnel	blockierter Windkanal m
chemotactic	chemotaktisch		
chemotaxis	Chemotaxis f	choke-free	krisisfrei
chemotron	Chemotron n, elektrochemischer Wandler m		
		choke modulation	s. constant-current modulation
chemotronics	Chemotronik f		
chemotropic curvature	chemotropische Krümmung f	choke piston (plunger)	s. shorting plunger <el.>
		choke plunger	s. movable-core choke
chemotropism	Chemotropismus m	choking	s. obstruction
chenier	s. beach ridge	choking coil	s. choke
Cherenkov effect	s. Čerenkov effect	choking Mach number	Blockierungs-Mach-Zahl f
cherry-red heat	Kirschrotglut f <850 ··· 900 °C>		
		choking region	Bereich m der kritischen Mach-Zahlen
Cheseaux' and Olbers' paradox, Cheseaux-Olbers paradox	s. photometric[al] paradox	cholesteric phase	cholesterische Phase f
chest of drawers argument	s. Dirichlet['s] principle	chopped bar recorder	s. point recorder
Chévenard dilatometer	Chévenardsches Dilatometer n, Chévenard-Dilatometer n	chopped beam	zerhackter Strahl m
		chopped wave, interrupted wave	zerhackte Welle f
Chew-Low equations	Chew-Lowsche Gleichungen fpl		
Chew-Mandelstam equations	Chew-Mandelstamsche Gleichungen fpl	chopper, vibrator, vibrating contactor, vibrating (pendulum) rectifier <el.>	Zerhacker[umformer] m, Pendelumformer m, Pendelwechselrichter m, Kontaktwechselrichter m, Wechsel[gleich]richter m, Pendelgleichrichter m
Chézy['s] formula, Chézy formula of hydraulics	Chézysche Formel f [der Hydraulik], Formel von Chézy		
chief ray <opt.>, principal ray	Hauptstrahl m <Opt.>		
chief series, chief-series	Hauptreihe f <Gruppentheorie>	chopper, mechanical chopper; neutron chopper, mechanical neutron chopper <nucl.>	Chopper m, mechanischer Unterbrecher m, mechanischer Zerhacker m, Zerhacker <Kern.>
chief valence, primary valence (valency), main valency	Hauptvalenz f		
Chikolev['s] method	Tschikolewsche Linienbildmethode f	chopper bar	Fallbügel m

chopper bar recorder	s. point recorder	chromaticity diagram, chromaticity chart, colour triangle	Farbtafel f, Farbdreieck n, Farbendreieck n
chopper disk method	s. Fizeau['s] method		
chopper spectrometer	Spektrometer n mit Chopper, Chopperspektrometer n	chromaticness	s. chromaticity
		chromatic over-correction	chromatische Überkorrektion f
chopping ⟨of the beam⟩	Zerhackung f [des Strahlenbündels]	chromatic parallax	Verfärbungsparallaxe f
		chromatic resolving power	s. resolving power ⟨of grating⟩
chopping	s. a. crushing ⟨mech.⟩	chromatics	s. theory of colours
choppy sea	leichtbewegte See f, kabbelige See, kleine Wellen fpl ⟨Stärke 3⟩	chromatic scale, chromatic tone scale	chromatische Tonleiter (Tonskala, Tonfolge) f
choppy wind, gusty (squally, puffy) wind; bumpy air	böiger Wind m	chromatic sensation, sensation of colour, colour sensation	Farbempfindung f
chord ⟨of the wing⟩; wing chord ⟨aero.⟩	Profilsehne f, Profiltiefe f, Flügelsehne f, Flügeltiefe f, Tiefe f des Tragflügels	chromatic tone scale	s. chromatic scale
		chromatic undercorrection	chromatische Unterkorrektion f
chord coil	Sehnenspule f	chromatic variation in [image] position	s. longitudinal chromatic aberration ⟨el., opt.⟩
chord length, length of the chord	Sehnenlänge f ⟨Profil⟩		
chord packing, radiate packing ⟨chem.⟩	Strahlenkörper m	chromatic variation of magnification	s. lateral chromatic aberration
C horizon	s. subsoil ⟨geo.⟩	chromatic variation of spherical aberration	s. spherochromatism
choroisotherm, choroisothermal line	Choroisotherme f		
		chromatid break	Chromatidbruch m
		chromatin rarefaction	Chromatinverdünnung f
Chrétien [mirror] system, Chrétien telescope	Spiegelsystem n von Chrétien, Chrétien-System n	chromatism	Chromasie f
		chromatograph, fractometer	Chromatograph m, Fraktometer m
Christiansen filter, Christiansen-type filter	Dispersions[licht]filter n, Christiansen-Filter n, Monochrom n	chromatographic adsorption	s. adsorption chromatography
		chromatology	s. theory of colours
Christiansen [radio] interferometer	Christiansen-Interferometer n, Radiointerferometer n nach Christiansen	chromatometer; colorimeter	Kolorimeter n; Farbmeßgerät n, Farbmesser m
		chromatometer	s. Newton['s] chromatometer
Christiansen-type filter	s. Christiansen filter		
Christmas-tree antenna, fishbone antenna	Tannenbaumantenne f	chromatometry ⟨chem.⟩	Chromatometrie f ⟨Chem.⟩
		chromatometry	s. a. colorimetry
Christmas-tree pattern	s. light band	chromic acid cell, bichromate cell	Chromsäureelement n
Christmas-tree pattern	s. Buchmann-and-Meyer pattern	chromidia	Chromidien pl
Christoffel symbol, [Riemann-Christoffel] three-index symbol, 3-index symbol	Christoffelsches Symbol n, [Christoffelsches] Dreiindizessymbol (Dreizeigersymbol) n, Christoffel-Symbol n, Christoffel-Affinität f, g-Klammer f, Koeffizient m des affinen Zusammenhangs, Drei-Index-Symbol n	chromogenic development	chromogene Entwicklung f
		chromophore, chromophore group	Chromophor m, chromophore Gruppe f, Farbträger m
		chromophoric electron	Chromophorelektron n
		chromoscope ⟨opt.⟩	Chromoskop n ⟨Opt.⟩
		chromosomal garniture	Chromosomengarnitur f
Christoffel symbol of the first ⟨or second⟩ kind, three-index symbol of the first ⟨or second⟩ kind	Christoffelsches Symbol n erster ⟨oder zweiter⟩ Art, Christoffelsche Klammer f erster ⟨oder zweiter⟩ Art	chromosome	s. root diagram ⟨math.⟩
		chromosome aberration	s. chromosome damage
		chromosome break[age]	Chromosomenbruch m
		chromosome damage, chromosome aberration	Chromosomenschaden m, Chromosomenaberration f
chroma ⟨Munsell system⟩	Sättigungsstufe f, Sättigungsgrad m ⟨DIN-System⟩	chromosome deficiency, chromosome deletion	Chromosomenstückausfall m, Chromosomendefizienz f
chromatic aberration, primary spectrum	chromatische Aberration (Abweichung) f, Farb[en]fehler m, Farbabweichung f, chromatischer Abbildungsfehler (Fehler) m	chromosome inversion	chromosomale Inversion f
		chromosome mating, chromosome pairing	Chromosomenpaarung f
		chromosome number	Chromosomenzahl f
chromatic aberration of position	s. longitudinal chromatic aberration	chromosome pairing, chromosome mating	Chromosomenpaarung f
chromatic adaptation	s. colour adaptation	chromosome translocation, translocation [of chromosome]	Chromosomenstückverlagerung f, Chromosomentranslokation f, Translokation f
chromatic colour, hue[d] colour	bunte (chromatische) Farbe f, Buntfarbe f		
chromatic correction	chromatische Korrektion f	chromospheric facula, plage, plage area	chromosphärische Fackel f
chromatic difference in [image] position	s. longitudinal chromatic aberration ⟨el., opt.⟩	chromospheric flare	chromosphärische Eruption f
chromatic difference of magnification	s. lateral chromatic aberration		
		chronaxie	Chronaxie f, Kennzeit f
chromatic distortion, distortion of colour ⟨opt.⟩	Farbverzerrung f; Farbwandlung f; Farbverschiebung f	chronic exposure, permanent exposure	chronische Strahlenbelastung (Bestrahlung) f, Dauerbestrahlung f, Dauereinwirkung f von Strahlung
chromatic equidensity	Buntäquidensite f, Farbäquidensite f		
chromaticity; chromaticness	Farbart f, Reizart f	chronogeometry	Chronogeometrie f
chromaticity chart	s. chromaticity diagram	chronogram	Chronogramm n
chromaticity co-ordinate	Farbwertanteil m, Eichreizanteil m; Farbmaßzahl f	chronograph, time recorder, time recording apparatus; time printer	Chronograph m, Zeitschreiber m, Zeitregistrierapparat m; Zeitdrucker m
chromaticity co-ordinate in the C.I.E. standard colorimetric system, C.I.E. chromaticity coordinate, standard chromaticity co-ordinate	Normfarbwertanteil m, Normalfarbwertanteil m, Normalreizanteil m		

chronoisotherm, chronoisothermal line	Chronoisotherme f	circle of convergence	Konvergenzkreis m
		circle of curvature, osculating circle	Krümmungskreis m, Schmiegkreis m, Schmiegungskreis m, Oskulationskreis m
chronological order	s. chronology		
chronological product, Wick['s] chronological product, time-ordered product	chronologisches (Wicksches, zeitgeordnetes) Produkt n, T-Produkt n	circle of geodesic curvature	geodätischer Krümmungskreis m (Kreis m zweiter Art)
chronological table	Zeittafel f	circle of inflexions <mech.>	Wendekreis m <Mech.>
chronology, time sequence; chronological order	Zeitfolge f, zeitliches Nacheinander n, Chronologie f; Zeitordnung f	cirde of least confusion	s. disk of aberration
		circle of position, position circle	Positionskreis m
chronology	s. a. time determination	circle polynomial	s. Zernike['s] orthogonal polynomial
chronology	s. a. time reckoning		
chronometer	s. time piece	circle property; transformation carrying circles into circles	Kreisverwandtschaft f; kreisverwandte Abbildung f
chronometry	s. measurement of time		
chronon	Chronon n		
chronophotography	Chronophotographie f	circle vector diagram	s. circle diagram <el.>
chronoscope	Chronoskop n, Kurzzeitmesser m	circling <round>	s. revolution <around, round>
chronotron	Chronotron n	circuit <el.>	Schaltung f <El.>
chute	Fallrinne f		
		circuit, electrical circuit, current circuit <el.>	[elektrischer] Stromkreis m, Kreis m <El.>
chute	s. a. rapids <of river>		
C.I.E.	s. International Commission on Illumination		
C.I.E. chromaticity co-ordinate	s. chromaticity co-ordinate in the C.I.E. standard colorimetric system	circuit; loop <techn.>	Kreislauf m, Kreis m; Schleife f <Techn.>
		circuit	s. a. closed curve <math.>
		circuital field	s. rotational field
C.I.E. colour stimulus [specification], standard colour stimulus [specification], colour stimulus [specification] in the C.I.E. standard colorimetric system	Normvalenz f, Normfarbvalenz f, Normalreiz m	circuit algebra	s. Boolean algebra
		circuital vector field	s. rotational field
		circuit analysis, network (electrical circuit) analysis	Netzwerkanalyse f, Netzanalyse f, Stromkreisanalyse f
		circuit analyzer, network analyzer	Netz[werk]analysator m, Netzmodell n, Netzwerkgleichungslöser m
C.I.E. colour system	s. C.I.E. standard system		
C.I.E. distribution coefficient, standard distribution coefficient, distribution coefficient in the C.I.E. standard colorimetric system	Normspektralwert m, spektraler Normalreizbetrag m	circuitation	s. circulatory integral
		circuit board	s. printed board
		circuit branching, current branching	Stromverzweigung f, Stromaufteilung f
		circuit breaker, [contact] breaker, interrupter, cut-out <el.>	Unterbrecher m, Stromunterbrecher m <El.>
C.I.E. distribution curve (function), standard distribution function (curve), distribution function (curve) in the C.I.E. standard colorimetric system	Normalspektralwertkurve f, Normspektralwertfunktion f		
		circuit breaker	s. a. switch
		circuit-breaking transient [phenomenon]	Ausschaltvorgang m
		circuit closer, switch, contactor	Einschalter m
C.I.E. standard colorimetric observer	farbmeßtechnischer (farbmetrischer) Normalbeobachter m CIE	circuit component	s. circuit element
		circuit constant	s. linear electrical constant
		circuit diagram	s. schematic circuit diagram
C.I.E standard [colorimetric] system, C.I.E trichromatic system, C.I.E. colour system	Norm[farb]valenzsystem n, CIE-Farbmaßsystem n, Normalfarbensystem n, Normalreizsystem n	circuit diagram	s. wiring diagram <el.>
		circuit element, element [of the circuit], [circuit] component, part <of the electrical circuit>; line element	Schaltungselement n, Schaltelement n; Stromkreiselement n; Leitungselement n
cilia movement, ciliary motion	Ziliarbewegung f, Zilienbewegung f, Cilienbewegung f	circuit fault	Schaltungsfehler m
		circuit gap admittance, gap admittance	Spaltleitwert m [des Kreises]
cilium	Zilie f, Wimper f, Cilie f	circuit model	s. test circuit
CI method	s. configuration-interaction method	circuit noise; line noise	Kreisrauschen n; Leitungsgeräusch n
cinema screen	s. projection screen		
cinematographic picture	s. moving picture	circuit of lower voltage	Unterspannungskreis m
		circuit regeneration	s. feedback
cinemicrographic camera	s. microcinematographic camera	circuit segment	Schaltsegment n
cinemicrography	s. microcinematography	circuit theory	s. theory of electric circuits
cineradiography, roentgen (X-ray) cinematography, radio-cinematography, Y-ray movies	Röntgenkinematographie f; Bioröntgenographie f	circuit variable	Schaltungsvariable f, Schaltvariable f
		circuit wiring, wiring; cabling; inter[-]wiring; connection, connecting[-up]	Verdrahtung f, Verkabelung f; Beschaltung f
cinetics	s. kinetics		
cine turret	s. turret head		
C-invariance	s. charge invariance		
circle <surface or line> <math.>; circumference <line>	Kreis m <Fläche oder Linie>; Kreislinie f	circuit with distributed elements	Schaltung f mit verteilten Parametern
circle circumscribed of …	s. circumcircle		
circle diagram, circle vector diagram <el.>	Kreisdiagramm n <El.>	circuit with lumped elements	s. lumped-constant circuit
		circulant	s. cyclic determinant
circle diagram	s. a. locus <control>	circular	kreisförmig, Kreis-; zirkular, zirkulär, Zirkular-
circle diagram of Mohr [for stress]	s. Mohr['s] circle		
circle diagram of Smith	s. Smith chart		
circle of confusion	s. disk of confusion	circular	s. a. circularly polarized

circular

circular accelerator, circular magnetic accelerator	Kreisbeschleuniger m, Ringbeschleuniger m, Zirkularbeschleuniger m
circular aperture; circular diaphragm; circular disk with a hole	Kreis[loch]blende f; Kreislochplatte f; kreisförmige Öffnung f
circular arc, arc (segment) of the circle	Kreisbogen m, Kreisbogenabschnitt m
circular birefringence	s. allogyric double refraction
circular Bloch line, annular Bloch line	Ring-Bloch-Linie f, Ringlinie f
circular bubble	s. circular level
circular chart, circular nomogram	Kreisnomogramm n, Kreistafel f
circular chart <stat.>	Kreisdiagramm n <Stat.>
circular chromatography, horizontal chromatography, circular technique of chromatography	horizontale Technik (Papierchromatographie, Chromatographie) f, Rundfilterchromatographie f, Zirkularchromatographie f, Ring[papier]chromatographie f
circular co-ordinate	isotrope Koordinate f, Minimalkoordinate f
circular current; circulating (ring) current	Ringstrom m; Kreisstrom m
circular current effect	Ringstromeffekt m
circular curvature	s. mean curvature
circular cylinder	Kreiszylinder m
circular cylindrical co-ordinates	s. cylindrical co-ordinates
circular diaphragm	s. circular aperture
circular dichroism, Cotton effect	zirkularer Dichroismus m, Rotationsdichroismus m, Zirkulardichroismus m, Cotton-Effekt m
circular disk with a hole	s. circular aperture
circular dividing, graduation (division) of the circular scale, graduation (division) of the circle	Kreisteilung f
circular dividing engine, circular engine	Kreisteilmaschine f
circular double refraction	s. allogyric double refraction
circular elliptic integral of the third kind	zirkuläres elliptisches Integral n dritter (3.) Gattung
circular engine	s. circular dividing engine
circular equilibrium orbit	s. equilibrium orbit
circular filter, round filter	Rundfilter n
circular function, trigonometric function	trigonometrische Funktion f, Kreisfunktion f
circular level, circular spirit level, circular bubble, box level	Dosenlibelle f
circularly polarized, circular	zirkular polarisiert
circularly polarized oscillation	s. circular oscillation
circular magnetic accelerator	s. circular accelerator
circular measure, radian measure	Bogenmaß n
circular motion	Kreisbewegung f, kreisförmige Bewegung f
circular neutral wedge, circular wedge	Kreisgraukeil m, Kreiskeil m
circular nomogram, circular chart	Kreisnomogramm n, Kreistafel f
circular orbit	s. circular path
circular oscillation; circularly polarized oscillation	zirkulare Schwingung f, Kreisschwingung f; zirkular polarisierte Schwingung
circular path, circular trajectory (orbit), orbit	Kreisbahn f, kreisförmige Umlaufbahn f
circular pendulum	Kreispendel n
circular permutation, cyclic permutation (interchange)	zyklische Vertauschung f; zyklische Permutation f
circular polariscope	Zirkularpolariskop n
circular polarization	zirkulare Polarisation f, Zirkularpolarisation f
circular ring, annulus	Kreisring m
circular scale	Kreisskala f, Kreisskale f
circular scale	s. a. graduated circle
circular sector, sector of the circle	Kreisausschnitt m, Kreissektor m
circular segment, segment of the circle	Kreisabschnitt m, Kreissegment n
circular shift	s. cyclic shift
circular spirit level	s. circular level
circular stage (table)	Rundtisch m
circular technique of chromatography	s. circular chromatography
circular trajectory	s. circular path
circular tube	Kreisrohr n, Rohr n mit kreisförmigem Querschnitt
circular velocity, elliptical velocity	erste kosmische Geschwindigkeit[sstufe] f, Kreisbahngeschwindigkeit f, elliptische Geschwindigkeit
circular vortex (vorticity)	s. circular whirl
circular wave number	s. wavelength constant
circular wave number vector	s. circular wave vector
circular wave vector, circular wave number vector, wave [number] vector, propagation vector	Kreiswellen[zahl]vektor m, Wellen[zahl]vektor m, Ausbreitungsvektor m, Fortpflanzungsvektor m
circular wedge, circular neutral wedge	Kreisgraukeil m, Kreiskeil m
circular whirl, circular vortex (vorticity)	zirkularer Wirbel m, Kreiswirbel m
circulating air; recirculated air	Umluft f
circulating beam	s. internal beam
circulating current	s. circular current
circulating flow	kreisende Strömung f
circulating fuel	umlaufender Brennstoff m
circulating memory	s. cycle store
circulating pump, circulation pump, circulator	Umwälzpumpe f, Umlaufpumpe f, Zirkulationspumpe f
circulating storage (store)	s. cycle storage
circulating system	s. circulatory system
circulation	Umlaufen n, Umlauf m; Kreisen n; Umwälzung f; Kreislauf m, Zirkulation f
circulation <aero., hydr.>	Zirkulation f <Aero., Hydr.>
circulation[/ with], circulatory, cyclic <hydr., aero.>	zirkulationsbehaftet, Zirkulations-, zyklisch <Hydr., Aero.>
circulation / without	s. circulation-free
circulation branch	Zirkulationsast m, Zirkulationszweig m
circulation coefficient	Zirkulationsbeiwert m
circulation constant	Zirkulationskonstante f, Umlaufgröße f
circulation flow	s. cyclic potential motion
circulation-free, without circulation, acyclic <of flow>	zirkulationsfrei, ohne Zirkulation, azyklisch <Strömung>
circulation index, index of circulation	Zirkulationsindex m
circulation layer	Zirkulationsschicht f, Umlaufschicht f
circulation loop	Umlaufleitung f, Umwälzleitung f, Umwälzschleife f
circulation of the magnetic intensity	magnetische Umlaufspannung f
circulation of the vector field	Zirkulation f des Vektorfeldes
circulation of water, water circulation	Wasserzirkulation f, Wasserumlauf m, Wasserkreislauf m
circulation pattern	Zirkulationsbild n
circulation-preserving motion	zirkulationserhaltende Bewegung f
circulation process	Zirkulationsgeschehen n

circulation pump	s. circulating pump	cirque, glacial cirque, corrie	Kar n, Karnische f; Gebirgsbecken n; Zirkustal n
circulation ring	Zirkulationsring m, Zirkulationsrad n		
circulation system	s. circulatory system		
circulation theorem	Zirkulationssatz m, Zirkulationstheorem n	cirque	s. a. lunar crater
circulation theorem	s. a. Kelvin['s] circulation theorem	cirque glacier, corrie glacier	Kargletscher m; Fußgletscher m
circulation thermostat	s. circulation-type thermostat	cirrocumulus [cloud], Cc	Cirrocumulus m, feine (hohe) Schäfchenwolke f, Federschichtwolke f, Federhaufenwolke f, Zirrokumulus m, Cc
circulation-type thermostat, circulation thermostat	Umwälzthermostat m, Flüssigkeitsumwälzthermostat m, Umlaufthermostat m		
circulation voltage	Umlaufspannung f	cirrostratus [cloud], Cs	Cirrostratus m, [hohe] Schleierwolke f, Zirrostratus m, Cs
circulator, microwave circulator, waveguide circulator	Zirkulator m, Mikrowellenzirkulator m, Richtungsgabel f, Ringleiter m, Umlenker m, Wellenleiterzirkulator m	cirrus, cirrus cloud, Ci	Cirrus m, [hohe] Federwolke f, hohe Eiswolke f, Zirrus m, Zirruswolke f, Ci
		cis-elimination	cis-Eliminierung f, cis-Abspaltung f
circulator	s. a. circulating pump		
circulatory	s. circulation <hydr., aero.>	cis-form	s. cis-isomer
circulatory flow	rollende Strömung f	cis-isomer[ide], cis-stereoisomer, cis-form	cis-Form f, cis-Isomer n
circulatory flow	s. a. cyclic potential motion		
circulatory integral, closed contour line integral, contour integral, circuitation	Randintegral n, Umlauf[s]integral n [um die Fläche], Linienintegral n längs der geschlossenen Kurve, Linienintegral über die Randkurve, geschlossenes Linienintegral	Cisotti['s] differential-difference equation	Cisottische Differential-Differenzen-Gleichung f
		cis-position, cis-situation	cis-Stellung f
		cis-stereoisomer	s. cis-isomer
		cis-tactic	cis-taktisch
circulatory system, circulation (circulating) system	Zirkulationssystem n	cistern barometer, reservoir [mercury] barometer, cup (bulb) barometer	Gefäßbarometer n, Gefäß-Quecksilberbarometer n
circulizer <in the stellarator>	Zirkulator m <im Stellarator>	cistern manometer	Gefäßmanometer n
circum-Antarctic basin	antarktischer Wasserring m	cistern of the thermometer, thermometer bulb	Thermometerkugel f, Thermometergefäß n
circumcircle, circumscribed circle, circle circumscribed of...	Umkreis m, umbeschriebener Kreis m, umschriebener Kreis	cis-trans isomer	s. geometric[al] isomer
		cis-trans isomerism	s. geometrical isomerism
		citrate cycle	s. Krebs cycle
circumcirculation, washing-round, lopping-round	Umspülung f	civilian transformation	= growth transformation or nucleation transformation
circumference	s. circle	civil twilight	bürgerliche Dämmerung f
circumference	s. periphery <math.>	civil year, calendar (artificial) year	bürgerliches Jahr n, Kalenderjahr n
circumference	s. perimeter <quantity, math.>	cladding, plating	Plattierung f
circumference factor <acc.>	Umfangsfaktor m <Beschl.>	cladding	s. a. canning <fuel elements>
circumference of orbit	s. orbit circumference	cladding	s. a. fuel element can
circumferential; peripheral	Umfangs-; peripher; Mantel-; Rand-	Clairaut['s] [differential] equation	s. differential equation of Clairaut
circumferential component, peripheral component	Umfangskomponente f	Clairaut['s] theorem	Clairautsches Theorem n
		clamp [circuit]	s. clamper <el.>
		clamper, clamper circuit, clamping [circuit], clamp, clamp circuit <el.>	Clampingschaltung f, Klemmschaltung f <El.>
circumferential direction	Umfangsrichtung f		
circumferential fault	s. boundary fault	clamping of the pendulum	Pendeleinspannung f, Einspannung f des Pendels
circumferential speed, peripheral speed (velocity)	Umfangsgeschwindigkeit f	clam-shell mark [in the fatigue fracture]	s. cyster shell marking
circumferential stress	s. tangential stress	clam shell markings <of fatigue crack>, conchoidal fracture (markings), arrest lines	Muschelbruch m <bei Ermüdung>
circumglobal radiation	Zirkumglobalstrahlung f		
circumgyration <about a free axis>; rotation	Rotation f, Drehung f; Rotieren n	Clapeyron-Clausius relation	s. Clausius-Clapeyron['s] equation
circumhorizontal arc	Zirkumhorizontalbogen m, unterer Berührungsbogen m des großen Ringes	Clapeyron['s] elastic body	Clapeyronsches elastisches Gebilde n
circumlunar orbit	Mondumlaufbahn f	Clapeyron['s] equation, Clapeyron relation	Clapeyronsche Gleichung (Zustandsgleichung) f
		Clapeyron equation	s. a. Clausius-Clapeyron['s] equation
circummeridian altitude	Zirkummeridianhöhe f	Clapeyron relation	s. Clapeyron['s] equation
circumnutation	Zirkumnutation f	Clapeyron['s] theorem	Clapeyronscher Arbeitssatz m
circumplanetary	zirkumplanetar		
circumpolar star	Zirkumpolarstern m	Clapeyron['s] theorem	s. a. equation of three moments
circumpolar vorticity, circumpolar whirl	Zirkumpolarwirbel m, zirkumpolarer Wirbel m	clapotis	Plätschern n; Plätscherwelle f, Clapotis f
circumrotation	s. revolution <around, round>	Clapp oscillator	Clapp-Oszillator m
		clarification, clarifying, clearing, cleaning	Klärung f
circumscribed circle	s. circumcircle	clarifying solution	Klärlösung f
circumscribed halo	umschriebener Halo m	Clark cell, Latimer-Clark cell	Clark-Element n, Clarksches Normalelement n, Clark-Standardelement n
circumsphere	Umkugel f, um[be]schriebene Kugel f		
circumzenithal arc	Zirkumzenitalbogen m, oberer Berührungsbogen m des großen Ringes, Zirkumzenitalkreis m	clarke, Clarke number (value)	Clarke-Zahl f, Clarke m, Verteilungsquotient m
		Clark rule	Clarksche Regel f
		class	s. set <math.>

class bound[ary], class limit	Klassengrenze f	Clausius-Mosotti-Lorentz-Lorenz equation (formula)	s. Lorentz-Lorenz formula
classes / between	s. interclass	Clausius-Rankine cycle	s. Rankine cycle
class frequency	Klassenhäufigkeit f, Klassenbesetzung f	Clausius['] theorem	Clausius-Gleichung f, Clausiussche Gleichung f, Satz m von Clausius
classical Boltzmann statistics	s. Maxwell-Boltzmann statistics	Clausius virial	Clausiussches Virial n
classical canonical form, Jordanian canonical form, first canonical form, Jordan normal form <of matrix>	Jordansche Normalform f, dritte Normalform <Matrix>	Clausius['] virial theorem	s. virial theorem
		Clayden effect	Clayden-Effekt m
		Clayton['s] period	Clayton-Periode f
		cleaning	s. clarification
		cleanliless; cleanness	s. purity
		clean-up	Aufzehrung f, „clean-up" n
		clean-up effect	„clean-up"-Effekt m, Aufzehrungseffekt m
classical electron radius, electron radius	[klassischer] Elektronenradius m	clear <of day, sky>	heiter <Tag, Himmel>
classical ensemble	s. Gibbsian ensemble	clear, limpid, transparent	klar, durchsichtig
classical formalism	Formalismus m der klassischen Theorien	clear air turbulence, C.A.T.	Klarluftturbulenz f, wolkenfreie Turbulenz f, Luftwirbel m bei klarem Wetter, CAT
classical mechanics, Newtonian (Newton['s]) mechanics	klassische Mechanik f, Newtonsche Mechanik	clearance	Lichtraumprofil n
classical Poisson bracket[s]	s. Poisson['s] bracket	clearance <bio.>	Clearance f, „clearance" f
classical principle of relativity	s. Galilean principle of relativity	clearance	s. a. gap <techn.>
classical scattering	s. Thomson scattering	clearing	s. clarification
classical statistics	s. Maxwell-Boltzmann statistics	clearing	s. brightening <opt.>
		clearing	s. release <el.>
classical theory of the electron	s. Lorentz['s] theory of electrons	clearing field, sweeping field, ion draw-out field	Reinigungsfeld n, Ziehfeld n, Ionenziehfeld n, Absaugfeld n
classical thermodynamics	klassische Thermodynamik f, mechanische Wärmetheorie f	clearing thickness	Aufhellungsdicke f
		clearing time	s. opening time
		clearing up <meteo.>	Aufklaren n, Klärung f
classification, classifying process, sizing, size separation, grading, sorting	Klassieren n [nach der Korngröße], Trennung f nach der Korngröße	clearing up	s. a. brightening <opt.>
		clearing up	s. a. elucidation
		clearing voltage, sweeping voltage, ion draw-out voltage	Ziehspannung f, Ionenziehspannung f, Absaugspannung f, Reinigungsspannung f
classification of high-temperature insulation	Wärmeklasse f		
classifying process	s. classification	clear overflow weir	s. free weir
class interval; class interval length, class length, class range <stat.>	Klassenintervall n; Klassenbreite f, Klassengröße f <Stat.>	cleavability	Spaltbarkeit f
		cleavage; schistosity, slaty cleavage; foliation <geo.>	Schieferung f <Geo.>
class limit	s. class bound		
class number	Klassenzahl f	cleavage <bio.>	Durchschnürung f <Bio.>
class of cloud	s. cloud species	cleavage, cleaving <cryst.>	Spaltung f <Krist.>
class of stars, star class, star type	Sternklasse f, Sterntyp m	cleavage brittleness, intercrystalline (intergranular) brittleness	interkristalline Brüchigkeit f, Spaltbrüchigkeit f
class of symmetry, symmetry class	Symmetrieklasse f	cleavage crack	Spaltungsriß m
class of the flare	s. importance of the flare	cleavage face	s. cleavage surface
class range	s. class interval	cleavage fracture, cleave (separation) fracture, rupture	Trennungsbruch m, Trennbruch m
class sum	Klassensumme f		
clastic rock, rubble	Trümmergestein n, klastisches Sedimentgestein n	cleavage of the ring	s. ring cleavage
clathrate	Klathrat n, Käfigeinschlußverbindung f	cleavage plane	Spaltebene f, Spaltungsebene f
clathration, imprisonment <chem.>	Einschließung f <Chem.>	cleavage strength	Spaltfestigkeit f, Spaltungsfestigkeit f
Claude air liquefier	Claudesche Luftverflüssigungsmaschine f, Luftverflüssigungsmaschine von Claude	cleavage surface (face), cleavage face	Spaltfläche f
		cleave fracture	s. cleavage fracture
Claude cycle	Claudescher Kreisprozeß m, Claude-Prozeß m	cleaving <cryst.>, cleavage	Spaltung f <Krist.>
clausius, Cl	Clausius n, Cl	Clebsch-Gordan coefficient, vector addition coefficient	Clebsch-Gordan-Koeffizient m, Vektoradditionskoeffizient m
Clausius-Clapeyron equation, Clausius-Clapeyron['s] relation, Clapeyron-Clausius relation, Clapeyron equation	Clausius-Clapeyronsche Gleichung (Differentialgleichung) f, Clausius-Clapeyron-Gleichung f, Gleichung von Clausius-Clapeyron, Clapeyron-Clausius-Gleichung f	Clebsch-Gordan expansion	Clebsch-Gordan-Zerlegung f
		Clebsch-Gordan rule	Clebsch-Gordansche Regel f, Clebsch-Gordan-Regel f
		Clebsch-Gordan series	Clebsch-Gordan-Reihe f, Gordansche Reihenentwicklung f
Clausius-Duhem inequality, principle of dissipation	Dissipationsprinzip n, Clausius-Duhemsche Ungleichung f	Clebsch['s] transformation, transformation of Clebsch	Clebsch-Transformation f, Clebschsche Transformation f
Clausius equation [of state]	Clausiussche Zustandsgleichung f	cleft <geo.>	Kluft f <Geo.>
Clausius inequality	Clausiussche Ungleichung f	cleft	s. a. rill
		cleft family, family of clefts	Kluftschar f
Clausius-Mosotti equation, Clausius-Mosotti relation	Clausius-Mosottische Formel (Beziehung, Gleichung) f, Clausius-Mosotti-Gleichung f, Clausius-Mosottisches Gesetz n	cleftiness <geo.>	Klüftung f, Zerklüftung f
		cleft system, system of clefts	Kluftsystem n

Clément-Desormes experiment	Clément-Desormesscher Versuch *m*	clock star	Zeitstern *m*
Clemmow-Mullally-Allis diagram, CMA diagram	CMA-Diagramm *n*, Clemmow-Mullally-Allis-Diagramm *n*	clockwise	im Uhrzeigersinn, in mathematisch negativem Sinn, in mathematisch negativer Richtung, in negativer Richtung, mathematisch negativ
clepsydra, water clock	Wasseruhr *f*, Klepsydra *f*		
Clerk Maxwell relation	s. Maxwell relation <opt.>		
click [pressure] gauge	Tickmanometer *n*		
cliff glacier	s. suspended glacier	clockwise circularly polarized	s. right-handed circular
cliff interferometer, cliff-top (sea) interferometer	Kliffinterferometer *n*	clockwise elliptically polarized	s. right-handed elliptically polarized
Clifford['s] algebra	Cliffordsche Algebra *f*, Clifford-Algebra *f*	clockwise polarized, right-handed polarized	rechtspolarisiert, rechtsdrehend polarisiert, rechtshändig polarisiert
Clifford number	Cliffordsche Zahl *f*		
cliff-top interferometer	s. cliff interferometer		
climagram	Klimogramm *n*	clockwise process, right-handed cycle	Rechtsprozeß *m*
climate province	Klimaprovinz *f*		
climatic fluctuation	Klimaschwankung *f*	clockwise rotation	s. dextrorotation
		clock-work, clockwork mechanism	s. clock movement
climatic pole	Klimapol *m*, klimatischer Pol *m*	close approach	s. encounter <e.g. of stars>
climatic zone	Klimazone *f*, Klimagürtel *m*	close binary	enger Doppelstern *m*
		close collision	Nahstoß *m*, Nahordnungsstoß *m*
climatological diagram	Klimadiagramm *n*	close coupling	s. tight coupling <el.>
climatological net, net of climatological stations	Klimanetz *n*	closed antenna	s. loop antenna
		closed channel [of reaction]	geschlossener Kanal (Reaktionskanal) *m*
climb	s. a. climbing motion	closed circuit <el.>	geschlossener Stromkreis (Kreis) *m* <El.>
climbing	s. climbing motion		
climbing ability (capacity)	Steigfähigkeit *f*	closed circuit, closed-circuit system; closed loop; closed cycle <therm.>	geschlossener Kreis[lauf] *m*; geschlossene Schleife *f* <Therm.>
climbing height, height of lift (climb, ascent)	Steighöhe *f*		
climbing motion, climb [-ing], non-conservative motion <of dislocations>	Klettern *n*, Kletterbewegung *f*, nichtkonservative Bewegung *f* <Versetzungen>, Versetzungsklettern *n*	closed-circuit arrangement	Ringschaltung *f*
		closed-circuit cooling	s. closed-loop cooling system
		closed-circuit current	s. resting current
climbing spark	Kletterfunke[n] *m*	closed-circuit system	s. closed circuit
		closed-circuit wind tunnel	s. return-flow wind tunnel
climbing speed (velocity), rate of climb (ascent), ascending velocity	Steiggeschwindigkeit *f*, Aufstiegsgeschwindigkeit *f*	closed cloud cover, closed cover of clouds	geschlossene (zusammenhängende) Wolkendecke *f*
clinoaxis	Klinoachse *f*	closed complex plane, extended [complex] plane	vollständige [komplexe] Zahlenebene *f*, abgeschlossene (volle) Zahlenebene, [ab]geschlossene komplexe Ebene *f*, [ab]geschlossene Ebene, Vollebene *f*
clinodiagonal	Klinodiagonale *f*		
clinogeotropism	Klinogeotropismus *m*		
clinographic	s. axonometric		
clinohedral class	s. hemihedry of the monoclinic system		
clinometer, bevel protractor; inclinometer; tilt meter	Neigungsmesser *m*, Gefäll[e]messer *m*; Inklinometer *n*; Fallwinkelmesser *m*, Klinometer *n*; Böschungsmesser *m*; Krängungsmesser *m*	closed contour	s. closed curve <math.>
		closed contour line integral	s. circulatory integral
		closed cover of clouds	s. closed cloud cover
		closed curve, circuit, closed contour (loop) <math.>	geschlossene Kurve (Linie) *f*; geschlossener Weg *m* <Math.>
clip-on ammeter, hook-on ammeter	Anlegerstrommesser *m*, Anlegeamperemeter *n*	closed cycle	s. closed circuit <therm.>
		closed domain	s. domain <math.>
clipper, pulse clipper, clipping circuit	Begrenzer *m*, Impulsbegrenzer *m*, Begrenzerkreis *m*	closed fault	s. compressive fault <geo.>
		closed form <cryst.>	geschlossene Form *f* <Krist.>
		closed interval, segment <math.>	abgeschlossenes Intervall *n*, Segment *n* <Math.>
clipper circuit	s. peak limiter		
clipping	Verstümmelung *f*	closed Jordan curve	s. simple closed curve
clipping	s. a. cut-off	closed loop	s. mesh <el.>
clipping circuit	s. clipper	closed loop	s. closed circuit <therm.>
clipping time	Zeitkonstante *f* des Begrenzerkreises, Klippzeit *f*	closed loop	s. closed curve <math.>
clock	s. time piece	closed-loop [automatic] control, feedback control, automatic control, control, backward-acting control	Regelung *f* [im geschlossenen Wirkungskreis], Rückwärtsregelung *f*; rückwärts geregelte Schaltung *f*
clock for comparison, comparison clock	Vergleichsuhr *f*		
clock generator	s. synchronizing pulse		
clock movement, movement of clock (watch); clockwork mechanism, drive mechanism [of the clock], clock-work	Uhrwerk *n*		
		closed-loop cooling system, closed-circuit cooling	Ringlaufkühlung *f*, Umlaufkühlung *f*
clock multivibrator	s. synchronizing pulse generator	closed-loop transfer function, transfer function of the closed-loop system, system function <control>	Übertragungsfunktion *f* des geschlossenen Regelkreises (Kreises, Regelsystems, Übertragungssystems, Systems), Übertragungsfunktion der geschlossenen Kette
clock paradox	Uhrenparadoxon *n*		
clock-pulse, timing pulse	Taktimpuls *m*		
clock reaction	s. slow reaction		
clock relay, timer, time switch	Schaltuhr *f*, Zeitschalter *m*, Zeitsteuergerät *n*; Zeitscheibe *f*		
		closed magnetic circuit *f* / with	eisengeschlossen
		closed-on-itself traverse	s. closed traverse
		closed orthogonal system	abgeschlossenes Orthogonalsystem *n*

closed phase	abgeschlossene Phase f	closure <math.>	[abgeschlossene] Hülle f, Abschluß m, Adhärenz f
closed pipe, stopped pipe	gedackte Pfeife f	closure <math., therm.>	Abgeschlossenheit f
closed set	abgeschlossene Menge f		
closed shell, filled shell, completed shell	abgeschlossene (vollbesetzte, besetzte, aufgefüllte) Schale f, [voll-]gefüllte Schale, Edelgasschale f	closure	s. a. closing
		closure domain, flux-closure domain, domain of closure <usually small>	Zusatzbezirk m, Zusatzbereich m, Zusatz-Elementarbereich m <zur Verminderung der Streuung in der Umgebung von Fremdeinschlüssen> <oft zipfelförmig>
closed simple curve	s. simple closed curve		
closed surface	geschlossene Fläche f		
closed surface integral, integral over a closed surface	Hüllenintegral n		
		closure of the shell; saturation of the shell; filling of the shell	Schalenabschluß m, Abschluß m der Schale; Auffüllen n der Schale
closed system <therm.>	abgeschlossenes (vollständiges) System n		
closed traverse, closed-on-itself traverse, traverse which closes on itself	geschlossener Polygonzug m	closure of the traverse, closing of the traverse	Abschluß m des Polygonzuges
closed [wind] tunnel	s. return-flow wind tunnel	cloth filter	s. filter cloth
close echo	Nahecho n	clothoid [curve]	s. Cornu['s] spiral
		clotting	s. coagulation
		cloud	s. star cloud <astr.>
close-in fallout	primärer radioaktiver Niederschlag m	cloud albedo, albedo of the clouds	Wolkenalbedo f
closely packed	s. close-packed	cloud amount	s. cloudiness <in eighths or octas>
closeness	s. environment		
close-packed, closely (densely) packed	dichtgepackt	cloud band, band of clouds	Wolkenband n
		cloud bank, bank of clouds	Wolkenbank f; Wolkenwand f
close-packed structure, closest-packed structure, closest packing	dichteste Packung f, dichteste gitterförmige Packung f, dichtestgepackte Struktur f, dichteste Packungsstruktur f; dichteste Kugelpackung[sstruktur] f, h. k. p.	cloud banner	Wolkenfahne f, Wolkenstreifen m
		cloud base	Wolkenuntergrenze f
		cloud base, base of the cloud	Unterseite f der Wolke, Wolkenunterseite f, Wolkenbasis f
close-packed structure, close packing	dichte Packung (Lagerung) f, Dichtpackung f; dichtgepackte Struktur f, dichte Packungsstruktur f	cloud burst	s. downpour
		cloud cap	Wolkenkappe f, Wolkenhaube f
close scanning	Feinabtastung f; Feinauflösung f	cloud ceilometer, ceilometer, ceiling ligh projector	Wolkenhöhenmesser m
closest approach	s. distance of closest approach	cloud chamber, fog chamber, fog-track chamber	Nebelkammer f
closest-packed	dichtestgepackt		
closest-packed structure	s. close-packed structure	cloud-chamber photograph	Nebelkammeraufnahme f
closest packing	s. close-packed structure		
close-talking response, close-talking sensitivity <of microphone>	Empfindlichkeit f [bei naher Besprechung], Übertragungsmaß n, [elektroakustischer] Übertragungsfaktor m	cloud-chamber track	s. cloud track
		cloud-cloud collision	Wolke-Wolke-Stoß m, Stoß m zweier Wolken
		cloud clutter, cloud echo	Wolkenecho n
close-up focusing	Naheinstellung f		
		cloud collision	Wolkenstoß m
close valley	Klause f, Klus[e] f; Engtalstrecke f	cloud column	s. smoke cloud
		cloud contour, cloud outline	Wolkenkontur f
closing, shutting, closure; stopping down <of diaphragm>	Schließen n	cloud-core collision	Wolke-Kern-Stoß m
closing	s. a. closure <geo.>	cloud cover	Wolkendecke f
closing arc, arc at make	Schließungsbogen m, Schließbogen m	cloud density measuring apparatus	Wolkendichtemesser m
		cloud depth	Wolkentiefe f
closing current, current [induced] at make	Schließungsstrom m, Schließstrom m	cloud development	Wolkenentwicklung f, Wolkenevolution f
closing error	s. misclosure	cloud discharge	s. cloud lightning discharge
closing of the traverse	s. closure of the traverse	cloud disk, cloud globe	Wolkenballen m
closing pressure, shutting pressure	Schließdruck m, Schließungsdruck m	cloud dome, cloud top, top of the cloud	Wolkenkuppe f
closing side <of polygon of forces>	Schlußlinie f <Kräftepolygon>	cloud echo	s. cloud clutter
		clouded glass	s. opal glass
closing spark, spark at make	Schließungsfunke m, Schließfunke m	cloud element, cloud particle	Wolkenelement n, Wolkenteilchen n
		cloud family	Wolkenfamilie f
closing the circuit, making of circuit	Schließen n des Stromkreises	cloud filter, yellow cloud filter	Wolkenfilter n
closing time <e.g. of shutter>	Schließzeit f, Schließdauer f <z. B. Verschluß>	cloud form, cloud shape	Wolkenform f
		cloud formation	Wolkengebilde n, Wolkenbildung f
closing yoke	Schlußjoch n	cloud formed during mixing of air masses	s. mixing cloud
closure, closing <geo.>	Abschlußrichtung f; Richtungsabschluß m; Schleifenschluß m <Geo.>		
		cloud gap	Wolkenloch n, Wolkenlücke f

cloud globe, cloud disk	Wolkenballen m	cloud width	s. width of cloud
cloud height, ceiling, main cloud base	Wolkenhöhe f, Bewölkungshöhe f; Hauptwolkenuntergrenze f	cloud wisp	s. rag of cloud
		cloudy	bewölkt, wolkig
		cloudy crystal ball [model]	s. semi-transparent model of nucleus
cloudiness	Bewölkung f	clover[-]leaf cyclotron	Kleeblattzyklotron n, Kleeblattypzyklotron n
cloudiness, cloud amount, amount of clouds <in eighths or octas>	Bedeckungsgrad m, Bedeckung f [des Himmels], Bewölkungsmenge f, Wolkenmenge f <in Achteln>		
		clue formation	s. formation of clues
		clue molecule, molecule convoluted to a clue, molecular coil	Knäuelmolekül n
clouding	Aufziehen n von Wolken (Bewölkung), Umwölkung f	Clusius[-Dickel] column	s. thermal diffusion column
		cluster, molecular cluster <molecules>	Molekülschwarm m, Molekülkomplex m, Molekülcluster m, Molekülgruppe f, ungleichzähliges Assoziat n, Cluster m [von Molekülen]
clouding of the lens	Linsentrübung f, Trübung f der Linse		
cloud layer	Wolkenschicht f		
cloudless	wolkenlos		
cloudlet	Wölkchen n		
cloud level	Wolkenetage f, Wolkenstockwerk n	cluster, nested sample <stat.>	Klumpenstichprobe f <Stat.>
		cluster	Cluster m, Schwarm m, Haufen m, Nest n
cloud lightning discharge, cloud discharge, air flash	Wolkenblitz m, Wolkenentladung f	cluster	s. a. complex ion
		cluster beam	Clusterstrahl m, Strahl m des kondensierten Gases
cloud limit	Schleiergrenze f, Nebelgrenze f, Nebelbildungsgrenzwert m	clustered; nested	nestartig, nest[er]förmig, haufenförmig
cloud limit	s. a. limit of the cloud	cluster expansion theory	Cluster-Entwicklungstheorie f, Clustermethode f
cloud mass	Wolkenmasse f		
cloud motion, cloud train	Wolkenzug m	cluster function	Clusterfunktion f
cloud of dislocations, dislocation cloud	Versetzungswolke f	clustering	Schwarmbildung f <in Flüssigkeiten>; Clusterbildung f, Nestbildung f, Haufenbildung f <Ionen>
cloud of droplets	Tröpfchenwolke f		
cloud of electrons	s. electron cloud		
cloud of ions	s. ion cloud <el., chem.>	clustering of galaxies, clustering of nebulae	Nebelhaufenbildung f
cloud of particles, swarm of particles	Teilchenwolke f		
		clustering of meteors	s. knot within a meteor stream
cloud of the volcano	s. cloud of volcanic ash		
cloud of vertical development	Wolke f mit vertikalem Aufbau, Wolke mit vertikaler Entwicklung	clustering of nebulae, clustering of galaxies	Nebelhaufenbildung f
		cluster integral	„cluster integral" n, Clusterintegral n
cloud of volcanic ash, cloud of the volcano	Eruptionswolke (Aschenwolke) f des Vulkans, Vulkanwolke f		
		cluster ion	s. complex ion
		cluster member	s. member of a cluster
cloud outline, cloud contour	Wolkenkontur f	cluster model	Clustermodell n
cloud particle, cloud element	Wolkenelement n, Wolkenteilchen n		
		cluster of galaxies (nebulae)	Nebelhaufen m
cloud physics	Physik f der Wolken, Wolkenphysik f	cluster of vacancies	s. vacancy cluster
		cluster parallax	s. moving-cluster parallax
cloud point	Trübungspunkt m, Trübepunkt m, Kristallisationsbeginn m	cluster point	s. accumulation point <math.>
		cluster star	s. member of a cluster
cloud pulse	Raumladungsimpuls m	cluster structure	Büschelstruktur f
cloud rag	s. rag of cloud		
cloud rake, comb nephoscope	Wolkenrechen m, Wolkenharke f	cluster theory	Clustertheorie f
cloud report	Wolkenmeldung f	cluster[-type] variable [star]	s. RR Lyrae star
cloud ribbon	s. rag of cloud		
cloud searchlight	Wolkenscheinwerfer m	clydonogram	s. klydonogram
		clydonograph	s. klydonograph
		clystron	s. klystron
		CMA diagram, Clemmow-Mullaly-Allis diagram	CMA-Diagramm n, Clemmow-Mullaly-Allis-Diagramm n
cloud seeding	Wolkensäen n		
cloud shape, cloud form	Wolkenform f		
Clouds of Magellan	s. Magellanic Clouds		
cloud sounding balloon, cloud test balloon	Wolkensonde f	cnoidal wave	cn^2-förmige Welle f, Flachwasserwelle f
cloud species, species (class) of cloud	Wolkengattung f	c-number	c-Zahl f
		C-number theory	Theorie f der C-Zahlen, C-Zahlen-Theorie f
cloud structure	Wolkenstruktur f, Wolkenaufbau m	coacervate droplet	Koazervattropfen m
cloud system	Wolkensystem n	coacervation	Koazervation f, Koazervierung f, Entmischung f
cloud test balloon, cloud sounding balloon	Wolkensonde f	co-activator	Koaktivator m
cloud theodolite	Wolkentheodolit m	co-adsorption	Koadsorption f, gemeinsame Adsorption f
cloud thickness, thickness of the cloud	Wolkenmächtigkeit f, Wolkendicke f	coagel	Koagel n
		coagulating, coagulation, clotting	Koagulation f, Gerinnung f
cloud top, cloud dome, top of the cloud	Wolkenkuppe f		
cloud track, cloud-chamber track, fog track	Nebelkammerspur f, Nebelspur f	coagulation heat, heat of coagulation	Koagulationswärme f
		coagulation point	Koagulationstemperatur f, Koagulationspunkt m
cloud train, cloud motion	Wolkenzug m		
cloud type	Wolkenart f, Wolkenbild n		
cloud veil, veil of cloud	Wolkenschleier m; Wolkenschirm m	coagulation zone	Koagulationszone f
cloud velocity gauging	Salzwolkenverfahren n	coagulum <pl.: coagula>	Koagulat n

coalescence	Koaleszenz f, Zusammenfließen n, Zusammenwachsen n, Verschmelzung f, Vereinigung f ‹kolloidaler Teilchen›	coating of the mirror	s. mirror coating
		coating thickness	s. thickness of layer
		coating thickness gauge (meter)	s. thickness meter
Coal Sack, coalsack nebula	Kohlensack m	coaxial conductor; coaxial line	Koaxialleitung f, koaxiale (konzentrische) Leitung f; Koaxialleiter m, koaxialer Leiter m
coaltitude, zenith[al] distance	Zenitdistanz f, Zenitabstand m		
Coanda effect	Coanda-Effekt m	coaxial line tube	s. Heil tube
coarse adjustment, rough adjustment, coarse setting (control)	Grobeinstellung f	coaxially packaged transistor	s. coaxial transistor
		coaxial resonant cavity	s. resonant cavity
coarse adjustment	s. a. coarse focusing mechanism ‹of microscope›	coaxial resonant cavity wavemeter	Topfkreiswellenmesser m
coarse adjustment	s. a. coarse focusing motion	coaxial transistor, transistor in coaxial packing, coaxially packaged transistor	Koaxialtransistor m
coarse control; shimming	Grobsteuerung f; Grobregelung f; Trimmen n		
		coaxing ‹of materials›	Trainieren n, Trainiereffekt m ‹Werkstoffe›
coarse control	s. a. coarse adjustment		
coarse control	s. a. coarse focusing mechanism	cobalt bomb, cobalt source ‹in gamma-ray therapy›	Kobaltquelle f, Kobalteinheit f, Kobaltkanone f, Kobaltbombe f
coarse control rod, shim rod	Trimmstab m, Grobregelstab m, Kompensationsstab m, Anpassungsstab m		
		cochlea ‹of ear›, snail	Schnecke f, Cochlea f ‹Ohr›
coarse-disperse	s. coarse-grain	cochlear microphonic, aural microphonic	Cochlearstrom m
coarse dust	Grobstaub m		
coarse-fine action mechanism; coarse-fine focusing mechanism	Grob-Fein-Trieb m	Cockcroft accelerator, Cockcroft and Walton generator, Cockcroft apparatus (generator), Cockcroft-Walton accelerator (apparatus, generator)	s. cascade generator
coarse focus control, coarse focusing	s. coarse focusing motion ‹of microscope›		
coarse focusing mechanism, coarse control (adjustment) ‹of microscope›	Grobtrieb m des Mikroskops	cock grease, grease for cocks	Hahnfett n
		cocking	s. straining
		cock[-]pit ‹geo.›	Cockpit n ‹Geo.›
coarse focusing motion, coarse focusing (focus control, adjustment) ‹of microscope›	Grobeinstellung f ‹Mikroskop›	cock plug, plug of the cock, faucet ‹US›	Hahnküken n, Küken n, Hahnkegel m
		cocontravariant tensor, mixed tensor	gemischter Tensor m
coarse grain	Grobkorn n	cocrystallization	Mitkristallisation f, gemeinsames Auskristallisieren n
coarse-grain, coarse grained; dispersoid, coarse-disperse	grobkörnig, Grobkorn-; grobdispers		
		co-current flow	s. parallel stream
coarse-grain annealing	s. high-temperature annealing	Codazzi equations [of surface], Codazzi-Gauss equations	s. Mainardi-Codazzi relations
coarse grained	s. coarse-grain		
coarse-grained density	grobe Dichte f	Coddington eyepiece	Coddington-Okular n
		Coddington position factor, position factor	Coddingtonscher Positionsfaktor m
coarse-grained density matrix (operator)	grobe Dichtematrix f, grober Dichteoperator m	Coddington shape factor, shape factor	Coddingtonscher Formfaktor m
coarse network [in the chromosphere]	chromosphärisches Netzwerk n	co-declination	s. north polar distance
coarsening ‹of grain›, grain coarsening	Kornvergröberung f, Vergröberung f [des Korns]; Kornvergrößerung f	coding theory, mathematical theory of communication, information theory [of Shannon-Weaver]	mathematische Theorie f der Nachrichtenübertragung, Informationstheorie f [von Shannon-Weaver]
		codirectional	s. parallel
coarse-pored	großporig, grobporig; weitporig	codirectional	s. same sense / in the
		codomain	s. range
coarse setting	s. coarse adjustment	coefficient comparison, comparison of coefficients [method]	Koeffizientenvergleich m
coarse structure term	Grobstrukturterm m		
coastal effect	Küsteneffekt m		
coastal refraction	Küstenbrechung f; Küstenpeilfehler m		
		coefficient in the expansion	s. coefficient of the expansion
coasting flight	s. inertial flight		
coastline, shoreline, shore line	Küstenlinie f	coefficient of advance, advance coefficient	Voreilungskoeffizient m
		coefficient of alienation	Alienationskoeffizient m, Zweideutigkeitsmaß n
coat, fog, cover	Beschlag m		
coat	s. a. coating ‹gen.›		
coated / becoming	s. covered with damp / getting		
coated method, coating method ‹radioautography›	„coated"-Methode f, Emulsionsmethode f ‹Autoradiographie›	coefficient of apparent expansion	relativer Ausdehnungskoeffizient m
		coefficient of association ‹stat.›	Abhängigkeitskoeffizient m von Yule, Yulescher Abhängigkeitskoeffizient
coated particle ‹reactor technology›	beschichtetes Teilchen n ‹Reaktortechnik›		
coating ‹with emulsion›	Aufgießen n, Vergießen n, Verguß m ‹Emulsion›; Beschichtung f	coefficient of asymmetry, asymmetry coefficient	Asymmetriebeiwert m, Asymmetriekoeffizient m
coating, coat, surface coat; covering, coverage; sheath; layer ‹gen.›	Überzug m, Schicht f, Überzugsschicht f; Beschichtung f; Belag m; Bedeckung f ‹allg.›	coefficient of attachment, attachment coefficient	Anlagerungskoeffizient m
		coefficient of capacitance, coefficient of capacity, capacitance coefficient	Kapazitätskoeffizient m; eigentlicher Kapazitätskoeffizient, eigentliche Kapazität f
coating	s. a. blooming ‹opt.›		
coating method ‹radioautography›, coated method	„coated"-Methode f, Emulsionsmethode f ‹Autoradiographie›		

coefficient of charge	Ladungsfaktor *m*	coefficient of linear extension, constant of elastic strain, reciprocal of Young's modulus	Dehn[ungs]zahl *f*, Dehnungskonstante *f*, Dehnungsgröße *f*, Dehnungskoeffizient *m*, Elastizitätskoeffizient *m*, Elastizitätszahl *f*
coefficient of chromatic difference in image position	s. longitudinal chromatic aberration ‹el., opt.›		
coefficient of compressibility, compressibility ‹quantity›	Kompressibilität *f*; Kompressibilitätskoeffizient *m*	coefficient of liquefaction, liquefaction coefficient	Verflüssigungskoeffizient *m*
coefficient of contraction	s. contraction coefficient	coefficient of mass conductivity	s. mass conductivity coefficient
coefficient of coupling	s. coupling coefficient ‹el.›	coefficient of measure	s. numerical measure
coefficient of cubic compressibility	s. cubic compressibility	coefficient of molecular association	Assoziationskonstante *f*
coefficient of diffusion	s. diffusion coefficient		
coefficient of dila[ta]tion	s. coefficient of thermal expansion	coefficient of momentum diffusion	s. eddy viscosity
coefficient of discharge	s. discharge coefficient	coefficient of mutual conductance	s. mutual conductance
coefficient of dispersion	s. dispersion coefficient		
coefficient of dynamic friction	s. coefficient of sliding friction	coefficient of mutual diffusion	Heterodiffusionskoeffizient *m*
coefficient of elasticity in shear	s. elastic shear modulus	coefficient of passage	s. coefficient of permeability
coefficient of evaporation	s. rate of evaporation	coefficient of performance, performance coefficient	Leistungsbeiwert *m*, Leistungsziffer *f*
coefficient of excess, excess; flatness factor, kurtosis ‹stat.›	Exzeß *m*; Koeffizient *m* des Exzesses, Kurtosis *f*, Steilheit *f*, Völligkeitsgrad *m*, Blockkoeffizient *m* ‹Stat.›		
		coefficient of performance, c.o.p. ‹of refrigerator›	Kälteleistungsziffer *f*, Nutzeffekt *m* ‹Kältemaschine›
coefficient of exchange, exchange coefficient	Austauschkoeffizient *m*		
coefficient of expansion	s. coefficient of thermal expansion	coefficient of performance ‹in refrigerating engineering›	Kältewirkungsgrad *m*, thermodynamischer Wirkungsgrad (Gütegrad) *m*, Gütegrad ‹Kältetechnik›
coefficient of feedback, feedback factor	Rückkopplungsfaktor *m*		
coefficient of fineness	Völligkeitsgrad *m* [der Verdrängung]	coefficient of permeability, coefficient of passage (transmission) ‹of a membrane›	Durchlässigkeitskoeffizient *m* ‹Membran›
coefficient of flow	s. flow coefficient		
coefficient of freedom, freedom coefficient	Freiheitskoeffizient *m*		
coefficient of friction, friction coefficient, frictional coefficient, friction factor	Reibungskoeffizient *m*, Reibungszahl *f*, Reibungsziffer *f*, Reibungsfaktor *m*, Reib[ungs]beiwert *m*, Reibwert *m*	coefficient of permeability	s. a. permeability coefficient
		coefficient of pitching moment	s. pitching moment coefficient
		coefficient of pivoting friction, coefficient of friction of pivoting	Koeffizient *m* der Bohrreibung (bohrenden Reibung), Bohrreibungskoeffizient *m*
coefficient of frictional resistance	s. friction coefficient ‹aero., hydr.›		
coefficient of friction at rest	s. coefficient of static friction		
		coefficient of polytropy	s. polytropic exponent
coefficient of friction of pivoting	s. coefficient of pivoting friction	coefficient of potential	Potentialkoeffizient *m*
		coefficient of probability	s. density in phase
coefficient of grain boundary diffusion	Korngrenzendiffusionskoeffizient *m*	coefficient of proportionality	s. factor of proportionality
coefficient of harmonic distortion, harmonic (nonlinear) distortion coefficient ‹of *n*-th order›	Klirrkoeffizient *m*, Teilklirrfaktor *m* ‹*n*-ter Ordnung›	coefficient of pseudoanomaly, pseudoanomaly coefficient	Pseudoanomaliekoeffizient *m*
		coefficient of rank correlation, Spearman['s] coefficient of rank correlation, rank correlation coefficient	Rangkorrelationskoeffizient *m*, Koeffizient *m* der Rangkorrelation, Spearmanscher Rangkorrelationskoeffizient
coefficient of heat conductivity	s. thermal conductivity		
coefficient of heat emission, heat emission coefficient	Wärmeabgabezahl *f*, Wärmeabgabeziffer *f*, Wärmeabgabekoeffizient *m* ‹in kcal/cm² s grd›		
		coefficient of recombination	s. recombination coefficient
		coefficient of remanent induction, remanence (remanent induction) coefficient	Nachwirkungsbeiwert *m*
coefficient of heat transfer	s. heat transfer coefficient		
coefficient of heat transfer ‹US›	s. heat[-]transmission coefficient		
		coefficient of resistance	s. friction coefficient
coefficient of heeling moment	s. rolling moment coefficient	coefficient of resistance	s. resistance coefficient
		coefficient of restitution	s. restitution coefficient
coefficient of increase of pressure	s. pressure coefficient		
		coefficient of rolling friction, coefficient of rolling resistance	Koeffizient *m* der rollenden Reibung, Rollreibungskoeffizient *m*, Rollreibungszahl *f*, Reibungsarm *m*
coefficient of induced magnetism	Koeffizient *m* des induzierten Magnetismus		
coefficient of induction, mutual capacitance	Influenz[ierungs]koeffizient *m*, Koeffizient *m* der gegenseitigen Kapazität, gegenseitige Kapazität *f*, Gegenkapazität *f*		
		coefficient of rolling moment	s. rolling moment coefficient
		coefficient of rolling resistance	s. coefficient of rolling friction
		coefficient of roughness	s. roughness coefficient
coefficient of inertia, inertial coefficient	Trägheitskoeffizient *m*		
coefficient of kinetic friction	s. coefficient of sliding friction	coefficient of selfdiffusion, self-diffusion (self-diffusing) coefficient, self-diffusivity	Selbstdiffusionskoeffizient *m*
coefficient of Knudsen diffusion	s. Knudsen diffusion coefficient		
		coefficient of selfinduction	s. inductance
coefficient of linear compressibility	s. linear compressibility		
coefficient of linear expansion, linear expansion coefficient, linear expansivity; linear thermal expansion coefficient	linearer Ausdehnungskoeffizient *m*, Längenausdehnungskoeffizient *m*, lineare Ausdehnungszahl *f*, Längen[aus]dehnungszahl *f*, Längsdehnungszahl *f*, Längsdehnungskoeffizient *m*; linearer Wärmeausdehnungskoeffizient *m*, lineare Wärmeausdehnungszahl *f*	coefficient of shear, shear[ing] coefficient, shear compliance	Schubgröße *f*, Schubkoeffizient *m*, reziproker Schubmodul *m*
		coefficient of sliding friction, coefficient of kinetic friction, coefficient of dynamic friction, friction constant	Gleitreibungskoeffizient *m*, Gleitreibungszahl *f*, Gleitreibungsbeiwert *m*, Reibungskoeffizient *m* der Bewegung, Koeffizient *m* der gleitenden Reibung, dynamischer Reibungskoeffizient

coefficient 106

coefficient of sound damping, sound damping (attenuation) coefficient (factor)	Schalldämpfungskonstante f	**coefficient of viscosity,** viscosity coefficient, shear viscosity coefficient, dynamic[al] viscosity, Newtonian viscosity, viscosity, internal friction factor, absolute viscosity η <quantity>	Viskosität f, [dynamische] Zähigkeit f, dynamische (Newtonsche) Viskosität, Koeffizient m der inneren Reibung, [innerer] Reibungskoeffizient m, Viskositätskoeffizient m, Zähigkeitskoeffizient m, Viskositäts[bei]wert m, Zähigkeits[bei]wert m, Viskositätsmaß n, Zähigkeitsmaß n, Viskositätskennziffer f, Zähigkeitskennziffer f, Konstante f der inneren Reibung, Viskositätskonstante f, Zähigkeitskonstante f, Zähigkeitszahl f, Zähigkeitsziffer f, η <Größe>
coefficient of specific heat	s. specific heat		
coefficient of specific heat at constant pressure, specific heat at constant pressure, isopiestic specific heat	spezifische Wärme f bei konstantem Druck		
coefficient of specific heat at constant volume	s. specific heat at constant volume		
coefficient of spin correlation, spin correlation coefficient	Koeffizient m der Spinkorrelation, Spinkorrelationskoeffizient m		
coefficient of stability	Stabilitätskoeffizient m	**coefficient of volume diffusion,** volume diffusion coefficient	Volum[en]diffusionskoeffizient m
coefficient of standard variation	s. standard deviation	**coefficient of volume expansion**	s. thermal coefficient of volume expansion
coefficient of static friction, coefficient of friction at rest, static coefficient of friction	Haftreibungskoeffizient m, Haftreibungszahl f, Haftreibungsbeiwert m, Reibungskoeffizient m der Ruhe, statischer Reibungskoeffizient	**coefficient of yawing moment**	s. yawing moment coefficient
		coefficient-setting potentiometer	Koeffizienten[einstell]-potentiometer n
		Coehn['s] law, Coehn['s] rule	Coehnsche Ladungsregel (Regel) f, Coehnsches Ladungsgesetz (Aufladungsgesetz) n
coefficient of stiffness, stiffness coefficient	Steifigkeitskoeffizient m, Steifekoeffizient m		
coefficient of surface expansion	Oberflächenausdehnungskoeffizient m, Flächenausdehnungskoeffizient m	**coercimeter,** coercive force meter, coercivity meter	Koerzitivfeldstärkemesser m, Koerzimeter n
coefficient of surface friction	s. friction coefficient <aero., hydr.>	**coercive field, coercive force;** coercivity	Koerzitivfeldstärke f, koerzitive Feldstärke f, Koerzitivkraft f
coefficient of the expansion [in a series], expansion coefficient, coefficient [of the variables] in the expansion	Entwicklungskoeffizient m	**coercive force meter**	s. coercimeter
		coercivity	s. coercive force
		coercivity meter	s. coercimeter
		coexisting phases	koexistente Phasen fpl
coefficient of thermal conductivity	s. thermal conductivity	**cofactor,** signed-minor, algebraic adjoint <math.>	algebraisches Komplement n, Kofaktor m, Adjunkte f, algebraische Adjungierte f <Math.>
coefficient of thermal diffusion	s. thermal diffusion coefficient		
coefficient of thermal expansion, [thermal] expansion coefficient, [thermal] coefficient of expansion, coefficient of dila[ta]tion, thermal expansivity	thermischer Ausdehnungskoeffizient m, Wärmeausdehnungskoeffizient m, Wärme[aus]dehnungszahl f, Wärmeausdehnungsbeiwert m, Wärmedehnzahl f, Ausdehnungszahl f, Wärme[aus]dehnungsvermögen n	**coffin**	s. flask <for shielding of radioactive materials>
		cogeoid, compensated geoid	Kogeoid n, kompensiertes Geoid n
		cogredient	kogredient
		cogredient automorphism, inner automorphism	innerer Automorphismus m
coefficient of thermometric conductivity	s. thermal diffusivity	**cog-wheel method**	s. Fizeau['s] method
		Cohen-Flatt method	Cohen-Flatt-Verfahren n
coefficient of the variables in the expansion	s. coefficient of the expansion	**coherence area**	Kohärenzgebiet n
		coherence condition	Kohärenzbedingung f
coefficient of total radiation	s. Stefan-Boltzmann['s] constant	**coherence distance,** coherence length	Kohärenzabstand m; Kohärenzlänge f, Interferenzlänge f
coefficient of transmission <of membrane>, coefficient of permeability (passage)	Durchlässigkeitskoeffizient m <Membran>	**coherence factor**	s. phase coherence factor
		coherence in time	s. time coherence
		coherence length	s. coherence distance
		coherence time	Kohärenzzeit f
coefficient of turbidity	s. turbidity coefficient	**coherency postulate,** postulate of coherency, Weyl['s] postulate	Kohärenzpostulat n, Weylsches Postulat n
coefficient of turbulence	s. eddy viscosity		
coefficient of utilization <el.>	Belastungsfaktor m, Lastfaktor m <El.>	**coherent baric systems**	kohärente Luftdrucksysteme (Luftdruckgebilde) npl
coefficient of utilization	s. a. utilization factor <opt.>	**coherent colloidal system**	s. gel
coefficient of utilization of the tunnel, tunnel coefficient	Kanalfaktor m <aero.>	**coherent cross-section**	s. coherent scattering cross-section
coefficient of variation, variation coefficient	Variationskoeffizient m, Variabilitätskoeffizient m, Variationsbeiwert m	**coherent detector**	s. lock-in detector
		coherent elastic scattering [of neutrons]	s. elastic coherent scattering
coefficient of velocity, velocity coefficient	Geschwindigkeitsziffer f, Geschwindigkeitsbeiwert m <Hydr.>; Geschwindigkeitsfaktor m <Vak.>	**coherent emission,** coherent radiation	kohärente Strahlung f
		coherent interface	s. composition plane
		coherent light conversion	kohärente Transformation f des Lichtes
coefficient of viscosity <in the general form of the equation of motion of a viscous fluid>	Viskositätskoeffizient m <im verallgemeinerten Newtonschen Schubspannungsansatz>	**coherent radiation**	s. coherent emission
		coherent scattering	kohärente Streuung f
		coherent scattering amplitude	kohärente Streuamplitude f, Amplitude f der kohärenten Streuung

coherent scattering cross-section, coherent cross-section, cross-section for coherent scattering	kohärenter Streuquerschnitt m, Wirkungsquerschnitt m für kohärente Streuung, Wirkungsquerschnitt der kohärenten Streuung	coincidence counter	Koinzidenzzähler m
coherent scattering factor	kohärenter Streukoeffizient m, Koeffizient m der kohärenten Streuung	coincidence criterion [of Berek], Berek['s] coincidence criterion	Koinzidenzkriterium n [von Berek]
		coincidence efficiency	Koinzidenzeffektivität f
coherent scattering length	kohärente Streulänge f	coincidence element	Koinzidenzelement n
coherent system of units	kohärentes Einheitensystem (Maßsystem) n, [aufeinander] abgestimmtes Einheitensystem	coincidence level	Koinzidenzlibelle f
		coincidence loss	Koinzidenzverlust m, Koinzidenzausfall m
coherent unit	kohärente (abgestimmte, wohlpassende) Einheit f, Systemeinheit f	coincidence magnetic spectrometer	s. magnetic coincidence spectrometer
		coincidence mixture	Koinzidenzmischung f
coherent waves, coherent wave trains	kohärente Wellenzüge mpl, kohärente Wellen fpl	coincidence of phases	s. phase coincidence
		coincidence rangefinder, coincidence reading rangefinder, coincidence telemeter, double-image (split-field, split-image, cut-image) rangefinder	Koinzidenz-Entfernungsmesser m; Mischbild-Entfernungsmesser m; Schnittbild-Entfernungsmesser m
coherer	Fritter m, Kohärer m		
coherer effect, Calzecchi-Onesti effect	Kohärereffekt m, Kohärerwirkung f		
cohesion	Kohäsion f		
		coincidence rate	Koinzidenz[zähl]rate f
		coincidence reading rangefinder	s. coincidence rangefinder
cohesional work, cohesion energy	s. cohesive energy	coincidence resolution time, coincidence resolving time	Auflösungszeit f der Koinzidenzschaltung, Koinzidenzauflösungszeit f
cohesion force, cohesive force	Kohäsionskraft f		
cohesion pressure	s. internal pressure		
cohesion strength, cohesive strength	Kohäsionsfestigkeit f	coincidence resolving power, resolving power of coincidence system	Koinzidenzauflösungsvermögen n, Auflösungsvermögen n des Koinzidenzsystems
cohesive energy, cohesion energy, work of cohesion, cohesional work	Kohäsionsenergie f		
		coincidence resolving time	s. coincidence resolution time
cohesive energy, binding energy <cryst.>	Bindungsenergie f <Krist.>	coincidence scintillation spectrometer	s. scintillation coincidence spectrometer
cohesive force	s. cohesion force		
cohesive strength	s. cohesion strength	coincidence spectrometer	Koinzidenzspektrometer n
cohobation	s. redistillation		
coil	s. winding pipe	coincidence spectrometry	Koinzidenzspektrometrie f
coil capacitance, distributed capacitance of the coil	Spulenkapazität		
		coincidence spectrum	Koinzidenzspektrum n
		coincidence stage	Koinzidenzstufe f
coil constant	s. Q	coincidence system	s. coincidence circuit
coil damping	Spulendämpfung f	coincidence telemeter	s. coincidence rangefinder
		coincidence tube, coincidence valve	Koinzidenzröhre f
coiled	s. helical		
coiled-coil filament, double helix <el.>	Doppelwendel f <El.>	coincidence width	Koinzidenzbreite f
		col, saddle	Sattel m
		col	s. a. saddle point <math.>
coiled-coil tungsten lamp	Wolframdoppelwendellampe f	colander	s. strainer
		colating, colation, straining <chem.>	Seihen n, Kolieren n <Chem.>
coil-loaded cable, pupinized (lump-loaded, coil-loaded) cable	Pupin-Kabel n	colature	Kolat n, Kolatur f, Seihfiltrat n
coil-loaded line [section]	Pupin-Leitung f		
		cold advection, cold air advection	Kälteadvektion f, Kaltluftadvektion f
coil loading	s. loading <of a line>		
coil loss	Spulenverlust m	cold air expansion machine	s. expansion machine
coil of Bitter type	s. Bitter coil	cold air film	Kaltlufthaut f
coil oscillator	s. coil-type oscillator	cold air wedge, wedge of cold air	Kaltluftkeil m
coil screen	Spulentopf m		
coil section	s. loading coil section	cold anticyclone, cold High	Kältehoch n
coil tap[ping]	Spulenabgriff m, Spulenanzapfung f, Spulenableitung f, Spulenabzweig m		
		cold approximation of plasma	kalte Näherung f des Plasmas
coil-type oscillator (vibrator), coil vibrator, coil oscillator	Spulenschwinger m	cold band	Kältebande f
		cold bath	Kältebad n, Kühlbad n
coincidence; superimposition <math.>	Deckung f <Math.>	cold-blooded animal, poikilotherm	Wechselwarmblüter m, Kaltblüter m, Poikilotherm m
coincidence analyzer	Koinzidenzanalysator m		
		cold-brittle, cold-short	kaltbrüchig
coincidence-anticoincidence telescope	Koinzidenz-Antikoinzidenz-Teleskop n	cold brittleness	s. cold-shortness
		cold calorimeter	s. Bunsen ice calorimeter
		cold capacitance	Kaltkapazität f
coincidence circuit; coincidence system <el.>	Koinzidenzkreis m; Koinzidenzschaltung f; Koinzidenzsystem n <El.>		
		cold cathode, dull emitter	Kaltkatode f, kalte Katode f
		cold-cathode arc	s. non-refractory arc
coincidence circuit operating in the nanosecond range	s. superfast coincidence circuit	cold-cathode discharge, cold-cathode gas discharge	Kaltkatodenentladung f, Kaltkatoden-Gasentladung f

cold-cathode discharge lamp, cold-cathode lamp <opt.>	Kaltkatodenlampe f <Opt.>	cold starting <of fluorescent lamp>	Kaltstart m
cold-cathode gas discharge, cold-cathode discharge	Kaltkatodenentladung f, Kaltkatoden-Gasentladung f	cold-start lamp	Kaltstart[-Leuchtstoff]-lampe f
cold cathode glow to arc transition	s. non-refractory electrode transition	cold stimulus	Kältereiz m
		cold trap, trap; refrigerated trap	Kühlfalle f, Kondensationsfalle f, Kaltfalle f; Ausfriertasche f
cold-cathode lamp, cold-cathode discharge lamp <opt.>	Kaltkatodenlampe f <Opt.>		
cold-cathode thyratron, cold-cathode tube, cold-cathode valve, grid-glow tube, relay valve	Glimmrelais n, Relaisröhre f, Kaltkatodenthyratron n, Kaltkatodenröhre f, Kleinthyratron n mit kalter Katode, Glimmröhrenrelais n	cold-type glacier, cold glacier	kalter Gletscher m
		cold-wall paradox	Kalte-Wand-Paradoxie f
		cold wave	Kältewelle f
		cold work	s. cold working
		cold work effect	s. strain hardening
cold conductor, resistor with high positive coefficient of temperature	Kaltleiter m	cold working, cold work	Kaltformgebung f, Kaltumformung f, Kaltverformung f, Kaltbearbeitung f
cold conductor bridge	Kaltleiterbrücke f	cold working, cold work	Kaltverstreckung f
		Cole-Cole diagram (plot)	Cole-Cole-Diagramm n
		collagen	Kollagen n, Leimbildner m
		collapsability, crushability	Zerdrückbarkeit f, Zerquetschbarkeit f
cold crack, hardening crack, quenching crack	Kaltriß m, Härteriß m, Riß m beim Erkalten	collapse	Zusammensturz m, Zusammenstürzen n, Zusammenfallen n, Kollaps m, Einsturz m
cold cracking, quench cracking	Kaltrißbildung f	collapse, decomposition, dying out <of field>	Abbau m; Zusammenbruch m <Feld>
cold day <temperature below −10 °C>	kalter Tag m, Kältetag m <Temperatur unter −10 °C>	collapse	s. a. breakdown <geo.>
		collapsed star	kollabierter Stern m
cold deformation	s. cold forming	collapse load	s. limit load
cold emission [of electrons]	s. field emission of electrons	collapse of the cavitation bubble	Zusammensturz m (Zusammenstürzen n) der Kavitationsblase
cold emission [of light]	s. chemiluminescence	collapse of the star, star collapse, gravitational collapse (concentration of the star contraction)	Zusammensturz m des Sterns, Sternzusammensturz m, Gravitationskollaps m, Zusammenziehung f durch die Gravitation, gravitationelle Zusammenziehung
cold finger, refrigerated finger	Kühlfinger m		
cold flow	kalter Fluß m, Kaltfließen n		
cold forming; cold deformation	Kalt[ver]formung f, Kaltumformung f	collapse of the voltage	s. voltage collapse
cold front line, line of cold front	Kaltfrontlinie f	collapsible	s. folding
		collapsing field	zusammenbrechendes Feld n
cold front occlusion, occlusion of cold front	Kaltfrontokklusion f	Collar triangle, aeroelastic triangle of forces	Collarsches Dreieck n
cold fusion	kalte Fusion f	collar vortex, vortex ring	Wirbelring m
cold glacier	s. cold-type glacier	collateral chain (family), collateral series	zugehörige (kollaterale) Zerfallsreihe f
cold hardiness	s. resistance to cold <bio.>	collateral motion	s. secondary motion
cold High, cold anticyclone	Kältehoch n	collateral series	s. collateral chain
cold-light mirror	s. cold mirror	collecting <opt.>, convergent, converging	sammelnd, kollektiv <Opt.>
cold mass, mass of cold air	Kaltluftmasse f	collecting electrode, collector electrode, gathering electrode	Sammelelektrode f, Fangelektrode f
cold mirror, cold-light mirror, heat transmitter	Kaltlichtspiegel m		
		collecting electrode	s. a. collector electrode
		collecting mirror	Fangspiegel m
cold neutron <$E_m < 0.0018$ eV>	kaltes (unterthermisches) Neutron n <mittlere Energie kleiner als 0,0018 eV>	collecting mirror	s. a. concave mirror
		collecting power <of lens>	Sammelvermögen n, Sammelkraft f
cold of evaporation	s. evaporative cold	collection chamber	Sammelkammer f, Sammelionisationskammer f
cold point, point of cold	Kältepunkt m		
cold pole, pole of cold	Kältepol m	collection efficiency	Sammelwirkungsgrad m, Sammelwirksamkeit f; Auffangausbeute f, Sättigungsgrad m
cold polymerization	Kaltpolymerisation f		
cold pool, kaltlufttropfen	Kaltlufttropfen m	collection of colour samples	Farbsammlung f
cold reactivity	Kaltreaktivität f, kalte Reaktivität f	collective electron model	Kollektivmodell n der Elektronen, kollektives Elektronenmodell n
cold receptor	Kälterezeptor m	collective electron theory	Kollektivtheorie f der Elektronen
		collective entropy	kollektive Entropie f <Zellenmodell der Flüssigkeiten>
cold resistance, resistance in the cold state	Kaltwiderstand m		
cold resistance	s. a. resistance to cold <bio.>	collective excitation state	kollektiver Anregungszustand m
cold run <of reactor>	Blindversuch m <am Reaktor>	collective free energy	kollektive freie Energie f <Zellenmodell der Flüssigkeiten>
cold-short, cold-brittle	kaltbrüchig		
cold-shortness, cold brittleness	Kaltbrüchigkeit f, Kaltsprödigkeit f	collective model [of nucleus]	s. unified model
		collective mode of motion	kollektive Bewegung f, Kollektivbewegung f
cold source	Kältequelle f		

collective nuclear model	s. unified model	collector residual current, collector leakage current	Kollektorreststrom m
collective rotational model	Kollektivrotationsmodell n, Modell n der kollektiven Rotation	collector ring	Kollektorring m
collective vibrational model	Kollektivschwingungsmodell n, Modell n der kollektiven Schwingung	collector segment, commutator segment	Kollektorlamelle f, Kommutatorlamelle f
collector <in flotation>	Sammler m, Kollektor m <Flotation>	collector space-charge layer (region)	Kollektorraumladungsschicht f; Kollektorraumladungszone f
collector, electron collector <of travelling-wave tube>	Elektronen[auf]fänger m, Auffangelektrode f, Auffängerelektrode f <Lauffeldröhre>	collector sparking collector-to-base capacitance, collector-base capacitance	s. sparking of brushes Kollektor-Basis-Kapazität f
collector, commutator <el.>	Kommutator m, Stromwender m; Kollektor m, Lamellenkommutator m	collector-to-base current gain	Stromverstärkungsfaktor m, Stromverstärkung f <in Emitterschaltung>
collector	s. a. collector electrode		
collector barrier [layer], collector transition region, collector transition layer [region], collector depletion layer	Kollektorrandschicht f, Kollektorgrenzschicht f, Kollektorübergangszone f; Kollektorsperrschicht f	collector-to-base voltage, collector-base voltage	Kollektor-Basis-Spannung f
		collector-to-emitter current gain	Stromverstärkungsfaktor m, Stromverstärkung f <in Basisschaltung>
collector barrier capacitance, collector barrierlayer capacitance, collector depletion layer capacitance, collector junction capacitance	Kollektorrandschichtkapazität f, Kollektorgrenzschichtkapazität f, Randschichtkapazität f des Kollektors; Kollektorsperrschichtkapazität f, Sperrschichtkapazität f des Kollektors	collector-to-emitter voltage, collector-emitter voltage	Kollektor-Emitter-Spannung f
		collector transition layer [region], collector transition region	s. collector barrier
		collector turnover voltage	Kollektordurchbruchspannung f, Kollektordurchschlagspannung f
collector-base capacitance, collector-to-base capacitance	Kollektor-Basis-Kapazität f	colliding-beam accelerator	„colliding-beam"-Beschleuniger m, Teilchenbeschleuniger m mit gegeneinanderlaufenden (entgegengesetzt umlaufenden) Teilchen, Kernmühle f
collector-base junction	Kollektor-Basis-Übergang m, Kollektorbasisübergang m		
collector-base leakage current, collector-base residual current	Kollektor-Basis-Reststrom m, Kollektorreststrom m für Basisschaltung		
collector-base space	Kollektor-Basis-Strecke f, Kollektorbasisstrecke f		
		colliding-beam experiment	„colliding-beam"-Experiment n
collector-base voltage	s. collector-to-base voltage	colliding galaxies	kollidierende (zusammenstoßende) Galaxien fpl
collector contact; collector lead	Kollektoranschluß m, Kollektorkontakt m	colliding[-particle] system	Stoßsystem n
collector cut-off current	Kollektorsperrstrom m	colligative	s. concentration-dependent
collector cut-off frequency	Kollektorgrenzfrequenz f	colligator	Kolligator m
collector depletion layer	s. collector barrier	collimated point source, unidirectional point source	kollimierte Punktquelle f, gerichtet strahlende Punktquelle
collector depletion layer capacitance	s. collector barrier capacitance		
collector diffusion capacitance	Kollektor-Diffusionskapazität f, Kollektordiffusionskapazität f, Diffusionskapazität f des Kollektors	collimating cone	Konuskollimator m, Kegelkollimator m
		collimating cylinder, cylindrical collimator (collector)	Zylinderkollimator m; Zylinderkollektor m
collector dissipation	Kollektorverlustleistung f	collimating lens	Kollimationslinse f, kollimierende Linse f
collector electrode, collecting electrode; collector <semi.>	Kollektorelektrode f; Kollektor m <Halb.>	collimating mark, sighting mark, sight graticule, measuring mark, target <opt.>	Zielmarke f, Abkommen n, Absehen n <Opt.>
collector electrode	s. a. collecting electrode		
collector-emitter leakage (residual) current	Kollektor-Emitter-Reststrom m, Kollektorreststrom m für Emitterschaltung	collimating ray	Zielstrahl m; Sehstrahl m
		collimating slit	Kollimatorschlitz m, Begrenzungsspalt m
collector-emitter voltage	s. collector-to-emitter voltage	collimating staff	Ziellatte f
collector-ground transistor	Transistor m in Kollektorschaltung, kollektorgeerdeter Transistor	collimation	Kollimation f, Kollimieren n, Bündelung f, Ausblendung f, Begrenzung f
		collimation axis, aiming axis, axis of collimation; collimation line, aiming line, line of collimation	Zielachse f, Kollimationsachse f; Ziellinie f, Absehlinie f, Kollimationslinie f
collector junction	Kollektorübergang m, Kollektorschicht f		
collector junction capacitance	s. collector barrier capacitance		
collector junction resistance	Kollektorsperrschichtwiderstand m	collimation constant	s. collimation error
collector lead; collector contact	Kollektoranschluß m, Kollektorkontakt m	collimation error, aiming error	Zielachsenfehler m, Kollimationsfehler m; Zielfehler m
collector leakage current, collector residual current	Kollektorreststrom m		
collector multiplication factor	Kollektorverstärkungsfaktor m	collimation line	s. collimation axis
collector path resistance, bulk resistance of collector	Kollektor-Bahnwiderstand m, Bahnwiderstand m des Kollektors	collimation plane	Kollimationsebene f
		collimator; collimator tube	Kollimator m; Kollimatorrohr n, Spaltrohr n
collector region	Kollektorzone f	collimator lens <of spectrograph>	Kollimatorlinse f <Spektrograph>

collimator 110

collimator mirror	Kollimatorspiegel m	collision mean free path, mean free path for collision	[mittlere freie] Stoßweglänge f, mittlere freie Weglänge f für Stoß, Stoßlänge f
collimator tube	s. collimator		
collinear, collineatory	kollinear	collision momentum	s. momentum of the impact
collinear antenna, Franklin antenna; Marconi-Franklin antenna	Franklin-Antenne f, Kollinearantenne f; Marconi-Franklin-Antenne f, Marconi-Franklin-System n	collision multiplication, multiplication by collision	Stoßvervielfachung f, Vervielfachung f durch Stöße
		collision number	s. number of collisions
collinear antenna [array], collinear array	Dipolreihe f	collision of the first kind	Stoß m erster Art
collineation	Kollineation f, kollineare Abbildung f	collision of the second kind, superelastic collision, hyperelastic collision	Stoß m zweiter Art, Klein-Rosseland-Stoß m, überelastischer (hyperelastischer, superelastischer) Stoß
collineatory	s. collinear		
collision; impact; shock; encounter; impinging	Stoß m; Zusammenstoß m; Kollision f; Zusammenprall m		
collision / without	s. collisionless	collision of two nuclei, nucleus-nucleus collision	Kern-Kern-Stoß m
collisional excitation, collision (impact) excitation, excitation by collision <of radiation>	Stoßanregung f, Anregung f durch Stoß <Strahlung>	collision operator	Stoßoperator m
		collision pair	Stoßpaar n
collisional multiplication [of carriers]	Stoßvervielfachung f [von Trägern]	collision parameter	s. impact parameter
		collision period	s. collision time
		collision point	s. point of collision
		collision probability	s. probability of collision
collision broadening, impact broadening, line broadening by impact	Stoßverbreiterung f, Linienverbreiterung f durch Stoßdämpfung	collision radiation, impact radiation	Stoßstrahlung f
		collision radiation	s. a. bremsstrahlung
		collision radius; neutron collision radius	Stoßradius m, Kollisionsradius m
collision chain, impact chain, chain [of collisions]	Stoßkette f	collision rate	s. probability of collision
collision coefficient	s. restitution coefficient	collision strength, shock strength	Stoßstärke f; Stoßleistung f
collision complex	Stoßkomplex m	collision term	Stoßterm m
collision cross-section, effective collision cross-section, cross-section for collision (impact), impact cross-section	Stoß[wirkungs]querschnitt m, Wirkungsquerschnitt m für Stoß, Wirkungsquerschnitt des Stoßes	collision theory; impact theory	Stoßtheorie f
		collision theory of Jeans'	s. encounter hypothesis <astr.>
		collision theory of Lorentz	s. Lorentz['s] collision theory
collision damping	Stoßdämpfung f	collision theory of Van Fleck and Weisskopf	s. Vleck-Weisskopf collision theory / Van
collision deactivation probability	Stoßentaktivierungswahrscheinlichkeit f	collision time, time of collision (impact), collision period	Stoßzeit f, Stoßdauer f
collision density	Stoß[zahl]dichte f, Kollisionsdichte f	collision transition probability	Stoßübergangswahrscheinlichkeit f
collision diagram, vector diagram of collision	Stoßdiagramm n, Vektordiagramm n des Stoßvorgangs	collision width	s. line width by collision damping
collision diameter, neutron collision diameter	Stoßdurchmesser m, Kollisionsdurchmesser m	collision with [the] wall	Wandstoß m
		collocation method <math.>	Kollokationsmethode f <Math.>
collision excitation	s. collisional excitation		
collision experiment <phys.>	Stoßversuch m <Phys.>	collocation point	Kollokationspunkt m
collision frequency, shock frequency	Stoßhäufigkeit f <Therm>; Stoßfrequenz f <El.>	collodion dry plate, dry collodion plate	trockene Kollodiumplatte f, Kollodiumtrockenplatte f
		collodion plate	Kollodiumplatte f
collision heating, heating by collision	Stoßaufheizung f		
		collodion wet plate, wet collodion plate	nasse Kollodiumplatte f, Kollodiumnaßplatte f, Naß[kollodium]platte f
collision-induced spectrum	stoßinduziertes Spektrum n	colloid, colloidal (colloid-disperse) system	Kolloid n, kolloid[disperses]es System n
collision integral	Stoßintegral n, Boltzmannsches Stoßintegral	colloid, colloidal, colloid-disperse	kolloiddispers, kolloid, kolloidal
collision invariant	Stoßinvariante f		
collision ionization	s. impact ionization	colloidal dispersion	Dispersionskolloid n, Phasenkolloid n
collision law, law of collision	Stoßgesetz n	colloidal electrolyte	Kolloidelektrolyt m
collisionless, without collision (shock), shock-free	stoßfrei	colloidal-labile, colloidally labile, colloidally unstable, colloidal-unstable	kolloid-labil, kolloidal-labil, kolloidalunstetig
collisionless plasma	stoßfreies Plasma n		
collisionless shock wave	Stoßwelle f im stoßfreien Plasma, stoßfreie Stoßwelle	colloidally stable, colloidal-stable	kolloid-stabil, kolloidal-stabil, kolloidalstetig
collision light	Stoßleuchten n	colloidally unstable	s. colloidally labile
		colloidal particle	kolloides Teilchen n, Kolloidteilchen n
collision loss, loss of energy due to collision (impact, choc), energy lost in an imperfect collision	Stoßverlust m	colloidal solution	kolloid[al]e Lösung f, Kolloidlösung f
		colloidal suspension	s. sol
		colloidal system	s. colloid
collision matrix, impact matrix	Stoßmatrix f	colloidal turbidity	kolloide Trübung f

colloidal-unstable	s. colloidally labile	colour deviation, colour difference	Farb[en]abweichung f; Farb[en]differenz f, Farbunterschied m
colloid analysis	Kolloidanalyse f		
colloid chemistry, colloid science, dispersoidology	Kolloidchemie f, Kolloidik f, Kolloidlehre f	colour discrimination	Farbunterscheidung f; Farbton-Unterschiedsempfindlichkeit f, Farbunterscheidungsvermögen n
colloid-disperse	s. colloid		
colloid-disperse system	s. colloid		
colloid meteorology	Kolloidmeteorologie f	colour disk; colour filter disk <tv.>	Farb[en]scheibe f; Farbfilterscheibe f <Fs.>
colloid mill	Kolloidmühle f	colour disk	s. a. Maxwell['s] disk
colloid optics	Kolloidoptik f	colour dosimeter, colourmetric dosimeter	Farbdosimeter n, kolorimetrisches Dosimeter n
colloid osmotic force	kolloidosmotische Kraft f	coloured afterimage	farbiges Nachbild n
colloid osmotic pressure, oncotic pressure	kolloidosmotischer (onkotischer) Druck m	coloured filter	Farbfilter n
		coloured fog	farbiger Schleier m, Farbschleier m
colloid physics	Kolloidphysik f	coloured glass	s. pigmented glass filter
colloid science	s. colloid chemistry	coloured halo, coloured ring	farbiger Halo (Ring) m, Farbring m
colloid-stable	s. colloidally stable		
cologarithm, colog N <= log (1/N)	negativer Logarithmus m <log (1/N) = −log N>	colouredness, colority	Farbigkeit f, Buntheit f
colongitude	= 180° − geographical longitude	coloured ring, coloured halo	farbiger Halo (Ring) m, Farbring m
Colonnetti['s] theorem	Colonnettisches Theorem n	coloured shadow	farbiger Schatten m, Farbschatten m
color <US>	s. colour	colour emissivity	Farbemissionsvermögen n
colorability <US>	s. colourability	colour-emitting phosphor dot	s. phosphor dot
colorant, colouring agent, colouring material; dye, dye stuff; stain	Farbmittel n, farbgebender Stoff m; Farbstoff m	colour equation	Farb[en]gleichung f
		colour equivalent	Farbäquivalent n
colorimeter; chromatometer	Kolorimeter n; Farbmeßgerät n, Farbmesser m	colour excess	Farb[en]exzeß m
		colour filter disk	s. colour disk <tv.>
colorimetric analysis, colorometry <chem.>	Kolorimetrie f, kolorimetrische Analyse f <Chem.>	colour flicker	Farbflimmern n, Farbenflimmern n
colorimetric purity	spektrale Farbdichte f, Farbdichte	colour fringe[s], bleeding	Farb[en]saum m, Farb[en]fransen fpl, Farbränder mpl
colorimetric standard illuminant	s. standard illuminant <A, B, or C>	colour geometry, colorimetry	niedere Farbmetrik f, Farbvalenzmetrik f, Farbreizmetrik f
colorimetry; chromatometry	Kolorimetrie f; Farbmessung f; Farbmeßtechnik f; Farbmetrik f	colour gradation, gradation of colours	Farbabstufung f, Farbenabstufung f
colorimetry	s. a. colour geometry	colour grating <opt.>	Farbgitter n <Opt.>
colorimetry	s. colorimetric analysis	colour group, black-[and-]white group	Schwarz-Weiß-Gruppe f, farbige Gruppe f, Farbgruppe f
colority	s. colouredness		
colour, color <US> <phys.>	Farbe f <Phys.>		
colourability, colorability <US>	Verfärbbarkeit f	colour group	s. a. magnetic point group
		colour group	s. a. magnetic space group
colour adaptation, chromatic adaptation <of eye>	Stimmung f, Farbstimmung f, chromatische (farbige) Adaptation f, Farbadaptation f; Farbumstimmung f; Farbverstimmung f <Auge>	colour hearing	Farbenhören n
		colour index	Farbenindex m
		colour indicator	s. acid-base indicator
		colouring	s. tinging
		colouring agent	s. colorant
		colouring curve	Verfärbungskurve f
colour analyzer	Farbanalysator m	colouring material	s. colorant
colouration	s. tinging	colour in reflected light	s. surface colour
colouration of cell nuclei	Kernfärbung f	colour in transmitted light	s. colour of the body in transmitted light
colouration of the body in reflected light	s. surface colour	colourless filter	Klarglasfilter n
colouration of the body in transmitted light	s. colour of the body in transmitted light	colourless halo, white halo	weißer Halo m, farbloser Halo
		colourless twilight	farbarme Dämmerung f
colouration spectrum, spectrum of colour[ation]	Verfärbungsspektrum n	colour-magnitude array	s. colour-magnitude diagram
colour atlas	Farb[en]karte f, Farb[en]atlas m	colour-magnitude diagram, colour-magnitude array, colour-brightness diagram	Farben-Helligkeits-Diagramm n, FHD
colour balance	Farbabstimmung f, Abstimmung f der Farben; Farbgleichgewicht n		
colour-brightness diagram	s. colour-magnitude diagram	colour match	Farb[en]gleichheit f
		colour matching	Farbabgleich m, Farbabgleichung f; farbige Angleichung f, Farbangleichung f; Farbanpassung f
colour cast, colour tinge	Farbstich m		
colour centre, F centre	Farbzentrum n, F-Zentrum n		
colour circle	Farbtonkreis m, Farb[en]kreis m, Ostwaldscher Farbenkreis	colourmetric dosimeter, colour dosimeter	Farbdosimeter n, kolorimetrisches Dosimeter n
		colour moment, leucocentric colour moment	Farbmoment n, Luthersches (leukozentrisches) Farbmoment, Buntmoment n
colour comparator	Farb[en]komparator m		
colour cone	[Ostwaldscher] Farbenkegel m; Farbtüte f	colour of the body in reflected light	s. surface colour
colour contrast, contrast in colour	Farbkontrast m; farbiger Kontrast m	colour of the body in transmitted light, colour (colouration of the body) in transmitted light, transmitted colour	Durchsichtfarbe f
colour correction factor <of photometer>	Farbkorrektionsfaktor m <Photometer>		
colour-correction filter	Farbkorrektionsfilter n, Farbkonversionsfilter n		
colour curve	Farbenindexkurve f	colour of the water	Gewässerfarbe f, Wasserfarbe f, Eigenfarbe f des Gewässers
colour deficiency	s. defective colour vision		

colour

colour phase contrast method	farbiges Phasenkontrastverfahren n	Columbus-type weight	s. torpedo sinker
colour phosphor dot	s. phosphor dot	column <mech.>; rod, bar	Stab m <Mech.>
colour point group	s. magnetic point group	column	s. a. measuring chain <geo.>
colour purity, purity of colour	Farbreinheit f, Reinheit f der Farbe	columnar, column-shaped	säulenförmig
colour pyramid	Farbenpyramide f, Farbpyramide f	columnar crystal	Stengelkristall m, säulenförmiger Kristall m
colour pyrometer	Farbpyrometer n	columnar crystallization	Stengelkristallisation f; Kolonnenkristallisation f
colour rainbow display, rainbow display	Regenbogenfarbmuster n	columnar glow-to-arc transition	s. column transition
colour reaction	Farbreaktion f	columnar granulation, transgranulation, transcrystallization	Transkristallisation f, Einstrahlung f <Krist.>
colour rendering, colour rendition	Farbwiedergabe f, Farbenwiedergabe f	columnar ice	Stengeleis n
colour scale	Farbskala f, Farbtonskala f, Farbskale f	columnar ionization	Kolonnenionisation f, Säulenionisation f
colour schlieren method, colour schlieren technique	Farbschlierenmethode f, Farbschlierenverfahren n	columnar recombination	Säulenrekombination f, Kolonnenrekombination f
colour screen process	s. screen process	columnar resistance	Säulenwiderstand m
colour selective mirror, reflecting dichroic mirror, dichroic mirror	dichroitischer (zweifarbiger, farbselektiv reflektierender) Spiegel m		
colour sensation	s. chromatic sensation	columnar structure	Säulenstruktur f
colour-sensitive part of the organ of vision	Farb[en]apparat m, Farbwahrnehmungsapparat m, Farbwahrnehmungsmechanismus m	columnar transition	s. column transition
		column chromatography	Säulenchromatographie f
		column diagram	s. histogram
colour separation	Farbtrennung f	column index, vertical row index	Spaltenindex m
colour separation	Farbauszug m, Teilauszug m, Teilfarbenauszug m	column matrix	Spaltenmatrix f
colour shade	s. tint	column of air, air column	Luftsäule f
colour shifter	s. wavelength shifter	column of gas in arc discharge, arc column	Bogensäule f, Lichtbogensäule f, Entladungsstrecke f des Bogens
colours of thin films (layers, plates)	Farben fpl dünner Blättchen, Schillerfarben fpl		
colour solid	Farbkörper m	column of mercury	s. mercury column
colour space	Farbenraum m, Vektorraum m der Farbvalenzen	column of microscope	s. microscope column
		column of water	s. water column
colour space group	s. magnetic space group	column rank	Spaltenrang m
colour specification	Farbbestimmung f; Farbenkennzeichnung f	column-shaped, columnar	säulenförmig
colour stimulus, stimulus	Farb[reiz]valenz f; Farbreiz m	column transition, columnar [glow-to-arc] transition	Säulenübergang m [der Glimmentladung in die Bogenentladung]
colour stimulus function	Farbreizfunktion f, relative spektrale Energieverteilung f	colure	Kolur m
		coma, tangential coma, meridian coma, meridional coma <opt.>	Koma f, Asymmetriefehler m, meridionale (tangentiale) Koma, Meridionalkoma f, Tangentialkoma f, Bildwölbung f, Zerstreuungsfigur f <Opt.>
colour stimulus [specification] in the C.I.E. standard colorimetric system	s. C.I.E. colour stimulus		
colour stimulus weight	s. tristimulus sum		
colour substance	Sehstoff m, Farbsubstanz f		
colour system	Farbsystem n	coma-free mirror, aplanatic mirror	komaf-:ier Spiegel m
colour temperature	Farbtemperatur f	coma of comet, shell of comet	Koma f des Kometen, Kernhülle f, Hülle f des Kometenkerns
colour temperature at wavelength λ	s. gradient temperature		
colour-temperature meter	Farbtemperaturmesser m	comatic circle	Zerstreuungsfigur f bei der Koma, Komafigur f
colour theory	s. theory of colours	combination <of spectral terms>	Interkombination f, Kombination f <Spektralterme>
colour thermoscope	Farbenthermoskop n		
colour threshold, threshold of colour	Farbschwelle f		
colour tinge	s. colour cast	combination <math.>, composition	Verknüpfung f <Math.>
colour tinge (tint)	s. tint	combination <of k out of n objects, of n things k at a time> <math.>	Kombination f <von n Elementen zur k-ten Klasse> <Math.>
colour transmission method	Farbtransformationsverfahren n, Farbübertragungsverfahren n		
		combination band	Kombinationsbande f
colour triangle	s. chromaticity diagram	combination conductance, total (overall) conductance	Kombinationsleitwert m, Gesamtleitwert m
colour trihedron	Farbdreikant n, Farbendreikant n		
colour value	s. tristimulus value	combination defect	Kombinationsfehler m, Kombinationsdefekt m
colour value sum	s. tristimulus sum		
colour vector, vector in colour space	Farbvektor m	combination difference	Kombinationsdifferenz f
colour velocity gauging	Farbverdünnungsverfahren n	combination frequency	Kombinationsfrequenz f
colour vision	Farbensehen n, Farbwahrnehmung f, Buntsehen n	combination law	s. prohibition of intercombinations
		combination line	Interkombinationslinie f, Kombinationslinie f
colour weight	s. tristimulus sum		
Colpitts circuit, Colpitts oscillator; three-point Colpitts circuit	Colpitts-Oszillator m; kapazitive Dreipunktschaltung f, Colpitts-Schaltung f	combination matrix, composition matrix	Verknüpfungsmatrix f
		combination oscillation, combination vibration	Kombinationsschwingung f

combination principle, [Rydberg-] Ritz['] combination principle	Ritzsches Kombinationsprinzip n, Kombinationsprinzip von [Rydberg-] Ritz	combustion heat, heat of combustion	Verbrennungswärme f
		combustion inhibitor	Verbrennungsverzögerer m
combination relation	Kombinationsbeziehung f	combustion plot	s. combustion diagram
		combustion potential	Verbrennungspotential n
combination scale	Verbundskala f	combustion residue, residue of combustion	Verbrennungsrückstand m
combination series	Kombinationsserie f, Interkombinationsserie f	combustion spectrum	Verbrennungsspektrum n
combination sound, combination tone	Kombinationston m	combustion temperature, temperature of combustion, flame temperature	Verbrennungstemperatur f
combination theory	s. combinatorial analysis		
combination tone, combination sound	Kombinationston m	combustion train	Verbrennungsanalysengerät n
combination vibration, combination oscillation	Kombinationsschwingung f	combustion tube	Verbrennungsrohr n
combination with water	s. hydration	combustion tube furnace	s. combustion furnace
combinatorial, combinatory	kombinatorisch	combustion velocity	s. rate of flame propagation
		combustion wave	Verbrennungswelle f
combinatorial analysis (theory), combinatory analysis, combination theory, theory of combinations	Kombinatorik f, Kombinationslehre f	combustion without flame, flameless combustion	stille Verbrennung f, flammenlose Verbrennung
		combustion zone	Verbrennungszone f
		cometary head	s. comet head
combinatory, combinatorial	kombinatorisch	cometary nucleus, nucleus [of the comet]	Kern m [des Kometen], Kometenkern m
combinatory analysis	s. combinatorial analysis	cometary orbit	Kometenbahn f
combined flow turbine	s. Francis turbine	cometary spectrum, comet spectrum	Kometenspektrum n
combined function	s. combined thermodynamic function	cometary tail, tail of the comet, comet tail	Kometenschweif m, Schweif m des Kometen
combined inversion	kombinierte Inversion f		
combined parity	kombinierte Parität f	comet associated with the shower	s. parent comet
combined rangefinder and viewfinder	s. range-viewfinder	comet head, cometary head, head of the comet	Kopf m des Kometen, Kometenkopf m
combined stress	zusammengesetzter Spannungszustand m	cometograph	Kometograph m
combined thermodynamic function, combined function	kombinierte [thermodynamische] Funktion f		
combined view and range finder	s. range-viewfinder	cometseeker	Kometensucher m
		comet spectrum, cometary spectrum	Kometenspektrum n
combining equivalent (weight)	s. equivalent weight	comet tail, tail of the comet, cometary tail	Kometenschweif m, Schweif m des Kometen
comb nephoscope, cloud rake	Wolkenrechen m, Wolkenharke f	comfort index	s. cooling power
comb-shaped, comb-type	kammförmig, Kamm-	comma <ac.>	Komma n <Ak.>
		command	s. instruction <num. math.>
combustibility, combustibleness	Brennbarkeit f; Verbrennbarkeit f	command	s. control <control>
		command [input]	s. command variable
combustion accelerator	s. combustion catalyst	command pulse	s. driving pulse <of gate>
combustion analysis	Verbrennungsanalyse f	command variable, control (command, reference) input, command, set point, controlling variable	Führungsgröße f, Sollgröße f, Sollwert m, Nutzsignal n
combustion at constant pressure	s. constant-pressure combustion		
combustion at constant temperature	s. constant-temperature combustion	commencement	s. initiation
combustion at constant volume	s. constant-volume combustion	commensurability	Kommensurabilität f
		commercially pure	s. engineering-grade
combustion boat	Verbrennungsschälchen n; Verbrennungsschiffchen n	comminution; grinding; milling <techn.>	Feinzerkleinerung f, Zerkleinerung f; Mahlen n, Zermahlung f; Brechen n <Techn.>
combustion calorimetry	Verbrennungskalorimetrie f	commissioning, putting into operation, start-up, starting	Inbetriebnahme f; Inbetriebsetzung f
combustion capillary	Verbrennungskapillare f		
combustion catalyst, combustion accelerator	Verbrennungsbeschleuniger m	Committee on Symbols, Units and Nomenclature [in Physics], S.U.N. Committee	Kommission f für Symbole, Einheiten und Nomenklatur [in der Physik], SUN-Kommission f
combustion centre	Verbrennungskern m, Verbrennungszentrum n	common-cathode amplifier	s. grounded-cathode amplifier
combustion chamber	Verbrennungskammer f; Verbrennungsraum m; Brennkammer f	common-collector circuit	s. grounded collector circuit
		common drain circuit (connection)	s. source follower circuit
combustion curve	Verbrennungskurve f, Verbrennungslinie f	common-emitter circuit (connection), grounded-emitter circuit (connection)	Emitter[grund]schaltung f, Emitterbasisschaltung f, Emitter-Basis-Schaltung f
combustion diagram, combustion plot	Verbrennungs[schau]bild n, Verbrennungsdiagramm n; Verbrennungsdreieck n		
		common gate circuit, common gate connection	Gate[-Basis]schaltung f, Tor-Basisschaltung f, Steuerelektroden-Basisschaltung f
combustion engine	s. internal-combustion engine		
combustion enthalpy, enthalpy of combustion	Verbrennungsenthalpie f	common helicoidal surface, Meusnier['s] helicoidal surface	Wendelfläche f, Minimalregelfläche f, flachgängige (gemeine, Meusniersche) Schraubenfläche f
combustion equation	Verbrennungsgleichung f		
combustion front	Verbrennungsfront f	common ion effect	Effekt m des gemeinsamen Ions
combustion furnace, combustion tube furnace	Verbrennungsofen m		
		common logarithm	s. Briggs['] logarithm
		common year	Gemeinjahr n

communal entropy	Gesamtentropie *f*	compactness <math.>	Kompaktheit *f* <Math.>
communicating vessels, connected vessels	kommunizierende Röhren *fpl* (Gefäße *npl*)	compactness of the crystal lattice	Dichtpackung *f* der Atome im Kristallgitter
communication, communications	Nachrichtenübermittlung *f*, Nachrichtenübertragung *f*, Kommunikation *f*	compact set, compact <math.>	kompakte Menge *f* <Math.>
		companding	Kompandierung *f*
communication channel, transmission channel, channel <el.>	Übertragungskanal *m*, Nachrichtenkanal *m*, Kanal *m*; Sprechstromkreis *m* <El.>	companion, secondary [component] <of binary star>	Begleiter *m* <Doppelsternsystem>
		comparability <e.g. of measuring results>	Vergleichbarkeit *f* <z. B. der Beobachtungsdaten>
communication engineering	s. telecommunication	comparable function	Vergleichsfunktion *f*
communication medium, transmission medium	Übertragungsmittel *n*, Übertragungsmedium *n*	comparative experiments	s. competitive experiments
communications	s. communication	comparative instrument, comparative measuring instrument	Vergleichsmeßgerät *n*, Vergleichsinstrument *n*, Vergleichsgerät *n*
communications engineering	s. telecommunication		
communication system, transmission (transfer) system, transducer	Kommunikationssystem *n*, Übertragungssystem *n*		
		comparative life[time], reduced lifetime, *ft* value	komparative (reduzierte) Lebensdauer *f*, *ft*-Wert *m*, modifizierter *f*-Wert *m*
communication theory	Kommunikationstheorie *f*, Nachrichtentheorie *f*		
commutability	s. permutability	comparative measurements, competitive (comparison) measurements, measurements for comparison	vergleichende Messungen *fpl*, Vergleichsmessungen *fpl*
commutant	s. commutator group		
commutant	s. centralizer		
commutating capacitor	Kommutierungskondensator *m*		
commutating factor	Kommutierungsfaktor *m*	comparative measuring instrument	s. comparative instrument
commutating field	Wendefeld *n*		
		comparative method	s. method of comparison
commutating function	Umschaltfunktion *f*, Umpolfunktion *f*	comparative quantity; comparative value	Vergleichsgröße *f*; Vergleichswert *m*
commutating [inter]pole, reversing pole, interpole <el.>	Wendepol *m*, Zwischenpol *m*, Hilfspol *m* <El.>	comparative resistance	s. comparison resistance
		comparative value	s. comparative quantity
commutating switch	s. changeover switch	comparator, cathetometer	Kathetometer *n*
commutating voltage	Stromwendespannung *f*	comparator, comparator circuit	Vergleichsschaltung *f*, Komparatorschaltung *f*
commutation <el.>	Kommutierung *f*, Stromwendung *f*, Kommutation *f* <El.>	comparator <opt.; techn.>	Komparator *m* <Opt.; Techn.>
commutation <math.>	Vertauschung *f* <Math.>	comparator bridge	Vergleichsbrücke *f*, Vergleichsmeßbrücke *f*
commutation relation	Vertauschungsrelation *f*		
		comparator circuit, comparator	Vergleichsschaltung *f*, Komparatorschaltung *f*
commutation rule	s. commutative law	comparator principle [of E. Abbe]	s. Abbe['s] comparator principle
commutation symmetry	s. permutation symmetry		
commutative	kommutativ	comparing rule, measuring rule, rule	Maßstab *m*, Maßstablineal *n*
commutative field	s. field <algebra>	comparison; intercomparison	Vergleich *m*; Gegenüberstellung *f*
commutative group	s. Abelian group		
commutative law, commutation rule	Kommutativgesetz *n*, kommutatives Gesetz *n*, Vertauschungsregel *f*, Vertauschungssatz *n*	comparison bridge	s. Wheatstone['s] bridge
		comparison calibration, calibration by comparison	Vergleichseichung *f*
		comparison capacitance	s. reference capacitance
commutator <math.>	Kommutator *m* <Math.>	comparison clock, clock for comparison	Vergleichsuhr *f*
commutator	s. a. double-throw switch	comparison electrode	s. reference electrode
commutator	s. a. collector <el.>	comparison element	s. error detector <control>
commutator group, commutator subgroup, commutant, derived group	Kommutatorgruppe *f*, abgeleitete Gruppe *f*, Ableitung *f*, Kommutant *m*	comparison ellipsoid	s. reference ellipsoid
		comparison eyepiece	s. reference eyepiece
		comparison inductance, reference inductance	Vergleichsinduktivität *f*
commutator segment	s. collector segment		
commutator segment voltage	s. segment voltage	comparison lamp	Vergleichslampe *f*
commutator sparking	s. sparking of brushes	comparison measurements	s. comparative measurements
commutator subgroup	s. commutator group	comparison method <math.>	Majorantenmethode *f* <bei gewöhnlichen Differentialgleichungen>
commutator switch	s. pole-changing switch		
commuting, permutable	[miteinander] vertauschbar, kommutierend		
compact <math.>, compact set	kompakte Menge *f* <Math.>	comparison method <of spectrographic analysis>	s. method of comparison with standards
compact	s. a. completely continuous	comparison microscope, microscope for comparison	Vergleichsmikroskop *n*
compactability; rammability <of the material>	Verdichtbarkeit *f*, Verdichtungsfähigkeit *f* <Material>		
compactedness	s. compactness	comparison of coefficients [method]	s. coefficient comparison
compact galaxy	Kompaktgalaxis *f*, Kompaktgalaxie *f*, kompakte Galaxie *f*	comparison prism	s. reference prism
		comparison radiator	s. reference radiator
compacting, compaction, densification, packing	Verdichtung *f* [von Material]	comparison ray	s. reference ray
		comparison resistance, comparative (reference) resistance	Vergleichswiderstand *m*
compacting (compaction) by vibration	s. vibrational compacting		
		comparison series	Vergleichsreihe *f*
compactness, compactedness	Kompaktheit *f*; Dichtheit *f*; Geschlossenheit *f* <Aufbau>	comparison solution, reference solution	Vergleichslösung *f*
		comparison standard	Vergleichsnormal *n*, Vergleichsmaß *n*

comparison star, reference star	Anschlußstern m, Vergleichsstern m	compensating pendulum	s. compensated pendulum
comparison surface	Vergleichsfläche f	compensating potentiometer	s. balancing potentiometer
comparison surface [of visual photometer]	Vergleichsfeld n [des visuellen Fotometers]	compensating pyrheliometer	s. compensation pyrheliometer
comparison test <for convergence>	Vergleichskriterium n, Majorantenkriterium n <für die Konvergenz von Reihen>	compensating stop, compensating diaphragm	Ausgleichblende f
		compensating voltage, compensator (bucking) voltage <el.>	Kompensationsspannung f <El.>
comparison theorem	Vergleichssatz m		
comparison voltage	s. reference voltage <el.>	compensating wave	s. spacing wave
compartment	s. chamber	compensation; balancing; equalization, equalizing; equilibration; neutralization; levelling; bucking; cancellation	Kompensation f; Kompensierung f; Ausgleich m; Abgleich m
compass; magnetic compass; box compass	Kompaß m; Magnetkompaß m; Bussole f		
compass card, card (scale) of the compass, dial card [of the compass], compass scale; wind rose	Kompaßrose f, Strichrose f; Windrose f		
		compensation, boost <el.>	Anheben n <El.>
compass scale	s. compass card	compensation	s. a. adjustment <math.>
compass theodolite	Bussolentheodolit m	compensation chamber	s. compensated chamber
compatibility	Kompatibilität f <Math.>; Verträglichkeit f <Math., Techn.>	compensation computation	s. computation of adjustment
		compensation magnetometer, compensating magnetometer	Kompensationsmagnetometer n
compatibility condition	s. integrability condition <math.>		
compatibility condition	s. compatibility equation	compensation method	s. Poggendorff['s] compensation method
compatibility equation, compatibility condition, condition of compatibility <mech.>	Kompatibilitätsbedingung f, Verträglichkeitsbedingung f, Kompatibilitätsrelation f, Kompatibilitätsgleichung f <Mech.>	compensation of damping	s. reversal of damping
		compensation of distortion	s. equalization <el.>
		compensation of disturbance variable, disturbance variable feed forward	Störwertaufschaltung f, Störgrößenaufschaltung f, Störaufschaltung f
compatibility problem	Verträglichkeitsproblem n, Problem n der Werkstoffwahl	compensation of friction torque, frictional compensation	Reibungskompensation f, Reibungsausgleich m
compatible	[miteinander] verträglich, kompatibel, [miteinander] vereinbar	compensation of potential[s]	s. equalization of potential
		compensation of thermal expansion	Wärmekompensation f, Wärmeausgleich m, Ausgleich m von Wärmedehnungen
compatible acceleration	s. Coriolis acceleration		
compensated chamber, compensated ionization chamber, compensation chamber	Kompensationskammer f, kompensierte Ionisationskammer f		
		compensation pendulum	s. compensated pendulum
		compensation pipes	Ausgleichsleitung f
compensated geoid, cogeoid	Kogeoid n, kompensiertes Geoid n	compensation point; compensating light <opt.>	Kompensationspunkt m; Kompensationslicht n <Opt.>
compensated ionization chamber	s. compensated chamber		
compensated micromanometer	Kompensationsmikromanometer n	compensation point	s. a. compensation temperature
		compensation pyrheliometer, compensating (Ångström['s]) pyrheliometer	Kompensationspyrheliometer n [nach Ångström], Ångström-Pyrheliometer n
compensated pendulum, compensation (compensating, grate) pendulum, grate compensation pendulum	Kompensationspendel n, Ausgleichspendel n, Rostpendel n, Minimalpendel n, Minimumpendel n		
		compensation temperature; compensation point	Kompensationstemperatur f; Kompensationspunkt m
compensated region, c region	Kompensationszone f, kompensierte Zone f, c-Zone f	compensation theorem	Kompensationssatz m, Satz m von der Kompensation
compensated scan	kompensierte Abtastung f	compensation viscometer	s. compensated viscometer
compensated semiconductor	Kompensationshalbleiter m		
		compensator, optical compensator <opt.>	[optischer] Kompensator m, Streckenkompensator m; Drehkeilpaar n <Opt.>
compensated viscometer, compensation viscometer	Kompensationsviskosimeter n		
		compensator	s. a. expansion tank
compensating achromat	Kompensationsachromat m, Achromat m mit Farbvergrößerungsfehler	compensator	s. a. potentiometer <el.>
		compensator of thermal expansion	s. heat compensator
		compensator plate	Kompensatorplatte f; Kompensationsplatte f
compensating amplifier	Kompensationsverstärker m		
compensating diaphragm	s. compensating stop	compensator voltage	s. compensating voltage <el.>
compensating eyepiece	Kompens[ations]okular n	compensatory movement <of crust>	Ausgleichsbewegung f <der Erdkruste>
compensating filter <opt.>	Ausgleichfilter n; Kompensationsfilter n <Opt.>	compensatory pause	kompensatorische Pause f <Extrasystole>
		compensatory pressure	Kompensationsdruck m
compensating illumination	Kompensationsbeleuchtung f	competing reaction, competitive reaction	konkurrierende Reaktion f, Konkurrenzreaktion f
compensating light	s. compensation point	competition principle of Dietzel	Konkurrenzprinzip n von Dietzel
compensating magnetometer, compensation magnetometer	Kompensationsmagnetometer n	competitive experiments, comparative experiments, experiments for comparison	vergleichende Versuche mpl, Vergleichsversuche mpl
compensating method	s. Poggendorff['s] compensation method		
compensating motion	Ausgleichbewegung f	competitive inhibition	kompetitive Hemmung (Hemmwirkung) f, Konkurrenzhemmung f, Verdrängungshemmung f
compensating osmometer	Kompensationsosmometer n [nach Lipatow]		

competitive measurements	s. comparative measurements	completely diffusing	vollkommen streuend
competitive reaction	s. competing reaction	completely integrable	vollständig integrabel
compilation [in a table]; tabulation; summarizing [in a table]	Tabulierung f; Tabell[aris]ierung f, Zusammenstellung f [in einer Tabelle]; Vertafelung f	completely integrated circuit	voll integrierte (vollständig integrierte) Schaltung f
		completely miscible, consolute	vollständig (unbeschränkt, lückenlos, vollkommen) mischbar
complanar forces	s. system of complanar forces	completely ordered state	vollständig geordneter Zustand m
complanarity, coplanarity	Komplanarität f, Koplanarität f	completely reducible representation, fully reducible representation	vollreduzible (vollständig reduzible) Darstellung f
complanatic, coplanatic	komplanatisch	completely regular Banach algebra	s. C*-algebra
complement	s. complementary set	completely rough regime	s. rough regime
complement	s. complementary operation	completely soluble	vollständig (unbeschränkt, unbegrenzt) löslich
complementariness of the Raman and infrared spectra for molecules with a centre of symmetry	Alternativverbot n	completely symmetric	vollsymmetrisch, vollständig (vollkommen) symmetrisch
		completely wetting	vollkommen benetzend, vollständig benetzend
complementarity principle	s. principle of complementarity	complete miscibility	vollständige (unbeschränkte, lückenlose) Mischbarkeit f
complementary acceleration	s. Coriolis acceleration	complete m.k.s. system	s. Giorgi system
complementary colour	Komplementärfarbe f, komplementäre (kompensative) Farbe f, Ergänzungsfarbe f; Kompensationsfarbe f, Kompensativfarbe f	completeness [of the system of functions]	Vollständigkeit f [des Funktionensystems]
		completeness relation	s. Parseval['s] formula
		complete normed algebra	s. Banach algebra
		complete normed space	s. Banach space
complementary emitter, complementary radiator	komplementärer Strahler m, Komplementärstrahler m	complete ordering	s. ordering
		complete orthogonal set	s. complete orthogonal system
complementary energy	Komplementärenergie f	complete orthogonal system, complete orthogonal set	vollständiges Orthogonalsystem n
complementary filter	Komplementärfilter n		
complementary instrument	s. supplementary apparatus		
complementary minor	s. minor	complete orthonormal system	vollständiges Orthonormalsystem n; vollständige Orthonormalfolge f
complementary modulus	Komplement n, komplementärer Modul m		
complementary operation, complementary symmetry operation, anti-operation, complement	Antisymmetrieoperation f		
		complete Paschen-Back effect	vollständiger Paschen-Back-Effekt m
		complete primitive	s. general solution
complementary radiator	s. complementary emitter	complete radiator	s. black body
complementary screen	komplementärer Schirm (Beugungsschirm) m	complete revolution; complete turn, turnover	volle (vollständige) Umdrehung f; voller (ganzer) Umlauf m, Vollumlauf m
complementary set, complement ⟨of a set⟩	Komplementärmenge f, komplementäre Menge f, Komplement n ⟨Menge⟩		
		complete series of mixed crystals, complete series of solid solutions, series of solid solutions, series of mixed crystals	lückenlose Mischkristallreihe f, Mischkristallreihe f
complementary space	komplementärer Raum m, Komplementärraum m		
complementary symmetry operation	s. complementary operation		
complementary wave length	kompensative Wellenlänge f		
		complete set	s. complete system ⟨math.⟩
		complete shadow, umbra, core shadow	Kernschatten m
complete continuity	Vollstetigkeit f	complete solubility	s. unlimited solubility
complete cycle; full circulation	Vollumlauf m, vollständiger (voller) Umlauf m	complete solution	s. complete integral
		complete space	vollständiger Raum m
complete Debye-Hückel equation	vollständige Debye-Hückelsche Gleichung f	complete symmetry	vollkommene (vollständige) Symmetrie f, Vollsymmetrie f
complete differential	s. exact differential		
completed shell	s. closed shell	complete synchrone	vollständige Synchrone f
complete elliptic integral ⟨of the first, second or third kind⟩	vollständiges elliptisches Integral n ⟨erster, zweiter oder dritter Gattung⟩	complete system; complete set ⟨math.⟩	vollständiges System n ⟨Math.⟩
		complete turn	s. complete revolution
		complete wave function	vollständige Wellenfunktion f
complete equilibrium	ungehemmtes (vollständiges) Gleichgewicht n	complex	s. complex compound
		complex	s. nucleus
complete graph, complete linear complex	vollständiger Graph m	complex alternating-current (a.c.) potentiometer	s. complex potentiometer
complete Hamiltonian, total Hamiltonian	vollständiger Hamilton-Operator m		
		complex bend	zusammengesetzte Biegung f
complete integral, Jacobi['s] complete integral, complete solution	[Jacobi] vollständiges Integral n, vollständige Lösung f	complex beta decay	komplexer Beta-Zerfall m
		complex beta[-ray] spectrum	komplexes Beta-Spektrum n
complete ionization	s. total ionization	complex coacervate	Komplexkoazervat n
complete linear complex, complete graph	vollständiger Graph m	complex compound, complex, Werner complex, co-ordination entity; co-ordination compound	Komplexverbindung f, Komplex m; Koordinationsverbindung f, semipolare Verbindung f
complete linear group, full linear group	volle lineare Gruppe f		
completely additive	vollständig additiv		
completely coherent	vollkohärent, vollkommen kohärent		
		complex conjugate, conjugate complex, conjugate [imaginary]	konjugiert[-]komplex, [komplex] konjugiert, konj. kom.
completely continuous, compact ⟨of operator⟩	vollstetig ⟨Operator⟩		
		complex contrast transmission function, CCTF	[komplexe] Kontrastübertragungsfunktion f, KKÜF, CCTF
completely degenerate	vollständig entartet		

complex coupling, reactance-capacitance coupling — komplexe Kopplung f, induktiv-kapazitive Kopplung

complex degree of coherence — s. phase coherence factor

complex formation, complexing — Komplexbildung f

complex-forming substance — s. complexing agent

compleximetry — s. chelatometry

complex impedance, complex resistance — komplexer Widerstand (Wechselstromwiderstand, Wellenwiderstand) m, Vektorimpedanz f

complexing, complex formation — Komplexbildung f

complexing agent, complex-forming substance — Komplexbildner m

complex ion, cluster ion, cluster — Komplexion n, komplexes Ion n, Clusterion n, Molion n

complex molecule, complicated molecule — Komplexmolekül n

complex of elements — Elementkomplex m

complexometry — s. chelatometry

complex optical potential — s. complex potential of the optical model

complex oscillation, composite oscillation — zusammengesetzte Schwingung f

complex particle — zusammengesetztes Teilchen n

complex plane, Argand plane, Gauss plane. Gaussian plane; Argand diagram — Gaußsche (Argand-Gaußsche) Zahlenebene f, Ebene f der komplexen Zahlen, [komplexe] Zahlenebene, konforme (komplexe) Ebene, z-Ebene, Argumentebene f

complex plane except the infinite point — punktierte Ebene f

complex potential model — s. semi-transparent model of nucleus

complex potential of the optical model, [complex] optical potential — komplexes Potential n des optischen Modells, optisches [komplexes] Potential

complex potentiometer, complex alternating-current (a.c.) potentiometer — komplexer Kompensator (Wechselstromkompensator) m

complex radiation — s. mixed radiation

complex resistance — s. complex impedance

complex salt, tutton salt — komplexes Salz n

complex sound — Tongemisch n

complex sound velocity — komplexe Schallgeschwindigkeit f

complex spectrum — komplexes Spektrum n

complex sphere, Riemann sphere — [Riemannsche] Zahlenkugel f

complex-valued — komplexwertig

complex velocity potential — komplexes Geschwindigkeitspotential n

compliance, mobility inertia — reziproke (Kehrwert m der) Steifigkeit f, Nachgiebigkeit f, Komplianz f

complicated molecule, complex molecule — Komplexmolekül n

component, part, element, [construction] unit, subassembly <of construction> — Bauelement n; Bauteil n; Baustein m; Teil n (m) <Bauteil>

component <of thermodynamic system> — Komponente f <thermodynamisches System>

component; projection <math.> — Komponente f; Bild n; Projektion f <Math.>

component <of the electrical circuit> — s. circuit element

component motion, component of motion — Bewegungskomponente f, Komponente f der Bewegung, Teilbewegung f

component of binary star — Komponente f des Doppelsterns, Doppelsternkomponente f

component of deformation — s. strain component

component of motion — s. component motion

component of strain — s. strain component

component of strain — s. principal strain

component of stress — s. stress component

component of the force — Kraftkomponente f, Komponente f der Kraft, Teilkraft f

component of the solution — Lösungskomponente f, Lösungsgenosse m

component of the velocity vector, velocity component, component of velocity — Geschwindigkeitskomponente f, Komponente f der Geschwindigkeit, Teilgeschwindigkeit f

component of the voltage — s. partial voltage

component of velocity — s. velocity component

component under examination — s. sample

composite cathode — zusammengesetzte Schichtkatode (Katode) f

composite decay curve — zusammengesetzte Zerfallskurve f, komplexe Zerfallskurve

composite Doppler effect — zusammengesetzter Doppler-Effekt m

composite filter — Verbundfilter n

composite float, ball and line float, depth (double, subsurface) float — Tiefenschwimmer m, Tiefschwimmer m

composite hypothesis — zusammengesetzte Hypothese f

composite lens, compound lens; composite objective — mehrlinsiges (viellinsiges, zusammengesetztes) Objektiv n, Mehrlinser m, Viellinser m, Verbundobjektiv n, zusammengesetzte Linse f, Verbundlinse f

composite nomogram, composite nomograph — zusammengesetztes Nomogramm n

composite objective — s. composite lens

composite oscillation, complex oscillation — zusammengesetzte Schwingung f

composite radiation — s. mixed radiation

composite reaction — Stufenreaktion f, zusammengesetzte Reaktion f

composite resistor — Massewiderstand m

composite rocket — s. multistage rocket

composite spectrum — überlagertes (zusammengesetztes) Spektrum n

composite strength, aggregate strength — zusammengesetzte Festigkeit f

composite tide, compound tide — Kombinationstide f, zusammengesetzte (gemischte) Tide f, Verbundtide f

composite tides — s. mixed tides

composition, [algebraic] operation, combination <math.> — Verknüpfung f, [algebraische] Operation f, Komposition f <Math.>

composition <math.> — Komposition f, Zergliederung f, Zerfällung f

composition, addition <process> <mech.> — Zusammensetzung f <Vorgang> <Mech.>

composition <result> — Zusammensetzung f; Bestand m <Ergebnis>

composition by mass, composition by weight — Massenzusammensetzung f, Gewichtszusammensetzung f

composition equation — Verknüpfungsgleichung f

composition matrix — s. combination matrix

composition of motions — Zusammensetzung f von Bewegungen

composition of sound, sound composition — Klangzusammensetzung f

composition plane, composition surface, coherent interface — Verwachsungsebene f, Verwachsungsfläche f

composition series — Kompositionsreihe f

composition surface — s. composition plane

compound/III-V, group III-V compound — III/V-Verbindung f, $A^{III}B^V$-Verbindung f

compound centrifugal force — s. Coriolis force

compound crystal — Verbindungskristall m

compound distribution, mixed distribution — zusammengesetzte Verteilung f

compound-elastic scattering — s. resonance scattering

compound eye, facetted eye — Facettenauge n, Komplexauge n

compound Fabry-Pérot étalon, compound Fabry-Pérot interferometer	Compoundinterferometer n [nach Houston]; Multiplex-Interferenzspektrometer n, Multiplex-Interferenzspektroskop n [nach Gehrcke und Lau]	compressible fluid motion compression	s. compressible flow Kompression f, Verdichtung f, Komprimieren n, Zusammendrückung f; Stauchung f
compound fold	zusammengesetzte Falte f, Spezialfalte f	compression compression compression	s. a. pression load s. a. flattening <math.> s. a. strain <mech.>
compound glass	s. laminated glass	compressional-dilatational wave, condensational-rarefactional wave	Verdichtungs-Verdünnungs-Welle f
compounding <el.>	Kompoundierung f <El.>		
compounding	s. a. mixing <mech.>		
compound lamp	Verbundlampe f		
compound lens	s. composite lens		
compound machine, compound-wound machine	Doppelschlußmaschine f, Gleichstrom-Doppelschlußmaschine f, [Gleichstrom-]Verbundmaschine f, [Gleichstrom-]Kompoundmaschine f, Compoundmaschine f	compressional oscillation, compression (compressive) oscillation, compressional vibration	Verdichtungsschwingung f, Kompressionsschwingung f, Druckschwingung f
		compressional stiffness	Kompressionssteifigkeit f
		compressional vibration	s. compressional oscillation
compound magnetic field	s. resultant magnetic field	compressional viscosity	s. bulk viscosity
compound motion, resultant motion	resultierende Bewegung f	compressional wave, compression (compressive, condensational) wave <aero., hydr.>	Verdichtungswelle f, Kompressionswelle f, Verdichtungslinie f <Aero., Hydr.>
compound nucleus, intermediate nucleus	Compoundkern m, Compoundsystem n, Zwischenkern m, Verbundkern m		
		compression cap	s. air cap
		compression cone	Kompressionstubus m
compound-nucleus formation cross-section, cross-section for compound nucleus formation	Compoundkern-Bildungsquerschnitt m, Wirkungsquerschnitt m für (der) Compoundkernbildung	compression creep	Kompressionskriechen n
		compression curve	Verdichtungskurve f
		compression diagram, compression plot	Verdichtungsdiagramm n
		compression due to creep, creep compression	Kriechstauchung f
compound-nucleus fragment	Zwischenkernfragment n		
compound nucleus mode, compound nucleus reaction [mode], indirect nuclear reaction	Compoundkernreaktion f, Kernreaktion f mit Compoundkernstadium, indirekte Kernreaktion	compression efficiency	Kompressionswirkungsgrad m, Verdichtungswirkungsgrad m
		compression gauge	s. McLeod gauge
		compression heat	s. heat of compression
compound-nucleus model, model of the compound nucleus	Compoundmodell n, Zwischenkernmodell n	compression heating, heating by compression	Kompressionsaufheizung f, Aufheizung f durch Kompression
compound nucleus reaction [mode]	s. compound nucleus mode	compression ignition	Verdichtungszündung f, Kompressionszündung f
compound-nucleus-type interaction	s. indirect interaction	compression-ignition engine	s. diesel
compound pendulum	s. physical pendulum	compression impact test	s. impact compression test
compound prism, Rutherfurd prism	Rutherfurd-Prisma n, Compoundprisma n	compression liquefying	Verdichtungsverflüssigung f
compound pulley	s. pulley [block]	compression loading	s. pressure load
compound rule of three	s. conjoined rule of three	compression loss	Verdichtungsverlust m, Kompressionsverlust m
compound semiconductor	Verbindungshalbleiter m, zusammengesetzter Halbleiter m		
compound state, intermediate state <nucl.>	Zwischenzustand m, Compoundzustand m, Verbundzustand m, Übergangszustand m <Kern.>	compression Mach wave	Machsche Kompressionswelle f
		compression manometer	s. McLeod gauge
compound tide	s. composite tide	compression modulus	s. bulk modulus
compound tides	s. mixed tides	compression of the geoid	s. flattening of the Earth
compound tube	s. multiple-unit tube		
compound-wound machine	s. compound machine	compression oscillation	s. compressional oscillation
comprehensibility	s. intelligibility	compression period, period of compression, compression time	Kompressionszeit f, Verdichtungszeit f, Verdichtungsperiode f
compressed-air atomization	Druckluftzerstäubung f		
compressed air technique, pneumonics	Pneumonik f	compression plot, compression diagram	Verdichtungsdiagramm n
compressed gas	s. pressurized gas	compression pressure	Verdichtungsdruck m, Verdichtungsspannung f
compressed gas lamp	Preßgaslampe f		
compressibility, volume elasticity, bulk elasticity, elasticity of bulk, volume compressibility <property> <therm.>	Kompressibilität f, Volum[en]elastizität f, Zusammendrückbarkeit f, Verdichtbarkeit f, Komprimierbarkeit f, Volum[en]kompressibilität f; Stauchbarkeit f <Eigenschaft> <Therm.>	compression ratio	Verdichtungsgrad m, Verdichtungsverhältnis n, Kompressionsgrad m, Kompressionsverhältnis n, Verdichtung f
		compression refrigerating machine	s. compression-type refrigerating machine
		compression resistance	s. pressure drag
compressibility, coefficient of compressibility <quantity>	Kompressibilität f, Kompressibilitätskoeffizient m <Größe>	compression shock, pressure shock, shock	Verdichtungsstoß m
compressibility factor	Kompressibilitätsfaktor m, Realfaktor m	compression speed	s. speed of compression
compressibility integral	Kompressibilitätsintegral n	compression strain	s. unit shortening
compressibility modulus	s. bulk modulus	compression stress	s. pressure load
compressibility stall	s. shock stall	compression stroke	Verdichtungstakt m, Verdichten n; Verdichtungshub m
compressible boundary layer	kompressible Grenzschicht f		
		compression test; upsetting test; crushing test	Stauchversuch m, Stauchprobe f, Stauchprüfung f, Druckversuch m, Druckprobe f, Druckprüfung f, Kompressionsversuch m
compressible flow, compressible fluid flow, compressible fluid motion	kompressible Strömung f; Strömung kompressibler Flüssigkeiten		
compressible fluid jet	kompressibler Strahl m	compression time	s. compression period

compression-type refrigerating machine, compression refrigerating machine	Kompressionskältemaschine f, Kompressionskühlmaschine f, Kaltdampfmaschine f	Compton wavelength
computation
computation
computation of adjustment	Compton-Wellenlänge f
s. rough calculation
s. evaluation <of dates>
s. calculus of observations
compression wave	s. compressional wave	computer programme	s. routine
compression work, work of compression	Verdichtungsarbeit f, Kompressionsarbeit f	computing amplifier
Comstock['s] refraction formula	s. operational amplifier
Refraktionsformel (Brechungsformel) f von Comstock, Comstocksche Refraktionsformel (Brechungsformel)
compressive cleaving	Druckspaltung f		
compressive dislocation	s. compressive fault <geo.>		
compressive elastic limit	s. elastic limit for compression		
compressive fault, compressive dislocation, conjunctive (closed) fault <geo.>	Pressung f, kompressive Dislokation f; Aufschiebung f <Geo.>	concatenation <chem.>
concave	s. cascade connection
konkav <Math., Opt.>; [rund]hohl <allg.>
		concave angle	konkaver (überstumpfer, hohler) Winkel m
compressive force	Stauchkraft f	concave cathode	s. cavity cathode
		concave grating	s. concave reflection grating
compressive force	s. a. pressure force	concave grating spectrograph	Konkavgitterspektrograph m
compressive loading	s. pressure load		
compressive oscillation	s. compressional oscillation	concave lens	Konkavlinse f, konkave Linse f, Hohllinse f; Minusglas n, Konkavglas n
compressive power	s. compressor power		
compressive resultant	Druckresultante f		
compressive shear	Reibungsdruck m, negative Reibungsspannung f	concave mirror, collecting mirror	Hohlspiegel m, Konkavspiegel m, Sammelspiegel m, konkaver Spiegel m
compressive strain	s. unit shortening		
compressive strength, resistance to compression	Druckfestigkeit f	concave plasmolysis
concave quartz plate	Konkavplasmolyse f
Hohlquarz m
		concave reflection grating, concave grating	[Rowlandsches] Konkavgitter n, Hohlgitter n, Rowland-Gitter n, Rowlandsches Reflexionsgitter n
compressive stress, pressure stress	Druckspannung f, Kompressionsspannung f		
compressive stress	s. a. pressure load	concavo-convex lens	s. converging meniscus
compressive twin	s. pressure twin	concealed motion	verborgene Bewegung f
compressive wave	s. compressional wave	concentrated couple <mech.>	Punktmoment n, konzentriertes Moment n
compressive yield point (strength), yield point (stress) in compression	Quetschgrenze f, Stauchgrenze f, Stauchfestigkeit f	concentrated force
concentrated load, single load, point load	s. point force
[punktförmig angreifende] Einzellast f, Punktlast f, konzentrierte Last f, Punktbelastung f
compressor, volume compressor <el.>	Dynamikpresser m, Presser m <El.>		
compressor power, compressive power	Verdichterleistung f, Verdichtungsleistung f	concentrated mass, particle mass, point mass
concentrated vortex (vorticity)	Punktmasse f, konzentrierte Masse f
Einzelwirbel m
comproportionation, comproportionation reaction, conproportionation	Komproportionierung f, Komproportionierungsreaktion f	concentrated wash
concentrating column	s. rill erosion
Verstärkungssäule f
Compton absorption coefficient	Compton-Absorptionskoeffizient m, Compton-Umwandlungskoeffizient m	concentrating cup, focusing cup
concentration; enrichment	Katodenbecher m
Anreicherung f; Konzentrierung f, Konzentration f
Compton collision	Compton-Stoß m	concentration osmotic value <bio.>,	osmotischer Wert m, Saugwert m <der Lösung> <Bio.>
Compton effect	Compton-Effekt m		
Compton effect cross-section	s. Compton scattering cross-section	concentration, reduction <by evaporation> <chem.>	Einengung f, Konzentrierung f <Chem.>
Compton electron	Compton-Elektron n		
Compton energy	Compton-Energie f	concentration <quantity>
concentration	Konzentration f <Größe>
s. a. focusing <opt.>
Compton-Getting effect	Compton-Getting-Effekt m	concentration by mass	s. mass concentration
Compton meter	s. Compton spectrometer	concentration by volume, volume (volumetric; bulk) concentration	Konzentration f in Volum[en]prozent, Volum[en]konzentration f
Compton proton	Compton-Proton n, Compton-Rückstoßproton n		
Compton recoil	Compton-Rückstoß m	concentration by weight	s. mass concentration
Compton recoil particle	Compton-Rückstoßteilchen n	concentration cell <with or without transference>	Konzentrationselement n; Konzentrationskette f <mit oder ohne Überführung>
Compton rule	Comptonsche Regel f		
Compton scatter[ing], modified scattering	Compton-Streuung f	concentration-dependent, dependent on concentration; colligative	konzentrationsabhängig
Compton scattering coefficient	Compton-Streukoeffizient m, Comptonscher Streukoeffizient m	concentration depolarization	Konzentrationsdepolarisation f
Compton scattering cross-section, Compton effect cross-section, cross-section for Compton scattering	Compton-Streuquerschnitt m, Wirkungsquerschnitt m für (der) Compton-Streuung, Wirkungsquerschnitt für Compton-Effekt, Wirkungsquerschnitt des Compton-Effekts	concentration difference, difference of concentrations	Konzentrationsunterschied m, Konzentrationsdifferenz f
		concentration effect	Konzentrationseffekt m
		concentration error, error due to concentration	Konzentrationsfehler m
		concentration factor	s. stress concentration factor
Compton shift	Compton-Verschiebung f	concentration gradient, gradient (drop) of concentration	Konzentrationsgradient m, Konzentrationsgefälle n
Compton-Simon['s] experiment	Compton-Simon-Versuch m, Versuch m von Compton und Simon		
Compton spectrometer, Compton meter	Compton-Spektrometer n	concentration inhomogeneity	Konzentrationsinhomogenität f
Compton sum spectrometer	Compton-Summenspektrometer n	concentration interval	Konzentrationsbereich m, Konzentrationsintervall n

concentration meter	Konzentrationsmesser m	condensation nucleus, nucleus of condensation, condensation germ (centre)	Kondensationskern m, Kondensationszentrum n, Kondensationskeim m; atmosphärischer Kondensationskern
concentration of [charge] carriers	s. charge carrier density		
concentration of impurities	s. impurity concentration	condensation-nucleus counter	Kondensationskernzähler m
concentration of intrinsic defects	Fehlordnungsgrad m	condensation number	Kondensationszahl f
		condensation point, point of condensation <math.>	Kondensationspunkt m, Verdichtungspunkt m
concentration of ions	s. ionic concentration	condensation point	s. a. liquefaction temperature
concentration of sound	s. focusing of sound	condensation polymerization	s. polycondensation
concentration of the beam	s. focusing <opt.>		
concentration of the tracks	s. track density	condensation psychrometer	Kondensationspsychrometer n
concentration overpotential; concentration polarization	Konzentrationsüberspannung f; Konzentrationspolarisation f	condensation pump	s. condensing pump
		condensation rate	Kondensationsgeschwindigkeit f
concentration polarization	s. concentration overpotential	condensation shock, condensation jump	Kondensationsstoß m
concentration potential	Konzentrationspotential n		
concentration profile	Konzentrationsprofil n	condensation space	s. condensation cavity
concentration quenching	s. self-quenching <of luminescence>	condensation surface, condensing surface	Kondensationsfläche f
concentration ratio, ratio of concentrations	Konzentrationsverhältnis n	condensation temperature	s. liquefaction temperature
concentration speck	s. sensitivity speck	condensation theory [of ground water]	Verdichtungstheorie f, Kondensationstheorie f, Verflüssigungstheorie f
concentration supercooling	Konzentrationsunterkühlung f		
concentric system, monocentric system <opt.>	monozentrisches (konzentrisches) System n <Opt.>	condensation trail, vapour trail	Kondensstreifen m
		condensation turbidity	s. turbidity due to condensation
concept of equipartition	s. law of equipartition <of energy>	condensation-type ion source, ion condensation-type source	Kondensationsionenquelle f
concept of physical quantity, quantity concept	[physikalischer] Größenbegriff m, Begriff m der physikalischen Größe		
		condensation water, condensate water, condensate	Kondens[ations]wasser n, Kondensat n, Schwitzwasser n
concert pitch	s. philharmonic pitch		
conchoid	Konchoide f, Muschellinie f	condensation within a meteor stream	s. knot within a meteor stream
conchoid of a circle	s. Pascal['s] limaçon		
conclusion [a posteriori]	Rückschluß m	condensator	s. condenser <techn.>
concord, consonance, consonancy	Konsonanz f, Gleichklang m, Ruheklang m	condensed film	s. condensate film
		condensed matter	kondensierte Materie f, Kondensat n, zusammenhängende Materie
concordance <geo.>	Konkordanz f <Geo.>		
concordant coast	Längsküste f	condensed matter physics, physics of condensed matter	Physik f der kondensierten Materie
concordant folding	s. harmonic folding		
concretion <geo.>	Konkretion f <Geo.>	condensed ring compound	s. fused ring compound
concurrent <math.>	durch einen Punkt gehend <Math.>	condensed spark	kondensierter Funke m, kondensierte Entladung f
concurrent centrifuge	s. flow-through centrifuge	condenser, condensator <techn.>	Kondensator m, Verflüssiger m. Kondensor m <Techn.>
concussion of the ground	Bodenschwingungen fpl, Bodenschütterung f		
condensance	s. capacitive reactance	condenser <opt.>	Kondensor m, Kollektor m <Opt.>
condensate <therm.>	Kondensat[ionsprodukt] n, niedergeschlagene Flüssigkeit f, Niederschlag m	condenser	s. a. capacitor <el.>
		condenser aperture	s. aperture of the illuminator's aperture stop
condensate	s. a. condensation water		
condensate film, condensed film	Kondensatfilm m	condenser coupling	s. capacitive coupling
		condenser current	s. residual current
condensate water	s. condensation water	condenser for transillumination, transmitted-light condenser	Durchlichtkondensor m
condensation <phys.; chem.>	Kondensation f <Phys.; Chem.>; Verdichtung f <Phys.>		
		condenser lens	Kondensorlinse f, Leuchtfeldlinse f, Kondensor m, Kollektor m
condensation	s. a. liquefaction <of gases or gels>		
condensation adiabat	s. adiabatic curve of condensation	condenser lens of microscope	s. microscope condenser
condensational-rarefactional wave	s. compressional-dilatational wave	condenser optics	Kondensoroptik f
condensational wave	s. compressional wave	condenser turret	Kondensorrevolver m
condensation cavity; condensation space	Kondensationshohlraum m; Kondensationsraum m	condenser with apertured diaphragm	s. diaphragm condenser
		condensing heat-rejection effect	Entropievermehrung f des Kühlwassers
condensation centre	s. condensation nucleus		
condensation cloud	Kondenswolke f	condensing pump, condensation pump	Kondensationspumpe f
condensation drip, condensation drop[let]	Kondensationströpfchen n, Kondensationstropfen m		
condensation during ascending motion	Hebungskondensation f	condensing refrigeration effect	Kondensationskühleffekt m
		condensing surface	s. condensation surface
condensation germ	s. condensation nucleus	condensing temperature	s. liquefaction temperature
condensation heat	s. heat of condensation	condensive susceptance, capacitive susceptance, capacitance <el.>	kapazitiver Blindleitwert (Leitwert) m, Kapazitanz f, kapazitive Suszeptanz f
condensation hygrometer	s. dew-point hygrometer		
condensation in momentum space	s. momentum space condensation		
		condition	s. supposition
condensation jump	s. condensation shock	conditional branch	s. conditional jump
condensation level, height of condensation	Kondensationsniveau n, Kondensationshöhe f	conditional break[-] point <num. math.>	Verzweigungspunkt m <num. Math.>

conditional convergence	bedingte (nichtabsolute) Konvergenz f	conductance cell, conductivity cell	Leitfähigkeitsmeßzelle f, Leitfähigkeitszelle f
conditional distribution [function]	bedingte Verteilung f, bedingte Verteilungsfunktion f	conductance characteristic, conductance diagram	Leitwertcharakteristik f, Leitwertkennlinie f, Leitwertdiagramm n
conditional entropy	bedingte Entropie f, Kontextentropie f	conductance coefficient	Leitwert[s]zahl f
conditional equation, equation of condition	Bestimmungsgleichung f	conductance coefficient, conductance ratio	Leitfähigkeitskoeffizient m, Leitfähigkeitsquotient m
conditional expectation	bedingter Erwartungswert m	conductance diagram	s. conductance characteristic
conditional instability	s. moist adiabatic instability	conductance measurement	s. conductometry
conditional jump, conditional branch, conditional transfer [of control]	bedingter Sprung m	conductance of skin	Hautleitwert m
		conductance per unit length	Leitwert[s]belag m
conditionally convergent	bedingt (nichtabsolut) konvergent	conductance ratio	s. conductance coefficient
conditionally periodic	bedingt[-]periodisch	conductance titration	s. conductimetric titration
conditional probability	bedingte Wahrscheinlichkeit f, Übergangswahrscheinlichkeit f	conductance water, conductivity water	Leitfähigkeitswasser n, ultrareines Wasser n
conditional stability	bedingte Stabilität f	conductimetric titration, conductometric titration, conductance titration, conductometry	konduktometrische Titration f, Leitfähigkeitstitration f, Konduktometrie f
conditional transfer [of control]	s. conditional jump		
conditioned reflex	bedingter Reflex m		
conditioned stimulus	bedingter Reiz m	conducting film (layer)	s. conductive layer
condition equation ‹triangulation›	Bedingungsgleichung f	conducting plate	s. flat conductor
condition for balance, balance condition ‹of the bridge›	Abgleichbedingung f ‹Brücke›	conducting salt	s. supporting electrolyte
		conduction	s. electrical conduction
		conduction band, conductivity band	Leitungsband n, Leit[fähigkeits]band n
condition for injection, injection condition ‹acc., semi.›	Einschlußbedingung f ‹Beschl.›; Injektionsbedingung f ‹Beschl., Halb.›	conduction by extrinsic carriers	s. extrinsic conduction
		conduction coefficient of heat transfer, conduction (conductive) heat transfer coefficient	Leitungstransportkoeffizient m
condition for monochromatism, condition of monochromatism	Monochromatizitätsbedingung f, Monochromasiebedingung f		
		conduction counter	s. crystal counter ‹nucl.›
condition for shock waves	s. shock condition	conduction current	Leitungsstrom m
condition for the angles	s. angular condition	conduction current density	Leitungsstromdichte f
conditioning	Konditionierung f, Herstellung f bestimmter (konstanter) Versuchsbedingungen	conduction current density four vector	Leitungs-Viererstromdichte f
conditioning of air	s. air conditioning	conduction electron, conductivity electron	Leitungselektron n, Leitfähigkeitselektron n
condition of achromatism	Achromasiebedingung f		
condition of adiabaticity, adiabatic condition	Adiabasiebedingung f, Adiabatenbedingung f	conduction heat transfer coefficient	s. conduction coefficient of heat transfer
condition of aplanatism	Aplanasiebedingung f	conduction loss, heat conduction loss, loss of heat by conduction	Wärmeleitungsverlust m, Leitungsverlust m
condition of compatibility	s. compatibility equation ‹mech.›		
condition of continuity, continuity condition ‹math.›	Stetigkeitsbedingung f ‹Math.›	conduction mechanism	s. mechanism of conductivity
		conduction of excitation	s. stimulus conduction
condition of continuity	s. a. continuity equation ‹hydr.›	conduction of heat	s. heat conduction
condition of isentropy	Isentropiebedingung f	conduction of sound, sound conduction	Schalleitung f
condition of isoplanatism, isoplanasic condition, Staeble-Lihotzki condition ‹opt.›	Isoplanasiebedingung f, Staeble-Lihotzkysche Bedingung f, Proportionalitätsbedingung f	conduction of stimulus	s. stimulus conduction
		conductive coupling	konduktive Kopplung f
		conductive heat transfer coefficient	s. conduction coefficient of heat transfer
condition of Lipschitz, Lipschitz condition	Lipschitz-Bedingung f	conductive layer, conducting layer, conducting film	Leitschicht f
condition of monochromatism	s. condition for monochromatism	conductivity, electric[al] conductivity, electroconductibility; specific conductance, specific conductivity ‹el.chem.›	[elektrische] Leitfähigkeit f, [elektrisches] Leitvermögen n, spezifischer Leitwert m; spezifische [elektrische] Leitfähigkeit ‹El.Chem.›
condition of no slip	s. no-slip condition		
condition of orthogonality (perpendicularity)	Orthogonalitätsbedingung f		
condition of plasticity	s. yield condition		
condition of tautochronism	Tautochroniebedingung f	conductivity at infinite dilution	Leitfähigkeit f in unendlicher Verdünnung
condition of Widerøe	s. Widerøe['s] flux condition		
condition of zero slip	s. no-slip condition		
conditions	s. state	conductivity band, conduction band	Leitungsband n, Leit[fähigkeits]band n
conductance	Wirkleitwert m, Konduktanz f	conductivity bridge	Leitfähigkeitsmeßbrücke f, Leitfähigkeitsbrücke f
conductance, electric conductance	Leitwert m, elektrischer Leitwert	conductivity by extrinsic carriers	s. extrinsic conduction
conductance ‹of vacuum line›	Leitfähigkeit f ‹Vakuumleitung›	conductivity cell	s. conductance cell
conductance bridge	Leitwertmeßbrücke f, Leitwertbrücke f, Konduktanz[meß]brücke f	conductivity counter	Leitfähigkeitszähler m

conductivity electron	s. conduction electron	confidence level	s. level of significance
conductivity ellipsoid	Leitfähigkeitsellipsoid n	confidence limit	Vertrauensgrenze f; Konfidenzgrenze f; Fiduzialgrenze f
conductivity measurement	s. conductometry	fiducial limit	
conductivity measuring instrument	s. conductivity meter	confidence limits, confidence interval, confidence region, fiducial limits	Vertrauensbereich m, Vertrauensgrenzen fpl, Vertrauensintervall n, Konfidenzbereich m, Konfidenzintervall n; Mutungsbereich m, Mutungsintervall n <beim indirekten Schluß>
conductivity mechanism	s. mechanism of conductivity		
conductivity meter, conductivity measuring instrument, conductometer	Leitfähigkeitsmesser m, Leitfähigkeitsmeßgerät n, Leitwertmesser m, Konduktometer n		
conductivity modulation	Leitfähigkeitsbeeinflussung f, Leitfähigkeitsmodulation f	confidence probability	s. level of significance
		confidence region	s. confidence limits
		configuration, [spatial] arrangement	Konfiguration f, [räumliche] Anordnung f
conductivity modulation transistor	Leitfähigkeitsmodulationstransistor m		
		configuration <opt.>, figuration	Figuration f, Konfiguration f <Opt.>
conductivity of the human body, body conductivity	Körperleitfähigkeit f	configurational energy	Konfigurationsenergie f
		configurational entropy	Konfigurationsentropie f
conductivity temperature coefficient, temperature coefficient of conductivity	Temperaturkoeffizient m der [elektrischen] Leitfähigkeit, Leitfähigkeits-Temperaturkoeffizient m	configurational free energy	freie Konfigurationsenergie f
		configurational heat capacity	Konfigurationswärme-[kapazität] f
conductivity tensor	Leitfähigkeitstensor m	configurational integral	s. configuration integral
conductivity water	s. conductance water	configurational luminescence	Konfigurationsleuchten n
conductometer	s. conductivity meter		
conductometric titration	s. conductimetric titration		
conductometry, conductivity measurement, conductance measurement	Konduktometrie f, Leitfähigkeitsmessung f	configurational parameter	Konfigurationsparameter m
		configurational relaxation	Konfigurationsrelaxation f
conductometry	s. a. conductimetric titration	configurational statistics	Konfigurationsstatistik f
conductor	Leiter m		
conductor	Konduktor m, Konduktorkugel f	configuration averaging	Konfigurationsmittelung f
conductor	s. a. line <el.>	configuration co-ordinate	Konfigurationskoordinate f
conductor of rectangular (square) section	s. rectangular conductor		
conductor's valve	s. štopcock	configuration co-ordinate model	Konfigurationskoordinatenmodell n [von Mott, Gurney und Seitz]
conduit tee	s. tee		
cone <of the eye>	Zapfen m, Zäpfchen n <Auge>		
cone-and-plate rheogoniometer	s. rheogoniometer	configuration integral, configurational integral	Konfigurationsintegral n, Verteilungsfunktion f der potentiellen Energie
cone diaphragm	Konusmembran f		
cone flow, conical flow	kegelige (kegelförmige, konische) Strömung f	configuration interaction, CI	Konfigurationswechselwirkung f, CI
cone-in-cone texture	Tütentextur f, Kegel-in-Kegel-Textur f		
		configuration-interaction method, CI method, antisymmetric molecular orbital configuration-interaction method, ASMO CI method	Konfigurationswechselwirkungsmethode f, Methode f der Konfigurationswechselwirkung, Verfahren n der Konfigurationswechselwirkung, ASMO-CI-Methode f, ASMO-CI-Verfahren n
cone of dispersion, cone of spread, dispersing (scattering) cone	Streukegel m, Streuungskegel m		
cone of escape	Entweichungskegel m		
cone of friction, friction cone	Reibungskegel m		
cone of light rays, light cone, luminous cone, ray cone, cone of radiation (rays)	Lichtkegel m, Strahlenkegel m		
		configuration mixture	Konfigurationsmischung f, Mischkonfiguration f
		configuration of equilibrium	s. equilibrium configuration
cone of nulls	s. cone of silence	configuration of planet	s. planetary configuration
cone of pressure relief, cone of pumping depression, cone of [water table] depression	Senkungstrichter m, Depressionstrichter m, Entnahmetrichter m	configuration polymorphy	Konfigurationspolymorphie f
		configuration purity	Konfigurationsreinheit f
cone of radiation	s. cone of light rays	configuration radiator	Konfigurationsstrahler m
cone of shearing stress	Schubspannungskegel m	configuration space	Konfigurationsraum m, Lagenraum m
cone of silence, cone of nulls	Schweigekegel m		
cone of spread	s. cone of dispersion		
cone of water table depression	s. cone of pressure relief	confined ground water	abgeschirmtes Grundwasser n
cone semi-angle, semi-vertex (semi-apex) angle [of the cone], semi-angle of the cone, semi-cone angle	[halber] Öffnungswinkel m des Kegels	confinement of plasma	s. plasma containment
		confinement time	Confinementzeit f, Einschließ[ungs]zeit f, Einschlußzeit f, Begrenzungszeit f
cone texture	s. zonal texture	confining bed (layer), confining stratum	Grundwassersohle f
confidence	s. level of significance		
confidence belt	Konfidenzgürtel m, Vertrauensgürtel m	confining liquid; sealing liquid, sealing fluid	Absperrflüssigkeit f; Sperrflüssigkeit f; Dichtungsflüssigkeit f
confidence coefficient	s. leve lof significance		
confidence interval	s. confidence limits		
confidence interval estimation	Konfidenzintervallschätzung f		

confining magnetic field	s. magnetic confining field	congo-red test paper	Kongo[rot]papier n
confining of plasma	s. plasma containment	congruence	Kongruenz f
confining stratum	s. confining bed		
confirmation, verification, corroboration <math.>	Bestätigung f, Erhärtung f, Verifizierung f <Math.>		
		congruent mapping	kongruente Abbildung f
confluence	Konfluenz f, Zusammenfluß m (Vereinigung f) gleichrangiger Ströme	congruent melting	kongruentes Schmelzen n
		congruent melting point	kongruenter Schmelzpunkt m, Kongruenzschmelzpunkt m
confluence of singular points	Konfluenz f singulärer Punkte		
confluent hypergeometric equation [of Kummer]	s. Kummer['s] [differential] equation	congruent transformation	s. orthogonal transformation
		conic, conic section	Kegelschnitt m
confluent hypergeometric function, Kummer['s] function; confluent hypergeometric series, Kummer['s] series	konfluente hypergeometrische Funktion f, Kummer[-Pochhammer]sche Funktion, Funktion des Drehparaboloids; konfluente hypergeometrische Reihe f	conical beaker	s. Philipps beaker
		conical co-ordinates	Kegelkoordinaten fpl
		conical flow	s. cone flow
		conical function	Kegelfunktion f
		conical horn [waveguide]	konisches Horn n, konischer Trichter m, Konushorn n, Konustrichter m, Kegelhorn n, Kegeltrichter m
confluent hypergeometric function of second kind	konfluente hypergeometrische Funktion f zweiter Art	conical horn loudspeaker	Konus[trichter]lautsprecher m, Kegeltrichterlautsprecher m, Trichterlautsprecher m
confluent hypergeometric series	s. confluent hypergeometric function		
confluent region, contact region <semi.>	Kontaktzone f; Kontaktenge f <Halb.>	conical indenter	Kegel[druck-Prüf]körper m, kegelförmiger Eindringkörper m <bei der Kegeldruck-Härteprüfung>
confocal, homofocal	konfokal, homofokal		
confocal co-ordinates	konfokale Koordinaten fpl		
		conically ground joint	Kegelschliff m
confocal ellipsoidal co-ordinates	s. ellipsoidal co-ordinates	conical mirror, conic mirror	Kegelspiegel m
confocal paraboloidal co-ordinates, parabolic co-ordinates	[ebene] parabolische Koordinaten fpl	conical pendulum	Kegelpendel n, konisches Pendel n
conformal	s. equiangular	conical point, first Lagrangian point, inner Lagrangian point	erster Lagrange-Punkt m, innerer Lagrange-Punkt
conformal co-ordinates	konforme Koordinaten fpl		
conformal curvature tensor	s. Weyl['s] tensor	conical refraction	konische Refraktion f
		conical scan	Quirlen n
conformal map[ping], conformal transformation (representation), isogonal (equiangular, anglepreserving) mapping	konforme Abbildung f, winkeltreue Abbildung, konforme Transformation f	conical shutter	Kegelblende f
		conical streamer	s. wind cone
		conical surface	Kegelfläche f
		conic mirror, conical mirror	Kegelspiegel m
conformal projection, equiangular projection, orthomorphic projection	winkeltreue (konforme) Projektion f, winkeltreuer (konformer) Entwurf m, Winkeltreuentwurf m, orthomorphe Projektion	conicoid	s. quadric <non-degenerate case>
		conic projection	Kegelprojektion f, konische Projektion f, Kegelentwurf m, konischer Entwurf m
conformal representation	s. conformal mapping		
conformal space-time	konforme Raumzeit f	conics	Theorie f der Kegelschnitte
conformal transformation	s. conformal mapping	conic section, conic	Kegelschnitt m
conformation, constellation <chem.>	Konformation f, Konstellation f <Chem.>	conisphere, konisphere	Konisphäre f
		conjoined rule of three, compound rule of three, chain rule	Kettenregel f
conformational analysis	Konformationsanalyse f		
conformation isomer, conformer, rotational isomer, rotamer	Konformer n, Konformationsisomer n, Rotamer n, Rotationsisomer n	conjugate	s. complex conjugate
		conjugate	s. adjoint space
		conjugate axis	Nebenachse f <Hyperbel>
conformity	s. isogonality <math.>	conjugate Bertrand curves	s. Bertrand curves
conformity principle	Konformitätsprinzip n		
conform tensor	s. Weyl['s] tensor	conjugate bonds	s. conjugate double bonds
confounding <stat.>	Vermengen n <Stat.>	conjugate complex	s. complex conjugate
		conjugate curves	s. Bertrand curves
confused sea, confuse sea	unregelmäßig bewegte See f, wilde See, Stampfsee f	conjugated [double] bonds	s. conjugate double bonds
		conjugate diameter	konjugierter Durchmesser m
confusion colour, mixed colour <opt.>	Mischfarbe f <Opt.>	conjugate double bonds, conjugate[d] bonds	konjugierte Doppelbindungen (Bindungen) fpl
congeal	s. congelation		
congealing point	s. solidification point		
congealing point	s. point of congelation <of oil>	conjugate function	konjugierte Potentialfunktion f (harmonische Funktion f), [harmonische] konjugierte Funktion
congelation, congeal, freezing-together	Zusammenfrieren n		
congelifraction	Kongelifraktion f, Frostsprengung f, Frostverwitterung f, Congelifraction f		
		conjugate imaginary	s. complex conjugate
		conjugate matrix	s. adjoint matrix
		conjugate nuclei, semimirror nuclei	konjugierte Kerne mpl
congelisol	s. permafrost		
congestion	s. accumulation	conjugate points	konjugierte Punkte mpl
congestus, cauliflower, con <meteo.>	congestus, blumenkohlförmig [aufgequollen], con <Meteo.>		
		conjugate points <of compound pendulum>	Aufhänge- und Schwingungsmittelpunkt m <physikalisches Pendel>
congestus cloud	s. cumulus		
conglomerate <chem., geo.>	Konglomerat n <Chem., Geo.>	conjugate quaternion	konjugierte Quaternion f
		conjugate solution	konjugierte Lösung f
conglomeration [of the grains]	Zusammenballung f [der Körner]		

conjugate space	s. adjoint space	conservation of moment of momentum	s. conservation of angular momentum
conjugating frequency	Knickpunktfrequenz f, Verknüpfungsfrequenz f	conservation of momentum, momentum conservation	Erhaltung f des Impulses, Impulserhaltung f, Erhaltung der Bewegungsgröße
conjugation, conjugation operator	Konjugation f, Konjugationsoperator m		
conjugation <math., chem., bio.>	Konjugation f <Math., Chem., Bio.>; Zuordnung f <allg.>	conservation of parity principle	s. law of conservation of parity
		conservation of particles	Erhaltung f der Teilchenzahl
conjugation energy	Konjugationsenergie f	conservation of volume	s. constancy of volume
conjugation operator, conjugation	Konjugation f, Konjugationsoperator m	conservative field [of force]	konservatives Feld (Kraftfeld) n
conjunction <astr.>	Konjunktion f, Gleichschein m <Astr.>	conservative force, potential force	konservative Kraft f, Potentialkraft f
conjunction, logic[al] product <math.>	Konjunktion f, logisches Produkt n <Math.>	conservative motion, slip motion <of dislocations>	konservative Bewegung f, Gleitbewegung f <Versetzung>
conjunctive fault	s. compressive fault <geo.>		
conjunctive matrix by a unitary transformation	s. unitary similar matrix	conserved quantity	Erhaltungsgröße f
conjunctive normal form	konjunktive Normalform f		
connected in series	s. series connected <el., gen.>	consideration of models	Modellbetrachtung f
connected load (value)	s. contact value <el.>	consistence	s. viscidity <chem.>
connected vessels	s. communicating vessels	consistency, self-consistency <math.>	Konsistenz f, Widerspruchsfreiheit f, Widerspruchslosigkeit f Verträglichkeit f <Math.>
connecting	s. circuit wiring		
connecting	s. switching <el.>		
connecting circuit	Verbindungsstromkreis m		
		consistency	s. a. viscidity <chem.>
connecting diagram	s. schematic circuit diagram	consistency curve	Konsistenzkurve f
connecting direction	Anschlußrichtung f; Richtungsanschluß m	consistency equation, constitutive equation	Konsistenzgleichung f; Materialgleichung f
connecting piece	s. nozzle	consistent <math.>	konsistent; widerspruchsfrei; permanent; verträglich <Math.>
connecting-up	s. circuit wiring		
connection, interconnection, hookup <el.>	Zusammenschaltung f <El.>		
connection	s. a. switching <el.>	consistent	s. a. viscid <chem.>
connection	s. a. nozzle	consistent estimate (estimator)	konsistente Schätzung (Schätzfunktion) f
connection across	s. bridging		
connection by flexible pipe (tube)	s. flexible pipe connection	consistent grease	s. grease
		consistometer	Konsistometer n, Konsistenzmesser m
connection by solder; solder, solder[ed] joint, solder[ed] connection; junction <semi.>	Lötstelle f; Lötverbindung f	console	s. indicator <el.>
		consolidation	Befestigung f
		consolidation <geo.>	Konsolidation f, Versteifung f; Verdichtung f; Pressung f <Geo.>
connection coefficient	Komponente f des affinen Zusammenhangs		
connection diagram	s. schematic circuit diagram	consolidation	s. a. pore fluid anelasticity
connection in cascade	s. cascade connection <el., chem.>	consolute, completely miscible	vollständig (unbeschränkt) mischbar
connection in parallel	s. parallel connection	consolute point	s. critical solution temperature
connection in series	s. series connection		
connection of networks, geodesic connection of networks	Netzanschluß m, Zusammenschluß m von Netzen	consonance, consonancy	s. concord
		consonant choir effect	chorischer Effekt m
		conspicuity <with the naked eye> <astr.>; visibility <meteo., astr.>; seeing <astr.>	Sichtbarkeit f <Meteo., Astr.>; Sicht f <Meteo.>; Sichtgrad m <Meteo.>
connection to the neutral conductor	Nullung f		
connexion	s. connection		
conode, tie line	Konode f, Konnode f	conspicuous	s. visible <astr.>
co-normal	Konormale f	constancy <math.>	Konstanz f <Math.>
conproportionation	s. comproportionation	constancy	s. a. permanence
Conrad discontinuity	Conradsche Diskontinuität[sfläche] f, Conrad-Diskontinuität f	constancy	s. a. stability <of instrument, source>
		constancy of light velocity	Konstanz f der Lichtgeschwindigkeit
Conrad['s] pendulum	Conrad-Pendel n		
consecutive <math.>	benachbart, konsekutiv	constancy of volume, volume constancy (conservation), conservation of volume	Volum[en]beständigkeit f, Volum[en]konstanz f, Raumbeständigkeit f, Raumkonstanz f
consecutive mean	s. moving average		
consecutive reaction, consequent reaction	Folgereaktion f		
consequent <geo.>	konsequent <Geo.>		
		constant	s. fixed value
		constant; invariable; unvarying; fixed	konstant; unveränderlich, invariabel; fest
consequent reaction, consecutive reaction	Folgereaktion f		
consequent river	konsequenter Fluß m, Folgefluß m	constant <of instrument, source>, stable	konstant, stabil <Gerät, Quelle>
conservation law	s. law of conservation	constant	s. a. steady
conservation law of isobaric spin	s. law of conservation of isobaric spin	constant acceleration	s. uniform acceleration
		constant amplitude recording	Aufzeichnung f mit konstanter Amplitude
conservation of angular momentum, conservation of moment of momentum	Erhaltung f des Drehimpulses, Drehimpulserhaltung f	constant boiling mixture	s. constant boiling-point mixture
		constant boiling-point mixture	s. azeotrope
conservation of [electric] charge, charge conservation	Erhaltung f der [elektrischen] Ladung, Ladungserhaltung f	constant by volume	volum[en]beständig, raumbeständig
		constant current	s. direct current <el.>
conservation of energy and momentum	Energie-Impuls-Erhaltung f, Erhaltung f von Energie und Impuls	constant-current arc, direct-current arc, d.c. arc	Gleichstrombogen m, Gleichstromlichtbogen m
		constant-current diagram	Konstantstromdiagramm n
conservation of energy principle	s. energy conservation law		
conservation of mass (matter) principle	s. law of conservation of mass	constant-current generator	s. electric generator

constant-current modulation, Heising modulation, choke modulation	Parallelröhrenmodulation f [nach Heising], Heising-Modulation f	constant-pressure combustion, combustion at constant pressure	Gleichdruckverbrennung f
		constant pressure cycle	s. Joule cycle
		constant[-]pressure gas thermometer	Gasthermometer n konstanten Drucks
		constant pressure line	s. isobar ‹therm., meteo.›
		constant-rate creep	s. quasiviscous creep
		constant-ratio head	Destillationsaufsatz m (Destillationsrohr n) mit konstantem Rückflußverhältnis
constant current source	s. stable current source		
constant-deviation dispersion prism, constant-deviation prism	Prismensystem (Dispersionsprisma, Prisma) n mit konstanter Ablenkung	constants of elasticity	s. elastic constants
		constant-strain-rate test	s. long-duration creep-rupture test
		constant temperature	konstante (gleichbleibende) Temperatur f
constant-deviation spectrometer	Prismenspektrometer (Spektrometer) n mit konstanter Ablenkung	constant-temperature bath	s. thermostatic bath
constant diameter hardness [number]	s. monotron hardness	constant-temperature combustion, combustion at constant temperature	Gleichtemperaturverbrennung f
constant displacement hydrometer	s. weight aerometer	constant temperature vessel	s. temperature control vessel
constant flow	s. steady flow	constant term, absolute term	Absolutglied n
constant-k general L network, constant-k L network	Grundhalbglied n, Zobelsches Grundhalbglied, Zobelsches Grundglied n, Wagner-Glied n	constant value control	s. automatic stabilization
		constant velocity recording	Aufzeichnung f mit konstanter Schnelle
		constant voltage generator	Gleichspannungsgenerator m
constant-gradient focusing	s. weak focusing	constant-volume combustion, combustion at constant volume	Gleichraumverbrennung f
constant in creep rate law	Konstante f im Kriechgesetz		
constant in Hölder['s] condition, Hölder constant	Hölder-Koeffizient m, [Hölderscher] Koeffizient m	constant-volume deformation	Deformation f ohne Volumänderung
constant-k filter	Grundfilter n	constant-volume gas thermometer	Gasthermometer n konstanten Volumens, Gasthermometer konstanter Dichte, Gasthermometer nach Jolly, Jollysches Gasthermometer
constant light	Gleichlicht n		
constant light method, constant light technique	Gleichlichtmethode f		
		constant-volume gas turbine	s. explosion turbine
		constant volume specific heat	s. specific heat at constant volume
constant magnetic field	magnetisches Gleichfeld n, konstantes magnetisches Feld n	constant wave method	Konstantwellenmethode f
constant motion, uniform [speed] motion	gleichförmige Bewegung f	constellation	Sternbild n
		constellation	s. a. conformation ‹chem.›
constant of anharmonicity	s. anharmonicity constant	constituent ‹chem.›	Bestandteil m, Anteil m, Konstituent m ‹Chem.›
constant of atomic physics	s. atomic constant	constituent of tide, tidal component	Gezeitenkomponente f, Gezeitenglied n
constant of Coulomb	s. elastic shear modulus	constitution ‹chem.›	Konstitution f ‹Chem.›
constant of elastic strain	s. coefficient of linear extension	constitution	s. a. structure
constant of electromagnetic field, field constant	Feldkonstante f	constitutional formula	s. structural formula
		constitutionally homogeneous	s. homogeneous structure / of
constant of gravitation, gravitational constant, gravitation constant	Gravitationskonstante f, Newtonsche Gravitationskonstante	constitutionally inhomogeneous	s. inhomogeneous structure / of
		constitutionally stable, structural-stable, structurally stable, of stable structure	strukturstabil, strukturbeständig
constant of heat exchange	s. heat-exchange constant		
constant of inertia	Trägheitskonstante f	constitutionally unstable	s. structural-unstable
constant of integration	Integrationskonstante f	constitutional water, water of constitution	Konstitutionswasser n
constant of magnetostrictive anisotropy	s. magnetostriction constant	constitution diagram	s. phase diagram
constant of mean refraction	s. refraction constant	constitution formula, structural (constitutional, graphic, rational) formula	Strukturformel f, Konstitutionsformel f, Valenzstrichformel f
constant of nutation, nutation constant	Nutationskonstante f		
constant of proportionality	s. factor of proportionality	constitutive constant	s. material constant
		constitutive equation	s. consistency equation
constant of refraction	s. refraction constant	constitutive equation	s. stress-strain relation
constant of renormalization	Renormierungskonstante f	constitutive parameter	s. material parameter
		constitutive property, structural property	Struktureigenschaft f; konstitutive Eigenschaft f
constant of surface tension	s. surface tension constant ‹nucl.›	constrained, forced ‹mech.›	zwang[s]läufig, Zwangs- ‹Mech.›
constant of the measuring instrument, measuring instrument constant	Meßgerätekonstante f, Gerätekonstante f, Instrumentenkonstante f, Apparat[e]konstante f	constrained distribution	Zwang[s]verteilung f
		constrained material point, constrained point, non-free point	gebundener Massenpunkt m, unfreier Punkt m, gebundener Punkt
constant of the meter, meter constant	Zählerkonstante f		
constant of thermodynamics	s. thermodynamic constant	constrained motion, forced motion	zwang[s]läufige (erzwungene; eingeschränkte) Bewegung f, Zwangsbewegung f, Zwang[s]lauf m
constant-potential accelerator	Beschleuniger m mit konstantem Potential		
constant pressure	konstanter Druck m, Gleichdruck m		

constrained 126

constrained oscillation	s. forced oscillation	contact detector	s. contact rectifier
constrained point	s. constrained material point	contact discontinuity	s. material discontinuity
constrained system	System n mit Zwang[sbedingungen], gebundenes [mechanisches] System, unfreies System	contact electromotive force, contact e.m.f.	Kontakt-EMK f, Kontaktspannung f
constraining force	s. reaction	contact electromotive series, contact series, contact potential series	Kontaktspannungsreihe f, elektrische Spannungsreihe f, Spannungsreihe der Kontaktpotentiale
constraint	Zwang[s]läufigkeit f, Zwang m		
constraint, constraints equation, restraining condition; constraint factor <mech.>	Zwangsbedingung f, Bedingung[sgleichung] f, Bindung f, Nebenbedingung f; Zwang m	contact equilibrium	Kontaktgleichgewicht n
		contact filtration	Kontaktfiltration f, Kontaktfilterung f
		contact force	Kontaktkraft f
constraint dependent on the time	s. rheonomic constraint	contact gap, contact clearance, contact spacing	Kontaktabstand m
constraint factor	s. constraint <mech.>		
constraint hypersurface	s. hypersurface of constraints	contact gettering	Kontaktgetterung f
constraint independent of time, non varying constraint, scleronomous binding	skleronome Bedingung f, starrgesetzliche Bedingung	contact goniometer, semicircular (angle) protractor, protractor	Anlegegoniometer n, Kontaktgoniometer n, Transporteur m
		contact halation (halo)	Kontakthof m
constraint of the first class	s. first class constraint	contact hygrometer	Kontakthygrometer n
		contacting	Kontaktierung f
constraint of the second class	s. second class constraint	contacting agent (material)	s. contact material
constraints equation	s. constraint	contacting unit	s. sensitive element
constriction; necking [down]; contraction of area; pinch, pinching; waist	Einschnürung f	contact interaction	Kontaktwechselwirkung f
		contact interface	s. surface of contact
		contact load	Berührungsbelastung f
constriction, abscission, segmentation	Abschnürung f	contact mass	s. contact <chem.>
constriction	s. a. contraction	contact material, contacting material, contacting agent	Kontaktwerkstoff m, Kontaktmittel n
constringence, reciprocal (inverse of) dispersive power, Abbe number	Abbesche Zahl f, Abbe-Zahl f, reziproke relative Dispersion f	contact-metamorphic rock	Kontaktgestein n
construction by Wulff, Wulff['s] construction	Wulffsche Konstruktion f	contact metamorphism	s. juxtaposition metamorphism
construction of the funicular (link) polygon	Seileckkonstruktion f	contact microradiography	Kontaktmikroradiographie f
construction unit	s. component <of construction>	contact noise, crackling noise	Kratzgeräusch n; Kontaktrauschen n; Kontaktgeräusch n
consumable electrode	verzehrbare Elektrode f		
consummation of errors	Fehlerabgleich[s]methode f	contact opening time	s. opening time
consumption <also chem.>; expense, expenditure; display	Verbrauch m; Aufwand m; Verzehrung f	contactor, circuit closer, switch	Einschalter m
		contactor <normally open or normally closed>, contactor relay; overload relay	Schütz n, Schalterschütz n <mit Arbeits- oder Ruhekontakten>
consumption, power consumption (absorption); power (horsepower) input; power requirement (demand), demand for power <el.>	Leistungsaufnahme f, Leistungsverbrauch m; Leistungsbedarf m; Leistungsaufwand m <El.>		
		contact panel, contact-bank, bank of contacts	Kontaktbank f, Bank f, Kontaktkranz m, Kontaktfeld n; Kontaktbahn f; Kontaktleiste f
consumption	s. a. burn <e.g. of electrodes>		
consumption density	Verbrauchsdichte f	contact path, contact travel	Kontaktweg m, Kontaktstrecke f, Kontaktbahn f
contact, contact mass, solid catalyst <chem.>	Feststoffkatalysator m, Kontakt[stoff] m, Kontaktmasse f <Chem.>	contact phenomenon	Kontakterscheinung f
		contact plate	Kontaktplättchen n, Bodenkontakt m
contact	s. a. contiguity <gen.>	contact potential	s. contact potential difference
contact angle	s. angle of contact		
contact area ratio	s. ratio of bearing contact area	contact potential barrier, potential barrier at the contact	Kontaktpotentialwall m
contact atomic battery (cell)	s. contact cell		
contact-bank	s. contact panel	contact potential difference, c.p.d., CPD; contact potential	Kontaktspannung f, Kontaktpotentialdifferenz f, Berührungsspannung f, Kontaktelektrizität f, Berührungselektrizität f; Kontaktpotential n
contact binary	Kontaktdoppelstern m, Kontaktsystem n		
contact blade	Kontaktmesser n		
contact bounce	Kontaktsprung m, Kontakt[rück]prall m, Kontaktprellung f		
		contact potential series	s. contact electromotive series
contact breaker	s. circuit breaker <el.>	contact problem <elast.>	Berührungsproblem n
contact-breaking spark	s. quenched spark	contact protection	s. shock-hazard protection
contact brush, brush, wiper	Schleifbürste f; Kontaktarm m; Kontaktbürste f	contact radioautography	Kontaktautoradiographie f
contact catalysis	s. heterogeneous catalysis	contact rectifier; contact detector	Kontaktgleichrichter m, Kontaktstromrichter m; Kontaktdetektor m
contact cell, contact atomic cell, contact atomic battery	Kontaktpotentialelement n; Kontaktpotentialbatterie f		
		contact rectifier	s. a. barrier-layer rectifier
contact clearance	s. contact gap	contact region	s. confluent region <semi.>
contact controller	s. step regulator	contact relation <therm.>	Kontaktrelation f <Therm.>
contact corrosion, deposit (meeting) corrosion	Kontaktkorrosion f, Berührungskorrosion f; Belagerungskorrosion f; Bedeckungseffekt m; Elementbildung f	contact resistance	Kontaktwiderstand m
		contact resistance, transition resistance <el. chem.>	Übergangswiderstand m <El. Chem.>
contact cup anemometer	Schalen[kreuz]kontaktanemometer n		

contact ring	s. slip ring <el>	content meter	Konzentrationsmesser m, Gerät n zur Gehaltsbestimmung
contact semiconductor-metal	Kontakt m Halbleiter—Metall, Halbleiter-Metall-Kontakt m	content of condensation nuclei	Kondensationskerngehalt m
contact semiconductor-semiconductor	Kontakt m Halbleiter—Halbleiter, Halbleiter-Halbleiter-Kontakt m	content of dust nuclei	Staubkerngehalt m
contact series	s. contact electromotive series	content of energy	s. energy content
contact set	Kontaktsatz m	content of isotope, isotope content	Isotopengehalt m
		contiguity; juxtaposition; contact <gen.>	Berührung f; Kontakt m <allg.>
contact spacing	s. contact gap	contiguity	s. a. vicinity
contact spot	Kontaktstelle f	continental air	s. continental mass
contact stimulation	Berührungsreizung f	continental climate	Landklima n, kontinentales Klima n, Kontinentalklima n, Binnenklima n
contact stimulus, thigmic stimulus, haptic stimulus	Berührungsreiz m, Kontaktreiz m, Tastreiz m, haptischer (thigmischer) Reiz m	continental drift, drift of continents	Kontinentaldrift f, Kontinentalverschiebung f
contact stress <mech.>	Berührungsspannung f <Mech.>	continental drift theory, Wegener['s] theory of continental drift	Kontinentalverschiebungstheorie f, Wegeners Theorie f der Kontinentalverschiebung, Kontinentaldrifttheorie f
contact surface, critical surface <according to Roche>	Kontaktfläche f [nach Roche]	continental glacier	Deckgletscher m, Grönlandtyp-Gletscher m
contact surface	s. a. surface of contact	continental ice, land ice, inland ice	Inlandeis n
contact thermoelectromotive force, contact thermoelectric e.m.f.	Kontakt-Thermo-EMK f, Kontaktanteil m der Thermo-EMK	continentality	Kontinentalität f
contact thermometer	Kontaktthermometer n, Berührungsthermometer n		
contact time	s. opening time	continental margin	Kontinentalrand m
contact to earth	s. short-circuit to earth	continental mass	Kontinentmasse f, Kontinentalmassiv n
contact[-] transformation	Berührungstransformation f	continental mass; continental air	Kontinentalluftmasse f, kontinentale Luftmasse f; Kontinentalluft f
		continental platform	Kontinentaltafel f
contact travel	Schaltweg m	continental shelf, shelf	Schelf m, Kontinentalsockel m, neritischer Bereich m
contact travel	s. a. contact path		
contact twin	s. juxtaposition twin		
contact value, connected load (value) <el.>	Anschlußwert m <El.>	continental slope	Kontinentalhang m, Kontinentalböschung f
contact variable <therm.>	Kontaktvariable f <Therm.>	continental undulation of the geoid	kontinentale Undulation f des Geoids
contagious distribution	Ansteckungsverteilung f	contingency <stat.>	Kontingenz f <Stat.>
container	s. transfer container	contingency table, $m \times n$ table	Kontingenztafel f, $m \times n$-Tafel f
containing a portion of black	s. non-zero black content / having		
containing a portion of black and white	s. non-zero black and white content / having	continuability	Fortsetzbarkeit f
containing a portion of white	s. non-zero white content / having	continual	s. steady
		continual creation, continuous creation	kontinuierliche Schöpfung f
containing sprinklings, scattered [here and there] <geo.>	eingesprengt, dispers; zerstreut <Geo.>	continual hypothesis (theory), continuum theory (hypothesis) <mech.>	Kontinuitätshypothese f, Kontinuitätstheorie f <Mech.>
containment	s. containment vessel	continuant	Kontinuante f, Kettenbruchdeterminante f
containment of plasma	s. plasma containment		
containment vessel, containment, safety container	Sicherheitsbehälter m, Containment n <Reaktor>; dichte Umschließung f <für radioaktive Stoffe>	continuation <math.>	Fortsetzung f <Math.>
		continuation lead	s. artificial line
		continued fraction <math.>	Kettenbruch m <Math.>
		continued fraction representation	s. expansion in terms of continued fractions
		continued product, infinite product	unendliches Produkt n
contaminant	Kontaminationsmittel n	continuity	Kontinuität f
contaminant	s. a. impurity		
contaminant	s. a. pollutant	continuity <math.>	Stetigkeit f <Math.>
contamination	s. radiocontamination	continuity concept	Stetigkeitsbegriff m
contamination	s. a. pollution	continuity condition, condition of continuity <math.>	Stetigkeitsbedingung f <Math.>
contamination density	s. impurity concentration		
contamination detector	s. contamination meter	continuity condition	s. a. continuity equation <hydr.>
contamination index	s. degree of pollution		
contamination meter, contamination detector	Kontaminationsmesser m, Kontaminationsmeßgerät n, Versuchungsmeßgerät n	continuity equation, equation of continuity, principle of continuity	Kontinuitätsgleichung f
content by mass	s. mass content		
content by per cent	s. relative content	continuity equation, equation (condition) of continuity, continuity condition <hydr.>	Kontinuitätsgleichung f, Kontinuitätsbedingung f, Inkompressibilitätsbedingung f <Hydr.>
content by volume, volume content	Gehalt m in Volumeneinheiten, Volum[en]gehalt m		
content by weight	s. mass content		

continuity of state[s], state continuity	Zustandskontinuität f, Kontinuität f der Zustandsübergänge
continuous, steady, permanent, constant, continual	ständig, stetig, permanent, Dauer-, kontinuierlich
continuous <math.>	stetig <Math.>
continuous	s. a. continuously operated
continuous absorption spectrum	s. absorption continuum
continuous action controller	s. continuous controller
continuous[-] action laser	s. continuous[-] wave laser
continuous[-] action maser	s. continuous[-] wave maser
continuous air monitor	kontinuierliches Luftüberwachungsgerät n
continuous amplification	s. continuous excitation <of oscillation>
continuous atomic spectrum above limit of the series	Grenzkontinuum n [der Serie], Seriengrenzkontinuum n
continuous beam	durchgehender (durchlaufender) Balken m, Durchlaufbalken m, Durchlaufträger m
continuous charge	s. continuous load <el.>
continuous coiling	durchlaufende Wendel f
continuous control	stetige (stetig wirkende) Steuerung f; stetige (stetig wirkende) Regelung f
continuous controller, continuous action controller	stetiger Regler m, stetig wirkender Regler
continuous convergence	stetige Konvergenz f
continuous corona	s. K corona
continuous creation, continual creation	kontinuierliche Schöpfung f
continuous current	s. direct current <el.>
continuous current amplifier	s. direct-current amplifier
continuous discharge	Dauerentladung f, kontinuierliche Entladung f
continuous distribution	stetige (geometrische) Verteilung f
continuous electronic spectrum, electron continuum	Elektronenkontinuum n
continuous electrophorus	s. influence machine
continuous emission spectrum	s. emission continuum
continuous excitation, amplification <of boundary layer>	Anfachung f
continuous excitation; continuous amplification; anti-damping <of oscillation>	Anfachung f der Schwingung, Schwingungsanfachung f
continuous expansion chamber, continuously sensitive expansion chamber	kontinuierliche Nebelkammer f
continuous-flow calorimeter, flow calorimeter	Strömungskalorimeter n, Durchströmungskalorimeter n
continuous group	s. topological group
continuous ingot casting	Strangguß m
continuous in operation	s. continuously operated
continuous laser	s. continuous[-] wave laser
continuous Lichtenberg figures	kontinuierliche Lichtenberg-Figuren fpl
continuous light	Dauerlicht n; Dauerbelichtung f
continuous load, continuous ratings (charge), steady (permanent) load	Dauerbelastung f, Dauerlast f <El.>
continuous load	s. a. permanent load <mech.>
continuous loading, krarupization	Krarupisierung f
continuously adjustable	stufenlos verstellbar, stufenlos einstellbar, stufenlos regelbar, regelbar, Regel-
continuously adjustable inductor	s. variometer
continuously deformable	stetig deformierbar
continuously differentiable	stetig differenzierbar
continuously loaded cable, Krarup cable	Krarup-Kabel n; Krarup-Leitung f
continuously operated, continuously operating, continuous [in operation]	kontinuierlich [arbeitend], mit kontinuierlichem Betrieb
continuously operated maser	s. continuous[-] wave maser
continuously operating	s. continuously operated
continuously operating laser	s. continuous[-] wave laser
continuously sensitive expansion chamber, continuous expansion chamber	kontinuierliche Nebelkammer f
continuous maser	s. continuous[-] wave maser
continuous medium, continuum <mech.>	deformierbares (kontinuierliches) Medium n, Kontinuum n <Mech.>
continuous metric variable <therm.>	kontinuierliche metrische Variable f <Therm.>
continuous molecular spectrum above band head	Grenzkontinuum n der Bande, Bandengrenzkontinuum n
continuous motion	kontinuierliche Bewegung f, Kontinuumsbewegung f
continuous on the left	linksseitig (rückwärts) stetig, linksstetig
continuous on the right	rechtsseitig (vorwärts) stetig, rechtsstetig
continuous oscillation	s. undamped oscillation
continuous phase, dispersion medium, external phase	Emulsionsmittel n, Dispersionsmittel n, kontinuierliche (äußere) Phase f
continuous radiation	s. white radiation
continuous rain; steady rain	Dauerregen m; Landregen m
continuous random variable	kontinuierliche Zufallsvariable (statistische) Variable) f
continuous ratings	s. continuous load <el.>
continuous regime flow	s. continuum flow
continuous regulation, stepless regulation; continuous variation	stufenlose Regelung f
continuous slowing down model, Fermi-age model	Fermi-Alter-Modell n, Modell n der kontinuierlichen Bremsung
continuous spectrum, continuum <opt.>	kontinuierliches Spektrum n, Kontinuum n <Opt.>
continuous spectrum <math.>	kontinuierliches Spektrum n, Streckenspektrum n, Häufungsspektrum n, Verdichtungsspektrum n <Math.>
continuous spectrum for extra-high pressure	s. extra-high pressure continuum
continuous time signal, permanent time signal	Dauerzeitzeichen n
continuous tone	Dauerton m
continuous tone	s. a. half-tone <opt.>
continuous transformation	kontinuierliche (stetige) Transformation f
continuous transition	kontinuierlicher Übergang m
continuous variability, quantitative (fluctuating) variability	kontinuierliche (fluktuierende, quantitative) Variabilität f
continuous variable	kontinuierliche Variable f <Therm.>; stetige Variable <Math.>
continuous variation	s. continuous regulation
continuous wave, undamped wave, cw, CW, C.W., c.w.	ungedämpfte Welle f, kontinuierliche Welle
continuous[-] wave laser, continuous laser, continuous[-] action laser, continuously operating laser, cw laser	kontinuierlicher Laser m, kontinuierlich arbeitender Laser, Laser mit kontinuierlichem Betrieb
continuous-wave magnetron	Dauermagnetron n

continuous[-] wave maser, continuous maser, continuous[-] action maser, continuously operated maser, cw maser	kontinuierlicher Maser m, kontinuierlich arbeitender Maser, Maser mit kontinuierlicher Strahlung (Anregung)	contracting-expanding nozzle	s. Laval nozzle
		contraction, shortening	Kontraktion f, Zusammenziehung f, Verkürzung f
continuous-wave power	Dauerstrichleistung f	contraction, transverse contraction <elast.>	Querkontraktion f, Querverkürzung f, Querkürzung f, Querzusammenziehung f, Kontraktion f
continuous X-radiation (X-ray radiation, X-rays)	s. bremsstrahlung		
continuum <pl.: continua> <math.>	Kontinuum n <pl.: Kontinua> <Math.>	contraction; shrinkage, shrinking; shortening	Schrumpfung f; Schwindung f, Schwinden n, Schwund m
continuum	s. a. continuous medium <mech.>		
continuum	s. a. continuous spectrum <opt.>		
continuum eigenfunction	Kontinuumeigenfunktion f	contraction, contraction of cross-section, thinning [-down] [of cross-section], weakening [of cross-section], narrowing, constriction <mech.>	Querschnittsvereng[er]ung f, Querschnitts[ver]schwächung f, Querschnittsverminderung f, Querschnittsabnahme f, Vereng[er]ung f [des Querschnitts], Verschwächung f [des Querschnitts], Schwächung f [des Querschnitts], Verminderung f [des Querschnitts], Abnahme f [des Querschnitts], Verdünnung f, Einengung f
continuum-emission storm, continuum storm	Kontinuumsturm m		
continuum flow, continuous regime flow	Kontinuumströmung f		
continuum hypothesis	s. continual theory <mech.>		
continuum infinite	s. power of the continuum / having the		
continuum mechanics	s. mechanics of the continuum		
continuum storm, continuum-emission storm	Kontinuumsturm m	contraction <of tensor>	Verjüngung f, Kontraktion f, Faltung f <Tensor>, Tensorverjüngung f <Math.>
continuum theory <e.g. of dislocations, nuclear reactions>	Kontinuumtheorie f <z. B. Versetzungen, Kernreaktionen>		
		contraction, inner multiplication, transvection <of tensor>	Überschiebung f [von Indizes] <Tensor>
continuum theory	s. a. continual theory <mech.>	contraction	s. a. muscular contraction
continuum theory	s. a. phenomenological theory	contraction coefficient, coefficient of contraction	Kontraktionskoeffizient m, Kontraktionsziffer f, Einschnürungszahl f, Einschnürungsziffer f
contour	s. outline <of steel>		
contour acuity, vernier acuity	Noniensehschärfe f, Breitenwahrnehmung f		
contour analysis	Umrißanalyse f	contraction crack, shrinkage (casting) crack	Schrumpfriß m, Schwind[ungs]riß m
contour chart	s. hypsometric map	contraction heat	s. heat of contraction
contour diagram, contourogram	Isoliniendiagramm n, Umrißdiagramm n	contraction hypothesis	Kontraktionstheorie f [von Helmholtz], Helmholtzsche Kontraktionstheorie, Kontraktionshypothese f, Schrumpfungstheorie f
contour ellipse	s. ellipse of correlation		
contour fringe	s. fringe of equal thickness		
contour height line	s. isobar <meteo.>		
contour integral, line integral; flow <e.g. of a tensor field, along a curve>	Kurvenintegral n, Linienintegral n		
		contraction in length, linear contraction	Längenkontraktion f, Längenschrumpfung f, lineare Kontraktion (Schrumpfung) f
contour integral	s. a. circulatory integral		
contour interpolation	Umrißinterpolation f		
contour line	s. isohypse		
contour line	s. equipotential line <el.>	contraction in volume	s. volume contraction
contour line of water table	s. water table contour	contraction of area; constriction; necking [down]; pinch, pinching; waist	Einschnürung f
contour map	s. hypsometric map		
contour of the [spectral] line	s. line profile		
		contraction of cross-section	s. contraction
contour of water table	s. water table contour	contraction of jet, contraction of the vein	Strahlkontraktion f; Strahleinschnürung f
contourogram, contour diagram	Isoliniendiagramm n, Umrißdiagramm n		
contour oscillation	s. flexural vibration	contraction of solidification	Erstarrungskontraktion f
contour plan	s. hypsometric map		
contour projector	s. profile projector	contraction of the cardiac muscle, contraction of the heart	Herzkontraktion f
contour survey, altimetric survey, survey of the relief	Höhenaufnahme f		
		contraction of the muscle	s. muscular contraction
contour vibration	s. flexural vibration	contraction of the pupil, myosis	Pupillenverengerung f, Miosis f
contracted column	kontrahierte Säule f; Schlauchentladung f		
		contraction of the vein	s. contraction of jet
contracted stream [of the liquid]	s. contracted vein	contraction pressure, shrinkage pressure, pressure due to shrinkage	Schrumpfdruck m
contracted tensor	verjüngter Tensor m		
contracted vein [of the liquid], contracted stream [of the liquid], vena contracta	vena f contracta, verengter Flüssigkeitsstrahl m		
		contraction ratio, narrowing ratio	Verjüngungsverhältnis n, Verengungsverhältnis n, Verengungszahl f, Kontraktionsverhältnis n
contracted weir, suppressed weir	Überfall m mit Seiteneinzwängung; Wehr n mit Seiteneinzwängung		
		contractive core	kontraktiver Kern m
		contracture	Kontraktur f
		contraflow	s. counter[-]flow
contractibility	s. contractility	contragredience	Kontragredienz f
contractile vacuole	pulsierende Vakuole f	contragredient automorphism, outer automorphism	äußerer Automorphismus m
contractility, contractibility	Kontrakti[bi]lität f, Zusammenziehbarkeit f		
contracting	s. wind tunnel contraction	contragredient co-ordinate	kontragrediente Koordinate f

contraharmonic 130

contraharmonic mean	kontraharmonisches Mittel n, kontraharmonischer Mittelwert m	control circuit	s. a. test circuit
		control coefficient	Regelfaktor m
contra-parallelogram	Gelenkantiparallelogramm n	control constant	s. restoration constant
		control contour, control line	Kontrollinie f
contrast	s. gamma ⟨quantity⟩		
contrast colour	Kontrastfarbe f		
contrast factor	s. gamma ⟨quantity⟩	control current, controlling current	Steuerstrom m, Stellstrom m
contrast filter	Kontrastfilter n		
contrast hue	s. relative hue	control device	s. final control element
contrast in brightness	s. luminance contrast	control electrode, modulator (guide; gate) electrode ⟨of the valve⟩	Steuerelektrode f
contrast in colour, colour contrast	Farbkontrast m; farbiger Kontrast m		
contrast in the interior of the surface far from its edges	Flächenkontrast m, Binnenkontrast m	control element	s. final control element
		control element	s. control member
		control error, error in control loops, error [deviation], deviation variable (value), deviation, departure, unbalance ⟨control⟩	Regelabweichung f ⟨Regelung⟩
contrast of details, detail contrast	Detailkontrast m		
contrast of eye	s. physiological contrast		
contrast of motion	Bewegungskontrast m, Kontrastbewegung f	control gear, stabilizer, ballast [unit] ⟨of discharge lamp⟩	Vorschaltgerät n ⟨Entladungslampe⟩
contrast of temperatures, temperature contrast	Temperaturgegensatz m		
contrast perceptibility function	Kontrastwahrnehmungsfunktion f	control grid	Steuergitter n
contrast perception, perception of contrast	Schwellenwahrnehmung f, Unterschiedswahrnehmung f, Kontrastwahrnehmung f	control grid	s. a. cathode grid
		control grid dissipation	Steuergitterbelastung f
		control grid modulation	Steuergittermodulation f
contrast phenomenon	Kontrastphänomen n, Kontrasterscheinung f	control grid of variable mu tube	Regelgitter n
contrast photometer	s. equality of contrast photometer		
contrast range, range of contrast	Kontrastumfang m	control hand, control pointer	Schleppzeiger m
contrast reduction, reduction of contrast	Kontrastminderung f	control input	s. command variable
		controlled area	kontrollierter Bereich m
contrast reduction factor	s. contrast transmission factor	controlled member	s. controlled system
		controlled member with several interacted controlled conditions, controlled plant with several interacted parameters ⟨US⟩	vermaschte Regelstrecke f
contrast rendition, rendition of contrast	Kontrastwiedergabe f		
contrast sensitivity	Kontrastempfindlichkeit f, Unterschiedsempfindlichkeit f		
contrast threshold [of eye]	Kontrastschwellenwert m [des Auges]	controlled nuclear reaction	gesteuerte Kernreaktion f
		controlled plant ⟨US⟩	s. controlled system
contrast transmission factor, contrast reduction factor	Kontrastübertragungsfaktor m	controlled plant with several interacted parameters ⟨US⟩	s. controlled member with several interacted controlled conditions
contrast transmission function, optical transfer function, frequency distribution function, response function, CTF, OTF	Kontrastübertragungsfunktion f, KÜF, CTF	controlled system, system to be controlled, controlled member ⟨GB⟩, controlled plant ⟨US⟩, plant ⟨US⟩ ⟨of the first or of higher order⟩	Regelstrecke f, Regelobjekt n ⟨erster oder höherer Ordnung⟩, Steuerstrecke f
contrasty, high-contrast, rich in contrast	kontrastreich		
contravariance	Kontravarianz f	controlled valency	gesteuerte Valenz f
contravariant component; contravariant co-ordinate	kontravariante Komponente f; kontravariante Koordinate f	controlled variable, regulated variable, regulated quantity	Regelgröße f
contravariant derivative	kontravariante Ableitung f	controller	Regler m
control; modulation	Aussteuerung f	controller; switchgear, switchgear installation	Schaltanlage f, Schaltapparat m
control, governing, command ⟨control⟩	Steuerung f, Vorwärtsregelung f; vorwärts geregelte Schaltung f ⟨Regelung⟩		
		controller without power amplification	s. self-operated controller
		controller with power amplification	s. relay-operated controller
control	s. a. closed-loop control	control line	s. control contour
control	s. a. monitoring	controlling current	s. control current
control	s. a. testing	controlling torque	Einstellmoment n
control and safety system	Steuer- und Schutzsystem n, SuS		
control area	Regelfläche f	controlling variable	s. command variable
control band	s. control range ⟨control⟩	control loop, control system, feedback control system, regulating system	Regelkreis m, Regelungskreis m, Regelsystem n; Steuersystem n
control button	s. focus control button ⟨e.g. of microscope⟩		
control characteristic, transfer characteristic	Steuerkennlinie f, Steuercharakteristik f; Steuerstabkennlinie f ⟨Reaktor⟩		
		control mechanism	s. switching gear ⟨mech.⟩
		control member, control element ⟨of the reactor⟩	Steuerorgan n, Steuerelement n ⟨Reaktor⟩
control check; check-back	Überprüfung f		
control circuit	Regelschaltung f	control member	s. a. final control element

control performance, performance of control	Regelgüte f, Güte f des Regelungssystems	convective flow; turbidity current <in dissolution of salts>	konvektive Strömung f, Konvektionsströmung f; Konvektionsstrom m
control point; minor control point; check point <geo.>	Paßpunkt m; Kontrollpunkt m <Geo.>	convective flow of heat, convective heat flow	konvektive Wärmeströmung f; konvektiver Wärmestrom m
control point	s. a. point of measurement <of thermocouple>	convective heat exchange	s. heat transfer by convection
control pointer, control hand	Schleppzeiger m	convective heat loss, convective loss of heat	konvektiver Wärmeverlust m
control pulse	s. command pulse	convective heat transfer coefficient	s. convection heat transfer coefficient
control range; control band	Regelbereich m, Regelhub m; Regelband n; Stellbereich m, Steuerbereich m, Steuerhub m	convective instability	konvektive Instabilität (Labilität) f
control range	s. a. drive range	convective layer, convective zone	Konvektionszone f, Konvektionsschicht f
control reactivity	Steuerreaktivität f	convective loss of heat, convective heat loss	konvektiver Wärmeverlust m
control register	s. programme register	convective mass transfer	s. convective transport
control rod	Steuerstab m	convective potential	s. convection potential
control sample	s. duplicate	convective precipitation	konvektiver Niederschlag m, Konvektionsniederschlag m
control signal	s. manipulated variable		
control specimen	s. duplicate		
control surface	Kontrollfläche f	convective transport, convective mass transfer, convection mass transfer	Konvektionstransport m, konvektiver Stoffaustausch (Transport) m
control system	s. control loop	convective transport coefficient	s. convection heat transfer coefficient
control theory	s. automatic control theory		
control value	s. manipulated variable	convective zone	s. convective layer
control voltage	Regelspannung f	conventional, interim	interimistisch, vereinbart, bedingt
		conventional circuit, conventional electric circuit	konventioneller Stromkreis m
control voltage, driving voltage, drive voltage, excitation voltage	Steuerspannung f, Steuersignalspannung f		
		conventional entropy	konventionelle Entropie f
control without power amplification	s. direct control	conventional magnetization	technische Magnetisierung f
control with power amplification	s. indirect control	conventional magnification	konventionelle Vergrößerung f
convected co-ordinates	mitgeschleppte (mitbewegte, mitgeführte) Koordinaten fpl	conventional millimetre of mercury	s. torr
convectional circulation	Konvektionskreislauf m	conventional millimetre of water [column]	s. millimetre of water
convection band	Konvektionsband n	conventional tropopause	konventionelle Tropopause f
convection by turbulence	s. turbulent convection		
convection cell	Konvektionszelle f	conventional unit	konventionelle Einheit f
convection cell	s. a. Bénard cell	conventional yield limit (point)	[technische] Dehngrenze f, Formdehngrenze f; technische Fließgrenze f
convection current, electric[al] convection current	[elektrischer] Konvektionsstrom m		
		convergence, converging <math., opt.>	Konvergenz f; Konvergieren n <Math., Opt.>
convection current density	Konvektionsstromdichte f, Dichte f des Konvektionsstromes	convergence	s. a. atmospheric convergence <meteo.>
		convergence almost everywhere	Konvergenz f fast überall
convection current density four vector	Konvektions-Viererstromdichte f	convergence circuit	Konvergenzschaltung f
		convergence factor	s. cut-off factor <math.>
convection diffusion	konvektive Diffusion f, Konvektionsdiffusion f	convergence in mean, strong convergence <of functions>	Konvergenz f im Mittel, limes m in medio, starke Konvergenz, Konvergenz bezüglich der starken Topologie, l. i. m. <von Funktionen>
convection heat transfer coefficient, convective transport (heat transfer) coefficient	Konvektionstransportkoeffizient m		
convection level	Konvektionshöhe f	convergence in measure	Konvergenz f dem Maß nach, asymptotische Konvergenz
convection mass transfer	s. convective transport		
convection modulus	s. Grashof['s] number	convergence in probability, probability (stochastic, weak) convergence	Konvergenz f nach Wahrscheinlichkeit, stochastische (schwache) Konvergenz
convection of heat, heat (thermal) convection, thermoconvection, heat flow[ing], thermal flow	Wärmekonvektion f, Wärmeströmung f, Thermokonvektion f, thermische Konvektion f		
		convergence limit	Konvergenzgrenze f
		convergence limit [of band progression]	Konvergenzstelle f der Bande, Bandenkonvergenz[stelle] f
convection potential, convective potential	Konvektionspotential n		
convection vector	Konvektionsvektor m	convergence line, convergent line	Konvergenzlinie f
convection voltage	Konvektionsspannung f		
convective clouds	Konvektionsbewölkung f, Konvektivbewölkung f, Konvektionswolken fpl	convergence magnet	Konvergenzmagnet m
		convergence method, Kratky['s] method [of convergence]	Konvergenzverfahren n [von Kratky], Kratkysches Konvergenzverfahren
convective condensation level	konvektives Kondensationsniveau n	convergence of lines, convergence of verticals	Stürzen n der Linien
convective derivative, Stokes operator	konvektive Ableitung f	convergence of meridians	Meridiankonvergenz f
convective equilibrium	konvektives Gleichgewicht n, Konvektionsgleichgewicht n	convergence of the beam	s. beam convergence
		convergence of verticals, convergence of lines	Stürzen n der Linien
convective exchange of heat	s. heat transfer by convection	convergence ratio	s. angular magnification
		convergence region	s. domain of convergence

convergence test	s. criterion of convergence	conversion element	Konvertierungseinheit f
convergency	s. convergence	conversion factor	s. reduction factor
convergent <e.g. nth, of a continued fraction>	Näherungsbruch m <z. B. n-ter, eines Kettenbruchs>	conversion filter	s. correction filter <opt.>
		conversion formula, inversion formula	Umkehrformel f
convergent, converging, collecting <opt.>	sammelnd, kollektiv <Opt.>	conversion fraction	s. internal conversion coefficient <nucl.>
convergent channel, converging channel	konvergenter (sich verengender) Kanal m	conversion gain	Mischverstärkung f, Transponierungsverstärkung f
convergent-divergent nozzle	s. Laval nozzle	conversion gain	s. a. breeding gain
		conversion into a soluble form, rendering soluble	Aufschließung f, Aufschluß m
convergent lens, converging lens, positive lens	Sammellinse f, Positivlinse f	conversion length	Konversionslänge f, Umwandlungslänge f
convergent light, converging [beam of] light	konvergentes Licht (Lichtstrahlenbündel) n	conversion line	s. conversion electron line
		conversion of energy	s. transformation of energy
convergent line, convergence line	Konvergenzlinie f	conversion of radiation, radiation conversion	Strahlungsumwandlung f, Strahlungswandlung f
convergent lines, converging lines	stürzende Linien fpl	conversion probability	s. internal conversion probability
convergent nozzle	konvergente Düse f	conversion ratio; breeding ratio	Konversionsgrad m, Konversionsfaktor m, Konversionsverhältnis n; Brutfaktor m, Brutverhältnis n
convergent nuclear chain reaction, subcritical nuclear chain reaction	konvergente Kernkettenreaktion f, unterkritische Kernkettenreaktion		
convergent point	s. vertex <astr.>	conversion ratio	s. a. internal conversion coefficient <nucl.>
convergent portion, converging portion <of nozzle>	konvergenter Teil m, Einlaufteil m <Düse>	conversion spectrum	s. internal conversion spectrum
		conversion transconductance	Mischsteilheit f, Konversionssteilheit f, Überlagerungssteilheit f, Umwandlungssteilheit f, Transponierungssteilheit f
convergent ring mirror	s. ring mirror		
convergent sequence	konvergente Folge f		
converging, convergent, collecting <opt.>	sammelnd, kollektiv <Opt.>		
converging	s. a. convergence	conversion transition	Konversionsübergang m, konvertierter Übergang m
converging beam of light	s. convergent light	converter, inverter, mutator <el.>	Stromrichter m, Mutator m <El.>
converging channel, convergent channel	konvergenter (sich verengender) Kanal m		
converging factor	s. cut-off factor <math.>	converter <el.>	Umformer m <El.>
converging lens	s. convergent lens		
converging light	s. convergent light	converter <el.>	Wandler m, Umwandler m, Konverter m; Mischröhre f <El.>
converging lines, convergent lines	stürzende Linien fpl		
converging meniscus, positive meniscus, concavo-convex lens	sammelnder (positiver) Meniskus m; konkav-konvexe Linse f	converter, converter (regenerative) reactor, regenerative converter, converter plant <nucl.>	Reaktorkonverter m, Konverterreaktor m, Konverter m, Konversionsreaktor m <Kern.>
converging portion	s. convergent portion	converter	s. a. inverter <el.>
converse	s. inversion <gen.>	converter	s. a. mixing stage <el.>
converse magnetostriction	s. inverse magnetostriction	converter	s. a. transducer <meas.>
converse of the Noether theorem	Umkehrung f des E. Noetherschen Satzes, umgekehrter Noetherscher Satz m	converter element <el.>	Mischelement n <El.>
		converter plant	s. converter <nucl.>
		converter reactor	s. converter <nucl.>
converse of the theorem, inverse theorem	Umkehrung f [des Satzes], Umkehrsatz m	converter stage	s. mixing stage <el.>
		converter tube, frequency changer, frequency changer valve, mixing valve, mixing tube	Doppelsteuermischröhre f, Mischoszillatorröhre f, Mischröhre f
converse piezoelectric effect	s. electrostriction		
conversion <el.>	Umformung f <El.>		
conversion; interconversion <el.>	Umwandlung f, Wandlung f, Konversion f <El.>		
conversion <math.>	Konvertierung f <Math.>		
conversion <nucl.; chem.>, converting <nucl.; chem.>	Konversion f, Umwandlung f <Kern>; Konvertierung f <Chem.>; Konversion f <Chem.>	converter unit	s. transcriber <num. math.>
		convertible lens; set of lenses	Satzobjektiv n; Objektivsatz m
conversion	s. a. converting <of fertile material>		
conversion	s. a. inversion <gen.>		
conversion	s. a. mixing <el.>		
conversion	s. a. transformation <of the equation> <math.>	convertible unsymmetrical anastigmat	halbsymmetrischer Anastigmat m
conversion coefficient <el.>	Umformungsfaktor m <El.>		
conversion coefficient	s. a. internal conversion coefficient <nucl.>	converting	s. breeding <of fertile material>
		converting	s. conversion <nucl., chem.>
conversion coefficient	s. a. reduction factor		
conversion conductance	Konversionsleitwert m	convex body, egg-shaped body	konvexer Körper m, Eikörper m
conversion efficiency	s. light output ratio of a fitting	convex corner	konvexe Ecke f
		convex hull	konvexe Hülle f
conversion electron, internal conversion electron, electron of internal conversion	Konversionselektron n, Elektron n der inneren Konversion (Umwandlung)	convexity <math.>	Konvexität f <Math.>
		convexity	s. a. bulging
		convex lens	konvexe Linse f, Konvexlinse f; Plusglas n, Konvexglas n
conversion electron line, conversion line	Konversions[elektronen]linie f, Umwandlungslinie f		
conversion electron spectroscopy	Konversionselektronenspektroskopie f	convex mirror	Wölbspiegel m, Konvexspiegel m, Zerstreuungsspiegel m
conversion electron spectrum	s. internal conversion spectrum	convexo-concave lens	s. diverging meniscus

convolution, folding, faltung <with> <of functions> <math.>	Faltung f <mit> <Funktionen> <Math.>	Cooper pairing, electron pairing	Elektronenpaarung f
		co-ordinate bond	s. dative bond
		co-ordinate condition of Einstein-Hilbert	s. Einstein-Hilbert condition
convolution	s. a. formation of clues	co-ordinate conditions of de Donder	s. Donder conditions / de
convolution	s. a. convolution integral		
convolution integral, convolution, faltung, resultant <math.>	Faltungsintegral n, Faltungsprodukt n, Faltung f <Funktionen, Distributionen>; Kompositionsprodukt n <Distributionen> <Math.>	co-ordinate formula	Komplexformel f
		co-ordinate grid, co-ordinate net, grid of co-ordinates	Koordinatennetz n, Koordinatengitter n
convolution theorem, faltung theorem	Faltungssatz m	co-ordinate line	Koordinatenlinie f
		co-ordinate measuring apparatus	s. co-ordinate measuring instrument
convolution theorem [of Laplace transform]	Faltungssatz m [der Laplace-Transformation]	co-ordinate measuring instrument, co-ordinate measuring apparatus, co-ordinatometer	Koordinatenmeßgerät n <Opt.> Koordinatenmeßapparat m <Astr.>
Conway['s] redox pump	Redoxpumpe f [nach Conway], Conwaysche Redoxpumpe		
cooked, overdeveloped	überentwickelt	co-ordinate microscope, co-ordinate reading microscope	Koordinatenmeßmikroskop n
Cooke lens, Taylor lens	Cooke-Linse f, „Cooke lens" f, Taylor-Linse f		
cooking <of the emulsion>	s. ripening	co-ordinate net	s. co-ordinate grid
coolant	s. heat-transfer agent	co-ordinate paper	Koordinatenpapier n
coolant	s. reactor coolant		
coolant circuit	s. coolant loop		
coolant loop, coolant circuit, heat-transfer circuit	Kühlkreislauf m, Kühlkreis m, Wärmeübertragungskreis[lauf] m	co-ordinate plane	Koordinatenebene f
		co-ordinate plotter	s. characteristic recorder
		co-ordinate potentiometer	s. co-ordinate type alternating-current potentiometer
coolant-moderator	s. moderator-coolant		
cooled stage	Kühltisch m		
cool flame	kalte Flamme f	co-ordinate reading microscope	s. co-ordinate microscope
Coolidge tube, Coolidge X-ray tube	Coolidge-Röhre f, Coolidge-Röntgenröhre f, Lilienfeld-Röhre f	co-ordinate representation, q-representation, Schrödinger representation, Schrödinger picture	Ortsdarstellung f, q-Darstellung f, Schrödinger-Darstellung f, Koordinatendarstellung f; Schrödinger-Bild n
cooling; refrigeration	Kühlung f; Abkühlung f		
cooling, cooling down, growing cold	Erkalten n, Abkühlung f		
cooling	s. a. dying out <of activity>	co-ordinates, co-ordinates [fixed] in space	s. space co-ordinates
cooling	s. a. lowering of temperature	co-ordinates in the plane	s. plane co-ordinates
		co-ordinates of the asymmetric ellipsoid	s. ellipsoidal co-ordinates
cooling	s. a. temperature drop		
cooling agent	s. heat-transfer agent	co-ordinates of the elliptic cylinder, elliptic[-]cylindrical co-ordinates, elliptic co-ordinates	Koordinaten fpl des elliptischen Zylinders, elliptische Zylinderkoordinaten fpl
cooling agent	s. reactor coolant		
cooling area	Kühlfläche f		
cooling by radiation	s. radiation cooling		
cooling coefficient	Kühlungskoeffizient m, Kühlziffer f, Kühlzahl f	co-ordinates of the parabolic cylinder, parabolic cylindrical co-ordinates	Koordinaten fpl des parabolischen Zylinders, parabolische Zylinderkoordinaten fpl
cooling coil, calandria	Schlangenkühler m		
		co-ordinates of the paraboloid of revolution	s. parabolic co-ordinates
cooling constant	Abkühlungskonstante f	co-ordinate space	Koordinatenraum m
cooling curve, recalescence curve	Abkühlungskurve f	co-ordinate system at rest relative to the Sun	in bezug auf die Sonne ruhendes Koordinatensystem n
cooling down	s. cooling		
cooling during ascending motion	Hebungsabkühlung f	co-ordinate transformation	s. transformation of co-ordinates
		co-ordinate trihedral	s. trihedral
cooling fluid	s. heat-transfer agent	co-ordinate type [alternating-current] potentiometer, co-ordinate type a.c. potentiometer, co-ordinate potentiometer	komplexer Kompensator m, Wechselstromkompensator m mit zusammengesetzter Vergleichsspannung, Koordinatenkompensator m, Koordinatenpotentiometer m
cooling jacket	Kühlmantel m		
cooling medium	s. heat-transfer agent		
cooling period, decay period <of radioactive substances>	Abklingzeit f, Abkühlzeit f <von Aktivitäten>		
		co-ordinate valence (valency)	s. co-ordination valence
cooling pond	s. pond for nuclear reactor	co-ordination bond	s. dative bond
cooling power [of the atmosphere], comfort index <kata factor divided by the cooling time>	Abkühlungsgröße f, Katawert m, Behaglichkeitsziffer f	co-ordination chemistry, co-ordination theory	Komplexchemie f; Koordinationslehre f, Koordinationstheorie f, Wernersche Theorie f
		co-ordination compound	s. complex compound
cooling stress	s. shrinkage stress	co-ordination entity	s. complex compound
cooling surface	s. heat-absorbent surface	co-ordination isomerism	Koordinationsisomerie f, Komplexisomerie f
cool lava, solidified lava	erstarrte Lava f		
co-operative assembly	kooperative Gesamtheit f	co-ordination number	Koordinationszahl f, Koordinationsziffer f
co-operative orientation	kooperative Orientierung f		
co-operative orientation effect	kooperativer Orientierungseffekt m	co-ordination number theory [of Linwood and Weyl]	Koordinationszahltheorie f [von Linwood und Weyl]
co-operative phenomena	kooperative Erscheinungen fpl	co-ordination polyhedron	Koordinationspolyeder n
Cooper effect	Cooper-Effekt m		
Cooper pair	Cooper-Paar n	co-ordination shell	Koordinationsschale f, Koordinationssphäre f

co-ordination 134

co-ordination theory	s. co-ordination chemistry	core of the section, core of the cross-section	Querschnittskern m
co-ordination valence (valency), co-ordinate valence (valency)	koordinative Wertigkeit f, Zähnigkeit f, Zähligkeit f <Chem.>	core of the shower, shower core	Schauerkern m
co-ordinative bond	s. dative bond	core of the vortex, vortex core (centre, nucleus)	Wirbelkern m, Wirbelzentrum n
co-ordinative valence (valency)	s. co-ordination valence	core-particle interaction	Rumpf-Teilchen-Wechselwirkung f
co-ordinatometer	s. co-ordinate measuring instrument	core polarization	Rumpfpolarisation f, Polarisation f des Atomrumpfes
co-oscillating tides	Mitschwingungsgezeiten pl		
co-oscillation	s. sympathetic oscillation	core shadow, umbra, complete shadow	Kernschatten m
Copernican system	kopernikanisches System n	core storage	s. core storage unit
cophasal state	Gleichphasigkeit f	core storage unit, core store	s. magnetic-core memory
coplanarity, complanarity	Komplanarität f, Koplanarität f	core tank	s. reactor vessel
coplanatic, complanatic	komplanatisch	core transformer, core-type transformer	Kerntransformator m
copolyaddition	Kopolyaddition f		
copper-block calorimeter	Kupfer[block]kalorimeter n	core tube, inner tube	Kernrohr n, Innenrohr n
copper-constantan thermocouple	Kupfer-Konstantan-Thermoelement n, Kupfer-Konstantan-Element n	core-type transformer	s. core transformer
		core velocity	Kerngeschwindigkeit f
copper-oxide photovoltaic cell	s. cuprous oxide photocell	coring	s. microscopic segregation
co[-]precipitation	Mitfällung f, gemeinsame Fällung f; induzierte Mitfällung f	Coriolis acceleration, acceleration of Coriolis, complementary (compatible) acceleration	Coriolis-Beschleunigung f, Rechtsablenkung f
copying on printing-out paper	s. printing-out <phot.>	Coriolis coupling, Coriolis interaction	Coriolis-Kopplung f, Coriolis-Wechselwirkung f
corallite, coral skeleton	Korallenskelett n		
co-range line of tide	Linie f gleicher Tidenhübe (Gezeitenhübe)	Coriolis effect	Coriolis-Effekt m
		Coriolis field	Coriolis-Feld n
Corbino disk	Corbino-Scheibe f		
Corbino effect	[Macaluso-]Corbino-Effekt m	Coriolis force, compound centrifugal force; geostrophic force	Coriolis-Kraft f, zusammengesetzte Zentrifugalkraft f, zweite Zusatzkraft f
Corbino magnetoresistance	magnetische Widerstandsänderung f in der Halbleiterplatte (Corbino-Scheibe)		
		Coriolis interaction	s. Coriolis coupling
		Coriolis parameter	Coriolisscher Parameter m
cord <in glass>	Schlierenband n <Glasfehler>	Coriolis perturbation	Coriolis-Störung f
		Coriolis splitting	Coriolis-Aufspaltung f
corded lava	Stricklava f; Fladenlava f; Gekröselava f	Coriolis term	Coriolis-Term m
cord galvanometer	s. string galvanometer	Coriolis['] theorem	Coriolisscher Satz m
cording diagram	s. schematic circuit diagram	corkscrew antenna, helical antenna	Wendelantenne f, Spulenantenne f, Schraubenantenne f, Helixantenne f, Spiralantenne f
core <of the line>, line centre	zentraler Kern m [der Spektrallinie], Linienkern m, Linienzentrum n, Linienmitte f		
		corkscrew field, screw field	Schraubenfeld n, schraubenförmiges Feld n
core <of the star>	Kern m [des Sterns]		
core, reactor core, active core, active lattice, reaction zone <of reactor>	Spaltzone f, aktive Zone f, Core n, Cor m (n), Reaktorcor[e] m (n), Kern m des Reaktors, Spaltraum m <Reaktor>	corkscrew rule, right-hand screw rule, thumb rule, Ampère['s] rule, Amperian float rule	Uhrzeigerregel f, Kork[en]zieherregel f, Maxwellsche Schraubenregel f, Daumenregel f, [Ampèresche] Schwimmerregel f, Ampèresche Regel f, Linke-Hand-Regel f
core <el., e.g. of coil>; limb <of magnet>	Kern m <El., z. B. Spule>		
core	s. a. atomic trunc	cornea	Hornhaut f, Cornea f
core conversion ratio	inneres Konversionsverhältnis n, Core-Konversionsverhältnis n, Konversionsverhältnis für die aktive Zone	corneal lens	Cornealschale f, Kornealschale f; Kontaktschale f, Haftschale f, Haftglas n, Kontaktglas n
		corner	s. vertex <geometry; cryst.>
core-core collision	Kern-Kern-Stoß m	corner cube, triple mirror, retrodirective mirror; central mirror	Tripelspiegel m; Zentralspiegel m
core cross-section	s. cross-section of the core		
cored carbon	Dochtkohle f		
core isomerism, nuclear core isomerism	Kernrumpfisomerie f, Rumpfisomerie f		
core magnetic field	s. internal field <geo.>	corner cube interferometer	„corner-cube"-Interferometer n, Tripelspiegel-Interferometer n
core-magnet-type instrument; core-magnet-type system	Kernmagnetinstrument n; Kernmagnetmeßwerk n, Kernmagnetsystem n		
		corner detail	Eckenschärfe f
core memory	s. magnetic-core memory	corner reflector, angled reflector, V reflector	Winkelreflektor m, Winkelspiegel m <El.>
core of the cross-section, core of the section	Querschnittskern m		
		corner vane	s. paddle <hydr.>
core of the Earth, Earth's core	Erdkern m, Zentrosphäre f	cornice	Wächte f, Gewächte f
core of the flow, middle of the flow	Kernströmung f; Strömungskern m	cornice glacier	s. suspended glacier
		Cornu; Cornu halfshade; Cornu prism	Halbschattenapparat m nach Cornu, Cornuscher Halbschattenpolarisator m; Cornusches Prisma n, [Quarz-]Cornu-Prisma n
core of the nucleon	s. nucleor		
core of the nucleus, trunc of the nucleus, nuclear core, nuclear trunc, nuclear frame	Kernrumpf m, Rumpf m des Atomkerns		
		Cornu['s] spiral, clothoid [curve], Euler['s] spiral	Cornusche Spirale f, Cornu-Spirale f, Spinnlinie f, Klothoide f

corona, corona discharge, corona ozonizer discharge, [corona] brushing, spray discharge, crown [discharge] — Koronaentladung f, Sprühentladung f, Korona[-erscheinung] f, Sprüherscheinung f, Sprühen n

corona, polar corona <of polar aurora> — Polarlichtkrone f, Korona f, Polarlichtfächer m

corona — s. a. solar corona

corona — s. a. aureole <opt., meteo.>

corona anemometer — Koronaanemometer n

corona brushing (discharge) — s. corona

corona effect — Koronaeffekt m

coronagraph, coronograph; coronavisor, extraeclipsing coronograph — Koronograph m [nach Lyot]

coronal, coronal prominence, coronal-type prominence — koronale Protuberanz f

coronal arch — Koronabogen m

coronal condensation — koronale Kondensation f

corona line — Koronalinie f

corona loss — Sprühverlust m, Koronaverlust m

coronal prominence (rain) — s. coronal

coronal ray (streamer) — Koronastrahl m

coronal-type prominence — s. coronal

corona of the Sun — s. solar corona

corona ozonizer discharge — s. corona

corona point, spray point, discharge point; active spot [of corona discharge] — Sprühspitze f, Koronaentladungsspitze f, Sprühstelle f, Sprühpunkt m

coronavisor — s. coronagraph

coronium — Koronium n

coronizing electrode — s. glow-discharge electrode

coronograph — s. coronagraph

corposant — s. Saint Elmo['s] fire

corpus — s. field <algebra>

corpuscle, material particle — Korpuskel n, Teilchen n, Materieteilchen n, Masseteilchen n

corpuscular-disperse — korpuskulardispers

corpuscular eclipse — korpuskulare Finsternis f

corpuscular nature — Korpuskelnatur f

corpuscular radiation, corpuscular rays, particle radiation — Korpuskularstrahlung f, Teilchenstrahlung f, Partikelstrahlung f, Materiestrahlung f

corpuscular stream, particle flow — Teilchenstrom m, Partikelstrom m, Korpuskelstrom m

corpuscular theory [of light], Newton['s] corpuscular theory, Newton['s] emission theory, Newton['s] theory of light — Korpuskulartheorie f [des Lichtes], Emissionstheorie f des Lichtes [von Newton], Emanationstheorie f, ballistische Lichttheorie f, Emissionshypothese f, Korpuskularhypothese f, Newtonsche Lichttheorie, Lichttheorie von Newton

corpusculum tactus — [Meißnersches] Tastkörperchen n, corpusculum n tactus

corradiation — s. beam convergence

corrasion — Korrasion f; Windschliff m, Windabschleifung f; Sandschliff m

correct — s. true-sided <of image>

corrected area [of sunspots], reduced area [of sunspots] — korrigierte Fleckenfläche f

corrected bearing — s. true bearing

correct figure <significant figure or leading zero> — gültige Ziffer f

correcting arrangement — s. corrective

correcting element — s. final control element

correcting stub — s. stub <el.>

correction; amendment — Korrektion f; Berichtigung f; Verbesserung f; Korrektur f <negativer Wert des Fehlers>

correction device — s. final control element

correction filter, conversion filter <opt.> — Konversionsfilter n, Korrektionsfilter n <Opt.>

correction for curvature — Niveaureduktion f, Höhenunterschiedsreduktion f

correction for edge effect, correction of edge effect, edge[-effect] correction — Randkorrektion f

correction for viscosity, viscosity correction — Viskositätskorrektion f, Zähigkeitskorrektion f

correction of distortion — s. compensation of distortion

correction of edge effect — s. correction for edge effect

correction of pin-cushion distortion — Kissenentzerrung f

correction of the hysteresis loop, shearing method — Scherungsmethode f

correction term, corrective term — Korrektionsglied n, Korrektionsterm m, Korrekturglied n, Korrekturterm m

correction to vacuum — Vakuumkorrektion f

corrective, correcting arrangement — Korrektiv n

corrective term — s. correction term

correctness — s. rightness <num. math.>

corrector [formula] — s. interpolation formula

corrector plate — s. Schmidt corrector plate

correlation <stat., geo.> — Korrelation f <Stat., Geo.>

correlation analysis — Korrelationsanalyse f

correlation between classes — s. interclass correlation

correlation calculus — Korrelationsrechnung f

correlation coefficient — Korrelationskoeffizient m

correlation ellipse — s. ellipse of correlation

correlation energy — Korrelationsenergie f

correlation factor — s. correlation coefficient

correlation frequency — Korrelationsfrequenz f

correlation function <ac.> — Korrelationsfunktion f, Einflußfunktion f <Ak.>

correlation function — s. a. autocorrelation function <stat.>

correlation length — Korrelationslänge f

correlation ratio — Korrelationsverhältnis n

correlation table — Korrelationstabelle f, Korrelationstafel f

correlation tensor — Korrelationstensor m, Kovarjanztensor m

correlation tensor of turbulence — s. velocity correlation tensor

correlative — Korrelate f

correlative equation — Korrelatengleichung f

correlative inhibition — korrelative Hemmung f, Korrelationshemmung f

correlative sediments — korrelate Ablagerungen fpl

correlatogram, correlogram — Korrelogramm n

correspondence principle, Bohr's correspondence principle, principle of correspondence — Korrespondenzprinzip n [von Bohr], Bohrsches Korrespondenzprinzip

corresponding points [of the retina] — korrespondierende Netzhautstellen fpl, korrespondierende Stellen fpl [der Netzhaut], konjugierte Netzhautstellen, korrespondierende Punkte mpl [der Netzhaut], konjugierte Punkte [der Netzhaut], [einander] entsprechende Netzhautstellen, Netzhautkorrespondenz f

corresponding states, correspondent states — übereinstimmende (korrespondierende) Zustände mpl

corresponding times — korrespondierende Zeiten fpl

corrie — s. cirque

corrie glacier, cirque glacier — Kargletscher m; Fußgletscher m

corroboration — s. confirmation <math.>

corrodent, corroding agent — Korrosionsmittel n

corroding 136

corroding	s. corrosion	cosine line	s. cosinusoid
corroding agent	s. corrodent	cosine source, cosine surface source, source emitting according to a cosine law	Kosinusquelle f [von Lambert], Lambertsche Kosinusquelle f
corrosion; corroding	Korrosion f; Korrosionsangriff m, Angriff m, Angreifen n; Zerfressung f		
corrosion behaviour; corrosion properties	Korrosionsverhalten n; Korrosionseigenschaften fpl, korrosive Eigenschaften fpl	cosinusoid, cosine curve, cosine line	Kosinuslinie f, Kosinuskurve f, kosinusförmige Kurve f
		cosmic abundance	kosmische Elementenhäufigkeit (Häufigkeit) f, relative Häufigkeit des Elements im Kosmos, relative Elementenhäufigkeit im Kosmos
corrosion cell, corrosion element	Korrosionselement n		
corrosion cracking	s. stress corrosion		
corrosion due to radiation [effect]	s. radiation corrosion		
corrosion effect	s. corrosive action	cosmical constant <Λ>	s. cosmologic[al] constant
corrosion element, corrosion cell	Korrosionselement n	cosmic chemistry	s. space chemistry
		cosmic dust	s. interstellar dust
corrosion endurance	s. corrosion fatigue	cosmic expansion, expansion of the universe	Expansion (Ausdehnung) f des Weltalls
corrosion endurance limit	s. corrosion fatigue limit	cosmic exploration	s. space research
corrosion fatigue, corrosion endurance	Korrosionsermüdung f	cosmic exposure age, exposure age	Bestrahlungsalter n <z. B. des Meteoriten>
		cosmic noise, extraterrestrial noise	kosmisches (extraterrestrisches) Rauschen n, Weltraumrauschen n
corrosion fatigue limit, corrosion endurance limit	Korrosionsermüdungsfestigkeit f, Korrosionsschwingungsfestigkeit f		
		cosmic radiation, cosmic rays	kosmische Strahlung (Höhenstrahlung) f, Höhenstrahlung, Höhenstrahlen mpl, [kosmische] Ultrastrahlung f, Heßsche Strahlung
corrosion-proof steel	s. stainless steel		
corrosion properties	s. corrosion behaviour		
corrosion rate	Korrosionsgeschwindigkeit f		
corrosion resistance, resistance to corrosion	Korrosionsbeständigkeit f; Korrosionsfestigkeit f; Korrosionswiderstand m; Rostbeständigkeit f	cosmic-ray background	kosmische Untergrundstrahlung (Hintergrundstrahlung) f, 3-K-Strahlung f
		cosmic-ray burst, cosmic-ray jet, sudden increase of cosmic-ray intensity	Höhenstrahlungseruption f, Höhenstrahlungsausbruch m, Ausbruch m der kosmischen Strahlung, Ultrastrahlungseruption f, Ultrastrahlungsausbruch m
corrosion-resistant steel	s. stainless steel		
corrosive action, corrosivity, corrosion effect	Korrosivität f, Korrosionswirkung f, korrosive Wirkung f, Korrosionseinfluß m, Aggressivität f		
		cosmic-ray jet, jet [in the emulsion]	Jet m [der kosmischen Strahlung] <in der Emulsion>
corrosive wear	korrosiver Verschleiß m	cosmic-ray particle	Teilchen n der kosmischen Strahlung, Höhenstrahlteilchen n, Ultrastrahl[ungs]teilchen n
corrosivity	s. corrosive action		
corrugated field	Runzelfeld n, Wellfeld n		
corrugated guide	s. corrugated waveguide	cosmic rays	s. cosmic radiation
corrugated mirror	Riffelspiegel m	cosmic-ray shower, shower, shower of cosmic radiation, shower of particles	Schauer m [der kosmischen Strahlung], kosmischer Schauer, Teilchenschauer m, Ultrastrahlungsschauer
corrugated structure (surface)	s. plane corrugated surface		
corrugated torus, diaphragmatic torus, disk torus, disk-loaded torus, iris torus, iris-loaded torus	Runzeltorus m		
		cosmic-ray star	durch kosmische Strahlung erzeugter Zertrümmerungsstern m, Zertrümmerungsstern [der kosmischen Strahlung], Höhenstrahlungsstern m, Ultrastrahlungsstern m
corrugated tube	Wellrohr n		
corrugated tube cooler	s. sylphon cooler	cosmic-ray telescope	Höhenstrahl[ungs]teleskop n
corrugated waveguide, corrugated guide, diaphragmatic waveguide, disk[-loaded] waveguide, iris[-loaded] waveguide	Runzelröhre f, Runzelleiter m, Hohlleiter m mit Blendenscheiben (Kreisblenden), gefalteter (gefältelter) Hohlleiter	cosmic refraction	kosmische (jährliche) Refraktion f, Courvoisier-Effekt m
		cosmic research	s. space research
		cosmic rocket, space probe, space rocket	kosmische Rakete f, Weltraumrakete f, Raumsonde f, Raumprobe f, künstlicher Planetoid m
corrugation; ripple; riffle	Riffelung f, Rippelung f; Wellung f; Faltung f; Riffelung f		
Corti['s] organ	Cortisches Organ n, Organon n spirale	cosmic-scale turbulence	Turbulenz f im kosmischen Maßstab
cosecant, cosec	Kosekans m, Kosekansfunktion f, cosec	cosmic setting	kosmischer Untergang m
coset <of group> <math.>	Nebenklasse f, Nebengruppe f, Nebenschar f, Restklasse f <der Gruppe> <Math.>	cosmic velocity	kosmische Geschwindigkeit[sstufe] f
		cosmochemistry	s. space chemistry
		cosmogonid	Kosmogonide f
coset	s. a. residue class <math.>	cosmological constant, cosmic[al] constant <Λ>	kosmologische Konstante f
cosine amplitude, cos am, cn	Cosinus m amplitudinis, cos am, cn	cosmological paradox	kosmologisches Paradoxon n
cosine capacitor	s. static phase advancer	cosmological red-shift	s. red shift
cosine curve	s. cosinusoid	cosmological term	kosmologischer Term m, kosmologisches Glied n
cosine emission law	s. cosine law [of diffusing surface]		
		cosolvency	Kosolvenz f
cosine formula	s. theorem of Carnot		
cosine integral, Ci	Integralkosinus m, Cosinus m integralis, Ci	cosolvent	Kosolvens n
		Costa de Ribeiro effect	s. thermodielectric effect
cosine law	s. theorem of Carnot <math.>	Coster-Kronig transition	Coster-Kronig-Übergang m
		cote, index number of altitude <of a point>	Kote f; Kotenzahl f
cosine law [of diffusing surface], Lambert['s] law [of diffusion], Lambert['s] law of emission, Lambert['s] cosine law, cosine emission law	Kosinusgesetz n [von Lambert], Lambertsches Kosinusgesetz f (cos-Gesetz, Ge-setz) n, cos-Gesetz, Lamberts Kosinusgesetz	coted projection, topographic projection	kotierte Projektion f, topographisches Verfahren n
		Cotes' quadrature formulae, Cotes' rule	[Newton-]Cotessche Formeln fpl, Formeln von Newton-Cotes

co[-]tidal line, line of simultaneous high tide	Flutstundenlinie *f*	Coulombian field, Coulomb field	Coulomb-Feld *n*, Coulombsches Kraftfeld *n*
Cotton balance	Cottonsche Waage *f*, Cotton-Waage *f*, Feldwaage *f* nach Cotton	Coulombian repulsion, Coulomb repulsion	Coulomb-Abstoßung *f*, Coulombsche Abstoßung *f*
Cotton effect	*s.* circular dichroism	coulombic integral, Coulomb integral	Coulomb-Integral *n*
Cotton-Mouton constant, magnetic birefringence constant	Cotton-Mouton-Konstante *f*	coulombic potential	*s.* Coulomb potential
		Coulomb integral	*s.* coulombic integral
Cotton-Mouton effect	Cotton-Mouton-Effekt *m*, magnetische Doppelbrechung *f*	Coulomb interaction	Coulombsche Wechselwirkung *f*, Coulomb-Wechselwirkung *f*
Cottrell atmosphere [of impurities], atmosphere ‹of dislocations›, Cottrell cloud	Cottrell-Wolke *f*, Cottrellsche Versetzungswolke *f*	Coulomb['s] law, Coulomb law of force, law of electrostatic attraction	Coulombsches Gesetz *n* [der Elektrostatik], Gesetz der elektrostatischen Anziehung, elektrisches Coulombsches Gesetz
Cottrell barrier	*s.* Cottrell['s] dislocation	Coulomb['s] law of friction	Coulombsches Reibungsgesetz *n*
Cottrell cloud	*s.* Cottrell atmosphere		
Cottrell['s] dislocation, Lomer-Cottrell dislocation, Lomer-Cottrell sessile dislocation, Lomer-Cottrell lock, Lomer-Cottrell barrier, Cottrell barrier	[Lomer-]Cottrell-Versetzung *f*, Cottrellsche Versetzung *f*, Lomer-Cottrellsche [unbewegliche] Versetzung, Lomer-Cottrellsches Versetzungshindernis *n*, Lomer-Cottrell-Versetzungshindernis *n*	Coulomb['s] law of magnetism	magnetisches Coulombsches Gesetz *n*, Coulombsches Gesetz des Magnetismus
		Coulomb logarithm	Coulombscher Logarithmus *m*, Coulomb-Logarithmus *m*
		coulombmeter, voltammeter, coulometer	Coulometer *n*, Voltameter *n*, Coulombmeter *n*
Cottrell effect	Cottrell-Effekt *m*	Coulomb multiple scattering	Coulombsche Vielfachstreuung *f*, Coulomb-Vielfachstreuung *f*, Vielfach-Coulomb-Streuung *f*
Cottrell force	Cottrell-Kraft *f*		
Cottrell hardening	Verfestigung *f* durch Cottrell-Effekt		
Cottrell locking	Cottrell-Blockierung *f*	Coulomb operator	Coulomb-Operator *m*
coudé column, coudé-type column	Kniesäule *f*, geknickte Säule *f*	Coulomb phase shift	Coulomb-Phasenverschiebung *f*
coudé focus, Coudé focus	Coudéfokus *m*, Coudé-Fokus *m*	Coulomb potential, coulombic potential	Coulomb-Potential *n*, Coulombsches Potential *n*
coudé mounting, coudé-type mounting	Knie[säulen]montierung *f*, Coudémontierung *f*, Montierung *f* mit Kniesäule [nach Repsold]	Coulomb radius	Coulomb-Radius *m*
		Coulomb repulsion	*s.* Coulombian repulsion
		Coulomb scattering	Coulomb-Streuung *f*, Coulombsche Streuung *f*
coudé telescope, coudé-type telescope	Coudéspiegel *m*, Spiegelteleskop *n* mit Cassegrain-Coudé-Strahlengang, knieförmig gebogenes Spiegelteleskop; geknicktes (knieförmig gebogenes) Fernrohr *n*, Coudéfernrohr *n*	Coulomb scattering angle	Coulomb-Streuwinkel *m*, Winkel *m* der Coulombschen Streuung
		Coulomb scattering by the residual gas	*s.* gas scattering
		Coulomb scattering cross-section, cross-section for Coulomb scattering	Wirkungsquerschnitt *m* für (der) Coulomb-Streuung, Coulomb-Streuquerschnitt *m*
coudé-type column, coudé column	Kniesäule *f*, geknickte Säule *f*		
coudé-type mounting	*s.* coudé mounting	Coulomb scattering matrix	*s.* matrix of Coulomb scattering
coudé-type telescope	*s.* coudé telescope		
Couette flow	Couette-Strömung *f*	Coulomb wave function	*s.* Whittaker['s] function
coulomb, C, ampere-second, As	Coulomb *n*, C, Coul, Cb, Amperesekunde *f*, As	coulometer, voltameter, coulombmeter	Coulometer *n*, Voltameter *n*, Coulombmeter *n*
Coulomb attraction, Coulombian attraction	Coulomb-Anziehung *f*, Coulombsche Anziehung *f*	coulometric titration	coulometrische Titration *f*
		coulometry	Coulometrie *f*, coulometrische Analyse *f*, Coulombmetrie *f*
Coulomb barrier	Coulombscher Potentialwall *m*, Coulomb-Wall *m*, Coulomb-Schwelle *f*, Coulombsche Potentialschwelle *f*, Coulomb-Barriere *f*		
		count, pulse, counter pulse, counting [im]pulse, c ‹nucl.›	Impuls *m*, Zählstoß *m*, Zähl[er]impuls *m*, Imp. ‹Kern.›
		count	Impulszahl *f*, gezählte Impulse *mpl*
Coulomb bond energy	Coulombsche Bindungsenergie *f*, Coulomb-Bindungsenergie *f*	countable	*s.* denumerable
		countable additivity, σ-additivity	Sigmaadditivität *f*, σ-Additivität *f*
Coulomb damping	Coulomb-Dämpfung *f*		
Coulomb degeneracy	Coulomb-Entartung *f*, Coulombsche Entartung *f*	countably additive, totally additive, absolutely additive	abzählbar[-]additiv, absolut additiv, total-additiv, voll-additiv
Coulomb energy	Coulomb-Energie *f*, Coulombsche Energie *f*	countably additive algebra, sigma-algebra, σ-algebra	Sigmaalgebra *f*, σ-Algebra *f*, Sigmaring *m*, σ-Ring *m*
Coulomb exchange energy	Coulomb-Austauschenergie *f*		
		count-down	„count-down" *m*
Coulomb excitation	Coulomb-Anregung *f*	count-down	*s. a.* pulse-rate division
Coulomb field, Coulombian field	Coulomb-Feld *n*, Coulombsches Kraftfeld *n*	counter, radiation counter, counter (counting) tube ‹nucl.›	Zählrohr *n*, Zähler *m*, Strahlungszählrohr *n* ‹Kern.›
Coulomb force	Coulomb-Kraft *f*, Coulombsche Kraft *f*	counter	*s. a.* pulse counter ‹nucl.›
		counter	*s. a.* register
Coulomb friction	Coulombsche Reibung *f*	counteraction, countereffect, reaction ‹mech.›	Gegenwirkung *f*, Reaktion *f*, „reactio" *f* ‹Mech.›
Coulomb gauge	Coulomb-Eichung *f*, Coulomb-Konvention *f*	counterbalance, counter[-] balance	*s.* counterweight
Coulombian attraction, Coulomb attraction	Coulomb-Anziehung *f*, Coulombsche Anziehung *f*	counter-balance	*s.* equilibrium / be in
		counter body, counter cathode ‹nucl.›	Zählrohrkatode *f*, Zählrohrgehäuse *n*, Zählergehäuse *n* ‹Kern.›

counterclockwise circularly polarized	s. left-handed circular	counter[-]stimulus	Gegenreiz m
counterclockwise direction, anti-clockwise direction	Gegenuhrzeigersinn m	countersun	s. anthelion
		counter telescope, telescope <nucl.>	Zählrohrteleskop n, Zählrohrkombination f, Zählerkombination f, Teleskop n <Kern.>
counterclockwise elliptically polarized	s. left-handed elliptic	counter time lag	s. counting time lag
counterclockwise polarized	s. left-handed polarized	counter-torque, opposite torque (moment of couple)	Gegendrehmoment n
counterlockwise rotation	s. laevorotation	countertrades	s. antitrades
counter component	s. opposite component	counter[-]tube	s. counting tube
counter-controlled	zählrohrgesteuert	counter tube	s. counter <nucl.>
countercoupling	s. reverse feedback	counter twilight	s. antitwilight
counter[-]current, rotary stream	Neerstrom m	counter-voltage	s. inverse voltage <el.>
		counter wall, wall of the counter [tube]	Zählrohrwand[ung] f
counter[-]current	s. a. reverse current <el.>	counterweight, counter[-] weight, counterbalance, counter[-] balance. counterpoise, bob-weight	Gegengewicht n; Ausgleichsgewicht n; Äquilibriergewicht n <El.>
countercurrent column	Gegenstromkolonne f		
countercurrent cooler	Gegenströmer m, Gegenstromapparat m; Gegenstromkühler m		
		counting	Zählung f
		counting assembly	s. pulse counter <nucl.>
countercurrent distillation	s. rectification <chem.>	counting chamber	Zählkammer f
countercurrent electrolysis	Gegenstromelektrolyse f	counting channel, pulse counting channel, channel	Zählkanal m, Impulszählkanal m, Kanal m
counter[-]current flow	s. counterflow	counting circuit	s. pulse counting circuit
counterdiffusion	Gegendiffusion f	counting decade, electronic counting decade	Zähldekade f, elektronische Zähldekade
countereffect, counteraction, reaction <mech.>	Gegenwirkung f, Reaktion f, „reactio" f <Mech.>		
counter efficiency, counting efficiency, efficiency of counter (counting), counter response, response [of the counter]	Zähl[rohr]ausbeute f, Ansprechwahrscheinlichkeit f, Effektivität f, Quantenausbeute f <des Zählrohrs>, Zählerausbeute f	counting diamond	Zähldiamant m
		counting efficiency	s. counter efficiency
		counting eyepiece	Zählokular n
		counting frequency meter, counter frequency meter	zählender Frequenzmesser m, Zählerfrequenzmesser m
counter electromotive force, counter-emf, back electromotive force, back-emf, back e.m.f.	gegenelektromotorische Kraft f, Gegen-EMK f	counting geometry, counter geometry	Zähl[rohr]geometrie f, Geometrie f des Zählrohrs
counter[-]example	Gegenbeispiel n	counting impulse	s. count
		counting ionization chamber	s. pulse ionization chamber
counter field, opposing field	Gegenfeld n	counting loss	Zählverlust m <Kern.>; Zählfehler m
counterflow, countercurrent flow, countercurrent, contraflow	Gegenströmung f	counting mechanism	s. register
		counting period, count period, counting time	Zählzeit f, Zähldauer f, Zählperiode f
counterforce	Gegenkraft f		
counter frequency meter	s. counting frequency meter	counting pulse	s. count
counter gas	Zählgas n. Zählrohrfüllgas n	counting rate; pulse rate, impulsing rate	Zählrate f, Zählgeschwindigkeit f; Impulsdichte f, Impulsrate f
counter geometry	s. counting geometry		
counterglow	Widerschein m <Dämmerungserscheinung>	counting-rate characteristic	s. counting rate-voltage characteristic
counterglow, gegenschein	Gegenschein m <Zodiakallicht>	counting-rate meter, rate[ ]meter, integrating instrument, integrator	Impulsdichtemesser m, Mittelwertmesser m, Integrator m, Ratemeter n
counterion, gegenion, opposer ion	Gegenion n		
countermovement, induced movement <opt.>	Gegenbewegung f; induzierte Bewegung f <Opt.>		
		counting rate-voltage characteristic, counting response, counting-rate characteristic	Zähl[rohr]charakteristik f, Impuls-Spannungs-Charakteristik f [des Zählrohres], Zählercharakteristik f
counter of nuclei, nuclei counter	Kernzähler m, Kondensationskernzähler m		
counter operating voltage	Zählrohrbetriebsspannung f		
counter overvoltage	s. overvoltage of the Geiger-Müller counter	counting statistics	Zählstatistik f
counterpoise	s. counterweight	counting technique, pulse counting technique	Zähltechnik f, Impulszähltechnik f
counter[-]potential	s. inverse voltage <el.>	counting technique [of microscopic particles]	Zählmethode f [mikroskopischer Teilchen]
counterpressure	s. backpressure		
counterpressure diagram, vacuum diagram	Unterdruckfigur f		
counterpressure trapezoid, vacuum trapezoid	Unterdrucktrapez n	counting time	s. counting period
		counting time lag, counter time lag, statistical counting (counter) time lag	Zählverzögerung f, statistische Zählverzögerung
counter probe	Zählrohrsonde f		
		counting tube, counter tube, countertube; electron[ic] counter; scaler tube	Zählröhre f; elektronischer Zähler m; Elektronenzähler m, Untersetzerröhre f
counter pulse	s. count		
counter quench[ing] circuit	Zählrohrlöschkreis m, Zählrohrlöschschaltung f		
counterradiation	s. sky back radiation	counting tube	s. a. counter
counter range [of the reactor]	Zählrohrbereich m, Anlaufbereich m, Anlaufgebiet n <Reaktor>	counting unit	s. pulse counter <nucl.>
		count period, counting period (time)	Zählzeit f, Zähldauer f, Zählperiode f
counter reaction	s. gegenreaction	country rock	Nebengestein n
counter resolving time	Zählrohrauflösungszeit f		
counter response	s. counter efficiency		
counter-slope	Gegengefälle n; Gegenböschung f	couple <of forces> force couple	Kräftepaar n, Drehkraft f

coupled-circuit filter	Koppelfilter *n*, Filterankopplung *f*	covalent bond	s. atomic bond
coupled oscillations	gekoppelte Schwingungen *fpl*	covalent compound	s. atomic compound
coupled pendulums	gekoppelte Pendel *npl*	covalent-ionic resonance	Resonanz *f* kovalenter Ionen
coupled reactions	gekoppelte (konjugierte, induzierte, sympathetische) Reaktionen *fpl*	covalent link[age]	s. atomic bond
		covalent molecule	s. atomic molecule
couple of instantaneous rotations	momentane Rotationspaar *n*	covalent radius [of atom], atomic radius	kovalenter Radius *m*, [kovalenter] Atomradius *m*
couple of rotations	Drehpaar *n*	covariance	Kovarianz *f*
couple of vectors, vector couple	Vektorpaar *n*; Stäbepaar *n* <Study>	covariance analysis, analysis of covariance	Kovarianzanalyse *f*, Mitstreuungszerlegung *f*
coupler	s. coupling element <el.>	covariance matrix, dispersion matrix <stat.>	Kovarianzmatrix *f*, Varianz-Kovarianz-Matrix *f*, Dispersionsmatrix *f*, Streuungsmatrix *f* <Stat.>
coupling <to; between> <gen., el.>; interconnection <el.>	Kopplung <mit; zwischen>; Verkopplung *f*; Ankopplung *f* <an>	covariance principle, principle of general covariance	Kovarianzprinzip *n*, Prinzip *n* der allgemeinen Kovarianz
coupling admittance	Koppelleitwert *m*, Kopplungsleitwert *m*	covariant	Kovariante *f*
coupling aperture	s. coupling window	covariant component; covariant co-ordinate	kovariante Komponente *f*; kovariante Koordinate *f*
coupling between phases, interphase coupling	Zwischenphasenkopplung *f*	covariant curvature tensor	s. Riemann-Christoffel tensor
coupling by hole, hole coupling	Lochkopplung *f*	covariant derivative	kovariante Ableitung *f*
coupling capacitance	Kopplungskapazität *f*	covariant differentiation	kovariante Differentiation *f*, Erweiterung *f* <Tensor>
coupling capacitor	Koppelkondensator *m*, Kopplungskondensator *m*, Kopplungskapazität *f*	covariant quantum field theory	kovariante Quantenfeldtheorie *f*
coupling cases [in molecular spectra], Hund['s] cases, Hund['s] coupling cases <a to e>	Hundsche Fälle (Kopplungsfälle) *mpl*, Kopplungsfälle (Kopplungsverhältnisse *npl*) nach Hund <a bis e>	cover, fog, coat	Beschlag *m*
		cover <geo.>	Decke *f* <Geo.>
		cover, covering <math.>	Überdeckung *f* <Math.>
		coverage	s. scanning
coupling coefficient, coefficient of coupling, coupling factor (value) <el.>	Kopplungsfaktor *m*, Kopplungsgrad *m*; Kopplungskoeffizient *m* <El.>	coverage	s. coating
		coverage	s. field of sight <of instrument>
		coverage diagram	s. radar coverage diagram
coupling constant	Kopplungskonstante *f*	covered with damp / getting, becoming coated, fogging	Anlaufen *n*; Beschlagen *n*
coupling effect <e.g. of electrons>, effect of coupling	Kopplungseffekt *m* <z. B. der Elektronen>		
		cover film	s. protective film
coupling element, coupler <el.>	Kopplungsglied *n*, Koppelglied *n*, Kopplungselement *n*, Koppelelement *n* <El.>	cover glass	Deckglas *n*
		covering, wrapping	Umhüllung *f*, Umwicklung *f*
coupling energy	Kopplungsenergie *f*		
coupling factor <of elastic oscillations>	Kopplungsfaktor *m* <elastische Schwingungen>	covering, cover <math.>	Überdeckung *f* <Math.>
		covering	s. a. coating <gen.>
coupling factor	s. a. coupling coefficient <el.>	covering capacity <of colour>	Deckkraft *f*
coupling impedance	Kopplungsimpedanz *f*, Koppelimpedanz *f*	covering group	Überlagerungsgruppe *f*
coupling index <acc.>	Kopplungsindex *m* <Beschl.>	covering manifold	Überlagerungsmannigfaltigkeit *f*
coupling inductance	Kopplungsinduktivität *f*		
coupling matrix	Kopplungsmatrix *f*	cover rock, cap rock	Deckgebirge *n*, Deckgestein *n*, Dach *n*
coupling medium	s. optical coupling		
coupling meter	Kopplungsmesser *m*		
coupling parameter <elast.>	Kopplungsparameter *n*, mikroskopische elastische Konstante *f*, Kraftkonstante *f* <Elast.>	coversine, covers *x*	= 1¹ − sin *x*
		covibration	s. sympathetic oscillation
		covibration	s. resonant vibration
		covolume, excluded volume	Kovolumen *n*, verbotenes Volumen *n*, Eigenvolumen *n* [der Moleküle]
coupling problem, Riemann-Hilbert problem	Kopplungsproblem *n*, Riemann-Hilbert-Problem *n*		
coupling ratio	Kopplungsverhältnis *n*	covolume of ion	s. ion covolume
coupling resistance; coupling resistor	Kopplungswiderstand *m*, Koppelwiderstand *m*	cow	s. isotopic generator
		Cowling['s] theorem	Satz *m* von Cowling, Cowlingscher Satz, Cowlingsches Theorem *n*
coupling resonance	Kopplungsresonanz *f*		
coupling scheme	Kopplungsschema *n*		
coupling slit	s. coupling window	c particle	s. Xi-hyperon
coupling stiffness	Kopplungssteifigkeit *f*	CP invariance	CP-Invarianz *f*
coupling term <math.>	Kopplungsglied *n*, Kopplungsterm *m* <Math.>		
coupling value	s. coupling coefficient <el.>	C.P.S. emitron, orthicon, orthicon tube, emitron	Orthikon *n*, Emitron *n*
coupling window, coupling aperture, coupling slit	Kopplungsfenster *n*, Koppelfenster *n*, Kopplungsschlitz *m*, Koppelschlitz *m*	CPT theorem, Lüders-Pauli theorem, TCP theorem	CPT-Theorem *n*, PTC-Theorem *n*, Lüders-Pauli-Theorem *n*, TCP-Theorem *n*
course <e.g. of clouds>	Zug *m*, Ziehen *n* <z. B. der Wolken>	CPT transformation	CPT-Transformation *f*
course	s. a. shape <of the curve>	CP violation	Verletzung *f* der CP-Invarianz
course-and-bearing indicator	s. direction finder		
course deviation	Kursabweichung *f*, Kursablage *f*	crack arrest temperature, CAT	Rißfangtemperatur *f*
course of adaptation, curve of adaptation	Adaptationskurve *f*	crack depth	Rißtiefe *f*
course of adaptation	s. a. adaptation process	crack detector; flaw detector, defectoscope, inspectoscope	Rißdetektor *m*, [magnetischer] Rissprüfer *m*, Rißprüfer *m*; Defektoskop *n*
course of the river	Flußlauf *m*; Stromlauf *m*		
covalence, covalency	Bindigkeit *f*, Bindungswertigkeit *f*		
covalence function	Kovalenzfunktion *f*	crack due to multiple hardening	s. repeated hardening crack
covalency	s. covalence		

cracked-carbon resistor	s. carbon resistor	creeping motion, trailing motion <of plant>; crawling motion <of animal> <bio.>	Kriechbewegung f <Bio.>
crack formation (generation)	s. cracking		
crack indicator	Rißsichtgerät n	creeping rubbish	Gekriech n, Kriechschutt m
crackiness	s. brittleness	creeping wave	Kriechwelle f
cracking, crack formation, crack generation; crazing <of polymer>	Rißbildung f; Aufreißen n, Rissigwerden n; Springen n	creep law, creep rate law (equation)	Kriechgesetz n
		creep limit, creep strength	Kriechgrenze f, Dauerdehngrenze f; Zeit[stand]kriechgrenze f
cracking resistance, crack resistance (strength)	Rißfestigkeit f, Rißbeständigkeit f	creep rate equation (law)	s. creep law
cracking spark, sparker	Knallfunke[n] m	creep rate limit	Kriechgeschwindigkeitsgrenze f
crackling noise	s. contact noise	creep recovery	s. elastic after-effect
"cracknel"	verknoteter Volltorus m, „Brezel" f	creep resistance	s. limiting creep stress
crack nucleus	Rißkeim m; Rißkeimzentrum n	creep-rupture test [at elevated temperature]	Zeitstandversuch m [bei erhöhter Temperatur]
crack resistance (strength)	s. cracking resistance	creep strain, creep elongation, elongation due to creep	Kriechdehnung f
crack toughness	s. fracture toughness	creep strength	s. creep limit
cracovian	Krakoviane f	creep viscosity	Kriechzähigkeit f
cradle-type mount	s. English mounting	c region	s. compensated region
crag surf	Klippenbrandung f	C region	s. transition region of mantle <geo.>
Cramer-Rao inequality, information inequality	Ungleichung f von Fréchet	Cremona [force] diagram, Cremona['s] polygon of forces	s. force diagram
Cramer['s] rule	Cramersche Regel f		
cranked lever	s. bent lever	crepe ring	s. crape ring
cranking model, Inglis['] model	Modell n von Inglis, Inglissches Modell, „cranking"-Modell n, Kurbelmodell n [von Inglis]	crepuscular rays	Dunststrahlung f, Dämmerungsstrahlen mpl
		crescent[-shaped]; cusped; falcated <astr.>	sichelförmig, halbmondförmig
crank lever	s. bent lever	crescent aerofoil (airfoil)	s. variable sweep wing
crape ring, ring C, crepe (gauze, dusky) ring	Kreppring m, Florring m, C-Ring m		
crater, pot-hole <geo.>; scour	Kolk m, Strudelloch n, Strudeltopf m, Strudelkessel m	crescent wing	s. variable sweep wing
		crest <of the wave>, wave crest, ripple crest, top of the wave, peak of the wave	Kamm m [der Welle], Wellenkamm m, Wellenberg m, Wellenscheitel m, Scheitel m [der Welle], Wellenkuppe[l] f, Wellenbogen m
cratering <geo.>	Auskolkung f, Kolkbildung f		
craterlet, small crater, crater pit	Kratergrube f		
crater of the Moon	s. lunar crater	crest <geo.>	Scheitel m <Geo.>
crater pit	s. craterlet	crest, mountain crest <geo.>	Kamm m, Gebirgskamm m; Grat m <Geo.>
craton <geo.>	Kraton n, Kratogen n; [alte] Masse f <Geo.>		
		crest	s. a. peak <gen.>
crawling [motion]	s. creeping motion <bio.>	crest	s. a. peak value <of variable quantity> <el.>
crawling speed	Schleichdrehzahl f, Schleichdrehgeschwindigkeit f, Schleichumdrehungsgeschwindigkeit f	crest / without	s. unmanned
		crest factor, peak factor, amplitude factor	Spitzenfaktor m, Scheitelfaktor m
c ray, seismic ray reflected upwards at the outer core boundary	c-Welle f, am Kern reflektierte Erdbebenwelle f		
		crest height <of wave>	Kammhöhe f <Welle>
craze	s. hair-line crack	crest length <of wave>	Kammlänge f <Welle>
crazing	s. cracking		
creation, production, formation, generation, birth	Bildung f, Erzeugung f, Generation f	crest of the dam (weir), dam (weir) crest	Wehrkrone f; Dammkrone f, Sperrmauerkrone f, Bekrönung f
		crest of the weir	Überfallkante f, Überströmkante f, Überfallscheide f; Wehrschwelle f, Wehrdrempel m
creation cross-section	s. production cross-section		
creation of poles	s. production of poles		
creation operator, emission (production) operator	Erzeugungsoperator m		
creation rate, pair creation rate	Paarbildungsrate f	crest-type mountains	s. mountain crests
		crest value	s. peak <gen.>
creation rate	s. a. production rate <nucl.>	crest value	s. peak value <of variable quantity> <el.>
creep; creepage, creeping	Kriechen n		
creep, meter creeping	Zählerleerlauf m	crevasse, glacier crevasse	Gletscherspalte f
creep	s. a. creep deformation		
creep	s. a. creep function		
creepage	s. creep	crevice corrosion	Spaltenkorrosion f, Rißkorrosion f
creepage spark	s. surface discharge spark		
creep buckling	plastisches Kriechen n	crew / with, manned, man-carrying	bemannt
creep compliance	Kriechnachgiebigkeit f		
creep compression, compression due to creep	Kriechstauchung f	crimp[ing]	s. squeeze
		crippling	s. local buckling
creep curve	Kriechkurve f	crippling force	s. critical force
creep deformation, creep	Kriechverformung f, Abgleitung f	crippling load, axial compression	Knickbeanspruchung f, Beanspruchung f auf Knickung
creep elongation	s. creep strain		
creep fluidity	Kriechfluidität f	crippling load	s. a. critical load of Euler
creep function, creep	Kriechfunktion f	crippling resilience (stress)	s. critical compressive stress
creeping	s. creep		
creeping current	s. surface leakage current	crippling test	s. buckling test
creeping flow	s. creeping motion	"crisis" of drag, striking drag reduction at the critical Reynolds number	Widerstandskrisis f, Krisis f der Strömung
creeping motion, very slow (small) motion, creeping (very slow), flow	schleichende Strömung (Bewegung, Flüssigkeitsbewegung, Bewegungsart) f		

crispening, stylizing, stylization	Umrißversteilerung f	critical free stream Mach number	kritische Mach-Zahl f in freier Strömung
crit, critical mass (amount), chain-reacting mass (amount) <nucl.>	kritische Masse f, kritische Menge f <Kern.>	critical frequency <ac.>	kritische Frequenz f <Ak.>
		critical frequency <of skin effect, of radio wave propagation, semi.>	kritische Frequenz f, Grenzfrequenz f <Skineffekt, Radiowellenausbreitung>; Entdämpfungsfrequenz f, Grenzfrequenz f <Halb.>
criterion for luminosity	Leuchtkraftkriterium n		
criterion for yield	s. yield condition		
criterion of convergence, test for (of) convergence, convergence test	Konvergenzkriterium n		
		critical frequency	s. a. limiting frequency
		critical frequency	s. a. cut-off frequency <of waveguide, of filter>
criterion of instability, instability criterion	Labilitätskriterium n	critical frequency of flicker, [critical] flicker frequency, [flicker] fusion frequency; minimum frame speed [for merging of pictures] <opt.>	kritische Frequenz f [des Flimmerns], Verschmelzungsfrequenz f, Verschmelzungsschwelle f, Flimmerfrequenz f, Frequenzgrenze f des Flimmerns <Opt.>
criterion of yielding	s. yield condition		
critical amount	s. crit <nucl.>		
critical angle <of total reflection>, critical angle of incidence	Grenzwinkel m [der Totalreflexion]		
critical angle of attack	s. angle of stall		
critical angle of incidence	s. critical angle	critical glide	Grenzgleitung f
critical angle refractometer	Totalreflektometer n, Total[reflexions]refraktometer n, Brechzahlmesser m mit Hilfe des Grenzwinkels der Totalreflexion	critical grid current	Gitterzündstrom m
		critical grid voltage	Gitterzündspannung f
		critical height of roughness	s. critical roughness
		critical isotherm	kritische Isotherme f
critical assembly	kritische Anordnung f	criticality	Kritizität f, Kritikalität f
critical chain reaction	s. selfsustained nuclear chain reaction	critical length, cut-off length	Grenzlänge f
critical charge radius	kritischer Radius m der Ladung	critical line, line of critical states	kritische Linie f, Linie der kritischen Zustände
critical coefficient	kritischer Koeffizient m	critical load	kritische Belastung f, Grenzlast f, Grenzbelastung f
critical compressive stress, critical stress [in buckling], crippling stress (resilience)	Knickspannung f, kritische Druckspannung f	critical load of Euler, Euler['s] load, Euler['s] critical (crippling) load, crippling load, buckling load, Euler force	Knicklast f, kritische Last f, Eulersche Knicklast
critical condition	kritische Bedingung f, Kritizitätsbedingung f		
critical constant	s. critical datum <therm.>	critical Mach number	kritische Mach-Zahl f
critical cooling rate, critical rate of cooling	kritische Abkühlungsgeschwindigkeit f	critical magnetic neutron scattering, critical magnetic scattering [of neutrons]	kritische magnetische Neutronenstreuung f, kritische magnetische Streuung f [der Neutronen]
critical coupling, optimum coupling	kritische Kopplung f		
critical curve	s. solubility curve	critical mass <of rocket>	kritische Masse f <Rakete>
critical damping	kritische Dämpfung f; Grenzdämpfung f	critical mass, limiting mass, mass-limit <of white dwarfs>	Grenzmasse f, kritische Masse f <weiße Zwerge>
critical datum, critical constant (parameter, quantity, value) <therm.>	kritisches Datum n, kritische Konstante (Zustandsgröße, Größe) f, kritischer Parameter (Wert) m <Therm.>	critical mass	s. a. crit <nucl.>
		critical melting point, critical temperature of melting	kritischer Schmelzpunkt m, kritische Schmelztemperatur f
critical density of conduction electrons	s. critical electron density	critical nuclear chain reaction	s. selfsustained nuclear chain reaction
critical depth [of channel]	kritische Tiefe f [des Kanals]	critical opalescence	kritische Opaleszenz f
critical dimensions	s. critical size <nucl., bio.>	critical parameter	s. critical datum <therm.>
critical discharge, critical flow	kritischer Abfluß m, kritische Strömung f	critical period of the reactor	Grenzperiode f des Reaktors
critical distance of ions	kritischer Ionenabstand m	critical point, arrest point, halt	Haltepunkt m, kritischer Punkt m
critical electron density, critical density of conduction electrons	Elektronenzünddichte f, kritische Elektronendichte f		
		critical point, stationary point <of function>	kritischer (stationärer) Punkt m <Funktion>
critical elongation	kritische Streckung f	critical point	s. a. singular point
critical energy <geo.; of cosmic ray>	kritische Energie f <Geo.; kosmische Strahlung>	critical point	s. a. transformation point <of steel>
critical equation	kritische Gleichung f	critical point	s. a. transition temperature <of superconductor>
critical excitation potential, critical potential <of atom>	kritisches Anregungspotential n, kritisches Potential n <Atom>	critical point of decalescence	s. decalescence point
critical explosion pressure	kritischer Explosionsdruck m	critical point of recalescence, recalescence point, transformation point on cooling, Ar point	Haltepunkt m der Abkühlungslinie, Haltepunkt (kritischer Punkt m) bei der Abkühlung
critical field, critical field strength, critical strength of [electric] field	kritische Feldstärke f, Grenzfeldstärke f		
		critical point of solution	s. critical solution temperature
		critical point of the flow	s. stagnation point <aero., hydr.>
critical field, threshold field <superconductivity>	kritisches Magnetfeld (Feld) n, kritische Feldstärke f <Supraleitfähigkeit>	critical potential	s. critical excitation potential <of atom>
critical field curve, threshold field curve	magnetische Schwell[en]wertkurve, Schwell[en]wertkurve f, kritische Feldkurve f	critical pressure ratio	kritisches Druckverhältnis n
		critical pressure rise	kritischer Druckanstieg m
critical flicker frequency	s. critical frequency of flicker	critical quantity	s. critical datum <therm.>
critical flow	s. critical discharge	critical radius	kritischer Radius m; Hallabstand m <Ak.>
critical force, crippling force	Knickkraft f		
		critical rate of cooling, critical cooling rate	kritische Abkühlungsgeschwindigkeit f
		critical Rayleigh number, R_{cr}	kritische Rayleigh-Zahl f (Rayleighsche Zahl) f

critical reaction	s. selfsustained nuclear chain reaction	Crocco variable	Croccosche Variable f
critical reactor	s. chain-reacting pile <nucl.>	Crocco-Vazsonyi equation	s. Crocco['s] equation
critical region, rejection region; rejection zone <stat.>	kritischer Bereich m, Ablehnungsbereich m; Ablehnungszone f <Stat.>	crochet method	s. Rozhdestvensky['s] method
critical resistance; boundary resistance; limit resistance	Grenzwiderstand m	Crookes['] dark space, Hittorf['s] dark space	Hittorfscher Dunkelraum m, Crookesscher Dunkelraum, innerer Dunkelraum, [zweiter] Katodendunkelraum m
critical Reynolds number, transition Reynolds number, trip Reynolds number	kritische Reynolds-Zahl (Reynoldssche Zahl, Re-Zahl) f, Umschlag-Reynolds-Zahl f	Crookes['] radiometer, vane radiometer	Lichtmühle f, [Crookessches] Radiometer n
critical roughness, critical height of roughness	kritische Rauhigkeitshöhe f	Crookes-Townsend radiometer	Crookes-Townsend-Radiometer n
		Crookes['] tube	Crookessche Röhre f, Crookessches Rohr n
critical shape of the drop	kritische Gestalt f des Tröpfchens	cross	Ergänzungsvektor m, Ergänzung f
critical shearing stress, critical shear stress	kritische Schubspannung f, kritische Schubkraft f	cross ampere-turns	Queramperewindungszahl f, Querdurchflutung f, Quererregung f
critical shear strain	kritische Scherung f	cross-arm	s. transverse beam <mech.>
critical shear stress	s. critical shearing stress	cross axis mounting, modified English mounting	englische Achsenmontierung f
critical shear stress law of Schmid	s. Schmid['s] law of critical shear stress		
critical size, critical dimensions <nucl., bio.>	kritische Größe f (Abmessungen fpl) <Kern., Bio.>	cross[-] bar	s. transverse beam <mech.>
		cross[-] beam	s. transverse beam <mech.>
critical solution point (temperature), critical temperature (point) of solution, plait (consolute) point, c.s.t.	kritische Lösungstemperatur f (Mischungstemperatur), kritischer Lösungspunkt (Mischungspunkt, Entmischungspunkt) m, Faltpunkt m	cross bending, transverse bending, bending in flexure	allgemeine Biegung f, Querkraftbiegung f
		cross Bloch line	Kreuz-Bloch-Linie f, Kreuzlinie f
		cross bombardment[s], cross fire	gekreuzte Kernreaktionen fpl, Kreuzbeschuß m
critical sound velocity	s. Laval velocity	cross bond[ing]	s. cross[-]linking
critical sphere, chain-reacting sphere	kritische Kugel f	cross-brace	s. diagonal member
critical stability	s. stability limit	cross breaking strength, buckling strength, resistance to buckling	Knickfestigkeit f
critical state <of reactor>	kritischer Zustand m, Kritischsein n <Reaktor>		
		cross coefficient	Kreuzkoeffizient m
critical state of flow	kritischer Strömungszustand m	cross-coil direction finder	s. crossed-loop direction finder
critical strength of [electric] field	s. critical field	cross-coil ohmmeter, electrodynamical ohmmeter	Kreuzspulenohmmeter n, Kreuzspulen-Widerstandsmesser m, elektrodynamisches Ohmmeter n
critical stress [in buckling]	s. critical compressive stress		
critical surface	s. contact surface <according to Roche>	cross component	s. transverse component
		cross correlation	s. cross correlation function
critical temperature	s. transformation point <of steel>	cross correlation coefficient	Kreuzkorrelationskoeffizient m, gegenseitiger Korrelationskoeffizient m
critical temperature	s. transition temperature <of superconductor>		
critical temperature of melting, critical melting point	kritischer Schmelzpunkt m, kritische Schmelztemperatur f	cross correlation function; cross correlation	Kreuzkorrelationsfunktion f, gegenseitige Korrelationsfunktion f; Kreuzkorrelation f, gegenseitige Korrelation f
critical temperature of solution	s. critical solution temperature		
critical tensile stress	kritische Zugspannung f	cross current	s. shunt current <el.>
critical value <in buckling>	Knickwert m	cross drift	Querdrift f
		crossed circuits	s. crossed currents
		crossed-coil antenna	s. crossed loops
critical value <math.>	kritischer Wert m <Math.>	crossed-coil direction finder	s. crossed-loop direction finder
critical value	s. a. critical datum <therm.>	crossed currents; crossed circuits	gekreuzte Ströme mpl; gekreuzte Stromkreise mpl
critical velocity; cut-off velocity; velocity limit, limit of velocity	Grenzgeschwindigkeit f, kritische Geschwindigkeit f		
		crossed disparity	gekreuzte (ungleichnamige) Disparation f
critical velocity, velocity of small shallow-water gravity wave <hydr.>	Schwallgeschwindigkeit f, Grundwellengeschwindigkeit f <Hydr.>	crossed dispersions	s. crossed spectra
		crossed grating, two-dimensional grating <opt.>	Kreuzgitter n, Flächengitter n, zweidimensionales Gitter n <Opt.>
critical viscous sublayer	kritische zähe Unterschicht f		
		crossed-grating interferometer	Kreuzgitterinterferometer n
critical wave, cut-off wave <of waveguide>	Grenzwelle f, kritische Welle f <Hohlleiter>	crossed-grating spectrograph	Kreuzgitterspektrograph m
critical wavelength	s. cut-off wavelength <of waveguide>	crossed-grating spectrum	Kreuzgitterspektrum n
		crossed lens	Linse f bester Form
Crocco['s] equation, Crocco['s] theorem, Crocco-Vazsonyi equation	Croccoscher Wirbelsatz m, Crocco-Vazsonyischer Wirbelsatz		
		crossed-loop antenna	s. crossed loops
Crocco['s] paradox	Croccosches Paradoxon n	crossed-loop direction finder, cross[ed]-coil direction finder	Kreuzrahmenpeiler m
Crocco['s] point	Croccoscher Punkt m		
Crocco stream function	Crocco Funktion f		
Crocco['s] theorem	s. Crocco['s] equation		
Crocco transformation	Croccosche Transformation f, Crocco-Transformation f	crossed loops, crossed-loop antenna, crossed-coil antenna	Kreuzrahmen m, Kreuzrahmenantenne f

crossed-mirror square, right-angle mirror square	Spiegelkreuz *n*; Kreuzspiegel *m*	**cross polarization**, transverse polarization	Querpolarisation *f*, transversale Polarisation *f*, Transversalpolarisation *f*
crossed Nicol prisms, crossed nicols	gekreuzte Nicols *npl*	**cross product**	*s.* vector product
crossed prism square, double prism square	Prismenkreuz *n*, Doppel[winkel]prisma *n*	**cross ratio**, double ratio, anharmonic ratio	Doppelverhältnis *n*
crossed seas	Kreuzsee *f*		
crossed spectra, crossed dispersions	gekreuzte Spektren *npl* (Dispersionen *fpl*)	**cross relaxation**, spinharmonic coupling	Kreuzrelaxation *f*, Cross-relaxation *f*
crossed tubular levels	Kreuzlibelle *f*	**cross-relaxation maser**	Kreuzrelaxationsmaser *m*
cross effect <therm.>	Überlagerungsprozeß *m* <Therm.>	**cross resistance (resistor)**	*s.* shunt resistance
cross effect	*s. a.* normal stress effect	**cross rule**	Mischungskreuz *n*, Andreas-Kreuz *n*
cross[-] elasticity	Elastizität *f* zweiter Ordnung	**cross[-]section** <phys.>	Wirkungsquerschnitt *m*, Querschnitt *m* <Phys.>
		cross-sectional area, sectional area; plan area	Querschnittsfläche *f*
cross fault, oblique fault	Schrägverwerfung *f*, Diagonalverwerfung *f*		
cross fault	*s. a.* transcurrent fault	**cross-sectional moment of inertia**	Trägheitsmoment *n* des Querschnitts
cross-field generator	Querfeldmaschine *f*; Querfeldgenerator *m*, Querfelddynamomaschine *f*	**cross-section for ...**	*s.* the special term
		cross-section for bound scattering	*s.* bound cross-section
cross fire	*s.* cross bombardment[s]	**cross-section for creation**	*s.* production cross-section
cross firing	Kreuzfeuerbestrahlung *f*	**cross-section for formation**	*s.* production cross-section
cross flow, cross-flow <hydr.>	Querstrom *m*, Querströmung *f*; Queranströmung *f* <Hydr.>	**cross-section for generation**	*s.* production cross-section
		cross-section for impact	*s.* collision cross-section
		cross-section for neutron transport	*s.* transport cross-section
cross flow type heat exchanger	Kreuzstrom[-Wärme]austauscher *m*, Kreuzströmer *m*	**cross-section for small angle inelastic collisions (scattering)**	Wirkungsquerschnitt *m* für unelastische Kleinwinkelstreuung
cross folding; cross folds	Vergitterung *f*; Querfalten *fpl*	**cross-section of carrier trapping**	*s.* trapping cross-section <semi.>
cross force, transverse (lateral) force <mech.>	Querkraft *f*, seitliche Kraft *f* <Mech.>	**cross-section of magnetic path in air**	*s.* air-magnetic cross-section
cross force	*s. a.* dynamic lift <aero., hydr.>	**cross-section of magnetic path in metal**	*s.* metal-magnetic cross-section
cross girder	*s.* transverse beam <mech.>	**cross-section of single turn**, turn cross-section	Windungsquerschnitt *m*
cross-hatching	[doppelte] Schraffierung *f*, Kreuzschraffierung *f*	**cross-section of the core**, core cross-section <el.>	Kernquerschnitt *m*; Eisenquerschnitt *m* <El.>
cross inductance, transverse inductance, shunt inductance	Querinduktivität *f*, Querinduktion *f*	**cross-section of the stream**	Wasserquerschnitt *m*, Flußquerschnitt *m*, Durchflußquerschnitt *m*, Abflußquerschnitt *m*, benetzter Querschnitt *m*; Strömungsquerschnitt *m*
cross induction	*s.* cross[-]talk		
crossing; transposition [by crossing] <of wires>	Kreuzung *f* <Leitungen>		
		cross-section paper	*s.* millimetre squared paper
crossing-over	Crossing-over *n*, Faktorenaustausch *m*, Erbfaktorenaustausch *m*, Segmentaustausch *m*	**cross-section under tension**	Zugquerschnitt *m*
crossing symmetry	Crossingsymmetrie *f*, „crossing"-Symmetrie *f*, Überkreuzsymmetrie *f*	**cross shrinkage**, transverse shrinkage	Querschrumpfung *f*
		cross slip	Quergleitung *f*
cross interlacing, interlacing, interlacement	Verschränkung *f*		
cross-line micrometer	*s.* filar micrometer	**cross slip line**	Quergleitlinie *f*
cross-line screen	Rastergitter *n*		
cross[-]link, cross linkage	*s.* cross[-]linking	**cross stay**	*s.* diagonal member
cross-linked molecule, network molecule	vernetztes Molekül *n*	**cross stratification**	Kreuzschichtung *f*
cross[-]linking, cross[-]link, cross linkage, cross bonding, cross bond	Vernetzung *f*, Querbindung *f*	**cross stripe**, transverse stripe; stripe running across	Querstreifen *m*
		cross table	*s.* stage
		crosstalk, spurious (magnetic) printing	Kopiereffekt *m*
cross linking agent	Vernetzungsmittel *n*, Vernetzer *m*	**cross[-]talk**, cross induction; side-to-side cross[-]talk	Übersprechen *n*; Nebensprechen *n*
cross magnetization, transverse (perpendicular) magnetization	Quermagnetisierung *f*, transversale Magnetisierung *f*	**crosstalk attenuation**	Übersprechdämpfung *f*; Nebensprechdämpfung *f*
cross modulation	Kreuzmodulation *f*	**crosstalk coupling**; side-to-side unbalance	Nebensprechkopplung *f*; Übersprechkopplung *f*
cross neutralization	Gegentakt-Neutralisationsschaltung *f*	**crosstalk meter**	Nebensprechdämpfungsmesser *m*
cross[-]over, cross-over point <el.opt.>	Cross[-]over *n*, Überkreuzungspunkt *m*, Strahlkreuzungspunkt *m*, Kreuzungspunkt *m*, Überkreuzungsstelle *f*, Einschnürungsstelle *f*, erste Konvergenzstelle *f*, Bündelknoten *m*, Brennfleck *m* <El.Opt.>	**cross viscosity**	quadratischer Viskositätskoeffizient *m*
		cross voltage, perpendicular voltage, transverse voltage	Querspannung *f*
cross[-]piece	*s.* transverse beam <mech.>	**crosswind force**	*s.* dynamic lift <aero., hydr.>
cross point	*s.* branch point <math.>		

cross-wire eyepiece	Fadenkreuzokular n	cryophorus	Kryophor m
cross-wire micrometer	s. filar micrometer	cryophysics, low-temperature physics	Kryophysik f, Tieftemperaturphysik f; Kältephysik f
Crova wavelength, effective wavelength, spectral position	wirksame (effektive) Wellenlänge f, Crova-Wellenlänge f	cryopump	s. cryogenic pump
crowded spectrum	überhäuftes Spektrum n	cryosar ‹cryoswitching by avalanche and recombination›	Kryosar m
crowdion	„crowdion" n, Crowdion n		
crow-flight distance, crow-fly distance	Luftlinienentfernung f, Entfernung f in Luftlinie	cryoscope	Kryoskop n, Gefrierpunktmesser m
crown [discharge]	s. corona	cryoscopic constant, molal (molecular, molar) depression of freezing point, molal (molecular, molar) lowering of freezing point, freezing point constant	kryoskopische Konstante f, molale (molekulare, molare) Gefrierpunktserniedrigung f
cruciform twin	Durchkreuzungszwilling m		
Crudeli['s] method	Crudelische Methode f		
crude moment, non-central moment	nichtzentrales Moment n		
crumbling	Zerbröckeln n; Bröckeln n ‹Opt.›	cryoscopic determination [of molecular weight], cryoscopic method, cryoscopy	Gefrierpunktverfahren n, Gefrierpunktmethode f, kryoskopische Molekulargewichtsbestimmung (Methode, Bestimmung) f, Kryoskopie f
crunode	s. double point		
crunode	s. node ‹of the curve›		
crush, crushing ‹geo.›	Zerrüttung f, Zerruschelung f ‹Geo.›		
crushability, collapsability	Zerdrückbarkeit f, Zerquetschbarkeit f	cryoscopic method	s. cryoscopic determination
		cryoscopy	s. cryoscopic determination
crush breccia	s. fault breccia	cryosistor	Kryosistor m
crushing, squashing; bruising	Zerdrückung f; Zerquetschung f; Zermalmung f	cryosphere	Kryosphäre f
		cryostat	Kryostat m, Kältebad n
		cryotron	Kryotron n, Cryotron n
		cryotronics	Kryotronik f
crushing, crush ‹geo.›	Zerrüttung f, Zerruschelung f ‹Geo.›	cryoturbation	Kryoturbation f, Mikrosolifluktion f
crushing, size reduction, mechanical subdivision, chopping ‹mech.›	Brechung f, Grobzerkleinerung f, Zerkleinerung f, Zerstückelung f ‹Mech.›	cryptocrystalline	kryptokristallin, dicht
		cryptogear	s. epicyclic gear
crushing strength of the cube	s. cube strength	cryptoionic bond	Kryptoionenbindung f
crushing test	s. compression test	cryptoionic intermediate state	kryptoionischer Zwischenzustand m
crush zone, zone of crush (fracture)	Zerrüttungszone f, Ruschelzone f, Zerrüttungsgebiet n		
		cryptomerous	kryptomer
crust, protective crust	Kruste f, Schutzrinde f	cryptomorphous	kryptomorph
crustal movement	s. diastrophism	cryptoscope, kryptoscope	Kryptoskop n
crustal shortening	Schrumpfung f der Kruste		
crusting	Krustenbildung f	cryptovolcanism	Kryptovulkanismus m
		crystal aggregate, crystalline aggregate	Kristallaggregat n, kristallines Aggregat n
crust magnetic field, magnetic field of the Earth's crust	Erdkrustenfeld n	crystal analysis	s. crystal-structure determination
crust of the Earth, Earth's crust	Erdkruste f	crystal analysis	s. X-ray crystallographic analysis
		crystal axis	s. axis of crystal
crust of weathering	Verwitterungskruste f, Verwitterungsrinde f, Verwitterungsdecke f	crystal beaded screen	s. beaded screen
		crystal blank, crystal block, blank, mother crystal	Rohkristall m, Kristallrohling m, Kristallblock m
cryogen	s. frigorific mixture		
cryogenic	kryogen[isch], Kryo-, Tieftemperatur-		
cryogenic bubble chamber	Tieftemperatur-Blasenkammer f	crystal boundary	Kristallgrenze f, Begrenzung f des Kristalls
cryogenic engineering, cryogenics	Kryotechnik f	crystal calibrator, quartz calibrator	Quarzeichgenerator m, Quarzeichoszillator m, Quarzeicher m
cryogenic lens	Kryolinse f		
cryogenic maser	Tieftemperaturmaser m	crystal chemistry	Kristallchemie f, Kristallstrukturkunde f
cryogenic pump, cryopump	Kryopumpe f, kryogene Pumpe f	crystal class, crystallographic class	Kristallklasse f
cryogenics	Lehre f von den tiefen Temperaturen, Kryogenik f, Tieftemperaturforschung f	crystal conduction counter	s. crystal counter ‹nucl.›
		crystal-controlled clock, quartz clock	Quarzuhr f
cryogenics	s. a. cryogenic engineering	crystal-controlled oscillator, quartz-[crystal-]controlled oscillator, quartz[-crystal] oscillator, crystal[-stabilized] oscillator, quartz-[crystal-]stabilized oscillator	quarzgesteuerter Oszillator m, quarzstabilisierter Oszillator, Quarzoszillator m, Kristalloszillator, Quarzgenerator m; Quarzsender m
cryogetter pump	Kryogetterpumpe f		
cryohydrate	Kryohydrat n		
cryohydric point	kryohydratischer Punkt m, Kryopunkt m		
cryoluminescence	Kryolumineszenz f		
cryomagnetic anomaly	kryomagnetische Anomalie f	crystal counter [tube], crystal detector, [crystal] conduction counter, photoconductivity counter ‹nucl.›	Kristallzähler m ‹Kern.›
cryometry	Kryometrie f, Tieftemperaturmessung f, Kältemessung f		
cryopedology	Kryopedologie f, Lehre f vom Frostboden, Frostbodenforschung f	crystal defect	s. crystal imperfection
		crystal defect	s. defect
		crystal detector	s. detector ‹el.›
		crystal detector	s. a. crystal counter ‹nucl.›
cryopedometer	Kryopedometer n, Bodenfrostmesser m	crystal diffraction, crystalline diffraction	Beugung f am Kristall, Kristallbeugung f

crystal diode	s. semiconductor diode	**crystallization polarization**	s. crystallization overpotential
crystal-diode detector	s. detector <el.>	**crystallization pressure,** crystallizing pressure	Kristallisationsdruck m
crystal direction	s. crystallographic direction	**crystallization tendency**	Kristallisationsfreudigkeit f, Kristallisationsneigung f
crystal domain, crystallographic domain, domain [of crystal], region (area) of crystal <cryst.>	Kristallbereich m <Krist.>		
crystal dosimeter	Kristalldosimeter n	**crystallizer [tank],** crystallizing tank	Kristallisator m, Kristallisierapparat m, Kristallierer m, Kristaller m
crystal druse	s. druse	**crystallizing [out]**	s. crystallization
crystal edge, edge of the crystal	Kristallkante f	**crystallizing pressure,** crystallization pressure	Kristallisationsdruck m
crystal effect	Einfluß m der Kristallstruktur, Einfluß des Kristallgitters, Kristalleffekt m, Kristallgefügeeinfluß m	**crystallizing tank**	s. crystallizer
		crystalloblastesis	Kristalloblastese f
		crystallochemical	kristallchemisch
crystal field	[inneres] Kristallfeld n	**crystallofluorescence**	s. crystal fluorescence
		crystallogenesis	Kristallogenese f
crystal field theory, crystalline-field theory	Kristallfeldtheorie f	**crystallogram**	s. X-ray pattern
crystal filter	s. quartz filter	**crystallographic axial ratio,** axial ratio, intercept ratio	[kristallographisches] Achsenverhältnis n
crystal fluorescence, fluorescence in crystal, crystallofluorescence	Kristallfluoreszenz f, Kristallofluoreszenz f	**crystallographic axis**	s. axis of crystal
crystal form, crystalline form, crystal shape	Kristallform f	**crystallographic change**	s. crystallographic transformation.
crystal formation	s. crystallization	**crystallographic class**	s. crystal class
crystal grain	s. grain <cryst.>	**crystallographic direction,** crystal direction	kristallographische Richtung f, Kristallrichtung f
crystal grating	s. crystal lattice		
crystal growing (growth)	s. growing of crystals	**crystallographic domain**	s. crystal domain <cryst.>
		crystallographic group	kristallographische Gruppe f
crystal growth, growth of crystal	Kristallwachstum n, Kristallvergrößerung f	**crystallographic index**	kristallographischer Index m
crystal habit	s. habit of the crystal	**crystallographic microscope**	Kristallographiemikroskop n
crystal holder, crystal-holding device	Kristallhalterung f, Kristallhalter m, Kristallträger m	**crystallographic orientation,** crystal orientation	kristallographische Orientierung f, Kristallorientierung f
crystal imperfection, crystal defect, imperfection of crystal	Kristall[bau]fehler m, Kristallbaustörung f, Kristalldefekt m, Baufehler m des Kristalls, Kristallstrukturfehler m		
		crystallographic plane, crystal plane	Kristallebene f
		crystallographic reorientation	s. recrystallization
crystal lattice, lattice, crystal grating <cryst.>	Kristallgitter n, Gitter n <Krist.>	**crystallographic symmetry**	s. crystal symmetry
crystal lattice defect (imperfection)	s. defect	**crystallographic transformation (transition),** crystallographic change	kristallographische Umwandlung f, kristallographischer Übergang m
crystalline aggregate, crystal aggregate	Kristallaggregat n, kristallines Aggregat n	**crystallographic zone**	s. zone [of crystal]
crystalline anisotropy energy	s. energy of magnetic anisotropy	**crystallographic zone axis,** zone axis	Zonenachse f, Zonenlinie f, Zonengerade f
crystalline diffraction	s. crystal diffraction	**crystallography**	Kristallographie f; Kristallkunde f, Kristallehre f; Kristallbeschreibung f
crystalline-field theory, crystal field theory	Kristallfeldtheorie f		
crystalline form, crystal form	Kristallform f	**crystallography**	s. a. crystal-structure determination
crystalline grain	s. grain <cryst.>	**crystallohydrate**	s. crystalline hydrate
crystalline hoar-frost	Haarfrost m	**crystalloid**	Kristalloid n
crystalline hydrate, crystallohydrate	Kristallhydrat n	**crystalloluminescence**	s. crystal luminescence
		crystallometer	Kristallmesser m
crystalline index	Kristallinitätsindex m	**crystallometry**	Kristallmessung f
crystalline lens	Augenlinse f, Kristallinse f	**crystallophosphorescence**	s. crystal phosphorescence
crystalline liquid	s. liquid crystal		
crystalline solid solution	s. solid solution	**crystal loudspeaker**	s. piezoelectric loudspeaker
crystalline state	kristalliner Zustand m	**crystal luminescence,** luminescence in crystal, crystalloluminescence	Kristallumineszenz f, Kristallumineszenz f
crystalline structure	s. crystal structure		
crystalline transition	kristalliner Übergang m	**crystal microphone**	s. piezoelectric microphone
crystallinity	Kristallinität f	**crystal momentum**	s. quasi-momentum
crystal liquid	s. liquid crystal	**crystal monochromator**	Kristallmonochromator m
crystallite, matted crystal	Kristallit m		
crystallizability	Kristallisationsfähigkeit f, Kristallisierbarkeit f	**crystal morphology,** morphology of crystals	Kristallmorphologie f
		crystal needle	s. whisker
		crystal nucleus	s. nucleus of crystal
crystallization, crystallizing; crystal formation; crystallizing out	Kristallisation f, Kristallisieren n; Kristallbildung f; Auskristallisieren n, Kornbildung f	**crystal optics**	Kristalloptik f
		crystal orientation	s. crystallographic orientation
		crystal oscillation	s. crystal vibration
crystallization center	s. nucleus of crystal	**crystal oscillator**	s. crystal-controlled oscillator
crystallization germ	s. germ of crystal		
crystallization from gas phase <from fluid or liquid phase, from solution, from melt, from solid phase>	Kristallisation f aus der Gasphase <flüssigen Phase oder Lösung, Schmelze, festen Phase>	**crystal oscillator**	s. oscillating quartz
		crystal periodicity, periodicity in space of the crystal, periodicity of lattice	Kristallperiodizität f, Periodizität f der Kristallstruktur, Periodizität des Gitters
crystallization heat, heat of crystallization	Kristallisationswärme f		
crystallization limit	Kristallisationsgrenze f	**crystal phosphorescence,** phosphorescence in crystal, crystallophosphorescence	Kristallphosphoreszenz f, Kristallophosphoreszenz f
crystallization overpotential; crystallization polarization	Kristallisationsüberspannung f; Kristallisationspolarisation f		
		crystal photoeffect, crystal photoelectric effect	Kristallphotoeffekt m

crystal 146

crystal physics	Kristallphysik f	cubic	s. a. cubic curve
crystal plane	s. crystallographic plane	cubical	s. a. three-dimensional
crystal plasticity	s. plasticity of crystals	cubical contents	s. volume
crystal plate, crystal slab	Kristallplatte f	cubical contraction	s. volume contraction
crystal platelet, crystal wafer	Kristallplättchen n, Kristallblättchen n	cubical dilatation, volumetric dilatation <elasticity>	Raumdehnung f, [kubische] Dilatation f, räumliche (kubische) Dehnung f <Elastizität>
crystal powder, powdered crystal	Kristallpulver n		
crystal pseudomorphism	s. pseudomorphism	cubical expansion	s. cubic dilatation
crystal pulling	s. pulling of crystals	cubical strain	s. general state of strain
crystal rectifier	s. detector <el.>	cubical stress	s. volume stress
crystal reflection	Kristallreflexion f	cubic body centred	s. body-centred cubic
crystal refractometer	Kristallrefraktometer n	cubic capacity	s. capacity
		cubic closed-packed structure	kubisch dichteste Kugelpackung f
crystal refractoscope	Kristallrefraktoskop n		
crystal resonator	s. piezoelectric resonator	cubic compressibility, coefficient of cubic compressibility	kubische Kompressibilität f, kubischer Kompressibilitätskoeffizient m
crystal shape	s. crystal form		
crystal size	Kristallgröße f		
crystal skeleton	s. dendrite	cubic crystal[lographic] system	s. cubic system
crystal slab, crystal plate	Kristallplatte f		
crystal space	Kristallraum m, Raum m des Kristallgitters	cubic curve, cubic	Kurve f dritter Ordnung, Kubik f, kubische Kurve
crystal spectrograph (spectrometer)	s. Bragg spectrometer	cubic dilatation, cubical expansion, volumetric (measure, volume) expansion, expansion by volume <therm.>	kubische (räumliche) Ausdehnung f, Raumausdehnung f, Volum[en]ausdehnung f, Volum[en]dehnung f <Therm.>
crystal spectroscopy	Kristallspektroskopie f		
crystal-stabilized oscillator	s. crystal-controlled oscillator		
crystal spectrum	Kristallspektrum n		
crystal stress	Kristallverspannung f	cubic expansion coefficient	s. thermal coefficient of volume expansion
crystal structure, crystalline structure	Kristallstruktur f, Kristallbau m, Kristallgefüge n, kristallographische Struktur f	cubic face-centred	s. face-centred cubic
		cubic intermodulation factor	kubischer Differenztonfaktor (Intermodulationsfaktor) m, Differenztonfaktor zweiter Ordnung
crystal-structure determination, crystal analysis, analysis of crystal structure, [structural] crystallography; structure analysis, structural analysis, structural research	Kristallstrukturanalyse, Kristallstrukturbestimmung f, Kristallgitterbestimmung f; Strukturanalyse f, Strukturbestimmung f, Strukturforschung f, Strukturuntersuchung f; Feinstrukturanalyse f, Feinstrukturbestimmung f, Feinstrukturuntersuchung f		
		cubic lattice	kubisches Gitter n
		cubicle; cell; element; cellule <of wing>	Zelle f
		cubic metre	Kubikmeter n, m³; Festmeter n, fm
crystal surface	Kristalloberfläche f	cubic point group	kubische Punktgruppe f
crystal symmetry, crystallographic symmetry, symmetry properties of the lattice, symmetry of lattice	Kristallsymmetrie f, kristallographische Symmetrie f, Gittersymmetrie f	cubic space-centred	s. body-centred cubic
		cubic symmetry	Würfelsymmetrie f, räumliche (kubische) Symmetrie f
crystal system, system of crystal symmetry	Kristallsystem n, Syngonie f	cubic system, cubic crystal[lographic] system, isometric system, isometric crystal[lographic] system, regular system, regular crystal[lographic] system	kubisches System (Kristallsystem) n, reguläres System (Kristallsystem), tesserales System (Kristallsystem), Tesseralsystem n, regelmäßiges System (Kristallsystem), isometrisches System
crystal system of lower symmetry	niederes Kristallsystem n		
crystal tetrode	s. semiconductor tetrode		
crystal texture	Kristalltextur f		
crystal tracht	s. tracht of the crystal		
crystal triode	s. transistor	cubing	s. cubage
crystal vibration, crystal oscillation	Kristallschwingung f	cuboid	s. rectangular parallelepiped
		cubo-octahedron	Kubooktaeder n
crystal wafer	s. crystal platelet	Culmann ellipsoid [of inertia]	s. ellipsoid of inertia of Culmann
crystal water, water of crystallization (hydration)	Kristallwasser n		
		culminating point	Kulminationspunkt m
crystal whisker	s. whisker	cumulant, semi-invariant <stat.>	Kumulante f, Halbinvariante f <Stat.>
crystal zone	s. zone [of crystal]		
C-shaped electrode	s. cee electrode	cumulation, cumulative process	Kumulation f, kumulativer Prozeß m
C star	s. carbon star		
C-type weight	s. torpedo sinker	cumulative distribution function	s. distribution function
cubage; cubature; cubing	Kubatur f, Inhaltsberechnung f, Volum[en]berechnung f		
		cumulative dose, accumulated dose	kumulative (akkumulierte) Dosis f, Summendosis f, Gesamtdosis f
cube, regular hexahedron, hexahedron	Würfel m, regelmäßiges Sechsflach (Hexaeder) n, regelmäßiger Sechsflächner m, Hexaeder		
		cumulative double bonds	kumulierte Doppelbindungen fpl
cube compressive (crushing) strength	s. cube strength	cumulative frequency	Summenhäufigkeit f, kumulative Häufigkeit f
cube root law	Kubikwurzelgesetz n	cumulative frequency curve	s. distribution curve
cube-shaped, cubic, cubical	würfelförmig		
		cumulative frequency function	s. distribution function
cube strength, cube crushing (compressive) strength, crushing strength of the cube	Würfeldruckfestigkeit f, Würfelfestigkeit f		
		cumulative ionization	lawinenartige (kumulative) Ionisation f, Lawinenionisation f
cube texture [in metals]	kubische Textur (Metallstruktur) f	cumulative probability function	s. distribution function
cubic, ³, cu.	Kubik-, ³, c, cb	cumulative process, cumulation	Kumulation f, kumulativer Prozeß m
cubic[al]	s. a. cube-shaped		

current

cumuliform cloud, heap cloud	haufenförmige (cumulusartige) Wolke f, Cumuliformisform f	current, electric current; strength (intensity) of current, current strength (intensity, volume), amperage <el.>	Strom m, elektrischer Strom; Stromstärke f, elektrische Stromstärke, Stromwert m <El.>
cumulonimbus [cloud], thundercloud, Cb	Cumulonimbus m, Kumulonimbus m, Gewitterwolke f, getürmte Haufenwolke f, Böenwolke f, Gewitterturm m, Kumulonimbuswolke f, Cb	current	s. a. stream
		current	s. a. flow
		current	s. a. thermodynamic flux
		current after injury	Verletzungsstrom m, Demarkationsstrom m
cumulus, cumulus cloud, congestus cloud, C	Cumulus m, Kumulus m, Schönwettercumulus m, Haufenwolke f, Quellwolke f, C	current algebra, algebra of currents	Stromalgebra f
		current amplification	Stromverstärkung f
cumulus arcus	Rollcumulus m, Rollkumulus m, Cumulus m arcus	current amplification factor	s. current gain
		current antinode, current loop	Strombauch m
cumulus cloud	s. cumulus	current at break	s. break current
cumulus fractus, fracto-cumulus	Fractocumulus m, zerrissene Quellwolke f	current at make	s. closing current
		current at the terminals, terminal current	Klemmenstrom m, Klemmstrom m
Cunningham factor	Cunninghamscher Faktor m, Cunningham-Faktor m	current balance	s. ampere balance
cup anemometer, rotating-cup anemometer	s. dish Schalenkreuzanemometer n; Schalenanemometer n	current balance equation	Strombilanzgleichung f
		current branching, circuit branching	Stromverzweigung f, Stromaufteilung f
cup barometer	s. cistern barometer	current carrier	Stromträger m
cup drawing test	s. cupping and drawing test	current-carrying, carrying a current, traversed by a current, live	stromführend; stromdurchflossen; unter Strom
cupellation, cupullation <met.>	Treibarbeit f, Treiben n, Abtreiben n, Kupellation f		
cupping and drawing test; cupping test, cup test, cup drawing test; drawing test	Tiefungs- und Ziehversuch m, Streckziehversuch m, Tiefziehversuch m, Tiefungsversuch m; Napfziehversuch m, Näpfchen[zieh]versuch m, Tiefzieh-Näpfchenversuch m, AEG-Verfahren n	current carrying capacity	Kontaktdauerstrom m
		current chamber, current ionization chamber	Stromkammer f, Stromionisationskammer f
		current characteristic, current diagram	Stromkennlinie f, Stromcharakteristik f, Stromkurve f, Stromdiagramm n
cuprous oxide cell, cuprous oxide photocell, copper-oxide photovoltaic cell	Kupferoxydulphotoelement n, Kupferoxydul[-Sperrschichtphoto]zelle f, Kupfer(I)-oxid-Photoelement n, Kupfer-Kupferoxydul-Zelle f	current circuit	s. circuit <el.>
		current circuit	s. current path <el.>
		current concentration <el.chem.>	Stromkonzentration f <El.Chem.>
		current conduction time	Stromführzeit f
cup test	s. cupping and drawing test	current coverage, ampere-turns per unit length	Strombelag m, Durchflutung f pro Längeneinheit
cupullation	s. cupellation		
cure	s. hardening <of concrete>		
cure	s. hardening <of plastics, resins>	current density, electric current density; current density vector <el.>	Stromdichte f, elektrische Stromdichte, elektrische Dichte f; Stromdichtevektor m <El.>
cure	s. vulcanization		
curie, Ci, c, C	Curie n, Ci, c, C		
Curie-Chéneveau balance	Curie-Waage f	current density <el.chem.>	Stromdichte f <El.Chem.>
Curie constant	Curie-Konstante f, Curiesche Konstante f	current density operator, operator of current density	Stromdichteoperator m
Curie cut	s. X cut		
Curie['s] equation, Curie['s] law	Curiesches Gesetz n	current density vector	s. current density <el.>
		current detector	s. current indicator
Curie point [of temperature], Curie temperature; ferromagnetic Curie point [of temperature], ferromagnetic Curie temperature, magnetic transformation (transition) temperature	Curie-Punkt m, Curie-Temperatur f, Curiescher Punkt m; ferromagnetischer Curie-Punkt	current determinant	Stromdeterminante f
		current diagram	s. current pattern
		current diagram	s. current characteristic
		current displacement	s. skin effect
		current displacement factor, displacement factor	Stromverdrängungsfaktor m
Curie['s] principle	s. Curie['s] theorem	current distribution control	Stromverteilungssteuerung f
Curie scale of temperature	Curiesche Temperaturskala f	current distribution noise	s. partition noise
Curie susceptibility	Curie-Suszeptibilität f, Kernsuszeptibilität f		
Curie['s] symmetry principle	s. Curie['s] theorem	current-dividing network	Stromteilernetzwerk n
Curie temperature	s. Curie point	current division, subdivision of the current	Stromteilung f
Curie['s] theorem, Curie['s] [symmetry] principle	Curiesches Prinzip n		
		current division factor	Stromteilerfaktor m
Curie-Weiss law	Curie-Weisssches Gesetz n	current due to friction[al electricity]	s. friction current
curing	= cure		
curium, ⁹⁶Cm	Curium n, ⁹⁶Cm	current efficiency	Stromwirkungsgrad m
curl, rotor, rotation, curl <math.>	Rotation f, vektorielle Rotation, Rotor m, Wirbel m, Quirl m, rot <Math.>		
Curl	s. areal curl	current efficiency current yield, <el.chem.>	Stromausbeute f <El.Chem.>
curl field	s. rotational field	current electrode	Stromelektrode f
curl of the tensor	Rotation f des Tensors, tensorielle Rotation	current equivalent, equivalent current	Stromäquivalent n
curly bracket	s. brace		
curoid	Curoid n		

current

current error <meas.>	Stromfehler *m* <Meß.>
current feed	Stromkopplung *f*, Einkopplung *f* im Strombauch
current feedback	Stromrückkopplung *f*; Stromrückführung *f*
current feedback, negative current feedback	Stromgegenkopplung *f*
current fission chamber	Strom-Spaltungskammer *f*
current flow	s. passage of current
current fluctuation, power fluctuation	Stromschwankung *f*
current follower	s. grounded-grid current
current function	s. stream function
current gain, current amplification factor	Stromverstärkungsfaktor *m*, Stromverstärkung *f*, Stromvergrößerung *f* Stromüberhöhungsfaktor *m*; Impedanzwandlung *f*
current generator cell	s. voltaic cell
current generator equivalent circuit, current source equivalent circuit, equivalent circuit with current generator	Einströmungsersatzschaltbild *n*, Stromquellenersatzschaltbild *n*
current heat	s. Joule heat
current impulse	s. impulse of current
current indicator; current detector	Stromanzeiger *m*, Stromindikator *m*; Stromnachweisgerät *n*
current induced at break	s. break current
current induced at make	s. closing current
current intensity	s. current <el.>
current in the branch	s. branch current <el.>
current ionization chamber, current chamber	Stromkammer *f*, Stromionisationskammer *f*
current law	s. Kirchhoff['s] current law
current limitation, current limiting	Strombegrenzung *f*
current-limiting reactor, protective reactance coil	Strombegrenzungsdrossel *f*, Kurzschlußdrossel *f*
current loop, current antinode	Strombauch *m*
current matrix	Strommatrix *f*
current meter, current velocity meter, device for measuring fluid flow velocities; rheometer	Strömungsgeschwindigkeitsmesser *m*, Strömungsmesser *m*; Rheometer *n*
current node	Stromknoten *m*
current noise	Stromrauschen *n*
current noise power	Stromrauschleistung *f*
current of accelerated particles	s. accelerated [particle] current <acc.>
current of dielectric convection	s. displacement current
current of precipitation	Niederschlagsstrom *m*
current of the corona discharge	Sprühstrom *m*
current of the lightning	Blitzstrom *m*
current operator	Stromoperator *m*
current passage	s. passage of current
current path, path of current, current circuit, series circuit <el.>	Strompfad *m*, Strombahn *f*, nichtverzweigter Stromkreis *m*, Stromkreis, Serien[strom]kreis *m* <El.>
current pattern, current diagram	Stromverteilungsbild *n*, Strombild *n*
current probe	Stromsonde *f*
current pulse	s. impulse of current
current ratio	s. current transformation
current regulator [tube]	s. barretter
current resonance, parallel resonance, parallel phase resonance, antiresonance	Parallelresonanz *f*, Stromresonanz *f*, Sperresonanz *f*, Antiresonanz *f*
current reverser	s. pole-changing switch
current r.m.s., current root-mean-square, root-mean-square [value of] current. r.m.s. current [value], effective current	Effektivwert *m* des Stromes, Effektivstrom *m*, Effektivwert der Stromstärke, effektive Stromstärke *f* [des Wechselstroms], Stromeffektivwert *m*
current rush	s. impulse of current
current sheet, stream sheet	Stromblatt *n*, Stromfläche *f*
current source	s. source of current
current source equivalent circuit	s. current generator equivalent circuit
current-stabilized	stromstabilisiert, stromkonstant
current stabilizer	Stromstabilisator *m*, Stromgleichhalter *m*, Stromkonstanthalter *m*
current stabilizer	s. a. barretter
current standard	Stromnormal *n*
current stop	s. mains failure
current strength	s. current <el.>
current supply	s. power supply
current surge	s. impulse of current
current system <of geomagnetism>	Stromsystem *n*, Strombasis *f* <Geomagnetismus>
current transfer	Stromübernahme *f*
current transformation [ratio], current ratio	Stromübersetzung *f*
current transformer, series transformer	Stromwandler *m*, Stromtransformator *m*
current vector	Stromzeiger *m*, Stromvektor *m*
current velocity	s. water current velocity
current velocity meter, current meter, device for measuring fluid flow velocities; rheometer	Strömungsgeschwindigkeitsmesser *m*, Strömungsmesser *m*; Rheometer *n*
current-voltage characteristic, volt-ampere characteristic, E-I characteristic, i-V characteristic; characteristic curve of the thermionic valve, characteristic [diagram] of the thermionic valve, valve characteristic, tube characteristic	Strom-Spannung[s]-Charakteristik *f*, Stromspannungskennlinie *f*, Strom-Spannung[s]-Kennlinie *f*, Strom-Spannung[s]-Diagramm *n*, Spannung-Strom-Charakteristik *f*, VA-Charakteristik *f*, I-U-Charakteristik *f*, VA-Kennlinie *f*, I-U-Kennlinie *f*; Kennlinie *f* der Elektronenröhre, Röhrenkennlinie *f*, Röhrencharakteristik *f*
current-voltage characteristic, voltage-current characteristic <of photocell>	Kennlinie *f*, Strom-Spannung[s]-Charakteristik *f*, lichtelektrische Charakteristik *f* <Photozelle>
current volume	s. current <el.>
current wave	Stromwelle *f*
current-wavelength characteristic <of photocell>	spektrale Empfindlichkeitskurve *f* <Photozelle>
current yield, current efficiency <el.chem.>	Stromausbeute *f* <El.Chem.>
cursor <e.g. of slide rule>	Läufer *m* <z. B. Rechenschieber>
cursor, cursor slide[r]	s. wiper <el.>
curtain	Abschirmfolie *f*, Neutronenfänger *m*
curtain	s. a. draperies
curtain [fading] shutter, curtain wipe	Vorhang[verschluß] *m*, Vorhangblende *f*
curtate distance	kurtierte Distanz *f*, distantia *f* curtata
Curtis stuge, velocity stage	Curtis-Stufe *f*, Geschwindigkeitsstufe *f*
Curtis turbine, Curtis-type turbine, velocity [stage] turbine	Curtis-Rad *n*, C-Rad *n*, Curtis-Turbine *f*, Geschwindigkeitsrad *n*
curunde	s. double point
curvature <of the triode characteristic>	Krümmung *f* [der Triode]
curvature, first curvature <of the curve>	Krümmung *f*, erste Krümmung, Biegung *f*, Flexion *f* <Kurve>
curvature	s. a. bending
curvature movement	Krümmungsbewegung *f*
curvature of field	s. field curvature
curvature of the bands	Verkippen *n* der Bänder
curvature of the Earth	Erdkrümmung *f*
curvature of the image field	s. field curvature
curvature of the path	Bahnkrümmung *f*

curvature of the second kind	Streckenkrümmung f, Streckenwirbel m	curve of shortest descent	s. brachistochrone
		curve of spectral distribution [of energy]	Kurve f der spektralen Energieverteilung, spektrale Energieverteilungskurve f
curvature of the spectral line	s. spectral line curvature		
curvature of the surface	Flächenkrümmung f	curve of stability	s. stability line
		curve of state, state curve	Zustandskurve f
		curve of sublimation	s. sublimation curve
curvature of vertical	Vertikal[en]krümmung f, Krümmung f der Vertikalen	curve of the equation of time	s. plot of the equation of time
curvature scalar	Krümmungsskalar m	curve of the thermo-electromotive force versus (vs.) temperature, thermoelectromotive force plotted against the temperature	Thermokurve f
curvature tensor	s. Riemann-Christoffel tensor		
curved bar	gekrümmter Stab m		
curved bar with large curvature	stark gekrümmter Stab m		
		curve of water level variation	s. water level curve
curved bar with small curvature	schwach gekrümmter Stab m	curvilinear co-ordinates (co-ordinate system), Gauss co-ordinates, curvilinear system [of co-ordinates]	krummlinige Koordinaten fpl, Gaußsche Koordinaten; krummliniges Koordinatensystem n
curved crystal, bent crystal	gebogener (gewölbter) Kristall m		
curved-crystal spectrometer	Spektrometer n mit gebogenem Kristall		
		curvilinear orthogonal co-ordinates	s. orthogonal curvilinear co-ordinates
curved mirror, bent mirror	gewölbter Spiegel m, gekrümmter Spiegel	curvilinear regression	nichtlineare Regression f
curved shock	gekrümmte Stoßfront f	curvilinear system [of co-ordinates]	s. curvilinear co-ordinates
curve factor	Ausbauchungsfaktor m	curvimeter	Kurvimeter n, Kurven[bogen]messer m; Krümmungsmesser m
curve family	s. family of characteristic[s]		
curve filling factor	Kurvenfüllbeiwert m, Kurvenfüllfaktor m	cusp, cuspidal point, stationary point, spinode; cuspidal value <of the curve>	Rückkehrpunkt m, Kuspidalpunkt m, Spitze f, stationärer Punkt m, Spitzpunkt m, Kehrpunkt m <Kurve>
curve fitting, fitting of the curve	Anpassung f der Kurve, Kurvenanpassung f		
curve length, arc length, Arcus; arc co-ordinate <math.>	Bogenlänge f <Math.>		
		cusp, extremity of the crescent <of the Moon or an inferior planet>	Hörnerspitze f
curve of adaptation, course of adaptation	Adaptationskurve f		
		cusped	s. crescent <astr.>
curve of [centres of] buoyancy	Auftriebskurve f, Formschwerpunktskurve f	cusped geometry	Sichelspiegelgeometrie f
curve of constant density	s. isopycnic	cuspidal point	s. cusp <of the curve>
curve of correction of the hysteresis loop, shearing curve	Scherungskurve f, Scherungslinie f, Scherungsgerade f	cuspidal point of the first kind, cusp of the first kind, simple cusp	Spitze f erster Art, Umkehrpunkt m erster Art
curve of deflection	s. bending line	cuspidal point of the second kind, cusp of the second kind	Spitze f zweiter Art, Schnabelspitze f, Umkehrpunkt m zweiter Art
curve of dispersion, dispersion curve	Dispersionskurve f; Dispersionsdiagramm n		
curve of double curvature, space curve, spatial curve; twisted curve, skew curve	Raumkurve f; doppeltgekrümmte Kurve f, Kurve doppelter Krümmung, nichtebene Kurve	cuspidal value	s. cusp <of the curve>
		cusp mirror	sichelförmiger Spiegel m, Sichelspiegel m
		cusp of the first (second) kind	s. cuspidal point of the first (second) kind
curve of equal altitude	s. isohypse	cut	s. notch
curve of equal density	s. equidensity	cut	s. truncation <of the series, math.>
curve of equal deviation	s. line of equal deviation		
curve of equal intensity	s. isoseism[al]	cut/45°; 45° section	45°-Schnitt m
curve of equal level	s. isohypse	cut-image rangefinder	s. coincidence rangefinder
curve of equal optical density	s. equidensity	cut-in	s. interconnection <el.>
		cut-off; clipping	Abschneidung f; Beschneidung f, Begrenzung f
curve of equal path difference, curve of equal relative retardation of optical paths	Gangunterschiedskurve f, Kurve f gleichen Gangunterschieds		
		cut-off, cut-off energy	Abschneideenergie f
curve of equal specific volume	s. isostere	cut-off <of the rocket>	Brennschluß m <infolge Zündungsaussetzung>, Abschaltung f des Triebwerks <Rakete>
curve of equal velocity	s. isotac		
curve of equilibrium	Gleichgewichtskurve f		
curve of floatation	Schwimmkurve f	cut-off	s. a. blocking <el.>
		cut-off	s. a. cut-off frequency <of waveguide, of filter>
curve of flux distribution	s. distribution of luminous flux		
		cut-off	s. a. burn-out
curve of intersection, line of intersection, intersection line	Schnittkurve f, Schnittlinie f	cut-off angle of current flow, electrode current averaging time <el.>	Stromflußwinkel m, Unsymmetriewinkel m, Brennzeit f <El.>
curve of light distribution	s. light distribution curve		
curve of magnetic flux	s. magnetic flux curve	cut-off angular frequency	s. angular cut-off frequency
curve of magnetic induction	s. magnetic induction curve		
curve of magnetization	s. magnetization curve	cut-off arc	Ausschaltlichtbogen m
curve of magnetization tips	s. tip curve		
curve of neutral stability	Indifferenzkurve f	cut-off bias, grid bias (cut-off voltage) <of the valve>	Gittersperrspannung f, Steuergittereinsatzspannung f <Röhre>
curve of normal distribution [of errors]	s. error curve		
curve of normal magnetization	s. tip curve		
curve of nucleation rate	Keimhäufigkeitskurve f	cut-off bias	s. a. cut-off voltage
		cut-off bias[ing potential]	s. reverse bias
curve of pursuit	Verfolgungskurve f, Hundekurve f, Fliehkurve f, Fluchtkurve f	cut-off current	s. reverse current <semi.>

cut-off 150

cut-off delay	s. disconnection delay <el.>	cycle efficiency, efficiency of the thermodynamic cycle	Prozeßwirkungsgrad m <Therm.>
cut-off energy, cut-off	Abschneideenergie f	cyclelog	s. time schedule controller
cut-off energy of beta spectrum	s. maximum energy of beta-ray spectrum	cycle of load	s. cycle of load stressing
cut-off factor; convergence (converging) factor <asymptotic expansion> <math.>	Konvergenzfaktor m <Math.>	cycle of load stressing, cycle of stress[es], stress cycle, cycle of load, load[ing] cycle	Lastspiel n, Lastwechsel m
cut-off factor <theory of fundamental particles>	„cut-off"-Faktor m, Abschneidefaktor m <Elementarteilchentheorie>	cycle of magnetization	Magnetisierungszyklus m
		cycle of stress[es]	s. cycle of load stressing
		cycle per second, cycle/second, cycle, hertz, cps, c/s, c, Hz	Hertz n, Hz
cut-off frequency	Abschneidefrequenz f; Debyesche Maximalfrequenz f <Festkörperphysik>	cycle rate counter	s. cycle counter
		cycle/second	s. cycle per second
cut-off frequency, cut-off, critical frequency <of waveguide, of filter>	Grenzfrequenz f <Hohlleiter, Filter>	cycles of limit load stressing	Grenzlastspielzahl f, Grenz[last]wechselzahl f
		cycles of load stressing, number of cycles of load stressing	Lastspielzahl f, Lastwechselzahl f, Lastspiele npl
cut-off frequency, gain-crossover frequency, gain cross-over frequency <control>	Schnittfrequenz f <Regelung>	cycles [of load stressing] per unit time	Lastspielfrequenz f, Lastwechselfrequenz f
cut-off frequency	s. a. limiting frequency	cycles per unit time	s. a. number of cycles
cut-off length	s. critical length	cycle storage (store), circulating storage (store, memory), cyclic store, cyclic memory, dynamic storage (store)	Umlaufspeicher m, periodischer Speicher m
cut-off method	Abschneidemethode f		
cut-off point, limit point	Grenzpunkt m		
cut-off radius	Abschneideradius m		
cut-off range	s. off-region		
cut-off rod	s. safety rod	cycle time	s. duration of cycle
cut-off time, switch-off period, off-period <semi.>	Sperrzeit f <Halb.>	cyclic; periodic[al]	periodisch [veränderlich]; zyklisch
cut-off velocity	s. critical velocity	cyclic <chem.>	zyklisch, ringförmig, cyclisch, cycl.; zyklisiert
cut-off voltage, cut-off bias	Sperrspannung f, Grenzspannung f; Einsatzspannung f; Unterdrückungsspannung f, Unterdrückungspotential n	cyclic <math.>	zyklisch <Math.>
		cyclic	s. a. circulation <hydr., aero.>
cut-off wave	s. critical wave <of waveguide>	cyclic accelerator, cyclic orbit accelerator	zyklischer Beschleuniger m, Mehrfachbeschleuniger m, Vielfachbeschleuniger m
cut-off wavelength, critical wavelength <of waveguide>	Grenzwellenlänge f, kritische Wellenlänge f, Abschneidewellenlänge f <Hohlleiter>	cyclical stress	s. cyclic stress
		cyclic balance	zyklisches Gleichgewicht n
		cyclic boundary condition	s. Born-von Kármán boundary condition
cut orientation, orientation of the cut	Schnittlage f	cyclic class, cyclic crystal class	zyklische Kristallklasse f
cut-out	s. circuit breaker <el.>	cyclic component	zyklische Komponente f
cut plane	s. plane of the section	cyclic co-ordinates	s. ignorable co-ordinates
cutting	s. notching	cyclic crystal class, cyclic class	zyklische Kristallklasse f
cutting force, force of cut	Schnittkraft f		
cutting reducer	s. subtractive reducer	cyclic determinant, circulant	zyklische Determinante f, Zirkulante f
cutting to size	Zuschnitt m		
c-w laser	s. continuous[-]wave laser	cyclic interchange	s. circular permutation
c-w maser	s. continuous[-]wave maser	cyclic irrotational motion	s. cyclic potential motion
cyanometer	Zyanometer n, Himmelsblaumesser m	cyclic loading	s. fatigue loading
cyanometry	Zyanometrie f, Himmelsblaumessung f	cyclic memory	s. cycle store
cybernetic accelerator	kybernetischer Beschleuniger m	cyclic motion	s. cyclic potential motion
cybotactic, cybotaxic	cybotaktisch, Nahordnungs-	cyclic orbit accelerator	s. cyclic accelerator
		cyclic permutation	s. circular permutation
		cyclic point <math.>	Scheitel m, zyklischer Punkt m <Math.>
cybotactic group	cybotaktische Gruppe f	cyclic potential motion, cyclic irrotational motion, cyclic motion, circulation flow, circulatory flow	Zirkulationsströmung f, zyklische Potentialströmung f, Potentialströmung mit Zirkulation, zirkulatorische Potentialströmung f, zikulatorische Strömung f
cybotactic state	cybotaktischer Zustand m		
cybotaxic	s. cybotactic		
cybotaxis	Cybotaxis f, Nahordnung f in Flüssigkeiten, cybotaktische Struktur f		
cycle	Zyklus m, Kreislauf m		
cycle <astr.>	Zyklus m, Zykel m, Zirkel m, Periode f <Astr.>		
cycle, nucleus, ring <chem.>	Ring m, Kern m, Zyklus m <Chem.>	cyclic shift, end-around (circular, nonarithmetic, ring) shift, register rotation, rotation of register <num. math.>	zyklische Vertauschung f, zyklische Verschiebung f <num. Math.>
cycle <mech.>, stroke	Takt m <Mech.>		
cycle, working cycle <therm.>	Kreisprozeß m, geschlossener Prozeß m <Therm.>		
cycle	s. a. cycle per second	cyclic storage (store)	s. cycle store
cycle	s. a. loop <num.math.>	cyclic stress[ing], cyclical (vibratory, vibrating, oscillating) stress	Schwingspannung f, Schwingungsspannung f, schwingende Spannung f
cycle counter, cycle rate counter	Periodenzähler m		
cycle criterion	Umlauf[s]zahl f, Umwälzzahl f, Zirkulationszahl f; Wasserumlauf[s]zahl f	cyclic structure <chem.>	Ringstruktur f, zyklische Struktur f <Chem.>

cyclic symmetry, cyclosymmetry	zyklische Symmetrie f	cyclonic situation	Tiefdruckwetterlage f, Tiefdrucklage f
cyclic variable [star]	zyklischer Veränderlicher m		
cyclic viscosity	zyklische Viskosität f	cyclonic thunderstorm	Wirbelgewitter n
cyclid[e]	Zyklide f	cyclonic trajectory	Zyklonenbahn f, Zyklonenzugstraße f, Zyklonenweg m
cycling	s. fatigue loading		
cycling [movement]	s. hunting		
cycling time	s. duration of cycle	cyclonic vorticity	s. cyclone low
cyclization, ring closure, ring formation	Zyklisierung f, Ringschluß m, Ringbildung f	cyclonium, Cy	= promethium, Pm
		Cyclopean eye	s. central eye
cycloconverter	Zyklokonverter m	cycloscope, cyclograph, polar co-ordinate oscilloscope, polar co-ordinate oscillograph	Polarkoordinatenoszillograph m, Polarkoordinatenoszilloskop n, Zyklograph m, Zykloskop n
cyclogenesis	Zyklogenesis f, Zyklonenbildung f; Tiefdrucktätigkeit f; Entwicklung f des Zyklons		
		cyclostrophic wind	zyklostrophischer Wind m
		cyclosymmetry, cyclic symmetry	zyklische Symmetrie f
cyclogenetic line	zyklogenetische Linie f	cyclosynchrotron	s. synchrocyclotron
cyclogram	Zyklogramm n	cyclotron	Zyklotron n, Cyclotron n, Cyklotron n
cyclograph	s. cycloscope		
cycloid, cycloidal curve	Zykloide[nkurve] f, Radlinie f, Radkurve f	cyclotron angular frequency	Zyklotronkreisfrequenz f
cycloidal pendulum, cycloid pendulum, Huyghens['] pendulum	Zykloidenpendel n		
		cyclotron beam energy	Zyklotronstrahlenergie f
cycloidal surface	Zykloidenfläche f		
cycloidal wave	Zykloidalwelle f	cyclotron damping	Zyklotrondämpfung f
cycloid pendulum	s. cycloidal pendulum	cyclotron dee	Zyklotronduant m, Zyklotrondee n, Zyklotronelektrode f
cycloinverter	Zyklowechselrichter m, Zykloumrichter m		
		cyclotron effect	Zyklotroneffekt m
cyclolysis	Zyklolyse f, Auflösung f der Zyklone	cyclotron frequency, cyclotron resonance frequency, gyromagnetic (Larmor) frequency	Zyklotron[resonanz]frequenz f, gyromagnetische Frequenz f, Larmor-Frequenz f
cyclometer	s. hodometer		
cyclometric function	s. antitrigonometric[al] function		
cyclonastic	zyklonastisch	cyclotron frequency of the electron	s. electron cyclotron frequency
cyclonasty	Zyklonastie f, Suchbewegung f, Cyclonastie f		
		cyclotron heating, cyclotron resonance heating	Zyklotronresonanz[auf]heizung f, Aufheizung f durch Zyklotronresonanz
cyclone, meteorological depression, depression, low-pressure area, Low, barometric minimum, dip, L <meteo.>	Tiefdruckgebiet n, Tief n, Zyklone f, barometrisches Minimum n, Minimum, Depression f, T <Meteo.>		
		cyclotronic [resonance] mass spectrometer	s. synchrometer
		cyclotron ion source	s. cyclotron-type ion source
cyclone	s. a. mobile cyclone <meteo.>	cyclotron mass spectrometer	s. synchrometer
cyclone	s. a. cyclone separator	cyclotron oscillation, cyclotron pulsation	Zyklotronschwingung f
cyclone	s. a. tropical cyclone		
cyclone dust extractor (separator)	s. cyclone separator	cyclotron radiation	s. synchrotron radiation
		cyclotron resonance, gyromagnetic resonance, gyroresonance; diamagnetic resonance	Zyklotronresonanz f, gyromagnetische Resonanz f, Gyroresonanz f; diamagnetische Resonanz
cyclone low, cyclonic vorticity	Tiefdruckwirbel m, Zyklonenwirbel m, zyklonaler Wirbel m, zyklonale Vorticity f		
		cyclotron resonance frequency	s. cyclotron frequency
cyclone regeneration	Zyklonenregeneration f		
cyclone separator, cyclone; cyclone dust extractor, cyclone dust separator	Zyklon m, Zyklonabscheider m, Zyklonenscheider m, Wirbelsichter m; Zyklonfilter n, Zyklonluftfilter n, Staubfänger m	cyclotron resonance heating	s. cyclotron heating
		cyclotron resonance mass spectrometer	s. synchrometer
		cyclotron-type ion source, cyclotron ion source, ion cyclotron-type source	Zyklotronionenquelle f
		cyclotron wave	Zyklotronwelle f
		cylinder, right circular cylinder, roller	gerader Kreiszylinder m, Walze f, Zylinder m
cyclonic activity	Tiefdrucktätigkeit f, Zyklonentätigkeit f		
		cylinder cathode	s. cylindrical cathode
cyclonic air current (stream)	zyklonale Luftströmung f	cylinder co-ordinates	s. cylindrical co-ordinates
		cylinder dial	Trommelskale f
cyclonic branch, low-pressure branch	Tiefdruckausläufer m, Tiefausläufer m		
cyclonic centre, centre of cyclonic pressure, centre of low-pressure [area], low-pressure centre, depression centre	Tiefdruckkern m, Kern m des Tief[druckgebiet]s, Tiefdruckschwerpunkt m, Tiefdruckzentrum n, zyklonales Zentrum (Druckzentrum) n	cylinder envelope <techn.>; lateral surface of the cylinder, lateral area of the cylinder <math.>	Zylindermantel m
		cylinder function	s. Bessel function
		cylinder glass	s. cylindrical spectacle lens
		cylinder lens	s. cylindrical lens
cyclonic precipitation	s. frontal precipitation	cylinder spectacle lens, cylindrical spectacle lens, cylindrical (cylinder) glass	Zylinderglas n, zylindrisches (astigmatisches) Brillenglas n
cyclonic rain	Zyklonenregen m		
		cylinder wave	s. cylindrical wave
cyclonic shear	zyklonale Scherung f, Zyklonalscherung f	cylindrical anamorphic lens	s. cylindrical lens
		cylindrical anode magnetron	s. diode magnetron

cylindrical

cylindrical barrage	s. roller weir	cytophotometry	Zytophotometrie f
cylindrical capacitor	Zylinderkondensator m	cytoplasm <bio.>	Zytoplasma n, Zellplasma n, Plasma n <Bio.>
cylindrical cathode, cylinder cathode, cathode cylinder	Hohlkatode f, Rundkatode f, Zylinderkatode f, zylindrische (zylinderförmige) Katode f	cytoplasmic membrane	Plasmamembran f
cylindrical chamber	s. cylindrical ionization chamber	cytoplasmic thread <bio.>	Plasmafaden m <Bio.>
cylindrical chronograph	Walzenchronograph m, Zylinderchronograph m	Czochralski['s] method, pulling technique of Czochralski, technique of Czochralski, method of Czochralski	Czochralski-Methode f, Czochralski-Verfahren n, Ziehen n von Kristallen [nach dem Czochralski-Verfahren], Kristallzüchtung f aus der Schmelze nach dem Czochralski-Verfahren
cylindrical coil	s. solenoid		
cylindrical collector (collimator)	s. collimating cylinder		
cylindrical condition	Zylinderbedingung f		
cylindrical co-ordinates, cylinder (cylindrical polar, semi-polar, circular cylindrical) co-ordinates	Zylinderkoordinaten fpl, Kreiszylinderkoordinaten fpl		

D

cylindrical core	s. pot-type core		
cylindrical counter [tube]	zylindrisches Zählrohr n, Zylinderzählrohr n; Topfzählrohr n, Topfzähler m	Dach photometer	s. roof photometer
		daily amount of rainfall	tägliche Niederschlagsmenge (Niederschlagshöhe) f, Tagesniederschlagshöhe f, Tagesmenge f, Tagesergiebigkeit f
cylindrical domain	Zylindergebiet n, Zylinderbereich m		
cylindrical domain	s. a. bubble domain <magn.>		
cylindrical flow	Zylinderströmung f, zylindrische Strömung f	daily amplitude	Tagesamplitude f, Tagesgangamplitude f
cylindrical function	s. Bessel function	daily average	s. daily mean
cylindrical glass	s. cylindrical spectacle lens	daily inequality, diurnal inequality	tägliche Ungleichheit (Ungleichung) f
cylindrical harmonic	s. Bessel function	daily lunar inequality	s. diurnal lunar inequality
cylindrical ionization chamber, cylindrical chamber	Zylinderionisationskammer f, Zylinderkammer f	daily map	Tageskarte f
cylindrical lens, cylinder lens; cylindrical anamorphic lens	Zylinderlinse f	daily mean [value], daily (diurnal) average, diurnal mean [value]	Tagesmittel n, Tagesmittelwert m; mi tlerer Tageswert m
		daily mean value of temperature	s. mean temperature of the day
cylindrically ground joint	Zylinderschliff m	daily periodicity, diurnal periodicity	Tagesperiodizität f, zirkadianer Rhythmus m
cylindrically symmetric, cylindrosymmetric	zylindersymmetrisch		
		daily rhythm; diurnal rhythm	Tagesrhythmus m
cylindrical mirror <opt.>	Zylinderspiegel m <Opt.>	daily runoff, runoff per day	Tagesabflußmenge f, Tagesabfluß m
cylindrical parabolic antenna	Zylinderparaboloidantenne f		
		daily solar inequality	s. diurnal solar inequality
		daily solifluction	Tageszeitensolifluktion f
cylindrical polar co-ordinates	s. cylindrical co-ordinates	daily value, diurnal value	Tageswert m
cylindrical projection	Zylinderprojektion f, Zylinderentwurf m, zylindrische Projektion f, zylindrischer Entwurf m, Zylinderriß m	daily variation	s. diurnal variation
		Dale-Gladstone refraction formula	s. Gladstone and Dale law
		Dalembertian	s. Alembertian / d'
		Dalitz pair	Dalitz-Paar n
cylindrical set	Zylindermenge f	Dalitz plot, phase space plot	Dalitz-Diagramm n, Dalitz-Plot n
cylindrical shell	Zylinderschale f, zylindrische Schale f		
		Dalitz-Tuan resonance	Dalitz-Tuan-Resonanz f
		dalton	Dalton n
cylindrical spectacle lens, cylindrical (cylinder) glass, cylinder spectacle lens	Zylinderglas n, zylindrisches (astigmatisches) Brillenglas n	<= 1,6601 · 10⁻²⁷ kg>	Dalton n $<= 1{,}6601 \cdot 10^{-27}$ kg>
		Dalton['s] equation [of evaporation], Dalton['s] law [of evaporation]	Daltonsche Verdunstungsgleichung f
cylindrical square	Winkeltrommel f	daltonide	Daltonid n, daltonide (Daltonsche) Verbindung f
cylindrical surface	Zylinderfläche f, zylindrische Fläche f		
cylindrical symmetry, cylindrosymmetry	Zylindersymmetrie f, zylindrische Symmetrie f	daltonism	Anerythropsie f, Rotgrünblindheit f, Daltonismus m
cylindrical ungula, ungula of the cylinder	Zylinderhuf m		
cylindrical universe	Zylinderwelt f	Dalton['s] law [of additive pressures]	s. Dalton['s] law [of partial pressures]
		Dalton['s] law [of evaporation]	s. Dalton['s] equation [of evaporation]
cylindrical wave, cylinder wave, two-dimensional wave	Zylinderwelle f, Kreiszylinderwelle f, zweidimensionale Welle f	Dalton['s] law [of partial pressure], Dalton['s] law [of additive pressures], Dalton['s] theory, law of partial pressures, Henry['s] law, Gibbs-Dalton law	Daltonsches Gesetz n, Gesetz der Partialdrücke
cylindrosymmetric, cylindrically symmetric	zylindersymmetrisch		
cylindrosymmetry, cylindrical symmetry	Zylindersymmetrie f, zylindrische Symmetrie f		
cymometer	s. wavemeter	Dalton['s] scale, Dalton['s] temperature scale	Daltonsche Temperaturskala f, Dalton-Skala f
cymoscope, wave indicator	Wellenanzeiger m, Wellenindikator m		
		Dalton['s] theory	s. Dalton['s] law [of partial pressures]
cyster shell marking [in the fatigue fracture], clam-shell mark [in the fatigue fracture], arrest line, fatigue crescent	Rastlinie f [am Dehnungsbruch]		
		dam, retaining dam (dike); weir <hydr.>	Talsperre f, Sperre f; Staudamm m, Staumauer f, Stauwerk n, Stauwehr n, Sperrdamm m, Sperrmauer f, Sperranlage f
cytokinesis	Zytokinese f, Zytoplasmateilung f, Plasmateilung f		

damage curve, damage line Schadenslinie *f*
damage of the material due to long-term alternating strain Zerrüttung *f* <Werkstoff>, Schädigung *f* durch Dauerschwingbeanspruchung
dam crest *s.* crest of the weir
dam embankment, embankment of the dam Wehrkörper *m*, Staumauerkörper *m*
Damköhler['s] first ratio, Damköhler number, Dam Damköhlerscher Koeffizient *m*, Damköhlersche Zahl *f*, Dam, *Da*
damming *s.* water-surface ascent
dam on bed of river *s.* submerged weir
damp *s.* humidity
damped oscillation, decadent oscillation gedämpfte Schwingung *f*
damped periodic instrument gedämpft schwingendes Meßgerät *n*
dampening *s.* humidification
damp haze *s.* drizzling fog
damping <process; quantity> Dämpfung *f* <Vorgang; Größe>
damping <el.>, one-over-Q value, 1/Q value, degree of damping <el.> Dämpfungsfaktor *m*, Dämpfungsgrad *m*, Dämpfung *f* <El.>
damping *s. a.* humidity
damping *s. a.* dying out <of an oscillation>
damping *s. a.* dimming <of light>
damping *s. a.* introduction of additional damping
damping *s.* fading
damping along the line *s.* attenuation along the line
damping capacity *s.* viscosity
damping capacity of the material *s.* mechanical hysteresis
damping coefficient *s.* damping exponent
damping coefficient *s.* acoustic absorption factor
damping constant *s. a.* damping exponent
damping diode *s.* efficiency diode
damping exponent (factor), damping constant (coefficient), attenuation constant (coefficient, factor), specific damping Dämpfungsexponent *m*, Dämpfungskonstante *f*, Dämpfungsmodul *m*, Dämpfungsziffer *f*, Dämpfungsfaktor *m*, Dämpfungskoeffizient *m*
damping factor *s. a.* ballistic factor
damping factor *s. a.* acoustic absorption factor <ac.>
damping force <damped oscillations> Dämpfungskraft *f*, Reibungskraft *f* <gedämpfte Schwingungen>
damping function Dämpfungsfunktion *f*
damping in the pass band, pass-band damping Lochdämpfung *f*, Durchlaßdämpfung *f*; Grunddämpfung *f*
damping material *s.* sound insulator <ac.>
damping moment Dämpfungsmoment *n*
damping of oscillations Schwingungsdämpfung *f*
damping of sound *s.* attenuation of sound
damping period Beruhigungszeit *f*
damping pole Dämpfungspol *m*, Unendlichkeitsstelle *f* der Wellendämpfung
damping ratio *s.* decrement
damping resistance (resistor) *s.* attenuator <el.>
damping term *s.* reaction force
dam with frames and needles *s.* needle dam
dam with lifting gates, weir with lifting gates Schützenwehr *n*
Dancoff-Ginzburg correction Dancoff-Ginzburg-Korrektion *f*
dangerous cross-section *s.* dangerous section
dangerous cylinder gefährlicher Zylinder *m*
dangerous diagram gefährliches Diagramm *n*
dangerous locus, dangerous surface gefährlicher Ort *m*, gefährliche Fläche *f*
dangerous section, dangerous cross-section, most strained section gefährlicher Querschnitt *m*, gefährdeter Querschnitt
dangerous surface *s.* dangerous locus

dangling bond *s.* unsaturated bond
daniell = 1,042 V°
Daniell cell, Daniell standard cell, double-fluid cell Daniell-Element *n*, Daniell-Normalelement *n*
Daniell tap Daniellscher Hahn *m*
daraf <= 1 V/C> Daraf *n* <= 1 V/C>
Darboux integral Darbouxsches Integral *n*
darcy, D, d Darcy *n*, D
Darcy['s] coefficient *s.* resistance coefficient <hydr.>
Darcy['s] equation, Darcy['s] formula, Darcy['s] law, hydraulic friction formula Darcysches Gesetz *n*, Filtergesetz *n*, hydraulische Reibungsformel *f*
Darcy impact-pressure tube Darcysches Staurohr *n*
Darcy['s] law *s.* Darcy['s] formula
dark absorption marking *s.* filament <in Sun spectrograms>
dark adaptation Dunkeladaptation *f*, Dunkelstimmung *f*
dark adaptation curve Dunkeladaptationskurve *f*
dark-adapted eye dunkeladaptiertes Auge *n*, Dunkelauge *n*
dark burn of the phosphor, fatigue of the phosphor Ermüdung *f* des Leuchtstoffs
dark cloud, dark nebula Dunkelnebel *m*, Dunkelwolke *f*
dark companion, invisible companion unsichtbarer (dunkler) Begleiter *m*
dark conduction Dunkelleitung *f*
dark conductivity Dunkelleitfähigkeit *f*
dark current Dunkelstrom *m*; photoelektrischer (lichtelektrischer) Dunkeleffekt *m*
dark discharge *s.* Townsend discharge
darkened circle, full circle voller (dunkler, schwarzer) Kreis *m*
Darken equations Darkensche Gleichungen *fpl*
darkening *s.* black[-]out
darkening towards the limb, limb darkening <opt., astr.> Randverdunklung *f* <Opt., Astr.>
dark field, dark ground Dunkelfeld *n*
dark-field condenser Dunkelfeldkondensor *m*
dark-field illumination Dunkelfeldbeleuchtung *f*
dark-field microscopy Dunkelfeldmikroskopie *f*
dark-field microscopy in transmitted light *s.* transmitted-light dark-field microscopy
dark-field vertical illumination Auflicht-Dunkelfeldbeleuchtung *f*, Außenbeleuchtung *f*
dark flame *s.* blue flame
dark flocculus *s.* filament <in Sun spectrograms>
dark ground *s.* dark field
dark hydrogen flocculus *s.* filament <in Sun spectrograms>
dark intensification *s.* blanking
dark interval, dark period Dunkelzeit *f*, Dunkelperiode *f*
dark lane dunkler Absorptionsstreifen (Streifen) *m*
dark light *s.* black light
dark-line spectrum *s.* absorption spectrum
dark marking *s.* filament <in Sun spectrograms>
dark nebula, dark cloud Dunkelnebel *m*, Dunkelwolke *f*
dark-orange heat Dunkelorangeglut *f* <1100 °C>
dark period, dark interval Dunkelzeit *f*, Dunkelperiode *f*
dark period <bio.> Dunkelperiode *f* <Bio.>
dark pulse Dunkelstromimpuls *m*, Dunkelimpuls *m*
dark radiation *s.* black light
dark radiation *s.* obscure radiation
dark reaction, Blackman reaction Dunkelreaktion *f*, Blackman-Reaktion *f*, chemische Reaktion *f* <Photosynthese>
dark-red heat, dull-red heat, low-red heat Dunkelrotglut *f* <700 °C>

dark resistance	Dunkelwiderstand *m*	Davis-Gibson colour filter	Davis-Gibson-Filter *n*
darkroom safelight filter	*s.* safelight filter	Davisson-Germer['s] experiment	Davisson-Germer-Versuch *m*, Versuch *m* von Davisson und Germer
dark segment¹	*s.* Earth's shadow		
dark space	Dunkelraum *m*		
dark space of the corona discharge	Rumpf *m* (Transportzone *f*) der Koronaentladung	Davis['] theory of cycles	Zykluslehre *f* von Davis
		Davydov splitting	Dawydow-Aufspaltung *f*
dark-trace screen	Leuchtschirm *m* der Dunkelschriftröhre	Davy['s] experiment	Davyscher Versuch *m*
		davyum	= rhenium
dark-trace tube	*s.* skiatron	Dawes limit	Dawes-Grenze *f*
dart leader	Pfeilleader *m*, pfeilförmig vordringende Vorentladung *f*, Pfeilleitblitz *m*	dawn	Morgendämmerung *f*
		dawn chorus	Dämmerungschor *m* <Whistler>
dart[-]over	*s.* spark[-]over		
Darwin-Fowler method	*s.* Fowler-Darwin method <therm.>	day, d	Tag *m*, d
		day airglow, day glow	Taghimmelsleuchten *n*
dash-dot line	*s.* dot-and-dash line		
dashed curve, dashed line, dash curve (line)	gestrichelte Linie *f*	daylight factor	Tageslichtquotient *m*, Tageslichtfaktor *m*
dashed curve (line)	*s. a.* dotted curve	daylight fluctuation	*s.* fluctuation of daylight illumination
dashing of the waves	*s. a.* dash curve		
dashing rule	*s.* beating	daylight illumination, daylighting	Tageslichtbeleuchtung *f*, Tagesbeleuchtung *f*, natürliche Beleuchtung *f*
dash[-]pot	Strichregel *f*		
dashpot dampening, oil damping	"dash-pot" *m*, Dämpfer *m* Öldämpfung *f*		
		daylight lamp	Tageslichtlampe *f*
data amplifier	Meßwertverstärker *m*	day-light meteor, day-time meteor	Tageslichtmeteor *n*
data printer	*s.* printer		
data processing	*s.* evaluation <of dates>	daylight photometer, hemaraphotometer	Tageslichtphotometer *n*
date line, international date line	Datumgrenze *f*, Datumsgrenze *f*, Datumslinie *f*		
		daylight spectrum	Tageslichtspektrum *n*
		daylight visibility [distance]	Tagessichtweite *f*, Tagessicht *f*
dating, age estimation (determination, measurement), determination of age	Altersbestimmung *f*, Datierung *f*		
		day-night effect	*s.* diurnal variation
		day period / 27-	*s.* twenty-seven-day recurrence effect
dative bond, dative covalence, mixed double bond co-ordinate (co-ordination, co-ordinative) bond, semipolar [double] bond, semi-ionic bond	koordinative (kovalentdative, semipolare) Bindung *f*, Koordinationsbindung *f*, semipolare (halbpolare) Doppelbindung *f*	day side	Tagseite *f*
		day-time meteor, day-light meteor	Tageslichtmeteor *n*
		day-time meteor shower, day-time stream	Tageslichtstrom *m* <Meteore>
dative bond	*s. a.* back donation	day-time train	Tageslichtschweif *m*, Tagschweif *m* <Meteor>
dative covalence	*s.* dative bond		
dative valence	Koordinationsvalenz *f*, semipolare Valenz *f*	day-time wave	Tag[es]welle *f*
		dazzle[ment]; glare; glare blinding	Blendung *f*
datum level (plane), reference datum; null plane	Nullebene *f*; Bezugsebene *f*		
		dazzle source, source of glare	Blendquelle *f*
datum point	Normalhöhepunkt *m*, N. H., NH	D-case, R-symmetric case	R-symmetrischer Fall *m*, D-Fall *m*
		D-D reaction	*s.* deuteron-deuteron reaction
Daubresse prism	Daubresse-Prisma *n*	de-acceleration	*s.* deceleration <mech.>
dauermodification, permanent modification	Dauermodifikation *f*	deactivation	*s.* inactivation
		de[-]activation cross-section, cross-section for de[-]activation	Entaktivierungs[wirkungs]querschnitt *m*, Desaktivierungs[wirkungs]querschnitt *m*, Wirkungsquerschnitt *m* für (der) Entaktivierung, Wirkungsquerschnitt für (der) Desaktivierung
daughter, decay product, disintegration product, progeny, daughter product <nucl.>	Zerfallsprodukt *n*, Folgeprodukt *n*, Nachfolgeprodukt *n*, Tochterprodukt *n*, Tochtersubstanz *f* <Kern.>		
daughter	*s. a.* daughter atom		
daughter	*s. a.* daughter element		
daughter	*s. a.* daughter nucleus	dead angle	toter Winkel *m*
daughter activity	Tochteraktivität *f*, Aktivität *f* des Folgeprodukts		
daughter atom	Folgeatom *n*, Atom *n* des Folgeprodukts, Tochteratom *n*	dead band	unwirksamer Bereich *m*
		dead-beat [aperiodical]	*s.* aperiodic
		dead centre, dead point	Totpunkt *m*, toter Punkt *m*; Umkehrpunkt *m*
daughter decay	Tochterzerfall *m*		
daughter element	Folgeelement *n*, Tochterelement *n*, Abkömmling *m*	deadened room	*s.* anechoic chamber <ac.>
		deadening	*s.* sound insulation
daughter fraction	Tochterfraktion *f*, Anteil *m* der Zerfallsprodukte	dead load	*s.* permanent load <mech.>
		dead point	*s.* dead centre
daughter nucleus	Folgekern *m*, Tochterkern *m*, Abkömmling *m*	dead point position	Totpunktlage *f*, Totlage *f*
		dead room	*s.* anechoic chamber <ac.>
daughter product	*s.* daughter <nucl.>	dead space	schädliches Volumen *n*, schädlicher (toter) Raum *m*, Totraum *m*
Dauphiné twin	Dauphinéer Zwilling *m*		
Dauphiné-type law	Dauphinéer Gesetz *n*	dead-stop titration, biamperometric titration	Stillstandtitration *f*, "dead-stop"-Titration *f*

dead tide	s. neap tide	Debye-Jauncey scattering	Debye-Jauncey-Streuung f
dead time ⟨of counter⟩	Totzeit f ⟨Zählrohr⟩	Debye-Keesom force	Debye-Keesom-Kraft f
dead time	s. a. hangover time	Debye length, Debye['s] shielding (screening) distance, screening radius, Debye-Hückel parameter, radius of the ionic atmosphere	Debye-Länge f, Debye-Radius m, Abschirmradius m, Debye[-Hückel]scher Radius m, Debye-Hückelscher Parameter m
dead time correction	s. resolving time correction		
dead time loss	Totzeitverlust m		
dead volcano, quiescent (dormant) volcano	untätiger Vulkan m		
dead water	s. wake space		
dead weight load	s. permanent load ⟨mech.⟩	Debye number	Debyesche Zahl f, Debye-Zahl f
dead-weight piston (pressure) gauge, dead-weight tester	s. manometric balance	Debye parameter	s. Debye temperature
		Debye-Picht formula	Debye-Pichtsche Formel f [der beugungsoptischen Abbildung]
dead zone	s. silent zone		
deaeration	Entlüftung f, Luftaustreibung f, Austreibung (Verdrängung) f der Luft, Luftverdrängung f	Debye potential	Debyesches Potential n, Debye-Potential n
		Debye-Ramm restriction of internal rotation	Debye-Rammsche Rotationsbehinderung f
deafening	s. sound insulation		
deamplification	s. fading	Debye-Scherrer-Hull method	s. Debye-Scherrer method
Dean number	Deansche Zahl f, Dean-Zahl f	Debye-Scherrer interference; Debye-Scherrer interference fringe	Debye-Scherrer-Interferenz f, Röntgenstrahlinterferenz f nach Debye-Scherrer
deaquation	s. dehydration		
deathnium ⟨semi.⟩	Rekombinationsstelle f, Rekombinationszentrum n, Deathnium n ⟨Halb.⟩		
		Debye-Scherrer line	Debye-Scherrer-Linie f, Debye-Scherrer-Kurve f
deattenuation	s. reduction of the damping		
débâcle	s. mud stream	Debye-Scherrer method, powder diffraction method, powder-crystal method [of X-ray diffraction], Debye-Scherrer-Hull method, powder photography, powder method (diffractometry)	Debye-Scherrer-Verfahren n, Debye-Scherrer-Methode f, Pulvermethode f, Pulververfahren n, Pulverbeugungsverfahren n, Debye-Scherrersche Methode f
deblocking ⟨ferromagnetism⟩	Entarretierung f ⟨Ferromagnetismus⟩		
Debot effect ⟨phot.⟩	Debot-Effekt m ⟨Phot.⟩		
debris cone, dejection cone, alluvial cone	Schutthalde f, Schuttkegel m, Ablagerungskegel m, Geschiebekegel m, Geröllkegel m, Schutthügel m; Schwemmkegel m, Schwemmfächer m		
		Debye-Scherrer pattern, powder[ed-crystal] pattern, powder diagram (photograph), [X-ray] powdered-crystal photograph	Debye-Scherrer-Aufnahme f, Debye-Scherrer-Diagramm n, Pulverdiagramm n, Pulverbeugungsaufnahme f, Debye-Aufnahme f, Debye-Diagramm n, Debyeogramm n
debris flow	s. mud stream		
debunching	Entpaketisierung f, Bündelzerstreuung f		
debye, Debye unit, D ⟨= 10⁻¹⁹ e.s.u.⟩	Debye n, D ⟨= 10⁻¹⁹ esE⟩	Debye-Scherrer-type neutron diffraction pattern	Neutronenbeugungsaufnahme f vom Debye-Scherrer-Typ
Debye approximation, Debye-Hückel approximation	Debyesche Näherung f, Debye-[Hückelsche] Näherung f	Debye screening distance	s. Debye length
Debye-Bromwich potential	Debye-Bromwich-Potential n	Debye-Sears cell	Debye-Sears-Zelle f
Debye characteristic temperature	s. Debye temperature	Debye-Sears effect	Debye-Sears-Effekt m, Beugung f des Lichtes an Ultraschallwellen
Debye['s] cube law, Debye['s] T^3-law, Debye T^3 approximation	Debyesches Gesetz n, T^3-Gesetz n [der spezifischen Wärmen], Debyesches T^3-Gesetz [der spezifischen Wärmen], Debyesche T^3-Näherung f	Debye-Sears pattern	Debye-Sears-Diagramm n
		Debye['s] shielding distance	s. Debye length
		Debye sphere	Debyesche Kugel f, Debye-Kugel f
Debye cut-off frequency	s. Debye frequency	Debye T^3 approximation	s. Debye['s] cube law
Debye['s] dipole theory	Debyesche Dipoltheorie f (Theorie f der Dipolorientierung)	Debye temperature, Debye characteristic temperature, characteristic [Debye] temperature, Debye Θ, Debye parameter	Debye-Temperatur f, charakteristische [Debyesche] Temperatur f, Debyesche charakteristische Temperatur, Debye-Parameter m
Debye effect	Debye-Effekt m		
Debye energy	s. induction energy		
Debye-Falkenhagen effect, dispersion of conductance	Debye-Falkenhagen-Effekt m, elektrolytischer Debye-Effekt m, Dispersionseffekt m der Leitfähigkeit		
		Debye['s] T^3-law	s. Debye['s] cube law
		Debye unit, debye, D ⟨= 10⁻¹⁹ e.s.u.⟩	Debye n, D ⟨= 10⁻¹⁹ esE⟩
Debye-formula, Langevin-Debye equation (formula)	[Langevin-]Debyesche Formel f	Debye-Waller factor, Debye-Waller temperature factor, Lamb-Mössbauer factor	Debye-Wallerscher Temperaturfaktor (Faktor) m, Debye-Waller-Faktor m, Debyescher Temperaturfaktor (Wärmefaktor m), Temperaturfaktor
Debye frequency, Debye cut-off frequency	Debye-Frequenz f, Debyesche Frequenz (Abschneidefrequenz) f		
Debye frequency spectrum	Debyesches Frequenzspektrum n		
Debye function	Debye-Funktion f, Debyesche Funktion f	Debye wave	Debye-Welle f
		deca..., da, D	Deka..., da
Debye-Hückel approximation	s. Debye approximation	decade average, decade mean, ten-days average	Dekadenmittel n, Zehntagemittel n
Debye-Hückel charge cloud	s. ion cloud ⟨el., chem.⟩		
Debye-Hückel equation (law, limiting law), Debye-Hückel-Onsager equation; Onsager conductivity equation	Debye-Hückel[-Onsager]-sche Gleichung f, Debye-Hückelsches Grenzgesetz n	decade bridge	Dekadenmeßbrücke f, Dekadenbrücke f
		decade capacitance box, capacitance decade [box]	Kapazitätsdekade f, dekadischer Kondensator m, Dekaden[normal]kondensator m, Stufenkondensator m, C-Dekade f
Debye-Hückel parameter	s. Debye length		
Debye-Hückel theory	Debye-Hückel-Theorie f, Debye-Hückel[-Falkenhagen]sche Theorie f	decade conductance box	dekadischer Wirkleitwert m, Leitwertdekade f

decade 156

decade-counter tube, decade counting tube	dekadische Zählröhre *f*, Dekadenzählröhre *f*, Dezimalzählröhre *f*	decay branch	s. branch of the radioactive family
decade inductance box, decadic inductance box, inductance decade	Induktivitätsdekade *f*, L-Dekade *f*, dekadische Induktivität *f*, 'Dekadeninduktivität *f*	decay chain	s. disintegration chain
		decay channel	Zerfallskanal *m*, Zerfallsrichtung *f*, Zerfallsweg *m*
decade mean	s. decade average	decay characteristic, persistence characteristic ‹of luminescence›	Abklingcharakteristik *f*, Abfallcharakteristik *f*, Zerfallscharakteristik *f* ‹Lumineszenz›
decadent oscillation	s. damped oscillation		
decade resistance box	Dekadenwiderstand *m*, Dekadenrheostat *m*, Widerstandsdekade *f*, R-Dekade *f*, Stufenwiderstand *m*	decay characteristic ‹nucl.›	Zerfallscharakteristik *f* ‹Kern.›
		decay coefficient	s. decay constant
decade scaler, decascaler, scale decade; scale of ten circuit	dekadischer Untersetzer *m*, Dekadenuntersetzer *m*, Dekadenzähler *m*, Zehnfachuntersetzer *m*, Untersetzungsdekade *f*; dekadische Untersetzungsschaltung *f*, Zehnfachuntersetzungsschaltung *f*	decay constant, disintegration constant, radioactive decay (disintegration) constant, decay coefficient (factor), transformation (transmutation) constant	Zerfallskonstante *f*, radioaktive Zerfallskonstante
		decay constant [of luminescence]	Abklingkonstante *f*, Geschwindigkeitskonstante (Zerfallskonstante) *f* der Lumineszenz
decade scaling	dekadische Untersetzung *f*, Zehnfachuntersetzung *f*, Dekadenzählung *f*	decay current	Ausschwingstrom *m*; Abfallstrom *m*
decadic digit	s. hartley	decay curve ‹of luminescence; oscillation›	Abklingkurve *f*, Abklingungskurve *f* ‹Lumineszenz; Schwingung›; Zerfallskurve *f* ‹Lumineszenz›
decadic inductance box	s. decade inductance box		
decadic molar absorptivity	dekadische molekulare Absorptionskonstante *f*, molekularer Absorptionsmodul *m*; dekadische molekulare Extinktionskonstante *f*, molekularer Extinktionsmodul *m*		
		decay curve, activity curve, disintegration curve ‹nucl.›	Zerfallskurve *f*, Aktivitätskurve *f* ‹Kern.›
decalescence	Dekaleszenz *f*		
decalescence point, critical point of decalescence, transformation point on heating	Haltepunkt *m* der Erhitzungslinie, Haltepunkt (kritischer Punkt *m*) bei der Erwärmung	decay electron, disintegration electron	Zerfallselektron *n*
		decay energy	s. disintegration energy
		decay factor	s. decay constant
decameter	Dekameter *n*, DK-Messer *m*	decay function ‹nucl.›	Zerfallsfunktion *f* ‹Kern.›
decametric wave	Dekameterwelle *f*	decay half-time, half-time of decay	Rückenhalbwertzeit *f*, Rückenhalbwertsdauer *f*
decametric wavelength [range]	s. high-frequency range	decaying current impulse	abklingender Stromimpuls *m*
decanning	s. dismantling		
decantation, decanting, settling, sedimentation ‹chem.›	Absitzenlassen *n*, Abstehenlassen *n*, Absetzenlassen *n*; Klärung *f*; Absitzen *n*, Absetzen *n*, Abstehen *n*; Stehenlassen *n* ‹Chem.›	decaying nucleus	s. radioactive nucleus
		decaying turbulence	abklingende Turbulenz *f*
		decay law, law of decay	Abklinggesetz *n*, Abklingungsgesetz *n*
decantation, decanting; pouring into another vessel ‹chem.›	Dekantieren *n*, Dekantation *f*, Abgießen *n*; Umgießen *n*, Umschütten *n*, Umfüllen *n* ‹Chem.›	decay law [of atomic nucleus]	s. law of radioactive disintegration
		decay luminescence	Zerfallsleuchten *n*, Zerfallslumineszenz *f*
decanting pipet[te]	Überlaufpipette *f*		
		decay mean free path, decay path	[mittlere freie] Zerfallsweglänge *f*, Zerfallsweg *m*
decarbonization	Entkarbonisierung *f*		
decarbonization, decarburization	Entkohlung *f*, Kohlenstoffentzug *m*; Frischen *n*	decay modulus	= reciprocal of damping exponent
decascaler	s. decade scaler	decay of field, field decay	Feldabfall *m*, Feldzerfall *m*, Abfall (Zerfall) *m* des Feldes
decay, decrease, diminution, fall, droop[ing], drop, degradation	Abfall *m*, Abnahme *f*, Absinken *n*, Fallen *n*, Kleinerwerden *n*, Rückgang *m*, Sinken *n*, Verminderung *f*, Verringerung *f*		
		decay of magnetic flux	s. magnetic decay
		decay of radioactivity, activity decay	Aktivitätsabfall *m*
		decay of sawtooth signal	Sägezahnrücklauf *m*
decay, ‹of atomic nucleus›, nuclear (radioactive, atomic) decay, disintegration [of atomic nucleus], nuclear (radioactive, atomic) disintegration	Zerfall *m* [des Atomkerns], Kernzerfall *m*, radioaktiver Zerfall, Atomzerfall *m*	decay of sunspot group	Auflösung *f* der Fleckengruppe
		decay of the mu-meson (muon), mu-meson decay, muon decay	Zerfall *m* des Myons, Myonzerfall *m*, μ-Zerfall *m*, My-Zerfall *m*, Muonzerfall *m*
		decay of the pi-meson, pi-meson decay, pion decay	Zerfall *m* des Pi-Mesons, Pionzerfall *m*, π-Zerfall *m*, Pi-Zerfall *m*
decay, dying out ‹of luminescence, fluorescence, or phosphorescence›; luminescent decay; fluorescent decay; phosphorescent decay	Abklingen *n*, Abfall *m*, Zerfall *m* ‹Lumineszenz, Fluoreszenz *oder* Phosphoreszenz›; Lumineszenzabfall *m*; Lumineszenzzerfall *m*; Fluoreszenzabfall *m*; Fluoreszenzzerfall *m*; Phosphoreszenzabfall *m*, Phosphoreszenzzerfall *m*	decay of vorticity (whirls)	s. dissipation of vorticity
		decay particle, disintegration particle	Zerfallsteilchen *n*
		decay path	s. decay mean free path
		decay period, cooling period ‹of radioactive substances›	Abklingzeit *f*, Abkühlzeit *f* ‹Aktivitäten›
decay	s. a. dying out		
decay	s. a. dying out ‹of activity›	decay period	s. a. transmutation period ‹nucl.›
decay	s. a. weathering	decay probability, disintegration probability	Zerfallswahrscheinlichkeit *f*
decay analysis, disintegration analysis	Zerfallsanalyse *f*		
		decay product	s. daughter ‹nucl.›

decay proton, disintegration proton	Zerfallsproton n	declination, magnetic declination (variation), angle of declination, declination angle, variation of the compass; magnetic deviation	Deklination f, magnetische Deklination, magnetische Mißweisung f, Mißweisung
decay rate	s. rate of decay		
decay rate	s. disintegration rate <nucl.>		
decay scheme	s. disintegration scheme		
decay series	s. disintegration series		
decay time, dying-out time, die-away time	Abklingzeit f, Abklingdauer f	declination <astr.>	Deklination f, Abweichung f <Astr.>
decay time <of pulse>	Abfallzeit f <Impuls>	declinational tide	Deklinationstide f
		declination angle	s. declination
decay time <of luminescence>	Zerfallszeit f, Abklingzeit f <Lumineszenz>	declination axis	Deklinationsachse f
decay time	s. a. transmutation period <nucl.>	declination chart, declination map, variation chart, variation map	Deklinationskarte f, Mißweisungskarte f, Karte f der magnetischen Mißweisungen, Variationskarte f
decay time	s. a. fall time <el.>		
decay time constant	Abklingzeitkonstante f		
		declination compass	s. declinatoire
		declination map	s. declination chart
decay towards the edge, decrease towards the edge	Randabfall m	declination variometer, D-variometer	Deklinationsvariometer n, D-Variometer n
decelerating electrode, retarding electrode, decelerator	Verzögerungselektrode f, Verlangsamungselektrode f, Bremselektrode f	declinatoire, decline compass, declination compass	Deklinatorium n, Deklinationsbussole f, Abweichungskompaß m
decelerating lens	s. delay lens	decline in potential	s. potential drop
decelerating rocket; braking rocket, brake rocket [engine], retrorocket, retrograde rocket	Bremsrakete f	declinometer	Deklinationsnadel f, Deklinationsmesser m, Deklinometer n
		declivity, slope <geo.>	Hang m <Geo.>
		decoherence	Entfrittung f
		decoherer	Dekohärer m, Entfritter m
deceleration, de-acceleration, negative acceleration, retardation, delay, drag acceleration <mech.>	Verzögerung f, Verlangsamung f, negative Beschleunigung f, Bremsung f <Mech.>	decohesion	Dekohäsion f, Aufhebung f der Kohäsionskräfte, Ablösung f, Lösung f
		decoloring <US>	s. decolouring
		decolorization <US>	s. decolourization
deceleration energy, running-out energy	Auslaufenergie f	decolorizing <US>	s. decolouring
		decolouring (decolourization)	s. discolouration
deceleration force	verzögernde Kraft f, Verzögerungskraft f	decomposable operator	zerlegbarer Operator m
deceleration parachute	s. retarding parachute	decomposable representation	zerlegbare (zerfallbare, vollreduzible, ganz reduzible) Darstellung f
deceleration radiation	s. bremsstrahlung		
decelerator <bio.>	Dezelerator m, Decelerator m <Bio.>	decomposed layer, weathered layer	Verwitterungsschicht f
decelerator	s. a. decelerating electrode	decomposition, dying out, collapse <of field>	Abbau m, Zusammenbruch m <Feld>
decelerometer	Verzögerungsmesser m, Dezelerometer n	decomposition <of representation>	Zerlegung f, Ausreduzierung f <Darstellung>
December solstice, winter solstice	Wintersolstitium n, Wintersonnenwende f	decomposition, degradation <chem.>	Abbau m, stufenweise Zerlegung f <Chem.>
dechannel[l]ing	Dekanalisierung f, „dechannel[l]ing" n	decomposition <of the vector into its components>, resolution, resolving	Zerlegung f <des Vektors in seine Komponenten>, Komponentenzerlegung f
deci..., d	Dezi..., d		
decibel, dB, db	Dezibel n, dB; db		
decibel per milliwatt, dBm, DBM	Dezibel n, bezogen auf 1 mW, dBm	decomposition	s. a. weathering
		decomposition	s. a. chemical decomposition <chem.>
decibel per watt, DBW, dbw	Dezibel n, bezogen auf 1 W, dBW	decomposition	s. a. chemical weathering <geo.>
decidability	Entscheidbarkeit f	decomposition	s. a. division
decile	Dezil n	decomposition by radiation	s. radiolysis
decimal absorption coefficient	s. decimal extinction coefficient <opt.>	decomposition halo	Zersetzungshof m
decimal absorption index	dekadischer Absorptionsindex m	decomposition heat	s. heat of decomposition
decimal digit	s. hartley	decomposition into factors	s. factoring
decimal extinction	s. internal optical density		
decimal extinction coefficient, extinction coefficient; [decimal] absorption coefficient, absorbance index <opt.>	[dekadischer] Extinktionsmodul m, dekadische Extinktionskonstante f; dekadische Absorptionskonstante f <Opt.>	decomposition into partial fractions, partial fraction expansion, expressing in partial fractions	Partialbruchzerlegung f
		decomposition of force[s]	s. resolution of force[s]
decimal extinction index	dekadischer Extinktionsindex m	decomposition of spectral line	Feinzerlegung f
decimal logarithm	s. Brigg['s] logarithm	decomposition of the molecule	s. molecular decomposition
decimal optical density	s. internal optical density		
decimal scaler; scale of 10^n circuit	Dezimaluntersetzer m, 10^nfach-Untersetzer m, Zehnfachuntersetzer m	decomposition of the motion, motion decomposition	Zerlegung f der Bewegung
decimal turbidity coefficient [of Ångström]	dekadischer Trübungskoeffizient m [nach Ångström]	decomposition of the space <in dissections>	Zerlegung f des Raumes <in Gebiete>
		decomposition of unity	Zerlegung f der Eins
decimetre wave	s. ultra-high frequency wave <100 — 10 cm>	decomposition point, decomposition temperature	Zersetzungspunkt m, Zersetzungstemperatur f, Zerfallstemperatur f, Z.
decimetric wavelength [range]	s. ultra-high frequency range	decomposition potential	Zersetzungspotential n
decinormal, tenth-normal, 0.1 N, N/10	zehntelnormal, dezinormal, 0,1 n, n/10		
decision content	s. information content	decomposition pressure	Zersetzungsdruck m, Zersetzungsspannung f
decision function	Entscheidungsfunktion f		
decladding	s. dismantling	decomposition temperature	s. decomposition point

decomposition

decomposition theorem	Zerlegungssatz m	de-emphasis, postemphasis	Deakzentuierung f, Deemphasis f
decomposition value	Zersetzungskoeffizient m	deenergization; de-energizing; de-excitation	Aberregung f, Entregung f, Schwingungsentregung f, Abregung f
decomposition voltage	Zersetzungsspannung f		
decompression	s. pressure relief		
decompression	s. expansion <of gases>	deep, deep of the river	Flußstrecke f, Tiefwasserstrecke f des Flusses
decompressor, expansion engine, expansion machine	Expansionsmaschine f, Ausdehnungsmaschine f, Detander m	deep acceptor level, deep-lying acceptor level	tiefliegendes Akzeptorniveau n
decontaminant, decontaminating agent, decontaminating substance	Dekontaminationsmittel n, Dekontaminierungsmittel n, Entseuchungsmittel n	deep current <in the oceans>	Tiefenströmung f; Tiefenstrom m <im Meer>
decontamination	Dekontamination f, Entseuchung f, Entaktivierung f	deep donor level, deep-lying donor level	tiefliegendes Donatorniveau n
decontamination factor	Dekontaminationsfaktor m, Dekontaminationsgrad m, Entseuchungsfaktor m, Entseuchungsgrad m	deep drawing in steps <met.>	Stufenzieh[verfahr]en n <Met.>
		deep drawing with pressure pads, deep drawing with prevention of wrinkling	Tiefziehen n mit Faltenhaltung, Tiefziehen mit Niederhalter
decontamination index	Dekontaminationsindex m, Entseuchungsindex m		
decontamination ratio	Dekontaminationsverhältnis n	deepening <of colour>; black[-]out, blacking-out; darkening; dimming, subduing <of light>; damping <of light> <opt.>	Verdunklung f; Abdunkeln n; Lichtdämpfung f <Opt.>
deconvolution, unfolding <of spectrum>	Dekonvolution f, Entfaltung f <Spektrum>, Rücktransformation f in das wahre Spektrum	deepening <of the depression>	Vertiefung f <der Depression>, Zyklonenverstärkung f, Zyklonenvertiefung f
decoration technique	Dekorationsverfahren n, „decoration"-Methode f		
decorporation	Dekorporierung f, Dekorporation f, Ausscheidung f	deepening of the front	Verschärfung f der Front
decoupling	Entkopplung f	deep fade, deep fading	Tiefschwund m
		deep-focus earthquake	Tiefenbeben n, Tief[herd]beben n
decrease	s. decay	deep ionization, ionization in depth	Tiefenionisation f
decrease	s. dying out <of an oscillation>	deep-lying acceptor level	s. deep acceptor level
decrease in brightness, loss in brightness, penumbral effect	Helligkeitsabfall m	deep-lying donor level	s. deep donor level
		deep-ocean, deep-water; abyssal	Tiefsee-; Abyssal-, abyssal, abyssisch
decrease in contrast, decrease of contrast	Kontrastabschwächung f; Kontrastabfall m	deep ocean	s. a. deep[-]sea
decrease in temperature	s. temperature drop	deep-ocean basin, deep-sea basin	Tiefseebecken n
decrease in volume, reduction in (of) volume, volumetric reduction, volume diminution	Volum[en]verminderung f, Volum[en]verringerung f, Volum[en]abnahme f, Raumverminderung f	deep ocean floor, deep-sea floor	Tiefseeboden m
		deep-ocean syncline, deep-sea syncline	Tiefseemulde f
decrease of contrast	s. decrease in contrast	deep of the river, deep	Flußstrecke f, Tiefwasserstrecke f des Flusses
decrease towards the edge	s. decay towards the edge	deep[-]sea, deep ocean	Tiefsee f
decreasing branch	s. descending branch <of a curve>		
decreasing characteristic	fallende Charakteristik (Kennlinie) f	deep-sea basin	s. deep-ocean basin
		deep-sea floor	s. deep ocean floor
decrement, decrement	Dämpfungsdekrement n, Schwingungsdekrement n, Dämpfungsverhältnis n, Amplitudenverhältnis n, Dekrement n	deep-sea lead	Tiefseelot n, Tieflot n
decrease, decrement of damping, damping ratio		deep-sea sounding [by lead and line], bathymetry	Tief[see]lotung f, Meerestiefenmessung f; Wassertiefenmessung f, Tiefenmessung f; Bathymetrie f
decremeter	Dämpfungsmesser m, Dekremeter n		
decrepitation, puffing	Dekrepitieren n	deep-sea syncline, deep-ocean syncline	Tiefseemulde f
decrescence	Dekreszenz f	deep surface	Tiefenfläche f
decrystallization	Entkristallisation f	deep water, bottom water <geo.>	Tiefenwasser n <Geo.>
decuplet, 10-multiplet	10-Multiplett n, Dekuplett n	deep-water	s. deep-ocean
Dedekind['s] pigeonhole principle	s. Dirichlet['s] principle	deep-water circulation	Tiefenzirkulation f
dedifferentiation	Dedifferenzierung f	deep-water wave	Tiefwasserwelle f
deduction	Deduktion f		
		de-excitation	s. deenergization
dedusting; dust separation; dust precipitation; removing of dust	Staubabscheidung f, Entstaubung f	de-excitation photon	Kern-Gamma-Quant n, Abregungsphoton n
		defect, lattice defect, crystal [lattice] defect, structural defect, structural irregularity, structural imperfection, [crystal] lattice imperfection, imperfection, structural failure, structural fault	Gitter[bau]fehler m, Gitterfehlstelle f, Gitterfehlordnung f, Fehlordnung f, Gitter[bau]störung f, Gitterdefekt m, Defekt m, Gitterstörstelle f, Gittereigenfehlstelle f, [physikalische] Störstelle f, Störung f, Fehlstelle f [des Gitters], Baufehler m, Strukturfehler m, Strukturstörung f, Strukturdefekt m, Kristallgitter[bau]fehler m, Kristallgitterstörung f
dE/dx counter, energy-loss detector	dE/dx-Zähler m, Δx-Zähler m, Energieverlustdetektor m		
dee; duant <gen.; of cyclotron>	Duant m, Dee n, D n, D-Elektrode f; Binant m <allg.; Zyklotron>		
de-electrification	Entelektrisierung f		
de-electrification factor	Entelektrisierungsfaktor m		

defect	*s. a.* aberration <e.g. of lens, eye>	deflecting plate, deflection plate, deflector <el.>	Ablenkplatte *f* <El.>
defect annealing	*s.* annealing <of radiation damage>	deflecting reflector, deflecting antenna <el.>	Umlenkreflektor *m*, Umlenkspiegel *m*, Umlenkantenne *f* <El.>
defect band, impurity band	Störband *n*, Störstellenband *n*	deflecting torque, driving torque	Meßmoment *n*
defect centre	*s.* impurity centre <semi.>		
defect concentration	*s.* impurity concentration	deflecting unit	*s.* deflector
defect conduction	*s.* extrinsic conduction	deflection; swing	Ablenkung *f*; Auslenkung *f*
defect conductivity	*s.* extrinsic conduction		
defect density	*s.* impurity concentration		
defective colour vision, colour deficiency	Farbenfeltlsichtigkeit *f*, Farbsinnstörung *f*, Farbsehstörung *f*; Farbsehschwächung *f*; Farbanomalie *f*	deflection; excursion <of a pointer, a needle>	Ausschlag *m*
		deflection, deviation <magn.>	Ablenkung *f*, Deviation *f* <Magn.>
defective contact	*s.* intermittent contact	deflection, elongation <mech.>	Elongation *f*, lineare Auslenkung *f*, Schwingungsausschlag *m*, Schwing[ungs]weg *m* <Mech.>
defective vision	*s.* ametropia		
defect level	*s.* impurity level		
defect mobility, impurity mobility	Störstellenbeweglichkeit *f*		
defectoscope	*s.* flaw detector	deflection	*s. a.* bowing under load <mech.>
defect site, impurity site	Störstellenplatz *m*		
		deflection	*s. a.* ejection <acc.>
defect state	*s.* impurity state	deflection	*s. a.* electrooptical scanning
defect state-to-band transition	Störstelle-Band-Übergang *m*	deflection	*s. a.* turn[-back]
defect term <semi.>, impurity term	Störterm *m*, Störstellenterm *m* <Halb.>	deflection aberration, spot distortion	Ablenkfehler *m*, Fleckverzerrung *f*
defensive reaction	Abwehrreaktion *f*		
		deflection angle of the valences	*s.* valence deflection angle
deferent	Deferent *m*, deferierender Kreis *m*	deflection around a corner	*s.* turn[-back]
deferred reaction, delayed reaction	verzögerte Reaktion *f*	deflection circuit	*s.* sweep circuit
deficiency index	Defektindex *m*	deflection coils, deflection yoke, scanning coils (yoke)	Ablenkspulen *fpl*, Ablenkjoch *n*
deficiency of discharge, deficit of discharge	Verdunstungsgröße *f*		
deficiency of mass	*s.* mass deficiency		
deficiency of vision	*s.* ametropia	deflection constant	Ablenkungskonstante *f*
deficient area	Unterschußfläche *f*	deflection current	*s.* deflecting current
deficient year, imperfect year, annus deficiens	mangelhaftes Gemeinjahr *n*	deflection curve	*s.* bending line
		deflection efficiency	Umlenkwirkungsgrad *m*
deficit of discharge	*s.* deficiency of discharge		
defining equation	Definitionsgleichung *f*	deflection function	Ablenkungsfunktion *f*
		deflection linearity error	*s.* aberration from linearity
defining relation	definierende Relation *f*, definierende (erzeugende) Gleichung *f*	deflection method	Ausschlag[s]verfahren *n*, Ausschlagsmethode *f*, Ausschlagsmeßmethode *f*
definite integral	bestimmtes Integral *n*		
definite kernel	definiter Kern *m*		
definiteness	Definitheit *f*	deflection modulus of the elastic support	*s.* modulus of deflection of the elastic support
definition <math.>	Definition *f* <Math.>	deflection of flap, angle of flap deflection	Klappenausschlag *m*
definition, sharpness <opt., phot.>	Definition *f*, Definitionskraft *f*, Schärfe *f*, Scharfzeichnung *f*	deflection of light rays [which pass close to a celestial body]	*s.* light-ray bending
definition	*s. a.* resolving power	deflection of plate	Plattendurchbiegung *f*
definition in depth	*s.* depth of field	deflection of the needle, needle deflection (throw)	Nadelausschlag *m*
definition range	*s.* zone of sharpness		
deflagration, slow combustion	Deflagration *f*, Verpuffung *f*, Abbrennen *n*, Ausbrennen *n*, Auskochen *n*	deflection of the needle	*s. a.* pointer deflection
		deflection of the plumb line, plumb-line deflection, plumb[-line] deviation, deviation of (from) the vertical	Lotabweichung *f*
deflagration pressure	Verpuffungsdruck *m*, Verpuffungsspannung *f*	deflection of the pointer	*s.* pointer deflection
deflagration rate	*s.* deflagration speed	deflection plate	*s.* deflecting plate <el.>
deflagration speed (velocity), deflagration rate	Verpuffungsgeschwindigkeit *f*, Deflagrationsgeschwindigkeit *f*	deflection potentiometer	Ausschlagkompensator *m*, Stufenkompensator *m*
		deflection sensitivity	Ablenkempfindlichkeit *f*
deflagration wave	Deflagrationswelle *f*, langsame Verbrennungswelle *f*		
		deflection space	Ablenkraum *m*
deflation, wind erosion, aeolian erosion	Deflation *f*, Ausblasung *f*, Abblasung *f*, Abhebung *f*, Winderosion *f*, äolische Erosion (Verwitterung) *f*, Windabtragung *f*, Windabtrag *m*		
		deflection spectrometer	*s.* Bragg spectrometer
		deflection speed, sweep speed (rate), sweep (time-base) velocity	Kippgeschwindigkeit *f*, Zeitablenkgeschwindigkeit *f*, Ablenkgeschwindigkeit *f*
		deflection surface <of the plate>	Biegungsfläche *f* <Platte>
deflecting antenna	*s.* deflecting reflector <el.>	deflection surface	*s. a.* stress quadric
deflecting capacitor <el., acc.>; deflector <acc.>; sweep capacitor <el.>	Ablenkkondensator *m*	deflection to the right	Rechtsabweichung *f*
		deflection-type bridge	Ausschlagsbrücke *f*, im Ausschlagsverfahren betriebene Brücke *f*
deflecting current, deflection current; sweep (breakover) current	Ablenkstrom *m*, Kippstrom *m*		
deflecting force	Ablenkungskraft *f*		

deflection 160

deflection wattmeter	s. electrodynamic wattmeter	deformation vector	Deformationsvektor m
deflection yoke	s. deflection coils	deformation vibration	s. bending vibration
deflector, deflecting unit	Ablenkteil m; Ablenkgerät n	deforming force	Umform[ungs]kraft f, Verformungskraft f, Formänderungskraft f
deflector ‹acc.›	Deflektor m, Auslenkvorrichtung f, Ablenkvorrichtung f, Ablenker m ‹Beschl.›	defo test, deformation test of Baader, Baader['s] deformation test	Defoprüfung f, Defoverfahren n [nach Baader], Deformationsverfahren n nach Baader, Baadersches Deformationsverfahren
deflector ‹acc.›	s. a. deflecting capacitor ‹el., acc.›	defrosting	s. deicing
deflector	s. a. deflecting plate ‹el.›	degasification, degassing, outgassing, extraction of gas	Entgasung f, Gasaustreibung f, Austreibung f von Gasen, Beseitigung f von Gasresten
deflector coils	s. orbit shift coils ‹acc.›		
deflocculation	Entflockung f		
defocusing ‹Us›, defocussing	Defokussierung f, Entbündelung f, Entfokussierung f	degassing by cavitation	Kavitationsentgasung f
defo elasticity	Defoelastizität f [nach Baader]	degaussing	s. demagnetization
		degaussing field, demagnetizing field	Entmagnetisierungsfeld n, entmagnetisierendes Feld n
defo hardness	Defohärte f [nach Baader]	degeneracy, degeneration	Entartung f; Ausartung f ‹Math.›
		degeneracy	s. a. degree of degeneracy ‹qu.›
defo[-]meter	Defo[meß]gerät n, Defometer n, Defoapparat m	degeneracy temperature, degeneration temperature	Entartungstemperatur f
deformability	Formänderungsfähigkeit f, Formänderungsvermögen n, Verformungsfähigkeit f, Verzerrungsfähigkeit f, Umformungsfähigkeit f, Deformierbarkeit f, Gestaltänderungsfähigkeit f, Gestaltänderungsvermögen n	degenerate distribution	s. singular distribution
		degenerate kernel	entarteter (ausgearteter) Kern m
		degenerate level	entartetes Niveau n
		degenerate motion	entartete Bewegung f
		degenerate star	entarteter Stern m
		degenerate state	entarteter Zustand m
		degeneration	s. degeneracy
deformable surface	verbiegbare Fläche f	degeneration of the cloud, melting[-away] of the cloud	Wolkenauflösung f, Auflösung f der Wolke
deformation; strain; change of form ‹mech.›	Verformung f, Form[ver]änderung f, Deformation f, Verzerrung f [der Form], Deformierung f ‹Mech.›	degeneration temperature, degeneracy temperature	Entartungstemperatur f
deformation band	Deformationsband n, Verformungsband n	degenerative feedback	s. reverse feedback
		degradation ‹of energy›	Energieverlust m ‹infolge Stoßes›; Abwertung (Entwertung) f der Energie, Energieentwertung f, Degradation f [der Energie], Energiedegradation f
deformation defect	Verformungsdefekt m, Verformungsbaufehler m		
deformation deviator	s. deviator of stretching		
deformation ellipsoid	s. strain ellipsoid		
deformation energy density	Deformationsenergiedichte f	degradation, degrading, shading ‹of band head›	Bandenabschattierung f, Abschattierung f ‹Bande›
deformation energy of nucleus	s. nuclear deformation energy	degradation	s. a. decay
deformation hypothesis	Verformungshypothese f	degradation	s. a. decomposition ‹chem.›
deformation loss, loss due to the deformation	Deformationsverlust m	degradation effect	Entartungseffekt m
		degradation of radiation	Strahlungsdegradation f
deformation matrix	s. strain matrix		
deformation measure	s. strain measure ‹mech.›	degradation to[wards] the red, red degradation	Rotabschattierung f
deformation method	s. slope deflection method		
deformation of areas	Flächendilatation f	degradation to[wards] the violet, violet degradation	Violettabschattierung f
deformation of convective type, exchange deformation	Austauschdeformation f, Rinnendeformation f, Deformation f vom konvektiven Typ; Rinneninstabilität f		
		degraded neutron	s. non-virgin neutron
		degraded radiation	degradierte Strahlung f, Strahlung mit verminderter Energie
deformation parameter, strain parameter, parameter of strain	Verformungsparameter m, Verzerrungsparameter m, Formänderungsparameter m, Deformationsparameter m	degraded to[wards] the red, shaded to[wards] the red, red-shaded	rotabschattiert
deformation parameter ‹nucl.›	Deformationsparameter m ‹Kern.›	degraded to[wards] the violet, shaded to[wards] the violet, violet-shaded	violettabschattiert
deformation period	s. period of deformation		
deformation point	[dilatometrischer] Erweichungspunkt m, [dilatometrische] Erweichungstemperatur f	degrading	s. degradation
		degree, rank, order, valence ‹of tensor›	Stufe f ‹Tensor›, Tensorstufe f
deformation polymorphism	Deformationspolymorphie f, Deformationsallotropie f	degree	s. a. degree of angle
		degree	s. a. degree of temperature ‹unit of temperature difference›
deformation potential	Deformationspotential n		
deformation rate	s. rate of strain		
deformation resistance	s. resistance to deformation	degree	s. a. degree of topological mapping
deformation tensor	s. strain tensor		
deformation test of Baader	s. defo test	degree absolute	s. kelvin
		degree Baumé, baumé, °Bé	Baumé-Grad m, Baumé n, °Bé
deformation texture, texture resulting from deformation	Verformungstextur f, Verzerrungstextur f	degree Brix ‹of sugar›	Brix-Grad m ‹Zucker›
		degree Cartier	Cartier-Grad m

degree Celsius (centigrade)	s. centigrade	degree of insensitivity, degree of insensitiveness	Unempfindlichkeitsgrad m
degree Fahrenheit, Fahrenheit, °F	Grad m Fahrenheit, Fahrenheit-Grad m, Fahrenheitsgrad m, °F	degree of instability	Labilitätsgrad m, Instabilitätsgrad m
degree Gay-Lussac, °GL	Grad m Gay-Lussac, °GL	degree of ionization, fractional ionization	Ionisierungsgrad m, Ionisationsgrad m
degree Kelvin	s. kelvin	degree of ionization	s. a. degree of dissociation
degree of absorption	s. acoustic absorption factor <ac.>	degree of irregularity	Ungleichförmigkeitsgrad m, Ungleichförmigkeitszahl f; Ungleichmäßigkeitsgrad m <Schlitzverschluß>
degree of accuracy, degree of precision, order of accuracy	Genauigkeitsgrad m	degree of irregularity	s. a. degree of stability
degree of accuracy	s. a. grade class of accuracy <of an instrument>	degree of liquidity	s. degree of fluidity
		degree of modulation	s. percentage modulation
degree of acidity	s. acidity	degree of mutual exchange	Umsetzungsgrad m
degree of admission	s. degree of filling		
degree of advancement <chemical reaction>	Fortschrittsgrad m der chemischen Reaktion	degree of obscuration	Verfinsterungsgrad m
degree of a map, degree [of topological mapping]	Abbildungsgrad m	degree of occupation, occupancy	Besetzungsgrad m
degree of angle, angular degree, degree, deg, °	Winkelgrad m, Grad m, Altgrad m, ° <Einheit des ebenen Winkels>	degree of order	Ordnungsgrad m
		degree of orientation	Orientierungsgrad m
degree of arc	Bogengrad m	degree of overlap	Überlappungsgrad m
degree of association, association factor	Assoziationsgrad m	degree of permeability	Durchlässigkeitsgrad m, Durchlässigkeitszahl f
degree of availability	s. availability	degree of polarization	s. polarization degree
degree of branching	Verzweigungsgrad m	degree of pollution, degree of contamination, contamination index	Verunreinigungsgrad m, Verschmutzungsgrad m
degree of coherence	s. phase coherence factor		
degree of confidence	s. level of significance		
degree of contamination	s. degree of pollution	degree of polymerization	Polymerisationsgrad m
degree of convolution	Knäuelungsgrad m	degree of porosity	Sinterungsgrad m
degree of coverage, fractional coverage <also geo.>	Bedeckungsgrad m	degree of precision	s. degree of accuracy
		degree of prismatic deviation	s. unit deviation of prism
degree of cross linking	Vernetzungsgrad m	degree of reliability, reliability	Sicherheitsgrad m, Zuverlässigkeitsgrad m
degree of damping	s. damping <el.>		
degree of damping	s. one-over-Q value	degree of reset	Rückstellgrad m
degree of deformation <mech.>	Formänderungsgrad m, Verformungsgrad m, Verzerrungsgrad m, Deformationsgrad m <in %> <Mech.>	degree of reversibility <therm.>	Gütezahl f, Reversibilitätsgrad m, Umkehrbarkeitsgrad m <Therm.>
		degree of roughness	s. roughness coefficient
		degree of saturation	Sättigungsgrad m
degree of degeneracy, degree of degeneration, degeneracy, statistical weight, weight <qu.>	Grad m der Entartung, Entartungsgrad m, statistisches Gewicht n, Gewicht <Qu.>	degree of saturation	s. a. V value <geo.>
		degree of selectivity, selectivity ratio	Selektionsgrad m
		degree of sensitiveness (sensitivity)	Empfindlichkeitsgrad m
degree of depolarization, depolarization factor <opt.>	Depolarisationsgrad m, Depolarisationsfaktor m <Opt.>	degree of sensitization	Sensibilisierungsgrad m
		degree of sharpness	Schärfegrad m
degree of dispersion	s. dispersity	degree of shear[ing]	Scherungsgrad m
degree of dissociation, degree of ionization	Dissoziationsgrad m	degree of solvation	Solvatationsgrad m
		degree of stability, degree of irregularity <control>	Stabilitätsgrad m, Stabilitätswert m <Regelung>
degree of distortion <el.>	Verzerrungsgrad m <El.>		
degree of enrichment	s. enrichment <of fuel, in %>	degree of statical indeterminacy	s. degree of hyperstaticity
degree of feeding	s. degree of filling	degree of supercooling	Unterkühlungsgrad m
degree of filling; degree of admission, degree of feeding	Füllungsgrad m	degree of superheating, superheating, number of degrees of superheat	Überhitzungsgrad m, Überhitzung f
degree of fluidity; degree of liquidity	Flüssigkeitsgrad m	degree of supersaturation	Übersättigungsgrad m
degree of forbiddenness, order of forbiddenness	Grad m des Verbots, Verbotenheitsgrad m, Verbotenheitsfaktor m, Ordnung f des Verbots	degree of swelling, swelling degree (capacity; value)	Quellungsgrad m; Quellwert m
degree of freedom <mech., stat.>	Freiheitsgrad m, Grad m der Freiheit <Mech., Stat.>	degree of symmetry [of the axis]	s. degree of the axis <cryst.>
		degree of temperature, degree, °K, °C, deg. K, deg. C, deg. <unit of temperature difference>	Temperaturgrad m, Wärmegrad m, Grad m, grd <Einheit der Temperaturdifferenz>
degree of freedom [in phase rule], number of degrees of freedom, variance <in phase rule>	Freiheit f, Freiheitsgrad m, Anzahl f der frei wählbaren Versuchsbedingungen <Phasenregel>		
		degree of the axis, degree of symmetry [of the axis], order of symmetry [of the axis] <cryst.>	Zähligkeit f [der Symmetrieachse], Symmetrieordnung f [der Achse], Symmetriegrad m [der Achse] <Krist.>
degree of geomagnetic activity	erdmagnetischer (geomagnetischer) Unruhegrad m		
degree of hardness	s. hardness <mech.>	degree of the International Sugar Scale	s. sugar degree
degree of homogeneity <of radiation>	Homogenitätsgrad m <Strahlung>	degree of thermal dissociation	thermischer Dissoziationsgrad m
degree of humidity, fractional humidity	Feuchtigkeitsgrad m	degree of topological mapping, degree of a map, degree	Abbildungsgrad m
degree of hyperstaticity (indeterminacy), degree of statical indeterminacy	Grad m der statischen Unbestimmtheit		
		degree of toughness <of the material>	Zähigkeitsgrad m <Werkstoff>

degree of turbidity	Trübungsgrad m, Trübegrad m	delay constant, L/R ratio	Verzögerungskonstante f, L/R
degree of turbulence	s. scale of turbulence	delay distortion	s. phase distortion
degree of vacuum	Güte f des Vakuums	delay echo	s. long-delay echo
degree of wear, wearability	Verschleißgrad m, Grad m des Verschleißes, Abnutzungsgrad m	delayed alpha-particle	verzögertes Alpha-Teilchen n
degree Rankine, °R, °Rank, deg. R	Grad m Rankine, Rankine-Grad m, °R, °Rank	delayed boiling	s. delay in boiling
degree Réaumur, °R	Grad m Réaumur, Réaumur-Grad m, °R	delayed coincidence	verzögerte Koinzidenz f
degree Scheiner, Scheiner rating	Scheiner-Grad m	delayed commutation	s. undercommutation
degree sugar, °S	Grad m Sugar, °S	delayed control	s. threshold control
degree Twaddle	s. Twaddle degree	delayed[-]critical	verzögert[-]kritisch
dehumidification, drying of air	Luftfeuchtung f, Lufttrocknung f		
dehumidification <removal of water from gas>	s. drying	delayed echo, retarded echo	Nachecho n
dehydrant, dehydrating agent	s. dehydrator	delayed elasticity, retarded elasticity	verzögerte Elastizität f
dehydration, shrinking	Entquellung f	delayed elasticity	s. a, elastic after-effect
dehydration <removal of water from substances>	s. drying	delayed equilibrium restoration	s. delayed restoration of equilibrium
dehydration, desiccation, dewatering, deaquation, removal (deprivation) of water <chem.>	Dehydratation f, Dehydratisierung f, Wasserabspaltung f, Wasserentzug m, Wasserentziehung f, Entwässerung f, Austrocknung f <Chem.>	delayed feedback, lagged feedback	Rückführung f mit Totzeit, verzögerte Rückführung f
		delayed fission neutron	s. delayed neutron
		delayed fluorescence	verzögerte Fluoreszenz f
dehydration	s. a. drying	delayed fracture	verzögerter Bruch m
dehydrator, dehydrating agent, dehydrant, desiccant, desiccative, drying agent, dryer, drier, siccative, exsiccant	Trockenmittel n, Trocknungsmittel n; Sikkativ n; Trockenstoff m	delayed gamma[-ray]	verzögertes Gamma-Quant n
		delayed neutron, delayed fission neutron	verzögertes Neutron (Spaltneutron) n, verspätetes Neutron
		delayed neutron emitter, precursor	Mutternuklid n (Mutterkern m, Urnuklid n) verzögerter Neutronen
		delayed neutron fraction	Anteil m der verzögerten Neutronen
dehydrogenation	Dehydrierung f, Abspaltung f von Wasserstoff		
deicing, defrosting	Enteisung f	delayed precipitation	Nachfällung f
deionization	Deionisation f, Deionisierung f, Entionisierung f	delayed reaction, deferred reaction	verzögerte Reaktion f
deionization potential	Deionisationspotential n, Deionisierungspotential n Entionisierungspotential n	delayed reactivity	verzögerte Reaktivität f
deionization potential	s. a. extinction voltage <of discharge>	delayed relay, delay-action relay, slow-operating relay	verzögertes Relais n, verzögert wirkendes Relais, träge wirkendes Relais, Verzögerungsrelais n
deionization rate	Entionisierungsgeschwindigkeit f		
deionization time	Deionisationszeit f, Deionisierungszeit f, Entionisierungszeit f, Löschzeit f	delayed restoration of equilibrium, delayed equilibrium restoration	verzögerte Gleichgewichtseinstellung f
deionization voltage	s. extinction voltage <of discharge>	delayed-supercritical, prompt-subcritical	prompt[-]unterkritisch, verzögert[-]überkritisch
deionizing grid	Deionisationsgitter n, Deionisierungsgitter n, Entionisierungsgitter n		
Dejardin window	Dejardin-Fenster n	delay element	s. delay-line element
dejection cone	s. debris cone	delay equalizer	s. phase corrector
dekatron method, dekatron technique [of measurement]	Zählröhrenverfahren n, Dekatronverfahren n	delay error	s. transit time error
		delay in boiling, delayed boiling	Siedeverzug m, Siedeverzögerung f; Verdampfungsverzug m
del, del vector, nabla, nabla vector, nabla operator, Hamiltonian, ∇ <math.>	Nabla n, Nablavektor m, Gradientvektor m, Nablaoperator m, Gradientoperator m, Operator m der räumlichen Differentiation, Hamiltonscher Operator, ∇ <Math.>	delay in condensation	Kondensationsverzug m
		delay in freezing	Gefrierverzug m
		delay lens, decelerating lens	Phasenverzögerungslinse f
		delay line, slow-wave structure; delay cable	Verzögerungsleitung f, Laufzeitleitung f, Laufzeitkette f, Verzögerungskette f, Verzögerungsanordnung f, Verzögerungslinie f, Verzögerungsstrecke f, Laufstrecke f; Verzögerungskabel n
Delaborne prism	Delaborne-Prisma n		
Delambre['s] analogies, Gauss analogies	Delambresche (Mollweidesche, Gaußsche) Formeln fpl <der sphärischen Trigonometrie>		
Delaunay['s] model	Delaunaysches Modell n		
Delaunay variable	Delaunaysche Koordinate f, Delaunaysches [kanonisches] Element n, Delaunaysches Bahnelement n	delay-line element, delay [-line] section, delay element	Laufzeitglied n
delay	s. time lag	delay-line helix; travelling-wave helix	Wendelleiter m als Verzögerungsleitung, Verzögerungswendel f
delay	s. deceleration <mech.>		
delay-action relay	s. delayed relay	delay-line section	s. delay-line element
delay cable	s. delay line	delay-line-shaped pulse	verzögerter Impuls m
delay capacitor	Verzögerungskondensator m		

delay-line storage, delay-line store	Laufzeitspeicher m, Verzögerungsleitungsspeicher m	deltoid, rhomboid	Deltoid n, Rhomboid n, Drachenfigur f, Drache m, ungleichseitig-schiefwinkliges Parallelogramm n
delay multivibrator	Verzögerungsmultivibrator m		
delay relay	s. time-delay relay	deltoid dodecahedron, deltohedron	Deltoiddodekaeder n, Deltoeder n
delay screen	Verzögerungsschirm m		
delay section	s. delay-line element	deltoid icositetrahedron	Deltoidikositetraeder n
delay time, incubation time; half-peak delay; peak delay	Verzögerungszeit f	delusion, illusion	Wahrnehmungsverzerrung f, Täuschung f
		del vector	s. del <math.>
		demagnetization, degaussing	Entmagnetisierung f, Demagnetisierung f
delay time <semi.; control>	Verzögerungszeit f <Halb.; Regelung>; Verzugszeit f <Übertragungsglied>	demagnetization coefficient	s. demagnetization factor
delay time constant	Verzögerungszeitkonstante f	demagnetization curve	Entmagnetisierungskurve f
		demagnetization energy	Entmagnetisierungsenergie f
Delbrück scattering [of photons]	s. scattering of light by Coulomb field	demagnetization factor, demagnetizing factor, demagnetization coefficient	Entmagnetisierungsfaktor m, Entmagnetisierungskoeffizient m <formabhängige Komponente des Entmagnetisierungstensors>
deliquescence	Zerfließlichkeit f		
deliquescence <of hygroscopic matter>	Zerfließen n [des hygroskopischen Stoffes], Zergehen n, Feuchtwerden n, Feuchtigkeitsanziehung f		
Delisle projection	Delislesche Schnittkegelprojektion f	demagnetization tensor	Entmagnetisierungstensor m
delivery of heat	s. heat output	demagnetizing factor	s. demagnetization factor
delivery of pump	s. exhausting power	demagnetizing field	s. degaussing field
delivery side <of the pump>, pressure side	Druckseite f [der Pumpe]	demal solution <1 g-equ. of solute per dm³>	Lösung f von 1 demal, Normallösung f <1 g-Äqu. Gelöstes/dm³>
Dellinger effect (fade-out)	s. radio fade-out	demand, requirement <for>	Forderung f <nach>, Anforderung f <an>
delocalization effect	Delokalisierungseffekt m	demand	s. a. requirements
delocalization energy, enlargement energy	Delokalisierungsenergie f	demand attachment	s. peak-reading meter
		demand for power	s. consumption <el.>
Delon rectifier circuit	s. Greinacher circuit	demand power, design power, rated power	Solleistung f
delta	s. delta operator		
delta amplitude, Δ am, dn	Delta amplitudinis, Delta-amplitude f, Δ am, dn	demarcation potential	s. injury potential
		dematerialization	Dematerialisation f, Entmaterialisierung f
delta bond, δ-bond	Delta-Bindung f, δ-Bindung f	Dember effect	Dember-Effekt m
		Dember potential	Dember-Potential n
Delta Cepheid-type [star], cepheid [variable star], cepheid variable	Delta Cephei-Stern m, Delta-Cephei-Veränderlicher m, Cepheid m, Cephei-Stern m, Blinkstern m; eigentlicher Delta Cephei-Stern	demigroup	s. semi-group
		demineralization of water	s. water softening
		demixing; separation; segregation; precipitation <of emulsion>	Entmischung f, Zerfall m <Gemisch>
delta connection, mesh (triangle) connection	Deltaschaltung f, Dreieckschaltung f	demixing surface	Entmischungsfläche f
		Demkina colorimeter	Dreifarbenmeßgerät n nach Djomkina
Delta-E effect, ΔE effect	ΔE-Effekt m, Delta-E-Effekt m	demodulation <el.>	Demodulation f <El.>
delta-electron	s. delta-ray	demodulation	s. a. rectification <el.>
delta function [of Dirac], Dirac delta function, [Dirac's] δ-function, Dirac function, Dirac delta distribution, Dirac measure, unit impulse function [of order one], spike function, delta operator	Delta-Funktion f [von Dirac], [Diracsche] δ-Funktion f, Dirac-Funktion f, Diracsche Funktion f, Dirac-Impuls m, Einheitsimpuls m, Nadelimpuls m, [normierte] Zackenfunktion f, Diracsches Funktional (Maß) n	demodulation effect	Gleichrichtungseffekt m, Demodulationseffekt m
		demodulator	s. rectifier <el.>
		Demoivre['s] theorem	s. Moivre['s] theorem
		demonstration, illustration	Veranschaulichung f
		demonstration	s. a. projecting <opt.>
		demonstration	s. a. proof <math.>
		demotion of quantum number	Abnahme f der Quantenzahl bei der Molekülaufspaltung
delta modulation	Deltamodulation f, Pulsdeltamodulation f	Dempster-type mass spectrometer	Dempstersches Massenspektrometer n, Massenspektrometer nach Dempster, Massenspektrometer mit Richtungsfokussierung
delta operator	s. laplacian		
delta operator	s. delta function		
delta-particle	s. delta-ray		
delta-particle track	s. delta track		
delta-ray, delta-particle, delta-electron, knocked-on electron, knock-on	Delta-Strahl m, Delta-Teilchen n, Delta-Elektron n, Anstoßelektron n	demulsification, breaking	Demulgieren n, Dismulgieren n, Entmischung f, Zerfall m <Emulsion>, Emulsionsspaltung f, Emulsionsentmischung f
delta reply, delta response, impulse reaction, negative derivative of the relaxation function	Impulsreaktion f, Deltaantwort f, negative Ableitung f der Relaxationsfunktion		
		demulsification agent, demulsifier, emulsion breaker	Demulgator m, Emulsionsspalter m
Delta Scuti-type star	Delta Scuti-Stern m	denaturation <chem.; bio.>; denaturation of the nuclear fuel <nucl.>	Vergällung f, Denaturierung f, Denaturation f <Chem.>; Denaturierung (Vergällung) des Kernbrennstoffs (Spaltstoffs) <Kern.>
delta-star connection	Dreieck-Stern-Schaltung f		
delta-track, delta-particle track, δ track	Deltaspur f, Delta-Spur f, Delta-Bahn f, δ-Spur f		
		denaturation theory	Denaturationstheorie f
delta voltage	s. mesh voltage	dendrite, dendrite crystal, crystal skeleton, skeleton [of crystal], skeleton crystal, pine crystal, fir tree crystal[lite], arborescent crystal	Dendrit m, dendritischer (moosähnlicher) Kristall m, Skelettkristall m, Kristallskelett n, Tannenbaumkristall m, Farnkristall m
delta wing, airfoil of delta shape	Deltaflügel m, deltaförmiger Tragflügel m, Dreieckflügel m		
delta-zigzag connection	Dreieck-Zickzack-Schaltung f		
deltohedron	s. deltoid dodecahedron		

dendritic crystallization	dendritische Kristallisation f, Dendritenbildung f; Skelettbildung f	density of heat flow	s. heat flow density
dendritic growth, skeleton growth	Skelettwachstum n, dendritisches Wachstum n, Dendrit[en]wachstum n	density of impurities	s. impurity concentration
		density of lines of force	s. field density
		density of magnetic charge, magnetic charge density	magnetische Ladungsdichte f
dendritic structure	dendritische Struktur f, Dendritstruktur f, Tannenbaumstruktur f	density of magnetic force	s. magnetic force density
		density of mass	s. density
dendrochronology	Dendrochronologie f, Baumringdatierung f	density of meteor stream	Meteoritendichte f im Strom
Dennison rule	Dennisonsche Isotopenregel f	density of nuclear matter	s. nuclear density
		density of particle pairs, particle pair density	Teilchenpaardichte f
denominate	benannt, dimensionsbehaftet	density of polarization charge, density of bound charges, polarization (bound) charge density	Polarisationsladungsdichte f, Dichte f der Polarisationsladungen
denominate scale	benannte Skala f		
dense <math.>, everywhere dense	überall dicht, dicht <Math.>		
dense cloud	schattige Wolke f, schattengebende Wolke	density of saturated phase (vapour)	s. saturation density
dense crown	Schwerkron n, Schwerkronglas n	density of solarization, solarization density	Solarisationsdichte f
dense flint	Schwerflint n, Schwerflintglas n	density of source distribution, density of sources	s. source density
densely packed	s. close-packed	density of states, state density	Zustandsdichte f
denseness	s. density		
dense opal [glass]	starkgetrübtes Glas n	density of stations, station density	Stationsdichte f
dense set	[in sich] dichte Menge f, insichdichte Menge	density of the shadow	Schattendichte f
densification	s. compacting	density of vapour[s]	s. vapour density
densimeter	s. areometer	density of volume charge	s. space charge density
densimetry, measurement of density, density measurement	Dichtebestimmung f, Dichtemessung f, Densimetrie f	density of vorticity, vorticity density	Wirbeldichte f
		density operator	s. density matrix
densitometer, opacimeter	Schwärzungsmesser m, Dens[it]ometer n	density range, density scale	Schwärzungsumfang m, Schwärzungsbereich m, Schwärzungsskala f
densitometry	Densitometrie f, Schwärzungsmessung f	density range of the negative, density volume of the negative, intensity range of the negative	Negativumfang m
density, density of mass, mass density, specific mass, specific density <in g/cm³ or kg/m³>	Dichte f, Dichte der Masse (räumlichen Massenbelegung), [mittlere] Massendichte f, Densität f, spezifische Masse f		
		density range of the positive, density volume of the positive, intensity range of the positive	Positivumfang m
density; denseness	Dichte f; Dichtheit f		
density	s. a. optical density <phot.>	density reference scale	Schwärzungsskala f
density after vibration, vibrational density	Rütteldichte f	density relief	Schwärzungsrelief n, Schwärzungsplastik f
density bottle	s. pyknometer		
density by volume	s. volume density	density relief, density relief method (technique)	Schwärzungsreliefverfahren n, Schwärzungsplastikverfahren n, Schwärzungsplastik f
density contrast	Schwärzungskontrast m		
		density scale	s. density range
density current	Konzentrationsströmung f	density temperature coefficient, temperature coefficient of density	Temperaturkoeffizient m der Dichte, Dichte-Temperaturkoeffizient m
density effect	Dichteeffekt m		
density function	s. stellar density function		
density function	s. probability density	density threshold	Schwärzungsschwelle f
density gauge, density meter	Dichtemesser m	density volume of the negative	s. density range of the negative
density gradation	Schwärzungsabstufung f	density volume of the positive	s. density range of the positive
density in phase, phase density, ensemble density, coefficient of probability	Phasendichte f; Wahrscheinlichkeitskoeffizient m	denudation	Denudation f, flächenhafte Abtragung f, Flächenabtragung f
		denudation level (plane)	s. plane of denudation
density matrix, von Neumann matrix, density operator, statistical operator (matrix)	Dichtematrix f, Dichteoperator m, statistischer Operator m	denumerable, enumerable, countable	abzählbar
		deoxidation	s. desoxidation
		deoxyribonucleic acid	s. desoxyribonucleic acid
		departure	s. control error
		departure	s. unconformity
		departure of frequency	s. frequency drift
		dependability [in service]	s. reliability
density measurement	s. densimetry		
density measurement by hydrometers	Spindelung f	dependence of permittivity on frequency, frequency dependence of permittivity	Frequenzabhängigkeit f der Dielektrizitätskonstante, Frequenzdispersion f
density meter	s. density gauge		
density-modulated, modulated in density	dichtemoduliert		
density of bound charges	s. density of polarization charge	dependence on direction, directional dependence, directionality, directivity	Richtungsabhängigkeit f
density of carriers	s. charge carrier density		
density of charge	s. charge density		
density of charge carriers	s. charge carrier density	dependency area	s. domain of dependence
		dependent equatorial co-ordinates; dependent equatorial system [of co-ordinates], first equatorial system [of co-ordinates], standard system	festes Äquatorialsystem n, Koordinaten fpl im Stundenwinkelsystem; Stundenwinkelsystem n
density of electric force	s. electric force density		
density of gas, vapour (gas) density, density of vapour[s]	Dampfdichte f, Gasdichte f		
density of haze particles	Dunstdichte f		
density of heat	s. heat density	dependent on concentration	s. concentration-dependent

dependent on structure, structure-sensitive, structure-dependent	strukturempfindlich, strukturabhängig
dependent on time	s. time-dependent <mech.>
dependent stochastic variable	stochastisch abhängige Variable f, abhängige Zufallsvariable f
dephlegmation, partial condensation	Teilkondensation f, partielle (teilweise) Kondensation f, Dephlegmation f
dephlegmator, refluxer, reflux exchanger, partial condenser	Rücklaufkondensator m [mit Teilkondensation], verstärkender Rücklaufkondensator, Rückflußkühler m [mit Teilkondensation], Rückflußkondensator m [mit Teilkondensation], Dephlegmator m
depleted; depopulated; emptied <semi.>	verarmt; erschöpft <Halb.>
depleted boundary layer	s. depletion layer <semi.>
depleted surface boundary layer, surface depletion layer	Verarmungsrandschicht f, Randverarmungszone f, Erschöpfungsrandschicht f, erschöpfte Randschicht f
depletion; exhaustion; impoverishment	Verarmung f; Erschöpfung f, Verbrauchen n
depletion; stripping <nucl.>	Verarmung f; Abreicherung f <Kern.>
depletion <of charge carriers> <semi.>	Verarmung f [an Ladungsträgern], Räumung f [von Ladungsträgern], Ausräumung f [der Ladungsträger], Erschöpfung f [der Ladungsträger] Verdrängung f [von Ladungsträgern]
depletion curve, recession curve <hydr.>	Trockenwetterabflußlinie f, Trockenwetterganglinie f <Hydr.>
depletion effect <semi.>	Verdrängungseffekt m <Halb.>
depletion layer <of barrier>, depleted boundary layer, depletion region, exhaustion layer, exhaustion region <semi.>	Verarmungsschicht f, Verarmungszone f, Verarmungsgebiet n, Verarmungsbereich m, erschöpfte Schicht f, Erschöpfungszone f, Raumladungsschicht f, Raumladungszone f <Halb.>
depletion layer	s. a. internal barrier layer <semi.>
depletion-layer capacitance	s. barrier-layer capacitance
depletion layer effect	s. barrier-layer effect
depletion-layer photo[electric] effect	s. photovoltaic effect
depletion layer transistor	Sperrschichttransistor m
depletion layer width	s. barrier width
depletion-mode insulated-gate field effect transistor	s. junction-gate field-effect transistor
depletion region	s. depletion layer <semi.>
depolarization coefficient <el.>	Depolarisationskoeffizient m <El.>
depolarization effect	Depolarisationseffekt m
depolarization factor	s. degree of depolarization <opt.>
depolarization field	Depolarisationsfeld n
depolarizer	Depolarisator m
depolarizing electrode	Depolarisationselektrode f
depolished glass	s. frosted glass
depolymerization	s. polymer degradation
depopulated	s. depleted
depopulation, emptying	Leeren n, Entleeren n, Depopularisieren n, Entpopularisierung f
deposit, sediment	Ablagerung f, Sediment n; Sinkstoff m
deposit	s. a. precipitate <chem.>
deposit attack; deposit corrosion, undermining pitting	Belagkorrosion f, Korrosionsangriff m unter Ablagerungen
deposit corrosion	s. a. contact corrosion
deposited moraine	Stapelmoräne f, abgelagerte Moräne f
deposition	s. settling
deposition	s. precipitation <chem.>
deposition	s. desublimation
depressant, depressing agent	Drücker m, Depressans n
depression <of land>; subsidence; immersion <geo.>	Senkung f, Depression f <Geo.>
depression	s. a. pit
depression	s. a. cyclone <meteo.>
depression	s. a. lowering
depression angle, angle of depression	Depressionswinkel m, negative Höhe f; Senkungswinkel m, Absenkungswinkel m
depression centre	s. cyclonic centre
depression contour, isokatabatic line	Isokatabase f
depression of the boiling point	s. lowering of the boiling point
depression of the freezing point, lowering of the freezing point, freezing-point depression	Gefrierpunktserniedrigung f, Gefrierpunkterniedrigung f
depression of the ice point, ice-point depression	Depression f des Eispunktes
depression of wet bulb	s. psychrometer difference
depression of zero	s. zero depression
deprivation of water	s. dehydration
depth contour [line]	s. isobath
depth definition	s. depth of field
depth developer	Tiefenentwickler m
depth dose	Tiefendosis f
depth erosion	Tiefenerosion f, Tiefenschurf m
depth finding	s. measurement of depth in ultrasonics
depth float	s. composite float
depth gauge; depth gauge micrometer, depth micrometer	Tiefenmaß n, Tiefenlehre f, Tiefenmesser m; Tiefentaster m; Tiefenmeßschieber m
depth measurement	s. measurement of depth <in ultrasonics>
depth micrometer	s. depth gauge
depth of Earth's core	Kerntiefe f
depth of fall	s. height of fall
depth of field, depth of focus, focal range, definition in depth, depth definition	Schärfentiefe f, Tiefenschärfe f, Abbildungstiefe f, Tiefe f der scharfen Abbildung, Fokustiefe f; Tiefenbereich m <Elektronenmikroskopie>
depth-of-field indicator, depth-of-field ring	Schärfentiefe[n]rechner m, Schärfentiefe[n]anzeiger m, Schärfentiefe[n]ring m
depth of focus, focal (hypocentral) depth, depth of origin (hypocentre) <geo.>	Herdtiefe f, Hypozentraltiefe f
depth of focus	s. a. depth of field
depth of friction, friction depth	Reibungstiefe f
depth of hardened layer, depth of hardening, hardening depth, depth of "penetration", hardness penetration	Einhärtungstiefe f, Härtetiefe f, Durchhärtung f
depth of hypocentre	s. depth of focus <geo.>
depth of immersion	s. submergence
depth of modulation	s. percentage modulation
depth of origin	s. depth of focus <geo.>
depth of penetration, penetration (penetrating) depth, penetration	Eindringtiefe f, Eindringungstiefe f; Eindringmaß n
depth of "penetration"	s. a. depth of hardened layer
depth of penetration	s. a. submergence
depth of rainfall	s. height of precipitation
depth of reflection, reflection depth	Reflexionstiefe f
depth of smoothness, levelling depth <hydr.>	Glättungstiefe f <Hydr.>

depth of the cup	Tiefung f, Tiefungswert m	derived set, derivative set, derivation	Ableitung f ‹einer Menge›, abgeleitete Menge f
depth of the potential well	s. potential well depth	derived unit	abgeleitete Einheit (Maßeinheit) f
depth resolution	s. resolution in depth		
depth resolving power	s. resolving power in depth	derived vector, tractor ‹math.›	derivierter Vektor m, Traktor m ‹Math.›
depth wave, wave in depth	Tiefenwelle f	dermatometry	Dermatometrie f
depupinization	Entspulung f, Entpupinisieren n		
dereflection	Entspiegelung f, Reflex[ver]minderung f, Reflexions[ver]minderung f	desactivation	s. deactivation
		desalination of water, water desalination	Wasserentsalzung f
derivability	Ableitbarkeit f	desaturation	s. dilution ‹of the solution›
derivability	s. a. differentiability	Descartes['] folium, Cartesian folium	kartesisches Blatt n
derivant, derivate	s. derivative ‹chem.›		
derivation, recording ‹of bioelectrical currents›	Ableitung f ‹bioelektrischer Ströme›	Descartes['] law	s. Snell['s] law
derivation, development ‹of formula›	Herleitung f, Ableitung f, Entwicklung f ‹Formel›	Descartes['] ray	Descartesscher (mindestgedrehter) Strahl m, Grenzstrahl m der Brechung
derivation	s. a. differentiation ‹math.›	Descartes['] rule of signs, rule of signs	Descartessche (Cartesische, Harriotsche) Zeichenregel f
derivation	s. a. derived set		
derivative, derivate, derivant ‹chem.›	Abkömmling m, Derivat n ‹Chem.›	descending branch, decreasing branch, descending portion ‹of a curve›	absteigender Ast m ‹Kurve›
derivative, differential coefficient (quotient) ‹math.›	Ableitung f, Differentialquotient m, Derivierte f	descending current ‹bio.›	absteigender Strom (Reizstrom) m ‹Bio.›
derivative	s. a. substitute	descending node	absteigender Knoten m
derivative action	s. rate action	descending portion	s. descending branch
derivative-action control	s. rate-action control	descending source, descending spring	absteigende Quelle f, Auslaufquelle f; Überlaufquelle f, Überfallquelle f, Sturzquelle f, Rheokrene f
derivative-action controller	s. rate-action controller		
derivative-action time, rate time	Vorhaltzeit f, Beschleunigungszeit f		
		descension ‹astr.›	Deszension f, Abstieg m ‹Astr.›
derivative control, rate control, differential control	Regelung f mit Differentialeinfluß, Regelung mit Vorhalt, Differentialregelung f, D-Regelung f	descent velocity, rate of [vertical] descent; sinking speed	Sinkgeschwindigkeit f, Abstiegsgeschwindigkeit f
derivative control	s. a. rate-action control		
derivative controller	s. rate-action controller	described area	überstrichene Fläche f
derivative following the fluid	s. material derivative	describing function	äquivalenter [komplexer] Verstärkungskoeffizient m, Beschreibungsfunktion f, äquivalenter [komplexer] Verstärkungsfaktor m
derivative matrix, R matrix	R-Matrix f, „derivative matrix" f, Hilfsmatrix f		
derivative of higher order, higher-order derivative	Ableitung f höherer Ordnung, höhere Ableitung	descriptive astronomy	s. uranography
		descriptive geometry	darstellende Geometrie f
derivative of the Dirac function	Ableitung f der Dirac-Funktion	desensitization	Desensibilisierung f ‹Phot.›; Phlegmatisierung f
derivative of the second order	s. second-order derivative	desensitizer, desensitizing dye	Desensibilisator m
derivative on the left	s. left-handed derivative		
derivative on the right	s. right-hand derivative	desert crust	Wüstenkruste f, Wüstenrinde f; Wüstenlack m
derivative polarographic titration; derivative polarography	derivative Polarographie f, Derivativpolarographie f; derivative polarographische Titration f		
		desiccant	s. dehydrator
		desiccation	s. dehydration ‹chem.›
derivative proportional control	s. proportional derivative control	desiccation	s. drying
		desiccation	s. drying out
derivative proportional controller	s. proportional and derivative action controller	desiccative	s. dehydrator
		design; proportioning; dimensioning; sizing; choice of parameters	Dimensionierung f, Bemessung f
derivative proportional integral control, proportional integral derivative control, P.I.D. control, three-term control	PID-Regelung f, Proportional-Integral-Regelung f mit Differentialeinfluß, Proportional-Integral-Regelung mit Vorhalt		
		design, plan, test programme ‹of the first or second order›	Versuchsplan m ‹erster oder zweiter Ordnung›
		design	s. a. version
		designation; notation; system of notation; symbolism	Bezeichnung f; Bezeichnungsweise f; Schreibweise f; Symbolik f
derivative proportional integral controller, proportional integral derivative controller, P.I.D. controller, three-term controller	PID-Regler m, Proportional-Integral-Regler m mit Differentialeinfluß, Proportional-Integral-Regler mit Vorhalt	design of experiment, planning of experiment	Versuchsplanung f
		design power, rated (demand) power	Solleistung f
		desired position, required (nominal) position	Sollstellung f
derivative set	s. derived set	desired value	s. set level
derivatives of all orders / having, infinitely differentiable	unendlich oft differenzierbar	desired value pointer, desired voltage indicator	Sollwertanzeiger m, Spannungslupe f, Voltlupe f
derivative thermogravimetric analysis, derivative thermogravimetry	s. differential thermogravimetry		
		desk calculating machine, desk-calculator, desk digital computer, calculator	[digitale] Tischrechenmaschine f, Tischhandrechenmaschine f
derivative with respect to time	s. time derivative		
derived current	Ableit[ungs]strom m, Zweigstrom m	Deslandres band scheme	s. Deslandres table
		Deslandres equation, Deslandres formula	Deslandressche Bandenformel (Formel) f, Bandenformel f
derived group	s. commutator group		
derived quantity, secondary quantity	abgeleitete Größe[nart] f	Deslandres['] laws	Deslandressche Gesetze npl

Deslandres scheme of band heads	s. Deslandres table
Deslandres table, Deslandres band scheme, Deslandres scheme of band heads	Kantenschema n
Deslandres term	Deslandrescher Term m
desmotrope	Desmotrop n
desmotrope	s.a. desmotropic
desmotropic, desmotrope, merotropic, merotrope	desmotrop
desmotropism	s. keto-enol tautomerism
desmotropism	s. tautomerism
desolvation energy	Desolvatationsenergie f
desorption	Desorption f
desorption isotherm	Desorptionsisotherme f
desoxidation, deoxidation	Desoxydation f, Sauerstoffentzug m; Beruhigung f ⟨Schmelze⟩
desoxyribonucleic acid, desoxyribose nucleic acid, deoxyribonucleic acid, DNA	Desoxyribonukleinsäure f, Desoxyribosenukleinsäure f, DNS
despiralization	Entspiralisierung f
desquamation ⟨bio.; geo.⟩; exfoliation ⟨bio.⟩	Abschuppung f, Desquamation f ⟨Bio., Geo.⟩
destrengthening, loss of strength, work-softening, softening	Entfestigung f
destrengthening annealing	s. relief annealing
Destriau effect, Destriau-type electroluminescence, electroluminescence produced by collision excitation process	Destriau-Effekt m, innere Elektrolumineszenz f, Destriau-Typ-Elektrolumineszenz f, Elektrolumineszenz vom Destriau-Typ
destruction of carriers	Vernichtung f von Ladungsträgern
destruction of fluorescence	Fluoreszenzabbau m, Abbau m der Fluoreszenz
destruction of surface ⟨by meteorites⟩	Oberflächenverwüstung f ⟨durch Meteoriteneinsturz⟩
destruction operator	s. annihilation operator
destruction rate, annihilation rate	Vernichtungsrate f
destructive distillation	Zersetzungsdestillation f
destructive form	Skulpturform f, Destruktionsform f, destruktive Form f
destructive hydrogenation	destruktive Hydrierung f
destructive structure	Abbaustruktur f
destructive testing [of materials]	Zerstörungsprüfung f, Werkstoffprüfung f mit Zerstörung der Probe
desublimation, solidensing	Desublimation f, Solidensieren n, Kondensation f fest, Deposition f, Sublimation f
desultory precipitations, scattered showers	vereinzelte Niederschläge (Schauer) mpl
deswelling ⟨of gel⟩	Abschwellung f, Entquellung f ⟨Gel⟩
detached binary; resolved binary	getrennter Doppelstern m, getrenntes System n; aufgelöster Doppelstern
detached bow wave	abgelöste Bugwelle f
detached shock[-wave]	abgelöster Verdichtungsstoß m, abgehobener Verdichtungsstoß, abgelöste Stoßwelle f
detachment, removal, liberation ⟨of electron⟩	Ablösung f, Auslösung f, Austritt m ⟨Elektron⟩
detachment	s.a. separation ⟨e.g. of flow, vortex, boundary layer⟩
detachment of binary	s. resolving of binary star
detail contrast	s. contrast of details
detailed balancing	detailliertes Gleichgewicht n, Gleichgewicht des Elementarprozesses
details / without	detaillos
detectability, detectivity	Nachweisbarkeit f; Erfassungsgrenze f, Nachweisgrenze f ⟨Chem.⟩
detectability of flaws	s. flaw detectability
detectable	meßbar groß, nachweisbar, erfaßbar
detecting action of electrolytic cell	elektrolytische Gleichrichterwirkung f, Gleichrichterwirkung (Ventilwirkung f) der elektrolytischen Zelle
detecting crystal, rectifying crystal	Detektorkristall m
detecting ink	s. magnetic paste
detecting instrument, detector ⟨gen.⟩	Detektor m, Nachweisgerät n, nachweisendes Gerät n, Nachweisinstrument n
detecting valve	s. rectifier valve
detecting valve	s. rectifier tube ⟨el.⟩
detection; tracing; tracking; proof; verification; evidence	Nachweis m, Detektion f, Detektierung f; Beobachtung f; Feststellung f; Entdeckung f; [experimenteller] Beweis m
detection	s. a. rectification ⟨el.⟩
detection efficiency, detection sensitivity	Nachweisempfindlichkeit f, Nachweiseffektivität f, Nachweisvermögen n
detection element	s. sensitive element
detection limit ⟨chem.⟩	Erfassungsgrenze f ⟨Chem.⟩
detection limit	s. a. threshold of sensitivity
detection range	Erfassungsreichweite f
detection sensitivity	s. detection efficiency
detection threshold, threshold of detection (detectability)	untere Nachweisgrenze f
detectivity ⟨nucl.⟩	= reciprocal of noise equivalent power
detectivity, detectability	Nachweisbarkeit f
detector, radiation detector, radiation detecting instrument	Detektor m, Strahlungsdetektor m, Strahlungsnachweisgerät n, Strahlendetektor m, Strahlennachweisgerät n
detector ⟨el.⟩	Detektor m, Richtleiter m ⟨El.⟩
detector, crystal detector, crystal-diode detector, crystal rectifier ⟨el.⟩	Detektor m, Kristalldetektor m, Detektorzelle f, Kristalldiode f; Kristallgleichrichter m ⟨El.⟩
detector	s. a. detecting instrument ⟨gen.⟩
detector	s. a. nuclear detector
detector	s. a. rectifier ⟨el.⟩
detector	s. a. detector/1/v
detector diode	s. rectifier diode
detector of sound	Schalldetektor m
detector tube (valve)	s. rectifier tube ⟨el.⟩
detention time	s. residence time
detergent	s. surface active agent
deterioration of catalyst	s. catalyst poisoning
deterioration of the phosphor	Zerstörung f des Leuchtstoffs, Zerstörung der Lumineszenz, Lumineszenzzerstörung f
deterioration of visibility	Sichtverschlechterung f
determinacy	Determiniertheit f
determinal equations	Periodengleichungen fpl, Periodenrelationen fpl
determinant ⟨of order n⟩	Determinante f ⟨n-reihige, n-ter Ordnung, der Ordnung n⟩
determinantal equation	Determinantengleichung f ⟨Determinante gleich Null gesetzt⟩
determinantal polynomial	s. secular determinant ⟨of matrix⟩
determinantal representation	Determinantendarstellung f

determinantal 168

determinantal wave function, Slater determinant	Slater-Determinante *f*	deuteron, deuton, d	Deuteron *n*, Deuton *n*, Deuteriumkern *m*, d
		deuteron-deuteron reaction, D-D reaction	Deuteron-Deuteron-Reaktion *f*, D-D-Reaktion *f*, (d,d)-Reaktion *f*
determinant of ladder network	*s.* iterative determinant		
determinant of the [transformation] coefficients	Koeffizientendeterminante *f*	deuteron-deuteron scattering	Deuteron-Deuteron-Streuung *f*
determinate	determiniert, bestimmt	deuteron fission, deuteron-induced fission, d,f reaction	deuteroninduzierte (deuteronausgelöste) Spaltung *f*, Spaltung (Kernspaltung *f*) durch ein Deuteron, (d,f)-Prozeß *m*, (d,f)-Reaktion *f*
determinate	*s. a.* statically determinate		
determination; assignment	Bestimmung *f*, Ermittlung *f*; Determination *f*		
determination of age	*s.* dating	deuteron photodisintegration	Photospaltung *f* (Photozerfall *m*) des Deuterons, Kernphotoeffekt *m* am Deuteron, Deuteronphotospaltung *f*, D(γ,n)-Prozeß *m*
determination of average age	*s.* averaging		
determination of crystal indices	*s.* indexing <cryst.>		
determination of gas density, manoscopy	Gasdichtebestimmung *f*	deuteron-proton process, (d,p) process	Deuteron-Proton-Reaktion *f*, (d,p)-Prozeß *m*
determination of length	*s.* measurement of length		
determination of moisture content	*s.* moisture-content determination		
determination of molecular weight, molecular weight determination	Molekulargewichtsbestimmung *f*	deuteron stripping	Deuteronstripping *n* <(d,p)- oder (d,n)-Reaktion>
		deuteroxide	*s.* deuterium oxide
		deuton	*s.* deuteron
determination of the distribution coefficients, distribution coefficient determination	Spektralwertbestimmung *f*, Spektrumseichung *f*	developable, evolvable <math.>	abwickelbar <Math.>
		devaporation	= condensation of vapours
		developable <in a series>	entwickelbar, zerlegbar <in eine Reihe>
determination of zero	Nullpunkt[s]bestimmung *f*	developable surface, torse	abwickelbare Fläche *f*, Torse *f*
determining function	*s.* original		
determining function <celestial mech.>	*s.* generating function	developer for X-ray film	Röntgenentwickler *m*
determining variable	*s.* regressor	developer liquid	*s.* solvent <chromatography>
detersion	Detersion *f*, Abschleifung *f* <Geo.>		
detonating agent (explosive)	*s.* initial detonating agent	developer stains, spots caused by developing agent	Entwicklerflecke *mpl*
detonating fireball	*s.* sound-emitting fireball		
detonation adiabatic [line]	Detonationsadiabate *f*	developing agent	Entwicklersubstanz *f*
detonation front	*s.* front of the detonation wave	development <of chromatogram>	Entwicklung *f*, Laufenlassen *n*, Chromatographieren *n* <Chromatogramm>
detonation limits	Detonationsgrenzen *fpl*		
detonation pressure	Detonationsdruck *m*	development, formation <e.g. of flow>	Ausbildung *f*, Entwicklung *f* <z. B. Strömung>
detonation velocity	Detonationsgeschwindigkeit *f*		
detour factor	Umwegfaktor *m*	development, derivation <of formula>	Entwicklung *f*, Herleitung *f*, Ableitung *f* <Formel>
detraction	Detraktion *f*, splitternde Erosion *f*	development <math.>	Abwicklung *f* <Math.>
detrition	Detrition *f*, reibender Verschleiß *m*	development <phot.>	Entwicklung *f* <Phot.>
		development adjacency effect	*s.* neighbourhood effect
detritus	Detritus *m*	development distance	*s.* length of run
		development factor	*s.* gamma <quantity>
		development in a series	*s.* expansion in a series
		development nucleus	Entwicklungskeim *m*, Vollkeim *m*
detuning / 45°	45°-Verstimmung *f*	development of gas	*s.* gas evolution
detuning filter	Verstimmungsfilter *n*	development of heat	*s.* heat release
detuning method, off-resonance method	Verstimmungsmethode *f*, Verstimmungsverfahren *n*	development of scallops	*s.* earing
		development of the coast, line of development of the coast	Verlauf *m* der Küste
detwinning	Entzwillingen *n*		
deuteranomalous vision	Deuteranomalie *f*, Grünschwäche *f*		
deuteranopia, green blindness	Deuteranopie *f*, Grünblindheit *f*	development of the spot group	Entwicklung *f* der Fleckengruppe
deuterated compound, deutero compound	Deuteroverbindung *f*, deuterierte Verbindung *f*	development reactor, pilot reactor	Versuchsreaktor *m*, Pilotreaktor *m*
		development time <chromatography>	Laufzeit *f* <Chromatographie>
deuteration	Deuterierung *f*	deviate	*s.* deviation
		deviating mirror	Umlenkspiegel *m*
deuterium, heavy hydrogen, D, $^2_1$H, ^{2}H	Deuterium *n*, schwerer Wasserstoff *m*	deviating prism, deviation prism, deviative prism	Ablenkprisma *n*, brechender Keil *m*, ablenkendes (brechendes) Prisma *n*; Schwenkkeil *m*
deuterium-moderated reactor	*s.* heavy water pile		
deuterium oxide, deuteroxide, heavy water, D$_2$O	schweres Wasser *n*, Schwerwasser *n*, Deuteriumoxid *n*, D$_2$O	deviation <magn.>, deflection	Ablenkung *f*, Deviation *f* <Magn.>
		deviation, deviate <from> <math., mech.>	Abweichung *f* <vom Mittelwert, vom Sollwert>; Deviation *f* <vom Mittelwert> <Math., Mech.>
deuterium-protium compound, HD	Deuteriumwasserstoff *m*, HD		
deuterium-protium oxide	*s.* semi-heavy water		
deuterium-substituted	deuteriumsubstituiert	deviation	*s. a.* control error
deutero compound, deuterated compound	Deuteroverbindung *f*, deuterierte Verbindung *f*	deviation	*s. a.* unconformity
		deviation detector	*s.* error detector <control>
		deviation from the vertical	*s.* deflection of the plumb line

deviation of the frequency	s. frequency deviation	dextrorotatory quartz, dextrogyric (dextrogyrate, right-handed) quartz	Rechtsquarz m
deviation of the vertical	s. deflection of the plumb line		
deviation prism	s. deviating prism	dextrorse	s. right-handed <techn.>
deviation ratio	Hubverhältnis n, Hubausnutzung f	dextrorse helix	s. right-twisted helix
		dextrorse screw	s. right-twisted helix
deviation to the east	Ostabweichung f	diabatic, non-adiabatic	nichtadiabatisch
deviation value (variable)	s. control error	diabatic flow, Rayleigh flow	diabatische Strömung f, Rayleigh-Strömung f
deviative prism	Umlenkprisma n		
deviative prism	s. deviating prism	diac	s. trigger diode
deviatoric [part of the] strain tensor	s. deviator of stretching	diacaustic [line]	Diakaustik f, diakaustische Linie f, diakaustische Kurve f
deviatoric [part of the] stress tensor	s. stress deviator	diacaustic	s. diacaustic surface
		diacaustic point, diapoint	diakaustischer Punkt m, Diapunkt m
deviator of stretching, deviator strain tensor, strain (deformation deviator, deviatoric [part of the] strain tensor	Deviator m der Streckung, Deviator des Dehnungstensors (Deformationstensors)	diacaustic surface, diacaustic	diakaustische Fläche f, Diakaustik f
		diacoustics, diaphonics	Diakustik f, Lehre f von der Schallbrechung
deviator stress tensor	s. stress deviator	diactinic, violet and ultraviolet transmitting	diaktinisch, violett- und ultraviolettdurchlässig
device fit to be put on <e.g. a microscope>	Aufsatzgerät n, Aufsetzgerät n <z. B. Mikroskop>		
device for measuring fluid flow velocities; current meter, current velocity meter, rheometer	Strömungsgeschwindigkeitsmesser m, Strömungsmesser m; Rheometer n	diad axis, 2-al axis, axis of order 2, two-fold axis [of symmetry], 2-fold axis [of symmetry], two-fold rotary axis	zweizählige (2zählige) Symmetrieachse f, zweizählige Drehungsachse (Drehachse, Rotationsachse, Achse) f, Digyre f
devitrification	Entglasung f, Devitrifikation f	diad axis of the second sort, 2-al [symmetry-] axis of the second sort, two-fold (2-fold) axis of the second sort, axis of the second sort of order 2	zweizählige Drehspiegelungsachse f, Digyroide f, zweizählige Gyroide f
devoid of matter; void of air	luftleer		
Dewar calorimeter, vacuum calorimeter	Vakuumkalorimeter n		
Dewar flask	s. Dewar vacuum flask		
Dewar structure, long-bond structure	Dewar-Struktur f		
Dewar vacuum flask, Dewar vessel, Dewar (vacuum, thermos) flask	Dewar-Gefäß n, Dewarsches (Weinholdsches) Gefäß n, Vakuum[mantel]gefäß n	diageotropic	diageotropisch
		diageotropism	Diageotropismus m
		diagnostic routine, error-detecting routine	Diagnoseprogramm n, Fehlersuchprogramm n
dewatering	s. dehydration <chem.>	diagnostics of plasma	s. plasma diagnostics
dew cap	Taukappe f	diagonal	s. principal diagonal
		diagonal astigmatism	Diagonalastigmatismus m
dew-drop	Tautropfen m		
dew measurer, drosometer	Drosometer n, Taumesser m	diagonal cleavage	Diagonalschieferung f
dew[-]point; dew-point temperature	Taupunkt m; Taupunkt[s]temperatur f	diagonal coast	Diagonalküste f, Schrägküste f
dew-point equation, equation for dew-point	Taupunktsgleichung f	diagonal current	s. transverse current
		diagonal element	Diagonalelement n; Diagonalglied n
dew-point hygrograph, dew-point recorder, dew-point writer	Taupunktschreiber m	diagonal eyepiece	gebrochenes Okular n, Zenitokular n
		diagonal form	Diagonalgestalt f, Diagonalform f
dew-point hygrometer, condensation hygrometer, hygrodeik, dew-point mirror	Taupunkthygrometer n, Kondensationshygrometer n, Taupunktspiegel m, Taupunktmesser m, Taupunktmeßgerät n	diagonalization	Diagonalisierung f
		diagonal matrix	Diagonalmatrix f
		diagonal member, web member <mech.>	Strebe f, Diagonalstab m <Mech.>
dew-point interval, dew-point region	Taupunktbereich m, Taupunktgebiet n	diagonal of the bridge containing the null indicator <meas.>	den Nullindikator enthaltende Brückendiagonale f, Nullzweig m <Meß.>
dew-point mirror	s. dew-point hygrometer		
dew-point recorder	s. dew-point hygrograph	diagonal operator	Diagonaloperator m
dew-point region, dew-point interval	Taupunktbereich m, Taupunktgebiet n	diagonal position	Diagonalstellung f, hellste Stellung f
dew-point temperature	s. dew[-]point	diagonal process	s. Cantor['s] diagonal process
dew-point writer	s. dew-point hygrograph	diagonal sequence	Diagonalfolge f
dextrogyrate	s. dextrogyric <opt.>		
dextrogyrate quartz	s. dextrorotatory quartz	diagonal stratification	Diagonalschichtung f
dextrogyric, dextrorota[to]ry, dextrogyrate, dextrogyrous, rotating the plane of polarization clockwise, D, d, D <opt.>	rechtsdrehend, dextrogyr, d, D <Opt.>	diagonal sum	s. trace <of matrix, operator>
		diagonal sum method	Diagonalsummenmethode f
		diagonal sum rule	Invarianz f der Spur einer Matrix von der Darstellung, Diagonalsummengesetz n
dextrogyric	s. a. right-handed <techn.>		
dextrogyric quartz	s. dextrorotatory quartz		
dextrogyrous	s. dextrogyric	diagonal web	s. strut bracing
dextroisomer, D-isomer, d-isomer	rechtsdrehendes Isomer n, D-Isomer n, d-Isomer n	diagram factor	s. relative efficiency <therm.>
		diagram line, series line	Serienlinie f, Diagrammlinie f
dextropolarization	s. right-handed polarization		
dextrorotary	s. dextrogyric <opt.>	diagram of bands	Bänderschema n, Bänderdiagramm n, Energiebänderschema n
dextrorotation, positive rotation, clockwise rotation	Rechtsdrehung f, positive Drehung f; Rechtslauf m		
		diagram of luminous flux	s. distribution of luminous flux
dextrorotatory	s. dextrogyric <opt.>	diagram of recrystallization	Rekristallisationsdiagramm n, Rekristallisationsschaubild n
dextrorotatory form, D-form, d-form	rechtsdrehende Form f, D-Form f, d-Form f		

diagram of reference, calibration plot	Eichdiagramm n, Bezugsdiagramm n	diaphragm	s. a. partition <chem.>
diagram of state	s. phase diagram	diaphragmatic torus	s. corrugated torus
diagram of velocities	Geschwindigkeitsdiagramm n, Geschwindigkeitsplan m, Geschwindigkeitsschaubild n	diaphragmatic waveguide	s. corrugated waveguide
		diaphragmation	s. diaphragming
		diaphragmation of solid angle, diaphragming of solid angle	Raumwinkelausblendung f
diagram tachometer	Diagrammtachymeter n, Kurventachymeter n	diaphragm capacitor, membrane capacitor	Membrankondensator m
diagrid	s. grate		
diakisdodecahedron	s. diplohedron	diaphragm condenser, condenser with aperturated diaphragm	Lochblendenkondensor m
dial, sundial, sun dial	Sonnenuhr f		
dial balance, bent-lever balance	Zeigerwaage f		
dial barometer, wheel barometer	Zeigerbarometer n	diaphragm current	Strömungsstrom m, Diaphragmenstrom m
dial card [of the compass]	s. compass card	diaphragm electricity	Strömungselektrizität f
dial compass, solar (sun) compass	Sonnenkompaß m	diaphragm for measuring stream velocity	s. travelling screen
dial gauge (indicator)	Meßuhr f	diaphragming, diaphragmation, irising	Ausblendung f; Abblendung f; Einführung f von Blendenscheiben <Wellenleiter>
dial indicator	s. a. pointer instrument		
dial strain gauge	Meßuhrdehnungsmesser m, Dehnungsmeßuhr f	diaphragming of solid angle	s. diaphragmation of solid angle
dialysate	Dialyseprodukt n, Dialysat n	diaphragm lens [for electrons]	Lochblendenlinse f
dialysis	Dialyse f		
dialytic telescope	dialytisches Fernrohr n		
dialyzer	Dialysator m, Dialysierzelle f		
diamagnetic, diamagnetic substance	Diamagnetikum n, diamagnetischer Stoff m	diaphragm photometer	Photometer n mit meßbar veränderlicher Blende, Blendenphotometer n
diamagnetic correction	diamagnetische Korrektion f		
diamagnetic resonance	s. cyclotron resonance	diaphragm pump	Membranpumpe f
diamagnetic screening, diamagnetic shielding	diamagnetische Abschirmung f	diaphragm technique	s. travelling screen technique
diamagnetic screening constant	diamagnetische Abschirmungskonstante f	diaphragm valve; membrane valve	Membranventil n; membranbetätigtes Ventil n
diamagnetic shielding	s. diamagnetic screening	diaphragm voltage	Strömungsspannung f
diamagnetic substance	s. diamagnetic		
diamagnetic susceptibility	diamagnetische Suszeptibilität f		
diamagnetometer	Diamagnetometer n	diapir fold[ing]; piercement folding	Quellfaltung f, Diapirfaltung f
diamer	s. diastereoisomer	diapoint	s. diacaustic point
diamerism	s. diastereoisomerism	diapositive, slide	Diapositiv n, Dia n
diameter error [of the divided circle]	Durchmesserfehler m [des Teilkreises]	diaprojection	s. still projection
		diaschistic rock	s. schizolite
diamond <acc.>	„diamond" m, Bereich m [für das Vorhandensein] periodischer Bahnen	diascopic projection	s. still projection
		diasolysis	Diasolyse f
		distereo[iso]mer, diamer	Diastereomer n, Diastereoisomer n
diamond lattice	s. diamond structure		
diamond principle	„diamond"-Prinzip n	diastereo[iso]merism, diamerism	Diastereomerie f, Diastereoisomerie f
diamond pyramid hardness	s. Vickers hardness number	diastolic pressure <Bio.>	diastolischer Druck m <Bio.>
diamond pyramid hardness test	s. Vickers hardness test	diastrophism, crustal movement	Bewegung f der Erdkruste, Krustenbewegung f, Diastrophismus m
diamond pyramid hardness testing machine	s. Vickers hardness testing machine	diathermal	s. diathermanous
diamond-shaped antenna, rhombic antenna, Bruce antenna	Rhombusantenne f, Rautenantenne f, Bruce-Antenne f	diathermance, diathermancy, permeability to heat <phenomenon>	Wärmedurchlässigkeit f, Diathermansie f, Diathermanität f; Temperaturdurchgriff m <Erscheinung>
diamond structure, diamond lattice	Diamantgitter n, Diamantstruktur f, Diamantgitterstruktur f	diathermanous, diathermic, diathermous, diathermal, permeable to heat, permitting radiant heat to pass through, heat-transmitting	diatherman, wärmedurchlässig, wärmedurchlassend, durchlässig [für Wärmestrahlung]
diamond thermometer	Diamantthermometer n		
dianegative	Dianegativ n		
digphaneity, diaphanousness, translucency	Diaphanität f	diathermometer	Diathermometer n
		diathermous	s. diathermanous
diaphanometer	Lichtdurchlässigkeitsprüfer m, Diaphanometer n	diatomaceous earth, diatomite	s. Kieselgur
diaphanoscope	Diaphanoskop n, Lufttrübungsmesser m von Scharonow	diatonic tone scale	diatonische Tonleiter (Tonskala, Tonfolge)
diaphanous, translucent	durchscheinend, diaphan		
		diaxiality, biaxiality	Zweiachsigkeit f
diaphanousness	s. diaphaneity		
diaphonics	s. diacoustics	dichotomy	Dichotomie f, Halbphase f <Astr.>; Gabelung f
diaphorimeter	Perspirationsmesser m	dichotomy	s. a. alternative variability <stat.>
diaphototropic	diaphototropisch		
diaphototropism	Diaphototropismus m	dichroic	dichroitisch
diaphragm	s. travelling screen		
diaphragm, iris	Blende[nscheibe] f, Runzel f <Hohlleiter>	dichroic, dichromatic, two-colour, bicolor, bicoloured; bichromatic	zweifarbig, bichromatisch, dichromatisch
diaphragm; stop; blind; shutter; septum <opt.>	Blende f, Diaphragma n <Opt.>		
diaphragm	s. a. aperturated diaphragm <opt.>	dichroic fog	dichroitischer (zweifarbiger) Schleier m, Lösungsschleier m

dichroic mirror	s colour selective mirror	dielectric strength, electric strength, disruptive strength; breakdown field, disruptive electric field strength, breakdown field strength	Durchschlagfestigkeit f, Durchschlagsfestigkeit f, Durchschlagsfeldstärke f, Durchbruchfeldstärke f, dielektrische Feldstärke (Festigkeit) f; Überschlagsfeldstärke f, Überschlagsfestigkeit f
dichroic ratio	dichroitisches Verhältnis n		
dichroism	Zweifarbigkeit f, Dichroismus m		
dichromatic	s. dichroic		
dichromatic vision, dichromatism, partial colour blindness	Dichromasie f, partielle Farbenblindheit f, Zweifarbenblindheit f, Dichromatopsie f		
dichroscopic magnifier	dichroskopische Lupe f, Dichroskop n; Haidingersche Lupe f	dielectric susceptibility	s. susceptibility <el.>
		dielectric tensor, permittivity tensor, tensor of permittivity	dielektrischer Tensor m, Tensor der Dielektrizitätskonstante, DK-Tensor m, Epsilontensor m. ε-Tensor m Dielektrizitätstensor m
Dicke radiometer	Dickesches Radiometer n		
diclinic	diklin		
di-digonal equatorial class	s. orthorhombic holohedry		
di-digonal polar class	s. hemimorphic hemihedry of the orthorhombic system	dielectric waveguide	dielektrischer Wellenleiter m
didymium, Di <neodymium-praseodymium mixture>	Didym n, Di <Neodym-Praseodym-Gemisch>	dielectrometry, measurement of permittivity (dielectric constant)	DK-Metrie f, Dielektrometrie f, Dekametrie f
die-away time	s. decay time	dielectronic recombination, two-electron recombination	Zweielektronenrekombination f, dielektrische Rekombination f
dielectric; dielectric fluid; [electric] insulator; non-conductor	Dielektrikum n; dielektrisches Medium n; [elektrischer] Isolator m; Nichtleiter m		
		dielectrophoresis	Dielektrophorese f
dielectric; non[-]conducting, non-conductive; insulating <el.>	dielektrisch; nichtleitend; isolierend <El.>	diesel, Diesel engine, compression-ignition engine	Gleichdruckmaschine f, Maschine f mit Gleichdruckverbrennung, Diesel[-Motor] m
dielectric amplifier	dielektrischer Verstärker m, Resonanzverstärker m	Diesel cycle, diesel cycle	Dieselscher Kreisprozeß m, Diesel-Prozeß m
dielectric antenna	s. dielectric rod antenna		
dielectric breakdown	s. breakdown		
dielectric conductance	dielektrischer Leitwert m	Diesel engine	s. diesel
		Diesselhorst [direct-current] potentiometer	Diesselhorst-Kompensator m, Kompensator m nach Diesselhorst
dielectric conductance	s. a. dielectric leakage		
dielectric constant	s. permittivity <of the material>	Dieterici['s] equation, Dieterici equation of state	Dietericische Gleichung (Zustandsgleichung) f, Dieterici-Gleichung f
dielectric constant	s. relative permittivity <of the material>		
dielectric displacement	s. electric displacement <el.>	dif, δ	rundes d, δ
		difference absorption	s. selective absorption
dielectric fatigue, dielectric remanence	dielektrische Nachwirkung f, dielektrische Remanenz f	difference band	Differenzbande f
		difference between saturation and real temperature	Unterkühlung f, Grädigkeit f, Differenz f zwischen Sättigungs- und tatsächlicher Temperatur
dielectric field	dielektrisches Feld n		
dielectric fluid	s. dielectric		
dielectric heating	dielektrische Erhitzung (Erwärmung) f, Dielektrikerhitzung f	difference-differential equation	Differenzen-Differentialgleichung f, Differential-Differenzengleichung f, Hystero-Differentialgleichung f
dielectric hysteresis	dielektrische Hysterese f, Nichtleiterhysterese f		
		difference equation	Differenzengleichung f
dielectric leakage, dielectric leakance	s. leakance		
dielectric loss	dielektrischer Verlust m	difference factorization method	Methode f der Differenzenfaktorisierung, Differenzenfaktorisierungsmethode f
dielectric loss angle, loss angle	dielektrischer Verlustwinkel m, Verlustwinkel [des Dielektrikums]		
dielectric loss coefficient (factor)	s. loss tangent	difference group	s. factor group
		difference in brightness (luminance), luminance (brightness) difference	Leuchtdichteunterschied m, Helligkeitsunterschied m
dielectric polarization, electric polarization, polarization vector, polarization [of dielectric] <el.>	elektrische Polarisation f [des Dielektrikums], dielektrische Polarisation, Vektor m der elektrischen Polarisation, Polarisationsvektor m, Polarisation [des Dielektrikums], Dipoldichte f, Elektrisierung f <El.>		
		difference in optical path	s. difference of path
		difference limen	s. difference threshold
		difference method	Differenz[meß]methode f, Differenz[en]verfahren n; Differenzenmethode f <Math.>
		difference number, neutron excess [number]	Neutronenüberschuß m
dielectric power factor	s. loss tangent	difference of concentrations	s. concentration difference
dielectric principal axis, principal axis of permittivity	dielektrische Hauptachse f	difference of level; altitude difference	Niveauunterschied m, Gefällhöhe f; Höhenunterschied m, Höhendifferenz f
dielectric relaxation; dipole relaxation	dielektrische Relaxation f, Dipolrelaxation f		
		difference of path, difference in optical path, path difference, relative retardation of optical paths, retardation <of rays>	Gangunterschied m, Gangdifferenz f, Wegunterschied m, Wegdifferenz f <Strahlen>
dielectric relaxation time	dielektrische Relaxationszeit f		
dielectric remanence	s. dielectric fatigue	difference of potential	s. electric tension
dielectric resistance	s. insulation resistance	difference of temperature, temperature difference	Temperaturdifferenz f, Temperaturunterschied m <in grd>
dielectric rigidity	s. dielectric strength		
dielectric rod antenna, dielectric rod radiator, rod radiator, dielectric antenna	Stielstrahler m, dielektrischer Stielstrahler, dielektrische Antenne f; dielektrischer Stabstrahler m, Stabstrahler	difference of the logarithm to base ten of internal optical density to unity	Diabatie f
		difference operator	Differenzenoperator m

difference

difference quotient	Differenzenquotient m
difference ring	s. residue[-]class ring
difference schema method	Differenzenschemaverfahren n
difference threshold, differential threshold, difference limen, just noticeable difference	Unterschiedsschwelle f, Wahrnehmungsschwelle f
difference[-]tone, differential tone	Differenzton m, Schwebungston m
different from zero	s. non-zero
differentiability, derivability	Differenzierbarkeit f
differential aberration	differentielle Aberration f
differential absorption ratio	differentielles Absorptionsverhältnis n
differential analysis	Differentialanalyse f; Komplexanalyse f <Geo.>
differential analyzer, differential-analyzer type of calculating machine <math.>	Integrieranlage f, Integriermaschine f, Differentialanalysator m <Math.>
differential block	s. differential pulley
differential bridge [of Jaumann], Jaumann differential bridge, Q bridge	Jaumann-Brücke f, Differentialmeßbrücke f nach Jaumann
differential-bridge-type spectrometer, Lippmann-Weber spectrometer	Spektrometer n mit Differentialbrücke [nach Lippmann und Weber], Brückenspektrometer n
differential calorimeter, twin calorimeter	Differentialkalorimeter n, Zwillingskalorimeter n
differential catalogue	Anschlußkatalog m
differential coefficient	s. derivative <math.>
differential-compound	gegenkompoundiert, Gegenverbund-
differential control	s. rate-action control
differential cross-section	differentieller Wirkungsquerschnitt (Querschnitt) m, Differential[-Wirkungs]querschnitt m
differential determination	s. relative determination <of star position or brightness>
differential discriminator	Differentialdiskriminator m, Differenzdiskriminator m
differential dissolution heat, differential heat of solution (mixing, dilution), heat of dilution	differentielle Lösungswärme f
differential effective emission	differentielle effektive Ausstrahlung f
differential equation of Clairaut, Clairaut['s] [differential] equation	Clairautsche Differentialgleichung f
differential equation of d'Alembert-Lagrange, d'Alembert['s] differential equation, Lagrange['s] differential equation	Differentialgleichung f von d'Alembert-Lagrange, d'Alembertsche Differentialgleichung, Lagrangesche Differentialgleichung
differential equation of Fuchsian type	s. Fuchs type [differential] equation
differential equation of Hill type	s. Hill['s] differential equation
differential equation of Riccati, Riccati['s] equation	[allgemeine] Riccatische Differentialgleichung f
differential equation of the elliptical type	s. elliptical differential equation
differential equation of the hyperbolic type	s. hyperbolic differential equation
differential equation of the parabolic cylinder function, Weber['s] differential equation	Differentialgleichung f der Funktion des parabolischen Zylinders, Webersche Differentialgleichung
differential equation of the parabolic type	s. parabolic equation
differential equation of the polytrope	Polytropendifferentialgleichung f, Differentialgleichung f der Polytrope
differential equation of Van der Pol	s. Pol['s] differential equation / Van der
differential extinction coefficient	differentieller Extinktionskoeffizient m
differential fading, selective fading	selektiver Schwund m, Selektivschwund m, Interferenzschwund m
differential filter, Jaumann filter	Differentialfilter n, Tangensfilter n, Jaumann-Filter n
differential flowmeter	Staudruckströmungsmesser m, Staurohr-Strömungsmesser m, Differenzdruckströmungsmesser m
differential form <math., also e.g. of a law>	Differentialform f <Math., auch z. B. eines Gesetzes>
differential gauge	s. differential manometer
differential heat of dilution (mixing, solution)	s. differential dissolution heat
differential impedance	s. internal resistance <of thermionic valve, triode>
differential instrument, differential measuring instrument	Differenzmesser m, Differentialmeßgerät n, differentielles Meßgerät n
differential invariant	Differentialinvariante f
differential ionization chamber	Differential[ionisations]kammer f, differentielle Ionisationskammer f
differential Joule-Thomson effect	differentieller Joule-Thomson-Effekt m
differential magnetograph	s. gradient variometer
differential magnetograph	s. magnetic gradiometer
differential manometer, differential [pressure] gauge	Differentialmanometer n, Differenzdruckmesser m, Feindruckmanometer n
differential measuring instrument, differential instrument	Differenzmesser m, Differentialmeßgerät n, differentielles Meßgerät n
differential of arc, element of length, linear element, line element	Bogenelement n, Bogendifferential n, Linienelement n
differential of area	s. element of area
differential operator	Differentialoperator m
differential parameter of the first order, two-parametric gradient	erster Beltramischer Differentialparameter (Differentiator) m
differential parameter of the second order	s. laplacian
differential permeability	Differentialpermeabilität f, differentielle Permeabilität f
differential pressure, pressure differential	Druckunterschied m, Druckdifferenz f; Differenzdruck m, Wirkdruck m, Differentialdruck m
differential pressure gauge, differential pressure indicator	Wirkdruckmesser m
differential pressure gauge	s. a. differential manometer
differential pressure indicator	s. differential pressure gauge
differential pressure producer (transmitter)	Wirkdruckgeber m, Wirkdruckwandler m
differential process	s. additive process
differential pulley, differential block	Differentialflaschenzug m
differential quotient	s. derivative <math.>
differential range spectrum	differentielles Reichweitenspektrum n, differentielle Reichweitenverteilung f
differential refractometer	Differenzrefraktometer n
differential resistance	s. internal resistance <of thermionic valve, triode>
differential rotation of the Galaxy	differentielle Rotation f des Milchstraßensystems
differential scanning calorimetry, DSC	Kalorimetrie f mit Differentialabtastung, Differentialscanningkalorimetrie f, DSK
differential theorem <of Laplace transform>	Differentiationssatz m
differential thermal analysis, DTA	Differentialthermoanalyse f, DTA

differential thermal e.m.f.	differentielle Thermo-EMK f, differentielle Thermospannung (Thermokraft) f	**diffraction grating,** grating <opt.>	Beugungsgitter n, [optisches] Gitter n <Opt.>
differential thermobalance	Differentialthermowaage f	**diffraction group**	Beugungsgruppe f
		diffraction image	s. diffraction pattern
differential thermocouple	Differentialthermoelement n	**diffraction index**	s. Miller index
		diffraction instrument, diffractometer, diffracting device	Beugungsgerät n, Diffraktometer n
differential thermogravimetric analysis	s. differential thermogravimetry	**diffraction line**	s. diffraction curve
differential thermogravimetry, derivative thermogravimetry, differential (derivative) thermogravimetric analysis, DTG	Differentialthermogravimetrie f, derivative Thermogravimetrie f, DTG	**diffraction loss**	Diffraktionsverlust m
		diffraction maximum, diffraction peak	Beugungsmaximum n
		diffraction microscopy	Diffraktionsmikroskopie f, Beugungsmikroskopie f
		diffraction mottle, diffraction spot	Beugungsfleck m
differential thermogravimetry / by (of), DTG	differentialthermogravimetrisch, DTG	**diffraction oscillation**	Beugungsschwingung f, Diffraktionsschwingung f
differential thermometer; aethrioscope	Differentialthermometer n, Differentialthermoskop n	**diffraction pattern,** diffraction image	Beugungserscheinung f, Beugungsbild n, Beugungsfigur f, Beugungsdiagramm n; beugungsoptische Abbildung f
differential threshold	s. difference threshold		
differential tone	s. difference[-]tone		
differential transducer	Differentialgeber m	**diffraction pattern,** diffraction photograph, diffractogram	Beugungsaufnahme f, Beugungsdiagramm n
		diffraction peak, diffraction maximum	Beugungsmaximum n
differential transformer	Differentialübertrager m, Differentialtransformator m; Ausgleichsübertrager m; Brückenübertrager m	**diffraction phenomenon**	Beugungserscheinung f
		diffraction photograph	s. diffraction pattern
		diffraction problem involving edges, problem involving edges	Kantenproblem n, Kantenbeugungsproblem n
differential wattmeter	s. Johnson power meter	**diffraction ring**	Beugungsring m
differential Zener resistance	s. break-through resistance		
differentiating circuit	s. differentiator	**diffraction scattering**	s. shadow scattering
differentiation <of pulses>, electric differentiation	Differentiation f, Differenzierung f, Differenzierung f <Impulse>, elektrische Differentiation	**diffraction spectrograph**	s. grating spectrograph
		diffraction spectrometer, grating spectrometer	Gitterspektrometer n, Beugungsspektrometer n
differentiation, derivation <with respect to> <math.>	Differentiation f, Ableitung f <nach> <Math.>	**diffraction spectroscope,** grating spectroscope	Beugungsspektroskop n, Gitterspektroskop n
differentiation	s. a. discrimination		
differentiation operator; differentiation symbol	Differentiationsoperator m; Differentiationssymbol n	**diffraction spectrum**	Beugungsspektrum n
		diffraction spot	s. diffraction mottle
		diffraction wave	s. diffracted wave
differentiation term by term, term-by-term differentiation	gliedweise Differentiation f	**diffractogram**	s. diffraction pattern
		diffractometer	s. diffraction instrument
		diffractometry	s. diffraction analysis
differentiator, differentiating circuit	Differenzierglied n, Differenzierteil n, Differentiator m, Differenziergerät n; Differenzierschaltung f	**diffusate**	Diffusat n
		diffuse band	diffuse Bande f
		diffused base transistor	Transistor m mit inhomogen-diffundierter Basis
differentiator <math.>	Differentiator m, Derivimeter n, Derivator m <Math.>	**diffused-base transistor**	s. a. diffusion transistor
		diffuse density	diffuse Schwärzung f
different phase / of	ungleichphasig, verschiedenphasig	**diffused junction,** diffused layer <semi.>	Diffusionsübergang m, Diffusionsschicht f, diffusionserzeugte Schicht f <Halb.>
diffluence <geo.>	Diffluenz f		
difform <difform system>	difform <difformes System>		
		diffused-junction transistor	Diffusionsflächentransistor m
diffracted wave, diffraction wave	gebeugte (abgebeugte) Welle f, Beugungswelle f		
diffracting device	s. diffraction instrument	**diffused layer**	s. diffused junction <semi.>
diffracting edge	beugende Kante f, Beugungskante f	**diffuse double layer,** Gouy layer, diffuse part of the double layer	diffuser Anteil m der elektrochemischen Doppelschicht, diffuse Doppelschicht f, Gouysche Schicht f, Gouy-Doppelschicht f
diffraction <from, by>	Beugung f <an>; Diffraktion f; Abbeugen n		
diffractional disk, diffraction disk	Beugungsscheibchen n, Beugungsscheibe f		
diffraction analysis, diffractometry	Beugungsanalyse f, Beugungsuntersuchung f, Diffraktometrie f	**diffused radiation,** imprisoned radiation	diffundierte Strahlung f, Diffusionsstrahlung f
		diffused transistor	s. diffusion transistor
diffraction angle	Beugungswinkel m	**diffuse edge,** smearing-out of boundary	Randauflockerung f, Randverschmierung f
diffraction broadening	Diffraktionsverbreiterung f, Verbreiterung f durch Beugung	**diffuse edge / having**	s. diffuse edges / with
		diffuse edges / with, having diffuse edge, tapered	randverschmiert
diffraction by grating	Gitterbeugung f, Beugung f am Gitter		
diffraction by passage through a slit	Beugung f am Spalt	**diffuse halation,** diffusion halation	Diffusionslichthof m
diffraction cone	Beugungskegel m	**diffusely scattered**	diffus gestreut
diffraction curve, diffraction line	Beugungskurve f, Beugungslinie f	**diffuse nebula**	diffuser Nebel m
diffraction disintegration of deuteron	Diffraktionsspaltung f des Deuterons	**diffuseness**	Eigenschaft f, diffus zu sein; diffuse Beschaffenheit f
diffraction disk, diffractional disk	Beugungsscheibchen n, Beugungsscheibe f	**diffuseness**	s. a. unsharpness <opt.>
		diffuseness of the line, unsharpness of the line, line unsharpness	Linienunschärfe f, Unschärfe f der Spektrallinie
diffraction dispersing system	s. dispersing system with diffraction grating		
diffraction fringe	Beugungsstreifen m; Beugungssaum m	**diffuse part of the double layer**	s. diffuse double layer

diffuser

diffuser ‹of light›, light diffuser ‹opt.›	lichtstreuender Körper m, Lichtstreu[ungs]körper m, Streukörper m ‹Licht›; Lichtdiffusor m; Weichstrahler m ‹Opt.›	diffusion by interchange	s. interchange mechanism of diffusion
		diffusion by turbulence	s. eddy diffusion
		diffusion capacitance	Diffusionskapazität f
diffuser ‹aero.›	Diffusor m ‹Aero.›	diffusion chamber, diffusion cloud chamber	Diffusionsnebelkammer f
diffuse radiation	s. scattered radiation		
diffuse reflectance ‹US›	s. diffuse reflection factor		
diffuse reflection, scattering, scattered (dispersed) reflection	diffuse (gestreute) Reflexion f, Streureflexion f; Remission f ‹Licht›	diffusion coefficient, coefficient of diffusion, diffusivity, diffusion constant	Diffusionskoeffizient m, Diffusionskonstante f
diffuse reflection factor, [diffuse] reflectance ‹US›	diffuser Anteil m des Reflexionsgrades, Grad m der diffusen (gestreuten) Reflexion; Remissionsgrad m, Remissionskoeffizient m	diffusion coefficient	s. a. scattering coefficient
		diffusion coefficient-mobility relation	s. Einstein['s] relation
		diffusion constant	Diffusionskonstante f
		diffusion constant	s. a. diffusion coefficient
diffuse-reflection photometer	Diffusionsphotometer n	diffusion-controlled limiting current	s. limiting current ‹el.chem.›
		diffusion cooling	Diffusionskühlung f
diffuse reflection spectrum, spectrum of diffuse reflection, reflectance spectrum	Spektrum n diffuser Reflexion, Remissionsspektrum n		
		diffusion cross-section	s. diffusion area
		diffusion current	s. limiting current ‹el.chem.›
diffuse refraction, scattered (dispersed) refraction	diffuse (gestreute) Brechung f, Streubrechung f	diffusion current density, diffusion flow	Diffusionsstromdichte f
diffuser grid	Verzögerungsgitter n, Verzögerungsprofilgitter n, Diffusorgitter n	diffusion depth	Diffusionstiefe f, Tiefe f der Diffusionsschicht
diffuser screen	s. light-diffusing screen		
diffuse scattering	s. disorder scattering	diffusion diameter, equivalent classical mean hard-spherical diameter	Diffusionsdurchmesser m
diffuse series	erste (diffuse) Nebenserie f, diffuse Serie f		
diffuse spectrum	diffuses Spektrum n	diffusion electrode, porous electrode	Diffusionselektrode f
diffuse spot	diffuser Schwärzungsfleck m	diffusion equation	s. Fick['s] second law
diffuse transmission, scattered (dispersed) transmission	gestreute (diffuse) Transmission f, gestreute (diffuse) Durchlassung f	diffusion equation of Beltrami	s. Beltrami['s] diffusion equation
		diffusion equilibrium	s. equilibrium of diffusion
diffuse transmission factor, diffuse transmittance ‹US›	diffuser (gestreuter) Anteil m des Durchlaßgrades, Grad m der gestreuten (diffusen) Durchlassung (Transmission), Durchlässigkeitsfaktor m	diffusion factor, diffusing (diffusion) power ‹of the secondary source›	Streuvermögen n ‹lichtstreuender Körper›
		diffusion flame	Diffusionsflamme f
diffusibility, diffusibleness	Diffusionsvermögen n, Diffusionsfähigkeit f	diffusion flow, flow of diffusing molecules	Diffusionsstrom m, Diffusionsströmung f
		diffusion flow	s. a. diffusion current density
diffusing; diffusion ‹into, through, in›; indiffusion	Diffundieren n; Einwanderung f, Eindiffundieren n; Durchwanderung f; Diffusion f	diffusion frequency	Diffusionsfrequenz f
		diffusion front	Diffusionsfront f
diffusing disk	s. diffusing lens	diffusion function	s. Mie['s] scattering function
diffusing filter	Streufilter n		
diffusing glass	s. opal glass	diffusion halation, diffuse halation	Diffusionslichthof m
diffusing lens, diffusing disk, Duto lens	Dutolinse f, Dutoscheibe f, Weichzeichnerscheibe f, Weichzeichner m, Streuscheibe f	diffusion hardening [of the neutron spectrum], neutron hardening by diffusion	Diffusionshärtung f [des Neutronenspektrums]
diffusing of the wave packet	Zerfließen n des Wellenpakets		
diffusing power	s. diffusion factor ‹of the secondary source›	diffusion heat, heat of transfer (transport)	Diffusionswärme f, Überführungswärme f
diffusing screen; incident light attachment ‹cpt.›	Streuscheibe f, Streuschirm m, Streuer m ‹Opt.›	diffusion hygrometer	Diffusionshygrometer n [nach Greinacher], Greinacher-Hygrometer n
diffusing time [of wave packet]	Zerflißzeit f [des Wellenpakets]	diffusion indicatrix	s. scattering indicatrix
		diffusion kernel, Yukawa kernel	Diffusions[integral]kern m
diffusion	s. diffusing	diffusion law	s. Fick['s] law
diffusion	s. scattering	diffusion layer ‹el.chem.›, Nernst diffusion layer	[Nernstsche] Diffusionsschicht f ‹El.chem.›
diffusion	s. scattering [of light]		
diffusion after-effect	s. Richter lag	diffusion length	Diffusionslänge f
diffusion-age approximation	Diffusions-Alters-Näherung f	diffusionless transformation, martensitic (martensite, shear-type, shear, military) transformation	Martensitumwandlung f, martensitische (diffusionslose, diffusionsfreie) Umwandlung f, Scherungsumwandlung f, Umwandlung ohne Diffusion
diffusional jog	Diffusionssprung m		
diffusional transformation	s. nucleation and growth transformation		
diffusion analysis	Diffusionsanalyse f		
diffusion annealing	Diffusionsglühen n	diffusion magnetic after-effect	s. Richter lag
diffusion approximation	Diffusionsnäherung f	diffusion mass-transfer	Diffusionstransport m
diffusion area, diffusion cross-section	Diffusionsquerschnitt[sfläche f] m		
diffusion area, square of neutron diffusion length ‹nucl.›	Diffusionsfläche f, Quadrat n der Neutronendiffusionslänge ‹Kern.›	diffusion mean free path, mean free path for diffusion, mean diffusion path	mittlere freie Diffusionsweglänge f, [mittlere] Diffusionsweglänge, mittlere freie Weglänge für Diffusion, mittlerer Diffusionsweg m
diffusion barrier	Diffusionsbarriere f, Diffusionsschranke f; Diffusionswand f	diffusion mobility	Diffusionsbeweglichkeit f
diffusion boundary layer	Diffusionsgrenzschicht f	diffusion of chemical impurities, diffusion of impurity atoms	Fremddiffusion f
diffusion breadth, diffusion width ‹of the track›	Diffusionsbreite f der Spur	diffusion of light	s. scattering ‹of light›
		diffusion of vorticity	s. eddy diffusion

diffusion overpotential; diffusion polarization	Diffusionsüberspannung f; Diffusionspolarisation f	dihedral angle, dihedron	Diederecke f, Zweiflach n, Dieder n
		dihedral group	Diedergruppe f
diffusion permeability	Diffusionspermeabilität f	dihedron, dihedral angle	Diederecke f, Zweiflach n, Dieder n
diffusion photo-e.m.f.	Diffusions-Photo-EMK f	dihexagonal alternating class	s. rhombohedral holohedry
diffusion polarization	s. diffusion overpotential	dihexagonal bipyramidal class, dihexagonal-dipyramidal [crystal] class, dihexagonal equatorial class	s. holohedry of the hexagonal system
diffusion potential, junction potential, liquid junction potential, potential of the diffusion force	Diffusionspotential n, Flüssigkeitspotential n		
		dihexagonal polar (pyramidal) class	s. hemimorphic hemihedry of the hexagonal system
diffusion potential difference, diffusion voltage, potential difference ‹semi.›	Diffusionsspannung f ‹Halb.›	diisotactic	diisotaktisch
		dilatancy, volume change by shear, Kelvin effect, viscous dilatancy	Dilatanz f, Volum[en]änderung f durch Scherung, Kelvin-Effekt m
diffusion power ‹of the secondary source›	s. diffusion factor	dilatation; extension; expansion	Dilatation f; Dehnung f; Ausdehnung f; Zerrung f; Ausweitung f
diffusion pressure	Diffusionsdruck m		
diffusion pressure deficit	Saugdruck m, Diffusionsdruckdefizit n	dilatational coefficient of friction	s. second viscosity coefficient
diffusion pump	Diffusionspumpe f; Diffusionsluftpumpe f	dilatational fissure, extension fissure (crevice)	Zugkluft f, Zugspalte f, Zerrspalte f
diffusion rate, rate (speed, rapidity) of diffusion, diffusion velocity	Diffusionsgeschwindigkeit f	dilatational shock, rarefaction[al] shock, shock of rarefaction	Verdünnungsstoß m
diffusion relaxation	Diffusionsrelaxation f	dilatational strain, volume (bulk) strain, strain of volume	relative Volum[en]änderung f, Volum[en]dilatation f, Dilatation f
diffusion resistance, resistance to diffusion ‹bio.›	Diffusionswiderstand m ‹Bio.›	dilatational strain, uniform dilatation, pure dilatational strain	gleichförmige Dilatation f, reine Volumenänderung f
diffusion resistance; resistance to spreading, spreading resistance ‹semi.›	Ausbreitungswiderstand m ‹Halb.›	dilatational wave, extensional (dilational) wave ‹mech.›	Dehnungswelle f, Dehnwelle f, Dilatationswelle f
diffusion ring	Diffusionsring m	dilatational wave	s. a. longitudinal wave
diffusion room	s. reverberation chamber	dilatational wave	s. a. rarefactional wave ‹aero., hydr.›
diffusion separating column	Diffusionstrennkolonne f	dilatational work, volume[tric] work	Volum[en]arbeit f
diffusion thermoeffect, Dufour effect	Diffusionsthermoeffekt m, Dufour-Effekt m	dilatation curve, dilatometric curve	Dilatationskurve f
diffusion time, thermal neutron lifetime	Diffusionszeit f	dilatation number; volume ratio; volume relation	Volum[en]verhältnis n
diffusion transistor, diffused-base transistor, diffused transistor	Diffusionstransistor m, diffundierter Transistor m	dilatation of the pupil, mydriasis	Pupillenerweiterung f, Mydriasis f
		dilatation wave	s. rarefactional wave ‹aero., hydr.›
diffusion velocity	s. diffusion rate	dilation	s. dilatation
diffusion viscosity	Diffusionsviskosität f	dilatometer	Dilatometer n, Wärme[aus]dehnungsmesser m, Ausdehnungsmesser m, Dehnungsmesser m
diffusion voltage ‹semi.›, [diffusion] potential difference	Diffusionsspannung f ‹Halb.›		
diffusion wave	Diffusionswelle f	dilatometric curve, dilatation curve	Dilatationskurve f
diffusion width ‹of the track›, diffusion breadth	Diffusionsbreite f der Spur	dilatometric measurement, dilatometry	Wärme[aus]dehnungsmessung f, Ausdehnungsmessung f, Dehnungsmessung f, dilatometrische Messung f, Dilatometrie f
diffusiophoresis	Diffusiophorese f		
diffusive equilibrium, equilibrium of diffusion, diffusion equilibrium	Diffusionsgleichgewicht n		
		diluent	Verdünnungsmittel n, Verdünner m
diffusivity ‹ac.›	Diffusität f ‹Ak.›	dilute colouration	dilute (aufgelöste, verdünnte) Färbung f
diffusivity	s. a. diffusion coefficient		
diffusivity [for heat]	s. thermal diffusivity	dilution, thinning, desaturation ‹of the solution›	Verdünnung f, Konzentrationsverminderung f ‹Lösung›
diffusivity for (of) momentum	s. eddy viscosity		
digamma function, psi-function	Digammafunktion f, [Gaußsche] Psi-Funktion f, [Gaußsche] Ψ-Funktion f	dilution analysis	Verdünnungsanalyse f
		dilution effect	Verdünnungseffekt m
digesting, digestion	Digerieren n		
digestion ‹bio.›	Verdauung f, Digestion f ‹Bio.›	dilution factor	Verdünnungsfaktor m, Verdünnung f ‹Größe›
digitizing	Digitalumsetzung f, Digitaldarstellung f	dilution gauging, dilution metering	Verdünnungsverfahren n [der Wassermengenmessung]
digonal	digonal		
digonal equatorial class	s. monoclinic holohedry		
digonal holoaxial class	s. enantiomorphous hemihedry of the orthorhombic system	dilution heat, heat of dilution	Verdünnungswärme f
		dilution metering	s. dilution gauging
digonal polar class	s. hemimorphic hemihedry of the monoclinic system	dim	s. mat
		dimension, dimensionality, dim ‹math., phys., techn.›	Dimension f, dim ‹Math., Phys., Techn.›; Größenart f ‹Phys.›
digraph	s. directed graph		
digression	[astronomische] Digression f	dimension	s. a. linear dimension ‹gen.›
dihedral angle	Kantenwinkel m, Flächenwinkel m, Diederwinkel m	dimensional, with (having a) dimension	dimensionsbehaftet

dimensional 176

dimensional analysis (consideration), method of dimensions	Dimensionsanalyse f, Dimensionsanalysis f, Dimensionsanalytik f, Dimensionalbetrachtung f, Dimensionsbetrachtung f	dioptric rule dioptrics, anaclastics	Visierplatte f, Visierlineal n Dioptrik f, Lehre f von der Brechung des Lichtes
dimensional equation, dimensional relation	Dimensionsgleichung f	dioptrometer	Dioptrienmesser m, Sphärometer n für Brillengläser; Dioptriemeter n
		diosmosis	Diosmose f, zweiseitige Osmose f
dimensional formula, measure formula	Dimensionszeichen n, Dimensionsformel f, Dimensionssymbol n, Dimensionsausdruck m	dip, sagging, dipping dip <of curve, surface>	Durchhängen n, Durchhang m; Durchbiegung f Einsattlung f <Kurve, Fläche>
dimensional invariance	dimensionelle Invarianz f	dip, fall of ground, downgoing <geo.>	Fallen n, Einfallen n <Geo.>
dimensionality	s. dimension <math., phys.>	dip	s. a. magnetic dip
dimensional perturbation	dimensionale Störung f	dip	s. a. dipping
dimensional quantity	dimensionsbehaftete Größe f	dip	s. a. cyclone <meteo.>
dimensional relation	s. dimensional equation	dip[-]circle, magnetic dip circle	Inklinatorium n
dimensional transformation	dimensionelle Transformation f	dip contact, dipping contact	Tauchkontakt m
dimensioning; proportioning; sizing; choice of parameters; design	Dimensionierung f, Bemessung f	dip gettering	Tauchgetterung f
		diphase region, two-phase region	Zweiphasenbereich m, Zweiphasengebiet n, heterogenes Gebiet n des Zweiphasengemisches
dimensionless, non[-]dimensional	dimensionslos, dimensionsfrei		
dimensionless group (number, parameter)	s. similarity parameter <therm.>	diplet	s. doublet
dimensionless number	s. a. pure number	diplohedron, diploid, disdodecahedron, diakisdodecahedron, dyakisdodecahedron	Diploeder n, Diploid n, Dyakisdodekaeder n, Disdodekaeder n
dimensionless quantity	s. relative quantity		
dimensionless specific speed, shape number	dimensionslose Schnelläufigkeitszahl f		
dimension product	Dimensionsprodukt n	diploidal [crystal] class	s. paramorphic hemihedry of the regular system
dimerism	Dimerie f		
dimetric	dimetrisch, monodimetrisch	dip needle, dipping needle	Inklinationsnadel f, Inklinationsbussole f, Inklinationskompaß m, Neigungskompaß m
dimetric projection	dimetrische Parallelperspektive (Projektion) f		
dimi..., dm <= 10^-4	Dimi..., dm <= 10^-4	dip of the horizon, apparent depression of horizon	Kimmtiefe f, Depression f des Horizonts, Verengung f des Horizonts
diminished interval <ac.>	vermindertes Intervall n <Ak.>		
diminishing	s. diminution		
diminishing factor, reduction factor	Verkleinerungsfaktor m		
diminution, optical diminution, diminishing, [optical] reduction <opt.>	Verkleinerung f, optische Verkleinerung <Opt.>	dipolar effect	s. dipole effect
		dipolar gas	s. dipole gas
		dipolar ion	s. amphoteric ion
		dipolar orientation, dipole orientation	Dipolorientierung f
diminution	s. a. decay	dipolar strength	Dipolstärke f
diminution	s. a. reduction	dipole	Dipol m
diminution factor	Abminderungsfaktor m	dipole <hydr.>, doublet source, doublet, dipole source	Doppelquelle f, Quellsenke f, Dipolquelle f, Dipol m <hydr.>
dimming	s. black[-]out <of light>		
dimness	s. turbidity		
dimorphism <bio.>	Dimorphismus m <Bio.>	dipole, dipole antenna (aerial), doublet [antenna] <el.>	Dipolantenne f, Dipol m <El.>
dimorphism <cryst.>	Dimorphie f <Krist.>		
Dimroth cooler	Dimroth-Kühler m	dipole absorption	Dipolabsorption f
Dines anemograph	Böenschreiber m, Universal-Windmeßgerät n	dipole aerial (antenna)	s. dipole <el.>
		dipole column	s. stacked dipoles
dineutron, bineutron	Dineutron n, Doppelneutron n	dipole crystal	Dipolkristall m
		dipole current flow	Dipolströmung f
Dini series	Dini-Reihe f		
diocotron effect	s. slipstream effect	dipole density	Dipoldichte f
diode, vacuum diode, diode tube, two-element tube (valve), two-electrode tube (valve)	Diode f, Zweipolröhre f, Zweielektrodenröhre f	dipole-dipole force	Dipol-Dipol-Kraft f
		dipole-dipole interaction	Dipol-Dipol-Wechselwirkung f
		dipole double layer	Dipoldoppelschicht f
diode characteristic	Diodenkennlinie f, Diodencharakteristik f		
diode magnetron, cylindrical diode magnetron, cylindrical anode magnetron	Nullschlitzmagnetron n, Magnetfeldröhre f mit Vollanode, ungeschlitzte Magnetfeldröhre, Rollkreismagnetron n	dipole effect, dipolar effect	Dipoleffekt m
		dipole elastic relaxation	dipolelastische Relaxation f
		dipole electric absorption	elektrische Dipolabsorption f
diode mixing	Diodenmischung f		
diode noise	Diodenrauschen n	dipole energy	Dipolenergie f
diode probe-type voltmeter, probe[-type] voltmeter	Taströhrenvoltmeter n, Tastvoltmeter n	dipole feed	Dipolspeisung f
diode tube	s. diode	dipole field	Dipolfeld n
diophantine approximation	diophantische Approximation f		
diophantine equation, indeterminate equation	diophantische Gleichung f, unbestimmte Gleichung	dipole force	Dipolkraft f
		dipole gamma-ray transition	Dipol-Gamma-Übergang m
diopter, dioptric, dpt, dptr	Dioptrie f, dpt, dptr	dipole gas, dipolar gas	Dipolgas n
diopter <instrument; optical medium>	Diopter n <Gerät; optisches Medium>	dipole group relaxation	Dipolgruppenrelaxation f
diopter square	Diopterinstrument n; Kreuzscheibe f		
dioptric	s. diopter		

dipole interaction energy, energy of dipole interaction	Dipolwechselwirkungsenergie f, Dipolenergie f
dipole lattice	Dipolgitter n
dipole layer, electric[al] double layer, electrochemical double layer	Dipolschicht f, Dipolzone f, elektr[ochem]ische Doppelschicht f
dipole meter	Dipolmeter n
dipole molecule, polar molecule	polares Molekül n, Dipolmolekül n
dipole moment, dipole momentum	Dipolmoment n
dipole orientation	s. dipolar orientation
dipole oscillation	Dipolschwingung f
dipole potential	Dipolpotential n
dipole-quadrupole force	s. dispersion force
dipole-quadrupole interaction	Dipol-Quadrupol-Wechselwirkung f
dipole radiation	Dipolstrahlung f
dipole radical relaxation	dipolradikale Relaxation f
dipole relaxation	s. dielectric relaxation
dipole relaxation loss	Dipolrelaxationsverlust m
dipole row, row of dipoles	Dipolzeile f
dipole singularity	Dipolsingularität f
dipole source, doublet source, doublet, dipole <hydr.>	Doppelquelle f, Quellsenke f, Dipolquelle f, Dipol m <Hydr.>
dipole transition	Dipolübergang m
dipole wave	Dipolwelle f
dipping, dip, plunging, plunge	Eintauchen n; Tauchung f
dipping, sagging, dip	Durchhängen n, Durchhang m; Durchbiegung f
dipping; moving in, insertion; plunging; immersion <of rods>	Einfahren n; Absenken n; Hinablassen n; Einschieben n; Eintauchen n <Stäbe>
dipping contact, dip contact	Tauchkontakt m
dipping electrode	Tauchelektrode f
dipping microscope	Eintauchmikroskop n
dipping needle	s. dip needle
dipping refractometer	Eintauchrefraktometer n
dip pole	s. magnetic dip pole
diproton	Diproton n, Doppelproton n
dip variometer	s. inclination variometer
diquark	Diquark n
Dirac['s] algebra	Diracsche Algebra f
Dirac bispinor	Diracscher Bispinor m
Dirac curve	s. Dirac lines
Dirac delta distribution (function), Dirac function	s. delta function
Dirac equation	Dirac-Gleichung f
Dirac function	s. delta function
Dirac h, h[-lbar, $\hbar$ $<=h/2\pi>$	Diracsches h n, Dirac-h n, h quer, $\hbar$ $<=h/2\pi>$
Dirac['s] hole theory	s. hole theory
Dirac interaction	Diracsche Wechselwirkung f
Dirac lines, Dirac curve	Dirac-Kurven fpl, Dirac-Linien fpl, Diracsche Linien fpl, Dirac-Diagramm n
Dirac matrix	s. Dirac spin matrix
Dirac measure	s. delta function
Dirac['s] pair theory	s. Dirac['s] hole theory
Dirac particle	Dirac-Teilchen n, Diracsches Teilchen n
Dirac spin matrix, spin matrix of Dirac, Dirac matrix, gamma matrix	Diracsche Spinmatrix (Matrix) f, Dirac-Matrix f, Spinmatrix von Dirac
Dirac spinor	Diracscher Spinor m
Dirac theory	Diracsche Theorie f [der Lichtemission], Diracsche Strahlungstheorie f
Dirac['s] theory of perturbations	s. time-dependent perturbation theory
Dirac wave	Dirac-Welle f
Dirac wave function	Diracsche Wellenfunktion f
direct <of motion>	rechtläufig <Bewegung>
direct-action controller	s. self-operated controller
direct-axis component of electromotive force	s. direct-axis electromotive force
direct-axis component of magnetomotive force	Längsdurchflutung f, Längs-MMK f
direct-axis electromotive force, direct-axis e.m.f., direct-axis component of electromotive force; direct-axis voltage	Längs-EMK f, Längsfeld-EMK f, Haupt-EMK f; Längsspannung f, Längsfeldspannung f
direct-axis subtransient electromotive force	subtransitorische Längs-EMK f, Subtransient-EMK f des Längsfeldes
direct-axis transient electromotive force	transitorische Längs-EMK f, Transient-EMK f des Längsfeldes
direct-axis voltage	s. direct-axis electromotive force
direct collision, direct encounter	direkter Stoß m
direct colorimetry, visual colorimetry	visuelle (subjektive) Farbmessung f
direct component	s. direct-current component
direct control, self-acting control, control without power amplification	Regelung f ohne Hilfsenergie, direkte Regelung, unmittelbare Regelung
direct control grid current, d.c. control grid current	Steuergitter-Gleichstrom m
direct controller	s. self-operated controller
direct conversion of energy	Energie-Direktumwandlung f, direkte Energieumwandlung f
direct correlation, positive correlation	positive Korrelation f
direct-coupled amplifier	s. direct-current amplifier
direct coupling, direct-current (galvanic, resistance, resistive, ohmic) coupling <of circuit>	direkte (ohmsche) Kopplung f, Direktkopplung f, galvanische Ankopplung f (Kopplung), Widerstandskopplung f <Leitungskreis>
direct current	Hinstrom m
direct current, constant (continuous, unidirectional) current, d.c., D.C., d-c, c.c. <el.>	Gleichstrom m <El.>
direct-current—alternating-current converter, d.c.-a.c. converter	Gleichstrom-Wechselstrom-Umformer m
direct-current—alternating-current inverter	s. inverter <el.>
direct-current ammeter, d.c. ammeter	Gleichstrommesser m, Gleichstrom-Amperemeter n
direct-current amplifier, d.c. amplifier, continuous current amplifier, direct-coupled amplifier	Gleichstromverstärker m, Gleichspannungsverstärker m
direct-current arc, constant-current arc, d.c. arc	Gleichstrombogen m, Gleichstromlichtbogen m
direct-current bridge, d.c. bridge	Gleichstrom[meß]brücke f
direct-current component, d.c. component, zero-frequency (direct) component	Gleichstromkomponente f; Gleichstromanteil m; Gleich[strom]wert m, Gleichstromgröße f
direct-current conductivity, d.c. conductivity	Gleichstromleitfähigkeit f
direct-current converter	s. direct-current to direct-current converter
direct-current coupled, d.c. coupled	galvanisch (direkt) gekoppelt, gleichstromgekoppelt
direct-current coupling	s. direct coupling
direct-current field, d.c. field	elektrisches Gleichfeld n, Gleichfeld

direct-current 178

direct-current-field synchrotron — s. FFAG synchrotron

direct-current grid modulation — Gittergleichstrommodulation f

direct current grid voltage — Gittergleichspannung f

direct-current Josephson effect, d.c. Josephson effect — Gleichstrom-Josephson-Effekt m, Josephson-Effekt m 1. Art

direct-current magnetic field, d.c. magnetic field — magnetisches Gleichfeld n

direct-current magnetization curve, d.c. magnetization curve — Gleichstrom-Magnetisierungskurve f

direct-current magnetohydrodynamic generator, DC MHD generator — Gleichstrom-MHD-Generator m, magnetohydrodynamischer Gleichstromgenerator m

direct-current mean, d.c. mean, electrolytic mean, galvanic mean — elektrolytischer (galvanischer) Mittelwert m, Gleichstrommittel n, Gleichstrommittelwert m

direct-current meter, d.c. meter — Gleichstromzähler m

direct-current potential — s. direct-current voltage

direct-current potentiometer, direct (d.c.) potentiometer — Gleichstromkompensator m

direct-current power transmission, d.c. power transmission — Gleichstrom-Energieübertragung f

direct-current source (supply), d.c. source, d.c. supply — Gleichstromquelle f

direct-current to alternating-current conversion, d.c.-a.c. conversion, inversion — Wechselrichtung f, Invertieren n

direct-current to alternating-current power converter — s. inverter <el.>

direct-current to direct-current converter, direct-current converter, d.c.-d.c. converter — Gleichstrom-Gleichstrom-Umformer m, Gleichstrom-Gleichstrom-Wandler m, Gleichstrom-Gleichstrom-Konverter m, Gleichstromumformer m

direct-current transformer, d.c. transformer — Gleichstromwandler m, Gleichstromtransformator m

direct-current voltage, d.c. (D.C., d-c, direct) voltage, direct[-current] potential — Gleichspannung f

direct-current voltage converter, d.c. voltage converter; direct-current (d.c.) voltage transformer — Gleichspannungswandler m; Gleichspannungsumformer m

direct-current voltage transducer, d.c. voltage transducer — Gleichspannungsgeber m, Gleichspannungsmeßwandler m

direct-current voltage transformer — s. direct-current voltage converter

direct-current voltmeter, d.c. voltmeter — Gleichspannungsmesser m, Gleichstromvoltmeter n

direct dye, substantive dye — Direktfarbstoff m, substantiver (direktziehender) Farbstoff m, Substantivfarbstoff m

directed, directional — gerichtet, gebündelt, Richt-

directed away from the Sun — von der Sonne abgewandt

directed beam, directional beam, directed ray — Richtstrahl m

directed graph, digraph, oriented graph — gerichteter (orientierter) Graph m

directed movement, unidirectional movement — geordnete Bewegung f, gerichtete Bewegung

directed quantity, vectored quantity — gerichtete Größe f, Richtungsgröße f

directed ray, directed beam — Richtstrahl m

directed towards the Sun, sunward — zur Sonne gerichtet, der Sonne zugewandt

directed valence — gerichtete Valenz f

direct encounter — s. direct collision

direct extrusion — Vorwärtsfließpressen n, Gleichfließpressen n

direct factor — direkter Faktor m

direct flux — Mitfluß m

direct glare — direkte Blendung f, Direktblendung f; Infeldblendung f

direct grid current — positiver Gitterstrom m

direct image — rechtläufige Abbildung f; direktes Bild n; direkt reflektiertes Bild

direct impact — gerader Stoß m

directing force — s. restoring force <mech.>

directing moment — s. restoring torque <meas.>

direct interaction, surface interaction <nucl.> — direkte Wechselwirkung f, Oberflächenwechselwirkung f <Kern.>

direct interaction [reaction] mode, direct interaction type of reaction, direct [nuclear] reaction, direct process, reaction proceeding directly <nucl.> — direkte Kernreaktion (Reaktion) f, Oberflächen[kern]reaktion f, Reaktion mit direkter Wechselwirkung <Kern.>

direction, sense, sense of direction — Richtungssinn m, Sinn m

directional, directed — gerichtet, gebündelt, Richt-

directional anomaly — Richtungsstörung f, Richtungsanomalie f

directional antenna array (network), antenna array — Richtantennennetz n, Richtantennenanordnung f, Richtantennensystem n

directional beam — s. directed beam

directional breakdown — Richtungsdurchschlag m

directional characteristic — s. radiation pattern

directional coincidence — Richtungskoinzidenz f

directional cooling, zone cooling — Zonenabkühlung f <stufenweise Abkühlung von einem Ende der Probe zum anderen>

directional correlation, angular (angle) correlation — Winkelkorrelation f, Richtungskorrelation f

directional counter — richtungsabhängiges Zählrohr n

directional coupler — Richtungskoppler m, Richtkoppler m

directional coupling — Richtungskopplung f, Richtkopplung f

directional degeneration, spatial (space) degeneration

directional dependence, dependence on direction, directionality, directivity — Richtungsabhängigkeit f

directional derivative — Richtungsableitung f

directional detector — richtungsabhängiger Detektor m, Richtungsdetektor m

directional diagram, directivity diagram (pattern), directional pattern <ac.> — Schalldruckdiagramm n <Ak.>

directional diagram — s. a. radiation pattern

directional diagram of loop antenna, directivity diagram of loop antenna — Rahmendiagramm n

directional differentiation — Richtungsdifferentiation f

directional distortion — Richtungsverzerrung f

directional distribution — s. angular distribution

directional effect, directionality [effect], directivity, directive effect — Richtwirkung f, Richteffekt m, Richtungswirkung f, Richtwirkungseffekt m

directional emissivity — [gerichteter] Emissionsgrad m

directional error, error of direction — Richtungsfehler m

directional field, direction field of lineal elements, field of tangents <math.> — Richtungsfeld n <Math.>

directional focusing	s. direction focusing <of the first, mech. second order>	direction of hard magnetization, hard direction	harte Richtung (Magnetisierungsrichtung) f
directional force	s. restoring force <mech.>	direction of magnetization, sense of magnetization	Magnetisierungsrichtung f
directional gain	s. directivity index <ac.>	direction of motion, direction of movement	Bewegungsrichtung f, Bewegungssinn m; Zugrichtung f
directional gyro[scope]	Kurskreisel m, Richtungskreisel m	direction of normal, normal direction	Normalenrichtung f
directional gyroscope	s. a. azimuth gyroscope	direction of plumb line, plumb-line direction	Lotrichtung f
directional isolator	s. isolator <el.>	direction of Poynting vector, ray direction, direction of ray	Strahlrichtung f, Richtung f des Poyntingschen Vektors
directionality, dependence on direction, directional dependence, directivity	Richtungsabhängigkeit f	direction of principal curvature, principal direction of curvature <math.>	Haupt[krümmungs]-richtung f <Math.>
directional[ity] effect, directivity, directive effect	Richtwirkung f, Richtungswirkung f, Richt[wirkungs]effekt m	direction of ray, ray direction, direction of Poynting vector	Strahlrichtung f, Richtung f des Poyntingschen Vektors
directionality, directivity	Richt[ungs]fähigkeit f, Richt[ungs]vermögen n, Richteigenschaft f, Richtungsbündelung f	direction of revolution	s. sense of rotation
		direction of rolling, rolling direction	Walzrichtung f
directionality effect, directional (directive) effect, directionality, directivity	Richtwirkung f, Richteffekt m, Richtungswirkung f, Richtwirkungseffekt m	direction of rotation	s. sense of rotation
		direction of screwing	s. orientation of the screw
		direction of sight, direction of view	Blickrichtung f
directional lighting	Beleuchtung f durch gerichtetes Licht	direction of slip[ping]	s. slip direction
directional microphone, unidirectional microphone	Richtmikrophon n, Mikrophon n mit Richtwirkung	direction of tension; direction of traction	Zugrichtung f
directional pattern	s. directional diagram <ac.>	direction of the screw	s. orientation of the screw
directional pattern	s. radiation pattern	direction of traction; direction of tension	Zugrichtung f
directional phase changer (shifter)	Richtungsphasenschieber m	direction of translation	s. slip direction
directional plane <math.>	Leitebene f, Richtebene f <Math.>	direction of transmission	s. forward direction
directional quantization	s. space quantization	direction of trend <geo.>	Streichrichtung f <Geo.>
directional radiation, direction radiation, directive radiation	Richtstrahlung f, gerichtete Strahlung f	direction of twinning, twinning direction	Zwillingsrichtung f, Verwachsungsrichtung f
		direction of view	s. direction of sight
directional receiver, unidirectional receiver	Richtempfänger m, Richtungsempfänger m	direction radiation	s. directional radiation
		direction uncertainty, uncertainty of direction	Richtungsunschärfe f
directional reflectance <US>	s. direct reflection factor	direction vector	s. unit vector
directional relay, back-current relay	Richtungsrelais n, Rückleistungsrelais n, Rückwattrelais n	directive coefficient <of antenna; ac.>, directivity factor	Richt[ungs]faktor m, Richtwirkungsfaktor m <Antenne; Ak.>
directional resistance	s. rectifier load resistance	directive effect	s. directional effect
directional respone	s. directional sensitivity	directive equation of the straight line, directive straight line equation	Richtungsgleichung f der Geraden
directional response pattern	s. radiation pattern		
directional sensitivity, angular sensitivity, directional response	richtungsabhängige Empfindlichkeit f, Richtungsempfindlichkeit f, Winkelempfindlichkeit f	directive field	Richtfeld n
		directive force	s. restoring force <mech.>
		directive gain	s. aerial gain
directional vision	Richtungssehen n	directive pattern	s. radiation pattern
direction angle; azimuth angle, azimuth, azimuthal angle	Richtungswinkel m; Azimutwinkel m, Azimut n (m), Seitenwinkel m	directive radiation	s. directional radiation
		directive straight line equation, directive equation of the straight line	Richtungsgleichung f der Geraden
direction cosine	Richtungskosinus m	directivity, directionality	Richt[ungs]fähigkeit f, Richt[ungs]vermögen n, Richteigenschaft f, Richtungsbündelung f
direction field of lineal elements, directional field, field of tangents <math.>	Richtungsfeld n <Math.>		
		directivity	s. a. dependence on direction
direction finder, bearing finder, direction-finding installation (system); course-and-bearing indicator; radar direction finder	Peiler m, Peilanlage f, Peilgerät n; Funkpeilgerät n	directivity	s. a. directional effect
		directivity diagram, directional diagram (pattern), directivity pattern <ac.>	Schalldruckdiagramm n <Ak.>
direction finder antenna, direction finder loop	Peilrahmen m	directivity diagram of direction finder	Peildiagramm n
direction finder triangle	s. direction finding triangle	directivity diagram of loop antenna, directional diagram of loop antenna	Rahmendiagramm n
direction finding	s. bearing		
direction-finding installation	s. direction finder		
direction-finding system	s. direction finder	directivity factor, directive coefficient <of antenna; ac.>	Richt[ungs]faktor m, Richtwirkungsfaktor m <Antenne; Ak.>
direction finding triangle, direction finder triangle	Peildreieck n		
direction focusing, directional (spatial, space, angular) focusing <of the first, second order>	Richtungsfokussierung f, Raumfokussierung f, räumliche Fokussierung f <erster, zweiter Ordnung>	directivity function	Richtfunktion f
		directivity index, directional gain <ac.>	Richtungsmaß n, Bündelungsindex m <Ak.>
direction of action <of a force>	Angriffsrichtung f <Kraft>	directivity pattern	s. directional diagram <ac.>
direction of conormal, transverse direction	Konormalenrichtung f	direct lattice	direktes Gitter n
		direct levelling <US>	s. levelling <geo.>
direction of easy magnetization	s. easy direction of magnetization	direct light	s. reflected light

direct-light microscope, reflection microscope, microscope arranged for vertical illumination	Auflichtmikroskop *n*	direct sense of motion, directness of motion	Rechtläufigkeit *f* der Bewegung
direct-light microscopy, investigation under the reflection microscope, investigation under a microscope arranged for vertical illumination; reflected-light (epi-illumination) mode of microscopic viewing	Auflichtmikroskopie *f*	direct-shadow method	*s.* shadow method
		direct steam, live steam	Frischdampf *m*
		direct stress	*s.* normal stress <mech.>
		direct sum	direkte Summe *f*
		direct transition	direkter (vertikaler) Übergang *m*
		direct transmission, regular transmission	gerichtete Transmission (Durchlassung) *f*
		direct transmission factor, direct transmittance, regular transmittance <US>	gerichteter Anteil *m* des Durchlaßgrades, Grad *m* der gerichteten Transmission (Durchlassung)
directly ionizing particle	direkt ionisierendes Teilchen *n*	direct vernier	nachtragender Nonius *m*
directly ionizing radiation	direkt ionisierende Strahlung *f*		
directly proportional; proportional	proportional, verhältnisgleich; direkt proportional	direct-view[ing] memory tube	Direktsicht-Speicherröhre *f*
direct magnetostriction, direct magnetostrictive effect	direkte Magnetostriktion *f*, direkter Magnetostriktionseffekt *m*	direct vision, foveal vision	direktes Sehen *n*, foveales Sehen
direct multiplication of matrices	direkte Multiplikation *f* von Matrizen, Übermatrixbildung *f*	direct-vision prism	Geradsichtprisma *n*, geradsichtiges Prisma *n*
		direct-vision spectroscope, spectroscope of direct vision	Geradsichtspektroskop *n*, geradsichtiges Spektroskop *n*
directness of motion	*s.* direct sense of motion	direct voltage	*s.* direct-current voltage
direct nuclear reaction	*s.* direct interaction type of reaction <nucl.>	direct voltage characteristic	Gleichspannungscharakteristik *f*, Gleichspannungskennlinie *f*
direct observation	unmittelbare (direkte) Beobachtung *f*, Direktbeobachtung *f*	direct-voltage component	Gleichspannungskomponente *f*
direct optical type [of] plotting machine	*s.* rectifier <opt.>	direct-voltage source, d.c. voltage source	Gleichspannungsquelle *f*
director	*s.* parasitic director <el.>	direct wave, forward wave <geo.>	direkte Welle *f* <Geo.>
direct photonuclear effect (reaction)	direkter Kernphotoeffekt *m*, Direkteffekt *m*	direct wave	*s. a.* surface wave
direct piezoelectric effect	*s.* piezoelectric effect	Dirichlet['s] boundary condition, boundary condition of the first kind, first boundary condition	Dirichletsche Randbedingung *f*, Randbedingung erster Art, erste Randbedingung
direct polarity	*s.* negative polarity		
direct potential	*s.* direct-current voltage		
direct potentiometer	*s.* direct-current potentiometer		
direct process	*s.* direct interaction type of reaction <nucl.>	Dirichlet['s] boundary [value] problem	*s.* Dirichlet['s] problem
direct product	direktes Produkt *n* <Gruppen, Algebren, Distributionen>; tensorielles Produkt <Algebren>; Tensorprodukt *n* <Matrizen, Distributionen>	Dirichlet['s] condition <of Fourier transformation>	Dirichletsche Bedingung *f*, Dirichlet-Bedingung *f* <Fourier-Transformation>
		Dirichlet['s] discontinuity factor	Dirichletscher diskontinuierlicher Faktor *m*, Diskontinuitätsfaktor *m*
direct product	*s. a.* Kronecker product	Dirichlet expansion, expansion in a Dirichlet series	Dirichlet-Entwicklung *f*
direct radiation, leakage radiation <of X-ray tube>	Leckstrahlung *f*, direkte Strahlung *f*, Direktstrahlung *f*	Dirichlet integral	Dirichletsches [singuläres] Integral *n*
direct-radiator loudspeaker, hornless loudspeaker	trichterloser Lautsprecher *m*		
		Dirichlet['s] principle, Dedekind['s] pigeon-hole principle, box principle, box argument, chest of drawers argument	Dirichletscher Schubkastensatz *m* Schubfachprinzip *n*, Dirichletsches Prinzip *n*
direct reaction, forward reaction	Hinreaktion *f*, Vorwärtsreaktion *f*		
direct reaction	*s. a.* direct interaction type of reaction <nucl.>	Dirichlet['s] principle <of potential theory>	Dirichletsches Prinzip *n*, Thomson-Dirichletsches Prinzip <Potentialtheorie>
direct-reading balance of Westphal, balance of Westphal, Mohr-Westphal balance	Mohrsche Waage *f*, Mohr-Westphalsche Waage *f*, Westphalsche Waage		
		Dirichlet['s] problem, Dirichlet['s] boundary problem, Dirichlet['s] boundary value problem, first boundary [value] problem, boundary value problem of the first kind	Dirichletsches Problem (Randwertproblem) *n*, Dirichlet-Problem *n*, Dirichletsche Randwertaufgabe *f*, erstes Randwertproblem *n*, erste Randwertaufgabe *f*, Randwertaufgabe (Randwertproblem) erster Art
direct-reading instrument	direktanzeigendes Meßgerät (Instrument) *n*, Meßgerät mit Direktablesung, Ablesegerät *n*, Skalen[meß]gerät *n*, Skaleninstrument *n*		
		Dirichlet['s] series	Dirichletsche Reihe *f*, Dirichlet-Reihe *f*
direct-reading sextant, scale sextant	Skalensextant *m*		
direct recombination	*s.* band-to-band recombination	Dirichlet['s] stability theorem, Dirichlet['s] theorem [of stability], stability theorem of Dirichlet, least-energy principle	Dirichletscher Stabilitätssatz *m*, Stabilitätssatz von Dirichlet
direct reduction	reines Reaktionsschmelzen *n*, direkte Reduktion *f*		
direct reflectance <US>	*s.* direct reflection factor		
direct reflection, regular reflection, specular reflection, reflection <opt.>	gerichtete (regelmäßige, reguläre, spiegelnde) Reflexion *f*, Spiegelreflexion *f*, Spiegelung *f*, Reflexion	dirigibility; navigability; maneuvrability, manoeuvrability	Lenkbarkeit *f*, Steuerbarkeit *f*; Manövrierfähigkeit *f*, Wendigkeit *f*
		disability glare	physiologische Blendung *f*; Relativblendung *f*; Adaptationsblendung *f*
direct reflection factor, direct (regular) reflectance, reflectance factor <US>, specular reflectivity	gerichteter Anteil *m* des Reflexionsgrades, Grad *m* der gerichteten Reflexion		
		disaccommodation	Desakkommodation *f*
		disadvantage factor	Disadvantagefaktor *m*, Absenkungsfaktor *m*
direct reflection spectrum, spectrum of direct reflection	Spektrum *n* spiegelnder Reflexion		
directrix <math.>	Leitlinie *f*, Direktrix *f*, Leitkurve *f*; Leitgerade *f* <Math.>	disaggregation; loosening; breaking-up	Auflockerung *f*, Lockerung *f*
		disaggregation <chem.>	Desaggregation *f* <Chem.>

disagreement — s. unconformity
disappearance, vanishing, dying-away — Verschwinden n, Auflösung f
disappearance, disappearing, immersion ‹behind the limb of the Moon or Sun› — Verschwinden n ‹hinter dem Mond- oder Sonnenrand›
disappearance of magnetism — Schwinden n des Magnetismus
disappearance of the meteor, extinction of the meteor — Verlöschen n des Meteors
disappearance of voltage ‹el.› — Ausfall m ‹Spannung›, Spannungsausfall m ‹El.›
disappearing — s. disappearance
disappearing [-] filament pyrometer — Kreuzfadenpyrometer n, Fadenpyrometer n, Glühfadenpyrometer n, Leuchtdichtepyrometer n
disassembly, dismantling, dismounting ‹e.g. of experiment› — Abbau m, Demontage f, Demontierung f ‹z. B. des Versuchs›
disassimilation — s. catabolism
disassociation, dissociation in molecules, molecular dissociation — Entassoziation f, Desassoziation f
discernibility, distinguishability — Unterscheidbarkeit f
discharge — Entladung f

discharge, outflow, outflux, efflux, effluence, effluent, issue ‹of liquid› — Ausströmung f, Ausfluß m, Ausfließen n, Abfluß m; Ablassen n ‹Flüssigkeit›
discharge, discharge rate, rate of discharge, run-off ‹per unit time› — Volum[en]abfluß m, Volum[en]ausfluß m, Volum[en]ergiebigkeit f, Abflußmenge f [je Zeiteinheit], Ausflußmenge f [je Zeiteinheit], Abfluß m
discharge avalanche — Entladungslawine f
discharge burst — s. discharge pulse
discharge capacity ‹el.› — Ableitvermögen n ‹El.›
discharge chamber, gas discharge chamber — Gasentladungskammer f, Entladungskammer f
discharge coefficient, coefficient of discharge — Ausflußkoeffizient m, Ausflußziffer f, Ausflußzahl f
discharge coefficient ‹of orifices, nozzles, venturis› — Durchflußkoeffizient m, Durchflußfaktor m, Durchflußzahl f ‹Blenden, Düsen, Meßrohre›
discharge coil, drainage coil — Erdungsdrossel, f Erdschlußdrosselspule f
discharge counter, gaseous discharge counter [tube] — Gasentladungszählrohr n
discharge current — Entladungsstrom m, Strom m im Gasentladungsrohr; Entladestrom m
discharge current ‹through the surge diverter› — Ableiterstrom m
discharge current — s. a. surface leakage current
discharge curve — s. discharge rating curve
discharge duration curve — Wassermengenabflußlinie f, Wassermengendauerlinie f
discharge factor — Entladungsfaktor m
discharge gap, discharge space — Entladungsstrecke f; Entladungsraum m
discharge gap, arrester ‹el.› — Spannungsableiter m, Ableiter m ‹El.›
discharge gettering — Entladungsgetterung f
discharge glow — s. glow
discharge head — Ausflußhöhe f
discharge in a gas — s. electric discharge
discharge in litre per second per square kilometre, specific flow (modulus) — Abflußspende f, spezifischer Abfluß m, Spende f Wasser[mengen]spende f
discharge lamp — Entladungslampe f
discharge luminescence — s. glow

discharge mass curve — Abflußsummenlinie f, Wassermengensummenganglinie f
discharge measurement — Wassermengenmessung f
discharge micrometer — Gasentladungsmikrometer n
discharge of turbine — s. admission of fluid to turbine blades
discharge of water, water yield, yield of water — Wasserabgabe f; Wasserergiebigkeit f
discharge on (over) the surface — s. surface discharge ‹el.›
discharge over weir — überfallende Menge f, Strömungsmenge f über Wehr, Überfallmenge f; Überlaufmenge f, Überströmmenge f
discharge path — Entladungsweg m, Entladungskanal m
discharge plasma, gas discharge plasma, plasma of gaseous discharge — Gasentladungsplasma n, Entladungsplasma n
discharge point; corona point, spray point, active spot [of corona discharge] — Sprühspitze f, Koronaentladungsspitze f, Sprühstelle f, Sprühpunkt m
discharge potential, discharge voltage — Entladespannung f, Abgabespannung f; Entladungsspannung f; Entladungspotential n; Spannung f an der Gasentladungsstrecke
discharge pressure — Austrittsdruck m
discharge pulse; discharge surge, discharge burst — Entladungsstoß m
discharger — s. spark gap
discharge rate, rate of discharge ‹of liquid› — Ausflußgeschwindigkeit f; Ausströmungsgeschwindigkeit f; Auslaßgeschwindigkeit f ‹Flüssigkeit›
discharge rate — s. a. discharge ‹per unit time›
discharge rating curve, discharge curve, [station] rating curve, stage-discharge relation — Schlüsselkurve f, Pegelschlüsselkurve f, Pegelcharakteristik f, Abfluß[mengen]kurve f, Wasserfrachtlinie f
discharge resistor — s. discharging resistor
discharge section line, discharge site, metering section — Abflußmeßstelle f
discharge space, discharge gap — Entladungsstrecke f; Entladungsraum m
discharge surge — s. discharge pulse
discharge through a gas — s. electric discharge
discharge time constant — Entladezeitkonstante f
discharge to earth (ground) — Erdentladung f
discharge tube; discharge vessel — Entladungsrohr n; Entladungsröhre f; Entladungsgefäß n
discharge voltage; residual voltage ‹US› ‹of surge diverter› ‹el.› — Restspannung f ‹El.›
discharge voltage — s. a. discharge potential
discharging nozzle — Ausflußdüse f
discharging resistance, earthing resistance, ground resistance, grounding resistance ‹US› — Erd[ungs]widerstand m, Entladewiderstand m, Durchgangswiderstand m, Übergangswiderstand m
discharging resistor, discharge resistor — Entladewiderstand m
discoloration ‹US› — s. discolouration
discolouration, discoloration ‹US›, decolourization, decolorization ‹US›, decolour[iz]ing, decolor[iz]ing ‹US› — Entfärbung f, Verfärbung f, Ausbleichung f
discomfort glare — psychologische Blendung f

discomposition, knocking-out, atomic displacement, displacement <of atoms> — Umlagerung f <Atome>, Atomumlagerung f, Einlagerung f, atomare Verschiebung f, Atomverschiebung f

discomposition effect, Wigner effect; knocking-out effect — Wigner-Effekt m; Atomumlagerung f durch Kernstoß

discone antenna — Scheibenkonusantenne f, Scheiben-Kegel-Antenne f, Diskonantenne f

disconnected, unconnected; totally disconnected <math.> — zusammenhangslos, punkthaft; total unzusammenhängend, total zusammenhangslos <Math.>

disconnecting — s. disconnection <el.>
disconnecting switch — s. switch
disconnection, disconnecting, breaking <el.> — Trennung f, Ausschaltung f, Abschaltung f <El.>

disconnection delay, cut-off delay <el.> — Abschaltverzögerung f <El.>

disconnect jack, break jack, transfer jack — Trennklinke f

discontinuity; jump, step, saltus — Sprung m, sprungartige (sprunghafte) Änderung f; Sprunghaftigkeit f; Diskontinuität f

discontinuity <of material>, material separation — Ungänze f
discontinuity, discontinuity surface <geo.> — Diskontinuität[sfläche] f <Geo.>

discontinuity <math.> — Unstetigkeit f <Math.>

discontinuity — s. a. point of discontinuity
discontinuity condition, jump condition — Unstetigkeitsbedingung f; Sprungbedingung f
discontinuity interaction, interaction of discontinuities — Unstetigkeitswechselwirkung f, Wechselwirkung f von Unstetigkeiten

discontinuity interval, interval of discontinuity — Unstetigkeitsstrecke f

discontinuity layer, thermocline — Temperatursprungschicht f, [thermische] Sprungschicht f

discontinuity line, line of discontinuity — Unstetigkeitslinie f, Diskontinuitätslinie f

discontinuity of tangential component, tangential discontinuity — Tangentialsprung m, Sprung m der Tangentialkomponente
discontinuity of the first kind — s. jump discontinuity
discontinuity of the second kind — Unstetigkeit f zweiter Art

discontinuity order, order of the discontinuity — Unstetigkeitsordnung f
discontinuity potential, potential of discontinuity — Unstetigkeitspotential n
discontinuity problem [of diffraction theory] — Sprungwertproblem n [der Beugungstheorie]
discontinuity surface <aero., hydr.> — Trenn[ungs]fläche f, freie Strahlgrenze f <Aero., Hydr.>

discontinuity surface, surface of discontinuity, singular surface <hydr., aero.> — Unstetigkeitsfläche f [im engeren Sinne], Diskontinuitätsfläche f <Hydr., Aero.>
discontinuity surface, surface of discontinuity <math.; phys.; met.> — Unstetigkeitsfläche f, Sprungfläche f, Diskontinuitätsfläche f <Math.; Phys.; Met.>

discontinuity surface — s. a. discontinuity <geo.>

discontinuity value, value of the discontinuity — Sprungwert m, Sprunggröße f

discontinuity wave; distortional wave — Unstetigkeitswelle f

discontinuous; jumplike; stepped, step-like; unsteady; sudden — sprunghaft; diskontinuierlich
discontinuous <math.> — unstetig <Math.>
discontinuous control, intermittent control — unstetige (unstetig wirkende) Steuerung f; unstetige (unstetig wirkende) Regelung f, Abtastregelung f

discontinuous precipitation — s. eutectoid reaction
discontinuous variability — s. alternative variability <stat.>
discontinuum — Diskontinuum n

discord, dissonance — Dissonanz f, Spaltklang m

discordance of stratification, stratigraphic discordance — Schichtungsdiskordanz f, Diskordanz f, ungleichsinnige Lagerung f
discordant folding, disharmonic folding — diskordante (disharmonische) Faltung f
discrepancy — s. unconformity
discrete band — diskrete Bande f
discrete-band spectrum — s. many-lined spectrum
discrete distribution — diskrete (arithmetische) Verteilung f
discrete energy level — diskretes Energieniveau n

discreteness — Diskretheit f

discrete pulse, single (isolated) pulse — Einzelimpuls m, diskreter Impuls m
discrete radio source, discrete source — diskrete Radioquelle f

discrete spectrum — diskretes Spektrum n
discrete spectrum — s. a. point spectrum
discrete state — diskreter Zustand m

discrete stochastic process — diskreter stochastischer Prozeß m
discriminant — Diskriminante f
discriminant function — s. discriminator <stat.>
discriminating element — s. error detector <control>
discrimination; distinction; differentiation; selectivity; selectance — Diskrimination f; Unterscheidung f, Unterschied m; Selektivität f; Trenn[ungs]vermögen n; Trennschärfe f; Selektanz

discrimination factor — Diskriminierungsfaktor m, Diskriminationsfaktor m
discrimination index — Diskriminanzfaktor m, Unterscheidungsfaktor m
discrimination level — Diskriminierpegel m, Diskriminationspegel m, Diskriminatorspannung f
discrimination of particles — Teilchendiskriminierung f, Teilchenunterscheidung f
discrimination of the filter, filter discrimination, selectivity [discrimination] — Selektivität f des Filters, Trennschärfe f des Filters

discrimination sensitivity — Unterschiedsempfindlichkeit f
discriminator, amplitude (pulse-amplitude, pulse-height, integral) discriminator — Diskriminator m, Amplitudendiskriminator m, Impulshöhendiskriminator m, Impulsamplitudendiskriminator m
discriminator, discriminant function <stat.> — Diskriminanzfunktion f, Unterscheidungsfunktion f, diskriminierende (diskriminatorische) Funktion f <Stat.>

discriminatory analysis — Diskriminanzanalyse f, Unterscheidungsanalyse f, Trennverfahren n <Math.>

disdodecahedron — s. diplohedron
disengagement — s. release
disentanglement of magnetic field lines — Entwirrung f der magnetischen Feldlinien
disequilibrium — s. non-equilibrium
disgregation energy — Disgregationsenergie f
dish, cup — Schale f, Schälchen n
dish, plate; platform — Teller m
dish — s. a. scale
disharmonic folding, discordant folding — diskordante (disharmonische) Faltung f
dish of the scales — s. scale
disintegration, sputtering <of cathode> — Zerstäubung f <Katode>

dislocation

disintegration <geo.>, physical weathering	mechanische (physikalische) Verwitterung f <Geo.>	disk-loaded torus	s. corrugated torus
disintegration	s. a. weathering <geo.>	disk-loaded waveguide	s. corrugated waveguide
disintegration	s. a. decay <nucl.>	disk method	Scheibenmethode f
disintegration	s. a. disintegration event		
disintegration analysis, decay analysis	Zerfallsanalyse f		
disintegration branch	s. branch of the radioactive family <nucl.>	disk of aberration, disk of [least] confusion, circle of [least] confusion, blur circle, aperture effect	Unschärfe[n]kreis m, Streu[ungs]kreis m, Streuscheibchen n, Streufigur f, Zerstreuungskreis m
disintegration chain	s. disintegration series <nucl.>		
disintegration constant	s. decay constant		
disintegration curve	s. decay curve <nucl.>	disk planimeter	Scheiben[rad]planimeter n, Scheibenrollplanimeter n
disintegration electron, decay electron	Zerfallselektron n		
disintegration energy, decay energy, nuclear disintegration energy	Zerfallsenergie f	disk population, disk-type (disklike) population, population I of the Galaxy	Scheibenpopulation f
disintegration event, disintegration	Zerfallsakt m, Zerfall m	disk-seal diode	Scheibendiode f
disintegration law [of atomic nucleus]	s. law of radioactive disintegration	disk-seal triode	Scheibentriode f
disintegration of atomic nucleus	s. decay <nucl.>	disk-seal tube, disk tube	Scheibenröhre f
disintegration of front, frontolysis	Frontolyse f, Frontenauflösung f, Auflösung f der Front		
disintegration of the comet; disruption of the comet	Auflösung f der Kometen; Zerfall m des Kometen	disk shutter	Scheibenverschluß m; Scheibenblende f
disintegration particle, decay particle	Zerfallsteilchen n	disk storage (store)	s. disk file memory
		disk torus	s. corrugated torus
		disk tube	s. disk-seal tube
disintegration period	s. transmutation period <nucl.>	disk-type electrometer	Scheibenelektrometer n
disintegration plane	Zerfallsebene f	disk-type electrostatic generator	Scheibengenerator m
disintegration probability, decay probability	Zerfallswahrscheinlichkeit f		
disintegration product	s. daughter		
disintegration proton, decay proton	Zerfallsproton n	disk-type electrostatic machine	Scheibenelektrisiermaschine f
disintegration rate, decay rate, transmutation rate, rate of decay (disintegration) <nucl.>	Zerfallsrate f, Umwandlungsrate f, Zerfallsgeschwindigkeit f, Umwandlungsgeschwindigkeit f <Kern.>		
		disk-type population	s. disk population
		disk-type winding, pie (pie-type, interleaved, sandwich coil) winding	Scheibenwicklung f
		disk valve, poppet (pocketed, plate, mushroom) valve	Tellerventil n, Kegelventil n, Scheibenventil n
disintegration scheme, decay scheme	Zerfallsschema n, Zerfallschema n		
disintegration series, decay series, transformation series, radioactive series, series; disintegration chain, decay chain, transformation chain; radioactive family, transformation family <nucl.>	Zerfallsreihe f, radioaktive Zerfallsreihe (Stammreihe f), Reihe f, radioaktiver Stammbaum m; Zerfallskette f, Zerfallsfolge f, Umwandlungskette f, Umwandlungsfolge f; radioaktive Familie f, Zerfallsfamilie f <Kern.>	disk waveguide	s. corrugated waveguide
		dislocation <cryst.>	Versetzung f <Krist.>
		dislocation <geo.>	Dislokation f, Störung f <Geo.>
		dislocation	s. a. displacement
		dislocation arrangement	s. dislocation array
		dislocation array, pattern of dislocation, dislocation pattern (arrangement, configuration)	Versetzungsanordnung f, Versetzungskonfiguration f
disintegrations per minute	s. transmutations per minute		
disintegrations per second	s. transmutations per second	dislocation cloud, cloud of dislocations	Versetzungswolke f
disintegration star	Zerfallsstern m	dislocation configuration	s. dislocation array
		dislocation core	s. dislocation kernel
disintegration time	s. transmutation period	dislocation density tensor, tensor of dislocation density	Versetzungsdichtetensor m, Tensor m der Versetzungsdichte
disjoint, non-overlapping <math.>	disjunkt, elementefremd, fremd, durchschnittsfremd <Math.>		
		dislocation dipole	Versetzungsdipol m
		dislocation dissociation	s. dissociation of the dislocation
disjunction, logic[al] sum	Disjunktion f, logische Summe f		
disjunction <geo.>	Teilbarkeit f <Geo.>	dislocation earthquake	s. tectonic earthquake
disjunctive dislocation (fault), gaping fault, open fault <geo.>	Zerrung f, disjunktive Dislokation f, Disjunktivstörung f <Geo.>	dislocation energy, energie of dislocation	Versetzungsenergie f
		dislocation forest	Versetzungswald m
		dislocation gliding, glide motion of the dislocation, gliding of the dislocation	Versetzungsgleiten n, Gleitbewegung f (Gleiten n) der Versetzung
disjunctive normal form, alternative normal form	disjunktive Normalform f, alternative Normalform		
disjunct motion	sprunghafte Bewegung f, sprungweise Bewegung	dislocation jog, jog	Versetzungssprung m, Sprung m <Versetzungstheorie>
disk anode, plate anode	Scheibenanode f, Telleranode f		
disk damping	Scheibendämpfung f	dislocation kernel, dislocation core, centre of dislocation	Versetzungskern m
disk discharger	Scheibenfunkenstrecke f	dislocation line, line of dislocation	Versetzungslinie f, Versetzungsgrenze f
disk electrophoresis	Diskelektrophorese f		
		dislocation loop, dislocation ring, loop-shaped dislocation, loop of dislocation	Versetzungsschleife f, Versetzungsring m, ringförmige Versetzung f
disk file memory, magnetic disk store (storage, memory), disk store (storage)	Scheibenreihenspeicher m, Magnetplattenspeicher m, Magnetscheibenspeicher m, Plattenspeicher m, Scheibenspeicher m		
		dislocation migration, migration of dislocation	Versetzungswanderung f, Wanderung f der Versetzung
disklike population	s. disk population	dislocation model	Versetzungsmodell n

dislocation 184

dislocation mountains	Schollengebirge n; Rumpfgebirge n, Rumpfschollengebirge n, Keilschollengebirge n	dispenser cathode, dispensed cathode	Vorratskatode f

		dispersal	s. dispersation
		dispersant	s. disperser
dislocation multiplication, multiplication of dislocations	Versetzungsvervielfachung f, Versetzungsmultiplikation f, Multiplikation f von Versetzungen	dispersation, dispersion, dispersal	Dispergieren n, Dispergierung f
		dispersed fibriform	fadenförmig dispers, fibrillär dispers
dislocation network, network of dislocations	Versetzungsnetzwerk n, Versetzungsgitter n	dispersed laminar	laminar dispers, blättchenförmig dispers
dislocation node	Versetzungsknoten m		
dislocation of higher order	Überversetzung f, Versetzung f höherer Ordnung	dispersed phase, disperse phase, internal phase	disperse Phase f, disperser Bestandteil m, Dispersum n
dislocation pattern	s. dislocation array	dispersed reflection	s. scattered reflection
dislocation "pipe"	Versetzungs-„röhre" f	dispersed reflection	s. diffuse reflection
		dispersed refraction	s. scattered refraction
dislocation pipe diffusion, pipe diffusion	„pipe diffusion" f, Röhrendiffusion f, Diffusion f in Röhren [längs der Versetzungslinien]	dispersed refraction	s. a. diffuse refraction
		dispersed transmission	s. diffuse transmission
		disperse field, magnetic disperse field	[magnetisches] Dispersionsfeld n
dislocation plane	Versetzungsebene f	disperse phase	s. dispersed phase
dislocation potential	Versetzungspotential n	disperser, dispersing agent, dispersant, dispersion (dispersive) agent	Dispergiermittel n, Dispersionsmittel n
dislocation relaxation	Versetzungsrelaxation f		
dislocation ring	s. dislocation loop	disperse system	s. dispersion
dislocation row, row of dislocations	Versetzungsreihe f	dispersing agent	s. disperser
dislocation screw, dislocation spiral	Versetzungsschraube f, Versetzungsspirale f	dispersing cone, cone of dispersion (spread), scattering cone	Streukegel m, Streuungskegel m
dislocation source	Versetzungsquelle f		
dislocation spiral	s. dislocation screw	dispersing medium, dispersive (dispersion) medium <opt.>	dispergierendes Medium n, Dispersionsmedium n <Opt.>
dislocation splitting	s. dissociation of the dislocation		
dislocation structure	Versetzungsstruktur f	dispersing power	s. a. reciprocal constringence
dislocation theory of melting	Versetzungstheorie f des Schmelzens	dispersing prism	s. dispersion prism
		dispersing system	Spektralapparat m, Spektralgerät n
dislocation velocity, velocity of dislocations	Versetzungsgeschwindigkeit f		
		dispersing system with diffraction grating, diffraction dispersing system	Gitterspektralapparat m, Gitterapparat m
dislocation wall, surface array of dislocations	Versetzungswand f		
dismantling, decanning, decladding	Enthülsung f; Entfernung f der Brennelementhüllen	dispersing system with prism, prism dispersing system	Prismenspektralapparat m, Prismenapparat m
dismantling	s. a. disassembly <e.g. of experiment>		
		dispersion	Dispersion f; Zerteilung f, Zerstreuung f, Streuung f
dismemberment; division	Gliederung f; Aufgliederung f; Zergliederung f; Zerlegung f	dispersion <of spectral apparatus)	Dispersion f <Spektralapparat>
dismounting	s. disassembly <e.g. of experiment>	dispersion, disperse system <chem.>	Dispersion f, disperses System n <Chem.>
dismutation [reaction]	s. oxidoreduction	dispersion, spectral dispersion, prismatic dispersion <opt.>	Dispersion f, Farbzerlegung f, [spektrale] Zerlegung f, Spektralzerlegung f
D-isomer, d-isomer, dextroisomer	rechtsdrehendes Isomer n, D-Isomer n, d-Isomer n		
disorder, defects, disarrangement of the structure <cryst.>	Fehlordnung f <Krist.>	dispersion, variance, square of the standard deviation, var <stat.>	Varianz f, Dispersion f, Streuungsquadrat n, Streuung f, var <Stat.>
disordered crystal	s. imperfect crystal		
disordered flow, disordered stream	ungeordnete Strömung f, Unordnungsströmung f	dispersion	s. a. dispersation
		dispersion	s. a. dispersity
disordered motion, random (irregular, chaotic) motion; random flight	ungeordnete (chaotische, regellose, statistische) Bewegung f	dispersional frequency	s. dispersion frequency
		dispersion analysis	Dispersionsanalyse f, Dispersoidanalyse f
		dispersion and mask (template) method	Spektralmaskenverfahren n, Staffelblendenverfahren n
disordered scattering	s. disorder scattering		
disordered stream, disordered flow	ungeordnete Strömung f, Unordnungsströmung f	dispersion and mask (template) photometer, template and dispersion photometer	Spektralmaskenphotometer n, Staffelblendenphotometer n
disorder energy	Unordnungsenergie f		
disorder-order transformation, disorder-order transition	Unordnungs-Ordnungs-Umwandlung f		
		dispersion caused by diffraction grating, dispersion due to diffraction	Beugungsdispersion f
disorder pressure	Entropiedruck m		
		dispersion coefficient, coefficient of dispersion	Dispersionskoeffizient m, Zerstreuungskoeffizient m
disorder scattering, disordered scattering, diffuse scattering	ungeordnete (diffuse) Streuung f, Diffusionsstreuung f, Unordnungsstreuung f	dispersion constant	Dispersionskonstante f
		dispersion current	Ausbreitungsstrom m
disorientation	Desorientierung f, Aufhebung f der Orientierung	dispersion curve, curve of dispersion	Dispersionskurve f; Dispersionsdiagramm n
dispansive <opt.>, diverging, divergent	zerstreuend, dispansiv <Opt.>	dispersion degree	s. dispersity
		dispersion diagram	s. scatter diagram <stat.>
disparity, fixation disparity, geometric disparity	Disparation f, geometrische Disparation	dispersion due to diffraction, dispersion caused by diffraction grating	Beugungsdispersion f
dispensed cathode	s. dispenser cathode		

dispersion ellipse	s. ellipse of correlation	**dispersoid**	Dispersoid n
dispersion error, error of dispersion	Zerstreuungsfehler m	**dispersoid**	s. a. coarse-grain
		dispersoid colloid	s. lyophilic colloid
dispersion force, dispersion interaction, London force, dipole-quadrupole force	Dispersionskraft f, Dispersionswechselwirkung f, London-Kraft f, Dipol-Quadrupol-Kraft f	**dispersoidology**, colloid chemistry (science)	Kolloidchemie f, Kolloidik f, Kolloidlehre f
		disphenoid	s. a. bisphenoid <cryst.>
		displaced atom	umgelagertes Atom n
		displaced liquid, liquid displaced	verdrängte Flüssigkeit f
dispersion formula; dispersion relation, dispersion law	Dispersionsformel f <Opt.>; Dispersionsbeziehung f, Dispersionsrelation f, Dispersionsgleichung f, Dispersionsgesetz n <Kern., Quantenfeldtheorie>	**displaced volume**, volume displaced, volume forced away, displacement <quantity>	verdrängtes Volumen n, eingetauchtes Volumen, Verdrängung f <Größe>
		displacement; substitution	Verdrängung f
		displacement, displacement (piston-swept) volume, volume of stroke	Hubraum m; Hubvolumen n
dispersion frequency, dispersional frequency	Dispersionsfrequenz f	**displacement**, schubweg, displacement distance	Schubweg m
dispersion hardening	s. age-hardening		
dispersion interaction	s. dispersion force		
dispersion law	s. dispersion formula	**displacement**, dislocation, shifting, shift, removal <gen.>	Verschiebung f, Verlagerung f <allg.>
dispersion lens	s. divergent lens		
dispersion line	Dispersionslinie f	**displacement**, shift <geo.>	Verschiebung f <Geo.>
dispersion matrix	s. covariance matrix <stat.>		
dispersion medium	Dispersionsmittel n, Dispergens n	**displacement**, water displacement <hydr.>	Wasserverdrängung f, Deplacement n, eingetauchtes Volumen n
dispersion medium	s. a. continuous phase		
dispersion medium	s. a. dispersing medium <opt.>	**displacement** <mech.>	Verrückung f, Verschiebung f <Mech.>
dispersion of conductance	s. Debye-Falkenhagen effect		
		displacement <mech.>, displacement vector	Verrückungsvektor m, Verschiebungsvektor m <Mech.>
dispersion of heat, heat dispersion; heat leak[age], leakage of heat	Wärmestreuung f; Wärmeverlust m, Wärmeundichtigkeit f	**displacement** <chem.>; refining	Treiben n, Austreiben n, Abtreiben n <Chem.>
dispersion of light	Lichtzerlegung f, Zerlegung f des Lichtes	**displacement**	s. a. displaced volume
dispersion of optical activity	s. rotatory dispersion	**displgcement**	s. a. displacement reaction
		displacement	s. a. discomposition <of atoms>
dispersion of optical axes	Dispersion f der optischen Achsen, Achsendispersion f	**displacement**	s. a. electric displacement
		displacement	s. a. path
dispersion of polarization, polychroism, pleochroism	Pleochroismus m, Polychroismus m	**displacement adsorption**	Verschiebungsadsorption f
		displacement angle, shift angle	Verschiebungswinkel m
dispersion of rotation	s. rotatory dispersion	**displacement angle** <el.>	Verstimmungswinkel m, Differenzwinkel m; Verdreh[ungs]winkel m
dispersion of sound, sound (acoustic) dispersion	Schalldispersion f		
dispersion photometer	Photometer n mit Zerstreuungslinse	**displacement by temperature effect**	s. temperature-induced shift
		displacement chromatographic analysis	s. displacement development
dispersion prism, dispersing prism	Dispersionsprisma n	**displacement chromatography**	s. displacement development
		displacement collision	Umlagerungsstoß m; Verlagerungsstoß m
dispersion profile, Lorentz profile	Dispersionsprofil n, Lorentz-Profil n		
		displacement co-ordinate	Verrückungskoordinate f, Verschiebungskoordinate
dispersion range	Dispersionsgebiet n, Dispersionsbereich m	**displacement correction**	Verdrängungskorrektion f
dispersion rate	s. dispersity	**displacement crack**	Verschiebungsspalte f
dispersion relation	s. dispersion formula	**displacement current**, polarization current, current of dielectric convection	Verschiebungsstrom m, [di]elektrischer Verschiebungsstrom, [dielektrischer] Polarisationsstrom m
dispersion spectrum, prismatic spectrum, prism (refraction) spectrum	Dispersionsspektrum n, Brechungsspektrum n, Prismenspektrum n, prismatisches Spektrum n		
dispersion surface	Dispersionsfläche f	**displacement current density**	Verschiebungsstromdichte f
dispersion tensor	Dispersionstensor m	**displacement derivative**	Verrückungsableitung f, Verschiebungsableitung f
dispersion term	Dispersionsterm m		
dispersity, dispersivity, degree of dispersion, dispersion degree (rate), dispersion	Dispersionsgrad m, Dispersitätsgrad m, Zerteilungsgrad m, Dispersität f	**displacement development**, displacement chromatography; displacement chromatographic analysis	Verdrängungschromatographie f, Bandenverdrängungschromatographie f, Verdrängungselution f; Verdrängungsanalyse f
dispersity, dispersiveness, dispersivity	Dispersität f		
dispersive agent	s. disperser		
dispersive lens	s. divergent lens		
dispersive medium	s. disperser	**displacement diagram**	s. Williot diagram
dispersive medium	s. dispersing medium <opt.>	**displacement distance**, schubweg, displacement	Schubweg m
dispersiveness, dispers[iv]ity	Dispersität f	**displacement electrophoresis**	Verdrängungselektrophorese f
dispersive power	Zerstreuungsvermögen n	**displacement error** <US>	s. phase angle
dispersive power	s. a. reciprocal constringence		
dispersive spectrometry	dispersive Spektrometrie f	**displacement factor**, current displacement factor	Stromverdrängungsfaktor m
dispersivity	s. dispersity		
dispersivity quotient	Materialdispersion f	**displacement field**	Verrückungsfeld n, Verschiebungsfeld n

displacement

displacement figure, Hollenberg['s] figure	Hollenbergsche Verdrängungsfigur f, Verdrängungsfigur	displacement transducer, displacement measuring transducer	Weggeber m, Wegmeßwandler m
displacement flow, displacement stream	Verdrängungsströmung f	displacement vector, displacement <mech.>	Verrückungsvektor m, Verschiebungsvektor m <Mech.>
displacement flux, electric flux	Verschiebungsfluß m, elektrischer Fluß m (Verschiebungsfluß)	displacement vector	s. a. electric displacement <el.>
displacement function	Verschiebungsfunktion f	displacement voltage <of electronic valve>	Verschiebungsspannung f <Röhre>
displacement generator	Verschiebeoszillator m	displacement volume	s. displacement
displacement gradient	Verrückungsgradient m, Verschiebungsgradient m	displacement wave	Versetzungswelle f
displacement gradient tensor, displacement tensor	Verrückungstensor m, Verschiebungstensor m	displacement work, work of displacement	Verdrängungsarbeit f
displacement in Brownian movement	Brownsche Schwankung (Bewegungsschwankung) f	displacer	Verdränger m, Verdrängungskörper m
displacement kernel, kernel of displacement	Verschiebungs[integral]kern m	displace-time diagram; path-time diagram	Weg-Zeit-Diagramm n, Weg-Zeit-Schaubild n
displacement law <of radioactive disintegration>	s. radioactive displacement law	display	s. consumption
		display	s. a. indication
		display	s. a. scope
		display	s. a. version
displacement law for complex spectra, law of spectroscopic (spectrometric) displacement, Kossel-Sommerfeld (Sommerfeld-Kossel) [displacement] law	spektroskopischer Verschiebungssatz m, Kossel-Sommerfeldscher Verschiebungssatz	display	s. a. plan-position indicator
		display of direction finder, cathode-ray display of direction finder, bearing indicator scope, scope of direction finder	Peilrohr n, Peilröhre f; Peilwinkeloszillograph m
displacement law of Soddy and Fajans	s. radioactive displacement law	display system	s. indicator <el.>
displacement law of Wien	s. Wien['s] displacement law	display tube, indicator tube	Übersichtsröhre f, Übersichtsbildröhre f
displacement line, line of displacement vector	Verschiebungslinie f, Feldlinie f des Vektors der dielektrischen Verschiebung	display unit	s. indicator <el.>
		disposal	s. removal
		disproportionation	s. oxidoreduction
displacement measuring transducer, displacement transducer	Weggeber m, Wegmeßwandler m	disruption, fragmentation <of the meteor>	Zerplatzen n, Zerspringen n, Zerstörung f <Meteor>
displacement modulation	s. pulse-position modulation	disruption of the comet; disintegration of the comet	Auflösung f des Kometen; Zerfall m des Kometen
displacement of Bloch wall	s. boundary movement	disruption of the molecule	s. molecular decomposition
displacement of current	s. skin effect		
displacement of equilibrium, equilibrium shift	Gleichgewichtsverschiebung f	disruption of the star cluster, dissociation of the cluster	Auflösung f des Sternhaufens
displacement of field, field displacement	Feldverdrängung f; Feldverdrängungseffekt m	disruptive breakdown (discharge)	s. breakdown
displacement of liquid	Flüssigkeitsverschiebung f	disruptive [electric field] strength	s. dielectric strength
displacement of spectral line	s. line shift	disruptive voltage	s. breakdown voltage
displacement of the centre of gravity (mass)	Schwerpunkt[s]verschiebung f, Schwerpunkt[s]verlagerung f	dissecting microscope	Präpariermikroskop n
		dissection	s. division
displacement of transport	Führungsverschiebung f	dissector [tube], image dissector [tube], multiplier-type [image] dissector	Sondenröhre f, Farnsworth-Röhre f, "dissector"-Röhre f
displacement operator	Verschiebungsoperator m		
"displacement" polarizability	Verschiebungspolarisierbarkeit f	dissimilar	s. opposite
		dissimilation	s. catabolism
"displacement" polarization, polarization [brought about] by atomic and electronic movement	Verschiebungspolarisation f	dissipated heat	s. lost heat
		dissipated power, dissipation power, lost power	Zerstreuungsleistung f, zerstreute (dissipierte) Leistung f; Verlustleistung f
displacement potential	Verrückungspotential n, Verschiebungspotential n	dissipated power in reverse direction	Sperrverlustleistung f
displacement reaction, displacement	Verdrängungsreaktion f	dissipated power of the control grid	Steuergitterverlustleistung f
displacement resistance, resistance to displacement	Verschiebungswiderstand m	dissipation <of energy or power>	Dissipation f, Zerstreuung f; Vernichtung f <Energie oder Leistung>
displacement resonance, amplitude resonance	Amplitudenresonanz f	dissipation constant	Dissipationskonstante f
displacement rule	Verschiebungsregel f	dissipation factor	Verlustfaktor m
displacement spike	"displacement spike" m, Umlagerungsbereich m, Umordnungsbereich m, Schmelzzone f	dissipation factor, acoustic (sound) dissipation factor <ac.>	Schalldissipationsgrad m, Dissipationsgrad m, Verwärmgrad m <Ak.>
displacement stream, displacement flow	Verdrängungsströmung f	dissipation function, dissipative function <mech.>	Dissipationsfunktion f, Zerstreuungsfunktion f <Mech.>
displacement surface, shift surface	Verschiebungsfläche f	dissipation function <therm.>	Dissipationsfunktion f, Energiedissipation f <Therm.>
displacement tensor, displacement gradient tensor	Verrückungstensor m, Verschiebungstensor m	dissipation function of Rayleigh	s. viscous dissipation function <hydr.>
displacement thickness [of boundary layer], boundary layer displacement thickness	Verdrängungsdicke f [der Grenzschicht], Grenzschicht-Verdrängungsdicke f	dissipation law, recombination law, law of recombination	Wiedervereinigungsgesetz n, Rekombinationsgesetz n

dissipationless line, zero-loss (no-loss, loss-free, lossless) line	verlustlose Leitung f, verlustfreie Leitung	**dissolution heat**	s. heat of solution
dissipation-loss resistance	s. loss resistance	**dissolution spectrum,** solution spectrum	Lösungsspektrum n
dissipation of heat, heat (thermal) dissipation	Wärmezerstreuung f, Wärmedissipation f, Wärmeableitung f	**dissolvent**	s. solvent
		dissolving	s. dissolution
		dissolving	s. dissolution <chem.>
dissipation of jet	Strahldissipation f	**dissonance,** discord	Dissonanz f, Spaltklang m
dissipation of matter in the universe	s. unrestricted dissipation of matter in the universe	**dissymmetrical**	s. asymmetric[al]
		dissymmetry	s. asymmetry
dissipation of the resistance	Widerstandsbelastung f	**dissymmetry factor**	s. anisotropy factor
		dissymmetry to earth	Erdunsymmetrie f, Erdkopplung f
dissipation of vorticity, decay of vorticity (whirls)	Wirbelzerstreuung f	**dissymmetry value**	Unsymmetriezahl f
		distance	s. path
		distance	s. gap
dissipation power	s. dissipated power	**distance appreciation**	s. appreciation of distance
dissipation rate	Dissipationsgeschwindigkeit f	**distance between atoms**	s. interatomic distance
		distance between electrodes	s. electrode separation
dissipation sphere	Dissipationssphäre f	**distance between pupils**	s. interocular distance
dissipative; lossy; leaky	verlustbehaftet	**distance control**	s. telecontrol
		distance covered	s. path
dissipative force	dissipative Kraft f	**distance fog,** atmospheric fog	Entfernungsschleier m
dissipative function <mech.>	s. dissipation function	**distance from focal point**	Brennpunktsweite f
dissipative line, lossy line	verlustbehaftete Leitung f, Verlustleitung f	**distance from the coast**	Küstenferne f, Meerferne f
dissipative operator	dissipativer Operator m	**distance from the screen**	Schirmabstand m
dissipative power loss	Dämpfungsverlust m	**distance function**	Abstandsfunktion f
		distance judgment	s. appreciation of distance
dissipative stress	dissipativer Spannungsanteil m	**distance meter,** [optical] rangefinder, [optical] telemeter, optical distance meter	[optischer] Entfernungsmesser m, Distanzmesser m, Telemeter n; Abstandsmesser m
dissipativity	Dissipativität f		
dissociation, splitting <of molecules>	Dissoziation f, Aufspaltung f, Zerlegung f <Moleküle>		
dissociation by rotation	Rotationsdissoziation f	**distance modulus**	Entfernungsmodul m
dissociation constant, ionization constant	Dissoziationskonstante f, Ionisationskonstante f	**distance of closest approach;** closest approach	geringster Abstand m bei der Annäherung; dichteste Annäherung f, größte Annäherung
dissociation continuum	Dissoziationskontinuum n	**distance of epicentre,** epicentral distance	Epizentraldistanz f, Epizentralentfernung f
dissociation energy, energy of dissociation <chem.>	Dissoziationsenergie f, Dissoziationsarbeit f, Trennungsarbeit f <Chem.>	**distance of fall**	Fallweg m
		distance of hearing, hearing distance, earshot, audible range	Hörweite f
dissociation equilibrium	Dissoziationsgleichgewicht n	**distance of horizon**	s. distance of visible horizon
		distance of hypocentre	s. hypocentral distance <geo.>
dissociation field effect	Dissoziationsspannungseffekt m [von M. Wien-Schiele], Dissoziationsfeldeffekt m, Wien-Schiele-Effekt m	**distance of most distinct vision,** distance of normal vision	Bezugssehweite f, Normsehweite f, deutliche Sehweite f
		distance of·punctum proximum, minimum distance of clear vision	Nahpunktabstand m <vom Hornhautscheitel aus gemessen>
dissociation in molecules	s. disassociation	**distance of punctum proximum from principal point of eye**	Nahpunktabstand m
dissociation limit	Dissoziationsgrenze f		
dissociation of the cluster, disruption of the star cluster	Auflösung f des Sternhaufens	**distance of punctum remotum,** maximum distance of clear vision	Fernpunktabstand m <vom Hornhautscheitel aus gemessen>
dissociation of the dislocation, splitting (slipping) of the dislocation, dislocation dissociation (splitting)	Versetzungsaufspaltung f, Aufspaltung f der Versetzung	**distance of punctum remotum from principal point of eye**	Fernpunktabstand m
		distance of sliding	Gleitweg m, Reibungsweg m
dissociation of water vapour, steam (water vapour) dissociation	Wasserdampfspaltung f	**distance of visible horizon,** distance of horizon	Kimmweite f, Aussichtsweite f, Kimmdistanz f, Kimmabstand m
dissociation potential	Dissoziationspotential n	**distance passed through**	s. path
dissociation pressure, dissociation tension	Dissoziationsdruck m, Dissoziationsspannung f, Dissoziationstension f	**distance-preserving,** preserving the separation	abstandstreu; zwischenstandstreu
dissociation theory of Arrhenius-Ostwald	Dissoziationstheorie f von Arrhenius-Ostwald, Arrhenius-Ostwaldsche Dissoziationstheorie	**distance setting,** meter setting	Entfernungseinstellung f
dissociative capture	dissoziative Anlagerung f	**distance thermometer,** telethermometer, remote thermometer	Fernthermometer n
dissociative ionization	dissoziative Ionisation f		
dissociative recombination	dissoziative Rekombination f	**distant action**	s. action at a distance
		distant collision	ferner Stoß m, Fernstoß m, Fernordnungsstoß m
dissolution, dissolving	Dissolution f, Auflösung f von Kolloidsystemen		
dissolution, dissolving, solution <chem.>	Lösung f, Auflösung f <Chem.>	**distant control**	s. telecontrol

distant earthquake, earthquake of distant origin, teleseism	Fernbeben *n*	**distortion correction**	*s.* compensation of distortion <el.>
distant field, far (radiation) field, remote radiation field	Fern[wirkungs]feld *n*	**distortion detector,** non-linear detector	nichtlinearer Detektor *m*, Verzerrungsdetektor *m*
distant-reading instrument	*s.* telemeter	**distortion due to multi-path transmission**	Mehrwegeverzerrung *f*
distant site error, site error; inter-site error	Standortfehler *m*; Standortumgebungsfehler *m*	**distortion ellipse** <geo.>, [Tissot] indicatrix	[Tissotsche] Indikatrix *f*, Verzerrungsellipse *f* <Geo.>
distant zone, radiation zone, wave zone, Fraunhofer['s] zone, Fraunhofer['s] region	Wellenzone *f*, Fernzone *f*, Strahlungszone *f*, Fraunhofersche Zone *f*, Fraunhofersches Gebiet *n*	**distortion energy**	*s.* strain energy due to the distortion
distant zone <el.>	Fernzone *f* <El.>	**distortion energy theory,** theory of strain energy of distortion	Gestaltänderungsenergiehypothese *f*
distex process	*s.* extractive distillation		
distillation, volatilization, vaporization, sublimation	Destillation *f*, Destillieren *n*, Siedetrennung *f*	**distortion factor,** harmonic distortion [factor], nonlinear distortion factor, overall coefficient of harmonic distortion, klirr factor, harmonic content	Klirrfaktor *m*, Gesamtklirrfaktor *m*, Klirrgrad *m*, Oberwellengehalt *m*, Oberschwingungsgehalt *m*, Verzerrungsfaktor *m*
distillation column, distillation tower, distilling column (tower)	Destillierkolonne *f*, Destilliersäule *f*		
distillation flask (retort, still), still, distilling flask	Blase *f*, Destillierblase *f*, Destillationsblase *f*, Destillierkolben *m*, Destillationskolben *m*	**distortion factor** <hydr.>	Distorsionsfaktor *m* <Hydr.>
		distortion factor meter	Klirrfaktormesser *m*
distillation tower	*s.* distillation column		
distillation tube, fractionating tube	Destillationsaufsatz *m*; Fraktionieraufsatz *m*, Aufsatz *m*	**distortion matrix**	*s.* strain matrix
		distortion noise, harmonic distortion noise	Klirrleistung *f*, Klirrgeräusch *n*
distilled water, dist. water	destilliertes Wasser *n*, aqua *f* destillata, dest. Wasser, aq. dest.	**distortion of colour,** chromatic distortion <opt.>	Farbverzerrung *f*; Farbwandlung *f*; Farbverschiebung *f* <Opt.>
distilling column	*s.* distillation column	**distortion of the emulsion**	Verzerrung *f* der Emulsion
distilling flask	*s.* distillation flask		
distilling off	Abdestillieren *n*	**distortion of the Sun** <rising *or* setting>, distortion	Zerrbild *n* [der Sonne] <aufgehend *oder* untergehend>
distilling tower	*s.* distillation column		
distinction	*s.* discrimination	**distortion of third order,** third-order distortion	kubische Verzerrung *f*, Verzerrung dritter Ordnung
distinctive feature	*s.* distinguishing feature		
distinctive line, sensitive (persistent) line, raie ultime, letzte linie	letzte Linie *f*, Restlinie *f*, beständige Linie, Nachweislinie *f*	**distortion power**	Verzerrungsleistung *f*
		distortion set	*s.* distortion analyzer
distinguishability, discernibility	Unterscheidbarkeit *f*	**distortion standard**	Verzerrungsvierpol *m*, Verzerrungsnormal *n*, Verklirrer *m*
distinguished sub-group	*s.* normal divisor		
distinguishing characteristic (feature), characteristic (distinctive) feature	Unterscheidungsmerkmal *n*	**distortion tensor**	Distorsionstensor *m*
		distortion tensor	*s. a.* strain tensor
		distributed, non concentrated	verteilt, stetig verteilt
distorted crystal	verzerrter Kristall *m*, gestörter Kristall	**distributed amplifier,** distributed line amplifier	Kettenverstärker *m*
distorted lattice	verzerrtes Gitter *n*, gestörtes Gitter		
distorted region	verzerrter (gestörter) Bereich *m*, Verzerrungsbereich *m*	**distributed capacitance**	verteilte Kapazität *f*
distorted wave	verzerrte Welle[nform] *f*	**distributed capacitance of the coil,** coil capacitance	Spulenkapazität *f*
distorted wave Born approximation, DWBA method	DWBA-Methode *f*, Bornsche Näherung *f* mit gestörter Welle, „distortedwave"-Born-Näherung *f*		
		distributed force	verteilte Kraft *f*
distorted wave[s] method, method of distorted waves	Störwellenmethode *f*, Methode *f* der gestörten Welle[n], „distortedwave[s]"-Methode *f*	**distributed inductance,** distributed self-induction	verteilte Induktivität *f*, verteilte Selbstinduktion *f*
		distributed line amplifier	*s.* distributed amplifier
distorting lens	*s.* anamorphotic lens	**distributed load**	verteilte Last *f*, [stetig] verteilte Belastung *f*, Streckenlast *f*
distortion <el., tv.>	Verzerrung *f*, Amplitudenverzerrung *f* <El.; Fs.>		
distortion <opt.>	Verzeichnung *f*, Verzeichnungsfehler *m* <Opt.>	**distributed parameters / with**	mit verteilten Elementen (Parametern)
distortion, distortion of the Sun <rising *or* setting>	Zerrbild *n* [der Sonne] <aufgehend *oder* untergehend>	**distributed resistance**	verteilter Widerstand *m*
		distributed resonant circuit	*s.* resonant circuit with distributed parameters
distortion	*s. a.* warping	**distributed roughness**	flächenhafte Rauhigkeit *f*
distortional strain energy	*s.* strain energy due to the distortion		
distortional wave; discontinuity wave	Unstetigkeitswelle *f*	**distributed self-induction**	*s.* distributed inductance
distorsional wave	*s. a.* shear wave	**distributed source**	verteilte Quelle *f*
distortion analyzer; distortion set	Verzerrungsmeßgerät *n*, Verzerrungsmesser *m*, Verzerrungsanalysator *m*; Verzerrungsmeßplatz *m*	**distributed suction**	verteiltes Absaugen *n*
		distribution; partition	Verteilung *f*
distortion analyzer, harmonic distortion analyzer	Klirranalysator *m*	**distribution** <in nature>	Verbreitung *f* <in der Natur>
distortion bridge, resonance bridge	Klirrfaktormeßbrücke *f*, Resonanzbrücke *f*, Oberwellenmeßgerät *n*, Resonanzmeßbrücke *f*	**distribution,** generalized function <math.>	Distribution *f*, verallgemeinerte Funktion *f*
		distribution analysis	Verteilungsanalyse *f*
distortion broadening	Verzerrungsverbreiterung *f*	**distribution chart,** distribution map, partition chart (map)	Verteilungskarte *f*
distortion by damping	Dämpfungsverzerrung *f*		

distribution coefficient, partition coefficient, distribution ratio (number), ratio of concentration	[Nernstscher] Verteilungskoeffizient m, Konzentrationsverhältnis n; Einbaukoeffizient m Spektralwert m <Opt.>	distribution of velocity distribution parameter distribution polygon distribution ratio distribution skew on the left, left-skew distribution distribution skew on the right, right-skew distribution distribution temperature	s. velocity distribution Verteilungsparameter m Verteilungspolygon n s. distribution coefficient linksschiefe Verteilung f, rechtssteile Verteilung rechtsschiefe Verteilung f, linkssteile Verteilung s. temperature corresponding to the spectral distribution of energy of the radiator
distribution coefficient <opt.>	
distribution coefficient determination	s. determination of the distribution coefficients
distribution coefficient in the C.I.E. standard colorimetric system	s. C.I.E. distribution coefficient
distribution curve, cumulative frequency curve; percentile curve, ogive	Verteilungskurve f, kumulative Verteilungskurve; Ogive f	distribution valve	Verteilungsschieber m
distribution curve <colorimetry>	s. a. distribution function	distributive law <math.>	Distributivgesetz n, distributives Gesetz n, Mischungsregel f <Math.>
distribution curve in the C.I.E. standard colorimetric system	s. C.I.E. distribution function	distributivity	Distributivität f
distribution density	s. probability density	distributor	Verteiler m; Verzweiger m
distribution factor, DF <health physics>	Verteilungsfaktor m, DF <Strahlenbiologie>	distributor control	Vertikalsteuerung f
distribution fluctuation[s]	
distribution[-]free test; non-parametric test, order test	verteilungsfreier (nichtparametrischer, parameterfreier) Test m; Anordnungstest m	
		disturbance, disturbing quantity	Störgröße f, Störungsgröße f, störende Größe f, Störung f
distribution function, probability (cumulative) distribution function, cumulative frequency (probability) function, probability function, partition function	Verteilungsfunktion f, kumulative Verteilungsfunktion f, Verteilung f, Summenfunktion f, Summen[häufigkeits]verteilung f	disturbance <astr., math.>, perturbation, perturbance	Störung f; Perturbation f <Astr., Math.>
		disturbance <control>	s. a. disturbance upset
		disturbance energy	s. perturbation energy
		disturbance field, disturbing field; external field; extraneous field; foreign field; interfering field, interference field <el.>	Störfeld n, Störungsfeld n; äußeres Feld n; Fremdfeld n <El.>
distribution function; distribution curve <colorimetry>	Spektralwertfunktion f; Spektralwertkurve f, spektrale Eichwertkurve f, Eichreizkurve f <Farbmessung>
distribution function	s. a. joint distribution	disturbance force, disturbing force, force of perturbation	Störkraft f, störende Kraft f, Störungskraft f
distribution function in the C.I.E. standard colorimetric system	s. C.I.E. distribution function
distribution graph	Häufigkeitskurve f	disturbance function	s. perturbing function <astr.>
distribution in altitude (height)	s. vertical distribution
distribution in frequency	s. frequency distribution	disturbance method	s. perturbation method
distribution in phase	s. phase spectrum	disturbance of equilibrium, perturbation of equilibrium, unbalance	Störung f des Gleichgewichts, Gleichgewichtsstörung f
distribution law, partition law	Verteilungsgesetz n
distribution law	s. Nernst distribution law	disturbances, microvariations, microscopic variations, trouble	Unruhe f
distribution law of Laplace	Laplacesches Verteilungsgesetz n
distribution map	s. distribution chart	disturbance transfer function	Störungsübertragungsfunktion f
distribution modulus	Verteilungsmodul m
distribution noise	s. partition noise
distribution number	s. distribution coefficient	disturbance upset (variable), disturbance <control>	Störgröße f <Regelung>
distribution of angles of attack	Anstellwinkelverteilung f
distribution of brightness	Leuchtdichteverteilung f, Helligkeitsverteilung f	disturbance variable feed forward, compensation of disturbance variable	Störwertaufschaltung f, Störgrößenaufschaltung f, Störaufschaltung f
distribution of lines of force, field distribution	Feldlinienverteilung f, Kraftlinienverteilung f	disturbance velocity, secondary (collateral) motion <turbulence>	Nebenbewegung f, Schwankungsbewegung f, Querbewegung f <Turbulenz>
distribution of luminous flux, luminous-flux distribution (diagram), curve of flux distribution, [polar] diagram of luminous flux	Lichtstromverteilung f, Lichtstromverteilungskurve f, Lichtstromdiagramm n
		disturbance vortex, interference vortex	Störwirbel m, Störungswirbel m
		disturbation theory	s. perturbation theory
		disturbed day, active day	gestörter Tag m
distribution of luminous intensity	s. light distribution	disturbed differential equation	gestörte Differentialgleichung f
		disturbed equilibrium	gestörtes Gleichgewicht n
distribution of mass, mass distribution	Massenverteilung f
		disturbed Sun, active Sun	gestörte Sonne f, aktive Sonne
distribution of nuclei size	s. size spectrum of nuclei	disturbing current	s. parasite current
		disturbing field	s. disturbance field <el.>
distribution of potential, potential distribution [curve]	Potentialverteilung[skurve] f, Potentialverlauf m	disturbing force, disturbance force, force of perturbation	Störkraft f, störende Kraft f, Störungskraft f
distribution of the wind waves, spectrum of the wind waves, wave spectrum	Windseeverteilung f, Windseespektrum n, Windwellenspektrum n	disturbing function, perturbing function, disturbance function <astr.>	Störungsfunktion f <Astr.>
		disturbing mass, perturbing mass	störende Masse f
distribution of turbidity	Trübungsverteilung f	disturbing quantity	s. disturbance
distribution of velocities	s. velocity distribution	dit	s. hartley
distribution of velocities [of flow]	Strömungsgeschwindigkeitsverteilung f, Verteilung f der Strömungsgeschwindigkeiten	ditesseral central class	s. holohedry of the regular system
		ditesseral polar class	s. hemimorphic hemihedry of the regular system

ditetragonal | **190**

ditetragonal alternating class	s. hemihedry of the second sort of the tetragonal system	diurnal variation, daily variation, diurnal turn; day-night effect	Tagesgang m, Tagesvariation f, tägliche Variation (Änderung, Schwankung) f, Tagesschwankung f, täglicher Gang m
ditetragonal bipyramidal class, ditetragonal-dipyramidal [crystal] class, ditetragonal equatorial class, holohedry (holohedral class) of the tetragonal system, tetragonal holohedry, normal class	Holoedrie f des tetragonalen Systems, ditetragonal-bipyramidale Klasse f, ditetragonal dipyramidale Klasse, tetragonale Holoedrie	diurnal wave of temperature, diurnal temperature wave	Tageswelle f der Temperatur
		diurnal yield, yield per day	Tagesausbeute f
		divacancy	s. double vacancy
		divariant system, bivariant system	bivariantes (divariantes) System n
ditetragonal polar class, ditetragonal-pyramidal class	s. hemimorphic hemihedry of the tetragonal system	divergence ⟨of series⟩	Divergenz f ⟨Reihe⟩
		divergence, div; ∇ ⟨of vector, tensor⟩	Divergenz f, Quelldichte f, Quellenstärke f, div; ∇ ⟨Vektor, Tensor⟩
ditrigonal bipyramidal [crystal] class, ditrigonal dipyramidal [crystal] class, ditrigonal equatorial class, trigonal holohedry [of the hexagonal system], trigonotype class, sphenoidal hemihedry, hemihedral class with threefold axis of the hexagonal system	Hemiedrie f II. Art des hexagonalen Systems, ditrigonal-bipyramidale Klasse f, trigonale Hemiedrie, ditrigonal dipyramidale Klasse	divergence ⟨geo.⟩, vergence	Vergenz f, Überfaltungsrichtung f ⟨Geo.⟩
		divergence ⟨meteo.⟩, atmospheric divergence	Divergenz f, Massendivergenz f ⟨Meteo.⟩
		divergence	s. a. unconformity
		divergence angle, angle of divergence	Divergenzwinkel m, Divergenz f; Streuungswinkel m; Spreiz[ungs]winkel m
ditrigonal polar class, ditrigonal pyramidal [crystal] class	s. hemimorphic hemihedry of the rhombohedral class	divergence difficulties	Divergenzschwierigkeiten fpl
		divergence line, divergent line	Divergenzlinie f
ditrigonal scalenohedron, hexagonal scalenohedron	ditrigonales Skalenoeder n	divergence loss	Divergenzverluste mpl
		divergence of fluid	Strömungsdivergenz f
ditrigonal scalenohedry	s. rhombohedral holohedry	divergence of the diffracted ray	Beugungsdivergenz f
diurnal aberration	tägliche Aberration f	divergence theorem	s. Green['s] theorem
diurnal arc	Tagbogen m	divergent, diverging, dispansive ⟨opt.⟩	zerstreuend, dispansiv ⟨Opt.⟩
diurnal average	s. daily mean value		
diurnal balance	Tageshaushalt m	divergent chain reaction, uncontrolled chain reaction	ungesteuerte (unbeherrschte, nicht gesteuerte) Kettenreaktion f, Kettenexplosion f
diurnal circle	Tagkreis m		
diurnal climate	Tageszeitenklima n		
diurnal inequality, daily inequality	tägliche Ungleichheit (Ungleichung) f	divergent flow	divergente Strömung f
diurnal insolation	Tagesinsolation f	divergent glass, diverging glass	Zerstreuungsglas n
diurnal libration, parallactic libration	tägliche (parallaktische) Libration f ⟨Mond⟩	divergent lens, negative lens, diverging lens, dispersion (dispersive) lens	Zerstreuungslinse f, Negativlinse f, Streu[ungs]linse f
diurnal lunar inequality, Moon's (lunar) diurnal inequality, Moon's (lunar) daily inequality, daily lunar inequality	tägliche lunare Ungleichheit f	divergent line, divergence line	Divergenzlinie f
		divergent nozzle, diverging portion (nozzle)	divergenter Teil m, Auslaufteil m
diurnal maximum of temperature, diurnal temperature maximum	Tageshöchsttemperatur f, höchste Temperatur f des Tages	divergent nuclear chain reaction, supercritical nuclear chain reaction	divergente Kernkettenreaktion f, überkritische Kernkettenreaktion
diurnal mean	s. daily mean [value]	divergent wave, propagating (diverging) wave	auslaufende Welle f, fortlaufende Welle
diurnal mean of temperature	s. mean temperature of the day	diverging, divergent, dispansive ⟨opt.⟩	zerstreuend, dispansiv ⟨Opt.⟩
diurnal mean value	s. daily mean value	diverging glass, divergent glass	Zerstreuungsglas n
diurnal minimum of temperature, diurnal temperature minimum	Tagestiefsttemperatur f, tiefste Temperatur f des Tages	diverging lens	s. divergent lens
		diverging meniscus, negative meniscus; convexo-concave lens	negativer (streuender) Meniskus m; konvexkonkave Linse f
diurnal motion of the Earth	Tagesbewegung (tägliche Bewegung) f der Erde		
diurnal parallax, geocentric parallax	tägliche (geozentrische) Parallaxe f, Höhenparallaxe f	diverging nozzle (portion)	s. divergent nozzle
		diverging tube	divergentes Rohr n
diurnal periodicity, daily periodicity	Tagesperiodizität f, zirkadianer Rhythmus m	diverging wave	s. propagating wave
		diversion	s. turn
		diversity	s. diversity reception
		diversity factor	Verschiedenheitsfaktor m
diurnal rhythm; daily rhythm	Tagesrhythmus m	diversity ratio	= maximum illuminance divided by minimum illuminance of a surface
diurnal rotation	tägliche Drehung f		
diurnal solar inequality, Sun's (solar) diurnal inequality, Sun's (solar) daily inequality, daily solar inequality	tägliche solare Ungleichheit f	diversity reception, diversity	Mehrfachempfang m, Diversityempfang m, „diversity"-Empfang m, Vielfachempfang m, Vielfachantennenempfang m; „diversity" n, Diversity n
diurnal sum	Tagessumme f		
diurnal temperature maximum	s. diurnal maximum of temperature	divertor ⟨plasma physics⟩	Divertor m
		divide ⟨US⟩, water[-]shed, watershed divide, line of separation between waters ⟨geo.⟩	Wasserscheide[linie] f, Scheide f, Scheitelung f; Kammwasserscheide f ⟨Geo.⟩
diurnal temperature minimum	s. diurnal minimum of temperature		
diurnal temperature wave	s. diurnal wave of temperature	divided arm Schering bridge	Spaltzweigbrücke f [nach Schering]
diurnal tides	ganztägige (eintägige, tägliche) Gezeiten pl, Eintagsgezeiten pl	divided circle	s. graduated circle
		divided circle error, error of division [of the circle], error in (of) circle graduation (division)	Teilkreisfehler m, Kreisteilungsfehler m, Teilungsfehler m [des Teilkreises]
diurnal turn	s. diurnal variation		
diurnal value, daily value	Tageswert m		

divided circular scale	s. graduated circle	domain <of the function>, domain of definition, set of definition, range [of validity], range of definition <math.>	Definitionsbereich m, Vorbereich m, Variabilitätsbereich m, Argumentbereich m, Urbildbereich m, Wirkungsbereich m <Math.>
divided difference [of the function]	dividierte (geteilte) Differenz f [der Funktion], Steigung f [der Funktion] Differenzenquotient m [der Funktion]		
divided scale error	s. error of division	domain	s. a. domain of integrity
divider	s. divider unit	domain	s. a. crystal domain <cryst.>
divider cube	s. dividing cube	domain	s. a. ferromagnetic domain <magn.>
divider unit; divider	Teilergerät n; Teiler m		
dividing back, series exposure slide, multiplying back	Belichtungsreihenschieber m, Multiplikator m	domain boundary, domain (Bloch) wall, ferro-magnetic (ferrimagnetic) domain wall	Bloch-Wand f, Blochsche Wand, Wand f, Übergangsbereich m <El.>, Domänengrenzfläche f, Domänengrenze f
dividing cube, divider cube	Teilungswürfel m, Strahlenteilungswürfel m, Trennwürfel m		
dividing engine, graduating engine	Teilmaschine f	domain boundary energy, wall energy	Wandenergie f, Bloch-Wand-Energie f
dividing line, separation (separating, split) line	Trennlinie f, Trennungslinie f	domain boundary energy density, domain boundary energy per unit area	spezifische Wandenergie f, Wandenergiedichte f
dividing partition	s. partition <chem.>		
dividing prism	Scheideprisma n		
dividing surface	s. interface	domain boundary friction, Bloch wall friction	Bloch-Wand-Reibung f
dividing wall	s. partition <chem.>		
diving moment, negative pitching moment	negatives Kippmoment n, kopflastiges Längsmoment n	domain energy	Anteil m der freien Energie bei der Gliederung in Elementarbereiche einheitlicher spontaner Magnetisierung, Domänenenergie f
division; decomposition; separation; dissection	Unterteilung f; Zerlegung f; Zerteilung f, Teilung f		
division; dismemberment	Gliederung f; Aufgliederung f; Zergliederung f; Zerlegung f	domain of closure	s. closure domain
		domain of convergence, region of convergence, convergence region	Konvergenzbereich m, Konvergenzgebiet n
division <of the scale>, scale division, division (graduation) line of the scale, scale graduation	Skalenteil m, Teilstrich m [der Skala], Teilungsstrich m, Strich m, Teilungsintervall n, Skt.	domain of crystal	s. crystal domain <cryst.>
		domain of definition	s. domain <math.>
		domain of dependence, dependency area, range of dependence	Abhängigkeitsgebiet n, Abhängigkeitszone f, Abhängigkeitsbereich m
division <math.>, subdivision	Unterteilung f <Math.>		
division	s. a. cell division <bio.>	domain of integrity, [integral] domain, integral ring	Integritätsbereich m, kommutativer Ring m [mit Eins] ohne Nullteiler
division algebra	Divisionsalgebra f		
division algorithm	s. Euclid['s] algorithm		
division factor [of scale]	Teilungsfaktor m [der Skala], Skalenteilungsfaktor m	domain of rationality	s. field <algebra>
		domain pattern	Domänenmuster n
		domain size, magnetic domain size	Domänengröße f
division in degrees, graduation	Gradteilung f, Gradeinteilung f	domain structure	Domänenstruktur f, Bereichsstruktur f, Bezirksstruktur f
division in two	s. bipartition		
division line (mark) of the circle	Teilkreisstrich m, Teilstrich m [des Teilkreises]	domain theory, Weiss['] theory [of ferromagnetism]	Weisssche Theorie f [des Ferromagnetismus], Domänentheorie f
division line of the scale	s. division <of the scale>		
division of layers, layer division	Schichtenteilung f	domain volume	Weiss-Volumen n, Volumen n des Weissschen Bezirks, Volumen des magnetischen Elementarbereichs, Domänenvolumen n
division of the circle (circular scale)	s. circular dividing		
division rate, cell division rate	Zellteilungsgeschwindigkeit f		
division ring	s. skew field	domain wall	s. domain boundary
divisor of zero	s. zero divisor	domain wall of the crystal	Kristallbereichswand f
Dixon theorem	Dixonscher Satz m		
D log E curve	s. characteristic curve	domatic class	s. hemihedry of the monoclinic system
D/L ratio, drag-lift ratio	Gleitzahl f		
Döbereiner['s] triad, triad	Triade f [nach Döbereiner], Döbereinersche Triade	dome <cryst.>	Doma n <pl: Domen> <Krist.>
docking	Ankoppeln n, „docking" n	dome	s. a. brachyanticlinal <geo.>
doctrine of catastrophe[s]	s. catastrophic theory	dominant mode, dominant wave, predominant mode, principal mode <of waveguide>	Grundwelle f, Grundmode f, Grundschwingung f, Grundschwingungstyp m, Grundschwingungsart f, vorherrschender Wellentyp (Schwingungstyp) m <Wellenleiter>
dodecahedral slip	Dodekaedergleitung f		
Doerner-Hoskins distribution law	Verteilungsgesetz n nach Doerner und Hoskins		
dog days	Hundstage mpl		
doldrum[s], zone of equatorial calmness	Mallung f, Doldrum n, Kalmengürtel m, Windstillengürtel m, Zone f der äquatorialen Windstillen	dominant wavelength	farbtongleiche (dominierende) Wellenlänge f
Dolezalek [two-segment] electrometer	s. two-segment electrometer	dominant wind; prevailing wind	vorherrschender Wind m; herrschender Wind
Dolph-Chebyshev array, Chebyshev array	Tschebyscheff-Netz n, Tschebyscheffsches Kurvennetz n, äquidistantes Kurvensystem n	dominating function, majorant [function]	Majorantenfunktion f, „dominating function" f
		Donder conditions / de, co-ordinate conditions of de Donder	de Dondersche Bedingungen fpl, Koordinatenbedingungen fpl von de Donder
Dolph-Chebyshev distribution	Dolph-Tschebyscheff-Verteilung f, Dolph-Tscheby-scheffsche Verteilung f		
		Donders['] law, Donders['] rule	Dondersche Regel f
domain; closed domain, range of definition (validity) <math.>	Bereich m <Algebra, Analysis>; abgeschlossenes Gebiet n <Analysis> <Math.>	Donnan distribution	Donnan-Verteilung f
		Donnan distribution coefficient	Donnanscher Verteilungskoeffizient m

Donnan 192

Donnan [membrane] equilibrium, Gibbs-Donnan equilibrium, membrane equilibrium — Donnan-Gleichgewicht n, Donnansches Gleichgewicht n

Donnan potential — Donnan-Potential n

donor, donor impurity, n-type impurity — Donator m, n-Typ-Verunreinigung f, Donor m

donor <bio.> — Spender m, Donor m <Bio.>

donor-acceptor bond — Donator-Akzeptor-Bindung f

donor bond — Donatorbindung f, Elektronendonatorbindung f

donor cell — Spenderzelle f, Donorzelle f

donor centre — Donatorzentrum n

donor impurity — s. donor

donor level — Donatorniveau n, Donatorterm m

donor spin resonance — Donatorspinresonanz f

donor state — Donatorzustand m

donut — s. doughnut <of betatron>

donutron — Donutron n, Käfigmagnetron n

dopant concentration, doping concentration — Dotierungskonzentration f

doping <with> <semi.> — Dotierung f, Dopen n <mit> <Halb.>

doping concentration — s. dopant concentration

Doppler averaged cross-section — [mittlerer] Doppler-Querschnitt m, Doppler-Wirkungsquerschnitt m

Doppler broadening, Doppler-effect broadening — Doppler-Verbreiterung f, Temperaturverbreiterung f, thermischer Doppler-Effekt m

Doppler coefficient of reactivity — Doppler-Koeffizient m der Reaktivität

Doppler displacement — s. Doppler shift

Doppler effect — Doppler-Effekt m

Doppler-effect broadening — s. Doppler broadening

Doppler effect in optics, optical Doppler effect — optischer Doppler-Effekt m, Doppler-Effekt in der Optik

Doppler effect of the first order, linear Doppler effect — Doppler-Effekt m erster Ordnung, linearer Doppler-Effekt

Doppler effect of the second order, quadratic Doppler effect — Doppler-Effekt m zweiter Ordnung, quadratischer Doppler-Effekt

Doppler frequency — Doppler-Frequenz f

Doppler frequency shift — s. Doppler shift

doppleron — Doppleron n

Doppler principle — Doppler-Prinzip n, Dopplersches Prinzip n

Doppler shift, Doppler displacement, Doppler frequency shift — Doppler-Verschiebung f, Doppler-Frequenzverschiebung f

Doppler shift attenuation method — Methode f der Verminderung der Doppler-Verschiebung

Doppler width — Doppler-Breite f

Dorgelo['s] method — Dorgelosche Methode f

dormant volcano, quiescent (dead) volcano — untätiger Vulkan m

Dorn effect, sedimentation potential — Sedimentationspotential n, Dorn-Effekt m, elektrophoretisches Potential n

Dorno radiation <280—315 um> — Dorno-Strahlung f

dorsal projection — s. AP view

dosage, dosing, allotment, proportioning — Dosierung f, Zumessung f

dosage measurement, dosimetry — Dosimetrie f, Dosismessung f

dosage rate, dose rate — Dosisleistung f

dosage system, dosing system, doser, dosimeter — Dosiervorrichtung f, Zumeßgerät n; Probeneinführungssystem n

dose build-up factor — Dosisaufbaufaktor m, Dosiszuwachsfaktor m

dose distribution — Dosisverteilung f

dose-effect curve, dose-response curve — Dosis-Wirkung-Kurve f, Dosis-Effekt-Kurve f; Strahlenschädigungskurve f

dose-effect method, tolerance analysis — Dosis-Wirkungs-Verfahren n, Toleranzanalyse f

dose equivalent, DE — Dosisäquivalent n, DE

dose-equivalent detector — dosisäquivalenter Detektor m

dose equivalent rate — Dosisäquivalentleistung f

dose field — Dosisfeld n

dose fractionation — Dosisfraktionierung f, Fraktionierung f der Dosis

dose metameter — Dosismetameter m

dose[-]meter — s. dosimeter

dose protraction — s. protraction [of dose]

doser — s. dosage system

dose rate, dosage rate — Dosisleistung f

dose rate meter — Dosisleistungsmesser m

dose reduction factor — Dosisverringerungsfaktor m, Dosisreduktionsfaktor m

dose-response curve — s. dose-effect curve

dosifilm, film dosimeter, film, photographic dosimeter — Filmdosimeter n

dosimeter, dose[-]meter, radiation dose meter — Dosimeter n, Dosismesser m

dosimeter — s. a. dosage system

dosimetric measurement, health measurement — Strahlenschutzmessung f, dosimetrische Messung f

dosimetry, dosage measurement — Dosimetrie f, Dosismessung f

dosing — s. dosage

dosing pump, metering pump — Dosierpumpe f

dosing system — s. dosage system

dot <sign of differentiation in math.> — Punkt m <Differentiationszeichen in der Math.>

dot-and-dash curve (line), dash-dot line, chain-dotted line — strich-punktierte Linie f

dot-bar pattern, dot pattern — punktförmiges Gitterraster n

dot interlace — s. dot interlacing

dot interlace system — s. dot interlacing system

dot interlacing, picture-dot interlacing, [picture-] dot interlace, dot interleave (interleaving) — Punktschachtelung f, Punktsprungabtastung f, Punktverflechtung f

dot interlacing system, dot interlace (interleave) system — Punktsprungverfahren n; Punktsprungsystem n

dot interleave — s. dot interlacing

dot interleave system — s. dot interlacing system

dot interleaving — s. dot interlacing

dot line — s. dotted line

dot pattern — s. dot-bar pattern

dot product — s. scalar product

dot recorder — s. point recorder

dot-sequential system — Punktfolgeverfahren n, Punktfolgesystem n

dotted curve, dotted line, broken line, dot line, dashed curve (line) — punktierte Linie f, punktierte Kurve f

dotting recorder — s. point recorder

double aerial cine camera [for serial shots] — s. twin serial camera

double amplitude [of the oscillation] — doppelte Schwingungsamplitude f, Schwing[ungs]breite f, Schwingungsbogen m

double-amplitude peak, peak-to-peak value, peak-to-peak [amplitude], total amplitude — Spitze-zu-Spitze-Wert m, Spitze-Spitze-Wert m, Spitze-zu-Spitze-Amplitude f, Spitze f zu Spitze

double astrograph	Doppelastrograph *m*	double-effect evaporator, two-effect evaporator	Zweistufenverdampfer *m*
double barrier [layer]	Doppelrandschicht *f*, Doppelgrenzschicht *f*, Doppelsperrschicht *f*	double exposure	Doppelbelichtung *f*
double-base transistor, two-basic transistor	Doppelbasistransistor *m* <Typ pnp oder npn>	double eyepiece	Doppelokular *n*, Demonstrationsokular *n*
		double fibre texture	Doppelfasertextur *f*
double-beam betatron, dual-beam (double-ray) betatron	Zweistrahlbetatron *n*	double field analyzer [of Lippich]	s. Lippich halfshade
double-beam cathode-ray tube	s. double-beam tube	double finder telescope, two-position viewfinder	Zweifachsucher *m*
double-beam oscillograph, double-beam oscilloscope, dual trace oscilloscope, two-beam oscilloscope	Zweistrahloszillograph *m*, Doppelstrahloszillograph *m*, Zweistrahloszilloskop *n*	double float, composite (ball and line, depth, subsurface) float	Tiefschwimmer *m*, Tiefschwimmer *m*
double-beam spectrometer	Zweistrahlspektrometer *n*	double-fluid cell	s. Daniell cell
		double-focusing mass spectrograph	doppel[t]fokussierender Massenspektrograph *m*
double-beam spectroscopy	Zweistrahlspektroskopie *f*	double-focusing mass spectrometer	doppel[t]fokussierendes Massenspektrometer *n*
double-beam tube, double-beam cathode-ray tube	Doppelstrahlröhre *f*, Zweistrahlröhre *f*	double-focus interference microscope	Doppelfokus-Interferenzmikroskop *n*
		double-focus tube	s. bifocal tube
double-beta decay (disintegration)	doppelter (dualer) Beta-Zerfall *m*	double force, elastic dipole	Doppelkraft *f*, elastischer Dipol *m*
double bond	s. double linkage	double Fourier transformation, two-dimensional Fourier transformation	zweifache Fourier-Transformation *f*
double bridge	s. Kelvin bridge		
double-cavity klystron, two-cavity (double-resonator) klystron	Zweikammerklystron *n*, Zweikreisklystron *n*	double fringe	Doppelstreifen *m*
double-centre theodolite, repeating theodolite	Repetitionstheodolit *m*, Repetiertheodolit *m*		
		double galaxy, double nebula	Doppelnebel *m*, Doppelsystem *n*
double-charged	s. doubly charged	double glide, duplex slip	Doppelgleitung *f*
double circle diagram	Doppelkreisdiagramm *n*	double-grating spectrograph	Doppelgitterspektrograph *m*
double circle reading	Doppelkreisablesung *f*	double grid	Doppelraster *m*
double cloud chamber	Doppelnebelkammer *f*		
		double-grid tube (valve)	s. tetrode
double cluster	Doppelhaufen *m*	double-gun cathode-ray tube	Zweikanonen-Elektronenstrahlröhre *f*
double coincidence	Doppelkoinzidenz *f*, Zweifachkoinzidenz *f*, Zweierkoinzidenz *f*		
		double helix <el.>	Gegenwendel *f* <El.>
double coincidence spectrometer	Doppelkoinzidenzspektrometer *n*, Zweifachkoinzidenzspektrometer *n*	double helix <el.>, coiled-coil filament	Doppelwendel *f* <El.>
		double helix <math.>	Doppelspirale *f*, Doppelhelix *f* <Math.>
double coincidence stage	Zweifachkoinzidenzstufe *f*, Zweifach-Rossi-Stufe *f*	double horizontal pendulum	Horizontaldoppelpendel *n*
double collector method <spectr.>	Doppelauffängermethode *f* <Spektr.>	double-humped, double-peaked; bimodal	zweihöckrig, zweispitzig, mit zwei Maxima; zweigipflig, bimodal
double-colour group, bicoloured group	zweifarbige Gruppe *f*, Schwarz-Weiß-Gruppe *f*		
double commutator	s. bicommutant	double-humped curve	zweihöckrige Kurve *f*
double Compton effect, double Compton scattering	doppelte Compton-Streuung *f*, doppelter Compton-Effekt *m*	double-humped response	s. double ripple
		double image, mixed image	Mischbild *n*
double conductor, double-conductor line	s. two-wire line	double image <opt.>	Doppelbild *n* <Opt.>
double-cone[-shaped] antenna	s. biconical antenna	double-image eyepiece	Doppelbildokular *n*
double control grid	Zweifachsteuergitter *n*	double-image micrometer	Doppelbildmikrometer *n*
double-control tube	Doppelsteuerröhre *f*, Doppelgitterröhre *f*	double[-] image polarizing prism, double[-] image prism	Polarisations-Doppelprisma *n*, zweiteiliges Polarisationsprisma *n*, Doppelbildprisma *n*
double-core flux-gate magnetometer	Doppelkernsonde *f*		
double curve <math.>	Doppelkurve *f*, Doppellinie *f*, Knotenlinie *f* <Math.>	double image prism due to Dove, Dove [polarizing] prism	Dove-Prisma *n*, Polarisationsprisma *n* nach Dove
double cusp	s. tacnode	double-image rangefinder	s. coincidence rangefinder
double-delta connection	Doppeldreieckschaltung *f*	double-injection diode	Doppelinjektionsdiode *f*
double-diffused transistor	Doppeldiffusionstransistor *m*, doppeltdiffundierter Transistor *m*	double integral	Doppelintegral *n*; Ebenenintegral *n*
double dipole	Doppeldipol *m*	double interference-filter spectroscope	Doppel-Interferenzfilterspektroskop *n*
double-edge variable-area recording	Doppelzackenschrift *f*		
		double internal conversion	s. e-e process

double | | | 194

double ionization chamber	s. back-to-back ionization chamber	double reflection [effect]	Doppelreflexion f
double isomorphism, isodimorphism	Isodimorphie f, Isodimorphismus m	double refraction, birefringence	Doppelbrechung f
double jog	Doppelsprung m	double-refracting	s. birefringent
double kink	Doppelknick m	double refraction due to rotation, rotation double refraction	Rotationsdoppelbrechung f
double labelling [technique]	Doppelmarkierung f, doppelte Markierung f		
double Laplace transform[ation]	doppelte (zweidimensionale) Laplace-Transformation f	double refraction in electrical fields	s. Kerr effect
double law of the mean	s. second mean value theorem of the differential calculus	double refraction in flow, flow (streaming, Maxwell) birefringence, Maxwell effect	Strömungsdoppelbrechung f
double layer	Doppelschicht f	double refraction in transverse magnetic field	s. magnetic double refraction
double-layer potential of Odqvist	Doppelschichtpotential n von Odqvist		
double lens	s. bilens	double refraction under pressure, piezobirefringence	Doppelbrechung f unter Druck[einwirkung]; Deformationsdoppelbrechung f
double lever, twin lever	Doppelhebel m		
double-line metal-dielectric type interference filter	Metalldoppelinterferenzfilter n, Doppellinienfilter n	double replica technique, two-step replica technique	Zwischenschichtverfahren n; zweistufiges Abdruckverfahren n; Mehrfachabdruckverfahren n
		double resistance box	[gleichläufiger] Doppelkurbelwiderstand m
double-line spectroscopic binary, spectrum binary	Doppelstern m mit den überlagerten Spektren beider Komponenten, Doppelstern mit zwei Spektren, Spektrumdoppelstern m	double resonance method [of Feher]	s. ENDOR
		double-resonance spectrograph	Doppelresonanzspektrograph m
		double-resonator klystron, double-cavity (two-cavity) klystron	Zweikammerklystron n, Zweikreisklystron n
double linkage, double linking, double bond, four-electron bond	Doppelbindung f, Zweifachbindung f, Vierelektronenbindung f	double rhombic antenna	Doppelrhombusantenne f
double logarithmic co-ordinates	doppeltlogarithmische Koordinaten fpl	double ring; Newton['s] double ring	Doppelring m; Newtonscher Doppelring
double microscope	Doppelmikroskop n [nach Lau]	double ripple; double-humped response; two-wave property	Doppelwelligkeit f, Zweiwelligkeit f
double mirror	Doppelspiegel m		
double mirror galvanometer	Doppelspiegelgalvanometer n	doubler stage; doubler	Verdoppler m; Verdopplerstufe f
double mirror square, double reflecting square	Doppelwinkelspiegel m	double scattering experiment	Zweifachstreuexperiment n, Doppelstreuversuch m
double modulation, pulse-time modulation	Doppelmodulation f; Zweistufenmodulation f	double serial camera	s. twin serial camera
double modulus	s. modulus of inelastic buckling	double series	Doppelreihe f, zweifach unendliche Reihe f
double molecule	Doppelmolekül n	double-shock diffuser	Zweistoßdiffusor m
double monochromator	Doppelmonochromator m, Doppelspiegelmonochromator m	double-sideband modulation	Zweiseitenbandmodulation f
		double-sided staff, staff (rod) graduated on both sides; two-sided level rod <US>	Wendelatte f
double nebula	s. double galaxy		
double observer rangefinder	s. long-baseline rangefinder		
double-peaked	s. double-humped	double slit	Doppelspalt m
double-peaked distribution, bimodal distribution	zweigipflige Verteilung f, bimodale Verteilung	double star, binary star, binary	Doppelstern m; Doppelsternsystem n
double pendulum	Doppelpendel n, sympathisches Pendel n	double stream amplifier, electron[-]wave tube	Elektronenwellenröhre f
double periodic function	doppeltperiodische Funktion f	double suspension	s. bifilar suspension
double photogrammetric chamber	Zweifachmeßkammer f, Doppelkammer f, Verbundkammer f	doublet, doublet lens, doublet lens system	Duplet n, Zweilinsensystem n, Zweilinser m
		doublet, objective doublet, doublet lens, doublet objective	Doppelobjektiv n, zweilinsiges Objektiv n, Zweilinsenobjektiv n, Zweilinser m
double point, crunode	Doppelpunkt m		
double Poisson distribution, Thomas distribution	doppelte Poisson-Verteilung f, Thomas-Verteilung f	doublet, dublet <spectr.>	Dublett n, Doppellinie f <Spektr.>
		doublet	s. a. dipole <el.>
double-prime[d]	zweigestrichen	doublet	s. a. doublet source <hydr.>
double prism	s. biprism	double-tail[ed] test, two-sided test	zweiseitiger Test m
double prism monochromator	Prismendoppelmonochromator m		
		doublet antenna	s. dipole <el.>
double prism square, crossed-prism square	Prismenkreuz n, Doppel[winkel]prisma n	double T-bridge [circuit], twin T-bridge	Doppel-T-Brücke f, Doppel-T-Meßbrücke f, T-T-Netzwerk n
double probe, dual probe, twin probe	Doppelsonde f	double tensor	s. second-order tensor
double pulse	Doppelimpuls m, Impulspaar n	double tensor field	Doppeltensorfeld n
double pulse generator	Doppelimpulsgenerator m	double-throw contact, two-way contact [with neutral position], changeover contact	Wechselkontakt m, Umschalt[e]kontakt m, Umschalterkontakt m
doubler; doubler stage	Verdoppler m; Verdopplerstufe f		
double ratio	s. cross ratio	double-throw switch, two-way switch; changeover (selector, commutating) switch, switch, commutator	Zweiweg[e]umschalter m, Zweistellungsumschalter m, Umschalter m [mit zwei Stellungen]; Umpolschalter m
double-ray betatron	s. dual-beam betatron		
double reflecting square, double mirror square	Doppelwinkelspiegel m		

drag-lift

double time Green['s] function, two-time Green['s] function — Greensche Zweizeitfunktion f, Zweizeit-Green-Funktion f
doublet interval, doublet separation — Dublettabstand m

doublet lens — s. doublet
doublet lens system — s. doublet
doublet objective — s. doublet
doublet separation — s. doublet interval
doublet source, doublet, dipole source, dipole <hydr.> — Doppelquelle f, Quellsenke f, Dipolquelle f, Dipol m <hydr.>
doublet spectrum — Dublettspektrum n
doublet spin state — Dublettspinzustand m

doublet splitting — Dublettaufspaltung f

doublet structure — Dublettstruktur f
doublet telescope, binocular [telescope], binoculars — Doppelfernrohr n, binokulares Fernrohr n, Binokel n
doublet term — Dubletterm m
double-tuned amplifier — Zweikreisverstärker m

double vacancy, divacancy, double-void, vacancy pair, pair of vacancies (voids) — Doppelleerstelle f, doppelte Leerstelle f, Leerstellenpaar n, Doppelvakanz f
double-valued, two-valued <math.> — zweiwertig, zweideutig <Math.>
double-valued function — zweideutige (zweiblättrige, zweiwertige) Funktion f
double-valuedness, two-valuedness <math.> — Zweiwertigkeit f, Zweideutigkeit f <Math.>
double valve — Doppelröhre f, Zweifachröhre f

double V[-]antenna, X[-]antenna — Spreizdipol m, X-Antenne f, Doppel-V-Antenne f

double variation method — Doppelvariationsmethode f

double-void — s. double vacancy
double-wall, double-walled — doppelwandig
double-wedge <opt.> — Doppelkeil m <Opt.>
double weighing, exchange method, Gauss method <of weighing> — Vertauschungsmethode f, Methode f der Doppelwägung, Doppelwägung f, Vertauschungsverfahren n <Wägen>

doubling time, breeding doubling time, fuel doubling time — Verdopplungszeit f, Brutverdopplungszeit f, Spaltstoffverdopplungszeit f
doubling time, neutron doubling time — Neutronenverdopplungszeit f, Verdopplungszeit f
doubly charged, double-charged — zweifach geladen
doubly coated, bilaterally coated, double-coated — doppelseitig (beidseitig, doppelt) beschichtet

doubly magic nucleus — doppeltmagischer Kern m

doubly photographed meteor — doppeltphotographiertes Meteor n, Doppelaufnahme f (stereoskopische Aufnahme f) eines Meteors

doubly refracting — s. birefringent
doubly refracting biplate, doubly refracting half-shade — doppelbrechende Halbschattenplatte f; Halbschattenapparat m mit doppelbrechender Platte

doubly stable — doppeltstabil
doughnut, vacuum doughnut, toroid, donut <of betatron> — Ringkammer f, Ringröhre f, [ringförmige] Vakuumkammer f <Betatron>

doughnut, [neutron] flux converter — Flußkonverter m, Flußumwandler m
doughy, pasty — teigartig, teigig
Dove['s] law — Dovesches Gesetz n, Drehungsgesetz n des Windes
Dove [polarizing] prism, double image prism due to Dove — Dove-Prisma n, Polarisationsprisma n nach Dove
Dove prism — s. reversing prism

Dowell interferometer — Dowell-Interferometer n
down-coming wave, space (spatial, sky, indirect, atmospheric) wave — Raumwelle f <El.>

down flow — s. backstreaming
downgoing — s. dip <geo.>
down[-]lead <of antenna>, downlead of aerial — Niederführung f [der Antenne], Antennenniederführung f, Antennenableitung f, Ableitung f der Antenne

down pipe, waste pipe — Fallrohr n, Fallröhre f <Hydr.>

downpour, violent downpour, cloud burst, heavy shower — Wolkenbruch m; Platzregen m
downslope wind — s. orographic downward wind
downstream; down the river — stromabwärts, stromab, mit der Strömung
downstream apron — s. downstream floor
downstream back; downstream face (facing) <of weir or dam> — Wehrrücken m; Überfallrücken m; Abfallmauer f
downstream floor, downstream apron — Sturzbett n [des Wehrs], Wehrsturzbett n, Absturzboden m, Sohle f der unteren Haltung, luftseitige Sohlenbefestigung f

down the river, downstream — stromabwärts, stromab, mit der Strömung
down time, shut-down time <of reactor> — Abschaltzeit f, Außerbetriebszeit f, Standzeit f
downward gust — Fallbö[e] f
downward induced transition — induzierter Übergang m nach unten
downward wind — s. katabatic wind
downwash <aero.> — Abwind m <Aero.>

downwash field — Abwindfeld n
draconitic month, draconitic period, nodical month — drakonitischer Monat m, drakonitischer Umlauf m
draft [of water], draught [of water] — Tiefgang m, Tauchung f

drag; traction; pull[ing]; drawing; tug — Ziehen n, Zug m, Fortziehen n; Schleppen n
drag, aerodynamic drag (resistance); air resistance, resistance of air; windage — Luftwiderstand m
drag, frontal resistance, resistance, aerodynamic drag (resistance), resistance to air flow — Widerstand m [in Richtung der Strömung], Strömungswiderstand m, Rücktrieb m <Aero.>
drag — s. a. carrying-away
drag acceleration — Mitführungsbeschleunigung f, Führungsbeschleunigung f, Fortführungsbeschleunigung f, Widerstandsbeschleunigung f
drag acceleration — s. a. deceleration <mech.>
drag axis, axis of drag — Widerstandsachse f

drag coefficient, dragging coefficient — Mitführungskoeffizient m, Mitbewegungskoeffizient m

drag coefficient <aero.> — Widerstandsbeiwert m, Beiwert m des Widerstandes, [aerodynamische] Widerstandszahl f, Widerstandskoeffizient m <Aero.>

drag due to lift — s. trailing-edge drag
drag flow — Widerstandsströmung f

drag force <aero.> — Widerstandskraft f, Rücktriebkraft f <Aero.>
drag force [of the flow] — Schleppkraft f [der Strömung]
drag from lift — s. trailing-edge drag
dragging — s. carrying-away
dragging coefficient, drag coefficient — Mitführungskoeffizient m, Mitbewegungskoeffizient m
dragging of light — Mitführung f des Lichts <im bewegten Medium>
dragging of the ether, ether drag — Äthermitführung f
drag head, resistance head — Widerstandshöhe f

drag-lift ratio, D/L ratio — Gleitzahl f

drag polar	Widerstandspolare *f*	drifting of the pole	Polwanderung *f*
drag-torque (drag-type) tachometer	*s.* eddy current tachometer	drifting snow	Schneefegen *n*; Schneetreiben *n*; Treibschnee *m*
drag-torque viscometer	*s.* rotational viscometer		
drag velocity	Mitführungsgeschwindigkeit *f*, Führungsgeschwindigkeit *f*	drift instability	Instabilität *f* durch Anregung von Driftwellen
		drift klystron	*s.* drift-tube klystron
drain ⟨semi.⟩	Drainelektrode *f*, Drain *m*, Abzugselektrode *f*, Abzug *m*, Abfluß *m*, d-Pol *m* ⟨Halb.⟩	drift meter, drift gauge, drift indicator	Abtriftmesser *m*
		drift mobility	Driftbeweglichkeit *f*, mittlere Driftgeschwindigkeit *f*
drainage ⟨geo.⟩, [river] basin, region of alimentation	Einzugsgebiet *n*; Stromgebiet *n*, Flußgebiet *n* ⟨Geo.⟩	drift of continents, continental drift	Kontinentaldrift *f*, Kontinentalverschiebung *f*
drainage area, drainage basin, catchment area, catchment	Einzugsgebiet *n*, Niederschlagsgebiet *n*, Abflußgebiet *n*; Zuflußgebiet *n*, Sammelgebiet *n*, Sammelbecken *n*	drift of ions	*s.* migration of ions
		drift of the continents from the poles	Polflucht *f* der Kontinente
drainage coil	*s.* discharge coil	drift soil, water-deposited soil, alluvial soil, warp	Anschwemmung *f*, Aufschüttung *f*, Schwemmland *n*, Spülboden *m*, Alluvialboden *m*, holozäner Boden *m*
drainage density ⟨geo.⟩	Flußdichte *f* ⟨Geo.⟩		
drain water	Dränagewasser *n*; Qualmwasser *n*; Kuverwasser *n*		
Draper catalog[ue]	*s.* Henry Draper catalog[ue]	drift space, drift tunnel, bunching region; drift tube	Laufraum *m*, Triftraum *m*
Draper effect	Draper-Effekt *m*		
draperies, curtain	Draperien *fpl*, Polarlichtdraperien *fpl*		
Draper law	*s.* Grotthus-Draper law		
Draper rule	Drapersche Regel *f*, Drapersches Gesetz *n*	drift speed, drift velocity ⟨of electrons⟩	Driftgeschwindigkeit *f*, Wander[ungs]geschwindigkeit *f*, mittlere Durchdringungsgeschwindigkeit *f* ⟨der Elektronen⟩
draught, draught of water, draft [of water]	Tiefgang *m*, Tauchung *f*		
draught gauge, draft gauge ⟨US⟩	Zugmesser *m*, Unterdruckmesser *m*	drift surface	Driftfläche *f*, Triftfläche *f*
		drift time ⟨of ions⟩	Driftzeit *f*, Wanderungszeit *f* ⟨Ionen⟩
draught of water, draught, draft [of water]	Tiefgang *m*, Tauchung *f*	drift transistor	Drifttransistor *m*, gedrifteter Transistor *m*
drawability	*s.* ductility		
drawable	*s.* ductile	drift tube	*s.* drift space
draw-down curve	*s.* recession curve ⟨hydr.⟩	drift tube	*s.* drift-tube klystron
drawing; traction; pull[ing]; tug; drag	Ziehen *n*, Zug *m*, Fortziehen *n*; Schleppen *n*	drift-tube klystron, floating-drift klystron, drift tube, drift klystron	Triftröhre *f*, Driftröhre *f*, Klystron *n*
drawing	*s. a.* tempering		
drawing ability	*s.* ductility		
drawing angle	Ziehwinkel *m*	drift tunnel	*s.* drift space
drawing eyepiece	Zeichenokular *n*	drift velocity	*s.* drift speed ⟨of electrons⟩
		drilitic, dry electrolytic capacitor	Trockenelektrolytkondensator *m*
drawing force	Ziehkraft *f*		
drawing-in	*s.* suction ⟨of pump⟩	drip[ping], dropping	Tropfen *n*, Tröpfeln *n*
drawing of glass	Ziehen *n* von Glas	dripping water, dropping water, trickling water	Tropfwasser *n*
drawing of samples	*s.* sampling		
drawing of tubes, tube drawing	Ziehen *n* von Rohren, Rohrziehen *n*, Rohrzug *m*		
drawing of wires, wire drawing	Ziehen *n* von Draht, Drahtziehen *n*	drip-proof, rain[-]proof	tropfwassergeschützt, tropfwasserdicht
drawing plane, plane of [the] paper	Zeichenebene *f*, Papierebene *f*		
drawing test	*s.* cupping and drawing test		
drawing texture	*s.* texture in drawn wires		
D-region	*s.* lower mantle ⟨D' and D''⟩		
Dresler photocell	*s.* filter photocell	drip-round condenser	Rieselkondensator *m*, Rieselkühler *m*
"dressed" particle	angezogenes Teilchen *n*		
Drew interferometer, shearing interferometer of Drew	Interferometer *n* nach Drew, Drew-Interferometer *n*	drive amplifier	Treiberverstärker *m*
		drive circuit, driving circuit	Treiberschaltung *f*
drier	*s.* dehydrator	drive coil	Treibspule *f*
drift	Drift *f*, Auswanderung *f*, Wanderung *f*, Weglaufen *n*	drive current, driving current	Treiberstrom *m*, Treibstrom *m*
drift ⟨ac.⟩	Schlupf *m* ⟨Ak.⟩	drive frequency	*s.* pilot frequency
drift, driftage; transit ⟨gen.; geo.⟩	Drift *f*; Abtrieb *m*, Abtrift *f*, Abdrift *f*; Rückdrift *f* ⟨allg.; Geo.⟩	drive mechanism [of the clock]	*s.* clock movement
		driven antenna	angeschlossenes Antennenelement *n*
drift angle	Driftwinkel *m*, Triftwinkel *m*; Abtriebswinkel *m*	driven dipole, active dipole, radiating dipole	Strahlungsdipol *m*, strahlender Dipol *m*, Dipolstrahler *m*
drift current ⟨el.⟩	Driftstrom *m*, Triftstrom *m* ⟨El.⟩		
drift current density	Driftstromdichte *f*	driven end	*s.* secondary drive
drift current theory [of Ekman]	Driftstromtheorie *f*, Triftstromtheorie *f* ⟨von Ekman⟩	driven multivibrator	*s.* synchronized multivibrator
		driven side	*s.* secondary drive
drift energy	Driftenergie *f*	drive pulse	*s.* driving pulse
drift field factor	Driftfeldfaktor *m*	driver	*s.* driver stage
		drive range, range of modulation (uniform control), control range	Aussteuer[ungs]bereich *m*, Aussteuerungsumfang *m*
drift gauge	*s.* drift meter		
drift ice line, limit of drift ice	Treibeisgrenze *f*		
drift indicator	*s.* drift meter	driver stage, driver, driving stage, drive unit	Treiberstufe *f*, Treiber *m*
drifting	Treiben *n*		
drifting	*s. a.* driving ⟨geo.⟩		

driver valve	Treiberröhre f	drop model; liquid-drop model, Volmer-Weber mechanism ‹cryst.›	Tröpfchenmodell n; Volmer-Weber-Mechanismus m ‹Krist.›
drive unit	s. driver stage		
drive voltage	s. control voltage	drop of concentration, concentration gradient, gradient of concentration	Konzentrationsgradient m, Konzentrationsgefälle n
driving ‹el.›	Treiben n ‹El.›		
driving, drifting, pushing forward, pushing ahead ‹geo.›	Vortrieb m ‹Geo.›	drop of potential	s. potential drop
		drop out, release, releasing ‹of relay›	Abfallen n, Abfall m
driving circuit, drive circuit	Treiberschaltung f	drop-out value ‹of relay›	Abfallwert m ‹Relais›
driving current, drive current	Treiberstrom n, Treibstrom m		
driving field strength	treibende elektrische Feldstärke f	dropper	s. drop counter
		dropper	s. dropping bottle
driving force, motive power, motive (living) force	Antriebskraft f, treibende Kraft f, Triebkraft f, bewegende Kraft f, Bewegungskraft f	dropping, drip, dripping	Tropfen n, Tröpfeln n
		dropping ball method	s. falling sphere method
		dropping bottle, dropping flask (glass, vessel, vial, tube), dropper	Tropfflasche f, Tropfglas n, Tropfgefäß n, Tropfrohr n
driving impedance ‹ac.›, driving-point impedance	Eingangs-Scheinwiderstand m, Eingangsscheinwiderstand m, Eingangsimpedanz f ‹Ak.›		
		dropping bottle	s. a. drop counter
		dropping cock, drop cock, drop tap	Tropfhahn m, Tropfenhahn m
driving point, point of connection; junction	Anschlußpunkt m	dropping electrode	Tropfelektrode f
driving point; feeding point, feed point	Speisepunkt m; Einspeisepunkt m; Einströmungspunkt m	dropping flask	s. dropping bottle
		dropping funnel	Tropftrichter m
		dropping glass	s. dropping bottle
driving-point admittance	s. input admittance	dropping liquid, liquid, liquor	tropfbare Flüssigkeit f, Flüssigkeit
driving-point impedance, driving impedance ‹ac.›	Eingangs-Scheinwiderstand m, Eingangsscheinwiderstand m, Eingangsimpedanz f ‹Ak.›	dropping[-]mercury electrode	Quecksilber-Tropfelektrode f, Quecksilbertropfelektrode f
		dropping point, drop point, drop[ping] temperature	Tropfpunkt m, Tropftemperatur f
driving-point impedance	s. a. input impedance ‹el.›		
driving potential	Treibpotential n	dropping resistor	s. series resistor
		dropping temperature, drop[ping] point, drop temperature	Tropfpunkt m, Tropftemperatur f
driving pulse	Treiberimpuls m		
driving pulse, drive (command, control) pulse; enabling pulse ‹of gate›	Steuerimpuls m	dropping test	s. spot test ‹chem.›
		dropping tube (vessel, vial)	s. dropping bottle
driving stage	s. driver stage	dropping water, dripping water, trickling water	Tropfwasser n
driving torque	Antriebsdrehmoment n		
driving torque, deflecting torque	Meßmoment n	drop point, dropping point, drop[ping] temperature	Tropfpunkt m, Tropftemperatur f
driving voltage	s. control voltage	drop-ratio method	Tropfenverhältnismethode f
drizzle, drizzling; fine rain, mizzle, mizzling	Sprühregen m, Staubregen m, Niesel[regen] m, Nieseln n; feiner Regen m		
		drops / by (in)	s. drop by drop
		drop-shaped schliere, drop	Tropfenschliere f
		drop size	Tropfengröße f
drizzling fog, mist, Scotch mist, damp haze	nieselnder (nässender) Nebel m, Nebelreißen n, Reißen n des Nebels, feuchter Dunst m, Nieseltröpfchen npl	drop tap, drop[ping] cock	Tropfhahn m, Tropfenhahn m
		drop temperature, drop[ping] point, dropping temperature	Tropfpunkt m, Tropftemperatur f
drone, booming, roaring, rumbling ‹ac.›	Dröhnen n ‹Ak.›	drop test	s. spot test ‹chem.›
droop[ing]	s. decay	drop weight method, drop method	Tropfengewichtsmethode f, Tröpfchenmethode f
drop, drop-shaped schliere	Tropfenschliere f		
drop	s. a. decay	dropwise	s. drop by drop
drop by drop, by drops, in drops, dropwise	tropfenweise	dropwise condensation, rain-like condensation	Tröpfchenkondensation f, Tropfenkondensation f, Kondensation f in Tropfenform
drop cock, dropping cock, drop tap	Tropfhahn m, Tropfenhahn m		
drop collector	Tropfkollektor m	drosometer, dew measurer	Drosometer n, Taumesser m
drop counter, dropper, dropping bottle; stalagmometer	Tropfenzähler m; Stalagmometer n	drosometer plate	Tauplatte f
		drowned spring, submerged spring, subaqueous spring	untermeerische (unterseeische) Quelle f, Untermeeresquelle f, Unterseequelle f
drop fall, fall of drops	Tropfenfall m		
drop in temperature	s. temperature drop		
droplet formation, formation of drop[let]s	Tropfenbildung f, Tröpfchenbildung f	drowned weir	s. submerged weir
		drowning	Übertönen n
droplet model	verfeinertes Tröpfchenmodell n	Drude law, Drude['s] relation	Drudesches Gesetz n, Drudesche Gleichung f
droplet spectrum	Tröpfchenspektrum n, Tropfenspektrum n	Drude['s] theory of optically active crystals	Drudesche Theorie f der optisch aktiven Kristalle
drop method, drop weight method	Tropfengewichtsmethode f, Tröpfchenmethode f		
		drum camera	Trommelkamera f
		drum cavity, tympanic cavity	Paukenhöhle f, cavum n tympani, Trommelhöhle f
drop method ‹el.›	Tropfenverfahren n ‹El.›		
drop method	s. a. spot test ‹chem.›	drum filter	Trommel[dreh]filter n

drumhead	s. tympanum	dry flash-over voltage	Trockendurchbruchspannung f, Trockendurchschlagspannung f
drum lens	Gürtellinse f		
drum memory	s. magnetic drum store	dry foam	Trockenschaum m
drum reading	Trommelablesung f	dry fog	trockener Nebel m; Höhenrauch m, Haarrauch m, Sonnenrauch m, Moorrauch m
drum scanner, mirror drum scanner, belt scanner	Spiegelradabtaster m, Trommelabtaster m		
		dry friction, solid friction	trockene Reibung f, Festkörperreibung f
		dry ice, carbon-dioxide ice, solid carbon dioxide	Trockeneis n, Kohlensäureschnee m, festes Kohlendioxid n
drum sextant	Trommelsextant m		
drumskin action	Vibration f der Wand als Ganzes		
drum storage (store)	s. magnetic drum store	drying <removal of water by heat>; dehydration, desiccation, exsiccation <removal of water from substances>; dehumidification, dehydration <removal of water from gas>	Trocknung f; Entfeuchtung f
drum-type counter mechanism	Rollenzählwerk n, Zahlenrollenwerk n, Zählwerkrolle f, Zahlenrolle f, Ziffernrolle f, Zahlenwalze f		
drum-type flowmeter, drum-type [fluid] meter	Trommelzähler m	drying agent	s. dehydrator
		drying of air, dehumidification, dehumidifying	Luftentfeuchtung f, Lufttrocknung f
Drüner camera	Drünersche Kamera f, Stereoskopkamera f		
druse, crystal druse	Druse f, Kristalldruse f; Kristallgruppe f; Kristallrasen m	drying out, desiccation	Austrocknung f
		drying properties	Trocknungsfähigkeit f, Trockenfähigkeit f
		dry lens[es]	s. dry objective
		dry matter	Trockensubstanz f, Trockenmasse f
druse cavity, cavity <geo.>	Drusenraum m <Geo.>	dry measure	s. capacity measure
		dry mounting	Trockenaufziehverfahren n
Druyvesteyn distribution	Druyvesteyn-Verteilung f	dry objective, dry lens[es]	Trockenobjektiv n, Trockensystem n
dry adiabat[ic curve], dry adiabatic line	Trockenadiabate f, Kondensationsadiabate f	dry photography	Trockenphotographie f
dry adiabatic gradient	s. dry adiabatic lapse rate	dry rectifier, semiconductor (bimetallic) rectifier, plate rectifier	Halbleitergleichrichter m, Trockengleichrichter m, Plattengleichrichter m
dry adiabatic instability	Trockenlabilität f, trockenadiabatische Labilität f		
dry adiabatic lapse rate, dry adiabatic temperature gradient, dry adiabatic gradient	trockenadiabatischer Temperaturgradient m	dry saturated steam; dry saturated vapour, dry steam (vapour)	trocken gesättigter Dampf m
		drysdale compensator	s. alternating-current potentiometer
dry adiabatic line, dry adiabat, dry adiabatic curve	Trockenadiabate f, Kondensationsadiabate f	dry shrinkage, air shrinkage	Trockenschwindung f
dry adiabatic stability	Trockenstabilität f, trockenadiabatische Stabilität f	dry snow avalanche, dust avalanche, powdery avalanche; slab avalanche	Trockenschneelawine f, trockene Lawine f, Trockenlawine f; Schneebrett n; Staublawine f
dry adiabatic temperature gradient	s. dry adiabatic lapse rate		
dry analysis (assay, assaying)	Trockenanalyse f	dry stable stratification	trockenstabile Schichtung f
dry beach	Trockenstrand m	dry stage [of convection]	Trockenstadium n [der Konvektion]
dry box, glove box	Handschuhbox f, Glovebox f	dry steam	Trockendampf m, trockener Dampf m
dry[-]bulb reading (temperature), reading on the dry-bulb thermometer	Temperatur f des trockenen Thermometers	dry steam	s. a. dry saturated steam
		dry suspension	Trockensuspension f
		dry tube, air-cooled tube, metall-cooled tube	luftgekühlte Röhre f, Luftkühlröhre f, Trockenröhre f, Metallkühlröhre f
dry[-]bulb thermometer	Trockenthermometer n, trockenes Thermometer n		
dry cell	Trockenelement n	dry unstable stratification	trockenlabile Schichtung f
dry collodion plate, collodion dry plate	trockene Kollodiumplatte f, Kollodiumtrockenplatte f	dry vapour	s. dry saturated steam
		dry weight	Trockengewicht n
dry colour	s. pigment		
dry condenser [lens]	Trockenkondensor m, Trockendunkelfeldkondensor m	dry writer	Trockenschreiber m
		dual-beam betatron, double-beam betatron, double-ray betatron	Zweistrahlbetatron n
dry content	Trockengehalt m		
dry deposit, radioactive dry deposit, dry fallout	trockener Fallout m, Fallout außerhalb der Niederschläge	dual circuit, dual network	duale Schaltung f, Dualschaltung f, duales Netzwerk n
		dual decay	dualer Zerfall f
dry development	s. xerographic development	dual integral equations	duale Integralgleichungen fpl
dry-disk rectifier	Trockenscheibengleichrichter m		
		dual ion	s. amphoteric ion
dry electrolytic capacitor, drilitic	Trockenelektrolytkondensator m	duality principle, principle of duality	Dualitätsprinzip n
dry emulsion	Trockenemulsion f	dual lattice, reciprocal lattice	reziprokes Gitter n, Reziprokgitter n, Dualgitter n, duales Gitter
dryer	s. dehydrator		
dry fallout	s. dry deposit		
dry film lubrication	Trocken[film]schmierung f	dual network	s. dual circuit
dry filter	Trockenfilter n	dual of the tensor, dual tensor	dualer Tensor m

dual potentiometer; tandem (gauged) potentiometer — Doppelpotentiometer n; Tandempotentiometer n

dual probe, double probe, twin probe — Doppelsonde f

dual-rate moon position camera, Markowitz['] moon camera — Mondkamera f von Markowitz

dual scaler, dual scaling circuit, scale-of-2^n circuit — Dualuntersetzerschaltung f; Dualuntersetzer m

dual sentence, reciprocal sentence — dualisierte Aussage f

dual space, adjoint space, conjugate [space] — adjungierter (konjugierter, polarer, dualer) Raum m, Dual m

dual spherical harmonics method, Yvon['s] method — Methode f von Yvon, Yvonsche Methode

dual-temperature process — Heiß-Kalt-Verfahren n, Zweitemperaturverfahren n, Zweitemperaturprozeß m

dual tensor, dual of the tensor — dualer Tensor m

dual trace oscilloscope — s. double-beam oscillograph

Duane and Hunt law, Duane-Hunt law — Duane-Huntsches Verschiebungsgesetz (Gesetz) n

Duane curve — Duanesche Kurve f

Duane-Hunt law — s. Duane and Hunt law

duant ⟨gen., of cyclotron⟩; dee — Duant m, Dee n, D n, D-Elektrode f; Binant m ⟨allg.; Zyklotron⟩

duant electrometer — s. two-segment electrometer

dubbing; rerecording, mixing ⟨of sound⟩ — Mischen n, Mischung f, Tonmischung f ⟨Ton⟩

Dubuat['s] paradox — Dubuatsches Paradoxon n

duct, wave duct, sound duct ⟨ac.⟩ — akustischer Wellenleiter m, Wellenleiter ⟨Ak.⟩

duct — s. a. hollow waveguide

duct — s. a. atmospheric duct

ductile, drawable, stretchable, tensile — duktil, ziehbar, ziehfähig, streckbar, bildsam, dehnbar, formbar, umformbar, verformbar ⟨unter Zugbeanspruchung⟩

ductile fracture; gliding fracture; sliding fracture (rupture); shear fracture (failure) — Verformungsbruch m; Gleit[ungs]bruch m; Schiebungsbruch m, Schiebebruch m, Verschiebungsbruch m; Zähbruch m, zäher Bruch m; Scherbruch m

ductility; drawing ability; drawability, stretchability; stringiness, tensility — Duktilität f, Ziehbarkeit f, Ziehfähigkeit f, Streckbarkeit f, Bildsamkeit f, Dehnbarkeit f, Formbarkeit f, Umformbarkeit f, Verformbarkeit f, Verformungsvermögen n ⟨durch Zug⟩

ductilometer — Duktilometer n

Duddell oscillograph — Duddell-Oszillograph m

Duffing equation — Duffingsche Differentialgleichung f

Duffin-Kemmer equation, Kemmer [wave] equation — Kemmersche Wellengleichung f, [Duffin-]Kemmersche Gleichung f

Dufour effect, diffusion thermoeffect — Diffusionsthermoeffekt m, Dufour-Effekt m

Duhamel['s] integral — Duhamelsches Integral n, Duhamel-Integral n

Duhem-Margules equation (relation) — [Gibbs-]Duhem-Margulessche Gleichung f, Gleichung von [Nernst-]Duhem-Margules, Duhemsche Gleichung

Duhem['s] theorem ⟨therm.⟩ — Duhemscher Satz m ⟨Therm.⟩

dull — s. a. mat

dull emitter — s. cold cathode

dull-emitting cathode — Sparkatode f

dull glass, opal glass, milk glass — Trübglas n, Opalglas n, Opakglas n, Milchglas n

dull-red heat — s. dark-red heat

Dulong and Petit['s] law [of atomic heats], Dulong-Petit law (rule) — Dulong-Petitsches Gesetz n, Dulong-Petitsche Regel f, Regel von Dulong und Petit

dumbbell model — Hantelmodell n

dumbbell molecule — Hantelmolekül n

dumbbell nebula — Hantelnebel m, Dumbbell-nebel m

dumbbell-shaped — hantelförmig

dummy, summation dummy; dummy (umbral, saturated) index, umbral suffix ⟨of tensor⟩ — Summationsindex m

dummy combination, pseudocombination — Scheinkombination f, Scheinbehandlung f

dummy dee — Gegendee n, Gegenduant m

dummy index — s. dummy

dummy load — Scheinbelastung f, fiktive Belastung f

dummy scale — Zapfenlinie f

dummy suffix notation (summation convention) — s. summation convention

dump — Schnellablaß m

dumping ground, burial ground, graveyard — [radioaktiver] Friedhof m, Vergrabungsstelle f, Abfallager n

dumpy level, level with fixed telescope — Nivellier[instrument] n mit festem Fernrohr [und umsetzbarer Libelle]

dune remnants — Kupsten pl

D unit [of Mallet] — D-Einheit f [nach Mallet]

duolateral coil, honeycomb coil, honeycomb-tube coil — Honigwabenspule f, Kreuzwickelspule f, Waben[wicklungs]spule f

duoplasmatron, duoplasmatron ion source, ion duoplasmatron source, Von Ardenne [ion] source — Duoplasmatron-Ionenquelle f [nach von Ardenne], Duoplasmatronquelle f

dupe negative, picture-dupe negative, duplicated negative — Duplikatnegativ n, Dupnegativ n

dupe positive, picture-dupe positive, duplicated positive — Duplikatpositiv n, Duppositiv n

Dupin indicatrix — Dupinsche Indikatrix f

duplet — s. doublet ⟨spectr.⟩

duplexer, two-way antenna — Zweiwegantenne f, Simultanantenne f

duplex slip, double glide — Doppelgleitung f

duplex star connection — Doppelsternschaltung f

duplicate, duplicate sample (specimen), control sample (specimen) — Kontrollprobe f, Vergleichsprobe f

duplicated negative — s. dupe negative

duplicated positive — s. dupe positive

duplicate sample (specimen) — s. duplicate

duplication formula — Verdopplungsformel f

dupligrammetry — Dupligrammetrie f, Dupligrammethode f

Dupré['s] equation — Duprésche Gleichung f

durability — s. permanence ⟨gen.⟩

duration during which the wind acts [on water surface], duration of wind [action] — Wirk[ungs]dauer f des Windes, Windwirk[ungs]dauer f, Winddauer f

duration of afterglow, persistence, time (duration) of persistence, afterglow picture — Nachleuchtdauer f, Nachleuchtzeit f

duration of ascent, time of climb — Steigzeit f, Steigdauer f

duration of bright sunshine, duration of sunshine — Sonnenscheindauer f, Sonnenscheinstunden fpl

duration of cast — s. duration of throw

duration of cycle, cycle time, cycling time	Zykluslänge *f*, Zyklusdauer *f*, Zyklus *m*; Wechseldauer *f*, Dauer *f* eines Wechsels	dust-laden	staubreich
duration of experiment; duration of test	Versuchsdauer *f*, Versuchszeit *f*	dust nebula	Staubnebel *m*
		dust nucleus	Staubkern *m*
		dust particle, speck of dust	Staubpartikel *f*, Staubteilchen *n*, Staubkorn *n*, Stäubchen *n*
duration of exposure, exposure time, exposure period ⟨opt.⟩	Expositionszeit *f*, Belichtungszeit *f*	dust precipitation	s. dedusting
		dust[-]proof, dust-tight	staubdicht, staubsicher; staubgeschützt
		dust separation	s. dedusting
		dust separator (settler)	s. dust collector
duration of full aperture	Offenzeit *f*	dust storm, sand storm	Sandsturm *m*; Samum *m*; Chamsin *m*, Khamsin *m*; Gibli *m*, Ghibli *m*; Sommerburan *m*, Karaburan *m*, schwarzer Buran *m*
duration of measurement	Meßzeit *f*, Meßdauer *f*		
		dust-tight, dust[-]proof	staubdicht, staubsicher; staubgeschützt
duration of overlap, overlap interval	Überlappungsdauer *f*, Überlappungsintervall *n*	dust train	Staubschweif *m*
		dust trap	s. dust collector
		dust turbidity, dust haze	Staubtrübung *f*
duration of peak, peak of the flash	Scheitelzeit *f*		
duration of persistence	s. persistence		
duration of sunshine, duration of bright sunshine	Sonnenscheindauer *f*, Sonnenscheinstunden *fpl*	Duto lens, diffusing lens, diffusing disk	Dutolinse *f*, Dutoscheibe *f*, Weichzeichnerscheibe *f*, Weichzeichner *m*, Streuscheibe *f*
duration of test	s. duration of experiment		
duration of throw, duration of cast	Wurfdauer *f*	duty cycle	s. pulse width-repetition ratio
duration of total eclipse	Totalitätsdauer *f*	D-variometer, declination variometer	Deklinationsvariometer *n*, D-Variometer *n*
duration of wind [action]	s. duration during which the wind acts	Dvořak['s] shadow method	Dvoraksches Schattenverfahren *n*
durchgriff	s. penetrance	dwarf, dwarf star, main-sequence star	Zwergstern *m*, Zwerg *m*, Hauptreihenstern *m*
durchmusterung ⟨astr.⟩	Durchmusterung *f* ⟨Astr.⟩		
durée utile ⟨bio.⟩	Nutzzeit *f*, minimale Reizzeit *f* ⟨Bio.⟩	dwarf galaxy, dwarf nebula	Zwerggalaxis *f*, Zwergnebel *m*, Gnomgalaxis *f*
duromer	s. thermosetting plastic		
durometer	s. hardness tester	dwarf red star, red dwarf	roter Zwerg *m*
Dushman['s] formula	Dushman-Formel *f*, Dushmansche Formel *f*		
		dwarf star, dwarf, main-sequence star	Zwergstern *m*, Zwerg *m*, Hauptreihenstern *m*
dusk, owl-light, twilight, gloaming	Abenddämmerung *f*		
		DWBA method	s. distorted wave Born approximation
dusky ring, crape ring, ring C, crepe ring, gauze ring	Kreppring *m*, Florring *m*, C-Ring *m*	dwelling lake	Reliktsee *m*
		dyadic	s. affinor
dust	s. fines ⟨geo.⟩	dyadic Green['s] function, Green['s] tensor, Green['s] matrix	Greenscher Tensor *m*, tensorielle Greensche Funktion *f*, Greensche Matrix *f*
dust avalanche	s. dry snow avalanche		
dustball	Staubball *m*		
		dyadic polynomial	s. affinor
dust catcher, dust collector, dust trap (settler, separator), duster	Staubsammler *m*, Staubfänger *m*, Staubfang *m*	dyakisdodecahedral class	s. paramorphic hemihedry of the regular system
		dyakisdodecahedron	s. diplohedron
		dye	s. colorant
dust concentration, dust density	Staubdichte *f*	dye experiment, Reynolds' experiment	Farbfadenversuch *m*, Reynoldsscher Farbfadenversuch
dust content, dustiness	Staubgehalt *m*		
		dyeing	s. tinging
dust core, moulded core, iron dust core, powdered core	Massekern *m*, Pulverkern *m*	dye line	Farbfaden *m*
		dye reducer	Farbabschwächer *m*
		dye-stuff; pigment	Pigment *n*, Körperfarbe *f*; Pigmentfarbstoff *m*
dust counter	s. konimeter		
dust counting, konimetry	Staubgehaltsmessung *f*, Staubmessung *f*, Konimetrie *f*	dye stuff	s. colorant
		dying-away, disappearance, vanishing	Verschwinden *n*, Auflösung *f*
		dying down	s. dying out ⟨of an oscillation⟩
		dying-down time	Ausschwingdauer *f*, Ausschwingzeit *f*
dust density, dust concentration	Staubdichte *f*		
dust devil	Staubsturm *m*, Staubwirbel[sturm] *m*; Staubtrombe *f*, Staubhose *f*, Staubteufel *m*	dying out, damping, decay, decrease, dying down ⟨of an oscillation⟩; free vibration	Abklingen *n* ⟨Schwingung⟩; Ausschwingen *n*; freie Schwingung *f*
		dying out, cooling, decay ⟨of activity⟩	Abklingen *n*, Abkühlung *f* ⟨Aktivität⟩
dust devil, sand devil, sand spout	Sandhose *f*; Haboob *m*, Habub *m*		
duster	s. dust collector	dying out, decomposition, collapse ⟨of field⟩	Abbau *m*, Zusammenbruch *m* ⟨Feld⟩
dust film	Staubhaut *f*		
dust filter, aerial dust filter	Staubfilter *n*	dying out	s. a. decay
		dying-out time	s. decay time
		dyke	s. eruptive vein
		dynameter, dynamometer ⟨opt.⟩	Dynameter *n* [nach Ramsden] ⟨Opt.⟩
dust-flow method	Schwebeteilchenmethode *f*		
		dynamic accuracy, dynamic precision (fidelity)	dynamische Genauigkeit *f*
dust haze	s. dust turbidity		
dustiness, dust content	Staubgehalt *m*	dynamic action of force	dynamische Wirkung *f* der Kraft, dynamische Kraftwirkung *f*

dynamical allotropy dynamische Allotropie f
dynamical analogy s. dynamical similarity
dynamical balancing dynamische Auswuchtung f
dynamical depth dynamische Tiefe f
dynamical ellipticity dynamische Elliptizität f
dynamical equation of state dynamische Zustandsgleichung f
dynamical method s. transpiration method
dynamical metre dynamisches Meter n, Berk n, berk
dynamical parallax [of binary star], dynamic parallax [of binary star] dynamische (hypothetische) Parallaxe f, Doppelsternparallaxe f
dynamical similarity, (similitude), dynamic[al] analogy dynamische Ähnlichkeit f
dynamical surface tension s. non-equilibrium surface tension
dynamical theory of tide dynamische Gezeitentheorie f
dynamical time scale dynamische Zeitskala f
dynamical viscosity s. coefficient of viscosity <quantity>
dynamic amplifier s. expander <el.>
dynamic analogy s. dynamical similarity
dynamic boundary condition dynamische (restliche) Randbedingung f
dynamic characteristic, characteristic, operating curve (line), working curve dynamische Kennlinie (Charakteristik) f, Arbeitskennlinie f, Arbeitskurve f
dynamic climatology dynamische Klimatologie f, Witterungsklimatologie f
dynamic coercitivity, dynamic coercive force dynamische Koerzitivfeldstärke f, dynamische Koerzitivkraft f
dynamic compliance, storage compliance Speicherkomplianz f, dynamische Nachgiebigkeit (Komplianz) f
dynamic elasticity, elastodynamics Elastodynamik f
dynamic elastic modulus, dynamic modulus dynamischer Modul (Elastizitätsmodul) m
dynamic electron multiplier, dynamic multiplier Pendelvervielfacher m, dynamischer Vervielfacher m
dynamic equilibrium s. transient equilibrium
dynamic error, potential correction vorübergehende Regelabweichung f
dynamic expander s. expander <el.>
dynamic fidelity, dynamic accuracy (precision) dynamische Genauigkeit f
dynamic freezing-in, relaxation freezing-in dynamisches Einfrieren n, Relaxationseinfrieren n
dynamic friction Bewegungsreibung f, dynamische Reibung f
dynamic head s. velocity head
dynamic height s. geopotential
dynamic hysteresis, flux-current loop, elastic hysteresis elastische Hysterese f, dynamische Hystereseschleife f, dynamische Hysterese
dynamic hysteresis s. a. alternating hysteresis
dynamic hysteresis curve, dynamic hysteresis loop dynamische Hystereseschleife (Hysteresiskennlinie, magnetische Zustandskurve, Kennlinie) f
dynamic induction dynamische Induktion f
dynamic isomerism s. tautomerism
dynamicizer, parallel to-series converter Parallel-Serie-Konverter m, Parallel-Serie-Umsetzer m
dynamic lift, aerodynamic lift, lifting force, thrust; normal force, cross[wind] force <aero., hydr.> dynamischer Auftrieb m; aerodynamischer Auftrieb; Quertrieb m, Querkraft f <Aero., Hydr.>
dynamic loading, impulse loading dynamische Belastung f
dynamic mean Sun, mean Sun [dynamische] mittlere Sonne f
dynamic metamorphism s. dynamometamorphism
dynamic method s. transpiration method <of vapour-pressure measurement>
dynamic microphone s. moving coil microphone
dynamic modulus, dynamic elastic modulus dynamischer Modul (Elastizitätsmodul) m

dynamic multiplier, dynamic electron multiplier Pendelvervielfacher m, dynamischer Vervielfacher m
dynamic nuclear polarization, dynamic polarization of nuclear spins dynamische Kernpolarisation f, dynamische Kernspinpolarisation f
dynamic parallax [of binary star] s. dynamical parallax [of binary star]
dynamic permeability Wechselpermeabilität f, Wechselfeldpermeabilität f, Wechselstrompermeabilität f, dynamische Permeabilität f
dynamic plate resistance s. dynamic resistance <of thermionic valve>
dynamic polarization of nuclear spins, dynamic nuclear polarization dynamische Kernpolarisation f, dynamische Kernspinpolarisation f
dynamic precision s. dynamic accuracy
dynamic pressure, hydrodynamic (stagnation, kinetic) pressure, pressure head Staudruck m, Geschwindigkeitsdruck m, dynamischer Druck m, Fließdruck m
dynamic range, volume range Dynamik f, Schalldruckumfang m, Aussteuerungsbereich m
dynamic resistance dynamischer Widerstand m
dynamic resistance, dynamic plate resistance <of thermionic valve> dynamischer Innenwiderstand m, Arbeitswiderstand m <Elektronenröhre>
dynamics Dynamik f, Lehre f von den Kräften
dynamic slope s. dynamic transconductance
dynamics of flight, flight dynamics Flugdynamik f
dynamic specific resistance <ac.> Strömungswiderstand m <Ak.>
dynamic specific speed dynamische Schnellläufigkeitszahl f
dynamic strain dynamische Verformung f
dynamic storage (store) s. cyclic storage
dynamic strength, resistance to vibrations, resistance to oscillations Schwingungsfestigkeit f
dynamic stress dynamische Spannung f
dynamic superplasticity s. phase transformation plasticity
dynamic surface tension s. non-equilibrium surface tension
dynamic susceptibility, Bloch susceptibility Blochsche (dynamische) Suszeptibilität f
dynamic system of units dynamisches Einheitensystem n
dynamic temperature coefficient dynamischer Temperaturkoeffizient m
dynamic temperature difference dynamischer Temperaturunterschied m
dynamic test dynamische Prüfung f, dynamisches Prüfverfahren n; dynamische Versuchsführung f
dynamic transconductance, dynamic (mutual) slope dynamische Steilheit f, Arbeitssteilheit f, Betriebssteilheit f
dynamic viscosity s. coefficient of viscosity
dynamo s. electric generator <el.>
dynamo effect Dynamoeffekt m
dynamo-electrical principle dynamoelektrisches Prinzip n, Dynamoprinzip n
dynamo-electric induction dynamoelektrische Induktion f
dynamo-electric machine s. electric generator
dynamograph, recording dynamometer Dynamograph m, Registrierdynamometer n
dynamometamorphism, dynamic metamorphism Dynamometamorphose f, Dislokationsmetamorphose f, Dynamometamorphismus m, Druckumwandlung f
dynamometer Dynamometer n, Kraftmesser m
dynamometer s. a. dynameter <opt.>
dynamo theory Dynamotheorie f

dynatron effect	s. secondary electron emission	earth['s] attraction, attraction of the Earth, force of gravity, gravity, gravitation force, gravitational force, gravitation	Erdanziehung f, Anziehungskraft f der Erde, Erdschwere f, Schwerkraft f, Schwere f
dynatron oscillator	Dynatronoszillator m, Dynatron n, Dynatronschaltung f		
dyne	Dyn n, dyn		
dyne per square centimetre, barye, microbar, ba, μbar, μb	Mikrobar n, μbar, μb <besonders Ak.>	earth capacitance; ground capacitance	Erdkapazität f
dynistor	Dynistor m	Earth-circling satellite	s. artificial Earth's satellite
Dynkin diagram	s. root diagram <math.>	earth connection	s. earth wire
dynode, secondary emitting dynode; secondary emission cathode; electron mirror	Dynode f, Prallelektrode f, Pralldynode f, Sekundäremissionskatode f, Sekundärelektronenkatode f, SE-Katode f, Sekundärelektronendynode f, Zwischenelektrode f, Sekundärelektronenanode f; Elektronenspiegel m	earth connection	s. mass connection
		Earth['s] core	s. core of the Earth
		earth contact	s. earth fault
		Earth['s] crust, crust of the Earth	Erdkruste f
		earth current, ground current	Erdstrom m; vagabundierender Strom m
dyon	Dyon n	earthdin, earthquake, earth tremors, temblor <US>	Erdbeben n, Beben n
dyotron	Dyotron n <Dreielektrodenmikrowellenröhre>		
		Earth['s] electric field, geoelectric field	elektrisches Erdfeld n, elektrisches Feld n der Erde, geoelektrisches Feld
Dyson['s] chronological operator, Dyson operator, time ordering operator, P symbol of time ordering, P operator	Dyson-Operator m, Dyson[-Wick]scher Operator (Zeitordnungsoperator) m, chronologischer (chronologisierender) Operator, P-Operator m, P-Symbol n [der chronologischen Ordnung]		
		earth ellipsoid, [mean] terrestrial ellipsoid, earth (terrestrial) spheroid	Erdellipsoid n, mittleres Erdellipsoid, Erdsphäroid n
		earth fault, earth leakage, accidental earth, earth contact; mass contact; body contact	Erdschluß m, Erdableitung f; Masseschluß m; Körperschluß m
Dyson['s] chronological product, P-product	P-Produkt n. Dysonsches Produkt n	Earth['s] flattening	s. flattening of the Earth
		Earth gyroscope	s. gravity controlled gyroscope
		Earth induction	s. geoinduction
Dyson effect	Dyson-Effekt m	earth-inductor, earth inductor	Erdinduktor m
Dyson operator	s. Dyson['s] chronological operator		
		earthing	s. mass connection
dysphotic zone	dysphotische (schwach beleuchtete) Zone f	earthing circuit (connection)	s. earth wire
dysprotid, proton donor, proton acid, prot[on]ic acid, acid [according to Brønsted]	Protonendonator m, Dysprotid n, Proton[en]säure f, Säure f [im Sinne von Brønsted]	earthing resistance	s. discharging resistance
		Earth['s] interior, interior of the Earth	Erdinneres n
		earth leakage	s. earth fault
		Earth light	Erdlicht n
dystectic, dystectic mixture	Dystektikum n, dystektisches Gemisch n	Earth['s] magnetic field	s. terrestrial magnetic field
		Earth['s] magnetic pole	s. magnetic dip pole
dystectic, dystectic point, dystectic temperature	dystektischer Punkt m	Earth['s] mantle, mantle of the Earth	Erdmantel m

E

		earth metal	Erdmetall n
		Earth['s] oblateness	s. flattening of the Earth
		Earth['s] orbit, terrestrial orbit	Erdbahn f
Eagle grating mounting, Eagle mounting [of diffraction grating]	Eaglesche Gitteraufstellung f		
		earth plate, ground plate; ground rod	Erder m, Erdungsleitung f; Erdelektrode f; Erdplatte f
eagre, tidal eagre, tidal bore	Springwelle f, Springflutwelle f		
eagre	s. high tide raised by a storm	earth potential, earth	Erdpotential n, Erde f
ear, scallop <met.>	Zipfel m, Falte f <Met.>	earthquake, earth tremors, earthdin, temblor <US>	Erdbeben n, Beben n
ear drum, tympanum	Trommelfell n		
earing, symmetrical waviness, development of scallops	Zipfelbildung f, Faltenbildung f, Wellung f der Oberfläche	earthquake due to collapse, subsidence earthquake	Einsturzbeben n, Einbruchbeben n
early atmosphere	Atmosphäre f im ersten Entwicklungsstadium	earthquake energy	Bebenenergie f, Erdbebenenergie f
Early effect, base thickness (width) modulation	Early-Effekt m, Basisbreitenmodulation f	earthquake focus	s. focus of earthquake
		earthquake intensity, intensity of earthquake	Erdbebenstärke f, Bebenstärke f, Stärke (Intensität) f des Bebens, Erdbebenintensität f
early-type star	Stern m vom frühen Spektraltyp, früher Typ m		
early-warning radar	Vorwarnradar n, Frühwarnradar n	earthquake magnitude	s. magnitude
		earthquake of distant origin, distant earthquake, teleseism	Fernbeben n
Earnshaw['s] theorem	Satz m von Earnshaw, Earnshawscher Satz m, Theorem n von Earnshaw	earthquake series	s. earthquake swarm
		earthquake shock, shock, earth tremor <geo.>	Erdstoß m, Bodenstoß m <Geo.>
earshot	s. hearing distance	earthquake swarm, earthquake series	Schwarmbeben n
earth	s. earth potential		
earth-air current	Schlechtwettervertikalstrom m, Schlechtwetterstrom m, luftelektrischer Vertikalstrom m bei Schlechtwetterlage, Erde-Luft-Strom m	earthquake wave, earth wave, seismic wave	Erdbebenwelle f, seismische Welle (Woge) f, Dislokationswoge f
		Earth['s] radiation	s. terrestrial radiation
		earth resistance meter	Erdungsmesser m

Earth['s] revolution, revolution of Earth	Erdumlauf m, Erdrevolution f	eccentric dipole [of the geomagnetic field]	exzentrischer Dipol m [des geomagnetischen Feldes]
Earth['s] rotation, rotary motion of the Earth, rotation of the Earth	Erddrehung f, Erdrotation f, Erdumdrehung f, Erdumschwung m	eccentric error <of division>, error of centering (centring)	Exzentrizitätsfehler m, exzentrischer Fehler m <Teilkreis>
Earth['s] satellite	s. artificial Earth's satellite	eccentricity <of conic>	[lineare] Exzentrizität f, Brennweite f <Kegelschnitt>
Earth['s] shadow, umbra of the Earth	Erdschatten m		
Earth['s] shadow, dark segment <twilight phenomenon>	dunkles Segment n, Erdschatten m <Dämmerungserscheinung>	eccentricity [of the orbit]	numerische Exzentrizität f [der Bahn]
		eccentric motion	Exzenterbewegung f, Revolution f
earth-shine, ashen light	aschgraues Mondlicht (Licht) n; Erdlicht n, Erdschein m	eccentric tension	exzentrischer (außermittiger) Zug m
earth spheroid	s. earth ellipsoid	eccentric vision, parafoveal vision	parafoveales (parazentrisches, exzentrisches) Sehen n
Earth['s] surface, earth-surface, surface of the Earth; terrene	Erdoberfläche f		
Earth['s] terminator	Erdterminator m, Terminator m des Erdschattens	Eccles-Jordan circuit (multivibrator)	s. flip-flop
earth tides, terrestrial tides, bodily tides	Gezeiten pl des Erdkörpers, Erdgezeiten pl	Eccles['] relation	Ecclessche Beziehung f
earth tremor	s. earthquake shock	échelette, échelette grating	Echelettegitter n
earth tremors	s. earthquake	échelle, échelle grating	Echellegitter n
earth wave	s. earthquake wave	échellegram	Echellegramm n
earth wire, ground wire, earth (ground, earthing) connection, ground, grounding (earthing) circuit <el.>	Erdleitung f, Erdungsleitung f <El.>	échelle grating, échelle	Echellegitter n
		échelle spectrograph	Echellespektrograph m
		échelon, Michelson échelon, échelon grating	[Michelsonsches] Stufengitter n, Echelon n, Michelson-Gitter n, Treppengitter n, treppenförmiges Gitter n
easily flowing liquid	leichtbewegliche Flüssigkeit f		
easily fusible (meltable)	s. low-melting	echelon fault	Staffelbruch m
easily volatilized	s. readily volatile		
eastern amplitude, ortive amplitude	Morgenweite f		
		échelon grating	s. échelon
Eastern European time, East-European time	osteuropäische Zeit f, OEZ	echelon lens, Fresnel lens, stepped lens	Fresnel-Linse f, Fresnelsche Linse f, Stufenlinse f
eastern spot	s. following spot <astr.>	echelon lens condenser	Stufenlinsenkondensor m
East-European time, Eastern European time	osteuropäische Zeit f, OEZ	echo, echo image	Echobild n, Echo n; Schattenbild n
east point [of the horizon]	Ostpunkt m		
east-west asymmetry <of cosmic rays>	Ost-West-Asymmetrie f <der kosmischen Strahlung>	echo; echo signal	Echo n; Echosignal n
		echo, re-echo, resounding, reverberation; woolliness	Widerhall m
east-west effect	Ost-West-Effekt m	echo box	Echobox f
easy axis [of magnetization], easy direction for [of] magnetization, direction of easy magnetization, axis of easy magnetization, preferred direction of magnetization	Richtung f der leichtesten Magnetisierbarkeit, magnetische Vorzugsrichtung f, Vorzugsrichtung der Magnetisierung, günstigste Magnetisierungsrichtung (Magnetisierungsachse) f, leichte Richtung	echo current attenuation, regularity attenuation, [structural] return loss	Rückflußdämpfung f; Echodämpfung f
		echo depth sounder	s. echo sounding device
		echo depth sounding, echo sounding	Echolotung f, akustische Echolotung
		echo effect	Echoeffekt m, Echowirkung f
easy-flow direction	s. forward direction	echogram; reflectogram	Echogramm n; Reflektogramm n
easy glide [region], stage I of work-hardening	„easy glide"-Bereich m, Bereich m I der Verfestigungskurve	echo image	s. echo
		echoing characteristic; reflection characteristic	Rückstrahlcharakteristik f
ebb-and-float, ebb and flood, ebb and flow	s. tides	echoing characteristic, reverberation curve (characteristic)	Nachhallkurve f, Nachhallcharakteristik f
Eberhard[t] effect, edge effect; Mackie lines; border effect; fringe effect <phot.>	Kanteneffekt m, Eberhard-Effekt m; [photographischer] Randeffekt m; Saumeffekt m <Phot.>	echo[-]meter	Echometer n
Ebert grating mounting, Ebert mounting [of diffraction grating]	Ebertsche Gitteraufstellung f	echo modulation, modulation of reflected signal	Rückstrahlmodulation f
ebullience	s. ebullition	echo pulse	Reflexionsimpuls m; Rückstrahlimpuls m; Echoimpuls m; Rücklaufimpuls m
ebulliometer	Ebulliometer n; Siedepunktmesser m		
ebullioscope	Ebullioskop n	echo room	s. reverberation chamber
ebullioscopic constant, molal (molecular, molar) elevation of boiling point, molal (molecular, molar) rise of boiling point	ebullioskopische Konstante f, molale (molekulare, molare) Siedepunktserhöhung f	echo sound altimeter	s. echo-sounding device
		echo sounding, echo depth sounding	Echolotung f, akustische Echolotung
ebullition; ebullience	Kochen n, heftiges Sieden n; Aufwallen n, Wallung f, Aufkochen n	echo-sounding device, echo depth sounder, echo sound altimeter, zonic depth finder, fathometer	Echolot n, Schallot n, Behm-Lot n
E capture [decay], EC	s. orbital-electron capture		
E capturer	s. electron capturer <nucl.>		
eccentric angle <of conic>	Exzentrizitätswinkel m <Kegelschnitt>	echo wave	Echowelle f
eccentric collision	exzentrischer Stoß m	Eckert number, E	Eckert-Zahl f, Eckertsche Zahl f, E
eccentric compression	exzentrischer (außermittiger) Druck m	eclipse	Finsternis f, Verfinsterung f; Eklipse f

eclipse comet	Finsterniskomet *m*	eddy conductivity, turbulent conductivity, turbulent thermal conductivity; apparent conductivity, apparent thermal conductivity	turbulente Wärmeleitfähigkeit (Wärmeleitzahl, Leitfähigkeit) *f*, Turbulenzwärmeleitfähigkeit *f*, Turbulenzwärmeleitzahl *f*, Wirbelleitfähigkeit *f*; Scheinleitfähigkeit *f*, Scheinwärmeleitfähigkeit *f*
eclipsed	in Stellung auf Deckung, verfinstert, ekliptisch		
eclipsed conformation	Deckungsstellung *f*, verfinsterte Stellung *f*, Verfinsterungsstellung *f*		
eclipse of the Moon, lunar eclipse	Mondfinsternis *f*		
eclipse of the Sun, solar eclipse	Sonnenfinsternis *f*		
eclipsing binary [star], eclipsing variable, photometric binary [star], occultation variable	Bedeckungsveränderlicher *m*, photometrischer Doppelstern *m*, Finsternisstern *m*	eddy current coefficient, Foucault current coefficient	Wirbelstrombeiwert *m*, Wirbelstromfaktor *m*
		eddy current damping	Wirbelstromdämpfung *f*, Induktionsdämpfung *f*
ecliptic[al] co-ordinates, ecliptic[al] system [of co-ordinates], celestial latitude and longitude	Ekliptikalsystem *n*, ekliptikales Koordinatensystem *n*, ekliptikale (ekliptische) Koordinaten *fpl*, Ekliptikkoordinaten *fpl*, Koordinaten im Ekliptikalsystem	eddy current effect, Faraday effect	Wirbelstromeffekt *m*
		eddy current energy <US>, eddy current loss	Wirbelstromverlust *m*, Foucault-Verlust *m*
		eddy current loss resistance	Wirbelstrom-Verlustwiderstand *m*
ecliptic[al] latitude, celestial latitude, latitude <astr.>	ekliptikale (ekliptische) Breite *f*, Breite <Astr.>		
		eddy current revolution counter	s. eddy current tachometer
ecliptic[al] longitude, [celestial] longitude <astr.>	ekliptikale (ekliptische) Länge *f*, Länge <Astr.>	eddy currents, Foucault currents <el.>	Wirbelströme *mpl*, Foucault-Ströme *mpl*, Foucaultsche Ströme *mpl* <El.>
ecliptic[al] stream	Ekliptikalstrom *m*		
ecliptic[al] system [of co-ordinates]	s. ecliptic[al] co-ordinates	eddy current tachometer, drag-type (drag-torque) tachometer; eddy current revolution counter	Wirbelstromtachometer *n*, Wirbelstromgeschwindigkeitsmesser *m*; Wirbelstromdrehzahlmesser *m*
ecliptic plane, plane of ecliptic	ekliptikale Ebene *f*, Ebene der Ekliptik, Erdbahnebene *f*		
economic coefficient, Pfeffer coefficient	Pfeffer-Koeffizient *m*, ökonomischer Koeffizient *m*	eddy diffusion, turbulent (vorticity) diffusion, diffusion of vorticity; apparent diffusion	turbulente Scheindiffusion (Diffusion) *f*, Turbulenzdiffusion *f*, Wirbeldiffusion *f*; Scheindiffusion *f*
economy <of ion source>	Güte[faktor *m*] *f*, Ökonomie *f* <Ionenquelle>		
economy circuit	Sparschaltung *f*	eddy diffusivity, turbulent diffusivity, turbulent thermal diffusivity; turbulent diffusion coefficient; apparent diffusivity	Koeffizient *m* der turbulenten Scheindiffusion (Diffusion), turbulente Diffusivität *f*, Turbulenzdiffusionskoeffizient *m*, Wirbeldiffusionskoeffizient *m*; Scheindiffusionskoeffizient *m*, Scheindiffusivität *f*; Koeffizient der atmosphärischen Turbulenz
economy of heat; heat gain, gain of heat, heat economy	Wärmegewinn *m*; Wärmeersparnis *f*		
economy principle, principle of economy	Sparsamkeitsregel *f* [von Pauling]		
economy resistor	Sparwiderstand *m*		
		eddy energy, turbulent energy, energy of turbulence, eddy kinetic energy	Turbulenzenergie *f*, turbulente Energie *f*; Wirbelungsenergie *f*, Wirbelungsarbeit *f*
ecotope	Ökotop *n*		
E counter	E-Zähler *m*, Restenergiezähler *m*		
ectropical region, ectropical zone, extropical region (zone)	Ektropen *pl*, außertropische Zone *f*	eddy-energy flow (flux)	Turbulenzenergiefluß *m*
EDA complex, adduct, electron-donor-acceptor complex	Addukt *m*, EDA-Komplex *m*, Elektronen-Donator-Akzeptor-Komplex *m*	eddy erosion	Wirbelerosion *f*
		eddy field	s. rotational field
		eddy flux	s. turbulent flux
		eddy flux conservation law	s. law of conservation of eddy flux
Eddington flow	Eddington-Strömung *f*	eddy formation	s. formation of vortices
		eddy freedom, absence of vortices (eddies), irrotationality	Wirbelfreiheit *f*, Wirbellosigkeit *f*
Eddington['s] [standard stellar] model	Eddingtonsches Standardmodell *n*		
Eddington['s] transfer equation	Eddingtonsche Transportgleichung *f*, Strahlungstransportgleichung *f* von Eddington	eddy generation	s. formation of vortices
		eddy heat conduction	s. eddy conduction
		eddy heat flux	s. eddy conduction
eddy <large-scale>; vortex <pl: vortices, vortexes>, whirl	Wirbel *m*, Wirbelgebilde *n*	eddying, whirling, swirling motion, eddy, turbulence	Wirbelung *f*, Verwirblung *f*; Durchwirbelung *f*
		eddying; vortical, vortex; eddy; whirling; vortex-like	Wirbel-; wirb[e]lig, wirbelnd; wirbelförmig, wirbelartig; wirbelbehaftet
eddy	s. a. whirling		
eddy	s. a. vortex <hydr.>		
eddy	s. a. vortex region	eddying	s. a. formation of vortices
eddy chamber, vortex chamber	Wirbelkammer *f*	eddying whirl	s. turbulent motion
		eddying whirl	s. a. vortex motion
eddy coefficient	s. effective turbulent diffusivity	eddy invariant; vortex invariant	Wirbelinvariante *f*
		eddy kinetic energy	s. eddy energy
eddy conduction [of heat], eddy heat conduction, turbulent conduction [of heat], turbulent heat conduction; apparent conduction [of heat], apparent heat conduction, eddy heat flux	turbulente Wärmeleitung *f*, turbulente Leitung *f*; Scheinwärmeleitung *f*, Scheinleitung *f*	eddy making, turbulent separation	turbulente Ablösung *f*
		eddy motion	s. vortex motion
		eddy motion	s. a. turbulent motion
		eddy motion of the water particles, standing wave, rinsing roller, roll <hydr.>	Wasserwalze *f* <Hydr.>

eddy motion of the water particles near the bottom, bottom standing wave	Grundwalze f	edge of cleavage crack, edge of crack	Rißrand m
		edge of regression	Rückkehrkante f, Rückkehrkurve f, Gratlinie f, Kuspidalkante f
eddy motion of the water particles near the surface, surface standing wave, ground roll[ing]	Deckwalze f	edge of the band	s. band head <opt.>
		edge of the bank	Uferkante f, Kante f des Ufers
eddy of fluid	s. vortex <hydr.>	edge of the crystal, crystal edge	Kristallkante f
eddy resistance	Wirbelwiderstand m	edge of the pulse, pulse front, front of the pulse	Impulsflanke f, Impulsfront f, Flanke f des Impulses
eddy sink, vortex sink, vortex sump, eddy sump	Wirbelsenke f	edge of water, strand[-]line, water edge	Strandlinie f, Küstenlinie f, Streichlinie f, Uferlinie f, Wasserspiegelrand m
eddy source, vortex source	Wirbelquelle f	edge-on structure	„edge-on"-Struktur f, Struktur f mit Bindung übereck
eddy space, vortex space	Wirbelraum m	edge point	Kantenpunkt m
eddy spectrum	s. spectrum of turbulence	edge resolution	s. edge acuity
eddy stress	s. Reynolds stress	edge scattering	Randstreuung f, Kantenstreuung f
eddy sump, vortex sink, vortex sump, eddy sink	Wirbelsenke f	edge shift	Kantenverschiebung f
eddy transfer	s. turbulent transfer	edge slope, pulse slope (steepness), edge steepness, slope (steepness) of edge	Impulsflankensteilheit f, Flankensteilheit f, Impulssteilheit f
eddy transfer coefficient	s. effective turbulent diffusivity		
eddy transport	s. turbulent transfer	edge spectrograph	s. wedge spectrograph
eddy velocity	s. fluctuation velocity	edge steepness	s. edge slope
eddy viscosity, eddy viscosity coefficient, turbulent viscosity, apparent turbulent kinematic viscosity, coefficient of turbulence, coefficient of momentum diffusion, diffusivity for (of) momentum; apparent viscosity, virtual viscosity	scheinbare (turbulente) Zähigkeit f, [turbulente] Scheinzähigkeit f, scheinbare (apparente, turbulente) Viskosität f, Diffusionsbeiwert m der Bewegungsgröße, Turbulenzkoeffizient m, Austausch m, [turbulente] Scheinreibung f, turbulente Reibung f, Turbulenzreibung f, turbulenter Scheinreibungskoeffizient m, virtuelle Zähigkeit, Wirbelzähigkeit f	edge structure <of X-ray spectra>	Kantenstruktur f <Röntgenspektren>
		edge tone, schneidenton	Schneidenton m; Hiebton m
		edge-type meter	s. edgewise meter
		edge water	Schichtwasser n
		edge wave	Kantenwelle f; Randwelle f
		edgewise meter, edgewise pattern instrument, edgewise pattern meter, edge-type meter	Profilgerät n, Profilinstrument n
		E-diagram	s. existence diagram
Eder solution	Edersche Lösung f, Edersche Flüssigkeit f	Edison effect	s. thermionic emission
		EEDOR	s. electron-electron double resonance
edge <of polyhedron>	Kante f <Vielflach>	E effect	s. electromeric effect
edge acuity; edge resolution, resolution of the edges; edge (marginal) definition	Randschärfe f; Randauflösung f	E effect	s. a. seismoelectric effect of the second kind
		e⁺e⁻ pair	s. positron-electron pair
edge condition	Kantenbedingung f	e-e process, double internal conversion	ee-Prozeß m, doppelte innere Umwandlung f
edge contrast, boundary contrast	Grenzkontrast m, Randkontrast m	effect; action; influence <on>	Wirkung f <auf>; Einfluß m <auf>; Einwirkung f <auf>; Effekt m; Beeinflussung f <von>
edge correction	s. correction for edge effect		
edge crack, [lap] edge fracture	Kanten[ein]riß m, Randriß m	effect carbon, flame carbon	Effektkohle f
edge damping; surface damping	Randdämpfung f	effecting; causing; inducing, induction; production	Verursachen n, Bewirken n, Bedingen n, Hervorrufen n; Auslösung f; Erzeugung f
edge definition	s. edge acuity		
edge diffraction, knife-edge diffraction	Kantenbeugung f, Beugung f an der Kante, Randbeugung f	effective absorbing (aerial) area	s. beam area
		effective aerial height	s. effective height of the antenna
edge discharge	s. point discharge	effective alternating-current resistance	s. resistance <el.>
edge dislocation, Taylor-Orowan dislocation; stair-rod dislocation	Stufenversetzung f, Kantenversetzung f, Längsversetzung f, 0°-Versetzung f	effective antenna temperature	s. effective temperature of the antenna
edge drag	s. trailing-edge drag <aero.>	effective aperture, aperture <of objective>	wirksame Öffnung f, Öffnung, Apertur f <Objektiv>
edge effect, boundary effect	Randeffekt m		
edge effect	s. a. Eberhard effect <phot.>	effective aperture ratio	effektives Öffnungsverhältnis n, effektive Lichtstärke f
edge-effect correction	s. correction for edge effect		
edge emission, boundary emission	Kantenemission f	effective area, useful area <opt.>	Nutzfläche f <Opt.>
edge emission spectrum	Kantenemissionsspektrum n	effective area of the antenna	s. beam area
edge field, fringing field, marginal field, margin of the field	Randfeld n	effective atomic number, effective nuclear charge, Z_{eff}	effektive Ordnungszahl (Kernladungszahl) f, Z_{eff}
edge filter	Kantenfilter n	effective attenuation	Wirkdämpfung f
edge focusing	Kantenfokussierung f, Randfokussierung f	effective cadmium cut-off	effektive Cadmium-Abschneideenergie f
edge fog	Randschleier m	effective collision cross-section	s. collision cross-section
edge fracture	s. edge crack		
edge growth	Kantenwachstum n	effective component	s. real component

effective conductance, real part of the admittance	Wirkleitwert m, Wirkanteil m des komplexen Gesamtleitwertes, Parallelwirkleitwert m	effective range [of instrument], effective part of scale, extent, instrument range, range [of the instrument]; measuring (measurement) range, range of measurements	Meßbereich m, Bereich m; Meßumfang m <Meß.>
effective cross-section	effektiver Wirkungsquerschnitt (Querschnitt) m		
effective cross-section <hydr., aero.>	wirksamer Querschnitt m <Hydr., Aero.>	effective range of nuclear forces	effektive Reichweite f der Kernkräfte
effective cross-section of carrier trapping	s. trapping cross-section <semi.>	effective reactance	s. reactance
effective current	s. current r. m. s.	effective resistance	s. resistance <el.>
effective electron mass, effective mass of electron	effektive Masse f des Elektrons, effektive Elektronenmasse f	effective singlet range	effektive Singulettreichweite f
		effective sound pressure	s. root-mean-square sound pressure
effective energetic efficiency	effektiver energetischer Wirkungsgrad m	effective surface area	effektive Oberfläche f
		effective temperature; bolometric radiation temperature, apparent temperature <astr.>	effektive Temperatur f; bolometrische Strahlungstemperatur f, Gesamtstrahlungstemperatur f, Äquivalenztemperatur f <Astr.>
effective focal spot	effektiver Brennfleck m		
effective gain	Wirkverstärkung f		
effective grid potential, effective potential of grid	Gittereffektivpotential n		
		effective temperature of the antenna	s. antenna temperature
effective half-life	effektive Halbwertzeit f	effective thermal cross-section, Westcott cross-section	effektiver thermischer Wirkungsquerschnitt (Querschnitt) m, Westcott-Querschnitt m, Westcott-Wirkungsquerschnitt m
effective height of the antenna, antenna effective height, effective aerial height, radiation height, virtual height	wirksame (effektive) Antennenhöhe f, Strahlungshöhe f [der Antenne], Strahlhöhe f [der Antenne], Antennen[wirk]höhe f, Wirk[sam]höhe f der Antenne, Effektivhöhe f der Antenne, Wirkantennenhöhe f, wirksame (effektive) Höhe f der Antenne		
		effective thermal efficiency	effektiver thermischer Wirkungsgrad m
		effective turbulent diffusivity, "austausch" (exchange, interchange, eddy, eddy transfer, turbulent transfer) coefficient	Austauschkoeffizient m
effective horse power	s. brake horse power	effective value	s. root-mean-square value
effective incidence	effektiver Anstellwinkel m	effective velocity	s. root-mean-square speed
effective length <of separation column>	Trennlänge f, effektive (wirksame) Trennlänge <Trennkolonne>	effective volt, volt effective	Volt n effektive Spannung, Volt effektiv
effective length of magnet, magnetic length	magnetische Länge f, wirksame Länge des Magneten	effective wavelength, Crova wavelength, spectral position	wirksame (effektive) Wellenlänge f, Crova-Wellenlänge f
effective mass	effektive (wirksame, wirkende) Masse f	effective work	s. useful work
effective mass, virtual (induced) mass, apparent additional mass	scheinbare Masse f, virtuelle Masse, induzierte Masse	effectiveness	s. efficiency
		effect of cavitation, cavitation phenomenon (effect)	Kavitationserscheinung f
effective mass of electron, effective electron mass	effektive Masse f des Elektrons, effektive Elektronenmasse f	effect of coupling, coupling effect <e.g. of electrons>	Kopplungseffekt m <z. B. der Elektronen>
effective mass tensor	s. tensor of effective mass	effect of exposure, exposure effect	Belichtungseffekt m
effective multiplication factor, K_{eff}	effektiver Multiplikationsfaktor m, k_{eff}	effect of light	Lichteffekt m, Lichtwirkung f
effectiveness	s. efficiency		
effective nuclear charge	s. effective atomic number	effect of nuclear spin, spin effect	Kernspineffekt m
effective number of fission neutrons, ν_{eff}	effektive Zahl f der Spaltneutronen, effektive Spaltneutronenzahl f, ν_{eff}	effect of ozone shadow, ozone shadowing	Ozonschatteneffekt m
effective output	s. actual output		
effective part of scale	s. effective range		
effective permeability	Wirkpermeabilität f, Effektivpermeabilität f, Wirkanteil m der komplexen Permeabilität, wirksame (effektive) Permeabilität f	effect of perspective <opt.>, stereoscopic effect	stereoskopischer (plastischer) Effekt m, Raumeffekt m, Raumwirkung f, räumliche (plastische) Wirkung f, 3-D-Effekt m <Opt.>
		effect of rejuvenation	Verjüngungseffekt m
effective potential of grid, effective grid potential	Gittereffektivpotential n	effector	Effektor m
		effects due to isotopic change of mass	s. mass effect
effective power, efficiency, axial refraction <of spectacle lens>	Hauptpunktsbrechwert m, Hauptpunktsrefraktion f, axiale Refraktion f, Brechkraft f <Brillenglas>	effects due to isotopic change of volume	s. volume effect
		efferent	efferent
		effervescence	Aufbrausen n, Aufschäumen n
effective principal quantum number	effektive Hauptquantenzahl f	efficacy	s. efficiency
		efficacy	s. a. output
effective proton-proton range	effektive Proton-Proton-Reichweite f	efficiency. effectiveness, effectiviness, efficacy	Effektivität f, Wirksamkeit f
		efficiency	Wirkungsgrad m, Nutzeffekt m; Güteverhältnis n; Ausbeute f
effective pyranometer	Effektivpyranometer n		
effective quantum energy	effektive Quantenenergie f	efficiency, efficacy; output, productivity; performance	Leistung[sfähigkeit] f, Produktionsleistung f, Produktivität f
effective radiation, useful radiation	Nutzstrahlung f	efficiency	s. a. utilization factor <opt.>
effective radius <bio.>	effektiver Radius m, Schädigungsradius m	efficiency	s. a. effective power

efficiency diode, booster diode, damping diode, series-efficiency diode	Schalterdiode f, Boosterdiode f, Spardiode f, Dämpfungsdiode f	Ehrenhaft effect, magnetophotophoresis	Magnetophotophorese f, Ehrenhaft-Effekt m
efficiency formula	Wirkungsgradformel f	Ehringhaus compensator	Ehringhaus-Kompensator m, Quarzplattenkompensator m nach Ehringhaus
		E-I characteristic	s. current-voltage characteristic
efficiency of Carnot['s] cycle	Carnot-Wirkungsgrad m, Carnotscher Wirkungsgrad m	eiconal	s. eikonal
		Eiffel chamber	Eiffel-Kammer f
efficiency of counter (counting)	s. counter efficiency	eigen angular momentum	s. spin angular momentum
		eigendifferential	Eigendifferential n
efficiency of fluid flow, fluid flow efficiency, flow efficiency	Strömungswirkungsgrad m	eigenellipse	Eigenellipse f
		eigenfield, proper field	Eigenfeld n
		eigenfrequency	s. natural frequency
efficiency of ionization, ionization efficiency	Ionisierungsausbeute f	eigenfunction, proper function; characteristic function	Eigenfunktion f; Eigenlösung f; Eigenelement n; Eigenvektor m
efficiency of [light] source	s. light output ratio <opt.>	eigenfunctional	Eigenfunktional n
efficiency of rectification	s. rectification ratio	eigenfunction expansion	Entwicklung f nach Eigenfunktionen
efficiency of space occupation	Raumausnutzung f	eigenmoment, proper moment	Eigenmoment n
		eigenperiod	Eigenperiode f
efficiency of the thermodynamic cycle, cycle efficiency	Prozeßwirkungsgrad m <Therm.>	eigenrotation, self-rotation, proper rotation	Eigenrotation f, Eigendrehung f
efficiency ratio	s. relative efficiency	eigenstate, characteristic state, proper state	Eigenzustand m
efficiency threshold, threshold of efficiency	Wirksamkeitsschwelle f, Effektivitätsschwelle f	eigenstate of radiation, mode of radiation	Eigenzustand m der Strahlung
efficient <stat.>, asymptotically efficient	effizient <Stat.>	eigentemperature, natural (intrinsic) temperature	Eigentemperatur f
efflorescence, efflorescency	Effloreszenz f, Ausblühen n, Auswitterung f	eigentensor	Eigentensor m
effluence, effluent	s. discharge <of liquid>	eigentone <ac.>	s. natural oscillation
effluogram	s. exhaustion diagram	eigentone <ac.>	s. a. vibrational mode
efflux	s. discharge <of liquid>	eigenvalue, proper (principal, characteristic) value; proper (characteristic) number; latent (characteristic) root <of a matrix>	Eigenwert m, charakteristischer Wert m; charakteristische Zahl f, charakteristische Wurzel f <Matrix>
efflux of energy	Energieabfluß m		
efflux velocity, jet velocity, exit velocity <of gas>	Strahlaustrittsgeschwindigkeit f, Ausström[ungs]geschwindigkeit f <Gas>		
efflux viscometer	s. gravity viscometer		
effort <of material>	Anstrengung f <Material>	eigenvalue equation	Eigenwertgleichung f
effuser	Ausströmer m		
effusiometer, Bunsen [-Schilling] effusiometer, Schilling-type effusion bottle <US>	Effusiometer [von Bunsen] n, Bunsensches Effusiometer, Dichtemesser (Gasdichtemesser) m von Bunsen-Schilling	eigenvalue of energy, characteristic (inherent) number (value) of energy	Energieeigenwert m
		eigenvalue problem, proper value problem	Eigenwertproblem n, Eigenwertaufgabe f
effusiometry	Effusiometrie f		
effusion	Effusion f; Ausströmung f; Erguß m <Geo.>		
effusion, gaseous diffusion, gas diffusion	Gasdiffusion f	eigenvalue spectrum	Eigenwertspektrum n
effusion law of Bunsen, Bunsen['s] law of effusion	Bunsensches Ausströmungsgesetz n	eigenvector, proper vector; latent vector, characteristic vector, modal column <of a matrix>	Eigenvektor m
effusion method	Ausströmungsmethode f		
effusive [rock], extrusive [rock]	Ergußgestein n, Ausbruchsgestein n, Extrusivgestein n, Vulkanit m, Effusivgestein n	eigenvolume of the ion, ion eigenvolume, proper volume of ion, ion proper volume	Ioneneigenvolumen n, Eigenvolumen n des Ions
e-folding time	Ver-e-fachungszeit f		
Ɛ-function of Weierstrass, Weierstrassian function Ɛ, Weierstrassian Ɛ-function	Weierstraßsche Ɛ-Funktion f, Exzeßfunktion f	Eigen-Wicke['s] partition function	Verteilungsfunktion f von Eigen und Wicke, Eigen-Wickesche Verteilungsfunktion
egg-shaped, oviform	eiförmig	eight-electrode tube, octode, eight-element tube, six-grid tube	Oktode f, Achtröhre f, Sechsgitterröhre f
egg-shaped body, convex body	konvexer Körper m, Eikörper m		
Ehn size, McQuaid-Ehn size	[McQuaid-]Ehn-Korngröße f, arteigene Korngröße f	eight-electron bond, quadruple bond, quadruple link[age]	Vierfachbindung f, Achtelektronenbindung f
		eight-electron shell, L-shell	L-Schale f, Achterschale f
Ehrenfest['s] adiabatic law, adiabatic law for quantized states [of Ehrenfest], Ehrenfest['s] theorem	[Ehrenfestsche] Adiabatenhypothese f, Ehrenfestsches Adiabatenprinzip n, Ehrenfestscher Adiabatensatz m	eight-element tube	s. eight-electrode tube
		eightfold twisting	s. spiral-eight twisting
		eightfold way / the, the 8-fold way, Gell-Mann – Ne'eman scheme, octet method	Der achtfache Weg m, Gell-Mann – Ne'eman-Schema n, Oktettmethode f, Klassifikation f nach Oktetts der SU(³)-Symmetrie
Ehrenfest['s] equations	s. Ehrenfest['s] relations		
Ehrenfest-Oppenheimer law	Ehrenfest-Oppenheimerscher Satz m		
Ehrenfest['s] relations, Ehrenfest['s] equations	Ehrenfestsche Gleichungen fpl		
		eight-pole network	s. eight-terminal network
		eight-segmented magnetron	Achtschlitzmagnetron n
Ehrenfest['s] theorem	Ehrenfestsche Sätze mpl, Sätze von Ehrenfest		
Ehrenfest['s] theorem	s. a. Ehrenfest['s] adiabatic law	eight-terminal circuit	Achtpolschaltung f
		eight-terminal network, octopole, octupole, eight-pole network <el.>	Achtpol m <El.>
Ehrenfest urn model	Ehrenfestsches Urnenmodell n		

EIH approximation method, Einstein-Infeld-Hoffmann approximation
EIH theory, Einstein-Infeld-Hoffmann theory

eikonal, eikonal function, point eikonal, [e]iconal; Hamilton['s] characteristic [function], characteristic function [of Hamilton], point characteristic function [of Hamilton], point characteristic [of Hamilton], two-point characteristic [function], Hamilton['s] two-point characteristic function
eikonal equation
eikonal function
einstein, quantum mole, E
Einstein['s] action principle, Einstein['s] principle of action
Einstein-Bose statistics
Einstein characteristic temperature
Einstein coefficient, Einstein probability (transition) coefficient; Einstein transition probability, transition probability of Einstein
Einstein condensation

Einstein constant [of gravitation]

Einstein['s] convention
Einstein crystal

Einstein-de Haas effect, rotation by magnetization, Richardson[-Einstein-de Haas] effect
Einstein-De Sitter model, model of Einstein and De Sitter, universe of Einstein and De Sitter
Einstein diffusion equation
Einstein displacement [of light], Einstein effect
Einstein effect
Einstein equation for diffusion in solids
Einstein['s] equation [for photoelectric emission], Einstein['s] photoelectric equation, photoelectric equation, Einstein['s] law

Einstein['s] equivalence principle
Einstein['s] field equations, field equations of Einstein
Einstein['s] formula

Einstein['s] formula of radition theory
Einstein function, Einstein specific heat function
Einstein['s] general theory of relativity
Einstein-Hilbert condition, co-ordinate condition of Einstein-Hilbert

EIH-Approximationsmethode f, Einstein-Infeld-Hoffmann-Approximation f
EIH-Theorie f, Einstein-Infeld-Hoffmannsche Theorie f

Eikonal n, Streckeneikonal n; charakteristische Funktion f [von Hamilton], Hamiltons Zweipunktcharakteristik f, Zweipunktcharakteristik von Helmholtz; zeitunabhängige Wirkungsfunktion f

Eikonalgleichung f
s. eikonal
Einstein n, E
Einsteinsches Wirkungsprinzip n

s. Bose-Einstein statistics
s. characteristic Einstein temperature

Einstein-Koeffizient m; Einsteinsche Übergangswahrscheinlichkeit f, Übergangswahrscheinlichkeit nach Einstein

s. Bose-Einstein condensation
Einsteinsche Gravitationskonstante f

s. summation convention
s. Einstein['s] model [of crystal]
[Richardson-]Einstein-de-Haas-Effekt m, magnetomechanischer Effekt m

Weltmodell n von Einstein und de Sitter, Einstein-de-Sitter-Welt f, Einstein-de-Sitter-Universum n
s. Einstein['s] relation

s. relativistic deflection of light

s. a. gravitational red-shift
s. Einstein['s] relation

Einsteinsche Gleichung f [der Photoelektrizität], [Einsteinsche] Gleichung für den photoelektrischen Effekt, Einsteinsche Gleichung des Photoeffekts, Grundgleichung f für den Photoeffekt (lichtelektrischen Effekt), Einstein-Beziehung f, lichtelektrische (photoelektrische) Gleichung, Lenard-Einstein-Gleichung f, Lenard-Einsteinsche Gleichung, Lenard-Einsteinsches Gesetz n
s. equivalence principle

Einsteinsche Feldgleichungen fpl, Feldgleichungen von Einstein
Einsteinsches Viskositätsgesetz n

s. Bohr['s] frequency condition
Einsteinsche Funktion f, Einstein-Funktion f
s. general theory of relativity

Einstein-Hilbertsche Koordinatenbedingung f, Koordinatenbedingung von Einstein-Hilbert

Einstein['s] hypothesis of light quanta, light-quantum hypothesis, light-quantum theory [of Einstein], quantum theory of light
Einstein['s] inertial moment
Einstein-Infeld-Hoffmann approximation, EIH approximation method
Einstein-Infeld-Hoffmann theory, EIH theory
einsteinium, $_{99}$Es
Einstein-Laub force density
Einstein['s] law of photochemical equivalence
Einstein['s] law
Einstein lift

Einstein['s] light deflection
Einstein['s] mass-energy relation[ship]
Einstein-Maxwell field equations
Einstein-Maxwell theory, Maxwell-Einstein theory
Einstein-Minkowski space
Einstein['s] model, Einstein['s] universe

Einstein['s] model [of crystal], Einstein crystal

Einstein pendulum
Einstein['s] photoelectric equation
Einstein['s] plus-minus relation

Einstein['s] principle of action, Einstein['s] action principle
Einstein['s] principle of equivalence
Einstein['s] principle of relativity
Einstein['s] principle of special relativity, principle of special relativity

Einstein probability coefficient
Einstein['s] pseudotensor, energy-momentum pseudotensor

Einstein red shift
Einstein['s] relation, [Einstein['s]] mass-energy relation[ship], mass-energy interrelation

Einstein['s] relation, Einstein relationship [between mobility and diffusion coefficient], Einstein diffusion equation, Einstein equation for diffusion in solids, diffusion coefficient-mobility relation, mobility-diffusion coefficient relation

Lichtquantentheorie f [von Einstein], Einsteinsche Lichtquantentheorie, Lichtquantenhypothese f, Photonentheorie f, Photonenhypothese f

Einsteinsches Inertialmoment n
EIH-Approximationsmethode f, Einstein-Infeld-Hoffmann-Approximation f
EIH-Theorie f, Einstein-Infeld-Hoffmannsche Theorie f
Einsteinium n, $_{99}$Es
Einstein-Laubsche Kraftdichte f
s. law of photochemical equivalence

s. Einstein['s] equation
Einsteinscher Kasten (Aufzug) m
s. relativistic deflection of light
s. Einstein['s] relation

Einstein-Maxwellsche Feldgleichungen fpl
Einstein-Maxwellsche Theorie f, Maxwell-Einsteinsche Theorie
s. space-time <math.>
Einstein-Universum n, Einsteinsches Weltmodell n, Einsteinsche Zylinderwelt f, Einstein-Welt f
Einstein-Modell n, Einsteinsches Kristallmodell n, Modell n des Einsteinschen Kristalls, Einsteinscher Kristall m, Einstein-Kristall n
Einsteinsches Pendel n
s. Einstein['s] equation [for photoelectric emission]
Plus-Minus-Relation f von Einstein, Einsteinsche Plus-Minus-Relation
Einsteinsches Wirkungsprinzip n

s. equivalence principle

Einsteinsches Relativitätsprinzip n
spezielles Relativitätsprinzip n, Einsteinsches [spezielles] Relativitätsprinzip, Relativitätsprinzip von Poincaré und Einstein
s. Einstein coefficient

Einsteinscher Pseudotensor m [der Impuls-Energie-Dichte], Energie-Impuls-Pseudotensor m, Energie-Impuls-Pseudotensordichte f
s. gravitational red shift
Einsteinsche Beziehung f [zwischen Masse und Energie], Einsteinsche Gleichung f, Einstein-Gleichung f, Energie-Masse-Beziehung f, Energie-Masse-Gleichung f, Masse-Energie-Beziehung f, Masse-Energie-Gleichung f
Einsteinsche Beziehung f [für den Diffusionskoeffizienten]

Einstein shift	s. gravitational red-shift	elastic axis, elastica, elastic line, neutral axis, neutral filament, central line <elasticity>	elastische Linie f, Elastika f, Biegelinie f, neutrale Linie (Achse f, Faser f), Nullachse f, Nullinie f, Mittellinie f <Elastizitätstheorie>
Einstein-Smoluchowski equation, equation of Einstein and Smoluchowski	Einstein-Smoluchowskische Gleichung f		
Einstein space	Einstein-Raum m, Einsteinsche Mannigfaltigkeit f, Einsteinscher Raum m	elastic body	s. perfectly elastic solid
		elastic buckling	elastische Knickung f
Einstein specific heat function	s. Einstein function	elastic coefficient	Elastizitätskoeffizient m, elastischer Koeffizient m
Einstein['s] spherical space	Einsteinscher Kugelraum m, Kugelraum	elastic coherent scattering, coherent elastic scattering [of neutrons]	kohärente elastische Streuung f [von Neutronen]
Einstein-Straus field equations	Einstein-Straussche Feldgleichungen fpl, Feldgleichungen von Einstein und Straus, schwaches Feldgleichungssystem n [von Einstein]	elastic collision, elastic impact, billard-ball collision	elastischer Stoß m
		elastic collision cross-section	s. elastic scattering cross-section
Einstein['s] summation convention	s. summation convention	elastic constant	s. restoring force <mech.>
		elastic constants, constants of elasticity	Elastizitätskonstanten fpl, elastische Konstanten fpl
Einstein temperature	s. characteristic Einstein temperature	elastic cross-section	s. elastic scattering cross-section
Einstein['s] tensor, Ricci['s] tensor	Ricci-Tensor m, Einstein-Tensor m	elastic deformation, elastic strain	elastische Deformation (Verformung, Formänderung) f
Einstein term	Einstein-Term m		
Einstein['s] theory of gravitation	Einsteinsche Gravitationstheorie f	elastic dipole, double force	Doppelkraft f, elastischer Dipol m
Einstein['s] theory of solids	Einsteinsche Theorie f der Festkörper	elastic distorsional potential	elastisches Verzerrungspotential n
Einstein['s] time dilation	s. time dilatation <rel.>	elastic elongation	elastische Dehnung f
Einstein transition coefficient (probability)	s. Einstein coefficient	elastic energy density	elastische Energiedichte f
		elastic energy flux	elastischer Energiefluß m
		elastic equilibrium	elastisches Gleichgewicht n
Einstein['s] unified field theory	Einsteinsche einheitliche Feldtheorie f, Relativitätstheorie f des unsymmetrischen Feldes	elastic ether model	elastisches Äthermodell n
		elastic failure, failing, failure <in theory of strength of materials>	Versagen n <Festigkeitslehre>
Einstein['s] universe, Einstein['s] model	Einstein-Universum n, Einsteinsches Weltmodell n, Einsteinsche Zylinderwelt f, Einstein-Welt f	elastic feedback	nachgebende (elastische, isodrome) Rückführung f
		elastic flexibility of support	elastische Nachgiebigkeit f der Stütze
Einthoven galvanometer	s. string galvanometer	elastic foundation	elastische Unterlage f
Einthoven['s] triangle	Einthovensches Dreieck n <Elektrokardiographie>	elastic hysteresis	s. elastic after[-]effect
		elastic hysteresis	s. a. dynamic hysteresis
einzel lens, unipotential lens, single [electron] lens	Einzellinse f, Dreielektrodenlinse f, elektrostatische Einzellinse	elastic hysteresis loop	mechanische (elastische) Hysteresisschleife f, Zug-Druck-Hysteresisschleife f
ejection, extraction, deflection <of the beam, particles> <acc.>	Ausschleusen n, Auslenkung f, Herausführung f, Ejektion f <Strahl, Teilchen>, Strahlherausführung f, Strahlauslenkung f <Beschl.>	elastic impact	s. elastic collision
		elasticity	Elastizität f
		elasticity ellipsoid	s. ellipsoid of elasticity
		elasticity in shape (shear)	s. shape elasticity
ejection <geo., astr.>	Auswurf m, Ejektion f <Geo., Astr.>	elasticity of bulk	s. compressibility
		elasticity of elongation (extension)	s. tensile elasticity
ejection <of air>, expulsion	Ausstoßen n <Luft>	elasticity of form (shape, shear)	s. shape elasticity
		elastic lag	s. elastic after[-]effect
ejection of matter, surge, surge prominence; mass ejection	Auswurf m (Ausschleudern n) von Materie, Materieauswurf m, Materieausbruch m	elastic limit, limit of [linear] elasticity	Elastizitätsgrenze f
		elastic limit for compression, compressive elastic limit	Druckelastizitätsgrenze f, Elastizitätsgrenze f gegenüber Druck
ejection theory	Auswurftheorie f		
ejector, impulsor, torsor <math.>	Impulsor m, Ejektor m, Torsor m <Math.>	elastic limit for tension, tensile elastic limit	Zugelastizitätsgrenze f, Elastizitätsgrenze f gegenüber Zug
ejector	s. a. air ejector	elastic line	s. elastic axis
ejector	s. a. beam extractor <acc.>	elastic material	elastischer Stoff (Werkstoff) m, Elastikum n <pl: Elastika>
eka-element	Eka-Element n		
Ekman flow	Ekmansche Strömung f		
Ekman spiral	s. spiral of Ekman	elastic modulus	s. Young['s] modulus
elaidinization	Elaidinisierung f	elastic-plastic, elasto-plastic	elastisch-plastisch, elastoplastisch
elastance, stiffness <el.>	Elastanz f, reziproke Kapazität f	elastic-plastic body, Prandtl[-]body	Prandtlscher (elastisch-plastischer) Körper m, elastisch-plastische Substanz f
elastica	s. elastic axis <elasticity>		
elastic after[-]effect, elastic hysteresis, elastic lag, creep recovery	elastische Nachwirkung f, elastische Nachwirkungserscheinung f	elastic-plastic deformation, elastic and plastic strain	elastisch-plastische Deformation f, elastoplastische Formänderung f
elastic after-effect function, after-effect function	Nachwirkungsfunktion f	elastic-plastic equilibrium	elastisch-plastisches Gleichgewicht n
elastic and plastic strain, elastic-plastic deformation	elastisch-plastische Deformation f, elastoplastische Formänderung f	elastic potential, specific potential energy of deformation <mech.>	elastisches Potential n [der Volumeneinheit], spezifische Formänderungsarbeit (Formänderungsenergie) f, Energiedichte f <Mech.>
elastic anisotropy	elastische Anisotropie f	elastic potential [per unit volume]	s. specific strain energy
elasticator	Elastikator m		

elastic 210

elastic potential per unit mass, strain energy per unit mass	elastisches Potential n pro Masseneinheit
elastic range	elastischer Bereich m, Elastizitätsbereich m, Elastizitätsgebiet n
elastic recovery; springback, springiness <US>	elastische Erholung f; Rückfederung f
elastic relaxation, release of elastic stresses	elastische Relaxation f
elastic scattering	elastische Streuung f
elastic scattering cross-section, elastic collision cross-section, elastic cross-section, cross-section for elastic scattering (collisions)	Wirkungsquerschnitt m für elastische Streuung, Wirkungsquerschnitt der elastischen Streuung, Wirkungsquerschnitt für elastischen Stoß, elastischer Streuquerschnitt (Stoßquerschnitt) m
elastic scattering sub-matrix, elastic S-submatrix, elastic submatrix	elastische Streuuntermatrix (S-Untermatrix, Untermatrix) f, Untermatrix der elastischen Streuung
elastic scattering with formation of compound nucleus	s. resonance scattering
elastic scattering without formation of compound nucleus, non-compound-elastic scattering	formelastische Streuung f, elastische Streuung ohne Compoundkernbildung
elastic shear modulus	s. shear modulus
elastic shell	elastische Schale f
elastic sol, Lethersich body, Jeffreys body, relaxing gel	elastisches Sol n, Lethersichscher (Jeffreysscher) Körper m, relaxierendes Gel n
elastic solid	s. perfectly elastic solid
elastic S-submatrix	s. elastic scattering submatrix
elastic stiffness	elastische Steifigkeit (Steifheit) f
elastic stiffness matrix	Tensor m der elastischen Koeffizienten, reziproker Hookescher Tensor, Matrix f der Elastizitätskoeffizienten
elastic strain	s. elastic deformation
elastic strain energy	s. total strain energy
elastic stress, elastic tension	elastische Spannung f
elastic stress	elastischer Spannungszustand m, elastisch gespannter Zustand m
elastic submatrix	s. elastic scattering submatrix
elastic support	elastische Stütze f
elastic tension	s. elastic stress
elastic tube pressure gauge	s. tube spring manometer
elastic-viscoplastic	elastisch-viskoplastisch
elastic wave, stress wave	elastische Welle f
elastivity	spezifische Elastanz f
elastodynamics, dynamic elasticity	Elastodynamik f
elastomechanics, theory of elasticity	Elastizitätstheorie f, Elastomechanik f
elastomer; elastomeric plastic, elastoplastic	Elastomer n, Elast m
elasto-osmometry	Elastoosmometrie f
elasto-plastic, elastic-plastic	elastisch-plastisch, elastoplastisch
elastoresistance	galvanoelastischer Effekt m
elastostatics	Elastostatik f
elastothiomer, polysulfide polymer (rubber), thioplast	Thioplast m, Elastothiomer n
elasto-viscosity	Elastoviskosität f
elasto-viscous solid	elastisch-viskoses Medium n, elastisch-zähflüssiger Körper m
E layer, Kennelly-Heaviside['s] layer, Heaviside['s] layer	E-Schicht f, Heaviside-Kennelly-Schicht f, Heaviside-Schicht f
elbow of the waveguide	s. waveguide elbow
electret	Elektret n

electric affinity	s. electron affinity
electrical analogy	elektrische Analogie f; Elektromodellierung f
electrical attenuation	elektrische Dämpfung f
electrical ballistic pendulum	elektroballistisches Pendel n
electrical breakdown in air, breakdown in air	Luftdurchschlag m, elektrischer Durchschlag m in Luft
electrical breakdown in vacuum, vacuum breakdown, vacuum sparking	Vakuumdurchschlag m, Durchschlag (Durchbruch) m im Vakuum
electrical capacitance	s. capacitance <el.>
electrical circuit	s. circuit <el.>
electrical circuit analysis	s. network analysis
electrical circuit constant, linear electrical constant, circuit constant	Leitungsparameter m, Leitungskonstante f
electrical conduction, conduction	[elektrische] Leitung f, Elektrizitätsleitung f
electrical conductivity	s. conductivity
electrical convection current	s. convection current
electrical defect [in crystals]	elektrische Fehlordnung f [in Kristallen]
electrical depolarization	elektrische Depolarisation f
electrical dipole transition	elektrischer Dipolübergang m
electrical double layer, dipole layer, electrochemical double layer	Dipolschicht f, Dipolzone f, elektr[ochem]ische Doppelschicht f
electrical double refraction	s. Kerr effect
electrical energy density	elektrische Energiedichte f
electrical equivalent of heat, proportionality coefficient in Joule's law of electric heating <= 0.239 cal/VAs>	elektrisches Wärmeäquivalent n
electrical form factor, form factor <el.>	[elektrischer] Formfaktor m <El.>
electrical image, electric[al] mirror image	elektrisches Spiegelbild (Bild) n
electrical image	s. a. electric image
electrical impedance	s. impedance <el.>
electrical inverter	s. inverter <el.>
electrical line	s. line <el.>
electrical load	s. load
electrically heated thermocouple, thermo[-] converter, thermal converter	Thermoumformer m
electrically measuring instrument	elektrisches Meßgerät n für nichtelektrische Größen
electrically negative, negative; negatively charged <el.>	negativ, elektrisch negativ; negativ [auf]geladen <El.>
electrically neutral, neutral, elektrisch neutral; uncharged, without charge, of zero charge <el.>	neutral, elektrisch neutral; ungeladen, ladungsfrei, ohne Ladung <El.>
electrically positive, positive; positively charged <el.>	positiv, elektrisch positiv; positiv [auf]geladen <El.>
electrical mirror image, electrical image	elektrisches Spiegelbild (Bild) n
electrical network reciprocity theorem	s. reciprocity theorem
electrical network synthesis, network synthesis, synthesis of electrical network	Netzwerksynthese f
electrical pumping	elektrisches Pumpen n
electrical resistance <el.>, resistance	Widerstand m, elektrischer Widerstand <El.>
electrical Senftleben effect	elektrischer Senftleben-Effekt m
electrical speech level, speech (vocal, volume) level	Sprachpegel m
electrical splitting of spectral lines	s. Stark splitting
electrical stimulation, Gudden-Pohl effect, electrophoto-luminescence	Gudden-Pohl-Effekt m, elektrische Ausleuchtung f

electrical strain, electrical stress	elektrische (dielektrische) Beanspruchung f	electric excitation	s. a. electric stimulation
electrical system of units	elektrisches Einheitensystem n	electric eye	s. photoelectric cell
electrical tension	s. voltage <el.>	electric field, electric space, field of electric intensity	elektrisches Feld n
electrical thermometer	elektrisches Temperaturmeßgerät (Thermometer) n	electric field	s. a. electric intensity
electrical time distribution system, time distribution system	Zentraluhrenanlage f	electric field energy	s. energy of electric field
		electric field intensity (strength)	s. electric intensity
electrical transient	s. transient	electric field strength due to the space wave	Raumfeldstärke f
electric arc, arc, voltaic arc <el.>	[elektrischer] Bogen (Lichtbogen) m	electric field vector	s. electric intensity
electric arc [in gas], arc discharge	Bogenentladung f	electric flux, displacement flux	Verschiebungsfluß m, elektrischer Fluß m (Verschiebungsfluß)
electric balance	elektrische Waage f	electric flux density	s. electric displacement
electric balance	elektrisches Gleichgewicht n	electric force density, density of electric force, force density in the electric field	Kraftdichte f im elektrischen Feld, elektrische Kraftdichte
"electric" Barkhausen discontinuity, ferroelectric Barkhausen discontinuity	„elektrischer" Barkhausen-Sprung m, ferroelektrischer Barkhausen-Sprung	electric forming	elektrisches Formieren n, elektrische Formierung f
		electric generator, generator, self-excited direct-current generator, self-excited constant-current generator, dynamoelectric machine, dynamo <el.>	elektrischer Generator m, Generator, Gleichstromgenerator m mit Selbsterregung, Dynamo m, Dynamomaschine f <El.>
electric bulb	s. incandescent lamp		
electric capacitance (capacity)	s. capacitance <el.>		
electric cell	s. voltaic cell		
electric charge	s. charge <el.>		
electric charge density, charge density	[elektrische] Ladungsdichte f, elektrische Dichte f	electric image, electrical image, potential image, image pattern	Potentialgebirge n, Potentialbild n; Ladungsbild n, Ladungsrelief n, Ladungsmosaik n, lichtelektrisches Emissionsbild n
electric conductance, conductance	Leitwert m, elektrischer Leitwert		
electric conduction of metals, metallic conduction	metallische Leitung (Leitfähigkeit) f, elektrische Leitung der Metalle	electric image force	elektrische Bildkraft f
		electric impedance	s. impedance
electric constant	s. permittivity of free space	electric induction, inducing electrostatic charges	Influenzieren n, elektrische Verteilung f, elektrostatische Induktion f
electric coupling	s. capacitive coupling		
electric current	s. current <el.>	electric induction	s. electrostatic induction
electric current density	s. current density <el.>	electric induction	s. a. electric displacement
electric current density of electrons	elektrische Stromdichte f von Elektronen	electric influence	s. electrostatic induction
electric current flowing through a closed surface	Durchflutung f, elektrische Durchflutung	electric insulator	s. dielectric
		electric intensity, electric field intensity (strength), [intensity of] electric field; electric [field] vector, E-vector	elektrische Feldstärke f, Stärke f des elektrischen Feldes, elektrisches Spannungsgefälle n; elektrischer Feld[stärke]vektor m, Vektor m der elektrischen Feldstärke, elektrischer Vektor
electric current sheet	elektromagnetisches Blatt n		
electric differentiation	s. differentiation <of pulses>		
electric dipole moment	elektrisches Dipolmoment n		
electric dipole radiation	elektrische Dipolstrahlung f	electricity of atmospheric precipitation	Niederschlagselektrizität f
		electric leakage tester	Leckstrommesser m
electric discharge	elektrische Entladung f	electric length [of the line]	elektrische Länge f [der Leitung], wirksame Länge [der Leitung], wirksame Leitungslänge f
electric discharge [in a gas], discharge in (through) a gas, gaseous discharge, gas discharge	Gasentladung f, Entladung f in einem Gas		
		electric lens	s. electrostatic lens
		electric migration	s. electromigration
electric displacement, dielectric displacement, displacement, electric induction, elektostatic induction; displacement vector, electric displacement vector, electric flux density	[di]elektrische Verschiebung f, Verschiebung, [di]elektrische Verschiebungsdichte f, Verschiebungsdichte, [di]elektrische Verschiebungsflußdichte, Verschiebungsflußdichte, spezifische Verschiebung, elektr[ostat]ische Induktion f, elektrostatischer Induktionsstrom m, elektrische (spezifische) Erregung f, Erregung, [elektrische] Erregungsdichte f, elektrische Felddichte (Dichte) f, Dichte f des elektrischen Feldes; [di-] elektrischer Verschiebungsvektor m, Verschiebungsvektor, Vektor m der [di]elektrischen Verschiebung <El.>	electric multipole moment	elektrisches Multipolmoment n
		electric multipole radiation	elektrische Multipolstrahlung (Strahlung) f, transversale magnetische Strahlung, TM-Strahlung f
		electric multipole transition	elektrischer Multipolübergang m
		electric network reciprocity theorem	s. reciprocity theorem
		electric osmosis, electro[end]osmosis	Elektroosmose f, Elektroendosmose f
		"electric" output of the reactor <in MW(e)>	„elektrische" Leistung f des Reaktors <in MW$_{el}$>
		electric parameters of soil	Erdbodenkonstanten fpl
		electric polarizability, polarizability	Polarisierbarkeit f, elektrische Polarisierbarkeit
electric displacement vector	s. electric displacement	electric polarization	s. dielectric polarization
electric-dust figure	s. Lichtenberg figure	electric potential	s. potential
electric electron lens, electrostatic lens, electric lens	elektrostatische Linse f, elektrische Elektronenlinse (Linse) f	electric potential atmosphere gradient	s. potential gradient in the air
electric excitation	elektrische Erregung f, elektrische Anregung f	electric potential in the air, potential in the air	luftelektrisches Potential n

electric precipitation, electric separation; electrofiltration — elektrische Gasreinigung *f*, EGR-Verfahren *n*, Cottrell-Möller-Verfahren *n*; elektrische Gasentstaubung *f*; Elektrofiltration *f*

electric precipitator, electrostatic precipitator, electr[ostat]ic separator, electrostatic filter — elektrostatischer Abscheider *m*, Elektrofilter *n*

electric quadrupole moment — elektrisches Quadrupolmoment *n*

electric quadrupole radiation — elektrische Quadrupolstrahlung *f*

electric resistance — s. resistance <el.>
electric scalar potential, scalar electric potential — skalares elektrisches Potential *n*

electric screening — elektrische Abschirmung *f*
electric separation — s. electric precipitation
electric separator — s. electric precipitator
electric space — s. electric field
electric stimulation, excitation by electric currents, electric excitation <bio.> — elektrische Reizung *f* <Bio.>

electric stimulus — elektrischer Reiz *m*

electric strength — s. dielectric strength
electric stress tensor — elektrischer Spannungstensor *m*
electric supply — s. power supply <el.>
electric susceptibility — s. susceptibility <el.>
electric time constant — elektrische Zeitkonstante *f*

electric transition, E-type transition — elektrischer Übergang *m*, E-Übergang *m*
electric vector — elektrischer Vektor *m*

electric wind — elektrischer Wind *m*
electrifiability — Elektrisierbarkeit *f*
electrification, electrifying, electrization — Elektrisierung *f*
electrifier — s. influence machine
electrino — Elektrino *n*
electrization, electrification, electrifying — Elektrisierung *f*
electro-acoustic analogy — elektroakustische Analogie *f*

electro-acoustic coupling impedance — s. electro-acoustic force factor
electro-acoustic efficiency — elektroakustischer Wirkungsgrad *m*

electro-acoustic force factor, electro-acoustic coupling impedance — elektroakustischer Umwandlungsfaktor (Übertragungsfaktor) *m*
electro-acoustic four-terminal network — elektroakustischer Vierpol *m*
electro-acoustic transducer — elektroakustischer Wandler *m*

electroanalysis, electroanalytical method, electrochemical analysis — Elektroanalyse *f*, elektrochemische Analyse *f*
electrocaloric effect — elektrokalorischer Effekt *m*

electrocalorimeter — Elektrokalorimeter *n*
electrocapillarity — Elektrokapillarität *f*
electrocapillary current — Elektrokapillarstrom *m*
electrocapillary curve — Elektrokapillarkurve *f*

electrocapillary phenomenon — elektrokapillare Erscheinung *f*
electrocatalysis — Elektrokatalyse *f*
electrocautery — Elektrokaustik *f*, Heißkaustik *f*, Thermokaustik *f*

electrochemical analysis, electroanalysis, electroanalytical method — Elektroanalyse *f*, elektrochemische Analyse *f*
electrochemical cell — s. voltaic cell
electrochemical corrosion — s. galvanic corrosion
electrochemical double layer — s. dipole layer
electrochemical electromotive series — s. electrochemical series

electrochemical equivalent — elektrochemisches Äquivalent *n*
electrochemical passivity — elektrochemische Passivität *f*
electrochemical potential gradient — elektrochemisches Potentialgefälle *n*
electrochemical series, electromotive [force] series, electrochemical electromotive series, standard electrode-potential series, potential series — elektrochemische Spannungsreihe *f*, Redoxpotentialreihe *f*, Redoxpotentialkette *f*, Spannungsreihe *f*

electrochemical transducer — elektrochemischer Wandler *m*
electrochemical valency — elektrochemische Wertigkeit *f*
electrochromatography — Elektrochromatographie *f*
electrochromatophoresis — Elektrochromatophorese *f*

electrocoagulation — Elektrokoagulation *f*, Kaltkaustik *f*
electroconductibility — s. electric[al] conductivity <el. chem.>

electrocorticogram — Elektrokortikogramm *n*
electrocrystallization — s. electrolytic crystallization
electrocution — Elektrokution *f*; elektrische Tötung *f*

electrode <of the first, second, third kind> — Elektrode *f* <erster, zweiter, dritter Art>

electrodecantation — Elektrodekantierung *f*
electrode connection — Elektrodenanschluß *m*

electrode current averaging time <el.>, cut-off angle of current flow — Stromflußwinkel *m*, Unsymmetriewinkel *m*, Brennzeit *f* <El.>
electrode distance — s. electrode separation
electrode gap — s. electrode separation
electrodeless discharge — elektrodenlose Entladung *f*
electrodeless [ionic] tube, nullode — Sperröhre *f*, Nullode *f*
electrodeposition, electrolytic deposition — elektrolytische Abscheidung (Aufbringung) *f*
electrodeposition — s. a. electrogravimetry
electrode potential — s. relative electrode potential
electrode process — Elektrodenvorgang *m*
electrode reaction — Elektrodenreaktion *f*
electrode separation, [inter]electrode distance (gap), distance (gap) between electrodes, auxiliary (analytical) gap; vane distance — Elektrodenabstand *m*; Plattenabstand *m*

electrode tension — s. relative electrode potential
electrode-to-skin distance — Elektrode-Haut-Abstand *m*
electrodialysis, electro-ultrafiltration — Elektrodialyse *f*
electrodialyzer — Elektrodialysator *m*
electrodiffusion — Elektrodiffusion *f*
electrodiffusion coefficient — Elektrodiffusionskoeffizient *m*
electrodisintegration — Elektron-Kern-Reaktion *f*, elektroneninduzierte Kernreaktion *f*, Elektrozerfall *m*

electrodispersion — Elektrodispersion *f*

electrodissolution — s. electrolytic dissolution
electrodynamical analogy — elektrodynamische Analogie *f*
electrodynamical ohmmeter — s. cross-coil ohmmeter
electrodynamic balance, ampere (Ampère, current) balance — Stromwaage *f*

electrodynamic balance — s. a. electrodynamic instrument
electrodynamic constant — s. velocity of light in vacuum
electrodynamic force — s. Lorentz force

electrodynamic instrument, electrodynamometer, electrodynamic balance — elektrodynamisches Meßgerät (Instrument, Meßinstrument) n, Elektrodynamometer n, Dynamometer n; elektrodynamisches (dynamometrisches) Meßwerk n

electrodynamic loudspeaker [of Rice-Kellogg], Rice-Kellogg loudspeaker — elektrodynamischer Lautsprecher m [nach Rice-Kellogg], Lautsprecher nach Rice-Kellogg, Rice-Kelloggscher Lautsprecher

electrodynamic microphone — s. moving-coil microphone

electrodynamics in vacuo, vacuum electrodynamics — Vakuumelektrodynamik f

electrodynamic theodolite — elektrodynamischer Theodolit m

electrodynamic wattmeter, deflection wattmeter — elektrodynam[ometr]ischer Leistungsmesser m, elektrodynamisches Wattmeter n, dynamometrischer Leistungsmesser

electrodynamometer — s. electrodynamic instrument

electroencephalogram, encephalogram, E.E.G. — Elektr[o]enzephalogramm n, EEG

electro-encephalograph, encephalograph — Enzephalograph m, Elektroenzephalograph m, Hirnstromschreiber m

electroencephalography, encephalography, E.E.G. — Elektroenzephalographie f, Elektrenzephalographie f, Enzephalographie f

electroendosmosis, electroosmosis, electric osmosis — Elektroosmose f, Elektroendosmose f

electrofiltration — s. electric precipitation

electrofluidodynamic — s. electrohydrodynamic

electrogasdynamic generator, EGD generator, EGDG — elektrogasdynamischer Generator m, EGD-Generator m

electrography — Elektrographie f, Effluviographie f

electrogravimetric analysis (determination), **electrogravimetry**, electrodeposition — Elektrogravimetrie f, elektrogravimetrische Analyse (Bestimmung) f

electrohydraulic effect — elektrohydraulischer Effekt m

electrohydrodynamic, electrofluidodynamic, electroplasmadynamic, EHD, EPD — elektrohydrodynamisch, elektrofluidodynamisch, elektroplasmadynamisch, EHD, EPD

electrohydrodynamics — Elektrohydrodynamik f

electrokinesis, **electrokinetic effect**, **electrokinetic phenomenon** — elektrokinetische Erscheinung f, elektrokinetischer Effekt m, Elektrokinese f

electrokinetic potential, zeta[-]potential, ζ-potential — elektrokinetisches Potential n, Zeta-Potential n, ζ-Potential n, diffuser Anteil m der Galvani-Spannung

electrokinetics — Lehre f von den elektrischen Strömen, Elektrokinetik f

electrokymograph — Elektrokymograph m

electroluminescence — Elektrolumineszenz f

electroluminescence produced by collision excitation process — s. Destriau effect

electrolysate, product of electrolysis — Elktrolyseprodukt n

electrolysis bath — s. electrolytic bath

electrolysis in the dry way, electrolysis of fused materials (salts), fusion (igneous, smelting-flux) electrolysis — Schmelzelektrolyse f, Schmelzflußelektrolyse f

electrolyte balance — Elektrolytgleichgewicht n

electrolytically deposited — elektrolytisch aufgebracht, elektrolytisch abgeschieden

electrolytical solution pressure (tension) — s. solution pressure

electrolytic apparatus, electrolytic cell, electrolyzer — Elektrolyseeinrichtung f, Elektrolyseapparatur f, Elektrolyseapparat m, Elektrolyseanlage f, Elektrolyseur m

electrolytic bath (cell), ionic (electrolysis) bath, electrolytic tank (through) — Elektrolyse[n]bad n, elektrolytischer Trog m

electrolytic cell, electrolytic couple, pot — Elektrolysezelle f, Elektrolysiergefäß n, Elektrolysegefäß n, elektrolytische Zelle f

electrolytic cell — s. a. electrolytic apparatus

electrolytic chromatography — elektrolytische Chromatographie f

electrolytic conduction — elektrolytische Leitung f, Elektrolytleitung f

electrolytic conductivity — elektrolytische Leitfähigkeit f

electrolytic conductor — elektrolytischer Leiter m

electrolytic corrosion — s. galvanic corrosion

electrolytic couple — s. electrolytic cell

electrolytic crystallization, electrocrystallization — elektrolytische Kristallisation f, Elektrokristallisation f

electrolytic deposition — s. electrodeposition

electrolytic detector, Schloemilch detector — elektrolytischer Detektor m, Elektrolytdetektor m, Schloemilch-Zelle f

electrolytic dissociation constant — elektrolytische Dissoziationskonstante f

electrolytic dissolution, electrodissolution — elektrolytische Auflösung f

electrolytic gas — s. oxyhydrogen gas

electrolytic hygrometer — Leitfähigkeitshygrometer n

electrolytic interrupter, Wehnelt interrupter — elektrolytischer Unterbrecher m, Wehnelt-Unterbrecher m

electrolytic mean — s. direct-current mean

electrolytic polarization, polarization in an electrolyte; galvanic polarization — Polarisation f [bei elektrolytischen Vorgängen], elektrochemische (reversible; elcktrolytische, galvanische; chemische) Polarisation, Abscheidungspolarisation f

electrolytic polishing — s. electropolishing

electrolytic reduction, cathodic reduction — elektrolytische (katodische) Reduktion f

electrolytic refining of metals — Metallraffination f

electrolytic separation — s. electroparting

electrolytic solution — elektrolytische Lösung f, Elektrolytlösung f

electrolytic solution pressure (tension) — s. solution pressure

electrolytic tank (through) — s. electrolytic bath

electrolytic tautomerism — s. electromerism

electrolyzer — s. electrolytic apparatus

electromagnetic cascade — elektromagnetische Kaskade f

electromagnetic c.g.s. system — s. electromagnetic system of units

electromagnetic component <of cosmic rays>, electron-photon component — Elektron-Photon-Komponente f

electromagnetic constant — s. velocity of light in vacuum

electromagnetic coupling — s. inductive coupling

electromagnetic energy, energy of electromagnetic field — Energie f des elektromagnetischen Feldes, elektromagnetische Feldenergie (Energie; Energiedichte) f

electromagnetic field tensor — s. four-tensor of electromagnetic field

electromagnetic fluctuation of the vacuum — s. electromagnetic vacuum fluctuation

electromagnetic galvanometer, moving-iron galvanometer, soft-iron galvanometer — Weicheisengalvanometer n, Dreheisengalvanometer n, elektromagnetisches Galvanometer n

electromagnetic geon — s. geon

electromagnetic inducing — s. inducing <el.>

electromagnetic induction

electromagnetic instrument — s. moving-iron instrument

electromagnetic 214

electromagnetic interrupter — s. Wagner interrupter

electromagnetic lens, magnetic lens — magnetische Linse f (Elektronenlinse) f

electromagnetic levitation, levitation by [forces of electromagnetic] induction — Magnetschwebeverfahren n, elektromagnetische Levitation f, Schweben n im elektromagnetischen Feld, Magnetkissenverfahren n

electromagnetic mass — elektromagnetische Masse f

electromagnetic mass separator, mass (electromagnetic, isotope) separator — [elektromagnetischer] Massentrenner m, Massenseparator m, Isotopentrenner m, Isotopenseparator m

electromagnetic moment <of magnet, body>, magnetic moment — magnetisches Moment n, elektromagnetisches Moment <Magnet, Körper>

electromagnetic momentum — elektromagnetischer Impuls m

electromagnetic radiation associated with electronic transition — s. electron radiation

electromagnetics — Elektromagnetik f, Lehre f von den Wechselwirkungen elektrischer und magnetischer Felder

electromagnetic screen — elektromagnetischer Schirm m <gegen äußere Wechselfelder>

electromagnetic separation of isotopes — s. separation of isotopes by electromagnetic method

electromagnetic separator — s. electromagnetic mass separator

electromagnetic shape factor — elektromagnetischer Formfaktor m

electromagnetic stress [tensor] — elektromagnetischer Spannungstensor m

electromagnetic system of units, electromagnetic c.g.s. system, c.g.s.e.m.u. (cgs emu) system, emu (e.m.u.) system [of units] — elektromagnetisches CGS-System (Einheitensystem, Maßsystem) n

electromagnetic theory of light, Maxwell['s] theory of light — elektromagnetische Lichttheorie f [von Maxwell], elektromagnetische Theorie f des Lichts [von Maxwell], Maxwellsche Theorie des Lichts

electromagnetic transition — elektromagnetischer Übergang m

electromagnetic unit, e.m.u., emu — elektromagnetische [CGS-]Einheit f, emE

electromagnetic unit of charge — elektromagnetische Ladungseinheit f

electromagnetic vacuum fluctuation, electromagnetic fluctuation of the vacuum, vacuum fluctuation of the electromagnetic field, zero-point electromagnetic field fluctuation — Nullounktschwankung f der Feldstärke, Nullfeldschwankung f, Vakuumschwankung f der Feldstärke, Vakuumschwankung des elektromagnetischen Feldes

electromagnetic wave vector — elektromagnetischer Wellenvektor m

electromagnetism — Elektromagnetismus m

electromechanical analogy of the first kind — elektromechanische Analogie f erster Art, Kraft-Spannungs-Analogie f

electromechanical analogy of the second kind — elektromechanische Analogie f zweiter Art, Kraft-Strom-Analogie f

electromechanical coupling impedance — s. electromechanical force factor

electromechanical efficiency — mechanisch-elektrischer Wirkungsgrad m

electromechanical force factor — elektromechanischer Umwandlungsfaktor m

electromechanical four-terminal network — elektromechanischer Vierpol m

electromechanical transducer — elektromechanischer Schallwandler (Wandler) m

electromeric effect, E effect — Mesomerieeffekt m, mesomerer Substituenteneffekt m, M-Effekt m, elektromerer Effekt m, Elektromerieeffekt m, E-Effekt m

electromeric energy, enotropic energy — elektromere (enotrope) Energie f

electromerism, electrolytic tautomerism — Elektromerie f, Elektronentautomerie f

electromerism — s. a. gasionization

electrometer — Elektrometer n, Elektrizitätsmesser m, Elektrizitätswaage f

electrometer amplifier — Elektrometer[röhren]verstärker m

electrometer bridge — Elektrometerbrücke f

electrometer tube (valve) — Elektrometerröhre f

electrometric analysis (titration) — s. potentiometry

electromigration, electric migration — Elektromigration f, Wanderung f im elektrischen Feld, Festkörperelektrolyse f

electromotive force, off-load voltage, open circuit voltage, e.m.f. — [eingeprägte] elektromotorische Kraft f, EMK, Urspannung f, Leerlauf[klemmen]spannung f, Ruhespannung f, innere (chemische) Spannung f

electromotive force of the cell, e.m.f. of the cell, cell electromotive force, cell e.m.f., cell voltage — elektromotorische Kraft f des galvanischen Elements, EMK f des galvanischen Elements, Zellen-EMK f, Zellspannung f, Zellenspannung f

electromotive [force] series — s. electrochemical series

electromyogram, EMG — Elektromyogramm n

electromyography — Elektromyographie f

electron; negatron, negative electron, e⁻ — Elektron n; Negatron n, negatives Elektron, e⁻

electron absorption coefficient — Elektronenabsorptionskoeffizient m

electron accelerator — Elektronenbeschleuniger m, Beschleuniger m für Elektronen

electron acceptor, electron sink <semi., chem.> — Elektronenakzeptor m, Elektronenfänger m <Halb., Chem.>

electron affinity, electric affinity — Elektronenaffinität f, Elektroaffinität f, EA

electron affinity spectrum — Elektronenaffinitätsspektrum n

electronasty, galvanonasty — Elektronastie f, Galvanonastie f

electronation <el.chem.> — s. reduction <chem.>

electron atmosphere <astr.> — Elektronenatmosphäre f <Astr.>

electron atmosphere — s. a. electron cloud

electron attachment, electron trapping — Elektronenanlagerung f

electron background — Elektronenuntergrund m, Elektronenrauschen n

electron beam, electronic beam; electron ray; cathode ray (beam); cathode ray pencil — Elektronenstrahl m, Elektronenbündel n; Katodenstrahl m; Katodenstrahlbündel n

electron beam circuit, electron-beam processed circuit — mit Elektronenstrahl aufgetragene Schaltung f, im Elektronenstrahlverfahren hergestellte Schaltung

electron-beam compass — Elektronenstrahlkompaß m

electron beam curing — Elektronenstrahlhärtung f

electron-beam device, electron-ray device — Elektronenstrahlgerät n

electron-beam interference; electron interference — Elektronenstrahlinterferenz f; Elektroneninterferenz f

electron-beam magnetron — s. electron-wave magnetron

electron beam parametric amplifier — parametrischer Elektronenstrahlverstärker m

electron-beam processed circuit — s. electron beam circuit

electron-beam tube — s. cathode-ray tube

electron-bombardment conductivity — elektroneninduzierte Leitfähigkeit f

electron bombardment furnace	Elektronenstrahlofen *m*	electron-donor-acceptor complex	*s.* EDA complex
		electron dose	Elektronendosis *f*
electron bridge	Elektronenbrücke *f*	electron drift, electron migration	Elektronenwanderung *f*
electron capture [decay], EC	*s.* orbital-electron capture		
electron capturer, E capturer <nucl.>	E-Fänger *m*, Elektronenfänger *m* <Kern.>	electronegative	elektronegativ
		electronegativeness, electronegativity	Elektronegativität *f*
electron carrier	Elektronenübertrager *m*, Elektronenträger *m*	electron ejection, electron extraction <acc.>	Elektronenextraktion *f*, Elektronenherausführung *f*, Elektronenausschleusung *f*, Herausführung *f* des Elektronenstrahls, Herausführung der Elektronen
electron cloud, electronic cloud, cloud of electrons, electron[ic] atmosphere	Elektronenwolke *f*, Elektronenatmosphäre *f*		
electron cluster	Elektronenpaket *n*		
electron collection	Elektronenabsaugung *f*; Elektronensammlung *f*	electron-electron double resonance, EEDOR	Elektron-Elektron-Doppelresonanz *f*, EEDOR
electron collection chamber	Elektronensammelkammer *f*	electron-electron scattering, Møller scattering	Elektron-Elektron-Streuung *f*, Møller-Streuung *f*
electron collector	*s.* collector <of travelling wave tube>		
electron compound	Elektronenverbindung *f*, „electron compound" *f*	electron-electron umklapp process, electron-electron U-process	Elektron-Elektron-Umklappprozeß *m*
electron concentration	*s.* electron density		
electron conduction	*s.* n-type conduction	electron emission source, electron source	Elektronenquelle *f*
electron conductivity, n-type conductivity	Elektronenleitfähigkeit *f*, Überschußleitfähigkeit *f*, n-Typ-Leitfähigkeit *f*	electron emitter	Elektronenstrahler *m*
		electron energy band	*s.* energy band
electron conductor, electronic conductor, first class conductor	Elektronenleiter *m*, Leiter *m* erster Ordnung (Klasse), Leiter I. Ordnung	electron energy in volts	Voltenergie *f*, Voltmaß *n* der Energie
		electron equivalent	Elektronenäquivalent *n*
electron configuration	Elektronenkonfiguration *f*	electron escape; electron tunneling	Elektronendurchtunnelung *f*; Überwindung *f* des Potentialwalls durch ein Elektron
electron continuum, continuous electronic spectrum	Elektronenkontinuum *n*		
electron counter	*s.* electronic counter	electro[-]neutrality	Elektroneutralität *f*
electron-coupled oscillator, eco, e.c.o.	Eco[-Oszillator] *m*, elektronengekoppelter Oszillator *m*, Eko-Schaltung *f*	electron excess	Elektronenüberschuß *m*
		electron exchange	Elektronenaustausch *m*
electron coupling	*s.* electronic coupling	electron exchanger	Elektronenaustauscher *m*
electron coupling	*s. a.* electron-pair bond		
electron crystal	Elektronenkristall *m*	electron extraction	*s.* electron ejection <acc.>
electron current	*s.* electronic current	electron faster than light	*s.* electron having a velocity faster than light
electron cyclotron	Elektronenzyklotron *n*		
electron cyclotron resonance, ECR	Elektronenzyklotronresonanz *f*	electron filter	Elektronenfilter *n*
electron cyclotron frequency, cyclotron frequency of the electron	Zyklotronfrequenz *f* des Elektrons, Zyklotronelektronenresonanzfrequenz *f*	electron fluid	Elektronenflüssigkeit *f*, Elektronenfluidum *n*
		electron flux, electronic flux	Elektronenfluß *m*
electron defect	*s.* electronic defect	electron friction	Elektronenreibung *f*
electron deficit	Elektronenunterschuß *m*, Elektronendefizit *n*, Elektronenmangel *m*	electron gas	Elektronengas *n*
		electron gun	Elektronenkanone *f*, Elektronenstrahl-Erzeugungssystem *n*, Strahl[erzeugungs]system *n*, Strahlerzeuger *m*; Elektronenschleuder *f*; Elektronenspritze *f* <Leckprüfgerät>
electron delivery	Elektronenabgabe *f*		
electron density; electron concentration	Elektronendichte *f*; Elektronenkonzentration *f*; Elektronenbelegung *f*		
electron detachment, electron liberation, electron removal, electron release	Elektronenablösung *f*, Elektronenauslösung *f*, Elektronenaustritt *m*, Elektronenabspaltung *f*, Elektronenbefreiung *f*	electron having a velocity faster than light	Überlichtelektron *n*
		electron heat conductivity, heat conductivity due to the electrons	elektronische (Elektronenanteil *m* der) Wärmeleitfähigkeit *f*
electron device	*s.* electronic device	electron hole	*s.* positive hole
electron diffraction apparatus, electron diffractometer	Elektronenbeugungsgerät *n*	electron-hole acoustical wave	Elektron-Defektelektron-Schallwelle *f*, Elektron-Loch-Schallwelle *f*
electron diffraction camera, camera for electron diffraction	Elektronenbeugungskamera *f*, Kamera *f* für Elektronenbeugungsaufnahmen	electron-hole interaction	Elektron-Loch-Wechselwirkung *f*, Elektron-Defektelektron-Wechselwirkung *f*
electron diffraction halo	Elektronenbeugungshalo *m*		
electron diffraction pattern, electronogram	Elektronenbeugungsbild *n*, Elektronenbeugungsaufnahme *f*	electron-hole pair, exciton, hole-electron pair	Exciton *n*, Exziton *n*, Elektron-Defektelektron-Paar *n*
electron diffraction spectrum	Elektronenbeugungsspektrum *n*	electron-hole pair generation (production), carrier pair generation	Elektron-Loch-Paarbildung *f*, Elektron-Defektelektron-Paarbildung *f*, Trägerpaargeneration *f*, Trägerpaarbildung *f*, Ladungsträgerpaargeneration *f*, Ladungsträgerpaarbildung *f*
electron diffractometer	*s.* electron diffraction apparatus		
electron discharge tube	Elektronenentladungsrohr *n*		
electron distribution function	Elektronenverteilungsfunktion *f*	electron-hole recombination	Elektron-Defektelektron-Rekombination *f*, Elektron-Loch-Rekombination *f*
electron donor, electron source, electronogen	Elektronendonator *m*, elektronischer Donator *m*, Elektronenspender *m*		

electronic

electronic aberration, electron-optical aberration	elektronischer Bildfehler *m*, elektronenoptische Aberration *f*
electronic atmosphere	s. electron atmosphere
electronic atomic heat, electronic heat	Elektronenwärme *f*, elektronische Atomwärme *f*
electronic band	Elektronen[sprung]bande *f*
electronic band of ozone, ozone band, absorption band of ozone	Ozonbande *f*
electronic band spectrum, electronic spectrum	Elektronenspektrum *n*, Elektronenbandenspektrum *n*
electronic beam	s. electron beam
electronic-beam current	Elektronenstrahlstrom *m*, Elektronenstrahlstromstärke *f*
electronic Bohr magneton	s. Bohr magneton
electronic charge, charge of the electron, elementary quantum of electricity, unit charge, elementary charge	[elektrische] Elementarladung *f*, Ladung *f* des Elektrons, Elektronenladung *f*, elektrisches Elementarquantum *n*, Elementarquantum *n* der Elektrizität
electronic charge-to-mass ratio	s. charge-to-mass ratio of the electron
electronic clock	Elektronenuhr *f*
electronic cloud	s. electron cloud
electronic compass	Elektronenkompaß *m*
electronic conduction	s. n-type conduction
electronic conductor	s. electron conductor
electronic counter	s. counting tube
electronic counting decade, counting decade	Zähldekade *f*, elektronische Zähldekade
electronic coupling, electron (beam) coupling	elektronische Ankopplung *f*, Elektronenkopplung *f*
electronic current, electron current	Elektronenstrom *m*; Glühkatodenstrom *m*
electronic defect	Elektronenfehlstelle *f*; Elektronenstörstelle *f*
electronic device, electron device	Elektronengerät *n*
electronic eigenfunction	Elektroneneigenfunktion *f*
electronic energy <of molecule>	Elektronenenergie *f* <Molekül>
electronic equidensity	elektronische Äquidensite *f*
electronic equilibrium	Elektronengleichgewicht *n*
electronic flash	s. electronic-flash lamp
electronic-flash lamp, electronic flash, flash tube, speedlight, high-voltage flash	Elektronenblitzentladungslampe *f*, Lichtblitzentladungslampe *f*, „flash tube" *f*, Blitzröhre *f*, Röhrenblitz *m*, Elektronenblitzgerät *n*, Hochspannungsblitzgerät *n*, Hochspannungsblitz *m*, Röhrenblitzgerät *n*, Röhrenblitzer *m*
electronic flux, electron flux	Elektronenfluß *m*
electronic formula, octet (polarity) formula	Elektronenformel *f*
electronic heat, electronic atomic heat	Elektronenwärme *f*, elektronische Atomwärme *f*
electronic image, electronic picture; cathode-ray tube display	Elektronenbild *n*
electronic image reproduction device	[elektronenoptisches] Abbildungsgerät *n*
electronic inductivity	s. permittivity <of the material>
electronic lens	s. electron lens
electronic masking	elektronisches Frequenzfilterverfahren *n*; Logetronographie *f*
electronic mass, mass of the electron, electron mass	Elektronenmasse *f*, Masse *f* des Elektrons
electronic mobility, mobility of electrons	Elektronenbeweglichkeit *f*
electronic molecular state, electronic state of the molecule	Elektronenzustand *m* des Moleküls
electronic noise factor	elektronische Rauschzahl *f*, elektronischer Rauschfaktor *m*
electronic optics	s. electron optics
electronic orbit, electron orbit	Elektronen[kreis]bahn *f*
electronic oscillation	s. electron oscillation
electronic partition function	Elektronenzustandssumme *f*
electronic picture	s. electronic image
electronic picture reproducing tube	s. picture tube
electronic polarizability, electron polarizability	elektronische Polarisierbarkeit *f*, Elektronen[verschiebungs]polarisierbarkeit *f*, Elektronenanteil *m* der Polarisierbarkeit
electronic polarization	elektronische Polarisation *f*, Elektronenverschiebungspolarisation *f*, Elektronenanteil *m* der dielektrischen Verschiebungspolarisation
electronic potentiometer, automatic potentiometer with electronic circuit	[selbsttätiger] Kompensator *m* mit elektronischem Verstärker, elektronisches Potentiometer *n*, Elektronenpotentiometer *n*, elektronische Meßbrücke *f*
electronic potentiometer recorder, recording electronic potentiometer	elektronischer Kompensograph *m*, Kompensationsschreiber *m* mit elektronischem Verstärker
electronic prism, electron-optical prism	Elektronenprisma *n*, elektronenoptisches Prisma *n*
electronic Raman effect, electronic Raman scattering	elektronischer Raman-Effekt *m*, elektronische Raman-Streuung *f*
electronic resonance	Elektronenresonanz *f*
electronics, radio-frequency unit, R.F. unit, radioelectronics	Hochfrequenzteil *m*, HF-Teil *m*, Elektronikteil *m*
electronic semiconductor	Elektronenhalbleiter *m*, elektronischer Halbleiter *m*
electronic shell, electron shell	Elektronenschale *f*
electronic shell	s. a. atomic electron shell
electronic shower	Elektronenschauer *m*
electronic specific heat	spezifische Elektronenwärme *f*, elektronische spezifische Wärme *f*
electronic spectrum, electronic band spectrum	Elektronenspektrum *n*, Elektronenbandenspektrum *n*
electronic state of the molecule, electronic molecular state	Elektronenzustand *m* des Moleküls
electronic telescope	Elektronenfernrohr *n*
electronic timer, timer, timing pulse generator	elektronischer Zeitgeber (Zeitschalter) *m*
electronic transition, electron transition (jump)	Elektronenübergang *m*, Elektronensprung *m*
electronic trap, electron trap	Elektronenhaftstelle *f*, Elektronenhaftterm *m*; Elektronenfalle *f*, Elektronentrap *m*
electronic valve	s. thermionic valve
electronic work function	s. work function
electron image tube	s. image[-]converter tube
electron impact ion source	Elektronenstoßionenquelle *f*
electron impact spectrum	Elektronenstoßspektrum *n*
electron-impact value of ionization potential, vertical ionization potential	vertikale Ionisierungsspannung *f*
electron injection	Elektroneneinschuß *m*, Elektroneninjektion *f*, Elektroneneinschleusung *f*

electron injector	Elektroneninjektor m, Elektroneneinschußsystem n	electron-optical aberration, electronic aberration	elektronischer Bildfehler m, elektronenoptische Aberration f
electron interchange	Elektronenaustausch m	electron-optical conversion of image	elektronenoptische Bild[um]wandlung f
electron interference; electron-beam interference	Elektronenstrahlinterferenz f; Elektroneninterferenz f	electron-optical image	elektronenoptische Abbildung f, elektronenoptisches Bild n
electron interferometer	Elektroneninterferometer n	electron-optical prism	s. electronic prism
electron interferometry	s. interferometry of electrons	electron-optical refraction law	elektronenoptisches Brechungsgesetz n
electron-ion collision	Elektron-Ion-Stoß m	electron optics, electronic optics	Elektronenoptik f
electron-ion Hamiltonian	Elektron-Ion-Hamilton-Operator m	electron orbit	s. electronic orbit
electron ionization	Elektronenionisation f	electron oscillation, electronic oscillation	Elektronenschwingung f
electron-ion recombination	Elektron-Ion-Rekombination f	electron oscillograph (oscilloscope), cathode-ray oscillograph (oscilloscope)	Elektronenstrahloszillograph m, Katodenstrahloszillograph m
electron isomerism	Elektronenisomerie f		
electron jump	s. electronic transition		
electron-lattice interaction	Elektron-Gitter-Wechselwirkung f	electron pair	s. positron-electron pair <nucl.>
electron lens, electronic lens	Elektronenlinse f, elektronenoptische Linse f	electron-pair bond	s. atomic bond
electron liberation	s. electron detachment	electron-pair hunting	Elektronenpaarpendelung f
electron linac, electron linear accelerator	Linearbeschleuniger m für Elektronen, Elektronenlinearbeschleuniger m	electron pairing, Cooper pairing	Elektronenpaarung f, Paarung f von Elektronen
electron line density	lineare Elektronendichte f, Linienelektronendichte f; Elektronenbelegung f	electron paramagnetic resonance	s. electron spin resonance
		electron paramagnetic resonance spectroscopy	s. electron spin resonance spectroscopy
electron luminescence	s. cathodoluminescence	electron-permeable, electron-transmitting	elektronendurchlässig
electron magnetic moment, magnetic moment of the electron	magnetisches Moment n des Elektrons	electron-phonon interaction energy	Elektron-Phonom-Wechselwirkungsenergie f
electron magnetic resonance	s. electron spin resonance		
electron magnetic resonance spectroscopy	s. electron spin resonance spectroscopy	electron-phonon umklapp process, electron-phonon U-process	Elektron-Phonon-Umklappprozeß m
electron mass	s. electronic mass	electron-photon component, electromagnetic component <of cosmic rays>	Elektron-Photon-Komponente f <kosmische Strahlung>
electron-mechanical transducer	s. mechanotron		
electron microgram	s. electron micrograph		
electron micrograph; electron microgram	elektronenmikroskopische Aufnahme f, elektronenmikroskopisches Bild n; Elektronenmikrogramm n	electron plasma	Elektronenplasma n
		electron plasma frequency	s. Langmuir frequency
electron microprobe analysis	s. electron-probe microanalysis	electron plasma oscillation	Elektronenplasmaschwingung f
electron microscope, ultramicroscope	Elektronen[über]mikroskop n, Übermikroskop n	electron polarizability	s. electronic polarizability
		electron-positron annihilation	s. electron-positron pair annihilation
electron-microscopical, ultramicroscopical, by electron microscopy	elektronenmikroskopisch, übermikroskopisch	electron-positron field	Elektron-Positron-Feld n
		electron-positron pair	s. positron-electron pair <nucl.>
electron microscopy	Elektronen[über]mikroskopie f, Übermikroskopie f	electron-positron pair annihilation, electron-positron annihilation, positron-electron annihilation	Elektron-Positron-Paarvernichtung f, Paarvernichtung f von Elektronen, Elektronenpaarvernichtung f, Zerstrahlung f des Elektron-Positron-Paares
electron microscopy / by	s. electron-microscopical		
electron microscopy by reflection	s. reflection electron microscopy		
electron migration, electron drift	Elektronenwanderung f		
electron mirror	s. dynode	electron-positron pair creation	Elektron-Positron-Paarbildung f, Elektronenpaarbildung f, Paarung f von Elektronen
electron-mirror image converter	Elektronenspiegelbildwandler m		
electron mirror telescope	Elektronenspiegelteleskop n	electron-positron scattering, Bhabha scattering	Elektron-Positron-Streuung f, Bhabha-Streuung f
electron multiplication	Elektronenvervielfachung f		
electron multiplier [tube]	s. photomultiplier	electron-positron vacuum	Elektron-Positron-Vakuum n, Elektronen-Positronen-Vakuum n
electron neutrino	s. neutrino in beta decay		
electron-neutrino field	Elektron-Neutrino-Feld n	electron pressure	Elektronendruck m
electron-neutron interaction	Elektron-Neutron-Wechselwirkung f	electron-probe [micro-] analysis, electron microprobe analysis	Elektronenstrahl-Mikroanalyse f
electron nuclear double resonance [technique]	s. ENDOR		
electron octet	Elektronenoktett n		
electron of internal conversion, [internal] conversion electron	Konversionselektron n, Elektron n der inneren Konversion (Umwandlung)	electron-probe microanalyzer, microanalyzer	Mikro[elektronen]sonde f, [Elektronenstrahl-] Mikroanalysator m
		electron pyrolysis	Elektronenbrennen n
electronogen	s. electron donor	electron radiation, electromagnetic radiation associated with electronic transition	Elektronenstrahlung f, elektromagnetische Strahlung f des Atoms bei Elektronenübergängen
electronogram	s. electron diffraction pattern		
electronography	Elektronenbeugungsuntersuchung f, Elektronographie f		
		electron radius	s. classical electron radius

electron 218

electron ray	s. electron beam	electron theory of valence	Elektronentheorie f der Valenz
electron-ray device	s. electron-beam device	electron-to-atom ratio, valence electron concentration	Valenzelektronenkonzentration f, Valenzelektronendichte f
electron-ray tube	s. cathode-ray tube		
electron release (removal)	s. electron detachment		
electron resonance breakdown, multipact[or] effect	Elektronenresonanzdurchschlag m, Elektronenresonanzdurchbruch m	electron transference number	Elektronenüberführungszahl f
electron resonance capture	Resonanzelektroneneinfang m	electron transfer reaction	Elektronentransferreaktion f, Elektronenüberführungsreaktion f
electron rest mass	Ruhemasse f des Elektrons, Elektronenruhmasse f	electron-transfer spectrum	Elektronenüberführungsspektrum n, Elektronentransferspektrum n, „electron-transfer"-Spektrum n
electron-scan[ning] microscope	s. scanning microscope		
electron scattering cross-section, cross-section for electron scattering	Elektronenstreuquerschnitt m		
		electron transition	s. electronic transition
		electron-transmitting, electron-permeable	elektronendurchlässig
electron screening, screening of nucleus, screening effect <nucl.>	Kernabschirmung f, Abschirmung f der Kernladung (des Atomkerns), atomare Abschirmung, Abschirm[ungs]wirkung f <Kern.>	electron trap, electronic trap	Elektronenhaftstelle f, Elektronenhaftterm m; Elektronenfalle f, Elektronentrap m
		electron trapped at the F-centre	Fehlstellenelektron n, F-Elektron n
electron-seeking, electrophilic, cationoid	elektrophil, elektronensuchend, elektronenfreundlich, kationoid	electron trapping, electron attachment	Elektronenanlagerung f
electron shell, electronic shell	Elektronenschale f	electron tube	s. thermionic valve
electron shell	s. a. atomic electron shell	electron tunneling; electron escape	Elektronendurchtunnelung f; Überwindung f des Potentialwalls durch ein Elektron
electron-shell structure; Pauli vacancy principle	Schalenstruktur f (Schalenbau m) der Elektronen im Atom, Schalenstruktur des Atoms, Elektronenschalenstruktur f; Schalenbau (Schalenstruktur) der Elektronenhülle, Hüllenstruktur f des Atoms		
		electron vacancy	s. positive hole
		electron valve	s. thermionic valve
		electron velocity in volts	Voltgeschwindigkeit f, Voltmaß n der Geschwindigkeit
electron sink <semi., chem.>, electron acceptor	Elektronenakzeptor m, Elektronenfänger m <Halb., Chem.>	electron[-] volt, eV	Elektronenvolt n, eV
		electron[-] voltaic effect	Elektron-Volta-Effekt m
electron site	Elektronenplatz m, Elektronenstelle f	electron wave	Elektronenwelle f
		electron wave field	Elektronenwellenfeld n
electron sound velocity	Elektronenschallgeschwindigkeit f	electron wave function	Elektronenwellenfunktion f, Elektronenzustandsfunktion f
electron source, electron emission source	Elektronenquelle f		
electron source	s. a. electron donor	electron wavelength	Elektronenwellenlänge f, De-Broglie-Wellenlänge f des Elektrons
electron specific charge	s. charge-to-mass ratio of the electron		
electron spectroscopy	Elektronoskopie f, Elektronenspektroskopie f	electron-wave magnetron, electron-beam magnetron	Elektronenwellen-Magnetfeldröhre f, Elektronenwellenmagnetron n, Elektronenstrahlmagnetron n
electron spectroscopy for chemical analysis	s. ESCA		
electron spin	Elektronenspin m, Elektronendrall m		
electron spin operator	Elektronenspinoperator m	electron wave number	Elektron[en]wellenzahl f
electron spin resonance, electron paramagnetic resonance, electron magnetic resonance, EPR, E.P.R., ESR, E.S.R.	Elektronenspinresonanz f, [para]magnetische Elektronenresonanz f, elektronen[para]magnetische Resonanz f, ESR, EPR, PR	electron[-] wave tube, double stream amplifier	Elektronenwellenröhre f
		electro-optic[al] [Kerr] effect	s. Kerr effect
		electrooptics	Elektrooptik f
		electroosmosis, electroendosmosis, electric osmosis	Elektroosmose f, Elektroendosmose f
electron spin resonance spectroscopy, electron paramagnetic resonance spectroscopy, electron magnetic resonance spectroscopy, EPR technique, ESR technique	Elektronen[spin]resonanzspektroskopie f, paramagnetische Resonanzspektroskopie f, Methode f der [para]magnetischen Elektronenresonanz, ESR-Methode f, ESR-Technik f, PR-Methode f, PR-Technik f	electroosmotic force	elektroosmotische Kraft f
		electroosmotic process (technique)	Osmoseverfahren n
		electroparting, electrolytic separation	elektrolytische Trennung f
		electropherogram	Elektropherogramm n, Pherogramm n
		electropherography, ionography, pherography	Elektropherographie f, Pherographie f, Trägerelektrophorese f
electron state	Elektronenzustand m		
electron stereomicroscope, stereo[scopic] electron microscope	Stereoelektronenmikroskop n [nach Kinder]	electrophilic, electron-seeking, cationoid	elektrophil, elektronensuchend, elektronenfreundlich, kationoid
electron stereomicroscopy, stereo[scopic] electron microscopy	Stereoelektronenmikroskopie f	electrophilic reactivity	Elektrophilität f, Elektrophilie f
electron stopping power	Elektronenbremsvermögen n	electrophilic rearrangement, electrophilic transposition, cationoid rearrangement (transposition)	elektrophile Umlagerung f, kationoide Umlagerung
electron swarm, swarm of electrons	Elektronenschwarm m		
electron synchrotron	Elektronensynchrotron n, Stoßelektronenschleuder f	electrophilic series	Elektrophilitätsreihe f, Elektrophiliereihe f
electron temperature	Elektronentemperatur f	electrophilic substitution, cationoid substitution	elektrophile (kationoide) Substitution f
electron term	Elektronenterm m	electrophilic transposition	s. electrophilic rearrangement
electron theory <of metals>	Elektronentheorie f <der Metalle>	electrophonic effect	elektrophonischer Effekt m

electrophoresis — [freie] Elektrophorese f
electrophoresis cell (chamber) — Elektrophoresezelle f, elektrophoretische Kammer f
electrophoretic currents — elektrophoretische Ströme mpl
electrophoretic effect — elektrophoretischer (kataphoretischer, longitudinaler) Effekt m
electrophoretic mobility — elektrophoretische Beweglichkeit f
electrophoretic potential — elektrophoretisches Potential n, elektrophoretische Spannung f
electrophorus — Elektrophor m
electrophotoconductography — Elektrophotokonduktographie f, Photoleitfähigkeitselektrophotographie f
electrophotography — Elektrophotographie f
electrophotoluminescence, photoelectroluminescence — Elektrophotolumineszenz f
electrophotoluminescence — s. a. electrical stimulation
electrophotophoresis — Elektrophotophorese f
electrophysics — Elektrizitätslehre f, Elektrik f, Elektrophysik f
electroplasmadynamic — s. electrohydrodynamic
electropolishing, electrolytic polishing — Elektropolierung f, elektrolytische Polierung f, elektrolytisches Polieren n, Elektropolieren n

electropositive — elektropositiv
electropositivity — Elektropositivität f
electroproduction [of elementary particles] — Elektroerzeugung f
electroreflectance spectrum — Elektro[nen]reflexionsspektrum n
electroretinogram, E.R.G. — Elektroretinogramm n
electro-saltatory transmission [of nerve impulse] — s. saltatory conduction
electroscope — Elektroskop n <ungeeichtes Elektrometer>
electrosol — Elektrosol n
electrostatic acceleration — elektrostatische Beschleunigung f, Spannungsbeschleunigung f, Beschleunigung durch Spannungsfelder, Wirbelbeschleunigung f
electrostatic accelerator — elektrostatischer Beschleuniger m, Spannungsbeschleuniger m, Wirbelbeschleuniger m
electrostatic attraction — elektrostatische Anziehung f
electrostatic biprism — elektrostatisches Biprisma n [nach Möllenstedt]
electrostatic bond — s. electrovalency bond
electrostatic c.g.s. system — s. electrostatic system of units
electrostatic charge, static charge, static electric charge, static — statische Ladung f, elektrostatische Ladung, elektrostatische Aufladung f
electrostatic coupling — s. electric coupling
electrostatic electron optics — elektr[ostat]ische Elektronenoptik f
electrostatic energy, energy of electrostatic field — Energie f des elektrostatischen Feldes, elektrostatische Energie
electrostatic field — elektrostatisches Feld n, statisches [elektrisches] Feld, Influenzfeld n
electrostatic filter — s. electric precipitator
electrostatic force density (per unit volume) — elektrostatische Kraftdichte f

electrostatic generator, statitron — elektrostatischer Generator m
electrostatic generator — s. a. influence machine
electrostatic image — elektrische Bildladung f, elektrostatisches Bild n

electrostatic induction, electric induction, electric influence — Influenz f, elektrische Influenz (Induktion) f, Influenzerscheinung f, elektrostatische Induktion, elektrische Verteilung f
electrostatic induction — s. a. electric displacement
electrostatic ion microscope, field-ion microscope — Feldionenmikroskop n, Felddesorptionsmikroskop n, Protonenmikroskop n
electrostatic lens, electric lens, electric electron lens — elektrostatische Linse f, elektrische Elektronenlinse (Linse) f
electrostatic machine — s. influence machine
electrostatic potential barrier — elektrostatischer Potentialwall m
electrostatic precipitator — s. electric precipitator
electrostatic pressure — elektrostatischer Druck m
electrostatic radius, proton radius <of nucleus> — elektrostatischer Radius m, Protonenradius m
electrostatic screen — elektrostatische Abschirmung f, elektrostatischer Schirm m
electrostatic screening (shielding) — elektrostatische Abschirmung f
electrostatic separator — s. electric precipitator
electrostatic storage tube, storage tube, memory tube — Speicherröhre f, Elektronenstrahl-Speicherröhre f

electrostatic system of units, electrostatic c.g.s. system, c.g.s.e.s.u. (cgs esu) system, esu (e.s.u.) system [of units] — elektrostatisches CGS-System (Einheitensystem, Maßsystem) n
electrostatic unit, e.s.u., esu — elektrostatische [CGS-]Einheit f, esE, el.stat. Einheit
electrostatic unit of charge — elektrostatische Ladungseinheit f, ESL
electrostatic unit of Duane, E unit [of Duane] — E-Einheit f [nach Duane], elektrostatische Einheit f [nach Duane]
electrostatic unit of electric tension, electrostatic unit of potential — elektrostatische Spannungseinheit (Potentialeinheit) f, cmgs-Potentialeinheit f, ESP
electrostatic valence — s. ionic valence
electrostatic valency — s. ionic valence
electrostatic voltmeter — [elektro]statisches Voltmeter n, [elektro]statischer Spannungsmesser m
electrostatic wave, Langmuir wave — elektrostatische (Langmuirsche) Welle f, Langmuir-Welle f
electrostenolysis — Elektrostenolyse f
electrostriction, converse piezoelectric effect, inverse piezoelectricity (pizoelectric effect) — Elektrostriktion f, reziproker piezoelektrischer Effekt m, umgekehrter Piezoeffekt m
electrostrictive transducer — elektrostriktiver Wandler m
electrotachyscope — Anschützscher Schnellseher m, Elektrotachyskop n
electrothermal analogy — elektrothermische Analogie f
electrothermal relay — s. thermal relay
electrothermal series, thermoelectric [electromotive] series, thermoelectric potential series — thermoelektrische Spannungsreihe f
electrothermic instrument — s. thermal instrument
electrothermics — Elektrothermie f
electrothermoluminescence — Elektrothermolumineszenz f
electrotonic force — elektrotonische Kraft f
electrotonus — Elektrotonus m
electrotropism, galvanotropism — Elektrotropismus m, Galvanotropismus m
electro-ultrafiltration, electrodialysis — Elektrodialyse f
electrovalence, electrovalency — s. ionic valence
electrovalency — s. a. charge number of the ion

electrovalency bond, electrovalent bond, [hetero]polar bond, ion[ic] bond, electrostatic (ionogenic, ion-dipole) bond, ionic (ion, heteropolar) binding, ionic link[age], heteropolar linkage	Ionenbeziehung *f*, Ionenbindung *f*, [hetero]polare Bindung *f*, elektrovalente Bindung, elektrostatische Bindung, ionogene Bindung, ionare Bindung, Elektrovalenzbindung *f*	element of climate element of composite symmetry	s. meteorological element zusammengesetzte Deckoperation *f*, Element *n* der zusammengesetzten Symmetrie
electroviscous effect	elektroviskoser Effekt *m*	element of diffraction grating	s. element of grating
		element of extension	s. element of volume
		element of grating, element of diffraction grating	Gitterelement *n* <Opt.>
element; cell, cubicle; cellule <of wing>	Zelle *f*	element of length, differential of arc, line[ar] element	Bogenelement *n*, Bogendifferential *n*, Linienelement *n*
element, link, section, segment, member <techn., el.>	Glied *n* <Techn., El.>		
element	s. a. component <of construction>	element of path, path element	Wegelement *n*
element <of the electrical circuit>	s. a. circuit element	element of slip, slip element, element of translation	Gleitelement *n*, Translationselement *n*
elemental; nascent <chem.>	atomar, elementar; naszierend <Chem.>	element of space symmetry, space symmetry element	Raumsymmetrieelement *n*
elementary act	s. event <nucl.>	element of the circuit	s. circuit element
elementary analysis, ultimate analysis	Elementaranalyse *f*	element of the orbit, orbital element	Bahnelement *n*
elementary antenna	Elementarantenne *f*; Elementarstrahler *m*	element of translation, slip element, element of slip	Gleitelement *n*, Translationselement *n*
elementary cell	s. unit cell <cryst.>		
elementary charge	s. electronic charge	element of turbulence, turbulence element; bubble of turbulence	Turbulenzelement *n*; Turbulenzballen *m*, Turbulenzkörper *m*, Turbulenzpfropfen *m*; Flüssigkeitsballen *m* [bei turbulenter Strömung]
elementary circulation	Elementarströmung *f*		
elementary complex	Elementkomplex *m*		
elementary cone	Elementarkegel *m*		
elementary crystal	Elementkristall *m*		
elementary current	s. molecular current		
elementary divisor	Elementarteiler *m*	element of volume, volume (space) element, element of extension	Volum[en]element *n*, Raumelement *n*
elementary event	s. event <nucl.>		
elementary geodesy, geodesy, inferior geodesy	Geodäsie *f*, niedere Geodäsie, Vermessungskunde *f*		
elementary geometry, solid [analytic] geometry	Elementargeometrie *f*	element of vortex, vortex element, elementary vortex	Wirbelelement *n*, Elementarwirbel *m*
elementary hypervolume	s. hypervolume element	element semiconductor	s. simple semiconductor
elementary intersection jog	Elementarsprung *m* <Platzwechsel>	element specific activity, gram[me]-element specific activity	spezifische Aktivität *f* des Elements
elementary lattice	Elementargitter *n*	element synthesis	s. nucleogenesis
elementary lattice cell	s. unit cell <cryst.>	elevated fog	Hochnebel *m*; gestiegener Nebel *m*
elementary length	Elementarlänge *f*, kleinste (elementare) Länge *f*		
elementary light wave	s. elementary wave	elevation, angle of elevation, angle of departure	Elevationswinkel *m*, Elevation *f*, Höhenwinkel *m*, Erhebungswinkel *m*, Erhebung *f*
elementary magnet; molecular magnet	Elementarmagnet *m*; Molekularmagnet *m*		
elementary particle, fundamental particle	Elementarteilchen *n*		
elementary particles of Sakata	s. Sakata particles	elevation <of star> <astr.>, altitude	Höhe *f*, Gestirnshöhe *f*, Sternhöhe *f* <Astr.>
		elevation <hydr.>	s. a. elevation
elementary pencil	Elementarbündel *n*	elevation	s. a. capillary rise
		elevation	s. a. increase
elementary process	infinitesimaler Prozeß *m*	elevation above ground, height (vertical distance) above ground	Höhe *f* über Grund, Höhe über dem Erdboden (Boden)
elementary process <nucl.>	Elementarprozeß *m* <Kern.>		
elementary process <phot.>	[photographischer] Elementarprozeß *m* <Phot.>	elevation above sea level	s. height above sea level
		elevation head, potential (geodesic) head, elevation <hydr.>	Ortshöhe *f* <Hydr.>
elementary quantum of action	s. Planck['s] constant		
elementary quantum of electricity	s. electronic charge	elevation of pressure, pressure rise (increase), increase of pressure	Druckerhöhung *f*, Drucksteigerung *f*; Druckanstieg *m*
elementary semiconductor	s. simple semiconductor	elevation of the boiling point, rising (raising) of the boiling point, boiling point elevation (rising, raising)	Siedepunktserhöhung *f*
elementary sone	einfacher Klang *m*		
elementary source	Elementarquelle *f*		
elementary time	Elementarzeit *f*, kleinste Zeit *f*		
elementary tone	einfacher Ton *m*	eleven-year cycle, eleven-year period	elfjährige Periode *f*
elementary unit	s. fundamental unit		
elementary vortex	s. element of vortex	eliminant, resultant <math.>	Resultierende *f*, Resultante *f* <Math.>
elementary wave, elementary light wave, secondary wave, secondary disturbance, S-wave, Huyghens wavelet, ray velocity surface	Elementarwelle *f*, Sekundärwelle *f*, Huygenssche Elementarwelle, sekundäre Kugelwelle *f*, sekundäre Welle *f*, S-Welle *f*	eliminate by transformation	s. remove by transformation
		elimination, filtering [out], filtration, selection <el.>	Siebung *f*, Sieben *n*, Aussiebung *f*, Filterung *f* <El.>
elementary work	Elementararbeit *f*, elementare (infinitesimale) Arbeit *f*	elimination cleavage	s. fragmentation [reaction]
		elimination filter, suppression (rejection, exclusion) filter	Sperrfilter *n* <El.; Opt.>; Okularsperrfilter *n* <Opt.>; Sperrsieb *n* <El.>
element at infinity, ideal element	uneigentliches Element *n*, unendlich[ ]fernes Element	elimination of group <chem.>	Eliminierung *f* einer Atomgruppe <Chem.>
		elimination of heat	s. heat removal
element of area, differential of area, areal element, surface element	Flächenelement *n*, Oberflächenelement *n*	elimination of image field curvature, flattening of image field	Bildfeldebnung *f*

eliminator	s. filter circuit	elliptical loading	elliptische Tiefenverteilung f, elliptische Belastung f
eliquation	s. segregation <met.>		
Ellerman bomb	Ellerman-Bombe f		
ellipse described by the light vector with the direction of rotation to the left	Schwingungsellipse f für links elliptisch polarisiertes Licht	elliptically polarized; elliptic	elliptisch polarisiert, elliptisch schwingend; elliptisch
		elliptical nebula, elliptical galaxy	elliptischer Nebel m
ellipse described by the light vector with the direction of rotation to the right	Schwingungsellipse f für rechts elliptisch polarisiertes Licht	elliptical orbit	elliptische Bahn f, Ellipsenbahn f
		elliptical oscillation	elliptische (elliptisch polarisierte) Schwingung f, Ellipsenschwingung f
ellipse of correlation, homothetic (dispersion, contour, correlation) ellipse	Korrelationsellipse f, Umrißellipse f, Streuungsellipse f, homothetische Ellipse f	elliptical point, elliptic point	elliptischer Punkt m
		elliptical velocity	s. circular velocity
ellipse of inertia, inertia (momental, moment) ellipse	Trägheitsellipse f, Momentenellipse f	elliptic comet	elliptischer Komet m, Komet mit elliptischer Bahn
ellipsograph, elliptic trammel, trammel	Ellipsograph m, Ellipsenzirkel m, Ovalzirkel m	elliptic compensator	s. quarter-wave plate compensator
ellipsoidal co-ordinates, confocal ellipsoidal co-ordinates, elliptical co-ordinates [of Lamé], co-ordinates of the asymmetric ellipsoid	Lamésche [elliptische] Koordinaten fpl, [allgemeine] elliptische Koordinaten, Koordinaten des dreiachsigen Ellipsoids	elliptic co-ordinates	s. elliptic cylindrical co-ordinates
		elliptic cylinder	elliptischer Zylinder m
		elliptic[-]cylindrical co-ordinates, co-ordinates of the elliptic cylinder, elliptic co-ordinates	Koordinaten fpl des elliptischen Zylinders, elliptische Zylinderkoordinaten fpl
ellipsoidal distribution of velocities	ellipsoidische Geschwindigkeitsverteilung f		
ellipsoidal function, Lamé['s] function	Lamésche Funktion f	elliptic halation, elliptic halo	elliptischer Halo m, eiförmiger Hof m (Halo)
ellipsoidal harmonic	Lamésches Produkt n	elliptic integral <of the first, second, third kind>	elliptisches Integral n <erster, zweiter, dritter Gattung>
ellipsoidal variable [star]	ellipsoidischer Veränderlicher m		
ellipsoidal wave function, Lamé['s] wave function	Lamésche Wellenfunktion f	elliptic integral of the first <second; third> kind in Legendre's normal form, Legendre['s] [standard] form of the elliptic integral of the first <second; third> kind, normal elliptic integral of the first <second; third> kind in Legendre's notation, Legendre['s] elliptic integral of the first (second; third) kind	elliptisches Normalintegral n erster <zweiter; dritter> Gattung [in der Legendreschen Normalform], Normalintegral erster <zweiter; dritter> Gattung [in der Legendreschen Normalform], Legendresche Normalform f des elliptischen Integrals erster <zweiter; dritter> Gattung
ellipsoidal zenith	ellipsoidischer Zenit m		
ellipsoid mirror	Ellipsoidspiegel m		
ellipsoid of comparison	s. reference ellipsoid		
ellipsoid of deformation, strain ellipsoid, deformation ellipsoid	Verzerrungsellipsoid n, Verformungsellipsoid n, Formänderungsellipsoid n, Deformationsellipsoid n		
ellipsoid of elasticity, elasticity (stress) ellipsoid	Elastizitätsellipsoid n, Spannungsellipsoid n, Stressellipsoid n		
		ellipticity	s. out-of-roundness
ellipsoid of elasticity	s. index ellipsoid <opt.>	elliptic paraboloid	elliptisches Paraboloid n
ellipsoid of error	Fehlerellipsoid n	elliptic partial differential equation	s. elliptical differential equation
ellipsoid of gyration, central ellipsoid, gyration ellipsoid	MacCullaghsches (reziprokes) Trägheitsellipsoid n, MacCullaghsches (zweites) Zentralellipsoid n, MacCullagh-Ellipsoid n, Gyrationsellipsoid n	elliptic pendulum	Ellipsenpendel n
		elliptic point	s. elliptical point
		elliptic polarization	elliptische Polarisation f
ellipsoid of inertia, inertia (momental, moment) ellipsoid	Trägheitsellipsoid n, Momentenellipsoid n, Trägheitsfläche f; Cauchysches Ellipsoid n <axiale Trägheitsmomente>	elliptic space, polar space	elliptischer Raum m
		elliptic trammel, ellipsograph, trammel	Ellipsograph m, Ellipsenzirkel m, Ovalzirkel m
		elliptic vortex of Kirchhoff	elliptischer Wirbel m von Kirchhoff
ellipsoid of inertia of Culmann, Culmann ellipsoid [of inertia]	Culmannsches Trägheitsellipsoid n	elongated chain	gestreckte Kette f
		elongation, absolute elongation, tensile deformation, longitudinal deformation, stretching strain, tension strain	Verlängerung f, Längenzunahme f, Längendilatation f, Dehnung f, Streckung f, Längung f, Längsverformung f
ellipsoid of Poinsot	s. Poinsot['s] ellipsoid		
ellipsoid of polarization	s. polarization ellipsoid		
ellipsoid of revolution, spheroid of revolution, spheroid	Rotationsellipsoid n, Drehellipsoid n, Umdrehungsellipsoid n, Rotationssphäroid n, Sphäroid n		
ellipsoid of wave normals	s. index ellipsoid <opt.>	elongation, percentage elongation, strain, stretch <in %>	Dehnung f, prozentuale Dehnung f <in %>
ellipsoid wave	Ellipsoidwelle f	elongation <of the celestial object> <astr.>	Elongation f <Astr.>
ellipsometry	Ellipsometrie f	elongation	s. a. deflection <mech.>
elliptic; elliptically polarized	elliptisch polarisiert, elliptisch schwingend; elliptisch	elongation 60°	Sextilschein m
		elongation 120°	Trigonalschein m
elliptical analyzer	elliptischer Analysator m, Glimmerkompensator m	elongation at break	s. breaking elongation
		elongation due to creep, creep strain, creep elongation	Kriechdehnung f
elliptical co-ordinates	elliptische Koordinaten fpl		
elliptical co-ordinates [of Lamé]	s. ellipsoidal co-ordinates	elongation matrix	s. strain matrix
		elongation per unit length	s. unit elongation
elliptical differential equation, elliptic partial differential equation, differential equation of the elliptic[al] type	elliptische Differentialgleichung (Gleichung) f, Differentialgleichung vom elliptischen Typ	elongation quadric, quadric of elongation, strain quadric	Elongationsfläche f, Tensorfläche (quadratische Form) f des Elongationstensors
elliptical element	elliptisches Element (Bahnelement) n	elongation tensor	s. strain tensor
elliptical galaxy, elliptical nebula	elliptischer Nebel m	Elster-Geitel effect, Geitel effect	[Elster-]Geitel-Effekt m
elliptical inequality	s. Sun's anomalistic inequality	eluate	Eluat n

elucidation

elucidation, clearing up	Aufklärung f, Klärung f	emersion; emergence <geo.>	Auftauchen n <Geo.>
elucidation	s. a. interpretation		
eluent, eluting agent (solvent)	Elutionsmittel n, Eluens n	emersion <of the star>	Emersion f; Wiederauftauchen n <des Sterns nach der Bedeckung>; Austritt m aus dem Planetenschatten <Astr.>
elution	Elution f, Eluieren n, Auswaschung f, Herausspülung f		
elution analysis (chromatography)	Elutionsanalyse f, Durchlaufchromatographie f	emersion time, emergence time	Übermeereszeit f
		emersion wave	Emersionswelle f
elutriating funnel	Schlämmtrichter m, Schlämmkegel m	Emerson effect	Emerson-Effekt m
elutriation	Schlämmung f, Aufschlämmung f, Abschlämmung f	emission, emission of radiation, radiation; release of radiation	Emission f; Abstrahlung f; Strahlung f, Strahlungsemission f, Strahlenemission f; Aussendung f [von Strahlung]
elutriation analysis	Schlämmanalyse f, Elutration f		
elutron	Elutron n <Beschleuniger, Mehrfachausnutzung des Linearbeschleunigers>	emission band	Emissionsbande f
		emission centre, centre of emission	Emissionszentrum n
eluvial soil, soil of weathering, uppermost layer of soil, surface soil	Oberboden m, Verwitterungsboden m, A-Horizont m, Eluvialhorizont m, Auswaschungshorizont m, Eluvium n	emission centre	s. a. photoelectric emission centre
		emission characteristic	Emissionscharakteristik f, Emissionskennlinie f, Emissionskurve f
Elverson oscilloscope	s. flash-type stroboscope	emission coefficient <in Planck's law of radiation>	Emissionskoeffizient m <Plancksches Strahlungsgesetz>
emagram, skew $T-\log p$ diagram	Emagramm n		
eman, E, Em <10^{-10} Ci/l>	Eman n, Em, eman <10^{-10} Ci/l>	emission constant	Emissionskonstante f <Konstante K der Richardson-Gleichung>
emanating power	Emaniervermögen n		
		emission continuum, continuous emission spectrum	Emissionskontinuum n, kontinuierliches Emissionsspektrum n
emanation, radioactive emanation	Emanation f, Emanieren n; Ausströmen n (Ausstrahlung f) radioaktiver Gase	emission current density	Emissionsstromdichte f
emanation, [radio]active emanation, radioactive noble gas	Emanation f, radioaktives Edelgas	emission discontinuity	s. emission edge
		emission drift effect	Emissionsdrifteffekt m
emanation, exhaustion, exit <of gas>	Ausströmung f, Emanation f <Gas>	emission edge, emission discontinuity (limit)	Emissionskante f, Emissionsbandenkante f
emanation	s. a. radon <element>	emission efficiency of cathode	Heizmaß n der Katode
emanation pump	Emanationspumpe f		
emanium	s. radon <element>	emission image	Emissionsbild n
emanometer	Emanometer n, Emanationsmesser m	emission layer, airglow layer, [glow-]emitting layer	Emissionsschicht f, Schicht f des Nachthimmelsleuchtens
emanon	s. radon		
embankment of the dam, dam embankment	Wehrkörper m; Staumauerkörper m	emission limit	s. emission edge
		emission line	Emissionslinie f
embedding, imbedding, merging	Einbettung f		
		emission microscope	Emissions[elektronen]mikroskop n
embedding medium	Einschlußmittel n, Einschlußmedium n, Einbettungsmittel n	emission microscope	s. a. field emission microscope
embolismic year	Schaltjahr n <jüdischer Kalender>	emission microscopy	Emissionsmikroskopie f
embossed lens film, lenticulated screen film, lens screen film <US>	Linsenrasterfilm m	emission nebula, emission nebulosity	s. gaseous nebula
		emission of heat	s. heat emission
embrace line, line of embrace	Umschlingungslinie f	emission of light	Lichtemission f, Lichtausstrahlung f, Lichtabgabe f, Lichtentwicklung f
embrittlement	Versprödung f		
embryo, crystal nucleus <cryst.>	Embryo m <Krist.>	emission of radiation	s. emission
		emission operator, creation (production) operator	Erzeugungsoperator m
embryo	s. a. nucleus of crystal <cryst.>		
Emden-Fowler equation	Emden-Fowlersche Differentialgleichung f	emission probability, emission rate	Emissionswahrscheinlichkeit f
Emden function, Emden polytropic function of index n, Lane-Emden function	Emdensche Funktion f vom Index n	emission rate	Emissionsrate f, Emissionshäufigkeit f, Emissionsgeschwindigkeit f
Emden['s] gaseous sphere	Emdensche Gaskugel f	emission spectrochemical analysis using X-rays, X-ray emission [spectrochemical] analysis	Röntgenemissionsspektralanalyse f
emergence	s. emersion		
emergence angle <geo.>	Emergenzwinkel m <Geo.>		
emergence time, emersion time	Übermeereszeit f	emission spectrometer, emission spectroscope	Emissionsspektrometer n, Emissionsspektroskop n
emergency shut-down, safety shut-down, scram <US> <of reactor>	Sicherheitsabschaltung f, Abschaltung f aus Sicherheitsgründen, Havariestop m, Notabschaltung f, Schnellschluß m, Schnellabschaltung f, Schnellstopp m <Reaktor>	emission-spectrometrical, emission-spectroscopical	emissionsspektroskopisch, emissionsspektrometrisch
		emission spectroscope	s. emission spectrometer
		emission-spectroscopical, emission-spectrometrical	emissionsspektroskopisch; emissionsspektrometrisch
emergency shut-down rod	s. safety rod		
emergent column (stem) correction	s. thermometric correction	emission spectroscopy	Emissionsspektroskopie f

emission spectrum, bright-line spectrum	Emissionsspektrum *n*	emitting area	Emissionsfläche *f*; Strahlungsfläche *f*; Abgabefläche *f*
emission star	s. star with expanding envelope	emitting electron	s. luminous electron
emission yield	Emissionsausbeute *f*	emitting layer	s. emission layer
emissive fission	Emissionsspaltung *f*, Spaltung *f* nach Abgabe eines Neutrons	emitting nucleon	s. luminous nucleon
		emitting power	s. emissivity
emissive material	Emissionsoxid *n*	emitting surface, radiating surface, radiation [emissive] surface, radiant surface	Emissionsfläche *f*, Strahlungsfläche *f*, emittierende Oberfläche *f*, Abstrahlfläche *f*
emissive power	s. emissivity		
emissive power for the wavelength λ	s. spectral emissivity		
emissivity, emissive (emitting, radiative) power, radiating power (capacity)	Emissionsvermögen *n*, Ausstrahlungsvermögen *n*, Strahlungsvermögen *n*, Emissionsverhältnis *n*, Emissionszahl *f*	emmetropia, normal vision	Normalsichtigkeit *f*, Rechtsichtigkeit *f*, Emmetropie *f*
		emmetropic eye	emmetropes Auge *n*
emissivity, hemispherical emissivity	halbräumliches (hemisphärisches) Emissionsvermögen *n*, halbräumlicher (hemisphärischer) Emissionsgrad *m*	E[-] mode, E[-] wave, mode of electric type, wave of electric type, TM[-] mode, TM[-] wave, transverse magnetic mode, transverse magnetic wave, transverse H[-] mode. transverse H[-] wave	E-Welle *f*, Welle *f* vom elektrischen Typ, TM-Welle *f*, transversal[-]magnetische Welle (Mode *f*), transversale magnetische Welle (Mode), transversale H-Welle *f*, Transversal-H-Welle *f*, E-Typ-Welle *f*, transversal[-] magnetischer Wellentyp *m*, E-Typ *m*, TM-Typ *m*, E-Mode *f*, TM-Mode *f*
emissivity	s. a. radiant emittance		
emissivity of cathode, cathode emissivity	Elektronenausbeute *f* <Elektronenröhre>		
emitron, orthicon, orthicon tube, C.P.S. emitron	Orthikon *n*, Emitron *n*		
emittance, spot size divergence <acc.>	Emittanz *f* <Beschl.>	E-mode function	E-Modenfunktion *f*, E-Wellen[typ]funktion *f*
emittance	s. a. radiant emittance	emollescence, softening, mollification	Erweichung *f*
emitter <nucl.>, radiator	Strahler *m* <Kern.>	empirical distribution	empirische Verteilung *f*
emitter	s. a. emitter electrode		
emitter	s. a. source of radiation	empirical formula, molecular formula, gross formula	Summenformel *f*, Bruttoformel *f*, empirische Formel *f*, Molekularformel *f*, Analysenformel *f*, Substanzformel *f*
emitter barrier [layer], emitter transition region, emitter transition layer [region]	Emitterrandschicht *f*, Emittergrenzschicht *f*, Emitterübergangszone *f*; Emittersperrschicht *f*		
		empirical standard deviation	empirische Streuung *f*
emitter barrier capacitance	s. emitter barrier-layer capacitance	empirical value	Erfahrungswert *m*
emitter barrier-layer capacitance, emitter barrier capacitance	Emitterrandschichtkapazität *f*, Emittergrenzschichtkapazität *f*, Randschichtkapazität *f* des Emitters; Emittersperrschichtkapazität *f*, Sperrschichtkapazität *f* des Emitters	empiric horopter, true horopter	wahrer Horopter *m*, empirischer Horopter
		empiric variance, sample variance	empirische Varianz *f*
		emprotid, proton acceptor, proton base, prot[on]ic base, base [according to Brønsted]	Protonenakzeptor *m*, Emprotid *n*, Proton[en]base *f*, Base *f* [im Sinne von Brønsted]
emitter-base diode	Emitter-Basis-Diode *f*		
emitter-base junction, emitter junction	Emitterübergang *m*, Emitter-Basis-Übergang *m*	emptied <semi.>, depleted; depopulated	verarmt; erschöpft <Halb.>
emitter bulk resistance, emitter path resistance	Emitter-Bahnwiderstand *m*, Bahnwiderstand *m* des Emitters	empty; unoccupied, non-occupied; unfilled; unpopulated; vacant	unbesetzt, nichtbesetzt; leer; vakant; frei
emitter contact, emitter terminal	Emitterkontakt *m*; Emitteranschluß *m*	empty band, empty [electron] energy band	unbesetztes Energieband (Band) *n*, leeres Energieband
emitter diffusion capacitance	Emitter-Diffusionskapazität *f*, Emitterdiffusionskapazität *f*, Diffusionskapazität *f* des Emitters		
		emptying, depopulation	Leeren *n*, Entleeren *n*, Depopularisieren *n*, Entpopularisierung *f*
emitter efficiency, emitter injection efficiency	Emitterergiebigkeit *f*; Emitterwirkungsgrad *m*	emptying, evacuation	Leeren *n*, Entleeren *n*
emitter electrode; emitter	Emitterelektrode *f*, Emissionselektrode *f*; Emitter *m*	emptying hole	Entleerungsöffnung *f*, Abflußloch *n*
		empty lattice site	s. vacant site <cryst.>
emitter follower	Emitterfolger *m*, Emitterverstärker *m*	empty level, unfilled level, unoccupied level	unbesetztes Niveau *n*
		empty magnification	leere Vergrößerung *f*, Übervergrößerung *f*, tote Vergrößerung *f*
emitter-ground transistor	Transistor *m* in Emitterschaltung, emittergeerdeter Transistor	empty place	s. vacant site <cryst.>
		empty place in the shell, shell vacancy, vacancy in the shell	Leerstelle *f* in der Schale
		empty set	s. null set
		empty site	s. vacant site <cryst.>
emitter injection efficiency	s. emitter efficiency	empty space	s. free space
emitter junction, emitter-base junction	Emitterübergang *m*, Emitter-Basis-Übergang *m*	empty state, unfilled state	unbesetzter Zustand *m*
emitter path resistance	s. emitter bulk resistance	emu (e.m.u.) system [of units]	s. electromagnetic system of units
emitter terminal	s. emitter contact	emulgator	s. emulsifying agent
emitter transition layer [region], emitter transition region	s. emitter barrier [layer]	emulsification	s. emulsifying
		emulsified liquid	emulgierte Flüssigkeit *f*, disperser Bestandteil *m*
emitting antenna	s. transmitting antenna <el.>	emulsifier	s. emulsifying agent

emulsifying, emulsification	Emulgierung f, Emulsionieren n, Emulsionsbildung f	**enantiomorphous hemihedry of the rhombohedral system**	s. trigonal holoaxial class
emulsifying agent, emulsifier, emulgator <chem.>	Emulgator m	**enantiomorphous hemihedry of the tetragonal system**, tetragonal holoaxial class, trapezohedral [crystal] class, tetragonal-trapezohedral [crystal] class, tetragonal enantiomorphy, enantiomorphous hemihedral class of the tetragonal system	enantiomorphe Hemiedrie f des tetragonalen Systems, tetragonale trapezoedrische Hemiedrie, tetragonal-trapezoedrische Klasse f, tetragonal trapezoedrische Klasse
emulsion; photographic emulsion, photoemulsion	Emulsion f; photographische Emulsion, Photoemulsion f, optische Emulsion		
emulsion breaker, demulsification agent	Demulgator m, Emulsionsspalter m		
emulsion fog	Emulsionsschleier m		
emulsion polymerization	s. pearl polymerization	**enantiomorphy**	s. enantiomorphism <cryst.>
emulsion shreds, shreds	Nudeln fpl <Emulsion>	**enantiotropes**	Enantiotrope mpl
emulsion star, nuclear star, star <nucl.>	Emulsionsstern m, Stern m [in der Kernspuremulsion] <Kern.>	**enantiotropism**, enantiotropy	Enantiotropie f
		encapsulated source	s. sealed source
emulsion stripping, stripping off the emulsion	Schichtablösung f	**encapsulating**, encapsulation, canning	Kapselung f, Verkapselung f
emulsion support	s. film base <phot.>		
emulsion technique	s. nuclear emulsion technique		
emulsion track, photolayer track	Photoschichtspur f		
emulsoid	s. lyophilic colloid	**encased magnet**, boxed (pot, shell-type) magnet	Mantelmagnet m
enabling pulse <of gate>; driving (drive, command, control) pulse	Steuerimpuls m	**encastré beam**	s. fixed-ended beam
		encephalogram, electroencephalogram, E.E.G.	Elektr[o]enzephalogramm n, EEG
enabling pulse	s. a. gating pulse	**encephalograph**, electroencephalograph	Enzephalograph m, Elektroenzephalograph m, Hirnstromschreiber m
enantiomer, enantiomorph, antimer, optical antimer (antipode, isomer, isomeride), mirror-symmetric isomer	Spiegelbildisomer n, [optischer] Antipode m, optische Modifikation f, Enantiomorph m, optisches Isomer n, Antimer n, Antilog n		
		encephalography, electroencephalography, E.E.G.	Elektroenzephalographie f, Enzephalographie f
enantiomorphic	s. enantiomorphous	**Encke['s] division**	Enckesche Teilung f
enantiomorphic symmetry	s. enantiomorphism <cryst.>	**enclosed arc lamp**, enclosed lamp	Dauerbrandbogenlampe f; Flammenbogenlampe f
enantiomorphic symmetry group	enantiomorphe Symmetriegruppe f, Spiegelsymmetriegruppe f	**enclosed area of hysteresis loop**, area of hysteresis loop	Hysteresisfläche f, Hystereseflāche f, Flächeninhalt m (Fläche f) der Hysteresisschleife
enantiomorphism, optical (mirror-symmetric) isomerism <chem.>	Spiegelbildisomerie f, optische Isomerie f, Enantiomorphie f <Chem.>	**enclosed lamp**	s. enclosed arc lamp
		enclosure	[ab]geschlossener Raum m
enantiomorphism, enantiomorphy, enantiomorphic (mirror) symmetry <cryst.>	Enantiomorphie f <Krist.>	**encounter**; collision; impact; shock; impinging	Stoß m; Zusammenstoß m; Kollision f; Zusammenprall m
		encounter, approach, close approach <e:g. of stars>	Begegnung f, Zusammentreffen n, Zusammenstoß m, Annäherung f, Begegnungsvorgang m
enantiomorphous, enantiomorphic, antimeric[al], mirror-symmetric <chem.>	spiegelbildisomer, optisch isomer, enantiomorph <Chem.>		
enantiomorphous hemihedral class of the cubic system	s. enantiomorphous hemihedry of the regular system	**encounter hypothesis**, collision theory of Jeans', Jeans' hypothesis of close approach <astr.>	Hypothese (Katastrophentheorie) f von Jeans, Begegnungstheorie f, Jeanssche Katastrophentheorie
enantiomorphous hemihedral class of the hexagonal system	s. enantiomorphous hemihedry of the hexagonal system	**encroaching [upon]**, washing-away, sweeping-away	Wegschwemmen n, Fortschwemmen n, Fortspülen n
enantiomorphous hemihedral class of the tetragonal system	s. enantiomorphous hemihedry of the tetragonal system	**encrustation**, incrustation	Verkrustung f, Überkrustung f, Krustenbildung f
enantiomorphous hemihedral class of the trigonal system	s. trigonal holoaxial class		
		end, endpoint, end point, terminus, terminal point <math.>	Endpunkt m <Math.>
enantiomorphous hemihedry of the hexagonal system, hexagonal holoaxial class, trapezohedral [crystal] class, hexagonal enantiomorphy, enantiomorphous hemihedral class of the hexagonal system, hexagonal trapezohedral [crystal] class	enantiomorphe Hemiedrie f des hexagonalen Systems, hexagonal-trapezoedrische Klasse f, trapezoedrische Hemiedrie	**end-around shift**	s. cyclic shift
		end block, end-measuring block (rod), end measure (standard); [precision] gauge block	Endmaß n; Parallelendmaß n
		end-cooled test	s. Jominy['s] end-quench test
		end-face flux, face-ring flux	Stirnfluß m
		end-face leakage, face-ring leakage, overhang leakage	Stirnstreuung f
enantiomorphous hemihedry of the orthorhombic system, digonal holoaxial class, [bi-]sphenoidal class, hemihedral class of the rhombic system	orthorhombische Hemiedrie f, rhombische Hemiedrie, bisphenoidische Klasse f, rhombisch-bisphenoidische Klasse, rhombisch-disphenoidische Klasse	**end-face leakage flux**, face-ring leakage flux	Stirnstreufluß m
		end-face stray field, face-ring stray field	Stirnstreufeld n
		end-fed vertical antenna, series-fed vertical antenna	fußpunktgespeiste Vertikalantenne f, Vertikalantenne mit Zuführung der Energie am Fußpunkt
enantiomorphous hemihedry of the regular system, tesseral holoaxial class, plagihedral class, gyroidal hemihedry, gyroidal [crystal] class, pentagon-icositetrahedral class, regular enantiomorphy, enantiomorphous hemihedral class of the cubic system	enantiomorphe Hemiedrie f des kubischen Systems, pentagonikositetraedrische Klasse f, plagiedrische Hemiedrie, gyroedrische Hemiedrie		
		end-fire [antenna] array, end-on directional array	Längsstrahler m; Längsgruppe f, Dipolgruppe f mit phasenverschoben geschalteten Elementen

end-fire couplet	Antennenanordnung f mit längskompensierter Speisung	endurance ratio	Ermüdungsverhältnis n
end gauge, rod gauge	Stichmaß n	endurance strength	s. endurance
end group	Endgruppe f, endständige Gruppe f	endurance strength at alternating (repeated) load, fatigue strength at alternating (repeated) load, endurance limit at repeated stress in one direction, fatigue strength at repeated stress in one direction, fatigue limit for fluctuating stress, natural strength (limit of stress)	Schwellfestigkeit f, Ursprungsfestigkeit f
end impedance, load impedance	Endimpedanz f, Abschlußimpedanz f		
endless screw, worm	Schnecke f, endlose Schraube f		
end measure, end-measuring block (rod)	s. end block		
end moraine, terminal moraine, frontal moraine	Endmoräne f, Stirnmoräne f, Moränenwall m		
		endurance tension-compression strength	s. fatigue strength for tension-compression
endoe[ne]rgic	s. endothermic	endurance test	s. fatigue experiment
end of the world	Weltuntergang m, Weltende n	endurance testing machine	s. fatigue testing machine
endogenous	endogen, innenbürtig	endurance torsion test	s. torsion endurance test
endomorph	endomorph	end window	Endfenster n, Stirnfenster n
endomorphism	Endomorphismus m, Endomorphie f <Math.>; Endomorphose f <Geo.>	end-window counter, end-window counter tube; bell counter	Endfensterzählrohr n; Glockenzählrohr n, Becherzählrohr n; Fensterzählrohr n
endomorphism ring	Endomorphismenring m	energetic albedo	Energiealbedo f
end-on directional array	s. end-fire array	energetically unfavourable	energetisch ungünstig
end-on observation	Beobachtung f in Achsenrichtung	energetic idling	energetischer Leerlauf m
end-on structure	„end-on"-Struktur f, Struktur f mit Bindung am Ende	energetic linkage	energetische Kopplung f
		energetic particle, high-energy (penetrating) particle	energiereiches (durchdringendes) Teilchen n, Teilchen hoher Energie
endoplasmic reticulum, ergastoplasm	Ergastoplasma n, endoplasmatisches Retikulum n	energetic quantity	Strahlungsgröße f, strahlungsphysikalische Größe f
ENDOR, ENDOR technique, electron nuclear double resonance [technique], double resonance method [of Feher]	ENDOR-Technik f, ENDOR-Methode f, Doppelresonanzmethode f [nach Feher], Elektron-Kern-Doppelresonanzmethode f	energetic state, state of energy, [energy] state	Energiezustand m, [energetischer] Zustand m
		energid	Energide f
ENDOR spectrometer	ENDOR-Spektrometer n	energizing	s. excitation
		energizing voltage	s. breakdown voltage
		energy	Energie f
ENDOR spectrum	ENDOR-Spektrum n	energy	s. a. power
ENDOR technique	s. ENDOR	energy	s. a. work
endosity, negative viscosity	Endosität f, negative Viskosität f	energy-absorbing	s. endothermic
endosmotic	endosmotisch	energy absorption build-up factor	Energieabsorptionsaufbaufaktor m
endotaxy	Endotaxie f		
endothermal, endothermic, heat-consuming, heat absorbing; endoergic, endoenergic, energy-absorbing, absorbing energy	endotherm, wärmeverbrauchend, wärmeverzehrend-endergonisch, endoenergetisch, energieverbrauchend, energieverzehrend, wärmeaufnehmend	energy absorption coefficient	s. absorption coefficient <nucl.>
		energy-accumulation electrode	s. energy storage electrode
		energy approximation	Energienäherung f
endpoint, end point, end, terminus, terminal point <math.>	Endpunkt m <Math.>	energy at the absolute zero of temperature	s. zero-point energy
		energy balance, balance of energy	Energiebilanz f; Energiegleichgewicht n; Energiehaushalt m
end[-]point <of titration>, titration end[-]point	Titrationsendpunkt m, Endpunkt m [der Titration]	energy band, [Bloch] band, electron energy band	Energieband n, Band n, Bloch-Band n
end-point energy	Endenergie f	energy band model	s. band model
end product, final product <of decay series>	stabiler Kern m, Schlußglied n <Zerfallsreihe>	energy barrier	s. energy threshold
		energy blur; indeterminacy of energy	Energieunschärfe f; Energieunbestimmtheit f
end-quench test	s. Jominy['s] end-quench test		
end radiation <of continuous X rays>	s. quantum limit	energy build-up factor	Energieaufbaufaktor m
end reaction, marginal force	Randkraft f	energy carrier	Energieträger m
end reactions	s. support reactions		
end scale value, maximum scale value, rating	Meßbereichsendwert m, Meßbereichendwert m	energy conservation law, principle of the conservation of energy, [conservation of] energy principle, energy equation, energy theorem	Energie[erhaltungs]satz m, Erhaltungssatz m der Energie, Satz m von der Erhaltung der Energie, Energieprinzip n, Energiegleichung f
end standard	s. end block		
end supports	Einspannbedingungen fpl		
endurance, endurance limit, endurance strength, fatigue limit, fatigue strength	Dauerfestigkeit f, Dauerschwingfestigkeit f, [untere] Ermüdungsgrenze f, Ermüdungsfestigkeit f		
		energy constant	Energiekonstante f <h>, Konstante f der lebendigen Kraft
endurance	s. a. fatigue	energy consumption	Energieverbrauch m; Energieverzehr[ung f] m
endurance limit at repeated stress in one direction	s. endurance strength at alternating load	energy-containing eddy	energiehaltiger Wirbel m
endurance limit for complete reversal of stress	s. fatigue strength [for completely reversed stress]	energy content, energy storage, potential energy, content of energy, amount of energy contained	Energieinhalt m, Energiegehalt m, Arbeitsinhalt m
endurance limit under [completely] reversed bending stress[es]	s. fatigue strength under [completely] reversed bending strength		

energy

energy content of quanta, quantum energy	Quantenenergie *f*
energy conversion	*s.* transformation of energy
energy conversion efficiency	Energieausbeute *f*, Wirkungsgrad *m* bezüglich Energie <Szintillator>
energy correcting arrangement, energy corrective	Energiekorrektiv *n*
energy decrement	Energiedekrement *n*
energy density	Energiedichte *f*
energy density of radiation	*s.* radiant energy density
energy dependence <of detector>	Energiegang *m*, Härtegang *m*, Gang *m* mit der Härte <Detektor>
energy diaphragm	Energieblende *f*
energy discrimination	Energiediskriminierung *f*
energy dispersion formula	Energiedispersionsformel *f*
energy efficiency; utilization of energy, energy utilization	energetischer Wirkungsgrad *m*; Energieausnutzung *f*
energy efficiency	*s. a.* energy output
energy ellipsoid	Energieellipsoid *n*
energy equation	*s.* energy conservation law
energy equivalent	Energieäquivalent *n*
energy exchange time, time of energy exchange	Energieaustauschzeit *f*
energy expended, expenditure of energy (work)	aufgewendete Energie (Arbeit) *f*; Energieaufwand *m*, Arbeitsaufwand *m*
energy exposure	*s.* quantity of radiation
energy exposure	*s. a.* radiant exposure
energy fault	Energiefehlordnung *f*
energy flow [density], energy flow per unit area, energy flow vector	*s.* energy flux density
energy fluctuation	*s.* spread in energy
energy fluence	Energiefluenz *f*
energy fluence build-up factor	Energiefluenzaufbaufaktor *m*
energy flux	*s.* energy flux density
energy flux density, intensity <bio.>	Energieflußdichte *f*, Intensität *f* <Bio.>
energy flux density, energy flux, flux, energy flow density, energy flow [per unit area], energy flow vector, power flow per unit area <gen., el.>; Poynting['s] vector; radiation vector <el.>	Energiestromdichte *f*, Energiefluß *m*, Energieströmung *f*, Energieflußdichte *f*, Energiestrom *m*, Energieströmungsvektor *m*, Flächendichte *f* der Leistung, Flächendichte des Leistungsflusses <allg., El.>; Poyntingscher Vektor *m*, Poynting-Vektor *m*, Strahlungsvektor *m* <El.>
energy flux of radiation	Strahlungsfluß *m*, Strahlungsenergiefluß *m*, Energiefluß *m* der Strahlung
energy function	Energiefunktion *f*
energy gap, energy gap parameter <in superconductivity>	Energielückenparameter *m*, Energielücke *f* <Supraleitfähigkeit>
energy gap	*s. a.* gap
energy-gap model	Energielückenmodell *n*
energy gap parameter	*s.* energy gap
energy gap width	*s.* width of the forbidden gap
energy generated in combustion, energy of (released by) combustion	Verbrennungsenergie *f*
energy generation, energy production; energy release (liberation); power production, power generation	Energieerzeugung *f*; Energiefreisetzung *f*; Erzeugung *f* nutzbarer Energie
energy group	Energiegruppe *f*
energy imparted by ionizing radiation, integral absorbed dose <bio.>	durch ionisierende Strahlung zugeführte Energie *f*, integrale Energiedosis *f* <Bio.>
energy increment	Energiezuwachs *m*, Energieinkrement *n*
energy in laboratory system	Laborenergie *f*, Energie *f* im Laborsystem
energy input	zugeführte Energie *f*
energy integral	Energieintegral *n*
energy isolation	energetische Isolation *f*
energy jump	Energiesprung *m*
energy level, level	Energieniveau *n*, Niveau *n*
energy level density, level density	Niveaudichte *f*, Energieniveaudichte *f*, Dichte *f* der Energieniveaus
energy-level diagram, energy-level scheme, energy scheme, level scheme, level diagram	Energie[niveau]schema *n*, Niveauschema *n*, Energieniveaudarstellung *f*, Energieniveaudiagramm *n*, Niveaudiagramm *n*
energy level of the molecule	*s.* molecular energy level
energy level of the nucleus, nuclear [energy] level	Kern[energie]niveau *n*, Energieniveau *n* des Kerns, Kernterm *m*
energy-level scheme	*s.* energy-level diagram
energy-level width, level width	Niveaubreite *f*, Breite *f* des Energieniveaus
energy liberation	*s.* energy generation
energy line <hydr.>	Energielinie *f* <Hydr.>
energy-loss detector	*s.* dE/dx counter
energy loss time	*s.* energy replacement time
energy lost in an imperfect collision	*s.* collision loss
energy matrix	Energiematrix *f*
energy meter, active-energy meter, watt-hour meter	Wattstundenzähler *m*, Wirkverbrauchszähler *m*, WV-Zähler *m*
energy migration	Energiewanderung *f*
energy-momentum density	Energie-Impuls-Dichte *f*
energy-momentum flux	Energie-Impuls-Fluß *m*
energy-momentum operator	Energie-Impuls-Operator *m*
energy-momentum pseudotensor	*s.* Einstein['s] pseudotensor
energy-momentum tensor, energy tensor, matter tensor, stress-energy-momentum tensor	Impuls-Energie-Tensor *m*, Energie-Impuls-Tensor *m* [der Materie], Materietensor *m*, Materie-Energie-Tensor *m*, Energietensor *m* [der Materie], Energie-Spannungs-Tensor *m*, Energie-Impulsdichte-Tensor *m*, vierdimensionaler Energie-Impuls-Spannungs-Tensor *m*, vierdimensionaler Spannungstensor *m*
energy momentum theorem, laws of conservation of energy and momentum	Energie-Impuls-Satz *m*, Energie-Impuls-Erhaltungssatz *m*, Satz *m* von der Erhaltung der Energie und des Impulses, Energie- und Impulssatz *m*, Erhaltungssatz *m* von Energie und Impuls
energy-momentum vector	*s.* four-momentum
energy necessary for separating a particle from the nucleus	*s.* separation energy
energy of absolute zero	*s.* zero-point energy
energy of absorption, absorption energy	Absorptionsenergie *f*
energy of activation	*s.* activation energy <therm., chem.>
energy of adhesion, work of adhesion	Adhäsionsarbeit *f*, Haftarbeit *f*
energy of adsorption, adsorbing energy	Adsorptionsenergie *f*
energy of association, association energy	Assoziationsenergie *f*
energy of attachment, attachment energy	Anlagerungsenergie *f*, Anlagerungsarbeit *f*

energy of charge exchange, charge exchange energy	Umladungsenergie *f*	energy of vibration, vibration[al] energy, oscillation energy	Schwingungsenergie *f* <z. B. Moleküle>; Oszillationsenergie *f*
energy of combustion, energy released by combustion, energy generated in combustion	Verbrennungsenergie *f*	energy of wind, wind energy	Windenergie *f*
energy of deformation	s. specific strain energy	energy operator	Energieoperator *m*
energy of dipole interaction, dipole interaction energy	Dipolwechselwirkungsenergie *f*, Dipolenergie *f*	energy oscillation	Energieschwingung *f*
energy of dislocation, dislocation energy	Versetzungsenergie *f*	energy output, energy yield (efficiency)	Energieausbeute *f*
energy of dissociation <chem.>, dissociation energy	Dissoziationsenergie *f*, Dissoziationsarbeit *f*, Trennungsarbeit *f* <Chem.>	energy output of the Sun, solar luminosity, solar energy output	Sonnenstrahlungsintensität *f*, Sonnenintensität *f* <in erg/s>
energy of distortion condition	s. Mises-Hencky flow condition	energy per unit volume of deformation	s. specific strain energy
energy of electric field, electric field energy	Energie *f* (Energieinhalt *m*) des elektrischen Feldes, elektrische Feldenergie *f*	energy principle	s. energy conservation law
energy of electromagnetic field	s. electromagnetic energy	energy principle of potential theory	Energieprinzip *n* der Potentialtheorie
energy of electrostatic field	s. electrostatic energy	energy production	s. energy generation
energy of form anisotropy, form anisotropy energy	Formanisotropieenergie *f*, Energie *f* der Formanisotropie	energy propagation	Energieausbreitung *f*, Energiefortpflanzung *f*
energy of generation, formation energy	Bildungsenergie *f*, Bildungsarbeit *f*	energy quantification (quantization)	Energiequantelung *f*
energy of grain boundary, grain boundary energy	Korngrenzenenergie *f*	energy quantum	s. quantum of energy
energy of instability	Labilitätsenergie *f*	energy quantum efficiency	s. quantum efficiency
energy of jogs	Sprungenergie *f*	energy quantum of lattice vibration, lattice vibration quantum	Gitterschwingungsquant *n*, Energiequant *n* der Kristallgitterschwingung
energy of light	s. light energy	energy radiation	s. radiation of energy
energy of magnetic anisotropy, magnetic-crystalline (magnetocrystalline) energy, [magnetocrystalline] anisotropy energy, crystalline anisotropy energy, [magnetic] anisotropic energy	[kristallographische] Anisotropieenergie *f*, Energie *f* der kristallographischen (magnetischen) Anisotropie, [magnetische] Kristallenergie *f*	energy reflection build-up factor	Energiereflexionsaufbaufaktor *m*
		energy release	s. energy generation
		energy released by combustion, energy of (generated in) combustion	Verbrennungsenergie *f*
		energy replacement time, energy loss time	Energieverlustzeit *f*
		energy resolution	Energieauflösung *f*, energetische Auflösung *f*, Energieauflösungsvermögen *n*, energetisches Auflösungsvermögen *n*
energy of magnetic field	s. magnetic energy	energy resonance curve	Energieresonanzkurve *f*
energy of magnetization, magnetization energy (work), work of magnetization, magnetic work	Magnetisierungsarbeit *f*, Magnetisierungsenergie *f*	energy-rich	energiereich
		energy scheme	s. energy-level diagram
		energy separation	Energieseparation *f*
		energy shell, energy surface <therm.>	Energieschale *f*, Energiefläche *f* <Therm.>
energy of magnetostatic field	s. magnetostatic energy		
energy of migration, migration energy	Wanderungsenergie *f*	energy shell ensemble, microcanonical assembly (ensemble)	mikrokanonische Gesamtheit *f*
energy of mixing	s. mixing energy		
energy of motion	s. kinetic energy	energy source	s. power source
energy of *n*-particle system	s. virial	energy state, state of energy, [energetic] state	Energiezustand *m*, [energetischer] Zustand *m*
energy of nuclear oscillations, nuclear oscillation energy	Kernschwingungsenergie *f*	energy state of the molecule, molecular [energy] state	Molekülzustand *m*, Energiezustand *m* des Moleküls
energy of quadrupole interaction, quadrupole interaction energy	Quadrupolwechselwirkungsenergie *f*, Quadrupolenergie *f*	energy state of the nucleus	s. nuclear state
		energy state term, energy term, term [of energy], state of energy term	Term *m*, Energieterm *m*, Energiestufe *f*
energy of radiation	s. radiant energy		
energy of rotation	s. rotational energy	energy storage	s. energy content
energy of stacking faults, stacking fault energy	Stapelfehlerenergie *f*	energy storage electrode, energy-accumulation electrode	Speicherelektrode *f*
energy of the impact	s. impact energy	energy straggling, spread in energy; energy fluctuation	Energiestreuung *f*; Energieschwankung *f*
energy of the nuclear reaction	s. Q value <nucl.>		
energy of the pulse, pulse energy	Impulsenergie *f*, Impulsarbeit *f*	energy-stress complex	Energie-Spannungs-Komplex *m*
energy of thermal motion	[kinetische] Energie *f* der Wärmebewegung, kinetische Wärmeenergie *f*		
energy of transfer, transfer energy <therm.>	Überführungsenergie *f* <Therm.>	energy surface	Energiefläche *f*, Fläche *f* gleicher Energie
energy of transformation (transition), transformation (transition) energy	Umwandlungsenergie *f*	energy surface	s. a. energy shell <therm.>
		energy tensor	s. energy-momentum tensor
		energy term	s. energy state term
energy of turbulence, turbulent energy, eddy energy, eddy kinetic energy	Turbulenzenergie *f*, turbulente Energie *f*; Wirbelungsenergie *f*, Wirbelungsarbeit *f*	energy term structure	s. level structure
		energy theorem	s. energy conservation law
		energy thickness <of or for boundary layer>	Energieverlustdicke *f*, Energiedicke *f*

energy threshold, threshold energy, threshold, energy barrier, barrier of energy	Energieschwelle f, Schwelle[nenergie] f, Schwell[en]wert m der Energie, Energieschwellenwert m
energy transfer by radiation	Strahlungstransport m der Energie, Energietransport m durch Strahlung, Strahlungsenergietransport m
energy transfer coefficient	Energieumwandlungskoeffizient m, Umwandlungskoeffizient m, wahrer Absorptionskoeffizient m, Energieübertragungskoeffizient m; Energieumsatz m
energy transfer equation	Energietransportgleichung f
energy transformation	s. transformation of energy
energy transformation coefficient	Energieumwandlungskoeffizient m
energy unit of dose <corresponds to an energy absorption of 93 erg per 1 g of tissue>	Energieeinheit f der Dosis <entspricht einer Energieabsorption von 93 erg/g Gewebe>
energy unit of Grey	Energieeinheit f von Grey
energy utilization	s. energy efficiency
energy velocity	s. ray velocity
energy well	Energiemulde f
energy yield	s. energy output
energy zero	Energienullpunkt m
e-neutrino	s. neutrino in beta decay
enforced dipole radiation, induced dipole radiation	erzwungene Dipolstrahlung f
Engesser-von Kármán theory [of buckling]	Engesser-von-Kármánsche Knicktheorie f, Knicktheorie von Engesser-Kármán
engineering-grade, commercially pure, practical grade <90—97%>	technisch rein, technisch
engineering mechanics, industrial mechanics	technische Mechanik f
engineering system [of units], technical system [of units], system of units used in engineering and technology	technisches Maßsystem n, technisches Einheitensystem n, technisches System n [von Maßeinheiten]
engineering system [of mechanical units], engineering system of units	s. metric gravitational system
engineering unit, industrial (technical) unit	technische Einheit f, technische Maßeinheit f
englacial, intraglacial	inglazial, intraglazial
englacial moraine, internal moraine	Innenmoräne f
Engler degree, Engler number, °E	Engler-Grad m, °E
Engler viscometer	Englersches Viskosimeter n, Engler-Prüfgerät n
English mounting, yoke-type mounting, cradle-type mount	englische Rahmenmontierung f, englische Montierung f
English statute mile, statute mile, mile, British mile, mi, st.Mi., m	englische Meile f, angelsächsische Meile <= 1609 m>
engram	Engramm n
engraved meander, entrenched meander	Talmäander m, Talschlinge f; eingesenkter Mäander m; Gleitmäander m
enhanced field, strong (high, high-intensity, high-strength) field	starkes Feld n, Starkfeld n
enhanced line	besonders intensive Linie f, sehr starke Linie, hervortretende (verbreiterte) Linie
enhancement, increase	Steigerung f
enhancement	s. a. increase
enhancement	s. a. amplification
enhancement effect; gain effect	Verstärkerwirkung f, Verstärkungswirkung f, Verstärkereffekt m, Verstärkungseffekt m
enharmonic	enharmonisch
enlargement <phot.>	Vergrößerung f <Phot.>
enlargement	s. a. widening <mech.>
enlargement energy	s. delocalization energy
enlargement factor	Vergrößerungsfaktor m; Tubusfaktor m
enlargement scale, scale of enlargement, enlarging scale	Vergrößerungsmaßstab m
enlarging coil, widening coil	Expansionsspule f
enlarging scale	s. enlargement scale
enneode	Enneode f, Neunpolröhre f
enograph	Enograph m
enotropic energy	s. electromeric energy
enriched [surface] boundary layer, enrichment layer	Anreicherungsrandschicht f
enrichment; concentration	Anreicherung f; Konzentrierung f, Konzentration f
enrichment, degree of enrichment <of fuel, in %>	Anreicherung f, Anreicherungsgrad m
enrichment factor <nucl.>	Anreicherungsfaktor m <Kern.>
enrichment layer	s. enriched surface boundary
enrichment on the surface	Anreicherung f an der Oberfläche
ensemble, Gibbsian (classical) ensemble	Gibbssche Gesamtheit f, [klassische] Gesamtheit
ensemble <qu.>	Ensemble n, Gesamtheit f <Qu.>
ensemble	s. a. set <math.>
ensemble average	s. phase space average
ensemble density	s. density in phase
Enskog['s] approximation	Enskogsche Näherung f, Enskog-Näherung f
Enskog-Chapman theory	Enskog-Chapmansche Theorie f [der Bremsung], Enskog-Chapman-Theorie f
Enskog series, Enskog['s] solution	Enskogsche Lösung (Entwicklung) f
entanglement, intertwining, interlacing, interlacement	Verschlingung f, Verflechtung f
entering; incidence; incoming, arrival <e.g. of wave>	Einfall m, Inzidenz f; Einlaufen n; Auftreffen n <z. B. Welle>
entering of penumbra	Eintritt m in den Halbschatten
enthalpometric titration	s. thermometric titration
enthalpy, heat content, total heat, Gibbs['] heat function, heat function <at constant pressure>	Enthalpie f, [Gibbssche] Wärmefunktion f, Wärmeinhalt m [bei konstantem Druck], Drosselfunktion f <bei konstantem Druck>
enthalpy, generalized heat content <generalized definition>	Enthalpie f, verallgemeinerter Wärmeinhalt m <verallgemeinerte Definition>
enthalpy-entropy chart, enthalpy-entropy diagram [of R. Mollier]	s. H-S diagram
enthalpy of activation, activation enthalpy	Aktivierungsenthalpie f
enthalpy of combustion, combustion enthalpy	Verbrennungsenthalpie f
enthalpy of formation, formation enthalpy	Bildungsenthalpie f
enthalpy of fusion	s. heat of fusion
enthalpy of magnetization	s. heat of magnetization
enthalpy of mixing, mixing enthalpy; heat of mixing, mixing heat; [thermodynamic] excess function	Mischungsenthalpie f; Mischungswärme f
enthalpy of reaction, reaction enthalpy	Reaktionsenthalpie f, Reaktionswärme f bei konstantem Druck
enthalpy of solution	s. heat of solution
enthalpy of sublimation	s. heat of sublimation
enthalpy thickness	Enthalpiedicke f
entire function	ganze Funktion f
entire function	s. a. integral function
entocentric projection	entozentrische Perspektive f; entozentrische Projektion f
entoptic phenomenon, phosphene	entoptische Erscheinung f
entotic	entotisch
entrainment; dragging, drag; carrying off, carrying away	Mitführung f, Mitbewegung f, Mitnahme f; Mitschleppen n, Mitreißen n; Mitgehen n
entrainment of air, air entrainment	Luftmitführung f
entrainment of sound, sound entrainment	Schallmitführung f

entrance <of the tube>, tube entrance	Rohreinlauf *m*, Einlauf *m* [des Rohres]	enucleation <bio.>	Enukleierung *f*, Enukleation *f* <Bio.>
entrance channel, initial channel	Eingangskanal *m*, Anfangskanal *m*	enumerable	s. denumerable
entrance port	s. entrance window	enumerably infinite dimensional space	abzählbar unendlichdimensionaler Raum *m*
entrance pupil, object-side pupil, iris	Eintrittspupille *f*	envelope, envelope curve, enveloping curve <line>	Einhüllende *f*, Enveloppe *f*, Hüllkurve *f*, Hüllgebilde *n*, Umhüllende *f* <Kurve>
entrance slit	Eintrittsspalt *m*; Spektrographenspalt *m*; Eingangsspalt *m*	envelope, envelope surface, enveloping surface <surface>	Hüllfläche *f*, Einhüllende *f*; Enveloppe *f*, Hüllhyperfläche *f*, Hüllgebilde *n* <Fläche>
entrance temperature	s. inlet temperature	envelope curve	s. envelope <line>
entrance velocity, inlet (intake, admission) velocity, velocity of inlet	Eintrittsgeschwindigkeit *f*, Geschwindigkeit *f* am Eingang, Einströmgeschwindigkeit *f*	envelope delay, envelope delay time, group delay, group delay time	Gruppenlaufzeit *f*
entrance window, entrance port	Eintrittsluke *f*, Ding[raum]luke *f*		
entrenched meander, engraved meander	Talmäander *m*; Talschlinge *f*, eingesenkter Mäander *m*; Gleitmäander *m*		
entropic efficiency	Entropiewirkungsgrad *m*		
		envelope delay-frequency distortion	s. phase distortion
entropy <therm.>	Entropie *f*, Verwandlungsgröße *f* <Therm.>	envelope delay time	s. envelope delay
entropy	s. a. average information content	envelope form	Envelopform *f*, Briefumschlagform *f*
entropy at the absolute zero of temperature	s. zero-point entropy	envelope surface	s. envelope <surface>
entropy balance equation	Entropiebilanzgleichung *f*	envelope velocity, group velocity	Gruppengeschwindigkeit *f*
entropy chart, entropy diagram	Entropiediagramm *n*	enveloping curve	s. envelope <line>
		enveloping surface	s. envelope <surface>
entropy concept	Entropiebegriff *m*	environment, vicinity	Umgebung *f*; Umwelt *f*
entropy constant	s. Sackur-Tetrode constant	environmental activity	Umgebungsaktivität *f*
entropy current	s. entropy flux	environmental conditions	Umweltbedingungen *fpl*, Umgebungsbedingungen *fpl*
entropy diagram	s. temperature-entropy diagram		
entropy diagram	s. a. entropy chart	environmental factor, influence of the surroundings	Umwelteinfluß *m*
entropy elasticity	s. caoutchouc elasticity		
entropy flow, entropy flux, entropy current	Entropiestromdichte *f*, Entropiefluß *m*, Entropieströmung *f*	environmental lighting, ambient illumination, ambient lighting	Umgebungsbeleuchtung *f*
entropy increase	Entropiezunahme *f*, Entropievermehrung *f*		
entropy inequality	Entropieungleichung *f*	environmental monitoring	Umgebungsüberwachung *f*
entropy integral	Entropieintegral *n*		
entropy law of Boltzmann	s. Boltzmann principle	environmental pollution	Umweltverschmutzung *f*
entropy of absolute zero	s. zero-point entropy	environmental temperature, ambient temperature, temperature of the surrounding air	Umgebungstemperatur *f*
entropy of activation, activation entropy	Aktivierungsentropie *f*		
entropy of adsorption, adsorption entropy	Adsorptionsentropie *f*		
entropy of formation, formation entropy	Bildungsentropie *f*	enzyme inactivator; enzyme inhibitor; substance poisoning an enzyme, poison of enzyme	Fermentgift *n*, Fermenthemmstoff *m*, Fermentinhibitor *m*
entropy of information source	s. average information content		
entropy of ions, ion[ic] entropy	Ionenentropie *f*	eolian accumulation	äolische Akkumulation *f*, Windablagerung *f*
entropy of mixing, mixing entropy	Mischungsentropie *f*	eolian deposit, wind-laid deposit, wind-borne sediment	äolisches Sediment *n*, Windsediment *n*, Windablagerung *f*
entropy of transfer, entropy of transport, transfer (transport) entropy	Überführungsentropie *f*		
		eolospheric model	Äolosphärenmodell *n*
entropy of transformation, entropy of transition, transformation (transition) entropy	Umwandlungsentropie *f*	eolotropic	s. aeolotropic
		eötvös, E	Eötvös *n*, Eötvös-Einheit *f*, E
		Eötvös['] balance	s. Eötvös torsion balance
		Eötvös constant	Eötvössche Zahl *f*
entropy of transport	s. entropy of transfer	Eötvös correction	Eötvös-Korrektion *f*
entropy per symbol, average information content per symbol	mittlerer Informationsbelag *m*, Informationsbelag *m*	Eötvös effect	Eötvös-Effekt *m*
		Eötvös equation	Eötvössche Gleichung *f*
entropy principle	s. second law	Eötvös['] experiment	Eötvösscher Versuch *m* [zum Vergleich von träger und schwerer Masse]
entropy production	s. production of entropy		
entropy source	Entropiequelle *f*		
entropy[-] temperature diagram (plot)	s. temperature-entropy diagram	Eötvös formula, Eötvös rule	Eötvössche Regel *f*, Eötvössche Formel *f*
entropy term	Entropieglied *n*, Entropieterm *m*	Eötvös torsion balance, Eötvös['] balance	Eötvös-Drehwaage *f*, Eötvössche Drehwaage *f*, Drehwaage von Eötvös
entropy vector	Entropievektor *m*		
entropy wave	Entropiewelle *f*	epact	Epakte *f*
entry <of a table>	Eingang *m* <Tabelle>	E peak	Maximum *n* der E-Schicht, E-Schicht-Maximum *n*
entry field	s. entry portal		
entry into the atmosphere	Eindringen *n* (Eintritt *m*, Eintauchen *n*) in die Atmosphäre	epeirogenesis	Ep[e]irogenese *f*
		ephemeral	ephemer, ephemerisch
entry portal, entry field	Einfallsfeld *n*, Einfallfeld *n*	ephemeris	Ephemeride *f*
		ephemeris second	Ephemeridensekunde *f*
		ephemeris time	Ephemeridenzeit *f*
entry rate (velocity)	s. velocity of entry		
enucleate[d] <bio.>	enukleiert, entkernt, kernlos <Bio.>	epicadmium neutron	Epikadmiumneutron *n*

epicentral distance, distance of epicentre	Epizentraldistanz f, Epizentralentfernung f
epicentre	Epizentrum n; Erdnullpunkt m
epicondenser	Epileuchte f, Epikondensor m
epicycle	Epizykel m, Epizyklus m
epicyclic gear, planet[ary] gear, cryptogear	Planetengetriebe n, Umlaufgetriebe n
epicycloidal motion	epizykloidische Bewegung f
epigenetic valley	epigenetisches Tal n
epi-illumination mode of microscopic viewing	s. direct-light microscopy
epilation dose	Epilationsdosis f
epilimnion	Epilimnion n
epimer, epimeride	Epimer n
epimerism, epimery	Epimerie f
epimorphic mapping, epimorphism	Epimorphismus m, epimorphe Abbildung f
epinasty	Epinastie f
epiparaclase, shove fault <geo.>	Überschiebung f <Geo.>
epiplanar transistor, epiplanar triode, epitaxial planar transistor, epitaxial planar triode, planar epitaxial transistor, planar epitaxial triode	Epiplanartransistor m, Epiplanartriode f, Epitaxial-Planartransistor m, Epitaxial-Planartriode f, Planar-Epitaxialtransistor m, Planar-Epitaxialtriode f
epipolar axis	Kernachse f
epipolar beam of rays	Kernstrahlenbündel n, Kernbündel n
epipolar pencil of rays	Kernstrahlenbüschel n, Kernbüschel n
epipolar plane, basal plane <US>	Kernebene f
epipolar point, epipole	Kernpunkt m
epipolar ray	Kernstrahl m
epipole	s. epipolar point
epirogenetic motion; undation	epirogenetische Bewegung f; Undation f
episcopic illumination	s. vertical illumination
episcopic projection	episkopische Projektion f, Epiprojektion f
episcotister	s. stroboscopic disk
epistasis	Epistase f
epitactic layer	epitaktische Schicht f
epitaxial growth	s. epitaxy
epitaxial junction	Epitaxialübergang m
epitaxial mesa transistor	Epitaxial-Mesatransistor m
epitaxial planar transistor (triode)	s. epiplanar transistor
epitaxial transistor	Epitaxialtransistor m
epitaxy, oriented overgrowth, oriented growth, oriented crystal growth, epitaxial growth	Epitaxie f, orientierte (gesetzmäßige) Verwachsung f, orientierte (kohärente) Aufwachsung f, Aufwachsung
epithermal <geo.>	epithermal <Geo.>
epithermal <nucl.>	epithermisch <kern.>
epithermal neutron	epithermisches Neutron n
epithermal reactor	epithermischer Reaktor m
epizone	Epizone f
E plane bend	E-Ebenen-Biegung f
epoch of osculation	Oskulationsepoche f
epoch of periastron, time of periastron passage	Zeit f des Periastrons, Periastronzeit f
Eppley pyrheliometer	Eppley-Pyrheliometer n

epsilon system, epsilon-tensor, e-tensor, Levi-Civita['s] tensor, Levi-Civita symbol, tensor identity of Levi-Civita, generalized Kronecker delta	Epsilontensor m, ε-Tensor m, Levi-Cività-Dichte f, Levi-Cività-Tensor m, Levi-Cività-Symbol n, Levi-Cività sches Symbol n, total (vollständig) antisymmetrischer Tensor m, Levi-Cività scher Fundamentaltensor m, Fundamentaltensor m von [Ricci und] Levi-Cività
Epstein['s] apparatus, Epstein frame (hysteresis tester)	Epstein-Apparat m, Epstein-Gerät n, Epstein-Rahmen m
equal <to>	gleich
equal accuracy / of	gleichgenau
equal-angle point	s. focal point
equal area / of, area-preserving, area-equivalent, equi-areal	flächentreu, inhaltstreu
equal-area projection	s. equivalent projection
equal-armed balance, equi-arm balance, lever balance (scale)	gleicharmige Waage f, Hebelwaage f
equal-arm[ed] lever; balance, bascule	gleicharmiger Hebel m; Wippe f
equal chromaticity stimulus	Farbvalenz f gleicher Farbart, Farbreizvalenz f gleicher Reizart
equal-energy source	energiegleiche Lichtquelle f
equal-energy white, equi-energy white	energiegleiches Weiß n, Weiß gleicher Energieanteile, Idealweiß n
equal-function line	s. isoline
equal-inclination fringe	s. fringe of equal inclination
equal in dimension, equidimensional	dimensionsgleich
equality of brightness photometer, luminosity photometer, equality of luminosity photometer	Gleichheitsphotometer n
equality of brightness principle, equality of luminosity principle	Gleichheitsprinzip n, Gleichheitsverfahren n
equality of contrast photometer, contrast photometer	Kontrastphotometer n
equality of contrast principle	Kontrastprinzip n
equality of heat	Wärmegleichheit f
equality of luminosity photometer	s. equality of brightness photometer
equality of luminosity principle, equality of brightness principle	Gleichheitsprinzip n, Gleichheitsverfahren n
equality of structure, structural equality	Strukturgleichheit f
equalization, levelling[-up]	Vergleichmäßigung f, Ausgleichung f, Einebnung f
equalization; rectification; compensation (correction) of distortion, distortion correction <el.>	Entzerrung f, Verzerrungskompensation f <El.>
equalization	s. a. equating
equalization	s. a. compensation
equalization of concentration	Konzentrationsausgleich m
equalization of potential[s], compensation of potential[s], potential equalization	Potentialausgleich m
equalization of temperature	s. heat balance
equalizing	s. compensation
equalizing of heat (temperature)	s. heat balance
equalizing pulse <tv.>	Ausgleich[s]impuls m, Trabant m, Gleichlaufimpuls m <Fs.>
equalizing pulse following frame synchronizing pulse	Nachtrabant m; Nachausgleichsimpuls m; Nachbegleiter m
equalizing pulse preceding frame synchronizing pulse	Vortrabant m; Vorausgleichsimpuls m; Vorbegleiter m; Vorausbegleiter m

equations

equal loudness contour, equal loudness curve, Fletcher-Munson curve	Fletcher-Munson-Kurve f, Kurve f gleicher Lautstärke [nach Fletcher und Munson], Kurve gleich'r Lautheit
equal-loudness curve (line)	s. isacoustic line
equally distributed	gleichverteilt
equally spaced, equispaced, equidistant, evenly spaced	äquidistant, abstandsgleich, gleichabständig, in gleichem Abstand
equally tempered interval, tempered interval	[gleichschwebend] temperiertes Intervall n
equally tempered scale, equal-tempered scale, tempered scale, equal temperament, temperament <ac.>	[gleichschwebend] temperierte Stimmung f, Temperatur f; gleichschwebende Tonleiter f, [gleichschwebend] temperierte Tonleiter, [gleichschwebend] temperierte Skala (Skale) f
equal of magnitude, but opposite of sign; of the same magnitude, but oppositely directed	entgegengesetzt gleich
equal phase / of	s. phase / in
equal-pressure line	s. isobar <therm., meteo.>
equal probability, equiprobability	Gleichwahrscheinlichkeit f, gleiche Wahrscheinlichkeit f
equal probability / of (with), equiprobable	gleichwahrscheinlich
equal structure / of	strukturgleich
equal temperament, equal-tempered scale	s. equally tempered scale <ac.>
equal-velocity curve (line)	s. isotach
equating, equalization	Gleichsetzen n
equating <math.>, fitting, matching, adapting	Anpassung f; Angleichung f <Math.>
equation between numerical values	Zahlenwertgleichung f
equation between quantities	Größengleichung f
equation between units	Einheitengleichung f
equation for dew-point, dew-point equation	Taupunktsgleichung f
equation for vapour pressure, vapour pressure equation	Dampfdruckgleichung f
equation of centre	Mittelpunktsgleichung f
equation of circulation	Zirkulationsgleichung f
equation of condition, conditional equation	Bestimmungsgleichung f
equation of continuity	s. continuity equation
equation of diffusion	s. Fick['s] second law
equation of Einstein and Smoluchowski, Einstein-Smoluchowski equation	Einstein-Smoluchowskische Gleichung f
equation of equilibrium	Gleichgewichtsgleichung f
equation of five moments	Fünfmomentengleichung f
equation of heat balance, heat equation	Wärmebilanzgleichung f; <Geo. auch> Wärme[haushalts]gleichung f
equation of heat conduction	s. heat equation
equation of hydrodynamics, fundamental equation of hydrodynamics, hydrodynamic fundamental equation	Grundgleichung f der Hydrodynamik, hydrodynamische Grundgleichung
equation of hydrostatics, fundamental equation of hydrostatics, hydrostatic fundamental equation, [basic] hydrostatic equation	Grundgleichung f der Hydrostatik, hydrostatische Grundgleichung
equation of light, light equation	Lichtgleichung f; Lichtzeit f
equation of material balance	Stoffbilanzgleichung f
equation of maximum work	s. Gibbs-Helmholtz relation
equation of maximum work	s. a. Helmholtz equation [of thermodynamics]
equation of mixed type	Gleichung f gemischten Typs
equation of momentum	Impulsgleichung f
equation of motion; ponderomotive law	Bewegungsgleichung f
equation of mutual exchange reaction	Umsetzungsgleichung f
equation of oscillation, oscillation equation, time-independent wave equation	Schwingungsgleichung f, zeitfreie Wellengleichung f, zeitunabhängige Schrödinger-Gleichung f
equation of reaction isotherm	s. law of mass action
equation of Robert Mayer, relation of J.R. Mayer, Mayer['s] equation	Gleichung f von J. R. Mayer, Beziehung f von Robert Mayer, Mayersche Beziehung
equation of state, state (characteristic) equation, pressure-volume-temperature relation <therm.>	Zustandsgleichung f <Therm.>
equation of string vibrations	s. equation of the vibrating string
equation of telegraphy, telegraph[ic] equation	Telegraphengleichung f
equation of tendency, tendency equation	Tendenzgleichung f
equation of the centre [of Moon], inequality [of the Moon] <astr.>	Mittelpunktsgleichung f, Große Ungleichung (Ungleichheit) f, Ungleichung [des Mondes], Ungleichheit [des Mondes] <Astr.>
equation of the fourth degree, biquadratic (quartic) equation	biquadratische Gleichung f, Gleichung vierten Grades
equation of the Fuchsian type	s. Fuchs type [differential] equation
equation of the Moon	Gleichung f des Mondes, Mondgleichung f
equation of the n-th degree	Gleichung f n-ten Grades
equation of the polytropic line, polytropic relation	Polytropenbeziehung f, Polytropengleichung f, Gleichung f der Polytrope
equation of the reaction, reaction equation (formula), formula of the reaction	Reaktionsgleichung f
equation of the trochoid, trochoid formula (equation)	Trochoidengleichung f, Trochoidenformel f
equation of the vibrating string, equation of string vibrations	Gleichung (Differentialgleichung) f der schwingenden Saite
equation of three moments, three moments equation, three-moment equation, theorem of three moments, Clapeyron['s] theorem	Dreimomentengleichung f, Clapeyronscher Dreimomentensatz (Arbeitssatz) m, Clapeyronsche Gleichung f, Clapeyronsches Theorem n
equation of tides, tide equation	Gezeitengleichung f
equation of time	Zeitgleichung f
equation of wave normals, Fresnel's equation of wave normals	Fresnelsches Gesetz n
equations of compatibility of strain	s. St. Venant['s] compatibility equations
equations of Gauss and Codazzi	s. Mainardi-Codazzi relations
equations of gravitational field, gravitational field equations	Feldgleichungen fpl der Gravitationstheorie, Gravitationsgleichungen fpl
equations of gyroscopic motion	Kreiselgleichungen fpl
equations of motion	s. Euler['s] equations of hydrokinetics
equations of Plucker	s. Plucker equations
equations of reaction isobars and isochores, van t'Hoff equations	van't Hoffsche Gleichungen fpl
equations of the network, system equations	Netzwerkgleichungen fpl, Systemgleichungen fpl

equatorial	Äquatoreal n, parallaktisch montiertes (aufgestelltes) Fernrohr n	equi-areal mapping	s. area-preserving mapping
		equi-arm balance	s. equal-armed balance
equatorial, sagittal, radial <opt.>	sagittal, äquatorial, felgenrecht, Sagittal-, Äquatoreal-, Äquatorial-	equiatomic	gleichatomig
		equicohesive temperature	Äquikohäsionstemperatur f
equatorial beam	s. sagittal pencil		
equatorial belt <of Jupiter>	Äquatorgürtel m, äquatorparallele Streifen mpl <Jupiter>	equiconcentration line	s. isoconcentrate
		equiconcentration surface, isoconcentrate surface, surface of equal concentration	Fläche f gleicher Konzentration
equatorial circle	Äquatorkreis m		
equatorial class	s. hemihedry of the monoclinic system		
equatorial coma, sagittal coma	Rinnenfehler m, sagittale (äquatoriale) Koma f, Sagittalkoma f	equicontinuous	gleichgradig stetig, gleichartig stetig
		equidense [linse]	s. isopycn
		equidense line	s. a. isodense
equatorial co-ordinates, equatorial system [of co-ordinates]	Äquatorialsystem n, Koordinaten fpl im Äquatorialsystem	equidensite	s. equidensity
		equidensitography	Äquidensitographie f
		equidensitometering	Äquidensitometrieren n
equatorial coudé	Äquatoreal coudé n	equidensitometry	Äquidensitometrie f
equatorial electrojet	äquatorialer Elektrojet m	equidensity, equidensite, line (curve) of equal [optical] density <of the first, second, ... order>	Äquidensite f, photographische Äquidensite <erster, zweiter, ... Stufe>
equatorial fan, sagittal fan, sagittal pencil [of rays], equatorial pencil [of rays]	Sagittalbüschel n, Äquatorealbüschel n, Äquatorialbüschel n		
		equidensography	Äquidensographie f
		equidensoscopy	Äquidensoskopie f
equatorial focal line, sagittal focal line	sagittale (äquatoriale) Brennlinie f	equidimensional, equal in dimension	dimensionsgleich
		equidirectional	s. same sense / in the
equatorial horizontal parallax	Äquatorialhorizontalparallaxe f	equidirectional	s. parallel
		equidirectional electric field	elektrisches Gleichfeld n, Gleichfeld
equatorial image point, sagittal image point	sagittaler (äquatorialer) Bildpunkt m	equidistance [of layers]	Schichtenabstand m, Schichtenäquidistanz f, Schichthöhe f, Äquidistanz f
equatorial moment of inertia	äquatoriales Trägheitsmoment n, Trägheitsmoment in bezug auf eine Achse, Trägheitsmoment bei Biegung		
		equidistant	s. equispaced
		equidistant projection	abweitungstreue (abstandstreue) Projektion f, Äquidistanzprojektion f, abweitungstreuer (abstandstreuer) Entwurf m, Äquidistanzentwurf m
equatorial moment of inertia of the line, axial moment of inertia of the line	axiales Linienträgheitsmoment n, äquatoriales Linienträgheitsmoment		
equatorial moment of resistance, equatorial (axial) resisting moment, axial moment of resistance	äquatoriales Widerstandsmoment n, axiales Widerstandsmoment	equidistribution	s. equipartition
		equi-energy spectrum	energiegleiches Spektrum n
		equi-energy white, equal-energy white	energiegleiches Weiß n, Weiß gleicher Energieanteile, Idealweiß n
equatorial mounting	s. parallactic mounting		
equatorial pencil [of rays]	s. equatorial fan	equigeopotential surface	s. geopotential surface
equatorial plane <geo., astr.>	Äquatorebene f, Äquatorialebene f <Geo., Astr.>	equilateral hyperbola, equiangular (rectangular) hyperbola	gleichseitige Hyperbel f
equatorial plate, metaphase plate	Äquatorialplatte f	equilibrant force	s. balancing force
equatorial projection	s. transverse projection	equilibration, balancing <mech.>	Auswuchtung f <Mech.>
equatorial quantum number	äquatoriale Quantenzahl f		
		equilibration	s. a. compensation
equatorial radius of gyration (inertia)	äquatorialer Trägheitsradius m	equilibrium, balance, equipoise	Gleichgewicht n
equatorial ray, sagittal ray	Sagittalstrahl m, Äquatorealstrahl m, Äquatorialstrahl m		
		equilibrium, balance; stability	Gleichgewicht n; Stabilität f
equatorial resisting moment	s. equatorial moment of resistance	equilibrium, balance	Bilanz f; Balance f; Gleichgewicht n
equatorial section, sagittal section	Sagittalschnitt m, zweiter Hauptschnitt m, Äquatorealschnitt m, Äquatorialschnitt m	equilibrium / be in, balance [each other]; counter-balance	im Gleichgewicht sein (stehen mit), sich im Gleichgewicht befinden, einander das Gleichgewicht halten
equatorial system [of co-ordinates], equatorial co-ordinates	Äquatorialsystem n, Koordinaten fpl im Äquatorialsystem		
		equilibrium accelerating voltage	Sollbeschleunigungsspannung f, Gleichgewichtsbeschleunigungsspannung f
equator line	Äquatorlinie f		
equiamplitude surface, surface of equal amplitude	Fläche f gleicher Amplitude		
		equilibrium altitude, equilibrium float altitude	Gleichgewichts[flug]höhe f
equi-angled, equiangular	gleichwinklig	equilibrium compliance	Gleichgewichtskomplianz f
equiangular, isogonal, isogonic, conformal, angle-preserving	winkeltreu, konform, isogonal, isogonisch, isogon	equilibrium concentration <chem.>	Gleichgewichtskonzentration f <Chem.>
equiangular hyperbola, equilateral (rectangular) hyperbola	gleichseitige Hyperbel f	equilibrium concentration	s. a. equilibrium density <semi.>
equiangular mapping	s. conformal mapping	equilibrium configuration, configuration of equilibrium	Gleichgewichtskonfiguration f
equiangular projection	s. conformal projection		
equiangular spiral, logarithmic (logistic) spiral	logarithmische Spirale f, gleichwinklige Spirale	equilibrium constant, mass action constant	Gleichgewichtskonstante f, Massenwirkungskonstante f, Konstante f des chemischen Gleichgewichts, Konstante des Massenwirkungsgesetzes, Gleichgewichtsgröße f, Massenwirkungsgröße f
equianharmonic point	äquianharmonischer Punkt m		
equi-areal, area-preserving, area-equivalent, of equal area	flächentreu, inhaltstreu		

equilibrium criterion	Gleichgewichtskriterium n	equilibrium shift, displacement of equilibrium	Gleichgewichtsverschiebung f
equilibrium density, equilibrium concentration <of carriers, electrons, holes, ions, majority carriers, minority carriers> <semi.>	Gleichgewichtsdichte f, Gleichgewichtskonzentration f <der Ladungsträger, Elektronen, Löcher, Ionen, Majoritätsträger, Minoritätsträger> <Halb.>	equilibrium slope, normal slope	Gleichgewichtsgefälle n, Normalgefälle n
		equilibrium spectrum of Heisenberg	Gleichgewichtsspektrum n von Heisenberg
		equilibrium state, state of equilibrium	Gleichgewichtszustand m
equilibrium diagram	s. phase diagram	equilibrium structure	Gleichgewichtsstruktur f
equilibrium diameter, equilibrium orbit diameter	Sollkreisdurchmesser m, Gleichgewichtsdurchmesser m	equilibrium surface	Gleichgewichtsfläche f
equilibrium distillation	s. flash distillation	equilibrium surface tension, static surface tension	Gleichgewichts-Oberflächenspannung f, statische Oberflächenspannung f
equilibrium distribution	Gleichgewichtsverteilung f		
equilibrium domain	Gleichgewichtsdomäne f		
equilibrium electron	Sollelektron n	equilibrium system	Gleichgewichtssystem n
equilibrium energy	Sollenergie f, Gleichgewichtsenergie f	equilibrium temperature, temperature of equilibrium	Gleichgewichtstemperatur f
equilibrium enthalpy entropy diagram	Gleichgewichts-Enthalpie-Entropie-Diagramm n		
equilibrium field [strength]	Gleichgewichtsfeldstärke f	equilibrium tide, statical tide	Gleichgewichtstide f, statische Tide f
equilibrium float altitude	s. equilibrium altitude	equilibrium time	Zeit f bis zur Einstellung des Gleichgewichts, Gleichgewichtszeit f, Relaxationszeit f
equilibrium form; type of equilibrium	Gleichgewichtsform f, Gleichgewichtsart f		
equilibrium gradient	Gleichgewichtsgradient m	equilibrium value, steady [-state] value	Gleichgewichtswert m, stationärer Wert m
equilibrium inner electrical potential	s. reversible relative potential at zero current		
equilibrium luminance	Gleichgewichtsleuchtdichte f	equilibrium vapour pressure	Gleichgewichtsdampfdruck m
equilibrium moisture [content], equilibrium water content, equilibrium water	Gleichgewichtsfeuchtigkeit f, Gleichgewichtsfeuchte f, Gleichgewichts-Feuchtigkeitsgehalt m	equilibrium water [content]	s. equilibrium moisture content
		equilux curve	s. isolux
		equimolar solution, equimolecular solution	äquimol[ekul]are Lösung f
equilibrium momentum	Sollimpuls m, Gleichgewichtsimpuls m	equimolecular mixture	äquimolekulares Gemisch n
		equimolecular solution, equimolar solution	äquimol[ekul]are Lösung f
equilibrium of diffusion, diffusive (diffusion) equilibrium	Diffusionsgleichgewicht n	equinoctial colure	Äquinoktialkolur m
		equinoctial point, equinox	Äquinoktialpunkt m
equilibrium of exchange	Austauschgleichgewicht n		
equilibrium of forces	Kräftegleichgewicht n, Gleichgewicht n der Kräfte	equinox	Tagundnachtgleiche f, Tag-und-Nacht-Gleiche f, Äquinoktium n
equilibrium of isotope exchange, isotopic exchange equilibrium	Isotopenaustauschgleichgewicht n	equinox	s. a. equinoctial point
		equipartition, equidistribution, rectangular distribution (partition)	Gleichverteilung f, Rechteckverteilung f, rechteckige Verteilung f
equilibrium orbit, synchronous (phase-stable, stable) orbit; circular equilibrium orbit	stabile Bahn f, Sollbahn f; Gleichgewichtsbahn f; Sollkreis m	equipartition	s. a. equipartition of energy
		equipartition law	s. law of equipartition <of energy>
equilibrium orbit contraction	Sollkreiskontraktion f		
equilibrium orbit diameter, equilibrium diameter	Sollkreisdurchmesser m, Gleichgewichtsdurchmesser m	equipartition of [kinetic] energy, equipartition	Gleichverteilung f der [kinetischen] Energie, Energiegleichverteilung f, Gleichverteilung
equilibrium orbit expansion	Sollkreisexpansion f		
equilibrium orbit radius, equilibrium radius	Sollkreisradius m, Gleichgewichtsradius m, Synchronradius m	equipartition principle (theorem)	s. law of equipartition <of energy>
		equiphase surface, surface of equal phase, surface of constant phase	Phasenfläche f, Fläche f gleicher Phase, Fläche konstanter Phase
equilibrium partial pressure	Gleichgewichtspartialdruck m		
equilibrium particle, phase-stable (phase-stationary, synchronous) particle	Sollteilchen n, Synchronteilchen n	equipoise	s. equilibrium
		equipollent	parallel und gleichgerichtet
		equipollent force systems, equivalent force systems	[mechanisch] äquivalente Kräftesysteme npl
equilibrium phase, charged particle equilibrium phase, synchronous phase	Sollphase f, Synchronphase f, Gleichgewichtsphase f	equipollent vectors	gleiche Vektoren mpl mit gleicher Trägergeraden
		equipotential cathode	Äquipotentialkatode f
equilibrium point, equilibrium region <astr.>	Balancepunkt m, Gleichgewichtspunkt m, Gleichgewichtszone f <Astr.>	equipotential connection	Ausgleichsleitung f, Ausgleichsverbindung f, Äquipotentialleitung f
equilibrium position, position of equilibrium	Gleichgewichtslage f, Ruhelage f	equipotential line, contour (potential) line <el.>; stress line <of elasticity>	Äquipotentiallinie f, Niveaulinie f, Potentiallinie f <El.; Elastizität>
equilibrium potential, potential of equilibrium	Gleichgewichtspotential n		
equilibrium pressure	Gleichgewichtsdruck m	equipotential surface, potential surface, surface of constant potential <also el.>	Äquipotentialfläche f, Potentialfläche f, Niveaufläche f, Schichtfläche f, Niveauschicht f <auch El.>; elektrische Niveaufläche f <El.>
equilibrium process; quasistatic process	quasistatischer Prozeß m; Gleichgewichtsprozeß m		
equilibrium profile, profile of equilibrium	Gleichgewichtsprofil n, Normalprofil n; Normalgefällekurve f <Geo.>		
equilibrium radius	s. equilibrium orbit radius	equipresence principle, principle of equipresence	Äquipräsenzprinzip n, Prinzip n der Äquipräsenz
equilibrium reaction	Gleichgewichtsreaktion f	equiprobability, equal probability	Gleichwahrscheinlichkeit f, gleiche Wahrscheinlichkeit f
equilibrium region	s. equilibrium point <astr.>		
equilibrium restoration, establishment of the equilibrium	Gleichgewichtseinstellung f, Einstellung f des Gleichgewichts	equiprobable, of (with) equal probability	gleichwahrscheinlich

equiscalar	äquiskalar	equivalent electrons	äquivalente Elektronen *npl*
equisignal	Gleichsignal *n*	equivalent focal length	Äquivalentbrennweite *f*, Äquivalenzbrennweite *f*
equisignal line; equisignal sector; equisignal zone, bi-signal zone	Leitstrahl *m*; Leitebene *f*, Leitstrahlebene *f*; Leitstrahlbereich *m*; Leitstrahlsektor *m*; Leitstrahllinie *f*	equivalent focus	äquivalenter Brennpunkt *m*, Äquivalentbrennpunkt *m*, Äquivalenzbrennpunkt *m*
equispaced, equally spaced, equidistant, evenly spaced	äquidistant, abstandsgleich, gleichabständig, in gleichem Abstand	equivalent force systems	s. equipollent force systems
		equivalent functions	asymptotisch gleiche (äquivalente) Funktionen *fpl*
equivalence class <math.>	Äquivalenzklasse *f*, Abstraktionsklasse *f*, Restklasse *f*, Klasse *f* <Math.>	equivalent gridleak resistance	äquivalenter Gitterwiderstand *m*
equivalence class of local fields	s. Borchers class	equivalent height [of reflection]	s. apparent height
equivalence coefficient, Guillet's coefficient [of equivalence]	Gleichwertigkeitskoeffizient *m*, Äquivalenzkoeffizient *m* [nach Guillet], Wertkoeffizient *m*	equivalent length of pendulum	s. reduced length
		equivalent line width, equivalent width [of the spectral line]	Äquivalentbreite *f* [der Spektrallinie], Äquivalentlinienbreite *f*
equivalence of mass and energy	s. mass equivalence of energy	equivalent loudness	s. loudness level <ac.>
equivalence of mass and energy principle, equivalence principle, principle of equivalence [of mass and energy], principle of mass-energy equivalence, mass-energy equivalence law (principle)	Masse-Energie-Äquivalenz [-prinzip *n*] *f*, Energie-Masse-Äquivalenz [prinzip *n*] *f*, Äquivalenzprinzip *n* von Masse und Energie, Prinzip *n* der Äquivalenz von Masse und Energie, Prinzip der Masse-Energie-Äquivalenz	equivalent mapping	s. equi-areal mapping
		equivalent network	s. equivalent circuit
		equivalent noise admittance, noise equivalent admittance	äquivalenter Rauschleitwert *m*
		equivalent noise resistance, noise equivalent resistance	äquivalenter Rauschwiderstand *m*, Äquivalentwiderstand *m*, Rauschersatzwiderstand *m*
equivalence point, neutralization point, point of neutralization <chem.>	Äquivalenzpunkt *m*, stöchiometrischer Punkt *m*, theoretischer Endpunkt *m*, Neutralpunkt *m*, Neutralisationspunkt *m* <Chem.>	equivalent nucleons	äquivalente Nukleonen *npl*
		equivalent of heat, thermal equivalent	Wärmeäquivalent *n*
		equivalent particles, identical particles	identische Teilchen *npl*, gleiche Teilchen
equivalence principle	s. equivalence of mass and energy principle	equivalent pendulum, equivalent simple pendulum, simple equivalent pendulum	korrespondierendes Pendel *n*
equivalence principle [of Einstein], Einstein's principle of equivalence, Einstein's equivalence principle	Äquivalenzprinzip *n* [von Einstein], Einsteinsches Äquivalenzprinzip *n*	equivalent potential	Ersatzpotential *n*
		equivalent potential temperature	äquivalentpotentielle Temperatur *f*, potentielle Äquivalenttemperatur *f*
equivalence problem	Äquivalenzproblem *n*		
equivalence relation	Äquivalenzrelation *f*		
equivalence theorem	Äquivalenztheorem *n*	equivalent projection, equal-area projection	flächentreue (äquivalente) Projektion *f*, flächentreuer (äquivalenter) Entwurf *m*
equivalence to tissue, tissue equivalence	Gewebeäquivalenz *f*		
equivalent amount, equivalent quantity	äquivalente Menge *f*, Äquivalentenmenge *f*	equivalent quantity, equivalent amount	äquivalente Menge *f*, Äquivalentenmenge *f*
equivalent bonds	Bindungen *fpl* gleicher Valenz	equivalent radius	Äquivalentradius *m*
equivalent capacitance	Ersatzkapazität *f*	equivalent refraction, refraction equivalent	Refraktionsäquivalent *n*
equivalent chain	äquivalente Kette *f*		
equivalent charge	Äquivalentladung *f*	equivalent representation	s. similar representation
equivalent circuit; equivalent network; replacement diagram, replacement scheme	Ersatz[schalt]bild *n*, Äquivalenzschaltbild *n*; Ersatzschaltung *f*, äquivalente Schaltung *f*; Ersatzstromkreis *m*, Ersatzkreis *m*	equivalent resistance	Ersatzwiderstand *m*; Äquivalentwiderstand *m*
		equivalent röntgen, roentgen equivalent	Röntgenäquivalent *n*
		equivalent simple pendulum	s. equivalent pendulum
equivalent circuit with current generator	s. current generator equivalent circuit	equivalent solid angle [of the antenna]	äquivalenter Raumwinkel *m* [der Antenne]
equivalent classical mean hard-spherical diameter, diffusion diameter	Diffusionsdurchmesser *m*	equivalent sparking distance	äquivalente Funkenschlagweite *f*
		equivalent stopping power	Bremsäquivalent *n*
equivalent combining weight	s. equivalent weight		
equivalent concentration	s. normality	equivalent thickness [of layer]	äquivalente Schichtdicke *f*, Äquivalentschichtdicke *f*
equivalent conductance, equivalent conductivity	Äquivalentleitfähigkeit *f*	equivalent tube, equivalent valve; replacement tube	Ersatzröhre *f*; Austauschröhre *f*
equivalent conductance (conductivity) at infinite dilution, equivalent conductance (conductivity) at zero concentration, limiting equivalent conductance	Äquivalentleitfähigkeit *f* bei unendlicher Verdünnung, Grenzleitfähigkeit *f*, Grenzäquivalentleitfähigkeit *f*	equivalent turbulence	gleichwertige Turbulenz *f*
		equivalent valve	s. equivalent tube
		equivalent veiling luminance	äquivalente Schleierleuchtdichte *f*
		equivalent weight; [equivalent] combining weight, combining equivalent	Äquivalentgewicht *n* <von Element, Ion, Radikal oder Verbindung>; Verbindungsgewicht *n*
equivalent constant potential	äquivalentes konstantes Potential *n*, äquivalente Gleichspannung *f*		
equivalent current, current equivalent	Stromäquivalent *n*		
equivalent diameter, hydraulic (hydraulically equivalent) diameter	hydraulischer (gleichwertiger, äquivalenter) Durchmesser *m*	equivalent width [of the spectral line], equivalent line width	Äquivalentbreite *f* [der Spektrallinie], Äquivalentlinienbreite *f*
equivalent diode [of a triode]	Ersatzdiode *f*, äquivalente Diode *f*	equivoluminal wave	s. shear wave
equivalent dose	äquivalente Dosis *f*	erasable storage	löschbare Speicherung *f*
equivalent echoing area	s. radar echo cross-section	erase time, erasing time	Löschzeit *f* <Oszilloskop>

erasure <of record>	Löschung f, Auslöschung f <Aufzeichnung, Speicherung>	error detector, deviation detector, error-sensing device, discriminating (comparison) element, measuring unit, summing point <control>	Meßglied n, Vergleichsorgan n, Vergleichselement n, Vergleichsglied n <Regelung>
Erdélyi['s] function	Erdélyische Funktion f	error deviation	s. control error
erect <of image>	aufrecht, rechtwendig <Bild>	error distribution curve	s. error curve
erecting eyepiece, terrestrial eyepiece, inverting eyepiece	terrestrisches Okular n, Okular mit Bildumkehr, Erdfernrohrokular n	error due to change of temperature	Temperaturfehler m
erecting lens, image erecting lens, lenticular erecting system	Umkehrlinse f	error due to concentration, concentration error	Konzentrationsfehler m
erecting prism	s. image erecting prism	error due to friction, frictional error	Reibungsfehler m
erecting system, image erecting system, [optical] inversion system	Umkehrsystem n, Bildaufrichtungssystem n, Aufrichtungssystem n	error due to unbalance, unbalance error	Unsymmetriefehler m
erecting telescope	s. image erecting telescope	error estimation, estimate of error	Fehlerabschätzung f
erection, rectification <of image> <opt.>	Aufrichten n, Bildrichtung f; Bilddrehung f <Opt.>	error first kind	s. error of the first kind
E region	s. outer core	error function, error integral, Gaussian error function, Gauss['] error function, Gaussian transcendental function; erf, erfi; Erf, Erfi	Fehlerfunktion f, Fehlerintegral n, Kramp[-La-place]sche Transzendente f, Gaußsche Transzendente (Funktion f), Krampsche Funktion, „error function" f; Fehlerwahrscheinlichkeitsfunktion f, Gaußsches Fehlerintegral n; erf; Erf
erg	Erg n, erg		
ergastoplasm, endoplasmic reticulum	Ergastoplasma n, endoplasmatisches Retikulum n		
ergodic condition, ergodicity condition	Ergodenbedingung f		
ergodic hypothesis, Boltzmann's ergodic hypothesis, principle of continuity of path	Ergodenhypothese f, Boltzmannsche Ergodenhypothese		
ergodicity	Ergodizität f		
ergodicity condition	s. ergodic condition	error function complement; erfc; Erfc	= 1 − error function
ergodic problem	Ergodenproblem n	error in amplitude measuring	Amplitudenfehler m
ergodic state	ergodischer Zustand m	error in circle division (graduation)	s. error of circle division
ergodic theorem	Ergodensatz m, Ergodentheorem n	error in control loops	s. control error
ergodic theorem in the mean	s. statistical ergodic theorem	error integral	s. error function
ergodic theory	Ergodentheorie f	error law, error-law distribution, [normal] law of errors, Gaussian law of error [distribution]	Fehlergesetz n, Gaußsches Fehlergesetz
ergograph	Ergograph m		
Erichsen cupping test, Erichsen test; Avery test; Olsen test <US>	Tiefungsversuch m [nach Erichsen], Einbeulversuch m [nach Erichsen], Erichsen-Tiefungsversuch m, Erichsen-Tiefung f, Erichsen-Probe f, Erichsen-Test m		
		error of approximation, procedural bias	Verfahrensfehler m
Ericsson cycle	Ericsson-Prozeß m, Ericssonscher Kreisprozeß m	error of centering (centring), eccentric error <of division>	Exzentrizitätsfehler m, exzentrischer Fehler m <Teilkreis>
eriscope	s. image iconoscope	error of circle division (graduation)	s. divided circle error
erlang, Erl	Erlang n, Erl	error of direction, directional error	Richtungsfehler m
Erlanger Programm, Klein['s] Erlanger programme	Erlanger Programm n		
Erlenmeyer flask	Erlenmeyer-Kolben m	error of dispersion, dispersion error	Zerstreuungsfehler m
erosion	Erosion f; Ausnagung f; Auswaschung f; Abtragung f; fluviatile Erosion	error of division, error of graduation <of the scale>, divided scale error, scale division error	Skalenteilungsfehler m, Teilungsfehler m [der Skala]
erosion corrosion	Erosionskorrosion f, Erosion-Korrosion f		
erosion due to cavitation	s. cavitation erosion	error of division [of the circle]	s. divided circle error
erosion of the bank, bank erosion	Uferabbruch m, Ufereinbruch m, Abbruch m des Ufers; Uferangriff m	error of division of the grating	Gitterfehler m, Teilungsfehler m des Gitters
erosive wear	erosiver Verschleiß m, Erosionsverschleiß m; Spülverschleiß m <Flüssigkeiten>; Strahlverschleiß m <Gase>	error of estimate	Schätzungsfehler m
		error of first kind	s. error of the first kind
		error of graduation	s. error of division <of the scale>
erratic	erratischer Block m, Findling m, Erratikum n	error of horizontal axis, horizontal axis error	Kippachsenfehler m
erratic block	erratische Scholle f, Deckenrest m		
erratic material, erratics	erratisches Geschiebe n, Erratika npl	error of measuring instrument	s. instrumental error <e.g. of theodolite>
error curve, [Gauss] error distribution curve, normal error (frequency, distribution, probability) curve, probability curve, Gaussian curve [of error], Gaussian error curve, Gauss['] error curve, bell-shaped curve, curve of normal distribution [of errors]	Gauß-Kurve f, Gaußsche Kurve f, Gaußsche Fehlerkurve f, Fehlerkurve, Gaußsche Glockenkurve f, Glockenkurve, Wahrscheinlichkeitskurve f, Normalverteilungskurve f, Normalkurve f	error of pointing <astrophotography>	Einstellungsfehler m <Astrophotographie>
		error of rounding	Rundungsabweichung f
		error of second kind	s. error of the second kind
		error of the first kind, error [of] first kind, type I error	Fehler m erster Art, Alpha-Fehler m, α-Fehler m
		error of the first <second> order, measuring error of the first <second> order	Meßfehler m erster <zweiter> Ordnung
error-detecting routine	s. diagnostic routine		

error of the second kind, error [of] second kind, type II error | Fehler *m* zweiter Art, Beta-Fehler *m*, β-Fehler *m*
error of vertical axis, vertical axis error | Stehachsenfehler *m*
error probability | s. level of significance
error propagation, propagation of error[s] | Fehlerfortpflanzung *f*
error propagation law (theorem) | s. propagation theorem
error rate | Fehlerhäufigkeit *f*
error second kind | s. error of the second kind
error-sensing device | s. error detector
error transfer function | Fehlerübertragungsfunktion *f*
Ertel-Rossby [convection] theorem | Ertel-Rossbyscher Konvektionssatz (Satz) *m*
Ertel['s] theorem, Ertel['s] vortex theorem | Ertelscher Wirbelsatz *m*, Wirbelsatz von (nach H.) Ertel
Ertel['s] theorem on circulating motions | Ertelscher Zirkulationssatz *m*
Ertel['s] vortex theorem | s. Ertel['s] theorem
eruption [of volcano], volcanic eruption | Ausbruch *m*, Eruption *f*, Vulkanausbruch *m*, Vulkaneruption *f*
eruption [on the Sun] | s. solar flare
eruptive prominence | eruptive Protuberanz *f*
eruptive rock, volcanic rock, volcanic igneous rock, igneous rock, volcanic | Magmagestein *n*, magmatisches (vulkanisches) Gestein *n*, Erstarrungsgestein *n*, Eruptivgestein *n*, Massengestein *n*, Magmatit *m*
eruptive vein, intrusive (igneous) vein, [igneous] dyke | Eruptivgang *m*, Gesteinsgang *m*
erythema, skin erythema, reddening of the skin | Erythem *n*, Hautrötung *f*
erythema caused by exposure to heat | Wärmeerythem *n*
erythema dose, threshold erythema dose | Erythemdosis *f*
erythemal efficiency | Erythemwirksamkeit *f*
erythemal wavelengths | Erythemalgebiet *n*, Erythemalbereich *m*
Esaki diode, tunnel diode | Tunneldiode *f*, Esaki-Diode *f*
ESCA, electron spectroscopy for chemical analysis | ESCA-Technik *f*, Röntgenstrahl-Elektronenspektroskopie *f*
escape factor | Escapefaktor *m*
escapement <of clock> | Hemmung *f*, Hemmwerk *n* <Uhr>
escape of neutrons, leakage, neutron leakage | Neutronenabfluß *m*, Neutronenausfluß *m*, Neutronenverlust *m*
escape of stars | Entweichen *n* von Sternen
escape peak, leakage peak | „escape"-Peak *m*, „escape peak" *m*, Restspitze *f*
escape speed, escape velocity [from Earth], velocity of escape, parabolic velocity, speed of escape | Entweich[ungs]geschwindigkeit *f*, parabolische Geschwindigkeit *f*, zweite kosmische Geschwindigkeit[sstufe] *f*, Fluchtgeschwindigkeit *f*
escape velocity from Galaxy | vierte kosmische Geschwindigkeit[sstufe] *f*
escape velocity from solar system | dritte kosmische Geschwindigkeit[sstufe] *f*
E-shaped core | E-Kern *m*
eskar, esker, osar | Os *n* (*m*) <*pl.*: Oser>, Äs *n* (*m*), Esker *m*, Wallberg *m*
Es-layer | s. sporadic E-layer
esperium | s. plutonium
essential boundary condition, geometric boundary condition | wesentliche (geometrische) Randbedingung *f*
essential constant | wesentliche Konstante *f*, wesentlicher Parameter *m*

essential singularity | s. irregular singularity
essential singular kernel | wesentlich singulärer Kern *m*
essential singular point | s. irregular singularity
establishment of the equilibrium, equilibrium restoration | Gleichgewichtseinstellung *f*, Einstellung *f* des Gleichgewichts
estimate; estimation | Abschätzung *f*; Schätzung *f*; Einschätzung *f*
estimator | Schätzfunktion *f*
esu (e.s.u.) system [of units] | s. electrostatic system of units
e-system | s. alternator
étalon, standard[ized] measure, standard; gage, gauge | Etalon *m*, Eichmaß *n*, Normal[maß] *n*, Meßnormal *n*, Eichnormal *n*, Norm *f*
étalon plate | Etalonplattenspektroskop *n*, Etalonplatte *f*
etchant, etching solution (reagent, medium) | Ätzmittel *n*, Ätzlösung *f*
etch cavity | s. etch pit
etched figure, etch[-] figure | Ätzfigur *f*, Lösungsfigur *f*, Korrosionsfigur *f*
etch hill[ock], hillock | Ätzhügel *m*
etching | Ätzung *f*; Anätzen *n*
etching-away | Wegätzen *n*, Abätzen *n*
etching channel | Ätzkanal *m*
etching medium (reagent, solution) | s. etchant
etch pattern | Ätzbild *n*
etch pit, pit | Ätzgrübchen *n*, Ätzgrube *f*
etch point | Ätzpunkt *m*
ether <opt.> | Äther *m*, Lichtäther *m*, Weltäther *m* <Opt.>
ether drag, dragging of the ether | Äthermitführung *f*
ether drag[ging] coefficient | Äthermitführungskoeffizient *m*
ether drift | s. ether wind
ether model | Äthermodell *n*
ether theory of light, Fresnel's theory [of light] | Äthertheorie *f* des Lichts [von Fresnel], Fresnelsche Theorie *f* [des Lichts], elastische Lichttheorie *f*
ether wind, ether drift | Ätherwind *m*, Ätherdrift *f*
ethylene isomerism | s. geometrical isomerism
Ettingshausen coefficient | Ettingshausen-Koeffizient *m*
Ettingshausen effect | Ettingshausen-Effekt *m*
E-type transition | s. electric transition
Eucken equation | s. Eucken relation
Eucken['s] equation of state | Euckensche Zustandsgleichung *f*
Eucken relation, Eucken equation | Euckensche Beziehung (Gleichung) *f*, Eucken-Formel *f*
Euclid['s] algorithm, division algorithm, Euclidean algorithm | euklidischer Algorithmus *m*, Kettendivision *f*, Divisionsalgorithmus *m*
Euclidean affine space | euklidisch-affiner Raum *m*, euklidisch-affine Mannigfaltigkeit *f*
Euclidean algorithm | s. Euclid['s] algorithm
Euclidean frame | euklidisches Bezugssystem *n*
Euclidean metric | euklidische Metrik *f*
Euclidean metric space | euklidisch-metrischer Raum *m*
Euclidean solid, rigid body; Euclid solid <rheology> | starrer Körper *m*
Euclidean space, euclidian space | euklidischer Raum *m*
Euclidean space-time | euklidisches Raum-Zeit-Kontinuum *n*, euklidische Raumzeit *f*
euclidian space | s. Euclidean space
Euclid solid <rheology>, rigid body; Euclidean solid | starrer Körper *m*
eucolloid, natural (true) colloid | Eukolloid *n*
eudiometer, explosion burette | Eudiometer[rohr] *n*, Explosionsbürette *f*
eudiometry | Eudiometrie *f*, eudiometrische Messung *f*
euhedral <cryst.> | s. idiomorphic

Euler acceleration	Eulersche Beschleunigung f
Euler['s] angle	s. Eulerian angle
Euler['s] buckling theory	Eulersche Theorie f der elastischen Knickung
Euler condition	Eulersche [notwendige] Bedingung f
Euler['s] constant, Euler-Mascheroni constant, Mascheroni['s] constant	Eulersche Konstante f, [Euler-]Mascheronische Konstante, Euler-Mascheroni-Konstante f
Euler['s] crippling (critical) load	s. critical load of Euler
Euler-d'Alembert paradox	s. hydrodynamic paradox of d'Alembert
Euler-d'Alembert principle; Lagrange-d'Alembert principle, d'Alembert-Lagrange variational principle, principle of Lagrange and d'Alembert	Euler-d'Alembertsches Prinzip n; Lagrangesches Prinzip, Lagrange-d'Alembertsches Prinzip, d'Alembert-Lagrangesches Variationsprinzip n, Prinzip von Lagrange und d'Alembert
Euler['s] diagram <therm.>	Eulersches Diagramm n, Euler-Diagramm n <Therm.>
Euler['s] differential equation, Euler['s] (homogeneous) equation	Eulersche Differentialgleichung f
Euler['s] dynamical equations, Euler equations [of motion], Euler's equations	dynamische Eulersche Gleichungen fpl
Euler['s] equation	Eulersche Gleichung (Polytropengleichung) f
Euler['s] equation, Lambert['s] equation	Lambertsche (Eulersche) Gleichung f, Lambertsches Theorem n <von der Bewegung der Himmelskörper>
Euler['s] equation	s. a. Euler-Lagrange equation
Euler['s] equation	s. a. Euler['s] differential equation
Euler['s] equations [for a rigid body], Euler's gyration equations	Eulersche Gleichungen fpl des starren Körpers, Eulersche Kreiselgleichungen fpl
Euler['s] equations of hydrokinetics (motion), equations of motion	Eulersche Bewegungsgleichungen fpl [der Hydromechanik]
Euler equations [of motion], Euler's dynamical equations	dynamische Eulersche Gleichungen fpl
Euler force	s. critical load of Euler
Euler['s] formula [for a polyhedron]	s. Euler's theorem on polyhedrons
Euler['s] formula, Euler['s] relation	Eulersche Formel (Gleichung) f, Euler-Moivresche Formel
Euler['s] formula	s. a. Euler['s] turbine formula
Euler['s] gas-dynamical equations	Eulersche gasdynamische Gleichungen fpl
Euler['s] gyration equations	s. Euler equations [for a rigid body]
Euler['s] hyperbola	Euler-Hyperbel f, Eulersche Hyperbel f
Eulerian angle, Euler['s] angle	Eulerscher Winkel m
Eulerian approach	s. Eulerian representation
Eulerian correlation coefficient	Eulerscher Korrelationskoeffizient m
Eulerian derivative	s. material derivative
Eulerian description	s. Eulerian representation
Eulerian free period	Eulersche Periode f, Eulers freie Periode
Eulerian integral	Eulersches Integral n, Euler-Integral n
Eulerian integral of the first kind	s. beta function
Eulerian integral of the second kind	s. gamma-function
Eulerian method of analysis	s. Eulerian representation
Eulerian parameter, Euler-Rodrigues parameter, parameter of Rodrigues	Eulerscher [symmetrischer] Parameter m, [Euler-]Rodriguesscher Parameter, Parameter von Rodrigues
Eulerian representation, Eulerian approach (description), Eulerian method of analysis	Eulersche Darstellung (Beschreibung, Methode) f
Eulerian turbulence scale	Eulerscher Turbulenzgrad m
Eulerian variable, Euler variable, spatial variable	Eulersche Variable f
Euler['s] kinematic relations	Eulersche kinematische Gleichungen fpl
Euler-Lagrange equation, Cauchy-Euler equation, Euler['s] equation	Euler-Lagrange-Gleichung f, Euler-Lagrangesche Gleichung f, Eulersche Differentialgleichung f
Euler-Lagrange equations	s. Lagrange['s] equations
Euler['s] law [of illumination]	Eulersches Beleuchtungsgesetz n
Euler['s] load	s. critical load of Euler
Euler-Maclaurin formula, Euler-Maclaurin sum formula, Euler['s] summation formula	Euler-Maclaurinsche Formel f, Euler-Maclaurinsche Summationsformel f
Euler-Mascheroni constant	s. Euler constant
Euler['s] method <math.>, point slope method	Polygonzugverfahren n <Math.>
Euler['s] multiplier, integrating factor	integrierender Faktor m, Eulerscher (integrierender) Multiplikator m
Euler['s] number, pressure coefficient, E, C_p	Eulersche Zahl f, Eu
Euler['s] relation	s. Euler['s] formula
Euler-Rodrigues parameter	s. Eulerian parameter
Euler['s] second integral	s. gamma-function
Euler['s] spiral	s. Cornu['s] spiral
Euler['s] stress tensor	Eulerscher Spannungstensor m
Euler['s] stretching tensor, stretching tensor of Euler	Eulerscher Streckungstensor m, Streckungstensor von Euler
Euler['s] summation formula	s. Euler-Maclaurin formula
Euler['s] theorem [for (on) homogeneous functions], theorem of Euler	Satz m von Euler, Eulerscher Satz <über homogene Funktionen>
Euler['s] theorem on polyhedrons, Euler['s] formula [for a polyhedron]	Eulersche Polyederformel f, [Descartes-]Eulerscher Polyedersatz m
Euler['s] turbine formula, Euler['s] formula	Eulersche Turbinengleichung f, Hauptgleichung f der Turbinentheorie
Euler variable	s. Eulerian variable
e unit <of Friedrich and Kroenig>	e-Einheit f [von Friedrich und Kroenig]
E unit [of Duane], electrostatic unit of Duane	E-Einheit f [nach Duane], elektrostatische Einheit f [nach Duane]
eupatheoscope	Eupatheoskop n
eupelagic region (zone)	eupelagischer Bereich m
euphotic zone	euphotische (reichlich beleuchtete) Zone f
euphotometric	euphotometrisch
eupolymer	s. high polymer
Eustachian tube	Eustachische Röhre (Tube) f, Ohrtrompete f
eustasy	Eustasie f
eustatic fluctuation of sea level	eustatische Meeresspiegelschwankung f
eustatism	Eustatismus m
eutectic, eutectic mixture	Eutektikum n, eutektisches Gemisch (Gemenge) n, eutektische Mischung f
eutectic halt, eutectic (monotectic) point	eutektischer (kryohydratischer) Punkt m
eutectic horizontal	Eutektikale f, eutektische Linie f
eutectic mixture	s. eutectic
eutectic point	s. eutectic halt
eutectic temperature	eutektische Temperatur f
eutectoid	Eutektoid n
eutectoid decomposition	s. eutectoid reaction
eutectoid halt	s. eutectoid point
eutectoid horizontal	Eutektoidale f, eutektoide Linie f

eutectoid 238

eutectoid point, eutectoid halt	eutektoider Punkt m	evaporation heat, heat of evaporation	Verdunstungswärme f
eutectoid reaction (transformation, transition), eutectoid decomposition, discontinuous precipitation	eutektoider Zerfall m	evaporation height, height of evaporation, amount of evaporation in mm	Verdunstungshöhe f
eutrophic	eutroph	evaporation intensity, intensity of evaporation	Verdunstungsstärke f, Verdunstungsintensität f, Verdunstungskraft f
eutropy	[katamere] Eutropie f		
evacuated space	s. vacuum space	evaporation in vacuo	s. metallization by vacuum evaporation
evacuated system, vacuum system	Vakuumsystem n		
evacuation; pumping out; rarefaction	Evakuierung f, Abpumpen n; Entlüftung f	evaporation meter	s. evaporimeter
		evaporation model	Verdampfungsmodell n, Ausdampf[ungs]modell n
		evaporation neutron	Verdampfungsneutron n
evacuation	s. a. emptying	evaporation nucleon	Verdampfungsnukleon n, Ausdampfnukleon n
evacuation of heat	s. heat removal		
evaluation; appraisal <US>;analysis; processing, treatment; calculation; computation <of dates>; data processing	Auswertung f; Analyse f; Verarbeitung f; Berechnung f <Daten>; Datenverarbeitung f	evaporation number <chem.>	Verdunstungszahl f <Chem.>
		evaporation of the nucleus, nuclear evaporation	Verdampfung f des Kerns, Kernverdampfung f
evaluation equipment	s. analyzer	evaporation pan	s. evaporimeter
evanescence, extinction <of luminescence>	Auslöschung f, Löschung f <Lumineszenz>	evaporation plant	s. evaporator
		evaporation psychrometer	s. psychrometer
evanescent mode	abklingender Schwingungstyp (Wellentyp) m, abklingende Mode f	evaporation pump	Verdampferpumpe f
evanescent wave	abklingende Welle f	evaporation rate, rate of evaporation (vaporization), vaporization rate, evaporative rate	Verdampfungsgeschwindigkeit f, Verdunstungsgeschwindigkeit f
Evans['] [root-locus] method	s. root locus method		
evapor	Evapor m	evaporation region, evaporation zone, region of evaporation	Verdampfungsteil m, Verdampferteil m, Verdampfungsgebiet n
evaporability, vaporizability, vaporability, evaporative capacity	Verdampfbarkeit f, Verdampfungsfähigkeit f, Verdampfungsvermögen n		
evaporability	Verdunstbarkeit f, Evaporabilität f	evaporation residue	Verdampfungsrückstand m, Verdunstungsrückstand m
evaporated filament	Verdampfungsheizfaden m	evaporation scales	Verdunstungswaage f
evaporated film; gaseous film	aufgedampfte Schicht f, Aufdampfschicht f; Gasfilm m, Gashaut f	evaporation star, nucleon star	Verdampfungsstern m, Zertrümmerungsstern m
evaporated metal [layer]	Metallaufdampfschicht f		
evaporating apparatus	s. evaporator		
evaporating basin	s. evaporating tank		
evaporating capacity, evaporativity, potential rate of evaporation	Verdunstungsvermögen n	evaporation supercooling	s. evaporative supercooling
evaporating dish	Verdampfungsschale f, Abdampfschale f; Verdunstungsschälchen n, Verdunstungsschale f	evaporation theory [of nucleons]	Verdampfungstheorie f, Ausdampftheorie f, Ausdampfungstheorie f
		evaporation to dryness, boiling down	Eindampfung f zur Trockne
evaporating flask (pan, pot)	s. evaporating tank	evaporation zone	s. evaporation region
evaporating tank, evaporating basin, evaporating flask, evaporating pot, evaporating pan	Verdampfungsgefäß n, Abdampfgefäß n, Verdampfungspfanne f; Verdunstungsgefäß n	evaporative ablation, evaporation ablation	Verdunstungsablation f
		evaporative capacity	s. evaporability
		evaporative cold, evaporation cold, cold of evaporation	Verdunstungskälte f
evaporating thermostat, evaporative thermostat	Verdampferthermostat m, Verdampfungsthermostat m	evaporative cooling, boiling (evaporation) cooling, vapour cooling	Verdunstungskühlung f; Verdunstungsabkühlung f, Siedekühlung f, Verdampfungskühlung f
evaporation <by ebullition>, vaporization	Verdampfung f		
		evaporative rate	s. evaporation rate
		evaporative supercooling, evaporation supercooling	Verdampfungsunterkühlung f
evaporation <from the surface>, surface evaporation	Verdunstung f; Evaporation f, unproduktive Verdunstung f; Ausdünstung f		
		evaporative thermostat	s. evaporating thermostat
evaporation	Eindampfung f, Abdampfung f	evaporativity, evaporating capacity, potential rate of evaporation	Verdunstungsvermögen n
evaporation <of nucleons>	Ausdampfung f, Verdampfung f <Nukleonen>	evaporator [unit]; evaporating apparatus; evaporation plant	Verdampfer m; Verdampf[ungs]apparat m; Verdampf[ungs]anlage f, Verdampferanlage f
evaporation ablation, evaporative ablation	Verdunstungsablation f		
evaporation centre	Verdampfungszentrum n		
evaporation coefficient	s. rate of evaporation	evaporigraph, atmograph	Atmograph m, Evaporigraph m
evaporation cold	s. evaporative cold		
evaporation cooling	s. evaporative cooling	evaporimeter, evaporometer, evaporation gauge (meter), evaporation pan; atmometer	Verdunstungsmesser m; Evaporimeter n; Atmometer n; Atmidometer n
evaporation curve; vaporization curve	Verdampfungskurve f; Verdunstungskurve f		
evaporation equilibrium, vaporization equilibrium	Verdampfungsgleichgewicht n	evapor-ion pump	Ionenverdampferpumpe f, Evapor-Ion-Pumpe f
evaporation exponent	Verdunstungsexponent m		
evaporation flux density	Verdampfungsstromdichte f		
		evaporizing getter	Verdampfungsgetter m, Verdampfgetter m
evaporation gauge	s. evaporimeter		
evaporation heat, [latent] heat of evaporation, vaporization heat, [latent] heat of vaporization	Verdampfungswärme f, Dampfbildungswärme f	evaporography	Evaporographie f
		evaporometer	s. evaporimeter

evapo[ro]transpiration	Evapotranspiration f	Ewing method, isthmus method	Isthmusmethode f, Isthmusverfahren n, Ewingsche Methode f
evection <in latitude, in longitude>	Evektion f <in Breite, in Länge>	Ewing theory of ferromagnetism	Ewingsche Theorie f des Ferromagnetismus
evection tide	Evektionstide f, Evektionswelle f	exact differential, total (perfect, complete) differential	vollständiges (totales, exaktes) Differential n
E-vector	s. electric intensity	exact [differential] equation	s. total differential equation
even-even nucleus; even-even nuclide	gg-Kern m, Gerade-gerade Kern m, doppelt gerader Kern m; gg-Nuklid n, Gerade-gerade-Nuklid n	exactness <e.g. of theory>	Exaktheit f <z. B. einer Theorie>
evening series	Abendgruppe f, Abendreihe f	exact solution, rigorous solution, strict solution	strenge Lösung f, exakte Lösung
evening star	Abendstern m		
evenly spaced	s. equispaced	exact χ^2-test	s. Fisher-Yates test
even molecule	gerades Molekül n, Molekül mit gerader Valenzelektronenzahl	exaltation of molecular refraction, optical exaltation	Exaltation f der Molekularrefraktion
even-odd nucleus; even-odd nuclide	gu-Kern m, Gerade-ungerade-Kern m; gu-Nuklid n, Gerade-ungerade-Nuklid n	examination <e.g. of the plate>	Durchsuche f, Durchmusterung f <z. B. Kernspurplatte>
		examination	s. a. testing
even parity, positive parity, parity + 1	gerade Parität f, Parität + 1, positive Parität	exaration	Exaration f
event, act, elementary act, elementary event <nucl.>	Ereignis n, Akt m, Einzelprozeß m, Elementarereignis n, Elementarakt m <Kern.>	exceeding, outnumbering	Übertreffen n, Übersteigen n, Größersein n
		exceeding, overrun, overshoot, passing-over, transgression	Überschreitung f <einer bestimmten, natürlichen Grenze>
event, world point, space-time point <rel.>	Ereignis n, Raumzeitpunkt m, Raum-Zeit-Punkt m, Weltpunkt m <Rel.>	exceeding probability, probability for exceeding	Überschreitungswahrscheinlichkeit f
event <stat.>, chance event	zufälliges Ereignis n, Ereignis <Stat.>	exceptional crystal	besonderer Kristall m
Eve number	Evesche Zahl f	exceptional direction	Ausnahmerichtung f
Everett['s] formula [of interpolation], Everett['s] interpolation formula	Everettsche Interpolationsformel f	exceptional plane, characteristic plane	charakteristische Ebene f
		excess	Exzeß m; Überschuß m
		excess	s. a. coefficient of excess <stat.>
ever-frost	s. permafrost		
evermoist	immerfeucht	excess absorption	Überschußabsorption f
eversafe	nuklear sicher	excess buoyancy	Auftriebsüberschuß m <Auftrieb − Gewicht>
Evershed effect	Evershed-Effekt m		
everywhere dense, dense <math.>	überall dicht, dicht <Math.>	excess carrier, excess charge carrier	Überschußladungsträger m, Überschußträger m
evidence	s. detection		
E-viton	E-Viton n	excess carrier concentration (density), excess concentration (density) of carriers, added carrier concentration	Überschußträgerkonzentration f, Überschußträgerdichte f, Überschußkonzentration f, Überschußdichte f
evoked potential	Erregungspotential n		
evolute [of curve]	Evolute f		
evolute [of surface], evolute surface, centre of curvature surface, central surface, surface of centres of the surface, centrosurface	Krümmungsmittelpunktsfläche f, Evolutenfläche f, Zentralfläche f		
		excess carrier resorption in the base	Überschußladungsträgerresorption f [in der Basis], Überschußträgerresorption f [in der Basis], Zurückgehen n der Überschußladungsträger
evolutionary phase	Entwicklungsstufe f, Entwicklungsphase f		
evolutionary track (trend)	Entwicklungsweg m		
evolution diagram	Entwicklungsdiagramm n	excess carrier storage in the base	Überschußladungsträgerspeicherung f [in der Basis], Überschußträgerspeicherung f [in der Basis]
evolution equation	Entwicklungsgleichung f		
evolution of gas	s. gas evolution		
evolution of heat	s. heat release		
evolution of stars, stellar evolution	Sternentwicklung f	excess charge	Überschußladung f
evolvable <math.>, developable	abwickelbar <Math.>	excess charge carrier	s. excess carrier
		excess concentration	Konzentrationsüberschuß m, Überschußkonzentration f
evolvent, involute	Evolvente f, Involute f, Filarevolvente f, Fadenevolvente f		
		excess concentration of carriers	s. excess carrier concentration
evolvent [function], involute [function], ev <math.>	Evolventenfunktion f, Evolvens m, ev <Math.>	excess conduction	s. n-type conduction
		excess current, overcurrent	Überstrom m, Überschußstrom m
evorsion <geo.>	Evorsion f, Ausstrudelung f, Auskolkung, Herausstrudeln n <Geo.>	excess density of carriers	s. excess carrier concentration
		excess electron, surplus electron	Überschußelektron n
Ewald['s] construction	Ewald-Konstruktion f, Ewaldsche Konstruktion f	excess entropy	Überschußentropie f
Ewald-Kornfeld method	Ewald-Kornfeldsches Verfahren n, Methode f von Ewald und Kornfeld	excess function <chem.>	Überschußfunktion f; Exzeßfunktion f, Zusatzfunktion f, Zusatzgröße f <Chem.>
Ewald['s] method	Ewaldsches Verfahren n, Methode f von Ewald		
Ewald['s] solution, pendellösung, pendulum solution	Pendellösung f, Ewaldsche Pendellösung	excess function	s. a. enthalpy of mixing
		excess heat, surplus heat	Überschußwärme f, überschüssige Wärme f, Wärmeüberschuß m
Ewald sphere, sphere of reflection	Ewaldsche Kugel f, Ausbreitungskugel f, Reflexionskugel f, Ewald-Kugel f	excessive load; overload, overloading, superloading	Überlast f; Über[be]lastung f, Mehrbelastung f
E[-] wave	s. E[-] mode	excessively acid	übersauer

excess minority carrier	Überschußminoritätsträger m
excess multiplication constant, excess multiplication factor	Überschußmultiplikationsfaktor m <k — 1>
excess noise factor, excess noise figure	zusätzliche Rauschzahl f, zusätzlicher Rauschfaktor m
excess of heat	Wärmeüberschuß m
excess pressure of sound, excess sound pressure	Überschalldruck m
excess reactivity, built-in reactivity	Reaktivitätsreserve f; Überschußreaktivität f, eingebaute Reaktivität f
excess reverse current	Übersperrstrom m, Überstrom m in Sperrichtung
excess semiconductor	s. n-type semiconductor
excess sound pressure, excess pressure of sound	Überschalldruck m
excess temperature, overtemperature	Übertemperatur f, Überschußtemperatur f
excess velocity, superspeed	Übergeschwindigkeit f
exchange, interchange	Austausch m; Wechsel m
exchange <between two stores>, exchanging	Umspeicherung f
exchange adsorption	Austauschadsorption f
exchange broadening, broadening of lines by exchange interaction	Austauschverbreiterung f
exchange capacity <bio.>	Austauschkapazität f <Bio.>
exchange chromatography	Austauschchromatographie
exchange coefficient. coefficient of exchange	Austauschkoeffizient m
exchange coefficient	s. a. effective turbulent diffusivity
exchange collision	Austauschstoß m
exchange constant	[wahre] Austauschkonstante f
exchange correction	Austauschkorrektion f
exchange correlation	Austauschkorrelation f
exchange coupling	Austauschkopplung f
exchange coupling	s. a. electron-pair bond
exchange current	Austauschstrom m
exchange current density	Austauschstromdichte f
exchange deformation	s. deformation of convective type
exchange degeneracy	Austauschentartung f
exchange diffusion	Austauschdiffusion f
exchange effect, exchange phenomenon	Austauscheffekt m
exchange energy	Austauschenergie f
exchange energy density	Austauschenergiedichte f
exchange field	Austauschfeld n
exchange force; position-exchange (platzwechsel) force	Austauschkraft f; Platzwechselkernkraft f
exchange frequency	Austauschfrequenz f
exchange gas	Austauschgas n
exchange Hamiltonian	Austausch-Hamilton-Operator m, Hamilton-Austauschoperator m
exchange integral	Austauschintegral n
exchange interaction	Austauschwechselwirkung f
exchange layer <meteo.> austausch region	Austauschschicht f <Meteo.>
exchange magnetic moment	magnetisches Austauschmoment n
exchange method	s. double weighing
exchange narrowing, narrowing of lines by exchange interaction	Austauschverschmälerung f
exchange of heat, heat exchange	Wärmeumsatz m
exchange of heat	s. a. heat transfer
exchange of heat	s. a. heat exchange
exchange of ions	s. ion exchange
exchange of momentum	Impulsaustausch m
exchange of site, interchange of sites; place exchange, platzwechsel; transposition of pairs, phantom transposition	Platzwechsel m
exchange of states, state exchange	Zustandsaustausch m
exchange of water	s. water exchange
exchange operator	Austauschoperator m
exchange phenomenon	s. exchange effect
exchange polarization, polarization by exchange	Austauschpolarisation f
exchange potential	Austauschpotential n
exchange rate	Austauschrate f; Austauschgeschwindigkeit f
exchange reaction	Austauschreaktion f
exchange reaction	s. a. interchange reaction
exchange resonance	Austauschresonanz f
exchange stiffness parameter, Bloch wall parameter	Bloch-Wand-Parameter m
exchange tensor	Austauschtensor m
exchange term	Austauschterm m, Austauschglied n, Austauschanteil m
exchange time	Austauschzeit f
exchanging, exchange <between two stores>	Umspeicherung f
excimer, excited dimer	Excimer n
excitant [of luminescence]	Lumineszenzerreger m, Erreger m [der Lumineszenz]
excitation, exciting; energizing; agitation; stimulation; activation	Anregung f; Erregung f; Aktivierung f
excitation; excitement, agitation <bio.>	Erregung f <Bio.>
excitation at break, break excitation	Öffnungsreiz m
excitation at make	Schließreizung f
excitation band	Anregungsband n
excitation by alternating current, alternating-current excitation, a.c. excitation	Wechselerregung f, Wechselstromerregung f
excitation by alternating currents <bio.>	Wechselstromreizung f
excitation by collision	s. collisional excitation <of radiation>
excitation by electric currents	s. electric stimulation <bio.>
excitation by electron impact	Elektronenstoßanregung f
excitation circuit	Erregerkreis m, Erregerstromkreis m
excitation collision	Anregungsstoß m
excitation conduction, excitation transmission	Erregungsleitung f
excitation cross-section, cross-section for excitation	Anregungsquerschnitt m, Wirkungsquerschnitt m für (der) Anregung, Anregungswirkungsquerschnitt m
excitation current	s. exciting current <bio.>
excitation curve	Anregungskurve f
excitation energy <bio.>, stimulus energy	Reizenergie f <Bio.>
excitation energy <nucl.>	Anregungsenergie f <Kern>
excitation function	Anregungsfunktion f
excitation in nerves, stimulation of nerve, nerve stimulation	Nervenreizung f
excitation in the parallel mode	Gleichtaktanregung f
excitation into the conduction band	Heben (Anheben) n ins Leitungsband

excitation level, excited level	angeregtes Niveau n, Anregungsniveau n	exciton state	Excitonenzustand m
excitation luminescence	Anregungsleuchten n	excitron, excitron valve	Excitron n, Excitronröhre f
excitation number	Anregungszahl f	excluded volume, covolume	Kovolumen n, verbotenes Volumen n, Eigenvolumen n [der Moleküle]
excitation of boundary layer, boundary layer excitation	Grenzschichtanfachung f, Anfachung f der Grenzschicht	exclusion area	strahlungsgefährdete Zone f, verbotene Zone
excitation of luminescence, luminescence excitation	Erregung (Anregung) f der Lumineszenz, Lumineszenzerregung f, Lumineszenzanregung f	exclusion filter	s. suppression filter
		exclusion filter	s. selective filter <opt.>
		exclusion of minority carriers	Exklusion (Feldverdrängung) f von Minoritätsträgern
excitation of oscillations, oscillation (vibration) excitation, excitation of vibrations; release of oscillations, oscillation release; generation of oscillations (vibrations), oscillation (vibration) generation	Schwingungserzeugung f, Erzeugung f von Schwingungen; Schwingungserregung f, Erregung f von Schwingungen, Anregung f von Schwingungen, Schwingungsanregung f	exclusion principle, Pauli['s] exclusion principle, Pauli['s] principle	[Paulisches] Ausschließungsprinzip n, Pauli-Prinzip n, Paulisches Prinzip (Eindeutigkeitsprinzip) n, Eindeutigkeitsprinzip, Pauli-Verbot n, Äquivalenzverbot n
		excretion <bio.>	Exkretion f; Ausscheidung f <Bio.>
excitation of sound	s. sound generation	excursion <e.g. of reactor>	Exkursion f <z. B. des Reaktors>
excitation of vibrations	s. excitation of oscillations	excursion	. a. deflection <of a pointer, needle>
excitation potential, excitation voltage	Anregungsspannung f, Anregungspotential n	execution	s. carrying out
excitation purity, purity	spektraler Farb[wert]anteil m, Farbanteil	exergy	Exergie f, technische Arbeitsfähigkeit f
excitation raising electrons from valency into the conduction band	s. intrinsic excitation	exerted moment	s. torque
		exfoliated mica	Glimmerschuppe f, Glimmerflocke f, Glimmerschüppchen n
excitatoin spectrum	Erregungsspektrum n, Erregungsverteilung f	exfoliation	Schichtspaltung f; Abschieferung f; Abblättern n
excitation state, excited state	angeregter Zustand m, Anregungszustand m	exfoliation	s. a. desquamation
		exhalation, volcanic exhalation	Exhalation f; Aushauchung f; Ausdünstung f <Geo.>
excitation threshold, threshold of stimulation (stimulus, irritation), stimulus threshold, threshold stimulus	Reizschwelle f, Schwellenreiz m, Nullschwelle f		
		exhalation <bio.>	Exhalation f, Ausatmung f <Bio.>
excitation time, stimulus time <bio.>	Reizzeit f, Reizdauer f <Bio.>	exhaust gas turbine	Abgasturbine f
excitation transmission, excitation conduction	Erregungsleitung f	exhausting power, delivery of pump, pump[ing] capacity, pumpage	Saugleistung f, Förderleistung f, Pumpleistung f
excitation voltage, excitation potential	Anregungsspannung f, Anregungspotential n	exhaustion; depletion; impoverishment	Verarmung f; Erschöpfung f, Verbrauchen n
excitation voltage	s. a. control voltage	exhaustion, extraction <e.g. of charged particles>	Absaugen n, Abziehen n, Abzug m, Extraktion f, Herausziehen n <z. B. geladene Teilchen>
excitation wave	Erregungswelle f		
excited dimer, excimer	Excimer n		
excited level, excitation level	angeregtes Niveau n, Anregungsniveau n	exhaustion, emanation, exit <of gas>	Ausströmung f, Emanation f
excited state, excitation state	angeregter Zustand m, Anregungszustand m	exhaustion diagram; effluogram	Ausströmdiagramm n
excited state, state of excitation <bio.>	Erregungszustand m <Bio.>	exhaustion layer	s. depletion layer <semi.>
excitement; excitation, agitation <bio.>	Erregung f <Bio.>	exhaustion of helium	Heliumbrennen n, Ausbrennen (Verbrennen) n des Heliums
exciter [of oscillations]	s. oscillator <el.>		
exciting	s. excitation	exhaustion of hydrogen	Wasserstoffbrennen n, Ausbrennen (Verbrennen) n des Wasserstoffs
exciting absorption	erregende Absorption f		
exciting agent, stimulation substance, exciting substance, stimulating agent	Reizmittel n, Reizstoff m, Stimulans n	exhaustion rate, rate of evacuation, pump speed, [relative] pumping speed <of pump>	Sauggeschwindigkeit f, Pumpgeschwindigkeit f, Fördergeschwindigkeit f, Volum[en]durchfluß m, Saugvermögen n <Pumpe>
exciting anode	s. starting anode	exhaustion region	s. depletion layer <semi.>
exciting coil	s. magnet coil	exhaust-steam turbine	Abdampfturbine f
exciting current, magnetizing current	Magnetisierungsstrom m	exhaust tube, pumping lead (stem)	Pump[en]rohr n, Pump[en]stengel m, Pumpstutzen m; Pumpzapfen m
exciting current, excitation (stimulating) current <bio.>	Reizstrom m, Reizstromstärke f <Bio.>	exhaust-type steam engine	Auspuffmaschine f
exciting field, magnetization field, magnetizing field	Magnetisierungsfeld n, Magnetisierfeld n, Erregerfeld n	existence diagram, E-diagram	Existenzdiagramm n
		existence theorem	Existenzsatz m
exciting force	Anregungskraft f	existential operator (quantifier), quantor of existence	Partikularisator m, Existentialoperator m, Existenzquantor n
exciting star	anregender Stern m		
exciting substance	s. exciting agent	exit	s. exhaustion <of gas>
exciting voltage <bio.>	Reizspannung f <Bio.>	exit channel	Ausgangskanal m
		exit dose	Austrittsdosis f
exciting winding	s. field winding	exit loss	Austrittsverlust m
exciton, electron-hole pair, hole-electron pair	Exciton n, Exziton n, Elektron-Defektelektron-Paar n	exit port	s. exit window <opt.>
		exit portal	Austrittsfeld n
exciton band	Excitonband n		
exciton level	Excitonenniveau n	exit probability <of electron>	Austrittswahrscheinlichkeit f <Elektron>

exit pupil, image-side pupil, Ramsden circle, eye-ring	Austrittspupille f, Augenkreis m, Ramsdenscher Kreis m, bildseitiges Blendenbild n der Öffnungsblende	**expansion by heat**	s. thermal expansion
		expansion by volume	s. cubic[al] expansion ‹therm.›
		expansion chamber ‹therm.›	Expansionskammer f, Expansionsraum m
exit slit, output aperture	Austrittsspalt m; Austrittsschlitz m; Ausgangsspalt m; Austrittsblende f	**expansion chamber**	s. a. surge tank
		expansion cloud chamber, Wilson['s] cloud (expansion) chamber, Wilson['s] chamber	Expansionsnebelkammer f, Wilsonsche Nebelkammer f, Nebelkammer f
exit temperature, outlet temperature	Austrittstemperatur f, Temperatur f am Ausgang, Temperatur beim Austritt, Ausgangstemperatur f	**expansion coefficient**	s. coefficient of thermal expansion
exit velocity	s. efflux velocity ‹of gas›	**expansion coefficient**	s. a. coefficient of the expansion [in a series]
exit window, exit port ‹opt.›	Austrittsluke f, Bildluke f, Bildraumluke f ‹Opt.›	**expansion coefficient**	s. a. expansion ratio
ex-nova, post-nova ‹pl.: ex-novae, post-novae›	Postnova f, Exnova f ‹pl.: Postnovae, Exnovae›	**expansion constant**, Hubble['s] constant	Hubble-Konstante f, Hubblesche Konstante f, Expansionskonstante f
ex-nova spectrum, post-nova spectrum	Postnovaspektrum n	**expansion cooling**	Expansionskühlung f
ex-nova state, post-nova state	Postnovazustand m	**expansion crack**	Dehnungsriß m; Treibriß m
exocyclic ‹chem.›	exozyklisch, exocyclisch ‹Chem.›		
exoelectron	Exoelektron n	**expansion curve**	Ausdehnungskurve f, Expansionslinie f
exoelectron[ic] emission, afteremission [of electrons], EEE	Elektronennachemission f, Exoelektronenemission f, Exoemission f, Kramer-Effekt m, EEE	**expansion efficiency**	Expansionswirkungsgrad m
		expansion engine, expansion machine, decompressor	Expansionsmaschine f, Ausdehnungsmaschine f, Detander m
exoenergetic, exo[en]ergic	s. exothermic	**expansion in a Dirichlet series**, Dirichlet expansion	Dirichlet-Entwicklung f
exogenetic, exogenous	exogen, außenbürtig		
exograph	s. radiograph	**expansion in an orthogonal series**, orthogonal expansion	Orthogonalentwicklung f, Entwicklung f in eine Orthogonalreihe
exomorphism	Exomorphose f		
exosmosis	Exosmose f	**expansion in a series**, series expansion, development in a series	Entwicklung f in eine Reihe, Zerlegung f in eine Reihe, Reihenentwicklung f
exosphere, spray region, fringe region	Exosphäre f, äußere Atmosphäre f		
exothermal, exothermic, heat-generating; exoenergetic, exoenergic, exoergic	exotherm, wärme[ab]-gebend, wärmeerzeugend, wärmeentbindend; exergonisch, exoenergetisch, energieabgebend	**expansion in Legendre polynomials**, Legendre polynomial expansion	Entwicklung f nach Legendreschen Polynomen, Entwicklung nach Kugelfunktionen
		expansion in plane waves, plane wave expansion	Entwicklung f nach ebenen Wellen
exotic atom	exotisches (fremdartiges) Atom n	**expansion instrument**, hot-wire instrument	Hitzdrahtinstrument n; Hitzdrahtmeßgerät n; Hitzdrahtmeßwerk n
exotic river	Fremdlingsfluß m		
exotropism	Exotropismus m	**expansion into (in terms of) continued fractions**, continued fraction representation	Kettenbruchentwicklung f, Kettenbruchdarstellung f
expander, tube expander	Aufweitedorn m, Rohraufweitedorn m, Streckdorn m, Aufweitestopfen m		
		expansion liquefying	Expansionsverflüssigung f
expander ‹el.›	Dehner m, Amplitudendehner m ‹El.›	**expansion machine**, cold air expansion machine	Kaltluftmaschine f, Kaltluft-Expansionsmaschine f
expander, volume expander, dynamic expander (amplifier) ‹el.›	Dynamikdehner m ‹El.›	**expansion machine**	s. a. expansion engine
		expansion Mach wave	Machsche Expansionswelle f
expanding envelope	expandierende Gashülle f	**expansion of the universe**, cosmic expansion	Expansion (Ausdehnung) f des Weltalls
expanding fan, fan of comet	fächerförmige Schweifstrahlen mpl, Fächer m		
expanding jet [of the comet], jet of the comet	Schweifstrahl m, fadenförmiger Schweifstrahl	**expansion parameter**	Entwicklungsparameter m
expanding universe	expandierendes Weltall n, „expanding universe" n	**expansion pyrometer**	s. bimetallic pyrometer
		expansion ratio, expansion coefficient	Expansionsverhältnis n, Expansionsgrad m, Expansionszahl f, Druckverhältnis n, Ausbreitungskoeffizient m
expansibility, expansibleness, expansiveness	Ausdehnbarkeit f, Ausdehnungsfähigkeit f, Expansionsfähigkeit f		
expansion; dilatation; extension	Dilatation f; Dehnung f; Ausdehnung f; Zerrung f, Ausweitung f		
		expansion tank	s. surge tank
		expansion theorem	Entwicklungssatz m
expansion; decompression ‹of gases›	Ausdehnung f, Expansion f, Expandieren n; Entspannung f ‹Gase›	**expansion theorem**	[Heavisidescher] Entwicklungssatz m
expansion ‹math.›	Entwicklung f ‹Math.›	**expansion thermometer**	Ausdehnungsthermometer n
expansion ‹mech.›, widening, broadening, enlargement	Erweiterung f ‹Mech.›		
expansion	s. a. widening	**expansion tong**	Zangenmanipulator m, Fernbedienungszange f
expansion accompanied by the doing of external work	Entspannung f unter äußerer Arbeitsleistung	**expansion vessel**	s. surge tank
		expansion wave	s. rarefactional wave ‹aero., hydr.›
expansion according to the [elements of the] j-th column ‹of determinant›	Entwicklung f nach der j-ten Spalte ‹Determinante›	**expansion wave**	s. expansive wave
		expansion work	Dehnungsarbeit f, Ausdehnungsarbeit f, Expansionsarbeit f
expansion bellows, bellows	Dehnbüchse f; Druck[ausgleichs]dose f; Dehnungsausgleicher m	**expansiveness**, expansibility, expansibleness	Ausdehnbarkeit f, Ausdehnungsfähigkeit f, Expansionsfähigkeit f

expansive wave, expansion wave, blast wave	Expansionswelle f, Druckwelle f	**explosion burette**, eudiometer	Eudiometer[rohr] n, Explosionsbürette f
expectancy, expectation	s. mathematical expectation <stat.>	**explosion centre**, centre of explosion	Explosionsherd m, Explosionszentrum n, Nullpunkt m <Explosion>
expectation of life <bio.>	Lebenserwartung f, mittlere Lebensdauer f <Bio.>	**explosion crater**	Explosionskrater m; Sprengkrater m, Explosionstrichter m
expectation (expected) value	s. mathematical expectation <stat.>	**explosion engine**	s. internal-combustion engine
expedance, negative impedance	negativer komplexer Wechselstromwiderstand m, negative Impedanz f, Expedanz f	**explosion focus**, hypocentre of the explosion	Sprengherd m
expenditure	s. consumption	**explosion gas pipette**, gas ignition pipette, gas-explosion tube	Explosionspipette f
expenditure of energy (work)	s. energy expended	**explosion heat**	s. heat of explosion
expense; consumption; expenditure; display	Verbrauch m; Aufwand m; Verzehrung f	**explosion limit**, explosive (explosivity) limit	Explosionsgrenze f
experience	Erfahrung f; Empirie f	**explosion limits** <US>	s. inflammability limits
experiment; run, test	Experiment n, Versuch m	**explosion line**, blast line	Sprenglinie f
experimental arrangement (assembly)	s. experimental set-up	**explosion motor**	s. internal-combustion engine
experimental check, experimental tests, experimental verification	experimentelle Nachprüfung (Prüfung, Bestätigung, Verifizierung) f	**explosion shock**, explosion wave	Explosionswelle f, Knallwelle f
experimental condition	Versuchsbedingung f	**explosion theory** <of Universe>	Explosionstheorie f <des Weltalls>
experimental fact	Erfahrungstatsache f	**explosion turbine**, constant-volume gas turbine	Verpuffungsturbine f, Explosionsturbine f, Gleichraum[verbrennungs]turbine f
experimental hole	Experimentierkanal m		
experimental loop, loop <of reactor>	Versuchsschleife f, Experimentierschleife f <Reaktor>		
experimental material	s. material under investigation		
experimental point, measuring point <e.g. in a diagram>	Meßpunkt m, Meßwert m <z. B. im Diagramm, auf der Skala>	**explosion wave**, explosion shock	Explosionswelle f, Knallwelle f
		explosion welding	s. explosive welding
		explosive	Explosivstoff m, Sprengstoff m
experimental reactor	Versuchsreaktor m; Experimentierreaktor m	**explosive**, high explosive, brisant explosive	[brisanter] Strengstoff m
		explosive flame	s. shooting flame
experimental result	s. result of measurement	**explosive force**	s. explosive power
experimental section, throat <e.g. of the wind tunnel>	Versuchsstrecke f, Versuchsstelle f; Versuchsplatz m <z. B. Windkanal>	**explosive limit**	s. explosion limit
		explosiveness	s. explosibility
experimental set-up, experimental arrangement, experimental assembly; test set-up	Versuchsanordnung f, Versuchsaufbau m, experimentelle Anordnung f	**explosive power**, explosive force	Sprengkraft f, Explosionskraft f
		explosive star	s. nova
		explosive welding, explosion welding	Sprengplattieren n, Explosionsschweißen n, Schockwellenplattieren n, Explosivplattieren n, Schockschweißen n, Sprengschweißen n
experimental tests	s. experimental check		
experimental value, measured value, value measured, test value	Meßwert m, experimentell ermittelter Wert m, experimenteller Wert		
		explosivity	s. explosibility
		explosivity limit	s. explosion limit
		exponent, index <math.>	Exponent m; Hochzahl f <math.>
		exponent	s. a. exponential curve
		exponential	s. exponential function
experimental verification	s. experimental check	**exponential curve**, exponent	Exponentialkurve f
experiment for observing interference	s. interference experiment		
experiment series, test series; series of tests	Versuchsreihe f, Versuchsserie f	**exponential decay**, exponential fall	exponentieller Abfall m
experiments for comparison, competitive (comparative) experiments	vergleichende Versuche mpl, Vergleichsversuche mpl	**exponential distribution**	Exponentialverteilung f
explanation, interpretation, elucidation	Interpretation f, Deutung f, Auslegung f, Erklärung f	**exponential experiment**	Exponentialexperiment n, Exponentialversuch m
explanatory variable	s. regressor	**exponential fall**	s. exponential decay
explement of angle	Ergänzungswinkel m zu 360°	**exponential filter**, power law filter	Potenzfilter n
exploded wire	s. exploding wire	**exponential function**, exponential	Exponentialfunktion f
exploded-wire continuum	Metalldrahtentladungskontinuum n		
exploded wire discharge	s. exploding wire	**exponential function**, exp, e	Exponentialfunktion f, e-Funktion f, exp, e
exploding galaxy	explodierende Galaxis f	**exponential horn**, logarithmic horn	Exponentialhorn n, logarithmisches Horn n, Exponentialtrichter m
exploding wire [discharge], exploded wire [discharge]	explodierender Draht m, Metalldrahtentladung f		
exploration of space	s. space research		
exploring <of image>, scansion, scanning	Bildfeldzerlegung f; Bildzerlegung f	**exponential integral**, exponential integral function, ei, Ei	Exponentialintegral n, Integralexponentialfunktion f, Integralexponentielle f, Ei, ei
exploring	s. a. scanning		
exploring disk, Nipkow disk, spiral disk, aperatured disk	Nipkow-Scheibe f, Abtastscheibe f, Spirallochscheibe f	**exponential line** <el.>, exponential transmission line	Exponentialleitung f <El.>
exploring electrode	s. active electrode	**exponentially growing flow**	exponentiell angefachte Strömung f
explosibility, explosiveness, explosivity	Explodierbarkeit f, Explosivität f, Sprengfähigkeit f		
explosion analysis	Explosionsanalyse f		

exponential pile (reactor)	Exponentialreaktor m	extended dislocation	aufgespaltene Versetzung f
exponential rising	exponentieller Anstieg m, Zunahme f nach einem Exponentialgesetz	extended mean value theorem	s. Taylor formula
exponential scale	Potenzskala f; Potenzskale f	extended mean value theorem	s. second mean value theorem of the differential calculus
exponential series	Exponentialreihe f	extended plane	s. closed complex plane
exponential transmission line, exponential line ‹el.›	Exponentialleitung f ‹El.›	extended point transformation	erweiterte Punkttransformation f
exponential well	Exponentialpotential n, exponentieller Potentialtopf m, Exponentialtopf m	extended shower	s. extensive shower
		extended source	ausgedehnte Quelle f
exponent in creep rate law	Exponent m im Kriechgesetz	extended surface	entwickelte Oberfläche f
		extended system ‹therm.›	erweitertes System n ‹Therm.›
expose ‹to an action›	aussetzen ‹einer Wirkung›	extended tip, stretched tip ‹of wing›	ausgezogene Spitze f ‹Tragflügel›
exposed	s. radiation-exposed	extended tube ‹qu.›	erweiterte Röhre f ‹Qu.›
exposed-stem correction, exposed-thread correction	s. thermometric correction	extensible	s. telescopic
		extensimeter	s. extensometer
expose to radiation	exponieren; bestrahlen; beschießen; belichten; aussetzen ‹Strahlung›	extension; dilatation; expansion	Dilatation f; Dehnung f; Ausdehnung f; Zerrung f, Ausweitung f
exposition meter	s. exposure meter	extension, spread[ing], stretch[ing]	Spreizung f
exposure; irradiation, illumination	Strahlenexponierung f, Exponierung f, Exposition f, Bestrahlung f; Belichtung f	extension ‹e.g. of field, operator› ‹math.›	Erweiterung f ‹z. B. Körper, Operator› ‹Math.›
		extension	s. a. extent
exposure ‹quantity› ‹bio.›	Exposure f, Exposition f, „exposure"-Leistung f; Strahlenbelastung f ‹Größe› ‹Bio.›	extensional oscillation (vibration), longitudinal vibration, longitudinal oscillation	Längsschwingung f, Dehnungsschwingung f, Longitudinalschwingung f, longitudinale Schwingung f
exposure ‹quantity›, quantity of illumination ‹opt.; phot.›	Belichtung f ‹Größe› ‹Opt.; Phot.›; Exposition f ‹Phot.›	extensional wave, dilatational wave ‹mech.›	Dehn[ungs]welle f, Dilatationswelle f ‹Mech.›
exposure	s. a. taking ‹phot.›	extension crevice (fissure)	s. dilatational fissure
exposure age	s. cosmic exposure age		
exposure calculator	Expositionsrechenschieber m	extension in configuration	Konfigurationsausdehnung f
exposure-density relationship	s. characteristic curve	extension in depth, extent in depth	Tiefenausdehnung f
exposure factor	Expositionsfaktor m		
exposure field, irradiation field	Bestrahlungsfeld n	extension in phase	Phasenausdehnung f
		extension in velocity	Geschwindigkeitsausdehnung f
exposure fog	Belichtungsschleier m	extension lead (line)	s. artificial line
exposure hole	s. irradiation channel	extension of effective part [of scale], range extension	Bereichserweiterung f, Meßbereichserweiterung f, Erweiterung f des Meßbereichs
exposure meter	Belichtungsmesser m		
exposure nucleus	Belichtungskeim m		
exposure period	s. exposure time ‹opt.›	extension of the crescent (horns of Venus)	Übergreifen n der Hörnerspitzen
exposure rate ‹bio.›	Exposureleistung f, Expositionsleistung f, „exposure"-Leistung f ‹Bio.›	extension of the tube, tube extension	Tubusauszug m
exposure rate	s. a. irradiance	extension pad	s. artificial line
		extension ring	Verlängerungsring m
exposure rate meter	Exposureleistungsmesser m, Expositionsleistungsmesser m	extension tube ‹opt.›	Ansatztubus m, Vergrößerungstubus, m, Verlängerungstubus m ‹Opt.›
exposure time, irradiation time	Expositionszeit f, Bestrahlungszeit f		
exposure time, exposure period, duration of exposure ‹opt.›	Expositionszeit f, Belichtungszeit f	extensive air shower	s. extensive shower
		extensive parameter (property, quantity)	s. extensive thermodynamic property
exposure value, light value	Lichtwert m, Belichtungswert m	extensive shower, extensive (extended) air shower, extended shower, giant air shower, Auger shower	ausgedehnter Luftschauer m, Auger-Schauer m, Riesenschauer m
expressing in partial fractions, partial fraction expansion, decomposition into partial fractions	Partialbruchzerlegung f		
		extensive thermodynamic property, extensive quantity (property), extensive parameter, magnitude ‹therm.›	extensive Variable (Größe) f, extensiver (additiver) Parameter m, Extensitätsvariable f, Extensitätsparameter m, Extensitätsgröße f, Quantitätsgröße f, generalisierte Koordinate f ‹Therm.›
expression for the variation of mass with velocity, relativistic mass equation	relativistische Massengleichung (Massenänderung) f, Lorentz[-Einstein]sche Gleichung f		
expression to be integrated	s. integrand		
expulsion, ejection ‹of air›	Ausstoßen n ‹Luft›	extensometer, extensimeter, strainometer	Dehnungsmesser m, Extensometer n
		extensometric; tensometric	extensometrisch; tensometrisch
exsiccant	s. dehydrator	extensometry, strain measurement (gauging)	Dehnungsmessung f
exsiccation	s. dehydration		
extended	ausgedehnt ‹flächenhaft oder räumlich›, nichtpunktförmig	extent, extension	Ausdehnung f, Erstreckung f
		extent	s. a. effective range
extended	s. a. three-dimensional	extent in depth, extension in depth	Tiefenausdehnung f
extended air shower	s. extensive shower		
extended complex plane	s. closed complex plane		

extent of accommodation	s. amplitude of accommodation	externally applied load	s. external force
extent of reaction	[molare] Reaktionslaufzahl f	external magnetic flux	Fremdfluß m
		external mirror coating	s. mirror surfacing
extenuation <of action>	s. fading	external modulation	äußere Modulation f
exterior <math.>	Äußeres n <Math.>	external normal pressure	äußerer Normaldruck m
exterior ballistics, external ballistics	äußere Ballistik f	external optical density, reflection [optical] density	Schwärzung (optische Dichte) f bei Reflexion, Reflexionsdichte f
exterior boundary value problem	äußeres Randwertproblem n		
exterior derivative	äußere Ableitung f		
exterior differential form	äußere Differentialform f	external parameter	äußerer Parameter m
		external phase	s. continuous phase
		external photoeffect (photoelectric effect)	s. photoemissive effect
exterior differentiation	äußere Differentiation f	external porosity, surface porosity	Oberflächenporosität f, Außenporosität f, Außenlunker m, bis zur Oberfläche reichender Mikrolunker m
exterior measure, upper measure	äußeres Maß n		
exterior multiplication	äußere Multiplikation f		
exterior normal derivative	äußere Normalableitung f, Ableitung f in Richtung der äußeren Normalen	external potential energy	äußere potentielle Energie f, Lagenenergie f, Energie der Lage
exterior pressure, pressure outside	äußerer Druck m, Außendruck m	external power	äußere Leistung f, Leistung äußerer Arbeit
exterior product	s. outer product		
exterior temperature, outside temperature, temperature outside	Außentemperatur f	external Q [factor]	äußere Kreisgüte f
		external quenching	Fremdlöschung f
exterior work, external work, work done by external forces	äußere Arbeit f, Arbeit äußerer Kräfte		
external-anode tube, external-anode valve	Außenanodenröhre f	external quenching [of luminescence]	Fremdauslöschung f [der Lumineszenz]
		external radiation	äußere Strahlung f
external aperture	äußere Apertur f	external resistance (resistor)	s. load resistance
external ballistics	s. exterior ballistics	external rotation	äußere Rotation f
external block effect	äußerer Blockeffekt m	external rotation partition function, partition function of external rotation	Zustandssumme f der äußeren Rotation
external breeding ratio	äußeres Brutverhältnis n		
external cathode counter [tube], Maze counter [tube], Maze tube counter	Maze-Zählrohr n, Zählrohr n mit Außenkatode		
		external shape of the crystal	s. habit of the crystal
external chord	äußere Profilsehne f	external twisting moment	s. torsional moment
external condition, external constraint	äußere Bedingung f		
		external variance	s. interclass variance
external conical refraction	äußere konische Refraktion f	external virial	äußeres Virial n
		external work	s. exterior work
external constraint	s. external condition	extinction, optical extinction (density), absorbance	[dekadische] Extinktion f, optische Dichte f, spektrales Absorptionsmaß n
external conversion	äußere Konversion f, äußere Umwandlung f		
external conversion electron	Elektron n der äußeren Umwandlung (Konversion)	extinction <of discharge>, quenching	Löschung f <Entladung>
external diffusion coefficient	äußerer Diffusionskoeffizient m	extinction <of light> <opt., astr.>	Extinktion f <Licht> <Opt., Astr.>
external dimensions	s. overall dimensions	extinction, evanescence <of luminescence>	Auslöschung f, Löschung f <Lumineszenz>
external drop [in potential]	äußerer Spannungsabfall m		
external excitation, independent (separate) excitation	Fremderregung f; äußere Erregung f	extinction	s. a. cancellation <of radiation> <gen.>
		extinction by steam, steam extinction	Wasserdampfextinktion f
external exposure, external irradiation	äußere Bestrahlung f, äußerliche Bestrahlung; Fremdbestrahlung f	extinction coefficient	s. decimal extinction coefficient
external field	äußeres Feld n	extinction coefficient at unit concentration	s. molar extinction coefficient
external field <of polarizing prism>, useful field of view measured externally	Gesichtsfeldwinkel m, Dingwinkel m <Polarisationsprisma>	extinction coefficient at unit density	s. specific extinction coefficient
		extinction coefficient for the atmospheric haze	Dunst-Extinktionskoeffizient m
external field	s. a. disturbance field <el.>		
external force; externally applied load	äußere Kraft f; von außen wirkende (aufgebrachte) Kraft, eingeprägte Kraft, Stützlast f	extinction coefficient for unit concentration	s. molar extinction coefficient
		extinction coefficient for unit density	s. specific extinction coefficient
external geomagnetic field	Außenfeld n, Erdaußenfeld n	extinction coefficient multiplied by the factor $\lambda/4\pi$; absorption coefficient multiplied by the factor $\lambda/4\pi$	Extinktionskoeffizient m; Absorptionskoeffizient m
external gravitational field	äußeres Gravitationsfeld n		
external heat of evaporation, external latent heat	äußere Verdampfungswärme f		
		extinction coefficient per unit concentration	s. molar extinction coefficient
external inductance	äußere Induktivität f, äußerer Selbstinduktionskoeffizient m	extinction coefficient per unit density	s. specific extinction coefficient
		extinction index	Extinktionsindex m
external irradiation	s. external exposure	extinction integral	Extinktionsintegral n
external kinetic energy	äußere kinetische Energie f	extinction of light in the air	s. atmospheric extinction
external latent heat	s. external heat of evaporation	extinction of the meteor, disappearance of the meteor	Verlöschen n des Meteors
external load, extrinsic load	äußere Belastung f		

extinction   246

extinction photometer s. star photometer
extinction position, Auslöschungsstellung *f*
  position of extinction
extinction potential s. extinction voltage
extinction power Extinktionsgrad *m*, Extinktionsvermögen *n*
extinction table Extinktionstabelle *f*
extinction theorem Extinktionssatz *m* ‹der Streuung von Teilchen›
  ‹in particle scattering›

extinction voltage, Löschspannung *f*
  extinction potential; ‹Entladung›
  deionization voltage,
  deionization potential
  ‹of discharge›

extinction voltage Löschspannung *f*
  ‹of ion tube› ‹Ionenröhre›
extinguished volcano erloschener Vulkan *m*
extinguishing s. cancellation
  ‹of radiation› ‹gen.›
extra-close coupling, extrem feste Kopplung *f*
  extremely close
  coupling
extractant, extraction Extraktionsmittel *n*, selektives (differenzierendes)
  solvent, extractive agent Lösungsmittel *n*

extractibility Extraktionsfähigkeit *f*; Extrahierbarkeit *f*
extracting electrode Saugelektrode *f*, Absaugelektrode *f*
extracting field Absaugfeld *n*

extraction ‹chem.› Extraktion *f*, Extrahieren *n*, Herauslösen *n*; Herausziehen *n* ‹Chem.›
extraction ‹e.g. of rods›, Ausfahren *n*, Herausziehen *n*; Anheben *n*
  withdrawal ‹z. B. Stäbe›
extraction s. *a.* exhaustion ‹e.g. of charged particles›
extraction s. *a.* ejection ‹of the beam›
extraction apparatus, Extraktionsapparat *m*, Extraktor *m*
  extractor
extraction by means of a Sondenextraktion *f*
  probe, probe extraction
extraction by shaking s. shaking
  with solvent
extraction coefficient Extraktionskoeffizient *m*
extraction of gas, Entgasung *f*, Gasaustreibung *f*, Austreibung *f* von Gasen, Beseitigung *f* von Gasresten
  degassing, outgassing,
  degasification
extraction of heat s. heat removal
extraction of ion beam, Ionenausschleusung *f*, Ionenextraktion *f*, Herausführung *f* des Ionenstrahls
  ion beam extraction,
  ion extraction
extraction of power, Leistungsentnahme *f*; Leistungsentzug *m*
  taking (removal) of
  power, power extraction
extraction potential s. extraction voltage
extraction solvent s. extractant
extraction turbine, Anzapfturbine *f*, Entnahmeturbine *f*
  pan-out turbine
extraction voltage, Absaugspannung *f*, Ziehspannung *f*; Saugspannung *f* ‹El.›
  extraction potential

extractive agent s. extractant
extractive distillation, Extraktivdestillation *f*, extraktive Destillation *f*, Extraktionsdestillation *f*, Distexprozeß *m*
  distex process
extractor, extraction Extraktionsapparat *m*, Extraktor *m*
  apparatus
extractor s. *a.* beam extractor ‹acc.›
extracurrent Extrastrom *m*
extra-dense crown Schwerstkron *n*, Schwerstkronglas *n*, SSK
extra-dense flint Schwerstflint *n*, Schwerstflintglas *n*, SSF

extraeclipsing corono- s. coronagraph
  graph
extra-excitation s. overexcitation
extra exposure, pre-exposure, preliminary [uniform] exposure, prefogging Vorbelichtung *f*

extra-foveal vision, indirektes (extrafoveales) Sehen *n*
  indirect vision
extragalactic, extragalaktisch, außergalaktisch, anagalaktisch
  anagalactic
extrahard s. extremely hard
extra-heavy aggregate, Schwerstbeton *m*, Beton *m* hoher Dichte
  extra-heavy[-aggregate] concrete, high-density concrete
extra-high-current Höchststromgenerator *m*
  generator, extra-high-output generator
extra-high energy, Höchstenergie *f*
  superhigh energy, very high energy
extra-high-energy Höchstenergiephysik *f*, Kernphysik (Physik) *f* höchster Energien
  [nuclear] physics,
  extremely high energy
  physics
extra-high frequency, Extrahochfrequenz *f*, Millimeterwellenfrequenz *f*, Höchstfrequenz (Frequenz) *f* im Millimeterwellenbereich, EHF ‹30 000 ··· 300 000 MHz›
  extremely high frequency,
  E.H.F., EHF, c.h.f., ehf
  ‹30,000 – 300,000 Mc/s›

extra-high frequency Millimeterwellenbereich *m*, Millimeterbereich *m*, Millibereich *m*, EHF-Bereich *m*, EHF
  range, range of extra-high (extremely high) frequency, extremely high frequency range, millimetric wavelength [range], E.H.F. range, E.H.F.
extra-high frequency Millimeterwelle *f*
  wave, millimetre wave, ‹1 ··· 10 mm›
  E.H.F. wave ‹1 – 10 mm›

extra-high-output s. extra-high-current
  generator generator
extra-high-power tube, Höchstleistungsröhre *f*
  ultra-high-power tube
extra-high pressure, very Höchstdruck *m*
  !high pressure, hyperpressure
extra-high pressure con- Höchstdruckkontinuum *n*
  tinuum, continuous spectrum for extra-high pressure
extra-high pressure Höchstdruckentladung *f*
  discharge
extra-high pressure Höchstdruck[entladungs]lampe *f*, Superhochdrucklampe *f*
  [discharge] lamp
extra high pressure Quecksilberhöchstdrucklampe *f*, Hg-Höchstdrucklampe *f*, Höchstdruck-Quecksilberdampflampe *f*
  mercury [vapour] lamp
extra-high pressure Xenon-Höchstdruckbogen *m*
  xenon arc, xenon extra-high pressure arc
extra-high temperature höchste Temperatur *f*, Höchsttemperatur *f*
extra-high-temperature Höchsttemperatur-Ionenquelle *f*
  ion source
extra-high tension, Höchstspannung *f*
  extra-high voltage, supervoltage, E.H.T., e.h.t., eht, E.H.V., e.h.v., ehv
extra-high-tension Höchstspannungsgenerator *m*
  generator, extra-high-voltage generator
extra-high-tension Höchstspannungsisolation *f*
  insulation, extra-high-voltage insulation
extra-high-tension Höchstspannungsisolator *m*
  insulator, extra-high-voltage insulator
extra-high-tension line, Höchstspannungsleitung *f*
  extra-high-voltage line
extra-high vacuum s. ultra-high vacuum
extra-high-voltage s. extra-high tension
extra-high-voltage s. extra-high-tension
  generator generator
extra-high-voltage Höchstspannungsisolation *f*
  insulation, extra-high-tension insulation
extra-high-voltage s. extra-high-tension
  insulator insulator
extra-high-voltage line s. extra-high-tension line
extra hole zusätzliches Defektelektron (Loch) *n*

extra-loose coupling, extrem lose Kopplung *f*
  extremely loose coupling
extra-low, extremely low extrem niedrig

extramolecular condensation	s. intermolecular condensation	extremely high frequency range	s. extra-high frequency range
extraneous field	s. disturbance field	extremely loose coupling, extra-loose coupling	extrem lose Kopplung f
extranuclear <bio., nucl.>; orbital, peripheral <nucl.>	extranuklear, Hüllen-, Bahn-, kernfern <Kern.>; extranuklear, extranukleăr <Bio.>	extremely low, extra-low	extrem niedrig
		extremely pure, extra[-]pure, high-purity, hyperpure	reinst
extranuclear electron, orbital electron, planetary electron	Hüllenelektron n, Bahnelektron n	extremely soft, extrasoft	extrem weich, extraweich
		extreme population I	Extreme Population f I
extraordinary Hall coefficient	außerordentlicher Hall-Koeffizient m	extreme red	äußerstes (extremes) Rot n
extraordinary high sea, extraordinary stormy sea	außergewöhnlich hohe (schwere) See f, gewaltig schwere See <Stärke 9>	extreme sensitivity, supersensitivity, ultrasensitivity	Höchstempfindlichkeit f, Superempfindlichkeit f, extreme Empfindlichkeit f
		extreme ultraviolet, E.U.V., euv	extremes Ultraviolett n, EUV
extraordinary ray	außerordentlicher (extraordinärer) Strahl m		
extraordinary stormy sea	s. extraordinary high sea	extreme ultraviolet radiation, E.U.V. (euv) radiation	EUV-Strahlung f, extreme Ultraviolettstrahlung f, Strahlung f im extremen Ultraviolett
extraordinary wave, X wave	außerordentliche Welle f		
extrapolated boundary	extrapolierte Grenze (Reaktorbegrenzung) f		
extrapolated range	extrapolierte Reichweite f	extreme value, extremum, extreme	Extremum n, Extremwert m
extrapolation chamber, extrapolation ionization chamber	Extrapolationskammer f	extreme-value problem, extremum problem	Extremwertproblem n, Extremalaufgabe f
		extreme violet	äußerstes (extremes) Violett n
extrapolation distance, linear extrapolation distance (length), augmentation distance; extrapolation length	Extrapolationslänge f, lineare Extrapolationslänge, Extrapolationsstrecke f, extrapolierte Länge f, extrapolierter Abstand m		
		extremity <of the vector>	Spitze f [des Vektors]
		extremity of the crescent <of the Moon or an inferior planet>, cusp	Hörnerspitze f
extrapolation ionization chamber	s. extrapolation chamber	extremum in the large, absolute (global) extremum	absolutes Extremum n, Extremum im Großen
extrapolation length	s. extrapolation distance		
extra[-]pure, high-purity, extremely pure, hyperpure	reinst	extremum of temperature	Temperaturextrem n
extra-pure material	s. extra-pure substance		
extra-pure substance, extra-pure material	Reinststoff m		
		extremum problem, extreme-value problem	Extremwertproblem n, Extremalaufgabe f
		extrinsic, impurity <semi.>	gitterfremd, materialfremd, stofffremd, Fremd-, Verunreinigungs-, störstellenhaltig, Stör-; störstellenleitend <Halb.>
extrasoft	s. extremely soft		
extra spectral line	zusätzliche Spektrallinie f, Zusatzlinie f		
extra-steep	übersteil		
extraterrestrial noise, cosmic noise	kosmisches (extraterrestrisches) Rauschen n, Weltraumrauschen n	extrinsic carrier	Störstellenladungsträger m
extraterrestrial physics	extraterrestrische Physik f	extrinsic colour mixture, improper colour mixture	äußere Farbmischung f, uneigentliche Farbmischung
extraterrestrial solar radiation	extraterrestrische Sonnenstrahlung f	extrinsic conduction, impurity (defect) conduction, conduction by extrinsic carriers, extrinsic (impurity, defect) conductivity, conductivity by extrinsic carriers	Störstellenleitung f, Störleitung f, Fehlordnungsleitung f, Fremdleitung f, Stör[stellen]leitfähigkeit f, Fehlordnungsleitfähigkeit f, Fremdleitfähigkeit f
extraterrestrial zone of radiation	s. Allen radiation belt / Van		
extra-thermal ionization	überthermische Ionisierung f		
extratropical region (zone)	s. ectropical region		
extra voltage	Extraspannung f	extrinsic conductivity, impurity conductivity <quantity>	Stör[stellen]leitfähigkeit f, Fehlordnungsleitfähigkeit f, Fremdleitfähigkeit f <Größe>
extra-wide-angle objective	Überweitwinkelobjektiv n		
extra-wide-angle photography	Überweitwinkelaufnahme f	extrinsic conductivity	s. a. extrinsic conduction
extremal	Extremale f	extrinsic ion	s. impurity ion
extremal property	Extremaleigenschaft f	extrinsic load, external load	äußere Belastung f, Belastung
extreme, extreme value, extremum	Extremum n, Extremwert m	extrinsic photoconduction, extrinsic photoconductivity	Störphotoleitung f, Störphotoleitfähigkeit f
extreme case; border-line case, limiting case	Grenzfall m; Extremfall m	extrinsic photoconductive effect	Störphotoleitungseffekt m
extreme fibre	Randfaser f	extrinsic photoconductivity <quantity>	Störphotoleitfähigkeit f <Größe>
extreme layer	Randfaserschicht f, äußerste Faserschicht f		
extremely close coupling, extra-close coupling	extrem feste Kopplung f	extrinsic photoconductivity	s. extrinsic photoconduction
extremely compact galaxy	äußerst (extrem) kompakte Galaxie (Galaxis) f	extrinsic property, structure-sensitive property	strukturempfindliche Eigenschaft f
extremely good visibility, visibility, vista	Fernsicht f	extrinsic property <semi.>	Störleitungseigenschaft f <Halb.>
extremely hard, extra-hard	überhart, extrem hart, extrahart	extrinsic semiconductor, impurity semiconductor	Störstellen[halb]leiter m, Stör[halb]leiter m, Fremd[halb]leiter m
extremely high energy physics	s. extra-high-energy physics		
extremely high frequency	s. extra-high frequency <30,000–300,000 Mc/s>	extrinsic source	Störstellenquelle f

extrinsic variable [star], pseudo[ ]variable [star], improper variable [star]	Pseudoveränderlicher m, uneigentlicher Veränderlicher m	Fabry-Pérot interferometry	Fabry-Pérot-Interferometrie f
extruded bar, extruded product <met.>	Strang m <Met.>	Fabry-Pérot laser, Fabry-Pérot optical maser, Fabry-Pérot-type laser, FP laser	Fabry-Pérot-Laser m, Laser m mit Fabry-Pérot-Resonator, FP-Laser m
extrusion	Strangpressen n; Fließpressen n; <Plaste auch> Extrudieren n		
extrusive [rock], effusive [rock]	Ergußgestein n, Ausbruchsgestein n, Extrusivgestein n, Vulkanit m, Effusivgestein n	Fabry-Pérot resonator, optical resonator	Fabry-Pérot-Resonator m, optischer Resonator m
exudation <geo.>	Exsudation f, Ausscheidung f <Geo.>	face, plane surface <of polyhedron>	Fläche f, Seite f, Seitenfläche f, [ebene] Randfläche f, [ebene] Begrenzungsfläche f, [ebene] Grenzfläche f <Polyeder>
eye	s. observation port		
eye and ear method	Aug-und-Ohr-Methode f	face-centred, face-centered <US>, all-face centred, plane-centred	[grenz]flächenzentriert, allseitig[-] flächenzentriert, f.z.
eyeglass	s. eyepiece lens		
eyehole	s. observation port		
eye horizon	Augenhorizont m	face-centred cubic, cubic face-centred, f.c.c., FCC	kubisch flächenzentriert, k.f.z., kfz
eyelens	s. eyepiece lens		
eye level	Augenhöhe f		
		face-centred cubic lattice, f.c.c. lattice, FCC lattice	kubisch flächenzentriertes Gitter n, k.f.z.-Gitter n, kfz-Gitter n
eye of the storm (tropical cyclone)	Auge n des tropischen Wirbelsturms		
eyepiece	Okular n	face hardening	s. surface hardening
eyepiece cup	Okularmuschel f	face-ring flux, end-face flux	Stirnfluß m
eyepiece filter, ocular filter	Okularsperrfilter n, Okularfilter n	face-ring leakage, end-face leakage, overhang leakage	Stirnstreuung f
eyepiece for comparison, reference (comparison) eyepiece	Vergleichsokular n	face-ring leakage flux, end-face leakage flux	Stirnstreufluß m
eyepiece goniometer, protractor ocular head, goniometer (goniometric) eyepiece	Goniometerokular n, Winkelmeßokular n, Okulargoniometer n	face-ring stray field, end-face stray field	Stirnstreufeld n
		facet	Facette f; Ommatidium n, Augenkeil m, Sehkeil m
		face terrace	s. shore terrace
eyepiece lens, eyelens, eyeglass, ocular	Okularlinse f; Einblicklinse f, Auglinse f	facet rock, facet stone; wind-carved pebble, wind kanter	Windkanter m, Kantengeschiebe n, Kantengeröll n; Facettengeschiebe n, Facettengeröll n
eyepiece micrometer, micrometer eyepiece, filar eyepiece	Okularmikrometer n		
		facetted eye	s. compound eye
eyepiece micrometer screw, screw micrometer eyepiece, screw eyepiece micrometer	Okularschraubenmikrometer n, Okularschraublehre f, Okularmeßschraube f	facilitated diffusion	geförderte Diffusion f; Huckepackdiffusion f
		facilitation	Bahnung f, Erleichterung f
		facility added	s. supplementary apparatus
		factorable	zerlegbar [in Faktoren]
eyepiece planimeter, planimeter eyepiece	Planimeterokular n, Okularplanimeter n	factor analysis	Faktoranalyse f, Faktorenanalyse f
eyepiece slide	Okularauszug m; Okularstutzen m	factor[-] group, quotient (difference) group	Faktorgruppe f, Restklassengruppe f; Differenzgruppe f
		factorial coefficient	s. Stirling['s] number
eyepiece spectroscope, ocular spectroscope, spectroscopic eyepiece	Okularspektroskop n	factorial function, factorial polynomial	Faktorielle f, verallgemeinerte Potenz f
		factorial function	s. a. gamma function
eyepiece turret, revolving eyepiece head	Okularrevolver m	factorial moment	faktorielles Moment n
		factorial number	s. Stirling['s] number
eyepiece with indicator, microscopic eyepiece with indicator	Zeigerokular n	factorial polynomial	s. factorial function
		factorial series	Fakultätenreihe f
eye position, centre of perspectivity, centre of projection	Perspektivitätszentrum n, Auge n, Blickzentrum n, Projektionszentrum n	factoring, factorization, decomposition into factors	Faktorisation f, Faktorisierung f, Faktor[en]zerlegung f
eye-ring	s. exit pupil		
eye separation	s. interocular distance		
eye sight	s. observation port	factorization method	Faktorisierungsmethode f
eye slit	Beobachtungsspalt m, Beobachtungsschlitz m	factor loading	s. saturation <stat.>
		factor model	Faktormodell n
		factor of merit	s. Q
eye spot, stigma	Augenfleck m, Stigma n	factor of proportionality, proportionality factor (coefficient; constant), coefficient (constant) of proportionality	Proportionalitätsfaktor m, Proportionalitätskoeffizient m; Proportionalitätskonstante f
eyestrain, strain of eye	Augenermüdung f, Ermüdung f des Auges		
Eyring equation	Eyringsche Gleichung f, Eyring-Gleichung f		
		factor of quality	s. Q
		factor of safety	s. safety factor
		factor of turbidity	s. turbidity factor
		factor of uncertainty	Unsicherheitsfaktor m
F			
		factor ring, residue[-] class ring, residue ring, difference ring	Restklassenring m, Faktorring m, Differenzring m
Fabry-Pérot étalon	s. a. lame étalon		
Fabry-Pérot étalon	Fabry-Pérot-Etalon m, Pérot-Fabry-Etalon m	facula <pl: -lae>, facula area <pl: -lae -as>, solar facula (mountain)	Sonnenfackel f, Fackel f; Fackelgebiet n
Fabry-Pérot interference spectroscope, Fabry-Pérot interferometer	Fabry-Pérot[-Interferometer] n, Fabry-Pérot-Interferenzspektroskop n, Luftplattenspektroskop n, Pérot-Fabry-Interferometer n, Interferometer n von Fabry-Pérot		
		Faddeyev['s] equation	Faddejew-Gleichung f
		fade [in motion pictures]	Überblendung f
		fade-out	s. radio fade-out
		fade slide	Schieberblende f

fading; damping; attenuation; deamplification; extenuation <of action>	Abschwächung f; Schwächung f; Dämpfung f	falling short [of the given value]	Unterschreitung f [des Sollwertes]
fading <el.>	Fading n, Schwund m, Schwinden n <El.>	falling speed, velocity (rate) of fall, velocity (rate) of descent	Fallgeschwindigkeit f
fading, fading of latent image, latent image fading, regression [of latent image] <phot.>	Abklingen n [des latenten Bildes], Regression f [des latenten Bildes], Rückgang m [des latenten Bildes] <Phot.>	falling sphere experiment, falling ball experiment; falling sphere (ball) test	Kugelfallversuch m; Kugelfallprobe f
fading <phot.>, bleaching out	Fading n, Abblassen n, Verblassen n, Ausbleichen n, Abklingen n <Phot.>	falling sphere method, falling (dropping) ball method	Fallkugelmethode f, Kugelfallmethode f
fading by absorption	Absorptionsschwund m	falling sphere sound source, falling ball sound source	Kugelfallschallquelle f
fading down; fading out	Ausblendung f	falling sphere test, falling sphere (ball) experiment; falling ball test	Kugelfallversuch m; Kugelfallprobe f
fading due to polar aurora, auroral fading	Polarlichtschwund m; Nordlichtschwund m	falling sphere viscometer, falling body (ball) viscometer	Fallkugelviskosimeter n, Fallkörperviskosimeter n, Kugelfallviskosimeter n
fading of latent image	s. fading <phot.>	falling star, shooting star	Sternschnuppe f
fading out	s. fading down	fall in temperature	s. temperature drop
fading period, period of fading	Schwundperiode f	fall of a meteorite, meteoritic fall	Meteoritenfall m
Fahrenheit, degree Fahrenheit, °F	Grad m Fahrenheit, Fahrenheit-Grad m, Fahrenheitsgrad m, °F	fall of drops, drop fall	Tropfenfall m
Fahrenheit [temperature] scale, F-scale	Fahrenheit-Skala f, Fahrenheit-Skale f	fall-off ratio, F.O.R.	Abfallverhältnis n
		fall of ground <geo.>	s. dip
		fall of potential	s. potential drop
failing, [elastic] failure <in theory of strength of materials>	Versagen n <Festigkeitslehre>	fall of temperature	s. temperature drop
		fall-out, fallout, radioactive fall-out	Fallout m, Ausfall m, radioaktiver Ausfall (Fallout, Niederschlag) m <aus der Atmosphäre>
failing strain	s. breaking elongation		
failing stress	s. fracture stress	fall streak, virga	Fallstreifen m
failure; breakdown <in reliability theory>	Versagen n, Ausfall m; Störung f <Zuverlässigkeitstheorie>	fall time, decay time <el.>	Rückdauer f; Abstiegszeit f; Abklingzeit f <El.>
failure	s. a. failing	fall velocity <hydr.>, sinking velocity	Sinkgeschwindigkeit f <Hydr.>
failure condition	s. fracture condition	false brinelling	s. fretting corrosion
failure criterion	Versagenskriterium n	false cleavage, pseudocleavage	Pseudoschieferung f
failure physics, physics of failures	Physik f des Versagens		
failure probability	Ausfallswahrscheinlichkeit f, Unzuverlässigkeitsfunktion f	false conclusion, fallacy	Trugschluß m
		false equilibrium, apparent equilibrium	scheinbares Gleichgewicht n
failure rate	Versagenshäufigkeit f, Ausfallshäufigkeit f, Ausfallsrate f	false front, apparent front, pseudofront	Scheinfront f
faint luminescence, feeble luminescence	schwache Lumineszenz f	false zodiacal light	falsches Zodiakallicht n
faint meteor	[licht]schwaches Meteor n	falsification	Falsifizierung f
fair[ed] curve	s. smooth curve	falsification <of the results>, alteration	Verfälschung f [der Meßergebnisse]
fairing	[strömungsgünstige] Verkleidung f	faltung	s. convolution integral <math.>
fair weather	Schönwetter n, schönes Wetter n	faltung	s. convolution <of functions> <math.>
faithful representation	treue Darstellung f	faltung theorem	s. convolution theorem
Fajans rules	Fajanssche Regeln fpl	family of aerofoil sections	Profilfamilie f, Profilsystem n
falcated <astr.>	s. crescent[-shaped]		
fall <mech.>	Fall m <Mech.>	family of characteristic[s], characteristics family, [characteristic] curve family, performance chart, set of characteristics	Kennlinienschar f; Kennlinienfeld n, Kennfeld n
fall	s. a. decay		
fall	s. a. sudden fall		
fallacy, false conclusion	Trugschluß m		
falling	Fallbewegung f		
falling ball experiment	s. falling sphere experiment	family of clefts, cleft family	Kluftschar f
falling ball method	s. falling sphere method	family of comets	Kometenfamilie f
falling ball sound source, falling sphere sound source	Kugelfallschallquelle f	family of curves, group (system) of curves	Kurvenschar f, Schar f [von Kurven]
falling ball test	s. falling sphere experiment	family of cyclones, series of cyclones	Zyklonenfamilie f, Zyklonenserie f
falling ball (body) viscometer	s. falling sphere viscometer	family of feedback characteristics	Rückkopplungs-Kennlinienfeld n
falling drop method, falling drop specific densimeter method	Tropfenfallmethode f, Methode f der fallenden Tropfen, Tröpfchenfallmethode f		
		family of oscillation characteristics, oscillation characteristic family	Schwingkennlinienfeld n
falling into dust <gen.>	Zerfallen n, Zerfall m <allg.>		
falling of the water level	Wasserspiegel[ab]senkung f, Spiegelabsenkung f, Absenkung (Senkung) f des Wasserspiegels, Spiegelsenkung f	family of surfaces, system of surfaces	Flächenschar f, Flächensystem n
		family of waves	Wellenfamilie f
falling out <of synchronism>, falling out of step	Außertrittfallen n	fan fader	Fächerblende f

fan

fan fold	Fächerfalte f
fanglomerate	Fanglomerat n, Schlammbrekzie f
Fankuchen cut	Fankuchen-Anschnitt m
fanning <e.g. of electronic beam>	Auffächern n, Ausfächern n <z. B. Elektronenstrahl>
Fanning equation	Fanning-Gleichung f, Fanningsche Gleichung f
fanning growth	Auffächerungswachstum n
Fanno curve, Fanno line	Fanno-Kurve f, Fannosche Kurve f
fan of comet, expanding fan	fächerförmige Schweifstrahlen mpl, Fächer m
fan of light beams	Lichtfächer m
fan of rays	s. beam <of radiation>
fan ray <of Sun corona>	Fächerstrahl m <Sonnenkorona>
Fanselau coil	Fanselau-Spule f
fan shooting	Fächerschießen n
fan wheel anemometer	s. vane anemometer
farad, F	Farad n, F
faraday	s. Faraday constant
Faraday balance	Faradaysche Torsionswaage f, Faraday-Waage f
Faraday cage, screened cage, Faraday screen, Faraday shield; Faraday cup, Faraday cylinder, ice-pail	Faraday-Käfig m, Faradayscher Käfig m; Faraday-Becher m, Faraday-Kasten m, Faraday-Zylinder m, Faradayscher Becher m
Faraday constant, faraday, F	Faraday n, Faraday-Konstante f, Faraday-Zahl f, Faradaysche Konstante (Zahl, Äquivalentladung, Ladung) f, F
Faraday cup	s. Faraday cage
Faraday current, faradic current	faradischer Strom m, Faradisationsstrom m
Faraday cylinder	s. Faraday cage
Faraday dark space	Faradayscher (zweiter) Dunkelraum m, zweiter Katodendunkelraum m
Faraday disk machine	Faradaysche Scheibenmaschine f, Scheibenmaschine nach Faraday
Faraday dispersion	Faraday-Dispersion f
Faraday effect	Faraday-Effekt m, Magnetrotation f, Magnetorotation f
Faraday effect, eddy current effect	Wirbelstromeffekt m
Faraday['s] experiment	Faradayscher Käfigversuch m (Becherversuch m; Rotationsversuch m)
Faraday isolator; Faraday rotator	Faraday-Isolator m
Faraday['s] law, Faraday laws of electrolysis	Faradaysches Gesetz n [der Elektrolyse], Faradaysches (elektrochemisches) Äquivalentgesetz n, Faradaysche Gesetze npl [der Elektrolyse]
Faraday['s] law of induction, law of induction, [Faraday-Neumann] law of electromagnetic induction, Faraday['s] theorem, induction theorem	Induktionsgesetz n [von Faraday], Faradaysches Induktionsgesetz, Faradaysche Induktionsregel f, zweite Maxwellsche Gleichung f, zweiter Maxwellscher Hauptsatz m
Faraday laws of electrolysis	s. Faraday['s] law
Faraday-Neumann law of electromagnetic induction	s. Faraday['s] law of induction
Faraday pendulum	Faraday-Pendel n
Faraday rotator; Faraday isolator;	Faraday-Isolator m
Faraday screen (shield)	s. Faraday cage
Faraday['s] theorem	s. Faraday['s] law of induction
Faraday's theory, proximity theory	[Faradaysche] Nahewirkungstheorie f
Faraday-Tyndall effect, Tyndall effect	[Faraday-]Tyndall-Effekt m; Tyndall-Phänomen n

Faraday-type magnetohydrodynamic generator, magnetohydrodynamic Faraday generator	MHD-Faraday-Generator m, Faraday-MHD-Generator m
farad bridge	s. capacitance bridge
faradic current	s. Faraday current
faradic stimulation, faradism	faradeische Reizung f, Faradisation f, Faradotherapie f
farad[ ]meter	s. capacitance meter
far field, distant (radiation) field	Fernfeld n, Fernwirkungsfeld n
far field pattern, Fraunhofer pattern	Fernfeldcharakteristik f, Fernfeld-Richtdiagramm n
far infra-red, far infrared <> 25 µm>	fernes Infrarot n, fernes Ultrarot n <> 25 µm>
far infra-red radiation	ferne Infrarotstrahlung f, Strahlung f im fernen Infrarot
far point of clear vision, punctum remotum <opt.>	Fernpunkt m, punctum n remotum; Fernpunkt im engeren Sinne, manifester Fernpunkt <Opt.>
far red irradiation	s. infra-red irradiation
far side of the Moon, other side of the Moon	Rückseite f des Mondes
far ultra[-]violet	fernes Ultraviolett n
far ultra[-]violet radiation	ferne Ultraviolettstrahlung f, Strahlung f im fernen Ultraviolett
farvitron	Farvitron n
far zone	s. radiation zone
far zone focusing	Weiteinstellung f
fast-acces memory (storage, store)	s. rapid-acces memory
fast approximation	schnelle Näherung f
fast breeder, fast breeder reactor, FBR	schneller Brüter m, schneller Brutreaktor m, SBR
fast chamber, fast ionization chamber	schnelle Ionisationskammer (Kammer) f
fast chamber, fast-compression cloud chamber	schnelle Nebelkammer f, schnelle Kammer f
fast chopper <el.>	Schnellunterbrecher m <El.>
fast chopper	s. a. fast neutron selector
fast-coincidence circuit (system)	schnelle Koinzidenzschaltung f
fast-compression cloud chamber, fast chamber	schnelle Nebelkammer f, schnelle Kammer f
fast cross-section, fast neutron cross-section, cross-section for fast neutrons	schneller Neutronen[wirkungs]querschnitt m, Wirkungsquerschnitt m für schnelle Neutronen, Wirkungsquerschnitt der schnellen Neutronen
fast detection, speedy detection	schneller Nachweis m
fast detector	schneller Detektor m, schnelles Nachweisgerät n
fast effect, fast fission effect	Schnellspaltungseffekt m, Einfluß m schneller Neutronen
fast electronics	schnelle Elektronik f
fastening with wedges, wedging, keying	Verkeilen n
faster-than-light particle	s. tachyon
fast fading	schneller Schwund m
fast fission, fast neutron fission	schnelle Spaltung f, Schnellspaltung f, Spaltung durch schnelle Neutronen

fatigue

fast fission cross-section, fast neutron fission cross-section, cross-section for fast fission	schneller Spaltquerschnitt *m*, Spaltquerschnitt für schnelle Neutronen, Wirkungsquerschnitt *m* für Spaltung durch schnelle Neutronen
fast fission effect, fast effect	Schnellspaltungseffekt *m*, Einfluß *m* schneller Neutronen
fast fission factor, fast multiplication factor	Schnellspalt[ungs]faktor *m*, Multiplikationsfaktor *m* für schnelle Neutronen
fast flow	s. shooting flow ⟨hydr.⟩
fast flux, fast neutron flux	Fluß *m* der schnellen Neutronen, schneller Fluß (Neutronenfluß) *m*
fast front wave	Schnelläufer *m*, schnelllaufende Welle *f*
fast group	schnelle Gruppe *f*
fast ion	s. small ion ⟨geo.⟩
fast ionization chamber, fast chamber	schnelle Ionisationskammer (Kammer) *f*
fast leakage	schneller Ausfluß (Abfluß, Verlust) *m*, Ausfluß schneller Neutronen
fast-motion effect (method)	s. low-speed photography
fast-motion picture[s], pictures in fast motion	Zeitrafferfilm *m*, Zeitrafferaufnahme *f*
fast multiplication factor, fast fission factor	Schnellspalt[ungs]faktor *m*, Multiplikationsfaktor *m* für schnelle Neutronen
fast neutron	schnelles Neutron *n*
fast neutron capture	s. r process ⟨astr.⟩
fast neutron cross-section	s. fast cross-section
fast-neutron detector	Detektor *m* für schnelle Neutronen
fast neutron fission	s. fast fission
fast neutron fission cross-section	s. fast fission cross-section
fast neutron flux, fast flux	Fluß *m* der schnellen Neutronen, schneller Fluß (Neutronenfluß) *m*
fast-neutron lifetime	s. slowing-down time
fast neutron reactor, fast reactor	schneller Reaktor *m*, Schnellreaktor *m*
fast neutron selector, fast chopper	schneller Geschwindigkeitsselektor (Chopper, Neutronenmonochromator) *m*
fast-neutron spectrometer	Spektrometer *n* für schnelle Neutronen
fast nova	schnelle Nova *f*
fast particle, high-speed particle	schnelles Teilchen *n*
fast process	s. r process ⟨astr.⟩
fast pulse amplifier	Breitbandimpulsverstärker *m*
fast reactor, fast neutron reactor	schneller Reaktor *m*, Schnellreaktor *m*
fast-slow coincidence	„fast-slow"-Koinzidenz *f*, „Schnell-langsam"-Koinzidenz *f*
fast-slow coincidence circuit	„fast-slow"-Koinzidenzkreis *m*, „Schnell-langsam"-Koinzidenzkreis *m*
fast state, fast surface trap, fast trap	schneller Oberflächenterm (Term, Oberflächenhaftterm, Haftterm, Oberflächenzustand, Zustand) *m*
fast storage (store)	s. rapid-acces memory
fatal dose, lethal dose, LD	Letaldosis *f*, letale (tödliche) Dosis *f*, LD
fathometer	s. echo-sounding device
fatigue, endurance	Ermüdung *f*
fatigue corrosion	Ermüdungskorrosion *f*
fatigue crack	Ermüdungsriß *m*; Daueranriß *m*
fatigue crescent	s. oyster shell marking
fatigue curve	s. Wöhler curve
fatigue effect; appearance of fatigue	Ermüdungserscheinung *f*
fatigue experiment, fatigue test, life test, endurance test ⟨US⟩	Ermüdungsversuch *m*, Dauerversuch *m*, Dauerprüfung *f*, dynamische Dauerfestigkeitsprüfung *f*
fatigue failure	s. fatigue fracture
fatigue fracture, fatigue failure	Dauerbruch *m*, Schwingungsbruch *m*, Dauerschwingungsbruch *m*, Ermüdungsbruch *m*
fatigue fracture at a stated number of cycles, fatigue fracture for limit life	Zeitschwingungsbruch *m*, Zeitbruch *m*
fatigue impact test	Dauerschlagversuch *m*, Dauerversuch *m*
fatigue impact testing machine	Dauerschlagwerk *n*
fatigue limit	s. endurance
fatigue limit [for (under) completely reversed stress]	s. fatigue strength ⟨for completely reversed stress⟩
fatigue limit for fluctuating stress	s. endurance strength at alternating load
fatigue loading, cyclic loading, cycling	Dauerschwingungsbeanspruchung *f*; Wechselbeanspruchung *f*; Schwellbeanspruchung *f*
fatigue notch factor	s. reduced factor of stress concentration
fatigue notch sensitivity, notch sensitivity	Kerbempfindlichkeit *f*, Kerbempfindlichkeitszahl *f*
fatigue of the phosphor, dark burn of the phosphor	Ermüdung *f* des Leuchtstoffs
fatigue-proof, fatigue-resistant, fatigue resisting	ermüdungsfest, ermüdungsbeständig, ermüdungsfrei
fatigue strength ⟨for completely reversed stress⟩, reversed fatigue strength, alternating tension and compression stress fatigue strength, fatigue limit [for (under) completely reversed stress], endurance limit for complete reversal of stress	Wechselfestigkeit *f*, Schwingungsfestigkeit *f*; Zug-Druck-Wechselfestigkeit *f*
fatigue strength	s. a. endurance
fatigue strength at alternating load, endurance (fatigue) strength at repeated load, endurance strength at alternating load	Schwellfestigkeit *f*
fatigue strength at alternating load	s. endurance strength at alternating load
fatigue strength at a stated number of cycles	s. fatigue strength for limit life
fatigue strength at repeated load (stress in one direction)	s. endurance strength at alternating load
fatigue strength for limit life, fatigue strength at a stated number of cycles, fracture range, time strength	Zeitschwingfestigkeit *f*, Zeitfestigkeit *f*
fatigue strength for tension-compression, tension-compression fatigue strength, endurance tension-compression strength	Zug-Druck-Dauerfestigkeit *f*
fatigue strength reduction factor	s. reduced factor of stress concentration
fatigue strength under [completely] reversed bending strength (stress); endurance limit under [completely] reversed bending stress[es]	Biegewechselfestigkeit *f*, Biegeschwingfestigkeit *f*
fatigue strength under repeated bending stress[es] in one direction, pulsating fatigue strength under bending stress[es], pulsating bending strength	Biegeschwellfestigkeit *f*
fatigue stress concentration factor	s. reduced factor of stress concentration

fatigue 252

fatigue test	s. fatigue experiment	Fechner colour, Benham colour	Benham-Farbe f, Fechner-Benhamsche Farbe f, Flimmerfarbe f, polyphäne Farbe
fatigue testing machine, endurance testing machine	Dauerschwing[ungs]prüfmaschine f, Schwingprüfmaschine f [für Dauerschwingversuche]; Pulsator m; Pulser m; Dauer[stand]prüfmaschine f	Fechner fraction	Fechner-Verhältnis n, reziproke Kontrastempfindlichkeit f
		Fechner['s] law; Mackenzie equation <ac.>	Fechnersches Gesetz n
		Feddersen oscillations	Feddersen-Schwingungen fpl
fatigue torsion test	s. torsion endurance test	feeble breeze <of Beaufort No. 3>, feeble (light) wind	schwache Brise f <Stärke 3>
fatigue wear, wear by fatigue	Ermüdungsverschleiß m	feeble current, weak current, [low-voltage] low current	Schwachstrom m; niedriger (geringer, schwacher) Strom m
fat splitting	Fettspaltung f		
faucet <US>, cock plug, plug of the cock	Hahnküken n, Küken n, Hahnkegel m	feeble luminescence, faint luminescence	schwache Lumineszenz f
fault, fracture <geo.>	Bruch m, Verwerfung f, Sprung m, Verwurf m; Spaltenverwerfung f <Geo.>	feeble solution, generalized solution <math.>	schwache (verallgemeinerte) Lösung f <Math.>
fault <cryst.>	s. a. stacking fault	feeble wind, feeble breeze, light wind <of Beaufort No. 3>	schwache Brise f <Stärke 3>
fault angle, angle of fault	Sprungwinkel m, Verwerfungswinkel m		
fault block	Bruchscholle f	feedback, feedback coupling, back coupling, reaction [coupling]; retroaction; [circuit] regeneration	Rückkopplung f; Rückführung f; Rückspeisung f; Rückleitung f; „feedback" n
fault-block valley, fault-line valley	Grabental n, Talgraben m		
fault breccia, crush breccia	Schuttbrekzie f		
fault current	Fehlerstrom m	feedback admittance	s. reaction conductance
fault detection (finding), fault hunting	Fehlersuche f	feedback amplifier	s. feedback-stabilized amplifier
faulted underfold	s. underthrust	feedback circuit	s. feedback loop
fault fissure	s. paraclase	feedback control	s. closed-loop control
fault height, height of the fault, amplitude of the fault <geo.>	Verwerfungshöhe f, Verwurf m, Sprunghöhe f <Geo.>	feedback control system	s. control loop
		feedback coupling	s. feedback
		feedback element, feedback section	Rückführ[ungs]glied n, Rückkopplungsglied n
fault hunting	s. fault detection	feedback factor, coefficient of feedback	Rückkopplungsfaktor m
fault line, fracture line <geo.>	Verwerfungslinie f, Bruchlinie f	feedback gain	Rückkopplungsverstärkungsfaktor m
fault-line valley	s. fault-block valley		
fault-line valley	s. a. rift [valley]	feedback inhibition	Endprodukthemmung f, Rückkopplungshemmung f
fault localization, localization of defects, localizing a fault	Fehlereingrenzung f, Eingrenzung f von Fehlern; Fehlerort[sbestimm]ung f		
		feedback loop, feedback circuit, regenerative [loop of the] circuit	Rückkopplungskreis m, Rückführ[ungs]kreis m, Rückkopplungsschleife f, Rückführ[ungs]schleife f, Rückführ[ungs]leitung f, Rückkopplungsleitung f
fault plane <geo.>	Sprungfläche f, Verwerfungsfläche f <Geo.>		
		feedback path; singing path	Rückkopplungsweg m, Rückführungsweg m, Rückführpfad m, Rückkopplungszweig m
fault region, fault zone	Bruchzone f, Verwerfungszone f, Sprungzone f		
fault spring	Verwerfungsquelle f	feedback ratio	Rückkopplungsgrad m, Rückführungsgrad m
fault water	s. fissure water		
fault zone, fault region	Bruchzone f, Verwerfungszone f, Sprungzone f	feedback section, feedback element	Rückführ[ungs]glied n, Rückkopplungsglied n
favourable geometry	günstige Geometrie f	feedback-stabilized amplifier, feedback amplifier	rückgekoppelter Verstärker m, Rückkopplungsverstärker m
favoured [forbidden] transition	s. superallowed transition		
favoured [forbidden] transition	s. a. unique transition		
Faxén['s] resistance formulae	Faxénsche Widerstandsformeln fpl	feedback system	rückgekoppeltes System n, System mit Rückführung
Faxén['s] theorems	Faxénsche Sätze mpl		
Faxén-Waller scattering	s. inelastic scattering by crystals	feedback time constant	Rückführzeitkonstante f, Rückkopplungszeitkonstante f
Faye effect, free[-]air effect	Freilufteffekt m, Faye-Effekt m, Faye-Wirkung f		
		feed equipment	s. power pack
		feedforward	s. positive feedback
Faye['s] reduction	s. free[-]air reduction	feeding in the parallel mode	Gleichtaktspeisung f
F-case, R-antisymmetric case	R-antisymmetrischer Fall m, F-Fall m		
F-centre	F-Zentrum n	feeding point, feed point; driving point	Speisepunkt m; Einspeisepunkt m; Einströmungspunkt m
F'-centre	F'-Zentrum n		
F-centre	s. a. colour centre	feed pipe, supply (inlet, intake) pipe, supply tube, lead; penstock <of turbine>	Zuleitungsrohr n, Zuführungsrohr n, Zuflußrohr n; Zulaufrohr n
F corona, Fraunhofer corona	F-Komponente f der Koronastrahlung, Fraunhofer-Komponente f, F-Korona f, Fraunhofer-Korona f		
F distribution	s. Fisher['s] distribution	feed point	s. feeding point
F.D.S. law	s. Fermi-Dirac-Sommerfeld velocity distribution law	feed point impedance	s. input impedance
		feed-point reactance, input reactance	Eingangsblindwiderstand m
Feather analysis, Feather method, method of the Feather plot	Methode f von Feather, Feather-Methode f, Feather-Analyse f	feed point resistance, input resistance	Eingangswiderstand m; Gitter-Katode-Widerstand m
Feather rule	Feathersches Gesetz n, empirische Formel f von Feather	feed power pack	s. power pack
		feed-through	s. bushing <el.>
featureless	s. smeared	feeler, probe, sound, sonde	Sonde f; Fühler m; Taster m; Spürgerät n
feature on the Moon's surface	s. formation on the Moon's surface		

feeling organ, touch organ	Tastsinnesorgan n, Tastorgan n, Tangorezeptor m, Fühlorgan n
Feller-Arley process, birth-and-death process	Feller-Arley-Prozeß m, Geburt- und Tod-Prozeß m, Geburten- und Todesprozeß m
femto ..., $f <= 10^{-15}$	Femto ..., $f <= 10^{-15}$
femtometre, fermi, fm	Femtometer n, Fermi n, fm
fence phenomenon, palisade (railing) phenomenon	Staketenphänomen n
Fermat['s] law, Fermat['s] principle <of stationary optical paths>, law of extreme path, principle of least time	Fermatsches Prinzip n [des kürzesten Lichtweges], Fermatscher Satz m [der geometrischen Optik], [Fermatscher] Satz der schnellsten Ankunft, Fernatsches Gesetz n, Gesetz des kürzesten Lichtweges, Prinzip der schnellsten Ankunft, Prinzip des kürzesten Weges (Lichtweges), Prinzip des ausgezeichneten Lichtweges, Prinzip vom ausgezeichneten Lichtweg
Fermat['s] principle in relativity, Fermat['s] principle of least proper time	s. principle of least proper time
fermentation	Gärung f; Fermentation f
ferment model, catalator	Katalator m, Fermentmodell n
fermi	s. femtometre
Fermi age <of neutron>, symbolic age [of neutron], neutron age, age <nucl.>	Fermi-Alter n, Neutronenalter n, Neutronen-„age" n, Alter n [des Neutrons], Age m, „age" n <Kern.>
Fermi-age model, continuous slowing down model	Fermi-Alter-Modell n, Modell n der kontinuierlichen Bremsung
Fermi analysis	Fermi-Analyse f
Fermi approximation	Fermi-Näherung f
Fermi characteristic energy level	s. Fermi limit <semi., met.>
Fermi circular wave vector, Fermi propagation vector	Ausbreitungsvektor m für Fermi-Energie, Fermi-Ausbreitungsvektor m
Fermi collision theory	Fermische Stoßtheorie f
Fermi constant, Fermi coupling constant, Fermi interaction constant	Kopplungskonstante f für den Beta-Zerfall, Fermi-Konstante f
Fermi degeneracy	Fermi-Entartung f
Fermi-Dirac commutation relations, anticommutation relations (rules)	Fermi-Diracsche Vertauschungsrelationen fpl
Fermi-Dirac distribution, Fermi-Dirac distribution function, Fermi distribution	Fermi-Verteilungsfunktion f, Fermi-Diracsche Verteilungsfunktion f, [Fermische] Besetzungsfunktion f; Fermi-[Dirac-]Verteilung f; Fermische Geschwindigkeitsverteilung f
Fermi-Dirac ensemble	Fermi-Dirac-Gesamtheit f
Fermi-Dirac gas	s. Fermi gas
Fermi-Dirac liquid	s. Fermi liquid
Fermi-Dirac particle	s. fermion
Fermi-Dirac perfect gas	s. Fermi gas
Fermi-Dirac probability, Fermi probability	Fermi-Dirac-Wahrscheinlichkeit f, Fermi-Wahrscheinlichkeit f
Fermi-Dirac-Sommerfeld velocity distribution law, F.D.S. law	Geschwindigkeitsverteilungsgesetz (Verteilungsgesetz) n von Fermi-Dirac-Sommerfeld, Fermi-Dirac-Sommerfeldsches Verteilungsgesetz n, FDS-Gesetz n
Fermi-Dirac statistics, Fermi statistics, FD statistics	Fermi-[Dirac-]Statistik f, Fermi-Diracsche Quantenstatistik f, FD-Statistik f
Fermi distribution	s. Fermi-Dirac distribution
Fermi energy <of the nucleon>	Fermi-Energie f, Fermische Energie f <Nukleon>
Fermi energy	s. a. Fermi level
Fermi function	Fermische Funktion f, Fermi-Funktion f
Fermi gas, Fermi-Dirac gas, Fermi-Dirac perfect gas	Fermi-[Dirac-]Gas n, Fermi-Diracsches ideales Gas n
Fermi-gas model, Thomas-Fermi model <of the nucleus>	Fermi-Gas-Modell n, Fermi-Gasmodell n, Thomas-Fermi-Modell n [des Kerns]
Fermi interaction	Fermi-Wechselwirkung f, Fermische Wechselwirkung f
Fermi interaction constant	s. Fermi constant
Fermi intercept, scattering length	Streulänge f
Fermi kernel	Fermi-Kern m, Fermi-Bremskern m
Fermi-Kurie plot	s. Kurie plot
Fermi level, Fermi limit; Fermi energy; Fermi characteristic energy level <semi., met.>	Fermische Grenzenergie (Energie) f, Fermi-Grenzenergie f, Grenzenergie von Fermi, Fermi-Energie f; Fermi-Grenze f, Fermi-Kante f, Fermi-Niveau n, kritisches Niveau n <Halb., Met.>
Fermi liquid, Fermi-Dirac liquid	Fermi-[Dirac-]Flüssigkeit f
Fermi momentum	[Fermischer] Grenzimpuls m, Grenzimpuls von Fermi, Fermi-Impuls m
fermion, Fermi[-Dirac] particle, particle with halfinteger spin	Fermion n, Fermi-Teilchen n
fermion-antifermion pair	Fermion-Antifermion-Paar n
Fermi operator	Fermi-Operator m
Fermi-Parker mechanism	Fermi-Parker-Mechanismus m
Fermi particle	s. fermion
Fermi plateau, polarization (ionization) plateau	Fermi-Plateau n
Fermi plot	s. Kurie plot
Fermi potential	Fermi-Potential n
Fermi pressure	Fermi-Druck m
Fermi probability, Fermi-Dirac probability	Fermi-[Dirac-]Wahrscheinlichkeit f
Fermi propagation vector, Fermi circular wave vector	Ausbreitungsvektor m für Fermi-Energie, Fermi-Ausbreitungsvektor m
Fermi pseudopotential, nuclear pseudopotential	Fermisches Pseudopotential n, Kernpseudopotential n
Fermi resonance, resonon	Fermi-Resonanz f, Resonon n
Fermi selection rules	Fermische Auswahlregeln fpl, Fermi-Auswahlregeln fpl
Fermi source	Fermi-Quelle f
Fermi spectrum	Fermi-Spektrum n
Fermi sphere	Fermi-Kugel f
Fermi statistics	s. Fermi-Dirac statistics
Fermi surface	Fermi-Fläche f, Fermi-Oberfläche f
Fermi temperature	Fermi-Temperatur f
Fermi term	Fermi-Wechselwirkungsterm m, Fermi-Term m, Fermi-Glied n
Fermi theory <of beta decay or of metal electrons>	Fermische Theorie f <des Beta-Zerfalls, der Beta-Umwandlung bzw. der Metallelektronen>
Fermi-Thomas atom	Fermi-Thomas-Atom n
Fermi-Thomas equation, Thomas-Fermi equation, Thomas-Fermi differential equation	Gleichung f von Fermi-Thomas, Fermi-Thomassche Gleichung, Thomas[-Fermi]sche Differentialgleichung f, Thomas-Fermi-Differentialgleichung f, Differentialgleichung von Thomas und Fermi, Thomas-Fermische Gleichung, Thomas-Fermi-Gleichung f

Fermi transition	Fermi-Übergang m	ferrogarnet	Ferrogranat m, Ferrit m mit Granatstruktur
fermium, $_{100}$Fm	Fermium n, $_{100}$Fm	ferromagnet[ic], ferromagnetic body; ferromagnetic material	Ferromagnetikum n, ferromagnetischer Stoff m; ferromagnetischer Körper m
Fermi['s] $1/v$ law, $1/v$ law	$1/v$-Gesetz n, Fermisches $1/v$-Gesetz		
Fermi zero	Fermischer Nullpunkt m		
Ferranti effect	Ferranti-Effekt m	ferromagnetic coupling	ferromagnetische Kopplung f
Ferraris instrument, induction instrument, induction-type instrument	Ferraris-Meßgerät n, Ferraris-Gerät n, Ferraris-Instrument n, Drehfeldmesser m, Induktionsmeßgerät n, Induktionsinstrument n; Ferraris-Meßwerk n, Induktionsmeßwerk n	ferromagnetic Curie point [of temperature], ferromagnetic Curie temperature	s. Curie point
		ferromagnetic domain, Weiss['] domain, domain, magnetic domain <magn.>	Weissscher Bezirk m, ferromagnetischer (Weissscher) Bereich m, [magnetischer] Elementarbereich m, Elementarbezirk m, Domäne f, Bezirk m <Magn.>
ferric induction	s. intensity of magnetization		
ferrimagnet, ferrimagnetic material (substance)	Ferrimagnetikum n, ferrimagnetischer Stoff m		
ferrimagnetic domain wall	s. domain boundary	ferro-magnetic domain wall	s. domain boundary
ferrimagnetic material, ferrimagnetic substance, ferrimagnet	Ferrimagnetikum n, ferrimagnetischer Stoff m	ferromagnetic electron resonance	ferromagnetische Elektronenresonanz f
		ferromagnetic material, ferromagnetic, ferromagnet; ferromagnetic body	Ferromagnetikum n, ferromagnetischer Stoff m; ferromagnetischer Körper m
ferrimagnetic resonance, resonance in ferrimagnetic materials	ferrimagnetische Resonanz f		
ferrimagnetic state	ferrimagnetischer Zustand m, Ferrizustand m	ferromagnetic powder, magnetic powder	Magnetpulver n
ferrimagnetic substance, ferrimagnetic material, ferrimagnet	Ferrimagnetikum n, ferrimagnetischer Stoff m	ferromagnetic resonance absorption	ferromagnetische Resonanzabsorption f
ferrimagnetism	Ferrimagnetismus m	ferromagnetic spin wave, ferromagnon	Ferromagnon n, Spinwelle f im Ferromagnetikum, ferromagnetische Spinwelle f
ferrite; ferrite material; alpha-iron	Ferrit n (m); Ferritwerkstoff m; Alpha-Eisen n, Alpha-Ferrit m	ferromagnetic state	ferromagnetischer Zustand m, Ferrozustand m
		ferromagnetism	Ferromagnetismus m
		ferromagnetoelectric	ferromagnetoelektrisch
ferrite amplifier	Ferritverstärker m, Ferritreaktanzverstärker m		
ferrite-core matrix	s. ferrite-toroid matrix	ferromagnon, ferromagnetic spin wave	Ferromagnon n, Spinwelle f im Ferromagnetikum, ferromagnetische Spinwelle
ferrite-core memory, ferrite memory	Ferritkernspeicher m		
ferrite material	s. ferrite	ferrometer	Ferrometer n
ferrite matrix	s. ferrite-toroid matrix	ferroprobe	Ferrosonde f
ferrite memory	s. ferrite-core memory		
ferrite ring	Ferritring m	ferroresonance	Ferroresonanz f
ferrite toroid	Ferritringkern m	ferroresonant circuit	Resonanzkreis m mit Eisen[kern]spule, Resonanzschaltung f mit Eisenkernspule
ferrite-toroid matrix; ferrite-core matrix, ferrite matrix, ferritic matrix	Ferritringmatrix f, Ferritringkernmatrix f; Ferritkernmatrix f		
		ferrospinel, spinel ferrite	Ferrospinell n, Ferrit m mit Spinellstruktur
ferritic matrix	Ferritmatrix f	ferrostatic pressure	ferrostatischer Druck m
ferritic matrix	s. a. ferrite-toroid matrix	ferrous sulfate dosimeter	s. Fricke dosimeter
ferroacoustic resonance	ferroakustische Resonanz f	Ferry-Porter law	Ferry-Portersches Gesetz n
		fertile	brutfähig, brütbar
ferrodynamic instrument	ferrodynamisches Meßgerät (Instrument) n, eisengeschlossenes elektrodynamisches Meßwerk n		
		fertile material, breeding material	Brutstoff m, Brutmaterial n
ferroelectric, ferroelectric material, Seignette electric	Ferroelektrikum n <pl.: ...ika>, Ferrodielektrikum n, ferroelektrischer Isolierstoff (Stoff) m, Seignette[di]elektrikum n	fertility	Brütbarkeit f, Brutfähigkeit f
		fertilization membrane	Befruchtungsmembran f
		fervor effect	Fervoreffekt m
ferroelectric, Seignetteelectric	ferroelektrisch, seignetteelektrisch		
ferroelectric Barkhausen discontinuity	s. "electric" Barkhausen discontinuity	fervorization	Fervorisieren n, Fervorisation f
ferroelectric ceramics	Seignettekeramik f	Féry autocollimating spectrograph	Féry-Spektrograph m
		Féry prism	Férysches Prisma n, Féry-Prisma n
ferroelectric hysteresis [curve], hysteresis curve for a ferroelectric material	ferroelektrische Hysteresis[kurve] f		
		Féry [radiation] pyrometer, total radiation [type] pyrometer	Féry-Pyrometer n, Gesamtstrahlungspyrometer n; Ardometer n
ferroelectricity, Seignette electricity	Ferroelektrizität f, Seignetteelektrizität f		
ferroelectric material	s. ferroelectric		
ferroelectric parametric amplifier	parametrischer Verstärker m mit Ferroelektrikum		
		Fessenden transmitter	Fessenden-Sender m
		Fessenkov['s] hypothesis	Fessenkowsche Theorie f
		festoon, bundle of water tubes	Siederohrbündel n

fetch	Streichlänge (Wirklänge, Wirkungslänge) f des Windes, Windwirk[ungs]länge f, wirksame Windbahn f, Einfluß m der Bestreichungslänge [windangefachter Wellen]	Fick['s] law [of diffusion], Fick's diffusion law, Fick equation, [Fickian] diffusion law, Fick['s] laws	Ficksches Gesetz n, Ficksches Diffusionsgesetz n, Gesetz von Fick; Ficksche Gesetze npl <erstes und zweites>
Feulgen procedure (reaction)	s. plasmal reaction	Fick['s] laws	s. Fick['s] law
Feussner generator	Feußner-Funkenerzeuger m, Feußner-Generator m	Fick['s] second law, equation of diffusion, general equation of diffusion, diffusion equation	zweites Ficksches Gesetz n, zweite Ficksche Gleichung f, [elementare] Diffusionsgleichung f, allgemeine Differentialgleichung f der Diffusion
Feussner polarizing prism, Feussner prism	Feußner-Prisma n, Polarisationsprisma n nach Feußner	fictitious binding energy	scheinbare Bindungsenergie f
Feynman diagram, Feynman graph	Feynman-Graph m, Feynman-Diagramm n	fictitious boundary, imaginary boundary	fiktive Begrenzung f, scheinbare Grenze f
		fictitious dose	scheinbare Dosis f, Scheindosis f
Feynman integral	Feynman-Integral n	fictitious dose ratio	Scheindosisverhältnis n
FFAG radial-ridge synchrotron, FFAG radial-sector synchrotron, radial-ridge (radial-sector) synchrotron	FFAG-Synchrotron n vom Radialtyp, Radialtyp m, Radialsektor-FFAG-Synchrotron n, Radialsektor-Ringphasotron n	fictitious force, apparent force	Scheinkraft f, fiktive Kraft f, Hilfskraft f, Ergänzungskraft f
		fictitious moment of inertia, reduced moment of inertia	reduziertes Trägheitsmoment n
FFAG spiral-ridge synchrotron, FFAG spiral-sector synchrotron, spiral-ridge synchrotron, spiral-sector synchrotron	FFAG-Synchrotron n vom Spiraltyp, Spiraltyp m, Spiralrücken-FFAG-Synchrotron n, Spiralrücken-Ringphasotron n, Spiralsektor-FFAG-Synchrotron n, Spiralsektor-Ringphasotron n	fictitious pendulum	hypothetisches Pendel n
		fictitious Sun moving along the ecliptic	s. first mean Sun
		fictitious Sun moving along the equator, second mean Sun	zweite mittlere Sonne f; [fiktive] mittlere Sonne, die sich gleichförmig im Äquator bewegt
		fictitious viscosity	s. apparent viscosity
FFAG stabilization, fixed-field alternating-gradient stabilizing	FFAG-Stabilisierung f	fictitious year, Besselian [fictitious] year	Besselsches Jahr n, annus fictus m
		fidelity [of reproduction], reproduction fidelity	naturtreue Wiedergabe f, Naturtreue f, Natürlichkeit f, Wiedergabetreue f, Wiedergabegenauigkeit f
FFAG synchrotron, fixed-field alternating-gradient synchrotron, direct-current-field synchrotron, d-c field synchrotron	FFAG-Synchrotron n, Festfeldsynchrotron n mit starker Fokussierung, Festfeld-AG-Synchrotron n, Ringphasotron n, ringförmiges Synchrozyklotron n	fiducial distribution	Fiduzialverteilung f
		fiducial indicator	Fühlhebelmikrometer n
		fiducial inference	Fiduzialschluß m
fiber <US>, fibre	Faser f; Fiber f <Bio., auch Opt.>		
fibering, fibrillation	Faserung f; Aufspaltung f [in Fasern]; Faserbildung f	fiducial limit	s. confidence limit
fibre bundle	Faserbündel n, Fiberbündel	fiducial limits	s. confidence limits
fibre bundle, bundle of optical fibres	Fiberoptik f, Faseroptik f	fiducial mark	Rahmenmarke f, Randmarke f
fibre cloud	faserige Wolke f		
fibre diagram	Faserdiagramm n	fiducial probability	Fiduzialwahrscheinlichkeit f
		fiducial temperature	Vergleichstemperatur f, Bezugstemperatur f
fibre electrometer, string electrometer, filament electrometer	Fadenelektrometer n, Saitenelektrometer n	fiducial value, reference value	Vergleichswert m, Bezugswert m
fibre optics	Fiberoptik f, Glasfaseroptik f, Faseroptik f	field <of a quantity> <phys.>	Feld n <einer Größe> <Phys.>
fibre strainmeter, string strainmeter	Saitendehnungsmesser m	field, field strength, field intensity	Feldstärke f, Feld n, Feldintensität f
fibre structure, fibrous (bacillary) structure	Faserstruktur f, Kettenstruktur f	field, domain of rationality, commutative field <algebra>	Körper m, Rationalitätsbereich m, kommutativer Körper <Algebra>
fibre texture	Fasertextur f	field; portable, portative	tragbar; Feld-
fibriform, fibrous, filamentous	faserig, faserartig, Faser-, fibrillär	field arc	s. non-refractory arc
fibril, fibrilla	Fibrille f	field aspect <of matter>	Feldbild n
fibrillar, fibrillary, fibrilliform, fibrillous <bio.>	fibrillär <Bio.>	field balance	s. magnetic balance
		field barometer	Feldbarometer n, Reisebarometer n
fibrillar structure, fibrillary structure	Fibrillarstruktur f	field breakdown, Zener breakdown	Zener-Durchbruch m, Zener-Durchschlag m, Felddurchbruch m, Felddurchschlag m
fibrillary	s. fibrillar <bio>		
fibrillary structure	s. fibrillar structure		
fibrillation	Herzflimmern n, Flimmern n <Bio.>	field capacity [of soil]	Feldkapazität f [des Bodens], F.K.
fibrillation	s. a. fibering		
fibrilliform, fibrillous, fibrillar[y] <bio.>	fibrillär <Bio.>	field coil	s. magnet coil
fibroelastic	fiberelastisch	field constant, constant of electromagnetic field	Feldkonstante f
		field-controlled transistor	s. field-effect transistor
fibrous, fibriform, filamentous	faserig, faserartig, Faser-, fibrillär	field curvature, curvature of [the image] field	Bild[feld]wölbung f, Bildflächenwölbung f; Bildfeldkrümmung f
fibrous fracture, woody fracture	Faserbruch m, Schieferbruch m, Holzfaserbruch m	field decay, decay of field	Feldabfall m, Feldzerfall m, Abfall (Zerfall) m des Feldes
fibrous protein	s. scleroprotein		
fibrous structure	s. fibre structure		
Fick['s] diffusion law, Fick equation	s. Fick['s] law	field density, density of lines of force	Felddichte f, Feldliniendichte f, Kraftliniendichte f
Fick['s] first law	[erstes] Ficksches Gesetz n		
Fickian diffusion	Ficksche Diffusion f		
Fickian diffusion equation (law)	s. Fick['s] law	field description	Feldbeschreibung f

field

field diaphragm	s. field stop	**field-ion microscope,** electrostatic ion microscope	Feldionenmikroskop n, Felddesorptionsmikroskop n, Protonenmikroskop n
field directivity pattern, field pattern	Spannungsrichtdiagramm n; Feldstärkediagramm n	**fieldistor**	Fieldistor m
field displacement, displacement of field	Feldverdrängung f; Feldverdrängungseffekt m	**field lens,** field flattener, flattening lens	Feldlinse f, Kollektivlinse f
field displacement isolator	Feldverdrängungsisolator m	**field lens**	s. a. front lens
field distribution	Feldverteilung f, Feldverlauf m	**fieldless,** field-free; zero-field	feldfrei
field distribution, distribution of lines of force	Feldlinienverteilung f, Kraftlinienverteilung f	**field line**	s. line of force
field distribution diagram	Felddiagramm n	**field luminance,** adaptation brightness, adaptation luminance	Adaptationshelligkeit f, Adaptationsintensität f, Adaptationsleuchtdichte f, Gesichtsfeldleuchtdichte f
field dose, surface dose	Oberflächendosis f	**field magnet**	Feldmagnet m
field effect	Feldeffekt m, F-Effekt m	**field map[ping]**	s. pattern of the field
field-effect transistor, field-controlled transistor, unipolar transistor, FET	Feldeffekttransistor m, Kanaltransistor m, Feldtransistor m, Unipolartransistor m, unipolarer Transistor m, FET	**field mass** <of the source particle>	Feldmasse f <des Quellteilchens>
		field measurement	Feldmessung f
		field moisture	s. soil moisture
		field of current	s. field of flow
		field of electric intensity	s. electric field
		field of extremals	Extremalenfeld n
		field of flow, field of current	Strömungsfeld n, Stromfeld n
		field of force[s], force field	Kraftfeld n, Kräftefeld n
		field of force	s. a. electric field
		field of gravity, gravitational (gravity) field	Gravitationsfeld n, Schwerefeld n, Schwerkraftfeld n
field electron discharge	Feldelektronenentladung f	**field of points**	Punktfeld n
field emission	s. field emission of electrons	**field of pressure gradient**	Druckgradientenfeld n
field-emission arc	s. non-refractory arc		
field emission current, autoelectronic current	Feldemissionsstrom m, Kaltemissionsstrom m	**field of sharpness,** sharp field	Schärfenfeld n
field emission electron	Feldemissionselektron n	**field of sight,** visual field, field of vision, coverage <of instrument>	Sichtfeld n, Gesichtsfeld n, Instrumentengesichtsfeld n; Bildkreis m <opt. Instrument>
field emission microscope, point projection electron microscope, emission microscope	Feldelektronenmikroskop n, Spitzen[über]mikroskop n, Feldemissions[-Elektronen]mikroskop n	**field of sight meter,** visual field meter, kampometer	Gesichtsfeldmesser m, Kampimeter n
field-emission microscopy	Feldelektronenmikroskopie f, Spitzenmikroskopie f, Feldemissions[-Elektronen]mikroskopie f	**field of tangents,** directional field, direction field of lineal elements <math.>	Richtungsfeld n <Math.>
field emission of electrons, field emission, cold emission [of electrons], autoelectronic emission	Feldemission f, Kaltemission f, kalte Emission f, Kaltkatodenemission f, Feldelektronenemission f, kalte Elektronenemission f, autoelektronischer Effekt m, Autoemission f	**field of velocity,** velocity field	Geschwindigkeitsfeld n
		field of view <opt.>	Blickfeld n, Kernfeld n <Opt.>
		field of vision	s. visual field
		field of vision	s. field of sight <of instrument>
		field-of-vision stop	s. field stop
		field of vorticity	s. rotational field
		field operator	Feldoperator m
field energy	Feldenergie f	**field oscillator method**	Methode f der Feldoszillatoren
field equations	Feldgleichungen fpl		
field equations of Einstein, Einstein's field equations	Einsteinsche Feldgleichungen fpl, Feldgleichungen von Einstein	**field particle**	Feldteilchen n
		field pattern, field directivity pattern	Spannungsrichtdiagramm n; Feldstärkediagramm n
field evaporation	Feldverdampfung f		
field flattener, field lens, flattening lens	Feldlinse f, Kollektivlinse f	**field pattern**	s. a. pattern of the field
		field photophoresis	Feldphotophorese f
field flutter	Feldflutter m	**field plotting,** graphical construction of field	graphische Feldermittlung (Feldausmessung, Feldkonstruktion, Feldberechnung) f, Feldausmessung f
field-free, fieldless, zero-field	feldfrei		
field function	Feldfunktion f	**field point**	s. point under consideration
field index, magnetic-field index, n value	[kritischer] Feldindex m, Magnetfeldindex m, Exponent m des Feldabfalls, Feldexponent m	**field quantity,** field variable	Feldgröße f, Feldvariable f
		field quantization	Feldquantelung f, Feldquantisierung f
field instrument, instrument for field measurements	Feldinstrument n, Feldmeßgerät n, Reiseinstrument n, Reisemeßgerät n; relatives Meßgerät n	**field quantum,** fundamental field particle	Feldquant n
		field raising, rise of field	Feldaufbau m, Aufbau m des Feldes
field intensity, field strength, field	Feldstärke f, Feld n, Feldintensität f	**field reduction**	Abschwächung f des Feldes, Feldreduzierung f, Feldschwächung f
field intensity indicator (meter), field strength meter	Feldstärkemesser m	**field regulator**	s. field rheostat
		field rheostat, field regulator	Feldsteller m, Magnetfeldregler m, Feldregler m
field ion emission	Feldionenemission f		
field ionization	Feldionisierung f, Feldionisation f, Ionisierung f im starken elektrischen Feld	**field rotor**	s. pole wheel
		field star, background star, non-cluster star, non-member of a cluster	Feldstern m

field stop, field diaphragm, field-of-vision stop	Feldblende f, Gesichtsfeldblende f, Sehfeldblende f; Leuchtfeldblende f <Mikroskopierbeleuchtung>
field strength, field intensity, field	Feldstärke f, Feld n, Feldintensität f
field strength meter	s. field intensity indicator
field tensor	s. four-tensor of electromagnetic field
field theodolite	Feldtheodolit m, Reisetheodolit m, „relativer" Theodolit m
field-theoretic	feldtheoretisch
field theory	Feldtheorie f
field theory of fundamental particles, generalized electrodynamics	Feldtheorie f der Elementarteilchen, verallgemeinerte Elektrodynamik f
field theory of Schrödinger, Schrödinger['s] field theory	Schrödingers rein affine Feldtheorie f, rein affine Feldtheorie [von Schrödinger]
field triangulation, triangulation grid, triangulation	Triangulationsnetz n
Field tube	Field-Rohr n
field variable, field quantity	Feldgröße f, Feldvariable f
field vector	Feldvektor m
field vector	s. a. bound vector
field winding, magnet (operating, induction, inductive) winding, exciting winding	Erregerwicklung f; Feldwicklung f; Magnetwicklung f; Polwicklung f
Fierz term	Fierz-Glied n
fifa	= fissions per initial fissile atom
figural after-effect	figurale Nachwirkung f
figuration, configuration <opt.>	Figuration f, Konfiguration f <Opt.>
figuratrix	Figuratrix f
figured lens	asphärische Linse f [geringer Deformation]
figure of merit	Gütemaß n, Gütezahl f
figure of merit	s. a. transconductance-to-capacitance ratio
figure of merit	s. a. Q
figure of merit of the tube	Gütezahl f der Röhre, Güte f der Röhre
figure of noise	s. noise factor
figuring of optic[al] parts	Feinoptik f; Fertigungstechnik f der Optik
filament; thread	Faden m
filament, heating filament, filamentary cathode, heater <of electron tube>	Heizfaden m, Heizdraht m, Heizer m, Brenner m; Glühfaden m, Glühdraht m; Leuchtdraht m, Leuchtfaden m
filament, dark [absorption] marking, dark [hydrogen] flocculus <in Sun spectrograms>	Filament n, dunkler Faden (Flocculus) m, dunkles Filament, dunkle Flocke f <auf Chromosphärenbildern>
filament, filament prominence <astr.>	Filament n, fadenförmige Protuberanz f <Sonneneruption>
filamentary	s. fibriform
filamentary cathode	s. filament <of electron tube>
filamentary nebula <astr.>	Fasernebel m, Filament n, filamentartiger Nebel m <Galaxis>
filamentary structure <astr.>	Filamentstruktur f, Faserstruktur f <Astr.>
filamentary transistor	Fadentransistor m
filament circuit, heater circuit	Heiz[strom]kreis m, Heizungskreis m
filament current; heater current, heating current	Heizstrom m; Heizfadenstrom m
filament current power	s. filament power <el.>
filament electrometer	s. string electrometer
filament-growth method	s. Arkel-De Boer technique
filament line in a fluid, liquid (fluid) filament	Flüssigkeitsfaden m
filament of the nebula	Filament n des Nebels, filamentartiger Nebelstreifen m
filament of water, water filament	Wasserfaden m
filamentous	s. fibrous
filamentous	s. a. fibriform
filament pipette	Glühdrahtpipette f
filament power, heater (heating) power; filament current power <el.>	Heizleistung f; Heizfadenleistung f <El.>
filament prominence	s. filament
filament rangefinder, range-finding telescope	Fadenentfernungsmesser m, Fadendistanzmesser m, Okularfadenentfernungsmesser m, Reichenbachscher Entfernungsmesser m, distanzmessendes Fernrohr n
filament resistance; filament rheostat	Heizwiderstand m; Fadenwiderstand m
filament thermometer	Fadenthermometer n
filament voltage, heater voltage, voltage of filament battery <el.>	Heizfadenspannung f, Fadenspannung f, Heizspannung f <El.>
filar eyepiece, eyepiece micrometer, micrometer eyepiece	Okularmikrometer n
filar micrometer, cross-wire (cross-line) micrometer	Fadenmikrometer n, Fadenkreuzmikrometer n
filiform, filamentous, filamentary, thread-shaped	fadenförmig
filing[s]	Feilspäne mpl
filled band, filled energy band	[voll]besetztes Energieband n, [voll]besetztes Band n
filled column, packed column (tower), filled tower	Füllkörperkolonne f, Füllkörpersäule f
filled energy band	s. filled band
filled level, occupied level	[voll]besetztes Niveau n, [voll]besetztes Energieniveau n
filled shell	s. closed shell
filled tower	s. filled column
filler ring, filling[-in] ring, packing ring	Füllring m
fill factor	s. space factor
filling <into, on>	Schüttung f
filling factor	s. space factor
filling gas	Füllgas n
filling-gas mixture	Füllgemisch n
filling gas of the chamber, chamber gas	Kammergas n, Füllgas n der Kammer
filling-in ring	s. filling ring
filling of the shell	s. closure of the shell
filling out factor <el.>	Völligkeitsgrad m <El.>
filling ring, packing (filler, filling-in) ring	Füllring m
filling up <of depression>	Auffüllung f <Depression>
fill-in light; broadside; booster light, kicker light	Aufheller m
fill-in screen	s. reflecting screen
film; thin layer; pellicle	dünne Schicht f, Haut f, Häutchen n, Film m
film	s. a. dosifilm
film badge, film pack	Strahlenschutzplakette f, Filmplakette f; Personenfilmdosimeter n, Filmpersonendosimeter n

film 258

film balance [introduced by **Langmuir**], Langmuir['s] film balance — Langmuirsche Waage (Filmwaage) f, Filmwaage von Langmuir

film base, base material, base, emulsion support, support, backing <of film> <phot.> — Schichtträger m, Emulsionsträger m, Filmträger m, Träger m [der Schicht], Filmunterlage f, Unterlage f [des Films]

film boiling, sheet boiling — Filmsieden n, Filmverdampfung f

film capacitor, film-type capacitor — Schicht[en]kondensator m

film cathode — Schichtkatode f

film coefficient, film heat-transfer coefficient, film transfer rate — Filmkoeffizient m, Wärmeübergangszahl f bei Filmkondensation

film condensation — s. filmwise condensation

film conductor, film-type conductor — Schichtenleiter m

film cooling — Filmkühlung f, Kühlung f durch äußere Berieselung

film corrosion, layer corrosion — Schichtkorrosion f

film creep [of helium], super surface film phenomenon [of helium] — Kriechen n dünner Flüssigkeitsschichten [von Helium]

film dosimeter — s. dosifilm

film dosimetry — Filmdosimetrie f

film evaporation — Dünnschichtverdampfung f, Filmverdampfung f

film formation — Oberflächenfilmbildung f

film-grain noise, grain noise — Kornrauschen n

film growth, growth of films — Schichtwachstum n

film heat-transfer coefficient, film coefficient, film transfer rate — Filmkoeffizient m, Wärmeübergangszahl f bei Filmkondensation

film pack — s. film badge

film pressure — Filmdruck m

film resistance, sheet resistance [of films] — Schichtwiderstand m

film resistor — Schichtwiderstand m

film ring — Filmring m, ringförmiges Filmdosimeter n, Fingerring m mit Filmeinlage

film shrinkage, shrinkage of the film — Filmschrumpfung f, Schrumpfung f des Films

film-strip and slide projector — s. still projector

film thickness — s. thickness of layer

film thickness gauge (meter) — s. thickness meter

film transfer rate, film [heat-transfer] coefficient — Filmkoeffizient m, Wärmeübergangszahl f bei Filmkondensation

film-type capacitor, film capacitor — Schicht[en]kondensator m

film-type conductor, film conductor — Schichtenleiter m

film-type variable resistor — Schichtdrehwiderstand m

film viscometer — Filmviskosimeter n

film viscosity — Filmviskosität f

filmwise condensation, film condensation — Filmkondensation f

Filon['s] formulae — Filonsche Formeln fpl

Filon theory — Filonsche Theorie f

filter, light filter, optical filter — Lichtfilter n, [optisches] Filter n; Lichtdrossel f

filter aid — Filterhilfsmittel n

filter analyzer, polarizing-filter analyzer — Filteranalysator m

filter attenuation band — s. stop band

filter bed — Filterschicht f, Filterbett n

filter bell — Filtrationsglocke f

filter bottom — Filterboden m

filter cake, solid residue — Filterkuchen m, Filterrückstand m

filter candle — Filterkerze f

filter capacitor — Siebkondensator m, Filterkondensator m

filter chain, ladder-type filter — Filterkette f, Siebkette f

filter circuit, filtering circuit, eliminator — Siebschaltung f, Filterschaltung f, Siebkreis m, Filterkreis m

filter cloth, cloth filter — Filtertuch n, Tuchfilter n

filter coil, retardation coil — Siebdrossel f, Siebspule f

filter crucible — Filtertiegel m

filter cuvet — Filterküvette f

filter difference — Filterdifferenz f

filter difference technique [of actinometry] — Filterdifferenzverfahren n [der Aktinometrie]

filter discrimination, discrimination of the filter, selectivity [discrimination] — Selektivität f des Filters, Trennschärfe f des Filters

filter element, trap <el.> — Siebglied n <El.>

filter flask, filtering flask — Saugflasche f

filter fluorometer — Filterfluorometer n

filtergram, spectroheliogram — Spektroheliogramm n

filter hardening [of the neutron spectrum], neutron hardening by filters — Filterhärtung f [des Neutronenspektrums]

filtering, filtration — Filtration f, Filtrierung f, Filterung f

filtering, filtering out, filtration, selection, elimination <el.> — Siebung f, Sieben n, Aussiebung f, Filterung f <El.>

filtering circuit — s. filter circuit

filtering flask, filter flask — Saugflasche f

filtering material (medium), filter medium — Filtermittel n, Filtermaterial n, Filterstoff m

filtering-off — Abfiltrieren n

filtering-off — Wegfiltern n <Strahlung>

filtering out, filtering, filtration, selection, elimination <el.> — Siebung f, Sieben n, Aussiebung f, Filterung f <El.>

filter medium, filtering medium (material) — Filtermittel n, Filtermaterial n, Filterstoff m

filter operator — Sieboperator m

filter photocell, Dresler photocell — Filterphotoelement n, Dreslersche Filterzelle f, Dresler-Zelle f

filter photometer — Filterphotometer n

filter plate; frit — Filterplatte f; Fritte f

filter range — s. pass[-]band

filter rejection (stop) band — s. stop band

filtration, filtering — Filtration f, Filtrierung f, Filterung f

filtration — s. filtering <el.>

filtration — s. a. percolation

filtration — s. a. infiltration

filtration flow — Unterströmung f

filtration theory — Filtrationstheorie f

fima — = fissions per initial metal atom

fin — s. stabilizing fin

final compression pressure — Verdichtungsenddruck m, Verdichtungsendspannung f

final control element, control element, positioning element, control member, control device, regulated unit, actuator, correcting element, correction device	Stellglied n, Steller m, Stellorgan n; Regelglied n, Regelelement n, Regelorgan n, Regulator m; Steuerglied n, Steuerelement n, Steuerorgan n
final magnification	Endvergrößerung f
final mass <of rocket>	Endmasse f <Rakete>
final nucleus	Endkern m
final product, end product <of decay series>	stabiler Kern m, Schlußglied n <Zerfallsreihe>
final speed	s. final velocity
final state <nucl.>	Endzustand m <Kern.>
final state	s. a. steady state
final temperature, permanent operating temperature	Beharrungstemperatur f, Dauertemperatur f, Endtemperatur f
final temperature of operation; working temperature, operating temperature	Betriebstemperatur f; Arbeitstemperatur f
final vacuum, ultimate vacuum, ultimate pressure	Endvakuum n
final velocity, terminal speed (velocity), final speed	Endgeschwindigkeit f
finder [telescope] <astr.>, finding telescope	Sucherfernrohr n, Sucher m <Astr.>
finding of a meteorite	Fund m eines Meteoriten, Meteoritenfund m
finding telescope, finder [telescope] <astr.>	Sucherfernrohr n, Sucher m <Astr.>
fine; finely ground; finely divided	feingemahlen; feinzerkleinert; feinzerteilt
fine	s. a. fine-grain
fine adjustment; fine control, regulation, regulating; fine focusing [adjustment] <opt.>	Feineinstellung f; Feinregelung f
fine-adjustment reading, minute (fine) reading	Feinablesung f
fine-adjustment scale, vernier [scale], microadjustment dial	Feineinstellskala f
fine control	s. fine adjustment
fine control rod, regulating rod	Regelstab m, Feinregelstab m
fine dust	Feinstaub m
fine focus, fine focusing adjustment, mechanism of fine adjustment: slow-motion drive (screw)	Feintrieb m; Feinstellschraube f, Feinbewegungsschraube f
fine focusing <opt.>	s. fine adjustment
fine focusing adjustment	s. fine focus
fine focusing adjustment	s. a. fine adjustment
fine focusing motion; micromotion, slow motion, micrometric displacement	Feinbewegung f
fine-focus tube	Feinfokus[röntgen]röhre f
fine grain	Feinkorn n
fine-grain, fine grained, finely granular, small-grained, short-grained	feinkörnig, kleinkörnig; Feinkorn-
fine-grain, fine grained, highly dispersed, fine	hochdispers
fine-grained density	feine Dichte f
fine gravel	s. fines
finely crystalline	feinkristallin[isch]
finely divided; fine; finely ground	feingemahlen; feinzerkleinert; feinzerteilt
finely granular	s. fine-grain
finely ground; fine; finely divided	feingemahlen; feinzerkleinert; feinzerteilt
fine mottle, fine mottling, spicule	Spiculum n, Spikule f <pl: Spicula, Spikulen>
fineness	Feingehalt m, Feinheit f, Feine f, Korn n
fineness of grain	Kornfeinheit f, Feinkörnigkeit f
fineness of grinding	Mahlfeinheit f; Mahlgrad m
fineness of sieving	Siebfeinheit f
fineness ratio <of aerofoil>	Gleitzahl f <Flügel>
fineness ratio <of body>, body fineness ratio	Schlankheitsgrad m <Körper>
fine pointed flame	s. shooting flame
fine-pored	feinporig
fine rain; drizzle, drizzling	Sprühregen m, Staubregen m, Niesel[regen] m, Nieseln n; feiner Regen m
fine range diffraction, selected area diffraction	Feinbereichsbeugung f
fine reading, minute (fine-adjustment) reading	Feinablesung f
fines; fine gravel; dust	Grus m; Staub m <Geo.>
fine-scale microinstability	s. microinstability
fine-scale mixing	s. phase mixing
fine silt	s. suspended load
fine slip, microslip	Feingleitung f, Elementarstruktur f im Gleitlinienbild
fine structure <of spectral line, curve>	Feinstruktur f <Spektrallinie, Kurve>
fine structure constant, Sommerfeld fine structure constant	Feinstrukturkonstante f [von Sommerfeld], Sommerfeldsche Feinstrukturkonstante, Sommerfeld-Konstante f
fine-structure splitting	Feinstrukturaufspaltung f
fine-structure term	Feinstrukturterm m
fine topology	feine Topologie f, „topologie fine" f
fine tuning; sharp tuning	Feinabstimmung f, Scharfabstimmung f, scharfe Abstimmung f; Feinabgleich m
fine vacuum <$1 - 10^{-3}$ Torr>	Feinvakuum n <$1 \cdots 10^{-3}$ Torr>
Finger['s] theorem <on strain and rotation>	Fingerscher Satz m <über Deformation und Drehung>
finite	endlich, [von] endlicher Größe; finit
finite difference method, lattice-point method	Differenzenverfahren n, Differenzenmethode f, Gitterpunktmethode f
finite dimensional space	endlichdimensionaler Raum m
finite displacement	endliche Verschiebung f
finite elasticity theory	s. non-linear theory of elasticity
finite element method	Elementenmethode f, Finit-Element-Methode f
finite equation	finite Gleichung f, endliche Gleichung
finite expression	finiter Ausdruck m
finite group	endliche Gruppe f
finite Hankel transform	endliche Hankel-Transformation f
finite movement	endliche Bewegung f, gebundene Bewegung
finiteness, finitude	Endlichkeit f, Finitheit f
finite norm operator	s. Hilbert-Schmidt operator
finite part, Hadamard['s] finite part	[Hadamardscher] endlicher Teil m

finite | **260**

finite size effect, nuclear volume effect	Effekt *m* der endlichen Kernausdehnung, Kernvolumeneffekt *m*, „finite-size"-Effekt *m*	**first detector stage** **first equation of Maxwell,** Ampère's law in the differential form	*s.* mixing stage <el.> erste Maxwellsche Gleichung (Feldgleichung) *f*, Durchflutungsgesetz (Erregungsgesetz) *n* in der Differentialform, Differentialform *f* des Durchflutungsgesetzes
finitude	*s.* finiteness		
Finkelstein grating mounting, Finkelstein mounting [of diffraction grating]	Finkelsteinsche Gitteraufstellung *f*		
finning, ribbing	Berippung *f*; Verrippung *f*	**first equatorial system [of co-ordinates]**	*s.* dependent equatorial co-ordinates
		first filter, prefilter	Vorfilter *n*
Finn['s] method	Finnsche Methode *f*		
Finsler space	Finslerscher Raum *m*, Finslersche Mannigfaltigkeit *f*	**first focal point,** object focus, front focus	Dingbrennpunkt *m*, dingseitiger (objektseitiger, vorderer) Brennpunkt *m*
fireball, bolide <astr.>	Feuerkugel *f*, Bolid *m* <Astr.>		
fireball <cosmic rays>	Feuerball *m*, „fireball" *m* <kosm. Strahlung>	**first forbidden,** forbidden of first order	einfach verboten, verboten von erster Ordnung
fireball <nucl.>, ball of fire	Feuerball *m* <Kern.>	**first Green formula,** Green's formula of the first kind	Greensche Formel *f* erster Art, erste Greensche Formel
fireball	*s. a.* ball lightning		
fireball model	Feuerballmodell *n*, „fireball"-Modell *n*	**first harmonic**	erste Harmonische *f*
fire point	*s.* ignition point	**first harmonic**	*s. a.* fundamental mode
fire-proof, fire-resistant, fire-resisting, refractory, resistant to fire (heat), flameproof, flame-retardant	feuerfest, feuerbeständig	**first-harmonic content**	Grundschwingungsgehalt *m*
		first integral	erstes Integral *n*, Vorintegral *n*
		first integral of motion	*s.* integral of motion <mech.>
firing, shot firing	Zündung *f* der Sprengladung	**first Kirchhoff law**	*s.* Kirchhoff['s] current law
		first Lagrangian point, conical point, inner Lagrangian point	erster Lagrange-Punkt *m*, innerer Lagrange-Punkt
firing	*s. a.* sintering <of ceramics>		
firing angle, ignition angle	Zündwinkel *m*, Zündverzögerungswinkel *m*	**first law** <of thermodynamics>	erster Hauptsatz *m*, erster Hauptsatz der Thermodynamik, erster Hauptsatz der Wärmelehre
firing current; ignition current; striking current	Zündstrom *m*; Zündstromstärke *f*, Zündungsstromstärke *f*		
firing delay, ignition delay (lag), firing lag, time lag of the ignition <of discharge>	Zündverzögerung *f*, Zündverzug *m* <Entladung>; Zündmomentverspätung *f* <Gleichrichter>	**first law of Kepler**	erstes Keplersches Gesetz *n*
		first law of Kirchhoff	*s.* Kirchhoff['s] current law
		first law of motion	*s.* Newton['s] first law
firing delay time, firing time, blocking period	Zündzeit *f*, Zündverzögerungszeit *f*	**first mean Sun,** fictitious Sun moving along the ecliptic	erste mittlere Sonne *f*; [fiktive] mittlere Sonne, die sich gleichförmig in der Ekliptik bewegt; Zwischensonne *f*
firing duration, burning time <of rocket>	Brennzeit *f* <Rakete>		
firing lag	*s.* ignition delay	**first meridian**	*s.* zero meridian
firing of the rocket	Zündung *f* der Rakete	**first moment of the surface,** static moment of the surface	statisches Flächenmoment *n* (Moment *n* der Fläche)
firing of thyratron, ignition of thyratron	Zündung *f* des Thyratrons		
firing point	*s.* ignition point	**first-order aberration,** primary aberration, Seidel aberration	Seidelscher Bildfehler *m*, Seidelscher Bildfeldfehler *m*, monochromatischer Bildfehler, Schärfenfehler *m*, Schärfefehler *m*
firing point (potential)	*s.* ionization potential		
firing pulse	*s.* ignition pulse		
firing time, firing delay time, blocking period	Zündzeit *f*, Zündverzögerungszeit *f*		
		first-order approximation, first approximation	erste Näherung *f*
firing voltage	*s.* striking voltage <of discharge *or* tube>		
firmament	*s.* vault of heaven	**first-order phase change**	*s.* first-order transition
firn, névé	Firn *m*, Firnschnee *m*	**first-order reaction**	*s.* reaction of first order
		first-order spectrum, primary spectrum	Primärspektrum *n*, Spektrum *n* erster Ordnung
firn basin, névé basin	Firnfeld *n*, Firnmulde *f*, Firnbecken *n*		
firn ice	Firneis *n*, Schnee-Eis *n*	**first-order temperature coefficient,** linear temperature coefficient	Temperaturkoeffizient *m* erster Ordnung, linearer Temperaturkoeffizient
firn line	*s.* snow[]line		
first approximation, first-order approximation	erste Näherung *f*	**first-order transformation (transition),** transition (transformation, phase change) of first order, first-order phase change, phase transformation (transition, change)	Umwandlung *f* erster (I.) Ordnung (Art), Übergang *m* erster (I.) Ordnung (Art), Phasenumwandlung *f*, Phasenübergang *m*
first boundary condition	*s.* Dirichlet['s] boundary condition		
first boundary [value] problem	*s.* Dirichlet['s] problem		
first canonical form	*s.* classical canonical form	**first-order wave,** billow, wave [of the first order]	Woge *f*, Welle *f* erster Ordnung
first class conductor	*s.* electron conductor		
first class constraint, constraint of the first class	Zwangsbedingung *f* der ersten Klasse	**first point of Aries,** vernal [equinox] point	Frühlingspunkt *m*, Widderpunkt *m*
first collision correction	Erststoßkorrektur *f*	**first point of Libra**	*s.* autumnal point
first collision kerma	„first-collision"-Kerma *f*, Erststoßkerma *f*	**first postulate of thermodynamics,** general law of thermodynamics	allgemeiner Hauptsatz *m* der Thermodynamik, erstes Postulat *n* der Thermodynamik
first condensate, primary condensate	Vorkondensat *n*		
first critical potential, resonance potential	Resonanzpotential *n*, erstes kritisches Potential *n*, Resonanzspannung *f*	**first quantum number,** principal (total, main) quantum number	Hauptquantenzahl *f*
		first runnings <chem.>, overhead product	Vorlauf *m* <Chem.>
first curvature	*s.* mean curvature		

first sound	„first sound" m, Wärmewelle f erster (1.) Art, Schall- und Wärmewellen fpl erster (1.) Art, Wärmewellenintensität f erster (1.) Art
first term	s. fixed term
first theorem of the mean <for integrals>	erster Mittelwertsatz m [der Integralrechnung]
first Townsend coefficient	erster Townsend-Koeffizient m
first Townsend discharge	primäre Townsend-Entladung f
first twilight arch	erster (leuchtender) Dämmerungsbogen m
fir tree crystal[lite]	s. dendrite
Fischer-Hinnen law	Fischer-Hinnensches Gesetz n
Fischer-Riesz theorem, Riesz-Fischer['s] theorem, Riesz representation theorem [for Hilbert spaces]	Fischer-Rieszscher Satz m, Riesz-Fischerscher Satz
Fischer-Schaffeld law	Fischer-Schaffeldsches Gesetz n
fishbone antenna, Christmas-tree antenna	Tannenbaumantenne f
Fisher['s] amount of information	Fisherscher Informationsbetrag m, Fishersches Integral n
Fisher['s] distribution; Fisher['s] F distribution, F distribution; Fisher['s] z-distribution	Fishersche Verteilung f, Fisher-Verteilung f; F-Verteilung f, Fishersche F-Verteilung; z-Verteilung f, Fishersche z-Verteilung
Fisher-Pitman test	s. randomization test
Fisher['s] test for independence, Fisher-Yates test, exact χ^2 test	Fisher-Yates-Test m, exakter Test m von R. A. Fisher, Fishers Test (exakter Unabhängigkeitstest m)
Fisher['s] z-distribution	s. Fisher['s] distribution
fisheye	Fischauge f; Flockenriß n
fisheye	s. a. Maxwell['s] fisheye
fishtail twin	Schwalbenschwanzzwilling m
fish-type body, streamlined body, body of good streamline shape	Stromlinienkörper m, stromlinienförmiger Körper m
Fiske step, Fiske wave	Fiske-Stufe f
fisser	s. fissionable material
fissile, fissionable <US> <nucl.>	spaltbar, spaltfähig <Kern.>
fissile material	s. fissionable material
fissility, fissionability <US> <nucl.>	Spaltbarkeit f <Kern.>
fissiography, fission-product radioautography	Spaltprodukt-Autoradiographie f
fission, nuclear fission <nucl.>	Spaltung f, Kernspaltung f <Kern.>
fission <of cell> <bio.>	s. a. cell division
fissionability <US> <nucl.>, fissility	Spaltbarkeit f <Kern.>
fissionable <US> <nucl.>, fissile	spaltbar, spaltfähig <Kern.>
fissionable material, fissile material, fissioner, fisser	Spaltmaterial n, Spaltstoff m, spaltbares Material n, spaltbarer Stoff m
fission barrier	Spaltungsbarriere f
fission bomb	Spalt[ungs]bombe f, Kernspaltungsbombe f
fission capture; useful capture	Spalteinfang m
fission capture cross-section, cross-section for fission capture	Spalteinfangquerschnitt m, Wirkungsquerschnitt m für Spalteinfang, Wirkungsquerschnitt des Spalteinfangs
fission chain, fission decay chain	Spalt[produkt]kette f, Spaltproduktreihe f
fission chain reaction, chain fissions	Spalt[ungs]kettenreaktion f, Kettenspaltung f, Kernspaltungskettenreaktion f, Kettenreaktion f der Kernspaltung
fission chamber, fission ionization chamber	Spaltungskammer f, Spaltkammer f
fission counter	Spalt[ungs]zähler m
fission counting rate	Spaltzählrate f
fission cross-section, nuclear fission cross-section, cross-section for nuclear fission, cross-section for fission	Spaltquerschnitt m, Wirkungsquerschnitt m für (der) Spaltung, Kernspaltungsquerschnitt m, Wirkungsquerschnitt für (der) Kernspaltung, Spaltungsquerschnitt m, Spalt[ungs]wirkungsquerschnitt m
fission cross-section for thermal neutrons	s. thermal fission cross-section
fission decay chain, fission chain	Spalt[produkt]kette f, Spaltproduktreihe f
fission energy	Spalt[ungs]energie f
fissioner	s. fissionable material
fission fragment	Spaltbruchstück n, Spaltfragment n
fission fragment separation	Trennung f der Spaltbruchstücke
fission gamma	Spaltgamma n, Spalt[ungs]-Gamma-Quant n, Spalt-Gamma-Strahl m
fission gas; volatile fission products	Spalt[ungs]gas n, gasförmige (flüchtige) Spaltprodukte npl
fission heat, heat of fission	Spaltungswärme f
fissioning distribution; fissioning spectrum	Energieverteilung f der die Spaltung verursachenden Neutronen; Energiespektrum n der die Spaltung verursachenden Neutronen
fission ionization chamber, fission chamber	Spaltungskammer f, Spaltkammer f
fission mean free path, mean free path for fission	[mittlere freie] Spaltweglänge f, [mittlere freie] Spaltungsweglänge f, mittlere freie Weglänge f für Spaltung
fission neutron	Spaltneutron n
fission neutron energy	[kinetische] Energie f der Spaltneutronen, Spaltneutronenenergie f
fission plasma reactor	Plasmaspaltungsreaktor m
fission poison	Spaltgift n
fission probability	Spaltwahrscheinlichkeit f
fission product	Spaltprodukt n
fission product activity	Spaltproduktaktivität f
fission product poisoning	s. poisoning of the nuclear reactor
fission product radiation	Spaltproduktstrahlung f
fission-product radioautography	s. fissiography
fission-product yield, fission yield	Spalt[produkt]ausbeute f, Ausbeute f der Spaltung
fission rate, rate of fission	Spaltrate f, Spalthäufigkeit f, Spaltungen fpl pro Zeiteinheit
fission reactor	Spaltungsreaktor m
fission recoil, fission recoil nucleus	Spaltbruchstück n im Augenblick der Trennung, Rückstoßkern m bei der Spaltung
fission spectrum	Spalt[neutronen]spektrum n, Energiespektrum n der Spaltneutronen
fission theory [of double stars] <astr.>	Theorie f der Spaltung eines Einzelsterns, Spaltungstheorie f [der Doppelsterne] <Astr.>
fission threshold	Spalt[ungs]schwelle f, Schwellenenergie f für Spaltung
fission track	Spur f des Spaltfragments
fission track dating (method), fission track technique	Festkörperspurverfahren n [der Altersbestimmung]

fission track detector	s. solid-state track detector	fixed echo	s. permanent echo
fission width	Spaltungsbreite f	fixed-ended arch	s. hingeless arch
fission yield, fission-product yield	Spalt[produkt]ausbeute f, Ausbeute f der Spaltung	fixed-ended beam, encastré beam	beiderseits eingespannter Balken m
fission yield curve	Spaltausbeutekurve f		
		fixed error	s. systematic error <stat.>
fissium, Fs	Fissium n, Fs	fixed field	Festfeld n, ruhendes Feld n
fissure; cleft	Klüftung f, Zerklüftung f	fixed-field alternating-gradient accelerator, FFAG accelerator	FFAG-Maschine f, FFAG-Beschleuniger m
fissure <geo.>	Bruchspalte f <Geo.>		
fissure eruption, linear eruption	Lineareruption f, Spalteneruption f, Spaltenerguß m, Spaltenausbruch m	fixed-field alternating-gradient stabilizing, FFAG stabilization	FFAG-Stabilisierung f
fissure source	Spaltenquelle f		
fissure water, fault water	Spaltenwasser n; Kluftwasser n	fixed-field alternating-gradient synchrotron	s. FFAG synchrotron
		fixed frame	festes Bezugssystem n
fitting, matching, adapting, equating <math.>	Anpassung f; Angleichung f <Math.>	fixed-frequency cyclotron, f-f cyclotron	Zyklotron n mit fester Frequenz, Festfrequenzzyklotron n
fitting condition <math.>	Anpassungsbedingung f, Anschlußbedingung f <Math.>		
fitting of the curve, curve fitting	Anpassung f der Kurve, Kurvenanpassung f	fixed frequency magnetron	Festfrequenzmagnetron n
Fitzgerald['s] experiment	[Fitzgeraldscher] Kondensatordrehversuch m	fixed frequency oscillator	Festfrequenzoszillator m
Fitzgerald-Lorentz contraction	s. Lorentz contraction	fixed ground water	s. adhesive water
Fitzgerald vector	Fitzgeraldscher Vektor	fixed in space, spatial	raumfest
five constants dispersion formula of Ketteler	Kettelersche Dispersionsformel f, Fünfkonstanten-Dispersionsformel f von Ketteler	fixed-in-the-earth [co-ordinate] system	erdgebundenes (erdfestes) Koordinatensystem n, erdfestes System n
		fixed load	s. permanent load <mech.>
five-days average, pentad average, pentad mean	Pentadenmittel n, Fünftagemittel n	fixed point <math.>	Fixpunkt m <Math.>
		fixed point <of temperature scale>, fixed thermometric point; fundamental point <therm.>	Fixpunkt m, Temperaturfixpunkt m, Temperaturfestpunkt m; Fundamentalpunkt m <Therm.>
five-dimensional	fünfdimensional		
five-membered ring, five ring	Fünferring m		
five-tensor	Fünfertensor m		
five-years' average (mean), lustrum (lustre) average	Lustrummittel n, Fünfjahresmittel n	fixed point <num. math.>	Festkomma n <num. Math.>
		fixed point	s. a. reference point
fixation, fixing <opt.; phot.; bio.>	Fixierung f <Phot.; Opt.; Bio.>; Fixation f <Opt.; Bio.>	fixed[-]point theorem	Fixpunktsatz m
		fixed pulley	feste Rolle f
fixation	s. a. localization	fixed ratio	Festverhältnis n
fixation at a line, localization in a line <of vector>	Linienflüchtigkeit f <Vektor>	fixed star, star, stellar body <astr.>	Fixstern m, Stern m; Gestirn n <Astr.>
fixation at a point, localization in a point <of vector>	Gebundenheit f <Vektor>	fixed system [of co-ordinates], fixed co-ordinate system	ortsfestes Koordinatensystem (System) n, festes System
fixation disparity, disparity, geometric disparity	Disparation f, geometrische Disparation	fixed term, first term	Grenzterm m, Festterm m, unveränderlicher Term m
fixed	fest, festgehalten, Fest-, Fix-in Ruhe, ruhend, fest, bewegungslos, unbewegt	fixed thermometric point	s. fixed point
fixed, at rest, non-moving, motionless		fixed value; constant; set value	Festwert m; Konstante f
fixed; stationary	stationär; unbeweglich, ortsfest, feststehend	fixed variable	festgehaltene Variable f, feste Variable
fixed; constant: invariable; unvarying	konstant; unveränderlich, invariabel, fest	fixed vector	s. bound vector
		fixed weir	festes Wehr n, festes Stauwerk n
fixed antenna direction finder	s. fixed direction finder	fixing	Einspannung f
fixed arch	s. hingeless arch	fixity, non-mobility	Unbeweglichkeit f
fixed axode, fixed cone of instantaneous axes	Spurkegel m, ruhende Achsenfläche f, fester Momentanachsenkegel m	fixity	s. a. non[-]volatility
		Fizeau['s] experiment	Fizeauscher Versuch m
		Fizeau['s] formula	Fizeausche Formel f
fixed bearing, rigid point of support	fester Stützpunkt m	Fizeau-Foucault fringes	Fizeau-Foucaultsche Streifen mpl
fixed-blade turbine	s. propeller turbine	Fizeau fringe	s. fringe of equal thickness
fixed capacitor	Festkondensator m		
		Fizeau['s] interference experiment	Fizeauscher Interferenzversuch m, Interferenzversuch von Fizeau
fixed centrode	s. herpolhode <mech.>		
fixed cone of instantaneous axes, fixed axode	Spurkegel m, ruhende Achsenfläche f, fester Momentanachsenkegel m	Fizeau['s] method, [Fizeau] rotating wheel method, toothed wheel method, cog-wheel method, chopper disk method	Zahnradmethode f, Methode f von Fizeau, Fizeausche Methode (Zahnradmethode)
fixed co-ordinate system, fixed system [of co-ordinates]	ortsfestes Koordinatensystem (System) n, festes System		
fixed curve of instantaneous centres	s. herpolhode <mech.>	Fizeau phenomenon	Fizeausche Erscheinung f
fixed direction finder, fixed antenna direction finder	Festrahmenpeiler m, Peiler m mit Festrahmen und Goniometer	Fizeau rotating wheel method	s. Fizeau['s] method
		flabbiness	s. slackness
		flabby, flaccid, untensioned, slack	schlaff, entspannt, ungespannt
		flageolet tone	Flageoletton m

flaky structure, flaky texture	Schuppenstruktur f, Schuppenbau m, Schuppung f	flange coupling, flanged connector, flanged joint, flange joint	Flanschverbindung f <Mech., El.>; Flanschanschluß m <Mech., El.>; Flansch[an]kopplung f <El.>
flame analysis	Flammenanalyse f	flange joint	s. flange coupling
flame arc, flaming arc	Flammenbogen m	flank angle	Flankenwinkel m
flame arc lamp	Beck-Hochleistungslampe f, Beck-Bogenlampe f	flank moraine, lateral (marginal, peripheral) moraine	Seitenmoräne f, Ufermoräne f, Randmoräne f
flame arc lamp	s. a. flame lamp	flap	s. camber changing flap <of airfoil>
flame calorimetry	Flammenkalorimetrie f		
flame carbon, effect carbon	Effektkohle f	flap attenuator, strip attenuator	Streifenabschwächer m
flame-carbon lamp, flame lamp	Effektbogenlampe f, Effektkohle[bogen]lampe f	flare, lens flare, reflex <phot.>	Reflex m, Reflexionsfleck m <Phot.>
flame collector	Flammensonde f, Flammenkollektor m	flare <pyrotechnics>	Fackel f <Pyrotechnik>
flame conduction	Flamm[en]leitung f	flare <on the Sun>	s. a. solar flare
flame-emission line, flame line	Flammenlinie f	flare angle, flaring angle; half-power width, lobe width <of antenna systems>	Öffnungswinkel m <Antennensysteme>
flame-emission spectrum, flame spectrum	Flammenspektrum n		
flame[-] front	Flammenfront f		
flame gauge, flame pressure gauge	Flammenmanometer n		
flame hardening	s. surface hardening		
flame ionization detector	Flammenionisationsdetektor m		
flame lamp, flame (flaming) arc lamp, alternating-current (a.c.) flame lamp	Flammenbogenlampe f, Wechselstrom-Flammenbogenlampe f; Wechselstrom-Effektbogenlampe f	flareback	s. light-back
		flare point	s. flash point
		flare star	s. UV Ceti-type variable
		flaring angle	s. flare angle
		flash, lightning [flash], flash of lightning, lightning stroke	Blitz m; Blitzstrahl m
flame lamp, flame-carbon lamp	Effektbogenlampe f, Effektkohle[bogen]lampe f	flash	s. a. photoflash
		flash	s. a. scintillation
		flash arc	s. Rocky-Point effect
flameless combustion, combustion without flame	stille Verbrennung f, flammenlose Verbrennung	flash[-]back	s. light-back
		flashback limit	Rückschlaggrenze f, Rückzündgrenze f
flameless combustion	s. a. catalytic combustion	flash boiler	Schnell[strom]verdampfer m
flame line, flame-emission line	Flammenlinie f		
flame-out of the rocket	Brennschluß m der Rakete		
		flash bulb	s. photoflash lamp
		flash distillation, equilibrium distillation	Gleichgewichtsdestillation f
flame photography	Flammenphotographie f		
flame photometer	Flammenphotometer n	flash duration	Leuchtzeit f, Leuchtdauer f <Elektronenblitz-Entladungslampe>
flame photometry	Flammenphotometrie f		
flame plasma	Flammenplasma n		
flame pressure gauge, flame gauge	Flammenmanometer n	flashed glass	Überfangglas n, überfangenes Glas n
flameproof	s. fire-resistant		
flameproof	s. non-inflammable	flashed opal [glass]; cased opal [glass]	Überfang[trüb]glas n, Opalüberfangglas n
flame propagation, propagation (spread) of flames, flame spread	Flammenausbreitung f, Flammenfortpflanzung f	flasher [device]	Würfelreflektor m
		flashers	s. windows <radar>
flame resistance	s. fireproofness	flash evaporation, flashing	Entspannungsverdampfung f, Einfachverdampfung f, Flashverdampfung f
flame-retardant	s. fire-resistant		
flame spectrometry, flame spectroscopy	Flammenspektroskopie f, Flammenspektrometrie f	flash getter	Verdampfungsgetter m, Verdampfergetter m, Abdampfgetter m
flame spectrophotometry	Flammenspektralphotometrie f		
flame spectroscopy, flame spectrometry	Flammenspektroskopie f, Flammenspektrometrie f	flashing, post-exposure	Nachbelichtung f
flame spectrum, flame-emission spectrum	Flammenspektrum n	flashing <opt., el.>; unsteadiness of light <emitted by a source>; flicker <e.g. of flame>	Flackern n <Opt., El.>; Aufflackern n <z. B. des Bogens>
flame speed	s. rate of flame propagation		
flame spread	s. flame propagation		
flame temperature	Flammentemperatur f	flashing	s. a. flash evaporation
		flashing point	s. flash point
flame temperature, combustion temperature, temperature of combustion	Verbrennungstemperatur f	flash lamp	s. photoflash lamp
		flashlight	s. photoflash
		flash of light	s. scintillation
flame velocity	s. rate of flame propagation	flash of lightning	s. flash
		flashometer	Lichtblitzanalysator m
flame zone	Flammenzone f		
flaming	s. inflammation	flash[-]over	s. spark[-]over
flaming arc, flame arc	Flammenbogen m	flashover voltage, sparkover voltage	Überschlagsspannung f
flaming arc lamp	s. a. flame lamp		
flaming aurora	flammendes Polarlicht n	flash photolysis	Blitzlichtphotolyse f, Lichtblitzphotolyse f, Flashphotolyse f
flammability	s. inflammability		
flammability limits <US>	s. inflammability limits	flash point, flashing point, flare point, F.P	Flammpunkt m, Entflammungstemperatur f, FP
flange	Flansch m		

flash radiography, ultra-high-speed radiography — Blitzaufnahme *f*, Röntgenblitzaufnahme *f*
flash spectrum — Flashspektrum *n*
flash to earth, lightning flash (discharge) to earth — Erdblitz *m*
flash tube — s. electronic-flash lamp
flash-type stroboscope, stroboscope; Elverson oscilloscope — Lichtblitzstroboskop *n*, Stroboskop *n*
flash-type stroboscopy — Lichtblitzstroboskopie *f*
flash X-ray tube, X-ray flash tube — Röntgenblitzröhre *f*
flask; bottle; jar — Flasche *f*, Fläschchen *n*
flask; vessel; receiver; receptacle; reservoir; basin — Behälter *m*, Behältnis *n*; Gefäß *n*, Bassin *n*, Becken *n*; Vorratsgefäß *n*; Vorratsbehälter *m*; Zulaufbehälter *m*; Reservoir *n*
flask, cask <US> <cylindrical>; shielded box <rectangular>; coffin, casket <for shielding of radioactive materials> — Transportkontainer *m*, Kontainer *m*, Container *m*, Transportbehälter *m*, Strahlenschutzbehälter *m*, Behälter *m* <für radioaktive Materialien>
flask; retort — Kolben *m*; Retorte *f*
flat, optically flat (plane), plane <opt.> — [optisch] eben, [optisch] flach <Opt.>
flat — s. a. planat
flat angle, straight angle — gestreckter Winkel *m*
flat anode — Plananode *f*
flat cast[ing] — s. flat throw <mech.>
flat channel, shallow-water channel — Flachwasserkanal *m*, Seichtwasserkanal *m*
flat coil, pancake (slab) coil — Flachspule *f*
flat-coil [measuring] instrument — Flachspulinstrument *n*, Flachspulmeßgerät *n*
flat conductor, plate [-shaped] conductor, conducting plate — plattenförmiger Leiter *m*, Plattenleiter *m*
flat-crested weir — s. broad-crested weir
flat curve — flache Kurve *f*
flat-die forging — s. smith forging
flat-ended tube, flat-faced cathode-ray tube — Elektronenstrahlröhre *f* mit Planschirm, Katodenstrahlröhre *f* mit ebener Bildfläche
flat jet — flacher Strahl *m*, Flachstrahl *m*
"flat" lens — Planglas *n* <als Brillenglas>
flat mirror, plane mirror — Planspiegel *m*, ebener Spiegel *m*, Flachspiegel *m*
flatness, planeness, smoothness — Ebenheit *f*, Glätte *f*
flatness factor — s. coefficient of excess
flat plate flow, flow over (past) a flat plate — Plattenströmung *f*, Plattenumströmung *f*
flat profile — Streckenprofil *n*
flat slab — s. slab
flat slap — s. a. plate
flat-slab buttress dam, Ambursen dam — Ambursenwehr *n*

flat space — ebener Raum *m*, nichtgekrümmter Raum
flat space-time — ebenes Raum-Zeit-Kontinuum *n*
flat surface grinding — Planschleifen *n*, Planschliff *m*
flattening, planishing <of the bump> — Ausbeulung *f*, Beulen *n*, Austreibung *f* der Beule
flattening, graduation <math.>; smoothing <math., el., techn.> — Glättung *f*, Ausgleichung *f* <Math., El., Techn.>; Glättungsprozeß *m* <Techn.>; Ebnung *f*
flattening, compression <math.> — Abplattung *f* <Math.>
flattening <met.> — Richten *n* <Met.>
flattening, flux flattening <nucl.> — Flußabflachung *f*, Glätten *n* der Flußverteilung <Kern.>
flattening, oblateness <quantity> — Abplattung *f* <Größe>
flattening lens — s. field lens
flattening of image field, elimination of image field curvature — Bildfeldebnung *f*
flattening of the Earth, Earth's oblateness (flattening), oblateness (polar flattening) of the Earth, compression of the geoid — Abplattung *f* der Erde, polare Abplattung der Erde, Erdabplattung *f*
flattening of the flood wave — Verflachung *f* der Hochwasserwelle
flattening of the wave — Wellenverflachung *f*
flattening reducer — s. superproportional reducer
flat throw, flat cast[ing] <mech.> — Flachwurf *m*, Flachschuß *m*, flacher Wurf *m*, flacher Schuß *m* <Mech.>
flat-top antenna, plane (sheet) antenna — Flächenantenne *f*
flat-topped fold, box fold — Kofferfalte *f*
flat trajectory, sweeping trajectory — Flachbahn *f*; gestreckte (rasante) Flugbahn *f*
flat tube — Flachrohr *n*
flat vibrator — s. plate-like vibrator
flaw, cavity <as a material defect> — Hohlraum *m*, Kaverne *f*
flaw detectability, detectability of flaws — Fehlererkennbarkeit *f*, Erkennbarkeit *f* von Fehlern
flaw detector — s. crack detector
flaw in the liquid — Aufreißung *f* in der Flüssigkeit
flaw of Smekal, Smekal defect (flaw), pore, loose place [of Smekal], lockerstelle — Lockerstelle *f* [nach Smekal], Smekalsche Lockerstelle, Lockerion *n*
F-layer, Appleton layer <el.> — F-Schicht *f*, Appleton-Schicht *f* <El.>
flecnodal tangent — Fleknodaltangente *f*, Ruhtangente *f*
flecnode — Wendeknoten *m*, Fleknodalpunkt *m*
flection — = second derivative
flection — s. bending
fleece cloud — s. alto-cumulus
fleet water — s. shallow water
Fleming['s] [first] rule — s. left-hand rule
Fleming['s] [second] rule — s. right-hand rule
Fletcher['s] indicatrix — s. index ellipsoid
Fletcher-Munson curve, equal loudness contour (curve) — Fletcher-Munson-Kurve *f*, Kurve *f* gleicher Lautstärke [nach Fletcher und Munson], Kurve gleicher Lautheit
Flettner rotor — Flettner-Rotor *m*
Flettner ship, rotor ship — [Flettnersches] Rotorschiff *n*, Flettner-Schiff *n*
flexibility, pliability — Biegsamkeit *f*, Biegungselastizität *f*, Flexibilität *f*
flexibility — s. a. slenderness ratio
flexible pipe connection, connection by flexible pipe (tube) — Schlauchverbindung *f*
flexible suspension — weiche (frei bewegliche) Aufhängung *f*
flexion — s. bending
flex point <of the curve> <math.>, point of inflexion (contrary flexure), inflexion point — Wendepunkt *m*, Inflexionspunkt *m* erster Ordnung; Inflexionspunkt <der Kurve> <Math.>
flexural buckling; buckling; lateral buckling — Knickung *f* [seitliche] Ausknickung *f*, seitliches Ausweichen *n*
flexural centre — s. shear centre
flexural couple — s. bending couple
flexural glide — Biegegleitung *f*
flexural load, bending stress — Biegebeanspruchung *f*
flexural loading fatigue testing machine — Biegeschwingungsmaschine *f*, Prüfmaschine *f* für Biegeschwingungsversuche
flexural mode [of oscillation] — s. flexural vibration

flexural moment	s. flexural torque	**floatation area**, water-plane area, water-line section	Schwimmfeld n, Schwimmfläche f, Wasserlinienfläche f
flexural plane, bending line plane, plane of flexure	Biegungsebene f	**floatation plane**, water-plane, plane of floatation	Schwimmebene f
flexural rigidity	s. bending stiffness	**floater**	s. float
flexural rigidity of the plate	s. rigidity of the plate	**float gauge**; float-type limnimeter	Schwimmerpegel m; Schwimmerlimnimeter n
flexural stiffness	s. bending stiffness	**float gauging**	Schwebekörperverfahren n der Durchflußmessung, Schwimmermethode f (Schwimmerverfahren n) der Wassermengenmessung, Durchflußmessung f nach der Schwimmermethode
flexural strength	s. bending strength		
flexural stress, bending (transverse) stress	Biegespannung f, Biegenormalspannung f		
flexural tensile strength	Biegezugfestigkeit f		
flexural torque, bending couple (moment), flexural moment (couple)	Biegemoment n, Biegungsmoment n	**floating**, floatation, flotation	Schwimmen n
flexural transverse strength	s. bending strength	**floating bell manometer**, bell manometer	Tauchglockendruckwaage f, Tauchglockenmanometer n, Glockenmanometer n
flexural vibration, flexure mode, flexural mode [of oscillation], thickness vibration, contour vibration (oscillation)	Biegeschwingung f, Querschwingung f, Dickenschwingung f, Biegungsschwingung f	**floating card compass**, immersed compass, fluid compass	Schwimmkompaß m
		floating crucible	schwimmender Tiegel m, Schwimmtiegel m
flexural wave, bending wave	Biegungswelle f, Biegewelle f	**floating-drift klystron**	s. drift-tube klystron
		floating-drift klystron (tube, tube type klystron)	s. single-cavity klystron
flexure <geo.>	Flexur f <Geo.>		
flexure, bending, flection, flexion, folding <mech.>	Biegung f <Mech.>		
		floating drop, suspended drop	schwebender Tropfen m
flexure	s. a. bowing under load <mech.>	**floating-drop method (technique)**	Methode f der schwebenden Tropfen
flexure crystal	Biegeschwinger m, Dickenschwinger m, Querschwinger m, Biegekristall m	**floating grid**	offenes Gitter n, freies Gitter
		floating mark	wandernde Marke f, Wandermarke f
flexure mode	s. flexural vibration	**floating point** <num. math.>	Gleitkomma n, gleitendes (bewegliches) Komma n <num. Math.>
flicker, flickering, fuzziness	Flimmern n		
flicker <e.g. of flame>; unsteadiness of light <emitted by a source>; flashing <opt., el.>	Flackern n <Opt., El.>; Aufflackern n <z. B. des Bogens>	**floating potential**	inneres Kontaktpotential n
		floating power	s. floatability
		floating speed	Stellgeschwindigkeit f
flicker effect	Funkeleffekt m, Flickereffekt m; Flackereffekt m <Photozelle>		
flicker [fusion] frequency	s. critical frequency of flicker <opt.>	**floating zenith telescope**	„floating zenith"-Teleskop n
flickering	s. flicker	**floating-zone melting (method, technique)**, vertical method of zone melting; zone floating [method]	tiegelfreies Zonenschmelzen (Zonenreinigen) n [in senkrechter Richtung], Fließzonentechnik f, „floating-zone"-Methode f, Schwimmzonenmethode f
flicker photometer	Flimmerphotometer n, Flackerphotometer n, Schwankungsphotometer n		
flight altitude	s. flying altitude		
flight dynamics	s. dynamics of flight		
flight height	s. flying altitude		
flight mechanics, mechanics (theory) of flight	Flugmechanik f	**float limnigraph; float mareograph**; float-type water-level recorder	schreibender Schwimmerpegel m, Schwimmerschreibpegel m
flight of the nebulae	s. recession of the nebulae		
flight path	s. trajectory		
flight time	s. time of flight <nucl.>	**float method (technique)**	s. flotation method
flip-flop, flip-flop generator (oscillator, multivibrator), Eccles-Jordan multivibrator, bistable multivibrator	Flip-Flop[-Generator] m, Flip-Flop-System n, bistabiler Multivibrator m, Dualstufe f, Bistabilelement n, Speicherelement n, Gedächtnis n	**float-type limnimeter**; float gauge	Schwimmerpegel m; Schwimmerlimnimeter n
		float-type pressure gauge	Schwimmermanometer n
		float-type water-level recorder; float mareograph; float limnigraph	schreibender Schwimmerpegel m, Schwimmerschreibpegel m
flip-flop, flip-flop circuit, Eccles-Jordan circuit	Flip-Flop-Schaltung f [nach Eccles-Jordan], bistabile Multivibratorschaltung f, Eccles-Jordan-Schaltung f	**flocculant, flocculating agent**	Flockungsmittel n, Flocker m
flip-flop generator (multivibrator, oscillator)	s. flip-flop	**flocculation**	Flockung f, Ausflockung f
flip-over of spin	s. spin flip	**flocculus** <pl: flocculi>, plage	Flocculus m <pl: Flocculi>, Flocke f <Astr.>
flip-over probability, flop-over (umklapp) probability	Umklappwahrscheinlichkeit f	**flood interval**, lunitidal (high-water) interval	Flutstunde f, Hafenzeit f, Hafenwasserintervall n
		floodlighting	Anleuchtung f, Flutlichtbeleuchtung f, Anstrahlung f; Flutlicht n
float	Schwimmer m; Schwimmkörper m; Schwebekörper m		
floatability, floatage, flo[a]tation; floating power	Schwimmfähigkeit f	**flood wave**	Hochwasserwelle f, Flutwelle f
floatation, floating, flotation	Schwimmen n	**floor of ocean**; ocean (sea) floor, ocean core	Meeresboden m, Meeresgrund m
floatation	s. a. floatability		
floatation	s. a. flotation	**flop**, total loss	Totalausfall m

flop-in method	„flop-in"-Methode *f*	flow condition	*s.* yield condition
flop-out method	„flop-out"-Methode *f*	flow condition of Hencky, Hencky's flow condition	Henckysche Fließbedingung *f*, Fließbedingung von Hencky
flop-over of spin	*s.* spin flip		
flop-over probability, flip-over (umklapp) probability	Umklappwahrscheinlichkeit *f*		
		flow condition of Mises	*s.* Mises yield condition
		flow cone	Strömungskegel *m*
flop-over process, umklapp process, U-process	Umklappprozeß *m*; Spinumklappprozeß *m*, Spin-„flip-flop"-Prozeß *m*, „flip-flop"-Prozeß *m*	flow counter, flow counter tube	Durchflußzähler *m*
		flow criterion	*s.* yield condition
		flow diagram, picture of flow, flow pattern	Strömungsbild *n*, Stromlinienbild *n*, Strömungsfigur *f*, Strömungsdiagramm *n*
Floquet['s] theorem	Theorem *n* (Satz *m*) von Floquet, Floquetscher Satz		
Flory-Huggins effect	Flory-Huggins-Effekt *m*	flow diagram	*s. a.* flow chart
Flory temperature, theta temperature of Flory	Theta-Temperatur *f* [von Flory], Florysche Temperatur *f*, Θ-Temperatur *f*	flow direction	*s.* forward direction
		flow-direction meter	Strömungsrichtungsmesser *m*
		flow drag	*s.* hydraulic resistance <hydr.>
flotation, floating, floatation	Schwimmen *n*		
		flow efficiency	*s.* efficiency of fluid flow
flotation, floatation; froth flotation	Flotation *f*, Schwimmaufbereitung *f*, Flotationsverfahren *n*, Flotieren *n*; Schaumschwimmverfahren *n*	flow ellipse	Strömungsellipse *f*
		flow energy	Strömungsenergie *f*
		flow figure, slip band, glide band, Lüders band, stretcher strain, strain figure	Gleitband *n*, Fließfigur *f*, Gleitfigur *f*, Lüderssches Band *n*, Lüdersscher Streifen *m*
flotation method, float method, float technique; temperature gradient method	Schwimmermethode *f*, Schwebemethode *f*		
		flow friction	*s.* fluid friction
		flow from sinks, sink flow	Senkenströmung *f*
flow; movement; streaming; fluid flow, current <gen.>	Strömung *f*, Strömen *n* <allg.>	flow from sources, source flow	Quellströmung *f*
		flow height	*s.* flow index
flow, flowing, flowage, fluxion, run, movement <of liquid>	Fließen *n*, Fluß *m* <Flüssigkeit>	flow in a rough tube	Rauhrohrströmung *f*, Rauhigkeitsströmung *f*
		flow index, flow height, index of flow	Abflußhöhe *f*
flow <of current through>	Fließen *n* <Strom durch>		
		flowing	*s.* flow <of liquid>
flow; contour integral, line integral <e.g. of a tensor field, along a curve>	Kurvenintegral *n*, Linienintegral *n*	flowing back	*s.* backstreaming
		flowing equilibrium, flux equilibrium, open system equilibrium, steady state <bio.>	Fließgleichgewicht *n*, Flußgleichgewicht *n* <Bio.>
flow	*s. a.* yield properties		
flow	*s. a.* rate of flow		
flow	*s. a.* yielding <of metal>	flowing point	*s.* yield point
flow	*s. a.* thermodynamic flux	flowing strength	*s.* yield strength
flow	*s. a.* stream	flow integral	Strömungsintegral *n*
flowability of solids	Fließvermögen *n* von Festkörpern	flow in three dimensions, three-dimensional flow	dreidimensionale Strömung *f*, räumliche Strömung
flow against the body	Anströmung *f*		
		flow layer	*s.* schliere
		flow limit	*s.* yield strength
flowage <hydr.>, flow regime	Strömungsart *f*, Bewegungsart *f* <Hydr.>	flow line, streamline, stream line, line of flow	Stromlinie *f*, Strömungslinie *f*
flowage	*s. a.* flow <of liquid>		
flow along a slab, plane flow	[Kirchhoffsche] Plattenströmung *f*, Strömung *f* längs einer ebenen Platte	flow machine, fluid kinetic machine, fluid flow engine	Strömungsmaschine *f*
		flow Mach number	*s.* free stream Mach number
flow around a body, flow over (past) a body, passing motion [around], streaming [around], streaming [round]	Umströmung *f*; Umfließen *n*	flowmeter	Mengenmeßgerät *n*, Mengenmesser *m*, Durchflußmengenmeßgerät *n*, Durchfluß[mengen]messer *m*, Strömungs[mengen]messer *m*, Durchflußmeßgerät *n*; Flüssigkeitsdurchflußmeßgerät *n*, Flüssigkeitsdurchflußmesser *m*; Verbrauchsmeßgerät *n*, Verbrauchsmesser *m*; Volum[en]meßgerät *n*, Volum[en]messer *m*; Durchflußstärkemeßgerät *n*, Durchflußstärkemesser *m*
flow around an edge	Kantenumströmung *f*		
flow around a parabola	Parabelumströmung *f*		
flow around the corner, flow past corner	Eckenumströmung *f*; Eckenströmung *f*		
flow at subsonic velocity, subsonic flow	Unterschallströmung *f*		
flow at supersonic velocity	*s.* supersonic flow		
flow at the lifting surface	Tragflächenströmung *f*		
		flow method <calorimetry>	Strömungsmethode *f* <Kalorimetrie>
flow behaviour	*s.* flow	flow near the wall	Wandströmung *f*, wandnahe Strömung *f*
flow birefringence, double refraction in flow, streaming (Maxwell) birefringence, Maxwell effect	Strömungsdoppelbrechung *f*		
		flow nozzle	Normdüse *f*, Düse *f* <Meßgerät>
		flow of charge carriers	*s.* carrier flow
		flow of diffusing molecules, diffusion flow	Diffusionsstrom *m*, Diffusionsströmung *f*
flow calorimeter	*s.* continuous-flow calorimeter		
flow chart, flow diagram, process chart <num. math.>	Flußdiagramm *n*, Programmablaufplan *m*, PAP <num. Math.>	flow of electric charge	elektrische Strömung *f*
		flow of heat	*s.* rate of heat flow
		flow of material, material flow	Werkstofffluß *m*
flow chart	*s. a.* flowsheet		
flow cleavage, basic cleavage	Fließschieferung *f*, Hauptschieferung *f*	flow of the river, river discharge (flow, runoff), stream[ ]flow <geo.>	Abfluß *m*, Abflußmenge *f* <Geo.>: Wasserführung *f* <Fluß>
flow coefficient, coefficient of flow, runoff coefficient (percentage)	Abflußkoeffizient *m*, Abflußfaktor *m*, Abflußbeiwert *m*, Abflußverhältnis *n*	flow of water, run-off [of water], water flow	Abfluß *m* <Wasser>, Wasserabfluß *m*, Wasserfracht *f*

flow over (past) a body s. flow around a body
flow over (past) a flat plate s. flat plate flow
flow past cascade s. cascade flow
flow pattern, picture of flow, flow diagram — Strömungsbild n, Stromlinienbild n, Strömungsfigur f, Strömungsdiagramm n
flow phenomenon Strömungserscheinung f
flow point s. yield point
flow potential Strömungspotential n, Fließpotential n
flow pressure Strömungsdruck m, Fließdruck m

flow properties s. yield properties
flow proportional counter Durchflußproportionalzähler m

flow pump, fluid flow pump, flow-type pump — Strömungspumpe f
flow rate, rate of flow, flow velocity, velocity of flow, stream velocity — Strömungsgeschwindigkeit f; Fließgeschwindigkeit f, Strömgeschwindigkeit f; Durchflußgeschwindigkeit f
flow rate s. a. rate of flow
flow rate of the gas s. rate of gas flow
flowrator <US> s. rotameter
flow re-attachment, re[-]attachment [of flow] — Wiederanlegen n der Strömung

flow regime, flowage <hydr.> — Strömungsart f, Bewegungsart f <Hydr.>

flow resistance s. hydraulic resistance <hydr.>
flowsheet, flow chart, technological layout — Fließbild n, Fließdiagramm n, Ablaufplan m, Ablaufschema n, Stammbaum m, schematischer Arbeitsplan

flow stress, yield stress — Fließspannung f

flow structure s. fluidal structure
flow through cascade s. cascade flow
flow-through centrifuge, concurrent centrifuge — Durchlaufzentrifuge f, Durchströmzentrifuge f

flow through pipes, pipe flow, tubular flow — Rohrströmung f
flow-through ultramicroscope, flow ultramicroscope — Durchflußultramikroskop n
flow-type pump, [fluid] flow pump — Strömungspumpe f
flow ultramicroscope, flow-through ultramicroscope — Durchflußultramikroskop n
flow vector Strömungsvektor m
flow velocity s. flow rate
flow visualization Sichtbarmachung f der Strömung
flow without separation Strömung f ohne Ablösung

fluctuating drop, oscillating [liquid] drop, fluctuating liquid drop — schwingender Tropfen m, schwingenderFlüssigkeitstropfen m
fluctuating light fluktuierendes Licht n
fluctuating liquid drop, oscillating [liquid] drop, fluctuating drop — schwingender Tropfen m, schwingender Flüssigkeitstropfen m
fluctuating variability, continuous (quantitative) variability — kontinuierliche (fluktuierende, quantitative) Variabilität f
fluctuation, statistical fluctuation — [statistische] Schwankung f, Fluktuation f
fluctuation, fluctuation spectrum — Schwankungsspektrum n
fluctuation after-effect s. Jordan lag
fluctuational quantity Schwankungsgröße f
fluctuation[-] dissipation theorem Schwankungs-Dissipations-Theorem n

fluctuation effect s. fluctuation phenomenon
fluctuation in radiation, radiation fluctuation — Strahlungsschwankung f

fluctuation in reverse direction, reverse fluctuation — Rückwärtsschwankung f

fluctuation in the main voltage s. main voltage fluctuation
fluctuation magnetic after-effect s. Jordan lag
fluctuation noise s. noise
fluctuation noise s. partition noise
fluctuation of daylight illumination, daylight fluctuation — Tageslichtschwankung f
fluctuation of the liquid drop s. liquid drop oscillation
fluctuation phenomenon (process), fluctuation effect, statistical fluctuation phenomenon (effect) — statistische Schwankungserscheinung f, Schwankungserscheinung, Schwankungseffekt m

fluctuation resistance Schwankungswiderstand m, differentieller Widerstand m
fluctuation spectrum, fluctuation — Schwankungsspektrum n
fluctuation theory of light scattering, Smoluchowski-Einstein theory — Schwankungstheorie f der Lichtstreuung, Fluktuationstheorie f der Wasserfarbe, von Smoluchowski-Finsteinsche Theorie f der Wasserfarben

fluctuation velocity, eddy velocity — Schwankungsgeschwindigkeit f
flue[]gas, smoke gas — Rauchgas n

flue gas analysis Rauchgasanalyse f

fluence, particle fluence <bio.> — Teilchenfluenz f, Fluenz f <Bio.>
fluence rate s. particle flux density <bio.>

flue pipe, labial pipe, blow pipe — Lippenpfeife f, Labialpfeife f
fluerics s. fluidics
fluid Fluid n, Fluidum n, Flüssigkeit-Gas n, Flüssigkeit f oder Gas n
fluid, fluidic — strömungsfähig, fluid
fluidal structure, fluidal texture, fluxion structure, flow structure — Fluidaltextur f, Fließstruktur f, Fließtextur f

fluid amplification s. fluidics
fluid bed s. fluidized bed
fluid carrier s. carrier liquid
fluid compass, floating card compass, immersed compass — Schwimmkompaß m

fluid converter, torque converter — Strömungsumwandler m

fluid coupling s. hydraulic coupling
fluid dynamics s. aerohydrodynamics
fluid energy mill, jet mill, micronizer — „jet"-Mühle f, Strahlmühle f, Düsenmühle f
fluid filament, liquid filament, filament line in a fluid — Flüssigkeitsfaden m

fluid flow; flow; movement; streaming <gen.> — Strömung f, Strömen n <allg.>
fluid flow efficiency s. efficiency of fluid flow
fluid flow engine s. fluid kinetic machine
fluid flow physics Strömungsphysik f

fluid flow pump, flow[-type] pump — Strömungspumpe f
fluid friction, flow friction, hydrodynamic friction — Flüssigkeitsreibung f

fluid friction damping, liquid damping — Flüssigkeitsdämpfung f

fluid gauge, liquid manometer, liquid-pressure gauge — Flüssigkeitsmanometer n

fluidic, fluidic element, fluid-jet element — digitales (pneumatisches) Strömungselement n, Strömungselement pneumatischer Art, Fluidelement n, „fluidic"-Schaltelement n, Strömungsregler m, Strömungsverstärker m

fluidic, fluid — strömungsfähig, fluid

fluidic

fluidic element	s. fluidic
fluidics, fluidonics, fluerics, fluid amplification	Fluidik f, Lehre f von den pneumatischen Strömungselementen (Strömungsreglern, Strömungsverstärkern)
fluidifiant	Fluidifiant m
fluidification	Fluidifikation f
fluidimeter	s. viscometer
fluidity	Flüssigkeitscharakter m, Fluidität f
fluidity, fluidity coefficient ⟨quantity⟩	Fluidität f ⟨Größe⟩
fluidization, fluidized-bed technique	Wirbelschichtverfahren n, Wirbelbettverfahren n, Wirbelfließverfahren n, Staubfließverfahren n, Fließbettverfahren n, Fluidatbettverfahren n, Fluidisation f, Fluidierung f
fluidized bed, fluid bed ⟨chem.⟩	Wirbelschicht f, Wirbelbett n, Fließbett n, Wanderschicht f, Wanderbett n, Bewegtbett n, Fluidatbett n ⟨Chem.⟩
fluidized bed technique	s. fluidization
fluid-jet element	s. fluidic
fluid kinetic machine, flow machine, fluid flow engine	Strömungsmaschine f
fluid lens	Flüssigkeitslinse f
fluid line, material line	flüssige Linie f, materielle Linie
fluid mechanics, science of fluid flow	Strömungsmechanik f, Strömungslehre f, Mechanik f der Flüssigkeiten und Gase
fluidmeter	s. viscometer
fluidonics	s. fluidics
fluid plastic	Fluidoplast m
fluid surface	flüssige Fläche f
fluid theory of heat	s. caloric theory
fluid-type instability	Instabilität f vom fluiden Typ, fluide Instabilität f
fluid wave	Flüssigkeitswelle f
flume	s. channel ⟨hydr.⟩
fluophotometer, fluorophotometer	Fluorophotometer n, Fluophotometer n, Fluoreszenzphotometer n
fluoradiography	s. fluorography
fluoren	Fluoren n
fluorescence	Fluoreszenz f
fluorescence analysis, fluorescence spectroscopy (spectrum analysis)	Fluoreszenzanalyse f, Fluoreszenzspektralanalyse f, Fluoreszenzspektrum n, Spektrofluorimetrie f
fluorescence destruction dosimetry	Fluoreszenzabbaudosimetrie f
fluorescence dosimeter	Fluoreszenzdosimeter n
fluorescence dosimetry	Fluoreszenzdosimetrie f
fluorescence efficiency	s. fluorescence yield
fluorescence in crystal, crystal fluorescence, crystallofluorescence	Kristallfluoreszenz f, Kristallofluoreszenz f
fluorescence lifetime	Fluoreszenzlebensdauer f
fluorescence line, fluorescent line	Fluoreszenzlinie f
fluorescence meter	s. fluorometer
fluorescence microscope	Fluoreszenzmikroskop n
fluorescence microscopy	Fluoreszenzmikroskopie f
fluorescence spectrum, fluorescent spectrum	Fluoreszenzspektrum n
fluorescence titration	s. volumetric fluorescence analysis
fluorescence yield, fluorescence efficiency	Fluoreszenzausbeute f
fluorescent decay	s. decay
fluorescent energy	Fluoreszenzenergie f
fluorescent indicator	Fluoreszenzindikator m, fluoreszierender Indikator m
fluorescent lamp, fluorescent tube ⟨US⟩	Leuchtstofflampe f, Leucht[stoff]röhre f; Fluoreszenzlampe f; Lumineszenzlampe f, Kaltlichtlampe f
fluorescent light	Fluoreszenzlicht n
fluorescent line	s. fluorescence line
fluorescent radiation	s. characteristic X-rays
fluorescent screen	Fluoreszenzschirm m, [fluoreszierender] Leuchtschirm m
fluorescent spectrum, fluorescence spectrum	Fluoreszenzspektrum n
fluorescent tube	s. fluorescent lamp
fluorimeter, fluorometer, fluorescence meter	Fluorometer n, Fluorimeter n, Fluoreszenzmesser m, Leuchtstoffmesser m; Fluoreszenzintensitätsmesser m; Fluoreszenzabklingzeitmesser m
fluorimetry, fluorometry; fluorophotometry	Fluorimetrie f, Fluorometrie f, Fluoreszenzmessung f; Fluoreszenzintensitätsmessung f; Fluorophotometrie f, Fluoreszenzabklingzeitmessung f
fluorite lattice, fluorite structure, fluorspar structure	Flußspatgitter n, Flußspatstruktur f, Fluoritstruktur f
fluorite lens, semiapochromat, fluorite system	Fluoritobjektiv n, Fluoritsystem n, Semiapochromat m, Halbapochromat m
fluorite structure	s. fluorite lattice
fluorite system, semiapochromat, fluorite lens	Fluoritobjektiv n, Fluoritsystem n, Semiapochromat m, Halbapochromat m
fluorogram	s. screen photograph
fluorography, photofluorography, photoroentgenography, fluoradiography, indirect radiography, mass miniature radiography	Schirmbildaufnahme f, Schirmbild[aufnahme]verfahren n, Schirmbildphotographie f, Röntgenschirmbildverfahren n, Röntgenschirmbildaufnahme f, Röntgenschirmbildaufnahmeverfahren n, Röntgenschirmbildphotographie f, Leuchtschirmphotographie f, Radiophotographie f
fluorometer	s. fluorimeter
fluorometry	s. fluorimetry
fluorophotometer, fluophotometer	Fluorophotometer n, Fluophotometer n, Fluoreszenzphotometer n
fluorophotometry	s. fluorimetry
fluoroscope, roentgenoscope, radioscope	Durchleuchtungsgerät n, Röntgendurchleuchtungsanlage f, Durchstrahlungsgerät n, Röntgendurchstrahlungsapparat m
fluoroscopy, radioscopy; roentgenoscopy, X-raying; skioscopy, radioexamination	Durchleuchtung f, Durchstrahlung f ⟨mit radioaktiver oder Röntgenstrahlung⟩, Radioskopie f, Fluoroskopie f; Röntgenoskopie f, Röntgen n, Röntgendurchleuchtung f, Röntgendurchstrahlung f
fluorspar structure	s. fluorite lattice
fluted spectrum	s. channelled spectrum
flute-type deformation, interchange[-type] deformation	Austauschdeformation f, Deformation f vom konvektiven Typ; Rinnendeformation f
flute-type instability	s. interchange instability
flutter	Flattern n, Flattererscheinung f, Flatterschwingungen fpl
flutter, flutter effect, undulation effect ⟨el.⟩	Flattereffekt m, Rauhigkeit f ⟨El.⟩
flutter ⟨aero.⟩	Flattern n ⟨Aero.⟩
flutter-analog[ue] machine	Analogierechenmaschine f (Analogrechner m) für Flügelflattern
flutter echo ⟨el.⟩, multiple echo	Mehrfachecho n, Mehrfachreflexion f, Vielfachreflexion f; Klangecho n
flutter effect	s. flutter ⟨el.⟩
fluviograph	Fluviograph m, Schreibpegel m

flux, flux of the vector, vector[ial] flux ‹through the surface›	Fluß m [des Vektors], Vektorfluß m ‹durch die Fläche›	**flying spot;** travelling spot	wandernder Lichtfleck m
flux ‹therm.›, thermodynamic flux	[thermodynamischer] Fluß m ‹Therm.›	**flying-spot recorder,** light-spot recorder	Lichtpunkt[linien]schreiber m, Lichtlinienschreiber m
flux	s. a. neutron flux		
flux	s. a. volume flow		
flux	s. a. energy flux density ‹el.›	**flying-spot scanner**	Lichtfleckabtaster m, Leuchtfleckabtaster m, Lichtpunktabtaster m; Lichtstrahlabtaster m
flux averaged cross-section	über den Fluß gemittelter Wirkungsquerschnitt m (Querschnitt m)	**flying-spot scanning;** light-spot scanning	Lichtfleckabtastung f, Leuchtfleckabtastung f; Lichtpunktabtastung f; Lichtstrahlabtastung f
flux-closure domain	s. closure domain		
flux converter, neutron flux converter, doughnut	Flußkonverter m, Flußumwandler m	**flywheel**	Schwungrad n; Schwungscheibe f; Schwungmasse f
flux-current loop	s. dynamic hysteresis	**flywheel circuit**	Schwungradschaltung f, Schwungradkreis m
flux density; specific discharge	Flußdichte f, Stromdichte f	**flywheel effect**	Schwungradeffekt m
flux density	s. a. particle flux density ‹bio.›		
flux density	s. a. radiant flux density	**flywheel moment,** moment of gyration	Schwungmoment n
flux depression	Flußabsenkung f, Flußabfall m		
flux displacement	Flußverdrängung f		
flux distribution, neutron flux distribution	Flußverteilung f, Verteilung f des Neutronenflusses	**f[-]m cyclotron**	s. synchrocyclotron
		f-number, f-ratio, stop number, focal ratio; speed ‹of camera lens›	Blendenzahl f, Blendennummer f, Öffnungszahl f
flux distribution ‹el.›	Flußlinienverteilung f, Flußverteilung f ‹El.›	**foam column**	Schaumsäule f
flux equilibrium, flowing equilibrium, open system equilibrium, steady state ‹bio.›	Fließgleichgewicht n, Flußgleichgewicht n ‹Bio.›	**focal,** focal line	Fokalkurve f, Fokale f
		focal axis	Fokalachse f
		focal collimator	Meßkollimator m
		focal curve	s. focal line
flux flattening, flattening ‹nucl.›	Flußabflachung f, Glätten n der Flußverteilung ‹Kern.›	**focal depth,** depth of focus (origin, hypocentre), hypocentral depth ‹geo.›	Herdtiefe f, Hypozentraltiefe f
fluxgate, flux[-] gate, flux gate detector	s. saturable-core magnetometer	**focal distance**	Brennpunktabstand m, Fokaldistanz f
fluxing	s. melting point depression		
fluxing, fluxion	s. plastification	**focal distance**	s. a. hypocentral distance ‹geo.›
fluxion	s. flow ‹of liquid›		
fluxion ‹math.›	= derivative	**focal distance of photogrammetric lens**	s. calibrated focal length
fluxion structure	s. fluidal texture		
flux linkage, magnetic linkage	Flußverkettung f, Spulenfluß m	**focal distance of the collimator lens**	Kollimatorkonstante f
flux[ ]meter, maxwellmeter	Fluxmeter n, Flußmesser m, Maxwellmesser m; Kriechgalvanometer n	**focal length**	Brennweite f, Fokalweite f, Fokusweite f
		focal length ratio	Brennweitenverhältnis n
fluxmeter	s. a. radiometer	**focal line,** focal [curve]	Fokalkurve f, Fokale f
flux of force ‹mech.›	Kraftfluß m ‹Mech.›	**focal line,** focal straight line	Brenngerade f, Fokalgerade f
flux of heat	s. rate of heat flow		
flux of magnetic induction vector	s. magnetic flux	**focal line**	Brennlinie f
		focal monochromator	Fokalmonochromator m
flux of particles, particle flux	Teilchenfluß m	**focal plane**	Brennebene f, Fokalebene f
		focal-plane shutter, slotted shutter	Schlitzverschluß m; Bildfensterverschluß m
flux of radiant energy	s. radiant flux		
flux of radiation	s. radiant flux	**focal point,** focus ‹pl: foci or focuses›, focusing point; equal-angle point	Brennpunkt m; Sammelpunkt m; Fokus m, Fokalpunkt m, winkeltreuer Punkt m ‹Meßbild›
flux of the tensor field	Fluß m des Tensorfeldes		
flux of the vector	s. flux		
flux of vorticity, vortex (vorticity) flux	Wirbelfluß m; Vorticityfluß m ‹Geo.›	**focal point,** spiral point, focus ‹math.›	Strudelpunkt m ‹Math.›
fluxoid	Fluxoid n, Zirkulationsquant n	**focal-point triangulation**	Fokalpunkttriangulation f
fluxoid [quantum], fluxon, magnetic flux quantum	Fluxoidquant n, Fluxon n, magnetisches Flußquant n	**focal power,** power, lens power (strenght), strenght of lens ‹opt.›	Brechkraft f, Brechwert m, Stärke f, reziproke Brennweite f ‹Opt.›; Refraktion f ‹Auge›; Brennpunktsrefraktion f ‹Auge›
flux ratio	Flußverhältnis n		
flux through single turn, turn flux	Windungsfluß m		
flux time, integrated flux, integrated neutron flux, time integral of flux ‹in n/cm²›	integraler Fluß (Neutronenfluß) m, Flußzeit f, Zeitintegral n des Neutronenflusses ‹in n/cm²›	**focal property** ‹e.g. of conics›	Brennpunktseigenschaft f ‹z. B. von Kegelschnitten›
		focal radius ‹of conics›	Brennstrahl m ‹Kegelschnitt›
fly['s] eye	Fliegenauge n	**focal range**	s. depth of field
fly['s] eye technique	Fliegenaugentechnik f	**focal ratio,** f-number, f-ratio, stop number	Blendenzahl f, Blendennummer f, Öffnungszahl f
flying altitude, [flight] altitude, flying (flight, true) height	Flughöhe f	**focal ray** ‹opt.›	Brennstrahl m ‹Opt.›
		focal refraction	Brennpunktsrefraktion f
flying asunder	Auseinanderfliegen n		
flying height	s. flying altitude	**focal region of earthquake**	s. focus of earthquake
flying saucer, unidentified flying object, UFO	unidentifiziertes fliegendes Objekt n, fliegende Untertasse f, UFO	**focal spot** ‹opt.›	Brennfleck m; punktförmiger Brennfleck ‹Opt.›
flying speed	Fluggeschwindigkeit f		

focal 270

focal straight line, focal line	Brenngerade f, Fokalgerade f	focusing impact chain	s. focusing chain
focal surface	Brennfläche f	focusing lens	Fokussierlinse f, Fokussierungslinse f, Bündelungslinse f; Brennlinse f
focimeter, focometer, vertometer	Fokometer n, Brennweitenmesser m	focusing magnifier	Einstellupe f
Fock-Klein-Gordon equation, Klein-Gordon equation, relativistic Schrödinger equation	Klein-Gordon-Gleichung f, relativistische Schrödinger-Gleichung f	focusing of sound, sound focusing, concentration of sound, sound (acoustic) concentration	Schallbündelung f, Schallkonzentrierung f, Schallkonzentration f, Schallfokussierung f
Fock representation; Fock space	Fock-Darstellung f, Focksche Darstellung f; Fock-Raum m	focusing on infinity	Unendlicheinstellung f, Einstellung f auf Unendlich
focometer, focimeter, vertometer	Fokometer n, Brennweitenmesser m	focusing plane	Einstellebene f
focometry, measurement of focal length	Fokometrie f, Brennweitenmessung f	focusing point	s. focus
		focusing screen, ground-glass screen, mat glass plate, ground glass	Mattscheibe f
focus <pl: foci or focuses>, focal point, focusing point; equalangle point	Brennpunkt m; Sammelpunkt m; Fokus m, Fokalpunkt m, winkeltreuer Punkt m <Meßbild>	focusing solenoid; focusing coil <acc.>	Fokussierspule f
		focusing system	s. separating system
focus, origin, hearth, seat [of origin], centre <geo., meteo.>	Herd m <Geo., Meteo.>	focusing telescope	Einstellfernrohr n, Beobachtungsokular n
		focusing wheel	Schärfeneinstellrädchen n
focus, spiral point, focal point <math.>	Strudelpunkt m <Math.>	focus of diffraction grating, grating focus	Gitterbrennpunkt m
focus	s. a. aerodynamic centre	focus of earthquake, focal region of earthquake, earthquake focus, seismic focus, hypocentre	Hypozentrum n, Erdbebenherd m, Herd m des Bebens
focus	s. a. principal focus		
focus [button]	s. focus control button		
focus control, focusing	Brennpunkteinstellung f, Fokuseinstellung f, Fokussierung f		
		focuson	Fokuson n
		focussing	s. focusing <opt.>
focus control button, focus [button], control (adjustment) button <e.g. of microscope>	Triebknopf m <z. B. Mikroskop>	focus-to-film distance	Fokus-Film-Abstand m
		focus-to-surface distance, FSD	Fokus-Oberfläche-Abstand m, FOA
focused collision sequence	s. focusing chain		
focused dynode	Schaufeldynode f	Foerster probe	s. Förster probe
focused multiplier phototube, focused photomultiplier [tube]	Schaufelvervielfacher m	fog	[dichter] Nebel m
		fog, coat, cover	Beschlag m
		fog, photographic fog	Schleier m, photographischer Schleier
		fog, ligasoid <chem.>	Nebel m, Flüssigkeitsaerosol n, Aerosol n mit flüssiger disperser Phase, Ligasoid n <Chem.>
focusing, focussing, focusing action, beam focusing, concentration, concentration of the beam <opt.>	Fokussierung f, Bündelung f, Sammlung f, Strahl[en]fokussierung f, Strahl[en]bündelung f, Strahl[en]konzentrierung f, Konzentrierung f [des Strahls] <Opt.>	fog attenuation	Nebeldämpfung f
		fog bow, white rainbow	Nebelbogen m, weißer Regenbogen m
focusing <of distance, definition>	Einstellung f <Entfernung, Schärfe>	fog caused by developers exposed to air, aerial fog	Luftschleier m
focusing	s. a. focus control	fog centre, fog nucleus	Schleierkeim m, Schleierzentrum n
focusing action	s. focusing <opt.>		
focusing acuity, acuity of focusing	Bündelungsschärfe f	fog chamber, cloud chamber, fog-track chamber	Nebelkammer f
focusing adjustment, sharp focusing (setting, adjustment); focusing control <opt.>	Scharfeinstellung f, Scharfstellung f, Fokussierung f <Opt.>	fog cooling	Schleierkühlung f
focusing chain, focusing impact chain, focused collision sequence	fokussierende Stoßkette f	fog density	Schleierschwärzung f, Schleierdichte f
		fog development; growth of fog	Schleierentwicklung f; Schleierwachstum n
focusing coil <acc.>; focusing solenoid	Fokussierspule f	fog due to stray light	Reflexschleier m
focusing collisions	fokussierende Stöße mpl	fog elimination, background eradication <phot.>	Schleierentfernung f <Phot.>
focusing condition	Fokussierungsbedingung f	fog frequency	Nebelhäufigkeit f
focusing control; sharp focusing (setting, adjustment), focusing adjustment <opt.>	Scharfeinstellung f, Scharfstellung f, Fokussierung f <Opt.>	foggant	s. fogging agent
		fogging, getting covered with damp, becoming coated	Anlaufen n; Beschlagen n
focusing cup, concentrating cup	Katodenbecher m	fogging; veiling effect <phot.>	Verschleierung f; Verschleierungseffekt m
focusing electrode	Fokussier[ungs]elektrode f; Bündelungselektrode f, Konzentrationselektrode f	fogging agent, foggant	Schleiermittel n
		fog grain	Schleierkorn n
focusing defect	Fokussierungsfehler m	fog inhibitor, antifoggant, fog prevention agent	schleierverhindernder Zusatz m, schleierverhinderndes Mittel n, Schleierschutzmittel n, Schleierverhütungsmittel n, schleierwidriges Mittel
focusing from close-up to infinity	Naheinstellung f auf Unendlich, Nah-Unendlich-Einstellung f		

fog in patches; swath of mist, streaks of fog — Nebelfetzen *m*; Nebelschwaden *m*
fog nucleus, fog centre — Schleierkeim *m*, Schleierzentrum *n*
fog prevention agent — *s.* antifoggant
fog track, cloud track, cloud-chamber track — Nebelkammerspur *f*, Nebelspur *f*

fog-track chamber, cloud chamber, fog chamber — Nebelkammer *f*
fog train, vapour train <of meteor> — Nebelschweif *m*, Dampfschweif *m* <Meteor>
foil activation — Sondenaktivierung *f*, Folienaktivierung *f*
foil detector — Foliendetektor *m*
foil electroscope — *s.* leaf electroscope
foil gauge — Folien-Dehnungsmeßstreifen *m*, Foliendehnungsmesser *m*
Foitzik photoelectric photometer, Foitzik photometer — lichtelektrisches Sichtphotometer *n* von Foitzik, Foitziksches Sichtphotometer, Foitzik-Photometer *n*
Fokker-Planck equation — Fokker-Planck-Gleichung *f*, Fokker-Plancksche Gleichung *f*, Einstein-Fokker-Plancksche (Planck-Fokkersche) Differentialgleichung *f*

fold <geo.> — Falte *f* <Geo.>
folded dipole — *s.* folded dipole antenna
folded dipole antenna, folded dipole — Faltdipol *m*, Schleifendipol *m*, Schleifenantenne *f*

folded filter, plaited (pleated, prefolded) filter — Faltenfilter *n*
folded magnetization — gefaltete Magnetisierung *f*

folded system <mech.> — Faltwerk *n*, räumliches Flächentragwerk *n* <Mech.>
folded unipole antenna — Faltunipol *m*

folding, plication <geo.> — Faltung *f* <Geo.>
folding <mech.>, bending, flexure — Biegung *f* <Mech.>

folding, collapsible — zusammenlegbar
folding — *s. a.* convolution <math.>
folding-up — *s.* contraction <of tensor>
Foldy effect — Foldy-Effekt *m*
Foldy-Wouthuysen transform[ation] — Foldy-Wouthuysen-Transformation *f*
foliaceous (foliate) texture — Blättchentextur *f*, Folientextur *f*
foliation — *s.* cleavage <geo.>
follower — *s.* following spot <astr.>
follower — *s. a.* repeater <el.>
follower control — *s.* follow-up system
following, tracking <in the trajectory> — Nachlauf *m* <in der Bahn>
following spot, f-spot, eastern spot, follower <astr.> — F-Fleck *m*, [nach]folgender Fleck *m* <Astr.>
follow-up control — Nachlaufsteuerung *f*, Nachlaufregelung *f*

follow-up system — *s.* servomechanism
foot <math., mech.> — Fußpunkt *m* <Math., Mech.>
foot of microscope, microscope base (foot), base of microscope — Mikroskopfuß *m*, Fuß *m* des Mikroskops
foot of the whirlwind, base of the whirlwind — Trombenfuß *m*
forbidden band, forbidden [electron] energy band, forbidden gap — *s.* gap
forbidden cone — *s.* Störmer cone
forbidden gap width — *s.* width of the forbidden gap
forbidden line, forbidden spectral line — verbotene Linie *f*, verbotene Spektrallinie *f*

forbiddenness due to a selection rule — Auswahlverbot *n*
forbiddenness of combination — *s.* prohibition of inter-combinations
forbidden of first order, first forbidden — einfach verboten, verboten von erster Ordnung
forbidden reflection — verbotener Reflex *m*
forbidden region <astr.> — verbotener Bereich *m* <Astr.>
forbidden spectral line, forbidden line — verbotene Linie *f*, verbotene Spektrallinie *f*

forbidden transition — verbotener Übergang *m*

Forbush decrease — Forbush-Abfall *m*

Forbush effect — Forbush-Effekt *m*

force acting on a body in a field — Feldkraft *f*
force arm — *s.* arm of the couple
force at a distance — *s.* long-range force
force at the support — *s.* supporting force
force coefficient <aero.> — Kraftbeiwert *m* <Aero.>

force constant — Kraftkonstante *f*
force constant [of the spring] — *s.* spring constant
force couple, couple <of forces> — Kräftepaar *n*, Drehkraft *f*
forced — erzwungen
forced — Zwang[s]-, Druck-

forced, constrained <mech.> — zwang[s]läufig, Zwangs- <Mech.>
forced circulation, induced circulation — Zwang[s]umlauf *m*, Zwang[s]zirkulation *f*, erzwungener Umlauf *m*

forced commutation — Zwang[s]kommutierung *f*

forced convection — erzwungene (aufgezwungene) Konvektion *f*, Druckkonvektion *f*
forced crystallization — Zwang[s]kristallisation *f*

forced diffusion — erzwungene Diffusion *f*
forced double refraction — *s.* stress birefringence
forced downward wind — *s.* orographic downward wind
force density, assigned force — Kraftdichte *f*
force density in the electric field, electric force density, density of electric force — Kraftdichte *f* im elektrischen Feld, elektrische Kraftdichte
force density in the magnetic field, magnetic force density, density of magnetic force — Kraftdichte *f* im magnetischen Feld, magnetische Kraftdichte
force dependent on position — ortsabhängige Kraft *f*
force dependent on velocity — geschwindigkeitsabhängige Kraft *f*
forced harmonic motion — *s.* forced vibration
force diagram, Cremona [force] diagram, Maxwell diagram, Cremona['s] polygon of forces, reciprocal force diagram — Cremonascher (reziproker) Kräfteplan *m*, Cremona-Plan *m*
forced meander — gezwungener Mäander *m*

forced motion — *s.* constrained motion
forced oscillation, forced vibration (harmonic motion), constrained oscillation — erzwungene Schwingung *f*

forced [radial-]synchrotron oscillation — erzwungene Synchrotronschwingung *f*
force due to mass — *s.* volume force
forced upward wind — *s.* orographic upward wind
forced vibration, forced (constrained) oscillation, forced harmonic motion — erzwungene Schwingung *f*
force field, field of force[s] — Kraftfeld *n*, Kräftefeld *n*
force-free, under [the action of] no forces, free from forces — kräftefrei, kraftfrei

force[-]function — Kräftefunktion *f*
force function for constant temperature — *s.* free energy <therm.>

force

force in the bar	Stabkraft f, Stabspannung f	foreshock wave	Vorläuferwelle f
force necessary to separate two bodies from one another	Abreißkraft f	foreshortening, perspective foreshortening	perspektivische Verkürzung f
force of attraction	s. attractive force	foreshortening, perspective exaggeration	perspektivische Übertreibung f
force of current interaction	s. Lorentz force	Forest-Palmer compensator / De	Kompensator m von de Forest und Palmer, De-Forest-Palmer-Kompensator m
force of cut	s. cutting force		
force of friction, friction[al] force, resistive force <mech.>	Reibungskraft f; Inhärenzkraft f <Mech.>	fore-vacuum, initial vacuum, preliminary vacuum, partial vacuum	Vorvakuum n, Anfangsvakuum n
force of gravity	s. earth's attraction		
force of inertia, inertia force, inertial force, d'Alembert['s] auxiliary force, inertia resistance, mass force	D'Alembert-Kraft f, d'Alembertsche Kraft (Trägheitskraft) f, d'Alembert-Kraft f, Trägheitskraft f, Trägheitswiderstand m, Scheinkraft f, Massenkraft f, Massendruck m	fore-vacuum line	Vorvakuumleitung f
		forging [residual] stress	Schmiedespannung f
		forked lightning	Linienblitz m
		forked lightning	Gabelblitz m
		forking	s. branching
		fork mounting, fork-type of mount	Gabelmontierung f
force of magnetic attraction, attractive force of magnet; magnetic attraction	magnetische Anziehung f; magnetische Anziehungskraft f	form, homogeneous polynomial, quantic <math.>	Form f, homogenes Polynom n <Math.>
		formability	s. workability
		formability limit [in deep-drawing]	Ziehverhältnis n, Ziehgrenze f
force of magnetic repulsion, repulsive (repelling) force of magnet; magnetic repulsion	magnetische Abstoßung f; magnetische Abstoßungskraft f	formal charge	formale Ladung f, Formalladung f
		formality <chem.>	Formalität f <Chem.>
		form anisotropy	s. anisotropy of form
force of perturbation, disturbing (disturbance) force	Störkraft f, störende Kraft f, Störungskraft f	formant	Formant[bereich] m, Teiltonkomponente f
		formant chart, formant diagram	Formantkarte f, Formantdiagramm n
force of repulsion, repulsive (repelling, repellent) force	Abstoßungskraft f, abstoßende Kraft f; Repulsivkraft f	formation, production, creation, generation, birth	Bildung f, Erzeugung f, Generation f
force of transport, force of transportation	Mitführungskraft f, Führungskraft f	formation, development <e.g. of flow>	Ausbildung f, Entwicklung f <z. B. Strömung>
force of transport, centrifugal force	Zentrifugalkraft f, Fliehkraft f, Schleuderkraft f	formation <of accumulator, condenser, cathode, pulse>; forming <semi.>	Formierung f <Akkumulatorplatte, Kondensator, Katode, Impuls; Halb.>; Formung f <Impuls>
force of transportation	s. force of transport		
force of wind	s. wind strength		
force operator, operator of force	Kraftoperator m, Operator m der Kraft	formation cross-section	s. production cross-section
		formation energy, energy of generation	Bildungsenergie f; Bildungsarbeit f
force pipe, pressure tube	Druckrohr n	formation enthalpy, enthalpy of formation	Bildungsenthalpie f
force polygon	s. polygon of forces		
force pump	s. press[ure] pump	formation entropy, entropy of formation	Bildungsentropie f
force[-] reflecting manipulator	Kraftübertragungsmanipulator m	formation heat, heat of formation	Bildungswärme f, Entstehungswärme f, Verbindungswärme f
force-voltage analogy	Analogie f Kraft-Spannung, Kraft-Spannung-Analogie f		
		formation of an atmospheric duct	Tunnelschichtbildung f
Ford-Wheeler approximation, rainbow scattering approximation	Ford-Wheeler-Näherung f, Ford-Wheelersche Näherung f		
		formation of clues, clue formation; convolution	Knäuelbildung f; Knäuelung f, Verknäuelung f
fore and aft overlap	s. longitudinal overlap		
forebay	s. upper pond	formation of drop[let]s, droplet formation	Tropfenbildung f, Tröpfchenbildung f
forecast[ing]; prediction; prognosis, prognostication	Vorhersage f, Voraussage f, Prognose f	formation of eddies	s. formation of vortices
		formation of elements	s. nucleogenesis
forecast period, period of forecast[ing]	Vorhersagezeitraum m, Prognosezeitraum m	formation of fronts, frontogenesis	Frontogenese f, Frontenbildung f
		formation of ions, ionization, ionizing	Ionisation f, Ionisierung f, Ionenbildung f
foreground collimating mark; foreground collimating point	Vordergrundmarke f, Bildvordergrundmarke f; Rahmen-Vordergrundmarke f		
		formation of nuclei, nucleation	Keimbildung f, Bildung f von Keimen, Kernbildung f
foreign atom	s. impurity atom <semi.>		
foreign body theory	s. inclusion theory of Kersten		
foreign field	s. disturbance field <el.>		
foreign ion	s. impurity ion		
foreign nucleus	Fremdkeim m		
Forel scale	Forel-Skala f		
forepump, pre-vacuum pump, preevacuation pump, backing pump, roughing pump	Vorpumpe f, Vorvakuumpumpe f, Vordruckpumpe f	formation of protective film, passivation, passivating	Passivierung f, Schutzschichtbildung f, Deckschichtbildung f
		formation of scale, scaling, scale formation	Verzunderung f, Zunderbildung f, Zunderung f
		formation of shadows, shadowing	Schattenbildung f
fore-runner, precursor <geo.>	Vorläufer m <Geo.>	formation of stars, star formation <astr.>	Sternentstehung f, Sternbildung f <Astr.>
forescatter, forward scatter[ing], forescattering	Vorwärtsstreuung f		
		formation of structures, structure formation	Strukturbildung f
forescatter angle, forward scattering angle, forescattering angle	Vorwärtsstreuwinkel m	formation of thermal cracks, heat cracking	Warmrißbildung f, Wärmerißbildung f, Brandrißbildung f
forescattered, scattered forward	vorwärts[]gestreut		
forescattering	s. forescatter	formation of vortices, formation of eddies, vortex (eddy) formation (generation), eddying	Wirbelbildung f, Wirbelentstehung f; Wirbelerzeugung f
forescattering angle	s. forescatter angle		
foreshock <of earthquake>	Vorschock m, Vorläuferstoß m <Erdbeben>		

formation of waves, wave formation; wave generation, generation of waves	Wellenerzeugung *f*; Wellenbildung *f*, Wellenentstehung *f*	forward conductance, forward transconductance, mutual conductance	Vorwärtssteilheit *f*
formation on the Moon's surface, lunar formation, lunar surface marking, feature on the Moon's surface	Oberflächenform *f* des Mondes	forward cone, future light cone	Vorwärtskegel *m*, Vorkegel *m*
		forward control	s. forward-acting control
		forward current	Durchlaßstrom *m*, Vorwärtsstrom *m*, Strom *m* in Durchlaßrichtung (Flußrichtung)
formation rate	s. production rate ‹nucl.›		
formative timelag ‹of discharge›	Aufbauzeit *f* ‹Gasentladung›	forward current density	Durchlaßstromdichte *f*, Vorwärtsstromdichte *f*, Stromdichte *f* in Flußrichtung
form birefringence, form double refraction	Formdoppelbrechung *f*		
form drag, form resistance, vortex resistance	Formwiderstand *m*	forward current transformation [ratio]	Stromübersetzung *f* vorwärts
		forward difference	aufsteigende Differenz *f*, rückwärts genommene Differenz *f*
form effect	s. anisotropy of form		
form factor ‹el.›, electrical form factor	Formfaktor *m*, elektrischer Formfaktor ‹El.›		
form factor, shape factor ‹nucl.›	Formfaktor *m* ‹Kern.›	forward difference quotient	vorderer Differenzenquotient *m*
forming	s. formation ‹semi.›	forward direction, easy-flow (low-resistance) direction; flow direction; transmission (transmitting) direction, direction of transmission	Durchlaßrichtung *f*; Flußrichtung *f*
form of bifurcation	Verzweigungsform *f*		
form of energy, kind of energy	Energieform *f*, Energieart *f*		
form of equilibrium, shape of equilibrium	Gleichgewichtsfigur *f*, Gleichgewichtsform *f*	forward-facing wave, forward wave	Vorwärtswelle *f*
form of oscillations (vibrations)	Schwingungsform *f*	forward motion	s. forward movement
form resistance	s. form drag	forward movement, forward motion, moving forward, advance, advancing; pushing forward (ahead); propulsion	Vorwärtsbewegung *f*; Vordringen *n*; Vorrücken *n*; Vorstoßen *n*, Vorstoß *m*, Vortrieb *m*; Antreiben *n*
formulae of [Serret-]Frenet	s. Frenet formulae		
formulae of the reaction	s. reaction equation		
formula for luminosity, luminosity formula	Leuchtkraftformel *f*		
formula of Blasius, Blasius' theorem, theorem of Blasius	Blasiusscher Satz *m*, Blasiussche Formel *f*, Blasius-Formel *f*	forward overlap	s. longitudinal overlap
		forward peak, forward scattering peak	Vorwärtspeak *m*, Vorwärts[streu]maximum *n*
		forward power	Vorwärtsleistung *f*
formula of conjugate points, imaging equation	Abbildungsgleichung *f*, Abbildungsformel *f*	forward radiation	Vorwärtsstrahlung *f*
		forward reaction	s. direct reaction
formula of discharge over weir, weir equation	Überfallgleichung *f*, Wehrformel *f*	forward resistance	Durchlaßwiderstand *m*, Widerstand *m* in Durchlaßrichtung (Flußrichtung), Flußwiderstand *m*
formula of Hankel	Hankelsche Formel *f*		
formula of state, state formula	Zustandsformel *f*	forward / reverse counter	s. bidirectional counter
formula of the concave mirror	Spiegelformel *f*, Spiegelgleichung *f*	forward scatter[ing], forescatter[ing]	Vorwärtsstreuung *f*
formula quantity, quantity in the formula	Formelgröße *f*	forward scattering angle, forescatter[ing] angle	Vorwärtsstreuwinkel *m*
formula representing the band edges	Kantenformel *f*	forward scattering peak, forward peak	Vorwärtspeak *m*, Vorwärts[streu]maximum *n*
formula weight	Formelgewicht *n*	forward shock	s. head wave
formula weight	s. a. mol	forward speed	Vorwärtsgeschwindigkeit *f*; Geradeausgeschwindigkeit *f*
Försterling prism train	Försterlingscher Dreiprismensatz *m*		
Förster photometer	Förstersher Lichtsinnprüfer *m*, Förstersches Photometer *n*	forward stagnation point	s. point of branching ‹hydr.›
		forward thrust	s. thrust
		forward transadmittance	s. transfer admittance
Förster probe, Foerster probe, second harmonic magnetic modulator	Förster-Sonde *f*	forward transconductance	s. forward conductance
fortin	s. kilogram[me]	forward transfer impedance	Leerlaufkernwiderstand *m* vorwärts; Übertragungswiderstand *m* vorwärts
Fortin barometer	[Fortinsches] Gefäßbarometer *n*, Fortinsches Barometer *n*		
		forward wave, forward-facing wave	Vorwärtswelle *f*
Fortrat diagram, Fortrat parabola	Fortrat-Diagramm *n*, Fortratsche Parabel *f*	forward wave	s. a. direct wave ‹geo.›
		fossile ice, subsurface ice	Steineis *n*, fossiles Bodeneis *n*
forward-acting control (regulation), forward control	Vorwärtsregelung *f*	Foster bridge	Foster-Brücke *f*
		Foster['s] reactance theorem, reactance theorem [of Foster]	Fostersches Reaktanztheorem *n*, Fosterscher Reaktanzsatz *m*, Reaktanzsatz [von Campbell und Foster]
forward airscrew, tractor airscrew, tractor screw, tractor propeller	Zugschraube *f*		
forward-backward counter	s. bidirectional counter	Foster-Seeley discriminator	s. phase discriminator
forward bias, forward biasing potential	Durchlaßvorspannung *f*, Vorspannung *f* in Durchlaßrichtung (Flußrichtung)	Föttinger converter	Strömungsumwandler *m* nach Föttinger, Föttingerscher Strömungsumwandler
forward conductance	Flußleitwert *m*, Durchlaßleitwert *m*, Vorwärtsleitwert *m*, Leitwert *m* vorwärts (in Durchlaßrichtung)	Foucault current coefficient, eddy current coefficient	Wirbelstrombeiwert *m*, Wirbelstromfaktor *m*
		Foucault currents	s. eddy currents ‹el.›

Foucault['s] gyroscope	Foucault-Gyroskop n, Foucaultsches Gyroskop n, Gyroskop n von Foucault, Bohnenbergsches Maschinchen n, Foucault-Kreisel m	four-dimensional current [density]	s. four-vector of electric current
		four-dimensional density, four-density, 4-density	Viererdichte f, vierdimensionale Dichte f
Foucault knife-edge	Foucaultsche Schneide f	four-dimensional density of force	s. four-density of force
Foucault knife-edge test, knife-edge test [of Foucault]	[Foucaultsches] Schneidenverfahren n, Schneidenprüfung f, Schneidenmethode f	four-dimensional force	s. four-force
		four-dimensional gradient, four-gradient, 4-gradient	Vierergradient m, vierdimensionaler Gradient m
Foucault['s] method, rotating mirrors method	Drehspiegelmethode f, Methode f von Foucault, Foucaultsche Methode (Drehspiegelmethode f, Meßmethode f der Lichtgeschwindigkeit), Foucaults Methode	four-dimensional momentum	s. four-momentum
		four-dimensional potential	s. four-potential
		four-dimensional tensor, four-tensor, 4-tensor, world tensor	Vierertensor m, vierdimensionaler Tensor m
Foucault['s] pendulum	Foucaultsches Pendel n, Foucault-Pendel n		
Foucault['s] pendulum experiment	Foucaultscher Pendelversuch m	four-dimensional vector	s. four vector
		four-dimensional velocity [vector]	s. four-velocity
Foucault prism	Foucaultsches Prisma n, Foucault-Prisma n	four-dimensional wave vector, four-wave vector, 4-wave vector	Viererwellenvektor m, vierdimensionaler Wellenvektor m
Foucault rotation	Foucaultsche Pendeldrehung f		
foundation slab, main foundation	Wehrsohle f, Wehrboden m, Wehrplatte f, Fundamentsohle f, Sohlenplatte f; Wehrfuß m	four-electrode tube (valve)	s. tetrode
		four-electron bond	s. double linkage
		four-element tube (valve)	s. tetrode
founding <of glass>	Schmelzen n <Glas>	four energy-level laser, four-level laser	Vierniveaulaser m
founding	s. a. heat <of metal>		
fount	s. spouting spring		
fountain effect	s. thermomechanical effect	four[-]factor formula (product)	Vierfaktorformel f, Vierfaktorenformel f
fountain model	Fontänenmodell n	four-fields correlation	Vierfelderkorrelation f
fountain-pen type pocket dosimeter, pen-type dosimeter	Füll[feder]halterdosimeter n, Ansteckdosimeter n		
four-acceleration, 4-acceleration, four-vector of acceleration, four-dimensional acceleration	Viererbeschleunigung f, Vierervektor m der Beschleunigung, vierdimensionale Beschleunigung f	four-fold axis [of symmetry]	s. tetrad axis
		four-fold axis of the second sort	s. tetrad axis of the second sort
		four-fold charged	vierfach geladen
		four[-]fold table, two-by-two contingency table, 2·2 table	Vierfeldertafel f, Zwei-mal-zwei-Tafel f, 2·2-Tafel f
four-angular momentum, 4-angular momentum, four-vector of angular momentum, four-dimensional angular momentum	Viererdrehimpuls m, Vierervektor m des Drehimpulses, vierdimensionaler Drehimpuls m		
		four-force, 4-force, four-vector of force, four-dimensional force, vector of four-dimensional force	Viererkraft f, Vierervektor m der Kraft, vierdimensionale Kraft f, Vektor m der Minkowski-Kraft
four-band system	Vierbandensystem n		
four-bar linkage	s. linked quadrilateral		
four-beam oscillograph	s. four-beam oscilloscope		
four-beam oscilloscope, four-beam oscillograph	Vierstrahloszillograph m, Vierstrahloszilloskop n	four-gradient, 4-gradient, four-dimensional gradient	Vierergradient m, vierdimensionaler Gradient m
four-body collision, four-particle collision	Viererstoß m, Vierfachstoß m, Vierteilchenstoß m	four-group	s. quadratic group
		Fourier analysis, harmonic analysis	Fourier-Analyse f, harmonische Analyse f, Oberwellenanalyse f
four-body decay	Zerfall m in vier Teilchen, Vierteilchenzerfall m, Vierkörperzerfall m	Fourier analyzer, harmonic analyzer, periodometer	harmonischer Analysator m, Fourier-Analysator m; Oberwellenanalysator m
four-centre five-electron approximation	Vierzentren-Fünfelektronen-Näherung f		
four colours problem	Vierfarbenproblem n	Fourier-Bessel function	s. Bessel function
		Fourier-Bessel series	Fourier-Bessel-Reihe f, Fourier-Reihe f mit Zylinderfunktionen
four-component spinor, spinor of four components	vierkomponentiger Spinor m		
		Fourier-Bessel transform	s. Hankel transform
four-component theory	Vierkomponententheorie f	Fourier-Bessel transform[ation]	s. Hankel transform[ation]
four-component vector of energy-momentum	s. four-momentum	Fourier coefficient	[Euler-]Fourier-Koeffizient m, Fourier-Konstante f, Entwicklungskoeffizient m, harmonischer Konstituent m
four-current	s. four-vector of current		
four-current density	s. four-vector of current		
four-cusped hypocycloid	s. astroid		
		Fourier component	s. harmonic
four-density, 4-density, four-dimensional density	Viererdichte f, vierdimensionale Dichte f	Fourier equation	s. Fourier['s] law of heat conduction
		Fourier expansion	s. harmonic expansion
four-density of force, 4-density of force, four-dimensional density of force	Viererkraftdichte f, vierdimensionale Kraftdichte f	Fourier['s] heat conduction equation	s. Fourier['s] law of heat conduction
		Fourier integral	Fourier-Integral n, Fouriersches Integral n
four-dimensional acceleration	s. four acceleration		
four-dimensional angular momentum	s. four-angular momentum	Fourier['s] integral theorem, integral theorem of Fourier	Fouriersche Integralformel (Integraldarstellung) f

Fourier integral transform	s. Fourier transform	**four-particle collision,** four-body collision	Viererstoß m, Vierfachstoß m, Vierteilchenstoß m
Fourier['s] inversion formula, Fourier['s] inversion theorem	Fourierscher Umkehrsatz m, Fouriersche Umkehrformel f	**four-pendulum support**	Vierpendelstativ n
Fourier kernel	Fourier-Kern m, Fourierscher Kern m	**four-pi counter; four-pi detector, four-pi pulse counting assembly;** 4π counter; 4π pulse counting assembly, 4π detector	4π-Zähler m, Vier-pi-Zähler m; 4π-Detektor m, Vier-pi-Detektor m
Fourier['s] law [of heat conduction], Fourier['s] heat conduction equation, Fourier equation	Fouriersches Gesetz n [der Wärmeleitung], Fouriersche Wärmeleitungsgleichung f (Differentialgleichung f der Wärmeleitung)		
		four-point electrode	Vierpunktelektrode f
Fourier number, Fo	Fouriersche Zahl f, Fourier-Zahl f, Fo	**four-point method, four-point technique**	Vierspitzenmethode f, Vierpunktverfahren n
Fourier series	Fourier-Reihe f, Fouriersche Reihe f	**four pole**	s. four-terminal network
Fourier series	s. a. trigonometric series	**four-pole characteristic**	s. four-pole parameter
Fourier space	Fourier-Raum m	**four-pole circuit,** four-terminal network, quadripole, four-pole network, four pole; two-terminal-pair network	Vierpol m, vierpoliges Netzwerk n, Zweiklemmenpaar n; echter Vierpol m
Fourier spectroscopy, harmonic spectroscopy	Fourier-Spektroskopie f		
Fourier spectrum, harmonic spectrum	Fourier-Spektrum n, harmonisches Spektrum n, Oberwellenspektrum n		
		four-pole coefficient	s. four-pole parameter
Fourier-Stieltjes transform	Fourier-Stieltjes-Transformierte f	**four-pole constant**	s. four-pole parameter
		four-pole equations	s. four-pole relations
Fourier-Stieltjes transform[ation]	Fourier-Stieltjes-Transformation f	**four-pole matrix,** characteristic matrix of the two-terminal-pair network, quadripole matrix	Vierpolmatrix f
Fourier synthesis, harmonic synthesis	harmonische Synthese f, Fourier-Synthese f		
Fourier transform, Fourier integral transform	Fourier-Transformierte f		
		four-pole network	s. four-terminal network
		four-pole parameter, four-pole constant (coefficient, characteristic)	Vierpolkoeffizient m, Vierpolkonstante f, Vierpolparameter m, Vierpol[kenn]größe f
Fourier transform, Fourier transformation	Fourier-Transformation f		
four-index symbol	s. Riemann-Christoffel symbol	**four-pole relations**	s. characteristic relations of the two-terminal-pair network
four-layer diode, Shockley diode, three-junction diode	Vierschichtdiode f, Vierschichtendiode f, Shockley-Diode f	**four-potential,** 4-potential, four-vector of potential, four-dimensional potential, charge-current potential	Viererpotential n, Vierervektor m des Potentials, vierdimensionales Potential n
four-layer n-p-n-p diode	s. n-p-n-p diode	**four-pronged star**	vierarmiger (vierstrahliger) Stern m, Vierspurenstern m
four-layer n-p-n-p transistor	s. n-p-n-p transistor		
four-layer p-n-p-n diode	s. p-n-p-n diode	**four-pulse generator**	Vierimpulsgenerator m
four-layer p-n-p-n transistor	s. p-n-p-n transistor	**four-quadrant power factor meter**	Vierquadrant[en]meßgerät n, Vierquadrant[en]-Leistungsfaktormesser m, Vierquadrant[en]-Phasenmesser m
four-layer structure	Vierschicht[en]struktur f		
four-layer transistor (triode), three-junction triode	Vierschicht[en]transistor m, Vierschicht[en]triode f, Kipptriode f		
		four ring, four-membered ring	Viererring m, Vierring m
four-leafed rose	Vierblatt n	**four-slot [cylinder] antenna**	Vierschlitzstrahler m
four-level laser, four energy-level laser	Vierniveaulaser m	**four-tensor,** 4-tensor, four-dimensional tensor, world tensor	Vierertensor m, vierdimensionaler Tensor m
four-level maser	Vierniveaumaser m	**four-tensor of dielectric polarization and magnetization intensity**	s. polarization-magnetization tensor
four-level solid-state laser	Vierniveau-Festkörperlaser m	**four-tensor of electromagnetic field,** electromagnetic field tensor, field tensor	[elektromagnetischer] Feldtensor m, [elektromagnetischer] Feldstärketensor m, Tensor m der Feldstärke, Vierertensor m (Tensor) des elektromagnetischen Feldes
four-matrix, 4-matrix	Vierermatrix f		
four-membered ring, four ring	Viererring m, Vierring m	**four-terminal impedance network**	Impedanzvierpol m
four-member index	viergliedriger Flächenindex m		
four-moment equation	Viermomentengleichung f	**four-terminal network,** quadripole, four-pole network (circuit), four pole; two-terminal-pair network	Vierpol m, vierpoliges Netzwerk n, Zweiklemmenpaar n; echter Vierpol
four-momentum, 4-momentum, momentum-energy vector, energy-momentum vector, four-vector of momentum-energy, four-component vector of energy-momentum, four-dimensional momentum	Viererimpuls[vektor] m, Impuls-Energie-Vektor m, Energie-Impuls-Vektor m, Energie-Impuls-Virervektor m, Vierervektor m von Impuls und Energie, vierdimensionaler Impuls m		
		fourth	Quarte f
		fourth harmonic point, harmonic conjugate	vierter harmonischer Punkt m
		four-vector, 4-vector, four-dimensional vector, world vector	Vierervektor m, vierdimensionaler Vektor m
four nuple, quadruped, tetrapod, vierbein	Vierbein n	**four-vector of acceleration**	s. four-acceleration

four-vector of angular momentum	s. four-angular momentum	fractionation	s. a. fractional distillation
four-vector of current [density], four-vector of electric current [density], four-current density, four-current, 4-current, four-dimensional current density, four-dimensional current, charge-current density [four vectors]	Vier[er]stromdichte f, Viererstrom m, Vierervektor m der elektrischen Stromdichte, Vierervektor des elektrischen Stromes, vierdimensionale Stromdichte f (Dichte f des elektrischen Stromes), Strom-Ladungsdichte f, Strom-Ladungsdichte-Vierervektor m	fraction exchange	Austauschfaktor m, Austauschquotient m
		fraction field	s. quotient field
		fraction of saturation	Sättigungsanteil m
		fracto cloud	s. fractus
		fracto[-]cumulus, cumulus fractus	Fractocumulus m, zerrissene Quellwolke f
		fractograph	s. fracture
		fractometer, chromatograph	Chromatograph m, Fraktometer n
		fracto[-]nimbus, nimbus fractus	Fractonimbus m, Nimbus m fractus, zerrissene Schlechtwetterwolke f
four-vector of force	s. four-force		
four-vector of momentum-energy	s. four-momentum		
four-vector of potential	s. four-potential	fracto[-]stratus, stratus fractus, scud	Fractostratus m, zerrissene Schichtwolke f
four-vector of velocity	s. four-velocity		
four-velocity, 4-velocity, four-vector of velocity, four-dimensional velocity [vector]	Vierergeschwindigkeit f, Vierervektor m der Geschwindigkeit, vierdimensionale Geschwindigkeit f	fractural cleavage, fracture cleavage	Bruchschieferung f
		fracture; rupture; fractograph; fracture (rupture) area; fracture surface, fractured face <mech.>	Bruch m, Bruchbild n; Bruchfläche f <Mech.>
four-wave vector, 4-wave vector, four-dimensional wave vector	Viererwellenvektor m, vierdimensionaler Wellenvektor m	fracture	s. a. fault <geo.>
		fracture across the grains, transcrystalline (transgranular) fracture	intrakristalliner Bruch m, Bruch quer durch Einzelkristalle
four-way cock	Vierwegehahn m, Kreuzhahn m	fracture area	s. fracture
		fracture cleavage	s. fractural cleavage
fovea [centralis], macula	Netzhautgrube f, Fovea f [centralis], Area f centralis	fracture condition, failure condition	Bruchbedingung f, Festigkeitsbedingung f
foveal vision, direct vision	direktes Sehen n, foveales Sehen	fractured face	s. fracture <mech.>
		fracture line	s. rupture line
foveola	Sehgrube f, Sehgrübchen n, Foveola f	fracture line	s. a. fault line <geo.>
		fracture load, breaking load, fracturing load	Bruchlast f; Höchstlast f; Reißlast f, Zerreißlast f
Fowler-Darwin method, Darwin-Fowler method, method of steepest descent[s], steepest descent method, saddle point method <therm.>	Darwin-Fowler-Methode f, Darwin-Fowlersche Methode f, Sattelpunktmethode f <Therm.>	fracture range	s. fatigue strength for limit life
		fracture strain	s. breaking elongation
		fracture strength	s. modulus of rupture
		fracture stress, breaking (failing, ultimate) stress, break strain	Bruchspannung f; Bruchbeanspruchung f
Fowler series	Fowler-Serie f		
FP laser	s. Fabry-Pérot-type laser	fracture surface	s. fracture
fraction, break, salient point; kink, knee <of the curve>	Knick m; Knie n; Abknicken n <Kurve>	fracture toughness, crack toughness	Bruchwiderstand m, Bruchzähigkeit f, Rißzähigkeit f
fractional absorbance (absorptance)	Teilabsorptionsvermögen n	fracture without displacement	Teilbarkeitskluft f, Ablösungskluft f, Absonderungskluft f
fractional centrifugation, fractionated centrifugation	fraktionierte Zentrifugierung f		
		fracturing load, breaking load, fracture load <mech.>	Bruchlast f; Höchstlast f; Reißlast f, Zerreißlast f
fractional condensation	fraktionierte Kondensation f		
fractional coverage <also geo.>, degree of coverage	Bedeckungsgrad m	fractus, fractus form, ragged cloud, fracto cloud	zerrissene Wolke f, Fractusform f, Fractowolke f
fractional crystallization	fraktionierte Kristallisation (Kristallisierung) f	fragility; brittleness; breakability; friability; shortness; crackiness; rottenness <of steel>	Sprödigkeit f, Brüchigkeit f, Zerbrechlichkeit f
fractional distillation, fractionation	fraktionierte Destillation f, Fraktionieren n		
		fragment	s. nuclear fragment
		fragmentation, disruption <of the meteor>	Zerplatzen n, Zerspringen n, Zerstörung f <Meteor>
fractional fissure	Bruchspalte f		
fractional humidity	s. degree of humidity	fragmentation, rhexis <bio.>	Fragmentation f, Chromosomenfragmentation f, Rhexis f <Bio.>
fractional ionization	s. degree of ionization		
fractional isotopic abundance	s. abundance of isotopes	fragmentation [of nucleus], nuclear explosion, atomic explosion, atomic fragmentation	„fragmentation"-Reaktion f, Kernexplosion f, Kernzertrümmerung f, Fragmentierung f, Atomzertrümmerung f
fractional linear transformation	s. homographic transformation		
fractional load, underload	Unterlast f, Teillast f; Unter[be]lastung f		
fractional solution	fraktionierte Lösung (Auflösung) f	fragmentation [reaction], elimination cleavage <chem.>	Fragmentierung f <Chem.>
fractional sublimation	fraktionierte Sublimation f	Frahm frequency meter	s. reed-type frequency meter
fractional yield	Ausbeute f je Stufe	frame, framed structure, frame structure <mech.>	Stabwerk n, Rahmen m, Rahmenwerk n <Mech.>
fractionated centrifugation	s. fractional centrifugation	frame <stat.>	Rahmen m, Auswahlgrundlage f, Erhebungsgrundlage f <Stat.>
fractionated irradiation	s. split-dose irradiation		
fractionated treatment, fractionating, fractionation	Fraktionierung f, Fraktionieren n, Fraktionisierung f	frame	s. a. rib
		frame amplifier	s. vertical amplifier
		frame antenna	s. loop antenna
fractionating column (tower), fractionation column	Fraktionierkolonne f; Fraktionieraufsatz m	frame deflection	s. image deflection
		framed structure, frame, frame structure	Stabwerk n, Rahmen m, Rahmenwerk n <Mech.>
fractionating tube	s. distillation tube	frame grid	Spanngitter n
fractionation, fractionating, fractionated treatment	Fraktionierung f, Fraktionisierung f	frame grid valve	Spanngitterröhre f

frame of reference, reference frame (system), system of reference, referential	Bezugssystem n	**frazil [ice]**	s. slush ice
		Fréchet differential	Fréchetsches Differential n
		Fredholm['s] determinant	Fredholmsche Determinante f
frame structure, frame, framed structure <mech.>	Stabwerk n, Rahmen m, Rahmenwerk n <Mech.>	**Fredholm['s] equation**	s. Fredholm['s] integral equation <of second kind>
framework, system of bars	Fachwerk n	**Fredholm['s] equation of the first kind**	s. integral equation of first kind
framing index; adjustment mark; index mark	Einstellmarke f	**Fredholm['s] integral equation** <of second kind>, Fredholm['s] equation [of the second kind], [linear] integral equation of the second kind	Fredholmsche Integralgleichung f [zweiter Art], Integralgleichung vom Fredholmschen Typ, Fredholmsche Gleichung f [zweiter Art], [lineare] Integralgleichung zweiter Art
Francis turbine, single-runner Francis turbine, radial-axial turbine, combined (mixed) flow turbine	Francis-Turbine f, Spiralturbine f		
Franck and Hertz experiments	Elektronenstoßversuche (Stoßversuche) mpl von Franck und Hertz, Franck-Hertzsche Elektronenstoßversuche (Versuche mpl), Franck-Hertz-Versuche mpl	**Fredholm['s] integral equation of the first kind**	s. integral equation of first kind
		Fredholm kernel (nucleus), kernel, nucleus	Fredholmscher Kern m
		free[-] air correction	s. free[-] air reduction
		free[-] air counter, open [air] counter, free counter	offenes Zählrohr n
Franck-Condon principle	Franck-Condon-Prinzip n		
		free[-] air dose, air dose, in-air dose	Dosis f „frei in Luft", Freiluftdosis f, Luftdosis f
Franck-Condon shift	Franck-Condon-Verschiebung f	**free[-] air effect**	s. Faye effect
Franck-Condon transition	Franck-Condon-Übergang m	**free[-] air geoid**	Freiluftgeoid n
Franck-Hertz law	Franck-Hertz-Regel f, Franck-Hertzsche Regel f	**free[-] air ionization chamber,** free (open-air) ionization chamber, air-[-filled] ionization chamber	Freiluft-Standardkammer f; Freiluft-Ionisationskammer f, offene (luftgefüllte) Ionisationskammer f, [offene] Luftionisationskammer f
Franck-Rabinowitch [cage] effect	s. Frank-Rabinowitch [cage] effect		
Françon eyepiece, interference eyepiece	Interferenzokular n [nach Françon]		
Frank half-dislocation, Frank partial dislocation	Franksche (nichtgleitfähige) unvollständige Versetzung f, Franksche Halbversetzung f	**free[-] air [over]pressure**	Überdruck m in freier Atmosphäre
		free[-] air reduction, Faye['s] reduction, free[-] air correction	Kondensationsreduktion f, Freiluftreduktion f, Faye-Reduktion f, Freiluftkorrektion f
Frankl['s] boundary value problem, Frankl['s] problem	Franklsches Randwrtproblem n		
franklin, statcoulomb, Fr	Franklin n, Fr	**free-body diagram**	Kräfteplan m, Kraftplan m, Krafteck n
Franklin antenna	s. collinear antenna	**free boundary**	freier Rand m, freie Berandung f, freie Grenzlinie f; freie Strahlgrenze f
Frankl['s] problem	s. Frankl boundary value problem		
Frank partial dislocation, Frank half-dislocation	Franksche (nichtgleitfähige) unvollständige Versetzung f, Franksche Halbversetzung f	**free-boundary flow**	Strömung f mit freier Berandung (Grenzlinie, Strahlgrenze)
		free-bound electron transition, free-bound transition	frei-gebundener Übergang m, Frei-Gebunden-Übergang m
Frank-Rabinowitch cage	Frank-Rabinowitsch-Käfig m		
Frank-Rabinowitch [cage] effect, Franck-Rabinowitch [cage] effect, cage effect	Frank-Rabinowitsch-Effekt m, Käfigeffekt m	**free-bound radiation**	s. recombination radiation
		free-bound transition, free-bound electron transition	frei-gebundener Übergang m, Frei-Gebunden-Übergang m
Frank-Read [dislocation] source, Frank-Read net, Frank-Read mill	Frank-Read-Quelle f, Frank-Read-Versetzungsquelle f, Frank-Readsche Versetzungsquelle (Quelle) f, Frank-Readsches Netzwerk n	**free charge,** true charge	freie Ladung f, ableitbare Ladung, wahre Ladung
		free colour, plain colour, surface colour	freie (unbezogene) Farbe f, Flächenfarbe f
		free conductance, short-circuit conductance	Kurzschlußleitwert m
Frank-Van der Merwe mechanism	s. rigid model <cryst.>	**free convection,** natural convection	freie Konvektion f, natürliche Konvektion
Franz-Keldys[c]h effect	Franz-Keldys[c]h-Effekt m	**free counter,** free[-] air counter, open [air] counter	offenes Zählrohr n
f-ratio, f-number, stop number, focal ratio	Blendenzahl f, Blendennummer f, Öffnungszahl f		
F ratio, F-statistic, variance ratio	Varianzquotient m, Quotient m F, F-Prüfzahl f	**free cross-section,** free scattering cross-section, cross-section for free scattering	Streuquerschnitt m von freien Atomen, Wirkungsquerschnitt m für (der) Streuung an freien Atomen
Fraunhofer corona	s. F corona		
Fraunhofer diffraction	Fraunhofersche Beugung f	**free discharge,** free-flow discharge	freies Ausströmen n, freier Auslauf m
Fraunhofer diffraction fringes	s. Fraunhofer diffraction phenomena	**freedom coefficient,** coefficient of freedom	Freiheitskoeffizient m
Fraunhofer diffraction phenomena; Fraunhofer pattern, Fraunhofer diffraction fringes	Fraunhofersche Beugungserscheinungen fpl	**freedom of action** (motion, movement)	Bewegungsfreiheit f
		free edge <of a plate>	freier Rand m <Platte>
		free electron theory [of metal]	Metallelektronentheorie f, Theorie f der freien Elektronen (Metallelektronen)
Fraunhofer line	Fraunhofer-Linie f, Fraunhofersche Linie f	**free energy,** Helmholtz['] free energy, Helmholtz['] function, work function, maximum work function, force function for constant temperature <therm.>	freie Energie f, Helmholtzsche freie Energie, Helmholtz-Funktion f <Therm.>
Fraunhofer pattern	s. Fraunhofer diffraction phenomena		
Fraunhofer pattern	s. a. far field pattern		
Fraunhofer['s] region	s. radiation zone		
Fraunhofer spectrum	Fraunhofer-Spektrum n, Fraunhofersches Spektrum n		
		free energy [for constant pressure]	s. free enthalpy
Fraunhofer['s] zone	s. radiation zone		

free energy of reaction	freie Reaktionsenergie f	free-molecule flow	s. molecular flow
free energy of the surface [per unit area]	s. surface energy	free nutation, Chandler's motion of the pole	Chandlersche Polbewegung f, Chandlersche Nutation f, freie Nutation
free enthalpy, Gibbs['] free energy, Gibbs['] function, Gibbs['] (total) thermodynamic potential, Gibbs['] potential, Gibbs['] free enthalpy, Gibbs['] chemical potential, free energy [for constant pressure], thermal potential	freie Enthalpie f, Gibbssche freie Energie f, Gibbssche Funktion (Wärmefunktion) f, Gibbs-Funktion f, Gibbssches thermodynamisches Potential n, Gibbssches [chemisches] Potential, freie Gibbssche Energie	free of stress (tension)	s. unstressed <mech.>
		free overfall weir	s. free weir
		free particle, unbound particle	freies (nichtgebundenes) Teilchen n
		free path, free path length	freie Weglänge f; freie Wegstrecke f
		free period, natural period [of oscillation]; characteristic period	Eigenperiode f, Eigenschwingungsdauer f
free fall	freier Fall m		
free-fall apparatus	Fallmaschine f	free point, free mass point, unconstrained point	freier Massenpunkt (Punkt) m
free-fall trajectory; free-flight trajectory	Trägheitsbahn f	free polynomial ring	freier Polynomring m
		free radial-synchrotron oscillation	freie Synchrotronschwingung f
free fall weir, free weir, free overfall weir, clear overflow weir, weir with free fall	vollkommener Überfall m; vollkommenes Wehr n, vollkommenes Überfallwehr n	free radical polymerization	Radikalpolymerisation f, radikalische Polymerisation f
		free rotation	s. free internal rotation
		free-running frequency	s. natural frequency
free-field calibration	Freifeldeichung f	free-running multivibrator	eigenerregter Multivibrator m, selbsterregter Multivibrator, selbstschwingender Multivibrator, ungetasteter Multivibrator
free-field current response (sensitivity)	Feldstromempfindlichkeit f, Freifeld-Stromübertragungsmaß n		
free-field voltage response (sensitivity)	Feldempfindlichkeit f, Feldübertragungsfaktor m, Freifeld-Spannungsübertragungsmaß n	free-running oscillator, self-oscillator	selbsterregter Oszillator m, eigenerregter Oszillator
free flight	s. inertial flight	free scattering cross-section	s. free cross-section
free-flight trajectory; free-fall trajectory	Trägheitsbahn f	free space, empty space, physical vacuum, absolute vacuum, vacuum [in the proper sense], space devoid of matter	freier Raum m, [luft]leerer Raum, physikalisches (absolutes) Vakuum n, Vakuum [im eigentlichen Sinne]; Luftleere f
free flight wind tunnel	s. open jet wind tunnel		
free flow	freie Strömung f		
free-flow discharge	s. free discharge		
free föhn	freier Föhn m, Föhn der freien Atmosphäre	free-space attenuation	Freiraumdämpfung f, Funkfelddämpfung f, Streckendämpfung f
free-free absorption	s. inverse bremsstrahlung		
free-free electron transition, free-free transition	frei-freier Übergang m, Frei-Frei-Übergang m	free-space pattern	Freiraumcharakteristik f, Freiraum-Richtdiagramm n
free from distortion, rectilinear, orthoscopic	verzeichnungsfrei, rektolinear, orthoskopisch, tiefenrichtig	free-space propagation	Freiraumausbreitung f
free from flares		free spinning, spinning, spin, tail spin	Trudeln n, Trudelbewegung f, Trudelflug m
	reflexfrei	free spinning [vertical] [wind] tunnel, spin[ning] wind tunnel, vertical [-axis] [spin] wind tunnel	senkrechter Windkanal m, Trudelkanal m, [senkrechter] Trudelwindkanal m
free from forces	s. force-free		
free from strain	s. unstrained <mech.>		
free ground water	s. phreatic water		
free group, word group	freie Gruppe f, Wortgruppe	free stream Mach number, flow Mach number	Anström-Mach-Zahl f
free gyroscope, space gyroscope	kräftefreier Kreisel m, Kreisel mit drei Freiheitsgraden		
		free stream total temperature	Gesamttemperatur f der freien Strömung
		free stream velocity	Anströmgeschwindigkeit f
free impedance, short-circuit impedance	[elektrische] Kurzschlußimpedanz f; Kurzschlußwiderstand m	free subscripts and superscripts	freie Indizes mpl
		free surface	freie Oberfläche f
free impedance	s. a. input impedance	free surface energy	s. surface energy
free internal rotation, free rotation	freie innere Rotation f, [freie] Drehbarkeit f <Molekülgruppe>	free surface of water	s. surface <hydr.>
		free surface vortex	trichterförmiger Wirbel m
		free time of flight	freie Flugzeit f
free ionization chamber	s. free[-] air ionization chamber	free torsion, St. Venant torsion	freie (de Saint-Venantsche) Torsion f
free jet, open jet, jet flow; stream[ ]flow	freier Strahl m, Freistrahl m, Strahlströmung f, Strahlausfluß m	free transmission range	s. pass[-]band
		free variability	freie Variabilität f
		free vibration	s. dying out <of an oscillation>
free-jet-type turbine	s. impulse turbine		
free jet[-] wind tunnel	s. open jet wind tunnel <aero.>	free volume	freies Volumen n
		free volume theory	s. lattice-cell theory <of liquids>
free length	s. reduced buckling length		
freely supported, simply supported	frei aufliegend (gelagert)	free vortex, potential vortex, point vortex	freier Wirbel m, abgehender Wirbel
freely supported bearing (end)	s. simply supported bearing	free vortex core	freier Wirbelkern m
free mass point	s. free point		
free meander	freier Mäander m	free vortex system, horseshoe vortex system	Hufeisenwirbelsystem n
free-molecule diffusion	Diffusion f freier Moleküle, Knudsen-Diffusion f		

free weir, free fall weir, free overall weir, clear overflow weir, weir with free fall — vollkommener Überfall *m*; vollkommenes Wehr *n*, vollkommenes Überfallwehr *n*

freeze-drying, lyophilization, lyophilizing — Gefriertrocknung *f*, Lyophilisation *f*, Lyophilisierung *f*

freeze-out — Ausfrieren *n*

freeze-up; freezing, freezing-in — Einfrieren *n*, Gefrieren *n*; Zufrierung *f*

freezing, solidification, solidifying; set, setting — Erstarrung *f*, Festwerden *n*, Verfestigung *f*

freezing <e.g. of magnetic field lines, electron gas, degrees of freedom> — Einfrieren *n* <z. B. magnetische Feldlinien, Elektronengas, Freiheitsgrade>

freezing[-in]; freeze-up — Einfrieren *n*; Gefrieren *n*; Zufrierung *f*

freezing-in temperature, glass (second order) transition temperature, vitrification temperature — Einfrier[ungs]temperatur *f*, Einfrierpunkt *m*, ET

freezing mixture — s. frigorific mixture

freezing nucleus, nucleus for the initiation of freezing — Gefrierkern *m*

freezing point — s. solidification point

freezing point constant — s. cryoscopic constant

freezing-point curve, liquidus, liquidus line (curve) — Liquiduslinie *f*, Liquiduskurve *f*

freezing-point depression — s. lowering of the freezing point

freezing-point diagram — Gefrierpunktdiagramm *n*

freezing point of antimony, antimony point — Erstarrungspunkt *m* (Erstarrungstemperatur *f*) des Antimons, Antimonpunkt *m*

freezing point of gold, gold point, point of freezing gold — Goldpunkt *m*, Erstarrungspunkt *m* des Goldes

freezing point of platinum, platinum point, point of freezing platinum — Platinpunkt *m*, Erstarrungspunkt *m* des Platins

freezing point of silver, silver point, point of freezing silver — Silberpunkt *m*, Erstarrungspunkt *m* (Erstarrungstemperatur *f*) des Silbers

freezing temperature, brittle point, brittle temperature — Sprödigkeitspunkt *m*, Sprödigkeitstemperatur *f*, Brittlepunkt *m*

freezing temperature — s. a. solidification point

freezing-together, congelation, congeal — Zusammenfrieren *n*

F region — s. transition region <geo.>

French calorie — s. kilogramme-calorie

French pitch <435 c/s> — s. philharmonic pitch

Frenet[-Serret] formulae, Serret-Frenet formulae, formulae of [Serret-]Frenet — Frenetsche Formeln *fpl*, Frenet-Formeln *fpl*, Serretsche Formeln

Frenkel defect; Frenkel disorder; Frenkel pair, interstitial-vacancy pair — Frenkel-Defekt *m*, Frenkel-Fehlstelle *f*; Frenkel-Paar *n*; Zwischengitteratom-Leerstellen-Paar *n*, Frenkel-Fehlordnung *f*, Frenkelsche Fehlordnung *f*

Frenkel exciton — Frenkel-Exciton *n*

Frenkel['s] theory of spontaneous fission — Frenkelsche Theorie *f* der spontanen Spaltung

freon[-filled bubble] chamber — Freonblasenkammer *f*

frequency, oscillation (oscillating, vibrational, vibration) frequency — Frequenz *f*, Schwingungszahl *f*, Schwingungsfrequenz *f*

frequency, <stat.> — Häufigkeit *f*, Frequenz *f*, Dichtigkeit *f*, Bestandsdichte *f*, Individuenabstand *m* <Stat.>

frequency analysis — Frequenzanalyse *f*

frequency band, frequency range — Frequenzband *n*, Frequenzbereich *m*, Frequenzgebiet *n*; Frequenzumfang *m*

frequency bridge — Frequenzmeßbrücke *f*

frequency change <el.>, mixing, conversion — Mischung *f*, Mischen *n* <El.>

frequency change — s. a. frequency translation <el.>

frequency changer — s. converter tube

frequency changer — s. frequency converter

frequency changer valve — s. converter tube

frequency characteristic — s. frequency response

frequency component, frequency fraction — Teilfrequenz *f*

frequency compression, bandwidth compression, bandwidth narrowing — Frequenzbandkompression *f*; Frequenzbandverschmälerung *f*

frequency conversion, transposition <el.> — Frequenztransponierung *f*, Transponierung *f*, Frequenzumsetzung *f*, Umsetzung *f*; Ummodelung *f* <El.>

frequency converter; frequency changer; frequency transformer <el.> — Frequenzwandler *m*, Periodenwandler *m*; Frequenzumformer *m*, Periodenumformer *m*; Frequenzumsetzer *m* <El.>

frequency converter, inverter, converter, power frequency converter <el.> — Umrichter *m*; Umkehrrohr *n* <El.>

frequency curve — Häufigkeitskurve *f*

frequency decade — Frequenzdekade *f*

frequency dependence of permittivity — s. dependence of permittivity on frequency

frequency deviation, deviation of the frequency, frequency swing; frequency sweep — Frequenzabweichung *f*; Frequenzhub *m*

frequency deviation meter — Frequenzhubmesser *m*

frequency distribution, frequency spectrum, distribution in frequency — Häufigkeitsverteilung *f*, Häufigkeitsspektrum *n*; Frequenzverteilung *f*

frequency distribution function — s. contrast transmission function

frequency divider, scaler — Frequenzteiler *m*, Untersetzer *m*

frequency-divider stage, scaling stage, step-down stage — Untersetzerstufe *f*, Teilerstufe *f*, Frequenzteilerstufe *f*

frequency division — Frequenzteilung *f*, Frequenzabbau *m*, Frequenzuntersetzung *f*, Untersetzung *f* der Frequenz

frequency drift, departure (pushing) of frequency, frequency pushing — Frequenzdrift *f*, Frequenzabwanderung *f*, Frequenzauswanderung *f*, Weglaufen *n* der Frequenz

frequency equation — s. characteristic equation

frequency factor, pre-exponential factor <in the Arrhenius equation> — Frequenzfaktor *m*

frequency fraction, frequency component — Teilfrequenz *f*

frequency function — s. probability frequency function

frequency-height curve — s. ionogram

frequency indicator — s. wavemeter

frequency instability, frequency sliding, mode shift — Frequenzgleiten *n*, Frequenzinkonstanz *f*, Frequenzinstabilität *f*

frequency interval, frequency spacing — Frequenzabstand *m*

frequency jumping — Frequenzsprung *m*

frequency meter — s. wavemeter

frequency method, frequency response method, method of Bode, Bode['s] method — Methode *f* des Bode-Diagramms, Frequenzgangmethode *f*

frequency-modulated cyclotron — s. synchrocyclotron

frequency multiplication	Frequenzvervielfachung f
frequency multiplier	Frequenzvervielfacher m
frequency of fadings	Schwundhäufigkeit f
frequency of haloes	Halohäufigkeit f
frequency of ionization, ionization frequency	Ionisationshäufigkeit f, Ionisierungshäufigkeit f
frequency of magnetic reversals	Ummagnetisierungshäufigkeit f
frequency of meteors	s. rate of shooting stars
frequency of mutations, mutation rate	Mutationshäufigkeit f, Mutationsrate f, Mutationsgeschwindigkeit f
frequency of nutation, nutation frequency	Nutationsfrequenz f
frequency of quadrupole transition, quadrupole frequency	Quadrupolübergangsfrequenz f, Quadrupolfrequenz f
frequency of ripple, hum frequency	Brummfrequenz f
frequency of thunderstorms, thunderstorm frequency	Gewitterhäufigkeit f
frequency parameter	Frequenzparameter m
frequency polygon	Häufigkeitspolygon n
frequency pulling, persistence of frequency, pulling into tune, pull-in, pulling ‹of oscillator, magnetron› ‹el.›	Mitnahme f, Mitziehen n, Frequenzmitnahme f, Frequenzmitziehen n, Frequenzziehen n, Ziehen n ‹El.›
frequency pushing	s. frequency drift
frequency range	s. frequency band
frequency range of audibility	s. frequency range of hearing
frequency range of hearing, frequency range of audibility, range of audibility (hearing), audibility range, audible spectrum; auditory sensation area	Hörbereich m, Hörfrequenzbereich m, hörbarer Frequenzbereich m; Hörfläche f
frequency response, frequency response characteristic, frequency response curve, frequency characteristic, harmonic response [characteristic], response	Frequenzgang m, Frequenzcharakteristik f, Frequenzkennlinie f, Frequenzverlauf m, Frequenzkurve f; Frequenzdurchlaßkurve f; Frequenzempfindlichkeitskennlinie f; Frequenzempfindlichkeit f; Frequenzwiedergabe f; Frequenzwiedergabekurve f
frequency response ‹control›	Frequenzgang m ‹Regelung›
frequency response characteristic (curve)	s. frequency response
frequency response in the diffuse [sound] field	Diffusfeldübertragungsmaß n
frequency response in the free [sound] field	Freifeldübertragungsmaß n
frequency response method, frequency method, method of Bode, Bode['s] method	Methode f des Bode-Diagramms, Frequenzgangmethode f
frequency selection	Frequenzwahl f
frequency selectivity	Frequenzselektivität f
frequency sharing [scheme]	Frequenzverteilung f, „frequency sharing" n
frequency shift	Frequenzverwerfung f, Frequenzwanderung f, Frequenzverschiebung f
frequency-shift theorem [of Laplace transform]	Dämpfungssatz m [der Laplace-Transformation]
frequency sliding, mode shift, frequency instability	Frequenzgleiten n, Frequenzinkonstanz f, Frequenzinstabilität f
frequency spacing	s. frequency interval
frequency spectrograph	Frequenzspektrograph m
frequency spectrum	Frequenzspektrum n, Frequenzgemisch n
frequency spectrum	s. a. frequency distribution
frequency standard	Frequenznormal n, Frequenzeichnormal n; Frequenzstandard m
frequency-statistical	häufigkeitsstatistisch
frequency sweep	s. wobbulation
frequency sweep	s. a. frequency deviation
frequency-swept oscillator	s. wobbler
frequency swing	s. frequency deviation
frequency synthesis	Frequenzsynthese f
frequency synthesizer	Frequenzerzeuger m
frequency theory ‹of Rutherford›, frequency theory of pitch, telephone theory [of Rutherford]	Telephontheorie f [des Hörens], Rutherfordsche Telephontheorie
frequency transformation	s. frequency translation ‹el.›
frequency transformer	s. frequency converter ‹el.›
frequency translation; frequency transformation; frequency change ‹el.›	Frequenzkonversion f; Frequenztransformation f; Frequenzumformung f; Frequenz[um]wandlung f; Frequenzänderung f ‹El.›
frequency-type telemetering	Fernmessung f mit Frequenzvariation
frequency wow	s. wow ‹el.›
fresh gale, gale ‹of Beaufort No. 8›	stürmischer Wind m ‹Stärke 8›
freshly fallen snow	Neuschnee m
fresh[ ]water	Süßwasser n, süßes Wasser
fresh wind ‹of Beaufort No. 5›	frische Brise f ‹Stärke 5›
fresnel $<= 10^{12}$/s	Fresnel $n <= 10^{12}$/s
Fresnel-Arago laws; Fresnel['s] laws	Fresnel-Aragosche Sätze mpl
Fresnel['s] biprism	Fresnelsches Doppelprisma (Biprisma) n, Biprisma von Fresnel
Fresnel['s] construction, Fresnel['s] method	Zonenkonstruktion von Fresnel, Fresnelsche Zonenkonstruktion (Methode) f
Fresnel['s] convection coefficient	s. Fresnel['s] dragging coefficient
Fresnel diffraction	Fresnelsche Beugung f
Fresnel diffraction fringes; Fresnel diffraction phenomena; Fresnel pattern	Fresnelsche Beugungserscheinungen fpl
Fresnel['s] double mirror, Fresnel['s] mirror, Fresnel mirrors, bimirror	Fresnelscher Spiegel m, Fresnelscher Doppelspiegel m
Fresnel['s] drag[ging] coefficient, Fresnel['s] convection coefficient	Fresnelscher Mitführungskoeffizient m, Mitführungskoeffizient m
Fresnel['s] ellipsoid, ray ellipsoid	Fresnelsches Ellipsoid (Ausbreitungsellipsoid) n, Strahlenellipsoid n
Fresnel['s] equation of wave normals, equation of wave normals	Fresnelsches Gesetz n
Fresnel['s] equations, Fresnel['s] relationships [for reflection and refraction], Fresnel['s] reflection formulae	Fresnelsche Formeln (Gleichungen, Reflexionsformeln) fpl, Reflexionsformeln von Fresnel
Fresnel['s] experiment	s. Fresnel['s] mirror experiment
Fresnel['s] hemilens, hemilens	Fresnelsche Halblinse f
Fresnel-Huygens['] principle	Fresnel-Huygens-Prinzip n, Fresnel-Huygenssches (Huygens-Fresnelsches) Prinzip n
Fresnel['s] integral	Fresnelsches Integral n
Fresnel['s] laws; Fresnel-Arago laws	Fresnel-Aragosche Sätze mpl, Fresnel-Integral n
Fresnel lens, echelon lens, step[ped] lens	Fresnel-Linse f, Fresnelsche Linse f, Stufenlinse f
Fresnel['s] method	s. Fresnel['s] construction

Fresnel['s] mirror, Fresnel['s] double mirror, Fresnel mirrors, bimirror — Fresnelscher Spiegel *m*, Fresnelscher Doppelspiegel *m*

Fresnel['s] mirror experiment, Fresnel['s] experiment — Fresnelscher Spiegelversuch (Interferenzversuch) *m*, Spiegelversuch (Interferenzversuch) von Fresnel

Fresnel mirrors — s. Fresnel['s] mirror

Fresnel['s] parallelepiped, Fresnel rhomb — Fresnelsches Parallelepiped *n*

Fresnel pattern <of antenna>, near field pattern — Nahfelddiagramm *n* <Antenne>

Fresnel pattern — s. a. Fresnel diffraction phenomena

Fresnel['s] principle, Huyghens-Fresnel principle — Fresnelsches Prinzip *n*

Fresnel['s] reflection coefficient, Fresnel['s] reflection factor, reflection factor (coefficient) <opt.> — Reflexionskoeffizient *m*, Fresnelscher Reflexionskoeffizient, Reflexionsfaktor *m* <Opt.>

Fresnel['s] reflection formulae — s. Fresnel['s] equations

Fresnel['s] region — s. near zone <ac.; el.>

Fresnel['s] relationships [for reflection and refraction] — s. Fresnel's equations

Fresnel rhomb, Fresnel['s] parallelepiped — Fresnelsches Parallelepiped *n*

Fresnel['s] theory [of light] — s. ether theory of light

Fresnel['s] wave surface — Fresnelsche Wellenfläche *f*

Fresnel['s] zone, half-period element (zone), Huyghens['] zone <opt.> — Fresnelsche Zone *f*, Fresnel-Zone *f* <Opt.>

Fresnel['s] zone — s. a. near zone <ac.; el.>

frettage, fretting corrosion, false brinelling; galling; chafing — Reib[ungs]korrosion *f*, Fraßkorrosion *f*, Reib[ungs]oxydation *f*, Passungsverschleiß *m*, Passungsrost *m*, Reibrost *m*

Freundlich['s] adsorption equation (isotherm) — s. Volmer['s] equation

Freundlich effect — Freundlich-Effekt *m*

Freundlich equation — Freundlichsche Isothermengleichung *f*

Freundlich['s] equation [for adsorption], Freundlich isotherm — s. Volmer['s] equation

Freystedt analyzer — Freystedt-Analysator *m*

friability; brittleness; breakability; fragility; shortness; crackiness; rottenness <of steel> — Sprödigkeit *f*, Brüchigkeit *f*, Zerbrechlichkeit *f*

friable — zerreiblich; morsch

Fricke dosimeter, ferrous sulfate dosimeter — Fricke-Dosimeter *n*, Ferrosulfatdosimeter *n*

frictiograph — Friktiograph *m*

friction — Reibung *f*

friction, tangential reaction — Tangentialreaktion *f*

frictional <hydr., aero.>, viscous — zäh. viskos, viskös, reibungsbehaftet <Hydr., Aero.>

frictional coefficient — s. coefficient of friction

frictional compensation, compensation of friction torque — Reibungskompensation *f*, Reibungsausgleich *m*

frictional current, friction current, current due to friction[al electricity] — Reibungsstrom *m*

frictional drag — s. surface-friction drag <aero., hydr.>

frictional electricity, friction electricity, triboelectricity — Reibungselektrizität *f*

frictional electric machine — s. friction-type electrostatic machine

frictional electrification, triboelectrification — Reibungselektrisierung *f*

frictional error, error due to friction — Reibungsfehler *m*

frictional flow — s. viscous flow

frictional force, friction force, force of friction, resistive force <mech.> — Reibungskraft *f*; Inhärenzkraft *f* <Mech.>

frictional heat, heat of friction, friction heat — Reibungswärme *f*

frictional loss, friction loss, loss due to friction — Reibungsverlust *m*

frictional motion — s. viscous flow

frictional ratio — Reibungsverhältnis *n*

frictional resistance, friction resistance <mech.> — Reibungswiderstand *m* <Mech.>

frictional resistance — s. a. skin friction

frictional term, friction term — Reibungsterm *m*, Reibungsglied *n*

frictional torque — s. friction torque

frictional work — s. work of friction

friction at rest — s. static friction

friction coefficient, coefficient of [frictional] resistance, coefficient of surface friction <aero., hydr.> — Reibungszahl *f*, Reibungswiderstandszahl *f* <Aero., Hydr.>

friction coefficient — s. a. coefficient of friction

friction cone, cone of friction — Reibungskegel *m*

friction constant, viscous damping coefficient <damped oscillations> — Reibungskonstante *f* <gedämpfte Schwingung>

friction constant — s. a. coefficient of sliding friction

friction current, frictional current, current due to friction[al electricity] — Reibungsstrom *m*

friction depth, depth of friction — Reibungstiefe *f*

friction drag — s. surface-friction drag <aero., hydr.>

friction electricity — Reibungselektrizität *f*, Triboelektrizität *f*

frictional electricity, triboelectricity

friction factor — s. coefficient of friction

friction factor — s. resistance coefficient <hydr.>

friction force, frictional (resistive) force, force of friction <mech.> — Reibungskraft *f*; Inhärenzkraft *f* <Mech.>

friction gauge — Reibungsmanometer *n*

friction head, loss of head due to friction — Reibungs[widerstands]höhe *f*, Reibungsgefälle *n*

friction heat, heat of friction, frictional heat — Reibungswärme *f*

friction layer — s. boundary layer <hydr.>

frictionless — s. non-viscous <of flow, liquid, gas>

frictionless instability, non-viscous instability, inviscid instability — reibungslose Instabilität *f*

frictionless seismograph — reibungsloser Seismograph *m*

friction loss, frictional loss, loss due to friction — Reibungsverlust *m*

friction loss coefficient, loss coefficient — Widerstandsziffer *f* des einzelnen hydraulischen Hindernisses

friction moment — s. friction torque

friction of motion — s. kinetic friction

friction of repose (rest) — s. static friction

friction of sliding, sliding friction — Gleitreibung *f*, gleitende Reibung *f*, Reibung der Bewegung

friction of the rope — s. rope friction

friction pulley, friction roller — Reibrolle *f*

friction resistance <mech.>, frictional resistance — Reibungswiderstand *m* <Mech.>

friction roller, friction pulley — Reibrolle *f*

friction stress — Reibungsspannung *f*

friction tensor — Reibungstensor *m*, Tensor *m* der Reibungsspannungen (Reibungsdrücke)

friction term, frictional term — Reibungsterm *m*, Reibungsglied *n*

friction torque, frictional torque, friction moment, moment of friction — Reibungsmoment *n*, Reibungsdrehmoment *n*

friction-type electrostatic machine, frictional electric machines	Reibungselektrisiermaschine *f*	frontal moraine, terminal moraine, end moraine	Endmoräne *f*, Stirnmoräne *f*, Moränenwall *m*
friction velocity	Schubspannungsgeschwindigkeit *f*	frontal precipitation, cyclonic precipitation	zyklonaler (frontaler) Niederschlag *m*, Zyklonenniederschlag *m*
Friedel['s] law	Friedelsches Gesetz *n*, Friedelsche Regel *f*	frontal projection	s. PA view
Friedel['s] sum rule	Friedelsche Summenregel (Beziehung) *f*	frontal resistance, drag, resistance ‹aero.›	Widerstand *m* [in Richtung der Strömung], Strömungswiderstand *m*, Rücktrieb *m* ‹Aero.›
Friedmann equation	Friedmannsche Differentialgleichung *f*		
Friedrichs['] rule	Friedrichsche Regel *f*	frontal squall, line squall	Frontbö *f*, Linienbö *f*
Friedrichs['] shallow-water expansion, shallow-water approximation	Flachwassernäherung *f*, Seichtwassernäherung *f*, Friedrichssche Seichtwasserentwicklung *f*	frontal surface	s. front ‹meteo.›
		frontal thunderstorm	s. front thunderstorm
		frontal zone	Frontalzone *f*
		front-coated mirror	s. surface-coated mirror
frigorific mixture, refrigerating (freezing) mixture, cryogen	Kältemischung *f*	front depth of field	Vordertiefe *f*
		front diaphragm, front shutter ‹phot.›; anterior shutter	Vorderblende *f*
frilling	s. stripping ‹of an emulsion, a coating›		
fringe, interference fringe, interference band	Interferenzstreifen *m*, Interferenz *f*, Interferenzerscheinung *f*	front edge	s. frontal edge
		front effect, front-layer effect	Vorderwandeffekt *m*
		front element	s. front lens
fringe counter	Interferenzzähler *m*	front focal length	s. object focal length
		front focus, object focus, first focal point	Dingbrennpunkt *m*, dingseitiger (objektseitiger, vorderer) Brennpunkt *m*
fringe effect	s. Eberhard effect ‹phot.›		
fringe howl; acoustical feedback; howling, howl	akustische Rückkopplung (Rückwirkung) *f*; Rückkopplungspfeifen *n*, Pfeifen *n*		
		frontier point, boundary point	Randpunkt *m*
fringe of constant optical thickness	s. fringe of equal thickness	front-layer effect	s. front effect
		front-layer photocell	s. front-wall photovoltaic cell
fringe of equal inclination, interference fringe of equal inclination, isoclinic fringe, equal-inclination fringe, uniform inclination fringe, ring to infinity; Haidinger['s] fringe (ring)	Haidingerscher Ring *m*, Interferenz *f* (Ring *m*, Streifen *m*, Kurve *f*) gleicher Neigung, Mascartscher (isokliner) Streifen, Planparallelitätsring *m*, Plattenring *m*, Lummer-Haidinger-Ring *m*	front lens, front element, field lens	Frontlinse *f*, Vorderlinse *f*
		front line	s. front ‹meteo.›
		front nodal point, object nodal point	Dingknotenpunkt *m*, dingseitiger (objektseitiger, vorderer) Knotenpunkt *m*
		front of the detonation wave, detonation front	Detonationswellenfront *f*, Chapman-Jouguetsche Ebene *f*
fringe of equal thickness, interference fringe of equal thickness, fringe of constant optical thickness, equal-thickness (isopachic, uniform thickness, contour, Fizeau) fringe	Interferenzstreifen *m* (Interferenz *f*, Kurve *f*) gleicher Dicke, Keilinterferenz *f*, Fizeauscher Streifen *m*, Fizeausche Interferenzkurve *f*	front of the pulse, pulse front, edge of the pulse	Impulsflanke *f*, Impulsfront *f*, Flanke *f* des Impulses
		frontogenesis, formation of fronts	Frontogenese *f*, Frontenbildung *f*
		frontolysis, disintegration of front	Frontolyse *f*, Frontenauflösung *f*, Auflösung *f* der Front
fringe of superposition	Überlagerungsstreifen *m*		
fringe pattern	Streifenbild *n*, Interferenzstreifenbild *n*	front passage, passage of front	Frontdurchgang *m*, Durchgang *m* der Front, Frontpassage *f*
fringe radiation, side-lobe radiation	Zusatzstrahlung *f*	front principal plane, object principal plane	Dinghauptebene *f*, dingseitige (objektseitige, vordere) Hauptebene *f*
fringe region, exosphere, spray region	Exosphäre *f*, äußere Atmosphäre *f*		
		front principal point, object principal point	Dinghauptpunkt *m*, dingseitiger (objektseitiger, vorderer) Hauptpunkt *m*
fringe structure	Fransenstruktur *f*		
fringing field, edge field, marginal field, margin of the field	Randfeld *n*		
		front projection, frontside projection	Aufprojektion *f*
frit; filter plate	Filterplatte *f*; Fritte *f*	front shock	s. head wave
		front shutter, front diaphragm ‹phot.›; anterior shutter	Vorderblende *f*
fritting	Frittung *f*		
		front side of the cyclone	Zyklonenvorderseite *f*
		frontside projection, front projection	Aufprojektion *f*
frog's leg experiment [of Galvani]	Froschschenkelexperiment *n* [von Galvani], Froschschenkelversuch *m*	front sight	s. foresight
		front silver coating	s. mirror surfacing
		front-silvered mirror	s. mirror surfacing
Fröhlich['s] Hamiltonian	Fröhlichscher Hamilton-Operator *m*	front silver surfacing	s. mirror surfacing
		front slot, front wing	Vorflügel *m*
Froissart['s] theorem	Froissartscher Satz *m*, Satz von Froissart	front stagnation point	s. point of branching ‹hydr.›
		front storm, front thunderstorm	Frontgewitter *n*
fronde thermometer	s. sling thermometer		
front, front[al] line ‹meteo.›	Front *f*, Frontlinie *f*, Störungslinie *f*, Bodenfront *f* ‹Meteo.›	front-surface mirror	s. surface-coated mirror
		front thunderstorm, frontal thunderstorm, front storm	Frontgewitter *n*
front, frontal surface ‹meteo.›	Front *f*, Frontfläche *f* ‹Meteo.›		
		front time	Stirnzeit *f*
front, object[-side] ‹opt.›	dingseitig, objektseitig, gegenstandsseitig, Gegenstands-, Ding-, Objekt-, vorderer ‹Opt.›	front-to-back ratio	s. front-to-rear ratio
		front-to-rear ratio, front-to-back ratio	Vor-Rück-Verhältnis *n*, Vor-Rückwärts-Verhältnis *n*
frontal edge, front edge, leading edge ‹hydr., aero.›	Vorderkante *f*, Anströmkante *f* ‹Hydr., Aero.›		
frontal fog	Frontnebel *m*		
frontal horopter	s. horopter		
frontal line	s. front ‹meteo.›		

front velocity, velocity of wave front	Frontgeschwindigkeit f	fuel assembly	Brennstoffkassette f
front vergence, object vergence	dingseitige (objektseitige) Vergenz f	fuel calorimeter	Verbrennungskalorimeter n
front vertex object distance	s. object distance from the vertex	fuel cell, galvanic fuel cell	Brennstoffelement n, elektrochemisches (galvanisches) Brennstoffelement, Brennstoffzelle f
front-view telescope	s. Herschelian telescope	front-wall cell	s. front-wall photovoltaic cell
front-wall photovoltaic cell, front-wall cell, front-layer photocell	Vorderwandzelle f, Vorderwandphotoelement n, Vorderwandelement n	fuel channel	Brennstoffkanal m, Brennelementenkanal m, Arbeitskanal m
		fuel charge, charge ⟨of reactor⟩	Brennstoffeinsatz m, Reaktorbeschickung f, Beschickung f des Reaktors, Reaktorcharge f
front wave	Frontwelle f	fuel cycle	Brennstoffzyklus m, Brennstoffkreislauf m
front wing, front slot	Vorflügel m	fuel doubling time, doubling time, breeding doubling time	Verdopplungszeit f, Brutverdopplungszeit f, Spaltstoffverdopplungszeit f
frost	Reif m		
frost day	Frosttag m		
frosted, mat, ground	matt		
frosted glass, mottled glass, depolished glass	Mattglas n; Eisglas n	fuel element ⟨nucl.⟩	Brenn[stoff]element n ⟨Kern.⟩
frosting	Reifbildung f, Rauhreifbildung f		
frosting, mottling, mat finishing, matting ⟨of glass⟩	Mattierung f ⟨Gläser⟩	fuel element can, can, canning, cladding ⟨of reactor⟩	Brennelement[en]hülle f, Brennstoffhülle f, Hülle f des Brennelements ⟨Reaktor⟩
frost limit, limit of frost	Frostgrenze f, Frosttiefe f		
frost[-]point; frost-point temperature	Reifpunkt m, Frostpunkt m; Reifbildungstemperatur f	fuel inventory	Brennstoffinvestition f, Brennstoffeinsatz m
		fuel lifetime	Brennstofflebensdauer f ⟨in MWd/t⟩
frost weathering	Frostverwitterung f, Frostsprengung f, Spaltenfrost m	fuel plate	s. plate-type fuel element ⟨of reactor⟩
froth flotation	s. flotation	fuel reprocessing, reprocessing of irradiated fuel	Brennstoff-Wiederaufarbeitung f, Wiederaufarbeitung f des bestrahlten Kernbrennstoffs
frothiness; frothing quality; frothing power	Schaumigkeit f, Schäumigkeit f; Schaumkraft f, Schaum[bildungs]vermögen n, Schäumvermögen n		
Froude law of similarity, Froude['s] law of similitude	Froudesches Ähnlichkeitsgesetz (Modellgesetz) n, Froudesche Modellregel (Regel) f	fuel rod	Brennstoffstab m
Froude['s] number, Froude parameter, F	Froudesche Zahl f, Froudesche Kennzahl f, Froude-Zahl f, Fr	fuel utilization	Brennstoffausnutzung f
Froude pendulum, pendulum swinging on a rotating shaft	Froudesches Pendel n, Reibungspendel n	fugacity, fugitiveness	Fugazität f, Flüchtigkeit f
Frowe magnetometer	Schwingspulen-Induktionsmagnetometer n, Frowe-Magnetometer n, Magnetometer n nach Frowe	Fulcher band	Fulcher-Bande f
		fulchronograph	Fulchronograph m
		fulcrum	s. point of support ⟨of lever⟩
frozen equilibrium	eingefrorenes (gehemmtes) Gleichgewicht n	fulcrum of suspension, point of suspension, suspension point	Aufhängepunkt m
frozen-in degree of freedom	eingefrorener Freiheitsgrad m	fulgurit	Fulgurit m, Blitzröhre f
frozen-in field lines ⟨into a material⟩	eingefrorene Feldlinien fpl ⟨in ein Material⟩	fulgurometer	Fulgurometer n
		full adaptation, state of full adaptation	vollendete Adaptation f, Adaptationszustand m
frozen soil	Frostboden m	full angle	s. perigon
F-scale	s. Fahrenheit [temperature] scale	full annealing, soft annealing, spheroidizing	Weichglühen n
F² series	s. Patterson synthesis		
f-spot	s. following spot ⟨astr.⟩		
F-statistic	s. variance ratio	full circle, darkened circle	voller (dunkler, schwarzer) Kreis m
f stop, stop value	Blendenwert m	full circulation; complete cycle	Vollumlauf m, vollständiger (voller) Umlauf m
f-sum rule of Kühn-Thomas-Reiche	s. Kühn-Thomas-Reiche sum rule		
F-test	s. variance ratio test	full[-] colour content	Vollfarbenanteil m, Vollfarbengehalt m
ft value	s. comparative life		
Fubini['s] theorem	Fubinischer Satz m	full[-] colour point	Vollfarbenpunkt m
		full deflection	s. full scale deflection ⟨meas.⟩
Fuchsian [differential] equation	s. Fuchs-type [differential] equation	full development	Ausentwicklung f
Fuchs' theorem, Fuchs's theorem	Satz m von Fuchs, Fuchsscher Satz	full excursion	s. full scale deflection ⟨meas.⟩
Fuchs-type [differential] equation, Fuchsian [differential] equation, differential equation of Fuchsian type, equation of the Fuchsian type	Differentialgleichung f vom Fuchsschen Typus, Differentialgleichung f der Fuchsschen Klasse	full inhomogeneous Lorentz group	volle inhomogene Lorentz-Gruppe f
		full ionization	s. total ionization
		full line, solid curve, solid line	ausgezogene Kurve f; fette Linie f
fuel	s. nuclear reactor fuel ⟨nucl.⟩	full linear group, complete linear group	volle lineare Gruppe f
fuel	s. a. propellant		

full Lorentz group, orthochronous Lorentz group	orthochrone (volle, vollständige) Lorentz-Gruppe *f*	**functional connection**	funktionaler Zusammenhang *m*
full modulation, total modulation	Vollaussteuerung *f*	**functional derivative**	*s.* variational derivative
full orthogonal group, orthogonal group	volle (erweiterte) orthogonale Gruppe *f*	**functional determinant**, Jacobian	Funktionaldeterminante *f*, Jacobische Determinante *f*
full radiator	*s.* black body	**functional-differential equation**	Funktionaldifferentialgleichung *f*
full radiator temperature	*s.* total radiation temperature	**functional equation**, operator equation	Operatorgleichung *f*, Funktionalgleichung *f*
full scale	*s.* full scale deflection <meas.>		
full scale deflection, full scale [travel], full deflection (excursion), limiting deflection	Vollausschlag *m*, voller Ausschlag *m*, Vollauslenkung *f*; Endausschlag *m* <Meß.>	**functional generator**, input table	Funktionstrieb *m*, Funktionswandler *m*
full scale reading	*s.* infinity	**functional group**, functioning group	funktionelle Gruppe *f*; Wirkungsgruppe *f* <Bio.>
full scale travel	*s.* full scale deflection <meas.>	**functional integral**	Funktionalintegral *n*
full scale value	*s.* infinity	**functional integration**	Funktionalintegration *f*
full sphere; solid sphere	Vollkugel *f*		
full wave	Vollwelle *f*	**functional matrix**, Jacobian matrix	Funktionalmatrix *f*, Jacobische Matrix *f*
		functional operator	Funktionaloperator *m*
full-wave antenna, full-wave dipole	Ganzwellendipol *m*, Ganzwellenantenne *f*	**functional potentiometer**	Funktionspotentiometer *n*
full-wave detector	*s.* full-wave rectifier	**function-element** <math.>	Funktionselement *n* <Math.>
full-wave dipole, full-wave antenna	Ganzwellendipol *m*, Ganzwellenantenne *f*	**function generator**	Funktionsgeber *m*, Funktionsgenerator *m*, Funktionsumformer *m*
full-wave rectification	Vollweggleichrichtung *f*, Zweiweggleichrichtung *f*, Gegentaktgleichrichtung *f*, Doppelweggleichrichtung *f*	**functioning group**	*s.* functional group
		function of bounded variation	Funktion *f* beschränkter Schwankung
full-wave rectifier, full-wave detector, push-pull detector, push-pull demodulator; full-wave rectifier circuit	Vollweggleichrichter *m*, Zweiweggleichrichter *m*, Doppelweggleichrichter *m*, Gegentaktgleichrichter *m*, Gegentaktdemodulator *m*; Vollweg-Gleichrichterschaltung *f*, Zweiweg[-Gleichrichter]-schaltung *f*	**function of cylindrical wedge**	zylindrische Keilfunktion *f*
		function of formal logic, truth function	Wahrheitsfunktion *f*
		function of state, state function	Zustandsfunktion *f*
		function of strain, strain function	Verformungsfunktion *f*, Verzerrungsfunktion *f*
		function of support, support[ing] function	Stützfunktion *f*
full-wave rectifier circuit	*s.* full-wave rectifier	**function of switching**	*s.* logic[al] operation
full width at half[-] maximum, half-width [of the peak], peak width, FWHM, fwhm, half-intensity width	Halbwert[s]breite *f*, Halbbreite *f*, Peakhalbwertsbreite *f*	**function of the network**, system function	Systemfunktion *f*, Netzwerkfunktion *f*
		function of the parabolic cylinder	*s.* parabolic cylinder function
full width at [one] quarter of maximum	Viertelwert[s]breite *f*	**function of the position [of the point]**	*s.* position function
full width at [one] tenth of maximum	Zehntelwert[s]breite *f*	**function of time *t* / as a**	*s.* time-dependent
		function series, series of functions	Funktionenreihe *f*, Funktionsreihe *f*
fully developed flow	*s.* steady flow	**function space**	Funktionalraum *m*, Funktionenraum *m*, Funktionsraum *m*
fully developed turbulence	vollausgebildete (volle, voll entwickelte) Turbulenz *f*, Vollturbulenz *f*		
fully elastic, perfectly elastic	vollkommen elastisch, ideal elastisch, völlig elastisch	**function theory**, theory of functions [of a complex variable]	Funktionentheorie *f*
fully elastic torsion, perfectly elastic torsion	vollkommen (völlig) elastische Torsion *f*	**function to be integrated**	*s.* integrand
fully inelastic	*s.* perfectly inelastic	**functor**	Funktor *m*
fully intermeshed network, intermeshed network, mesh network	Maschennetz *n*, vermaschtes Netz *n*, vermaschtes Netzwerk *n*	**fundamental**	*s.* fundamental mode
		fundamental absorption, absorption in the matrix lattice, lattice absorption	Grundgitterabsorption *f*
fully plastic	*s.* perfectly plastic		
fully plastic torsion, perfectly plastic torsion	vollkommen plastische Torsion *f*, völlig plastische Torsion	**fundamental absorption edge**	*s.* lattice absorption edge
		fundamental angular frequency	*s.* natural angular frequency
fully protective tube housing	*s.* X-ray tube housing	**fundamental band**	Grundschwingungsbande *f*, Grundbande *f*
fully reducible representation	*s.* completely reducible representation	**fundamental case**, ordinary case, normal case	Normalfall *m*
fully reversed cycle	Wechsel[beanspruchungs]-lastspiel *n*		
fully-rough flow	ausgebildete Rauhigkeitsströmung (Rauhrohrströmung) *f*	**fundamental colour**	*s.* primary colour
		fundamental dimension	*s.* fundamental quantity
		fundamental doublet	Grunddublett *n*
fully soft, perfectly soft	vollkommen weich, völlig weich, ideal weich	**fundamental ensemble**	Grundgesamtheit *f*
		fundamental equation, principal equation, basic equation	Grundgleichung *f* <Phys.>; Fundamentalgleichung *f*, charakteristische Gleichung *f* <Math.>
fumarole	Fumarole *f*		
fuming acid	rauchende Säure *f*		
functional analysis	Funktionalanalysis *f*	**fundamental equation of hydrodynamics**	*s.* equation of hydrodynamics
functional calculus	*s.* predicate calculus	**fundamental equation of hydrostatics**	*s.* equation of hydrostatics
functional circuit	Funktionsschaltung *f*		

fundamental equation of non-equilibrium thermodynamics Grundgleichung f der Thermodynamik irreduzibler Prozesse, Gleichung f der Entropieerzeugung

fundamental equation of rocket motion, Ziolkovsky['s] formula Grundgleichung f der Raketenbewegung, Ziolkowskische Gleichung f, Ziolkowski-Formel f, Ziolkowski-Gleichung f

fundamental field particle, field quantum Feldquant n

fundamental form, metric form, ground form <math.> Grundform f, Fundamentalform f; Urform f <Math.>

fundamental frequency, basic (primary) frequency Grundfrequenz f, Fundamentalfrequenz f

fundamental frequency, normal frequency <of coupled systems> Normalfrequenz f, Fundamentalfrequenz f, Eigenfrequenz f, normale Frequenz f, Hauptfrequenz f <gekoppelte Systeme>

fundamental frequency s. a. natural frequency
fundamental harmonic s. fundamental mode
fundamental integral Grundintegral n, Extremalintegral n

fundamental interval, separation of fundamental points Fundamentalabstand m

fundamental lattice, [matrix] lattice, host [crystal] lattice Grundgitter n, Wirtsgitte n

fundamental lattice absorption edge s. lattice absorption edge

fundamental law of algebra, fundamental theorem of algebra Fundamentalsatz m der Algebra, Hauptsatz m der Algebra

fundamental law of crystallography s. law of rational indices

fundamental level, normal (ground) level Grundniveau n

fundamental metric tensor, fundamental tensor, metric tensor [metrischer] Fundamentaltensor m, metrischer Tensor m, Maßtensor m

fundamental mode, fundamental, fundamental harmonic, fundamental oscillation, fundamental vibration, first harmonic Grundschwingung f, Fundamentalschwingung f, Fundamentale f

fundamental oscillation, normal mode [of vibration] <of coupled systems> Normalschwingung f, Eigenschwingung f, Fundamentalschwingung f, Hauptschwingung f <gekoppelter Systeme>

fundamental oscillation s. a. fundamental mode
fundamental particle, elementary particle Elementarteilchen n
fundamental particles of Sakata s. Sakata particles
fundamental period s. primitive period
fundamental periodic parallelogram, primitive period parallelogram Periodenparallelogramm n, Fundamentalparallelogramm n, Elementarparallelogramm n

fundamental point, basic point <math.> Grundpunkt m

fundamental point s. a. fixed point [of temperature scale]
fundamental polygon Fundamentalpolygon n
fundamental polyhedron Fundamentalpolyeder n
fundamental quantity, primary quantity, basic quantity; fundamental dimension Grundgröße[nart] f, Basisgröße[nart] f, Ausgangsgröße[nart] f, Fundamentalgröße[nart] f, Grunddimension f

fundamental research, "basic research" Grundlagenforschung f

fundamental resonance Grundresonanz f

fundamental rotation[al] band Grundrotationsbande f, Rotationsgrundbande f

fundamental sequence s. Cauchy sequence

fundamental series, series of fundamental stars, Küstner series <astr.> Fundamentalreihe f, Fundamentalsternreihe f, Küstnersche Reihe f <Astr.>

fundamental series, Bergmann series <spectr.> Bergmann-Serie f, Fundamentalserie f <Spektr.>

fundamental set, fundamental system <math.> Fundamentalsystem n [von Lösungen], kanonisches Fundamentalsystem, Hauptsystem n [von Lösungen], Integralbasis f

fundamental solution, principal solution Grundlösung f, Fundamentallösung f, Fundamentalintegral n

fundamental sound, fundamental tone Grundton m

fundamental standard s. primary standard
fundamental star Fundamentalstern m
fundamental state s. ground state <nucl.>
fundamental system, system of fundamental stars <astr.> Fundamentalsystem n <Astr.>

fundamental system s. a. fundamental set <math.>

fundamental tensor, metric tensor, fundamental metric tensor Fundamentaltensor m, metrischer Fundamentaltensor, metrischer Tensor m, Maßtensor m

fundamental term, ground (normal) term, term of ground state Grundterm m, Term m des Grundzustandes

fundamental theorem <rel.> s. centre of mass theorem

fundamental theorem of algebra, fundamental law of algebra Fundamentalsatz m der Algebra, Hauptsatz m der Algebra

fundamental tone, fundamental sound, primary tone Grundton m

fundamental unit, basic (primary, elementary) unit Grundeinheit f, Basiseinheit f, Ausgangseinheit f

fundamental vibration s. fundamental mode
fundamental vibrational band Grundschwingungsbande f, Schwingungsgrundbande f

fundamental wave Grundwelle f
fundamental wavelength Grundwellenlänge f

funicular curve (line) s. catenary
funicular polygon, link polygon, string polygon Seilpolygon n, Seileck n

funnel, pipe [of ingot] <met.> trichterförmiger Lunker (Schwindungslunker) m

funnel antenna s. horn <el.>
funnel cloud Trombenschlauch m, Trombentrichter m, [trichterartiger] Schlauch m, Schlauchwolke f, schlauchförmige (trichterförmige) Wolke f, Trichterwolke f

funnel diaphragm, funnel-type diaphragm Einhängeblende f, Trichterblende f

funnel effect Trichtereffekt m
funnelling Trichterbildung f
funnel of the vortex (whirl) Wirbeltrichter m
funnel-shaped (funnel-type) antenna s. horn <el.>
funnel-type diaphragm, funnel diaphragm Einhängeblende f, Trichterblende f

funnel[-type] viscometer Trichterviskosimeter n

furcation s. branching
furious sea rollende See f, hochgehende See; Rollen n <See>

furrow, rill, rille, groove, cleft <on the Moon's surface> Rille f <auf der Mondoberfläche>

Furry process Furryscher Prozeß m
Furry theorem Satz m (Theorem n) von Furry, Furrysches Theorem <für Feynman-Graphen>

furstenau, F
further decay, further disintegration Fürstenau n, F
Weiterzerfall m

fuse <of glass> Schmelze f <Glas>

fused electrolyte	Schmelz[fluß]elektrolyt m; Schmelzbad n	future light cone, forward cone	Vorwärtskegel m, Vorkegel m
fused electrolyte cell	Hochtemperaturelement n	fuzziness	s. flicker
fused junction	Rekristallisationsübergang m, Rekristallisationsschicht f	f-value, oscillator strength	Oszillator[en]stärke f, f-Wert m

G

fused metal, liquid metal, molten metal, melt of metal	Metallschmelze f, Flüssigmetall n, geschmolzenes Metall n
fused-on	zugeschmolzen
fused ring compound, condensed ring compound	kondensiertes Ringsystem n
fused salt, molten salt, liquid salt	Salzschmelze f
fusibility, meltability, meltableness	Schmelzbarkeit f; Schmelzflüssigkeit f
fusible cone	s. pyrometric cone
fusing <opt.>, fusion	Fusion f, Verschmelzung f <Opt.>
fusing into ..., fusion into ...	Einschmelzung f, Verschmelzung f in ...; reine Einschmelzung
fusing point	s. melting point
fusion, blending	Verschmelzung f
fusion, fusing <opt.>	Fusion f, Verschmelzung f <Opt.>
fusion, thermonuclear	thermonuklear, Fusions-, Kernfusions-, Verschmelzungs-
fusion	s. a. alloying
fusion	s. a. melting
fusion	s. a. nuclear fusion <nucl.>
fusionable material	thermonuklearer Brennstoff m, Fusionsstoff m
fusion cone	s. pyrometric cone
fusion curve, melting [pressure] curve, solidification curve; ice line	Schmelzkurve f
fusion diagram	Schmelzdiagramm n
fusion electrolysis	s. electrolysis in the dry way
fusion energy, nuclear fusion energy; thermonuclear energy	Fusionsenergie f, Kernverschmelzungsenergie f, Kernfusionsenergie f, Verschmelzungsenergie f; thermonukleare Energie f (Fusionsenergie)
fusion enthalpy	s. heat of fusion
fusion frequency	s. critical frequency of flicker
fusion heat	s. heat of fusion
fusion hypothesis	Verschmelzungshypothese f
fusion limit, limit of fusion	Fusionsgrenze f, Doppelbildschwelle f
fusion of beams	Strahlenvereinigung f
fusion phenomenon, phenomenon of fusion	Verschmelzungsphänomen n
fusion process	s. fusion reaction
fusion range	s. melting range
fusion reaction, fusion process	Fusionsreaktion f, Kernverschmelzungsreaktion f, Kernfusionsreaktion f, Verschmelzungsreaktion f, Fusionsprozeß m, Kernfusionsprozeß m, Kernverschmelzungsprozeß m, Verschmelzungsprozeß m
fusion reactor, nuclear fusion reactor; thermonuclear reactor	Fusionsreaktor m, Kernfusionsreaktor m; thermonuklearer Reaktor m
fusion temperature, melting point, melting temperature, fusing point, m.p., f.p.	Schmelzpunkt m, Schmelz[punkt]temperatur f, Fließpunkt m, Schmp., Fp., F.; Schmelzgrenze f
fusion temperature, nuclear fusion temperature <nucl.>	Fusionstemperatur f, Kernverschmelzungstemperatur f, Kernfusionstemperatur f, Verschmelzungstemperatur f <Kern.>
fusion welding, welding together	Verschweißen n <z. B. beim Verschleiß>
fusion zone, melting zone	Schmelzzone f

gabble	Schnattern n
Gabor method, Gabor technique, microscopy by reconstructed wave fronts	Gabor-Verfahren n, Mikroskopie f mittels rekonstruierter Wellenfronten
Gaede['s] mercury pump	Gaedesche Quecksilberpumpe f, Quecksilberpumpe nach Gaede
Gaede['s] molecular pump, molecular air (drag) pump	Molekularluftpumpe f [nach Gaede], Gaedesche Molekularluftpumpe
Gaede['s] molvacuummeter	Gaedesches Molvakuummeter n
Gaede['s] vacuscope	Gaedesches Vakuskop n
gage <US>	s. gauge
gain, amplifier (available) gain, gain ration, amplification (gain, intensifying, multiplication, speed, voltage) factor <el.>	Verstärkungsfaktor m, Verstärkung f, Gewinn m <El.>
gain, saving	Einsparung f; Ersparnis f
gain	s. a. increase
gain area, gain-bandwidth product	Verstärkungsfläche f
gain characteristic, amplifier characteristic	Verstärkerkennlinie f, Verstärkercharakteristik f, Verstärkerkurve f, Verstärkungsverlauf m
gain cross-over frequency, gain-cross-over frequency	s. cut-off frequency <control>
gain effect; enhancement effect	Verstärkerwirkung f, Verstärkungswirkung f, Verstärkereffekt m, Verstärkungseffekt m
gain factor	s. gain
gain factor of photoconductivity	Gewinnfaktor m der Photoleitfähigkeit
gain instability factor <for pumping>	Verstärkerinstabilitätsfaktor m
gain loss	Verstärkungsabfall m
gain margin, amplitude margin	Amplitudenrand m, Amplitudenabstand m
gain of antenna	s. aerial gain
gain of heat, heat gain; economy of heat, heat economy	Wärmegewinn m; Wärmeersparnis f
gain parameter	Gewinnparameter m
gain-phase characteristic	Amplituden-Phasen-Charakteristik f, Hodograph m des Frequenzgangs
gain point	Verstärkungspunkt m
gain ratio	s. gain
gal <= 1 cm/s²	Gal n, Galilei n, gal <= 1 cm/s²
galactic centre	galaktisches Zentrum n, Zentrum des Milchstraßensystems, Milchstraßenzentrum n
galactic cluster, galactic star cluster	galaktischer Haufen m, galaktischer Sternhaufen m
galactic co-ordinates; galactic system [of co-ordinates]	galaktisches System (Koordinatensystem) n; Koordinaten fpl im galaktischen System, galaktische Koordinaten
galactic corona, galactic halo	galaktische Korona f, Koronakomponente f der Radiofrequenzstrahlung, [galaktischer] Halo m
galactic disk	galaktische Scheibe f
galactic ground noise, galactic radio-frequency radiation	galaktische Radiofrequenzstrahlung f, galaktisches Rauschen n
galactic halo	s. galactic corona
galactic nuclear region, galactic nucleus, nucleus of the galaxy	galaktischer Kern m, Kern [des Milchstraßensystems], Milchstraßenkern m

galactic parallactic angle	galaktische Parallaxe f	galling; scuffing; seizure, seizing	adhäsiver Verschleiß m; örtliche Verschweißung f; Kommabildung f; Fressen n; Festfressen n
galactic pericentre, pericentre <astr.>	Perigalaktikum n <Astr.>		
galactic plane	galaktische Ebene f, Milchstraßenebene f, Symmetrieebene f des Milchstraßensystems	galling	s. a. fretting corrosion
		Galton['s] apparatus (board), Galtonian board; pinball board	Galtonsches Brett n, Galton-Brett n
galactic pole	galaktischer Pol m	Galton['s] whistle	Galtonsche Pfeife f, Galton-Pfeife f, Grenzpfeife f
galactic radio-frequency radiation, galactic ground noise	galaktische Radiofrequenzstrahlung f, galaktisches Rauschen n	galvanic cell	s. voltaic cell
		galvanic corrosion, electrochemical (electrolytic) corrosion	galvanische (elektrolytische, elektrochemische) Korrosion f
galactic rotation	galaktische Rotation f, Milchstraßenrotation f, Rotation f des Milchstraßensystems, Rotation der Milchstraße	galvanic coupling	s. direct coupling
		galvanic current	galvanischer Strom m
		galvanic electromotive series, galvanic series	galvanische Spannungsreihe f
galactic star cluster	s. galactic cluster	galvanic fuel cell	s. fuel cell
galactic structure	Milchstraßenstruktur f, galaktische Struktur f, Struktur des Milchstraßensystems	galvanic half-cell, half-cell	Halbzelle f, Halbelement n, galvanisches Halbelement, elektrochemische Elektrode f
galactic system, stellar system, galaxy, system of stars, island universe	Sternsystem n, Galaxie f, Galaxis f <pl.: Galaxien>	galvanic mean	s. direct-current mean
		galvanic polarization	s. electrolytic polarization
		galvanic series, galvanic electromotive series	galvanische Spannungsreihe f
galactic system [of co-ordinates]	s. galactic co-ordinates	galvanic stimulation, galvanism, galvanization	Galvanisation f, galvanische Reizung f
galactic window	galaktisches Fenster n		
		galvanic theodolite	galvanischer Theodolit m
		Galvani potential, inner electrical potential	Galvani-Potential n, Galvani-Spannung f, galvanische Spannung f, inneres elektrisches Potential n
gqlaxy, galactic system, stellar system, system of stars, island universe	Sternsystem n, Galaxie f, Galaxis f <pl.: Galaxien>		
Galaxy, Milky Way System, Milky Way	Milchstraßensystem n, Galaxis f, Milchstraße f	galvanism	Galvanismus m
		galvanism, galvanization	s. a. galvanic stimulation
Galaxy brightness	galaktische Helligkeit f	galvanocautery	Galvanokaustik f
galaxy of galaxies	s. metagalaxy	galvanoluminescence	Galvanolumineszenz f
gale, fresh gale <of Beaufort No. 8>	stürmischer Wind m <Stärke 8>	galvanomagnetic effect, magnetoelectric effect	galvanomagnetischer (magnetoelektrischer) Effekt m
gale, strong gale <of Beaufort No. 9>	Sturm m <Stärke 9>	galvanomagnetic hysteresis	galvanomagnetische Hysteresis f
gale, whole gale <of Beaufort No. 10>	schwerer Sturm m <Stärke 10>		
Galerkin['s] method	Galerkinsche Methode f	galvanomagnetic semiconductor device, Hall effect device, Hall device	Hall-Gerät n, Hall-Effekt-Gerät n, galvanomagnetisches Halbleitergerät n
Galilean co-ordinate system	s. Galilean frame of reference		
Galilean frame of reference, Galilean system of reference (co-ordinates), Galilean reference (co-ordinate) system	Galileisches Bezugssystem (Koordinatensystem) n, Inertialsystem n <in der klassischen Mechanik>	galvanometer constant, static galvanometer constant	Galvanometerkonstante f, statischer Reduktionsfaktor m, Stromkonstante f
		galvanometer constant	s. ballistic constant
		galvanometer of the mechanical oscillograph, loop galvanometer of the mechanical oscillograph	Schleifenschwinger m, Schleifenschwingergalvanometer n, Schwinger m des Schleifenoszillographen
Galilean group	Galilei-Gruppe f		
Galilean invariance	Galilei-Invarianz f, Galileische Invarianz f	galvanometer with moving magnet, needle (moving-magnet) galvanometer	Nadelgalvanometer n, Drehmagnetgalvanometer n
Galilean metric	Galileische Metrik f		
Galilean number	s. Galileo['s] number	galvanometer with optical pointer, lightspot galvanometer, luminous pointer galvanometer	Lichtmarkengalvanometer n, Lichtzeigergalvanometer n, Lichtpunktgalvanometer n
Galilean observer	Galileischer Beobachter m		
Galilean principle of relativity, classical principle of relativity	Galileisches (Newtonsches, klassisches) Relativitätsprinzip n, Galileis Relativitätsprinzip (Prinzip n der Relativität)		
		galvanonasty, electronasty	Elektronastie f, Galvanonastie f
		galvanostatic	galvanostatisch
Galilean reference system	s. Galilean frame of reference	galvanotaxis	Galvanotaxis f
		galvanotropism, electrotropism	Elektrotropismus m, Galvanotropismus m
Galilean space-time	Galileisches Raum-Zeit-Kontinuum n, Galileische Raumzeit f	games theorie	s. theory of games
		gamma, $\gamma = 1\,\mu g$	Gamma n, $\gamma = 1\,\mu g$
Galilean system of co-ordinates (reference)	s. Galilean frame of reference	gamma, gamma unit, γ <= 1 nT> <geo.>	Kleingauß n, γ <= 1 nT> <Geo.>
Galilean telescope, Galileo['s] telescope	Galileisches (holländisches) Fernrohr n, Galilei-Fernrohr n	gamma, gamma value, contrast factor, contrast, photographic contrast, development factor <quantity> <phot.>	Gamma-Wert m, γ-Wert m, photographischer Kontrast m, Kontrastfaktor m, Entwicklungsfaktor m, Steilheit f, mittlerer Gradient m <Größe> <Phot.>
Galilean transformation	Galilei-Transformation f		
Galileo['s] law of inertia	Galileisches Trägheitsgesetz n		
Galileo['s] number, Galilean number, Ga	Galilei-Zahl f, Galileische Kennzahl f, Ga	gamma	s. a. gamma quantum
		gamma	s. a. ratio of the specific heats
Galitzin pendulum, long period vertical seismometer	Galitzin-Pendel n	gamma	$= 10^{-5}$ Oe $= 10^{-2}/4\Pi$ A/m
		gamma absorption thickness gauge	s. gamma-ray absorption thickness gauge

gamma-active

gamma-active, gamma-radioactive	gamma-aktiv	gamma-ray activity, gamma activity, gamma radioactivity	Gamma-Aktivität f
gamma activity, gamma-ray activity, gamma radioactivity	Gamma-Aktivität f	gamma-ray astronomy	Gamma-Astronomie f, Gamma-Strahlen-Astronomie f
gamma backscattering thickness gauge	s. gamma-ray backscattering thickness gauge	gamma-ray autoradiography, gamma-ray radioautography	Gamma-Autoradiographie f
gamma-camera	s. scintillation camera		
gamma cascade, gamma-ray cascade	Gamma-Kaskade f, Gamma-Gamma-Kaskade f	gamma-ray background; background gamma radiation	Gamma-Untergrund m, Gamma-Strahlenuntergrund m; Untergrund-Gamma-Strahlung f; Gamma-Hintergrund m
gamma constant	s. specific gamma-ray constant		
gamma counter	s. gamma-ray counter	gamma-ray backscattering; gamma-ray reflection	Gamma-Rückstreuung f; Gamma-Reflexion f
gamma decay, gamma disintegration	Gamma-Zerfall m, Gamma-Umwandlung f		
gamma dose, gamma-ray dose	Gamma-Strahl[en]dosis f, Gamma-Dosis f	gamma-ray backscattering gauge	Gamma-Rückstreumeßgerät n
gamma dose meter, gamma-ray dosimeter	Gamma-Dosimeter n, Gamma-Strahldosimeter n		
		gamma-ray backscattering gauging, gamma-ray backscattering thickness gauging	Gamma-Rückstreu-Dickenmessung f, Gamma-Reflexionsdickenmessung f
gamma emitter, gamma-ray emitter, gamma radiator	Gamma-Strahler m		
gamma-escape, gamma-ray emission	Gamma-Emission f, Gamma-Strahlenemission f, Gamma-Strahlung f	gamma-ray backscattering thickness gauge, gamma backscattering thickness gauge	Gamma-Rückstreu-Dickenmesser m, Gamma-Reflexionsdickenmesser m
gamma-function, gamma function, factorial function, Eulerian integral of the second kind, Euler['s] second integral, Γ-function	Gammafunktion f, Fakultätenfunktion f, Eulersches Integral n zweiter Art (Gattung), Euler-Integral n zweiter (2.) Art, vollständige Gammafunktion f, Γ-Funktion f	gamma-ray backscattering thickness gauging, gamma-ray backscattering gauging	Gamma-Rückstreu-Dickenmessung f, Gamma-Reflexionsdickenmessung f
		gamma-ray camera	s. scintillation camera
		gamma-ray cascade, gamma cascade	Gamma-Kaskade f, Gamma-Gamma-Kaskade f
gammagram, gamma-radiogram	Gamma-Radiogramm n, Gammagramm n, Gamma-Radiographie f	gamma-ray counter, gamma counter	Gamma-Zählrohr n; Gamma-Zähler m
gammagraphy, radiography by gamma-rays, gamma-[ray]radiography	Gammagraphie f, Gamma-Radiographie f		
		gamma-ray deexcitation	Gamma-Deexzitation f, Gamma-Abregung f
gamma heating	Gamma-Aufheizung f, Erwärmung f durch Gamma-Strahlung	gamma-ray detector	Gamma-Detektor m, Detektor m für Gamma-Strahlung
gamma-irradiation, gamma-ray irradiation (exposure)	Gamma-Bestrahlung f	gamma-ray dose, gamma dose	Gamma-Strahl[en]dosis f, Gamma-Dosis f
		gamma-ray dose-rate constant	s. specific gamma-ray constant
gamma lifetime	Gamma-Lebensdauer f	gamma-ray dosimeter, gamma dose meter	Gamma-Dosimeter n, Gamma-Strahldosimeter n
gamma matrix	s. Dirac spin matrix		
gamma-meter, gamma radiation meter	Gamma-Strahlungsmesser m, Gammameter n	gamma-ray dosimetry	Gamma-Dosimetrie f, Gamma-Strahldosimetrie f
gammametry	Gammametrie f		
gamma network	s. general Γ network	gamma-ray electroscope	Gamma-Strahlenelektroskop n
gamma permanence rule, Γ permanence rule, Landé['s] Γ-permanence rule	Gamma-Permanenzregel f, Γ-Permanenzregel f, Permanenzregel f für die Γ-Werte		
		gamma-ray emission	s. gamma-escape
		gamma-ray emitter, gamma emitter, gamma radiator	Gamma-Strahler m
gamma photon, gamma quantum, gamma-ray quantum, gamma-ray [photon], gamma <nucl.>	Gamma-Quant n, Gamma-Photon n, Gamma-Strahl m, Gamma n <Kern.>		
		gamma-ray energy	Gamma-Energie f
gamma radiation	s. gamma rays	gamma-ray exposure	s. gamma-irradiation
gamma radiation meter, gamma meter	Gamma-Strahlungsmesser m, Gammameter n	gamma-ray induced nuclear reaction	s. photodisintegration
gamma radiator, gamma emitter, gamma-ray emitter	Gamma-Strahler m	gamma-ray irradiation	s. gamma-irradiation
		gamma-ray material testing, gamma-ray materiology	s. gamma-radiographic testing
gamma-radioactive, gamma-active	gamma-aktiv		
gamma radioactivity, gamma[-ray] activity	Gamma-Aktivität f	gamma-ray photon (quantum), gamma photon (quantum), gamma[-ray] <nucl.>	Gamma-Quant n, Gamma-Photon n, Gamma-Strahl m, Gamma n <Kern.>
gamma-radiogram	s. gammagram		
gamma-radiographic testing, gamma-ray material testing, gamma-ray materiology	Gamma-Werkstoffprüfung f, [zerstörungsfreie] Werkstoffprüfung f mittels Gamma-Strahlung, Gamma-Defektoskopie f, Gamma-Prüfung f	gamma-ray radioautography	s. gamma-ray autoradiography
		gamma-ray radiography	s. gammagraphy
		gamma-ray reflection; gamma-ray backscattering	Gamma-Rückstreuung f; Gamma-Reflexion f
		gamma-ray resonance, gamma resonance	Resonanz f mit Gamma-Emission, Gamma-Resonanz f
gamma-radiography	s. gammagraphy		
gamma-ray	s. gamma quantum <nucl.>	gamma-ray resonance spectroscopy	s. Mößbauer spectrometry
gamma-ray absorption thickness gauge, gamma absorption thickness gauge	Gamma-Absorptionsdickenmesser m	gamma rays, gamma radiation, radioactive gamma-rays	Gamma-Strahlung f, radioaktive Gamma-Strahlung, Gamma-Strahlen mpl

gamma-ray scintillation spectrometer, scintillation gamma-ray spectrometer	Szintillations-Gamma-Spektrometer n	gap; space <between>; play; clearance; allowance; backlash; slackness <techn.>	Spiel n; Zwischenraum m; Spalt m <Techn.>
gamma-ray shield, gamma-shield	Abschirmung f gegen Gamma-Strahlung, Gamma-Abschirmung f, Gamma-Strahlenschutz m, Gamma-Schild m	gap gap gap admittance, circuit gap admittance gap between electrodes gap between poles, pole gap	s. a. spark gap s. a. magnet gap <magn.> Spaltleitwert m des Kreises s. electrode separation Pollücke f
gamma-ray source, gamma source	Gamma-Quelle f, Gamma-Strahlungsquelle f	gap counting gap density	Lückenzählung f Lückendichte f
gamma-ray spectrometer, gamma-spectrometer	Gamma-Spektrometer n, Gamma-Strahlspektrometer n		
gamma-ray spectroscopy, gamma spectroscopy	Gamma-Spektroskopie f	gap field	Schlitzfeld n, Spaltfeld n
gamma-ray spectrum, gamma spectrum	Gamma-Spektrum n, Gamma-Strahlenspektrum n	gaping fault, disjunctive fault (dislocation), open fault <geo.>	Zerrung f, disjunktive Dislokation f, Disjunktivstörung f <Geo.>
gamma resonance gamma-shield gamma source	s. gamma-ray resonance s. gamma-ray shield s. gamma-ray source	gap leakage	Spaltstreuung f
gamma-space, gas-space, γ-space, Γ-space	Gamma-Raum m, Gasraum m, Gibbsscher Phasenraum m, γ-Raum m, Γ-Raum m	gap length, width (length) of air gap, [air-]gap width	Polschuhabstand m, Luftspaltlänge f, Luftspaltbreite f
gamma-spectrometer, gamma-ray spectrometer	Gamma-Spektrometer n, Gamma-Strahlspektrometer n	gap length <nucl.> gapped ring gap width, width (length) of air gap, air-gap width, gap length	Lückenlänge f <Kern.> s. split ring Polschuhabstand m, Luftspaltlänge f, Luftspaltbreite f
gamma spectroscopy, gamma-ray spectroscopy	Gamma-Spektroskopie f	gap width	s. a. width of the forbidden gap
gamma spectrum, gamma-ray spectrum	Gamma-Spektrum n, Gamma-Strahlenspektrum n	Garabedian['s] iteration method	Garabediansche Iterationsmethode f
gamma sum rule [due to Goudsmit], Goudsmit gamma sum rule, Goudsmit['s] Γ sum rule	Goudsmitscher Gamma-Summensatz m, Gamma-Summensatz [von Goudsmit], Γ-Summensatz m, Summensatz m (Summenregel f) für die Γ-Werte	Gardon radiometer Garton effect gas absorption, gas clean-up gas adsorption chromatography gas amplification, gas multiplication	Gardon-Radiometer n Garton-Effekt m Gasaufzehrung f; Gasabsorption f s. gas-solid chromatography Gasverstärkung f
gamma unit gamma value Gammel-Thaler force	s. gamma s. gamma <quantity> Gammel-Thaler-Kraft f		
		gas amplification factor	Gasverstärkungsfaktor m, Gasverstärkung f
Gammel-Thaler potential	Gammel-Thaler-Potential n, Potential n der Gammel-Thaler-Kräfte	gas analysis; gasometry gas-and-dust nebula	Gasanalyse f Gas- und Staubnebel m, gas-staub-förmiger Nebel m, Gas-Staub-Nebel m, Emissions-Reflexions-Nebel m
Gamow barrier, Gamow wall	Gamow-Berg m, Gamow-Wall m, Gamow-Potentialwall m		
Gamow factor Gamow-Teller selection rule	s. penetration probability Gamow-Teller-Auswahlregel f, Gamow-Tellersche Auswahlregel f	gas balance gas ballast gas ballast method	Gaswaage f Gasballast m Gasballastverfahren n [von Gaede]
Gamow-Teller transition Gamow wall, Gamow barrier	Gamow-Teller-Übergang m Gamow-Berg m, Gamow-Wall m, Gamow-Potentialwall m	gas ballast pump, surplus gas pump gas bottle gas bubble chamber	Gasballastpumpe f s. washing bottle Gasblasenkammer f
gamut, scale, tone scale, musical scale <ac.>	Tonleiter f, Tonskala f, Tonreihe f <Ak.>		
ganged potentiometer Gantmakher-Kaner oscillation, GKO	s. dual potentiometer Gantmakher-Kaner-Schwingung f	gas calorimeter gas calorimetry gas cell, gas couple, gaseous couple	Gaskalorimeter n Gaskalorimetrie f Gaskette f, Gaselement n
gap; interspace; interstice, interstitial space; interval; opening; hole; distance	Lücke f; Zwischenraum m; Strecke f; Abstand m; Intervall n	gas centrifuge gas chromatogram gas-chromatographic, by gas chromatography	Gaszentrifuge f Gaschromatogramm n gaschromatographisch
gap; space; slit; slot	Spalt m; Schlitz m	gaschromathermography	s. thermo gas chromatography
gap; orifice; opening; hole; port[hole]	Öffnung f; Loch n; Kanalmündung f, Kanalöffnung f, Kanal m; Durchführung f	gas chromatography, GC gas chromatography / by, gas-chromatographic	Gaschromatographie f, GC gaschromatographisch
gap, band gap, energy gap, forbidden gap, forbidden energy band, forbidden electron energy band, forbidden band <in band model>	verbotene Zone f, verbotenes Energieband (Band) n, verbotener Energiebereich m, Energielücke f, Lücke f, Energieabstand m <Bändermodell>	gas clean-up, gas absorption gas constant, gas constant per mole, universal gas constant, molar gas constant, universal gas constant per mole	Gasaufzehrung f; Gasabsorption f Gaskonstante f, universelle Gaskonstante, ideale Gaskonstante, molare Gaskonstante
gap <of commensurability> <astr.> gap, lacuna <math.>	Kommensurabilitätslücke f, Lücke f <Astr.> Lücke f <Math.>		
		gas constant per gramme	s. specific gas constant

gas

gas counter, gaseous counter	Gaszählrohr n
gas couple	s. gas cell
gas current, ion current <in electron tubes>	Gasstrom m, Gasionenstrom m, Ionenstrom m <Röhren>
gas density	s. vapour density
gas-density balance	Gasdichtewaage f [nach Martin]
gas detector, gas indicator	Gasspürgerät n
gas diffusion, gaseous diffusion, effusion	Gasdiffusion f
gas discharge	s. electric discharge
gas discharge chamber, discharge chamber	Gasentladungskammer f, Entladungskammer f
gas-discharge electron source	Gasentladungs-Elektronenquelle f
gas-discharge gap, gas gap	Gasentladungsstrecke f, Gasstrecke f
gas-discharge gauge, gas-discharge manometer	Gasentladungsmanometer n
gas discharge plasma, discharge plasma, plasma of gaseous discharge	Gasentladungsplasma n, Entladungsplasma n
gas discharge track chamber (detector), track delineating chamber	Gasspur[en]kammer f, Gasentladungs-Spurdetektor m
gas dispersion	Gasdispersion f
gas[-]dynamical	gasdynamisch
gas-dynamic equation	gasdynamische Gleichung f
gas dynamics	Gasdynamik f
gas economy	Gasökonomie f
gaseity, gas state, gaseous state, gaseousness	gasförmiger Zustand m, Gaszustand m
gas electrode	Gaselektrode f
gaseous cavitation	unechte Kavitation f, Gaskavitation f
gaseous counter	s. gas counter
gaseous couple, oxyhydrogen couple, hydrogen-oxygen cell	Knallgaskette f, Knallgaselement n, Wasserstoff-Sauerstoff-Kette f, Gaselement n, Gaskette f
gaseous couple	s. a. gas cell
gaseous diffusion, gas diffusion, effusion	Gasdiffusion f
gaseous diffusion cascade, [isotope] separation cascade, cascade [of separating units], Hertz['] cascade	Trennkaskade f [nach G. Hertz], Hertzsche Trennkaskade, Diffusions[trenn]kaskade f, Gasdiffusions[trenn]kaskade f, Kaskade f
gaseous discharge	s. electric discharge
gaseous discharge counter [tube], discharge counter	Gasentladungszählrohr n
gaseous discharge tube	Gasentladungsrohr n, Gasentladungsröhre f
gaseous envelope	Gashülle f, gasförmige Hülle f
gaseous equilibrium, gas equilibrium	Gasgleichgewicht n
gaseous film	s. evaporated film
gaseous fluid <phys.>, gas medium	gasförmiges Medium n <Phys.>
gaseous inclusion, gas pocket	Gasblase f, Gaseinschluß m
gaseous ionization; gas ionization, electromerism	Gasionisation f, Gasionisierung f
gaseous laser, gas laser, gaseous-state laser	Gaslaser m
gaseous medium, medium, atmosphere <chem.>	Atmosphäre f, gasförmiges Milieu n
gaseous nebula, emission nebula, emission nebulosity	Gasnebel m, Emissionsnebel m, Emissionsgasnebel m
gaseousness	s. gas state
gaseous phase radiochromatography	Radiogaschromatographie f, Gasradiochromatographie f
gaseous radiospectrometer	Radiofrequenzgasspektrometer n
gaseous ring	Gasring m
gaseous state	s. gas state
gaseous-state laser	s. gas laser
gaseous train	Gasschweif m
gas equilibrium	s. gaseous equilibrium
gaser <gamma radiation amplification by stimulated emission of radiation>	Gaser m, Gamma-Strahlenmaser m
gas evolution, evolution (generation, development) of gas, gas formation; gassing	Gasentwicklung f, Gasfreisetzung f; Gasen n
gas-expansion thermometer, gas thermometer	Gasthermometer n
gas-explosion tube, gas ignition pipette, explosion gas pipette	Explosionspipette f
gas-filled ionization chamber	Ionisationskammer f mit Gasfüllung, gasgefüllte Ionisationskammer
gas-filled pentode, three-grid ion tube, ion pentode	Gaspentode f
gas-filled photocell, photoemissive gas-filled cell	Gaszelle f, Edelgaszelle f, gasgefüllte Photozelle f
gas-filled tube rectifier, gas tube, gasotron, gas rectifier	gasgefüllte Gleichrichterröhre f, Gasgleichrichterröhre m, Gasotron n, Gas[entladungs]ventil n
gas flame, gas jet, gas light	Gasflamme f
gas-flow counter [tube], gas-flow radiation detector	Gasdurchflußzähler m, Gasdurchflußzählrohr n
gas flowmeter	Gasmengenmesser m, Gasströmungsmesser m
gas-flow radiation detector	s. gas-flow counter
gas flow rate	s. rate of gas flow
gas focusing	Gasfokussierung f, Gaskonzentrierung f
gas formation	s. gas evolution
gas friction	Gasreibung f
gas gap, gas-discharge gap	Gasentladungsstrecke f, Gasstrecke f
gas-gas immiscibility	Gas-Gas-Unmischbarkeit f
gas gauge, gas manometer	Gasdruckmesser m, Gasmanometer n
gas hydrate	Gashydrat n, Eishydrat m
gasification, gasifying	Vergasung f
gas ignition pipette	s. explosion gas pipette
gas indicator	s. gas detector
gas interferometer, interferometer for gases	Gasinterferometer n
gas ionization, gaseous ionization, electromerism	Gasionisation f, Gasionisierung f
gas jet, gas flame, gas light	Gasflamme f
gas jet pump	s. jet pump
gasket	s. packing
gasketed ring, gasket ring	Dichtungsring m
gas-kinetic	gaskinetisch
gas-kinetic cross-section, molecular cross-section	Molekülquerschnitt m, gaskinetischer Querschnitt m, Stoßquerschnitt m
gas kinetics	Gaskinetik f
gas lamp; incandescent gas light, gas light	Gasglühlicht n, Gaslicht n
gas laser, gaseous laser, gaseous-state laser	Gaslaser m
gas law	s. Boyle-Charles law
gas leak detector	Gasspürgerät n, Gassucher m
gas light; incandescent gas light, gas lamp	Gasglühlicht n, Gaslicht n
gas light, gas flame, gas jet	Gasflamme f
gas light paper	s. contact printing paper
gas-liquid chromatography, GLC	Gas-Flüssigkeits-Chromatographie f, Gas[-Flüssigkeits]-Verteilungschromatographie f

gas-liquid interface	s. liquid-gas interface	gate electrode	s. a. gate ‹semi.›
gas lubrication	Gasschmierung f	gate element	s. gating unit
gas manometer	s. gas gauge	gate pulse, gating (antiparalysis, opening, enabling) pulse	Öffnungsimpuls m
gas mantle, Welsbach mantle, mantle, incandescent mantle	Auer-Glühkörper m, AuerStrumpf m, Glühkörper m, Glühstrumpf m, Gasglühstrumpf m	gate stage, gating stage	Durchlaßsteuerstufe f, Torstufe f, Torsteuerstufe f
gas medium, gaseous fluid ‹phys.›	gasförmiges Medium n ‹Phys.›	gate valve, gating valve	Torröhre f
gas multiplication	s. gas amplification		
gas noise, ionization noise, ion noise	Ionisationsrauschen n, Ionenrauschen n		
gasomagnetron	gasgefüllte Magnetfeldröhre f, gasgefülltes Magnetron n	gate voltage	Torspannung f, Torsteuerspannung f
gasometry; gas analysis	Gasanalyse f	gate width	Durchlaßbreite f
gasotron	s. gas-filled tube rectifier		
gas pocket, gaseous inclusion	Gasblase f, Gaseinschluß m	gate width	Auftastimpulsbreite f, Auftastimpulsdauer f ‹Öffnungs- bzw. Sperrzeit in der Torschaltung›
gas porosity	Gasporosität f		
gas ratio	s. vacuum factor		
gas recombination	Gasrekombination f, Gaswiedervereinigung f		
gas-recombining apparatus	Gasrekombinator m, Knallgasrekombinator m	gathering	s. trapping
		gathering electrode	s. collecting electrode
gas rectifier	s. gas-filled tube rectifier	gating	Durchlaßsteuerung f; Austastung f; Strahlsperrung f ‹Fs.›
gas refrigerating machine	Gaskältemaschine f		
gas scale of temperature, ideal gas scale of temperature, perfect-gas scale	Gasskala f der Temperatur, ideale Gasskala	gating circuit	s. gate circuit
		gating electrode	s. gate ‹semi.›
		gating element	s. gating unit
		gating multivibrator	s. univibrator
gas scattering, Coulomb scattering by the residual gas	Coulomb-Streuung f am Restgas, Gasstreuung f	gating pulse, gate (antiparalysis, opening, enabling) pulse	Öffnungsimpuls m
gasschaukel, trennschaukel, swing separator	Gasschaukel f [nach Clusius], Clusiussche Gasschaukel (Trennschaukel f), Trennschaukel [nach Clusius]	gating pulse, gate	Auftastimpuls m
gas scrubbing, gas washing	Gaswäsche f, Gaswaschung f, Gasberieselung f		
		gating stage, gate stage	Durchlaßsteuerstufe f, Torstufe f, Torsteuerstufe f
gassing; gas evolution (formation), evolution (generation, development) of gas	Gasentwicklung f, Gasfreisetzung f; Gasen n		
		gating unit, gating element, gate element	Torelement n, Torschaltungselement n
gas-solid chromatography, gas adsorption chromatography, GSC	Gas-Fest[körper]-Chromatographie f, Gas-Adsorptionschromatographie f, Adsorptionschromatographie f	gating valve, gate valve	Torröhre f
		g-atom, gramme-atom, gram-atom, gramatomic weight	Grammatom n, Atomgramm n, g-Atom n, gAtom f
gas-solid interface	s. solid-gas interface	Gaugain coil	Gaugain-Spule f, Gaugainsche Spule f
gas-space	s. gamma-space		
gas state, gaseous state, gaseousness, gaseity	gasförmiger Zustand m, Gaszustand m	gauge, gage ‹US›, measuring instrument (apparatus), measurer, meter	Meßgerät n, Meßinstrument n, Messer m, Meßapparat m
gas streamline, streamline of gas	Gasfaden m		
gas thermometer, gas-expansion thermometer	Gasthermometer n	gauge, pressure gauge (meter), pressure-measuring device, manometer	Druckmesser m, Manometer n
gas triode	s. thyratron		
gas tube	s. gas-filled tube rectifier		
gas-type gravimeter	Gasgravimeter n		
gas-walled chamber, gas-walled ionization chamber	Gaswändekammer f, gasäquivalente Ionisationskammer f	gauge ‹field theory›	Eichung f ‹Feldtheorie›
		gauge	s. a. water scale ‹hydr.›
		gauge	s. a. étalon
gas washing, gas scrubbing	Gaswäsche f, Gaswaschung f, Gasberieselung f	gauge	s. a. vernier caliper
		gauge block	s. end block
gas-washing bottle	s. washing bottle	gauge condition	Eichbedingung f
gate, gate electrode, gating electrode ‹semi.›	Gateelektrode f, Gate n, Tor n, Torelektrode f, Steuerelektrode f, Steuerkontakt m, Sperrelektrode f, g-Pol m, Gatter n ‹Halb.›	gauge covariance	Eichungskovarianz f, Eichkovarianz f
		gauge covariant	eichungskovariant, eichkovariant
		gauged potentiometer	s. dual potentiometer
gate	s. a. gating pulse	gauge factor, calibration factor	Eichfaktor m
gate [circuit], gating circuit	Torschaltung f, Impulstorschaltung f, Impulstor n, Tor n, Torkreis m, Torkreisschaltung f, Gateschaltung f, „gate"-Schaltung f; Durchlaßschaltung f; Gatter n, Gatterschaltung f	gauge glass, water-gauge glass, water glass	Standglas n, Wasserstand[s]glas n, Wasserstand[s]rohr n
		gauge group	Eichgruppe f
gate current	Torstrom m, Torsteuerstrom m	gauge head	s. measuring head
		gauge[-]invariance	Eichinvarianz f
gate electrode; control (modulator, guide) electrode ‹of the valve›	Steuerelektrode f		
		gauge-invariant	eichinvariant

gauge 292

gauge measuring interferometer; length measuring interferometer	Interferenzkomparator m
gauge probe	s. measuring head
gauge transformation <of the first or second kind>	Eichtransformation f, Umeichung f <erster oder zweiter Art>
gauge weight, standard weight, gauging weight	Eichgewicht n
gauging, calibration	Eichung f; Kalibrierung f; Einmessen n
gauging tensor	Eichtensor m
gauging weight, standard (gauge) weight	Eichgewicht n
Gaunt factor	Gaunt-Faktor m
gauss, G, Γ <= 10^{-4} T>	Gauß n, Großgauß n, G, Gs, Γ <= 10^{-4} T>
gaussage	= magnetic induction in gauss
Gauss analogies	s. Delambre['s] analogies
Gauss-Bonnet formula (theorem)	[Gauß-]Bonnetsche Integralformel f, Gauß-Bonnetsche Formel f, Formel von [Gauß-]Bonnet
Gauss-Codazzi equations	s. Mainardi equations
Gauss conformal projection	s. transverse Mercator projection
Gauss co-ordinates	s. curvilinear co-ordinates
Gauss curvature, Gaussian (specific, total) curvature	Gaußsche Krümmung f, Gaußsches Krümmungsmaß n
Gauss distribution	s. Gaussian distribution
Gauss['] divergence theorem	s. Green['s] theorem
Gauss-Doolittle method, abbreviated Doolittle method	Gauß-Doolittle-Methode f, verkürzte Doolittle-Methode f
Gauss['] elimination method, Gaussian elimination (algorithm)	Gaußsches Eliminationsverfahren n, Gaußscher Algorithmus m
Gauss['] equation, Theorema egregium	Gaußsche Gleichung f, Theorema n egregium
Gauss equation in celestial mechanics	Gaußsche Gleichung f in der Himmelsmechanik
Gauss['] error curve	s. error curve
Gauss error distribution curve	s. error curve
Gauss['] error function	s. error function
Gauss eyepiece	Gaußsches Okular n
Gauss flux theorem, Gauss['] theorem; Gauss law	Gaußscher Satz m [der Elektrostatik], [Gaußscher] Flußsatz m
Gauss formula	Formel f von Gauß, Gaußsche Formel
Gauss['] formula <in geometric optics>	Gaußsche Gleichung f <in der geometrischen Optik>
Gauss['] formula of interpolation, Gauss['] interpolation formula, Gaussian interpolation formulas, Newton-Gauss formulas	Gaußsche Interpolationsformel f
Gauss['] hypergeometric [differential] equation	s. hypergeometric differential equation
Gauss hypergeometric function, hypergeometric function	[Gaußsche] hypergeometrische Funktion f
Gaussian	s. Gaussian distribution
Gaussian algorithm	s. Gauss['] elimination method
Gaussian approximation	s. Gaussian optics
Gaussian constant [of gravitation]	Gaußsche Gravitationskonstante f, Gravitationskonstante (Attraktionskonstante f) des Sonnensystems, Anziehungskraft f der Sonne
Gaussian curvature	s. Gauss curvature
Gaussian curve [of error]	s. error curve
Gaussian differential equation	s. hypergeometric differential equation
Gaussian distribution, Gauss distribution, normal distribution, Gaussian probability distribution, normal distribution law, Gaussian	Gauß-Verteilung f, Gaußsche Verteilung f, Normalverteilung f, Gaußsche Normalverteilung, Gaußsche Wahrscheinlichkeitsverteilung f, Normalverteilungsgesetz n
Gaussian elimination	s. Gauss['] elimination method
Gaussian equatorial constants	Gaußsche Konstanten fpl
Gaussian error curve	s. Gaussian curve
Gaussian error function	s. error function
Gaussian hypergeometric series, hypergeometric series	[Gaußsche] hypergeometrische Reihe f
Gaussian image point, paraxial image point	Gaußscher (paraxialer, idealer; axialer) Bildpunkt m
Gaussian interpolation formulas	s. Gauss['] formula of interpolation
Gaussian kernel	s. Gauss kernel
Gaussian law of errors (error distribution)	s. error law
Gaussian lens equation	s. Gauss lens formula
Gaussian noise	Gaußsches Rauschen n
Gaussian optics, Gaussian approximation	Gaußsche Dioptrik f, Gaußsche Optik f, Gaußsche Abbildung f, Gaußsche Näherung f, Gaußsche Approximation f
Gaussian parameter, Gauss parameter	Gaußscher Parameter m
Gaussian plane	s. complex plane
Gaussian position, Gauss position	Gaußsche Lage f, Gaußsche Hauptlage f
Gaussian probability distribution	s. Gaussian distribution
Gaussian process	Gaußscher Prozeß m
Gaussian pulse	s. bell-shaped pulse
Gaussian quadrature formula	s. Gauss mechanical quadrature
Gaussian representation	s. spherical mapping
Gaussian system [of units]	Gaußsches Einheitensystem (Maßsystem, System) n, symmetrisches CGS-System n
Gaussian theorem	s. Green theorem
Gaussian transcendental function	s. error function
Gaussian variable	normalverteilte Variable f
Gaussian variation	Gaußsche Variation f
Gaussian wave group	Gaußsches Wellenpaket n
Gaussian well, Gauss potential	Gauß-Potential n, Gaußsches Potential n, Gaußscher Potentialtopf m, Gaußsche Potentialmulde f
Gaussian width	Gaußsche Breite f, Gauß-Breite f
Gauss['] interpolation formula	s. Gauss['] formula of interpolation
Gauss kernel, Gaussian kernel	Gaußscher Integralkern m, Gaußscher Bremskern m
Gauss-Krüger co-ordinates	Gauß-Krügersche Koordinaten fpl; Gauß-Krügersche Meridianstreifen mpl
Gauss-Krüger projection	s. transverse Mercator projection
Gauss-Lambert projection	winkeltreue Kegelprojektion f [nach Gauß-Lambert], winkeltreuer Kegelentwurf m [nach Gauß-Lambert], Gauß-Lambertsche winkeltreue Kegelprojektion
Gauss law; Gauss['] theorem, Gauss flux theorem	Gaußscher Satz m [der Elektrostatik], [Gaußscher] Flußsatz m
Gauss lens formula, lens formula, [Gaussian] lens equation, Gauss optics formulae	allgemeine Linsenformel f, Linsenformel, Gaußsche Linsenformel, Linsengleichung f
Gauss mean value theorem [for potential functions], theorem of the mean for harmonic functions	Gaußscher Mittelwertsatz m [der Potentialtheorie], Mittelwertsatz der Potentialtheorie (harmonischen Funktionen); Gaußscher Satz vom arithmetischen Mittel

Gauss mechanical quadrature, Gaussian quadrature formula	Gaußsche mechanische Quadratur f, Gaußsche Quadraturformel f	**Gehrcke-Lau method**	Gehrcke-Lausche Methode f
gaussmeter	Gaußmeter n, Gaußmesser m	**geiger,** Geiger counter, Geiger tube ‹in popular usage›	Geiger-Zähler m ‹GM-Zählrohr + elektronische Ausrüstung›
Gauss method	s. double weighing	**Geiger counting region**	s. Geiger region
Gauss moment	Gauß-Moment n	**Geiger formula,** Geiger law	Geigersches Reichweitengesetz n
Gauss optics formulae	s. Gauss lens formula	**Geiger-Klemperer counter**	Geiger-Klemperer-Zählrohr n
Gauss paper, normal probability paper	Gaußsches Papier n, Gaußsches Wahrscheinlichkeitspapier n, Wahrscheinlichkeitspapier	**Geiger law,** Geiger formula	Geigersches Reichweitengesetz n
Gauss parameter, Gaussian parameter	Gaußscher Parameter m	**Geiger-Marsden's experiment**	Geiger-Marsdenscher Versuch m, Versuch von Geiger und Marsden
Gauss plane	s. complex plane	**Geiger-Müller counter [tube], Geiger-Müller counting tube,** GM counter [tube], Geiger-Müller tube, GM tube	Geiger-Müller-Zählrohr n, GM-Zählrohr n, Geiger-Müllersches Zählrohr n, [Geiger-Müller-]Auslösezählrohr n
Gauss point	s. principal point		
Gauss position	s. Gaussian position		
Gauss potential	s. Gaussian well		
Gauss ray, paraxial ray	Paraxialstrahl m, paraxialer Strahl m; Nullstrahl m		
Gauss region, paraxial region	paraxiales (Gaußsches, achsennahes) Gebiet n, fadenförmiger Raum m	**Geiger-Müller region**	s. Geiger region
		Geiger-Müller tube	s. Geiger-Müller counter
Gauss-Seidel method, single-step iteration [for solving linear equations], Seidel['s] method	[Gauß-]Seidelsches Iterationsverfahren n, Gauß-Seidelsches Verfahren n, Iterationsverfahren von Gauß-Seidel, Gauß-Seidel-Verfahren n	**Geiger-Nuttall relation, Geiger-Nuttall rule**	Geiger-Nuttallsche Reichweitebeziehung (Regel, Beziehung, Formel) f, Geiger-Nuttall-Regel f, Geiger-Nuttall-Beziehung f, Geiger-Nuttallsches Gesetz n
Gauss['] theorem, Gauss flux theorem; Gauss law	Gaußscher Satz m [der Elektrostatik], [Gaußscher] Flußsatz m	**Geiger plateau,** plateau of the counter, voltage plateau ‹of the counter›	Plateau n, Geiger-Plateau n, Plateaubereich m ‹Zählrohrcharakteristik›
Gauss['] theorem	s. a. Green theorem	**Geiger point counter**	Geigerscher Spitzenzähler m
Gauss-type lens, Gauss-type objective	Photoobjektiv n vom Gauß-Typ, Gauß-Typ m		
Gauss-Weingarten equations	Gauß-Weingartensche Gleichungen fpl	**Geiger region,** Geiger-Müller region, Geiger counting region	Auslösebereich m, Geiger-Bereich m, Geiger-Gebiet n
gauze lens, mesh electron lens	Netzlinse f	**geigerscope,** spinthariscope	Spinthariskop n
gauze ring, crape (crepe, dusky) ring, ring C	Kreppring m, Florring m, C-Ring m	**Geiger threshold**	Geiger-Schwelle f, Einsatzspannung f
gauze sound, howling tone, howling sound	Heulton m		
Gay-Lussac experiment	Gay-Lussacscher Versuch (Drosselversuch, Überströmungsversuch) m, Drosselversuch von L. J. Gay-Lussac	**Geissler tube**	Spektralröhre f, Geißlersche (Plückersche) Röhre f, Geißler-Röhre f
		Geitel effect	s. Elster-Geitel effect
Gay-Lussac-Humboldt law, Gay-Lussac law [of combining volumes]	Gay-Lussacsches Gesetz n der einfachen Gasvolumina, Gay-Lussac-Humboldtsches Gesetz, Gasvolumengesetz n	**gel,** jell, jelly, coherent colloidal system	Gel n, kohärentes kolloidales System n
		gelatification, gelatination	s. gelation
		gelatine dry photographic plate	Trockenplatte f, photographische Trockenplatte
Gay-Lussac law [of expansion], Charles law	Gay-Lussacsches Gesetz n, Gay-Lussac-Gesetz n	**gelatine effect**	Gelatineeffekt m, Ross-Effekt m
G-band ‹194—212 or 3,950—5,850 Mc/s›	G-Band n ‹194 ··· 212 oder 3 950 ··· 5 850 MHz›	**gelatine formation**	s. gelation
		gelatine relief	Gelatinerelief n
		gelatinform	s. gelatinous
geanticline, geoanticline	Geantiklinale f	**gelatinform state,** gelatinous state	Gelzustand m
		gelatin[iz]ation	s. gelation
gear, gearing	Getriebe n	**gelatinous,** gelatinform, gel-like, jelly[-]like, jelatinous	gelartig, Gel-; gelatinös, gelatineartig; gallertartig
gear ‹of steam engine›, gearing	Steuerung f ‹Dampfmaschine›		
gear pump	Zahnradpumpe f	**gelatinous state,** gelatinform state	Gelzustand m
gear ratio, transmission ratio	Übersetzung f, Übersetzungsverhältnis n		
gedanken experiment	s. imaginary experiment	**gelation,** gelling, gelatification, gelatin[iz]ation, jelling, gel[atine] formation	Gelieren n, Gelbildung f, Gelatinierung f
Gegenbauer['s] function, ultraspherical function	Gegenbauersche (metasphärische, ultrasphärische) Funktion f		
Gegenbauer['s] polynomial, ultraspherical polynomial	Gegenbauersches (ultrasphärisches) Polynom n, ultrasphärische Funktion f, p-dimensionale zonale Kugelfunktion f	**gelation water**	Quellungswasser n
		gel chromatography, gel permeation chromatography, gel filtration, GPC, restricted diffusion chromatography	Gel-Permeations-Chromatographie f, Gelchromatographie f, Anschlußchromatographie f, Gelfiltration f, GPC
gegenion, counterion, opposer ion	Gegenion n		
gegenion exchange	Gegenionenaustausch m		
gegenreaction, counter reaction, opposing	Gegenreaktion f		
		gel electrophoresis	Gelelektrophorese f
gegenschein, counterglow	Gegenschein m ‹Zodiakallicht›	**gel filtration**	s. gel chromatography
		gel formation	s. gelation
Géhéniau-Komar scalar	Géhéniau-Komarscher Skalar m	**gel fraction,** gel skeleton	Gelfraktion f
Gehloff telephotometer	Telephotometer n von Gehloff, Gehloff-Telephotometer n	**Gelhoff-Schering photometer**	Photometer n von Gelhoff-Schering, Gelhoff-Schering-Photometer n

gel-like	s. gelatinous
gelling	s. gelation
gelling point, gel point	Gelbildungstemperatur f, Gel[atin]ierungstemperatur f
gelling property	Gelierfähigkeit f, Gelierkraft f
Gell-Mann and Brueckner method	Gell-Mann-Bruecknersche Methode f
Gell-Mann equation	Gell-Mann-Gleichung f
Gell-Mann-Ne'eman scheme	s. eightfold way / the
Gell-Mann tetrahedron	Gell-Mannsches Tetraeder n
Gell-Mann theory	Gell-Mannsche Theorie f, Gell-Mann-Theorie f
gel particle	Gelteilchen n
gel permeation	Gelpermeation f
gel permeation chromatography	s. gel chromatography
gel skeleton, gel fraction	Gelfraktion f
gel-sol change (transformation), solation	Gel-Sol-Umwandlung f
genealogic coefficient	Abstammungskoeffizient m, genealogischer Koeffizient m
gene locus, locus	Genort m, Genlocus m, Locus m <pl.: Loci>
genemotor <US>	s. rotary converter
gene mutation, point mutation	Genmutation f, Punktmutation f
general balance, general conservation law	allgemeiner Erhaltungssatz m, Generalbilanz f
General Catalogue, general star catalogue	Generalkatalog m
General Conference of the International Bureau of Weights and Measures, C.G.P.M.	Generalkonferenz f für Maß und Gewicht, CGPM
general conservation law, general balance	allgemeiner Erhaltungssatz m, Generalbilanz f
general co-ordinates, generalized co-ordinates, Lagrange['s] generalized co-ordinates, Lagrange['s] variables, Lagrange['s] co-ordinates parameters of the system	verallgemeinerte (generalisierte, allgemeine) Koordinaten fpl, Lagrangesche [verallgemeinerte] Koordinaten, Lagrangesche Variable f, Systemkoordinaten fpl
general corrosion, surface corrosion	diffuse (gleichmäßige) Korrosion f, gleichmäßiger Angriff m von der Oberfläche her
general covariance	allgemeine Kovarianz f
general diffused light, uniform light	gleichförmiges Licht n
general diffused lighting, uniform lighting	gleichförmige Beleuchtung f
general equation of diffusion	s. Fick['s] second law
general function	generelle Funktion f
general gravitation	s. gravitation
generality	Allgemeingültigkeit f
generality quantifier, quantor of generality, universal quantifier	Generalisator m, Alloperator m, Allquantor m
generalization	Verallgemeinerung f, Erweiterung f <Math.>; Generalisierung f <Statistik>; Generalisieren n <Kartographie>; Ausdehnung f, Erweiterung f <allg.>
generalized acceleration	verallgemeinerte (generalisierte, allgemeine) Beschleunigung f
generalized acceleration vector, vector of generalized acceleration	verallgemeinerter Beschleunigungsvektor m
generalized acting force	verallgemeinerte eingeprägte Kraft f
generalized affinity	s. affinity <chem., el.chem., therm.>
generalized compliances	generalisierte Elastizitätskoeffizienten mpl
generalized component of momentum	s. generalized momentum
generalized co-ordinates	s. general co-ordinates
generalized co-ordinate vector	verallgemeinerter Koordinatenvektor m
generalized displacement	verallgemeinerte Verschiebung f
generalized electrodynamics, field theory of fundamental particles	Feldtheorie f der Elementarteilchen, verallgemeinerte Elektrodynamik f
generalized energy	verallgemeinerte (generalisierte, allgemeine) Energie f
generalized force	verallgemeinerte (generalisierte, allgemeine, Lagrangesche) Kraft f
generalized force	s. affinity <chem., el.chem., therm.>
generalized function, distribution <math.>	Distribution f, verallgemeinerte Funktion f <Math.>
generalized heat content, enthalpy <generalized definition>	Enthalpie f, verallgemeinerter Wärmeinhalt m <verallgemeinerte Definition>
generalized H-theorem	verallgemeinertes (generalisiertes) H-Theorem n
generalized Kronecker delta	s. epsilon-tensor
generalized mean value theorem	s. second mean value theorem of the differential calculus
generalized mean value theorem	s. a. Taylor['s] formula
generalized momentum, generalized component of momentum	verallgemeinerter Impuls m, generalisierter Impuls, allgemeiner Impuls, Impulskoordinate f
generalized momentum corresponding to an ignorable co-ordinate	zyklischer Impuls m
generalized Newtonian liquid	s. non-Newtonian liquid
generalized Nyquist-Cauchy criterion [of stability]	s. Nyquist-Cauchy criterion
generalized point group	s. magnetic point group
generalized potential	verallgemeinertes (generalisiertes, allgemeines) Potential n
generalized projection	verallgemeinerte Projektion f
generalized ratio test	s. Cauchy's ratio test
generalized seniority	verallgemeinerte Seniorität f
generalized shear	generalisierte Scherung f
generalized solution, feeble solution <math.>	schwache (verallgemeinerte) Lösung f <Math.>
generalized space group	s. magnetic space group
generalized spherical harmonic, Wigner function	Wigner-Funktion f, Wignersche Funktion f, verallgemeinerte Kugelfunktion f
generalized stability criterion of Nyquist-Cauchy	s. Nyquist-Cauchy criterion
generalized strain	verallgemeinerte (generalisierte, allgemeine) Verformung f
generalized stress	verallgemeinerte (generalisierte, allgemeine) Spannung f
generalized symmetric group	volle monomiale Gruppe f, Symmetrie f [vom Grad l/l], verallgemeinerte symmetrische Gruppe
generalized Talmi coefficient, Balashov coefficient	Balaschow-Koeffizient m, verallgemeinerter Talmi-Koeffizient m
generalized velocity	verallgemeinerte (generalisierte, allgemeine) Geschwindigkeit f
generalized velocity [vector], vector of generalized velocity	verallgemeinerter Geschwindigkeitsvektor m
general law of thermodynamics, first postulate of thermodynamics	allgemeiner Hauptsatz m der Thermodynamik, erstes Postulat n der Thermodynamik

general lighting	Allgemeinbeleuchtung f	generation process <semi.>	Generationsprozeß m <Halb.>
general lighting service lamp	Allgebrauchslampe f, Glühlampe f für Allgebrauchszwecke	generation rate <semi.>	Erzeugungsrate f, Erzeugungsgeschwindigkeit f
general map	Übersichtskarte f	generation time, neutron generation time	Generationsdauer f der Neutronen, mittlere Lebensdauer f der Neutronengeneration
general mean value theorem	s. Taylor['s] formula		
general Γ network, Γ network, gamma network	Γ-Glied n, Gamma-Glied n	generator, producer	Generator m, Erzeuger m, Sender m
general perturbation theory	allgemeine Störungsrechnung f	generator <of a group>	Erzeugende f <Gruppe>
general position / in	[in] allgemeiner Lage	generator, generatrix, ruling <of a surface>	Erzeugende f <Fläche>
general precession	allgemeine Präzession f	generator	s. a. electric generator <el.>
general product, outer product, product <of tensors>	[allgemeines] Tensorprodukt n, direktes Produkt n <Tensoren>	generator	s. a. oscillator <el.>
		generator of sound	s. sound generator
general-purpose manipulator	Universalmanipulator m	generator pulse time zero	Nullzeitimpuls m
general radio-frequency radiation	allgemeine Radiofrequenzstrahlung f	generatrix, generator <of a surface>	Erzeugende f <Fläche>
		generic phase	generelle Phase f
General Relativity	s. general theory of relativity	genetic dose	genetische Dosis (Strahlungsdosis, Strahlungsbelastung) f
general solution, most general solution, complete primitive	allgemeine Lösung f, allgemeinste Lösung	genetic effect of radiation	genetische Strahlenwirkung f, genetischer Strahlungseffekt (Effekt) m
general star catalogue, General Catalogue	Generalkatalog m	Geneva mechanism (motion, movement)	s. Maltese cross
general state of strain, tri-axial strain, three-dimensional strain, cubic[al] strain, volume strain	räumlicher (dreiachsiger) Verzerrungszustand m, räumlicher (dreiachsiger) Formänderungszustand m, räumliche Verzerrung (Formänderung, Verformung, Deformation) f	genome segregation	Genomsegregation f, Genomsonderung f
		gentle slope	leichtes Gefälle n
		genuine cavitation	s. true cavitation
		genuine coincidence, true coincidence	echte Koinzidenz f
		genuine [spectral] line	reelle Linie f, Mutterlinie f
general state of stress	s. volume stress	genus <math.>	Geschlecht n <Math.>
general synoptic situation	s. general weather situation	geoacoustics	Geoakustik f
		geoanticline	s. geanticline
general theory	allgemeine (globale) Theorie f	geocentric co-ordinates, geocentric system [of co-ordinates]	geozentrisches Koordinatensystem n, geozentrische Koordinaten fpl
general theory of relativity, [Einstein['s] general] theory of relativity, General Relativity	[Einsteinsche] allgemeine Relativitätstheorie f, Theorie f der Relativität der Beschleunigungen	geocentric distance	geozentrische Distanz (Zenitdistanz) f
		geocentric horizon, true (geometrical, celestial) horizon	wahrer Horizont m, geozentrischer Horizont
general theory of shells	Biegetheorie f der Schalen	geocentric longitude	s. oblique ascension
general virial equation, virial equation of state	viriale Zustandsgleichung f, Virialform f der thermischen Zustandsgleichung	geocentric parallax, diurnal parallax	tägliche (geozentrische) Parallaxe f, Höhenparallaxe f
		geocentric system <of co-ordinates>	s. geocentric co-ordinates
general weather situation, [general] synoptic situation, state of the weather	Gesamtwetterlage f, Wetterlage f	geocentric system <of Universe>, geocentric world system	geozentrisches System (Weltsystem, Weltbild) n
		geochronology	Geochronologie f
generating circle	s. rolling circle		
generating function; determining function <celestial mech.>	erzeugende Funktion f, Erzeugende f	geocinetics, geokinetics	Geokinetik f, Lehre f von den rezenten Bewegungen der Erdrinde
generating functional	erzeugendes Funktional n	geocorona	Geokorona f
generating transformation	erzeugende Operation (Transformation) f	geode, vug[g] <geo.>	Geod n, Sekretion f, Lösungshohlraum m, Geode f <Geo.>
generation; production; formation; creation; birth	Bildung f; Erzeugung f; Generation f	geodesic, geodesic line	Geodätische f, geodätische (geradeste) Linie f, Geodäte f
generation <of neutrons, nuclei>	Generation f <Neutronen, Kerne>	geodesic application of gravity	geodätische Gravimetrie f, Anwendung f von Schweremessungen in der Geodäsie
generation <semi.>	Generation f <Halb.>		
generation cross-section	s. production cross-section		
generation current <semi.>	Generationsstrom m <Halb.>	geodesic azimuth, spheroidal azimuth	geodätisches Azimut n
generation model	Generationsmodell n	geodesic base comparator	s. surveying tape comparator
generation of gas, gas evolution (formation), evolution (development) of gas; gassing	Gasentwicklung f, Gasfreisetzung; Gasen n	geodesic circle, geodesic distance-circle	geodätischer Entfernungskreis m (Kreis m erster Art)
generation of heat	s. heat release	geodesic connection of networks, connection of networks	Netzanschluß m, Zusammenschluß m von Netzen
generation of neutrons	Neutronengeneration f		
generation of oscillations	s. excitation of oscillations	geodesic co-ordinates, geodesic parameters	geodätische Koordinaten fpl, Zentralkoordinaten fpl
generation of sound	s. sound generation	geodesic curvature, tangential curvature	geodätische Krümmung f, Abwickelkrümmung f, Tangentialkrümmung f
generation of vibrations	s. excitation of oscillations		
generation of waves, wave generation; wave formation, formation of waves	Wellenerzeugung f; Wellenbildung f, Wellenentstehung f	geodesic displacement	s. parallel displacement
		geodesic distance	geodätische Entfernung f

geodesic

geodesic distance-circle, geodesic circle	geodätischer Entfernungskreis *m* (Kreis *m* erster Art)	**geometrical horizon**	*s.* true horizon
geodesic field	geodätisches Feld (Röhrenfeld) *n*, Röhrenfeld	**geometrical incidence**, aerodynamic angle of incidence (attack)	geometrischer Anstellwinkel *m*, aerodynam.-scher Anstellwinkel
geodesic head, elevation (potential) head, elevation ⟨hydr.⟩	Ortshöhe *f* ⟨Hydr.⟩	**geometrical isomer[id]**, geometric[al] stereoisomer[id], cis-trans isomer	cis-trans-Isomer *n*, geometrisches Isomer *n*
geodesic level, levelling instrument, surveyor's level	Nivellier *n*, Nivellierinstrument *n*	**geometrical isomerism**, geometric[al] stereoisomerism, cis-trans isomerism; alloisomerism; ethylene isomerism	cis-trans-Isomerie *f*, geometrische Isomerie *f*; Alloisomerie *f*; Äthylenisomerie *f*
geodesic levelling	*s.* levelling ⟨geo.⟩		
geodesic line	*s.* geodesic		
geodesic parameters	*s.* geodesic co-ordinates	**geometrical mechanics**	geometrische Mechanik *f*
geodesic tape comparator	*s.* surveying tape comparator	**geometric[al] optics**, ray optics	geometrische Optik *f*, Strahlenoptik *f*
geodesic torsion	geodätische Windung (Torsion) *f*	**geometrical optics**, geometric-optical, geometric optics	geometrisch-optisch
geodesic visibility distance	geodätische Sichtweite *f*	**geometrical-optics approximation**, geometric-optical approximation	geometrisch-optische Näherung *f*
geodesy; inferior geodesy, elementary geodesy	Geodäsie *f*; niedere Geodäsie, Vermessungskunde	**geometrical-optics expansion**	geometrisch-optische Reihenentwicklung *f*
geodetic	*s.* geodesic		
geodimeter	Geodimeter *n*	**geometrical-optics field**, geometric-optical field	geometrisch-optisches Feld *n*
geodynamics	Geodynamik *f*		
geoelectric effect, GEE	geoelektrischer Effekt *m*, GEE	**geometrical optics limit**, limiting case of geometrical optics	geometrisch-optischer Grenzfall *m*, Grenzfall der geometrischen Optik
geoelectric field	*s.* Earth electric field	**geometrical seismology**	geometrische Seismologie (Seismik) *f*
geoelectrics	Geoelektrik *f*		
geoepinasty	Geoepinastie *f*	**geometrical series**	*s.* geometric series
geogony	Geogonie *f*, Geogenie *f*, Erdentstehungslehre *f*	**geometrical stereoisomer[id]**	*s.* geometrical isomer
geographical mile ⟨= 7,420.44 m⟩	geographische Meile *f* ⟨= 7 420,44 m⟩	**geometrical stereoisomerism**	*s.* geometrical isomerism
geographical visibility distance	geometrische (geographische) Sichtweite *f*	**geometrical theory of diffraction**	geometrische Beugungstheorie *f*
geographic north	Geographisch-Nord *n*	**geometric average**, geometric mean	geometrisches Mittel *n*
geographic sphere	geographische Hülle *f*, geographische Sphäre *f*	**geometric boundary condition**, essential boundary condition	wesentliche Randbedingung *f*, geometrische Randbedingung
geoidal azimuth	*s.* azimuth ⟨astr.⟩	**geometric buckling**, geometric laplacian	Geometriebuckling *n*, geometrische Flußwölbung *f*, geometrischer Parameter *m*
geoidal surface	Geoidfläche *f*, Meeresfläche *f*		
geoid undulation, geoid warping	Geoidundulation *f*		
geoinduction, Earth induction	Geoinduktion *f*, Erdinduktion *f*	**geometric capacitance**	geometrische Kapazität *f*
geoisotherm; geoisothermal line	Geoisotherme *f*, Geotherme *f*	**geometric disparity**, disparity, fixation disparity	Disparation *f*, geometrische Disparation
geokinetics	*s.* geocinetics	**geometric distortion**	Geometrieverzerrung *f*
geomagmatic cycle, magmatic cycle	geomagmatischer Zyklus *m*		
geomagnetic activity, geomagnetic microvariation	erdmagnetische Unruhe (Aktivität) *f*, geomagnetische Unruhe	**geometric distortion** ⟨opt.⟩	geometrische Verzeichnung *f* ⟨Opt.⟩
geomagnetic axis, magnetic axis [of the Earth]	magnetische Achse *f* [der Erde], Magnetachse *f* [der Erde], magnetische Erdachse *f*	**geometric extent**	geometrischer Fluß *m*
geomagnetic cycle	geomagnetischer Zyklus *m*	**geometric factor**, geometry factor	Geometriefaktor *m*, geometrischer Faktor *m*
geomagnetic effect	*s.* latitude effect	**geometric horopter**, mathematical horopter	mathematischer (geometrischer) Horopter *m*
geomagnetic field	*s.* terrestrial magnetic field	**geometric isomerism**	*s.* geometrical isomerism
geomagnetic index	geomagnetischer Index *m*	**geometric laplacian**	*s.* geometric buckling
geomagnetic microvariation, geomagnetic activity	erdmagnetische Unruhe (Aktivität) *f*, geomagnetische Unruhe	**geometric levelling**	*s.* levelling ⟨geo.⟩
geomagnetic pole, magnetic axis pole	geomagnetischer Pol *m*, theoretischer magnetischer Pol [der Erde]	**geometric libration**, optical libration	optische (geometrische) Libration *f* ⟨Mond⟩
geomagnetics	Geomagnetik *f*, Magnetik *f*	**geometric locus**, locus ⟨math.⟩	[geometrischer] Ort ⟨pl.: Örter⟩ ⟨Math.⟩
geomagnetic storm	*s.* magnetic storm		
geomagnetic tides	geomagnetische Gezeiten *pl*	**geometric mean**	*s.* geometric average
geomagnetic time	geomagnetische Zeit *f*	**geometric-optical**, geometrical optics	geometrisch-optisch
geomagnetic variation	erdmagnetische (geomagnetische) Variation *f*		
geomagnetism, terrestrial magnetism	Geomagnetismus *m*, Erdmagnetismus *m*	**geometric-optical approximation**, geometrical-optics approximation	geometrisch-optische Näherung *f*
geometric aberration	*s.* monochromatic aberration		
geometric acoustics, ray acoustics	geometrische Akustik *f*, Strahlenakustik *f*	**geometric-optical field**	*s.* geometrical-optics field
geometric addition, vector addition	Vektoraddition *f*, geometrische Addition *f*	**geometric optics**	*s.* geometrical optics
		geometric stereoisomerism	*s.* geometrical isomerism
geometrical albedo, Lambert['s] albedo	geometrische Albedo *f* [nach Lambert], Lambertsche Albedo	**geometric stress concentration factor**	*s.* stress concentration factor
		geometric sum, vector[ial] sum	geometrische Summe *f*, Vektorsumme *f*
geometrical broadening [of spectral lines]	geometrische Linienverbreiterung *f*	**geometric temperature gradient**	*s.* vertical temperature gradient
geometrical head, position head, gravity head	wirkliche Höhe *f*, Höhenlage *f*	**geometrization**	Geometrisierung *f*
		geometrodynamics	Geometrodynamik *f*
		geometrography	Geometrographie *f*

geometry factor, geometric factor	Geometriefaktor m, geometrischer Faktor m	**getter tablet,** tablet getter	Gettertablette f
geometry of position	s. projective geometry	**getting over the potential barrier**	s. tunnelling through the [potential] barrier
geometry programme	Geometrieprogramm n	**g-factor**	s. Landé['s] g-factor
geon, electromagnetic geon	Geon n, elektromagnetisches Geon	**G-function**	G-Funktion f
		ghost [image], spectral grate ghost <in grating spectra>	Geist m, Gittergeist m, falsche Linie f <im Beugungsspektrum>
geonegative	geonegativ		
geonomy	Geonomie f	**ghost pulse**	s. spurious pulse
geo-perception	Geoperzeption f	**ghost scattering,** spurious scattering	„spurious scattering" n, unechte Streuung f, falsche Streuung
geophotogrammetry, ground photogrammetry	Geophotogrammetrie f, terrestrische Photogrammetrie f, Erdbildmessung f	**ghost signal**	s. spurious signal
		ghost structure, banded (striated) structure	Bänderstruktur f, Streifenstruktur f
geopositive	geopositiv	**giant,** giant star, giant-stream star	Riesenstern m, Riese m, Gigant m
geopotential, geopotential height, dynamic height	Geopotential n, dynamische Höhe f [des Erdpunktes]	**giant air shower**	s. extensive shower
		giant bolide, superbolide	Überbolid m, Riesenmeteorit m
geopotential (geopotential energy	geopotentielle Energie f	**giant-cell model**	Riesenzellenmodell n
geopotential height	s. geopotential	**giant galaxy,** giant nebula	Riesengalaxie f, Riesennebel m
geopotential metre	geopotentielles Meter n	**giant ion**	Riesenion f
geopotential surface, equigeopotential (level) surface	Geopotentialfläche f	**giant molecule**	s. high polymer
		giant nebula, giant galaxy	Riesengalaxie f, Riesennebel m
geostatic pressure	eostatischer Druck m	**giant planet**	s. major planet
geostatics	Geostatik f, Erdstatik f	**giant-pulse generation**	s. giant-pulse laser action
geostationary satellite	s. stationary satellite	**giant-pulse laser**	Riesenimpulslaser m
geostrophic flow	geostrophische Strömung f		
geostrophic force	s. Coriolis force	**giant-pulse laser action,** giant-pulse generation	Riesenimpulserzeugung f
geostrophic wind, gradient current due to. geostrophic forces	geostrophischer Wind m		
		giant resonance	Riesenresonanz f
geosyncline	Geosynklinale f	**giant sequence,** giant stream	Riesenast m, Nebenast m
geotaxis	Geotaxis f		
		giant star, giant, giant-stream star	Riesenstern m, Riese m, Gigant m
		giant stream, giant sequence	Riesenast m, Nebenast m
geotectonic cycle, tectonic cycle	geotektonischer Zyklus m	**giant-stream star,** giant star, giant	Riesenstern m, Riese m, Gigant m
geothermal degree	s. geothermal gradient		
geothermal flux, vertical conducted heat flow	geothermischer Fluß m	**giant trap**	Riesenhaftstelle f, Riesentrap m
geothermal (geothermic) gradient, geothermal degree, thermal gradient	geothermischer Gradient m; geothermische Tiefenstufe f	**Gibbs['] adsorption equation,** Gibbs['] adsorption formula, Gibbs['] adsorption isotherm, adsorption equation of Gibbs, adsorption formula of Gibbs, adsorption isotherm of Gibbs	Gibbssches Adsorptionsgesetz n, Gibbssche Adsorptionsgleichung (Adsorptionsformel, Adsorptionsisotherme, Isothermengleichung, Gleichung für die Adsorption) f, Adsorptionsgleichung (Adsorptionsformel, Adsorptionsisotherme, Isothermengleichung) von Gibbs
geothermics	Geothermik f, geothermische Untersuchungen fpl		
geothermometer	Geothermometer n		
geothermy	Geothermie f		
geotorsion	Geotorsion f		
geotropic curvature	geotropische Krümmung f		
geotropism	Geotropismus m, Gravitropismus m		
		Gibbs['] chemical potential	s. free enthalpy
Gerber['s] parabola	Gerber-Parabel f, Gerbersche Parabel f	**Gibbs-Curie-Wulff principle**	Gibbs-Curie-Wulffsches Prinzip n
Gerdien arc	Gerdien-Bogen m		
Germain-Liger transformation	Germain-Ligersche Transformation f		
germanium [barrage] photocell, germanium p-n junction photovoltaic cell	Germaniumphotoelement n, Germaniumsperrschicht-[photo]zelle f	**Gibbs-Curie-Wulff theorem**	Gibbs-Curie-Wulffsches Theorem n, Theorem von Gibbs-Curie-Wulff
		Gibbs-Dalton law	s. Dalton['s] law [of partial pressure]
German mounting	deutsche Montierung f	**Gibbs['] diagram**	Gibbssches Diagramm n
germinating microcrack	Mikroanriß m	**Gibbs['] distribution,** canonical distribution	Gibbssche Verteilung f, Gibbs-Verteilung f, kanonische Verteilung
germ <cryst.>	s. nucleus		
germ of crystal[lization], crystallization germ	Kristallkeim m, Kristallisationskeim m	**Gibbs-Donnan equilibrium**	s. Donnan equilibrium
Gerstner['s] wave	Gerstnersche Welle f, Gerstner-Welle f	**Gibbs-Duhem equation,** Gibbs-Duhem relation	[Gibbs-]Duhemsche Gleichung f, Duhem-Gibbssche Gleichung, Gibbs-Duhemsche Relation f
		Gibbs effect	s. Gibbs['] phenomenon
		Gibbs['] equation	Gibbssche Gleichung f
		Gibbs['] equation	s. a. Gibbs relation
		Gibbs['] free energy (enthalpy), Gibbs['] function	s. free enthalpy
getter, gettering agent	Getter[stoff] m, Gettermetall n, Fangstoff m, Gettermaterial n, getternder Stoff m		
getter backing	Getterspiegel m	**Gibbs['] fundamental equation,** Gibbs relation, Gibbs['] equation	Gibbssche Fundamentalgleichung f
gettering	Getterung f, Gasbindung f, Restgasbindung f		
gettering agent	s. getter	**Gibbs' general equation,** Liouville['s] equation	Liouville-Gleichung f, Liouvillesche Gleichung f
getter-ion pump, sorption pump, ion getter pump	Ionengetterpumpe f, Ionen-Getterpumpe f, Getterionenpumpe f		
getter pump	s. sorption pump		

Gibbs['] heat function	s. enthalpy	**glacier flow**	Fließen *n* des Gletschers, Gletscherfluß *m*
Gibbs-Helmholtz equations, [Gibbs-] Helmholtz relations	[Gibbs-]Helmholtzsche Gleichungen *fpl*, Gibbs-Helmholtz-Gleichungen	**glacier mill**	Gletschermühle *f*
		glacier table	Gletschertisch *m*
Gibbs-Helmholtz relation, equation of maximum work	Gibbs-Helmholtzsche Gleichung *f* für die freie und die innere Energie	**glacier tongue**, tongue of the glacier	Gletscherzunge *f*
		glacier wind	Gletscherwind *m*
Gibbs-Helmholtz relations	s. Gibbs-Helmholtz equations	**glacilimnetic**	glazilimnisch
Gibbsian ensemble, [classical] ensemble	Gibbssche Gesamtheit *f*, [klassische] Gesamtheit	**glacimarine**	glazimarin
Gibbs-Konovalov rule, Gibbs-Konovalov theorem	Gibbs-Konowalowscher Satz *m*, Gibbs-Konowalowsche Regel *f*	**Gladstone and Dale law, Gladstone-Dale law**, Dale-Gladstone refraction formula	Gladstone-Dalesches Gesetz *n*, Dale-Gladstonesche Refraktionsformel *f*
Gibbs['] layer	Gibbssche Schicht *f*		
Gibbs['] paradox	Gibbssches Paradoxon *n*	**Gladstone['s] law**	Gladstonesches Gesetz *n*
Gibbs['] phase integral, phase integral of Gibbs	Gibbssches Phasenintegral *n*		
Gibbs['] phase rule	s. phase rule		
Gibbs['] phenomenon, Gibbs effect	Gibbssches Phänomen *n*, Gibbssche Erscheinung *f*	**Glagolev['s] point counter**, point counter of Glagolev	Pointcounter *m* nach Glagolev, Glagolevscher Pointcounter
Gibbs['] potential	s. free enthalpy		
Gibbs relation, Gibbs['] [fundamental] equation	Gibbssche Fundamentalgleichung *f*	**GLAG theory**, Ginzburg-Landau-Abrikossov-Gorkov theory	GLAG-Theorie *f*, Ginsburg-Landau-Abrikossow-Gorkowsche Theorie *f* [der Supraleitung]
Gibbs['] statistics	Gibbssche Statistik *f*, Gibbs-Statistik *f*		
Gibbs['] theorem	Gibbssches Theorem *n*, Gibbsscher Satz *m*	**glancing**, grazing	Streifen *n*
Gibbs['] thermodynamic potential	s. free enthalpy	**glancing angle**, Bragg reflection angle, Bragg angle, grazing angle	Glanzwinkel *m*, Braggscher Reflexionswinkel (Winkel) *m*, Winkel der Braggschen Reflexion, Beugungswinkel *m*
Gibbs['] vector algebra, vector algebra of Gibbs	Gibbssche Vektoralgebra *f*, Vektoralgebra von Gibbs		
giga ..., G, B	Giga ..., G		
gilbert, Gb	Gilbert *n*, Gb		
Gill-Morell oscillation	Gill-Morell-Schwingung *f*	**glancing collision**, small-angle collision	Kleinwinkelstoß *m*
gimbal, gimbal mounting (suspension), mounting in gimbals, cardanic suspension, Cardan['s] suspension, universal mounting (suspension)	kardanische Aufhängung *f*, Kardan-Aufhängung *f*, Cardanische Aufhängung	**glancing entrance**, grazing entrance, method of glancing (grazing) entrance	streifender Eintritt *m*, Methode *f* des streifenden Eintritts
		glancing exit, grazing exit, method of glancing (grazing) exit	streifender Austritt *m*, Methode *f* des streifenden Austritts
Ginzburg-Landau-Abrikossov-Gorkov theory, GLAG theory	GLAG-Theorie *f*, Ginsburg-Landau-Abrikossow-Gorkowsche Theorie *f* [der Supraleitung]	**glancing illumination**, grazing illumination	streifende Beleuchtung *f*, Streiflicht *n*
		glancing incidence, grazing incidence	streifender Einfall *m*
g-ion	s. gramme-ion		
gion	s. graviton	**Glan[-Thompson] prism**, Glazebrook prism	Glan-Thompson-Prisma *n*, Glansches Prisma *n*, Prisma von Glazebrook
Giorgi system [of units], m.k.s.a. system [of units], complete m.k.s. system, MKSA system, system of absolute electrical units	Giorgisches Einheitensystem (System, Maßsystem) *n*, MKSA-System *n*, absolutes elektrisches Einheitensystem, Meter-Kilogramm-Sekunde-Ampère-System *n*, Giorgi-System *n*, Vierersystem *n*		
		glare; glare blinding; dazzle[ment]	Blendung *f*
		glare effect	Blendwirkung *f*
		glare index	Blendungsexponent *m*
		Glaser lens, solenoid[al] lens	Glaser-Linse *f*, Solenoidlinse *f*
		glass-calomel electrode [couple]	Glas-Kalomel-Elektrode *f*
giraffe, boom <in the emulsion>	Giraffe *f* <in der Emulsion>	**glass dosemeter (dosimeter)**	Glasdosimeter *n*
girder; beam <mech.>	Balken *m*; Träger *m*, Tragbalken *m*; Fachwerkträger *m* <Mech.>	**glass dosimetry**	Glasdosimetrie *f*
		glass electrode	Glaselektrode *f*, Glashalbzelle *f*
given	s. preʃ-]set		
given value of argument in interpolation, interpolation node	Stützstelle *f*, Stützwert *m*, Grundpunkt *m*, Interpolationsknoten *m*, Knoten *m* <Interpolation>	**glass filter funnel**, suction filter	Glasfilternutsche *f*
		glass formation	s. vitrification
		glass former, glass-forming substance	Glasbildner *m*
glacial avalanche	Eislawine *f*		
glacial basin, rock basin	Gletschertopf *m*	**glass gob**, gob	Glasrohling *m*, Rohling *m* <Glas>
glacial cirque	s. cirque		
glacial cosmogony	Welteislehre *f*	**glass grating**	Glasgitter *n*
glacial erosion	Glazialerosion *f*, Gletschererosion *f*	**glass helix**	Glaswendel *f*
glacial eustasy	Eiseustasie *f*, Glazialeustasie *f*		
glacial isostasy	Eisisostasie *f*, Glazialisostasie *f*	**glassiness**	Glasigkeit *f*
		glass plug, glass stopper	Glasstopfen *m*
glacial scratches, striae	Gletscherschliff *m*, Gletscherschrammen *fpl*, Kritzer *mpl*	**glass sight**	s. sighting telescope
		glass spectrograph	Glas[prismen]spektrograph *m*
glaciation	Vergletscherung *f*	**glass stopper**, glass plug	Glasstopfen *m*
glaciation	s. a. icing		
glacieolian	glaziäolisch	**glass structure**	Glasstruktur *f*
		glass-to-metal seal	s. metal-glass seal
glacier crevasse, crevasse	Gletscherspalte *f*	**glass transition**, vitrification, glass formation	Vitrifizierung *f*, Vitrifikation *f*, Verglasung *f*, Übergang *m* in den Glaszustand, Glasbildung *f*
glacieret, second order glacier	Gletscher *m* zweiter Ordnung	**glass transition temperature**	s. freezing-in temperature

glass ultraviolet	Glasultraviolett n, Glas-UV m	**glimmer, glint**	s. gleam
		glissile dislocation	s. slip dislocation
glassy, vitreous	glasig, glasartig	**glissile interface**	gleitfähige Phasengrenzfläche f
		glitter	s. twinkle
		gloaming	s. dusk
glassy sea, smooth sea, unrippled sea	spiegelglatte See f, [vollkommen] glatte See, Meeresstille f <Stärke 0>	**global**	s. non-local <math.>
		global extremum, absolute extremum, extremum in the large	absolutes Extremum n, Extremum im Großen
glassy state, vitreous state	Glaszustand m, glasartiger Zustand m	**global fallout**	globaler Fallout m
Glauert factor, Glauert number	Glauertsche Zahl f, Glauert-Zahl f	**global radiation**	Globalstrahlung f
Glauert rule	Glauertsche Regel f		
glaze	s. glazed frost	**globar**	Globar m, Silitstift m, Silitheizstab m
Glazebrook prism, Glan-Thompson prism, Glan prism	Glan-Thompson-Prisma n, Glansches Prisma n, Prisma von Glazebrook		
glazed frost, glaze	Glatteis n	**globe lightning**, ball lightning	Kugelblitz m
glazing, photographic glazing	Satinage f, Satinieren n	**globe photometer**, sphere photometer	Kugelphotometer n
gleam, bloom; glimmer; glint, shimmer	Schimmern n; Schimmer m	**globe photometer**	s. a. photometric integrator
		globe thermometer	Kugel[strahlungs]thermometer n
glide, gliding flight, volplane	Gleitflug m; Segelflug m	**globular cloud**	ballenförmige Wolke f, Globulusform f
glide	s. a. gliding	**globular cluster**, globular star cluster	Kugelsternhaufen m, Kugelhaufen m
glide band	s. slip band		
glide direction	s. slip direction		
glide ellipse, slip ellipse	Gleitellipse f	**globular projection**	Globularprojektion f
glide lamella	Gleitlamelle f	**globular protein**	s. spheroidal protein
		globular star cluster, globular cluster	Kugelsternhaufen m, Kugelhaufen m
glide line	s. slip line		
glide motion	s. slip <cryst.>	**globule**	Globule f <Astr.>
glide motion of the dislocation, gliding of the dislocation, dislocation gliding	Versetzungsgleiten n, Gleitbewegung f (Gleiten n) der Versetzung	**gloriole**	s. glory
		glory, phantom ring; heiligenschein	Glorie f; Heiligenschein m, Gloriole f
		gloss; glossiness; lustre, luster <US>	Glanz m
glide path, glide slope	Gleitweg m		
glide path reception, glide slope reception	Gleitstrahlempfang m, Gleitwegempfang m	**gloss** <quantity>	Glanzzahl f, Glanz m
		glossimeter	s. glossmeter
		glossiness	s. gloss
		glossmeter, glossimeter	Glanzmesser m
glide plane, slip (shearing) plane, plane of slip <cryst.>	Gleitebene f, Translationsebene f <Krist.>	**glottic catch (cleft), glottis**	Glottis f, Stimmritze f
		glove box, dry box	Handschuhbox f, Glovebox f
glide plane <cryst.>, glide-reflection plane	Gleitspiegelebene f, Gleitebene f <Krist.>	**glow**, glow light, discharge glow (luminescence)	Glimmlicht n, Glimmen n
glider <hydr.>; slip surface, sliding surface, gliding surface	Gleitfläche f	**glow**, incandescence, heat, glowing	Glut f, Glühen n
		glow	Glut f, Gluthitze f, Glühhitze f
glider, skimming boat, planing boat, hydroplane	Gleitboot n, Wassergleiter m	**glow cathode**	s. hot cathode
		glow column, luminous column	Glimmsäule f
glide reflection, gliding reflection	Gleitspiegelung f		
		glow current, luminous current	Glimmstrom m
glide-reflection plane, glide plane <cryst.>	Gleitspiegelebene f, Gleitebene f <Krist.>	**glow curve**, thermal glow curve, thermoluminescence curve	Thermolumineszenzkurve f; Glowkurve f
glide slope	s. glide path		
glide slope reception, glide path reception	Gleitstrahlempfang m, Gleitwegempfang m	**glow discharge**, luminous [current] discharge	Glimmentladung f
glide stage	Gleittisch m	**glow discharge anemometer**	Glimmentladungsanemometer n
		glow-discharge cathode	Glimmkatode f
glide step	Gleitstufe f, Gleitschritt m		
glide system, slip system	Gleitsystem n		
glide vector, slip vector	Gleitvektor m	**glow-discharge electrode**, coronizing electrode	Glimmelektrode f
gliding, slipping[-down], slipping, sliding, slide	Rutschen n, Gleiten n; Abgleiten n; Abrutschen n		
		glow-discharge-excited oscillation	Glimmlichtschwingung f
gliding, slipping <geo.>	Abgleitung f <Geo.>	**glow discharge gauge (manometer)**	Glimmentladungsmanometer n
gliding	s. a. slip <cryst.>		
gliding	s. a. slippage	**glow-discharge lamp**	s. negative glow lamp
gliding angle <aero.>	Gleitwinkel m <Aero.>	**glow-discharge stabilizer [tube]**; neon stabilizer [tube]	Glimm[strecken]stabilisator m, Glimmspannungsstabilisator m, Glimmröhre f zur Spannungsstabilisierung, Glimmstabilisatorröhre f, Stabilisatorglimmröhre f
gliding flight	s. glide		
gliding fold, sliding fold, slip fold	Gleitfalte f		
gliding fracture	s. ductile fracture		
gliding of the dislocation, glide motion of the dislocation, dislocation gliding	Versetzungsgleiten n, Gleitbewegung f (Gleiten n) der Versetzung		
		glow discharge thyratron	Glimmthyratron n
gliding reflection	s. glide reflection	**glow-emitting layer**, airglow (emitting, emission) layer	Emissionsschicht f, Schicht f des Nachthimmelsleuchtens
gliding surface	s. glider		

glow gap	Glimmstrecke f	goniometer eyepiece, protractor ocular head, eyepiece goniometer, goniometric eyepiece	Goniometerokular n, Winkelmeßokular n, Okulargoniometer n
glow heat	s. glowing heat		
glowing cathode	s. hot cathode		
glowing heat, incalescence, incandescence, white heat, glow heat	Weißglut f, Weißglühen n, Weißglühhitze f, Weißgluthitze f, Inkaleszenz f <1 300 °C und mehr>	goniometer technique, X-ray goniometry	Röntgengoniometerverfahren n, Röntgengoniometrie f
		goniometric eyepiece	s. protractor ocular head
		good geometry	gute (günstige) Geometrie f
glow lamp	s. incandescent lamp	good heat conductor	guter Wärmeleiter m
glow lamp	s. a. negative glow lamp		
glow light	s. glow		
glow peak, thermal glow peak	Glowmaximum n, Glow-peak m	Goodman['s] diagram, Goodman line	Spannungshäuschen n; Goodman-Diagramm n, Dauerfestigkeitsschaubild n nach [Gerber, Launhardt-Weyrauch,] Goodman; Dauerfestigkeitsschaubild nach Kommerell [und Roß]
glow potential	s. breakdown voltage		
glow-to-arc transition	Übergang m Glimmstrom–Lichtbogen, Umschlagen n der Glimmentladung in die Bogenentladung, Glimmbogen m		
		goodness of fit test	s. chi-square test
glucinum	= beryllium, Be	good quantum number	gute Quantenzahl f
glue, size	Leim m	good visibility	gute Sicht f
glueing, gluing	Leimen n	Goos-Hänchen effect	Goos-Hänchen-Effekt m
		Gordon['s] wave operator, wave operator	Wellenoperator m, Gordonscher Wellenoperator
glycolytic coefficient	glykolytischer Koeffizient m	Gorsky effect	Gorsky-Effekt m
GM tube, GM counter [tube]	s. Geiger-Müller counter	Gorter-Mellink friction	Gorter-Mellinksche Reibung f
gnomon	Gnomon m, Schattenstab m	Görtzel-Greuling kernel	s. Greuling-Goertzel kernel
		Goss texture	Goss-Textur f
gnomonic projection, orthodromic projection	Gnomonprojektion f, gnomonische (gnomische, orthodromische) Projektion f, Geradwegprojektion f, Zentralprojektion f	"go to" statement	s. jump <num. math.>
		Göttingen-type wind tunnel	Göttinger Windkanal m
		Goubau-Harms wave, Goubau wave	Goubau-Harmssche Oberflächenwelle f
		Goubau line	Goubauscher Wellenleiter (Oberflächenleiter) m, Goubau-Draht m, Goubau-System n, [Harms-]Goubau-Leitung f
gnomonic rule	gnomonisches Lineal n		
goal	Zielpunkt m, Ziel n		
gob, glass gob	Glasrohling m, Rohling m <Glas>		
goblet, stellar embryo	Sternembryo m	Goubau wave, Goubau-Harms wave	Goubau-Harmssche Oberflächenwelle f
Goertzel-Greuling kernel	s. Greuling-Goertzel kernel	Goudsmit gamma sum rule	s. gamma sum rule
going critically <of pile>	Kritischwerden n <Reaktor>	Goudsmit-Uhlenbeck assumption	Goudsmit-Uhlenbecksche Hypothese f
going round of the wind	s. veering of wind [to]		
Golay cell (detector, pneumatic cell), pneumatic receiver	Golay-Zelle f, Golay-Detektor m ,pneumatischer Strahlungsempfänger m [nach Golay], Strahlungsempfänger (Luftthermometer n) von Golay	Gould['s] belt [of bright stars]	Gould-Gürtel m
		Goulier prism	s, pentagonal prism
		Gouy balance	Gouy-Waage f, Gouysche Waage f
		Gouy layer	s. diffuse double layer
		Gouy principle	Gouysches Prinzip n, Prinzip von Gouy
Goldansky-Karyagin effect	Goldanski-Karjagin-Effekt m	Gouy['s] theorem	Satz m von Gouy, Gouyscher Satz
Goldberg postulate	Goldberg-Bedingung f	governing	s. control <control>
Goldberg wedge	Goldberg-Keil m	governing error	größter Fehler m, Hauptfehler m
Goldberg wedge analysis, neutral wedge analysis	Graukeilanalyse f	governing parameter	maßgebender (bestimmender) Parameter m
golden rule, rule of three, rule of proportion	Regeldetri f, Dreisatz m	g permanence rule	g-Permanenzregel f, Permanenzregel f für den g-Faktor
golden rule of mechanics	goldene Regel f der Mechanik	GP zone	s. Guinier-Preston zone
golden section	Goldener Schnitt m, stetige Teilung f	Graaff [accelerator] / Van de	s. Graaff generator / Van de
		Graaff generator / Van de, Van de Graaff [accelerator], belt-type generator, insulating moving belt electrostatic accelerator	Van-de-Graaff-Generator m, van de Graaffscher Generator m, Bandgenerator m, Van-de-Graaff-Beschleuniger m
gold-leaf electrometer (electroscope)	Goldblattelektroskop n, Goldblattelektrometer n, Goldblattvoltmeter n		
gold point, freezing point of gold, point of freezing gold	Goldpunkt m, Erstarrungspunkt m des Goldes		
Goldstein['s] solution	Goldsteinsche Lösung f	Graaff neutron generator / Van de, Graaff type neutron generator / Van de	Van-de-Graaff-Neutronengenerator m, van de Graaffscher Neutronengenerator m
Goldstone diagram	Goldstone-Diagramm n		
Goldstone theorem	Goldstone-Theorem n, Satz m von Goldstone	grad	s. grade
		grad	s. a. gradient <math.>
Golgi apparatus, Golgi complex	Golgi-Apparat m	Grad	s. a. surface gradient
		gradation <gen.>, grading	Stufung f, Abstufung f, Gradation f <allg.>
gon	s. grade		
goniasmometer	Goniasmometer n	gradation, steepness of gradation <phot.>	Gradation f, Steilheit f, Gradationssteilheit f <Phot.>
goniometer; angle measuring instrument; angle protractor, protractor	Goniometer n; Winkelmeßinstrument n, Winkelmeßgerät n, Winkelmesser m	gradation	s. a. vignetting <phot.>
		gradation of colours, colour gradation	Farbabstufung f, Farbenabstufung f
		grad coil, gradient coil	Gradientspule f
goniometer <for single-crystal X-ray diffraction>, X-ray goniometer	Röntgengoniometer n, Goniometer n, Winkelmeßkammer f	grade, gon, ᵍ, gr	Gon n, Neugrad n, ᵍ

grade, sort	Güteklasse *f*; Gütegrad *m*; Sorte *f*	**graduated plate**	Teilplatte *f*
grade, grain-size class	Kornklasse *f*	**graduated spring,** measuring spring	Meßfeder *f*
grade <of matrix>; rank <math.>	Rang *m*; Rangzahl *f* <Math.>	**graduated staff;** levelling staff <*pl.*: staves>, level rod, stadia rod <US>	Nivellierlatte *f*
grade class of accuracy, degree of accuracy <of an instrument>	Genauigkeitsklasse *f* <Gerät>	**graduating engine,** dividing engine	Teilmaschine *f*
graded [interference] filter, wedge-shaped multilayer dielectric interference filter, multilayer dielectric interference filter with shaped distance layer	Verlauffilter *n*, Verlaufinterferenzfilter *n*, verlaufendes Interferenzfilter *n*, Interferenzfilter mit keilförmigen Schichten	**graduation,** scale, scale mark, scale division (graduation)	Skalenteilung *f*, Skaleneinteilung *f*
		graduation, division in degrees	Gradteilung *f*, Gradeinteilung *f*
		graduation	s. a. calibration
		graduation	s. a. smoothing
graded junction <semi.>	nichtabrupter (stetiger, kontinuierlicher, allmählicher, abgestufter) Übergang *m* <Halb.>	**graduation line of the scale**	s. a. division <of the scale>
		graduation of the circle (circular scale)	s. circular dividing
grade grid, map grid	Kartennetz *n*, Gradnetz *n* [der Karte]	**Graeffe['s] method, Graeffe['s] root-squaring method**	Gräffesche Näherungsmethode *f*, Gräffesches (Graeffesches) Verfahren *n*, Graeffe-Verfahren, Verfahren der quadrierten Wurzeln
gradient	Gradient *m*, Gefälle *n*		
gradient, slope, ascent, angular coefficient <of the curve>	Anstieg *m*, Richtungskoeffizient *m*, Steigung *f*, Neigung *f* <Kurve>		
gradient <of a scalar>, grad <math.>	Gradient *m* [eines Skalars], grad <Math.>	**Graetz bridge-type rectifier**	s. Graetz rectifier
gradient acceleration	Gradientbeschleunigung *f*	**Graetz number**	Graetz-Zahl *f*, Graetzsche Kennzahl (Zahl) *f*, Gz
gradient coil, grad coil	Gradientspule *f*		
gradient coupling	Gradientkopplung *f*	**Graetz rectifier,** Graetz bridge-type rectifier, bridge rectifier, bridge rectifier circuit	Graetz-Schaltung *f*, Graetz-Gleichrichter *m*, Graetz-Brücke *f*, Brückengleichrichter *m*, Gleichrichter (Meßgleichrichter) *m* in Brückenschaltung, Gleichrichterbrücke *f*, Graetzsche Vollwegschaltung *f*
gradient current	Gradientströmung *f*, Druckgefällsströmung *f*		
gradient current, gradient wind	Gradientwind *m*		
gradient current due to geostrophic forces, geostrophic wind	geostrophischer Wind *m*		
gradient elution	Gradientenelution *f*		
gradient force	Gradient[en]kraft *f*, Gefällskraft *f*		
gradient layer chromatography, gradient TLC	Gradientschichtchromatographie *f*, dreidimensionale Dünnschichtchromatographie *f*	**graft[ed] [co]polymer**	Pfropf[ko]polymer *n*, Graftkopolymer *n*
		graft[ed] [co]polymerization	Pfropf[ko]polymerisation *f*, Graftkopolymerisation *f*, Zweigkopolymerisation *f*, Zweig[-Misch]polymerisation *f*
gradient of concentration	s. concentration gradient		
gradient of heat, heat gradient	Wärmegradient *m*; Wärmegefälle *n*		
gradient of refractive index	Brechungsgefälle *n*, Brechzahlgefälle *n*, Brechungsindexgradient *m*	**Graham['s] law [of diffusion]**	Grahamsches Gesetz *n*
		grain, crystal grain, crystalline grain <cryst.>	Korn *n*, Kristallkorn *n* <Krist.>
gradient of the thermocline, thermocline gradient	Sprungschichtgradient *m*	**grain boundary**	Korngrenze *f*
gradient of wind, wind gradient	Windgradient *m*, Windgefälle *n*		
gradient reflection	Gradientenreflexion *f*		
gradient temperature, colour temperature at wavelength λ	Gradationstemperatur *f*	**grain boundary conduction**	Korngrenzenleitung *f*, Korngrenzenleitfähigkeit *f*
		grain boundary conductivity	Korngrenzenleitfähigkeit *f*
gradient tensor	Gradiententensor *m*, Gradientaffinor *m*	**grain boundary diffusion**	s. grain boundary migration
gradient TLC	s. gradient layer chromatography	**grain boundary energy,** energy of grain boundary	Korngrenzenenergie *f*
gradient variometer	s. magnetic variometer		
gradient variometer	s. a. magnetic gradiometer	**grain-boundary flow**	Korngrenzenfließen *n*
gradient wind, gradient current	Gradientwind *m*	**grain-boundary fracture**	s. intergranular fracture
grading, classification, sizing, size separation, sorting, classifying process	Klassieren *n* [nach der Korngröße], Trennung *f* nach der Korngröße	**grain boundary migration,** migration of grain boundaries; grain boundary diffusion, intergranular diffusion	Korngrenzenwanderung *f*, Korngrenzenverschiebung *f*, Korngrenzendiffusion *f*
grading, gradation <gen.>	Stufung *f*, Abstufung *f*, Gradation *f* <allg.>		
gradiometer, gravitational variometer, gravity variometer	Gradiometer *n*, Gradientvariometer *n*, Schwerevariometer *n*, Schweremesser *m*	**grain boundary thickness**	Korngrenzenbreite *f*
		grain coarsening	s. coarsening <of grain>
		grain counting	Kornzählung *f*
gradiometer	s. a. magnetic gradiometer	**grain depth development**	Korntiefenentwicklung *f*
Grad['s] method of moments	s. method of moments		
gradometer	s. magnetic gradiometer	**grain form,** grain shape	Kornform *f*
gradually applied load	s. progressive load	**grain fraction,** size fraction	Kornfraktion *f*, Korngrößenfraktion *f*
graduated arc	s. graduated circle		
graduated circle, divided circle, divided circular scale, circular scale; graduated arc	Teilkreis *m*, Kreisteilung *f*; Meßkreis *m*; Limbus *m*; Gradbogen *m*	**graininess**	s. granulation
		graininess	s. a. grain structure
		graining, pelletizing, granulating, granulation	Pelletisieren *n*, Granulieren *n*
		graining out	s. salting out
		grain noise, film-grain noise	Kornrauschen *n*

grain of glacier ice	Gletscherkorn n	granular material, granulate[d material], pellets	Granulat n, Granalien pl, Pellets pl
grain permeability	Kornpermeabilität f	granulating, pelletizing, granulation, graining	Pelletisieren n, Granulieren n
grain raster	Kornraster m		
grain refinement (refining), refinement (refining) of grains	Kornverfeinerung f, Kornfeinung f	granulation, granularity [of emulsion], graininess	Körnung f, Granulation f, Körnigkeit f; Grobkörnigkeit f
grain shape, grain form	Kornform f		
grain size, size [of grain]; granulation size	Korngröße f	granulation, pelletizing, granulating, graining	Pelletisieren n, Granulieren n
grain-size class	s. grade		
grain-size distribution curve	s. granulometric curve	granulation <of photosphere>, photospheric granulation	Granulation f [der Photosphäre]
grain structure, graininess	Kornstruktur f, Korngefüge n	granulation analysis	s. particle-size analysis
grain structure <of image>	Kornstruktur f <Bild>	granulation size; grain size, size [of grain]	Korngröße f
grain structure of fracture, structural fracture	Bruchgefüge n		
grain surface development	Kornoberflächenentwicklung f	granule, granular element <astr.>	Granulum n <pl.: Granula, Granulen>, Element n der Granulation <Astr.>
grainy ice	Korneis n		
gram <US>	s. gramme	granulometric analysis	s. particle-size analysis
Gram determinant, Gramian	Gramsche Determinante f	granulometric curve, grain-size distribution curve, particle-size distribution curve	Körnungskennlinie f, Körnungslinie f, Kornverteilungskurve f, Siebkurve f, Sieblinie f
gramme, gram <US>, g, gm., gr.	Gramm n, g, Massengramm n		
gramme-atom[ic weight], gramatom[ic weight], g-atom	Grammatom n, Atomgramm n, g-Atom n, gAtom n, Tom n, Atol n	graph, topologic graph	topologischer Graph m, Graph
gramme-atomic percentage, atom percent, atomic percent, atom%, at.%	A·omprozent n, Atom-%, At.-%	graph <of operator, transformation>	Graph m <Operator, Transformation>
		graph	s. a. graphical representation
		grapher	s. recorder
gramme-calorie	s. international steam-table calorie	graphical construction, graphical solution	graphische Lösung f, zeichnerische Lösung
gramme-calorie, gramme-calory	s. calorie	graphical construction	s. a. graphical representation
gramme-element specific activity	s. element specific activity	graphical construction of field	s. field plotting
gramme-equivalent, gram-equivalent, val, g-equ.	Val n, Grammäquivalent n, Äquivalent n, val, g-Äqu.	graphical representation, plot, graphical construction, graph <of a function>	[graphische] Darstellung f, Kurvendarstellung f, Kurvenbild n <Funktion>
gramme-force	s. gramme-weight	graphical solution, graphical construction	graphische Lösung f, zeichnerische Lösung
gramme-ion, gram[-]ion, g-ion	Grammion n, g-Ion n, gIon n	graphical statics, graphostatics, graphic statics	graphische Statik f, Graphostatik f
gramme-mole, gramme-molecular weight, gramme-molecule	s. mol		
		graphic formula	s. structural formula
		graphic instrument	s. graph recorder
gramme[-]rad, gram[-]rad, g rad	Grammrad n, Gramm-Rad n, g rd	graphic statics, graphostatics, graphical statics	graphische Statik f, Graphostatik f
gramme roentgen, gram roentgen, gram[me]-röntgen, g R	Grammröntgen n, Gramm-Röntgen n, g R	graphite layer structure, graphite structure	Graphitstruktur f, Graphitschichtstruktur f
gramme-röntgen	s. gramme roentgen	graphitization, graphitizing	Graphit[is]ieren n, Graphitisation f
gramme-weight, gram weight, gram[me]-force, gf, G, pond, p	Pond n, p		
		grapho-analytical method (technique)	graphisch-analytische Methode f
Gram-Schmidt orthogonalization [procedure], Gram-Schmidt orthogonalization process, Gram-Schmidt process, Schmidt['s] [orthogonalization] process	[Hilbert-]Schmidtsches Orthogonalisierungsverfahren n, Orthogonalisierungsverfahren von Erhard Schmidt, Schmidtscher Orthogonalisierungsprozeß m	graphostatics, graphic[al] statics	graphische Statik f, Graphostatik f
		graph paper	s. squared paper
		graph plotter	s. X-Y plotter
		graph recorder	s. recorder
		Grashof['s] number, convection modulus, Gr	Grashof-Zahl f, Grashofsche Kennzahl (Zahl) f, Gr
granatohedron, rhombododecahedron, rhombic dodecahedron	Rhombendodekaeder n, Granatoeder n	Grassmann[¹s] laws	Graßmannsche Gesetze npl; farbmetrisches Grundgesetz n
grand canonical distribution, T-μ distribution	große kanonische Verteilung f	Grassot fluxmeter	Grassotsches Fluxmeter n
		grate, grating, diagrid, grid	Gitterrost m, Rost m
grand canonical ensemble, grand ensemble	große kanonische Gesamtheit f, große Gesamtheit, große Gibbssche Gesamtheit	grate [compensation] pendulum	s. compensated pendulum
		graticule <opt.>, groove grating, grating	Strichgitter n <Opt.>
grand canonical partition function, T-μ partition function	große kanonische Verteilungsfunktion f	graticule <opt.>	Strichplatte f <Opt.>
grand ensemble	große Gesamtheit f		
grand ensemble	s. a. grand canonical ensemble	grating; rubbing; smearing; wiping	Reiben n; Wischen n
grand partition function, grand partition sum	große Verteilungsfunktion f	grating, wire grating <gauze, grid> <el.>	Drahtnetz n, Netz n, Drahtgitter n <El.>
grand potential	großes Potential n	grating, diffraction grating <opt.>	Beugungsgitter n, optisches Gitter n, Gitter <Opt.>
Grand Tour <Earth-Jupiter-Saturn-Uranus-Neptune>	Grand Tour f, „Mehrzweckfahrt" f	grating, groove grating, graticule <opt.>	Strichgitter n <Opt.>
granular element	s. granule	grating	s. a. grate
granularity [of emulsion]	s. granulation	grating aperture	Gitteröffnung f

grating autocollimating spectrograph	Autokollimations-Gitterspektrograph *m*	gravitational collapse (concentration of the star, contraction)	s. collapse of the star
grating constant	s. separation <opt.>	gravitational constant	s. constant of gravitation
grating diaphragm	Gitterblende *f*	gravitational displacement of spectral lines	s. gravitational red-shift
grating equation, grating formula	Gittergleichung *f*	gravitational distribution law	s. barometric equation
grating focus, focus of diffraction grating	Gitterbrennpunkt *m*	gravitational energy	Gravitationsenergie *f*
grating formula	s. grating equation	gravitational field, field of gravity, gravity field	Gravitationsfeld *n*, Schwerefeld *n*, Schwerkraftfeld *n*
grating line	s. groove		
grating monochromator	Gittermonochromator *m*	gravitational field equations, equations of gravitational field	Feldgleichungen *fpl* der Gravitationstheorie, Gravitationsgleichungen *fpl*
grating reflector	Drahtnetzreflektor *m*, Rasterreflektor *m*		
grating spectrograph, diffraction spectrograph	Gitterspektrograph *m*, Beugungsspektrograph *m*	gravitational field [strength]	Gravitationsfeldstärke *f*
grating spectrometer, diffraction spectrometer	Gitterspektrometer *n*, Beugungsspektrometer *n*	gravitational force	s. earth's attraction
		gravitational force	s. gravitation
		gravitational geon	Gravitationsgeon *n*
grating spectroscope, diffraction spectroscope	Beugungsspektroskop *n*, Gitterspektroskop *n*	gravitational interaction	Gravitationswechselwirkung *f*, gravitative Wechselwirkung *f*
		gravitational lens	Gravitationslinse *f*
		gravitational mass	s. heavy mass
grating spectrum; normal spectrum	Gitterspektrum *n*; Normalspektrum *n*	gravitational measurement	s. gravimetry
		gravitational moment	Gravitationsmoment *n*
		gravitational paradox, Seeliger's paradox	Gravitationsparadoxon *n*, Neumann-Seeligersches Paradoxon *n*
graupel	s. ice pellet		
gravel filter	Kiesfilter *n*		
gravel[ly] soil, gritty soil	Skelettboden *m*, Grusboden *m*	gravitational potential	Gravitationspotential *n*
graveyard	s. burial ground		
gravics = theory of gravitational fields		gravitational potential	Potential *n* der Schwerkraft der Erde, Schwerepotential *n*, Schwerkraftpotential *n*
gravimeter, gravitometer, gravity meter	Gravimeter *n*, Schweremesser *m*, Schwerkraftmesser *m*		
		gravitational quantum	s. graviton
gravimètre	Dichtemesser *m* für Flüssigkeiten, Flüssigkeitsdichtemesser *m*	gravitational radiation	Gravitationsstrahlung *f*
		gravitational red-shift, relativity displacement of spectral lines, gravitational displacement of spectral lines, Einstein [red] shift, Einstein effect	Rotverschiebung *f* im Schwerefeld (Gravitationsfeld), [allgemein-] relativistische Rotverschiebung, Einstein-Verschiebung *f*, Einsteinsche Rotverschiebung (Spektralverschiebung *f*), Einstein-Effekt *m*, Gravitations-Rotverschiebung *f*
gravimetric analysis	s. gravimetry <chem.>		
gravimetric correction, gravity correction	Schwerekorrektion *f*, Schwerkraftkorrektion *f*		
gravimetric map, gravity contour map	Schwerekarte *f*, Schwerebild *n*		
gravimetric measurement	s. gravimetry		
gravimetric network, gravity network	Schwerenetz *n*	gravitational shift	Gravitationsverschiebung *f*
		gravitational system of units	Gravitationseinheitensystem *n*
gravimetric station	Schwerestation *f*	gravitational variometer	s. gradiometer
gravimetric variometer	Gravitationsvariometer *n*	gravitational wave	Gravitationswelle *f*, Schwerewelle *f*
gravimetry, gravity survey, gravity (gravitational, gravimetric) measurement	Gravimetrie *f*, Schweremessung *f*, Schwerkraftmessung *f*, Schwerevermessung *f*	gravitational wave	s. a. gravity wave
		gravitational wave surface	Gravitationswellenfläche *f*
		gravitation constant	s. constant of gravitation
gravimetry, gravimetric analysis <chem.>	Gravimetrie *f*, gravimetrische Analyse *f*, Gewichtsanalyse *f*	gravitation dynamics	Gravitationsdynamik *f*
		gravitation force	s. earth's attraction
gravisphere	Gravisphäre *f*	gravitation force	s. gravitation
gravitating gas	gravitierendes Gas *n*	gravitation law, law of universal gravitation, law of gravitation	allgemeines Gravitationsgesetz *n*, Gravitationsgesetz
gravitation, universal gravitation, general gravitation, gravitational attraction, mass potential; gravitational force, gravitation force, world force	[allgemeine] Gravitation *f*, [allgemeine] Massenanziehung *f*, universelle Gravitation, gravitative Anziehung *f*; [Newtonsche] Gravitationskraft *f*, Massenanziehungskraft *f*, Weltkraft *f*		
		gravitation law [of Newton]	s. law of gravitation
		gravitino, graviton, quantum of gravitational radiation, gravitational quantum, gion	Graviton *n*, Gravitationsquant *n*, Gravitino *n*, Quant *n* des Gravitationsfeldes
gravitation	s. a. earth['s] attraction	gravitometer, gravimeter, gravity meter	Gravimeter *n*, Schweremesser *m*, Schwerkraftmesser *m*
gravitational aberration [of light]	s. relativistic deflection of light		
gravitational acceleration	s. acceleration of gravity	graviton, gravitino, quantum of gravitational radiation, gravitational quantum, gion	Graviton *n*, Gravitationsquant *n*, Gravitino *n*, Quant *n* des Gravitationsfeldes
gravitational anomaly, gravity anomaly	Schwereanomalie *f*, Schwerestörung *f*, Anomalie *f* der Schwerkraft		
		gravitophotoresis	Gravitophotorese *f*
		gravity	s. earth's attraction
gravitational attraction	s. gravitation	gravity acceleration	s. acceleration of gravity
gravitational coagulation	Schwerekoagulation *f*, Koagulation *f* durch die Schwerkraft	gravity anomaly, gravitational anomaly	Schwereanomalie *f*, Schwerestörung *f*, Anomalie *f* der Schwerkraft

gravity axis, centroid axis, axis of gravity — Schwerlinie f, Schwerpunkt[s]achse f, Schwerachse f, Impulsachse f, raumfeste Impulsachse

gravity barometer, weight barometer — Waagenbarometer n

gravity bob, sensitivity nut — Empfindlichkeitseinstellschraube f, Reguliergewicht n ‹Waage›

gravity bottle — s. pyknometer

gravity-capillary wave — Schwerekapillarwelle f

gravity constant — s. acceleration of gravity

gravity contour map, gravimetric map — Schwerekarte f, Schwerebild n

gravity controlled gyroscope, Earth gyroscope, barygyroscope — schwerer Kreisel m

gravity correction, gravimetric correction — Schwerekorrektion f, Schwerkraftkorrektion f

gravity dam — Schwergewichts[stau]mauer f, Gewichts[stau]mauer f

gravity field, gravitational field, field of gravity — Gravitationsfeld n, Schwerefeld n, Schwerkraftfeld n

gravity flow — Gravitationsströmung f

gravity formula — Schwereformel f

gravity head, position head, geometrical head — wirkliche Höhe f, Höhenlage f

gravity measurement — s. gravimetry

gravity meter, gravimeter, gravitometer — Gravimeter n, Schweremesser m, Schwerkraftmesser m

gravity network, gravimetric network — Schwerenetz n

gravity-operated ‹techn.› — frei fallend, freifallend ‹Techn.›

gravity pendulum — Schwerependel n, Gravitationspendel n

gravity plane, plane of gravity — Schwerebene f

gravity pressure, pressure due to gravity (the own weight) — Schweredruck m

gravity reduction — Schwerereduktion f, Massenreduktion f

gravity segregation — Schwereseigerung f, Schwerkraftseigerung f

gravity separation — Schweretrennung f, Massenkraftklassierung f, Klassieren (Trennung) f nach der Masse, Trennung im Schwerefeld

gravity survey — s. gravimetry

gravity variometer — s. gradiometer

gravity viscometer, efflux viscometer — Ausflußviskosimeter n

gravity wave, gravitational wave — Schwerewelle f

gray ‹US› — s. grey

grazing, glancing — Streifen n

grazing angle — s. glancing angle

grazing entrance, glancing entrance, method of glancing (grazing) entrance — streifender Eintritt m, Methode f des streifenden Eintritts

grazing exit, glancing exit, method of glancing (grazing) exit — streifender Austritt m, Methode f des streifenden Austritts

grazing illumination, glancing illumination — streifende Beleuchtung f, Streiflicht n

grazing incidence, glancing incidence — streifender Einfall m

grazing occultation — streifende Bedeckung f

grease, consistent (lubricant) grease, solid lubricant, albany grease — Schmierfett n, Schmierfeststoff m, fester Schmierstoff m, Starrschmiere f

grease — erstes Gefrierstadium n des Wassers

grease for cocks, cock grease, tap grease — Hahnfett n

grease spot photometer, Bunsen photometer — Fettfleckphotometer n [von Bunsen], Bunsen-Photometer n

great circle — Großkreis m, größter Kreis (Kugelkreis) m, Hauptkreis m der Kugelfläche

great circle line, orthodrome — Orthodrome f

greatest common divisor, highest common factor, G.C.D. — größter gemeinschaftlicher (gemeinsamer) Teiler m, ggT

greatest lower bound, infimum, inf — untere Grenze f, Infimum n, inf

great fall, sudden fall, fall — Sturz m

great fireball, bright fireball — heller Bolid m, großer Bolid

great metacentre — großes Metazentrum n

great planet — s. major planet

green blindness, deuteranopia — Deuteranopie f, Grünblindheit f

Green['s] deformation tensor, strain tensor of Green — Greenscher Deformationstensor m, Deformationstensor von Green

green flash — grüner Strahl m, grünes Flämmchen n

Green['s] formula[e] — s. Green['s] theorem

Green['s] formula of the first kind, first Green formula — Greensche Formel f erster Art, erste Greensche Formel

Green['s] formula of the second kind, second Green formula — Greensche Formel f zweiter Art, zweite Greensche Formel

Green['s] function, source function — Greensche Funktion f, Einflußfunktion f, Quellenfunktion f

Green['s] function [in quantum field theory] — s. quantum Green['s] function ‹qu.›

Green['s] function of the first ‹second› kind — Greensche Funktion f erster ‹zweiter› Art

greenhouse effect, terrestrial greenhouse effect — Glashauseffekt m, Glashauswirkung f der Atmosphäre, Treibhauseffekt m, Treibhauswirkung f der Atmosphäre, Gewächshauseffekt m, Greenhouseeffekt m; Glashausprinzip n

Green['s] identity — s. Green['s] theorem

green line of solar corona — grüne Koronalinie f

Green['s] matrix, Green['s] tensor, dyadic Green['s] function — Greenscher Tensor m, tensorielle Greensche Funktion f, Greensche Matrix f

Green['s] reciprocity theorem — Greenscher Reziprozitätssatz m, Greensches Reziprozitätstheorem n

green segment — grünes Segment n

green shadow — Grünschatten m

green strength — Grünfestigkeit f, Grünstandfestigkeit f

Green['s] stress tensor — Greenscher Spannungstensor m

Green['s] symmetrical theorem, integral theorem of Green, Green['s] theorem (formulae, formula, identity) — Greenscher Satz m, Greensche Sätze mpl, Greensche Formeln fpl

Green['s] tensor, dyadic Green['s] function, Green['s] matrix — Greenscher Tensor m, tensorielle Greensche Funktion f, Greensche Matrix f

Green['s] theorem, Green['s] transformation, Ostrogradsky['s] theorem, divergence theorem, Gauss['] divergence theorem, integral theorem of Gauss, Gaussian theorem, Gauss['] theorem, integration by parts — Gaußscher Satz m [der Vektoranalysis], Gaußscher Satz der Integralrechnung, Gaußsche (Greensche) Integralformel f, Integralformel (Integralsatz m) von Gauß, Gauß[-Ostrogradski]scher Integralsatz, Ostrogradskische Formel f (Integralformel), Gauß-Ostrogradskische (Gaußsche, Greensche) Formel, Divergenzsatz m, Fundamentalsatz m der Vektoranalysis

Green['s] theorem	s. a. Green['s] symmetrical theorem	grey tone	Grauton m
Green['s] theorem for n = 2, Riemann['s] theorem	Gaußsche Integralformel f im Fall n = 2, Greensche Integralformel, Integralformel von Green, Riemannsche Integralformel (Formel) f, Gaußscher Integralsatz m im Fall n = 2	grey track, grey prong	„graue" Spur f
		grey value	Grauwert m
		grey veiling, veiling (masking, shading) by grey, grey masking (shading)	Grauverhüllung f, Vergrauung f
		grey wedge, neutral wedge, wedge	Graukeil m, Neutralkeil m, Keil m
Green['s] transformation	s. Green['s] theorem	grey-wedge exposure meter, wedge exposure meter	Keilbelichtungsmesser m
Greenwich astronomical time	s. Greenwich Mean Astronomical Time		
Greenwich civil time	s. Universal time	grey wedge pyrometer	Graukeilpyrometer n
Greenwich Mean Astronomical Time, Greenwich Mean time, Greenwich astronomical time, G.M.T., GMT, G.M.A.T., GMAT	mittlere astronomische Zeit f Greenwich (Grw.), mittlere Zeit Greenwich (Grw.), MaZGr	grid; net; lattice	Kurvennetz n, Liniennetz n, Netz n
		grid <el.>	Gitter n <El.>
		grid, rectangular coordinate system <geo.>	Gitternetz n, Gitter n, Gauß-Krüger-Koordinaten fpl, Gauß-Krügersche Koordinaten fpl (Meridianstreifen mpl) <Geo.>
Greenwich meridian	s. zero meridian		
G region	s. inner core		
Gregorian calendar	gregorianischer Kalender m		
Gregorian instrument, Gregorian [reflecting] telescope	Gregorysches Spiegelteleskop n, Spiegelteleskop nach Gregory	grid, blade grid, vane grid <hydr., aero.>	Schaufelgitter n, Flügelgitter n, Gitter n
		grid	s. a. modulator
Gregorian year	gregorianisches Jahr n	grid	s. a. screen
Gregory['s] backward formula, Newton['s] interpolation formula with backward differences	Newtonsche Interpolationsformel f mit aufsteigenden Differenzen, zweite Gregory-Newtonsche Formel f	grid	s. a. stationary grid
		grid	s. a. grate
		grid-anode capacitance, grid-plate capacitance (capacity)	Gitter-Anode[n]-Kapazität f, Gitteranodenkapazität f
Gregory['s] formula, Gregory-Newton formula	Gregorysche Integrationsformel f	grid-anode conductance <of thermionic valve>, reaction conductance	Rückwirkungsleitwert m
Gregory['s] forward formula, Newton['s] interpolation formula with forward differences	Newtonsche Interpolationsformel f mit absteigenden Differenzen, erste Gregory-Newtonsche Formel f	grid-anode gap, grid-plate gap	Gitter-Anoden-Strecke f
		grid-anode space, grid-plate space	Gitter-Anoden-Raum m
Gregory['s] interpolation formulae	s. Newton['s] interpolation formulae	grid bias, cut-off bias, grid cut-off voltage <of the valve>	Gittersperrspannung f, Steuergittereinsatzspannung f <Röhre>
Gregory-Newton formula	s. Gregory['s] formula		
Gregory['s] series	Arkustangensreihe f, arctan-Reihe f		
Greinacher accelerator	s. cascade generator	grid bias	s. a. grid bias voltage
Greinacher circuit, Greinacher doubling circuit, Latour circuit, Delon rectifier circuit, voltage doubling circuit [of Greinacher], Liebenow circuit	Greinacher-Schaltung f, Greinacher-Stufe f, Spannungsverdopplerschaltung f [nach Greinacher], Stabilovoltschaltung f, Latour-Schaltung f, Delon-Schaltung f, Liebenow-Schaltung f	grid bias	s. a. grid-bias voltage
		grid bias detector	s. anode detector
		grid-bias modulation	Gitterspannungsmodulation f
		grid-bias voltage, grid bias, bias voltage, bias, grid polarization (priming) voltage, priming grid voltage	Gittervorspannung f, Gitterverschiebungsspannung f, Steuergittervorspannung f
Greinacher-Cockcroft [-Walton] generator	s. cascade generator		
Greinacher doubling circuit	s. Greinacher circuit	grid capacitance	s. input capacitance
		grid-cathode capacitance, grid-to-cathode capacitance, grid-filament capacitance	Gitter-Katode-Kapazität f, Gitter-Katoden-Kapazität f, Gitterkatodenkapazität f
Grenet variometer	Grenetsches Variometer n		
grenz ray region	Grenzstrahlgebiet n		
grenz rays, infra-Röntgen rays, Bucky rays	Grenzstrahlen mpl, Bucky-Strahlen mpl	grid-cathode gap	Gitter-Katoden-Strecke f
		grid-cathode space	Gitter-Katoden-Raum m
grenz tube	Grenzstrahlröhre f	grid characteristic	Gitterstrom-Gitterspannungs-Kennlinie f, Gitterstromcharakteristik f, Gitterkennlinie f, Gittercharakteristik f, I_g-U_g-Kennlinie f
Greuling-Goertzel kernel, Goertzel-Greuling (Görtzel-Greuling) kernel	Greuling-Goertzel-Kern m		
grey atmosphere	graue Atmosphäre f		
grey body, gray body <US>, non-selective radiator	Graustrahler m, grauer Strahler (Körper) m, nichtselektiver Strahler	grid control	Gittersteuerung f
		grid current	Gitterstrom m
		grid current pulse	Gitterstromimpuls m
grey body radiation	graue Strahlung f, Graustrahlung f	grid-current starting point	Gitterstromeinsatzpunkt m
grey filter	Unechtgraufilter n	grid cut-off voltage	s. grid bias
grey fog	Grauschleier m	gridded chamber, grid ionization chamber	Ionisationskammer f mit Gitter, Gitterionisationskammer f
grey group	graue Gruppe f		
grey heat	Grauglut f <400 °C>		
		gridded dynode	Netzdynode f
grey masking	s. veiling by grey		
grey prong, grey track	„graue" Spur f		
grey scale, grey series	s. progressive series of greys	gridded electrode	Netzelektrode f; Gitterelektrode f
grey shaded	s. non-zero black and white content / having <of chromatic colour>	grid-dip meter	Grid-Dip-Meter n, Grid-dip-Oszillator m, Griddipper m
grey shading	s. veiling by grey		
grey step wedge	s. neutral step wedge		

grid dissipation	Gitterbelastung f, Gitterverlustleistung f	Griffith crack	Griffithscher Riß m, Griffith-Riß m
grid energy, lattice [binding] energy	Gitterenergie f	grignardizing; Grignard reaction, Grignard synthesis	Grignard-Synthese f, Grignardsche Synthese f, Grignard-Reaktion f, Grignardsche Reaktion f; Grignardierung f
grid-filament capacitance	s. grid-cathode capacitance	Grimm-Sommerfeld['s] compound, Grimm-Sommerfeld phase	Grimm-Sommerfeld-Phase f, Grimm-Sommerfeldsche Phase (Verbindung) f
grid-glow tube	s. cold-cathode valve		
grid hum	Gitterbrumm n	Grimm-Sommerfeld['s] rule	Grimm-Sommerfeldsche Regel f
grid ionization chamber, gridded chamber	Ionisationskammer f mit Gitter, Gitterionisationskammer f	Grimsehl['s] method	Grimsehls Methode f
		grinding	Schleifen n, Schliff m
grid leak, grid leak resistance; grid leak resistor, bias resistor	Gitterableitwiderstand m, Gitterableitung f, äußerer Gitterwiderstand m	grinding	s. a. comminution <techn.>
		grinding	s. a. rubbing [to powder]
		grinding-down	s. grinding
		grinding-in	Einschleifen n
grid line	Gitter[netz]linie f, Gittergerade f	grinding to powder	s. grinding
		grind plane	Schlifffläche f
grid mesh, mesh	Gittermasche f, Masche f des Gitters	gritty soil, gravel soil, gravelly soil	Skelettboden m, Grusboden m
grid method	Rastermethode f, Rasterverfahren n, Rastertechnik f <Exponierung in Eichfeldern>	Grodzinski hardness test	Grodzinski-Härteprüfung f
		groove, groove of grating; grating line	Furche f, Gitterfurche f, Strich m, Gitterstrich m <Beugungsgitter>
grid micrometer	Netzmikrometer n; Okularnetzmikrometer n		
grid nephoscope, grid-type nephoscope	Wolkengitter n	groove, rill, rille, furrow, cleft <on the Moon's surface>	Rille f <auf der Mondoberfläche>
grid net	quadratisches Netz n, Quadratnetz n	groove angle	Rillenwinkel m
grid noise	Gitterrauschen n		
grid north	Gitternord m, Gitter-Nord m	groove depth	Furchentiefe f
		groove form	Furchenform f
grid of co-ordinates, co-ordinate grid (net)	Koordinatennetz n, Koordinatengitter n	groove grating, grating, graticule <opt.>	Strichgitter n <Opt.>
grid of points, point grid	Punktnetz n, Punktgitter n; Zahlengitter n	groove grating spectrograph	Strichgitterspektrograph m
grid optics, raster optics	Rasteroptik f	groove-needle resonance	Rille-Nadel-Resonanz f
grid-plate capacitance (capacity), grid-anode capacitance	Gitter-Anode[n]-Kapazität f, Gitteranodenkapazität f	groove of grating, groove; grating line	Furche f, Gitterfurche f, Strich m, Gitterstrich m <Beugungsgitter>
grid-plate characteristic	Anodenstrom-Gitterspannungs-Kennlinie f, I_a-U_g-Kennlinie f	groove of the notch, notch groove, root (base) of the notch	Kerbgrund m
		groove spacing, separation [of the elements of grating] <opt.>	Gitterkonstante f [des Beugungsgitters] <Opt.>, optische Gitterkonstante
grid-plate gap, grid-anode gap	Gitter-Anoden-Strecke f		
grid-plate space, grid-anode space	Gitter-Anoden-Raum m	gross balance	Bruttobilanz f
		gross beta activity	s. total beta activity
grid-plate transconductance	s. transconductance	gross calorific value, gross heating value <US>, gross heat of combustion, higher (upper) calorific value, G.C.V., G.H.V. <techn.>	oberer Heizwert m, Brennwert m, Verbrennungswärme f, Ho <Techn.>
grid point, lattice point <math.>	Gitterpunkt m; Stützstelle f <Math.>		
grid polarization voltage	s. grid-bias voltage		
grid potential, grid voltage <el.>	Gitterspannung f, Gitterpotential n <El.>	gross formula	s. empirical formula
		gross instability	s. magnetohydrodynamic instability
grid priming voltage	s. grid-bias voltage	gross refrigerating capacity	Bruttokälteleistung f
grid ratio	Rasterverhältnis n	gross register ton	Bruttoregistertonne f, BRT
		gross tonnage	Bruttotonnage f, Bruttoregistertonnenzahl f, BRT-Zahl f
grid resistance, incremental [grid] resistance, resistance of grid circuit	innerer Gitterwiderstand m, Gitterwiderstand, Gitterkreiswiderstand m		
		Gross transformation	Gross-Transformation f, Grosssche Transformation f
grid spacing	Rasterkonstante f, Rasterteilung f		
grid structure, cellular network, reticular structure	Netzstruktur f, Netzverband m	gross weight	Bruttomasse f; Bruttogewicht n
		Grotrian diagram	Grotrian-Diagramm n, Diagramm n nach Grotrian
grid support	Gittersteg m, Gitterstrebe f		
grid sweep, grid swing	Gitteraussteuerung f	Grotthus-Draper law, law of Grotthus and Draper, Draper law	[Grotthus-]Drapersches Gesetz n, Grotthus-Draper-Gesetz n, Gesetz von Grotthus und Draper
grid-to-cathode capacitance	s. grid-cathode capacitance		
grid transparency	s. penetrance	ground; mass, body <el.>	Masse f, Körper m; Erde f <El.>
grid-type nephoscope, grid nephoscope	Wolkengitter n	ground, mat, frosted	matt
		ground	s. a. mass connection
grid voltage, grid potential <el.>	Gitterspannung f, Gitterpotential n <El.>	ground	s. a. earth wire <el.>
		ground absorption	Erdbodenabsorption f, Bodenabsorption f
grid voltage pulse	Gitterspannungsimpuls m		
gridwork	s. cellular network	ground antenna	Erdantenne f

ground avalanche	s. humid snow avalanche	ground plate; earth plate, ground rod	Erder m, Erdungsleitung f; Erdelektrode f; Erdplatte f
ground breaker, ground roll[ing], roller	Roller m, Brander m, auflaufende Welle f		
ground capacitance; earth capacitance	Erdkapazität f	ground pressure	Bodendruck m
ground connection	s. earth wire <el.>	ground reflection	Bodenreflexion f, Bodenrückstrahlung f
ground contact	s. mass connection		
ground current, earth current	Erdstrom m; vagabundierender Strom m	ground resistance	s. discharging resistance
		ground rod; earth plate, ground plate	Erder m, Erdungsleitung f; Erdelektrode f; Erdplatte f
grounded anode amplifier	s. cathode follower		
grounded-base circuit	Basisschaltung f, Basisgrundschaltung f	ground roll[ing], ground breaker, roller	Roller m, Brander m, auflaufende Welle f
grounded-cathode amplifier, common-cathode amplifier; grounded-cathode stage	Katodenbasisverstärker m; Katodenbasisstufe f	ground roll[ing]	s. a. eddy motion of the water particles near the bottom
		ground sample	s. metallographic specimen
		ground state, normal state, fundamental state, g.s., g	Grundzustand m, Normalzustand m
grounded-cathode circuit, grounded-cathode-type circuit, see-saw circuit	Katodenbasisschaltung f, KB-Schaltung f, KBS	ground stopper; ground[-] glass stopper	Schliffstopfen m, eingeschliffener Stopfen m; eingeschliffener Glasstopfen m
grounded-cathode stage	s. grounded-cathode amplifier	ground swell <hydr.>	Grundwelle f <Hydr.>
grounded-cathode-type circuit	s. grounded-cathode circuit	ground temperature	Temperatur f am Boden, Temperatur in Bodennähe, Bodentemperatur f
grounded collector circuit, common collector circuit	Kollektor[grund]schaltung f, Kollektorbasisschaltung f, Kollektor-Basis-Schaltung f	ground term, normal (fundamental) term, term of ground state	Grundterm m, Term m des Grundzustandes
grounded-emitter circuit (connection)	s. common-emitter circuit	ground water	s. soil water
		ground water	s. underground water
grounded-grid amplifier	Gitterbasisverstärker m	ground-water basin	Grundwasserbecken n
		ground-water contour [line]	s. water table contour
		ground-water divide, ground-water watershed	Grundwasserscheide f
grounded-grid circuit (stage), grounded-grid-type circuit, grounded grid, current follower	Gitterbasisschaltung f, GB-Schaltung f, GBS, Gitterbasisstufe f	ground-water floor	Grundwasserstockwerk n
		ground-water level	s. level of ground water
		ground-water reservoir, water-bearing stratum; aquifer	wasserführende Schicht f, Grundwasserleiter m
grounded grid, current follower	s. grounded-grid circuit	ground-water watershed, groundwater divide	Grundwasserscheide f
grounded ice; ground ice; anchor ice	Grundeis n; Ankereis n	ground-water wave	Grundwasserwelle f
ground fog	Bodennebel m; Wiesennebel m	ground wire	s. earth wire <el.>
		group, main (periodic) group, Mendeleev['s] [periodic] group <in the periodic table>	Hauptgruppe f, Gruppe f, Familie f <im Periodensystem>
ground form	s. fundamental form		
ground[-] glass; ground joint; ground glass joint	Schliffverbindung f; Schliff m; Glasschliff m		
ground glass	s. a. groundglass screen	group, grouping, rest <chem.>	Gruppe f <Chem.>
groundglass image	Mattscheibenbild n		
ground glass joint; ground joint; ground[-] glass	Schliffverbindung f; Schliff m; Glasschliff m	group, point[-] group [of symmetry], point symmetry group <cryst.>	Punktsymmetriegruppe f, Punktgruppe f <Krist.>
groundglass plane	s. image plane	group <math.>	Gruppe f <Math.>
groundglass rangefinder	s. reflex-prism split image rangefinder	group algebra, group ring	Gruppenalgebra f, Gruppenring m
groundglass screen, focusing screen, mat glass plate, ground glass	Mattscheibe f	group averaged cross-section	über die Gruppen gemittelter Wirkungsquerschnitt m (Querschnitt m)
ground[-] glass stopper	s. ground stopper		
ground ice; anchor ice; grounded ice	Grundeis n; Ankereis n		
grounding	s. mass connection	group character, character	Gruppencharakter m, Charakter m
grounding circuit	s. earth wire <el.>	group character, group property	Gruppeneigenschaft f
grounding resistance	s. discharging resistance		
ground inversion, surface inversion	Bodeninversion f	group III—V compound, III—V compound	IIIV/V-Verbindung f, $A^{III}B^V$-Verbindung f
ground joint; ground glass joint; ground[]glass	Schliffverbindung f; Schliff m; Glasschliff m	group constant	Gruppenkonstante f
		group delay	s. envelope delay
ground-joint female part	s. socket [of ground-in joint]	group delay / frequency characteristic	s. phase response
ground-joint male part	s. male part [of ground-in joint]	group delay time	s. envelope delay
ground leak, short-[-circuit] to earth, contact to earth, accidental ground	Erdschluß m	group-diffusion method, group method	Gruppendiffusionsmethode f, Gruppenmethode f
ground level, normal (fundamental) level	Grundniveau n	group frequency	Gruppenfrequenz f
		group index, group refractive index	Gruppenbrechungsindex m, Gruppen-Brechungsindex m
ground-level air	s. near-ground air		
ground moraine, subglacial moraine	Grundmoräne f; Moränendecke f	grouping, group <chem.>	Gruppe f <Chem.>
		grouping <stat.>	Klasseneinteilung f <Stat.>
		grouping [of electrons]	s. a. bunching
ground photogrammetry	s. geophotogrammetry	group method	s. group-diffusion method
ground-plane antenna; horizontally polarized antenna	„ground-plane"-Antenne f; horizontal polarisierte Antenne f	group of curves, family of curves, system (set) of curves	Kurvenschar f, Schar f [von Kurven]

group   308

group of isometry   Isometriegruppe *f*

group of isotropy, isotropy group   Isotropiegruppe *f*

group of movement, movement group   Bewegungsgruppe *f*

group of plates   Plattensatz *m*

group of restricted homogeneous Lorentz transformation   s. proper Lorentz group

group of rotation   s. rotation[s] group

group of similarity transformations   Gruppe *f* der Ähnlichkeitstransformationen

group of sunspots, spot group   Fleckengruppe *f*, Sonnenfleckengruppe *f*

group of translations, translation[al] group   Translationsgruppe *f*

group property   s. group character

group radiator   Gruppenstrahler *m*

group refractive index, group index   Gruppenbrechungsindex *m*, Gruppen-Brechungsindex *m*

group relaxation   s. block relaxation

group removal cross-section, removal cross section   Removalquerschnitt *m*, „removal"-Querschnitt *m*, Ausscheidquerschnitt *m*

group ring   s. group algebra

groups / between group[-]theoretical   s. interclass gruppentheoretisch

group theory <math.>   Gruppentheorie *f* <Math.>

group transfer scattering cross-section   Gruppenübergangsquerschnitt *m*

group velocity, envelope velocity   Gruppengeschwindigkeit *f*

group wavelength   Gruppenwellenlänge *f*

growing   s. growing of crystals

growing cold, cooling, cooling down   Erkalten *n*, Abkühlung *f*

growing from the melt [of crystals]   s. pulling of crystals

growing of crystals, [crystal] growing, growth of crystals, crystal growth   Züchtung *f* [von Kristallen], Kristallzüchtung *f*

growing warm, heating, heat; warming   Aufheizung *f*; Ausheizung *f*; Erhitzung *f*; Erwärmung *f*

grown junction, pulled junction   gezogener Übergang *m*

grown-junction transistor   gezogener Transistor *m*, Wachstumstransistor *m*

growth <cryst.; nucl.; bio.>   Wachstum *n* <Krist.; Kern.; Bio.>

growth <of the function>, order of the function   Wachstumsordnung *f* [der Funktion], Ordnung *f* [der Funktion]

growth   s. a. increase

growth curve <nucl.>   Nachbildungskurve *f*, Anstiegskurve *f*, Wachstumskurve *f* <Kern.>

growth curve   s. a. law of growth <stat.>

growth defect   Wachstumsbaufehler *m*, Wachstumsfehler *m*

growth face, growth plane   Wachstumsfläche *f*

growth factor   Wachstumsfaktor *m*

growth formula (function)   s. law of growth <stat.>

growth habit   s. habit of the crystal

growth layer   Wachstumsschicht *f*

growth line   Wachstumsgerade *f*

growth of crystal, crystal growth   Kristallwachstum *n*, Kristallvergrößerung *f*

growth of crystals   s. growing of crystals

growth of films, film growth   Schichtwachstum *n*

growth of fog; fog development   Schleierentwicklung *f*; Schleierwachstum *n*

growth of the germs (nuclei)   Kernwachstum *n*; Keimwachstum *n*

growth operator, increase operator, operator of increase   Zuwachsoperator *m*

growth plane, growth face   Wachstumsfläche *f*

growth point, point of growth <math.>   Wachstumspunkt *m* <Math.>

growth rate, rate of growth, growth velocity <cryst.; bio.>   Wachstumsgeschwindigkeit *f*, Wachstumsrate *f* <Krist.>; Wachstumsschnelligkeit *f* <Bio.>

growth spiral   Wachstumsspirale *f*

growth step   Wachstumstreppe *f*; Wachstumsstufe *f*, Wachstumskante *f*

growth texture, secondary recrystallization texture   Wachstumstextur *f*

growth theory [of crystals]   Wachstumstheorie *f* [der Kristalle]

growth twin   Wachstumszwilling *m*

growth velocity; rate of growth, growth rate <cryst.; bio.>   Wachstumsgeschwindigkeit *f*, Wachstumsrate *f* <Krist.>; Wachstumsschnelligkeit *f* <Bio.>

Grüneisen-Borelius relation   Grüneisen-Boreliussche Beziehung *f*

Grüneisen['s] constant, Grüneisen gamma, Grüneisen number   Grüneisen-Konstante *f*, Grüneisensche Konstante *f*, Grüneisenscher Parameter (Koeffizient) *m*

Grüneisen equation of state, Mie-Grüneisen equation of state   Grüneisensche Zustandsgleichung (Beziehung) *f*, Grüneisen-Beziehung *f*

Grüneisen['s] first rule   erste Grüneisensche Regel *f*

Gruneisen formula   s. Bloch-Grüneisen equation

Grüneisen gamma   s. Grüneisen['s] constant

Grüneisen['s] law, Grüneisen['s] rule (relation), Grüneisen['s] second rule, Grüneisen['s] two-constant formula   Grüneisensche Regel (Ausdehnungsregel, Zweiparameterformel) *f*, zweite Grüneisensche Regel, Grüneisensches Gesetz *n*

Grüneisen number   s. Grüneisen['s] constant

Grüneisen['s] relation ([second] rule), Grüneisen['s] two-constant formula   s. Grüneisen['s] law

G star, solar star, sun-type star   G-Stern *m*, Sonnenähnlicher *m*

g sum rule, g-sum rule, Pauli['s] g-sum rule   g-Summensatz *m*, Summensatz *m* (Summenregel *f*) für den g-Faktor

G-test   s. substitute *t*-test

guard cell   Schließzelle *f*

guard digit, guarding figure, security digit; guard position <num. math.>   Schutzziffer *f*; Schutzstelle *f* <num. Math.>

guard electrode   Schutzelektrode *f*

guarding figure   s. guard digit <num. math.>

guard position   s. guard digit <num. math.>

guard ring <el.>   Schutzring *m*; Hilfselektrode *f* <z. B. Ionisationskammer> <El.>

guard-ring detector   Schutzringdetektor *m*

Guchmann number   Guchmann-Zahl *f*, Guchmannsche Kennzahl *f*

Gudden and Pohl primary current   Gudden-Pohlscher Primärstrom *m*

Gudden-Pohl effect, electrical stimulation, electrophotoluminescence   Gudden-Pohl-Effekt *m*, elektrische Ausleuchtung *f*

Gudermannian, gd, Gd <arctan (sh)>   Gudermann-Funktion *f*, gd <arctan (sinh)>

Guest['s] theory, maximum shear theory   Schubspannungshypothese *f*, Maximalscherungstheorie *f*, Hypothese *f* der größten Schubspannung von Guest

Guggenheim['s] mixing law   Guggenheimsches Mischungsgesetz *n*

Guggenheim['s] rule   Guggenheimsche Regel *f*

guidance   Lenkung *f*; Führung *f*; Steuerung *f*

guidance; guide way; guide; guiding arrangement; locating arrangement   Führung *f*; Führungsbahn *f*; Führungseinrichtung *f*

guidance plane	Leitebene *f*	Gullstrand['s] formula	Gullstrandsche Formel (Fundamentalgleichung) *f*, Linsenformel *f* von Gullstrand
guide; guidance; guide way; guiding arrangement; locating arrangement	Führung *f*; Führungsbahn *f*; Führungseinrichtung *f*	gully due to erosion	Erosionsschlucht *f*, Erosionsgraben *m*
guide	s. hollow waveguide	gully erosion	Grabenspülung *f*, Grabenerosion *f*
guide beam, guiding (localizer) beam	Leitstrahl *m*	gum	Gummi *n*
guide centre	s. guiding centre	gum [resin]	Gummiharz *n*
guided rocket	lenkbare Rakete *f*; gesteuerte Rakete; ferngesteuerte Rakete	Gunn diode	Gunn-Diode *f*
		Gunn effect	Gunn-Effekt *m*
guided wave, channel wave <geo.>	Kanalwelle *f*, geführte Welle *f* <Geo.>	Gunn oscillator	Gunn-Oszillator *m*
guided wave, wave in the waveguide	Hohlleiterwelle *f*, Hohlrohrwelle *f*, Rohrwelle *f*, Hohlraumwelle *f*, geleitete (geführte) Welle *f*	Gurevich effect	Gurevich-Effekt *m*
		Gurwitsch radiation (rays)	s. mitogenetic radiation
		gust <of wind>; blast of wind	Windstoß *m*
guide electrode	s. control electrode	gustiness [of wind]	Windbögigkeit *f*, Böigkeit *f* [des Windes], Windunruhe *f*, Unruhe *f* des Windes
guide field, guiding field	Führungsfeld *n*		
guide number	Leitzahl *f*		
guide-pulley	s. idler	gusty wind, choppy (squally, puffy) wind; bumpy air	böiger Wind *m*
guider, guiding telescope	Leitfernrohr *n*, Leitrohr *n*		
guide-ring, guide wheel <hydr.>	Leitrad *n*, Leitapparat *m*, Leitvorrichtung *f* <Hydr.>	Gutowsky['s] rule	Gutowskysche Regel *f*, Aufspaltungsregel *f* von Gutowsky
guide roller, idler, idler wheel, guide-pulley	Umlenkrolle *f*		
		guttation	Guttation *f*
		Guye['s] hypothesis	Guyesche Hypothese *f*
		guyot	Guyot *m*, Tiefenhügel *m*
guide star, reference star	Leitstern *m*, Haltestern *m*		
guide telescope	s. guiding telescope	Guyot-Bjerknes effect	Guyot-Bjerknes-Effekt *m*
guide wave	s. matter wave		
guide way; guidance; guide; guiding arrangement; locating arrangement	Führung *f*; Führungsbahn *f*; Führungseinrichtung *f*	G-value, G value, G; radiation-chemical yield	G-Wert *m*, 100-eV-Ausbeute *f*; strahlenchemische Ausbeute *f*, Strahlungsausbeute *f*
guide wheel, guide-ring <hydr.>	Leitrad *n*, Leitapparat *m*, Leitvorrichtung *f* <Hydr.>	gypsum plate	Gipskeil *m*, Gipsblättchen *n*, Gipsplättchen *n*
guiding <of telescope>; star tracking	Nachführung *f* <Fernrohr>	gyration, movement of the top, movement of gyro, gyroscopic (gyratory) motion	Kreiselbewegung *f*, Drehung *f* um einen Punkt, sphärische Bewegung (Rotation) *f*, Gyration *f*
guiding arrangement; guidance; guide way; guide; locating arrangement	Führung *f*; Führungsbahn *f*; Führungseinrichtung *f*		
		gyration centre	s. centre of rotation
guiding beam, guide beam, localizer beam	Leitstrahl *m*	gyration constant	Gyrationskonstante *f*
		gyration ellipsoid	s. ellipsoid of gyration
guiding centre, guide centre <mech.>	Führungszentrum *n* <Mech.>	gyration modulus, planar radius of inertia	planarer Trägheitsradius *m*
guiding error	Führungsfehler *m*, Nachführungsfehler *m*	gyration radius	s. radius of gyration
guiding [magnetic] field, guiding field	[magnetisches] Führungsfeld *n* <Beschl.>	gyration radius of atom, radius of gyration of the atom	mittlerer Radius *m* der Elektronenhülle, mittlerer Elektronenhüllenradius *m*, Gyrationsradius *m* des Atoms
guiding field	s. a. guide field		
guiding of light	Lichtleitung *f*, Lichtfortleitung *f*		
		gyration surface	Gyrationsfläche *f*
		gyration vector	Gyrationsvektor *m*
guiding of the beam, beam guidance	Strahlführung *f*	gyrator, Y circulator, waveguide Y circulator	Gyrator *m*, Y-Zirkulator *m*, Y-Richtungsgabel *f*
guiding telescope, guider, star tracker	Leitfernrohr *n*, Leitrohr *n*	gyratory motion	s. gyration
		gyro	s. gyroscopic instrument
Guild colorimeter	Dreifarbenmeßgerät *n* [nach Guild-Bechstein]	gyro	s. top
		gyroaxis, gyroscope axis, axis of the top, spin axis	Kreiselachse *f*
Guillemin effect	Guillemin-Effekt *m*		
Guillery impact test, Guillery['s] test	Einbeulversuch *m* nach Guillery	gyro[-]compass, gyroscopic compass, gyrostatic compass	Kreiselkompaß *m*, Einkreiselkompaß *m*
Guillet['s] coefficient [of equivalence], equivalence coefficient	Gleichwertigkeitskoeffizient *m*, Äquivalenzkoeffizient *m* [nach Guillet], Wertkoeffizient *m*		
		gyrocompass with two degrees of freedom	Kreiselkompaß *m* mit zwei Freiheitsgraden
guillotine factor	Guillotinefaktor *m*	gyrodamping, gyro damping	Kreiseldämpfung *f*, Gyrodämpfung *f*
guillotine shutter	Guillotineverschluß *m*		
Guinier-Preston zone, GP zone	Guinier-Preston-Zone *f*, Guinier-Prestonsche Zone *f*, GP-Zone *f*	gyrohedron	s. pentagonal icositetrahedron
		gyrohorizon	s. artificial horizon
Gülcher thermopile	Gülchersche Säule *f*	gyroidal [crystal] class, gyroidal hemihedry	s. enantiomorphous hemihedry of the regular system
Guldberg['s] rule	Guldbergsche Regel *f*		
Guldberg-Waage law	s. law of mass action	gyroide	s. rotation-reflection axis
Guldin['s] rule (theorem), centrobaric rule, Pappus['] theorem	Guldinsche Regel *f*, Guldinsches Theorem *n*	gyro[-]interaction	Kreiselwechselwirkung *f*, Gyrowechselwirkung *f*
Gulf magnetometer, rotary vane magnetometer	Gulf-Magnetometer *n*, Rotationsflügelmagnetometer *n*, Magnetometer *n* mit Rotationsflügelnachsteuerung	gyromagnetic; magneto[-]mechanic[al]	gyromagnetisch, kreiselmagnetisch, rotationsmagnetisch; magnetomechanisch

gyromagnetic effect; gyromagnetic phenomenon, magnetomechanical effect	gyromagnetischer Effekt m, gyromagnetische Erscheinung f; magnetomechanischer Effekt	habit [of the crystal], crystal habit, growth habit, [external] shape of the crystal	Habitus m [des Kristalls], Kristallhabitus m, Gesamtgestalt f des Kristalls
gyromagnetic frequency	s. cyclotron frequency	habit[-] plane	Habitusebene f
gyromagnetic phenomenon, gyromagnetic effect; magnetomechanical effect	gyromagnetischer Effekt m, gyromagnetische Erscheinung f; magnetomechanischer Effekt	Hackethal wire hackly fracture	Hackethal-Draht m zackiger Bruch m, hakiger Bruch
gyromagnetic ratio	gyromagnetisches Verhältnis n	Hadamard['s] determinantal inequality	s. Hadamard['s] determinant theorem
gyromagnetic resonance	s. cyclotron resonance	Hadamard['s] determinant theorem; Hadamard['s] [determinantal] inequality	Hadamardscher Determinantensatz m; Hadamardsche Ungleichung (Abschätzung) f
gyromechanical factor	gyromechanischer Faktor m		
gyro pendulum, gyroscope pendulum	Kreiselpendel n, gyroskopisches Pendel n		
gyro-relaxation	gyromagnetische Relaxation f, Gyrorelaxation f	Hadamard['s] finite part, finite part	[Hadamardscher] endlicher Teil m
gyroresonance	s. cyclotron resonance	Hadamard['s] inequality	s. Hadamard['s] determinant theorem
gyroscope, gyro; top	Kreisel m	Hadamard['s] three-circles theorem, three-circles theorem	[Hadamardscher] Dreikreisesatz m, Hadamard-Faber-Blumenthalscher Dreikreisesatz
gyroscope, gyroscopic instrument, gyro	Gyroskop n, Kreiselgerät n, Kreiselinstrument n		
gyroscope axis	s. gyroaxis		
gyroscope pendulum, gyro pendulum	Kreiselpendel n, gyroskopisches Pendel n	hadron	Hadron n
gyroscopic compass	s. gyro[-]compass		
gyroscopic couple	s. gyrostatic moment	hadronic decay, non-leptonic decay	nichtleptonischer Zerfall m, hadronischer Zerfall
gyroscopic horizon	s. artificial horizon		
gyroscopic instrument, gyroscope, gyro	Gyroskop n, Kreiselgerät n, Kreiselinstrument n	haematological state	Differentialblutbild n, differentielles Blutbild n
gyroscopic moment	s. gyrostatic moment	haemodynamics	Blutdynamik f
gyroscopic motion	s. movement of the top		
gyroscopic stabilization, gyrostabilization	Kreiselstabilisierung f, gyrostatische Stabilisierung f	Häffner effect	Häffner-Effekt m
		Hagenbach['s] correction	Hagenbachsche Korrektion (Korrektur) f, Hagenbach-Korrektur f
gyroscopic stabilizer	s. gyro[-]stabilizer		
gyroscopic term	gyroskopischer Term m, gyroskopisches Glied n	Hagen-Poiseuille equation (law)	s. Poiseuille law
		Hagen-Rubens equation (relation)	Hagen-Rubens-Beziehung f, Hagen-Rubenssche Beziehung f
gyroscopic theory, theory of tops, theory of gyroscope	Kreiseltheorie f, Theorie f des Kreisels		
gyrosphere	[Schuler-]Anschützscher Zweikreiselkompaß m, Zweikreiselkompaß [von Anschütz]	hahnium, bohrium <element 105, proposed names>	Hahnium n, Bohrium n
		Hahn-Metcalf drift tube	Hahn-Metcalf-Röhre f
gyrostabilization	s. gyroscopic stabilization	Haidinger brush	Haidingersches Büschel n
gyro[-]stabilizer, gyroscopic stabilizer	Stabilisierungskreisel m; Schiffskreisel m	Haidinger['s] fringe (interference fringe, ring)	s. fringe of equal inclination
		Haigh['s] diagram [of fatigue strength]	Dauerfestigkeitsschaubild n nach Haigh, Haigh-Diagramm n
		hail	Hagel m
gyrostat	Gyrostat m	hail shower (squall)	Hagelschauer m
gyrostatic compass	s. gyro[-]compass		
gyrostatic moment, gyroscopic moment, gyroscopic couple	Kreiselmoment n, Kreiselkraft f, Gyralmoment n, Gyralkraft f, Deviationswiderstand m, aufrichtendes Drehmoment n	hailstone	Hagelkorn n, Hagelstein m; Schloße f
		hail storm, hailstorm	Hagelwetter n, Hagelschlag m
gyrostatic pressure	Deviationsdruck m	hair crack	s. hair-line crack
		hair hygrometer, [de] Saussure['s] hygrometer	Haarhygrometer n
gyrostatics	Gyrostatik f		
gyrostatic thermometer	s. sling thermometer	hairline, hair-line crack, hair crack, capillary crack (flaw), craze	Haarriß m
gyrosynchrotron radiation, magnetic bremsstrahlung, magnetobremsstrahlung	magnetische Bremsstrahlung f, Magnetobremsstrahlung f, Gyrosynchrotronstrahlung f		
		hairpin cathode	Haarnadelkatode f
		hairpin filament	Haarnadelwendel f
gyrotropic	gyrotrop	hairpin galvanometer	Haarnadelgalvanometer n
		halation, halo, photographic halo, aureola	Lichthof m, photographischer Lichthof, Hof m
		Hale reflector, Mount Palomar telescope, Palomar telescope	Hale-Teleskop n, Palomar-Teleskop n, Hale-Reflektor m

H

Haag field	Haag-Feld n	half amplitude	halbe Schwingungsweite (Amplitude) f
Haar measure	Haarsches Maß m		
Haas-Shubnikov effect / de	s. Shubnikov-de Haas effect	half-bounded operator	halbbeschränkter Operator m
Haas-van Alphen effect / de	de Haas-van Alphenscher Effekt m, De-Haas-van-Alphen-Effekt m	half-cell, galvanic half-cell	Halbzelle f, [galvanisches] Halbelement n, elektrochemische Elektrode f
Habann magnetron	s. two-segmented magnetron	half-chord	halbe Flügelsehne f
Habann oscillation	Habann-Schwingung f	half-circulation	halber Umlauf m
Habann oscillator	Habann-Generator m	half-closed interval, half-open interval, partly open interval	halboffenes Intervall n
Habann tube	s. two-segmented magnetron		
Haber-Born cycle	s. Born-Haber cycle	half-cycle, half cycle, half-period, semiperiod, semi-period	Halbperiode f, halbe Periode f
Haber-Kerschbaum equation	Haber-Kerschbaumsche Formel f		

half-cylinder	Halbzylinder *m*	**half-space**, infinite half-space, semi-infinite space	Halbraum *m*, unendlicher Halbraum
half dislocation, **half-dislocation**, partial dislocation	Halbversetzung *f*, Teilversetzung *f*, unvollständige (partielle) Versetzung *f*	**half-space problem**	*s*. Boussinesq's problem
half-fine	halbfein	**half-step**	*s*. half-tone <ac.>
half[-] image <opt.>	Halbbild *n*, stereoskopisches Halbbild <Opt.>	**half-thickness**	*s*. half-value layer
		half-tide level	*s*. mean tide
half-integer, half-integral, half-odd[-integral], half numberly, semi-integer, semi-integral	halbzahlig	**half-time of decay**, decay half-time	Rückenhalbwertzeit *f*, Rückenhalbwertsdauer *f*
		half-time of exchange	Halbwertzeit *f* des Austausches, Austauschhalbwertzeit *f*
half-intensity width	*s*. full width at half-maximum	**half-tone**, semitone, semit, half-step <ac.>	Halbton *m*, halber Ton *m* <Ak.>
half jog	Halbsprung *m*	**half-tone**, middle tone, continuous tone, semi-tone <opt.>	Halbton *m* <Opt.>
half-life	*s*. half-life period		
half-life	*s*. *a*. radioactive half-life		
half life of a first-order chemical reaction	Halbwertzeit *f* einer Reaktion 1. Ordnung	**half-tone picture**	Halbtonbild *n*
		half-value angle	Halbwertswinkel *m*
		half-value depth, tissue half-value depth, HVD, $D_{1/2}$	Gewebe-Halbwerttiefe *f*, GHT, $D_{1/2}$
half-life period, half-life	Halbwertzeit *f*, Halbwertszeit *f*	**half-value depth, half-value layer (thickness)**, half-thickness, HVL, HVT	Halbwert[s]schicht *f*, Halbwert[s]schichtdicke *f*, Halbwert[s]dicke *f*, Halbdicke *f*, HWS
half-line, ray <math.>	Halbgerade *f*, Strahl *m* <Math.>		
half-metal	*s*. semi-metal	**half-wave**	Halbwelle *f*
half-moment theory	Halbmomententheorie *f*	**half-wave antenna**	*s*. half-wave dipole
		half-wave circuit	Einwegschaltung *f*, Halbwellenschaltung *f*
half numberly half-odd [-integral], half-integral, half-integer	halbzahlig	**half-wave dipole**, half-wave antenna, semi-wave antenna	Halbwellendipol *m*, Halbwellenantenne *f*
half-open interval	*s*. half-closed interval		
half-peak delay	*s*. delay time	**half-wavelength plate**	*s*. half-wave plate
half-peak divergence, half-peak spread <US>	Halbstreuwinkel *m*	**half-wave line**, λ/2-line, half-wave transmission line	Halbwellenleitung *f*, λ/2-Leitung *f*
half-period, semiperiod, semi-period, half-cycle, half cycle	Halbperiode *f*	**half-wave plate**, half-wavelength plate, λ/2 plate	Halbwellen[längen]plättchen *n*, λ/2-Wellenlängenplättchen *n*, λ/2-Plättchen *n*, λ/2-Blättchen *n*, Lambda-Halbe-Plättchen *n*, Lambda-Halbe-Blättchen *n*
half-period element (zone)	*s*. Fresnel zone		
half-plane	Halbebene *f*		
half-power beam width	*s*. lobe width <for antennas>		
half-power width	*s*. flare angle	**half-wave potential**	Halbstufenpotential *n*, Halbwellenpotential *n*
half power width of lobe	*s*. lobe width <for antennas>	**half-wave radiator**	Halbwellenstrahler *m*
half-range, half-width, semi-range <stat.>	halbe Spannweite *f*, halbe Breite *f* <Stat.>	**half-wave rectification**, one-half period rectification, single-wave (single-way) rectification	Halbwellengleichrichtung *f*, Halbweggleichrichtung *f*, Einweggleichrichtung *f*, Einphasengleichrichtung *f*
half-regular variable [star], semi-regular variable [star]	halbperiodischer (halbregelmäßiger) Veränderlicher *m*		
half-section	Halbglied *n*	**half-wave rectifier**, single-wave rectifier, single-way rectifier, single-phase rectifier	Halbwellengleichrichterschaltung *f*, Halbwellengleichrichter *m*, Halbweggleichrichter *m*, Einweggleichrichter *m*, Einphasengleichrichter *m*
half shade, penumbra, partial (half, incomplete) shadow	Halbschatten *m*, Penumbra *f*		
halfshade, halfshade plate, half-shadow plate	Halbschattenplatte *f*		
halfshade	*s*. half-shadow device	**half-wave slit**	Halbwellenschlitz *m*
halfshade analyzer, half-shadow analyzer	Halbschattenanalysator *m*	**half-wave transmission line**, half-wave line, λ/2-line	Halbwellenleitung *f*, λ/2-Leitung *f*
halfshade compensator, half-shadow compensator	Halbschattenkompensator *m*	**half-width**, half-range, semi-range <stat.>	halbe Spannweite *f*, halbe Breite *f* <Stat.>
halfshade plate	*s*. halfshade	**half-width [of the peak]**	*s*. full width at half[-] maximum
halfshade polarizer, half-shadow polarizer	Halbschattenpolarisator *m*	**half-width of the spectral line**	*s*. line width
half shadow	*s*. half shade		
half-shadow analyzer, halfshade analyzer	Halbschattenanalysator *m*	**halide**, halogenide, haloid [salt]	Halogenid *n*, Halid *n*, Haloid *n*
half-shadow angle	Halbschatten *m*, Halbschattenwinkel *m*	**halide leak detector**	Halogenleckfinder *m*
half-shadow compensator, halfshade compensator	Halbschattenkompensator *m*	**Hall angle**	Hall-Winkel *m*, Hallscher Winkel *m*
half-shadow device, half-shadow polarimeter, halfshade	Halbschattenapparat *m*, Halbschattenpolarimeter *n*, Halbschattenvorrichtung *f*	**Hall coefficient, Hall constant**	Hall-Koeffizient *m*, Hall-Konstante *f*
		Hall current	Hall-Strom *m*
		Hall device, Hall effect device, galvanomagnetic semiconductor device	Hall-Gerät *n*, Hall-Effekt-Gerät *n*, galvanomagnetisches Halbleitergerät *n*
half-shadow plate	*s*. halfshade	**Hall effect**	Hall-Effekt *m*
half-shadow polarimeter	*s*. half-shadow device		
half-shadow polarizer, halfshade polarizer	Halbschattenpolarisator *m*	**Hall effect device**, Hall device, galvanomagnetic semiconductor device	Hall-Gerät *n*, Hall-Effekt-Gerät *n*, galvanomagnetisches Halbleitergerät *n*
half-shadow prism	Halbschattenprisma *n*	**Hall-effect magnetometer**	Hall-[Effekt-]Magnetometer *n*
half-silvered	halbdurchlässig verspiegelt	**Hall electric field**, Hall field, Hall field intensity, Hall field strength	Hall-Feldstärke *f*
half-sinusoid	halbe Sinuswelle *f*		

Hall

Hall electromotive force, Hall c.m.f., Hall voltage (tension)	Hall-Spannung f
Halley['s] comet	Halleyscher Komet m
Hall field	Hall-Feld n
Hall field, Hall field intensity (strength)	s. Hall electric field
Hall generator	Hall-Generator m
Hall['s] halo, Hall's ring	Halo m von Hall
Hall mobility	Hall-Beweglichkeit f
Hall probe	Hall-Sonde f, Feldsonde f
Hall['s] ring	s. Hall['s] halo
Hall tension	s. Hall electromotive force
Hall-type magnetohydrodynamic generator, magnetohydrodynamic Hall generator	MHD-Hall-Generator m, Hall-MHD-Generator m
Hall voltage	s. Hall electromotive force
Hallwachs effect	s. photoemissive effect
halo <pl.: haloes, halos>	Halo m <pl.: Halos>
halo, photographic halo, halation, aureola	Lichthof m, photographischer Lichthof, Hof m
halochromic	halochrom
halochromism	Halochromie f
halo effect	Haloeffekt m
halogen	Halogen n, Salzbildner m
halogen counter	s. halogen-quenched counter
halogen effect	Halogeneffekt m
halogenide, halide, haloid [salt]	Halogenid n, Halid n, Haloid n
halogen-quenched counter [tube], halogen counter	Halogenzählrohr n
haloid [salt]	s. halogenide
halometer, salinometer	Salzspindel f, Salz[gehalt]messer m, Salinometer n
halo of 22°, 22°-ring, 22°-halo	kleiner Ring m, 22°-Halo m, 22°-Ring m, gewöhnlicher Halo m, kleiner Halo
halo of 46°, 46°-ring, 46°-halo	großer Ring m, großer Halo m, 46°-Ring m, 46°-Halo m
halo of the comet	Halo m des Kometen
halo phenomenon	Haloerscheinung f; Halophänomen n
halo[-type] population, population II of the Galaxy	Halopopulation f; Halo m
Halpern-Johnson['s] theory	Halpern-Johnsonsche Theorie f
halt	s. critical point
halving	s. bipartition
Hamburger['s] law (theorem), law of Hamburger	Satz m von Hamburger, Hamburgerscher Satz
Hamel flow	Hamelsche Strömung f
Hamel spiral, spiral of Hamel	Spirale f von Hamel, Hamelsche Spirale, Hamel-Spirale f
Hamilton['s] angle characteristic [function]	s. angle characteristic T
Hamilton['s] canonical equations [of motion], canonical equations [of motion], Hamilton['s] equations, Hamiltonian system of differential equations	[Hamiltonsche] kanonische Bewegungsgleichungen fpl, [Hamiltonsche] kanonische Gleichungen fpl, Hamiltonsche Gleichungen (der Dynamik), Hamiltonsche Bewegungsgleichungen (gewöhnliche Differentialgleichungen fpl), Hamiltonsche (kanonische) Differentialgleichungen, kanonisches (Hamiltonsches) Differentialgleichungssystem n, kanonisches Gleichungssystem n
Hamilton-Cayley theorem	s. Cayley-Hamilton theorem
Hamilton['s] characteristic [function]	s. eikonal
Hamilton['s] equations	s. Hamilton['s] canonical equations
Hamilton formalism	s. Hamiltonian formalism
Hamilton['s] function, Hamiltonian function, Hamiltonian	Hamilton-Funktion f, Hamiltonsche Funktion f
Hamiltonian	s. del <math.>
Hamiltonian	s. a. Hamiltonian function
Hamiltonian	s. a. Hamiltonian operator
Hamiltonian action	Hamiltonsche Wirkung f
Hamiltonian analogy	Hamiltonsche Analogie f
Hamiltonian density	Hamiltonsche Dichte f, Hamilton-Dichte f
Hamiltonian form, canonical form	kanonische Gestalt (Form) f, Hamiltonsche Form (Gestalt)
Hamiltonian formalism, Hamilton formalism	Hamilton-Formalismus m, Hamiltonscher Formalismus m, Formalismus der Hamiltonschen Gleichungen
Hamiltonian function, Hamilton['s] function, Hamiltonian	Hamilton-Funktion f, Hamiltonsche Funktion f
Hamiltonian line	Hamiltonsche Linie f
Hamiltonian operator, Hamilton operator, Hamiltonian	Hamilton-Operator m, Hamiltonscher Operator m
Hamiltonian surface	Hamiltonsche Fläche f
Hamiltonian system of differential equations	s. Hamilton's canonical equations
Hamilton-Jacobi [differential] equation, Hamilton-Jacobi partial differential equation[s] Hamilton['s] partial differential equation[s], partial differential equation of Hamilton-Jacobi	Hamilton-Jacobische [partielle] Differentialgleichung f, Hamilton-Jacobi-Gleichung f, Hamiltonsche partielle Differentialgleichung[en fpl]
Hamilton-Jacobi theorem	Hamilton-Jacobischer Satz m
Hamilton-Jacobi theory	Hamilton-Jacobische Theorie f
Hamilton['s] mixed characteristic function W	s. mixed eikonal
Hamilton operator	s. Hamiltonian operator
Hamilton['s] partial differential equation[s]	s. Hamilton-Jacobi [differential] equation
Hamilton['s] principal function	s. principal function
Hamilton['s] principle, principle of least action [of Hamilton]	Hamiltonsches Prinzip n [der kleinsten Wirkung], Hamilton-Prinzip n [der kleinsten Wirkung], Hamilton-Prinzip der stationären Wirkung, Prinzip von Hamilton, Prinzip der kleinsten Wirkung [von Hamilton]
Hamilton['s] two-point characteristic function	s. Hamilton's characteristic function
hammer <bio.; el.>	Hammer m
hammer forging, hammering	s. smith forging
hammer interrupter	s. Wagner interrupter
Hammer projection	Hammersche Projektion f, Hammers flächentreuer Entwurf m, Hammers flächentreue Planisphäre f
hammer track	Hammerspur f, Hammerstern m, T-Spur f
Hammett equation	Hammettsche Gleichung f
Hampson level indicator, hydrostatic gauge, hydrostatic level gauge	Hampsometer n, mittelbar wirkender Flüssigkeitsstandanzeiger m, Flüssigkeitsstandanzeiger mit heruntergezogenen Flüssigkeitsständen
hand capacitance	Handkapazität f
hand-capacitance effect, hand effect	Handempfindlichkeit f, Handeffekt m
H. and D. curve <phot.>	s. characteristic curve
hand dosimeter	Armbanddosimeter n, Handdosimeter n
hand effect, hand-capacitance effect	Handempfindlichkeit f, Handeffekt m
hand goniometer	Freihandwinkelmesser m
hand level	Freihandnivellier n, Handlevel n

handling; manipulation; operation ⟨gen.⟩	Handhabung f, Umgang m ⟨mit⟩; Hantieren n; Arbeitsgang m; Betätigung f, Operation f; Bedienung f, Manipulation f ⟨allg.⟩	**hardening** ⟨of electronic tube⟩	Hartwerden n ⟨Röhre⟩
		hardening, tannage ⟨of emulsion⟩	Härtung f, Gerbung f ⟨Emulsion⟩
		hardening ⟨of metals⟩	Härtung f ⟨Metalle⟩
handling; processing; working; treatment	Verarbeitung f	**hardening**, curing, cure ⟨of plastics, resins⟩	Härtung f ⟨Kunststoffe, Harze⟩
		hardening ⟨of radiation⟩	Härtung f, Energieheraufsetzung f ⟨Strahlung⟩
hand microtelephone, microtelephone, HMT	Mikrotelephon n	**hardening agent**	s. hardener
		hardening and tempering, tempering after hardening, temper hardening ⟨met.⟩	Vergütung f ⟨Met.⟩
hand spectroscope	Handspektroskop n		
hanging level, suspended level	Hängelibelle f		
hanging theodolite	Hängetheodolit m	**hardening bath**	s. hardener bath
		hardening by immersion, immersion hardening, liquid hardening	Tauchhärtung f
hangover	s. time lag		
hangover time, dead time; partial restoring time	Nachwirkzeit f, Nachwirkungszeit f; Teilsperrzeit f, Teilnachwirkzeit f	**hardening capacity**	s. hardenability
		hardening constituent	Härtebildner m
Hankel approximation	Hankelsche Näherung f, Hankel-Approximation f	**hardening crack**, cold crack, quenching crack	Kaltriß m, Härteriß m, Riß m beim Erkalten
Hankel function	s. Bessel function of the third kind	**hardening depth**, depth of hardened layer, depth of "penetration", hardness penetration	Einhärtungstiefe f, Härtetiefe f, Durchhärtung f
Hankel function of the first ⟨second⟩ kind	Hankelsche Funktion f erster ⟨zweiter⟩ Art		
Hankel inversion theorem	Hankelscher Umkehrsatz m	**hardening fixing bath**	Härtefixierbad n
		hardening of the neutron spectrum, neutron hardening	Härtung f des Neutronenspektrums, Neutronenhärtung f
Hankel transform, Fourier-Bessel transform	Hankel-Transformierte f		
Hankel transformation, Fourier-Bessel transform[ation]	Hankel-Transformation f	**hardening of the radiation**, radiation hardening	Strahlenhärtung f, Strahlungshärtung f
Hanle effect	Hanle-Effekt m		
Hansen diaphragm	Stufenblende f nach Hansen, Hansen-Blende f	**hard focus lens**	Hartzeichner m
Hansen['s] law, Ohm['s] law of light flux	Ohmsches Gesetz n für den Lichtfluß, Hansensches Gesetz		
		hard landing, rough landing	harte Landung f
haptic	Haptik f		
haptic lens	Sclerocornealschale f, Scleralschale f	**hard [magnetic] material**, magnetically hard material	hartmagnetischer (magnetisch harter) Werkstoff m; Dauermagnetwerkstoff m
haptic reaction	s. haptoreaction		
haptic stimulus, contact stimulus, thigmic stimulus	Berührungsreiz m, Kontaktreiz m, Tastreiz m, haptischer (thigmischer) Reiz m	**hardness**, hardness number, degree of hardness ⟨mech.⟩	Härte f, Härtezahl f, Härtegrad m ⟨Mech.⟩
		hardness ⟨of water⟩	Härte f, Härtegrad m ⟨Wasser⟩
haptogenic membrane	haptogene Membran f	**hardness**	s. a. penetrating power
haptonasty	Haptonastie f	**hardness due to magnesium**, magnesia hardness	Magnesiahärte f [des Wassers], Magnesiumhärte f [des Wassers]
haptoreaction, haptic reaction	Haptoreaktion f, haptische Reaktion f, Thigmoreaktion f		
haptotropism	Haptotropismus m	**hardness factor**	Härtefaktor m
		hardness gauge	s. hardness tester
hard ball	s. hard sphere	**hardness number**	s. hardness ⟨mech.⟩
hard component	s. penetrating component	**hardness penetration**	s. depth of hardened layer
hard-core model, hard-core-type model ⟨nucl.⟩	Modell n mit „hartem Kern", Modell mit undurchdringlichem Kern, Modell mit „hard core", „hard core"-Modell n ⟨Kern⟩	**hardness test**, hardness testing	Härteprüfung f
		hardness tester, hardness testing machine; hardness gauge, durometer	Härteprüfgerät n, Härteprüfer m, Härteprüfmaschine f, Härtemesser m
hard-core potential	Potential n mit „hard core", „hard-core"-Potential n		
		hardness testing, hardness test	Härteprüfung f
hard-core-type model	s. hard-core model ⟨nucl.⟩	**hardness testing machine**	s. hardness tester
hard direction [for magnetization], direction of hard magnetization	harte Richtung (Magnetisierungsrichtung) f	**hardness test using rolling balls**, rolling ball test	Rollhärteprüfung f
hardenability, hardening capacity	Härtbarkeit f		
hardenable at elevated temperatures, hardenable by heat treatment	s. thermosetting	**hardness test with conical indenter**, Ludwik test	Kegeldruck-Härteprüfung f
hardener, hardening agent	Härter m, Härtungsbeschleuniger m, Härtungsmittel n, Härtmittel n	**hard radiation**, penetrating radiation	harte (durchdringende, energiereiche) Strahlung f
		hard-radiation region	Hartstrahlgebiet n
		hard rays	s. hard X-rays
hardener, water hardener (hardening material)	Wasserhärter m, Wasserhärtungsmittel n	**hard shower**, penetrating shower	harter (durchdringender, energiereicher) Schauer m, Schauer durchdringender Teilchen
hardener bath, hardening bath	Härtebad n		
hardening; set, setting, cure ⟨of concretes⟩	Erhärtung f, Verfestigung f; Verhärtung f; Abbinden n; Anziehen n	**hard sphere**, billiard ball, hard ball	harte Kugel f, Billardkugel f

hard-sphere 314

hard-sphere collision, Harte-Kugel-Stoß *m*
hard-sphere-type collision

hard-sphere [lattice] gas, hard-sphere model, "billiard ball" model, rigid sphere gas (model) Harte-Kugel-Modell *n*, Billardkugelmodell *n*

hard-sphere-type collision *s.* hard-sphere collision

hard superconductor, harter (nichtidealer) Supraleiter *m*
non-ideal superconductor

hard vacuum forciertes Vakuum *n*
hardware model reales Modell *n*

hard X-rays, hard rays harte Strahlen *mpl*, harte Röntgenstrahlung *f*, Hartstrahlen *mpl*, Hartstrahlung *f*

hard X-ray tube Hartstrahlröhre *f*, Hartstrahl-Röntgenröhre *f*, harte Röntgenröhre *f*

Hardy-Schulze rule *s.* Schulze-Hardy rule
Hargrave kite Hargravescher Kastendrachen *m*, Kastendrachen [nach Hargrave]

Harker cut, Harker section Harkerscher Schnitt *m*
Harker function Harkersche Funktion *f*
Harker line, Harker peak Harkersche Linie *f*, Harker-Maximum *n*
Harker section, Harker cut Harkerscher Schnitt *m*

Harkins-Jura equations of adsorption, H-J equation Harkins-Jurasche Adsorptionsgleichungen *fpl*

Harkins['] rule Harkinssche Regel *f*
harmonic, [harmonic] component, Fourier component, harmonic oscillation, harmonic wave Harmonische *f*, Fourier-Komponente *f*, harmonische Komponente *f*, [harmonische] Oberschwingung *f*, [harmonische] Oberwelle *f*, Obertonschwingung *f*

harmonic, harmonic sound, harmonic overtone <ac.> Harmonische *f*, harmonischer Oberton *m*, harmonische Oberschwingung *f* <Ak.>

harmonic analysis, Fourier analysis Fourier-Analyse *f*, harmonische Analyse *f*
harmonic analyzer, Fourier analyzer, periodometer harmonischer Analysator *m*, Fourier-Analysator *m*; Oberwellenanalysator *m*
harmonic antenna Oberwellenantenne *f*
harmonic average, harmonic mean harmonisches Mittel *n*, harmonischer Mittelwert *m*

harmonic-balance method, method of harmonic balance Methode *f* der harmonischen Balance, Krylow-Bogoljubowsche Methode
harmonic component *s.* harmonic
harmonic conjugate, fourth harmonic point vierter harmonischer Punkt *m*
harmonic constant harmonische Konstante *f*
harmonic content *s.* distortion factor
harmonic co-ordinate system *s.* harmonic system of co-ordinates
harmonic curve; sinusoidal curve (line), sinusoid, sine curve Sinuskurve *f*, Sinuslinie *f*; harmonische Kurve *f*
harmonic dial Amplitude-Phase-Diagramm *n*

harmonic distortion *s.* distortion factor
harmonic distortion analyzer, distortion analyzer Klirranalysator *m*
harmonic distortion coefficient *s.* coefficient of harmonic distortion
harmonic distortion factor *s.* distortion factor
harmonic distortion noise, distortion noise Klirrleistung *f*, Klirrgeräusch *n*
harmonic echo Oberwellenecho *n*, harmonisches Echo *n*

harmonic expansion, Fourier expansion Entwicklung *f* in eine Fourier-Reihe, Fourier-Entwicklung *f*, Fourier-Zerlegung *f*, Orthogonalentwicklung *f*

harmonic filter, harmonic suppressor Oberwellensperre *f*, Oberwellensieb *n*, Oberwellenfilter *n*

harmonic folding, concordant folding konkordante Faltung *f*

harmonic frequency Oberschwingungsfrequenz *f*
harmonic function, potential function, potential <math.> Potentialfunktion *f*, Potential *n*, harmonische Funktion *f*
harmonic generation Oberwellenerzeugung *f*

harmonic generator, harmonic synthesizer Fourier-Generator *m*, Oberwellengenerator *m*, Oberwellenerzeuger *m*

harmonic mean, harmonic average harmonisches Mittel *n*, harmonischer Mittelwert *m*

harmonic mean energy harmonischer Mittelwert *m* der Energie

harmonic mode [quartz] crystal Oberwellenquarz *m*
harmonic motion; harmonic oscillation harmonische Bewegung *f*; harmonische Schwingung *f*

harmonic of the voltage, voltage harmonic Spannungsoberwelle *f*

harmonic order of frequency Vielfaches *n* der Grundfrequenz
harmonic oscillation *s.* harmonic
harmonic oscillation *s.* harmonic motion
harmonic oscillator harmonischer Oszillator *m*

harmonic overtone *s.* harmonic <ac.>
harmonic pencil harmonisches Strahlenbüschel *n*
harmonic points, harmonic range harmonische Punkte *mpl*
harmonic response [characteristic] *s.* frequency response
harmonic series, overtone series, partial series harmonische Tonreihe (Reihe) *f*, Naturtonreihe *f*, Obertonreihe *f*, Partialtonreihe *f*

harmonic sound *s.* harmonic <ac.>
harmonic spectroscopy, Fourier spectroscopy Fourier-Spektroskopie *f*

harmonic spectrum, Fourier spectrum Fourier-Spektrum *n*, harmonisches Spektrum *n*, Oberwellenspektrum *n*
harmonic suppressor, harmonic filter Oberwellensperre *f*, Oberwellensieb *n*, Oberwellenfilter *n*
harmonic synthesis, Fourier synthesis harmonische Synthese *f*, Fourier-Synthese *f*
harmonic synthesizer, harmonic generator Fourier-Generator *m*, Oberwellengenerator *m*, Oberwellenerzeuger *m*
harmonic system of co-ordinates, harmonic co-ordinate system harmonisches Koordinatensystem *n*
harmonic wave, sinusoidal wave, sine wave Sinuswelle *f*, sinusförmige (harmonische) Welle *f*
harmonic wave *s. a.* harmonic
Harress['] experiment Harressscher Versuch *m*, Versuch von Harress
Harris['] function Harris-Funktion *f*
har-h Harsch *m*
hartley, decadic (decimal) digit, dit <= 3.219 bits> Hartley *n*, dit <= 3,219 bit>
Hartley band Hartley-Bande *f*
Hartley circuit *s.* Hartley oscillator
Hartley oscillator, three-point Hartley circuit, Hartley circuit induktive Dreipunktschaltung *f*, Hartley-Schaltung *f*, Hartley-Oszillator *m*

Hartmann dispersion formula	s. Hartmann wave-length formula	Hay bridge	Hay-Brücke f, Haysche Brücke f
Hartmann flow	Hartmann-Strömung f, Hartmannsche Strömung	Hayford['s] ellipsoid, Hayford spheroid	s. international ellipsoid
Hartmann formula	s. Hartmann wave-length formula	Hayford zone	Hayfordsche Zone f
Hartmann generator, Hartmann oscillator, Hartmann's whistle	Hartmann-Generator m, Hartmannsche Pfeife f, Gasstromgenerator m	haze, atmospheric haze haze haze haze drop haze extinction	[atmosphärischer] Dunst m s. a. fog s. a. mist Dunsttröpfchen n Dunstextinktion f
Hartmann layer	Hartmannsche Schicht f		
Hartmann['s] line	s. slip line	haze nucleus	Dunstkern m
Hartmann['s] method, Hartmann test <opt.>	Hartmannsche Extrafokalmethode (Methode) f, Extrafokalmethode [von Hartmann]	haze particle	Dunstteilchen n, Dunstpartikel f
		haze scattering, scattering by haze particles	Dunststreuung f
Hartmann number	Hartmann-Zahl f, Hartmannsche Kennzahl (Ähnlichkeitszahl) f	haziness, non-visibility, lack of visibility	Unsichtigkeit f; Dunstigkeit f, Diesigkeit f
Hartmann oscillator, Hartmann generator, Hartmann's whistle	Hartmann-Generator m, Hartmannsche Pfeife f, Gasstromgenerator m	H balance, horizontal field balance	Feldwaage f zur Messung der Horizontalintensität, H-Waage f
		H band <7,05 − 10 Gc/s>	H-Band n <7,05 ··· 10 GHz>
Hartmann paper	Hartmannsches Dispersionspapier n; Hartmannsches Netz n, Dispersionsnetz n		
		h bar, h-bar	s. Dirac h
		H-body	s. perfectly elastic solid
Hartmann problem	Hartmann-Problem n, Hartmannsches Problem n	H-D curve	s. characteristic curve <phot.>
Hartmann test	s. Hartmann['s] method	head	s. pressure head
Hartmann wave-length formula; Hartmann [dispersion] formula	Hartmannsche Dispersionsformel f, Dispersionsformel von Hartmann	head	s. measuring head
		head	s. plate <chem.>
		head amplifier; pre[-]amplifier, pre[-]amp	Vorverstärker m, Anfangsstufenverstärker m; Kopfverstärker m
Hartmann['s] whistle	s. Hartmann oscillator		
Hartree approach (approximation)	Hartree-Näherung f, Hartreesche Näherung f	head of a liquid, liquid column	Flüssigkeitssäule f
Hartree-Fock approach, individual-particle approach	Hartree-Focksche Näherung f, Einzelteilchennäherung f	head of pressure above atmospheric, positive pressure head	Überdruckhöhe f
		head of the band	s. band head <opt.>
Hartree-Fock-Dirac self-consistent-field method, Hartree-Fock method, self-consistent-field method, method of self-consistent field	Hartree-Focksche Methode f, Hartree-Fock-Methode f, „self-consistent field"-Methode f [von Hartree-Fock], Methode des „self-consistent field", Hartreesche Methode, Focksche Methode	head of the comet, comet[ary] head	Kopf m des Kometen, Kometenkopf m
		head of water	s. water column
		head-on collision, central impact, central collision	zentraler Stoß m, Zentralstoß m, gerader Stoß
		head-on type photomultiplier tube	Sekundärelektronenvervielfacher m mit Stirnflächenphotokatode
Hartree-Fock model [of nucleus]	s. shell model [of nucleus]	head on weir	Überfallhöhe f, Stauhöhe f
Hartree-Fock potential	Hartree-Fock-Potential n	head shock wave	s. head wave
Hartree harmonic	s. space harmonic	head-to-head arrangement (structure of polymer)	Kopf-Kopf-Verknüpfung f
Hartree['s] law	Hartreesches Seriengesetz (Gesetz) n		
Hartree system [of units]	s. system of atomic units	head-to-tail arrangement (structure of polymer)	Kopf-Schwanz-Verknüpfung f
Hartree unit, atomic unit, natural unit	Hartree-Einheit f, atomare (natürliche) Einheit f		
		head water	s. a. upper pool
Hartshorn bridge	Hartshorn-Brücke f, Hartshornsche Brücke f	head waters, upper course (waters) <of river>	Oberlauf m <Fluß>
Harvard classification, Harvard system <of spectral classification>, Harvard system of spectral classes	Harvard-Klassifikation f	head wave, head shock wave, Mintrop wave; forward (front, nose, bow) shock; ballistic wave	Kopfwelle f <Geschoß>, Stoßwelle f vor der Nase, Verdichtungsstoß m am Kopfende
Harvey harmonic analyzer	Harvey-Analysator m, harmonischer Analysator m von Harvey		
		head weight	größtes Gewichtsstück n in einem Gewichtssatz
hatch	Schraffe f, Bergstrich m		
		health measurement, dosimetric measurement	Strahlenschutzmessung f, dosimetrische Messung f
hatchet planimeter	Beilplanimeter n, Hatchet-Planimeter n, Schneiden[rad]planimeter n, Schleppe f, Stangenplanimeter n		
		health monitoring, protection survey, radiation survey(monitoring)	Strahlenschutzüberwachung f
hatching	Schraffierung f; Schraffur f, Schraffen n	health physicist	Strahlenschutzphysiker m, Gesundheitsphysiker m
Hathaway oscillograph	Hathaway-Oszillograph m, Zwölfschleifenoszillograph m [nach Hathaway]		
		health physics; health precaution	Strahlenschutzphysik f, physikalischer Strahlenschutz m, Gesundheitsphysik f; Strahlenschutzüberwachungsdienst m, Strahlenüberwachungsdienst m
Hausdorff measure	Hausdorffsches Maß n		
Hausdorff [topological] space, T_2-space, separated [topological] space	Hausdorffscher Raum m, T_2-Raum m, H-Raum m, separierter Raum		
Hauy law	s. law of rational indices		
Havelock['s] law	Havelocksches Gesetz n		
Havemann balance	Magnetwaage f nach R. Havemann, Havemann-Waage f		
haversine	= $(1 - \cos x)/2$	heap cloud, cumuliform cloud	haufenförmige (cumulusartige) Wolke f, Cumuliformisform f
Hawkins cell	Hawkins-Element n		

hearing, sense of hearing	Gehör n	heat capacity per unit volume, volume (volumetric) heat capacity, volumetric specific heat, specific heat per unit volume	Wärmekapazität f, bezogen auf die Volumeneinheit; Volumenwärmekapazität f, spezifische Wärme f [, bezogen auf die Volumeneinheit]
hearing acuity	s. acuity of hearing		
hearing distance, distance of hearing, earshot, audible range	Hörweite f		
hearing sensitivity, auditory sensitivity	Hörempfindlichkeit f		
hearing volume, limits of hearing	Gehörumfang m	heat capacity ratio	s. ratio of the specific heats
heart action, heart beat	Herzschlag m	heat capacity standard	Wärmekapazitätsnormal n
heart action current	s. action current due to the heart	heat change	s. heat effect
		heat coefficient	Wärmekoeffizient m
heart beat, heart action	Herzschlag m	heat colour	Glühfarbe f
heart contour	s. heart shape	heat compensation	s. heat balance
hearth, focus, origin, seat [of origin], centre ‹geo., meteo.›	Herd m ‹Geo., Meteo.›	heat compensator, compensator of thermal expansion	Wärmeausgleicher m, Wärmeausgleichvorrichtung f, Wärmekompensator m, Dehnungsausgleicher m, Kompensator m
heart line	s. heart shape		
heart pacemaker	s. pacemaker		
heart shape, cardioid [curve], heart contour (line)	Kardioide f, Herzkurve f, Herzlinie f	heat concentration	Wärmekonzentration f
		heat concept, notion of heat	Wärmebegriff m
heat; hotness; warmth ‹gen.; geo.›	Wärme f ‹allg.; Geo.›	heat-conducting, heat conductive, thermally conducting	wärmeleitend
heat	Hitze f		
heat, incandescence, glowing, glow	Glut f, Glühen n	heat conducting power	s. thermal conductivity
		heat conduction, conduction of heat, thermal conduction	Wärmeleitung f, innere Wärmeleitung, Wärmeleitfähigkeit f ‹Vorgang›
heat	s. a. heating		
heat	s. a. melt		
heat	s. a. melting		
heat	s. a. heat capacity	heat conduction damping	Wärmeleitungsdämpfung f
heat	s. a. heat energy		
heat abduction	s. heat removal	heat conduction equation, heat equation, Biot-Fourier equation, equation of heat conduction	Wärmeleitungsgleichung f, Wärmeleitgleichung f
heat-absorbent surface, cooling surface; radiating surface	Kühlfläche f, Abkühlungs[ober]fläche f		
heat absorber, heat (thermal) accumulator, heat reservoir	Wärmespeicher m, Wärmeakkumulator m, Wärmeabsorber m		
		heat conduction loss	s. conduction loss
		heat conductive	s. heat-conducting
heat absorbing	s. endothermal	heat conductivity [coefficient]	s. thermal conductivity
heat absorption, absorption of heat	Wärmeaufnahme f, Wärmeabsorption f, Wärmebindung f; Wärmevernichtung f; Wärmeeinnahme f		
		heat conductivity due to the electrons, electron heat conductivity	elektronische Wärmeleitfähigkeit f, Elektronenanteil m der Wärmeleitfähigkeit
heat absorption coefficient	Wärmeabsorptionskoeffizient m		
		heat conductivity due to the lattice	s. lattice heat conductivity
heat absorption filter	Wärmeabsorptionsfilter n	heat conductivity method	Wärmeleitfähigkeitsmethode f, Wärmeleit[ungs]verfahren n
heat absorption ratio	Wärmeaufnahmeverhältnis n		
heat absorptivity	s heat capacity	heat conductivity tensor	s. tensor of heat conductivity
heat abstraction	s. heat removal	heat conductor, thermal conductor	Wärmeleiter m
heat accumulation, accumulation of heat	Wärmestauung f, Wärmestau m		
heat accumulation	s. a. heat storage	heat constant	Wärmekonstante f
heat action	s. action of heat	heat-consuming	s. endothermal
heat adduction	s. heat input	heat consumption	Wärmeverbrauch m; Wärmedurchsatz m; Wärmeaufwand m
heat advection	Wärmeadvektion f		
heat ageing, thermal ageing	thermische Alterung f, Wärmealterung f		
		heat contact	s. thermal contact
		heat content	s. enthalpy
heat balance, thermal balance	Wärmebilanz f	heat convection	s. convection of heat
		heat crack	s. hot crack
heat balance, equalizing of heat (temperature), heat (temperature) compensation, equalization of temperature	Wärmeausgleich m, Temperaturausgleich m	heat cracking, formation of thermal cracks	Warmrißbildung f, Wärmerißbildung f, Brandrißbildung f
		heat current	s. rate of heat flow
		heat current density	s. heat flow density
		heat death	Wärmetod m
heat balance [of the atmosphere], heat budget ‹geo.›	Wärme[gehalts]haushalt m, Wärmebilanz f, thermische Bilanz f ‹Geo.›	heat delivery, heat output, delivery of heat, heat yield	Wärmeabgabe f, Wärmeabfluß m; Wärmeausbeute f
heat barrier, thermal barrier	Hitzebarriere f, Hitzemauer f, Wärmemauer f	heat density, density of heat; heat transferred per unit area	Wärmedichte f; Heizflächenbelastung f
heat bridge	Wärmebrücke f		
heat budget, heat balance [of the atmosphere] ‹geo.›	Wärme[gehalts]haushalt m, Wärmebilanz f, thermische Bilanz f ‹Geo.›	heat devaluation	Wärmeabwertung f, Abwertung f der Wärme
heat calculation	Wärmerechnung f	heat development	s. heat release
heat capacity, heat, capacity for (of) heat, calorific (thermal) capacity, thermal capacitance; thermal (heat) absorptivity	Wärmekapazität f, Wärme f; Wärmeaufnahmevermögen n, Wärmeaufnahmefähigkeit f	heat diffusivity	s. thermal diffusivity
		heat dilation indicator, heat expansion indicator	Wärme[aus]dehnungsanzeiger m
		heat dispersion	s. dispersion of heat
		heat dissipated, loss of heat, heat loss	Wärmeverlust m
heat capacity at constant pressure, isobaric heat capacity	Wärmekapazität f bei konstantem Druck, isobare Wärmekapazität	heat dissipated in the reflector, reflector heat	Reflektorwärme f
		heat dissipating device	s. heat dissipator
heat capacity at constant volume, isochoric heat capacity	Wärmekapazität f bei konstantem Volumen, isochore Wärmekapazität	heat dissipation, dissipation of heat, thermal dissipation	Wärmezerstreuung f, Wärmedissipation f, Wärmeableitung f
heat capacity per unit mass	s. specific heat [capacity]		

heat dissipation loss [of the transducer] — Wärmeableitungsverlust m
heat dissipator, heat dissipating device — Wärmeableit[ungs]vorrichtung f, Wärmezerstreuungseinrichtung f
heat dynamometer — Wärmedynamometer n
heat economy — s. heat gain
heated wire, hot wire, heating wire — Hitzdraht m, Heißdraht m, Heizdraht m

heat effect, heat change, heat of reaction, reaction heat, heat tonality — Wärmetönung f [der chemischen Reaktion], Reaktionswärme f

heat effect <bio.> — Hitzewirkung f <Bio.>
heat effect — s. a. action of heat
heat effect method, method of measurement based on heat effect — Wärmetönungsverfahren n
heat efficiency, utilization of heat, heat utilization — Wärmeausnutzung f, Wärmenutzung f
heat efficiency — s. a. thermal efficiency
heat-eliminating, heat-removing — wärmeabgebend, wärmeabführend
heat elimination — s. heat removal
heat emission, emission of heat — Wärmeausstrahlung f, Wärmeabstrahlung f, Wärmeabgabe f durch Strahlung

heat emission coefficient, coefficient of heat emission — Wärmeabgabezahl f, Wärmeabgabeziffer f, Wärmeabgabekoeffizient m <in kcal/cm² s grd>

heat emission loss — Wärmeabstrahlungsverlust m
heat endurance — s. thermal stability
heat energy, thermal (calorific) energy, thermal (heat) work, heat — Wärmeenergie f, thermische Energie (Arbeit) f, Wärmearbeit f, Wärme f
heat engine, heat motor, thermodynamic machine — Wärmekraftmaschine f, kalorische Maschine f
heat equation, heat conduction equation, Biot-Fourier equation, equation of heat conduction — Wärmeleitungsgleichung f, Wärmeleitgleichung f

heat equation, equation of heat balance — Wärmebilanzgleichung f; <Geo. auch> Wärme[haushalts]gleichung f
heat equivalent [of the work done], thermal value — kalorisches Arbeitsäquivalent n, Wärmewert m [der Arbeitseinheit]
heater, heating device — Heizer m; Heizung f; Heizkörper m; Heizapparat m; Heizvorrichtung f; Erhitzer m
heater, heating conductor, heating element — Heizleiter m
heater — s. a. heating filament <of electron tube>
heater circuit, filament circuit — Heiz[strom]kreis m, Heizungskreis m
heater current; filament current; heating current — Heizstrom m; Heizfadenstrom m

heater power, heating power; filament [current] power <el.> — Heizleistung f; Heizfadenleistung f <El.>
heater voltage, filament voltage, voltage of filament battery <el.> — Heizfadenspannung f, Fadenspannung f, Heizspannung f <El.>
heat evacuation — s. heat removal
heat evolution — s. heat release
heat exchange, exchange of heat — Wärmeumsatz m
heat exchange, heat interchange, exchange (interchange) of heat <direct heat transfer without intermediate accumulation> — Wärmeaustausch m, Wärmetausch m <direkter Wärmeübergang ohne Zwischenspeicherung>

heat exchange — s. a. heat transfer
heat exchange by conduction — s. heat transfer by conduction
heat exchange by convection — s. heat transfer by convection
heat exchange by electromagnetic waves, heat exchange by radiation — s. heat transfer by radiation

heat-exchange constant, constant of heat exchange — Wärmeaustauschkonstante f
heat exchange efficiency — Wärmeaustauscheffektivität f, Wärmeaustausch-Effektivitätszahl f
heat exchanger, heat interchanger, interchanger — Wärme[aus]tauscher m, Wärmeaustauschapparat m
heat-exchange surface, heat exchanging surface — Wärmeaustauschfläche f
heat expansion curve — Wärmeausdehnungskurve f
heat expansion indicator, heat dilation indicator — Wärmedehnungsanzeiger m, Wärmeausdehnungsanzeiger m
heat extraction — s. heat removal
heat-fast — s. heat-proof
heat fastness, heat-fast quality — s. thermal stability
heat filter — Wärmefilter n
heat filtering — Wärmefilterung f
heat flash — Wärmeblitz m
heat flow — s. heat convection
heat flow — s. rate of heat flow
heat flow density, density of heat flow, heat current density, heat flux density — Wärmestromdichte f
heat flow diagram — Wärmeschaltbild n, Schaltbild n, Wärme[schalt]schema n, Wärmeschaltung f, Wärme[fluß]bild n, Wärmeflußdiagramm n

heat flow function — Wärmestromfunktion f
heat flowing — s. heat convection
heat flow line, line of heat flow [vector] — Wärmestromlinie f
heat flow meter — Wärmeflußmesser m, Wärmestrommesser m
heat flow rate — s. rate of heat flow
heat flow theory — Wärmeströmungstheorie f
heat flow transformation, transformation of heat flow — Wärmeflußtransformation f
heat flow vector, thermal (heat) flux vector — Wärmeflußvektor m, Wärmestromvektor m
heat flux — s. rate of heat flow
heat flux density — s. heat flow density
heat flux vector — s. heat flow vector
heat forming, hot working — Warmumformung f, Warmformgebung f, Warm[ver]formung f, Warmformverfahren n

heat function — s. enthalpy
heat gain, gain of heat; economy of heat, heat economy — Wärmegewinn m; Wärmeersparnis f
heat-generating — s. exothermic
heat generation — s. generation of heat
heat gradient, gradient of heat — Wärmegradient m; Wärmegefälle n
heat hardening — s. hot hardening
heat index <astr.> — Wärmeindex m <Astr.>
heat influx — s. heat input
heating — Heizung f, Heizen n; Beheizen n
heating, heat; warming, growing warm — Aufheizung f; Ausheizung f; Erhitzung f; Erwärmung f
heating <e.g. of nucleus, chromosphere, corona> — Aufheizung f <z. B. Kern, Chromosphäre, Korona>
heating bath, bath — Heizbad n, Wärmebad n

heating by collision, collision heating — Stoßaufheizung f

heating by compression, compression heating — Kompressionsaufheizung f, Aufheizung f durch Kompression
heating by conduction — Erwärmung f durch Wärmeleitung
heating circuit — s. heater circuit
heating coil <therm.> — Heizschlange f <Therm.>

heating conductor, heating element, heater	Heizleiter m	heat loss coefficient	Wärmeverlustziffer f
heating crack, hot crack, heat crack	Temperaturriß m, Warmriß m, Wärmeriß m, Vielhärtungsriß m	heat measurement; calorimetry; calorimetering	Kalorimetrie f, Wärme[mengen]messung f; Kalorimetrieren n
heating current; filament current; heater current	Heizstrom m; Heizfadenstrom m	heat measuring device	Wärmemeßgerät n, Wärmemeßeinrichtung f, Wärmemesser m
heating curve	Erwärmungskurve f, Wärmekurve f	heat meter	Wärmemengenzähler m, Wärmezähler m, Wärmeverbrauchszähler m
heating device	s. heater		
heating effect	Heizeffekt m, Heizwirkung f	heat motion	s. thermal agitation
heating effect	s. a. heat action	heat motor, heat engine, thermodynamic machine	Wärmekraftmaschine f, kalorische Maschine f
heating efficiency	s. heat output		
heating efficiency	s. a. thermal efficiency	heat of absorption, absorption heat	Absorptionswärme f
heating element	Heizelement n		
heating element	s. a. heating conductor	heat of activation	s. activation energy <therm., chem.>
heating filament	s. filament <of electron tube>	heat of adhesion, adhesion heat	Adhäsionswärme f
heating microscope	Heiztischmikroskop n; Erhitzungsmikroskop n, Hochtemperaturmikroskop n	heat of adsorption, adsorption heat	Adsorptionswärme f
		heat of coagulation	s. coagulation heat
		heat of combination	s. heat of formation
heating of plasma, plasma heating	Plasmaaufheizung f, Aufheizung f des Plasmas	heat of combustion, combustion heat	Verbrennungswärme f
heating of the wall	Wandaufheizung f	heat of compression, compression heat	Verdichtungswärme f, Kompressionswärme f
heating pattern; variation of temperature, temperature variation	Temperaturgang m; Temperaturverlauf m	heat of condensation, latent heat of condensation, condensation heat, heat of liquefaction	Kondensationswärme f, Verflüssigungswärme f
heating period	s. warm-up time		
heating power	s. heat output		
heating power	s. heater power <el.>	heat of contraction, contraction heat	Verkürzungswärme f, Kontraktionswärme f
heating power	s. net calorific value		
heating stage [of microscope]; hot stage [of microscope]	Heiztisch m, Mikroskopheiztisch m	heat of crystallization, crystallization heat	Kristallisationswärme f
heating surface	Heizfläche f	heat of decomposition, decomposition heat <chem.>	Zersetzungswärme f, Zerfallswärme f <Chem.>
		heat of dilution, dilution heat	Verdünnungswärme f
heating time, heating-up period <of tube>	Anheizzeit f <Röhre>	heat of dilution	s. a. differential dissolution heat
heating time	s. a. warm-up time		
heating time constant	Wärmezeitkonstante f	heat of disintegration, heat of radioactivity	Zerfallswärme f
		heat of dissipation	Dissipationswärme f
heating-up period	Einbrennzeit f	heat of dissociation	Dissoziationswärme f
heating-up period	s. a. heating time		
heating value	s. net calorific value	heat of dissolution	s. heat of solution
heating wire, hot wire, heated wire	Hitzdraht m, Heißdraht m, Heizdraht m	heat of evaporation, evaporation heat	Verdunstungswärme f
		heat of evaporation	s. a. evaporation heat
heat input, heat supply, heat influx, heat adduction	Wärmezufuhr f, Wärmezuführung f; Wärmezufluß m, Wärmezustrom m; Wärmeeinströmung f, Wärmeeinstrom m; Wärmeeinfall m	heat of explosion, explosion heat	Explosionswärme f
		heat of fission, fission heat	Spaltungswärme f
		heat of formation, formation heat, heat of combination	Bildungswärme f, Entstehungswärme f, Verbindungswärme f
heat-insulated, heat-isolated	wärmeisoliert		
heat-insulating	wärmedämmend, wärmeisolierend	heat of friction, friction[al] heat	Reibungswärme f
heat-insulating material	s. heat insulator		
heat insulation, thermal insulation, insulation, lagging <therm.>	Wärmedämmung f, Wärme[schutz]isolierung f, [thermische] Isolierung f, Wärmeisolation f, Wärmeschutz m <Therm.>	heat of fusion, latent heat of fusion, fusion (melting) heat, [latent] heat of melting; enthalpy of fusion, fusion (melting) enthalpy	Schmelzwärme f, latente Schmelzwärme; Schmelzenthalpie f
		heat of hydration, hydration heat	Hydratationswärme f
heat insulator, heat-insulating material	Wärmedämmstoff m, Wärmeisolierstoff m, Wärmeisoliermaterial n, Wärmeisolator m, Wärmeschutzstoff m, Wärmedämmschutz m	heat of ignition, heat of inflammation	Zündwärme f
		heat of imbibition, heat of swelling, swelling heat	Quellungswärme f
heat intensity	Wärmeintensität f	heat of inflammation, heat of ignition	Zündwärme f
heat interchange	s. heat exchange	heat of ionization	Ionisationswärme f
heat interchanger, heat exchanger, interchanger	Wärme[aus]tauscher m, Wärmeaustauschapparat m		
		heat of isomerization, isomeric (isomerization) heat	Isomerisationswärme f
heat-isolated, heat-insulated	wärmeisoliert	heat of isothermal compression, isothermal heat of compression	isotherme Kompressionswärme f
heat leak[age], leakage of heat; dispersion of heat, heat dispersion	Wärmestreuung f, Wärmeverlust m, Wärmeundichtigkeit f		
heat lightning, heat thunderstorm	Wärmegewitter n, Luftmassengewitter n	heat of isothermal expansion, isothermal heat of expansion	isotherme Expansionswärme f
heat lightning, sheet (summer) lightning	Wetterleuchten n	heat of linkage	Bindungswärme f
heat load[ing], thermal load[ing], thermal stress	Wärmebelastung f, Wärmebeanspruchung f	heat of liquefaction	s. heat of condensation
heat loss, loss of heat, heat dissipated	Wärmeverlust m		

heat of magnetization, magnetization heat (enthalpy), enthalpy of magnetization — Magnetisierungswärme f; Magnetisierungsenthalpie f

heat of melting — s. heat of fusion
heat of mixing — s. enthalpy of mixing
heat of mutual exchange [reaction] — Umsetzungswärme f
heat of neutralization, neutralization heat — Neutralisationswärme f
heat of phase transformation (transition) — s. heat of transformation
heat of physical adsorption — physikalische Adsorptionswärme f
heat of racemization, racemization heat — Razemisierungswärme f
heat of radioactivity, heat of disintegration — Zerfallswärme f
heat of reaction — s. heat effect
heat of remagnetization — s. hysteresis heat
heat of separation — Trenn[ungs]wärme f
heat of solidification, latent heat of solidification, solidification heat — Erstarrungswärme f; Erstarrungsenthalpie f
heat of solution, heat of dissolution, [dis]solution heat; solution enthalpy, enthalpy of solution — Lösungswärme f; Lösungsenthalpie f
heat of stirring — Rührungswärme f
heat of subcooling, subcooling (supercooling) heat, heat of supercooling — Unterkühlungswärme f
heat of sublimation, enthalpy (latent heat) of sublimation, sublimation heat (enthalpy) — Sublimationswärme f; Sublimationsenthalpie f
heat of supercooling, subcooling (supercooling) heat, heat of subcooling — Unterkühlungswärme f
heat of swelling, swelling heat, heat of imbibition — Quellungswärme f
heat of transfer, diffusion heat, heat of transport — Diffusionswärme f, Überführungswärme f
heat of transformation, heat of transition, transformation heat, transition heat, latent heat, heat of phase transformation (transition); transformation enthalpy, transition enthalpy — Umwandlungswärme f, latente Wärme f; Umwandlungsenthalpie f

heat of transport, diffusion heat, heat of transfer — Diffusionswärme f, Überführungswärme f
heat of vaporization — s. evaporation heat
heat of wetting, wetting heat — Benetzungswärme f
heat output, calorific power, caloric power, heating power, thermal power, heating efficiency — Wärmeleistung f, Wärme f

heat output, heat delivery, delivery of heat, heat yield — Wärmeabgabe f, Wärmeabfluß m; Wärmeausbeute f
heat output recorder — Wärmeleistungsschreiber m
heat overload — Wärmeüberbeanspruchung f
heat passage — s. transmission of heat
heat penetration, penetration of heat — Wärmeeindringung f, Wärmedurchdringung f
heat penetration coefficient — Wärmeeindringzahl f
heat phenomenon, thermal phenomenon — Wärmeerscheinung f
heat physics, physics of heat — Wärmephysik f
heat pipe — s. heat tube
heat pole; source of heat, heat source — Wärmequelle f; Wärmepol m; Wärmespender m
heat polymerization — Wärmepolymerisation f

heat position finder; heat range finder — Wärmepeiler m

heat potential — Wärmepotential n
heat-pressure gauge, thermogauge — Thermomanometer n
heat production — s. generation of heat
heat-proof, heat-resisting, heat-resistant, resistant to heat, heat-fast, heat-stable; high-temperature resistant; temperature-resistant; thermally stable, thermostable — hitzebeständig, hitzefest, hitzesicher; hochwarmfest, hochtemperaturbeständig, hochwarmbeständig; warmfest, wärmebeständig, wärmefest, wärmeresistent, wärmesicher, temperaturbeständig, temperaturfest, thermisch stabil

heat-proof — s. a. athermanous
heat proofness, heat-proof quality — s. thermal stability
heat propagation, propagation of heat — Wärmeausbreitung f, Wärmefortpflanzung f, Wärmefortleitung f
heat pulse — Wärmeimpuls m

heat pump — Wärmepumpe f

heat quantity, quantity (amount) of heat — Wärmemenge f, Wärme f
heat radiation, thermal radiation, radiation of heat; calorific radiation, caloric radiation; incandescence — Wärmestrahlung f, thermische Strahlung f, Temperaturstrahlung f

heat radiation detector, heat radiation receiver — Wärmestrahlungsempfänger m

heat radiation pyrometer — s. radiation pyrometer
heat radiation receiver — s. heat radiation detector
heat radiation sensing device, heat radiation sensor — Wärmestrahlungsfühler m
heat radiation spectrum, heat (thermal) spectrum — Wärmestrahlungsspektrum n, Wärmespektrum n
heat range finder; heat position finder — Wärmepeiler m
heat ray — Wärmestrahl m

heat received — Wärmeeinstrahlung f

heat receptor, thermoreceptor — Thermorezeptor m, Wärmerezeptor m
heat-reflecting filter — s. heat reflector
heat-reflecting glass — Wärmeschutzglas n

heat reflection, reflection of heat — Wärmerückstrahlung f, Wärmereflexion f
heat reflector, heat-reflecting filter — Wärmeschutzfilter n, Wärmereflexionsfilter n; Wärmeflußsperre f

heat regeneration, regeneration of heat — Wärmerückgewinnung f, Wärmerückgewinn m, Wärmeregeneration f
heat regenerator — s. regenerator
heat rejection — s. heat removal
heat release, heat evolution (development), release (evolution, development) of heat; generation (production) of heat, heat generation (production) — Wärmeentwicklung f, Wärmeentbindung f, Wärmefreisetzung f; Wärmeerzeugung f, Wärmebildung f, Wärmeproduktion f
heat removal, heat elimination (evacuation, extraction, abstraction, abduction, rejection), removal (elimination, evacuation, extraction, abstraction, abduction, rejection) of heat — Wärmeabfuhr f, Wärmeabführung f; Wärmeableitung f; Wärmeentziehung f, Wärmeentzug m; Wärmeentnahme f
heat-removing, heat-eliminating — wärmeabgebend, wärmeabführend
heat requirement for heating — Erhitzungswärme f

heat reservoir — Wärmereservoir n

heat reservoir — s. a. heat absorber
heat resistance — s. thermal stability

heat-resistant

heat-resistant, heat-resisting	s. heat-proof
heat-resisting quality	s. thermal stability
heat-retaining capacity	Wärmehaltevermögen n, Wärmerückhaltevermögen n
heat retention	Wärmehaltung f
heat-retention coefficient	Wärmehaltungskoeffizient m
heat sensitivity	s. sensitivity to heat
heat shield	s. thermal shield
heat sink, sink of heat	Wärmesenke f; Wärmeabfuhrelement n
heat source, source of heat; heat pole	Wärmequelle f; Wärmepol m; Wärmespender m
heat spectrum, heat radiation spectrum, thermal spectrum	Wärmestrahlungsspektrum n, Wärmespektrum n
heat spike theory, theory of Seitz	Seitzsche Wärmespitzentheorie f, Wärmespitzentheorie [von Seitz]
heat stability	Wärmestabilität f
heat-stable	s. heat-proof
heat storage, heat accumulation, storage (accumulation) of heat	Wärme[auf]speicherung f, Wärmestauung f, Wärmestau m
heat-storage capacity	Wärmespeicher[ungs]fähigkeit f, Wärmespeicher[ungs]vermögen n
heat stroke ‹bio.›	Hitzschlag m ‹Bio.›
heat sum	Wärmesumme f
heat supply	Wärmeversorgung f, Wärmelieferung f
heat supply	s. a. heat input
heat system	Wärmesystem n
heat technology, science of heat	Wärmelehre f, Kalorik f
heat test, hot test, test at elevated temperature	Warmversuch m, Warmprobe f, Warmprüfung f, Hochtemperaturversuch m, Hitzeprüfung f, Temperaturprüfung f
heat theorem	s. third law ‹of thermodynamics›
heat thunderstorm, heat lightning	Wärmegewitter n; Luftmassengewitter n
heat-tight	s. athermanous
heat tonality	s. heat effect
heat transfer, heat transmission (exchange), transfer (transference, transmission, exchange) of heat	Wärmeübertragung f, Wärmeübergang m, Wärmeaustausch m
heat transfer, heat transport	Wärmetransport m, Wärmeübertragung f, Wärmeverfrachtung f, Wärmeüberführung f
heat transfer	s. a. transfer of heat
heat-transfer agent, heat-transfer fluid, heat-transfer medium; coolant, cooling agent, cooling fluid, cooling medium	Wärmeträger m, Wärmeüberträger m, Wärmeübertragungsmittel n; Kühlmittel n, Kühlstoff m, Kühlmedium n
heat-transfer area; heat-transfer surface	Wärmeübertragungsfläche f; Wärmeübergangsfläche f; Wärmedurchgangsfläche f
heat transfer by conduction, heat transmission by conduction, heat exchange by conduction	Wärmeübertragung f (Wärmeübergang m, Wärmeaustausch m) durch Leitung, Wärmeüberleitung f
heat transfer by convection, heat transmission by convection, heat exchange by convection, convective heat exchange, convective exchange of heat	Wärmeübertragung f durch Konvektion (Mitführung, Berührung), Wärmeübergang m durch Konvektion (Mitführung, Berührung), Wärmeaustausch m durch Konvektion (Mitführung, Berührung), konvektive Wärmeübertragung, konvektiver Wärmeübergang (Wärmeaustausch)
heat transfer by electromagnetic waves	s. heat transfer by radiation
heat transfer by forced convection	Wärmeübertragung f (Wärmeübergang m, Wärmeaustausch m) bei erzwungener Konvektion, Wärmeübertragung (Wärmeübergang, Wärmeaustausch) bei aufgezwungener Strömung
heat transfer by free convection	Wärmeübertragung f (Wärmeübergang m, Wärmeaustausch m) bei freier Konvektion
heat transfer by radiation, heat transfer by electromagnetic waves, heat transmission by radiation (electromagnetic waves), heat exchange by radiation (electromagnetic waves), radiative heat transfer (transmission, exchange), radiative transfer [of heat]	Wärmeübertragung f durch Strahlung, Wärmeübergang m durch Strahlung, Wärmeaustausch m durch Strahlung
heat-transfer circuit, coolant loop, coolant circuit	Kühlkreislauf m, Kühlkreis m, Wärmeübertragungskreis[lauf] m
heat-transfer coefficient, transfer coefficient, coefficient of heat transfer ‹by convection, forced convection, free convection, radiation›	Wärmeübergangszahl f ‹in kcal/m² h grd› ‹bei Konvektion oder Mitführung, erzwungener Konvektion oder aufgezwungener Strömung, freier Konvektion, Strahlung›
heat-transfer factor ‹of heat pump›	Wärmewirkungsgrad m, Wärmeziffer f ‹Wärmepumpe›
heat-transfer fluid	s. heat-transfer agent
heat-transfer loss, loss due to heat transfer	Wärmeübertragungsverlust m, Wärmeübergangsverlust m
heat-transfer medium	s. heat-transfer agent
heat transferred per unit area	s. heat density
heat-transfer resistance	s. reciprocal of heat-transfer coefficient
heat-transferring, heat-transmitting	wärmeübertragend
heat-transfer surface; heat-transfer area	Wärmeübertragungsfläche f; Wärmeübergangsfläche f; Wärmedurchgangsfläche f
heat transformation	Wärmetransformation f
heat transformer	Wärmetransformator m
heat transition	s. transfer of heat
heat transmission	s. heat transfer
heat transmission	s. transmission of heat
heat transmission by ...	s. heat transfer by ...
heat[-] transmission coefficient, over[-]all heat-transfer coefficient, over[-]all coefficient [of heat transfer], thermal transmittance, coefficient of heat transfer ‹US›, u value ‹US›	Wärmedurchgangszahl f ‹in kcal/m² h grd›
heat-transmission resistance, reciprocal of heat-transmission coefficient	Wärmedurchgangswiderstand m
heat transmission resistance	Wärmeleitungswiderstand m, Wärmedurchlaßwiderstand m, Wärmedämmzahl f ‹Wanddicke/Wärmeleitfähigkeit, in m² h °C/kcal›
heat transmitter, cold mirror, cold-light mirror	Kaltlichtspiegel m
heat-transmitting, heat-transferring	wärmeübertragend
heat-transmitting	s. a. diathermanous
heat transport, heat transfer	Wärmetransport m, Wärmeübertragung f, Wärmeverfrachtung f, Wärmeüberführung f
heat-transport phenomenon	Wärmetransporterscheinung f
heat treatment, temperature treatment	Wärmebehandlung f

heat tube, heat pipe	Wärmerohr n	heavy mass, gravitational (ponderable) mass	schwere Masse f
heat unit, unit of heat, caloric (thermal) unit	Wärmemengeneinheit f, Wärmeeinheit f	heavy-media aggregate separation	Schwerflüssigkeitsaufbereitung f, Schwertrübeaufbereitung f, Schwertrübescheidung f, Dichtesortierung f, Schwimm- und Sinkverfahren n
heat-unsteady	s. thermolabile		
heat utilization, utilization of heat, heat efficiency	Wärmeausnutzung f, Wärmenutzung f		
heat value	s. net calorific value		
heat-variable resistor	s. thermistor	heavy meson	s. K-meson
heat wave <meteo.>	Hitzewelle f <Meteo.>	heavy metal, high-density metal	Schwermetall n
heat work	s. heat energy	heavy nucleus, heavy element atomic nucleus	schwerer Kern m
heat yield	s. heat output		
heaviness, ponderosity, ponderability	Schwere f		
heaving [motion]; vertical motion (movement)	Hebung f; Vertikalbewegung f	heavy-particle synchro-, tron, protonsynchrotron, synchrophasotron	Synchrophasotron n, Protonensynchrotron n, Synchrotron n für schwere geladene Teilchen
Heaviside calculus	s. operator calculus	heavy rain	Starkregen m, starker Regen m
Heaviside['s] expansion theorem	Heavisidescher Entwicklungssatz m		
Heaviside['s] function	s. Heaviside['s] unit function	heavy shower	s. downpour
		heavy track, heavy branch, black prong, black track	schwere Spur f, schwarze Spur, dicke Spur
Heaviside['s] layer, ionosphere, thermosphere	Ionosphäre f, Thermosphäre f, Heaviside-Schicht f, Ionisationsschicht f	heavy water, deuterium oxide, deuteroxide, D_2O	schweres Wasser n, Schwerwasser n, Deuteriumoxid n, D_2O
Heaviside['s] layer	s. a. E Layer		
Heaviside-Lorentz system [of units], Lorentz-Heaviside system [of units], Lorentz-Heaviside units, Heaviside system of units	Lorentzsches Einheitensystem n, Heaviside-Lorentzsches Einheitensystem (Maßsystem n), Lorentz-Heavisidesches Einheitensystem, Lorentz-Heavisidesche Einheiten fpl, Heavisidesches Einheitensystem (Maßsystem)	heavy[-] water [moderated] pile, heavy water reactor; deuterium-moderated reactor	Schwerwasserreaktor m; schwerwassermoderierter Reaktor m
		Heber['s] approximation	Heber-Näherung f, Hebersche Näherung f
		hecto..., h	Hekto.... h
		hectometer wave, hectometric wave, medium-frequency wave	Mittelwelle f, Hektometerwelle f
Heaviside-Lorentz unit, Heaviside unit	Heaviside[-Lorentz]sche Einheit f	hectometer wavelength range	s. medium frequency range
Heaviside operational calculus	s. operator calculus	hectometric wave, hectometer wave, medium-frequency wave	Mittelwelle f, Hektometerwelle f
Heaviside['s] partial fraction rule	Heavisidesche Partialbruchregel f	Hecuba gap	Hecuba-Lücke f
Heaviside system of units	s. Heaviside-Lorentz system	Hecuba problem	Hecuba-Problem n
Heaviside unit	s. Heaviside-Lorentz unit	hedgehog transformer	Igeltransformator m, Igelumformer m
Heaviside['s] unit function, unit function [of Heaviside], unit step [function], unit pulse function, Heaviside['s] function	Heaviside-Funktion f, Heavisidesche Funktion (Einheitsfunktion) f, [Heavisidesche] Sprungfunktion f, Heavisidesche Stufenfunktion f, Einheitssprung m	hedgerow prominence	s. quiescent prominence
		Hedvall effect	Hedvall-Effekt m
		Heegner circuit; Heegner oscillator	Heegner-Schaltung f
		heel, still bottom heel, still bottoms, tailings, bottoms, leavings	Destillierrückstand m, Blasenrückstand m, Destillationsrückstand m
		heel effect	„heel"-Effekt m, „Fersen-effekt" m
heavy-aggregate [concrete], heavy concrete, loaded concrete	Schwerbeton m, Strahlenschutzbeton m	heeling moment coefficient	s. rolling moment coefficient
heavy anode, solid anode, non-split anode	Vollanode f, massive Anode f	Heesch-Shubnikov group	s. magnetic space group
		hefner, Hefner candle, Hefner-Kerze <= 0.903 cd>	Hefner-Kerze f, HK <= 0,903 cd>
heavy anode tube, solid anode tube	Vollanodenröhre f		
heavy-bodied	s. viscid <chem.>	Hefner lamp	Hefner-Lampe f, Amylazetatlampe f
heavy body	schwerer Körper m		
heavy branch, heavy track, black prong, black track	schwere Spur f, schwarze Spur, dicke Spur	Hehl['s] law	Hehlsches Gesetz n
		hei	s. hei-function
heavy chain	schwere Kette f	Heiden['s] halo, Heiden['s] ring	Halo m von Heiden
heavy concrete	s. heavy-aggregate		
heavy current, power current	Starkstrom m	hei-function, Kelvin hei function, hei	Kelvinsche (Thomsonsche) hei-Funktion f, hei-Funktion f, hei
heavy-duty	hochbelastbar, hochbeanspruchbar, Hochlast-, Hochleistungs-	height, true height, absolute height	wahre Höhe f, absolute Höhe, Höhe
		height above ground, vertical distance above ground, elevation above ground	Höhe f über Grund, Höhe über dem Erdboden (Boden)
heavy-duty electrode	Hochleistungselektrode f		
heavy electronics	Schwerelektronik f	height above sea level, orthometric height, vertical distance above sea level, elevation above sea level	Höhe f über Normalnull, Höhe über NN, Höhe über dem Meeresspiegel, Höhe ü. d. M., orthometrische Höhe, Höhe über NN
heavy element atomic nucleus	s. heavy nucleus		
heavy-gas approach (approximation)	Schwergasnäherung f		
heavy hydrogen, deuterium, $D, {}_1^2H, {}^2H$	Deuterium n, schwerer Wasserstoff m		
		height adjustment, vertical adjustment (motion)	Höhenverstellung f
heavy ice	schweres Eis n, gefrorenes Schwerwasser n		
heavy ion	s. large ion <geo.>	height correction	Höhenkorrektion f
heavy-ion linear accelerator, hilac	Schwerionen-Linearbeschleuniger m		
heavy liquid bubble chamber, heavy liquid chamber, HLBC	Schwerflüssigkeits-Blasenkammer f, Schwerflüssigkeitskammer f	height equivalent to a theoretical plate (stage), height of packing equivalent to one theoretical plate, HETS, HETP	theoretische Trennstufenhöhe f, Trennstufenhöhe, Bodenwert m, äquivalente Füllkörperhöhe f, HETP-Wert m

height

height equivalent to 1 Torr of pressure drop	s. barometric gradient	height of the viscosity pole, viscosity pole height	Viskositätspolhöhe f
height finder, height indicator; altimeter, altitude meter (measuring instrument)	Altimeter n, Höhenmesser m; Höhenfinder m, Höhensucher m	height of the wave, wave height	Wellenhöhe f
height-finding radar	Höhenbestimmungsradar n, Höhenfinderradar n	height of throw, height of projection <height to which the body thrown will ascend>	Wurfhöhe f, Steighöhe f
		height of tropopause	Tropopausenhöhe f
height-gain function	Höhengewinnfunktion f	height of waters	Pegelstand m
height gauge	Höhenlehre f	height of weir, weir height	Wehrhöhe f, Dammhöhe f, Höhe f der Dammkrone
		heiligenschein; glory, phantom ring, gloriole	Glorie f; Heiligenschein m, Gloriole f
height indicator	s. height finder	Heiligtag effect	Heiligtag-Effekt m
height mark; reference mark	Höhenmarke f, Höhenkote f	Heil tube, coaxial line tube	Heilscher Generator (Auskoppelgenerator) m, Zweischlitz-Einkammer-Klystron n, Zweispalt-Einkammer-Klystron n
height measurement	s. hypsometry		
height measuring barometer, barometric altimeter, pressure altimeter	barometrischer Höhenmesser m, Höhenbarometer n	Heine-Borel['s] theorem	Heine-Borelscher Überdeckungssatz (Satz) m, Satz (Überdeckungssatz) von Heine-Borel
height of ascent	s. height of capillary rise	Heisenberg['s] field theory [of fundamental particles]	s. Heisenberg['s] non-linear field theory
height of ascent	s. a. height of lift		
height of a transfer unit, HTU	Wirkungshöhe f [der Kolonne]	Heisenberg force, Heisenberg interactive force, charge exchange force	Heisenberg-Kraft f, Ladungsaustauschkraft f
height of capillary rise	s. capillary rise		
height of climb, height of lift (ascent), climbing height	Steighöhe f	Heisenberg['s] formula	s. Heisenberg['s] non-linear field theory
		Heisenberg interactive force	s. Heisenberg force
height of condensation, condensation level	Kondensationsniveau n, Kondensationshöhe f	Heisenberg['s] [matrix] mechanics	s. matrix mechanics
height of drop	s. height of fall	Heisenberg['s] non-linear field theory [of fundamental particles], Heisenberg['s] field theory [of fundamental particles]; Heisenberg['s] formula	Heisenbergsche Feldtheorie f der Elementarteilchen, nichtlineare Spinortheorie f [von Heisenberg]; Heisenbergsche Weltformel f, Weltformel [von Heisenberg], Weltgleichung f [von Heisenberg], Gleichung f für die Materie
height of evaporation, evaporation height, amount of evaporation in mm	Verdunstungshöhe f		
height of fall, height of the fall, height of drop, space which the body falls, depth of fall	Fallhöhe f		
height of inversion [layer]	Inversionshöhe f		
height of lift, height of climb (ascent), climbing height	Steighöhe f	Heisenberg['s] operator, charge exchange operator	Heisenberg-Operator m, Operator m der Heisenberg-Kräfte, Ladungsaustauschoperator m
height of lift, suction height (lift) <of the pump>	Förderhöhe f, Saughöhe f <Pumpe>	Heisenberg picture, Heisenberg representation	Heisenberg-Darstellung f, Heisenbergsche Darstellung f, Heisenberg-Bild n, Energiedarstellung f, Matrixdarstellung f
height of potential barrier, barrier height	Höhe f des Potentialwalls, Walltiefe f		
height of precipitation; rain height; amount of rainfall, depth of rainfall, rainfall	Niederschlagshöhe f, Regenhöhe f; Niederschlagsmenge f, Regenmenge f	Heisenberg['s] potential, charge exchange potential	Heisenberg-Potential n, Potential n der Heisenberg-Kräfte
		Heisenberg['s] principle of uncertainty	s. uncertainty principle
		Heisenberg['s] quantum mechanics	s. matrix mechanics
		Heisenberg representation	s. Heisenberg picture
		Heisenberg resonance	Heisenberg-Resonanz f
height of projection, height of throw <height to which the body thrown will ascend>	Wurfhöhe f, Steighöhe f		
		Heisenberg ring	Heisenberg-Ring m
height of rebound, rebound	Rückprallhöhe f, Rücksprunghöhe f	Heisenberg['s] theory of ferromagnetism	Heisenbergsche Theorie f des Ferromagnetismus
height of reflection	Reflexionshöhe f		
height of rise	s. height of capillary rise	Heisenberg['s] uncertainty principle	s. uncertainty principle
height of roughness, roughness height	Rauhigkeitshöhe f	Heising modulation	s. constant-current modulation
height of shell	s. sag	Heitler-London approximation	Heitler-London-Näherung f, Heitler-Londonsche Näherung f
height of snow	Schneehöhe f; Schneetiefe f		
		Heitler-London covalence (electron pair) theory, Heitler-London method, Heitler-London theory [of electron-pair bond]	Heitler-London-Verfahren n, Heitler-London-Methode f
height of the breast / in the, waist-level	in Brusthöhe		
height of the fall, height of fall (drop), space which the body falls, depth of fall	Fallhöhe f		
height of the fault	s. fault height <geo.>	Heitler-London model	Heitler-London-Modell n, Heitler-Londonsches Modell n
height of the horizon	Horizonthöhe f		
height of the shell (vault)	s. sag	Heitler-London-Slater-Pauling theory	s. valence-bond theory

Heitler-London theory [of electron-pair bond], Heitler-London theory of valence, Heitler-London covalence (electron pair) theory, Heitler-London method, spin-valence theory	Heitler-London-Verfahren n, Heitler-London-Methode f	**helicoidal displacement (motion)**	s. screw displacement
		helicoidal surface	s. helicoid
		helicon	Heliconwelle f, Helicon n, Helikon n
		helicon-acoustical nuclear resonance	helikon-kernakustische Resonanz f
Heitler unit	s. cascade unit	**helimagnetism**	Helimagnetismus m
Hele-Shaw analogy	Hele-Shaw-Analogie f	**heliocentric co-ordinates,** heliocentric system of co-ordinates	heliozentrische Koordinaten fpl, heliozentrisches Koordinatensystem n
Hele-Shaw apparatus, Hele-Shaw cell	Hele-Shaw-Apparat m		
Hele-Shaw cell, Hele-Shaw apparatus	Hele-Shaw-Apparat m	**heliocentric parallax,** annual parallax, parallax	jährliche (heliozentrische) Parallaxe f; Parallaxe
Hele-Shaw['s] experiment	Hele-Shaw-Versuch m, Versuch m von Hele Shaw	**heliocentric system**	s. heliocentric world system
		heliocentric system of co-ordinates	s. heliocentric co-ordinates
Hele-Shaw flow	Hele-Shaw-Strömung f	**heliocentric theory**	s. heliocentric world system
heliacal rising	kosmischer Aufgang m; heliakischer Aufgang	**heliocentric world system,** heliocentric system [of the world]; heliocentric theory	heliozentrisches Weltsystem (System) n, heliozentrisches Weltbild n; heliozentrische Theorie f
heliacal setting	heliakischer Untergang m		
heliacal year	heliakisches Jahr n		
helical, screw, screw-like, coiled, helicoidal	schraubenförmig, Schrauben[linien]-; wendelförmig	**heliograph,** sunshine recorder	Heliograph m, Sonnenscheinautograph m, Sonnenscheinschreiber m
helical, spiral, planispiral	Spiral-, spiralförmig, spiralig	**heliographic co-ordinates,** heliographic system of co-ordinates	heliographische Koordinaten fpl, heliographisches Koordinatensystem n
helical accelerator	s. helix accelerator		
helical antenna, corkscrew antenna	Wendelantenne f, Spulenantenne f, Schraubenantenne f, Helixantenne f, Spiralantenne f	**helion,** helium nucleus <^{4}He>; alpha particle (ray)	Alpha-Teilchen n; Helion n, Heliumkern m
		heliophotography, solar photography	Sonnenphotographie f
helical-blade stirrer	Schneckenrührwerk n, Schneckenrührer m, Schraubenflügelrührer m	**heliophysics,** physics of the Sun, solar physics	Sonnenphysik f, Physik f der Sonne
		helioscope; solar eyepiece	Sonnenokular n, helioskopisches Okular n; Helioskop n, Sonnenfernrohr n
helical coiling	Schraubenwindung f		
helical conductor, helix conductor, helix, spiral <el.>	Wendelleitung f, Helix f, Wendelleiter m, Wendel f <El.>	**helioscope glass**	Sonnenglas n
helical configuration	s. helical structure		
helical curve	s. helix		
helical deformation	Spiraldeformation f	**heliotrope,** surveyor's heliotrope <instrument>	Heliotrop n, Sonnenspiegel m <Instrument>
helical disk, spiral disk	Spiralscheibe f	**heliotropic wind**	heliotropischer Wind m
helical dislocation, spiral dislocation	Spiralversetzung f, spiralförmige Versetzung f	**heliotropism,** phototropism	Phototropismus m, Heliotropismus m
helical field, spiral field	Spiralfeld n	**helipot**	s. helical potentiometer
		helium age	geologisches Alter n nach der Heliummethode, Heliumalter n
helical flow	schraubenförmige Strömung f		
helical instability	Instabilität f gegen Spiraldeformation	**helium cycle**	Heliumzyklus m
		helium film, Rollin film	Heliumschicht f, Heliumfilm m, Rollin-Film m
helical line	s. helix		
helical motion	s. screw displacement	**helium-group gas**	s. rare gas
helical potentiometer, helipot	Wendelpotentiometer n	**helium leak detector**	Heliumleckfinder m, Heliumlecksucher m, Heliumleckprüfer m
helical scanning, spiral scanning	Schraubenlinienabtastung f, Schraubenlinienzerlegung f, Spiralabtastung f, Spiralablenkung f	**helium nucleus**	Heliumkern m <$^4_2$He, $^3_2$He oder $^6_2$He>
		helium nucleus	s. a. helion <^{4}He>
		helium permeation	Heliumdurchlässigkeit f
		helium thermometer	Heliumthermometer n
helical structure, helical configuration, helix <gen., also bio.>	Spiralstruktur f, Helikalstruktur f, Helixstruktur f <allg., auch bio.>	**helium vapour pressure thermometer**	Heliumdampfdruckthermometer n
		helix, spiral, spire	Spirale f <ebene Kurve>
helical surface, helicoid, helicoidal surface	Schraubenfläche f, Helikoid n	**helix,** helical curve, helical line, spiral line, slope line	Schraubenlinie f, Schnekkenlinie f, Böschungslinie f <Raumkurve>
helical symmetry	Schraubensymmetrie f		
helical trajectory	schraubenförmige Bahn f, Schraubenbahn f		
helical waveguide	Wendelleiter m, schraubenförmiger Wellenleiter m		
helicity <quantum number; acc.>	Helizität f, „helicity" f, Schraubensinn m <Quantenzahl>; Spiralität f, Helizität f <Beschl.>	**helix,** travelling wave helix, helix waveguide <acc.>	Wendel f, Helix f, Hohlleiterwendel f, Wendelhohlleiter m <Beschl.>
helicity	s. a. orientation of the screw	**helix** <bio., chem.>	Helix f, Strukturwendel f, Schraubenkette f <Bio., Chem.>
helicoid, helical surface, helicoidal surface	Schraubenfläche f, Helikoid n	**helix**	s. a. helical conductor
helicoidal	s. helical	**helix**	s. a. helical structure

helix accelerator; helical accelerator	Wendelbeschleuniger m, Wendel-Linearbeschleuniger m, Helixbeschleuniger m	Helmholtz['] place theory, Helmholtz['] resonance theory, place theory [of Helmholtz], resonance theory [of Helmholtz], localization (resonator) theory, Helmholtz['] theory <of hearing>	Einortstheorie f, Resonanztheorie f [von Helmholtz], Helmholtzsche Resonanztheorie, Resonatorentheorie f <des Hörens>
helix conductor	s. helical conductor <el.>	Helmholtz-Rayleigh dissipation theorem	Helmholtz-Rayleighscher Dissipationssatz m
helix model	Helixmodell n	Helmholtz['s] reciprocity principle (theorem)	Helmholtzscher Reziprozitätssatz m, Helmholtzsches Reziprozitätsgesetz n
helix waveguide, travelling-wave helix, helix <acc.>	Wendel f, Helix f, Hohlleiterwendel f, Wendelhohlleiter m <Beschl.>	Helmholtz['] relation	s. Lagrange['s] theorem
		Helmholtz relations, Gibbs-Helmholtz equations (relations)	[Gibbs-]Helmholtzsche Gleichungen fpl, Gibbs-Helmholtz-Gleichungen fpl
Helmert-Pearson distribution, χ_n^2 distribution	Helmert[-Pearson]sche Verteilung f, χ_n^2-Verteilung f	Helmholtz['] resonance theory	s. Helmholtz['] place theory
helmholtz <= 1 debye / sq. ångström>	Helmholtz n <= 1 Debye / Å²>	Helmholtz['] resonator, spherical resonator	Helmholtz-Resonator m, Helmholtzscher Resonator m, Kugelresonator m
Helmholtz['] air wave	Helmholtzsche Luftwoge f, Luftwoge nach Helmholtz	Helmholtz['] second theorem [/ von], Helmholtz['s] second vorticity theorem	zweiter Helmholtzscher Wirbelsatz m, Helmholtzscher zweiter Wirbelsatz, zeitlicher Erhaltungssatz m der Wirbeltheorie, Satz m von der Erhaltung der Wirbelstärke [eines Wirbelfadens]
Helmholtz ampere balance, Helmholtz balance	Stromwaage f nach Helmholtz, Helmholtzsche Stromwaage, Helmholtz-Stromwaage f		
Helmholtz coils	Helmholtzsche Spule[n] f [pl], Helmholtz-Spulen fpl		
Helmholtz dissipation theorem	Helmholtzscher Dissipationssatz m	Helmholtz['] theorem	Helmholtzscher Satz m (Überlagerungssatz) m, Helmholtzsches Theorem n, Helmholtz-Theorem n, Satz von Helmholtz
Helmholtz['] double layer [of ions]	Helmholtzsche Doppelschicht (Ionendoppelschicht) f, Helmholtz-Doppelschicht f		
Helmholtz['] equation, [reduced] wave equation	Helmholtzsche Gleichung (Schwingungsgleichung) f	Helmholtz['] theorem	s. a. Thévenin['s] theorem
		Helmholtz['] theorem for fluids	s. Helmholtz['] first theorem
Helmholtz['] equation [for a reversible electrolyte cell]	s. Helmholtz['] equation [of thermodynamics]	Helmholtz['] theory <of hearing>	s. Helmholtz['] place theory
Helmholtz['] equation [for optical magnification]	s. Lagrange['s] theorem	Helmholtz['] theory of colour vision	Helmholtzsche Farbentheorie f
Helmholtz['] equation [for vorticity]	Helmholtzscher Wirbelsatz m	Helmholtz['] wave, shear wave	Helmholtzsche Welle f, Helmholtz-Welle f
Helmholtz['] equation [of thermodynamics], equation of maximum work; Helmholtz['] equation [for a reversible electrolyte cell], Helmholtz['] formula of galvanic cell	Helmholtzsche Gleichung f [der Thermodynamik], Gibbs-Helmholtzsche Gleichung, Helmholtz-Gleichung f; Helmholtzsche Gleichung des galvanischen Elementes	helvetium	= astatine, At
		hemaraphotometer, daylight photometer	Tageslichtphotometer n
		hemeralopia, night blindness, noctalopia	Nachtblindheit f, Dämmerungsblindheit f, Tagessichtigkeit f, Hemeralopie f, Hemeropie f
		hemianopsia	s. half-blindness
		hemicolloid, semicolloid, mesocolloid	Semikolloid n, Hemikolloid n, Mesokolloid n
Helmholtz['] first theorem [/ von], Helmholtz['] theorem [for fluids]	erster Helmholtzscher Wirbelsatz m, räumlicher Erhaltungssatz m der Wirbeltheorie, Satz m von der Erhaltung der Wirbellinien	hemigroup	s. semigroup
		hemihedral	hemiedrisch, halbflächig
		hemihedral class of the monoclinic system	s. hemihedry of the monoclinic system
		hemihedral class of the rhombic system	s. enantiomorphous hemihedry of the orthorhombic system
Helmholtz flow, linear flow	Helmholtzsche Strömung f, lineare Strömung	hemihedral class of the triclinic system	s. hemihedry of the triclinic system
Helmholtz flow	s. a. Kirchhoff-Helmholtz flow	hemihedral class with inversion axis of the tetragonal system	s. hemihedry of the second sort of the tetragonal system
Helmholtz['] formula for Huyghens principle, Helmholtz formulation of Huyghens principle	Helmholtzsche Formel f für das Huygenssche Prinzip	hemihedral class with threefold axis of the hexagonal system	s. trigonal holohedry [of the hexagonal system]
		hemihedral form, hemihedron	Hemieder n, Halbflächner m, Hälftflächner m, Teilflächner m
Helmholtz['] formula of galvanic cell	s. Helmholtz['] equation [of thermodynamics]	hemihedrism	s. hemihedry
Helmholtz formulation of Huyghens principle	s. Helmholtz['] formula for Huyghens principle	hemihedron, hemihedral form	Hemieder n, Halbflächner m, Hälftflächner m, Teilflächner m
Helmholtz['] free energy, Helmholtz['] function	s. free energy <therm.>	hemihedry, hemihedrism	Hemiedrie f, Hemihedrie f, domatische Klasse f
Helmholtz instability	s. shearing instability		
Helmholtz-Kelvin theory	Helmholtz-Kelvinsche Theorie f	hemihedry of the monoclinic system, equatorial (clinohedral, domatic) class, monoclinic hemihedry, hemihedral class of the monoclinic system	monokline Hemiedrie f, domatische Klasse f, monoklin domatische Klasse
Helmholtz-Ketteler [dispersion] formula, Ketteler-Helmholtz formula	[Ketteler-]Helmholtzsche Dispersionsformel f		
Helmholtz-Lagrange formula	s. Lagrange['s] theorem		

hemihedry of the second sort of the tetragonal system, tetragonal hemihedry of the second sort, ditetragonal alternating class, sphenoidal (scalenohedral) class, tetragonal-scalenohedral [crystal] class, hemihedral class with inversion axis of the tetragonal system	Hemiedrie f II. Art des tetragonalen Systems, sphenoidische Hemiedrie, tetragonal-skalenoedrische Klasse f, tetragonal skalenoedrische Klasse	**hemimorphic hemihedry of the rhombohedral class,** ditrigonal polar class, rhombohedral hemimorphic class, ditrigonal pyramidal [crystal] class, rhombohedral hemimorphy, hemimorphic hemihedral class of the trigonal system	hemimorphe Hemiedrie f des rhomboedrischen Systems, ditrigonal-pyramidale Klasse f, trigonale Hemimorphie f, ditrigonal pyramidale Klasse
hemihedry of the triclinic system, triclinic hemihedry, asymmetric (hemipinakoidal, pedial, triclinic hemihedral) class, hemihedral class of the triclinic system	trikline Hemiedrie f, pediale Klasse f, asymmetrische Klasse	**hemimorphic hemihedry of the tetragonal system,** ditetragonal polar class, hemimorphic (ditetragonal-pyramidal) class, tetragonal hemimorphy, hemimorphic hemihedral class of the tetragonal system	hemimorphe Hemiedrie f des tetragonalen Systems, ditetragonal-pyramidale Klasse f, ditetragonale Hemimorphie f, ditetragonal pyramidale Klasse
hemilens	s. Fresnel['s] hemilens		
hemimorphic	hemimorph	**hemimorphism, hemimorphy,** hemimorphic class	Hemimorphie f, hemimorphe Symmetrieklasse f
hemimorphic class, hemimorphism, hemimorphy	Hemimorphie f, hemimorphe Symmetrieklasse f	**hemipelagic region,** hemipelagic zone	hemipelagischer Bereich m
hemimorphic class	s. a. hemimorphic hemihedry of the hexagonal system	**hemipinakoidal class**	s. hemihedry of the triclinic system
hemimorphic class	s. a. hemimorphic hemihedry of the orthorhombic system	**hemipyramid**	Hemipyramide f, Prisma n allgemeinster Lage
hemimorphic class	s. a. hemimorphic hemihedry of the tetragonal system	**hemispheric, hemi-spherical**	Halbkugel-, halbkugelförmig, hemisphärisch; halbräumlich
hemimorphic class [of the monoclinic system]	s. hemimorphic hemihedry of the monoclinic system	**hemispherical chamber,** hemispherical ionization chamber	Halbkugelkammer f, Halbkugel-Ionisationskammer f
hemimorphic class of the rhombic system	s. hemimorphic hemihedry of the orthorhombic system	**hemispherical emissivity**	s. emissivity
hemimorphic hemihedral class of the cubic system	s. hemimorphic hemihedry of the regular system	**hemispherical intensity**	hemisphärische (halbräumliche) Lichtstärke f
hemimorphic hemihedral class of the hexagonal system	s. hemimorphic hemihedry of the hexagonal system	**hemispherical ionization chamber,** hemispherical chamber	Halbkugelkammer f, Halbkugel-Ionisationskammer f
hemimorphic hemihedral class of the tetragonal system	s. hemimorphic hemihedry of the tetragonal system	**hemispherical lens,** semicircular lens	Halbkugellinse f
hemimorphic hemihedral class of the trigonal system	s. hemimorphic hemihedry of the rhombohedral class	**hemispherical mirror**	Halbkugelspiegel m
		hemispherical stage	s. spherical stage
		hemitrisoctahedron	s. triakisdodecahedron
		hemitrope	s. twin <cryst.>
hemimorphic hemihedry	hemimorphe Hemiedrie f	**hemitropism,** twinning, twin formation <cryst.>	Zwillingsbildung f, Zwillingsverwachsung f, Verzwillingung f <Krist.>
hemimorphic hemihedry of the hexagonal system, dihexagonal polar (pyramidal) class, hemimorphic class, hexagonal hemimorphy, hemimorphic hemihedral class of the hexagonal system	hemimorphe Hemiedrie f des hexagonalen Systems, dihexagonal-pyramidale Klasse f	**HE-mode**	s. hybrid wave
		hemolysis	Hämolyse f
		Hempel gas pipette	Hempel-Pipette f, Hempelsche Pipette (Gaspipette) f
		Hencky['s] flow condition, flow condition of Hencky	Henckysche Fließbedingung f, Fließbedingung von Hencky
		Henning['s] formula	Henningsche Wasserdampfdruckformel f
		Henrici analyzer	Henrici-Analysator m
		henry, H	Henry n, H
hemimorphic hemihedry of the monoclinic system, digonal polar class, monoclinic hemimorphy, hemimorphic class [of the monoclinic system]	monokline Hemimorphie f, sphenoidische Klasse f	**Henry-Dalton law,** Henry['s] law	[Henry-]Daltonsches Gesetz n
		Henry Draper catalog[ue], Draper catalog[ue], HD	[Henry-]Draper-Katalog m, HD
		Henry['s] law, Dalton['s] law [of solubility of gases]	Henrysches Gesetz (Löslichkeitsgesetz, Absorptionsgesetz) n, [Henryscher] Verteilungssatz m
hemimorphic hemihedry of the orthorhombic system, didigonal polar class, pyramidal (hemimorphic) class, orthorhombic hemimorphy, hemimorphic class of the rhombic system	orthorhombische Hemimorphie f, rhombische Hemimorphie, pyramidale Klasse f, rhombisch-pyramidale Klasse	**Henry['s] law**	s. a. Henry-Dalton law
		Henry['s] law constant	Henry-Koeffizient m, Henryscher Koeffizient (Absorptionskoeffizient) m, reziproker Löslichkeitskoeffizient m
		henrymeter, inductance meter, inductometer	Induktivitätsmesser m, Induktivitätsmeßgerät n
hemimorphic hemihedry of the regular system, inclined hemihedry, regular hemimorphy, hemimorphic hemihedral class of the cubic system, [hexakis]tetrahedral, hexatetrahedral [crystal] class, ditesseral polar class	hemimorphe Hemiedrie f des kubischen Systems, tetraedrische Hemiedrie, geneigtflächige Hemiedrie, hexakistetraedrische Klasse f	**Henry['s] substantial law**	substantielles Henrysches Gesetz n
		Henry volumetric law	volumetrisches Henrysches Gesetz n
		her	s. her-function
		Herbert pendulum	Herbert-Pendel n
		Herbig-Haro object	Herbig-Haro-Objekt n
		hereditary defect	Erbschaden m

hereditary material, material with memory	Material n mit Nachwirkung	Hertz effect	Hertz-Effekt m
hereditary unit, heredity determinant	Erbeinheit f	Hertz['] experiment	Hertzscher Gitterversuch m
her-function, Kelvin her function, her	Kelvinsche (Thomsonsche) her-Funktion f, her [-Funktion]	Hertzian dipole (doublet), Hertz dipole, elementary dipole, Hertz oscillator	Hertzscher (elementarer) Dipol m, Elementardipol m, linearer elektrischer Oszillator m, Hertzscher Oszillator (Schwingungskreis) m, Kurzdipol m, cos β-Dipol m
Hering['s] law	Heringsches Gesetz n		
Hering['s] rule	Heringsche Regel f		
Hering['s] theory [of colour vision]	s. "opponent" theory of colour vision	Hertzian problem	Kontaktproblem n
Hermann-Mauguin notation	Hermann-Mauguinsche Bezeichnung[sweise] f	Hertzian reflector	Hertzscher Spiegel (Antennenspiegel) m, Antennenspiegel
Hermann-Mauguin symbol	Hermann-Mauguinsches Symbol n	Hertzian vector, Hertz vector, polarization potential	Hertzscher Vektor m, [elektrisches] Polarisationspotential n, Hertzsches Potential n
Hermann['s] theory [of low currents]	Hermannsche Strömchentheorie f, Strömchentheorie		
hermetical; hermetically enclosed; hermetically sealed	hermetisch; hermetisch dicht (abgeschlossen; verschlossen)	Hertzian wave	s. Hertz wave
		Hertz oscillator	s. Hertzian dipole
		Hertz['] principle	s. principle of least curvature
hermetic enclosure	hermetisch abschließendes Gefäß n	Hertzsprung gap	Hertzsprung-Lücke f
hermetic seal[ing]	hermetischer Verschluß m	Hertzsprung-Russell diagram, Russell diagram, spectrum-luminosity relation, H-R diagram, star (stellar) spectrum-luminosity relation	Hertzsprung-Russell-Diagramm n, Russell-Diagramm n, Zustandsdiagramm n, stellares Hauptdiagramm n, HRD
Hermitean	s. Hermitian		
Hermite function	Hermitesche Funktion f, Hermite-Funktion f		
Hermite [orthogonal] polynomial, orthogonal Hermite polynomial, Hermitian polynomial	[Tschebyscheff-]Hermitesches Polynom n, [Tschebyscheff-]Hermite-Polynom n		
Hermitian, Hermitean	hermitesch, hermitisch	Hertz vector, Hertzian vector, polarization potential	Hertzscher Vektor m, [elektrisches] Polarisationspotential n, Hertzsches Potential n
Hermitian conjugate	hermitesch konjugiert		
Hermitian conjugate <of an operator>	hermitesch Konjugierte f [eines Operators], hermitesch konjugierter Operator m	Hertz wave, Hertzian wave	Hertzsche Welle f
		Hess diagram	Heß-Diagramm n, Heßsches Diagramm n
Hermitian conjugate [matrix]	s. adjoint matrix	Hesse['s] determinant, Hessian	Hessesche Determinante (Kovariante) f, Hesse-Determinante f
Hermitian form	Hermitesche Form f		
Hermitian kernel [of an integral equation]	hermitescher Kern m [einer Integralgleichung]	Hesse['s] normal (standard) form, normal equation of Hesse	Hessesche Normalform f
Hermitian matrix, self-adjoint matrix	hermitesche Matrix f, selbstadjungierte Matrix, Hermite-Matrix f	Hessian, Hesse['s] determinant	Hessesche Determinante (Kovariante) f, Hesse-Determinante f
Hermitian operator, symmetrical operator	hermitescher Operator m, symmetrischer Operator, Hermite-Operator m	Hessian matrix	Hessesche Matrix f
Hermitian part	hermitescher Anteil m	Hess['] law [of heat summation], law of Hess, law of constant heat summation	Heßscher Satz m (Heßsches Gesetz n) [von den konstanten Wärmesummen], Regel f von Heß, Heßsche Regel, Satz (Gesetz) der konstanten Wärmesummen, Satz von der Konstanz der Wärmesumme, Gesetz von den konstanten Wärmesummen
Hermitian polynomial	s. Hermite polynomial		
Hermitian scalar product	Hermitesches Skalarprodukt n		
Hermitian transformation	hermitesche Transformation f		
hermiticity	Hermitezität f		
Hero['s] fountain	Heronsball m, Heronsbrunnen m		
Heroult [electric arc] furnace	Heroult-Ofen m, Heroult-Lichtbogenofen m		
herpolhode, herpolhodie, fixed centrode, fixed curve of instantaneous centres <mech.>	Herpolhodie[kurve] f, Spurkurve f, Rastpolkurve f, Spurbahn f, Serpoloide f, ruhende Zentrode (Polkurve) f, feste Momentanzentrenkurve f <Mech.>	Hess viscosimeter	Hess-Instrument n, Röhrenviskosimeter n [nach Hess]
		Hestia gap	Hestia-Lücke f
		heteroatom, heterocyclic atom	Heteroatom n
		heteroatomic	s. heterocyclic
		heteroatomic chain, heterochain	Heterokette f, heteroatomare Kette f
herpolhode cone, space cone	Herpolhodiekegel m, Rastpolkegel m; Ruhekegel m, Festkegel m, raumfester Drehkegel m	heteroatomic ring	s. heterocycle
		heteroazeotrope	heteroazeotropes Gemisch n
herpolhodie	s. herpolhode <mech.>	heterochain	s. heteroatomic chain
herpolhodograph	Herpolhodograph m	heterocharge	Heteroladung f
Herschel['s] condition	Herschel-Bedingung f, Herschelsche Bedingung f	heterochromatic, heterochromous	heterochrom. verschiedenfarbig, heterochromatisch
		heterochromatic	s. a. heterogeneous <of radiation>
Herschel effect; latent Herschel effect	Herschel-Effekt m		
Herschel fringe	Herschel[-Ketteler]scher Streifen m, Herschelsche Interferenz f	heterochromatic photometry	heterochrome (verschiedenfarbige, heterochromatische) Photometrie f, Photometrie farbigen Lichtes
Herschelian telescope, front-view telescope	Spiegelteleskop n nach Herschel, Herschelsches Spiegelteleskop, Frontviewteleskop n [nach Herschel]		
		heterochromous	s. heterochromic
		heterocondensation polymerization, heteropolycondensation	Heteropolykondensation f
Hershberger['s] method	Hershbergersches Meßverfahren f	heterocycle; heteronucleus, heterocyclic nucleus, heteroatomic (heterocyclic, heterogeneous) ring	Heterozyklus m; Heteroring m
hertz	s. cycle per second		
Hertz['s] cascade	s. gaseous diffusion cascade		
Hertz dipole	s. Hertzian dipole		

heterocyclic; heteronuclear; heteroatomic	heterozyklisch; heteronuklear, verschiedenkernig; heteroatomar	heterojunction	Heteroübergang m
heterocyclic atom	s. heteroatom	heterolysis, heterolytic reaction (split)	Heterolyse f
heterocyclic nucleus (ring)	s. heterocycle	heterolyte	Heterolyt m
heterodesmic structure	heterodesmische Struktur f	heterolytic addition, ionic (polar) addition	ionische (polare, heterolytische) Addition f
		heterolytic reaction (split)	s. heterolysis
heterodisperse, polydisperse	polydispers, heterodispers	heteromeric	heteromer
heterodromous reversibility	heterodrome Reversibilität f	heteromerism, heteromery	Heteromerie f
heterodyne, heterodyne oscillator, heterodyne warbler oscillator, beat frequency oscillator, b.f.o.	Schwebungssummer m, Schwebungsoszillator m, Schwebungsgenerator m, Überlagerungsoszillator m, Überlagerungsgenerator m, Überlagerungssummer m; Heterodyneschaltung f	heterometry	s. nephelometric titration
		heteromorphic <opt.>	heteromorph, raumverzerrt <Opt.>
		heteromorphic transformation	heteromorphe Umwandlung f
		heteromorphism	Heteromorphie f, Heteromorphismus m
		heteronuclear	s. heterocyclic
heterodyne action, heterodyning <el.>	Überlagerung f <El.>	heteronucleus	s. heterocycle
		heteroparametric excitation	heteroparametrische Erregung f
heterodyne beat method, beat method	Schwebungs[ton]verfahren n, Schwebungsmethode f, „heterodyne beat"-Methode f	heterophase fluctuation	heterophasige Fluktuation f
		heteropolar	heteropolar, wechselpolig
heterodyne frequency meter, heterodyne wavemeter	Überlagerungswellenmesser m, Interferenzwellenmesser m; Schwebungswellenmesser m; Überlagerungsfrequenzmesser m, Interferenzfrequenzmesser m, Schwebungsfrequenzmesser m		
		heteropolar binding (bond)	s. electrovalent bond
		heteropolar compound, ionic compound, polar compound	Ionenverbindung f, ionogene (heteropolare, polare) Verbindung f
		heteropolar induction	Wechselpolinduktion f
heterodyne interference	s. superheterodyne interference		
heterodyne klystron	Überlagerungsklystron n	heteropolarity	Heteropolarität f
heterodyne note, heterodyne tone, beat tone (note); interference note	Schwebungston m, Überlagerungston m; Interferenzton m	heteropolar linkage	s. electrovalent bond
		heteropolar molecule, ionic molecule	Ionenmolekül n, heteropolares Molekül n
		heteropolycondensation, heterocondensation polymerization	Heteropolykondensation f
heterodyne oscillator	s. heterodyne		
heterodyne tone	s. heterodyne note	heteroscedastic	heteroskedastisch [verbunden]
heterodyne warbler oscillator	s. heterodyne		
heterodyne wavemeter	s. heterodyne frequency meter	heterosphere	Heterosphäre f
		heterostatic circuit, heterostatic method	Quadrantschaltung f, heterostatische Schaltung f
heterodyne whistle	s. superheterodyne interference		
heterodyning, heterodyne action <el.>	Überlagerung f <El.>	heterostatic method, heterostatic circuit	Quadrantschaltung f, heterostatische Schaltung f
heteroenergetic	s. heterogeneous		
hetero[-]epitaxy	Heteroepitaxie f	heterotaxial phenomenon, heterotaxy	Heterotaxie f
heterogeneity, inhomogeneity, heterogeneousness, inhomogeneousness, non-uniformity	Heterogenität f, Inhomogenität f, Ungleichförmigkeit f, Ungleichartigkeit f, Verschiedenartigkeit f	heterotaxy, heterotaxial phenomenon	Heterotaxie f
		heterotopic; non-isotopic	nichtisotop[isch]; heterotop
heterogeneous, inhomogeneous, heterogenetic	inhomogen, heterogen, ungleichartig, verschiedenartig, ungleichförmig	heterotopy <bio.>	Heterotopie f <Bio.>
		heterotrophy	Heterotrophie f
		heterotropic	heterotrop
		heuristic	heuristisch
heterogeneous; heteroenergetic; heterochromatic; polyenergetic, non-monoenergetic; polychromatic <of radiation>	heterogen; heteroenergetisch; heterochromatisch; polyenergetisch; polychromatisch <Strahlung>	Heusler alloy	Heuslersche Legierung f
		Hevel['s] halo (ring)	Halo m von Hevel
		hexad axis, 6-al axis, axis of order 6, six-fold axis [of symmetry], 6-fold axis	sechszählige Symmetrieachse (Drehungsachse, Achse) f, Hexagyre f, 6zählige Symmetrieachse f
heterogeneous beam <of electrons>	weißer Strahl m <von Elektronen>		
heterogeneous catalysis, contact catalysis	heterogene Katalyse f, Oberflächenkatalyse f, Kontaktkatalyse f	hexad axis of the second sort, 6-al [symmetry-]axis of the second sort, six-fold (6-fold) axis of the second sort, axis of the second sort of order 6	sechszählige Drehspiegelungsachse f, Hexagyroide f
heterogeneous combustion	heterogene Verbrennung f		
heterogeneous equilibrium	heterogenes Gleichgewicht n		
heterogeneous lattice	heterogenes Gitter n	hexad symmetry, 6-al symmetry, symmetry of order six (6)	sechszählige Symmetrie f, 6zählige Symmetrie
heterogeneous mixture	Gemenge n, heterogenes Gemisch n; Haufwerk n		
heterogeneousness	s. heterogeneity	hexagonal alternating class	s. hexagonal tetartohedry of the second sort
heterogeneous pile, heterogeneous reactor	heterogener Reaktor m, Heterogenreaktor m	hexagonal bipyramidal class	s. paramorphic hemihedry of the hexagonal system
heterogeneous radiation	s. white radiation	hexagonal close-packed, hcp, HCP, H.C.P.	hexagonal dichtgepackt (dichtest)
heterogeneous reactor, heterogeneous pile	heterogener Reaktor m, Heterogenreaktor m	hexagonal close-packed structure, hexagonal close packing	hexagonal dichteste Kugelpackung (Packung) f, hexagonale Kugelpackung
heterogeneous ring	s. heterocycle		
heterogenetic	s. heterogeneous		
heteroion, ion-molecule complex	Ion-Molekül-Komplex m, Heteroion n	hexagonal condition	s. St. Venant-Tresca yield condition

hexagonal 328

hexagonal crystal system, hexagonal system	hexagonales System (Kristallsystem) *n*	**hidden co-ordinates** **hidden edge; hidden line**	*s.* ignorable co-ordinates unsichtbare Kante *f*, verdeckte Kante
hexagonal-dipyramidal [crystal] class	*s.* paramorphic hemihedry of the hexagonal system	**hidden parameter, hidden variable**	verborgener Parameter *m*
hexagonal enantiomorphy	*s.* enantiomorphous hemihedry of the hexagonal system	**hierarchic structure of the Universe**	hierarchische Struktur *f* der Welt
hexagonal equatorial class	*s.* paramorphic hemihedry of the hexagonal system		
hexagonal hemimorphy, hemimorphic hemihedry (hemihedral class) of the hexagonal system, dihexagonal polar (pyramidal) class, hemimorphic class	hemimorphe Hemiedrie *f* des hexagonalen Systems, dihexagonalpyramidale Klasse *f*	**High**, high-pressure area, anticyclone, barometric maximum, maximum of atmospheric pressure, H	Hoch *n*, Hochdruckgebiet *n*, barometrisches Maximum *n*, H
		high-accuracy instrument	*s.* precision instrument
hexagonal holoaxial class	*s.* enantiomorphous hemihedry of the hexagonal system	**high activity** **high-altitude chamber** **high-altitude flow** **high-altitude observatory**	*s.* high-level activity *s.* low-pressure chamber *s.* high-altitude stream Höhenobservatorium *n*
hexagonal holohedry	*s.* holohedry of the hexagonal system	**high-altitude[-research] rocket**	*s.* altitude rocket
hexagonal ogdohedry	*s.* trigonal pyramidal [crystal] class	**high-altitude stream**, altitude stream,	Höhenströmung *f*
hexagonal paramorphy	*s.* paramorphic hemihedry of the hexagonal system	[high-]altitude flow **high-altitude wind**, upper wind; aloft wind	Höhenwind *m*
hexagonal polar class	*s.* tetartohedry of the hexagonal system	**high-angle grain boundary**	*s.* large-angle grain boundary
hexagonal prism	hexagonales (sechsseitiges) Prisma *n*	**high-aperture** **high atmosphere**	*s.* high-power <opt.> *s.* upper atmosphere
hexagonal-pyramidal [crystal] class	*s.* tetartohedry of the hexagonal system	**high-boiling**	hochsiedend, schwersiedend
hexagonal-scalenohedral [crystal] class	*s.* rhombohedral holohedry		
hexagonal scalenohedron, ditrigonal scalenohedron	ditrigonales Skalenoeder *n*	**high-boiling fraction** **high-boiling-liquid cooling**, high-temperature liquid cooling	Schwersiedende *n*, Hochsiedende *n* Heißkühlung *f*
hexagonal structure	hexagonale Struktur *f*, Hexagonalstruktur *f*		
hexagonal symmetry	hexagonale Symmetrie *f*	**high cloud**	hohe Wolke *f*
hexagonal system	*s.* hexagonal crystal system		
hexagonal tetartohedry	*s.* tetartohedry of the hexagonal system	**high concentration**	hohe (starke) Konzentration *f*
hexagonal tetartohedry of the second sort <rhombohedric system>, hexagonal alternating class, trirhombohedral class, rhombohedral tetartohedry, paramorphic hemihedral class of the trigonal system	paramorphe Hemiedrie *f* des rhomboedrischen Systems, rhomboedrische Klasse *f*, rhomboedrische Tetartoedrie *f*	**high-contrast**, contrasty, rich in contrast **high-contrast developer** **high-current accelerator**, high-intensity accelerator	kontrastreich hart arbeitender Entwickler *m* Hochstrombeschleuniger *m*
		high-current arc, high-current carbon arc; high-intensity carbon arc, high-intensity arc	Hochstrom[licht]bogen *m*, Hochstromkohlebogen *m*; Hochintensitäts[licht]-bogen *m*, HI-Bogen *m*, HI-Lichtbogen *m*, Hochleistungs[licht]bogen *m*
hexagonal trapezohedral [crystal] class	*s.* enantiomorphous hemihedry of the hexagonal system		
hexagonal yield condition	*s.* St. Venant-Tresca yield condition		
hexahedron	Hexaeder *n*, Sechsflach *n*, Sechsflächner *m*	**high-current arc [lamp]**, high-intensity arc lamp; high-intensity carbon arc lamp, high-intensity carbon arc	Hochstrom-Kohlebogenlampe *f*; Hochintensitäts-Bogenlampe *f*, Hochintensitäts-Lichtbogenlampe *f*; Flammenbogenlampe *f*
hexahedron	*s. a.* cube		
hexakisoctahedral class	*s.* holohedry of the regular system		
hexakisoctahedron	Hexakisoktaeder *n*, 48-Flächner *m*, Achtundvierzigflächner *m*		
hexakistetrahedral class	*s.* hemimorphic hemihedry of the regular system	**high-current carbon arc** **high-current discharge**	*s.* high-current arc Starkstromentladung *f*, Entladung *f* mit hoher Stromdichte
hexakistetrahedron	Hexakistetraeder *n*, 24-Flächner *m*, Vierundzwanzigflächner *m*		
hexatetrahedral [crystal] class	*s.* hemimorphic hemihedry of the regular system	**high-current electron accelerator of Steenbeck** **high-current generator**, high-output (high-yield) generator	Starkstrom-Elektronenbeschleuniger *m* nach Steenbeck Hochstromgenerator *m*
hexoctahedral [crystal] class	*s.* holohedry of the regular system		
H.F.	*s.* high-frequency		
H-filter, H-section (H-type) filter	H-Filter *n*	**high-current ion source**, ion high-current (high-yield) source, high-yield ion source	Hochstrom-Ionenquelle *f*
H form, hydrogen form	H-Form *f*, Wasserstoffform *f*		
		high-definition	*s.* high-resolution
H.F. titration	*s.* high-frequency titration	**high-definition image**, point image; sharp image <opt.>	Punktabbildung *f*, punktförmige Abbildung *f*; scharfe Abbildung, scharfes Bild *n* <Opt.>
H-function [of Boltzmann], Boltzmann['s] H-function, Boltzmann['s] function, Boltzmann['s] triple integral function of H (t)	H-Funktion *f*, Boltzmannsche H-Funktion *f*, Boltzmanns H-Funktion *f*		
		high-definition lens, sharp-focus lens	Scharfzeichner *m*, scharfzeichnendes Objektiv *n*
H-function of Kotchine, Kotchine['s] H-function	H-Funktion *f* von Kotschin, Kotschinsche H-Funktion	**high-delivery head**, high head	Hochgefälle *n*
		high-delivery pump	Hochleistungspumpe *f*
H.-H. (H-H) reaction	*s.* proton-proton reaction		
Hick['s] [series] formula	Hicksche Serienformel (Formel) *f*, Hick-Formel *f*	**high-density concrete**	*s.* extra-heavy aggregate

high-density metal, heavy metal	Schwermetall *n*	**high-frequency photograph**	*s.* high-speed photograph
high-elastic[ity], superelastic	hochelastisch	**high-frequency photography**	*s.* high-speed cinematography
high[-]elasticity	Hochelastizität *f*	**high frequency range,** range of high frequency, decametric wavelength [range], H.F. range, H.F.	Dekameterwellenbereich *m*, Dekameterbereich *m*, Dekabereich *m*, Hochfrequenzbereich *m*, HF-Bereich *m*, HF
high-emission cathode	Hochleistungskatode *f*		
high-energy accelerator, high-power (high-output, high-energy-radiation) accelerator	Hochenergiebeschleuniger *m*, Beschleuniger *m* für hohe Energien	**high-frequency record[ing]**	*s.* high-frequency photograph
high-energy collision	energiereicher Stoß *m*	**high-frequency schlieren photograph,** high-speed schlieren photograph	Hochgeschwindigkeits-Schlierenaufnahme *f*, Hochfrequenz-Schlierenaufnahme *f*
high-energy electron diffraction, HEED	Hochenergie-Elektronenbeugung *f*	**high-frequency sound,** H.F. sound	Hochfrequenzschall *m*, HF-Schall *m*
high-energy nuclear physics	*s.* high-energy physics	**high-frequency sound wave**	hochfrequente Schallwelle *f*, Schallwelle hoher Frequenz
high-energy particle, penetrating particle, energetic particle	energiereiches (durchdringendes) Teilchen *n*, Teilchen hoher Energie	**high-frequency titration,** radio-frequency (H.F., R.F.) titration	Hochfrequenztitration *f*, HF-Titration *f*
high-energy physics, high-energy nuclear physics	Hochenergie[kern]physik *f*, hochenergetische Kernphysik *f*, Kernphysik (Physik *f*) hoher Energien	**high-frequency titrator,** H.F. titrator	Hochfrequenztitrimeter *n*, HF-Titrimeter *n*
		high-gain amplifier	Hochleistungsverstärker *m*
high-energy-radiation accelerator	*s.* high-energy accelerator	**high-grade,** highly enriched	hochangereichert
higher calorific value	*s.* gross calorific value	**high head,** high-delivery head	Hochgefälle *n*
higher-degree term, term of higher order (degree), higher order term	Glied *n* höherer Ordnung	**high-impedance,** highohmic, high-resistance, high-resistivity, high-resistive	hochohmig
higher harmonic, upper harmonic, ultraharmonic	höhere Harmonische *f*, Harmonische höherer Ordnung	**high-impedance valve voltmeter**	Hochohmröhrenvoltmeter *n*, hochohmiges Röhrenvoltmeter *n*
higher-order derivative, derivative of higher order	Ableitung *f* höherer Ordnung, höhere Ableitung	**high-intensity accelerator**	*s.* high-current accelerator
higher order term, term of higher order (degree), higher degree term	Glied *n* höherer Ordnung	**high-intensity arc**	*s.* high-current arc
		high-intensity arc lamp	*s.* high-current arc lamp
higher voltage, superior voltage	Oberspannung *f*	**high-intensity carbon**	Hochintensitätskohle *f*, HI-Kohle *f*, Hochleistungskohle *f*
highest coefficient, leading coefficient	höchster Koeffizient *m* <Polynom>	**high-intensity carbon arc**	*s.* high-current arc
highest common factor, greatest common divisor, G.C.D.	größter gemeinschaftlicher (gemeinsamer) Teiler *m*, ggT	**high-intensity carbon arc [lamp]**	*s.* high-current arc lamp
		high-intensity field, strong (high) field, high-strength (enhanced) field	starkes Feld *n*, Starkfeld *n*
high explosive	*s.* explosive		
high field, strong field, high-intensity (high-strength, enhanced) field	starkes Feld *n*, Starkfeld *n*	**high-level**	*s.* highly radioactive
		high-level activity, high activity, hot activity	hohe Aktivität *f*, heiße Aktivität
high-field emission arc	Feldbogen *m*		
		high-level dosimetry	Dosimetrie *f* hoher Aktivitäten, „highlevel"-Dosimetrie *f*
high-flux reactor, high-flux-type nuclear reactor	Reaktor *m* mit hohem Neutronenfluß, Hochflußreaktor *m*	**high-level waste**	*s.* hot waste
high frequency, H.F., h.f., HF; radio-frequency, R.F., r.f.	Hochfrequenz *f*, HF	**highly compressed**	hochverdichtet, hochkomprimiert
high-frequency cinematography	*s.* high-speed cinematography	**highly concentrated**	hochkonzentriert
high-frequency conductivity, radio-frequency (H.F., R.F.) conductivity	Hochfrequenzleitfähigkeit *f*, HF-Leitfähigkeit *f*	**highly degenerate**	stark entartet, hochentartet, hochgradig entartet
		highly dilute	hochverdünnt
high-frequency energy, radio-frequency energy, R.F. energy, H.F. energy	Hochfrequenzenergie *f*, HF-Energie *f*	**highly dilute gas,** highly rarefied gas	hochverdünntes Gas *n*
high-frequency magnetic mirror, radio-frequency magnetic mirror, R.F. magnetic mirror	[magnetischer] Hochfrequenzspiegel *m*, Hochfrequenzpfropfen *m*, HF-Spiegel *m*, HF-Pfropfen *m*	**highly dispersed,** fine-grain, fine [grained]	hochdispers
		highly enriched, high-grade	hochangereichert
high-frequency mass spectrometer, radio-frequency (H.F., R.F.) mass spectrometer	Hochfrequenz-Massenspektrometer *n*, Radiofrequenz-Massenspektrometer *n*, HF-Massenspektrometer *n*	**highly excited level; highly excited state**	hohes Anregungsniveau *n*; hochangeregter Zustand *m*
		high-lying level (state)	*s.* shallow level
high-frequency oscillation, radio-frequency oscillation, R.F. (H.F.) oscillation	Hochfrequenzschwingung *f*, HF-Schwingung *f*	**highly ionized,** stripped	hochionisiert
		highly ionized plasma	hochionisiertes Plasma *n*
high-frequency permeability, radio-frequency permeability, H.F. permeability, R.F. permeability	Hochfrequenzpermeabilität *f*, HF-Permeabilität *f*	**highly radioactive,** high-level, hot <nucl.>	hochaktiv, hochgradig (stark) radioaktiv, heiß <Kern.>

highly rarefied gas, highly dilute gas	hochverdünntes Gas *n*	**high-pressure incandescent lamp**	Hochdruckglühlampe *f*
highly stabilized (stable), high-stability	hochkonstant, hochstabil	**high-pressure ionization chamber**	Hochdruckionisationskammer *f*
highly symmetric, high-symmetric, of high order of symmetry	hochsymmetrisch	**high-pressure lamp,** high-pressure discharge lamp	Hochdruck[entladungs]- lampe *f*, Hochdruck-Gasentladungslampe *f*
highly viscous liquid	s. high-viscosity liquid	**high pressure mercury lamp,** high pressure mercury vapour lamp	Quecksilberhochdrucklampe *f*, Hg-Hochdrucklampe *f*, Hochdruck-Quecksilberdampflampe *f*, Quecksilberhochdruckbrenner *m*, Quecksilberdampf-Hochdruckbrenner *m*
high-melting, refractory, sluggish, viscous	schwerschmelzbar, schwerschmelzend, hochschmelzend, schwerflüssig, strengflüssig		
high Miller indices / of	hochindiziert		
high-molecular, high molecular weight / of, macromolecular	hochmolekular, makromolekular		
		high-pressure mercury pump	Quecksilberhochdruckpumpe *f*
high-ohmic, high-resistance, high-resistivity, high-resistive, high-impedance	hochohmig, Hochohm-	**high pressure mercury vapour lamp**	s. high pressure mercury lamp
		high-pressure physics	Physik *f* der hohen Drücke, Physik hoher Drücke, Hochdruckphysik *f*
high-order electrodynamics of Bopp-Podolsky, Bopp-Podolsky electrodynamics [of higher order]	Elektrodynamik *f* höherer Ordnung von Bopp-Podolsky, Bopp-Podolskysche Elektrodynamik höherer Ordnung	**high-pressure pipe line**	s. pressure line
		high pressure surface, lower surface, pressure side <of the airfoil>	Flügelunterseite *f*, Unterseite *f* <des Flügels>
high order of symmetry / of, high-symmetric, highly symmetric	hochsymmetrisch	**high-pressure vessel**	s. pressure vessel
		high-pressure zone, zone of high pressure	Hochdruckgürtel *m*, Hochdruckzone *f*, Hochdruckring *m*
high-order white, white of higher order	Weiß *n* höherer Ordnung		
		high-purity, extra[-]pure, extremely pure, hyperpure	reinst
high-output accelerator	s. high-energy accelerator		
high-output generator	s. high-current generator	**high-radiation field**	starkes Strahlungsfeld *n*
high-output instrument, high-performance instrument, instrument of high performance	Hochleistungsgerät *n*, Hochleistungsinstrument *n*	**high-resistance,** high-ohmic, high-resistivity high-resistive, high-impedance	hochohmig
high-pass, high-pass filter <el.>	Hochpaß *m*, Hochpaßfilter *n*, Kondensatorkette *f* <El.>	**high-resistance direction**	s. reverse direction <semi.>
high-performance instrument, instrument of high performance, high-output instrument	Hochleistungsgerät *n*, Hochleistungsinstrument *n*	**high resistance meter**	Hochohmmeter *n*
		high-resistive, high-resistivity	s. high-ohmic
high pitch	s. concert pitch <450 c/s>	**high-resolution,** high-resolving, with high resolving power, high-definition	hochauflösend
high polymer, eupolymer; macromolecule, macromol, giant molecule	Hochpolymer[e] *n*, Makropolymer[e] *n*, hochpolymerer (makropolymerer) Stoff *m*, Makrolar[e] *n*, Hochmolekulare *n*; Makromolekül *n*, Riesenmolekül *n*	**high-resolution detector**	Nachweisgerät *n* mit hohem Auflösungsvermögen, hochauflösender Detektor *m*, Hochauflösungsdetektor *m*
		high-resolution spectrometer	s. spectrometer with high resolving power
high-potential electrode, high-voltage electrode	Hochspannungselektrode *f*	**high-resolving**	s. high-resolution
high-power, high-aperture <opt.>	lichtstark <Opt.>	**high-resolving oscillograph**	Hochleistungsoszillograph *m*
high-power accelerator	s. high-energy accelerator	**high resolving power / with**	s. high-resolution
high-power klystron	s. power klystron	**high seas**	hohe See *f*, hoch[]gehende See, hoher Seegang *m*, hoher (großer) Wellengang *m*, hohe (große) Wellen *fpl* <Stärke 7>
high-power pulse generator	Hochleistungsimpulsgenerator *m*		
high-power test generator	Leistungsmeßsender *m*		
high-power X-ray tube	Hochleistungs-Röntgenröhre *f*		
		high-sensitive gas analyzer	Gasspurenanalysator *m*
high-preferred orientation	s. preferred orientation		
high pressure, h. p.	Hochdruck *m*, hoher Druck *m*, H. D.	**high-speed camera,** rapid sequence camera; high-speed cinematograph	Hochgeschwindigkeitskamera *f*, Hochfrequenzkamera *f*, Hochgeschwindigkeitskinematograph *m*, Hochfrequenzkinematograph *m*
high-pressure arc	Hochdruckbogen *m*, Hochdrucklichtbogen *m*		
high-pressure area	s. High		
high-pressure branch, anticyclonic branch	Hochdruckausläufer *m*		
		high-speed camera	s. a. slow-motion camera
high-pressure centre	s. anticyclonic centre		
high-pressure counter	Hochdruckzählrohr *n*	**high-speed camera shooting,** slow-motion [camera] shooting, slow-motion record, shooting for high-speed (slow-motion) effect, high-speed shooting for low-speed projection	Zeitlupenaufnahme *f*, Zeitdehneraufnahme *f*, Aufnahme *f* in Zeitlupe, zeitgedehnte Aufnahme
high-pressure discharge	Hochdruck-Gasentladung *f*, Hochdruckentladung *f*		
high-pressure discharge lamp, high-pressure lamp	Hochdruck[entladungs]- lampe *f*, Hochdruck-Gasentladungslampe *f*		
high-pressure gauge	Druckmesser *m*, Hochdruckmeßgerät *n*, Hochdruckmesser *m*, Meßgerät *n* für hohe Drücke, Druckmanometer *n*	**high-speed centrifuge,** ultracentrifuge, supercentrifuge	Ultrazentrifuge *f*
		high-speed cinematograph	s. high-speed camera

high-speed cinematography, high-frequency cinematography; high-speed photography, high-frequency photography — Hochgeschwindigkeitskinematographie f, Hochfrequenzkinematographie f; Hochgeschwindigkeitsphotographie f, Hochfrequenzphotographie f; Hochgeschwindigkeitsaufnahme f, Hochfrequenzaufnahme f

high-speed cinematography [for low-speed projection] s. high-speed photography

high-speed computer, high-speed electronic computer schneller Rechner m, Schnellrechner m, schnelle elektronische Rechenmaschine f

high-speed particle, fast particle — schnelles Teilchen n

high-speed pen recorder; high-speed recorder (self-recording instrument) — Schnellschreiber m

high-speed photograph, high-speed record[ing], high-frequency photograph, high-frequency record[ing] — Hochgeschwindigkeitsaufnahme f, Hochfrequenzaufnahme f, Hochgeschwindigkeitsphotographie f, Hochfrequenzphotographie f

high-speed photography s. high-speed cinematography

high-speed photography [for low-speed projection], high-speed cinematography [for low-speed projection], slow-motion method (effect), time magnifying — Zeitlupenkinematographie f, Zeitlupenphotographie f, Zeitlupenverfahren n, Zeitdehnungsverfahren n, Zeitlupeneffekt m, Zeitdehnungseffekt m, Zeitlupe f, Zeitdehnung f

high-speed physics Kurzzeitphysik f

high-speed printer Schnelldrucker m, Schnelldruckwerk n

high-speed reaction Hochgeschwindigkeitsreaktion f, Kurzzeitreaktion f

high-speed record[ing] s. high-speed photograph

high-speed recorder, high-speed self-recording instrument; high-speed pen recorder — Schnellschreiber m

high-speed schlieren photograph, high-frequency schlieren photograph — Hochgeschwindigkeits-Schlierenaufnahme f, Hochfrequenz-Schlierenaufnahme f

high-speed self-recording instrument, high-speed recorder; high-speed pen recorder — Schnellschreiber m

high-speed shooting for low-speed projection s. high-speed camera shooting

high-speed storage (store) s. rapid acces memory

high-speed wind tunnel Hochgeschwindigkeits-Windkanal m

high-spin complex, spin-free complex, outer-orbital complex — Normalkomplex m, magnetisch normaler Komplex m, [„normaler"] Anlagerungskomplex m

high-stability, highly stable, highly stabilized — hochkonstant; hochstabil

high-strength field, strong (high, high-intensity) field, enhanced field — starkes Feld n, Starkfeld n

high-symmetric, highly symmetric, of high order of symmetry — hochsymmetrisch

high-temperature annealing, coarse-grain annealing — Hochglühen n, Grobkornglühen n

high-temperature approach, high-temperature solution — Hochtemperaturentwicklung f, Lösung f für hohe Temperaturen

high-temperature arc, high-temperature electric arc — Hochtemperaturbogen m, Hochtemperaturlichtbogen m

high-temperature creep Hochtemperaturkriechen n

high-temperature creep test s. tensile test at elevated temperature

high-temperature electric arc, high-temperature arc — Hochtemperaturbogen m, Hochtemperaturlichtbogen m

high-temperature emitter, high-temperature radiator — Hochtemperaturstrahler m

high-temperature liquid cooling s. high-boiling-liquid cooling

high-temperature microscope Erhitzungsmikroskop n, Hochtemperaturmikroskop n

high-temperature physics, physics of high temperature — Hochtemperaturphysik f

high-temperature plasma physics, nuclear fusion physics — Hochtemperatur-Plasmaphysik f, Kernfusionsphysik f, Fusionsphysik f

high-temperature radiator, high-temperature emitter — Hochtemperaturstrahler m

high-temperature reactor, HTR — Hochtemperaturreaktor m, HTR

high-temperature resistance s. thermal stability

high-temperature resistant s. heat-proof

high-temperature solution, high-temperature approach — Hochtemperaturentwicklung f, Lösung f für hohe Temperaturen

high-temperature strength s. thermal stability

high tension, high voltage, H.V., h.v., H.T., h.t. <el.> — Hochspannung f <El.>

high-tension arc, high-voltage arc — Hochspannungsbogen m, Hochvoltbogen m

high-tension atomic battery, high-voltage atomic battery — Hochspannungs-Radionuklidbatterie f, Hochspannungs-Isotopenbatterie f

high-tension current, high-voltage current — Hochspannungsstrom m, Hochvoltstrom m

high-tension line, high-voltage line, high-tension transmission line — Hochspannungsleitung f, Hochvoltleitung f

high-tension [power] supply, high-voltage power supply, high-voltage supply — Hochspannungsnetz[anschluß]gerät n, Hochspannungsstromversorgung f

high-tension transmission line, high-voltage line, high-tension line — Hochspannungsleitung f, Hochvoltleitung f

high-tension voltmeter Hochspannungsvoltmeter n

high tide, total tide, high water — Hochwasser n, Gezeitenhochwasser n, Tidehochwasser n

high tide raised by a storm; eagre; bore — Sturmflut f

high-upper atmosphere s. upper atmosphere

high vacuum, microvac[uum] — Hochvakuum n <$10^{-3} \cdots 10^{-8}$ Torr>

high-vacuum breakdown Hochvakuumdurchschlag m

high-vacuum cock, high-vacuum cut-off — Hochvakuumhahn m

high-vacuum deposition [by evaporation], metallizing by high-vacuum evaporation — Hochvakuumbedampfung f, Hochvakuumaufdampfung f

high-vacuum discharge Hochvakuumentladung f

high-vacuum discharge spectrum Hochvakuumentladungsspektrum n

high-vacuum photocell s. vacuum photocell

high-vacuum physics Hochvakuumphysik f

high-vacuum pump Hochvakuumpumpe f

high-vacuum

high-vacuum rectifier s. vacuum valve
high-velocity pyrometer <US>, suction pyrometer, high-velocity thermocouple <US> — Ansaugepyrometer n, Aspirationspyrometer n
high-velocity star <astr.> — Schnelläufer m <Astr.>

high-velocity thermocouple <US>, suction pyrometer, high-velocity pyrometer <US> — Ansaugepyrometer n, Aspirationspyrometer n
high-viscosity liquid, highly viscous liquid — hochviskose Flüssigkeit f
high voltage, high tension, H.V., h.v., H.T., h.t. <el.> — Hochspannung f <El.>
high-voltage acceleration tube, high-voltage tube <acc.> — Hochspannungsrohr n <Beschl.>

high-voltage accelerator — Hochspannungsbeschleuniger m, Hochvoltbeschleuniger m
high-voltage arc, high-tension arc — Hochspannungsbogen m, Hochvoltbogen m
high-voltage atomic battery, high-tension atomic battery — Hochspannungs-Radionuklidbatterie f, Hochspannungs-Isotopenbatterie f
high-voltage current, high-tension current — Hochspannungsstrom m
high-voltage electrode, high-potential electrode — Hochspannungselektrode f
high-voltage electrolytic capacitor — Hochvolt-Elektrolytkondensator m
high-voltage flash s. electronic-flash lamp
high-voltage generator — Hochspannungsgenerator m, Hochspannungserzeuger m, Hochvoltgenerator m
high-voltage glow discharge tube — Hochspannungs[-Glimm]röhre f, Hochvoltglimmlampe f
high-voltage instrument — Hochspannungs[meß]gerät n, Hochspannungsinstrument n
high-voltage line, high-tension [transmission] line — Hochspannungsleitung f, Hochvoltleitung f
high-voltage power supply s. high-tension power supply
high-voltage pulse generator — Hochspannungsimpulsgenerator m, Impulshochspannungsgenerator m
high-voltage supply s. high-tension power supply
high-voltage tube s. high-voltage acceleration tube <acc.>
high-voltage tubular discharge lamp s. tubular discharge lamp
high-voltage unit — Hochspannungsanlage f, Hochvoltanlage f
high water, total tide, high tide — Hochwasser n, Gezeitenhochwasser n, Tidehochwasser n
high water <of river> — Hochwasser n; Schwellhochwasser n; Stauhochwasser n <Fluß>
high-water interval, lunitidal interval, flood interval — Flutstunde f, Hafenzeit f, Hafenwasserintervall n
high water of spring tide — Spring[flut]hochwasser n, Springtidenhochwasser n
high-yield generator s. high-current generator
high-yield ion source s. high-current ion source
hilac s. heavy-ion linear accelerator
Hilbert expansion — Hilbertsche Entwicklung f
Hilbert['s] matrix — Hilbert-Matrix f, H-Matrix f
Hilbert['s] method — Hilbertsche Methode f

Hilbert parallelotope — Hilbertscher Quader m

Hilbert-Schmidt kernel, normalizable kernel — normierbarer (Hilbert-Schmidtscher, quadratisch integrierbarer) Kern m
Hilbert-Schmidt operator, finite norm operator — Hilbert-Schmidtscher Operator m, Hilbert-Schmidt-Operator m
Hilbert space — Hilbert-Raum m
Hilbert transform[ation] — Hilbert-Transformation f

Hilborn detector, neutron-beta detector, n-ß detector — Hilborn-Detektor m, Stromelement n, Neutron-Beta-Detektor m, n-ß-Detektor m
Hildebrand['s] equation — Hildebrandsche Gleichung f
Hildebrand rule — Hildebrandsche Regel f
hill and dale recording, vertical recording — [Aufzeichnung f in] Tiefenschrift f, Edisonschrift f
Hill['s] differential equation, differential equation of Hill type — Hillsche Differentialgleichung f, Differentialgleichung vom Hillschen Typ
Hill['s] equation <bio.> — Hillsche Gleichung f <Bio.>
hillock, etch hill[ock] — Ätzhügel m

Hill['s] problem — Hillsches Mondproblem n, Hillsches Problem n
Hill['s] reaction — Hillsche Reaktion f, Hill-Reaktion f
hill shading, shading — Schummerung f
hillside upcurrent s. orographic upward wind
Hill['s] system [of differential equations] <astr.> — Hillsche Differentialgleichungen fpl, Hillsches System n [von Differentialgleichungen] <Astr.>
Hill['s] theory [of the Moon] — Hillsche Mondtheorie f
Hill['s] variational orbit, variational orbit — Hillsche Variationsbahn f, Variationsbahn
Hilsch tube, Hilsch['s] vortex tube, [Ranque-Hilsch] vortex tube — Hilschsches Wirbelrohr n, [Ranque-Hilsch-] Wirbelrohr, Hilschsche Wirbelröhre f, Hilsch-Rohr n
Hiltner-Hall effect — Hiltner-Hall-Effekt m
hindcasting of storm — Entwicklungsgeschichte f des Sturms, Sturmentwicklungsgeschichte f
hindered diffusion — behinderte Diffusion f
hindered falling — Fall m im beengten («eingeengten) Raum, eingeengter Fall
hindered internal rotation — behinderte innere Rotation f
hindered rotation — behinderte Rotation f
hindered settling — verzögerte Fällung f, verzögerte Absetzung f
hindered torsion — Wölbkrafttorsion f, Torsion f bei behinderter Querschnittsverwölbung, behinderte Verwölbung f, Biegeverdrehung f
hindering, hindrance — Behinderung f
hindrance factor — „hindrance"-Faktor m, Widerstandsfaktor m
hinged electromagnet — Scharnierelektromagnet m
hinge joint s. pin joint
hingeless arch, fixed[-ended] arch, rigid arch, build-in arch — eingespannter Bogen m, gelenkloser Bogen, Bogen mit eingespannten Enden
hinge moment — Rudermoment n, Scharniermoment n, Betätigungsmoment n
Hirn cycle — Hirnscher Kreisprozeß m

His['] bundle — Hissches Bündel n
hiss, hissing <e.g. of microphone> — Zischen n <z. B. des Mikrophons>

hiss effect — Zischeffekt m

hissing, hiss <e.g. of microphone>	Zischen n <z. B. des Mikrophons>	hodoscope	Hodoskop n, Conversi-Zähler m
hissing arc	zischender Bogen (Lichtbogen) m, Zischbogen m	Hoeppler viscosimeter	Höpplersches Viskosimeter n, Höppler-Viskosimeter n
hissing of the arc	Zischen n des Lichtbogens	Hoff['s] equation / van't Hoff equations/ van't, equations of reaction isobars and isochores	s. Hoff['s] law / van't van't Hoffsche Gleichungen fpl
histogram, bar diagram, bar chart; column diagram	Histogramm n, Treppenpolygon n; Säulendiagramm n <dreidimensional>; Streifendiagramm n <zweidimensional>; Rechteckdarstellung f, Rechteckzug m, Rechteckstufenkurve f; Staffelbild n		
		Hoff['s] equilibrium box / van't, van't Hoff['s] reaction box	van't Hoffscher Gleichgewichtskasten m
		Hoff['s] factor / van't	van't Hoffscher Faktor m, Van't-Hoff-Faktor m
historadioautography	Histoautoradiographie f	Hoff['s] formula / van't	s. Hoff['s] law / van't
history, prehistory	Vorgeschichte f	Hoff isochore / van't	s. reaction isochore
hit <radiobiology>	Treffer m <Strahlenbiologie>	Hoff['s] law / van't	van't Hoffsche Regel f, RGT-Regel f
hit of nucleus, nuclear event	Kerntreffer m, [kernphysikalisches] Ereignis n	Hoff['s] law / van't, van't Hoff['s] relation, van't Hoff['s] equation (formula) <for osmotic pressure>	[Avogadro-]van't Hoffsches Gesetz n, Gesetz von Avogadro-van't Hoff <für den osmotischen Druck>
hit theory; target theory	Treffertheorie f, Depottheorie f; Treffbereichstheorie f		
Hittorf['s] dark space, Crookes' dark space	Hittorfscher Dunkelraum m, Crookesscher Dunkelraum, innerer Dunkelraum, zweiter Katodendunkelraum m	Hoff-Le Chatelier principle / van't	van't Hoff-Le Chateliersches Prinzip m
		Hoff['s] reaction box / van't, van't Hoff['s] equilibrium box	van't Hoffscher Gleichgewichtskasten m
Hittorf['s] principle, short-path principle	Hittorfsches Prinzip m	Hoff reaction isobar / van't	s. reaction isobar
Hittorf tube	Hittorfsche Röhre f	Hoff reaction isochore / van't	s. reaction isochore
H-J equation, Harkins-Jura equations of adsorption	Harkins-Jurasche Adsorptionsgleichungen fpl	Hoff['s] relation / van't	s. Hoff['s] law / van't
Hα line [of hydrogen], H_a line [of hydrogen], hydrogen alpha line	Hα-Linie f [des Wasserstoffs], H_a-Linie f [des Wasserstoffs], Wasserstoff-Alpha-Linie f	Hofmann['s] rule	Hofmannsche Regel f
		Hofmeister series, lyotropic series	lyotrope (Hofmeistersche) Reihe f, Quellungsreihe f
H-magnetometer, horizontal magnetometer	H-Magnetometer n; Horizontal[intensitäts]-magnetometer n	Hofstadter['s] experiments	Hofstadtersche Versuche mpl
h-matrix, hybrid matrix	Hybridmatrix f, h-Matrix f	Hohlborn circuit	Hohlborn-Schaltung f
H meson	s. K-meson	Hohle alternating-current potentiometer, Hohle potentiometer	Hohle-Kompensator m, Kompensator m nach Hohle
H-M-H method	s. molecular orbitals method		
H[-] mode, H[-]wave, mode of magnetic type, wave of magnetic type, TE[-] mode, TE[-] wave, transverse electric mode, transverse electric wave, transverse E[-] mode, transverse E[-] wave	H-Welle f, Welle f vom magnetischen Typ, TE-Welle f, transversal[-]elektrische Welle (Mode f), transversale elektrische Welle (Mode), transversale E-Welle f, Transversal-E-Welle f, H-Typ-Welle f, transversal[-]elektrischer Wellentyp m, H-Typ m, TE-Typ m, H-Mode f, TE-Mode f	Hohle circuit	Hohle-Schaltung f, Hohle-Brücke f
		Hohle potentiometer, Hohle alternating-current potentiometer	Hohle-Kompensator m, Kompensator m nach Hohle
		hohlraum	s. hollow space
		Hohmann ellipse	Hohmann-Ellipse f
		Hohmann transfer orbit	Hohmannsche Übergangsbahn f
		hoist[ing]	s. lifting
		hoisting work	s. stroke work
		hold-back, hold-up, retention; prehension	Zurückhaltung f, Retention f; Festhalten n
H-mode function	H-Modenfunktion f, H-Wellen[typ]funktion f	hold-back agent; hold-back carrier	Rückhalteträger m
H-network, H-type network, H-section	H-Schaltung f, H-Glied n		
hoar frost, hoar-frost; hoar frost deposit, white frost	Rauhreif m	holder; support; mount, mounting support	Halterung f, Halter m
hoar-frost line; sublimation curve, curve of sublimation	Sublimations[druck]kurve f, Sublimationslinie f	Hölder['s] condition	Hölder-Bedingung f, H-Bedingung f
Hockin['s] condition	Hockinsche Bedingung f, Herschelsche Forderung f	Hölder constant	s. constant in Hölder['s] condition
hodograph <hydr., geo.>	Hodograph m, Hodographenkurve f, Geschwindigkeitskurve f, Hodogramm n <Hydr., Geo.>	Hölder continuity	Hölder-Stetigkeit f, Höldersche Stetigkeit f, H-Stetigkeit f
		Hölder continuous	Hölder-stetig, H-stetig
hodograph characteristic, characteristic in the hodograph plane	Hodographencharakteristik f	Hölder index	s. order in the condition of Lipschitz
hodograph equation	Hodographengleichung f	Hölder['s] transformation	Höldersche Transformation f, Hölder-Transformation f
hodograph method	Hodographenmethode f		
hodograph plane	Hodographenebene f	holding <of relay>	Halten n <Relais>
hodograph transformation	Hodographentransformation f	holding [at a temperature]	Halten n [bei einer Temperatur]
hodograph variable	Hodographenvariable f	holding capacity	s. capacity
		holding current	Haltestrom m
hodometer, odometer; pedometer; perambulator; cyclometer	Hodometer n; Schrittzähler m, Schrittzahlmesser m, Schrittmesser m; Wegmesser m; Meßrad n; Zyklometer n	holding force; holding power	Haltekraft f; Haltevermögen n
		holding in storage	s. hold-up
		holding potential	Haltepotential n
		holding power; holding force	Haltekraft f; Haltevermögen n

holding — 334

holding time	s. residence time	hollow conductor	s. hollow waveguide
holding voltage	Haltespannung f	hollow conical antenna	Hohlkegelantenne f
holdor, holographic date storage	holographischer Datenspeicher m, Holdor m	hollow crystal	Hohlkristall m
		hollow cylinder	Hohlzylinder m
hold range	s. pull-in range	hollow cylinder source, tubular source	hohlzylinderförmige Quelle f, Hohlzylinderquelle f, rohrförmige Quelle
hold[-]up	Materialeinsatz m, Inhalt m <Anlage>		
hold-up, hold-back, retention; prehension	Zurückhaltung f, Retention f; Festhalten n	hollow dam, buttress dam	Pfeilerstaumauer f, aufgelöste Staumauer f
hold-up; storage; holding in storage; keeping; preservation	Lagerung f; Aufbewahrung f, Lagerhaltung f	hollow discharge lamp, hollow discharge [light] source, hollow discharge tube	s. hollow-cathode discharge tube
hold-up time	s. residence time	hollow enclosure	s. hollow space
hole; orifice; opening; gap, port [hole]	Öffnung f; Loch n; Kanalmündung f, Kanalöffnung f, Kanal m; Durchführung f	hollow-pipe waveguide	s. hollow waveguide
		hollow shell	Hohlschale f
hole <in the structure of a liquid>	Loch n <Flüssigkeitsstruktur>	hollow space, hollow enclosure (box, chamber), hohlraum, black-body furnace	Hohlraumkörper m, Hohlraumstrahler m, Hohlraum m
hole <geo.>	Schurf m, Schürfloch n <Geo.>		
hole	s. a. gap	hollow vortex	Hohlwirbel m
hole	s. a. positive hole		
hole and slot anode magnetron, hole-and-slot magnetron	Schlitz-und-Loch-Magnetron n, Zylinder-Spalt-Magnetron n	hollow waveguide, hollow-pipe waveguide, hollow (tubular) conductor, [wave]guide, duct, waveguide [transmission] line	Hohl[rohr]leiter m, Hohlrohr n, Hohlraum-[wellen]leiter m; Hohl[rohr]leitung f
hole burning	Lochbrennen n		
hole conduction	s. p-type conduction	Holmgreen circuit	Holmgreen-Schaltung f
hole conductivity, p-type conductivity	Defekt[elektronen]leitfähigkeit f, Löcherleitfähigkeit f, p-[Typ-]Leitfähigkeit f	holocrystalline	holokristallin, vollkristallin
		hologram, holograph	Hologramm n
		holograph, hologram	Hologramm n
hole coupling, coupling by hole	Lochkopplung f	holographic date storage, holdor	holographischer Datenspeicher m, Holdor m
hole current	Defektelektronenstrom m, Löcherstrom m	holographic interferometry	holographische Interferometrie f
hole diffusion	s. vacancy diffusion	holography	Holographieren n, Holographie f
hole diffusion current	Defektelektronen-Diffusionsstrom m, Löcherdiffusionsstrom m	holohedral	holoedrisch, vollflächig
		holohedral class of the cubic system	s. holohedry of the regular system
hole-electron pair, exciton, electron-hole pair	Exciton n, Exziton n, Elektron-Defektelektron-Paar n	holohedral class of the hexagonal system	s. holohedry of the hexagonal system
hole in the energy continuum	Lücke f im Kontinuum der besetzten Energieniveaus	holohedral class of the monoclinic system, monoclinic holohedry, holohedry of the monoclinic system, digonal equatorial class, normal (prismatic) class	monokline Holoedrie f, prismatische Klasse f
hole model <of liquids>	Löchermodell n <der Flüssigkeiten>		
hole semiconductor	s. p-type semiconductor		
hole theory [of electron], Dirac['s] hole theory, Dirac['s] pair theory, pair theory	Löchertheorie f [von Dirac] Diracsche Löchertheorie, , Löchertheorie des Elektrons, Positronentheorie f, Paartheorie f	holohedral class of the rhombic system	s. orthorhombic holohedry
		holohedral class of the tetragonal system	s. holohedry of the tetragonal system
hole theory of liquids	Löchertheorie f der Flüssigkeiten	holohedral class of the triclinic system	s. holohedry of the triclinic system
hole trap	Defektelektronenhaftstelle f, Defektelektronenhaftterm m; Defektelektronenfalle f, Defektelektronentrap m, Löchertrap m, Löcherfalle f, Leuchtzentrum n, „hole trap" m	holohedral class of the trigonal system	s. rhombohedral holohedry
		holohedrism	s. holohedry
		holohedron	Vollflächner m, Holoeder n
		holohedry, holohedrism	Holoedrie f; holoedrische Klasse f; Vollflächigkeit f
Hollenberg['s] figure, displacement figure	Hollenbergsche Verdrängungsfigur f, Verdrängungsfigur	holohedry of the hexagonal system, dihexagonal equatorial class, normal class, dihexagonal bipyramidal class, dihexagonal-dipyramidal [crystal] class, hexagonal holohedry, holohedral class of the hexagonal system	Holoedrie f des hexagonalen Systems, dihexagonal-bipyramidale Klasse f, hexagonale Holoedrie, dihexagonal dipyramidale Klasse
hollow	hohl		
hollow	s. cavity		
hollow-anode tube, hollow-anode X-ray tube	Hohlanoden-Röntgenröhre f, Hohlanodenröhre f		
Holloway['s] formula	Hollowaysche Reichweitenbeziehung f für Alpha-Teilchen		
hollow beam	Hohlstrahl m, Rohrstrahl m	holohedry of the monoclinic system	s. monoclinic holohedry
hollow box	s. hollow space	holohedry of the orthorhombic system	s. orthorhombic holohedry
hollow-cathode discharge	Hohlkatodenentladung f	holohedry of the regular system, ditesseral central class, normal class, hexakisoctahedral class, hexoctahedral [crystal] class, regular holohedry, holohedral class of the cubic system	Holoedrie f des kubischen Systems, hexakisoktaedrische Klasse f, kubische Holoedrie, kubisch-holoedrische Klasse
hollow-cathode discharge tube, hollow-cathode lamp, hollow discharge tube; hollow discharge lamp; hollow discharge [light] source	Hohlkatoden-Gasentladungsröhre f, Hohlkatoden[-Entladungs]-röhre f; Hohlkatodenlampe f; Hohlkatodenlichtquelle f		
hollow chamber	s. hollow space	holohedry of the rhombohedral system	s. rhombohedral holohedry

holohedry of the tetragonal system, tetragonal holohedry, ditetragonal equatorial class, ditetragonal bipyramidal class, ditetragonal-dipyramidal [crystal] class, holohedral class of the tetragonal system, normal class — Holoedrie f des tetragonalen Systems, ditetragonal-bipyramidale Klasse f, ditetragonal dipyramidale Klasse, tetragonale Holoedrie

holohedry of the triclinic system, triclinic holohedry, centrosymmetric (normal, pinacoidal) class, holohedral class of the triclinic system, triclinic holohedral class — trikline Holoedrie f, pinakoidale Klasse f, triklinpinakoidale Klasse

holohyaline — holohyalin
holometer — Holometer n
holomict — holomikt
holomorphic, regular <geo., math.>; regular analytic <math.> — holomorph, regulär <Geo., Math.>; regulär analytisch <Math.>
holomorphic function, regular [analytic] function — holomorphe (regulär analytische) Funktion f
holonomic constraint — holonome Bedingung (Zwangsbedingung, Bindung, Bedingungsgleichung) f
holonomic co-ordinates, true co-ordinates — holonome Koordinaten fpl, wahre Koordinaten
holonomo-scleronomic system — holonomes skleronomes System n
holonomy — Holonomie f
holonomy group — Holonomiegruppe f

holospheric isanomal — holosphärische Isanomale f
holospheric temperature — holosphärische Temperatur f

Holtsmark broadening — Holtsmark-Verbreiterung f
Holtsmark distribution — Holtsmarksche Wahrscheinlichkeitsverteilung (Verteilung) f, Holtsmark-Verteilung f
Holtz['] continuous electrophorus — Holtzsche Influenzmaschine f
Holtz-type generator, Toepler-Holtz generator — Toepler-Holtz-Generator m

Holzknecht unit, H — Holzknecht-Einheit f, H
homal — homal
homenergic, isoenergetic, homoenergetic — isoenergetisch

homentropic flow (motion) — s. isentropic flow
homeo[-]epitaxy — s. isentropic flow
homeomorphic <math., opt.>; topologically equivalent <math.> — homöomorph; topologisch äquivalent <Math.>; raumähnlich <Opt.>
homeomorphism, isomorphism <cryst.> — Isomorphie f, kristallographische Isomorphie, Homöomorphie f <Krist.>
homeomorphism — s. a. bicontinuous mapping <math.>
homeostasis — Homöostasis f
homeostat — Homöostat m
homeostatic — homöostatisch
homeostrophic — homöostrophisch
homeotectic — s. homotectic
homeothermal, homo[io]thermal, homo[io]thermic, warm-blooded — homöotherm, homoiotherm, warmblütig, gleichwarm
home position — s. position of rest
homing guidance; auto-guidance — Heimfindungslenkung f; Zielfluglenkung f; Selbstlenkung f; Selbstannäherung f

homoatomic ring — s. homocycle
homoazeotrope — homoazeotropes Gemisch n

homocentric beam, stigmatic beam — homozentrisches Bündel (Strahlenbündel) n
homocharge — Homöoladung f

homochromatic, isochromatic, homochrome — gleichfarbig, isochrom, homochrom, isochromatisch

homochromatic photometry — isochrome (gleichfarbige) Photometrie f
homochrome — s. homochromatic
homochronism — Homochronie f

homocline, monocline — Monoklinale f

homocycle, homocyclic nucleus (ring), homoatomic ring, isocyclic nucleus, isocycle — Isozyklus m, Homozyklus m, isozyklischer Ring m, homozyklischer Ring
homodesmic structure — homodesmische Struktur f

homodisperse — s. monodisperse
homodromous reversibility — homodrome Reversibilität f
homodyne reception, zero-beat reception — Homodyneempfang m

homoenergetic — s. isoenergetic
homoentropic flow (motion) — s. isentropic flow
homofocal, confocal — konfokal, homofokal
homogenate — Homogenisat n, Homogenisierungsprodukt n
homogeneity, homogeneousness, homogeny — Homogenität f, Gleichartigkeit f, Gleichförmigkeit f
homogeneization, homogenization, homogenizing — Homogenisierung f, Homogenisation f
homogeneous — homogen, gleichartig, gleichmäßig, einheitlich
homogeneous — s. a. monochromatic <of electromagnetic or corpuscular radiation>
homogeneous anisotropy — homogene Anisotropie f
homogeneous carbon, plain carbon, pure carbon, retort carbon — Homogenkohle f, Reinkohle f, Retortenkohle f, Reindochtkohle f
homogeneous combustion, uniform combustion — homogene Verbrennung f
homogeneous co-ordinates — homogene Koordinaten fpl
homogeneous deformation, homogeneous strain — homogene Verformung (Formänderung, Deformation, Verzerrung) f
homogeneous differential equation — s. homogeneous linear differential equation
homogeneous differential system — s. homogeneous system of differential equations
homogeneous elongation; inflation — homogene Dehnung f, homogene Dilatation f
homogeneous equation — homogene Gleichung f
homogeneous equation — s. a. homogeneous linear differential equation
homogeneous equation — s. a. Euler['s] differential equation
homogeneous glide — homogene Gleitung f
homogeneous-heterogeneous catalysis — homogen-heterogene Katalyse f, Homogen-Heterogen-Katalyse f
homogeneous-heterogeneous process of combustion — homogen-heterogener Verbrennungsprozeß m
homogeneous immersion — homogene Immersion f
homogeneous in structure — s. homogeneous structure / of
homogeneous isotropic turbulence; isotropic turbulence — isotrope Turbulenz f
homogeneous kinetics, kinetics of homogeneous systems — Homogenkinetik f
homogeneous linear differential equation, homogeneous linear equation, homogeneous differential equation, homogeneous equation — homogene [lineare] Differentialgleichung f, homogene Gleichung f; zugehörige homogene [lineare] Differentialgleichung, verkürzte [lineare] Differentialgleichung, verstümmelte Differentialgleichung

homogeneous Lorentz group — homogene Lorentz-Gruppe f

homogeneous

homogeneous Lorentz transformation	homogene Lorentz-Transformation f
homogeneous magnetic field, uniform magnetic field	homogenes Magnetfeld (magnetisches Feld) n
homogeneous mixture, mixture, [uniform] mix; intermixture	[homogenes] Gemisch n, [homogene] Mischung f
homogeneousness	s. homogeneity
homogeneous polynomial, form <math.>	Form f, homogenes Polynom n <Math.>
homogeneous reactor	homogener Reaktor m, Homogenreaktor m, Lösungsreaktor m
homogeneous region, one-phase region	Einphasenbereich m, homogenes Gebiet n
homogeneous shear	homogene Scherung f
homogeneous shortening	homogene Verkürzung f
homogeneous strain	homogener Verformungszustand m
homogeneous strain	s. a. homogeneous deformation
homogeneous stress	homogener Spannungszustand m
homogeneous structure / of, structural-homogeneous, structurally (constitutionally) homogeneous, homogeneous in structure	strukturhomogen
homogeneous system, one-phase system, monophase system	homogenes System n, Einphasensystem n, einphasiges System
homogeneous system of differential equations, homogeneous differential system	homogenes Differentialgleichungssystem n; verkürztes Differentialgleichungssystem; verstümmeltes System n
homogeneous tension	homogener Zug m
homogeneous turbulence	homogene Turbulenz f
homogenization, homogenizing, homogeneization	Homogenisierung f, Homogenisation f
homogenizing	Diffusionsglühen n, Homogenisierungsglühen n
homogeny	s. homogeneity
homographic function	[gebrochen] lineare Funktion f
homographic transformation, homography, Möbius['] transformation, [bi]linear transformation, bilinear mapping, fractional linear transformation, linear [fractional] transformation	Homographie f, gebrochen lineare Transformation (Substitution) f, Möbius-Transformation f, lineare Transformation (Substitution), lineare Abbildung f, Kollineation f
homoiothermal, homoiothermic, hom[e]othermal, homothermic, warm-blooded	homöotherm, homoiotherm, warmblütig, gleichwarm
homojunction	Homoübergang m
homolog, homologue; homologous compound	Homologe n; homologe Verbindung f
homologation [reaction]	Homologisierungsreaktion f
homologous compound; homologue, homolog	Homologe n; homologe Verbindung f
homologous lines, homologous pair of lines	homologes Linienpaar n, homologe Linien fpl
homologous points	homologe Punkte mpl
homologous polymeric compound	s. polymer-homologue
homologous series	homologe Reihe f
homologue, homolog; homologous compound	Homologe n; homologe Verbindung f
homology <math., chem., bio.>	Homologie f <Math., Chem., Bio.>
homolytic addition, radical addition	radikalische (homolytische) Addition f
homolytic reactivity	homolytische Reaktivität f
homomerism	Homöomerie f
homometric pair	homometrisches Paar n
homometric structure	homometrische Struktur f
homomorphic, homomorphous <math.>	homomorph, isomorph, meroedrisch (mehrstufig) isomorph <Math.>
homomorphic mapping	s. homomorphism
homomorphic state / in the	zustandshomomorph
homomorphism, homomorphic mapping	Homomorphismus m, homomorphe Abbildung f
homomorphous	s. homomorphic
homonuclear molecule	gleichkerniges Molekül n, homonukleares Molekül
homopause	Homopause f
homophase fluctuation	homophasige Fluktuation f
homophotic image	homophotisches Bild n
homopolar; unipolar <chem., el.>	homöopolar <Chem., El.>; gleichpolig, Gleichpol-, unipolar, Unipolar- <El.>
homopolar binding	s. atomic bond
homopolar bond	s. atomic bond
homopolar compound	s. atomic compound
homopolar crystal	s. atomic crystal
homopolar direct-current generator, homopolar dynamo, homopolar generator	Gleichpolgenerator m, Gleichpol[dynamo]maschine f, Unipolarmaschine f, Unipolargenerator m
homopolar induction	unipolare Induktion f, Unipolarinduktion f, Gleichpolinduktion f
homopolar link[age]	s. atomic bond
homopolar molecule	s. atomic molecule
homopolar region	UM-Gebiet n, unipolares Gebiet n
homopolar valency	s. covalence
homoscedastic	homoskedastisch [verbunden]
homoseismal	Homoseiste f
homosphere	Homosphäre f
homotactic	homotaktisch
homotaxis	Homotaxis f
homotectic, homeotectic	homöotektisch
homothermal, homothermic	s. homeothermal
homothetic <math.>	homothetisch, ähnlich und ähnlich gelegen <Math.>
homothetic ellipse	s. ellipse of correlation
homothetic transformation, transformation of similitude, similitude, similarity transformation <math.>	Homothetie f, Ähnlichkeitsabbildung f, Ähnlichkeitstransformation f <Math.>
homotopic, reconcilable	homotop
homotopy	Homotopie f
homotropic	homotrop
Höner rhomb	Hönersches Parallelepiped n
honeycomb, honeycomb straightener, honeycomb grill <hydr.>	Zellen[körper]gleichrichter m, Wabengleichrichter m, Wabenstruktur f, Stromgleichrichter m, Gleichrichter m <Hydr.>
honeycomb	wabenartig, wabenförmig, Waben-
honeycomb coil, honeycomb-tube coil, duolateral coil	Honigwabenspule f, Kreuzwickelspule f, Waben-[wicklungs]spule f
honeycomb condenser	Wabenkondensor m
honeycomb corrosion	s. tubercular corrosion
honeycombed structure, honeycomb structure	Wabenstruktur f, Honigwabenstruktur f
honeycomb grill	s. honeycomb <hydr.>
honeycombing	s. tubercular corrosion
honeycomb mirror	Wabenspiegel m
honeycomb straightener	s. honeycomb <hydr.>
honeycomb structure, honeycombed structure	Wabenstruktur f, Honigwabenstruktur f
honeycomb-tube coil, honeycomb coil, - duolateral coil	Honigwabenspule f, Kreuzwickelspule f, Waben-[wicklungs]spule f
honeycomb weathering	Wabenverwitterung f

Hönl-Kronig rules	Hönl-Kronigsche Regeln *fpl*	horizontal candle power	s. mean horizontal intensity <opt.>
hood; cap <techn.>	Aufsatz *m*; Haube *f*; Glocke *f*; Kappe *f* <Techn.>	horizontal cast[ing], horizontal throw	horizontaler Wurf *m*, waagerechter Wurf
		horizontal characteristic	Horizontalcharakteristik *f*
hook-collector transistor	s. four-layer transistor	horizontal chromatography	s. circular chromatography
Hookean body	s. perfectly elastic solid		
Hookean deformation	Hookesche Deformation *f*	horizontal circle, horizontal, limb <of theodolite> <astr.>	Horizontalkreis *m*, Horizontal *m*, Limbus *m* <Theodolit> <Astr.>
Hookean solid, Hooke['s] body, Hookeian solid	s. perfectly elastic solid	horizontal-component seismograph	s. horizontal seismograph
Hooke['s] law [of elasticity]	Hookesches Gesetz *n*	horizontal co-ordinates, horizontal system [of co-ordinates]	Horizontalsystem *n*, Azimutsystem *n*, horizontales Koordinatensystem *n*, System *n* des Horizonts, Koordinaten *fpl* im Horizontalsystem, Horizontalkoordinaten *fpl*, horizontale Koordinaten
Hooke potential	Hookesches Potential *n*		
Hooker telescope	Hooker-Teleskop *n*, Hooker-Spiegelteleskop *n*		
Hooke['s] solid	s. perfectly elastic solid		
Hooke['s] tensor	Hookescher Tensor *m*, Tensor der elastischen Konstanten		
hook gauge	Hakenstechpegel *m*	horizontal definition	s. horizontal resolution
		horizontal deflecting electrode	s. horizontal plate
Hookian solid	s. perfectly elastic solid	horizontal deflection, X deflection; horizontal sweep, line sweep, line scanning	Horizontalablenkung *f*, Waagerechtablenkung *f*; X-Ablenkung *f* <Oszillograph>; Zeilenablenkung *f*, Zeilenabtastung *f*, Zeilenkipp *m* <Fs.>
hook method [of Rozhdestvensky]	s. Rozhdestvensky['s] method		
hook-on ammeter, clip-on ammeter	Anlegerstrommesser *m*, Anlegeamperemeter *n*		
hook transistor	s. four-layer transistor		
hoop	Reifen *m*		
hoop drop recorder	s. point recorder	horizontal-deflection amplifier	s. horizontal amplifier
hoop stress	s. tangential stress	horizontal deflection electrode	s. horizontal plate
hop	s. discontinuity		
Hope['s] apparatus	Hopescher Apparat *m*	horizontal-deflection oscillator, horizontal oscillator; horizontal-scanning generator; line oscillator	Horizontal[ablenk]oszillator *m*, Horizontal[ablenk]-generator *m*; Zeilen[ablenk]oszillator *m*, Zeilen[ablenk]generator *m*, Zeilenkippgenerator *m*
Hopf['s] theory of turbulence	Hopfsche Turbulenztheorie *f*		
Hôpital['s] rule / l'	s. Hospital['s] rule / [De] l'		
Hopkinson effect	Hopkinson-Effekt *m*		
Hopkinson['s] law, Ohm['s] law for magnetic circuits, Ohm['s] law of magnetism	Hopkinsonsches Gesetz *n* [des magnetischen Kreises], Ohmsches Gesetz des Magnetismus, Ohmsches Gesetz für magnetische Kreise, magnetisches Ohmsches Gesetz		
		horizontal-deflection plate	s. horizontal plate
		horizontal-deflection unit, horizontal sweep unit, line sweep unit, line deflection set	Horizontalablenkgerät *n*, Zeilenablenkgerät *n*, Zeilenablenkteil *n* (*m*), Zeilenkippgerät *n*, Zeilenkippteil *n* (*m*)
Hopkinson test	Hopkinson-Test *m*		
Hopkins['] oscillator	Hopkins-Generator *m*, Hopkinsscher Generator *m*, Hopkins-Schaltung *f*		
		horizontal deflector	s. horizontal plate
hopping conductivity	„hopping"-Leitfähigkeit *f*	horizontal displacement, horizontal shift <geo.>	Horizontalverschiebung *f*, Blattverschiebung *f*, söhlige Verschiebung *f*, Blatt *n* <Geo.>
hopping model	„hopping"-Modell *n*, Hüpfmodell *n*		
		horizontal distance	Horizontaldistanz *f*, Horizontalabstand *m*
hopping process	„hopping"-Prozeß *m*, Hüpfprozeß *m*	horizontal exchange coefficient	horizontaler Austauschkoeffizient *m*, Gleitaustauschkoeffizient *m*
horizon camera	Horizontkammer *f*	horizontal field balance, H balance	Feldwaage *f* zur Messung der Horizontalintensität, H-Waage *f*
horizon of sources	Quellhorizont *m*		
horizontal	s. isohypse	horizontal-force variometer	s. horizontal-intensity variometer
horizontal	s. horizontal circle <of theodolite> <astr.>	horizontal geomagnetic field strength	s. mean horizontal intensity <geo.>
horizontal adjustment, horizontal and vertical adjustment of the instrument axes	Horizontieren *n*		
		horizontal fringes	Horizontalstreifen *mpl*
		horizontal horopter, transverse horopter	Querhoropter *m*, Horizontalhoropter *m*
		horizontal hunting	Zeilenzittern *n*
horizontal amplifier, horizontal-deflection amplifier; horizontal sweep amplifier, X amplifier, X-axis amplifier; line amplifier	Horizontalverstärker *m*, Horizontalablenkverstärker *m*, X-Verstärker *m*; Zeilen[ablenk]verstärker *m*	horizontal intensity	s. mean horizontal intensity <opt.>; geo.>
		horizontal-intensity variometer, horizontal [-force] variometer, H-variometer	Horizontal[intensitäts]-variometer *n*, H-Variometer *n*
		horizontal line	s. isohypse
		horizontally mounted (operated) camera	s. horizontal camera
horizontal and vertical adjustment of the instrument axes	s. horizontal adjustment	horizontally polarized antenna; ground-plane antenna	„ground-plane"-Antenne *f*; horizontal polarisierte Antenne *f*
horizontal aperture	Horizontalapertur *f*		
horizontal axis, horizontal trunnion axis, trunnion axis <of theodolite>	Kippachse *f*, Horizontalachse *f* <Theodolit>	horizontal magnetic balance	magnetische Horizontalwaage *f*
		horizontal magnetometer, H-magnetometer	H-Magnetometer *n*, Horizontalintensitätsmagnetometer *n*, Horizontalmagnetometer *n*
horizontal axis error	s. error of horizontal axis		
horizontal camera, horizontally operated (mounted) camera	Horizontalkamera *f*		
		horizontal magnification	Horizontaldehnung *f*

horizontal

horizontal oscillator	s. horizontal-deflection oscillator	**horn,** horn[-type] antenna, horn aerial; funnel[-type] antenna, funnel-shaped antenna, inverted-pyramid antenna <el.>	Horn n, Hornantenne f; Hornstrahler m; Trichterantenne f; Trichterstrahler m <El.>
horizontal parallax	Horizontalparallaxe f		
horizontal part of the pulse, pulse tilt, pulse top, top [of the pulse]	Impulsdach n, Dach n		
horizontal pattern, horizontal-plane directional pattern, azimuth radiation pattern	Horizontaldiagramm n, Horizontal-Strahlungsdiagramm n	**horn,** horn loudspeaker, horn-type loudspeaker	Trichterlautsprecher m, Hornlautsprecher m, Trichterstrahler m
		horn aerial (antenna)	s. horn <el.>
		horn arrester; horn lightning arrester	Hörnerableiter m; Hörnerblitzableiter m
horizontal pendulum	Horizontalpendel n	**Hornbostel-Wertheimer effect,** binaural effect	Binauraleffekt m, Hornbostel-Wertheimer-Effekt m
horizontal plane	Horizontebene f, Horizontalebene f		
horizontal-plane directional pattern, horizontal (azimuth radiation) pattern	Horizontaldiagramm n, Horizontal-Strahlungsdiagramm n	**Horner['s] method (process, scheme)**	Hornersches Schema n, Horner-Schema n
		horn-fed paraboloid	Hornparabol n, Hornparabolantenne f, horngespeistes Parabol n
horizontal plate, X plate, horizontal deflecting (deflection) electrode, horizontal deflector, horizontal-deflection plate	Horizontalablenkplatte f, X-Platte f	**horn feed**	Hornspeisung f
		hornito	Spratzkegel m
		hornless loudspeaker	s. direct-radiator loudspeaker
horizontal projection; top view	Horizontalprojektion f; Grundriß m; Draufsicht f	**horn lightning arrester,** horn arrester	Hörnerableiter m; Hörnerblitzableiter m
horizontal refraction	Horizontalrefraktion f, Horizontrefraktion f	**horn loudspeaker,** horn-type loudspeaker, horn	Trichterlautsprecher m, Hornlautsprecher m, Trichterstrahler m
horizontal resolution, horizontal definition	Horizontalauflösung f, Waagerechtauflösung f	**horn mouth**	Trichteröffnung f; Trichtermündung f
		horn of the loudspeaker, loudspeaker horn	Lautsprechertrichter m
		horn throat	Trichterhals m
		horn-type antenna	s. horn <el.>
		horn-type loudspeaker, horn loudspeaker, horn	Trichterlautsprecher m, Hornlautsprecher m, Trichterstrahler m
		horopter, horopter curve, frontal horopter	Horopter m, Horopterkurve f
horizontal scanning, horizontal sweep	Horizontalabtastung f, Horizontalscanning n	**horse latitudes**	s. subtropical calmbelt
horizontal-scanning generator	s. horizontal-deflection oscillator	**horse[-]shoe base**	Hufeisenfuß m
horizontal seismograph, horizontal-component seismograph	Horizontalseismograph m	**horse-shoe magnet**	Hufeisenmagnet m
		horse-shoe mounting	Hufeisenmontierung f, Hale-Teleskop-Montierung f
horizontal shift	s. horizontal displacement <geo.>	**horse-shoe vortex**	Hufeisenwirbel m
horizontal shot, straight-on angle shot	Horizontalaufnahme f, Waagerechtaufnahme f	**hose,** flexible tube (pipe)	Schlauch m
		hospital physics	Krankenhausphysik f; Klinikphysik f
horizontal solar telescope, horizontal telescope	Horizontalteleskop n	**Hospital['s] rule,** Hospital['s] rule / [De] l', Bernoulli-l'Hospital['s] rule, Bernoulli-De-l'Hospital['s] rule, Hôpital['s] rule /l'	[de] l'Hospitalsche Regel f, Bernoulli-[de-]l'Hospitalsche Regel, Regel von [de] l'Hospital, Regel von Bernoulli-[de-] L'Hospital
horizontal stratification	horizontale (schwebende; söhlige) Schichtung f		
horizontal sweep, horizontal scanning	Horizontalabtastung f, Horizontalscanning n		
horizontal sweep	s. a. horizontal deflection	**host,** host material	Wirt[s]substanz f, Grundsubstanz f, Wirt[s]material n, Grundmaterial n, Wirt m
horizontal sweep amplifier	s. horizontal amplifier		
horizontal sweep unit	s. horizontal-deflection unit	**host atom**	Wirt[s]atom n
horizontal system [of co-ordinates]	s. horizontal co-ordinates	**host crystal,** oikocryst	Wirt[s]kristall m, Grundkristall m, Mutterkristall m
horizontal telescope, horizontal solar telescope	Horizontalteleskop n		
horizontal throw, horizontal cast[ing]	horizontaler Wurf m, waagerechter Wurf	**host crystal lattice,** matrix (fundamental) lattice, lattice	Grundgitter n, Wirtsgitter n
horizontal thrust of arch, thrust of arch	Horizontalschub (Seitenschub) m des Bogens		
horizontal trunnion axis, horizontal axis, trunnion axis <of theodolite>	Kippachse f, Horizontalachse f <Theodolit>	**host material,** host	Wirt[s]substanz f, Grundsubstanz f, Wirt[s]material n, Grundmaterial n, Wirt m
horizontal variometer	s. horizontal-intensity variometer	**hot,** highly radioactive, high-level <nucl.>	heiß, hochaktiv, hochgradig radioaktiv, stark radioaktiv <Kern.>
horizontal visibility [distance]	horizontale Sichtweite f, Horizontalsicht f, horizontale Sicht f	**hot activity**	s. high-level activity
		hot age hardening	s. hot work hardening
		hot-air engine, thermomotor	Heißluftmotor m, Heißluftmaschine f
horn, acoustic horn, sound funnel <ac.>	Schalltrichter m, Trichter m <Ak.>		

hot atom	heißes Atom n, hochangeregtes Atom	hot source (spa)	s. thermal spring
hot-atom chemistry, hot chemistry, recoil chemistry	heiße Chemie f, Chemie hochangeregter (hochradioaktiver, heißer) Atome, Rückstoßchemie f, Heiße-Atom-Chemie f, Chemie der Rückstoßatome	hot-spark technique	Methode f der heißen Funken
		hot spot <nucl.>	heiße Stelle f <Kern.>
		hot spot	s. a. hot point
		hot spot factor; hot channel factor <nucl.>	Überlastfaktor m; Kühlkanalfaktor m, Unsicherheitsfaktor m der Kanalüberhitzung <Kern.>
"hot" band	„heiße" Bande f „hot band" f	hot spring	s. thermal spring
hot-brittle, hot brittleness	s. hot-short s. hot shortness	hot stage [of microscope]; heating stage [of microscope]	Heiztisch m, Mikroskopheiztisch m
hot-carrier diode, Schottky barrier diode	Schottky-Barriere-Diode f, Metall-Halbleiter-Diode f	hot-start lamp	Glühstartlampe f, Warmstartlampe f
hot cathode, thermionic cathode, incandescent cathode, glow[ing] cathode	Glühkatode f	hot straightening	Warmrichten n
		hot straining, hot drawing down	Warmrecken n
		hot test	s. heat test
		hot trap	Warmfalle f
hot-cathode discharge, semi-self-sustained discharge	Glühkatodenentladung f, halbselbständige Entladung f	hot up[-]set [forging], hot up[-]setting, hot crimping	Warmstauchung f
hot-cathode lamp	Glühkatodenlampe f	hot waste, high-level waste	hochaktiver Abfall m, heißer Abfall
hot-cathode tube (valve), thermionic tube, thermionic valve	Glühkatodenröhre f, Glühkatodenrohr n	hot weather <meteo.>	Hitze f <Meteo.>
		hot wire, heated wire, heating wire	Hitzdraht m, Heißdraht m, Heizdraht m
hot cave, hot cell	heiße Zelle f, heiße Kammer f	hot wire	s. a. Pirani gauge
		hot-wire anemometer	s. hot-wire velocity meter
hot channel effect	Kanalüberhitzung f	hot-wire galvanometer, thermo[-]galvanometer, thermocouple[-type] galvanometer	Thermogalvanometer n, Hitzdrahtgalvanometer n
hot channel factor, hot factor <nucl.>	Überlastfaktor m; Kühlkanalfaktor m, Unsicherheitsfaktor m der Kanalüberhitzung <Kern.>	hot-wire gauge	s. Pirani gauge
		hot-wire ignition	Glühdrahtzündung f
hot chemistry	s. hot-atom chemistry	hot-wire instrument, expansion instrument	Hitzdrahtinstrument n, Hitzdrahtmeßgerät n; Hitzdrahtmeßwerk n
Hotchkiss super-dip	Feldwaage f nach Hotchkiss, Hotchkiss-Waage f		
hot crack, heating crack, heat crack	Temperaturriß m, Warmriß m, Wärmeriß m, Vielhärtungsriß m	hot-wire manometer	s. Pirani gauge
		hot[-] wire microphone, thermal microphone, thermomicrophone	Hitzdrahtmikrophon n, thermisches Mikrophon n, Thermomikrophon n
hot crimping, hot up[-]set [forging], hot up[-]setting	Warmstauchung f		
hot critical	heißkritisch	hot[-] wire process (technique)	s. Arkel process / Van
hot day	heißer Tag m		
hot drawing	Warmziehen n	hot-wire velocity meter, hot-wire anemometer	Hitzdrahtanemometer n, Hitzdrahtwindmesser m
hot drawing down	s. hot straining		
hot ductility	Warmbiegsamkeit f		
		hot workability	Warmumformbarkeit f, Warm[ver]formbarkeit f
hot electrode	Glühelektrode f	hot-work hardening, hot age hardening, age hardening at elevated temperature[s], ageing with increased temperatures <of metals>	Warmhärtung f, Warmverfestigung f <Metalle>
Hotelling['s] distribution, Hotelling['s] generalized Student distribution; Hotelling['s] T, T² distribution	Hotelling-Verteilung f; Hotellings T n, T²-Verteilung f		
hot hardening <of plastics>, heat hardening	Warm[aus]härtung f, Wärmehärtung f, Heißhärtung f, Hitzehärtung f <Kunststoffe>	hot working	Warmbearbeitung f, Warmbehandlung f
		hot working, heat forming	Warmumformung f, Warmformgebung f, Warm[ver]formung f, Warmformverfahren n
hot hardness	Warmhärte f	hour, h, hr.	Stunde f, h, Std.
		hour, time	Uhrzeit f, Uhr f, h
hot junction	heiße (warme) Lötstelle f, Heißlötstelle f	hour [angle], sideral hour angle	Stundenwinkel m
hot laboratory	heißes Labor[atorium] n	hour axis, polar axis <astr.>	Stundenachse f, Pol[ar]achse f, Rektaszensionsachse f <Astr.>
hotness; heat; warmth <gen.; geo.>	Wärme f <allg.; Geo.>	hour circle, right ascension circle	Stundenkreis m, Himmelsmeridian f
hot point, hot spot	Wärmestaustelle f, Wärmenest n, Wärmepunkt m	hour-glass	Sanduhr f
hot probe	Glühsonde f	hourly average (mean)	Stundenmittel n
hot quenching	s. martempering	hourly rate of meteors	s. rate of shooting stars
hot-short, hot-brittle; red-short	warmbrüchig, rotbrüchig	housing; case, casing; box	Gehäuse n
hot shortness, hot brittleness; red shortness	Warmbrüchigkeit f, Warmsprödigkeit f; Rotbrüchigkeit f; Rotbruch m	Houston function	Houstonsche Funktion f
		hovercraft; air-cushion craft (vehicle), ACV; surface-effect ship	Luftkissenboot n; Luftkissenfahrzeug n

hovering [flight]	Schweben n, Schwebeflug m	Hugoniot relation	Hugoniotsche Beziehung f
Hove space-time correlation function / Van	Van-Hove-Raum-Zeit-Korrelationsfunktion f	Hugoniot['s] theorem	Hugoniotscher Satz m
		hula-loop antenna, ring antenna, ring dipole	Ringdipol m, Ringantenne f, Ringdipolantenne f
		Hull diagram	Hull-Diagramm n
Howarth transformation	Howarthsche Transformation f, Howarth-Transformation f	Hull magnetron	Hull-Magnetron n, Hullsches Magnetron n
howl[ing], acoustical feedback; fringe howl	akustische Rückkopplung (Rückwirkung) f; Rückkopplungspfeifen n, Pfeifen n	hull of the ship, ship hull	Schiffskörper m, Schiffsrumpf m, Körper (Rumpf) m des Schiffes
howl[ing] <ac.>	Heulen n <Ak.>	Hulthén function, Hulthén-type function	Funktion f vom Hulthénschen Typ, Hulthénsche Funktion
howling sound (tone), gauze sound	Heulton m	Hulthén potential	Hulthén-Potential n
h-parameter, hybrid parameter	Hybridparameter m, h-Parameter m	Hulthén-type function, Hulthén function	Funktion f vom Hulthénschen Typ, Hulthénsche Funktion
H particle	s. proton		
H plane bend	H-Ebenen-Biegung f	hum; ripple; alternating-current (mains line, power line) hum	Brumm m, Brummen n; Netzbrumm m, Netzbrummen n
H process	s. proton-proton reaction		
H ray	s. proton beam		
H-R diagram	s. Hertzsprung-Russell diagram	human-body counter (radiation meter, spectrometer)	s. whole-body counter
H I region	H I-Gebiet n		
H II region, H+ region, Strömgren sphere	H II-Gebiet n, Wasserstoff-Emissionsgebiet n	hum due to emission	Emissionsbrummen n, Emissionsbrumm m
H-S diagram, enthalpy-entropy diagram [of R. Mollier], Mollier['s] enthalpy-entropy diagram, Mollier['s] diagram, Mollier['s] chart, enthalpy-entropy chart	Mollier-Diagramm n, Molliersches Diagramm n, Enthalpie-Entropie-Diagramm n [von R. Mollier], J,S-Diagramm n, JS-Diagramm n, Mollier-Enthalpie-Entropie-Diagramm n	humectant	Feuchthaltemittel n
		Hume-Rothery phase	Hume-Rothery-Phase f, Hume-Rothersche Phase f
		Hume-Rothery rule, 8-N rule	Hume-Rothersche Regel f
		hum factor, ripple factor (ratio), hum level, percentage ripple voltage	Brummabstand m, Brummfaktor m, Brummspannungsverhältnis n
H-section	s. H-network		
H-section filter, H-type filter, H-filter	H-Filter n	hum frequency, frequency of ripple	Brummfrequenz f
Hα spectroheliogram, hydrogen Hα line spectroheliogram, hydrogen spectroheliogram	Hα-Spektroheliogramm n, Wasserstoff-Spektroheliogramm n	humid <of climate>	humid; vollhumid <Klima>
		humid heat	feuchte Wärme f
H-theorem [of Boltzmann and Lorentz], Boltzmann's H-theorem	Boltzmannsches H-Theorem n, H-Theorem n, Boltzmannscher H-Satz m	humidification, moistening, wetting, dampening	Befeuchtung f, Anfeuchtung f; Durchfeuchtung f; Netzung f; Benetzung f
H-type filter	s. H-section filter		
H-type network, H-network, H-section	H-Schaltung f	humidistat	Humidistat m, Feuchteregler m, Feuchtigkeitsregler m
Hubble['s] constant, expansion constant	Hubble-Konstante f, Hubblesche Konstante f, Expansionskonstante f	humidity; wetness; wet humidity <of climate>	Nässe f Humidität f <Klima>
Hubble['s] effect	s. red shift		
Hubble['s] law, velocity-distance relation	Hubblesches Gesetz n, Hubblesche Beziehung f, Geschwindigkeit-Abstand-Beziehung f	humidity <of air, atmosphere>; moisture content; damp; moisture <of a substance>	Feuchte f, Feuchtigkeit f; Feuchtigkeitsgehalt m, Feuchtegehalt m
Hubble['s] red-shift	s. red shift	humidity-mixing ratio, mixing ratio <meteo.>	Mischungsverhältnis n, spezifische Mengenfeuchtigkeit f <Meteo.>
Huber-Mises-Hencky yield criterion	s. Mises-Hencky flow condition		
Hübl number	Hübl-Zahl f	humidor	Feuchtlagerraum m, Lagerraum m konstanter Luftfeuchte
Hückel['s] approximation	Hückelsche Approximation (Näherung) f		
hue, quality <of colour>	Farbton m, Ton m [der Farbe], Qualität f <Farbe>	humid snow avalanche; ground avalanche	Feuchtschneelawine f; Naßschneelawine f, nasse Lawine f; Grundlawine f
hue[d] colour	s. chromatic colour		
hueless colour	s. achromatic colour	humid temperature	s. wet-bulb reading
hue ray	Farbtonstrahl m	hum level	s. hum factor
Huet prism	Huetsches Prisma n	Hummel circuit	Hummel-Schaltung f
Huggins band	Huggins-Bande f	hummock	Hummock m
Huggins-Bingham formula	Huggins-Binghamsche Formel f	hummocked ice, old pack, pack, pack-ice	Packeis n
Hughes relay	Hughes-Relais n		
Hugoniot	s. Rankine-Hugoniot curve	hump <of the curve>	Buckel m, Höcker m <Kurve>
Hugoniot adiabatic curve [for detonations and deflagrations]	Hugoniotsche Verbrennungskurve f	Humphreys series	Humphreys-Serie f
		Humphries['] equation	Humphriessche Gleichung f
Hugoniot curve	s. Rankine-Hugoniot curve	Hund['s] cases, Hund['s] coupling cases <a to e>, coupling cases [in molecular spectra]	Hundsche Fälle (Kopplungsfälle) mpl, Kopplungsfälle (Kopplungsverhältnisse npl) nach Hund <a bis e>
Hugoniot curve for condensation shock, adiabatic curve of condensation, condensation adiabat	Kondensationsadiabate f, Hugoniotsche Kurve f für Kondensationsstoß		
		Hund-Mulliken-Hückel method	s. molecular orbitals method
Hugoniot-Duhem theorem	Hugoniot-Duhemscher Satz m	Hund-Mulliken-Lennard Jones-Hückel theory	s. molecular orbital theory
Hugoniot-elastic limit	Hugoniot-elastische Grenze f, HEL, dynamische Elastizitätsgrenze f	hundredth-normal, centinormal 0.01 N, N/100	hundertstelnormal, zentinormal, 0,01 n, n/100
Hugoniot equation	Hugoniot-Gleichung f		

hundredth-normal solution, centinormal solution, 0.01 N solution
Hundertstelnormallösung f, 0,01 n Lösung f

hundredth-value layer, hundredth value thickness
Hundertstelwertschicht [-dicke] f, Hundertstelwert[s]breite f, Hundertstelwertdicke f

Hund['s] rule Hundsche Regel f
hunting, cycling, cycling movement
Pendelung f <um die Gleichgewichtslage, um den Mittelwert>

hunting Schwingneigung f, Schwingungsneigung f
hunting s. a. overshoot <control>
hunting electron s. oscillating electron
hunting of temperature s. temperature fluctuation
hurricane <Atlantic and Caribbean>; tropical cyclone (revolving storm), cyclone; typhoon <West Pacific>; willy-willy <Australia>
tropischer Wirbelsturm m, Wirbelsturm, Zyklon m; Hurrikan m; Taifun m; Willy-Willy m

hurricane <of Beaufort No. 12> Orkan m <Stärke 12>
hurricane path, path of the hurricane
Asgardweg m, Asgardsweg m, zerstörende Bahn f der Trombe

Hurst dosimeter, Hurst-type dosimeter
Hurst-Dosimeter n, Dosimeter n vom Hurst-Typ

Hurter and Driffield curve, Hurter-Driffield curve
s. characteristic curve <phot.>

Hurter-Driffield degree Hurter-Driffield-Grad m

Hurwitz['s] criterion [of stability], stability criterion of Hurwitz
Hurwitzsches Stabilitätskriterium (Kriterium) n, Stabilitätskriterium nach Hurwitz, Hurwitz-Stabilitätskriterium n, Hurwitz-Kriterium n, Kriterium von Hurwitz

Hurwitz['] equation Hurwitzsche Gleichung f
Huth-Kühn oscillation Huth-Kühn-Schwingung f
Huth-Kühn oscillator Huth-Kühn-Schaltung f

Huyghenian eyepiece, Huyghens['] eyepiece, negative eyepiece
Huygenssches Okular n, Huygens-Okular n, negatives Okular, Okular nach Huygens

Huyghens['] construction
Huygenssche Konstruktion (Enveloppenkonstruktion) f, Huygens' Konstruktion

Huyghens['] equation Huygenssche Differentialgleichung f

Huyghens['] eyepiece, Huyghenian eyepiece, negative eyepiece
Huygenssches Okular n, Huygens-Okular n, negatives Okular, Okular nach Huygens

Huyghens-Fresnel principle s. Fresnel['s] principle
Huyghens['] pendulum, cycloid[al] pendulum
Zykloidenpendel n

Huyghens['] principle Huygenssches Prinzip n, Huygens' Prinzip, Huygensscher Satz m

Huyghens['] source Huygenssche Quelle f, Quellpunkt m der Elementarwellen, [elementare] Huygenssche Strahlungsquelle f

Huyghens['] tensor Huygensscher Tensor m
Huyghens tractory, tractrix, tractory of Huyghens
Traktrix f, Schleppkurve f, Traktorie f von Huygens, Hundekurve f

Huyghens['] undulation theory s. wave theory of light

Huyghens['] vectorial principle, vectorial Huyghens['] principle
vektorielles Huygenssches Prinzip n

Huyghens wavelet s. elementary wave
Huyghens['] zone s. Fresnel zone
H-variometer, horizontal-intensity (horizontal [force]) variometer
Horizontal[intensitäts]variometer n, H-Variometer n

H-vector s. magnetic field vector
H[-] wave s. H[-] mode
hyaline, vitrophyric glasig, hyalin, vitrophyrisch

hyalocrystalline hyalokristallin[isch]
hybrid, junction point, junction <of waveguides>
Verzweigung[sstelle] f, Verzweigungspunkt m <Wellenleiter>

hybrid s. hybrid orbital <qu.>
hybrid binding, hybrid bond
Hybridbindung f, Zwitterbindung f

hybrid circuit, discrete-component circuit
Hybridschaltung f, hybride Schaltung f

hybrid computer, analog-digital computer
Hybridrechner m, Analog-Digital-Rechner m, kombinierte Rechenmaschine f

hybrid field hybrides Feld n, Hybridfeld n
hybrid four-terminal network, hybrid network
Hybridvierpol m

hybrid function Hybridfunktion f
hybrid ion, amphoteric ion, zwitterion, dipolar ion, dual ion, amphion, inner salt
Zwitterion n, amphoteres Ion n, Ampho-Ion n

hybridization, hybridizing <qu.>
Hybridisierung f, Hybridisation f, Bastardisierung f, Mischung f von Valenzzuständen <Qu.>

hybridized orbital s. hybrid orbital
hybrid junction hybride Kopplung (Verbindung) f, Hybridkopplung f, hybrider Übergang m, Hybridübergang m, Hybridverbindung f, „hybrid junction" n

hybrid matrix, h-matrix Hybridmatrix f, h-Matrix f
hybrid mode s. hybrid wave
hybrid network, hybrid four-terminal network
Hybridvierpol m

hybrid orbital, hybridized orbital, hybrid <qu.>
hybrid[isiert]es Orbital n, Hybrid[orbital] n, Zwitterorbital n <Qu.>

hybrid parameter, h-parameter
Hybridparameter m, h-Parameter m

hybrid resonance Hybridresonanz f
hybrid T, hybrid tee [junction], hybrid T [waveguide] junction
s. magic T

hybrid wave, mixed wave; hybrid mode, mixed mode, HE[-]mode
hybride Welle f, Hybridwelle f, HE-Welle f; hybride Mode f, Hybridmode f, gemischter Wellentyp (Schwingungstyp) m, gemischte Mode, HE-Mode f

hydatogenesis Hydatogenese f
hydatogenic hydatogen
hydratation s. hydration
hydrated form Hydratform f
hydrated ion, aquo-ion Hydration n, Ionenhydrat n
hydrate envelope Hydrathülle f
hydrate isomerism Hydratisomerie f
hydrate water s. water of hydration
hydratic weathering allitische (hydratische) Verwitterung f

hydration, hydratization, hydratation, combination with water
Hydratation f, Hydratisierung f, Hydration f, Wasseranlagerung f

hydration-dehydration theory
Hydratations-Dehydratations-Theorie f

hydration heat s. heat of hydration
hydration number, hydration value
Hydratationszahl f

hydration series Hydratationsreihe f
hydration value s. hydration number
hydration water s. water of hydration
hydratization s. hydration
hydrature Hydratur f
hydraulically equivalent diameter s. hydraulic diameter
hydraulically rough, rough <hydr.>
rauh, hydraulisch rauh <Hydr.>

hydraulically   342

hydraulically smooth, smooth ‹hydr.› — glatt, hydraulisch glatt ‹Hydr.›

hydraulic analogy — hydraulisches Analogon n, hydraulische Analogie f
hydraulic clutch — s. hydraulic coupling
hydraulic conductivity — Strömungsleitfähigkeit f, hydraulische Leitfähigkeit f
hydraulic conductivity, permeability [coefficient] ‹in Darcy's law› — Durchlässigkeit f ‹im Darcyschen Gesetz›
hydraulic coupling, fluid coupling, hydraulic clutch — Strömungskupplung f, hydraulische (hydrodynamische) Kupplung f, Flüssigkeitskupplung f
hydraulic diameter, [hydraulically] equivalent diameter — hydraulischer (gleichwertiger, äquivalenter) Durchmesser m
hydraulic discriminant, characteristic hydraulic number — hydraulische Kennzahl f
hydraulic dynamometer — hydraulisches Dynamometer n, hydraulischer Zugkraftmesser m
hydraulic efficiency — hydraulischer Wirkungsgrad m

hydraulic friction — hydraulische Reibung f
hydraulic friction factor — s. resistance coefficient ‹hydr.›
hydraulic friction formula — s. Darcy's law
hydraulic grade, hydraulic gradient ‹hydr.› — Druckgefälle n, Gefäll[s]verlust m, [relatives] Gefälle n, hydraulischer Gradient m, hydraulisches Gefälle ‹Hydr.›
hydraulic head, hydraulic pressure head — hydraulische Höhe f, Strömungsenergie f ‹Energiekonstante in der Bernoullischen Gleichung›
hydraulic head, water column pressure — Wassersäulendruck m
hydraulic jump, water jump — Wassersprung m, hydraulischer Sprung m, Wasserschwall m, Wechselsprung m
hydraulic loss — hydraulischer Verlust m
hydraulic mean depth — s. hydraulic radius
hydraulic module (modulus) — hydraulischer Modul m
hydraulic power — s. water power
hydraulic pressure — hydraulischer Druck m
hydraulic pressure head — s. hydraulic head
hydraulic radius, mean hydraulic depth, hydraulic mean depth — hydraulischer Radius m, Profilradius m, Umfangstiefe f
hydraulic ram, water ram — hydraulischer Widder m, Stoßheber m

hydraulic resistance, flow resistance, flow drag, resistance to flow, resistance, hydraulic resistivity, resistance to liquid flow ‹hydr.› — Strömungswiderstand m, hydrodynamischer Widerstand m, hydraulischer Widerstand, Fließwiderstand m, Widerstand ‹Hydr.›

hydraulic resistance, local feature ‹hydr.› — einzelnes Hindernis n, Einzelhindernis n ‹Hydr.›
hydraulic resistivity — spezifischer Strömungswiderstand (hydraulischer Widerstand) m
hydraulic resistivity — s. a. hydraulic resistance ‹hydr.›
hydraulics — Hydraulik f, Hydrodynamik f des Stromfadens ‹eindimensionale Strömungslehre›

hydraulic screw, water screw — Wasserschraube f, Wasserschnecke f
hydraulic seal — s. liquid seal
hydraulic shock — hydraulischer Stoß m
hydraulic tachometer, velocity-head tachometer — Staudrucktachometer n

hydraulic test, water-pressure test, water test — Wasser[druck]prüfung f, Wasser[druck]probe f, Wasser[druck]versuch m, Druckwasserprüfung f, Druckwasserprobe f, hydraulische Probe f

hydrion — s. hydrogen ion
hydroacoustic range finder, hydrolocator — Unterwasser-Schallortungsgerät n

hydroacoustics, hydro-acoustics, underwater acoustics — Hydroakustik f, Unterwasserakustik f, Unterwasserschallehre f; Wasserschalltechnik f
hydroacoustic wave — hydroakustische Welle f
hydroballistics — Hydroballistik f, Unterwasserballistik f
hydrocal — hydrodynamischer Simulator m

hydrodiascope ‹opt.› — Hydrodiaskop n, Wasserkammer f ‹Opt.›
hydroduct — Troposphärenkanal m, der sich durch Feuchtigkeitsänderungen ausgebildet hat
hydrodynamical analogy, hydrodynamical analogy in torsion — hydrodynamische Analogie f, hydrodynamisches Analogon (Gleichnis, Ähnlichkeitsgesetz) n, Strömungsgleichnis n
hydrodynamical derivative — s. material derivative
hydrodynamical equation — hydrodynamische Bewegungsgleichung f
hydrodynamical model [of the nucleus], hydrodynamical nuclear model, two-liquid model [of the nucleus], two-liquid nuclear model — hydrodynamisches Modell n [des Atomkerns], hydrodynamisches Kernmodell n, Zweiflüssigkeitenmodell n [des Atomkerns]
hydrodynamic approximation — hydrodynamische Näherung f [des kollektiven Modells], kollektives Tröpfchenmodell n
hydrodynamic buoyancy, vertical hydrodynamic force — hydrodynamischer Auftrieb m
hydrodynamic density — hydrodynamische Dichte f
hydrodynamic effect — hydrodynamischer Effekt m
hydrodynamic force — hydrodynamische Kraft f
hydrodynamic friction — s. fluid friction
hydrodynamic fundamental equation — s. equation of hydrodynamics
hydrodynamic long-range force, long-range hydrodynamic force — hydrodynamische Fernkraft f, Bjerknes-Kraft f
hydrodynamic paradox [of d'Alembert], d'Alembert's paradox, Euler-d'Alembert paradox, paradox of Euler and d'Alembert — hydrodynamisches Paradoxon n [von d'Alembert], [Euler-]d'Alembertsches Paradoxon, Paradoxon von Euler und d'Alembert, Dirichletsches Paradoxon
hydrodynamic potential — hydrodynamisches Potential n
hydrodynamic pressure — hydrodynamischer Druck m
hydrodynamic pressure — s. a. dynamic pressure
hydrodynamic radiation — hydrodynamische Strahlung f
hydrodynamic spectrum — hydrodynamisches Spektrum n
hydrodynamic velocity — hydrodynamische Geschwindigkeit f
hydroelectric cell, wet cell — nasses Element n, Naßelement n, hydroelektrisches Element

hydroelectrometer — Hydroelektrometer n
hydroenergetic — hydroenergetisch
hydrofoil — Wasserflügel m, Unterwasserflügel m; Tragflügelboot n

hydrogel — Hydrogel n
hydrogen alpha line, Hα line [of hydrogen], H$_a$ line [of hydrogen] — H$_a$-Linie f [des Wasserstoffs], Hα-Linie f [des Wasserstoffs], Wasserstoff-Alpha-Linie f

hydrogen

hydrogen analyzer, hydrogen gas analyzer	Wasserstoffmesser *m*
hydrogen arc	Wasserstoffbogen *m*, Wasserstoff-Lichtbogen *m*
hydrogenation, hydrogenizing	Hydrierung *f*, Wasserstoffanlagerung *f*
hydrogen atmosphere, atmosphere of hydrogen	Wasserstoffatmosphäre *f*
hydrogen atom transfer [reaction], proton transfer reaction	Protontransferreaktion *f*, Wasserstoffatom-Transferreaktion *f*
hydrogen attack, hydrogen evolution corrosion	Wasserstoffkorrosion *f*
hydrogen blister	s. pitting
hydrogen blistering, hydrogen embrittlement	Wasserstoffporenbildung *f*, Wasserstoffversprödung *f*
hydrogen bond, H-bond; hydrogen bridge bond; hydrogen bridge, H-bridge	Wasserstoffbindung *f*; Wasserstoffbrückenbindung *f*; Wasserstoffbrücke *f*, H-Brücke *f*, Protonbrücke *f*
hydrogen bond association, association by hydrogen bonds	Wasserstoffbrückenassoziation *f*
hydrogen bridge	s. hydrogen bond
hydrogen brittleness, hydrogen embrittlement	Wasserstoffsprödigkeit *f*
hydrogen [bubble] chamber, hydrogen-filled bubble chamber, HBC	Wasserstoff-Blasenkammer *f*
hydrogen chamber, hydrogen-filled cloud chamber	wasserstoffgefüllte Nebelkammer *f*, Wasserstoff-Nebelkammer *f*
hydrogen cloud	Wasserstoffwolke *f*, Wolke *f* von interstellarem Wasserstoff
hydrogen containing, hydrogenous	wasserstoffhaltig
hydrogen-containing shield	wasserstoffhaltige Abschirmung *f*
hydrogen convection zone	Wasserstoff-Konvektionszone *f*
hydrogen disease	Wasserstoffkrankheit *f*
hydrogen electrode, hydrogen gas electrode	Wasserstoffelektrode *f*
hydrogen embrittlement, hydrogen brittleness	Wasserstoffsprödigkeit *f*
hydrogen embrittlement	s. a. hydrogen blistering
hydrogen equivalent	Wasserstoffäquivalent *n*
hydrogen evolution	Wasserstoffentwicklung *f*
hydrogen evolution corrosion, hydrogen attack	Wasserstoffkorrosion *f*
hydrogen exchange [reaction]	Wasserstoffaustausch[reaktion *f*] *m*
hydrogen exponent	s. pH
hydrogen-filled bubble chamber	s. hydrogen bubble chamber
hydrogen-filled cloud chamber, hydrogen chamber	wasserstoffgefüllte Nebelkammer *f*, Wasserstoff-Nebelkammer *f*
hydrogen-filled discharge lamp	s. hydrogen lamp
hydrogen flame detector	Wasserstoffflammendetektor *m*
hydrogen flocculi	Wasserstoffflocculi *mpl*
hydrogen form, H form	H-Form *f*, Wasserstoffform *f*
hydrogen gas analyzer, hydrogen analyzer	Wasserstoffmesser *m*
hydrogen gas electrode, hydrogen electrode	Wasserstoffelektrode *f*
hydrogen glow discharge	Wasserstoffglimmentladung *f*
hydrogen half-cell	Wasserstoffhalbzelle *f*
hydrogen-helium-metal ratio	Häufigkeitsverhältnis *n* Wasserstoff:Helium:Metalle
hydrogen Hα line spectroheliogram, Hα-spectroheliogram, hydrogen spectroheliogram	H_α-Spektroheliogramm *n*, Wasserstoff-Spektroheliogramm *n*
hydrogen index	s. pH
hydrogen ion, hydrion	Wasserstoffion *n*
hydrogen ion activity	Wasserstoffionenaktivität *f*, Protonenaktivität *f*, Hydroniumionenaktivität *f*
hydrogen ion concentration	Wasserstoffionenkonzentration *f*
hydrogen ion exponent	s. pH
hydrogenizing	s. hydrogenation
hydrogen lamp, hydrogen-filled discharge lamp	Wasserstoff[-Entladungs]lampe *f*, Wasserstoffstrahler *m*, Wasserstoff-Gasentladungslampe *f*, Wasserstoff-Entladungsrohr *n*, Wasserstoff-Entladungsröhre *f*
hydrogen-like atom; hydrogen-like ion	wasserstoffähnliches Atom (Ion) *n*
hydrogen-like function, hydrogen-like wave function	wasserstoffähnliche Wellenfunktion *f*
hydrogen-like ion, hydrogen-like atom	wasserstoffähnliches Atom (Ion) *n*
hydrogen-like spectrum	wasserstoffähnliches Spektrum *n*
hydrogen-like system, one-electron system, lone electron	Ein[zel]elektronensystem *n*, wasserstoffähnliches System *n*
hydrogen-like wave function, hydrogen-like function	wasserstoffähnliche Wellenfunktion *f*
hydrogen line, line of hydrogen	Wasserstofflinie *f*
hydrogen liquefaction	Wasserstoffverflüssigung *f*
hydrogen liquefier	Wasserstoffverflüssiger *m*
hydrogen nebula	Wasserstoffnebel *m*
hydrogen nucleus	Wasserstoffkern *m*
hydrogen number	s. pH
hydrogenolysis	Hydrogenolyse *f*
hydrogenous, hydrogen-containing	wasserstoffhaltig
hydrogen overpotential (overtension, overvoltage)	Wasserstoffüberspannung *f*, Überspannung *f* des Wasserstoffs
hydrogen-oxygen fuel cell, hydrox cell	Wasserstoff-Sauerstoff-Brennstoffelement *n*
hydrogen peroxide theory	Wasserstoffperoxidtheorie *f*
hydrogen promotion	Begünstigung *f* durch Wasserstoff
hydrogen radius	Wasserstoffradius *m*
hydrogen reaction, hydrogen thermonuclear reaction	thermonukleare Reaktion *f* mit Wasserstoffisotopen, Wasserstoffbombenreaktion *f*, Wasserstoffbombenprozeß *m*, Wasserstoff[-Kern]reaktion *f*
hydrogen scale [of temperature]	s. international hydrogen scale
hydrogen [spectral] series	Wasserstoffserie *f*
hydrogen spectroheliogram, Hα spectroheliogram, hydrogen Hα line spectroheliogram	H_α-Spektroheliogramm *n*, Wasserstoff-Spektroheliogramm *n*
hydrogen spectrum	Wasserstoffspektrum *n*
hydrogen standard electrode	s. standard hydrogen electrode
hydrogen target; proton target	Wasserstofftarget *n*; Protonentarget *n*

hydrogen 344

hydrogen temperature, Wasserstofftemperatur f
  liquid hydrogen
  temperature
hydrogen term Wasserstoffterm m
hydrogen thermonuclear s. hydrogen reaction
  reaction
hydrogen thyratron Wasserstoffthyratron n, Wasserstoffthyratronröhre f, Wasserstoffstromtor n
hydrogen transfer Wasserstofftransfer m, Wasserstoffübertragung f
hydrogen-unlike, wasserstoffunähnlich
  unhydrogen-like
hydrogen valence s. valency
hydrogen voltameter Wasserstoffcoulometer n, Wasserstoffvoltameter n
hydrography; hydrology Gewässerkunde f; Hydrologie f; Hydrographie f, Lehre f vom Oberflächenwasser
hydroisobath Hydroisobathe f
hydroisohypse Hydroisohypse f
hydrokinematics Hydrokinematik f
hydrokinetics Hydrokinetik f
hydrol Hydrol n
hydrolocation, Unterwasserschallortung f, Unterwasserortung f
  subaqueous sound
  ranging
hydrolocator, hydroacoustic range finder Unterwasser-Schallortungsgerät n
hydrological year Abflußjahr n
hydrologic cycle Kreislauf m des Wassers, Wasserkreislauf m
hydrology; hydrography Gewässerkunde f; Hydrologie f; Hydrographie f, Lehre f vom Oberflächenwasser
hydrolysate, hydrolyzate Hydrolysat n, Hydrolyseprodukt n
hydrolysis, hydrolyzation, aquolysis Hydrolyse f; Aquatisierung f
hydrolysis constant Hydrolysenkonstante f
hydrolyte Hydrolyt m
hydrolytic decomposition hydrolytische Zerlegung f, Zerlegung durch Hydrolyse
hydrolytic destruction of polymers hydrolytischer Abbau m von Polymeren
hydrolytic weathering hydrolytische Verwitterung f; water repellency
hydrolyzate s. hydrolysate
hydrolyzation, hydrolysis, aquolysis Hydrolyse f; Aquatisierung f
hydromagnetic, magnetohydrodynamic, MHD, M.H.D., m.h.d., MH, M.H., m.h. magnetohydrodynamisch, hydromagnetisch, MHD, magnetofluidodynamisch
hydromagnetic dynamo, magnetohydrodynamic dynamo magnetohydrodynamischer Dynamo m, hydromagnetischer Dynamo, MHD-Dynamo m
hydromagnetic equations s. magnetohydrodynamic equations
hydromagnetic instability s. magnetohydrodynamic instability
hydromagnetics, magnetohydrodynamics Magnetohydrodynamik f, Hydromagnetik f, Magnetofluidodynamik f
hydromagnetic shock wave s. magnetohydrodynamic shock wave
hydromagnetic wake, magnetohydrodynamic wake magnetohydrodynamischer Nachlauf m
hydromagnetic wave, magnetohydrodynamic wave, MHD wave, m.h.d. wave magnetohydrodynamische Welle f, hydromagnetische Welle, MHD-Welle f
hydromechanical similarity hydromechanische Ähnlichkeit f
hydromechanics Hydromechanik f
hydrometallurgy Naßmetallurgie f, Hydrometallurgie f

hydrometamorphism Hydrometamorphose f; Hydrometamorphismus m
hydrometeor Hydrometeor n
hydrometeorology Hydrometeorologie f
hydrometer Hydrometer n, Flüssigkeitsmengenmesser m
hydrometer s. a. areometer
hydrometric channel hydrometrische Rinne f
hydrometric cradle hydrometrische Wiege f
hydrometric current meter s. hydrometric vane <hydr.>
hydrometric seismograph Hydrometerseismograph m
hydrometric vane, [water-measuring] vane, hydrometric (propellertype) current meter Flügelradanemometer n, Meßflügel m, [hydrometrischer] Flügel m <Hydr.>
hydrometry Hydrometrie f, Wasser[mengen]messung f, Wassermeßwesen n, Wassermeßkunst f, Wassermeßlehre f, Wassermessungslehre f; Durchflußmengenmessung f, Flüssigkeitsmengenmessung f
hydronasty Hydronastie f
hydronium ion, hydroxonium ion, oxonium ion, H_3O^+ Oxoniumion n, Hydroniumion n, H_3O^+
hydronium ion concentration Hydroniumionenkonzentration f
hydrooptics Gewässeroptik f, Hydrooptik f, Optik f der Gewässer; Optik der Binnengewässer
hydrophilic, hydrophilous, water-loving hydrophil, wasserfreundlich, wasserliebend, wasseranziehend
hydrophilic group hydrophile Gruppe f
hydrophilic nature (property), hydrophily Hydrophilie f
hydrophiling, hydrophilization Hydrophilieren n
hydrophilous, hydrophilic, water-loving hydrophil, wasserfreundlich, wasserliebend, wasseranziehend
hydrophily, hydrophilic nature (property) Hydrophilie f
hydrophobic, water-hating hydrophob, wasserfeindlich
hydrophobic nature (property), hydrophoby Hydrophobie f
hydrophobing, hydrophobization Hydrophobieren n
hydrophoby, hydrophobic nature (property); water repellency Hydrophobie f; Wasserabstoßung f, Unbenetzbarkeit f
hydrophone; subaqueous microphone, underwater (submarine) microphone Hydrophon n, Unterwasser-Horchgerät n; Unterwasserschallempfänger m, Unterwasserempfänger m; Unterwassermikrophon n
hydrophore Hydrophor m
hydrophysics Hydrophysik f
hydroplane s. skimming boat
hydropneumatolytic hydropneumatolytisch
hydroquinol electrode, hydroquinone electrode Hydrochinonelektrode f
hydroseal s. liquid seal
hydrosol Hydrosol n
hydrosphere Hydrosphäre f, Wasserhülle f [der Erde]
hydrostatical s. hydrostatic
hydrostatic approximation, quasi-hydrostatic approximation (assumption) hydrostatische Näherung f
hydrostatic balance hydrostatische Waage f
hydrostatic buoyancy, buoyancy, vertical hydrostatic force, [hydro]static lift, buoyant lift, upthrust <hydr.> hydrostatischer Auftrieb m, statischer Auftrieb, Auftrieb <Hydr.>

hydrostatic equation	s. equation of hydrostatics	hygroscopicity	Hygroskopizität f, Wasserbindungsvermögen n; Feuchtigkeitsaufnahmezahl f, Hygroskopizitätszahl f
hydrostatic equilibrium, mechanical equilibrium	mechanisches Gleichgewicht n, hydrostatisches Gleichgewicht		
hydrostatic fundamental equation	s. equation of hydrostatics	hygroscopic moisture	hygroskopische Feuchtigkeit f
hydrostatic gauge	hydrostatisches Manometer n	hygroscopic water	hygroskopisches Wasser n, Adsorptionswasser n
hydrostatic [level] gauge	s. Hampson level indicator	hygrostat	Hygrostat m
		hygrothermograph	Hygrothermograph m
hydrostatic levelling	hydrostatisches Nivellement n	hygrothermoscope	Hygrothermoskop n
hydrostatic lift	s. hydrostatic buoyancy	Hylleraas['] method, method of Hylleraas	Hylleraassche Methode (Näherungsmethode) f, Methode von Hylleraas
hydrostatic paradox	s. Stevin's paradox		
hydrostatic pressure, hydrostatic tension	hydrostatischer Druck m	hylotropy	Hylotropie f
		hypabyssal	hypabyssisch
hydrostatic pressure chamber	hydrostatische Druckkammer f	hyperabrupt junction	hyperabrupter Übergang m
		hyperballistics	Hyperballistik f
hydrostatic stress	hydrostatischer Spannungszustand m	hyperbola rule	s. product rule <bio.>
		hyperbolical distance	hyperbolischer Abstand m
hydrostatic tension, hydrostatic pressure	hydrostatischer Druck m	hyperbolic comet	hyperbolischer Komet m, Komet mit hyperbolischer Bahn
hydrostatic weighing	hydrostatische Wägung f		
		hyperbolic cosecant, csch, cosech	Hyperbelkosekans, hyperbolischer Kosekans m, cosecans m hyperbolicus, cosech, csch, Cofec
hydrotaxis	Hydrotaxis f		
hydrotherm	Hydrotherme f		
hydrothermal solubility	hydrothermale Löslichkeit f		
hydrothermal synthesis	Hydrothermalsynthese f	hyperbolic cosine, arc-hyperbolic cosine, ch, cosh	Hyperbelkosinus m, hyperbolischer Kosinus m, cosinus m hyberbolicus, cosh, ch, Ch, Cof
hydrotimetric degree	Wasserhärtegrad m, hydrotimetrischer Grad m		
hydrotropic action	hydrotrope Wirkung f	hyberbolic cotangent, arc-hyperbolic cotangent, cth, coth, ctgh	Hyperbelkotangens m, hyperbolischer Kotangens m, cotangens m hyperbolicus, coth, cth, Cth, ctgh, Ctg
hydrotropic compound	hydrotrope Verbindung f		
hydrotropism <bio.>	Hydrotropismus m <Bio.>		
hydrotropy	Hydrotropie f		
hydrox cell, hydrogen-oxygen fuel cell	Wasserstoff-Sauerstoff-Brennstoffelement n	hyperbolic cylinder	hyperbolischer Zylinder m
		hyperbolic decay	hyperbolischer Abfall m
hydroxonium ion, hydronium ion, oxonium ion, H_3O^+	Hydroniumion n, Oxoniumion n, H_3O^+	hyperbolic differential equation, hyperbolic equation, hyperbolic partial differential equation, differential equation of the hyperbolic type	hyperbolische (total-hyperbolische, normalhyperbolische) Differentialgleichung f, Differentialgleichung vom hyperbolischen Typ, hyperbolischer Typ m
hydroxyl, OH group	Hydroxylgruppe f, OH-Gruppe f		
hydroxyl ion, OH^-	Hydroxylion n, OH^-		
hydroxyl-ion exponent, pOH, pOH value, pOH factor	pOH-Wert m, pOH <nur in Verbindung mit dem Zahlenwert>, Hydroxylionenexponent m		
		hyperbolic function	Hyperbelfunktion f, hyperbolische Funktion f
hyetograph	s. pluviograph	hyperbolic geometry, Lobachevskian geometry	hyperbolische Geometrie f, Lobatschewskische Geometrie
hyetography	s. pluviography		
hyetometer	s. rain gauge		
hyetometry	s. pluviometry		
hygric continentality	hygrische Kontinentalität f	hyperbolic logarithm	s. natural logarithm
		hyperbolic magnetic bottle	hyperbolische Flasche f.
hygric season	hygrische Jahreszeit f		
hygrochasy	Hygrochasie f	hyberbolic metric	hyperbolische Metrik f
hygrodeik	s. dew-point hygrometer	hyperbolic mirror	Hyperbolspiegel m, hyperbolischer Spiegel m
hygrogram	Hygrogramm n		
hygrograph, moist-o-graph	Hygrograph m, Feuchtigkeitsschreiber m, Feuchteschreiber m, Luftfeuchtigkeitsschreiber m	hyperbolic motion	hyperbolische Bewegung f, Hyperbelbewegung f
		hyperbolic orbit	hyperbolische Bahn f, Hyperbelbahn f
hygrometer, hygroscope	Hygrometer n, Feuchtigkeitsmesser m, Feuchtemesser m, Luftfeuchtigkeitsmesser m, Hygroskop n	hyperbolic paraboloid	hyperbolisches Paraboloid n, Sattelfläche f
		hyperbolic partial differential equation	s. hyperbolic differential equation
hygrometric state	s. relative humidity	hyperbolic plane, Lobachevski plane	hyperbolische (Lobatschewskische) Ebene f
hygrometry, air moisture measurement	Hygrometrie f, Luftfeuchtigkeitsmessung f, Feuchtemessung f, Feuchtigkeitsmessung f, Messung f der Luftfeuchtigkeit (Feuchtigkeit); Feuchtemeßkunde f		
		hyperbolic point, saddle point, col <math.>	Sattelpunkt m, hyperbolischer Punkt m <Math.>
		hyperbolic secant, sch, sech	Hyperbelsekans m, hyperbolischer Sekans m, secans m hyperbolicus, sech, sch, Sec
hygrophilic, hygrophilous	hygrophil, feuchtigkeitsliebend		
hygroscope	s. hygrometer		
hygroscopic, hygr.	hygroskopisch, Feuchtigkeit anziehend, wasseranziehend, wasseraufsaugend, wasserbindend, wasserbindungsfähig, wassergierig, wasserziehend, hygr., hy	hyperbolic sine, arc-hyperbolic sine, sh, sinh	Hyperbelsinus m, hyperbolischer Sinus m, sinus m hyperbolicus, sinh, sh, Sh, Sin
		hyperbolic space, Lobachevski space	hyperbolischer Raum m, Lobatschewskischer Raum
hygroscopic coefficient	hygroskopischer Koeffizient m	hyperbolic spiral, reciprocal spiral	hyperbolische Spirale f

hyperbolic 346

hyperbolic tangent, arc-hyperbolic tangent, th, tanh, tgh	Hyperbeltangens m, hyperbolischer Tangens m, tangens m hyperbolicus, tanh, th, tgh, Th, $\mathfrak{Tg}$	**hypergeometric function,** Gauss hypergeometric function	[Gaußsche] hypergeometrische Funktion f
hyperboloid of one sheet	einschaliges Hyperboloid n	**hypergeometric function of second kind**	hypergeometrische Funktion f zweiter Art
hyperboloid of two sheets, two-sheet (parted) hyperboloid	zweischaliges Hyperboloid n	**hypergeometric series,** Gaussian hypergeometric series	[Gaußsche] hypergeometrische Reihe f
hypercentric perspective	hyperzentrische Perspektive f	**hypergeostrophic**	hypergeostrophisch
hypercharge	Hyperladung f	**hypergol**	Hypergol n
hyperchrom[at]ic	hyperchrom	**hypergolic;** self-inflammable, self-igniting, self-ignitable; pyrophoric	selbstentzündlich, selbstentflammbar; pyrophor; selbstzündend
hyperchromism	Hyperchromie f	**hyperhomology**	Hyperhomologie f
hypercohomology	Hyperkohomologie f	**hypermatrix,** partitioned matrix, matrix of matrices	Hypermatrix f, Übermatrix f, Matrix f von Matrizen; in Kästchen eingeteilte Matrix
hypercomplex number	hyperkomplexe Zahl f, extensive Zahl		
hypercomplex system, algebra	Algebra f; hyperkomplexes System n, assoziative K-Algebra f, assoziative R-Algebra f	**hypermetropia,** hyperopia	Übersichtigkeit f, Hyper[metr]opie f
hypercone	Hyperkegel m	**hypermetropic,** long-sighted	übersichtig, hypermetropisch
hyper-conical horn	hyperkonisches Horn n	**hypermicroscope**	s. ultramicroscope
hyperconjugation, Baker-Nathan effect, no-bond resonance	Hyperkonjugation f, Baker-Nathan-Effekt m, Konjugation f zweiter (2.) Ordnung	**hypermultiplet,** supermultiplet	Supermultiplett n, Hypermultiplett n
		hyperneutral symmetry	hyperneutrale Symmetrie f
hyperelastic body	hyperelastischer Körper m	**hypernucleus**	s. hyperfragment
hyperelastic collision	s. collision of the second kind	**hyperon**	Hyperon n
		hyperon decay	Hyperonenzerfall m
hyperelliptic function	hyperelliptische Funktion f	**hyperon gas**	Hyperonengas n
hyper[-]eutectic	übereutektisch, hypereutektisch	**hyperplane**	Hyperebene f
hyper[-]eutectoid	übereutektoid, hypereutektoid	**hyperpolarizability tensor,** tensor of hyperpolarizability	Tensor m der Hyperpolarisierbarkeit, Hyperpolarisierbarkeitstensor m
hyperexponential horn	s. hypex horn	**hyperpolarization**	Hyperpolarisation f
hyperfiltration	s. reverse osmosis	**hyperpressure**	s. very high pressure
hyperfine coupling	Hyperfein[struktur]kopplung f	**hyperpure,** extra[-]pure, high-purity, extremely pure	reinst
hyperfine energy	Hyperfein[struktur]energie f	**hyperquantization,** second quantization	zweite Quantelung f, Hyperquantelung f, Hyperquantisierung f, zweite Quantisierung f
hyperfine field	Hyperfeinfeld n		
hyperfine interaction	Hyperfein[struktur]wechselwirkung f	**hypersensitization,** supersensitization	Übersensibilisierung f, Supersensibilisierung f, Hypersensibilisation f, [photographische] Hypersensibilisierung f
hyperfine quantum number	Gesamtdrehimpulsquantenzahl f [einschließlich Kernspin] <Atom oder Molekül>		
hyperfine spectrum	Hyperfeinspektrum n	**hypersensitizer,** supersensitizer	Übersensibilisator m, Supersensibilisator m, Hypersensibilisator m
hyperfine splitting, hyperfine structure splitting	Hyperfeinstrukturaufspaltung f, Hyperfeinaufspaltung f	**hypersonic aerodynamics**	Hyperschallaerodynamik f
		hypersonic flow	Hyperschallströmung f
hyperfine structure, hfs	Hyperfeinstruktur f, HFS	**hypersonic range,** hypersonic region	hoher Überschallbereich m, hohes Überschallgebiet n, hypersonischer Bereich m, hypersonisches Gebiet n, Hyperschallbereich m
hyperfine structure effect	Hyperfeinstruktureffekt m		
hyperfine structure multiplet	Hyperfeinstrukturmultiplett n	**hypersonic shock tube,** hypersonic shock tunnel	Hyperschall-Stoßwellenrohr n
hyperfine structure operator	Hyperfeinstrukturoperator m	**hypersonic speed,** hypersonic velocity	hohe Überschallgeschwindigkeit f, hypersonische Geschwindigkeit f, Hyperschallgeschwindigkeit f
hyperfine structure splitting, hyperfine splitting	Hyperfeinstrukturaufspaltung f, Hyperfeinaufspaltung f		
		hypersonic wave	Hyperschallwelle f, thermische Schallwelle f
hyperfine [structure] transition	Hyperfein[struktur]übergang m	**hypersonic wind tunnel**	Hyperschallwindkanal m
hyperfluidity	Hyperfluidität f	**hypersorption [process]**	Hypersorption[sverfahren n] f, Hypersorptionsprozeß m, stetige Adsorption f
hyperfocal distance	Hyperfokale f		
hyperfragment; hypernucleus	Hyperfragment n	**hypersound**	Hyperschall m
hyperfrequency wave	s. microwave	**hypersound absorption**	Hyperschallabsorption f
hypergalaxy, metagalaxy, supergalaxy, supercluster, galaxy of galaxies	Metagalaxis f, Hypergalaxis f, Metagalaxie f, Superhaufen m, Supergalaxis f	**hyperspace**	Hyperraum m
		hypersphere <math.>	Hyperkugel f; Hypersphäre f, Sphäre f <Math.>
hypergene	hypergen	**hyperstatic**	statisch überbestimmt
hypergeometric differential equation, Gaussian differential equation, Gauss['] hypergeometrie [differential] equation	hypergeometrische Differentialgleichung (Gleichung) f, Gaußsche Differentialgleichung	**hyperstatic**	s. a. statically indeterminate
		hyperstaticity, static indeterminateness	statische Unbestimmtheit f
		hypersurface of constraints, constraint hypersurface	Hyperfläche f der Zwangsbedingungen, Zwangsbedingungenhyperfläche f

hypersynchronous, supersynchronous	übersynchron
hyperthermia	Hyperthermie f
hyperthermocouple	Feinthermoelement n
hypertonicity	Hypertonie f
hypertonic solution	hypertonische Lösung f
hypervelocity	s. superrelativistic velocity
hypervolume	Hypervolumen n
hypervolume element, elementary hypervolume	Hypervolumenelement n <Math.>
hypex horn, hyperexponential horn	Hyperexponentialhorn n, Hyperexponentialtrichter m
hypidiomorphic, hypidiomorphous	hypidiomorph
hypocentral depth, depth of focus (origin, hypocentre), focal depth <geo.>	Herdtiefe f, Hypozentraltiefe f
hypocentral distance, focal distance, distance of hypocentre <geo.>	Herddistanz f, Herdentfernung f, Hypozentraldistanz f, Hypozentralentfernung f <Geo.>
hypocentre	s. focus of earthquake
hypocentre of the explosion, explosion focus	Sprengherd m
hypochromic	hypochrom
hypochromism	Hypochromie f
hypocrystalline, partly crystalline	hypokristallin
hypoelastic	hypoelastisch
hypoelasticity, hypo-elasticity	Hypoelastizität f, hypoelastisches Verhalten n
hypoelliptic	hypoelliptisch
hypoeutectic	untereutektisch, hypoeutektisch
hypoeutectoid	untereutektoid, hypoeutektoid
hypogene	hypogen
hypogeostrophic	hypogeostrophisch
hypoid [gear]	Hypoidzahnrad n; Schraub-Kegelradgetriebe n, Kegel-Schraubgetriebe n, Hypoidgetriebe n
hypolimnion	Hypolimnion n
hypometamorphism	Hypometamorphose f; Hypometamorphismus m
hypomorphic	hypomorph
hyponasty	Hyponastie f
hyposynchronous	s. subsynchronous
hypothermia	Hypothermie f
hypothesis <stat.>	Hypothese f <Stat.>
hypothesis of plane cross-sections	s. Bernoulli's hypothesis
hypothesis of the heat death of the universe	Wärmetodtheorie f
hypothesis of wall similarity, law of the wall	Wandgesetz n
hypothesis tested, null hypothesis, nullhypothesis	Nullhypothese f
hypotonicity	Hypotonie f
hypotonic solution	hypotonische Lösung f
hypotrochoid	Hypotrochoide f, Hypotrochoidale f
hypsochrome, hypsochromic	hypsochrom; farberhöhend
hypsochromic displacement	hypsochrome Verschiebung f
hypsochromic effect, hypsochromism	Farberhöhung f, Hypsochromie f
hypsogram of transmission	Übertragungsplan m
hypsographic curve, hypsometric curve	hypsometrische (hypsographische) Kurve f, Höhenverteilungskurve f
hypsometer, hypsometric altimeter; hypsothermometer, boiling-point thermometer	Hypsometer n; Hypsothermometer n, Höhenthermometer n, Siedebarometer n, Siedethermometer n
hypsometric chart	s. hypsometric map
hypsometric curve	s. hypsographic curve
hypsometric distribution, vertical distribution, distribution in height (altitude)	Höhenverteilung f
hypsometric map, map (chart) of isohypses, contour map (chart), outline map (chart), contour plan, hypsometric chart, altimetric[al] chart (map), isohypsic chart (map)	Höhenlinienkarte f, Höhenkarte f, Höhenschichtenkarte f, Höhenschichtkarte f, Schichtlinienplan m, Umrißkarte f, Konturkarte f, Schichtenkarte f, Isolinienkarte f
hypsometric temperature, altitude temperature, temperature aloft	Höhentemperatur f
hypsometry, altimetry, measurement of altitude (height), altitude (height) measurement	Hypsometrie f, Höhenmessung f
hypsothermometer	s. hypsometer
hypsotonic	hypsotonisch, grenzflächeninaktiv
hysteresigraph	s. hysteresisograph
hysteresimeter	s. hysteresis meter
hysteresis <also quantity>	Hysterese f, Hysteresis f, Nachhinken n <auch Größe>
hysteresis	s. a. magnetic hysteresis
hysteresis branch, hysteresis curve, hysteretic curve	Hysteresekurve f, Hysteresiskurve f, Hystereseast m, Hysteresisast m
hysteresis coefficient	s. hysteresis loss coefficient
hysteresis current	Hysteresisstrom m, Hysteresestrom m
hysteresis curve, hysteresis branch, hysteretic curve	Hysteresekurve f, Hysteresiskurve f, Hystereseast m, Hysteresisast m
hysteresis curve for a ferroelectric material	s. ferroelectric hysteresis curve
hysteresis cycle	s. hysteresis loop <el.>
hysteresis effect	Hystereseerscheinung f, Hysteresiseffekt m, Rückstandserscheinung f
hysteresis energy, hysteresis work; remagnetization energy (work)	Hysteresearbeit f, Hystereseenergie f, Hysteresisarbeit f, Hysteresisenergie f, Ummagnetisierungsarbeit f, Ummagnetisierungsenergie f
hysteresis factor	s. hysteresis coefficient
hysteresisgraph, hysteresisograph, hysteresigraph	Hystereseschreiber m, Hystereseschleifenschreiber m
hysteresis heat, hysteretic heat; heat of remagnetization	Hysteresiswärme f, Hysteresewärme f; Ummagnetisierungswärme f
hysteresis loop, hysteretic loop (cycle), hysteresis cycle; B-H loop, B/H loop, magnetization loop <el.>	Hystereseschleife f, Hysteresisschleife f, Hysteresezyklus m; Magnetisierungsschleife f <El.>
hysteresis loss, hysteretic loss	Hysteresisverlust m, Hystereseverlust m, Energieverlust m durch Hysteresis, Hysteresisverlustleistung f, Hystereseverlustleistung f, Hysteresisverlustarbeit f, Hystereseverlustarbeit f, Nachwirkungsverlust m
hysteresis loss angle	magnetischer Verlustwinkel m, Hystereseverlustwinkel m, Hysteresisverlustwinkel m
hysteresis loss coefficient, hysteresis coefficient, hysteresis factor	Hystereseverlustziffer f, Hysteresisverlustziffer f, [magnetische] Verlustziffer f, Verlust[bei]wert m, Hysteresekoeffizient m, hysteretischer Koeffizient m, Hysteresebeiwert m, Hysteresisbeiwert m
hysteresis meter, hysteresimeter	Hysteresemesser m
hysteresis of capillary condensation	Kapillarkondensationshysterese f

hysteresisograph,
  hysteresisgraph,
  hysterisigraph
Hystereseschreiber m,
  Hystereseschleifen-
  schreiber m

hysteresis part of complex permeability
Hysteresisanteil m der komplexen Permeabilität

hysteresis-type, hysteretic
hystereseartig

hysteresis work s. hysteresis energy
hysteretic, hysteresis-type hystereseartig
hysteretic curve s. hysteresis curve
hysteretic cycle s. hysteresis loop
hysteretic heat s. hysteresis heat
hysteretic loop s. hysteresis loop
hysteretic loss s. hysteresis loss
hysterocrystallization Hysterokristallisation f
hyzone s. tritium

I

iaser s. iraser
iatron Iatron n

I band, isotropic band, I-disk
I-Streifen m, isotroper Streifen m <Muskel>, isotrope Scheibe f

icaroscope Ikaroskop n
iceberg covered with snow, snowberg schneebedeckter Eisberg m
ice blink, blink of ice Eisblink m, Blinken n des Eises, Eisreflexion f
ice-bulb temperature s. wet-bulb reading
ice calorimeter s. Bunsen Ice calorimeter
ice cloud Eiswolke f, Eisnadelwolke f
ice day Eistag m
ice formation s. icing
ice in soil Bodeneis n
Iceland crystal (spar), calcareous spar, spar, spath, calcite $CaCO_3$
Kalkspat m, Doppelspat m, Spat m, Calcit m, Kalzit m, Islandspat m, isländischer Doppelspat m $CaCO_3$

ice line; melting (fusion, melting pressure, solidification) curve
Schmelzkurve f

ice lobe Eislobus m, Lobus m
ice melting point s. ice point
i-centre, interstitial centre i-Zentrum n

ice nucleus Eiskeim m
ice nucleus, icy nucleus <of comet> Eiskern m, gefrorener Kern m <Komet>
ice-pail s. Faraday cage
ice pellet, graupel, sleet <US> Frostgraupel f, Graupel f
ice point, ice melting point Eispunkt m

ice-point depression s. depression of the ice point
ice push s. shove <geo.>
ice pyrheliometer Eispyrheliometer n
ichnography <of particle tracks>
Ichnographie f <Aufnahme von Korpuskularspuren>

icing; ice formation; glaciation
Vereisung f; Eisbildung f

icing index Vereisungsindex m
ICI observer, standard observer
Normalbeobachter m, CIE-Normalbeobachter m

ICI photometric standard observer, photometric standard observer
photometrischer Normalbeobachter m

iconal s. eikonal
iconoscope, storage-type camera tube, image-storing tube
Bildspeicherröhre f, Ikonoskop n

icosahedral group Ikosaedergruppe f
icosahedron Ikosaeder n, Zwanzigflach n, Zwanzigflächner m, 20-Flächner m

icositetrahedron s. pentagonal icositetrahedron
icy nucleus <of comet>, ice nucleus
Eiskern m, gefrorener Kern m <Komet>
icy rain Eisregen m

ideal <math.> Ideal n <Math.>
ideal antenna ideale (isotrope verlustfreie) Antenne f

ideal black body s. black body
ideal condition <without friction>
ideale Zwangsbedingung f <ohne Reibung>
ideal conductivity, perfect conductivity
vollkommene (ideale) Leitfähigkeit f
ideal conductor, perfect conductor
idealer Leiter m, Idealleiter m
ideal crystal, perfect crystal
Idealkristall m, idealer (fehlerfreier) Kristall m
ideal cyclone Idealzyklone f, junge Zyklone f

ideal drag, profile drag Profilwiderstand m

ideal element, element at infinity
uneigentliches Element n, unendlich[]fernes Element

ideal fluid s. ideal liquid
ideal gas, perfect gas ideales Gas n, vollkommenes Gas
ideal gas law s. Boyle-Charles law
ideal gas scale of temperature, gas scale of temperature, perfect-gas scale
Gasskala f der Temperatur, ideale Gasskala

ideal irregularity, ideal non-uniformity
Grenzungleichmäßigkeit f, ideale Ungleichmäßigkeit f

idealization; simplification; reduction
Vereinfachung f; Idealisierung f
idealized fluid idealisierte Flüssigkeit f

idealized fluid of Kármán and Tsien, Kármán-Tsien fluid
Kármán-Tsiensche Flüssigkeit f, Kármán-Tsien-Flüssigkeit f, idealisierte Flüssigkeit von Kármán und Tsien

idealized fluid of Tomotika and Tamada, Tomotika-Tamada fluid
Tomotika-Tamada-Flüssigkeit f, Tomotika-Tamadasche Flüssigkeit f, idealisierte Flüssigkeit von Tomotika und Tamada

ideal line, line at infinity
uneigentliche (unendlich[]ferne) Gerade f, Ferngerade f

ideal liquid, perfect liquid, Pascalian liquid; ideal fluid, perfect fluid, inviscid fluid
ideale (vollkommene) Flüssigkeit f, vollkommener (idealer) flüssiger Körper m

ideally conducting, perfectly conducting
ideal leitend
ideally imperfect crystal
idealer Mosaikkristall m, ideal fehlgeordneter Kristall m

ideally plastic s. perfectly plastic
ideal magnetization curve, anhysteretic magnetization curve
ideale Magnetisierungskurve f, hysteresefreie Magnetisierungskurve

ideal non-uniformity, ideal irregularity
Grenzungleichmäßigkeit f, ideale Ungleichmäßigkeit f

ideal plane, plane at infinity
uneigentliche (unendlich[]ferne) Ebene f, Fernebene f

ideal plasticity s. perfect plasticity
ideal point, point at infinity <math.>
uneigentlicher (unendlich[ ]ferner) Punkt m, Fernpunkt m

ideal pole arc ideeller Polbogen m
ideal process factor, ideal separation factor
theoretischer Trennfaktor m

ideal simple process factor
theoretischer elementarer Trennfaktor m, theoretischer Trennfaktor einer Stufe

ideal solution, perfect solution
ideale Lösung f, vollkommene Lösung
ideal viscous liquid s. Newtonian fluid
idemfactor s. unit tensor

idempotent [element]	idempotentes Element n, Idempotent n	idler wheel	s. idler
		idle transition	blinder Übergang m
identically equal [to], ≡	identisch gleich, ≡	idle voltage	s. reactive voltage
identical particles, equivalent particles	identische Teilchen npl, gleiche Teilchen	idling, idle running, running without load, no-load [operation], nil-load <e.g. of motor>	Leerlauf m <z. B. Motor>
identical transformation, identity <math.>	identische Transformation f		
identifiable design, optotype; [optical] test object <opt.>	Sehzeichen n, Optotype f; Testobjekt n <Opt.>	idling reaction <bio.>	Leerlaufreaktion f <Bio.>
		I effect	s. seismoelectric effect of the first kind
identification	Identifizierung f, Identifikation f; Bestimmung f; Zuordnung f; Erkennung f	ierfc	= [integral of] error function complement
		if and only if, iff	wenn und nur wenn; dann und nur dann, wenn; genau wenn
identification range	Erkennungsreichweite f, Erkennungsbereich m	igneous dyke	s. igneous vein
identifying line, analytical line, important identifying line <spectr.>	Analysenlinie f, Hauptlinie f, Hauptnachweislinie f <Spektr.>	igneous electrolysis	s. electrolysis in the dry way
		igneous rock	s. eruptive rock
identity <gen.>	Identität f; Gleichartigkeit f <allg.>	igneous vein, eruptive vein, intrusive vein, igneous dyke, dyke	Eruptivgang m, Gesteinsgang m
identity <math.>	identische Operation f, Identität f, Identitätsoperation f <Math.>		
		ignitability	s. inflammability
identity	s. a. identical transformation <math.>	ignitability limit	s. inflammability limit
		ignitable	s. inflammable
identity [element], unit element, unity, unity element, unit; neutral element <math.>	Einheit f, Einheitselement n, Einselement n, Eins f, neutrales Element n <Math.>	igniter [electrode]	s. ignition rod
		igniting anode	s. starting anode
		igniting flame, ignition flame, pilot flame	Zündflamme f, Lockflamme f
identity matrix, unit matrix	Einheitsmatrix f		
		igniting pulse	s. ignition pulse
identity operator, unity operator, unit operator	Identitätsoperator m, Einheitsoperator m	ignition; inflammation, initiation of combustion <chem.>	Entzündung f, Zündung f; Entflammung f <Chem.>
identity period	Identitätsperiode f, Identitätsabstand m	ignition angle, firing angle	Zünd[verzögerungs]winkel m
identity principle of microparticles	Prinzip n der Identität von Mikroteilchen, Identitätsprinzip n [von Mikroteilchen]	ignition anode	s. starting anode
		ignition by contact	Berührungszündung f
		ignition by contact breaking	Abreißzündung f
identity problem, word problem	Identitätsproblem n, Wortproblem n		
		ignition by incandescence	Glühzündung f
identity tensor	s. unit tensor		
identity theorem	Identitätssatz m	ignition characteristic of thyratron	s. starting characteristic of thyratron
idiochromatic <cryst.>	eigenfarbig, idiochromatisch, farbig <Krist.>	ignition current; striking current; firing current	Zündstrom m; Zündstromstärke f, Zündungsstromstärke f
idiochromatic colouration, idiochromatism	idiochromatische Färbung f, Eigenfärbung f		
		ignition delay, ignition lag, firing delay (lag), time lag of the ignition <of discharge>	Zündverzögerung f, Zündverzug m <Entladung>; Zündmomentverspätung f <Gleichrichter>
idiocyclophanic crystal	idiozyklophaner (ideozyklophaner) Kristall m		
idiomorphic, idiomorphous, automorphic, automorphous, euhedral <cryst.>	idiomorph, automorph <Krist.>	ignition device, starting device <of the discharge lamp>	Zündvorrichtung f, Zündeinrichtung f, Zündanlage f <Entladungslampe>
idiophanic (idiophanous) [interference] ring	idiophaner Ring m	ignition electrode, starting electrode	Zündelektrode f
		ignition energy	Zündenergie f
		ignition filament	Zündfaden m
idiostatic circuit, idiostatic method [of Joubert]	idiostatische Schaltung f [nach Joubert]	ignition flame, igniting (pilot) flame	Zündflamme f, Lockflamme f
I-disk	s. I band		
I divergence, information for discrimination	I-Divergenz f, diskriminierende Information f	ignition lag, time lag of the ignition, ignition delay, spark lag	Zündverzögerung f, Zündverzug m; Funkenverzögerung f
idle, wattless, reactive <el.>	Blind-, wattlos, leistungslos <El.>		
		ignition lag	s. a. ignition delay
idle component	s. reactive component	ignition limit	s. inflammability limit
idle current; open-circuit (no-load) current	Leerlaufstrom m; Leerstrom m	ignition limits	s. inflammability limits
		ignition loss	s. loss of ignition
idle current	s. a. reactive current	ignition of the discharge, initiation of the discharge	Zündung f der Entladung
idle power	s. reactive power		
idler, idler wheel, guide roller, guide-pulley	Umlenkrolle f	ignition of thyratron, firing of thyratron	Zündung f des Thyratrons
idler circuit	Hilfskreis m, „idler"-Kreis m <Halbleiterdiodenverstärker>	ignition oscillation, starting oscillation	Zündschwingung f
		ignition overvoltage, breakdown overvoltage	Zündüberspannung f
idler frequency	Frequenz f des Hilfskreises, „idler"-Frequenz f <Halbleiterdiodenverstärker>	ignition peak	Zündspitze f
		ignition peak fluctuation	Zündspitzenschwankung f, Zündspitzenfluktuation f
idle running	s. idling		

ignition

ignition point, ignition temperature, fire point <chem.>	Entzündungstemperatur f, Entzündungspunkt m, Zündtemperatur f, Zündpunkt m, Entzündung f; Gaszündpunkt m; Tropfzündpunkt m; Brennpunkt m, Brandpunkt m <Chem.>
ignition point, firing point <e.g. of discharge, thyratron>	Zündeinsatz[punkt] m, Zünd[zeit]punkt m, Zündmoment m <z. B. Entladung, Thyratron>
ignition potential	s. striking voltage <of discharge or tube>
ignition pulse, firing pulse, starting pulse, igniting pulse	Zündstoß m, Zündimpuls m; Zündsteuerimpuls m <Thyratron>
ignition quality	s. inflammability
ignition range	s. inflammability limits
ignition rate	s. rate of flame propagation
ignition residue	s. residue on ignition
ignition rod, ignitor [electrode], igniter [electrode]	Zündstift m, Ignitronzündstift m, Ignitronstift m, Ignitor m
ignition source	Zündquelle f
ignition spark, pilot spark	Zündfunke m
ignition temperature	s. ignition point <chem.>
ignition threshold	s. striking voltage <of discharge or tube>
ignition velocity	s. rate of flame propagation
ignition voltage	s. striking voltage <of discharge or tube>
ignition zone, inflammation zone, zone of inflammation	Zündzone f; Zündnest n
ignitor [electrode]	s. ignition rod
ignitron	Ignitron n, Zündstiftröhre f, Ignitronröhre f, Zündstiftgerät n, Zündstiftgefäß n
ignorable co-ordinates, cyclic (hidden, kinosthenic) co-ordinates	zyklische (ignorable, verborgene) Koordinaten fpl, zyklische Variable fpl
ignoration of co-ordinates, Routh method	Routhsche Methode f
ikonal	s. eikonal
i layer	s. intrinsic region
Ilkovic equation	Ilkovič-Gleichung f, Gleichung f von Ilkovič
Illiovici bridge	Illiovici-Brücke f, Brücke f von Illiovici
illuminance, illuminancy, intensity of illumination, illumination [intensity] lightness <quantity>	Beleuchtungsstärke f
illuminating flash	s. scintillation
illuminating power	s. luminosity
illumination, lighting, light	Beleuchtung f
illumination	s. a. illuminance
illumination	s. a. irradiation
illumination device, illuminator, illumination system	Beleuchtungsapparat m, Illuminator m
illumination efficiency	s. utilization factor <opt.>
illumination for scotopic vision; illumination referred to dark-adapted eye	Dunkelbeleuchtungsstärke f
illumination from stars, star light	Sternlicht n
illumination function	Illuminationsfunktion f
illumination in reflected light	s. vertical illumination
illumination in transmitted light	s. transillumination
illumination meter, illumination photometer, illuminometer, light meter; luxometer, lux meter	Beleuchtungsmesser m; Luxmeter n
illumination of the slit, slit illumination	Spaltbeleuchtung f; Spaltausleuchtung f
illumination photometer, illumination meter, illuminometer, light meter; luxometer, lux meter	Beleuchtungsmesser m; Luxmeter n
illumination referred to dark-adapted eye; illumination for scotopic vision	Dunkelbeleuchtungsstärke f
illumination system	s. illuminator
illuminator, illumination device, illumination system	Beleuchtungsapparat m, Beleuchtungssystem n, Illuminator m
illuminator	s. a. vertical illuminator
illuminometer, illumination photometer (meter), light meter; luxometer, lux meter	Beleuchtungsmesser m; Luxmeter n
illusion, delusion	Wahrnehmungsverzerrung f, Täuschung f
illusion of depth, plastic effect, plastic	Plastik f
illusory correlation; nonsense correlation	Scheinkorrelation f; Nonsenskorrelation f
illustration, demonstration	Veranschaulichung f
illuvial soil, illuvium, B horizon, lower layer of soil <geo.>	Unterboden m, B-Horizont m, Illuvialhorizont m, Anreicherungshorizont m, Einschwemmungshorizont m, Illuvium n <Geo.>
image, mirror image, reflected image	Spiegelbild n
image <opt.>	Abbildung f; Abbild n <Opt.>
image <math.>	Bild n <Math.>
image	s. a. transform <math.>
image admittance, characteristic admittance <of four-terminal network>	Wellenleitwert m <Vierpol>
image antenna	Bildantenne f
image attenuation coefficient, image attenuation constant	Spiegeldämpfungskoeffizient m
image attenuation constant, image attenuation factor, quadripole attenuation	Vierpoldämpfungsfaktor m, Vierpoldämpfung f, Wellendämpfung f [des Vierpols], Wellendämpfungsmaß n; Spannungsdämpfung f
image brightness, brightness of the image	Bildhelligkeit f; Bildleuchtdichte f
image channel selectivity, image selectivity	Spiegelselektion f
image charge	Bildladung f, Spiegelbildladung f, Spiegelladung f
image[-]converter [tube], image-viewing tube, image tube, electron image tube	Bildwandler m, elektronenoptischer Bildwandler, Bildwandlerröhre f, Bildverstärker m
image current [transfer] ratio	Wellenstromübersetzung f [vorwärts]
image defect	s. aberration
image deflection	s. vertical deflection
image dissector [tube]	s. dissector
image distance <from image principal point>, image intercept	Bildweite f
image distance from the vertex [of the lens], back vertex image distance, lens / image distance	bildseitige Schnittweite f, Bildschnittweite f, hintere Schnittweite; Schnittweite, optische Schnittweite <Objektiv>

image erecting lens, erecting lens, lenticular erecting system	Umkehrlinse f	**image plane;** groundglass plane, plane of ground glass	Bildebene f, Gaußsche Bildebene <Opt.>; Mattscheibenebene f, Auffangebene f <Phot.>
image erecting prism, erecting prism, inversion prism, reversing prism, inverting prism	Umkehrprisma n, Stürzprisma n	**image point** <opt.>	Bildpunkt m <Opt.>
image erecting system, erecting system, [optical] inversion system	Umkehrsystem n, Bildaufrichtungssystem n, Aufrichtungssystem n	**image point coordinates**	Bildkoordinaten fpl, Bildkoordinatensystem n
		image position <opt.>	Bildlage f <Opt.>
image erecting telescope, erecting (inversion) telescope, [image] reversing telescope	Umkehrfernrohr n, aufrichtendes Fernrohr n, bildaufrichtendes Fernrohr	**image power ratio,** image transfer power ratio	Wellenleistungsübersetzung f
		image principal plane, back principal plane	Bildhauptebene f, bildseitige (hintere) Hauptebene f
image field, image field of sight (view)	Bild[sicht]feld n, bildseitiges Gesichtsfeld n, Austrittssichtfeld n	**image principal point,** rear principal point, internal perspective centre	Bildhauptpunkt m, bildseitiger (hinterer) Hauptpunkt m
		image ratio <el.>	Spiegelverhältnis n <El.>
image field dissection	s. scansion		
image field stop	Bildfeldblende f; Austrittsblende f	**image ray,** ray from image point	Bildstrahl m
image flicker	Bildflimmern n	**image reactor**	Bildreaktor m
image focal length, back focal length	Bildbrennweite f, bildseitige (hintere) Brennweite f	**image reversal,** solarization <phot.>	Solarisation f, Bildumkehrung f <Phot.>
image focus, back focus, second focal point	Bildbrennpunkt m, bildseitiger (hinterer) Brennpunkt m	**image reversing prism**	s. reversing prism
		image reversing telescope	s. image erecting telescope
image force, mirror-image force	Bildkraft f, Spiegelbildkraft f	**image rotation spectrograph**	Spektrograph m mit Bildrotation
image formation, imaging, imagery <opt.>	Abbilden n; Bilderzeugung f	**imagery**	s. image formation
image formed by diverging lens	Zerstreuungsbild n	**image selectivity,** image channel selectivity	Spiegelselektion f
		image sharpness, precision of image	Bildschärfe f, Schärfe f des Bildes, Zeichenschärfe f, Zeichnungsschärfe f
image forming system, imaging system	abbildendes System n		
		image-side pupil	s. exit pupil
image frequency, second channel frequency	Spiegelfrequenz f; Bild[punkt]frequenz f	**image source,** virtual source	Bildquelle f, virtuelle Quelle f
		image space	Bildraum m
image function <opt.>	Bildfunktion f <Opt.>		
image function	s. a. transform <math.>	**image-storing tube,** storage-type camera tube, iconoscope	Bildspeicherröhre f, Ikonoskop n
image iconoscope, supericonoscope; supereriscope, eriscope	Superikonoskop n, Zwischenbildikonoskop n; Ikonoskop n mit Vorabbildung, Image-Ikonoskop n; Supereriscope n, Eriscope n		
		image surface	Bildschale f; Bildfläche f
		image transfer coefficient, image transfer constant, quadripole propagation factor	Vierpolübertragungsmaß n, Übertragungsmaß n des Vierpols, Wellenübertragungsmaß n [des Vierpols]
image impedance	s. characteristic impedance <of four-terminal network>		
image intercept	s. image distance	**image transfer power ratio,** image power ratio	Wellenleistungsübersetzung f
image inversion	Bildumkehr[ung] f		
image line	Spiegelleitung f, Spiegelleiter m	**image-transfer storing tube**	Vorabbildungs-Bildspeicherröhre f
image measuring apparatus, photogrammetric apparatus	Bildmeßgerät n	**image tube**	s. image[-] converter tube
image method	s. method of images	**image vergence,** rear (back) vergence	bildseitige Vergenz f, Bildvergenz f
image nodal point, back nodal point	Bildknotenpunkt m, bildseitiger (hinterer) Knotenpunkt m	**image-viewing tube**	s. image[-] converter tube
		image voltage ratio, image voltage transfer ratio	Wellenspannungsübersetzung f [vorwärts]
image of coarse grain	Grobkornbild n		
image of interference	s. interference pattern	**image wave,** mirror wave	Spiegelwelle f
image of the slit, slit image	Spaltbild n, Schlitzbild n, Spaltabbildung f	**imaginary axis,** axis of imaginaries	imaginäre Achse f
image orthicon, superorthicon; superemitron	Superorthikon n, Zwischenbildorthikon n, Image-Orthicon n; Superemitron n	**imaginary axis**	s. a. conjugate axis
		imaginary boundary, fictitious boundary	fiktive Begrenzung f, scheinbare Grenze f
		imaginary component	s. reactive component
image parameter theory	Spiegelparametertheorie f	**imaginary current**	s. reactive current
image pattern	s. electric image	**imaginary experiment,** mental (gedanken, thought) experiment	Gedankenversuch m, Gedankenexperiment n
image phase constant, image phase factor, quadripole phase constant, phase factor (constant), [unit] wavelength constant	Vierpolwinkelmaß n, Vierpolphasenfaktor m, Vierpolphasenkonstante f, Winkelmaß n [des Vierpols]		
		imaginary part	Imaginärteil m
		imaginary part of complex permeability, reactive permeability	Reihenwiderstandspermeabilität f, Blindpermeabilität f, Imaginärteil m der komplexen Permeabilität

imaginary 352

imaginary power	s. reactive power	immersion thermostat, immersion-type thermostat	Tauchthermostat m
imaginary voltage	s. reactive voltage		
imaging	s. image formation		
imaging equation, formula of conjugate points	Abbildungsgleichung f, Abbildungsformel f	immersion-type electrode, immersion electrode	Tauchelektrode f
imaging system	s. image-forming system	immersion-type pyrometer, immersion pyrometer	Tauchpyrometer n; Tauchthermoelement n
imbalance	s. instability		
imbedding, embedding, merging	Einbettung f		
imbedding <of a space> <math.>	Einbettung f <Raum> <Math.>	immersion-type thermostat, immersion thermostat	Tauchthermostat m
imbibition, absorption, sucking [up], suction	Aufsaugen n, Aufnahme f; Einsaugung f; Absorption f	immersion[-type] viscometer	Tauchviskosimeter n
imbibition [of texture]	Imbibition f [der Textur]	immersion washing	Standwässerung f
imbibition	s. a. swelling	immiscibility, non-miscibility	Nichtmischbarkeit f, Unmischbarkeit f, Unvermischbarkeit f
imbibitional force	Quellungskraft f		
imbibition method, Ambronn's imbibition method	Imbibitionsverfahren n [nach Ambronn], Ambronnsche Imbibitionsmethode f	immittance	Immittanz f <Blindwiderstand + -leitwert>
imbibition pressure, swelling pressure	Quellungsdruck m	immobile <astr.>, stationary	stationär, stillstehend <Astr.>
imitation; simulation	Modellierung f, Nachbildung f; Simulation f; Nachahmung f	immobile wave; standing wave; stationary wave; standing (stationary) vibration	stehende Welle f, Stehwelle f; stehende Schwingung f
immediate-acces storage (store)	s. zero-acces storage		
immediate effect of irradiation	Frühfolgen fpl der Bestrahlung	immovable	unbewegbar, unverrückbar
		immunodiffusion	Immundiffusion f, Geldiffusion f
immersed, inserted <of rods>	eingetaucht	immunoelectrophoresis	Immunelektrophorese f
immersed compass, floating card compass, fluid compass	Schwimmkompaß m	impact; collision; shock; encounter; impinging	Stoß m; Zusammenstoß m; Kollision f; Zusammenprall m
		impact; shock; percussion; stroke; blow; push; shove; impulse	Schlag m; Stoß m, Anstoß m
immersion	Immersion f		
immersion <geo.>	s. depression <of land>		
immersion <behind the limb of the Moon or Sun>, disappearance, disappearing	Verschwinden n <hinter dem Mond- oder Sonnenrand>	impact, bound, bounce, shock, knock-on, impingement, impinging	Aufschlag m, Aufprall m, Anprall m, Prall m
		impact <astr.>	Einsturz m, Aufsturz m <Astr.>
immersion	s. a. moving in <of rods>	impact, impulsive	stoßartig
immersion colorimeter	Eintauchkolorimeter n [nach Duboseq], Duboseq-Kolorimeter n	impact bending strength	Schlagbiegefestigkeit f
immersion condenser	Immersions[dunkelfeld]-kondensor m		
immersion counter	Eintauchzählrohr n, Tauchzählrohr n, Tauchzähler m		
immersion depth	s. submergence	impact bending strength; impact toughness (resilience) <of plastics>	Schlagbiegezähigkeit f, Schlagzähigkeit f
immersion dose	Immersionsdosis f		
immersion electrode, immersion-type electrode	Tauchelektrode f	impact brittleness	Schlagsprödigkeit f
		impact broadening	s. collision broadening
immersion electron microscope, immersion microscope	Immersions[elektronen]-mikroskop n	impact chain, collision chain, chain of collisions, chain	Stoßkette f
immersion hardening, hardening by immersion, liquid hardening	Tauchhärtung f	impact coefficient	s. restitution coefficient
		impact compression test, compression impact test	Schlagstauchversuch m, Schlagdruckversuch m
immersion lens	Immersionslinse f		
immersion method, immersion technique	Immersionsmethode f, Immersionsverfahren n, Immersionstechnik f, Einbettungsmethode f	impact cross-section	s. collision cross-section
		impact elasticity	s. rebound elasticity
		impact electron	Stoßelektron n
immersion method	s. a. immersion technique	impact endurance test, repeated-load impact test	Vielschlagversuch m
immersion microscope, immersion electron microscope	Immersions[elektronen]-mikroskop n	impact energy, energy of the impact; striking energy	Stoßenergie f; Schlagenergie f
immersion objective	Immersionsobjektiv n, Immersion f		
immersion oil	Immersionsöl n	impact excitation, shock (repulse, impulse, pulse) excitation <of oscillation>	Stoßanregung f, Stoßerregung f <Schwingung>
immersion pyrometer, immersion-type pyrometer	Tauchpyrometer n; Tauchthermoelement n		
		impact excitation	s. a. collisional excitation <of radiation>
immersion refractometer	Eintauchrefraktometer n	impact fatigue strength	Dauerschlagfestigkeit f, Dauerschlagarbeit f, Schlagermüdungsgrenze f
immersion refractometry	Eintauchrefraktometrie f		
		impact figure, impact pattern, percussion figure	Schlagfigur f
immersion system	Immersionssystem n		
immersion technique, immersion method	Tauchverfahren n, Tauchmethode f <Techn.>	impact fluorescence	Stoßfluoreszenz f
immersion technique	s. a. immersion method	impact force	Stoßkraft f; Schlagkraft f

impact fracture	Stoßbruch *m*	impact theory; collision theory	Stoßtheorie *f*
impact hardness	Stoßhärte *f*, Schlaghärte *f*	impact torsion test, torsion impact test	Schlagverdrehversuch *m*, Schlagtorsionsversuch *m*, Schlagdrehversuch *m*
impact hardness testing	Schlaghärteprüfung *f*	impact toughness	s. impact bending strength
		impact transfer, shock transfer	Stoßübertragung *f*
		impact transition temperature	Versprödungstemperatur *f*
impact hypothesis, meteoric theory, meteoritic theory	Einsturztheorie *f*, Meteoritentheorie *f*, Aufsturztheorie *f*	impact tube, pressure tube, impact pipe ‹meas.›	Stau[druck]rohr *n*, Staudruckmesser *m*; Staudruckfahrtmesser *m* ‹Meß.›
impact ionization, collision ionization, ionization by collision	Stoßionisation *f*, Stoßionisierung *f*	impact tube	s. a. Pitot tube
		impact value	s. notch impact strength
		impact value	s. a. impact strength
impact ionization coefficient	Stoßionisationskoeffizient *m*	impact wave, shock wave, blast	Stoßwelle *f*
impact ionization probability, impact ionization rate	Stoßionisationswahrscheinlichkeit *f*	impact wear, wear by impacts, brinelling	Stoßverschleiß *m*
		impact work	s. impulsive work
impact ionization rate, impact ionization probability	Stoßionisationswahrscheinlichkeit *f*	impedance, electric[al] impedance, apparent resistance, alternating-current resistance, skin resistance, resistance operator, a.c. resistance ‹el.›	[elektrischer] Scheinwiderstand *m*, [komplexer] Wechselstromwiderstand *m*, [elektrische] Impedanz *f*, scheinbarer Widerstand *m*, Scheinwert *m* des Wechselstromwiderstandes, Widerstandsoperator *m*, Richtwiderstand *m* ‹El.›
impact load, impulsive load, shock load (stress), sudden [change of] load; impact stress	schlagartige Beanspruchung *f*, Schlagbeanspruchung *f*, Beanspruchung *f* auf Schlag; Stoßbeanspruchung *f*, stoßartige (stoßweise) Beanspruchung *f*; Stoßbelastung *f*, stoßweise Belastung *f*; Stoßlast *f*		
		impedance	s. a. acoustic impedance ‹ac.›
		impedance bridge, skeleton-type bridge	Impedanz[meß]brücke *f*, Scheinwiderstands-[meß]brücke *f*
impact machine	Schlagwerk *n*	impedance-capacitance coupling	Kondensator-Drossel-Kopplung *f*
impact matrix, collision matrix	Stoßmatrix *f*	impedance-capacitance coupling	s. a. inductance-capacitance coupling ‹of thermionic tubes›
impact momentum	s. momentum of the impact		
impact neutron	Anstoßneutron *n*		
impact normal, shock normal	Stoßnormale *f*	impedance converter; impedance transformer	Impedanzwandler *m*
impactor	Impaktor *m*		
impact parameter, collision parameter	Stoßparameter *m*		
		impedance coupling; choke coupling	Drosselkopplung *f*
impact parameter approximation	Stoßparameternäherung *f*	impedance function	Impedanzfunktion *f*
		impedance locus	Widerstandsortskurve *f*
impact pattern, impact figure	Schlagfigur *f*	impedance matrix ‹el., therm.›	Impedanzmatrix *f* ‹El., Therm.›
impact pipe	s. impact tube		
impact point	s. point of collision		
impact pressure, shock pressure	Stoßdruck *m*, Stoßkraft *f*	impedance matrix, Z matrix ‹of waveguide›	Wellenwiderstandsmatrix *f*, Z-Matrix *f* ‹Wellenleiter›
impact process, knock-on process	Anstoßprozeß *m*		
		impedance meter, impedometer	Scheinwiderstandsmesser *m*, Scheinwiderstandsprüfer *m*, Impedanzmesser *m*, Impedanzmeßgerät *n*
impact radiation, collision radiation	Stoßstrahlung *f*		
impact resilience	s. impact bending strength		
impact resistance	s. notch impact strength		
impact resistance	s. a. impact strength		s. input impedance
impact sound; impulsive sound; strike note	Schlagton *m*; Schallstoß *m*	impedance of driving-point	
impact spectrum	Stoßspektrum *n*	impedance of grid circuit	Gitterimpedanz *f*, Gitterkreisimpedanz *f*
		impedance operator, symbolic impedance	Operatorimpedanz *f*
impact strength, impact value, impact resistance, toughness, shock resistance, shock stability, resistance to impact (shock), shock strength	Schlag[formänderungs]festigkeit *f*; Schlagelastizitätsgrenze *f*; Schlagstreckgrenze *f*; Schlagstauchgrenze *f*, spezifische Schlagarbeit *f*, Stoßfestigkeit *f*		
		impedance phase angle	Widerstandsphasenwinkel *m*
		impedance transformation	s. resistance transformation
		impedance transformer; impedance converter	Impedanzwandler *m*
impact strength	s. a. notch impact strength		
impact stress	s. impact load		
impact tensile strength, tensile impact strength	Schlagzugfestigkeit *f*		
		impedance triangle, triangle of impedance, vector diagram of impedance	Widerstandsdreieck *n*
impact tension test[ing]	s. tension impact test		
impact test ‹techn.›	Schlagversuch *m*, Schlagprobe *f*, Schlagprüfung *f*, Stoßversuch *m* ‹Techn.›		
		impedance-type partial-fraction network	Widerstands-Partialbruchschaltung *f*
impact testing machine	Schlagprüfgerät *n*		
		impedance unbalance measuring set, return loss measuring set	Fehlerdämpfungsmesser *m*, Nachbild[ungs]messer *m*
impact test using progressive load; test using progressive load	Stufenversuch *m*; Stufenschlagversuch *m*		
		impedometer	s. impedance meter

impedor	Impedanz f, Scheinwiderstand m, Impedor m <Bauelement>	impossible displacement	unmögliche Verrückung f
impeller <of pump>; runner <of water turbine>	Laufrad n, Kreiselrad n, Rotor m, Läufer m <Turbine, Pumpe>	impossible velocity, velocity incompatible with the constraints	unmögliche Geschwindigkeit f
impeller	s. a. propeller	impoverishment; depletion; exhaustion	Verarmung f; Erschöpfung f, Verbrauchen n
impeller pump	s. rotodynamic pump	impregnated carbon	imprägnierte Kohle f
impenetrability	s. tightness		
impenetrable	s. tight	impregnated cathode	imprägnierte Katode (Vorratskatode) f
imperfect crystal, real crystal, non-ideal crystal, disordered crystal	Realkristall m, realer (nichtidealer, fehlerhafter, fehlgeordneter) Kristall m, Fehlkristall m	impregnation; soaking	Imprägnieren n; Tränken n; Durchtränken n
imperfect elasticity	unvollkommene Elastizität f	impress	s. indentation
imperfect gas	s. real gas	impressed electromotive force, impressed e.m.f.	eingeprägte (innere) Feldstärke f, eingeprägte elektromotorische Kraft f, eingeprägte EMK f
imperfection, non-ideality	Unvollkommenheit f, Nichtidealität f, nichtideales Verhalten n		
		impressed field	eingeprägtes Feld n
imperfection, defect <cryst.>	Fehlstelle f, Defekt m, Fehlordnung f <Krist.>	impressed force, acting force, active force	eingeprägte Kraft f
imperfection	s. a. defect	impressed voltage	aufgedrückte Spannung f
imperfection of crystal	s. crystal imperfection	impression, visual impression <opt.>	Sehbild n, Anschauungsbild n, Eindruck m <Opt.>
imperfect resonance	unvollständige (unvollkommene) Resonanz f		
imperfect year, deficient year, annus deficiens	mangelhaftes Gemeinjahr n	impression	s. a. sensation
		impression of depth	s. space impression
		imprimitive	imprimitiv
imperial inch, inch, international inch, Canadian inch, in., " <= 25,4 mm>	Zoll n, " <= 25,4 mm>	imprisoned radiation, diffused radiation	diffundierte Strahlung f, Diffusionsstrahlung f
		imprisonment, clathration <chem.>	Einschließung f <Chem.>
imperial [standard] yard	s. yard	imprisonment of resonance radiation, radiation diffusion (trapping, capture), resonance radiation trapping (capture)	Strahlungsdiffusion f, Resonanzstrahlungseinfang m
impermeability	s. tightness		
impermeability to light; opacity, opaqueness, blackness; non-transparency	Lichtundurchlässigkeit f, Undurchlässigkeit f für Licht; Undurchsichtigkeit f		
impermeable	s. tight	improper action variable, improper phase integral	uneigentliche Wirkungsvariable f
impermeable stratum, aquifuge	wasserundurchlässige Schicht f, Wassertrennungsschicht f		
		improper angle variable	uneigentliche Winkelvariable f
impermeable to heat	s. athermanous	improper cavitation	unechte Kavitation f
impermeable to light; opaque; non-transparent, not transparent	lichtundurchlässig, undurchlässig für Licht; opak; undurchsichtig, nicht durchsichtig	improper colour mixture, extrinsic colour mixture	äußere Farbmischung f, uneigentliche Farbmischung
		improper function	uneigentliche Funktion f
		improper integral	uneigentliches Integral n
impersonal equation	unpersönliche Gleichung f	improper mapping, improper transformation	uneigentliche Transformation (Abbildung) f
impersonal micrometer	unpersönliches Mikrometer n		
impervious [to]	s. tight	improper orthogonal mapping, improper orthogonal transformation, reversal, reflexotation, improper rotation, rotary reflection <math.>	uneigentliche orthogonale Transformation (Abbildung) f, Drehung f und Spiegelung f, Drehspiegelung f, Umlegung f, Umwendung f <Math.>
imperviousness	s. tightness		
impetus <geo.>	Impetus m <Geo.>		
impingement	s. bound		
impingement attack (erosion), rain erosion	Tropfenschlagerosion f; Regenerosion f, Tropfenschlagkavitation		
impinging; collision; impact; shock; encounter	Stoß m; Zusammenstoß m; Kollision f; Zusammenprall m	improper phase integral, improper action variable	uneigentliche Wirkungsvariable f
impinging	s. a. bound	improper rearrangement, improper transposition	unechte Umlagerung f, Umlagerung im weiteren Sinn
implant	Spickungspräparat n, Spickung f		
implementation	s. carrying out	improper rotation	unechte Drehung f
implicit function theorem	Auflösungssatz m	improper rotation	s. a. improper orthogonal mapping <math.>
implosion	Implosion f		
imponderability, imponderableness	Unwägbarkeit f, Imponderabilität f; Gewichtslosigkeit f	improper transformation, improper mapping	uneigentliche Transformation (Abbildung) f
imponderability	s. a. absense of gravity	improper transposition, improper rearrangement	unechte Umlagerung f, Umlagerung im weiteren Sinn
imponderable, weightless, agravic	schwerelos		
imponderable, weightless, unponderable, unweighable	unwägbar [gering], Spuren-; gewichtslos	improper variable [star], pseudo[]variable [star], extrinsic variable [star]	Pseudoveränderlicher m, uneigentlicher Veränderlicher m
imponderableness	s. imponderability		
importance	Neutroneneinfluß m, Einfluß m [der Neutronen], Neutroneninhalt m	improved Euler-Cauchy method	verbessertes Euler-Cauchy-Verfahren n
<of neutrons>, neutron importance		improved Euler (point slope) method	verbessertes Polygonzugverfahren n
importance function <nucl.>	Einflußfunktion f <Kern.>	improvement factor	Verbesserungsfaktor m
importance of the flare, class of the flare	Intensitätsklasse f der Sonneneruption	impulse, impulse of force, time integral of force <mech.>	Impuls m, Kraftstoß m, Kraftimpuls m, Zeitintegral n der Kraft
important identifying line, analytical (identifying) line <spectr.>	Analysenlinie f, Hauptlinie f, Hauptnachweislinie f <Spektr.>	impulse	s. a. impact
		impulse	s. a. pulse
impossibility principle	Unmöglichkeitsprinzip n	impulse amplifier	s. pulse amplifier
impossibility theorem	Unmöglichkeitssatz m	impulse approximation	Impulsnäherung f

impulse breakdown	Stoßdurchschlag m, Stoßdurchbruch m, elektrischer Durchschlag (Durchbruch) m bei Stoßspannung, Stoßüberschlag m	impulse-type telemetering	Impulsfrequenz[-Fernmeß]verfahren n, Impulsfernmessung f, Impulsfrequenz-Fernmessung f
impulse breakdown voltage	Stoßdurchschlagspannung f, Stoßdurchbruchspannung f, Stoßüberschlagspannung f	impulse ultrasound, impulse sound, pulse ultrasound (sound)	Impulsschall m
impulse contact	Wischkontakt m, Impulskontakt m	impulse voltage breakdown strength	s. impulse electric strength
		impulse voltage generator, pulse (surge) voltage generator	Stoßspannungsgenerator m, Stoßspannungserzeuger m
impulse corona	s. burst pulse corona	impulse water turbine, action water turbine	Freistrahlturbine f, hydraulische Aktionsturbine f
impulse counter	s. pulse counter <nucl.>	impulse wheel	s. impulse turbine
impulse current generator, pulse (surge) current generator	Stoßstromgenerator m, Stoßstromerzeuger m	impulsing, pulsing, [im]pulse sending	Impulsgebung f, Impulsgabe f
impulse direction finding, pulse direction finding, impulse (pulsed, pulse) radar	Impulspeilverfahren n, Impulspeilung f, Impulsradar n	impulsing rate, counting rate; pulse rate	Zählrate f, Zählgeschwindigkeit f; Impulsdichte f, Impulsrate f
impulse discharge	s. impulsive discharge	impulsive, impact	stoßartig
impulse electric strength, impulse voltage breakdown strength	Stoßdurchbruchfestigkeit f, Stoßdurchschlagfestigkeit f, Stoßüberschlagfestigkeit f, Impulsdurchschlagsfestigkeit f	impulsive burst	impulsiver Burst m
		impulsive discharge, pulsed discharge, [im]pulse discharge	Stoßentladung f, Impulsentladung f
impulse exciter	s. impulser	impulsive force, instantaneous force, momentary force	momentan wirkende Kraft f, Stoßkraft f, Momentankraft f
impulse function, pulse function	Stoßfunktion f, Impulsfunktion f, Nadelfunktion f	impulsive load	s. impact load
impulse generator, pulse generator, pulse generating device	Impulsgenerator m, Stoßgenerator m; Impulserzeuger m; Wanderwellengenerator m	impulsive moment	Stoßmoment n
		impulsive moment	s. a. angular impulse
		impulsive motion, impulse motion	Anlaufströmung f, Anlaufbewegung f
impulse loading	s. dynamic loading	impulsive sound	s. impact sound
impulse magnetization, pulse magnetization	Stoßmagnetisierung f	impulsive work, impact work	Stoßarbeit f; Schlagarbeit f
impulse motion, impulsive motion	Anlaufströmung f, Anlaufbewegung f.	impulsor, ejector, torsor <math.>	Impulsor m, Ejektor m, Torsor m <Math.>
impulse noise, pulse noise	Impulsrauschen n	impurity; adulterant; admixture; contaminant	Verunreinigung f; Beimischung f, Beimengung f; Fremdbestandteil m, Fremdstoff m, Fremdbaustein m
impulse of current, pulse (rush) of current, current [im]pulse, current rush (surge), surge	Stromstoß m, Stromimpuls m		
impulse of force	s. impulse	impurity, chemical impurity, lattice impurity <cryst., semi.>	[chemische] Störstelle f, Fremdstörstelle f, Fremdbeimischung f, Beimischung f, Verunreinigung f, Beimengung f
impulse of recoil, recoil impulse	Rückstoßimpuls m		
impulse of tension	s. impulse of voltage		
impulse of voltage, pulse of voltage, voltage impulse (pulse), impulse (pulse) of tension, voltage surge	Spannungsstoß m, Spannungsimpuls m	impurity	s. a. extrinsic <semi.>
		impurity addition	Fremdatomzusatz m
		impurity adsorption, adsorption of impurities	Fremdadsorption f
impulse oscillator, pulse oscillator	Impulsoszillator m	impurity atom, foreign atom <semi.>	Störatom n, Störstellenatom n, Fremdatom n, Störstelle f, gitterfremdes Atom n, Verunreinigungsatom n; Fremdstörstelle f <Halb.>
impulse permeability	Impulspermeabilität f		
impulse phase (position), pulse position, pulse phase	Impulslage f, Impulsphase f		
impulser, pulse modulator, pulser	Impulsmodulator m	impurity band; defect band	Störband n, Störstellenband n
		impurity band conduction	Störbandleitung f
impulser, pulser, [im]pulse sender, impulse exciter	Impulsgeber m	impurity centre, defect centre <semi.>	Störstellenzentrum n, Störzentrum n, Verunreinigungszentrum n <Halb.>
impulse radar	s. impulse direction finding		
impulse ratio	Stoßverhältnis n, Impulsverhältnis n	impurity concentration, concentration (density) of impurities, impurity density, defect concentration (density), contamination density	Störstellendichte f, Störstellenkonzentration f, Verunreinigungsdichte f, Verunreinigungskonzentration f
impulse reaction	s. delta reply		
impulse response	s. unit[-] impulse response		
impulse sender	s. impulser		
impulse sending	s. impulsing		
impulse sequence (series)	s. pulse train		
impulse sound, impulse ultrasound, pulse ultrasound (sound)	Impulsschall m	impurity conduction (conductivity)	s. extrinsic conduction
		impurity conductivity	s. extrinsic conductivity
		impurity content <semi.>	Störstellengehalt m, Verunreinigungsgehalt m <Halb.>; Fremdstoffgehalt m
impulse spectrum, pulse spectrum <el.>	Impulsspektrum n <El.>		
impulse strength, strength of the impulse, pulse strength	Impulsstärke f, Fläche f unter der Impulskurve	impurity density	s. impurity concentration
		impurity diffusion	Störstellendiffusion f, Verunreinigungsdiffusion f
impulse test[ing], pulse test (testing)	Impulsprüfverfahren n; Impuls-Echo-Prüfung f	impurity effect	Verunreinigungseffekt m
impulse train	s. pulse train		
impulse turbine, free-jet-type turbine; action turbine, [single-wheel] Pelton turbine; Pelton [water-]wheel, impulse wheel	Freistrahlturbine f, Gleichdruckturbine f; Aktionsturbine f, Pelton-Turbine f, Becherturbine f; Pelton-Rad n	impurity ion, extrinsic (foreign, added) ion	Störion n, Fremdion n
		impurity level, defect level; impurity state, defect state	Stör[stellen]niveau n, Verunreinigungsniveau n; Stör[stellen]zustand m, Verunreinigungszustand m

impurity level population	Störniveaubesetzung *f*	**incident particle,** bombarding particle, projectile	Beschußteilchen *n*, Geschoßteilchen *n*, einfallendes (einlaufendes) Teilchen *n*
impurity mobility, defect mobility	Störstellenbeweglichkeit *f*	**incident wave,** incoming wave	einlaufende Welle *f*, einfallende Welle
impurity semiconductor	s. extrinsic semiconductor	**incipient crack (flaw)**	Anriß *m*
impurity site, defect site	Störstellenplatz *m*		
impurity state	s. impurity level	**incipient plasmolysis,** liminal plasmolysis	Grenzplasmolyse *f*
impurity term, defect term <semi.>	Störterm *m*, Störstellenterm *m* <Halb.>	**incircle,** inscribed circle	Inkreis *m*, einbeschriebener Kreis *m*
impurity-vacancy pair	Verunreinigungs-Leerstellen-Paar *n*, Störstelle-Loch-Paar *n*	**incision**	Einschnitt *m*, Einschneiden *n*
impurity zone <semi.>	Störstellenzone *f*, Störzone *f* <Halb.>	**inclination,** slope; incline; tilt	Neigung *f*; Gefälle *n*; Steigung *f*
imref <US>, quasi-Fermi level	Quasi-Fermi-Niveau *n*, Quasi-Fermi-Kante *f*	**inclination,** angle of inclination; tilt angle, angle of tilt, angle of slope, slope angle	Neigungswinkel *m*, Neigung *f*; Fallwinkel *m*
inaccessibility	Unzugänglichkeit *f*		
inaccessibility axiom [of Carathéodory]	s. principle of inaccessibility	**inclination** <to>; tilting	Neigung *f* <gegen, zu>; Schrägstellung *f*
inaccuracy of measurement, measurement (measuring) inaccuracy	Meßunsicherheit *f*	**inclination**	s. a. inclination of orbit
		inclination	s. a. magnet dip
		inclination balance	Neigungswaage *f*
inactivating, inactivation, deactivation, desactivation	Inaktivierung *f*, De[s]aktivierung *f*, Entaktivierung *f*	**inclination factor,** obliquity factor	Fresnelscher Neigungsfaktor *m*, Neigungsfaktor
inactivation <bio.>	Inaktivierung *f* <Bio.>		
inactive, passive, reactionless <chem.>	passiv, Passiv-, inaktiv, reaktionsträge <Chem.>		
		inclination joint <of microscope>	Kippe *f* <Mikroskop>
inactive, stable; nonactive, non-radioactive; cold <nucl.>	stabil; inaktiv, nichtaktiv, nichtradioaktiv; kalt <Kern.>	**inclination of orbit;** path inclination	Bahnneigung *f*
inactive, optically inactive <opt.>	optisch inaktiv, inaktiv <Opt.>	**inclination of orbit,** inclination to ecliptic, inclination <astr.>	Neigung *f* der Bahnebene, Bahnneigung *f* [gegen die Ekliptik], Inklination *f* <Astr.>
inactive carrier	s. stable carrier		
inactive radical, radicaloid	Radikaloid *n*, inaktives Radikal *n*	**inclination variometer,** dip variometer, I-variometer	Inklinationsvariometer *n*, I-Variometer *n*
inactive vibration	inaktive Schwingung *f*	**incline;** slope; inclination, tilt	Neigung *f*; Gefälle *n*; Steigung *f*
inactivity, inertness, reactionlessness <chem.>	chemische Trägheit *f*, Reaktionsträgheit *f*, Inaktivität *f* <Chem.>	**inclined**	s. oblique
in-air dose, free air dose, air dose	Dosis *f* „frei in Luft", Freiluftdosis *f*, Luftdosis *f*	**inclined body tube**	Schrägtubus *m*, Schrägeinblick[tubus] *m*
inaudible sound	unhörbarer Schall *m*	**inclined dispersion**	geneigte Dispersion
incalescence, incandescence, white heat (glow), glowing heat, glow heat	Weißglut *f*, Weißglühen *n*, Weißglühhitze *f*, Weißgluthitze *f*, Inkaleszenz *f* <1300 °C und mehr>	**inclined flow**	Schrägströmung *f*
		inclined hemihedry	s. hemimorphic hemihedry of the regular system
incandescence, heat, glowing, glow	Glut *f*, Glühen *n*	**inclined plane,** oblique plane	schiefe Ebene *f*
incandescence	s. a. incalescence	**inclined shower,** lateral shower	Seitenschauer *m*; schräg einfallender Schauer *m*
incandescence	s. a. heat radiation		
incandescent bulb	s. incandescent lamp	**inclined throw,** oblique projection <mech.>	schiefer Wurf *m* <Mech.>
incandescent cathode	s. hot cathode		
incandescent-filament lamp	Glühfadenlampe *f*		
incandescent gas light	s. gas light	**inclined track**	geneigte Spur *f*, schräg einfallende Spur, Schrägbahn *f*
incandescent lamp, incandescent bulb, electric bulb, glow lamp	Glühlampe *f*	**inclined tube manometer,** tilting manometer	Schrägrohrmanometer *n*, Flüssigkeitsmanometer *n* mit geneigtem Schenkel
incandescent light	Glühlicht *n*, weißes Licht *n*		
incandescent mantle	s. Welsbach mantle	**inclinometer**	s. clinometer
incandescent tube	Glühröhrchen *n*	**inclusion** <in a crystal>	Einschluß *m*, Inklusion *f* <in einem Kristall>
inch, international inch, imperial inch, Canadian inch, in., " <= 25,4 mm>	Zoll *n*, " <= 25,4 mm>	**inclusion** <math.>	Inklusion *f*, Enthaltenseinsbeziehung *f* <Math.>
incidence; entering; incoming, arrival <e.g. of wave>	Einfall *m*, Inzidenz *f*; Einlaufen *n*; Auftreffen *n* <z. B. Welle>	**inclusion compound**	Einschlußverbindung *f*
incidence / at <plate>	angestellt <Platte>	**inclusion model of Kersten,** Kersten['s] inclusion model	Fremdkörpermodell *n* [von Kersten], Kerstensches Fremdkörpermodell
incidence angle	s. angle of incidence		
incident dose	Einfallsdosis *f*	**inclusion of additional points**	Neupunkteinschaltung *f*, Punkteinschaltung *f*, Einschaltung *f* <Geo.>
incident light	s. reflected light		
incident light attachment, diffusing screen <opt.>	Streuscheibe *f*, Streuschirm *m*, Streuer *m* <Opt.>		
incident light condenser	s. vertical illuminator	**inclusion of air,** trapping of air	Lufteinschluß *m*
incident light illumination	s. vertical illumination		

inclusion theorem	Einschließungssatz *m*	incongruent saturated solution	*s.* incongruently saturated solution
inclusion theory of Kersten, Kersten['s] inclusion theory, foreign body theory	Kerstensche Theorie *f*, Fremdkörpertheorie *f* von Kersten	incongruous <math.>, incongruent	inkongruent <Math.>
incoherence, non-coherence	Inkohärenz *f*, Nichtkohärenz *f*	inconsistence, inconsistency	Inkonsistenz *f*
incoherent addition [of light beams]	inkohärente Addition *f* [von Lichtstrahlen]	inconstancy, non-constancy <math.>	Inkonstanz *f*, Nichtkonstanz *f* <Math.>
incoherent colloidal system	*s.* sol	inconstancy, instability, non-constancy <meas.>	Inkonstanz *f*, Instabilität *f* <Meß.>
incoherent cross-section	*s.* incoherent scattering cross-section	in-core detector	Incoredetektor *m*, „in-core"-Detektor *m*
incoherent radiation	inkohärente Strahlung *f*	incorporation <bio.>	Inkorporieren *n*, Inkorporation *f* <Bio.>
incoherent scattering cross-section, incoherent cross-section, cross-section for incoherent scattering	inkohärenter Streuquerschnitt *m*, Wirkungsquerschnitt *m* für inkohärente Streuung, Wirkungsquerschnitt der inkohärenten Streuung	incorporation	*s. a.* introduction <e.g. of impurities>
		increase; growth; rise, rising; augmentation; increment; accretion; gain; ascent; enhancement; build-up; elevation	Zunahme *f*; Anstieg *m*; Anwachsen *n*; Vergrößerung *f*, Erhöhung *f*, Steigen *n*, Wachsen *n*, Wachstum *n*; Zuwachs *m*, Inkrement *n*; Heraufsetzung *f*
incoherent unit, non-coherent unit	nichtkohärente (inkohärente, systemfreie, systemfremde) Einheit *f*	increase, enhancement	Steigerung *f*
incombustibility	Unbrennbarkeit *f*, Unverbrennbarkeit *f*	increase in temperature	*s.* temperature increase
incombustible	*s.* non[-]combustible	increase of pressure, pressure rise, elevation of pressure	Druckerhöhung *f*, Drucksteigerung *f*; Druckanstieg *m*
incoming, incidence; entering; arrival <e.g. of wave>	Einfall *m*, Inzidenz *f*; Einlaufen *n*; Auftreffen *n* <z. B. Welle>	increase of slope	Versteilerung *f*
incoming pulse, input pulse	Eingangsimpuls *m*, ankommender Impuls *m*	increase of temperature	*s.* temperature increase
incoming wave, incident wave	einlaufende Welle *f*, einfallende Welle	increase of tensile strength	Reißverfestigung *f*
incommensurability	Inkommensurabilität *f*	increase of the period of seismic waves	Periodenverlängerung *f* (Verlängerung *f* der Periode) seismischer Wellen
incompatibility tensor	Inkompatibilitätstensor *m*		
incompatible	unvereinbar, unverträglich, nicht miteinander verträglich, inkompatibel, disjunkt	increase of volume, volume increase; bulking	Volum[en]zunahme *f*, Volum[en]vergrößerung *f*
incompatible events, mutually exclusive events	disjunkte (unvereinbare) Ereignisse *npl*	increase operator, growth operator, operator of increase	Zuwachsoperator *m*
incomplete beta[-] function	unvollständige Betafunktion *f*, $B(x, \alpha, \beta)$	increment	*s.* increase
		incremental control	*s.* step control
incomplete breakdown, partial breakdown	Teildurchschlag *m*	incremental grid resistance	*s.* grid resistance
incomplete circuit	*s.* open circuit	incremental impulse	zusätzlicher Impuls *m*, Zusatzimpuls *m*, Zuwachsimpuls *m*
incomplete combustion, partial combustion	unvollständige Verbrennung *f*, Teilverbrennung *f*		
incomplete elliptical integral	unvollständiges elliptisches Integral *n*	incremental inductance, additional inductance	zusätzliche Induktivität *f*, Zusatzinduktivität *f*, Zuwachsinduktivität *f*
incomplete evaporation, partial evaporation	Teilverdampfung *f*, unvollständige Verdampfung *f*	incremental permeability	Amplitudenpermeabilität *f*; Wechselpermeabilität *f*, bezogen auf den Scheitelwert der Wechselgrößen; Überlagerungspermeabilität *f*, permanente (zusätzliche) Permeabilität *f*, Zusatzpermeabilität *f*, Zuwachspermeabilität *f*
incomplete gamma[-] function	unvollständige Gammafunktion *f*, $\Gamma(x, p)$		
incomplete miscibility	*s.* partial miscibility		
incompleteness	Unvollständigkeit *f*		
incomplete reflection	unvollkommene Spiegelung *f*		
incomplete shadow	*s.* penumbra		
incomplete shell, unfilled shell	nichtabgeschlossene (nichtbesetzte, nicht vollbesetzte, nicht aufgefüllte, unvollständige) Schale *f*		
		incremental resistance	*s.* grid resistance
		incremental resistance	*s.* internal resistance < of thermionic valve, triode>
incomplete wetting	unvollkommene (unvollständige) Benetzung *f*	incrustation, encrustation	Verkrustung *f*, Überkrustung *f*, Krustenbildung *f*
incompressibility	Inkompressibilität *f*, Nichtzusammendrückbarkeit *f*, Nichtzusammenpreßbarkeit *f*, Nichtkomprimierbarkeit *f*, Unzusammendrückbarkeit *f*		
		incubation [period], incubation time; latent (latency) period, latent (latency) time <of a disease> <bio.>	Inkubationszeit *f*, Inkubation *f*; Latenzzeit *f*, Latenz *f* <Krankheit> <Bio.>
incompressibility coefficient	Inkompressibilität[skoeffizient *m*] *f*		
incompressible flow	inkompressible Strömung *f*; inkompressibles Fließen *n*	incubation time; delay time, half-peak delay; peak delay	Verzögerungszeit *f*
incongruent, incongruous <math.>	inkongruent <Math.>		
		indecomposable matrix	*s.* non-decomposable matrix
incongruently saturated solution, incongruent saturated solution	inkongruent gesättigte Lösung *f*, inkongruente gesättigte Lösung	indecomposable representation	unzerlegbare Darstellung *f*
		indefinite	*s.* smeared
incongruent melting	inkongruentes Schmelzen *n*	indefinite integral	unbestimmtes Integral *n*
incongruent melting point	inkongruenter Schmelzpunkt *m*	indefinite integral, antiderivative, primitive	Stammfunktion *f*, primitive Funktion *f*, [unbestimmtes] Newtonsches Integral *n*
incongruent phase	inkongruente Phase *f*		
		indefinite metric	indefinite Metrik *f*

indefiniteness 358

indefiniteness; indeterminateness, indeterminedness, undeterminedness <math.>	Unbestimmtheit f <Math.>	**indeterminateness, indeterminedness,** undeterminedness; indefiniteness <math.>	Unbestimmtheit f <Math.>
indefinite quadratic form	indefinite quadratische Form f	**indeterminateness, indeterminedness,** undeterminedness <mech.>	Unbestimmtheit f <Mech.>
indent[ation], pit, recess, depression	Aussparung f, Ausschnitt m, Vertiefung f, Höhlung f, Einbuchtung f	**index,** index of the crystal face, symbol of the crystal face <cryst.>	Flächenindex m, Flächensymbol n, Symbol n der Kristallfläche <Krist.>
indentation; impress	Eindrückung f, Eindringen n; Eindruck m	**index** <of the curve>, number of turns	Windungszahl f, Umlaufszahl f, Index m <Kurve>
indentation	s. a. notch	**index** <of the subgroup>	Index m <Untergruppe>
indentation hardness	Eindruckhärte f, Eindringhärte f, Druckhärte f, Härte f gegenüber dem Eindringen	**index**	s. a. subscript or superscript <math.>
indentation problem	Kerbproblem n	**index**	s. a. exponent <math.>
indented	s. toothed	**index**	s. a. indicator
indenter	Eindruckprüfkörper m, Eindringkörper m	**index catalogue**	Indexkatalog m
		index correction <e.g. of theodolite>; instrument correction	Instrumentenkorrektion f, Instrumentalkorrektion f; Indexkorrektion f <z. B. Theodolit>
indenting, notching, cutting	Kerbung f, Einkerbung f; Nutung f	**index ellipsoid,** Fletcher['s] indicatrix, optical indicatrix, indicatrix of refraction, wavenormal ellipsoid, ellipsoid of wave normals, reciprocal ellipsoid, ellipsoid of elasticity <opt.>	Indexellipsoid n, Brechungsindexellipsoid n, Fletchersches Ellipsoid n, Indikatrix f, Fletchersche (optische) Indikatrix, Normal[en]ellipsoid n, reziprokes Ellipsoid, Elastizitätsellipsoid n <Opt.>
independence of temperature; temperature stability	Temperaturunabhängigkeit f; Temperaturkonstanz f, Temperaturstabilität f		
independence theorem	Unabhängigkeitsprinzip n [der Kraftwirkungen], viertes Newtonsches Gesetz n, [Newtons] Lex f quarta		
		index error	s. instrumental error
independent decay product	primäres Zerfallsprodukt n	**indexing,** indexing of crystal faces, determination of crystal indices <cryst.>	Indizierung f [von Kristallflächen], Bestimmung f der Indizes <Krist.>
independent equatorial co-ordinates, independent equatorial system [of co-ordinates], second equatorial system [of co-ordinates]	Rektaszensionssystem n, bewegliches Äquatorialsystem n, Koordinaten fpl im Rektaszensionssystem	**indexing** <math.>	Indizierung f; Bezeichnung f mit Indizes <Math.>
		indexing error, accumulated error <of division>	Summenteilfehler m; akkumulierter Fehler m
		indexing of crystal faces	s. indexing <cryst.>
independent excitation, external (separate) excitation	Fremderregung f; äußere Erregung f	**index mark;** reference mark	Strichmarke f
		index mark, adjustment mark; framing index	Einstellmarke f
independent fission yield, primary fission yield	primäre Spalt[produkt]ausbeute f, Fragmentausbeute f	**index number** <stat.>	Indexzahl f <Stat.>
		index number of altitude	s. cote
independent of direction, non-directional, non-directive, non-directed	richtungsunabhängig, ungerichtet	**index of circulation,** circulation index	Zirkulationsindex m
		index of flow, flow index, flow height	Abflußhöhe f
independent of structure	s. structure-insensitive	**index of inertia [of quadratic form]**	Trägheitsindex m [der quadratischen Form]
independent of the path	wegunabhängig		
independent of time, time-independent; scleronomous, scleronomic[al] <mech.>	zeitunabhängig, zeitfrei; skleronom <Mech.>	**index of Miller,** Miller [crystallographic] index	Miller-Index m, Millerscher Index m
		index of refraction	s. refractive index
independent pair model	Modell n unabhängiger Paare, ,,independent pair"-Modell n	**index of the crystal edge,** symbol of the crystal edge	Kantenindex m, Kantensymbol n, Symbol n der Kristallkante, Zonensymbol n
independent particle model [of nucleus]	Einzelteilchenmodell n, Einzelnukleonen-Kernmodell n	**index of the crystal face,** index, symbol of the crystal face <cryst.>	Flächenindex m, Flächensymbol n, Symbol n der Kristallfläche <Krist.>
independent stochastic variable	stochastisch unabhängige Variable f, unabhängige Zufallsvariable f	**index of the stream activity**	Index m (Kennzahl f) der Stromtätigkeit
		index sphere	Indexkugel f
independent variable, argument <math.>	unabhängige Variable (Veränderliche) f, Argument n	**index surface**	Indexfläche f
		index tensor	Indextensor m
indestructibility, indestructibleness	Unzerstörbarkeit f	**india-rubber ball,** rubber ball	Gummiball m
indestructibleness of the vortex	Wirbelunzerstörbarkeit f	**indicated power**	indizierte Leistung f, Indikatorleistung f
indeterminacy	Indeterminiertheit f	**indicated pressure**	indizierter Druck m
indeterminacy, uncertainty <phys.>	Unsicherheit f, Ungenauigkeit f, Unbestimmtheit f, Unschärfe f, Ungewißheit f <Phys.>	**indicated thermal balance**	indizierte Wärmebilanz f
		indicated work	indizierte Arbeit f, Indikatorarbeit f
indeterminacy of energy; energy blur	Energieunschärfe f; Energieunbestimmtheit f	**indicating goniometer;** pin-and-arc indicator	Winkelanzeigegerät n, Winkelindikator m; 1 in and Arc n
indeterminacy principle	s. uncertainty principle		
indeterminate	s. statically indeterminate	**indicating instrument,** indicator, indicator gauge <meas.>	anzeigendes Meßgerät n, Anzeigegerät n, Indikator m, Zeiger m
indeterminate equation, diophantine equation	diophantische Gleichung f, unbestimmte Gleichung f		
indeterminate form	unbestimmter Ausdruck m, unbestimmte Form f	**indicating liquid,** manometer liquid, manometric liquid (fluid)	Manometerflüssigkeit f

induced

indicating range	Anzeigebereich *m*	indirect controller	s. relay-operated controller
		indirect coupling	indirekte Kopplung *f*
indication, taking an indicator diagram <mech.>	Indizierung *f*, Aufnahme *f* eines Indikatordiagramms <Mech.>	indirect demonstration	s. indirect proof
		indirect excitation	Umweganregung *f*, indirekte Anregung *f*
indication, display	Anzeige *f*; Indikation *f*	indirect extrusion, inverted extrusion	Rückwärtsfließpressen *n*, Gegenfließpressen *n*
indication; signalling	Signalisierung *f*; Meldung *f*	indirect glare	indirekte Blendung *f*, Indirektblendung *f*; Umfeldblendung *f*
indication-background ratio	Anzeige-Nulleffekt-Verhältnis *n*		
indication of absolute (real) value, absolute (real) value indication	Istwertanzeige *f*, Absolutwertanzeige *f*	indirect interaction, compound-nucleus-type interaction	indirekte Wechselwirkung *f*, Wechselwirkung mit Compoundkernstadium
indicator, pointer, needle; index <of measuring instrument>	Zeiger *m* <allg.; Meßgerät>	indirect interstitial mechanism	s. interstitially mechanism
		indirect lighting	indirekte Beleuchtung *f*, Umfeldbeleuchtung *f*
indicator, visual indicator; visualizer, display unit (system), viewing unit; console <el.>	Sichtgerät *n* <El.>		
		indirectly heated cathode, separately heated cathode	indirekt geheizte Katode *f*
indicator, tracer, labelled atom, tagged atom, marker <nucl.>	Tracer *m*, markiertes Atom *n*, Indikator *m* <Kern.>	indirectly ionizing particle	indirekt ionisierendes Teilchen *n*
indicator	s. a. acid-base indicator	indirectly ionizing radiation	indirekt ionisierende Strahlung *f*
indicator	s. a. indicating instrument <meas.>	indirect nuclear reaction	s. compound nucleus mode
indicator	s. a. plan-position indicator <radar>	indirect observation	s. mediating observation
		indirect proof, reductio[n] ad absurdum proof, indirect demonstration	indirekter Beweis *m*, Widerspruchsbeweis *m*
indicator diagram, work diagram, performance chart; steam pressure diagram, vapour diagram, steam diagram	Indikatordiagramm *n*, *p,V*-Diagramm *n*, *pv*-Diagramm *n*, Druckdiagramm *n*, Arbeitsdiagramm *n*, Arbeitsschaubild *n*; Dampfdruckdiagramm *n*		
		indirect radiation	indirekte Strahlung *f*, Indirektstrahlung *f*
indicator gauge	s. indicating instrument <meas.>	indirect radiography	s. fluorography
		indirect vision, extrafoveal vision	indirektes (extrafoveales) Sehen *n*
indicator interval	s. transition interval	indirect wave, space (spatial, sky) wave, atmospheric (downcoming) wave <el.>	Raumwelle *f* <El.>
indicator paper, reaction (test) paper	Indikatorpapier *n*, Reagenzpapier *n*		
indicator range	s. transition interval		
indicator solution <chem.>	Indikatorlösung *f* <Chem.>	indirect wave, reflected wave <geo.>	reflektierte (indirekte) Welle *f* <Geo.>
indicator tube, display tube	Übersichtsröhre *f*, Übersichtsbildröhre *f*	indiscernibility, indistinguishability	Ununterscheidbarkeit *f*, Nichtunterscheidbarkeit *f*
		indissoluble, indissolvable, insoluble, undissolving	unlöslich, nichtlöslich; unangreifbar
indicatrix, Tissot indicatrix, distortion ellipse <geo.>	Tissotsche Indikatrix *f*, Indikatrix, Verzerrungsellipse *f* <Geo.>	indistinct, smeared, blurred, indefinite, featureless, structureless, washed-out, weakened	verwaschen, verschwommen, undeutlich, unscharf, wenig ausgeprägt
indicatrix <variational calculus>	Indikatrix *f* <Variationsrechnung>		
indicatrix	s. a. Dupin['s] indicatrix	indistinguishability, indiscernibility	Ununterscheidbarkeit *f*, Nichtunterscheidbarkeit *f*
indicatrix of diffusion	s. scattering indicatrix		
indicatrix of refraction	s. index ellipsoid	indistinguishability principle, principle of indistinguishability	Ununterscheidbarkeitsprinzip *n*
indicial admittance	Kennleitwert *m*		
		individual dosimetry, personal dosimetry	Personendosimetrie *f*, individuelle Dosimetrie *f*, Individualdosimetrie *f*
indicial equation	determinierende Gleichung (Fundamentalgleichung) *f*		
indicial response	s. unit[-] step response	individual ergodic theorem, Birkhoff ergodic theorem	individueller Ergodensatz *m*, Ergodensatz von Birkhoff
indifferent	indifferent		
indifferent; insensible; unfeeling <bio.>	unempfindlich <Bio.>	individual error, personal error	persönlicher Fehler *m*
indifferent electrode	indifferente Elektrode *f*	individual H theorem	individuelles *H*-Theorem *n*
indifferent equilibrium, neutral equilibrium (stability)	indifferentes Gleichgewicht *n*, stetiges Gleichgewicht	individual-particle approach, Hartree-Fock approach	Hartree-Fock-Näherung *f*, Hartree-Focksche Näherung *f*, Einzelteilchennäherung *f*
indifferent gas, neutral gas	indifferentes Gas *n*, Neutralgas *n*, neutrales Gas	individual-particle model [of nucleus]	Mehrteilchen-Schalenmodell *n* [des Atomkerns]
indifferent zone	Indifferenzzone *f*		
indiffusible; non-diffusible, non-diffusing	nichtdiffusibel, indiffusibel; nichtdiffundierend	individual-particle wave function	Einzelteilchen-Wellenfunktion *f*, Einteilchen-Wellenfunktion *f*, Einzelteilchenfunktion *f*
indiffusion	s. diffusing		
indirect-action controller	s. relay-operated controller	indivisibility	Unteilbarkeit *f*
indirect colorimetry, physical colorimetry	objektive Farbmessung *f*, physikalische Farbmessung	indoor <of apparatus>	Innenraum-, Innen-; Zimmer- <Gerät>
indirect control, control with power amplification	Regelung *f* mit Hilfsenergie, indirekte Regelung, mittelbare Regelung	induced absorption, stimulated absorption, Stoicheff absorption	induzierte (stimulierte, erzwungene) Absorption *f*, Stoicheff-Absorption *f*
		induced activity	s. induced radioactivity
		induced angle of attack	induzierter Anstellwinkel *m*

induced bremsstrahlung	induzierte Bremsstrahlung f	inducing, causing; effecting; induction; production	Verursachen n, Bewirken n, Bedingen n, Hervorrufen n; Auslösung f; Erzeugung f
induced charge, inductive charge	Influenzladung f, influenzierte (induzierte) Ladung f	inducing, induction; initiation, starting, commencement; introducing, introduction	Auslösung f, Einleitung f, Induzierung f; Initiierung f; Zündung f
induced circulation, forced circulation	Zwang[s]umlauf m, Zwang[s]zirkulation f, erzwungener Umlauf m	inducing, [electromagnetic] induction <el.>	Induzieren n, [elektromagnetische] Induktion f <El.>
induced conductivity	induzierte Leitfähigkeit f	inducing electrostatic charges, electric induction	Influenzieren n, elektrische Verteilung f, elektrostatische Induktion f
induced current, induction current	Induktionsstrom m, induzierter Strom m; Influenzstrom m	inductance; self-induction coefficient, coefficient of self-induction, self[-]inductance	Induktivität f; Selbstinduktionskoeffizient m, Koeffizient m der Selbstinduktion, Induktionskoeffizient m, Eigeninduktivität f, Selbstinduktivität f, Selbstinduktion f
induced decay	s. induced nuclear disintegration		
induced dipole radiation, enforced dipole radiation	erzwungene Dipolstrahlung f		
induced disintegration	s. induced nuclear disintegration	inductance box	Induktivitätskasten m [für Meßzwecke]
induced downwash	induzierter Abwind m	inductance box with plugs, plug inductance box	Stöpselinduktivität f
induced drag	s. trailing-edge drag <aero.>		
induced electromotive force, induced e.m.f., induced voltage, induction voltage	induzierte EMK, induzierte elektromotorische Kraft f, induzierte Spannung f, Induktionsspannung f	inductance bridge	Induktivitätsmeßbrücke f, Induktivitätsbrücke f
		inductance-capacitance coupling, impedance-capacitance coupling, choke coupling, L-C coupling <of thermionic tubes>	Drosselkopplung f, Drosselkondensatorkopplung f, Drosselkapazitätskopplung f, L/C-Kopplung f, LC-Kopplung f <Röhren>
induced emission [of light]	s. stimulated emission [of light]		
induced fission	induzierte Spaltung (Kernspaltung) f, künstliche Spaltung (Kernspaltung)	inductance coefficient	Induktivitätsfaktor m
induced force	s. magnetic field intensity	inductance coil, induction coil, inductor, self-inductor	Induktionsspule f, Induktivität f, Selbstinduktionsspule f
induced mass, virtual (effective, apparent, additional) mass	scheinbare Masse f, virtuelle Masse, induzierte Masse		
induced movement, countermovement <opt.>	Gegenbewegung f; induzierte Bewegung f <Opt.>	inductance decade	s. decade inductance box
		inductance meter, henrymeter, inductometer	Induktivitätsmesser m, Induktivitätsmeßgerät n
induced movement	s. a. stimulation movement <bio.>		
induced noise	Influenzrauschen n	inductance per unit length	Induktivitätsbelag m, Induktionsbelag m; induktiver Belag m
induced nuclear decay (disintegration), induced disintegration (decay), induced [nuclear] transformation	induzierte Kernumwandlung f, induzierter Kernzerfall m, induzierte Umwandlung f	inductance-resistance low pass [filter]	LR-Tiefpaß m
		inductance standard	s. standard inductance
		inductance transducer	s. inductive tranducer
		inductance tube, inductance valve	Induktanzröhre f
induced nuclear reaction, induced reaction	induzierte Kernreaktion f, induzierte Reaktion f		
		induction <bio.>	Induktion f, Auslösung f <Bio.>
induced nuclear transformation	s. induced nuclear disintegration	induction <math.>	Induktion f <Math.>
induced paramagnetism	induzierter Paramagnetismus m	induction	s. a. inducing
		induction	s. a. inducing <el.>
induced photoelectric effect	induzierter Photoeffekt (lichtelektrischer Effekt) m	induction	s. a. magnetic induction <el.>
		induction accelerator	s. betatron <acc.>
induced predissociation	induzierte Prädissoziation f	induction balance; magnetic balance, field balance	Feldwaage f, magnetische Waage f, Magnetwaage f; Induktionswaage f
induced quadrupole moment	induziertes Quadrupolmoment n	induction coil	s. inductance coil
		induction coil	s. inductorium
		induction compass	Induktionskompaß m
induced radiation	s. stimulated radiation	induction current, induced current	Induktionsstrom m, induzierter Strom m; Influenzstrom m
induced radioactivity, induced activity	induzierte Radioaktivität f; induzierte Aktivität f		
induced Raman effect, stimulated Raman effect	stimulierter Raman-Effekt m, induzierter Raman-Effekt	induction drag	s. inductive drag
		induction effect	Induktionseffekt m, induktiver Effekt m, I-Effekt m
induced reaction	s. induced nuclear reaction		
induced reactions	s. coupled reactions	induction electron accelerator	s. betatron
induced topology	induzierte Topologie f		
induced transformation	s. induced nuclear disintegration	induction energy, Debye energy	Debyesche Energie f, Debye-Energie f
		induction field	Induktionsfeld n
induced transition, stimulated transition	induzierter (stimulierter, erzwungener) Übergang m		
		induction flowmeter <bio.>	Induktionsflowmeter n Induktions-Blutströmungsmesser m, induktiver Blutstromstärkemesser m <Bio.>
induced velocity	induzierte Geschwindigkeit f		
induced voltage	s. induced electromotive force	induction flux	s. magnetic flux

induction force	Induktionskraft *f*	**inductive transducer,** inductance transducer	induktiver Wandler *m*; induktiver Meßgeber *m*, induktiver Geber *m*
induction generator	Induktionsgenerator *m*, induktive Stromquelle *f*	**inductive trouble**	*s.* induction interference
induction heating	Induktionsheizung *f*, induktive Heizung *f*; induktive Erhitzung (Erwärmung, Warmbehandlung) *f*	**inductive winding**	*s.* magnet winding
		inductivity	*s.* permittivity ‹of the material›
		inductometer	*s.* variometer
		inductometer	*s. a.* inductance meter
induction hypothesis	Induktionsannahme *f*, Induktionsvoraussetzung	**inductor**	Induktor *m*
		inductor ‹bio.›	Induktor *m* ‹Bio.›
induction instrument	*s.* Ferraris instrument	**inductor**	*s. a.* choke
induction interaction	Induktionswechselwirkung *f*	**inductor**	*s. a.* inductance coil
induction interference, inductive trouble (interference)	Induktionsstörung *f*, induktorische Beeinflussung *f*	**inductorium,** induction coil; spark coil; Ruhmkorff['s] [induction] coil	Induktionsapparat *m*, Induktorium *n*; Funkeninduktor *m*; Ruhmkorff-Spule *f*, Ruhmkorff-Induktor *m*
induction machine	Induktionsmaschine *f*, Asynchronmaschine *f*	**inductor magnetometer,** induction magnetometer	Induktionsmagnetometer *n*
induction magnetometer, inductor magnetometer	Induktionsmagnetometer *n*	**industrial mechanics,** engineering mechanics	technische Mechanik *f*
induction meter	Induktionszähler *m*, Ferraris-Zähler *m*	**industrial physics,** technological physics	technische Physik *f*
induction period, induction time ‹chem., phot.›	Induktionsperiode *f*, Induktionszeit *f*; Inkubationszeit *f*, Latenzzeit *f* ‹Chem., Phot.›	**industrial telescope**	technisches Fernrohr *n*
induction shock	Induktionsstoß *m*; Induktionsschlag *m* ‹Induktorium›	**industrial unit,** engineering unit, technical unit	technische Einheit *f*, technische Maßeinheit *f*
		ineffectivity, inefficiency	Unwirksamkeit *f*
induction tensor	Induktionstensor *m*, Erregungstensor *m*	**inefficient estimator**	nichtwirksame (ineffiziente) Schätzfunktion *f*
induction theorem	*s.* Faraday['s] law of induction	**inefficient statistics**	nichtwirksame (ineffiziente) Statistik *f*
induction time	*s.* induction period ‹chem., phot.›	**inelastic,** non-elastic ‹mech.›	unelastisch, inelastisch, nichtelastisch ‹Mech.›
induction-type instrument	*s.* Ferraris instrument	**inelastic ‹nucl.›**	unelastisch, inelastisch ‹Kern.›
induction variometer	Induktionsvariometer *n*	**inelastically scattered**	unelastisch (inelastisch) gestreut
induction vector, vector of induction	Induktionsvektor *m*	**inelastic buckling,** plastic buckling, non-elastic buckling	plastische Knickung *f*, unelastische Knickung
induction voltage	*s.* induced voltage		
induction winding, magnet (operating, inductive) winding, field (exciting) winding	Erregerwicklung *f*; Feldwicklung *f*; Magnetwicklung *f*; Polwicklung *f*	**inelastic collision,** inelastic event (phenomenon, impact) ‹nucl.›	unelastischer Stoß *m*, inelastischer Stoß ‹Kern.›
induction zone	*s.* near zone ‹ac.; el.›	**inelastic collision cross-section**	*s.* inelastic scattering cross-section
inductive ‹math.; el.›	induktiv ‹Math.; El.›; induktorisch ‹El.›	**inelastic continuum**	unelastisches (inelastisches) Kontinuum *n*
inductive acceleration	Induktionsbeschleunigung *f*, induktive Beschleunigung *f*	**inelastic cross-section**	*s.* inelastic scattering cross-section
inductive accelerometer	induktiver Beschleunigungsmesser *m*	**inelastic event,** inelastic collision (phenomenon, impact) ‹nucl.›	unelastischer Stoß *m*, inelastischer Stoß ‹Kern.›
inductive capacity	*s.* permittivity ‹of the material›		
inductive charge	*s.* induced charge	**inelastic impact**	*s.* inelastic collision
inductive coupling, mutual-inductance (magnetic, jigger, electromagnetic) coupling	induktive Kopplung *f*, magnetische Kopplung; induktive Ankopplung *f*	**inelastic impact**	*s.* perfectly inelastic impact ‹mech.›
		inelasticity, non-elasticity	Inelastizität *f*, inelastisches (unelastisches, nichtelastisches) Verhalten *n*, Unelastizität *f*, Nichtelastizität *f*
inductive, drag, induction drag ‹aero.›	elektromagnetische Viskosität (Bremswirkung) *f*, elektromagnetischer (induktiver) Widerstand *m*, induktiver „drag" *m*, Bremswirkung durch induzierte Wirbelströme ‹Aero.›	**inelastic phenomenon**	*s.* inelastic collision
		inelastic range	*s.* plastic range
		inelastic scattering by crystals, thermal (temperature) diffuse scattering, Faxén-Waller scattering	unelastische Streuung *f* an Kristallen, Faxén-Waller-Streuung *f*, thermische Diffusionsstreuung *f*, temperaturdiffuse Streuung *f*
inductive drop, inductive drop in potential, inductive drop of voltage	induktiver Spannungsabfall *m*		
		inelastic scattering cross-section, inelastic collision cross-section, inelastic cross-section, cross-section for inelastic scattering (collisions)	Wirkungsquerschnitt *m* für unelastische Streuung, Wirkungsquerschnitt der unelastischen Streuung, Wirkungsquerschnitt für unelastischen Stoß, unelastischer (inelastischer) Streuquerschnitt *m*, unelastischer (inelastischer) Stoßquerschnitt *m*
inductive interference	*s.* induction interference		
inductive loop	Induktionsschleife *f*		
inductive method, inductive technique ‹meas.›	Wirbelstromverfahren *n* ‹Meß.›		
inductive reactance; inductive resistance; positive reactance ‹el.›	induktiver [elektrischer] Widerstand *m*; induktiver Blindwiderstand *m*, Induktanz *f*, induktive Reaktanz *f* ‹El.›		
		inequality, unevenness; topographic inequality	Unebenheit *f*
inductive susceptance	induktiver Blindleitwert *m*, Suszeptanz *f*, induktive Suszeptanz *f*	**inequality**	Ungleichheit *f*, Störung *f* ‹Astr.›; Ungleichung *f* ‹Astr.; Math.›
inductive technique, inductive method ‹meas.›	Wirbelstromverfahren *n* ‹Meß.›	**inequality**	*s. a.* equation of the centre ‹astr.›

inequality

inequality in height [of tide]	Ungleichheit f in Höhe
inequality in time	Ungleichheit f in Zeit
inequality of Harnack	Harnacksche Ungleichung f
inequality of the lengths of arms	Ungleicharmigkeit f
inequality of the Moon	s. equation of the centre <astr.>
inequilateral; scalene, scalenous	ungleichseitig
iners	s. kilogram[me]
inert <chem.>	inert, Inert-, Schutz- <Chem.>
inert	s. a. inertial
inert atmosphere, protective atmosphere (medium), inert medium	Schutz[gas]atmosphäre f, Inertgasatmosphäre f; Schutzgaspolster n
inert gas; protective gas	inertes Gas n, Inertgas n; Schutzgas n
inert gas	s. a. rare gas
inertia, vis inertia, inertness	Trägheit f, Beharrungsvermögen n, Beharrung f
inertia <phot.>	Inertia f <Phot.>
inertia	s. a. inertial
inertia centre	s. centre of mass
inertia ellipse, ellipse of inertia, momental ellipse, moment ellipse	Trägheitsellipse f, Momentenellipse f
inertia ellipsoid	s. ellipsoid of inertia
inertia force	s. force of inertia
inertia head	Trägheitsdruckhöhe f
inertial, inertia, inert; sluggish; slow-response	träg[e]
inertial coefficient, coefficient of inertia	Trägheitskoeffizient m
inertial compression	Trägheitskompression f
inertial co-ordinate system	s. inertial frame
inertialess	trägheitslos, trägheitsfrei
inertialessness, non-inertia, absence of inertia	Trägheitslosigkeit f
inertialess variable	trägheitslose Variable f
inertial field	Trägheitsfeld n
inertial flight, free flight, passive flight, coasting flight	Trägheitsflug m, antriebsloser Flug m, passiver Flug, freier Flug
inertial force	s. force of inertia
inertial frame [of reference], inertial reference frame, inertial system [of co-ordinates], inertial co-ordinate system	Inertialsystem n; inertiales Koordinatensystem n
inertial guidance	Trägheitslenkung f, Trägheitssteuerung f
inertial mass, inert mass	träge Masse f, Inertialmasse f, Impulsmasse f, Masse der Bewegung
inertial oscillation	Trägheitsschwingung f
inertial parameter, parameter of inertia	Trägheitsparameter m
inertial property	Inertialeigenschaft f
inertial reference frame, inertial system [of co-ordinates]	s. inertial frame
inertial tensor, moment of inertia tensor, inertia tensor, tensor of inertia	Trägheitstensor m
inertial term, inertia term	Trägheitsglied n, Trägheitsterm m
inertial time	Inertialzeit f
inertial transformation	Inertialtransformation f
inertial wave	Trägheitswelle f
inertia of mass, mass inertia	Massenträgheit f, Trägheit f der Masse
inertia pressure	Trägheitsdruck m
inertia resistance	s. force of inertia
inertia rod, rod of inertia	Trägheitsstab m
inertia stress	Trägheitsbeanspruchung f, Trägheitsbelastung f, Belastung f durch Trägheitskräfte
inertia tensor, moment of inertia tensor, inertial tensor, tensor of inertia	Trägheitstensor m
inertia term, inertial term	Trägheitsglied n, Trägheitsterm m
inert mass	s. inertial mass
inert medium, protective atmosphere, protective medium, inert atmosphere	Schutzgasatmosphäre f, Schutzatmosphäre f, Inertgasatmosphäre f; Schutzgaspolster n
inertness, inactivity, reactionlessness <chem.>	chemische Trägheit f, Reaktionsträgheit f, Inaktivität f <Chem.>
inertness	s. a. inertia
inert solvent, latent solvent	indifferentes (latentes) Lösungsmittel n
inert zone	Unempfindlichkeitsbereich m, Unempfindlichkeitszone f
inessential singularity	s. regular singularity
inexpansibility	Unausdehnbarkeit f
inextensible string	undehnbarer Faden m
inf	s. greatest lower bound
infection of air	s. atmospheric pollution
inferior atmospheric layer, lower atmospheric layer	Grundschicht f [der Troposphäre]
inferior conjunction	untere Konjunktion f
inferior geodesy, geodesy, elementary geodesy	Geodäsie f, niedere Geodäsie, Vermessungskunde f
inferior layer	s. underlayer <geo.>
inferior limit	s. lower limit <math.>
inferior mirage	untere Luftspiegelung f, Luftspiegelung nach unten; Schwebung f, Kimmung f
inferior planet, inner planet	innerer Planet m, unterer Planet
in-field	einfallendes Feld n, „in"-Feld n
infiltration, percolation, influent seepage, filtration, oozing away	Infiltration f, Einströmung f, Eindringen n, Einsickern n, Einlagerung f, Versickerung f, Sickerung f
infiltration rate	s. percolation rate
infiltrometer	Versickerungsmesser m, Infiltrometer n
infimum	s. greatest lower bound
infinite	unendlich groß; unendlich ausgedehnt; unbegrenzt; unendlich, ∞
infinite dilution	unendliche Verdünnung f <Lösung>
infinite dimension / of, infinite-dimensional	unendlichdimensional, ∞-dimensional
infinite group	unendliche Gruppe f
infinite half-space, half-space, semi-infinite space	Halbraum m, unendlicher Halbraum
infinitely adjacent	s. adjacent
infinitely differentiable, having derivatives of all orders	unendlich oft differenzierbar
infinitely dilute solution	unendlich verdünnte Lösung f
infinitely divisible distribution	unbeschränkt teilbare Verteilung f
infinitely divisible random variable	unbeschränkt teilbare Zufallsvariable f
infinitely rare medium	unendlich verdünntes Medium n
infinitely safe geometry	s. always safe geometry
infinitely slow	unendlich langsam
infinitely thick	unendlich dick
infinitely thin, infinitesimally thin	unendlich dünn
infinite matrix	unendliche Matrix f
infinite motion, infinite movement	infinite Bewegung f, ungebundene Bewegung
infinite multiplication constant, infinite multiplication factor	Multiplikationsfaktor m für unendlich ausgedehntes Medium, Multiplikationsfaktor für die unendlich ausgedehnte Anordnung, Multiplikationsfaktor k_∞, unendlicher Multiplikationsfaktor

infinite product, continued product	unendliches Produkt *n*	**inflectional tangent,** stationary tangent	Wendetangente *f*, stationäre Tangente *f*
infinite reactor	unendlich ausgedehnter Reaktor *m*, unbegrenzter Reaktor, Reaktor mit unendlichen Abmessungen	**inflector**	Inflektor *m*
		inflexibility; stiffness, rigidity	Steifigkeit *f*, Steifheit *f*, Steife *f*
		inflexion, inflection	Wendung *f*; Inflexion *f*
infinite reflux [ratio]	unendliches Rücklaufverhältnis *n*	**inflexion point**	s. point of inflexion <of the curve> <math.>
infinite series	unendliche Reihe *f*	**inflow,** influx; water inflow	Zufluß *m*, Zustrom *m*; Einströmung *f*; Zuflußmenge *f*
infinitesimal	infinitesimal, unendlich klein		
infinitesimal-amplitude wave, infinitesimal wave	Welle *f* infinitesimaler Amplitude, infinitesimale Welle	**inflow**	Versinkung *f*
infinitesimal analysis, infinitesimal calculus, calculus	Differential- und Integralrechnung *f*, Infinitesimalrechnung *f*	**inflow and outflow,** tides, ebb and flood (flow), ebb-and-float	Gezeiten *pl*, Tiden *fpl*, Ebbe *f* und Flut *f*
infinitesimal deformation, infinitesimal strain	infinitesimale Verformung (Deformation) *f*	**inflow curve, inflow plot**	Zuflußmengenlinie *f*
infinitesimal displacement	infinitesimale Verrückung *f*	**influence** <on>; effect; action	Wirkung *f* <auf>; Einfluß *m* <auf>; Einwirkung *f* <auf>; Effekt *m*; Beeinflussung *f* <von>
infinitesimally thin, infinitely thin	unendlich dünn	**influence coefficient,** influence number	Einflußzahl *f*, Maxwellsche Einflußzahl, Einflußkoeffizient *m*
infinitesimal mapping	infinitesimale Abbildung *f*		
infinitesimal oscillation	infinitesimale (unendlich kleine) Schwingung *f*	**influence factor,** limiting factor	Einflußfaktor *m*; Beeinflussungsfaktor *m*
infinitesimal rotation	infinitesimale (elementare) Drehung *f*, infinitesimale (elementare) Rotation *f*	**influence function,** obliviator <gen., elasticity>	Einflußfunktion *f*, Obliviator *m* <allg., Elastizität>
infinitesimal strain, infinitesimal deformation	infinitesimale Verformung (Deformation) *f*	**influence line**	Einflußlinie *f*
infinitesimal transformation	infinitesimale Transformation *f*, infinitesimaler Operator *m*	**influence machine,** continuous electrophorus, electrostatic machine (generator), electrifier	Influenzmaschine *f*; Elektrisiermaschine *f*
infinitesimal uniqueness	infinitesimale Eindeutigkeit *f*	**influence number**	s. influence coefficient
		influence of heat	Wärmeeinfluß *m*
infinitesimal wave	s. infinitesimal-amplitude wave	**influence of space charge,** space-charge effect	Raumladungseinfluß *m*, Raumladungseffekt *m*, Raumladungswirkung *f*
infinite-slab geometry, slab geometry	Geometrie *f* der unendlich ausgedehnten Platte, Plattengeometrie *f*	**influence of the surroundings,** environmental factor	Umwelteinfluß *m*
infinite system of equations	unendliches Gleichungssystem *n*	**influence of the walls,** action of the walls, wall action, wall influence	Wandeinfluß *m*, Wandwirkung *f*
infinite-valued	unendlich vieldeutig		
infinity, scale end value, full scale value, full scale reading	Skalenendwert *m*, Endwert *m*	**influence on weather /** having an, influencing the weather	wetterwirksam
		influence surface	Einflußfläche *f*
		influencing function	Eingriffsfunktion *f*
		influencing the weather, having an influence on weather	wetterwirksam
infinity / at	im Unendlichen		
inflammability, flammability <US>, inflammableness, ignitability; ignition quality	Zündbarkeit *f*, Entzündlichkeit *f*, Entzündbarkeit *f*, Zündfähigkeit *f*, Zündempfindlichkeit *f*; Entflammbarkeit *f*	**influent seepage**	s. infiltration
		influx	s. inflow
		information	s. statement
		information carrier	Informationsträger *m*
inflammability limit, ignition limit, ignitability limit, limit of inflammability (ignition, ignitability)	Zündgrenze *f*	**information content,** amount of information, set of information, quantity of information, volume of information, information volume; decision content	Informationsgehalt *m*, Informationsbetrag *m*, Informationsmenge *f*, Informationsumfang *m*, Informationsvolumen *n*, Anzahl *f* der Einzelnachrichten, Informationsinhalt *m*; Nachrichtenmenge *f*, Nachrichtengehalt *m*
inflammability limits, limits of inflammability, ignition limits (range), flammability limits <US>, explosion limits <US>	Zündbereich *m*, Zündgrenzen *fpl*, Explosionsbereich *m*		
		information efficiency	Informationswirkungsgrad *m*
inflammable, inflammatory, ignitable	entflammbar; entzündlich, entzündbar, zündfähig, zündbar		
inflammableness	s. inflammability	**information for discrimination,** I divergence	I-Divergenz *f*, diskriminierende Information *f*
inflammation, flaming; ignition, initiation of combustion <chem.>	Entzündung *f*, Zündung *f*; Entflammung *f* <Chem.>		
		information gain	Informationsgewinn *m*
		information inequality, Cramer-Rao inequality	Ungleichung *f* von Fréchet
inflammation zone, ignition zone, zone of inflammation	Zündzone *f*; Zündnest *n*	**information parameter,** parameter of information	Informationsparameter *m*
inflammatory	s. inflammable		
inflation; homogeneous elongation	homogene Dehnung *f*, homogene Dilatation *f*	**information rate**	Informationsrate *f*, Informationsgeschwindigkeit *f*, Informationsfluß *m*; Nachrichtenfluß *m*, Nachrichtenstrom *m*
inflection; inward bend	Einbeulung *f*; Einbiegung *f*		
inflection, inflexion <math.>	Wendung *f*; Inflexion *f* <Math.>		

information redundance, redundancy, redundancy	Redundanz f, Informationsüberschuß m
information ribonucleic acid, iRNA	s. messenger ribonucleic acid
information theory [of Shannon-Weaver], coding theory, mathematical theory of communication	mathematische Theorie f der Nachrichtenübertragung, Informationstheorie f [von Shannon-Weaver]
information transfer (transmission)	Informationsübertragung f
information volume	s. information content
infra-acoustic, infrasonic, subaudic, subsonic	Infraschall-, infraakustisch, unter dem Hörbereich
infraluminescence	Infralumineszenz f
infra[-]red, I.R., IR, i.r., ir	infrarot, Infrarot-, ultrarot, Ultrarot-, IR-, UR-
infra-red	s. a. infrared-radiation
infra-red	s. a. infra-red range
infra-red absorption, I.R. absorption	Infrarotabsorption f, IR-Absorption f
infra-red absorption analysis, I.R. absorption analysis	Infrarot-Absorptionsanalyse f, IR-Absorptionsanalyse f
infra-red absorption analyzer	s. infra-red absorption gas analyzer
infra-red absorption band, I.R. absorption band	Infrarot-Absorptionsbande f, IR-Absorptionsbande f
infra-red absorption gas analyzer, infra-red absorption analyzer, I.R. absorption analyzer	Infrarot-Absorptionsanalysengerät n, IR-Absorptionsanalysengerät n
infra-red absorption recorder, I.R. absorption recorder	Infrarotabsorptionsschreiber m, Ultrarotabsorptionsschreiber m, Uras
infra-red absorption spectrometry (spectroscopy), I.R. absorption spectroscopy, I.R. absorption spectrometry	Infrarot-Absorptionsspektroskopie f, Infrarot-Absorptionsspektrometrie f, IR-Absorptionsspektroskopie f, IR-Absorptionsspektrometrie f
infra-red absorption spectrum, I.R. absorption spectrum	Infrarot-Absorptionsspektrum n, IR-Absorptionsspektrum n
infra-red active, infrared[-]active, I.R. active	infrarot[-]aktiv, IR-aktiv
infra-red analysis, I.R. analysis	Infrarotanalyse f, IR-Analyse f
infra-red A region, infra-red region A <0.76−1.4 μm>	IR-A-Gebiet n, Infrarot-A-Gebiet n <0,76 ··· 1,4 μm>
infra-red band, I.R. band	Infrarotbande f, IR-Bande f
infra-red band spectrum, I.R. band spectrum	Infrarot-Bandenspektrum n, IR-Bandenspektrum n
infra-red bolometer, I.R. bolometer	Infrarotbolometer n, IR-Bolometer n
infra-red B region, infra-red region B <1.4−3.0 μm>	IR-B-Gebiet n, Infrarot-B-Gebiet n <1,4 ··· 3,0 μm>
infra-red catastrophe, infra-red problem (divergence), I.R. catastrophe, I.R. problem, I.R. divergence	Infrarotkatastrophe f, Infrarotdivergenz f, IR-Katastrophe f, IR-Divergenz f
infra-red cutting filter, I.R. cutting filter	Infrarotschutzfilter n, IR-Schutzfilter n, Infrarotsperrfilter n, IR-Sperrfilter n
infra-red detector	s. infra-red radiation detector
infra-red dissipation of space charges	s. infra-red removal of space charges
infra-red divergence	s. infra-red catastrophe
infra-red effect, infra-red radiation effect, I.R. [radiation] effect	Infrarot[strahlen]wirkung f, IR-Strahlenwirkung f, IR-Wirkung f
infra-red emission, I.R. emission	Infrarotemission f, IR-Emission f
infra-red emulsion	s. infrared-sensitive emulsion
infra-red excitation	s. infra-red stimulation
infra-red film	s. infrared sensitive film
infra-red filter, I.R. filter	Infrarotfilter n, IR-Filter n
infra-red glass, I.R. glass	Infrarotglas n, IR-Glas n
infra-red illumination	s. infra-red irradiation
infra-red image converter, infra-red telescope, sniperscope, I.R. image converter, I.R. telescope	Infrarotbildwandler m, Infrarotfernrohr n, Infrarotteleskop n, Sniperscope n, IR-Bildwandler m, IR-Fernrohr n, IR-Teleskop n, Infrarot-Beobachtungsgerät n, IR-Beobachtungsgerät n
infrared[-] inactive, IR inactive	infrarot-inaktiv, IR-inaktiv
infra-red irradiation, infra-red illumination, far red irradiation, I.R. irradiation, I.R. illumination	Infrarotbestrahlung f, IR-Bestrahlung f
infra-red lamp, infra-red source, infra-red radiator, I.R. lamp, I.R. source, I.R. radiator	Infrarotstrahler m, Infrarotlichtquelle f, Infrarotlampe f, IR-Strahler m, IR-Lichtquelle f, IR-Lampe f
infra-red light	s. infra-red radiation
infra-red line, I.R. line	Infrarotlinie f, IR-Linie f
infra-red location, I.R. location; infra-red position finding	Infrarotortung f, IR-Ortung f
infra-red locator, I.R. locator; infra-red position finder	Infrarot-Ortungsgerät n, IR-Ortungsgerät n
infra-red magnitude, infra-red stellar magnitude, I.R. magnitude <of the star>	Infrarothelligkeit f, IR-Helligkeit f <Gestirn>
infra-red maser <infra-red amplification by stimulated emission of radiation>, iraser, iaser	Iraser m, Infrarotmaser m, IR-Maser m
infra-red microscope, I.R. microscope	Infrarotmikroskop n, IR-Mikroskop n
infra-red microscopy, I.R. microscopy	Infrarotmikroskopie f, IR-Mikroskopie f
infra-red microspectrograph, I.R. microspectrograph	Infrarot-Mikrospektrograph m, IR-Mikrospektrograph m
infra-red microspectrography, I.R. microspectrography	Infrarot-Mikrospektrographie f, IR-Mikrospektrographie f
infra-red microspectrometer, I.R. microspectrometer	Infrarot-Mikrospektrometer n, IR-Mikrospektrometer n
infra-red microspectrometry	s. infra-red microspectroscopy
infra-red microspectrophotometer, I.R. microspectrophotometer	Infrarot-Mikrospektralphotometer n, IR-Mikrospektralphotometer n

infra-red microspectrophotometry, I.R. microspectrophotometry — Infrarot-Mikrospektralphotometrie f, IR-Mikrospektralphotometrie f

infra-red microspectroscope, I.R. microspectroscope — Infrarot-Mikrospektroskop n, IR-Mikrospektroskop n

infra-red microspectroscopy, I.R. microspectroscopy, infra-red microspectrometry, I.R. microspectrometry — Infrarot-Mikrospektroskopie f, IR-Mikrospektroskopie, Infrarot-Mikrospektrometrie f, IR-Mikrospektrometrie f

infra-red monochromator, monochromator for infra-red radiation, I.R. monochromator — Infrarotmonochromator m, IR-Monochromator m

infra-red part — s. infra-red range

infra-red permeability — s. infra-red transparency

infra-red photocell, infrared-sensitive photocell, I.R. photocell — Infrarotphotozelle f, IR-Photozelle f, Infrarotzelle f, IR-Zelle f

infra-red photograph, infra-red image, I.R. photograph, I.R. image — Infrarotaufnahme f, Infrarotbild n, Infrarotphotographie f, IR-Aufnahme f, IR-Bild n, IR-Photographie f

infra-red photography, I.R. photography — Infrarotphotographie f, IR-Photographie f

infra-red photometer, I.R. photometer — Infrarotphotometer n, IR-Photometer n

infra-red photometry, I.R. photometry — Infrarotphotometrie f, IR-Photometrie f

infra-red photomicrography, I.R. photomicrography — Infrarot-Mikrophotographie f, IR-Mikrophotographie f

infra-red physics, I.R. physics — Infrarotphysik f, IR-Physik f

infra-red plate, infrared-sensitive plate, I.R. [sensitive] plate — Infrarotplatte f, infrarotempfindliche Platte f, IR-[empfindliche] Platte f

infra-red polarization — s. atomic polarization

infra-red portion — s. infra-red range

infra-red position finder — s. infra-red locator

infra-red position finding; infra-red (I.R.) location — Infrarotortung f, IR-Ortung f

infra-red problem — s. infra-red catastrophe

infra-red quenching [of photoconductivity] — Infrarotlöschung f [der Photoleitfähigkeit], IR-Löschung f [der Photoleitfähigkeit]; Infrarottilgung f [der Photoleitfähigkeit], IR-Tilgung f [der Photoleitfähigkeit]

infra-red radiation, infra-red, infra-red rays, infra-red light, I.R. radiation, I.R. — Infrarotstrahlung f, infrarote Strahlung f, Infrarotstrahlen mpl, infrarote Strahlen mpl, Infrarot[licht] n, infrarotes Licht n, IR-Strahlung f, IR

infra-red radiation detector, infra-red detector, I.R. [radiation] detector — Infrarotdetektor m, Infrarot-Strahlungsmeßgerät n, Infrarot-Strahlungsmesser m, IR-Detektor m, IR-Strahlungsmeßgerät n, IR-Strahlungsmesser m

infra-red radiation effect, infra-red effect, I.R. [radiation] effect — Infrarot[strahlen]wirkung f, IR-Strahlenwirkung f, IR-Wirkung f

infra-red radiation receiver, infra-red receiver, I.R. [radiation] receiver — Infrarotempfänger m, IR-Empfänger m, Infrarot-Strahlungsempfänger m, IR-Strahlungsempfänger m

infra-red radiation temperature — infrarote Strahlungstemperatur f

infra-red radiator — s. infra-red lamp

infra-red range, infra-red portion, infra-red part, infra-red region <of the electromagnetic spectrum>, infra-red, I.R., I.R. range, I.R. portion — Infrarotbereich m, Infrarotgebiet n, infraroter Bereich m, infrarotes Gebiet n <des elektromagnetischen Spektrums>, infraroter Spektralbereich m, infrarotes Spektralgebiet n, Infrarot n, IR, IR-Bereich m, IR-Gebiet n

infra-red rangefinder, I.R. rangefinder — Infrarot-Entfernungsmesser m, IR-Entfernungsmesser m, Ultrarot-Entfernungsmesser m, UR-Entfernungsmesser m

infra-red rays — s. infra-red radiation

infra-red receiver — s. infra-red radiation receiver

infra-red region, region of the infra-red spectrum, I.R. region — Infrarotgebiet n, Gebiet n des infraroten Spektrums, IR-Gebiet n

infra-red region — s. a. infra-red range

infra-red region A, infra-red A region <$0.76-1.4\,\mu m$> — IR-A-Gebiet n, Infrarot-A-Gebiet n <$0,76\cdots 1,4\,\mu m$>

infra-red region B, infra-red B region <$1.4-3.0\,\mu m$> — IR-B-Gebiet n, Infrarot-B-Gebiet n <$1,4\cdots 3,0\,\mu m$>

infra-red removal of space charges, infra-red dissipation of space charges — Infrarotbeseitigung f von Raumladungen, IR-Beseitigung f von Raumladungen

infra-red rotation[al] band — Infrarot-Rotationsbande f, IR-Rotationsbande f

infra-red sensitive — s. sensitive to infra-red

infrared-sensitive emulsion, infra-red emulsion, I.R. sensitive emulsion, I.R. emulsion — infrarotempfindliche Emulsion f, I. R. empfindliche Emulsion, Infrarotemulsion f, IR-Emulsion f

infrared-sensitive film, infra-red film, I.R. sensitive film, I.R. film — infrarotempfindlicher Film m, Infrarotfilm m, IR-empfindlicher Film, IR-Film m

infrared-sensitive photocell — s. infra-red photocell

infrared-sensitive plate, infra-red plate, I.R. [sensitive] plate — Infrarotplatte f, infrarotempfindliche Platte f, IR-[empfindliche] Platte f

infra-red sensitivity, sensitivity to infra-red rays, I.R. sensitivity — Infrarotempfindlichkeit f, IR-Empfindlichkeit f

infra-red sensitization, I.R. sensitization — Infrarotsensibilisierung f, IR-Sensibilisierung f

infra-red sensitizer, I.R. sensitizer — Infrarotsensibilisator m, IR-Sensibilisator m

infra-red shadow, I.R. shadow — Infrarotschatten m, IR-Schatten m

infra-red source — s. infra-red lamp

infra-red spectrograph, I.R. spectrograph — Infrarotspektrograph m, IR-Spektrograph m

infra-red spectrography, I.R. spectrography — Infrarotspektrographie f, IR-Spektrographie f

infra-red spectrometer, I.R. spectrometer — Infrarotspektrometer n, IR-Spektrometer n

infra-red spectrometry — s. infra-red spectroscopy

infra-red spectrophotometer, recording infra-red spectrometer, I.R. spectrophotometer — Infrarot-Spektralphotometer n, registrierendes Infrarotspektrometer (IR-Spektrometer) n, IR-Spektralphotometer n

infra-red spectroscope, I.R. spectroscope — Infrarotspektroskop n, IR-Spektroskop n

infra-red spectroscopy, I.R. spectroscopy, infra-red spectrometry, I.R. spectrometry — Infrarotspektroskopie f, IR-Spektroskopie f, Infrarotspektrometrie f, IR-Spektrometrie f, Spektroskopie f der Infrarotspektren

infra-red spectrum, I.R. spectrum	Infrarotspektrum *n*, IR-Spektrum *n*, infrarotes Spektrum *n*	**inhibiting action,** inhibitory action (effect)	Hemmwirkung *f*
infra-red standard, standard infra-red, I.R. standard	Infrarotstandard *m*, Infrarotnormal *n*, IR-Standard *m*, IR-Normal *n*	**inhibiting value,** inhibition index	Hemmungsindex *m*
infra-red stellar magnitude, infra-red (I.R.) magnitude <of the star>	Infrarothelligkeit *f*, IR-Helligkeit *f* <Gestirn>	**inhibition, anticatalysis,** negative catalysis <chem.>	Inhibition *f*, Hemmung *f*, Verzögerung *f*, Antikatalyse *f*, negative Katalyse *f* <Chem.>
infra-red stimulation, infra-red excitation, I.R. stimulation, I.R. excitation	Infrarotstimulierung *f*, Infraroterregung *f*, Infrarotanregung *f*, IR-Stimulierung *f*, IR-Erregung *f*, IR-Anregung *f*	**inhibition index** **inhibitor,** anticatalyst, anticatalyzer, passivator, passivating agent, paralyst, paralyzer, retardant, retarder <chem.>	s. inhibiting value Inhibitor *m*, Hemmstoff *m*, Hemmungsmittel *n*, Passivator *m*, Antikatalysator *m*, negativer Katalysator *m*, Katalysatorgift *n*, Verzögerer *m*, Verzögerungsmittel *n* <Chem.>
infra-red telephony, I.R. telephony	Infrarottelephonie *f*, IR-Telephonie *f*	**inhibitory action,** inhibiting action, inhibitory effect	Hemmwirkung *f*
infra-red telescope	s. infra-red image converter	**inhibitory activity**	Hemmungsaktivität *f*
infra-red transmittance	s. infra-red transparency	**inhibitory effect**	s. inhibitory action
infra-red transmitting, infra-red transparent, transparent to infra-red [rays], I.R. transmitting	infrarotdurchlässig, IR-durchlässig	**inhibitory impulse** <bio.> **inhomogeneity**	Hemmungsimpuls *m* <Bio.> s. heterogeneity
infra-red transparency, I.R. transparency, infra-red permeability, I.R. permeability; infra-red transmittance, I.R. transmittance	Infrarotdurchlässigkeit *f*, IR-Durchlässigkeit *f*, Durchlässigkeit *f* im infraroten Spektralbereich	**inhomogeneity in glass** **inhomogeneity theory** **inhomogeneous,** heterogeneous, heterogenetic	Glasfehler *m* Inhomogenitätstheorie *f* inhomogen, heterogen, ungleichartig, verschiedenartig, ungleichförmig
infra-red transparent	s. infra-red transmitting	**inhomogeneous differential equation**	inhomogene Differentialgleichung *f*, inhomogene Gleichung *f*
infra-red vibration[al] band, I.R. vibration[al] band	Infrarot-Schwingungsbande *f*, IR-Schwingungsbande *f*		
		inhomogeneous Galilean group	inhomogene Galileische Gruppe *f*
		inhomogeneous in structure	s. inhomogeneous structure / of
infra-Röntgen rays	s. grenz rays	**inhomogeneous integral equation** <of the first, second kind>	inhomogene Integralgleichung *f* <erster, zweiter Art>
infrasonic, subaudio, subsonic, infra-acoustic, subacoustic	Infraschall-, infraakustisch, unter dem Hörbereich		
infrasonic frequency, subaudio frequency, subsonic frequency	Infraschallfrequenz *f*	**inhomogeneous line** **inhomogeneous linear differential equation**	inhomogene Leitung *f* inhomogene lineare Differentialgleichung *f*, vollständige lineare Differentialgleichung
infrasonic [frequency] region, subsonic [frequency] region	Infraschallbereich *m*		
infrasonics, infrasound, infrasonic vibrational wave	Infraschall *m*, Beben *n*	**inhomogeneous Lorentz group,** Poincaré group	inhomogene Lorentz-Gruppe *f*, Poincaré-Gruppe *f*
infrasonic source	Infraschallquelle *f*	**inhomogeneous magnetic field,** non-uniform magnetic field	inhomogenes Magnetfeld *n*
infrasonic vibration	Infraschallschwingung *f*		
infrasonic vibrational wave, infrasound	s. infrasonics	**inhomogeneousness** **inhomogeneous structure / of,** structural-inhomogeneous, structurally (constitutionally) inhomogeneous, inhomogeneous in structure	s. heterogeneity strukturinhomogen
infusion	Infusion *f*		
infusion <chem.>	Ansatz *m*; Aufguß *m* <Chem.>		
infusorial earth	s. kieselguhr		
Inglis['] model	s. cranking model		
ingot; pig, bar	Barren *m*; Massel *f*	**inhomogeneous system of differential equations**	inhomogenes (erweitertes) Differentialgleichungssystem *n*
ingression	Ingression *f*		
inherent capacitance, self-capacitance	Eigenkapazität *f*		
inherent density, natural density	Eigendichte *f*	**inhomogeneous wave;** transversally damped wave	inhomogene Welle *f*; quergedämpfte Welle; schräggedämpfte Welle
inherent feedback	innere Rückkopplung *f*		
inherent filtration, self-filtering	Eigenfilterung *f*, Selbstfilterung *f*	**in[-]hour,** inhour value, inverse hour	Inhour *f*, reziproke Stunde *f*, inhour
inherent frequency	s. natural frequency	**inhour formula**	„inhour"-Formel *f*
inherent inductance	Eigeninduktivität *f*	**inhour value,** in[-]hour, inverse hour	Inhour *f*, reziproke Stunde *f*, inhour
inherent noise; set noise	Eigengeräusch *n*	**ininflammable**	s. non-inflammable
		initial atmosphere, protoatmosphere	Uratmosphäre *f*, Protoatmosphäre *f*
inherent noise figure	s. noise factor	**initial body retention,** retention coefficient	Retentionsfaktor *m* <Bio.>
inherent number of energy	s. eigenvalue of energy		
inherent regulation	s. self-regulation	**initial breakdown voltage,** initial ignition voltage	Erstzündspannung *f*
inherent rigidity, natural rigidity	Formstarrheit *f*		
inherent safety, intrinsic safety	inhärente (innere) Sicherheit *f*, Eigensicherheit *f*	**initial channel,** entrance channel	Eingangskanal *m*, Anfangskanal *m*
inherent stability	Eigenstabilität *f*	**initial conditions,** initial data (values), Cauchy data <math.>	Anfangsbedingungen *fpl*; Anfangswerte *mpl* <Math.>
inherent tension	s. internal stress	**initial creep**	s. transient creep
inherent value of energy	s. eigenvalue of energy	**initial current,** starting current	Anfangsstrom *m*; Anzugsstrom *m*; Anlaßstrom *m*

initial current curve (law)	s. residual current law	initial transconductance	Anschwingsteilheit f
initial current of emission, residual current <of diode>	Anlaufstrom m		
initial curve of magnetization	s. virgin curve of magnetization	initial turbulence	Vorturbulenz f
		initial vacuum	s. fore-vacuum
initial data, initial conditions (values), Cauchy data <math.>	Anfangsbedingungen fpl; Anfangswerte mpl <Math.>	initial value <of a quantity, also math.>	Anfangswert m <auch Math.>; Ausgangswert m <Größe>
initial deformation; initial strain	Anfangsverformung f	initial[-] value problem, Cauchy problem	Anfangswertproblem n, Anfangswertaufgabe f; Cauchysches Problem n, Cauchysches Anfangswertproblem; Wurfproblem n <Zweikörperbewegung>
initial detonating agent, initiating explosive, priming explosive, primer, detonating agent (explosive)	Initialsprengstoff m, Initialexplosivstoff m, Zündsprengstoff m		
initial flow	s. transient creep		
initial heat	initiale Wärme f <Muskelkontraktion>	initial values, initial conditions (data), Cauchy data <math.>	Anfangsbedingungen fpl; Anfangswerte mpl <Math.>
initial ignition	Initialzündung f	initial voltage	s. initial potential <el.>
		initial vortex	s. cast-off vortex
initial ignition voltage, initial breakdown voltage	Erstzündspannung f	initial wave	Initialwelle f
		initial weight	s. amount weighed
		initiating explosive	s. initial detonating agent
		initiating particle	erzeugendes Teilchen n, auslösendes Teilchen
initial inverse voltage	Sprungspannung f		
initial ionization	Anfangsionisation f, Anfangsionisierung f	initiating pulse, release pulse; trigger pulse, triggering pulse	Auslöseimpuls m, Startimpuls m; Triggerimpuls m; Austastimpuls m
initial ionizing event, primary ionizing event	primäres Ionisationsereignis n	initiating reaction	s. starting reaction
		initiating the chain	s. chain initiation <chem.>
initial ion pair, primary (original) ion pair	primäres Ionenpaar n	initiation, inducing, induction; starting, commencement; introducing, introduction	Auslösung f, Einleitung f, Induzierung f; Initiierung f; Zündung f
initial load, preload, minor load	Vorlast f		
initial magnetization	Erstmagnetisierung f	initiation [of chain]	s. chain initiation
initial magnetization curve	s. virgin curve of magnetization	initiation of combustion	s. ignition
initial mass <of rocket>	Anfangsmasse f, Startmasse f <Rakete>	initiation of fracture, nucleation of fracture	Einsetzen n des Bruchs
initial meridian	s. zero meridian	initiation of the discharge, ignition of the discharge	Zündung f der Entladung
initial modulus	Anfangsmodul m, Initialmodul m		
initial onset method, vanishing current method	Nullstrommethode f	initiator [for polymerization]; accelerator of polymerization, polymerization accelerator, polymerization catalyst	Initiator m [der Polymerisation], Polymerisationsanreger m, Polymerisationsinitiator m, Anreger m, Starter m; Polymerisationsbeschleuniger m, Polymerisationskatalysator m
initial particle	s. primary particle		
initial permeability, initial relative permeability	Anfangspermeabilität f		
initial perturbation	Anfangsstörung f	injecting system <acc.>	Einschußsystem n, Injektionssystem n <Beschl.>
initial phase, starting phase	Anfangsphase f; Initialphase f <Bio.>		
initial point, origin; starting point <e.g. of the motion>; point of emergency	Anfangspunkt m, Ausgangspunkt m	injection <of particles> <acc.>	Einschießen n, Einschuß m, Injektion f, Einschleusen n, Einbringen n, Einspritzen n <Teilchen> <Beschl.>
initial position	Anfangslage f; Ausgangslage f; Ausgangsstellung f	injection <bio., chem.>	Injektion f, Einspritzung f <Bio., Chem.>
initial potential	s. sparking potential <el.>	injection <geo.>	Injektion f, Einschub m <Geo.>
initial quantity	Ausgangsgröße f		
initial radiation	Initialstrahlung f	injection <semi.>	Injektion f <Halb.>
initial recombination [of ions]	Initialrekombination f [von Ionen]	injection condition <acc., semi.>, condition for injection	Einschußbedingung f <Beschl.>; Injektionsbedingung f <Beschl., Halb.>
initial relative permeability	s. initial permeability	injection cooling	Einspritzkühlung f
initial resistance	Ruhewiderstand m	injection current <acc., semi.>	Einschußstrom m <Beschl.>; Injektionsstrom m <Beschl., Halb.>
initial strain; initial deformation	Anfangsverformung f		
initial strain	Anfangsbeanspruchung f; Anfangsbelastung f	injection efficiency <acc., semi.>	Einschußwirkungsgrad m <Beschl.>; Injektionswirkungsgrad m <Beschl., Halb.>
initial stress	Anfangsspannung f, Eigenspannung f, Vorspannung f <Mech.>		
		injection electroluminescence, injection-type electroluminescence	Injektionselektrolumineszenz f
initial strip	Anfangsstreifen m		
initial susceptibility	Anfangssuszeptibilität f	injection energy <acc.>	Einschußenergie f, Injektionsenergie f <Beschl.>
initial system	Ausgangssystem n, ursprüngliches System n		
initial thrust	Startschub m, Anfangsschub m	injection laser	s. semiconducting laser
		injection luminescence	Injektionsleuchten n
initial torque, starting torque	Anzugs[dreh]moment n, Anlaufdrehmoment n, Startdrehmoment n, Stillstandsmoment n; Anfahr[dreh]moment n; Hochlaufmoment n	injection luminescence diode, light-emitting diode, LED	Injektionslumineszenzdiode f, Lumineszenzdiode f, Leuchtdiode f, Lichtdiode f

injection moment <acc.>	Einschußmoment m, Einschußzeitpunkt m, Einschießungszeitpunkt m, Injektionsmoment m, Injektionszeitpunkt m <Beschl.>	inner-orbital complex, low-spin complex, spin-paired (penetration, sandwich) complex	Durchdringungskomplex m, magnetisch anomaler Komplex m
injection of plasma	s. plasma injection	inner partition	s. partition <chem.>
injection of propellant	Einspritzen n des Treibstoffs	inner planet, inferior planet	innerer Planet m, unterer Planet
injection optics <acc.>	Einschußoptik f, Injektionsoptik f, Injektoroptik f <Beschl.>	inner point <math.>	innerer Punkt m <Math.>
		inner pole machine	s. revolving field machine
		inner potential, intrinsic potential <of crystal>	inneres Potential n <Kristall>
injection transistor	s. bipolar transistor	inner product	s. scalar product
injection-type electroluminescence, injection electroluminescence	Injektionselektrolumineszenz f	inner quantum number, quantum number of the total angular momentum, total angular momentum quantum number, internal quantum number	Gesamtdrehimpulsquantenzahl f, innere Quantenzahl f, Quantenzahl des Gesamtdrehimpulses der Elektronenhülle
injection voltage <acc.>	Einschußspannung f, Injektionsspannung f <Beschl.>		
injector, [steam] jet pump, steam injector	Dampfstrahlpumpe f, Wasserdampfstrahlpumpe f, Injektor m	inner radiation belt, inner radiation zone, inner Van Allen [radiation] belt	innerer Strahlungsgürtel m
injector <of jet engine>	Einspritzdüse f <Raketenmotor>	inner ring, ring B	Innenring m, B-Ring m
injector <acc.>	Injektor m, Injektionsgerät n, Einschußgerät n <Beschl.>	inner salt	s. amphoteric ion
		inner-shell electron, inner electron	inneres Elektron n, Innenelektron n, Elektron einer inneren Schale, Rumpfelektron n
injury potential, lesion potential, demarcation potential	Verletzungspotential n, Verletzungsspannung f, Demarkationspotential n		
injury potential at rest, rest injury potential	Verletzungsruhepotential n	inner total reflection	innere Totalreflexion f
ink recorder, pen-and-ink recorder	Tintenschreiber m; Tintenschreibwerk n	inner tube, core tube	Kernrohr n, Innenrohr n
		inner Van Allen [radiation] belt	s. inner radiation zone
		inner work function	innere Austrittsarbeit f
ink-vapour recorder	Tintenstrahlschreiber m	inoculating crystal	s. seed crystal
		inoculation, inoculum	s. seeding
		in-operator, "in"-operator	„in"-Operator m, in-Operator m
inland ice	s. continental ice	in-parallel connection	s. parallel connection
inlet pipe	s. supply pipe	in-phase component	„in-phase"-Komponente f
inlet side, suction side	Saugseite f, Saugende n	in-phase element, active element, real element	Wirkelement n
inlet temperature, entrance temperature	Eintrittstemperatur f, Temperatur f am Eingang, Temperatur beim Eintritt, Eingangstemperatur f	in-pile experiment, in-pile test	Bestrahlungsversuch (Versuch) m innerhalb des Reaktors
		in-plane vibration	ebene Schwingung f
		input, input power	Eingangsleistung f
inlet velocity, entrance (intake, admission) velocity, velocity of inlet	Eintrittsgeschwindigkeit f, Geschwindigkeit f am Eingang; Einströmgeschwindigkeit f	input, input terminals <el.>	Eingang m, Eingangsklemmen fpl <El.>
		input <control>	Eingangsgröße f <Regelung>
inner accommodation	innere Akkommodation f, innerer Akkommodationsanteil m	input <num. math.>	Eingabe f, Dateneingabe f, Input m <num. Math.>
		input	s. a. input unit
inner automorphism, cogredient automorphism	innerer Automorphismus m	input admittance; driving point admittance, admittance of driving-point	Eingangsadmittanz f, Eingangsscheinleitwert m; Wellenleitwert m des Anschlußpunktes
inner bremsstrahlung, internal bremsstrahlung	innere Bremsstrahlung f		
inner capacity	innere Kapazität f	input admittance of the tube	Röhreneingangsleitwert m, Eingangsleitwert m der Röhre, Gesamteingangsleitwert m der Röhre
inner-complex compound (salt)	innerer Komplex m, Innerkomplexverbindung f, inneres Komplexsalz n		
inner conductor	Innenleiter m	input capacitance; input grid capacitance, grid capacitance	Eingangskapazität f; Gitter[kreis]kapazität f, Eingangsgitterkapazität f
inner cone [of flame]	Flammenkern m, Innenkern m, grüner Kern m		
inner core, G region <of Earth>	innerer Kern m, G-Schale f, G-Schicht f <Erde>	input conductance	Eingangswirkleitwert m
		input control	Vorregelung f, Vorsteuerung f
inner ear	Innenohr n		
inner electrical potential	s. Galvani potential	input current	Eingangsruhestrom m, Inputstrom m
inner electron, inner-shell electron	inneres Elektron n, Innenelektron n, Elektron einer inneren Schale	input device (equipment)	s. input unit
		input grid capacitance, grid capacitance; input capacitance	Eingangskapazität f; Gitter[kreis]kapazität f, Eingangsgitterkapazität f
inner energy, internal energy	innere Energie f		
inner Lagrangian point, conical point, first Lagrangian point	erster Lagrange-Punkt m, innerer Lagrange-Punkt	input impedance; driving-point impedance, impedance of driving-point; feed point impedance; free impedance; sending end impedance	Eingangsimpedanz f, Eingangsscheinwiderstand m, Eingangswiderstand m; Wellenwiderstand m des Anschlußpunktes
innermost electron	Elektron n der innersten Schale, kernnächstes (innerstes) Elektron		
inner multiplication, contraction, transvection <of tensor>	Überschiebung f [von Indizes] <Tensor>		
		input noise resistance	Eingangsrauschwiderstand m

input power, input	Eingangsleistung f	insolubilizing	Überführung f in die unlösliche Form
input power	zugeführte Leistung f	insoluble, indissoluble, indissolvable, undissolving	unlöslich, nichtlöslich; unangreifbar
input pulse, incoming pulse	Eingangsimpuls m, ankommender Impuls m	insoluble fraction, insoluble part	Unlösliche n
input reactance, feed-point reactance	Eingangsblindwiderstand m	inspection	s. testing
input resistance, feed point resistance	Eingangswiderstand m; Gitter-Katode-Widerstand m	inspection hole	s. observation port
		inspection instrument	s. testing instrument
		inspectoscope	s. crack detector
input resonator	s. buncher <of the klystron>	inspissation; thickening; bodying; livering <chem.>	Eindicken n, Verdickung f, Verdichtung f <Chem.>
input table, functional generator	Funktionstrieb m, Funktionswandler m	instability, imbalance, unstability; lability	Instabilität f, Unstabilität f; Labilität f
input terminals, input <el.>	Eingang m, Eingangsklemmen fpl <El.>	instability, unstability <chem.>	Unbeständigkeit f, Instabilität f <Chem.>
input time constant	Eingangszeitkonstante f	instability, inconstancy, non-constancy <meas.>	Inkonstanz f, Instabilität f <Meß.>
input tube	Eingangsröhre f; Vorröhre f	instability <meteo.>	Instabilität f <Meteo.>
		instability constant	Unbeständigkeitskonstante f, Instabilitätskonstante f
input unit, input equipment, input device, input	Eingabewerk n, Eingabegerät n	instability criterion, criterion of instability	Labilitätskriterium n
		instability of plasma [column], plasma instability	Plasmainstabilität f, Instabilität f der Plasmasäule
inrush current	s. transient current		
inscattering, scattering-in	Hineinstreuung f	instability region	Instabilitätsbereich m, Instabilitätsgebiet n
inscattering correction	Korrektion f für Hineinstreuung	instability shower	Instabilitätsschauer m
inscribed angle	Peripheriewinkel m, Umfangswinkel m		
inscribed circle	s. incircle	instability stop band, stop band, stopband, unstable stop band <acc.>	Stoppband n [im Diamanten], instabiler Streifen m <Beschl.>
insensible; indifferent; unfeeling <bio.>	unempfindlich <Bio.>	installation of chokes	Verdrosselung f
insensitive; unreactive <of instrument>	unempfindlich <Gerät>	instant, instant of time, time, moment, epoch	Zeitpunkt m, Zeit f, Moment m, Augenblick m
insensitive interval, paralysis time, paralysis period, insensitive time	Sperrzeit f, Unempfindlichkeitszeit f, Totzeit f	instantaneous acceleration	Momentanbeschleunigung f, momentane (instantane) Beschleunigung f
insensitive plane, insensitivity plane	Unempfindlichkeitsebene f, unempfindliche Ebene f	instantaneous acoustic density of kinetic energy	s. instantaneous acoustic kinetic energy per unit volume
insensitive time, paralysis time (period), insensitive interval	Sperrzeit f, Unempfindlichkeitszeit f, Totzeit f	instantaneous acoustic density of potential energy	s. instantaneous acoustic potential energy per unit volume
insensitive to structure	s. structure-insensitive	instantaneous acoustic kinetic energy per unit volume, instantaneous acoustic density of kinetic energy	momentane Dichte f der kinetischen Schallenergie
insensitivity plane, insensitive plane	Unempfindlichkeitsebene f, unempfindliche Ebene f		
inseparable <math.>	nichtseparierbar; nichttrennbar, untrennbar <Math.>		
		instantaneous acoustic potential energy per unit volume, instantaneous acoustic density of potential energy	momentane Dichte f der potentiellen Schallenergie
inseqoent river	insequenter Fluß m		
in-series connection	s. series connection		
insert	s. insert lattice		
inserted; immersed <of rods>	eingetaucht	instantaneous acoustic power [across a surface element], sound energy flux	momentane Schalleistung f
insertion	s. moving in <of rods>		
insertion	s. introduction <e.g. of impurities>		
insertion attenuation, insertion loss	Einfügungsdämpfung f, Einfügungsverlust m	instantaneous acoustic power per unit area, instantaneous sound energy flux per unit area	momentane Schallintensität f
insertion gain	Einfügungsgewinn m		
insertion loss, insertion attenuation	Einfügungsdämpfung f, Einfügungsverlust m	instantaneous adaptation; adaptation of the cones	Sofortadaptation f; Momentadaptation f; Zäpfchenanpassung f
insertion of electrons	Elektroneneinbau m	instantaneous altitude of the pole	instantane Polhöhe f
inside, interior <math.>	Inneres n; offener Kern m <Punktmenge> <Math.>	instantaneous angular velocity	momentane Winkelgeschwindigkeit f
inside calipers, internal calipers, internal caliper gauge	Innentaster m, Innenfeinmeßgerät n, mechanischer Taster m	instantaneous angular velocity [vector]	momentaner Winkelgeschwindigkeitsvektor m
		instantaneous axis [of rotation]	Momentanachse f [der Drehung], Momentandrehachse f, momentane (instantane, augenblickliche) Drehachse f, instantane Rotationsachse f
inside concentration	Binnenkonzentration f		
inside pressure	s. internal pressure		
inside temperature	Innentemperatur f		
insolameter, insolation meter	Besonnungsmesser m, Insolameter n		
insolation <meteo.>	Insolation f, Sonneneinstrahlung f, Einstrahlung f, Sonnenbestrahlung f, Besonnung f <Meteo.>	instantaneous beam current	momentaner Strahlstrom m
		instantaneous beam intensity, instantaneous (beam) intensity <acc.>	[momentane] Strahlstärke f, [momentane] Strahlintensität f <Beschl.>
insolation meter, insolameter	Besonnungsmesser m, Insolameter n		
insolation weathering, thermal weathering	Insolationsverwitterung f, Temperaturverwitterung f	instantaneous breakdown	Sofortdurchschlag m
		instantaneous centre	s. instantaneous centre of rotation

instantaneous   370

instantaneous centre of accelerations, centre of instantaneous accelerations	momentaner Beschleunigungspol m, Momentanbeschleunigungspol m, momentanes Beschleunigungszentrum n, Momentanbeschleunigungszentrum n	**instantaneous sound pressure**	momentaner Schalldruck m
		instantaneous space	momentaner Raum m
		instantaneous storage (store)	s. zero-acces storage
		instantaneous strain	momentane Verformung f
instantaneous centre of rotation, instantaneous centre	Momentanpol m, Geschwindigkeitspol m, momentaner Drehpol m, Momentanzentrum n, momentanes Drehzentrum n	**instantaneous system [of co-ordinates]**	Momentansystem n, Instantansystem n
		instantaneous twist	s. instantaneous screw motion
		instantaneous value, momentary value	Momentanwert m, Augenblickswert m
instantaneous centre of velocities, centre of instantaneous velocities	momentaner Geschwindigkeitspol m, Momentangeschwindigkeitspol m, momentanes Geschwindigkeitszentrum n, Momentangeschwindigkeitszentrum n	**instantaneous velocity**	Momentangeschwindigkeit f, momentane (instantane) Geschwindigkeit f
		instantaneous voltage; transient voltage	Augenblicksspannung f, Augenblickswert m der Spannung, Moment[an]spannung f
instantaneous current	Augenblicksstrom m, Augenblickswert m des Stromes, Momentanstrom m		
		instant of time	s. instant
		in-state	„in"-Zustand m
instantaneous density of sound energy, instantaneous sound energy density	momentane Schallenergiedichte f	**instruction,** order, command <num. math.>	Befehl m <num. Math.>
		instrumental altitude of the pole	instrumentelle Polhöhe f
instantaneous element	instantanes Element (Bahnelement) n	**instrumental azimuth**	Instrumentalazimut n, Instrumentazimut n
instantaneous flow, instantaneous rate of flow	momentane Durchflußmenge f, Augenblicksbelastung f	**instrumental error,** error of measuring instrument, [measuring] instrument error, meter error; index error <e.g. of theodolite>	Instrumentenfehler m, Instrumentalfehler m, Gerätefehler m, Apparatefehler m, Apparatefehler m; Indexfehler m <z. B. Theodolit>
instantaneous force	s. impulsive force		
instantaneous frequency	Momentanfrequenz f, momentane Frequenz f, Augenblicksfrequenz f		
instantaneous ignition	Sofortzündung f		
instantaneous ignition lamp	Sofortstartlampe f	**instrumental neutron activation analysis,** INAA	instrumentelle Neutronenaktivierungsanalyse f, INAA
instantaneous intensity, [instantaneous] beam intensity <acc.>	[momentane] Strahlstärke f, [momentane] Strahlintensität f <Beschl.>	**instrumental optics**	Instrumentelle Optik f
		instrumental parallax	Einstellparallaxe f
instantaneous load, momentary load <el.>	Momentanbelastung f, Augenblicksbelastung f, momentane Belastung f <El.>	**instrumental refraction**	Instrumentenrefraktion f
instantaneous modulus	s. unrelaxed modulus	**instrumental seismology**	instrumentelle Seismologie (Seismik) f
instantaneous motion	momentane (instantane) Bewegung f, Momentanbewegung f	**instrumental stimulus,** matching stimulus, primary	Meßvalenz f
instantaneous orbit	Momentankreis m, Momentanbahn f, momentane Bahn f	**instrumental width [of the line],** line width due to the apparatus used	Apparatebreite f
instantaneous orbital plane	instantane Bahnebene f	**instrumentation**	s. measuring equipment
instantaneous photograph	s. instantaneous shot	**instrument capable of plotting from aerial photographs**	s. aerocartograph
instantaneous photography	Momentphotographie f, Momentaufnahme f	**instrument capsule**	Instrumentenkapsel f
instantaneous power	Momentanleistung f, momentane Leistung f, Augenblicksleistung f		
instantaneous rate of flow, instantaneous flow	momentane Durchflußmenge f, Augenblicksbelastung f	**instrument-carrying rocket,** instrumented rocket	instrumententragende Rakete f
instantaneous rotation	Momentandrehung f, momentane (instantane) Drehung f, momentane (instantane) Rotation f	**instrument correction;** index correction <e.g. of theodolite>	Instrumentenkorrektion f, Instrumentalkorrektion f; Indexkorrektion f <z. B. Theodolit>
instantaneous screw axis	momentane (instantane) Schraubenachse f	**instrumented rocket,** instrument-carrying rocket	instrumententragende Rakete f
instantaneous screw motion, instantaneous twist	Schrotung f, Axoidbewegung f, momentane (instantane) Schraubenbewegung f	**instrumented satellite**	Meßsatellit m
instantaneous shortcircuit current, mechanical short-time current rating <US>	Stoßkurzschlußstrom m, dynamischer Grenzstrom m	**instrument error**	s. instrumental error
		instrument for field measurements, field instrument	Feldinstrument n, Feldmeßgerät n, Reiseinstrument n Reisemeßgerät n; relatives Meßgerät n
instantaneous shot, instantaneous photograph, pistolgraph. snapshot	Momentaufnahme f, Augenblicksaufnahme f, Schnappschuß m		
instantaneous shutter	Momentverschluß m	**instrument head**	s. measuring head
		instrument hole <of reactor>	Instrumentenkanal m, Meßkanal m <Reaktor>
instantaneous sound energy density, instantaneous density of sound energy	momentane Schallenergiedichte f	**instrument load**	Instrumentenlast f
instantaneous sound energy flux per unit area, instantaneous acoustic power per unit area	momentane Schallintensität f	**instrument movement,** meter movement, movement of the instrument; measuring system	Meßwerk n; Meßsystem n

instrument of high performance, high-performance (high-output) instrument	Hochleistungsgerät n, Hochleistungsinstrument n	intake ‹into the organ›, uptake [by the organ]	Aufnahme f [durch das Organ], Organaufnahme f, Einbau m [in das Organ], Inkorporation f
instrument probe	s. measuring head	intake chamber	s. surge chamber ‹hydr.›
instrument range	s. effective range ‹meas.›	intake line	s. suction line
instrument screen, instrument shelter, screen, shelter	Schutzhäuschen f, Instrumentenschutzhäuschen n, Instrumenten[schutz]hütte f, Schutzhütte f, Hütte f, Wetterhäuschen n, Wetterhütte f	intake of water	s. water intake
		intake pipe	s. supply pipe
		intake pressure, suction pressure	Saugdruck m; Ansaugdruck m
		intake stroke, suction stroke	Ansaugtakt m
instrument transformer	s. transducer ‹meas.›	intake velocity	s. inlet velocity
instrument transformer load, load of instrument transformer	Bürde f, Belastung f des Meßwandlers	integer, integral number, rational integer	ganze [rationale] Zahl f, ganzrationale Zahl
instrument with locking device, relay-type recording instrument	Fallbügelinstrument n, Meßgerät n mit Fallbügel	integrability condition, compatibility condition ‹math.›	Integrabilitätsbedingung f, Verträglichkeitsbedingung f, Kompatibilitätsbedingung f ‹Math.›
		integrable	integrierbar; integrabel ‹System partieller Differentialgleichungen, Pfaffsche Form›
instrument with magnetic screening, iron-screened instrument	eisengeschirmtes Meßgerät n		
		integrable connection, integrable transfer	integrable Übertragung f
instrument with optical pointer, optical (luminous) pointer instrument, light-spot (mirror) instrument	Lichtmarkeninstrument n, Lichtmarkenmeßgerät n, Lichtzeigerinstrument n, Lichtzeiger[meß]gerät n	integral absorbed dose	s. energy imparted by ionizing radiation ‹bio.›
		integral action time, reset[ting] time	Nachstellzeit f, Nachlaufzeit f, Nachgebezeit f
		integral bias summing coincidence spectrometer	s. sum-peak spectrometer
instrument with suppressed zero	s. suppressed zero instrument		
insulance	s. insulation resistance	integral control, astatic control	Integralregelung f, I-Regelung f, astatische Regelung f
insulant, insulating material, insulator	Isolierstoff m, Isoliermaterial n		
insular climate, maritime climate, oceanic climate	Seeklima n, maritimes Klima n, ozeanisches Klima		
insulated-gate metal-oxide semiconductor field[-] effect transistor, IGFET	isolierter Kanaltransistor (Feldeffekttransistor) m, Feldeffekttransistor m mit isolierter Torelektrode, IKT	integral controller, astatic controller	Integralregler m, I-Regler m, astatischer Regler m
		integral cross-section, integrated cross-section	integraler (integrierter) Wirkungsquerschnitt m
insulated wall, insulating wall, adiabatic wall	wärmeundurchlässige Wand f, adiabatische Wand	integral curve, mass curve	Summen[gang]linie f, Integralkurve f, Inhaltslinie f
insulating; dielectric; non[-]conducting, non-conductive ‹el.›	dielektrisch; nichtleitend; isolierend ‹El.›	integral curve ‹math.›	Integralkurve f, Lösungskurve f ‹Math.›
insulating material, insulator, insulant	Isolierstoff m, Isoliermaterial n	integral discriminator	s. discriminator
		integral dissolution heat	s. integral heat of solution
insulating material	s. a. sound insulator ‹ac.›	integral domain, domain of integrity, [integrity] domain, integral ring	Integritätsbereich m, kommutativer Ring m [mit Eins] ohne Nullteiler
insulating moving belt electrostatic accelerator	s. Graaff generator / Van de		
		integral dose	Integraldosis f, integrale Dosis f
insulating strength	Isolationsfestigkeit f	integral equation method	Integralgleichungsmethode f
insulating transformer	Trenntransformator m, Maschenentkoppler m; Zweigentkoppler m; Potentialentkoppler m	integral equation of Schwarzschild and Milne, Schwarzschild-Milne equation	Schwarzschild-Milnesche Integralgleichung f
insulating wall	s. insulated wall	integral equation of the first kind, linear integral equation of the first kind, Fredholm['s] [integral] equation of the first kind	[lineare] Integralgleichung f erster Art, Fredholmsche Integralgleichung (Gleichung f) erster Art
insulation ‹el.›	Isolation f; Isolierung f		
insulation	s. a. heat insulation ‹therm.›		
insulation hum	Isolationsbrumm n, Isolationsbrummen n		
insulation loss	Isolationsverlust m	integral equation of the second kind	s. Fredholm['s] integral equation
insulation material	s. sound insulator ‹ac.›	integral equation of the third kind, linear integral equation of the third kind	Integralgleichung f dritter Art, lineare Integralgleichung dritter Art
insulation resistance, dielectric resistance, insulance	Isolationswiderstand m, dielektrischer Widerstand m		
		integral extinction	integrale Auslöschung f
insulation test voltage	Stehstoßspannung f	integral form	Integralform f
		integral function, entire function	ganze Funktion f
		integral heat of [dis-]solution, integral [dis-]solution heat	integrale Lösungswärme f
insulativity	spezifischer Isolationswiderstand m		
		integral inflow curve	Zuflußsummenkurve f, Zuflußsummenganglinie f
insulator	s. dielectric	integral invariant	[vollständige] Integralinvariante f
insulator	s. a. insulating material		
insulator-type transformer	Topfstromwandler m, Topfwandler m	integral ionization, integrated ionization	integrale Ionisation f, Auslaufionisation f
		integral Joule-Thomson effect	integraler Joule-Thomson-Effekt m
intact	antiklastisch, intakt	integral kernel	s. kernel ‹of integral equation›

integral

integral luminance	integrale Leuchtdichte *f*; integrale Strahldichte *f*	integrating factor, Euler's multiplier	integrierender Faktor *m*, ·Eulerscher (integrierender) Multiplikator *m*
integral number	*s.* integer	integrating gyro[scope]	Summenkreisel *m*
integral of areas	*s.* principle of conservation of areas	integrating instrument, integrating measuring instrument, meter <meas.>	integrierendes Meßgerät (Gerät, Instrument) *n*, zählendes Meßgerät (Gerät, Instrument), Zähler *m*, Zähluhr *f*, Uhr *f* <Meß.>
integral of motion, first integral of motion <mech.>	erstes Integral *n* der Bewegung[sgleichung], intermediäres Integral [der Bewegungsgleichungen], Integral der Bewegung[sgleichungen], Bewegungsintegral *n*		
		integrating instrument	*s. a.* counting-rate meter
		integrating ionization chamber	integrierende Ionisationskammer *f*
integral of refraction	Refraktionsintegral *n*	integrating measuring instrument	*s.* integrating instrument
integral of state, integral over states	Zustandsintegral *n*	integrating network	*s.* integrating circuit
		integrating network	*s.* integrating unit
integral operator of Bergman	Bergmanscher Integraloperator *m*, Integraloperator von Bergman	integrating photometer	Integralphotometer *n*, integrierendes Photometer *n*
integral over a closed surface, closed surface integral	Hüllenintegral *n*	integrating photometer (sphere)	*s. a.* photometric integrator
		integrating system	integrierendes System *n*, I-System *n*
integral over states, integral of state	Zustandsintegral *n*	integrating unit, integrating network	Integrationsglied *n*, Integrierglied *n*
		integration <meas.>	Integration *f*, Mittelwertmessung *f* <Meß.>
integral part	größte ganze Zahl *f*, größtes Ganzes *n*, ganzer Teil *m*	integration by parts, integration per parts, partial integration	partielle (unvollständige, teilweise) Integration *f*, Integration nach Teilen, Teilintegration *f*, Produktintegration *f*
integral principle, [integral] variational principle <mech.; qu.>	Variationsprinzip *n*, Integralprinzip *n*, Extremalprinzip *n* <Mech.; Qu.>		
integral rational function, polynomial	Polynom *n*, ganze rationale Funktion *f*	integration by parts	*s. a.* Green theorem
		integration method of Hamilton and Jacobi	Hamilton-Jacobische Integrationsmethode *f*
integral representation	Integraldarstellung *f*; quellenmäßige Darstellung *f* <Rel.>		
integral ring	*s.* integral domain	integration method of velocity measurement	Ablaufverfahren *n*, Integrationsmethode *f* der Geschwindigkeitsmessung
integral sign	Integralzeichen *n*		
integral solution heat	*s.* integral heat of solution		
integral spin	ganzzahliger Spin *m*		
integral sum, Riemann sum	Integralsumme *f*		
integral theorem <of Laplace transform>	Integrationssatz *m*	integration of impulses, integration of pulses	Impulsintegration *f*, Integration *f* von Impulsen
integral theorem of Fourier, Fourier['s] integral theorem	Fouriersche Integralformel (Integraldarstellung) *f*	integration per parts	*s.* integration by parts
		integration term by term, term-by-term integration	gliedweise Integration *f*
integral theorem of Gauss	*s.* Green theorem		
integral theorem of Green	*s.* Green['s] symmetrical theorem	integration time	Integrationszeit *f*, Integrierzeit *f*
integral theorem of Stokes	*s.* Stokes['] theorem	integration time constant	Integrationszeitkonstante *f*
integral variational principle, variational (integral) principle <mech.; qu.>	Variationsprinzip *n*, Integralprinzip *n*, Extremalprinzip *n* <Mech.; Qu.>	integrator <element of computer>	Integrator *m* <Element des Analogrechners>
		integrator	*s. a.* counting-rate meter
		integrator	*s. a.* integraph
integrand, function to be integrated, expression to be integrated	Integrand *m*	integrator circuit	*s.* integrating circuit
		integrity, wholeness	Ganzheit *f*
		integrity domain	*s.* integral domain
		integro-differential equation	Integrodifferentialgleichung *f*, Integro-Differentialgleichung *f*
integraph, integrator	Integraph *m*, Integrator *m*		
integrated circuit	integrierte Schaltung *f*	integrometer, moment planimeter	Integrimeter *n*
integrated cross-section, integral cross-section	integraler (integrierter) Wirkungsquerschnitt *m*	intelligibility, relative articulation, articulation, comprehensibility	Sprachdeutlichkeit *f*, Sprachverständlichkeit *f*, [relative] Verständlichkeit *f*, Deutlichkeit *f*
integrated current, summated current	Integralstrom *m*, Integralstromstärke *f*		
integrated flux, integrated neutron flux, flux time, time integral of flux <in n/cm²>	integraler Fluß (Neutronenfluß) *m*, Flußzeit *f*, Zeitintegral *n* des Neutronenflusses <in n/cm²>	intelligibility of characters, legibility of characters	Zeichenlesbarkeit *f*, Lesbarkeit *f* der Zeichen
		intelligible crosstalk, uninverted crosstalk	verständliches Nebensprechen *n*
integrated ionization	*s.* integral ionization	intense line, strong line	starke Linie *f*, intensive Linie
integrated neutron flux	*s.* integrated flux		
integrated power spectrum	*s.* spectral function <stat.>	intensification, photographic intensification, intensification of the photographic image	photographische Verstärkung *f*, Verstärkung [des photographischen Bildes]
integrated reflection	integrierte Reflexion *f*, Gesamtreflexion *f*		
		intensification	*s. a.* amplification
integrated voltage, summated voltage	Integralspannung *f*	intensification factor, intensifying factor, speed factor <phot.>	Verstärkungsfaktor *m* <Phot.>
integrating circuit, integrating network; integrator circuit	Integrierschaltung *f*, Integrierkreis *m*, Integrationsschaltung *f*, Integratorschaltung *f*, integrierendes Netzwerk *n*		
		intensification of latent image, latent image intensification, latensification	Latensifikation *f*, Verstärkung *f* des latenten Bildes
integrating denominator	integrierender Nenner *m*		
integrating dose meter	integrierendes Dosimeter *n*	intensification of the photographic image, [photographic] intensification	photographische Verstärkung *f*, Verstärkung [des photographischen Bildes]

intensifier, photographic intensifier <phot.> — photographischer Verstärker *m*, Verstärker <Phot.>
intensifier electrode, intensifier ring, post-accelerating (post-accelerator) electrode, second gun electrode — Nachbeschleunigungselektrode *f*
intensifying factor, intensification (speed) factor <phot.> — Verstärkungsfaktor *m* <Phot.>
intensifying factor — *s. a.* gain
intensifying screen — Verstärkerfolie *f*, Verstärkerschirm *m*, Verstärkungsfolie *f*, Verstärkungsschirm *m*
intensimeter <ac.> — Intensimeter *n* <Ak.>
intensitometer <for X-rays> — Intensimeter *n* <für Röntgenstrahlung>
intensity <gen.>; magnitude <of force> — Intensität *f*; Stärke *f* <allg.>
intensity, energy flux density <bio.> — Energieflußdichte *f*, Intensität *f* <Bio.>
intensity — *s. a.* lightness
intensity alternation, alternation of intensity — Intensitätswechsel *m*
intensity-controlling electrode — Lichtsteuerelektrode *f*
intensity diagram of light, intensity image of light — Lichtgebirge *n*
intensity factor — *s.* intensive variable <therm.>
intensity image of light, intensity diagram of light — Lichtgebirge *n*
intensity level — *s.* loudness level <ac.>
intensity level — *s. a.* sound intensity level <ac.>
intensity maximum, light maximum — Lichtmaximum *n*
intensity meter — Intensitätsmesser *m*
intensity millicurie, Sievert unit, ImC — Sievert-Einheit *f*, ImC
intensity minimum, light minimum — Lichtminimum *n*
intensity modulation, light modulation, modulation of light — Modulation *f* des Lichtes, Lichtmodulation *f*, Lichtsteuerung *f*
intensity of backscattered radiation, backscatter intensity — Rückstreuintensität *f*, Rückstrahlintensität *f*
intensity of continuous load — spezifische Belastung *f*
intensity of current — *s.* current <el.>
intensity of distributed load — *s.* intensity of load
intensity of earthquake, earthquake intensity — Erdbebenstärke *f*, Bebenstärke *f*, Stärke (Intensität) *f* des Bebens, Erdbebenintensität *f*
intensity of electric field — *s.* electric intensity
intensity of emission — Emissionsstärke *f*
intensity of evaporation, evaporation intensity — Verdunstungsstärke *f*, Verdunstungsintensität *f*, Verdunstungskraft *f*
intensity of flow — *s.* rate of flow
intensity of illumination — *s.* illuminance <quantity>
intensity of light — *s.* light intensity
intensity of load, intensity of distributed load — Belastungsstärke *f*, Belastungsintensität *f*
intensity of luminescence — *s.* luminescence intensity
intensity of magnetic field — *s.* magnetic field intensity
intensity of magnetization, magnetic [dipole] moment per unit volume, magnetic pole strength per unit volume, magnetic moment density, magnetization; intrinsic (ferric) induction; magnetization vector, vector of magnetization — Magnetisierung *f*, magnetisches Moment (Dipolmoment) *n* der Volumeneinheit, eingeprägte (innere) Induktion *f*, Magnetisierungsstärke *f*, Magnetisierungskraft *f*; Magnetisierungsvektor *m*
intensity of radiation, radiation intensity, radiant intensity — Strahlungsintensität *f*, Intensität *f* [der Strahlung], Strahlenintensität *f*
intensity of radioactivity — *s.* activity <nucl.>
intensity of sensitization, sensitizing intensity — Sensibilisierungsintensität *f*

intensity of sound — *s.* sound intensity
intensity of stress, stress intensity — Spannungsintensität *f*
intensity of terrestrial radiation — terrestrische Strahlungsintensität *f*
intensity of the band — Bandenintensität *f*, Intensität *f* der Bande
intensity of the beam current, beam current — Strahlstrom *m*, Strahlstromstärke *f*
intensity of the spectral line, [spectral] line intensity, spectrum line intensity, line strength, strength of line — Intensität *f* der Spektrallinie, Linienintensität *f*, Linienstärke *f*, Spektrallinienintensität *f*
intensity of torsional strain (stress) — *s.* torsional stress
intensity of turbulence, turbulence intensity — Turbulenzstärke *f*
intensity of wave, wave intensity — Intensität *f* der Welle
intensity of wind — *s.* wind intensity
intensity range of the negative, density range (volume) of the negative — Negativumfang *m*
intensity range of the positive, density range (volume) of the positive — Positivumfang *m*
intensity ratio versus voltage characteristic of Kerr cell — Licht-Spannung-Kennlinie *f*, Lichtspannungskennlinie *f*
intensity spectrum <ac.> — Intensitätsspektrum *n*
intensity sum rule — Intensitätssummenregel *f*, Summenregel *f* für die Intensität[en]
intensity wave — Intensitätswelle *f*
intensive parameter — *s.* intensive variable <therm.>
intensive property — intensive Eigenschaft *f*
intensive property (quantity, thermodynamic property) — *s.* intensive variable <therm.>
intensive variable, intensive quantity, intensive parameter, intensive [thermodynamic] property, intensity factor, thermodynamic tension <therm.> — intensive Variable (Größe) *f*, intensiver Parameter *m*, Intensitätsvariable *f*, Intensitätsparameter *m*, generalisierte Kraft *f*, [thermodynamische] Intensitätsgröße *f*
interaccelerator, intermediate accelerator — Zwischenbeschleuniger *m*
interact — wechselwirken, in Wechselwirkung treten (stehen), aufeinander einwirken, miteinander reagieren
interacting control, multivariable control, multielement control, multiple control — vermaschte Regelung *f*; Mehrfachregelung *f*; Mehrfachsteuerung *f*

interacting field — wechselwirkendes Feld *n*
interaction; mutual interaction, reciprocal action, interreaction, mutual action — Wechselwirkung *f*; wechselseitige Beeinflussung *f*, gegenseitige Wechselwirkung, Wechselspiel *n*
interaction, interconnection — Vermaschung *f*, Verkopplung *f*
interaction assembly [of nuclei] — Wechselwirkungsgruppe *f* [von Kernen]
interaction between nucleons, nucleon-nucleon interaction — Nukleon-Nukleon-Wechselwirkung *f*
interaction constant — Wechselwirkungskonstante *f*
interaction cross-section, cross-section for interaction — Wechselwirkungsquerschnitt *m*, Wirkungsquerschnitt *m* für (der) Wechselwirkung
interaction effect — „interaction"-Effekt *m*, Wechselwirkungseffekt *m*
interaction factor — Wechselwirkungsfaktor *m*

interaction

interaction force	Wechselwirkungskraft f	interchange, mutual exchange	Umtausch m; Auswechslung f; Vertauschung f
interaction Hamiltonian	Wechselwirkungs-Hamilton-Operator m; Wechselwirkungs-Hamilton-Funktion f	interchange, changeover switching, switching-over, switching, change <el.>	Umschaltung f; Umstellung f <El.>
interaction Lagrangian	Wechselwirkungs-Lagrange-Dichte f	interchange	s. a. exchange
interaction law	s. Newton['s] third law [of motion]	interchange	s. a. mixing <mech.>
interaction length	s. interaction mean free path	interchangeable, replacement <of a meter>	austauschbar, auswechselbar, Austausch- <Gerät>
interaction loss	Wechselwirkungsverlust m	interchangeable condensor [lens]	Wechselkondensor m
		interchange coefficient	s. effective turbulent diffusivity
interaction mean free path, mean free path for interaction, interaction length	[mittlere freie] Wechselwirkungslänge f, mittlere freie Weglänge f für die Wechselwirkung	interchange deformation, interchange-type deformation; flute-type deformation	Austauschdeformation f, Deformation f vom konvektiven Typ; Rinnendeformation f
		interchange diffusion, interchange mechanism of diffusion, diffusion by interchange	Diffusion f durch Platzwechsel, Platzwechselmechanismus m der Diffusion
interaction of discontinuities, discontinuity interaction	Unstetigkeitswechselwirkung f, Wechselwirkung f von Unstetigkeiten	interchange instability; flute-type instability	Instabilität f gegen Austauschdeformation, Austauschinstabilität f, konvektive Instabilität; Rinneninstabilität f
interaction operator	Wechselwirkungsoperator m		
interaction parameter	Wechselwirkungsparameter m		
interaction picture	s. interaction representation		
interaction picture equation, Tomonaga-Schwinger['s] equation	Tomonaga-Schwinger-Gleichung f, Tomonaga-Schwingersche Gleichung f	interchange mechanism of diffusion, interchange diffusion, diffusion by interchange, site-hopping mechanism, activated mechanism	Diffusion f durch Platzwechsel, Platzwechselmechanismus m der Diffusion, Platzaustauschmechanismus m [der Oberflächendiffusion], [direkter] Platzaustausch m
interaction potential	Wechselwirkungspotential n		
interaction range	Wechselwirkungsbereich m		
interaction representation, interaction picture, Tomonaga-Schwinger picture	Wechselwirkungsdarstellung f, Wechselwirkungsbild n, Tomonaga-Bild n, Tomonaga-Darstellung f	interchange model [of diffusion]	Platzwechselmodell n [der Diffusion]
		interchange of heat	s. heat exchange
		interchange of radiant energy	Strahlungsenergieaustausch m, Strahlungsaustausch m
interaction space	Wechselwirkungsraum m		
interaction splitting	Wechselwirkungsaufspaltung f	interchange of radiant heat, radiant heat interchange	Strahlungswärmeaustausch m
interaction strength, strength of the interaction	Stärke f der Wechselwirkung, Wechselwirkungsstärke f	interchange of sites; exchange of site, place exchange, platzwechsel; transposition of pairs, phantom transposition	Platzwechsel m
interaction term	Wechselwirkungsterm m		
interaction time	Wechselwirkungszeit f		
interaction type, mode of interaction, type of interaction	Wechselwirkungstyp m, Wechselwirkungsart f, Art f der Wechselwirkung	interchange process, process of interchange [of sites]	Platzwechselvorgang m
interatomic distance, distance between atoms, atomic spacing	interatomarer Abstand m, Atomabstand m	interchanger, heat exchanger, heat interchanger	Wärme[aus]tauscher m, Wärmeaustauschapparat m
interatomic force	interatomare (zwischenatomare) Kraft f	interchange reaction, exchange reaction	Platzwechselreaktion f
interatomic Stark effect	interatomarer Stark-Effekt m		
interatomic Stark effect broadening	interatomare Stark-Effekt-Verbreiterung f	interchange theory [of viscosity]	Platzwechseltheorie f [der Viskosität], Platzwechseltheorie von Eyring
interattraction	s. mutual attraction	interchange-type deformation, interchange deformation; flute-type deformation	Austauschdeformation f, Deformation f vom konvektiven Typ; Rinnendeformation f
interband, intermediate band	Zwischenband n		
interband level	Zwischenbandniveau n; Zwischenbandterm m		
interband recombination	s. band-to-band recombination	interclass correlation, between-class correlation, correlation between classes	Zwischenklassenkorrelation f, Interklaßkorrelation f, Interklassenkorrelation f
interband scattering	s. band-to-band scattering		
interband transition	s. band-to-band transition		
intercalary day, leap day, adding day	Schalttag m	interclass variance, between-group variance, between-class variance, variance between classes (treatments), external variance	Varianz f zwischen den Klassen (Gruppen), Zwischen[klassen]varianz f, äußere Varianz, Interklaßvarianz f, Interklassenvarianz f
intercarrier [sound] system	Differenzträgerverfahren n, Intercarrierverfahren n, Interferenztonempfang m		
		intercombination law	s. prohibition of intercombinations
		intercombination line	Interkombinationslinie f
intercellular substance	Zwischenzellsubstanz f	intercomparison; comparison	Vergleich m; Gegenüberstellung f
intercept	s. point of intersection	interconnected	s. intermeshed
interception, taking of a bearing	Anpeilung f	interconnected coil leakage field	Zickzackstreufeld n
interception <e.g. of free electrons, a beam>	Abfangen n <z. B. freie Elektronen, Strahl>		
		interconnection, interaction	Vermaschung f, Verkopplung f
interception	s. a. intersection		
interception	s. a. trapping		
interception range	s. pull-in range		
intercept ratio	s. crystallographic axial ratio	interconnection <el.>; coupling <to; between> <gen., el.>	Kopplung f <mit; zwischen>; Verkopplung f; Ankopplung f <an>
intercept receiver, listening device	Horchgerät n		

interconnection, connection, hookup <el.>	Zusammenschaltung *f* <El.>	interfacial diffusion	Grenzflächendiffusion *f*
interconnection; interposition; cut-in <el.>	Zwischenschaltung *f* <El.>	interfacial energy	Grenzflächenenergie *f*, Grenzflächenarbeit *f*
interconnection	s. a. linkage	interfacial film	Grenzflächenfilm *m*
interconversion <el.>; conversion	Umwandlung *f*, Wandlung *f*, Konversion *f* <El.>		
interconvertible	ineinander umformbar, gegenseitig umformbar		
intercoolant, intermediate coolant <e.g. of nuclear reactors>; intermediate heat-transfer agent	Zwischenkühlmittel *n* <z. B. des Kernreaktors>; Zwischenwärmeträger *m*, Zwischenwärmeüberträger *m*	interfacially active	s. surface-active
		interfacial membrane	Grenzflächenmembran *f*
		interfacial phenomenon	Grenzflächenerscheinung *f*
		interfacial polarization, Maxwell-Wagner polarization	Grenzflächenpolarisation *f*, Grenzschichtpolarisation *f*, Polarisation *f* in Grenzflächen
intercooler, intermediate cooler	Zwischenkühler *m*		
		interfacial potential	Grenzflächenpotential *n*
		interfacial surface energy	s. interfacial tension
intercrescence, intergrowth, overgrowth <cryst.>	Verwachsung *f* <Krist.>	interfacial tension, interfacial surface energy	Grenzflächenspannung *f*
intercrystalline brittleness, intergranular (cleavage) brittleness	interkristalline Brüchigkeit *f*, Korngrenzenbrüchigkeit *f*, Spaltbrüchigkeit *f*		
intercrystalline corrosion, intergranular corrosion	interkristalline Korrosion *f*; Korngrenzenkorrosion *f*, Kornzerfall *m*	interfacial tension	s. a. surface tension
		interfacial viscosity	Grenzflächenviskosität *f*
		interfacial wave	s. boundary wave
intercrystalline cracking, intergranular cracking	interkristalline Rißbildung *f*	interfc	= [integral of] error function complement
intercrystalline cracking due to stress corrosion	s. intercrystalline stress corrosion cracking	interference <of waves>	Interferenz *f*, Überlagerung *f* <von Wellen>
intercrystalline failure (fracture)	s. intergranular fracture	interference <aero.>	Interferenz *f* <Aero.>
intercrystalline precipitation, intergranular precipitation	Korngrenzenausscheidung *f*	interference <gen.>	Störung *f* <allg.>
intercrystalline solidification, intergranular solidification	Korngrenzenverfestigung *f*, Spannungsverfestigung *f*	interference	s. a. parasitics <el.>
		interference absorber	Interferenzabsorber *m*
intercrystalline stress corrosion cracking, intercrystalline cracking due to stress corrosion	interkristalline Spannungsrißkorrosion *f*	interference band, interference fringe, fringe	Interferenzstreifen *m*, Interferenz[erscheinung] *f*
		interference characteristic	Störcharakteristik *f*
		interference colour	Interferenzfarbe *f*
interdecile range	Dezilabstand *m*	interference colour with polarized light	Polarisationsfarbe *f*
interdiffusion	Interdiffusion *f*	interference contrast	Interferenzkontrast *m*
interdiffusion coefficient, chemical diffusion coefficient	Interdiffusionskoeffizient *m*	interference current	s. parasite current
		interference drag <aero.>	Interferenzwiderstand *m* <Aero.>
interdigital line	Doppelkammleitung *f*, Interdigitalleitung *f*	interference experiment, experiment for observing interference	Interferenzversuch *m*
interdigital magnetron	Doppelkammagnetron *n*, Interdigitalmagnetron *n*		
interdiurnal variability	interdiurne Veränderlichkeit *f*	interference eyepiece, Françon eyepiece	Interferenzokular *n* [nach Françon]
interdot scan[ning]	Zwischenpunktabtastung *f*	interference factor, perturbance factor <gen.>	Störfaktor *m* <allg.>
interelectrode capacitance, tube (total electrode) capacitance	Elektrodenkapazität *f*, [innere] Röhrenkapazität, Zwischenelektrodenkapazität *f*	interference fading	Interferenzschwund *m*, Interferenzfading *n*, Flackerschwund *m*, Flackerfading *n*
interelectrode conductivity	Zwischenelektrodenleitfähigkeit *f*	interference field	Interferenzfeld *n*
interelectrode distance (gap)	s. electrode separation	interference field	s. a. disturbance field <el.>
interelectrode transit time	Zwischenelektrodenlaufzeit *f*	interference figure <of crystals in the polarizing microscope>, bisectrix interference figure	Achsenbild *n* <von Kristallen>
interelement effect	Interelementeffekt *m*		
interface, boundary [surface], surface of separation, bounding (separation, parting, dividing) surface	Grenzfläche *f*, Phasengrenzfläche *f*; Grenzschicht *f*; Trennfläche *f*, Trennungsfläche *f*; Zwischenfläche *f*	interference figure	s. a. interference pattern
		interference filter	Interferenz[licht]filter *n*
		interference filter spectroscope	Interferenzfilterspektroskop *n*
interface, junction [transition] region, transition region <semi.>	Übergangszone *f*, Übergangsgebiet *n*, Übergangsbereich *m* <Halb.>	interference fringe, fringe, interference band	Interferenzstreifen *m*, Interferenz[erscheinung] *f*
interface	s. a. intermediate layer	interference fringe by reflection, interference fringe in reflected light, reflected fringe	Interferenzerscheinung *f* bei Auflichtbeobachtung
interface	s. a. interplanar crystal spacing		
interface layer	s. intermediate layer		
interface normal	Grenzflächennormale *f*		
interface region, boundary layer region	Grenzschichtgebiet *n*, Grenzschichtbereich *m*	interference fringe by transmission, interference fringe in transmitted light, transmitted fringe	Interferenzerscheinung *f* bei Durchlichtbeobachtung
interfacial angle <of crystals>	Grenzflächenwinkel *m* <Kristall>		

interference

interference fringe in reflected light	s. interference fringe by reflection	interference spectroscopy, interferometric spectroscopy, interference spectrometry	Interferenzspektroskopie f, Interferenzspektrometrie f
interference fringe in thin films; interference in thin films	Interferenzerscheinung f an dünnen Blättchen; Interferenz f an dünnen Blättchen		
interference fringe in transmitted light	s. interference fringe by transmission	interference spectrum	Interferenzspektrum n
interference fringe of equal inclination	s. fringe of equal inclination	interference spectrum <el.>	Störspektrum n <El.>
interference image	s. interference pattern	interference spot	Interferenzfleck m
interference in thin films	s. interference fringe in thin films	interference suppression device, rejector (rejection, stopper) circuit	Sperrkreis m; Drosselkreis m
interference limiter; noise limiter	Rauschbegrenzer m; Geräuschbegrenzer m, Störbegrenzer m, Störbegrenzerkreis m	interference surface	Interferenzfläche f
		interference susceptibility	Störempfindlichkeit f, Störanfälligkeit f
interference magnifier	Interferenzlupe f		
interference maximum	Interferenzmaximum n	interference term	Interferenzterm m; Störterm m
interference method <of the first, second, third kind>	Interferenzmethode f, Interferenzverfahren n <erster, zweiter, dritter Art>	interference total reflection	Interferenztotalreflexion f
		interference transit instrument	Interferenzdurchgangsinstrument n
interference microscope, microinterferometer	Interferenzmikroskop n, Mikrointerferometer n, Beugungsmikroskop n	interference voltage, parasitic voltage, noise voltage	Störspannung f
interference microscopy	Interferenzmikroskopie f, Mikrointerferometrie f, Beugungsmikroskopie f; Mehrfachreflexinterferometrie f	interference voltage meter, parasitic voltage meter	Störspannungsmeßgerät n, Störspannungsmesser m
		interference vortex, disturbance vortex	Störwirbel m, Störungswirbel m
interference minimum	Interferenzminimum n	interference wedge	Interferenzkeil m
interference note	s. heterodyne note	interferential polarizational filter	s. Lyot filter
interference of diffracted light, interference of diffuse light, Whewell fringe, Quetelet fringe	Interferenz f des gebeugten Lichtes, Interferenz diffusen Lichts, Newtonscher Staubring (Farbenring) m, Farbe f dicker Platten, Whewellscher Streifen m, Queteletscher Streifen (Ring m)	interferential refractometer	Interferenzrefraktometer n, Interferentialrefraktometer n, Vierplattenrefraktometer n, Interferenzrefraktor m, Interferentialrefraktor m
		interfering energy	Störenergie f
interference pattern, interference image, image of interference; interference figure	Interferenzbild n; Interferenzfigur f	interfering field	s. disturbance field <el.>
		interfering frequency	s. spurious frequency
		interfering signal	s. spurious signal
		interferogram	Interferogramm n
interference phenomenon, phenomenon of interference	Interferenzerscheinung f	interferometer <opt.>	Interferometer n, Interferenzgerät n, Interferenzapparat m <Opt.>
interference photograph	Interferenzaufnahme f	interferometer	s. a. radio interferometer <astr.>
interference photometer	Interferenzphotometer n [nach Fuchs und Lummer]	interferometer base, aerial spacing	Antennenabstand m; Interferometerbasislänge f, Interferometerbasis f, Basislänge f
interference photometry	Interferenzphotometrie f	interferometer effect	Interferometereffekt m
interference plate	Interferenzplatte f	interferometer for gases, gas interferometer	Gasinterferometer n
interference point	Interferenzpunkt m	interferometric dilatometer	Interferenzdilatometer n, Interferenzdehnungsmesser m
interference prism	Interferenzprisma n		
interference pulse	Störimpuls m, Störpuls m	interferometric heliometer	Interferenzheliometer n [nach Linnik]
interference radiation	s. perturbing radiation <el.>	interferometric spectroscopy	s. interference spectroscopy
interference rainbow	s. secondary rainbow	interferometry of electrons, electron interferometry	Elektroneninterferometrie f
interference rangefinder	Interferenzentfernungsmesser m		
interference ring	Interferenzring m	interfibrillar space	Interfibrillarraum m
interference spectrograph	Interferenzspektrograph m	interflow	Deckschichtabfluß m
		intergalactic matter	intergalaktische (internebulare) Materie f
interference spectrometer, interference spectroscope	Interferenzspektroskop n, Interferenzspektrometer n	interglacial period	Interglazialzeit f, Interglazial n, Zwischeneiszeit f
interference spectrometry, interference spectroscopy, interferometric spectroscopy	Interferenzspektroskopie f, Interferenzspektrometrie f	intergranular brittle fracture	s. intergranular fracture
		intergranular brittleness	s. intercrystalline brittleness
		intergranular corrosion, intercrystalline corrosion	interkristalline Korrosion f; Korngrenzenkorrosion f, Kornzerfall m
interference spectroscope, interference spectrometer	Interferenzspektroskop n, Interferenzspektrometer n	intergranular cracking, intercrystalline cracking	interkristalline Rißbildung f
		intergranular diffusion	s. grain boundary migration

intergranular fracture, intercrystalline failure (fracture), intergranular brittle fracture, grain-boundary fracture — interkristalliner Bruch *m*, Korngrenzenbruch *m*

intergranular precipitation, intercrystalline precipitation — Korngrenzenausscheidung *f*

intergranular solidification — s. intercrystalline solidification

intergrowth, intercrescence, overgrowth <cryst.> — Verwachsung *f* <Krist.>

interim, conventional — interimistisch, vereinbart, bedingt

interim stage — s. intermediate stage

interionic attraction — Anziehung *f* der Ionen untereinander, interionare Anziehung

interionic interaction energy — interionare Wechselwirkungsenergie *f*

interionic theory of electrolytes — interionische Theorie *f* der Elektrolyte

interior, inside <math.> — Inneres *n*; offener Kern *m* <Punktmenge> <Math.>

interior ballistics, internal ballistics — innere Ballistik *f*

interior boundary value problem — inneres Randwertproblem *n*

interior derivative — innere Ableitung *f*

interior force, total stress — Spannkraft *f*

interior measure, lower measure — inneres Maß *n*

interior of the Earth, Earth's interior — Erdinneres *n*

interkinesis, interphase — Interkinese *f*, Interphase *f*

interlacement — s. interlacing

interlacing, cross interlacing, interlacement — Verschränkung *f*

interlacing, entanglement, intertwining, interlacement, tangling — Verschlingung *f*, Verflechtung *f*

interlattice, intermediate lattice — Zwischengitter *n*

interlattice plane distance — s. interplanar crystal spacing

inter[]layer — s. intermediate layer

interleaved winding — s. pie winding

interlevel transition — s. transition between levels

interlinked current, line current, system current — verketteter Strom *m*

interlinked flux — verketteter Fluß *m*

interlinked phases — verkettete Phasen *fpl*

interlinked voltage — s. line voltage

interlinking — s. linkage

interlinking angle, angle of interlinking — Verkettungswinkel *m*

interlinking factor — Verkettungsfaktor *m*, Verkettungszahl *f*

interlinking point — Verkettungspunkt *m*

interlock — s. interlocking

interlocked multiplets — verkettete Multipletts *npl*

interlocking, locking; blocking; latching — Blockierung *f*, Blockung *f*; Verblockung *f*; Sperrung *f*; Verriegelung *f*

interlocking — s. a. blocking <el.>

interloper — systemfremder Stern *m*, Fremdstern *m*

interloper — s. a. quasar

intermediary metabolism — intermediärer Stoffwechsel *m*, Zwischenstoffwechsel *m*, Zwischenmetabolismus *m*

intermediary orbit, intermediate orbit — intermediäre Bahn *f*

intermediary value, intermediate value — Zwischenwert *m*

intermediate, intermediate product — Zwischenprodukt *n*

intermediate — s. a. intermediate stage

intermediate accelerator, interaccelerator — Zwischenbeschleuniger *m*

intermediate annealing, process annealing — Zwischenglühung *f*

intermediate anticyclone, intermediate High — Zwischenhoch *n*, Zwischenhochdruckgebiet *n*, Zwischenhochgebiet *n*

intermediate axis — Zwischenachse *f*

intermediate ballistics — Zwischenballistik *f*

intermediate band, interband — Zwischenband *n*

intermediate basis circuit — Zwischenbasisschaltung *f*

intermediate beat, intermediate oscillation — Zwischenschwingung *f*

intermediate calculation — Zwischenrechnung *f*

intermediate-circuit coupling — Zwischenkreiskopplung *f*

intermediate cloud — mittelhohe Wolke *f*

intermediate compound — Zwischenstoff *m*, Zwischenverbindung *f*, intermediäre Verbindung *f*

intermediate continent — Kontinentalbrücke *f*

intermediate contour — Hilfshöhenlinie *f*

intermediate coolant — s. intercoolant

intermediate cooler, intercooler — Zwischenkühler *m*

intermediate corona — Übergangskorona *f*

intermediate coupling — intermediäre Kopplung *f*

intermediate cyclone — Zwischentief *n*, Zwischentief[druck]gebiet *n*, Zwischenzyklone *f*

intermediate differential, partial differential — partielles Differential *n*

intermediate earthquake — intermediäres (mitteltiefes) Erdbeben (Beben) *n*

intermediate energy; medium energy; moderate energy — mittlere Energie *f*, Mittelenergie *f*

intermediate film technique — Zwischenfilmverfahren *n*, Zwischenfilmmethode *f*

intermediate focus — Zwischen[bild]fokus *m*, Zwischenbrennpunkt *m*

intermediate-focus beta-ray spectrometer — s. Siegbahn-Slätis spectrometer

intermediate focusing — Zwischenbildfokussierung *f*

intermediate-focusing spectrometer, intermediate-image spectrometer — Zwischenbild[fokus]spektrometer *n*, Spektrometer *n* mit Zwischenbildfokussierung

intermediate frequency, superheterodyne frequency, I.F., IF, i.f., if — Zwischenfrequenz *f*, ZF

intermediate-frequency band filter, I.F. band filter — Zwischenfrequenzbandfilter *n*, ZF-Bandfilter *n*

intermediate-frequency bandwidth, I.F. bandwidth — Zwischenfrequenzbandbreite *f*, ZF-Bandbreite *f*

intermediate-frequency trap, I.F. trap — Zwischenfrequenzsaugkreis *m*, ZF-Saugkreis *m*

intermediate-frequency trap, I.F. trap — Zwischenfrequenzsperrkreis *m*, ZF-Sperrkreis *m*

intermediate heat-transfer agent — s. intercoolant

intermediate High, intermediate anticyclone — Zwischenhoch *n*, Zwischenhochdruckgebiet *n*, Zwischenhochgebiet *n*

intermediate high-pressure wedge, intermediate wedge of high pressure — Zwischenhochkeil *m*

intermediate illumination — Übergangsbeleuchtung *f*

intermediate image — Zwischenbild *n*; Zwischenabbildung *f*

intermediate-image spectrometer — s. intermediate-focusing spectrometer

intermediate integral <math.> — Zwischenintegral *n*, intermediäres Integral *n*, intermediäre Lösung *f*, Zwischenlösung *f* <Math.>

intermediate interaction	intermediäre Wechselwirkung f	intermeshed, interconnected, interacting, multi-loop	vermascht
intermediate ion	Zwischenion n, Mittelion n		
intermediate lattice, interlattice	Zwischengitter n	intermeshed network	s. fully intermeshed network
intermediate layer, inter[]layer; sandwich; interface layer, interface; substratum	Zwischenschicht f; Zwischenlage f	intermetallic compound, intermetallic phase; intermediate phase, interphase	intermetallische Verbindung (Phase) f; intermediäre Phase, Zwischenphase f
intermediate layer, inter[]layer, internal stratum <geo.>	Zwischenlage f, Zwischenmittel n, Zwischenschicht f, Einlagerung f <Geo.>	intermicellar force of attraction	intermizellare Anziehungskraft f
		intermicellar water	intermizellares Wasser n
intermediate matching network	ebnender Zwischenvierpol m	intermittence, intermittency	Aussetzen n, zeitweilige Unterbrechung f, Intermittenz f
intermediate matrix	Zwischenmatrix f	intermittence effect, intermittency effect <phot.>	Unterbrechungseffekt m, Intermittenzeffekt m <Phot.>
intermediate negative	Zwischennegativ n, Internegativ n		
intermediate neutron <0.5 eV − 200 keV>	mittelschnelles (intermediäres) Neutron n	intermittency factor	Intermittenzfaktor m
intermediate nucleus, compound nucleus	Compoundkern m, Compoundsystem n, Zwischenkern m, Verbundkern m	intermittent	intermittierend, turnusmäßig, [periodisch] aussetzend, zeitweilig unterbrochen, mit Unterbrechungen
intermediate orbit, intermediary orbit	intermediäre Bahn f		
intermediate oscillation, intermediate beat	Zwischenschwingung f	intermittent, jerky	ruckartig
intermediate phase, intermetallic compound, intermetallic phase; interphase	intermetallische Verbindung (Phase) f; intermediäre Phase, Zwischenphase f	intermittent contact, loose contact, defective contact	Wackelkontakt m
		intermittent control	s. discontinuous control
		intermittent current	intermittierender Strom m
		intermittent flow	intermittierende Strömung f
intermediate point	Zwischenpunkt m, Einschaltpunkt m, eingeschalteter Punkt m	intermittent illumination <opt.>	intermittierende Beleuchtung f <Opt.>
intermediate population [II]	Zwischenpopulation f [II]	intermittent jet	s. pulse jet
		intermittent light	Lichtsignal n, das in gewissen zeitlichen Abständen aufleuchtet; intermittierendes Lichtsignal
intermediate pressure	Zwischendruck m		
intermediate product	s. intermediate		
intermediate reaction	Zwischenreaktion f		
intermediate reactor, intermediate spectrum reactor	mittelschneller Reaktor m, intermediärer Reaktor	intermittent light, light-dark cycle <bio.>	intermittierendes Licht n, Licht-Dunkel-Wechsel m <Bio.>
intermediate reading	Zwischenablesung f	intermittent light in which the light and dark periods are equal, isophase light	Gleichtaktfeuer n
intermediate result; subtotal	Zwischenergebnis n		
intermediate rock, neutral rock	intermediäres Gestein n	intermittent motion	ruckartige Bewegung f, Ruckbewegung f
intermediate spectrum reactor, intermediate reactor	mittelschneller Reaktor m, intermediärer Reaktor	intermittent operation, intermittent service	turnusmäßiger Betrieb m, aussetzender Betrieb, Aussetzbetrieb m, intermittierender Betrieb, diskontinuierlicher Betrieb
intermediate stage, interim stage, interstage; buffer stage; intermediate step; intermediate	Zwischenstadium n, Zwischenstufe f; Zwischenschritt m		
intermediate state, compound state <nucl.>	Zwischenzustand m, Compoundzustand m, Verbundzustand m, Übergangszustand m <Kern.>	intermittent river, intermittent stream	intermittierender Fluß m
		intermittent service	s. intermittent operation
intermediate state <of super conductor>	Zwischenzustand m, intermediärer Zustand m <Supraleitung>	intermittent source	intermittierende Quelle f
		intermittent stimulus	intermittierender Reiz m
intermediate step; intermediate (interim) stage, interstage; buffer stage	Zwischenstadium n, Zwischenstufe f; Zwischenschritt m	intermixture	s. mixture
		intermodulation	Intermodulation f, Differenztonbildung f, Zwischenmodulation f
intermediate structure	Zwischenstruktur f		
intermediate support	Zwischenstütze f		
intermediate temperature	Zwischentemperatur f		
intermediate temperature, medium (moderate) temperature	mittlere Temperatur f	intermodulation factor	Differenztonfaktor m, Intermodulationsfaktor m, Intermodulationsgrad m, Modulationsfaktor m
intermediate tone	Zwischenton m		
intermediate twilight	Zwischendämmerung f	intermolecular condensation, extramolecular condensation, self-condensation, autocondensation	intermolekulare (extramolekulare) Kondensation f, Selbstkondensation f, Autokondensation f
intermediate value, intermediary value	Zwischenwert m		
intermediate-value theorem	Zwischenwertsatz m		
intermediate vector boson	intermediäres Vektorboson n	intermolecular force	zwischenmolekulare Kraft f, intermolekulare Kraft
intermediate water	Zwischenwasser n	intermolecular migration	s. intermolecular rearrangement
intermediate wave	Zwischenwelle f	intermolecular potential	s. potential of the intermolecular forces
intermediate wedge of high pressure, intermediate high-pressure wedge	Zwischenhochkeil m	intermolecular rearrangement, intermolecular transposition (migration)	intermolekulare Umlagerung f, zwischenmolekulare Umlagerung

intermolecular reduction	intermolekulare Reduktion f	**internal degree of freedom**	innerer Freiheitsgrad m
intermolecular tension	zwischenmolekulare Spannung f	**internal development nucleus,** intragranular development nucleus	Innenkeim m
intermolecular transition probability	intermolekulare Übergangswahrscheinlichkeit f	**internal disturbance,** internal trouble	Eigenstörung f
intermolecular transposition	s. intermolecular rearrangement	**internal dose,** internal radiation dose; internal exposure	innere Dosis (Strahlungsdosis, Bestrahlungsdosis) f
internal absorptance <US>, internal absorption factor	Reinabsorptionsgrad m	**internal drop [in potential]**	innerer Spannungsabfall m
internal absorption	s. self-absorption	**internal electron-positron pair**	Konversionselektronenpaar n, Elektron-Positron-Paar n der inneren Umwandlung
internal absorption factor, internal absorptance <US>	Reinabsorptionsgrad m		
internal absorption factor of unit length	s. absorptivity	**internal energy**	s. inner energy
internal adsorption	innere Adsorption f	**internal exposure,** internal irradiation	inner[lich]e Bestrahlung f, Bestrahlung von innen
internal aerodynamics	innere Aerodynamik f		
		internal exposure	s. a. internal dose
		internal field	inneres Feld n <Dipolflüssigkeit>; Innenfeld n <Magnet>
internal aperture	innere Apertur f, Grenzapertur f		
internal ballistics	s. interior ballistics	**internal field,** internal magnetic field [of the Earth], internal geomagnetic field, core magnetic field, magnetic field of the earth core <geo.>	magnetisches Innenfeld n der Erde, Erdinnenfeld n, Innenfeld n <Geo.>
internal barrier layer, barrier [layer], [internal] blocking layer, depletion layer <semi.>	Sperrschicht f, Feldzone f, innere Randschicht f <Halb.>		
internal beam, circulating beam	innerer (interner, umlaufender) Strahl m, innerer (interner, umlaufender) Teilchenstrahl m, inneres (internes, umlaufendes) Bündel n, inneres (internes, umlaufendes) Teilchenbündel n		
		internal field emission	s. Zener effect
		internal force	innere Kraft f
		internal friction	s. viscosity
		internal friction factor	s. coefficient of viscosity
		internal geomagnetic field	s. internal field <geo.>
internal block effect	innerer Blockeffekt m		
internal blocking layer	s. internal barrier layer <semi.>	**internal heat of evaporation,** internal latent heat	innere Verdampfungswärme f
internal breeding ratio	inneres Brutverhältnis n		
internal bremsstrahlung	s. inner bremsstrahlung	**internal impedance** <of the conductor>	innerer Wellenwiderstand m [des Leiters]
internal caliper gauge, internal calipers	s. inside calipers	**internal impedance**	s. a. internal resistance <of thermionic valve, triode>
internal chord	innere Profilsehne f	**internal indicator**	interner Indikator m
internal circuit	innerer Stromkreis m; innere Schaltung f		
internal coherence	innerer Zusammenhang m	**internal inductance**	innere Induktivität f, innerer Selbstinduktionskoeffizient m
internal-combustion engine, combustion engine, explosion engine; explosion motor	Verbrennungs[kraft]maschine f; Verbrennungsmotor m, Explosionsmotor m		
		internal induction	s. magnetic polarization
		internal injection <acc.>	Inneneinschuß m, innere Injektion f <Beschl.>
internal combustion engine	s. a. Otto engine		
internal compensation	innere Kompensation f	**internal irradiation,** internal exposure	inner[lich]e Bestrahlung f, Bestrahlung von innen
internal Compton effect	innerer Compton-Effekt m		
internal condensation, intramolecular condensation	innere Kondensation f, intramolekulare Kondensation	**internal latent heat**	s. internal heat of evaporation
		internally focused lens	Wanderlinse f
internal conductance	s. transconductance		
internal conical refraction	innere konische Refraktion f	**internal magnetic field [of the Earth]**	s. internal field <geo.>
internal conversion	innere Konversion (Umwandlung) f	**internal memory,** internal storage, temporary storage, working storage	innerer Speicher m, Arbeitsspeicher m
internal conversion coefficient, conversion coefficient, conversion ratio; conversion fraction <nucl.>	Koeffizient m der inneren Konversion (Umwandlung), Konversionskoeffizient m, Konversionsfaktor m, Umwandlungskoeffizient m, Umwandlungsfaktor m <Kern.>		
		internal micrometer	Mikrometerstichmaß n
		internal mirror coating	s. mirror lining
		internal mode; intrinsic property <math.>	innere Eigenschaft f
		internal moraine, englacial moraine	Innenmoräne f
internal conversion electron, conversion electron, electron of internal conversion	Konversionselektron n, Elektron n der inneren Konversion (Umwandlung)		
		internal mould lubricant	s. lubricant
		internal noise, self-noise	Eigenrauschen n
internal conversion electron spectrum	s. internal conversion spectrum	**internal noise voltage**	Eigenrauschspannung f
internal conversion peak	Konversionslinie f, Linie f der inneren Umwandlung	**internal optical density,** decimal optical density, decimal extinction	innere Schwärzung f, dekadische Extinktion f
internal conversion probability, conversion probability	Konversionswahrscheinlichkeit f, Wahrscheinlichkeit f für innere Konversion		
		internal optical density defined by natural logarithm	s. Napierian optical density
internal conversion spectrum, [internal] conversion electron spectrum, conversion spectrum	Konversions[elektronen]spektrum n, Umwandlungsspektrum n, Spektrum n der Elektronen der inneren Konversion		
		internal oxidation	innere (intramolekulare) Oxydation f
internal co-ordinate	innere Koordinate f	**internal pair coefficient**	Koeffizient m der inneren Paarbildung

internal pair creation, internal pair production	innere Paarbildung f	international candle power, candle power, I.C.P., ICP <= 1.019 cd>	internationale Kerze f, IK <= 1,019 cd>
internal parameter	s. internal variable	international colour index	internationaler Farbenindex m
internal perspective centre	s. rear principal point	International Commission on Illumination, ICI, C.I.E.	Internationale Beleuchtungskommission f, IBK
internal phase, dispersed phase, disperse phase	disperse Phase f, disperser Bestandteil m, Dispersum n		
internal photoeffect, internal photoelectric effect, photoconductive effect, photoelectric conduction, photoconduction, intrinsic photoeffect, photoresistance, photoresistive effect	innerer Photoeffekt (lichtelektrischer Effekt) m, innere lichtelektrische Wirkung f, Halbleiterphotoeffekt m, Photoleitungseffekt m	international date line international electrical system of units, international system of units of electricity International Electrotechnical Commission, IEC	s. date line internationales elektrisches Einheitensystem n, m-s-V_{int}-A_{int}-System n <bis 1947 gültig> Internationale Elektrotechnische Kommission f, IEC, IEK
internal pole machine	s. revolving field machine	international ellipsoid, Hayford's ellipsoid, Hayford spheroid	internationales Erdellipsoid (Referenzellipsoid) n, Hayfordsches Rotationsellipsoid n, Hayford-Ellipsoid n
internal porosity	innere Porosität f, Innenporosität f, Innenlunker m		
internal potential energy	innere potentielle Energie f, [elastische] Formänderungsenergie f		
internal pressure, inside pressure, pressure inside	innerer Druck m, Innendruck m	International Geophysical Year, IGY	Internationales Geophysikalisches Jahr n, IG J
internal pressure, cohesion pressure	Kohäsionsdruck m, Binnendruck m	international gravity formula	internationale Schwereformel f
internal quantity	s. internal variable		
internal quantum number	s. inner quantum number		
internal quenching, self-quenching, self-quenching action	Selbstlöschung f	international hydrogen scale, hydrogen scale [of temperature]	internationale Wasserstoffskala f, Wasserstoffskala f [der Temperatur], Wasserstofftemperaturskala f
internal radiation dose	s. internal dose		
internal reference	s. internal standard		
internal reflection	innere Reflexion f	international inch, inch, imperial inch, Canadian inch, in., " <= 25,4 mm>	Zoll n, " <= 25,4 mm>
internal resistance, [anode] differential resistance, incremental resistance, internal (differential) impedance <of thermionic valve, triode>	innerer Widerstand m, differentieller Widerstand, Innenwiderstand m, differentieller Innenwiderstand m	international knot, US knot, knot, kn, int.kn.	Knoten m, kn
		international magnetic character figure [for the day]	internationale magnetische Charakterzahl f [des Tages], internationale Charakterzahl [des Tages], internationale erdmagnetische Charakterzahl [des Tages]
internal resistance <of source>, source resistance	Innenwiderstand m, innerer Widerstand m, Eigenwiderstand m		
internal rotation	innere Rotation		
internal rotation partition function, partition function of internal rotation	Zustandssumme f der inneren Rotation	international mile, sea mile, US-nautical mile, nautical mile, intern. mile <= 1 852 m>	Seemeile f, internationale Seemeile, sm <= 1852 m>
internal rupture	innere Zerreißung f		
internal scattering	s. resonance scattering	international ohm, Board of Trade ohm, [unit] legal ohm <= 1,000 50 Ω>	internationales Ohm n <= 1,000 50 Ω>
internal standard, internal reference	innerer Standard m		
internal standard method	leitprobenfreies Verfahren n [der Spektralanalyse]	international photon, luxon, photon, troland	Troland n, internationales Photon n, Photon, Luxon n
internal storage	s. internal memory		
internal stratum	s. intermediate layer <geo.>	international pitch	s. philharmonic pitch <440 c/s>
internal stress	innerer Spannungszustand m, innere Verspannung f		
internal stress, internal (inherent) tension, residual [machining] stress, locked-up stress <mech.>	innere (verbleibende) Spannung f, Eigenspannung f, Bearbeitungsspannung f, Restspannung f, Nachspannung f <Mech.>	international prototype meter, prototype meter, metre des archives, primary (standard) meter	Urmeter n
		international quiet day	international ruhiger Tag m
internal structure	innere Struktur f	international standard atmosphere, standard international atmosphere, ISA	internationale Standardatmosphäre (Normalatmosphäre) f, ISA, INA
internal surface	innere Oberfläche (Fläche) f, Innen[ober]fläche f		
internal tension	s. internal stress <mech.>	international steamtable calorie, steamtable calorie, gram[me]calorie, cal$_{IT}$ <= 4,186 84 J>	internationale Tafelkalorie f, Tafelkalorie f, Grammkalorie f, cal$_{IT}$ <= 4,186 84 J>
internal tides	innere Gezeiten pl		
internal transmission factor, internal transmittance <US>	Durchsichtigkeitsgrad m, internaler Transmissionsgrad m		
internal transmission factor of unit length	s. transmissivity	international system of units, SI system [of units]	internationales [praktisches] Einheitensystem n, internationales Maßsystem n, Système n International, SI-System n, SI, MKSAKC-System n
internal transmittance <US>, internal transmission factor	Durchsichtigkeitsgrad m, Reintransmissionsgrad m		
internal trouble, internal disturbance	Eigenstörung f		
internal variable, intrinsic variable, internal quantity (parameter)	innere Variable f, innere Größe f, innerer Parameter m	international system of units of electricity, international electrical system of units	internationales elektrisches Einheitensystem n, m-s-V_{int}-A_{int}-System n <bis 1947 gültig>
internal virial	inneres Virial n		
internal volume	Eigenvolumen n	International Union of Pure and Applied Physics, I.U.P.A.P.	Internationale Union f für Reine und Angewandte Physik, IUPAP
internal water, underground water	Tiefenstandwasser n	intern. mile	s. international mile <= 1 852 m>
internal wave <geo.>	s. bodily seismic wave		
internal waviness of glass	s. waviness in glass	internodal interval	Internodialstrecke f, Internodium n
International Bureau of Weights and Measures, IBWM	Internationales Büro n für Maß und Gewicht, IBMG	internuclear	internuklear, zwischennuklear

internuclear axis	Verbindungslinie *f* der Kerne, Kernverbindungslinie *f*	interrupter	*s.* circuit breaker <el.>
internuclear distance, nuclear separation (spacing, distance)	Kernabstand *m*, Atomkernabstand *m*	interrupter	*s.* switch <el.>
		interrupting time, total break time <US>	[elektrische] Ausschaltdauer *f*
		interrupting voltage	Schaltspannung *f*
interocular distance, interocular spacing, eye separation; inter-pupil[l]ary distance, distance between pupils	Augenabstand *m*; Pupillendistanz *f*, PD	interruption <phot.>	Unterbrechung *f* <Phot.>
		interruption arc	Abreiß[licht]bogen *m*, Unterbrechungslichtbogen *m*, Abschaltlichtbogen *m*, Schaltlichtbogen *m*, Schaltbogen *m*
interparticular force	zwischen den Teilchen wirkende Kraft *f*, Kraft zwischen den Teilchen	interruption of chain	*s.* chain interruption <chem.>
interpenetrating samples	ineinandergreifende Stichproben *fpl*, überlagerte Stichproben	interruption of current	Stromunterbrechung *f*
interpenetration	Durchwachsung *f*	interruption of the arc	Abreißen *n* (Erlöschung *f*) des Lichtbogens
interpenetration, penetration, intersection <math.>	Durchdringung *f* <Math.>	interruption voltage	Abreißspannung *f*, Erlöschungsspannung *f*
		intersecting point	*s.* point of intersection
interpenetration twin	*s.* penetration twin	intersection; interception; traversing, piercing	Schneiden *n*, Schnitt *m*; Durchstoßen *n*
interphase	*s.* interkinesis	intersection <of dislocations>	Durchschneiden *n* <Versetzungen>
interphase	*s.* intermediate phase		
interphase	*s.* phase boundary		
interphase coupling, coupling between phases	Zwischenphasenkopplung *f*	intersection <geo.>	Einschneiden *n*, Streckeneinschnitt *m* <Geo.>
		intersection <geo.>	Vorwärtseinschneiden *n*, Vorwärts[ein]schnitt *m* <Geo.>
interphase line, phase-boundary line	Phasengrenzlinie *f*		
interphase nucleus	Interphasenkern *m*	intersection, [inter-]penetration <math.>	Durchdringung *f* <Math.>
interplanar crystal spacing, interplanar spacing, interlattice plane distance, interface	Netzebenenabstand *m*, Abstand *m* der Kristallebenen	intersection	*s. a.* point of intersection
		intersectional jog	*s.* intersection jog
		intersection angle, angle of intersection	Schnittwinkel *m*
interplanetary dust	interplanetarer Staub *m*	intersection condition	Schnittlinienbedingung *f*
interplanetary gas	interplanetares Gas *n*, gasförmiger Anteil *m* der interplanetaren Materie	intersection jog, intersectional jog	Durchschneidungssprung *m*
		intersection line	*s.* curve of intersection
interplanetary matter	interplanetare Materie *f*	intersection photogrammetry, photogrammetry by intersection, photogrammetric intersection, two-image photogrammetry	photogrammetrisches Vorwärtseinschneiden *n*, Zweibildmessung *f*; Einschneidephotogrammetrie *f*, Meßtischphotogrammetrie *f*, Bildmessung *f*
interpolated extrasystole	interpolatorische Extrasystole *f*		
interpolating field	interpolierendes Feld *n*		
interpolating function	Interpolationsfunktion *f*		
		intersection point	*s.* point of intersection
		intersection ray	Schnittstrahl *m*
interpolation	Interpolation *f*, Interpolieren *n*, Einschalten *n* [von Funktionswerten]	intersection theorem, single intersection theorem	Schnittpunktsatz *m* [von Serrin]
interpolation error	Interpolationsfehler *m*	inter-site error, site error; distant site error	Standortfehler *m*; Standortumgebungsfehler *m*
interpolation formula, corrector [formula] <in numerical solution of differential equations>	Interpolationsformel *f*	intersolid diffusion	Diffusion *f* zwischen Festkörpern, Festkörperdiffusion *f*
		interspace	*s.* gap
		interstadial period	Interstadialzeit *f*, Interstadial *n*
interpolation node	*s.* given value of argument in interpolation	interstage	*s.* intermediate stage
interpolation polynomial	Interpolationspolynom *n*, Schaltpolynom *n*	interstage attenuator	Zwischenabschwächer *m*
interpolation series	Interpolationsreihe *f*	interstage coupling	Kopplung *f* zwischen Stufen, Stufenkopplung *f*
interpole	*s.* commutating pole <el.>		
interposition	*s.* interconnection <el.>	interstellar absorption line, interstellar [spectral] line, stationary absorption line	interstellare Absorptionslinie *f*
interpretation; explanation, elucidation	Interpretation *f*, Deutung *f*, Auslegung *f*; Erklärung *f*		
interpretation of aerial photographs	*s.* restitution from aerial photographs	interstellar continuous absorption	kontinuierliche interstellare Absorption *f*
interpretoscope	Interpretoskop *n*	interstellar dust, interstellar grains, cosmic dust	interstellarer Staub *m*, kosmischer Staub
interpulse interval	*s.* pulse separation		
interpupil[l]ary distance	*s.* interocular distance	interstellar line	*s.* interstellar absorption line
interreaction	*s.* interaction	interstellar line absorption	interstellare Linienabsorption *f*
interreflection	Interreflexion *f*, gegenseitige Reflexion *f*	interstellar material (matter, medium)	interstellare Materie *f*
interreflection ratio	Interreflexionswirkungsgrad *m*		
		interstellar reddening, space reddening	interstellare Verfärbung *f*
interrupted continuous wave, ICW, I.C.W., i.c.w.	ungedämpfte unterbrochene Welle *f*; getastete ungedämpfte Welle	interstellar spectral line	*s.* interstellar absorption line
		interstellar wind	interstellarer Wind *m*
interrupted direct current	zerhackter Gleichstrom *m*, gehackter Gleichstrom	interstice, interstitial site, interstitial lattice site, interstitial position	Zwischengitterplatz *m*, Zwischengitterlage *f*, Zwischengitterpunkt *m*
interrupted quenching	*s.* martempering	interstice	*s. a.* gap
interrupted wave, chopped wave	zerhackte Welle *f*	interstitial, interstitial defect	Zwischengitterfehlstelle *f*

interstitial, interstitial atom	Zwischengitteratom n, Atom n auf Zwischengitterplatz, Lückenatom n	intertwining, entanglement, interlacing, interlacement, tangling	Verschlingung f, Verflechtung f
interstitial alloy	Zwischengitterlegierung f	interval, mesh size, step size <in numerical integration>	Schrittweite f, Schrittgröße f, Maschenweite f, Tafelintervall n, Tafelschritt m, Spanne f, Integrationsintervall n <numerische Integration>
interstitial atom	s. interstitial		
interstitial centre, i-centre	i-Zentrum n		
interstitial compound	Zwischengitterverbindung f, interstitielle Verbindung f, Einlagerungsverbindung f	interval, region, range <gen.>	Intervall n, Bereich m, Gebiet n <allg.>
		interval <math.>	Intervall n <Math.>
interstitialcy, interstitial formation	Zwischengitter[atom]bildung f, Zwischengitterplatzbildung f	interval, separation [of two events], separation between events <rel.>	Intervall n, Weltintervall n, Abstand m zwischen zwei Ereignissen (Weltpunkten) <Rel.>
interstitialcy, interstitial pair	Zwischengitterpaar n	interval	s. a. gap
interstitialcy mechanism, [indirect] interstitial mechanism	Zwischengitter[platz]-mechanismus m, indirekter Zwischengittermechanismus	interval analyzer, pulse interval analyzer, time sorter	Impulsintervallanalysator m, Intervallanalysator m
		interval factor	s. Landé g-factor
		interval function	Intervallfunktion f
interstitialcy migration, interstitial migration	Zwischengitterwanderung f, Zwischengitteratomwanderung f	intervalley effect	„intervalley"-Effekt m
interstitial defect	s. interstitial		
interstitial diffusion	Zwischengitterdiffusion f, Zwischengitteratomdiffusion f	intervalley scattering	„intervalley"-Streuung f
		interval of discontinuity, discontinuity interval	Unstetigkeitsstrecke f
interstitial fluid <bio.>	interstitielle Flüssigkeit f, Zwischenflüssigkeit f <Bio.>	intervalometer, time interval meter [unit]	Zeitintervallmesser m, Zeitintervallmeßgerät n
interstitial formation, interstitialcy	Zwischengitter[atom]bildung f, Zwischengitterplatzbildung f	intervalometer	Zeitfolgeregler m, Bildfolgeregler m, Intervalometer n
interstitial ion	Zwischengitterion n	interval rule, Landé['s] interval rule	Intervallregel f, Landésche (spektroskopische) Intervallregel, Landésche Regel f
interstitial jog	Zwischengittersprung m		
interstitial lattice site, interstitial site, interstitial position, interstice	Zwischengitterplatz m, Zwischengitterlage f, Zwischengitterpunkt m	interval timer	Zeitintervallschreiber m, Intervallschreiber m
		intervalve coupling	Röhrenkopplung f, Kopplung f zwischen Röhren
interstitial mechanism	s. interstitialcy mechanism	intervening strata	s. interstratification
interstitial migration, interstitialcy migration	Zwischengitterwanderung f, Zwischengitteratomwanderung f	inter[-]wiring	s. circuit wiring
		interzone transition	s. band-to-band transition
		intimate contact	inniger Kontakt m
interstitial pair, interstitialcy	Zwischengitterpaar n	intraclass correlation	Paarkorrelation f, Innerklassenkorrelation f, Intraklaßkorrelation f
interstitial position	s. interstitial site		
interstitial pressure	Porendruck m	intraclass variance	s. within-group variance
		intracrustal	intrakrustal, innerkrustal
interstitial site, interstitial lattice site, interstitial position, interstice	Zwischengitterplatz m, Zwischengitterlage f, Zwischengitterpunkt m	intracrystalline; intragranular	intrakristallin
		intraglacial, englacial	inglazial, intraglazial
interstitial solid solution, interstitial solution	Einlagerungsmischkristalle mpl, interstitiäre Mischkristalle mpl, Überschußmischkristalle mpl	intragranular; intracrystalline	intrakristallin
		intragranular development nucleus, internal development nucleus	Innenkeim m
interstitial space	s. gap		
interstitial state	Zwischengitterzustand m		
interstitial structure	Zwischengitterstruktur f	intragranular dislocation	intrakristalline Versetzung f
interstitial type Schottky defect	s. Schottky defect		
interstitial-vacancy pair	s. Frenkel defect	intra-mercurial planet	intramerkurieller Planet m
interstitial water, capillary water	Kapillarwasser n, Porenwasser n	intramolecular condensation	s. internal condensation
		intramolecular degree of freedom	innermolekularer Freiheitsgrad m
interstratification, intervening strata <geo.>	Zwischenschicht[bild]ung f, Zwischenlagerung f; Wechsellagerung f, wechselweise Schichtung f <Geo.>	intramolecular force	innermolekulare Kraft f
		intramolecular isotope effect	intramolekularer Isotopieeffekt m
intertropical convergence, ITC	innertropische Konvergenz f, ITC	intramolecular migration, intramolecular rearrangement, intramolecular transposition, molecular transposition (rearrangement)	innere Umlagerung f, innermolekulare Umlagerung, innermolekulare Umordnung f, intramolekulare Umlagerung, Molekülumlagerung f
intertropical convergence zone, intertropical front, i.t.c.z., itcz	Bereich m der innertropischen Konvergenz, Intertropikfront f, ITCZ		
interturn capacitance	Windungskapazität f	intramolecular transformation	innermolekulare Umwandlung f
interturn short circuit	Windungsschluß m	intramolecular transposition	s. intramolecular rearrangement

intransitive	intransitiv	intrinsic multipole moment	inneres Multipolmoment n
intranuclear <bio.>	intranukleār, intranuklear <Bio.>	intrinsic nuclear quadrupole moment, intrinsic quadrupole moment of nucleus	inneres Kernquadrupolmoment n, inneres Quadrupolmoment n des Kerns
intranuclear <nucl., chem.>	innernuklear, intranuklear, innerhalb des Kerns <Kern., Chem.>	intrinsic parity	innere Parität f
intranuclear attraction, nuclear attraction	innernukleare (intranukleare) Anziehung f, Kernanziehung f	intrinsic photoconduction	Eigenphotoleitung f, innere Photoleitung f, Intrinsicphotoleitung f, Eigenphotoleitfähigkeit f
intranuclear repulsion, nuclear repulsion	innernukleare (intranukleare) Abstoßung f, Kernabstoßung f	intrinsic photoconductivity	Eigenphotoleitfähigkeit f, innere Photoleitfähigkeit f, Intrinsicphotoleitfähigkeit f
intrapermafrost water	Grundwasser n im Dauerfrostboden		
intravalley scattering	„intravalley"-Streuung f	intrinsic photoconductor	Eigenphotoleiter m
intrinsic <semi.>	gittereigen, eigenleitend, materialeigen, stoffeigen, Eigen-, Eigenleitungs- <Halb.>	intrinsic photoeffect	s. internal photoeffect
		intrinsic potential	s. inner potential
intrinsic accuracy	Eigengenaugkeit f	intrinsic property, structure-insensitive property	strukturunempfindliche Eigenschaft f
intrinsic activation, self-activation	Eigenaktivierung f, Selbstaktivierung f	intrinsic property; internal mode <math.>	innere Eigenschaft f
intrinsically variable star, physical variable [star], proper (intrinsic) variable	physischer Veränderlicher m, eigentlicher Veränderlicher	intrinsic Q, unloaded Q, unloaded Q factor	Güte f (Gütefaktor m) des unbelasteten Resonanzkreises
intrinsic angular momentum	s. spin angular momentum	intrinsic quadrupole moment of nucleus	s. intrinsic nuclear quadrupole moment
intrinsic angular momentum of atomic nucleus	s. nuclear spin	intrinsic range	eingeprägte Reichweite f
intrinsic-barrier transistor, intrinsic-region transistor, p-n-i-p transistor	pnip-Transistor m	intrinsic region, region of intrinsic conduction, i region; intrinsic layer, layer of intrinsic conduction (material), i layer	Eigenleitungszone f, i-Zone f; Eigenleitungsschicht f, i-Schicht f
		intrinsic-region transistor	s. intrinsic-barrier transistor
		intrinsic resistance, umklapp resistance	Umklappwiderstand m, innerer Widerstand m
		intrinsic safety	s. inherent safety
		intrinsic semiconduction	s. intrinsic conduction
intrinsic carrier	Eigenleitungsträger m	intrinsic semiconductivity	s. intrinsic conductivity <semi., el.chem.>
intrinsic conduction, intrinsic semiconduction (conductivity)	Eigenleitung f, Eigenhalbleitung f, Eigenleitfähigkeit f	intrinsic semiconductor, i-type semiconductor	Eigenhalbleiter m, Eigenleiter m, i-Typ-Halbleiter m, i-Halbleiter m, i-Leiter m
intrinsic conductivity <semi., el.chem.>	Eigenleitfähigkeit f, innere Leitfähigkeit f, Intrinsicleitfähigkeit f <Halb., El.Chem.>		
intrinsic conductivity	s. a. intrinsic conduction		
intrinsic contrast	wahrer Helligkeitskontrast m, Eigenkontrast m	intrinsic temperature, eigentemperature, natural temperature	Eigentemperatur f
intrinsic co-ordinates	eingeprägte Koordinaten fpl	intrinsic temperature <semi.>	Eigenleitungstemperatur f <Halb.>
intrincis co-ordinates	s. a. natural co-ordinates	intrinsic theory of strain	Eigentheorie f der Verformung
intrinsic defect	Eigenstörstelle f; Eigenfehlordnung f	intrinsic variable, physical variable [star], proper variable, intrinsically variable star	physischer Veränderlicher m, eigentlicher Veränderlicher
intrinsic displacement	innere Verrückung f		
intrinsic double refraction	Eigendoppelbrechung f		
intrinsic electric quadrupole moment	inneres elektrisches Quadrupolmoment n	intrinsic variable	s. a. internal variable
		intrinsic viscosity, limiting viscosity	Grenzviskosität f, Grundviskosität f; Eigenviskosität f, K-Wert m, „intrinsic viscosity" f, innere Viskosität f
intrinsic energy, characteristic energy	Eigenenergie f, innere Energie f		
intrinsic equation [of the curve]	s. natural equation [of the curve]	introducing, introduction; inducing, induction; initiation, starting, commencement	Auslösung f, Einleitung f, Induzierung f; Initiierung f; Zündung f
intrinsic excitation, excitation raising electrons from valency into the conduction band	Grundgitteranregung f, Grundgittererregung f, Valenzband-Leitungsband-Anregung f, direkte Anregung f vom Valenzins Leitungsband	introduction; location, placing	Einbringen n; Einführung f
		introduction <of a correction>	Anbringen n <Korrektion>
intrinsic hue	freie Farbe f, unbezogene Farbe	introduction, incorporation, insertion <e.g. of impurities>	Einbau m, Einbauen n, Einlagerung f <z. B. Fremdatome>
intrinsic induction	s. intensity of magnetization		
intrinsic intensity <of lamp>	s. luminance	introduction of additional damping, damping	Bedämpfung f
intrinsic internal energy	eigentliche innere Energie f		
intrinsic layer	s. intrinsic region	intrusion	Intrusion f <auch Geo.>; Werkstoffeinsenkung f
intrinsic luminous intensity <of lamp>	s. luminance	intrusion; invasion; irruption; wedging <meteo.>	Einbruch m; Durchbruch m <Meteo.>
intrinsic magnetic moment	magnetisches Eigenmoment n, inneres magnetisches Moment n	intrusive rock, abyssal rock, plutonic rock, plutonite	Tiefengestein n, Intrusivgestein n, plutonisches Gestein n, Plutonit m
intrinsic magnetization, spontaneous magnetization	spontane Magnetisierung f, Spontanmagnetisierung f		
intrinsic mass, self mass, proper mass <qu.>	Selbstmasse f, Eigenmasse f <Qu.>	intrusive vein, eruptive vein, igneous vein, igneous dyke, dyke	Eruptivgang m, Gesteinsgang m
intrinsic mass	s. a. mechanical mass		

intuitionistic 384

intuitionistic logic	intuitionistische Logik *f*	inverse cotangent, anticotangent, arc cotangent, arc cot, arc ctg, cot⁻¹, ctg⁻¹	Arkuskotangens *m*, arc cot
inundation area	s. overflow area		
"in vacuo" thermometer	s. black-bulb thermometer		
invariable; constant; unvarying; fixed	konstant; unveränderlich, invariabel; fest	inverse current	s. reverse current ⟨el.⟩
		inverse current ratio	Stromübersetzung *f* rückwärts, Rückwärtsübersetzung *f* [des Stroms]
invariable pendulum	invariables Pendel *n*		
invariable plane ⟨astr.⟩	unveränderliche (invariable, invariante) Ebene *f*, UVE ⟨Astr.⟩	inverse diode, blocking diode	Sperrdiode *f*, Sperrschichtdiode *f*
		inverse element	s. inverse ⟨math.⟩
		inverse emitter current, reverse emitter current	Emitterrückstrom *m*
invariance of translation	Translationsinvarianz *f*	inverse feedback	s. reverse feedback
invariant	Invariante *f*	inverse fluorescence	umgekehrte Fluoreszenz *f*
invariant, scalar, scalar quantity, scalar tensor, scalar invariant	Skalar *m*, skalare Größe *f*, skalarer Tensor *m*, skalare Invariante *f*	inverse frequency, inversion frequency	Umkehrfrequenz *f*
		inverse function	Umkehrfunktion *f*, inverse Funktion *f*
invariant decomposition	invariante Zerlegung *f*	inverse grid current, reverse[d] grid current, backlash	Gitterrückstrom *m*, negativer Gitterstrom *m*
invariant embedding method	Matrizenmethode *f* [des Gammastrahlungstransports]		
invariant of refraction, Abbe invariant	Abbesche Invariante *f*, Invariante der Brechung	inverse grid potential (voltage), reverse grid voltage, back-lash potential	Gittergegenspannung *f*
invariant of strain, strain invariant	Deformations[tensor]invariante *f*, Invariante *f* des Verformungstensors (Deformationszustandes, Formänderungszustandes, Verzerrungszustandes), Verzerrungsinvariante *f*, Verformungsinvariante *f*, Formänderungsinvariante *f*	inverse hour, in[-]hour, inhour value	Inhour *f*, reziproke Stunde *f*, inhour
		inverse hyperbolic cosine, antihyperbolic cosine, arch, ch⁻¹, cosh⁻¹	Areakosinus *m*, Areacosinus *m* hyperbolicus, ar cos, arch, Ar Cos
invariant of stress, stress invariant	Spannungstensorinvariante *f*, Invariante *f* des Spannungszustandes	inverse hyperbolic cotangent, antihyperbolic cotangent, arcth, ar cot, cth⁻¹, coth⁻¹	Areakotangens *m*, Areacotangens *m* hyperbolicus, ar cot, arcth, Ar Ctg
invariant plane ⟨cryst.⟩	invariante Ebene *f* ⟨Krist.⟩		
invariant property	Invarianzeigenschaft *f*	inverse hyperbolic function	s. antihyperbolic function
invariant sub-group	s. normal divisor	inverse hyperbolic sine, antihyperbolic sine, sh⁻¹, sinh⁻¹, arsh	Areasinus *m*, Areasinus hyperbolicus, ar sin, arsh, Ar Sin
invariant system	nonvariantes System *n*, invariantes System		
invariant theory, theory of invariants	Invariantentheorie *f*	inverse hyperbolic tangent, antihyperbolic tangent, th⁻¹, tanh⁻¹, arth	Areatangens *m*, Areatangens hyperbolicus, ar tan, arth, Ar Tg
invariant under rotation	s. rotation-invariant		
invasion	s. intrusion ⟨meteo.⟩		
invasion coefficient	spezifischer Absorptionsfaktor *m*	inverse ignition	s. backfire ⟨of rectifier⟩
invasion of cold air	Kaltlufteinbruch *m*, Kälteeinbruch *m*; Kaltluftvorstoß *m*	inverse image, preimage, antecedent ⟨math.⟩	Urbild *n*, Original *n* ⟨Math.⟩
		inverse induced Raman effect, inverse stimulated Raman effect	inverser stimulierter (induzierter) Raman-Effekt *m*
invasion of warm air	Warmlufteinbruch *m*, Wärmeeinbruch *m*; Wärmevorstoß *m*	inverse isotope effect	inverser Isotopieeffekt *m*
invasion of water; water burst; water breaking-in	Wasserdurchbruch *m*, Wassereinbruch *m*	inverse K-capture, inverse K-electron capture	inverser K-Einfang *m*
inventory	Einsatz *m*, Gesamtmenge *f*, Gesamtzahl *f*	inverse Landau effect	umgekehrter Landau-Effekt *m*
inverse; inversion; change; conversion; converse ⟨gen.⟩	Umkehrung *f*; Umkehr *f*; Wechsel *m*; Inversion *f* ⟨allg.⟩	inverse lattice vector, reciprocal vector	reziproker Vektor *m*, inverser Gittervektor *m*
		inversely proportional	umgekehrt proportional
inverse, inverse element ⟨math.⟩	Inverse *n*, inverses Element *n* ⟨Math.⟩	inverse magnetism	umgekehrter Magnetismus *m*
		inverse magnetization	umgekehrte Magnetisierung *f*, Inversmagnetisierung *f*
inverse ⟨of the matrix⟩, inverse (reciprocal, adjugate) matrix	inverse Matrix *f*, Kehrmatrix *f*, Inverse *f* [der Matrix], reziproke Matrix *f*, Reziproke *f* [der Matrix]	inverse magnetostriction, converse magnetostriction	umgekehrte Magnetostriktion *f*
		inverse matrix	s. inverse ⟨of the matrix⟩
inverse astigmatism	s. astigmatism against the rule	inverse multiplet	verkehrtes Multiplett *n*, Multiplett mit verkehrter Termordnung
inverse ballistic problem	umgekehrtes ballistisches Problem *n*	inverse nuclear reaction, inverse reaction	inverse Kernreaktion (Reaktion) *f*, umgekehrte Reaktion, Umkehrreaktion *f*
inverse basis, reciprocal basis	reziproke Basis *f*, Basisvektoren *mpl* des reziproken Gitters		
inverse beta transformation	inverse Beta-Umwandlung *f*, inverser Beta-Zerfall *m*, umgekehrter Beta-Zerfall	inverse of dispersive power	s. constringence
		inverse of the operation, inverse operation	Umkehroperation *f*, Umkehrung *f* der Operation, inverse Operation *f*
inverse bremsstrahlung, free-free absorption	inverse Bremsstrahlung *f*, Frei-Frei-Absorption *f*		
inverse circular function	s. antitrigonometric[al] function	inverse open-circuit transfer voltage ratio	Leerlauf-Spannungsübertragungsfaktor *m* vorwärts
inverse collision	inverser Stoß *m*	inverse operation	s. inverse of operation
inverse Compton effect	inverser Compton-Effekt *m*	inverse order of terms	Termumkehr *f*, umgekehrte (verkehrte) Termordnung *f*, Umkehrung *f* der Termordnung
inverse correlation, negative correlation	negative Korrelation *f*		
inverse cosine, anticosine, arc cosine, arc cos, cos⁻¹	Arkuskosinus *m*, arc cos	inverse Overhauser effect	umgekehrter Overhauser-Effekt *m*

inverse photoelectric effect	inverser Photoeffekt *m*	**inversion** <chem.; semi.>	Inversion *f* <Chem.; Halb.>
inverse piezoelectricity (piezoelectric effect)	s. electrostriction	**inversion,** inversion with respect to a point <cryst.>	Inversion *f*, Abbildung *f* an einem Punkt <Krist.>
inverse pole figure	reziproke Polfigur *f*, inverse Polfigur	**inversion; inverse; change; conversion;** converse <gen.>	Umkehrung *f*; Umkehr *f*; Wechsel *m*; Inversion *f* <allg.>
inverse predissociation	inverse Prädissoziation *f*	**inversion,** inversion of relief <geo.>	Inversion *f*, Reliefumkehr *f* <Geo.>
inverse probability, a posteriori probability, posterior probability, probability a posteriori	inverse Wahrscheinlichkeit *f*, a posteriori-Wahrscheinlichkeit *f*, aposteriorische Wahrscheinlichkeit, Rückschlußwahrscheinlichkeit *f*, Wahrscheinlichkeit a posteriori, Endwahrscheinlichkeit *f*	**inversion**	s. a. mathematical inversion <math.>
		inversion	s. a. inverting <math.>
		inversion	s. a. temperature inversion <meteo.>
inverse probability theorem	s. Bayes[']' theorem	**inversion** <el.>	s. a. direct-current to alternating-current conversion
inverse problem	Umkehrproblem *n*		
inverse Raman effect	inverser Raman-Effekt *m*	**inversion axis**	Inversionsachse *f*
inverse ratio	s. reciprocal ratio	**inversion clouds**	Inversionsbewölkung *f*
inverse reaction	s. inverse nuclear reaction	**inversion curve**	Inversionskurve *f* [des Joule-Thomson-Effekts]
inverse segregation, inverted segregation	umgekehrte Blockseigerung *f*	**inversion density**	Inversionsdichte *f*
inverse short-circuit transfer current ratio	Kurzschluß-Stromübertragungsfaktor *m* vorwärts	**inversion doublet**	Umkehrdublett *n*, Inversionsdublett *n*
		inversion doubling	Inversionsaufspaltung *f*, Umkehrverdopplung *f*, Inversionsverdopplung *f*
inverse sine, antisine, arc sine, arc sin, sin⁻¹	Arkussinus *m*, arc sin		
inverse spinel, magnetite	Inversspinell *m*, Magnetit *m*	**inversion factor**	Inversionsfaktor *m*
inverse spinel structure	inverse Spinellstruktur *f*	**inversion formula,** conversion formula	Umkehrformel *f*
inverse-square law	[quadratisches] Abstandsgesetz *n*, [quadratisches] Entfernungsgesetz *n*, Entfernungsquadratgesetz *n*, umgekehrt-quadratisches Gesetz *n*	**inversion formula,** inversion integral <in Laplace transformation>	Umkehrformel *f*, Umkehrintegral *n* <Laplace-Transformation>
		inversion formulae of Hankel	Hankelsche Umkehrformeln *fpl*
inverse-square law of photometry	photometrisches Grundgesetz (Entfernungsgesetz) *n*, optisches Entfernungsgesetz, quadratisches Entfernungsgesetz der Photometrie	**inversion frequency,** inverse frequency	Umkehrfrequenz *f*
		inversion in molecular vibration	Inversionsschwingung *f*
		inversion integral, inversion formula <in Laplace transformation>	Umkehrformel *f*, Umkehrintegral *n* <Laplace-Transformation>
inverse stimulated Raman effect, inverse induced Raman effect	inverser stimulierter (induzierter) Raman-Effekt *m*	**inversion layer** <meteo.; semi.>	Inversionsschicht *f* <Meteo.; Halb.>; Umkehrschicht *f*, Temperaturumkehrschicht *f* <Meteo.>
inverse stratification	s. inverse thermal stratification		
inverse tangent, antitangent, arc tangent, arc tg, arc tan, tg⁻¹, tan⁻¹	Arkustangens *m*, arc tan, arc tg		
inverse theorem, converse of the theorem	Umkehrung *f* [des Satzes], Umkehrsatz *m*	**inversion matrix**	Inversionsmatrix *f*
		inversion multiplet	Umkehrmultiplett *n*, Inversionsmultiplett *n*
inverse thermal stratification, inverse stratification	inverse (verkehrte) Temperaturschichtung *f*, inverse (verkehrte) Schichtung *f*	**inversion of coordinates**	Inversion *f* des Koordinatensystems
inverse Thomson effect, Benedicks effect	[1.] Benedicks-Effekt *m*	**inversion of phase**	s. phase reversal <el.>
		inversion of phases, phase reversal, phase inversion <chem.>	Inversion *f* der Phasen, Phasenumkehr *f* <Chem.>
inverse transfer current ratio	Stromübertragungsfaktor *m* vorwärts	**inversion of relief,** inversion <geo.>	Inversion *f*, Reliefumkehr *f* <Geo.>
inverse transfer voltage ratio	Spannungsübertragungsfaktor *m* vorwärts	**inversion of space**	s. space reflection
inverse transform	s. original	**inversion of the point**	s. mathematical inversion <math.>
inverse transform	s. a. inverse transformation		
inverse transformation, inverse transform	inverse Transformation *f*; inverse Abbildung *f*, Umkehrabbildung *f*; Rücktransformation *f*	**inversion point**	s. stagnation point
		inversion prism	s. image erecting prism
inverse transition	reziproker Übergang *m*	**inversion region,** transition region	Inversionszone *f*, Inversionsbereich *m*, Inversionsgebiet *n*
inverse trigonometric[al] function	s. antitrigonometrical function		
inverse voltage, counter[-]voltage, bucking (back-off) voltage, counter[-] potential, back (reverse) potential <el.>	Gegenspannung *f*; Schleusenspannung *f* <El.>	**inversion spectrum,** reversal spectrum	Umkehrspektrum *n*, Inversionsspektrum *n*
		inversion state	s. negative temperature state
		inversion surface, surface of inversion	Inversionsfläche *f*
inverse voltage, return voltage <el.>	Rückspannung *f*, Rückflußspannung *f*; Fehlphasenspannung *f* <El.>	**inversion symmetry**	Inversionssymmetrie *f*
		inversion system, [image] erecting system, optical inversion system	Umkehrsystem *n*, Bildaufrichtungssystem *n*, Aufrichtungssystem *n*
inverse voltage, reverse voltage <semi.>	Sperrspannung *f*, Grenzspannung *f* <Halb.>		
inverse voltage ratio	Spannungsübersetzung *f* rückwärts, Rückwärtsübersetzung *f* [der Spannung]	**inversion telemeter,** invert-type rangefinder, invert[ed-image] rangefinder	Kehrbild-Entfernungsmesser *m*, Invert-Entfernungsmesser *m*
		inversion telescope	s. image erecting telescope
inverse Zeeman effect	umgekehrter (inverser) Zeeman-Effekt *m*	**inversion temperature,** Joule-Thomson inversion temperature	Inversionstemperatur *f*, thermischer Umkehrpunkt *m*
inversion <for permutation>	Inversion *f* <Permutation>	**inversion with respect to a point**	s. inversion <cryst.>

inversion 386

inversion with respect to the circle (sphere)	s. mathematical inversion <math.>	inward bend; inflection	Einbeulung f; Einbiegung f
inversor, reversing (reciprocating) device <math.; opt.>	Inversor m	inward normal	innere Normale f
inverted, [reversed] upside-down <of image>	kopfstehend, umgekehrt, verkehrt <Bild>	iodide process	s. hot wire process
		iodine voltameter	Jodcoulometer n, Jod-Titrationscoulometer n
inverted diode	Inversionsdiode f	iodine well	Jodmulde f
inverted extrusion	s. indirect extrusion	iodopsin	Jodopsin n, Sehviolett n
inverted fold, overturned fold, overfold; overfolding, reversed fold	überkippte Falte f; vergente Falte; Überfaltung f	ion accelerator	Ionenbeschleuniger m, Ionenbeschleunigungsanlage f
inverted-image rangefinder	s. invert-type rangefinder	ion acoustic oscillation	s. ion sound
		ion-acoustic wave	Ionenschallwelle f
inverted microscope, Le Chatelier microscope	Le-Chatelier-Mikroskop n, gestürztes (umgekehrtes) Mikroskop n	ion activity	Ionenaktivität f
		ional concentration	ionale Konzentration f
inverted multiplet	umgekehrtes Multiplett n	ion association, ionic association	Ionenassoziation f
inverted population	inverse (invertierte) Besetzung f; umgekehrter Besetzungszustand m	ion association	Ionenassoziat n
		ion avalanche	Ionenlawine f
inverted position [of frequencies]; lower side band position	Kehrlage f [der Frequenzen], Frequenzkehrlage f	ion-beam current	Ionenstrahlstrom m, Ionenstrahlstromstärke f
		ion beam extraction, extraction of ion beam, ion extraction	Ionenausschleusung f, Ionenextraktion f, Herausführung f des Ionenstrahls
inverted-pyramid antenna	s. funnel antenna <el.>		
inverted right to left	s. reversed right to left <of image>	ion-beam maser	Ionenstrahlmaser m
inverted segregation, inverse segregation	umgekehrte Blockseigerung f	ion beam scanning	[massenspektrometrische] Ionenstrahlanalyse f, Ionenstrahlscanning n
inverted top to bottom	s. reversed top to bottom		
inverter, invertor, electrical inverter, direct-current−alternating-current inverter, d.c.-a.c. inverter, direct-current to alternating-current power converter, d.c.-a.c. power converter <el.>	Wechselrichter m, Gleichstrom-Wechselstrom-Konverter m, Umkehrstromrichter m <El.>	ion-beam tube	Ionenstrahlröhre f
		ion binding (bond)	s. electrovalent bond
		ion burn[ing], ion spot	Ionen[brenn]fleck m
		ion capillary-arc source, ion capillary-type source, capillary-arc ion source	Kapillarbogen-Ionenquelle f
		ion chain	Ionenkette f
		ion cloud, ionic cloud, cloud of ions, ionic atmosphere, Debye-Hückel charge cloud <el. chem.>	Ionenwolke f, Ionenatmosphäre f, statistische Ionenverteilung f <El. Chem.>
inverter, converter, [power] frequency converter <el.>	Umrichter m; Umkehrrohr n <El.>		
inverter, invertor <el.>	Inverter m, Nichtkreis m		
inverter	s. a. converter <el.>		
inverter stage, phase inverter stage, reversal stage	Phasenumkehrstufe f, Umkehrstufe f	ion cloud effect	Ionenwolkeneffekt m
		ion cloud equilibrium	Ionenwolkengleichgewicht n
inverter tube, phase inverter, phase inverter tube	Umkehrröhre f, Phasenumkehrröhre f	ion cloud relaxation	Ionenwolkenrelaxation f
		ion cluster	Ionencluster m, Ionennest n, Ionenschwarm m
		ion collection	Ionensammlung f
invertible matrix, non-singular matrix, regular matrix	reguläre (invertierbare, umkehrbare, nichtsinguläre, nichtausgeartete) Matrix f	ion collection chamber	Ionensammelkammer f
		ion collection time	Ionensammelzeit f
inverting, inversion <math.>	Invertierung f <Math.>	ion column	Ionensäule f
inverting eyepiece, terrestrial eyepiece, erecting eyepiece	terrestrisches Okular n, Okular mit Bildumkehr, Erdfernrohrokular n	ion complex, ionic complex	Ionenkomplex m
		ion complex formation	Komplexionbildung f
inverting prism	s. image erecting prism		
invertor	s. inverter <el.>	ion concentration	s. ionic concentration
invert[-type] rangefinder, inverted-image rangefinder, inversion telemeter	Kehrbild-Entfernungsmesser m, Invert-Entfernungsmesser m	ion condensation	Kondensation f an Ionen
		ion condensation-type source, condensation-type ion source	Kondensationsionenquelle f
investigation under the reflection microscope	s. direct-light microscopy	ion conduction, ionic conduction	Ionenleitung f, Ionenleitfähigkeit f
inviscid	s. non-viscous <of flow, liquid, gas>	ion conductivity, ionic conductivity	Ionenleitfähigkeit f <Halb., El.Chem.>; Ionenäquivalentleitfähigkeit f <El.Chem.>
inviscid fluid	s. ideal liquid		
inviscid instability	s. frictionless instability		
invisible companion, dark companion	unsichtbarer (dunkler) Begleiter m	ion conductor, ionic conductor, second-class conductor	Ionenleiter m, Leiter m zweiter Ordnung (Klasse), Leiter II. Ordnung
invisible radiation, ultraphotic rays	unsichtbare Strahlung f, Strahlung im unsichtbaren Spektralbereich		
		ion core	Ionenrumpf m
involute, evolvent	Evolvente f, Involute f, Filarevolvente f, Fadenevolvente f	ion counter	Ionenzähler m
		ion covolume, covolume of ion, ionic covolume	Ionenkovolumen n, Kovolumen (Eigenvolumen) n des Ions
involute [function], evolvent [function], ev <math.>	Evolventenfunktion f, Evolvens m, ev <Math.>		
		ion current, gas current <in electron tubes>	Gasstrom m, Gasionenstrom m, Ionenstrom m <Röhren>
involution	Involution f		
involutory	involutorisch	ion current integrator	Ionenstromintegrator m, Ionenstrom-Mittelwertmesser m
invulnerability to jamming	Störunempfindlichkeit f, Stabilität f gegenüber Störungen		
		ion cyclotron frequency	Ionenzyklotronfrequenz f

ion cyclotron heating, ion cyclotron resonance heating	Ionenzyklotronresonanzaufheizung *f*	**ion hose,** ion sheath, ion layer	Ionenschlauch *m*; Ionenschicht *f*
ion cyclotron resonance, ICR	Ionenzyklotronresonanz *f*	**ionic cctivity coefficient**	Ionenaktivitätskoeffizient *m*, Aktivitätskoeffizient *m* der Ionen
ion cyclotron resonance heating	s. ion cyclotron heating	**ionic addition,** polar (heterolytic) addition	ionische (polare, heterolytische) Addition *f*
ion cyclotron-type source, cyclotron[-type] ion source	Zyklotronionenquelle *f*	**ionic association**	s. ion association
ion density	Ionendichte *f*	**ionic atmosphere,** ion[ic] cloud, cloud of ions, Debye-Hückel charge cloud <el.chem.>	Ionenwolke *f*, Ionenatmosphäre *f*, statistische Ionenverteilung *f* <El.Chem.>
ion device	s. ionic device		
ion dipole	Ionendipol *m*	**ionic bath,** electrolytic bath, electrolytic cell (tank, trough)	Elektrolyse[n]bad *n*, elektrolytischer Trog *m*
ion-dipole bond	Ion-Dipol-Bindung *f*		
ion-dipole bond	s. a. electrovalent bond	**ionic binding (bond)**	s. electrovalent bond
ion discharge, ionic discharge	Ionenentladung *f*	**ionic centrifuge**	Ionenzentrifuge *f*
ion-dispersed	ionendispers	**ionic cloud,** ion cloud, cloud of ions, ionic atmosphere, Debye-Hückel charge cloud <el.chem.>	Ionenwolke *f*, Ionenatmosphäre *f*, statistische Ionenverteilung *f* <El.Chem.>
ion dose <used in Germany, more general than: exposure>	Ionendosis *f*	**ionic complex**	s. ion complex
ion dose rate	Ionendosisleistung *f*	**ionic compound,** heteropolar compound, polar compound	Ionenverbindung *f*, ionogene (heteropolare, polare) Verbindung *f*
ion draw-out field	s. clearing field	**ionic concentration,** ion concentration, concentration of ions	Ionenkonzentration *f*
ion draw-out voltage, clearing voltage, sweeping voltage	Reinigungsspannung *f*, Ziehspannung *f*, Ionenziehspannung *f*, Absaugspannung *f*	**ionic conduction,** ion conduction	Ionenleitung *f*, Ionenleitfähigkeit *f*
ion duoplasmatron source	s. duoplasmatron ion source	**ionic conductivity,** ion conductivity	Ionenleitfähigkeit *f* <Halb.; El.Chem.>; Ionenäquivalentleitfähigkeit *f* <El.Chem.>
ion eigenvolume, eigenvolume (proper volume) of the ion, ion proper volume	Ioneneigenvolumen *n*, Eigenvolumen *n* des Ions	**ionic conductor,** ion conductor, second-class conductor	Ionenleiter *m*, Leiter *m* zweiter Ordnung (Klasse), Leiter II. Ordnung
ion-electron emission	Ion-Elektron-Emission *f*	**ionic covolume**	s. ion covolume
		ionic crystal, polar crystal	Ionenkristall *m*, polarer Kristall *m*
ion entropy, ionic entropy, entropy of ions	Ionenentropie *f*	**ionic deformation**	Ionendeformation *f*
ion exchange, exchange of ions, ionic replacement	Ionenaustausch *m*; Ionenumtausch *m* <im Boden>	**ionic device,** ion device	Ionengerät *n*
		ionic discharge	s. ion discharge
ion exchange adsorption	Ionenaustauschadsorption *f*	**ionic double-electric layer, ionic double layer**	Ionenanteil *m* der elektrochemischen Doppelschicht
ion-exchange bed, ion-exchanger bed	Austauscherbett *n*, Ionenaustauscherbett *n*	**ionic drift**	s. migration of ions
		ionic entropy	s. ion entropy
ion-exchange chromatography	Austauschchromatographie *f*, Ionenaustauschchromatographie *f*, heteropolare Chromatographie *f*	**ionic equilibrium**	Ionengleichgewicht *n*
		ionic equivalent [weight]	Ionenäquivalentgewicht *n*
		ionic etching	Ionenätzung *f*, ionische Ätzung *f*
ion-exchange column	Ionenaustauschersäule *f*, Ionenaustauscherkolonne *f*, Austauschersäule *f*, Austauscherkolonne *f*	**ionic formula**	Ionenformel *f*
		ionic friction	Ionenreibung *f*
		ionic function	Ionenfunktion *f*
		ionic gas model	Ionengasmodell *n*
ion-exchange filter	Ionenaustauschfilter *n*, Austauschfilter *n*	**ionic impurity**	Ionenstörstelle *f*
ion-exchange membrane	Ionenaustauschermembran *f*, ionenaustauschende Membran *f*	**ionic interaction**	Ionenwechselwirkung *f*
		ionicity, ionicness	Ionizität *f*, Ionencharakter *m*
		ionic lattice, ion grid, ion lattice	Ionengitter *n*
ion exchanger, ionite	Ionenaustauscher *m*, Austauscher *m*, Ionit *m*	**ionic link[age]**	s. electrovalent bond
		ionic liquid	Ionenflüssigkeit *f*
ion-exchanger bed, ion-exchange bed	Austauscherbett *n*, Ionenaustauscherbett *n*	**ionic loudspeaker**	Ionenlautsprecher *m*
ion-exchange resin	Ionenaustausch[er]harz *n*, Austausch[er]harz *n*, Ionenaustauscher *m* auf Kunstharzbasis	**ionic mean free path,** mean free path of the ion	mittlere freie Weglänge *f* des Ions
		ionic micell	Ionenmizelle *f*, Ionenmizell *n*
ion exchanger in the H[-] form	Ionenaustauscher *m* in der H-Form	**ionic microphone**	Ionenmikrophon *n*, ionisches Mikrophon *n*
ion-exchanging surface	Ionenaustauschfläche *f*	**ionic migration**	s. migration of ions
ion exclusion [technique]	Ionenausschlußverfahren *n*, Elektrolytvorlaufverfahren *n*	**ionic migration ratio**	Ionenwanderungsverhältnis *n*
ion extraction	s. ion beam extraction	**ionic mobility,** ion mobility, mobility of ions	Ionenbeweglichkeit *f*, Beweglichkeit *f* der Ionen
ion flow, ion flux	Ionenfluß *m*	**ionic molecule,** heteropolar molecule	Ionenmolekül *n*, heteropolares Molekül *n*
ion gauge	s. ionization gauge		
ion getter pump	s. getter-ion pump	**ionic movement**	s. ionic migration
ion grid	s. ionic lattice	**ionicness,** ionicity	Ionizität *f*, Ionencharakter *m*
ion guide <acc.>	Ionenleiter *m* <Beschl.>		
ion gun	Ionenkanone *f*, Ionenstrahler *m*	**ionic plasma,** ion plasma	Ionenplasma *n*
ion heating	Ionenaufheizung *f*, ionische Aufheizung *f*	**ionic polarizability**	Ionen[verschiebungs]polarisierbarkeit *f*, ionische (elektrochemische) Polarisierbarkeit *f*, Polarisierbarkeit bei Ionen
ion high-current (high-yield) source	s. high-current ion source		

ionic polarization	ionische Polarisation f, Ionen[verschiebungs]polarisation f	ionization colorimeter, ionocolorimeter	Ionisationskolorimeter n
ionic product, ion product	Ionenprodukt n	ionization constant	s. dissociation constant
		ionization constant	s. Townsend ionization coefficient
ionic pump, ion pump	Ionenpumpe f	ionization continuum	Ionisationskontinuum n, Ionisierungskontinuum n
ionic radius, ion radius	Ionenradius m, scheinbarer Ionenradius		
ionic Raman effect	Ionen-Raman-Effekt m	ionization core	s. ionization nucleus
ionic replacement	s. ion exchange	ionization cross-section, cross-section for ionization	Ionisierungsquerschnitt m, Wirkungsquerschnitt m für (der) Ionisierung, Ionisierungswirkungsquerschnitt m, Ionisations[wirkungs]querschnitt m
ionic screen	Ionenschirm m		
ionic selectivity	Ionenselektivität f		
ionic semiconductor	Ionenhalbleiter m		
ionic solid	Ionenfestkörper m	ionization current	Ionisationsstrom m, Ionisierungsstrom m
ionic solution	Ionenlösung f	ionization density	Ionisationsdichte f, Ionisierungsdichte f
ionic spectrum, spectrum produced by ionized atoms	Spektrum n ionisierter Atome	ionization detector	Ionisationsdetektor m
		ionization dosimeter	Ionisationsdosimeter n
ionic state, state of ions	Ionenzustand m		
ionic strength	Ionenstärke f		
ionic theory of excitation	Ionentheorie f der Erregung	ionization efficiency, efficiency of ionization	Ionisierungsausbeute f
		ionization efficiency curve	Ionisierungsausbeutekurve f
ionic valence (valency), electrostatic valence (valency), electrovalence, electrovalency	Ionenwertigkeit f, Ionenvalenz f, heteropolare Wertigkeit (Valenz) f, Elektrovalenz f, Ionenladungszahl f	ionization energy, ionization potential, ionizing energy <in eV>	Ionisierungsenergie f, Ionisationsenergie f, Ionisierungsarbeit f, Ionisationsarbeit f
ionic valve	Ionenventil n	ionization equilibrium	s. ionization balance
ionic weight	Ionengewicht n	ionization event	s. ionizing event
ionic wind	Ionenwind m	ionization flue gas indicator	Ionisations-Rauchgasmelder m, „elektronische Nase" f
ionic yield	s. ion yield		
ionic yield	s. ion-pair yield		
ion impact	Ionenstoß m	ionization fraction	Ionisierungsbruchteil m
ion impact ionization	Ionenstoßionisierung f	ionization frequency, frequency of ionization	Ionisationshäufigkeit f, Ionisierungshäufigkeit f
ion implantation	Ionenimplantation f	ionization function	Ionisierungsfunktion f
		ionization gauge, ion gauge, ionization pressure (vacuum) gauge, vacuum ionization gauge, ionization manometer	Ionisationsmanometer n, Ionisationsvakuummeter n
ion-ion emission	Ion-Ion-Emission f		
ion-ion recombination, ionic recombination	Ion-Ion-Rekombination f		
		ionization glow	Elektronenstoßleuchten n
ionite, ion exchanger	Ionenaustauscher m, Austauscher m, Ionit m	ionization impact	s. ionizing impact
		ionization in depth, deep ionization	Tiefenionisation f
ionium age	Ioniumalter n, nach der Ioniummethode bestimmtes geologisches Alter n	ionization in two stages	Zweistufenionisierung f, Zweistufenionisation f
		ionization isomerism	Ionisationsisomerie f
		ionization kernel, ionization nucleus (core)	Ionisationskern m
ionizability	Ionisierbarkeit f	ionization limit	Ionisierungsgrenze f
		ionization manometer	s. ionization gauge
ionization, ionizing, formation of ions	Ionisation f, Ionisierung f, Ionenbildung f	ionization mean free path, mean free path for ionization	[mittlere freie] Ionisierungsweglänge f, [mittlere freie] Ionisationsweglänge f, mittlere freie Weglänge f für Ionisation (Ionisierung)
ionization anemometer, ionized gas anemometer	Ionisationsanemometer n		
ionization balance, ionization equilibrium	Ionisationsgleichgewicht n, Ionisierungsgleichgewicht n		
		ionization method, ionization technique	Ionisationsverfahren n, Zählrohrverfahren n, Zählrohrmethode f
ionization burst	s. burst		
ionization by charge exchange, ionization by electron transfer	Ladungsaustauschionisation f	ionization noise, ion noise, gas noise	Ionisationsrauschen n, Ionenrauschen n
		ionization nucleus, ionization kernel (core)	Ionisationskern m
ionization by collision	s. impact ionization		
ionization by electron impact	Elektronenstoßionisation f	ionization number, number of ionizations	Ionisierungszahl f
ionization by electron transfer, ionization by charge exchange	Ladungsaustauschionisation f	ionization of air, atmospheric ionization, air ionization	Luftionisation f, Luftionisierung f, Ionisierung (Ionisation) f der Luft, atmosphärische Ionisation, Ionisation der Atmosphäre
ionization by pressure, pressure ionization	Druckionisation f		
ionization by single impact, single impact ionization	Ionisierung f durch Einzelstoß, Einzelstoßionisierung f	ionization path, ionization track	Ionisierungsbahn f, Ionisierungsspur f
		ionization plateau, polarization plateau, Fermi plateau	Fermi-Plateau n
ionization chamber	Ionisations[meß]kammer f, Ionenkammer f		
ionization chamber detector	Ionisationskammerdetektor m, Strahlungsnachweisgerät (Nachweisgerät) n mit Ionisationskammer	ionization potential, ionizing potential; firing potential, firing point <in V>	Ionisationsspannung f, Ionisierungsspannung f, Ionisierungspotential n, Ionisationspotential n <in V>
ionization coefficient	s. Townsend ionization coefficient	ionization potential	s. a. ionization energy <in eV>
ionization coefficient, n_+/n_D	Ionisierungskoeffizient m, n_+/n_D	ionization pressure	Ionisierungsdruck m
ionization collision	s. ionizing impact	ionization pressure gauge	s. ionization gauge

ionization probability, probability of ionization	Ionisationswahrscheinlichkeit f, Ionisierungswahrscheinlichkeit f	ionogram, ionospheric characteristic, frequency-height curve	Ionogramm n, Durchdrehaufnahme f; Durchdrehbeobachtung f, Ionosphärendurchdrehaufnahme f
ionization pulse ‹of ionization detector›	Ionisationsstoß m, Ionisationsimpuls m ‹Ionisationsdetektor›		
ionization pump	Ionisationspumpe f		
ionization range	Ionisierungsreichweite f, Ionisationsreichweite f	ionography	s. electropherography
		ionoluminescence	Ionolumineszenz f
		ionometer	Ionometer n
ionization rate	Ionisierungsgeschwindigkeit f, Ionisationsgeschwindigkeit f, Ionisierungsrate f ‹in Ionen/cm³ s›	ionometer, roentgenometer	Röntgenstrahlintensitätsmesser m, Ionometer n
		ionometric technique of materials testing	radiometrische Defektoskopie f, ionometrisches Verfahren n der Werkstoffprüfung
ionization stopping	Ionisationsbremsung f		
ionization technique, ionization method	Ionisationsverfahren n, Zählrohrverfahren n, Zählrohrmethode f	ionopause	Ionopause f
		ionophilic	ionophil
ionization temperature	Ionisationstemperatur f	ionophone	Ionophon n
ionization time	Ionisationszeit f, Ionisierungszeit f	ionophoresis, iontophoresis	Ionophorese f, Iontophorese f
		ion-optical	ionenoptisch
ionization track, ionization path	Ionisierungsbahn f, Ionisierungsspur f	ion orbit; ion trajectory, ion path	Ionenbahn f
ionization vacuum gauge	s. ionization gauge	ion oscillation, positive-ion oscillation	Ionenschwingung f, Schwingung f der positiven Ionen
ionization volume density, volume density of ionization	Volum[en]ionisationsdichte f, Volum[en]ionisierungsdichte f, Ionisationsdichte f pro Volum[en]einheit, Ionisierungsdichte f pro Volum[en]einheit, Volum[en]dichte f der Ionisation (Ionisierung)	ionosonde	Ionosonde f
		ionosphere, thermosphere, Heaviside layer	Ionosphäre f, Thermosphäre f, Heaviside-Schicht f, Ionisationsschicht f
ionized gas anemometer	s. ionization anemometer	ionospheric characteristic	s. ionogram
ionizing	s. ionization		
ionizing action, ionizing effect	ionisierende Wirkung f, Ionisationswirkung f, Ionisationseffekt m	ionospheric conductivity	Ionosphärenleitfähigkeit f
		ionospheric current system	ionosphärisches Stromsystem n
ionizing capacity	s. ionizing power	ionospheric disturbance	ionosphärische Störung f, Ionosphärenstörung f
ionizing collision	s. ionizing impact		
ionizing effect, ionizing action	ionisierende Wirkung f, Ionisationswirkung f, Ionisationseffekt m	ionospheric echo	Ionosphärenecho n
		ionospheric eclipse	ionosphärische Finsternis f
ionizing electrode	Ionisierungselektrode f	ionospheric model	Ionosphärenmodell n
ionizing energy	s. ionization energy ‹in eV›	ionospheric noise storm, ionospheric storm	Ionosphärensturm m
ionizing event, ionization event	Ionisierungsereignis n, Ionisierung[sakt m] f, Ionisationsereignis n, Ionisation f	ionospheric physics, physics of ionosphere	Ionosphärenphysik f
		ionospheric plasma wavelength, plasma wavelength	Plasmawellenlänge f
ionizing field	Ionisierungsfeld n		
ionizing impact, ionization impact; ionizing collision, ionization collision; ionizing shock ‹plasma›	Ionisierungsstoß m, Ionisationsstoß m, ionisierender Stoß m	ionospheric research	Ionosphärenforschung f
		ionospheric scattering	ionosphärische Streuung f
		ionospheric sounding	Ionosphären[echo]lotung f
		ionospheric storm, ionospheric noise storm	Ionosphärensturm m
		ionospheric tides	Ionosphärengezeiten pl, Gezeiten pl der Ionosphäre
ionizing potential	s. ionization potential ‹in V›		
ionizing power, ionizing capacity	Ionisierungsvermögen n, Ionisationsvermögen n; Ionisierungsfähigkeit f	ionospheric wave	Ionosphärenwelle f
		ionospheric weather, weather of ionosphere	Ionosphärenwetter n
ionizing radiation, ionizing rays	ionisierende Strahlung f, ionisierende Strahlen mpl	ionotropic	ionotrop
		ionotropy	Ionotropie f, Tautomerie f mit Platzwechsel des Wasserstoffions
ionizing shock	s. ionizing impact		
ion lattice	s. ionic lattice		
ion layer, ion hose, ion sheath	Ionenschlauch m; Ionenschicht f	ion output, ion yield, ionic yield	Ionenausbeute f
ion lens	Ionenlinse f	ion pair, ion twin; associated ion pair	Ionenpaar n, Ionenzwilling m; assoziiertes Ionenpaar n
ion magnetron	Ionenmagnetron n		
ion magnetron heating	Ionenmagnetronaufheizung f	ion pairing, ion pair production	Ionenpaarbildung f, Ionenpaarerzeugung f
ion microprobe	Ionenmikrosonde f	ion-pair yield, ionic yield	Ionenpaarausbeute f
ion microscope	Ionenmikroskop n	ion path; ion orbit; ion trajectory	Ionenbahn f
ion microscopy	Ionenmikroskopie f		
ion migration	s. ionic migration	ion pentode, three-grid ion tube, gas-filled pentode	Gaspentode f
ion mobility	s. ionic mobility		
ion-molecule complex	s. heteroion		
ion movement	s. ionic migration	ion photography	Ionenphotographie f
ion noise	s. ionization noise	ion plasma, ionic plasma	Ionenplasma n
ionocolorimeter	s. ionization colorimeter	ion plasma frequency	Ionenplasmafrequenz f, Plasmafrequenz f der Ionen
ion of similar radius	diadoches Ion n		
ionogenic	ionogen		
ionogenic bond	s. electrovalency bond		

ion

ion product	s. ionic product	iron dust core	s. dust core
ion proper volume	s. eigenvolume of the ion	iron fill factor, iron space factor	Eisenfüllfaktor m
ion-propulsed rocket, ion rocket	Ionenrakete f	iron-free	eisenarm; eisenlos, eisenfrei
ion pump, ionic pump	Ionenpumpe f	iron-free betatron, air-core betatron	„eisenloses" Betatron n, Luftspulenbetatron n, Betatron mit Luftspulen
ion radius, ionic radius	Ionenradius m, scheinbarer Ionenradius	iron-hydrogen barretter, barretter	Eisenwasserstoffwiderstand m, Eisenwiderstand m
ion recombination	Ionenrekombination f		
ion repeller, repeller ‹of mass spectrometer›	Repeller m, Repellerplatte f, Ionenrepeller m ‹Massenspektrometer›	iron loss	Eisenverluste mpl, Eisenkernverluste mpl
ion[-repulsed] rocket	Ionenrakete f	iron meteorite, siderite	Eisenmeteorit m, Siderit m
ion scintillation detector	Szintillationsionenzähler m, Szintillationsionendetektor m	iron needle instrument, permanent-magnet moving-coil instrument	Eisennadelinstrument n, Eisennadelmeßgerät n, Dreheiseninstrument n mit Magnet
ion sheath, ion hose, ion layer	Ionenschlauch m; Ionenschicht f	iron screen	Eisen[ab]schirmung f
ion slip	Ionenschlupf m	iron-screened instrument, instrument with magnetic screening	eisengeschirmtes Meßgerät n
ion sound, ion acoustic oscillation	Ionenschall m, Ionenschallschwingung f, Longitudinalschwingung f der Ionen im Plasma		
ion sound velocity	Ionenschallgeschwindigkeit f	iron space factor, iron fill factor	Eisenfüllfaktor m
ion source	Ionenquelle f	irradiance, exposure rate, irradiancy	Bestrahlungsstärke f
ion spectrum	Ionenspektrum n		
ion spot, ion burn, ion burning	Ionenfleck m, Ionenbrennfleck m	irradiance	s. a. radiance
ion synergism	Ionensynergismus m	irradiancy	s. irradiance
ion temperature	Ionentemperatur f	irradiated; radiation-exposed, exposed	strahlenexponiert, bestrahlt; strahlenbelastet
iontophoresis, ionophoresis	Ionophorese f, Iontophorese f		
ion trajectory, ion path; ion orbit	Ionenbahn f	irradiation; illumination; exposure	Strahlenexponierung f, Exponierung f, Exposition f; Bestrahlung f; Belichtung f
ion transfer[ence] number	Ionenüberführungszahl f	irradiation	Irradiation f, Überstrahlung f
ion trap	Ionenfalle f		
ion triplet	Ionendrilling m, Ionentriplett n	irradiation, radiation ‹upon›	Einstrahlung f
iontron	Iontron n, Ionstron n	irradiation	s. a. radiant exposure
ion tube	Ionenröhre f; Ionenrohr n	irradiation by ultrasonic waves	Durchschallung f
ion twin	s. ion pair		
ion vacancy	Ionenleerstelle f, Ionenfehlstelle f, Ionenloch n, Ionenlücke f	irradiation channel, exposure hole	Bestrahlungskanal m ‹zur Bestrahlung im Reaktor›
ion yield, ionic yield, ion output	Ionenausbeute f		
iraser, infra-red maser, I.R. maser, iaser ‹infrared amplification by stimulated emission of radiation›	Iraser m, Infrarotmaser m, IR-Maser m	irradiation facility	s. irradiation plant
		irradiation field, exposure field	Bestrahlungsfeld n
		irradiation plant, irradiation facility, irradiation rig	Bestrahlungsanlage f
I ray, seismic ray reflected downwards at the inner core boundary	I-Welle f, am inneren Kern gebrochene Erdbebenwelle f	irradiation reactor	Bestrahlungsreaktor m
		irradiation rig, irradiation source, irradiator	Strahler m, Strahlungsquelle f ‹für Bestrahlungen›
i region	s. intrinsic region	irradiation rig	s. a. irradiation plant
iridescence, irisation	Irisieren n	irradiation source, irradiation rig, irradiator	Strahler m, Strahlungsquelle f ‹für Bestrahlungen›
		irradiation time, exposure time	Expositionszeit f, Bestrahlungszeit f
iridescence, schillerization	Schillern n	irradiator, irradiation source, irradiation rig	Strahler m, Strahlungsquelle f ‹für Bestrahlungen›
iridescent cloud, mother-of-pearl cloud	irisierende Wolke f, Perlmutterwolke f	irrational dispersion	irrationale Dispersion f
iris, entrance pupil, object-side pupil	Eintrittspupille f	irrational equation	Wurzelgleichung f
		irrational twin	irrationaler Zwilling m
iris, iris diaphragm	Irisblende f, Iris f	irreducibility	Irreduzibilität f
irisation	s. iridescence	irreducible	irreduzibel
iris diaphragm, iris	Irisblende f, Iris f	irreducible case	Casus m irreducibilis
		irreducible representation, simple representation	irreduzible Darstellung f
irising	s. diaphragming		
iris-loaded torus	s. corrugated torus	irregular astigmatism	unregelmäßiger Astigmatismus m, Astigmatismus irregularis
iris-loaded waveguide	s. corrugated waveguide		
iris photometer	Irisphotometer n	irregular doublet	irreguläres Dublett n, Abschirmungsdublett n
iris torus	s. corrugated torus		
iris waveguide	s. corrugated waveguide	irregular galaxy, irregular nebula	unregelmäßiges (irreguläres) Sternsystem n, unregelmäßiger (irregulärer) Nebel m
iRNA	s. nuclear ribonucleic acid		
iron arc	s. Pfund arc		
iron arc lamp	Eisenbogenlampe f	irregularity	Ungeordnetheit f
iron-clad galvanometer	s. shielded galvanometer	irregularity	s. a. non-uniformity
iron-cored type instrument, iron-core instrument	Eisenkerninstrument n, eisengeschlossenes Meßgerät n	irregularity coefficient ‹control›	Ungleichförmigkeitsgrad m ‹Regelung›

irregularity of flow, non-uniformity of flow	Strömungsungleichheit *f*	**isanemon[e]**	Isanemone *f*
irregular motion	s. disordered motion	**isanomal, isanomal curve (line)**	s. isoanomal
irregular nebula	s. irregular galaxy	**isenerg[e]**	Isenerge *f*, Linie *f* gleicher innerer Energie
irregular photophoresis, trembling effect	irreguläre (unregelmäßige) Photophorese *f*	**isenerg[et]ic**	s. isoenergetic
irregular singularity, irregular singular point, essential singularity, essential singular point, point of indetermination	wesentlich[e] singuläre Stelle *f*, [singuläre] Stelle der Unbestimmtheit, Unbestimmtheitsstelle *f*, wesentliche (irreguläre) Singularität *f*, stark singuläre Stelle	**isenthalp, isenthalpic line,** line of equal enthalpy	Isenthalpe *f*, Drossellinie *f*, Drosselkurve *f*
		isenthalpic change [of state]	isenthalpische Zustandsänderung (Änderung) *f*, Zustandsänderung bei konstanter Enthalpie
irreversibility, non-reversibility	Irreversibilität *f*, Nichtumkehrbarkeit *f*	**isenthalpic line**	s. isenthalp
irreversible adsorption	s. chemisorption	**isentrop[e], isentropic line**	Isentrope *f*
irreversible boundary movement, irreversible displacement of the Bloch wall	irreversible Wandverschiebung *f*	**isentropic change [of state]**	isentrope Zustandsänderung (Änderung) *f*, Zustandsänderung bei konstanter Entropie
irreversible change [of state]	irreversible Änderung (Zustandsänderung) *f*		
irreversible cycle	irreversibler Kreisprozeß *m*, nicht umkehrbarer Kreisprozeß	**isentropic chart**	s. adiabatic chart
		isentropic compressibility, adiabatic [coefficient of bulk] compressibility	adiabatische Kompressibilität *f*, adiabatischer Kompressibilitätskoeffizient *m*
irreversible displacement of the Bloch wall, irreversible boundary movement	irreversible Wandverschiebung *f*		
irreversible electrode	irreversible Elektrode *f*	**isentropic flow,** hom[o]entropic flow, hom[o]entropic motion, homeo[-]epitaxy	isentrop[isch]e Strömung *f*, homöoentrope Bewegung *f*, Homöoepitaxie *f*
irreversible permeability	irreversible Permeabilität *f*		
		isentropic line	s. isentrop[e]
		isentropic surface	Isentropenfläche *f*
irreversible thermodynamics, non-equilibrium thermodynamics	Thermodynamik *f* irreversibler Prozesse, irreversible Thermodynamik	**isentropy**	Isentropie *f*
		Ising model	Ising-Modell *n*
		island <el.>	Insel *f* <El.>
irreversible transformation, irreversible transition	irreversibler Übergang *m*, irreversible Umwandlung *f*; irreversible Überführung *f*	**island effect**	Inseleffekt *m*, Inselbildung *f*
		island ice	Eiskappe *f*, Eisschild *m*, Inseleis *n*
irritant, stimulus <bio.>	Reiz *m* <Bio.>	**island model,** Mott['s] island model	Mottsches Inselmodell *n*, Inselmodell
irritation plasmolysis, stimulative plasmolysis	Reizplasmolyse *f*	**island of isomerism**	Isomerieinsel *f*
irrotational, potential	wirbelfrei, Potential-, drehungsfrei, rotationsfrei, rotorlos	**island universe,** galactic (stellar) system, galaxy, system of stars	Sternsystem *n*, Galaxie *f*, Galaxis *f* <*pl.*: Galaxien>
irrotational field, non-rotational field, non-circuital field, lamellar [vector] field, non-vortical field, vector field derivable from a scalar potential, potential field	wirbelfreies Feld (Vektorfeld) *n*, potentiales Vektorfeld, Gradientenfeld *n*, rotationsfreies (drehungsfreies) Feld (Vektorfeld), lamellares Vektorfeld (Feld), laminares Vektorfeld (Feld), Potentialfeld *n*, wirbelfreies (reines) Quellenfeld *n*, Quellenfeld	**isoallobar**	s. isallobar
		isoallobaric wind, isallobaric wind	isallobarer Wind *m*, isallobarischer Wind
		isoamplitude [curve], isoamplitude line, isogram of amplitude	Isoamplitude[nlinie] *f*, Linie *f* gleicher Amplitude, Isamplitude *f*
		isoanabase, isanabase, isobase	Isanabase *f*, Isobase *f*
irrotational flow	s. potential flow	**isoanakatabar**	Isanakatabare *f*
irrotationality, absence of vortices (eddies), eddy freedom	Wirbelfreiheit *f*, Wirbellosigkeit *f*	**isoanomal, isoanomalous curve (line),** magnetic isoanomalous line, isanomal line (curve), isanomal, isabnormal [line]	Isanomale *f*, Linie *f* gleicher Anomalie, Linie gleicher magnetischer Anomalie, Linie gleicher Abweichung
irrotationality, potentiality	Wirbelfreiheit *f*, Drehungsfreiheit *f*		
irrotational motion	s. irrotational flow		
irrotational vector, potential vector	wirbelfreier Vektor *m*, Potentialvektor *m*; wirbelfreies Vektorfeld *n*		
		isoaurore	s. isochasm
irrotational vortex, potential vortex	Potentialwirbel *m*	**isobar,** isobaric curve (line), constant-pressure line, equal-pressure line, line of equal pressure <therm., meteo.>; contour height line <meteo.>	Isobare *f*, Isobarenlinie *f*, Gleichdrucklinie *f*, Kurve *f* gleichen Drucks, Isopieste *f* <Therm., Meteo.>
irruption	s. intrusion		
isabnormal [line]	s. isoanomal		
isacoustic curve, isacoustic line, equal-loudness curve (line, contour), loudness[-level] contour	Isakuste *f*, Isoakuste *f*, Linie *f* gleicher Lautstärke, Kurve *f* gleicher Lautstärke		
		isobar, nuclear isobar, nucleonic isobar	Isobar *n*, Kernisobar *n*
isallobar, isallobaric line, isoallobar	Isallobare *f*	**isobaric analog state,** analog state	[isobarer] Analogzustand *m*
isallobaric wind, isoallobaric wind	isallobarer Wind *m*, isallobarischer Wind	**isobaric change [of state]**	isobare Zustandsänderung (Änderung) *f*, Zustandsänderung bei konstantem Druck
isallohypse, isallopotential [curve]	Isallopotential[linie *f*] *n*, Isallohypse *f*		
isallotherm	Isallotherme *f*	**isobaric compressibility**	isobare Kompressibilität *f*
		isobaric curve	s. isobar <therm., meteo.>
isametral	Isametrale *f*	**isobaric expansion coefficient**	isobarer Ausdehnungskoeffizient *m*
isanabase, iso[ana]base	Isanabase *f*, Isobase *f*		

isobaric

isobaric heat capacity, heat capacity at constant pressure	Wärmekapazität f bei konstantem Druck, isobare Wärmekapazität	**isobary,** isobarism **isobase** **isobath,** depth contour line, depth contour	Isobarie f s. isoanabase Isobathe f, Tiefenlinie f, Tiefenkurve f, Wassertiefenlinie f, Wassertiefenisobathe f
isobaric-isosteric line, isobar-isostere	isobar-isostere Linie f, Isobare-Isostere f, Isobaren-Isosteren-Linie f	**isobathytherm** **isobestic point** **isoboson** **isobront**	Isobathytherme f isobestischer Punkt m Isoboson n Isobronte f
isobaric laws, isobar rules	Isobarensätze mpl [von Mattauch], [Mattauchsche] Isobarenregeln fpl, Mattauchsche Regeln fpl	**isocandela curve,** isocandela line <US>, isocandle curve	Isocandelakurve f, Linie (Kurve) f gleicher Lichtstärke
isobaric line **isobaric number** **isobaric retrograde condensation,** retrograde condensation of the second kind	s. isobar <therm., meteo.> s. neutron excess retrograde Kondensation f zweiter Art, isobare retrograde Kondensation	**isocandela diagram** **isocandela line,** isocandle curve **isocandle diagram** **isocatabase**	s. light distribution curve s. isocandela curve s. light distribution curve Isokatabase f
isobaric space, isotopic space, charge space, iso-spin space, isospace	Iso[topen]spinraum m, isotoper Spinraum m, Isoraum m, isotoper Raum m, Isobarenspinraum m, isobarer Spinraum m, Ladungsraum m	**isocatanabar** **isochasm,** isoaurore	Isokatanabare f Isochasme f
isobaric spin, iso[topic] spin, isotopic variable	Iso[topen]spin m, isotoper (isobarer) Spin m, Isobarenspin m. Ladungsspin m	**isocheim[e], isochimene**	Isochimene f
isobaric spin conservation law	s. law of conservation of isobaric spin	**isochion** **isochiot**	s. isohion Isochiote f
isobaric spin co-ordinate, isotopic spin co-ordinate, isospin (charge) co-ordinate	Isospinkoordinate f, Isotopenspinkoordinate f, Ladungskoordinate f	**isochor[e],** isometric [line], isovolumic (isosteric) line, isophere, isostere, isopycn	Isochore f, Linie f konstanten Volumens, isometrische Linie, Isophere f, Isostere f, Isopykne f
isobaric spin doublet, isotopic spin doublet, isodoublet, charge doublet	Isospindublett n, Isodublett n, Isotopenspindublett n, Ladungsdublett n	**isochore of reaction** **isochoric change [of state]**	s. reaction isochore isochore Zustandsänderung (Änderung) f, Zustandsänderung bei konstantem Volumen
isobaric spin group, isotopic spin group, isospin group	Isospingruppe f, Isotopenspingruppe f	**isochoric heat capacity,** heat capacity at constant volume	Wärmekapazität f bei konstantem Volumen, isochore Wärmekapazität
isobaric spin matrix, isotopic spin matrix, isospin matrix	Isospinmatrix f, Isotopenspinmatrix f	**isochrom[atic]** **isochromatic,** isochromatic curve, isochromatic line	s. line of equal colour Isochromate f, isochromatische Kurve f, Farbgleiche f; Schubgleiche f; Strahlungsisochromate f
isobaric spin multiplet, isotopic spin multiplet, isomultiplet, charge multiplet	Isospinmultiplett n, Isomultiplett n, Isotopenspinmultiplett n, Ladungsmultiplett n	**isochromatic,** homochromatic, homochrome	gleichfarbig, isochrom, homochrom, isochromatisch
isobaric spin operator, isotopic spin operator, isospin operator	Isospinoperator m, Isotopenspinoperator m	**isochromatic curve, isochromatic line,** isochromatic	Isochromate f, isochromatische Kurve f, Farbgleiche f; Schubgleiche f; Strahlungsisochromate f
isobaric spin quantum number, isotopic spin quantum number, isospin quantum number, isotopic variable	Isospinquantenzahl f, Isotopenspinquantenzahl f	**isochromatic surface,** surface of constant phase difference **isochromatism** **isochrone,** isochronous curve **isochronism**	isochromatische Fläche f Isochromasie f Isochrone f, Gleichzeitenkurve f Isochronie f, Isochronismus m
isobaric spin selection, isotopic spin selection	Isospinauswahl f, Isotopenspinauswahl f		
isobaric spin selection rule, isotopic spin selection rule	Isospinauswahlregel f, Isotopenspinauswahlregel f		
isobaric spin singlet, isotopic spin singlet, isosinglet, charge singlet	Iso[topen]spinsingulett n, Isosingulett n, Ladungssingulett n		
isobaric spin triplet, isotopic spin triplet, isotriplet, charge triplet	Isospintriplett n, Isotriplett n, Isotopenspintriplett n, Ladungstriplett n	**isochronous curve** **isochronous cyclotron** **isochronous radius** **isochronous revolution** **isoclinal, isoclinal fold**	s. isochrone s. AVF cyclotron Isochronradius m isochroner Umlauf m Isoklinalfalte f, Isoklinale f
isobaric spin vector, isotopic spin vector, vector of isobaric (isotopic) spin, isospin vector	Isospinvektor m, Isotopenspinvektor m	**isoclinal structure** **isocline, isoclinic, isoclinic line**	Isoklinalstruktur f Isokline f; Richtungsgleiche f; Linie f gleicher Inklination; Linie gleicher Neigung, Isoklinale f
isobaric surface, surface of equal pressure, surface of constant pressure	Isobarenfläche f, Gleichdruckfläche f, Fläche f gleichen Drucks, isobare Fläche		
isobaric triad, isobaric triplet	isobares Tripel n, drei aufeinanderfolgende stabile Isobare npl	**isoclinic fringe**	s. fringe of equal inclination
isobarism, isobary	Isobarie f	**isoclinic line** **isoclinotropism** **isocolloid**	s. isocline Isoklinotropismus m Isokolloid n
isobar-isostere, isobaric-isosteric line	isobar-isostere Linie f, Isobare-Isostere f, Isobaren-Isosteren-Linie f	**isoconcentrate,** line of equal concentration, line of constant concentration, equiconcentration line	Isokonzentrate f, Linie f gleicher Konzentration
isobar-isosteric solenoid	isobar-isosteres Rohr n		
isobar of reaction **isobar rules**	s. reaction isobar s. isobaric laws	**isoconcentrate surface** **isocorrelate**	s. equiconcentration surface Isokorrelate f

isocosm, isocosmic line	Isokosme *f*
isocount [contour]	*s.* isopulse
isocrym	Isokryme *f*
isocurlus	Linie *f* gleicher Wirbelstärke
isocycle, isocyclic nucleus, homocycle, homocyclic nucleus (ring), homoatomic ring	Isozyklus *m*, Homozyklus *m*, isozyklischer Ring *m*, homozyklischer Ring
isocylindrical projection	*s.* Lambert projection
isodense	*s.* isopycn
isodensitometer	Isodensitometer *n*, Äquidensitometer *n*
isodesmic	isodesmisch
isodiaphere	Isodiapher *n*
isodimorphism, double isomorphism	Isodimorphie *f*, Isodimorphismus *m*
isodisperse, monodisperse, homodisperse	isodispers, monodispers, homodispers
isodose, isodose contour (curve, line)	Isodosenkurve *f*, Isodosiskurve *f*, Isodosis *f*
isodose chart	Isodosenkarte *f*, Isodosendiagramm *n*, Isodosentafel *f*, Isodosenplan *m*
isodose contour (curve, line)	*s.* isodose
isodose surface	Isodosenfläche *f*
isodoublet	*s.* isobaric spin doublet
isodrome, isodromic line	Isodrome *f*
isodynam, isodynamic line, magnetic isodynam	Isodyname *f*, magnetische Isodyname, Linie *f* gleicher magnetischer Feldstärke
isodynamic change [of state]	isodynamische Zustandsänderung *f*, isodynamische Änderung *f*
isodynamic line	*s.* isodynam
isodyne	Isodyne *f*
isoelectric point	isoelektrischer Punkt *m*
isoelectric temperature	isoelektrische Temperatur *f*
isoelectr[on]ic sequence [of atoms]	isoelektronische Reihe *f*, isoelektronische Atome *npl*
isoenergetic, isoenergic, isenerg[et]ic, homoenergic, homoenergetic	isoenergetisch
isoenergetic change [of state]	isoenergetische Zustandsänderung *f*, isoenergetische Änderung *f*
isoenergetic surface, surface of equal energy	Fläche *f* gleicher Energie, isoenergetische Fläche
isofamily	Isofamilie *f*
isofermion	Isofermion *n*
isogal	Isogale *f*
isogam, isogamme	Isogamme *f*
isogeopotential	Isogeopotential[lini]e *f*
isogeopotential surface	Isogeopotentialfläche *f*
isogeotherm	Isogeotherme *f*
isogeothermal surface	Isogeotherme[nfläche] *f*
isoglacihypse	Isoglazihypse *f*
isogon, isogonal, isogonic [line], isogonal line	Isogone *f*, Linie *f* gleicher Deklination
isogonal	*s. a.* equiangular
isogonality, conformity, preservation of angles <math.>	Winkeltreue *f*, Isogonalität *f*, Konformität *f* <Math.>
isogonal line	*s.* isogon
isogonal mapping	*s.* conformal mapping
isogonic	*s.* isogon
isogonic	*s.* equiangular
isogonic line	*s.* isogon
isogonic zero line	*s.* agonic line
isograd[e]	Isograde *f*
isogradient	Isogradient *m*
isogram	Isogramme *f*
isogram	*s. a.* isoline
isogram of amplitude	*s.* isoamplitude line
isogrive	Isogrive *f*
isogyre, achromatic (neutral) line, brush	Isogyre *f*
isohaline, isosalinity line	Isohaline *f*
isohel	Isohelie *f*, Isohele *f*
isohion, isochion, isonival line	Isohione *f*, Isochione *f*
isohydrometric line	isohydrometrische Kurve *f*
isohyet[al], isohyetose	Isohyete *f*, Regengleiche *f*
isohygromen, isohygromenic line	Isohygromene *f*
isohygrotherm	Isohygrotherme *f*
isohypse, isohypse line, horizontal [line], altitude line (curve), curve of equal altitude, level line (curve), curve of equal level, contour line, line of level	Isohypse *f*, Höhen[schicht]linie *f*, Höhengleiche *f*, Höhenkurve *f*, Horizontale *f*, Horizontallinie *f*, Horizontalkurve *f*, Schicht[en]linie *f*, Niveaulinie *f*, Niveaukurve *f*
isohypsic chart (map)	*s.* hypsometric map
isoinversion	Isospiegelung *f*
isoionic point	isoionischer Punkt *m*
isokatabatic line, depression contour	Isokatabase *f*
isolated; solitary; sporadic	isoliert; vereinzelt; sporadisch
isolated point, isolated singular point	isolierter [singulärer] Punkt *m*, Einsiedlerpunkt *m*, isolierte Singularität *f* (singuläre Stelle *f*)
isolated pulse, single pulse, discrete pulse	Einzelimpuls *m*, diskreter Impuls *m*
isolated singular point	*s.* isolated point
isolated vortex	isolierter Wirbel *m*
isolation	*s.* separation <chem.>
isolation material	*s.* sound insulator <ac.>
isolator, directional isolator, microwave isolator <el.>	Isolator *m*, Richtungsleitung *f*, Richt[ungs]leiter *m*, Richtungsisolator *m*, Mikrowellenisolator *m* <El.>
isoline, equal-function line, isogram	Isolinie *f*, Isarithme *f*, Gleiche *f*, Isogramm *n*, Linie *f* gleichen Wertes
isolog, isologue	Isolog[es] *n*
isologous series	isologe Reihe *f*
isologue	*s.* isolog
isoluminance curve	Kurve *f* gleicher Leuchtdichte
isolux, isolux curve (line), equilux curve	Isoluxe *f*, Isoluxkurve *f*
isolychn	Isolychne *f*
isomagnetic	*s.* isomagnetic line
isomagnetic chart, isomagnetic map	isomagnetische Karte *f*
isomagnetic jump	isomagnetischer Sprung *m*
isomagnetic line, isomagnetic	isomagnetische Kurve (Linie) *f*, Isomagnetik *f*
isomagnetic map, isomagnetic chart	isomagnetische Karte *f*
isomer, nuclear isomer	Kernisomer *n*, Isomer *n*
isomer[e], isomeride <chem.>	Isomer[e] *n* <Chem.>
isomeric branching	isomere Verzweigung *f*
isomeric colours	unbedingt-gleiche Farben *fpl*, isomere Farben
isomeric heat, isomerization heat, heat of isomerization	Isomerisationswärme *f*
isomeric shift	Isomerieverschiebung *f*

isomeric transition, I.T.	isomerer Übergang m, isomere Umwandlung f, i. Ü., I.T.	isophenological line	isophänologische Linie f
isomeride, isomer[e] <chem.>	Isomer[e] n <Chem.>	isophot, isophot curve, isophot[ic] line	Isophote f, Linie (Kurve) f gleicher Helligkeit am Objekt, Kurve (Linie) gleicher Beleuchtungsstärke, Beleuchtungsgleiche f, Lichtgleiche f
isomerism, isomery	Isomerie f; Lagerungsisomerie f		
isomerism of atomic nucleus, nuclear isomerism	Kernisomerie f, Isomerie f des Atomkerns		
		isophot wavelength	isophote Wellenlänge f
isomerization heat, isomeric heat, heat of isomerization	Isomerisationswärme f	isopiestic	isopiestisch
		isopiestic specific heat	s. specific heat at constant pressure
isomeromorphism	Isomeromorphie f	isoplanasic	isoplanatisch
isomery	s. isomerism	isoplanasic condition	s. condition of isoplanatism
isometabolic line	Isometabole f	isoplanatism	Isoplanasie f
		isoplere	s. isochore
isometric	s. isochore	isopleth, isoplethal	Isoplethe f
isometric, length-preserving <math.>	isometrisch; längentreu, maßstabgerecht <Math.>	isopleth	s. a. net chart
		isoplethal, isopleth	Isoplethe f
isometric co-ordinate	s. isothermal parameter	isopolar, line of equal polarization	Isopolare f
isometric crystal[lographic] system	s. cubic system		
isometric lines	s. isochore	isopolymorphism	Isopolymorphismus m, Isopolymorphie f
isometric lines	s. isothermal lines		
isometric mapping, length-preserving mapping	längentreue Abbildung f, Abwicklung f, Abwickelung f	isopor[ic line]	Isopore f, Isovariationskurve f, Linie f gleicher säkularer Variation
isometric parameter	s. isothermal parameter	isopotential change [of state]	isopotentielle Zustandsänderung f; isopotentielle Änderung f
isometric projection	isometrische Parallelperspektive f; isometrische Projektion f		
		isopotential curve, isopotential line	Isopotentiallinie f, Isopotentiale f
isometric specific heat	s. specific heat at constant volume	isopotential surface	Isopotentialfläche f
isometric system	s. cubic system	isopter	Isoptere f
isometry	Isometrie f, isometrische Abbildung (Transformation) f	isopulse, isopulse contour, isopulse curve, isocount, isocount contour	Isoimpulskurve f, Linie f gleicher Zählrate
isomonimic line	Isomonime f		
		isopycn	s. isochore
isomorphic; isomorphous; isostructural	isomorph; isostrukturell	isopycn[al], isopycnic, isopycnic line, curve of constant density, line of equal density, isodense, equidense	Isopykne f, Linie f gleicher Dichte, Isodense f, äquidense Kurve f
isomorphic <math.>	isomorph <Math.>		
isomorphic mapping	s. isomorphism <math.>		
isomorphic state / in the	zustandsisomorph		
isomorphism, homeomorphism <cryst.>	Isomorphie f, kristallographische Isomorphie, Homöomorphie f <Krist.>	isopycnic surface	Isopyknenfläche f, isopyknische Fläche f, Fläche gleicher Dichte
isomorphism, isomorphic mapping <math.>	Isomorphismus m, Isomorphie f, isomorphe Abbildung f <Math.>	isoquot	Isoquote f
		isorad, isorad line	Isoradlinie f, Isoradkurve f
		isorad map	Isoradkarte f
isomorphous; isomorphic; isostructural	isomorph; isostrukturell	isorotation	Isorotation f
		isosalinity line, isohaline	Isohaline f
isomorphous insertion	isomorpher Einbau m	isoscalar	Isoskalar m
isomorphous replacement	isomorphe Substitution f, isomorphe Ersetzung f	isoscalar cloud	Isoskalarwolke f
		isoscalar resonance	isoskalare Resonanz f, Isoskalarresonanz f
isomultiplet	s. isobaric spin multiplet		
isoneph	Isonephe f	isosceles triangle	gleichschenkliges Dreieck n
isonival line	s. isohion		
iso-ombral line, line of equal (constant) evaporation	Isoombre f	isoseism[al], isoseist, curve of equal intensity	Isoseiste f, Linie f gleicher Erdbebenstärke
isoorthotherm	Isoortotherme f	isosinglet	s. isobaric spin singlet
isoosmotic solution, isotonic (isosmotic) solution	isotonische (isosmotische) Lösung f	isosmotic solution	s. isotonic solution
		isospace	s. isobaric space
		isospin	s. isobaric spin
isopac[h], isopachyte	Isopache f, Isopachyte f	isostasy, isostatics	Isostasie f, Massenkompensation f
		isostath	Isostate f
isopag	Isopage f	isostatic compensation	isostatische Ausgleichsbewegung (Kompensation) f
isoparaclase	Isoparaklase f		
isopause	Isopause f	isostatic equilibrium, buoyant stability	isostatisches Gleichgewicht n, Schwimmgleichgewicht n
isopectic, isopectic line	Isopekte f		
isoperibol microcalorimeter	s. isothermal microcalorimeter	isostatic geoid	isostatisches Geoid n
		isostatic reduction	isostatische Korrektion (Reduktion) f <nach Airy-Heiskanen>
isoperimetric problem	isoperimetrisches Problem n		
		isostatics	s. isostasy
		isostatic surface	isostatische Fläche (Ausgleichsfläche) f
isophane	Isophane f		
		isostere, isosteric line, curve of equal specific volume	Isostere f, isostere Kurve f
isophase, line of constant phase	Isophase f, Linie f gleicher Phase		
isophase light	s. intermittent light in which the light and dark period are equal	isostere	s. a. isochore
		isosteric heat of adsorption	isostere Adsorptionswärme f
		isosteric line, isostere	Isostere f
isophase surface	Isophasenfläche f, Fläche f gleicher Phase	isosteric surface	s. surface of equal specific volume

isosterism — Isosterie f
isostilb, isostilb curve (line) — Isostilbe f
isostructural — s. isomorphous
isosurface — Isofläche f
isotac — Isotake f
isotac, isovel, equal-velocity curve (line), line of equal (constant) velocity, curve of equal velocity — Isotache f, Linie f gleicher Geschwindigkeit

isotachyte — Isotachyte f
isotactic polymer — isotaktisches Polymer n
isotalantose — Isotalantose f

isothere — Isothere f
isotherm[al], isothermal line, line of constant (equal) temperature — Isotherme f, Wärmegleiche f
isothermal calorimeter — isothermes Kalorimeter n

isothermal change [of state] — isotherme Zustandsänderung f, Zustandsänderung bei konstanter Temperatur; isotherme Änderung (Veränderung) f
isothermal coefficient of bulk compression — s. isothermal compressibility
isothermal compressibility; isothermal coefficient of bulk compression — isotherme Kompressibilität f; isothermer Kompressibilitätskoeffizient m

isothermal conditions, isothermy, isothermality — Isothermie f
isothermalcy — Stabilität f auf Grund isothermer Schichtung

isothermal elastic potential — isothermes elastisches Potential n
isothermal electric conductivity — isotherme elektrische Leitfähigkeit f
isothermal Hall effect — isothermer Hall-Effekt m

isothermal heat conductivity — isotherme Wärmeleitfähigkeit f
isothermal heat of compression, heat of isothermal compression — isotherme Kompressionswärme f
isothermal heat of expansion, heat of isothermal expansion — isotherme Expansionswärme f
isothermality — s. isothermy
isothermal-jacket microcalorimeter — s. isothermal microcalorimeter
isothermal Joule-Thomson coefficient — isothermer Joule-Thomson-Koeffizient m

isothermal line — s. isothermal
isothermal lines, isometric lines, isothermal system of curves; isothermal net <on the surface> <math.> — Isothermenschar f, Isothermensystem n; isothermes Kurvennetz n, isometrisches Netz n <auf der Fläche> <Math.>

isothermally jacketted microcalorimeter — s. isothermal microcalorimeter
isothermal microcalorimeter; isothermal-jacket microcalorimeter, isothermal-shell microcalorimeter, isothermally jacketted microcalorimeter, isoperibol microcalorimeter — isothermes Mikrokalorimeter n

isothermal modulus of elasticity — isothermer Elastizitätsmodul m
isothermal Nernst effect — isothermer Nernst-Effekt m

isothermal Nernst-Ettingshausen effect — isothermer Nernst-Ettingshausen-Effekt m
isothermal net — s. isothermal lines <on a surface>
isothermal parameter, isothermic parameter, isometric parameter, isometric co-ordinate — isothermer (thermischer) Parameter m, isometrischer Parameter, isometrische Koordinate f
isothermal path — isothermer Weg m
isothermal phase change — isotherme Phasenänderung (Phasenumwandlung) f

isothermal piezoelectric coefficient — isothermer piezoelektrischer Koeffizient m
isothermal quenching, quench hardening — Abschreckhärtung f, Umwandlungshärtung f
isothermal-shell microcalorimeter — s. isothermal microcalorimeter
isothermal speed of sound, isothermal velocity of sound — isotherme Schallgeschwindigkeit f
isothermal surface — isotherme Fläche f, Isothermenfläche f; Isothermfläche f <Math.>
isothermal system of curves — s. isothermal lines <on a surface>
isothermal unattainability — isotherme Unerreichbarkeit f
isothermal velocity of sound, isothermal speed of sound
isothermic — s. isothermal
isothermobath — Isothermobathe f

isotherm of reaction — s. law of mass action
isotherm of swelling, swelling isotherm — Quellungsisotherme f
isothermohypse — Isothermohypse f
isothermy, isothermality, isothermal conditions — Isothermie f
isotomeograph — Isotomeograph m
isotone — Isoton n
isotone — s. a. isotonic
isotone abundance — Isotonenhäufigkeit f

isotonic, isotone, monotonically (monotone) increasing <math.> — [monoton] wachsend, nicht abnehmend, isoton <Math.>
isotonic coefficient — isotonischer Koeffizient m

isotonicity <bio.> — Isotonie f <Bio.>
isotonic solution, is[o]osmotic solution — isotonische (isosmotische) Lösung f
isotonism, isotony — Isotonie f <Kern.>
isotope — Isotop n
isotope — s. a. nuclide
isotope analysis, isotopic analysis (assay) — Isotopenanalyse f
isotope balance — Isotopenbilanz f
isotope chart, isotope table, chart of nuclides — Isotopentafel f, Isotopentabelle f, Nuklidtabelle f, Nuklidtafel f, Nukliddiagramm n

isotope content, content of isotope — Isotopengehalt m
isotope dating, isotopic dating — Altersbestimmung f mittels Isotopen, Datierung f mit Hilfe von Isotopen
isotope dilution analysis, isotopic dilution analysis — Isotopenverdünnungsanalyse f
isotope dilution method, isotopic dilution method — Isotopenverdünnungsmethode f
isotope dosimetry — Isotopendosimetrie f
isotope effect, isotopic effect — Isotopieeffekt m, Isotopeneffekt m
isotope emitting low-energy radiation — s. soft radiator
isotope-enriched, isotopically enriched — isotopenangereichert

isotope exchange, isotopic exchange — Isotopenaustausch m
isotope-excited X-ray fluorescence analysis — s. a. d ioisotope-excited X-ray fluorescence analysis
isotope filter — Isotopenfilter n
isotope fractionation — Isotopenfraktionierung f

isotope incoherence — isotopische Inkohärenz f
isotope incoherent scattering — isotopisch-inkohärente Streuung f, isotopische Streuung

isotope mass effect — s. mass effect
isotope method — s. tracer method
isotope mixture — s. isotopic mixture
isotope powered thermoelectric generator — s. thermoelectric battery
isotope-producing reactor — Isotopenproduktionsreaktor m, Produktionsreaktor m zur Isotopenherstellung, Reaktor m zur Isotopenproduktion

isotope production	s. radioisotope production	isotopic spin	s. isobaric spin
isotope retention	Isotopenretention f	isotopic splitting	isotope Aufspaltung f, Isotopieaufspaltung f
isotope rule, Aston rule, Aston isotope rule	Astonsche Isotopenregel f, Isotopenregel [von Aston]	isotopic substitution	s. isotopic replacement
isotope separation, separation of isotopes, separation ⟨of isotopes⟩	Isotopentrennung f, Trennung f ⟨Isotope⟩	isotopic system	isotopes System n
isotope separation cascade	s. gaseous diffusion cascade	isotopic tagging	s. labelling [with isotope] ⟨nucl.⟩
isotope separation factor	s. separation factor	isotopic tracer, tracer isotope, isotope tracer, isotopic indicator, isotopic marker, marker	Tracerisotop n, Leitisotop n, Indikatorisotop n, isotoper Indikator m, Markierungsisotop n
isotope separation plant	Isotopentrennanlage f		
isotope separator	s. electromagnetic mass separator		
isotope shift, isotopic shift	Isotopieverschiebung f, Isotopieverschiebungseffekt m, Isotopenverschiebung f, isotope Verschiebung f	isotopic variable	s. isobaric spin
		isotopic variable	s. isobaric spin quantum number
		isotopic volume effect	s. volume effect
		isotopic weight	s. atomic mass
isotope specific activity ⟨per gramme⟩	spezifische Aktivität f des Isotops ⟨pro Gramm⟩	isotopism ⟨nucl.⟩; isotopy ⟨math.⟩	Isotopie f
isotope structure	Isotopiestruktur f, Isotopiehyperfeinstruktur f	isotrimorphism, triple isomorphism	Isotrimorphie f, Isotrimorphismus m
isotope table	s. isotope chart	isotriplet	s. isotopic spin triplet
isotope tracer	s. isotopic tracer	isotron	Isotron n
isotope transport	Isotopentransport m	isotropic antenna	s. spherical antenna
isotope volume effect	s. volume effect	isotropic band	s. I band
isotope weight	s. atomic mass	isotropic chamber, isotropic spark chamber, track delineating chamber	isotrope Funkenkammer f
isotopic abundance	s. abundance of isotopes		
isotopically enriched, isotope-enriched	isotopenangereichert		
		isotropic conductivity	isotrope Leitfähigkeit f
		isotropic curve, minimal curve	isotrope Kurve f, Minimalkurve f, Kurve der Länge Null
isotopically labelled	s. labelled		
isotopically labelled compound	s. tracer compound		
isotopically replaced (substituted), replaced (substituted) by an isotope	isotopensubstituiert	isotropic elasticity	isotrope Elastizität f
		isotropic plane	[einfach] isotrope Ebene f, Minimalebene f
		isotropic point	isotroper Punkt m
		isotropic radiator	s. spherical radiator
isotopically tagged	s. labelled	isotropic spark chamber, isotropic chamber, track delineating chamber	isotrope Funkenkammer f
isotopic analysis (assay), isotope analysis	Isotopenanalyse f		
isotopic carrier	isotoper Träger m		
		isotropic turbulence, homogeneous isotropic turbulence	isotrope Turbulenz f
isotopic composition	isotope Zusammensetzung f, Isotopenzusammensetzung f		
		isotropic vector	isotroper Vektor m, lichtartiger Vektor
isotopic dating, isotope dating	Altersbestimmung f mittels Isotopen, Datierung f mit Hilfe von Isotopen	isotropism, isotropy	Isotropie f
		isotropy criterion	Isotropiekriterium n
isotopic dilution analysis	s. isotope dilution analysis	isotropy group, group of isotropy	Isotropiegruppe f
isotopic dilution method, isotope dilution method	Isotopenverdünnungsmethode f	isotypic ⟨cryst.⟩	isotyp
isotopic effect	s. isotope effect	isotypism, isotypy	Isotypie f
isotopic exchange, isotope exchange	Isotopenaustausch m	isovector	Isovektor m
		isovector cloud	Isovektorwolke f
isotopic exchange equilibrium, equilibrium of isotope exchange	Isotopenaustauschgleichgewicht n	isovector resonance	Isovektorresonanz f, isovektorielle Resonanz f
		isovel	s. isotach
		isovolume specific heat	s. specific heat at constant volume
isotopic exchange rate, isotopic rate of exchange	Isotopenaustauschgeschwindigkeit f		
		isovolumic line	s. isometric line
isotopic exchange reaction, atom-transfer reaction	Isotopenaustauschreaktion f	isovolumic specific heat	s. specific heat at constant volume
		issue	s. discharge ⟨of liquid⟩
isotopic generator, radioisotope generator, milking system (battery), cow	Isotopengenerator m, Generatorsäule f, Melksystem n	isthmus method, Ewing method	Isthmusmethode f, Isthmusverfahren n, Ewingsche Methode f
		ITAE criterium	= integral of time-multiplied absolute value of error criterion
isotopic indicator	s. isotopic tracer		
isotopic invariance	Isotopieinvarianz f, isotopische Invarianz f	item	Informationseinheit f, Einzelnachricht f
isotopic labelling	s. labelling [with isotope] ⟨nucl.⟩	iterated ⟨of function⟩, iterated function	Iterierte f ⟨Funktion⟩
isotopic marker	s. isotopic tracer	iterated fission	Mehrfachspaltung f, Vielfachspaltung f
isotopic mass effect	s. mass effect		
isotopic mixture, isotope mixture	Isotopengemisch n	iterated fission expectation, iterated fission probability	asymptotische Spalterwartung f, iterierte Spalterwartung f
isotopic multiplet	Isotopenmultiplett n, isotopes Multiplett n		
isotopic number	s. neutron excess		
isotopic parity	Isotopenparität f		
isotopic pleiade, pleiade of isotopes	Plejade f, Isotopenplejade f		
isotopic power generator	s. atomic battery	iterated function, iterated ⟨of function⟩	Iterierte f ⟨Funktion⟩
isotopic rate of exchange	s. isotopic exchange rate	iterated integral, multiple integral; multiple iterated integral	mehrfaches Integral n, Mehrfachintegral n, Vielfachintegral n; iteriertes Integral
isotopic ratio	s. relative isotopic abundance		
isotopic replacement, isotopic substitution	Isotopensubstitution f, isotope Substitution f		
isotopic shift	s. isotope shift	iterated kernel	iterierter Kern m

iterated limit	sukzessiver Grenzübergang m
iterated logarithm	iterierter Logarithmus m
iterated network	s. ladder network
iterated series	iterierte Reihe f
iterating, iteration	s. successive approximation
iteration method	s. iterative method
iteration step, step of iteration	Iterationsschritt m
iterative attenuation [constant]	Kettendämpfung f, Kettendämpfungsfaktor m
iterative current ratio	Kettenstromübersetzung f
iterative determinant, chain determinant, determinant of ladder network	Kettendeterminante f
iterative impedance	Ketten[dämpfungs]widerstand m, Kettenimpedanz f
iterative matrix, chain matrix, matrix of ladder network	Kettenmatrix f, Strom-Spannungs-Kettenmatrix f
iterative method, iteration method, method of successive approximations, Picard['s] method	Iterationsverfahren n, Iterationsmethode f, iteratives Verfahren n, Methode der Iteration[en], Methode (Verfahren) der sukzessiven Approximation[en]; Methode der kontraktiven Abbildung, Prinzip n der kontrahierenden Abbildung
iterative phase constant, iterative phase factor	Kettenwinkelmaß n, Kettenphasenfaktor m
iterative propagation constant	Kettenübertragungsmaß n
iterative structure	s. ladder network
iterative voltage ratio	Kettenspannungsübersetzung f
itinerary	Routenaufnahme f, Itinerar n
i-type semiconductor	s. intrinsic semiconductor
I-variometer, inclination variometer, dip variometer	Inklinationsvariometer n, I-Variometer n
i-V characteristic	s. current-voltage characteristic
ixodynamics	Ixodynamie f
Izod impact bend test, Izod impact test, Izod test	Izod-Kerbschlag[biege]versuch m, Izod-Versuch m, Kerbschlag[biege]versuch m nach Izod, Schlagversuch m nach Izod
Izod specimen	Izod-Probe f, Izod-Kerbschlag[biege]probe f, Kerbschlag[biege]probe f nach Izod
Izod test	s. Izod impact test

J

jack, latch <el.>	Klinke f <El.>
jacket, sheath <techn.>	Mantel m <Techn.>
jacket of the calorimeter, calorimeter jacket	Kalorimeterisolierung f, Isolierung f des Kalorimeters
jacketing, canning, cladding <fuel elements>	Umhüllung f, Einhülsung f, Einhüllung f, Kapselung f <Brennelemente>
Jacobian, functional determinant	Funktionaldeterminante f, Jacobische Determinante f
Jacobian action	Jacobische Wirkung f
Jacobian amplitude, am <math.>	Amplitude f, am <Math.>
Jacobian ellipsoid, Jacobi ellipsoid, Jacobi's figure of equilibrium	Jacobisches Ellipsoid n, Jacobi-Ellipsoid n
Jacobian [elliptic] function, Jacobi['s] elliptic function	Jacobische [elliptische] Funktion f
Jacobian matrix	s. functional matrix
Jacobi['s] bracket	Jacobische Klammer f, Jacobischer Klammerausdruck m
Jacobi['s] canonical co-ordinate	s. Jacobi['s] co-ordinate
Jacobi['s] complete integral	s. complete integral
Jacobi['s] condition	Jacobische Bedingung f
Jacobi['s] constant	Jacobische Konstante f
Jacobi['s] co-ordinate, Jacobi['s] canonical co-ordinate	Jacobische Koordinate f, Jacobische kanonische Koordinate
Jacobi ellipsoid, Jacobian ellipsoid, Jacobi's figure of equilibrium	Jacobisches Ellipsoid n, Jacobi-Ellipsoid n
Jacobi['s] elliptic function	s. Jacobian [elliptic] function
Jacobi['s] equation	Jacobische Gleichung f; Jacobische Differentialgleichung f
Jacobi['s] figure of equilibrium, Jacobi[an] ellipsoid	Jacobisches Ellipsoid n, Jacobi-Ellipsoid n
Jacobi['s] identity, Jacobi['s] relation	Jacobische Identität f
Jacobi['s] multiplicator, multiplicator of Jacobi	Jacobischer Multiplikator m
Jacobi['s] polynomial	Jacobisches Polynom n
Jacobi['s] principle [of least action]	Jacobisches Prinzip n [der kleinsten Wirkung], Jacobi-Prinzip n
Jacobi['s] relation, Jacobi['s] identity	Jacobische Identität f
Jacobi['s] theorem	Jacobischer Satz m, Satz von Jacobi <über geodätische Linien>; Jacobisches Theorem n <Methode der kleinsten Quadrate>; Jacobischer Knotensatz m, Satz von der Elimination der Knoten, Jacobisches Theorem <Dreikörperproblem>
Jacobi['s] theta function, theta function, ϑ function <of the first, second, third, fourth kind>	Jacobische (elliptische) Theta-Funktion f, Theta-Funktion [von Jacobi], ϑ-Funktion f <erster, zweiter, dritter, vierter Art>
Jacobi['s] zeta function, zeta function of Jacobi, zn	Zeta-Funktion f von Jacobi, Jacobische Zeta-Funktion f, zn
Jahn-Teller effect	Jahn-Teller-Effekt m
Jahn-Teller rule, Jahn-Teller theorem	Jahn-Teller-Theorem n, Theorem n von Jahn-Teller, Satz m von Jahn-Teller, Jahn-Tellersche Regel f
Jamin compensator, Babinet compensator	Babinet-Kompensator m, Babinetscher Kompensator m
Jamin effect	Jamin-Effekt m
Jamin interferometer, Jamin refractometer	Jamin-Interferometer n, Jamins[ches] Interferometer n, Jaminscher Interferenzrefraktor m, Interferenzrefraktometer n
jamming	s. parasitics <el.>
jamming alpha-particles together, [triple-]alpha process, Salpeter process	Heliumreaktion f, Salpeter-Prozeß m, Alpha-Prozeß m
jamming modulation	s. noise modulation
Janka hardness [number]	Janka-Härte f

Janossy density	Janossy-Dichte *f*	jet pressure	Strahldruck *m*
Jansen circuit	Jansen-Schaltung *f*	jet propulsion	s. reaction propulsion
Janski noise	= cosmic noise	jet pump; gas jet pump	Strahlpumpe *f*; Treibmittelpumpe *f*; Gasstrahlpumpe *f*
Janzen-Rayleigh iteration, Janzen-Rayleigh method	Janzen-Rayleigh-Methode *f*, Janzen-Rayleighsche Iteration[smethode] *f*	jet re[-]attachment, re[-]attachment of the jet	Wiederanlegen *n* des Strahles
Japan twin	Japaner Zwilling *m*		
jar; bottle; flask	Flasche *f*, Fläschchen *n*	jet separation	Strahlablösung *f*, Ablösung *f* des Strahles
Jaumann differential bridge, differential bridge [of Jaumann], Q bridge	Jaumann-Brücke *f*, Differentialmeßbrücke *f* nach Jaumann	jet stream [in the atmosphere]; jet stream current <geo.>	Strahlströmung *f*, Strahlstrom *m*, „jet stream" *m* [in der Atmosphäre] <Geo.>
Jaumann filter, differential filter	Differentialfilter *n*, Tangensfilter *n*, Jaumann-Filter *n*	jettison[ing]	Abwerfen *n*, Abwurf *m*, Ablösung *f*, Abtrennung *f*
Javan laser	Javan-Laser *m*	jet velocity, efflux velocity, exit velocity <of gas>	Strahlaustrittsgeschwindigkeit *f*, Ausström[ungs]geschwindigkeit *f* <Gas>
J band <53—82 Gc/s>	J-Band *n* <53 ⋯ 82 GHz>		
Jeans['] equation of viscosity, Jeans['] viscosity equation	Jeanssche Viskositätsgleichung *f*, Viskositätsgleichung von Jeans	jet water, sprayed water, water jets	Spritzwasser *n*
Jeans' hypothesis of close approach	s. encounter hypothesis <astr.>	jigger, jigger transformer	Jigger *m*
Jeans['] [radiation] law	s. Rayleigh-Jeans['] law	jigger coupling	s. inductive coupling
Jeans['] viscosity equation, Jeans['] equation of viscosity	Jeanssche Viskositätsgleichung *f*, Viskositätsgleichung von Ieans	jigger transformer	s. jigger
		j-j coupling, (j-j) coupling	jj-Kopplung *f*, j-j-Kopplung *f*
Jeffery flow	Jefferysche Strömung *f*	j-j coupling shell model	s. one-body model of nucleus
Jeffreys body, elastic sol, Lethersich body, relaxing gel	elastisches Sol *n*, Lethersichscher (Jeffreysscher) Körper *m*, relaxierendes Gel *n*	j-L coupling, Racah coupling	Racah-Kopplung *f*, jL-Kopplung *f*
		jockey weight	s. rider
jelatinous	s. gelatinous	Joffé effect	Joffé-Effekt *m*
jell	s. jelly	jog, dislocation jog	Versetzungssprung *m*, Sprung *m* <Versetzungstheorie>
Jellet, Jellet halfshade, Jellet prism	Prisma *n* von Jellet, Prisma von Jelliet		
Jellet-Cornu [prism]	s. Jellet-Cornu halfshade	jog formation, kink formation	Sprungbildung *f*
Jellet-Cornu halfshade; Jellet-Cornu prism; Jellet-Cornu	Halbschattenapparat *m* nach Jellet und Cornu, Jellet-Cornuscher Halbschattenpolarisator *m*; Jellet-Cornu-Prisma *n*, Jellet-Cornusches Prisma *n*	jog line <cryst.>	Sprunglinie *f* <Krist.>
		jog pair formation, kink pair formation	Sprungpaarbildung *f*
		Johansson gauge, slip gauge, block gauge, parallel gauge	Parallelendmaß *n*
Jellet halfshade, Jellet prism, Jellet	Prisma *n* von Jellet, Prisma von Jelliet	Johnson and Lark-Horowitz formula	Formel *f* von Johnson und Lark-Horowitz
jelling	s. gelation	Johnson effect	Johnson-Effekt *m*, thermisches Widerstandsrauschen *n*
jellium	Jellium *n*		
jelly, lyogel, jell	Lyogel *n*, Gallerte *f*		
jelly	s. a. gel	Johnson noise, thermal noise, thermal agitation noise	thermisches Rauschen *n*, Wärmerauschen *n*, Wärmegeräusch *n*
jelly[-]like	s. gelatinous		
jerk; jolt, sudden push; tug	Ruck *m* <Ableitung der Beschleunigung>		
		Johnson power meter, differential wattmeter	Differentialleistungsmesser *m*, Differentialwattmeter *n*, Differenzleistungsmesser *m*, Differenzwattmeter *n*
jerky, intermittent	ruckartig		
jerky flow, jerky motion <hydr.>	ruckartige Strömung *f*, ruckartige Bewegung *f* <Hydr.>		
		Johnson-Rahbek effect	Johnson-Rahbek-Effekt *m*
jet; vein; stream <aero., hydr.>	Strahl *m* <Aero., Hydr.>	joint, weld	Klebstelle *f*
jet	s. a. cosmic-ray jet	joint, joint connection <of system of bars>; node <of frame>; panel point <of truss>	Knoten *m*, Knotenpunkt *m*, Knotenverbindung *f* <Fachwerk>
jet	s. a. jet nozzle		
jet boundary <aero., hydr.>	Strahlgrenze *f* <Aero., Hydr.>		
jet deflector <hydr.>	Strahlablenker *m* <Hydr.>	joint	s. a. waveguide joint
jet diffuser <hydr.>	Strahlzerstreuer *m*, Zerstreuer *m* <Hydr.>	joint	s. a. union <of sets>
		joint connection	s. joint
jet flame	s. shooting flame	joint cumulative distribution function	s. joint distribution
jet flow, free jet, open jet; stream[ ]flow	freier Strahl *m*, Freistrahl *m*, Strahlströmung *f*, Strahlausfluß *m*		
		joint distribution, multivariate distribution, [multivariate] distribution function, joint-probability distribution [function], joint [cumulative] distribution function	mehrdimensionale Verteilung (Wahrscheinlichkeitsverteilung) *f*, gemeinsame (mehrdimensionale) Verteilungsfunktion *f*, Ver[bindungsver]teilungsfunktion *f*, multivariable Verteilung (Verteilungsfunktion)
jet formation	Strahlbildung *f*, Strahlausbildung *f*		
jet impingement attack (corrosion)	s. rain erosion		
jet in the emulsion, cosmic-ray jet, jet	Jet *m* [der kosmischen Strahlung] <in der Emulsion>		
jet mill, fluid energy mill, micronizer	„jet"-Mühle *f*, Strahlmühle *f*, Düsenmühle *f*		
jet model	„jet"-Modell *n*, Jetmodell *n*	joint distribution density	gemeinsame (mehrdimensionale) Verteilungsdichte *f*
jet nozzle, propelling nozzle, nozzle, jet	Schubdüse *f*, Strahldüse *f*, Düse *f*		
		joint distribution function	s. joint distribution
jet of flame	s. shooting flame	jointing-rule, straight-edge rule	Richtlatte *f*; Richtscheit *n*
jet of the comet, expanding jet [of the comet]	Schweifstrahl *m*, fadenförmiger Schweifstrahl		
		joint moment	s. product moment
		joint of waveguide	s. waveguide joint

joint-probability distribution [function]	s. joint distribution
joliot-curium, jolium	s. nobelium
Jolly['s] balance	Jollysche Federwaage f
jolt	s. jerk
Joly block photometer (screen), wax block [photometer]	Joly-Photometer n, Jolysches Photometer n
Jominy end-cooled test, Jominy['s] end-quench test, end-quench test, end-cooled test	Stirnabschreckversuch m, Jominy-Probe f, Jominy-Versuch m, Jominyscher Stirnabschreckversuch m
Jones hardness [number]	Jones-Härte f
Jones zone	Jones-Zone f
Jong-Bouman camera / de	[De-]Jong-Bouman-Kammer f, Röntgengoniometer n nach de Jong und Bouman
Jordan algebra	Jordan-Algebra f
Jordan-Brouwer theorem	Jordan-Brouwerscher Satz m
Jordan curve, simple curve	Jordan-Kurve f, Jordansche Kurve f, Jordan-Bogen m, einfacher Kurvenbogen m, Bogen m
Jordan-Hölder[-Schreier-Zassenhaus] theorem	Satz m von Jordan-Hölder
Jordanian canonical form	s. classical canonical form
Jordan lag, fluctuation after-effect, fluctuation magnetic after-effect	thermische Nachwirkung f, Fluktuationsnachwirkung f, Jordan-Nachwirkung f, Jordansche Nachwirkung, irreversible Nachwirkung
Jordan['s] law, Jordan['s] theorem	Jordanscher Hilfssatz (Satz) m, Satz (Lemma n) von Jordan
Jordan matrix	Jordan-Matrix f
Jordan normal form	s. classical canonical form
Jordan sunshine recorder	Jordan-Sonnenschreiber m, Sonnenscheinautograph m nach Jordan
Jordan['s] theorem	Jordanscher Kurvensatz m
Jordan['s] theorem, Jordan['s] law	Jordanscher Hilfssatz (Satz) m, Satz (Lemma n) von Jordan
Jordan-Wigner commutation rule	Jordan-Wignersche Vertauschungsrelation f
Jordan-Wigner matrix	Jordan-Wignersche Matrix f
Josephson contact, Josephson junction, tunnel contact	Josephson-Kontakt m, Tunnelkontakt m
Josephson effect	Josephson-Effekt m
Josephson junction	s. Josephson contact
Joshi effect	Joshi-Effekt m
Jost function	Jost-Funktion f
Jost point	Jost-Punkt m
Joubert['s] disk	Joubertsche Scheibe f
Jouguet['s] theorem	Jouguetscher Satz m
Joukowski airfoil	s. Joukowski profile
Joukowski condition	s. Kutta-Joukowski condition
Joukowski formula	Joukowskische Formel f
Joukowski function	Joukowskische Funktion f
Joukowski['s] hypothesis	s. Kutta-Joukowski condition
Joukowski profile, Joukowski airfoil	Joukowski-Profil n, Joukowskisches Flügelprofil n
Joukowski['s] rule	Joukowskische Regel f
Joukowski theorem	Joukowskischer Satz m
Joukowski transformation	Joukowski-Abbildung f
joule, joule absolute, newton meter, watt[-]second, absolute joule, J, N m, Ws	Joule n, Newtonmeter n, Wattsekunde f, absolutes Joule, Joule absolut, Großerg n, J, N m, W s
Joulean heat	s. Joule heat
Joule-Clausius velocity	Joule-Clausiussche Geschwindigkeit f, Joule-Clausius-Geschwindigkeit f
Joule coefficient	Joule-Koeffizient m, Joulescher Koeffizient
Joule current heat	s. Joule heat
Joule cycle, constant pressure cycle, Joule-Thomson process, Brayton cycle	Joulescher Kreisprozeß m, Joule-Prozeß m
Joule effect	Joule-Effekt m
Joule effect, Joule-Thomson effect, Joule-Kelvin effect	Joule-Thomson-Effekt m, Thomson-Joule-Effekt m, [isenthalpischer] Drosseleffekt m
Joule effect	s. a. Joule heat
Joule effect <of magnetostriction>	s. Joule magnetostriction effect
Joule effect loss in the winding	Wicklungsverlust m
Joule expansion	Joulesche Ausdehnung f
Joule['s] experiment	Joulescher Versuch m, Versuch von Joule
Joule heat, Joulean heat, Joule effect, [Joule] current heat	Joulesche Wärme f, [Joulesche] Stromwärme f
Joule heating	s. ohmic heating <of plasma>
Joule-Kelvin effect	s. Joule-Thomson effect
Joule-Kelvin throttling experiment, Joule-Thomson experiment, throttling experiment [of Joule and Kelvin]	Joule-Thomson-Versuch m, Joule-Thomsonscher Drosselversuch (Überleitungsversuch) m, Drosselversuch von Joule-Thomson
Joule law <therm.>	Joulesches Gesetz n <Therm.>
Joule['s] law [of electric heating] <el.>	Joule[-Lenz]sches Gesetz n <El.>
Joule magnetostriction effect, Joule effect [of magnetostriction]	Effekt m (Erscheinung f) der Magnetostriktion, Magnetostriktionseffekt m, magnetostriktive Erscheinung f, [magnetoelastischer] Joule-Effekt m, magnetoelastischer Effekt von Joule
Joule-Thomson coefficient	Joule-Thomson-Koeffizient m
Joule-Thomson effect, Joule[-Kelvin] effect	Joule-Thomson-Effekt m, Thomson-Joule-Effekt m, [isenthalpischer] Drosseleffekt m
Joule-Thomson expansion	s. throttling
Joule-Thomson experiment	s. Joule-Kelvin throttling experiment
Joule-Thomson inversion temperature	s. inversion temperature
Joule-Thomson process, Joule cycle, constant pressure cycle, Brayton cycle	Joulescher Kreisprozeß m, Joule-Prozeß m
Jourdain['s] principle	Jourdain-Prinzip n, Jourdainsches Prinzip n
journal [bearing] friction	Zapfenreibung f
journal support, pivot support	Zapfenlagerung f
journey of air masses, transfer of air masses	Luftmassentransport m, Luftmassenverfrachtung f, Luftmassenversetzung f
Jovian planet	s. major planet
Jovignot test	Jovignot-Versuch m, Jovignot-Prüfung f, Jovignot-Probe f
J ray, S ray in the inner core	J-Welle f, S-Welle f im inneren Kern
judgment of distance	s. appreciation of distance
Julian calendar	julianischer Kalender m
Julian century	julianisches Jahrhundert n
Julian date	Julianisches Datum n
Julian year	Julianisches Jahr n
Julius wave machine	Juliussche Wellenmaschine f
jump, jump discontinuity, ordinary discontinuity, discontinuity of the first kind <math.>	Unstetigkeit f erster Art, Sprung m <Math.>
jump, branch, transfer [of control]; jump order, jump instruction, "go to" statement, transfer command <num. math.>	Sprung m; Sprungbefehl m, Sprunganweisung f <num. Math.>
jump, transition, jumping <qu.>	Übergang m, Sprung m <Qu.>

jump	s. a. discontinuity	junction transistor, junction-type triode, semiconductor junction transistor	Flächentransistor m, Halbleiterflächentransistor m, Schicht[kristall]transistor m
jump characteristic	s. transient response		
jump condition; discontinuity condition	Unstetigkeitsbedingung f; Sprungbedingung f		
jump discontinuity	s. jump <math.>	junction transition region, interface, junction (transition) region <semi.>	Übergangszone f, Übergangsgebiet n, Übergangsbereich m <Halb.>
jump distance, average distance from interstice to interstice, width of the potential barrier <of ions in glass>	Sprungdistanz f <von Ionen im Glas>		
		junction-type triode	s. junction transistor
		junction width	s. barrier width
jump frequency, transition frequency	Sprungfrequenz f	June solstice, summer solstice	Sommersolstitium n, Sommersonnenwende f
jump front	Sprungfront f	Junkers['] calorimeter, Junkers-type gas calorimeter, water-flow calorimeter	Kalorimeter n mit Wasserdurchfluß, Junkerssches Kalorimeter
jump function, step function	Sprungfunktion f, Schrittfunktion f		
jumping	s. jump <qu.>		
jumping up, upsetting	Stauchung f; Anstauchung f		
		Jurin['s] law, Jurin rule	Jurinsches Gesetz n
jump instruction	s. jump <num. math.>	just noticeable difference	s. difference threshold
jump-like; stepped, step-like; discontinuous; unsteady; sudden	sprunghaft; diskontinuierlich	juvenile water	juveniles Wasser n, Juvenilwasser n
		juxtaposed spectra	nebeneinandergestellte Spektren npl
jump method	Sprungstellenverfahren n		
jump moment	Sprungmoment n	juxtaposition	Juxtaposition f, Anlagerung f, Aneinanderlagerung f, Nebeneinanderlagerung f
jump order	s. jump <num. math.>		
jump quantity	Sprunggröße f		
jump relation, relation for the jumps	Sprungrelation f		
		juxtaposition	s. a. contiguity <gen.>
		juxtaposition metamorphism, contact metamorphism	Kontaktmetamorphose f
junction <of thermocouple>	Lötstelle f, Verbindungsstelle f <Thermoelement>		
junction, junction point, hybrid <of waveguides>	Verzweigung[sstelle] f, Verzweigungspunkt m <Wellenleiter>	juxtaposition twin, contact twin	Berührungszwilling m, Kontaktzwilling m, Juxtapositionszwilling m
junction, semiconductor junction <semi.>	Flächenübergang m, Übergang m, Halbleiterübergang m, Übergangsschicht f, Schicht f, „junction" f <Halb.>		

K

junction	s. a. driving point	K-absorption limit, K edge	K-Absorptionskante f
junction	s. a. solder <semi.>	Kaiser effect	Kaiser-Effekt m
junction	s. a. waveguide joint	kaleidophon[e]	Tonschwingungsspiegel m, Kaleidophon n, Wheatstonesches (phonisches) Kaleidoskop n, Lissajous-Apparat m
junction area	Sperrschichtfläche f; Fläche f des Übergangs		
junction capacitance	s. barrier-layer capacitance		
junction cell	s. photovoltaic cell	kaleidoscope prism	Vierfachprisma n
junction depletion layer	Übergangssperrschicht f	kaltlufttropfen, cold pool	Kaltlufttropfen m
junction diode, p-n junction diode, semi-conductor junction diode	Halbleiterflächendiode f, Flächendiode f, pn-Diode f, Schichtdiode f, pn-Flächendiode f	Kaluza-Klein-Fock theory, Kaluza-Klein theory	Kaluza-Kleinsche einheitliche Feldtheorie f, Kaluza-Klein[-Fock]sche Theorie f, einheitliche Feldtheorie von Kaluza und Klein
junction field effect transistor	s. junction-gate field-effect transistor		
junction-gate field-effect transistor, junction field effect transistor, bulk junction[-gate] field effect transistor, IFET; depletion-mode insulated-gate field effect transistor	Shockley-Feldeffekttransistor m, Sperrschicht-Feldeffekttransistor m, IFET, „junction-gate"-Feldeffekttransistor m	Kaluza['s] theory [of electricity]	Kaluzasche Theorie f
		Kamerlingh-Onnes['] equation of state	Kamerlingh-Onnessche Zustandsgleichung f, Zustandsgleichung von Kamerlingh-Onnes
		kampometer	s. field of sight meter
		Kant['s] and Laplace['s] cosmogenies, Kant-Laplace['s] hypothesis	Kant-Laplacesche Theorie f
junction loss	Verbindungsverlust m	kaon	s. K-meson
		Kapitza balance	Kapitza-Waage f, Kapitzasche Waage f
junction luminescence	Übergangslumineszenz f	Kapitza['s] cycle	Kapitza-Prozeß m, Kapitzascher Prozeß (Kreisprozeß) m
junction photocell	s. photovoltaic cell		
junction point	Kontaktspitze f		
junction point, junction, hybrid <of waveguides>	Verzweigung[sstelle] f, Verzweigungspunkt m <Wellenleiter>	Kapitza['s] experiments	Kapitzasche Versuche mpl, Experimente npl von Kapitza
		Kapitza['s] law	Kapitzasches Gesetz n, Gesetz von Kapitza
junction potential <semi.>	Übergangspotential n <Halb.>	Kapitza liquefier	Verflüssiger m nach Kapitza, Kapitzascher Verflüssiger
junction potential	s. a. diffusion potential		
junction rectifier	s. barrier-layer rectifier <semi.>	Kapitza resistance	s. Kapitza thermal resistance
junction region, interface, [junction] transition region <semi.>	Übergangszone f, Übergangsgebiet n, Übergangsbereich m <Halb.>	Kapitza temperature jump	Kapitzascher Temperatursprung m
		Kapitza thermal resistance, Kapitza resistance, thermal boundary resistance	Kapitzascher Wärmewiderstand m
junction resistance	s. barrier-layer resistance		
junction temperature	Temperatur f der Lötstelle, Lötstellentemperatur f, Verbindungsstellentemperatur f		
		Kaplan['s] airfoil	Kaplanscher Tragflügel m, Kaplan-Flügel m
junction temperature	s. a. barrier layer temperature	Kaplan turbine	Kaplan-Turbine f
junction tetrode	Transistorflächentetrode f, Flächentetrode f	kappa flow	s. quasiviscous creep
		Kapp['s] diagram, Kapp['s] plot (line)	Kappsches Diagramm n, Kapp-Diagramm n
junction thickness	s. barrier width		

Kapp['s] law	Kappsches Gesetz n
Kapp['s] line (plot), Kapp['s] diagram	Kappsches Diagramm n, Kapp-Diagramm n
Kapp['s] triangle	Kappsches Dreieck n
Kapteyn['s] integral, Kapteyn['s] trigonometric integral	Kapteyns trigonometrisches Integral n
Kapteyn['s] schedule, Kapteyn['s] scheme	Kapteynsches Schema n
Kapteyn['s] selected area, selected area	Kapteynsches Eichfeld n, Eichfeld, „selected area" n, ausgewähltes Feld n
Kapteyn['s] series	Kapteynsche Reihe f
Kapteyn['s] trigonometric integral, Kapteyn['s] integral	Kapteyns trigonometrisches Integral n
Kapteyn['s] universe	Kapteynsches Weltmodell (Universum) n
karat	s. metric carat
Kármán boundary-layer theorem, momentum theorem of boundary layer theory, momentum integral equation	Kármánsche Integralbedingung f, Impulssatz m (Impulsintegralgleichung f) der Grenzschichttheorie
Kármán['s] constant, Kármán['s] factor	s. Kármán['s] universal constant
Kármán flow	Kármánsche Strömung f
Kármán['s] formula	Kármánsche Formel f
Kármán['s] function	Kármánsche Funktion f
Kármán-Howarth equation	Kármán-Howarthsche Gleichung f
Kármán momentum integral equation, Kármán-Pohlhausen method	Kármán-Pohlhausensche Methode (Näherungsmethode) f, Kármánsches Näherungsverfahren n
Kármán No. [/ von], Kármán number [/ von]	s. Kármán's universal constant
Kármán-Pohlhausen method, Kármán momentum integral equation	Kármán-Pohlhausensche Methode (Näherungsmethode) f, Kármánsches Näherungsverfahren n
Kármán rule	Kármánsche Regel f
Kármán['s] similarity theory	Kármánsche Ähnlichkeitstheorie f
Kármán['s] street	s. Kármán['s] vortex street
Kármán['s] theory of rolling [/ von]	[von] Kármánsche Walztheorie f, Walztheorie von Kármán
Kármán-Trefftz profile	Kármán-Trefftz-Profil n
Kármán-Tsien compressibility correction formula, Kármán-Tsien compressibility rule, Kármán-Tsien relation	Kármán-Tsiensche Kompressibilitätsregel f
Kármán-Tsien fluid, idealized fluid of Kármán and Tsien	Kármán-Tsiensche Flüssigkeit f, Kármán-Tsien-Flüssigkeit f, idealisierte Flüssigkeit von Kármán und Tsien
Kármán-Tsien method	Kármán-Tsiensche Methode f
Kármán-Tsien relation	s. Kármán-Tsien compressibility correction formula
Kármán-Tsien transonic similarity number	transsonische Ähnlichkeitszahl f, Ähnlichkeitszahl für schallnahe Strömungen
Kármán['s] universal constant, Kármán['s] constant (factor), [von] Kármán number, [von] Kármán No., k, Ka	Kármán-Zahl f, Von-Kármán-Zahl f, Kármánsche Konstante f, Kármánsche Kennzahl f, Ka
Kármán['s] vortex path, Kármán['s] vortex street, Kármán['s] vortices, Kármán['s] street, vortex street	Kármánsche Wirbelstraße f, Kármán-Wirbel mpl
K-Ar method	s. argon method
Karolus cell	Karolus-Zelle f, Lichtsteuerzelle f [von Karolus]
Karolus['] method	Intensitätsverfahren n nach Karolus, Karolussches Intensitätsverfahren
Karolus-Mittelstaed method	Karolus-Mittelstaedsche Methode f, Methode von Karolus und Mittelstaed
karyokinesis	s. mitosis
karyoklasis <bio.>	Karyoklasie f, Fragmentation f <Bio.>
Kasper polyhedron	Kasper-Polyeder n
katabatic wind, downward wind	katabatischer Wind m, Abwind m; Fallwind m
katabolism	s. catabolism
kata factor, katathermometer factor	Gerätekonstante f des Katathermometers, Katawert m, Katathermometerfaktor m
katafront	s. catafront
katamorphism	Katamorphose f
katathermometer, Kata-thermometer, catathermometer	Katathermometer n [nach Hill]
katathermometer factor, kata factor	Gerätekonstante f des Katathermometers, Katawert m, Katathermometerfaktor m
Kater pendulum	Katersches Pendel n
katharometer	s. catharometer
katharometric cell, catharometric cell	Wärmeleitfähigkeitsmeßzelle f
katharometry, catharometry, catarometry	Katharometrie f, Katarometrie f, Wärmeleitfähigkeitsmessung f
katisallobar, catisallobar	Katisallobare f
K Auger electron	K-Auger-Elektron n
Kautsky effect	Kautsky-Effekt m
kayser, K	Kayser n, K
K band <18,0—26 or 11—33 Gc/s>	K-Band n <18,0···26 oder 11···33 GHz>
K-binding energy	K-Bindungsenergie f, Bindungsenergie f des K-Elektrons, Bindungsenergie eines Elektrons auf der K-Schale
K-body	s. Kelvin['s] body
K-capture, K-electron capture	K-Einfang m
K-conversion	[innere] Konversion f an der K-Schale, K-Konversion f, K-Umwandlung f, Umwandlung f an der K-Schale
K-conversion coefficient, K-conversion ratio	Koeffizient m der inneren Konversion an der K-Schale, Konversionskoeffizient m der K-Schale, K-Konversionskoeffizient m
K-conversion line	K-Konversionslinie f, K-Umwandlungslinie f
K-conversion ratio	s. K-conversion coefficient
K corona, continuous corona	K-Komponente f der Koronastrahlung, kontinuierliche Komponente (Korona) f, K-Korona f
K edge	s. K-absorption limit
keenness, sharpness <of the cutting edge>	Schärfe f <Schneide>
keenness [of vision]	s. visual acuity
keeping; storage; holding in storage; hold-up; preservation	Lagerung f; Aufbewahrung f
Keesom force	Keesom-Kraft f
Keesom potential	Keesom-Potential n
K-effect, K term	K-Effekt m, K-Term m
Kê['s] grain boundary model	Kêsches Korngrenzenmodell n
kei[-function], Kelvin kei function	Kelvinsche (Thomsonsche) kei-Funktion f, kei-Funktion, kei
Keith-Flack['s] node, sino-auricular node	[Keith-Flackscher] Sinusknoten m, Keith-Flackscher Knoten m
Kekulé structure	Kekulé-Struktur f
K[-]electron	s. K-shell electron
K-electron capture, K-capture	K-Einfang m
Kell factor	Kell-Faktor m

Kellner['s] eyepiece, achromat zed Ramsden eyepiece — Kellner-Okular n, Kellnersches Okular (Mikroskopokular) n, Okular n nach (von) Kellner

kelvin, K, *obsolete*: degree Kelvin (absolute, °K, deg K) — Kelvin n, K, *veraltet*: Grad m Kelvin, Kelvin-Grad m, °K

Kelvin absolute electrometer, absolute (Kelvin, attracted disk) electrometer — [Kelvinsches] Absolutelektrometer n, absolutes Elektrometer n, Spannungswaage f

Kelvin['s] absolute temperature scale — s. Kelvin temperature scale

Kelvin ampere balance, Kelvin balance — Stromwaage f nach Kelvin, Kelvinsche (Thomsonsche) Stromwaage, Kelvin-Stromwaage f, Thomson-Stromwaage f, Thomson-Waage f

Kelvin['s] body, K-body, Kelvin[-Voigt] model, Voigt model, Voigt material, Voigt unit, Kelvin['s] solid, Kelvin material — Kelvinscher (Voigtscher) Körper m, K[elvin-]Körper m, [Kelvin-]Voigtsches Modell n, Voigt-Modell n, Voigtsches Element n, Voigt-Element n

Kelvin bridge, Thomson double bridge, double bridge — Thomson-Brücke f, Thomsonsche Doppelbrücke (Brücke, Meßbrücke) f, Thomson-Meßbrücke f, Doppel[meß]brücke f, Thomsonsche Brückenschaltung f, Thomson-Brückenschaltung f, Thomson-Schaltung f

Kelvin['s] circulation theorem, Kelvin['s] theorem, Thomson['s] circulation theorem, Thomson['s] theorem, circulation theorem <hydr.> — [Thomsonscher] Zirkulationssatz m, Thomsonscher Satz m [von der Erhaltung der Zirkulation], Thomsonscher Erhaltungssatz m, Kelvinsches Zirkulationstheorem n, Kelvinscher Zirkulationssatz, Thomson-Bjerknessches Zirkulationstheorem, Zirkulationssatz nach Kelvin, Zirkulationstheorem nach Kelvin <Hydr.>

Kelvin contraction theory [of stars], theory of Kelvin [and Helmholtz] — Kelvin-Helmholtzsche Kontraktionstheorie (Theorie) f, Theorie von Kelvin-Helmholtz

Kelvin effect, dilatancy, volume change by shear, viscous dilatancy — Dilatanz f, Volum[en]änderung f durch Scherung, Kelvin-Effekt m

Kelvin effect — s. a. skin effect

Kelvin effect — s. a. Thomson effect

Kelvin electrometer — s. Kelvin absolute electrometer

Kelvin equation [for the capillary pressure], Kelvin relation — Kelvinsche Kapillardruckgleichung f, Kelvin-Beziehung f

Kelvin['s] formulation of the second law of thermodynamics — s. second law [of thermodynamics]

Kelvin['s] function, Thomson['s] function <ber, bei, her hei, ker or kei> — Thomsonsche Funktion <ber, bei, her, hei, ker oder kei>

Kelvin function of the first kind, bei-function, bei — Kelvinsche (Thomsonsche) Funktion f erster Art, bei-Funktion f, bei

Kelvin function of the second kind, ber-function, ber — Kelvinsche (Thomsonsche) Funktion f zweiter Art, ber-Funktion f, ber

Kelvin hei function, hei-function, hei — Kelvinsche (Thomsonsche) hei-Funktion f, hei-Funktion, hei

Kelvin-Helmholtz theorem — Kelvin-Helmholtzscher Satz m

Kelvin her function, her-function, her — Kelvinsche (Thomsonsche) her-Funktion f, her-Funktion, her

Kelvin kei function — s. kei-function

Kelvin ker function, ker-function, ker — Kelvinsche (Thomsonsche) ker-Funktion f, ker-Funktion, ker

Kelvin['s] law — Thomsonsches (Kelvinsches) Gesetz n

Kelvin material — s. Kelvin['s] body

Kelvin['s] minimum energy theorem, Kelvin['s] principle — Kelvinsches Prinzip n der kleinsten (minimalen) kinetischen Energie, Thomsonscher Minimalsatz m

Kelvin model — s. Kelvin['s] body

Kelvin['s] principle — s. Kelvin['s] minimum energy theorem

Kelvin relation, Kelvin equation [for the capillary pressure] — Kelvinsche Kapillardruckgleichung f, Kelvin-Beziehung f

Kelvin scale — s. absolute temperature scale

Kelvin skin effect — s. skin effect

Kelvin['s] solid — s. Kelvin['s] body

Kelvin['s] statement [of the second law of thermodynamics] — s. second law [of thermodynamics]

Kelvin temperature, absolute temperature, temperature on the Kelvin scale — absolute Temperatur f, Kelvin-Temperatur f

Kelvin temperature scale — s. absolute temperature scale [of Kelvin]

Kelvin['s] theorem — Kelvinscher Satz m

Kelvin['s] theorem — s. a. Kelvin['s] circulation theorem <hydr.>

Kelvin transform — Kelvin-Transformierte f, Thomson-Transformierte f

Kelvin['s] transformation, Thomson['s] transformation — Kelvin-Transformation f, Thomson-Transformation f

Kelvin['s] transformation, Stokes['] theorem, integral theorem of Stokes — Stokesscher Satz (Integralsatz) m, Integralsatz von Stokes, Stokessche Integralformel (Formel) f

Kelvin-Voigt model — s. Kelvin['s] body

K-emission, K-radiation — K-Strahlung f

K-emitter — K-Strahler m

Kemmer equation, Kemmer wave equation — s. Duffin-Kemmer equation

Kennard electrode — Kennard-Elektrode f

Kennelly-Heaviside['s] layer — s. E layer

kenotron — Glühventil n, Hochvakuum-Diodengleichrichterröhre f, Kenotron n

Kent and Lawson photoelectric analyzer, Kent-Lawson photoelectric analyzer, photoelectric analyzer of Kent and Lawson — Kent-Lawson-Analysator m, photoelektrischer Analysator m nach Kent und Lawson

Kê pendulum — Kê-Pendel n

kepler — s. kilogram[me]

Kepler['s] area law — s. principle of conservation of areas

Kepler['s] equation — Keplers[che] Gleichung f, Kepler-Gleichung f

Keplerian ellipse, orbital ellipse — Kepler-Ellipse f

Keplerian elliptic motion, Keplerian motion, two-body motion — Kepler-Bewegung f, Keplersche Bewegung f, Kegelschnittsbewegung f, Zweikörperbewegung f

Keplerian orbit — Kepler-Bahn f, Keplersche Bahn f, Kegelschnittbahn f, Kegelschnittsbahn f

Keplerian time equation — Keplersche Zeitgleichung f

Kepler['s] laws — Keplersche Gesetze npl

Kepler problem — s. two-body problem

Kepler['s] second law — s. principle of conservation of areas

Kepler telescope, astronomical telescope — astronomisches (Keplersches) Fernrohr n, Kepler-Fernrohr n

Kepler['s] third law — drittes Keplersches Gesetz n

ker — s. ker-function

keratometer; Wessely keratometer — Scheitelabstandsmesser m; Wesselysches Keratometer n, Keratometer [nach Wessely]

keratoscope — Keratoskop n [nach Placido], Placido-Scheibe f

Kerber['s] eyepiece	Kerber-Okular n, Kerbersches Okular (Mikroskopokular) n, Planokular n vom Kerberschen Typ, Okular nach (von) Kerber	K-factor, multiplication factor, multiplication constant	Multiplikationsfaktor m, Vermehrungsfaktor m, k-Faktor m
		K-forbiddenness	K-Verbot n
		K-forbidden transition	K-verbotener Übergang m
ker-function, Kelvin ker function, ker	Kelvinsche (Thomsonsche) ker-Funktion f, ker-Funktion, ker	Khinchine['s] structure function	Khintchinesche (Chintchinsche) Strukturfunktion f
		Khurgin['s] refraction	Churginsche Brechung f, Churgin-Brechung f
kerma, kinetic energy released in mater (material)	Kerma f	kick	s. discontinuity
		kick[back]	s. pip
		kickback	s. rebound
kerma rate	Kermaleistung f	kicker light; fill-in light; broadside; booster light	Aufheller m
kernel <of integral equation>, integral kernel, kernel function, nucleus	Kern m [der Integralgleichung], Integralkern m; Kernfunktion f <Laplace-Transformation>		
		kicksorter	s. pulse-amplitude analyzer
		kienboeck, kienboeck unit, X	Kienboeck n, Kienboeck-Einheit f, X
kernel, Fredholm kernel (nucleus), nucleus	Fredholmscher Kern m	kieselguhr, diatomaceous earth, diatomite, infusorial earth, siliceous earth, tripoli	Kieselgur n, Infusorienerde f, Diatomeenerde f, Tripel m, Polierschiefer m
kernel function	s. kernel		
kernel of displacement, displacement kernel	Verschiebungs[integral]-kern m		
kernel of the spectrum, spectrum kernel	Spektralkern m	Kihara['s] potential	Kihara-Potential n, Kiharasches Potential n
		Kikuchi band	Kikuchi-Band n
		Kikuchi envelope	Kikuchi-Enveloppe f
Kerr cell, optical lever	Kerr-Zelle f	Kikuchi line	Kikuchi-Linie f
		Kikuchi['s] method	Kikuchi-Methode f, Methode f der Wegwahrscheinlichkeiten [nach Kikuchi]
Kerr constant, Kerr electro-optic[al] constant	Kerr-Konstante f		
Kerr effect, Kerr electro-optic[al], electro-optic[al] [Kerr] effect, electrical double refraction, double refraction in electrical fields	Kerr-Effekt m, elektrooptischer Kerr-Effekt m, elektrische Doppelbrechung f, Doppelbrechung im elektrischen Feld	killer, luminescence killer, scotophor	Killer m, Lumineszenzkiller m, Lumineszenzgift n
Kerr electro-optic[al] constant	s. Kerr constant	killer centre	Killerzentrum n
		killing	s. sacrificing
Kerr electro-optic[al] effect	s. Kerr effect	Killing field	Killingsches Feld n
		kiln-dried	ofengetrocknet
Kerr['s] electro-optic[al] law, Kerr['s] law	Kerrsches Gesetz n	kilo..., k	Kilo..., k
		kilo[-]calorie, kilogram[me][-] calorie, kcal <= 4,186.84 J>.	Kilokalorie f, Kilogrammkalorie f, kcal <= 4186,84 J>
Kerr magnetic effect, Kerr magneto-optic[al] effect, magnetooptic[al] [Kerr] effect, magnetic Kerr effect	magnetooptischer Kerr-Effekt m, magnetischer Kerr-Effekt		
		kilogram <US>	s. kilogramme
		kilogramme, kilogram, kilogram[me] mass, kg	Kilogramm n, Massenkilogramm n, kg
Kerr relation	Kerrsche Beziehung f	kilogramme[-]calorie	s. kilo[-]calorie
Kersten['s] inclusion model, inclusion model of Kersten	Fremdkörpermodell n [von Kersten], Kerstensches Fremdkörpermodell	"kilogramme des archives", kilogram des archives	Urkilogramm n, „kilogramme n des archives"
Kersten['s] inclusion theory, inclusion theory of Kersten, foreign body theory	Kerstensche Theorie f, Fremdkörpertheorie f von Kersten	kilogramme-force, kilogram-force, kilogram[me] weight, kilogram[me]-weight, kgf, kG	Kilopond n, kilogramme-force n, kp, kgf, kG
Kerst oscillation	s. betatron oscillation		
Kerst-Serber stability	Kerst-Serber-Stabilität f	kilogramme-force-meter	s. kilogramme-meter
		kilogramme mass	s. kilogramme
ket, ket vector	ket-Vektor m, ket n	kilogramme-metre, kilogram-meter, kilogram[me]-force-meter, kgf·m, kGm, kgm	Kilopondmeter n, Meterkilopond n, kpm, mkp
keto-enol tautomerism; desmotropism, merotropy	Keto-Enol-Tautomerie f; Desmotropie f		
Ketteler-Helmholtz formula	s. Helmholtz-Ketteler formula	kilogramme-mole[cule]	s. kilomol[e]
		kilogramme-weight	s. kilogramme-force
ket vector, ket	ket-Vektor m, ket n	kilohyl, metrical technical unit of mass, metric slug, khyl	technische Masse[n]einheit f, metrische Masseeinheit, ME, TME, techma, Kilohyl n, khyl
Keuffel and Esser colour analyzer	Spektralphotometer n von Keuffel und Esser		
Kew barometer	s. Kew-pattern barometer	kilometre wave	s. low-frequency wave
Kew-pattern barometer, Kew pattern of barometer, Kew barometer	Barometer n Modell Kew, Kew-Barometer n, Kewsches Barometer	kilometric wavelength [range]	s. low frequency range
		kilomol, kilomole, kilogram[me]-molecule, kilogram[me]-mole, kmol, kmole	Kilomol n, Kilogrammol n, Kilogrammolekül n, Kilogramm-Molekül n, kmol, kMol
key, key button	Taste f; Taster m		
keyed instrument	Tasteninstrument n	kilon	s. kilogramme
		kilopond	s. kilogramme-force
Keyes['] equation	Keyessche Gleichung f	kind of energy, form of energy	Energieform f, Energieart f
key-hole observation	Schlüssellochbeobachtung f		
keying	Tastung f	kind of particle, sort of particle; type of particle	Teilchensorte f; Teilchenart f
keying	Umtastung f	kind of stimulus, stimulus	Reizart f
keying, fastening with wedges, wedging	Verkeilen n		
keystone distortion, trapezoidal distortion, trapezium distortion	trapezförmige Verzeichnung (Verzerrung) f, Trapezverzeichnung f, Trapezverzerrung f, Trapezfehler m	kinematic, kinematical	kinematisch <auf die Bewegung bezüglich>
		kinematical compatibility condition	kinematische Kompatibilitätsbedingung f
		kinematical constraint	kinematische Bedingung f, kinematische Bindung f
k factor	s. thermal conductivity		
k-factor	s. specific gamma-ray constant		

kinematical

kinematical derivative	kinematische Ableitung *f*
kinematical effect of Lorentz transformation	kinematischer Effekt *m* der Lorentz-Transformation
kinematically admissible	kinematisch zulässig
kinematically determinate	kinematisch bestimmt
kinematically indeterminate	kinematisch unbestimmt
kinematically similar	kinematisch ähnlich
kinematical north pole [of the Earth]	kinematischer Nordpol *m* [der Erde]
kinematical quantity	kinematische Größe *f*
kinematical relativity	kinematische Relativitätstheorie *f* <Milne>
kinematical similitude	kinematische Ähnlichkeit *f*
kinematical viscosity, kinematic (kinetic) viscosity	kinematische Zähigkeit (Viskosität) *f*, Maxwellscher kinematischer Reibungskoeffizient *m*
kinematic exchange tensor	kinematischer Austauschtensor *m*
kinematic potential	s. Lagrangian function <mech.>
kinematic programme	Kinematikprogramm *n*
kinematics, pure kinematics, phoronomics, phoronomy, theory of motion	Kinematik *f*, reine Kinematik, Phoronomie *f*, Lehre *f* von der Bewegung, Bewegungslehre *f*
kinematics [of mechanisms]	technische Kinematik *f*, Getriebelehre *f*
kinematic specific speed	kinematische Schnelläufigkeitszahl *f*
kinescope	s. picture tube
kinestate	Kinestat *m*
kinetic	kinetisch <auf die Bewegung materieller Systeme, speziell der Atome oder Moleküle, bezüglich>
kinetic, reaction[-] kinetic <chem.>	reaktionskinetisch, kinetisch <Chem.>
kinetically determinate	kinetisch bestimmt
kinetically indeterminate	kinetisch unbestimmt
kinetic analogy in buckling of bars	Kirchhoffsche kinetische Analogie *f*
kinetic Boltzmann equation	kinetische Boltzmann-Gleichung *f*
kinetic chain length	kinetische Kettenlänge *f*
kinetic coefficient, phenomenological coefficient, Onsager coefficient	kinetischer (phänomenologischer, Onsagerscher) Koeffizient *m*, Onsager-Koeffizient *m*
kinetic current	kinetischer Strom *m*
kinetic energy, energy of motion, actual energy, vis viva	kinetische Energie *f*, Bewegungsenergie *f*, Energie der [fortschreitenden] Bewegung
kinetic energy coefficient, kinetic energy correction factor	Coriolisscher Korrektionsfaktor *m*, Bewegungsenergiebeiwert *m*
kinetic energy head	s. velocity head
kinetic energy released in matter (material), kerma	Kerma *f*
kinetic equation	s. balance equation <el.>
kinetic equation of reactor	kinetische Gleichung *f* des Reaktors, kinetische Reaktorgleichung *f*
kinetic equilibrium	s. transient equilibrium
kinetic friction, friction of motion	Bewegungsreibung *f*, kinetische Reibung *f*
kinetic head	s. velocity head
kinetic instability, microinstability, microscopic instability, fine-scale microinstability	kinetische Instabilität *f*, Instabilität vom kinetischen Typ
kinetic isotope effect	s. chemical-kinetic isotope effect
kinetic mass	kinetische Masse *f*
kinetic momentum	kinetischer Impuls *m*
kinetic potential	s. Lagrangian function <mech.>
kinetic power theorem	kinetisches Leistungstheorem *m*
kinetic pressure <of plasma>	kinetischer Druck *m* <Plasma>
kinetic pressure	s. a. dynamic pressure
kinetic rolling friction	Bewegungsreibung *f* beim Rollen
kinetics	Kinetik *f*, Lehre *f* von den Bewegungen materieller Systeme
kinetics of aggregation	Aggregationskinetik *f*
kinetics of homogeneous systems, homogeneous kinetics	Homogenkinetik *f*
kinetics of reaction, reaction kinetics, chemical kinetics	Reaktionskinetik *f*, chemische Reaktionskinetik, chemische Kinetik *f*
kinetic temperature	kinetische Temperatur *f*
kinetic theory of fluids	kinetische Theorie *f* der Flüssigkeiten
kinetic theory of gases	kinetische Gastheorie *f*
kinetic theory of heat	kinetische Wärmetheorie *f*
kinetic viscosity	s. kinematic viscosity
kinetochore	Kinetochor *m*
kinetostatically determinate	kinetostatisch bestimmt
kinetostatically indeterminate	kinetostatisch unbestimmt
kinetostatics	Kinetostatik *f*
Kingsbury curve	Kingsbury-Kurve *f*
kink	s. break <of the curve>
kink band	Knickband *n*
kink band density	Knickbanddichte *f*
kinked plate	geknickte Platte *f*
kink formation, jog formation	Sprungbildung *f*
kinking	s. buckling
kink instability	Instabilität *f* gegen Knickung (Knickdeformation), Knickinstabilität *f*, „kink"-Instabilität *f*
kink pair formation, jog pair formation	Sprungpaarbildung *f*
kinosthenic co-ordinates	s. ignorable co-ordinates
Kipp gas generator	Kippscher Apparat (Gasentwickler) *m*
Kirchhoff['s] approach (approximation)	Kirchhoffsche Näherung *f*
Kirchhoff['s] balance, Kirchhoff['s] potential balance	Kirchhoffsche Potentialwaage (Waage) *f*, Potentialwaage nach Kirchhoff
Kirchhoff['s] boundary conditions	Kirchhoffsche Randbedingungen *fpl*
Kirchhoff-Bunsen spectroscope	Spektroskop *n* von Kirchhoff und Bunsen
Kirchhoff-Clausius theorem	Kirchhoff-Clausisscher Satz *m*
Kirchhoff['s] current law, current law, first Kirchhoff law, first law of Kirchhoff	erster Kirchhoffscher Satz *m*, erste Kirchhoffsche Regel *f*, Verzweigungspunktregel *f*, Knotenpunktregel *f*, erstes Kirchhoffsches Gesetz *n*, Knotenpunktgesetz *n* [von Kirchhoff], [Kirchhoffscher] Verzweigungssatz *m*, Kirchhoffsches Verzweigungsgesetz *n*
Kirchhoff['s] equation[s] [for the heat of reaction]	Kirchhoffsche Gleichung *f*, Kirchhoffsches Gesetz *n* [in der physikalischen Chemie], Kirchhoffscher Satz *m* [von der Temperaturabhängigkeit der Wärmetönungen]
Kirchhoff['s] experiment	Kirchhoffscher Versuch (Grundversuch) *m*, Kirchhoffs Grundversuch
Kirchhoff['s] formula <of diffraction theory>	Kirchhoffsche Formel *f* [der Beugungstheorie], Kirchhoffsche Beugungsformel *f*, Kirchhoffsches Beugungsgesetz *n*, Kirchhoffsche Wellenformel *f*
Kirchhoff['s] formula for edge capacitance	Kirchhoffsche Formel *f* für die Randkorrektion der Kapazität
Kirchhoff-Helmholtz flow, Helmholtz flow	Helmholtzsche Strömung *f*
Kirchhoff['s] integral	Kirchhoffsches Integral *n*
Kirchhoff['s] law [of emission], Kirchhoff['s] law of radiation	Kirchhoffsches Gesetz *n* [für schwarze Strahler], Kirchhoffsches Strahlungsgesetz *n*, Kirchhoffscher Satz *m* [der Temperaturstrahlung]

Kirchhoff['s] laws ‹of electrical circuits›, Kirchhoff['s] laws of networks (current)	Kirchhoffsche Sätze *mpl* [der Netzwerke], Kirchhoffsche Sätze der Stromverzweigung, Kirchhoffsche Regeln *fpl*, Kirchhoffsche Gesetze *npl* [der Netzwerke]	**Klein-Nishina formula**	Klein-Nishina-Formel *f*
		Klein-Nishina scattering	Klein-Nishina-Streuung *f*
		Klein-Nishina scattering cross-section	s. Klein-Nishina cross-section
Kirchhoff['s] laws in acoustics	Kirchhoffsche Sätze *mpl* (Gesetze *npl*) in der Akustik	**Klein['s] paradox**	Kleinsches Paradoxon *n*
		Klein['s] parameter	Kleinscher Parameter *m*
Kirchhoff['s] laws of current (networks)	s. Kirchhoff['s] laws ‹of electrical circuits›	**Klein['s] principle**	Kleinsches Prinzip *n*
		Klein['s] quadratic group, quadratic group, Klein['s] four-group, Klein['s] 4-group, four-group, Klein['s] group, vierer group ‹math.›	Kleinsche Vierergruppe *f*, Vierergruppe ‹Math.›
Kirchhoff-Lorenz solution, Kirchhoff['s] solution [of scalar wave equation]	Kirchhoffsche Lösung *f* [der Wellengleichung], Kirchhoff-Lorenzsche Lösung		
Kirchhoff-Planck function	Kirchhoff-Planck-Funktion *f*		
Kirchhoff-Planck['s] law	Kirchhoff-Plancksches Gesetz *n*	**Klein-Rosseland relation**	Klein-Rosselandsche Beziehung *f*, Klein-Rosseland-Gleichung *f*
Kirchhoff['s] potential balance, Kirchhoff['s] balance	Kirchhoffsche Potentialwaage (Waage) *f*, Potentialwaage nach Kirchhoff	**Klein['s] surface**, Klein['s] bottle	Kleinscher Schlauch *m*
		K-line ‹K_α, K_β etc.›	K-Linie *f*, K-Röntgenlinie *f*, Röntgen-K-Linie *f* ‹K_α, K_β usw.›
Kirchhoff['s] problem	Kirchhoffsches Problem *n*		
Kirchhoff['s] second law	s. Kirchhoff['s] voltage law		
Kirchhoff['s] solution [of scalar wave equation], Kirchhoff-Lorenz solution	Kirchhoffsche Lösung *f* [der Wellengleichung], Kirchhoff-Lorenzsche Lösung	**Klinger['s] theory**	Klingersche Theorie *f*
		klinostat	Klinostat *m*
		klirr factor	s. distortion factor
Kirchhoff['s] theory [of diffraction]	Kirchhoffsche Theorie *f* [der Beugung], Kirchhoffsche Beugungstheorie *f*	**K/L ratio**	K/L-Verhältnis *n*
Kirchhoff['s] voltage law, voltage law, Kirchhoff['s] second law, second law of Kirchhoff	zweiter Kirchhoffscher Satz *m*, zweite Kirchhoffsche Regel *f*, Maschenpunktregel *f*, Maschenregel *f*, zweites Kirchhoffsches Gesetz *n*	**klydonograph**	Klydonograph *m*, Gleitfunkenmeßstrecke *f*
		klystron, clystron, McNally (Shepart) tube	Klystron *n*, Mehrkreistriftröhre *f*, geschwindigkeitsgesteuerte Laufzeitröhre *f*
Kirchner number, *Ki*	Kirchner-Zahl *f*, *Ki*		
Kirkendall effect	Kirkendall-Effekt *m*	**klystron amplifier**	Klystronverstärker *m*
Kirkwood and Monroe's theory of melting	Kirkwood-Monroesche Schmelztheorie *f*	**klystron generator**, klystron oscillator	Klystronoszillator *m*
Kirkwood and Yvon's theory, Kirkwood-Yvon theory	Kirkwood-Yvonsche Theorie *f*	**klystron multiplier**	Vervielfacherklystron *n*
Kirkwood['s] approximation	Kirkwoodsche Näherung *f*	**klystron oscillator**, klystron generator	Klystronoszillator *m*
Kirkwood['s] equations ‹of the first, second kind›	Kirkwoodsche Gleichungen *fpl* ‹erster, zweiter Art›	**K-meson**, kaon, heavy meson, H meson	K-Meson *n*, schweres Meson *n*, Kaon *n*
Kirkwood-Müller equation	Kirkwood-Müller-Gleichung *f*, Kirkwood-Müllersche Gleichung *f*	**knee** ‹of the curve›, break, fraction, salient point; kink	Knick *m*; Knie *n*; Abknicken *n* ‹Kurve›
Kirkwood['s] solutions ‹of the Bloch equation›	Kirkwoodsche Lösung *f* ‹der Blochschen Gleichung›	**knee lever**	Kniehebel *m*
		knee lever	s. a. bent lever
Kirkwood['s] theory	Kirkwoodsche Theorie *f*	**knee of the pipe, knee-piece [of the pipe]**	Rohrkrümmer *m*, Rohrknie *n*, Rohrbogen *m*
Kirkwood-Yvon theory, Kirkwood and Yvon's theory	Kirkwood-Yvonsche Theorie *f*	**knee-toggle lever**	s. bent lever
		knee voltage, bottoming voltage	Kniespannung *f*
Kirpitchev No., Kirpitchev number	Kirpitschow-Zahl *f*	**Kneser dispersion**	Kneser-Dispersion *f*, Knesersche Dispersion *f*
Kistyakovski['s] rule	Kistjakowskische Regel *f*, Regel von Kistjakowski		
kite	Drachen *m*	**knife edge** ‹in the Töpler method›	Schlierenblende *f*
Kjeldahl method, Kjeldahl technique	Kjeldahl-Aufschluß *m*, Kjeldahlsche Stickstoffbestimmung *f*	**knife[-] edge** ‹of balance, pendulum›	Schneide *f*, Schneidenlager *n* ‹Waage, Pendel›
Klein['s] bottle	s. Klein['s] surface	**knife[-] edge** ‹opt.›	Schneide *f* ‹Opt.›
Klein['s] catastrophe	Kleinsche Katastrophe *f*, Klein-Katastrophe *f*	**knife-edge balance**	Schneidenwaage *f*
		knife-edge bearing, blade bearing, steel-prism bearing	Schneidenlagerung *f*, Schneidenlager *n*
Kleinen / im, in the small, locally ‹math.›	im Kleinen, lokal ‹Math.›		
Klein['s] Erlanger programme, Erlanger Programm	Erlanger Programm *n*	**knife-edge diffraction**, edge diffraction	Kantenbeugung *f*, Beugung *f* an der Kante, Randbeugung *f*
Klein['s] four-group	s. Klein['s] quadratic group	**knife-edge effect**	Messerschneideneffekt *m*
Klein-Gordon equation, Fock-Klein-Gordon equation, relativistic Schrödinger equation	Klein-Gordon-Gleichung *f*, relativistische Schrödinger-Gleichung *f*		
		knife-edge test [of Foucault]	s. Foucault knife-edge test
		knife-edge vacuum seal	Schneidendichtung *f*, Messerschneiden-Vakuumdichtung *f*
Klein-Gordon field	Klein-Gordon-Feld *n*		
Klein['s] group	s. Klein['s] quadratic group	**knife-line corrosion**	Messerlinienkorrosion *f*
Klein['s] lemma ‹therm.›	Kleinsches Lemma *n* ‹Therm.›	**Knight shift**	Knightshift *m*, Knight-„shift" *m*, Knight-Verschiebung *f*
Klein-Nishina absorption	Klein-Nishina-Absorption *f*	**knocked-on atom**	angestoßenes Atom *n*, Anstoßatom *n*, „knocked-on"-Atom *n*
Klein-Nishina cross-section, Klein-Nishina scattering cross-section	Klein-Nishina-Streuquerschnitt *m*, Klein-Nishina-Querschnitt *m*, Klein-Nishina-Wirkungsquerschnitt *m* für (der) Klein-Nishina-Streuung	**knocked-on electron**	s. delta-ray
		knocking	Klopfen *n*

knocking-on,
knocking-out
knocking-out
Herausstoßen n, Anstoßen n, Herausschlagen n
s. a. discomposition <of atoms>

knocking-out effect, Wigner effect; discomposition effect
Wigner-Effekt m, Atomumlagerung f durch Kernstoß

knock-on, bound, bounce, shock, impact, impingement, impinging
Aufschlag m, Aufprall m, Anprall m, Prall m

knock-on
s. a. delta-ray

knock-on process, impact process
Anstoßprozeß m

Knoop hardness [number]
Knoop-Härte f

Knoop hardness (indentation) test
Knoop-Härteprüfung f

Knop['s] solution
Knopsche Lösung f, Knopsche Nährlösung f

knot, international knot, US knot, kn, int.kn.
Knoten m, kn

knot of the prominence, prominence knot
Protuberanzenknoten m

knot within a meteor stream, condensation within a meteor stream, clustering of meteors
Meteorschwarm m, Sternschnuppenschwarm m

knot within cometary tail, tail condensation
Schweifwolke f

Knudsen absolute manometer, Knudsen gauge, Knudsen radiometer-vacuummeter
Knudsen-Manometer n, Knudsensches [Radiometer-]Vakuummeter n, Molekularvakuummeter n, Wärmeableitungsmanometer n

Knudsen cosine law, **Knudsen cosine rule**
Knudsensche Kosinusregel f, Kosinusregel (Kosinusgesetz n) von Knudsen

Knudsen diffusion
Knudsensche Diffusion f, Knudsen-Diffusion f

Knudsen diffusion coefficient, coefficient of Knudsen diffusion
Knudsenscher Diffusionskoeffizient m, Knudsen-Diffusionskoeffizient m

Knudsen effect, thermal molecular flow, thermomolecular flow
Knudsen-Effekt m, thermomolekularer Knudsen-Effekt m, thermische Molekularströmung f, thermomolekulare Strömung f

Knudsen flow, non[-]continuum flow
Knudsen-Strömung f, Knudsensche Strömung f, Nichtkontinuumsströmung f, Gemischtströmung f

Knudsen gas
Knudsen-Gas n

Knudsen gauge
s. Knudsen absolute manometer

Knudsen['s] laws
Knudsensche Gesetze npl

Knudsen layer
Knudsen-Schicht f

Knudsen number, Knudsen similarity number
Knudsensche Zahl f, Knudsensche Zahl (Kennzahl, Ähnlichkeitskennzahl) f, K

Knudsen radiometer-vacuummeter
s. Knudsen absolute manometer

Knudsen similarity number
s. Knudsen number

knurled[-head] screw, milled[-head] screw
Rändelschraube f

Koch['s] equation [of state]
Kochsche Zustandsgleichung f, Zustandsgleichung nach Koch

Koch instrument, Koch microphotometer
Kochsches Mikrophotometer n, Mikrophotometer nach Koch

Kohaut['s] method
Kohaut-Verfahren n

Kohler['s] curve, **Kohler['s] diagram**
Kohler-Diagramm n, Kohlersches Diagramm n

Kohler['s] equation (formula), Kohler['s] relation (rule)
Kohlersche Regel (Formel) f, Kohlersche Beziehung f

Köhler['s] illumination, **Köhler['s] method**
Köhler-Beleuchtung f, Köhlersche Beleuchtung f, Köhlersches Beleuchtungsprinzip (Prinzip) n

Kohler['s] principle
Kohlersches Prinzip n

Kohler['s] relation (rule), Kohler['s] formula, Kohler['s] equation
Kohlersche Regel (Formel) f, Kohlersche Beziehung f

Kohlrausch[s] law
s. Kohlrausch square-root law

Kohlrausch['s] law [of the independent migration of ions]
s. law of the independent migration of ions

Kohlrausch['s] square-root law, Kohlrausch['s] law, square-root law [of Kohlrausch]
Kohlrauschsches Quadratwurzelgesetz (Gesetz) n, Quadratwurzelgesetz [von Kohlrausch]

Kohn effect
Kohn-Effekt m

Kolk['s] method / Van der, method of oblique illumination
van der Kolksche Methode f, Methode von Schröder van der Kolk

Kolmogoroff['s] distribution function
Kolmogorowsche Verteilungsfunktion f

Kolmogoroff['s] ergodic theorem, maximum ergodic theorem
maximaler Ergodensatz m, Ergodensatz von Kolmogorow

Kolmogoroff interval, Kolmogoroff region
Kolmogorow-Bereich m

Kolmogoroff microscale
Kolmogorowsche Mikrolänge f, inneres (lokales) Maß n der Turbulenz

Kolmogoroff region, Kolmogoroff interval
Kolmogorow-Bereich m

Kolmogoroff similarity hypothesis, local similarity hypothesis; universal equilibrium hypothesis
Kolmogorowsche Ähnlichkeitshypothese f

Kolmogoroff-Teller equation
Kolmogorow-Teller-Gleichung f

Kolmogoroff['s] theory [of turbulence], theory of locally isotropic turbulence
Theorie f der lokal isotropen Turbulenz, Kolmogorowsche Turbulenztheorie f

Kondo effect
Kondo-Effekt m

könig, König unit
König-Einheit f

König-Martens spectrophotometer, Martens spectrophotometer
Spektralphotometer n von König-Martens

König unit, könig
König-Einheit f

konimeter, dust counter
Konimeter n, Staubzähler m; Staubgehaltsmesser m, Staubgehaltsmeßgerät n, Staubmesser m

konimetry
s. dust counting

koniscope
Koniskop n

konisphere, conisphere
Konisphäre f

konoscopic figure
konoskopische Figur f

Konowaloff rule
Konowalowsche Regeln fpl

Koopmans['] theorem
Koopmanssches Theorem n

Koppe['s] theory
Koppesche Theorie f

Kopp['s] law
Koppsche Regel f

Kopp-Neumann['s] law
s. Neumann-Kopp rule

Korringa['s] formula
Korringa-Beziehung f, Beziehung f von Korringa

Korte['s] laws
Kortesche Gesetze npl

Koschmieder['s] [viscibility] formula, Koschmieder['s] relation
Sichtweitenformel f [von Koschmieder], Koschmiedersche Sichtweitenformel; Luftlichtformel f [von Koschmieder], Koschmiedersche Luftlichtformel

Kossel cone
Kossel-Kegel m, Kosselscher Kegel m

Kossel effect
Kossel-Effekt m

Kossel line
Kossel-Kurve f, Kossel-Linie f, Kosselsche Linie f

Kossel-Sommerfeld [displacement] law
s. displacement law for complex spectra

Kossel-Stranski['s] theory [of crystal growth]
Kossel-Stranskische Wachstumstheorie f

Kossel['s] theory of valence
Kosselsche Valenztheorie f (Theorie f der chemischen Bindung)

Köster effect
Köster-Effekt m

Kösters biprism
s. beam splitting prism

Kösters gauge-measuring interferometer, Kösters interferometer
Interferenzkomparator m nach Kösters

Kösters['] interference double prism	s. beam splitting prism	Kruskal-Shafranov condition	s. Kruskal['s] condition
Kösters interferometer, Kösters gauge-measuring interferometer	Interferenzkomparator m nach Kösters	Krüss bilateral slit, bilateral slit of Krüss	Krüßscher Doppelspalt m, Bilateralspalt m [nach Krüß]
Kostinsky effect <phot.>	Kostinsky-Effekt m <Phot.>	kryptoscope, cryptoscope	Kryptoskop n
Kotchine['s] H-function, H-function of Kotchine	H-Funktion f von Kotschin, Kotschinsche H-Funktion	K series limit	K-Seriengrenze f, K-Grenze f, Grenze f der K-Serie
Kotchine['s] theorem	Kotschinscher Satz m	K-shell, two-electron shell	K-Schale f, K-Schale f, Zweierschale f
Kovalevskaya['s] gyroscope	Kowalewskajascher (Kowalewskischer) Kreisel m		
Kovats index	s. retention index		
Kowalewski's integral	Kowalewskisches Integral n	K-shell electron, K[-] electron	Elektron n der K-Schale, K-Elektron n, K-Schalenelektron n
K-radiation, K-emission	K-Strahlung f		
Krafft point	Krafft-Punkt m	k-space, wave-vector space	k-Raum m, Wellen[zahl]-vektorraum m, Wellenzahlraum m
Kramer effect	Kramer-Effekt m		
Kramers['] absorption coefficient	Kramersscher Absorptionskoeffizient m		
Kramers['] degeneracy, Kramers['] degeneration	Kramers-Entartung f, Kramerssche Entartung f	K spectroheliogram, calcium K line, spectroheliogram	K-Spektroheliogramm n, Calcium-Spektroheliogramm n, Kalzium-Spektroheliogramm n
Kramers - De Kronig relations	s. Kramers-Kronig relations	K term	s. K-effect
Kramers['] doublet	Kramers-Dublett n, Kramerssches Dublett n	Kubo-Tomita theory	Kubo-Tomita-Theorie f, Theorie f von Kubo und Tomita
Kramers['] equation, Kramers['] formula	Kramerssche Formel (Gleichung) f	Kuene['s] coefficient of absorption	Kuenescher Absorptionskoeffizient m
Kramers-Heisenberg dispersion formula	s. Kramers-Kronig relations	Kühle circuit	Kühle-Schaltung f
Kramers-Kronig relations, Kramers-De Kronig relations; Kramers-Heisenberg dispersion formula	Kramers-Kronigsche Dispersionsbeziehungen fpl, Kramers-de-Kronigsche Relationen fpl, Kronig-Kramerssche Beziehungen fpl, Dispersionsrelationen fpl; Kramers-Heisenberg-Relationen fpl, Kramers-Heisenbergsche Dispersionsformel f	Kuhn and Rittmann's hypothesis, Kuhn-Rittmann['s] hypothesis	Kuhn-Rittmannsche Hypothese f, Hypothese von Kuhn und Rittmann
		Kuhn [power] law	Kuhnsches Potenzgesetz n
		Kuhn-Rittmann['s] hypothesis, Kuhn and Rittmann's hypothesis	Kuhn-Rittmannsche Hypothese f, Hypothese von Kuhn und Rittmann
		Kuhn-Thomas-Reiche [f-]sum rule, Kuhn-Thomas-Reiche f-sum rule, f-sum rule of Kuhn-Thomas-Reiche	Summenregel f von Kuhn-Thomas-Reiche, Kuhn-Thomas-Reichesche Summenregel, f-Summensatz m von Thomas-Reiche-Kuhn
Kramers['] law	Kramerssches Gesetz n		
Kramers['] operator	Kramersscher Zeitumkehroperator (Operator) m		
Kramers['] superexchange, superexchange	Superaustausch m [nach Kramers]	Kuiper['s] hypothesis	Kuipersche Theorie f, Theorie von Kuiper
Kramers['] theorem	Satz m (Theorem n) von Kramers, Kramers-Theorem n, Kramerssches Theorem	Kummer['s] [differential] equation, confluent hypergeometric equation [of Kummer], Pochhammer-Barnes equation	Kummersche (konfluente hypergeometrische) Differentialgleichung f
Krarup cable, continuously loaded cable	Krarup-Kabel n; Krarup-Leitung f		
krarupization, continuous loading	Krarupisierung f	Kummer['s] function	s. confluent hypergeometric function
Kratky[s] method [of convergence]	s. convergence method	Kummer['s] series	s. confluent hypergeometric function
K ray, seismic ray reflected downwards at the outer core boundary	K-Welle f, am Kern gebrochene Erdbebenwelle f	Kundt['s] dust figure	Kundtsche Staubfigur f, Staubfigur
Krebs cycle, Krebs tricarboxylic acid cycle, tricarboxylic acid cycle, citrate cycle	Krebs-Zyklus m, Zitronensäurezyklus m, Trikarbonsäurezyklus m, Citronensäurezyklus m, Tricarbonsäurezyklus m	Kundt effect	Kundt-Effekt m
		Kundt['s] experiment	[Kundtscher] Teilungsversuch m
Kries theory of colour vision / von	von Kriessche Zonentheorie f, Zonentheorie nach von Kries	Kundt['s] law of abnormal dispersion	Kundtsches Gesetz n der anomalen Dispersion
		Kundt['s] manometer	Kundtsches Manometer n
		Kundt['s] mirror	Kundtscher Spiegel m
Kronecker delta, Kronecker symbol	[Kroneckersches] Deltasymbol n, Kronecker-Symbol n, Kroneckersches Symbol n (Delta n, δ), Einheitstensor m zweiter Stufe	Kundt['s] prism	Kundtsches Prisma n, Farbstoffprisma n
		Kundt['s] rule	Kundtsche Regel f
		Kundt['s] tube	Kundtsches Rohr n, Kundtsche Röhre f, Kundt-Rohr n
Kronecker product, direct product <of representations>	Kronecker-Produkt n, tensorielles (Kroneckersches) Produkt n, Tensorprodukt n	Kunsman anode	Kunsman-Anode f
		Küpfmüller['s] criterion [of stability], stability criterion of Küpfmüller	Küpfmüllersches Stabilitätskriterium (Kriterium) n, Stabilitätskriterium nach Küpfmüller, Küpfmüller-Stabilitätskriterium n, Küpfmüller-Kriterium n, Kriterium von Küpfmüller
Kronecker symbol	s. Kronecker delta		
Kronecker tensor	s. unit tensor		
Kronig-Penney model	Kronig-Penney-Modell n, Kronig-Penneysches Modell n		
Krukowski [alternating-current] potentiometer, Krukowski [a.c.] potentiometer	Krukowski-Kompensator m, Phasenschieberkompensator m nach Krukowski	Küpfmüller['s] law	Zeitgesetz n von Küpfmüller, Küpfmüllersches Zeitgesetz
		kurchatovium, rutherfordium, $_{104}$Ku	Kurtschatowium n, Rutherfordium n, $_{104}$Ku
Kruskal['s] condition (criterion), Kruskal-Shafranov condition	Kruskal-Schafranow-Bedingung f, Kruskal-Bedingung f	Kurie plot, Fermi-Kurie plot, Fermi plot	Fermi-Plot n, Fermi-Kurve f, Kurie-Plot n, Fermi-Diagramm n, Kurie-Diagramm n
Kruskal limit	Kruskal-Grenze f		
		kurtosis	s. coefficient of excess <stat.>

Küstner dosimeter	Küstner-Dosimeter n, Küstner-Eichstandgerät n	lack of definition, lack of focus, unsharpness, diffuseness, blur[ring] <opt.>	Unschärfe f <Opt.>
Küstner series, fundamental series, series of fundamental stars <astr.>	Fundamentalreihe f, Fundamentalsternreihe f, Küstnersche Reihe f <Astr.>	lack of generality / without	s. loss of generality / without
Kutta flow	Kutta-Strömung f	lack of mass, mass deficiency, deficiency of mass	Massendefizit m, Massenunterschuß m
Kutta-Joukowski condition, Joukowski['s] hypothesis, Joukowski condition	[Kutta-]Joukowski-Bedingung f, Kuttasche Abflußbedingung f, Hinterkantenbedingung f [von Kutta-Joukowski], Bedingung f von Kutta-Joukowski	lack of parallelism, parallelism error	Parallelitätsfehler m
		lack of uniformity	s. non-uniformity
		lack of visibility	s. non-visibility
		lacquer replica	Lackabdruck m
Kutta-Joukowski formula	s. Kutta-Joukowski law		
Kutta-Joukowski hypothesis	Kutta-Joukowskische Hypothese f	lactam-lactim tautomerism	Laktam-Laktim-Tautomerie f
Kutta-Joukowski law (lift formula), Kutta-Joukowski theorem, Kutta-Joukowski formula	Kutta-Joukowskische Auftriebsformel (Formel) f, Kutta-Joukowskischer Satz m, Satz von Kutta-Joukowski, Kutta-Joukowski-Gleichung f	lactescence	Milchtrübe f
		lacuna	s. gap <math.>
		lacunary <math.>	lakunär, Lücken- <Math.>
		lacustrine	s. limnetic
		ladder approximation	Leiternäherung f
k-vector density	k-Vektordichte f	ladder diagram	Leitertafel f, Leiterdiagramm n
k-vector field <math.>	k-Vektorfeld n <Math.>	ladder line; ladder network; iterative structure	Kettenleiter m, [elektrische] Kette f; Kettenschaltung f, Hintereinanderschaltung f von Vierpolen; Kettenbruchschaltung f, Abzweigschaltung f; Impulskette f
K X-ray radiation, K X-rays	K-Röntgenstrahlung f, Röntgen-K-Strahlung f		
kymogram	Kymogramm n		
kymograph	s. roentgen kymograph		
Kyropoulos['] method	Kyropoulos-Verfahren n, Kyropoulos-Methode f, Kristallzüchtung f aus der Schmelze nach dem Kyropoulos-Verfahren		
		ladder-type filter, filter chain	Filterkette f, Siebkette f
		Ladenburg['s] law	Ladenburgsches Gesetz n
		laevogyrate	s. laevogyric <opt.>
		laevogyrate quartz, laevorotatory (laevogyric, left-handed) quartz	Linksquarz m

L

label	s. tag	laevogyratory, laevogyric, laevogyrous, laevorotatory, laevorotary, laevogyrate, rotating the plane of polarization anticlockwise, levogyric, l, L <opt.>	linksdrehend, lävogyr, l, L <Opt.>
label[l]ed, labelled with isotope, labeled [with isotope], isotopically labelled (tagged), tagged [with isotope]	markiert [mit einem Isotop], isotop[]markiert		
labelled atom, tracer, tagged atom, indicator, marker <nucl.>	Tracer m, markiertes Atom n, Indikator m <Kern.>	laevogyric quartz, laevorotatory (laevogyrate, left-handed) quartz	Linksquarz m
labelled compound	s. tracer compound	laevoisomer, L-isomer, l-isomer	linksdrehendes Isomer n, L-Isomer n, l-Isomer n
labelled with isotope	s. labelled	laevorotary	s. laevogyric <opt.>
labelled with radioactive isotope, tagged with radioactive isotope	radioaktiv markiert, markiert mit einem radioaktiven Isotop	laevorotation, levorotation, negative (counterclockwise) rotation	Linksdrehung f, negative Drehung f; Linkslauf m
labelled with stable isotope	stabilisotop markiert	laevorotatory	s. laevogyric <opt.>
labelling [with isotope], isotopic labelling, tagging [with isotope], isotopic tagging; tracing <nucl.>	Markierung f, isotope Markierung <Kern.>	laevorotatory form, L-form, l-form	linksdrehende Form f, L-Form f, l-Form f
		laevorotatory quartz, laevogyric (laevogyrate, left-handed) quartz	Linksquarz m
lab frame	s. laboratory system	lag	s. time lag
labial pipe, flue pipe, blow pipe	Lippenpfeife f, Labialpfeife f	lag angle, angle of lag; retardation angle	Nacheil[ungs]winkel m; Verzögerungswinkel m
labile equilibrium	s. unstable equilibrium	lag correlation	Lagkorrelation f
labile frame; labile truss; unstable frame; unstable truss	labiles Fachwerk n, kinematisch unbestimmtes Fachwerk	lagged feedback, delayed feedback	Rückführung f mit Totzeit, verzögerte Rückführung
lability; instability, imbalance, unstability	Instabilität f, Unstabilität f; Labilität f	lagging	s. heat insulation
		lagging	s. a. lining
		lagging edge	s. trailing edge
lability energy	Labilitätsenergie f	lagging of phase	s. phase lagging
laboratory co-ordinates (co-ordinate system)	s. laboratory system	lag in magnetization, magnetization lag, magnetic lag (retardation)	Magnetisierungsverzug m, Magnetisierungsverzögerung f
laboratory experiment	Laborversuch m, Laboratoriumsversuch m, Laboruntersuchung f		
laboratory frame	s. laboratory system	lag of release, releasing (release) time	Auslösezeit f
laboratory scale	Labormaßstab m		
laboratory system [of co-ordinates], laboratory co-ordinates (frame, co-ordinate system), L[-]system, L frame, lab frame	Laborsystem n, Laborkoordinaten fpl, L-System n, Laborkoordinatensystem n, Beobachtersystem n	lag of thermometer	Nachhinken n des Thermometers
		Lagrange bracket	Lagrange-Klammer f, Lagrangesche Klammer f, Lagrangescher Klammerausdruck m
laboratory test	Laborprüfung f, Labor[atoriums]versuch m	Lagrange['s] co-ordinates	s. general co-ordinates
labyrinth <ac.>	Labyrinth n <Ak.>		
labyrinth gland (packing, seal)	Labyrinthdichtung f	Lagrange['s] criterion	Lagrangesches Kriterium n

Lagrange-d'Alembert principle	s. Euler-d'Alembert principle	Lagrangian derivative	s. variational derivative
Lagrange density	s. Lagrangian density	Lagrangian dynamics	Lagrangesche Dynamik f
Lagrange['s] differential equation	s. differential equation of d'Alembert-Lagrange	Lagrangian equations of motion	s. Lagrange['s] equations <of the second kind>
Lagrange['s] equation <in celestial mechanics>	Lagrangesche Schlüsselgleichung (Gleichung) f <Himmelsmechanik>	Lagrangian form	Lagrangesche Form f
		Lagrangian formalism	Lagrange-Formalismus m, Lagrangescher Formalismus m
Lagrange['s] equations <of the first kind>	Lagrangesche Bewegungsgleichungen (Gleichungen) fpl erster Art, Lagrange-Gleichungen fpl erster Art, Lagrangesche Gleichungen 1. Art	Lagrangian formulation	s. Lagrangian method
		Lagrangian function <of variational problem>	Lagrange-Funktion f, Lagrangesche Funktion f, Grundfunktion f <Variationsproblem>
Lagrange['s] equations <of the second kind>, Lagrange['s] equations of motion, Lagrangian equations of motion, Euler-Lagrange equations	Lagrangesche Bewegungsgleichungen (Gleichungen) fpl zweiter Art, Lagrange-Gleichungen fpl zweiter Art, Lagrangesche Gleichungen 2. Art	Lagrangian function, Lagrangian, kinetic potential, kinematic potential <mech.>	Lagrange-Funktion f, Lagrangesche Funktion f, kinetisches Potential n; freie Energie f <bei skleronomen Systemen> <Mech.>
		Lagrangian matrix, Lagrange['s] matrix	Lagrange-Matrix f
Lagrange factor	s. Lagrange['s] multiplier	Lagrangian method [of analysis], Lagrangian picture, Lagrangian representation, Lagrangian formulation	Lagrangesche Darstellung (Methode) f, Lagrangesches Bild n
Lagrange['s] formula	Lagrangesche Formel f		
Lagrange['s] formula	s. a. Lagrange['s] theorem		
Lagrange['s] formula of interpolation, Lagrange's interpolation formula	Lagrangesche Interpolationsformel f		
Lagrange['s] generalized co-ordinates	s. general co-ordinates	Lagrangian surface	Lagrangesche Fläche f
		Lagrangian turbulence scale	Lagrangescher Turbulenzgrad m
Lagrange gyroscope	Lagrangesches Gyroskop n	Lagrangian wave	s. long wave <hydr.>
Lagrange-Helmholtz equation (formula, invariant, law)	s. Lagrange['s] theorem	lag theorem [of Laplace transform]	s. time-shift theorem
		Laguerre['s] [differential] equation	Laguerresche Differentialgleichung f
Lagrange['s] identity	Lagrangesche Identität f	Laguerre['s] function	Laguerresche Funktion f, Laguerre-Funktion f
Lagrange['s] interpolation formula, Lagrange['s] formula of interpolation	Lagrangesche Interpolationsformel f	Laguerre['s] polynomial	[Tschebyscheff-]Laguerresches Polynom n, [Tschebyscheff-]Laguerre-Polynom n, Kummersches (Lagrange-Abelsches) Polynom
Lagrange invariant	s. Lagrange['s] theorem		
Lagrange['s] law	s. Lagrange['s] theorem		
Lagrange['s] matrix, Lagrangian matrix	Lagrange-Matrix f	Lainer effect	Lainer-Effekt m
Lagrange['s] multiplier, Lagrange factor, [Lagrange's] undetermined multiplier	Lagrangescher Multiplikator m, Lagrange-Faktor m	lake of cold air, local region of cold air	Kaltluftsee m, Kältesee m, Frostloch n
Lagrange['s] periodical solution	Lagrangesche periodische Lösung f		
		Lalande cell	Lalande-Element n
		Lallemand['s] formula	Lallemandsche Formel f, Formel von Lallemand
Lagrange['s] polynomial	Lagrangesches Polynom n	Lamb curve	Lambsche Kurve f
Lagrange['s] theorem, Lagrange['s] formula (law), Smith-Helmholtz law (equation), Lagrange-Helmholtz equation (formula, invariant, law), Helmholtz-Lagrange formula, Helmholtz['] relation, Helmholtz['] equation [for optical magnification], Lagrange invariant	Helmholtz-Lagrangesche Invariante (Gleichung) f, [Huygens-]Helmholtzsche Gleichung, Helmholtz-Gleichung f, Smith-Lagrangesche Gleichung, Satz m von Helmholtz-Lagrange, Helmholtz-Lagrangescher Satz		
		lambda doubling	s. lambda-type doubling
		lambda hyperon, Λ-hyperon	Λ-Hyperon n, Lambda-Hyperon n
		lambda leak, Onnes effect	Lambda-Leck n, [Kamerlingh-]Onnes-Effekt m
		lambda line, λ-line	λ-Linie f, Lambda-Linie f
		lambda meson	s. lambda hyperon
		lambda particle	s. lambda hyperon
		lambda phenomenon, λ-phenomenon	λ-Phänomen n, Lambda-Phänomen n
Lagrange['s] theorem <in celestial mechanics, mech., analysis, group theory>	Lagrangescher Satz m, Satz von Lagrange	lambda plate, λ plate	Lambdaplättchen n, Lambdablättchen n, Wellenlängenblättchen n, λ-Plättchen n, λ-Blättchen n; <aus Gips> Gipsrot n I. Ordnung
Lagrange['s] three-body problem	Lagrangescher Spezialfall m [des Dreikörperproblems], Lagrangesches Dreikörperproblem n		
		lambda point, λ-point	λ-Punkt m, Lambda-Punkt m
Lagrange['s] undetermined multiplier	s. Lagrange['s] multiplier		
Lagrange['s] variables	s. general co-ordinates	lambda-point transition, λ-transition, lambda transition, λ-point transition	λ-Übergang m, Lambda-Übergang m
Lagrangian <in field theory>	Lagrange-Funktion f, Lagrange-Funktional n <Feldtheorie>		
		lambda shock [wave]	s. bifurcated shock
Lagrangian	s. a. Lagrangian function <mech.>	lambda-transformation of Einstein, λ-transformation of Einstein	Einsteinsche Lambda-Transformation f, Einsteinsche λ-Transformation f
Lagrangian action	Lagrangesche Wirkung f		
		lambda transition, λ-transition, λ-point transition, lambda-point transition	λ-Übergang m, Lambda-Übergang m
Lagrangian autocorrelation	Lagrangesche Autokorrelationsfunktion f		
Lagrangian correlation coefficient	Lagrangescher Korrelationskoeffizient m	lambda-transition	s. a. second order transition
Lagrangian density [function], Lagrange density	Lagrange-Dichte f, Lagrangesche Dichtefunktion f, differentielle Lagrange-Funktion f	lambda-type doubling, lambda doubling	Lambda-Aufspaltung f, Lambda-Typ-Aufspaltung f
		lambda-type shock wave	s. bifurcated shock

lambert 410

lambert, la, La <= 10⁻⁴ asb>
   Lambert *n*, la, La <= 10⁻⁴ asb>

Lambert['s] albedo
   s. geometric albedo

Lambert-Beer law
   s. Beer['s] law

Lambert conformal [conic] projection, Lambert['s] conical orthomorphic projection, Lambert projection
   winkeltreuer Entwurf *m* [nach Gauß-Lambert], Gauß-Lambertscher winkeltreuer Entwurf, Lamberts winkeltreuer [echter] Kegelentwurf *m* <mit einem bzw. zwei längentreuen Breitenkreisen>, Lamberts winkeltreue Kegelprojektion *f*

Lambert['s] cosine law
   s. cosine law [of diffusing surface]

Lambert['s] equation
   s. Euler['s] equation

Lambert['s] equivalent projection
   Lamberts flächentreue Azimutalprojektion *f*

Lambertian radiator
   s. surface emitting according to the cosine law

Lambertian surface
   s. uniform diffuser

Lambert['s] law <of absorption>
   s. Bouguer-Beer law

Lambert['s] law <of diffusion, of emission>
   s. cosine law [of diffusing surface]

Lambert projection, isocylindrical projection
   sozylindrischer Entwurf *m* [nach J. H. Lambert], Lambertsche Projektion *f*, flächentreuer Zylinderentwurf *m* mit längentreuem Äquator

Lambert projection
   s. a. Lambert conformal [conic] projection

Lambert series
   Lambertsche Reihe *f*

Lambert['s] theorem
   Lambertscher Satz *m* <über die Krümmung der scheinbaren Bahn>

Lamb-Mössbauer factor
   s. Debye-Walter factor

Lamb-Retherford['s] experiment
   Lamb-Retherford-Versuch *m*, Versuch *m* von Lamb und Retherford

Lamb-Retherford shift, Lamb shift, radiative frequency shift
   Lamb-[Retherford-]Verschiebung *f*, Lambsche Verschiebung *f*, Lamb-Shift *m*, Lambshift *m*

Lamb vector
   Lambscher Vektor *m*

Lamb wave
   Lamb-Welle *f*, Plattenwelle *f*

Lamé['s] coefficient
   Laméscher Koeffizient *m*, Lamé-Koeffizient *m*

Lamé['s] cone of shearing stress
   Lamésche Schubspannungskegel *m*

Lamé['s] constant
   s. Lamé['s] elastic constant

Lamé['s] differential parameter
   Laméscher Differential-parameter *m*

Lamé['s] elastic constant, Lamé['s] constant
   Lamésche Elastizitätskonstante *f*, Laméscher Elastizitätsmodul *m*, Lamésche [elastische] Konstante *f*, Lamésche Konstante der Elastizität

Lamé['s] equation
   Lamésche Differentialgleichung *f*; Lamésche Wellengleichung *f*

lame étalon, Fabry-Pérot étalon, air wedge, wedge-shaped layer of air
   Lame-étalon *f*, Lamé-étalon'' *f*, Luftkeil *m*, keilförmige Luftschicht *f*, keilförmige Luftplatte *f*, Luftplatte, Fabry-Pérot-Etalon *m*

Lamé['s] function, ellipsoidal function
   Lamésche Funktion *f*

Lamé['s] function of the first kind
   Lamésche Funktion *f* erster Gattung <1., 2., 3. *oder* 4. Art>

Lamé['s] function of the second kind
   Lamésche Funktion *f* zweiter (2.) Gattung, zugeordnete Lamésche Funktion *f*

lamellar field
   s. irrotational field

lamellar structure
   s. laminated structure

lamellar vector field
   s. irrotational field

Lamé-Maxwell equations
   Lamé-Maxwellsche Gleichungen *fpl*

Lamé['s] polynomial
   Lamésches Polynom *n*

Lamé['s] sphere
   Lamé-Kugel *f*

Lamé['s] stress ellipsoid, stress ellipsoid
   Lamé-Spannungsellipsoid *n*, Lamésches Spannungsellipsoid

Lamé['s] wave function, ellipsoidal wave function
   Lamésche Wellenfunktion *f*

lamina <*pl.*: laminae>, plastic sheet
   Plastfolie *f*

laminar aerofoil section, laminar airfoil section, laminar flow section
   Laminarprofil *n*

laminar flow, streamline flow, laminated flow
   laminare Strömung (Bewegung) *f*, Laminarströmung *f*, Laminarbewegung *f*, schlichte Strömung (Flüssigkeitsströmung *f*, Bewegung, Flüssigkeitsbewegung *f*), Schichtenströmung *f*, Bandströmung *f*, Überlagerungsströmung; laminares Fließen *n*, Gleiten *n* <Geo.>

laminar flow section
   s. laminar airfoil

laminar friction
   laminare Reibung *f*

laminar grating
   Laminargitter *n*

laminarization
   Laminarhaltung *f*

laminar separation
   laminare Ablösung *f*

laminar structure
   laminare Struktur *f*

laminar sublayer, laminar sub-layer, viscous sub-layer
   laminare Unterschicht *f*

laminar thermal convection in the atmosphere, thermal convection, thermic upwash, thermal
   Thermik *f*, gleichmäßige Konvektion *f*, thermische Konvektion

laminate, laminated fabric, laminated material, laminated [plastic] sheet, resin-bond laminated fabric, multi-layer plastic material
   Schichtstoff *m*; Schichtpreßstoff *m*; Hartgewebe *n*

laminated flow
   s. laminar flow

laminated glass, compound glass
   Verbundsicherheitsglas *n*, Mehrschichtenglas *n*, Mehrschichten-Sicherheitsglas *n*

laminated growth
   Lamellenwachstum *n*

laminated lens, multi-layer lens
   geschichtete Linse *f*, Schichtlinse *f*

laminated magnet
   Blättermagnet *m*, Lamellenmagnet *m*, Lamellarmagnet *m*

laminated material
   s. laminate

laminated paper
   Hartpapier *n*, Schichtpreßpapier *n*

laminated [plastic] sheet
   s. laminate

laminated structure, lamellar structure; layer structure, stratiform structure
   Blätterstruktur *f*, Lamellarstruktur *f*, Lamellenstruktur *f*, Lamellenschichtung *f*; Schichtstruktur *f*, Schichtaufbau *m*, Schichten[auf]bau *m*; Schichtgefüge *n*

laminated window
   Lamellenfenster *n*

lamination; piling; stacking; stratification; layering
   Schichtung *f*, Schichten *n*; Schichtbildung *f*, Stratifikation *f*

lamination stack; stratification; striation
   Schichtung *f*

laminograph, planigraph, stratigraph, tomograph, body section device
   Tomograph *m*, Stratigraph *m*, Planigraph *m*

laminography
   s. body section roentgenography

La Mont nozzle
   La-Mont-Düse *f*

Lamont['s] position [of magnet]
   Lamontsche Lage (Hauptlage) *f* [des Magneten], Lamont-Lage *f* [des Magneten]

Lamont['s] theodolite
   Theodolit *m* nach Lamont, Lamontscher Theodolit, Lamont-Theodolit *m*

lamp producing white light, white lamp
   Weißlichtlampe *f*, Weißlampe *f*

lamp with solid carbons; carbon arc lamp
   Reinkohlebogenlampe *f*, Reinkohlenlampe *f*; Kohlebogenlampe *f*

Lanczos['] unitary field theory, unitary field theory [of Lanczos] — unitäre Feldtheorie f [von Lanczos]

Landahl curve — Landahl-Kurve f

Landau damping, Landau-Lifshitz damping — Landau-Dämpfung f, Landau-Lifshitzsche Dämpfung f

Landau diagram — Landau-Diagramm n

Landau diamagnetism — Landauscher Diamagnetismus m, Landau-Diamagnetismus m

Landau effect — Landau-Effekt m

Landau equation — Landausche Gleichung f, Landau-Gleichung f

Landau fluctuations — Landau-Schwankungen fpl, Landau-Fluktuationen fpl

Landau level — Landau-Niveau n

Landau-Lifshitz damping — s. Landau damping

Landau-Lifshitz damping parameter — Dämpfungsparameter m von Landau-Lifshitz, Landau[-Lifshitz]scher Dämpfungsparameter

Landau-Lifshitz equation — Landau-Lifshitzsche Gleichung f

Landau-Lifshitz gravitational pseudotensor — Landau-Lifshitzscher Gravitationspseudotensor m

Landau model, non-branching model — Landau-Modell n [des Zwischenzustandes]

Landau-Placzek formula — Landau-Placzeksche Formel f

Landau quantization — Landau-Quantelung f

Landau-Silin['s] theory of electron gas — Landau-Silinsche Theorie f des Elektronengases

Landau-Stanyoukovich equation of state — Zustandsgleichung f von Landau-Stanjukowitsch, Landau-Stanjukowitschsche Zustandsgleichung

Landau-Zener equation — Landau-Zenersche Gleichung f

land breeze, land wind, off-shore wind — Landwind m

Land camera — s. Polaroid-Land camera

land chain, measuring chain, surveyor's chain, column <geo.> — Meßkette f <Geo.>

Landé['s] g-factor, atomic g-factor, g-factor, Landé['s] splitting factor, spectroscopic splitting factor, splitting factor, interval factor — [Landéscher] g-Faktor m, Atom-g-Faktor m, Elektronen-g-Faktor m, Landé-Faktor m, Landéscher Faktor m, Aufspaltungsfaktor m [der Hyperfeinaufspaltung], Landéscher (spektroskopischer) Aufspaltungsfaktor

Landé['s] interval rule — s. interval rule

Landen['s] transformation — Landensche Transformation f

Landé['s] Γ-permanence rule — s. gamma permanence rule

Landé['s] splitting factor — s. Landé g-factor

landfall — s. soil slip

land ice, continental ice — Inlandeis n

landing on water, water landing, alighting [on water], surfacing — Landung f auf dem Wasser, Wasserlandung f, Wasserung f

landing rocket — landende Sonde (Rakete) f, Landungsrakete f

Landolt band (fringe) — Landoltscher Streifen m

Landolt-Oudeman law, Oudeman['s] law, law of Oudeman — Oudemansches Gesetz n, Landolt-Oudemansches Gesetz

Landolt ring — Landoltscher Ring m

landslide, landslip — s. soil slip

land survey[ing], mapping, topographic mapping — Landesvermessung f, Landesaufnahme f, Landeskartierung f, Mappierung f

land wind — s. land breeze

lane — Nullhyperbel f

Lane-Emden function, Emden function, Emden polytropic function of index n — Emdensche Funktion f vom Index n

Lane['s] law — Lanesches Gesetz n

Lange cell — s. photovoltaic cell

Lange effect — Lange-Effekt m

Langevin['s] approximation — Langevin-Näherung f

Langevin-Born theory — Langevin-Bornsche Theorie f

Langevin-Debye equation (formula), Debye-formula — Debyesche Formel f, Langevin-Debyesche Formel

Langevin['s] [diamagnetism] equation — Langevinsche Gleichung f

Langevin['s] formula — Langevinsche Formel f

Langevin['s] function — Langevin-Funktion f, Langevinsche Funktion

Langevin ion — s. large ion

Langevin-Pauli formula — Langevin-Paulische Formel f

Langevin pressure — Langevin-Druck m, Langevinscher Schallstrahlungsdruck m

Langhans['] layer, layer of Langhans — Langhans-Schicht f

langley, ly, Ly, lan <= 1 cal/cm² — Langley n, ly, Ly, lan <= 1 cal/cm²

Lang['s] method, Lang['s] technique — Langsche Methode f, Lang-Verfahren n, Langsches Verfahren n, Lang-Technik f, Röntgentopographie f

Langmuir['s] adsorption equation, Langmuir['s] adsorption isotherm, Langmuir['s] equation, adsorption formula of Langmuir, adsorption isotherm of Langmuir, Langmuir['s] isotherm — Isothermengleichung (Adsorptionsisotherme) f von Langmuir, Langmuirsche Adsorptionsisotherme (Adsorptionsgleichung f, Gleichung f für die Adsorption), Langmuir-Volmersche Adsorptionsgleichung f

Langmuir-Child three-halves power law — s. Langmuir['s] law

Langmuir curve, Langmuir diagram — Langmuir-Diagramm n, Langmuir-Kurve f

Langmuir-Dushman molecular gauge — s. Langmuir manometer

Langmuir effect, Langmuir-Taylor effect — Langmuir-Taylor-Effekt m, Langmuir-Effekt m

Langmuir['s] equation — s. Langmuir['s] adsorption equation

Langmuir['s] film balance, film balance [introduced by Langmuir] — Langmuirsche Waage (Filmwaage) f, Filmwaage von Langmuir

Langmuir frequency, electron plasma frequency, plasma frequency — Langmuir-Frequenz f, Elektronenplasmafrequenz f, Plasmafrequenz f [der Elektronen]

Langmuir gauge — s. Langmuir manometer

Langmuir['s] isotherm — s. Langmuir['s] adsorption equation

Langmuir['s] law, [Langmuir-Child] three-halves power law, Langmuir-Child law, $3/2$ power law, space charge law — Raumladungsgesetz n, Langmuirsches Raumladungsgesetz, Langmuirsches Gesetz n, Langmuirsches $3/2$-Gesetz n, Langmuirsche Formel f, Drei-Halbe-Gesetz n, $U^{3/2}$-Gesetz n

Langmuir manometer, Langmuir gauge, Langmuir-Dushman molecular gauge, rotating-disk vacuum gauge, rotating viscometer gauge — Langmuir-Manometer n, Langmuirsches Manometer n, Reibungsmanometer n mit rotierender Scheibe, Langmuir-Dushmansches Molekularmanometer n, rotierende Scheibe f

Langmuir oscillation, longitudinal electronic oscillation — Langmuir-Schwingung f, longitudinale Elektronenschwingung f [im Plasma], Langmuirsche Elektronenschwingung

Langmuir paradox — Langmuirsches Paradoxon n

Langmuir probe, Langmuir-type probe — Langmuir-Sonde f

Langmuir-Saha equation — Langmuir-Saha-Gleichung f, Langmuir-Sahasche Gleichung f

Langmuir-Schottky law, Schottky-Langmuir law — Gesetz *n* von Langmuir und Schottky, Langmuir-Schottkysches Raumladungsgesetz *n* (Gesetz), Langmuir-Schottkysche Formel *f*, Schottky-Langmuirsche Raumladungsgleichung *f*

Langmuir-Taylor effect, Langmuir effect — Langmuir-Taylor-Effekt *m*, Langmuir-Effekt *m*

Langmuir torch — Langmuir-Fackel *f*
Langmuir trough — Langmuir-Trog *m*
Langmuir-type probe — *s.* Langmuir probe
Langmuir wave — *s.* electrostatic wave
Lang probe — Lang-Sonde *f*
Langsdorf counter — Langsdorf-Zähler *m*

Lang['s] technique — *s.* Lang['s] method
lantern slide — Diapositivplatte *f*
lantern-slide projector — *s.* still projector
lanthanide contraction — Lanthanidenkontraktion *f*
lanthanide elements (group) — *s.* lanthanides
lanthanides, lanthanide series, lanthanoids, lanthanide elements (group) — Lanthan[o]iden *npl*, Gruppe *f* der Lanthaniden

lap edge fracture — *s.* edge crack
lapilli, volcanic pellets — Lapilli *mpl* <*sing.*: Lapillo>, Rapilli *mpl* <*sing.*: Rapillo>

Laplace azimuth — Laplacesches Azimut *n*
Laplace azimuth station, Laplace station (point), azimuth station — Laplacescher Punkt *m*, astronomische Station *f*

Laplace['s] coefficient, surface spherical harmonic — Laplacescher Koeffizient *m*

Laplace['s] constant, capillary constant, specific cohesion, capillary tension — Kapillarkonstante *f*, Kapillaritätskonstante *f*, Kapillarspannung *f*

Laplace['s] demon — Laplacescher Dämon *m*
Laplace['s] differential equation, Laplace['s] equation, potential equation — Laplacesche Differentialgleichung (Potentialgleichung) *f*, Potentialgleichung, Laplacesche Gleichung *f*

Laplace['s] differential operator — *s.* laplacian
Laplace distribution — Laplace-Verteilung *f*, Laplacesche Verteilung *f*
Laplace equation <ac.; geo.> — Laplacesche Gleichung *f*, Laplace-Gleichung *f* <Ak.; Geo.>

Laplace['s] equation — *s. a.* Laplace['s] differential equation

Laplace['s] expansion of determinant <math.> — Laplacescher Entwicklungssatz *m* <Math.>

Laplace['s] formula <for capillary pressure> — Laplace-Gleichung *f* <für den Kapillardruck>

Laplace['s] hypothesis [of primeval nebula], Laplace['s] theory — Nebularhypothese *f* [von Laplace], Laplacesche Theorie, Rotationshypothese *f*

Laplace['s] integral, Laplace['s] vector — Laplace-Integral *n*, Laplacesches Integral *n*, Laplacescher Vektor *m*

Laplace['s] law — *s.* Laplace's theorem <el.>
Laplace observation — Laplace-Beobachtung *f*, Laplacesche Beobachtung *f*

Laplace['s] operator — *s.* laplacian
Laplace point — *s.* Laplace station
Laplace['s] series — Laplacesche Reihe *f*
Laplace['s] spherical function (harmonic) — *s.* surface harmonic
Laplace station, [Laplace] azimuth station, Laplace point — Laplacescher Punkt *m*, astronomische Station *f*

Laplace['s] theorem, Biot-Savart['s] law, Laplace's law, Ampère['s] law, Biot-Savart relation — Biot-Savartsches Gesetz *n*, Laplacesches Gesetz <El.>

Laplace-Stieltjes transform[ation] — Laplace-Stieltjes-Transformation *f*

Laplace['s] theorem <hydr., aero.> — Laplacescher Satz *m* <Hydro., Aero.>
Laplace['s] theory — *s.* Laplace's hypothesis

Laplace transform — Laplace-Transformierte *f*, Unterfunktion *f*, Bildfunktion *f* <Laplace-Transformation>

Laplace transform, Laplace transformation — Laplace-Transformation *f*, Laplacesche Transformation *f*, Transformation nach Laplace

Laplace['s] vector — *s.* Laplace['s] integral
laplacian, Laplacian derivative, Laplace['s] operator, Laplace['s] differential operator, delta operator, delta, differential parameter of the second order, Δ — Laplace-Operator *m*, Laplacescher Operator *m*, Delta-Operator *m*, Delta *n*; Laplacescher Differentialausdruck (Ausdruck) *m*; Laplacesche Ableitung *f*; zweiter Beltramischer Differentialparameter *m*, zweiter Differentialparameter von Lamé, Differentialparameter *m* zweiter Ordnung, Δ

laplacian — = negative buckling <in reactor theory>
Laplacian determinism — Laplacescher Determinismus *m*

Laporte parity rule, Laporte['s] rule, Laporte selection rule — Laportesche Regel *f*, Auswahlregel (Regel) *f* von Laporte

lapping — Läppen *n*, Läppung *f*, Läppschliff *m*
lapse — *s.* time behaviour
lapse rate, temperature lapse [rate] — vertikaler Temperaturgradient *m*, vertikales Temperaturgefälle *n*

large / in the — *s.* non-local
large-angle grain boundary, high-angle grain boundary — Großwinkelkorngrenze *f*

large-angle scattering — *s.* wide-angle scattering
large-area contact, area contact — Flächenkontakt *m*

large-area-contact rectifier — *s.* surface-contact rectifier
large-area photomultiplier — Großflächen-Photovervielfacher *m*

large-area scintillation counter — großflächiger Szintillationszähler *m*, Großflächen-Szintillationszähler *m*

large calorie — *s.* kilo-calorie
large ion, macro-ion, Langevin ion, show (heavy) ion <geo.> — Großion *n*, großes Ion *n*, Makroion *n*

Large Magellanic Cloud — Große Magellansche Wolke *f*
large scale <geo.> — weiträumig <Geo.>

large-scale turbulence, macroturbulence — großräumige (weiträumige, großmaßstäbliche) Turbulenz *f*, Großturbulenz *f*, Makroturbulenz *f*

large-scale turbulent flame — turbulente Flamme *f* im Großen, großmaßstäblich turbulente Flamme

large-signal amplification; large-signal gain — Großsignalverstärkung *f*

large-signal current amplification; large-signal current gain — Großsignalstromverstärkung *f*

large-signal gain; large-signal amplification — Großsignalverstärkung *f*

large-signal theory — Großsignaltheorie *f*

Larmor [angular] frequency, Larmor precession frequency, angular frequency (velocity) of Larmor precession — Larmor-Kreisfrequenz *f*, Larmor-Frequenz *f*, Larmor-Präzessionsfrequenz *f*, Kreisfrequenz *f* der Larmor-Präzession

Larmor frequency — *s. a.* cyclotron frequency
Larmor period, Larmor precession period (time) — Larmor-Präzessionszeit *f*

Larmor precession — Larmor-Präzession *f*, Larmorsche Präzession *f*

Larmor precession frequency — *s.* Larmor angular frequency

Larmor precession period (time), Larmor period — Larmor-Präzessionszeit *f*

Larmor radius	Larmor-Radius m, Larmorscher Radius m	**latent heat of fusion (melting)**	s. heat of fusion
Larmor['s] theorem	Larmorscher Satz m, Satz (Theorem n) von Larmor, Larmor-Theorem n	**latent heat of solidification**, heat of solidification, solidification heat	Erstarrungswärme f; Erstarrungsenthalpie f
laryngophone, throat microphone	Kehlkopfmikrophon n	**latent heat of sublimation**	s. heat of sublimation
		latent heat of vaporization	s. evaporation heat
laser, optical maser ⟨light amplification by (through) stimulated emission of radiation⟩	Laser m, optischer Maser m, Lichtkanone f	**latent Herschel effect**; Herschel effect	Herschel-Effekt m
		latent image, latent photographic image, [photographic] sub-image	latentes Bild n, latentes photographisches Bild
		latent image fading	s. fading ⟨phot.⟩
laser amplifier, optical maser amplifier	Laserverstärker m, Molekularverstärker m im optischen Bereich, optischer Molekularverstärker (Quantenverstärker m)	**latent image intensification**, intensification of latent image, latensification	Latensifikation f, Verstärkung f des latenten Bildes
		latent injury; **latent lesion**; latent damage	latente Schädigung f, Spätschaden m
		latent period, latency period, latency, latent (latency) time ⟨e.g. in irradiation⟩ ⟨bio.⟩	Latenzzeit f, Latenz f ⟨z. B. bei der Bestrahlung⟩ ⟨Bio.⟩
laser beam, laser light beam	Laserstrahl m		
laser diode, laser-effect diode	Laserdiode f, Lasereffektdiode f	**latent period**	s. a. incubation period ⟨bio.⟩
laser light beam, laser beam	Laserstrahl m	**latent-period shortening**	Latenzverkürzung f
laser mode	Lasermode f, Laserwelle f	**latent photographic image**, latent image	latentes Bild n, latentes photographisches Bild
laser oscillator	Lasergenerator m, Laseroszillator m, Laser m, Lichtgenerator m	**latent punctum remotum**	latenter Fernpunkt m
		latent root	s. eigenvalue ⟨of matrix⟩
		latent solvent, inert solvent	indifferentes (latentes) Lösungsmittel n
		latent time	s. incubation period ⟨of a disease⟩ ⟨bio.⟩
laser radar, optical radar, lidar ⟨light detection and ranging⟩	Laserradar n, optischer Sucher m	**latent time**	s. a. latent period ⟨e.g. in irradiation⟩ ⟨bio.⟩
laser radiation	Laserstrahlung f	**latent vector**, characteristic vector ⟨of a matrix⟩; eigenvector, proper vector, model column	Eigenvektor m
laser rangefinder, laser ranger	Laser-Entfernungsmeßgerät n, Laser-Entfernungsmesser m, Entfernungsmesser m mit Lasergerät	**latent xerographic image**	s. latent electrical image
		late radiation death	Spättod m [nach Bestrahlung]
laser rotation rate sensor	s. optical quantum gyroscope		
laser spectroscopy	Laserspektroskopie f	**late radiation effect**, late effect	Spätschaden m, Strahlenspätschaden m, Strahlungsspätschaden m, Spätfolge f der Bestrahlung, Spätwirkung f [der Bestrahlung]
laser spike, spike of the laser	Laserblitz m		
laser unit	Lasergerät n		
last collision correction	Letztstoßkorrektion f		
last multiplier	letzter Multiplikator m	**lateral aberration**	s. transverse ray aberration
last runnings ⟨chem.⟩	Nachlauf m ⟨Chem.⟩	**lateral aberration of the ray**	laterale Strahlaberration f
		lateral area, lateral surface ⟨math.⟩	Mantel m, Mantelfläche f ⟨Math.⟩
latch, jack ⟨el.⟩	Klinke f ⟨El.⟩	**lateral area of the cylinder**	s. lateral surface of the cylinder ⟨math.⟩
latched relay	s. locked-in relay		
latching; interlock[ing], locking; blocking	Blockierung f, Blockung f; Verblockung f; Sperrung f; Verriegelung f	**lateral buckling**; buckling; flexural buckling	Knickung f; [seitliche] Ausknickung f, seitliches Ausweichen n
latching relay	s. lock-in relay	**lateral capacitance**	Seitenkapazität f
late effect	s. late radiation effect	**lateral chain**	s. side chain
latency [period]	s. incubation period ⟨bio.⟩	**lateral chemical potential**	laterales chemisches Potential n
latency period	s. a. latent period ⟨bio.⟩		
latency time ⟨of detector⟩	Latenzzeit f ⟨Detektor⟩	**lateral chromatic aberration**, transverse chromatic aberration, chromatic variation of magnification, chromatic difference of magnification	Farbvergrößerungsfehler m, chromatische Vergrößerungsdifferenz (Queraberration, Querabweichung) f, Farbquerfehler m, Farbfehler m des Hauptstrahls, Farbenfehler m der Bildvergrößerung (Bildgröße), Farbmaßstabsfehler m
latency time	s. a. latency period ⟨e.g. in irradiation⟩ ⟨bio.⟩		
latency time	s. a. incubation period ⟨of a disease⟩ ⟨bio.⟩		
latensification, latent image intensification, intensification of latent image	Latensifikation f, Verstärkung f des latenten Bildes		
latent damage	s. latent injury	**lateral deflection**	s. lateral deviation
latent electrical image, latent xerographic image, residual charge pattern [recording the image in xerography], potential relief	latentes elektrisches Bild n [bei der Elektrophotographie], Potentialrelief n	**lateral deviation**; lateral deflection	seitliche Ablenkung f; seitliche Abweichung f, Seitenabweichung f; seitliche Auslenkung f, Auslenkung f
		lateral displacement, side thrust	Lateralverschiebung f, laterale (seitliche) Verschiebung f
latent heat	s. heat of transformation		
latent heat of condensation, heat of condensation (liquefaction), condensation heat	Kondensationswärme f, Verflüssigungswärme f	**lateral erosion**, side wash	Seitenerosion f, Lateralerosion f, Seitenschurf m
latent heat of evaporation	s. evaporation heat	**lateral eruption**	Flankeneruption f

lateral extensometer	s. thickness gauge	latitude pair	Breitenpaar n
lateral force	s. cross force <mech.>	latitude quantum number	Breitenquantenzahl f
lateral force	s. a. shear force	latitude series	Breitengruppe f
lateral force coefficient	Querkraftbeiwert m	Latour circuit	s. Greinacher circuit
lateral force density	Querkraftdichte f	lattice <of flow>	Gitter n <Strömung>
lateral geotropism	Lateralgeotropismus m	lattice, structure <math.>	Verband m <Math.>
lateral illumination, side illumination, side lighting; half-back	Seitenbeleuchtung f, seitliche Beleuchtung f		
lateral intersection	Seitwärtseinschneiden n, Seitwärtseinschnitt m	lattice, latticing network, web network <mech.>	Fachwerk[netz] n, Füllungsstäbe mpl <im Raumfachwerk> <Mech.>
lateral inversion of image, reversion right to left	Seitenumkehr f des Bildes	lattice	s. a. crystal lattice <cryst.>
		lattice	s. a. grid
lateral load, transverse load	seitliche Belastung f, Belastung in der Querrichtung, Querbelastung f	lattice	s. a. matrix lattice
		lattice absorption	s. absorption in the matrix lattice
laterally inverted (transposed)	s. reversed right to left <of image>	lattice absorption edge, fundamental absorption edge, fundamental lattice absorption edge	Grundgitter[-Absorptions]-kante f, Grundabsorptionskante f, Absorptionskante f des Kristalls, Gitterabsorptionskante f
laterally uninverted, true-sided, correct <of image>	seitenrichtig <Bild>		
lateral magnification	s. magnification <opt.>		
lateral moraine, flank (marginal, peripheral) moraine	Seitenmoräne f, Ufermoräne f, Randmoräne f	lattice binding	Gitterbindung f
lateral oblique [photograph]	seitliche Schrägaufnahme f, seitliches Schrägbild n	lattice binding energy, lattice energy, grid energy	Gitterenergie f
lateral oscillation, transverse vibration (oscillation), lateral vibration	transversale Schwingung f, Transversalschwingung f, Querschwingung f	lattice cell	Gitterzelle f
		lattice-cell theory, cell theory, free volume theory <of liquids>, cell model [of the liquid state]	Zellentheorie f, Theorie f des freien Volumens <der Flüssigkeiten>
lateral overlap	Querüberdeckung f		
lateral pressure, side (transverse) pressure, side thrust	Seitendruck m, seitlicher Druck m, Querdruck m	lattice collision	Gitterstoß m, Zusammenstoß m mit dem Gitter
lateral record	s. lateral recording	lattice complex	Gitterkomplex m
lateral recording, lateral record	[Aufzeichnung f in] Seitenschrift f, Berliner-Schrift f, Querschrift f	lattice conductivity	s. lattice heat conductivity
		lattice constant	s. lattice parameter <cryst.>
		latticed	gitterförmig
lateral refraction	Seitenrefraktion f, Lateralrefraktion f, laterale Refraktion f	lattice defect	s. defect
		lattice diffusion	Gitterdiffusion f
lateral resolving power	laterales Auflösungsvermögen n	lattice dislocation	Gitterversetzung f
		lattice distortion	Gitterverzerrung f, Gitterstörung f, Gitterverbiegung f
lateral shower, inclined shower	Seitenschauer m; schräg einfallender Schauer m		
lateral spherical aberration	s. transverse ray aberration	lattice dynamics	Gitterdynamik f
lateral spread <of cosmic-ray shower>	laterale Ausdehnung (Ausbreitung) f, seitliche Ausdehnung, Schauerbreite f	lattice element <cryst.>	Gitterbaustein m <Krist.>
lateral strain	s. transverse strain	lattice emission	Gitterleuchten n
lateral structure function	laterale Strukturfunktion f	lattice energy, lattice binding energy, grid energy	Gitterenergie f
lateral surface; lateral area <math.>	Mantel m, Mantelfläche f <Math.>	lattice entropy	Gitterentropie f
		lattice expansion	Gitteraufweitung f, Gitterdehnung f
lateral surface of the cylinder, lateral area of the cylinder <math.>; cylinder envelope	Zylindermantel m	lattice force	Gitterkraft f
		lattice gas	Gittergas n
		lattice heat	Gitterwärme f
lateral tangential arc to 22°-halo, arc of Lowitz	seitlicher Berührungsbogen m des kleinen Ringes, Lowitzscher [schiefer] Bogen m	lattice heat conductivity, heat conductivity due to the lattice, lattice [thermal] conductivity	Gitterwärmeleitfähigkeit f, Gitteranteil m der Wärmeleitfähigkeit, [thermische] Gitterleitfähigkeit f
lateral tangential arc to 46°-halo	seitlicher Berührungsbogen m des großen Ringes	lattice hole	s. vacant site
		lattice imperfection	s. defect
lateral vibration, transverse vibration (oscillation), lateral oscillation	transversale Schwingung f, Transversalschwingung f, Querschwingung f	lattice impurity, impurity, chemical impurity <cryst., semi.>	[chemische] Störstelle f, Fremdstörstelle f, Fremdbeimischung f, Beimischung f, Verunreinigung f, Beimengung f <Krist., Halb.>
late-type star	Stern m vom späten Spektraltyp, später Typ m		
lather	Seifenschaum m		
Latimer-Clerk cell	s. Clerk cell	lattice inclusion compound	s. lattice-type inclusion compound
Latin square	lateinisches Quadrat n		
latitude, latitude angle <as a co-ordinate>	Breite f, Breitengrad m, Breitenwinkel m <als Koordinate>	lattice ion	Gitterion n
		lattice matrix	Gittermatrix f
		lattice mobility	Gitterbeweglichkeit f
latitude <of an emulsion>, range of sensitivity	Empfindlichkeitsbereich m		
latitude	s. a. ecliptical latitude <astr.>	lattice motion	Gitterbewegung f
latitude angle, latitude <as a co-ordinate>	Breite f, Breitengrad m, Breitenwinkel m <als Koordinate>	lattice network, bridge circuit, bridge connection	Brückenschaltung f
latitude effect, geomagnetic effect <of cosmic rays>	Breiteneffekt m, Poleffekt m, geomagnetischer Effekt m <der kosmischen Strahlung>	lattice network [structure]; lattice-type connection; lattice-type section, X-quadripole	X-Schaltung f, Kreuzschaltung f, Kreuzverbindung f; Kreuzglied n, Vierpolkreuzglied n, X-Vierpol m, X-Glied n
latitude line	s. line of equal latitude		

lattice of lines, line lattice (screen)	Linienraster m, Liniengitter n	Laue['s] equations, Laue['s] conditions	Laue-Bedingungen fpl, Lauesche Gleichungen (Fundamentalgleichungen, Bedingungen) fpl, Laue-Gleichungen fpl
lattice optics, optics of crystalline lattice	Gitteroptik f		
lattice parameter, unit cell dimension, lattice constant, lattice spacing <cryst.>	Gitterkonstante f [des Kristalls], kristallographische Gitterkonstante, Kristallgitterkonstante f, Gitterparameter m, Gitterabstand m <Krist.>	Laue film, Laue X-ray film	Laue-Film m
		Laue-Friedrich-Knipping theory, Laue theory	Lauesche Theorie f, Laue-Friedrich-Knippingsche Theorie
lattice pitch, lattice spacing	Gitterschritt m, Gitterteilung f, Gitterabstand m	Laue group, Laue symmetry group	Laue-Gruppe f, Lauesche Symmetriegruppe f, Laue-Symmetriegruppe f
lattice plane	s. atomic plane <cryst.>		
lattice point <cryst.>	Gitterpunkt m <Krist.>	Laue index	Laue-Index m
		Laue interference	Laue-Interferenz f, Röntgenstrahlinterferenz f nach Laue
lattice point, grid point <math.>	Gitterpunkt m, Stützstelle f <Math.>	Laue method	Laue-Verfahren n, Laue-Methode f, [von] Lauesche Methode f
lattice-point method, finite difference method	Differenzenverfahren n, Differenzenmethode f, Gitterpunktmethode f	Laue pattern	s. Laue diffraction pattern
		Laue pattern made by use of focusing geometry	fokussiertes Laue-Diagramm n
lattice position	s. lattice site		
lattice potential <cryst.>	Gitterpotential n <Krist.>	Laue photograph	s. Laue diffraction pattern
		Laue photography	Laue-Aufnahme f, Laue-Photographie f
lattice scattering	Gitterstreuung f, Streuung f am Gitter		
lattice site, atom[ic] site, site [in the lattice], lattice position	Gitterplatz m, Gitterstelle f	Laue spike	Laue-Stachel m
		Laue spot	Laue-Fleck m, Laue-Reflex m, Interferenzfleck m <im Laue-Diagramm>
lattice spacing, lattice pitch	Gitterschritt m, Gitterteilung f, Gitterabstand m		
lattice spacing	s. a. lattice parameter <cryst.>	Laue symmetry	Laue-Symmetrie f
		Laue symmetry group	s. Laue group
lattice structure	Gitterstruktur f, Gitteraufbau m, Gitterbau m	Laue theory, Laue-Friedrich-Knipping theory	Lauesche Theorie f, Laue-Friedrich-Knippingsche Theorie
lattice temperature	Gittertemperatur f	Laue X-ray diffraction pattern	s. Laue diffraction pattern
lattice theory <math.>	Verbandstheorie f, Theorie f der Verbände <Math.>	Laue X-ray film, Laue film	Laue-Film m
lattice thermal conductivity	s. lattice heat conductivity	Laue X-ray pattern	s. Laue diffraction pattern
lattice translation	Gittertranslation f	launch, launching; liftoff, rise <of rocket, aircraft>	Start m, Aufstieg m <Rakete, Flugzeug>; Abschuß m; Abheben n [von der Startrampe] <Rakete>
lattice-type connection	s. lattice network		
lattice-type inclusion compound, lattice inclusion compound	Gittereinschlußverbindung f	launch emplacement	s. launching emplacement
		launching	s. launch
lattice-type section	s. lattice network	launching acceleration	Startbeschleunigung f
lattice unit	s. unit cell <cryst.>		
lattice vacancy	s. vacant site <cryst.>		
lattice vector	Gittervektor m	launching base	s. launching site
lattice vibration	Gitterschwingung f	launching booster	s. carrier rocket
		launching emplacement, launch emplacement, launching platform	Abschußplattform f, Startplattform f
lattice vibrational spectrum	Gitterschwingungsspektrum n		
lattice vibration quantum, energy quantum of lattice vibration	Gitterschwingungsquant n, Energiequant n der Kristallgitterschwingung	launching pad	s. launching site
		launching platform	s. launching emplacement
		launching rack, launching ramp	Abschußrampe f, Startrampe f
lattice wave	Gitterwelle f		
lattice wave vector	Gitterwellenvektor m		
latticing network	s. lattice <mech.>	launching rails, launching tracks	Startschienen fpl
latus rectum <of conic section>	Parameter m <Kegelschnitt>		
Laue asterism	Laue-Asterismus m		
Laue back-reflection method	s. back-reflection method	launching ramp	s. launching rack
		launching range	s. launching site
		launching rocket	s. carrier rocket
Laue back-reflection photogram (photograph)	s. back-reflection Laue pattern	launching site, launching base, launching pad, launching range	Abschußbasis f, Startplatz m
Laue back-reflection photography	s. back-reflection method	launching speed	Startgeschwindigkeit f
Laue chamber, Laue diffraction chamber	Laue-Kammer f, Laue-Beugungskammer f		
Laue['s] conditions	s. Laue['s] equations	launching tower, servicing tower	Startturm m
Laue diffraction	Laue-Beugung f, Lauesche Beugung f		
Laue diffraction chamber, Laue chamber	Laue-Kammer f, Laue-Beugungskammer f	launching tracks	s. launching rails
		launching vehicle	s. carrier rocket
Laue diffraction pattern, Laue pattern, Laue photograph, Laue X-ray [diffraction] pattern	Laue-Diagramm n, Laue-Aufnahme f, Laue-Beugungsdiagramm n, Einkristalldiagramm n	Laurent['s] expansion	Laurent-Entwicklung f, Laurentsche Entwicklung f
		Laurent halfshade; Laurent half-shade plate, Laurent plate	Halbschattenapparat m mit Laurent-Platte; Laurent-Platte f

Laurent series	Laurent-Reihe f, Laurentsche Reihe f	law of conservation of power, power conservation law	Arbeitssatz m, Leistungs[erhaltungs]satz m, Satz m von der Erhaltung der Leistung, Erhaltungssatz m der Leistung
Lauritsen electroscope	Lauritsen-Elektroskop n		
Laval density	Laval-Dichte f, kritische Dichte f	law of constancy of angles, law of constant angles	Winkelkonstanzgesetz n, Winkelbeständigkeitsgesetz n, Gesetz n der Winkelbeständigkeit (Winkelkonstanz, Konstanz der Flächenwinkel), Steno[sches] Gesetz, Stenosche Regel f
Laval nozzle, Laval valve, convergent-divergent nozzle, contracting-expanding nozzle	Laval-Düse f, konvergent-divergente Düse f		
Laval pressure	Laval-Druck m		
Laval state	Laval-Zustand m		
Laval temperature	Laval-Temperatur f	law of constant heat summation	s. Hess['] law
Laval valve	s. Laval nozzle		
Laval velocity, critical sound velocity	Laval-Geschwindigkeit f, kritische Schallgeschwindigkeit f	law of constant proportions, law of definite proportions (composition)	Gesetz n der konstanten Proportionen (Verhältnisse, Gewichtsverhältnisse)
lava plateau	Lavaplateau n, Übergußtafelland n		
Laves phase	Laves-Phase f	law of constant proportions of volume, law of definite proportions of volume	Gesetz n der konstanten Volumenverhältnisse
law for ideal gas	s. Boyle-Charles law		
law of action and reaction	s. Newton['s] third law [of motion]		
law of additive volumes	s. Amagat['s] law	law of correspondent (corresponding) states	s. theorem of corresponding states
law of areas	s. principle of conservation of areas	law of cosine['s], theorem of Carnot, cosine formula (law) <math.>	Kosinussatz m <Math.>
law of associated production	Gesetz n der assoziierten Erzeugung		
law of averages	s. law of the mean	law of decay, decay law	Abklinggesetz n, Abklingungsgesetz n
law of Cailletet and Mathias	s. Cailletet-Mathias law	law of definite composition (proportions)	s. law of constant proportions
law of chance	Zufallsgesetz n	law of definite proportions of volume, law of constant proportions of volume	Gesetz n der konstanten Volumenverhältnisse
law of collision, collision law	Stoßgesetz n		
law of composition, rule of composition	Zusammensetzungsvorschrift f; Verknüpfungsgesetz n	law of degradation of energy	. second law
law of conjugate points <opt.>	Abbildungsgesetz n	law of electromagnetic induction	s. Faraday['s] law of induction
law of connected vessels	Gesetz n der kommunizierenden Gefäße	law of electrostatic attraction, Coulomb's law, Coulomb law of force	Coulombsches Gesetz n [der Elektrostatik], Gesetz der elektrostatischen Anziehung, elektrisches Coulombsches Gesetz
law of conservation, conservation law	Erhaltungssatz m, Erhaltungsgesetz n		
law of conservation of angular momentum	s. angular momentum conservation law	law of energetics	s. law of thermodynamics
law of conservation of baryon number	s. baryon number conservation law	law of equality of incidence and refraction plane	allgemeines Brechungsgesetz n, Satz m der Gleichheit von Einfalls- und Durchlaßebene
law of conservation of charge, charge conservation law, law (principle) of conservation of electric charge	Satz m von der Erhaltung der Ladung, Ladungserhaltungssatz m, Erhaltungssatz m der [elektrischen] Ladung	law of equipartition [of energy], principle of equipartition [of energy], equipartition theorem (law), equipartition principle, concept of equipartition of energy	Gleichverteilungssatz m [der Energie], Gleichverteilungssatz der kinetischen Energie, Energiegleichverteilungssatz m, Gleichverteilungsgesetz n, Gleichverteilungsprinzip n, Äquipartitionstheorem n
law of conservation of circulation	Erhaltungssatz m der Zirkulation		
law of conservation of eddy flux, eddy flux conservation law, vorticity flux conservation law	Satz m von der Erhaltung des Wirbelflusses		
law of conservation of electric charge	s. law of conservation of charge	law of equivalence, theorem of equivalence <opt., theory of four-terminal network>	Äquivalenzsatz m <Opt., Vierpoltheorie>
law of conservation of energy	s. energy conservation law	law of equivalent proportions, law of reciprocal proportions	Gesetz n der äquivalenten Proportionen
law of conservation of entropy	Erhaltungssatz m der Entropie	law of errors	s. error law
law of conservation of isobaric spin, conservation law of isobaric spin, isobaric spin conservation law	Isospinerhaltungssatz m, Erhaltungssatz m des Isospins, Satz m von der Erhaltung des Isospins	law of excluded middle, law of the excluded middle, tertium exclusum, tertium non datur	Satz m vom ausgeschlossenen Dritten, tertium n non datur
law of conservation of mass (matter), mass conservation law, principle of conservation of mass (matter), conservation of mass principle, conservation of matter principle	Satz m von der Erhaltung der Masse, Masse[n]erhaltungssatz m, Massenbilanzgleichung f, Gesetz n von der Erhaltung der Masse (Materie), Erhaltungssatz m der Masse (Materie)	law of extreme path	s. Fermat['s] principle
		law of falling bodies	Fallgesetz n
		law of gravitation, Newton['s] law of gravitation, gravitation law [of Newton], Newton['s] law of universal gravitation	Gravitationsgesetz n [von Newton], Newtonsches Gravitationsgesetz, [Newtonsches] Massenanziehungsgesetz n, Newtonsches Gesetz n
law of conservation of moment of momentum	s. angular momentum conservation law	law of gravitation	s. a. law of universal gravitation
law of conservation of momentum	s. momentum conservation law	law of Grotthus and Draper	s. Grotthus-Draper law
law of conservation of parity, parity conservation law, principle of conservation of parity, conservation of parity principle	Satz m von der Erhaltung der Parität, Paritätserhaltungssatz m, Erhaltungssatz m der Parität	law of growth <cryst.>	Wachstumsgesetz n <Krist.>
		law of growth; growth formula; growth function; growth curve <stat.>	Wachstumsgesetz n; Wachstumsformel f; Wachstumsfunktion f; Wachstumskurve f <Stat.>
law of conservation of particle number	s. particle number conservation law		

law of Hamburger, Hamburger['s] law (theorem)	Satz *m* von Hamburger, Hamburgerscher Satz
law of Hess	*s.* Hess['] law
law of homogeneous circuit	*s.* Magnus['] law
law of induction	*s.* Faraday['s] law of induction
law of inertia <of quadratic forms>	Trägheitsgesetz *n* [der quadratischen Formen], Sylvestersches Trägheitsgesetz
law of inertia	*s. a.* Newton['s] first law
law of large numbers	Gesetz *n* der großen Zahlen
law of lever	*s.* lever principle
law of light sums	Lichtsummengesetz *n*
law of Magnus	*s.* Magnus['] law
law of Malus, Malus['] [cosine-squared] law, Malus-Daupin theorem, Malus['] theorem	Satz *m* (Gesetz *n*) von Malus, Malusscher Satz
law of mass action, mass[-action] law, mass action expression, isotherm of reaction, [equation of] reaction isotherm, Guldberg-Waage law	[Guldberg-Waagesches] Massenwirkungsgesetz *n*, Gesetz *n* von Guldberg und Waage, Reaktionsisotherme *f*, Gleichung *f* der Reaktionsisothermen, MWG
law of moment of momentum <hydr.>	Drehimpulssatz *m*, allgemeiner Flächensatz *m* [der Hydromechanik], Impulsmomentensatz *m* [der Hydromechanik], Drallsatz *m*, Drehmomentensatz *m* <Hydr.>
law of motion	Bewegungsgesetz *n*
law of multiple proportions	Gesetz *n* der multiplen Proportionen (Verhältnisse, Gewichtsverhältnisse), Gesetz der mehrfachen Proportionen (Verhältnisse, Gewichtsverhältnisse), Daltonsches Gesetz der multiplen Proportionen (Verhältnisse, Gewichtsverhältnisse), chemisches Grundgesetz *n*
law of multiple proportions of volume, law of volumes	Gesetz *n* der multiplen Volumenverhältnisse
law of mutuality of phases	Satz *m* der koexistierenden Phasen
law of nature, natural law	Naturgesetz *n*, Weltgesetz *n*
law of Oudeman, Oudeman['s] law, Landolt-Oudeman law	Oudemansches Gesetz *n*, Landolt-Oudemansches Gesetz
law of parallel axes	*s.* parallel axis theorem
law of partial pressures	*s.* Dalton['s] law
law of Paschen, Paschen['s] law	Paschensches Gesetz *n*
law of pendulum motion (oscillation), pendulum law	Pendelgesetz *n*
law of photochemical equivalence, photochemical equivalence law, Einstein['s] law of photochemical equivalence, Stark-Einstein['s] law	[Stark-Einsteinsches] Äquivalentgesetz *n*, Quantenäquivalentgesetz *n*, [Stark-Einsteinsches] Äquivalenzgesetz *n*, Gesetz *n* der photochemischen Äquivalenz, photochemisches Äquivalenzgesetz *n*, Einsteins photochemisches Äquivalentgesetz, Einsteinsches Äquivalentgesetz
law of planetary distances, Bode['s] law, Titius-Bode law	Titius-Bodesche Regel (Reihe) *f*, Bodesches Gesetz *n*, Abstandsgesetz *n*
law of probability, probability law	Wahrscheinlichkeitsgesetz *n*
law of proximity theory	Nahewirkungsgesetz *n*, Nahwirkungsgesetz *n*
law of radiation, radiation law, radiant law, radiation formula	Strahlungsgesetz *n*, Strahlungsformel *f*
law of radioactive decay	*s.* law of radioactive disintegration
law of radioactive disintegration, law of radioactive decay, radioactive disintegration law, disintegration law [of atomic nucleus], radioactive decay law, decay law [of atomic nucleus]	Zerfallsgesetz *n* [der Radioaktivität], radioaktives Zerfallsgesetz, Gesetz *n* des radioaktiven Zerfalls
law of rational indices, law of rational intercepts, law of rationality, rationality law, fundamental law of crystallography, Hauy law	Rationalitätsgesetz *n* [der Flächenindizes], Haüysches Gesetz *n*, Gesetz der rationalen Achsenabschnitte (Doppelverhältnisse, Indizes, Parameter), Parametergesetz *n*, Grundgesetz *n* der Kristallographie
law of reaction	*s.* Newton['s] third law
law of reaction	*s.* Le Chatelier['s] principle <therm.>
law of reaction rate	Geschwindigkeitsgleichung *f*, Geschwindigkeitsgesetz *n*, Zeitgesetz *n* der Reaktion
law of reciprocal proportions	*s.* law of equivalent proportions
law of reciprocity	*s.* Bunsen-Roscoe reciprocity law
law of recombination, recombination law, dissipation law	Wiedervereinigungsgesetz *n*, Rekombinationsgesetz *n*
law of reflection	Reflexionsgesetz *n*, Spiegel[ungs]gesetz *n*
law of refraction, refraction law	Brechungsgesetz *n*
law of resistance for turbulent flow, turbulent law of resistance	turbulentes Widerstandsgesetz *n*
law of Retgers, Retgers['] law	Retgerssches Gesetz *n*
law of shearing stress, law of torsion stress	Schubspannungsansatz *m*, Schubspannungsgesetz *n*
law of similarity, similarity principle, similarity law	Ähnlichkeitsgesetz *n*, Ähnlichkeitsprinzip *n*, Similaritätsprinzip *n*
law of similarity transformation, similarity principle <of Laplace transformation>	Ähnlichkeitssatz *m* <Laplace-Transformation>
law of sines, sine law <of trigonometry *or* spherical trigonometry>	Sinussatz *m* <der ebenen *oder* sphärischen Trigonometrie>
law of small numbers	Gesetz *n* der kleinen Zahlen, Gesetz der seltenen Ereignisse
law of specific energies	*s.* Müller['s] law
law of spectrometric (spectroscopic) displacement	*s.* displacement law for complex spectra
law of stress	*s.* Newton['s] third law
law of superposition	*s.* principle of superposition
law of the excluded middle, law of excluded middle, tertium exclusum, tertium non datur	Satz *m* vom ausgeschlossenen Dritten, tertium *n* non datur
law of the independent migration of ions, Kohlrausch['s] law [of the independent migration of ions]	Gesetz *n* [von] der unabhängigen Ionenwanderung, Kohlrauschsches Gesetz [von der unabhängigen Ionenwanderung]
law of the linear change of bending stress	Geradliniengesetz *n*, Naviersches Geradliniengesetz
law of the mean, mean value theorem, law of averages	Mittelwertsatz *m*
law of the mean, mean value theorem <of the differential calculus>	erster Mittelwertsatz *m* [der Differentialrechnung], Mittelwertsatz der Differentialrechnung
law of the propagation of errors	*s.* propagation theorem
law of the rectilinear diameter	*s.* Cailletet-Mathias law
law of thermal equilibrium, zeroth law of thermodynamics	nullter Hauptsatz *m* der Thermodynamik, Gesetz *n* des thermischen Gleichgewichts, zweites Postulat *n* der Thermodynamik

law of thermodynamics, law of energetics	Hauptsatz m der Thermodynamik	L-cathode, Lemmens diffusion cathode	Lemmens-Katode f, L-Katode f
law of the transmissibility of pressure	s. Pascal['s] law	L-C circuit, L-C network, L-C section	LC-Glied n
law of the wall, hypothesis of wall similarity	Wandgesetz n	L-C coupling	s. inductance-capacitance coupling <of thermionic tubes>
law of torsion stress, law of shearing stress	Schubspannungsansatz m, Schubspannungsgesetz n	L circuit; L section, L network	L-Glied n; L-Schaltung f
law of universal gravitation, law of gravitation, gravitation law	allgemeines Gravitationsgesetz n, Gravitationsgesetz	L-C network, L-C circuit, L-C section	LC-Glied n
law of velocity addition	Gesetz n der Addition der Geschwindigkeiten	L-conversion	[innere] Konversion f an der L-Schale, L-Konversion f, L-Umwandlung f, Umwandlung f an der L-Schale
law of volumes	s. law of multiple proportions of volume		
law of vortex motion	Turbulenzgesetz n, Wirbelgesetz n, Gesetz n der Wirbelbewegungen	L-conversion coefficient, L-conversion ratio	Koeffizient m der inneren Konversion an der L-Schale, Konversionskoeffizient m der L-Schale, L-Konversionskoeffizient m, L-Umwandlungskoeffizient m
law of zones, Spoerer['s] law, zone law	Spörersches Gesetz n, Zonengesetz n		
lawrencium, $_{103}$Lw	Lawrencium n, Lawrentium n. $_{103}$Lw		
laws of conservation of energy and momentum	s. energy momentum theory	L-conversion line	L-Konversionslinie f, L-Umwandlungslinie f
lay, twist	Drallänge f, Schlaglänge f, Drall m	L-conversion ratio	s. L-conversion coefficient
layer, coat	Beschichtung f	L corona	L-Komponente f der Koronastrahlung, L-Korona f
layer	s. a. coating		
layer cathode, multi-layered cathode, multilayer cathode	Mehrschichtkatode f, Vielschichtkatode f, Schichtenkatode f, vielschichtige Katode f	LC oscillator	LC-Generator m, LC-Oszillator m
layer chromatography, spread layer chromatography	Schichtchromatographie f	L/C ratio	L/C-Verhältnis n
		L-C section	s. L-C network
layer cloud	s. stratiform cloud	L/D ratio	s. lift-drag ratio
layer corrosion	s. film corrosion	LD 50 time	s. median lethal time
layer division, division of layers	Schichtenteilung f	leaching; lixiviation; solid-liquid extraction	Laugung f, Auslaugung f, Auswaschung f, Festflüssig-Extraktion f
layer division technique, technique of layer division	Schichtenteilungsmethode f, Schichtenteilungsverfahren n	lead, prediction <control>	Vorhalt m <Regelung>
layer impermeable to underground water	Grundwasserstauer m, grundwasserstauende Schicht f	lead	s. a. leading
		lead	s. a. pitch
		lead	s. a. supply pipe
layering	s. lamination	lead age	Bleialter n
layer lattice, layer structure	Schichtengitter n, Schichtgitter n	lead amalgam normal (standard) cell	Bleielement n
layer line <cryst.>	Schichtlinie f <Krist.>	lead angle, angle of lead, [phase-]advance angle <control>	Vorhaltwinkel m, Vorhaltewinkel m <Regelung>
layer line method, layer line technique	Schichtlinienverfahren n, Schichtlinienmethode f		
		lead angle	s. a. angle of lead
layer of charge; sheet of charge	Ladungsschicht f	lead brick	Bleiziegel m, Bleibaustein m
layer of fluid, liquid layer, liquid film	Flüssigkeitsschicht f; Flüssigkeitslamelle f; Flüssigkeitshaut f; Flüssigkeitsfilm m	lead castle	liegende Bleikammer f, Blei[meß]kammer f
		lead circuit, phase-advance circuit	Vorhaltkreis m, Vorhaltekreis m
layer of intrinsic conduction (material)	s. intrinsic region	lead dating method, lead method of dating	Bleimethode f, Bleiisotopenmethode f
layer of Langhans, Langhans['] layer	Langhans-Schicht f		
layer of mixing, mixing layer, mixed layer	Mischungsschicht f, Vermischungsschicht f	lead door	Tür f mit Bleieinlage
layer of stability, stability layer	Stabilitätsschicht f	lead equivalent, protective value	Bleiäquivalent n, Bleigleichwert m
layer of troubling, troubling layer	Trübschicht f, Trübungsschicht f		
		leader	Leader m
		leader	s. a. preceding spot
layer structure, layer lattice	Schichtengitter n, Schichtgitter n	leader channel, return stroke channel	Blitzkanal m, Entladungskanal m des Blitzes
layer structure	s. a. laminated structure	leader formation	Leaderbildung f, Kanalkopfbildung f
layer thickness	s. thickness of layer		
layout	s. version	lead glass	Bleiglas n
L band <0,4 — 1,6 or 390—1,550 Mc/s>	L-Band n <0,4 ··· 1,6 oder 390 ··· 1550 MHz>	lead-in	s. lead-through <el.>
		lead inductance	Zuleitungsinduktivität f
		leading, lead; advance, advancing; speed-up	Voreilung f
L-binding energy	L-Bindungsenergie f, Bindungsenergie f des L-Elektrons, Bindungsenergie eines Elektrons auf der L-Schale	leading coefficient, highest coefficient	höchster Koeffizient m <Polynom>
		leading current	voreilender Strom m
LCAO approximation, LCAO method, LCAO-MO method, linear combination of atomic orbitals approximation	LCAO-MO-Methode f, LCAOMO-Methode f, LCAO-MO-Näherung f	leading diagonal, principal diagonal, [main] diagonal	Hauptdiagonale f, Hauptdiagonale f, Hauptschräge f
L-capture, L-electron capture	L-Einfang m, L-Elektroneneinfang m	leading echo, pre-echo	Vorecho n

leading edge, frontal edge, front edge ‹hydr., aero.›	Vorderkante *f*, Anströmkante *f* ‹Hydr., Aero.›	**leakage impedance,** stray impedance	Streuimpedanz *f*
leading edge [of the pulse], leading front [of the pulse]	Vorderflanke *f* [des Impulses], Impulsvorderflanke *f*	**leakage inductance, leakage inductive,** stray inductance	Streuinduktivität *f*
leading edge vortex	Vorderkantenwirbel *m*	**leakage inductance (inductive)**	*s. a.* leakance
leading front [of the pulse]	*s.* leading edge [of the pulse]	**leakage loss**	Leckverlust *m*; Gasverlust *m*
leading note	Leitton *m*	**leakage of heat**	*s.* dispersion of heat
leading of phase, phase lead[ing], advance of phase, phase advance	Phasenvoreilung *f*	**leakage operator**	Verlustoperator *m*
		leakage path ‹el.›	Streuweg *m*, Streuflußweg *m* ‹El.›
leading phase	voreilende Phase *f*	**leakage path; tracking path** ‹el.›	Kriechweg *m*; Kriechstrecke *f* ‹El.›
leading [sun]spot	*s.* preceding spot	**leakage peak**	*s.* escape peak
leading through	*s.* lead-through	**leakage radiation,** direct radiation ‹of X-ray tube›	Hüllenausfallstrahlung *f*, Leckstrahlung *f*, direkte Strahlung *f*, Direktstrahlung *f*
leading zero	führende Null *f*		
lead method of dating, lead dating method	Bleimethode *f*, Bleiisotopenmethode *f*		
lead rubber	Bleigummi *m*	**leakage radiation**	*s. a.* leakage
		leakage rate	*s.* leak rate
lead screw [of micrometer], micrometer screw, micrometric screw	Meßspindel *f*, Mikrometerschraube *f*; Feinmeßschraube *f* ‹z. B. beim Mikroskop›	**leakage reactance**	Streublindwiderstand *m*, Streureaktanz *f*
		leakage resistance	Ableit[ungs]widerstand *m*
		leakage resonance ‹el.›	Streuresonanz *f* ‹El.›
lead-through, leading through, lead-in; bushing; feed-through ‹el.›	Durchführung *f* ‹El.›	**leakage spectrum**	Abflußspektrum *n*, Ausflußspektrum *n*
lead tree, arbor Saturni	Bleibaum *m*	**leakage survey,** leak hunting, search for leaks, leak detection, checking for gas leaks	Lecksuche *f*, Aufsuchen *n* von Undichtheiten
leaf ‹of Riemann surface›	Blatt *n* ‹Riemannsche Fläche›		
leaf electroscope, foil electroscope	Blättchenelektroskop *n*, Blattelektroskop *n*	**leakage test**	*s.* leak test
leafing	*s.* peeling off	**leakage voltage**	*s.* reactance voltage
leaf shutter	Lamellenverschluß *m*, Segmentverschluß *m*, Segmentblende *f*	**leakance,** leakage inductance (inductive), dielectric leakage (leakance)	Ableitung *f*, dielektrische Ableitung ‹Leitung, Isolator›
		leakance per unit length	Ableitungsbelag *m*, kilometrischer Belag *m*
leak; leakage; leaky area	Leck *n*; Undichtigkeit[sstelle] *f*, Undichte *f*, Leckstelle *f*, Leckschadenstelle *f*; Leckage *f*; Drosselstelle *f*	**leak detection,** leak hunting, search for leaks, leakage survey; checking for gas leaks	Lecksuche *f*, Aufsuchen *n* von Undichtheiten
leak ‹el.›	Ableitung *f* ‹El.›	**leak detector; leak tester**	Lecksucher *m*, Lecksuchgerät *n*, Leckfinder *m*, Leckspürgerät *n*; Leckprüfer *m*; Schadensucher *m*
leak	*s. a.* magnetic leakage ‹el.›		
leakage; loss	Verlust *m*; Einbuße *f*		
leakage, neutron leakage, escape of neutrons	Neutronenabfluß *m*, Neutronenausfluß *m*, Neutronenverlust *m*	**leak hunting,** search for leaks, leak detection, leakage survey; checking for gas leaks	Lecksuche *f*, Aufsuchen *n* von Undichtheiten
leakage, leakage radiation, radiation leakage	Sickerstrahlung *f*, Leckstrahlung *f*, Leakage *f*		
leakage ‹of electric charge›	Abfließen *n*, Abfluß *m* ‹von Ladungen›	**leakiness,** untightness	Undichtigkeit *f*, Undichtheit *f*
leakage	*s. a.* surface leakage ‹el.›	**leaking[out], leakage;** spillage, spilling	Lecken *n*; Auslaufen *n*; Durchsickern *n*; Undichtwerden *n*
leakage	*s. a.* leak		
leakage	*s. a.* leaking		
leakage	*s. a.* magnetic leakage ‹el.›	**leakproof**	*s.* tight
leakage coefficient	Leckbeiwert *m*, Undichtigkeitszahl *f*	**leak rate,** leakage rate, rate of leakage	Undichtheit *f*, Undichtigkeit *f*, Leckrate *f*; Leckverlust *m*, Undichtigkeitsverlust *m*, Undicht[heits]verlust *m*
leakage coefficient	*s. a.* magnetic leakage factor		
leakage conductance	[ohmscher] Leckleitwert *m*		
leakage current, stray current[s]	Irrstrom *m*; Fehlstrom *m*; Leckstrom *m* ‹auch Halb.›; Ableit[ungs]strom *m*; Isolationsstrom *m*	**leak resistance**	*s.* shunt resistance
		leak test, leakage test, leak testing, proofing	Leckprüfung *f*, Dicht[igkeits]prüfung *f*, Dichtigkeitsprobe *f*
leakage current	*s. a.* surface leakage current		
leakage current	*s. a.* residual current ‹of electrolytic capacitor›	**leak tester;** leak detector	Lecksucher *m*, Lecksuchgerät *n*, Leckfinder *m*, Leckspürgerät *n*; Leckprüfer *m*; Schadensucher *m*
leakage current path, path of leakage current ‹el.›	Leckweg *m*, Irrweg *m* ‹El.›		
leakage damping	Ableitungsdämpfung *f*	**leak testing**	*s.* leak test
		leak-tight	*s.* tight
leakage factor	*s.* magnetic leakage factor ‹el.›	**leaky;** lossy; dissipative	verlustbehaftet
leakage field	*s.* magnetic stray field	**leaky area**	*s.* leak
leakage flux, magnetic leakage flux, stray flux	magnetischer Streufluß *m*, Streufluß	**leaky-pipe antenna, leaky waveguide**	*s.* slotted cylinder antenna
		leap	= jump
leakage flux density, stray flux density	Streuflußdichte *f*	**leap day,** intercalary day, adding day	Schalttag *m*
leakage hardening [of the neutron spectrum], neutron hardening by leakage	Ausflußhärtung *f* [des Neutronenspektrums]	**leap distance**	*s.* skip distance
		leap year, abundant year	Schaltjahr *n* ‹Gregorianischer Kalender›
		learning machine	lernende Maschine *f*

learning system	lernendes System *n*	lee wave flow, lee-side flow	Leewellenströmung *f*, Leeströmung *f*
least action principle	s. principle of least action		
least common denominator, lowest common denominator	Hauptnenner *m*, Generalnenner *m*	lee wave theory	Leewellentheorie *f*
		left / on the, sinistrorse; left-handed <math.>	linksseitig; Links- <Math.>
least common multiple	kleinstes gemeinsames Vielfaches *n*, KGV	left derivative	s. left-handed derivative
least-energy principle	s. Dirichlet['s] stability theorem	left-handed, sinistrorse; on the left <math.>	linksseitig; Links- <Math.>
least mean square error	s. root-mean-square error	left-handed, sinistrogyric <techn.>	linksgängig, linksdrehend, Links-; linksläufig; linkswendig <Techn.>
least squares estimator	Gaußsche Schätzfunktion *f*		
least squares method, method (principle) of least squares	Methode *f* der kleinsten Quadrate (Quadratsummen), Fehlerquadratmethode *f*	left-handed circular[ly polarized], counterclockwise circularly polarized	zirkular linkspolarisiert, linkszirkular [polarisiert], linksdrehend zirkular polarisiert, linkspolarisiert zirkular
least upper bound, supremum, sup	obere Grenze *f*, Supremum *n*, sup	left-handed circular polarization	zirkulare Linkspolarisation *f*, linkszirkulare Polarisation *f*
least work	kleinste Arbeit (Formänderungsarbeit) *f*	left-handed co-ordinate system, left-handed system [of co-ordinates], left system [of co-ordinate axes]	Linkssystem *n*, linkshändiges Koordinatensystem *n*, linkshändiges System *n*
leaving of penumbra	Austritt *m* aus dem Halbschatten		
leavings	s. still bottom heel		
Lebesgue integral	Lebesguesches Integral *n*, L-Integral *n*		
Lebesgue measure	Lebesguesches Maß *n*	left-handed cycle, anticlockwise process	Linksprozeß *m*
Lebesgue space	Lebesguescher Raum *m*	left-handed derivative, left derivative, derivative on the left	linksseitige Ableitung *f*
Lebesgue-Stieltjes integral	Lebesgue-Stieltjessches Integral *n*		
Lebesgue['s] theorem	Lebesguescher Satz *m*	left-handed elliptic[ally polarized], counterclockwise elliptically polarized	elliptisch linkspolarisiert, linkselliptisch [polarisiert], linksdrehend elliptisch polarisiert, linkspolarisiert elliptisch
Le Chatelier-Braun principle	s. Le Chatelier['s] principle		
Le Chatelier-Guertler rules	le Chatelier-Guertlersche Regeln *fpl*		
Le Chatelier microscope, inverted microscope	Le-Chatelier-Mikroskop *n*, gestürztes (umgekehrtes) Mikroskop *n*	left-handed elliptical polarization	elliptische Linkspolarisation, *f* linkselliptische Polarisation *f*
Le Chatelier['s] principle, Le Chatelier['s] rule, principle of Le Chatelier, Le Chatelier-Braun principle, principle of Le Chatelier and Braun, principle of the least constraint; law of reaction <therm.>	le Chatelier[-Braun]sches Prinzip *n*, Le Chatelier- und Braun-Prinzip *n*, Prinzip vom kleinsten Zwang, Prinzip des kleinsten Zwanges, Prinzip von le Chatelier, Le Chatelier-Braunscher Satz *m*, Satz von le Chatelier-Braun, Satz vom Prinzip des kleinsten Zwanges	left-handed helix	s. left-twisted helix
		left-handed polarization	Linkspolarisation *f*, linkshändige Polarisation *f*
		left-handed polarized, counterclockwise polarized	linkspolarisiert, linksdrehend (linkshändig) polarisiert
		left-handed quartz, laevorotatory (laevogyric, laevogyrate) quartz	Linksquarz *m*
Le Chatelier thermocouple	s. platinum/platinumrhodium thermocouple	left-handed screw[ing]	s. left-twisted helix
		left-handed system [of co-ordinates]	s. left-handed co-ordinate system
Lecher circuit	s. resonant circuit with distributed parameters	left-hand helix	s. left-twisted helix
Lecher frame, Lecher system, Lecher wires, radio-frequency two-wire line	Lecher-System *n*, Lecher-Leitung *f*, Lecher-Drähte *mpl*, Hochfrequenz-Paralleldrahtsystem *n*, Hochfrequenz-Doppeldrahtsystem *n*	left-hand lay, left-hand twist	Linksdrall *m*
		left-hand limit, limit on the left	linksseitiger Grenzwert *m*, linksseitiger Limes *m*
		left-hand rule, Fleming['s] [first] rule	Dreifingerregel *f* der linken Hand, Linke-Hand-Regel *f*, Linkehandregel *f*
Leclanché cell, Leclanché dry cell	Leclanché-Element *n*, Leclanché-Trockenelement *n*, Braunsteinelement *n*, Salmiakelement *n*		
		left-hand screw	s. left-twisted helix
ledge	Sprunglinie *f*, „ledge" *f*	left-hand side, left side <of the equation>	linke Seite *f* <Gleichung>
Leduc effect	s. Righi-Leduc effect		
Leduc law, Amagat-Leduc law (rule), Amagat law	Amagat-Leducsche Regel *f*	left-hand twist, left-hand lay	Linksdrall *m*
		left-invariant	linksinvariant
Lee model	Lee-Modell *n*	left inverse	Linksinverse *n*
lee-side flow	s. lee wave flow		
lee-side vortex, leeward vortex, lee vortex	Leewirbel *m*	left multiplication	s. premultiplication
		left side, left-hand side <of the equation>	linke Seite *f* <Gleichung>
lee-side wave	s. lee wave		
lee-side wave equation	s. lee wave equation	left-skew distribution, distribution skew on the left	linksschiefe Verteilung *f*, rechtssteile Verteilung
Leeuwen['s] theorem / Van	van Leeuwensches Theorem *n*, Van-Leeuwen-Theorem *n*, Theorem (Satz *m*) von van Leeuwen		
		left system [of co-ordinate axes]	s. left-handed co-ordinate system
		left-to-right reversed	s. reversed right to left <of image>
lee[ward] vortex	s. lee-side vortex		
lee wave, lee-side wave	Leewelle *f*	left-twisted helix, left-twisted screw, left-hand[ed] helix, sinistrorse helix (screw), left-hand[ed] screw, left-handed screwing	Linksschraube *f*
lee wave equation, lee-side wave equation	Leewellengleichung *f*		

leg <el.>	Schenkel m, Jochschenkel m <El.>	Leibniz['s] formula (rule, theorem), Leipnitz['s] formula (rule, theorem) <for the nth derivative of a product>	Leibnizsche Formel f [für die Ableitungen höherer Ordnungen eines Produktes], Leibnizsche Produktenregel f
legal metrology	gesetzliches Meßwesen n		
legal ohm	s. international ohm	Leibniz['] rule (test, theorem), Leibnitz['s] rule (test, theorem) <for convergence>	Leibnizsche Regel f, Leibnizscher Satz m, Leibnizsches Konvergenzkriterium n, Leibnizsches Kriterium n
legal time, standard time	Normalzeit f, Nationalzeit f		
Legendre['s] associated function [of the first kind]	s. associated Legendre function [of the first kind]		
		Leidenfrost['s] phenomenon, calefaction	Leidenfrostsches Phänomen n, Leidenfrost-Phänomen n
Legendre['s] associated function of the second kind	s. associated Legendre function of the second kind		
Legendre['s] coefficient	s. Legendre polynomial	Leiden jar, Leyden jar	Leidener (Kleistsche, Leydener) Flasche f, Glaskondensator m
Legendre['s] condition	Legendresche Bedingung f		
Legendre['s] elliptic integral of the first <second; third> kind	s. elliptic integral of the first <second; third> kind in Legendre's normal form	Leithäuser circuit	Leithäuser-Schaltung f
		Leitz dilatometer	Leitz-Dilatometer n
		L-electron	L-Elektron n, Elektron n der L-Schale
Legendre['s] [differential] equation	Legendresche Differentialgleichung f, Legendresche Gleichung f	L-electron capture, L-capture	L-Einfang m, L-Elektroneneinfang m
		Lemaître-Eddington model, model of Lemaître and Eddington	Lemaître-Eddingtonsches Modell n
Legendre['s] form of elliptical integral	s. Legendre['s] integral		
Legendre['s] form of the elliptical integral of the first <second; third> kind	s. elliptic integral of the first <second; third> kind in Legendre's normal form	Lemaître['s] model	Lemaîtresches Modell n, [Friedmann-]Lemaître-Welt f
		Leman prism	Leman-Prisma n, Sprenger-Prisma n
Legendre function	Legendresche Funktion f, Legendresche Kugelfunktion f	Lemmens diffusion cathode, L-cathode	Lemmens-Katode f, L-Katode f
Legendre function of the first kind, spherical harmonic of the first kind	Legendresche Funktion (Kugelfunktion) f erster Art, Kugelfunktion erster (1.) Art	Lenard effect, beaking drop effect, balloelectric effect	Wasserfalleffekt m, Lenard-Effekt m; Wasserfallelektrizität f, Balloelektrizität f
Legendre function of the second kind, spherical harmonic of the second kind, surface zonal harmonic of the second kind	Legendresche Funktion f zweiter Art, Legendresche Kugelfunktion f zweiter Art, Kugelfunktion zweiter (2.) Art	Lenard['s] law [of absorption]	Lenardsches Massenabsorptionsgesetz (Massengesetz, Gesetz) n
		Lenard['s] method of opposing field, retarding potential method	Lenardsche Gegenfeldmethode f, Gegenfeldmethode f [nach Lenard]
Legendre['s] integral, Legendre['s] standard integral; Legendre['s] form (normal form, standard form) of elliptical integral	Legendresches Normalintegral n, Legendresches Integral n; Legendresche Normalform f des elliptischen Integrals	Lenard ray	Lenard-Strahl m
		Lenard tube	Lenard-Rohr n, Lenard-Röhre f
		Lenard window	Lenard-Fenster n, Lenardsches Fenster n
		length	s. magnitude <of vector>
Legendre['s] normal form of elliptical integral	s. Legendre['s] integral	lengthening; prolongation; production protraction [of the line]	Verlängerung f
Legendre operator	Legendrescher Operator m	length measurement	s. measurement of length
Legendre polynomial, Legendrian, zonal spherical harmonic, zonal harmonic [function], spherical harmonic of the first kind	Legendresches Polynom n, Legendrescher Koeffizient m, Kugelfunktion f erster Art, zonale Kugelfunktion (Harmonische f)	length measurement by interferometric method	Interferenzlängenmessung f
		length measuring	s. measurement of length
		length measuring interferometer; gauge measuring interferometer	Interferenzkomparator m
Legendre polynomial expansion	s. expansion in Legendre polynomials	length-measuring machine, length measuring machine	Längenmeßmaschine f
Legendre potential, Legendre transformed potential	Legendresches Potential n		
		length of air gap, width of air gap, [air-]gap width, gap length	Polschuhabstand m, Luftspaltlänge f, Luftspaltbreite f
Legendre series	Legendresche Reihe f		
Legendre['s] standard form of elliptical integral	s. Legendre['s] integral		
		length of arc gap, arc length	Lichtbogenlänge f; Bogenlänge f
Legendre['s] standard form of the elliptic integral of the first <second; third> kind	s. elliptic integral of the first <second; third> kind in Legendre['s] normal form	length of break	s. break
		length of moderation, slowing-down length, moderation length	Bremslänge f
Legendre['s] standard integral	s. Legendre['s] integral	length of path	s. orbit circumference
Legendre['s] theorem	Legendrescher Satz m	length of plateau, plateau length	Plateaulänge f
Legendre transform	Legendre-Transformierte f		
Legendre transform, Legendre transformation	Legendresche Transformation f, Berührungstransformation f von Legendre	length of run, development distance	Laufstrecke f, Gesamtlaufstrecke f, Entwicklungsstrecke f, Wanderungsstrecke f, Wanderungsweite f
Legendre transformed potential, Legendre potential	Legendresches Potential n	length of span	s. span <mech.>
		length of the chord, chord length	Sehnenlänge f <Profil>
Legendrian	s. Legendre polynomial		
legibility of characters	s. intelligibility of characters	length of the equivalent simple pendulum, length of the simple equivalent pendulum	s. reduced length [of the pendulum]
Lehmann ellipse	Lehmann-Ellipse f		
Leibnitz ...	s. Leibniz ...		

length

length of the spin angular momentum vector	Betrag m des Spindrehimpulses (Eigendrehimpulses), Spindrehimpulslänge f
length-preserving, isometric <math.>	isometrisch; längentreu, maßstabgerecht <Math.>
length-preserving mapping, isometric mapping	längentreue Abbildung f, Abwicklung f, Abwickelung f
length standard, standard of length	Längennormal n
length strength parameter, power <of electronic lens>	Lichtstärke f <Elektronenlinse>
lengthwise stratified	s. longitudinally stratified
Lennard-Jones equation of state	Lennard-Jonessche Zustandsgleichung f
Lennard-Jones model	Lennard-Jones-Modell n, Lennard-Jonessches Modell n
Lennard-Jones potential, Lennard-Jones potential function <e.g. Lennard-Jones six-twelve (6,12) potential function>	Lennard-Jones-Potential n, Lennard-Jonessches Potential n <z. B. Lennard-Jones-(6,12)-Potential>
lens action, lens effect	Linsenwirkung f
lens antenna, radio lens	Linsenantenne f
lens astrograph, refracting astrograph	Linsenastrograph m
lens barrel	s. lens mount
lens blooming, blooming of the lens, lens coating	Linsenvergütung f, Blauung f der Linse
lens cap	s. protective cap
lens casing	s. lens mount
lens cementing	Linsenkittung f, Linsenverkittung f
lens centre, optical centre of the lens	Linsenmittelpunkt m, optischer Mittelpunkt m der Linse
lens chain	Linsenkette f
lens coating	s. lens blooming
lens combination, lens system	Linsensystem n, Linsenkombination f
lens condenser	Linsenkondensor m
lens cover	s. protective cap
lens disk	Linsenscheibe f
lens drum	Linsenkranz m, Linsentrommel f
lens drum scanner	Linsenkranzabtaster m
lens effect	s. lens action
lens equation	s. Gauss lens formula
Lense-Thirring effect	Lense-Thirring-Effekt m
lens flare, flare, reflex <phot.>	Reflex m, Reflexionsfleck m <Phot.>
lens for high definition effects, hard focus lens	Hartzeichner m
lens for microwaves, microwave lens	Mikrowellenlinse f
lens formula	s. Gauss lens formula
lens guard	s. protective cap
lens hood, lens shade, lens shield, sun shade	Lichtkappe f [des Objektivs]; Sonnenblende f, Sonnenschutz m; Gegenlichtblende f
lens / image distance	s. image distance from the vertex
lens lid	s. protective cap
lens-line disk	linsenförmige Scheibe f
lens-mirror system, catadioptric system	Spiegellinsensystem n, Spiegellinse f, katadioptrisches System n
lens mount, lens barrel, lens seating, lens casing, setting of lens	Linsenfassung f
lens / object distance	s. object distance from the vertex
lens of Luneberg, Luneberg['s] lens	Luneberg-Linse f, Lunebergsche Linse f, Linse von Luneberg
lens power	s. focal power
lens screen film <US>, embossed lens film, lenticulated screen film	Linsenrasterfilm m
lens seating	s. lens mount
lens shade, lens hood, lens shield, sun shade	Lichtkappe f [des Objektivs]; Sonnenblende f, Sonnenschutz m; Gegenlichtblende f
lens-shaped, lenticular, lentiform	linsenförmig
lens shield, lens hood, lens shade, sun shade	Lichtkappe f [des Objektivs]; Sonnenblende f, Sonnenschutz m; Gegenlichtblende f
lens spectrometer <opt.>	Linsenspektrometer n
lens spectrometer	s. a. magnetic lens spectrometer
lens strength	s. focal power
lens system, lens combination	Linsensystem n, Linsenkombination f
lens telescope, refractor, refracting telescope <astr.>	Refraktor m, Linsenfernrohr n, Linsenteleskop n <Astr.>
lens turret	s. turret head
lens vertex, vertex of the lens	Linsenscheitel m; Linsenpol m
lenticular, lentiform, lens-shaped	linsenförmig
lenticular cloud, altocumulus lenticularis	Lenticulariswolke f, Altocumulus m lenticularis, Ac lenticularis, linsenförmige Wolke f, Lenticularisform f
lenticular erecting system, [image] erecting lens	Umkehrlinse f
lenticular screen, lenticulated screen	Riffelwand f, Linsenraster m; Linsenfarbraster m
lenticulated screen film, embossed lens film, lens screen film <US>	Linsenrasterfilm m
lentiform	s. lenticular
lenz, L	Lenz n, L
Lenz['s] law, Lenz['s] rule	Lenzsche Regel f, Regel von Lenz, Lenzsches Gesetz n, Hemmungsgesetz n
Leonhard['s] criterion [of stability]	s. Michailov['s] criterion
Leontovich['s] approximative boundary condition, Leontovich['s] condition	Leontowitsch-Bedingung f, Leontowitschsche Bedingung f, genäherte Grenzbedingung f von Leontowitsch
lepton	Lepton n
lepton charge, lepton number	Leptonenladung f, Leptonenzahl f
lepton decay, leptonic decay	leptonischer Zerfall m, Leptonenzerfall m
lepton number, lepton charge	Leptonenzahl f, Leptonenladung f
Leray['s] method	Leraysche Methode f
Lerch['s] theorem	Lerchscher Satz m
lesion <bio.>	Verletzung f <Bio.>
lesion potential, injury potential, demarcation potential	Verletzungspotential n, Verletzungsspannung f Demarkationspotential n
Leslie['s] cube	Lesliescher Würfel m
lessening	s. reduction
lessivation	Lessivierung f, Durchschlämmung f, Illimerisation f
less luminous supergiant	schwächerer Überriese m
lethal, lethal factor (gene)	Letalfaktor m
lethal dose, fatal dose, LD	Letaldosis f, letale (tödliche) Dosis f, LD
lethal factor (gene)	s. lethal
lethality	Tödlichkeit f, Letalität f, Sterbewahrscheinlichkeit f <für eine bestimmte Krankheit>
lethargy group	Lethargiegruppe f
lethargy of the neutron, neutron lethargy, lethargy variable	Neutronenlethargie f, Lethargie f des Neutrons

lethargy pitch	Lethargieschrittweite *f*	levelling bottle (bulb)	*s.* levelling vessel
lethargy variable	*s.* lethargy of the neutron	levelling depth, depth of smoothness ‹hydr.›	Glättungstiefe *f* ‹Hydr.›
Lethersich body	*s.* elastic sol		
letter scales	Briefwaage *f*	levelling instrument, surveyor's level, geodesic level, level	Nivellier *n*, Nivellierinstrument *n*
letzte linie, sensitive (persistent, distinctive) line, raie ultime	letzte Linie *f*, Restlinie *f*, beständige Linie, Nachweislinie *f*	levelling net	Nivellementsnetz *n*
leucitohedron	*s.* pentagonal icositetrahedron	levelling of discharge section line, levelling of metering section	Wasserwägung *f*
leuco-centric colour moment, colour moment	Farbmoment *n*, Lutherches Farbmoment, leukozentrisches Farbmoment, Buntmoment *n*	levelling staff ‹pl.: staves›, graduated staff; level rod, stadia rod ‹US›	Nivellierlatte *f*
leucocrate	leukokrat		
leucometer	Leukometer *n*	levelling tube	*s.* levelling vessel
leucosol	Leukosol *n*	levelling-up, equalization, levelling	Vergleichmäßigung *f*, Ausgleichung *f*, Einebnung *f*
level, energy level	Energieniveau *n*, Niveau *n*		
		levelling vessel; levelling bottle; levelling bulb; levelling tube	Ausgleichsgefäß *n*; Niveaukugel *f*; Niveaurohr *n*
level, spirit level, water level, bubble level, water balance	Libelle *f*; Wasserwaage *f*; Richtwaage *f*; Libellenwaage *f*		
level ‹gen.›	Pegel *m*, Stand *m*, Standhöhe *f*, Füllstand *m*, Behälterstand *m*, Höhe *f*, Füllhöhe *f*, Niveau *n* ‹allg.›; Ebene *f* ‹allg.›; Spiegel *m* ‹allg.›; Pegel ‹allg.; El.›		
		level measurement ‹el.›	Pegeln *n*, Pegelmessung *f* ‹El.›
level	*s. a.* levelling instrument	level measuring	Niveaumessung *f*, Füllstandsmessung *f*, Behälterstandsmessung *f*, Pegel[stands]messung *f*
level	*s. a.* term		
level	*s. a.* level of significance ‹stat.›		
level above threshold	*s.* sensation level		
level adjustment; level setting	Einpegeln *n*; Pegeleinstellung *f*	level meter	*s.* level indicator
		level of discomfort	*s.* upper threshold of hearing
level analysis, term analysis, analysis of energy levels	Termanalyse *f*	level of ground water, ground-water level	Grundwasserspiegel *m*; Grundwasserstand *m*
level axis	Libellenachse *f*	level of loudness	*s.* loudness level ‹ac.›
level broadening	Niveauverbreiterung *f*	level of significance, significance level, error probability	Irrtumswahrscheinlichkeit *f*, Überschreitungswahrscheinlichkeit *f*, Sicherheitswahrscheinlichkeit *f*
level constant, value of level division, sensitiveness of the level	Parswert *m*, Teilwert *m* (Angabe *f*, Empfindlichkeit *f*) der Libelle		
level-controlled	pegelgesteuert		
level-crossing technique	*s.* Hanle effect	level of significance, confidence level, level, degree of confidence, confidence probability, confidence coefficient, confidence ‹stat.›	statistische Sicherheit *f*, Sicherheitsschwelle *f*, Sicherheitsgrad *m*, Vertrauenskoeffizient *m*, Konfidenzkoeffizient *m*, Konfidenzniveau *n*, Konfidenz[wahrscheinlichkeit] *f*, Bedeutsamkeitsstufe *f* ‹in %›, Niveau *n*, Grad *m* ‹Stat.›
level curve	*s.* isohypse		
level density, energy level density	Niveaudichte *f*, Energieniveaudichte *f*, Dichte *f* der Energieniveaus		
level diagram	Pegeldiagramm *n*, Pegellinie *f*, Pegelkurve *f* ‹Geo., El.›; Pegelschaulinie *f* ‹El.›; Pegelplan *m* ‹El.›		
		level of upper pond, level of upper pool	Stauspiegel *m*, gestauter Wasserspiegel *m*, Wehrspiegel *m*
level diagram	*s. a.* energy-level diagram		
level displacement, level shift, term displacement (shift)	Termverschiebung *f*, Niveauverschiebung *f*, Levelshift *m*	level order, order of terms (levels), term order	Termordnung *f*
		level oscillation, capillary-level oscillation	Kapillarniveauschwingung *f*
level drift	Pegeldrift *f*		
level error, altitude error	Höhenfehler *m*	level pendulum	Niveaupendel *n*
		level population	*s.* population
level error	Neigungsfehler *m*	level position, term position; position of level	Termlage *f*; Niveaulage *f*
level gauge, barometric (atmospheric) pressure, air pressure	atmosphärischer Druck *m*, barometrischer Druck, Luftdruck *m*	level recorder, recording transmission-measuring set ‹el.›	Pegelschreiber *m* ‹El.›
level indicator, level meter	Niveauanzeiger *m*, Niveauindikator *m*, Füllstand[s]anzeiger *m*, Füllhöhenmesser *m*, Höhenstandsanzeiger *m*, Behälterstandsanzeiger *m*, Pegelanzeiger *m*, Füllstandsmesser *m*	level rod, stadia rod ‹US›; levelling staff ‹pl.: staves›, graduated staff	Nivellierlatte *f*
		level rod ‹US›, topographic stadia rod, stadia rod	Tachymeterlatte *f*
		level scheme	*s.* energy-level diagram
		level setting; level adjustment	Einpegeln *n*; Pegeleinstellung *f*
level line	*s.* isohypse		
levelling; geometric levelling, geodesic levelling; direct levelling ‹US› ‹geo.›	Nivellement *n*; Nivellierung *f*, Höhenaufnahme *f*, Einwägung *f*; geometrisches Nivellement, geometrische Höhenmessung *f* ‹Geo.›	level shift, level displacement, term displacement (shift)	Termverschiebung *f*, Niveauverschiebung *f*, Levelshift *m*
		level shift rule	Termverschiebungsregel *f*
		level spacing	Niveauabstand *m*, Niveaudistanz *f*, Energieniveauabstand *m*
levelling ‹of the instrument›	Horizontierung *f*; Horizontaleinstellung *f*, Waagerechteinstellung *f*; Horizontalaufstellung *f*, Waagerechtaufstellung *f*		
		level spheroid	Niveausphäroid *n*
		level splitting, splitting ‹of energy level›	Niveauaufspaltung *f*, Aufspaltung *f* ‹Energieniveau›
levelling	*s. a.* compensation		
levelling	*s. a.* levelling-up		

level structure, energy term structure, term structure	Niveaustruktur f, Niveauaufbau m; Termstruktur f	libration ‹in longitude, in latitude›	Libration f ‹in Länge, in Breite›
level surface	s. geopotential surface	librational wave	Librationswelle f
level trier	Libellenprüfer m	libration cloud	Librationswolke f
level tube, tubular level	Röhrenlibelle f	libration period	Librationsperiode f
level tube bubble	Libellenblase f	libration point, point of libration	Librationspunkt m, Librationszentrum n, Gleichgewichtspunkt m, abarischer Punkt m; Lagrangescher Dreieckspunkt m, Lagrangesches Librationszentrum
level width, energy-level width	Niveaubreite f, Breite f des Energieniveaus		
level with fixed telescope, dumpy level	Nivellier[instrument] n mit festem Fernrohr [und umsetzbarer Libelle]		
		libron	Libron n
		Lichnerowicz['] theorem	Theorem n von Lichnerowicz, Lichnerowiczsches Theorem
leverage [ratio], lever transmission	Übersetzung f, Übersetzungsverhältnis n ‹Hebel›; Hebelarmverhältnis n	Lichtenberg figure, electric-dust figure	Lichtenbergsche Figur (Gleitentladungsfigur) f
lever arm, lever bar	Hebelarm m	Lichtenstein['s] method	Lichtensteinsche Methode f
lever balance	s. equal-armed balance		
lever bar	s. lever arm	lid	Verschlußdeckel m, Deckel m
lever dynamometer	Hebeldynamometer n	lidar	s. laser radar
lever principle, principle of the lever, law of lever	Hebelgesetz n, Hebelsatz m, Momentensatz m	Lie algebra, Lie ring	Lie-Ring m, Liescher Ring m, Liesche Algebra f, infinitesimale Gruppe f
lever rule ‹chem.›	Hebelgesetz n [der Phasenmengen], Hebelbeziehung f der Phasenmengen, Hebelarmbeziehung f ‹Chem.›	Liebenow circuit	s. Greinacher circuit
		Lieben tube	Lieben-Röhre f
lever scale	s. equal-armed balance	Lieberkuehn mirror, Lieberkühn mirror	Lieberkühn-Spiegel m, Lieberkühnscher Spiegel m
lever transmission	s. leverage		
lever wind camera, rapid wind lever camera	Schnellaufzugkamera f	Liebig condenser	Liebig-Kühler m
Levi-Civita symbol, Levi-Civita['s] tensor	s. epsilon-tensor	Liebmann['s] approximation method, Liebmann['s] method [of approximation]	Liebmann-Verfahren n, Liebmannsches Näherungsverfahren n, Liebmannsche Methode f
levigation	s. decantation		
levitation, suspension in space	Levitation f, [freies] Schweben n		
levitation by [forces of electromagnetic] induction	s. electromagnetic levitation	Liebmann diagram	Liebmann-Diagramm n
		Liebmann effect	Liebmann-Effekt m
levo-	s. laevo-		
Lévy-Mises material	s. Saint Venant-Mises material	Lie derivative	Liesche Ableitung f, Liesches Differential n, Variationstransformation f
Lewis acid; aniophile	Lewis-Säure f, Antibase f; Anionenakzeptor m		
		Lie group	Liesche Gruppe f
		Liénard['s] equation	Liénardsche Gleichung f
Lewis and Randall rule	s. Lewis rule [of fugacities]	Liénard-Wiechert potential	s. Wiechert potential
Lewis base; catiophile	Lewis-Base f; Kationenakzeptor m	Liepmann number	Liepmannsche Zahl f, Liepmann-Zahl f
		Lie-Riemann-Helmholtz[-Hilbert] problem of the foundations of geometry	Riemann-Helmholtz-Liesches Raumproblem n
Lewis-Langmuir formula	Lewis-Langmuirsche Formel f		
Lewis No., Lewis number, Le	Lewis-Zahl f, Lewissche Kennzahl f, Le	Lie ring, Lie algebra	Lie-Ring m, Liescher Ring m, Liesche Algebra f, infinitesimale Gruppe f
Lewis-Randall rule, Lewis rule [of fugacities], Lewis and Randall rule	Fugazitätenregel f [von Lewis], Lewissche Fugazitätenregel (Regel f)		
		Liesegang banded precipitate	s. Liesegang rings
Leyden jar	s. Leiden jar	Liesegang effect	s. periodic precipitation
l-forbiddenness	l-Verbot n	Liesegang phenomenon	s. Liesegang rings
l-forbidden transition	s. unfavoured transition	Liesegang periodic precipitate, Liesegang rings, Liesegang banded precipitate, Liesegang phenomenon	Liesegangsche Ringe mpl, Liesegang-Ringe mpl
L-form, l-form, laevorotatory form	linksdrehende Form f, L-Form f, l-Form f		
L frame	s. laboratory system		
L.F. wave	s. low-frequency wave	Lie series	Lie-Reihe f
Liapunov conditions	Ljapunow-Bedingungen fpl	life	s. lifetime
Liapunov['s] first method	erste Methode f von Ljapunow, Ljapunows erste Methode	life characteristic	Lebensdauerkennlinie f, Lebensdauercharakteristik f, Lebensdauerkurve f, Lebensdauerverhalten n
Liapunov function	Ljapunowsche Funktion f	life test	Lebensdauerprüfung f; Brenndauerprüfung f ‹für Lichtquellen›
Liapunov['s] second method	zweite (direkte) Methode f von Ljapunow, Ljapunows zweite Methode		
		life test	s. a. fatigue experiment
		lifetime, life	Lebensdauer f
Liapunov['s] theorem [of stability], stability theorem of Liapunov	Ljapunowscher Stabilitätssatz m, Stabilitätssatz von Ljapunow		
lib	s. kilogramme		
liberation; release; setting free; disengagement	Freisetzung f; Freiwerden n; Auslösung f; Ablösung f; Abgabe f; Entbindung f	lifetime, life, serviceable life ‹techn.›	Lebensdauer f; Betriebsdauer f; Brenndauer f ‹Techn.›
liberation	s. a. detachment ‹of an electron›	life-time dose	Lebensdosis f
libra	s. kilogramme		

lift; stroke	Hub *m*	light band; optical pattern, Christmas-tree pattern	Lichtband *n*
lift, aerodynamic lift, lift[ing] force; buoyancy [force], buoyant force ‹aero., hydr.›; useful resistance ‹aero.›	Auftrieb *m* ‹Aero., Hydr.›	light-band instrument	Lichtbandinstrument *n*
lift axis	Auftriebsachse *f*	light barrier	s. photoelectric relay
lift coefficient	Auftriebsbeiwert *m*, Auftriebszahl *f*	light beam, beam of light; pencil of light, light[-ray] pencil	Lichtbündel *n*; Lichtbüschel *n*
lift curve diagram, lift / incidence curve	Auftriebskurve *f*	light beam	s. a. ray of light
lift-drag ratio, L/D ratio	reziproke Gleitzahl *f*, Verhältnis *n* von Auftrieb zu Widerstand	light-beam instrument	Lichtstrahl[meß]gerät *n*, Lichtstrahlinstrument *n*
lifted block	Hochscholle *f*	light beam localizer	Lichtvisier *n*
lift force	s. lift ‹aero., hydr.›	light-beam oscillograph	s. loop oscillograph
lift / incidence curve, lift curve diagram	Auftriebskurve *f*	light-beam pointer, optical pointer, luminous pointer, light pointer; light spot, spot	Lichtzeiger *m*, Leuchtzeiger *m*, Lichtmarke *f*
lifting ‹to, into›, raising ‹to, into›; hoisting ‹to›	Heben *n*, Hebung *f* ‹auf, in›		
lifting, uplift, upthrust, upheaval ‹geo.›	Hebung *f* ‹Geo.›	light-beam recorder	Lichtstrahl-Linienschreiber *m*, Lichtschreiber *m*, Lichtstrahlschreiber *m*
lifting	s. a. ascending motion		
lifting force	s. dynamic lift ‹aero., hydr.›		
lifting force	s. lift ‹aero., hydr.›	light-beam recording	s. optical recording
lifting force moment, lifting moment	Auftriebsmoment *n*	light box, negatoscope, negative viewer, spotting box	Negatoskop *n*, Negativschaukasten *m*, Negativbetrachter *m*
lifting height; stroke; stroke length	Hubweg *m*; Hublänge *f*; Hubhöhe *f*	light breeze, breeze, light wind ‹of Beaufort No. 2›	leichte Brise *f*, leichter Zug (Wind) *m* ‹Stärke 2›
lifting[-]line	tragende Linie *f*, Traglinie *f*	light centre ‹of lamp›	Lichtschwerpunkt *m*, Lichtzentrum *n*, Lichtmittelpunkt *m* ‹Lichtquelle›
lifting line theory	Traglinientheorie *f*		
lifting moment	s. lifting force moment	light centre length	Lichtschwerpunktabstand *m*, Lichtzentrumabstand *m*
lifting power ‹aero.›	Tragkraft *f* ‹Aero.›		
		light conditions, lighting conditions, light situation	Lichtverhältnisse *npl*
lifting surface	tragende Fläche *f*, Tragfläche *f*	light conductance	s. optical flux
lifting surface ‹hydr.›	Auftriebsfläche *f* ‹Hydr.›	light cone, light-cone, null cone ‹rel.›	Lichtkegel *m*, Kausalitätskegel *m*, Nullkegel *m* ‹Rel.›
lifting-surface theory	Tragflächentheorie *f*	light cone	s. a. cone of light rays
lifting vortex line theory	Theorie *f* der tragenden Wirbellinie	light converter	Lichtwandler *m*
lifting work	s. stroke work	light corpuscle	s. photon
liftoff	s. launch	light cross	Lichtkreuz *n*
lift of the valve, valve lift	Ventilhub *m*, Hub *m* des Ventils, Ventilerhebung *f*	light crown	Leichtkron *n*, Leichtkronglas *n*
lift parabola	s. metacentric parabola	light curve	Lichtkurve *f*
ligand, ligand group	Ligand *m*		
ligand field	Ligandenfeld *n*	light cut, light [inter]section, light sectioning	Lichtschnitt *m*
ligand field theory	Ligandenfeldtheorie *f*	light-cut method (technique)	s. light-intersection technique
ligand group, ligand	Ligand *m*	light-dark	Helldunkel *n*
ligasoid ‹chem.›, fog	Nebel *m*, Flüssigkeitsaerosol *n*, Aerosol *n* mit flüssiger disperser Phase, Ligasoid *n* ‹Chem.›	light-dark control	Hell-Dunkel-Steuerung *f*
		light-dark cycle, intermittent light ‹bio.›	intermittierendes Licht *n*, Licht-Dunkel-Wechsel *m* ‹Bio.›
light, light radiation, visible radiation	Licht *n*, sichtbare Strahlung *f*, sichtbares Licht	light deficiency	Lichtmangel *m*
		light demand	s. light requirement
		light detector, photodetector, light receiver	Lichtempfänger *m*, Lichtdetektor *m*
light, lighting, illumination	Beleuchtung *f*	light diffuser	s. diffuser
light; luminous signal; optical signal	Lichtsignal *n*, optisches Signal *n*	light-diffusing screen, diffuser screen	Weichzeichnerfolie *f*, Weichzeichner *m*, Streufolie *f*
light, light fitting	Beleuchtungskörper *m*	light distribution, distribution of luminous intensity, luminous-intensity distribution	Lichtverteilung *f*, Lichtstärkeverteilung *f*
light aberration	s. aberration of light		
light absorption spectrometry	Absorptionsspektrometrie *f* im sichtbaren Bereich		
light accumulator, light store	Lichtakkumulator *m*, Lichtspeicher *m*	light distribution curve, curve of light distribution, polar diagram of luminous intensity, isocandela diagram, isocandle diagram	Lichtstärkeverteilungskurve *f*, Lichtverteilungskurve *f*, Lichtverteilungsdiagramm *n*, Diagramm *n* gleicher Lichtstärke[n], Isocandeladiagramm *n*
light adaptation, bright adaptation, adaptation to light, photoadaptation	Helladaptation *f*, Hellstimmung *f*, Lichtstimmung *f*		
light-adapted eye	helladaptiertes Auge *n*, Hellauge *n*		
light air	s. very light breeze	light-emitting diode, LED	s. injection luminescence diode
light amplification, amplification of light; light gain	Lichtverstärkung *f*	light energy, energy of light	Lichtenergie *f*, Energie *f* des Lichts
		light equation, equation of light	Lichtgleichung *f*; Lichtzeit *f*
light amplifier	Lichtverstärker *m*	light equivalent	Lichtäquivalent *n*
		light field	Lichtfeld *n*
light-back, flash[-]back, flareback, back-fire, back firing, back flash	Rückschlag *m*, Flammenrückschlag *m*, Zurückschlagen *n* der Flamme	light filter, optical filter, filter	Lichtfilter *n*, [optisches] Filter *n*, Lichtdrossel *f*

light fitting, light	Beleuchtungskörper m	lightning discharge	Blitzentladung f, atmosphärische Entladung f
light flash	s. scintillation		
light flint	Leichtflint m, Leichtflintglas n	lightning discharge to earth, [lightning] flash to earth	Erdblitz m
light flux, luminous flux	Lichtstrom m, Lichtleistung f, Lichtfluß m		
light frost	Frostbeschlag m	lightning flash; lightning; flash [of lightning]	Blitz m; Blitzstrahl m
light gain; light amplification, amplification of light	Lichtverstärkung f		
		lightning flash to earth, flash (lightning discharge) to earth	Erdblitz m
light gathering power, light grasp <of optical instrument, e.g. telescope>	Lichtstärke f, Helligkeit f <optisches Instrument, z. B. Fernrohr>		
		lightning protection, protection against lightning	Blitzschutz m
light guide, light pipe, light line	Lichtleiter m; Lichtleitstab m		
		lightning protector, rare-gas lightning arrester	Luftleerblitzableiter m
Lighthill-Eppler method	Lighthill-Epplersches Verfahren n		
Lighthill gas	Lighthill-Gas n	lightning protector (rod)	s. a. surge diverter
Lighthill['s] method	s. Poincaré-Lighthill-Kuo method	lightning stepped leader	s. stepped leader
		lightning stroke	s. lightning
Lighthill['s] potential [function]	Lighthillsche Potentialfunktion f, Lighthill-Potential n	light optics	Lichtoptik f
		light-orange heat	Hellorangeglut f <1200 °C>
lighthouse tube	Leuchtturmröhre f, „lighthouse"-Röhre f		
light hydrogen, protium, ¹H	leichter Wasserstoff m, Protium n, ¹H	light output ratio, luminous efficiency, luminosity <of a source>, efficiency of [light] source <opt.>	Lichtausbeute f, Lichtleistung f <Lichtquelle> <Opt.>
lighting	Lichttechnik f		
lighting, light, illumination	Beleuchtung f		
lighting conditions, light conditions (situation)	Lichtverhältnisse npl		
lighting engineering; lighting technique (technology)	Beleuchtungstechnik f	light output ratio of a fitting, conversion efficiency, luminaire (luminary) efficiency <US>	Leuchtenwirkungsgrad m; Betriebswirkungsgrad m
light intensity, luminous intensity [of light], candle power, intensity of light <of source>	Lichtstärke f, Lichtintensität f, Intensität f <Lichtquelle>	light particle	s. photon
		light path	s. optical distance
		light pencil, pencil of light, light-ray pencil; beam of light, light beam	Lichtbüschel n; Lichtbündel n
light intersection, light section, light cut, light sectioning	Lichtschnitt m		
		light period	Hellperiode f, Hellzeit f
light-intersection method, light-intersection technique, light-section (light-cut, light-slit) technique, light-cut (light-slit) method	Lichtschnittverfahren n [nach Schmaltz], Lichtschnittechnik f	light permeability; permeability to light; transmission of light, light transmission	Lichtdurchlässigkeit f; Lichtdurchlassung f
		light phase	s. light reaction
		light phenomenon, luminous phenomenon	Leuchterscheinung f; Lichterscheinung f
light ion	s. small ion <geo.>		
light line, light pipe, light guide	Lichtleiter m; Lichtleitstab m	light pipe, light guide, light line	Lichtleiter m; Lichtleitstab m
light line, null line <rel.>	Nullinie f, Lichtlinie f, Kausalitätslinie f <Rel.>	light pointer	s. light-beam pointer
lightly irradiated, slightly irradiated	schwachbestrahlt	light-positive, photoconducting, photoconductive, photopositive	lichtelektrisch leitend (positiv), lichtpositiv, photoleitend, photopositiv
light maximum, intensity maximum	Lichtmaximum n		
light meson, L meson <μ or π>	leichtes Meson n, L-Meson n <μ oder π>	light pressure, pressure of light	Lichtdruck m <Phys.>
		light probe	Lichtsonde f
light meter, illumination photometer (meter), illuminometer; luxometer, lux meter	Beleuchtungsmesser m; Luxmeter n	light-producing, photogenic	lichterzeugend
		light-proof, lightproof, light-tight, lighttight	lichtdicht
light microscope, optical microscope	Lichtmikroskop n, optisches Mikroskop n	light quantity, photometric quantity	photometrische (lichttechnische) Größe f
light microscopy, optical microscopy	Lichtmikroskopie f, optische Mikroskopie f	light quantum	s. photon
		light-quantum hypothesis, light-quantum theory [of Einstein]	s. Einstein['s] hypothesis of light quanta
light-microsecond	Lichtmikrosekunde f		
light minimum, intensity minimum	Lichtminimum n		
light modulation, modulation of light, intensity modulation	Modulation f des Lichtes, Lichtmodulation f, Lichtsteuerung f	light radiation, light, visible radiation	Licht n, sichtbare Strahlung f, sichtbares Licht
light modulator; light relay; light valve	Lichthahn m, Lichtmodulator m; Lichtrelais n; Lichtventil n, Lichtsteuerröhre f; Lichtsteuergerät n; Lichtschleuse f	light ray, ray of light	Lichtstrahl m
		light-ray bending, bending of light [rays], deflection of light rays [which pass close to a celestial body]	Krümmung f von Lichtstrahlen, Krümmung der Lichtstrahlen, Lichtkrümmung f, Lichtablenkung f
		light-ray pencil	s. light pencil
		light reaction, light phase <in photosynthesis>	Lichtreaktion f, Lichtphase f <Photosynthese>
light-negative, photoresistive, photoresisting, photoresistant, photonegative	lichtelektrisch negativ, lichtnegativ, photonegativ, photoresistiv	light reaction	s. a. photochemical reaction
		light receiver	s. photodetector
		light-red heat	Hellrotglut f <950 °C>
lightness <of surface colour>; brightness, subjective brightness, quantity, intensity, luminosity	Farbhelligkeit f, Farbquantität f, Farbintensität f, Helligkeit f, Quantität f, Intensität f		
		light relay	s. light modulator
lightness	s. a. illumination <quantity>	light relay	s. a. photoelectric relay
lightness contrast	s. luminance contrast	light requirement, light demand	Lichtbedürfnis n; Lichtbedarf m
lightning; flash [of lightning], lightning flash (stroke)	Blitz m; Blitzstrahl m		
		light scatter[ing]	s. scattering
		light scattering function [for spherical particles]	s. Mie['s] scattering function
lightning arrester (conductor)	s. surge diverter		

light-screening photographic layer	s. anti[-]halation backing	light wind, feeble wind (breeze) <of Beaufort No. 3>	schwache Brise f <Stärke 3>
light section[ing]	s. light intersection	light wind	s. a. light breeze
light-section technique	s. light-intersection technique	light-year, light year, l.y.	Lichtjahr n, Lj.
light sensation, sensation of light	Lichtempfindung f; Lichteindruck m	like, of the same polarity (sign), having the same polarity (sign), similarly charged (electrified)	gleichnamig, gleicher Polarität, gleichen Vorzeichens
light sense, sense of sight	Lichtsinn m, Gesicht n	likelihood, plausibility	Likelihood f, Plausibilität f
light sense organ	s. organ of vision	likelihood equation	Likelihoodgleichung f
light-sensitive	s. photosensitive <phot.>	likelihood function	Likelihoodfunktion f
light situation	s. lighting conditions		
light-slit method (technique)	s. light-intersection technique	likelihood ratio	Likelihoodquotient m
light source, source of light, luminous source	Lichtquelle f	likelihood ratiotest, probability ratio test	Likelihoodverhältnistest m, [Maximum-]Likelihood-Quotienten-Test m, „likelihood ratio test" m, Likelihood Ratio Test m, Wahrscheinlichkeitsverhältnistest m
light source of microscope [illumination], source of illumination <of microscope>	Mikroskopierleuchte f, Mikroleuchte f		
light spectrograph, optical spectrograph	Lichtspektrograph m, optischer Spektrograph m		
light spectrography, optical spectrography	Lichtspektrographie f, optische Spektrographie f	like poles	gleichnamige Pole mpl
light spectrometer (spectroscope), optical spectrometer (spectroscope)	Lichtspektrometer n, Lichtspektroskop n, optisches Spektrometer (Spektroskop) n	Lilienfeld glow	Lilienfeld-[Seemannsches] Leuchten n
		Lilienthal['s] polar diagram	Lilienthalsches Polardiagramm n
light spectrometry, (spectroscopy), optical spectroscopy (spectrometry)	Lichtspektroskopie f, Lichtspektrometrie f, optische Spektroskopie (Spektrometrie) f	Lill['s] construction, Lill['s] method	Lillsche Konstruktion (Methode) f, Lillsches Verfahren n
		lim	s. limit <math.>
		lim	s. lower limit
light spectrum, optical (visible, luminous) spectrum	Lichtspektrum n, sichtbares (optisches) Spektrum n	lim	s. upper limit
		limaçon, Pascal['s] limaçon	Pascalsche Schnecke f
light speed	s. velocity of light	limb	s. horizontal circle <astr.>
light spot	Lichtfleck m; Lichtpunkt m	limb	s. a. core <el.>
light spot	s. a. light-beam pointer	limb brightening, brightening towards the limb	Randaufhellung f
light-spot galvanometer, galvanometer with optical pointer, luminous pointer galvanometer	Lichtmarkengalvanometer n, Lichtzeigergalvanometer n, Lichtpunktgalvanometer n		
		limb darkening, darkening towards the limb <opt., astr.>	Randverdunklung f <Opt., Astr.>
light-spot instrument	s. luminous pointer instrument		
light-spot recorder, flying-spot recorder	Lichtpunktlinienschreiber m, Lichtpunktschreiber m, Lichtlinienschreiber m	limb flare	Randeruption f
		limb of the Sun, solar limb, Sun's limb	Rand m der Sonnenscheibe, Sonnen[scheiben]rand m
light-spot scanning	s. flying-spot scanning		
light stimulus, stimulus of light, luminous (optical) stimulus	Lichtreiz m	limb of the U-tube	Schenkel m des U-Rohres
		liminal plasmolysis, incipient plasmolysis	Grenzplasmolyse f
light store	s. light accumulator	liminal value <bio.>	Grenzwert m <Bio.>
light sum	Lichtsumme f		
		liminal value	s. a. threshold <bio.>
light-tight, lighttight, light-proof, lightproof	lichtdicht	lim inf	s. lower limit
light transmission, transmission of light; permeability to light, light perviousness, light permeability	Lichtdurchlässigkeit f; Lichtdurchlassung f	limit, limitation; boundary, bound; margin; rim	Grenze f; Begrenzung f; Rand m; Berandung f
		limit, lim <math.>	Grenzwert m, Grenze f, Limes m, <Math.>
		limitation, restriction	Einschränkung f; Beschränkung f; Begrenzung f
light trap	Lichtfalle f	limitation, limit; boundary, bound; margin; rim	Grenze f; Begrenzung f; Rand m; Berandung f
light trapping	Lichteinfang m		
light tube	Lichtröhre f	limitational motion	Limitationsbewegung f
light unit, photometric unit	photometrische (lichttechnische) Einheit f	limitation diaphragm, barn doors, snoot	Strahlenbegrenzungsblende f
light utilization	Lichtausnutzung f	limitation of the beam	s. beam limiting
light value, exposure value	Lichtwert m, Belichtungswert m	limit bridge, tolerance bridge	Toleranzmeßbrücke f, Toleranzbrücke f
		limit cycle	Grenzzykel m
light valve	s. light modulator	limit depolarization	Grenzdepolarisation f
light-valve paradox of Wien, Wien['s] paradox	Lichtventilparadoxon n von Wien, Wiensches Lichtventilparadoxon (Paradoxon n)		
		limit design	Traglastverfahren n
light variation, variation in light	Lichtwechsel m	limit distribution	Grenzverteilung f
light vector	Lichtvektor m	limited discharge	behinderte (beschränkte) Entladung f
		limited elasticity	beschränkte Elastizität f
light velocity	s. velocity of light	limited linear	begrenzt linear
light water, ^1H_2O	leichtes Wasser n, Leichtwasser n <Wasser, das kein Deuterium und Tritium enthält>		
		limited proportionality	begrenzte Proportionalität f
light water	s. a. ordinary water		
light water reactor, LWR	Leichtwasserreaktor m, LWR		
light watt	s. photometric radiation equivalent	limited space-charge accumulation diode, LSA diode	LSA-Diode f
light-wave train	Lichtwellenzug m	limited swelling	beschränkte Quellung f

limited

limited to the left	nach unten beschränkt
limited to the right	nach oben beschränkt
limited variation, bounded variation	beschränkte Gesamtschwankung (Schwankung, Variation) *f*
limit element	*s.* accumulation point <math.>
limiter; limiting stage	Begrenzer *m*; Begrenzerstufe *f*
limiter diode	Begrenzerdiode *f*
limit function	Grenzfunktion *f*
limit gauge	Toleranzlehre *f*, Toleranzmaß *n*, Grenzlehre *f*
limit inferior	*s.* lower limit <math.>
limiting angle [of friction]	*s.* angle of friction
limiting case, borderline case; extreme case	Grenzfall *m*; Extremfall *m*
limiting case of geometrical optics, geometrical optics limit	geometrisch-optischer Grenzfall *m*, Grenzfall der geometrischen Optik
limiting concentration, limiting dilution	Grenzkonzentration *f*, Verdünnungsgrenze *f*, GK
limiting conductance (conductivity)	Grenzleitfähigkeit *f*
limiting creep stress, creep resistance, resistance to creep, limiting stress, long-time strength	Zeitstandfestigkeit *f*, Dauerstandfestigkeit *f*, Standfestigkeit *f*, Kriechfestigkeit *f*
limiting current, diffusion[-controlled limiting] current <el.chem.>	Grenzstrom *m*, Diffusions[grenz]strom *m*, [elektrochemischer] Sättigungsstrom *m* <El.Chem.>
limiting current density	Grenzstromdichte *f*, Sättigungsstromdichte *f*
limiting curve, border curve	Grenzkurve *f*
limiting deflection	*s.* full scale deflection <meas.>
limiting dilution	*s.* limiting concentration
limiting equivalent conductance	*s.* equivalent conductance at infinite dilution
limiting factor, influence factor	Einflußfaktor *m*, Beeinflussungsfaktor *m*
limiting factor <bio.>	begrenzender Faktor *m* <Bio.>
limiting flow	Grenzströmung *f*
limiting form of equilibrium	Gleichgewichtsgrenzform *f*
limiting frequency, threshold (critical, cut-off) frequency	Grenzfrequenz *f*, Schwellenfrequenz *f*
limiting frequency <of continuous X-rays>	*s.* quantum limit
limiting frequency of electrolysis	Grenzfrequenz *f* der Elektrolyse
limiting friction	*s.* static friction
limiting hysteresis loop, outermost hysteresis loop	Grenzschleife *f*, Grenzkurve *f*, äußerste Hystereseschleife *f*
limiting ionic conductance	Grenzionenleitfähigkeit *f*
limiting isoseist	Grenzisoseiste *f*
limiting law [for strong electrolytes]	*s.* Debye-Hückel equation
limiting Mach wave	Grenz-Mach-Welle *f*
limiting mass, critical mass, mass-limit <of white dwarfs>	Grenzmasse *f*, kritische Masse *f* <weiße Zwerge>
limiting mobility	Grenzbeweglichkeit *f*
limiting parabola	Grenzparabel *f*
limiting point	Häufungsgrenze *f*, Hauptlimes *m*, Unbestimmtheitsgrenze *f*
limiting point	*s. a.* accumulation point <math.>
limiting polarization	Grenzpolarisation *f*
limiting process, passing to the limit	Grenzübergang *m*
limiting quantity	Einflußgröße *f*
limiting regulator	Grenzwertregler *m*, Grenzwertgerät *n*, Grenzregler *m*
limiting sensitivity	*s.* threshold of sensitivity
limiting set <math.>	Grenzmenge *f* <Math.>
limiting slenderness ratio	Grenzschlankheit *f*
limiting speed, limiting velocity, terminal speed <mech., hydr.>	Grenzgeschwindigkeit *f*
limiting stage	*s.* limiter
limiting stress	*s.* limiting creep stress
limiting surface of rupture (yield), yield surface	Fließspannungsfläche *f*
limiting trajectory	Grenzbahn *f*
limiting vacuum	Grenzvakuum *n*
limiting velocity, terminal (limiting) speed <mech., hydr.>	Grenzgeschwindigkeit *f*
limiting viscosity	*s.* intrinsic viscosity
limiting viscosity number, viscosity number, viscosity value	Grenzviskositätszahl *f*, Viskositätszahl *f*, Staudinger-Index *m*
limit line of total reflection	Grenzlinie *f* der Totalreflexion
limit load; collapse load; yield load	Traglast *f*
limit micrometer	Toleranzmikrometer *n*
limit of audibility (audition)	Hörgrenze *f*, Grenze *f* des Hörbereichs
limit of backwater	Staugrenze *f*
limit of detectability	*s.* threshold of sensitivity
limit of drift ice, drift ice line	Treibeisgrenze *f*
limit of elasticity	*s.* limit of linear elasticity
limit of error, margin of error; maximum error	Fehlergrenze *f*; Grenzfehler *m*, Maximalfehler *m*, maximaler Fehler *m*
limit of frost, frost limit	Frostgrenze *f*, Frosttiefe *f*
limit of fusion, fusion limit	Fusionsgrenze *f*, Doppelbildschwelle *f*
limit of ignitability (ignition, inflammability)	*s.* inflammability limit
limit of integration	Integrationsgrenze *f*
limit of linear elasticity, elastic limit, limit of elasticity	Elastizitätsgrenze *f*
limit of proportionality	*s.* proportionality limit
limit of reaction, reaction limit	Reaktionsgrenze *f*
limit of resolution, resolution limit	Auflösungsgrenze *f*
limit of response	*s.* threshold of sensitivity
limit of saturation, saturation point (limit)	Sättigungspunkt *m*, Sättigungsgrenze *f*
limit of sensibility (sensitivity)	*s.* threshold of sensitivity
limit of stability, stability limit, critical stability	Stabilitätsgrenze *f*
limit of strength	*s.* strength <mech.>
limit of submersion	Inundationsgrenze *f*
limit of the Balmer series, Balmer limit	Balmer-Grenze *f*
limit of the cloud, cloud limit <meteo.>	Wolkenbegrenzung *f*; Wolkengrenze *f* <Meteo.>

limit of the series, series limit (cut-off, edge)	Seriengrenze f	Lindenbaum['s] postulate	Lindenbaumsches Postulat n
limit of tides, tidal limit	Tidegrenze f	Lindenblad antenna	Lindenblad-Antenne f, Lindenblad-Strahler m
limit of velocity; critical velocity; cut-off velocity; velocity limit	Grenzgeschwindigkeit f, kritische Geschwindigkeit f	line; peak; maximum	Peak m; Linie f; [scharfes] Maximum n; Gipfel m; Berg m, Spitze f <Chromatographie>
limit of vision	Sichtgrenze f	line, electrical line; wire; wiring; conductor <el.>	[elektrische] Leitung f, [elektrischer] Leiter m
limit on the left, left-hand limit	linksseitiger Grenzwert (Limes) m	line, spectral line, spectrum line <opt.>	Spektrallinie f, Linie f <Opt.>
limit on the right, right-hand limit	rechtsseitiger Grenzwert (Limes) m	line, straight line <math.>	Gerade f, gerade Linie f <Math.>
limit point, cut-off point	Grenzpunkt m	line	s. a. linear
limit point	s. a. accumulation point <math.>	lineac	s. linear accelerator
limit probability	Grenzwahrscheinlichkeit f	line advance, line spacing, scanning separation (pitch)	Zeilenabstand m
limit resistance; critical resistance; boundary resistance	Grenzwiderstand m	lineage	s. lineage structure
		lineage boundary	Verzweigungsgrenze f
limits [of application]	s. limits of validity	lineage structure, lineage	Verzweigungsstruktur f, „lineage"-Struktur f, Verzweigung f, „lineage" n
limits of error / within the	innerhalb der Fehlergrenzen		
limits of hearing, hearing volume	Gehörumfang m	lineal motion, one-dimensional motion	eindimensionale (lineale) Bewegung f
limits of inflammability	s. inflammability limits	lineal scale length, scale length, scale span	Skalenlänge f
limits of validity, limits, range of validity; limits (range) of application	Gültigkeitsgrenzen fpl; Gültigkeitsbereich m		
limit structure	Grenzstruktur f	line amplifier	s. horizontal amplifier
limit superior	s. upper limit	linear; line; line-shaped; one-dimensional, unidimensional	linear; Linien-; linienförmig; linienartig; linienhaft, linienhaft verteilt (ausgedehnt); eindimensional
limit switch; over-travel switch	Endschalter m, Endlagenschalter m, Endausschalter m; Grenzschalter m		
		linear absorption coefficient, linear energy absorption coefficient	linearer Absorptionskoeffizient (Energieabsorptionskoeffizient) m
limit theorem	Grenzwertsatz m	linear absorption coefficient, Napierian absorption coefficient, [natural] absorption coefficient <in Lambert's law>	[natürliche] Absorptionskonstante f, Absorptionskoeffizient m, natürlicher Absorptionsmodul m <im Lambertschen Absorptionsgesetz>
limit theorem of Laplace <stat.>	Laplacescher Grenzwertsatz m <Stat.>		
limit theorem of Poisson	Poissonscher Grenzwertsatz m		
limit volume	Grenzvolumen n, Limitvolumen n	linear absorption index, Napierian (natural) absorption index	natürlicher Absorptionsindex m
limnetic, lacustrine	limnisch, lakustrisch; limnetisch	linear acceleration	Linearbeschleunigung f
limnigraph, limnograph, water-level recorder, recording gauge	Schreibpegel m, schreibender Pegel m, Registrierpegel m, Limnigraph m, Limnograph m, Limnimeter n	linear accelerator, linac, lineac	Linearbeschleuniger m, Einfachbeschleuniger m, linearer Beschleuniger m, LB
		linear acoustics	lineare Akustik f
		linear activity	linienhaft verteilte Aktivität f, Linienaktivität f; lineare Aktivität
limp	s. untensioned		
limp-diaphragm pressure gauge	Manometer n mit weicher Membran	linear amplifier, proportional amplifier	Linearverstärker m, linearer (proportionaler) Verstärker m, Proportionalverstärker m
limpid, clear, transparent <e.g. of water>	klar, durchsichtig <z. B. Wasser>		
lim sup	s. upper limit	linear antenna array, linear array	lineare Dipolanordnung f, lineares Antennensystem n, lineare Antennenanordnung (Dipolkombination) f
linac	s. linear accelerator		
linatron	Linatron n		
Linde air liquefier, Linde liquefier	Lindesche Luftverflüssigungsmaschine (Kältemaschine, Maschine) f		
		linear attenuation coefficient	linearer Schwächungskoeffizient m
Lindeck potentiometer, Lindeck-Rothe potentiometer, photoelectric potentiometer	Lindeck-Rothe-Kompensator m, Lindeck-Potentiometer n, Photozellenkompensator m	linear attenuation coefficient	s. a. linear extinction coefficient
		linear birefringence, linear double refraction	lineare Doppelbrechung f
		linear bolometer	Linearbolometer n
Linde cycle; Linde liquefaction process	Linde-Prozeß m, Lindescher Kreisprozeß m; Linde-Verfahren n	linear chain, non-branching chain	lineare Kette f
Linde liquefier, Linde air liquefier	Lindesche Luftverflüssigungsmaschine (Kältemaschine, Maschine) f	linear charge	Linienladung f, lineare (linear verteilte) Ladung f
		linear charge density, linear density of [electric] charge	Linienladungsdichte f, Liniendichte f der Ladung, lineare Ladungsdichte f
Lindemann electrometer	Lindemann-Elektrometer n		
Lindemann frequency	Lindemannsche Frequenz f, Lindemann-Frequenz f		
Lindemann glass	Lindemann-Glas n	linear closure	lineare Hülle f
Lindemann melting point formula	Lindemannsche Schmelzpunktformel f (Formel f für den Schmelzpunkt)	linear colloid	Linearkolloid n
		linear combination	Linearkombination f
		linear combination of atomic orbitals approximation, LCAO approximation, LCAO method, LCAO-MO method	LCAO-MO-Methode f, LCAOMO-Methode f, LCAO-MO-Näherung f
Lindemann relation	Lindemannsche Beziehung f		
Lindemann['s] theory of melting point	Lindemannsche Schmelzpunkttheorie f		
Lindemann window	Lindemann-Fenster n		

linear communication	Informationskette f, Nachrichtenkette f, lineare Informationsübertragung (Nachrichtenübertragung) f	**linear extinction index,** Napierian (natural) extinction index	natürlicher Extinktionsindex m
linear compressibility; coefficient of linear compressibility	lineare Kompressibilität f; linearer Kompressibilitätskoeffizient m	**linear extrapolation distance (length)**	s. extrapolation distance
linear compression	s. unit shortening	**linear flow,** Helmholtz flow	Helmholtzsche Strömung f, lineare Strömung
linear connection <differential geometry>	linearer Zusammenhang m <Differentialgeometrie>	**linear focus,** line focus	Strichfokus m, Götze-Fokus m
linear contraction, contraction in length	Längenkontraktion f, Längenschrumpfung f, lineare Kontraktion (Schrumpfung) f	**linear form**	Linearform f
		linear fractional transformation	s. homographic transformation
linear correlation	lineare Korrelation f	**linear functional**	lineares Funktional n
linear density of [electric] charge, linear charge density	Linienladungsdichte f, Liniendichte f der Ladung, lineare Ladungsdichte f	**linear grating,** linear diffraction grating	lineares Beugungsgitter n
		linear harmonic oscillation	s. simple harmonic motion
linear detector, linear response detector	linearer Detektor m, Detektor mit linearer Charakteristik (Anzeige)	**linear harmonic oscillator,** linear oscillator, simple harmonic oscillator	linearer harmonischer Oszillator m
linear detector	s. a. linear rectifier	**linear heat expansion**	s. linear thermal expansion
linear diameter, true diameter <of star>	wahrer Durchmesser m, linearer Durchmesser <Gestirn>	**linear integral equation of the first kind**	s. integral equation of the first kind
linear differential equation <with constant or variable coefficients>	lineare Differentialgleichung f <mit konstanten oder variablen Koeffizienten>	**linear integral equation of the second kind**	s. Fredholm['s] integral equation [of the second kind]
		linear integral equation of the third kind, integral equation of the third kind	Integralgleichung f dritter Art, lineare Integralgleichung dritter Art
linear differential expression (form)	s. Pfaffian differential form		
linear diffraction grating, linear grating	lineares Beugungsgitter n	**linear in time,** time-proportional, proportional to time	zeitlinear; zeitproportional
linear dilatation	s. linear expansion		
linear dimension, linear extension, dimension, size <gen.>	[lineare] Abmessung f, Längenabmessung f, Längsabmessung f, Längenausdehnung f, Längsausdehnung f, Ausdehnung f, Dimension f <allg.>	**linearity circuit,** linearizing circuit	Linearisierungsschaltung f
		linearity error; aberration from linearity; deflection linearity error	Linearitätsabweichung f; Linearitätsfehler m
linear dispersion	Lineardispersion f, lineare Dispersion f	**linearization,** linearizing action	Linearisierung f
linear dividing engine	Längenteilmaschine f	**linearization parameter**	Linearisierungsparameter m
linear Doppler effect, Doppler effect of the first order	Doppler-Effekt m erster Ordnung, linearer Doppler-Effekt	**linearizing action,** linearization	Linearisierung f
		linearizing circuit	s. linearity circuit
linear double refraction, linear birefringence	lineare Doppelbrechung f	**linearizing resistance**	Linearisierungswiderstand m
linear dune	Strichdüne f	**linearly elastic**	linear[-]elastisch
linear electrical constant, [electrical] circuit constant	Leitungsparameter m, Leitungskonstante f	**linearly graded junction**	linear abgestufter Übergang m
		linearly ordered set	s. ordered set <math.>
linear electro-optical effect	s. Pockels effect	**linearly polarized,** plane polarized	linear polarisiert, geradlinig polarisiert
linear element, differential of arc, element of length, line element	Bogenelement n, Bogendifferential n, Linienelement n	**linearly polarized oscillation**	s. plane polarized oscillation
		linearly viscoelastic	linear[-]viskoelastisch
		linearly viscous	linear[-]viskos
linear energy absorption coefficient	s. linear absorption coefficient	**linear macromolecule,** linear molecule, thread-like molecule	Fadenmolekül n, lineares Molekül (Makromolekül) n, Linearmolekül n
linear energy transfer, LET, restricted linear collision stopping power	linearer Energietransfer m, „linear energy transfer" m, LET, LET-Faktor m, lineare Energieübertragung f, linearer Energieübertragungsfaktor m, lineares Energieübertragungsvermögen n, LEÜ	**linear magnetostriction**	lineare Magnetostriktion f, Längenmagnetostriktion f
		linear magnification	s. magnification <opt.>
		linear manifold	s. linear subspace
		linear mapping	lineare Abbildung f
		linear mean [value] <el.>	Gleichrichtwert m, Gleichwert m, linearer Mittelwert m <El.>
linear eruption	s. fissure eruption		
linear expansion, linear dilatation; unidirectional tension, simple elongation	lineare Ausdehnung f, Längenausdehnung f, Längendilatation f, Längs[aus]dehnung f, Längsdilatation f; einachsige Dehnung f	**linear measure**	Längenmaß n
		linear measurement	s. measurement of length
		linear molecule, linear macromolecule, thread-like molecule	Fadenmolekül n, lineares Molekül (Makromolekül) n, Linearmolekül n
linear expansion	s. a. linear thermal expansion	**linear moment,** static[al] moment, moment of first order, mass moment	statisches Moment n, Moment erster Ordnung, lineares Moment
linear expansion coefficient	s. coefficient of linear expansion		
linear expansivity	s. coefficient of linear expansion	**linear moment of inertia,** moment of inertia of a line	Linienträgheitsmoment n
linear extension	s. linear dimension		
linear extinction coefficient, Napierian extinction coefficient, natural extinction coefficient, linear attenuation coefficient	Extinktionskonstante f, natürliche Extinktionskonstante, natürlicher Extinktionsmodul m	**linear momentum;** momentum, quantity of motion <mech.>	Impuls m, Bewegungsgröße f; linearer Impuls <Mech.>
		linear momentum operator	s. momentum operator
		linear [multiterminal] network	lineares Netzwerk n, lineares Netz n

linear motor	Linearmotor *m*, Linear-Elektromotor *m*	**line broadening by damping**	*s.* natural broadening
		line broadening by impact	*s.* collision broadening
linear neutral wedge	linearer Graukeil *m*	**line broadening by radiation damping**	*s.* natural broadening
linear operation limits	*s.* range of linearity	**line broadening function**	Linienverbreiterungsfunktion *f*, LVF
linear ordering	*s.* ordering <math.>		
linear oscillation	*s.* linearly polarized oscillation	**line centre**, core <of the line>	zentraler Kern *m* [der Spektrallinie], Linienkern *m*, Linienzentrum *n*, Linienmitte *f*
linear oscillation	*s. a.* simple oscillation		
linear oscillator, simple (linear) harmonic oscillator	linearer harmonischer Oszillator *m*	**line conic, line-conic**	Kurve *f* zweiter Klasse
		line contour	*s.* line profile
linear perspective	Linearperspektive *f*	**line co-ordinates**	*s.* Plucker co-ordinates
linear pinch [effect]	linearer Pinch *m*, linearer Pincheffekt *m*	**line current**, system (interlinked) current	verketteter Strom *m*
		line curvature <of prismatic spectrum>	Linienkrümmung *f* <im Prismenspektrum>
linear polarization, plane polarization	lineare (geradlinige) Polarisation *f*, Linearpolarisation *f*	**line defect**, one-dimensional disorder	eindimensionale Fehlordnung (Fehlstelle) *f*
		line deflection set	*s.* horizontal-deflection unit
linear Raman effect, spontaneous Raman effect (scattering)	linearer Raman-Effekt *m*, spontaner Raman-Effekt	**line depression**, trough line <meteo.>	Troglinie *f* <Meteo.>
		line dipole	Liniendipol *m*, linearer Dipol *m*
linear range <of particle>	Reichweite *f* in cm <Teilchen>, lineare Reichweite [des Teilchens]	**line displacement**	*s.* line shift
		line element	*s.* linear element
		line element	*s.* circuit element
linear range	*s. a.* range of linearity	**line element of Schwarzschild**	Schwarzschildsches Linienelement *n*
linear rate	*s.* linear velocity		
linear rectifier, perfect rectifier, linear detector	geradliniger (linearer) Gleichrichter *m*, idealer Gleichrichter	**line emitted by neutral atom**	Neutralatomlinie *f*
linear regression	lineare Regression *f*	**line energy**	Linienenergie *f*
linear resonance accelerator	linearer Resonanzbeschleuniger *m*	**line error [of graduated circle]**	Strichfehler *m* [des Teilkreises]
linear response detector, linear detector	linearer Detektor *m*, Detektor mit linearer Charakteristik (Anzeige)	**line filament**	linienförmiger Leuchtkörper *m*
		line focus, linear focus	Strichfokus *m*, Götze-Fokus *m*
linear section of the programme, unbranched section of the programme	unverzweigtes Programmstück *n*, gerades Programmstück	**line focus tube**	Strichfokusröhre *f*
		line force	Linienkraft *f*
		line frequency	*s.* power-line frequency
linear source	*s.* line source	**line impedance**	Leitungsimpedanz *f*
linear space, vector space, linear vector space	Vektorraum *m*, Vektorgebilde *n*, linearer Raum		
		line index, row index	Zeilenindex *m*
linear specific ionization	*s.* specific ionization	**line integral**, contour integral; flow <e.g. of a tensor field, along a curve>	Kurvenintegral *n*, Linienintegral *n*
linear stopping power	lineares Bremsvermögen *n*		
linear strain	*s.* unit elongation	**line integral of the force**	Wegintegral *n* der Kraft
linear subspace, linear manifold	linearer Unterraum *m*, lineare Mannigfaltigkeit *f*		
linear system with constant coefficients	*s.* d'Alembert equation	**line intensity**	*s.* intensity of the spectral line
		line intersection method, method of line intersection	Linienschnittverfahren *n*
linear temperature coefficient, first-order temperature coefficient	Temperaturkoeffizient *m* erster Ordnung, linearer Temperaturkoeffizient		
		line lattice, lattice of lines, line screen	Linienraster *m*, Liniengitter *n*
linear tensor	linearer Tensor *m*, kovarianter Multivektor *m*	**line loss**, mains leakage <el.>	Leitungsverlust *m*; Längsverlust *m* <El.>
linear tensor density	lineare (kovariante alternierende) Tensordichte *f*	**line micrometer**	Strichmikrometer *n*
linear thermal expansion, linear heat expansion, linear expansion	lineare Wärmeausdehnung *f*, lineare [thermische] Ausdehnung *f*	**line microphone**, machine-gun microphone	lineare (gerade) Mikrophongruppe *f*, lineares Mikrophon *n*
linear thermal expansion coefficient	*s.* coefficient of linear expansion	**line narrowing**, spectral line narrowing, narrowing of the spectral line, spectral narrowing	Linienverschmälerung *f*, Linienverengerung *f*, Spektrallinienverschmälerung *f*, Spektrallinienverengerung *f*, Verschmälerung (Verengerung) *f* der Spektrallinie, spektrale Verengerung (Verschmälerung)
linear thermopile	lineare Thermosäule *f*, Linearthermosäule *f*		
linear-to-logarithmic converter [unit]	linear-logarithmischer Konverter (Wandler) *m*		
linear transformation	*s.* homographic transformation		
linear vector space, vector space, linear space	Vektorraum *m*, Vektorgebilde *n*, linearer Raum *m*	**line noise**, mains noise	Netzrauschen *n*, Netzgeräusch *n*, Netzton *m*
linear velocity <mech.>; linear rate	Lineargeschwindigkeit *f*, lineare Geschwindigkeit *f*	**line noise**	*s. a.* circuit noise
		line noting the valence, valence line, bond line	Valenzstrich *m*, Bindungsstrich *m*
linear velocity, velocity vector	Geschwindigkeitsvektor *m*		
linear viscosity	lineare Viskosität *f*	**line of action [of the force], line of application [of the force]**	Angriffslinie *f*, Wirkungslinie *f* <Kraft>
line at infinity, ideal line	uneigentliche (unendlich[] ferne) Gerade *f*, Ferngerade *f*	**line of application**	*s.* position <of sliding vector>
		line of apsides, apse line	Apsidenlinie *f*
line breadth	*s.* line width		
line broadening, spectral line broadening, broadening (widening) of the spectral line, [spectral] line widening	Linienverbreiterung *f*, Spektrallinienverbreiterung *f*, Verbreiterung *f* der Spektrallinie	**line of centres**, centre line <of the force system>	Zentrallinie *f* [des Kräftesystems]

line of centres, centre line <math.>	Zentrale *f* <Math.>	**line of level**	*s.* isohypse
		line of longitude	*s.* meridian
line of cold front, cold front line	Kaltfrontlinie *f*	**line of magnetic field strength**, magnetic line of force	magnetische Feldlinie *f*, Magnetfeldlinie *f*, magnetische Kraftlinie *f*
line of collimation	*s.* collimation line	**line of magnetic flux (induction)**	*s.* magnetic line of induction
line of constant concentration	*s.* isoconcentrate	**line of magnetization**	*s.* magnetization curve
line of constant evaporation, iso-ombral line, line of equal evaporation	Isoombre *f*	**line of maximum shearing stress**	*s.* shear line
line of constant phase	*s.* isophase	**line of nodes**, nodal line <astr., mech.>	Knotenlinie *f* <Astr., Mech.>; Knotenachse *f*
line of constant temperature, isothermal, isotherm[al line], line of equal temperature	Isotherme *f*, Wärmegleiche *f*	**line of numerus**	*s.* uniform scale
		line of position	*s.* position line
		line of principal stresses	*s.* trajectory of principal stresses
line of constant velocity	*s.* isotach	**line of regression**, regression line	Regressionsgerade *f*, Ausgleichsgerade *f*, Beziehungsgerade *f*, ausgleichende Gerade *f*
line of critical states, critical line	kritische Linie *f*, Linie der kritischen Zustände		
line of curvature	Krümmungslinie *f*	**line of separation between waters**, water[-]shed, watershed divide, divide <US> <geo.>	Wasserscheide *f*, Scheide *f*, Scheitelung *f*; Wasserscheidelinie *f*; Kammwasserscheide *f* <Geo.>
line of development of the coast, development of the coast	Verlauf *m* der Küste		
line of direction	Richtungslinie *f*, Lichtrichtung[slinie] *f*; Sehrichtung *f*	**line of shock**, shock line	Stoßlinie *f*
		line of sight, sighting line	Visierlinie *f*
line of discontinuity	*s.* discontinuity line	**line of sight**	Blicklinie *f*
line of dislocation, dislocation line	Versetzungslinie *f*, Versetzungsgrenze *f*	**line of sight**	*s. a.* line of vision
		line-of-sight distance	*s.* visibility
line of displacement vector, displacement line	Verschiebungslinie *f*, Feldlinie *f* des Vektors der dielektrischen Verschiebung	**line of sight method [of ray analysis]**	Methode *f* des kürzesten Strahlungsweges [der Strahlanalyse], Analyse *f* des kürzesten Strahlungsweges
line of electric flux	*s.* line of flux		
line of embrace, embrace line	Umschlingungslinie *f*	**line-of-sight velocity**, radial velocity <of star>	Radialgeschwindigkeit *f* <Himmelskörper>
line of equal colour, isochrom[atic]	Farbniveaulinie *f*, Linie *f* gleicher Farbe, Isochrome *f*	**line of simultaneous high tide**	*s.* co[-]tidal line
line of equal concentration	*s.* isoconcentrate	**line of single normal velocity**	*s.* primary optic axis
line of equal deformation	Linie *f* gleicher Deformation	**line of single ray velocity**	*s.* secondary optic axis
line of equal density	*s.* equidensity	**line of slope**, line of greatest slope <geo.>	Gefällskurve *f*; Gefällinie *f*, Fallinie *f*, Linie *f* der Maximalneigung <Geo.>
line of equal density	*s. a.* isopycn		
line of equal deviation, curve of equal deviation	Isokampte *f*, Kurve *f* gleicher Ablenkung		
line of equal enthalpy	*s.* isenthalp	**line of sources**, source line	Quellinie *f*, Quellfaden *m*
line of equal evaporation, iso-ombral line, line of constant evaporation	Isoombre *f*	**line of stability**, stability line, curve of stability, stability curve	Stabilitätslinie *f*, Stabilitätskurve *f*
line of equal latitude, latitude line, parallel	Breitengleiche *f*, Linie *f* gleicher Breite	**line of stress**, stress line, stress trajectory, line of tension	Spannungslinie *f*
line of equal longitude, longitude line	Längengleiche *f*, Linie *f* gleicher Länge	**line of strike**	*s.* line of trend
line of equal optical density	*s.* equidensity	**line of support**	Stützgerade *f*
		line of symmetry, symmetry line	Symmetriegerade *f*, Symmetrale *f*
line of equal polarization, isopolar	Isopolare *f*	**line of tension**, stress line, stress trajectory, line of stress	Spannungslinie *f*
line of equal pressure	*s.* isobar <therm., meteo.>		
line of equal stream function	*s.* line of flow	**line of thrust**	*s.* thrust line
line of equal temperature	*s.* line of constant temperature	**line of time** <rel.; math.>	Zeitlinie *f* <Rel.; Math.>
line of equal velocity	*s.* isotach	**line of trend**, line of strike <geo.>	Streichlinie *f* <Geo.>
line of field [strength]	*s.* line of force		
line of flexure, streamline, stream line, flow line, line of equal stream function	*s.* bending line	**line of vector**, vector line	Vektorlinie *f*, Feldlinie *f* des Vektorfeldes
line of flow, streamline, stream line, flow line, line of equal stream function	Stromlinie *f*, Strömungslinie *f*	**line of vision**, visual line, radius of vision; line of sight	Gesichtslinie *f*, Sichtlinie *f*, Visionsradius *m*
		line of warm front, warm front line	Warmfrontlinie *f*
		line optics	Linienoptik *f*
line of flux <el.>, line of electric flux	Induktionslinie *f*, Flußlinie *f*, Kraftflußlinie *f* <El.>	**line oscillator**	*s.* horizontal-deflection oscillator
line of force, line of field [strength], field line	Feldlinie *f*, Kraftlinie *f* [des Feldes], Feldstärkelinie *f*	**line profile**, profile of the [spectral] line, line contour, contour of the [spectral] line, line shape, shape of the [spectral] line, spectral line profile (contour, shape)	Linienform *f*, Spektrallinienform *f*, Form *f* der Spektrallinie, Linienkontur *f*, Kontur *f* der Spektrallinie, Linienprofil *n*, Spektrallinienprofil *n*, Liniengestalt *f*, Profil *n* (Gestalt *f*) der Spektrallinie
line of fracture, rupture line	Bruchlinie *f*		
line of greatest slope	*s.* line of slope <geo.>		
line of heat flow [vector], heat flow line	Wärmestromlinie *f*		
line of hydrogen, hydrogen line	Wasserstofflinie *f*		
line of hydrostatic pressure, water pressure line	Wasserdruckfigur *f*, Wasserdrucklinie *f*		
		liner	Liner *m*
		line reversal	*s.* spectral line reversal
line of induction	*s.* magnetic line of indutcion	**line scanning**	*s.* horizontal sweep
line of intersection	Schnittgerade *f*	**line screen**	*s.* lattice of lines
line of intersection	*s. a.* curve of intersection	**line segment**, segment <math.>	Strecke *f* <Math.>
line of latitude	*s.* parallel		

line shape	s. line profile	linkage, linking[-up]; interlinking; interconnection	Verkettung f
line-shaped	s. linear		
line-shaped source	s. line source		
line shape function, shape function of the line	Linienformfunktion f		
line shift, shift of spectral line, line displacement, displacement of spectral line, spectral shift	Linienverschiebung f, Verschiebung f der Spektrallinie, Spektral[linien]verschiebung f, spektrale Verschiebung	linkage <mech.>	Gelenkkette f, Gelenksystem n <Mech.>
		linkage force	s. binding force
		link coupling; low-impedance coupling	Linkkopplung f
line simulator	s. artificial line	linked quadrangle (quadrilateral), articulated quadrangle (quadrilateral), four-bar linkage	Gelenkviereck n
line source, line-shaped source, linear source; straight[-]line source	Linienquelle f, linienartige Quelle f, linienförmige Quelle, lineare Quelle; geradlinige Quelle		
line spacing, line advance, scanning separation (pitch)	Zeilenabstand m	Linke['s] factor of turbidity	s. turbidity factor [of Linke]
line spectrum	Linienspektrum n	Linke-Feussner actinometer, shielded actinometer, panzeractinometer	Panzeraktinometer n [nach Linke und Feußner], Linke-Feußner-Aktinometer n
line splitting, splitting <of the spectral line>	Linienaufspaltung f, Aufspaltung f <Spektrallinie>		
		Linke['s] turbidity factor (parameter)	s. turbidity factor [of Linke]
line splitting by charge exchange	s. charge-exchange splitting	linking	s. linkage
line squall, frontal squall	Frontbö f, Linienbö f	linking-up	s. linkage
		link line	Linkleitung f
line standard, line-standard comparator	Strichmaß n; Strichlehre f; Strichnormal n	link of chain, chain segment (element), segment of chain	Kettenglied n, Glied n der Kette
line standard dilatometer	Strichmaßdehnungsmesser m	link polygon, funicular polygon, string polygon	Seilpolygon n, Seileck n
line storage tube, single-beam line storage tube	Linienspeicherröhre f		
		Linnik interferometer, Linnik-type two-beam instrument	Auflicht-Interferenzmikroskop n nach Linnik, Linniksches Mikrointerferometer n
		linotron	Linotron n
line strength	s. intensity of the spectral line	Liouville damping	Liouville-Dämpfung f, Liouvillesche Dämpfung f
line stress, line tension	Linienspannung f	Liouville density	Liouville-Dichte f
line structure	Linienstruktur f, linienhafte Struktur f	Liouville['s] equation, Gibbs' general equation	Liouville-Gleichung f, Liouvillesche Gleichung f
line sweep	s. horizontal sweep	Liouville['s] formula <for Wronskian>	Liouvillesche Formel f <Wronski-Determinante>
line sweep unit	s. horizontal-deflection unit		
line tension	s. line stress	Liouville-Neumann series, Neumann's series	Neumannsche Reihe f
line termination	Leitungsabschluß m		
line texture	Linientextur f	Liouville['s] principle	s. Liouville['s] theorem <stat.>
line theory, theory of transmission lines	Leitungstheorie f	Liouville['s] theorem <for analytical functions>	Liouvillescher Satz m <für analytische Funktionen>
line transmission	Leitungsübertragung f		
line-turn, Maxwell turn	Maxwellwindung f	Liouville['s] theorem, Liouville['s] principle, principle of conservation of density-in-phase <stat.>	Liouvillescher Satz m, Liouville-Boltzmannscher Satz
line unsharpness, diffuseness (unsharpness) of the line	Linienunschärfe f, Unschärfe f der Spektrallinie		
line voltage, mains input, mains (supply) voltage, voltage of the main	Netzspannung f	lipoid-sieve theory [of permeability]	Lipoidfilterhypothese f [der Permeabilität]
		lipoid solubility	Lipoidlöslichkeit f
line voltage, system (interlinked, phase-to-phase) voltage	verkettete Spannung f, Leiterspannung f, Leitungsspannung f		
		lipoid theory of narcosis	Lipoidtheorie f der Narkose
line voltage change	s. variation in the mains voltage	lipophilic nature (property), lipophily	Lipophilie f
line vortex	s. vortex line	Lippich [halfshade]; Lippich prism, double field analyzer [of Lippich], Lippich-type polarimeter	Doppelfeldanalysator m, Halbschattenpolarimeter n von Lippich, Halbschattenapparat m nach [dem Prinzip von] Lippich, Polarimeter n mit Halbschattenprisma, Lippich-Prisma n, Prisma n von Lippich
line widening	s. line broadening		
line width, width of the spectral line, line breadth, breadth of the spectral line; half-width of the spectral line, whole half-width	Linienbreite f, Spektrallinienbreite f, Breite f der Spektrallinie; Halbwertsbreite f der Spektrallinie (Linie)		
line width by collision damping, collision width	Stoßbreite f		
		Lippich['s] theorem	Lippichscher Satz m
		Lippich-type polarimeter	s. Lippich halfshade
line width due to the apparatus used, instrumental width [of the line]	Apparatebreite f	Lippmann['s] [capillary] electrometer	s. capillary electrometer
lingering, residence	Verweilen n, Aufenthalt m	Lippmann equation	Lippmannsche Gleichung f
lingering sound (tone)	s. reverberation	Lippmann fringe	Lippmannscher Streifen m
lining; lagging	Auskleidung f, innerer Überzug m; Plattieren n	Lippmann plate	Lippmann-Platte f
lining-up; preparation	Herstellung f, Bereitung f, Präparation f, Vorbereitung f	Lippmann-Schwinger formalism	Lippmann-Schwingerscher Formalismus m
link, element; section; segment; member <techn., el.>	Glied n <Techn., El.>	Lippmann-Weber spectrometer	s. differential-bridge-type spectrometer

Lipschitz condition, condition of Lipschitz — Lipschitz-Bedingung f

Lipschitz constant — Lipschitz-Konstante f, Lipschitzsche Konstante f

Lipschitz continuous function — Lipschitz-stetige Funktion f

liquation <geo.> — Liquation f <Geo.>

liquation — s. a. microscopic segregation <met.>

liquefacient — s. liquefier

liquefaction <of gases or gels>; condensation <of gases> — Verflüssigung f

liquefaction coefficient, coefficient of liquefaction — Verflüssigungskoeffizient m

liquefaction point — s. liquefaction temperature

liquefaction pressure — Verflüssigungsdruck m

liquefaction temperature, liquefaction point, temperature of liquefaction; condensation temperature (point), temperature of condensation, condensing temperature — Verflüssigungstemperatur f, Verflüssigungspunkt m; Kondensationstemperatur f, Kondensationspunkt m

liquefier — Verflüssiger m, Verflüssigungsmaschine f

liquefier, liquefying agent, liquefacient — Verflüssigungsmittel n

liquid, dropping liquid, liquor — tropfbare Flüssigkeit f, Flüssigkeit

liquid — tropfbar[-]flüssig, tropfbar

liquid — s. a. melt

liquid-air trap — Kühlfalle f mit flüssiger Luft

liquid at its bubble point, orthobaric (saturated) liquid — orthobare Flüssigkeit f

liquid barometer — Flüssigkeitsbarometer n

liquid calorimeter, usual (water; mixture) calorimeter — Flüssigkeitskalorimeter n, Wasserkalorimeter n; Mischungskalorimeter n

liquid carrier — s. carrier liquid

liquid chromatography — s. stream chromatography

liquid column, head of a liquid — Flüssigkeitssäule f

liquid coolant — Kühlflüssigkeit f

liquid counter [tube] — Flüssigkeitszähler m; Flüssigkeitszählrohr n

liquid crystal, crystalline liquid, crystal liquid, mesomorphic phase, mesomorphous phase — flüssiger Kristall m, kristalline Flüssigkeit f, mesomorphe (liquokristalline) Phase f, Kristallchenflüssigkeit f

liquid damping, fluid friction damping — Flüssigkeitsdämpfung f

liquid displaced, displaced liquid — verdrängte Flüssigkeit f

liquid drop fluctuation — s. liquid drop oscillation

liquid droplet — Flüssigkeitströpfchen n

liquid-drop model, drop model; Volmer-Weber mechanism <cryst.> — Tröpfchenmodell n; Volmer-Weber-Mechanismus m <Krist.>

liquid drop model [of nucleus], liquid drop nuclear model — Tröpfchenmodell n [des Atomkerns]

liquid drop oscillation, oscillation (fluctuation) of the liquid drop, liquid drop fluctuation — Tröpfchenschwingung f

liquid-drop theory of the nucleus — Tröpfchentheorie f des Atomkerns

liquid element — Flüssigkeitselement n

liquid-expansion thermometer, liquid[-filled] thermometer; liquid-in-glass thermometer — Flüssigkeitsthermometer n

liquid filament, fluid filament, filament line in a fluid — Flüssigkeitsfaden m

liquid-filled thermometer — s. liquid-expansion thermometer

liquid film, liquid layer, layer of fluid — Flüssigkeitsschicht f; Flüssigkeitslamelle f; Flüssigkeitshaut f; Flüssigkeitsfilm f

liquid-film coefficient — Filmkoeffizient m der Flüssigkeit

liquid-film lubrication, liquid lubrication — Flüssigkeitsschmierung f

liquid filter <opt.> — Flüssigkeitsfilter n

liquid-flow counter — Flüssigkeitsdurchflußzähler m

liquid friction — Flüssigkeitsreibung f, Schmiermittelreibung f

liquid-gas interface, gas-liquid interface — Flüssigkeit / Gas - Grenzfläche f, Gas / Flüssigkeit - Grenzfläche f, Grenzfläche f Flüssigkeit — Gas, Grenzfläche Gas — Flüssigkeit, Grenzfläche flüssig — gasförmig, Grenzfläche gasförmig — flüssig

liquid hardening, immersion hardening, hardening by immersion — Tauchhärtung f

liquid helium temperature — Heliumtemperatur f

liquid hydrogen temperature, hydrogen temperature — Wasserstofftemperatur f

liquid-in-glass thermometer; liquid-expansion thermometer, liquid thermometer, liquid-filled thermometer — Flüssigkeitsthermometer n

liquidity — s. liquid state

liquid jet pump — Flüssigstrahlpumpe f

liquid junction potential — s. diffusion potential

liquid laser, liquid-state laser, liquid-state optical maser — Flüssigkeitslaser m

liquid layer, layer of fluid, liquid film — Flüssigkeitsschicht f; Flüssigkeitslamelle f; Flüssigkeitshaut f; Flüssigkeitsfilm m

liquid level; liquid surface, surface of the liquid — Flüssigkeitsstand m, Flüssigkeitsniveau n, Flüssigkeitspegel m; Flüssigkeitsspiegel m; Flüssigkeitsoberfläche f

liquid-level gauge (indicator, meter), liquidometer — Flüssigkeitsstandanzeiger m, Füllstandanzeiger m für Flüssigkeiten

liquid-liquid chromatography — Flüssig-flüssig-Chromatographie f

liquid-liquid chromatography — s. a. partition chromatography

liquid-liquid extraction — Flüssig-Flüssig-Extraktion f

liquid-liquid interface — Flüssigkeit / Flüssigkeit-Grenzfläche f, Grenzfläche f Flüssigkeit — Flüssigkeit, Grenzfläche flüssig — flüssig

liquid lubricant, lubricating oil, luboil — Schmieröl n

liquid lubrication, liquid-film lubrication — Flüssigkeitsschmierung f

liquid-magnetic — liquidmagnetisch

liquid manometer — s. fluid gauge

liquid medium — s. medium <chem.>

liquid meniscus, meniscus [of liquid] <mech.> — Meniskus m; Flüssigkeitsmeniskus m <Mech.>

liquid metal, molten metal, fused metal, melt of metal — Metallschmelze f, Flüssigmetall n, geschmolzenes Metall n

liquid mirror, liquid mirror surface	Flüssigkeitsspiegel m	liquid-vapour interface	Flüssigkeit/Dampf-Grenzfläche f, Grenzfläche f Flüssigkeit—Dampf
liquid mirror method	Methode f des „flüssigen" Spiegels	liquid-vapour mixture	Flüssigkeit-Dampf-Gemisch n
liquid mirror surface, liquid mirror	Flüssigkeitsspiegel m	liquid waste	Abfallösung f, flüssige Abfallstoffe mpl; Abwasser n
liquidness	s. liquid state		
liquidometer	s. liquid-level gauge	liquid water	tropfbares Wasser n, Tröpfchenwasser n
liquid-penetrant testing process, penetrant method	Eindringverfahren n, Diffusionsverfahren n <Werkstoffprüfung>	liquid whistle, ultrasonic fluid whistle	Flüssigkeitspfeife f
liquid phase	flüssige Phase f, Flüssigkeitsphase f, Flüssigphase f; Trennflüssigkeit f <Trennprozeß>	liquid window	flüssigkeitsgefülltes Schutzfenster n
		liquor	s. liquid
liquid-pressure gauge	s. fluid gauge	lisoloid	feste Emulsion f, Lisoloid n
liquid prism	Flüssigkeitsprisma n		
liquid-propellant motor, liquid-propellant rocket engine	Raketenmotor m mit Flüssigbrennstoff, Raketentriebwerk n mit flüssigem Brennstoff	L-isomer, l-isomer, laevoisomer	linksdrehendes Isomer n, L-Isomer n, l-Isomer n
		Lissajous['] curves, Lissajous['] figure[s], Lissajous['] pattern	Lissajous-Figur[en fpl] f Lissajous-Bahnen fpl
liquid-propellant rocket	Flüssigkeitsrakete f	Li star, lithium star	Lithiumstern m
liquid-propellant rocket engine, liquid-propellant motor	Raketenmotor m mit Flüssigbrennstoff, Raketentriebwerk n mit flüssigem Brennstoff	listening device, intercept receiver	Horchgerät n
		Listing['s] rule	Listingsche Regel f
		liter <US>	s. litre
liquid radioactive waste, liquid radwaste	radioaktive Abfallösung f, flüssiger radioaktiver Abfall m, radioaktives Abwasser n	lithium-chloride moisture meter	Lithiumchlorid-Feuchtigkeitsmesser m; Lithiumchlorid-Taupunktfühler m
liquid range	Flüssigkeitsgebiet n, Flüssigkeitsbereich m	lithium star, Li star	Lithiumstern m
		lithogenesis	Lithogenese f
liquid resistor	Flüssigkeitswiderstand m	lithogenetic, lithogenic	lithogen
liquid salt, molten salt, fused salt	Salzschmelze f	lithophysa	Lithophyse f
		lithosiderite, stony-iron meteorite	Stein-Eisen-Meteorit m, Lithosiderit m
liquid scintillation counter	Flüssigkeitsszintillationszähler m	lithosphere	Lithosphäre f
		litmus paper, litmus test paper	Lackmuspapier n
liquid scintillator, scintillating liquid	flüssiger Szintillator m, Szintillationsflüssigkeit f	litre, liter <US>, l, l.	Liter n, l, l
		litre atmosphere, lat	[technische] Literatmosphäre f, lat
liquid seal, hydraulic seal, water seal, packing water seal, hydroseal	Flüssigkeitsverschluß m, Tauchverschluß m, hydraulischer Verschluß m; Flüssigkeitsdichtung f, hydraulische Dichtung f, Wasserabschluß m, Wasser[ver]schluß m, Wasservorlage f, wasserdichter Abschluß m	litre atmosphere, physical litre atmosphere, latm	[physikalische] Literatmosphäre f, latm
		little crystal, small crystal	Kriställchen n
		"Little Green Man"	s. pulsar
		little metacentre	kleines Metazentrum n
		littoral, littoral zone, sea-shore zone	Litoral n, Uferregion f, Uferzone f, Gezeitenzone f, Strandbereich m
liquid shrinkage	s. piping		
liquid-solid chromatography, LSC	s. adsorption chromatography	littoral current	Uferströmung f
liquid-solid interface	s. solid-liquid interface		
liquid state, liquidity, liquidness	[tropfbar-]flüssiger Zustand m, Flüssigkeitszustand m; Tropfbarkeit f	littoral zone, littoral, sea-shore zone	Litoral n, Uferregion f, Uferzone f, Gezeitenzone f, Strandbereich m
		Littrow mirror	Littrow-Spiegel m
liquid-state laser	s. liquid laser	Littrow mounting	Aufbau (Prismenaufbau) m nach Littrow, Littrowscher Prismenaufbau
liquid-state optical maser	s. liquid laser		
liquid structure	Flüssigkeitsstruktur f	Littrow prism	Littrow-Prisma n
liquid surface	s. a. liquid level	Littrow spectrograph	Littrow-Spektrograph m
liquid-surface interferometer	Flüssigkeitsspiegelinterferometer n	lituus	Lituus m <Inverses der Fermatschen Spirale>
liquid surface wave, surface wave on liquids, wave on the surface of liquids	Oberflächenwelle f auf Flüssigkeiten, Welle f auf Flüssigkeitsoberflächen	litzendraht [wire]; litz wire, strand, stranded wire	Litze f
liquid thermometer	s. liquid-expansion thermometer	live	spannungsführend, unter Spannung
liquidus, boiling-point curve <in condensation of mixed vapours>	Siedekurve f, Siedelinie f, Verdampfungskurve f, untere (linke) Grenzkurve f; Destillationskurve f	live	s. a. current-carrying
		live load, moving (travelling, rolling) load	bewegliche Belastung f
liquidus, liquidus curve (line), freezing-point curve	Liquiduslinie f, Liquiduskurve f	live load, varying load <statics>	wechselnde Belastung f, Wechselbelastung f <Statik>
liquidus temperature	Liquidustemperatur f	livering	s. inspissation <chem.>
liquid-vapour equilibrium, vapour-liquid equilibrium	Dampf-Flüssigkeit-Gleichgewicht n, Flüssigkeit/Dampf-Gleichgewicht n, Gleichgewicht n Flüssigkeit—Dampf, Flüssigkeit und Dampf m im Gleichgewicht, Dampf m und Flüssigkeit im Gleichgewicht	live steam, direct steam	Frischdampf m
		live-voice audiometer, speech audiometer	Sprachaudiometer n
		living force	s. motive power
		living polymer	lebendes Polymer n
		lixiviation; leaching; solid-liquid extraction	Laugung f, Auslaugung f, Auswaschung f, Festflüssig-Extraktion f
		Ljungstroem turbine, Ljungström turbine	Ljungström-Turbine f

Llewellyn-Peterson equations	Llewellyn-Petersonsche Gleichungen *fpl*	loading in steps	s. progressive load[ing]
Lloyd['s] experiment	Lloydscher Spiegelversuch *m*	loading point <chem.>	Belastungsgrenze *f* <Chem.>
Lloyd mirror	Lloyd-Spiegel *m*, Lloydscher Spiegel *m*	loading point <el.>	Spulenpunkt *m* <El.>
L meson, light meson <µ or π>	leichtes Meson *n*, L-Meson *n* <µ oder π>	loading point, load limit	s. maximum permissible load
L/M ratio	L/M-Verhältnis *n*	load line	s. load curve
		load moment, moment of load	Lastmoment *n*
L network, L section; L circuit	L-Glied *n*; L-Schaltung *f*	load of instrument transformer, instrument transformer load	Bürde *f*, Belastung *f* des Meßwandlers
load, electrical load <el.>	[elektrische] Belastung *f*, [elektrische] Last *f*, <El.>	load on the valve	Ventilbelastung *f*
		load polygon	s. polygon of forces
load <mech.>	Last *f*, Belastung *f* <Mech.>	load resistance, ballast resistance, external resistance; load resistor, ballast resistor, external resistor	Verbraucherwiderstand *m*; Lastwiderstand *m*, Belastungswiderstand *m*; Außenwiderstand *m*, äußerer Widerstand *m*; Arbeitswiderstand *m*
load	s. a. strain <mech.>		
load admittance	Belastungsscheinleitwert *m*, Lastscheinleitwert *m*, Belastungsadmittanz *f*, Lastadmittanz *f*		
		load resistance	s. a. terminal resistance
load angle	Lastwinkel *m*	load resistance of the rectifier, rectifier load resistance	Richtwiderstand *m*
load arm of the lever	Lastarm *m*, Arm *m* der Last		
load at rupture	s. breaking load	load resistor	s. load resistance
load border	s. maximum permissible load	load varying between zero and maximum positive strain	s. pulsating load
load capacitance	Belastungskapazität *f*, Lastkapazität *f*	Lobachevskian geometry, hyperbolic geometry	hyperbolische Geometrie *f*, Lobatschewskische Geometrie
load capacity, load carrying capacity, load factor <mech., el.>	Belastbarkeit *f*		
		Lobachevski plane, hyperbolic plane	hyperbolische Ebene *f*, Lobatschewskische Ebene
load characteristic; load diagram	Lastcharakteristik *f*, Lastkurve *f*, Holbrook-Dixon-Kurve *f*, Belastungscharakteristik *f*, Belastungsdiagramm *n*, Belastungskennlinie *f*	Lobachevski space, hyperbolic space	hyperbolischer Raum *m*, Lobatschewskischer Raum
		lobe <in the directivity diagram>	Strahlungslappen *m*, Lappen *m*, Strahlungskeule *f*, Keule *f*, Strahlungszipfel *m*, Zipfel *m*, Strahlenlappen *m*, Strahlenkeule *f*, Strahlenzipfel *m* <im Richtdiagramm>
load coefficient	s. load factor <mech., el.>		
load-coil spacing, loading coil spacing	Spulenfeldlänge *f*, Spulenabstand *m*, Spulenabwicklung *f*		
load current	Laststrom *m*		
		lobed flowmeter	s. propeller-type flowmeter
load curve, load line	Belastungskurve *f*, Belastungslinie *f*	lobed impeller meter, rotating lobe meter	Drehkolbenzähler *m*
load cycle	s. cycle of load stressing	lobe pattern	s. radiation pattern
load diagram	s. load characteristic	lobe switching, antenna (aerial) switching	Antennenumschaltung *f*, Antennenumtastung *f*
loaded concrete	s. heavy-aggregate concrete		
loaded impedance	Eingangsimpedanz *f* bei Sollabschluß	lobe switching	s. beam switching
		lobe switching [radio] interferometer	„lobe switching"-Interferometer *n*
loaded Q, loaded Q factor	Güte *f* (Gütefaktor *m*) des belasteten Resonanzkreises		
		lobe width, [half-power] beam width, half-power width of lobe <for antennas>	Lappenbreite *f*, Halbwertsbreite *f* des Strahlungslappens <Antenne>
load-extension diagram	s. stress-strain curve		
load factor, load coefficient <mech., el.>	Belastungszahl *f*, Belastungsfaktor *m*, Belastungsziffer *f* <Mech., El.>; Lastfaktor *m* <El.>		
		lobe width	s. a. flare angle <of antenna system>
		lobing	s. beam switching
load factor <mech., el.>	s. a. load capacity	local adaptation	Lokaladaptation *f*
load function, loading function	Belastungsfunktion *f*	local analysis	s. local spectrochemical analysis
load impedance, end impedance	Endimpedanz *f*, Abschlußimpedanz *f*	local anode	Lokalanode *f*
		local attack	s. localized corrosion
load impedance	s. a. terminal impedance	local average	örtliches Mittel *n*, lokales Mittel
load index	Belastungsverhältnis *n*, Lastverhältnis *n*		
		local boiling, subcooled boiling	örtliches Sieden *n*, lokales Sieden
loading <in the reactor>	Beladung *f* mit Bestrahlungsgut, Einführung *f* von Bestrahlungsgut in den Reaktor	local buckling, crippling	Bculen *n*
		local cathode	Lokalkatode *f*
loading <of a line>, coil loading, pupinization	Bespulung *f*, Pupinisierung *f*	local cell, local element, local couple	Lokalelement *n*
loading; stressing; straining <mech.>	Beanspruchung *f*; Belastung *f* <Mech.>	local chromatic adaptation	s. local colour adaptation
		local climate	s. mesoclimate
loading coil, Pupin coil	Pupin-Spule *f*	local colour adaptation, local chromatic adaptation	farbige Lokaladaptation *f*; lokale Umstimmung *f*
loading coil section, coil section, pupinization section	Spulenfeld *n*, Ladungsabschnitt *m*		
		local compensation	lokale Kompensation (Ausgleichsbewegung) *f*
loading coil spacing, load-coil spacing	Spulenfeldlänge *f*, Spulenabstand *m*, Spulenabwicklung *f*		
		local corrosion	s. localized attack
		local couple	s. local cell
loading cycle	s. load cycle	local dosage, local dose	Ortsdosis *f*, Lokaldosis *f*, lokale Dosis *f*
loading density	Belastungsdichte *f*; Ladedichte *f* <Explosion>		
loading function, load function	Belastungsfunktion *f*	local earthquake	Ortsbeben *n*, Lokalbeben *n*

local electrode	Lokalelektrode f	local magnetic dip pole, local pole	lokaler Pol m, lokaler Magnetpol m
local element ‹astr.›	lokales Element n ‹Astr.›		
local element	s. a. local cell	local maximum	s. relative maximum
local extremum	s. relative extremum	local meridian	Ortsmeridian m
local fallout, local radioactive fallout	lokaler Fallout (Ausfall, radioaktiver Niederschlag) m	local minimum	s. relative minimum
local feature, hydraulic resistance ‹hydr›	einzelnes Hindernis n, Einzelhindernis n ‹Hydr.›	local perturbation	lokale Störung f
local field	s. local field intensity ‹el.›	local pole, local magnetic dip pole	lokaler Pol m, lokaler Magnetpol m
local field intensity, local field, Lorentz local field ‹el.›	lokales Feld n, Lorentzsches Lokalfeld n, Lokalfeld ‹El.›	local radioactive fallout, local fallout	lokaler Fallout (Ausfall, radioaktiver Niederschlag) m
local field theory	lokale Feldtheorie f	local refraction	Saalrefraktion f
local function	s. position function		
local Galilean system [of co-ordinates]	s. local inertial system	local region of cold air	s. lake of cold air
local glaciation	Lokalvergletscherung f	local rigidity	lokale Starrheit f
local group [of galaxies] ‹astr.›	lokale Gruppe f, lokales Supersystem n ‹Astr.›	local shower, passing shower, transient shower	Strichregen m
local heat transfer coefficient	lokale Wärmeübergangszahl f	local similarity hypothesis	s. Kolmogoroff similarity hypothesis
local horizon	s. apparent horizon	local sonic speed	s. local speed of sound
local inertial system [of co-ordinates], locally geodesic system [of co-ordinates], local Galilean system [of co-ordinates]	lokales Inertialsystem n, lokalgeodätisches Koordinatensystem n, lokalgeodätisches System n, lokal-Galileisches Bezugssystem n	local spectral analysis	s. local spectrochemical analysis
		local spectrochemical analysis, local [spectral] analysis	Lokalanalyse f
		local speed of sound, local sonic speed	lokale Schallgeschwindigkeit f
		local star-stream, moving cluster, moving star cluster	Bewegungssternhaufen m, Bewegungshaufen m, lokaler Sternstrom m
local invariant ‹astr.›	lokale Invariante f ‹Astr.›	local stellar system, local system ‹astr.›	lokales Sternsystem n ‹Astr.›
localizability	Lokalisierbarkeit f		
		local stress	örtliche Spannung f, lokale Spannung
localization; fixation; location; position determination, position finding; position fixing	Lokalisierung f, Ortsbestimmung f, Lagebestimmung f; Eingrenzung f, Begrenzung f; Ortung f; Lokalisation f ‹Math., physiologische Optik›; Standortbestimmung f; Positionsbestimmung f	local stress	lokaler (örtlicher) Spannungszustand m
		local system, local stellar system ‹astr.›	lokales Sternsystem n ‹Astr.›
		local thermodynamic[al] equilibrium	lokales thermodynamisches Gleichgewicht n
localization in a line	s. fixation at a line ‹of vector›	local time	Ortszeit f
		local transfer theory	lokale Übertragungstheorie f
localization in a point, fixation at a point ‹of vector›	Gebundenheit f ‹Vektor›	local variation; space dependence	Ortsabhängigkeit f
localization in space and time, space and time localization	räumliche und zeitliche Lokalisierung f	local variometer	Lokalvariometer n
localization of defects, fault localization; localizing a fault	Fehlereingrenzung f, Eingrenzung f von Fehlern; Fehlerort[sbestimm]ung f	locating arrangement; guidance; guide way; guide; guiding arrangement	Führung f; Führungsbahn f; Führungseinrichtung f
localization theory	s. Helmholtz['] place theory		
localized attack (corrosion), local corrosion (attack), location-action corrosion	örtliche (lokale) Korrosion f, örtlicher Angriff m, Lokalkorrosion f, örtliche Anfressung f	location, storage location, storage cell, memory cell, storage unit	Speicherzelle f; Speicherplatz m, Speicherstelle f
localized corrosion	s. pitting	location	s. a. introduction
localized fringes (interferences)	lokalisierte Interferenzen fpl	location	s. a. localization
		location-action corrosion	s. localized corrosion
localized level, localized term	lokalisiertes Niveau n, lokalisierter Term m	location finder, locator, position finder	Ortungsgerät n, Ortungsinstrument n; Ortungsanlage f
localized particle	lokalisiertes Teilchen n		
localized term	s. localized level		
localized vector, bound vector, fixed vector, field vector	gebundener Vektor m	location of black, black point	Farbort m des Schwarz, Schwarzpunkt m
		location of poles and zeros, pole-zero configuration	P-N-Verteilung f, P-N-Bild n, Pol-Nullstellen-Verteilung f, Pol-Nullstellen-Bild n
localizer beam, guide beam, guiding beam	Leitstrahl m	location of white, white point	Farbort m des Weiß, Weißpunkt m
localizing a fault	s. localization of defects	location sketch, area sketch, sketch	Kroki n
locally, in the small, im Kleinen ‹math.›	im Kleinen, lokal ‹Math.›		
locally analytic[al]	lokalanalytisch, lokal analytisch		
locally connected	lokal (im Kleinen) zusammenhängend	locator	s. location finder
		locked-up stress	s. internal stress ‹mech.›
locally convex space	lokalkonvexer Raum m	lockerstelle, Smekal defect (flaw), pore, flaw of Smekal, loose place [of Smekal]	Lockerstelle f [nach Smekal], Smekalsche Lockerstelle, Lockerion n
locally Euclidean, locally flat	lokal-euklidisch, lokal eben, lokaleben, lokal-eben		
locally geodesic system [of co-ordinates]	s. local inertial system	lock-in amplifier	„lock-in"-Verstärker m, Kohärenzverstärker m
local Mach number	lokale Mach-Zahl f	lock-in band	Mitnahmeband n

lock-in detector, coherent detector — Kohärenzgleichrichter *m*, „lock-in"-Gleichrichter *m*

locking, anchoring, blocking, pinning down <of dislocations> — Auflaufen *n*, Blockierung *f* <Versetzungen>

locking — s. a. interlock
locking — s. a. blocking <el.>
locking cam [of the Maltese cross] — Stiftscheibe *f*
locking of [grain] **boundaries** — Blockierung *f* der Korngrenzenwanderung, Korngrenzenblockierung *f*
locking range — s. pull-in range
locking relay — s. lock-in relay
lock-in range — s. pull-in range
lock-in relay, lock-on relay, locking relay, latched relay, latching relay — Haftrelais *n*, selbsthaltendes Relais *n*, Selbsthalterelais *n*, Sperrelais *n*

locomotion; movement — Fortbewegung *f*, Bewegung *f*, Fahren *n*, Fahrt *f*; Lokomotion *f* <Bio.>

locus <pl.: loci>, locus of point, point of colour <in chromaticity diagram> — Farbort *m*, Farbpunkt *m*
locus — s. gene locus
locus; vector diagram; circle diagram <control> — Ortskurve *f* <Regelung>

locus, geometric locus <math.> — [geometrischer] Ort *m* <pl.: Örter> <Math.>
locus fictus <astr.> — „locus fictus" *m* <Astr.>
locus of point — s. locus
locus of stimuli with zero luminosity — s. alychn
locus of the vortices — s. vortex line <opt.>
Loepelmann-Matthes formula — Loepelmann-Matthessche Formel *f*
loess sand — Lößsand *m*, Sandlöß *m*, Flottsand *m*, Schleppsand *m*

Loewe ring, Löwe ring — Löwescher Ring *m*
Loewner transformation — Loewnersche Transformation *f*
Loftin-White coupling, voltaic coupling <of thermionic valves> — galvanische Kopplung *f*, Loftin-White-Kopplung *f* <Röhren>
log, sillometer — Log *n*, Logge *f*, Fahrtgeschwindigkeitsmesser *m*
logarithm, log <to base a: $\log_a$> — Logarithmus *m*, log <zur Basis a: $^a\log, \log_a$>
logarithmic capacitor — Mittellinienkondensator *m*
logarithmic convexity — logarithmische Konvexität *f*
logarithmic co-ordinate paper, logarithmic paper — Logarithmenpapier *n*
logarithmic decrement [of damping], logarithmic decrement of attenuation, log.dec. — logarithmisches Dämpfungsdekrement *n*, logarithmisches Dekrement *n*
logarithmic derivative — logarithmische Ableitung *f*
logarithmic energy decrement — logarithmisches Energiedekrement *n*, logarithmischer Energieverlust *m*, logarithmisches Dekrement *n* der Energie
logarithmic horn, exponential horn — Exponentialhorn *n*, logarithmisches Horn *n*, Exponentialtrichter *m*
logarithmic increment — logarithmisches Inkrement *n*
logarithmic integral, logarithmic-integral function, li — Integrallogarithmus *m*, logarithmus *m* integralis, li, Li
logarithmic mean temperature difference, LMTD — mittlerer logarithmischer Temperaturunterschied *m*, LMTD-Wert *m*
logarithmic neutral wedge — logarithmischer Graukeil *m*

logarithmic normal distribution, logarithmico-normal distribution, log[-]normal distribution — logarithmisch normale Verteilung *f*, logarithmisch-normales Verteilungsgesetz *n*, logarithmische Normalverteilung *f*, Lognormalverteilung *f*, Normalverteilung zweiter (2.) Art

logarithmic paper, logarithmic co-ordinate paper — Logarithmenpapier *n*
logarithmic residue — logarithmisches Residuum *n*
logarithmic singularity — logarithmische Singularität *f*, logarithmisch-singulärer Punkt *m*
logarithmic spiral, equiangular (logistic) spiral — logarithmische Spirale *f*, gleichwinklige Spirale
logarithm of the reciprocal distortion factor — Klirrdämpfung *f*, Klirrabstand *m*
logarithm to base e — s. natural logarithm
logarithm to base 10 — s. Brigg['s] logarithm
logatom articulation, articulation for logatoms, syllabic articulation, articulation for syllables — Silbenverständlichkeit *f*, Logatomverständlichkeit *f*
log-counting meter — s. log meter
logetronography — Logetronographie *f*, elektronisches Frequenzfilterverfahren *n*
logger, log-counting meter, log meter — Meßgerät *n* mit logarithmischer Anzeige
logger — s. a. recorder
logic[al] circuit module — s. logic[al] element
logic[al] combination, logic[al] composition — logische Verknüpfung *f*

logic[al] element, logic[al] circuit module, switching element, switching member — logisches Element *n*, Logikelement *n*, Verknüpfungselement *n*, Verknüpfungsglied *n*, Schaltglied *n*
logic[al] function — s. logic[al] operation
logic[al] operation, logic[al] function; switching operation (function), function of switching — logische Operation *f*, [logische] Verknüpfungsoperation *f*, logische Funktion *f*; Schaltfunktion *f*
logic[al] product, conjunction — Konjunktion *f*, logisches Produkt *n*
logic[al] sum, disjunction — Disjunktion *f*, logische Summe *f*
logic[al] sum — s. a. union <of sets>
logistic curve, logistic growth curve, Pearl-Reed curve — logistische Kurve (Funktion) *f*, logistisches Wachstumsgesetz *n*; Robertsonsche Wachstumsfunktion *f*
logistics — s. mathematical logic
logistic spiral — s. logarithmic spiral
log-log paper — doppelt[]logarithmisches Papier *n*, Potenzpapier *n*, log-log-Papier *n*

log meter, log-counting meter, logger — Meßgerät *n* mit logarithmischer Anzeige
log[-]normal distribution — s. logarithmico-normal distribution
logometer — s. ratio[-] meter
Löhle photometer, Löhle visual photometer — visuelles Sichtphotometer *n* nach Löhle, Löhlesches Sichtphotometer
lolly ice — s. slush ice
Lomer-Cottrell barrier (dislocation, lock) — s. Cottrell['s] dislocation
Lomer-Cottrell reaction — Lomer-Cottrell Reaktion *f*, Lomer-Cottrellsche Versetzungsreaktion *f*
Lomer-Cottrell sessile dislocation — s. Cottrell['s] dislocation
Lommel['s] function — Lommelsche Funktion *f*
Lommel['s] law — Lommelsches Gesetz *n*
Lommel-Seeliger law — Lommel-Seeligersches Gesetz *n*
London constant — Londonsche Konstante *f*, London-Konstante *f*
London dipole theory — Londonsche Dipoltheorie *f*
London equation [for superconductors], London superconductivity equation — Londonsche Gleichung *f*, London-Gleichung *f*
London force — s. dispersion force
London formula, London relation — Londonsche Beziehung *f*
London['s] law — s. London's r^{-6} law

London relation	s. London formula	**long-half-life,** long-lived, long-life <nucl.>	langlebig, [mit] großer Halbwertzeit <Kern.>
London['s] r^{-6} **law,** London['s] law	Londonsches r^{-6}-Gesetz n	**long-handed tool;** remote handling device (equipment)	Fernbedienungsgerät n; Gerät n mit verlängertem Griff
London superconductivity equation	s. London equation	**longimetry**	s. measurement of length
London tensor	Londonscher Tensor m	**longitude,** longitude angle <as a co-ordinate>	Länge f, Längengrad m, Längenwinkel m <als Koordinate>
London theory [of superconductivity]	Londonsche Theorie f [der Supraleitfähigkeit]	**longitude**	s. a. ecliptic[al] longitude <astr.>
lone electron, one-electron system, hydrogen-like system	Einelektronensystem n, Einzelelektronensystem n, wasserstoffähnliches System n	**longitude angle**	s. longitude <as a co-ordinte>
lone electron, single electron	Einzelelektron n	**longitude effect**	Längeneffekt m
lone-pair, lone-pair electrons	einsames Elektronenpaar n, freies Elektronenpaar	**longitude line,** line of equal longitude	Längengleiche f, Linie f gleicher Länge
		longitude of periastron	Länge f des Periastrons, Periastronlänge f
"long anode" cavity magnetron, Boot magnetron	Langanodenmagnetron n, Langanodenmagnetfeldröhre f, Boot-Magnetron n	**longitude of the ascending node**	Länge f des [aufsteigenden] Knotens, Knotenlänge f, Knoten m
long-base[line] rangefinder, double observer rangefinder, rangefinder of the double observer type, two-station rangefinder	Zweistand-Entfernungsmesser m, Langbasis-Entfernungsmesser m	**longitudinal beam (girder);** stringer <mech.>	Längsträger m <Mech.>
		longitudinal chromatic aberration, chromatic aberration of position, chromatic difference (variation) in [image] position; coefficient of chromatic difference in image position <el.opt.>	Farb[en]ortsfehler m, Farbenfehler m des Bildortes, Farblängsfehler m, chromatische Längsaberration f, chromatische Längsabweichung f, Farbschnittweitenfehler m
long-bond structure, Dewar structure	Dewar-Struktur f		
long-coil vibrating galvanometer	Langspulen-Vibrationsgalvanometer n		
long counter	„long counter" m, „langes" Zählrohr n, Langzählrohr n, Hanson-McKibben-Zählrohr n	**longitudinal comparator,** subdividing comparator	Longitudinalkomparator m
		longitudinal conductivity	Longitudinalleitfähigkeit f, longitudinale Leitfähigkeit f, Längsleitfähigkeit f
long-crested	langkämmig	**longitudinal contraction**	s. unit shortening
long-crested weir	s. broad-crested weir	**longitudinal coupling**	Längskopplung f
long-delay echo, longduration echo, long echo, delay echo	Langlaufzeitecho n, Langzeitecho n, Hals-Störmer-Echo n	**longitudinal crevasse**	Längsspalte f
		longitudinal crystal	längsschwingender Kristall m
long-distance communication	Weitverkehrsverbindung f	**longitudinal-current carbon microphone, longitudinal-current microphone**	Längsstrommikrophon n
long-distance control	s. telecontrol		
long distance line	s. long distance transmission line <el.>		
long-distance propagation, long-range propagation	Weitbereich[s]ausbreitung f	**longitudinal damping**	Längsdämpfung f
		longitudinal deformation	s. elongation
long-cistance thermometer	s. telethermometer	**longitudinal diffusion**	Diffusion f in Längsrichtung, Längsdiffusion f
long-distance transmission; remote transfer; remote transmission	Fernübertragung f	**longitudinal disparity**	Längsdisparation f
		longitudinal Doppler effect	longitudinaler Doppler-Effekt m
long distance transmission line, long distance line; trunk circuit, trunk junction line <el.>	Fernleitung f <El.>	**longitudinal dune**	Reihendüne f, Längsdüne f
		longitudinal electronic oscillation	s. Langmuir oscillation
long-duration creeprupture test, long-duration stress-rupture test, constant-strain-rate test, long-time test, long-time creep test, long-run test, long-duration test, creep-rupture test	Zeitstandversuch m, Zeitstandprüfung f, Zeitstandprobe f, Langzeit[stand]versuch m, Dauerstandversuch m, Stand[zeit]versuch m, Standprobe f, Standprüfung f, Standprüfverfahren n, Langzeitverfahren n	**longitudinal electrooptical effect**	s. Pockels effect
		longitudinal electrostatic wave	longitudinale elektrostatische Welle f
		longitudinal extension per unit length	s. axial elongation
		longitudinal flow	Längsströmung f
long-duration echo	s. long-delay echo	**longitudinal flow** <around>	Längsanströmung f
long-duration irradiation, persistent (longtime) irradiation	Langzeitbestrahlung f	**longitudinal force**	Längskraft f
		longitudinal force	s. a. axial force
long-duration reaction	Zeitreaktion f	**longitudinal force [of the lines of force]**	Längszug m [der Kraftlinien]
long-duration [stressrupture] test	s. long-duration creep-rupture test	**longitudinal galvanomagnetic effect**	galvanomagnetischer Longitudinaleffekt m
long echo	s. long-delay echo	**longitudinal horopter,** vertical horopter	Längshoropter m, Vertikalhoropter m
longeron	s. spar		
longevity, long life <el.>	lange Lebensdauer f, Langlebensdauer f <El.>	**longitudinal impact,** axial impact	axialer Stoß m, Längsstoß m, longitudinaler Stoß
longevity, long life[time] <nucl.>	Langlebigkeit f, große (lange) Lebensdauer f <Kern.>	**longitudinally damped wave**	längsgedämpfte Welle f
		longitudinally homogeneous	längshomogen
long focal length lens, long-focus lens	Langfokuslinse f, langbrennweitige Linse f, Linse großer Brennweite	**longitudinally magnetized,** magnetized in longitudinal direction	längsmagnetisiert, in Längsrichtung magnetisiert
long-focus magnetic lens	magnetische Lang[fokus]-linse f		

longitudinally polarized neutrino	s. two-component neutrino	**longitudinal spherical aberration,** longitudinal ray aberration	Längsaberration f, sphärische Längsaberration
longitudinally stratified, piled up longitudinally (lengthwise), lengthwise stratified	längsgeschichtet	**longitudinal stability [of charged particle]**	Längsstabilität f [des Teilchens]
longitudinal magnetic field	magnetisches Längsfeld n, longitudinales Magnetfeld n	**longitudinal stratification;** longitudinal piling	Längsschichtung f
longitudinal magnetoresistance	longitudinaler magnetoresistiver Effekt m, longitudinale magnetische Widerstandsänderung f, longitudinale Widerstandsänderung im Magnetfeld	**longitudinal stress (tension)** <mech.>	Längsspannung f <Mech.>
		longitudinal tension coefficient of resistivity	longitudinaler Spannungskoeffizient m des spezifischen Widerstandes
		longitudinal transfer	Längsübertragung f, longitudinale Übertragung f
longitudinal magnetostriction	longitudinale Magnetostriktion f, Längsmagnetostriktion f	**longitudinal velocity,** velocity of longitudinal waves <ac.>	Ausbreitungsgeschwindigkeit f longitudinaler Schallwellen, Longitudinalgeschwindigkeit f <Ak.>
longitudinal magnification	s. axial magnification		
longitudinal mass	longitudinale Masse f	**longitudinal vibration,** extensional vibration (oscillation), longitudinal oscillation	Längsschwingung f, Dehnungsschwingung f, Longitudinalschwingung f, longitudinale Schwingung f
longitudinal metacentre	großes Metazentrum n, Längenmetazentrum n, Längsmetazentrum n		
longitudinal mode	longitudinaler Schwingungstyp m (Wellentyp) m, longitudinale Mode f, Longitudinalmode f, Längsmode f	**longitudinal vibration,** longitudinal oscillation	Longitudinalschwingung f, longitudinale Schwingung f, Verdichtungsschwingung f, Kompressionsschwingung f
longitudinal mode	s. a. axial mode		
longitudinal modulus of elasticity, relaxed (long-term) modulus of elasticity	dauernder Elastizitätsmodul m	**longitudinal Villari effect**	longitudinaler Villari-Effekt m
longitudinal moment, pitch moment, pitching moment <of wing> <aero.>	Längsmoment n, Kippmoment n [des Tragflügels] <Aero.>	**longitudinal wave, L wave,** dilatational wave	Longitudinalwelle f, longitudinale Welle f, Längswelle f, Verdichtungswelle f, Kompressionswelle f, L-Welle f
longitudinal Nernst-Ettingshausen coefficient	longitudinaler Nernst-Ettingshausen-Koeffizient m	**longitudinal wave, P ray,** P wave <geo.>	P-Welle f, Longitudinalwelle f <Geo.>
longitudinal Nernst-Ettingshausen effect	longitudinaler (zweiter) Nernst-Ettingshausen-Effekt m	**longitudinal wave once-reflected downwards at the Earth's outer surface,** PP ray, PP wave	PP-Welle f, einfach reflektierte Longitudinalwelle f
longitudinal oscillation, longitudinal vibration	Longitudinalschwingung f, longitudinale Schwingung f, Verdichtungsschwingung f, Kompressionsschwingung f		
		longitudinal Zeeman effect	longitudinaler Zeeman-Effekt m
longitudinal oscillation	s. a. extensional vibration	**long-lens spectrometer**	Langlinsenspektrometer n
longitudinal oscillation of plasma, longitudinal plasma oscillation	longitudinale Plasmaschwingung f	**long life,** longevity <el.>	lange Lebensdauer f, Langlebensdauer f <El.>
longitudinal overlap, forward overlap, fore and aft overlap	Vorwärtsüberdeckung f, Längsüberdeckung f	**long-life,** long-lived, long-half-life <nucl.>	langlebig, [mit] großer Halbwertzeit <Kern.>
		long life[time], longevity <nucl.>	Langlebigkeit f, große Lebensdauer f, lange Lebensdauer <Kern.>
longitudinal part <e.g. of the Hamiltonian>	longitudinaler Anteil m <z. B. des Hamilton-Operators>	**long-life tube**	Langlebensdauerröhre f
longitudinal part of the vertex function	Longitudinalkomponente f des Vertex		
longitudinal phonon	longitudinales Phonon n	**long-line effect**	Langleitungseffekt m
longitudinal photon	longitudinales (longitudinal polarisiertes) Photon n		
longitudinal piezoelectric effect	longitudinaler Piezoeffekt (piezoelektrischer Effekt) m	**long-lived,** long[-half]-life <nucl.>	langlebig, [mit] großer Halbwertzeit <Kern.>
longitudinal piling; longitudinal stratification	Längsschichtung f	**long-lived radiation**	langlebige Strahlung f
longitudinal plasma oscillation, longitudinal oscillation of plasma	longitudinale Plasmaschwingung f	**long-period average,** long-time average	langjähriges Mittel n
longitudinal profile, longitudinal section	Längsprofil n	**long-period comet**	langperiodischer Komet m
longitudinal ray aberration, longitudinal spherical aberration	Längsaberration f, sphärische Längsaberration	**long-periodic oscillation**	langperiodische Schwingung f
longitudinal relaxation	Längsrelaxation f	**long-period inequality**	langperiodische Ungleichheit f
longitudinal relaxation time	s. spin-lattice relaxation time	**long-period term,** term of long period	langperiodischer Term m, langperiodisches Glied n
longitudinal rigidity	Dehnungssteife f, Dehnsteife f	**long-period tides**	langperiodische Gezeiten pl
longitudinal section, longitudinal profile	Längsprofil n	**long-period variable,** long-period variable star	langperiodischer Veränderlicher m
longitudinal section wave	Längsschnittwelle f	**long-period variable of Mira Ceti-type,** Mira variable, Mira Ceti[-type] star, Mira star	Mira-Stern m, Mira-Veränderlicher m
longitudinal sound velocity	longitudinale Schallgeschwindigkeit f		
longitudinal sound wave	longitudinale Schallwelle f		
longitudinal space-charge wave parametric amplifier	parametrischer Verstärker m mit longitudinaler Raumladungswelle	**long-period variable star**	s. long-period variable
		long period vertical seismometer, Galitzin pendulum	Galitzin-Pendel n

long-persistence screen	Speicherschirm m, Schirm m mit großer Nachleuchtdauer, Leuchtschirm (Lumineszenzschirm) m mit langanhaltendem Nachleuchten	long wave, L <geo.>	lange Welle f, Longa f, Unda f longa, L <Geo.>
		long wave, shallow-water wave, Lagrangian wave <hydr.>	lange Welle f, Seichtwasserwelle f, seichte Welle <Hydr.>
		long wave	s. a. low-frequency wave
long[-]range	fernwirkend, Fernwirkungs-, Fern-; weitreichend, Langstrecken-, mit großem Aktionsradius	long-wave approximation, long-wavelength approximation	langwellige Näherung f
long-range	weitreichend, [von] großer Reichweite	long-wave atmospheric radiation to earth	Gegenstrahlung f
long-range action	s. action at a distance		
long-range alphaparticle	Alpha-Teilchen n großer Reichweite, weitreichendes Alpha-Teilchen	long-wavelength approximation, long-wave approximation	langwellige Näherung f
long-range Coulomb potential	fernwirkendes (weitreichendes) Coulomb-Potential n	long wavelength tail [of the absorption spectrum], absorption tail, tail [of absorption spectrum]	Ausläufer m [des Absorptionsspektrums], langwelliger Ausläufer [des Absorptionsspektrums], Ausläuferbande f
long-range effect	s. action at a distance		
long-range force, force at a distance	Fernwirkungskraft f, fernwirkende (weitreichende) Kraft f, Fernkraft f	long-wave phase [of earthquake]	langwellige Phase f [des Erdbebens]
long-range forecast	s. long-term prediction	long-wave radiation	langwellige Strahlung f, Langwellenstrahlung f
long-range hydrodynamic force	s. hydrodynamic longrange force		
long-range ionospheric propagation, nonstandard ionospheric propagation	ionosphärische Überreichweite f	long-wave range, long waves	Langwellenbereich m, Langwelle f, LW
		long-wave solar radiation, red solar radiation	Rotstrahlung f der Sonne
long-range navigation system, loran	Langstreckennavigationsradar n, Loran n		
long[-]range order	Fernordnung f	long-wave X-rays	s. soft X-rays
		long-wire antenna	Langdrahtantenne f
long-range ordering degree	Fernordnungsgrad m	looming, superior mirage	obere Luftspiegelung f, Luftspiegelung nach oben
long-range order[ing] parameter	Fernordnungsparameter m	Loomis-Wood diagram, Loomis-Wood pattern	Loomis-Wood-Diagramm n, Loomis-Woodsches Diagramm n
long-range prognosis	s. long-term prediction		
long-range propagation, long-distance propagation	Weitbereich[s]ausbreitung f	loop, antinode, antinodal point <of oscillation, standing wave>	Schwingungsbauch m; Wellenbauch m, Bauch m [der stehenden Welle]
long-range propagation	s. a. non-standard propagation	loop, experimental loop <of reactor>	Versuchsschleife f, Experimentierschleife f <Reaktor>
long-range triangulation, trilateration	Trilateration f		
long-range tropospheric propagation, nonstandard tropospheric propagation	troposphärische Überreichweite f	loop, loop of the routine, cycle <num.math.>	Schleife f [des Programms], Zyklus m [des Programms] <num. Math.>
long-run test	s. long-duration creeprupture test	loop <techn.>; circuit	Kreislauf m, Kreis m; Schleife f <Techn.>
long scale, long time[-] scale	lange Zeitskala f, lange Skala f	loop	s. a. loop antenna
		loop	s. a. loop prominence
longshore current	küstenparallele Strömung f	loop	s. a. mesh <el.>
		loop antenna, square loop antenna, loop, frame (closed) antenna	Rahmenantenne f
long-sighted, hypermetropic	übersichtig, hypermetropisch		
long-term accuracy	Langzeitgenauigkeit f	loop antenna, loop	Schleifenantenne f
long-term error, long-time error	Langzeitfehler m	loop antenna with goniometer, loop goniometer	Rahmengoniometer n
		loop circuit	s. two-wire line
long-term forecast (prediction), long-range forecast, long-range prognosis	langfristige Vorhersage f	loop direction finder	Rahmenpeiler m
long-term modulus of elasticity	s. longitudinal modulus of elasticity	loop gain	Schleifenverstärkung f
long-term stability	Langzeitkonstanz f, Langzeitstabilität f		
long-time average, long-period average	langjähriges Mittel n	loop galvanometer, single-loop[-type] galvanometer	Schleifengalvanometer n, Schleife f
long-time behaviour	Langzeitverhalten n	loop galvanometer of the mechanical oscillograph	s. galvanometer of the mechanical oscillograph
long-time creep test	s. long-duration creeprupture test		
long-time error, long-term error	Langzeitfehler m	loop goniometer, loop antenna with goniometer	Rahmengoniometer n
		loop of dislocation	s. dislocation loop
long-time fading	s. blackout	loop of the river, meander	Mäander m, Flußschleife f
long-time-interval measuring device, long-time-interval meter	Langzeitmeßgerät n, Langzeitmesser m		
		loop of the routine, loop, cycle <num.math.>	Schleife f [des Programms], Zyklus m [des Programms] <num. Math.>
long-time irradiation	s. persistent irradiation		
long time[-] scale, long scale	lange Zeitskala f, lange Skala f		
long-time strength	s. limiting creep stress	loop oscillogram	Schleifenoszillogramm n
long-time test	s. long-duration creeprupture test		
long tube effect	Rohrlängeneffekt m		

loop oscillograph, bifilar oscillograph, oscillograph with bifilar suspension, mechanical (rotating-mirror, light-beam) oscillograph — Schleifenoszillograph m, Lichtstrahloszillograph m

loop prominence, loop — gekrümmte Protuberanz f, Bogenprotuberanz f, Loopprotuberanz f

loop-shaped dislocation — s. dislocation loop

loop-type vibration galvanometer, loop wire vibration galvanometer — Schleifenvibrationsgalvanometer n

loose; in bulk — aufgelockert, locker, lose

loose — s. a. untensioned

loose contact, intermittent contact, defective contact — Wackelkontakt m

loose coupling, weak coupling, undercritical coupling <el.> — lose Kopplung f, unterkritische Kopplung <El.>

loosely bound — locker gebunden

looseness — s. slackness

loosening; breaking-up; disaggregation — Auflockerung f, Lockerung f

loosening; slackening — Lockerung f; Auflockerung f; Erschlaffen n, Nachlassen n

loose packed — lose gepackt, nicht dichtgepackt

loose place [of Smekal], Smekal defect (flaw), pore, flaw of Smekal, lockerstelle — Lockerstelle f [nach Smekal], Smekalsche Lockerstelle, Lockerion n

loose rock, scall — Lockergestein n, unverfestigtes Gestein n

loose snow — Lockerschnee m

lopper — s. peak limiter

lopping-round, circumcirculation, washing-round — Umspülung f

loran — s. long-range navigation system

Lorentz broadening [of spectral line] — Lorentz-Verbreiterung f

Lorentz['s] collision theory, collision theory of Lorentz — Lorentzsche Stoßtheorie f, Stoßtheorie von Lorentz

Lorentz condition, Lorentz gauge — Lorentz-Konvention f, Lorentz-Eichung f, Lorentz-Bedingung f, Lorentzsche Bedingung f

Lorentz contraction, Lorentz-Fitzgerald contraction, relativistic contraction — Lorentz-[Fitzgerald-]Kontraktion f, Fitzgerald-Lorentz-Kontraktion f, Lorentz-Verkürzung f, relativistische Kontraktion (Verkürzung) f

Lorentz contraction factor $\langle\sqrt{1-\beta^2}\rangle$ — Einsteinscher Faktor m der Zeitdilatation, Einstein-Faktor m

Lorentz['s] contraction hypothesis, Lorentz['s] hypothesis [of contraction] — Lorentzsche Kontraktionshypothese f, Lorentzsche Hypothese f

Lorentz covariance, relativistic covariance — relativistische Kovarianz f, Lorentz-Kovarianz f

Lorentz-covariant — Lorentz-kovariant

Lorentz curve, Lorentz plot — Lorentz-Kurve f

Lorentz density of force, Lorentz force density — Lorentzsche Kraftdichte f

Lorentz dispersion term — Lorentzscher Dispersionsterm m, Dispersionsterm von Lorentz

Lorentz dissociation — Lorentz-Dissoziation f

Lorentz double refraction — Lorentzsche Doppelbrechung f, Lorentz-Doppelbrechung f

Lorentz['] dragging coefficient — Lorentzscher Mitführungskoeffizient m

Lorentz electron — Lorentz-Elektron n, Lorentzsches Elektron n

Lorentz equations of motion, ponderomotive equations — Lorentzsche (klassische) Bewegungsgleichungen fpl [des Elektrons]

Lorentz factor — Lorentz-Faktor m

Lorentz field — Lorentz-Feld n, Lorentzsches Feld n

Lorentz-Fitzgerald contraction — s. Lorentz contraction

Lorentz force; electrodynamic force, force of current interaction — Lorentz-Kraft f; elektrodynamische Kraft f, Stromkraft f, magnetische Wirbelkraft f; elektrodynamische magnetische Kraft

Lorentz force density — s. Lorentz density of force

Lorentz['s] formula — Lorentzsche Formel f

Lorentz gas — Lorentz-Gas n

Lorentz gauge, Lorentz condition — Lorentz-Konvention f, Lorentz-Eichung f, Lorentz-Bedingung f, Lorentzsche Bedingung f

Lorentz group — Lorentz-Gruppe f

Lorentz-Heaviside system [of units], **Lorentz-Heaviside units** — s. Heaviside-Lorentz system

Lorentz['s] hypothesis [of contraction], Lorentz['s] contraction hypothesis — Lorentzsche Kontraktionshypothese f, Lorentzsche Hypothese f

Lorentz internal field — inneres Lorentzsches Feld n

Lorentz invariance, relativistic invariance — Lorentz-Invarianz f, relativistische Invarianz f

Lorentz invariant, world invariant — Lorentz-Invariante f

Lorentz-invariant, lorentz invariant, world-invariant — Lorentz-invariant, lorentz-invariant, relativistisch invariant

Lorentz ionization — Lorentz-Ionisation f, Lorentz-Ionisierung f

Lorentz local field — s. local field intensity <el.>

Lorentz-Lorenz effect — Lorentz-Lorenz-Effekt m

Lorentz-Lorenz equation (formula, relation), Lorenz-Lorentz formula, Clausius-Masotti-Lorentz-Lorenz equation (formula) <opt., mol.> — Lorentz-Lorenzsche Gleichung (Refraktionsformel, Formel) f, Lorentz-Lorentzsche Gleichung, (Refraktionsformel, Formel), Refraktionsformel nach (von) Lorentz-Lorenz (Opt., Mol.)

Lorentz['] metric — Lorentzsche Metrik f

Lorentz model — Lorentzsches Modell n, Modell von Lorentz

Lorentz plot, Lorentz curve — Lorentz-Kurve f

Lorentz profile, dispersion profile — Dispersionsprofil n, Lorentz-Profil n

Lorentz['s] reciprocity theorem — Lorentzscher Reziprozitätssatz m, Lorentzsches Reziprozitätstheorem n

Lorentz splitting — s. Zeeman splitting

Lorentz['s] theory of electrons, classical theory of the electron — Lorentzsche Elektronentheorie f, klassische Elektronentheorie

Lorentz['s] theory of the Zeeman effect — Lorentzsche Theorie f des Zeeman-Effekts

Lorentz transform[ation] — Lorentz-Transformation f

Lorentz triplet — s. Zeeman triplet

Lorentz unit, L — Lorentz-Enheit f, L

Lorenz constant, Lorenz number (ratio) — Lorenz-Zahl f, Lorenzsches Verhältnis n, L

Lorenz cycle — Lorenz-Prozeß m, Lorenzscher Kreisprozeß m

Lorenz law — s. Wiedemann-Franz-Lorenz law

Lorenz-Lorentz formula — s. Lorenz-Lorentz equation

Lorenz number (ratio) — s. Lorenz constant

Lorenz rule — Lorenzsche Regel f

Loschmidt['s] constant, Loschmidt['s] number <in cm⁻³> — Avogadrosche Zahl f, Avogadrosche Konstante f

Loschmidt method	Loschmidtsche Methode *f*
Loschmidt['s] number	*s.* Loschmidt['s] constant <in cm⁻³>
Loschmidt['s] reversibility paradox, reversibility paradox [of Loschmidt], umkehreinwand	Loschmidtscher Umkehreinwand *m*, Umkehreinwand von Loschmidt
loss; leakage	Verlust *m*; Einbuße *f*
loss angle, dielectric loss angle	dielektrischer Verlustwinkel *m*, Verlustwinkel [des Dielektrikums]
loss angle meter	Verlustwinkelmeßgerät *n*, Verlustwinkelmesser *m*
loss characteristic, loss curve	Verlustkurve *f*
loss coefficient, friction loss coefficient	Widerstandsziffer *f* des einzelnen hydraulischen Hindernisses
loss compliance	Verlustkomplianz *f*
loss cone	Verlustkegel *m*
loss current to earth (ground)	*s.* short-circuit current to earth
loss curve, loss characteristic	Verlustkurve *f*
loss due to friction, frictional loss, friction loss	Reibungsverlust *m*
loss due to heat transfer, heat-transfer loss	Wärmeübertragungsverlust *m*, Wärmeübergangsverlust *m*
loss due to range	Reichweitenverlust *m*
loss due to slippage	Schlupfverlust *m*
loss due to the deformation, deformation loss	Deformationsverlust *m*
loss due to wall friction, wall friction loss	Wandreibungsverlust *m*
Lossev effect	Lossew-Effekt *m*
loss factor	*s.* loss tangent
loss factor <US>	= product of relative permittivity and sine of loss angle
loss factor meter	Verlustfaktormeßgerät *n*, Verlustfaktormesser *m*
loss-free line, dissipationless (zero-loss, no-loss) line, lossless line	verlustlose Leitung *f*, verlustfreie Leitung
loss function, weight function <stat.>	Verlustfunktion *f* <Stat.>
loss in brightness, decrease in brightness, penumbral effect	Helligkeitsabfall *m*
loss in energy due to collision	Carnotscher Energieverlust *m*
loss in lift, loss of buoyancy	Auftriebsverlust *m*
loss in mixing, mixing loss	Vermischungsverlust *m*
loss in reverse direction	Sperrverlust *m*
loss in suppressed band, loss in suppressed range	Sperrdämpfung *f*
lossless line, dissipationless (zero-loss, no-loss, loss-free) line	verlustlose Leitung *f*, verlustfreie Leitung
loss modulus	Verlustmodul *m*
loss of buoyancy	*s.* loss in lift
loss of contrast	Kontrastverlust *m*
loss of energy due to choc (collision, impact)	*s.* collision loss
loss of energy due to ordinary beta decay, URCA process	URCA-Prozeß *m*
loss of flow	Strömungsverlust *m*
loss of generality /without, without lack of generality	ohne Beschränkung der Allgemeinheit (Allgemeingültigkeit), o. B. d. A.°
loss of head, loss of pressure head	Druckhöhenverlust *m*
loss of head due to friction, friction head	Reibungshöhe *f*, Reibungswiderstandshöhe *f*, Reibungsgefälle *n*
loss of heat, heat loss, heat dissipated	Wärmeverlust *m*
loss of heat by conduction	*s.* conduction loss
loss of light	Lichtverlust *m*
loss of pressure, pressure loss	Druckverlust *m*
loss of pressure head, loss of head	Druckhöhenverlust *m*
loss of remanent induction, remanence loss, residual loss	Nachwirkungsverlust *m*
loss of strength	*s.* destrengthening
loss of time	*s.* time required
loss of vacuum	Verschlechterung *f* des Vakuums
loss on ignition, ignition loss	Glühverlust *m*
loss parameter	Verlustparameter *m*
loss rate	Verlustrate *f*
loss ratio	Verlustverhältnis *n*
loss resistance, dissipation-loss resistance, wasteful resistance	Verlustwiderstand *m*
loss tangent, dielectric loss coefficient, dielectric loss factor, dielectric power factor, loss factor, tan δ	dielektrischer Verlustfaktor *m*, Verlustfaktor [des Dielektrikums], dielektrische Verlustziffer *f*, Verlustziffer [des Dielektrikums], dielektrische Verlustzahl *f*, Verlustzahl [des Dielektrikums], dielektrischer Verlust *m*, Verlust im Dielektrikum, tan δ
loss time, lost time	Verlustzeit *f*
lossy; leaky; dissipative	verlustbehaftet
lossy flow	Verlustströmung *f*, verlustbehaftete Strömung *f*
lossy line, dissipative line	verlustbehaftete Leitung *f*, Verlustleitung *f*
lost count	nichtgezählter Impuls *m*
lost current	Veruststrom *m*
lost energy, unavailable energy	verlorene Energie *f*
lost force	verlorene Kraft *f*
lost head	Verlusthöhe *f*, verlorene Höhe *f*
lost heat, dissipated heat	Verlustwärme[menge] *f*
lost mountain	*s.* monadnock
lost power	*s.* dissipated power
lost time, loss time	Verlustzeit *f*
lost work	Verlustarbeit *f*, verlorene Arbeit *f*; Arbeit der Bewegungswiderstände
Lo Surdo['s] method	Lo-Surdo-Methode *f*, Methode *f* von Lo Surdo
loudness <in sones>	Lautheit *f* <in Sone>
loudness	*s. a.* loudness level <ac.>
loudness contour	*s.* isacoustic curve
loudness level, [equivalent] loudness, level of loudness, intensity level, volume [of sound] <in phons> <ac.>	Lautstärke *f*, Lautklasse *f*, Volumen *n*, Tonvolumen *n* <in Phon> <Ak.>
loudness-level contour	*s.* isacoustic curve
loudness level indicator	*s.* volume indicator
loudness measurement, measurement of loudness	Lautstärkemessung *f*
loudness ratio	Lautstärkeverhältnis *n*
loudspeaker horn, horn of the loudspeaker	Lautsprechertrichter *m*
louver-type dynode, Venetian blind dynode	Jalousiedynode *f*

louver-type prism	Jalousieprisma n	**lower consolute temperature**	unterer kritischer Entmischungspunkt m
louver-type trap	Jalousiefänger m	**lower culmination**	untere Kulmination f, unterer Kulminationspunkt m
louvre, spill shield	Raster m, Lichtraster m <lichttechnisches Bauelement>	**lower Darboux integral**	Unterintegral n, unteres Darbouxsches Integral n
Love['s] displacement function	Lovesche Verschiebungsfunktion f	**lower Darboux sum**	[Darbouxsche] Untersumme f
Love number	Lovesche Zahl f	**lower explosion limit**	untere Explosionsgrenze f
Love['s] wave, Q wave	Love-Welle f, Lovesche Welle f, Q-Welle f	**lower half-plane**	untere Halbebene f
Lovibond tintometer, tintometer	Lovibondsches Farbmeßgerät n, Dreifarbenmeßgerät n nach Lovibond, [Lovibondsches] Tintometer n	**lower hemispherical flux**	unterer halbräumlicher (hemisphärischer) Lichtstrom m
		lower index	s. subscript
		lowering, depression	Senkung f; Absenkung f; Depression f; Erniedrigung f
Low	s. cyclone		
low-activity, low-level, warm <nucl.>	niedrigaktiv, „low-level"-, geringaktiv, schwachaktiv, warm <Kern.>	**lowering** <of an index>	Herunterziehen n <Index>
low-angle [grain] boundary	s. small-angle grain boundary	**lowering**	s. a. reduction
low-angle X-ray scattering	s. X-ray small-angle scattering	**Löwe ring,** Loewe ring	Löwescher Ring m
low-aspect-ratio wing, wing of small aspect ratio	Tragflügel (Flügel) m kleiner Streckung	**lowering of pressure,** reduction of pressure	Druckerniedrigung f, Druckabsenkung f, Druckminderung f, Druckreduzierung f
low binding <chem.>	lockere Bindung f, schwache Bindung <Chem.>	**lowering of temperature;** cooling	Temperaturerniedrigung f, Temperatursenkung f, Absenkung f der Temperatur; Abkühlung
low boiling, low boiling point / of	niedrigsiedend, leichtsiedend	**lowering of the boiling point,** depression of the boiling point, boiling point depression	Siedepunktserniedrigung f
low cloud	niedrige (untere; tiefhängende, tiefe) Wolke f	**lowering of the freezing point,** depression of the freezing point, freezing-point depression	Gefrierpunktserniedrigung f, Gefrierpunkterniedrigung f
low concentration, weak concentration	niedrige (geringe, schwache) Konzentration f		
low current, weak (feeble) current, low-voltage low current	Schwachstrom m; niedriger Strom m, geringer Strom, schwacher Strom	**lowering of the melting point**	s. melting point depression
		lowering of the water by wind effect	Windsenkung f des Wasserspiegels
low-current amplifier	Schwachstromverstärker m	**lowering of vapour pressure,** vapour pressure lowering	Dampfdruckerniedrigung f, Dampfdruckverminderung f
low-density flow	s. molecular flow	**lower inversion**	untere Inversion f
low-energy; nonpenetrating; soft <of radiation>	energiearm, niederenergetisch, Niederenergie-; nichtdurchdringend, weich <Strahlung>		
		lower ionosphere	niedere (tiefe) Ionosphäre f
		lower layer of soil	s. illuvial soil <geo.>
		lower limit <gen.>	Untergrenze f <allg.>
low-energy component, soft component	weiche Komponente f [der kosmischen Strahlung]; weiche Sekundärstrahlung f	**lower limit,** inferior limit, limit inferior, lim inf, lim <math.>	limes m inferior, unterer Limes (Hauptlimes) m, untere Häufungsgrenze (Unbestimmtheitsgrenze) f, lim inf, lim
low-energy electron diffraction, LEED	Niederenergie-Elektronenbeugung f, LEED		
low-energy nuclear physics, low-energy physics	niederenergetische Kernphysik f, Niederenergie[kern]physik f, Kernphysik (Physik f) niedriger Energien	**lower limit of audibility,** lower limit of hearing	untere Hörgrenze f
		lower limit of detection, LLD	untere Nachweisgrenze f
low-energy particle <E ≤ 30 MeV>	energiearmes Teilchen n <E ≤ 30 MeV>	**lower limit of the integral**	untere Integrationsgrenze f, untere Grenze f des Integrals
low-energy physics	s. low-energy nuclear physics	**lower mantle [of Earth],** D region <D' and D''>	innerer Erdmantel m, untere Mantelschicht f, unterer Mantel m (Teil m des Mantels), Untermantel m, D-Schicht f, D-Schale f <D' und D''>
low-energy radiation; soft radiation	weiche (energiearme) Strahlung f, Weichstrahlung f		
low-energy region <0—30 MeV>	Niederenergiegebiet n, Bereich m niedriger Energien <0 ··· 30 MeV>	**lower measure,** interior measure	inneres Maß n
		lower moraine	Untermoräne f
low-enriched, low-enrichment	leichtangereichert, leicht angereichert, schwachangereichert, geringangereichert	**lower paraselena,** under-moon	Untermond m
		lower parhelion, under-sun, underparhelion	Untersonne f; Nebensonne f der Untersonne
lower antitwilight	untere Gegendämmerung f	**lower part of the characteristic curve**	s. toe [of the characteristic curve]
lower atmosphere	innere (untere, niedere) Atmosphäre f, untere Schichten fpl der Atmosphäre	**lower pond (pool),** lower reach, tail water, after bay, tail race, underwater	untere Haltung f, Unterhaltung f, Unterwasser n, Talseite f
lower atmospheric layer, inferior atmospheric layer	Grundschicht f [der Troposphäre]		
lower bound	untere Schranke f		
		lower pool elevation	Unterwasserspiegel m, Unterwasserstand m, Unterwasserhöhe f, Unterspiegelhöhe f
lower calorific value	s. net calorie power		
lower central series	absteigende (unterste) Zentralfolge f, untere Zentralreihe f		
lower chromosphere	untere Chromosphäre f	**lower reach**	s. lower pool

lower semicontinuous function	unterhalbstetige (nach unten halbstetige) Funktion f	**low-melting**, easily meltable, easily fusible, non-refractory	niedrigschmelzend, leichtflüssig, leichtschmelzend, mit niedrigem Schmelzpunkt, leicht verdampfbar
lower side band position	s. inverted position		
lower stratosphere	s. tropopause	**low-molecular, low-molecular weight**	niedermolekular
lower surface, high pressure surface, pressure side ‹of the airfoil›	Flügelunterseite f, Unterseite f ‹des Flügels›	**low-noise**; noiseless, noise-free	rauscharm; rauschfrei, rauschlos
lower tangential arc	unterer Berührungsbogen m	**low-pass filter**, upper limiting filter	Tiefpaß m, Tiefpaßfilter n, Spulenleitung f, Spulenkette f, Drosselkette f
lower threshold of hearing	s. threshold of hearing		
lower triangular matrix	s. subdiagonal matrix	**low-pass R-C filter**, low-pass resistance-capacitance filter	Tiefpaß-RC-Filter n
lower troposphere, low troposphere	niedere (untere) Troposphäre f		
lower voltage	Unterspannung f	**low pitch**	s. international pitch ‹435 c/s›
lower yield point [stress]	untere Streckgrenze f	**low-potential**	s. low-voltage
		low-power lens (objective), low-speed lens, slow lens	lichtschwaches Objektiv n, schwaches Objektiv
lowest common denominator	s. least common denominator		
lowest usable frequency, LUF	niedrigste brauchbare Frequenz (Übertragungsfrequenz) f, LUF	**low-power reactor**	Reaktor m geringer Leistung, Niederleistungsreaktor m, Kleinreaktor m
lowest water level	Mindestwasser n, niedrigster Niedrigwasserstand m	**low pressure**, l.p.	Niederdruck m, ND, N.D.; niedriger (tiefer) Druck m, Tiefdruck m
low-excited state	schwachangeregter Zustand m		
low explosive	Schießstoff m, Schießmittel n, Treibmittel n	**low-pressure area**	s. cyclone ‹meteo.›
		low-pressure branch, cyclonic branch	Tiefdruckausläufer m, Tiefausläufer m
low-flux reactor	Niederflußreaktor m, Reaktor m mit geringem Neutronenfluß	**low-pressure centre**	s. cyclonic centre
		low-pressure chamber, high-altitude chamber, altitude chamber	Unterdruckkammer f, Barokammer f
low frequency, L.F., LF l.f., lf ‹30 – 300 kc/s›	Niederfrequenz f, Kilometerwellenfrequenz f, Frequenz f im Kilometerwellenbereich, LF, NF ‹30 ⋯ 300 kHz›		
		low-pressure discharge, low-pressure gaseous discharge	Niederdruckentladung f, Niederdruck-Gasentladung f
low frequency, L.F., LF l.f., lf ‹‹ 3 kc/s›	Niederfrequenz f, NF ‹‹ 3 kHz›	**low-pressure discharge lamp**, low-pressure lamp	Niederdruck[entladungs]lampe f, Niederdruck-Gasentladungslampe f
low frequency	s. a. audio[-] frequency		
low-frequency, l.f.; L.F., LF, lf	niederfrequent, Niederfrequenz-, NF-	**low-pressure gaseous discharge**, low-pressure discharge	Niederdruckentladung f, Niederdruck-Gasentladung f
low-frequency amplifier	s. audio amplifier		
low-frequency filter	s. audio-frequency filter	**low-pressure gauge**	Niederdruckmanometer n
low-frequency generator, low-frequency oscillator, l.f. generator, l.f. oscillator	Niederfrequenzgenerator m, NF-Generator m	**low-pressure lamp**, low-pressure discharge lamp	Niederdruck[entladungs]lampe f, Niederdruck-Gasentladungslampe f
		low-pressure mercury [vapour] lamp	Quecksilberniederdrucklampe f, Hg-Niederdrucklampe f, Niederdruck-Quecksilberdampflampe f, Niederdruck-Quecksilber[dampfentladungs]lampe f
low frequency range, range of low frequency, kilometric wavelength [range], L.F. range, L.F.	Kilometer[wellen]bereich m, Kilobereich m, Niederfrequenzbereich m, NF-Bereich m, LF-Bereich m, LF, NF		
		low-pressure physics	Physik f der niedrigen Drücke, Physik niedriger Drücke, Niederdruckphysik f
low-frequency rejection	s. audio-frequency filter		
low-frequency technique	niederfrequentes Verfahren n, Elongationsverfahren n	**low-pressure plasma**	Niederdruckplasma n
low-frequency wave, kilometre wave, long wafe, L.F. wave ‹1 – 10 km›	Kilometerwelle f ‹1 ⋯ 10 km›; Langwelle f ‹600 ⋯ 2 000 m im engeren Sinne, › 200 m allg.›	**low-pressure range**	Niederdruckbereich m, Niederdruckgebiet n
		low pressure surface, upper surface of the airfoil, suction side of the airfoil	Flügeloberseite f, Oberseite f des Tragflügels
low-impedance; low-resistance	niederohmig	**low probability / of**	wenig[]wahrscheinlich, gering[]wahrscheinlich
low-impedance coupling; link coupling	Linkkopplung f	**low radiation / of**	strahlungsarm
		low-red heat, dark-red heat, dull-red heat	Dunkelrotglut f ‹700 °C›
low-index	niedrig indiziert		
low-intensity arc	Niederstrombogen m		
		low-resistance; low-impedance	niederohmig
low-intensity irradiation	Schwachbestrahlung f	**low-resistance contact**	s. ohmic contact
		low-resistance direction	s. forward direction
low-intensity spark discharge	Glimmfunke m, Glimmlichtfunke m	**low seas**	schwach[]bewegte See f, ruhige See ‹Stärke 2›
low-level, low-activity, warm ‹nucl.›	niedrigaktiv, „low-level"-, geringaktiv, schwachaktiv, warm ‹Kern.›	**low solubility**	Schwerlöslichkeit f, geringe Löslichkeit f
low-level cyclone, low-level depression	flaches Tief[druckgebiet] n	**low-speed cinematography [for high-speed projection]**	s. low-speed photography
low-load hardness test	Kleinlast-Härteprüfung f		
low-loss line	verlustarme Leitung f	**low-speed lens**, low-power objective (lens), slow lens	lichtschwaches Objektiv n, schwaches Objektiv
low magnetic field, weak magnetic field	schwaches Magnetfeld n		

low-speed photography [for high-speed projection], low-speed cinematography [for high-speed projection], time lapse photography (cinematography), fast-motion method (effect), quick-motion method (effect), time compression [technique]	Zeitrafferkinematographie f, Zeitrafferphotographie f, Zeitraffungsverfahren n, Zeitraffverfahren n, Zeitraff[ungs]effekt m, Zeitraffung f	low-voltage current low-voltage gaseous discharge low-voltage lamp low-voltage low current, weak (feeble, low) current low-voltage radioactive battery low water, low tide low water [level]	Niederspannungsstrom m Niedervoltgasentladung f, Niederspannungs-Gasentladung f Niedervolt-Glühlampe f, Niedervoltlampe f, Niederspannungslampe f Schwachstrom m; niedriger (geringer, schwacher) Strom m s. low-voltage atomic battery Niedrigwasser n, Gezeitenniedrigwasser n, Tideniedrigwasser n Flußniedrigwasser n, Niedrigwasser n, Niederwasser n, Kleinwasser n, Minimalwasser n
low-speed shooting for high-speed projection	s. time-lapse camera shooting		
low speed stor[ag]e	s. slow storage		
low-spin complex, spin-paired complex, inner-orbital complex, sandwich complex	Durchdringungskomplex m magnetisch anomaler Komplex m		
low temperature	tiefe (niedrige) Temperatur f, Tieftemperatur f	loxodrome [curve], loxodromic curve (line, spiral), rhumb (Rhumb) line <on Earth>	Loxodrome f, Kursgleiche f, Schieflaufende f, Rhumblinie f
low-temperature approach, low-temperature approximation	Tieftemperaturnäherung f		
low-temperature band	Tieftemperaturbande f	loxodromic transformation	loxodromische Abbildung (Transformation) f
low-temperature calorimeter	Tieftemperaturkalorimeter n	L/R ratio, delay constant	Verzögerungskonstante f, L/R
low-temperature corrosion	Tieftemperaturkorrosion f	LSA diode, limited space-charge accumulation diode	LSA-Diode f
low-temperature crystallization	Tieftemperaturkristallisation f	L-S coupling, (L,S) coupling	s. Russell-Saunders coupling
low-temperature emitter, low-temperature radiator	Tieftemperaturstrahler m	L section, L network; L circuit	L-Glied n; L-Schaltung f
low-temperature engineering	Tieftemperaturtechnik f	L-series L-shaped curve	L-Serie f L-Kurve f
low-temperature fluorescent lamp	Tieftemperaturlampe f, kältefeste Leuchtstofflampe f	L-shell, eight-electron shell, octet shell	L-Schale f, Achterschale f
		L[-]system	s. laboratory system
		luboil	s. lubricating oil
low-temperature laboratory, refrigeration laboratory	Kältelaboratorium n, Tieftemperaturlaboratorium n	lubricant; internal mould lubricant, luboil	Schmiermittel n, Schmierstoff m; Gleitmittel n
low-temperature phenomenon	Tieftemperaturerscheinung f	lubricant film	Schmierfilm m, Schmierschicht f
low-temperature physics, cryophysics	Kryophysik f, Tieftemperaturphysik f, Kältephysik f	lubricant grease lubricating oil, liquid lubricant	s. grease Schmieröl n
low-temperature radiator, low-temperature emitter	Tieftemperaturstrahler m	lubricating power, lubricity	Schmierfähigkeit f, Schmiereigenschaften fpl
low-temperature state	Niedertemperaturzustand m	lubrication lubricity	Schmierung f Lubrizität f, Schlüpfrigkeit f
low-temperature thermometry	Tieftemperaturmessung f	lubricity lucimeter	s. a. lubricating power s. luminance meter
low tension	s. low voltage	Lüder band	s. Lüders band
low-tension voltmeter	Niederspannungsmesser m, Niederspannungsvoltmeter n	Lüders band, slip band, glide band, stretcher strain, strain figure, flow figure	Gleitband n, Fließfigur f, Gleitfigur f, Lüderssches Band n, Lüdersscher Streifen m
low tide, low water	Niedrigwasser n, Gezeitenniedrigwasser n, Tideniedrigwasser n	Lüders glide, Lüders slip	Lüders-Gleitung f
low tone	tiefer Ton m	Lüders['] line	s. slip line
low troposphere, lower troposphere	niedere (untere) Troposphäre f	Lüders-Pauli theorem Lüders slip, Lüders glide	s. CPT theorem Lüders-Gleitung f
low-vacuum tube (valve)	Niedervakuumröhre f	Ludwig-Soret effect Ludwik hardness [number]	s. Soret effect Ludwik-Härte f
low velocity layer	langsame Schicht f, Gutenbergscher Geschwindigkeitskanal (Kanal)m	Ludwik test, hardness test with conical indenter	Kegeldruck-Härteprüfung f
low viscosity / of	wenig[]zäh, schwach viskos	lug Luggin capillary	s. nozzle Luggin-Kapillare f
low volatility	Schwerflüchtigkeit f	Luggin-Haber electrode	Luggin-Haber-Elektrode f
low-volatility	schwerflüchtig	lukewarm, tepid	lauwarm
low voltage, low tension, low-tension voltage	Niederspannung f	lumen, lm	Lumen n, lm
low voltage, safe voltage	Kleinspannung f	lumen-erg, lumerg, lm erg	Lumenerg n, Lumerg n, lm erg
low-voltage, low-potential	niedervoltig, Niedervolt-, Niederspannungs-	lumen meter, lumete	Lichtstrommesser m, Lumenmeter n, Lichtstrommeßgerät n
low-voltage arc	Niedervoltbogen m, Niederspannungsbogen m		
low-voltage arc discharge	Niedervoltbogenentladung f, Niederspannungs-Bogenentladung f	lumerg, lumen-erg, lm erg lumeter	Lumenerg n, Lumerg n, lm erg s. lumen meter
		luminaire efficiency <US>	s. light output ratio of a fitting
low-voltage atomic battery, low-voltage radioactive battery	Niederspannungs-Radionuklidbatterie f, Niederspannungs-Isotopenbatterie f	luminance, luminance for photopic vision, luminancy; intrinsic [luminous] intensity <of lamp>	Leuchtdichte f, Flächenhelle f; Flächenhelligkeit f

luminance coefficient	s. luminance factor	**luminescent activator**	s. activator
luminance contrast; luminosity contrast; lightness contrast; brightness contrast, contrast in brightness	Leuchtdichtekontrast m, Helligkeitskontrast m	**luminescent bacterium,** luminous bacterium	Leuchtbakterium n, Leuchtbakterie f, leuchtendes Bakterium n
		luminescent band	Lumineszenzbande f
luminance curve	Remissionskurve f	**luminescent centre**	s. luminescence centre
luminance difference, difference in luminance (brightness), brightness difference	Leuchtdichteunterschied m, Helligkeitsunterschied m	**luminescent chamber**	Lumineszenzkammer f
		luminescent decay	s. decay <of luminescence>
		luminescent dosimeter, luminescence dosimeter	Lumineszenzdosimeter n, Kristallphosphordosimeter n
luminance difference threshold	Leuchtdichteunterschiedsschwelle f, Unterschiedsschwelle f für Leuchtdichte, Helligkeitsschwelle f	**luminescent emitting intensity**	s. luminescence intensity
		luminescent glass	luminiszierendes Glas n
		luminescent grade	lumineszenzrein
luminance factor, luminance coefficient	Hellbezugswert m, Leuchtdichtefaktor m	**luminescent indicator**	Lumineszenzindikator m
luminance fluctuation, brightness fluctuation	Helligkeitsschwankung f	**luminescent light**	Lumineszenzlicht n
luminance for photopic vision, luminance, luminancy; intrinsic [luminous] intensity <of lamp>	Leuchtdichte f, Flächenhelle f; Flächenhelligkeit f	**luminescent material,** luminophor, lumophor; luminous compound; phosphor	Luminophor m, Lumineszenzstoff m, Lumineszenzstrahler m, Lumineszenzlichtquelle f, kalte Lichtquelle f; Leuchtstoff m, Leuchtsubstanz f, Leuchtmaterial m, Leuchtmasse f; Phosphor m, Kristallphosphor m; Gitterstrahler m
luminance for scotopic vision, luminance referred to dark-adapted eye	Dunkelleuchtdichte f; Leuchtdichte f, bezogen auf das dunkeladaptierte Auge		
luminance indicatrix	Leuchtdichteindikatrix f		
luminance meter, lucimeter; stilbmeter	Leuchtdichtemesser m, Helligkeitsmesser m; Stilbmeter n		
		luminescent microscope	s. luminescence microscope
		luminescent microscopy	s. luminescence microscopy
		luminescent radiation	Lumineszenzstrahlung f
luminance range, brightness range, range of luminance	Helligkeitsumfang m	**luminescent screen,** luminous (phosphor, actinic) screen	Lumineszenzschirm m, Leucht[stoff]schirm m
luminance ratio	Leuchtdichteverhältnis n		
luminance referred to dark-adapted eye, luminance for scotopic vision	Dunkelleuchtdichte f; Leuchtdichte f, bezogen auf das dunkeladaptierte Auge	**luminescent-screen tube**	Leuchtschirmröhre f
		luminescent spectrum, luminescence spectrum	Lumineszenzspektrum n
luminance temperature	s. radiation temperature	**luminescent spot,** luminous spot, spot on a cathode-ray tube	Leuchtfleck m, Leuchtpunkt m
luminance temperature	s. a. black-body temperature		
luminancy	s. luminance		
luminant current discharge	s. glow discharge	**luminogen**	lumineszenzaktivierend, luminogen; lumineszenzerzeugend
luminary efficiency	s. light output ratio of a fitting		
luminescence	Lumineszenz f, kaltes Leuchten (Licht) n	**luminogen**	s. a. activator
		luminography	Luminographie f
luminescence activation, activation <of luminescence>	Aktivierung f [der Lumineszenz], Lumineszenzaktivierung f	**luminophor**	s. luminescent material
		luminosity, brightness, subjective brightness, brilliance, brilliancy <US>	Helligkeit f, Eindruckshelligkeit f, Helligkeitseindruck m, subjektive Helligkeit
luminescence activator	s. activator		
luminescence analysis	Lumineszenzanalyse f		
luminescence centre, luminescent centre, centre	Lumineszenzzentrum n, Leuchtzentrum n, Zentrum n	**luminosity**	Lumineszenzfähigkeit f, Luminosität f
luminescence dosimeter, luminescent dosimeter	Lumineszenzdosimeter n, Kristallphosphordosimeter n	**luminosity,** luminosity of a star, stellar luminosity, luminous (illuminating) power	Leuchtkraft f [eines Gestirns]
luminescence efficiency	s. quantum efficiency	**luminosity** <of a source>	s. light output ratio <opt.>
luminescence emission	Lumineszenzemission f	**luminosity** <of radiation>	s. a. luminous efficiency <of radiation>
luminescence excitation	s. excitation of luminescence	**luminosity**	s. a. lightness <of colour>
		luminosity	s. a. radiance
luminescence in crystal, crystal luminescence, crystalloluminescence	Kristallolumineszenz f, Kristallumineszenz f	**luminosity class**	Leuchtkraftklasse f
		luminosity contrast; luminance contrast; lightness contrast; brightness contrast, contrast in brightness	Leuchtdichtekontrast m, Helligkeitskontrast m
luminescence intensity, luminescent emitting intensity, intensity of luminescence	Lumineszenzintensität f, Lumineszenzstärke f		
		luminosity factor [of radiation]	s. photometric radiation equivalent
luminescence killer	s. killer	**luminosity formula,** formula for luminosity	Leuchtkraftformel f
luminescence mechanism, luminous mechanism, radiative mechanism	Leuchtmechanismus m [der Lumineszenz]	**luminosity function**	Leuchtkraftfunktion f
		luminosity-mass relation, mass-luminosity relation, mass-luminosity law, stellar mass-luminosity relation	Masse-Leuchtkraft-Beziehung f, Masse-Helligkeits-Beziehung f, Masse-Leuchtkraft-Gesetz n
luminescence microscope, luminescent microscope	Lumineszenzmikroskop n		
luminescence microscopy, luminescent microscopy	Lumineszenzmikroskopie f		
luminescence of the sea	Meeresleuchten n	**luminosity of a star**	s. luminosity
luminescence photography	Lumineszenzphotographie f	**luminosity photometer,** equality of luminosity (brightness) photometer	Gleichheitsphotometer n
luminescence-producing reaction	Leuchtreaktion f		
luminescence spectrum, luminescent spectrum	Lumineszenzspektrum n	**luminous bacterium,** luminescent bacterium	Leuchtbakterium n, Leuchtbakterie f, leuchtendes Bakterium n
luminescence spectrum analysis	Lumineszenzspektralanalyse f	**luminous band** <opt.>	Leuchtstreifen m <Opt.>

luminous 448

luminous body, luminous element	Leuchtkörper m
luminous column	s. glow column
luminous compound	s. luminescent material
luminous cone	s. cone of light rays
luminous crystal, luminous quartz	Leuchtquarz m; Leuchtkristall m
luminous current	s. glow current
luminous current discharge	s. glow discharge
luminous discharge	s. glow discharge
luminous discharge sheath [of corona]	Koronahaut f
luminous efficiency <of radiation>, luminosity [of radiation], visibility [of radiation], visual [luminous] efficiency [of radiation]	visueller Wirkungsgrad m [der Strahlung], visueller Nutzeffekt m [der Strahlung]
luminous efficiency	s. a. light output ratio <opt.>
luminous efficiency of visible radiation, visual [luminous] efficiency of visible radiation	visueller Wirkungsgrad m der sichtbaren Strahlung, visueller Nutzeffekt m der sichtbaren Strahlung
luminous electron, optical[ly active] electron, emitting electron	Leuchtelektron n, strahlendes Elektron n
luminous element, luminous body	Leuchtkörper m
luminous emittance, luminous exitance	spezifische Lichtausstrahlung (Leuchtstärke) f
luminous energy, quantity of light	Lichtmenge f, Lichtarbeit f
luminous energy intensity	s. radiant intensity
luminous environment	Farbklima n
luminous exitance	s. luminous emittance
luminous factor [of radiation]	s. photometric radiation equivalent
luminous flame, yellow flame <US>	leuchtende Flamme f, Leuchtflamme f
luminous flux, light flux	Lichtstrom m, Lichtleistung f, Lichtfluß m
luminous-flux diagram (distribution)	s. distribution of luminous flux
luminous flux for scotopic vision, luminous flux referred to dark-adapted eye	Dunkellichtstrom m; Lichtstrom m, bezogen auf das dunkeladaptierte Auge
luminous intensity <of light>, light intensity, candle power <of source>	Lichtstärke f, Lichtintensität f, Intensität f <Lichtquelle>
luminous intensity	s. a. radiant intensity
luminous-intensity distribution	s. light distribution
luminous intensity × exposure time <in cd · s>	Belichtungsgröße f <Lichtstärke × Belichtungszeit, in cd·s>
luminous mechanism, luminescence mechanism, radiative mechanism	Leuchtmechanismus m [der Lumineszenz]
luminous night cloud	s. noctilucent cloud
luminous nucleon, optical (emitting) nucleon	Leuchtnukleon n
luminous organ	Leuchtorgan n
luminous phenomenon, light phenomenon	Leuchterscheinung f; Lichterscheinung f
luminous pointer	s. light-beam pointer
luminous pointer galvanometer, light-spot galvanometer, galvanometer with optical pointer	Lichtmarkengalvanometer n, Lichtzeigergalvanometer n, Lichtpunktgalvanometer n
luminous pointer instrument	s. instrument with optical pointer
luminous power	s. luminosity
luminous power	s. a. radiant intensity
luminous quartz; luminous crystal	Leuchtquarz m; Leuchtkristall m
luminous reflectance	Lichtreflexionsgrad m, Lichtreflexionskoeffizient m; Lichtreflexionsvermögen f
luminous screen	s. luminescent screen
luminous signal; light; optical signal	Lichtsignal n, optisches Signal n
luminous source	s. light source
luminous spectrum, optical (visible, light) spectrum	Lichtspektrum n, sichtbares (optisches) Spektrum n
luminous spot, luminescent spot, spot on a cathode-ray tube	Leuchtfleck m, Leuchtpunkt m
luminous standard	Standardlampe f
luminous standard	s. a. primary standard
luminous vibration	Lichtschwingung f
Lummer-Brodhun contrast head	s. Lummer-Brodhun photometer head
Lummer-Brodhun cube, photometric cube, Swan cube	Photometerwürfel m [nach Lummer und Brodhun], Lummer-Brodhun-Würfel m, idealer Fettfleck m, Brodhunscher Würfel m
Lummer-Brodhun photometer	s. Lummer-Brodhun photometer head
Lummer-Brodhun photometer head, Lummer-Brodhun contrast head; Lummer-Brodhun photometer, Swan photometer	Photometeraufsatz m nach Lummer und Brodhun; Lummer-Brodhun-Photometer n
Lummer fringe	Lummerscher Doppelstreifen (Streifen) m, Doppelring m von Lummer
Lummer-Gehrcke plate	Lummer-Gehrcke-Platte f, Lummer-Platte f, Interferenzspektroskop n von Lummer-Gehrcke, Glasplattenspektroskop n, Lummer-Gehrcke-Interferenzplatte f
Lummer-Kurlbaum law	Lummer-Kurlbaumsches Gesetz n
Lummer-Kurlbaum standard	Lummer-Kurlbaum-Standard m
Lummer-Pringsheim black-body furnace, black-body furnace of Lummer-Pringsheim	Hohlraumstrahler m nach Lummer und Pringsheim, Modell n des schwarzen Strahlers von Lummer und Pringsheim
lumophor	s. luminescent material
lumped <of constants>	konzentriert <Parameter>
lumped circuit	zusammengezogener (aus Funktionsblöcken aufgebauter) Stromkreis m, Stromkreis mit konzentrierten Schaltelementen
lumped constant	konzentrierter (diskreter) Parameter m
lumped-constant [electric] circuit, circuit with lumped elements	Schaltung f mit konzentrierten (diskreten) Parametern
lumped dispersion	konzentrierte Dispersion f
lumped element	konzentriertes (diskretes) Schaltelement n
lump-loaded cable	s. coil-loaded cable
lumpy sea, rippling, rips	Kabbelung f, Kabbelsee f, kabbelige See f
lunar anomalistic inequality	s. lunar parallactic inequality
lunar aureole, lunar corona	Mondkranz m
lunar base	Mondbasis[station] f
lunar calendar	Mondkalender m
lunar corona, lunar aureole	Mondkranz m
lunar crater, crater of the Moon; cirque, ring mountain	Mondkrater m; Ringgebirge n
lunar cross	Mondkreuz n
lunar cycle, Metonic cycle	Metonischer Zyklus m, Mondzirkel m, Mondzyklus m
lunar daily inequality	s. diurnal lunar inequality
lunar daily variation [of magnetic field]	s. lunar magnetic variation
lunar day	Mondtag m
lunar disk, Moon's disk	Mondscheibe f
lunar diurnal inequality	s. diurnal lunar inequality
lunar diurnal variation [of magnetic field]	s. lunar magnetic variation
lunar echo	Mondecho n
lunar eclipse, eclipse of the Moon	Mondfinsternis f

lunar excursion module; lunar module; LEM	Mondauto *n*; Mondlandefahrzeug *n*, Mondlandefähre *f*, LEM *n* (*f*)
lunar formation	s. formation on the Moon's surface
lunar gravity, Moon['s] gravity	Mondschwerkraft *f*, Schwerkraft *f* des Mondes
lunar halo	Mondhalo *m*; Mondhof *m*, Mondring[halo] *m*
lunar landing	Mondlandung *f*
lunar magnetic variation, lunar variation; lunar daily variation [of magnetic field], lunar diurnal variation [of magnetic field]	lunare Variation *f*, lunare magnetische Variation; mondtäglicher Gang *m*, mondentägiger Gang, tägliche lunare Variation, L-Variation *f*
lunar map	Mondkarte *f*
lunar module	s. lunar excursion module
lunar month	s. synodic month
lunar mountains	Mondgebirge *n*
lunar occultation, occultation of the star [by the Moon]	Sternbedeckung *f* [durch den Mond]
lunar orbit, Moon's orbit, Moon's path	Mondbahn *f*
lunar orbit, selenocentric orbit	Mondumlaufbahn *f*, selenozentrische Umlaufbahn *f*
lunar parallactic inequality	s. Moon's parallactic inequality
lunar probe, Moon rocket	Mondsonde *f*, Mondrakete *f*, Lunik *m*
lunar rainbow	Mondregenbogen *m*
lunar ray, lunar streak, ray	Strahl *m*, heller Strahl <Oberflächenform des Mondes>
lunar shadow, Moon's shadow	Mondschatten *m*
lunar streak, lunar ray, ray	Strahl *m*, heller Strahl <Oberflächenform des Mondes>
lunar surface marking	s. formation on the Moon's surface
lunar terminator, terminator	Terminator *m*, Schattengrenze *f*
lunar theory	Mondtheorie *f*, Theorie *f* des Erdmondes
lunar tidal wave, lunar wave	Mondflutwelle *f*, Mondgezeitenwelle *f*, Mondwelle *f*
lunar tides	Mondgezeiten *pl*, Mondtiden *fpl*
lunar variation	s. lunar magnetic variation
lunar wave, lunar tidal wave	Mondflutwelle *f*, Mondgezeitenwelle *f*, Mondwelle *f*
lunar year, Moon's year	Mondjahr *n*
lunation	s. synodic month
lune	Zweieck *n*
Luneberg distribution	Luneberg-Verteilung *f*
Luneberg-Kline method	Luneberg-Klinesche Methode *f*, Methode von Luneberg und Kline
Luneberg['s] lens, lens of Luneberg	Luneberg-Linse *f*, Lunebergsche Linse *f*, Linse von Luneberg
Lunge scale	s. Baumé hydrometer scale
luni-solar	lunisolar, Lunisolar-
luni-solar precession	Lunisolarpräzession *f*
luni-solar semi-diurnal inequality, semi-diurnal [luni-solar] inequality	halbtägige Ungleichheit *f*, halbtägige lunisolare Ungleichheit
luni-solar year	Lunisolarjahr *n*, gebundenes Mondjahr *n*
lunitidal interval, flood (high-water) interval	Flutstunde *f*, Hafenzeit *f*, Hafenwasserintervall *n*
lusec	= 1 l/s at 10⁻⁶ torr
luster <US>, **lustre;** gloss; glossiness	Glanz *m*
lustre average	s. lustrum average
lustrum average, fiveyears' average (mean), lustre average	Lustrummittel *n*, Fünfjahresmittel *n*
Luther['s] condition	Luther-Bedingung *f*, Luthersche Bedingung *f*
Luther-Nyberg colour solid, Nyberg-Luther colour solid	Luther-Nybergscher (Nyberg-Lutherscher) Farbkörper *m*, Farbkörper nach Luther-Nyberg
Luther trichromatic coefficient (measuring number)	Luthersche Maßzahl (Farbmaßzahl) *f*, Luther-Maßzahl *f*
lux, metre-candle, lx	Lux *n*, lx
Luxembourg effect, Tellegen effect	Luxemburg-Effekt *m*
lux meter, luxometer; illumination photometer (meter), illuminometer, light meter	Beleuchtungsmesser *m*; Luxmeter *n*
luxon, international photon, photon, troland	Troland *n*, internationales Photon *n*, Photon, Luxon *n*
L wave	s. longitudinal wave
L X-rays	L-Röntgenstrahlung *f*, Röntgen-L-Strahlung *f*
lying fold	liegende Falte *f*
Lykov number	Lykow-Zahl *f*, Lykowsche Kennzahl *f*
Lyman ghost	Lyman-Geist *m*
Lyman line	Lyman-Linie *f*
Lyman series	Lyman-Serie *f*, Lymansche Serie *f*
Lyman ultraviolet	Lyman-Ultraviolett *n*, Lyman-Gebiet *n*
lyogel, jell[y]	Lyogel *n*, Gallerte *f*
lyolysis	s. solvolysis
lyolytic equilibrium	lyolytisches Gleichgewicht *n*
lyonium ion	Lyoniumion *n*
lyophile, lyophilic, solvent-loving	lyophil, lösungsmittelanziehend
lyophilic colloid; emulsoid	lyophiles Kolloid *n*; Emulsionskolloid *n*, Emulsoid *n*, kolloide Emulsion *f*
lyophilic nature, lyophilic property	Lyophilie *f*
lyophilization, lyophilizing	s. freeze-drying
lyophobe, lyophobic, solvent-hating	lyophob, lösungsmittelabstoßend
lyophobic colloid; dispersoid colloid, colloidal dispersion	lyophobes Kolloid *n*; Dispersionskolloid *n*, Phasenkolloid *n*
lyophobic nature, lyophobic property	Lyophobie *f*
lyophobization, lyophobizing	Lyophobisierung *f*
lyosol	Lyosol *n*
lyosorption	Lyosorption *f*
lyosphere	Lyosphäre *f*
Lyot filter, interferential polarizational filter, polarization interference filter	Polarisationsinterferenzfilter *n*, Lyot-Filter *n*, Lyotsches Filter *n*, Interferenzschichtpolarisator *m*
lyotropic effect	lyotroper Effekt *m*
lyotropic numbers	lyotrope Zahlen *fpl*
lyotropic series, Hofmeister series	lyotrope (Hofmeistersche) Reihe *f*, Quellungsreihe *f*
Lysholm grid	s. stationary grid
lysimeter	s. percolation gauge
lysis <bio.>	Auflösung *f*, Lysis *f*, Lyse *f* <Bio.>
lytic	lytisch

M

Macdonald['s] function, Mcdonald['s] function, modified Bessel function of the second kind, Basset['s] function	modifizierte Hankel-Funktion *f*, M[a]cdonald-Funktion *f*, Macdonaldsche (Bassetsche) Funktion *f*, Basset-Funktion *f*, modifizierte Bessel-Funktion *f* zweiter Art [mit nichtganzzahligem rein imaginärem Argument]
Macé de Lépinay halfshade; Macé de Lépinay wedge	Halbschattenapparat *m* nach Macé de Lépinay; Keil *m* nach Macé de Lépinay, Macé-de-Lépinayscher Keil

maceration	Mazeration f, Maceration f, Auslaugung f	macro attachment	Makrovorsatz m
Mach	s. Mach number		
Mach angle	Machscher Winkel m, Mach-Winkel m	macroaxis	Makroachse f, Makrodiagonale f
Mach cone, Mach front, Mach stem	Machscher Kegel m	macro Brownian movement	makro-Brownsche Bewegung f, makrobrownsche Bewegung
		macrocanonical ensemble, canonical assembly (ensemble)	kanonische Gesamtheit f, makrokanonische Gesamtheit
Mach['s] criterion	Machsches Kriterium n	macrocausality	Makrokausalität f
Mach disk	Machsche Scheibe f	macroclimate	Makroklima n, Groß-[raum]klima n
Mache unit	Mache-Einheit f, ME		
Mach fringe	Machscher Kontrastring m, Machscher Streifen m	macroclimatology	Makroklimatologie f, allgemeine Klimatologie f
Mach front	s. Mach cone	macrocrack	Makroriß m
machinability, ability to be cut	Zerspanbarkeit f	macrocrystalline	makrokristallin, grobkörnig
machine	s. atomic particle accelerator		
machine cycle; machine time	Maschinenzeit f	macroetch; macroetching	Makroätzung f
machine evaluation; mechanical evaluation	Maschinenauswertung f		
machine-gun microphone, line microphone	lineare (gerade) Mikrophongruppe f, lineares Mikrophon n	macrogeometrical shape, shape of the surface, macroshape	Oberflächengestalt f, makrogeometrische Gestalt f, Makrogestalt f, Oberflächenform f
machine plotting photogrammetric photographs	s. aerocartograph	macrograph, macrophotograph	Makroaufnahme f, Makrographie f, Makrophotographie f, Makrobild n
machine programme	s. routine		
machine source	s. neutron generator	macrography, macrophotography, macro photography	Makrophotographie f, Makrographie f, Makroaufnahme f
machine time; machine cycle	Maschinenzeit f		
machining	s. processing <mech.>	macrohardness	Makrohärte f
Mach line	Machsche Linie f	macro-ion, large ion, Langevin ion, slow ion, heavy ion <geo.>	Großion n, großes Ion n, Makroion n <Geo.>
		macromol[ecule]	s. high polymer
Machmeter, machmeter, mameter, M meter	Mach-Zahl-Messer m, Machmeter n	macromolecular	s. high-molecular
		macronucleus <bio.>	Makronukleus m, Großkern m <Bio.>
Mach net, principal net of the flow	Hauptnetz n der Strömung, Machsches Netz n	macroparameter, macroscopic variable, macroscopic parameter	makroskopischer Parameter m, makroskopische Variable f, Makroparameter m, Makrovariable f
Mach number, Mach, M	Mach-Zahl f, Machsche Zahl f, Mach n, M, Ma		
		macroparticle	Makroteilchen n
Mach pendulum	Machsches Pendel n	macrophotograph, macrograph	Makroaufnahme f, Makrographie f, Makrophotographie f, Makrobild n
Mach quadrangle	Machsches Viereck n		
Mach scale law	Machsches Ähnlichkeitsgesetz n	macrophotography, macro photography, macrography	Makrophotographie f, Makrographie f, Makroaufnahme f
Mach stem	s. Mach cone		
Mach wave	Machsche Welle f	macroporosity	Makroporosität f, Großporigkeit f
Mach wave machine	Machsche Wellenmaschine f	macropsia, macropsy, megalopsy	Vergrößertsehen n, Makropsie f, Megalopsie f
Mach-Zehnder interferometer; Mach-Zehnder refractometer	Mach-Zehnder-Interferometer n; Mach-Zehnder-Interferenzrefraktometer n	macrorheology	Makrorheologie f
		macroscale, macroscopic scale	Makromaßstab m, makroskopischer Maßstab m
Mach-Zehnder microinterferometer	Mikro-Mach-Zehnder-Anordnung f	macro-scale weather, macroweather	Großraumwetter n, Großwetter n
Mach-Zehnder refractometer	s. Mach-Zehnder interferometer	macroscopic absorption cross-section, Σ_a	makroskopischer Absorptionsquerschnitt m, Σ_a
Mackenzie equation; Fechner's law <ac.>	Fechnersches Gesetz n		
Mackerel sky	Makrelenhimmel m	macroscopic cross-section, Σ	makroskopischer Wirkungsquerschnitt m, makroskopischer Querschnitt m, Σ
Mackie lines	s. Eberhard effect <phot.>		
Maclaurin-Cauchy test	s. Cauchy['s] integral test [for convergence]		
Maclaurin ellipsoid	MacLaurinsches Ellipsoid n	macroscopic parameter	s. macroscopic variable
Maclaurin['s] expansion	MacLaurin-Entwicklung f, Entwicklung f in eine MacLaurinsche Reihe	macroscopic scale, macroscale	Makromaßstab m, makroskopischer Maßstab m
Maclaurin['s] formula, tangent (midpoint) formula, tangent-trapezoid[al] formula	Tangenten[trapez]regel f, Maclaurinsche Formel (Quadraturformel) f, Tangenten[trapez]formel f	macroscopic scattering cross-section, Σ_s	makroskopischer Streuquerschnitt m, Σ_s
		macroscopic section, macrosection	Makroschliff m, Makroschliffbild n
Maclaurin['s] series	MacLaurinsche Reihe f, Maclaurinsche Reihe	macroscopic segregation, macrosegregation, normal segregation, segregation <met.>	Blockseigerung f, Zonenseigerung f, Makroseigerung f <Met.>
macle	s. twin <cryst.>		
macroacervation	Makroazervation f		
macroanalysis	Makroanalyse f, Grammmethode f	macroscopic state, macrostate	Makrozustand m, makroskopischer Zustand m
macroatom	Makroatom n		

macroscopic variable, macroscopic parameter, macroparameter	makroskopischer Parameter *m*, makroskopische Variable *f*, Makroparameter *m*, Makrovariable *f*	**magnet case, magnet casing**	Magnetgehäuse *n*, magnetischer Leiter *m*, Magnetleiter *m*
macroscopic X-ray analysis	Röntgengrobstrukturuntersuchung *f*, Röntgengrobstrukturanalyse *f*	**magnet [cloud] chamber,** magnetic [cloud] chamber	Nebelkammer *f* mit Magnetfeld, Magnetnebelkammer *f*
macrosection, macroscopic section	Makroschliff *m*, Makroschliffbild *n*	**magnet coil,** magnetic coil, field coil, exciting coil, operating coil	Feldspule *f*, Erregerspule *f*, Magnetspule *f*
macrosegregation	s. macroscopic segregation		
macroseismic phenomenon, macroseisms	makroseismische Bewegung *f*; Makrobeben *n*	**magnet gap** **magnetic,** magnetic medium, magnetic material	s. air gap <magn.> Magnetikum *n*, magnetisches Medium (Material) *n*, magnetischer Stoff (Werkstoff) *m*
macroshape, shape of the surface, macrogeometrical shape	Oberflächengestalt *f*, makrogeometrische Gestalt *f*, Makrogestalt *f*, Oberflächenform *f*	**magnetic accomodation**	magnetische Akkomodation *f*
macrosolifluction	Makrosolifluktion *f*	**magnetic-active**	s. magnetically disturbed <geo.>
macrosonics	s. non-linear acoustics	**magnetic after-effect**	s. magnetic viscosity
macrostage [of microscope]	Makrotisch *m*, Großobjekttisch *m* <Mikroskop>	**magnetic ageing, magnetic aging**	magnetische Alterung *f*
macrostate, macroscopic state	Makrozustand *m*, makroskopischer Zustand *m*		
macrostructure	Makrogefüge *n*, Grobstruktur *f*, Makrostruktur *f*	**magnetically active**	s. magnetically disturbed <geo.>
macrosynoptic situation	Großwetterlage *f*, Großraum-Wetterlage *f*	**magnetically active plasma,** magnetic plasma, magnetoplasma	magnetisch aktives Plasma *n*, Magnetoplasma *n*, magnetfeldbehaftetes Plasma
macroturbulence	s. large-scale turbulence	**magnetically calm**	s. magnetically quiet <geo.>
macroviscosity	Makroviskosität *f*		
macroweather, macroscale weather	Großraumwetter *n*, Großwetter *n*	**magnetically disturbed,** magnetically active, magnetic-active <geo.>	magnetisch gestört, magnetisch aktiv, aktivmagnetisch <Geo.>
macula	s. fovea		
macula lutea	s. yellow spot		
Maddox['] method	Maddox-Verfahren *n*	**magnetically disturbed region**	magnetisches Störungsgebiet *n*, Störungsgebiet
Madelung constant	Madelungsche Zahl *f*, Madelung-Konstante *f*		
Madelung energy	Madelung-Energie *f*, Madelungsche Energie *f*	**magnetically hard material,** hard [magnetic] material	hartmagnetischer (magnetisch harter) Werkstoff *m*; Dauermagnetwerkstoff *m*
Madelung sum	Madelung-Summe *f*, Madelungsche Summe *f*		
madistor	Madistor *m*	**magnetically quiet,** magnetically calm, quiet, calm <geo.>	magnetisch ruhig, ruhig <Geo.>
maelstrom	Mahlstrom *m*, Mallstrom *m*		
magamp, magnetic amplifier	Magnetverstärker *m*, magnetischer Verstärker *m*, Transduktor *m*		
Magdeburg hemispheres	Magdeburger Halbkugeln *fpl* <O. von Guericke>	**magnetically soft material,** soft [magnetic] material	weichmagnetischer (magnetisch weicher) Werkstoff *m*
Magellanic Clouds, Magellan's Clouds, Clouds of Magellan	Magellansche Wolken *fpl*	**magnetic amplifier,** magamp, transducer	Magnetverstärker *m*, magnetischer Verstärker *m*, Transduktor *m*
magenta separation	s. red separation		
Maggi-Righi-Leduc effect	Maggi-Righi-Leduc-Effekt *m*	**magnetic analyzer,** analyzing magnet	magnetischer Analysator *m*, Magnetanalysator *m*, Analysiermagnet *m*
magic eye, "Magic Eye" tube, magic fan, tuning indicator, tunoscope	Abstimmanzeigeröhre *f*, magisches Auge (Band) *n*, magischer Fächer *m*; Abstimmanzeige *f*	**magnetic anisotropic energy**	s. energy of magnetic anisotropy
magic lantern	Laterna *f* magica, Hexenleuchte *f*	**magnetic anisotropy constant**	s. magnetocrystalline anisotropy constant
magic neutron number	magische Neutronenzahl *f*	**magnetic atom[ic] form factor,** magnetic form factor	magnetischer Formfaktor (Atomformfaktor) *m*
magic nucleus	magischer Kern *m*	**magnetic attraction;** force of magnetic attraction, attractive force of magnet	magnetische Anziehung *f*; magnetische Anziehungskraft *f*
magic number	magische Zahl *f*, magische Nukleonenzahl *f*		
magic proton number	magische Protonenzahl *f*		
magic T, magic tee [junction], magic T [waveguide] junction, hybrid T, hybrid T [waveguide] junction, hybrid tee [junction]	magisches T[-Glied] *n*, Serienverzweigung *f*, Wellenleiterweiche *f*, Hohlleiterweiche *f*, gemischte (hybride) T-Kopplung *f*, Hybrid-T-Kopplung *f*	**magnetic axis [of the Earth],** geomagnetic axis	magnetische Achse *f* [der Erde], Magnetachse *f* [der Erde], magnetische Erdachse *f*
		magnetic axis pole, geomagnetic pole	geomagnetischer Pol *m*, theoretischer magnetischer Pol [der Erde]
magmaplasma model	Magmaplasmamodell *n*, Magmaplasma-Verformungsmodell *n*	**magnetic balance,** field balance; induction balance	Feldwaage *f*, magnetische Waage *f*, Magnetwaage *f*; Induktionswaage *f*
magmatic cycle, geomagmatic cycle	geomagmatischer Zyklus *m*	**magnetic bar**	s. bar magnet
magmatic focus, volcanic focus	Vulkanherd *m*, vulkanischer Herd *m*, Magmaherd *m*	**magnetic barrier**	s. magnetic mirror
magnaflux inspection	s. magnetic particle inspection	**magnetic barrier layer effect**	s. Welker effect
		magnetic barrier trap	s. mirror machine
magnescope <el.>	Magneskop *n*, Vorsatzlinse *f* <El.>	**magnetic bay,** bay disturbance	Baystörung *f*, Baistörung *f*, Buchtstörung *f*
magnesia hardness, hardness due to magnesium	Magnesiahärte *f* [des Wassers], Magnesiumhärte *f* [des Wassers]	**magnetic bearing,** magnetic radio bearing	mißweisende Peilung *f*

magnetic

magnetic bias[ing], bias magnetization; magnetic displacement — Vormagnetisierung *f*; magnetische Verschiebung *f*

magnetic birefringence — s. magnetic double refraction

magnetic birefringence constant — s. Cotton-Mouton constant

magnetic blowing, magnetic blow-out — magnetische Blasung *f*, magnetische Beblasung *f*

magnetic bottle — s. mirror machine

magnetic breakdown (breakthrough) — magnetischer Durchbruch *m*

magnetic bremsstrahlung, gyrosynchrotron radiation, magnetobremsstrahlung — magnetische Bremsstrahlung *f*, Magnetobremsstrahlung *f*, Gyrosynchrotronstrahlung *f*

magnetic buzzer — Magnetsummer *m*

magnetic chamber, magnetic cloud chamber, magnet [cloud] chamber — Nebelkammer *f* mit Magnetfeld, Magnetnebelkammer *f*

magnetic character figure [for the day], character figure [for the day], magnetic figure [for the day] — magnetische Charakterzahl *f* [des Tages], Charakterzahl [des Tages], erdmagnetische Charakterzahl [des Tages], erdmagnetische Kennziffer [des Tages]

magnetic charge, quantity of magnetism — magnetische Ladung *f*

magnetic charge density — s. density of magnetic charge

magnetic chart, magnetic map — magnetische Karte *f*

magnetic circuit — magnetischer Kreis *m*, Magnetkreis *m*

magnetic class — s. magnetic crystal class

magnetic cloud chamber, magnetic chamber, magnet [cloud] chamber — Nebelkammer *f* mit Magnetfeld, Magnetnebelkammer *f*

magnetic coating — magnetische Beschichtung *f*, Magnetbeschichtung *f*

magnetic coil — s. magnet coil

magnetic coincidence spectrometer, coincidence magnetic spectrometer — magnetisches Koinzidenzspektrometer *n*

magnetic colatitude — Komplement *n* der magnetischen Breite

magnetic compass — s. compass

magnetic conductance, permeance — magnetischer Leitwert *m*, magnetische Leitfähigkeit *f*, Permeanz *f*

magnetic confinement [of plasma], magnetic plasma confinement, magnetic isolation of plasma — magnetische Einschließung *f*, magnetische Plasmaeinschließung *f*

magnetic confining field, confining magnetic field — magnetisches Begrenzungsfeld (Plasmabegrenzungsfeld) *n*

magnetic constant — s. relative permeability

magnetic convergence — Nadelabweichung *f*, magnetische Konvergenz *f*, Abweichung *f* von Gitternord

magnetic cooling, paramagnetic cooling — magnetische Kühlung (Abkühlung) *f*, Abkühlung durch adiabatische Entmagnetisierung

magnetic-core memory, magnetic-core storage (store), core storage [unit], core memory (store) — Magnetkernspeicher *m*, Kernspeicher *m*

magnetic coupling — s. inductive coupling

magnetic creep[ing] — s. magnetic viscosity

magnetic creeping — s. viscous hysteresis

magnetic criterion [of bond type] <of Pauling>, Pauling rule — magnetisches Kriterium *n* [von Pauling], Paulingsches Kriterium, Paulingsche Regel *f*

magnetic crochet — Haken *m* im Magnetogramm

magnetic cross-section — magnetischer Querschnitt *m*

magnetic crystal class, magnetic [crystallographic] class — magnetische Kristallklasse *f*, magnetische Klasse *f*

magnetic-crystalline energy — s. energy of magnetic anisotropy

magnetic-crystalline energy [density] — s. magnetocrystalline anisotropy energy density

magnetic crystallographic class — s. magnetic crystal class

magnetic current — magnetischer Strom *m*

magnetic current density — magnetische Stromdichte *f*

magnetic cushion — Magnetkissen *n*

magnetic damping — magnetische Dämpfung *f*

magnetic decay, decay of magnetic flux — magnetischer Schwund *m*

magnetic declination — s. declination

magnetic demodulation, magnetic detection — magnetische Demodulation (Gleichrichtung) *f*

magnetic deviation — s. declination

magnetic dilution — magnetische Verdünnung *f*

magnetic dip, dip, inclination, magnetic inclination, angle of [magnetic] inclination — Inklination *f*, magnetische Inklination, Inklinationswinkel *m*

magnetic dip circle, dip circle, dip-circle — Inklinatorium *n*

magnetic dipole field — magnetisches Dipolfeld *n*

magnetic dipole moment — magnetisches Dipolmoment *n*

magnetic dipole moment of the nucleus — s. magnetic moment of the nucleus

magnetic dipole moment per unit volume — s. intensity of magnetization

magnetic dipole radiation — magnetische Dipolstrahlung *f*

magnetic dipole sheet — s. magnetic shell

magnetic dip pole, dip pole, pole of magnetic dip, magnetic pole [of the Earth], Earth's (terrestrial) magnetic pole — magnetischer Pol *m* der Erde

magnetic disaccommodation — s. time decrease of permeability

magnetic disk — Magnetplatte *f*, Magnetscheibe *f*; Magnetschallplatte *f*

magnetic disk memory (storage, store) — s. disk file memory

magnetic disperse field, disperse field — magnetisches Dispersionsfeld *n*, Dispersionsfeld

magnetic dispersion — s. magnetic leakage

magnetic displacement — s. magnetic bias

magnetic domain — s. ferromagnetic domain <magn.>

magnetic domain size, domain size — Domänengröße *f*

magnetic double layer, magnetic shell (dipole sheet) — magnetisches Blatt *n*, magnetische Doppelfläche (Doppelschicht) *f*

magnetic double refraction, double refraction in transverse magnetic field, magneto-optic[al] birefringence (double refraction), magnetic birefringence — [transversale] magnetische Doppelbrechung *f*, magneto-optische Doppelbrechung

magnetic doublet — magnetisches Dublett *n*

magnetic drag, magnetic pull — magnetischer Zug *m*

magnetic drum store, drum store (storage, memory) — Magnettrommelspeicher *m*, Trommelspeicher *m*

magnetic dynamics of gas, magnetogasdynamics — Magnetogasdynamik *f*

magnetic electron microscope, magnetic microscope — [elektro]magnetisches Elektronenmikroskop *n*, Elektronenmikroskop mit magnetischen Linsen

magnetic electron optics — [elektro]magnetische Elektronenoptik *f*

magnetic energy, magnetic field energy, energy of magnetic field — magnetische Energie (Feldenergie) *f*, Energie (Energieinhalt *m*) des magnetischen Feldes

magnetic energy density	magnetische Energiedichte f	**magnetic induction,** induction, magnetic flux density, flux density; vector of magnetic induction <el.>	[magnetische] Induktion f, [magnetische] Flußdichte f, Magnetflußdichte f, [magnetische] Kraftflußdichte f, [magnetische] Kraftliniendichte f, magnetische Dichte f; Vektor m der magnetischen Induktion <El.>
magnetic energy product	Energiewert m, Energiedichteprodukt n, Energiedichte f <Produkt $(BH)_{max}$>		
magnetic energy quantum, magnon	Magnon n		
magnetic fatique	s. magnetic viscosity		
magnetic field; magnet space	Magnetfeld n, magnetisches Feld n	**magnetic induction curve,** curve of magnetic induction	Feldkurve f
magnetic field	s. a. magnetic field intensity	**magnetic induction flux**	s. magnetic flux
magnetic field balance	s. vertical-intensity magnetometer	**magnetic inertia**	magnetische Trägheit f
magnetic field energy	s. magnetic energy		
magnetic-field index	s. field index	**magnetic inspection**	s. non-destructive magnetic testing
magnetic field intensity, magnetic intensity (field strength), [intensity of] magnetic field, induced force, magnetizing force; magnetic field vector, H-vector	magnetische Feldstärke (Erregung) f, Magnetfeldstärke f, magnetisches Spannungsgefälle n, Stromkraft f; Vektor m der magnetischen Feldstärke	**magnetic intensity**	s. magnetic field intensity
		magnetic interrupter	s. Wagner interrupter
		magnetic isoanomalous line	s. isoanomalous line
		magnetic isodynam, isodynam, isodynamic line	Isodyname f, magnetische Isodyname, Linie f gleicher magnetischer Feldstärke
magnetic field of the earth core	s. internal field <geo.>		
magnetic field of the Earth's crust, crust magnetic field	Erdkrustenfeld n	**magnetic isolation of plasma**	s. magnetic confinement
		magnetic isotherm[al]	magnetische Isotherme f, Magnetisotherme f
magnetic field of the ship, ship magnetic field	Schiffsfeld n	**magnetic isthmus**	magnetischer Isthmus m
magnetic-field probe, magnetic probe	Magnetfeldsonde f, magnetische Sonde f	**magnetic Kerr effect**	s. Kerr magnetic effect
		magnetic lag	s. lag in magnetization
magnetic field strength	s. magnetic field intensity	**magnetic lag**	s. a. magnetic viscosity
magnetic field vector	s. magnetic field intensity	**magnetic latitude**	magnetische Breite f
magnetic figure [for the day]	s. magnetic character figure	**magnetic lattice force,** magnetic force of lattice	magnetische Gitterkraft f
magnetic flux, flux of magnetic induction vector, induction flux, magnetic induction flux	magnetischer Fluß (Induktionsfluß) m, Induktionsfluß, [magnetischer] Kraftfluß m, Kraftlinienfluß m, Magnetfluß m, Magnetfeldwert m, Wert m des Magnetfeldes, Anzahl f der Kraftlinien	**magnetic leakage,** leakage, leak, stray[ing]; magnetic dispersion <el.>	magnetische Streuung (Ausstreuung) f, Streuung des magnetischen Kraftflusses <El.>
		magnetic leakage factor, leakage factor, leakage coefficient <el.>	Streu[fluß]faktor m, Streuziffer f, Streugrad m, Streukoeffizient m, Streuungsfaktor m <El.>
		magnetic leakage field	s. magnetic stray field
magnetic flux curve, curve of magnetic flux	Felderregerkurve f, Durchflutungskurve f, Erregerkurve f	**magnetic leakage flux,** leakage flux, stray flux	magnetische Streufluß m, Streufluß
magnetic flux density	s. magnetic induction	**magnetic length,** effective length of magnet	magnetische Länge f, wirksame Länge des Magneten
magnetic flux in the air gap	Luftfluß m, Luftkraftfluß m, Luftfeld n		
magnetic flux quantum	s. fluxoid quantum	**magnetic lens,** electromagnetic lens	magnetische Linse f (Elektronenlinse) f
magnetic force	magnetische Kraft f, Kraft im magnetischen Feld	**magnetic lens spectrometer,** lens spectrometer	magnetisches Linsenspektrometer n, Magnetlinsenspektrometer n, Linsenspektrometer n, Spektrometer n mit magnetischen Linsen
magnetic force density, density of magnetic force, force density in the magnetic field	Kraftdichte f im magnetischen Feld, magnetische Kraftdichte		
magnetic force of lattice, magnetic lattice force	magnetische Gitterkraft f	**magnetic linear dichroism**	s. Voigt-Cotton-Moutton effect
magnetic form factor, magnetic atom[ic] form factor	magnetischer Formfaktor m, magnetischer Atomformfaktor m	**magnetic line of force,** line of magnetic field strength	magnetische Feldlinie (Kraftlinie) f, Magnetfeldlinie f
magnetic friction	magnetische Reibung f	**magnetic line of induction,** line of [magnetic] induction, line of magnetic flux	magnetische Induktionslinie f, Induktionslinie f
magnetic gate	magnetisches Tor n		
magnetic gradiometer, gradient variometer, differential magnetograph, gradiometer, gradometer	Gradiometer n, Gradientanlage f, Gradientmesser m, Differenzmesser m, Gradientvariometer n; Differentialmagnetograph m, Gradiograph m, Differenzschreiber m		
		magnetic linkage	s. flux linkage
		magnetic longitude	magnetische Länge f
		magnetic loss	Magnetisierungsverlust m; Ummagnetisierungsverlust m
magnetic hardness	magnetische Härte f	**magnetic map,** magnetic chart	magnetische Karte f
magnetic hardness coefficient	Koeffizient m der magnetischen Härte, magnetische Härte f, magnetischer Härtekoeffizient m	**magnetic mass**	s. magnetic pole strength
		magnetic material	s. magnetic
		magnetic matrix memory (storage, store), matrix memory (store, storage)	magnetischer Matrixspeicher m, Matrixspeicher, Magnetkernmatrixspeicher m
magnetic Hertzian vector	magnetischer Hertzscher Vektor m		
magnetic history	magnetische Vorgeschichte f		
		magnetic medium	s. magnetic
magnetic horizontal intensity	s. mean horizontal intensity	**magnetic meridional plane**	magnetische Meridianebene f
magnetic hum, magnetic ripple	magnetisches Brummen n, magnetischer Brumm m	**magnetic microscope**	s. magnetic electron microscope
magnetic hysteresis, hysteresis	magnetische Hysteresis (Hysterese) f, Hysterese, Nachhinken n der Induktion	**magnetic midnight**	magnetische Mitternacht f
		magnetic mirror, magnetic barrier; mirror region <plasma physics>	magnetischer Spiegel m; Spiegelgebiet n, magnetischer Pfropfen m, Pfropfen <Plasmaphysik>
magnetic image	magnetisches Bild n		
magnetic inclination	s. magnetic dip		

magnetic moment, electromagnetic moment <of magnet, body> — magnetisches Moment n, elektromagnetisches Moment <Magnet, Körper>
magnetic moment density — s. intensity of magnetization
magnetic moment of the atom — s. atomic magnetic moment
magnetic moment of the electron, electron magnetic moment — magnetisches Moment n des Elektrons
magnetic moment of the nucleus, nuclear magnetic moment; magnetic dipole moment of the nucleus, nuclear magnetic dipole moment — magnetisches Moment n des Kerns (Atomkerns), magnetisches Kernmoment n; magnetisches Dipolmoment n des Kerns (Atomkerns), magnetisches Kerndipolmoment n
magnetic moment of the proton, proton magnetic moment — magnetisches Moment n des Protons
magnetic moment per unit volume — s. intensity of magnetization
magnetic multipole moment — magnetisches Multipolmoment n
magnetic multipole radiation — magnetische Multipolstrahlung f
magnetic multipole transition — magnetischer Multipolübergang m
magnetic neutron scattering, magnetic scattering <nucl.> — magnetische Streuung f [der Neutronen], magnetische Neutronenstreuung f <Kern.>
magnetic noise — magnetisches Rauschen n
magnetic north — Magnetisch-Nord n (m)
magnetic paradox — magnetisches Paradoxon n
magnetic particle inspection, magnetic particle test, magnetic powder inspection, magnaflux inspection — Magnetpulververfahren n [der zerstörungsfreien Werkstoffprüfung], Magnetpulverprüfung f
magnetic particle rigidity — s. magnetic rigidity
magnetic particle test — s. magnetic particle inspection
magnetic paste, wet method paste, magnetic suspension; detecting ink — nasses Magnetpulver n, Magnetöl n, Magnet[pulver]suspension f, Magnetpulveraufschlämmung f
magnetic permeability, permeability — [magnetische] Permeabilität f, magnetische Durchlässigkeit f
magnetic plasma, magnetically active plasma, magnetoplasma — magnetisch aktives Plasma n, Magnetoplasma n, magnetfeldbehaftetes Plasma
magnetic plasma confinement — s. magnetic confinement
magnetic plasma frequency — magnetische Plasmafrequenz f, Hybridfrequenz f
magnetic point group, generalized point group, colour [point] group — magnetische Punktgruppe f
magnetic point pole, point pole — Punktpol m, magnetischer Punktpol
magnetic polarizability — s. magnetic susceptibility
magnetic polarization; magnetic polarization vector, internal induction, vector of magnetic polarization — magnetische Polarisation f; Vektor m der magnetischen Polarisation, magnetischer Polarisationsvektor m
magnetic pole [of the Earth] — s. magnetic dip pole
magnetic pole strength, strength of magnetic pole, pole strength, magnetic mass — [magnetische] Polstärke f, Stärke f des magnetischen Pols, magnetische Menge (Substanz) f, Magnetismusmenge f
magnetic pole strength per unit volume — s. intensity of magnetization
magnetic potential — s. magnetic scalar potential
magnetic potential [difference] — magnetische Spannung f, Durchflutung f, magnetische Durchflutung

magnetic potentiometer — magnetischer Spannungsmesser m
magnetic powder, ferromagnetic powder — Magnetpulver n
magnetic powder inspection — s. magnetic particle inspection
magnetic power — magnetische Leistung f
magnetic Prandtl number — magnetische Prandtl-Zahl f
magnetic pressure — magnetischer Druck m
magnetic printing, spurious printing, crosstalk — Kopiereffekt m
magnetic prism — magnetisches Prisma n
magnetic probe — s. magnetic-field probe
magnetic pull, magnetic drag — magnetischer Zug m
magnetic pumping — magnetisches Pumpen n
magnetic quadrupole moment — magnetisches Quadrupolmoment n
magnetic quadrupole radiation — magnetische Quadrupolstrahlung f
magnetic quantum number; axial quantum number — magnetische Quantenzahl f; Achsenquantenzahl f, axiale Quantenzahl f
magnetic quenching — magnetische Löschung f
magnetic radiation vector — magnetischer Strahlungsvektor m
magnetic radio bearing, magnetic bearing — mißweisende Peilung f
magnetic recording, recording on magnetic tape, tape recording — Magnetbandaufzeichnung f, Bandaufzeichnung f, Magnetton m, Tonbandaufzeichnung f, Magnettonbandaufzeichnung f
magnetic refrigerator — magnetisches Kühlaggregat n, magnetischer Kühler m, magnetische Kühlvorrichtung f
magnetic region — s. magnetic mirror
magnetic remanence — s. remanence
magnetic repulsion; force of magnetic repulsion, repulsive force of magnet, repelling force of magnet — magnetische Abstoßung f; magnetische Abstoßungskraft f
magnetic resistance, reluctance — magnetischer Widerstand m, Reluktanz f
magnetic resonance absorption — magnetische Resonanzabsorption f
magnetic resonance frequency — magnetische Resonanzfrequenz f
magnetic resonance method — s. Rabi['s] method
magnetic retardation — s. lag in magnetization
magnetic retentivity — s. retentivity
magnetic return path; magnetic yoke, transformer-core yoke — magnetische Rückleitung f, magnetischer Rückschluß m, Rückschlußjoch n; Rückschlußschenkel m
magnetic reversal — s. remagnetization
magnetic Reynolds number — magnetische Reynolds-Zahl f
magnetic rigidity, magnetic particle rigidity, particle rigidity; $B r$ value — magnetische Steifigkeit f, Steifigkeit des Teilchens <magnetische Feldstärke×Krümmungsradius>; magnetische Ablenkungsgröße f, Magnetfeldkrümmung f, RB-Wert m <magnetische Induktion×Krümmungsradius>
magnetic ripple — s. magnetic hum
magnetic rotary power — s. Verdet['s] constant
magnetic rotating field, rotating magnetic field — magnetisches Drehfeld n
magnetic rotation [of the plane of polarization], — magnetische Drehung f [der Polarisationsebene], magnetische Drehung

magneto-optic[al] rotation [of the plane of polarization]	der Polarisationsrichtung, magnetooptische Drehung [der Polarisationsebene], magnetooptische Drehung der Polarisationsrichtung	magnetic survey <geo.>	Magnetaufnahme f, magnetische Aufnahme (Vermessung) f <Geo.>
magnetic rotation spectrum	magnetisches Rotationsspektrum n	magnetic susceptibility, magnetic polarizability	magnetische Suszeptibilität (Polarisierbarkeit) f
magnetics	Magnetik f, Lehre f von den magnetischen Erscheinungen	magnetic susceptibility tensor, susceptibility tensor, [tensor of magnetic] susceptibility	Suszeptibilitätstensor m, Tensor m der magnetischen Suszeptibilität, Suszeptibilität f
magnetic saturation of the iron	Eisensättigung f	magnetic suspension	s. magnetic paste
magnetic scalar potential, magnetostatic potential, magnetic potential, scalar magnetic potential	skalares magnetisches Potential n, magnetisches Skalarpotential n, magnetostatisches (magnetisches) Potential	magnetic system period, magnet period	Periode f des magnetischen Systems, Periodizitätselement n
		magnetic tape store, tape store	Magnetbandspeicher m, Bandspeicher m
magnetic scale of temperature, magnetic temperature scale	magnetische Temperaturskala f	magnetic temperature	magnetische Temperatur f
		magnetic temperature scale, magnetic scale of temperature	magnetische Temperaturskala f
magnetic scattering	s. magnetic neutron scattering	magnetic test[ing]	s. non-destructive magnetic testing
magnetic scattering amplitude	magnetische Streuamplitude f	magnetic texture	magnetische Textur f
magnetic screening effect	magnetischer Abschirmeffekt m, magnetische Abschirmwirkung (Schirmwirkung) f	magnetic theodolite	Magnettheodolit m, magnetischer Theodolit m
		magnetic thermal insulation [of plasma]	magnetische Thermoisolation f [des Plasmas]
magnetic sector field, sector magnetic field	magnetisches Sektorfeld n	magnetic thermometry	magnetische Thermometrie (Temperaturmessung) f
magnetic secular variation, secular magnetic variation	magnetische Säkularvariation f, säkulare magnetische Variation f	magnetic time constant	magnetische Zeitkonstante f
magnetic Senftleben-Beenakker effect of viscosity	s. Senftleben-Beenakker effect		
magnetic separation	Magnetscheidung f; magnetische Trennung f	magnetic time lag	s. magnetic viscosity
magnetic shearing	s. shear of the magnetic field	magnetic $T^{3/2}$ law, Bloch['s] law, Bloch['s] $T^{3/2}$ law for magnetization	Blochsches Gesetz n, magnetisches $T^{3/2}$-Gesetz n
magnetic shell, magnetic double layer, magnetic dipole sheet	magnetisches Blatt n, magnetische Doppelfläche (Doppelschicht) f		
magnetic shunt	magnetischer Nebenschluß m (Shunt m), Eisenschluß m	magnetic torsion balance, torsion variometer	Torsionsvariometer n, magnetische Drehwaage (Torsionswaage) f
magnetic space group, generalized space group, [Heesch-]Shubnikov group, colour [space] group, black-and-white [space] group, black-white group	magnetische Raumgruppe f, Heesch-Schubnikow-Gruppe f, Schubnikow-Gruppe f, Schwarz-Weiß-Gruppe f	magnetic track	Magnettonspur f; Magnetspur f
		magnetic transformation (transition) temperature	s. Curie point
		magnetic trap	magnetische Falle f
		magnetic-type ion source	s. Penning ion source
magnetic spectrograph	Magnetspektrograph m, magnetischer Spektrograph m	magnetic variable [star]	Magnetfeldveränderlicher m, magnetischer Veränderlicher m
magnetic spectrometer	Magnetspektrometer n, magnetisches Spektrometer n	magnetic variation	magnetische Variation f, Variation des Magnetfeldes, Variation der erdmagnetischen Elemente
magnetic spectroscopy	Magnetspektroskopie f, magnetische Spektroskopie f		
magnetic spin quantum number, spin magnetic quantum number	magnetische Spinquantenzahl f, Magnetspinquantenzahl f, Spinmagnetismus m	magnetic variation	s. a. declination
		magnetic variometer, gradient variometer	Magnetvariometer n, magnetisches Variometer n
magnetic stability, magnetostability	Magnetostabilität f	magnetic vector	magnetischer Vektor m
magnetic standard	Magnetetalon n; Standardmagnet m	magnetic vector potential, vector magnetic potential	magnetisches Vektorpotential n
magnetic star	magnetischer Stern m		
magnetic stimulation	magnetische Ausleuchtung f		
magnetic stirrer	magnetisches Rührwerk n, magnetischer Rührer m	magnetic viscosity; magnetic after-effect (time lag, lag, creep[ing], fatigue)	magnetische Nachwirkung (Viskosität, Zähigkeit) f
magnetic storm, geomagnetic storm	[geo]magnetischer Sturm m, magnetisches Gewitter n		
magnetic stray field, stray magnetic field, stray field, [magnetic] leakage field	magnetisches Streufeld n, Streufeld, Magnetstreufeld n, magnetisches Störfeld n	magnetic wire	Magnetdraht m; Magnettondraht m
		magnetic wire store, wire store	Magnetdrahtspeicher m, Drahtspeicher m
magnetic stress tensor	magnetischer Spannungstensor m	magnetic work	s. energy of magnetization
magnetic structure determination by neutron diffraction	magnetische Strukturuntersuchung f mittels Neutronen[strahl]beugung, magnetische Neutronographie f	magnetic yoke, magnetic return path; transformer-core yoke	magnetische Rückleitung f, magnetischer Rückschluß m, Rückschlußjoch n; Rückschlußschenkel m
		magnetite, inverse spinel	Inversspinell m, Magnetit m
magnetic surface charge, magnetization charge	Magnetisierungsladung f, magnetische Flächenladung f	magnetizability, ability to be magnetized	Magnetisierbarkeit f
magnetic surface density	magnetische Oberflächendichte (Flächendichte) f		

magnetization

magnetization, magnetizing, magnetization process	Magnetisierung *f* <als Vorgang>	energy density, magnetic-crystalline energy [density]	Anisotropiedichte *f*, Energiedichte *f* der kristallographischen Anisotropie, Kristall-energiedichte *f*
magnetization	*s. a.* intensity of magnetization	magnetocrystalline energy	*s.* energy of magnetic anisotropy
magnetization by rotation	*s.* Barnett effect	magnetodielectric	Magnetodielektrikum *n*
magnetization by rubbing (stroke, touch)	Strichmagnetisierung *f*	magnetodynamics magnetoelastic anisotropy, strain anisotropy	Magnetodynamik *f* Spannungsanisotropie *f*
magnetization characteristic	*s.* magnetization curve	magnetoelastic constant	magnetoelastische Konstante *f*
magnetization charge, magnetic surface charge	Magnetisierungsladung *f*, magnetische Flächenladung *f*	magnetoelastic coupling constant	magnetoelastische Kopplungskonstante *f*
magnetization curve, curve (line) of magnetization, *B-H* curve, *B/H* curve, magnetization characteristic (line)	Magnetisierungskurve *f*, Magnetisierungs-[kenn]linie *f*, magnetische Zustandskurve *f*	magnetoelastic effect	magnetoelastischer Effekt *m*, magnetoelastische (elastisch-magnetische) Erscheinung *f*
magnetization energy	*s.* energy of magnetization	magnetoelastic energy	Spannungsenergie *f*, Spannungsanisotropieenergie *f*, Energie *f* der Spannungsanisotropie, magnetoelastische Kopplungsenergie *f* (Energie)
magnetization enthalpy	*s.* heat of magnetization		
magnetization field, magnetizing field; exciting field	Magnetisierungsfeld *n*, Magnetisierfeld *n*; Erregerfeld *n*		
magnetization heat	*s.* heat of magnetization	magnetoelastic energy density	Spannungsanisotropie [-Energiedichte] *f*, Spannungsenergiedichte *f*, Energiedichte *f* der Spannungsanisotropie
magnetization jump	Magnetisierungssprung *m*		
magnetization lag	*s.* lag in magnetization		
magnetization line	*s.* magnetization curve		
magnetization loop	*s.* hysteresis loop <el.>	magnetoelastic field	magnetoelastisches Feld *n*, Spannungsanisotropiefeld *n*
magnetization of permanent magnet	Permanenz *f*		
magnetization process	*s.* magnetization	magnetoelastic hysteresis, magnetomechanical hysteresis	magnetoelastische (magnetomechanische) Hysteresis (Hysterese) *f*
magnetization vector	*s.* intensity of magnetization		
magnetization work	*s.* energy of magnetization		
magnetized in longitudinal direction, longitudinally magnetized	längsmagnetisiert, in Längsrichtung magnetisiert	magnetoelastic wave	magnetoelastische Welle *f*
		magnetoelectric	Magnetoelektrikum *n*
magnetizing	*s.* magnetization		
magnetizing coil	Magnetisierungsspule *f*	magnetoelectric effect, galvanomagnetic effect	galvanomagnetischer (magnetoelektrischer) Effekt *m*
		magnetoelectric generator, magneto, magnetogenerator, magneto inductor	magnetelektrischer Generator *m*; Kurbelinduktor *m*; Magnetinduktor *m*
magnetizing current, exciting current	Magnetisierungsstrom *m*		
		magnetoelectric pyrometer	Galvanopyrometer *n*, magnetoelektrisches Pyrometer *n*
magnetizing field; magnetization field, exciting field	Magnetisierungsfeld *n*, Magnetisierfeld *n*; Erregerfeld *n*		
		magnetoelectric semiconductor device, magnetoelectric transducer	magnetoelektrischer Wandler *m*, magnetoelektrisches Halbleitergerät *n*
magnetizing force	Magnetisierungskraft *f*, Magnetisierkraft *f*		
magnetizing force	*s. a.* magnetic field intensity	magnetofluidodynamic	*s.* magnetohydrodynamic
magneto, magnetogenerator, magnetoelectric generator, magneto inductor	magnetelektrischer Generator *m*; Kurbelinduktor *m*; Magnetinduktor *m*	magnetofluidodynamics	*s.* magnetohydrodynamics
		magnetogasdynamic	magnetogasdynamisch
		magnetogasdynamics, magnetic dynamics of gas	Magnetogasdynamik *f*
magneto-acoustic heating	magnetoakustische Aufheizung (Heizung) *f*		
		magnetogenerator	*s.* magneto
magneto-acoustic mode	*s.* magneto-acoustic wave	magnetogram	Magnetogramm *n*
magneto-acoustic resonance	magnetoakustische Resonanz *f*	magnetograph	Magnetograph *m*
		magnetographic inspection	*s.* non-destructive magnetic testing
magneto-acoustic wave; magneto-acoustic mode, magnetosonic mode	magnetoakustische Welle *f*, Magnetoschallwelle *f*, magnetoakustische Mode *f*	magnetohydrodynamic, hydromagnetic, magnetofluidodynamic, MHD, M.H.D., m.h.d., MH, M.H., m.h., MFD, M.F.D.	magnetohydrodynamisch, hydromagnetisch, magnetofluidodynamisch, MHD, MFD
magneto-aerodynamics	Magnetoaerodynamik *f*		
magneto-bremsstrahlung	*s.* magnetic bremsstrahlung		
magnetocaloric effect	magnetokalorischer Effekt *m*	magnetohydrodynamic approximation	magnetohydrodynamische Näherung *f*, MHD-Näherung *f*
magnetocatalytic effect	magnetokatalytischer Effekt *m*		
magnetochemistry	Magnetochemie *f*	magnetohydrodynamic boundary layer	magnetohydrodynamische Grenzschicht *f*
magnetoconductivity	*s.* magnetic conductance		
magnetocrystalline anisotropy constant, [magnetic] anisotropy constant, anisotropy coefficient	Konstante *f* der kristallographischen Anisotropie, [kristallographische] Anisotropiekonstante *f*	magnetohydrodynamic conversion, magnetohydrodynamic generation of electricity	magnetohydrodynamische Erzeugung *f* von Elektroenergie
magnetocrystalline anisotropy energy	*s.* energy of magnetic anisotropy		
magnetocrystalline anisotropy energy density, anisotropy	[kristallographische] Anisotropieenergiedichte *f*, kristallographische	magnetohydrodynamic dynamo, hydromagnetic dynamo	magnetohydrodynamischer Dynamo *m*, hydromagnetischer Dynamo, MHD-Dynamo *m*

magnetohydrodynamic equations, hydromagnetic equations — Grundgleichungen *fpl* der Magnetohydrodynamik, magnetohydrodynamische (hydromagnetische) Gleichungen *fpl*

magnetohydrodynamic Faraday generator, Faraday-type magnetohydrodynamic generator — MHD-Faraday-Generator *m*, Faraday-MHD-Generator *m*

magnetohydrodynamic generation of electricity — *s.* magnetohydrodynamic conversion

magnetohydrodynamic generator, magnetoplasmadynamic generator, MHD generator, MPD generator — magnetohydrodynamischer (magnetoplasmadynamischer, plasmadynamischer) Generator *m*, Magnetohydrodynamikgenerator *m*, MHD-Generator *m*, MPD-Generator *m*

magnetohydrodynamic Hall generator, Hall-type magnetohydrodynamic generator — MHD-Hall-Generator *m*, Hall-MHD-Generator *m*

magnetohydrodynamic instability, hydromagnetic (gross) instability — magnetohydrodynamische Instabilität *f*, MHD-Instabilität *f*

magnetohydrodynamics, hydromagnetics, magnetofluidodynamics — Magnetohydrodynamik *f*, Hydromagnetik *f*, Magnetofluidodynamik *f*

magnetohydrodynamic shock wave, MHD shock wave, hydromagnetic shock wave — magnetohydrodynamische Stoßwelle *f*, MHD-Stoßwelle *f*

magnetohydrodynamic turbulence — *s.* magnetoturbulence

magnetohydrodynamic wake, hydromagnetic wake — magnetohydrodynamischer Nachlauf *m*

magnetohydrodynamic wave, MHD wave, m.h.d. wave, hydromagnetic wave — magnetohydrodynamische Welle *f*, hydromagnetische Welle, MHD-Welle *f*

magnetohydrostatic — magnetohydrostatisch

magneto inductor — *s.* magneto

magneto-ionic birefringence (double refraction) — magnetoionische Doppelbrechung *f*

magneto-ionic effect — magnetoionischer Effekt *m*

magneto-ionic theory of radiowave propagation — magnetoionische Theorie *f* der Radiowellenausbreitung

magneto-ionic wave — magnetoionische Welle *f*

magneto[-]mechanical, gyromagnetic — gyromagnetisch, kreiselmagnetisch, rotationsmagnetisch; magnetomechanisch

magnetomechanical effect; gyromagnetic phenomenon, gyromagnetic effect — gyromagnetischer Effekt *m*, gyromagnetische Erscheinung *f*; magnetomechanischer Effekt *m*

magnetomechanical factor, magnetomechanical ratio — magnetomechanisches Verhältnis *n*, magnetomechanischer Faktor *m* <reziprokes gyromagnetisches Verhältnis>

magnetomechanical hysteresis — *s.* magnetoelastic hysteresis

magnetomechanical parallelism — magnetomechanischer Parallelismus *m*

magnetomechanical ratio — *s.* magnetomechanical factor

magnetometer — Magnetometer *n*

magnetometric zero balance [of LaCour] — BMZ *n* [nach La Cour], magnetometrische Nullwaage *f*

magnetomotance — *s.* magnetomotive force

magnetomotive force, magnetomotance, m.m.f., M.M.F. — magnetomotorische Kraft *f*, magnetische Randspannung *f*, Randspannung *f*, MMK, Magneto-EMK *f*

magneton — Magneton *n*

magneto-optic[al] birefringence (double refraction) — *s.* magnetic double refraction

magneto-optic[al] [Kerr] effect — *s.* Kerr magneto-optic[al] effect

magneto-optic[al] rotation [of the plane of polarization] — *s.* magnetic rotation [of the plane of polarization]

magneto[-]optics — Magnetooptik *f*

magneto-oscillatory absorption effect, oscillatory magneto-band absorption — oszillatorische (oszillierende) Magneto[band]absorption *f*

magnetopause — Magnetopause *f*

magnetophotophoresis, Ehrenhaft effect — Magnetophotophorese *f*, Ehrenhaft-Effekt *m*

magnetopiezoresistance — Magneto-Piezo-Widerstand[sänderung *f*] *m*

magnetoplasma, magnetically active plasma, magnetic plasma — magnetisch aktives Plasma *n*, Magnetoplasma *n*, magnetfeldbehaftetes Plasma

magnetoplasmadynamic, MPD, M.P.D., m.p.d., MP, M. P., m.p. — magnetoplasmadynamisch, MPD

magnetoplasmadynamic generator — *s.* magnetohydrodynamic generator

magnetoplasmadynamics, magnetoplasma dynamics — Magnetoplasmadynamik *f*

magnetoresistance; magnetoresistance effect, magnetoresistive effect, magnetoresistivity [effect] — magnetische Widerstandsänderung *f*, Widerstandsänderung im Magnetfeld, Magnetoresistenz *f*, magnetowiderstand *m*; W.-Thomson-Effekt *m*, Thomson-Effekt *m*, Gauß-Effekt *m*

magnetoscope — Magnetoskop *n*

magneto-Seebeck effect — Magneto-Seebeck-Effekt *m*

magnetosonic mode — *s.* magneto-acoustic mode

magnetosphere — Magnetosphäre *f*

magnetostability — *s.* magnetic stability

magnetostable state — magnetostabiler Zustand *m*

magnetostatic energy, energy of magnetostatic field — magnetostatische Energie (Selbstenergie) *f*, Energie (Energieinhalt *m*) des magnetostatischen Feldes

magnetostatic energy density — Formanisotropie[-Energiedichte] *f*, magnetostatische Energiedichte *f*

magnetostatic field, static magnetic field — magnetostatisches Feld *n*, statisches Magnetfeld *n*, statisch-magnetisches Feld

magnetostatic induction — magnetische Influenz *f*

magnetostatic oscillation, Walker oscillation — magnetostatische Schwingung *f*, Walker-Schwingung *f*

magnetostatic potential — *s.* magnetic scalar potential

magnetostatics — Magnetostatik *f*

magnetostatic stress tensor — magnetostatischer Spannungstensor *m*

magnetostatic unit, m.s.u. — magnetostatische CGS-Einheit *f*, msE

magnetostriction — Magnetostriktion *f*

magnetostriction constant, constant of magnetostrictive anisotropy — Konstante *f* der magnetostriktiven Anisotropie (Verspannung), Magnetostriktions[-Anisotropie]-konstante *f*

magnetostriction delay line — Magnetostriktions-Verzögerungsleitung *f*, magnetostriktive Verzögerungsleitung *f*, magnetostriktives Laufzeitglied *n*

magnetostriction hysteresis — magnetostriktive Hysteresis (Hysterese) *f*

magnetostriction oscillator, magnetostrictive oscillator, magnetostrictor, magnetostrictive generator — Magnetostriktionsschwinger *m*, magnetostriktiver Schwinger (Schwingungserzeuger) *m*, Magnetostriktionsoszillator *m*, Magnetostriktionsgenerator *m*

magnetostriction oscillator, magnetostrictive oscillator, magnetostrictive transducer — Magnetostriktionssender *m*, magnetostriktiver Schallgeber (Ultraschallgeber, Ultraschallerzeuger, Ultraschallgenerator, Wandler) *m*

magnetostriction receiver — magnetostriktiver Empfänger (Schallempfänger) *m*, Magnetostriktionsempfänger *m*

magnetostrictive generator — *s.* magnetostriction oscillator

magnetostrictive manometer — Magnetostriktionsmanometer *n*, magnetostriktives Manometer *n*

magnetostrictive oscillator — *s.* magnetostriction oscillator

magnetostrictive strain	magnetostriktive Verzerrung (Deformation) f	magnification ratio <opt.>	Vergrößerung f, Vergrößerungszahl f, subjektive Vergrößerung <Opt.>
magnetostrictive stress	magnetostriktive Verspannung f	magnification ratio <of projector>	Verstärkungsfaktor m, Verstärkungszahl f, Leuchtenwirkungsgrad m <Scheinwerfer>
magnetostrictive transducer	magnetostriktiver Meßgeber m	magnified <of image>	vergrößert <Bild>
magnetostrictive transducer	s. a. magnetostriction oscillator	magnifier, magnifying glass	Lupe f, einfaches Mikroskop n, Vergrößerungsglas n
magnetostrictor	s. magnetostriction oscillator	magnifier	Vergrößerungsvorsatz m
magnetothermal analysis	magnetothermische Analyse f	magnifying glass magnifying power <of negative>	s. magnifier Vergrößerungsfähigkeit f [des Negativs]
magnetothermal diagram	magnetothermisches Diagramm n	magnifying power	s. a. angular magnification
magnetothermal effect	magnetothermischer Effekt m	magnistor magnitude, size	Magnistor m Größe f
		magnitude <of earthquake>, earthquake magnitude	Magnitude f [des Erdbebens]
magnetothermoelectric effect	magnetothermoelektrischer Effekt m	magnitude <of force>; intensity <gen.>	Intensität f; Stärke f <allg.>
magnetotropic	magnetotropisch	magnitude, value, length <of vector>	Betrag m, Länge f <Vektor>
magnetotropism	Magnetotropismus m	magnitude	s. a. stellar brightness
magnetoturbulence, magnetohydrodynamic turbulence	magnetohydrodynamische Turbulenz f, MHD-Turbulenz f	magnitude magnitude of alternating current	s. a. extensive variable Wechselstromgröße f, Wechselstromwert m
magneto-vibrational scattering [of neutrons], neutron magneto-vibrational scattering	magnetische Neutronenstreuung f an Gitterschwingungen (Phononen)	magnitude of angular velocity magnitude of the Sun, solar magnitude	s. angular speed Sonnenhelligkeit f
magnetoviscous	magnetoviskos	magnitude relation	Größenverhältnis n
magnet period, magnetic system period	Periode f des magnetischen Systems, Periodizitätselement n	magnon, magnetic energy quantum magnon dispersion curve	Magnon n Magnonendispersionskurve f
magnetron; cavity magnetron, resonator magnetron	Magnetron n; Magnetfeldröhre f [mit Hohlraumresonatoren], Magnetronröhre f, Hohlraummagnetron n	magnon drag magnon-magnon interaction	Magnon „drag" m, Elektronenmitführung f durch Magnonen Magnon-Magnon-Wechselwirkung f
magnetron amplifier magnetron diode, magnetron-type diode magnetron ion source	Magnetronverstärker m Magnetrondiode f, Magnetron-Typ-Diode f Magnetronionenquelle f	magnon spectrum Magnus effect Magnus['] law, law of Magnus (homogeneous circuit)	Magnonspektrum n, Magnonenspektrum n Magnus-Effekt m Magnussches Gesetz n
magnetron oscillator	Schwingmagnetron n, Magnetronoszillator m, Magnetrongenerator m	Mainardi-Codazzi relations, Mainardi equations, [Gauss-]Codazzi equations [of the surface], Codazzi-Gauss equations, equations of Gauss and Codazzi	Mainardi[-Codazzi]sche Gleichungen fpl, Codazzi[-Gauß]sche Gleichungen
magnetron-type diode, magnetron diode	Magnetrondiode f, Magnetron-Typ-Diode f		
magnet space; magnetic field	Magnetfeld n, magnetisches Feld n		
magnet space magnet tuning, permeability tuning	s. a. magnet gap <magn.> magnetische Abstimmung f, Permeabilitätsabstimmung f, M-Abstimmung f	main axis of dilatation (expansion) main band main cloud base, cloud height, ceiling	Dilatationshauptachse f Hauptbande f Wolkenhöhe f, Bewölkungshöhe f; Hauptwolkenuntergrenze f
magnet winding, operating (induction, inductive, field, exciting) winding	Erregerwicklung f; Feldwicklung f; Magnetwicklung f; Polwicklung f	main cone main device, main unit	Hauptkegel m Hauptgerät n
magnet yoke	Magnetjoch n	main diagonal sum, trace, diagonal sum, spur, tr <of matrix, operator>	Spur f, Diagonalsumme f, Sp <Matrix, Operator>
magnification, optical magnification, linear magnification, transverse magnification, lateral magnification <opt.>	Vergrößerung f, optische (laterale, transversale, lineare) Vergrößerung, Abbildungsmaßstab m, Seitenmaßstab m, Seitenverhältnis n, Seitenvergrößerung f, Breitenvergrößerung f, Lateralvergrößerung f, Transversalvergrößerung f, Quervergrößerung f, Abbildungsverhältnis n <Opt.>	main discharge main discharge gap, main gap main echo	Hauptentladung f Hauptentladungsstrecke f Hauptecho n
		main flow, mainstream	Grundströmung f, Hauptströmung f
		main foundation, foundation slab	Wehrsohle f, Wehrboden m, Wehrplatte f, Fundamentsohle f, Sohlenplatte f; Wehrfuß m
magnification changer, magnification change revolver	Vergrößerungswechsler m	main fraction main gap, main discharge gap	Hauptlauf m Hauptentladungsstrecke f
magnification factor magnification of area	s. resonance sharpness Flächenvergrößerung f	main geomagnetic field reversal, reversal of the main geomagnetic field	Umkehr f des geomagnetischen Hauptfeldes
magnification of the microscope	Mikroskopvergrößerung f, Vergrößerung f des Mikroskops	main ground water table	s. main water table
magnification range	Vergrößerungsbereich m	main group	s. group <in the periodic table>

main lobe, principal lobe, major [radiation] lobe, antenna major lobe	Hauptlappen *m*, Hauptkeule *f*, Hauptzipfel *m*, Hauptmaximum *n* <Richtdiagramm>	**majorant** **majorant [function],** dominating function **majorant series**	Majorante *f* Majorantenfunktion *f*, „dominating function" *f* Majorantenreihe *f*, Majorante *f*, Oberreihe *f*
main quantum number, principal (total, first) quantum number	Hauptquantenzahl *f*	**major axis** **majority carrier,** majority charge carrier	große Achse *f* Majoritäts[ladungs]träger *m*, Hauptladungsträger *m*, Mehrheitsträger *m*, Majorität *f*
main river, main stream	Hauptfluß *m*, Stammfluß *m*, Mutterfluß *m*	**majority[-] carrier contact**	Majoritätsträgerkontakt *m*
mains antenna	Lichtnetzantenne *f*	**majority[-] carrier emitter,** majority emitter	Majoritätsträgeremitter *m*, Majoritätsemitter *m*
mains connection **mains electricity supply** **main sequence** <astr.>	*s.* power supply *s.* power supply <el.> Hauptreihe *f*, Zwergenast *m*, Hauptast *m*, Hauptfolge *f*, Hauptsequenz *f* <Astr.>	**majority charge carrier** **majority decision element** **majority decision function**	*s.* majority carrier Schwellenwertelement *n* Schwell[en]wertfunktion *f*
main-sequence star, dwarf star, dwarf	Zwergstern *m*, Zwerg *m*, Hauptreihenstern *m*	**majority emitter,** majority[-] carrier emitter **majorization,** **majorizing**	Majoritätsträgeremitter *m*, Majoritätsemitter *m* Majorisierung *f*
mains failure, current stop	Netzausfall *m*	**major lobe** **major planet,** giant planet, Jovian planet, great planet	*s.* main lobe Riesenplanet *m*, jupiterähnlicher Planet *m*, großer Planet
mains fluctuation **mains frequency,** [power-]line frequency, [power] supply frequency	*s.* mains voltage fluctuation Netzfrequenz *f*	**major radiation lobe** **major second** **major spot** **make-and-break ignition**	*s.* main lobe große Sekunde *f* Hauptfleck *m* Abreißzündung *f*, Berührungszündung *f*
mains input, line (mains, supply) voltage, voltage of the main	Netzspannung *f*		
mains leakage, line loss <el.>	Leitungsverlust *m*; Längsverlust *m* <El.>	**make contact, make-contact unit,** making contact, normally open interlock <US>, operating contact	Arbeitskontakt *m*, Schließ[ungs]kontakt *m*, Schließer *m*
mains line hum, alternating-current hum, power line hum; hum; ripple	Brumm *m*, Brummen *n*; Netzbrumm *m*, Netzbrummen *n*	**make impulse** **make pulse,** transient pulse **make pulse,** make impulse **make ready time**	*s.* make pulse Einschaltstoß *m*, Einschaltstromstoß *m* Schließungsimpuls *m*, Stromschließungsstoß *m* Vorbereitungszeit *f*
mains noise, line noise	Netzrauschen *n*, Netzgeräusch *n*, Netzton *m*		
mainspring	Uhrfeder *f*, Triebfeder *f* [der Uhr]		
mains supply **main stream,** main river	*s.* power supply <el.> Hauptfluß *m*, Stammfluß *m*, Mutterfluß *m*	**make time**	*t* Einschaltverzögerung[szeit] *f*, Einschaltverzug *m*
mainstream **main stroke,** return stroke <of lightning>	*s. a.* main flow Hauptentladung *f*, Rückentladung *f*, Aufwärtsblitz *m* <Blitz>		
mains unit **mains variation** **mains voltage** **mains voltage fluctuation (variation)** **main tail** **maintaining voltage**	*s.* power pack *s.* main voltage fluctuation *s.* mains input *s.* main voltage fluctuation Hauptschweif *m* *s.* burning voltage <of discharge, arc>	**making** **making capacity** **making contact** **making current** **making deep furrows,** wrinkling **making of circuit** **making oversize,** oversizing	*s.* carrying out Einschaltvermögen *n* *s.* make contact *s.* transient current Zerfurchung *f* *s.* closing the circuit Überbemessung *f*, Überdimensionierung *f*
maintenance factor, reciprocal depreciation factor	Verminderungsfaktor *m* <Beleuchtungsanlage>		
main tide **main twilight arch,** second twilight arch	Stammtide *f* zweiter Dämmerungsbogen *m*, Hauptdämmerungsbogen *m*	**Maksutov camera (reflector, system, telescope)**	*s.* meniscus system
main unit, main device	Hauptgerät *n*	**male part [of ground-in joint],** ground-joint male part	Schliffkern *m*
main valency **main voltage fluctuation,** mains [voltage] fluctuation, fluctuation in the main voltage; variation in the mains voltage, mains [voltage] variation, line voltage change	*s.* primary valence Netzspannungsschwankung *f*, Netzschwankung *f*; Netzspannungsänderung *f*	**malleability,** forgeability **malleableizing,** malleablizing **malleable pig iron**	Schmiedbarkeit *f*; Hämmerbarkeit *f* Glühfrischen *n* Temperrohguß *m*
		malleablizing, malleableizing **Malter effect**	Glühfrischen *n*; Tempern *n* Malter-Effekt *m*
main water table, main ground water table, phreatic surface (nappe)	Grundwasserspiegel *m*, Grundwasseroberfläche *f*, Grundwasserfläche *f*; Hauptgrundwasserspiegel *m*	**Maltese cross, Maltese mechanism,** Geneva movement, Geneva motion, Geneva mechanism	Malteserkreuz *n*, Malteserkreuzanordnung *f*, Malteserkreuzschaltung *f*, Malteserkreuzgetriebe *n*; Malteserkreuzantrieb *m*
Majorana effect	Majorana-Effekt *m*		
Majorana force, space-exchange force	Majorana-Kraft *f*, Ortsaustauschkraft *f*	**Malus['] [cosine-squared] law,** Malus-Daupin theorem, Malus['] theorem, law of Malus	Satz *m* von Malus, Malusscher Satz, Gesetz *n* von Malus
Majorana operator, space-exchange operator	Majorana-Operator *m*, Ortsaustauschoperator *m*, Operator *m* der Majorana-Kräfte		
Majorana particle **Majorana potential,** space-exchange potential, potential of Majorana forces	Majorana-Teilchen *n* Majorana-Potential *n*, Ortsaustauschpotential *n*, Potential *n* der Majorana-Kräfte	**mameter** **mammatus cloud** **mammoth pump**	*s.* Machmeter Mammatuswolke *f* Mammutpumpe *f*, Druckluftwasserheber *m*
Majorana representation	Majorana-Darstellung *f*	**mamu**	*s.* millimass unit

man-carrying, manned, with crew	bemannt	mantle, Welsbach mantle, gas mantle, incandescent mantle	Auer-Glühkörper m, Auer-Strumpf m, Glühkörper m, Glühstrumpf m, Gasglühstrumpf m
Mandel'shtam ...	s. Mandelstam ...	mantle of the Earth, Earth's mantle	Erdmantel m
Mandelstam branch point	Mandelstam-Verzweigung f		
Mandelstam-Brillouin doublet	Mandelstam-Brillouin-Dublett n	manufacture	s. production
		manufacture of gratings, ruling [of gratings], ruling technique	Gitterteilung f, Gitterherstellung f, Gitterschneidetechnik f
Mandelstam[-Brillouin] effect	Mandelstam-Brillouin-Effekt m	manufacturer, producer	Hersteller[werk n] m
Mandelstam-Papalexi['s] method, method of Mandelstam and Papalexi	Methode f von Mandelstam und Papalexi, Mandelstam-Papalexi-Methode f	manufacturing	s. production
		manufacturing of sources, source production	Quellenherstellung f
Mandelstam representation	Mandelstam-Darstellung f	many-body force, many-particle force; many-nucleon force, multi-nucleon force	Mehrkörperkraft f, Mehrteilchenkraft f; Mehrnukleonenkraft f; Vielkörperkraft f, Vielteilchenkraft f; Vielnukleonenkraft f
mandrel drawing, plug drawing	Stopfenzug m, Ziehen n über einen Stopfen, Ziehen über eine Nuß		
mandrel drawing, bar drawing	Stangenzug m, Ziehen n über einen Dorn		
		many-body model of nucleus	Vielteilchenmodell n [des Kerns]
Manebach twin	Manebacher Zwilling m	many-body potential	s. many-nucleon potential
Manebach type law	Manebacher Gesetz n	many-body problem	Mehrkörperproblem n; Vielkörperproblem n
maneuvrability	s. dirigibility		
Mangin mirror	Mangin-Spiegel m	many-channel reaction, multichannel reaction	Mehrkanalreaktion f, Vielkanalreaktion f, Vielweg[e]reaktion f
Mangler['s] transformation	Manglersche Transformation f		
manifold <math.>	Mannigfaltigkeit f <Math.>	many-conductor system	s. multiconductor system
		many-degrees-of-freedom system	System n mit mehreren Freiheitsgraden
manifold; multiple, repeated <math.; gen.>	mehrfach, vielfach <Math.; allg.>	many-electron approximation	s. multi-electron approximation
manifold	s. a. set <math.>	many-electron centre, multi-electron centre	Mehrelektronenzentrum n; Vielelektronenzentrum n
manipulated variable, regulated condition, action control, control signal, control value	Stellgröße f	many-electron problem, multi-electron problem	Mehrelektronenproblem n; Vielelektronenproblem n
		many-electron representation, multi-electron representation	Mehrelektronendarstellung f; Vielelektronendarstellung f
manipulation	s. handling <gen.>		
manipulator	Manipulator m, Ferngreifer m, Fernbedienungsgerät n	many-electron spectrum, multi-electron spectrum, poly-electron spectrum	Mehrelektronenspektrum n; Vielelektronenspektrum n
Manley-Rowe relations	Manley-Rowe-Gleichungen fpl		
man-made Earth's satellite	s. artificial Earth's satellite	many-level resonance formula	Vielniveauresonanzformel f
man-made satellite	s. artificial satellite		
manned, man-carrying, with crew	bemannt	many-line[d] fluorescence, multi-line fluorescence, multiple-line fluorescence	Mehrlinienfluoreszenz f; Viellinienfluoreszenz f
Mannkopff spectrograph	Mannkopff-Spektrograph m		
Mann-Whitney test, Wilcoxon['s] test	Wilcoxon-Test m, Wilcoxonscher Test m, Mann-Whitney-Test m	many-line[d] spectrum, multi-line spectrum, multiple-line spectrum, discrete-band spectrum	Mehrlinienspektrum n; Viellinienspektrum n
manoeuvrability	s. dirigibility		
manograph	s. pressure recorder		
manometer, pressure gauge (meter), pressure-measuring device, gauge	Druckmesser m, Manometer m	many-nucleon configuration, multi-nucleon configuration	Vielnukleonenkonfiguration f, Mehrnukleonenkonfiguration f
manometer capsule	manometrische Kapsel f, Dosenmanometer n, Manometerdosensatz m	many-nucleon force	s. many-particle force
		many-nucleon potential, many-particle potential, many-body potential	Mehrnukleonenpotential n; Mehrteilchenpotential n, Mehrkörperpotential n; Vielnukleonenpotential n; Vielteilchenpotential n, Vielkörperpotential n
manometer liquid	s. manometric fluid		
manometric balance, manometric scale <US>, dead-weight pressure (piston) gauge, dead-weight pressure tester, piston pressure gauge, piston gauge <US>	Druckwaage f, manometrische Waage f; Kolbenmanometer n; Belastungsmanometer n, gewichtsbelastetes Kolbenmanometer n		
		many-particle description	Vielteilchenbeschreibung f, Mehrteilchenbeschreibung f
		many-particle force	s. many-body force
		many-particle potential	s. many-nucleon potential
manometric bomb	manometrische Bombe f	many-particle resonance	Mehrteilchenresonanz f
manometric fluid, manometric liquid, indicating (manometer) liquid	Manometerflüssigkeit f	many-particle resonance width	Mehrteilchenresonanzbreite f
manometric scale <US>	s. manometric balance	many-particle Schrödinger equation	s. many-particle wave equation
manometry, volumetric manometry	Manometrie f, volumetrische Manometrie; Manometermessung f, manometrische Messung f	many-particle Schrödinger function	s. many-particle wave function
		many-particle state	Mehrteilchenzustand m, Vielteilchenzustand m
manoscopy, determination of gas density	Gasdichtebestimmung f		
manostat	Manostat m, Druckhalter m	many-particle system	Mehrteilchensystem n, Vielteilchensystem n
manovacuummeter, mano-vacuum-meter	Manovakuummeter n		
		many-particle wave equation, many-particle Schrödinger equation	Vielteilchen-Wellengleichung f, Mehrteilchen-Wellengleichung f, Vielteilchen-Schrödinger-Gleichung f, Mehrteilchen-Schrödinger-Gleichung f
mantissa	Mantisse f; numerische Mantisse <num. Math.>		

many-particle wave function, many-particle Schrödinger function	Mehrteilchen-Wellenfunktion f, Mehrteilchen-Schrödinger-Funktion f, Vielteilchen-Wellenfunktion f, Vielteilchen-Schrödinger-Funktion f	marginal crevasse	Randspalte f; Randkluft f; Bergschrund m
many-quanta transition	Mehrquantenübergang m	marginal definition	s. edge acuity
		marginal density function	Randwahrscheinlichkeitsdichte f, Randverteilungsdichte f
		marginal discharge	Randentladung f
many-sheeted Riemannian space	mehrblättriges Riemannsches Gebiet n, mehrblättriger Riemannscher Raum m	marginal distribution	Marginalverteilung f, „marginal distribution" f
many-sheeted Riemann surface	mehrblättrige Riemannsche Fläche f	marginal distribution function	Randverteilungsfunktion f
many-spin system, multispin system	Vielspinsystem n	marginal field, fringing field, edge field, margin of the field	Randfeld n
many-time formalism	Mehrzeitformalismus m, „many-time"-Formalismus m	marginal force, end reaction	Randkraft f
many-time theory	mehrzeitige Theorie f, Mehrzeittheorie f	marginal moraine, lateral (flank) moraine, peripheral moraine	Seitenmoräne f, Ufermoräne f, Randmoräne f
many-to-many	mehrmehrdeutig, vielvieldeutig	marginal part, boundary part	Randpartie f
many-valley semiconductor, multivalley semiconductor	Mehrtalhalbleiter m, Vieltalhalbleiter m	marginal porosity	Randporigkeit f
		marginal ray, peripheral (rim) ray	Randstrahl m
many-valued, multiple-valued, multi[-]valued	mehrdeutig, vieldeutig; mehrwertig <Math.>	marginal region	s. peripheral region
		marginal stability	Randstabilität f
		marginal vortex	s. tip vortex
		marginal zone	s. peripheral region
		margin of energy	Energiereserve f, Energievorrat m
many-valued function	s. multivalent function	margin of error	s. limit of error
many-valued logic, multi-valued logic	mehrwertige Logik f	margin of safety	s. safety factor
		margin of safety against singing	Pfeifsicherheit f; Pfeifpunktabstand m
many-valuedness, multivaluedness, multiple valuedness <math.>	Mehrdeutigkeit f, Vieldeutigkeit f; Mehrwertigkeit f <Math.>	margin of the field, fringing field, edge field, marginal field	Randfeld n
map	s. mapping <math.>	Margoulis number, Mg	s. Stanton number
map grid, grade grid	Kartennetz n, Gradnetz n [der Karte]	Margules equation	Margulessches Gesetz n, Margulessche Gleichung (Gleichgewichtsbedingung) f
map of isohyets, chart of isohyets	Regenkarte f, Isohyetenkarte f		
map of isohypses	s. hypsometric map	marine barometer	Schiffsbarometer n
mapping, topographic mapping, land survey[ing]	Landesvermessung f, Landesaufnahme f, Landeskartierung f, Mappierung f	marine chronometer	Schiffschronometer n
		marine current, ocean[ic] current	Meeresströmung f
mapping, map, representation <math.>	Abbildung f <Math.>	marine erosion	s. abrasion <geo.>
mapping	s. a. topographic mapping	marine forecast, sea forecast	Wellenvorhersage f, Wellenprognose f
map projection, cartographic projection	Kartenprojektion f, Kartennetzentwurf m, kartographischer Entwurf m̄	marine magnetometer	Seemagnetometer n
		marine optics, optics of the sea	Meeresoptik f
maraging	s. age-hardening	marine physics, physical oceanography, physics of the ocean	physikalische Ozeanographie f, Physik f des Meeres
Marangoni effect	Marangoni-Effekt m		
Marangoni-Gibbs effect	Marangoni-Gibbs-Effekt m	mariograph	s. mareograph
marbling	Marmorierung f, Äderung f	Mariotte['s] law	Mariottesches Gesetz n
		Mariotte['s] law	s. a. boyle['s] law
		maritime climate, oceanic climate, insular climate	Seeklima n, maritimes Klima n, ozeanisches Klima
Marconi antenna	Marconi-Antenne f		
Marconi-Franklin antenna	s. collinear antenna	maritime polar air, polar maritime air	maritime Polarluft f, polare Meeresluft f
mare <pl.: maria>, sea <on the Moon>	Mare n <pl.: maria>, Mondmeer n	maritime tropical air, tropical maritime air	maritime Tropikluft f, tropische Meeresluft f
mareograph, mariograph, water-level recorder	Mareograph m, selbstregistrierender Flutmesser m, Schreibpegel m, schreibender Pegel m, Registrierpegel m, Wasserstandsschreiber m, Wasserspiegelschreiber m	maritimity	Maritimität f
		mark, marking, marker	Marke f, Markierung f; Markierungsstrich m; Impulsmarke f
mare's-tail [cloud]	Pferdeschwanzwolke f, Haarwolke f, Federwolke f, Windbaum m	mark: mira; azimuth mark	Mire f; Testmarke f
		marker, marker generator, marking generator	Markengeber m, Markengenerator m, Markierungsgenerator m
Margenau distribution	Margenau-Verteilung f	marker	s. a. mark
margin; boundary, bound; limit, limitation; rim	Grenze f; Begrenzung f; Rand m; Berandung f	marker	s. a. isotopic tracer
		marker	s. a. tracer
margin	Sicherheit f, Reserve f, Spielraum m	marker generator	s. marker
		marking	s. blanking <of a pulse>
margin	s. a. tolerance	marking	s. a. mark
marginal <geo.>	marginal, randlich <Geo.>	marking gauge	s. surface gauge
marginal coefficient	Randkoeffizient m, Leckfaktor m	marking generator, marker, marker generator	Markengeber m, Markengenerator m, Markierungsgenerator m

marking of minimum beam, Wolter['s] method	Minimumstrahlkennzeichnung f, Woltersche Methode f der Minimumstrahlkennzeichnung, Methode von Wolter	maser oscillation	Maserschwingung f
		maser oscillator, moser, quantum oscillator; molecular oscillator (generator)	Masergenerator m, Maseroszillator m, Quantengenerator m; Molekulargenerator m, Molekularoszillator m
marking-out, pegging-out ⟨US⟩, staking ⟨US⟩	Verpflockung f, Verpfählung f		
Markoff chain, Markov[ian] chain	Markowsche Kette f, Markoffsche Kette	maser radiation	Maserstrahlung f
Markoff distribution, Markovian distribution	Markow-Verteilung f, Markoffsche Verteilung f		
Markoff process, Markovian process, Markovian stochastic process	Markowscher [stochastischer] Prozeß m, Markowscher Vermehrungsprozeß m, Markoffscher Prozeß	maser ray	s. maser beam
		maser transition	Maserübergang m
		mask, printing mask	Maske f, Abdeckmaske f, Abdeckblende f, Kopiermaske f
Markov[ian] chain, Markoff chain	Markowsche Kette f, Markoffsche Kette	masked by black ⟨of chromatic colour⟩	s. non-zero black content / having
Markovian distribution	s. Markoff distribution	masked by grey ⟨of chromatic colour⟩	s. non-zero black and white content / having
Markovian process, Markovian stochastic process, Markoff process	Markowscher [stochastischer] Prozeß m, Markowscher Vermehrungsprozeß m, Markoffscher Prozeß	masked by white ⟨of chromatic colour⟩	s. non-zero white content / having
		masked front, masque front	maskierte Front f
Markowitz['] moon camera, dual-rate moon position camera	Mondkamera f von Markowitz	masking, veiling, shading ⟨of chromatic colours by a portion of white and/or black⟩	Verhüllung f [bunter Farben]
Markownikoff rule	Markownikowsche Regel f		
mark-to-space ratio	s. pulse width — repetition ratio	masking ⟨chem.⟩	Maskierung f ⟨Chem.⟩
marquenching	s. martempering	masking ⟨of front⟩ ⟨meteo.⟩	Maskierung f [der Front] ⟨Meteo.⟩
marsch source, marsch spring	Helokrene f, Sickerquelle f, Sumpfquelle f	masking	s. a. aural masking ⟨ac.⟩
		masking	s. a. masking technique
martempering, marquenching, interrupted quenching, hot quenching	Warmbadhärtung f, Stufenhärtung f	masking agent	Maskierungsmittel n
		masking audiogram	Verdecktıngsaudiogramm n
Martens and Heyn hardness [number], Martens hardness [number]	Martens-Härte f, Martens-Heyn-Härte f	masking by black, veiling (shading) by black, black veiling (masking, shading)	Schwarzverhüllung f, Verschwärzlichung f
		masking by grey, veiling (shading) by grey, grey veiling (masking, shading)	Grauverhüllung f, Vergrauung f
Martens degree	Martens-Grad m, Martens-Zahl f		
Martens hardness [number], Martens and Heyn hardness [number]	Martens-Härte f, Martens-Heyn-Härte f	masking by white, veiling (shading) by white, white veiling (masking, shading)	Weißverhüllung f, Verweißlichung f
Martens hardness test[ing]	Martens-Härteprüfung f, Kugeldruck-Härteprüfung f nach Martens		
		masking effect	s. aural masking ⟨ac.⟩
		masking method	s. masking technique
martensite point	Martensitpunkt m	masking technique, masking method, masking ⟨phot.⟩	Maskenverfahren n, Masken-Kopierverfahren n; Frequenzfilterverfahren n, Kontrastkontrollverfahren n; Maskierung f, Abdeckung f, Teilabdeckung f ⟨Phot.⟩
martensite (martensitic) transformation	s. diffusionless transformation		
Martens-Kennedy strain gauge	Dehnungsmesser m nach Martens-Kennedy, Martens-Kennedyscher Dehnungsmesser		
Martens['] [polarization] photometer	Polarisationsphotometer n von Martens, Martenssches Polarisationsphotometer		
		mason's level	s. striding level
		masque front	s. masked front
		mass	Masse f
Martens spectrophotometer, König-Martens spectrophotometer	Spektralphotometer n von König-Martens	mass, body; ground ⟨el.⟩	Masse f, Körper m; Erde f
		mass; massif ⟨geo.⟩	Massiv n, Massengebirge n, massiges Gebirge n; Gebirgsstock m, Stock m
Martens strain gauge, tilting-mirror [Martens] gauge	Martenssches Spiegelgerät n, Spiegelfeinmeßgerät n nach Martens	mass	s. a. material
		mass/having, mass/with, possessing mass	massebehaftet, massenbehaftet
Martens['] wedge	Martensscher Keil m		
martingale	Martingal n	mass absorption coefficient, mass energy absorption coefficient	Massenabsorptionskoeffizient m, Massen-Energieabsorptionskoeffizient m
Martyn['s] absorption theorem	Martynsches Absorptionstheorem n, Absorptionstheorem von Martyn		
Marx circuit; Marx generator	Marx-Schaltung f; Marxscher Stoßgenerator m	mass abundance	s. mass concentration
		mass acceleration	Massenbeschleunigung f
		mass action	Massenwirkung f
		mass action constant	s. equilibrium constant
Marx effect, regression effect	Marx-Effekt m	mass action expression, mass-action law	s. law of mass action
Marx generator	s. Marx circuit	mass analysis	Massenanalyse f
Marzetti plasticity	Marzetti-Plastizität f, Plastizität f nach Marzetti	mass analyzer	Massenanalysator m
		mass at rest, rest[-] mass, proper mass	Ruhemasse f, Ruhmasse f
Mascart-Jamin['s] experiment	Mascart-Jaminscher Versuch m, Versuch von Mascart und Jamin	mass attenuation coefficient	Massenschwächungskoeffizient m
Mascheroni['s] constant	s. Euler['s] constant		
maser ⟨microwave amplification by or through stimulated emission of radiation⟩, maser amplifier, quantum amplifier	Maser m, Maserverstärker m, Quantenverstärker m	mass attenuation coefficient for pair production	s. pair-production mass attenuation coefficient
		mass attenuation coefficient for coherent scattering	Rayleigh mass scattering coefficient
maser beam, maser ray	Maserstrahl m		

Massau['s] semi-graphical technique — Massausche halbzeichnerische Methode *f*
mass balance — Massenbilanz *f*; Massenhaushalt *m* <Meteo.>
mass centre — s. centre of mass
mass centre integral, centre-of-mass integral — Schwerpunktsintegral *n*

mass concentration, concentration by mass (weight), weight concentration, mass abundance — Konzentration *f* in Masseprozent (Gewichtsprozent), Masse[n]konzentration *f*, Gewichtskonzentration *f*
mass conductivity coefficient, coefficient of mass conductivity — Massenleitzahl *f*
mass connection, earth connection, body contact, mass contact, ground contact, earth contact, earthing, ground[ing] <US> — Anschluß *m* an Masse, Masseanschluß *m*, Massekontakt *m*, Verbindung *f* mit Masse (Erde); Masseverbindung *f*, Erdverbindung *f*, Erdanschluß *m*, Erdung *f*
mass conservation law — s. law of conservation of mass
mass contact — s. mass connection
mass content, content by mass, weight content, content by weight — Gehalt *m* in Masseneinheiten, Masse[n]gehalt *m*, Gewichtsgehalt *m*
mass conversion factor, atomic mass conversion factor — Smythe-Faktor *m*, Smythescher Faktor *m* <= 1,000275, Umrechnungsfaktor zwischen Atomgewicht und ME>
mass coulometer — s. weight coulometer
mass curve, integral curve — Summenganglinie *f*, Summenlinie *f*, Integralkurve *f*, Inhaltslinie *f*
mass decrement — Massendekrement *n*
mass defect, mass deficit, packing defect (loss, effect) <nucl.> — Massendefekt *m*, Kernschwund *m* <Kern.>
mass deficiency, deficiency (lack) of mass — Massendefizit *n*, Massenunterschuß *m*
mass deficit — s. mass defect
mass density — s. density
mass dipole — Massendipol *m*, Monopol-Dipol-Teilchen *n*, Pol-Dipol-Teilchen *n*
mass dispersion — Massendispersion *f*

mass distribution, distribution of mass — Massenverteilung *f*

mass doublet — Massendublett *n*
mass effect, isotope (isotopic) mass effect, effects due to isotopic change of mass; mass-sensitive isotope shift — Kernmasse[n]effekt *m*, Massenisotopieeffekt *m*, massenabhängige Isotopieverschiebung *f*, massenabhängiger Isotopie[verschiebungs]effekt *m*; Mitbewegung *f* des Kerns [bei der Isotopieverschiebung], Mitbewegungseffekt *m*
mass effect, packing effect <nucl.> — Masseneffekt *m*, Packungseffekt *m* <Kern.>
mass ejection, surge, surge prominence; ejection of matter — Auswurf *m* (Ausschleudern *n*) von Materie, Materieauswurf *m*, Materieausbruch *m*
mass energy absorption coefficient — s. mass absorption coefficient
mass-energy equivalence — s. mass equivalence of energy
mass-energy equivalence law (principle) — s. equivalence of mass and energy principle
mass-energy equivalent, mass equivalent of energy — Masse[n]äquivalent *n* der Energie, Masse-Energie-Äquivalent *n*, Energie-Masse-Äquivalent *n*
mass-energy interrelation, mass-energy relation[ship] — s. Einstein['s] relation
mass energy transfer coefficient — Massen-Energieumwandlungskoeffizient *m*, Massen-Energieübertragungskoeffizient *m*

mass equivalence of energy, mass-energy equivalence, equivalence of mass and energy — Äquivalenz *f* von Masse und Energie, Masse-Energie-Äquivalenz *f*, Energie-Masse-Äquivalenz *f*

mass equivalent of energy, mass-energy equivalent — Masse[n]äquivalent *n* der Energie, Masse-Energie-Äquivalent *n*, Energie-Masse-Äquivalent *n*
mass excess — Massenüberschuß *m*
Massey formula — Masseysche Formel *f*
Massey-Mohr formulae — Massey-Mohrsche Formeln *fpl*
mass filter — Massenfilter *n* [von Bennett]
mass flow, mass flow rate, mass flux, rate of mass flow, mass rate of flow (stream) <mass per unit time> — Durchfluß *m* [in Masseeinheiten], Durchflußmenge *f* [je Zeiteinheit], Durchflußstärke *f*, Mengen[durch]fluß *m*, Mengenstrom *m*, momentane Stromstärke *f*, Massen[durch]fluß *m*, Massenstrom *m*, Durchflußmasse *f* [je Zeiteinheit], Durchsatz *m* [in Masseeinheiten], Durchsatzmenge *f* [je Zeiteinheit], Mengendurchsatz *m*, Massendurchsatz *m*, Massenströmungsdichte *f* <Masse/Zeiteinheit>

mass flow ratio, mass ratio — relative Durchflußmenge *f*
mass force — s. force of inertia
mass flux — s. mass flow
mass fraction, weight fraction, mass ratio, weight ratio — Massenbruch *m*, Masseanteil *m*, Massefraktion *f*, Gewichtsanteil *m*, Gewichtsfraktion *f*, Gewichtsprozentsatz *m*
mass function [of binary stars] — Massenfunktion *f* [von Doppelsternen]
Massieu function — Massieusche Funktion *f*
Massieu-Planck function — Massieu-Plancksche Funktion *f*
massif; mass — Massiv *n*, Massengebirge *n*, massiges Gebirge *n*, Gebirgsstock *m*, Stock *m*
mass inertia, inertia of mass — Massenträgheit *f*, Trägheit *f* der Masse
mass law — s. law of mass action
massless, zero-mass — masselos, mit der Masse 0

mass limit, critical mass, limiting mass <of white dwarfs> — Grenzmasse *f*, kritische Masse *f* <weiße Zwerge>
mass-luminosity diagram — Masse-Leuchtkraft-Diagramm *n*, Masse-Helligkeits-Diagramm *n*
mass-luminosity law, mass-luminosity relation, luminosity-mass relation, stellar (star) mass-luminosity relation — Masse-Leuchtkraft-Beziehung *f*, Masse-Helligkeits-Beziehung *f*, Masse-Leuchtkraft-Gesetz *n*
mass miniature radiography — s. fluorography
mass moment, static[al] moment, moment of first order, linear moment — statisches Moment *n*, Moment erster Ordnung, lineares Moment
mass moment of inertia, moment of inertia, M.I. — Trägheitsmoment *n*, Massenträgheitsmoment *n*, Drehmasse *f*
mass monochromator — Massenmonochromator *m*
mass motion — Massenbewegung *f*, Bodenversetzung *f*

mass multipole — Massenmultipol *m*, Monopol-Multipol-Teilchen *n*

mass number, rough atomic weight, nuclear (nucleon) number *A* — Massenzahl *f*, Nukleonenzahl *f A, M*
mass of cold air, cold mass — Kaltluftmasse *f*

mass of displaced liquid — verdrängte Flüssigkeitsmasse *f*
mass of neutral atom, neutral mass — neutrale Masse (Atommasse) *f*, Masse des neutralen Atoms
mass of radiation — Masse *f* der Strahlung

mass of the atom, atomic mass — Masse *f* des Atoms, Atommasse *f*
mass of the electron, electron[ic] mass — Elektronenmasse *f*, Masse *f* des Elektrons
mass of the neutron, neutron mass — Neutronenmasse *f*, Masse *f* des Neutrons

mass of the proton, proton mass	Protonenmasse f, Masse f des Protons
mass of the resonance	Masse f der Resonanz
mass on chemical scale, chemical mass	Masse f nach der chemischen Skala
Masson disk	Massonsche Scheibe f
mass on physical scale, physical mass	Masse f nach der physikalischen Skala
mass operator	Massenoperator m
mass parameter	Massenparameter m, Massenkoeffizient m
mass peak, peak of mass spectrum	Massenlinie f, Massenpeak m, Linie f im Massenspektrum
mass percent, weight percent, mass %, wt.%	Masseprozent n, Gewichtsprozent n, Masse-%, Masse%, Gew.-%, Gew.%
mass percents	s. percentage by mass
mass per unit area, surface density (mass), thickness ⟨in g/cm²⟩	Flächenmasse f, Flächengewicht n, Flächendichte f, Flächenbelegung f; Dicke ⟨in g/cm²⟩
mass per unit length; weight per unit length	Massenbelag m, Massenbelegung f, Längengewicht n, Längenmasse f
mass photoelectric attenuation coefficient	Massenschwächungskoeffizient m für den Photoeffekt
mass point	s. material point
mass point mechanics, point mechanics	Punktmechanik f, Massenpunktmechanik f, Mechanik f des Massenpunktes
mass potential	s. gravitation
mass quadrupole	Massenquadrupol m, Monopol-Quadrupol-Teilchen n
mass radiator	Massenstrahler m
mass-radius relation	Masse-Radius-Beziehung f
mass range [of particle]	Reichweite f in g/cm² ⟨Teilchen⟩
mass rate of flow (stream)	s. mass flow rate
mass ratio, Ziolkovsky number ⟨rocket⟩	Massenverhältnis n, Ziolkowsky-Zahl f ⟨Rakete⟩
mass ratio	s. a. mass flow ratio
mass ratio	s. a. mass fraction
mass renormalization, renormalization of mass	Massenrenormierung f, Renormierung f der Masse
mass resistivity	spezifischer Widerstand m, bezogen auf die Masse; spezifischer Massewiderstand m
mass resolution	s. mass resolving power
mass resolving power, mass resolution	Massenauflösungsvermögen n, Massenauflösung f
mass scattering coefficient	Massenstreukoeffizient m
mass-sensitive isotope shift	s. mass effect
mass separation, separation of masses	Massentrennung f
mass separation	Zerlegung f in unterkritische Teilmassen
mass separator	s. electromagnetic mass separator
mass shell	Massenschale f
mass spectrogram	Massenspektrogramm n
mass spectrograph	Massenspektrograph m
mass spectrometer	Massenspektrometer n
mass spectrometer method	s. mass-spectrometric technique
mass-spectrometer used with a leak detector, mass-spectrometric leak detector	Lecksucher m mit Massenspektrometer
mass-spectrometric method, mass-spectrometric technique, mass spectrometer method	massenspektrometrische Methode f, Massenspektrometermethode f, Massenspektrometertechnik f
mass spectrometry, mass spectroscopy	Massenspektrometrie f, Massenspektroskopie f
mass spectrum	Massenspektrum n
mass standard	Masseneinheitsnormal n, Massennormal n
mass stopping power	Massenbremsvermögen n ⟨Energieverlust/Flächendichte⟩
mass surface, nuclear mass surface	Massenfläche f, Kernmassenfläche f ⟨Z, N-Koordinaten⟩
mass susceptibility	s. specific magnetic susceptibility
mass synchrometer	s. synchrometer
mass tensor	Massentensor m
mass-to-thrust ratio, weight-to-thrust ratio	Masse-Schub-Verhältnis n
mass transfer	Stoffaustausch m, Massenaustausch m, Stofftransport m, Massentransport m; Stoffübergang m, Massenübergang m; Stoffübertragung f, Massenübertragung f; Stoffaustrag m; Stoffabtragung f
mass transfer	s. a. transport of solids ⟨e.g. by rivers⟩ ⟨geo.⟩
mass transfer coefficient	Austauschzahl f, Stoffaustauschzahl f, Stoffübergangszahl f, Massenübergangszahl f
mass transfer potential	Massenübertragungspotential n
mass transfer rate	Stoffaustauschgeschwindigkeit f, Stoffübertragungsgeschwindigkeit f, Massenaustauschgeschwindigkeit f, Massenübergangsgeschwindigkeit f, Massenübertragungsgeschwindigkeit f
mass transport	s. transport of solids ⟨e.g. by rivers⟩ ⟨geo.⟩
mass transport equation	Massentransportgleichung f
mass velocity ⟨density×velocity⟩	Massenstromdichte f, Massenflußdichte f, Massenströmungsdichte f, Mengenstromdichte f, Mengenflußdichte f, Mengenströmungsdichte f ⟨Dichte×Geschwindigkeit⟩
mass-velocity relation[ship]	Masse-Geschwindigkeit-Beziehung f, Geschwindigkeit-Masse-Beziehung f
mass voltameter	s. weight coulometer
master clock	Hauptuhr f; Mutteruhr f
master curve	Leitkurve f, Leitbahn f
master equation	Mastergleichung f, „master equation" f
master-excited multivibrator	s. synchronized multivibrator
master frequency	Mutterfrequenz f
master gauge, standard gauge	Kontrollehre f, Normallehre f, Urlehre f, Paßlehre f, Prüflehre f
master handle ⟨of manipulator⟩	Steuergriff m, Betätigungsgriff m, Bedienungsgriff m ⟨Manipulator⟩
master potentiometer, standard potentiometer	Normalpotentiometer n; Normalkomparator m

master programme	Leitprogramm n, Hauptprogramm n
master pulse	Leitimpuls m, Hauptimpuls m, Steuerimpuls m, Masterimpuls m
master reaction	Schrittmacherreaktion f, Leitreaktion f, „master reaction" f
master-slave manipulator	Parallelmanipulator m, magische Hände fpl, „master-slave"-Manipulator m, Kopiermanipulator m
master sweep generator	s. wobbler
master telephone-transmission reference system	Ureichkreis m, SFERT
masurium, Ma	= technetium
mat, matte[d], frosted, dull, dim, ground	matt, glanzlos, trüb
matched junction	Verzweigung f mit Anpassung, angepaßte Verzweigung
matched termination, non-reflecting termination	reflexionsfreier Abschluß m
matching, fitting, adapting, equating <math.>	Anpassung f; Angleichung f
matching efficiency	Anpassungswirkungsgrad m
matching equivalent	s. standing wave ratio
matching for maximum current transfer, undermatching	Unteranpassung f
matching impedance	Anpassungswiderstand m, Anpassungsimpedanz f
matching stimulus, instrumental stimulus, primary	Meßvalenz f
matching stub	s. stub
material; matter; substance; mass	Stoff m; Werkstoff m; Substanz f; Material n; Masse f
material acceleration, substantial acceleration	substantielle Beschleunigung f
material balance	Stoffbilanz f, Materialbilanz f, Materialgleichgewicht n
material buckling	Materialbuckling n, materielle (materiell bestimmte) Flußwölbung f, Materialflußwölbung f, materielles Buckling n, Materiebuckling n, materieller Parameter m
material characteristic	s. material parameter
material constant, matter constant, constitutive constant	Materialkonstante f, Stoffkonstante f
material continuity equation	materielle Kontinuitätsgleichung f
material co-ordinates, substantial co-ordinates	substantielle (materielle, massenfeste, materialfeste) Koordinaten fpl
material curve	materielle Kurve f
material damping	s. mechanical hysteresis
material derivative, particle derivative, substantial derivative, Eulerian derivative, hydrodynamical derivative, derivative following the fluid, tota derivative	substantielle Ableitung f, Eulersche Ableitung f, materielle Ableitung, massenfeste Ableitung, materialfeste Ableitung
material discontinuity	substantielle Unstetigkeit f
material economy	Materialausnutzung f, Materialökonomie f
material field	materielles Feld n
material flow, flow of material	Werkstofffluß m
material for sound absorption	s. sound absorber
material [frame-]indifference principle, principle of material frame indifference	Unabhängigkeit f der Materialgleichungen vom Beobachter, Prinzip n der Bezugsindifferenz
material inventory	Materialeinsatz m
materialization	Materialisation f
material line	s. fluid line
material parameter, matter parameter, constitutive parameter, material characteristic	Materialparameter m, Stoffparameter m; Werkstoffkenngröße f, Werkstoffparameter m
material particle, corpuscle	Korpuskel n, Teilchen n, Materieteilchen n, Masseteilchen n
material pick-up, pick-up, material transfer, transfer	Werkstoffübertragung f, Übertragung f von Werkstoffen
material point, mass point, particle	Massenpunkt m, materieller Punkt m, Teilchen n <Mech.>
material separation	s. discontinuity <of material>
materials processing reactor	Werkstoffbestrahlungsreaktor m, Materialbestrahlungsreaktor m
materials testing, testing of materials, materiology	Werkstoffprüfung f, Materialprüfung f
materials testing reactor, testing reactor	Materialprüf[ungs]reaktor m, Prüfreaktor m
material surface	materielle Fläche f
material to be studied	s. material under investigation
material transfer	s. material pick-up
material transmitting pressure only	druckübertragender Stoff m, Füllstoff m, Flud m
material transmitting traction only	zugübertragender Stoff m, Hüllstoff m, Track m
material under investigation, material to be studied, experimental material	Untersuchungsmaterial n, Untersuchungssubstanz f
material under measurement (test)	Meßgut n
material volume	materielles Volumen n
material with memory	s. hereditary material
materiology	s. materials testing
mat finishing, frosting, mottling, matting <of glass>	Mattierung f <Gläser>
mat glass plate, focusing screen, groundglass screen, ground glass	Mattscheibe f
mathematical-astronomical geography	mathematisch-astronomische Geographie f
mathematical climatic zone, solar climatic zone	solare Klimazone f, mathematische Klimazone
mathematical expectation, expectation [value], expected value, expectancy, mean; mean of population, population mean <stat.>	[mathematischer] Erwartungswert m, mathematische Erwartung (Hoffnung) f, Mittelwert m, Durchschnitt m <Stat.>
mathematical horopter, geometric horopter	mathematischer (geometrischer) Horopter m
mathematical inversion, inversion [of the point]; inversion with respect to the circle (sphere) <math.>	Abbildung (Transformation) f durch reziproke Radien, Inversion f; Inversion (Spiegelung f) am Kreis; Inversion (Spiegelung) an der Kugel <Math.>
mathematical logic	mathematische Logik f
mathematical operation, operation <math.>	Operation f, Rechenoperation f <Math.>
mathematical pendulum, plane mathematical pendulum, simple pendulum	mathematisches Pendel n, Punktkörperpendel n
mathematical postulate of relativity of inertia	s. postulate of relativity of inertia
mathematical procedure, method of calculation	Rechengang m, Rechnungsgang m

mathematical 466

mathematical relationship; relation; relationship	Relation f; Beziehung f, Zusammenhang m	matter	Materie f
		matter; material; substance; mass	Stoff m; Werkstoff m; Substanz f; Material n; Masse f
mathematical rigor	mathematische Strenge f	matter constant, material constant, constitutive constant	Materialkonstante f, Stoffkonstante f
mathematical theory of communication, coding theory, information theory [of Shannon-Weaver]	mathematische Theorie f der Nachrichtenübertragung, Informationstheorie f [von Shannon-Weaver]		
		matter parameter	s. material parameter
		matter tensor	s. energy-momentum tensor
mathematization	Mathematisierung f	matter wave, de Broglie wave	Materiewelle f, De-Broglie-Welle f, de Brogliesche Welle f, De-Broglie-Materiewelle f
Mathiessen['s] rule	s. Matthiessen['s] rule		
Mathieu['s] canonical transformation	s. Mathieu transformation		
Mathieu['s] differential equation, Mathieu['s] equation	Mathieusche Differentialgleichung (Gleichung) f, Differentialgleichung der Funktionen des elliptischen Zylinders	matte surface	s. mat surface
		Matteucci effect	Matteucci-Effekt m
		Matthiessen['s] law	Matthießensches Gesetz n
		Matthiessen['s] rule	Matthießensche (Matthiessensche) Regel f; Matthießen-Nernstsche Regel
Mathieu['s] function	Mathieusche Funktion f, elliptische Zylinderfunktion f, Funktion des elliptischen Zylinders		
		matting	s. mat finishing <of glass>
Mathieu transformation, Mathieu['s] canonical transformation, canonical transformation of Mathieu	homogene (Mathieusche) kanonische Transformation f, homogene Berührungstransformation f	mattress antenna, mattress array of dipoles	Dipolebene f, Dipolwand f, Matratzenantenne f
		mattress reflector	Reflektorwand f
matrix	s, relief image <phot.>	mattress-type weathering, mattress weathering	Matratzenverwitterung f; Wollsackverwitterung f
matrix algebra; ring of matrices	Matrixalgebra f, Matrizenalgebra f; Matrixring m, Matrizenring m	maturing	s. ripening
		Maue['s] [integral] equations	Mauesche Integralgleichungen fpl
matrix calculus	Matrizenrechnung f, Matrizenkalkül m	Maupertuis action	s. Maupertuis['] principle
matrix element	Matrixelement n	Maupertuis['] principle [of least action], principle of least action [of Maupertuis), principle of Maupertuis, principle of the least action [of Maupertuis], Maupertuis action	[Euler-]Maupertuissches Prinzip n [der kleinsten Wirkung], [Euler-] Maupertuis-Prinzip n, Prinzip der kleinsten Wirkung [von Maupertuis], Prinzip von Maupertuis
matrixing	Matrizierung f		
matrix lattice, fundamental lattice, host [crystal] lattice, lattice	Grundgitter n, Wirtsgitter n		
matrix mechanics, Heisenberg['s] matrix mechanics, Heisenberg['s] quantum mechanics, Heisenberg mechanics	Matrizenmechanik f [von Heisenberg], Heisenbergsche Matrizenmechanik (Quantenmechanik) f, Heisenbergs Matrizenmechanik, quantenmechanische Methode f von Heisenberg		
		mavar, parametric (reactance) amplifier <mixer amplification by variable reactance>	parametrischer Verstärker m, Reaktanzverstärker m, Mavar m
		maximal	s. maximum
		maximizing	Maximierung f, Maximisierung f
matrix memory	s. magnetic matrix memory		
matrix notation	Matrizenschreibweise f, Matrixschreibweise f		
matrix of Coulomb scattering, Coulomb scattering matrix	Matrix f der Coulomb-Streuung, Coulomb-Streumatrix f	maximum; maximum value, maximal value	Maximum n; Maximalwert m, Höchstwert m
matrix of ladder network	s. iterative matrix		
matrix of matrices	s. hypermatrix	maximum, peak, line	Peak m, Linie f, [scharfes] Maximum n, Gipfel m; Berg m, Spitze f <Chromatographie>
matrix of the coefficients (system)	Koeffizientenmatrix f		
matrix of the transformation, transformation matrix	Transformationsmatrix f, Koeffizientenmatrix f der Transformation	maximum and minimum thermometer, Six's thermometer, maximum-minimum thermometer	Maximum-Minimum-Thermometer n, Maximum- und Minimumthermometer n
matrix operator	Matrixoperator m		
matrix product	Matrizenprodukt n	maximum boiling point	höchster (maximaler) Siedepunkt m, Maximalsiedepunkt m
matrix replica	Matrizenabdruck m		
matrix representation	Matrixdarstellung f <Operator>; Matrizendarstellung f <Ring>	maximum condition	Maximumbedingung f; Maximalbedingung f <Math.>
matrix storage	s. magnetic matrix memory	maximum corona	Maximumskorona f
matrix storage tube	Matrizenröhre f		
matrix store	s. magnetic matrix memory	maximum credible accident, MCA	größter anzunehmender Unfall m, GAU
mat surface, matte [surface] <opt.>	matte Oberfläche (Fläche) f <Opt.>	maximum deflection	maximale Ablenkung f, Ablenkweite f, Ablenkamplitude f
Mattauch-Herzog-type analyzer	Mattauch-Herzog-Analysator m, Analysator m vom Mattauch-Herzogschen Typ		
		maximum deflection, maximum deviation	maximaler Ausschlag m, Maximalausschlag m
		maximum deflection	s. a. sag
Mattauch-Herzog-type mass spectrograph	Massenspektrograph m vom Mattauch-Herzogschen Typ, Mattauch-Herzogscher Massenspektrograph, doppelfokussierender Massenspektrograph nach Mattauch-Herzog	maximum deviation	s. maximum deflection
		maximum deviation <control>	größte Regelabweichung f, Überschwing[ungs]weite f, maximale Nachstellung f <Regelung>
matte	s. mat surface		
matte[d]	s. mat	maximum direction finding, maximum technique of direction finding	Maximumpeilung f, Maximumpeilverfahren n
matted crystal, crystallite	Kristallit m		

maximum discharge	Maximalabfluß *m*	**maximum permissible body burden, M.P.B.B.**	maximal zulässige Körperbelastung *f*, MZKB
maximum discharge [in second-litre per square kilometre], maximum rate of runoff	höchste Hochwasserspende *f*		
maximum distance of clear vision, distance of punctum remotum	Fernpunktabstand *m* <vom Hornhautscheitel aus gemessen>	**maximum permissible concentration, M.P.C.**	maximal zulässige Konzentration *f*, höchstzulässige Konzentration, MZK
maximum distortion energy theory, theory of maximum strain energy due to distortion	Hypothese *f* der größten Gestaltänderungsarbeit	**maximum permissible current**	Strombelastbarkeit *f*
maximum energy of beta-ray spectrum, cut-off energy of beta spectrum	Grenzenergie *f* des Beta-Spektrums, Maximalenergie *f* des Beta-Spektrums	**maximum permissible dose,** maximum permissible level, M.P.D.	maximal zulässige Dosis (Strahlungsdosis, Strahlungsbelastung) *f*, maximale Strahlungsbelastung, höchstzulässige Dosis (Strahlungsdosis), MZD
maximum ergodic theorem, Kolmogoroff['s] ergodic theorem	maximaler Ergodensatz *m*, Ergodensatz von Kolmogorow		
maximum error	s. limit of error		
maximum fading	Schwundspitze *f*, Schwundmaximum *n*		
maximum freezing point	höchster (maximaler) Erstarrungspunkt *m*, Maximalerstarrungspunkt *m*	**maximum permissible dose equivalent, M.P.D.E.**	maximal zulässiges Dosisäquivalent *n*, MPDÄ
maximum frequency <of continuous X rays>	s. quantum limit	**maximum permissible flux density**	maximal zulässige Flußdichte *f*, maximale Flußdichte
maximum gust, peak gust	Spitzenbö *f*	**maximum permissible level**	s. maximum permissible dose
maximum height	Scheitelhöhe ; maximale Höhe *f*	**maximum permissible load,** maximum (peak) load, load limit (border), loading point <el.>	Höchstbelastung *f*, Höchstlast *f*, Höchstleistung *f*, Belastungsgrenze *f*, höchstzulässige Belastung *f* <El.>
maximum humidity [of air], saturation humidity	Sättigungsfeuchte *f*, maximale Luftfeuchtigkeit *f*		
maximum indication, maximum (peak) reading; peak indication	Maximumanzeige *f*	**maximum permissible organ content**	maximal zulässiger Organgehalt *m*
maximum indicator	s. peak-reading meter	**maximum permissible unbalance**	Schiefbelastbarkeit *f*
maximum induced shear stress, maximum intensity of shear	Grenzschubspannung *f*		
maximum likelihood	Maximum „likelihood" *f*, maximale Stichprobenwahrscheinlichkeit *f*	**maximum phase angle deviation,** phase deviation	Phasenhub *m*
		maximum pressure, pressure maximum	Druckmaximum *n*, Druckberg *m*; Höchstdruck *m*, Maximaldruck *m*
maximum likelihood estimator	Maximum-Likelihood-Schätzung *f*, plausibelste Schätzung *f*	**maximum principal stress theory**	s. maximum stress theory
maximum likelihood method, method of maximum likelihood	Maximum „likelihood"-Methode *f*, Maximum-Likelihood-Methode *f*, Maximal[e]-Stichprobenwahrscheinlichkeitsmethode *f*, Methode *f* der maximalen Stichprobenwahrscheinlichkeit	**maximum principle,** principle of the maximum; maximum-modulus principle	Maximumprinzip *n*; Prinzip *n* vom Maximum, Satz *m* vom Maximum
		maximum rate of runoff, maximum discharge [in second-litre per square kilometre]	höchste Hochwasserspende *f*
maximum load	s. maximum permissible load	**maximum reading,** peak reading; maximum (peak) indication	Maximumanzeige *f*
maximum-minimum thermometer, Six's thermometer, maximum and minimum thermometer	Maximum-Minimum-Thermometer *n*, Maximum- und Minimumthermometer *n*	**maximum retention time**	s. storage time <num.math.>
		maximum retentivity	maximal erreichbare Remanenz *f*
maximum-modulus principle	s. maximum principle	**maximum scale value,** end scale value, rating	Meßbereichsendwert *m*, Meßbereichendwert *m*
maximum normal stress theory, maximum [principal] stress theory	Hypothese *f* der größten Normalspannung	**maximum shearing stress**	maximale Schubspannung *f*
maximum observation	s. pure case	**maximum shearing stress condition,** maximum shearing-stress yield condition (criterion)	s. St. Venant-Tresca yield condition
maximum of atmospheric pressure	s. High		
maximum overshoot	Überschwingweite *f*, Überschwingungsweite *f*		
		maximum shear theory	s. Guest['s] theory
		maximum strain energy theory, strain energy theory	Hypothese *f* der größten Formänderungsarbeit
maximum permeability	Maximalpermeabilität *f*, maximale Permeabilität *f*	**maximum strain theory**	s. St. Venant['s] theory
maximum permissible alternating-current voltage	Stehspannung *f*	**maximum stress theory,** Rankine['s] theory	Theorie *f* der Maximalbelastung, Theorie von Rankine, Rankinesche Theorie
		maximum stress theory, maximum principal (normal) stress theory	Hypothese *f* der größten Normalspannung
maximum permissible amount, M.P.A.	maximal zulässige Menge *f*, höchstzulässige Menge, MZM	**maximum technique of direction finding,** maximum direction finding	Maximumpeilung *f*, Maximumpeilverfahren *n*

maximum thermometer	Maximumthermometer n	Maxwell element, Maxwellian element	Maxwell-Element n
maximum thrust	Maximalschub m, Grenzschubkraft f	Maxwell['s] energy-stress tensor	Maxwellscher Energie-Spannungs-Tensor m, Energie-Spannungs-Tensor von Maxwell
maximum torque, tilting moment, overturning moment	Kippmoment n		
		Maxwell equation [for refractive index]	s. Maxwell relation
maximum transferable energy	maximal übertragbare Energie f	Maxwell['s] equations, Maxwell['s] relations <el.>	Maxwellsche Gleichungen fpl <El.>
maximum turning value	s. relative maximum	Maxwell['s] equations, Maxwell['s] relations, reciprocal relations <therm.>	Maxwellsche Beziehungen fpl, Maxwellsche Relationen fpl <Therm.>
maximum usable frequency, MUF	maximale [brauchbare] Übertragungsfrequenz f, höchste benutzbare Frequenz f, MUF		
maximum value	s. maximum	Maxwell['s] equilibrium distribution [law]	s. Maxwellian distribution
maximum with constraints	Maximum n mit Nebenbedingungen	Maxwell field, Maxwellian field	Maxwell-Feld n, Maxwellsches Feld n
maximum work, maximal work	maximale Arbeit f, Maximalarbeit f	Maxwell['s] fisheye, fisheye	[Maxwellsches] Fischauge n
maximum work function	s. free energy	Maxwell formula <bio.>	Maxwellsche Gleichung f <Bio.>
maximum work principle, principle of maximum work	Prinzip n der maximalen Arbeit	Maxwellian cross-section	thermischer Neutronenquerschnitt m bei Maxwell-Verteilung der Energie
maxwell, M, Mx <= 10^{-8} Wb = 10^{-8} Vsec>	Maxwell n, M, Mx <= 10^{-8} Wb = 10^{-8} Vs>		
Maxwell and Betti reciprocity theorem	s. Betti['s] reciprocal theorem	Maxwellian disk	s. Maxwell['s] disk
Maxwell birefringence	s. double refraction in flow	Maxwellian distribution, Maxwell['s] distribution [of velocities], Maxwell-Boltzmann distribution [law], Maxwell['s] equilibrium distribution [law], Maxwell['s] velocity distribution [law], Maxwellian equilibrium distribution, Maxwell['s] distribution law, Maxwell-Boltzmann law, Maxwell law, Maxwell['s] distribution function, Maxwellian velocity distribution	Maxwell-Verteilung f, Maxwellsche Verteilung (Geschwindigkeitsverteilung, Gleichgewichtsverteilung) f, Maxwell-Boltzmann-Verteilung f, Maxwell-Boltzmannsche Verteilung, Maxwell[-Boltzmann]sche Verteilungsfuntion, Maxwell[Boltzmann]sches Verteilungsgesetz, Maxwellsches Geschwindigkeitsverteilungsgesetz n
Maxwell body, Maxwell solid (material), M-body	Maxwellscher Körper m, M-Körper m		
Maxwell-Boltzmann distribution [law]	s. Maxwellian distribution		
Maxwell-Boltzmann distribution law	s. a. Boltzmann distribution		
Maxwell-Boltzmann equation	s. Boltzmann['s] equation		
Maxwell-Boltzmann law	s. Maxwellian distribution		
Maxwell-Boltzmann law of energy distribution	Maxwell-Boltzmannsches Gesetz n der Energieverteilung		
Maxwell-Boltzmann statistics, Boltzmann statistics, classical [Boltzmann] statistics	[Maxwell-]Boltzmann-Statistik f, klassische Statistik f [Boltzmanns]		
		Maxwellian elastico-viscous liquid, Maxwellian fluid	Maxwell-Flüssigkeit f, Maxwellsche Flüssigkeit f
Maxwell-Boltzmann transport equation	s. Boltzmann['s] transport equation	Maxwellian element	s. Maxwell element
Maxwell-Boltzmann velocity distribution law, M.B. law	Geschwindigkeitsverteilungsgesetz (Verteilungsgesetz) n von Maxwell-Boltzmann, Maxwell-Boltzmannsches Verteilungsgesetz n	Maxwellian equilibrium distribution	s. Maxwellian distribution
		Maxwellian field	s. Maxwell field
		Maxwellian fluid, Maxwellian elastico-viscous liquid	Maxwell-Flüssigkeit f, Maxwellsche Flüssigkeit f
Maxwell bridge	Maxwell-Brücke f, Maxwellsche Brücke (Meßbrücke) f, Maxwell-Meßbrücke f		
		Maxwellian function	Maxwellsche Funktion f
		Maxwellian gas	Maxwell-Gas n, Maxwellsches Gas n
Maxwell['s] colour triangle	Maxwell-Helmholtzsches Farbendreieck (Farbdreieck, Dreieck) n, Newtonsches (Maxwellsches) Dreieck	Maxwellian molecule	Maxwellsches Molekül n, Maxwell-Molekül n
		Maxwellian relaxation time	Maxwellsche Relaxationszeit f
Maxwell['s] constant	Maxwell-Konstante f, Maxwellsche Konstante f	Maxwellian stress, Maxwell['s] stress	Maxwellsche Spannung f, Faraday-Maxwellsche Spannung
Maxwell['s] construction [of streamlines]	Maxwellsche Konstruktion f [der Stromlinien]		
Maxwell['s] demon	Maxwellscher Dämon m, Dämon von Maxwell	Maxwellian stress tensor	s. Maxwell['s] stress tensor
		Maxwellian velocity distribution	s. Maxwellian distribution
Maxwell['s] diagonal method	Maxwellsche Diagonalmethode f, Maxwellsches Diagonalverfahren n	Maxwellian view <in optical instruments>	Maxwellsche Beobachtung (Beobachtungsmethode, Methode) f <Opt.>
Maxwell diagram	s. force diagram		
Maxwell['s] disk, Maxwellian disk, Newton['s] chromatometer (colour circle, [colour] disk), colour disk	Farb[en]kreisel m, Ostwaldscher Farbenkreisel f, Farbenscheibe f, Maxwellsche Scheibe f, [Newtonsches] Chromatometer n	maxwellization	Maxwellisierung f
		Maxwell law	s. Maxwellian distribution
		Maxwell['s] law of viscosity	Maxwellsches Viskositätsgesetz n, Viskositätsgesetz von Maxwell
Maxwell['s] distribution [function], Maxwell['s] distribution law	s. Maxwellian distribution	Maxwell-Lorentz equations	Maxwell-Lorentzsche Gleichungen fpl, Maxwell-Lorentzsches Gleichungssystem n
Maxwell effect	s. double refraction in flow	Maxwell-Lorentz theory	Maxwell-Lorentzsche Theorie f
Maxwell-Einstein equations	Einstein-Maxwellsche Feldgleichungen fpl, Maxwell-Einsteinsche Feldgleichungen (Gleichungen) fpl		
		Maxwell material	s. Maxwell body
		maxwellmeter	s. flux[] meter
Maxwell-Einstein theory, Einstein-Maxwell theory	Einstein-Maxwellsche Theorie f, Maxwell-Einsteinsche Theorie	Maxwell-Minkowski equation	Maxwell-Minkowskische Differentialgleichung f

Maxwell['s] model, Maxwell['s] relaxation model	Maxwellsches Relaxationsmodell n, Maxwellsches Modell n	**McLeod gauge, McLeod pressure gauge**, compression gauge, compression manometer	McLeodsches Manometer (Vakuummeter) n, McLeod[-Manometer] n, [Mc]Leod-Vakuummeter n, Kompressionsmanometer n [nach McLeod], Leod-Vakuummeter n
Maxwell['s] problem	Maxwellsches Problem n		
Maxwell['s] reciprocal theorem, Maxwell['s] theorem	Satz m von der Gegenseitigkeit der Verschiebung[en], Maxwellscher Reziprozitätssatz m		
		McNally tube	s. klystron
Maxwell relation [between dielectric constant and index of refraction], Clerk Maxwell relation, Maxwell equation [for refractive index] <opt.>	Maxwellsche Beziehung f, Maxwellsche Relation f <Opt.>	**McQuaid-Ehn size**, Ehn size	McQuaid-Ehn-Korngröße f, Ehn-Korngröße f, arteigene Korngröße f
		M-discontinuity	s. Mohorovičić discontinuity
		Meacham oscillator	Meacham-Generator m, Meacham-Oszillator m
		mean, mean value, average value, average	Mittelwert m, Mittel n
Maxwell['s] relations, Maxwell['s] [thermodynamic] equations, reciprocal relations <therm.>	Maxwellsche Beziehungen fpl, Maxwellsche Relationen fpl <Therm.>	**mean**	s. a. mathematical expectation.
		mean	s. a. sample mean <stat.>
		mean acceleration [vector]	Vektor m der mittleren Beschleunigung, mittlere Beschleunigung f
Maxwell relaxation equation	Maxwellsche Relaxationsgleichung f		
Maxwell['s] relaxation model, Maxwell['s] model	Maxwellsches Relaxationsmodell n, Maxwellsches Modell n	**mean activity** <nucl.; of electrolyte>	mittlere Aktivität f <Kern.; Elektrolyt>; mittlere Ionenaktivität f <Elektrolyt>
Maxwell['s] rule, Maxwell['s] theorem [for isotherms] <therm.>	Maxwellsche Regel f, Maxwellsches Kriterium n <Therm.>	**mean activity coefficient**	mittlerer Ionenaktivitätskoeffizient (Aktivitätskoeffizient) m
Maxwell solid, Maxwell body (material), M-body	Maxwellscher Körper m, M-Körper m	**mean aerodynamic chord**	s. reference chord
Maxwell['s] stress	s. Maxwellian stress	**mean air temperature**, mean temperature of air	mittlere Lufttemperatur f
Maxwell['s] stress tensor, Maxwellian stress tensor	Maxwellscher Spannungstensor m	**mean angular motion**	s. mean motion <astr., mech.>
		mean annual discharge	s. mean annual runoff
Maxwell['s] theorem	s. Maxwell['s] reciprocal theorem	**mean annual runoff**, normal annual runoff, mean (normal) annual discharge	mittlerer Jahresabfluß m, mittlerer jährlicher Abfluß m
Maxwell['s] theorem [for isotherms]	s. a. Maxwell['s] rule <therm.>		
Maxwell['s] theorems in geometric optics	Maxwellsche Sätze mpl der geometrischen Optik	**mean approximation**	Approximation f im Mittel
Maxwell['s] theory	Maxwellsche Theorie f, Maxwell-Hertzsche Theorie	**mean binding energy per nucleon**	s. binding fraction
		mean camber, camber <of the wing>	Flügelwölbung f, Wölbung f des Tragflügels, Wölbungspfeil m des Tragflügels
Maxwell['s] theory of light	s. electromagnetic theory of light		
Maxwell['s] thermodynamic equations	s. Maxwell['s] relations <therm.>	**mean camber line**	s. skeleton line
		mean chain life	mittlere Kettenlebensdauer f
Maxwell turn, line-turn	Maxwellwindung f, Mxw	**mean charge density**	s. mean density of charge
Maxwell['s] velocity distribution [law]	s. Maxwellian distribution	**mean collision frequency**	mittlere Stoßhäufigkeit (Stoßzahl f pro Zeiteinheit)
Maxwell-Wagner polarization	s. interfacial polarization	**mean collision number**	mittlere Stoßzahl f
Maxwell-Wien bridge	Maxwell-Wien-Brücke f, Maxwell-Wiensche Brücke (Meßbrücke) f		
		mean collision time, mean free time	mittlere Stoßzeit f (freie Zeit f, Zeit zwischen zwei Stößen)
mayer	Mayer n		
Mayer-Bogolyoubov['s] equation [of state]	Mayer-Bogoljubowsche Gleichung (Zustandsgleichung) f	**mean cosmic abundance of elements**	mittlere kosmische Elementenhäufigkeit f
Mayer['s] equation, relation of J. R. Mayer, equation of Robert Mayer	Gleichung f von J. R. Mayer, Beziehung f von Robert Mayer, Mayersche Beziehung	**mean curvature [of surface]**, mean normal curvature, circular (first) curvature	mittlere Krümmung f, mittlere Flächenkrümmung f
Mayer['s] theory of condensation	Mayersche Kondensationstheorie f, Kondensationstheorie von J. R. Mayer	**mean density of charge**, average density of charge, mean (average) charge density	mittlere Ladungsdichte f
maze	s. radiation maze		
Maze counter [tube], Maze tube counter, external cathode counter [tube]	Maze-Zählrohr n, Zählrohr n mit Außenkatode	**meander**, loop of the river	Mäander m, Flußschleife f
M band <10 – 15 Gc/s>	M-Band n <10 ··· 15 GHz>	**meandering**	Mäandrierung f
M.B. law	s. Maxwell-Boltzmann velocity distribution law		
		meandering river	mäandrierender Fluß m
M-body, Maxwell body, Maxwell solid (material)	Maxwellscher Körper m, M-Körper m	**meander pattern**	Mäandermuster n
		meander profile	Mäanderprofil n
M-carcinotron, M-type carcinotron, M-type backward wave tube	Carcinotron n vom M-Typ, Rückwärtswellen-Magnetfeldröhre f, M-Typ-Rückwärtswellenröhre f, Rückwärtswellenröhre f vom M-Typ	**mean deviation**, average deviation	durchschnittliche (mittlere) Abweichung f
		mean differential cross-section [of the reaction]	mittlerer differentieller Wirkungsquerschnitt m [der Reaktion]
		mean diffusion path	s. diffusion mean free path
McBain-Bakr quartz spring balance, quartz spring balance	Quarzfederwaage f	**mean dispersion** <of glass>	Grunddispersion f, mittlere Dispersion f <Glas>
McBain sorption balance	McBainsche Sorptionswaage f		
		mean distance, semimajor axis [of orbit] <element of orbit>	große Halbachse f <Bahnelement>
Mcdonald['s] function	s. Macdonald['s] function		
McIntosh effect	McIntosh-Effekt m		
McLeod['s] equation	McLeodsche Gleichung (Regel) f	**mean distance between levels**	s. mean level spacing

mean diurnal motion	mittlere tägliche Bewegung (Bahnbewegung) f
mean eccentric anomaly	mittlere exzentrische Anomalie f
mean effective value, mean square value, root-mean-square value, r.m.s. value <el.>	Effektivwert m, quadratischer Mittelwert m <der Wechselgröße> <El.>
mean element of orbit, mean (average) orbital element, average element of orbit	mittleres Bahnelement n
mean energy decrement, average energy decrement, average decrement of energy	mittlerer Energieverlust m, mittleres Energiedekrement n
mean energy expended per ion pair formed	s. average energy expended in the gas per ion pair formed
mean error, average error	durchschnittlicher (einfacher mittlerer) Fehler m
mean error	s. a. root-mean-square error
mean free path	mittlere freie Weglänge f
mean free path for absorption, absorption mean free path	[mittlere freie] Absorptionsweglänge f, mittlere freie Weglänge f für Absorption
mean free path for attenuation	s. attenuation mean free path
mean free path for capture	s. capture mean free path
mean free path for collision, collision mean free path	[mittlere freie] Stoßweglänge f, mittlere freie Weglänge f für Stoß, Stoßlänge f
mean free path for diffusion	s. diffusion mean free path
mean free path for fission, fission mean free path	[mittlere freie] Spaltweglänge f, [mittlere freie] Spaltungsweglänge f, mittlere freie Weglänge f für Spaltung
mean free path for interaction	s. interaction mean free path
mean free path for ionization	s. ionization mean free path
mean free path for recoil, recoil mean free path	[mittlere freie] Rückstoßweglänge f, Rückstoßlänge f, mittlere freie Weglänge f für Rückstoß
mean free path for scattering, scattering mean free path	[mittlere freie] Streuweglänge f, mittlere freie Weglänge f für Streuung, mittlerer Streuweg m
mean free path for transport	s. transport mean free path
mean free path of low energy electrons moving through a gas, Ramsauer-Townsend collision free path	mittlere freie Weglänge f langsamer Elektronen im Gas
mean free path of the ion, ionic mean free path	mittlere freie Weglänge f des Ions
mean free time, mean collision time	mittlere Stoßzeit f (freie Zeit f, Zeit f zwischen zwei Stößen)
mean free time of flight, mean free transit time	mittlere freie Flugzeit f
mean geodesic curvature	mittlere geodätische Krümmung f
mean hemispherical candle power, mean hemispherical intensity	mittlere hemisphärische (halbräumliche) Lichtstärke f
mean high tide, mean high-tide level	mittleres Hochwasser n, Mittelhochwasser n
mean horizontal candle power, mean horizontal intensity, horizontal intensity (candle power)	mittlere horizontale Lichtstärke f, horizontale Lichtstärke <Opt.>
mean horizontal intensity, horizontal intensity (geomagnetic field strength), magnetic horizontal intensity	[mittlere] Horizontalintensität f <Geo.>
mean hydraulic depth	s. hydraulic radius
meaningful	sinnvoll, vernünftig
meaningful significant figure	s. significant digit
meaningless	sinnlos
mean integral cross-section [of the reaction]	mittlerer integraler Wirkungsquerschnitt m [der Reaktion]
mean internuclear separation (spacing)	mittlerer Kernabstand m
mean ionization energy, average ionization energy	mittlere Ionisierungsenergie f, mittlere Ionisationsenergie f
mean level distance, mean level spacing, mean distance between levels	mittlerer Niveauabstand m; mittlerer Termabstand m
mean life, mean lifetime, average life[time]	mittlere Lebensdauer f
mean life of the neutron	s. neutron lifetime
mean lifetime, mean life, average life, average lifetime	mittlere Lebensdauer f
mean line, bisectrix <pl.: -ices>, bisector <crystal optics>	Bisektrix f, Mittellinie f <Kristalloptik>
mean line of the profile	s. skeleton line
mean logarithmic energy decrement (loss)	s. average logarithmic energy decrement
mean longitude at zero epoch, zero epoch mean longitude	mittlere Länge f zur Epoche Null
mean lower hemispherical candle power, mean lower hemispherical intensity	mittlere untere hemisphärische (halbräumliche) Lichtstärke f
mean low tide, mean low-tide level	mittleres Niedrigwasser n, Mittelniedrigwasser n
mean mass velocity	s. barycentric velocity
mean mean longitude	mittlere mittlere Länge f
mean molar (molecular) quantity, molar quantity <of mixture> <therm.>	mittlere molare Größe f, molare Größe <Mischung> <Therm.>
mean motion, mean angular motion <astr., mech.>	mittlere Bewegung (Bahnbewegung, Winkelgeschwindigkeit) f <Astr., Mech.>
mean motion <hydr.>	mittlere Bewegung f, Hauptbewegung f <Hydr.>
mean neutron yield per fission	s. neutron yield per fission
mean noon	mittlerer Mittag m
mean normal curvature, mean curvature [of surface], circular (first) curvature	mittlere Krümmung f, mittlere Flächenkrümmung f
mean number of neutrons per absorption	s. neutron yield per absorption
mean number of neutrons per fission	s. neutron yield per fission
mean of population	
mean of sample, sample mean, mean <stat.>	Stichprobenmittel[wert m] n, Mittelwert m der Stichprobe, empirischer Mittelwert, Mittel n <Stat.>
mean orbital element, mean (average) element of orbit, average orbital element	mittleres Bahnelement n
mean path length of light	mittlere Reichweite f des Lichtes
mean place [of the star], mean position [of the star], mean star place (position)	mittlerer Ort m [des Gestirns], mittlerer Sternort m
mean power of the pulse, mean pulse power, average output of the pulse, average pulse output	Impulsdurchschnittsleistung f, Durchschnittsleistung f der Impulsschwingung, [mittlere] Impulsleistung f
mean range	mittlere Reichweite f
mean range of tide	mittlerer Gezeitenhub m, mittlerer Tidenhub m

mean refraction	mittlere Refraktion f	mean variability, average variability	mittlere Veränderlichkeit f
mean roughness	mittlere Rauheit f, mittlere Rauhigkeit[shöhe] f	mean velocity [vector]	Vektor m der mittleren Geschwindigkeit; mittlere Geschwindigkeit f
mean-sea-level, mean sea level, sea level, [elevation]	[mittlere] Meereshöhe f, [mittleres] Meeresniveau n, [mittlerer] Meeresspiegel m; Normalnull n, Normalnullpunkt m, N.N., NN	measurable <math.>; mensurable <geometry>	meßbar <Math.>
		measurable set	meßbare Menge f
		measurable variable, measurand, quantity to be measured	Meßgröße f, zu messende Größe f
mean sidereal day, average sidereal day	mittlerer Sterntag m	measure; solid measure	Maß n; körperliches Maß n, Maßverkörperung f
mean sidereal time, uniform sidereal time	mittlere Sternzeit f	measure, numerical measure, coefficient of measure, numerical value	Zahlenwert m, Maßzahl f, numerischer Wert m
mean solar day, average solar day	mittlerer Sonnentag m		
mean solar second	mittlere Sonnensekunde f		
mean solar time	mittlere Sonnenzeit f	measure, time <ac.>	Takt m, Zeitmaß n <Ak.>
mean spherical candle power, mean spherical intensity	mittlere sphärische (räumliche) Lichtstärke f	measure analysis	s. volumetric analysis
		measured quantity, quantity measured	gemessene Größe f, Meßgröße f
mean square	mittleres Quadrat n	measured result	s. result of measurement
		measured value	s. experimental value
mean square [deviation]	mittleres Abweichungsquadrad n, MQ	measure expansion	s. cubic[al] expansion <therm.>
mean square distance, root-mean-square distance	mittlerer quadratischer Abstand m, quadratisch gemittelter Abstand	measure formula, dimensional formula	Dimensionszeichen n, Dimensionsformel f, Dimensionssymbol n, Dimensionsausdruck m
mean square error	s. root-mean-square error		
mean square fluctuation	mittleres Schwankungsquadrat n		
mean square of distance	mittleres Abstandsquadrat n	measurement, measuring; metering; taking off	Messung f; Ausmessung f; Vermessung f; experimentelle Bestimmung f
mean square of velocity	mittleres Geschwindigkeitsquadrat n	measurement accuracy	s. accuracy of (in) measurement
mean square sound pressure	s. root-mean-square sound pressure	measurement amplifier	Meßverstärker m
mean square value, mean effective value, root-mean-square value, r.m.s. value <el.>	Effektivwert m, quadratischer Mittelwert m <der Wechselgröße> <El.>	measuring (test) amplifier, phantom repeater	
		measurement device; measuring device, measurement (measuring) system; measuring set-up	Meßeinrichtung f; Meßanordnung f; Meßvorrichtung f
mean square velocity	s. root-mean-square velocity		
mean star place (position), mean place [of the star], mean position [of the star]	mittlerer Ort m [des Gestirns], mittlerer Sternort m	measurement equipment	s. measuring equipment
		measurement inaccuracy, inaccuracy of measurement, measuring inaccuracy	Meßunsicherheit f
mean Sun	s. dynamic mean Sun		
mean temperature difference, MTD	mittlerer Temperaturunterschied m, mittlere Temperaturdifferenz f		
		measurement method	s. method of measurement
		measurement of altitude	s. hypsometry
mean temperature of air, mean air temperature	mittlere Lufttemperatur f	measurement of area, area (surface) measurement; planimetering, planimetration	Planimetrierung f; Flächen[aus]messung f
mean temperature of the day, diurnal mean of temperature, daily mean value of temperature	Tagesmitteltemperatur f, mittlere Tagestemperatur f		
		measurement of atmospheric pressure, barometry	Luftdruckmessung f, Barometrie f
mean-term forecast (prediction), medium-term forecast (prediction)	mittelfristige Vorhersage f, Mittelfristprognose f	measurement of bearing and distance to centre	Ablotung f
mean terrestrial ellipsoid	s. earth ellipsoid	measurement of density, densimetry, density measurement	Dichtebestimmung f, Dichtemessung f, Densimetrie f
mean tide, mean tide level, half-tide level	Tidemittelwasser n, mittleres Hochwasser n, Tidehalbwasser n, Mittelwasser n	measurement of depth, depth measurement (finding) <in ultrasonics>	Tiefenmessung f, Tiefenlotung f, Dickenmessung f, Abstandmessung f, Entfernungsmessung f <Ultraschalltechnik>
mean time between failures, m.t.b.f., MTBF	mittlere Lebensdauer f [des Bauteils], MTBF-Zeit f		
mean-type star	Stern m vom mittleren Spektraltyp, mittlerer Typ m	measurement of dewpoint	Taupunktsbestimmung f
		measurement of dielectric constant, dielectrometry, measurement of permittivity	DK-Metrie f, Dielektrometrie f, Dekametrie f
mean upper hemispherical candle power, mean upper hemispherical intensity	mittlere obere halbräumliche Lichtstärke f, mittlere obere hemisphärische Lichtstärke f		
		measurement of distance <passed through>	Wegmessung f
mean value	s. mean		
mean value of the scale, scale mean value	Skalenmittelwert m	measurement of distance	s. a. range finding
mean value theorem, law of the mean, law of averages	Mittelwertsatz m	measurement of elevation, angle of elevation measurement	Vertikalwinkelmessung f, Höhenwinkelmessung f
mean value theorem, law of the mean <of the differential calculus>	erster Mittelwertsatz m [der Differentialrechnung], Mittelwertsatz der Differentialrechnung	measurement of focal length, focometry	Fokometrie f, Brennweitenmessung f
		measurement of height	s. hypsometry

measurement 472

measurement of length, length (linear) measurement, length measuring, longimetry, determination of length — Längenmessung *f*, Längenbestimmung *f*

measurement of lengths — Streckenmessung *f*

measurement of loudness, loudness measurement — Lautstärkemessung *f*

measurement of moisture content — s. moisture-content determination

measurement of nuclear induction (resonance absorption) — s. nuclear magnetic resonance measurement

measurement of permittivity — s. measurement of dielectric constant

measurement of rock magnetism — Petromagnetik *f*

measurement of surface finish — Oberflächenprüfung *f*, Oberflächenprüfverfahren *n*

measurement of the first kind — Messung *f* erster Art

measurement of the second kind — Messung *f* zweiter Art

measurement of time, time measurement, timing, chronometry; time[-]keeping — Zeitmessung *f*, Chronometrie *f*; Zeitnahme *f*; Aufnahme *f* von Zeitmarken

measurement of turbidity, turbidimetry — Trübungsmessung *f*, Turbidimetrie *f*

measurement of volume — Volum[en]messung *f*, Raummessung *f*

measurement precision — s. accuracy of measurement

measurement process, process of measurement, measuring process — Meßprozeß *m*, Meßvorgang *m*

measurement range — s. measuring range

measurement result — s. result of measurement

measurements for comparison — s. comparative measurements

measurement system, measuring (measurement) device, measuring system; measuring set-up — Meßeinrichtung *f*; Meßanordnung *f*; Meßvorrichtung *f*

measurement technique — s. method of measurement

measurement transmitter, measuring (test) transmitter; [standard-]signal oscillator; [standard-]signal generator, measuring generator, test oscillator — Meßsender *m*; Meßgenerator *m*; Meßoszillator *m*

measurement weir, measuring weir, notched weir, weir — Meßüberfall *m*, Meßwehr *n*, Wehr *n*

measure of area, square measure — Flächenmaß *n*

measure of capacity — s. capacity measure

measure of dispersion — Streuungsmaß *n*, Variabilitätsmaß *n*

measure of distortion — Verzerrungsmaß *n* <El.>

measure of location — Maßzahl *f* der Lage

measure of skewness — Schiefheitsmaß *n*

measure of strain, strain measure, deformation measure <mech.> — Verzerrungsmaß *n*, Verformungsmaß *n*, Formänderungsmaß *n* <Mech.>

measure of turbidity, turbidity measure, turbidity parameter — Trübungsmaß *n*

measure preserving <math.> — maßtreu <Math.>

measurer — s. measuring instrument

measure theory — Maßtheorie *f*

measuring — s. measurement

measuring amplifier, measurement (test) amplifier, phantom repeater — Meßverstärker *m*

measuring apparatus — s. measuring instrument

measuring arrangement, arrangement (array) for measuring — Meßanordnung *f*

measuring assembly, radiation measuring assembly; radiation meter, radiometric instrument, radiation [measuring] instrument, radiometer — Meßplatz *m*, Strahlungsmeßplatz *m*, Kernstrahlungsmeßplatz *m*; Strahlungsmeßgerät *n*, Kernstrahlungsmeßgerät *n*, Strahlungsmesser *m*

measuring bead — Meßperle *f*

measuring bridge with glow indicator tube — Glimmbrücke *f*, Glimmmeßbrücke *f*

measuring bridge with telephone, telephone bridge — Telephonmeßbrücke *f*, Telephonbrücke *f*

measuring capsule, meter box, measuring cell — Meßdose *f*

measuring cascade <el.> — Meßkette *f* <El.>

measuring cell, meter box, measuring capsule — Meßdose *f*

measuring chain, land chain, surveyor's chain, column <geo.> — Meßkette *f* <Geo.>

measuring channel — Meßkanal *m*

measuring circuit — Meßschaltung *f*

measuring coil, search coil — Meßspule *f*, Suchspule *f*, Prüfspule *f*

measuring device, measurement device; measurement (measuring) system; measuring set-up — Meßeinrichtung *f*; Meßanordnung *f*; Meßvorrichtung *f*

measuring electrode, test electrode — Meßelektrode *f*

measuring equipment, measurement equipment, metering equipment, instrumentation — Meßplatz *m*; Meßausrüstung *f*, Meßapparatur *f*; Instrumentierung *f*, instrumentelle Ausrüstung *f*; Instrumentarium *n*

measuring error of the first <second> order, error of the first <second> order — Meßfehler *m* erster <zweiter> Ordnung

measuring eyepiece — Meßokular *n*

measuring gap; measuring slit — Meßspalt *m*

measuring generator — s. measurement transmitter

measuring head, [sensing] head, instrument (gauge, probe) head; [measuring] probe, instrument (gauge, sensing) probe — Meßkopf *m*, Kopf *m* des Meßgerätes; Meßsonde *f*, Sonde *f* [des Meßgeräts]

measuring inaccuracy, inaccuracy of measurement, measurement inaccuracy — Meßunsicherheit *f*

measuring instrument, measuring apparatus, measurer, meter; gauge, gage — Meßgerät *n*, Meßinstrument *n*, Messer *m*, Meßapparat *m*

measuring instrument constant — s. constant of the measuring instrument

measuring instrument employing vacuum tubes, vacuum-tube measuring instrument — Röhrenmeßgerät *n*, Röhrengerät *n*

measuring instrument error — s. instrumental error <e.g. of theodolite>

measuring jaw — Meßschnabel *m*, Meßschenkel *m*

measuring junction <of thermocouple>; point of measurement, measuring point; control point — Meßstelle *f*, Meßort *m*, Meßpunkt *m*

measuring loop — s. test loop

measuring machine — Meßmaschine *f*

measuring magnifier, precision magnifier, scale magnifying glass — Feinmeßlupe *f*, Meßlupe *f*

measuring mark, collimating mark, sighting mark, sight graticule, target <opt.> — Zielmarke *f*, Abkommen *n*, Absehen *n* <Opt.>

measuring method — s. method of measurement

measuring microscope, travelling microscope — Meßmikroskop *n*; Feinmeßmikroskop *n*

measuring nozzle, tuyere — Meßdüse *f*

measuring oscillograph, measuring oscilloscope — Meßoszillograph *m*, Meßoszilloskop *n*

measuring peak — Meßspitze *f*; Meßkuppe *f*

measuring point, point of measurement; control point; measuring junction — Meßstelle *f*, Meßort *m*, Meßpunkt *m*

measuring point	s. a. experimental point <e.g. in a diagram>	mechanical equilibrium, hydrostatic equilibrium	mechanisches (hydrostatisches) Gleichgewicht n
measuring point	s. a. measuring station	mechanical equivalent of heat	mechanisches (mechanisch-elektrisches) Wärmeäquivalent n, mechanischer Wärmewert m
measuring potentiometer	Meßpotentiometer n		
measuring probe	s. measuring head	mechanical equivalent of light, mechanical light equivalent	mechanisches Lichtäquivalent n, energetisches Lichtäquivalent
measuring procedure	s. method of measurement		
measuring process, process of measurement, measurement process	Meßprozeß m, Meßvorgang m	mechanical evaluation; machine evaluation	Maschinenauswertung f
measuring pulse	s. test pulse		
measuring range	s. effective range [of instrument]	mechanical flattening	mechanische Abplattung f
measuring room, test room, testing room, testing floor	Meßraum m, Meßzimmer n	mechanical hysteresis [effect], attenuation (damping capacity) of the material, material damping	Werkstoffdämpfung f
measuring rule, comparing rule, rule	Maßstab m, Maßstablineal n	mechanical impedance	mechanische Impedanz (Schallimpedanz) f, mechanischer Widerstand (Scheinwiderstand) m
measuring set-up	s. measuring device		
measuring slit; measuring gap	Meßspalt m	mechanical kinematics, theory of linkages	Zwang[s]laufiehre f, Getriebelehre f, Theorie f der Getriebe
measuring spectrum projector	Spektrenmeßprojektor m, Meßprojektor m		
measuring spring, graduated spring	Meßfeder f	mechanical length of tube	s. mechanical tube length
		mechanical light equivalent	s. mechanical equivalent of light
measuring station, measuring point	Meßstelle f, Meßstation f	mechanical loss angle	mechanischer Verlustwinkel m, Winkel m der mechanischen Verluste
measuring system	s. instrument movement		
measuring system	s. measuring device	mechanical loss factor	mechanischer Verlustfaktor m
measuring tape, tape measure, surveyor's tape, tape[line]	Bandmaß n, Meßband n	mechanically driven interrupter, motor [-driven] interrupter; motor[-driven] breaker	Motorunterbrecher m
measuring technique	s. method of measurement		
measuring transducer	s. transducer	mechanically similar	mechanisch ähnlich
measuring transformer	s. transducer <meas.>	mechanical manometer, mechanical pressure gauge	mechanisches Manometer n, elastisches Manometer
measuring transmitter	s. measurement transmitter		
measuring unit	s. error detector		
measuring vessel of the rain gauge, vessel of the rain gauge	Regenmessergefäß n	mechanical mass, intrinsic mass, bare mass	mechanische Masse f, nackte Masse, eingeprägte Masse
measuring viewfinder	s. range-viewfinder	mechanical monochromator, mechanical neutron monochromator	mechanischer Neutronenmonochromator m, mechanischer Monochromator m
measuring waveguide, waveguide slotted line	Hohlleitermeßleitung f, Hohlrohr-Meßleitung f, Wellenleiter-Meßleitung f, Meßhohlleiter m		
		mechanical neutron chopper	s. neutron chopper
measuring weir, measurement weir, notched weir, weir	Meßüberfall m, Meßwehr n, Wehr n	mechanical neutron monochromator, mechanical monochromator	mechanischer Neutronenmonochromator m, mechanischer Monochromator m
mechanical-acoustical coupling, mechano-acoustic coupling	mechanisch-akustische Kopplung f	mechanical neutron selector, mechanical velocity selector, mechanical selector	mechanischer Geschwindigkeitsselektor m, mechanischer Neutronenselektor m, mechanischer Selektor m
mechanical-acoustical efficiency, mechano-acoustic efficiency	mechanisch-akustischer Wirkungsgrad m		
mechanical-acoustical transducer, mechano-acoustic transducer	mechanisch-akustischer Wandler m	mechanical ohm	mechanisches Ohm n
		mechanical oscillation	mechanische Schwingung f
mechanical admittance	mechanische Admittanz f, mechanischer Leitwert m	mechanical oscillator, oscillator <mech.>	[mechanischer] Oszillator m, mechanische Schwingungsvorrichtung f <Mech.>
mechanical agitation, mechanical stirring	mechanisches Rühren n, mechanische Bewegung (Durchmischung) f		
mechanical agitator, mechanical stirrer	mechanischer Rührer m, mechanisches Rührwerk n	mechanical oscillograph, loop (bifilar) oscillograph, oscillograph with bifilar suspension	Schleifenoszillograph m, Lichtstrahloszillograph m
mechanical analogue	mechanische Analogie f	mechanical pantograph manipulator, pantograph manipulator	Storchschnabelmanipulator m, Scherenmanipulator m
mechanical automatic potentiometer	s. mechanical potentiometer		
mechanical axis <cryst.>	Elastizitätsachse f <Krist.>	mechanical passivity	mechanische Passivität f
mechanical backing pump	s. rotary slide valve vacuum pump	mechanical perpetual motion machine, mechanical perpetuum mobile	mechanisches Perpetuum n mobile
mechanical centring [of image]	mechanische Zentrierung f [des Bildes]		
mechanical chopper	mechanischer Zerhacker m	mechanical potentiometer, mechanical automatic potentiometer, automatic potentiometer with servo[mechanism]	mechanischer Kompensator m, mechanischer selbsttätiger Kompensator
mechanical chopper	s. a. chopper		
mechanical comparator	mechanischer Komparator m		
mechanical dividing head	mechanischer Teilkopf m, Teilkopf		
mechanical efficiency	mechanischer Wirkungsgrad m	mechanical potentiometer recorder, mechanical recording potentiometer	mechanischer Kompensograph m, mechanischer Kompensationsschreiber m
mechanical-electrical amplifier, mechano-electric amplifier	mechanisch-elektrischer Verstärker m	mechanical pressure gauge	s. mechanical manometer

mechanical pump	mechanische Pumpe f	mechanical work	mechanische Arbeit f, Gravitationsarbeit f
mechanical reactance, mechanical rectilinear (rectilinear) reactance	mechanische Reaktanz f, mechanischer Blindwiderstand m	mechanics of continuous media	s. mechanics of the continuum
		mechanics of flight, flight mechanics, theory of flight	Flugmechanik f
mechanical recorder, mechanical register	mechanischer Schreiber m, mechanisches Schreibgerät (Registriergerät) n	mechanics of the continuum, mechanics of continuous media, continuum mechanics	Kontinuumsmechanik f, Mechanik f der deformierbaren Medien (Körper), Mechanik der Kontinua
mechanical recording [of sound], mechanical sound recording	Nadeltonaufzeichnung f, Nadelton m, Nadeltonverfahren n	mechanics of the rocks, rock mechanics	Felsmechanik f, Gesteinsmechanik f
mechanical recording potentiometer	s. mechanical potentiometer recorder	mechanism of conductivity, conductivity (conduction) mechanism	Leitungsmechanismus m, Leitfähigkeitsmechanismus m
mechanical recovery, recovery of mechanical properties	mechanische Erholung f	mechanism of fine adjustment	s. fine focus
mechanical rectilineal (rectilinear) reactance	s. mechanical reactance	mechanization	Mechanisierung f
mechanical register	mechanischer Zähler m, mechanisches Zählwerk n	mechano-acoustic coupling, mechanical-acoustical coupling	mechanisch-akustische Kopplung f
		mechano-acoustic efficiency, mechanical-acoustical efficiency	mechanisch-akustischer Wirkungsgrad m
mechanical register, mechanical recorder	mechanischer Schreiber m, mechanisches Schreibgerät (Registriergerät) n	mechano-acoustic transducer, mechanical-acoustical transducer	mechanisch-akustischer Wandler m
mechanical relaxation	mechanische Relaxation f	mechanocaloric effect, mechano-caloric effect	mechanokalorischer (mechanisch-kalorischer) Effekt m; Daunt-Mendelssohn-Effekt m ‹Helium›
mechanical relaxation	s. a. viscosity		
mechanical resistance	mechanische Resistanz f, mechanischer Wirkwiderstand m		
mechanical rotational compliance, rotational compliance	Torsionsfederung f	mechano-chemical engine	mechanochemische Maschine f
mechanical rotational impedance, rotational [mechanical] impedance	Torsionsimpedanz f, komplexer Torsionswiderstand m, Torsionsscheinwiderstand m	mechano-chemical reaction	mechano-chemische Reaktion f
		mechano-chemistry	Mechanochemie f
		mechano-electric amplifier, mechanical-electrical amplifier	mechanisch-elektrischer Verstärker m
mechanical rotational reactance, rotational [mechanical] reactance	Torsionsreaktanz f, Torsionsblindwiderstand m	mechano-electric impedance	mechanisch-elektrische (mechano-elektrische) Impedanz f
		mechanostriction	Mechanostriktion f
mechanical rotational resistance, rotational [mechanical] resistance	Torsionswirkwiderstand m, Torsionswiderstand m, Torsionsresistanz f	mechanotron, electron-mechanical transducer	Mechanotron n
		Mechau['s] method	Mechau-Verfahren n
mechanical selector	s. mechanical neutron selector	Mechau projector	Mechau-Projektor m
		medial, medial telescope	Medial n, Medialfernrohr n
mechanical short-time current rating ‹US›	s. instantaneous short-circuit current	medial moraine	Mittelmoräne f
mechanical similitude	mechanische Ähnlichkeit f, dynamische Ähnlichkeit	medial telescope, medial	Medial n, Medialfernrohr n
mechanical sound recording, mechanical recording [of sound]	Nadeltonaufzeichnung f, Nadelton m, Nadeltonverfahren n	median, median line; middle line; centre line	Mittellinie f
		median	Seitenhalbierende f, Mediane f
mechanical stirrer, mechanical agitator	mechanischer Rührer m, mechanisches Rührwerk n		
mechanical stirring	s. mechanical agitation	median, median value ‹stat.›	Zentralwert m, Median m, Medianwert m ‹Stat.›
mechanical strength	mechanische Festigkeit f		
mechanical subdivision, crushing, size reduction, chopping ‹mech.›	Brechung f, Grobzerkleinerung f, Zerkleinerung f, Zerstückelung f ‹Mech.›		
mechanical system of units	mechanisches Einheitensystem n	median lethal dose, MLD, LD 50	LD₅₀ f, mittlere Letaldosis f, letale Dosis f für 50 % der Exponierten, Halbwertsdosis f, HWD
mechanical testing [of materials]	mechanische Prüfung (Werkstoffprüfung, Materialprüfung) f		
mechanical tube length, mechanical length of tube	mechanische Tubuslänge f	median lethal time, MLT, LD 50 time	mittlere Letalzeit f, mittlere Absterbezeit f
mechanical turbidity	mechanische Trübung f		
mechanical turbulence	mechanische Turbulenz f	median line, median; middle line; centre line	Mittellinie f
mechanical twin	mechanischer Zwilling m	median plane	Medianebene f
		median section ‹hydr.›	Mittelquerschnitt m ‹Hydr.›
mechanical twinning	mechanische Zwillingsbildung f	median test	Mediantest m
mechanical type [of] plotting machine	s. transformation drawing apparatus	median value	s. median ‹stat.›
		mediating observation, indirect observation	vermittelnde (mittelbare, indirekte) Beobachtung f
mechanical velocity selector	s. mechanical neutron selector		
mechanical viscosity	mechanische Viskosität f	medical physicist	medizinischer Physiker m
mechanical wave resistance	mechanischer Wellenwiderstand m	medical physics	medizinische Physik f

medical radiology, radiology	medizinische Radiologie *f*, Radiologie	**megaseisms**	Weltbeben *n*, Megaseismen *pl*
Mediterranean climate	Mittelmeerklima *n*, Etesienklima *n*, subtropisches Winterregenklima (Klima) *n*, Subtropenklima *n*		
		mega-undation	Mega-Undation *f*
		megawatt-day, MWd	Megawatt-Tag *m*, MWd
		megerg, mega-erg, Merg $<\approx 0.1$ J>	Megaerg *n*, Megerg *n*, Merg
medium, gaseous medium, atmosphere <chem.>	Atmosphäre *f*, gasförmiges Milieu *n*	**megohm,** mega-ohm, MΩ	Megaohm *n*, Megohm *n*, MΩ
medium, liquid medium, solution <chem.>	Lösung *f*, flüssiges Milieu *n*, flüssiges Medium *n* <Chem.>	**mehrstellen method**	Mehrstellenverfahren *n*
medium at rest	ruhendes Medium *n*	**Meidinger cell**	Meidinger-Element *n*
medium-distant earthquake	mittelweites Beben *n*, mittelweites Erdbeben *n*	**Meissner circuit;** Meissner oscillator	Meißner-Schaltung *f*, Meißnersche Rückkopplungsschaltung *f*; Meißner-Oszillator *m*
medium energy; moderate energy; intermediate energy	mittlere Energie *f*, Mittelenergie *f*		
medium-energy nuclear physics	Kernphysik *f* der mittleren Energien, Mittelenergiephysik *f*	**Meissner effect;** **Meissner-Ochsenfeld effect**	Meißner-Ochsenfeld-Effekt *m*; Meißner-Effekt *m*
		Meissner oscillator	s. Meissner circuit
medium frequency, M.F., MF, m.f., mf <300—3,000 kc/s>	Frequenz *f* im Mittelwellenbereich (Hektometerwellenbereich), Mittelwellenfrequenz *f*, Hektometerwellenfrequenz *f*, MF <300 ··· 3 000 kHz>	**Meixner['s] formulation**	Meixnersche Form *f*
		Meixner['s] rule	Meixnersche Regel *f*
		Méker burner, **Meker burner**	Méker-Brenner *m*, Meker-Brenner *m*
		mel	Mel *n*, mel
		Melde['s] experiment	Meldescher Versuch *m*
medium frequency <100—300 kc/s or 0.2—10 kc/s>	Mittelfrequenz *f* <100 ··· 300 kHz *oder* 0,2 ··· 10 kHz>	**meldometer**	s. melting point apparatus
		Mellin['s] inversion formula	s. Mellin['s] inversion integral
medium frequency range, range of medium frequencies, hectometer wavelength range, medium frequency wavelength [range], M.F. range, M.F.	Mittelwellenbereich *m*, Mittelwelle *f*, Hektometerwellenbereich *m*, Hektometerbereich *m*, MW-Bereich *m*, MW	**Mellin['s] inversion integral; Mellin['s] inversion theorem,** Mellin['s] inversion formula	Mellinsches Umkehrintegral *n*; Mellinsche Umkehrformel *f*, Fourier-Mellinscher Satz *m*
		Mellin['s] transform[ation]	Mellin-Transformation *f*, Mellinsche Transformation *f*
medium-frequency wave, hectometer wave, hectometric wave	Mittelwelle *f*, Hektometerwelle *f*	**Melloni thermopile**	Mellonische Thermosäule *f*
medium frequency wavelength [range]	s. medium frequency range	**melt;** heat; batch of metal; liquid <in the phase diagram>	Schmelze *f* <auch im Zustandsdiagramm>; Schmelzfluß *m*
medium-hard X-rays	mittelharte Röntgenstrahlung *f*	**meltability,** meltableness, fusibility	Schmelzbarkeit *f*; Schmelzflüssigkeit *f*
medium-heavy nucleus, medium nucleus	mittelschwerer Kern *m*, mittlerer Kern	**melted,** in the molten state, molten	schmelzflüssig
medium-high frequency wave	Grenzwelle *f*	**melting,** fusion, smelting; heat, founding <of metal>	Schmelzen *n*, Schmelzung *f*, Abschmelzen *n*; Schmelze *f*, Abtauen *n* <Schnee, Eis>
medium nucleus, medium-heavy nucleus	mittelschwerer Kern *m*, mittlerer Kern		
medium of propagation	Ausbreitungsmedium *n*, Fortpflanzungsmedium *n*, Fortpflanzungsmittel *n*	**melting-away of the cloud,** degeneration (melting) of the cloud	Wolkenauflösung *f*, Auflösung *f* der Wolke
		melting cone	s. pyrometric cone
medium pressure, middle pressure, M.P., m.p.	Mitteldruck *m*, mittlerer Druck *m*, MD, M. D.	**melting crucible,** melting pot	Schmelztiegel *m*
		melting curve, fusion (melting pressure, solidification) curve; ice line	Schmelzkurve *f*
medium-pressure synthesis	Mitteldrucksynthese *f*		
medium temperature, intermediate (moderate) temperature	mittlere Temperatur *f*	**melting enthalpy**	s. heat of fusion
		melting equilibrium	Schmelzgleichgewicht *n*
medium-term forecast (prediction), mean-term forecast (prediction)	mittelfristige Vorhersage *f*, Mittelfristprognose *f*	**melting figure**	Schmelzfigur *f*
		melting heat	s. heat of fusion
		melting ice	schmelzendes Eis *n*
medium voltage <1—45 kV>	Mittelspannung *f* <1 ··· 45 kV>	**melting-in**	Einschmelzen *n*
		melting isotherm	Schmelzisotherme *f*
meeting corrosion	s. contact corrosion	**melting loss**	Schmelzverlust *m*
mega…, M	Mega…, M		
megacycle [per second], megahertz, Mc/s, Mcps, MHz	Megahertz *n*, MHz	**melting of the cloud,** degeneration (melting-away) of the cloud	Wolkenauflösung *f*, Auflösung *f* der Wolke
mega-erg, megerg, Merg	Megaerg *n*, Megerg *n*, Merg	**melting phenomenon**	s. order-disorder transformation
megahertz	s. megacycle [per second]	**melting point,** melting temperature, temperature of melting, fusion temperature, fusing point, m.p., f.p.	Schmelzpunkt *m*, Schmelz[punkt]temperatur *f*, Fließpunkt *m*, Schmp., Fp., F.; Schmelzgrenze *f*
megalopsy, macropsia, macropsy	Vergrößertsehen *n*, Makropsie *f*, Megalopsie *f*		
megalosphere	Megalosphäre *f*		
mega-ohm, megohm, MΩ	Megaohm *n*, Megohm *n*, MΩ	**melting point,** melting temperature, temperature of melting <of glass>	Erweichungstemperatur *f* <Glas>
megaparsec, Mpc	Megaparsec, Mpc		
		melting point apparatus, meldometer	Schmelzpunktapparat *m*, Meldometer *n*
megaphone	Megaphon *n*, Schallverstärker *m*, Schalltrichter *m*		
megaphone, speaking tube	Sprachrohr *n*		

melting

melting point curve	Schmelzpunktkurve f, Schmelzpunktdiagramm n	membrane stress	Membranspannungszustand m; Membranspannung f
melting point depression (lowering), lowering of the melting point, fluxing	Schmelzpunkt[s]erniedrigung f, Schmelzpunktdepression f	membrane theory of excitation	Membrantheorie f der Erregung
melting point tube	Schmelzpunktröhrchen n, Schmelzpunktbestimmungsröhrchen n	membrane theory of [thin] shells	Membrantheorie f der Schalen
melting pot, melting crucible	Schmelztiegel m		
melting pressure, pressure of melting	Schmelzdruck m	membrane valve; diaphragm valve	Membranventil n; membranbetätigtes Ventil n
melting pressure curve, melting (fusion) curve, solidification curve; ice line	Schmelzkurve f	membrane wall, membranous wall	Membranwand f
		membrane wave	Membranwelle f
melting range, fusion range	Schmelzbereich m, Schmelzintervall n	membranous labyrinth	häutiges Labyrinth n, Labyrinthus m membranaceus
		membranous wall, membrane wall	Membranwand f
melting temperature	s. melting point	Mémery period	Mémery-Periode f
melting together, alloying, alloyage, fusion <met.>	Legieren n, Zu[sammen]schmelzung f, Verschmelzung f <Met.>	memistor	Memistor m
melting zone, fusion zone	Schmelzzone f	memory	s. storage
		memory capacity, storage capacity, memory size	Speicherkapazität f, Speichervermögen n; Speichergröße f
melt of metal, liquid metal, molten metal, fused metal	Metallschmelze f, Flüssigmetall n, geschmolzenes Metall n	memory cell	s. storage location
melt-water, thawing water, snowmelt	Schmelzwasser n	memory circuit	Speicherschaltung f
member; link, element; section; segment <techn., el.>	Glied n <Techn., El.>	memory effect	Memoryeffekt m, Gedächtniseffekt m, Nachwirkungsfehler m
member of a cluster, cluster star, cluster member	Haufenstern m; Mitgliedsstern m [des Haufens]	memory effect; aftereffect, remanence	Nachwirkung, Nachwirkungseffekt m, Nachwirkungserscheinung f
member of a radioactive chain, radioactive chain product	Glied n einer radioaktiven Zerfallsreihe	memory function	Gedächtnisfunktion f, Erinnerungsvermögen n
member of the system, star of the system	Systemstern m, Mitgliedsstern m [des Systems]	memory size	s. memory capacity
		memory time	Erinnerungszeit f
membrane	Membran f; Haut f	memory tube	s. electrostatic storage tube
		Mendeléef['s] classification [of the elements]	s. periodic system
membrane analogy [in torsion]	s. soap film analogy	Mendeléef['s] [periodic] law, periodic law [of Mendeléef], Mendeleyev['s] periodic law	Periodengesetz n [von Mendelejew], Periodengesetz von Mendelejeff
membrane behaviour	Membranverhalten n		
membrane capacitor, diaphragm capacitor	Membrankondensator m		
membrane conductance	s. membrane permeability	Mendeléef['s] periodic table	s. periodic system
membrane conductivity	Membranleitfähigkeit f	Mendeleev['s] [periodic] group	s. group <in the periodic table>
membrane current	Membranstrom m	mendelevium, 101Md, Mv	Mendelevium n, 101Md
membrane duct	Membranleiter m	Mendeleyev['s] periodic law	s. Mendeléef['s] [periodic] law
membrane electrode	Membranelektrode f		
membrane electrophoresis	Membranelektrophorese f	Mendelian segregation	Mendel-Spaltung f
membrane equation	Membrangleichung f	mengenlehre	s. theory of sets
membrane equilibrium	Membrangleichgewicht n	meniscus, liquid meniscus, meniscus of liquid <mech.>	Meniskus m, Flüssigkeitsmeniskus m <Mech.>
membrane equilibrium	s. a. Donnan [membrane] equilibrium		
membrane filter, ultrafilter, ultrafine filter	Membranfilter n, Ultrafilter n, Ultrafeinfilter n	meniscus, meniscus lens <opt.>	Meniskus m, Meniskuslinse f; Halbmuschel[-Brillen]glas n <Opt.>
membrane method, method of rubber membrane	Membranmethode f	meniscus depression, capillary depression	Kapillardepression f; kapillare Senkung f
membrane model	s. rubber membrane model	meniscus lens	s. meniscus <opt.>
membrane model [of Prandtl]	s. soap film analogy	meniscus of liquid, meniscus, liquid meniscus <mech.>	Meniskus m, Flüssigkeitsmeniskus m <Mech.>
membrane of the cell, cell membrane	Zellmembran f; Plasmamembran f		
membrane permeability, permeability of the membrane, membrane conductance	Membranpermeabilität f, Membrandurchlässigkeit f	meniscus reflector, meniscus system, meniscus telescope, Maksutov system, Maksutov telescope, Maksutov reflector; Maksutov camera	Meniskussystem n, Maksutow-Spiegel m, Maksutow-Spiegelsystem n; Meniskusteleskop n, Meniskus-Spiegelteleskop n, Maksutow-Spiegelteleskop n
membrane potential	Membranpotential n		
membrane radiometer	Membranradiometer n		
membrane resistance	Membranwiderstand m	mensuration, metric determination	Maßbestimmung f
membrane semipermeability	Membransemipermeabilität f	mensuration <e.g. of lengths, surfaces, bodies> <geometry>	Messung f, Berechnung f <z. B. Längen, Flächen, Körper> <Geometrie>

mental delusion	Sinnestäuschung f	mercury spectral lamp, spectral mercury [vapour] lamp	Quecksilberspektraldampflampe f, Quecksilberspektrallampe f
mental experiment	s. imaginary experiment		
mer, monomeric unit <chem.>	Grundbaustein m <Chem.>	mercury switch, mercury interrupter, mercury circuit breaker	Quecksilber[aus]schalter m, Quecksilberwippe f, Quecksilbertauchunterbrecher m, Quecksilberschaltröhre f, Schaltrohr n
Mercalli scale	Mercalli-Skala f		
Mercator mapping, Mercator projection	Mercator-Projektion f, Mercator-Entwurf m, Projektion f der wachsenden Breiten, Merkator-Projektion f, Merkator-Entwurf m		
		mercury thermometer, mercury-in-glass thermometer	Quecksilberthermometer n
Mercator-Sanson projection	Mercator-Sansonsche Projektion f	mercury vacuum gauge	Quecksilbervakuummeter n
		mercury vacuum pump	s. mercury air pump
mercurial pressure gauge, mercury gauge (manometer)	Quecksilbermanometer n	mercury vapour blast pump	Quecksilberdampfstrahl[luft]pumpe f
		mercury vapour lamp	s. mercury lamp
mercury absolute pressure barometer	Absolutdruckmesser m, Manobarometer n	mercury vapour pump, mercury diffusion pump	Quecksilberdiffusionspumpe f
mercury air pump, mercury [vacuum] pump	Quecksilberluftpumpe f, Quecksilber[vakuum]pumpe f	mercury voltameter, mercury coulometer	Quecksilbercoulometer n, Quecksilbervoltameter n
		Merg	s. megerg
mercury arc	Quecksilberbogen m, Quecksilberlichtbogen m	merging	s. embedding
		meridian, meridian line, line (meridian) of longitude	Meridian m, Meridianlinie f, Längenkreis m
mercury barometer	Quecksilberbarometer n		
mercury battery	s. mercury cell	meridian, tangential, meridional <opt.>	Meridional-, Tangential-, meridional, tangential, speichenrecht <Opt.>
mercury cell, mercury oxide cell; mercury battery	Quecksilberelement n; Quecksilberbatterie f		
		meridianal	s. peripheral
mercury circuit breaker	s. mercury switch	meridian beam, meridian pencil [of rays], tangential pencil [of rays], tangential beam	Meridional[strahlen]bündel n, Tangential[strahlen]bündel n
mercury[-] column, column of mercury, Hg	Quecksilbersäule f, Hg		
mercury contact thermometer	Quecksilberkontaktthermometer n	meridian circle, transit-circle, meridian instrument	Meridiankreis m
mercury coulometer, mercury voltameter	Quecksilbercoulometer n, Quecksilbervoltameter n	meridian coma	s. coma
		meridian curvature of the image field	s. meridional curvature of the image field
mercury cut-off <of vacuum system>	Quecksilberventil n <Vakuumanlagen>	meridian curve	Meridiankurve f
mercury diffusion pump, mercury vapour pump	Quecksilberdiffusionspumpe f	meridian ellipse	Meridianellipse f
		meridian fan, tangential fan, meridian pencil [of rays], tangential pencil [of rays]	Meridionalbüschel n, Tangentialbüschel n
mercury electrolytic meter, stiameter	Stiazähler m, Quecksilberelektrolytzähler m, Quecksilberzähler m, Stiameter n		
		meridian focal line, meridional (tangential) focal line, meridional (tangential, primary) focus	meridionale Brennlinie f, tangentiale Brennlinie; meridionaler Brennpunkt m, Meridionalbrennpunkt m
mercury gauge, mercury manometer, mercurial pressure gauge	Quecksilbermanometer n		
mercury horizon	Quecksilberhorizont m		
mercury-in-glass thermometer, mercury thermometer	Quecksilberthermometer n	meridian focal plane, meridional plane, tangential [focal] plane, meridional [focal] plane <opt.>	Meridionalebene f, Tangentialebene f, Meridianebene f <Opt.>
mercury interrupter	s. mercury switch	meridian gyro[scope]	Vermessungskreisel m, Meridianweiser m, Meridiankreisel m
mercury jet cathode	Quecksilberstrahlkatode f		
mercury jet pump	Quecksilberstrahlpumpe f	meridian image point, meridional (tangential) image point	meridionaler Bildpunkt m, tangentialer Bildpunkt
mercury kipp relay	Quecksilberkipprelais f, Quecksilberkippkontakt m		
mercury lamp, mercury vapour lamp	Quecksilberdampflampe f, Quecksilber[bogen]lampe f, Quecksilberbrenner m, Quecksilberdampfröhre f	meridian instrument, meridian circle, transit-circle	Meridiankreis m
		meridian line	Mittagslinie f, Nord-Süd-Linie f, Nord-Süd-Achse f
mercury manometer, mercury gauge, mercurial pressure gauge	Quecksilbermanometer n	meridian line	s. a. meridian
		meridian of Greenwich	s. zero meridian
mercury-mercurous chloride electrode	s. calomel electrode	meridian of longitude	s. meridian
		meridian passage	s. meridian transit
mercury oxide cell, mercury cell; mercury battery	Quecksilberelement n; Quecksilberbatterie f	meridian pencil [of rays], tangential pencil [of rays], meridian beam, tangential beam	Meridional[strahlen]bündel n, Tangential[strahlen]bündel n
mercury pool	Quecksilberteich m		
mercury pool electrode	Quecksilberteichelektrode f	meridian pencil [of rays]	s. meridian fan
		meridian plane, plane of the meridian, meridional plane	Meridianebene f
		meridian plane, meridian focal plane, tangential [focal] plane, meridional [focal] plane <opt.>	Meridionalebene f, Tangentialebene f, Meridianebene f <Opt.>
Mercury precession	Merkurpräzession f		
mercury pump	s. mercury air pump		
mercury resonance lamp	Quecksilberresonanzlampe f	meridian quantum number	Meridianquantenzahl f
mercury rotating pump	s. rotary mercury pump	meridian ray, meridional ray, tangential ray	Meridionalstrahl m, Tangentialstrahl m
mercury scale of temperature	Quecksilber-Temperaturskala f	meridian section	Meridianschnitt m
mercury seal; mercury-sealed joint	Quecksilberverschluß m; Quecksilberdichtung f	meridian section, meridional (tangential) section <opt.>	Meridionalschnitt m, Tangentialschnitt m <Opt.>
mercury-sealed joint; mercury seal	Quecksilberverschluß m; Quecksilberdichtung f	meridian seeker	Meridiansucher m

meridian telescope	Meridianfernrohr n	**mesh refinement,** refinement [of the mesh] <math.>	Verfeinerung f [der Unterteilung] <Math.>
meridian transit, meridian passage, transit (passage, passing) through the meridian	Meridiandurchgang m, Durchgang m durch den Meridian	**mesh size,** mesh spacing; mesh aperture	Maschenweite f; Maschenbreite f
meridional, meridian, tangential <opt.>	Meridional-, Tangential-, meridional, tangential, speichenrecht <Opt.>		
meridional coma	s. coma	**mesh size**	s. a. interval <in numerical integration>
meridional curvature of the image field, meridian (tangential) curvature of the image field	tangentiale Bildfeldwölbung (Bildfeldkrümmung) f, meridionale Bildfeldwölbung (Bildfeldkrümmung)	**mesh spacing**	s. mesh size
		mesh voltage, delta voltage	Dreieckspannung f, Deltaspannung f
meridional focal line	s. meridian focal line		
meridional focal plane, meridian [focal] plane, tangential [focal] plane, meridional plane <opt.>	Meridionalebene f, Tangentialebene f, Meridianebene f <Opt.>		
meridional focus	s. meridian focal line	**mesh-wire plate,** mesh anode, meshed anode	Gazeanode f, Maschenanode f
meridional height	Mittagshöhe f	**meshwork** <bio.>	Maschenwerk n <Bio.>
		mesic atom, mesonic atom	Meson[en]atom n, Mesoatom n
meridional image point, meridian (tangential) image point	meridionaler Bildpunkt m, tangentialer Bildpunkt	**mesic Auger effect,** mesonic Auger effect	mesonischer Auger-Effekt m
meridional plane, plane of the meridian, meridian plane	Meridianebene f	**mesic bremsstrahlung,** mesonic bremsstrahlung	Mesonenbremsstrahlung f
meridional plane, meridian [focal] plane, tangential [focal] plane, meridional focal plane <opt.>	Meridionalebene f, Tangentialebene f, Meridianebene f <Opt.>	**mesic charge,** mesonic charge	Mesonenladung f, mesische Ladung f, mesonische Ladung
		mesic decay, mesonic decay	mesonischer Zerfall m
meridional ray, meridian ray, tangential ray	Meridionalstrahl m, Tangentialstrahl m	**mesic force,** meson force	Meson[en]kraft f, mesonische Kraft f
meridional section, meridian section, tangential section <opt.>	Meridionalschnitt m, Tangentialschnitt m <Opt.>	**mesic K series,** mesonic K series	mesonische K-Serie f
		mesic Lamb shift, mesonic Lamb shift	mesonischer Lamb-Shift m
meridional stress	Meridionalspannung f	**mesic L series,** mesonic L series	mesonische L-Serie f
merocrystalline	merokristallin		
		mesic molecule, mesonic molecule	Meson[en]molekül n, Mesomolekül n
merohedral	meroedrisch, minderflächig	**mesic potential,** meson potential	Mesonenpotential n
merohedrism, merohedry	Meroedrie f	**mesic resonance,** meson resonance	mesonische Resonanz f, Mesonenresonanz f
merohedron	Meroeder n		
merohedry, merohedrism	Meroedrie f	**mesic shift,** mesonic shift	mesonische Verschiebung (Linienverschiebung) f
meromict	meromikt[isch]		
meromorphic function	meromorphe Funktion f	**mesic state,** mesonic state	Mesonquantenzustand m, Mesonzustand m
merotrope, merotropic	s. desmotropic		
merotropy	s. desmotropism	**mesic X rays,** mesonic X rays	mes[on]ische Röntgenstrahlung f, Röntgenstrahlung der Mesonatome
Merton vector	Mertonscher Vektor m		
Merz slit	Merzscher Spalt m		
mesa <semi.>	Kollektorinsel f, Mesa f <Halb.>		
mesa diode	Mesadiode f	**mesionic,** meso-ionic	mesoionisch
mesa structure	Mesastruktur f	**Mesny circuit, Mesny oscillator**	Mesny-Schaltung f, Mesny-Oszillator m
mesa transistor	Mesatransistor m	**mesobar,** mesobaric line	Mesobare f
		mesoclimate; local climate	Mesoklima n; Geländeklima n; Lokalklima n, lokales Klima n, Standortklima n
MESFET	s. surface-barrier field effect transistor		
mesh, grid mesh	Gittermasche f, Masche f des Gitters	**mesocolloid**	s. semicolloid
mesh, sieve mesh	mesh n, Masche f, Siebmasche f, Sieböffnungen fpl auf 25 mm Länge	**mesodesmic structure**	mesodesmische Struktur f
mesh, [closed] loop <el.>	Masche f <El.>	**mesodynamics**	s. meson dynamics
		meso form	Mesoform f
mesh	s. a. screen		
mesh analysis	s. particle-size analysis	**meso-ionic,** mesionic	mesoionisch
mesh anode, mesh-wire plate, meshed anode	Gazeanode f, Maschenanode f	**mesolyte**	Mesolyt m
mesh aperture	s. mesh size	**mesomerism,** structural resonance, resonance <chem.>	Mesomerie f, Strukturresonanz f, Resonanz f <Chem.>
mesh chamber, mesh ionization chamber	Ionisationskammer f mit Netzwandung		
mesh connection	s. delta connection	**mesometamorphic**	mesometamorph
mesh current	Maschenstrom m	**mesomorphic phase**	s. liquid crystal
		mesomorphism	Mesomorphie f
meshed anode	s. mesh anode	**mesomorphous phase**	s. liquid crystal
mesh electron lens, gauze lens	Netzlinse f	**mesomorphous state**	mesomorpher (liquokristalliner) Zustand m
mesh equation	Maschengleichung f	**meson-active**	mesonaktiv
mesh impedance matrix	Maschenimpedanzmatrix f	**meson cloud**	Mesonenwolke f
mesh ionization chamber, mesh chamber	Ionisationskammer f mit Netzwandung	**meson component**	Mesonenkomponente f
		meson dynamics, mesodynamics	Mesonendynamik f, Mesondynamik f, Mesodynamik f
mesh multiplier	s. Venetian blind multiplier		
mesh network	s. fully intermeshed network		

meson factory	Mesonenfabrik *f*, Mesonengenerator *m*
meson field	Meson[en]feld *n*, mes[on]isches Feld *n*, Kernkraftfeld
meson field theory	s. meson theory
meson force, mesic force	Meson[en]kraft *f*, mesonische Kraft *f*
mesonic	s. mesic
mesonic bremsstrahlung	s. mesic bremsstrahlung
mesonium	Mesonium *n*
meson-meson effect, meson-meson interaction	Meson-Meson-Effekt *m*, Meson-Meson-Wechselwirkung *f*
meson-nucleon scattering	Meson-Nukleon-Streuung *f*
meson octet	Mesonenoktett *n*
meson of the nucleus	s. nuclear π-meson
meson physics	Mesonphysik *f*, Mesonenphysik *f*
meson plural production, plural production of mesons	Mehrfacherzeugung *f* von Mesonen, plurale Mesonenerzeugung *f*
meson potential, mesic potential	Mesonenpotential *n*
meson resonance, mesic resonance	mesonische Resonanz *f*, Mesonenresonanz *f*
meson shower	Mesonenschauer *m*, Mesonengarbe *f*
meson spectrum, boson spectrum	Meson[en]spektrum *n*, Boson[en]spektrum *n*
meson theory, meson field theory	Mesonentheorie *f*, Mesonenfeldtheorie *f*
meson theory of nuclear forces	Mesonentheorie *f* der Kernkräfte
meson threshold	Mesonenschwelle *f*
mesonuclear resonance	Mesokernresonanz *f*
meson wave function	Mesonenwellenfunktion *f*, mesonische Wellenfunktion *f*
mesopause	Mesopause *f*
mesopic vision	Dämmerungssehen *n*, Zwielichtsehen *n*, Übergangssehen *n*, mesopisches Sehen *n*
mesoplankton	Mesoplankton *n*
mesoplasma breakdown	Mesoplasmadurchbruch *m*
meso-position	meso-Stellung *f*
mesoracemic	mesorazemisch
mesosiderite	Mesosiderit *m*
mesosphere	Mesosphäre *f*, [obere] Durchmischungsschicht *f*, Hochstratosphäre *f*
mesospheric cloud	s. noctilucent cloud
mesostasis	Mesostasis *f*
mesothermal	mesothermal
mesotrophic	mesotroph
mesozone	Mesozone *f*
message register, call meter, call-counting meter	Gesprächszähler *m*, Telephongesprächszähler *m*
messenger ribonucleic acid, messenger RNA, mRNA, template ribonucleic acid, template RNA	Boten-Ribonukleinsäure *f*, Messenger-Ribonukleinsäure *f*, Boten-RNS *f*, Messenger-RNS *f*, mRNS, Matrix-Ribonukleinsäure *f*, Matrix-RNS
meta-, m- ‹chem.›	meta-, m- ‹Chem.›
metabelian group	[2stufig] metabelsche Gruppe *f*
metabolic activity	Stoffwechselaktivität *f*
metabolic potential	Stoffwechselpotential *n*
metabolism	Stoffwechsel *m*, Metabolismus *m*
metabolite; product of metabolism	Metabolit *m*; Stoffwechselprodukt *n*
metacentre, centre of pressure	Metazentrum *n*
metacentric height	metazentrische Höhe *f*, Metazentrumhöhe *f*
metacentric parabola, stability (lift) parabola, parabola of stability	Auftriebsparabel *f*, Metazenterparabel *f*, Stabilitätsparabel *f*
metacentric radius	metazentrischer Halbmesser *m*, metazentrische Anfangshöhe *f*
metachromatic effects, metachromaticity, metachromatism	Metachromasie *f*
meta-compound, meta-substitution compound	meta-Verbindung *f*
metacontrast	Metakontrast *m*, metaphotischer Kontrast *m*
metadyne, metadyne dynamo, metadyne generator	Metadyne *f*, Metadyn[e]generator *m*, Querfeldmaschine *f*, Zwischenbürstenmaschine *f*, Metadyn[e]maschine *f*
meta-element, transition metal (element), transitional element, galaxy of galaxies	Übergangsmetall *n*, Übergangselement *n*
metagalaxy, hypergalaxy, supergalaxy, supercluster	Metagalaxis *f*, Hypergalaxis *f*, Metagalaxie *f*, Superhaufen *m*, Supergalaxis *f*
meta-ionic bond	Metaionenbindung *f*, metaionische Bindung *f*
metaisomer, meta isomeride, metameride ‹chem.›; metamer ‹bio., chem.›	Metamer[e] *n* ‹Bio., Chem.›; Metaisomer *n* ‹Chem.›
meta-isomerism ‹chem.›; metamerism ‹bio., chem.›	Metamerie *f* ‹Bio., Chem.›
metalanguage	Metasprache *f*
metalation, metallation	Metallierung *f*
metal backing	Metallspiegel *m*, metallische Verspiegelung *f*
metal backing; aluminium backing	Metallhinterlegung *f*; Aluminisierung *f*, Aluminiumhinterlegung *f*
metal barometer	s. aneroid barometer
metal bath, molten metal bath	Metallbad *n*
metal bellows	Metallbalg *m*, Wellrohr *n*, metallischer Faltenbalg *m*, Faltenbalg aus Metall, Wellrohrmembran *f*
metal biscuit, biscuit, metallic sponge	Metallschwamm *m*, Bisquit *m*, reduziertes Metall *n*
metal-capillary cathode	Metall-Kapillar-Katode *f*, MK-Katode *f*
metal-ceramic mixture	s. cermet
metal-ceramic seal, metal-to-ceramic seal, ceramic-to-metal seal	Metall-Keramik-Dichtung *f*, Metall-Keramik-Verbindung *f*
metal-ceramic tube, ceramic-metal tube	Metall-Keramik-Röhre *f*
metal-clad, metal-enclosed ‹apparatus›	metallisch gekapselt ‹Gerät›
metal cladding (coating), metallic coat[ing]	metallischer Überzug *m*, Metallüberzug *m*; Metallbelag *m*
metal coating by spraying	s. metal spraying
metal-cone picture tube	Metallkonus-Bildröhre *f*, Metallkolben-Bildröhre *f*
metal-cooled tube, air-cooled tube, dry tube	luftgekühlte Röhre *f*, Luftkühlröhre *f*, Trokkenröhre *f*, Metallkühlröhre *f*
metal dielectric filter, metal-dielectric interference filter, metal-dielectric type [interference] filter, metallic interference filter	Metallinterferenzfilter *n*, Linienfilter *n*, Interferenzlinienfilter *n*, Monochromat-Interferenzfilter *n*
metal electron	Metallelektron *n*
metalescence	s. metallic lustre

metalescent | s. metalline
metal-enclosed, metal-clad <apparatus> | metallisch gekapselt <Gerät>

metal-envelope tube | s. metal tube
metal filament lamp | Metallfaden[glüh]lampe f, Metalldrahtlampe f
metal film resistor; metal oxide film resistor; metallized film resistor | Metallschichtwiderstand m, Metallwiderstand m, Folienwiderstand m

metal finishing | s. metallization
metal fog, metal mist | Metallnebel m
metal foil, metallic foil | Metallfolie f
metal-glass seal, metal-to-glass seal, glass-to-metal seal | Metall-Glas-Dichtung f, Metall-Glas-Verbindung f, Glas-Metall-Verbindung f, Glas-Metall-Verschmelzung f
metal grating <opt.>; metal (metallic)lattice <cryst.> | Metallgitter n
metal-hydrogen shield | s. metal-water shield
metalimnion, thermocline <of lake> | Sprungschicht f, Metalimnion n <See>
metal-insulator-semiconductor field effect transistor, MISFET | MISFET, Metall-Isolator[-Halbleiter]-Feldeffekttransistor m, MIS-Transistor m
metallation | s. metalation
metal lattice, metallic lattice <cryst.>; metal grating <opt.> | Metallgitter n
metallic, metallic particle | Metallteilchen n
metallic arc | Metallichtbogen m

metallic bond, metallic link[age] | metallische Bindung f, Metallbindung f
metallic calorimeter | Metallkalorimeter n
metallic coat[ing], metal coating (cladding) | metallischer Überzug m, Metallüberzug m; Metallbelag m
metallic compound | Metallverbindung f
metallic conduction, electric conduction of metals | metallische Leitung (Leitfähigkeit) f, elektrische Leitung der Metalle
metallic conductor (conduit), metallic line | metallischer Leiter m, Metalleiter m, metallische Leitung f, Metalleitung f
metallic dust | Metallstaub m
metallic foil, metal foil | Metallfolie f
metallic interference filter | s. metal dielectric filter
metallic lattice, metal lattice <cryst.>; metal grating <opt.> | Metallgitter n
metallic line | s. metallic conductor
metallic-line star, metal line star | Metalliniensterm m

metallic link[age], metallic bond | metallische Bindung f, Metallbindung f
metallic lustre, metallic sheen, metalescence | Metallglanz m, metallischer Glanz m
metallic mirror, metal mirror <opt.> | Metallspiegel m <Opt.>
metallic particle, metallic | Metallteilchen n
metallic phase of hydrogen | metallische Phase f des Wasserstoffs
metallic pyrometer | s. bimetallic pyrometer
metallic radius | metallischer Radius m

metallic rectifier, tank rectifier, metallic valve | Metallgleichrichter m

metallic rectifier | s. a. barrier-layer rectifier
metallic reflection | metallische Reflexion f, Metallreflexion f
metallic sheen | s. metallic lustre
metallic sponge, biscuit, metal biscuit | Metallschwamm m, Bisquit m, reduziertes Metall n

metallic structure | Metallgefüge n; Metallstruktur f, metallische Struktur f

metallic thermometer, bimetallic thermometer | Metallthermometer n, Bimetallthermometer n

metallic valve, metallic rectifier, tank rectifier | Metallgleichrichter m

metalline, metalescent | metallisch glänzend, metallisch blank
metal-line star | s. a. metallic-line star
metallization, metallizing; metal finishing | Metallisierung f, Metallauftrag m, Metallaufbringung f, Metallbelegung f, Metallbelag m, Aufbringung f von metallischen Überzügen

metallization | s. a. mirror coating
metallization by high vacuum evaporation, vacuum metallization, metal vacuum evaporation, vacuum evaporation, vacuum coating, evaporation in vacuo, vacuum deposition | Aufdampfung f [im Vakuum], Vakuumaufdampfung f [von metallischen Überzügen], Vakuumbedampfung f, Metallisierung f durch Aufdampfung im Vakuum; Vakuumverdampfung f

metallized, mirrored, mirror lined, mirror coated | verspiegelt

metallized film resistor | s. metal film resistor
metallized paper capacitor | Metallpapierkondensator m, MP-Kondensator m

metallized screen <opt.> | Metallwand f <Opt.>

metallizing, mirror coating, mirroring, metallization | Verspiegelung f, Spiegelbelegung f, Spiegelbelag m

metallizing | s. a. metallization
metallizing by high-vacuum evaporation, high-vacuum deposition [by evaporation] | Hochvakuumbedampfung f, Hochvakuumaufdampfung f
metallographic[al] microscope, metallomicroscope, metallurgical microscope | Metallmikroskop n
metallographic investigation | Metallgefügeuntersuchung f, metallographische Untersuchung f
metallographic microscopy, micrography, metallomicroscopy, microscopy of metals | Metallmikroskopie f, Mikrogefügeuntersuchung f, Gefügebestimmung f

metallographic specimen, ground sample, microsection, polished sample (section), section | Schliff m, Mikroschliff m, Metallschliff m; Anschliff m
metallography | Metallographie f, Gefügelehre f, Metallgefügeuntersuchung f

metalloid, non-metal, antimetal | Nichtmetall n, Metalloid n

metalloid | s. a. semimetal
metallomagnetic cross-section | s. metal-magnetic cross-section
metallomicroscope, metallographic[al] microscope, metallurgical microscope | Metallmikroskop n
metallomicroscopy | s. metallographic microscopy
metallo-optical, metal-optic[al] | metalloptisch
metallo-optics, optics of metals | Metalloptik f

metallo-organic compound, metalorganic compound, organometallic compound	metallorganische Verbindung *f*, Metallorganyl *n*, Organometallverbindung *f*	**metal vapour lamp**	Metalldampflampe *f*
metallothermal (metallothermic) process	*s.* metallothermics	**metal-walled chamber, metal-walled ionization chamber**	Metallwändekammer *f*, Ionisationskammer *f* mit Metallwänden, Kammer *f* mit Metallwänden
metallothermics, metallothermy; metallothermic (metallothermal) process	Metallothermie *f*; metallothermisches Verfahren *n*	**metal-water shield,** metal-hydrogen shield	Metall-Wasser-Abschirmung *f*, Metall-Wasser-Schutz *m*, Metall-Wasser-Schirm *m*
metallurgical analysis	metallkundliche Analyse *f*		
metallurgical equilibrium diagram	*s.* phase diagram		
metallurgical microscope, metallographic[al] microscope, metallomicroscope	Metallmikroskop *n*	**metal working** <met.>	Umformung *f*, Formgebung *f*, Verformung *f* <Met.>
metallurgical phase diagram	*s.* phase diagram	**metamagnetism**	Metamagnetismus *m*
metallurgical structure	*s.* microstructure	**metamer** <bio., chem.>; metameride, metaisomer, meta isomeride <chem.>	Metamer[e] *n* <Bio., Chem.>; Metaisomer *n* <Chem.>
metal-magnetic cross-section, metallomagnetic cross-section, cross-section of magnetic path in metal	metallmagnetischer Querschnitt *m*	**metameric colours**	bedingt-gleiche Farben *fpl*, metamere Farben
metal mirror, metallic mirror <opt.>	Metallspiegel *m* <Opt.>	**metameric match**	bedingte Farbgleichheit *f*, metamere Farbgleichheit
metal mist, metal fog	Metallnebel *m*	**metameride,** metaisomer, meta isomeride <chem.>; metamer <bio., chem.>	Metamer[e] *n* <Bio., Chem.>; Metaisomer *n* <Chem.>
metal-optical, metallo-optic[al]	metalloptisch		
metalorganic compound	*s.* metallo-organic compound	**metamerism** <bio., chem.>; meta-isomerism <chem.>	Metamerie *f* <Bio., Chem.>
metal oxide film resistor	*s.* metal film resistor	**metamict decay**	metamikter Zerfall *m*
metal-oxide-semiconductor [field effect] transistor, metal[-]oxide surface field effect transistor, insulated-gate metal-oxide semiconductor field effect transistor, MOST, MOSFET, MISFET	Metall-Oxid-[Halbleiter-]Feldeffekttransistor *m*, Metall-Oxid-Halbleiter-Transistor *m*, Feldeffekttransistor mit isolierender Zwischenschicht, MOS-Feldeffekttransistor *m*, MOS-Transistor *m*, MOSFET, MOST; MIS-Transistor *m*, MISFET	**metamict state**	metamikter (pyrognomischer) Zustand *m*
		metamorphic rock	metamorphes (metamorphoses) Gestein *n*, Metamorphit *m*, Metamorph *n*
		metamorphism; metamorphosis	Metamorphose *f*; Metamorphismus *m*
		metamorphopsy	Verzerrtsehen *n*, Metamorphopsie *f*
metal physics, physics of metals	Metallphysik *f*	**metamorphosis**	*s.* metamorphism
metal[-] plate lens	metallische Linse *f*, Metallinse *f*, Metallplattenlinse *f*, Rohr[leiter]linse *f*	**metaosmotic**	metaosmotisch
		metaphase plate, equatorial plate	Äquatorialplatte *f*
metal prism	Metallprisma *n*	**metaphotic image**	metaphotisches Bild *n*
metal pulverization	*s.* metal spraying		
metal rectifier	*s.* barrier-layer rectifier	**metapole** <phot.>	Fokalpunkt *m*, Metapol *m* <Phot.>
metal science	*s.* science of metals	**meta position**	meta-Stellung *f*, Metastellung *f*
metal-semiconductor barrier, semiconductor-metal barrier	Metall-Halbleiter-Sperrschicht *f*; Metall-Halbleiter-Randschicht *f*	**metarheology**	Metarheologie *f*
metal-semiconductor contact; semiconductor-metal contact	Halbleiter-Metall-Kontakt *m*; Metall-Halbleiter-Kontakt *m*	**metasomatism, metasomatosis,** replacement	Metasomatose *f*, Verdrängung *f* im Großen <Geo.>
		metastable equilibrium	metastabiles Gleichgewicht *n*
metal-semiconductor interface, semiconductor-metal interface	Metall-Halbleiter-Grenzschicht *f*, Metall-Halbleiter-Grenzfläche *f*, Halbleiter-Metall-Grenzschicht *f*, Halbleiter-Metall-Grenzfläche *f*	**metastable equilibrium position**	metastabile Gleichgewichtslage *f*
		metastable level	metastabiles Niveau *n*
		metastable nucleus	metastabiler Kern *m*
		metastable state	metastabiler Zustand *m*
		metastable supersaturation	metastabile Übersättigung *f*
metal-semiconductor junction, semiconductor-metal junction	Metall-Halbleiter-Übergang *m*, Halbleiter-Metall-Übergang *m*	**metastate**	Metazustand *m*, meta-Zustand *m*
metal specimen	Metallprobe *f*	**metastatic electron**	metastatisches Elektron *n*
		meta-substitution compound, meta-compound	meta-Verbindung *f*
metal spraying, metal coating by spraying, metal pulverization, schooping, Schoop process, schoop-plating	Metallspritzen *n*, Metallisierung *f* durch Spritzen, Spritzmetallisieren *n*, Schoopisierung *f*, Schoopierung *f*, Aufspritzen *n* des Metalls, Spritzen *n* des metallischen Überzugs	**metathesis**	[chemische] Austauschreaktion *f*, Umsetzung *f* <Chem.>
		meteor	Meteor *n* (*m*)
		meteor activity	Meteortätigkeit *f*
		meteor astronomy	Meteorastronomie *f*
metal-to-ceramic seal, metal-ceramic seal, ceramic-to-metal seal	Metall-Keramik-Dichtung *f*, Metall-Keramik-Verbindung *f*	**meteor body,** meteoric body, meteoroid	Meteorkörper *m*, Meteoroid *n*, Meteorit *m*
		meteor echo	Meteorecho *n*
metal-to-glass seal	*s.* metal-glass seal		
metal-to-salt contact	Metall-Salz-Kontakt *m*	**meteor flare**	Lichtausbruch *m* <Meteor>
metal tube, metal-envelope tube, metal valve	Metallkolbenröhre *f*, Metallröhre *f*; Stahlröhre *f*		
		meteoric body, meteor body, meteoroid	Meteorkörper *m*, Meteoroid *n*, Meteorit *m*
metal vacuum evaporation	*s.* metallization by vacuum evaporation	**meteoric dust,** meteoritic dust; micrometeorite	Mikrometeorit *m*; meteoritischer Staub *m*, Meteorstaub *m*
metal valve	*s.* metal tube		
metal vapour	Metalldampf *m*	**meteoric patrol,** meteor patrol	Meteorüberwachung *f*

meteoric phenomenon	meteorische Erscheinung *f*, Meteorerscheinung *f*	**meteor path**, trajectory of the meteor	Bahn *f* des Meteors, Meteorbahn *f*
meteoric shower	*s.* meteor shower	**meteor patrol**, meteoric patrol	Meteorüberwachung *f*
meteoric theory, impact hypothesis, meteoritic theory	Einsturztheorie *f*, Meteoritentheorie *f*, Aufsturztheorie *f*	**meteor radiant**, radiant <of meteor stream>	Radiant *m*, Ausstrahlungspunkt *m*, Radiationspunkt *m* <Meteorstrom, Meteor>
meteorite, uranolith	Meteorit *m*, Uranolith *m*	**meteor radiation**	Meteorleuchten *n*, Meteorstrahlung *f*
meteorite crater, meteoritic crater	Meteoritenkrater *m*	**meteor radioastronomy**	Meteor-Radioastronomie *f*
meteorite impact	Meteoriteneinschlag *m*, Meteoritenaufschlag *m*, Einsturz *m* eines Meteoriten	**meteor shower**, meteoric shower	Meteorfall *m*, Sternschnuppenfall *m*
meteoritic astronomy, meteoritics	Meteoritenkunde *f*, Meteoritenastronomie *f*	**meteor spectrum**	Meteorspektrum *n*
meteoritic crater, meteorite crater	Meteoritenkrater *m*		
meteoritic dust, meteoric dust; micrometeorite	Mikrometeorit *m*; meteoritischer Staub *m*, Meteorstaub *m*	**meteor stream**	Meteorstrom *m*
		meteor trail, trail of the meteor	Spur *f* des Meteors, Meteorspur *f*
meteoritic fall, fall of a meteorite	Meteoritenfall *m*	**meteor train**, train of the meteor	Schweif *m* des Meteors, Meteorschweif *m*
meteoritics, meteoritic astronomy	Meteoritenkunde *f*, Meteoritenastronomie *f*	**meteor train spectrum**, spectrum of the meteor train	Schweifspektrum *n* des Meteors, Spektrum *n* des Meteorschweifs, Meteorschweifspektrum *n*
meteoritic seism	Bodenerschütterung *f* durch Meteoriteneinsturz, meteoritisches Beben *n*	**meteor with train**	Meteor *n* mit Schweif
meteoritic stone, aerolite, stony meteorite, meteorolite	Steinmeteorit *m*, Aerolith *m*, Meteorstein *m*, Asiderit *m*	**meter**, measuring instrument, measuring apparatus, measurer; gauge, gage	Meßgerät *n*, Meßinstrument *n*, Messer *m*, Meßapparat *m*
meteoritic theory, impact hypothesis, meteoric theory	Einsturztheorie *f*, Meteoritentheorie *f*, Aufsturztheorie *f*	**meter** <US>	*s. a.* metre
meteor light curve	Lichtkurve *f* des Meteors	**meter**	*s. a.* integrating instrument <meas.>
meteor nucleus, nucleus [of the meteor]	Kern *m* [des Meteors], Meteorkern *m*	**meter box**, measuring capsule, measuring cell	Meßdose *f*
meteor observer	Meteorbeobachter *m*	**meter bridge**	Meterbrücke *f*
meteorogram	Meteorogramm *n*	**meter constant**, constant of the meter	Zählerkonstante *f*
meteorograph	Meteorograph *m*, Baro-Thermo-Hygrograph *m*	**meter creeping**, creep	Zählerleerlauf *m*
meteoroid, meteor body, meteoric body	Meteorkörper *m*, Meteoroid *n*, Meteorit *m*	**meter error**, instrument[al] error, error of measuring instrument, measuring instrument error; index error <e.g. of theodolite>	Instrumentenfehler *m*, Instrumentalfehler *m*, Gerätefehler *m*, Apparatefehler *m*, Apparatfehler *m*; Indexfehler *m* <z. B. Theodolit>
meteorolite, aerolite, stony meteorite, meteoritic stone	Steinmeteorit *m*, Aerolith *m*, Meteorstein *m*, Asiderit *m*		
meteorological airplane	Wetterflugzeug *n*	**metering**	*s.* measurement
meteorological chart	*s.* synoptic map	**metering equipment**	*s.* measuring equipment
meteorological depression	*s.* cyclone	**metering pump**	*s.* dosing pump
meteorological divide	*s.* weather limit	**metering section**, discharge site (section line)	Abflußmeßstelle *f*
meteorological element, weather element (factor), element of climate	meteorologisches Element *n*, Wetterelement *n*, Wetterfaktor *m*, Klimaelement *n*	**meter movement**	*s.* instrument movement
		meter setting, distance setting	Entfernungseinstellung *f*
meteorological front, synoptic front	Wetterfront *f*		
		method, technique; process; procedure	Verfahren *n*; Technik *f*; Methode *f*
meteorological limit	*s.* weather limit	**method by repetition [of measurement of angles]**, repetition, repetition method	repetitionsweise Winkelmessung *f*, Repetitionswinkelmessung *f*, Repetition *f*
meteorological optical range, meteorological (standard) visibility	meteorologische (atmosphärische) Sichtweite *f*, Normsichtweite *f*		
meteorological optics, atmospheric optics	atmosphärische Optik *f*, Optik der Atmosphäre, meteorologische Optik	**method of associated particles**, associated particles method	Methode *f* der assoziierten Teilchen
meteorological rocket	meteorologische Rakete *f*, Wetterrakete *f*	**method of atomic orbitals**, atomic orbital method, AO method	Atomorbitalmethode *f*, AO-Methode *f*
meteorological satellite, weather satellite, weather-eye satellite	Wettersatellit *m*, Wetterbeobachtungssatellit *m*	**method of axial sections**	Achsenschnittverfahren *n*, Schneidenmessung *f*
		method of balayage	„balayage"-Verfahren *n*
meteorological ship, weather ship	Wetterbeobachtungsschiff *n*, Wetterschiff *n*	**method of Bode**, frequency [response] method, Bode['s] method	Methode *f* des Bode-Diagramms, Frequenzgangmethode *f*
meteorological tide	meteorologische Tide *f*	**method of calculation**, mathematical procedure	Rechengang *m*, Rechnungsgang *m*
meteorological tropic	meteorologischer Wendekreis *m*	**method of capacitor field**, capacitor field method	Kondensatorfeldmethode *f*
meteorological visibility	*s.* meteorological optical range		
meteorologic conditions, weather, atmospheric conditions	Witterung *f*, Wetterbedingungen *fpl*, Wetterverhältnisse *npl*, Witterungsverhältnisse *npl*	**method of central differences**	Verfahren *n* der zentralen Differenzen
		method of characteristic curves; method of determining flow lines by means of Mach characteristics	Charakteristikenverfahren *n*, Methode *f* der charakteristischen Kurven; Massausche Gitterkonstruktion *f*
meteorologic phenomenon, synoptic phenomenon, weather phenomenon	meteorologische Erscheinung *f*, meteorologisches Phänomen *n*, Wettererscheinung *f*; Witterungserscheinung *f*		
		method of Clément and Desormes	Clément-Desormes-Methode *f*, Clément-Desormessche Methode *f*, Clément-Desormesscher Versuch *m*, Clément-Desormes-Versuch *m*
meteorotropic	meteorotrop[isch]		
meteorotropism	Meteorotropismus *m*		

method of comparison, comparative method	Vergleichsmethode f, Vergleichsverfahren n	method of minimum squares	s. method of least squares
		method of mixtures	Mischungsmethode f
method of comparison with standards, comparison method [of spectrographic analysis]	leitprobengebundenes Verfahren n [der Spektralanalyse]	method of moments, Grad['s] method of moments, moments method	[Gradsche] Momentenmethode f, [Gradsches] Momentenverfahren n, Gradsche Methode f
method of conjugate gradients	Methode f der konjugierten Gradienten, cg-Methode f	method of neutral pseudoatoms, neutralpseudoatom method	Methode f der neutralen Pseudoatome
method of corresponding heights	Methode f der korrespondierenden Höhen	method of nodal voltages, nodal voltage method	Knotenspannungsmethode f, Methode f der Knotenspannungen
method of Czochralski	s. pulling technique of Czochralski	method of nuclear resonance absorption	s. nuclear induction technique
method of determining flow lines by means of Mach characteristics	s. method of characteristic curves	method of oblique illumination	s. Kolk['s] method / Van der
method of dimensions	s. dimensional analysis	method of Olaf Roemer, Römer['s] method, Roemer['s] method	Methode f von Olaf (Ole, Olaus) Römer. Römers Methode
method of discrete ordinates	s. Wick['s] method		
method of distorted waves	s. distorted waves method	method of opposing fields, opposing fields method	Gegenfeldmethode f
method of electrical analogy in hydrodynamics	Methode f der elektrischen Analogie [für inkompressible Potentialströmungen], elektrische Analogie f in der Hydrodynamik	method of parabolas, parabola method [of J. J. Thomson], Thomson['s] parabola method	Parabelmethode f [von J. J. Thomson], Thomsonsche Parabelmethode
method of Evans	s. root locus method	method of partial waves	s. partial wave method
method of falling particles	Fallmethode f <Viskositätsmessung>	method of perturbations	s. perturbation method
		method of phase diagram, phase diagram method	Phasendiagrammethode f, Methode f des Phasendiagramms
method of false position, regula falsi, rule of false position	Regula f falsi, Eingabeln n der Nullstelle, Sekantenverfahren n	method of prisms	Prismenmethode f
method of glancing (grazing) entrance	s. glancing entrance	method of residual activity	s. residual activity method
method of glancing (grazing) exit	s. glancing exit	method of residual rays, reststrahlen method	Reststrahlenmethode f [von Rubens], Reststrahlmethode f
method of harmonic balance, harmonic-balance method	Methode f der harmonischen Balance, Krylow-Bogoljubowsche Methode	method of rubber membrane, membrane method	Membranmethode f
method of homologous pairs of lines; two-line method	Verfahren n der homologen Linienpaare	method of Runge and Kutta	s. Runge-Kutta method
method of hydrodynamic images, principle of hydrodynamic images, method of images [in hydrodynamics]	Prinzip n der hydrodynamischen Bilder, Methode f der hydrodynamischen Bilder	method of saddle points	s. method of steepest descents <for complex integrals>
		method of scales, step method	Methode f der Stufenschätzung, [Argelandersche] Stufenschätzungsmethode f, Stufenschätzung f
method of Hylleraas, Hylleraas['] method	Hylleraassche Methode f, Näherungsmethode f, Methode von Hylleraas		
method of image charges, method of images, image method	Methode f der [elektrischen] Bilder, Bild[er]methode f, Spiegelbildmethode f, Methode (Prinzip n, Verfahren n) der Spiegelbilder, Spiegelungsmethode f, Spiegelpunktmethode f, elektrische Spiegelung f	method of sections	s. Ritter['s] method of sections
		method of self-consistenf field	s. Hartree-Fock method
		method of separation, separation method (technique; process)	Trenn[ungs]verfahren n, Trenn[ungs]methode f; Trenn[ungs]prozeß m
		method of sigma-monogenic functions	Methode f der sigma-monogenen Funktionen
method of images [in hydrodynamics]	s. method of hydrodynamic images	method of small disturbances (perturbations)	s. perturbation method
method of inversion	Inversionsmethode f		
method of investigation	Untersuchungsmethode f, Untersuchungsmethodik f	method of sources, source-[and-]sink method, sink-source method; small source theory <nucl.>	Quelle-Senken-Methode f, Quelle-Senken-Verfahren n
method of isochromatic curves	Isochromatenmethode f		
method of labelled atoms	s. tracer method	method of statistical testing, Monte[-] Carlo method, Monte[-] Carlo technique	Monte-Carlo-Methode f, Monte-Carlo-Verfahren n, Monte-Carlo-Technik f, Monte-Carlo-Rechnung f
method of least squares, least squares method	Methode f der kleinsten Quadrate (Quadratsummen), Fehlerquadratmethode f		
method of line intersection, line intersection method	Linienschnittverfahren n	method of steepest descent, steepest[-] descent method, method of steepest descents <numerical analysis>	Methode f des steilsten Abstiegs, Prinzip n des steilsten Abstiegs <numerische Analysis>
method of Mandelstam and Papalexi, Mandelstam-Papalexi['s] method	Methode f von Mandelstam und Papalexi, Mandelstam-Papalexi-Methode f		
		method of steepest descent[s]	s. Fowler-Darwin method
method of maximum likelihood	s. maximum likelihood method	method of steepest descents, steepest descent method, saddle-point method, method of saddle points, saddle point approximation <for complex integrals>	Sattelpunktmethode f, Paßmethode f Methode f der Sattelpunkte <für komplexe Integrale>
method of measurement, measurement method, measuring method	Meßmethode f, Meßmethodik f		
method of measurement, technique of measurement, measurement method (technique), measuring method (technique, procedure)	Meßverfahren n, Meßmethode f, Meßtechnik f		
		method of steepest descents	s. a. method of steepest descent <numerical analysis>
method of measurement based on heat effect, heat effect method	Wärmetönungsverfahren n	method of straight lines	Streckenzugverfahren n
		method of subject range, subject range method	Objektumfangmethode f

method 484

method of successive approximations	s. iterative method
method of successive elimination[s]	Methode f der schrittweisen Eliminierung
method of summation, summation method <math.>	Summationsverfahren n, Summationsmethode f, Limitierungsverfahren n, Summierungsverfahren n <Math.>
method of the Feather plot, Feather method, Feather analysis	Methode f von Feather, Feather-Methode f, Feather-Analyse f
method of three tripods	Zwang[s]zentrierung f
method of undetermined coefficients	Methode f der unbestimmten Koeffizienten
method of Weiss and Forrer, Weiss-Forrer method	Methode f von Weiß und Forrer, Weiß-Forrersche Methode
methorics	Methorik f
Metonic cycle, lunar cycle	Metonischer Zyklus m, Mondzirkel m, Mondzyklus m
metre, meter <US>, m	Meter n <schweiz.: m>, m
metre ampere	Meterampere n
metre-angle	Meterwinkel m, mw
metre-candle	s. lux
metre convention	Meterkonvention f
metre des archives, [international] prototype meter, primary meter	Urmeter n
metre-kilogramme-second-degree Kelvin system [of units]	s. m.k.s. degree Kelvin system of units
metre-kilogramme-second system [of units]	s. m.k.s. system [of mechanical units]
metre-ton-second system [of units], m.t.s. system [of units], MTS system [of units]	MTS-System n, MTS-Einheitensystem n, MTS-Maßsystem n, Meter-Tonne-Sekunde-System n
metre wave	s. very high frequency wave <1−10 m>
metric	Metrik f
metrical intransitivity <therm.>	metrische Intransitivität f <Therm.>
metrically transitive	metrisch transitiv
metrical technical unit of mass, metric slug, kilohyl, khyl	technische Masse[n]einheit f, metrische Masseeinheit ME, TME, techma, Kilohyl n, khyl
metrical transitivity <therm.>	metrische Transitivität f <Therm.>
metric carat, carat metric, carat, karat k, kk, c	metrisches Karat n, Karat, k <= 200 mg>
metric coherence	metrischer Zusammenhang m
metric determination, mensuration	Maßbestimmung f
metric energy-momentum tensor	Abrahamscher (metrischer) Energie-Impuls-Tensor m, metrischer Impuls-Energie-Tensor m, metrischer Materietensor m
metric form	s. fundamental form
metric fundamental form	metrische Fundamentalform f
metric gravitational system [of units], engineering system [of units], engineering system of mechanical units	technisches Einheitensystem n [der Mechanik], Meter-Kilopond-Sekunde-System n, m-kp-s-System n
metric purity	metrische Reinheit f
metric slug	s. metrical technical unit of mass
metric system [of units]	metrisches Einheitensystem (Maßsystem, System) n, Dezimalsystem n
metric tensor, fundamental tensor, fundamental metric tensor	[metrischer] Fundamentaltensor m, metrischer Tensor m, Maßtensor m
metric ton, tonne, millier, t	Tonne f, t
metric topology, strong topology	starke Topologie f
metric wavelength [range]	s. very high frequency range
metrization	Metrisierung f
metrological comparator	metrologischer Komparator m <für Meßlängen von 1 ... 4 m>
metrology	Meßkunde f, Metrologie f, Maß- und Gewichtskunde f; Meßwesen n
metronome, time keeper	Metronom n
Meunier...	s. Meusnier...
Meusnier['s] helicoidal surface	s. common helicoidal surface
Meusnier['s] theorem, theorem of Meusnier	Meusnierscher Satz m, Satz von Meusnier
Meyer expansion	Meyersche Expansion f
Meyer hardness, Meyer hardness number (value)	Meyer-Härte f
Meyer hardness test[ing]	Meyer-Härteprüfung f, Kugeldruck-Härteprüfung f nach Meyer
Meyer-Neldel rule	Meyer-Neldelsche Regel f
M.F. range	s. medium frequency range
M function, spinor S-matrix, spinorial S-matrix	M-Funktion f, Spinor-S-Matrix f, spinorielle S-Matrix f
MHD	s. magnetohydrodynamic
mica combination	Glimmerkombination f
mica disk, mica washer	Glimmerscheibe f
mica end-window counter	Glockenzählrohr n mit Glimmerfenster, Glimmer-Endfensterzählrohr n
mica plate	Glimmerblättchen n, Glimmerplättchen n
mica washer	s. mica disk
micell, micella	s. micelle
micellar colloid	s. association colloid
micellar structure	Mizellarstruktur f
micelle, micell, micella <pl.: micelles, micellae>	Mizelle f, Micelle f, Mizell n
Michaelis constant, Michaelis-Menten constant	Michaelis[-Menten]sche Konstante f, Michaelis-Menten-Konstante f
Michaelis-Menten equation	Michaelis-Mentensche Gleichung f, Michaelis-Menten-Gleichung f
Michailov['s] criterion [of stability], Michailov-Leonhard criterion [of stability], stability criterion of Michailov, stability criterion of Michailov-Leonhard, Leonhard['s] criterion [of stability], stability criterion of Leonhard	Michajlow-Leonhardsches Stabilitätskriterium (Kriterium) n, Stabilitätskriterium nach Michajlow [-Leonhard], Michajlow-[Leonhard-]Stabilitätskriterium n, Michajlow-[Leonhard-]Kriterium n, Kriterium von Michajlow[-Leonhard], Michajlowsches Stabilitätskriterium (Kriterium), Leonhardsches Stabilitätskriterium (Kriterium), Stabilitätskriterium nach Leonhard, Leonhard-Stabilitätskriterium n, Leonhard-Kriterium n, Kriterium von Leonhard
Michel coefficient	Michel-Koeffizient m
Michel-Lévy compensator, quartz-wedge compensator	Quarzkeilkompensator m [nach Michel-Lévy], Michel-Lévy-Kompensator m
Michelson actinometer	s. Robitzsch bimetallic actinometer
Michelson and Morley['s] ether drift experiment	s. Michelson-Morley['s] experiment
Michelson échelon	s. échelon
Michelson experiment	Michelsonscher Spiegelversuch m
Michelson experiment	s. a. Michelson-Morley['s] experiment
Michelson-Gale['s] experiment	Erddrehungsversuch (Versuch) m von Michelson und Gale, Michelson-Galescher Erddrehungsversuch
Michelson interferometer	Michelson-Interferometer n, Michelsons Interferometer n
Michelson line	Michelsonsche Gerade f <Detonation>
Michelson microinterferometer	Mikro-Michelson-Anordnung f

Michelson-Morley['s] experiment, Michelson and Morley['s] ether drift experiment; Michelson experiment — Interferenzversuch *m* von Michelson und Morley, Michelson-Morleyscher Interferenzversuch, Michelson-Morley-Versuch *m*; Michelson-Versuch *m*, Michelsonscher Versuch *m*, Versuch von Michelson

Michelson['s] rotating mirror — Michelsonscher Drehspiegel *m*

Michelson stellar interferometer, stellar interferometer — [Michelsonsches] Sterninterferometer *n*, Michelson-Sterninterferometer *n*

micro . . . , μ — Mikro . . . , μ

microadjustment dial, vernier [scale], fine-adjustment scale — Feineinstellskala *f*

micro[-]alloy diffused transistor, MADT — Transistor *m* mit mikrolegierter und diffundierter Basis

micro[-]alloy junction — Mikrolegierungsübergang *m*

micro-alloy transistor, microalloy transistor — Mikrolegierungstransistor *m*

microanalysis, microchemical analysis — Mikroanalyse *f*, Milligrammethode *f*

microanalyzer, electron-probe microanalyzer — Mikro[elektronen]sonde *f*, [Elektronenstrahl-]Mikroanalysator *m*

microanaphoretic — Mikroanaphorese-, mikroanaphoretisch

micro-assembly — Mikromontage *f*

micro attachment — Mikroansatz *m*, Mikroskopansatz *m*

microautograph — s. microautoradiogram

microautography, microautoradiography — Mikroautoradiographie *f*, Mikroautographie *f*

microautoradiogram, microautoradiograph, microautograph — Mikroautoradiographie *f*, Mikroautoradiogramm *n*

microautoradiography, microautography — Mikroautoradiographie *f*, Mikroautographie *f*

microbalance — Mikrowaage *f*

microbar, barye, dyne per square centimetre, ba, μbar, μb <especially ac.> — Mikrobar *n*, μbar, μb <besonders Ak.>

microbarogram — Mikrobarogramm *n*

microbarograph — Mikrobarograph *m*, Variograph *m*

microbarometer — Mikrobarometer *n*, Variometer *m*

microbeam — Feinstrahl *m*, Mikrostrahl *m*, Mikrostrahlenbündel *n*, Mikrobündel *n*; Strahlenstich *m*

microbeam of X-rays — Mikroröntgenstrahl *m*

micro Brownian movement — mikrobrownsche Bewegung *f*, mikro-Brownsche Bewegung

microburet[te] — Mikrobürette *f*

microburner — Mikrobrenner *m*

microcalorimetry — Mikrokalorimetrie *f*

microcanonical assembly, microcanonical ensemble, energy shell ensemble — mikrokanonische Gesamtheit *f*

microcanonical average, microcanonical mean — mikrokanonisches Mittel *n*

microcanonical ensemble — s. microcanonical assembly

microcanonical mean, microcanonical average — mikrokanonisches Mittel *n*

microcapillary — mikrokapillarer Raum *m*

microcard, microphotographic print, microphotocopy — Mikro[photo]kopie *f*, Mikrographie *f*, Mikroaufnahme *f*

microcataphoretic — Mikrokataphorese-, mikrokataphoretisch

microcator — Mikrokator *m*

microcausality — Mikrokausalität *f*

microcavity — Mikrohohlraum *m*

microchemical analysis, microanalysis — Mikroanalyse *f*, Milligrammethode *f*

microchemistry <GB>, trace chemistry <US> — Mikrochemie *f*, Spurenchemie *f*

microchronometer; short-time-interval meter — Kurzzeitmesser *m*

microcinematographic camera, cinemicrographic camera — mikrokinematographische Kamera *f*

microcinematography, cinemicrography — Mikrokinematographie *f*

microcircuit, microelectronic circuit; microcircuitry — Mikroschaltung *f*, mikroelektronische Schaltung *f*

microcircuit module — s. micromodule

microcircuitry — s. microcircuit

microclimatology, applied climatology — angewandte Klimatologie *f*, Mikroklimatologie *f*, Kleinklimatologie *f*

microcoacervation — Mikrokoazervation *f*

microconvection — Kleinkonvektion *f*, Mikrokonvektion *f*

microcorrosion — Mikrokorrosion *f*

microcoulometer, microvoltameter — Mikrocoulometer *n*, Mikrovoltameter *n*

microcrack, microscopic crack — Mikroriß *m*, mikroskopischer Riß *m*

microcreep — Mikrokriechen *n*

microcrystal — Mikrokristall *m*, Mikrokristallit *m*

microcrystalline — mikrokristallin, kleinkörnig

microcrystalline structure — s. microstructure

microcurrent, microflow — Mikroströmung *f*

microdensitometry — Mikrodensitometrie *f*, Mikroschwärzungsmessung *f*

microdissection — Mikrodissektion *f*, Mikrurgie *f*

microelectronic circuit — s. microcircuit

microelectrophoretic apparatus; microelectrophoretic cell, microelectrophoretic chamber — Mikroelektrophoresegerät *n*

microelement — s. tracer element <bio.>

microetch — s. microetching

microetching; microetch — Mikroätzung *f*

microexamination — s. microscopic examination

micro-eyepiece, microscope eyepiece — Mikroskopokular *n*, Mikrookular *n*

microfield — Mikrofeld *n*

microfilming, microfilm recording — Mikrofilmaufnahme *f*

microfilter — Mikromter *n*

micro-filtration, ultrafiltration — Ultrafiltration *f*

microfine structure — Mikrofeinstruktur *f*

microflare, subflare — Suberuption *f*, Mikroeruption *f*

microflaw — s. microporosity

microflow, microcurrent — Mikroströmung *f*

microfocus tube — Mikrofokusröhre *f*, Mikrofokus-Röntgenröhre *f*

microfractography — Mikrofraktographie *f*

microgram[me] method, ultramicro method — Ultramikroverfahren *n*

micrograph — Mikroschliffbild *n*, Gefügebild *n*, Mikro[gefüge]bild *n*

micrography, metallographic microscopy, metallomicroscopy, microscopy of metals — Metallmikroskopie *f*, Mikrogefügeuntersuchung *f*, Gefügebestimmung *f*

micrography, photomicrography	Mikrophotographie f	**micromodule assembly**	Mikromodulbaueinheit f
		micromodule circuit	Mikromodulschaltung f
micrography	s. a. microphotographic printing	**micromolecular solution**	mikromolekulare Lösung f
microhardness, small hardness	Mikrohärte f	**micromotion,** slow motion, micrometric displacement; fine focusing motion	Feinbewegung f
microhardness indentation	Mikrohärteeindruck m		
microhardness test, microhardness testing, micro indentation hardness test[ing]	Mikrohärteprüfung f	**micron** ‹particle in chem.›	Mikron n ‹Teilchen in der Chem.›
		micronizer, jet mill, fluid energy mill	„jet"-Mühle f, Strahlmühle f, Düsenmühle f
microhardness tester	Mikrohärteprüfer m, Mikrohärteprüfgerät n, Mikrohärtemesser m	**micron realm,** microscopic realm	mikroskopischer Bereich m, Mikronbereich m
		micronucleus	Mikronukleus m, Kleinkern m
microhardness testing, micro identation hardness test[ing]	s. microhardness test	**microobject,** microscopical object (specimen)	mikroskopisches Objekt n, Mikroobjekt n
microinstability, fine-scale microinstability, kinetic instability, microscopic instability	kinetische Instabilität f, Instabilität vom kinetischen Typ	**microobjective,** microscope objective (lens), micro lens, microlens	Mikroskopobjektiv n, Mikroobjektiv n
		micro-oscillation	Mikroschwingung f
microinterferometer, interference microscope	Interferenzmikroskop n, Mikrointerferometer n, Beugungsmikroskop n	**microoscillograph**	Mikrooszillograph m
		microoosmometer	Mikroosmometer n
		microparticle	Mikroteilchen n
microionophoretic	Mikroionophorese-, mikroionophoretisch	**microphone burning,** microphone noise; transmitter noise	Mikrophonrauschen n, Mikrophongeräusch n
micro lens, microlens, microscope objective (lens), microobjective	Mikroskopobjektiv n, Mikroobjektiv n	**microphone current** ‹el.›	Mikrophonstrom m ‹El.›
		microphone diaphragm; transmitter diaphragm	Mikrophonmembran f
microlite, microlith	Mikrolith m	**microphone effect**	s. microphonic effect
		microphone effect, microphonic action ‹bio.›	Mikrophoneffekt m ‹Bio.›
micromagnetic anomaly	mikromagnetische Anomalie f		
micromanipulator	Mikromanipulator m, Feinmanipulator m	**microphone noise,** microphone burning; transmitter noise	Mikrophonrauschen n, Mikrophongeräusch n
micromanometer, micro-pressure gauge	Mikromanometer n, Mikrodruckmesser m, Feindruckmanometer n	**microphone quality**	s. sound transmission quality
		microphonic action, microphone effect ‹bio.›	Mikrophoneffekt m ‹Bio.›
micrometeor, ultra-telescopic meteor	Mikrometeor n, ultrateleskopisches Meteor n	**microphonic effect,** microphone effect, microphonics, microphony, microphonism, pinging noise ‹El.›	Mikrophonie f, Mikrophon[ie]effekt m; Mikrophonbrodeln n; Röhrenklingen n, Klingen n; Krachen n ‹El.›
micrometeorite; meteoritic dust, meteoric dust	Mikrometeorit m; meteoritischer Staub m, Meteorstaub m		
micrometer ‹mech.›	Mikrometer n, Meßschraube f, Mikrometerschraube f, Dickenmesser m ‹Mech.›	**microphonic flame,** [sound-]sensitive flame	[schall]empfindliche Flamme f
		microphonics, microphonism, microphony	s. microphonic effect ‹el.›
micrometer, optical [type of] micrometer ‹opt.›	optisches Mikrometer n, Mikrometer ‹Opt.›	**microphony coefficient**	Klingkoeffizient m
micrometer caliper	s. screw gauge		
micrometer eyepiece, eyepiece micrometer, filar eyepiece	Okularmikrometer n	**microphony electromotive force,** microphony e.m.f.	s. microphony voltage
micrometer screw, micrometric screw, lead screw [of micrometer]	Meßspindel f, Mikrometerschraube f; Feinmeßschraube f ‹z. B. beim Mikroskop›	**microphony voltage,** voltage of microphonic effect, microphony electromotive force, microphony e.m.f.	Kling-EMK f, Klingurspannung f, Klingspannung f
micrometer thimble, thimble of micrometer	Mikrometertrommel f, Trommel f des Mikrometers; Meßtrommel f	**microphotocopy,** microcard, micrographic print	Mikrokopie f, Mikrophotokopie f, Mikrographie f, Mikroaufnahme f
micrometric displacement, micromotion, slow motion; fine focusing motion	Feinbewegung f	**microphotogram**	Mikrophotogramm n
		microphotogrammetry	Mikrophotogrammetrie f
micrometric screw, micrometer screw, lead screw [of micrometer]	Meßspindel f, Mikrometerschraube f; Feinmeßschraube f ‹z. B. beim Mikroskop›	**microphotographic print,** microcard, microphotocopy	Mikrokopie f, Mikrophotokopie f, Mikrographie f, Mikroaufnahme f
micrometric spark discharger, spark meter	Funkenmikrometer n	**microphotographic printing,** microphotography, micrography	Mikrographie f, Photomikrographie f, Mikrokopieren n, Mikrophotokopieren n, Mikroaufnahme f
micrometron [automatic microscope]	Mikrometron n	**microphotography**	s. a. photomicrography
micromicro . . .	s. pico . . .	**microphotometry**	Mikrophotometrie f
microminiature circuit, microminiaturized circuit	Mikrominiaturschaltung f	**microphysics**	Mikrophysik f
		micropipe	s. microporosity
		micropipet[te]	Mikropipette f
microminiature electronics	Mikrominiaturelektronik f	**microplasma density**	Mikroplasmadichte f
		micropiastometer	Mikroplastometer n
microminiaturized circuit, microminiature circuit	Mikrominiaturschaltung f	**microplate**	Mikroplatte f
		micropore	Mikropore f
		microporosity; micropipe, microflaw	Mikroporosität f, Mikrolunker m
micromodule, microcircuit module	Mikromodul[baustein] m, Mikroschaltungsbaustein m, Mikroschaltungsmodul m, Kompaktbaustein m, MM-Baustein m		
		microporous, mipor	mikroporös
		micropot[entiometer]	Mikropotentiometer n, Zwergpotentiometer n

micro-pressure gauge, micromanometer	Mikromanometer n, Mikrodruckmesser m, Feindruckmanometer n	microscopical object, microscopical specimen, microobject	mikroskopisches Objekt n, Mikroobjekt n
microprobe	Mikrosonde f	microscopic ash analysis	mikroskopische Aschenanalyse f, Mikroveraschung f, Schnittveraschung f
microprobing	Mikrosondierung f		
microprojection apparatus, microprojector	Mikroprojektionsgerät n, Mikroprojektor m, Mikroprojektionsapparat m	microscopic crack, microcrack	Mikroriß m, mikroskopischer Riß m
micropsy	Verkleinertsehen n, Mikropsie f	microscopic cross-section, σ	mikroskopischer Wirkungsquerschnitt (Querschnitt) m, σ
micropulsation	Mikropulsation f, Mikropulsierung f		
micropulser	s. square-wave generator	microscopic examination, microexamination	mikroskopische Untersuchung f; Mikroskopieren n
microradiogram, microradiograph	mikroradiographische Aufnahme f, Mikroradiogramm n, Mikroröntgenogramm n, Mikroradiographie f, Mikroröntgenographie f		
		microscopic eyepiece with indicator, eyepiece with indicator	Zeigerokular n
		microscopic field	mikroskopisches Feld n
microradiography	Mikroradiographie f, Radiographie f von Dünnschliffen	microscopic instability, microinstability, kinetic instability, fine-scale microinstability	kinetische Instabilität f, Instabilität vom kinetischen Typ
microradiometer	Mikroradiometer n		
micro[-]reciprocal degree, mired, M	Mired n, Miredwert m, M	microscopic periodicity	mikroskopische Periodizität f
microresistor	Mikrowiderstand m, Zwergwiderstand m	microscopic realm, micron realm	mikroskopischer Bereich m, Mikronbereich m
		microscopic reversibility	mikroskopische Reversibilität (Umkehrbarkeit) f
microrheology	Mikrorheologie f		
microroughness	Mikrorauhigkeit f		
microscope arm, arm of the microscope	Tubusträger m	microscopic segregation, microsegregation; coring; liquation <met.>	Kristallseigerung f, Kornseigerung f, Dendritenseigerung f, Mikroseigerung f <Met.>
microscope arranged for transillumination, transmitted-light (transmission) microscope	Durchlichtmikroskop n		
microscope arranged for vertical illumination	s. direct-light microscope	microscopic state, microstate	Mikrozustand m, mikroskopischer Zustand m
		microscopic variations, microvariations, disturbances, trouble	Unruhe f
microscope base, base (foot) of microscope, microscope foot	Mikroskopfuß m, Fuß m des Mikroskops	microscopy by reconstructed wave fronts	s. Gabor method
microscope body, body of microscope	Mikroskopstativ n, Stativ n des Mikroskops	microscopy by reflection	s. reflection electron microscopy
microscope column, column of microscope	Mikroskop[stativ]säule f, Stativsäule f des Mikroskops	microscopy by transmission	s. transmission electron microscopy
microscope condenser [lens], condenser lens of microscope	Mikroskopkondensor m	microscopy in transmitted light	s. transmitted-light microscopy
		microscopy of metals	s. micrography
microscope eyepiece, micro-eyepiece	Mikroskopokular n, Mikrookular n	microsection, thin section <bio.>	Dünnschnitt m <Bio.>
microscope foot, microscope base, base (foot) of microscope	Mikroskopfuß m, Fuß m des Mikroskops	microsection	s. a. metallographic specimen
		microsegregation	s. microscopic segregation <met.>
microscope for comparison, comparison microscope	Vergleichsmikroskop n	microseismic, microseismology	Mikroseismik f
microscope for examining nuclear tracks, microscope for the examination of nuclear tracks	Kernspurmeßmikroskop n, Kernspurmikroskop n	microseisms	seismische Unruhe f, Mikrobeben n, mikroseismische Bewegungen (Erschütterungen) fpl, Feinbewegungen fpl <Geo.>
microscope illumination	Mikroskopierbeleuchtung f	microslip, fine slip	Feingleitung f, Elementarstruktur f im Gleitlinienbild
		microslip line	Feingleitlinie f
microscope lens, microscope objective, microobjective, micro lens, microlens	Mikroskopobjektiv n, Mikroobjektiv n	microsolifluction	Mikrosolifluktion f
		microspectrometry, microspectroscopy	Mikrospektroskopie f, Mikrospektrometrie f
microscope micrometer	Schraubenmikroskop n	microspectrophotometer	Mikrospektrophotometer n
		microspectroscopy, microspectrometry	Mikrospektroskopie f, Mikrospektrometrie f
microscope objective, microscope lens, microobjective, micro lens, microlens	Mikroskopobjektiv n, Mikroobjektiv n	microsphere	Mikrosphäre f
		microstate, microscopic state	Mikrozustand m, mikroskopischer Zustand m
microscope slide	s. slide	micro-strain	Mikrodehnung f
microscope stage (table), stage, object (specimen) stage; cross table	Objekttisch m, Objektträgertisch m, Mikroskoptisch m; Kreuztisch m	microstress	Mikrospannung f
		microstrip	s. strip line
		microstrip technique	Mikrostriptechnik f
microscope theodolite	Mikroskoptheodolit m		
microscope tube, tube of microscope	Mikroskoptubus m, Tubus m des Mikroskops	microstructure; microcrystalline structure, metallurgical structure <of material>	Mikrostruktur f, Feinbau m, Feinstruktur f, Kleinstruktur f; Gefüge n, Feingefüge n, Mikrogefüge n <Werkstoff>
microscope with built-in photomicrographic ♦camera, camera microscope	Kameramikroskop n		

microsynoptic situation	Kleinwetterlage f	microwave oscillator, microwave generator	Mikrowellengenerator m, Mikrowellenoszillator m
microtasimeter	Mikrotasimeter n		
microtelephone, hand microtelephone, HMT	Mikrotelephon n	microwave parametric oscillator	parametrischer Mikrowellenoszillator m
microtherm	s. calorie	microwave radiation	Mikrowellenstrahlung f
microtome	Mikrotom n		
microtomy	Mikrotomie f	microwave region, microwave field	Mikrowellenbereich m, Mikrowellengebiet n
microtoroid, micro-toroid	Mikroringkern m	microwave resonance	Mikrowellenresonanz f
microtron ‹acc.›	Mikrotron n, Elektronenzyklotron n ‹Beschl.›		
microtube	Mikroröhre f	microwave resonance absorption	Mikrowellenresonanzabsorption f
microturbulence	s. small-scale turbulence	microwave resonator, microwave cavity	Mikrowellenhohlraum m, Mikrowellenresonator m
microvac[uum]	s. high vacuum		
microvariations, microscopic variations, disturbances, trouble	Unruhe f	microwave spectrometer	Mikrowellenspektralapparat m, Mikrowellenspektrometer n
microvariometer	Mikrovariometer n		
microvibrograph	Mikrovibrograph m	microwave spectroscopy, ultra-high frequency spectroscopy	Mikrowellenspektroskopie f, Höchstfrequenzspektroskopie f
microviscosity	Mikroviskosität f		
microvoltameter, microcoulometer	Mikrocoulometer n, Mikrovoltameter n		
microvolter	s. alternating-current microvoltmeter	microwave spectrum	Mikrowellenspektrum n
microvortex	Mikrowirbel m	microwave strip	s. strip line
microwave, hyperfrequency wave	Mikrowelle f, Höchstfrequenzwelle f, Zwergwelle f	microwave technique	s. microwave method
		microwave tube, microwave valve	Mikrowellenröhre f
microwave amplification	Mikrowellenverstärkung f, Höchstfrequenzverstärkung f	microweather	Kleinwetter n, Mikrowetter n
		micro-zone melting	Mikrozonenschmelzen n
microwave amplifier	Mikrowellenverstärker m, Höchstfrequenzverstärker m	mid-band frequency	Mittenfrequenz f, Mittelfrequenz f ‹des Bandes›, Bandmittenfrequenz f
microwave antenna	Mikrowellenantenne f	middle atmosphere	mittlere Atmosphäre f
		middle course [of river]	Mittellauf m
microwave breakdown	Mikrowellendurchschlag m	middle ear	Mittelohr n
		Middle[-]European time, Central[-]European time, C.E.T., CET	Mitteleuropäische Zeit f, MEZ
microwave cavity, microwave resonator	Mikrowellenhohlraum m, Mikrowellenresonator m		
microwave circuit	Mikrowellenschaltung f	middle-eye, central eye, Cyclopean eye	imaginäres Deckauge n, Mittelauge n, Zyklopenauge n, sensorisches Doppelauge f
microwave circulator	s. circulator		
microwave conductivity	Mikrowellenleitfähigkeit f	middle line; median [line]; centre line	Mittellinie f
		middle line of the profile	s. skeleton line
microwave discharge	Mikrowellenentladung f	middle of the flow	s. core of the flow
		middle plane, midplane; middle surface	Mittelebene f; Mittelfläche f
microwave electronics	Mikrowellenelektronik f		
microwave energy	Mikrowellenenergie f	middle pressure, medium pressure, M.P., m.p.	Mitteldruck m, mittlerer Druck m, MD, M. D.
microwave engineering; ultra-high frequency engineering	Höchstfrequenztechnik f; Mikrowellentechnik f	middle-shot water wheel	mittelschlächtiges Wasserrad n
microwave field, microwave region	Mikrowellenbereich m, Mikrowellengebiet n	middle surface	s. middle plane
		middle surface of the shell	Schalenmittelfläche f
microwave frequency	Mikrowellenfrequenz f	middle tone, half-tone, continuous tone, semitone ‹opt.›	Halbton m ‹Opt.›
		Middleton telephotometer	Sicht-Telephotometer n [von Middleton], Middleton-Telephotometer n
microwave generator, microwave oscillator	Mikrowellengenerator m, Mikrowellenoszillator m		
		mid-frequency, centre frequency ‹for frequency modulation›	Mittelfrequenz f, Mittenfrequenz f ‹Frequenzmodulation›
		midget	Kleinstanlage f
microwave interferometer	Mikrowelleninterferometer n	midget tube (valve), sub-miniature tube (valve)	Subminiaturröhre f, Gnomröhre f, Kleinströhre f
		mid[-]infrared	mittleres Infrarot n
microwave interferometry	Mikrowelleninterferometrie f	midnight Sun, polar day	Mitternachtssonne f, Polartag m
microwave isolator	s. isolator ‹el.›	mid-ocean[ic] ridge, ocean ridge	Tiefseerücken m, Meeresrücken m
microwave lens, lens for microwaves	Mikrowellenlinse f		
microwave magnetron	Mikrowellenmagnetron n		
		midperpendicular	Mittelsenkrechte f
microwave method, microwave technique; ultra-high frequency method, ultra-high frequency technique	Mikrowellentechnik f, Mikrowellenmethode f; Höchstfrequenzmethode f, Höchstfrequenztechnik f	midplane	s. middle plane
		mid-point	s. neutral point ‹el.›
		mid-point conductor	s. neutral point ‹el.›
		midpoint formula	s. Maclaurin[’s] formula

mid[-]range	Spannweitenmitte f, Mitte f des Variationsintervalls	milled[-head] screw, knurled[-head] screw	Rändelschraube f
mid troposphere	mittlere Troposphäre f	Miller-Bravais index, Bravais-Miller index	Bravais-Symbol n
Mie atmosphere	Mie-Atmosphäre f	Miller circuit	Miller-Kreis m
Mie coefficient	Mie-Koeffizient m	Miller crystallographic index, Miller index, index of Miller, diffraction index	Miller-Index m, Millerscher Index m
Mie['s] diffusion function	s. Mie['s] scattering function		
Mie effect	Mie-Effekt m	Miller effect	Miller-Effekt m
		Miller face	Millersche Netzebene f
Mie function	s. Mie['s] scattering function	Miller index, Miller crystallographic index, index of Miller, diffraction index	Miller-Index m, Millerscher Index m
Mie-Grüneisen equation of state	s. Grüneisen equation of state		
Mie resonance	Mie-Resonanz f		
Mie scattering	Mie-Streuung f		
Mie scattering coefficient, scattering coefficient [in Mie's theory]	Streukoeffizient m der Mie-Streuung, Miescher Streukoeffizient	Miller integrator, Miller transitron	Miller-Transitron n, Miller-Integrator m; Miller-Integratorschaltung f
Mie['s] scattering function, Mie function, light scattering function [for spherical particles], spherical vector wave function, Mie['s] diffusion function, diffusion function	Streufunktion f der Mie-Streuung, Miesche Streufunktion	milli..., m	Milli..., m
		millibar, tor, mb	Millibar n, Tor n, mb
		millier	s. metric ton
		Milligoat counter, non-directional counter [tube]	richtungsunabhängiges Zählrohr n, Milligoat-Zählrohr n, Milligoatsches Zählrohr
Mie scattering parameter	Streuparameter m [der Mie-Streuung]	Millikan capacitor	Millikanscher Kondensator m, Millikan-Kondensator m, Schwebekondensator m
Mie series	Miesche Reihe f		
Mie theory [of the optical effects of small particles]	Miesche Theorie f [der Streustrahlung], Miesche Beugungstheorie f	Millikan['s] experiment, Millikan['s] method; oil-drop experiment [of Millikan]	Millikanscher Öltröpfchenversuch m, Öltröpfchenversuch (Versuch m) von Millikan, Millikanscher Versuch m [mit dem schwebenden Öltröpfchen], Schwebetropfenversuch m, Schwebeversuch m, Schwebemethode f, Millikansche Bestimmung f des Elementarquantums [mit der Öltröpfchenmethode]; Öltröpfchenmethode f
migma	Migma n		
migmatite	Migmatit m, Mischgestein n		
migrating arc	wandernder Lichtbogen m		
migrating layer, moving layer	wandernde Schicht f		
migration	Wanderung f, Migration f, Bewegung f		
migration area	Migrationsfläche f, Wanderfläche f		
migration energy, energy of migration	Wanderungsenergie f		
migration enthalpy	Wanderungsenthalpie f	Millikan ultraviolet	Millikan-Ultraviolett n, Millikan-Gebiet n
migration length	Migrationslänge f, Wanderlänge f		
migration loss	Wanderungsverlust m	millimass unit, mamu <= $1.659\,790 \times 10^{-30}$ kg>	tausendstel [atomare] Masseneinheit f, TME <= $1,660 \cdot 10^{-30}$ kg>
migration of dislocation, dislocation migration	Versetzungswanderung f, Wanderung f der Versetzung		
		millimetre of mercury	s. torr
migration of grain boundaries, grain boundary migration; grain boundary diffusion	Korngrenzenwanderung f, Korngrenzendiffusion f, Korngrenzenverschiebung f	millimetre of water [column], conventional millimetre of water [column], mm of water, mm H_2O	Millimeter n Wassersäule, mm WS, mm H_2O
migration of ions, ion[ic] migration, ionic drift, drift (movement) of ions, ion[ic] movement	Ionenwanderung f, Ionendrift f, Ionenbewegung f	millimetre squared paper, squared (scale) paper, cross-section paper	Millimeterpapier n
		millimetre wave, extra-high frequency wave, E.H.F. wave <1 — 10 mm>	Millimeterwelle f <1 ··· 10 mm>
migration of spot zone	Verlagerung f der Fleckenzone, Wanderung f der Fleckenzone	millimetre-wavelength interferometry	Millimeterwelleninterferometrie f, Millimeter-Wellenlänge-Interferometrie f
migration of strand line	Strandverschiebung f		
migration of the earthquake foci (focuses)	Wanderung f der Bebenherde	millimetre-wavelength klystron, one-millimetre klystron	Millimeterwellenklystron n
migration of vacancies, vacancy migration, vacancy motion	Leerstellenwanderung f	millimetric wavelength [range]	s. extra-high frequency range
		millimicro..., mµ	s. nano..., n
migration rate (speed)	Wanderungsgeschwindigkeit f; Laufgeschwindigkeit f, Fließgeschwindigkeit f <Chromatographie>	milling	s. comminution <techn.>
		milliosmol[e]	Milliosmol n
		millitherm	s. kilo[-]kalorie
migratory depression	s. mobile cyclone <meteo.>	Mills cross aerial, pencil-beam interferometer	Mills-Kreuz n, Mills-Kreuzantenne f
migratory High, mobile anticyclone, anticyclone	Antizyklone f, wanderndes Hoch n, wanderndes Hochdruckgebiet n		
		Mills-Nixon effect, bond fixation	Mills-Nixon-Effekt m
Milankovitch['s] curve, radiation curve	Strahlungskurve f [von Milankovitch]	Milne-Eddington approximation	Milne-Eddington-Näherung f
mile, statute mile, English statute mile, British mile, mi, st.Mi., m <= 1,609 m>	englische Meile f, Meile, angelsächsische Meile <= 1 609 m>	Milne['s] kinematical cosmology	Milnesche kinematische Kosmologie f, kinematische Kosmologie von Milne
military transformation	s. diffusionless transformation		
milk glass, opal glass, dull glass	Trübglas n, Opalglas n, Opakglas n, Milchglas n	Milne probability	Milnesche Wahrscheinlichkeit f, Milne-Wahrscheinlichkeit f
milking battery (system)	s. isotopic generator		
Milky Way, Via Lactea	Milchstraße f	Milne['s] problem	Milnesches Problem n
Milky Way [System], Galaxy	Milchstraßensystem n, Galaxis f, Milchstraße f	mimetic	mimetisch, pseudomeroedrisch, pseudosymmetrisch

mimic diagram	Blindschaltbild *n*, Blindschema *n*
min	*s.* minute
min	*s.* minute <of angle>
Minami-indeterminacy	Minami-Unsicherheit *f*
mincing	*s.* rubbing
mineral crust	Gesteinskruste *f*, mineralische Kruste *f*
mineralization	Mineralisation *f*; Vererzung *f*
mineralizer	Mineralisator *m*, Kristallisator
mineralogical hardness, Mohs['] hardness [number]	Mohs-Härte *f*, Mohssche Härte *f*, Härtegrad *m* nach Mohs
minerogenic	minerogen, anorganogen
miner's inch	= 7 l/s *or* 0.7 l/s
miniature bulb, miniature lamp, pygmy lamp	Zwerglampe *f*, Zwergglühlampe *f*
miniature camera	Kleinbildkamera *f*
miniature Edison screw cap	Mignonsockel *m*
miniature lamp	*s.* miniature bulb
miniature tube (valve); bantam tube (valve)	Kleinröhre *f*, Miniaturröhre *f*
miniaturization	Miniaturisierung *f*
minimal curve, isotropic curve	isotrope Kurve *f*, Minimalkurve *f*
minimal polynomial, minimum function	Minimalpolynom *n*
minimal surface	Minimalfläche *f*
minimax principle	Mini-Max-Prinzip *n*, Minimaxprinzip *n*, Minimum-Maximum-Prinzip *n*
minimax solution	minimaxe Lösung *f*
minimeter	Minimeter *n*
minimization, minimizing	Minimierung *f*, Minimalisierung *f*, Minimisierung *f*, Vereinfachung *f*
minimum, minimum value; valley <of the curve>	Minimum *n*, Minimalwert *m*; Mindestwert *m*; Tal *n* <Kurve>
minimum B configuration	Minimum-B-Konfiguration *f*
minimum beam	Minimumstrahl *m*
minimum breakdown voltage <of a gas>	Mindestdurchschlagspannung *f*, Mindestspannung *f* der Spitzenentladung; Mindestspannungsfestigkeit *f*
minimum breakdown voltage of a gap	*s.* sparking potential <el.>
minimum condition	Minimumbedingung *f*; Minimalbedingung *f* <Math.>
minimum corona	Minimumskorona *f*
minimum deviation	Minimum *n* der Ablenkung, Minimalablenkung *f*, minimale Ablenkung *f*
minimum distance of clear vision, distance of punctum proximum	Nahpunktabstand *m* <vom Hornhautscheitel aus gemessen>
minimum duration of measurement	Mindestmeßzeit *f*
minimum entropy principle, principle of minimum entropy	Prinzip *n* der minimalen Entropie
minimum frame speed [for merging of pictures]	*s.* critical frequency of flicker <opt.>
minimum function, minimal polynomial	Minimalpolynom *n*
minimum ionization	Minimumionisation *f*, Minimumionisierung *f*, minimale Ionisation (Ionisierung) *f*, Minimalionisierung *f*, Minimalionisation *f*
minimum number of theoretical plates (stages)	theoretische Mindestbodenzahl *f*
minimum perceptible increment of loudness	Lautstärkeschwelle *f*
minimum permissible cross-section	Mindestquerschnitt *m*
minimum-phase-shift system	Phasenminimumsystem *n*
minimum potential energy theorem, theorem of minimum potential, principle of potential energy, principle of minimum strain energy <elasticity>	Minimalprinzip *n* für die Verschiebungen eines elastischen Körpers
minimum pressure, pressure minimum	Druckminimum *n*, Drucktal *n*, Mindestdruck *m*
minimum principle, principle of minimum	Minimumprinzip *n*; Minimalprinzip *n* <Math., Mech.>
minimum problem	Minimumproblem *n*
minimum reflux ratio	Mindestrücklaufverhältnis *n*
minimum schlieren method	Minimumschlierenverfahren *n*
minimum starting moment	Sattelmoment *n*
minimum suction quantity	Mindestabsaugmenge *f*
minimum temperature, temperature minimum	Tiefsttemperatur *f*, tiefste (minimale) Temperatur *f*, Temperaturminimum *n*
minimum thermometer	Minimumthermometer *n*
minimum threshold of hearing	*s.* threshold of hearing
minimum-to-maximum stress ratio <mech.>	Spannungsverhältnis *n* <Mech.>
minimum turning value	*s.* relative minimum
minimum value	*s.* minimum <of the curve>
minimum variance estimate	Minimalschätzung *f*
minimum water level	Immerwasser *n*, niedrigstes Niedrigwasser *n*
minimum wavelength of bremsstrahlung	Grenzwellenlänge *f* der Bremsstrahlung
minimum work	Mindestarbeit *f*
minimum working current	Ansprechstrom *m*, Ansprechstromstärke *f*
Minkowskian co-ordinates, Minkowskian space and time co-ordinates	Minkowskische Koordinaten (Raum- und Zeitkoordinaten) *fpl*
Minkowskian four-space	*s.* space-time <math.>
Minkowskian geometry, Minkowski geometry	Minkowskische Geometrie *f*
Minkowskian space	*s.* space-time <math.>
Minkowskian space and time co-ordinates, Minkowskian co-ordinates	Minkowskische Koordinaten (Raum- und Zeitkoordinaten) *fpl*
Minkowskian universe	*s.* space-time <math.>
Minkowski force	Minkowski-Kraft *f*
Minkowski geometry, Minkowskian geometry	Minkowskische Geometrie *f*
Minkowski['s] inequality	Minkowskische Ungleichung *f*
Minkowski space (universe, world)	*s.* space-time <math.>
minor, minor determinant, subdeterminant; complementary minor	Unterdeterminante *f*, Minor *m*, Subdeterminante *f*; komplementärer Minor *m*
minorant	Minorante *f*
minor axis, transverse axis; secondary axis <cryst.>	kleine Achse *f*; Nebenachse *f* <Krist.>
minor control	*s.* polygonal method
minor control point	Brechpunkt *m* [des Polygonzuges], Polygonpunkt *m*
minor control point; control point; check point <geo.>	Paßpunkt *m*; Kontrollpunkt *m* <Geo.>

minor determinant, minor, subdeterminant; complementary minor	Unterdeterminante f, Minor m, Subdeterminante f	mirror coated mirror coating, mirroring, metallizing, metallization	s. mirrored Verspiegelung f, Spiegelbelegung f, Spiegelbelag m
minor graduation	Nebenteilung f, Nebenskalenteilung f	mirror coating, reflector coating, coating of the mirror; mirror silvering	Spiegelbelag m, Belag m des Spiegels
minority carrier	Minoritäts[ladungs]träger m, Minderheits[ladungs]träger m, Minorität f	mirror coating mirror condenser [lens]	s. a. mirror surfacing Spiegelkondensor m
minority electron	Minoritätselektron n	mirror dislocation	Spiegelversetzung f
minority emitter	Minoritätsträgeremitter m, Minoritätsemitter m	mirror drum, mirror wheel, polygonal mirror	Spiegelrad n, Spiegeltrommel f, Polygonspiegel m
minority hole	Minoritätsdefektelektron n, Minoritätsloch n	mirror drum scanner, drum scanner, belt scanner	Spiegelradabtaster m, Trommelabtaster m
minor load, preload, initial load	Vorlast f		
minor load Rockwell hardness test, preload Rockwell hardness test	Vorlast-Härteprüfung f	mirrored, metallized, mirror lined, mirror coated	verspiegelt
minor lobe	s. side lobe		
minor planet, asteroid, planetoid, small planet	Planetoid m, Asteroid m, Kleiner Planet m, Zwergplanet m	mirrored scale, mirror scale mirror extensometer	Spiegelskala f, Spiegelskale f Spiegel-Dehnungsmeßgerät n, Spiegeldehnungsmesser m, Spiegel[feinmeß]gerät n <nach Bauschinger>
minor planet, terrestrial planet	erdähnlicher (terrestrischer) Planet m		
minor second	kleine Sekunde f		
Mintrop wave	s. head wave		
minus, negative pole	Minuspol m, negativer Pol m, Minus m	mirror galvanometer, reflecting galvanometer	Spiegelgalvanometer n, Reflex[ions]galvanometer n
minus mark, minus sign (symbol), negative sign; subtraction sign	Minuszeichen n; negatives Vorzeichen n	mirror glass, plate glass	Spiegelglas n
minus material	s. undersize	mirror image, reflected image, image	Spiegelbild n
minus sight	Vorwärtsvisur f, Vorwärtsvisieren n		
minus sign (symbol), minus mark, negative sign; subtraction sign	Minuszeichen n; negatives Vorzeichen n	mirror-image force mirror image function	s. image force Spiegelbildfunktion f
minus wave	Minuswelle f	mirroring	s. mirror coating
minute, min	Minute f, min	mirror instrument	Spiegelinstrument n, Spiegelmeßgerät n
minute, minute of arc, angular minute, sexagesimal minute, ', min <of angle>	Minute f [im Bogenmaß], Winkelminute f, Bogenminute f, Altminute f, <Winkelmaß>	mirror instrument	s. a. luminous pointer instrument
minute[s] pendulum / 84-, Schuler['s] pendulum, 84 min pendulum	Schuler-Pendel n, 84-min-Pendel n, 84-Minuten-Pendel n	mirror lens, catoptric objective, catoptric lens, mirror objective	Spiegelobjektiv n, katoptrisches Objektiv n, Reflexionsobjektiv n; katoptrisches Mikroskopobjektiv n
minute reading, fine[-adjustment] reading	Feinablesung f	mirror-lens objective mirror-lens telescope	s. catadioptric lens Linsenfernrohr n mit Spiegelkompensation, Spiegel-Linsen-System n, Spiegellinsenfernrohr n
minute respiration rate, minute ventilation	Ventilationsgröße f, Atemminutenvolumen n, Minutenvolumen n, AMV		
minutes period / 84.4-, Schuler period, 84.4 min period	Schuler-Frequenz f, 84,4-Minuten-Periode f, 84,4-min-Periode f	mirror-lined, backward mirror-coated	innenverspiegelt; rückwärtig verspiegelt, spiegelhinterlegt, spiegelunterlegt
minute ventilation, minute respiration rate	Ventilationsgröße f, Atemminutenvolumen n, Minutenvolumen n, AMV	mirror lined mirror lining, internal mirror coating; rear silver surfacing, rear silver coating	s. a. mirrored Innenverspiegelung f; Spiegelhinterlegung f, Spiegelunterlegung f, Verspiegelung f an der Rückfläche, rückwärtige Verspiegelung
minute volume [of the heart], cardiac output	Herzminutenvolumen n, Minutenvolumen n		
miobar, miobaric line	Miobare f		
mipor, microporous	mikroporös		
mira	s. mark		
Mira Ceti[-type] star	s. Mira star		
mirage	Luftspiegelung f, Mirage f		
mirage, blaze	„blaze" n, Spiegelung f; „blaze"-Winkel m	mirror machine, magnetic bottle, adiabatic trap, magnetic barrier trap, pyrotron	Spiegelmaschine f, magnetische Spiegelmaschine, magnetische Flasche f, Falle f mit magnetischen Barrieren, adiabatische Falle, magnetische Falle, Pyrotron n
Mira star (variable), Mira Ceti[-type] star, long-period variable of Mira Ceti-type	Mira-Stern m, Mira-Veränderlicher m		
mired, micro[-]reciprocal degree, M	Mired n, Miredwert m, Chromazität f, M	mirror microscope, mirror-type electron microscope	Spiegel[elektronen]mikroskop n, Elektronenspiegelmikroskop n
mirror <of microscope>	Kippspiegel m <Mikroskop>	mirror monochromator, monochromator having a mirror optics	Spiegelmonochromator m
mirror <opt.>	Spiegel m <Opt.>		
mirror	s. a. reflector	mirror nephoscope, reflecting nephoscope; nephoscope	Nephoskop n; Wolkenspiegel m
mirror and scale technique	Methode f der Neigungsänderung		
mirror antenna	reflektierende Antenne f	mirror nuclei, mirror pair of nuclei	Spiegelkerne mpl
mirror aperture, reflector aperture	Spiegelöffnung f	mirror nuclei of the first order	Spiegelkerne mpl erster (1.) Ordnung
mirror arc <of the scale>	Spiegelbogen m <der Skala>	mirror nuclides	Spiegelnuklide npl
mirror arc lamp, reflector arc lamp	Spiegelbogenlampe f		
mirror-bright	spiegelblank	mirror objective	s. mirror lens

mirror oscillograph, mirror oscilloscope	Spiegeloszillograph *m*	**misalignment**, offset, shift[ing]	Versetzung *f*, Verschiebung *f*, Versatz *m*
		mischmetal	Mischmetall *n*
mirror pair of nuclei	s. mirror nuclei	**miscibility gap**	Mischungslücke *f*
mirror plane, plane of mirror [reflection symmetry], reflection plane	Spiegelebene *f*		
mirror point	Spiegelpunkt *m*	**miscible**	mischbar
mirror polygon	Spiegelpolygon *n*		
mirror projector	Spiegelscheinwerfer *m*, Spiegelstrahler *m*; Spiegelanstrahler *m*	**misclosure**, closing error	Schlußfehler *m*, Abschlußfehler *m*; Abschlußwiderspruch *m*
mirror ratio	Spiegelverhältnis *n*		
mirror reading, mirror scale reading	Spiegelablesung *f*; [Gauß-]Poggendorffsche Spiegelablesung	**Mises['] flow equation [/von]**, [von] Mises['] plasticity equation	[von] Misessche Plastizitätsgleichung *f*
mirror reflector, viewing mirror	Spiegelreflektor *m*	**Mises-Hencky flow condition, Mises-Hencky yield condition / von**	s. Mises yield condition
mirror-reflex attachment, reflex attachment	Spiegelreflexaufsatz *m*, Spiegelreflexansatz *m*, Spiegelreflexvorsatz *m*	**Mises ideal plastic body, Mises material,** St. Venant-Mises (Saint Venant-Mises) material	Misesscher plastischer Körper *m*
mirror-reflex camera, reflex camera	Spiegelreflexkamera *f*, Reflexkamera *f*	**Mises['] plasticity equation [/von]**, [von] Mises['] flow equation	[von] Misessche Plastizitätsgleichung *f*
mirror region <plasma physics>; magnetic mirror	magnetischer Spiegel *m*; Spiegelgebiet *n*, [magnetischer] Pfropfen *m* <Plasmaphysik>	**Mises quadratic condition / von**	s. Mises yield condition
mirror scale, mirrored scale	Spiegelskala *f*; Spiegelskale *f*	**Mises['] theorem [/von]**	von Misesscher Satz *m*
mirror scale reading	s. mirror reading	**Mises['] transformation [/von]**	[von] Misessche Transformation *f*
mirror screw	Spiegelschraube *f*	**Mises yield condition (criterion)**, flow condition of Mises, yield criterion of von Mises, von Mises quadratic condition, quadratic yield condition; Mises-Hencky flow condition, von Mises-Hencky yield condition, energy of distortion condition; Huber-Mises-Hencky yield criterion	von Misessche Fließbedingung *f*, Misessche Fließbedingung, Misessche Bedingung *f*, Fließbedingung von Mises, quadratische Fließbedingung; Mises-Henckysche Fließbedingung *f*; Huber-Mises-Henckysche Fließbedingung
mirror sextant; sextant	Sextant *m*, Spiegelsextant *m*		
mirror silvering; mirror (reflector) coating, coating of the mirror	Spiegelbelag *m*, Belag *m* des Spiegels		
mirror surface, specular surface	Spiegelfläche *f*, spiegelnde Fläche *f*		
mirror surfacing, mirror coating, external mirror coating; front silver surfacing, front silver coating	Außenverspiegelung *f*; Verspiegelung *f* an der Frontfläche	**MISFET**	s. metal-insulator-semiconductor field effect transistor
		misfit	s. mismatch
		misfit angle	Fehlanpassungswinkel *m*
		misfit energy	Fehlanpassungsenergie *f*
mirror-symmetric, specular, reverse	spiegel[bild]symmetrisch, spiegelbildlich, spiegelverkehrt, spiegelrecht	**mismatch**, mismatching; mistermination; misfit	Fehlanpassung *f*
mirror-symmetric, enantiomorphous, enantiomorphic, antimeric[al] <chem.>	spiegelbildisomer, optisch isomer, enantiomorph <Chem.>	**mismatched**	nichtangepaßt; fehlangepaßt
		mismatch factor	Anpassungsfehler *m*
mirror-symmetric group	Spiegelsymmetriegruppe *f*	**mismatching**	Fehlanpassung *f* <Größe>
mirror-symmetric isomer	s. optical antimer	**mismatching**	s. a. mismatch
mirror-symmetric isomerism, enantiomorphism, optical isomerism <chem.>	Spiegelbildisomerie *f*, optische Isomerie *f*, Enantiomorphie *f* <Chem.>	**mismatch loss** <el.>	Stoßdämpfung *f* <El.>
		misorientation	Orientierungsfehler *m*; Fehlorientierung *f*
mirror symmetry, specular symmetry	Spiegelsymmetrie *f*	**misphasing**	s. phase shift
mirror symmetry, enantiomorphism, enantiomorphy, enantiomorphic symmetry <cryst.>	Enantiomorphie *f* <Krist.>	**missile**, projectile	Projektil *n*, Geschoß *n*
		mist, thin fog, haze	[leichter] Nebel *m*
		mist	s. a. drizzling fog
		mistake, blunder <math.>	grober Fehler *m* <Math.>
mirror telescope	s. reflecting telescope	**mistake** <num. math.>	Irrtum *m* <num. Math.>
mirror transit instrument, broken transit instrument	Durchgangsinstrument *n* mit geknicktem Fernrohr	**mistermination**	s. mismatch
		mist layer	Dunstschicht *f*; Dunstglocke *f*
mirror transition	Spiegelübergang *m*	**Mitchel float**	Treibboje *f* nach Mitchel, Mitchel-Schwimmer *m*
mirror-type electron microscope, mirror microscope	Spiegel[elektronen]mikroskop *n*, Elektronenspiegelmikroskop *n*	**mitogenetic radiation**, Gurwitsch radiation (rays)	mitogenetische Strahlung *f*
mirror-type precision instrument, precision mirror instrument	Spiegelfeinmeßgerät *n*	**mitosis**, karyokinesis	Mitose *f*, Karyokinese *f*, mitotische Teilung *f*, indirekte Kernteilung *f*, Äquationsteilung *f*
mirror wave, image wave	Spiegelwelle *f*	**mitotic index**	Mitoseindex *m*
mirror wheel, mirror drum, polygonal mirror	Spiegelrad *n*, Spiegeltrommel *f*, Polygonspiegel *m*	**mitotic poison**	Mitosegift *n*

mitotic spindle, spindle, spindle apparatus <of mitosis> — Kernspindel *f*, Teilungsspindel *f*, Spindel *f*, Spindelapparat *m* <Mitose>
mitre angle — 45°-Winkel *m*
mitre square — s. reflecting square
mitron — Mitron *n*
Mitscherlich['s] law — Mitscherlichsches Gesetz *n*
Mitscherlich phenomenon — Mitscherlich-Phänomen *n*
Mittag-Leffler['s] theorem — Mittag-Lefflerscher Satz (Partialbruchsatz; Anschmiegungssatz) *m*
mix, [homogeneous] mixture, uniform mix; intermixture — [homogenes] Gemisch *n*, [homogene] Mischung *f*
mix-crystal — s. solid solution
mixed bed — Mischbett *n*
mixed bed filter, mixed bed ion exchanger — Mischbettfilter *n*, Mischbettaustauscher *m*
mixed bond, polarized atomic bond — gemischte Bindung *f*, polarisierte Atombindung *f*
mixed boundary conditions — gemischte Randbedingungen *fpl*
mixed boundary value problem, mixed problem — gemischtes Randwertproblem (Problem) *n*, Anfangs-Randwertproblem *n*, Anfangswert-Randwert-Problem *n*, gemischte Randwertaufgabe *f*
mixed catalyst, multicomponent catalyst — Mehrstoffkatalysator *m*, Mischkatalysator *m*
mixed characteristic [function] — s. mixed eikonal
mixed chromatography — kombinierte Chromatographie *f*
mixed cloud — Mischwolke *f*
mixed colour, confusion colour <opt.> — Mischfarbe *f* <Opt.>
mixed condensation — Mischkondensation *f*
mixed conduction, mixed electrical conduction — gemischte [elektrische] Leitung *f*, Gemischtleitung *f*, Mischleitung *f*
mixed conductor — Gemischtleiter *m*, Mischleiter *m*, gemischter Leiter *m*
mixed coupling — gemischte Kopplung *f*
mixed crystal — s. solid solution
mixed crystallization — Mischkristallisation *f*
mixed derivative — gemischte Ableitung *f*
mixed distribution — s. compound distribution
mixed double bond — s. dative bond
mixed eikonal; mixed characteristic [function], Hamilton's mixed characteristic function *W* — gemischtes Eikonal *n*; gemischte charakteristische Funktion *f* [von Hamilton], Hamiltons gemischte charakteristische Funktion *W*
mixed electrical conduction, mixed conduction — gemischte [elektrische] Leitung *f*, Gemischtleitung *f*, Mischleitung *f*
mixed ensemble <stat.> — gemischte Gesamtheit *f*, Gemisch *n* <Stat.>
mixed film lubrication — Mischschmierung *f*
mixed flow — gemischte Strömung *f*
mixed flow turbine — s. Francis turbine
mixed fracture — Mischbruch *m* <Gleit- und Trennbruch>
mixed friction, semifluid friction — Mischreibung *f*, gemischte Reibung *f*
mixed gas laser — Mischgaslaser *m*
mixed grain [photographic] emulsion — Mischkornemulsion *f*
mixed illumination; mixed lighting — Mischbeleuchtung *f*
mixed image, double image — Mischbild *n*
mixed interaction — gemischte Wechselwirkung *f*
mixed isomorphic crystal — s. solid solution
mixed layer — s. layer of mixing

mixed level system — gemischtes Niveausystem *n*
mixed light — Mischlicht *n*
mixed lighting; mixed illumination — Mischbeleuchtung *f*
mixed light lamp, blended lamp — Mischlichtlampe *f*, Mischlichtstrahler *m*
mixed mode — s. hybrid wave
mixed problem — s. mixed boundary value problem
mixed product — s. parallelepipedal product
mixed radiation, composite radiation, complex radiation — Strahlungsgemisch *n*, Strahlengemisch *n*, zusammengesetzte Strahlung *f*, Mischstrahlung *f*
mixed rain and snow — s. rain and snow
mixed reflection — gemischte Reflexion *f*
mixed resonator — gemischter Resonator *m*
mixed-salt catalyzer — Mischsalzkatalysator *m*
mixed semiconductor — gemischter Halbleiter (Leiter) *m*, Gemischt[halb]leiter *m*, Misch[halb]leiter *m*
mixed series — Reihe *f* von Fundamental- und Anschlußsternen
mixed tensor, cocontravariant tensor — gemischter Tensor *m*
mixed term — gemischtes Glied *n*
mixed tides, compound tides, composite tides — gemischte (zusammengesetzte) Gezeiten *pl*
mixed transmission — gemischte Transmission (Durchlassung) *f*
mixed wave — s. hybrid wave
mixed waves — Wellengemisch *n*
mixer — s. mixing stage <el.>
mixer circuit, mixing circuit — Mischschaltung *f*
mixer diode — Mischdiode *f*
mixer-settler — Mixer-Settler *m*, Extraktionsapparat *m* vom Typ Mischen-Klären
mixer stage — s. mixing stage <el.>
mixing, dubbing <of sound>; rerecording — Mischen *n*, Mischung *f*, Tonmischung *f* <Ton>
mixing, conversion, frequency change <el.> — Mischung *f*, Mischen *n* <El.>
mixing <math.> — Mischen *n*, Mischung *f* <über die Indizes> <Math.>
mixing, compounding; mixing thoroughly; interchange; blending <e.g. of plastics> <mech.> — Mischen *n*, Mischung *f*, Vermischung *f*; Vermengen *n*; Durchmischung *f* <Mech.>
mixing circuit, mixer circuit — Mischschaltung *f*
mixing cloud, cloud formed during mixing of air masses — Mischungswolke *f*
mixing coefficient — Vermischungskoeffizient *m*
mixing efficiency — Homogenisierungsausbeute *f*; Mischwirkungsgrad *m*
mixing energy, mixing work, energy of work — Vermischungsarbeit *f*, Vermischungsenergie *f*
mixing enthalpy — s. enthalpy of mixing
mixing entropy — s. entropy of mixing
mixing heat — s. enthalpy of mixing
mixing layer — s. layer of mixing
mixing length, Prandtl['s] mixing length — [Prandtlscher] Mischungsweg *m*, [Prandtlsche] Mischungslänge *f*
mixing length theory — Mischungswegansatz *m*, Mischungsweghypothese *f*
mixing length vector — Mischungswegvektor *m*
mixing loss, loss in mixing — Vermischungsverlust *m*
mixing parameter — Mischparameter *m*

mixing proportion	s. mixture proportion	mobility tensor	Beweglichkeitstensor m
mixing rate, mixing speed	Vermischungsgeschwindigkeit f	Möbius band, Möbius strip	Möbiussches Band n
mixing ratio	s. humidity-mixing ratio	Möbius['] crystal	Möbius-Kristall m
mixing speed	s. mixing rate	Möbius['] law [of refraction]	Möbiussches Brechungsgesetz n, Brechungsgesetz von Möbius
mixing stage, mixer stage, mixer, first detector stage, converter stage, converter <el.>	Mischstufe f <El.>	Möbius net	Möbius-Netz n
		Möbius strip	s. Möbius band
mixing thoroughly	s. mixing <mech.>	Möbius['] transformation	s. homographic transformation
mixing tube (valve)	s. converter tube	mock antenna	s. artificial antenna
mixing work, mixing energy, energy of mixing	Vermischungsarbeit f, Vermischungsenergie f	mocksun, parhelion, sun-dog	Nebensonne f
mixture, homogeneous mixture, [uniform] mix; intermixture	[homogenes] Gemisch n, [homogene] Mischung f	mock-up	Modell n 1:1, Nachbildung f <in natürlicher Größe>
mixture calorimeter	s. liquid calorimeter	mock-up test	Scheinversuch m
mixture curve	Mischungslinie f, Mischungskurve f, Mischungsdiagramm n	modal column	s. eigenvector
		modal value	s. mode <stat.>
		mode, tonality <ac.>	Tonart f <Ak.>
mixture fog	Mischungsnebel m	mode, most probable value, modal value <stat.>	wahrscheinlichster (häufigster, plausibelster, dichtester) Wert m, Dichtemittel n, Dichtewert m, Gipfelwert m, Mode m, Modus m, Modalwert m Scheitel[wert] m <Stat.>
mixture law, mixture rule	Mischungsregel f [von Richmann]	mode	s. a. vibrational mode
mixture proportion (ratio), [mixing] proportion, mixing ratio, ratio of components	Mischungsverhältnis n	mode	s. a. mode of vibration
		mode admittance	Wellenleitwert m für den Schwingungstyp
		mode changer, mode transducer, mode transformer	Wellentypwandler m, Wellentypumformer m, Wellen[typum]wandler m, Wellentyptransformator m
mixture rule, mixture law	Mischungsregel f [von Richmann]		
mixture temperature	Mischtemperatur f	mode conversion, wave mode conversion, mode transformation, wave mode transformation	Wellentypumwandlung f, Wellentypumformung f, Wellentyptransformation f, Wellenformumwandlung f
mizzle, mizzling	s. drizzle		
MKK system, Yerkes system, Morgan-Keenan-Kellman system	MKK-System n, System n von Morgan-Keenan-Kellman		
MKSA system, m.k.s.a. system [of units]	s. Giorgi system [of units]	mode coupler	Wellentypkoppler m, Mode[n]koppler m
m.k.s. degree Kelvin system [of units], metre-kilogramme-second-degree Kelvin system [of units]	m-kg-s-°K-System n, Meter-Kilogramm-Sekunde-Grad Kelvin-System n	mode coupling theory	Theorie f der Modekopplung
		mode crossing	Wellen[typ]kreuzung f, Modenkreuzung f
		mode filter, wave-mode filter	Wellentypfilter n, Schwingungstypfilter n, Modenfilter n
m.k.s. (mks) system <of mechanical units>, M.K.S. system <of units>, metre-kilogramme-second system [of units]	MKS-System n, MKS-Maßsystem n, Meter-Kilogramm-Sekunde-System n [der Mechanik]	mode filter slot <el.>	Schlitzwellenfilter n, Schlitzblende f <El.>
		mode function	Modenfunktion f, Wellen[typ]funktion f
m.k.s. unit, M.K.S. unit	MKS-Einheit f	mode impedance	Wellenwiderstand m für den Schwingungstyp
MK-system, Morgan-Keenan system	MK-System n, System n von Morgan und Keenan		
M meter	s. Machmeter	mode in guide	s. waveguide mode
M/N ratio, yield per ion pair	M/N-Verhältnis n, Ausbeute f pro Ionenpaar	model atmosphere, model of atmosphere	Modellatmosphäre f, Atmosphärenmodell n
		model circuit	Modellschaltbild n
m × n table, contingency table	Kontingenztafel f, m × n-Tafel f	model experiment, model test[ing], model study; scale-model test[ing]	Modellversuch m, Versuch m am Modell
mobile	beweglich, transportabel, fahrbar, ortsveränderlich <komplett oder im Betrieb>		
		model flow, scale-model flow	Modellströmung f
		model law	Modellgesetz n, Modellregel f
mobile anticyclone, anticyclone, migratory High	Antizyklone f, wanderndes Hoch n, wanderndes Hochdruckgebiet n	model[l]ing	s. simulation
		model[l]ing	s. a. replica method
		model of atmosphere, model atmosphere	Modellatmosphäre f, Atmosphärenmodell n
mobile cyclone, cyclone, migratory depression <meteo.>	Zyklone f, wanderndes Tief[druckgebiet] n, [atmosphärische] Störung f <Meteo.>	model of Einstein and De Sitter, Einstein-De Sitter model, universe of Einstein and De Sitter	Weltmodell n von Einstein und de Sitter, Einstein-de-Sitter-Welt f, Einstein-de-Sitter-Universum n
mobile phase, moving phase	mobile (bewegliche) Phase f, Mobilphase f	model of energy bands	s. band model
mobile phase	s. a. solvent	model of Lemaître and Eddington, Lemaître-Eddington model	Lemaître-Eddingtonsches Modell n
mobility	Beweglichkeit f		
mobility <mech.>	Verschiebbarkeit f, Verschieblichkeit f <Mech.>	model of nucleus, nuclear model	Kernmodell n, Modell n des Atomkerns
mobility-diffusion coefficient relation	s. Einstein['s] relation	model of oscillating liquid drop, model of the fluctuating liquid drop	Modell n des schwingenden Tropfens
mobility inertia	s. compliance		
mobility of electrons	s. electronic mobility	model of rotating nucleus	Rotationsmodell n [des Atomkerns], Modell n des rotierenden Kerns
mobility of ions, ionic mobility, ion mobility	Ionenbeweglichkeit f, Beweglichkeit f der Ionen		
mobility resistance	s. responsivity		

model of the compound nucleus, compound-nucleus model	Zwischenkernmodell n, Compoundkernmodell n
model of the fluctuating liquid drop, model of oscillating liquid drop	Modell n des schwingenden Tropfens
model of the universe	Welt[all]modell n
model of united atom, united atom model	Modell n des vereinigten Atoms
model representation	Modellvorstellung f
model study, model test[ing], model experiment; scale-model test[ing]	Modellversuch m, Versuch m am Modell
mode of decay (disintegration), mode of radioactive decay	Zerfallstyp m, Zerfallsart f
mode of electric type	s. E[-] mode
mode of frequency	s. mode of vibration
mode of interaction, type of interaction, interaction type	Wechselwirkungstyp m, Wechselwirkungsart f, Art f der Wechselwirkung
mode of magnetic type	s. H[-] mode
mode of operation, regime	Betriebsweise f, Betriebsart f, Betrieb m, Betriebsregime n, Betriebsverhältnisse npl, Regime n; Fahrweise f
mode of operation, principle of operation, operating mode <of apparatus, instrument>	Wirkungsweise f, Funktionsweise f, Funktionsprinzip n, Wirkungsprinzip n; Wirkungsschema n
mode of oscillation	s. mode of vibration
mode of radiation, eigenstate of radiation	Eigenzustand m der Strahlung
mode of radiation, type (character, nature) of radiation	Strahlungsart f, Strahlenart f
mode of radioactive decay, mode of decay (disintegration)	Zerfallstyp m, Zerfallsart f
mode of tropospheric propagation, tropospheric mode	troposphärischer Schwingungstyp (Wellentyp) m, troposphärische Schwingungsart (Mode) f
mode of vibration, mode of wave, mode of oscillation (frequency), mode, wave mode	Schwingungs[wellen]typ m, Schwingungsart f, Schwingungsmode f, Mode f, Schwingungsmodus m, Modus m, Rasse f, Wellenart f, Wellentyp m, Welle f, Eigenzustand m der Schwingung
mode of wave	s. a. vibrational mode
moderated neutron	abgebremstes Neutron n, Bremsneutron n
moderated reactor	moderierter Reaktor m
moderate energy	s. medium energy
moderate gale, strong wind <of Beaufort No. 7>	steifer Wind m <Stärke 7>
moderate sea	mäßig bewegte See f, mäßige See, mäßiger Wellengang m, mäßige Wellen fpl <Stärke 4>
moderate-strong interaction	mittelstarke Wechselwirkung f
moderate temperature, intermediate (medium) temperature	mittlere Temperatur f
moderate wind <of Beaufort No. 4>	mäßige Brise f <Stärke 4>
moderating column	Moderatorsäule f, Bremssäule f
moderating material	s. moderator
moderating power, slowing-down power <for neutrons>	Bremsvermögen n, Bremskraft f <Neutronen>
moderating ratio	Bremsverhältnis n
moderation, slowing-down, slow down <of neutrons>	Bremsung f, Abbremsung f, Moderierung f <Neutronen>
moderation area	s. slowing-down area
moderation length, length of moderation, slowing-down length	Bremslänge f
moderator, moderating material	Moderator m, Bremsmittel n, Bremsstoff m, Bremssubstanz f, Neutronenbremse f
moderator-coolant, coolant-moderator	Kühlbremsmittel n, Kühlmittel-Moderator m, Kühlmittel n und Moderator m
moderator heat	Moderatorwärme f
moderator-reflector, reflector-moderator	Moderator-Reflektor m, Reflektor-Moderator m
mode shift, frequency sliding, frequency instability	Frequenzgleiten n, Frequenzinkonstanz f, Frequenzinstabilität f
mode transducer	s. mode changer
mode transformation, mode conversion, wave mode conversion, wave mode transformation	Wellentypumwandlung f, Wellentypumformung f, Wellentyptransformation f, Wellenformumwandlung f
mode transformer	s. mode changer
modification, variation <e.g. of experimental arrangement>	Modifizierung f, Abänderung f, Abwandlung f <z. B. Versuchsanordnung>
modification, variety <bio.>	Abart f, Varietät f, Spielart f, var.; Rasse f <Bio.>
modification <chem.; cryst.>	Modifikation f
modified Bessel function <of the first kind>	modifizierte Bessel-Funktion f [erster Art], modifizierte Besselsche Funktion f [erster Art], modifizierte Zylinderfunktion f erster Art
modified Bessel function of the second kind	s. Macdonald['s] function
modified conical projection	unechte Kegelprojektion f, pseudokonische (unechtkonische) Projektion f, unechter Kegelentwurf m, pseudokonischer (unechtkonischer) Entwurf m
modified cylindrical projection	unechte Zylinderprojektion f, pseudozylindrische (unecht-zylindrische) Projektion f, unechter Zylinderentwurf m, pseudozylindrischer (unecht-zylindrischer) Entwurf m
modified English mounting, cross axis mounting	englische Achsenmontierung f
modified index of refraction	modifizierter Brechungsindex m
modified length	s. reduced buckling length
modified Mathieu function	modifizierte Mathieusche Funktion f
modified Mercalli intensity scale [of 1931], scale of seismic intensity, seismic scale	Erdbebenskala f [von Mercalli-Sieberg-Cancani], Skala f von Mercalli-Sieberg-Cancani
modified projection, non-perspective projection	unechte (nichtperspektivische) Projektion f
modified Rayleigh number	modifizierte Rayleigh-Zahl f
modified scattering, Compton scatter[ing]	Compton-Streuung f
modulability	s. modulation capability
modular angle	Modularwinkel m
modular design principle	s. modular principle
modular equation	Modulargleichung f
modular function	Modulfunktion f
modular group	Modulgruppe f
modular principle [of construction], module principle [of construction], unit principle [of construction], unitized principle [of construction], modular design principle, units construction principle, UCP; module technique	Baukastenprinzip n, Baukastenbauweise f, Bausteinprinzip n
modular unit	s. module
modulated in density, density-modulated	dichtemoduliert
modulating current	Modulationsstrom m

modulating

modulating voltage	Modulationsspannung f	modulus of dilatation	s. bulk modulus [of elasticity]
modulating wave	Modulationswelle f	modulus of elasticity	s. Young['s] modulus
		modulus of elasticity for (in) tension	Zugelastizitätsmodul m, Elastizitätsmodul m für Zug
modulation	Modulation f, Modelung f; Einmodulieren n	modulus of elasticity in shear	s. shear modulus
modulation; control	Aussteuerung f	modulus of elongation (expansion, extension)	s. Young['s] modulus
modulation bridge	s. balanced modulator	modulus of inelastic buckling, reduced modulus [of elasticity], double modulus	Knickmodul m [nach Kármán], Knickzahl f, Kármánscher Knickmodul m
modulation capability, modulability	Modulationsfähigkeit f, Modulierbarkeit f		
modulation capacity	Modulationsumfang m, Modulationskapazität f; Aussteuerbarkeit f		
modulation coefficient, modulation factor	Modulationsfaktor m; Modulationsgrad m <AM>	modulus of periodicity, periodicity modulus	Periodizitätsmodul m, zyklische Konstante f
modulation conductance	Modulationsleitwert m	modulus of precision	Genauigkeitszahl f, Genauigkeitsmodul m, Präzisionsmaß n, Maß n der Präzision
modulation depth	s. percentage modulation		
modulation factor, modulation coefficient	Modulationsfaktor m; Modulationsgrad m <AM>		
modulation frequency	Modulationsfrequenz f, Modulierfrequenz f	modulus of resilience	spezifische Formänderungsarbeit f bis zur Elastizitätsgrenze, Resilienz f
modulation gain, transmission gain	Sendegewinn m [für Modulationsverfahren]	modulus of resistance, strength coefficient	Festigkeitskennwert m, Festigkeitszahl f, Festigkeitsziffer f, Festigkeitsmodul m
modulation grid	s. modulator <e.g. of electron gun>		
modulation hum	Modulationsbrumm[en n] m	modulus of rigidity	s. shear modulus
		modulus of rupture, modulus of stretch, rupture (stretch, tension) modulus, ultimate (fracture, absolute) strength, breaking point <mech.>	Bruchfestigkeit f, Bruchgrenze f, statische Zerreißfestigkeit f, Bruchmodul m, Zerreißmodul m, Zugmodul m <Mech.>
modulation index, phase modulation index	Modulationsindex m, Phasenwinkelhub m; Nullphasenwinkelhub m		
modulation noise, flicker noise	Modulationsrauschen n, Funkelrauschen n, Flickerrauschen n, 1/f-Rauschen n		
modulation of light, light modulation, intensity modulation	Modulation f des Lichtes, Lichtmodulation f, Lichtsteuerung f	modulus of stiffness, stiffness modulus	Steifigkeitsmodul m
		modulus of stretch	s. modulus of rupture
modulation of reflected signal, echo modulation	Rückstrahlmodulation f	modulus of the foundation	Bettungszahl f, Flächenbettungszahl f
modulation transfer function, MTF	Modulationsübertragungsfunktion f, MÜF, MTF	modulus of torsion	s. shear modulus
modulation trapezoid	Modulationstrapez n	modulus of volume elasticity (expansion)	s. bulk modulus [of elasticity]
modulator	Modulator m, Modler m; Modulationsgerät n; Tastsender m, getasteter Sender m	Moebius counter	s. twisted ring scaling circuit
		Moessbauer ...	s. Mössbauer ...
		mofette	Mofette f; Säuerling m
modulator, modulator electrode, modulation grid, grid, Wehnelt cylinder, Wehnelt modulator, Wehnelt grid <e.g. of electron gun>	Wehnelt-Zylinder m, Wehnelt-Blende f, Wehnelt-Elektrode f, Steuerzylinder m, Steuerscheibe f, Gitter n 1 <z. B. Elektronenkanone>	Mohn effect	Mohn-Effekt m
		Moho	s. Mohorovičić discontinuity
		Mohorovičić discontinuity, Moho, M-discontinuity	Mohorovičić-Diskontinuität f, Moho f
		Mohr['s] area moment circle, area moment circle. Mohr['s] circle for inertia	Trägheitskreis m, Mohrscher Trägheitskreis
modulator electrode, control (guide) electrode; gate electrode <of the valve>	Steuerelektrode f		
		Mohr['s] circle [diagram], circle diagram of Mohr [for stress], Mohr['s] circle for stress	Mohrscher Spannungskreis (Spannungs- und Verzerrungskreis, Kreis) m, Spannungskreis
modulator electrode	s. a. modulator <e.g. of electron gun>		
module, modular unit, module standard unit; module component; module assembly	Modul m, Modulschaltung f; Modulbaustein m; Modulbauelement n	Mohr['s] circle for inertia	s. Mohr's area moment circle
		Mohr['s] circle for stress	s. Mohr['s] circle
		Mohr['s] envelope of rupture	Mohrsche Bruchlinie (Hüllkurve) f
module / by	dem Betrage nach	Mohr-Land area moment circle	Mohr-Landscher Trägheitskreis m
module assembly (component)	s. module	Mohr['s] litre	Mohrsches Liter n
module of periods, period module	Periodenmodul m	Mohr['s] [strength] theory, theory of limiting stress condition	Hypothese f des elastischen Grenzzustandes [von Mohr]
module of plastic strain, plasticity modulus	Modul m der plastischen Formänderung		
module principle [of construction]	s. modular principle	Mohr-Westphal balance, [direct-reading] balance of Westphal	Mohrsche Waage f, [Mohr-]Westphalsche Waage f
module standard unit	s. module		
module technique	s. modular principle	Mohs['] hardness [number], mineralogical hardness	Mohs-Härte f, Mohssche Härte f, Härtegrad m nach Mohs
moduli of elasticity	Elastizitätsmoduln mpl, elastische Widerstandszahlen fpl		
modulo, mod	modulo, mod	Mohs['] hardness scale, Mohs['] scale, Mohs['] scale of hardness, Mohs['] table	Härteskala f nach Mohs, Mohs-Härte-Skala f, Mohssche (Mohs', Bruhnsche) Härteskala
modulus <of elliptic integral>	Modul m <des elliptischen Integrals>		
modulus	s. a. absolute value <of a real or complex number>	moiré, Moiré, moiré effect, moiré fringes, moiré pattern	Moiréeffekt m, Moirésstreifen mpl, Moiré[interferenz]-muster n, Moiré n
modulus of compression (cubic compressibility)	s. bulk modulus [of elasticity]		
modulus of deflection of the elastic support, deflection modulus of the elastic support	Nachgiebigkeitsmodul m der elastischen Unterlage (Stütze)	moiré method, moiré technique, technique of moiré fringes	Moirémethode f, [interferometrisches] Isopachenverfahren n
		moiré pattern	s. moiré

moiré technique — s. moiré method
moist adiabat, moist adiabatic curve (line), saturation (wet) adiabat, pseudoadiabat, pseudoadiabatic line — Feuchtadiabate f, Pseudoadiabate f
moist adiabatic, wet adiabatic, pseudoadiabatic — feuchtadiabatisch, kondensationsadiabatisch, pseudoadiabatisch
moist adiabatic curve — s. moist adiabat
moist adiabatic instability (lability), conditional instability — Feuchtlabilität f, feuchtadiabatische Labilität f
moist adiabatic lapse rate — s. saturated adiabatic lapse rate
moist adiabatic line — s. moist adiabat
moistening — s. humidification
moist-labile, wet-labile, pseudo-labile — feuchtlabil, pseudolabil
moist-o-graph, hygrograph — Hygrograph m, Feuchtigkeitsschreiber m, Feuchteschreiber m, Luftfeuchtigkeitsschreiber m
moist stability, saturated adiabatic stability — Feuchtstabilität f, feuchtadiabatische Stabilität f
moist-stable, wet-stable — feuchtstabil
moisture — s. humidity
moisture absorbing power, moisture absorptivity — Wasserdampfaufnahmevermögen n, Feuchtigkeitsaufnahmevermögen n
moisture absorption, absorption of moisture — Feuchtigkeitsaufnahme f, Aufnahme f von Feuchtigkeit
moisture absorptivity — s. moisture absorbing power
moisture capacity — s. water-holding capacity
moisture conductivity [coefficient] — Feuchtigkeitsleitzahl f
moisture content — s. humidity
moisture-content determination (measurement), determination (measurement) of moisture content — Feuchtemessung f, Feuchtebestimmung f, Feuchtigkeitsmessung f, Feuchtigkeitsbestimmung f
moisture-content measuring device — s. moisture meter
moisture-holding capacity — s. water-holding capacity
moisture meter; moisture-content measuring device — Feuchtemeßgerät n, Feuchtigkeitsmeßgerät n, Feuchtemesser m, Feuchtigkeitsmesser m
moisture of steam, steam moisture, steam wetness — Feuchtigkeit (Nässe) f des Dampfes, Dampffeuchtigkeit f, Dampfnässe f, Dampffeuchte f
moisture separator — s. separator
Moivre-Laplace['s] limit theorem — Moivre-Laplacescher Grenzwertsatz m
Moivre['s] theorem, Demoivre['s] theorem — Moivrescher Lehrsatz (Satz) m, Moivresche Formel f, Satz von Moivre, Moivre-Formel f
Mokroushin['s] formula — Mokroushinsche Formel f
mol, mole, molar unit; gramme-mole[cule], gram-mol[ecule], gram[me]-molecular weight, formula weight — Mol n; Grammol n, Grammolekül n, Gramm-Molekül n, Formelgewicht n, mol
molal concentration — s. molality
molal depression of freezing point — s. cryoscopic constant
molal elevation of boiling point — s. ebullioscopic constant
molality, molal concentration, mole-per-weight concentration — Molalität f, Kilogrammmolarität f, molale Konzentration f, Gewichtsmolarität f
molal lowering of freezing point — s. cryoscopic constant
molal rise of boiling point — s. ebullioscopic constant
molal solution — molale Lösung f
molar, M ‹chem.; phys. also: of order of magnitude of moles› — molar, m, M ‹Chem.; Phys. auch: von der Größenordnung Mol›; teilchenmengenbezogen
molar absorbancy index, molar absorptivity — s. molar extinction coefficient
molar concentration — s. molarity
molar conductance, molar conductivity — s. molecular conductivity
molar depression of freezing point — s. cryoscopic constant
molar dispersion (dispersivity) — s. molecular dispersion ‹opt.›
molar elevation of boiling point — s. ebullioscopic constant
molar enthalpy — molare Enthalpie f, Molenthalpie f
molar entropy — molare Entropie f, Molentropie f
molar extinction coefficient, molecular extinction coefficient, extinction coefficient for (per, at) unit concentration, molar absorptivity (absorbancy index) — molekulare Extinktionskonstante f, molare Extinktionskonstante, spezifische Extinktionskonstante, molarer [dekadischer] Extinktionskoeffizient m, Molarextinktion f
molar fraction, mole fraction, mol[e]fraction, molecular fraction — Molenbruch m
molar free energy, molar Helmholtz['] free energy — molare freie Energie f, Potential n
molar gas constant — s. gas constant
molar heat [capacity] — s. molecular heat [capacity] ‹at constant pressure or at constant volume›
molar heat of transformation (transition), molar transformation (transition) heat — molare Umwandlungswärme f; molare Umwandlungsenthalpie f
molar Helmholtz['] free energy, molar free energy — molare freie Energie f, Potential n
molarity, mol[ecul]ar concentration, mole-per-litre concentration, mol concentration ‹US› — Molarität f, Litermolarität f, molare Konzentration f, Konzentration in Mol/Liter, Volumenmolarität f
molar lowering of freezing point — s. cryoscopic constant
molar mass — molare Masse f, Molmasse f
molar parachor — Molparachor m
molar polarizability, molar polarization — s. molecular polarizability
molar quantity ‹therm.› — molare Größe f ‹Therm.›
molar quantity — s. a. mean molar quantity ‹of mixture› ‹therm.›
molar ratio, mole ratio, molecular ratio — Molverhältnis n, Molenverhältnis n
molar refraction, molecular refraction — Molekularrefraktion f, Molrefraktion f
molar rise of boiling point — s. ebullioscopic constant
molar rotation — s. molecular rotary power
molar solution, 1 M solution — molare Lösung f, m-Lösung f, 1 m Lösung
molar sound velocity, molar speed of sound, molar velocity of sound — molare Schallgeschwindigkeit f
molar susceptibility — Molsuszeptibilität f, molare Suszeptibilität f
molar transformation (transition) heat — s. molar heat of transformation
molar unit — s. mol
molar velocity of sound, molar speed of sound, molar sound velocity — molare Schallgeschwindigkeit f
molar volume, molecular volume — Molvolumen n, mol[ekul]ares Volumen n, Mol[ekul]arvolumen n
molar weight — s. molecular weight
molar yield, molecular yield — Molausbeute f
molcohesion, molecular cohesion — Molkohäsion f, Molekülkohäsion f
mol concentration ‹US› — s. molarity
mole — s. mol
molectronics, molecular electronics — Molekularelektronik f, Molektronik f
molecular ‹phys. also: of order of magnitude of a molecule› — Molekular-, Molekül-, molekular ‹Phys. auch: von der Größenordnung eines Moleküls›
molecular absorption coefficient — molekularer Absorptionskoeffizient m
molecular absorption spectroscopy — Absorptions-Molekülspektroskopie f
molecular abundance — s. mole fraction

molecular

molecular acid, neutral acid	Molekülsäure f, Neutralsäure f	**molecular disorder**, molecular chaos	molekulare Unordnung f, molekulares Chaos n
molecular acoustic absorption, molecular sound absorption	molekulare Schallabsorption f	**molecular-disperse system**, molecular dispersion	molekulardisperses System n
molecular acoustics	Molekularakustik f	**molecular dispersion**, molar dispersion, molecular dispersivity, molar dispersivity, specific dispersivity <opt.>	Molekulardispersion f, Moldispersion f, molekulare Dispersion f <Opt.>
molecular adsorption, monomolecular adsorption, unimolecular adsorption	monomolekulare Adsorption f, Adsorption in molekularer Schicht		
molecular aerodynamics	s. superaerodynamics	**molecular dispersivity**	s. molecular dispersion
molecular aggregate	s. molecule aggregate	**molecular disruption**	s. molecular decomposition
molecular air pump, Gaede['s] molecular pump, molecular drag pump	Molekularluftpumpe f [nach Gaede], Gaedesche Molekularluftpumpe	**molecular dissociation**, disassociation, dissociation in molecules	Entassoziation f, Desassoziation f
molecular amplifier	Molekularverstärker m	**molecular dissociation**	s. a. molecular decomposition
molecular association	s. association of molecules		
molecular attraction; molecular attraction force	Molekülanziehung f; Molekülanziehungskraft f	**molecular dissymmetry due to hindered rotation**	s. rotational isomerism
molecular band, spectral band, band	Spektralbande f, Bande f, Molekülbande f	**molecular distillation**, projective distillation, short-path distillation	Molekulardestillation f, Kurzwegdestillation f, Freiwegdestillation f, Hochvakuumdestillation f
molecular base, neutral base	Molekülbase f, Neutralbase f	**molecular drag pump**	s. Gaede['s] molecular pump
molecular beam, molecular ray	Molekularstrahl m, Molekülstrahl m, Molekularstrahl[en]bündel n, Molekülstrahl[en]bündel n	**molecular effusion**	Molekulareffusion f
molecular-beam maser	Molekularstrahlmaser m	**molecular electronics**, molectronics	Molekularelektronik f, Molektronik f
molecular-beam spectrometer	Molekularstrahlspektrometer n, Molekularstrahlresonanzapparatur f	**molecular elevation of boiling point**	s. ebullioscopic constant
molecular-beam spectroscopy	Molekularstrahlspektroskopie f	**molecular emission spectroscopy**	Emissions-Molekülspektroskopie f
molecular biology	Molekularbiologie f		
		molecular energy level, energy level of the molecule, molecular level; molecular term	Molekülniveau n, Energieniveau n des Moleküls; Molekülterm m
molecular bond	Molekülbindung f, molekulare Bindung f		
molecular chaos, molecular disorder	molekulare Unordnung f, molekulares Chaos n		
molecular circuit	Molekularschaltung f, molekularelektronische Schaltung f	**molecular energy state**, molecular state; energy state of the molecule	Molekülzustand m, Energiezustand m des Moleküls
molecular clock	Molekuluhr f, Molekularuhr f	**molecular extinction coefficient**	s. molar extinction coefficient
molecular cluster	s. cluster <of molecules>	**molecular field**	s. Weiss internal field
molecular cohesion, molcohesion	Molkohäsion f, Molekülkohäsion f	**molecular field coefficient**, Weiss field constant, molecular field constant	Weissscher Koeffizient m, Weiss-Koeffizient m, Weissscher Proportionalitätsfaktor m, Konstante f des molekularen Weissschen Feldes
molecular coil	s. clue molecule		
molecular colloid	Molekülkolloid n		
molecular compound	Molekülverbindung f, Molekülkomplex m, gleichzähliges Assoziat n		
molecular concentration	s. molarity	**molecular field constant**	s. molecular field coefficient
molecular conductance	s. molecular conductivity		
molecular conductivity, molecular conductance, molar conductivity, molar conductance	molare (molekulare) Leitfähigkeit f, Molekularleitfähigkeit f	**molecular flow**, free-molecule flow, molecule flow, low-density flow	freie Molekularströmung f, Molekularströmung f, molekulare Strömung f
molecular conductivity at infinite dilution	molare Leitfähigkeit f bei unendlicher Verdünnung, Grenzleitfähigkeit f	**molecular fluorescence**	Molekülfluoreszenz f
molecular cross-section	s. gas-kinetic cross-section	**molecular force**	Molekularkraft f
molecular crystal	Molekülkristall m, Molekülgitterkristall m, molekularer Kristall m	**molecular force field**	Molekularkraftfeld n
		molecular formula	s. empirical formula
molecular crystal structure	Molekülkristallstruktur f	**molecular fraction**, mole fraction, molfraction, molar fraction, molefraction	Molenbruch m
molecular current, Ampère['s] molecular current, elementary current	Molekularstrom m, Ampèrescher Molekularstrom (Ringstrom m, Kreisstrom m), Elementarstrom m, molekularer Kreisstrom		
		molecular free path	s. molecular mean free path
		molecular friction	Molekülreibung f, molekulare Reibung f
molecular decomposition, molecular disruption, molecular dissociation, disruption (decomposition) of the molecule	Moleküldissoziation f	**molecular gas**	Molekülgas n
		molecular gauge	s. molecular vacuum gauge
		molecular generator	s. maser oscillator
		molecular genetics	Molekulargenetik f
		molecular group	Molekülgruppe f \
molecular degree of freedom	molekularer Freiheitsgrad m	**molecular heat [capacity]**, molar heat [capacity] <at constant pressure or at constant volume>	molare Wärmekapazität f, Molwärme f, Molekularwärme f <bei konstantem Druck oder bei konstantem Volumen>
molecular depression of freezing point	s. cryoscopic constant		
molecular diagram	Moleküldiagramm n		
molecular diffusion	Molekulardiffusion f	**molecular heat conduction**	molekulare Wärmeleitung f
molecular diffusion coefficient	molekularer Diffusionskoeffizient m		

molecular heat conductivity	molekulare Wärmeleitfähigkeit f	molecular reflection coefficient	molekularer Reflexionskoeffizient m
molecular ion, molecule[-]ion	Molekülion n	molecular refraction, molar refraction, molecular refractivity, refractivity	Molrefraktion f, Molekularrefraktion f
molecularity [of the reaction]	Molekularität f [der Reaktion], Reaktionsmolekularität f	molecular refractivity	s. molecular refraction
molecular jump	Molekülsprung m	molecular rise of boiling point	s. ebullioscopic constant
molecular-kinetic isotope effect	molekularkinetischer Isotopieeffekt m	molecular rotary power, molecular rotation, molar rotation	molekulares Drehvermögen n, Molekulardrehung f, molekulare Drehung f, Molekularrotation f
molecular lattice	Molekülgitter n		
molecular level	s. molecular energy level	molecular rotation, rotation of molecules	Molekülrotation f
molecular lowering of freezing point	s. cryoscopic constant		
molecular magnet; elementary magnet	Elementarmagnet m; Molekularmagnet m	molecular roughness	molekulare Rauhigkeit f
molecular magnetism	Molekularmagnetismus m	molecular scattering	Molekularstreuung f, molekulare Streuung f, Molekülstreuung f
molecular mass	Molekülmasse f, absolutes Molekulargewicht n	molecular shell	Molekülschale f
molecular mean free path, molecular free path	molekulare mittlere freie Weglänge f, mittlere freie Weglänge der Moleküle	molecular sieve	Mol[ekular]sieb n
		molecular sieve effect	Molekularsiebeffekt m
molecular mechanics	molekulare Mechanik f	molecular sieving	Molekularsiebung f
molecular mode	Schwingungsfreiheitsgrad m im Molekül		
molecular model	Molekülmodell n	molecular solution, true solution	echte Lösung f, molekulare Lösung
molecular motion, molecular movement, thermal agitation of molecules, thermal (random, chaotic) motion of the molecules	Molekularbewegung f, Molekülbewegung f, molekulare Bewegung f, thermische Molekularbewegung, Wärmebewegung f der Moleküle	molecular sound absorption, molecular acoustic absorption	molekulare Schallabsorption f
		molecular space	s. mu space
		molecular spectroscopy	Molekülspektroskopie f
molecular number	Molekülzahl f <Summe der Kernladungszahlen der Atome eines Moleküls>	molecular spectrum	Molekülspektrum n
		molecular speed, molecular velocity	Molekulargeschwindigkeit f, Molekülgeschwindigkeit f
molecular orbit	s. molecular orbital		
molecular orbital, MO, molecular orbit	Molekülorbital n (m), MO, Molekularbahn f, molekulare Bahn f, Molekülbahn f, Molekülzustand m	molecular speed ratio	Molekulargeschwindigkeitsverhältnis n
molecular orbital[s] method, MO method, Hund-Mulliken-Hückel method, H-M-H method	Molekülorbitalmethode f, MO-Methode f, Molekülbahnmethode f, Methode f des Molekülorbitals, „molecularorbitals"-Methode f	molecular state, molecular energy state, energy state of the molecule	Molekülzustand m; Energiezustand m des Moleküls
		molecular statistics	molekulare Statistik f
molecular orbital theory, MO theory, Hund-Mulliken-Lennard Jones-Hückel theory	Molekülorbitaltheorie f, MO-Theorie f, Molekülbahntheorie f, Hund-Mulliken-Lennard Jones-Hückelsche Theorie f	molecular still	Molekulardestilliergerät n, Freiwegdestilliergerät n
		molecular stopping power	molekulares Bremsvermögen n
		molecular structure; structure of the molecule	molekulare Sruktur f, Molekularstruktur f, molekulares Gefüge n, Molekulargefüge n; Molekülbau m, Molekülstruktur f
molecular order	molekulare Ordnung f		
molecular oscillator	s. maser oscillator		
molecular physics	Molekularphysik f, Molekülphysik f		
molecular plane, μ plane	Phasenebene f, Molekülebene f, My-Ebene f, μ-Ebene f	molecular structure theory	Molekulartheorie f vom Aufbau der Materie
		molecular sublimation	Molekularsublimation f
molecular polarizability, molecular polarization, molar polarization, molar polarizability, polarizability of the molecule	Molpolarisation f, molare Polarisation f, molekulare Polarisierbarkeit f, molekulare elektrische Polarisierbarkeit, molekulare Polarisation, Molekularpolarisation f	molecular term	s. molecular energy level
		molecular theory of ferromagnetism	Molekulartheorie f des Ferromagnetismus
		molecular thermal pressure, thermomolecular pressure, thermal molecular pressure	Thermomolekulardruck m, thermomolekularer Druck m, thermischer Molekulardruck m
molecular polarization	s. a. orientation polarization	molecular transposition	s. intramolecular rearrangement
molecular position vector	Molekülortsvektor m		
molecular pressure gauge	s. molecular vacuum gauge	molecular vacuum gauge, molecular [pressure] gauge	Molekularvakuummeter n, Molekularmanometer n
molecular pump, molecular vacuum pump	molekularkinetische Vakuumpumpe f, Molekularpumpe f	molecular vacuum pump, molecular pump	molekularkinetische Vakuumpumpe f, Molekularpumpe f
molecular radius	Molekülradius m		
molecular ratio, mole ratio, molar ratio	Molverhältnis n, Molenverhältnis n	molecular velocity, molecular speed	Molekulargeschwindigkeit f, Molekülgeschwindigkeit f
		molecular velocity vector	Molekülgeschwindigkeitsvektor m
molecular ray, molecular beam	Molekularstrahl m, Molekülstrahl m, Molekularstrahl[en]bündel n, Molekülstrahl[en]bündel n	molecular vibration, vibration of the molecules, molecule vibration	Molekülschwingung f
molecular reaction	Molekülreaktion f		
molecular rearrangement	s. intramolecular rearrangement	molecular viscosity	molekulare Zähigkeit f
		molecular volume	Molekülvolumen n

molecular

molecular volume, molar volume	Molvolumen n, molares Volumen n, Molarvolumen n, molekulares Volumen, Molekularvolumen n
molecular weight, relative molecule mass, molar weight	Molekulargewicht n, relative Molekülmasse f, relatives Molekulargewicht n, Mol[ar]gewicht n, Mol.Gew., MG
molecular weight determination, determination of molecular weight	Molekulargewichtsbestimmung f
molecular yield, molar yield	Molausbeute f
molecule aggregate, molecular aggregate, supermolecule	Molekülaggregat n, Übermolekül n, Übermolekel f
molecule convoluted to a clue, clue molecule, molecular coil	Knäuelmolekül n
molecule flow	s. molecular flow
molecule[-] ion, molecular ion	Molekülion n
molecule space	s. mu space
molecule vibration, vibration of the molecules, molecular vibration	Molekülschwingung f
mole[ ]fraction, molfraction, molar fraction, molecular fraction, molecular abundance	Molenbruch m
Molenbroek-Chaplygin transformation, Chaplygin-Molenbroek transformation	Molenbroek-Tschaplygin-Transformation f, Molenbroek-Tschaplyginsche Transformation f
mole per cent, mole %	Molprozent n, Mol.%, Mol.-%
mole-per-litre concentration	s. molarity
mole-per-weight concentration	s. molality
mole ratio, molar ratio, molecular ratio	Molverhältnis n, Molenverhältnis n
moletron	Moletron n
molfraction	s. mole fraction
Möller prism	Möller-Prisma n
Møller scattering, electron-electron scattering	Elektron-Elektron-Streuung f, Møller-Streuung f
Møller wave matrix	Møllersche Wellenmatrix f
Mollier['s] chart	s. H-S diagram
Mollier['s] diagram	s. H-S diagram
Mollier['s] enthalpy-entropy diagram	s. H-S diagram
mollification, softening, emollescence	Erweichung f
mollisol, tabet soil	Auftauboden m, Mollisol m
Moll thermopile	Mollsche Thermosäule f
Moll vacuojunction	Mollsches Vakuumthermoelement n
Mollweide projection	Mollweidesche Projektion f, Mollweidescher [flächentreuer kartographischer] Entwurf m, homalographische Projektion f, [Babinetscher] homalographischer Entwurf
Mollwo relation	Mollwosche Gleichung f, Mollwo-Gleichung f
molten, in the molten state, melted	schmelzflüssig
molten metal, liquid metal, fused metal, melt of metal	Metallschmelze f, Flüssigmetall n, geschmolzenes Metall n
molten metal bath	s. metal bath
molten salt, fused salt, liquid salt	Salzschmelze f
molten-salt bath, salt bath	Salzbad n
molten-salt extraction	Salzschmelzflußextraktion f
molten state / in the, molten, melted	schmelzflüssig
moment, instant [of time], time, epoch	Zeitpunkt m, Zeit f, Moment m, Augenblick m
moment about the mean, central moment	zentrales Moment n, Zentralmoment n
momental diagram	s. moment diagram
momental ellipse, ellipse of inertia, inertia ellipse, moment ellipse	Trägheitsellipse f, Momentenellipse f
momental ellipsoid	s. ellipsoid of inertia
momental ellipsoid	s. a. Poinsot['s] ellipsoid
moment area	s. area of moments
moment arm	s. arm of the force
momentary force	s. impulsive force
momentary load	s. instantaneous load
momentary overload	kurzzeitige Überlastung f
momentary value, instantaneous value	Momentanwert m, Augenblickswert m
moment at point of support, moment at the support	Stützmoment n, Stützenmoment n
moment coefficient	Momentenbeiwert m, Momentenzahl f
moment diagram, momental diagram, bending moment diagram; moment curve (line)	Momentendiagramm n, Momentenplan m; Momentencharakteristik f, Momentenkurve f, Momentenlinie f, Momentenverlauf m
moment distribution method	Momentenausgleichsverfahren n [nach Cross]
moment ellipse, ellipse of inertia, inertia ellipse, momental ellipse	Trägheitsellipse f, Momentenellipse f
moment ellipsoid	s. ellipsoid of inertia
moment equation	Momentengleichung f
moment of aerodynamic forces	aerodynamisches Moment n
moment of circulation	Zirkulationsmoment n
moment of couple	s. torque
moment of distribution	Moment n der Verteilung
moment of first order, static[al] moment, linear moment, mass moment	statisches Moment n, Moment erster Ordnung, lineares Moment
moment of flexure	s. bending couple
moment of force	Moment n der Kraft, Kraftmoment n, Moment n <Betrag des Drehmoments>
moment of friction, friction[al] torque, friction moment	Reibungsmoment n, Reibungsdrehmoment n
moment of gravitation	Schweremoment n
moment of gyration	s. flywheel moment
moment of inertia, mass moment of inertia, M.I.	Trägheitsmoment n, Massenträgheitsmoment n, Drehmasse f
moment of inertia about a line, moment of inertia about an axis, moment of inertia with respect to an axis, axial moment of inertia	axiales (äquatoriales) Trägheitsmoment n, Trägheitsmoment in bezug auf eine Linie (Achse, Gerade)
moment of inertia of a line, linear moment of inertia	Linienträgheitsmoment n
moment of inertia of the line with respect to a point, polar moment of inertia of the line	polares Linienträgheitsmoment n
moment of inertia tensor, inertial (inertia) tensor, tensor of inertia	Trägheitstensor m
moment of inertia with respect to an axis	s. moment of inertia about a line
moment of interception	Abfangzeitpunkt m, Abfangaugenblick m
moment of load	s. load moment
moment of momentum, angular momentum, twist; angular momentum vector	Drehimpuls m, Impulsmoment n; Drehimpulsvektor m, Drall m, Schwung m
moment of percussion	Drehstoß m, Zeitintegral n des Drehmoments

moment of pivoting friction, pivoting friction torque	Bohrreibungsmoment n	momentum of the photon, photon momentum	Photonenimpuls m, Lichtquantenimpuls m, Lichtimpuls m, Impuls m des Lichtes
moment of plane area	s. angular impulse	momentum operator, linear momentum operator	Impulsoperator m
moment of resistance [of the beam section]	s. section modulus		
moment of rolling friction, rolling friction torque	Rollreibungsmoment n	momentum representation, p representation	Impulsdarstellung f, p-Darstellung f
moment of rotation	s. torque	momentum space	Impulsraum m
moment of rupture	s. breaking moment		
moment of sliding friction, sliding friction torque	Gleitreibungsmoment n		
moment of the mass	Massenmoment n		
moment of torsion	s. torsional moment	momentum space condensation, condensation in momentum space	Impulsraumkondensation f
moment planimeter, integrometer	Integrimeter n		
moment problem, problem of moments	Momentenproblem n	momentum-space integral	Impulsraumintegral n
moments method	s. method of moments	momentum-space representation	Impulsraumdarstellung f
momentum, quantity of motion; linear momentum <mech.>	Impuls m, Bewegungsgröße f; linearer Impuls <Mech.>	momentum spectrum <mech.>	Impulsspektrum n <Mech.>
momentum coefficient	Impulsbeiwert m	momentum sphere	Impulskugel f
momentum compaction factor	„momentum compaction"-Faktor m	momentum tensor	Impulstensor m
momentum conservation, conservation of momentum	Erhaltung f des Impulses, Impulserhaltung f, Erhaltung der Bewegungsgröße	momentum theorem	Momentensatz m, zweiter Impulssatz m
		momentum theorem	s. a. momentum equation <mech., hydr.>
momentum conservation law, law of conservation of momentum, principle of conservation of linear momentum, principle of conservation of momentum	Impulssatz m, Impulserhaltungssatz m, Erhaltungssatz m des Impulses, Satz m von der Erhaltung des Impulses, Prinzip n von der Erhaltung der Bewegungsgröße	momentum theorem of boundary layer theory	s. Kármán boundary-layer theorem
		momentum thickness [of boundary layer], momentum thickness, momentum deficit thickness, momentum-loss thickness	Impulsverlustdicke f, Impulsdicke f [der Grenzschicht]
		momentum transfer, transfer of momentum, momentum transport, transport of momentum <mech.>	Impulstransport m, Impulsübertragung f <Mech.>
momentum deficit thickness	s. momentum thickness of boundary layer		
momentum density [of electromagnetic field]	Impulsdichte f, elektromagnetische Impulsdichte		
momentum density tensor, tensor of momentum density	Impulsdichtetensor m	momentum transfer equation	Impulstransportgleichung f
momentum distribution <mech.>	Impulsverteilung f <Mech.>	momentum transport	s. momentum transfer <mech.>
momentum ellipse	Impulsellipse f	momentum vector	Impulsvektor m
momentum ellipsoid	Impulsellipsoid n	MO method	s. molecular orbital[s] method
		monacid	s. monobasic acid
momentum-energy radiation	Energie-Impuls-Strahlung f	monadnock; lost mountain	Härtling m, Monadnock m; Fernling m, Restberg m; Mosor m; Auslieger m, Zeugenberg m, Zeuge m
momentum-energy space, space of momentum and energy	Energie-Impuls-Raum m, Impuls-Energie-Raum m	monaural audition (hearing; listening)	einohriges Hören n
momentum-energy vector	s. four-momentum	Monge-Ampère equation	Monge-Ampèresche Gleichung f, Monge-Ampèresche Differentialgleichung f
momentum equation	s. principle of linear momentum		
momentum flow tensor, momentum flux tensor	Impulstransporttensor m	Monge cone	Mongescher Kegel m, Richtungskegel m, Elementarkegel m
momentum flux	Impulsfluß m	Monge equation	Mongesche Gleichung (Differentialgleichung) f
momentum flux tensor	s. momentum flow tensor	Monge['s] method	Zweitafelverfahren n, Zweitafelprojektion f
momentum flux vector	Impulstransportvektor m		
momentum integral	Impulsintegral n		
momentum integral equation	s. Kármán boundary-layer theorem	Monge['s] potential	Mongesches Potential n
		monitor, monitor receiver, monitoring receiver, monitoring unit	Monitor m, Kontrollempfänger m, Kontrollgerät n
momentum law	s. principle of linear momentum		
momentum-loss thickness	s. momentum thickness of boundary layer	monitor, warning device	Warngerät n
momentum of the impact, impact momentum, shock momentum, collision (striking) momentum	Schlagimpuls m, Stoßimpuls m	monitor	s. a. radiation monitor
		monitor chamber, monitor ionization chamber	Kontrollkammer f, Monitorkammer f, Überwachungsionisationskammer f

monitoring, survey, control, supervision	Überwachung f, Kontrolle f
monitoring feedback, stabilizing feedback	stabilisierende Rückführung f, Dämpfungsreflexschaltung f
monitoring instrument	s. radiation monitor
monitoring receiver (unit), monitor receiver, monitor	Monitor m, Kontrollempfänger m, Kontrollgerät n
monitor ionization chamber, monitor chamber	Kontrollkammer f, Monitorkammer f, Überwachungsionisationskammer f
monitor receiver, monitoring receiver; monitoring unit, monitor	Monitor m, Kontrollempfänger m, Kontrollgerät n
monkey chatter, monkey-chatter interference; adjacent-channel interference	Nachbarkanalstörung f
monkey chatter [interference]	s. sideband interference
monkey-chatter interference	s. monkey chatter
monoacid	s. monobasic acid
monoacid base, monobase	einsäurige Base f
monobasic acid, mon[o]acid	einbasische Säure f
monocentric system, concentric system <opt.>	monozentrisches System n, konzentrisches System <Opt.>
monochord, sonometer	Monochord n, Sonometer n
monochroic	monochroitisch
monochroism	Monochroismus m, isotrope Lichtabsorption f
monochromat, monochromatic lens, monochromatic objective	Monochromat n (m)
monochromatic, homogeneous, single-frequency, single-wavelength, monofrequent <of electromagnetic or corpuscular radiation>; monoenergetic, monoergic, monokinetic <of corpuscular radiation>	monochromatisch, homogen, einwellig, einfarbig <elektromagnetische oder Korpuskularstrahlung>; monoenergetisch, energiehomogen, monoergisch <Korpuskularstrahlung>
monochromatic aberration, geometric aberration	monochromatische Aberration f, monochromatischer Abbildungsfehler m, monochromatischer Fehler m, geometrische Aberration f
monochromatic emissive power	s. spectral emissivity [of a thermal radiator]
monochromatic extinction coefficient	spektraler Extinktionskoeffizient m
monochromatic eyepiece	Monochromatokular n
monochromatic filter	Monochromatfilter n
monochromaticity, monochromatism	Monochromatizität f, Einfarbigkeit f, Einwelligkeit f, Monochromasie f; Energieschärfe f
monochromatic lens	s. monochromat
monochromatic radiance, monochromatic radiant intensity per unit area	spektrale Strahldichte f
monochromatic radiant flux, monochromatic radiant power, spectral radiant power, spectral radiant flux	spektraler Strahlungsfluß m, spektrale Strahlungsleistung f
monochromatic radiant intensity, spectral radiant intensity	spektrale Strahlstärke f
monochromatic radiant intensity per unit area	s. monochromatic radiance
monochromatic radiant power, monochromatic radiant flux, spectral radiant power, spectral radiant flux	spektraler Strahlungsfluß m, spektrale Strahlungsleistung f
monochromatic vision, monochromatism	Monochromasie f, Zapfenfarbenblindheit f
monochromating crystal	Monochromatorkristall m, monochromatisierender Kristall m, Kristallmonochromator m
monochromatism, monochromatism, monochromatic vision	s. monochromaticity Monochromasie f, Zapfenfarbenblindheit f
monochromator for infra-red radiation, infra-red monochromator, I.R. monochromator	Infrarotmonochromator m, IR-Monochromator m
monochromator having a mirror optics, mirror monochromator	Spiegelmonochromator m
monochrome bandwidth	Schwarz-Weiß-Bandbreite f, Einfarben-Bandbreite f
monoclinal valley	Monoklinaltal n, monoklinales Tal n
monocline, homocline	Monoklinale f
monocline, monoclinic	monoklin <Krist.>
monoclinic crystal system	s. monoclinic system
monoclinic hemihedry	s. hemihedry of the monoclinic system
monoclinic hemimorphy	s. hemimorphic hemihedry of the monoclinic system
monoclinic holohedry, holohedry of the monoclinic system, digonal equatorial class, normal (prismatic) class, holohedral class of the monoclinic system	monokline Holoedrie f, prismatische Klasse f
monoclinic system, monosymmetric system, monoclinic crystal system	monoklines (monosymmetrisches) System n, monoklines Kristallsystem n
monocrystal, single crystal	Einkristall m
monocrystalline monocular	monokristallin; Einkristall-Monokular n; Monokel n
monocular; single-lens	einäugig; monokular
monocular dominance	Äugigkeit f, monokulare Dominanz f
monocular field of view	monokulares Blickfeld n
monocular rangefinder	Entfernungsmesser m mit einäugiger Beobachtung, Einstand-Entfernungsmesser m mit monokularer Beobachtung
monocular tube	Monokulartubus m
monocular visual field	monokulares Gesichtsfeld n
monodirectional	s. unidirectional
monodisperse, isodisperse, homodisperse	isodispers, monodispers, homodispers
monoenergetic	s. monochromatic
monoenergid cell	monoenergide Zelle f
monoergic	s. monochromatic
monofrequent	s. monochromatic
monofuel, monopropellant	homogener Treibstoff m
monogenic analytic function, monogenic function	monogene analytische Funktion f, monogene Funktion, vollständige analytische Funktion, vollständige Funktion
monoid	Monoid n, Halbgruppe f mit neutralem Element, Monoide f
monoid	s. a. semi-group
monoisotopic	isotopenrein, einisotopig, einisotop, monoisotopisch, ein Isotop enthaltend, ein stabiles Isotop besitzend
monoisotopic element, pure element	Reinelement n, isotopenreines (monoisotopisches, anisotropes) Element n
monokinetic	s. monochromatic
monolayer, monomolecular film (layer), unimolecular film (layer)	monomolekulare Schicht (Adsorptionsschicht) f, Monoschicht f, Einfachschicht f
monolayer model	Einschichtmodell n
monomer[ic]	monomer
monomeric unit	s. mer
monomial	Monom n
monomial group	monomiale Gruppe f
monomode waveguide	Eintypwellenleiter m
monomolecular adsorption, unimolecular adsorption, molecular adsorption	monomolekulare Adsorption f, Adsorption in molekularer Schicht

monomolecular decay	monomolekularer Zerfall m, monomolekulare Abklingung f	monsoonal phenomenon, monsoon-like phenomenon	Monsunerscheinung f; Monsunität f, monsunartige Erscheinung f
monomolecular film (layer), monolayer, unimolecular film (layer)	monomolekulare Schicht (Adsorptionsschicht) f, Monoschicht f, Einfachschicht f	monsoonal rain, monsoon rain	Monsunregen m
		monsoon current, monsoonal current	Monsunströmung f, Monsunstrom m
monomolecular recombination	monomolekulare Rekombination f	monsoon-like phenomenon, monsoonal phenomenon	Monsunerscheinung f; Monsunität f, monsunartige Erscheinung f
monomorphism <math.>	Monomorphismus m, Isomorphismus m in..., injektiver Homomorphismus m <Math.>	monsoon rain, monsoonal rain	Monsunregen m
monophase action potential	monophasische Aktionsspannung f	Monte[-] Carlo method, Monte[-] Carlo technique, method of statistical testing	Monte-Carlo-Methode f, Monte-Carlo-Verfahren n, Monte-Carlo-Technik f, Monte-Carlo-Rechnung f
monophase system, homogeneous system, one-phase system	homogenes System n, Einphasensystem n, einphasiges System		
monoplane filament <US>, uniplanar filament	flächenförmiger Leuchtkörper m	monte-jus	Montejus n, Druckbirne f, Druckbehälter m, Druckheber m
monopole	Monopol m	monthly amount	Monatsmenge f
		monthly average, monthly mean	Monatsmittel n, Monatsmittelwert m
monopole oscillation	Monopolschwingung f	monthly sum	Monatssumme f
monopole radiation	Monopolstrahlung f	Montigny['s] principle, principle of Montigny	Montignysches Prinzip n, Prinzip von (nach) Montigny
monopole source	einfache Quelle f, Monopolquelle f	Montsinger['s] law	Montsingersches Lebensdauergesetz n
monopole transition	Monopolübergang m	Moody diagram	Moody-Diagramm n
monopole wave	Monopolwelle f	Moon <of Earth>	Mond m, Erdmond m, Erdtrabant m
monopropellant	s. monofuel		
monostable, monostable circuit, monostable connexion	monostabile Schaltung f	moon, satellite <of a planet>	Mond m, Nebenplanet m, Satellit m, Trabant m, natürlicher Begleiter m <eines Planeten>
		Mooney['s] equation	Mooneysche Gleichung f
monosubstituted	einfachsubstituiert	Mooney plasticity, Mooney viscosity	Mooney-Plastizität f, Plastizität f nach Mooney
monosymmetric system	s. monoclinic system	Mooney plastometer	Mooney-Gerät n [zur Plastizitätsmessung]
monotectic, monotectic alloy, monotectic mixture	Monotektikum n, monotektische Legierung f, monotektisches Gemisch n	Mooney viscosity	s. Mooney plasticity
		moon-light effect	Mondscheineffekt m
monotectic point	s. eutectic halt	moonquake	Mondbeben n
monotone	s. monotonic <math.>	Moon rocket, lunar probe	Mondsonde f, Mondrakete f, Lunik m
monotonic, monotone <math.>; monotonous <ac.>	monoton	Moon's anomalistic inequality	s. Moon's parallactic inequality
		Moon's daily inequality	s. diurnal lunar inequality
monotonic[ally] decreasing, monotone decreasing <math.>	monoton fallend, fallend, [monoton] abnehmend, nicht zunehmend, antiton <Math.>	Moon's disk, lunar disk	Mondscheibe f
		Moon's diurnal inequality	s. diurnal lunar inequality
monotonic[ally] increasing, monotone increasing, isotonic <math.>	monoton wachsend, wachsend, nicht abnehmend, isoton <Math.>	Moon['s] gravity	s. lunar gravity
		Moon's gravity acceleration	s. acceleration due to lunar gravity
		Moon's limb	Mondrand m
monotonicity, monotony monotonicity theorem	Monotonie f Monotoniesatz m	Moon's orbit, lunar orbit, Moon's path	Mondbahn f
monotonic model, monotonic universe <of the first or second kind>	monotone Welt f, Modell n einer monotonen Welt <erster oder zweiter Art>	Moon's parallactic inequality, [lunar] parallactic inequality, Moon's (lunar) anomalistic inequality	lunare anomalistische Ungleichheit f, monatliche Ungleichheit, parallaktische Ungleichheit (Ungleichung f, Gleichung f)
monotonous <ac.>; monotonic, monotone <math.>	monoton	Moon's path, Moon's orbit, lunar orbit	Mondbahn f
monotony, monotonicity	Monotonie f	Moon's shadow, lunar shadow	Mondschatten m
monotron	Monotron n, Monotron-Härteprüfgerät n	Moon's year, lunar year	Mondjahr n
monotron <el.>	Monotron n, Müller-Rostas-Generator m <EL>	Moore light	Moore-Licht n, Moore-Lampe f, Tageslichtkohlensäurelampe f
monotron hardness [number], constant diameter hardness [number]	Monotronhärte f, CD-Härte f	mooring	Vermurung f
monotron hardness test[ing], monotron test[ing]	Monotron-Härteprüfung f	Morera['s] theorem	Satz m von Morera
		Morgan-Keenan-Kellman system, Yerkes system, MKK system	MKK-System n, System n von Morgan-Keenan-Kellman
monotropic	monotrop		
monotropy	Monotropie f		
monovalent, univalent <chem.>	monovalent, einwertig, einbindig <Chem.>	Morgan-Keenan system, MK-system	MK-System n, System n von Morgan und Keenan
monovariant, univariant	univariant, monovariant	Morgan['s] theorem /De Morgan['s] theorem	de Morgansches Theorem n, Theorem von de Morgan
monovariant equilibrium, univariant equilibrium	monovariantes (univariantes, einfachfreies, vollständiges) Gleichgewicht n	morning series	Morgengruppe f, Morgenreihe f
monovibrator	s. univibrator	morphology of crystals, crystal morphology	Kristallmorphologie f
monsoonal current, monsoon current	Monsunströmung f, Monsunstrom m	morphotropic series	morphotrope Reihe f

morphotropism, morphotropy, topotropism	Morphotropie f, Topotropie f	Mössbauer spectrometry (spectroscopy), [nuclear] gamma-ray resonance spectroscopy	Mößbauer-Spektrometrie f Resonanzspektroskopie f von Gamma-Strahlung
Morse alphabet, Morse code	Morse-Alphabet n; Morse-Kode m		
Morse code, Morse alphabet	Morse-Alphabet n; Morse-Kode m	Mössbauer spectrum	Mößbauer-Spektrum n
Morse curve	Morsesche Kurve f		
Morse equation	Morse-Gleichung f, Morsesche Gleichung f	Mossotti['s] model [of the molecule]	Mossottisches Modell n [des Moleküls], Mossottisches Molekülmodell n
Morse function, Morse potential [energy function]	Morsesche Funktion f, Morsesche Potentialfunktion f, Morsesches Potential n, Morse-Potential n	Moss relation	Moss-Relation f, Msssche Relation f, Msssche Beziehung f
Morse rule	Morsesche Regel f	MOST	s. metal-oxide semiconductor field effect transistor
mortality [rate]	Mortalität f, Sterblichkeit f, Sterbewahrscheinlichkeit f		
mortar	Mörser m, Reibschale f	most disturbed day	meistgestörter Tag m
mosaic, "air photo mosaic" <photogrammetry>	Bildskizze f, Luftbildskizze f, Mosaik n <Photogrammetrie>	most general solution, general solution	allgemeine Lösung f, allgemeinste Lösung
		most luminous supergiant	heller Überriese m
mosaic <e.g. of signal plate>	Mosaik n <z. B. der Speicherplatte>	most powerful test	trennschärfster Test m
mosaic	s. a. mosaic element	most probable error	wahrscheinlichster Fehler m, günstigster Fehler
mosaic	s. a. mosaic screen	most probable value	s. mode <stat.>
mosaic block	Mosaikblock m, Gitterblock m	most strained section, dangerous section, dangerous cross-section	gefährlicher Querschnitt m, gefährdeter Querschnitt
mosaic [block] boundary	Mosaikgrenze f	most stringent critical region <stat.>	strengster kritischer Bereich m <Stat.>
mosaic crystal	Mosaikkristall m	most stringent test	strengster Test m
mosaic electrode	s. mosaic screen	MO theory	s. molecular orbital theory
mosaic element, photoemissive mosaic element, mosaic photocathode, mosaic	Mosaikphotokatode f, Mosaikelement n	mother crystal	s. crystal blank
		mother liquid, mother liquor	s. mother solution
mosaic film, mosaic photographic film	Mosaikfilm m	mother-of-pearl cloud, nacreous cloud, iridescent cloud	irisierende Wolke f, Perlmutterwolke f
mosaic filter	Mosaikfilter n, Abstimmfilter n	mother rock	Muttergestein n
mosaic photocathode	s. photoemissive mosaic element	mother solution (water), mother liquor, mother liquid	Mutterlauge f, Mutterlösung f, Endlauge f, Endlösung f
mosaic photographic film, mosaic film	Mosaikfilm m	motility <bio.>	Motilität f <Bio.>
mosaic screen, mosaic electrode, mosaic, signal plate, pick-up plate	Speicherplatte f, Speichermosaik n, Speicherelektrode f, Mosaikelektrode f, Mosaikschirm m, Mosaik n, Signalplatte f	motion, run, running, movement	Gang m, Lauf m
		motion, movement	Bewegung f <Mech.>
		motional impedance	Bewegungsimpedanz f, kinetische Impedanz f, kinetischer Scheinwiderstand m
mosaic screen	Rasterschirm m; Rasterbildwand f	motion along a helix	s. screw displacement
mosaic structure, block structure, substructure	Mosaikstruktur f, Mosaiktextur f, Substruktur f	motion decomposition, decomposition of the motion	Zerlegung f der Bewegung
Moscow time	Moskauer Zeit f	motion in a straight line, rectilinear motion, straight line motion	geradlinige Bewegung f
Moseley['s] curve, Moseley['s] diagram, [for X-ray levels], Moseley['s] straight line	Moseley-Diagramm n, Moseleysches Diagramm n; Moseley-Gerade f, Moseleysche Gerade f, Moseley-Kurve f, Moseleysche Kurve f	motion in space	s. space motion
		motion in three dimensions	s. space motion
		motionless, at rest, non-moving, fixed	in Ruhe, ruhend, fest, bewegungslos, unbewegt
Moseley['s] law	Moseleysches Gesetz n, Moseleysche Formel f, Moseleysche Beziehung f	motionless satellite, [geo]stationary satellite	[geo]stationärer Satellit m, Satellit in geostationärer Umlaufbahn
Moseley['s] straight line	s. Moseley['s] diagram	motion of rotation	s. rotary motion
moser	s. maser oscillator	motion of the nucleus	s. nuclear movement
MOSFET	s. metal-oxide semiconductor field effect transistor	motion of the pendulum, pendular motion, pendulum motion, pendulum movement	Pendelbewegung f, Pendelschwingung f, Pendelung f
Mössbauer absorption	Mößbauer-Absorption f, Absorption f durch Mößbauer-Effekt, rückstoßfreie Resonanzabsorption (Absorption) f, rückstoßfreie Kernresonanzabsorption f von Gamma-Strahlung		
		motion of the sea, sea-way, sea	Seegang m, See f, Wellengang m
		motion of translation	s. translational movement
		motion of transport	Führungsbewegung f
Mössbauer clock	Mößbauer-Uhr f	motion picture projector	s. cinematograph projector
Mössbauer effect, nuclear gamma[-ray] resonance, NGR	Mößbauer-Effekt m	motive force, motive power, living force, moving force, driving force, propellant, propellent	Antriebskraft f, treibende Kraft f, Triebkraft f
Mössbauer effect spectrometer	Mößbauer-Spektrometer n		
		motoelectric effect	motoelektrischer Effekt m
Mössbauer line	Mößbauer-Linie f	motor <el.>; engine, mover <techn.>	Motor m
Mössbauer source	Mößbauer-Quelle f	motor <as a system of two straight lines, mech.>	Motor m, Schraubung f <als System zweier Geraden, Mech.>

motor-breaker	s. mechanically driven interrupter	movable, sliding; translatory	beweglich; [gegeneinander] verschiebbar, verschieblich
motor-converter	s. rotary converter	movable barrage, movable dam (weir)	bewegliches Wehr n
motor-driven breaker	s. mechanically driven interrupter	movable bearing, movable support	bewegliches Auflager n, beweglicher Stützpunkt m
motor-driven interrupter	s. mechanically driven interrupter		
motor ending	s. motor end[ ]plate	movable-core choke, choke plunger	Tauchkernspule f, Tauchkerndrossel[spule] f, Tauchspule f
motor end[-]plate, motoric end[]plate, motor ending, myoneural junction	motorische Endplatte f		
motor for automatic zero balance, automatic zero balance motor, automatic zeroing motor	Nullmotor m	movable-core transformer, sliding-core transformer, moving-coil (sliding-coil) transformer	Schiebetransformator m, Schubtransformator m, Schiebertransformator m; Gleittransformator m
motoric end[-]plate	s. motor end[-]plate		
motor-interrupter	s. mechanically driven interrupter	movable dam, movable barrage, movable weir	bewegliches Wehr n
motor symbolism	Motorrechnung f	movable pulley	lose Rolle f
Mott barrier [layer]	Mottsche Randschicht f	movable singularity	verschiebbare Singularität f, bewegliche Singularität
Mottelson-Valatin effect	Mottelson-Valatin-Effekt m	movable support	s. movable bearing
Mott exciton	Mott-Exciton n, schwach gebundenes Exciton n	movable weir, movable dam, movable barrage	bewegliches Wehr n
Mott['s] formula, Mott['s] scattering formula	Mottsche Streuformel f, Streuformel von Mott	movement; locomotion	Fortbewegung f, Bewegung f, Fahren n, Fahrt f; Lokomotion f <Bio.>
Mott['s] group theory	Mottsche Gruppentheorie f	movement	s. a. run
Mott['s] island model, island model	Mottsches Inselmodell n, Inselmodell	movement	s. a. flow
mottled, spotted, spotty, stained	fleckig	movement	s. a. motion <mech.>
mottled glass, frosted (depolished) glass	Mattglas n	movement blur	s. moving blur
mottling, frosting, mat finishing, matting <of glass>	Mattierung f <Gläser>	movement group, group of movement	Bewegungsgruppe f
		movement of clock	s. clock movement
mottling, mottling effect	Melierung f, Meliereffekt m	movement of gyro	s. movement of the top
Mott['s] model	Mottsches Modell n	movement of ions	s. migration of ions
Mott['s] scattering	Mottsche Streuung f, Mott-Streuung f	movement of the clock, movement of the watch	Gang m der Uhr
Mott['s] scattering formula, Mott['s] formula	Mottsche Streuformel f, Streuformel von Mott	movement of the instrument	s. instrument movement
moulded core	s. dust core	movement of the pointer; pointer deflection, needle deflection, deflection of the needle (pointer)	Zeigerausschlag m, Zeigerauslenkung f
mount; holder; support, mounting support	Halterung f, Halter m		
mountain-building, orogenesis, mountainous formation, orogeny; revolution	Orogenese f, Gebirgsbildung f, Umwälzung f	movement of the pole, polar motion, polar wandering	Polbewegung f, Polschwankung f, Polwanderung f, Polverschiebung f, Polverlagerung f
mountain chain, mountain range	Kettengebirge n		
mountain crest, crest <geo.>	Kamm m, Gebirgskamm m; Grat m <Geo.>	movement of the top, movement of gyro, gyration, gyroscopic motion, gyratory motion	Kreiselbewegung f, Drehung f um einen Punkt, sphärische Bewegung (Rotation) f, Gyration f
mountain crests, crest-type mountains, mountain ridges	Kammgebirge n		
mountainous formation	s. orogenesis	movement of the watch, movement of the clock	Gang m der Uhr
mountain range, mountain chain	Kettengebirge n	movement of watch	s. clock movement
mountain ridges	s. mountain crests	movement picture (plan)	Bewegungsplan m
mountain slip	s. soil slip	movie	s. moving picture
mountain wind	Bergwind m	movie projector	s. cinematograph projector
mounted in line, arranged in line, tandem-joined	hintereinander angeordnet	moving average, consecutive (overlapping, running) mean, sliding average	gleitender Durchschnitt m, gleitendes Mittel n
mounting <of telescope>	Montierung f <Fernrohr>		
mounting <of diffraction grating>	Gitteraufstellung f, Aufstellung f [des Beugungsgitters]	moving average [method]; use of moving averages	gleitende Durchschnittsbildung f; Gleitmittelverfahren f
mounting in gimbals	s. gimbal	moving axode, moving cone of instantaneous axes	Polhodiekegel m, Gangpolkegel m, Polkegel m, Laufkegel m
mounting method <of autoradiography>	Montiermethode f <Autoradiographie>	moving beam radiation therapy, moving beam therapy	Therapie f bei (mit) bewegtem Strahlenbündel, Bewegungstherapie f
mounting pillar <el.>	Steig[e]leitung f <El.>		
mounting support, holder; support; mount	Halterung f, Halter m	moving bed	Bewegtbett n
		moving blur, movement blur	Bewegungsunschärfe f
Mount Palomar telescope, Hale reflector, Palomar telescope	Hale-Teleskop n, Palomar-Teleskop n, Hale-Reflektor m	moving-boundary method	Methode f der bewegten Grenze
		moving centrode	s. polhode <mech.>
moustaches	s. spark <opt.>	moving circle	s. rolling circle
mouth; orifice, muzzle	Mündung f	moving cluster, moving star cluster, local starstream	Bewegungssternhaufen m, Bewegungshaufen m, lokaler Sternstrom m
mouth of the valley	Talausgang m, Talmündung f		
mouthpiece; nozzle	Mundstück n <z. B. der Düse>; Düsenmundstück n, Austrittsöffnung f der Düse	moving-cluster parallax, cluster parallax	Sternstromparallaxe f

moving coil; oscillator coil; vibrating coil	Oszillatorspule f; Schwingspule f, Vibrationsspule f	moving layer, migrating layer	wandernde Schicht f
		moving load	s. live load
		moving magnet, vibrating magnet	Schwingmagnet m
moving coil, rotating coil	Rotationsspule f, Drehspule f	moving-magnet galvanometer, needle galvanometer, galvanometer with moving magnet	Nadelgalvanometer n, Drehmagnetgalvanometer n
moving coil	s. a. voice coil		
moving-coil galvanometer, D'Arsonval galvanometer	Drehspulgalvanometer n, Spulengalvanometer n		
		moving magnet instrument	Drehmagnetinstrument n, Drehmagnetmeßgerät n
		moving mass-point	bewegter Massenpunkt m
moving-coil gradiometer	Rotationsspulengradiometer n	moving medium	bewegtes Medium n
moving-coil instrument	s. permanent-magnet moving-coil instrument	moving moraine	Wandermoräne f, bewegte Moräne f
moving-coil magnetometer	Rotationsspulenmagnetometer n		
moving coil microphone, moving-coil-type microphone, moving-conductor microphone, [electro]dynamic microphone	Tauchspul[en]mikrophon n, elektrodynamisches (dynamisches) Mikrophon n, Mikrophon mit beweglicher Spule	moving observer	bewegter Beobachter m
		moving phase	s. mobile phase
		moving phase	s. a. solvent
		moving phase band, band of moving phase, solvent front	Laufmittelfront f, Front f des Laufmittels, Fließmittelfront f
moving coil of the variometer, variometer rotor	drehbare Variometerspule f	moving picture, animated (cinematographic) picture, movie	Laufbild n
moving-coil pointer galvanometer	Drehspulzeigergalvanometer n	moving pictures camera; recording camera	Registrierkamera f, Aufnahmekamera f
moving-coil reflecting galvanometer	Drehspulspiegelgalvanometer n	moving prism	Wanderprisma f
		moving punch problem	s. problem of moving punch
moving-coil transformer	s. movable-core transformer	moving source	bewegte Quelle f
moving-coil-type microphone	s. moving coil microphone	moving space	begleitender Raum m
moving-coil variometer	Drehspul[en]variometer n, Variometer n mit drehbarer Spule, Drehdrossel f, Rotationsspulenvariometer n	moving trihedral, moving trihedron	begleitendes Dreibein n, Hauptdreikant n, begleitendes Dreikant n
moving-coil vibrating galvanometer	Drehspul-Vibrationsgalvanometer n, Spulenvibrationsgalvanometer n	MPD generator	s. magnetohydrodynamic generator
		M-region	M-Gebiet n, M-Region f
		Mrozowski filter	Mrozowski-Filter n
moving cone of instantaneous axes, moving axode, polhode (polhodic) cone	Polhodiekegel m, Gangpolkegel m, Polkegel m, Laufkegel m	m.t.s. system [of units], MTS system [of units], metre-ton-second system [of units]	MTS-System n, MTS-Einheitensystem n, MTS-Maßsystem n, Meter-Tonne-Sekunde-System n
moving curve of instantaneous centres	s. polhode <mech.>	mT-type L network	Zobelsches mT-Halbglied n, mT-Halbglied
moving dislocation, wandering dislocation; sweeping dislocation	wandernde Versetzung f, bewegte Versetzung	M-type backward wave tube, M-type carcinotron	s. M-carcinotron
moving-field radiotherapy	Bewegungstherapie f, Bewegungsstrahlentherapie f	m-type L network	[Zobelsches] m-Halbglied n, Zobelsches Halbglied n, Zobel-Halbglied n; Zobel-Glied n
moving force	s. motive force		
moving forward	s. forward movement		
moving frame of reference	bewegtes Bezugssystem n; begleitendes Bezugssystem n	$m\pi$-type L network	Zobelsches $m\pi$-Halbglied n, $m\pi$-Halbglied
moving grid, reciprocating grid, Potter-Bucky grid, Potter-Bucky, Bucky grid, Bucky, antidiffusion (antidiffusing) grid, antidiffusion screen, antidiffusing screen, Bucky screen	Streustrahlenraster m, beweglicher Raster m; [bewegliche] Streustrahlenblende f, Bucky-Blende f, Potter-Bucky-Blende f, Streustrahlenblende nach Bucky (Potter-Bucky), Laufblende f: Laufrasterblende f	Mu Cephei[-type] star	My Cephei-Stern m, μ Cephei-Stern m
		much larger than	groß gegen[über]
		much smaller than	klein gegen[über]
		mud; slime; sludge; slurry	Schlamm m; Mudd m; Mudde f
moving in, insertion; dipping; plunging; immersion <of rods>	Einfahren n; Absenken n; Hinablassen n; Einschieben n; Eintauchen n	mud and rock stream, mud avalanche	s. mud stream
		mud cone	Schlammkegel m
moving-iron galvanometer, soft-iron galvanometer, electromagnetic galvanometer	Weicheisengalvanometer n, Dreheisengalvanometer n, elektromagnetisches Galvanometer n	mud crack	Trockenriß m, Trocknungsriß m; Netzleiste f, Leistennetz n
		mud flow	s. mud stream
		mudlump, mud volcano	Schlammvulkan m, Schlammsprudel m, Salse f
moving-iron instrument, soft-iron instrument, electromagnetic instrument	Weicheisen[meß]gerät n, Weicheisen[meß]instrument n, Dreheisen[meß]gerät n, Dreheisen[meß]instrument n, elektromagnetisches Meßgerät n (Meßinstrument n, Instrument n, Gerät n)	mud stream, mud flow (avalanche), debris flow, mud and rock stream	Mure f, Murgang m, Ruff m, Rüffe f, Gieße f; Schlammstrom m
		mud volcano, mudlump	Schlammvulkan m, Schlammsprudel m, Salse f
moving-iron microphone	s. electromagnetic microphone	Mueller coefficient	Mueller-Koeffizient m, Muellerscher Koeffizient m
moving-iron oscillograph, soft iron oscillograph	Dreheisenoszillograph m, Weicheisenoszillograph m		

Mueller matrix	Muellersche Matrix *f*, Mueller-Matrix *f*
MUF	*s.* maximum usable frequency
MUF-factor	MUF-Faktor *m*
muffle [furnace], muffler	Muffelofen *m*
muffler	*s. a.* sourdine
muggy	schwül
muggy	*s. a.* warm and muggy
mulching	Selbstmulcheffekt *m*, Mulchen *n*; Mulchung *f*
Müller circle	Vieth-Müllerscher Kreis (Horopterkreis) *m*, Müllerscher Kreis, geometrischer Totalhoropter *m*
Müller fringe	Müllerscher Streifen *m*
Müller['s] law, law of specific energies	Gesetz *n* der spezifischen Sinnesenergien, Müllersches Gesetz *n*
Multhopp['s] method	Multhoppsches Verfahren *n*, Multhoppsches Quadraturverfahren *n*
multi-access computing	*s.* time sharing [scheme] <num.math.>
multianode rectifier, multi-anode rectifier	mehranodige Gleichrichterröhre *f*, mehranodiger Ventilgleichrichter *m*, mehranodiges Gleichrichterventil *n*, Mehranodenventil *n*, Mehranodengleichrichter *m*; Mehranodengefäß *n*, Mehranoden-Stromrichtergefäß *n*
multi-aperture core, multi-apertured core, multi-hole core	Mehrlochkern *m*, Viellochkern *m*
multiband antenna, multiple-tuned antenna	Mehrbandantenne *f*
multi-beam oscillograph	*s.* multiple-beam oscillograph
multi-beam oscillographic tube	*s.* multiple-beam oscillographic tube
multi-beam oscilloscope	*s.* multi-beam oscillograph
multi-beam oscilloscope tube	*s.* multi-beam oscillographic tube
multi-beam source, multiple source, multiple-beam source	Mehrfachquelle *f*, mehrfache Quelle *f*, Mehrstrahlquelle *f*
multi-beam tube	*s.* multiple-beam tube
multicavity klystron, multiple-cavity klystron	Mehrkammerklystron *n*, Vielkammerklystron *n*
multicavity magnetron, multiresonator magnetron, multisegment magnetron	Mehrkammermagnetron *n*, Vielkammermagnetron *n*, Vielresonatormagnetron *n*, Mehrresonatormagnetron *n*, Vielfachmagnetron *n*, Resotank *m*
multicellular counter [tube]	Multizellularzählrohr *n*
multicellular horn, sectoral horn, sectoral horn waveguide	Multizellularhorn *n*, Mehrkammerhorn *n*, Mehrzellenhorn *n*, Mehrzellentrichter *m*, mehrzelliges (sektorielles) Horn *n*, mehrzelliger (sektorieller) Trichter *m*, Sektorhorn *n*, Sektortrichter *m*
multicellular screen	Zellenbildschirm *m*
multicellular voltmeter, multiple electrometer	Multizellularvoltmeter *n*, Multizellularelektrometer *n*
multichannel amplifier	Mehrkanalverstärker *m*, Vielkanalverstärker *m*
multichannel analysis	Vielkanalanalyse *f*, Mehrkanalanalyse *f*
multichannel analyzer	Vielkanalanalysator *m*, Mehrkanalanalysator *m*
multichannel discriminator	Vielkanaldiskriminator *m*, Mehrkanaldiskriminator *m*
multichannel instrument	Mehrkanal[meß]gerät *n*, Mehrkanalinstrument *n*, Vielkanal[meß]gerät *n*, Vielkanalinstrument *n*
multichannel-multichannel two-parametric analysis	Vielkanal-Vielkanal-Methode *f*
multichannel oscillograph (oscilloscope)	*s.* multichannel recording oscillograph
multichannel probe, multiple probe	Vielkanalsonde *f*, Vielfachsonde *f*
multichannel pulse-height analyzer, channel pulse-height analyzer	Vielkanal-Impulshöhenanalysator *m*, Mehrkanal-Impulshöhenanalysator *m*
multichannel pulse transmission	Mehrkanal-Impulsübertragung *f*, Vielkanal-Impulsübertragung *f*
multichannel reaction, many-channel reaction	Mehrkanalreaktion *f*, Vielkanalreaktion *f*, Mehrweg[e]reaktion *f*
multichannel recorder	Mehrkanal[meß]schreiber *m*, Mehrkanalschreibgerät *n*, Mehrkanalregistriergerät *n*, Vielkanal[meß]schreiber *m*, Vielkanalschreibgerät *n*, Vielkanalregistriergerät *n*
multichannel recording oscillograph, multichannel oscillograph, multichannel oscilloscope	Mehrschleifenoszillograph *m*
multichannel scattering	Mehrkanalstreuung *f*, Vielkanalstreuung *f*
multichannel spectrograph	Vielkanalspektrograph *m*, Mehrkanalspektrograph *m*
multichannel spectrometer	Vielkanalspektrometer *n*, Mehrkanalspektrometer *n*
multichannel transmission	Mehrkanalübertragung *f*, Vielkanalübertragung *f*; Mehrkanalausstrahlung *f*, Vielkanalausstrahlung *f*
multicircuit filter, multiple-circuit filter	Mehrkreisfilter *n*, Vielkreisfilter *n*
multiclone, multicyclone	Multizyklon *m*, Multiklon *m*
multi[-]collector transistor, multiple-collector transistor	Multikollektortransistor *m*, Mehrfachkollektortransistor *m*
multicollinearity	Multikollinearität *f*
multi-colour photometry	Mehrfarbenphotometrie *f*
multi-colour point recorder, multi-colour recorder	Mehrfarbenschreiber *m*, Mehrfarben-Punktschreiber *m*
multi-colour printer	Mehrfarbendrucker *m*
multi-colour recorder	*s.* multi-colour point recorder
multicomponent alloy, polynary alloy	Mehrstofflegierung *f*, polynäre Legierung *f*
multicomponent catalyst, mixed catalyst	Mehrstoffkatalysator *m*, Mischkatalysator *m*
multicomponent system, polynary system	Mehrstoffsystem *n*, polynäres System *n*
multiconductor system, multiple-conductor system, many-conductor system	Mehrleitersystem *n*; Vielleitersystem *n*
multicyclone, multiclone	Multizyklon *m*, Multiklon *m*
multidecision problem	multiples Entscheidungsproblem *n*
multi-dee cyclotron, multiple-dee cyclotron	Mehrelektrodenzyklotron
multidigit	*s.* multiplace
multidimensional, of more than one dimension	mehrdimensional, vieldimensional
multidimensional analysis, multi-parameter analysis	Multiparameteranalyse *f*, Mehrparameteranalyse *f*, mehrparametrige (mehrdimensionale) Analyse *f*

multidimensional

multidimensional analyzer, multi-parameter analyzer	Multiparameteranalysator m, Mehrparameteranalysator m, mehrdimensionaler Analysator m	multilayer adsorption, multimolecular adsorption	multimolekulare (polymolekulare) Adsorption f, Adsorption in mehrfachmolekularer Schicht, Mehrschichtenadsorption f, Mehrfachschichtadsorption f, Viel[fach]schichtenadsorption f
multidomain structure	Mehrbereichstruktur f, Vielbereichstruktur f	multilayer cathode	s. multi-layered cathode
multielectrode lens, multitube lens	Mehrelektrodenlinse f, Mehrzylinderlinse f, Vielelektrodenlinse f	multilayer conductor	vielschichtiger Leiter m, Schichtleiter m
multielectrode tube, polyode [valve]	Mehrelektrodenröhre f, Mehrpolröhre f, Vielelektrodenröhre f, Vielpolröhre f, Polyode f	multilayer crystal, multi-layered crystal	Schichtkristall m
multi-electron approximation; many-electron approximation	Mehrelektronennäherung f, Vielelektronennäherung f	multilayer dielectric interference filter, multilayer interference filter, all-dielectric filter, multilayer filter	Mehrschichten-Interferenzfilter n, Mehrfachschicht-Interferenzfilter n [mit nichtabsorbierenden dielektrischen Schichten], Mehrschichtenfilter n
multi-electron atom, polyelectronic atom	Mehrelektronenatom n; Vielelektronenatom n		
multi[-]electron centre, many-electron centre	Mehrelektronenzentrum n; Vielelektronenzentrum n	multilayer dielectric interference filter with shaped distance layer	s. graded interference filter
multi-electron problem, many-electron problem	Mehrelektronenproblem n; Vielelektronenproblem n	multi-layered cathode, multilayer cathode, layer cathode	Mehrschichtkatode f, Vielschichtkatode f, Schichtenkatode f, vielschichtige Katode f
multi-electron representation, many-electron representation	Mehrelektronendarstellung f; Vielelektronendarstellung f		
multi-electron spectrum, many-electron spectrum, poly-electron spectrum	Mehrelektronenspektrum n; Vielelektronenspektrum n	multi-layered crystal	s. multilayer crystal
		multilayer film	Mehrschichtenfilm m, Mehrschichtfilm m
multielement control	s. interacting control		
multielement interferometer	Vielfachinterferometer n [von Christiansen]	multilayer [interference] filter	s. multilayer dielectric interference filter
multielement tube (valve)	s. multigrid tube	multilayer lens, laminated lens	geschichtete Linse f, Schichtlinse f
multi[-]emitter transistor, multiple-emitter transistor	Multiemittertransistor m, Mehrfachemittertransistor m	multilayer plastic material	s. laminate
multi-flap shutter	Jalousieverschluß m	multilayer structure	Mehrschichtenstruktur f, Vielschichtenstruktur f
multiflex galvanometer	Multiflexgalvanometer n		
multifocal lens	Mehrstärkenglas n, Multifokalglas n	multilayer winding	Mehrlagenwicklung f, Mehrschichtenwicklung f, Mehrschichtwicklung f, Schichtwicklung f
multifocal viewfinder, multifoc (multi-focus) finder, multifoc viewfinder	s. universal finder		
		multi-level maser	Mehrniveaumaser m
multigrid tube, multiple-grid tube, multiple-grid valve, multielement tube (valve)	Mehrgitterröhre f, Vielgitterröhre f	multi-level storage machine	Maschine f mit mehrstufigem Speichersystem
multigroup method	Mehrgruppenmethode f; Vielgruppenmethode f	multi-line fluorescence	s. many-line fluorescence
		multi-line spectrum, many-line[d] spectrum, multiple-line (discreteband) spectrum	Mehrlinienspektrum n; Viellinienspektrum n
multigroup model	Mehrgruppenmodell n; Vielgruppenmodell n		
multigroup neutron diffusion theory, multigroup theory [of neutron diffusion]	Mehrgruppentheorie f [der Neutronendiffusion], Mehrgruppendiffusionstheorie f, Vielgruppentheorie f [der Neutronendiffusion], Vielgruppendiffusionstheorie f	multilobe	vielzipflig, mehrzipflig, viellappig, mehrlappig
		multi-loop, intermeshed, interconnected, interacting	vermascht
		multimeter	s. multi-range instrument
multigun cathode-ray tube	s. multiple-beam tube	multimeter	s. multi-range multipurpose instrument
multi-hit process, multiple-hit (multitarget) process	Mehrtreffervorgang m, Mehrtrefferprozeß m	multimetering, multiple metering, multiple registration	Mehrfachablesung f, Vielfachablesung f; Mehrfachzählung f, Vielfachzählung f
multi-hit target theory, multi[ple-hit] target theory	Mehrtreffertheorie f		
		multimodal distribution	mehrgipflige Verteilung f
multi-hole core, multiapertured core, multiaperture core	Mehrlochkern m, Viellochkern m	multimode propagation	Vieltypausbreitung f
multi-isotopic element	Mischelement n, mehrisotopiges Element n	multimode waveguide	Vieltypwellenleiter m
multijet condenser	Vielstrahlkondensator m, Mehrstrahlkondensator m	multimolecular adsorption	s. multilayer adsorption
multilateral sound track	Vielzackenschrift f, Mehr[fach]zackenschrift f, Mehramplitudenschrift f	multimolecular layer, multilayer, polymolecular layer	Mehrfachschicht f, mehrfachmolekulare (multimolekulare, polymolekulare) Schicht f
		multinodal seiche	mehrknotige Seiche f
multilayer, multimolecular layer, polymolecular layer	Mehrfachschicht f, mehrfachmolekulare (multimolekulare, polymolekulare) Schicht f	multinomial	s. polynomial in several variables

multinomial distribution, polynomial distribution	[Bernoullische] Polynomialverteilung *f*, multinomiale (polynomische) Verteilung *f*, Multinomialverteilung *f*	**multiple action potential**, multiple potential of action	Mehrfach-Aktionspotential *n*, Vielfach-Aktionspotential *n*
multinuclear, multinucleate, polynuclear, polynucleate ‹chem., bio.›; polycyclic, multiring ‹chem.›	Mehrkern-, mehrkernig, Vielkern-, vielkernig ‹Chem., Bio.›; polyzyklisch ‹Chem.›	**multiple alleles**	multiple Allele *npl*
		multiple annihilation, multiple absorption	Vielfachvernichtung *f*, Mehrfachvernichtung *f*
multinuclear complex [compound]	mehrkerniger Komplex *m*, Mehrkernkomplex *m*	**multiple antenna**	*s*. multi-unit antenna
		multiple backscattering	Mehrfachrückstreuung *f*; Vielfachrückstreuung *f*
multinucleate	*s*. multinuclear		
multinucleon configuration, many-nucleon configuration	Vielnukleonenkonfiguration *f*, Mehrnukleonenkonfiguration *f*	**multiple band-elimination filter**	Mehrfachbandsperrfilter *n*
		multiple band-pass filter	Mehrfachbandpaßfilter *n*
multinucleon force	*s*. many-body force		
multinucleon model of nuclear disintegration	Vielnukleonenmodell *n* des Kernzerfalls	**multiple-beam cathode-ray tube**	*s*. multiple-beam tube
multipact[or]ing, multipact[or] effect, multipactoring effect; multipactor breakdown, electron resonance breakdown	„multipactor"-Effekt *m*, „multipact[or]ing" *m*; Elektronenresonanzdurchschlag *m*, Elektronenresonanzdurchbruch *m*	**multiple-beam interference**, multiple interference	Mehrstrahlinterferenz *f*, Mehrfach[strahl]interferenz *f*, Vielstrahlinterferenz *f*, Vielfach[strahl]interferenz *f*
		multiple-beam interference microscope	Mehrstrahl-Interferenzmikroskop *n*
multi-parameter analysis, multidimensional analysis	Multiparameteranalyse *f*, Mehrparameteranalyse *f*, mehrparametrige (mehrdimensionale) Analyse *f*	**multiple-beam interferometer**	Mehrstrahlinterferometer *n*
		multiple-beam interferometry, multiple interferometry	Mehrstrahlinterferometrie *f*, Mehrfachinterferometrie *f*
multi-parameter analyzer, multidimensional analyzer	Multiparameteranalysator *m*, Mehrparameteranalysator *m*, mehrdimensionaler Analysator *m*	**multiple-beam oscillograph**, multi-beam (multiple) oscillograph, multi[ple]-beam oscilloscope	Mehrstrahloszillograph *m*, Mehrstrahloszilloskop *n*
multipass heat exchanger	Vielstufen-Wärmeaustauscher *m*		
multipath propagation, multipath transmission, multipath transmission effect	Mehrwegeausbreitung *f*, Mehrfachwegausbreitung *f*, Mehrfachwegeeffekt *m*, Mehrwegeeffekt *m*, Mehrfachwege *mpl*	**multiple-beam oscillographic tube**, multi-beam oscillographic tube, multi[ple]-beam oscilloscope	Mehrstrahl-Oszillographenröhre *f*
		multiple-beam oscilloscope	*s*. multiple-beam oscillograph
		multiple-beam oscilloscope tube	*s*. multiple-beam oscillographic tube
		multiple-beam source, multiple source, multi-beam source	Mehrfachquelle *f*, mehrfache Quelle *f*, Mehrstrahlquelle *f*
multipath reception, multiple reception	Mehrwegeempfang *m*, Mehrfachempfang *m*, Vielfachempfang *m*, Mehrkanalempfang *m*, Vielwegeempfang *m*, Vielkanalempfang *m*	**multiple-beam tube**, multi-beam tube, multiple-beam cathode-ray tube, multiple electron beam tube, multiple-gun tube, multigun cathode-ray tube	Mehrstrahlröhre *f*
multipath transmission	*s*. multipath propagation		
multipath transmission effect	*s*. multipath propagation		
multiphase mixture	Mehrphasengemisch *n*	**multiple bond**, multiple link[age]	Mehrfachbindung *f*, Vielfachbindung *f*
multiphase structure	Mehrphasenstruktur *f*	**multiple capacitor**, multiple unit capacitor	Mehrfachkondensator *m*
multiphonon scattering	Mehrphononenstreuung *f*; Vielphononenstreuung *f*		
multiphonon transition	Mehrphononenübergang *m*; Vielphononenübergang *m*	**multiple-cavity klystron**, multicavity klystron	Mehrkammerklystron *n*, Vielkammerklystron *n*
multiplace, multidigit, with more than one figure	mehrstellig	**multiple circuit**	Mehrfachstromkreis *m*
multiplate capacitor	Vielplattenkondensator *m*		
multiplate chamber, multiplate cloud (expansion) chamber	Vielplatten[-Nebel]kammer *f*, Platten[nebel]kammer *f*, Mehrplattenkammer *f*	**multiple-circuit filter**, multicircuit filter	Mehrkreisfilter *n*, Vielkreisfilter *n*
		multiple coefficient of correlation, multiple correlation coefficient	multipler (mehrfacher) Korrelationskoeffizient *m*
multiplate generator	Vielplattengenerator *m*	**multiple coincidence**	Vielfachkoinzidenz *f*, Mehrfachkoinzidenz *f*
multiple, manifold; repeated ‹math.; gen.›	mehrfach, vielfach ‹Math.; allg.›	**multiple-coincidence circuit**	Vielfachkoinzidenzschaltung *f*, Mehrfachkoinzidenzschaltung *f*
multiple ‹consisting of a large number of events›; plural ‹consisting of a few events› ‹phys.› ‹use is often confused›	vielfach, Vielfach-, Viel- ‹aus vielen Einzelprozessen bestehend›; mehrfach, Mehrfach-, Mehr- ‹aus wenigen Einzelprozessen bestehend› ‹Phys.› ‹im Gebrauch oft keine klare Unterscheidung›	**multiple-coincidence counter**	Vielfachkoinzidenzzähler *m*, Mehrfachkoinzidenzzähler *m*
		multiple-collector transistor	*s*. multi[-]collector transistor
		multiple collision	Mehrfachstoß *m*; Vielfachstoß *m*
multiple absorption, multiple annihilation	Vielfachvernichtung *f*; Mehrfachvernichtung *f*	**multiple-conductor line**, multiple-wire line, multi[-]wire line	Mehrfachleitung *f*, Vielfachleitung *f*
multiple acceleration	Mehrfachbeschleunigung *f*, Vielfachbeschleunigung *f*		

multiple-conductor

multiple-conductor system, multiconductor system, many-conductor system — Mehrleitersystem n, Vielleitersystem n

multiple configuration approximation — Mehrfachkonfigurationsnäherung f

multiple contrast — Mehrfachkontrast m

multiple control — s. interacting control

multiple corona — mehrfacher Kranz m

multiple correlation — mehrfache Korrelation f, Mehrfachkorrelation f

multiple correlation coefficient, multiple coefficient of correlation — multipler (mehrfacher) Korrelationskoeffizient m

multiple Coulomb scattering — Coulomb-Vielfachstreuung f, Vielfach-Coulomb-Streuung f

multiple count, multiple tube count — mehrfach gezählter Impuls m

multiple creation — s. multiple production

multiple cross-hairs — Vielfachstrichkreuz n

multiple-crystal spectrometer — Mehrkristallspektrometer n, Vielkristallspektrometer n

multiple decay — s. multiple disintegration

multiple-dee cyclotron, multi-dee cyclotron — Mehrelektrodenzyklotron n

multiple delay discriminator — Vielfachverzögerungsdiskriminator m, Mehrfachverzögerungsdiskriminator m

multiple delay line — Vielfachverzögerungsleitung f, Mehrfachverzögerungsleitung f

multiple diffraction — Mehrfachbeugung f, Vielfachbeugung f

multiple discharges <of lightning> — Blitz m mit mehreren Teilentladungen

multiple disintegration, multiple decay, branching decay, branching <nucl.> — Mehrfachzerfall m, radioaktive Verzweigung f, Verzweigung <Kern.>

multiple dislocation — mehrfache Versetzung f, Mehrfachversetzung f

multiple echo, multiple reflection; flutter echo <el.> — Mehrfachecho n, Mehrfachreflexion f, Vielfachreflexion f; Klangecho n; Flatterecho n, Flatterwiderhall m <El.>

multiple-effect evaporation, multiple-stage evaporation — Mehrstufenverdampfung f, Mehrfachverdampfung f, stufenweise Verdampfung f, Stufenverdampfung f, Mehrkörperverdampfung f, Vielkörperverdampfung f

multiple-effect evaporator, multiple-stage evaporator — Mehrfachverdampfer m, Mehrfach-Verdampfungsanlage f, Mehrstufenverdampfer m, Mehrkörperverdampfer m, Vielkörperverdampfer m, Vielkörperverdampfungsanlage f

multiple electrometer, multicellular voltmeter — Multizellularvoltmeter n, Multizellularelektrometer n

multiple electron beam tube — s. multiple-beam tube

multiple-emitter transistor — s. multi[-]emitter transistor

multiple excitation — Mehrfachanregung f

multiple expansion — multiple Ausdehnung f, Mehrfachausdehnung f

multiple expansion engine — Mehrfachexpansionsmaschine f

multiple fibre — Mehrfachfiber f

multiple-filament lamp — Mehrfadenlampe f

multiple formation — s. multiple production

multiple Fourier series — mehrfache Fourier-Reihe f

multiple Fourier transform[ation] — mehrfache Fourier-Transformation f

multiple-frequency oscillator — Mehrfachgenerator m; Mehrfrequenzgenerator m

multiple galaxy <astr.> — Mehrfachgalaxie f, Mehrfachnebel m, Mehrfachsystem n <Astr.>

multiple grating, ultrasonic cross (multiple) grating — ebenes Ultraschallgitter n

multiple-grid tube, multiple-grid valve, multigrid tube, multielement tube (valve) — Mehrgitterröhre f, Vielgitterröhre f

multiple-gun tube — s. multiple-beam tube

multiple-hit process, multi-hit (multitarget) process — Mehrtreffervorgang m, Mehrtrefferprozeß m

multiple-hit target theory, multi[-hit] target theory — Mehrtreffertheorie f

multiple integral; iterated integral, multiple iterated integral — mehrfaches Integral n, Mehrfachintegral n, Vielfachintegral n; iteriertes Integral

multiple interference — s. multiple-beam interference

multiple interferometry, multiple-beam interferometry — Mehrstrahlinterferometrie f, Mehrfachinterferometrie f

multiple intersection — Mehrfacheinschneiden n

multiple ionization — Mehrfachionisation f, Mehrfachionisierung f, Vielfachionisation f, Vielfachionisierung f

multiple iterated integral; multiple integral; iterated integral — mehrfaches Integral n, Mehrfachintegral m, Vielfachintegral n; iteriertes Integral

multiple labelling, multiple tagging — mehrfache Markierung f

multiple-lap-type winding — Wendelwicklung f

multiple-line fluorescence — s. many-line fluorescence

multiple-line spectrum, many-line[d] spectrum, multi-line (discrete-band) spectrum — Mehrlinienspektrum n; Viellinienspektrum n

multiple link[age], multiple bond — Mehrfachbindung f, Vielfachbindung f

multiple mapping, multiple transformation, repeated mapping (transformation) — Mehrfachabbildung f, mehrfache Abbildung (Transformation) f, Mehrfachtransformation f

multiple Maxwell model — Vielfachmodell n nach Maxwell

multiple metering, multimetering, multiple registration — Mehrfachablesung f, Vielfachablesung f; Mehrfachzählung f, Vielfachzählung f

multiple oscillograph — s. multiple-beam oscillograph

multiple parallel winding, multiplex lap — mehrgängige Parallelwicklung f

multiple particle reaction — Mehrteilchenreaktion f

multiple pendulum — Mehrfachpendel n, Vielfachpendel n

multiple photogrammetric chamber — Mehrfach[meß]kammer f, Mehrfachaufnahmekammer f, Mehrbildkammer f, Vielfach[meß]kammer f

multiple point — mehrfacher Punkt m, p-facher Punkt, Kreuzungspunkt m, mehrfache (multiple) Stelle f

multiple-point recorder — Mehrpunktschreiber m

multiple potential of action — s. multiple action potential

multiple probe, multichannel probe — Vielkanalsonde f, Vielfachsonde f

multiple process; plural process — Vielfachprozeß m; Mehrfachprozeß m

multiple production, multiple creation, multiple formation — Vielfacherzeugung f, Vielfachbildung f

multiple proportions — multiple Proportionen fpl

multiple-range instrument — s. multi-range instrument

multiple-range meter	s. multi-range instrument
multiple reception	s. multipath reception
multiple recorder, multiple recording apparatus	Mehrfachschreiber m, Vielfachschreiber m, Mehrfachregistriergerät n, Vielfachregistriergerät n, Mehrfachaufzeichnungsgerät n, Vielfachaufzeichnungsgerät n
multiple rectifier [circuit], multiple screen	Mehrfachstromrichter m, Mehrfachgleichrichter m, Mehrfach-Gleichrichterschaltung f, Vielfachgleichrichter m
multiple reflection ⟨opt.⟩	mehrfache Reflexion f, Mehrfachreflexion f, Vielfachreflexion f; mehrfache Spiegelung f, Mehrfachspiegelung f, Vielfachspiegelung f ⟨Opt.⟩
multiple reflection	s. a. multiple echo ⟨el.⟩
multiple-reflection gravimeter	Mehrfachreflexionsgravimeter n
multiple registration, multimetering, multiple metering	Mehrfachablesung f, Vielfachablesung f; Mehrfachzählung f, Vielfachzählung f
multiple regression	Partialregression f, partielle (mehrfache) Regression f
multiple replica	Mehrfachabdruck m
multiple resonance	mehrfache Resonanz f, Mehrfachresonanz f, Vielfachresonanz f
multiple rhombic antenna, multiple-unit steerable antenna, musa antenna, muse antenna	mehrdrähtige Rhombusantenne f, vieldrähtige Rhombusantenne f, Mehrfachrautenantenne f, Mehrfachrhombusantenne f
multiple root, repeated root	mehrfache Nullstelle f; mehrfache Wurzel f
multiple-scale instrument (meter)	s. multi-range instrument
multiple scatter[ing]	Vielfachstreuung f
multiple screen	s. multiple rectifier
multiple series	mehrfache Reihe f
multiple slip, polyslip	Mehrfachgleitung f, Mehrfachgleitprozeß m
multiple solution, repeated solution	mehrfache Lösung f
multiple source, multiple-beam source, multi-beam source	Mehrfachquelle f, mehrfache Quelle f, Mehrstrahlquelle f
multiple[-] spark gap	Mehrfachfunkenstrecke f, Mehrfachhörnerableiter m, Vielfachfunkenstrecke f, Vielfachfunkenableiter m, Serienfunkenstrecke f
multiple stabilization	multiplikative Stabilisierung f
multiple-stage demagnetization	Mehrstufenentmagnetisierung f, mehrstufige Entmagnetisierung f
multiple-stage evaporation	s. multiple-effect evaporation
multiple-stage evaporator	s. multiple-effect evaporator
multiple star	Mehrfachstern m, Vielfachstern m
multiplet	Multiplett n, Linienkomplex m
multiple tagging, multiple labelling	mehrfache Markierung f
multiple tail	mehrfacher Schweif m
multiplet component	Multiplettkomponente f
multiple thermal spike	mehrfacher „thermal spike" m, mehrfacher Störungsbereich m
multiplet level, multiplet term	Multiplettterm m
multiplet line	Multiplettlinie f
multiplet of terms, term multiplet	Termmultiplett n
multiple transformation	s. multiple mapping
multiple transition	Mehrfachübergang m, mehrfacher (vielfacher) Übergang m, Vielfachübergang m
multiplet series	Multiplettserie f
multiplet splitting	Multiplettaufspaltung f
multiplet structure	Multiplettstruktur f
multiplet system, multiplet term system	Multipletttermsystem n, Multiplizitätssystem n, Multiplettsystem n
multiplet term, multiplet level	Multiplettterm m
multiplet term system, multiplet system	Multipletttermsystem n, Multiplizitätssystem n, Multiplettsystem n
multiplet theory, theory of multiplets	Multipletttheorie f, Theorie f der Multipletts
multiple tube count, multiple count	mehrfach gezählter Impuls m
multiple-tubed manometer	s. multitube manometer
multiple-tuned antenna, multiband antenna	Mehrbandantenne f
multiple twin	s. polysynthetic twin ⟨cryst.⟩
multiple[-] twin cable; multiple twin quad	Viererkabel n; Dieselhorst-Martin-Vierer m, Dieselhorst-Martin-Kabel n, DM-Vierer m
multiple twin formation	Dieselhorst-Martin-Verseilung f, DM-Verseilung f
multiple twin quad	s. multiple-twin cable
multiple-unit antenna	s. multi-unit antenna
multiple unit capacitor, multiple capacitor	Mehrfachkondensator m
multiple-unit steerable antenna	s. multiple rhombic antenna
multiple-unit tube, multi-unit tube; compound tube	Mehrfachröhre f, Vielfachröhre f, Verbundröhre f
multiple vacancy	mehrfache Leerstelle f, Mehrfachleerstelle f, Vielfachleerstelle f
multiple-valued, many-valued, multi[-]valued ⟨math.⟩	mehrdeutig, vieldeutig; mehrwertig ⟨Math.⟩
multiple-valued function	s. multivalent function
multiple valuedness, many-valuedness, multi-valuedness ⟨math.⟩	Mehrdeutigkeit f, Vieldeutigkeit f; Mehrwertigkeit f ⟨Math.⟩
multiple viewfinder	s. universal finder
multiple Voigt model	Vielfachmodell n nach Voigt
multiple-wire antenna, multi-wire antenna	Mehrdrahtantenne f, Mehrleiterantenne f, Vieldrahtantenne f, Vielleiterantenne f
multiple-wire line, multiple-conductor line, multi[-]wire line	Mehrfachleitung f, Vielfachleitung f
multiplex échelon	Multiplex-Stufengitter n
multiplexing	Mehrfachausnutzung f [von Leitungen], Vielfachausnutzung f [von Leitungen]
multiplex lap, multiple parallel winding	mehrgängige Parallelwicklung f
multiplex type plotting equipment	Stereokartiergerät n Multiplex
multiplication	Vervielfachung f; Verstärkung f; Vervielfältigung f
multiplication ⟨of neutrons⟩	Multiplikation f, Vermehrung f ⟨Neutronen⟩
multiplication ⟨bio.⟩	Vermehrung f ⟨Bio.⟩
multiplication ⟨math.⟩	Multiplikation f ⟨Math.⟩
multiplication by collision, collision multiplication	Stoßvervielfachung f, Vervielfachung f durch Stöße

multiplication

multiplication circuit, multiplier circuit	Vervielfachungsschaltung f; Vervielfacherschaltung f
multiplication constant	s. multiplication factor
multiplication density, reactivity density	Reaktivitätsdichte f
multiplication factor, K-factor, multiplication constant	Multiplikationsfaktor m, Vermehrungsfaktor m, k-Faktor m
multiplication factor	s. a. gain
multiplication length	Multiplikationslänge f
multiplication of dislocations, dislocation multiplication	Versetzungsvervielfachung f, Versetzungsmultiplikation f, Multiplikation f von Versetzungen
multiplication shower	s. cascade <nucl.>
multiplication table, Cayley['s] table	Kompositionstafel f; Multiplikationstabelle f, Multiplikationstafel f; Produkttafel f; Gruppentafel f, Cayleysche Tafel f
multiplication theorem [of probabilities]	Multiplikationssatz m [der Wahrscheinlichkeitsrechnung], Multiplikationssatz der Wahrscheinlichkeiten, Multiplikationsgesetz n [der Wahrscheinlichkeitsrechnung], Multiplikationstheorem n [der Wahrscheinlichkeitsrechnung]
multiplicative axiom	s. axiom of choice
multiplicative mixing <el.>	multiplikative Mischung f <El.>
multiplicative principle	s. axiom of choice
multiplicator of Jacobi, Jacobi['s] multiplicator	Jacobischer Multiplikator m
multiplicity <cryst.>	Zähligkeit f <Krist.>
multiplicity <math.>	Vielfachheit f, Multiplizität f <Math.>
multiplicity	s. a. multiplicity of terms
multiplicity factor <cryst.>	Formfaktor m <Krist.>
multiplicity of terms	Multiplizität f [der Terme], Vielfachheit f [der Terme]
multiplier	Vervielfacher m
multiplier, multiplier unit	Multipliziertrieb m
multiplier <math.>	Multiplikator m <Math.>
multiplier	s. a. photomultiplier
multiplier circuit, multiplication circuit	Vervielfachungsschaltung f; Vervielfacherschaltung f
multiplier circuit electrostatic accelerator	s. cascade generator
multiplier diode, multiplying diode	Vervielfacherdiode f
multiplier gain	Verstärkungsfaktor m des Photovervielfachers
multiplier gain-versus-voltage power law, multiplier gain-vs-voltage power law, photomultiplier characteristic	Photovervielfachercharakteristik f, Spannungsabhängigkeit f des Verstärkungsfaktors [beim Sekundärelektronenvervielfacher]
multiplier phototube	s. photomultiplier
multiplier stage, multiplying stage, stage of multiplication	Vervielfacherstufe f, Vervielfachungsstufe f
multiplier tube	s. photomultiplier
multiplier-type [image] dissector	s. dissector
multiplier unit	s. multiplier
multiply branched solution	mehrfach verzweigte Lösung f
multiply branching network	Vielfachabzweignetz n
multiply charged	mehrfach geladen, vielfach geladen
multiply connected	mehrfach zusammenhängend
multiplying back, series exposure slide, dividing back	Belichtungsreihenschieber m, Multiplikator m
multiplying diode	s. multiplier diode
multiplying stage	s. multiplier stage
multiplying system	multiplizierendes System n
multiply ionized	mehrfach ionisiert
multiply periodical	mehrfach periodisch
multiply scattered	vielfach gestreut
multipolarity, multipole order	Multipolordnung f, Multipolarität f
multipole expansion	Multipolentwicklung f, Entwicklung f nach Multipolen
multipole field	Multipolfeld n
multipole lens	Multipollinse f
multipole moment	Multipolmoment n
multipole of order n, 2^n pole, multipole with order n	2^n-Pol m, Multipol m der Ordnung n
multipole order, multipolarity	Multipolordnung f, Multipolarität f
multipole parameter	Multipolparameter m
multipole potential	Multipolpotential n
multipole radiation	Multipolstrahlung f
multipole transition	Multipolübergang m
multipole with order n, 2^n pole, multipole of order n	2^n-Pol m, Multipol m der Ordnung n
multiport, n-port	Mehrtor n, n-Tor n
multi-purpose instrument	s. universal instrument
multi-range instrument, multiple-range instrument, multi[ple]-scale instrument, multi[ple]-range meter, multi[ple]-scale meter, multimeter	Mehrbereich[s]meßgerät n, Mehrbereich[s]instrument n, Mehrfach[meß]gerät n, Mehrfachinstrument n, Vielbereich[s]meßgerät n, Vielfach[meß]gerät n, Vielfachinstrument n
multi-range measuring transformer	s. multi-range transformer
multi-range meter	s. multi-range instrument
multi-range multi-purpose instrument	s. universal instrument
multi-range transformer, multi-range measuring transformer	Mehrfach[meß]wandler m, Vielfach[meß]wandler m
multi-range voltmeter, multivoltmeter	Mehrbereichvoltmeter n, Mehrbereich-Spannungsmesser m, Vielbereichvoltmeter n, Vielbereich-Spannungsmesser m
multireflex klystron	Multireflex[ions]klystron n
multi-region reactor	Mehrzonenreaktor m, Mehrgebietreaktor m, Vielzonenreaktor m, Vielgebietreaktor m
multiresonator magnetron	s. multicavity magnetron
multiring, polycyclic <chem.>; multinuclear, multinucleate, polynuclear, polynucleate <chem., bio.>	Mehrkern-, mehrkernig, Vielkern-, vielkernig <Chem., Bio.>; polyzyklisch <Chem.>
multirotation, mutarotation, birotation	Mutarotation f, Multirotation f, Birotation f
multi-scale instrument (meter)	s. multi-range instrument
multiscaler	Mehrfachuntersetzer m, Vielfachuntersetzer m, Universaluntersetzer m
multisegment magnetron	s. multicavity magnetron
multishock compression	Mehrstoßkompression f
multislot magnetron	Vielschlitzmagnetron n, Mehrschlitzmagnetron n, Vielschlitz[magnetfeld]-röhre f

multisphere magnetron, wheel magnetron — Radmagnetron n
multispin system, many-spin system — Vielspinsystem n
multistable multivibrator — s. univibrator
multistage amplifier — mehrstufiger Verstärker m, Mehrstufenverstärker m
multistage compression — mehrstufige Kompression f
multistage expansion — mehrstufige Expansion f
multistage rocket, composite rocket, staged rocket, step-rocket — mehrstufige Rakete f, Mehrstufenrakete f, Raketenzug m, Stufenrakete f
multistimulus theory ‹e.g. of Hartridge› — Mehrfarbentheorie f ‹z. B. von Hartridge›
multitarget process, multi[ple]-hit process — Mehrtreffervorgang m; Mehrtrefferprozeß m
multitarget theory, multi[ple]-hit target theory — Mehrtreffertheorie f
multitone, multitone [sound] generator, Barrow generator — Multiton-Schallsender m, Multitongenerator m, Multiton m
multitube lens, multielectrode lens — Mehrelektrodenlinse f, Mehrzylinderlinse f, Vielelektrodenlinse f
multitube manometer, multiple-tubed manometer — Vielfachröhrenmanometer n
multiturn potentiometer — mehrgängiges Potentiometer n
multi-unit antenna, multiple-unit antenna, multiple antenna — Mehrfachdipol m, Mehrfachantenne f, Vielfachdipol m, Vielfachantenne f, Mehrelementantenne f, mehrelementige (vielelementige) Antenne f; Strahlergruppe f
multi-unit tube — s. multiple-unit tube
multivalent — s. polyvalent ‹chem.›
multivalent function, multiple-valued function, many-valued function ‹function theory› ‹math.› — mehrwertige (mehrblättrige, p-wertige, multivalente, p-valente, mehrdeutige) Funktion f ‹Funktionentheorie› ‹Math.›
multivalley semiconductor — s. many-valley semiconductor
multi[-]valued, multiple-valued, many-valued ‹math.› — mehrdeutig, vieldeutig; mehrwertig ‹Math.›
multi-valued logic, many-valued logic — mehrwertige Logik f
multi-valuedness, many-valuedness, multiple valuedness ‹math.› — Mehrdeutigkeit f, Vieldeutigkeit f; Mehrwertigkeit f ‹Math.›
multivariable control — s. interacting control
multivariate distribution [function] — s. joint distribution
multivector, alternating tensor, p-vector ‹math.› — Multivektor m, p-Vektor m, vollständig alternierender Tensor m, zusammengesetzte Größe f, Komplexgröße f ‹Math.›
multivibrator — Multivibrator m, Impulskipp m
multivibrator circuit — Multivibratorschaltung f, Multivibratorkippschaltung f, Kippstufe f
multivoltmeter — s. multi-range voltmeter
multi-wire antenna — s. multiple-wire antenna
multi[-]wire counter — Zählrohr n mit mehreren Zähldrähten, Mehrdrahtzählrohr n, Vieldrahtzählrohr n
multi[-]wire line, multiple-conductor line, multiple-wire line — Mehrfachleitung f, Vielfachleitung f
multi[-]wire proportional counter — Proportionalzählrohr n mit mehreren Zähldrähten
mu-mesic atom, mu-mesonic atom, μ-mesic atom, muonic atom — Myonatom n, μ-Mesonatom n, μ-Mesoatom n, μ-Meson-Atom n, Muonatom n, My-Mesonatom, My-Mesonenatom n, My-Mesoatom n

mu meson — s. muon
mu-meson decay, decay of the mu-meson, muon decay — Zerfall m des Myons, Myonzerfall m, μ-Zerfall m, My-Zerfall m
mu-meson field — My-Meson-Feld n, Myonfeld n, Muonfeld n
mu-mesonic atom — s. mu-mesic atom
mu-neutrino — s. neutrino in mu-meson decay
Munk['s] theorem — Munksches Verschiebungsgesetz n
Munroe effect — Munroe-Effekt m
Munsell system — Munsell-System n
muon, μ meson, mu meson, American meson — Myon n, μ-Meson n, My-Meson n, Müon n, Muon n
muon decay — s. mu-meson decay
muonic atom — s. mu-mesic atom
muonium — Myonium n
muon neutrino — s. neutrino in mu-meson decay
muon number — Myonenzahl f
mural circle (quadrant) — Mauerquadrant m
mural comparator — s. surveying tape comparator
murky day, overcast day — trüber Tag m
murky sky, wan sky — trüber Himmel m
Murnaghan['s] formula — Murnaghansche Formel f
Murphree plate efficiency, plate efficiency [factor] — Bodenwirkungsgrad m, Verstärkungsverhältnis n ‹Chem.›
Murphy['s] formula — Murphysche Formel f
musa antenna — s. multiple rhombic antenna
muscle contraction — s. muscular contraction
muscle fiber — Muskelfaser f
muscular contraction, muscle contraction, contraction [of the muscle] — Muskelzuckung f, Zuckung f [des Muskels], Muskelkontraktion f
muscular relaxation, relaxation of muscle — Muskelerschlaffung f, Erschlaffung f des Muskels
muscular tonus — Muskeltonus m
muscular work — Muskelarbeit f
muse antenna — s. multiple rhombic antenna
mush — s. parasitics
mush area, nuisance area — Störempfangsgebiet n
mushroom [cloud] — Staubpilz m, Rauchpilz m, Wolkenpilz m, Pilz m, pilzförmige Wolke f
mushroom valve — s. disk valve
musical acoustics — Musikakustik f
musical frequency — s. audio[-] frequency
musical instrument — Musikinstrument n
musical interval, [acoustic] interval ‹ac.› — musikalisches Intervall n, Intervall n ‹Ak.›
musical pitch ‹ac.› — musikalische Tonhöhe f ‹Ak.›
musical pitch, pitch ‹ac.› — Stimmung f ‹Ak.›
musical scale, gamut, scale, tone scale ‹ac.› — Tonleiter f, Tonskala f, Tonreihe f ‹Ak.›
musical sound, sound, tone ‹ac.› — Klang m ‹Ak.›
musical spark, singing spark — tönender Funke m
musical system — Tonsystem n
Muskhelishvili potential [function], potential function of Muskhelishvili — Potentialfunktion f von Muschelswili, Muschelischwilisches Potential n, Muschelischwilische Potentialfunktion
mu space, μ-space, molecule space, molecular space — μ-Raum m, My-Raum m, Molekülraum m, kleiner Phasenraum m, Molekülphasenraum m
mutable — mutabel, mutationsfähig
mutamer — Mutamer n
mutamerism — Mutamerie f
mutant — Mutante f

mutarotation, multirotation, birotation	Mutarotation f, Multirotation f, Birotation f	myopia, myopy, short-sightedness, near-sightedness	Kurzsichtigkeit f, Myopie f, Brachymetropie f
mutation action	s. interaction	myosis, contraction of the pupil	Pupillenverengerung f, Miosis f
mutation constant	Mutationskonstante f	myria..., ma $<= 10^4$>	Myria..., ma $<= 10^4$>
mutation due to radiation, radiomutation, radiation-induced mutation	strahlungsbedingte (strahlungsinduzierte) Mutation f, Mutation als Folge einer Strahleneinwirkung	myriametre wave	s. very-low frequency wave
		myriametre wavelength [range]	s. very low frequency range
mutation rate, frequency of mutations	Mutationshäufigkeit f, Mutationsrate f, Mutationsgeschwindigkeit f	myriotic field	myriotisches Feld n
mutator	s. converter <el.>		
mute	s. sourdine		
mutual action	s. interaction		
mutual attraction, interattraction	gegenseitige Anziehung f		
mutual capacitance	s. coefficient of induction		
mutual characteristic, transconductance characteristic	Steilheitskennlinie f, Steilheitscharakteristik f		
mutual conductance	s. transconductance		
mutual conductance	s. forward conductance		
mutual diffusion	gegenseitige Diffusion f		
mutual exchange, interchange	Umtausch m; Auswechslung f; Vertauschung f		
mutual exchange, mutual exchange reaction <chem.>	[chemische] Umsetzung f, Umsetzungsreaktion f <Chem.>		
mutual friction <He II>	gegenseitige Reibung f <He II>		
mutual impedance	gegenseitige Impedanz f, Wechselimpedanz f		
mutual inductance, coefficient of mutual conductance, mutual inductivity	Gegeninduktivität f, Kopplungsinduktionskoeffizient m, Wechselinduktionskoeffizient m, Koeffizient m der gegenseitigen Induktion, Gegeninduktionskoeffizient m, Wechselinduktivität f		
mutual-inductance coupling	s. inductive coupling		
mutual inductance per unit length	Gegeninduktivitätsbelag m		
mutual induction	Gegeninduktion f, gegenseitige (wechselseitige) Induktion f, Wechselinduktion f		
mutual inductivity	s. mutual inductance		
mutual information, synentropy	Synentropie f, gegenseitige (wechselseitige, übertragene) Information f		
mutual interaction	s. interaction		
mutually disjoined	paarweise disjunkt		
mutually exclusive events	s. incompatible events		
mutual repulsion	gegenseitige Abstoßung f		
mutual slope	s. dynamic transconductance		
mutual solubility	gegenseitige Löslichkeit f		
mutual solubility curve	s. solubility curve		
muzzle; orifice, mouth	Mündung f		
muzzle blast (report, sound)	Mündungsknall m		
mydriasis, dilatation of the pupil	Pupillenerweiterung f, Mydriasis f		
myelin fibre, myelin thread	Myelinfaden m		
myelin form	Myelinfigur f, Myelinform f		
myelin sheath	Myelinscheide f		
myelin thread, myelin fibre	Myelinfaden m		
myofibril	Myofibrille f, Muskelfibrille f		
myofilament	Myofilament n		
myogram	Myogramm n		
myoneural junction	s. motor end[]plate		
myope, short-sighted person	Kurzsichtige m, Myop m		

N

Nabarro-Herring model	Nabarro-Herring-Modell n
nabla, nabla operator (vector)	s. del <math.>
Nachet prism, tetrahedral prism	Nachet-Prisma n, Tetraederprisma n
Nachet['s] vertical illuminator	Vertikalilluminator m nach Nachet, Prismenilluminator m [nach Nachet], Prisma n
Nacken-Kyropoulos method, Nacken method	Nacken-[Kyropoulos-]Verfahren n, Nacken-[Kyropoulos-]Methode f, Kristallzüchtung f aus der Schmelze nach dem Nacken-Kyropoulos-Verfahren
nacreous cloud	s. mother-of-pearl cloud
Nadenenko dipole	Nadenenko-Antenne f, Nadenenko-Strahler m
nadir, plumb point, nadir point <of aerophotogram>	Nadirpunkt m, Bildnadir m <Luftmeßbild>
nadiral distance, nadir distance	Nadirdistanz f, Bildneigung f, Nadirabstand m
nadir point, plumb point, nadir <of aerophotogram>	Nadirpunkt m, Bildnadir m <Luftmeßbild>
nadir point triangulation, plumb-point triangulation	Nadirpunkttriangulation f, Nadirtriangulation f
naive model	einfaches Modell n
Nakamura biplate; Nakamura halfshade; Nakamura plate, Nakamura rotating biplate	Nakamura-Platte f; Halbschattenapparat m nach Nakamura
naked eye, unaided eye	unbewaffnetes Auge n, bloßes (freies) Auge
naked pile, naked reactor, bare reactor, bare pile	unreflektierter Reaktor m, Reaktor ohne Reflektor, nackter Reaktor
n-al axis	s. symmetry axis of order n
n-al axis of the second sort, n-al symmetry axis of the second sort, symmetry [axis] of the second sort of order n	n-zählige Drehspiegelungsachse f
naled	Naled f, Naljod f, Aufeisbildung f; Taryn f
n-al rotation axis	s. symmetry axis of order n
n-al screw axis, n-fold screw axis, screw axis of order n	n-zählige Schraubenachse f
n-al symmetry, n-fold symmetry, symmetry of order n	n-zählige Symmetrie f, n-Zähligkeit f, Symmetrie f der Ordnung n, Zähligkeit f n
n-al symmetry axis of the second sort	s. n-al axis of the second sort
nano..., n, millimicro..., mμ	Nano..., n
nanophotogrammetry	Nanophotogrammetrie f
nanosecond pulse	Impuls m im Nanosekundenbereich, Nanosekundenimpuls m
nanosecond pulse technique, nanosecond technique	Nanosekundenimpulstechnik f, Nanosekunden[meß]technik f
Nansen bathometer, Nansen bottle	Nansen-Flasche f
Naperian digit, nepit, nit <= 1.44 bits>	Nepit n, nepit, nit <= 1,44 bit>
Naperian logarithm	s. natural logarithm
Napier['s] analogies, Neper's analogies	Nepersche Analogien fpl, Napiersche Analogien
Napierian absorption coefficient	s. linear absorption coefficient <in Lambert's law>
Napierian absorption index, linear absorption index, natural absorption index	natürlicher Absorptionsindex m
Napierian extinction	s. Napierian optical density
Napierian extinction coefficient	s. linear extinction coefficient
Napierian extinction index	s. linear extinction index
Napierian logarithm	s. natural logarithm
Napierian optical density, Napierian extinction, natural [optical] extinction, internal optical density defined by natural logarithm	
Napier['s] logarithm	s. natural logarithm
nappe, overflowing sheet	überschießender Strahl m, Strahl, Überfallamelle f; Nappe f
nappe <geo.>	Überschiebungsdecke f, tektonische Decke f, Decke; Deckenüberschiebung f <Geo.>
nappe	s. a. sheet <math.>
narrow angle lighting fitting	Tiefstrahler m, tiefstrahlende Leuchte f
narrow band amplifier	Schmalbandverstärker m
narrow-band axis	Schmalbandachse f
narrow-band filter <opt., el.>	Schmalbandsperre f <El.>
narrow-band frequency modulation, NFM	Schmalband-Frequenzmodulation f
narrow-band noise	schmalbandiges Rauschen n
narrow-band noise generator	Schmalbandrauschgenerator m
narrow-band phase modulation, NPM	Schmalband-Phasenmodulation f
narrow beam	schmales Bündel n, enges Bündel, enges Strahlenbündel n; streustrahlenfreies Bündel; Fadenstrahl m
narrow-beam absorption	Absorption f unter der Bedingung des schmalen Bündels, Kleinfeldabsorption f, Schmalstrahlabsorption f
narrow-beam condition	Bedingung f des schmalen Bündels, Kleinfeldbedingung f
narrow-beam measurement	Messung f mit schmalem Bündel, Messung bei schmalem Bündel, Kleinfeldmessung f
narrow cut filter <opt.>	Schmalbandfilter n; tonrichtiges Filter n <Opt.>
narrow flame	s. shooting flame
narrowing	s. contraction
narrowing of lines by exchange interaction, exchange narrowing	Austauschverschmälerung f
narrowing of lines due to motion	Bewegungsverschmälerung f
narrowing of the forbidden zone	Verengerung (Verschmälerung) f des Bandabstandes
narrowing of the spectral line	s. line narrowing
narrowing ratio	s. contraction ratio
narrow pulse	schmaler Impuls m
narrow shower	schmaler Schauer m
nascent; elemental <chem.>	atomar, elementar; naszierend <Chem.>
nascent state, status nascens	naszierender Zustand m, Status m nascendi
Nasmyth reflector, Nasmyth telescope	Nasmyth-Teleskop n, Spiegelteleskop n nach Nasmyth
nastic movement, nastic reaction, nasty	Nastie f, nastische Bewegung f
natural absorption coefficient	s. linear absorption coefficient <in Lambert's law>
natural absorption index, linear (Napierian) absorption index	natürlicher Absorptionsindex m
natural abundance	natürliche Häufigkeit f
natural admittance	s. characteristic admittance <of transmission line>
natural angular frequency, fundamental (characteristic) angular frequency	Eigenkreisfrequenz f
	natürliche Extinktion f

natural

natural background radiation; background radiation; natural radiation background, radiation background, background	natürliche Untergrundstrahlung (Strahlung) f, natürlicher Strahlenpegel m; Untergrundstrahlung, Grundstrahlung f, Strahlungsuntergrund m; Umgebungsstrahlung f; Raumstrahlung f
natural breadth of energy level	s. natural width of energy level
natural broadening, radiation broadening, line broadening by [radiation] damping, broadening by damping	natürliche Linienverbreiterung f, Strahlungsverbreiterung f, f, Linienverbreiterung (Verbreiterung f) durch Strahlungsdämpfung, Linienverbreiterung durch Dämpfung, Dämpfungsverbreiterung f
natural capacitance	s. self-capacitance
natural circulation	Naturumlauf m, natürlicher Umlauf m
natural colloid, eucolloid, true colloid	Eukolloid n
natural convection, free convection	freie Konvektion f, natürliche Konvektion
natural co-ordinates; intrinsic co-ordinates; natural system [of co-ordinates], natural frame	natürliche Koordinaten fpl; natürliches Koordinatensystem n, natürliches System n
natural density, inherent density	Eigendichte f
natural diaphragm	natürliche Blende f
natural equation [of the curve], intrinsic equation [of the curve]	natürliche Gleichung f [der Kurve]
natural extinction	s. Napierian optical density
natural extinction coefficient	s. linear extinction coefficient
natural extinction index	s. linear extinction index
natural frame	s. natural co-ordinates
natural frequency, fundamental (inherent, characteristic) frequency, self-frequency, eigenfrequency, free-running frequency	Eigenfrequenz f, Resonanzfrequenz f, Eigenschwingungszahl f
natural hour	natürliche Stunde f <3 862 s der mittleren Zeit>
natural hydrogen, ordinary hydrogen	gewöhnlicher (natürlicher) Wasserstoff m
natural impedance, characteristic (surge) impedance <of the transmission line>	Wellenwiderstand m <Leitung>, Leitungswellenwiderstand m
natural isotopic mixture	natürliches Isotopengemisch n
natural law, law of nature	Naturgesetz n
natural level breadth (width)	s. natural width of energy level
natural light	natürliches Licht n
natural limit of stress	s. endurance strength at alternating load
natural line width, natural width of line, natural spectral line width, natural whole half width	natürliche Linienbreite f (Breite f der Spektrallinie)
natural logarithm, logarithm to base e, Napierian (Naperian, Napier's, hyperbolic) logarithm, ln, $\log_e$	natürlicher (Neperscher, Napierscher, hyperbolischer) Logarithmus m, ln, $^e\log$, $\log_e$
naturally occurring uranium, natural uranium, unenriched uranium	Natururan n, natürliches Uran n, nicht angereichertes Uran
naturally radioactive nuclide, natural radioactive nuclide, natural radionuclide	natürliches Radionuklid n, natürliches radioaktives Nuklid n, natürlich radioaktives Nuklid
natural nuclear transformation	s. spontaneous transformation
natural optical extinction	s. Napierian optical density
natural oscillation	s. vibrational mode
natural oscillation of antenna	Antenneneigenschwingung f, Eigenschwingung f der Antenne
natural parallelism	natürlicher Parallelismus m
natural period [of oscillation], free period; characteristic period	Eigenperiode f, Eigenschwingungsdauer f
natural phenomenon	Naturerscheinung f
natural pitch	natürliche Stimmung f
natural radiation background	s. natural background radiation
natural radioactive nuclide	s. naturally radioactive nuclide
natural radioactivity	natürliche Radioaktivität f
natural radionuclide	s. naturally radioactive nuclide
natural resonance	Eigenresonanz f
natural rigidity, inherent rigidity	Formstarrheit f
natural scatter[ing]	natürliche Streuung f
natural science	Naturwissenschaft f
natural slope	s. slope of repose
natural sound, eigentone	Eigenton m
natural spectral line width	s. natural line width
natural strength	s. endurance strength at alternating load
natural system [of co-ordinates]	s. natural co-ordinates
natural system of units	s. system of atomic units
natural temperature, eigentemperature, intrinsic temperature	Eigentemperatur f
natural time; relaxation time	Relaxationszeit f, Zeitkonstante f; Abklingzeit f; Einstellzeit f; Erholungszeit f
natural trajectory	wirkliche Bahn f
natural transformation	s. natural nuclear transformation
natural unit, atomic unit; Hartree unit	Hartree-Einheit f; atomare (natürliche) Einheit f
natural uranium, naturally occurring uranium, unenriched uranium	Natururan n, natürliches Uran n, nicht angereichertes Uran
natural velocity	s. proper velocity
natural vibration	s. vibrational mode
natural vibrational co-ordinates	natürliche Schwingungskoordinaten fpl
natural voltage <el.>	Eigenspannung f <El.>
natural water, ordinary water	gewöhnliches (natürliches, leichtes) Wasser n
natural wave	Eigenwelle f
natural wavelength	Eigenwellenlänge f, natürliche Wellenlänge f
natural whole half width	s. natural line width
natural width of [energy] level, natural breadth of energy level, natural level width, natural level breadth	natürliche Niveaubreite f, natürliche Breite f des Energieniveaus
natural width of line	s. natural line width
nature of radiation	s. type of radiation
Naumann['s] index	Naumannscher Flächenindex m
nautical astronomy	nautische Astronomie f
nautical mile	s. international mile <= 1,852 m>
Navier-Stokes equation of motion, Navier-Stokes equations	Navier-Stokessche Gleichungen fpl (Bewegungsgleichung f)
navigability	s. dirigibility
navigational aid	Navigationshilfsmittel n, Navigationsmittel n
navigational computer	s. navigation computer
navigational instrument	s. navigation instrument
navigational triangle	s. polar triangle
navigation computer, navigational computer	Navigationsrechner m, Navigationsrechenanlage f

navigation instrument, navigational instrument	Navigationsinstrument n, Navigationsgerät n
navigation satellite	Navigationssatellit m
N band <15—22 Gc/s>	N-Band n <15···22 GHz>
N-body	s. Newtonian fluid
n-body problem, problem of n bodies	n-Körper-Problem n
N.C. contact	s. rest contact
N-component, nuclear-active component, nuclear interacting component, nuclear component	kernaktive Komponente (Gruppe) f, N-Komponente f, Komponente der kernverwandten Teilchen, nukleare Komponente, Kernwechselwirkungskomponente f
n-compound, normal compound	normale Verbindung f, n-Verbindung f
n-conducting, N-conducting, n-type, N-type	n-leitend, n-, n-Typ-, überschußleitend
neap rise (tide), dead tide	Nippflut f, Nadirflut f, taube Flut f; Nipptide f, Nadirtide f, taube Tide f, Taubezeit f, Quadratur f
near-critic[al]	fastkritisch
near earthquake, neighbouring earthquake	Nahbeben n
nearest neighbour, neighbour of the first sphere	nächster Nachbar m, Nachbar erster Sphäre
nearest-neighbour interaction	Wechselwirkung f nächster Nachbarn
near field <ac.; el.>	Nahfeld n <Ak.; El.>
near field pattern, Fresnel pattern <of antenna>	Nahfelddiagramm n <Antenne>
nearfield region	s. near zone
near-forward scattering	Fastvorwärtsstreuung f
near-ground air [layer]	s. near-soil atmospheric layer
near infra-red [region] <2.5—25 μ>	mittleres Infrarot[gebiet] n, mittleres IR [-Gebiet] n, Infrarot-C-Gebiet n, IR-C-Gebiet n, mittleres Ultrarot n <3,0···25 μm>
near limit <phot.>	Nahpunkt m <Phot.>
nearly circular orbit	kreisnahe Bahn f
nearly parabolic orbit	parabelnahe Bahn f
nearly symmetric top, quasisymmetric top	quasisymmetrischer Kreisel m
near-magic	fastmagisch
near point of clear vision, punctum proximum	Nahpunkt m, punctum n proximum; Nahpunkt im engeren Sinne, manifester Nahpunkt
near-prompt	fastprompt
near-sightedness, myopia, myopy, short-sightedness	Kurzsichtigkeit f, Myopie f, Brachymetropie f
near singing, tendency to sing	Pfeifneigung f
near-soil atmospheric layer, bottom layer, near-ground air [layer], ground-level air, surface air, air close to the soil surface <meteo.>	bodennahe Luft[schicht] (Atmosphärenschicht) f, Bodenschicht f, Hautschicht f <Meteo.>
near-surface	s. surface
near-surface flow; surface flow, surface current	Oberflächenströmung f; oberflächennahe Strömung f
near-surface wave	s. surface wave
near the surface	s. surface
near-threshold stimulus	schwellennaher Reiz m
near ultraviolet	s. black light
near ultraviolet [region]	s. black-light region
near zone, induction zone, Fresnel['s] zone, nearfield region, Fresnel['s] region, Huyghens['] zone <ac.; el.>	Nahzone f, Nahwirkungsgebiet n, Nahfeld n, Induktionszone f, Fresnelsches Gebiet n, Fresnelsche Zone f, Fresnel-Zone f <Ak.; El.>
near-zone focusing, short-range focusing	Nahfeldeinstellung f
nebula; nebulosity <astr.>	Nebel m, Nebelfleck m <Astr.>
nebular hypothesis <established by Kant>	Meteoritenhypothese f [von Kant]
nebular line, nebulium line	Nebellinie f
nebular ring	Nebelring m
nebular shell, nebulous shell	Nebelhülle f
nebular spectrograph	Nebelspektrograph m
nebular stage <of nova>	Nebelstadium n <Nova>
nebular variable, T Tauri star, RW Aurigae-type star	RW Aurigae-Stern m, T Tauri-Stern m, Nebelveränderlicher m
nebulium	Nebulium n
nebulium line, nebular line	Nebellinie f
nebulosity	s. nebula <astr.>
nebulous cloud, nebulous stratus	schleierartige Wolke f, Nebulosusform f, Stratus m nebulosus
nebulous shell, nebular shell	Nebelhülle f
nebulous stratus, nebulous cloud	schleierartige Wolke f, Nebulosusform f, Stratus m nebulosus
necessary condition	notwendige Bedingung f
neck	Hals m, Einschnürung f
neck <of bottle>	Hals m <an Gefäßen>, Füllansatz m
neck, volcanic neck <geo.>	Vulkanschlot m, Schlot m, Schlotgang m, Schußkanal m, Eruptionskanal m, Stielgang m; Neck m <Geo.>
necking [down]	s. constriction
necking in tension, reduction of area in tension	Brucheinschnürung f, Bruchquerschnittsverminderung f
neck of areometer	Aräometerspindel f
neck of the meander lobe	Mäanderhals m, Schleifenhals m
needle, pointer <of measuring instrument>; indicator, index	Zeiger m <allg.; Meßgerät>
needle counter [tube]	Nadelzählrohr n
needle dam, needle weir, dam with frames and needles	Nadelwehr n
needle deflection, deflection of the needle, needle throw	Nadelausschlag m
needle deflection, pointer deflection, deflection of the needle (pointer); movement of the pointer	Zeigerausschlag m, Zeigerauslenkung f
needle effect of electrostatics, point effect of electrostatics	Spitzenwirkung f der Elektrostatik, Spitzeneffekt m der Elektrostatik
needle electrode	Nadelelektrode f
needle electrometer	Nadelelektrometer n
needle galvanometer, moving-magnet galvanometer, galvanometer with moving magnet	Nadelgalvanometer n, Drehmagnetgalvanometer n
needle gap	Spitzenfunkenstrecke f, Spitzenentladungsstrecke f, Spitzenzündstrecke f, Nadelfunkenstrecke f

needle

needle ice, candle ice	Kammeis n, Nadeleis n; Haareis n, Pipcrake n; Eisnadeln fpl	**negative feedback ratio**	Gegenkopplungsgrad m, Gegenkopplungsverhältnis n
needle oscillograph	Nadeloszillograph m	**negative flame**, cathodic flame	negative (katodische) Flamme f, Katodenflamme f
needle radiation	Nadelstrahlung f	**negative frequency part**	Teil m mit negativen Frequenzen
needle scratch, surface noise, scratch	Nadelgeräusch n, Nadelrauschen n, Kratzen n der Nadel	**negative glow**	negatives Glimmlicht n, negative Glimmschicht f; negatives Büschel n <Bogenentladung>
needle-shaped crystal	s. whisker		
needle throw, deflection of the needle, needle deflection	Nadelausschlag m	**negative glow lamp**, glow lamp	Glimmlampe f
needle-type suspension, point-type suspension	Spitzenlagerung f, Nadellagerung f	**negative-going pulse**, negative pulse	negativer Impuls m, Minusimpuls m, Negativimpuls m
needle weir, needle dam, dam with frames and needles	Nadelwehr n	**negative image**	s. negative
		negative impedance, expedance	negativer komplexer Wechselstromwiderstand m, negative Impedanz f, Expedanz f
Néel point, Néel temperature, antiferromagnetic Curie point (temperature)	Néel-Punkt m, Néel-Temperatur f, Néelsche Asymptotentemperatur f, antiferromagnetischer Curie-Punkt m, antiferromagnetische Übergangstemperatur f	**negative ion column**	negative Ionensäule f
		negative[-] ion vacancy, anion vacancy	Anionenleerstelle f, Anionenfehlstelle f, Anionenlücke f
Néel wall	Néel-Wand f	**negative lens**, divergent lens, diverging lens, dispersion (dispersive) lens	Zerstreuungslinse f, Negativlinse f, Streu[ungs]linse f
negative; negative image	Negativ n, photographisches Negativ; Negativbild n		
negative, electrically negative; negatively charged <el.>	negativ, elektrisch negativ; negativ [auf]geladen <El.>	**negative lift**	Untertrieb m, negativer Auftrieb m
negative absolute temperature, negative thermodynamic temperature	negative absolute Temperatur f	**negative limb**, negative terminal	Minusklemme f, negative Klemme f, Minuspol m
negative absorption	s. stimulated emission		
negative acceleration	s. deceleration <mech.>	**negatively charged**	s. negative <el.>
negative beta decay, β⁻ decay	β⁻-Zerfall m, Elektronenzerfall m	**negative meniscus**, diverging meniscus; convexo-concave lens	negativer (streuender) Meniskus m; konvexkonkave Linse f
negative binomial [series] distribution	s. Pólya['s] distribution	**negative modulation**	Negativmodulation f
negative boosting transformer	Saugtransformator m	**negative nodal point**, antinodal point	negativer Knotenpunkt m
negative branch, P-branch	P-Zweig m, negativer Zweig m	**negative osmosis**	negative Osmose f
negative bridge feedback	Brückengegenkopplung f	**negative parity**, odd parity, parity − 1	ungerade Parität f, Parität − 1, negative Parität
negative catalysis	s. inhibition <chem.>		
negative charge feedback	Ladungsgegenkopplung f	**negative pitching moment**, diving moment	negatives Kippmoment n
negative conductance transistor[ized] amplifier	NLT-Verstärker m <negative Leitung mit Transistoren>	**negative polarity**, direct polarity	Minuspolung f, negative (direkte) Polung f, negative Polarität f
negative correlation; inverse correlation	negative Korrelation f	**negative pole**, minus	Minuspol m, negativer Pol m, Minus n
negative crystal	negativer Kristall m	**negative position [of crystal]**	Subtraktionsstellung f
negative current feedback	s. current feedback		
negative definite	negativ[-] definit	**negative-positive process**, negative-positive technique	Negativ-Positiv-Prozeß m, Negativ-Positiv-Verfahren n
negative density, DN	Negativschwärzung f, Negativdichte f	**negative pressure**	s. underpressure
negative developer	Negativentwickler m	**negative pressure wave** <hydr.>	Gegenwelle f, reflektierte Welle f <Hydr.>
negative distortion	s. barrel distortion		
negative electricity	s. resinous electricity	**negative principal point**, antiprincipal point	negativer Hauptpunkt m
negative electron, negatron; e⁻ electron	Elektron n; Negatron n, negatives Elektron, e⁻	**negative process**	Negativprozeß m, Negativverfahren n
negative element of telephoto lens	Telenegativ n		
negative emulsion	Negativemulsion f	**negative pulse**, negative-going pulse	negativer Impuls m, Minusimpuls m, Negativimpuls m
negative energy state; negative term	negativer Energiezustand m; negativer Term m	**negative rain**	negativer Regen m
negative entropy	s. average information content		
negative excess	negativer Überschuß m	**negative reactance**	s. capacitive reactance
negative excess	s. a. platikurtosis	**negative reactivity**	negative Reaktivität f
negative eyepiece, Huyghenian eyepiece, Huyghens['] eyepiece	Huygensches (negatives) Okular n, Huygens-Okular n, Okular nach Huygens	**negative refraction**	negative Brechung f
negative feedback	s. reverse feedback	**negative resistance**	negativer [differentieller] Widerstand m, Negwid m
negative feedback amplifier	gegengekoppelter Verstärker m		
negative feedback factor	Gegenkopplungsfaktor m	**negative resistance diode**	Negativwiderstanddiode f

negative resistance effect	Negativwiderstandeffekt m, Negwideffekt m
negative rotation, laevorotation, levorotation, counterclockwise rotation	Linksdrehung f, negative Drehung f; Linkslauf m
negative semidefinite	negativ semidefinit
negative sequence component	Gegenkomponente f
negative sequence impedance, opposition impedance	Gegenimpedanz f, Gegenscheinwiderstand m, gegenläufige Impedanz f, Impedanz des gegenläufigen Feldes
negative sequence system, negative system	Gegensystem n
negative sequence system vector, negative system vector	Gegensystemvektor m
negative series feedback	Reihen[schluß]gegenkopplung f
negative sign, minus sign (symbol, mark); subtraction sign	Minuszeichen n; negatives Vorzeichen n
negative skewness	negative Schiefe f
negative stability	s. unstable equilibrium
negative system	s. negative sequence system
negative system vector, negative sequence system vector	Gegensystemvektor m
negative temperature coefficient, NTC	negativer Temperaturkoeffizient m
negative temperature coefficient resistor	s. thermistor
negative temperature state, inversion state	Zustand m mit negativer [absoluter] Temperatur
negative term; negative energy state	negativer Energiezustand m; negativer Term m
negative terminal, negative limb	Minusklemme f, negative Klemme f, Minuspol m
negative thermodynamic temperature, negative absolute temperature	negative absolute Temperatur f
negative viewer, negatoscope, light box, spotting box	Negatoskop n, Negativschaukasten m, Negativbetrachter m
negative viscosity, endosity	Endosität f, negative Viskosität f
negative voltage feedback	Spannungsgegenkopplung f
negativity wave	Negativitätswelle f
negaton	s. negatron
negatoscope, negative viewer, light box, spotting box	Negatoskop n, Negativschaukasten m, Negativbetrachter m
negatron, negative electron, e$^-$; electron	Elektron n; Negatron n, negatives Elektron, e$^-$
negatron ‹thermionic valve›	Negatron n ‹Elektronenröhre›
negentropy	s. average information content
neglect, neglection; omission	Vernachlässigung f; Fortlassung f, Weglassung f
negligible ‹with respect to›, **negligibly small** ‹in comparison with›	vernachlässigbar ‹gegen›, zu vernachlässigen, vernachlässigbar klein
Negretti thermometer	Negretti-Thermometer n
neighbor ‹US›	s. neighbour
neighborhood ‹US›	s. vicinity
neighbour, neighbor ‹US›	Nachbar m
neighbour, neighbouring atom	Nachbaratom n, Nachbar m
neighbourhood ‹math.›	Umgebung f ‹Math.›
neighbourhood	s. a. vicinity
neighbourhood effect, [development] adjacency effect	Nachbareffekt m [der Entwicklung]
neighbouring atom, neighbour	Nachbaratom n, Nachbar m
neighbouring earthquake, near earthquake	Nahbeben n
neighbouring group participation	Nachbargruppeneffekt m
neighbour of the first sphere	s. next neighbour
neighbour of the second sphere	s. next-nearest neighbour
Neil's parabola	s. semicubical parabola
nekton	Nekton n
nematic [crystal], nematic phase	nematische Phase f, pl-Phase f, nematische kristalline Flüssigkeit f, nematischer Kristall m
nematic state	nematischer Zustand m
Nemets effect	Nemets-Effekt m
neon bulb, neon lamp, neon tube	Neonglimmlampe f, neongefüllte Glimmlampe f, Glimmlampe mit Neonfüllung
neon lamp, neon tube	Neonlampe f, Neonröhre f
neon stabilizer [tube]	s. glow-discharge stabilizer tube
neon tube	s. neon bulb
neon tube	s. a. neon lamp
NEP	s. noise equivalent power
neper, Np, N	Neper n, Np, N
Neper['s] analogies, Napier's analogies	Nepersche Analogien fpl, Napiersche Analogien
Neperian logarithm	s. natural logarithm
neper meter	Nepermeter n
nephelauxetic effect	nephelauxetischer Effekt m
nephelometer	Nephelometer n, Trübungsmesser m
nephelometric titration, heterometry	nephelometrische Titration f, Heterometrie f, Trübungstitration f
nephelometry	Nephelometrie f, Trübungsmessung f
nephelometry in its proper sense	s. tyndallimetry
nephograph	Nephograph m
nephology	Lehre f von den Wolken, Wolkenkunde f
nephometer	Nephometer n, Bewölkungsmengenmesser m, Wolken[mengen]messer m
nephoscope; mirror (reflecting) nephoscope	Nephoskop n; Wolkenspiegel m
nepit, nit, Naperian digit ‹ = 1.44 bits›	Nepit n, nepit, nit ‹ = 1,44 bit›
neptunium, $_{93}$Np	Neptunium n, $_{93}$Np
neptunium [radioactive] family	s. neptunium series
neptunium [radioactive] series, $4n + 1$ series; neptunium family, neptunium radioactive family, radioactive family of neptunium, $4n + 1$ family	Neptuniumzerfallsreihe f, Neptuniumreihe f, ($4n + 1$)-Zerfallsreihe f, Zerfallsreihe f des Neptuniums; radioaktive Familie f des Neptuniums, Neptuniumfamilie f
Nernst approximation [formula]	Nernstsche Näherung[sformel] f
Nernst calorimeter	Nernstsches Metallkalorimeter (Kalorimeter) n, Nernst-Kalorimeter n
Nernst coefficient	Nernst-Koeffizient m
Nernst detector, Nernst-effect detector	Nernst-Detektor m, Nernst-Effekt-Detektor m
Nernst diffusion layer, diffusion layer ‹el.chem.›	[Nernstsche] Diffusionsschicht f ‹El.chem.›
Nernst distribution law, Nernst partition law, partition law [of Nernst], distribution law [of Nernst]	Nernstscher Verteilungssatz m
Nernst effect	Nernst-Effekt m
Nernst-effect detector	s. Nernst detector
Nernst-Einstein relation	Nernst-Einsteinsche Beziehung f
Nernst equation ‹for e.m.f.›	Nernstsche Gleichung f; Nernstsche Formel f, Formel von Nernst
Nernst equation ‹bio.›	Nernstsches Gesetz n ‹Bio.›

Nernst-Ettingshausen effect	Nernst-Ettingshausen-Effekt *m*, Ettingshausen-Nernst-Effekt *m* <1. und 2.>	**net loss**, net [transmission] equivalent, overall [line] attenuation, overall equivalent; net-loss factor	Restdämpfung *f*
Nernst factor	Nernst-Faktor *m*	**net loss** <gen.>	Gesamtverlust *m* <allg.>
Nernst field	Nernst-Feld *n*	**net-loss factor**	s. net loss
Nernst filament, Nernst glower	Nernst-Stift *m*, Nernst-Brenner *m*	**net magnetic field**	s. resultant magnetic field
Nernst['s] heat theorem	s. third law of thermodynamics	**net mass**	s. net
Nernst lamp	Nernst-Lampe *f*	**net multiplier**	s. Venetian blind multiplier
Nernst['s] law	s. third law of thermodynamics	**net of climatological stations**, climatological net	Klimanetz *n*
Nernst partition law	s. Nernst distribution law	**net of slip lines**	Gleitliniennetz *n*
Nernst['s] theorem	s. third law of thermodynamics	**net of Wulff**, Wulff['s] net, stereographic net	Wulffsches Netz *n*
Nernst-Thompson rule	Nernst-Thompsonsche Regel *f*	**net plane**, atomic plane, lattice plane, net <cryst.>	Netzebene *f*, Gitterebene *f* <Krist.>
Nernst transport number, true transport (transference) number	wahre Überführungszahl *f*, Nernstsche Überführungszahl	**net register ton**	Nettoregistertonne *f*, NRT
nerve conductance, nerve conduction, propagation of the nerve impulse	Nervenleitung *f*	**net tonnage**	Nettotonnage *f*, Nettoregistertonnenzahl *f*, NRT-Zahl *f*
nerve ending	Nervenendigung *f*	**net torque**, resulting torque, resultant torque	Gesamtdrehmoment *n*, resultierendes Drehmoment *n*
nerve excitation	Nervenerregung *f*	**net transmission equivalent**	s. net loss
nerve impulse, nervous impulse	Nervenimpuls *m*	**net velocity**, resultant velocity	resultierende Geschwindigkeit *f*
nerve stimulation, stimulation of nerve, excitation in nerves	Nervenreizung *f*	**net voltage of interference**	Reststörspannung *f*
nervous impulse	s. nerve impulse	**net weight**	s. net
nervus opticus, optic nerve	Sehnerv *m*, Nervus *m* opticus, Fasciculus *m* opticus	**network**, network of lines, system <el.>	Netzwerk *n*, Netz *n*, Streckenkomplex *m* <El.>
nesistor	Nesistor *m*, Zweipolfieldistor *m*	**network** <cryst.; in glass>	Netzwerk *n* <Krist.; in Gläsern>
nested	verschachtelt, geschachtelt, ineinandergeschachtelt	**network**, network of stations, réseau <geo.>	Stationsnetz *n* <Geo.>
nested; clustered	nestartig, nest[er]förmig, haufenförmig	**Γ network**	s. general Γ network
nested sample, cluster <stat.>	Klumpenstichprobe *f* <Stat.>	**network analysis**, circuit analysis, electrical circuit analysis	Netzwerkanalyse *f*, Netzanalyse *f*, Stromkreisanalyse *f*
nesting	Schachtelung *f*, Verschachtelung *f*	**network analyzer**, circuit analyzer	Netz[werk]analysator *m*, Netzmodell *n*, Netzwerkgleichungslöser *m*
nest of intervals <math.>	Intervallschachtelung *f*, Schachtelung *f* <Math.>	**network element**, system element; network(system) parameter	Netz[werk]element *n*; Netz[werk]parameter *m*
nest of pipes, bundle of pipes (tubes)	Rohrbündel *n*	**network-forming ion**	netzwerkbildendes Ion *n*
net; net weight; net mass	Eigengewicht *n*; Eigenmasse *f*, Nettomasse *f*; Nettogewicht *n*, Reingewicht *n*	**network-modifying ion**	netzwerk[ver]änderndes Ion *n*
net	s. a. atomic plane <cryst.>	**network molecule**	s. cross-linked molecule
net	s. a. grid	**network node**	s. node <el.>
net acceleration, resultant acceleration	Gesamtbeschleunigung *f*, resultierende Beschleunigung *f*	**network of dislocations**, dislocation network	Versetzungsnetzwerk *n*, Versetzungsgitter *n*
net caloric power (value), net calorific power (value), calori[fi]c power, lower calorific value, net heating value (power), heat[ing] value, heating power	Heizwert *m*, unterer Heizwert, Brennwert *m*	**network of lines**	s. network <el.>
		network of stations, network, réseau <geo.>	Stationsnetz *n* <Geo.>
		network parameter	s. network element
		network structure	Netzwerkstruktur *f*
net chart, nomogram with radial lines, isopleth	Netztafel *f*, Isoplethentafel *f*, Isoplethenkarte *f*	**network synthesis**, electrical network synthesis, synthesis of electrical network	Netzwerksynthese *f*
net damping, resultant damping; total damping	Gesamtdämpfung *f*; resultierende Dämpfung *f*	**network theory**, theory of electrical networks	Netzwerktheorie *f*
net density	Netzdichte *f*	**network theory**, theory of four-terminal networks	Vierpoltheorie *f*
net efficiency	s. overall efficiency	**network transformation**, transfiguration (transformation) of network	Netztransfiguration *f*, Netzumwandlung *f*
net equivalent	s. net loss	**network transmission equivalent**, transmission equivalent	Netzwerkbezugsdämpfung *f*, Netzwerk-Übertragungsäquivalent *n*
net force, resultant, resultant force <mech.>	resultierende Kraft *f*, Resultierende *f*, Resultante *f* <Mech.>	**Neuber-Papkovich solution**	s. Boussinesq-Papkovich solution
net gain, overall gain, overall amplification	Gesamtverstärkung *f*, Gesamtverstärkungsfaktor *m*	**Neuhaus['] method [of crystal growth]**	Kammerverfahren *n* [nach Neuhaus], Neuhaussches Kristallzüchtungsverfahren *n*
net heating power (value)	s. net calorific value	**Neumann['s] algebra /** von, W^*-algebra	von Neumannsche Algebra, Neumann-Algebra *f*, W^*-Algebra *f*
net level of interference	Reststörpegel *m*		

Neumann band, twin band — Neumannsches Band n, Zwillingsstreifen m
Neumann['s] Bessel function [of the second kind] — s. Bessel function of the second kind
Neumann['s] boundary condition, boundary condition of the second kind, second boundary condition — Neumannsche Randbedingung f, Randbedingung zweiter Art, zweite Randbedingung
Neumann['s] boundary [value] problem — s. Neumann['s] problem
Neumann['s] constant — Neumannsche Konstante f
Neumann['s] ergodic theorem / von Neumann['s] formula [of mutual inductance] — s. statistical ergodic theorem
Neumann['s] formula [of mutual inductance] — Neumannsche Formel f [für die Gegeninduktion]
Neumann['s] function — s. Bessel function of the second kind
Neumann-Kopp rule, Kopp-Neumann['s] law — Neumann-Koppsche Regel f, Joule-Koppsche Regel, Kopp-Neumannsche Regel, Regel von Kopp-Neumann
Neumann['s] law — s. Faraday['s] law of induction
Neumann line — Neumannsche Linie f
Neumann matrix / von Neumann['s] permeameter — s. density matrix
Neumann['s] permeameter — Neumann-Joch n
Neumann['s] polynomial — Neumannsches Polynom n
Neumann potential — Neumannsches Potential n, Neumann-Potential n
Neumann['s] principle — Neumannsches Prinzip n
Neumann['s] problem, Neumann['s] boundary [value] problem, second boundary [value] problem, boundary value problem of the second kind — Neumannsches Problem (Randwertproblem) n, Neumann-Problem n, Neumannsche (zweite) Randwertaufgabe f, zweites Randwertproblem, Randwertproblem (Randwertaufgabe) zweiter Art
Neumann['s] recorder, Neumann[s] sound pressure-reverberation time recorder — Neumann-Schreiber m, Neumann-Pegelschreiber m, Neumannscher Pegelschreiber m, Dämpfungsschreiber m [nach Neumann]
Neumann['s] series, Liouville-Neumann series — Neumannsche Reihe f
Neumann['s] triangle — Neumannsches Dreieck n
Neumayer screen — Neumayersche Hütte f
neurilemma, Schwann['s] sheath — Schwannsche Scheide f, Neurolemma n, Neurilemma n
neuristor — Neuristor m
neurite, axon — Axon n, Neurit m, Achsenzylinder m
neuron — Neuron n
neuston — Neuston n
neutral, neutral particle, uncharged particle — Neutrales n, neutrales (ungeladenes) Teilchen n, Neutralteilchen n, neutrale Partikel f
neutral — s. a. neutral point
neutral, electrically neutral; uncharged, without (of zero) charge <el.> — neutral, elektrisch neutral; ungeladen, ladungsfrei, ohne Ladung <El.>
neutral absorber — s. neutral filter
neutral acid, molecular acid — Molekülsäure f, Neutralsäure f
neutral axis — s. elastic axis <elasticity>
neutral base, molecular base — Molekülbase f, Neutralbase f
neutral conductor — s. neutral point
neutral cross-section, neutral section — neutraler Querschnitt m, Fließscheide f
neutral density filter — s. neutral filter
neutral diffuser, non-selective diffuser — neutral (grau, nichtselektiv, aselektiv) streuender Körper m, Neutralstreuer m
neutral drag — mechanische Bremswirkung f durch neutrale Luftpartikeln <Satellit>
neutral electrode <ECG> — indifferente Elektrode f
neutral element — s. identity [element]
neutral equilibrium, neutral stability, indifferent equilibrium — indifferentes Gleichgewicht n, stetiges Gleichgewicht

neutral filament
neutral filter, neutral absorber (density filter, grey non-selective filter), non-selective absorber (filter)
neutral gas
neutral glass, non-selective glass, smoked glass
neutral grey filter
neutral hue
neutral illumination, optically (physically) neutral illumination
neutrality condition
neutrality principle
neutralization, neutralizing, neutrodynization <el.>
neutralization
neutralization heat, heat of neutralization
neutralization point
neutralizing, neutralization, neutrodynization <el.>
neutralizing bridge circuit
neutralizing capacitance
neutralizing capacitor
neutralizing circuit, neutrodyne circuit neutrodyne [connection]
neutralizing resistor
neutralizing titration, acid-base titration
neutral layer, neutral surface, neutral plane <elasticity, elastic bending>
neutral line
neutral mass, mass of neutral atom
neutral meson, neutret[to]
neutral particle
neutral pi-meson, neutral pion, π^0 meson, π^0
neutral plane
neutral point, neutral; mid-point [conductor]; star[-]point, star zero point, zero point of the star, centre point, neutral conductor <el.>
neutral point <of atmospheric polarization>
neutral point, neutral temperature <of the thermocouple>
neutral point
neutral point voltage, star point voltage, voltage to neutral
neutral potential, potential independent of isobaric spin
neutral-pseudoatom method, method of neutral pseudoatom
neutral pseudoscalar [meson] theory

— s. elastic axis <elasticity>
— Neutralfilter n, Graufilter n, Schwächungsfilter n, neutrales (aselektives) Filter n, Echtgraufilter n
— s. indifferent gas
— Neutralglas n, neutrales Glas n, Grauglas n, Rauchglas n, Schwächungsglas n
— s. neutral filter
— neutraler Farbton m
— neutrale Beleuchtung f, optisch (physikalisch) neutrale Beleuchtung
— Neutralitätsbedingung f
— Neutralitätsprinzip n
— Neutralisation f <El.>
— s.a. compensation
— Neutralisationswärme f
— s. equivalence point <chem.>
— Neutralisation f <El.>
— Neutralisationsbrückenschaltung f, Neutralisationsschaltung f
— Neutralisationskapazität f, Neutrodynkapazität f
— Neutralisationskondensator m, Neutrodynkondensator m, Neutrodyn[-kondensator] m
— Neutrodynschaltung f, Neutrodyn[e] n, Neutralisationsschaltung f
— Nullpunkt[s]widerstand m, künstlicher Widerstand m
— Neutralisationstitration f, Neutralisationsanalyse f, Säure-Base-Titration f
— neutrale Schicht (Faserschicht, Fläche, Ebene) f, Nullschicht f <Elastizität, elastische Biegung>
— s. isogyre
— neutrale Masse (Atommasse) f, Masse des neutralen Atoms
— neutrales Meson n, Neutretto n
— s. neutral
— neutrales Pi-Meson (Pion, π-Meson) n, π^0-Meson n, π^0
— s. neutral layer
— neutraler Punkt (Leiter) m, Neutralpunkt m, Nullpunkt m, Nulleiter m; Sternpunkt m, Mittelpunkt m, [neutraler] Mittelleiter m, Mittelpunktleiter m; Sternpunktleiter m <El.>
— neutraler Punkt m, Neutralpunkt m <Himmelslichtpolarisation>
— neutraler Punkt m, neutrale Temperatur f <Thermoelement>
— s. a. centre of compression and twist
— Sternpunktspannung f
— neutrales Potential n
— Methode f der neutralen Pseudoatome
— neutrale pseudoskalare Mesonentheorie (Mesonenfeldtheorie, Theorie) f

neutral

neutral red	Neutralrot n, Toluylenrot n	neutron activation	Neutronenaktivierung f, Aktivierung f durch Neutronen
neutral rock, intermediate rock	intermediäres Gestein n	neutron activation analysis, NAA	Neutronenaktivierungsanalyse f
neutral salt	Neutralsalz n, neutrales Salz	neutron activation analysis / by	neutronenaktivierungsanalytisch
neutral scalar field	neutrales skalares Feld n		
neutral scalar meson theory, neutral scalar theory	neutrale skalare Mesonentheorie (Mesonenfeldtheorie, Theorie) f	neutron age, Fermi age [of neutron], symbolic age [of neutron], age <nucl.>	Fermi-Alter n, Neutronenalter n, Neutronen„age" n, Alter n [des Neutrons], Age m, „age" n <Kern.>
neutral section, neutral cross-section	neutraler Querschnitt m, Fließscheide f		
neutral stability	s. neutral equilibrium	neutron attenuation cross-section, cross-section for neutron attenuation	Neutronenschwächungsquerschnitt m, Wirkungsquerschnitt m für (der) Neutronenschwächung, Schwächungsquerschnitt m für Neutronen
neutral step wedge, step wedge, grey step wedge, sensitometric tablet	Stufengraukeil m, Stufenkeil m, Grautreppe f, Stufengrautafel f, Graustufenkeil m		
neutral surface	s. neutral layer	neutron balance	Neutronenbilanz f; Neutronengleichgewicht n
neutral temperature, neutral point <of the thermocouple>	neutraler Punkt m neutrale Temperatur f <Thermoelement>		
		neutron bath, neutron field	Neutronenfeld n
neutral theory [of nuclear forces]	neutrale Theorie f, Neutraltheorie f <der Kernkräfte>	neutron beam; neutron ray	Neutronenstrahl m; Neutronenbündel n
neutral wave	s. stable wave	neutron-beta detector	s. Hilborn detector
neutral wedge, grey wedge, wedge	Graukeil m, Neutralkeil m, Keil m, Schwärzungstreppe f	neutron binding energy	Bindungsenergie f des Neutrons, Neutronenbindungsenergie f
neutral wedge analysis, Goldberg wedge analysis	Graukeilanalyse f	neutron bombardment; neutron irradiation	Neutronenbestrahlung f; Neutronenbeschuß m
neutral wedge method	Graukeilverfahren n		
neutral wire	Nullungsleiter m		
neutret[to], neutral meson	neutrales Meson n, Neutretto n	neutron booster, neutron multiplicator	Neutronenmultiplikator m, Neutronenvervielfacher m
neutret[to]	s. a. neutrino in mu-meson decay	neutron burst	s. neutron pulse
neutrino bremsstrahlung	Neutrinobremsstrahlung f	neutron capture cross-section, cross-section for neutron capture	Neutroneneinfangquerschnitt m, Einfangquerschnitt m für Neutronen, Wirkungsquerschnitt m für Neutroneneinfang, Neutroneneinfangwirkungsquerschnitt m
neutrino charge, neutrino number	Neutrinoladung f, Neutrinozahl f		
neutrino field	Neutrinofeld n		
neutrino hypothesis	Neutrinohypothese f	neutron capture gamma-rays, capture gamma-rays, capture gamma radiation, capture gammas	Einfang-Gamma-Quanten npl, Einfang-Gamma-Strahlung f, Gamma-Strahlung f beim (n, γ)-Prozeß
neutrino in beta decay, electron neutrino, e-neutrino, v_e	e-Neutrino n, Elektron[en]neutrino n, beim Positronenzerfall (Beta-Zerfall) entstehendes Neutrino, zum Elektron gehörendes Neutrino, Neutrino der Theorie des Beta-Zerfalls, v_e		
		neutron-capture reaction	Neutroneneinfangreaktion f, Neutroneneinfangprozeß m <speziell: (n, γ)-Prozeß>
neutrino in mu-meson decay, neutrino in muon decay, muon neutrino, mu-neutrino, μ-neutrino, neutret[to], v_μ	μ-Neutrino n, My-Neutrino n, Myon[nen]neutrino n, beim My-Mesonen-Zerfall entstehendes Neutrino n, zum My-Meson gehörendes Neutrino, Muon[en]neutrino n, Müonenneutrino n, myonverwandtes Neutrino, Neutretto n, v_μ	neutron chain reaction	Neutronenkettenreaktion f
		neutron chamber, neutron irradiation chamber	Neutronenbestrahlungskammer f, Neutronenkammer f
		neutron chamber, neutron ionization chamber	Neutronenkammer f, Neutronenionisationskammer f, Ionisationskammer f für Neutronen
		neutron chopper	s. chopper <nucl.>
neutrino lens	Neutrinolinse f	neutron collimator; neutron howitzer	Neutronenkollimator m
neutrino luminosity	Neutrinohelligkeit f		
neutrino number, neutrino charge	Neutrinoladung f, Neutrinozahl f	neutron collision diameter, collision diameter	Stoßdurchmesser m, Kollisionsdurchmesser m
neutrino operator, operator of neutrino	Neutrinooperator m, Operator m des Neutrinos	neutron collision radius, collision radius	Stoßradius m, Kollisionsradius m
neutrino physics	Neutrinophysik f	neutron component	Neutronenkomponente f
neutrino radiation	Neutrinostrahlung f	neutron concentration	s. neutron density
neutrino theory of beta decay	Neutrinotheorie f des Beta-Zerfalls	neutron converter	Neutronenkonverter m, Neutronentransformator m, Neutronenumwandler m
neutrodyne [circuit], neutrodyne connection, neutralizing circuit	Neutrodynschaltung f, Neutrodyn[e] n, Neutralisationsschaltung f		
		neutron corrosion	Korrosion f durch Neutroneneinwirkung
neutrodynization	s. neutralization <el.>	neutron count	s. neutron pulse
neutron absorber, neutron sponge	Neutronenabsorber m, Neutronenfänger m	neutron counter	Neutronenzählrohr n
neutron absorption analysis	Neutronenabsorptionsanalyse f	neutron cross-section, cross-section for neutrons	Neutronen[wirkungs]querschnitt m, Wirkungsquerschnitt m für Neutronen
neutron absorption cross-section, cross-section for neutron absorption	Neutronenabsorptionsquerschnitt m, Absorptionsquerschnitt m für Neutronen, Wirkungsquerschnitt m für (der) Neutronenabsorption, Neutronenabsorptionswirkungsquerschnitt m	neutron crystal monochromator	Kristall[neutronen]monochromator m, Neutronenkristallmonochromator m
		neutron current	Neutronenstrom m, Neutronendiffusionsstrom m

neutron current density	Neutronenstromdichte f	neutron flux distribution, flux distribution	Flußverteilung f, Verteilung f des Neutronenflusses
neutron cycle	Neutronenzyklus m, Generationenfolge f der Neutronen	neutron flux meter	Neutronenflußmesser m
neutron deficiency	Neutronendefizit n	neutron gas	Neutronengas n
neutron-deficient	neutronenarm, neutronendefizit, mit Neutronendefizit	neutron generation	Neutronengeneration f
		neutron generation, neutron production	Neutronenerzeugung f
neutron density, neutron concentration <n/cm³>	Neutronenzahldichte f, Neutronendichte f, Neutronenkonzentration f <n/cm³>	neutron generation time, generation time	Generationsdauer f der Neutronen, mittlere Lebensdauer f der Neutronengeneration
neutron detector	Neutronendetektor m, Neutronennachweisgerät n	neutron generator, neutron producer, machine source	Neutronengenerator m, Neutronenerzeuger m; Neutronenerzeugungsreaktor m, Kleinreaktor m zur Neutronenerzeugung
neutron diffraction	Neutronen[strahl]beugung f, Neutronendiffraktion f	neutron[ ]graphy, neutron radiography, neutronography	Neutronenradiographie f
neutron diffraction meter	s. neutron diffractometer	neutron[ ]graphy	s. neutron-diffraction study
neutron diffraction pattern, neutronogram	Neutronenbeugungsbild n, Neutronenbeugungsaufnahme f, Neutronenbeugungsdiagramm n, Neutronogramm n	neutron group, neutron diffusion group, neutron energy group	Neutronengruppe f, Neutronendiffusionsgruppe f, Neutronenenergiegruppe
		neutron guide, neutron pipe	Neutronenleiter m
neutron-diffraction study, neutron diffractometry; neutron[ ]graphy	neutronendiffraktometrische Untersuchung f, Neutronenstrukturuntersuchung f, Neutronen[strahl]beugungsuntersuchung f; Neutronographie f	neutron hardening, hardening of the neutron spectrum	Härtung f des Neutronenspektrums, Neutronenhärtung f
		neutron hardening by absorption, absorption hardening [of the neutron spectrum]	Absorptionshärtung f [des Neutronenspektrums]
neutron diffractometer, neutron diffraction meter	Neutronenbeugungsanordnung f, Neutronenbeugungsgerät n, Neutronendiffraktometer n, Neutronenspektrometer n	neutron hardening by diffusion, diffusion hardening [of the neutron spectrum]	Diffusionshärtung f [des Neutronenspektrums]
		neutron hardening by filters, filter hardening [of the neutron spectrum]	Filterhärtung f [des Neutronenspektrums]
neutron diffractometry	s. neutron-diffraction study	neutron hardening by leakage, leakage hardening [of the neutron spectrum]	Ausflußhärtung f [des Neutronenspektrums]
neutron diffusion	Neutronendiffusion f		
neutron diffusion group, neutron group, neutron energy group	Neutronengruppe f, Neutronendiffusionsgruppe f, Neutronenenergiegruppe f	neutron heating	Neutronenaufheizung f
		neutron howitzer; neutron collimator	Neutronenkollimator m
neutron diffusion law	Neutronendiffusionsgesetz n, Gesetz n der Neutronendiffusion	neutronics <especially in nuclear reactor systems>; neutron physics	Neutronenphysik f
neutron diffusion length	s. diffusion length	neutron image intensifier [tube]	Neutronenbildverstärker m
neutron diffusion tensor	Neutronendiffusionstensor m		
neutron dose	Neutronendosis f	neutron importance, importance, importance of neutrons	Neutroneneinfluß m, Einfluß m [der Neutronen], Neutroneninhalt m
neutron dosemeter	Neutronendosimeter n, Neutronendosismesser m		
neutron doubling time, doubling time	Neutronenverdopplungszeit f, Verdopplungszeit f	neutron-induced fission	s. neutron fission
neutron economy	Neutronenökonomie f	neutron-induced reaction, neutron reaction	Neutronenreaktion f, neutroneninduzierte (durch ein Neutron ausgelöste) Reaktion f
neutron-electron interaction	Neutron-Elektron-Wechselwirkung f		
		neutron interference	Neutronen[strahl]interferenz f
neutron emitter	Neutronenstrahler m	neutron inventory	Gesamtzahl f der zu gegebener Zeit vorhandenen freien Neutronen, Neutroneninventar n, Neutroneninhalt m
neutron energy group, neutron group, neutron diffusion group	Neutronengruppe f, Neutronendiffusionsgruppe f, Neutronenenergiegruppe f		
neutron evaporation	Neutronenverdampfung f	neutron ionization chamber	s. neutron chamber
neutron excess [number], difference number, isobaric (isotopic) number	Neutronenüberschuß m	neutron irradiation; neutron bombardment	Neutronenbestrahlung f; Neutronenbeschuß m
neutron field, neutron bath	Neutronenfeld n	neutron irradiation chamber, neutron chamber	Neutronenbestrahlungskammer f, Neutronenkammer f
neutron filter	Neutronenfilter n		
neutron fission, neutron-induced fission, (n,f) reaction	neutroneninduzierte (neutronenausgelöste) Spaltung f, Spaltung durch ein Neutron, Kernspaltung f durch ein Neutron, (n,f)-Prozeß m, (n,f)-Reaktion f	neutron leakage, leakage, escape of neutrons	Neutronenabfluß m, Neutronenausfluß m, Neutronenverlust m
		neutron lethargy, lethargy of the neutron, lethargy variable	Neutronenlethargie f, Lethargie f des Neutrons
neutron flux, neutron flux density, flux	Neutronenfluß m, Fluß m <n/cm²s>, Neutronenflußdichte f	neutron lifetime, mean life of the neutron	Neutronenlebensdauer f, [mittlere] Lebensdauer f des Neutrons, mittlere Neutronenlebensdauer
neutron flux converter, flux converter, doughnut	Flußkonverter m, Flußumwandler m	neutron magneto-vibrational scattering	s. magneto-vibrational scattering [of neutrons]
neutron flux density	s. neutron flux		

neutron mass, mass of the neutron	Neutronenmasse f, Masse f des Neutrons	neutron reflector, neutron[-reflecting] mirror	Neutronenreflektor m, Neutronenspiegel m
neutron mean free path, neutron path length	mittlere freie Weglänge f des Neutrons, Neutronenweglänge f	neutron-rich	neutronenreich, mit Neutronenüberschuß
neutron migration length	s. migration length	neutron richness	Neutronenüberschuß m
neutron mirror	s. neutron reflector	neutron scattering factor	Neutronenstreukoeffizient m
neutron moment	Moment n des Neutrons, Neutronenmoment n	neutron scintillator	Neutronenszintillator m
neutron multiplication	Neutronenmultiplikation f, Neutronenvermehrung f	neutron self-radiation	Neutroneneigenstrahlung f
neutron multiplicator, neutron booster	Neutronenmultiplikator m, Neutronenvervielfacher m	neutron-sensitive, sensitive to neutrons	neutronenempfindlich, empfindlich gegen[über] Neutronen
neutron-neutron force	Neutron-Neutron-Kraft f	neutron shell	Neutronenschale f
neutron-neutron scattering, n-n scattering	Neutron-Neutron-Streuung f, n-n-Streuung f	neutron shield	Neutronenschild m, Neutronenschutz m, Abschirmung f gegen Neutronen
neutron number	Neutronenzahl f, Anzahl f der Neutronen im Kern	neutron shower	Neutronenschauer m
		neutron slowing-down length	s. slowing-down length
neutronogram	s. neutron diffraction pattern	neutron slowing-down spectrum	Neutronenbremsspektrum n
neutronography	s. neutron radiography	neutron source strength	Neutronenquellstärke f
neutron-optical	neutronenoptisch		
neutron optics	Neutronenoptik f	neutron spectrometer	Neutronenspektrometer n
neutron path length	s. neutron mean free path	neutron spectrometry, neutron spectroscopy	Neutronenspektrometrie f, Neutronenspektroskopie f
neutron period, neutron rate	Neutronenflußperiode f		
neutron-physical	neutronenphysikalisch	neutron spectrum	Neutronenspektrum n
neutron physics; neutronics ‹especially in nuclear reactor systems›	Neutronenphysik f	neutrons per absorption	s. neutron yield per absorption
neutron pile, Simpson['s] pile	Neutronenzählrohrteleskop n, Simpsonsche Säule f	neutrons per fission, ν	Gesamtzahl f der Neutronen je Spaltung ‹einschließlich der verzögerten›, ν
neutron pipe, neutron guide	Neutronenleiter m	neutrons per fission	s. neutron yield per fission
neutron poison, nuclear poison, reactor poison	Reaktorgift n, Neutronengift n, starker Neutronenabsorber m	neutron sponge, neutron absorber	Neutronenabsorber m, Neutronenfänger m
neutron poison effect, neutron poisoning	s. poisoning of the nuclear reactor	neutron standard [source], standard neutron source	Standardneutronenquelle f, Neutronenstandard m; Neutronenvergleichsquelle f
neutron probe	Neutronensonde f, Neutronenmeßkopf m		
neutron producer	s. neutron generator	neutron star	Neutronenstern m
neutron production, neutron generation	Neutronenerzeugung f	neutron state	Neutronenzustand m
neutron productivity, productivity [of neutrons]	Produktivität f [von Neutronen], Neutronenproduktivität f	neutron streaming	Neutronentransport m durch Spalte
		neutron temperature	Neutronentemperatur f
neutron projection operator	Neutronenprojektionsoperator m		
neutron proportional counter	Neutronenproportionalzählrohr n	neutron therapy	Neutronentherapie f
		neutron thermocouple	Neutronenthermoelement n
neutron-proton diagram	Neutron-Proton-Diagramm n	neutron thermopile	Neutronenthermosäule f
neutron-proton exchange force, neutron-proton force	Neutron-Proton-Kraft f, Neutron-Proton-Austauschkraft f	neutron-tight	neutronendicht, neutronenundurchlässig
neutron-proton ratio	Neutronen/Protonen-Verhältnis n, Verhältnis n von Neutronen- zu Protonenzahl	neutron total cross-section, total neutron cross-section	totaler Neutronenwirkungsquerschnitt (Wirkungsquerschnitt m für Neutronen), Gesamtneutronenquerschnitt m, Neutronengesamtquerschnitt m
neutron-proton reaction	s. (n,p) reaction		
neutron-proton scattering, n-p scattering	Neutron-Proton-Streuung f, n-p-Streuung f		
		neutron transition	Neutronenübergang m
		neutron transmission	Neutronendurchgang m, Neutronentransmission f, Neutronendurchstrahlung f
neutron pulse, neutron burst; neutron count	Neutronenimpuls m		
neutron radiation, neutron rays	Neutronenstrahlung f	neutron transparency	Neutronendurchlässigkeit f
neutron radiography, neutron[ ]graphy, neutronography	Neutronenradiographie f	neutron transport	Neutronentransport m
neutron radius [of nucleus]	Neutronenradius m [des Kerns], Kernkraftradius m	neutron transport cross-section	s. transport cross-section
neutron rate, neutron period	Neutronenflußperiode f	neutron transport theory, transport theory	Transporttheorie f, Neutronentransporttheorie f, kinetische Diffusionstheorie f
neutron-ray; neutron beam	Neutronenstrahl m; Neutronenbündel n		
neutron rays, neutron radiation	Neutronenstrahlung f	neutron trap	Neutronenfalle f, Neutronenauffänger m
neutron reaction	s. neutron-induced reaction	neutron vacancy	Neutronenleerstelle f, Neutronenloch n
neutron-reflecting mirror	s. neutron reflector		

neutron velocity selector	Neutronengeschwindigkeitsselektor m, Geschwindigkeitsselektor m für Neutronen	Newton['s] first law [of motion], first law of motion, Newton['s] law of inertia, law of inertia	erstes Newtonsches Gesetz (Axiom) n, [Newtonsches] Trägheitsgesetz n, [Newtons] Lex f prima, [allgemeines] Beharrungsgesetz n, Trägheitsprinzip n
neutron wave	Neutronenwelle f		
neutron wavelength	Neutronenwellenlänge f		
neutron width	Neutronenbreite f	Newton['s] formula <stat.>	Newtonsche Formel f <Stat.>
neutron yield	Neutronenausbeute f		
neutron yield per absorption, mean number of neutrons per absorption, neutrons per absorption, η	[mittlere] Spaltneutronenausbeute f pro absorbiertes Neutron, [mittlere] Anzahl (Zahl) f der pro absorbiertes Neutron emittierten Spaltneutronen, [mittlere] Spaltneutronenzahl f pro absorbiertes Neutron, η	Newton['s] formula	s. a. Newton['s] law of conjugate points
		Newton-Gauss formulas	s. Gauss['] formula of interpolation
		Newtonian absolute time, absolute time	absolute Zeit f, Newtonsche absolute Zeit
		Newtonian attraction	Newtonsche Attraktion f, Newtonsche Anziehung f
neutron yield per fission, mean neutron yield per fission, [mean] number of neutrons per fission, neutrons per fission, ν	[mittlere] Spaltneutronenausbeute f pro Spaltung, [mittlere] Anzahl (Zahl) f der pro Spaltung emittierten Spaltneutronen, mittlere Spaltneutronenzahl f, [mittlere] Spaltneutronenzahl pro Spaltung, mittlere Anzahl (Zahl) der Spaltneutronen [bei einer Spaltung], mittlere Anzahl (Zahl) der Spaltneutronen [pro Spaltung], ν	Newtonian attraction force	Newtonsche Anziehungskraft f
		Newtonian cosmology, Newton['s] cosmology	Newtonsche Kosmologie f
		Newtonian dynamics	Newtonsche Dynamik f
		Newtonian field of forces	Newtonsches Kraftfeld n
		Newtonian flow	Newtonsche Strömung f
		Newtonian fluid, Newtonian liquid, ideal viscous liquid, N-body	Newtonsche (ideale zähe) Flüssigkeit f, N-Körper m, idealviskose (rein[ ]viskose) Flüssigkeit
neutropause	Neutropause f		
neutrosphere	Neutrosphäre f		
névé, firn	Firn m, Firnschnee m	Newtonian focus, prime focus	Newton-Fokus m, Primärfokus m
névé basin, firn basin	Firnfeld n, Firnmulde f, Firnbecken n	Newtonian gas	Newtonsches Gas n, Newton-Gas n
névé line	s. snow[]line		
never frozen soil	Niefrostboden m	Newtonian interference colour, normal interference colour	normale Interferenzfarbe f, Newtonsche Interferenzfarbe
new atmosphere, atmosphere, at	technische Atmosphäre f, at		
new candle	s. candela	Newtonian liquid	s. Newtonian fluid
Newcomb['s] constant, precessional constant, Newcomb['s] precession constant	Newcombsche Präzessionskonstante f, Newcombsche Konstante f, Präzessionskonstante	Newtonian mechanics, classical mechanics, Newton['s] mechanics	klassische Mechanik f, Newtonsche Mechanik
		Newtonian motion	Newtonsche Bewegung f
Newcomb['s] period	Newcombsche Periode f	Newtonian principle of relativity	Relativitätsprinzip n der [klassischen] Mechanik, mechanischen (Newtonsches) Relativitätsprinzip
Newcomb['s] precession constant, precessional constant, Newcomb['s] constant	Newcombsche Präzessionskonstante f, Newcombsche Konstante f, Präzessionskonstante		
		Newtonian reflector	s. Newtonian telescope
Newlands['] law of octaves	Newlands' Gesetz n der Oktaven, Gesetz der Oktaven [von Newlands], Oktavengesetz n [von Newlands]	Newtonian relativity	s. Galilean principle of relativity
		Newtonian telescope, Newtonian reflector	Newtonsches Spiegelteleskop (Teleskop) n, Newton-Spiegel m, Spiegelteleskop nach Newton, Newton-Teleskop n
new Moon	Neumond m, Interlunium n		
new star, nova <pl.: novae>, explosive star	Nova f <pl.: Novae>, Neuer Stern m	Newtonian time	Newtonscher Zeitbegriff m, Newtonsche Zeit f
newton, N	Newton n, N	Newtonian viscosity	s. coefficient of viscosity <quantity>
Newton['s] approximation formula	s. Newton-Raphson algorithm		
Newton['s] axioms [of motion], Newton['s] laws [of motion]	Newtonsche Axiome npl [der Mechanik], Newtonsche Gesetze npl	Newton['s] interpolation formulae, Gregory['s] interpolation formulae	Newtonsche Interpolationsformeln fpl, Gregory-Newtonsche Formeln fpl
Newton['s] chromatometer	s. Maxwell['s] disk	Newton['s] interpolation formula with backward differences	s. Gregory['s] backward formula
Newton['s] colour circle	s. Maxwell['s] disk		
Newton['s] colour disk, Newton['s] disk	Newtonsche Farbenscheibe f	Newton['s] interpolation formula with forward differences	s. Gregory['s] forward formula
Newton['s] colour disk	s. a. Maxwell['s] disk		
Newton['s] cooling equation	s. Newton['s] law of cooling	Newton['s] law	s. Newton['s] second law
		Newton['s] law for heat loss	s. Newton['s] law of cooling
Newton['s] corpuscular theory	s. corpuscular theory		
Newton['s] cosmology, Newtonian cosmology	Newtonsche Kosmologie f	Newton['s] law of conjugate points, Newton['s] formula, Newton['s] equation [for conjugate distances]	Newtons[che] Abbildungsgleichung f, Grundgleichung f für die brechende Kugelfläche, Newtonsche Form f [der Grundgleichung für die brechende Kugelfläche], Newtons Form; Newtonsche Gleichungen fpl
Newton['s] diagram	Newtonsches Diagramm n, Puiseux-Diagramm n, Puiseuxsches Diagramm		
Newton['s] disk	s. Maxwell['s] disk		
Newton['s] disk	s. a. Newton['s] colour disk		
Newton['s] double ring; double ring	Doppelring m; Newtonscher Doppelring		
Newton['s] emission theory	s. corpuscular theory		
Newton['s] equation	s. Newton['s] law of conjugate points	Newton['s] law of cooling, Newton['s] law for heat loss, Newton['s] cooling equation	Newtonsches Abkühlungsgesetz n, Newtonsche Abkühlungsgleichung f, Newtonscher Ansatz m für den Wärmeübergang
Newton['s] extrapolation formula	Newtonsche Extrapolationsformel f		
Newton['s] finder, Newton['s] viewfinder, optical direct viewfinder	Linsendurchsichtsucher m, Newton-Sucher m, Galilei-Sucher m	Newton['s] law of fluid resistance	s. Newton['s] law of hydrodynamic resistance

Newton['s] law of friction	Newtonscher Reibungsansatz (Schubspannungsansatz, Ansatz) *m*	**new turbidity factor [of Linke]**	neuer Trübungsfaktor *m* [nach Linke]
Newton['s] law of friction	*s. a.* Newton['s] law of hydrodynamic resistance	**next-nearest neighbour,** second neighbour, neighbour of the second sphere	Nachbar *m* zweiter Sphäre, zweitnächster Nachbar
Newton['s] law of gravitation	*s.* law of gravitation	**Neyman['s] [contagious] distribution**	Neyman-Verteilung *f*, Neymansche Verteilung *f*
Newton['s] law of hydrodynamic resistance, Newton['s] law of [fluid] resistance, Newton['s] law of friction	Newtonsches Gesetz *n* für den hydrodynamischen Widerstand, Newtonsches Widerstandsgesetz *n*	**n-fold axis [of symmetry]**	*s.* symmetry axis of order *n*
		n-fold screw axis, *n*-al screw axis, screw axis of order *n*	*n*-zählige Schraubenachse *f*
Newton['s] law of inertia	*s.* Newton['s] first law	**n-fold symmetry,** *n*-al symmetry, symmetry of order *n*	*n*-zählige Symmetrie *f*, *n*-Zähligkeit *f*, Symmetrie *f* der Ordnung *n*, Zähligkeit *f n*
Newton['s] law of resistance	*s.* Newton['s] law of hydrodynamic resistance		
Newton['s] law of similarity	Newtonsches Ähnlichkeitsgesetz *n*	**Nicad**	*s.* nickel-cadmium cell
Newton['s] law of universal gravitation	*s.* law of gravitation	**Nichols['] locus**	Nichols-Ortskurve *f*
		Nicholson['s] hydrometer	Nicholsonsche Senkwaage *f*
Newton['s] laws [of motion], Newton['s] axioms [of motion]	Newtonsche Axiome *npl* [der Mechanik], Newtonsche Gesetze *npl*	**nick**	*s.* notch
Newton['s] mechanics, classical mechanics, Newtonian mechanics	klassische Mechanik *f*, Newtonsche Mechanik	**nick and bend test,** nick-break test	Kerbbruchversuch *m*
		nickel-cadmium battery (cell), Nicad	Nickel-Kadmium-Akkumulator *m*
newton meter	*s.* joule	**nickel-iron battery,** nickel-iron cell	Nickel-Eisen-Akkumulator *m*
Newton['s] method	*s.* Newton-Raphson method		
Newton No.	*s.* Newton number	**nicol, Nicol polarizing prism,** Nicol['s] prism	Nicol *n* (*m*), Nicolsches Prisma (Doppelprisma) *n*, Polarisationsprisma (Doppelprisma) *n* nach Nicol, Nicol-Prisma *n*, Nikol *n* (*m*)
Newton number, Newton No., *Ne* Newton similarity number	Newton-Zahl *f*, Newtonsche Kennzahl *f*, Newtonsche Ähnlichkeitszahl *f*, *Ne*		
Newton['s] potential	Newtonsches Potential *n*		
Newton['s] prism, quadratic prism	Newton-Prisma *n*	**Nier-type mass spectrometer**	Niersches Massenspektrometer *n*, Massenspektrometer vom Nierschen Typ
Newton-Raphson algorithm (formula, method), second-order (quadratically convergent) Newton-Raphson process, Newton['s] method, Newton['s] approximation formula	Newton-Raphsonsche Methode *f*, Newtonsches Näherungsverfahren (Verfahren) *n*, Newtonsche Näherungsmethode *f*		
		nieve penitente	*s.* penitentes
		nife [core]	Nife *n*, Nifekern *m*
		night airglow, night[] glow, nightglow emission, permanent aurora, night sky luminescence	Nachthimmelsleuchten *n*
Newton['s] ring	Newtonscher Ring *m*, Berührungsring *m*, Newton-Ring *m*, Ring (Streifen *m*) gleicher Dicke		
		night blindness, hemeralopia, noctalopia	Nachtblindheit *f*, Dämmerungsblindheit *f*, Tagessichtigkeit *f*, Hemeralopie *f*, Hemeropie *f*
Newton['s] second law [of motion], second law of motion, Newton['s] law	[zweites] Newtonsches Gesetz *n*, Newtonsches Grundgesetz *n* der Mechanik, Grundgesetz der Mechanik [für die fortschreitende Bewegung], Newtonsches Beschleunigungsgesetz *n*, Newtonsche Bewegungsgleichung (Gleichung) *f*, [Newtons] Lex *f* secunda, Newtonsches Kraftgesetz *n*, dynamische Grundgleichung *f*, Grundgleichung der Dynamik	**night effect; night error,** polarization error, twilight effect <el.>	Dämmerungseffekt *m*, Nachteffekt *m*; Nachteffektfehler *m*, Nachtfehler *m* <El.>
		night field intensity, night strength of field	Nachtfeldstärke *f*
		night glass	Nachtglas *n*, Nachtbeobachtungsglas *n*
		night[]glow, nocturnal glow	Nachtschein *m*
		nightglow [emission]	*s.* night airglow
		night myopia	Nachtmyopie *f*, Nachtkurzsichtigkeit *f*
Newton similarity number	*s.* Newton number	**night presbyopia**	Nachtpresbyopie *f*, Nachtalterssichtigkeit *f*
Newton-Stirling interpolation formula	*s.* Stirling['s] interpolation formula		
Newton['s] theory of light	*s.* corpuscular theory	**night range**	Nachtreichweite *f*
Newton['s] third law [of motion], third law of motion, principle of action and reaction, law of action and reaction, interaction law, law of reaction, law of stress	drittes Newtonsches Gesetz *n*, Wechselwirkungsgesetz *n*, Gegenwirkungsprinzip *n*, Prinzip *n* von Wirkung und Gegenwirkung, Prinzip von Aktion und Reaktion, Newtonsches Aktionsprinzip *n*, Reaktionsprinzip *n*, Wechselwirkungsprinzip *n*, Gesetz der Gleichheit von Aktion und Reaktion, actio *f* = reactio *f*, [Newtons] Lex *f* tertia	**night side;** shadow (shady) side	Nachtseite *f*; Schattenseite *f*
		night sky light	Nachthimmelslicht *n*
		night sky luminescence	*s.* night airglow
		night sky spectrograph	Nachthimmelsspektrograph *m*
		night sky spectrum	Nachthimmelsspektrum *n*
		night strength of field, night field intensity	Nachtfeldstärke *f*
		night-time [meteor] shower	Nachtstrom *m* <Meteore>
Newton['s] three-eights rule	*s.* three-eights rule		
Newton['s] viewfinder, Newton['s] finder, optical direct viewfinder	Linsendurchsichtsucher *m*, Newton-Sucher *m*, Galilei-Sucher *m*	**night twilight**	Nachtdämmerung *f*
		night twilight arch	Nachtdämmerungsbogen *m*, äußerster Dämmerungsbogen *m*

night visibility [distance], night visual range, visibility at night	Nachtsichtweite f, Nachtsicht f	nodal distance	Knotenabstand m
Nikuradse diagram	Nikuradsesches Schaubild n, Nikuradse-Diagramm n	nodal distance ⟨opt.⟩	Nodaldistanz f, Abstand m der Hauptpunkte ⟨Opt.⟩
nil-load	s. idling	nodal line, line of nodes ⟨astr., mech.⟩	Knotenlinie f ⟨Astr., Mech.⟩; Knotenachse f ⟨Mech.⟩
nilpotent element	nilpotentes Element n		
nilpotent matrix	nilpotente Matrix f	nodal plane	Knotenebene f
Nilsson model	Nilsson-Model n	nodal point, node ⟨of oscillation, standing wave⟩	Schwingungsknoten m; Wellenknoten m, Knoten m [der stehenden Welle]
Nilsson potential	Nilsson-Potential n, Nilssonsches Potential n	nodal point, node, branch[ing] point, break point, vertex ⟨el.⟩	Knoten m, Knotenpunkt m, Leitungsknoten[punkt] m, Verzweigungspunkt m ⟨El.⟩
nimbostratus, Ns	Nimbostratus m, Regenschichtwolke f, Ns		
nimbus, rain cloud	Nimbus m, Regenwolke f		
nimbus fractus, fracto[-]nimbus	Fractonimbus m, Nimbus m fractus, zerrissene Schlechtwetterwolke f	nodal point ⟨opt.⟩	Knotenpunkt m ⟨Opt.⟩
		nodal potential	Knotenpunktpotential n, Knotenpotential n
niphablepsia, niphotyphlosis	Niphablepsie f, Schneeblindheit f, Gletscherkatarrh m, ophthalmia f photoelectrica, photophthalmia f electrica	nodal shift	Knotenverschiebung f
		nodal-shifting method	Knotenverschiebungsmethode f
		nodal singularity, node ⟨for differential equations⟩	Knotenpunkt m ⟨Differentialgleichungen⟩
Nipkow disk, spiral disk, exploring disk, aperturered disk	Nipkow-Scheibe f, Abtastscheibe f, Spirallochscheibe f		
		nodal sphere	Knotenkugel f
		nodal surface	Knotenfläche f
Nissen bifilar electrometer	Zweifadenelektrometer n nach Nissen, Nissensches Zweifadenelektrometer	nodal value, node ⟨geo.⟩	Sattelpunkt m ⟨Geo.⟩
		nodal voltage method, method of nodal voltages	Knotenspannungsmethode f, Methode f der Knotenspannungen
nit, nepit, Naperian digit ⟨= 1.44 bits⟩	Nepit n, nepit, mt ⟨= 1,44 bit⟩		
nit	s. a. candela per square meter ⟨opt.⟩	nodding, nutation ⟨astr.; mech.⟩	Nutation f, reguläre (regelmäßige) Präzession f ⟨Astr.; Mech.⟩; Nutationsbewegung f
nitometer	Nitometer n		
niton, NT	s. radon ⟨element⟩	node, crunode ⟨of the curve⟩	Knotenpunkt m ⟨Kurve⟩
nitrating, nitration	Nitrieren n		
nitridation, nitriding, nitrogen case hardening ⟨of steel⟩	Nitrierhärtung f, Nitrieren n, Aufsticken n ⟨Stahl⟩	node, nodal singularity ⟨for differential equations⟩	Knotenpunkt m ⟨Differentialgleichungen⟩
		node ⟨of frame⟩	s. joint ⟨of system of bars⟩
nitrification	Nitrifikation f	node, nodal point, vibration (wave) node ⟨of oscillation, standing wave⟩	Schwingungsknoten m; Wellenknoten m, Knoten m [der stehenden Welle]
nitrogen-carbon cycle	s. carbon-nitrogen cycle		
nitrogen case hardening	s. nitridation ⟨of steel⟩		
nitrogen catastrophe	Stickstoffkatastrophe f		
nitrogenous metabolism	Stickstoffstoffwechsel m, N-Stoffwechsel m	node ⟨astr.⟩	Knoten m ⟨Astr.⟩
		node, nodal point, branch[ing] point, break point, vertex, network node ⟨el.⟩	Knoten m, Knotenpunkt m, Leitungsknoten[punkt] m, Verzweigungspunkt m ⟨El.⟩
nitrogen star	Stickstoffstern m		
nival climate, snow climate	nivales Klima n; vollnivales Klima		
nivation	Nivation f, Schnee-Erosion f, Firnerosion f	node, nodal value ⟨geo.⟩	Sattelpunkt m ⟨Geo.⟩
		node beam	Knotenstrahl m
		node of longitudinal wave	Druckknoten m
n-leg	n-Bein n		
N.L.S. wave	s. non-linear polarization source wave	node of potential, potential node	Spannungsknoten m
NMR	s. nuclear magnetic resonance	node of Ranvier, Ranvier node	Ranvierscher Schnürring (Schnürknoten) m
n-n junction, n-n+ junction	nn-Übergang m, nn+-Übergang m	node of the acoustic wave	Schallknoten m
n-n scattering	s. neutron-neutron scattering	node of the Moon's orbit	Drachenpunkt m, Knoten m der Mondbahn
nobelium, ₁₀₂No, jolium, joliot-curium, Jo	Nobelium n, ₁₀₂No, Jolium n, Jo	nodical month, draconitic month, draconitic period	drakonitischer Monat m, drakonitischer Umlauf m
Nobili['s] interference ring, Nobili['s] ring	Nobilischer Farbenring m	nodical year	drakonitisches Jahr n
		no-echo condition	s. polar blackout
		Noether['s] theorem	[E.] Noetherscher Satz m, Noethersches Theorem n, Noether-Theorem n
noble gas	s. rare gas		
noble metal	Edelmetall n		
no-bond resonance	s. hyperconjugation	no-failure probability	Zuverlässigkeitsfunktion f
noctalopia, night blindness, hemeralopia	Nachtblindheit f, Dämmerungsblindheit f, Tagessichtigkeit f, Hemeralopie f, Hemeropie f		
		no-field track	Nebelspur f in der feldfreien Nebelkammer
noctilucent cloud, luminous night cloud, mesospheric cloud	leuchtende Nachtwolke f, mesosphärische Wolke f		
		no forces / under, under the action of no forces, force-free, free from forces	kräftefrei, kraftfrei
noctilucent train ⟨of meteor⟩	Nachtschweif m ⟨Meteor⟩		
noctovision, scotopic vision	Nachtsehen n, Dämmerungssehen n, Dunkelsehen n, Stäbchensehen n, skotopisches Sehen n	noise ⟨ac.⟩	Geräusch n; Lärm m
		noise, random noise, fluctuation noise, statistical noise ⟨of thermionic valve⟩	Rauschen n, statistisches Rauschen ⟨Elektronenröhre⟩
nocturnal arc	Nachtbogen m		
nocturnal glow, night[]glow	Nachtschein m	noise abatement	Lärmbekämpfung f
nodal cone	Knotenkegel m	noise admittance	Rauschleitwert m
nodal cylinder	Knotenzylinder m	noise amplitude	Rauschamplitude f

noise

noise audiogram	Geräuschaudiogramm n
noise background ⟨el.⟩	Störuntergrund m; Störnebel m ⟨El.⟩
noise barometer	Lärmbarometer n
noise cancelling	s. noise suppression
noise characteristic	Rauschcharakteristik f, Rauschkennlinie f, Rausch[ausschlag]kurve f, Rauschamplitudenkurve f
noise current	Rauschstrom m
noise current component	Rauschstromanteil m, Rauschstromkomponente f
noise diode	Rauschdiode f
noise effect	s. shot effect
noise energy	Rauschenergie f
noise equivalent admittance	s. equivalent noise admittance
noise equivalent circuit	Rauschersatzschaltbild n, Rauschersatzschaltung f, Rauschersatzschema n
noise equivalent power, NEP	äquivalente Rauschleistung f
noise equivalent resistance	s. equivalent noise resistance
noise equivalent source	äquivalente Rauschquelle f
noise factor, inherent noise figure, noise figure, figure of noise, signal-to-noise merit	Rauschzahl f, Rauschfaktor m; Rauschgüte f; Geräuschverhältnis n, Geräuschfaktor m
noise factor meter	Rauschzahlmesser m, Rauschfaktormesser m
noise figure	s. noise factor
noise filter	Geräuschfilter n, Bewertungsfilter n, Rauschfilter n
noise filter	Störschutzfilter n, Störfilter n
noise-free	s. noiseless
noise function	Rauschfunktion f
noise generator	Rauschgenerator m, Rauscherzeuger m; Geräuscherzeuger m, Geräuschgenerator m
noise immunity, antijamming ability, noise stability	Störstabilität f, Störfestigkeit f, Störsicherheit f; Störspannungsfestigkeit f
noise keying	s. noise suppression
noiseless, noise-free; low-noise	rauscharm; rauschfrei, rauschlos
noise level, background level	Rauschpegel m, Rauschhöhe f; Störpegel m, Geräuschpegel m, Störspiegel m, Störniveau n
noise level ⟨ac.⟩	Geräuschpegel m ⟨Ak.⟩
noise level	s. a. noise voltage ⟨el.⟩
noise level meter	s. noise meter ⟨ac.⟩
noise limiter; interference limiter	Rauschbegrenzer m; Geräuschbegrenzer m, Störbegrenzer m, Störbegrenzerkreis m
noise matching	Rauschanpassung f
noise measuring meter, noise meter, psophometer ⟨el.⟩	Geräuschspannungsmesser m, Psophometer n, Geräuschmesser m ⟨El.⟩
noise meter, noise level meter ⟨ac.⟩	Geräuschmesser m ⟨Ak.⟩
noise modulation, jamming modulation	Störmodulation f; Rauschmodulation f
noise output	s. noise power ⟨el.⟩
noise pattern	Rauschbild n
noise performance	s. noise power ⟨el.⟩
noise potential	s. noise voltage ⟨el.⟩
noise power, noise performance; output noise power, noise [power] output ⟨el.⟩	Rauschleistung f [am Ausgang], Geräuschleistung f ⟨El.⟩
noise power ⟨of reactor⟩	Rauschleistung f, Leistung f zwischen den Impulsen ⟨Reaktor⟩
noise power output	s. noise power ⟨el.⟩
noise power ratio, noise ratio, NR	Rauschleistungsverhältnis n
noise power spectrum	Rauschleistungsspektrum n
noise pulse	Rauschimpuls m
noise region	Rauschgebiet n
noise resistance	Rauschwiderstand m
noise source ⟨el.; nucl.⟩	Rauschquelle f ⟨El.; Kern.⟩; Geräuschquelle f ⟨El.⟩
noise source ⟨el.⟩	Störquelle f, Störer m ⟨El.⟩
noise spectrum	Rauschspektrum n; Störspektrum n ⟨El.⟩
noise stability, antijamming ability, noise immunity	Störstabilität f, Störfestigkeit f, Störsicherheit f; Störspannungsfestigkeit f
noise storm	Radiosturm m, Geräuschsturm m, Rauschsturm m
noise suppression; parasitic suppression; noise keying; noise cancelling, silencing	Rauschunterdrückung f, Geräuschunterdrückung f, Krachtötung f, Krachunterdrückung f; Störungsunterdrückung f; Störaustastung f
noise suppressor capacitor	Störschutzkondensator m
noise temperature	Rauschtemperatur f
noise thermometer	Rauschthermometer n, Geräuschthermometer n
noise threshold	Rauschschwelle f
noise tube	Rauschröhre f
noise twoport, noisy four-terminal network	Rausch[quellen]vierpol m, rauschender Vierpol m
noise voltage, noise potential, psophometric voltage, noise level ⟨el.⟩	Rauschspannung f, Geräuschspannung f, Geräuschpegel m ⟨El.⟩
noise voltage, parasitic (interference) voltage	Störspannung f
noise-voltage source	Rauschspannungsquelle f
noisy four-terminal network, noise twoport	Rausch[quellen]vierpol m, rauschender Vierpol m
no-lift angle, zero lift angle	Nullauftriebswinkel m, Nullanstellwinkel m
no-lift line, zero lift line, axis of zero lift	Nullauftriebslinie f, Nullinie f des Profils, erste Achse f des Profils, Nullauftriebsachse f
no-load, unloaded ⟨el.⟩	unbelastet ⟨El.⟩
no-load	s. a. idling
no-load admittance, open-circuit admittance	Leerlaufleitwert m, Leerlaufadmittanz f, Leeradmittanz f
no-load capacitance, open-circuit capacitance	Leerkapazität f, Leerlaufkapazität f
no-load characteristic, open-circuit characteristic	Leerlaufcharakteristik f, Leerlaufkennlinie f
no-load condition	s. open circuit / being on ⟨el.⟩
no-load current, open-circuit current; idle current	Leerlaufstrom m; Leerstrom m
no-load gain	s. open-circuit gain
no-load impedance	s. open-circuit impedance
no-load inductance, open-circuit inductance	Leerlaufinduktivität f, Leerinduktivität f
no-load input impedance	s. open-circuit input impedance
no-load input power, no-load power	Leerlaufleistung f
no-load loss	Leerlaufverlust m; Leerverlust m
no-load operation	s. idling
no-load output	s. open-circuit output admittance
no-load output impedance	s. open-circuit output impedance
no-load power, no-load input power	Leerlaufleistung f
no-load resistance	s. open-circuit resistance
no-load voltage	s. open-circuit voltage

no-loss line, dissipationless (zero-loss) line, loss-free (lossless) line	verlustlose Leitung f, verlustfreie Leitung	**noncircuital field**	s. irrotational field
nominal A-bomb	s. nominal atomic bomb	**non-closed**, open	offen, nichtgeschlossen; nichtabgeschlossen
nominal atomic bomb, nominal A-bomb <$\triangle$ 20,000 t trinitrotoluene>	nominelle Atombombe f <$\triangle$ 20 000 t Trinitrotoluol>	**non-cluster galaxis, non-cluster nebula**	Feldnebel m
		non-cluster star, field star, background star, non-member of a cluster	Feldstern m
nominal circuit voltage, rated temperature-rise voltage, temperature rise voltage <of an instrument>	maximal zulässige Betriebsspannung f <Meßgerät>	**non-coherence**, incoherence	Inkohärenz f, Nichtkohärenz f
		non-coherent unit, incoherent unit	nichtkohärente (inkohärente, systemfreie, systemfremde) Einheit f
nominal position, desired (required) position	Sollstellung f	**non-combining terms**	nichtkombinierende Terme mpl
nominal power, rated power [output], rated output (burden), rating	Nennleistung f, Nominalleistung f	**non[-]combustible**, incombustible	nichtbrennbar, unbrennbar; unverbrennbar
nominal range of use	Nennbereich m	**non-commutability**, non-commutativity	Nichtvertauschbarkeit f, Nichtkommutativität f
		non-commutative group, non[-]abelian group	nichtkommutative (nichtabelsche) Gruppe f
nominal transformation ratio	Nennübersetzung f	**non-commutativity**, non-commutability	Nichtvertauschbarkeit f, Nichtkommutativität f
		non-compact group	nichtkompakte Gruppe f
		non-competitive inhibition	nichtkompetitive Hemmung f
		non-compound-elastic scattering	s. elastic scattering without formation of compound nucleus
nominal value, rating, rated value	Nennwert m, Nominalwert m	**non concentrated**, distributed	verteilt, stetig verteilt
		non[-]conducting, non-conductive; dielectric; insulating <el.>	dielektrisch; nichtleitend; isolierend <El.>
nominal value of the resistor	Nennwert m des Widerstandes, Nennwiderstand m	**non-conductor**	s. dielectric
		non-conservation of parity, violation of parity, parity non-conservation (violation)	Nichterhaltung f der Parität, Paritätsverletzung f
nomogram, nomograph, nomographic chart, abac	Nomogramm n, Rechentafel f, graphische Rechentafel, Abakus m		
nomogram with moving transparents, slide-rule nomogram	Flächenschieber m, Schiebeblattnomogramm n, Gleitflächentafel f, Nomogramm n mit beweglichen Transparenten	**non-conservative force**	nichtkonservative Kraft f
		non-conservative motion	s. climbing motion <of dislocations>
		non-constancy, inconstancy <math.>	Inkonstanz f, Nichtkonstanz f <Math.>
nomogram with radial lines, net chart, isopleth	Netztafel f, Isoplethentafel f, Isoplethenkarte f	**non-constancy**, instability, inconstancy <meas.>	Inkonstanz f, Instabilität f <Meß.>
nomograph[ic chart]	s. nomogram	**non[-]cónsumable electrode**	unverzehrbare Elektrode f
nomographic scale of a function	Funktionsskala f, Funktionsleiter f	**non-contact piston**	s. shorting plunger <el.>
non[-]abelian group, non-commutative group	nichtkommutative (nichtabelsche) Gruppe f	**non-contact[ing] thickness gauging**	berührungslose Dickenmessung f
non 1/v absorber	Nicht-1/v-Absorber m	**non-continuable** <math.>	nicht fortsetzbar <Math.>
		non-continuous	nichtstetig; nichtkontinuierlich
non-accelerated	s. accelerationless	**non[-]continuum flow**	s. Knudsen flow
non-accelerated frame of reference	unbeschleunigtes Bezugssystem n	**non-contrasty picture**, soft (uncontrasty) picture	weiches Bild n, kontrastloses (flaues) Bild
non-active	s. inactive	**non-correlated**	nichtkorreliert, korrelationsfrei
non-active carrier	s. stable carrier		
non-adiabatic, diabatic	nichtadiabatisch	**non-corrodible, non-corroding, non-corrosive**	nichtkorrodierend, nichtangreifbar, unangreifbar
nonarithmetic shift	s. cyclic shift		
non-artesian water	s. phreatic water	**non-corrosive**	nichtkorrodierend, nichtkorrosiv, nichtangreifend
non-associated liquid	s. normal liquid		
non-autonomous inverter	fremdgeführter (netzerregter) Wechselrichter m		
non-axial collision	nichtachsennaher Stoß m	**non-corrosive steel**	s. stainless steel
non-1/v behaviour	Nicht-/1v-Verhalten n, Abweichung f vom 1/v-Gesetz	**non-critical amount, non-critical mass**	nichtkritische Menge f, nichtkritische Masse f
non-black body, non-black radiator	nichtschwarzer Körper (Strahler) m	**non-crossing rule**	Neumann-Wignersche Regel f [für die Potentialenergie zweiatomiger Moleküle], Nichtüberkreuzungsregel f, Überkreuzungsverbot n, Überschneidungsverbot n
non-bonding electron	nichtbindendes (spinabgesättigtes) Elektron n		
non-bonding orbital	s. antibonding orbital		
non-branching chain	s. linear chain		
non-branching model	s. Landau model		
non[-]browning glass, stabilized glass	stabilisiertes Glas n	**non-crystalline liquid**	nichtkristalline Flüssigkeit f
non-causality	Akausalität f	**non-cyclic co-ordinate**, palpable co-ordinate	nichtzyklische Koordinate f
		non-Daltonian compound, non-daltonide	s. berthollide
non-central force, tensor force	Tensorkraft f, Nichtzentralkraft f, nichtzentrale Kraft f	**non-decomposable matrix**, indecomposable matrix	unzerlegbare Matrix f
non-central moment, crude moment	nichtzentrales Moment n	**non-decremental conduction**	Leitung f ohne Dekrement
non-central potential	nichtzentrales Potential n	**non-deformable**	unverformbar, nicht deformierbar
non-central t-distribution	nichtzentrale t-Verteilung f	**non-deformation of pulse shape**	Impulsformtreue f
non-centric, acentric	azentrisch, nichtzentrisch; nichtzentriert	**non[-]degeneracy**	Nichtentartung f

non-degenerate	nichtentartet; nichtausgeartet <Math.>	non-equilibrium	Nichtgleichgewichts-, nicht im Gleichgewicht [befindlich]
non-degenerate semiconductor	gewöhnlicher (nichtentarteter) Halbleiter m	non-equilibrium carrier density, non-equilibrium concentration (density)	Nichtgleichgewichtsdichte f, Nichtgleichgewichtskonzentration f
non-degenerate state	nichtentarteter Zustand m		
nondense, nowhere dense <math.>	nirgendsdicht	non-equilibrium effect, non-equilibrium phenomenon	Nichtgleichgewichtserscheinung f
non-dense cloud	lockere Wolke f	non-equilibrium ionization	Nichtgleichgewichtsionisierung f
non-destructive magnetic test[ing], magnetic testing, magnetic inspection, magnetographic inspection	magnetisches Prüfverfahren n [der zerstörungsfreien Werkstoffprüfung], magnetische Prüfung f, [zerstörungsfreie] magnetische Werkstoffprüfung f, Magnetdefektoskopie f	non-equilibrium plasma	Nichtgleichgewichtsplasma n, nicht im thermodynamischen Gleichgewicht befindliches Plasma n
		non-equilibrium process, non-static process	Nichtgleichgewichtsprozeß m, nichtstatischer Prozeß m
non-destructive materials testing, non-destructive testing [of materials]; NDT	zerstörungsfreie Werkstoffprüfung f, zerstörungsfreie Prüfung f, zerstörungsfreie Materialprüfung f, zerstörungsfreies Prüfverfahren n, Defektoskopie f	non-equilibrium state	Nichtgleichgewichtszustand m
		non-equilibrium surface tension, dynamic[al] surface tension	dynamische Oberflächenspannung f
		non-equilibrium thermodynamics, irreversible thermodynamics	Thermodynamik f irreversibler Prozesse, irreversible Thermodynamik
non-developed shower	nichtentwickelter Schauer m	non-erasable storage	nichtlöschbare Speicherung f
non-diagonal element, off-diagonal element	Nichtdiagonalelement n		
non-diagram line, satellite [X-ray] line, satellite [in X-ray spectrum]	Nichtdiagrammlinie f, Satellitenlinie f, Satellit m, Röntgensatellit m	nonet	Nonett n
		non-euclidean, non-Euclidean, non-euclidian, non-Euclidian	nichteuklidisch, nicht-Euklidisch
non-diathermic	s. athermanous	non-euclidean distance	nichteuklidischer Abstand m
non-diffusible; non-diffusing; indiffusible	nichtdiffusibel, indiffusibel; nichtdiffundierend	non-euclidean motion	nichteuklidische Bewegung f, Bewegung im nichteuklidischen Raum
non-dilatational strain, pure non-dilatational strain, change of shape	[reine] Gestalt[s]änderung f, Deformation f ohne Volumenänderung	non-Euclidean translation	nichteuklidische Schiebung f
non[-]dimensional, dimensionless	dimensionslos, dimensionsfrei	non-euclidian, non-Euclidian	s. non-euclidean
nondimensional group (quantity)	s. similarity parameter	non-evanescent wave	nichtabklingende Welle f
non-dipole field	Nichtdipolfeld n	non evaporating	s. non-volatile
non-directed	s. non-directional	non-faradaic current	s. residual current
non-directed bond	ungerichtete Bindung f	non-favoured beta transition, non-favoured transition, normal allowed transition	nichtbegünstigter Übergang m, normalerlaubter [Beta-]Übergang m, normaler Übergang
non-directed graph	ungerichteter Graph m		
non-directed radiation, undirected radiation, omnidirectional radiation	ungerichtete Strahlung f		
		non[-]ferrous metal	Nichteisenmetall n, NE-Metall n; Buntmetall n
non-directional, non-directive, independent of direction, non-directed	richtungsunabhängig, ungerichtet		
		non-fission capture	s. non[-]productive capture
non-directional counter [tube], Milligoat counter	richtungsunabhängiges Zählrohr n, Milligoat-Zählrohr n, Milligoatsches Zählrohr	non-flammable, non-inflammable, ininflammable, flameproof	nichtentflammbar, unentzündlich, unentflammbar
		non-flip scattered wave	Streuwelle f mit ungeänderter Spinrichtung
non-directional microphone, omnidirectional (astatic) microphone	Kugelmikrophon n, Mikrophon n mit Kugelcharakteristik, ungerichtetes Mikrophon		
		non-free body	unfreier Körper m
non-directive	s. non-directional	non-free point	s. constrained material point
non-directive antenna	s. omnidirectional antenna	non-gaseous	s. non-volatile
non-dispersive spectrometry	nichtdispersive Spektrometrie f	non-genuine vibration	unechte (uneigentliche) Schwingung f
non-echo chamber	s. anechoic chamber <ac.>	non-heat-conducting	nichtwärmeleitend
non-elastic, inelastic <mech.>	unelastisch, inelastisch, nichtelastisch <Mech.>	non-heat-isolated	nichtwärmeisoliert
non-elastic buckling, plastic buckling, inelastic buckling	plastische Knickung f, unelastische Knickung	non-holonomic constraint, anholonomic constraint	nichtholonome Zwangsbedingung (Bedingung) f, anholonome Bedingung, nichtholonome Bindung (Bedingungsgleichung) f
non-elastic collision	s. inelastic collision		
non-elastic impact	s. perfectly inelastic impact <mech.>	non-holonomic coordinate, quasi coordinate, pseudo co-ordinate	nichtholonome Koordinate f, Pseudokoordinate f, Quasikoordinate f
non-elasticity	s. inelasticity		
non-elastic range	s. plastic range		
non[-]elastic scattering	nonelastische Streuung f		
non-electrolysable, anelectric	nichtelektrolysierbar, anelektrisch	non-holonomic co-ordinate of velocity, non-holonomic velocity co-ordinate	nichtholonome Geschwindigkeitskoordinate f, nichtholonomer Geschwindigkeitsparameter m, Pseudoparameter m der Geschwindigkeit
non-electrolyte, anelectrolyte	Nichtelektrolyt m, Anelektrolyt m		
non-electrolyte complex	Nichtelektrolytkomplex m		
non-electromagnetic mass	nichtelektromagnetische Masse f	non-Hookian, non-linearly elastic	nichtlinear elastisch
non-empty; non-vacuum; non-void <math.>	nichtleer	non-ideal crystal	s. imperfect crystal
non-enumerable, uncountable	nichtabzählbar, überabzählbar, unabzählbar	non-ideality	s. imperfection
non-equilibrium, disequilibrium	Nichtgleichgewicht n; gestörtes Gleichgewicht n, Ungleichgewicht n	non-ideal superconductor, hard superconductor	harter Supraleiter m, nichtidealer Supraleiter

nonignitable s. non-inflammable
non-inductive induktivitätsarm; induktionsfrei
non-inductive resistance; non-inductive resistor induktionsfreier (eigeninduktivitätsfreier) Widerstand m
non-inertia, inertialessness, absence of inertia Trägheitslosigkeit f
non-inertial system Nichtinertialsystem n
non-inflammable, ininflammable, nonflammable, flameproof, nonignitable nichtentflammbar, unentzündlich, unentflammbar
non-interacted, non-interconnected unvermascht
non-interacting nichtwechselwirkend, nicht in Wechselwirkung tretend (stehend), ohne Wechselwirkung, wechselwirkungsfrei
non-interchangeable; non-reversible <el.> unverwechselbar
non-interconnected s. non-interacted
non-ionic, non-ionic detergent (tenside) nichtionogenes Tensid n, nichtionogener Stoff m, Nichtionogen n
non-ionic bond nichtionische Bindung f, Nichtionenbindung f
non-ionic detergent (tenside), non-ionic nichtionogenes Tensid n, nichtionogener Stoff m, Nichtionogen n
non-isentropic flow, anisentropic flow nichtisentrope Strömung f
non-isothermal plasma nichtisothermes Plasma n
non-isotopic; heterotopic nichtisotop[isch]; heterotop
non-isotopic carrier nichtisotoper Träger m, mechanischer Träger
non-isotopic labelling nichtisotope Markierung f
nonius, vernier Nonius m
non-leakage probability Verbleibwahrscheinlichkeit f
non-leptonic decay, hadronic decay nichtleptonischer Zerfall m, hadronischer Zerfall
non-linear acoustics, macrosonics nichtlineare Akustik f
non-linear detector, distortion detector nichtlinearer Detektor m, Verzerrungsdetektor m
non[-]linear distortion nichtlineare Verzerrung f, Klirrverzerrung f, Klirren n
nonlinear distortion coefficient s. coefficient of harmonic distortion <of n-th order>
nonlinear distortion factor s. distortion factor
non-linear elastic theory s. non-linear theory of elasticity
non-linear electrodynamics [of Born-Infeld] nichtlineare Elektrodynamik f [von Born und Infeld], Born-Infeldsche nichtlineare Elektrodynamik
non-linearly elastic, non-Hookian nichtlinear elastisch
non-linearly viscous fluid nichtlineare viskose Flüssigkeit f
non-linear mechanics, theory of non-linear vibrations Theorie f der nichtlinearen Schwingungen, nichtlineare Mechanik f
non-linear Newtonian liquid s. non-Newtonian liquid
non-linear oscillation s. non-linear vibration
non-linear oscillator, anharmonic oscillator anharmonischer (nichtharmonischer, nichtlinearer) Oszillator m
non-linear polarization source wave, N.L.S. wave NLS-Welle f, Welle f der nichtlinearen Polarisationsquellen
non-linear-resistance arrester Ventilableiter m
non-linear semiconducting dipole s. varistor
non-linear theory of elasticity, non-linear elastic theory, finite elasticity theory nichtlineare Elastizitätstheorie f

non-linear vibration, non-linear oscillation, pseudoharmonic oscillation, pseudoharmonic vibration nichtlineare Schwingung f, pseudoharmonische Schwingung
non-Liouville damping Nicht-Liouville-Dämpfung f, nicht-Liouvillesche Dämpfung f
non-local; global; in the large <math.> nichtlokal; global; im Großen <Math.>
non[-]localizable theory nichtlokalisierbare Theorie f
non-localized bond nichtlokalisierte Bindung f
non-localized fringes, non-localized interferences nichtlokalisierte Interferenzen fpl
non-localized molecular orbital, non-localized orbital nichtlokalisiertes Orbital n, nichtlokalisierte Molekülbahn f
non-localized vector s. sliding vector
non-local quantum field theory nichtlokale Quantenfeldtheorie f
non-luminous flame s. blue flame
non-magnetic scattering nichtmagnetische Streuung f
non-magnetic steel unmagnetisierbarer (unmagnetischer) Stahl m
non-1/v material Nicht-1/v-Material n <Stoff mit einem Einfangquerschnitt, der dem 1/v-Gesetz nicht genügt>
non-member of a cluster, field star, background star, non-cluster star Feldstern m
non-mes[on]ic decay nichtmesonischer Zerfall m
non-metal, metalloid, antimetal Nichtmetall n, Metalloid n
non-miscibility, immiscibility Nichtmischbarkeit f, Unmischbarkeit f, Unvermischbarkeit f
non-mobility, fixity Unbeweglichkeit f
non-moderator Nichtmoderator m, Material n mit kleinem Bremsquerschnitt
non-monoenergetic s. heterogeneous <of radiation>
non-moving, at rest, motionless, fixed in Ruhe, ruhend, fest, bewegungslos, unbewegt
non-moving observer, observer at rest ruhender Beobachter m
non-Newtonian, structural-viscou strukturviskos, nicht-Newtonsch, anomal fließend
non-Newtonian liquid, non-linear (generalized) Nwtonian liquid nicht-Newtonsche (anomal fließende, strukturviskose) Flüssigkeit f, nicht-Newtonscher Stoff m
non-occupied, unoccupied; unfilled; unpopulated; empty; vacant unbesetzt, nichtbesetzt; leer; vakant; frei
non-ohmic nichtohmsch
non-orientable surface, one-sided (unilateral) surface einseitige Fläche f, nichtorientierbare Fläche
non-orientation, absence of orientation Unorientiertheit f, Fehlen n einer Orientierung
non-oriented graph, ordinary graph nichtorientierter Graph m
non-orthogonality integral Nichtorthogonalitätsintegral n
non-oscillating s. aperiodic
non-overflow dam s. dam on bed of river
non-overlapping, disjoint <math.> disjunkt, elementefremd, fremd, durchschnittsfremd <Math.>
non-overloading amplifier nichtübersteuernder Verstärker m
non-paralyzable counter nichtblockierendes Zählrohr n
non-parametric test, distribution[-]free test, parameter-free test; order test verteilungsfreier (nichtparametrischer, parameterfreier) Test m; Anordnungstest m
non-penetrating s. low-energy <of radiation>
non-penetrating electron orbit, non-penetrating orbit Nichttauchbahn f, nichttauchende Elektronenbahn f
non-periodic s. aperiodic

non-perspective projection, modified projection	unechte (nichtperspektivische) Projektion f	**non-salient pole rotor**	Vollpolläufer m
non-photographic photogrammetry	nichtphotographische Photogrammetrie f	**non-saturated**, unsaturated	ungesättigt <auch Chem.>; nichtgesättigt; nichtabgesättigt; nicht voll ausgebildet
non-planar molecule	nichtebenes Molekül n		
non-planar network	nichtebenes Netzwerk n	**non-saturating**	nichtabsättigbar
non-polar, apolar	nichtpolar, apolar	**non-screen film**	folienloser Film m
nonpolarizable electrode, unpolarizable (unpolarized) electrode	unpolarisierbare Elektrode f	**non-seismic region**	s. aseismic region
		non-selective absorber	s. neutral filter
non-polar liquid	s. normal liquid	**non-selective diffuser**, neutral diffuser	neutral (grau, nichtselektiv, aselektiv) streuender Körper m, Neutralstreuer m
non-porous	porenfrei, porendicht, nichtporös		
non-potential force	Nichtpotentialkraft f	**non-selective filter**	s. neutral filter
		non-selective glass	s. neutral glass
non-primitive cell	nichtprimitive Gitterzelle f	**non-selective radiator**, grey body, gray body <US>	Graustrahler m, grauer Strahler (Körper) m, nichtselektiver Strahler
non[-]productive capture, non-fission capture	unproduktiver Einfang, nichtproduktiver Einfang, Verlusteinfang m		
		non-self-luminous object, non-self-luminous surface	Nichtselbstleuchter m, nichtselbstleuchtendes Objekt n, nichtselbstleuchtende Fläche f
non-productive evaporation	unproduktive Verdunstung		
non-radiative capture, radiationless capture	strahlungsloser (nichtstrahlender) Einfang m	**non-self-maintained conduction, non-self-maintained conductivity**, non-self-maintained electronic conduction (conductivity)	unselbständige Elektronenleitung f, unselbständige Leitung f, unselbständige Elektrizitätsleitung f, unselbständige Stromleitung f
non-radiative centre	strahlungsloses Zentrum n		
non-radiative recombination, radiationless recombination	Dreierstoßrekombination f, Rekombination f im Dreierstoß, strahlungslose (nichtstrahlende) Rekombination		
		non-self-maintained discharge; semi-self-sustained discharge	unselbständige Gasentladung (Entladung) f
non-radiative transition, radiationless (Auger) transition	strahlungsloser Übergang m, Auger-Übergang m	**non-self-maintained electronic conduction (conductivity)**	s. non-self-maintained conduction
non-radioactive	s. inactive	**non-self-quenching counter**	nichtselbstlöschendes Zählrohr n
non-reactive circuit	reaktionslose Schaltung f		
non-reactive resistance	winkelfreier Widerstand m, phasenfreier Widerstand	**nonsense correlation**	s. illusory correlation
		non-separable <chem.>	nichttrennbar, untrennbar <Chem.>
non-real <math.>	nichtreell <Math.>	**non-shower meteor**, sporadic, sporadic meteor	sporadisches Meteor n
non-recommended	nicht empfohlen		
non-rectifying contact	s. ohmic contact	**non-singular matrix**, invertible matrix, regular matrix	reguläre (invertierbare, umkehrbare, nichtsinguläre, nichtausgeartete) Matrix f
non-rectifying electrode	sperr[schicht]freie Elektrode f		
non-rectifying junction	sperr[schicht]freier Übergang m	**non-slipping**	schlupflos, schlupffrei; gleitfrei
non-reflecting	s. reflectionless	**non-smooth**	nichtglatt
non-reflecting termination, matched termination	reflexionsfreier Abschluß m	**non-solidified**, unsolidified	unverfestigt
		non-solvent, nonsolvent	Nichtlösungsmittel n
non-reflection	Reflexionsfreiheit f	**non-solving space**	nichtlösender Raum m
non-reflection attenuation	Anpassungsdämpfung f	**non-specific labelling**	s. physical labelling
non-refractory	s. low-melting	**non-specific tracer**	s. physical tracer
non-refractory arc, cold-cathode arc, field-emission arc, field arc	Feldbogen m, Feldlichtbogen m	**non-spherical**, aspherical	nichtsphärisch, nichtkugelförmig, nichtkuglig, asphärisch
		non-split anode	s. heavy anode
non-refractory cathode	leicht verdampfbare Katode f	**non-standard ionospheric propagation**, long-range ionospheric propagation	ionosphärische Überreichweite f
non-refractory electrode transition, cold cathode glow to arc transition	Übergang m Glimmstrom — Lichtbogen bei leicht verdampfbaren Elektroden		
		non-standard propagation, anomalous propagation, long-range propagation, overshoot[ing]	Überreichweite f
non-relativistic approximation	nichtrelativistische Näherung f		
non-relativistic region	nichtrelativistisches Gebiet n, NR-Gebiet n	**non-standard tropospheric propagation**, long-range tropospheric propagation	troposphärische Überreichweite f
non-resonance scattering	Nichtresonanzstreuung f		
non-resonant feeder, untuned feeder	unabgestimmte Speiseleitung f	**non-static process**	s. non-equilibrium process
		non-stationary; non-steady, unsteady[-state]	nichtstationär, instationär
non-reversibility, irreversibility	Irreversibilität f, Nichtumkehrbarkeit f		
non-reversible; non-interchangeable <cl.>	unverwechselbar	**non-stationary**	s. a. mobile
		non-stationary	s. a. time-dependent
non-Riemannian geometry	nicht-Riemannsche Geometrie f	**non-stationary current**, non-stationary state of current	nichtstationärer Strom m
non-rigid rotator	nichtstarrer (unstarrer) Rotator m		
non-rotational field	s. irrotational field	**non-stationary flow, (motion)**, non-steady flow, unsteady flow (motion)	instationäre (nichtstationäre) Strömung f; nichtstationäres Fließen n; instationäre (nichtstationäre) Bewegung f
non-salient pole machine	Vollpol[synchron]maschine f, Volltrommel[synchron]maschine f		
		non-stationary state of current	s. non-stationary current

non-steady, unsteady [-state]; non-stationary — nichtstationär, instationär
non-steady behaviour <e.g. of reactor> — nichtstationäres Verhalten n <z. B. des Reaktors>
non-steady flow — s. non-stationary flow
non-stoichiometric compound — nichtstöchiometrische Verbindung f
non-streamlined body — schlecht umströmbarer Körper m
non-substituted — unsubstituiert
nonsymmetrical, asymmetric[al], unsymmetric[al], dissymmetric[al] — asymmetrisch, unsymmetrisch, nichtsymmetrisch
non-symmetric halo — unsymmetrischer Halo m
nonsymmetry — s. asymmetry
non-thermal emission, non-thermal [radiofrequency] radiation — nichtthermische Radiofrequenzstrahlung f, nichtthermische Strahlung f
non-topographic photogrammetry — nichttopographische Photogrammetrie f; Nahbildmessung f
non-tracking, track resistant — kriechstromfest

non-tracking quality, tracking resistance — Kriechstromfestigkeit f, Gleichstrom-Kriechstromfestigkeit f

non-translucent, adiaphanous — adiaphan, nicht durchscheinend
non-transparency; impermeability to light; opacity, opaqueness, blackness — Lichtundurchlässigkeit f, Undurchlässigkeit f für Licht; Undurchsichtigkeit f
non-transparent; impermeable to light; opaque; not transparent — lichtundurchlässig, undurchlässig für Licht; opak; undurchsichtig, nicht durchsichtig
non-trivial solution, non-vanishing solution — nichttriviale Lösung f
non-turbulent — turbulenzfrei, nichtturbulent, nichtwirbelnd
non-uniformity, irregularity, lack of uniformity — Ungleichförmigkeit f, Ungleichmäßigkeit f
non-uniformity — s. a. heterogeneity
non-uniformity [of chain length], non-uniformity of polymer — Uneinheitlichkeit f [des Polymers]
non-uniformity of flow, irregularity of flow — Strömungsungleichheit f
non-uniform load <el.> — ungleichförmige (ungleichmäßige) Belastung f, Ungleichbelastung f <El.>
non-uniform magnetic field, inhomogeneous magnetic field — inhomogenes Magnetfeld n
non-uniform motion — ungleichförmige Bewegung f
non-uniform strain, unequal strain — ungleichmäßige Verformung (Deformation) f
non-uniform stress — s. unequal stress <mech.>
non-vacuum — s. non-empty
non-vanishing, non-zero, different from zero — nichtverschwindend, ungleich Null, verschieden von Null

non-vanishing solution, non-trivial solution — nichttriviale Lösung f

non-variant — nonvariant

non varying constraint, constraint independent of time, scleronomous binding — skleronome Bedingung f, starrgesetzliche Bedingung
non-virgin neutron; degraded neutron — nichtjungfräuliches Neutron n; degradiertes Neutron

non-viscous, inviscid, frictionless <of flow, liquid, gas> — reibungsfrei, reibungslos <Strömung, Flüssigkeit, Gas>
non-viscous instability, frictionless (inviscid) instability — reibungslose Instabilität f
non-visibility, lack of visibility; haziness, zero visibility — Unsichtigkeit f; Dunstigkeit f, Diesigkeit f
nonvoid — s. non-empty
nonvolatile — nichtflüchtiger Stoff m
non-volatile; nonevaporating; non-gaseous — nichtflüchtig; nichtgasförmig
nonvolatile storage — leistungsloser Speicher m
non[-]volatility, fixity — Nichtflüchtigkeit f
non-vortical field — s. irrotational field
non[-]wettability — Nichtbenetzbarkeit f
non-wetting — Nichtbenetzung f
non-wetting liquid — nichtbenetzende Flüssigkeit f
non-zero, non-vanishing, different from zero — nichtverschwindend, ungleich Null, verschieden von Null

non-zero black and white content / having, containing a portion of black and white, masked by grey, veiled by grey, shaded by grey, grey shaded <of chromatic colour> — grauverhüllt, vergraut

non-zero black content / having, containing a portion of black, masked (veiled, shaded) by black, black shaded <of chromatic colour> — schwarzverhüllt, verschwärzlicht

non-zero white content / having, containing a portion of white, masked (veiled, shaded) by white, white shaded <of chromatic colour> — weißverhüllt, verweißlicht

Norbury['s] rule — Norburysche Regel f
Nordheim['s] relation — Nordheimsche Beziehung (Relation) f
Nordheim['s] rules — Nordheimsche Regeln fpl, Nordheim-Regeln fpl
Nordström['s] theory of gravitation — Nordströms[che] Gravitationstheorie f, Gravitationstheorie von Nordström

norm; standard — Standard m; Norm f
norm <of the quaternion> — Norm f <Quaternion>
norm; bound <of operator> — Norm f <Math.>
normal, perpendicular [line], vertical line, plumb line — Senkrechte f, Lot n, Normale f
normal, normal to the surface, surface normal, normal of surface — Flächennormale f, Normale f der Fläche
normal — normal, regelmäßig, regelrecht, regulär
normal; perpendicular — senkrecht; normal; seiger, saiger; lotrecht

normal, standard — Standard, Normal-, normal
normal, N; n- <chem.> — normal, n, N; n- <Chem.>
normal acceleration, normal component of acceleration; centripetal [component of] acceleration — Normalbeschleunigung f, Normalkomponente f der Beschleunigung; Zentripetalbeschleunigung f
normal acoustic impedance, normal impedance <ac.> — Normalwiderstand m, normale Widerstandskomponente f <Ak.>
normal allowed transition, non-favoured [beta] transition — nichtbegünstigter (normaler) Übergang m, normalerlaubter [Beta-]Übergang m
normal annual discharge (runoff) — s. mean annual runoff

normal astrograph	Normalastrograph *m*	normal electrode, standard electrode	Normalelektrode *f*
normal atom	normales Atom *n* ‹alle Elektronen im Grundzustand›	normal electron, quasiparticle of the superconductor	Quasiteilchen *n* des Supraleiters, Normalelektron *n*
normal band, valence [electron] band, valence-bond band	Valenzband *n*, V-Band *n*, Valenzelektronenband *n*	normal elliptic integral of the first ‹second; third› kind in Legendre's notation	s. elliptic integral of the first ‹second; third› kind in Legendre's normal form
normal band	Normalbande *f*, Normalband *n* ‹dem Grundzustand entsprechend›	normal energy level ‹of atom *or* molecule›	niedrigstes Energieniveau *n*; Grundterm *m*; Grundzustand *m*, normaler Energiezustand *m* ‹Atom *oder* Molekül›
normal calomel electrode, standard calomel electrode, Ostwald['s] electrode	Normalkalomelelektrode *f*, Ostwald-Elektrode *f*	normal energy level ‹of electron›	Grundwert *m* der Energie, normaler Energiezustand *m*, Normalzustand *m* ‹Elektron›
normal case, ordinary case, fundamental case	Normalfall *m*	normal equation, standard equation	Normalgleichung *f*
normal cathode fall	normaler Katodenfall *m*	normal equation of Hesse, Hesse's standard (normal) form	Hessesche Normalform *f*
normal cell, standard [voltage] cell	Normalelement *n*	normal equivalent deviate, normal equivalent deviation, NED, N.E.D., n.e.d.	Normalfraktil *n*, NED *n*
normal class	s. monoclinic holohedry	normal error curve	s. error curve
normal class	s. orthorhombic holohedry	normal eye, standard eye	mittleres, normales menschliches Auge *n*; Normalauge *n*, normales Auge, Standardauge *n*
normal class	s. holohedry of the hexagonal system		
normal class	s. holohedry of the regular system		
normal class	s. holohedry of the tetragonal system	normal fold, symmetric fold	stehende (aufrechte) Falte *f*
normal class	s. holohedry of the triclinic system	normal force, perpendicular force; normal component of force	Normalkraft *f*; Normalkomponente *f* der Kraft
normal colour, standard colour	Normalfarbe *f*		
normal component of acceleration, normal acceleration; centripetal [component of] acceleration	Normalbeschleunigung *f*, Normalkomponente *f* der Beschleunigung; Zentripetalbeschleunigung *f*	normal force	s. dynamic lift ‹aero., hydr.›
		normal form of Weierstrass	Weierstraßsche Normalform *f*
		normal form transformation	Normalformtransformation *f*, Transformation *f* auf die Normalform
normal component of force; normal force, perpendicular force	Normalkraft *f*; Normalkomponente *f* der Kraft	normal frequency	s. fundamental frequency ‹of coupled systems›
normal component of strain, normal strain	Normalkomponente *f* der Verformung, normale Verformung *f*	normal frequency	s. a. standard frequency
		normal frequency curve	s. error curve
normal component of stress	s. normal stress	normal giant, normal giant star	normaler Riesenstern *m*, normaler Riese *m*
normal compound, n-compound	normale Verbindung *f*, n-Verbindung *f*		
normal conditions	s. standard conditions	normal glow discharge, normal [rate of] discharge	normale Glimmentladung (Entladung) *f*, Normalentladung *f*
normal conductor	Normalleiter *m*		
normal contact	s. rest contact		
normal co-ordinate analysis	Normalkoordinatenanalyse *f*	normal glow regime	Gebiet *n* der normalen Glimmentladung (Entladung)
normal co-ordinates, orthogonal trajectory co-ordinates	Normalkoordinaten *fpl*, Hauptkoordinaten *fpl*, Rayleighsche Koordinaten *fpl*	normal hydrogen	Normalwasserstoff *m*
		normal hydrogen electrode	s. standard hydrogen electrode
normal coupling, weak coupling ‹nucl.›	schwache Kopplung *f*, normale Kopplung ‹Kern.›	normal impedance, normal acoustic impedance ‹ac.›	Normalwiderstand *m*, normale Widerstandskomponente *f* ‹Ak.›
normal curvature vector	Normalkrümmungsvektor *m*	normal incidence, vertical incidence	senkrechter (normaler) Einfall *m*, Normaleinfall *m*
normal curve of magnetization	s. virgin curve of magnetization		
normal cut, X-cut, X cut	X-Schnitt *m*	normal induction	normale Induktion *f*
normal density	s. standard density ‹20 °C, 760 Torr›	normal interference colour, Newtonian interference colour	normale Interferenzfarbe *f*, Newtonsche Interferenzfarbe
normal derivative	Normalableitung *f*, Ableitung *f* in Normalenrichtung		
		normal isotope effect	normaler (regulärer) Isotopieeffekt *m*
normal developer, standard developer	Normalentwickler *m*, Standardentwickler *m*	normality, equivalent concentration	Normalität *f*, Äquivalentkonzentration *f*, Äquivalenzkonzentration *f*, Grammäquivalent *n* je Liter
normal direction, direction of normal	Normalenrichtung *f*		
normal discharge	s. normal glow discharge	normality factor ‹chem.›	Normalitätsfaktor *m*, Korrektionsfaktor *m*, Korrekturfaktor *m*
normal dispersion	normale Dispersion *f*		
normal distribution	s. Gaussian distribution	normalizable function, quadratically integrable function	normierbare Funktion *f*, quadratisch integrierbare Funktion
normal distribution curve	s. error curve		
normal distribution law	s. Gaussian distribution	normalizable kernel, Hilbert-Schmidt kernel	normierbarer Kern *m*, Hilbert-Schmidtscher Kern, quadratisch integrierbarer Kern
normal divisor, invariant sub-group, normal sub-group, self-conjugate sub-group, distinguished sub-group	Normalteiler *m*, invariante (ausgezeichnete, selbstkonjugierte) Untergruppe *f*		
		normalization	Normierung *f*
normal E-layer	normale E-Schicht *f*	normalization, normalizing [heat treatment]	Normalglühen *n*, Normalisierung *f*

normalization <num. math.>	Normalisierung f <num. Math.>	**normal permeability**	s. absolute permeability
normalization condition	Normierungsbedingung f, Normierungsbeziehung f	**normal photoelectric effect (emission)**	s. photoemissive effect
normalization factor, normalizing factor	Normierungsfaktor m	**normal plane**	Normalebene f
		normal polarogram	Normalpolarogramm n
		normal position, standard position	Normalstellung f; Normallage f
normalized algebra	normierte Algebra f	**normal position**	s. a. position of rest
normalized basis	normierte Basis f	**normal potential**	s. standard electrode potential
normalized co-ordinates, normed co-ordinates	normierte Koordinaten fpl	**normal pressure**	s. standard pressure <760 Torr>
normalized function	normierte Funktion f	**normal pressure and temperature**	s. standard electrode conditions
normalized impedance, reduced impedance, normalized wave impedance, reduced wave impedance	normierter (reduzierter) Wellenwiderstand m, normierter (reduzierter) Feldwellenwiderstand m	**normal-pressure drag,** pressure drag <aero.>	Druckwiderstand m <Aero.>
		normal probability curve	s. error curve
		normal probability paper	s. Gauss paper
normalized orthogonal system	s. orthonormal system	**normal process,** N process	N-Prozeß m, Normalprozeß m, normaler Prozeß m
normalized quaternion, versor	Versor m, normierte Quaternion f, genormte Quaternion	**normal product**	Normalprodukt n
normalized space, normed space	normierter Raum m	**normal rate of discharge,** normal [glow] discharge	normale Glimmentladung (Entladung) f, Normalentladung f
normalized unit	normierte Einheit f, reduzierte Einheit	**normal ray,** perpendicular ray	Normalstrahl m
normalized vector	s. unit vector	**normal ray**	s. a. ordinary ray
normalized wave impedance	s. normalized impedance	**normal reaction**	Normalreaktion f
		normal recession curve	s. recession curve <hydr.>
normalizing, normalizing heat treatment, normalization	Normalglühen n, Normalisierung f	**normal representation**	normale Darstellung f
		normal room temperature, room (ordinary) temperature	Raumtemperatur f, Zimmertemperatur f
normalizing factor, normalization factor	Normierungsfaktor m	**normal saline [solution]**	s. physiological salt solution
normalizing heat treatment	s. normalizing	**normal schliere,** standard schliere, reference schliere	Normalschliere f
normal law of errors	s. error law		
normal level, ground (fundamental) level	Grundniveau n	**normal segregation**	s. macroscopic segregation
normal liquid, non-associated liquid, unassociated liquid, non-polar liquid	nichtassoziierte (nichtangelagerte, nichtpolare, normale) Flüssigkeit f, Normalflüssigkeit f	**normal sensitivity f of,** of average sensitivity	normalempfindlich
		normal series	Normalreihe f
		normal shock	Normalstoß m, normaler Stoß m
normal Lorentz triplet, normal Zeeman triplet	normales Zeeman-Triplett n, normales Lorentz-Triplett n, normales Zeemansches Triplett n	**normal slope,** equilibrium slope	Gleichgewichtsgefälle n, Normalgefälle n
		normal solution, standard solution, 1 N solution	Normallösung f, n-Lösung f, normale Lösung f, 1 n Lösung
normally closed contact (interlock)	s. rest contact	**normal sound**	Normalschall m
normally distributed variable	normalverteilte Variable f	**normal spectrum**	s. grating spectrum
		normal spinel	Normalspinell m
normally open interlock <US>	s. make contact	**normal standard cell**	s. Weston normal standard cell
normally ordered aggregate, well-ordered set, well-ordered aggregate	wohlgeordnete Menge f, vollständig geordnete Menge, Wohlordnung f	**normal state,** standard state, state under normal conditions	Norm[al]zustand m, Zustand m unter Normalbedingungen
normal magnetization curve	s. virgin curve of magnetization	**normal state**	s. ground state
normal magnification	Normalvergrößerung f, normale Vergrößerung f; Pupillengleiche f <beim Fernrohr>	**normal-state disintegration energy**	Zerfallsenergie f für den Grundzustand
		normal-state energy	Energie f des Grundzustandes
normal mass effect	normaler Kernmasseneffekt m [der Isotopie]	**normal steam**	s. standard steam
normal matrix	normale Matrix f; Normalmatrix f	**normal stereogram**	Normalstereogramm n
		normal strain, normal component of strain	Normalkomponente f der Verformung, normale Verformung f
normal mode, <of vibration>, normal vibration <of microwaves>	Normalschwingung f, normale Mode f, Normalmode f <Mikrowellen>	**normal strain**	s. unit elongation
		normal stress	Normalspannungszustand m
normal mode <of vibration>, fundamental oscillation <of coupled systems>	Normalschwingung f, Eigenschwingung f, Fundamentalschwingung f, Hauptschwingung f <gekoppelter Systeme>	**normal stress,** normal component of stress, direct stress <mech.>	Normalspannung f <Mech.>
		normal stress <mech.>	Normalbeanspruchung f; Normalanstrengung f
normal multiplet, regular multiplet	regelrechtes (reguläres, normales) Multiplett n, Multiplett mit normaler Termordnung	**normal stress**	s. a. tensile stress
		normal stress effect, cross effect	Normalspannungseffekt m
normal of surface, normal to the surface, [surface] normal	Flächennormale f, Normale f der Fläche	**normal stress law**	Normalspannungshypothese f, Normalspannungsgesetz n [von Sohncke]
		normal sub-group	s. normal divisor
normal operator	normaler Operator m	**normal surface,** wave-normal surface, wave velocity surface	Normalenfläche f, Wellen[normalen]fläche f, Wellengeschwindigkeitsfläche f
normal order of terms	normale Termordnung f		
normal oxidation-reduction potential	s. standard oxidation-reduction potential	**normal temperature,** standard temperature	Normtemperatur f, Normaltemperatur f

normal temperature and pressure	s. standard conditions	nose shock	s. head wave
normal tensor	Normaltensor m, Normalaffinor m	no-signal potential	s. resting potential
		nosing	s. nose
normal term, ground term, fundamental term, term of ground state	Grundterm m, Term m des Grundzustandes	no-sky line	Himmelslichtgrenzlinie f
		no-slip condition, condition of no (zero) slip	Haftbedingung f
normal to the reflecting surface, axis (perpendicular) of incidence, perpendicular	Einfallslot n, Einfallsnormale f	notation; designation; system of notation; symbolism	Bezeichnung f; Bezeichnungsweise f; Schreibweise f; Symbolik f
normal to the surface, [surface] normal, normal of surface	Flächennormale f, Normale f der Fläche	notch, nick; indentation; cut	Kerbe f, Einkerbung f, Kerb m; Einschnitt m; Aussparung f; Scharte f
normal transformation	normale Transformation f	notch bar	s. notch specimen
normal unit vector	s. unit normal	notch bar bending test	Kerbbiegeversuch m, Kerbbiegeprüfung f
normal valence <chem.>	normale Wertigkeit f, normale Valenz f <Chem.>	notch bar impact resistance	s. notch impact strength
normal variable	Normalvariable f	notch bar impact test, notch beam impact test, notch bend test	Kerbschlagbiegeversuch m, Kerbschlagversuch m
normal vector	Normalenvektor m		
normal vibration, normal mode [of vibration] <of microwaves>	Normalschwingung f, normale Mode f, Normalmode f <Mikrowellen>	notch brittleness	Kerbsprödigkeit f
normal vibration of the molecule	Normalschwingung (Eigenschwingung) f des Moleküls	notch brittleness (ductility)	s. a. notch impact strength
		notched bar	s. notch specimen
normal vision, emmetropia	Normalsichtigkeit f, Rechtsichtigkeit f, Emmetropie f	notched effect	s. notch effect
		notched impact strength (value)	s. notch impact strength
normal Wien effect, Wien['s] effect	Wien-Effekt m normaler Wien-Effekt, Feldstärkeeffekt m [von Wien]	notched specimen	s. notch specimen
		notched weir, measuring weir, measurement weir, weir	Meßüberfall m, Meßwehr n, Wehr n
normal year	Normaljahr n		
normal Zeeman effect	normaler Zeeman-Effekt m, Zeeman-Effekt der Singulettsysteme	notch effect, notched effect	Kerbwirkung f
normal Zeeman triplet, normal Lorentz triplet	normales Zeeman-Triplett (Lorentz-Triplett, Zeemansches Triplett) n		
normatron	Normatron n		
normed co-ordinates	s. normalized-co-ordinates	notch [fatigue] factor	s. reduced factor of stress concentration
normed space, normalized space	normierter Raum m	notch groove, groove (root, base) of the notch	Kerbgrund m
Nörremberg['s] polarizer (polarizing apparatus)	Nörrembergscher Polarisationsapparat m	notch impact resistance	s. notch impact strength
		notch impact strength (value), [notched] impact strength (value), notch ductility, [notch] toughness, notch brittleness, notch [bar] impact resistance, impact resistance	Kerbschlagzähigkeit f, Kerbzähigkeit f, Kerbschlagwert m, Kerbschlagbiegezähigkeit f, Kerbfestigkeit f, spezifische Schlagarbeit f
north celestial pole, [celestial] north pole <astr.>	Himmelsnordpol m, nördlicher Himmelspol m, Nordpol m [des Himmels], Weltpol m <Astr.>		
northern autumnal equinox	s. autumnal equinox		
northern autumnal equinox	s. autumnal point		
northern dawn	s. northern lights	notching, indenting, cutting	Kerbung f, Einkerbung f; Nutung f
northern hemisphere	Nordhalbkugel f; nördliche Hemisphäre (Halbkugel) f, Nordhemisphäre f	notch sensitivity, fatigue notch sensitivity	Kerbempfindlichkeit f, Kerbempfindlichkeitszahl f
northern [polar] lights, aurora borealis, northern dawn	Nordlicht n, Aurora f borealis	notch specimen, notch bar, notched bar (specimen)	gekerbte Probe f, Kerbschlag[biege]probe f, gekerbter Probestab m, Kerbstab m
northern vernal equinox, vernal equinox, spring equinox	Frühlingsäquinoktium n, Frühlings-Tagundnachtgleiche f		
		notch toughness	s. notch impact strength
north magnetic pole	magnetischer Nordpol m	notch-type depression, V-depression, vee depression	V-Depression f, V-förmige Senke f
north point [of the horizon]	Nordpunkt m	not close-packed structure	nichtdichte Packung f
north polar distance, polar distance, co-declination, P.D., PD	Poldistanz f, Polabstand m, Nordpolabstand m, Polardistanz f	note amplifier	s. audio amplifier
		note frequency, beat frequency (rate)	Schwebungsfrequenz f, Schwebungszahl f
north polar sequence, polar sequence	Polsequenz f, Nordpolarsequenz f, Polfolge f	notion of heat, heat concept	Wärmebegriff m
north pole	s. north celestial pole <astr.>	not stratified, unstratified	ungeschichtet
north-south asymmetry	Nord-Süd-Asymmetrie f		
north-south effect	Nord-Süd-Effekt m	not transparent; impermeable to light; opaque; non-transparent	lichtundurchlässig, undurchlässig für Licht; opak; undurchsichtig, nicht durchsichtig
Norton['s] theorem	Satz m von H. F. Mayer, Nortonscher Satz		
Norwegia-type glacier, plateau glacier	Plateaugletscher m, Hochlandeis n, norwegischer Gletschertyp m	Nouy tensiometer / du	Adhäsionswaage f [nach Lecomte du Nouy]
		nova <pl.: novae>, new star, explosive star	Nova f <pl.: Novae>, Neuer Stern m, temporärer Veränderlicher m
nose; nosing	Nase f; Schnauze f; Vorderteil n; Bug m		
nose[]heaviness	Kopflastigkeit f; Vorderlastigkeit f	nova explosion, nova outburst, outburst of nova	Novaausbruch m, Helligkeitsausbruch (Lichtausbruch) m einer Nova
		Nowotny phase	Nowotny-Phase f
nose piece <e.g. of microscope>	s. turret head	nox, nx	Nox n, nx
		noxious surface	schädliche Fläche f

nozzle; mouthpiece	Mundstück n ‹z. B. der Düse›; Düsenmundstück n, Austrittsöffnung f der Düse	**n-type ionic conduction**	Ionenüberschußleitung f
		n-type ionic conductor	Ionenüberschußleiter m
nozzle	Düse f	**n-type metallic conduction**	metallische Elektronenleitung f
nozzle, flanged nozzle (socket), connecting piece, connection, lug	Stutzen m, Rohransatz m, Rohransatzstück n, Rohrstutzen m	**n-type semiconductor,** excess semiconductor, n-type conductor	Überschuß[halb]leiter m, n-[Typ-]Halbleiter m, n-Leiter m, Reduktions[halb]leiter m, Leiter (Störstellenhalbleiter) m vom n-Typ, Störelektronenleiter m, Donatorenleiter m
nozzle, spout ‹of waveguide›	Austrittsöffnung f [des Wellenleiters], Wellenleiter[-Austritts]öffnung f		
nozzle	s. a. jet nozzle		
nozzle flow	Düsenströmung f		
		nuclear	Kern-, Nuklear-, nuklear
nozzle separator, separation nozzle	Trenndüse f, Schäldüse f	**nuclear,** nucleonic, nuclear-physical, in (of, by) nuclear physics	kernphysikalisch
nozzle throat, throat of the nozzle	Düsenhals m, Hals m (Verengung f) der Düse, kritischer Düsenquerschnitt m	**nuclear acoustic resonance,** NAR	kernakustische Resonanz f, akustische Kernresonanz f, NAR
n-particle problem	n-Teilchen-Problem n	**nuclear-active component**	s. N-component
n-p junction	np-Übergang m, np-Verbindung f, np-Kontakt m	**nuclear-active particle**	kernaktives (kernverwandtes) Teilchen n
n-p-n-junction transistor, n-p-n-type transistor, n-p-n- transistor	npn-Transistor m, npn-Flächentransistor m	**nuclear adiabatic demagnetization,** nuclear cooling	nukleare adiabatische Abkühlung f, adiabatische Abkühlung eines Kernspinsystems, [adiabatische] Kernabkühlung f, Kernkühlung f, adiabatische Kernentmagnetisierung f
n-p-n-p diode, four-layer n-p-n-p diode	npnp-Diode f, npnp-Flächendiode f, npnp-Vierschichtdiode f	**nuclear alignement;** nuclear orientation	Kernorientierung f; Kernausrichtung f
		nuclear angular momentum	s. nuclear spin
n-p-n-p transistor, four-layer n-p-n-p transistor	npnp-Transistor m, npnp-Flächentransistor m, npnp-Vierschichttransistor m	**nuclear astrophysics**	Astrokernphysik f, Lehre f von der Entstehung der chemischen Elemente
		nuclear attraction, intranuclear attraction	innernukleare (intranukleare) Anziehung f, Kernanziehung f
n-p-n[-type] transistor	s. n-p-n junction transistor	**nuclear barrier**	Potentialwall m des Atomkerns
n-port, multiport	Mehrtor n, n- Tor n	**nuclear battery**	s. atomic battery
(n,p) process, (n,p) reaction, (n,p) type reaction, (n,p) type process, reaction of (n,p) type, neutron-proton reaction	(n,p)-Reaktion f, (n,p)-Prozeß m, Neutron-Proton-Reaktion f	**nuclear binding energy,** nucleus bond energy	Bindungsenergie f des Atomkerns (Kerns), Kernbindungsenergie f
		nuclear blast (burst)	s. atomic blast
		nuclear capture [of particles]	Kerneinfang m ‹(x, γ)-Prozeß›
N process, normal process	N-Prozeß m, Normalprozeß m, normaler Prozeß m	**nuclear cascade process**	Kaskadenkernreaktion f, Kaskaden[kern]prozeß m
n-p scattering	s. neutron-proton scattering	**nuclear chain reaction,** chain reaction ‹nucl.›	Kernkettenreaktion f, Kettenkernreaktion f
NPT	s. standard conditions		
(n,p) type process (reaction)	s. (n,p) reaction	**nuclear charge,** Ze	Kernladung f, Ze
n-region	n-leitende Zone f, n-leitender Bereich m n-Gebiet n, n-Zone f, n-Schicht f	**nuclear charge,** nucleonic charge	Nukleonenladung f, nukleare Ladung f, Kernladung f
		nuclear charge quantum number, charge quantum number	Ladungsquantenzahl f
N.T.C. resistor	s. thermistor		
n-th forbidden	n-fach verboten	**nuclear chemistry**	Kernchemie f, Chemie f der Kernreaktionen
n-th forbidden transition	n-fach verbotener Übergang m	**nuclear classification,** nuclear systematics	Kernsystematik f
n-th order transformation (transition), transition (transformation) of n-th order	Umwandlung f n-ter Ordnung (Art), Übergang m n-ter Ordnung (Art)	**nuclear collision**	Kernstoß m
		nuclear component	s. N-component
		nuclear constant	Kernkonstante f, kernphysikalische Konstante f
n-tuple	n-tupel n	**nuclear constituent,** nucleon; nuclear particle	Nukleon n, Kernbaustein m, Kernbestandteil m; Kernteilchen n
n-type, N-type, n-conducting, N-conducting	n-leitend, n-, n-Typ-, überschußleitend	**nuclear constitution,** nuclear structure	Kern[auf]bau m, Kernstruktur f, Bau m des Atomkerns
n-type conduction, electronic conduction, electron conduction, excess conduction, surplus conduction	Überschußleitung f, n-[Typ-]Leitung f, Elektronen[halb]leitung f, elektronische Halbleitung f, Donatorenleitung f, Störelektronenleitung f, Störstellenleitung f vom n-Typ, Zusatzelektronenleitung f, Zwischen[gitter]platzleitung f	**nuclear cooling**	s. nuclear adiabatic demagnetization
		nuclear core, core (trunk) of the nucleus, nuclear trunk (frame)	Kernrumpf m, Rumpf m des Atomkerns
		nuclear core isomerism, core isomerism	Kernrumpfisomerie f, Rumpfisomerie f
		nuclear criticality safety	Kritizitätssicherheit f
n-type conductivity, electron conductivity	Elektronenleitfähigkeit f, Überschußleitfähigkeit f, n-Typ-Leitfähigkeit f	**nuclear decay**	s. decay
		nuclear deformation energy, deformation energy of nucleus	Deformationsenergie f des Kerns, Kerndeformationsenergie f
n-type conductor	s. n-type semiconductor		
n-type impurity	s. donor	**nuclear democracy**	s. bootstrap

nuclear 538

nuclear density, density of nuclear matter	Dichte f der Kernmaterie, Kerndichte f, Materiedichte (Massendichte) f im Atomkern, Dichte des Atomkerns	nuclear force	Kernkraft f, Kernfeldkraft f, starke Kraft f
nuclear detector, detector	Kernstrahlungsdetektor m, Kernstrahlungsnachweisgerät n, kernphysikalisches Nachweisgerät n, Detektor m	nuclear force meson, π meson, pi meson, pion, British meson <π^+, π^0, π^->	π-Meson n, Pi-Meson n, Pion n <π^+, π^0, π^->
		nuclear form factor	Kernformfaktor m
		nuclear fragment, fragment, chip, splinter <nucl.>	Kernbruchstück n, Bruchstück n, Kernfragment n, Fragment n <Kern.>
nuclear dipole moment	Kerndipolmoment n		
nuclear disintegration	s. decay	nuclear frame	s. core of the nucleus
nuclear disintegration energy, decay (disintegration) energy	Zerfallsenergie f	nuclear fuel	s. nuclear reactor fuel <nucl.>
		nuclear fusion, fusion, nucleosynthesis <nucl.>	Kernfusion f, Fusion f, Kernsynthese f, Kernverschmelzung f, Kernaufbau m, Kernvereinigung f, Verschmelzung f [von Kernen] <Kern.>
nuclear distance	s. internuclear distance		
nuclear doublet	Kerndublett n		
nuclear electric moment	elektrisches Moment n des Atomkerns		
nuclear electric quadrupole moment	elektrisches Kernquadrupolmoment n		
nuclear electron	Kernelektron n	nuclear fusion energy	s. fusion energy
nuclear electronics	Kernelektronik f, kernphysikalische Elektronik f	nuclear fusion physics, high-temperature plasma physics	Hochtemperatur-Plasmaphysik f, Kernfusionsphysik f, Fusionsphysik f
nuclear emulsion, nuclear photographic emulsion	Kernspuremulsion f, Kernemulsion f, kernphysikalische Emulsion f	nuclear fusion reactor, fusion reactor; thermonuclear reactor	Fusionsreaktor m, Kernfusionsreaktor m; thermonuklearer Reaktor m
nuclear emulsion technique, photographic emulsion technique, emulsion technique, photographic plate technique	Plattentechnik f, Photoplattenmethode f, Photoplattentechnik f, Emulsionstechnik f, Kernemulsionstechnik f, Kernemulsionsmethode f	nuclear fusion temperature	s. fusion temperature <nucl.>
		nuclear gamma[-ray] resonance, NGR	s. Mössbauer effect
		nuclear gamma[-ray] resonance spectroscopy	s. Mössbauer spectrometry
		nuclear geophysics	Kerngeophysik f
		nuclear g-factor	Kern-g-Faktor m, g-Faktor m des Kernspins (Kerns)
nuclear energy	Kernenergie f, Atomkernenergie f	nuclear-grade, nuclear pure	nuklearrein
		nuclear gyromagnetic ratio	gyromagnetisches Verhältnis n des Atomkerns
nuclear energy level, nuclear level, energy level of the nucleus	Kern[energie]niveau n, Energieniveau n des Kerns, Kernterm m	nuclear gyroscope	Kern[spin]gyroskop n
nuclear energy-level diagram	Kernniveauschema n, Kerntermschema n	nuclear heating	nukleare Erwärmung (Aufheizung) f, Kernerwärmung f, Kernaufheizung f
nuclear energy state	s. nuclear state		
nuclear engine	Kernenergieantrieb m, Kernenergietriebwerk n, Atommotor m	nuclear inactive particle	kerninaktives Teilchen n, kernfremdes Teilchen
nuclear entropy	Kernentropie f	nuclear induction	s. nuclear magnetic resonance
nuclear envelope, nuclear (nucleus) membrane	Kernmembran f	nuclear induction technique; method of nuclear resonance absorption, technique of nuclear resonance absorption, NMR technique	Kerninduktionsmethode f; Methode f der magnetischen Kernresonanz [-absorption], Kernresonanzmethode f, NMR-Methode f
nuclear equation, nuclear reaction equation (formula)	Kernreaktionsformel f, Kernreaktionsgleichung f		
nuclear equivalent	s. nucleoid <bio.>		
nuclear evaporation, evaporation of the nucleus	Verdampfung f des Kerns, Kernverdampfung f		
		nuclear installation, nuclear plant (facility)	Kernanlage f
nuclear event; hit of nucleus	[kernphysikalisches] Ereignis n; Kerntreffer m	nuclear interacting component	s. N-component
nuclear excitation	Kernanregung f	nuclear interaction	Kernwechselwirkung f, Wechselwirkung f zwischen (mit) Kernen
nuclear explosion	s. atomic blast		
nuclear explosion	s. fragmentation [of nucleus]	nuclear investigation, nuclear study	kernphysikalische Untersuchung f
nuclear explosion test (trial)	s. atomic blast	nuclear isobar, [nucleonic] isobar	Isobar n, Kernisobar n
nuclear facility	s. nuclear installation	nuclear isomer, isomer	Kernisomer n, Isomer n
nuclear ferromagnetism	Kernferromagnetismus m	nuclear isomerism, isomerism of atomic nucleus	Kernisomerie f, Isomerie f des Atomkerns
nuclear field, nucleonic field	Kernfeld n, Kraftfeld n des Atomkerns, Feld n des Kerns, Nukleonenfeld n	nuclear level, nuclear energy level, energy level of the nucleus	Kernniveau n, Kernenergieniveau n, Energieniveau n des Kerns, Kernterm m
nuclear film	Kernspurfilm m, Film m für Kernspuraufnahmen		
nuclear fission, fission	Spaltung f, Kernspaltung f <Kern.>	nuclear magnetic alignment	magnetische Kernausrichtung f (Orientierung f der Kerne)
nuclear fission cross-section	s. fission cross-section		
nuclear fluid	Kernflüssigkeit f	nuclear magnetic dipole moment	s. magnetic moment of the nucleus
		nuclear magnetic induction	s. nuclear magnetic resonance
nuclear fluorescence, nuclear resonance fluorescence	Kernresonanzfluoreszenz f, Kernfluoreszenz f	nuclear magnetic moment	s. magnetic moment of the nucleus

nuclear magnetic resonance, nuclear resonance absorption, nuclear magnetic resonance absorption, NMR, n.m.r. <Purcell>; nuclear induction, nuclear magnetic induction <Bloch>
magnetische Kernresonanz f, magnetische Kernresonanzabsorption f, Kernspinresonanz f, Kernresonanzabsorption, kernmagnetische Resonanz f, NMR <nach Purcell>; Kerninduktion f <nach Bloch>

nuclear magnetic resonance absorption s. nuclear magnetic resonance

nuclear magnetic resonance measurement, measurement of nuclear induction, measurement of nuclear resonance absorption, NMR measurement
Kernresonanzmessung f, magnetische Kernresonanzmessung f, Kerninduktionsmessung f, NMR-Messung f

nuclear magnetic resonance phenomenon, NMR phenomenon
Kernresonanzeffekt m, Kernspinresonanzeffekt m, magnetischer Kernresonanzeffekt, Resonanzeffekt m, NMR-Effekt m

nuclear magnetic resonance signal s. nuclear resonance signal

nuclear magnetic resonance spectrograph, nuclear resonance absorption spectrograph, nuclear resonance spectrograph, NMR spectrograph
Kernresonanzspektrograph m, magnetischer Kernresonanzspektrograph m, Kerninduktionsspektrograph m, NMR-Spektrograph m

nuclear magnetic resonance spectrometer, nuclear resonance spectrometer, nuclear resonance absorption spectrometer, NMR spectrometer
Kernresonanzspektrometer n, magnetisches Kernresonanzspektrometer, Kerninduktionsspektrometer n, NMR-Spektrometer n

nuclear magnetic resonance spectroscopy, NMR spectroscopy
Kernresonanzspektroskopie f, magnetische Kernresonanzspektroskopie, NMR-Spektroskopie f

nuclear magnetic resonance spectrum, nuclear resonance spectrum, nuclear resonance absorption spectrum, NMR spectrum
Kernresonanzspektrum n, magnetisches Kernresonanzspektrum, Kerninduktionsspektrum n, NMR-Spektrum n

nuclear magnetism Kernmagnetismus m, Magnetismus m des Atomkerns

nuclear magneton Kernmagneton n, KM

nuclear mass; nuclear rest mass Kernmasse f; Ruhemasse f des Atomkerns

nuclear mass surface, mass surface Massenfläche f, Kernmassenfläche f <Z, N-Koordinaten>

nuclear matrix element Kernmatrixelement n

nuclear matter Kernmaterie f

nuclear medicine Nuklearmedizin f

nuclear membrane, nucleus membrane, nuclear envelope Kernmembran f

nuclear meson s. nuclear pi-meson

nuclear model, model of nucleus Kernmodell n, Modell n des Atomkerns

nuclear model of the atom Kernmodell n des Atoms

nuclear moment Kernmoment n, Moment n des Atomkerns

nuclear motion s. nuclear movement

nuclear movement, nuclear motion; motion of the nucleus Kernbewegung f; Mitbewegung f des Kerns, Kernmitbewegung f

nuclear multiplet Kernmultiplett n
nuclear number s. mass number
nuclear orientation; nuclear alignment Kernorientierung f; Kernausrichtung f

nuclear oscillation, oscillation of molecule nuclei Kernschwingung f [der Moleküle]

nuclear oscillation energy, energy of nuclear oscillations Kernschwingungsenergie f

nuclear Overhauser effect Kern-Overhauser-Effekt m

nuclear paramagnetic resonance s. nuclear magnetic resonance

nuclear paramagnetism Kernparamagnetismus m, Paramagnetismus m des Atomkerns

nuclear parent, parent nuclide. parent; parent nucleus, original nucleus Mutternuklid n, Ausgangsnuklid n; Ausgangskern m, Mutterkern m, Elternkern m

nuclear particle s. nucleon
nuclear particle track s. nuclear track
nuclear permeability Kernpermeabilität f <Bio.> <bio.>

nuclear phase displacement, nuclear phase shift Kernphasenverschiebung f

nuclear photodisintegration (photoeffect, photoelectric effect) s. photodisintegration

nuclear photographic emulsion s. nuclear emulsion

nuclear photography Kernphotographie f, Kernspurphotographie f

nuclear photomagnetic effect, γ,n reaction (γ,n)-Prozeß m. photomagnetischer Effekt m am Kern

nuclear photoreaction s. photodisintegration
nuclear-physical s. nuclear
nuclear physicist Kernphysiker m

nuclear physics f **by (in, of),** nuclear, nucleonic, nuclear-physical kernphysikalisch

nuclear pile s. nuclear reactor
nuclear pile neutron, pile neutron, reactor neutron Reaktorneutron n

nuclear pile oscillator, pile oscillator, reactivity oscillator, reactor oscillator Reaktoroszillator m, Pileoszillator m

nuclear pi-meson, nuclear π-meson, nuclear meson, meson [of the nucleus], Yukawa particle, Yukawa meson, yukon Kern-π-Meson n, Kern-pi-Meson n, Kernmeson n, Meson n [des Kerns], Yukawasches Kernmeson, Yukawa-Teilchen n, Yukon n, Yukawa-Quant n

nuclear plant s. nuclear installation
nuclear plate Kernplatte f, Kernspurplatte f, Kernemulsionsplatte f, Kernspur[en]emulsionsplatte f, Kernphotoplatte f

nuclear poison, neutron poison, reactor poison Reaktorgift n, Neutronengift n, starker Neutronenabsorber m

nuclear polarization Kernpolarisation f
nuclear potential, potential of nuclear forces Kernkraftpotential n, Potential n der Kernkräfte, Kernpotential n

nuclear potential energy potentielle Energie f des Atomkerns

nuclear power [nutzbare] Kernenergie f, Kernkraft f

nuclear-powered, nuclear propelled kernenergiegetrieben, mit Kernenergieantrieb, Reaktor-, Kern-, Atom-

nuclear-powered rocket, nuclear rocket Rakete f mit Ausnutzung von Kernenergie zur Beschleunigung einer Stützmasse, Kernrakete f

nuclear power plant Kernenergieanlage f, Leistungsreaktoranlage f

nuclear

nuclear power production	Kernenergieerzeugung f, Kernenergiegewinnung f, Kernenergiefreisetzung f
nuclear precession	Kernpräzession f
nuclear precession magnetometer	s. proton magnetometer
nuclear process; nuclear reaction	Kernreaktion f; Kernprozeß m, Kernumwandlungsprozeß m
nuclear propelled, nuclear-powered	kernenergiegetrieben, mit Kernenergieantrieb, Reaktor-, Kern-, Atom-
nuclear proton	Kernproton n
nuclear pseudopotential, Fermi pseudopotential	Fermisches Pseudopotential n, Kernpseudopotential n
nuclear pure, nuclear-grade	nuklearrein
nuclear purification	nukleare Feinreinigung f
nuclear purity	nukleare Reinheit f, Kernreinheit f
nuclear quadruplet	Kernquadruplett n
nuclear quadrupole coupling	Kernquadrupolkopplung f
nuclear quadrupole moment	Kernquadrupolmoment n
nuclear quadrupole resonance, NQR	Kernquadrupolresonanz f
nuclear quadrupole resonance frequency	Kernquadrupolresonanzfrequenz f
nuclear quadrupole resonance spectrograph	Kernquadrupolresonanzspektrograph m
nuclear quadrupole spectrum	Kernquadrupolspektrum n
nuclear radiation	Kernstrahlung f
nuclear radius	Kernradius m
nuclear reaction; nuclear process	Kernreaktion f; Kernprozeß m, Kernumwandlungsprozeß m
nuclear reaction cross-section	s. reaction cross-section
nuclear reaction energy	s. Q value <nucl.>
nuclear reaction equation, nuclear reaction formula	s. nuclear equation
nuclear reaction proceeding through (via) a compound nucleus	Zwischenkernreaktion f, Zwischenkernprozeß m, Kernreaktion f mit Compoundkernstadium, Reaktion f mit Compoundkernstadium, Compoundkernreaktion f
nuclear reaction yield, reaction yield	Ausbeute f der Kernreaktion, Reaktionsausbeute f
nuclear reactor, reactor, pile, nuclear pile, chain-reacting pile <nucl.>	Reaktor m, Kernreaktor m, Pile m <Kern.>
nuclear reactor fuel, nuclear fuel, fuel <nucl.>	Kernbrennstoff m, Brennstoff m, Spaltstoff m <Kern.>
nuclear reactor period	s. period
nuclear reactor reactivity	s. reactivity <nucl.>
nuclear recoil	Kernrückstoß m
nuclear relaxation	Kernrelaxation f
nuclear repulsion, intranuclear repulsion	innernukleare (intranukleare) Abstoßung f, Kernabstoßung f
nuclear resonance	Kernresonanz f
nuclear resonance absorption	s. nuclear magnetic resonance
nuclear resonance absorption spectrograph	s. nuclear magnetic resonance spectrograph
nuclear resonance absorption spectrometer	s. nuclear magnetic resonance spectrometer
nuclear resonance absorption spectrum, nuclear [magnetic] resonance spectrum, NMR spectrum	[magnetisches] Kernresonanzspektrum n, Kerninduktionsspektrum n, NMR-Spektrum n
nuclear resonance cryoscopy	Kernresonanzkryoskopie f
nuclear resonance fluorescence, nuclear fluorescence	Kernresonanzfluoreszenz f, Kernfluoreszenz f
nuclear resonance integral	s. resonance integral
nuclear resonance maser	Kernresonanzmaser m
nuclear resonance scattering	s. resonance scattering
nuclear resonance scattering cross-section, resonance scattering cross-section, cross-section for resonance scattering	Resonanzstreuquerschnitt m, Wirkungsquerschnitt m für (der) Resonanzstreuung
nuclear resonance signal, nuclear magnetic resonance signal, NMR signal	Kernresonanzsignal n, Kerninduktionssignal n, magnetisches Kernresonanzsignal n, NMR-Signal n
nuclear resonance spectrograph	s. nuclear magnetic resonance spectrograph
nuclear resonance spectrometer	s. nuclear magnetic resonance spectrometer
nuclear resonance spectrum	s. nuclear magnetic resonance spectrum
nuclear resonant scattering	s. resonance scattering
nuclear rest mass; nuclear mass	Kernmasse f; Ruhemasse f des Atomkerns
nuclear ribonucleic acid, nuclear RNA, nRNA	Kernribonukleinsäure f, Kern-RNS f, nukleäre Ribonukleinsäure f
nuclear rocket, nuclear-powered rocket	Rakete f mit Ausnutzung von Kernenergie zur Beschleunigung einer Stützmasse, Kernrakete f
nuclear rotation	Kernrotation f
nuclear rotational level	Kernrotationsniveau n, Rotationsniveau n des Atomkerns
nuclear rydberg	nukleares Rydberg n
nuclear saturation, saturation of nuclear matter	Kernsättigung f, Sättigung f der Kernmaterie
nuclear scattering amplitude	Kernstreuamplitude f, Amplitude f der Kernstreuung
nuclear science	Kernwissenschaft f
nuclear separation	s. internuclear distance
nuclear shell	Kernschale f
nuclear shell model	s. shell model
nuclear shell structure	s. shell structure of nucleus
nuclear size resonance	Kerngrößenresonanz f, Resonanzstruktur f des totalen Neutronenwirkungsquerschnitts
nuclear space <math.; bio.>	nuklearer Raum m <Math.; Bio.>; Kernraum m <Bio.>
nuclear spacing	s. internuclear distance
nuclear species, nuclide, atomic species, sort of atom	Nuklid n, Kernart f, Kernsorte f, Atomart f, Atomsorte f
nuclear spectrometer	Kernspektrometer n; Kernstrahlungsspektrometer n, Kernstrahlenspektrometer n
nuclear spectroscopy	Kernspektroskopie f
nuclear spectrum	Kernspektrum n, Gamma-Linienspektrum n
nuclear spin, nuclear angular momentum, intrinsic angular momentum of atomic nucleus	Kernspin m, Kerndrehimpuls m; Gesamtdrehimpuls (Drehimpuls) m des Atomkerns, mechanischer Drehimpuls des Atomkerns, mechanischer Gesamtdrehimpuls des Kerns, Kerndrall m, Kerndrallwert m
nuclear spin echo	Kernspinecho n
nuclear spin entropy	Kernspinentropie f
nuclear spin function	Kernspinfunktion f
nuclear spin-lattice relaxation, spin-lattice relaxation	Spin-Gitter-Relaxation f

nuclear spin operator, operator of nuclear spin	Kernspinoperator m, Operator m des Kernspins	nucleation rate, rate of nucleation	Keimbildungshäufigkeit f, Keimbildungsgeschwindigkeit f, Bildungsgeschwindigkeit f der Keime, Kernbildungsgeschwindigkeit f
nuclear spin quantum number	Kernspinquantenzahl f, Spinquantenzahl f des Atomkerns		
nuclear spin-spin relaxation, spin-spin relaxation	Spin-Spin-Relaxation f	nucleic acid, nuclein	Nukleinsäure f, Nucleinsäure f, Nuklein n
nuclear spin system	Kernspinsystem n	nuclei counter, counter of nuclei	Kernzähler m, Kondensationskernzähler m
nuclear stability	Kernstabilität f	nuclein	s. nucleoproteide
nuclear stability curve	Kernstabilitätskurve f	nuclein	s. a. nucleic acid
nuclear stability rules	Kernstabilitätsregeln fpl, Stabilitätsgesetze npl für die Nuklide	nucleogenesis, element synthesis, formation of elements	Elementenentstehung f, Elementenaufbau m, Elementaufbau m, Elementensynthese f, Nukleogenese f
nuclear star	s. emulsion star ‹nucl.›		
nuclear state, nuclear energy state, energy state of the nucleus	Kernzustand m, Energiezustand m des Atomkerns (Kerns), Kernenergiezustand m	nucleohiston	Nukleohiston n
		nucleoid, nuclear equivalent ‹bio.›	Nukleoid n, Karyoid n, Kernäquivalent n ‹Bio.›
		nucleolus	Nukleolus m, Nukleole f, Kernkörperchen n
nuclear statistics	Kernstatistik f		
nuclear structure, nuclear constitution	Kernbau m, Kernstruktur f, Bau m des Atomkerns, Kernaufbau m	nucleon, nuclear constituent; nuclear particle	Nukleon n, Kernbaustein m, Kernbestandteil m; Kernteilchen n
nuclear study	s. nuclear investigation	nucleon binding, nucleon coupling	Nukleonenkopplung f, Nukleonenbindung f
nuclear superheating	nukleare Überhitzung f	nucleon cascade	Nukleonenkaskade f
nuclear surface; border of the nucleus	Kernoberfläche f; Kernrand m	nucleon core, nucleor, bare nucleon, core of the nucleon	Nukleor n, Nukleonkern m, nacktes Nukleon n, innerster Bezirk m des Nukleons
nuclear surface energy, nuclear surface tension, surface energy of the nucleus	Oberflächenenergie (Oberflächenspannung) f des Kerns, Kernoberflächenenergie f, Kernoberflächenspannung f		
		nucleon coupling	s. nucleon binding
		nucleon field	s. nuclear field
nuclear surface oscillation, surface oscillation of the nucleus	Oberflächenschwingung f des Kerns, Kernoberflächenschwingung f	nucleon gas	Nukleonengas n
		nucleonic	kernelektronisch
		nucleonic, nuclear, nuclear-physical, in (of, by) nuclear physics	kernphysikalisch
nuclear surface tension	s. nuclear surface energy		
nuclear susceptibility	Kernsuszeptibilität f	nucleonic charge, nuclear charge	Nukleonenladung f, nukleare Ladung f, Kernladung f
nuclear systematics, nuclear classification	Kernsystematik f		
nuclear temperature	Kerntemperatur f	nucleonic component	Nukleonenkomponente f
		nucleonic device	s. nucleonic instrument
nuclear test	s. atomic blast	nucleonic field	s. nuclear field
nuclear thermodynamics, thermodynamics of the nucleus	Kernthermodynamik f, Thermodynamik f des Atomkerns	nucleonic instrument, nucleonic measuring instrument, nucleonic measuring device, nucleonic device	kernphysikalisches Meßgerät n; kernelektronisches Meßgerät; kerntechnisches Gerät n, kerntechnisches Meßgerät
nuclear track, track in nuclear emulsion, [charged] nuclear particle track; track of the nucleus	Kernspur f, Spur f in der Kernemulsion, Emulsionsspur f		
		nucleonic isobar	s. isobar
nuclear track chamber (detector)	s. track detector	nucleonic measuring device	s. nucleonic measuring instrument
nuclear track photograph, track photograph	Kernspuraufnahme f, Spuraufnahme f	nucleonic measuring instrument	s. nucleonic instrument
		nucleonics	Nukleonik f, angewandte Kernphysik f ‹soweit sie die Labor- und Meßtechnik betrifft›
nuclear transformation, transformation [of nucleus], atomic transformation, nuclear transmutation, transmutation [of nucleus], atomic transmutation ‹nucl.›	Kernumwandlung f, Umwandlung f [des Atomkerns], Atomumwandlung f, Transmutation f ‹Kern.›		
		nucleon isobar	Nukleonenisobar n
		nucleon-meson coupling constant	Nukleon-Meson-Kopplungskonstante f
nuclear transformation probability, transmutation probability, transmutation rate ‹nucl.›	Umwandlungswahrscheinlichkeit f ‹Kern.›	nucleon moment	s. orbital angular momentum of the nucleon
		nucleon-nucleon collision, nucleon-nucleon encounter	Nukleon-Nukleon-Stoß m
nuclear transition	Kernübergang m	nucleon-nucleon interaction, interaction between nucleons	Nukleon-Nukleon-Wechselwirkung f
nuclear transmutation	s. nuclear transformation		
nuclear trial	s. atomic blast		
nuclear trunk	s. core of the nucleus	nucleon-nucleon scattering	Nukleon-Nukleon-Streuung f, Streuung f von Nukleonen an Nukleonen
nuclear volume effect	s. finite size effect		
nucleate boiling (bubbling)	s. bulk boiling		
nucleation, formation of nuclei	Keimbildung f, Bildung f von Keimen, Kernbildung f	nucleon-nucleus collision	Nukleon-Kern-Stoß m
		nucleon-nucleus scattering	Nukleon-Kern-Streuung f
nucleation and growth transformation, diffusional transformation, civilian transformation	diffusionsbedingte (diffusionsartig verlaufende) Umwandlung f, Umwandlung durch Keimbildung und Wachstum	nucleon number	s. mass number
		nucleon orbital angular momentum	s. orbital angular momentum of the nucleon
		nucleon shell	Nukleonenschale f
nucleation cavity	Keimhöhle f	nucleon spin, spin of the nucleon	Spin m des Nukleons, Nukleonspin m, Nukleonenspin m
nucleation of fracture, initiation of fracture	Einsetzen n des Bruchs		

nucleon star	s. evaporation star	**nucleus of the meteor,** meteor nucleus, nucleus	Kern m [des Meteors], Meteorkern m
nucleon vertex function	Eckenfunktion f der Nukleonen	**nucleus of the planetary nebula,** central star	Zentralstern m [des planetarischen Nebels]
nucleon width	Nukleonenbreite f	**nuclide,** nuclear species, atomic species, sort of atom	Nuklid n, Kernart f, Kernsorte f, Atomart f, Atomsorte f
nucleophilic, anionoid	nukleophil, kernsuchend, kernfreundlich, anionoid		
nucleophilic addition	nukleophile Addition f, anionoide Addition		
nucleophilic reactivity	Nukleophilität f, Nukleophilie f	**nuclide emitting soft radiation**	s. soft radiator
		nuclidic mass	Nuklidmasse f <Masse des neutralen Atoms in ME>
nucleophilic rearrangement, nucleophilic transposition	nukleophile Umlagerung f, anionoide Umlagerung	**nuisance area,** mush area	Störempfangsgebiet n
		nuisance parameter	lästiger Parameter m
nucleophilic series	Nukleophilitätsreihe f, Nukleophiliereihe f	**null,** zero <of function, curve>	Nullstelle f <Funktion, Kurve>
nucleophilic substitution	nukleophile Substitution f, anionoide Substitution	**null amplifier**	Nullverstärker m
nucleophilic transposition	s. nucleophilic rearrangement	**null-balance indicator**	s. null detector
		null balancing, zero balancing, zero balance	Nullabgleich m
nucleoplasm	Karyolymphe f, Nucleoplasma n, Kernplasma n, Enchylem n, Kernsaft m	**null cone,** light cone, light-cone <rel.>	Lichtkegel m, Kausalitätskegel m, Nullkegel m <Rel.>
nucleoproteide, nucleoprotein, nuclein	Nukleoproteid n, Nuklein n	**null detector,** null indicator, null-balance indicator; null instrument, balancing instrument, null-type meter, balance meter	Nullanzeiger m, Nullindikator m, Nulldetektor m; Nullinstrument n, Nullgerät n, Nullmesser m
nucleor, nucleon core, bare nucleon, core of the nucleon	Nukleor n, Nukleonenkern m, nacktes Nukleon n, innerster Bezirk m des Nukleons		
nucleosynthesis	s. nuclear fusion		
nucleotide sequence	Nukleotidsequenz f		
nucleus, atomic nucleus, nucleus of atom	Atomkern m, Kern m [des Atoms]	**null element,** zero [element] <math.>	Nullelement n, Null f <Math.>
nucleus, cometary nucleus, nucleus of the comet	Kern m [des Kometen], Kometenkern m	**null galvanometer**	Nullgalvanometer n
nucleus, meteor nucleus, nucleus of the meteor	Kern m [des Meteors], Meteorkern m	**null[-] geodesic**	Nullgeodätische f
nucleus, Fredholm kernel (nucleus), kernel	Fredholmscher Kern m	**null[-]gravity**	s. absence of gravity
		null hypothesis, nullhypothesis, hypothesis tested	Nullhypothese f
nucleus, nucleus of cell, cell nucleus <bio.>	Zellkern m, Kern m [der Zelle], Nukleus m, Nucleus m, Karyon n <Bio.>		
		null indicator (instrument)	s. null detector
nucleus, cycle, ring <chem.>	Ring m, Kern m, Zyklus m <Chem.>	**nullity** <math.>	Rangdefekt m, Rangabfall m, Nullität f, Defekt m <Math.>
nucleus <cryst.; therm.>; germ, complex <cryst.>	Keim m <Krist.; Therm.>; Kern m, Komplex m <Krist.>	**null line,** light line <rel.>	Nullinie f, Lichtlinie f, Kausalitätslinie f <Rel.>
nucleus at rest, stationary nucleus, static nucleus	ruhender Kern m, stationärer Kern	**null line [gap]**	s. origin of the band
		null matrix, zero matrix	Nullmatrix f
nucleus bond energy, nuclear binding energy	Bindungsenergie f des Atomkerns, Bindungsenergie des Kerns, Kernbindungsenergie f	**null method,** zero method, balancing method	Nullmethode f; Nullabgleichmethode f
nucleus-cytoplasm relation	Kern-Plasma-Relation f, Kern-Plasma-Verhältnis n		
		nullode	s. electrodeless ionic tube
		null of directivity pattern, antenna null	Nullstelle f der Richtcharakteristik
nucleus for the initiation of freezing, freezing nucleus	Gefrierkern m		
nucleus membrane	s. nuclear membrane		
nucleus-nucleus collision, collision of two nuclei	Kern-Kern-Stoß m	**null operator**	Nulloperator m
		null plane; datum plane (level), reference datum	Nullebene f; Bezugsebene f
nucleus of atom	s. atomic nucleus		
nucleus of cell	s. nucleus		
nucleus of condensation	s. condensation nucleus		
nucleus of crystal, nucleus of crystallization, crystal nucleus, embryo, centre of crystallization, crystallization centre	Kristallisationskeim m, Kristallkeim m; Embryo m, Kristallisationskern m, Kristallkern m; Kristallisationszentrum n	**null representation**	Nulldarstellung f
		null sequence	s. sequence tending to zero
		null set, set of measure zero, empty set	Nullmenge f, Menge f vom Maß Null
		null system, zero-system <math.>	Nullsystem n, Nullkorrelation f <Math.>
		null transformation	Nulltransformation f
nucleus of the comet, cometary nucleus, nucleus	Kern m [des Kometen], Kometenkern m	**null-type meter**	s. null detector
		null vector	s. zero vector <also rel.>
		number	s. atomic charge
nucleus of the galaxy	s. galactic nucleus	**number**	s. similarity parameter <therm.>

number average	Zahlenmittel *n*
number average molecular weight	Zahlenmittel *n* des Molekulargewichts
number axis	*s.* uniform scale
number characteristic, characteristic	Charakterzahl *f*
number density, number density of particles, number of particles per unit volume	Anzahldichte *f*, Teilchenanzahldichte *f*, Teilchenzahldichte *f*, Teilchendichte *f*, Partikeldichte *f*
number density of molecules, number of molecules per unit volume	Molekülanzahldichte *f*, Molekülzahldichte *f*
number density of particles	*s.* number density
number display tube	Zahlenanzeigeröhre *f*
number-distance curve	Anzahl-Abstand[s]-Kurve *f*
number generator	Zahlengeber *m*
number of alternations	Polwechselzahl *f*
number of alternations	*s. a.* number of cycles
number of ampere turns	*s.* number of turns <el.>
number of collisions, collision number	Stoßzahl *f*
number of collisions with the wall	Wandstoßzahl *f*
number of condensation nuclei	Kondensationskernzahl *f*, Kernzahl *f*
number of cycles, cycles per unit time; number of alternations	Wechselzahl *f*, Anzahl *f* der Wechsel, Wechsel *mpl*
number of cycles of load stressing, cycles of load stressing	Lastspielzahl *f*, Lastwechselzahl *f*, Lastspiele *npl*
number of cycles of overstress	Überlastungsspielzahl *f*
number of degrees of freedom	Anzahl *f* der Freiheitsgrade, Zahl *f* der Freiheitsgrade, Freiheitszahl *f*
number of degrees of freedom	*s. a.* degree of freedom
number of degrees of superheat	*s.* degree of superheating
number of drops	Tropfenzahl *f*
number of exceeding values	Überschreitungszahl *f*
number of exchanges	*s.* number of interchanges
number of grooves per unit length, number of rulings per unit length	Strichzahl *f* <Beugungsgitter>
number of interchanges, number of exchanges	Platzwechselzahl *f*
number of ionizations, ionization number	Ionisierungszahl *f*
number of meteors per hour, rate of shooting stars, hourly rate of meteors, frequency of meteors	Häufigkeit *f* der Meteore, Anzahl *f* der Meteore pro Stunde
number of molecules per unit volume, number density of molecules	Molekülanzahldichte *f*, Molekülzahldichte *f*
number of moles	Molzahl *f*, Molenzahl *f*
number of nearest neighbours	Anzahl (Zahl) *f* der nächsten Nachbarn
number of neighbours	Nachbarzahl *f*, Anzahl *f* der Nachbarn
number of neutrons per fission	*s.* neutron yield per fission
number of nuclei	Keimzahl *f*, Anzahl *f* der Keime, Kernzahl *f*
number of nuclei per unit volume	Anzahl *f* der Kerne pro Volum[en]einheit, Zahl *f* der Kerne pro Volum[en]einheit, Kernanzahldichte *f*
number of particles, particle number; particulate number <of aerosol>	Teilchenzahl *f*
number of particles per unit volume	*s.* number density
number of places	Stellenzahl *f*
number of practical plates, number of real plates	praktische Bodenzahl *f*
number of revolutions, number of turns	Umdrehungszahl *f*, Drehzahl *f*, Tourenzahl *f*, Umlaufzahl *f*
number of revolutions per minute	*s.* revolutions per minute
number of revolutions per unit time	*s.* speed
number of rulings per unit length, number of grooves per unit length	Strichzahl *f* <Beugungsgitter>
number of secondary turns	Sekundärwindungszahl *f*
number of stages [of separation]	Trennstufenzahl *f*
number of theoretical plates (trays), NTP	Zahl *f* der theoretischen Böden, [theoretische] Bodenzahl *f*, NTP-Wert *m*
number of transfer units, NTU	[theoretische] Austauschzahl *f*, NTU-Wert *m*
number of turns, number of revolutions	Umdrehungszahl *f*, Drehzahl *f*, Tourenzahl *f*, Umlaufzahl *f*
number of turns, index <of the curve>	Windungszahl *f*, Umlaufszahl *f*, Index *m* <Kurve>
number of turns, number of ampere turns, ampere turns <el.>	Windungszahl *f*, Anzahl *f* der Windungen, Amperewindungszahl *f*, Stromwindungszahl *f*, elektrische Durchflutung *f* <El.>
number of turns per unit length	Windungszahl *f* pro Längeneinheit, Windungszahldichte *f*, Windungsdichte *f*
number of turns per unit time	*s.* speed
number operator, numerical operator	Zahlenoperator *m*
number reflection build-up factor	Quantenreflexions-Aufbaufaktor *m*
number representation <num. math.>	Zahlendarstellung *f*, Zahldarstellung *f* <num. Math.>
number system, system of numbers, numeration	Zahlensystem *n*
number triple, triple of numbers	Zahlentripel *n*
numeration	*s.* number system
numerator [of the fraction]	Zähler *m* [des Bruches]
numerical aperture, N.A., NA	numerische Apertur *f*, Apertur
numerical axis	*s.* uniform scale
numerical check <num. math.>	Probe *f* <num. Math.>
numerical coefficient, numerical factor	Zahlenfaktor *m*
numerical constant	Zahlenkonstante *f*
numerical data, numerics	numerische Werte *mpl*, Zahlenwerte *mpl*, Zahlenangaben *fpl*
numerical display tube	Ziffernanzeigeröhre *f*
numerical distance	numerischer Abstand *m*, numerische Entfernung *f*
numerical example	Zahlenbeispiel *n*, numerisches Beispiel *n*
numerical factor, numerical coefficient	Zahlenfaktor *m*
numerical integration	numerische Integration *f*
numerical line	*s.* uniform scale
numerical measure, measure, coefficient of measure, numerical value	Zahlenwert *m*, Maßzahl *f*, numerischer Wert *m*
numerical operator, number operator	Zahlenoperator *m*
numerical value	*s.* numerical measure

numerics	s. numerical data	Nyquist flank	Nyquist-Flanke f
nunatak	Nunatak m <pl.: -takr, -takker>	**Nyquist['s] formula**, Nyquist['s] theorem	Nyquistsche Rauschformel (Formel) f, Nyquist-Formel f
Nusselt equation	Nußeltsche Gleichung f	**Nyquist frequency**, turnover frequency	Nyquist-Frequenz f
Nusselt group	s. Nusselt number	**Nyquist locus**	s. transfer locus
Nusselt-Kraussold relation	Nußelt-Kraussoldsche Beziehung f	**Nyquist-Michailov criterion [of stability]**	s. Nyquist['s] criterion
Nusselt No.	s. Nusselt number	**Nyquist plot**	s. transfer locus
Nusselt number, Nusselt No., Nusselt group, Biot modulus (number), Nu, Bi	Nußelt-Zahl f [erster (1.) Art], Nußeltsche Kennzahl f, Nußeltsche Zahl f, Biot-Zahl f, Biotsche Kennzahl f, Nu	**Nyquist['s] rule**	s. Nyquist['s] criterion
		Nyquist['s] theorem	s. Nyquist['s] formula
		nystagmus	Nystagmus m, Augenzittern n
Nusselt sphere	Nußeltsche Kugel f	**Nyström extrapolation**	Nyström-Extrapolation f
Nusselt['s] theory [of filmwise condensation]	Nußeltsche Wasserhauttheorie f, Wasserhauttheorie von Nußelt		
nutating-disk flowmeter, nutating-disk [fluid] meter	Scheiben[rad]zähler m; Scheibenmengenmesser m, Scheibenradmesser m		
nutation, nodding <astr.; mech.>	Nutation f; reguläre Präzession f, regelmäßige Präzession <Astr.; Mech.>; Nutationsbewegung f	**O**	
		Oakes-Yang's problem	Oakes-Yangsches Problem n
nutation <bio.>	Nutationsbewegung f, Wachstumsbewegung f <Bio.>	**O association**	O-Assoziation f
		Obach cell	Obach-Element n
nutational ellipse, nutation ellipse	Nutationsellipse f	**object**; target	Ziel n
nutation angle	Nutationswinkel m	**object** <gen., opt., bio.>; specimen <gen., especially in electron microscopy>	Objekt n <Allg., Opt., Bio.>; Gegenstand m, Ding n <Allg., Opt.>; Gesichtsobjekt n, Sehding n, Sehobjekt n <physiol. Opt.>
nutation cone	Nutationskegel m		
nutation constant, constant of nutation	Nutationskonstante f		
nutation ellipse, nutational ellipse	Nutationsellipse f	**object**, object-side, front <opt.>	dingseitig, objektseitig, gegenstandsseitig, Gegenstands-, Ding-, Objekt-, vorderer <Opt.>
nutation frequency, frequency of nutation	Nutationsfrequenz f		
nutation in longitude	Nutation f in Länge	**object airlock**, specimen airlock	Objektschleuse f
nutation in obliquity [of ecliptic]	Nutation f in Schiefe	**object damage**, specimen damage	Objektschaden m
nutrient, nutrient material	Nährgut n	**object distance** <from object principal point>	Dingweite f, Gegenstandsweite f, Objektweite f
nutrient [liquid]	s. a. nutrient solution		
nutrient material	s. nutrient		
nutrient solution, nutrient liquid, nutrient	Nährlösung f	**object distance**	s. a. target distance
		object distance from the vertex [of the lens], front vertex object distance, lens / object distance	Dingschnittweite f, dingseitige (objektseitige, vordere, gegenstandsseitige) Schnittweite f
nutsche [filter], nutsch filter	Nutsche f, Filternutsche f, Nutsch[en]filter n		
Nutting-Scott-Blair equation	Nutting-Scott-Blairsche Gleichung f		
nuvistor	Nuvistor m	**object field**	Dingfeld n, Objektfeld n
n value	s. field index	**object field of sight**, object field of view	Dingfeld n, dingseitiges Gesichtsfeld n, Eintrittssichtfeld n, Dingsichtfeld n
n-valued logic[al calculus]	n-wertige Logik f		
Nyberg-Luther colour solid	s. Luther-Nyberg colour solid	**object field stop**	Dingfeldblende f, Objektfeldblende f, Eintrittsblende f
nyctalopia	Nyktalopie f, Tagblindheit f, Nachtsichtigkeit f	**object focal length**, front focal length	Dingbrennweite f, dingseitige (objektseitige, gegenstandsseitige, vordere) Brennweite f, Objektbrennweite f, Gegenstandsbrennweite f
nyctonasty	Nyktonastie f, nyktonastische Bewegung f, Schlafbewegung f		
Nyquist-Cauchy criterion [of stability], generalized Nyquist-Cauchy criterion [of stability], stability criterion of Nyquist-Cauchy, generalized stability criterion of Nyquist-Cauchy	[verallgemeinertes] Nyquist-Cauchysches Stabilitätskriterium n, [verallgemeinertes] Stabilitätskriterium nach Nyquist-Cauchy, [verallgemeinertes] Nyquist-Cauchy-Stabilitätskriterium n, Nyquist-Cauchy-Kriterium n, Nyquist-Cauchysches Kriterium n, [verallgemeinertes] Kriterium von Nyquist-Cauchy	**object focus**, front focus, first focal point	Dingbrennpunkt m, dingseitiger (objektseitiger, vorderer) Brennpunkt m
		object for estimating visibility	Sichtziel n
		object fouling	Objektverschmutzung f
		object function <opt.>	Objektfunktion f <Opt.>
		object holder	s. slide
		objectifiability [in quantum mechanics]	Objektivierbarkeit f [in der Quantenmechanik]
Nyquist['s] criterion [for a control system], Nyquist['s] criterion of stability, stability criterion of Nyquist, Nyquist-Michailov criterion [of stability], stability criterion of Nyquist-Michailov, topographical criterion [for a control system], Nyquist rule	Nyquist[-Michajlow]sches Stabilitätskriterium (Kriterium) n, Stabilitätskriterium nach Nyquist, Nyquist[-Michajlow]-Stabilitätskriterium n, Nyquist[-Michajlow]-Kriterium n, Kriterium von Nyquist[-Michajlow], Nyquist[-Michajlow]-Bedingung f, Nyquist[-Michajlow]sche Stabilitätsbedingung, Nyquist-Effekt m, Stabilitätskriterium von Nyquist-Michajlow	**objective colorimeter**	s. photoelectric colorimeter
		objective colorimetry	s. photoelectric colorimetry
		objective doublet, doublet, doublet lens, doublet objective	Doppelobjektiv n, zweilinsiges Objektiv n, Zweilinsenobjektiv n, Zweilinser m
		objective function	Zielfunktion f
		objective glossmeter, photoelectric glossmeter	lichtelektrischer (photoelektrischer, objektiver) Glanzmesser m
		objective grating	Objektivgitter n
Nyquist filter	Nyquist-Filter n	**objective mirror**; primary mirror <of telescope>	Hauptspiegel m <Fernrohr>

objective photometer, photoelectric photometer	lichtelektrisches (photoelektrisches, objektives) Photometer n	oblique illumination	Schrägbeleuchtung f, schiefe (schräge) Beleuchtung f, Schräglichtbeleuchtung f, Schräglicht n
objective prism	Objektivprisma n	oblique illuminator	Schräg[licht]illuminator m, Schräglichtkondensor m
object[-] micrometer	Objektmikrometer n		
object-mount	s. slide	oblique impact	schiefer Stoß m
object nodal point, front nodal point	Dingknotenpunkt m, dingseitiger (objektseitiger, vorderer) Knotenpunkt m	oblique incidence	schräger (schiefer) Einfall m
		oblique observation	Schrägbeobachtung f
object plane, specimen plane	Dingebene f, Gegenstandsebene f, Objektebene f	oblique photography	Schrägaufnahme f
object point <opt.>	Dingpunkt m, Gegenstandspunkt m, Objektpunkt m <Opt.>		
		oblique plane, inclined plane	schiefe Ebene f
object principal plane, front principal plane	Dinghauptebene f, dingseitige (objektseitige, vordere) Hauptebene f	oblique position; tilt; obliquity	Schräglage f, schräge Lage f, Neigung f; Schiefstellung f; Schrägstellung f; Verkippung f
object principal point, front principal point	Dinghauptpunkt m, dingseitiger (objektseitiger, vorderer) Hauptpunkt m	oblique projection, inclined throw <mech.>	schiefer Wurf m <Mech.>
object ray, ray from object point	Dingstrahl m	oblique projection	s. a. skew projection
		oblique ray	s. skew ray
object-side	s. object <opt.>	oblique reflection technique	Schrägreflexionsverfahren n
object-side pupil	s. entrance pupil		
object size	Dinggröße f, Gegenstandsgröße f, Objektgröße f	oblique shock	schiefer Verdichtungsstoß m
		oblique stratification	Schrägschichtung f
object slide	s. slide	oblique visibility [distance]	Schrägsichtweite f, Schrägsicht f
object space	s. original space <math.>		
object space <opt.>	Dingraum m, Gegenstandsraum m, Objektraum m <Opt.>	obliquity; oblique position; tilt	Schräglage f, schräge Lage f, Neigung f; Schiefstellung f; Schrägstellung f; Verkippung f
object stage	s. stage	obliquity, tilt	Schiefe f, Schräge f
object to be measured, object under measurement (test), test object	Meßobjekt n, Meßling m; Prüfobjekt n, Prüfling m; Testobjekt n	obliquity factor	s. inclination factor
		obliquity of [the] ecliptic	Schiefe f der Ekliptik
object to be studied, object under investigation	Untersuchungsgegenstand m, Untersuchungsobjekt n	obliviator	s. influence function <gen., elasticity>
		oblong, prolate	verlängert, gestreckt; länglich
object under measurement (test)	s. object to be measured	oblong basin, prolate basin <geo.>	Wanne f <Geo.>
object vergence, front vergence	dingseitige (objektseitige) Vergenz f	O branch	O-Zweig m
oblate ellipsoid of revolution, oblate spheroid	abgeplattetes Rotationsellipsoid n	Obreimov-Shubnikov method	Obreimow-Schubnikow-Verfahren n, Methode f von Obreimow-Schubnikow
oblateness	s. flattening <quantity>		
oblateness of the Earth	s. flattening of the Earth	obscured glass	s. opal glass
oblate spheroid	s. oblate ellipsoid of revolution	obscure radiation, dark radiation	Dunkelstrahlung f
oblate spheroidal co-ordinates	abgeplattet-rotationselliptische Koordinaten fpl, Koordinaten des abgeplatteten Rotationsellipsoids	obsequent river	obsequenter Fluß m
		observability	Beobachtbarkeit f
		observable	Observable f, beobachtbare Größe f
		observance	Beachtung f, Befolgung f
oblique; inclined; skew; slant; angled	schräg; schief; verkantet	observational equation, observation equation	Fehlergleichung f, Verbesserungsgleichung f
oblique, oblique[-] angled	schiefwinklig	observation hole	s. observation port
oblique, slant, skew <opt.>	schräg einfallend, schräg, schief <Opt.>	observation port, observation hole, viewing window, eyehole, eye sight, eye, peephole, inspection hole	Beobachtungsfenster n; Beobachtungsöffnung f; Schauloch n; Schauöffnung f; Einblickfenster n
oblique aerial survey	Luftbild-Schrägaufnahme f		
oblique[-] angled	s. oblique		
oblique anode	Schräganode f		
oblique ascension, geocentric longitude	Schrägaszension f, geozentrische Länge f	observation telescope, scope	Beobachtungsfernrohr n, Betrachtungsfernrohr n
oblique bending	schiefe (schräge) Biegung f	observed threshold	beobachteter Schwellenwert m, empirische Schwelle f
oblique bundle, slant bundle	schiefes Bündel n		
oblique co-ordinates	schiefwinklige Koordinaten fpl	observer at rest, non-moving observer	ruhender Beobachter m
oblique cylinder	schiefer Zylinder m	observing slit [of the dome]	Kuppelspalt m
oblique fault, cross fault	Schrägverwerfung f, Diagonalverwerfung f		
oblique flow	Schräganströmung f	obstacle, obstruction	Hindernis n; Schrank f; Widerstand m
		obstacle cloud; orographic cloud	Hinderniswolke f; orographische Wolke f
oblique fold, asymmetric fold	schiefe Falte f	obstacle gain	Wellenverstärkung f am Hindernis, Hindernisverstärkung f

obstacle

obstacle wave; orographic wave	Hinderniswelle *f*; Hinderniswoge *f*; orographische Welle *f*	**ocean wave,** sea wave	Meereswelle *f*, Meereswoge *f*
obstruction; choking	Verstopfung *f* ‹auch Medizin›; Verschließung *f*; Stauung *f*	**ocellus**	Ocellus *m*, Ozelle *f*
		o-compound, ortho-compound, ortho-substitution compound	ortho-Verbindung *f*, Orthoverbindung *f*, o-Verbindung *f*
obstruction, obstacle	Hindernis *n*; Schrank *f*; Widerstand *m*	**ocosphere**	Okosphäre *f*
obtained by a parallel displacement	parallel verschoben parallel übertragen	**octad symmetry,** 8-al symmetry, symmetry of order eight (8)	achtzählige Symmetrie *f*, 8zählige Symmetrie
obtuse, obtuse-angled	stumpfwinklig		
obtuse bisectrix	stumpfe (zweite) Bisektrix *f*, stumpfe (zweite) Mittellinie *f*	**octahedral environment**	Oktaederumgebung *f*
		octahedral group	Oktaedergruppe *f*
Obukhoff['s] theory, theory of Obukhoff	Obuchowsche Theorie *f*, Theorie von Obuchow	**octahedral invariant**	Oktaederinvariante *f*
obversion ‹math.›	Umkehrung *f* ‹Math.›	**octahedral plane**	Oktaederebene *f*
O-carcinotron, O-type carcinotron, O-type backward wave tube	Carcinotron *n* vom O-Typ, O-Typ-Rückwärtswellenröhre *f*, Rückwärtswellenröhre *f* vom O-Typ	**octahedral shear stress**	oktaedrale Schubspannung *f*, Schubspannung in Oktaederfläche, Oktaeder[schub]spannung *f*
occasive amplitude, western amplitude	Abendweite *f*	**octahedral shear-stress law**	Oktaeder[schub]spannungsgesetz *n*
occluded gas	okkludiertes Gas *n*	**octahedral site**	s. B site
occluding cyclone	okkludierende Zyklone *f*	**octahedral symmetry**	Oktaedersymmetrie *f*
occlusion ‹also meteo.›	Okklusion *f* ‹auch Meteo.›	**octahedron**	Oktaeder *n*, Achtflächner *m*, Achtflach *n*
occlusion of cold front, cold front occluison	Kaltfrontokklusion *f*	**octahedron structure**	Oktaederstruktur *f*
occlusion of warm front, warm front occlusion	Warmfrontokklusion *f*	**octal representation**	oktale Darstellung *f*, Oktaldarstellung *f*
		octane level (number)	s. octane ratio
occultation ‹astr.›	Bedeckung *f*, Verfinsterung *f* durch ein Gestirn ‹Astr.›	**octane rating,** octane ratio, octane value, octane number, octane level	Oktanzahl *f*, Klopffestigkeitswert *m*, Klopffestigkeit[szahl] *f*, Klopfzahl *f*, Klopffestigkeitsgrad *m*, OZ
occultation of the star [by the Moon], lunar occultation	Sternbedeckung *f* [durch den Mond]		
occultation variable	s. eclipsing variable	**octantal, octantal error, octantal in form**	Oktantfehler *m*
occulting light	unterbrochenes Feuer *n*		
occupancy	s. degree of occupation	**octave analyzer (band filter),** octave filter	Oktavsieb *n*, Oktavbandpaß *m*, Oktavfilter *n*
occupancy probability, occupation probability	Besetzungswahrscheinlichkeit *f*		
occupied level	s. filled level	**octave-band [sound] pressure level,** octave pressure level	Schalldruckpegel *m* der Oktave
occupation	Besetzung *f*		
occupational exposure, occupational irradiation	berufliche Bestrahlung *f*, berufsbedingte Bestrahlung (Strahlenexponierung) *f*	**octave filter**	s. octave analyzer
		octave pressure level	s. octave-band sound pressure level
occupation function	Besetzungsfunktion *f*, Zustandsbesetzungsfunktion *f*	**octet**	Oktett *n*
		octet formula, electronic formula, polarity formula	Elektronenformel *f*
occupation number	Besetzungszahl *f*		
occupation probability, occupancy probability	Besetzungswahrscheinlichkeit *f*	**octet method**	s. eightfold way / the
		octet rule, rule of eight	Oktettregel *f*, Langmuirsche Oktettregel, Regel *f* der maximalen Bindigkeit
occupation rule	Besetzungsvorschrift *f*		
occupied area, occupied space	Strahlungsbereich *m*, in dem sich Personen aufhalten dürfen	**octet shell**	s. L-shell
		octet theory ‹of G. N. Lewis›	Okttheorie *f* [von G. N. Lewis]
occupied state	besetzter Zustand *m*		
occurence of fading, appearance of fading	Schwundeinbruch *m*	**octode,** eight-electrode (eight-element, six-grid) tube	Oktode *f*, Achtpolröhre *f*, Sechsgitterröhre *f*
ocean basin	Ozeanbecken *n*	**octopole**	s. octupole
ocean core	s. ocean floor	**octupole,** octopole ‹nucl.›	Oktupol *m*, Oktopol *m* ‹Kern.›
ocean current, oceanic current, marine current	Meeresströmung *f*	**octupole**	s. a. eight-terminal network ‹el.›
ocean floor, floor of ocean, sea floor; ocean core	Meeresboden *m*, Meeresgrund *m*	**octupole excitation**	Oktupolanregung *f*
		octupole field	Oktupolfeld *n*
oceanic climate, maritime climate, insular climate	Seeklima *n*, maritimes Klima *n*, ozeanisches Klima	**octupole moment**	Oktupolmoment *n*
		octupole radiation	Oktupolstrahlung *f*
oceanic current, ocean (marine) current	Meeresströmung *f*	**octupole transition**	Oktupolübergang *m*
		ocular, eyepiece lens, eyelens, eyeglass	Okularlinse *f*; Einblicklinse *f*, Auglinse *f*
ocean of air	Luftozean *m*, Luftmeer *n*		
oceanography; oceanology	Ozeanographie *f*, Meereskunde *f*; Meeresforschung *f*	**ocular estimate,** visual estimate	visuelle Schätzung *f*, Schätzung
		ocular filter, eyepiece filter	Okularsperrfilter *n*, Okularfilter *n*
ocean ridge	s. mid-ocean ridge		
ocean troposphere	Troposphäre *f* des Ozeans, ozeanische Troposphäre	**ocular prism,** prismatic eyepiece	Okularprisma *n*
		ocular spectroscope, eyepiece spectroscope, spectroscopic eyepiece	Okularspektroskop *n*
ocean trough	Ozeangraben *m*, Meeresgraben *m*		

odd-even nucleus, odd-even nuclide	ug-Kern m, Ungerade-gerade-Kern m, ug-Nuklid n, Ungerade-gerade-Nuklid n	ohm, Ω ohmad, British Association Unit, British Association ohm, B.A.U. < = 0.988 Ω>	Ohm n, Ω Ohmad n, British Association Unit f, B.A.U. < = 0,988 Ω>
odd-even rule of nuclear stability	Ungerade-gerade-Regel f der Kernstabilität	ohmage	Widerstand[swert] m in Ohm, Ohmwert m
odd-even spin	Spin m eines ug-Kerns, ug-Spin m	Ohmart cell	Ohmart-Zelle f
odd function	ungerade Funktion f	ohmic, resistive, resistance <el.>	ohmsch, ohmisch <El.>
odd molecule	ungerades Molekül n, Molekül mit ungerader Valenzelektronenzahl	ohmic branch ohmic bulk resistance	s. resistance branch ohmscher Bahnwiderstand m
odd nucleus	ungerader Kern m, Kern ungerader Massenzahl	ohmic component, active (resistive) component	Wirkstromkomponente f, ohmsche Komponente f
odd-odd nucleus, odd-odd nuclide	uu-Kern m, Ungerade-ungerade-Kern m, doppelt ungerader Kern m, uu-Nuklid n, Ungerade-ungerade-Nuklid n	ohmic component of the attenuation constant	Widerstandsdämpfung f
odd-odd spin	Spin m eines uu-Kerns, uu-Spin m		
odd parity, negative parity, parity − 1	ungerade Parität f, Parität − 1, negative Parität	ohmic contact, non-rectifying contact, low-resistance contact	ohmscher (sperrfreier, sperrschichtfreier) Kontakt m, Kleinwiderstandskontakt m
odometer	s. hodometer		
Odqvist['s] method	Odqvistsche Methode f	ohmic coupling	s. direct coupling <of circuit>
oedometer	Oedometer n		
oersted, Oe, O < = 79,577 A/m>	Oersted n, Oe < = 79,577 A/m>	ohmic drop [in potential], ohmic drop of voltage, ohmic potential drop, resistive drop [of voltage], resistive drop in potential	ohmscher Spannungsabfall m
oersted meter	Oerstedmesser m		
Oersted phenomenon	Oersted-Effekt m, Oersted-Phänomen n		
off-axis, abaxial	außeraxial		
off-centre collision (impact)	nichtzentraler Stoß m		
off condition	s. off state	ohmic heating, resistive heating, Joule heating <of plasma>	ohmsche Heizung (Aufheizung) f, Joule-Effekt-Aufheizung f, Joulesche Aufheizung, Widerstandsheizung f <Plasma>
off critical amount	Differenz f zur kritischen Masse		
off-diagonal element	s. non-diagonal element	ohmic load	s. active load
offense against the selection rule	s. violation of the selection rule	ohmic loss, resistance loss	ohmscher Verlust m
offense against the sine condition, OSC	Verletzung f (Abweichung f von) der Sinusbedingung		
off-line equipment	selbständige Einheit f, Peripherieeinheit f	ohmic overpotential; ohmic polarization, resistive polarization	Widerstandsüberspannung f; Widerstandspolarisation f
off-load voltage	s. electromotive force	ohmic potential drop	s. ohmic drop
off-period, cut-off time, switch-off period <semi.>	Sperrzeit f <Halb.>	ohmic resistance	ohmscher Widerstand m Gleichstromwiderstand m
off-position	Ausschaltstellung f, „Aus"-Stellung f	Ohm['s] law	[elektrisches] Ohmsches Gesetz n
off-position	s. a. rest position <e.g. of relay>	Ohm['s] law for magnetic circuits	s. Hopkinson['s] law
off-region	s. stop band	Ohm['s] law of acoustics	Ohmsches Gesetz n der Akustik, Ohmscher Satz m, akustisches Ohmsches Gesetz <für Schallschnelle oder Schallwellenwiderstand>
off-resonance attenuation	Verstimmungsdämpfung f		
off-resonance method, detuning method	Verstimmungsmethode f, Verstimmungsverfahren n		
offset, shift[ing], misalignment	Versetzung f, Verschiebung f, Versatz m	Ohm['s] law of hearing	Ohmsches Gesetz n der Akustik, Ohm-Helmholtzsches Gesetz
offset, position error <control>	P-Abweichung f, Proportionalabweichung f, statische Nachstellung f, bleibende Abweichung f <Regelung>	Ohm['s] law of light flux, Hansen['s] law	Ohmsches Gesetz n für den Lichtfluß, Hansensches Gesetz
		Ohm['s] law of magnetism	s. Hopkinson['s] law
offset current	Offsetstrom m, Eingangsnullstromabweichung f	oikocryst oil air pump	s. host crystal s. oil pump
off-shell particle	Teilchen n außerhalb der Massenschale, „off-shell"-Teilchen n	oil artificial horizon, oil horizon oil bath	Ölhorizont m Ölbad n
offshoot of the traverse, open (unclosed) traverse; spur of the traverse	offener Polygonzug m, offener Zug m	oil capacitor oil damping, dashpot dampening	Ölkondensator m Öldämpfung f
off-shore wind	s. land breeze		
off-spring, secondary [particle]	Sekundärteilchen n, Sekundäres n	oil diffusion pump	Öldiffusionspumpe f
off state, off condition, blocking state (condition)	Sperrzustand m, gesperrter Zustand m		
ogdohedry	Ogdoedrie f, Achtelflächigkeit f		
ogive, percentile curve; distribution curve, cumulative frequency curve	Verteilungskurve f, kumulative Verteilungskurve; Ogive f	oil-drop experiment [of Millikan] oiled paper, oil[]paper oil-filled	s. Millikan['s] experiment Ölpapier n s. oil-immersed <of instrument>
ogive <aero., hydr.>	Kopf m; Spitze f; Spitzbogen m <Aero., Hydr.>		
OH group, hydroxyl	Hydroxylgruppe f, OH-Gruppe f	oil film	Ölfilm m, dünne Ölschicht f

oil fog	s. oil mist	once-through cooling	Kühlung f mit einmaligem Kühlmitteldurchlauf, Durchlaufkühlung f
oil horizon, oil artificial horizon	Ölhorizont m		
oil-immersed, oil-filled <of instrument>	ölgefüllt, unter Öl, Öl- <Gerät>	once-through cooling [by pump]	Zwang[s]durchlaufkühlung f, Zwang[s]laufkühlung f
oil immersion	Ölimmersion f	oncotic pressure	s. colloid osmotic pressure
oiliness	Öligkeit f	ondograph	Ondograph m, Wellenschreiber m, Wellenlinienschreiber m
oil-in-water emulsion	Öl-in-Wasser-Emulsion f, O/W-Emulsion f		
oil manometer	s. oil pressure gauge	ondometer	s. wavemeter
oil mist, oil fog, airborne oil fog	Ölnebel m	ondoscope	s. oscillograph
		one-armed balance	einarmige Waage f
oil[]paper	s. oiled paper	one-armed lever	einarmiger Hebel m
oil pressure gauge, oil manometer	Ölmanometer n, Öldruckmesser m, Öldruckmanometer n	one-body model of nucleus, single-particle model, j-j coupling shell model	Einteilchen[-Schalen]-modell n, Schalenmodell n mit einfacher jj-Kopplung der äußeren Teilchen, Schalenmodell mit jj-Kopplung
oilproof seal	s. oil seal		
oil pump, oil vacuum pump, oil air pump	Ölluftpumpe f, Ölvakuumpumpe f, Ölpumpe f		
		one-body problem, single-body problem	Einkörperproblem n
oil seal, oilproof seal	Öldichtung f		
oil separator	Ölabscheider m	one-centre approximation	Einzentrennäherung f
		one-circle goniometer	Einkreisgoniometer n, Einkreis-Reflex[ions]-goniometer n, einkreisiges Goniometer n
oil test cell; test cell	Ölprüfgerät n, Ölprüfeinrichtung f; Gerät n für Durchschlagprüfungen an Flüssigkeiten		
		one-component system, unicomponent system, unitary (unary) system	Einstoffsystem n, unitäres (unäres) System n, Einkomponentensystem n
oil vacuum pump	s. oil pump		
oil vapour	Öldampf m		
oil vapour pump	Öldampfstrahlpumpe f	one-cycle engine	s. one-stroke engine
Okubo['s] formula	Formel f von Okubo, Okubosche Formel	one-determinantal wave function	Eindeterminanten-Wellenfunktion f
Olbers['] hypothetical planet	hypothetischer Planet m nach Olbers	one-dimensional	s. linear
		one-dimensional disorder, line defect	eindimensionale Fehlordnung (Fehlstelle) f
Olbers['] paradox	s. photometrical paradox		
older population I	Ältere Population f I	one-dimensional distribution	s. univariate distribution
		one-dimensional flow	Fadenströmung f
		one-dimensional motion, lineal motion	eindimensionale (lineale) Bewegung f
old nova	s. ex-nova		
old pack, hummocked ice, pack, pack-ice	Packeis n	one-domain particle, single-domain particle	Einbereichspartikel f, Einbereichsteilchen n, Eindomänenteilchen n
old quantum theory	s. quantum theory	one-domain size	Einbereichsgröße f
oleometer	Ölaräometer n, Oleometer n	one-electron approximation	Einelektronennäherung f, Einelektronnäherung f
oleorefractometer	Ölrefraktometer n	one-electron bond, single-electron bond, semivalence, semivalency	Einelektronbindung f, Einelektronenbindung f
oleosol	Oleosol n		
oligodynamic effect, oligodynamics	Oligodynamie f, oligodynamische Wirkung f		
		one-electron model	Einelektronenmodell n
oligomer, oligopolymer	Oligomer[e] n, Oligopolymer[e] n	one-electron orbital wave function	s. orbital
oligotrophic	oligotroph		
olive	Olive f	one-electron problem, single-electron problem	Einelektronenproblem n
Ollard test	Ollardsches Verfahren n, Ollard-Verfahren n, Ollard-Test m	one-electron spectrum	Einelektronenspektrum n
		one-electron state	Einelektronenzustand m
Ollendorf['s] formula	Formel f von Ollendorf, Ollendorfsche Formel	one-electron system, hydrogen-like system, lone electron	Ein[zel]elektronensystem n, wasserstoffähnliches System n
Olsen test <US>	s. Erichsen cupping test		
ombrogram, pluviogram	Pluviogramm n, Ombrogramm n, Niederschlagsdiagramm n, Niederschlagskurve f	one-electron term	Einelektronenterm m
		one-electron theory	Einelektronentheorie f
ombrograph	s. pluviograph	one-electron wave function associated with the electronic configurations	s. orbital
ombrography	s. pluviography		
ombrometer	s. rain gauge		
ombrometry	s. pluviometry		
omission	s. neglect	one-group approximation	Eingruppennäherung f
omnidirectional antenna, omnidirective antenna	Rundstrahler m, rundstrahlende Antenne f, Rundstrahlantenne f		
		one-group method	Eingruppenmethode f
		one-group model	Eingruppenmodell n
omnidirectional microphone	s. non-directional microphone	one-group theory	Eingruppentheorie f
		one-half period rectification	s. half-wave rectification
omnidirectional radiation	s. non-directed radiation		
		one-kick multivibrator	s. univibrator
omnidirective antenna	s. omnidirectional antenna	one-level approximation, single-level approximation	Einniveau[an]näherung f
on-and-off switch, two-position switch, two-way switch	Schalter m mit zwei Stellungen, Zweistellungsschalter m, Zweiweg[e]schalter m, Ein-Aus-Schalter m		
		one-level formula, single-level formula	Einniveauformel f, Einniveau-Resonanzformel f
once-through, once-through circulation <techn.>	Zwang[s]durchlauf m, Zwang[s]lauf m <Techn.>		
		one-meson approximation	Einmesonnäherung f

one-millimetre klystron, millimetre-wavelength klystron	Millimeterwellenklystron *n*	**one-to-one mapping,** one-to-one correspondence, one-one mapping, bi-unique mapping, (1,1) correspondence, bijection, bijective mapping	eineindeutige Abbildung (Zuordnung) *f,* umkehrbar eindeutige Abbildung (Zuordnung)
one-mode resonance system	Resonanzsystem *n* mit einer Schwingungsmode		
one-one mapping	*s.* one-to-one mapping	**one-valued function,** single-valued function	eindeutige Funktion *f*
one-over-Q value, 1/Q value, damping, degree of damping <El.>	Dämpfungsfaktor *m,* Dämpfungsgrad *m,* Dämpfung *f* <El.>	**one-velocity transport theory**	Eingeschwindigkeits-Transporttheorie *f*
one-over-v law, 1/v-law	Eins-durch-v-Gesetz *n,* 1/v-Gesetz *n*	**one-wattmeter method**	Einwattmetermethode *f*
one-parameter	einparametrig	**one-way stress**	*s.* pulsating stress
one-particle equation, single-particle equation	Einteilchengleichung *f*	**"onion" diagram,** Sanson['s] net	Sanson-Netz *n,* Sansonsches Netz *n*
one-particle Green['s] function, single-particle Green['s] function	Greensche Einteilchenfunktion *f,* Einteilchen-Green-Funktion *f*	**-onium compound**	Oniumverbindung *f,* -onium-Verbindung *f*
		on-line computer	*s.* process computer
one-particle state	Ein[zel]teilchenzustand *m*	**on-line equipment**	angeschlossene Einheit *f,* „on-line"-Einheit *f*
one-particle structure	Einteilchenstruktur *f*	**on line-isotope (mass) separator**	*s.* on-line separator
one-pass gain	Durchgangsverstärkung *f*	**on-line mass spectrometer**	„on-line"-Massenspektrometer *n*
one-phase region, homogeneous region	Einphasenbereich *m,* homogenes Gebiet *n*	**on-line method**	*s.* on-line technique
one-phase system, homogeneous (monophase) system	homogenes (einphasiges) System *n,* Einphasensystem *n*	**on-line separator,** on-line isotope (mass) separator	„on-line"-Massentrenner *m,* „on-line"-Separator *m*
		on-line technique, on-line method	„on-line"-Methode *f*
one-phonon interaction, single-phonon interaction	Einphononwechselwirkung *f*	**Onnes effect**	*s.* lambda leak
		Onnes temperature, temperature of the zero field transition	Onnes-Temperatur *f*
one-port, two-terminal network, one-port network, two-pole network	Zweipol *m*		
		on-off	„Ein" — „Aus"
one-port cavity maser, reflection-type cavity maser	Reflexionsmaser *m,* Einstrahlmaser *m*	**on-off control,** two-step action [control], two-step control, two-position action [control], two-position (two-state) control, bang-bang servo	Zweipunktregelung *f,* Zweistellungsregelung *f,* Schwarz-Weiß-Regelung *f,* Ein-Aus-Regelung *f*
one-port network	*s.* one-port		
one-quarter wave skirt, quarter-wave transformer	Viertelwellenumformer *m*		
one-region reactor, single region reactor	Einzonenreaktor *m,* Eingebietreaktor *m*	**on-off control[ler]**	*s.* two-step action control[ler]
		on-off switch, single-throw switch	Ein-Aus-Schalter *m*
one-shot [multivibrator]	*s.* univibrator	**on-position**	Einschaltstellung *f,* „Ein"-Stellung *f*
one-side coated, single-side coated	einseitig beschichtet		
one-sided surface, unilateral surface, non-orientable surface	einseitige Fläche *f,* nichtorientierbare Fläche *f*	**on-position** <of relay>	Arbeitsstellung *f,* „Ein"-Stellung *f* <Relais>
one-sided test, single-tailed test, single tail test	einseitiger Test *m*	**Onsager['s] approximation**	Onsagersche Näherung *f,* Onsager-Näherung *f*
		Onsager-Casimir equations, Onsager-Casimir [reciprocity] relations	Onsager-Casimirsche Reziprozitätsbeziehungen (Reziprozitätsrelationen) *fpl*
one-slot antenna	*s.* one-slot cylinder antenna		
one-slot cylinder antenna, one-slot antenna	Einschlitzstrahler *m*	**Onsager coefficient**	*s.* kinetic coefficient
		Onsager conductivity equation	*s.* Debye-Hückel equation
		Onsager['s] correction	Onsager-Korrektion *f,* Onsagersche Korrektion *f*
one-step photograph	Minutenphotographie *f,* Minutenaufnahme *f,* Polaroid-Land-Aufnahme *f*	**Onsager['s] coupling matrix,** Onsager['s] matrix	Onsagersche Kopplungsmatrix *f,* Onsager-Matrix *f*
		Onsager['s] equation	Onsager-Gleichung *f*
one-step photographic camera, Polaroid-Land camera, Polaroid camera, Land camera	Landsche Ein-Minuten-Kamera *f,* Polaroid-Land-Kamera *f,* Polaroid-Kamera *f*	**Onsager['s] equation** <for conductance>	Onsagersche Gleichung *f* <für den elektrischen Leitwert>
		Onsager['s] equation [for dielectric constant]	*s.* Onsager['s] formula <for the dielectric constant>
one-step photographic process, one-step photography, while-you-wait photography	Minutenphotographie *f,* Polaroid-Land-Verfahren *n,* Ein-Minuten-Photographie *f,* „one-step photographic process" *m,* Schnellphotographie *f*	**Onsager equations,** Onsager relations, [Onsager] reciprocity relations, Onsager['s] reciprocal relations, Onsager symmetry relations	Onsager-Beziehungen *fpl,* Onsagersche Reziprozitätsbeziehungen (Beziehungen, Symmetriebeziehungen, Reziprozitätsrelationen, Relationen) *fpl*
one-step reaction	*s.* simple reaction		
one-stroke cycle engine	*s.* one-stroke engine		
one-stroke engine, one-[stroke] cycle engine, single-stroke [cycle] engine, single-cycle engine	Eintaktmotor *m,* Eintaktmaschine *f,* Eintakter *m*	**Onsager['s] formula** <for the dielectric constant>, Onsager['s] equation [for dielectric constant]	Onsagersche Formel *f* <für die Dielektrizitätskonstante>
one-tenth-peak divergence (spread), tenth-peak divergence (spread)	Zehntelstreuwinkel *m*	**Onsager-Lagrange function**	Onsager-Lagrange-Funktion *f*
one-to-one correspondence	*s.* one-to-one mapping	**Onsager['s] matrix,** Onsager['s] coupling matrix	Onsagersche Kopplungsmatrix *f,* Onsager-Matrix *f*

Onsager['s] principle [of symmetry], Onsager['s] symmetry principle
Onsager['s] reaction field, reaction field
Onsager['s] reciprocal (reciprocity) relations
Onsager['s] reciprocity theorem, Onsager['s] theorem
Onsager relations
Onsager['s] spherical model
Onsager['s] symmetry principle, Onsager['s] principle [of symmetry]
Onsager symmetry relations
Onsager['s] theorem, Onsager['s] reciprocity theorem
onset of superfluidity, superfluidity onset
on-shore breakers, surf on shore, sea breaking on shore
on-shore wind, sea breeze, sea wind

oolitic
Oort constant

Oort rotation formulae

ooze, silt

oozing, seepage, trickling through
oozing away
opacimeter
opacity; impermeability to light; opaqueness; non-transparency, blackness
opacity <quantity>

opacity of stellar interior, stellar opacity

opacus cloud
opalescence; opalizing
opalescent glass

opal glas, milk (dull, bone, clouded, obscured, diffusing) glass
opalizing; opalescence
opal lamp
opaque; impermeable to light; non-transparent, not transparent
opaque cloud, opacus cloud
opaque colour
opaque illuminator
opaque medium, radiopaque medium

opaqueness
opaque pigment
open <el.>

open, non-closed

open, open-type <of instrument>

open air counter, free[-] air counter, open counter, free counter

open-air ionization chamber
open arc
open-band semiconductor

Onsagersches Reziprozitätsprinzip (Prinzip, Symmetrieprinzip) *n*
Reaktionsfeld *n* [von Onsager]
s. Onsager equations

Onsagerscher Reziprozitätssatz *m*

s. Onsager equations
Onsagersches sphärisches Modell *n*
Onsagersches Reziprozitätsprinzip (Prinzip, Symmetrieprinzip) *n*
s. Onsager equations

Onsagerscher Reziprozitätssatz *m*

Einsetzen *n* der Suprafluidität
Strandbrandung *f*

Seewind *m*

oolithisch
Oortsche Konstante *f*

Oortsche Rotationsformeln *fpl*

Schlick *m*

Durchsickern *n*, Eindringen *n*
s. infiltration
s. densitometer
Lichtundurchlässigkeit *f*, Undurchlässigkeit *f* für Licht; Undurchsichtigkeit *f*
Opazität *f*, reziproker Durchlaßgrad *m* <Größe>

Sternopazität *f*

s. opaque cloud
Opaleszenz *f*; Opalisieren *n*
mitteltrübes Glas *n*, Opaleszenzglas *n*, Opaleszentglas *n*
Trübglas *n*, Opalglas *n*, Opakglas *n*, Milchglas *n*

Opaleszenz *f*; Opalisieren *n*
Opallampe *f*
lichtundurchlässig, undurchlässig für Licht; opak; undurchsichtig, nicht durchsichtig
undurchsichtige Wolke *f*, Opacusform *f*
s. body colour
s. vertical illuminator
Kontrastmittel *n*, Röntgenkontrastmittel *n*

s. opacity
s. body colour
offen <El.>

offen, nichtgeschlossen; nichtabgeschlossen
offen <gegen zufällige Berührung nicht geschützt> <Gerät>
offenes Zählrohr *n*

s. free[-] air ionization chamber
s. open-flame arc
Offenbandhalbleiter *m*

open channel <hydr.>

open channel [of the reaction] <nucl.>

open circle, unshaded circle <in a figure>
open circuit, incomplete circuit <el.>

open circuit

open circuit / being on; open-circuit condition, (operation, function), no-load condition <el.>

open-circuit admittance, no-load admittance

open-circuit capacitance, no-load capacitance
open-circuit characteristic; no-load characteristic
open-circuit condition
open-circuit current, no-load current; idle current
open-circuited line
open-circuit electromotive force
open-circuit function
open-circuit gain; no-load gain

open-circuit impedance, no-load impedance, open-end impedance; blocked impedance

open-circuit inductance, no-load inductance
open-circuit input impedance, no-load input impedance

open-circuit operation
open-circuit output admittance, no-load output admittance

open-circuit output impedance, no-load output impedance

open-circuit photoelectromotive force
open-circuit photomagnetoelectric voltage
open-circuit photovoltage, open-circuit photoelectromotive force, open-circuit photo-e.m.f.

open-circuit potential
open-circuit resistance, no-load resistance

open-circuit reverse voltage transfer
open-circuit transfer impedance

offenes Gerinne *n*, offener Kanal *m* <Hydr.>
offener Kanal *m* [der Reaktion], offener Reaktionskanal *m* <Kern.>
heller Kreis *m*, offener Kreis <in der Abbildung>
offener Stromkreis *m*, offener Kreis *m* <El.>

s. a. open[-] jet wind tunnel <aero.>
Leerlauf *m*; Leerlaufzustand *m*; Leerlaufbedingung *f* <El.>

Leerlaufleitwert *m*, Leerlaufadmittanz *f*, Leeradmittanz *f*
Leerkapazität *f*, Leerlaufkapazität *f*

Leerlaufcharakteristik *f*, Leerlaufkennlinie *f*

s. open circuit / being on
Leerlaufstrom *m*; Leerstrom *m*

leerlaufende Leitung *f*
s. open-circuit voltage

s. open circuit / being on
Leerlaufverstärkung *f*; Leerlaufverstärkungsfaktor *m*

Leerlaufimpedanz *f*, Leerlauf-Scheinwiderstand *m*, Leerlaufwiderstand *m*

Leerlaufinduktivität *f*, Leerinduktivität *f*
Leerlauf-Eingangswiderstand *m*

s. open circuit / being on
Leerlauf-Ausgangsleitwert *m*

Leerlauf-Ausgangswiderstand *m*

s. open-circuit photovoltage
photomagnetoelektrische Leerlaufspannung *f*
Leerlaufspannung *f* des Photoelements, Leerlauf-Photo-EMK *f*, Leerlauf-Photospannung *f*

s. open-circuit voltage
Leerlaufwirkwiderstand *m*, Leerlaufwiderstand *m*

Leerlauf-Spannungsrückwirkung *f*
Leerlauf-Kernwiderstand *m*

open-circuit transfer voltage ratio	Leerlauf-Spannungsübertragungsfaktor *m* rückwärts	**open manometer**, open gauge, open liquid manometer	offenes Flüssigkeitsmanometer *n*, offenes Manometer *n*
open-circuit voltage, open-circuit electromotive force, open-circuit e.m.f., open-circuit potential; no-load voltage	Leerlaufspannung *f*, Leerlauf-EMK *f*; Urspannung *f*, eingeprägte Spannung *f*, Leerlaufspannung des Generators	**open model [of the universe]**, open universe	offene Welt *f*, offenes Modell (Weltmodell) *n*
open-circuit voltage	s. a. electromotive force	**open phase**	offene (nichtabgeschlossene) Phase *f*
open cluster, open star cluster	offener Sternhaufen *m*	**open pipe**	offene Pfeife *f*
open counter, free[-] air counter, open air counter, free counter	offenes Zählrohr *n*	**open position**	s. vacant site
		open sector, sector aperture	Hellsektor *m*
open crystal form, open form	offene Form *f*	**open set**	offene Menge *f*
open end barometer, baroscope	Baroskop *n*	**open shade**, shade	Schatten *m*
open-end impedance	s. open-circuit impedance	**open star cluster**, open cluster	offener Sternhaufen *m*
open fault	s. disjunctive fault		
open-flame arc, open arc	offener (nackter) Lichtbogen *m*	**open system equilibrium**	s. flux equilibrium
open form	s. open crystal form	**open-throat wind tunnel**	s. open[-] jet wind tunnel <aero.>
open gauge, open manometer, open liquid manometer	offenes Flüssigkeitsmanometer *n*, offenes Manometer *n*	**open traverse**, unclosed traverse; spur (offshoot) of the traverse	offener Polygonzug *m*,.; offener Zug *m*
		open-type, open <of instrument>	offen <gegen zufällige Berührung nicht geschützt> <Gerät>
opening; orifice; hole; gap; port [hole]	Öffnung *f*; Loch *n*; Kanalmündung *f*, Kanalöffnung *f*, Kanal *m*; · Durchführung *f*	**open universe**, open model [of the universe]	offene Welt *f*, offenes Modell *n*, offenes Weltmodell *n*
opening, break	Öffnen *n*	**open wind tunnel**	s. open[-] jet wind tunnel <aero.>
opening <mech.>	Öffnung *f* <Mech.>	**open wire**, overhead conductor, overhead wire	Freileiter *m*
opening	s. a. gap		
opening area of the valve, valve [opening] area	[freier] Ventilquerschnitt *m*, Ventilöffnungsquerschnitt *m*	**opera glass[es]**	Opernglas *n*, Theaterglas *n*
opening current	s. break current	**operand**	Rechengröße *f*, Operand *m*
opening of the ring	s. ring cleavage		
opening of the valve, valve opening	Ventilöffnung *f*	**operating characteristic**, working characteristic, performance characteristic	Betriebskennlinie *f*, Betriebscharakteristik *f*
opening period, time of partial shutter opening <phot.>	Öffnungszeit *f* <Phot.>	**operating characteristic** <num. math.>	Operationscharakteristik *f*, O-C-Funktion *f* <num. Math.>
opening pulse	s. gating pulse	**operating characteristics**	s. operating parameters
opening spark	s. break spark	**operating coil**	s. magnet coil
opening time, contact opening time; contact time; clearing time <el.>	Ausschaltverzögerung *f*, Ausschaltverzug *m*, Öffnungszeit *f* <El.>	**operating contact**	s. make contact
		operating current, running (working) current	Betriebsstrom *m*, Arbeitsstrom *m*
		operating curve	s. dynamic characteristic
		operating data	s. operating parameters
		operating line	s. dynamic characteristic
		operating mode	s. mode of operation <of apparatus, instrument>
opening time, break time <el.>	Öffnungszeitpunkt *m* <El.>	**operating parameters**, operating characteristics, operating data, technical data	technische Daten *pl*, Betriebsdaten *pl*
open interval <math.>	offenes Intervall *n* <Math.>		
open jet, free jet, jet flow; stream[ ]flow	freier Strahl *m*, Freistrahl *m*, Strahlströmung *f*, Strahlausfluß *m*	**operating point**, working point	Arbeitspunkt *m*
open[-] jet wind tunnel, free[-] jet wind tunnel; free flight wind tunnel, open[-throat] wind tunnel, wind tunnel with open working section, open circuit <aero.>	Windkanal *m* mit freier Meßstrecke, Windkanal mit freiem Strahl, Freistrahlwindkanal *m*, offener Windtunnel *m* (Windkanal) <Aero.>	**operating temperature**	s. working temperature
		operating time <of relay>	Schaltzeit *f* <Relais>
		operating time	s. a. time of operation <of relay>
		operating voltage	s. burning voltage <of discharge, arc>
		operating winding operation	s. magnet winding Betrieb *m*
open liquid manometer	s. open gauge	**operation**, mathematical operation <math.>	Operation *f*, Rechenoperation *f* <Math.>
open-loop stable	stabil bei offenem Regelkreis		
open-loop transfer function, transfer function of the open-loop system	Übertragungsfunktion *f* des aufgeschnittenen (offenen) Regelsystems (Übertragungssystems, Systems, Regelkreises), Übertragungsfunktion der offenen Kette	**operation**	s. a. handling <gen.>
		operation	s. a. composition <math.>
		operational amplifier, computing amplifier	Funktionsverstärker *m*, Operationsverstärker *m*, Rechenverstärker *m*
		operational calculus	s. operator calculus

operational

operational element	Funktionselement n	opposed	s. opposite
operational research	s. operations research	opposer ion, counterion, gegenion	Gegenion n
operation of switch	s. switching <el.>	opposing connection, series-opposed (series-opposing) connection, series opposition	Gegenreihenschaltung f, Gegen[einander]-schaltung f, Gegensinnreihenschaltung f
operations analysis	s. operations research		
operations research, operations analysis <US>, operational research	mathematische Planungsforschung f, [betriebswirtschaftliche] Operationsforschung f, Unternehmensforschung f, „operations research" n	opposing field, counter field	Gegenfeld n
		opposing fields method, method of opposing fields	Gegenfeldmethode f
operator <math.>	Operator m <Math.>	opposing reaction, gegenreaction, counter reaction	Gegenreaktion f
operator	s. a. operator gene <bio.>		
operator	s. a. quantifier	opposite, of opposite polarity (sign), having opposite polarity (sign), opposed, unlike, dissimilar	ungleichnamig, ungleicher Polarität, ungleichen Vorzeichens
operator calculus, operational calculus, Heaviside [operational] calculus	[Heavisidesche] Operatorenrechnung f, Operatorenkalkül m, Heaviside-Kalkül m		
operator equation, functional equation	Operatorgleichung f, Funktionsgleichung f	opposite	s. a. antiparallel
		opposite and equal	s. same magnitude / of the
		opposite component, counter component	Gegenkomponente f <Nulleitersystem>; gegenläufige Komponente f
operator function, operator-valued function	Operatorfunktion f		
operator gene, operator <bio.>	Operatorgen n, Operator m <Bio.>	opposite direction / of, opposite in direction, oppositely directed	s. antiparallel
operator isomorphism	Operatorisomorphie f, Operatorisomorphismus m	opposite moment of couple	s. opposite torque
operator of antineutrino, antineutrino operator	Antineutrinooperator m, Operator m des Antineutrinos	opposite phase, antiphase, reversed phase	Gegenphase f
operator of charge density, charge density operator	Ladungsdichteoperator m		
operator of current density, current density operator	Stromdichteoperator m	opposite polarity / having (of), opposite sign / having (of)	s. opposite
operator of force, force operator	Kraftoperator m, Operator m der Kraft	opposite torque, opposite moment of couple, counter-torque	Gegendrehmoment n
operator of increase, growth (increase) operator	Zuwachsoperator m	opposition <astr.>	Opposition f, Gegenschein m
operator of neutrino, neutrino operator	Neutrinooperator m, Operator m des Neutrinos	opposition, opposition of phase, phase opposition, opposition shift	180°-Phasenverschiebung f, Phasenverschiebung um 180°, Phasenopposition f, entgegengesetzte Phasenlage f
operator of nuclear spin, nuclear spin operator	Kernspinoperator m, Operator m des Kernspins		
operator of orbital angular momentum, orbital angular momentum operator	Bahndrehimpulsoperator m		
		opposition / in	s. antiphase
		opposition impedance	s. negative sequence impedance
operator of particle number, particle number operator	Teilchenzahloperator m	opposition in right ascension	Opposition f in Rektaszension
operator of rest energy, rest energy operator	Ruhenergieoperator m, Ruheenergieoperator m	opposition method	Gegenschaltungsmethode f, halbpotentiometrische Schaltung (Methode) f
operator of time reversal, time reversal operator	Operator m der (für die) Zeitumkehr, Zeitumkehroperator m		
operator of total angular momentum, total angular momentum operator	Gesamtdrehimpulsoperator m, Operator m des Gesamtdrehimpulses	opposition of phase, opposition shift	s. opposition
		O-P process	s. Oppenheimer-Phillips process
operator of velocity, velocity operator	Geschwindigkeitsoperator m, Operator m der Geschwindigkeit	optic-acoustic effect	s. optico-acoustic phenomenon
operator-valued distribution	Operatordistribution f	optical activity, rotatory polarization, rotary polarization, opticity	optische Aktivität f, optisches Drehvermögen n, Rotationspolarisation f, Drehung f der Polarisationsebene (Schwingungsebene), optische Drehung, Drehvermögen n, Gyration f
operator-valued function, operator function	Operatorfunktion f		
operator wave function	Operatorwellenfunktion f	optical analysis of gas mixtures, optical gas analysis	optische Gasanalyse f (Analyse f von Gasgemischen)
operon	Operon n		
ophthalmic lens	s. spectacle lens	optical antimer (antipode)	s. enantiomer
ophthalmometer	Ophthalmometer n		
ophthalmoscope	Augenspiegel m, Ophthalmoskop n	optical axial plane	s. optic axial plane
		optical axis	optische Achse f
ophthalmoscopy	Ophthalmoskopie f, Augenspiegeln n	optical axis of eye	Augenachse f, optische Achse f des Auges
o-position, ortho-position	ortho-Stellung f, o-Stellung f	optical axis of the lens, axis of the lens	Linsenachse f, optische Achse f der Linse
Oppenheimer-Phillips process (relation), O-P process	Oppenheimer-Phillips-Prozeß m	optical balance, optical compensation	optischer Ausgleich m, optische Kompensation f
„opponent" theory of colour vision, Hering['s] theory [of colour vision]	[Heringsche] Gegenfarbentheorie f, Heringsche Vierfarbentheorie f, Vierfarbentheorie [von Hering]	optical bearing, optical direction finding	Sichtpeilverfahren n
		optical bench	optische Bank f
		optical binary, optical double star	optischer Doppelstern m

optical branch <of the elastic spectrum>	optischer Zweig m [des elastischen Spektrums]	**optical electron** **optical emptiness,** optical voidness, optical purity	s. luminous electron optische Reinheit f, optische Leere f
optical branch of lattice vibrations, optical lattice vibration	optische Gitterschwingung f, optischer Zweig m der Gitterschwingungen	**optical exaltation,** exaltation of molecular refraction	Exaltation f der Molekularrefraktion
optical brightener, brightener	optischer Aufheller m, optisches Bleichmittel n, Weißtöner m, „brightener" m	**optical exposure meter** **optical extensometer,** optical type extensometer	optischer Belichtungsmesser m optischer Dehnungsmesser m, optisches Dilatometer n
optical calculation	Optikrechnen n, optisches Rechnen n	**optical extent** **optical extinction,** extinction, optical density, absorbance, absorbancy	s. optical flux dekadische Extinktion f, optische Dichte f, spektrales Absorptionsmaß n
optical camera length, optical length of camera	optische Kameralänge f, optische Länge f der Kamera		
optical centre	optischer Mittelpunkt m; Sehzentrum n, optisches Zentrum (Wahrnehmungszentrum) n, Sehsphäre f	**optical filter,** light filter, filter	Lichtfilter n, [optisches] Filter n; Lichtdrossel f
		optical flat, plane parallel glass, plane glass, sheet of glass	planparallele Platte (Glasplatte) f, Planparallelplatte f, Plan[parallel]glas n, Planglasplatte f
optical centre of the lens, lens centre	Linsenmittelpunkt m, optischer Mittelpunkt m der Linse		
optical centring device **optical character**	s. optical plummet optischer Charakter m	**optical flux,** optical extent, light conductance	optischer Fluß m, Lichtleitwert m
optical chart **optical colouration**	s. optical test chart optische Färbung f, Kontrastfarbenbeleuchtung f	**optical foam** **optical gas analysis,** optical analysis of gas mixtures	optischer Schaum m optische Gasanalyse f, optische Analyse f von Gasgemischen
optical comparator	optischer Komparator m; [optisches] Längenmeßgerät n	**optical illusion,** pseudopsy	geometrisch-optische Wahrnehmungsverzerrung f, [geometrisch-] optische Täuschung f
optical compensation, optical balance	optischer Ausgleich m, optische Kompensation f		
optical compensator, compensator <opt.>	Kompensator m, optischer Kompensator <Opt.>	**optical image;** optical picture; optical mapping **optical indicatrix** **optical inversion system,** [image] erecting system, inversion system	optisches Bild n; optische Abbildung f s. index ellipsoid Umkehrsystem n, Bildaufrichtungssystem n, Aufrichtungssystem n
optical conductivity	optische Leitfähigkeit f		
optical constant **optical contact** **optical contrast** **optical coupling;** coupling medium, optical contact	optische Konstante f s. optical coupling optischer Kontrast m optischer Kontakt m; optisches Kontaktmittel n		
		optical isolator **optical isomer[ide]** **optical isomerism,** enantiomorphism, mirror-symmetric isomerism <chem.>	optischer Isolator m s. enantiomer Spiegelbildisomerie f, optische Isomerie f, Enantiomorphie f <Chem.>
optical density, density, blackening, blacking, photographic transmission density, transmission [optical] density <phot.>	[photographische] Schwärzung f, Filmschwärzung f, [optische] Dichte f, Deckung f <Phot.>		
		optical lattice vibration, optical branch of lattice vibrations	optische Gitterschwingung f, optischer Zweig m der Gitterschwingungen
optical density **optical density in reflected light**	s. a. optical extinction Aufsichtschwärzung f, Aufsichtdichte f		
optical depth **optical depth** **optical diminution,** diminution, diminishing, [optical] reduction	optische Tiefe f s. a. optical thickness Verkleinerung f, optische Verkleinerung <Opt.>	**optical law of refraction** **optical length** **optical length of camera,** optical camera length	s. Snell['s] law s. optical distance optische Kameralänge f, optische Länge f der Kamera
		optical length of ray **optical length of tube,** optical tube length	s. optical distance optische Tubuslänge f
optical direction finder	Sichtpeilgerät n, Sichtpeilanlage f, Sichtfunkpeiler m, Sichtpeiler m	**optical lever,** optimeter, refractionometer **optical lever** **optical levitation**	Optimeter n, optischer Fühlhebel m s. a. Kerr cell optisches Schweben n, optische Levitation f
optical direction finding, optical bearing	Sichtpeilverfahren n		
		optical libration, geometric libration	optische Libration f, geometrische Libration <Mond>
optical direct viewfinder, Newton['s] [view]finder	Linsendurchsichtsucher m, Newton-Sucher m, Galilei-Sucher m		
optical dissociation **optical distance,** optical length [of ray], optical path length, optical path, light path	optische Dissoziation f optische (reduzierte) Weglänge f, Lichtweg m, optischer (reduzierter) Weg m; Charakteristik f <in der geometrischen Optik>	**optically active electron** **optically empty,** optically void (pure) **optically flat,** flat, [optically] plane <opt.> **optically flat surface,** plane surface <opt.>	s. luminous electron optisch rein, optisch leer optisch eben, eben, optisch flach, flach <Opt.> Planfläche f <Opt.>
		optically inactive, inactive <opt.> **optically negative**	optisch inaktiv, inaktiv <Opt.> optisch negativ
optical distance **optical distance meter** **optical dividing head**	s. a. visibility s. rangefinder optischer Teilkopf m		
		optically neutral illumination, [physically] neutral illumination	neutrale Beleuchtung f, optisch (physikalisch) neutrale Beleuchtung
optical Doppler effect, Doppler effect in optics	optischer Doppler-Effekt m, Doppler-Effekt in der Optik		
optical double star, optical binary	optischer Doppelstern m	**optically plane,** optically flat, flat, plane <opt.>	optisch eben, eben, optisch flach, flach <Opt.>
optical doublet	optisches Dublett n, Doppellinie f		
optical eclipse **optical efficiency [of radiation]**	optische Finsternis f optischer Nutzeffekt m [einer Strahlung], optischer Wirkungsgrad m, Lichtwirkungsgrad m	**optically positive**	optisch positiv
		optically pure **optically uniaxial,** uniaxial	s. optically void optisch einachsig, einachsig
		optically void, optically empty, optically pure	optisch rein, optisch leer

optical magnification	s. magnification	optical scanning system	Abtastoptik f
optical magnon	optisches Magnon n		
optical mapping; optical image; optical picture	optisches Bild n; optische Abbildung f	optical sight	s. sighting telescope
		optical signal; luminous signal; light	Lichtsignal n, optisches Signal n
optical maser	s. laser	optical siren	optische Sirene f, Lichtsirene f
optical maser amplifier	s. laser amplifier		
optical-mechanical	optisch-mechanisch	optical slide rule, variopter	optischer Rechenstab m, Variopter m
optical micrometer, [optical type of] micrometer <opt.>	optisches Mikrometer n, Mikrometer <Opt.>	optical sound technique	Lichttonverfahren n
optical microscope, light microscope	Lichtmikroskop n, optisches Mikroskop n	optical sound track; optical sound tracking	Lichttonaufzeichnung f; Lichttonspur f
optical microscopy, light microscopy	Lichtmikroskopie f, optische Mikroskopie f	optical spectrograph, light spectrograph	Lichtspektrograph m, optischer Spektrograph m
optical mode	optischer Schwingungstyp (Wellentyp, Schwingungsfreiheitsgrad) m, optische Schwingungsart (Mode) f	optical spectrography, light spectrography	Lichtspektrographie f, optische Spektrographie f
optical model <of particle scattering>, optical model of nucleus	s. semi-transparent model of nucleus	optical spectrometer, optical spectroscope, light spectrometer (spectroscope)	Lichtspektrometer n, Lichtspektroskop n, optisches Spektrometer (Spektroskop) n
optical multiplication	optische Vervielfachung f [von Meßstrecken]	optical spectrometry, optical spectroscopy, light spectroscopy (spectrometry)	Lichtspektroskopie f, Lichtspektrometrie f, optische Spektroskopie (Spektrometrie) f
optical neutrality, physical neutrality	optische Neutralität f, physikalische Neutralität	optical spectrum, visible (luminous, light) spectrum	Lichtspektrum n, sichtbares (optisches) Spektrum n
optical nucleon, luminous nucleon, emitting nucleon	Leuchtnukleon n	optical square, square	Winkelinstrument n; Rechtwinkelinstrument n <für 90°>; Flachwinkelinstrument n <für 180°>; Winkelkreuz n
optical output ratio	optischer Wirkungsgrad m		
optical parallax	optische Parallaxe f; Einstellparallaxe f; Ableseparallaxe f	optical stimulation, photostimulation	Photoausleuchtung f, optische Ausleuchtung f
		optical stimulus	s. light stimulus
optical path [length], optical distance, optical length [of ray], light path	optische (reduzierte) Weglänge f, Lichtweg m, optischer (reduzierter) Weg m; Charakteristik f <in der geometrischen Optik>	optical system; optics	optisches System n; Optik f
		optical system for the projection, optical system of projection	s. projection optics
optical pattern	s. light band	optical system of the Schmidt telescope	s. Schmidt['s] optical system
optical phonon	optisches Gitterschwingungsquant (Phonon) n	optical telemeter, telemeter, [optical] rangefinder, [optical] distance meter	[optischer] Entfernungsmesser m, Distanzmesser m, Telemeter n; Abstandsmesser m
optical picture; optical image; optical mapping	optisches Bild n; optische Abbildung f		
optical plummet, optical centring device	optisches Lot n; optische Zentriervorrichtung f; Firstabloter m	optical telephone	optisches Telephon n, Lichttelephon n
		optical test	Sehprobe f
		optical test chart, optical test plate, optical chart, test chart, proof plate	Sehprobentafel f, Testplatte f, Testtafel f
optical pointer	s. light-beam pointer		
optical pointer instrument	s. instrument with optical pointer		
optical potential	s. complex potential of the optical model	optical test object	s. optotype
		optical test plate	s. optical test chart
optical printing <phot.>	Umkopieren n <Phot.>	optical theorem	optischer Satz m, optisches Theorem n
optical pumping	optisches Pumpen n	optical thickness, optical depth	optische Dicke f
		optical transfer function	s. contrast transmission function
optical purity	s. optical voidness	optical tube length, optical length of tube	optische Tubuslänge f
optical pyrometer	s. radiation pyrometer		
optical quantum gyroscope, laser rotation rate sensor	Lasergyrometer n	optical type extensometer, optical extensometer	optischer Dehnungsmesser m, optisches Dilatometer n
optical quenching	optische Tilgung f, Phototilgung f; optische Auslöschung (Löschung) f, Photo[aus]löschung f	optical type of micrometer, [optical] micrometer <opt.>	optisches Mikrometer n, Mikrometer <Opt.>
		optical variable [star]	optischer Veränderlicher m
optical radar	s. laser radar		
optical radial table	optischer Rundtisch m	optical voidness, optical emptiness, optical purity	optische Reinheit f, optische Leere f
optical range	s. visibility	optical wedge, wedge [interferometer] <opt.>	Keil m, optischer Keil <Opt.>
optical rangefinder	s. optical telemeter		
optical record	s. photographic recording	optical window [in Earth's atmosphere]	optisches Fenster n
optical recording, light-beam recording	Licht[strahl]registrierung f, Lichtschrift f	optic angle	s. angle of sight
		optic [axial] angle, axial angle	[optischer] Achsenwinkel m, wahrer Achsenwinkel
optical reduction	s. optical diminution		
optical resonator	s. Fabry-Pérot resonator	optic axial plane, axial plane, plane of optic[al] axes	Achsenebene f, optische Achsenebene
optical rotary dispersion	s. rotary dispersion		
optical rotatory power, rotatory power, specific rotatory power, specific rotation <quantity>	spezifische Drehung f [der Polarisationsebene], optisches Drehvermögen n, Drehvermögen <Größe>	optic axis (binormal)	s. primary optic axis
		optic biradial	s. secondary optic axis
		opticity	s. optical activity

optic nerve, nervus opticus	Sehnerv *m*, Nervus *m* opticus, Fasciculus *m* opticus	orbital, peripheral <nucl.>, extranuclear <bio., nucl.>	extranuklear, Hüllen-, Bahn-, kernfern <Kern.>; extranuklear, extranukleär <Bio.>
optico-acoustic gas analysis	optisch-akustische Gasanalyse *f*	orbital angular momentum of the nucleon, nucleon orbital angular momentum, nucleon moment	Bahndrehimpuls *m* des Nukleons, Bahnimpuls *m* (Moment *n*) des Nukleons, Nukleonmoment *n*, Nukleonenmoment *n*
optico-acoustic phenomenon, optic-acoustic (Tyndall-Röntgen) effect	optisch-akustische Erscheinung *f*, optisch-akustischer Effekt *m*, Tyndall-Röntgen-Effekt *m*		
optics	*s.* optical system	orbital angular momentum, orbital moment [of momentum], orbital momentum	Bahndrehimpuls *m*, Bahnmoment *n*, Bahnimpuls *m*
optics of crystalline lattice, lattice optics	Gitteroptik *f*		
optics of metals, metallo-optics	Metalloptik *f*	orbital angular momentum operator, operator of orbital angular momentum	Bahndrehimpulsoperator *m*
optics of moving media	Optik *f* bewegter Medien (Körper)		
optics of polarized light, polarization optics	Polarisationsoptik *f*	orbital angular momentum vector	Bahndrehimpulsvektor *m*
optics of the sea, marine optics	Meeresoptik *f*	orbital degeneracy, orbital degeneration	Bahnentartung *f*
optimal code, optimum code	Optimalcode *m*, Optimalkode *m*	orbital diamagnetism	Bahndiamagnetismus *m*
optimal colour	Optimalfarbe *f*		
optimalizing control	*s.* pick-holding control	orbital electron, planetary electron, extranuclear electron	Hüllenelektron *n*, Bahnelektron *n*
optimally coded programme, optimum programme	optimales Programm *n*, Schnellprogramm *n*, Bestzeitprogramm *n*		
optimeter, optical lever, refractionometer	Optimeter *n*, optischer Fühlhebel *m* <zur Längenmessung>	orbital-electron capture, electron capture [decay], E capture [decay], ε, EC	E-Einfang *m*, Elektroneneinfang *m*, Einfang *m* eines Hüllenelektrons, Bahnelektroneneinfang *m*, ε
optimization, optimizing	Optimierung *f*		
optimizing control	*s.* pick-holding control	orbital element, element of the orbit	Bahnelement *n*
optimum, optimum value	Optimalwert *m*, Optimum *n*, Bestwert *m*, günstigster Wert *m*	orbital ellipse, Keplerian ellipse	Kepler-Ellipse *f*
optimum code	*s.* optimal code	orbital equation, orbit equation	Bahngleichung *f*
optimum control	Optimalregelung *f*, optimale Regelung *f*; optimale Steuerung *f*	orbital magnetic moment	magnetisches Bahnmoment *n*, bahnmagnetisches Moment *n*, Bahnmagnetismus *m*
optimum control	*s. a.* pick-holding control		
optimum coupling, critical coupling	kritische Kopplung *f*	orbital moment [of momentum], orbital momentum, orbital angular momentum	Bahndrehimpuls *m*, Bahnmoment *n*, Bahnimpuls *m*
optimum estimator	optimale Schätzung *f*		
optimum programme, optimally coded programme	optimales Programm *n*, Schnellprogramm *n*, Bestzeitprogramm *n*	orbital motion (movement)	*s.* orbiting
optimum transfer function	Standardübertragungsfunktion *f*, optimale Übertragungsfunktion *f*, SÜF	orbital oscillation	Bahnoszillation *f*, Oszillation *f* um die mittlere Bahn
optimum value, optimum	Optimalwert *m*, Optimum *n*, Bestwert *m*, günstigster Wert *m*	orbital paramagnetism	Bahnparamagnetismus *m*
optional quenching circuit	einstellbare Löschschaltung *f*, wählbarer Löschkreis *m*	orbital path	*s.* orbit
		orbital period, period, period of revolution, time of one revolution <astr.>	Umlaufzeit *f*, Umlaufzeit *f*, Umlauf[s]dauer *f*, Umlauf[s]periode *f* <Astr.>
opto-electronic amplifier	optoelektronischer Verstärker *m*		
opto-electronics	Optoelektronik *f*, Optronik *f* <Licht-Elektronen-Wechselwirkung in Festkörpern>	orbital plane, orbit plane, plane of the orbit, plane of motion	Bahnebene *f*
		orbital quantum number	*s.* secondary quantum number
opto-electronic transducer	optoelektronischer Wandler *m*	orbital rocket, orbiting rocket	in eine Umlaufbahn gebrachte Sonde *f*, orbitale Sonde, orbitale Rakete *f*
optogram	Optogramm *n*		
optokinesis	Optokinese *f*		
opto-mechanical analogy	optisch-mechanische (optomechanische) Analogie *f*	orbital stability, orbit stability, stability of the orbit	orbitale Stabilität *f*, Bahnstabilität *f*
optometry, refractionometry	Optometrie *f*		
optotype, [optical] test object, identifiable design <opt.>	Sehzeichen *n*, Optotype *f*; Testobjekt *n* <Opt.>	orbital velocity; path velocity, velocity of motion along the path, velocity of flight	Bahngeschwindigkeit *f*
orange heat	Orangeglut *f*	orbital velocity	erste kosmische Geschwindigkeit[sstufe] *f*, Kreisbahngeschwindigkeit *f*, Orbitalgeschwindigkeit *f*
orange peel model	Apfelsinenschalenmodell *n*		
orbiform curve	Orbiforme *f*, ebener Körper *m* konstanter Breite, Gleichdick *n*, gleichdicke Kurve *f*	orbital wave function	Bahnwellenfunktion *f*
		orbit circumference, circumference of orbit, path length, length of path	Bahnlänge *f*, Bahnumfang *m*
orbit, orbital path	Umlaufbahn *f*, [geschlossene] Bahn *f*, Orbit *m* <um einen Zentralkörper>	orbit contractor, particle-orbit contractor	Teilchenbahnkontraktor *m*, Bahnkontraktor *m*
orbit	*s. a.* circular path	orbit equation	*s.* orbital equation
orbital, one-electron orbital wave function, one-electron wave function associated with the electronic configurations	Orbital *n* (*m*), Einzelelektronenzustand *m*; Einelektronen-Wellenfunktion *f*	orbit expander, particle-orbit expander	Teilchenbahndehner *m*, Bahndehner *m*, Teilchenbahnexpander *m*, Bahnexpander *m*

orbiting

orbiting, orbital motion, orbital movement, revolutionary motion, rotary motion	Bahnbewegung f; Umlauf[s]bewegung f, Bahnumlauf m, Kreisen n, orbitale Bewegung f <um einen Zentralkörper>; Kreisbahnbewegung f, Orbitalbewegung f <z. B. von Flüssigkeitsteilchen in Wasserwellen>
orbiting	s. a. revolution <around, round>
orbiting rocket, orbital rocket	in eine Umlaufbahn gebrachte Sonde f, orbitale Sonde (Rakete) f
orbiting the Moon	Mondumlauf m, Bahnumlauf m um den Mond, Umfliegen n des Mondes in einer geschlossenen Bahn, Umkreisen n des Mondes
orbit of planet, planetary orbit	Planetenbahn f
orbit-orbit interaction	Bahn-Bahn-Wechselwirkung f
orbit plane, plane of the orbit, orbital plane, plane of motion	Bahnebene f
orbit shift coils, deflector coils <acc.>	Ablenkspulen fpl <Beschl.>
orbit-spin coupling	s. spin-orbit coupling
orbit stability	s. orbital stability
order, order of magnitude; tenth power, power of ten	Größenordnung f; Zehnerpotenz f
order, order of spectrum, order of diffraction	Beugungsordnung f, Gitterordnung f, Ordnungszahl f [des Spektrums], Ordnung f des Beugungsspektrums (Spektrums)
order, rank, degree, valence <of tensor>	Stufe f <Tensor>, Tensorstufe f
order, instruction <num. math.>	Befehl m <num. Math.>
order	s. a. ordering <math.>
order	s. a. order of sequence
order / in the, in the order of, order-of-magnitude	größenordnungsmäßig, in der Größenordnung [von]
order-disorder phenomenon	Fernordnungserscheinung f, Ordnungs-Unordnungs-Erscheinung f
order-disorder transformation, order-disorder transition, phenomenon of melting, melting phenomenon	Ordnungs-Unordnungs-Umwandlung f, Ordnungs-Unordnungs-Übergang m, Übergang m vom Ordnungs-Unordnungs-Typ, Schmelzerscheinung f
ordered alloy	geordnete Legierung f
ordered by increasing ...	geordnet nach wachsendem ...
ordered scattering	s. Bragg scattering
ordered set, linearly ordered set <math.>	[einfach-]geordnete Menge f, k-geordnete (kettenmäßig geordnete, strenggeordnete, strikt geordnete, linear geordnete) Menge, Kette f, linearer Verband (Verein) m <Math.>
ordered set	s. a. partially ordered set <math.>
ordered solid solution	geordneter Mischkristall m
ordering, linear (total, complete, simple) ordering, order <math.>	[einfache] Ordnung f, lineare (totale, vollständige, konnexe, kettenmäßige) Ordnung, k-Ordnung f, Anordnung f <Math.>
ordering domain, ordering region	Ordnungsdomäne f, Ordnungsbereich m, Ordnungsgebiet n
ordering energy	Ordnungsenergie f
ordering phenomenon	Ordnungserscheinung f
ordering region	s. ordering domain
order in the condition of Lipschitz, Hölder index	Hölder-Exponent m, [Hölderscher] Exponent m
order of accuracy, degree of accuracy (precision)	Genauigkeitsgrad m
order of chemical reaction, order of reaction, reaction order	Reaktionsordnung f, Ordnung f der Reaktion
order of diffraction	s. order
order of forbiddenness, degree of forbiddenness	Grad m des Verbots, Verbotenheitsgrad m, Verbotenheitsfaktor m, Ordnung f des Verbots
order of interference	Ordnung f der Interferenz, Ordnungszahl f der Interferenz
order of levels	s. order of terms
order of magnitude, order; tenth power, power of ten	Größenordnung f; Zehnerpotenz f
order-of-magnitude, in the order [of]	größenordnungsmäßig, in der Größenordnung [von]
order of reaction, order of chemical reaction, reaction order	Reaktionsordnung f, Ordnung f der Reaktion
order of reflection, reflection order	Reflexionsordnung f, Ordnung f der Reflexion
order of sequence; order; sequence; succession	Reihenfolge f; Folge f; Ordnung f; Anordnung f
order of spectrum	s. order
order of superposition, stratigraphic sequence	Schicht[en]folge f, Schichtenkomplex m, Schichtengruppe f, Schichtenreihe f, Schichtserie f, Schichtensystem n
order of symmetry [of the axis]	s. degree of the axis <cryst.>
order of terms, term order, order of levels, level order	Termordnung f
order of the bond, bond order	Bindungsordnung f, Ordnung f der Bindung
order of the discontinuity	s. discontinuity order
order of the function	s. growth <of the function>
order of the pole	Polordnung f
order parameter	Ordnungsparameter m
order relaxation, Zener relaxation	Ordnungsrelaxation f, Zener-Relaxation f
order state, state of order	Ordnungszustand m
order statistic	Ranggröße f
order statistics	Ordnungsstatistik f
order test; non-parametric test, distribution[-]free test	verteilungsfreier (nichtparametrischer, parameterfreier) Test m; Anordnungstest m
ordinal number	s. atomic charge <nucl.>
ordinary bond	s. single bond
ordinary case, normal case, fundamental case	Normalfall m
ordinary component of double refraction	s. ordinary ray
ordinary differential equation	gewöhnliche Differentialgleichung f
ordinary diffusion	gewöhnliche Diffusion f
ordinary discontinuity	s. jump <math.>
ordinary finite difference method	gewöhnliches Differenzenverfahren n
ordinary force, Wigner force	Wigner-Kraft f, Wignersche Kraft f
ordinary graph	s. non-oriented graph
ordinary Hall coefficient	ordentlicher Hall-Koeffizient m
ordinary hydrogen, natural hydrogen	gewöhnlicher (natürlicher) Wasserstoff m
ordinary link[age]	s. single bond
ordinary ray, normal ray; ordinary wave; ordinary component of double refraction	ordentlicher (ordinärer) Strahl m; ordentliche (ordinäre) Welle f; ordentliche (ordinäre) Komponente f der Doppelbrechung
ordinary system, ordinary thermodynamic system	gewöhnliches [thermodynamisches] System n
ordinary temperature, room temperature, normal room temperature	Raumtemperatur f, Zimmertemperatur f
ordinary thermodynamic system	s. ordinary system

ordinary velocity of wave, ordinary wave velocity	ordentliche (ordinäre) Wellengeschwindigkeit *f*	oriented	orientiert; ausgerichtet; vorzugsgerichtet
ordinary water, natural water, light water	gewöhnliches (natürliches, leichtes) Wasser *n*	oriented circle <math.>	gerichteter (orientierter) Kreis *m*, Zykel *m* <Math.>
ordinary water level, ordinary water stage <hydr.>	gewöhnlicher Wasserstand *m*, Zentralwert *m*, ZW <Hydr.>	oriented crystal growth	*s.* epitaxy
		oriented graph	*s.* directed graph
		oriented [over]growth	*s.* epitaxy
ordinary wave	*s.* ordinary ray	orienting, orientation <geo.>	Orientierung *f* <Geo.>
ordinary wave velocity, ordinary velocity of wave	ordentliche (ordinäre) Wellengeschwindigkeit *f*	orienting compasses	Orientier[ungs]bussole *f*, Orientierungskompaß *m*
ordo-symbol	Landau-Symbol *n*, Landausches Symbol <O oder o>	orientometer	Orientometer *n*
Orear region [of momentum transfer]	Orearsches Gebiet *n*	orifice; opening; hole; gap; port [hole]	Öffnung *f*; Loch *n*; Kanalmündung *f*, Kanalöffnung *f*, Kanal *m*; Durchführung *f*
oreometry, orometry	Orometrie *f*		
organ dose	Organdosis *f*		
organic correlation	organische Korrelation *f*	orifice, mouth; muzzle	Mündung *f*
organic glass	organisches Glas *n* <Handelsnamen: Plexiglas, Lucit, Perspex, Pontalit, Diakon usw.>	orifice plate, plate orifice [meter], static plate	Meßblende *f*, Durchflußmeßblende *f*, Normblende *f*, Drosselscheibe *f*, Stauscheibe *f*, Blen-de[nscheibe] *f*, Staurand [-Strömungsmesser] *m*, Staudruckströmungsmesser *m*
organic moderator	organischer Moderator *m*, organische Bremsflüssigkeit *f*		
organic phosphor, organophosphor	Organophosphor *m*, organischer Leuchtstoff *m*	orificing	Drosselung *f*
organic regression	organische Regression *f*	origin, origination, source; parentage	Ursprung *m*, Entstehung *f*, Bildung *f*; Herkunft *f*, Zustandekommen *n*
organic scintillating solution	flüssiger organischer Szintillator *m*, organische Szintillationslösung *f*	origin, initial point; starting point <e.g. of the motion>; point of emergency	Anfangspunkt *m*, Ausgangspunkt *m*
organ of equilibrium	Gleichgewichtsorgan *n*		
organ of sight (vision), visual (light sense) organ	Sehorgan *n*, Lichtsinnesorgan *n*		
organogel	Organogel *n* (*m*)	origin, focus, hearth, seat [of origin], centre <geo., meteo.>	Herd *m* <Geo., Meteo.>
organometallic compound, metallo-organic compound, metalorganic compound	metallorganische Verbindung *f*, Metallorganyl *n*, Organometallverbindung *f*	origin	*s. a.* origin of co-ordinates
		origin	*s. a.* point of action
		original, original function, superior function, determining function; inverse transform	Oberfunktion *f*, Originalfunktion *f*, Stammfunktion *f*, Objektfunktion *f*, determinierende Funktion *f*; Rücktransformierte *f*
organophosphor, organic phosphor	Organophosphor *m*, organischer Leuchtstoff *m*		
organosol	Organosol *n*		
orientability	Orientierbarkeit *f*	original fission	Primärspaltung *f*, Erstspaltung *f*
orientable surface, two-sided surface	zweiseitige Fläche *f*, orientierbare Fläche		
orientation, orienting <geo.>	Orientierung *f* <Geo.>	original function	*s.* original
		original ion pair, primary ion pair, initial ion pair	primäres Ionenpaar *n*
orientation <math.>	Orientierung *f* <Math.>	original nucleus	*s.* parent nuclide
orientation; alignment <phys., chem.>	Orientierung *f*; Ausrichtung *f* <Phys., Chem.>	original particle	*s.* primary particle
		original rock	*s.* primary rock
orientational polarizability	*s.* orientation polarization	original space, superior space, object space <math.>	Objektbereich *m*, Objektraum *m*, Oberbereich *m*, Originalbereich *m*, Originalraum *m* <Math.>
orientation birefringence, orientation double refraction	Orientierungsdoppelbrechung *f*		
orientation disorder	Orientierungsunordnung *f*	origination, origin, source; parentage	Ursprung *m*, Entstehung *f*, Bildung *f*; Herkunft *f*, Zustandekommen *n*
orientation double refraction	*s.* orientation birefringence	origin distortion	*s.* zero variation
orientation effect	Orientierungseffekt *m*, Einfluß *m* der Orientierung	origin of co-ordinates, origin	Koordinatenursprung *m*, Anfangspunkt (Nullpunkt) *m* des Koordinatensystems, Koordinatenanfang[spunkt] *m*, Koordinatennullpunkt *m*
orientation factor	Orientierungsfaktor *m*		
orientation-imperfect crystal	Orientierungsfehlkristall *m*		
orientation movement <bio.>	Einstellbewegung *f* <Bio.>	origin of the band, band origin; zero line, null line; zero (null) line gap	Nullinie *f*; Nullücke *f* <Opt.>
orientation of the cut, cut orientation	Schnittlage *f*		
orientation of the screw, screw orientation, direction of the screw, screw direction, direction of screwing, screw[-]sense, screw sense, helicity	Schraubensinn *m*, Schraubungssinn *m*	origin of the force	*s.* point of action
		origin of the wave, wave centre, centre of the wave	Wellenzentrum *n*
		origin of turbulence, transition to turbulence	Turbulenzentstehung *f*
orientation ordering	Orientierungsordnung *f*	Orion[-type] star, Orion variable [star]	Orionveränderlicher *m*
orientation polarization, molecular polarization, orientational polarizability	Orientierungspolarisation *f*	Orlich bridge	Orlich-Brücke *f*
		ornithopter	Schlagflügelflugzeug *n*
		Ornstein and Zernike's integral equation	Ornstein-Zernikesche Integralgleichung *f*
orientation polymorphism	Orientierungspolymorphie *f*	Ornstein-Uhlenbeck process	Ornstein-Uhlenbeck-Prozeß *m*
orientation quantum number	Orientierungsquantenzahl *f*	orogen	Orogen *n*
orientation relation	Orientierungsbeziehung *f*	orogenesis, mountain-building, mountainous formation, orogeny; revolution	Orogenese *f*, Gebirgsbildung *f*; Umwälzung *f*
orientation triangle	Orientierungsdreieck *n*		

orogenesis

orogenesis, tectogenesis orogenic thrust	Tektogenese f, Orogenese f Gebirgsschub m
orogeny	Orogenie f
orogeny	s. a. orogenesis
orographic cloud; obstacle cloud	Hinderniswolke f; orographische Wolke f
orographic downward wind, downslope (forced downward) wind	Hangabwind m, Fallwind m
orographic effect of the wind	s. orographic wind effect
orographic elevation	orographische Hebung f
orographic isobar	orographische Isobare f
orographic obstacle	orographisches Hindernis n
orographic precipitation, orographic rainfall	orographischer Niederschlag (Regen) m, Geländeregen m; Steigungsregen m; Stauungsregen m
orographic snow[-]line	s. snow[-]line
orographic upward	s. up-stream
orographic upward wind, hillside upcurrent, forced upward wind	Hangaufwind m, Hangwind m
orographic wave; obstacle wave	Hinderniswelle f; Hinderniswoge f; orographische Welle f
orographic wind effect, orographic effect of the wind	orographischer Windeffekt m
orometry, oreometry	Orometrie f
O-R potential	s. oxidation-reduction potential
O-R process	s. oxidation-reduction process
orrery, planetarium	Planetarium n
Orr-Sommerfeld disturbance (perturbation) equation, Orr-Sommerfeld['s] equation, stability equation of Orr and Sommerfeld	Orr-Sommerfeldsche Störungsgleichung f, Orr-Sommerfeldsche Gleichung f
Orsat apparatus	Orsat-Apparat m
Orsat pipette	Orsat-Pipette f
orthicon [tube], [C.P.S.] emitron	Orthikon n, Emitron n
ortho axis, orthodiagonal axis	Orthoachse f, Orthodiagonale f
orthobaric density	orthobare Dichte f
orthobaric line	orthobare Kurve f, Orthobare f
orthobaric liquid, saturated liquid, liquid at its bubble point	orthobare Flüssigkeit f
orthobaric volume	orthobares Volumen n
orthochromatism	Orthochromasie f
orthochronous Lorentz group, full Lorentz group	orthochrone (volle, vollständige) Lorentz-Gruppe f
orthocomplement, orthogonal complement	orthogonales Komplement n
ortho-compound, orthosubstitution compound, o-compound	ortho-Verbindung f, Orthoverbindung f, o-Verbindung f
orthodiagonal axis, ortho axis	Orthoachse f, Orthodiagonale f
orthodiagraphy, orthoradioscopy	Orthoröntgenoskopie f, Orthodiagraphie f
orthodrome, great circle line	Orthodrome f, Großkreisbogen m
orthodromic projection	s. gnomonic projection
orthogeosyncline	Orthogeosynklinale f
orthogeotropism	Orthogeotropismus m
orthogonal	orthogonal, sich rechtwinklig schneidend, senkrecht aufeinanderstehend
orthogonal complement, orthocomplement	orthogonales Komplement n
orthogonal co-ordinates	rechtwinklige (orthogonale) Koordinaten fpl, Orthogonalkoordinaten fpl
orthogonal co-ordinate system, orthogonal system [of co-ordinates], orthogonal set [of co-ordinates]	rechtwinkliges Koordinatensystem n, orthogonales Koordinatensystem, Orthogonalsystem n
orthogonal curvilinear co-ordinates, curvilinear orthogonal co-ordinates	krummlinige Orthogonalkoordinaten fpl, orthogonale krummlinige Koordinaten fpl
orthogonal expansion, expansion in an orthogonal series	Orthogonalentwicklung f, Entwicklung f in eine Orthogonalreihe
orthogonal families of curves	orthogonale Kurvenscharen fpl
orthogonal group	s. full orthogonal group
orthogonal Hermite polynomial	s. Hermite polynomial
orthogonality	s. perpendicularity
orthogonality of error method	Fehlerorthogonalitätsmethode f
orthogonality relation	Orthogonalitätsrelation f, Orthogonalitätsbeziehung
orthogonalization and normalization	s. orthonormalization
orthogonalized plane wave, O.P.W.	orthogonalisierte ebene Welle f, OPW, OEW
orthogonal linear transformation, orthogonal mapping	s. orthogonal transformation
orthogonal matrix	orthogonale (orthonormierte) Matrix f
orthogonal normalized system	s. orthonormal system
orthogonal projection, orthographic projection	rechtschnittige (orthogonale, normale) Projektion f, rechtschnittiger [kartographischer] Entwurf m, Orthogonalprojektion f, Normalprojektion f
orthogonal set [of co-ordinates]	s. orthogonal co-ordinate system
orthogonal stochastic process	orthogonaler Prozeß m <Stat.>
orthogonal system [of co-ordinates]	s. orthogonal co-ordinate system
orthogonal trajectory	orthogonale Trajektorie f, Orthogonaltrajektorie f
orthogonal trajectory co-ordinates, normal co-ordinates	Normalkoordinaten fpl, Hauptkoordinaten fpl, Rayleighsche Koordinaten fpl
orthogonal transformation, orthogonal linear transformation, congruent transformation, orthogonal mapping	orthogonale Transformation f, orthogonale Abbildung f
orthographic projection	orthographische Projektion f, Parallelprojektion f der Erde
orthographic projection	s. a. orthogonal projection
orthoheliotropism	Orthoheliotropismus m
ortho[-]hydrogen, ortho hydrogen	Orthowasserstoff m, o[rtho]-Wasserstoff m
orthokinetic coagulation	orthokinetische Koagulation f
orthometamorphic rock, orthorock	Orthogestein n
orthometric correction	orthometrische Verbesserung f
orthometric height	s. height above sea level
orthomorphic	orthomorph, raumrichtig, tautomorph
orthomorphic projection	s. conformal projection
orthonormality	Orthonormiertheit f, Orthonormalität f
orthonormalization, orthogonalization and normalization	Orthonormierung f, Orthogonalisierung f und Normierung f
orthonormal system, orthogonal normalized system, normalized orthogonal system	Orthonormalsystem n, normiertes Orthogonalsystem n
orthonormal wave function	orthonormierte Wellenfunktion f
ortho-para conversion	Ortho-Para-Umwandlung f
ortho-para equilibrium	Ortho-Para-Gleichgewicht n
ortho-para ratio	Ortho-Para-Verhältnis n
orthopolar method	Orthopolarenverfahren n
ortho-position, o-position	ortho-Stellung f, o-Stellung f
ortho[-]positronium, triplet positronium	Orthopositronium n
orthoradioscopy, orthodiagraphy	Orthoröntgenoskopie f, Orthodiagraphie f
orthorhombic crystal system	s. rhombic crystal system
orthorhombic hemimorphy	s. hemimorphic hemihedry of the orthorhombic system

orthorhombic holohedry, holohedry of the orthorhombic system, holohedral class of the rhombic system, di-digonal equatorial class, bipyramidal (normal) class

orthorhombische Holoedrie f, rhombische Holoedrie, rhombisch-bipyramidale Klasse f, bipyramidale Klasse, rhombisch-dipyramidale Klasse

orthorhombic system s. rhombic crystal system
orthorock, orthometamorphic rock Orthogestein n
orthoscopic, free from distortion, rectilinear verzeichnungsfrei, rektolinear, orthoskopisch, tiefenrichtig

ortho-state, ortho state Orthozustand m
orthostatic orthostatisch
orthostigmat Orthostigmat n
ortho-substitution compound, ortho-compound, o-compound ortho-Verbindung f, Orthoverbindung f, o-Verbindung f
ortho term Orthoterm m
orthotomic orthotom
orthotomy, property of being orthotomic Orthotomie f
orthotropic plate orthotrope Platte f
orthotropism, orthotropy Orthotropie f
ortive amplitude, eastern amplitude Morgenweite f
Orton cone <US> s. pyrometric cone
O/R value, reduction oxidation index, oxidation-reduction index (value) Redoxindex m, O/R-Wert m

osar s. eskar
osar centre Oskern m, Oszentrum n
oscillating arc schwingender Lichtbogen m
oscillating circuit, oscillating electronic circuit, oscillator[y] circuit, oscillator [tank] <el.> Schwing[ungs]kreis m, elektr[omagnet]ischer Schwingkreis; schwing[ungs]fähiger Kreis m <El.>
oscillating-coil potentiometer Schwenkspulenkompensator m, Taumelspulenpotentiometer n
oscillating contact, vibrating contact Schwingkontakt m
oscillating crystal Schwenkkristall m
oscillating crystal <el.> Schwingkristall m, Schwinger m <El.>

oscillating crystal s. a. oscillating quartz
oscillating-crystal method, oscillation photography Schwenkmethode f, Schwenkkristallmethode f, Schwenkkristallverfahren n
oscillating current Schwingstrom m
oscillating drop s. oscillating liquid drop
oscillating electron, hunting electron Pendelelektron n
oscillating electronic circuit s. oscillating circuit
oscillating electron ion source s. Penning ion source
oscillating field, vibrating field Schwingungsfeld n
oscillating force Rüttelkraft f
oscillating frequency, [oscillation] frequency, vibration[al] frequency Frequenz f, Schwingungszahl f, Schwingungsfrequenz f
oscillating klystron, oscillator klystron Oszillatorklystron n
oscillating liquid drop, oscillating drop, fluctuating [liquid] drop schwingender Tropfen m, schwingender Flüssigkeitstropfen m
oscillating load, vibrating (vibration, vibratory) load; oscillating (vibrating, vibration, vibratory) strain Schwing[ungs]belastung f, schwingende Belastung f; schwingende Beanspruchung f, Schwing[ungs]beanspruchung f
oscillating mirror, vibrating mirror, oscillatory mirror Schwingspiegel m; Wackelspiegel m
oscillating model, oscillating universe <of the first or second kind> oszillierende (pulsierende) Welt f, Modell n einer oszillierenden Welt <erster oder zweiter Art>

oscillating quantity Schwinggröße f, Schwingungsgröße f
oscillating quantity, alternating quantity <el.> Wechselgröße f, Schwingung f <El.>
oscillating quartz [crystal], oscillating crystal, oscillator crystal, vibrating quartz [crystal], quartz-crystal oscillator, crystal oscillator, piezoid Schwingquarz m, schwingender Quarz[kristall] m, Piezoid n
oscillating rod, vibrating rod schwingender Stab m
oscillating rotator s. vibrating rotator
oscillating strain s. oscillating load
oscillating stress, cyclic[al] stress, vibratory (vibrating) stress Schwingspannung f, Schwingungsspannung f, schwingende Spannung f
oscillating system s. oscillation system
oscillating universe, oscillating model <of the first or second kind> oszillierende (pulsierende) Welt f, Modell n einer oszillierenden Welt <erster oder zweiter Art>
oscillation Schwingung f; Oszillation f; [periodische] Schwankung f
oscillation; swinging Schwenkung f
oscillation <of a real-valued function> <math.> Schwankung f, Oszillation f <einer reellen Funktion> <Math.>
oscillation s. a. pendular oscillation
oscillation amplitude s. amplitude <of vibration, oscillation>
oscillation characteristic family, family of oscillation characteristics Schwingkennlinienfeld n
oscillation energy, vibration[al] energy, energy of vibration Schwingungsenergie f <z. B. Moleküle>; Oszillationsenergie f
oscillation equation, equation of oscillation, time-independent wave equation Schwingungsgleichung f, zeitfreie Wellengleichung f, zeitunabhängige Schrödinger-Gleichung f
oscillation excitation s. excitation of oscillations
oscillation frequency, frequency, oscillating (vibrational, vibration) frequency Frequenz f, Schwingungszahl f, Schwingungsfrequenz f
oscillation generation s. excitation of oscillations
oscillation impedance Schwingwiderstand m, Schwingungswiderstand m
oscillation kernel Oszillationskern m
oscillation magnetometer Schwingmagnetometer n
oscillation matrix Oszillationsmatrix f
oscillation of coupled circuits Koppelschwingung f, Kopplungsschwingung f
oscillation of molecule nuclei, nuclear oscillation Kernschwingung f [der Moleküle]
oscillation of temperature about the mean value s. temperature fluctuation
oscillation of the first <second; third> kind Schwingung f erster <zweiter; dritter> Art
oscillation of the liquid drop s. liquid drop oscillation
oscillation period s. period of oscillation
oscillation photograph, X-ray oscillation photograph Schwenkkristallaufnahme f, Schwenkaufnahme f
oscillation photography s. oscillating-crystal method
oscillation quantum number s. vibration quantum number
oscillation range, vibration range Schwingbereich m, Schwingungsbereich m, Schwinggebiet n
oscillation release s. excitation of oscillations
oscillation rotation oszillierende Rotation f

oscillation

oscillation spectrum, vibrational spectrum, vibration spectrum	Schwingungsspektrum n
oscillation spike	Generationsspitze f, Oszillationsspitze f
oscillation stop	Schwingloch n
oscillation system, oscillating (oscillatory, vibrating) system	Schwing[ungs]system n, schwingendes System n; schwing[ungs]fähiges System
oscillation threshold	Generationsschwelle f
oscillation tube	s. oscillator valve
oscillation vector, vector of oscillation	Schwingungsvektor m
oscillation viscometer, oscillatory viscometer	Schwingungsviskosimeter n
oscillator; vibrator	Oszillator m, schwingendes (schwingfähiges) Gebilde n
oscillator, vibration generator, generator; exciter, exciter of oscillations <el.>	Oszillator m, Schwingungsgenerator m, Generator m, Schwingungserreger m, Schwingungserzeuger m, Schwinger m <El.>
oscillator <mech.>, mechanical oscillator	[mechanischer] Oszillator m, mechanische Schwingungsvorrichtung f <Mech.>
oscillator [circuit]	s. oscillating circuit <el.>
oscillator coil; moving coil; vibrating (vibration) coil	Oszillatorspule f; Schwingspule f, Vibrationsspule f
oscillator co-ordinates	Oszillatorkoordinaten fpl
oscillator crystal	s. oscillating quartz
oscillator drift	Oszillatordrift f, Frequenzauswanderung f des Oszillators
oscillator klystron, oscillating klystron	Oszillatorklystron n
oscillator model	Oszillatormodell n
oscillator potential	Oszillatorpotential n
oscillator radiation	Oszillatorausstrahlung f, Oszillator[ab]strahlung f, Oszillatorstörstrahlung f
oscillator strength, f-value	Oszillator[en]stärke f, f-Wert m
oscillator tank	s. oscillating circuit <el.>
oscillator tube (valve), oscillation tube	Oszillatorröhre f, Schwingröhre f
oscillator wave function	Oszillatorwellenfunktion f, oszillatorische Wellenfunktion f
oscillatory circuit	s. oscillating circuit <el.>
oscillatory discharge	oszillatorische Entladung (Funkenentladung) f
oscillatory instability, vibrational instability	Schwingungsinstabilität f
oscillatory magnetoband absorption, magneto-oscillatory absorption effect	oszillatorische (oszillierende) Magneto[band]absorption f
oscillatory mirror	s. oscillating mirror
oscillatory motion, oscillatory movement	Schwing[ungs]bewegung f, schwingende Bewegung f, Oszillationsbewegung f
oscillatory power	Schwingleistung f
oscillatory system	s. oscillation system
oscillatory viscometer, oscillation viscometer	Schwingungsviskosimeter n
oscillion, triode oscillator	Triodenoszillator m, Triodengenerator m
oscillistor	Oszillistor m, Oszillatortransistor m
oscillogram, oscillograph	Oszillogramm n, Oszillographenbild n, Schwingungsbild n, Wellenbild n
oscillograph, oscilloscope, ondoscope	Oszilloskop n, Oszillograph m
oscillograph	s. a. oscillogram
oscillograph bridge	Oszillographenbrücke f
oscillographic polarography	oszillographische Polarographie f
oscillographic representation	s. oscillography
oscillographic tube, oscilloscope tube, oscillotron	Oszillographenröhre f, Oszilloskopröhre f, Oszillotron n
oscillograph loop	Oszillographenschleife f
oscillograph spectrometer	Oszillographenspektrometer n
oscillograph with bifilar suspension	s. loop oscillograph
oscillography, oscilloscopy, oscillographic representation	Oszillographie f, oszillographische Darstellung f, Oszilloskopie f
oscillometry	Oszillometrie f; Hochfrequenzindikation f, HF-Indikation f
oscilloscope	s. oscillograph
oscilloscope tube	s. oscillographic tube
oscilloscopy	s. oscillography
oscillotron	s. oscillographic tube
osculating centre	Schmiegungsmittelpunkt m, Schmiegmittelpunkt m
osculating circle	s. circle of curvature
osculating curve	oskulierende Kurve f
osculating element [of orbit]	oskulierendes Element n [der Bahn]
osculating ellipse	oskulierende Ellipse f
osculating Euclidean metric	oskulierende euklidische Metrik f
osculating Euclidean space	oskulierender euklidischer Raum m
osculating Kepler ellipse	oskulierende Kepler-Ellipse f
osculating orbit	oskulierende Bahn f
osculating parabola	Schmieg[ungs]parabel f
osculating paraboloid	Schmieg[ungs]paraboloid n
osculating plane, plane of curvature	Schmieg[ungs]ebene f, Oskulationsebene f
osculating sphere, sphere of curvature	Schmieg[ungs]kugel f, Oskulationskugel f
osculating surface	oskulierende Fläche f
osculation <also astr.>; superosculation	Berührung f <Math.>; Oskulation f, Schmiegung f <Math., Astr.>; Hyperoskulation f <Math.>
Oseen['s] approximation	Oseensche Näherung f
Oseen['s] equation	Oseensche Gleichung (Formel) f
Oseen['s] flow	Oseensche Strömung f
Oseen['s] flow in three dimensions	Oseensche dreidimensionale Strömung f
Oseen['s] integral equation	Oseensche Integralgleichung f
Oseen['s] problem	Oseensches Problem n
Oseen['s] unsteady flow	Oseensche nichtstationäre Strömung f
Oseen['s] wake	Oseenscher Nachlauf m
osmolar concentration	Osmolarität f
osmometer due to Berkeley and Hartley, Berkeley-Hartley osmometer	Osmometer n nach Berkeley und Hartley, Berkeley-Hartley-Osmometer n
osmophilic	osmophil, osmiophil
osmophobic	osmophob
osmophor[e], osmophoric group	osmophore Gruppe f, Osmophor m
osmoregulation	Osmoregulation f
osmose; osmosis	Osmose f
osmose paper	s. osmotic paper
osmosis, osmose	Osmose f
osmotaxis	Osmotaxis f, Osmotaxe f
osmotic barrier	osmotische Barriere f
osmotic cell, osmotic-pressure cell	Osmosezelle f
osmotic coefficient	osmotischer Koeffizient m
osmotic constant, osmotic unit	osmotische Zustandsgröße (Konstante) f
osmotic energy	osmotische Energie f
osmotic equivalent	osmotisches Äquivalent n
osmotic exchange	osmotischer Austausch m
osmotic force	osmotische Kraft f
osmotic gradient	osmotischer Gradient m

osmotic pape., osmose paper	Osmosepapier n	outer automorphism, contragredient automorphism	äußerer Automorphismus m
osmotic potential	osmotisches Potential n	outer bremsstrahlung	äußere Bremsstrahlung f
osmotic pressure	osmotischer Druck m		
osmotic-pressure cell, osmotic cell	Osmosezelle f	outer capacity	äußere Kapazität f
		outer conductor, outer wire	Außenleiter m
osmotic shock	osmotischer Schock m		
osmotic solution	osmotische Lösung f	outer core [of Earth], E region	äußerer Kern (Erdkern) m, äußere Kernschale f (Schale f des Kerns), E-Schale f
osmotic term	osmotisches Glied n		
osmotic unit	s. osmotic constant		
osmotic value, concentration <bio.>	osmotischer Wert m, Saugwert m <der Lösung> <Bio.>		
		outer electrical potential	s. Volta potential difference
osmotic work	osmotische Arbeit f	outer measure	s. upper measure
osmotropism	Osmotropismus m	outermost hysteresis loop, limiting hysteresis loop	Grenzschleife f, Grenzkurve f, äußerste Hystereseschleife f
Ossanna circle, Ossanna diagram	Ossanna-Diagramm n, Ossanna-Kreis m		
Ossipov-King polarizing prism, Ossipov-King prism	Ossipow-King-Prisma n, Polarisationsprisma n von Ossipow und King	outermost orbit, outer (peripheral, valence) orbit	Valenzbahn f, kernfernste Bahn f, äußerste Elektronenbahn f
Ostrogradsky's theorem	s. Green theorem	outermost shell	s. valence shell
		outer multiplication of tensors	s. tensor multiplication
Ostwald['s] adsorption isotherm	Ostwaldsche Adsorptionsisotherme f	outer nucleon	s. peripheral nucleon
Ostwald body	Ostwaldscher Körper m, Körper mit Fließelastizität	outer orbit	s. outermost orbit
		outer-orbital complex, high-spin complex, spin-free complex	Normalkomplex m, magnetisch normaler Komplex m, [„normaler"] Anlagerungskomplex m
Ostwald colour atlas	Ostwaldscher Farbenatlas m		
Ostwald colour system, Ostwald system	Ostwald-System n, Ostwaldsches Farbsystem n		
		outer planet, superior planet	äußerer Planet m, oberer Planet
Ostwald curve	Ostwald-Kurve f	outer point	äußerer Punkt m
Ostwald-De Waele relation	Ostwald-de Waelesche Beziehung f	outer product, exterior (wedge) product	äußeres Produkt n
Ostwald['s] dilution law	Ostwaldsches Verdünnungsgesetz n, Ostwaldsches Verdünnungssatz m	outer product, general product, product <of tensors>	[allgemeines] Tensorprodukt n, direktes Produkt n <Tensoren>
Ostwald['s] electrode, standard (normal) calomel electrode	Normalkalomelelektrode f, Ostwald-Elektrode f	outer product	s. a. vector product
		outer radiation belt (zone), outer Van Allen [radiation] belt	äußerer Strahlungsgürtel m
Ostwald['s] power law	Ostwaldsches Potenzgesetz n, Potenzgesetz nach Ostwald		
		outer ring, ring A	äußerer Ring m, A-Ring m
Ostwald ripening	Ostwald-Reifung f, Rekristallisation f	outer shell	s. valence shell
Ostwald['s] rule	Ostwaldsche Stufenregel f	outer shell electron	s. bonding electron
Ostwald['s] solubility coefficient	s. solubility coefficient	outer Van Allen [radiation] belt, outer radiation zone (belt)	äußerer Strahlungsgürtel m
Ostwald['s] viscometer	Ostwaldsches Kapillarviskosimeter n, Ostwald-Viskosimeter n	outer wire	s. outer conductor
		outer work function	äußere Austrittsarbeit f
Ostwald system, Ostwald colour system	Ostwald-System n, Ostwaldsches Farbsystem n	outer zone	s. peripheral region
		out-field, outgoing field	auslaufendes Feld n, „out"-Feld n
other side of the Moon, far side of the Moon	Rückseite f des Mondes	outflow, outflux	s. discharge <of liquid>
		outgassing, degassing, degasification, extraction of gas	Entgasung f, Gasaustreibung f, Austreibung f von Gasen, Beseitigung f von Gasresten
otolith, statolith	Statolith m, Hörstein m, Gehörsteinchen n, Otolith m, Otokonie f, Statokonie f		
		outgoing field, out-field	auslaufendes Feld n, „out"-Feld n
Otto cycle	Ottoscher Kreisprozeß m, Otto-Prozeß m	outgoing radiation	Ausstrahlung f [der Erde]
		outgrowth; overgrowth <cryst.>	Überwachung f <Krist.>
Otto engine, internal combustion engine, spark-ignition engine	Otto-Motor m, Gleichraummaschine f, Maschine mit Gleichraumverbrennung, Verbrennungsmotor m mit Fremdzündung	out impedance	s. output impedance
		outlet, outcome, portal, outlet orifice	Austrittsöffnung f, Ausflußöffnung f, Ablaßöffnung f
O-type backward wave tube, O-type carcinotron, O-carcinotron	Carcinotron n vom O-Typ, O-Typ-Rückwärtswellenröhre f, Rückwärtswellenröhre f vom O-Typ	outlet, output <el.>	Ausgang m <El.>
		outlet orifice	s. outlet
		outlet pressure; discharge pressure	Austrittsdruck m, Druck m am Ausgang, Druck beim Austritt, Ausgangsdruck m
Oudeman['s] law, law of Oudeman, Landolt-Oudeman law	Oudemansches Gesetz n, Landolt-Oudemansches Gesetz	outlet pressure	Mündungsdruck m
outbreak	s. intrusion <meteo.>		
outburst of nova, nova outburst, nova explosion	Novaausbruch m, Helligkeitsausbruch (Lichtausbruch) m einer Nova		
		outlet temperature, exit temperature	Austrittstemperatur f, Temperatur f am Ausgang, Temperatur beim Austritt, Ausgangstemperatur f
outcome, outlet, portal, outlet orifice	Austrittsöffnung f, Ausflußöffnung f, Ablaßöffnung f		
outdiffusion, postalloy diffusion	Ausdiffusion f	outline, contour; planform; structural shape <of steel>	Kontur f; Umrißlinie f; Begrenzungslinie f; Umriß m; Bildgrenze f; Profilform f
outdoor apparatus; outdoor device	Freiluftgerät n; Freiluftanlage f		
		outline chart (map)	s. hypsometric map

outnumbering, exceeding	Übertreffen n, Übersteigen n, Größersein n	overall dimensions, external dimensions	Gesamtabmessung f, größte Abmessungen fpl; Größe f über alles; äußere Abmessungen, Außenmaße npl
out-of-balance	s. a. unbalance <mech.>		
out-of-balance bridge	s. unbalanced bridge		
out-of-phase, phase-shifted	außer Phase, phasenfalsch, phasenverschoben	overall efficiency, net efficiency; brake thermal efficiency	Gesamtwirkungsgrad m, Nettowirkungsgrad m
out-of-phase component	„out-of-phase"-Komponente f	overall efficiency of sound reproducer, acoustic-mechanical efficiency	akustisch-mechanischer Wirkungsgrad m
out-of-pile experiment, out-of-pile test	Bestrahlungsversuch (Versuch) m außerhalb des Reaktors	overall equivalent	s. net loss
out-of-plane vibration	nichtebene Schwingung f	overall gain, net gain; overall amplification	Gesamtverstärkungsfaktor m; Gesamtverstärkung f
out-of-roundness; ellipticity	Unrundheit f, Unrunde f; Elliptizität f	over[-]all heat-transfer coefficient	s. heat[-]transmission coefficient
out-of-step domain, antiphase domain	Antiphasenbereich m, antiphasiger Bereich m, Anti[phasen]domäne f	overall impulse	s. overall momentum
		overall line attenuation	s. net loss
out-operator	„out"-Operator m	overall loudness, summation loudness	Gesamtlautstärke f, Summenlautstärke f
output, productivity; efficiency, efficacy; performance	Leistung[sfähigkeit] f, Produktionsleistung f, Produktivität f	overall magnification, total magnification	Gesamtvergrößerung f
output, output power, power output	Ausgangsleistung f, Output m, Leistungsabgabe f, abgegebene Leistung f	overall momentum, total momentum (impulse), overall impulse	Gesamtimpuls m; resultierender Impuls m
output <chem.>	entnommene Fraktion f, Entnahmeprodukt n, Produkt n <Chem.>	overall plate efficiency, plate efficiency, plate efficiency factor	Gesamtbodenwirkungsgrad m <Verhältnis der Anzahl der notwendigen theoretischen Böden zur Anzahl der wirklich erreichten>
output, outlet <el.>	Ausgang m <El.>		
output <num. math.>	Output m, Ausgabe f, Datenausgabe f	overall rate-of reaction	Zeitgesetz n der Reaktion
output	s. a. power delivery	overall separation factor	Gesamttrennfaktor m
output	s. a. secondary drive	overall species	Gesamttrasse f
output admittance	Ausgangs[schein]leitwert m, Ausgangsadmittanz f	overall width [of grating], total width of grating	Gitterbreite f, Gesamtbreite f des Beugungsgitters
output aperture, exit slit	Austrittsspalt m; Austrittsschlitz m; Ausgangsspalt m; Austrittsblende f	overbar, overline	Strich m über ...
output capacitance	Ausgangskapazität f	overbarred quantity	überstrichene Größe f
output gap	Auskoppelschlitz m, Auskoppelspalt m	over-blowing	Überblasen n
		overblow tone	Überblaston m
output impedance, out impedance	Ausgangsimpedanz f, Ausgangsscheinwiderstand m, Outimpedanz f, „out"-Impedanz f	overbunching	überkritische Ballung f
		overcast	bedeckt; eingetrübt
output meter	Ausgangsleistungsmesser m, Leistungsmesser m, Outputmeter n	overcast day, murky day	trüber Tag m
		overclimb, stall, stalling, burbling, overzoom <aero.>	Überziehen n, Abkippen n, Abrutschen n, Durchsacken n <Aero.>
output noise power, noise [power] output; noise power (performance) <el.>	Rauschleistung f [am Ausgang], Geräuschleistung f <El.>		
		overcoming the potential barrier	s. tunnelling through the [potential] barrier
output power, output, power output	Ausgangsleistung f, Output m, Leistungsabgabe f, abgegebene Leistung f	overcommutation, accelerated commutation	Überkommutierung f, beschleunigte Kommutierung (Stromwendung) f
output quantity <el.>	Ausgangsgröße f <El.>	overcompensation	Überkompensierung f
output resistance	Ausgangswiderstand m; Ausgangswirkwiderstand m	overcompound excitation	Überverbunderregung f
output transformer	Ausgangstransformator m; Ausgangsübertrager m, Nachübertrager m	overcompounding	Überkompoundierung f
outside temperature	s. exterior temperature	overcompression, overpressure	Überkompression f, Überverdichtung f
out-state	„out"-Zustand m	overcompression ratio	Überkompressionsverhältnis n, Überkompression f
outward normal, outward pointing normal	äußere Normale f	overcorrection	Überkorrektion f
outward winding of the spiral arms	Öffnung f der Spiralwindungen nach außen	overcoupling, overcritical coupling	s. tight coupling <el.>
oval cross-section	ovaler Querschnitt m, Zitronenquerschnitt m	overcurrent, excess current	Überstrom m, Überschußstrom m
oval of Cassini, Cassinian oval (curve), cassinoid	Cassinische Kurve f, Cassinische Linie f	overcurrent cutout, overload cutout, overcurrent trip-out	Grenzstrom[aus]schalter m, Überstromschalter m, Überlastschalter m
ovaloid	Ovaloid n, Rotationsovaloid n	overcurrent factor	Überstrom[kenn]ziffer f, Überstromfaktor m
oval window	ovales Fenster n		
ovary ellipsoid, prolate spheroid, prolate ellipsoid [of revolution]	verlängertes Rotationsellipsoid n, gestrecktes Rotationsellipsoid	overcurrent relay	Überstromrelais n, Maximalstromrelais n, Maximalrelais n, Überlastungsrelais n, Überlastrelais n
overall amplification	s. overall gain		
overall attenuation	s. net loss		
over[-]all coefficient [of heat transfer]	s. heat[-] transmission coefficient	overcurrent trip-out, overload cutout, overcurrent cutout	Grenzstrom[aus]schalter m, Überstromschalter m, Überlastschalter m
overall coefficient of harmonic distortion	s. distortion factor		
overall contrast ratio	Gesamtkontrast m		

overdamming	Überstauung f, Überstau m	overfolding hypothesis, overfolding theory	Überfaltungstheorie f
		overgrowth, intergrowth, intercrescence <cryst.>	Verwachsung f <Krist.>
overdamped forced oscillation	überkritisch gedämpfte erzwungene Schwingung	overgrowth	s. a. outgrowth
overdamping, supercritical damping	überkritische Dämpfung f, Überdämpfung f	overhang; salient, projection	Ausladung f; Überhängen n; Auskragung f; Vorsprung m
		overhang, overhanging beam (end)	s. cantilever
overdeepening	Übertiefung f	overhang leakage	s. face-ring leakage
overdense	überdicht <Elektronendichte > 10^{12} e/cm>	Overhauser effect	Overhauser-Effekt m
		overhead, overhead distillate	Obendestillat n
		overhead conductor, overhead wire, open wire	Freileiter m
overdepth	Übertiefe f	overhead distillate	s. overhead
overdesign	s. oversizing	overhead distillate, overhead product, first runnings <chem.>	Vorlauf m <Chem.>
overdetermined system [of equations]	überbestimmtes Gleichungssystem n		
overdetermination	Überbestimmung f	overhead wire	s. overhead conductor
		overheat	s. overheating
overdetermination	Überbestimmtheit f	overheated steam, superheated steam, superheat; superheated vapour	Heißdampf m <Wasser>; überhitzter Dampf m
overdeveloped, cooked	überentwickelt		
overdimensioning	s. oversizing		
overdistillation	Überdestillieren n	overheating <el.>	Überheizung f <El.>
overdose	Überdosis f		
overdriven amplifier	übersteuerter Verstärker m	overheating, overheat, superheating, superheat	Überhitzung f; Überwärmung f; Wärmestauung f, Wärmestau m
		overirradiation	s. overexposure
		overland flow	s. surface discharge
overdriving; overriding; overloading, overload; overexcitation; overmodulation; blasting	Übersteuerung f; Impulsübersteuerung f	overlap, overlapping <with>	Überlappung f, Übergreifen n, Übereinandergreifen n, Überdeckung f, Überschneiden n <mit>
over-estimate	Überschätzung f	overlap, overlap of photographs	Überdeckung f [der Bilder]
overexcitation, extraexcitation, superexcitation	Übererregung f	overlap angle, angle of overlap	Überlappungswinkel m
		overlap factor	Überlappungsfaktor m
overexcitation	s. a. overdriving	overlap integral	Überlappungsintegral n
overexpansion	Überexpansion f		
overexposure, overirradiation	Überbestrahlung f, Überexponierung f, Überdosierung f der Strahlung	overlap interval, duration of overlap	Überlappungsdauer f, Überlappungsintervall n
overexposure, photographic overexposure <phot.>	Überexposition f, Überbelichtung f <Phot.>	overlap of energy bands	Überlappung f der Energiebänder
		overlap of photographs, overlap	Überdeckung f [der Bilder]
overfall, overflow	Überlauf m; Ablauf m; Abfluß m; Überlaufrinne f	overlap of strata	Übergreifen n der Schichten
		overlapping	s. overlap <with>
overfault, thrust fault, centrifugal (reversed) fault <geo.>	Aufschiebung f, widersinnige Verwerfung f <Geo.>	overlapping, [of interference orders]	Überlagerung f [von Interferenzordnungen]
		overlapping mean	s. moving average
overflow, overfall	Überlauf m; Ablauf m; Abfluß m; Überlaufrinne f	overlap ratio	Überdeckungsverhältnis n; Überdeckungsgrad m, Profilüberdeckung f, Eingriffsdauer f <Mech.>
overflow <num.math.>	Überlauf m <num. Math.>		
		overlap region, region of overlap	Überlappungsbereich m, Überlappungsgebiet n
overflow	s. a. overflowing	overline	s. overbar
overflow area, inundation area, submerged area	Überschwemmungsfläche f, Überschwemmungsgebiet n, Inundationsfläche f, Inundationsgebiet n	overload, excessive load; overloading, superloading	Überlast f; Über[be]lastung f, Mehrbelastung f
		overload	s. a. overdriving
		overload capacity	Überlastbarkeit f; Überlastfaktor m, Überlastungsfaktor m; Überlastungsfähigkeit f
overflow dam	s. overflow weir		
overflowing, overflow, overrun[ning], spill-over	Überlaufen n, Überströmen n		
		overload current	Überlast[ungs]strom m
		overload cutout, overcurrent cutout, overcurrent trip-out	Grenzstrom[aus]schalter m, Überstromschalter m, Überlastschalter m
overflowing sheet, nappe	[überschießender] Strahl m, Überfallamelle f; Nappe f		
overflow plate	Überlaufboden m	overloading, overload, excessive load; superloading	Überlast f; Über[be]lastung f, Mehrbelastung f
overflow reservoir, overflow tank	Überlaufgefäß n		
overflow tube, spillway	Überlaufrohr n	overloading	s. a. overdriving
		overload level <ac.>	Überlastungsgrenze f, Belastungsgrenze f <Ak.>
		overload point	Überlastungspunkt m, Überlastungsstelle f
overflow weir, overflow dam, spillway, spillway dam (weir)	Überfallwehr n, offenes Wehr n; Überfall[stau]mauer f	overload rating	s. permissible overload
		overload relay; contactor <normally open or normally closed>, contactor relay	Schütz n, Schaltschütz n <mit Arbeits- oder Ruhekontakten>
overfold; overfolding; inverted fold. overturned fold	überkippte Falte f; vergente Falte; Überfaltung f		

overload

overload resistance	Übersteuerungsfestigkeit f
overlying, super[im]position, super[im]posing	Superposition f, Überlagerung f
overmatching	Überanpassung f
overmodulation	Übermodulation f, Übermodelung f
overmodulation	s. a. overdriving
overpopulation	Überbesetzung f; Übervölkerung f
overpotential, overvoltage, overtension <el. chem.>	Überspannung f, Polarisation f, Überspannungspolarisation f, elektrische (galvanische, elektrolytische, irreversible) Polarisation <El.Chem.>
overpressure, superpressure, superatmospheric pressure, positive pressure	Überdruck m; Mehrdruck m
overpressure	s. a. overcompression
overpressure diagram	Überdruckdiagramm n
overpressure gauge, positive pressure gauge	Überdruckmanometer n, Überdruckmesser m
overpressure wind tunnel	Überdruckwindkanal m, Überdruckkanal m
overranging	s. overrun
over[-]relaxation	Überrelaxation f
overresonance	Überresonanz f
overriding	s. overdriving
overripening	Überreifen n
overrun, overranging, overshoot, exceeding, passing-over, transgression	Überschreitung f <einer bestimmten, natürlichen Grenze>
overrun[ing], overflowing, overflow, spill-over	Überlaufen n, Überströmen n
oversaturation, supersaturation	Übersättigung f
oversea refraction, overwater refraction	Überwasserrefraktion f
oversensitivity, supersensitivity	Überempfindlichkeit f
overshoot, overshooting, overswing, blip <of pulse>	Überschwingen n <Impuls>
overshoot, overshooting, overtravel, hunting <control>	Überschwingen n <Regelung>
overshoot	s. a. overshooting
overshoot	s. a. overrun
overshoot curve	überschwingende Kurve f
overshoot distortion	Übermodulationsverzerrung f, Übersteuerungsverzerrung f
overshooting, overshoot, overswing; ballistic factor, damping factor <US> <of measuring instrument>	Überschwingung f <Meßgerät>
overshooting	s. a. non-standard propagation
overshooting ratio, overshoot ratio	Überschwing[ungs]faktor m, Überschwing[ungs]verhältnis n
overshot water wheel	oberschlächtiges Wasserrad n
oversize	s. screenings
oversizing, making oversize; overdimensioning; overdesign	Überbemessung f, Überdimensionierung f
over[-]speed	Überdrehzahl f
overstability	Überstabilität f
overstable oscillation	überstabile Schwingung f
overstraining, overstressing	Überbeanspruchung f
overstress <mech.>; overvoltage <el.>	Überspannung f
overstressing, overstraining	Überbeanspruchung f
overswing	s. overshooting
overswing	s. a. overshoot <of pulse>
overtemperature, excess temperature	Übertemperatur f, Überschußtemperatur f
overtension	s. overpotential
overthrust	Tauchdecke f
overthrust	s. a. overthrust of folds
overthrust fold	überkippte Falte f; Deck[en]falte f; Überschiebungsfalte f; Tauchfalte f
overthrust of folds <geo.>	Faltenüberschiebung f <Geo.>
overthrust surface, thrust surface (plane)	Überschiebungsfläche f
overtone, upper partial <ac.>	Oberton m <Ak.>
overtone, partial, partial tone <ac.>	Teilton m, Partialton m, Oberton m <Ak.>
overtone	s. a. upper harmonic
overtone band	Obertonbande f
overtone series	s. harmonic series
overtravel, overshoot, overshooting, hunting <control>	Überschwingen n <Regelung>
over-travel switch	s. limit switch
overturn, tilting over, canting, upturning <geo.>	Überkippung f, Kippung f <Geo.>
overturned fold, inverted fold, overfold; overfolding	überkippte Falte f; vergente Falte; Überfaltung f
overturning moment	s. maximum torque
overturning moment coefficient	s. pitching moment coefficient
overturning sea, overturning wave	Übersturzsee f
overturn of the wave	Umkippen (Kentern) n der Welle
overvoltage <el.>; overstress <mech.>	Überspannung f
overvoltage	s. a. overpotential
overvoltage circuit breaker, overvoltage protective device	Überspannungs[schutz]gerät n, Überspannungsschutz m
overvoltage factor	Überspannungsfaktor m
overvoltage of the Geiger-Müller counter, counter overvoltage	Überspannung f des Geiger-Müller-Zählrohres, Zählrohrüberspannung f
overvoltage-proof, resistant to overvoltage, self-protecting	überspannungsfest, überspannungssicher
overvoltage protection, transient protection, surge protection	Überspannungsschutz m
overvoltage protective device, overvoltage circuit breaker	Überspannungs[schutz]gerät n, Überspannungsschutz m
overvoltage relay	Überspannungsrelais n
overvoltage suppressor	s. surge diverter
overvoltage transient (wave)	s. surge <el.>
overwater refraction, oversea refraction	Überwasserrefraktion f
overzoom, stall, stalling, burbling, overclimb <aero.>	Überziehen n, Abkippen n, Abrutschen n, Durchsacken n <Aero.>
oviform, egg-shaped	eiförmig

ovionic	Ovionic[-Bauelement] *n*
Ovshinsky effect	Ovshinsky-Effekt *m*
Owen bridge	Owen-Brücke *f*, Owen-Induktivitätsmeßbrücke *f*
Owens-Rutherford unit	Owens-Rutherford-Einheit *f*, O.-R.-Einheit *f*
owl-light, dusk, twilight, gloaming	Abenddämmerung *f*
own radiation <of a planet>	Eigenstrahlung *f* <Planet>
oxenium ion	Oxeniumion *n*
oxidability, oxidizability, oxidizing capacity (power), ability of oxidizing, oxidation susceptibility	Oxydierbarkeit *f*, Oxydationsvermögen *n*, Oxydationsfähigkeit *f*
oxidant, oxidizing agent (substance, chemical), oxidizer	Oxydationsmittel *n*, Oxydans *n* <pl.: Oxydanzien>
oxidation accelerator	s. oxidation catalyst
oxidation affinity per unit charge, oxidation potential	Oxydationspotential *n*
oxidation catalyst, oxidation accelerator	Oxydationsbeschleuniger *m*, Oxydationskatalysator *m*
oxidation film, oxide film, oxidic film, oxide skin, oxide coating; oxide layer	Oxidhaut *f*; Oxidschicht *f*
oxidation inhibitor	s. antioxidant
oxidation number, oxidation value, oxidation state, electrochemical valency, charge number of the ion	Oxydationszahl *f*, Oxydationsstufe *f*, Oxydationswert *m*, Ladungswert *m*, elektrochemische Wertigkeit *f*, Wertigkeit *f* des Ions
oxidation potential, oxidation affinity per unit charge	Oxydationspotential *n*
oxidation preventive	s. antioxidant
oxidation-reduction	s. oxidoreduction
oxidation-reduction chain, redox chain	Redoxkette *f*
oxidation-reduction cycle, redox cycle	Redoxzyklus *m*
oxidation-reduction electrode, redox electrode	Redoxelektrode *f*
oxidation-reduction equilibrium, redox equilibrium	Redoxgleichgewicht *n*, Reduktions-Oxydations-Gleichgewicht *n*
oxidation-reduction fuel cell, redox fuel cell	Redox-Brennstoffelement *n*
oxidation-reduction index, reduction-oxidation index, oxidation-reduction value, O/R value	Redoxindex *m*, O/R-Wert *m*
oxidation-reduction indicator, redox indicator	Redoxindikator *m*
oxidation-reduction ion exchanger, redox [ion] exchanger	Redoxaustauscher *m*, Redox-Ionenaustauscher *m*
oxidation-reduction potential, redox potential, O-R potential	Redoxpotential *n*, Oxydations-Reduktions-Potential *n*, Redoxspannung *f*
oxidation-reduction process, redox process, O-R process	Redoxprozeß *m*, Redoxvorgang *m*, Reduktions-Oxydations-Prozeß *m*, Oxydations-Reduktions-Prozeß *m*
oxidation-reduction reaction, redox reaction, reduction-oxidation reaction	Redoxreaktion *f*, Reduktions-Oxydations-Reaktion *f*
oxidation-reduction system, redox system	Redoxsystem *n*, Reduktions-Oxydations-System *n*
oxidation-reduction titration	s. oxidimetry
oxidation-reduction value, reduction-oxidation index, oxidation-reduction index, O/R value	Redoxindex *m*, O/R-Wert *m*
oxidation retarder	s. antioxidant
oxidation state	s. oxidation number
oxidation susceptibility	s. oxidability
oxidation value	s. oxidation number
oxidation zone	Oxydationszone *f*, Eiserner Hut *m*
oxidative weathering, weathering by oxidation	Oxydationsverwitterung *f*
oxide[-coated] cathode	Oxidkatode *f*, Wehnelt-Katode *f*; Dampfkatode *f*
oxide coating; oxide film, oxidic film, oxide skin, oxidation film, oxide layer	Oxidhaut *f*; Oxidschicht *f*
oxide layer	s. oxide film
oxide replica	Oxidabdruck *m*
oxide skin, oxidic film, oxide film, oxidation film, oxide coating; oxide layer	Oxidhaut *f*; Oxidschicht *f*
oxidimetry, oxidation-reduction (redox) titration	Oxydimetrie *f*, Redoxanalyse *f*, Redoxtitration *f*, Oxydations-Reduktions-Titration *f*
oxidizability	s. oxidability
oxidizer, oxidizing agent	s. oxidant
oxidizing capacity	s. oxidability
oxidizing chemical	s. oxidant
oxidizing flame	Oxydationsflamme *f*, oxydierende Flamme *f*
oxidizing fusion	oxydierendes Schmelzen *n*, Oxydationsschmelze *f*
oxidizing power	s. oxidability
oxidizing substance, oxidant, oxidizing agent (chemical), oxidizer	Oxydationsmittel *n*, Oxydans *n* <pl.: Oxydanzien>
oxidoreduction, oxidation-reduction; dismutation [reaction]; disproportionation	Oxydation-Reduktion *f*, Oxydoreduktion *f*, Dismutation *f*, Disproportionierung *f*
oximetry	Oxymetrie *f*, Sauerstoffmessung *f* <im Blut>
oxonium ion, hydronium ion, hydroxonium ion, H_3O^+	Hydroniumion *n*, Oxoniumion *n*, H_3O^+
oxycalorimeter	Sauerstoffkalorimeter *n*
oxygen bridge	Sauerstoffbrücke *f*
oxygen deficiency	Sauerstoffmangel *m*
oxygen dept	Sauerstoffhunger *m*
oxygen diffusion electrode	Sauerstoffdiffusionselektrode *f*
oxygen displacement	Sauerstoffverschiebung *f*
oxygen effect	Sauerstoffeffekt *m*
oxygen-ion conduction	Sauerstoffionenleitung *f*
oxygen octahedron	Sauerstoffoktaeder *n*
oxygen overvoltage	Sauerstoffüberspannung *f*
oxygen point, temperature of equilibrium between liquid oxygen and its vapour	Sauerstoffpunkt *m*
oxygen polarography	Sauerstoffpolarographie *f*
oxygen tetrahedron	Sauerstofftetraeder *n*
oxygen voltameter	Sauerstoffcoulometer *n*, Sauerstoffvoltameter *n*
oxyhydrogen, oxyhydrogen gas, electrolytic gas	Knallgas *n*
oxyhydrogen coulombmeter	s. oxyhydrogen voltameter
oxyhydrogen couple, gaseous couple, hydrogen-oxygen cell	Knallgaskette *f*, Knallgaselement *n*, Wasserstoff-Sauerstoff-Kette *f*, Gaselement *n*, Gaskette *f*

oxyhydrogen

oxyhydrogen gas, oxyhydrogen, electrolytic gas	Knallgas n
oxyhydrogen reaction	Knallgasreaktion f
oxyhydrogen voltameter, oxyhydrogen coulombmeter	Knallgascoulometer n, Knallgasvoltameter n
oxyluminescence	Oxylumineszenz f
oxyty	= concentration of dissolved oxygen
ozone band, absorption (electronic) band of ozone	Ozonbande f
ozone layer, ozonosphere <of atmosphere>	Ozonosphäre f, Ozonschicht f <Atmosphäre>
ozone shadow	Ozonschatten m
ozone shadowing, effect of ozone shadow	Ozonschatteneffekt m
ozonide	Ozonid n
ozonizer <e.g. of Siemens or Brodie>	Ozonisator m <z. B. von Siemens oder Brodie>
ozonolysis	Ozonspaltung f, Ozonolyse f
ozonometer	Ozonmesser m
ozonosphere, ozone layer <of atmosphere>	Ozonosphäre f, Ozonschicht f <Atmosphäre>

P

pA, pA number, pA value	pA-Wert m, pA
pace; step; stride	Schritt m; Stufe f
pacemaker, heart (cardiac) pacemaker	Herzschrittmacher m, „pacemaker" m
pack, hummocked ice, old pack, pack-ice	Packeis n
pack	s. a. packing <of column>
pack[age]	s. a. bunch <e.g. of waves, particles>
package	s. portable
packaged magnetron	Magnetron n mit Feldmagnet, Feldmagnet-Magnetron n
packaging, packing	Packung f; Feststampfen n; Stopfen n; Füllung f
packaging <of type A or type B> <nucl.>	Verpackung f <vom Typ A oder B> <Kern.>
packed column, packed tower, filled column, filled tower	Füllkörperkolonne f, Füllkörpersäule f
packed density	s. apparent density
packed tower	s. packed column
packet	s. bunch <e.g. of waves, particles>
packet emulsion, packet photographic emulsion	Mehrschichtenemulsion f, Vielschichtenemulsion f, Mehrfachschichtemulsion f, Vielfachschichtemulsion f
pack-ice, hummocked ice, old pack, pack	Packeis n
packing, packaging	Packung f; Feststampfen n; Stopfen n; Füllung f
packing, packing material, padding, gasket	Dichtung f, Packung f, Packungsmaterial n; Füllung f, Dichtungsmaterial n; Stampfmasse f
packing, compacting, compaction, densification	Verdichtung f [von Material]
packing, pack, filling <of column>	Füllkörper m [der Kolonne]; Aufsatz m
packing <cryst.; num. math.>	Packung f <Krist.; num. Math.>
packing defect, mass defect (deficit), packing loss (effect) <nucl.>	Massendefekt m, Kernschwund m <Kern.>
packing density	Informationsdichte f
packing density <cryst.>	Packungsdichte f <Krist.>
packing effect	s. mass effect <nucl.>
packing effect	s. packing defect <nucl.>
packing fraction; packing index	Packungsanteil m
packing loss	s. packing defect <nucl.>
packing material	s. packing
packing of cylinders, system of cylinders	Zylinderpackung f
packing of spheres, system of spheres	Kugelpackung f
packing ring, filling[-in] ring, filler ring	Füllring m
packing water seal	s. liquid seal
padder	s. padding capacitor
padding	s. packing
padding capacitor, padder	Paddingkondensator m, Serientrimmer m
paddle	Schaufel f
paddle [board], corner vane, baffle <hydr.>	Leitblech n, Leitschaufel f, Umlenkschaufel f, Schaufel f, schaufelförmiger Einbau m, Prallblech n, Umlenkblech n, Prallplatte f <Hydr.>
Padé['s] table	Padésche Tafel f, Padé-Entwicklung f
Paetow effect	Pätow-Effekt m
paint	Anstrichfarbe f, Farbe f, Anstrichstoff m
pain threshold of hearing	s. upper threshold of hearing
pair annihilation	Paarvernichtung f, Paarannihilation f, Paarzerstrahlung f
pair annihilation to neutrinos	Neutrinoerzeugung f durch Paarvernichtung
pair conversion	Paarkonversion f, Paarumwandlung f
pair-correlation function	Paarkorrelationsfunktion f
pair correlation model	Paarkorrelationsmodell n
pair creation, pair production (formation, emission, generation), pairing	Paarbildung f, Paarerzeugung f, Paarung f
pair-creation coefficient, pair-production coefficient	Paarbildungskoeffizient m, Schwächungskoeffizient m für den Paarbildungseffekt
pair creation rate	s. creation rate
pair density	Paardichte f
pair distribution function	Paarverteilungsfunktion f, Zweiteilchen-Verteilungsfunktion f
pair distribution matrix	Paarverteilungsmatrix f, Zweiteilchen-Verteilungsmatrix f
paired dislocation, super-extended dislocation	gepaarte Versetzung f, Versetzungspaar n
pair emission	s. pair creation
pair force	Paarkraft f
pair formation (generation), pairing	s. pair creation
pairing effect	Paarungseffekt m
pairing energy	Paarbildungsenergie f, Paarungsenergie f
pairing operator	Paarungsoperator m
pairing peak	Paarpeak m, Paarbildungslinie f
pair interaction	Paarwechselwirkung f

pair model	Paarmodell n
pair of data; pair of values	Wertepaar n
pair of scales, scales <US also sing.>; balance	Waage f
pair of stars	Sternpaar n
pair of vacancies	s. double vacancy
pair of values; pair of data	Wertepaar n
pair of voids	s. double vacancy
pair-producing collision	paarerzeugender Stoß m
pair production	s. pair creation
pair-production absorption	[Gamma-]Absorption f durch Paarbildung
pair-production coefficient	s. pair-creation coefficient
pair-production cross-section, cross-section for pair creation (production, generation, formation)	Paarbildungsquerschnitt m, Wirkungsquerschnitt m für (der) Paarbildung, Paarbildungswirkungsquerschnitt m
pair-production energy transfer coefficient	Paarumwandlungskoeffizient m, Paarbildungs-Umwandlungskoeffizient m
pair-production mass attenuation coefficient, mass attenuation coefficient for pair production	Massenschwächungskoeffizient m für den Paarbildungseffekt, Massen-Paarbildungskoeffizient m
pairs / in, pairwise	paarweise
pair spectrograph	Paarspektrograph m
pair spectrometer	Paarspektrometer n
pair theory	s. hole theory
pairwise, in pairs	paarweise
Pais['] equation	Paissche Gleichung f, Pais-Gleichung f
palaeo-astrobiology	Paläoastrobiologie f
palaeoclimate	Paläoklima n
palaeomagnetism	Paläomagnetismus m
palaeotemperature	Paläotemperatur f
Palatini['s] method (procedure)	Palatinisches Verfahren n
paleo ...	s. palaeo ...
palisade phenomenon, railing (fence) phenomenon	Staketenphänomen n
palladium-platinum thermocouple, pallaplat thermocouple, Pd-Pt thermocouple	Pallaplat-Thermoelement n, Pallaplatelement n, Palladium-Platin-Thermoelement n, Pd-Pt-Thermoelement n
Pall ring	Pall-Ring m
Palomar telescope, Hale reflector, Mount Palomar telescope	Hale-Teleskop n, Palomar-Teleskop n, Hale-Reflektor m
palpable co-ordinate, non-cyclic co-ordinate	nichtzyklische Koordinate
pan, [weighing] scale, scale pan, weighing dish, dish [of the scales]	Waagschale f, Waageschale f
panactinic	panaktinisch
pancake coil, slab coil, flat coil	Flachspule f
pancake ice, cake ice	Tellereis n, Pfannkucheneis n
pancaking <aero.>	Absacken n, Durchsacken n <Aero.>
panchromatic filter, panchromatic vision filter, P.V. filter	Panfilter n, panchromatisches Filter n
panchromatism, sensitivity to all colours	Panchromatismus m, Allfarbenempfindlichkeit f, Panchromasie f
pancratic condenser [lens]	pankratischer Kondensor m
pancratic telescope	pankratisches Fernrohr n
panel cabinet	Schaltschrank m
panel point	s. joint <of truss>
Paneth['s] [adsorption] rule	Panethsches Gesetz n
pan head, panoramic head, panoramic top	Panoramakopf m
panidiomorphic	panidiomorph
panning	Panoramieren n
Panofsky lens	Panofsky-Linse f
Panofsky ratio	Panofsky-Verhältnis n
panorama; panoramic view	Rundsicht f; Rundblick m; Panorama n
panoramic camera	Panoramakamera f, Rundbildaufnahmekammer f; Rundbildkamera f
panoramic cinematography	Panoramakinematographie f
panoramic effect	Panoramaeffekt m, Panoramawirkung f
panoramic exposure	Karussellaufnahme f, Panoramaaufnahme f
panoramic head, panoramic top, pan head	Panoramakopf m
panoramic photogram, panoramic survey	Panoramameßbild n, Rundblickmeßbild n
panoramic photograph, panoramic picture <phot.>	Panoramaaufnahme f, Rundbild n, Rundaufnahme f, Rundbildaufnahme f <Phot.>
panoramic photography, panoramic shot; pan-shot <phot.>	Panoramaaufnahme f, Rund[bild]aufnahme f <Phot.>
panoramic picture	s. panoramic photograph <phot.>
panoramic radar, panoramic surveillance radar, all-round looking radar, panoramic unit	Rundsuchradar n, Rundblickradar n, Rundsichtradar n, Panoramagerät n, Panoramafunkmeßgerät n
panoramic shot	s. panoramic photography <phot.>
panoramic surveillance radar	s. panoramic radar
panoramic survey, panoramic photogram	Panoramameßbild n, Rundblickmeßbild n
panoramic telescope	Panoramafernrohr n, Rundblickfernrohr n, Rundsichtfernrohr n
panoramic top	s. panoramic head
panoramic unit	s. panoramic radar
panoramic view; panorama	Rundsicht f; Rundblick m; Panorama n
pan-out turbine	s. extraction turbine
panphotometric	panphotometrisch
panradiometer	Panradiometer n
pan-shot	s. panoramic photography <phot.>
pantograph	Pantograph m, Storchschnabel m
pantograph arm	Scherenarm m, Storchschnabelarm m
pantograph manipulator	s. mechanical pantograph manipulator
Panum['s] area, area of single vision, region of single vision	Panum-Bereich m, Panum-Kreis m, Zone f des binokularen Einfachsehens, Zone der binokularen Verschmelzung f
pA number, pA, pA value	pA-Wert m, pA
Panum effect	Panum-Effekt m
Panum['s] theorem	Panumscher Satz m, Satz von Panum
Panum['s] vision, [binocular] single vision	Panum-Sehen n, beidäugiges Einfachsehen n
panynological analysis	s. pollen analysis
panzeractinometer, Linke-Feussner actinometer, shielded actinometer	Panzeraktinometer n [nach Linke und Feußner], Linke-Feußner-Aktinometer n
paper carriage	Papier[transport]walze f; Registrierwalze f; Schreibwagen m; Papierträger m, Registrierstreifenträger m, Schreibstreifenträger m
paper chromatogram	Papierchromatogramm n
paper chromatography, paper partition chromatography, papyrography	Papierchromatographie f, Papyrographie f
paper electropherogram	Papierelektropherogramm n

paper electropherography	Papierelektropherographie f	parabolic point	parabolischer Punkt m
paper electrophoresis	Papierelektrophorese f	parabolic potential	Parabelpotential n
paper feed	Papiervorschub m, Papiertransport m	parabolic quantum number	parabolische Quantenzahl f
paper feed mechanism	Papiervorschub m, Papiervorschubvorrichtung f, Papierschubwerk n	parabolic reflector, paraboloid[al] reflector; parabolic-reflector antenna <el.>	Parabolreflektor m, parabolischer Reflektor m; Parabol[oid]spiegel m, Parabol[oidspiegel]-antenne f <El.>
paper ionopherography	Papierionopherographie f	parabolic-reflector antenna	s. parabolic reflector <el.>
paper ionophoresis	Papierionophorese f	parabolic rule	s. Simpson['s] rule
paper partition chromatography	s. paper chromatography	parabolic stage of hardening	parabolische Verfestigung f
paper radiochromatograph	Radiopapierchromatograph m, Papierradiochromatograph m	parabolic trajectory, parabolic orbit	parabolische Bahn f
paper radiochromatography	Radiopapierchromatographie f, Papierradiochromatographie f	parabolic velocity	s. escape velocity
		parabolic velocity profile, Poiseuille velocity profile	parabolisches Geschwindigkeitsprofil n
paper strip electrophoresis	Papierstreifenelektrophorese f	parabolic waveform current, parabolic current	Parabelstrom m
paper tape storage, punched tape storage	Lochstreifenspeicher m	paraboloid[al] condenser, single-mirror condenser	Einspiegelkondensor m, Paraboloidkondensor m
Papin['s] [steam] digester	Papinscher Topf m, Dampfdrucktopf m	paraboloid[al] co-ordinates	parabolische Koordinaten fpl <konfokale Paraboloide>
Papkovich solution, Boussinesq-Papkovich solution, Neuber-Papkovich solution	Boussinesq-Papkowitsch-Lösung f, Papkowitsch-Lösung f	paraboloid[al] reflector	s. parabolic reflector <el.>
Papperitz['s] equation	s. Riemann['s] differential equation	paraboloid of revolution	Rotationsparaboloid n, Umdrehungsparaboloid n
P_n approximation	P_n-Approximation f	paraboson	Paraboson n
Pappus['] theorem	s. Guldin['s] rule	parachor	Parachor m [nach Sudgen], P
PA projection	s. PA view	parachute landing	Fallschirmlandung f
papyrography	s. paper chromatography	parachute recovery	Fallschirmbergung f
parabola method [of J. J. Thomson], Thomson['s] parabola method, method of parabolas	Parabelmethode f [von J. J. Thomson], Thomsonsche Parabelmethode	paraclase, fault fissure	Verwerfungskluft f, Verwerfungsspalte f, Sprungkluft f, Sprungspalte f, Paraklase f
parabola of safety	Sicherheitsparabel f		
parabola spectrograph	Parabelspektrograph m	para-compound, para-substitution compound, p-compound	para-Verbindung f, p-Verbindung f
parabolic comet	parabolischer Komet m, Komet mit parabolischer Bahn	paraconductivity	Paraleitfähigkeit f
		paracontrast	Parakontrast m
parabolic co-ordinates, confocal paraboloidal co-ordinates	parabolische Koordinaten fpl, ebene parabolische Koordinaten	paracrystal	Parakristall m
		paracrystalline	parakristallin, pseudoamorph
parabolic co-ordinates, co-ordinates of the paraboloid of revolution	rotationsparabolische (spezielle parabolische) Koordinaten fpl, Koordinaten des Rotationsparaboloids	paradox of Euler and d'Alembert	s. hydrodynamic paradox of d'Alembert
		paradox of Stokes, Stokes['] paradox	Stokessches Paradoxon n, Paradoxon von Stokes
parabolic creep	parabolisches Kriechen n	paradox of the space traveller, twin paradox	Zwillingsparadoxon n
parabolic current, parabolic waveform current	Parabelstrom m	paraelastic effect	paraelastischer Effekt m
parabolic cylinder function, function of the parabolic cylinder	Funktion f des parabolischen Zylinders, parabolische Zylinderfunktion f, Weber[-Hermite]sche Funktion	paraelastic resonance	paraelastische Resonanz f
		para-electric, para-electric material	Paraelektrikum n, paraelektrischer Stoff m
		para[-]electric, parelectric	paraelektrisch, parelektrisch
parabolic cylindrical co-ordinates, co-ordinates of the parabolic cylinder	Koordinaten fpl des parabolischen Zylinders, parabolische Zylinderkoordinaten fpl	para-electric material	s. para-electric
		paraelectric resonance, PER	paraelektrische Resonanz f, PER
		para-electric susceptibility	paraelektrische Suszeptibilität f
parabolic differential equation	s. parabolic equation	parafermion	Parafermion n
parabolic dune	Parabeldüne f	paraffin phantom	Paraffinphantom n
parabolic equation, parabolic [partial] differential equation, differential equation of the parabolic type	parabolische Differentialgleichung f, Differentialgleichung vom parabolischen Typ	parafoveal vision, eccentric vision	parafoveales (parazentrisches, exzentrisches) Sehen n
		paragenesis <geo.>	Paragenese f, Mineralparagenese f, Assoziation f <Geo.>
		paraheliotropism	Paraheliotropismus m
		parahelium, parhelium	Parahelium n, Parhelium n
		para-hydrogen, para hydrogen	Parawasserstoff m
parabolic flow, parabolic motion <hydr.>	Parabelströmung f <Hydr.>	paralic	paralisch
		parallactic angle, angle of situation	parallaktischer Winkel m, Parallaxenwinkel m
parabolic mirror, paraboloid[al] mirror <opt.>	Parabol[oid]spiegel m, parabolischer Spiegel (Hohlspiegel) m <Opt.>	parallactic difference	s. binocular parallax
		parallactic ellipse	parallaktische Ellipse f
parabolic motion	s. parabolic flow <hydr.>	parallactic error, parallax error, parallax displacement	Parallaxenfehler m
parabolic orbit, parabolic trajectory	parabolische Bahn f		
parabolic partial differential equation	s. parabolic equation		

parallactic inequality	s. Moon's parallactic inequality	parallel capacitor, shunt[ing] capacitor, by-pass capacitor	Parallelkondensator m, parallelgeschalteter (parallelliegender) Kondensator m, Nebenschlußkondensator m, Querkondensator m, Überbrückungskondensator m, Ableitkondensator m
parallactic libration, diurnal libration	tägliche (parallaktische) Libration f <Mond>		
parallactic mounting, equatorial mounting	parallaktische (äquatoriale) Fernrohrmontierung f, parallaktische (äquatoriale) Montierung f, parallaktische (äquatoriale) Aufstellung f		
		parallel circle	s. parallel <geo.>
		parallel cleavage	s. primary cleavage
parallactic rule, triquetra	parallaktisches Lineal n	parallel-coil movement	Parallelspulmeßwerk n
parallactic shift	parallaktische Verschiebung f		
parallactic triangle	s. polar triangle	parallel coil of wattmeter, wattmeter parallel coil	Wattmeterspannungsspule f
parallactoscopy	Parallaktoskopie f		
parallax; annual parallax, heliocentric parallax	Parallaxe f; jährliche (heliozentrische) Parallaxe	parallel computer	s. parallel machine
		parallel conductivity, parallel electric conductivity	Parallelleitfähigkeit f
parallax adjustment, parallax compensation, parallax correction	Parallaxenausgleich m		
parallax compensator	Parallaxenausgleich[er] m	parallel connection, connection in parallel, in-parallel (shunt) connection, paralleling	Parallelschaltung f, Nebeneinanderschaltung f
parallax computer	Parallaxenrechner m		
parallax correction, parallax compensation, parallax adjustment	Parallaxenausgleich m	parallel co-ordinates; parallel co-ordinate system, set of parallel co-ordinates	Parallelkoordinaten fpl, affine Koordinaten fpl; Parallelkoordinatensystem n, affines Koordinatensystem n
parallax displacement, parallax error, parallactic error	Parallaxenfehler m		
		parallel co-ordinates	s. a. Cartesian co-ordinates
		parallel co-ordinate system	s. parallel co-ordinates
parallax of one second, parsec, pc	Parsec n, Parallaxensekunde f, Sternweite f, Parsek n, pc	parallel current	s. parallel flow <hydr.>
		parallel cut, Y cut, Y-cut	Y-Schnitt m
parallax of reading	Ableseparallaxe f	parallel discharge gap; parallel [spark] gap	Parallelfunkenstrecke f
parallaxometer	Parallaxenmeßgerät n		
parallax photogrammetry	Parallaxenphotogrammetrie f	parallel displacement, parallel propagation (shift) <of vectors>	Parallelübertragung f, Parallelverschiebung f <Vektoren>
parallax refractometer	Parallaxenrefraktometer n		
		parallel displacement	s. a. translation <mech.>
parallax stereogram	Parallaxenstereogramm n	parallel division	Parallelteilung f
		parallel electric conductivity	s. parallel conductivity
parallel, parallel of latitude, line of latitude, parallel circle <geo.>	Breitenkreis m, Parallelkreis m, Parallel m <Geo.>	parallelepiped	s. parallelepipedon
		parallelepipedal deformation, parallelepipedal strain	parallelepipedische Verformung f
parallel, parallel line	Parallele f		
parallel; equidirectional, codirectional	parallel; gleichgerichtet	parallelepipedal product, triple product [of three vectors], scalar triple product, triple scalar product, mixed product	Spatprodukt n, skalares Dreierprodukt n, gemischtes Produkt n
parallel	s. a. line of equal latitude		
parallel access [computer] store	s. parallel store		
parallel adder	Paralleladdierschaltung f, Paralleladdierwerk n	parallelepipedal strain, parallelepipedal deformation	parallelepipedische Verformung f
		parallelepipedon, parallelepiped, parallelopiped[on]	Parallelepiped[on] n, Parallelflach n, Spat n
parallel addition	Paralleladdition f	parallel excitation, parallel field excitation	Parallelerregung f, Parallelfelderregung f
parallel admittance	Parallelleitwert m	parallel experiment	s. replicated experiment
parallel [antenna] array	Dipolgruppe f	parallel-faced hemihedry	s. paramorphic hemihedry of the regular system
		parallel field <of forces>	Parallelfeld n
parallel[-]axiom	Parallelenaxiom n	parallel field excitation, parallel excitation	Parallelerregung f, Parallelfelderregung f
		parallel flow, parallel stream, co-current flow	Parallelströmung f, Parallelstrom m, Translationsströmung f
parallel axis theorem, theorem of parallel axes, law of parallel axes, transfer theorem for moment of inertia, Steiner['s] theorem	Steinerscher Satz m, Satz von Steiner, Satz von Huygens, Huygensscher Satz		
		parallel flow	Schichtenströmung f
		parallel flow, parallel current <techn.>	Gleichstrom m <Techn.>
parallel band	Parallelbande f, ||-Bande f	parallel[-] flow exchanger	Gleichstrom-Wärmeaustauscher m; Gleichstrom[aus]tauscher m
parallel beam, parallel pencil of rays, bundle of rays parallel to each other, parallel rays	Parallelstrahlenbündel n, Parallelstrahlen mpl	parallel[-] flow principle, principle of parallel flow	Gleichstromprinzip n
		parallel[-] flow turbine, axial turbine	Axialturbine f
parallel beam of light	Parallellichtbündel n	parallel gap, parallel spark (discharge) gap	Parallelfunkenstrecke f
		parallel gauge, slip gauge, block gauge, Johansson gauge	Parallelendmaß n
parallel capacitance; shunt capacitance, shunt arm capacitance	Parallelkapazität f, Querkapazität f		
		parallel impedance	s. shunt impedance

paralleling

paralleling, parallel connection, connection in parallel	Parallelschaltung *f*, Nebeneinanderschaltung *f*
parallelism	Parallelismus *m*, Parallelität *f*
parallelism, plane parallelism	Planparallelität *f*
parallelism error, lack of parallelism	Parallelitätsfehler *m*
parallelizability	Parallelisierbarkeit *f*
parallel line, parallel	Parallele *f*
parallel machine, parallel computer	Parallelmaschine *f*, Parallelrechenmaschine *f*
parallel marking off	parallele Abtragung *f*
parallel of altitude	s. almucantar
parallel of latitude, parallel, line of latitude, parallel circle <geo.>	Breitenkreis *m*, Parallelkreis *m*, Parallel *m* <Geo.>
parallelogram law, principle of the parallelogram of forces	Parallelogrammregel *f*, Parallelogrammgesetz *n*, Satz *m* vom Parallelogramm der Kräfte
parallelogram of forces	Parallelogramm *n* der Kräfte, Kräfteparallelogramm *n*
parallelogram of motion (velocities)	Parallelogramm *n* der Geschwindigkeiten (Bewegung)
parallelogram pendulum	Parallelogrammpendel *n*
parallelohedron	Paralleloeder *n*
parallel operation	Parallelbetrieb *m*
parallelopiped[on]	s. parallelepipedon
parallelotope	Parallelotop *n*
parallel pencil of rays	s. parallel beam
parallel perspective	s. parallel projection
parallel phase resonance	s. parallel resonance
parallel[-] plane, plane[-]parallel	planparallel
parallel plate capacitor	s. plate capacitor
parallel plate chamber, parallel-plate spark chamber	Parallelplattenkammer *f*, Parallelplatten-Funkenkammer *f*
parallel plate chamber, parallel plate ionization chamber	Platten[ionisations]kammer *f*, Parallelplatten[-Ionisations]kammer *f*
parallel plate counter	Plattenzähler *m*, Parallelplattenzähler *m*
parallel plate electrodes	Parallelplattenelektroden *fpl*, Plattenelektroden *fpl*
parallel plate guide, parallel plate waveguide	Plattenwellenleiter *m*, Parallelplattenwellenleiter *m*, planparalleler Wellenleiter *m*
parallel plate ionization chamber	s. parallel plate chamber
parallel plate lens	Parallelplattenlinse *f*
parallel plate spark chamber	s. parallel plate chamber
parallel plate spark counter	Parallelplatten-Funkenzähler *m*
parallel plate waveguide	s. parallel plate guide
parallel projection, parallel perspective	Parallelprojektion *f*, Parallelperspektive *f*, Parallelriß *m*
parallel propagation, parallel displacement <of vectors>	Parallelübertragung *f*, Parallelverschiebung *f* <Vektoren>
parallel pumping effect	Parallelpumpeffekt *m*
parallel push-pull [cascade], single-ended push-pull [cascade]	eisenlose Gegentaktschaltung (Gegentaktstufe) *f*, Parallel-„push-pull"-Schaltung *f*, „single-ended push-pull"-Schaltung *f*
parallel rays	s. parallel beam
parallel reactance	Parallelblindwiderstand *m*, Parallelreaktanz *f*
parallel reaction	s. side reaction
parallel resistance	Paralleldämpfungswiderstand *m*
parallel resistance	s. a. shunt resistance
parallel resonance, parallel phase resonance, current resonance, antiresonance	Parallelresonanz *f*, Stromresonanz *f*, Sperresonanz *f*, Antiresonanz *f*
parallel resonant circuit	Parallelresonanzkreis *m*, Stromresonanzkreis *m*, Parallelschwingkreis *m*
parallel-resonant circuit amplifier	schwingkreisgekoppelter Verstärker *m*
parallel-resonant frequency	Parallelresonanzfrequenz *f*, Stromresonanzfrequenz *f*
parallel resonant impedance	s. shunt impedance
parallel-rod tank circuit	Lecher-Kreis *m*, Lecher-Resonanzkreis *m*, Parallel-Leistungsschwingkreis *m*
parallel sectioning	Parallelschnittverfahren *n*
parallel-series circuit, parallel-series connection	Parallelreihenschaltung *f*, Parallelserienschaltung *f*
parallel-series matrix	Parallelreihenmatrix *f*, Parallelserienmatrix *f*
parallel shift	s. parallel displacement <of vectors>
parallel shift	s. a. translation <mech.>
parallel spark gap, parallel [discharge] gap	Parallelfunkenstrecke *f*
parallel storage, parallel store, parallel access [computer] store	Parallelspeicher *m*, Rechenspeicher *m* mit Parallelzugriff
parallel stream, parallel flow, co-current flow	Parallelströmung *f*, Parallelstrom *m*, Translationsströmung *f*
parallel structure	Parallelstruktur *f*
parallel texture	Paralleltextur *f*
parallel-to-series converter, dynamicizer	Parallel-Serie-Konverter *m*, Parallel-Serie-Umsetzer *m*
parallel-tube amplifier, push-push amplifier	Gleichtaktverstärker *m*
parallel-wire line	s. two-wire line
parallel-wire wavemeter	Paralleldrahtwellenmesser *m*
paralysis; blocking; interlocking, locking; cut-off; rejection; blackout; bottoming <el.>	Sperrung *f* <El.>
paralysis circuit <of counter>	Sperrkreis *m* <Zählrohr>
paralysis period (time), insensitive interval (time)	Sperrzeit *f*, Unempfindlichkeitszeit *f*, Totzeit *f*
paralyst, paralyzer	s. inhibitor <chem.>
paralyzable counter	blockierendes Zählrohr *n*
paramagnet[ic], paramagnetic material, paramagnetic substance	Paramagnetikum *n*, paramagnetischer Stoff *m*
paramagnetic amplifier	paramagnetischer Verstärker *m*
paramagnetic cooling	s. magnetic cooling

paramagnetic Curie point [of temperature], Weiss constant	paramagnetische Curie-Temperatur f, paramagnetischer Curie-Punkt m, Weisssche Konstante f, Weiss-Konstante f
paramagnetic dispersion	paramagnetische Dispersion f
paramagnetic maser [amplifier]	Maser m mit paramagnetischem Material, paramagnetischer Quantenverstärker m
paramagnetic material	s. paramagnet
paramagnetic moment of the atom	s. atomic magnetic moment
paramagnetic permeability	paramagnetische Permeabilität f, Permeabilität des Paramagnetikums
paramagnetic relaxation	paramagnetische Relaxation f
paramagnetic resonance absorption	paramagnetische Resonanzabsorption f
paramagnetic resonance phenomenon	paramagnetische Resonanzerscheinung f
paramagnetic rotation [of the plane of polarization]	paramagnetische Drehung f [der Polarisationsrichtung]
paramagnetic scattering	paramagnetische Streuung f
paramagnetic screening, paramagnetic shielding	paramagnetische Abschirmung f
paramagnetic screening constant	paramagnetische Abschirmungskonstante f
paramagnetic shielding, paramagnetic screening	paramagnetische Abschirmung f
paramagnetic substance, paramagnet[ic], paramagnetic material	Paramagnetikum n, paramagnetischer Stoff m
paramagnetic susceptibility	paramagnetische Suszeptibilität f
parametamorphic rock, pararock	Paragestein n
parameter, characteristic, characteristic value, datum, characteristic datum <gen.>	Parameter m, Kennwert m, Kenngröße f, Kenndatum n, Kennziffer f, Charakteristik f, Charakteristikum n, charakteristischer Wert m, Bestimmungsgröße f; Nebenvariable f, Hilfsvariable f <allg.>
parameter change, parameter transformation	Parameteränderung f, Parametertransformation f
parameter curve, parametric curve	Parameterkurve f, Parameterlinie f
parameter-free test	s. non-parametric test
parameter invariance	s. adiabatic invariance
parameterization	s. parametrization
parameterized	parametrisiert
parameter of inertia, inertial parameter	Trägheitsparameter m
parameter of information, information parameter	Informationsparameter m
parameter of live steam	Frischdampfparameter m
parameter of Rodrigues	s. Eulerian parameter
parameter of state, variable of state, state parameter, state variable, thermodynamic co-ordinate (property)	Zustandsgröße f, Zustandsparameter m, Zustandsvariable f, Zustandsveränderliche f
	s. deformation parameter
parameter of strain	
parameter of the screw, pitch of the wrench	Parameter m der Dyname, Pfeil m der Schraube
parameter of velocity	Geschwindigkeitsparameter m
parameter scattering	Parameterstreuung f
parameters of the system	s. general co-ordinates
parameter transformation, parameter change	Parameteränderung f, Parametertransformation f
parametral face, parametral plane	Parameterfläche f, Parameterebene f
parametric amplification, reactance amplification	parametrische Verstärkung f, Reaktanzverstärkung f
parametric amplifier; reactance amplifier, mavar <mixer amplification by variable reactance>	parametrischer Verstärker m; Reaktanzverstärker m, Mavar m
parametric circuit	parametrischer Kreis m; parametrische Schaltung f
parametric curve	s. parameter curve
parametric diode	s. varactor
parametric equation, parametric representation	Parameterdarstellung f
parametric equation	Parametergleichung f
parametric excitation	parametrische Erregung f
parametric hypothesis	Parameterhypothese f, parametrische Hypothese
parametric line	s. parameter curve
parametric oscillation	parametrische Schwingung f
parametric oscillator	parametrischer Oszillator m
parametric representation, parametric equation	Parameterdarstellung f
parametric resonance	parametrische Resonanz f
parametric travelling-wave amplifier, travelling-wave parametric amplifier	parametrischer Wanderfeldverstärker (Wanderwellenverstärker) m
parametrix, singularity function	Parametrix f, Levische Funktion f, Singularitätenfunktion f, Singularität[s]funktion f
parametrization, parameterization	Parametrisierung f
parametron oscillation	Parametronschwingung f
para-molecule	para-Molekül n, Paramolekül n
paramorph	paramorphe Form f
paramorphic	paramorph
paramorphic hemihedral class of the cubic system	s. paramorphic hemihedry of the regular system
paramorphic hemihedral class of the hexagonal system	s. paramorphic hemihedry of the hexagonal system
paramorphic hemihedral class of the tetragonal system	s. paramorphic hemihedry of the tetragonal class
paramorphic hemihedral class of the trigonal system	s. hexagonal tetartohedry of the second sort
paramorphic hemihedry of the hexagonal system, hexagonal equatorial class, pyramidal class, hexagonal bipyramidal class, hexagonal-dipyramidal [crystal] class, hexagonal paramorphy, paramorphic hemihedral class of the hexagonal system	paramorphe Hemiedrie f des hexagonalen Systems, hexagonal-bipyramidale Klasse f, pyramidale Hemiedrie, hexagonal dipyramidale Klasse
paramorphic hemihedry of the regular system, tesseral central class, pyritohedral class, parallelfaced (pentagonal) hemihedry, dyakisdodecahedral class, regular paramorphy, paramorphic hemihedral class of the cubic system, diploidal [crystal] class	paramorphe Hemiedrie f des kubischen Systems, disdodekaedrische Klasse f, pentagonale Hemiedrie, parallelflächige Hemiedrie
paramorphic hemihedry of the tetragonal system, tetragonal paramorphy, paramorphic hemihedral class of the tetragonal system, tetragonal equatorial class, [bi]pyramidal class, tetragonal-dipyramidal [crystal] class	paramorphe Hemiedrie f des tetragonalen Systems, tetragonal-bipyramidale Klasse f, tetragonal dipyramidale Klasse, tetragonale pyramidale Hemiedrie
paramorphism, paramorphosis	Paramorphose f, Umlagerungspseudomorphose f
paranthelion	Nebengegensonne f
parantiselena	Nebengegenmond m

paraphase 572

paraphase amplifier	Verstärker m mit Phasenumkehr[ung], Phasenumkehrstufe f, Zweitaktverstärker m, Paraphasenverstärker m	paraxial image point, Gaussian image point	Gaußscher (paraxialer, idealer) Bildpunkt m; axialer Bildpunkt
paraphase amplifier	s. a. push-pull amplifier	paraxial optics	Gaußsche Dioptrik f, Lehre f von der optischen Abbildung mit Hilfe des fadenförmigen Raumes
para-position, p-position	para-Stellung f, p-Stellung f		
para[-]positronium, singlet positronium	Parapositronium n	paraxial ray, Gauss ray	Paraxialstrahl m, paraxialer Strahl m; Nullstrahl m
pararock, parametamorphic rock	Paragestein n	paraxial region, Gauss region	paraxiales (Gaußsches, achsennahes) Gebiet n, fadenförmiger Raum m
paraselena	Nebenmond m	paraxial Schroedinger equation	paraxiale Schrödinger-Gleichung f
parasite	s. parasitic element		
parasite current, parasitic current; interference current; disturbing (perturbing) current; sneak current; stray (vagabond) current	Störstrom m; Fremdstrom m; Streustrom m, vagabundierender Strom m	paraxial single-surface equation <opt.>	Gaußsche Gleichung f <Opt.>
		paraxial trajectory	paraxiale Bahn f, Paraxialbahn f
		parelectric	s. para[-]electric
		parent	s. parent atom
parasite drag (resistance), parasitic (passive, resistance) drag, passive (wasteful, prejudicial) resistance	schädlicher Widerstand m	parent	s. a. parent nuclide
		parent	s. a. parent element
		parentage	s. origin
		parental magma	s. primordial magma
parasitic absorption	parasitäre Absorption f	parent atom, parent	Ausgangsatom n, Mutteratom m
parasitic[ally excited] antenna	s. parasitic element		
parasitic antenna array, parasitic array	Antenne f mit Reflektoren und Direktoren	parent comet, comet associated with the shower	erzeugender Komet m, Mutterkomet m
parasitic capture [of neutrons]	parasitärer Einfang (Neutroneneinfang) m	parent element, parent <nucl.>	Ausgangselement n, Mutterelement n <Kern.>
parasitic capture-to-fission ratio	Verhältnis n der parasitären Einfänge zur Anzahl der Spaltungen	parent fraction	Ausgangsfraktion f, Anteil m der Ausgangssubstanz
		parenthesis, round bracket <math.>	[runde] Klammer f <Math.>
parasitic current	s. parasite current	parent mass peak, parent peak	Ausgangslinie f, Bezugslinie f im Massenspektrum <zum undissoziierten Molekül gehörig>
parasitic director, director, wave director <el.>	Direktor m, Wellenrichter m, Richtdipol m, Führungsantenne f, Leitantenne f <El.>		
parasitic drag	s. parasite drag	parent-molecule <in comet head>	Muttermolekül n <im Kometenkopf>
parasitic effect, perturbing action (influence, effect)	Störwirkung f, Störeinfluß m, Störeffekt m		
parasitic electromotive force, parasitic e.m.f.	Stör-EMK f, störende elektromotorische Kraft f	parent nucleus	s. parent nuclide
parasitic element [of antenna], radiation coupled element, parasitic antenna, passive antenna, parasitically excited antenna, passive element of antenna, parasite	strahlungsgekoppeltes (passives) Element n [der Antenne], strahlungsgekoppelte Antenne f, nichtangeschlossenes Zusatzelement n für Dipolantennen. Zusatzelement [der Antenne]	parent nuclide, [nuclear] parent; parent (original) nucleus	Mutternuklid n, Ausgangsnuklid n; Ausgangskern m, Mutterkern m, Elternkern m
		parent peak	s. parent mass peak
		parent population	s. population <stat., gen.>
		parhelic circle <halo>	Horizontalkreis m, Horizontalring m, Nebensonnenkreis m, Nebensonnenring m <Halo>
parasitic feedback	Streurückkopplung f	parhelion, mocksun, sun-dog	Nebensonne f
parasitic oscillation, undesired oscillation	Störschwingung f	parhelion of 22°, 22°-parhelion	Nebensonnenhalo m, Nebensonne f von 22°
parasitic oscillation	s. a. spurious oscillation	parhelium, parahelium	Parahelium n, Parhelium n
parasitic radiation	s. spurious radiation	parity	Parität f; Spiegelungsmoment n, Signatur f
parasitic reactance, spurious reactance	Störblindwiderstand m, Störreaktanz f	parity + 1, even parity, positive parity	gerade Parität f, Parität + 1, positive Parität
parasitic reflector, reflector, radiation-coupled reflector <el.>	Reflektor m <El.>	parity − 1, odd parity, negative parity	ungerade Parität f, Parität − 1, negative Parität
		parity check <num.math.>	Paritätsprüfung f <num. Math.>
parasitic resonance	Störresonanz f, parasitäre Resonanz f	parity coefficient	Paritätskoeffizient m
		parity conjugation [operation]	Paritätskonjugation f
parasitics; interference; jamming; mush <el.>	Störung f; Störgeräusch n <El.>	parity conservation law	s. law of conservation of parity
		parity favoured [forbidden] transition	s. unique transition
parasitic signal	s. spurious signal	parity non-conservation	s. non-conservation of parity
parasitic suppression	s. noise suppression		
parasitic voltage, interference (noise) voltage	Störspannung f	parity operator	Paritätsoperator m
		parity selection rule	Paritätsauswahlregel f
parasitic voltage meter, interference voltage meter	Störspannungsmeßgerät n, Störspannungsmesser m	parity unfavoured [forbidden] transition	s. unfavoured transition
parasitic wave	s. spurious wave	parity violation	s. non-conservation of parity
para-state, para state	Para-Zustand m		
parastatistics	Parastatistik f	Parker effect	Parker-Effekt m
parastrophe	Parastrophe f	parkerization, parkerizing	Parkerisieren n, Parker-Verfahren n
para-substitution compound, para-compound, p-compound	para-Verbindung f, p-Verbindung f	Parker['s] solution	Parker-Lösung f, Parkersche Lösung f
paraterm	Paraterm m	Parker-Washburn boundary	Parker-Washburn-Korngrenze f, Parker-Washburnsche Korngrenze f
paraxial	paraxial, achsennah		

parkesization, parkesizing	s. Parkes process	partial differential, intermediate differential	partielles Differential n
Parkes process (technique) [for desilvering lead], parkesizing, parkesization	Parkes-Verfahren n, Parkesieren n	partial differential coefficient, partial derivative	partielle Ableitung f
paroxysmal eruption	paroxysmale Eruption f, paroxysmaler Ausbruch m	partial differential equation	partielle Differentialgleichung f
Parr['s] principle	Parrsches Prinzip n	partial differential equation of Hamilton-Jacobi	s. Hamilton-Jacobi equation
Parry['s] arc	Parrys Halo m		
parsec, parallax of one second, pc	Parsec n, Parallaxensekunde f, Sternweite f, Parsek n, pc	partial diffusion coefficient	partieller Diffusionskoeffizient m
Parseval['s] equation, Parseval['s] formula, Parseval['s] theorem, completeness relation	Parsevalsche Formel (Gleichung) f, Abgeschlossenheitsrelation f, Vollständigkeitsrelation f, Parsevalscher Satz m, Parsevalsches Theorem n	partial dilution heat, partial heat of dilution	partielle Verdünnungswärme f
		partial discharge	Teilentladung f
		partial disintegration constant	partielle Zerfallskonstante f
		partial dislocation	s. half[-] dislocation
		partial dispersion	partielle Dispersion f
Parshall['] measuring flume	Parshall-Gerinne n, Parshall-Kanal m	partial domain	s. subdomain <math.>
Parsons turbine	s. reaction turbine	partial eclipse, penumbral eclipse	partielle Finsternis f, teilweise Verfinsterung f, Halbschattenfinsternis f
part, subset, sub-aggregate <math.>	Untermenge f, Teilmenge f, Teil m <Math.>		
part	s. a. circuit element <of the electrical circuit>	partial eclipse of the Sun	s. partial solar eclipse
part	s. a. component <of construction>	partial emissivity, partial emittance	Teilstrahlungsvermögen n
part by mass, part by weight	Masseteil m, Gewichtsteil m	partial energy	Partialenergie f
		partial entropy	Partialentropie f
part by volume	Volum[en]teil m, Raumteil m, Volum[en]anteil m, Raumanteil m	partial equilibrium	Teilgleichgewicht n, partielles Gleichgewicht n, Partialgleichgewicht n
part by weight	s. part by mass	partial evaporation, incomplete evaporation	Teilverdampfung f, unvollständige Verdampfung f
parted hyperboloid, two-sheet hyperboloid, hyperboloid of two sheets	zweischaliges Hyperboloid n		
		partial excitation	Teilerregung f
Parthasarathy['s] rule	Parthasarathysche Regel f	partial exposure, partial body irradiation	Teilkörperbestrahlung f, Teilbestrahlung f
partial, partial tone, partial overtone, overtone <ac.>	Teilton m, Partialton m, Oberton m <Ak.>	partial fraction	Partialbruch m
partial air force, aerodynamic derivative, resistance derivative	partielle Ableitung f von aerodynamischen Kräften <oder Momenten>	partial fraction expansion, expressing in partial fractions, decomposition into partial fractions	Partialbruchzerlegung f
partial analysis	Teilanalyse f		
partial association <stat.>	partielle Assoziation f <Stat.>	partial-fraction network	Partialbruchschaltung f
partial body irradiation, partial exposure	Teilkörperbestrahlung f, Teilbestrahlung f	partial heat of dilution	s. partial dilution heat
		partial horopter	Partialhoropter m, Linienhoropter m, partieller Horopter m
partial breakdown, incomplete breakdown	Teildurchschlag m		
partial capacitance	[Breisigsche] Teilkapazität f	partial image, split image	Teilbild n
partial coherence	partielle Kohärenz f		
partial colour blindness, dichromatic vision, dichromatism	Dichromasie f, partielle Farbenblindheit f, Dichromatopsie f, Zweifarbenblindheit f	partial inductance	Teilinduktivität f
		partial integration	s. integration by parts
		partial internal energy	innere Partialenergie f
partial combustion, incomplete combustion	unvollständige Verbrennung f, Teilverbrennung f	partial ionization	Teilionisation f, Teilionisierung f, teilweise (partielle) Ionisierung f
partial compensation of loss	s. reversal of damping		
partial condensation, dephlegmation	Teilkondensation f, partielle (teilweise) Kondensation f, Dephlegmation f	partial level width, partial width	Partialbreite f, partielle Niveaubreite f
		partial load; sub-load	Teillast f, Teilbelastung f
partial condenser	s. dephlegmator	partial luminous flux	Teillichtstrom m
partial contingency	partielle Kontingenz f		
partial conversion coefficient	partieller Konversionsfaktor m	partially coherent	teilkohärent, teilweise (partiell) kohärent
partial correlation	partielle (bereinigte) Korrelation f, Partialkorrelation f, Teilkorrelation f	partially crystalline	partiell kristallin
		partially degenerate	teilweise entartet
		partially dissoluble, partially soluble	teillöslich, teilweise (unvollständig, partiell) löslich
partial correlation coefficient	partieller (bereinigter) Korrelationskoeffizient m		
partial cross-section	partieller Wirkungsquerschnitt m, Partialquerschnitt m	partially enclosed, screened <of apparatuses>	gegen zufällige Berührung geschützt <Geräte>
		partially evacuated	teilevakuiert
partial current density	Teilstromdichte f		
partial deformation	Teilverformung f	partially miscible, partly miscible	teilweise (unvollständig, partiell) mischbar
partial degeneracy	teilweise Entartung f, Teilentartung f		
		partially occupied band	teilbesetztes Energieband n, teilweise besetztes Energieband
partial demagnetization	partielle Entmagnetisierung f		
partial derivative, partial differential coefficient	partielle Ableitung f	partially ordered set, ordered set, partly ordered set <math.>	halbgeordnete (partiell geordnete, teilweise geordnete, t-geordnete) Menge f, Verein m <Math.>
partial difference quotient	partieller Differenzenquotient m		

partially ordered state	teilweise geordneter Zustand *m*, teilgeordneter Zustand	partial sum	Partialsumme *f*, Teilsumme *f*
partially polarized	teilweise polarisiert, teilpolarisiert	partial suppression of sideband, partial sideband suppression	Seitenbandbeschneidung *f*
partially reflected	partiell (teilweise) reflektiert, teilreflektiert	partial thermodynamic potential	s. partial potential <of *n*-th order>
partially soluble, partially dissoluble	teillöslich, teilweise (unvollständig, partiell) löslich	partial tide	Partialtide *f*, partielle Tide *f*, Teiltide *f*, Teilgezeit *f*, Teilwelle *f* <Geo.>
partially transmitting, semi-transparent, semi-opaque <opt.>	halbdurchlässig, teildurchlässig, teilweise durchlässig <Opt.>	partial tone, partial [overtone], overtone <ac.>	Teilton *m*, Partialton *m*, Oberton *m* <Ak.>
partial matrix, submatrix	Untermatrix *f*, Teilmatrix *f*	partial transference (transport) number	partielle Überführungszahl *f*
partial miscibility, incomplete miscibility	unvollständige (teilweise, partielle) Mischbarkeit *f*, Teilmischbarkeit *f*	partial vacuum	s. fore-vacuum
		partial vacuum	s. underpressure
partial mode; partial wave; subwave	Teilwelle *f*, Partialwelle *f*	partial valence, partial valency, residual valence (valency)	Partialvalenz *f*, Restvalenz *f*, Teilvalenz *f*, Teilwertigkeit *f*
partial molal free energy	s. chemical potential	partial valence	s. a. secondary valence
partial molar heat	partielle Molwärme *f*	partial valence theory	Partialvalenztheorie *f*
partial molar quantity	partielle molare Größe *f*	partial valency	s. partial valence
partial node	Teilknoten *m*	partial vibration, partial oscillation	Partialschwingung *f*, Teilschwingung *f*
partial ordering	Halbordnung *f*, Partialordnung *f*, teilweise Ordnung *f*, t-Ordnung *f*		
partial oscillation, partial vibration	Partialschwingung *f*, Teilschwingung *f*	partial voltage, voltage fraction (component), component of the voltage	Teilspannung *f*
		partial voltage polygon	Teilspannungspolygon *n*
partial overtone	s. partial <ac.>	partial volume	Partialvolumen *n*, partielles Volumen *n*
partial Paschen-Back effect	partieller Paschen-Back-Effekt *m*	partial wave; partial mode; subwave	Teilwelle *f*, Partialwelle *f*
partial pitch	s. partial step		
partial polarization	Teilpolarisation *f*, teilweise (partielle) Polarisation *f*	partial wave method, method of partial waves	Partialwellenmethode *f*, Teilwellenmethode *f*, Methode *f* der Partialwellen
partial pole	Teilpol *m*		
partial potential, partial thermodynamic potential <of *n*-th order>	partielles [thermodynamisches] Potential *n*, Teilpotential *n* <*n*-ter Ordnung>	partial wave solution	Partialwellenlösung *f*, Teilwellenlösung *f*
		partial width, partial level width	Partialbreite *f*, partielle Niveaubreite *f*
partial pressure	Partialdruck *m*, partieller Druck *m*, Teildruck *m*; Partialdampfdruck *m*	particle	Teilchen *n*; Partikel *f* <*pl.*: Partikeln>
		particle	s. a. material point
partial pressure gradient	Partialdruckgefälle *n*	particle accelerator	s. atomic particle accelerator
partial problem, subproblem	Teilproblem *n*	particle aspect <of matter>	Teilchenbild *n*, Teilchenaspekt *m*, Partikelbild *n*, Partikelaspekt *m* <der Materie>
partial pulse	Teilimpuls *m*		
partial racemate	s. quasi[-] racemate		
partial racemization	partielle Razemisierung *f*	particle beam, beam <acc.>	Teilchenstrahl *m*, Strahl *m* <Beschl.>
partial radiation	Teilstrahlung *f*		
partial radiation pyrometer	Teilstrahlungspyrometer *n*	particle capture <acc.>	Teilcheneinfang *m* <Beschl.>
partial radiation thermometer	Teilstrahlungsthermometer *n*	particle current, accelerated [particle] current, current of accelerated particles <acc.>	Teilchenstrom *m* <Beschl.>
partial range, quasi range	partielle Spannweite *f*		
partial reaction	Teilreaktion *f*		
partial reaction width, channel width <nucl.>	Kanalbreite *f*, Partialbreite *f* des Kanals <Kern.>	particle displacement <ac.>	Schallausschlag *m*, Teilchenverschiebung *f* <Ak.>
partial reflection	partielle (teilweise) Reflexion *f*, Teilreflexion *f*	particle dynamics	Teilchendynamik *f*, Dynamik *f* der Teilchen
partial resonance	s. subresonance		
partial restoring time	s. hangover time	particle family	Teilchenfamilie *f*
partial reversal of damping	s. reversal of damping	particle flow, corpuscular stream	Teilchenstrom *m*, Partikelstrom *m*, Korpuskelstrom *m*
partial saturation	partielle Sättigung *f*, Teilsättigung *f*	particle fluence, fluence <bio.>	Teilchenfluenz *f*, Fluenz *f* <Bio.>
partial scattering cross-section	partieller Streuquerschnitt *m*	particle fluence build-up factor	Teilchenfluenz-Aufbaufaktor *m*
partial series	s. harmonic series	particle flux, flux of particles	Teilchenfluß *m*
partial shadow, penumbra, half shade (shadow)	Halbschatten *m*, Penumbra *f*	particle flux [density]	Teilchenstromdichte *f*; Teilchenflußdichte *f*, Teilchenfluß *m*
partial sideband suppression, partial suppression of sideband	Seitenbandbeschneidung *f*	particle flux density, flux density, fluence rate <bio.>	Teilchenflußdichte *f*, Flußdichte *f*, Fluenzleistung *f* <Bio.>
partial solar eclipse, partial eclipse of the Sun	partielle Sonnenfinsternis *f*		
partial solarization	Teilsolarisation *f*	particle function, particle wave function	Teilchen[wellen]funktion *f*, Wellenfunktion *f* des Teilchens
partial specific Gibbs function	s. chemical potential		
partial specific quantity	partielle spezifische Größe *f*	particle-hole theorem	Teilchen-Loch-Theorem *n*
partial step; partial pitch	Teilschritt *m*	particle level width, particle width	Teilchenniveaubreite *f*, Teilchenbreite *f*

particle localization	Teilchenort[s]messung f, Teilchenlokalisierung f	**particulate number** <of aerosol>; number of particles, particle number	Teilchenzahl f
particle mass	Teilchenmasse f	**particulate of aerosol**	s. aerosol particulate
particle mass, point (concentrated) mass	Punktmasse f, konzentrierte Masse f	**parting**; separation, separation of sizes	Scheidung f
particle momentum	Teilchenimpuls m	**parting**	s. a. separation
		parting	s. a. partition <chem.>
particle number, number of particles; particulate number <of aerosol>	Teilchenzahl f	**parting agent**	s. abherent
		parting surface	s. interface
particle number conservation law, law of conservation of particle number	Satz m von der Erhaltung der Teilchenzahl, Teilchenzahlerhaltungssatz m, Erhaltungssatz m der Teilchenzahl	**partition**, partitioning, segmentation, sectionalization, subdivision	Unterteilung f
		partition, dividing (inner) partition, partition wall, dividing wall, parting; diaphragm; baffle; septum <chem.>	Trennwand f, Trennungswand f, Scheidewand f, Zwischenwand f; Diaphragma n <Chem.>
particle number density operator	Teilchen[anzahl]dichteoperator m, Operator m der Einteilchen-Dichtematrix		
particle number operator, operator of particle number	Teilchenzahloperator m	**partition** <math.>	Partition f <Math.>
		partition	s. a. distribution
particle of air, air particle	Luftpartikel f, Luftteilchen n	**partition**	s. a. separation
		partition chart, distribution chart (map), partition map	Verteilungskarte f
particle of finite rest mass	Teilchen n endlicher Ruhemasse		
particle optics	Korpuskularoptik f	**partition chromatography**, liquid-liquid chromatography, partography	Verteilungschromatographie f
particle-orbit contractor, orbit contractor	Teilchenbahnkontraktor m, Bahnkontraktor m		
particle-orbit expander, orbit expander	Teilchenbahndehner m, Bahndehner m, Teilchenbahnexpander m, Bahnexpander m	**partition coefficient**	s. distribution coefficient
		partitioned matrix	s. hypermatrix
particle pair density, density of particle pairs	Teilchenpaardichte f	**partition function**, sum over states, sum-over-states, zustandssumme, state sum <therm.>	Zustandssumme f [von Planck], Plancksche Zustandssumme, Verteilungsfunktion f <Therm.>
particle production [in nuclear collisions]	Teilchenerzeugung f [durch Kernstöße]		
		partition function	s. a. distribution function
		partition function of external rotation, external rotation partition function	Zustandssumme f der äußeren Rotation
particle pulse, pulse of particles	Teilchenimpuls m		
particle radiation	s. corpuscular radiation	**partition function of internal molecular motions**	Zustandssumme f der inneren Molekülbewegungen
particle-rich shower	teilchenreicher Schauer m		
particle rigidity	s. magnetic rigidity	**partition function of internal rotation**, internal rotation partition function	Zustandssumme f der inneren Rotation
particle size	Teilchengröße f, Partikelgröße f		
particle-size analysis, granulation (granulometric, sieve, sieving, screen) analysis, sieve (screen) test, mesh analysis	Siebanalyse f, Körnungsanalyse f, Siebversuch m	**partition function of the molecule**	Zustandssumme f des Moleküls, Molekülzustandssumme f
		partition-function ratio	Zustandssummenverhältnis n
particle size distribution, size distribution	Korn[größen]verteilung f, Körnung f, Kornzusammensetzung f	**partitioning**	s. partition
		partition law, distribution law	Verteilungsgesetz n
particle-size distribution curve	s. granulometric curve	**partition law [of Nernst]**	s. Nernst distribution law
particle spectrum	Teilchenspektrum n	**partition map**, distribution chart (map), partition chart	Verteilungskarte f
particle track	s. track [of the particle]		
particle transfer (transport)	Teilchenübertragung f, Teilchentransport m	**partition method**, barrier diffusion method	Trennwanddiffusionsverfahren n, Isotopentrennung f durch Diffusion durch eine poröse Wand
particle velocity, acoustic[al] particle velocity, sound particle velocity, acoustic[al] velocity <ac.>	Schallschnelle f <Ak.>		
		partition noise, [current] distribution noise, fluctuation noise, distribution fluctuation[s]	Stromverteilungsrauschen n, Verteilungsrauschen n
particle wave function, particle function	Teilchen[wellen]funktion f, Wellenfunktion f des Teilchens		
particle width, particle level width	Teilchenniveaubreite f, Teilchenbreite f	**partition ratio**	Stromübernahmeverhältnis n
particle with half-integer spin, fermion, Fermi[-Dirac] particle	Fermion n, Fermi[-Dirac]-Teilchen n	**partition wall**	s. partition <chem.>
		partly crystalline, hypocrystalline	hypokristallin
particle with spin, spin particle	Teilchen n mit Spin, Spinteilchen n	**partly miscible**, partially miscible	teilweise (unvollständig, partiell) mischbar
particle with spin $\frac{1}{2}$, spin $\frac{1}{2}$ particle	Spin-$\frac{1}{2}$-Teilchen n, Teilchen n mit dem Spin $\frac{1}{2}$	**partly open interval**	s. half-closed interval
		partly ordered set	s. partially ordered set
particle with spin 1, spin 1 particle	Spin-1-Teilchen n, Teilchen n mit dem Spin 1	**partly transistorized**, part-transistorized	teiltransistorisiert, teilweise transistorbestückt
particular case, special case	Spezialfall m, spezieller Fall m, Sonderfall m	**part of reflected intensity**	s. reflected intensity
particular integral	s. particular solution	**part of the spectrum**	s. spectral region
particular solution, particular integral	partikuläre (spezielle, individuelle) Lösung f, partikuläres Integral n, Einzellösung f, Partiallösung f	**part of transmitted intensity**	s. transmitted intensity
		partography	s. partition chromatography
		parton	Parton n
particulate	s. aerosol particulate	**part per billion**, p.p.b., ppb <= 10^{-9} ≙ 10^{-7} vol.%>	Teil m pro Milliarde, part per billion, ppb <= 10^{-9} ≙ 10^{-7} Vol.-%>

part per million, p.p.m., ppm <= 10^{-6} △ 10^{-4} vol.%>	Teil m pro Million, part per million, ppm <= 10^{-6} △ 10^{-4} Vol.-%>	**passive,** inactive, reactionless <chem.>	passiv, Passiv-, inaktiv, reaktionsträge <Chem.>
part-transistorized, partly transistorized	teiltransistorisiert, teilweise transistorbestückt		
		passive-active cell	Passiv-Aktiv-Element n
pascal, Pa <= 1 N/m²	Pascal n, Pa <= 1 N/m²	**passive antenna**	s. parasitic element
Pascal['s] distribution	s. Pólya['s] distribution	**passive drag**	s. parasite drag
Pascalian liquid	s. ideal liquid	**passive element of antenna**	s. parasitic element
Pascal['s] law [of the transmissibility of hydrostatic pressure], principle of Pascal, law of the transmissibility of pressure, theorem on the isotropy of pressure	Pascalsches Gesetz n, Druckfortpflanzungsgesetz n	**passive film,** passive layer	Passivschicht f
		passive flight	s. inertial flight
		passive gravitational mass	passive schwere Masse f
		passive layer, passive film	Passivschicht f
Pascal['s] limaçon	s. limaçon	**passive mass** <of rocket>	passive Masse f <Rakete>
Pascal['s] rule	Pascalsche Regel f, Regel von P. Pascal	**passive past**	passive Vergangenheit f
		passive resistance	s. parasite drag
Pascal['s] triangle	Pascalsches Zahlendreieck n, Pascalsches Dreieck n	**passive slip plane**	nichtbetätigte Gleitebene f
Paschen-Back effect	Paschen-Back-Effekt m, magnetischer Verwandlungseffekt m	**passive transducer**	passiver Wandler m, passiver Transduktor m
		pass range	s. pass[-] band
Paschen circle	Paschen-Kreis m	**pastagram,** Bellamy pastagram	Bellamy-Diagramm n, Pastagramm n
Paschen curve	Paschen-Kurve f	**paste cathode**	Pastekatode f
Paschen['s] law, law of Paschen	Paschensches Gesetz n	**pasted-plate accumulator**	Bleiakkumulator m mit gepasteten Gitterplatten, Akkumulator m mit Gitterplatten
Paschen-Runge grating mounting, Paschen-Runge mounting [of diffraction grating]	Runge-Paschensche Gitteraufstellung f, Paschen-Rungesche Gitteraufstellung		
		pastel	Pastellfarbe f
		paste reactor	Pastenreaktor m
Paschen series	Paschen-Serie f	**pasting**	Pastierung f
		pasty, doughy	teigartig, teigig
pass, passage <of piece in rolling>	Stich m, Walzstich m, Durchgang m <Walzen>	**pasty state**	teigiger Zustand m
		patch; spot <also el.>; speck	Fleck m
passage, passing	Durchzug m, Vorbeizug m, Vorüberzug m; Vorbeigang m; Vorbeilaufen n	**path,** pathway, way; distance [passed through], distance covered, space passed through; travel; displacement	Weg m; Laufweg m; Flugweg m; Wegstrecke f, Laufstrecke f, Flugstrecke f, durchlaufene Strecke f, Strecke, zurückgelegter Weg
passage, transit <of a star>	Durchgang m; Vorübergang m <Gestirn>		
passage	s. a. pass <of piece in rolling>		
passage	s. a. passing		
passage grid controllance	s. penetrance	**path,** path length	Weglänge f
passage instrument	s. transit instrument <astr.>	**path**	s. a. trajectory
passage of current, current passage, current flow	Stromdurchgang m, Stromdurchfluß m, Stromfluß m	**path amplitude**	Wegamplitude f
		path analysis	s. path coefficient method
		path attenuation	Streckendämpfung f, Funkfelddämpfung f
passage of front, front passage	Frontdurchgang m, Durchgang m der Front, Frontpassage f	**path coefficient method,** path analysis	Pfadkoeffizientenmethode f, Pfadanalyse f
passage of heat	s. transmission of heat	**path contraction**	Bahnkontraktion f, Bahneinengung f
passage of zero [point]	s. zero passage		
passage through the meridian	s. meridian transit	**path difference**	s. difference of path <of rays>
pass[-] band, filter range; pass range; transmission range, free transmission range; transmission band	Durchlässigkeitsbereich m, Durchlässigkeitsband n, Durchlaßbereich m; nutzbare Bandbreite f	**path element,** element of path	Wegelement n
		path group	Wegegruppe f
		path inclination; inclination of orbit	Bahnneigung f
pass-band damping, damping in the pass band	Lochdämpfung f, Durchlaßdämpfung f; Grunddämpfung f	**path length,** path	Weglänge f
passing, passage	Durchzug m, Vorbeizug m, Vorüberzug m; Vorbeigang m; Vorbeilaufen n	**path length**	s. a. orbit circumference
		path line	s. trajectory
		path of conduction <bio.>	Leitungsbahn f <Bio.>
passing, passage, transmission, transit, traversing <of light, particles>	Durchgang m, Durchlaufung f, Durchlaufen n, Passieren n, Passage f, Durchgehen n, Durchtritt m, Durchsetzen n, Durchqueren n, Hindurchgehen n <Licht, Teilchen>	**path of current**	s. current path <el.>
		path of integration	Integrationsweg m
		path of leakage current, leakage current path <el.>	Leckweg m, Irrweg m <El.>
		path of rays, run of rays, ray[-] trajectory; trace of rays <US>	Strahlengang m, Strahlenverlauf m, Strahlenweg m, Strahlenbahn f
passing electron, transelectron	Transelektron n	**path of the hurricane,** hurricane path	Asgardweg m, Asgardsweg m, zerstörende Bahn f der Trombe
passing motion [around]	s. flow around a body		
passing-over	s. overrun	**pathologic system**	pathologisches System (Sternsystem) n
passing shower, transient (local) shower	Strichregen m		
passing through the meridian	s. meridian transit	**path resistance,** bulk resistance	Bahnwiderstand m
passing to the limit, limiting process	Grenzübergang m	**path-time diagram;** displace-time diagram	Weg-Zeit-Diagramm n, Weg-Zeit-Schaubild n
passivating	s. passivation		
passivating agent	s. inhibitor <chem.>		
passivation, passivating, formation of protective film	Passivierung f, Schutzschichtbildung f, Deckschichtbildung f		
passivation potential	Passivierungspotential n, Passivierungsspannung f		
passivator	s. inhibitor <chem.>		

path-time law, space-time law	Weg-Zeit-Gesetz n		pA value, pA, pA number	pA-Wert m, pA
path velocity	s. orbital velocity		PA view, PA projection, posterior-anterior view, anterior projection, frontal projection	Projektion f von hinten nach vorn
pathway	s. trajectory			
pathway of the reaction	Reaktionsbahn f			
pattern	s. screen			
pattern	s. version		pawl and ratchet motion, ratchet motion, ratchet wheel drive, rack wheel	Zahngesperre n, Klinkengesperre n, Klinkenschaltwerk n, Zahnklinkenschaltwerk n
patterned sampling, systematic sampling	systematische Probennahme f; systematisches Stichprobenverfahren n			
pattern of dislocation	s. dislocation array		pawl wheel, ratchet wheel	Sperrad n
pattern of the field, field pattern, lines of force; field mapping; field map	Feld[linien]bild n, Feldlinien fpl, Kraftlinienbild n, [bildliche] Darstellung f des Feldes durch Feldlinien		Pawsey stub	Pawseyscher Symmetriertopf m, Pawsey-Symmetriertopf m
			payload ‹of the rocket›	Nutzlast f ‹Rakete›
Patterson [diagram]	s. Patterson map		payload ratio	Nutzlastverhältnis n
Patterson['s] function, P-function	Pattersonsche Funktion f, Patterson-Funktion f, P-Funktion f			
			P band ‹0.225–0.39 or 12.4–18 Gc/s›	P-Band n ‹0,225···0,39 oder 12,4···18 GHz›
Patterson-Harker method, Patterson['s] method	Patterson[-Harker]sches Verfahren n, Patterson-[Harker-]Verfahren n, Pattersonsche Methode f			
			P-branch, negative branch	P-Zweig m, negativer Zweig m
			PC invariance	PC-Invarianz f
Patterson map, Patterson, Patterson diagram	Pattersonsche Karte f, Patterson-Karte f, Patterson-Diagramm n		p-compound, para-compound, para-substitution compound	para-Verbindung f, p-Verbindung f
			p-conducting, p-type	p-leitend, p-, p-Typ-, defektleitend
Patterson['s] method	s. Patterson-Harker method		P. control	s. proportional control
Patterson peak	Patterson-Maximum n, Pattersonsches Maximum n		P. controller	s. proportional controller
			P Cygni star	P Cygni-Stern m
Patterson projection	Pattersonsche Projektion f, Patterson-Projektion f		P.D. control	s. proportional derivative control
			P.D. controller	s. proportional and derivative action controller
Patterson section	Patterson-Schnitt m, Pattersonscher Schnitt m			
			pD value, pD	pD-Wert m, pD
Patterson series	s. Patterson synthesis		Peach-Koehler equation	Peach-Koehler-Gleichung f
Patterson space	Patterson-Raum m			
			peak, line, maximum	Peak m, Linie f, [scharfes] Maximum n, Gipfel m; Berg m, Spitze f ‹Chromatographie›
Patterson synthesis, Patterson series, F^2 series	Pattersonsche Synthese f, Patterson-Synthese f, Patterson-Reihe f, Pattersonsche Reihe f, F^2-Reihe f			
			peak, peak value, crest [value] ‹US›, apex, summit ‹gen.›	Scheitelwert m, Gipfelwert m, Scheitel m ‹allg.›
paucimolecular film, paucimolecular layer	paucimolekulare Schicht f, paucimolekularer Film m		peak ammeter	s. peak-reading ammeter
			peak amplitude	s. peak value
Pauli['s] algebra	Paulische Algebra f		peak counting rate	Peakzählrate f
Pauli approximation	Pauli-Näherung f, Paulische Näherung f			
Pauli equation	Pauli-Gleichung f, Paulische Gleichung f		peak current, peak value of current	Stromscheitelwert m, Scheitelwert m des Wechselstroms (Stroms), Scheitelstrom m; Stromspitzenwert m, Spitzenwert m des Wechselstroms (Stroms), Spitzenstrom m
Pauli['s] exclusion principle	s. exclusion principle			
Pauli function	Pauli-Funktion f, Paulische Funktion f			
Pauli['s] g-sum rule	s. g sum rule		peak delay	s. delay time
Pauli-Gürsey transformation	Pauli-Gürsey-Transformation f, Pauli-Gürseysche Transformation f		peak deviation of frequency	s. peak frequency deviation
			peakedness	Hochgipfligkeit f, positiver Exzeß m
Pauli-Jordan commutation function	Pauli-Jordansche Vertauschungsfunktion f		peak efficiency	Peakeffektivität f
Pauli line, Pauli straight line	Pauli-Gerade f		peaker [circuit]	s. peaking circuit
Pauli matrix	s. Pauli spin matrix		peaker strip	Differenzierspule f
Pauli rule, magnetic criterion [of bond type] ‹of Pauling›	magnetisches Kriterium n [von Pauling], Paulingsches Kriterium, Paulingsche Regel f		peak factor	s. crest factor
			peak factor bridge	Scheitelfaktormeßbrücke f
Pauli operator, Pauli spin operator	Pauli-Operator m, Paulischer Operator m		peak factor meter	Scheitelfaktormesser m, Scheitelfaktormeßgerät n
Pauli paramagnetism	Pauli-Paramagnetismus m, Paulischer Paramagnetismus m		peak force, peak mechanomotive force	Spitzenwert m der mechanomotorischen Kraft
Pauli['s] principle	s. exclusion principle			
Pauli representation	Pauli-Darstellung f, Paulische Darstellung f		peak frequency deviation, peak deviation of frequency	Maximalhub m [der Frequenz]
Pauli spin matrix, spin matrix [of Pauli], [two-by-two] Pauli matrix	Paulische Spinmatrix (Matrix) f, Spinmatrix [von Pauli], Pauli-Matrix f			
Pauli spin susceptibility	s. spin susceptibility		peak gust, maximum gust	Spitzenbö f
Pauli straight line, Pauli line	Pauli-Gerade f		peak height	Linienhöhe f, Peakhöhe f
Pauli system	Pauli-System n			
Pauli['s] theorem	Pauli-Theorem n, Paulisches Theorem n, Satz m von Pauli			
Pauli vacancy principle	s. electron-shell structure			

peak indication; maximum (peak) reading; maximum indication	Maximumanzeige f	peak value peak-value indicator peak value of current peak value of magnification, resonance ratio	s. a. peak s. peak-reading meter s. peak current Resonanzüberhöhung f der Amplitude
peaking circuit, peaker circuit, peaker	Spitzenkreis m		
peak inverse voltage	Scheitelsperrspannung f, Spitzensperrspannung f, Spitzenwert m der Spannung in Sperrichtung	peak value of voltage peak voltage, peak value of voltage	s. peak voltage Spannungsscheitelwert m, Scheitelwert m der Wechselspannung (Spannung), Scheitelspannung f; Spannungsspitzenwert m, Spitzenwert m der Wechselspannung (Spannung), Spitzenspannung f
peak limiter, amplitude limiter, clipper circuit, [amplitude] lopper	Amplitudenbegrenzer m		
peak load	Spitzenlast f; Spitzenbelastung f	peak voltmeter peak white; white peak	s. peak-reading voltmeter Weißspitze f, Spitzenweiß n, Maximum n an Weiß, hellste Stelle f des Bildes
peak load	s. a. maximum permissible load		
peak making current	Scheitelwert m des Einschaltstromes, Einschalt[strom]spitze f		
peak mechanomotive force	s. peak force	peak width	s. full width at half[-] maximum
peak of mass spectrum, mass peak	Massenlinie f, Massenpeak m, Linie f im Massenspektrum	pearlitic point, pearlitic temperature pearlitic structure	Perlitpunkt m perlitisches Gefüge n, Perlitgefüge n
peak of the atmospheric layer, top of the atmospheric layer	Gipfel m (Maximum n) der Atmosphärenschicht		
peak of the flash, duration of peak	Scheitelzeit f	pearlitic temperature pearl necklace pearl polymerization, bead polymerization; slurry polymerization [process], suspension polymerization; emulsion polymerization	s. pearlitic point s. bead lightning Perlpolymerisation f, Kornpolymerisation f, Suspensionspolymerisation f, Polymerisation f in Dispersion; Emulsionspolymerisation f, Polymerisation in Emulsion
peak of the wave	s. crest [of the wave]		
peakology	„peakology"-Methode f, Peakologie f, Peakanalyse f		
peak power meter	Spitzenleistungsmesser m		
peak pulse power	Impulsspitzenleistung f	Pearl-Reed curve, logistic curve, logistic growth curve	logistische Kurve (Funktion) f, logistisches Wachstumsgesetz n, Robertsonsche Wachstumsfunktion f
peak reading, maximum reading; maximum (peak) indication	Maximumanzeige f		
		pearl-string model	Perlschnurmodell n, Perlenkettenmodell n <Makromoleküle>
peak-reading ammeter, peak ammeter	Spitzen[wert]strommesser m, Scheitel[wert]strommesser m, Höchstwertstrommesser m, Maximumstromanzeigegerät n, Maximumstrom[an]zeiger m		
		pearshaped, pyriform pear[-]shaped figure [of equilibrium]	birnenförmig Poincarésche Birne f, birnenförmige Gleichgewichtsfigur f
peak-reading indicator, peak-reading meter, peak-value indicator, maximum indicator; demand attachment	Höchstwertanzeiger m, Höchstwertmesser m, Maximumanzeiger m, Maximumzeiger m, Spitzenwertmesser m, Scheitelwertmesser m	pearson['s] coefficient [of correlation] Pearson['s] distribution	s. Bravais correlation coefficient Pearsonsche Verteilung f
		Pearson-Lee-Fisher function peasant's proverb, peasant's saying pebble-bed reactor, pebble reactor	Pearson-Lee-Fisher-Funktion f Bauernregel f, Volkswetterregel f Kugelhaufenreaktor m, Pebblereaktor m
peak-reading voltmeter, peak voltmeter	Spitzenspannungsmesser m, Spitzen[wert]voltmeter n, Scheitel[wert]spannungsmesser m, Höchstwertvoltmeter n		
		pecky sea, rough sea, angry sea	[ziemlich] grobe See f, ziemlich hoher Wellengang m, ziemlich hohe Wellen fpl <Stärke 5>
peak selector	[automatischer] Linienwähler m		
peak-to-peak	[von] Spitze zu Spitze, Spitze-Spitze-, zwischen Maximum und Minimum	Péclet['s] number, Pe	Péclet-Zahl f, Pécletsche Kennzahl f, Pe
peak-to-peak [amplitude], peak-to-peak value, double-amplitude peak, total amplitude	Spitze-[zu-]Spitze-Wert m, Spitze-zu-Spitze-Amplitude f, Spitze f zu Spitze	pectization peculiar motion	s. coagulation Pekuliarbewegung f
		peculiar star	Pekuliarstern m, Peculiarstern m
peak-to-peak volt, volt peak-to-peak	Volt n Scheitelspannung, Volt Spitze-Spitze	pedal [curve], pedal locus, pedal locus line	Fußpunkt[s]kurve f
peak-to-valley ratio	Maximum/Minimum-Verhältnis n, Maximum-zu-Minimum-Verhältnis n	pedal surface	Fußpunkt[s]fläche f
peak-to-zero	[von] Spitze zu Null, Spitze-Null-, zwischen Maximum und Null	Pedersen ray pedestal <el.>	Pedersen-Strahl m Schulter f <El.>
peak-to-zero [value]	Spitze-[zu-]Null-Wert m, Spitze f zu Null	pedial class	s. hemihedry of the triclinic system
peak / trough ratio	Berg / Tal-Verhältnis n	pediment	Pediment n, Pedimentfläche f
peak value, peak amplitude, crest [value] <US> <of variable quantity> <el.>	Scheitelwert m, Amplitude f; Spitzenwert m <Wechselgröße> <El.>	pedion <cryst.>	Pedion n <Krist.>
		pedometer Peek['s] formula	s. hodometer Peeksche Formel f

peeler	Abschäler m, ,,peeler" m	pencil glide, pencil gliding, pencil slip[ping]	Stäbchengleitung f, ,,pencil glide" n, begrenztes Gleiten n
peeling [off]	Schälen n	pencil of light, light[-ray] pencil; beam of light, light beam	Lichtbündel n; Lichtbüschel n
peeling [off] <from>	s. stripping <of an emulsion, a coating>	pencil slip[ping]	s. pencil glide
peeling off; spalling; leafing	Abblättern n, Abplatzen n, <schichtweise> Ablösung f	Penck['s] limit	[Pencksche] Trockengrenze f
peening	s. smith forging	pendellösung, pendulum solution, Ewald['s] solution	Pendellösung f, Ewaldsche Pendellösung
peephole	s. observation port	pendular motion, pendulum motion (movement), motion of the pendulum, pendulation	Pendelbewegung f, Pendelschwingung f, Pendelung f
peg, stone <meas.>	Meßstab m, Meßstange f, Stab m <Meß.>		
pegging-out <US>, marking-out, staking <US>	Verpflockung f, Verpfählung f	pendular oscillation, [pendulum] oscillation <mech.>	Pendelschwingung f <Mech.>
Peierls['] equation, Peierls['] integral equation	Peierls-Gleichung f, Peierlssche Integralgleichung f, Integralgleichung von Peierls	pendulation	s. pendular motion
		pendulous body	s. bob of the pendulum
		pendulum	Pendel n
Peierls['] equation[s]	Peierlssche Gleichungen fpl	pendulum anemometer	s. pressure-plate anemometer
Peierls['] integral equation	s. Peierls['] equation	pendulum balance	s. pendulum weighing system
Peierls lattice force, Peierls-Nabarro force	Peierls-[Nabarro-]Kraft f, Peierls-Nabarrosche Kraft f	pendulum bob	s. bob of the pendulum
		pendulum deflection, pendulum swing	Pendelausschlag m
Peierls model	Peierlssches Modell n		
Peierls-Nabarro force, Peierls lattice force	Peierls-[Nabarro-]Kraft f, Peierls-Nabarrosche Kraft f	pendulum dynamometer	s. pendulum manometer
		pendulum effect	Pendeleffekt m
Peierls potential	Peierls-Potential n	pendulum equation	Pendelgleichung f
Peierls stress	Peierls-Spannung f, Peierlssche Spannung f	pendulum exposure, pendulum irradiation	Pendelbestrahlung f
pelagial, pelagic region, pelagic zone	Pelagial n, pelagischer Bereich m	pendulum hardness	Pendelhärte f
pelagian, pelagic	pelagisch, pelagial		
pelagic region (zone)	s. pelagial		
Pell['s] equation, Pellian equation	Pellsche Gleichung f		
pellet	Pellet n, Granulatkorn n, Granalie f, Kügelchen n,	pendulum hardness test	Pendelhärteprüfung f, Pendelschlaghärteprüfung f
pellet getter	Pillengetter m, Getterpille f		
pelletizing, granulating, granulation, graining	Pelletisieren n, Granulieren n	pendulum hardness tester (testing machine)	Pendelhärteprüfgerät n
		pendulum horizon	Pendelhorizont m
pellets, granulated (granular) material, granulate	Granulat n, Granalien pl, Pellets pl	pendulum inclinometer	Pendelneigungsmesser m
		pendulum instrument	Pendelgerät n, Pendelapparat m
Pellian equation	s. Pell['s] equation	pendulum irradiation, pendulum exposure	Pendelbestrahlung f
pellicle; thin layer; film	dünne Schicht f; Haut f, Häutchen n; Film m		
pellicle stack	Emulsionspaket n, Emulsionsstapel m	pendulum law, law of pendulum oscillation (motion)	Pendelgesetz n
pellicular water, adhesive water	Haftwasser n, Grundfeuchtigkeit f; Bergfeuchtigkeit f	pendulum level	s. pendulum weighing system
Pellin-Broca prism, Abbe prism	Abbe-Prisma n, Pellin-Broca-Prisma n	pendulum magnetometer	Pendelmagnetometer n
pellucidity, pellucidness	Pelluzidität f	pendulum manometer, pendulum[-type] dynamometer	Pendelmanometer n
pelorus	Pelorus m		
Peltier cell	Peltier-Zelle f	pendulum meter	Pendelzähler m, Aron-Zähler m, [Aronscher] Uhrzähler m
Peltier coefficient	Peltier-Koeffizient m		
Peltier cooling	s. Peltier effect cooling		
Peltier effect	Peltier-Effekt m		
Peltier effect cooling, Peltier cooling	Peltier-Kühlung f, Peltier-Effekt-Kühlung f	pendulum motion (movement), pendular motion, motion of the pendulum	Pendelbewegung f, Pendelschwingung f, Pendelung f
Peltier electromotive force, Peltier e.m.f.	Peltier-EMK f	pendulum oscillation	s. pendular oscillation <mech.>
Peltier heat	Peltier-Wärme f	pendulum rectifier	s. chopper <el.>
		pendulum seismometer	Pendelseismometer n
Pelton turbine, Pelton [water-]wheel	s. impulse turbine	pendulum sextant	Pendelsextant m
PEM effect	s. photoelectromagnetic effect	pendulum solution, pendellösung, Ewald['s] solution	Pendellösung f, Ewaldsche Pendellösung
penalty constant	Penaltykonstante f		
penalty function	Penaltyfunktion f, Straffunktion f	pendulum suspension, rocking suspension	Pendelaufhängung f
pen-and-ink recorder	s. ink recorder	pendulum swing, pendulum deflection	Pendelausschlag m
pencil <of rays>; beam <of radiation>	Strahlenbündel n, Bündel n, Strahl m; Strahlenbüschel n <in der Ebene>		
		pendulum swinging on a rotating shaft, Froude pendulum	Froudesches Pendel n, Reibungspendel n
pencil-beam antenna	s. superdirective antenna	pendulum-type dynamometer	s. pendulum manometer
pencil-beam interferometer, Mills cross aerial	Mills-Kreuz n, Mills-Kreuzantenne f	pendulum-type impact testing machine	Pendelschlagwerk n, Pendelhammer m, Schlagpendel n

pendulum viscometer	Pendelviskosimeter n	penetration twin, interpenetration twin, penetrating twin	Durchdringungszwilling m, Durchwachsungszwilling m, Penetrationszwilling m, Ergänzungszwilling m
pendulum weighing system, pendulum balance (level)	Pendelwaage f		
peneplain	Fastebene f, Peneplain f	penetrativeness	s. penetrating power
		penetrometer	s. qualimeter
peneseismic	peneseismisch	peniotron	Peniotron n
penetrability	Durchdringungsfähigkeit f; Durchdringbarkeit f; Durchdringlichkeit f	penitentes, nieve penitente	Zackenfirn m, Büßerschnee m, Penitentes pl
penetrability [of the barrier]	s. barrier factor	Penning discharge, Penning gas discharge, PIG discharge	Penning-Entladung f
penetrable, transparent <to particles>	durchlässig <für Teilchen>	Penning effect	Penning-Effekt m
penetrable, permeable <to gases>	durchdringbar, durchlässig, permeabel <für Gase>	Penning gas discharge	s. Penning discharge
		Penning [ionization] gauge, Philips gauge, Philips ion gauge, Philips ionization gauge, Penning vacuummeter, Philips vacuummeter, P.I.G.	Philips-Manometer n, Penning-Manometer n, Gasentladungsmanometer n nach Penning, Philips-Vakuummeter n, Penningsches Vakuummeter n
penetrameter	Penetrameter n		
penetrance, penetration [factor], reciprocal of amplification factor, grid transparency, passage grid contollance, transparence, durchgriff, penetration coefficient, transgrid action <el.>	Durchgriff m; Rückgriff m		
		Penning ion source, Penning type [ion] source, Philips ion gauge [arc] source, PIG ion (type) source, oscillating electron ion source, magnetic-type ion source	Penning-Ionenquelle f, PIG-Ionenquelle f, Pendelionenquelle f, Ionenquelle f vom PIG-Typ
penetrant method, liquid-penetrant testing process	Eindringverfahren n, Diffusionsverfahren n <Werkstoffprüfung>		
penetrating component, hard component <of cosmic rays>	harte (durchdringende) Komponente f <kosmische Strahlung>; harte Sekundärstrahlung f	Penning vacuummeter	s. Penning ionization gauge
		penstock [pipe] <of turbine>; supply (feed, inlet, intake) pipe, supply tube, lead	Zuleitungsrohr n, Zuführungsrohr n, Zuflußrohr n; Zulaufrohr n
penetrating depth	s. depth of penetration		
penetrating [electron] orbit	Tauchbahn f	pentad average, pentad mean, five-days' average	Pentadenmittel n, Fünftagemittel n
penetrating particle, high-energy (energetic) particle	energiereiches (durchdringendes) Teilchen n, Teilchen hoher Energie	pentadodecahedron, pentagonal dodecahedron, pyritohedron	Pentagondodekaeder n, Pyritoeder n
penetrating power, penetration power, penetrativeness	Eindringvermögen n		
		pentagonal hemihedry	s. paramorphic hemihedry of the regular system
penetrating power [of radiation], [radiation] hardness, penetration power <of radiation, especially of X-rays>	Durchdringungsvermögen n [der Strahlung], Strahlungshärte f, Strahlenhärte f, Härte f <Strahlung, speziell Röntgenstrahlen>	pentagonal icositetrahedron, icositetrahedron, trapezohedron, gyrohedron, leucitohedron, 24-hedron, deltoid icositetrahedron	Deltoidikositetraeder n, Pentagonikositetraeder n, Ikositetraeder n, Gyroeder n, Plagieder n, Vierundzwanzigflächner m, 24-Flächner m, Leuzitoeder n
penetrating radiation, hard radiation	harte (durchdringende, energiereiche) Strahlung f		
		pentagonal mirror, penta mirror	Pentaspiegel m
penetrating shower	s. hard shower	pentagonal prism, penta prism, Goulier prism	Penta[gon]prisma n, Goulier-Prisma n, Prandtl-Prisma n, Fünfseitenprisma n
penetrating twin	s. penetration twin		
penetration, piercing	Durchdringung f; Durchgang m; Eindringen n		
penetration <e.g. for lubricating oils>	Penetration f <z. B. Schmieröle>	pentagon-dodecahedral class	s. tetartohedry of the regular system
		pentagon-icositetrahedral class	s. enantiomorphous hemihedry of the regular system
penetration, interpenetration, intersection <math.>	Durchdringung f <Math.>		
penetration	s. a. depth of penetration	pentagrid converter	Pentagridkonverter m, Fünfgitterumformer m; Pentagridmischröhre f
penetration	s. a. penetrance		
penetration coefficient	s. barrier factor		
penetration coefficient	s. a. penetrance <el.>	pentahedron	Pentaeder n, Fünfflach n, Fünfflächner m
penetration complex	s. low-spin complex		
penetration corrosion	s. through corrosion	penta mirror, pentagonal mirror	Pentaspiegel m
penetration depth	s. depth of penetration		
penetration depth [in skin effect], skin depth	Eindringtiefe f [beim Skineffekt], Hauttiefe f, Hautdicke f, Skintiefe f, Skindicke f	pentane candle <= 1.001 cd>	Pentankerze f <= 1,001 cd>
		pentane lamp	Pentanlampe f
penetration factor	s. penetrance <of electron tube>		
		pentane thermometer	Pentanthermometer n
penetration factor	s. a. barrier factor	penta prism	s. pentagonal prism
penetration meter	s. qualimeter	pentaprism eye-level viewfinder, reflex focusing device	Prismeneinsatz m, Prismenaufsatz m
penetration of heat, heat penetration	Wärmeeindringung f, Wärmedurchdringung f		
penetration potential	Durchdringungspotential n		
penetration power	s. penetrating power	pentode, pentode tube (valve), five-electrode tube, three-grid valve	Pentode f, Fünfpolröhre f, Fünfelektrodenröhre f, Dreigitterröhre f
penetration power	s. a. penetrating power [of radiation]		
		pen-type dosimeter, fountain-pen type pocket dosimeter	Füll[feder]halterdosimeter n, Ansteckdosimeter n
penetration probability, potential-barrier penetration probability, probability of tunnelling; Gamow factor	Durchdring[ungs]wahrscheinlichkeit f; Gamow-Faktor m		
		penumbra, partial (incomplete) shadow, half shade (shadow)	Halbschatten m, Penumbra f
penetration resistance <bio.>	Penetrationswiderstand m, Permeationswiderstand m	penumbra, spot penumbra	Penumbra f (Hof m) des Sonnenflecks

penumbral eclipse s. partial eclipse
penumbral effect, Helligkeitsabfall m
  decrease (loss) in brightness
peplopause Peplopause f
peptizing agent, resolver Peptisator m, Peptisationsmittel n
PER s. paraelectric resonance
perambulator s. hodometer
percentage advance prozentuale Voreilung f
percentage bearing s. ratio of bearing contact area
  contact area
percentage by mass, Massenprozentsatz m, Gewichtsprozentsatz m
  percentage by weight,
  mass percents, weight
  percents, %wt., w/w
percentage composition, prozentuale Zusammensetzung f
  percent composition, percentage
percentage content, Prozentgehalt m, prozentualer Gehalt m
  relative content, content
  by per cent
percentage depth dose prozentuale Tiefendosis f, Tiefendosis f in Prozenten der Oberflächendosis
percentage distortion, relative Verzeichnung f, Verzeichnung <in %>
  relative distortion
percentage elongation s. elongation <in %>
percentage error; relativer Fehler m; prozentualer Fehler
  relative error
percentage modulation, Aussteuerungsgrad m; Aussteuerungskoeffizient m; Modulationstiefe f
  degree (depth) of modulation, modulation depth
percentage of moisture, relative Feuchtigkeit (Feuchte) f, prozentuale Feuchtigkeit, Feuchtigkeitsgrad m
  relative humidity, hygrometric state, saturation ratio
percentage of water, Wasserprozentgehalt m, prozentualer Wassergehalt m
  water ratio
percentage probability s. branching ratio <nucl.>
percentage reduction s. reduction of cross-sectional area
percentage reduction of Brucheinschnürung f, relative Brucheinschnürung, Einschnürung f <in %>
  area
percentage ripple voltage s. hum factor
percentage supersaturation prozentuale Übersättigung f
percentage yield; unit Stauchung f, relative Verkürzung f
  shortening, linear compression, longitudinal
  contraction
per cent by volume, Volum[en]prozent n, Vol.-%, Vol.%
  volume percentage,
  volume per cent, % vol.,
  vol. %, v/v
percent composition s. percentage composition
percentile, centile Perzentil n, Prozentil n, Zentil n
percentile curve, ogive; Verteilungskurve f, kumulative Verteilungskurve; Ogive f
  distribution curve,
  cumulative frequency
  curve
per cent ripple Welligkeitsgrad m
perceptibility Wahrnehmbarkeit f
perception <bio.> Wahrnehmung f <Bio.>
perception <bio.> s. a. reception
perception of brightness, Helligkeitswahrnehmung f
  perception of luminosity
perception of contrast, Schwellenwahrnehmung f, Unterschiedswahrnehmung f
  contrast perception
perception of depth, Raumwahrnehmung f, Tiefenwahrnehmung f, Raumsehen n, Tiefensehen n
  space perception
perception of luminosity s. perception of brightness
perception of movements, vision of movements Bewegungswahrnehmung f, Bewegungssehen n
perched [ground] water gespannter Grundwasserspiegel m
  table
percolate Perkolat n

percolating water, water Sickerwasser n, Senkwasser n, Sinkwasser n
  of infiltration
percolation Perkolieren n, Perkolation f; Durchseihung f
percolation s. a. infiltration
percolation coefficient, Durchsickerungskoeffizient m
  percolation factor
percolation gauge Lysimeter n
  (meter), lysimeter
percolation rate, per- Perkolationsgeschwindigkeit f, Durchsickerungsgeschwindigkeit f, Sickergeschwindigkeit f, Versickerungsgeschwindigkeit f
  colation velocity,
  seepage velocity, infiltration rate
percussion; impact; Schlag m, Stoß m, Anstoß m
  shock; stroke; blow;
  push; shove
percussion s. a. shaking
percussion figure s. impact figure
percussion instrument, Schlaginstrument n; Anschlaginstrument n
  struck instrument
percussive sound s. impact sound
Percy-Buck effect Percy-Buck-Effekt m
perdeuterated perdeuteriert, vollständig deuteriert
perennial source, perennierende Quelle f, Dauerquelle f
  perennial spring
Pérès['] method Pérèssche Methode f
Pérès['] wave Pérèssche Welle f
Perey effect Perey-Effekt m
perfect conductivity, vollkommene (ideale) Leitfähigkeit f
  ideal conductivity
perfect conductor, ideal idealer Leiter m, Idealleiter m
  conductor
perfect correlation, total totale (vollkommene) Korrelation f
  correlation
perfect crystal, ideal Idealkristall m, idealer (fehlerfreier) Kristall m
  crystal
perfect crystal lattice, ideales Gitter (Kristallgitter) n, Idealgitter n
  perfect lattice
perfect differential, exact vollständiges (totales, exaktes) Differential n
  (total, complete) differential
perfect diffuser vollkommen mattweiße Fläche f, vollkommen mattweißer Körper m
perfect diffusion vollkommene Streuung f
perfect dislocation vollständige (vollkommene) Versetzung f
perfect elasticity vollkommene (völlige, ideale) Elastizität f
perfect flexibility vollkommene Biegsamkeit f
perfect fluid s. ideal liquid
perfect fluidity vollkommene Fluidität f
perfect gas, ideal gas ideales Gas n, vollkommenes Gas
perfect gas equation [of s. Boyle-Charles law
  state], perfect gas law
perfect-gas scale, [ideal] Gasskala f der Temperatur, ideale Gasskala
  gas scale of temperature
perfect Helmholtz vollkommene Helmholtzsche Flüssigkeit f
  liquid
perfect lattice, perfect ideales Gitter (Kristallgitter) n, Idealgitter n
  crystal lattice
perfect liquid s. ideal liquid
perfectly conducting, ideal leitend
  ideally conducting
perfectly elastic, fully vollkommen (ideal, völlig) elastisch
  elastic
perfectly elastic body s. perfectly elastic solid
perfectly elastic impact vollkommen (völlig) elastischer Stoß m, elastischer Stoß <Mech.>
  <mech.>
perfectly elastic material Hookescher Körper m, Hookescher Festkörper m, H-Körper m, vollkommen elastischer Körper, ideal elastischer Körper, elastischer Körper
  (solid), elastic solid,
  Hookean (Hookeian,
  Hookian, Hooke['s])
  solid, [perfectly] elastic
  body, Hookean body,
  Hooke['s] body, H-body
perfectly elastic torsion, vollkommen (völlig) elastische Torsion f
  fully elastic torsion
perfectly inelastic, fully vollkommen unelastisch, völlig unelastisch, ideal unelastisch
  inelastic

perfectly inelastic collision, perfectly inelastic impact, plastic impact, plastic collision, inelastic (non-elastic) impact <mech.>	vollkommen unelastischer Stoß m, [völlig] unelastischer Stoß, plastischer Stoß <Mech.>	performance operator, transfer function	Übertragungsfunktion f, ÜF
		pergelisol, permafrost, perpetually frozen soil, ever-frost, tjaele	Dauerfrostboden m, [ewige] Gefrornis f, Permafrost m, Pergelisol m, Kongelisol m, Congelisol m
		perhapsatron	Perhapsatron n
perfectly mat	vollkommen matt	perhumid <of climate>	perhumid <Klima>
perfectly plastic, fully (ideally) plastic	vollkommen (völlig) plastisch, ideal[-]plastisch	periastron	Periastron n, Sternnähe f
		pericentre, galactic pericentre <astr.>	Perigalaktikum n <Astr.>
perfectly plastic torsion, fully plastic torsion	vollkommen (völlig) plastische Torsion f	pericentre <mech.>	Perizentrum n <Mech.>
perfectly polished	s. perfectly smooth	pericline	s. brachyanticlinal
perfectly rough	vollkommen rauh	pericynthion	s. perilune
perfectly smooth, perfectly polished	vollkommen glatt	perigean velocity	Perigäumsgeschwindigkeit f
		perigee	Perigäum n, Erdnähe f
perfectly soft, fully soft	vollkommen (völlig, ideal) weich	perigee altitude	Perigäumshöhe f
		perigee distance	Perigäumsdistanz f, Perigäumsabstand m, Perigäumsentfernung f
perfect mosaic crystal	vollkommener (idealer, vollständiger) Mosaikkristall m	perigon [angle], round angle, full angle	[ebener] Vollwinkel m
perfect plasticity, ideal plasticity; St. Venant (Saint-Venant) plasticity	vollkommene (völlige, ideale) Plastizität f	perihelic distance	s. perihelion distance
		perihelic velocity	Perihelgeschwindigkeit f
perfect rectifier, linear rectifier, linear detector	geradliniger (linearer, idealer) Gleichrichter m	perihelion	Perihel n, Perihelium n, Sonnennähe f
		perihelion distance, perihelic distance	Periheldistanz f, Perihelabstand m, Perihelentfernung f
perfect reflecting diffuser	vollkommen mattweißer Körper m bei Reflexion		
perfect resonance	vollständige Resonanz f, vollkommene Resonanz	perihelion motion	s. advance of perihelion
		perihelion passage	Periheldurchgang m
perfect rigidity	absolute (vollkommene) Starrheit f		
perfect set	perfekte Menge f	perikinetic coagulation	perikinetische Koagulation f
perfect solution, ideal solution	ideale Lösung f, vollkommene Lösung		
perfect transmitting diffuser	vollkommen mattweißer Körper m bei Transmission	perilune, pericynthion	Perilunium n, Mondnähe f
		perilymph	Perilymphe f, Gehörwasser n
perfect year, abundant year, annus abundans	überzähliges Gemeinjahr n <im jüdischen Kalender>	perimeter <opt.>	Perimeter n <Opt.>
perflectometer [comparator]	Perflekto[meter]komparator m	perimeter; circumference <quantity, math.>	Umfang m; Perimeter n <Größe, Math.>
perforated disk	s. apertured disk	perimeter	s. a. periphery
perforated plate, sieve plate	Siebboden m; Siebplatte f	perimorphism, peri-morphogenesis, perimorphosis	Perimorphose f, Umhüllungspseudomorphose f
perforated-plate column	s. sieve-plate column		
perforated screen; apertured (pinhole) diaphragm, diaphragm <opt.>	Lochblende f <Opt.>	period, period of the reactor, [nuclear] reactor period, time constant of nuclear reactor, reactor time constant, rise time <of nuclear reactor>	Periode f des Reaktors, Reaktorperiode f; Reaktorzeitkonstante f
perforated steel plate	Röhrchenplatte f		
perforation, punching; sprocket hole	Lochung f; Perforation f, Stanzloch n	period, period of revolution, orbital period, time of one revolution <astr.>	Umlaufszeit f, Umlaufzeit f, Umlauf[s]dauer f, Umlauf[s]periode f <Astr.>
perforation <chem.>	Perforieren n <Chem.>		
perforation	s. a. through corrosion	period <math.>	Periode f <Math.>
perforation pitch, pitch of the perforation	Perforationsabstand m, Perforationsschritt m, Loch[mitten]abstand m, Lochschritt m		
		period	s. a. radioactive half-life
		period	s. a. period of oscillation
		period	s. a. periodic time
performance; output, productivity; efficiency, efficacy	Leistung[sfähigkeit] f, Produktionsleistung f, Produktivität f	periodic adsorption	periodische Adsorption f
		periodic[al]; cyclic	periodisch [veränderlich]; zyklisch
performance	s. a. behaviour		
performance	s. a. making	periodically changing potential, periodic potential	periodisches (periodisch veränderliches) Potential n
performance	s. a. useful work		
performance characteristic, performance curve	Leistungscharakteristik f, Leistungs[kenn]linie f, Leistungskurve f	periodic boundary condition	s. Born-von Kármán boundary condition
performance characteristic	s. a. operating characteristic	periodic classification [of the elements]	s. periodic system
performance chart	s. indicator diagram	periodic disturbance	s. periodic perturbation
performance chart	s. a. family of characteristic[s]	periodic fluctuations of light (luminous flux)	Lichtwelligkeit f
performance coefficient, coefficient of performance	Leistungsbeiwert m, Leistungsziffer f		
performance criterion	Gütekriterium n		
performance curve, performance characteristic	Leistungscharakteristik f, Leistungs[kenn]linie f, Leistungskurve f	periodic focusing	Wechselfeldfokussierung f
performance factor <of relay>	Gütefaktor m <Relais>	periodic group, torsion group	periodische (ordnungsfinite) Gruppe f, Torsionsgruppe f
performance index	Güteindex m	periodic group	s. a. group <in the periodic table>
performance of control, control performance	Regelgüte f, Güte f des Regelungssystems	periodic inequality	s. periodic perturbation

periodic in the mean	im Mittel periodisch, periodisch im Mittel	**period of forecast[ing]**, forecast period, period of validity of forecast	Vorhersagezeitraum *m*, Prognosezeitraum *m*
periodicity condition	Periodizitätsbedingung *f*		
periodicity in space of the crystal, crystal periodicity, periodicity of lattice	Kristallperiodizität *f*, Periodizität *f* der Kristallstruktur, Periodizität des Gitters	**period of full opening [of shutter]**	Volloffenzeit *f*
		period of oscillation, period of vibration, oscillation period, vibration period, period	Schwingungsdauer *f*, Schwingungsperiode *f*, Periode *f*, Periodendauer *f*, Schwingdauer *f*, Schwing[ungs]zeit *f*
periodicity modulus, modulus of periodicity	Periodizitätsmodul *m*, zyklische Konstante *f*		
periodicity of lattice, crystal periodicity, periodicity in space of the crystal	Kristallperiodizität *f*, Periodizität *f* der Kristallstruktur, Periodizität des Gitters	**period of recession**, recessional period; stage of retreat	Rückzugsperiode *f*, Rückzugsstadium *n*
periodic law [of Mendeléef], Mendeléef['s] periodic law, Mendeléef['s] law, Mendeleyev['s] periodic law	Periodengesetz *n* [von Mendelejew], Periodengesetz von Mendelejeff	**period of recording**	s. recording period
		period of regression, regression period	Regressionsperiode *f*
		period of rest, state of rest <bio.>	Ruhezustand *m*, Ruheperiode *f* <Bio.>
periodic orbit	periodische Bahn *f*	**period of restitution**	Wiederherstellungsperiode *f*
periodic perturbation, periodic disturbance (inequality)	periodische Störung *f*	**period of revolution**, [orbital] period, time of one revolution <astr.>	Umlaufzeit *f*, Umlaufzeit *f*, Umlauf[s]dauer *f*, Umlauf[s]periode *f* <Astr.>
periodic potential, periodically changing potential	periodisches (periodisch veränderliches) Potential *n*		
periodic precipitation, Liesegang effect, rhythmic precipitation	Liesegang-Effekt *m*, periodische (rhythmische) Fällung *f*	**period of revolution (rotation)**	s. rotation period
		period of sunspots, sunspot cycle, sunspots cycle, sunspot period	Sonnenfleckenzyklus *m*, Fleckenzyklus *m*, Sonnenfleckenperiode *f*, Fleckenperiode *f*
periodic pulse train	s. recurrent pulses		
periodic sinusoidal flow	periodische sinusoidale Strömung *f*		
periodic solution <of the first, second, third kind>	periodische Lösung *f* <erster, zweiter, dritter Gattung>	**period of the reactor**	s. period
		period of validity of forecast	s. period of forecast
periodic source; rhythmic source	periodisch fließende Quelle *f*; episodisch fließende Quelle; Hungerquelle *f*	**period of vibration**	s. period of oscillation
		periodogram	Periodogramm *n*
periodic specimen, periodic structure	periodisches Objekt *n*	**periodogram analysis**	Periodogrammanalyse *f*, Periodogrammrechnung *f*
periodic square-wave pulse train	Rechteckpuls *m*, Rechteckstoßschwingung *f*, periodisch wiederkehrende Rechteckimpulsfolge *f*	**periodometer**	s. Fourier analyzer
		period range, time constant range <of reactor>	Periodenbereich *m*, Zeitkonstantenbereich *m* <Reaktor>
periodic stream	periodischer Meteorstrom *m*		
		period-spectrum relation	Periode[n]-Spektrum-Beziehung *f*
periodic structure	periodische Struktur *f*	**peripheral**; circumferential, meridianal	Umfangs-; peripher; Mantel-; Rand-
periodic structure	s. a. periodic specimen		
periodic system [of the elements], **periodic table [of the elements]**, periodic chart [of the elements], periodic classification [of the elements], Mendeléef['s] classification [of the elements], Mendeléef['s] periodic table	Periodensystem *n* [der Elemente], periodisches System *n* [der Elemente]; Tafel *f* des Periodensystems [der Elemente], Tabelle *f* des Periodensystems [der Elemente], Periodentafel *f*, Periodentabelle *f*	**peripheral**, meridianal, mer- <chem.>	peripheral, meridianal, mer- <Chem.>
		peripheral	s. a. extranuclear
		peripheral component, circumferential component	Umfangskomponente *f*
		peripheral electron	s. bonding electron <chem., nucl.>
		peripheral emission	Peripherieemission *f*
periodic time, period	Periodendauer *f*, Periode *f*, Periodenlänge *f*	**peripheral gas**	Mantelgas *n*
		peripheral layer, surface layer	Randschicht *f*, periphere Schicht *f*, Mantelschicht *f*
periodic variable; regular variable	regelmäßiger Veränderlicher *m*; periodischer Veränderlicher; Pulsationsveränderlicher *m*		
		peripheral moraine, lateral (flank, marginal) moraine	Seitenmoräne *f*, Ufermoräne *f*, Randmoräne *f*
period-luminosity relation	Periode[n]-Leuchtkraft-Beziehung *f*, Periode[n]-Helligkeits-Beziehung *f*		
		peripheral nucleon, outer nucleon	äußeres (peripheres) Nukleon *n*, Randnukleon *n*, Nukleon außerhalb der besetzten Schalen
period meter	Schwingungszeitmesser *m*, Schwingungszeitmeßanordnung *f*, Schwingungszeitmeßanlage *f*		
		peripheral orbit, outermost orbit, outer orbit, valence orbit	Valenzbahn *f*, kernfernste Bahn *f*, äußerste Elektronenbahn *f*
period meter, reactor period meter	Periodenmesser *m*, Reaktorperiodenmesser *m*		
period module, module of periods	Periodenmodul *m*	**peripheral ray**	s. marginal ray
period of advance	Vorstoßperiode *f*	**peripheral region**, peripheral zone, periphery, marginal region, marginal zone, border zone, outer zone	Randzone *f*, Randgebiet *n*, periphere Zone *f*, peripherer Bereich *m*, Peripherie *f*
period of beat, beat period, beat cycle	Schwebungsperiode *f*, Schwebungsdauer *f*		
period of compression, compression period, compression time	Kompressionszeit *f*, Verdichtungszeit *f*, Verdichtungsperiode *f*		
		peripheral shell	s. valence shell
		peripheral speed, circumferential speed, peripheral velocity	Umfangsgeschwindigkeit *f*
period of deformation, deformation period	Deformationszeit *f*, Verformungszeit *f*, Verzerrungszeit *f*		
		peripheral stress (tension)	Umfangsspannung *f*, Randspannung *f*
period of excitation	Anregungsdauer *f*	**peripheral unit**	s. supplementary apparatus
		peripheral velocity, circumferential (peripheral) speed	Umfangsgeschwindigkeit *f*
period of fading, fading period	Schwundperiode *f*		

peripheral velocity	Randgeschwindigkeit f, Mantelgeschwindigkeit f	permanent magnet	Permanentmagnet m, Dauermagnet m, permanenter Magnet m
peripheral vision	peripheres Sehen n	permanent[-] magnetic	permanentmagnetisch, dauermagnetisch
peripheral zone	s. peripheral region	permanent[-]magnetic circuit	permanent[]magnetischer Kreis m, Dauermagnetkreis m
peripheric fault, boundary (circumferential) fault	Randverwerfung f, Randstörung f	permanent-magnetic field	permanentes Magnetfeld n, Permanentmagnetfeld n
periphery; circumference; perimeter <math.>	Peripherie f, Umfangslinie f, Umfang m <Math.>	permanent-magnetic lens	permanent[ ]magnetische Linse f
periphery surface	s. surface	permanent-magnetic material	permanentmagnetischer Werkstoff m, Dauermagnetwerkstoff m
periplanatic	periplanatisch		
peri-position	peri-Stellung f	permanent magnetism	permanenter Magnetismus m, Permanentmagnetismus m, Dauermagnetismus m
periscopic lens	periskopisches Glas n		
periscopic lens <objective>	Periskop n <Photoobjektiv>	permanent magnetization [vector]	permanente Magnetisierung f
perisphere	Perisphäre f		
peristrophe	Peristrophe f	permanent-magnet moving-coil instrument, moving-coil instrument	Drehspulinstrument n, Drehspulmeßgerät n
peritectic	Peritektikum n; peritektische Legierung f; peritektisches Gefüge n		
peritectic point; peritectic temperature	peritektischer Punkt m; peritektische Temperatur f; Peritektikale f		
peritectoid	Peritektoid n	permanent-magnet moving-coil instrument, iron needle instrument	Eisennadelinstrument n, Eisennadelmeßgerät n, Dreheiseninstrument n mit Magnet
peritectoid point, peritectoid temperature	peritektoider Punkt m, peritektoide Temperatur f		
Perkin['s] phenomenon	Perkin-Phänomen n	permanent memory	s. permanent store
permafrost, perpetually frozen soil, ever-frost, pergelisol, tjaele	Dauerfrostboden m, [ewige] Gefrornis f, Permafrost m, Pergelisol m, Kongelisol m, Congelisol m	permanent modification, dauermodifikation	Dauermodifikation f
		permanent nova, recurrent nova, repeated nova	[periodisch] wiederkehrende Nova f, Novula f <pl.: Novulae>
permanence, permanency, durability, constancy <gen.>	Permanenz f, Unveränderlichkeit f, Dauerhaftigkeit f, Beständigkeit f, Beharrungszustand m, Konstanz f <allg.>	permanent operating temperature, final temperature	Beharrungstemperatur f, Dauertemperatur f, Endtemperatur f
		permanent set	s. plastic deformation
permanence of matter	Permanenz f der Materie	permanent short-circuit current	Dauerkurzschlußstrom m
permanence of the functional equation, persistence of the functional equation	Permanenz f der Funktionalgleichung	permanent store, permanent memory	permanenter Speicher m, Totspeicher m
permanence of vision	s. persistence of vision	permanent stream	permanenter Meteorstrom m
permanence principle	Permanenzprinzip n		
permanence principle of binding energy	Prinzip n der Konstanz der Bindungsenergie	permanent time signal, continuous time signal	Dauerzeitzeichen n
permanence principle of light velocity	Prinzip n der Konstanz der Lichtgeschwindigkeit	permanent wave	s. stable wave
permanency	s. permanence	permeability, magnetic permeability	[magnetische] Permeabilität f, magnetische Durchlässigkeit f
permanent	s. steady		
permanent aurora	s. night airglow	permeability, perviousness <of a solid>	Durchlässigkeit f, Permeabilität f <Festkörper>
permanent axis of rotation, stable axis [of rotation]	permanente (spontane) Drehachse f, stabile Achse f		
		permeability	s. a. permeability coefficient <Darcy's law>
permanent blip	s. permanent echo		
permanent charging	Dauerladung f	permeability	s. a. permeability coefficient <bio.>
permanent deformation	s. plastic deformation	permeability	s. a. absolute permeability
		permeability bridge	Permeabilitäts[meß]brücke f, Permeameter n
permanent echo, fixed echo, permanent blip	Festzielecho n, Festzeichen n, Festzacke f, Fixecho n, Dauerecho n	permeability coefficient, coefficient of permeability, permeability <bio.>	Permeabilitätskoeffizient m, Durchlässigkeitskoeffizient m <Bio.>
permanent elongation	s. residual elongation		
permanent excitation <e.g. of luminescence>	Dauererregung f <z. B. von Lumineszenz>	permeability coefficient, hydraulic conductivity, permeability <in Darcy's law>	Durchlässigkeit f <Darcysches Gesetz>
permanent exposure	s. chronic exposure	permeability constant <bio.>	Permeabilitätskonstante f, Permeationskonstante f <Bio.>
permanent filtration <bio.>	Vorfilterung f <Bio.>		
permanent gas	permanentes Gas n, Permanentgas n	permeability curve	Permeabilitätskurve f
permanent geomagnetic field	beharrliches Magnetfeld n der Erde	permeability factor, Vitamin P	Permeabilitätsfaktor m, Vitamin n P, Vitamin-P-Gruppe f, Permeabilitätsvitamin n, Citrin n
permanent hardness [of water]	bleibende (permanente) Härte f, Nichtkarbonathärte f, NKH <Wasser>		
		permeability for water, permeability to water, water permeability	Wasserdurchlässigkeit f, Wasserpermeabilität f <Bio.>
permanent load; continuous load; steady load; dead [weight] load, fixed load <mech.>	Dauerbelastung f; konstante (ständige, bleibende) Belastung f; Dauerlast f, ruhende Last f; ständige Last <Mech.>		
		permeability line	Permeabilitätsgerade f
		permeability matrix	Permeabilitätsmatrix f
permanent load	s. a. continuous load <el.>	permeability model	Durchlässigkeitsmodell n

permeability of free space, permeability of vacuum, absolute permeability of free space, absolute permeability of vacuum — [absolute] Permeabilität f des Vakuums, [absolute] Permeabilität des freien Raumes, Vakuumpermeabilität f, magnetische Permeabilität des Vakuums, magnetische Feldkonstante f, Induktionskonstante f, Permeabilitätskonstante f

permeability of the barrier — s. barrier factor

permeability of the membrane, membrane permeability (conductance) — Membranpermeabilität f, Membrandurchlässigkeit f

permeability of the toroidal core, toroidal-core permeability — Ringkernpermeabilität f, Werkstoffpermeabilität f

permeability of vacuum — s. permeability of free space

permeability series — Permeabilitätsreihe f

permeability tensor, tensor of permeability — Permeabilitätstensor m, Durchlässigkeitstensor m, Tensor m der Durchlässigkeit

permeability tensor <magn.> — Permeabilitätstensor m <Magn.>

permeability theory of narcosis — Permeabilitätstheorie f der Narkose

permeability to gas — Gasdurchlässigkeit f

permeability to heat — s. diathermance <phenomenon>

permeability to light, light permeability (perviousness); transmission of light, light transmission, photopermeability — Lichtdurchlässigkeit f; Lichtdurchlassung f

permeability to water, perviousness to water, permeability for water, water permeability — Wasserdurchlässigkeit f; Wasserpermeabilität f <Bio.>

permeability tuning, magnet tuning — magnetische Abstimmung f, Permeabilitätsabstimmung f, M-Abstimmung f

permeable, penetrable <to gases> — durchdringbar, durchlässig, permeabel <für Gase>

permeable to heat — s. diathermanous

permeable to light — s. transparent

permeameter — Permeabilitätsmesser m, Permeameter n, Eisenmeßgerät n, Meßjoch n

permeance, magnetic conductance — magnetischer Leitwert m, magnetische Leitfähigkeit f, Permeanz f

permeating light, transmitted (translucent) light — Durchlicht n

permeation <e.g. of gases> — Durchlaß m, Durchlassung f <Gase>

permeation <bio.> — Permeation f <Bio.>

permeation pressure — Permeationsdruck m

permeation rate — Durchlaßgeschwindigkeit f, Permeationsgeschwindigkeit f, Eindringgeschwindigkeit f

permissibility, allowedness, permission — Erlaubtheit f

permissible concentration, tolerance concentration — zulässige (verträgliche) Konzentration f, Toleranzkonzentration f

permissible dose — s. tolerance dose

permissible function — zulässige Funktion f [bei der Eigenwertaufgabe]

permissible limits — s. permissible tolerance

permissible overload, overload rating — zulässige Überlastung (Überbelastbarkeit) f, Überlastungsgrenze f, Überlastbarkeitsgrenze f

permissible reverse voltage — Sperrspannungsfestigkeit f

permissible stress, permissible (allowable) working stress, working (safe) stress — zulässige Spannung f; zulässige Beanspruchung f

permissible tolerance, tolerance, allowance, permissible (allowable) limits, margin — Toleranz f, Maßtoleranz f, zulässige Abweichung f, zulässiger Fehler m, Spielraum m

permissible tolerance [dose] — s. tolerance dose

permissible working stress — s. permissible stress

permission — s. permissibility

permittance — s. capacitance <el.>

permitting radiant heat to pass through — s. diathermanous

permittivity, absolute permittivity, dielectric constant, [specific] inductive capacity, specific (electronic, relative) inductivity, inductivity <of the material> — Dielektrizitätskonstante f, absolute Dielektrizitätskonstante, dielektrische Leitfähigkeit f, Induktionsvermögen n, Permittivität f, DK <des Mediums>

permittivity of free space, permittivity of vacuum, electric constant — [absolute] Dielektrizitätskonstante f des Vakuums, Influenzkonstante f, Verschiebungskonstante f, elektrische Feldkonstante f, absolute Dielektrizitätskonstante für den freien Raum, elektrostatische (dielektrische) Grundkonstante f

permittivity tensor — s. dielectric tensor

permselective membrane — permselektive Membran f

permutability, commutability — Vertauschbarkeit f, Kommutierbarkeit f

permutable, commuting — [miteinander] vertauschbar, kommutierend

permutation <gen.>; rearrangement; transposition — Umlagerung f, Verlagerung f; Umordnung f; Umstellung f; Umsetzung f; Vertauschung f <allg.>

permutation <math.> — Permutation f; Anordnung f <Math.>

permutation group — Permutationsgruppe f

permutation matrix — Vertauschungsmatrix f, Permutationsmatrix f

permutation of lines — Vertauschung f der Zeilen, Zeilenvertauschung f

permutation operator — Permutationsoperator m, Vertauschungsoperator m, Austauschoperator m

permutation symbol, alternator, e-system — Levi-Cività-Dichte f, Tensordichte f von Levi-Cività, Levi-Cività'sche Tensordichte f

permutation symmetry, commutation symmetry — Vertauschungssymmetrie f

permutation test — s. randomization test

permutit[e] ion exchange arrangement — Permutitentsalzungsanlage f, Permutitanlage f

permutit method, permutit process — Permutitverfahren n [der Wasserenthärtung]

permutoid reaction — permutoide Reaktion f

perovskite structure — Perowskitstruktur f

peroxide bridge — Peroxidbrücke f

perpendicular, perpendicular line, normal, vertical line, plumb line — Senkrechte f, Lot n, Normale f

perpendicular; normal — senkrecht; normal; seiger, saiger; lotrecht

perpendicular — s. a. perpendicular of incidence

perpendicular band — Senkrechtbande f, $\perp$-Bande f

perpendicular force; vertical force — senkrecht angreifende (wirkende) Kraft f, Senkrechtkraft f

perpendicular force, normal force; normal component of force — Normalkraft f; Normalkomponente f der Kraft

perpendicularity; squareness; rectangularity; orthogonality — Rechtwinkligkeit f; Rechteckigkeit f, Rechteckförmigkeit f; Orthogonalität f

perpendicular line — s. perpendicular

perpendicular

perpendicular magnetization, cross (transverse) magnetization	Quermagnetisierung f, transversale Magnetisierung f	**personal equation**	persönliche Gleichung f
perpendicular of incidence, axis of incidence, perpendicular, normal to the reflecting surface	Einfallslot n, Einfallsnormale f	**personal error**, individual error	persönlicher Fehler m
		personal probability, subjective probability	subjektive Wahrscheinlichkeit f
perpendicular ray, normal ray	Normalstrahl m	**personnel monitoring**	Strahlenschutzüberwachung f des Betriebspersonals, Personalüberwachung f
perpendicular vibration	Senkrechtschwingung f		
perpendicular voltage, cross voltage, transverse voltage	Querspannung f	**persorption**	Persorption f
		perspective, central perspective, central projection	Perspektive f, Zentralperspektive f, Zentralprojektion f
perpetual calendar	immerwährender Kalender m	**perspective**, in central perspective, in central projection	perspektiv, perspektivisch, zentralperspektivisch
perpetually frozen soil, permafrost, ever-frost, pergelisol, tjaele	Dauerfrostboden m, ewige Gefrornis f, Gefrornis, Permafrost m, Pergelisol m, Kongelisol m, Congelisol m	**perspective exaggeration**	s. foreshortening
		perspective foreshortening	s. foreshortening
perpetual motion [engine], **perpetual motion machine**, **perpetuum mobile** <of the first, second kind>	Perpetuum n mobile <erster, zweiter Art> <pl.: Perpetua mobilia, Perpetuum mobile>	**perspective picture**, picture <of perspective projection>	perspektivisches Bild n, Bild <Perspektive>
		perspective projection, true projection	perspektivische (echte, wahre) Projektion f, perspektivischer (echter, wahrer) Entwurf m
perpetual snow[-]line	s. snow[-]line	**perspectivity**	Perspektivität f, Zentralkollineation f, zentrale Kollineation f, Homologie f <Geometrie>
Perrin['s] rule	Perrinsche Regel f		
per-salt	Persalz n		
		perspiration	Perspiration f, Hautatmung f
persistence, time of persistence, duration of persistence (afterglow), afterglow duration	Nachleuchtdauer f, Nachleuchtzeit f	**perspiration corrosion**	Schwitzwasserkorrosion f
		perturbance	s. perturbation
		perturbance factor, interference factor <gen.>	Störfaktor m <allg.>
persistence <also chem.>	Persistenz f < auch Chem.>		
persistence <gen.>	Dauer f, Fortdauer f <allg.>; Durchhaltevermögen n <Stat.>	**perturbation**, disturbance, perturbance <astr., math.>	Störung f; Perturbation f <Astr., Math.>
persistence	s. a. afterglow <of screen>	**perturbation energy**, disturbance energy	Störungsenergie f
persistence characteristic	Nachleuchtcharakteristik f, Nachleuchtkurve f	**perturbation equation**	Störungs[differential]gleichung f
persistence characteristic, decay characteristic <of luminescence>	Abklingcharakteristik f, Abfallcharakteristik f, Zerfallcharakteristik f <Lumineszenz>	**perturbation field theory**	Störfeldtheorie f, Störungsfeldtheorie f
		perturbation Hamiltonian	Störungs-Hamilton-Operator m
persistence length	Persistenzlänge f		
persistence of frequency	s. frequency pulling		
persistence of state	Persistenz f des Zustandes		
		perturbation-insensitive physical property	störungsunempfindliche physikalische Eigenschaft f
persistence of the functional equation, permanence of the functional equation	Permanenz f der Funktionalgleichung		
		perturbation matrix	Störungsmatrix f
persistence of velocity	Persistenz f der Geschwindigkeit	**perturbation method**, disturbance method, method of [small] perturbations (disturbances)	Störungsmethode f
persistence of vision, permanence (retentivity) of vision	Nachbildwirkung f, Nachbildeffekt m, Trägheit f des Auges, Augenträgheit f		
		perturbation of equilibrium	s. disturbance of equilibrium
		perturbation operator	Störoperator m, Störungsoperator m
		perturbation potential, perturbing potential	Störpotential n, Störungspotential n
		perturbation-sensitive physical property	störungsempfindliche physikalische Eigenschaft f
persistence screen, persistent screen, phosphorescent screen, afterglow screen	Nachleuchtschirm m, Leuchtschirm (Lumineszenzschirm) m mit mittellangem Nachleuchten	**perturbation series**	Störungsreihe f
		perturbation term	s. perturbing term
persistency	s. persistence	**perturbation theory**, theory of perturbations, disturbation theory	Störungsrechnung f; Störungstheorie f
persistent current	Dauerstrom m		
persistent irradiation, long-duration (long-time) irradiation	Langzeitbestrahlung f	**perturbed angular correlation**, PAC	gestörte Winkelkorrelation f
		perturbed series	gestörte Serie f
persistent line, sensitive line, distinctive line, raie ultime, letzte linie	letzte Linie f, Restlinie f, beständige Linie, Nachweislinie f	**perturbing action**, perturbing influence (effect), parasitic effect	Störwirkung f, Störeinfluß m, Störeffekt m
persistent radiation	Dauerstrahlung f	**perturbing co-ordinates**	Störungskoordinaten fpl
persistent screen	s. persistence screen		
persisting elongation	s. residual elongation	**perturbing current**	s. parasite current
persistor	Persistor m	**perturbing effect**	s. perturbing action
persistotron	Persistotron n	**perturbing field intensity meter**	s. perturbing field strength meter
personal dose	Personendosis f, individuelle Dosis f, Individualdosis f		
personal dosemeter	Personendosimeter n, individuelles Dosimeter n, Individualdosimeter n	**perturbing field strength**; radio noise field intensity	Störfeldstärke f
personal dosimetry, individual dosimetry	Personendosimetrie f, individuelle Dosimetrie f, Individualdosimetrie f	**perturbing field strength meter**, perturbing field intensity meter	Störfeldstärkemesser m, Störfeldstärkemeßgerät n

perturbing function, disturbing (disturbance) function <astr.>	Störungsfunktion f <Astr.>	**pH,** pH number, pH value, hydrogen [ion] exponent, hydrogen index, hydrogen number	pH-Wert m, pH <nur in Verbindung mit dem Zahlenwert: pH = 7 usw.>, Wasserstoffexponent m, Wasserstoffzahl f, Säurestufe f
perturbing influence	s. perturbing action		
perturbing mass, disturbing mass	störende Masse f		
perturbing potential, perturbation potential	Störpotential n, Störungspotential n	**pH adjustment,** pH control	pH-Einstellung f, Einstellung f des pH-Wertes
perturbing radiation, interference radiation, spurious radiation, spurious emission, stray radiation <el.>	Störstrahlung f, Störemission f; Nebenausstrahlung f, ungewollte Ausstrahlung f; Nebenwellenausstrahlung f <El.>	**phakometer, phako- scope**	Phakometer n, Phakoskop n
		phanerocrystalline	phanerokristallin
		phantom	Phantom n
perturbing term, perturbation term	Stör[ungs]glied n, Störungsterm m	**phantom**	s. a. phantom circuit
		phantom chamber	Phantomkammer f
perturbing vector	Störungsvektor m	**phantom circuit,** phantom	Phantom[strom]kreis m, Vierer m; Phantomleitung f, Viererleitung f; Phantomschaltung f, Viererschaltung f
perveance, space-charge factor	Perveanz f, Raumladungskonstante f, Raumladungsfaktor m		
		phantom [circuit loading] coil	Phantomspule f, Phantom-Pupin-Spule f, Viererspule f
perversor	Perversor m, Kehrversor m		
perviousness	s. permeability	**phantom formation,** phantoming	Phantombildung f, Viererbildung f, Phantomschaltung f, Viererschaltung f
perviousness to water	s. permeability to water		
pervious wall	durchlässige Wand f		
Petersen coil, Petersen grounding coil	Petersen-Spule f, Erdschlußlöschspule f, Erdschlußspule f	**phantom material,** tissue-equivalent material	gewebeäquivalentes Material n, Gewebeäquivalent n, Phantomsubstanz f
Peters factor	Peters-Faktor m	**phantom repeater,** measuring (measurement, test) amplifier	Meßverstärker m
petit ensemble	kleine Gesamtheit f		
Petri dish	Petri-Schale f	**phantom ring;** glory, heiligenschein, gloriole	Glorie f; Heiligenschein m, Gloriole f
petrifaction, petrification	Versteinerung f; Petrefakt m; Petrifikation f		
petticoat insulator, bell-shaped insulator	Glockenisolator m; Deltaisolator m	**phantom transposition,** transposition of pairs <el.>	Schleifenkreuzung f <El.>
petticoat insulator, double-petticoat (double-shed) insulator	Doppelglockenisolator m	**phantom transposition**	s. a. interchange of sites
		pharmaceutical balance, tare balance	Tarierwaage f
Petzval['s] condition	s. Petzval sum	**pharoid**	Pharoid n, Strahlenköcher m
Petzval curvature	Petzval-Krümmung f	**phase,** phase of oscillation, phase angle <of oscillation>	Schwingungsphase f, Phasenwinkel m, Phase f <Schwingung>
Petzval sum; Petzval['s] condition; Petzval['s] theorem	Petzval-Summe f; Petzvalsche Bedingung f, Petzvalsche Bedingung f, Petzval-Coddingtonsches Gesetz n; Petzvalscher Satz m, Petzvalsches Theorem n		
		phase l **in,** of equal phase	in Phase, gleichphasig, phasengleich, konphas
		phase acceleration	Phasenbeschleunigung f
Petzval surface	Petzval-Fläche f, Petzval-Schale f, Petzvalsche Bildschale f	**phase advance,** phase lead[ing], leading (advance) of phase	Phasenvoreilung f
Peukert['s] equation	Peukertsche Gleichung f	**phase-advance angle,** lead angle, angle of lead, advance angle <control>	Vorhaltwinkel m, Vorhaltewinkel m <Regelung>
Pfaff['s] expression, Pfaffian	s. Pfaffian differential form		
Pfaffian differential equation	s. total differential equation	**phase-advance circuit,** lead circuit	Vorhaltkreis m, Vorhaltekreis m
Pfaffian [differential] form, Pfaffian, Pfaff['s] expression, linear differential expression (form)	Pfaffsche Form f, Pfaffscher Ausdruck m, lineare Differentialform f, linearer Differentialausdruck m	**phase advancer,** advancer	Phasenschieber m, Verschiebungstransformator m
Pfaff['s] system of equations	Pfaffsches Gleichungssystem n	**phase angle,** phase angle error, displacement error <US>	Fehlwinkel m, Phasenwinkelfehler m
Pfeffer cell, Pfeffer osmometer	Pfeffersche Zelle f, Pfeffersches Osmometer n, Osmometer nach Pfeffer	**phase angle,** phase of oscillation, phase <of oscillation>	Schwingungsphase f, Phasenwinkel m, Phase f <Schwingung>
Pfeffer coefficient, economic coefficient	Pfeffer-Koeffizient m, ökonomischer Koeffizient m	**phase angle** <astr.>	Phasenwinkel m <Astr.>
Pfeffer osmometer	s. Pfeffer cell	**phase angle** <of alternating quantity> <el.>	Phasenwinkel m <Wechselgröße> <El.>
Pflüger's laws	Pflügersche Zuckungsgesetze npl		
Pfotzer curve, Pfotzer line	Pfotzer-Kurve f	**phase-angle bridge**	Phasenbrücke f
Pfrenger['s] theory	Pfrengersche Theorie f, Theorie von Pfrenger		
P-function	s. Patterson['s] function	**phase angle error**	s. phase angle
Pfund arc, iron arc	Eisen[licht]bogen m, Pfund-Bogen m	**phase-angle modulation,** angle modulation	Phasenwinkelmodulation f, Pendelmodulation f
Pfund grating mounting, Pfund mounting [of diffraction grating]	Pfundsche Gitteraufstellung f	**phase annulus**	Phasenring m; ringförmiger Phasenstreifen m, Zernike-Ring m
Pfund series	Pfund-Serie f	**phase anomaly**	Phasenanomalie f, Phasensprung m
pF value, pF	pF-Wert m, pF	**phase average**	s. phase space average

phase

phase balance	s. phase coincidence	phase constant, wavelength (phase-shift) constant, wave parameter, phase [change] coefficient <el.>	Phasenkonstante f, Wellenlängenkonstante f, Phasenbelag m; Phasenmaß n <El.>
phase belt, belt <el.>	Strang m, Wicklungsstrang m <El.>		
phase belt voltage, phase-to-neutral voltage; star voltage, Y-voltage	Phasenspannung f, Sternspannung f, Strangspannung f	phase constant <of homogeneous line>	Winkelmaß n [der homogenen Leitung]
		phase constant	s. a. image phase constant
		phase contrast	Phasenkontrast m
		phase contrast combination	s. phase contrast device
phase boundary, phase limit, interphase, phase interface	Phasengrenze f, Phasengrenzfläche f, Phasengrenzschicht f	phase contrast condenser, phase condenser	Phasenkontrastkondensor m, Phasenkondensor m
		phase contrast device (equipment), phase contrast combination	Phasenkontrasteinrichtung f
phase-boundary line, interphase line	Phasengrenzlinie f	phase contrast image	Phasenkontrastbild n
phase-boundary potential	Phasengrenzpotential n	phase contrast method	Phasenkontrastverfahren n
phase bunching, phase grouping, [radio-frequency] bunching	Phasenbündelung f	phase contrast microscope, phase microscope	Phasenkontrastmikroskop n
		phase contrast microscopy, phase microscopy	Phasenkontrastmikroskopie f
phase capture region, capture region	Phaseneinfangbereich m	phase contrast photometer	Phasenkontrastphotometer n
phase cell	s. phase-space cell		
phase centre	Phasenmitte f	phase-contrast test due to F. Zernike, Zernike['s] phase contrast test (method)	Phasenkontrastverfahren n nach F. Zernike, Zernikesches Phasenkontrastverfahren
phase change	Phasenänderung f		
phase change, transition, transformation, change <met.>	Umwandlung f, Übergang m, Phasenumwandlung f, Phasenübergang m <Met.>		
		phase converter, phase transformer	Phasenumformer m, Arno-Umformer m
phase change	s. a. first-order transition <met.>		
		phase co-ordinate	Phasenkoordinate f
phase change coefficient	s. phase constant <el.>		
phase change of first order	s. first-order transition	phase correction <opt.>	Phasenkorrektion f <Opt.>
phase changer, phase shifter	Phasenschieber m, Phasenregler m	phase correction	s. a. phase compensation
		phase corrector, phase equalizer, delay equalizer, phase compensator	Phasenkorrektionseinrichtung f, Phasenentzerrer m, Laufzeitentzerrer m
phase characteristic	s. phase response		
phase coefficient <astr.>	Phasenkoeffizient m <Astr.>		
phase coefficient	s. a. phase constant <el.>	phase-correlated transition	phasenkorrelierter Übergang m
phase coherence	Phasenkohärenz f	phase current	Phasenstrom m
phase coherence factor, coherence factor, [complex] degree of coherence	Kohärenzgrad m, komplexer Kohärenzgrad, Interferenzfähigkeit f	phase curve	Phasenkurve f
		phase definition, phase resolution, phase resolving power	Phasenauflösung f, Phasenauflösungsvermögen n
phase-coherent	phasenkohärent		
phase coincidence, phase balance, coincidence (balance, synchronism) of phases	Phasengleichheit f, Phasenübereinstimmung f	phase delay [time]	Phasenlaufzeit f
		phase delay	s. a. phase lagging
		phase demodulator	s. phase discriminator
phase comparator	Phasenvergleicher m	phase density	s. density in phase
		phase detector	Phasendetektor m, Φ-Detektor m, Phi-Detektor m
phase-comparing network	s. phase comparison circuit		
phase comparison	Phasenvergleich m	phase deviation, maximum phase angle deviation	Phasenhub m
phase comparison circuit, phase-comparing network	Phasenvergleichsschaltung f		
phase-compensating filter	Phasenausgleichsfilter n	phase diagram, metallurgical phase diagram, [metallurgical] equilibrium diagram, constitution (state) diagram, diagram of state, thermodynamic [phase] diagram	Zustandsdiagramm n, therm[odynam]isches Zustandsdiagramm, Zustandsschaubild n, Phasendiagramm n, Gleichgewichtsdiagramm n
phase-compensating network	s. phase-equalizing network		
phase compensation; phase equalization; phase correction	Phasenentzerrung f; Phasenausgleich m <Fs.>; Phasenkompensierung f, Phasenkompensation f; Phasenschieben n		
		phase diagram, phase pattern <math.>	Phasendiagramm n, Phasenbild n <Math.>
phase compensation network	s. phase-equalizing network	phase diagram method, method f of phase diagram	Phasendiagrammmethode f, Methode f des Phasendiagramms
phase compensator	s. phase corrector		
phase condenser, phase contrast condenser	Phasenkontrastkondensor m, Phasenkondensor m	phase discriminator, phase demodulator, Foster-Seeley discriminator	Phasendiskriminator m, Diskriminator m nach Foster und Seeley, Foster-Seeley-Demodulator m, Riegger-Demodulator m, Riegger-Kreis m
phase condition	Phasenbedingung f		
phase conductor	Phasenleiter m		

phase displacement <acc.>	Versetzung f von Phasenraumelementen außerhalb des „buckets", Verdrängung f von Phasenraumelementen <Beschl.>	phase lag angle	Phasennacheilungswinkel m, Phasenverzögerungswinkel m
phase displacement	s. a. phase shift	phase lagging, phase lag, lagging of phase; phase delay, retardation of phase, phase retardation	Phasennacheilung f; Phasenverzögerung f; Phasenverlust m
phase distortion, transit time distortion, delay distortion; rise-time distortion; envelope delay-frequency distortion	Phasenverzerrung f, Laufzeitverzerrung f	phase lead	s. phase leading
		phase lead angle	Phasenvoreilungswinkel m
phase distribution, phase spectrum, distribution in phase	Phasenspektrum n, Phasenverteilung f	phase leading, phase lead (advance), leading (advance) of phase	Phasenvoreilung f
phase diversity	Phasendiversity f; Phasendiversityempfang m	phase limit	s. phase boundary
		phase-locked [to]	phasenstarr [mit], phasensynchronisiert, phasenverriegelt
phase divider, phase splitter	Phasenspalter m, Phasenteiler m, Phasentrenner m	phase margin	Phasenrand m, Phasenabstand m, Phasenreserve f
phase division; phase splitting <el.>	Phasenaufspaltung f, Phasenteilung f; Phasentrennung f <El.>	phase meter	s. power-factor meter
		phase microscope, phase contrast microscope	Phasenkontrastmikroskop n
phase equalization	s. phase compensation		
phase equalizer	s. phase corrector	phase microscopy, phase contrast microscopy	Phasenkontrastmikroskopie f
phase-equalizing network, phase-compensating network, phase compensation network	Phasenentzerrungskette f		
		phase mixing, fine-scale mixing	Phasenmischung f, Feinmischung f
		phase modulation, PM	Phasenmodulation f, PM
phase equation	Phasengleichung f	phase modulation index, modulation index	Modulationsindex m; Phasenwinkelhub m; Nullphasenwinkelhub m
phase equilibrium	Phasengleichgewicht n		
phase equivalent	Phasenäquivalent n		
phase error	Phasenfehler m	phase noise	Phasenrauschen n
		phase object, phase specimen	Phasenobjekt n
phase factor	Phasenfaktor m	phase of oscillation, phase angle, phase <of oscillation>	Schwingungsphase f, Phasenwinkel m, Phase f <Schwingung>
		phase of tide	Gezeitenphase f
phase factor	s. a. image phase constant	phase operator	Phasenoperator m
phase fluctuation	Phasenschwankung f	phase opposition	s. opposition [of phase]
phase focusing	Phasenfokussierung f, Phaseneinsortierung f; Phasenaussortierung f	phase opposition / in	s. antiphase
		phase oscillation	Phasenschwingung f
		phase patte.n, phase diagram <math.>	Phasendiagramm n, Phasenbild n <Math.>
phase focusing <acc.>	Phasenfokussierung f <Beschl.>	phase picture	s. phase portrait
phase-focusing principle, principle of phase stability	Prinzip n der Phasenstabilität (selbständigen Phasenstabilisierung)	phase plate	Phasenplatte f, Phasenkontrastplatte f, Phasenplättchen n
phase formulae	Phasenformeln fpl	phase point, representative point	Phasenpunkt m, Phasenbildpunkt m
phase frequency	Phasenfrequenz f	phase polarization	Phasenpolarisation f
phase function	Phasenfunktion f	phase portrait, phase picture	Phasenbild n, Bild n im Phasenraum
phase grating	Phasengitter n	phase position	Phasenlage f
phase grouping, bunching, phase bunching, radio-frequency bunching	Phasenbündelung f	phase problem	Phasenproblem n
		phase quadrature	s. quadrature [of phase]
phase hologram	Phasenhologramm n	phase quadrature / in, in quadrature	[um] 90° phasenverschoben
phase hyperspace	s. phase space	phaser, phonon maser	Phaser m, Phonon[en]maser m, Maser m im Tonfrequenzbereich
phase index, phase refractive index	Phasenbrechungsindex m, Phasen-Brechungsindex m		
phase integral	Phasenintegral n	phase reference information	Phasenbezugsinformation f
phase integral of Gibbs, Gibbs['] phase integral	Gibbssches Phasenintegral n	phase refractive index, phase index	Phasenbrechungsindex m, Phasen-Brechungsindex m
phase-integral relation	Phasenintegralbeziehung f		
phase interface	s. phase boundary	phase relation, phase relationship	Phasenbeziehung f, Phasenverhältnis n
phase inversion	s. phase reversal		
phase inverter	s. inverter tube	phase resolution, phase resolving power, phase definition	Phasenauflösung f, Phasenauflösungsvermögen n
phase-inverter circuit, phase reverter stage	Phasenumkehrschaltung f, Phasenumkehrstufe f, Phasenumkehrkreis m		
		phase resonance, velocity resonance	Phasenresonanz f
		phase response, phase-shift/frequency characteristic, phase characteristic, group delay/frequency characteristic	Phasenfrequenzgang m, Phasengang m, Phasen-Frequenz-Charakteristik f, Phasen-Frequenz-Kennlinie f
phase inverter stage	s. inverter stage		
phase inverter tube	s. inverter tube		
phase jump, sudden phase shift	Phasensprung m	phase retardation	s. phase lagging
		phase reversal, inversion of phases, phase inversion <chem.>	Inversion f der Phasen, Phasenumkehr f <Chem.>
phase lag	Phasenanschnitt m		
phase lag	s. a. phase lagging		

phase reversal, phase inversion, inversion of phase <el.>	Phasenumkehr f, Phasenumkehrung f <El.>
phase reversal transformer, phase-reversing transformer	Phasenumkehrübertrager m, Umkehrübertrager m
phase reverter stage	s. phase-inverter circuit
phase rotation	Phasendrehung f
phase rule, Gibbs['] phase rule	Gibbssche Phasenregel f, Phasenregel [von Gibbs], Gibbssches Phasengesetz n, Phasengesetz von Gibbs
phase-sensitive detection (rectification)	phasenempfindliche Gleichrichtung f
phase separation, segregation <bio.>	Segregation f, Sonderung f, Aufspaltung f, Entmischung f <Bio.>
phase separation <therm.>	Phasentrennung f <Therm.>
phase sequence, sequence of phases	Phasenfolge f
phase-sequence indicator	Drehfeldrichtungsanzeiger m, Phasenfolgeanzeiger m
phase shift, phase displacement; misphasing	Phasenverschiebung f, Phasendrehung f
phase-shift analysis	Analyse f der Phasenverschiebungen, Phasen[verschiebungs]analyse f, Phasenwinkelanalyse f
phase-shift angle	Phasenverschiebungswinkel m
phase-shift capacitor	s. static phase advancer
phase-shift circuit, phase-shifting circuit	Phasenschieberschaltung f
phase-shift constant	s. phase constant <el.>
phase-shifted, out-of-phase	außer Phase, phasenfalsch, phasenverschoben
phase shifter	s. phase changer
phase-shift / frequency characteristic	s. phase response
phase-shifting capacitor	s. static phase advancer
phase-shifting circuit, phase-shift circuit	Phasenschieberschaltung f
phase-shift oscillator	Phasenschiebergenerator m
phase-shift section	Phasendrehglied n
phase space, phase hyperspace	Phasenraum m
phase space average, ensemble average, phase average	Scharmittel n, Scharmittelwert m, Phasen[raum]mittel n, Phasenmittelwert m
phase-space cell, phase cell	Phasenraumzelle f
phase space distribution, angular distribution	Phasenraumverteilung f, Winkelverteilung f im Phasenraum
phase space element	Phasenvolumenelement n, Phasenraumelement n
phase space plot	s. Dalitz plot
phase-space volume, phase volume	Phasenvolumen n
phase spacing	Phasenabstand m
phase specimen, phase object	Phasenobjekt n
phase spectrum, phase distribution, distribution in phase	Phasenspektrum n, Phasenverteilung f
phase spectrum of the pulse, pulse-phase spectrum	Impulsphasenspektrum n, Phasenspektrum n des Impulses, Spektrum n der Impulsphasen
phase splitter, phase divider	Phasenspalter m, Phasenteiler m, Phasentrenner m
phase splitting; phase division <el.>	Phasenaufspaltung f, Phasenteilung f; Phasentrennung f <El.>
phase stability	Phasenstabilität f; Phasenkonstanz f
phase stability, self-stability [of phase], phase stabilization <acc.>	Phasenstabilität f, Autophasierung f, Synchrotronprinzip n, [selbständige] Phasenstabilisierung f, automatische Phasenstabilisierung <Beschl.>
phase stability region, bucket, phase-stable bucket	stabiler Phasenbereich m, phasenstabiler Bereich m, Phasenstabilitätsbereich m, „bucket" n
phase stabilization	s. phase stability <acc.>
phase-stable bucket	s. phase stability region
phase-stable orbit	s. equilibrium orbit
phase-stable particle, equilibrium particle, phase-stationary (synchronous) particle	Sollteilchen n, Synchronteilchen n
phase standard	Phasennormal n
phase state	Phasenzustand m
phase-stationary particle	s. phase-stable particle
phase structure	Phasenstruktur f
phase-swept interferometer, swept-lobe interferometer	„swept-lobe"-Interferometer n, Phasendrehinterferometer n
phase-switching interferometer	Phasenschaltinterferometer n, Ryle-Interferometer n
phase-switching method, Ryle['s] method	Phasenschaltverfahren n, Ryle-Verfahren n
phase theory [of excitation]	Phasentheorie f [der bioelektrischen Potentiale]
phase titration	Phasentitration f
phase-to-neutral voltage, phase belt voltage; star voltage, Y-voltage	Phasenspannung f, Sternspannung f, Strangspannung f
phase-to-phase voltage	s. line voltage
phase trajectory	Phasenbahn f, Phasentrajektorie f, Phasenkurve f
phase transformation <el.>	Phasenumformung f <El.>
phase transformation	s. a. first-order transition
phase transformation plasticity, dynamic superplasticity	dynamische Superplastizität f
phase transformer	Phasentransformator m
phase transformer, phase converter	Phasenumformer m, Arno-Umformer m
phase transition	s. first-order transition
phase unbalance	Phasenungleichgewicht n, Phasenungleichheit f
phase variable	Phasenvariable f
phase velocity, wave phase (propagation) velocity, propagation (wave) velocity, velocity of the wave	Phasengeschwindigkeit f, Ausbreitungsgeschwindigkeit f, Wellengeschwindigkeit f, Fortpflanzungsgeschwindigkeit f
phase velocity	s. a. wave normal velocity
phase volume	s. phase-space volume
phase wave	Phasenwelle f
phase wavelength	Phasenwellenlänge f
phasing	In-Phase-Bringen n, Phaseneinstellung f, Phasierung f
phasing capacitor	Phasenkondensator m
phasing chain, phasing network	Phasenkette f
phasitron	Phasitron n
phasometer	s. power factor indicator
phasotron	s. synchrocyclotron
pH change	pH-Änderung f, pH-Wert-Änderung f
pH control, pH adjustment	pH-Einstellung f, Einstellung f des pH-Wertes
pH-controller, pH-meter, pH-instrument	pH-Messer m
pH effect	pH-Effekt m
phenological season	phänologische Jahreszeit f

phenomenological coefficient	s. kinetic coefficient	phonometer, acoustimeter	Schallstärkemesser m, Akustimeter n
phenomenological electrodynamics	phänomenologische Elektrodynamik f	phonometry	Phonometrie f, Schallmessung f
phenomenological equations (relations) <therm.>	phänomenologische Gleichungen fpl <Therm.>	phonon, sound quantum, quantum of acoustic wave energy	Phonon n, Schallquant n
phenomenological theory, continuum theory	phänomenologische Theorie f, Kontinuumstheorie f	phonon bottleneck effect	Flaschenhalseffekt m [der Phononen]
phenomenon of diffraction, diffraction phenomenon	Beugungserscheinung f	phonon distribution	Phononenverteilung f, Schallquantenverteilung f
phenomenon of excitation	Reizerscheinung f	phonon drag	Phonon,,drag" m
phenomenon of fusion, fusion phenomenon	Verschmelzungsphänomen n	phonon entropy	Phononenentropie f, Schallquantenentropie f
phenomenon of interference, interference phenomenon	Interferenzerscheinung f	phonon exchange	Phononenaustausch m
		phonon excitation	Phononenanregung f
phenomenon of melting	s. order-disorder transformation	phonon frequency shift	s. phonon shift
		phonon gas	Phononengas n
phenomenon of turbulent fluctuation, turbulent fluctuation	turbulente Schwankungserscheinung f	phonon maser, phaser	Phaser m, Phonon[en]-maser m, Maser m im Tonfrequenzbereich
phenomenon of variability <bio.>	Variationserscheinung f <Bio.>	phonon part	Phononenanteil m
phenometry	Phänometrie f	phonon-phonon umklapp process, phonon-phonon U-process	Phonon-Phonon-Umklappprozeß m
pherography	s. electropherography		
phial, vial	Phiole f, Fläschchen n		
philharmonic pitch, American Standard pitch, standard pitch <440 c/s>; concert pitch, high pitch <450 c/s>; international pitch, low pitch, French pitch <435 c/s>	Kammerton m, Kammertonhöhe f, Normal-a' n, Normstimmton m <440 Hz>; internationale Stimmung f <435 Hz>	phonon shift, phonon frequency shift	Phononenverschiebung f
		phonon spectrum	Phononenspektrum n, Schallquantenspektrum n
		phonon width	Phononenbreite f
		phonosynthesis	Phonosynthese f
		phonozenograph	Phonogoniometer n
Philipps beaker, conical beaker	Philipps-Becher m, Erlenmeyersches Becherglas n, Nonnenglas n; konisches Becherglas n	phoronomics	s. kinematics
		phoronomy	s. kinematics
		phosphene	s. entoptic phenomenon
Philips cycle	Philips-Prozeß m	phosphor	s. luminescent material
Philips [ion] gauge	s. Penning ionization gauge	phosphor-bronze thermometer, resistance thermometer of phosphor-bronze	Widerstandsthermometer n aus Phosphorbronze f, Phosphorbronzethermometer n
Philips ion gauge [arc] source	s. Penning ion source		
Philips ionization gauge, Philips vacuummeter	s. Penning ionization gauge	phosphor dot, colour [-emitting] phosphor dot	Leuchtstoffpunkt m
Philpot-Svensson curve	Philpot-Svensson-Kurve f, Philpot-Svensson-Registrierkurve f	phosphorescence centre, phosphorescent centre	Phosphoreszenzzentrum n
Philpot-Svensson method	Philpot-Svenssonsche Methode f, Methode f von Philpot-Svensson	phosphorescence in crystal, crystal phosphorescence, crystallophosphorescence	Kristallphosphoreszenz f, Kristallophosphoreszenz f
pH indicator	s. acid-base indicator		
pH-instrument	s. pH-meter	phosphorescence spectrum, phosphorescent spectrum	Phosphoreszenzspektrum n
phlebostatic axis	phlebostatische Achse f		
phlegma	s. reflux		
phlogiston	Phlogiston n	phosphorescent centre, phosphorescence centre	Phosphoreszenzzentrum n
phlogiston theory, Stahl['s] phlogiston theory	Phlogistontheorie f	phosphorescent decay	s. decay
		phosphorescent screen, persistence screen, persistent screen, afterglow screen	Nachleuchtschirm m, Leuchtschirm (Lumineszenzschirm) m mit mittellangem Nachleuchten
pH-meter, pH-instrument; pH-controller	pH-Messer m		
pH number	s. pH		
phobo-phototaxis	Phobophototaxis f	phosphorescent spectrum, phosphorescence spectrum	Phosphoreszenzspektrum n
phobotactic reaction	phobotaktische Reaktion f		
phobotaxis	Phobotaxis f	phosphorimetry	Phosphorimetrie f, Phosphoreszenzmessung f
phon	Phon n, phon		
phonics	Phonik f, Schallehre f; Klanglehre f, Lautlehre f	phosphorogen	s. activator
		phosphorography	Phosphorographie f
phonic wheel, tone wheel	phonisches Rad n, Tonrad n		
phoning	s. telephony	phosphoroscope [of Becquerel], Becquerel (two-disk) phosphoroscope	Phosphoroskop n, Becquerel-Phosphoroskop n
phonocardiogram	Phonokardiogramm n, Herzschallbild n		
phonocardiography	Phonokardiographie f, Herzschallaufzeichnung f	phosphor screen, luminescent (luminous) screen, actinic screen	Lumineszenzschirm m, Leuchtschirm m, Leuchtstoffschirm m
phonogram, sound record	Phonogramm n, Schallaufzeichnung f		
phonograph cartridge, pick-up, playback (reproducing) head, pick-up cartridge <ac.>	Abtaster m, Tonabnehmerkopf m <Ak.>	phot, ph <= 10^4 lx>	Phot n, ph <= 10^4 lx>
		photism	Photismus m
phonolysis	Phonolyse f	photistor, phototransistor, transistor structure as a photoelectric cell, phototriode	Phototransistor m, lichtempfindlicher Transistor m, Phototriode f
phonometer	Schallmesser m, Schallmeßgerät n, Geräuschmesser m, Phonmeter n; Phonometer n, Hörschärfemesser m		

photoabsorption, photoelectric absorption — Photoabsorption f, photoelektrische (lichtelektrische) Absorption, Absorption durch Photoeffekt

photoabsorption band — Photoabsorptionsbande f

photoabsorption coefficient — s. photoelectric attenuation coefficient

photoabsorption cross-section, cross-section for photoabsorption — Photoabsorptions[wirkungs]querschnitt m, Wirkungsquerschnitt m für (der) Photoabsorption, Wirkungsquerschnitt für photoelektrische Absorption, Wirkungsquerschnitt der photoelektrischen Absorption

photoactivation — Photoaktivierung f; Lichtaktivierung f

photo-adaptation — s. light adaptation

photoaddition, photochemical addition — photochemische Anlagerung f

photoag[e]ing — Lichtalterung f

photobiology — Photobiologie f

photocarrier, photoinduced carrier — photoinduzierter Ladungsträger m, Phototräger m

photocatalysis, photochemical catalysis — Photokatalyse f, photochemische Katalyse f

photocatalyst, photochemical catalyst — Photokatalysator m, photochemischer Katalysator m

photocathode, photoelectric (photoemissive, photosensitive) cathode, photoemitter — Photokatode f

photocell — s. photoelectric cell

photocell — s. a. photoemissive cell

photocell noise — Photozellenrauschen n

photocentre — Lichtzentrum n

photochemical action — s. photochemical effect

photochemical addition, photoaddition — photochemische Anlagerung f

photochemical assimilation, assimilation — Assimilation f, photochemische Assimilation

photochemical autoxidation — Photoautoxydation f, photochemische Autoxydation f

photochemical catalysis, photocatalysis — Photokatalyse f, photochemische Katalyse f

photochemical catalyst, photocatalyst — Photokatalysator m, photochemischer Katalysator m

photochemical decomposition — s. photodissociation

photochemical destruction, photodestruction <of polymers> — photochemischer Abbau m <Polymere>

photochemical dissociation — s. photodissociation

photochemical effect, photochemical action — photochemische Wirkung f

photochemical equivalence law — s. law of photochemical equivalence

photochemical isomerization, photoisomeric change, photoisomerization — Photoisomerisation f, photochemische Isomerisation f

photochemical method of isotope separation — photochemische Methode f der Isotopentrennung

photochemical polymerization — s. photopolymerization

photochemical quantum yield — s. photochemical yield

photochemical reaction, photoreaction, light reaction — photochemische Reaktion f, Photoreaktion f, Lichtreaktion f

photochemical rearrangement — Photoumlagerung f, photochemische Umlagerung f

photochemical sensitization, photosensitization — photochemische Sensibilisierung f, Photosensibilisierung f

photochemical yield, quantum efficiency, photochemical quantum yield, quantum yield — Quantenausbeute f, photochemische Quantenausbeute, photochemische Ausbeute f

photoconductance — Photoleitwert m

photoconducting, photoconductive, photopositive, light-positive — lichtelektrisch leitend (positiv), lichtpositiv, photoleitend, photopositiv

photoconducting cell — s. photoconductive cell

photoconducting detector — s. photoconductive detector

photoconduction, photoelectric conduction, photoconductivity — Photoleitung f, photoelektrische Leitung f, lichtelektrische Leitung f, Photoleitfähigkeit f

photoconduction — s. a. internal photoeffect

photoconduction response (sensitivity), photoconductive sensitivity — Photoleitungsempfindlichkeit f

photoconductive — s. photoconducting

photoconductive cell, photoconducting cell, photoresistance, photoresistor, photoresistance cell, photoelectric resistance cell; photovaristor; photoconductive detector, photoconducting detector — Widerstands[photo]zelle f, Photowiderstandszelle f, Photowiderstand m, Photoleit[ungs]zelle f, lichtelektrischer (photoelektrischer) Widerstand m, Lichtwiderstand m, Halbleiter[-Photo]zelle f, Halbleiter-Photoelement n, Kristallphotozelle f; auf dem inneren lichtelektrischen Effekt beruhender Strahlungsempfänger m, Photoleitungsdetektor m

photoconductive compensator, photoresistance compensator — Photowiderstandskompensator m

photoconductive detector — s. photoconductive cell

photoconductive effect — s. internal photoeffect

photoconductive sensitivity — s. photoconduction response

photoconductive time constant — lichtelektrische (photoelektrische) Zeitkonstante f

photoconductivity, photoelectric conductivity — Photoleitfähigkeit f, photoelektrische (lichtelektrische) Leitfähigkeit f

photoconductivity — s. a. photoconduction

photoconductivity counter — s. crystal counter <nucl.>

photoconductor — Photoleiter m

photoconstriction coefficient — Photokonstriktionskoeffizient m

photoconstriction effect — Photokonstriktionseffekt m

photocreep — Photokriechen n

photocurrent, photoelectric current — Photo[elektronen]strom m, photoelektrischer (lichtelektrischer) Strom m

photocurrent coefficient — Photostromkoeffizient m

photocurrent stimulation — Photostromanregung f

photodecomposition — s. photodissociation

photodestruction, photochemical destruction <of polymers> — photochemischer Abbau m <Polymere>

photodetachment [of electrons] — Photoablösung f [von Elektronen], Elektronenablösung f durch Photonen[absorption], lichtelektrische Elektronenabspaltung f

photodetection — s. photographic detection

photodetector, light detector (receiver) — Lichtempfänger m, Lichtdetektor m

photodetector — s. a. photoelectric radiation detector

photodeuteron	Photodeuteron n	**photoelectric cell**	s. a. photoemissive cell
photodichroism	Photodichroismus m	**photoelectric colorimeter**, objective colorimeter	lichtelektrisches (photoelektrisches, objektives) Kolorimeter n; lichtelektrischer (photoelektrischer, objektiver) Farbmesser m
photodielectric effect	photodielektrischer (lichtdielektrischer) Effekt m		
photodiffusion voltage	Photodiffusionsspannung f		
photodinesis	Photodinese f	**photoelectric colorimetry**, objective colorimetry	lichtelektrische (photoelektrische, objektive) Kolorimetrie f; lichtelektrische (photoelektrische, objektive) Farbmessung f
photodiode, semiconductor photodiode	Photodiode f, Halbleiterphotodiode f		
photodisintegration, nuclear photodisintegration, photonuclear reaction, nuclear photoreaction, nuclear photoelectric effect, nuclear photoeffect, gamma-ray induced nuclear reaction, photoninduced nuclear reaction, γ,x reaction	Kernphotoeffekt m, Kernphotoreaktion f, Kernphotoprozeß m, Photokernreaktion f, Photokernprozeß m, Photozerfall m, photonukleare Reaktion f, gamma-induzierte Kernreaktion f, photoninduzierte Kernreaktion, (γ,x)-Prozeß m, (γ,x)-Reaktion f, Photoumwandlung f	**photoelectric compensator**, Lindeck-Rothe compensator	Lindeck-Rothe-Kompensator m, Photozellenkompensator m
		photoelectric conduction, photoconduction, photoconductivity	Photoleitung f, photoelektrische Leitung f, lichtelektrische Leitung, Photoleitfähigkeit f
		photoelectric conduction	s. a. internal photoeffect
		photoelectric conductivity, photoconductivity	Photoleitfähigkeit f, photoelektrische (lichtelektrische) Leitfähigkeit f
photodisintegration	s. a. photodissociation	**photoelectric constant**	photoelektrische (lichtelektrische) Konstante f
photodisintegration cross-section	s. photonuclear cross-section		
photodissociation, photochemical dissociation, photolysis, photochemical decomposition, photodecomposition, photodisintegration	Photodissoziation f, Photolyse f, photochemische Dissoziation f, photochemische Zersetzung f	**photoelectric current**, photocurrent	Photo[elektronen]strom m, photoelektrischer Strom m, lichtelektrischer Strom
		photoelectric densitometer for comparison	Vergleichsschwärzungsmesser m
		photoelectric detector	s. photoelectric radiation detector
photodynamic effect	photodynamischer Effekt m, Lichtsensibilisation f	**photoelectric dissociation**	lichtelektrische (photoelektrische) Dissoziation f
photoeffect	s. photoelectric effect		
photoelastic, stress-optic[al]	spannungsoptisch; photoelastisch	**photoelectric effect**, photoeffect, photoelectric phenomenon	Photoeffekt m, lichtelektrischer (photoelektrischer) Effekt m, lichtelektrische (photoelektrische) Wirkung f
photoelastic bench	spannungsoptische Bank f		
photoelastic coefficient, stress-optical coefficient	spannungsoptischer Koeffizient m	**photoelectric efficiency**, photoemissive efficiency, photoemissive yield, quantum efficiency [of photoelectric effect], photoelectric yield	lichtelektrische (photoelektrische) Quantenausbeute f, Quantenausbeute [des Photoeffekts], lichtelektrischer (photoelektrischer) Wirkungsgrad m, Photoelektronenausbeute f, Photoemissionsausbeute f
photoelastic constant, stress-optic[al] constant, stress optic constant	spannungsoptische Konstante f, photoelastische Konstante		
photoelastic fringe pattern, stress fringe pattern	spannungsoptisches Streifenbild n, Spannungsstreifenbild n		
photoelasticimetry, photoelastic investigation	s. photoelastic method		
		photoelectric emission	s. photoemissive effect
photoelasticity	Spannungsoptik f, Elastooptik f, Photoelastizität f	**photoelectric emission centre**, photoemissive centre, emission centre	lichtelektrisches Emissionszentrum (Zentrum) n, photoelektrisches Emissionszentrum (Zentrum) n
photoelastic method, photoelastic investigation, photoelasticimetry	spannungsoptische Untersuchung (Messung, Methode) f, photoelastische Methode, Photoelastizimetrie f		
		photoelectric emissivity, photoemissivity	Photoemissionsvermögen n
		photoelectric energy transfer coefficient	Photoumwandlungskoeffizient m, Energieumwandlungskoeffizient m für den Photoeffekt
photoelastic [stress] pattern, stress pattern	Isochromatenbild n, Spannungsmodell n		
photoelectret	Photoelektret n	**photoelectric equation**	s. Einstein['s] equation
photoelectric absorption	s. photoabsorption	**photoelectric exposure meter**	photoelektrischer Belichtungsmesser m, lichtelektrischer Belichtungsmesser
photoelectric absorption coefficient	s. photoelectric attenuation coefficient		
photoelectric activity, photoelectric sensitivity, photosensitivity, photoresponse	lichtelektrische (photoelektrische) Empfindlichkeit f, Photoempfindlichkeit f	**photoelectric fatigue**	lichtelektrische (photoelektrische) Ermüdung f; lichtelektrische Erregung f
		photoelectric flow meter	lichtelektrischer (photoelektrischer) Strömungsmesser m
photoelectric aftereffect	lichtelektrische (photoelektrische) Nachwirkung f	**photoelectric fringe counter**	photoelektrischer (lichtelektrischer) Interferenzzähler m
photoelectric analyzer of Kent and Lawson	s. Kent-Lawson photoelectric analyzer		
photoelectric atomic battery, photoelectric battery, photoelectric isotopic power generator	photoelektrische Batterie f, photoelektrische Radionuklidbatterie f	**photoelectric glossmeter**, objective glossmeter	lichtelektrischer (photoelektrischer, objektiver) Glanzmesser m
		photoelectric isotopic power generator	s. photoelectric atomic battery
photoelectric attenuation coefficient, photoelectric absorption coefficient, photoabsorption coefficient	Photoabsorptionskoeffizient m, Schwächungskoeffizient m für den Photoeffekt, photoelektrischer Absorptionskoeffizient m	**photoelectricity**	Photoelektrizität f, Lichtelektrizität f
		photoelectric line, photoelectric straightline	photoelektrische Gerade f
photoelectric battery	s. photoelectric atomic battery	**photoelectric luxmeter**	lichtelektrischer (photoelektrischer) Beleuchtungsmesser m, lichtelektrisches (photoelektrisches) Luxmeter n
photoelectric cathode	s. photocathode		
photoelectric cell, photocell, electric eye	lichtelektrische (photoelektrische) Zelle f, lichtelektrischer (photoelektrischer) Strahlungsempfänger m, lichtelektrischer (photoelektrischer) Wandler m, Photozelle f		
		photoelectric magnitude, photoelectric stellar magnitude	photoelektrische Helligkeit f, lichtelektrische Helligkeit <Gestirn>

photoelectric mass absorption (attenuation) coefficient — Massen-Photoabsorptionskoeffizient m, Massenschwächungskoeffizient m für den Photoeffekt, photoelektrischer Massenabsorptionskoeffizient m

photoelectric mass energy transfer coefficient — Massen-Photoumwandlungskoeffizient m

photoelectric multiplier s. photomultiplier

photoelectric peak, photopeak — Photopeak m, Photolinie f

photoelectric phenomenon s. photoelectric effect

photoelectric photometer, objective photometer — lichtelektrisches (photoelektrisches, objektives) Photometer n

photoelectric potentiometer s. Lindeck-Rothe potentiometer

photoelectric proportionality law — lichtelektrisches Proportionalitätsgesetz n, Gesetz n von Stoletow, Stoletowsches Gesetz

photoelectric radiation detector, photoelectric detector, photodetector — photoelektrisches (lichtelektrisches) Strahlungsmeßgerät n, photoelektrisches (lichtelektrisches) Strahlungsnachweisgerät n, photoelektrischer (lichtelektrischer) Detektor m, Photodetektor m

photoelectric relay, photorelay, photoswitch; light barrier, light relay — Lichtrelais n, lichtelektrisches Relais n; Lichtschranke f, Strahlenschranke f

photoelectric resistance cell s. photoconductive cell

photoelectric scanning s. photoelectric sensing

photoelectric semiconduction — Photohalbleitung f, lichtelektrische (photoelektrische) Halbleitung f

photoelectric semiconductor device — Photobauelement n, photoelektrisches Bauelement n, lichtelektrisches (photoelektrisches) Halbleitergerät n, lichtelektrische (photoelektrische) Halbleiterzelle f

photoelectric sensing, photoelectric scanning — lichtelektrische (photoelektrische) Abtastung f, Photoscanning n

photoelectric sensitivity, photosensitivity, photoresponse, photoelectric activity — lichtelektrische (photoelektrische) Empfindlichkeit f, Photoempfindlichkeit f

photoelectric sensitization — lichtelektrische (photoelektrische) Sensibilisierung f

photoelectric stellar magnitude, photoelectric magnitude — photoelektrische Helligkeit f, lichtelektrische Helligkeit <Gestirn>

photoelectric straight-line, photoelectric line — photoelektrische Gerade f

photoelectric threshold, photoelectric threshold energy, threshold energy of normal photoelectric effect — Grenzenergie f des äußeren Photoeffekts, Photoschwelle f, photoelektrische Aktivierungsenergie (Schwellenenergie) f, photoelektrischer Schwellenwert m, photoelektrische Schwelle f, lichtelektrische Aktivierungsenergie (Schwellenenergie), lichtelektrischer Schwellenwert, lichtelektrische Schwelle

photoelectric transition — photoelektrischer (lichtelektrischer) Übergang m

photoelectric tube s. photoelectric cell

photoelectric voltage, photovoltage — Photospannung f, photoelektrische (lichtelektrische) Spannung f

photoelectric work function — Austrittsarbeit f der Photoelektronen

photoelectric yield s. photoelectric efficiency

photoelectroluminescence s. electrophotoluminescence

photoelectromagnetic effect, PEM effect, photogalvanomagnetic effect — photoelektromagnetischer Effekt m, PEM-Effekt m, Kikoin-Noskow-Effekt m, photogalvanomagnetischer Effekt

photo-electromotive force, photo-e.m.f. — Photo-EMK f, photoelektromotorische Kraft f

photoelectron discharge — Photoelektronenentladung f

photoelectronics — Photoelektronik f

photoelectronic travelling-wave tube — Photoelektronen-Wanderfeldröhre f

photoelectron spectroscopy — Photoelektronenspektroskopie f

photoelectron spectrum — Photoelektronenspektrum n

photo-electron-stabilized photicon, rieseliconoscope — Rieselikonoskop n

photo-e.m.f., photo-electromotive force — Photo-EMK f, photoelektromotorische Kraft f

photoemission s. photoemissive effect

photoemissive cathode s. photocathode

photoemissive cell, photoemissive element, photoemissive tube; phototube, photovalve, photoelectric cell, photocell; photoemissive detector — Photozelle f [mit äußerem Photoeffekt], Emissionsphotozelle f, Photoemissionszelle f; auf dem äußeren lichtelektrischen Effekt beruhender Strahlungsempfänger m, Photoemissionsdetektor m

photoemissive centre s. photoelectric emission centre

photoemissive detector s. photoemissive cell

photoemissive effect, external photoelectric effect, normal photoelectric effect, external photoeffect, Hallwachs effect; normal emission, photoelectric emission, photoemission — äußerer lichtelektrischer Effekt m, äußerer Photoeffekt m (photoelektrischer Effekt), Photoemissionseffekt m, Hallwachs-Effekt m, Righi-Effekt m, normaler lichtelektrischer Effekt, normaler Photoeffekt (photoelektrischer Effekt); lichtelektrische Elektronenemission f, Photo[elektronen]emission f, photoelektrische (lichtelektrische) Emission

photoemissive efficiency s. photoelectric efficiency

photoemissive element s. photoemissive cell

photoemissive gas-filled cell s. gas-filled photocell

photoemissive mosaic element, mosaic element, mosaic photocathode, mosaic — Mosaikphotokatode f, Mosaikelement n

photoemissive tube s. photoemissive cell

photoemissive vacuum cell s. vacuum photocell

photoemissive yield s. photoelectric efficiency

photoemissivity, photoelectric emissivity — Photoemissionsvermögen n

photoemitter — Photoemitter m, Photoelektronenemitter m

photoemitter s. a. photocathode

photoemulsion, emulsion, photographic emulsion — Emulsion f, photographische Emulsion, Photoemulsion f, optische Emulsion

photoexcitation — Photoanregung f, Anregung f durch Photonenabsorption

photoexcitation cross-section, cross-section for photoexcitation — Photoanregungsquerschnitt m, Wirkungsquerschnitt m für Photoanregung, Photoanregungswirkungsquerschnitt m

photoexciton — Lichtexciton n, Photoexciton n

photo[-]eyepiece, projection eyepiece — Projektionsokular n, Photookular n, Projektiv n, mikrophotographisches Okular n

photofinish camera — Zielphotokamera f

photofission, photonuclear fission — Photospaltung f, (γ, f)-Prozeß m

photofission cross-section, cross-section for photofission — Photospalt[ungs]querschnitt *m*, Wirkungsquerschnitt *m* für Photospaltung, Photospaltungswirkungsquerschnitt *m*

photofission threshold — Schwellenenergie *f* der Photospaltung, Photospaltungsschwelle *f*

photoflash, flash, flashlight — Photoblitz *m*, Blitzlicht *n*

photoflash lamp, flash lamp, flash bulb, regular flash — Blitzlampe *f*, Vakublitz *m*, Vakublitzgerät *n*, Vakublitzleuchte *f*, Vakuumblitzlichtlampe *f*, Kolbenblitz *m*, Birnenblitz *m*

photoflood lamp, photographic lamp — Photoaufnahmelampe *f*, Photolampe *f*

photofluorogram — s. screen photograph

photofluorograph, photofluorographic unit, photo-roentgen unit, PR unit — Schirmbildgerät *n*, Röntgenschirmbildgerät *n*

photofluorography — s. fluorography

photogalvanomagnetic effect — s. photoelectromagnetic effect

photogel — Photogel *n*

photogenic, light-producing — lichterzeugend

photogoniometer — s. phototheodolite

photogram — Photogramm *n*, Meßbild *n*

photogrammetrical plotting, photogrammetrical restitution, plotting — Bildauswertung *f*, photogrammetrische Bildauswertung (Auswertung *f*), Auswertung

photogrammetric apparatus, image measuring apparatus — Bildmeßgerät *n*

photogrammetric chamber — Meßkammer *f*, Meßbild[aufnahme]kammer *f*; Meßbild[aufnahme]gerät *n*

photogrammetric intersection — s. intersection photogrammetry

photogrammetric map, photomap; aerophotogrammetric map; aerotopographic map — Bildplan *m*; Bildkarte *f*; Luftbildplan *m*, Luftbildkarte *f*

photogrammetric objective — photogrammetrisches Objektiv *n*; Meßobjektiv *n*

photogrammetric plotting instrument — s. aerocartograph

photogrammetric stereocamera — s. stereophotogrammetric camera

photogrammetric theodolite — s. phototheodolite

photogrammetric triangulation — s. phototriangulation

photogrammetry, phototopography — Photogrammetrie *f*, Bildmessung *f*, Phototopographie *f*

photogrammetry by intersection — s. intersection photogrammetry

photographically catalyzed nucleation, photonucleation, photographic nucleation — Photokeimbildung *f*

photographic astrometry — photographische Astrometrie *f*

photographic contrast — s. gamma <quantity>

photographic detection, photodetection, photographic method [of detection] — photographischer Nachweis *m*; photographische Methode *f*

photographic detector — photographischer Detektor (Strahlungsempfänger, Empfänger) *m*

photographic dosimeter — s. dosifilm

photographic effect — photographischer Effekt *m*

photographic emulsion, emulsion, photoemulsion — [photographische] Emulsion *f*, Photoemulsion *f*, optische Emulsion

photographic emulsion technique — s. nuclear emulsion technique

photographic fog, fog — Schleier *m*, photographischer Schleier

photographic glazing, glazing — Satinage *f*, Satinieren *n*

photographic halo, halo, halation, aureola — Lichthof *m*, photographischer Lichthof, Hof *m*

photographic intensification, intensification [of the photographic image] — photographische Verstärkung *f*, Verstärkung [des photographischen Bildes]

photographic intensifier, intensifier <phot.> — photographischer Verstärker *m*, Verstärker <Phot.>

photographic lamp, photoflood lamp — Photoaufnahmelampe *f*, Photolampe *f*

photographic layer — s. photolayer <phot.>

photographic magnitude, photographic stellar magnitude — photographische Helligkeit *f*, Blauhelligkeit *f* <Gestirn>

photographic method [of detection] — s. photographic detection

photographic nucleation, photonucleation, photographically catalyzed nucleation — Photokeimbildung *f*

photographic overexposure, overexposure <phot.> — Überexposition *f*, Überbelichtung *f* <Phot.>

photographic plane — Meßflugzeug *n*; Bildmeßflugzeug *n*

photographic plate, photoplate, plate <phot.> — Platte *f*, photographische Platte, Photoplatte *f* <Phot.>

photographic plate technique — s. nuclear emulsion technique

photographic radiation temperature — photographische Strahlungstemperatur *f*

photographic record, photographic recording, optical record — photographische Registrierung *f*, photographische Aufzeichnung *f*

photographic redevelopment — s. redevelopment

photographic reducer, reducer — Abschwächer *m*, photographischer Abschwächer

photographic reduction, reduction <phot.> — photographische Verkleinerung *f*, Verkleinerung <Phot.>

photographic sensitizer, sensitizer <phot.> — Photosensibilisator *m*, [photographischer] Sensibilisator *m* <Phot.>

photographic shutter, shutter <phot.> — Verschluß *m*, photographischer Verschluß <Phot.>

photographic sound recording; sound-on-film recording — photographische Schallaufzeichnung *f*

photographic stellar magnitude, photographic magnitude — photographische Helligkeit *f*, Blauhelligkeit *f* <Gestirn>

photographic sub-image — s. latent image

photographic surface photometry — photographische Großflächenphotometrie *f*

photographic telescope — s. astrograph

photographic transmission density — s. optical density <phot.>

photographic turbidity — s. turbidity <phot.>

photographic underexposure, underexposure; underexposition — Unterexposition *f*; Unterbelichtung *f*

photographing — s. taking <phot.>

photographone — Photographon *n*, Lichtsprechgerät *n*

photography of spectra — s. spectroscopic photography

photogyration	Photogyration f, photogyroskopischer Effekt m	photometric determination; photometric record[ing]	Ausphotometrierung f
photohole	Photodefektelektron n, Photoloch n	photometric end-point detection	s. photometric titration
photoimpact	Quantenstoß m, Photostoß m	photometric equivalence	s. photometric radiation equivalent
photo-inactivation	Photoinaktivierung f	photometric eyepiece, photometer eyepiece	Photometerokular n
photo-induced carrier, photocarrier	photoinduzierter Ladungsträger m, Phototräger m	photometric integrator, integrating (Ulbricht) sphere, integrating (sphere) photometer, [Ulbricht's] globe photometer	Ulbrichtsche Kugel f, Ulbricht-Kugel f, Ulbricht-Photometer n, U-Kugel f, Kugelphotometer n
photoinduction	Photoinduktion f		
photoinjection	Photoinjektion f		
photo-ionization, photoionization, atomic photoelectric effect	Photoionisation f, Photoionisierung f, photoelektrische (lichtelektrische) Ionisation f, Ionisation durch Photonen[absorption]		
		photometric lamp, photometer lamp, standard [photometric] lamp	Normallampe f, Photometerlampe f, Photometernormal n
		photometric magnitude	s. photometric stellar magnitude
photoionization cross-section, cross-section for photoionization	Photoionisationsquerschnitt m, Wirkungsquerschnitt m für (der) Photoionisation, Photoionisationswirkungsquerschnitt m	photometric parallax	photometrische Parallaxe f, Helligkeitsparallaxe f
		photometric quantity, light quantity	photometrische (lichttechnische) Größe f
photoionization efficiency	Photoionisationsausbeute f	photometric radiation equivalent, photometric equivalence, relative luminous efficiency, luminosity factor [of radiation], luminous factor [of radiation], visibility factor [of radiation], light watt	photometrisches Strahlungsäquivalent n
photoionizing radiation	photoionisierende Strahlung f		
photoisomeric change, photoisomerization, photochemical isomerization	Photoisomerisation f, photochemische Isomerisation f		
		photometric record[ing]	s. photometric determination
photokinesis	Photokinesis f	photometric standard observer, ICI photometric standard observer	photometrischer Normalbeobachter m
photokinetic threshold	photokinetische Schwelle f		
photolabile	photolabil		
photolayer, photosensitive layer, photographic (sensitive) layer <phot.>	Photoschicht f, photographische (lichtempfindliche, photoempfindliche) Schicht f <Phot.>	photometric stellar magnitude, photometric magnitude (brightness)	photometrische Helligkeit f <Gestirn>
		photometric titration, photometric end-point detection	photometrische Titration (Endpunktbestimmung) f
photolayer track, emulsion track	Photoschichtspur f		
photology, physical optics, science of light	physikalische Optik f, Lehre f vom Licht	photometric unit, light unit	photometrische (lichttechnische) Einheit f
		photometry	Photometrie f, Lichtmessung f
photoluminescence	Photolumineszenz f		
photolysis	s. photodissociation	photomicrogram, photomicrograph	Mikrophotographie f, Mikrobild n, Mikroaufnahme f, mikrophotographische Aufnahme f
photomagnetic effect <semi.>	photomagnetischer Effekt m <Halb.>		
photomagnetoelectric effect	photomagnetoelektrischer Effekt m	photomicrographic apparatus, photomicrographic equipment	mikrophotographisches Gerät n
photomap	s. photogrammetric map		
photomechanical effect	photomechanischer Effekt m		
photomeson	Photomeson n	photomicrography, micrography	Mikrophotographie f
photometer constant, photometric constant	Photometerkonstante f		
photometer eyepiece, photometric eyepiece	Photometerokular n	photomultiplier, photomultiplier tube, multiplier phototube, multiplier tube, multiplier, electron multiplier [tube], secondary emission multiplier, photoelectric multiplier, photomultiplier cell	Photovervielfacher m, Sekundärelektronenvervielfacher m, SEV m, Sekundär[emissions]vervielfacher m, Sekundäremissions-Verstärkerröhre f, Elektronenvervielfacher m, Photoelektronenvervielfacher m, Photomultiplier m, Multiplier m, photoelektr[on]ischer Vervielfacher m, Vervielfacher, Elektronenvervielfachungsröhre f, Photovervielfacherröhre f, Vervielfacherröhre f, Photovervielfachungsröhre f, Vervielfacher[photo]zelle f, photoelektrische Vervielfacherzelle f
photometer field	Photometerfeld n		
photometer for visibility measurement	Sichtphotometer n		
photometer head	Photometerkopf m; Photometeraufsatz m		
photometering	Photometrierung f		
photometer lamp, photometric lamp, standard [photometric] lamp	Normallampe f, Photometerlampe f, Photometernormal n		
photometer ped	s. photometer head		
photometer screen (test plate), test plate <of photometer>	Photometerschirm m, Auffangschirm m, Meßplatte f <des Photometers>		
photometrical paradox, Olbers['] (Cheseaux-Olbers, Cheseaux and Olbers') paradox	photometrisches Paradoxon n, Olberssches Paradoxon		
		photomultiplier cell	Photovervielfacherzelle f
photometric bench	Photometerbank f,		
photometric binary [star]	s. eclipsing variable		
photometric brightness	s. photometric stellar magnitude		
photometric brightness contrast	photometrischer Helligkeitskontrast m	photomultiplier cell	s. a. photomultiplier
photometric colour contrast	photometrischer Farbkontrast m	photomultiplier characteristic, multiplier gain-v[ersu]s-voltage power law	Photovervielfachercharakteristik f, Spannungsabhängigkeit f des Verstärkungsfaktors [beim Sekundärelektronenvervielfacher]
photometric constant, photometer constant	Photometerkonstante f		
photometric cube	s. Lummer-Brodhun cube		
photometric curve	Photometrierungskurve f	photomultiplier tube	s. photomultiplier

photomuon | Photomyon n, My-Photomeson n, μ-Photomeson n

photon, light quantum, light particle, light corpuscle, quantum of light | Photon n, Lichtquant n, Lichtteilchen n, Lichtkorpuskel n, Lichtatom n

photon, radiation quantum, quantum | Photon n, Strahlungsquant n, Quant n
photon, luxon, international photon, troland | Troland n, [internationales] Photon n, Luxon n
photon annihilation; quantum annihilation | Photonenvernichtung f; Quantenvernichtung f

photonastic | photonastisch
photonasty | Photonastie f
photon component | Photonenkomponente f
photon converter | Photonenwandler m

photon counter, quantum counter | Licht[quanten]zähler m, Lichtzählrohr n
photon echo | Photonecho n, Photonenecho n
photon echo method | Photonenechomethode f
photonegative | s. photoresistive
photonegative effect | Photonegativeffekt m
photon emission | s. photon radiation
photon emission curve | Photonenemissionskurve f

photoneutrino effect, photoneutrino process | Photoneutrinoeffekt m, Photoneutrinoprozeß m

photoneutron cross-section, cross-section for photoneutron emission | Photoneutronenquerschnitt m, Wirkungsquerschnitt m für (der) Photoneutronen[emission], Wirkungsquerschnitt für (γ,n)-Prozeß, Wirkungsquerschnitt des (γ,n)-Prozesses

photoneutron deuterium source | Deuterium-Photoneutronenquelle f
photoneutron source, photosource of neutrons | Photoneutronenquelle f

photon field | Photonenfeld n

photon flux | Photonenfluß m, Photonenstrom m
photon flux density | Photonenflußdichte f, Photonenstromdichte f

photon gas | Photonengas n
photon-induced nuclear reaction | s. photodisintegration
photon momentum, momentum of the photon | Photonenimpuls m, Licht[quanten]impuls m, Impuls m des Lichtes

photon-phonon interaction | Photon-Phonon-Wechselwirkung f
photon-photon scattering | s. scattering of light by light
photon population | Photonenbesetzung f

photon radiation; photon emission | Photonenstrahlung f; Photonenemission f

photon rocket | Photonenrakete f, Lichtdruckrakete f
photon transition | Photonenübergang m
photonuclear cross-section, photodisintegration cross-section | Wirkungsquerschnitt m für (der) Photokernreaktion, Wirkungsquerschnitt für Kernphotoeffekt, Wirkungsquerschnitt des Kernphotoeffekts, Photo[wirkungs]querschnitt m

photonuclear fission | s. photofission
photonuclear reaction | s. photodisintegration
photonuclear threshold | Schwellenenergie f für Kernphotoeffekt, photo-nuklearer Schwellenwert m

photonucleation, photographic nucleation, photographically catalyzed nucleation | Photokeimbildung f

photooxidation | Photooxydation f
photopeak, photoelectric peak | Photopeak m, Photolinie f

photoperiodism | Photoperiodismus m
photopermeability | s. permeability to light
photophoby | Photophobie f
photophoresis | Photophorese f
photopic vision | Tagessehen n, Zapfensehen n, photopisches Sehen n
photopiezoelectric effect | photopiezoelektrischer Effekt m
photopion | Photopion n, Pi-Photomeson n, π-Photomeson n

photoplasticimetry | s. photoplastic measurement
photoplasticity | Photoplastizität f
photoplastic measurement, photoplasticimetry | photoplastische Untersuchung f, Photoplastizimetrie f
photoplate | s. plate <phot.>
photopolymerization, photochemical polymerization | Photopolymerisation f, photochemische Polymerisation f

photopositive, photoconducting, photoconductive, light-positive | lichtelektrisch leitend (positiv), lichtpositiv, photoleitend, photopositiv
photopotential | Photopotential n
photoproduction cross-section, cross-section for photoproduction | Wirkungsquerschnitt m für (der) Photoerzeugung, Photoerzeugungs[wirkungs]querschnitt m

photoproduction of mesons | Photoerzeugung f von Mesonen, Photomesonenerzeugung f

photopsy | Photopsie f
photoreaction, photochemical reaction, light reaction | photochemische Reaktion f, Photoreaktion f, Lichtreaktion f

photo[-]reactivation, photo[-]restoration, photo[-]recovery, photo[-]reversal | Photoreaktivierung f
photoreception | Lichtreizaufnahme f, Photorezeption f

photoreceptor <bio.> | Lichtempfänger m, Photorezeptor m <Bio.>

photo[-]recovery, photo[-]reactivation, photo[-]restoration, photo[-]reversal | Photoreaktivierung f
photo[-]reduction | Photoreduktion f

photorelay, photoelectric relay, photoswitch; light barrier | Lichtrelais n, lichtelektrisches Relais n; Lichtschranke f, Strahlenschranke f
photoresistance | s. internal photoeffect
photoresistance [cell] | s. photoconductive cell
photoresistance compensator, photoconductive compensator | Photowiderstandskompensator m

photoresistant, photoresisting, photoresistive, photonegative, light-negative | lichtelektrisch negativ, lichtnegativ, photonegativ, photoresistiv
photoresistive effect | s. internal photoeffect
photoresistor | s. photoconductive cell
photoresonance | Photoresonanz f
photoresponse, photoelectric sensitivity (activity), photosensitivity | lichtelektrische (photoelektrische) Empfindlichkeit f, Photoempfindlichkeit f
photoresponsive | s. photosensitive
photo[-]restoration, photo[-]reversal, photo[-]reactivation, photo[-]recovery | Photoreaktivierung f
photoroentgenography | s. fluorography
photo-roentgen unit, photofluorograph, photofluorographic unit, PR unit | Schirmbildgerät n, Röntgenschirmbildgerät n
photoscanner | Photoabtaster m, Photoscanner m

photoscintigram | s. scintiphotogram
photosensibilisator | s. photosensitizer
photosensitive, sensitive to light, light-sensitive; photoresponsive; sensitized <phot.> | lichtempfindlich, photoempfindlich; photosensibel <Bio.>

photosensitive cathode	s. photocathode	photovoltaic effect, barrier-layer photoeffect, barrier-layer photoelectric (photovoltaic) effect, depletion-layer photo[-electric] effect, p-n junction photovoltaic effect	Sperrschicht-Photoeffekt m, Sperrschicht[photo]effekt m, Photo-Volta-Effekt m, Photospannungseffekt m, Photovolteffekt m, Randschichtphotoeffekt m, Raumladungsphotoeffekt m, Photospannung f
photosensitive layer	s. photolayer <phot.>		
photosensitive surface	s. photosurface		
photosensitivity, photoelectric sensitivity (activity), photoresponse	lichtelektrische (photoelektrische) Empfindlichkeit f, Photoempfindlichkeit f		
photosensitization, photochemical sensitization	photochemische Sensibilisierung f, Photosensibilisierung f		
photosensitizer	Photosensibilisator m	photovoltaic effect	s. a. Becquerel effect
photosource of neutrons	s. photoneutron source	photovoltaic junction	photovoltaischer Übergang m, Sperrschicht-Photoübergang m
photospallation	Photospallation f		
		photovoltaic process	Sperrschichtphotoprozeß m
photosphere	Photosphäre f	photronic [photo]cell	s. photovoltaic cell
photospheric facula	photosphärisches Fackelgebiet n, photosphärische Fackel f	Phragmén['s] theorem	Phragménscher Satz m
		phreatic nappe (surface)	s. main water table
photospheric granulation, granulation <of photosphere>	Granulation f [der Photosphäre]	phreatic water, non-artesian water, free ground water	ungespanntes Grundwasser n, freies Grundwasser
photospheric radiation	photosphärische Strahlung f, Photosphärenstrahlung f	phreatic zone	phreatischer Bereich m
		pH-stat	pH-Stat m
		pH titration	s. potentiometry
photostimulation, optical stimulation	Photoausleuchtung f, optische Ausleuchtung f	phugoid	Phugoid n
		pH value	s. pH
photostrophism	Photostrophismus m	physical acoustics, wave acoustics	Wellenakustik f
photosurface, photosensitive surface	strahlenempfindliche Fläche (Oberfläche) f, photoempfindliche Fläche		
		physical adsorption	s. physisorption
		physical age determination (estimation)	s. physical dating
photoswitch	s. photoelectric relay	physical atmosphere	s. standard atmosphere <unit>
photosynthetic	photosynthetisch		
phototactic	phototaktisch	physical atomic weight	physikalisches Atomgewicht n
phototaxis	Phototaxis f		
phototheodolite, photogrammetric theodolite, photogoniometer	Bildmeßtheodolit m, Bildtheodolit m, Phototheodolit m, Erdbildaufnahmegerät n, Erdbildaufnahme-Meßkammer f	physical atomic weight scale	s. physical scale
		physical chemistry, physicochemistry	physikalische Chemie f, Physikochemie f
		physical circuit, real (side) circuit, physical line	Stammleitung f
photothermoelasticity	Photothermoelastizität f		
photothermomagnetic	photothermomagnetisch	physical climatic zone	physische (wirkliche) Klimazone f, physische Zone f, Landschaftsgürtel m
photothermometry	Photothermometrie f		
photo[]timer	Photozeitschalter m, [photoelektrischer] Zeitschalter m, Phototimer m; Photoschaltuhr f; photoelektrischer Belichtungsautomat m; photoelektrischer (lichtelektrischer) Bestrahlungsautomat m		
		physical colorimetry, indirect colorimetry	objektive (physikalische) Farbmessung f
		physical component, physical tensor component	physikalische Komponente (Tensorkomponente) f
		physical constant	physikalische Konstante f
phototonus	Phototonus m		
phototopography, photogrammetry	Photogrammetrie f, Bildmessung f, Phototopographie f	physical dating, physical age determination (estimation)	physikalische Altersbestimmung f
		physical deterioration of the fuel material, deterioration of fuel	Abbrennen (Ausbrennen) n des Kernbrennstoffs, Spaltstofferschöpfung f
phototransistor, phototransistor, transistor structure as a photoelectric cell, phototriode	Phototransistor m, lichtempfindlicher Transistor m, Phototriode f		
		physical dimension	physikalische Dimension f
		physical double star, binary, binary star	physischer Doppelstern m
phototriangulation, photogrammetric triangulation	Bildtriangulation f, photogrammetrische Triangulation f		
		physical electronics	physikalische Elektronik f
phototriode	s. phototransistor	physical evaporimeter	physikalischer Verdunstungsmesser m
phototronics	Phototronik f		
phototropic	phototrop[isch]		
		physical geodesy	physikalische Geodäsie f
phototropism, heliotropism	Phototropismus m, Heliotropismus m	physical geography, physiography	physische (physikalische) Geographie f
phototropy	Phototropie f	physical half-life	s, radioactive half-life
phototube, photovalve	s. photoemissive cell	physical hydration, secondary hydration	sekundäre (physikalische) Hydratation f
phototube, photovalve	s. a. vacuum photocell		
photovaristor	s. photoconductive cell	physical labelling, non-specific labelling	nichtspezifische (physikalische) Markierung f
photovisual magnitude, photovisual stellar magnitude	photovisuelle Helligkeit f, Gelbhelligkeit f <Gestirn>		
		physical libration	physikalische Libration f <Mond>
photovoltage, photoelectric voltage	Photospannung f, photoelektrische Spannung f, lichtelektrische Spannung		
		physical line, real (side, physical) circuit	Stammleitung f
photovoltaic [barrier-layer] cell, photovoltaic detector, barrier layer [photo]cell, barrier-layer photoelectric (photovoltaic) cell, blocking layer [photo]cell, barrage [photo]cell, Lange cell, rectifier [photo]cell, photronic [photo]cell, semiconductor cell, junction [photo]cell; barrier layer detector	Photoelement n, Sperrschicht[-Photo]zelle f, Sperrschicht[-Photo]element n, Gleichrichter[-Photo]element n, Gleichrichter[-Photo]zelle f, Lichtelement n; auf dem Sperrschicht-Photoeffekt beruhender Strahlungsempfänger m, photovoltaischer Strahlungsempfänger (Strahlungsdetektor) m, photovoltaischer Detektor m, Photospannungsdetektor m, Sperrschichtdetektor m		
		physical litre atmosphere, litre atmosphere, latm	(physikalische) Literatmosphäre f, latm
		physically neutral illumination, [optically] neutral illumination	[optisch] neutrale Beleuchtung f, physikalisch neutrale Beleuchtung
		physical magnitude, [physical] quantity	[physikalische] Größe f; Größenart f
		physical mass	s. mass on physical scale
		physical mass scale	physikalische Massenskala f
		physical mass unit	s. atomic mass unit

physical metallurgy	s. science of metals	physics of high temperature, high-temperature physics	Hochtemperaturphysik f
physical methods of nondestructive testing	physikalische Methoden fpl der zerstörungsfreien Werkstoffprüfung, Defektoskopie f	physics of ionosphere, ionospheric physics	Ionosphärenphysik f
physical neutrality, optical neutrality	optische Neutralität f, physikalische Neutralität	physics of metals, metal physics	Metallphysik f
physical nutation	physikalische Nutation f	physics of solids, solid state physics	Festkörperphysik f
physical oceanography, marine physics, physics of the ocean	physikalische Ozeanographie f, Physik f des Meeres	physics of superhigh energies, superhigh energy physics	Höchstenergiephysik f
physical optics, wave optics	Wellenoptik f, physikalische Optik f	physics of the Earth's interior	Physik f des Erdinnern
physical optics, photology, science of light	physikalische Optik f, Lehre f vom Licht	physics of the ocean, physical oceanography, marine physics	physikalische Ozeanographie f, Physik f des Meeres
physical pendulum, compound pendulum, rigid body pendulum	physi[kali]sches Pendel n, Starrkörperpendel n, zusammengesetztes Pendel	physics of the orbital electrons	s. atomic physics
physical photometer	physikalisches (objektives) Photometer n	physics of the Sun, solar physics, heliophysics	Sonnenphysik f, Physik f der Sonne
physical photometry	physikalische (objektive) Photometrie f	physics of X-radiation, X-ray physics	Röntgenphysik f, Physik f der Röntgenstrahlen
physical pitch	physikalische Stimmung f	physiography, physical geography	physische (physikalische) Geographie f
physical quantity, quantity, physical magnitude	Größe f, physikalische Größe; Größenart f	physiological colorimetry	höhere Farb[en]metrik f, Farbempfindungsmetrik f
physical ripening ‹phot.›	physikalische Reifung f, Vorreifung f ‹Phot.›	physiological contrast, contrast of eye	physiologischer Kontrast (Helligkeitskontrast) m, Kontrast des Auges, funktioneller Kontrast, Wahrnehmungskontrast m, Kontrasterscheinung f, Kontrastempfindung f, Kontrastfunktion f
physical roentgen equivalent	s. roentgen equivalent		
physical scale [of atomic masses], physical scale of atomic weights, physical atomic weight scale	physikalische Atomgewichtsskala f, physikalische Skala f	physiological salt solution, physiological solution, normal saline [solution]	physiologische Kochsalzlösung f
physical second	s. atomic second	physiological solution	s. physiological salt solution
physical solvation	s. secondary solvation	physisorption, physical adsorption, reversible adsorption, Van der Waals adsorption	Physisorption f, physikalische (reversible) Adsorption f, Van-der-Waals-Adsorption f, van der Waalssche Adsorption
physical space ‹in biological optics›	Außenraum m, Objektraum m, [objektiver] physikalischer Raum m ‹biologische Optik›		
physical spectrophotometer	physikalisches (objektives) Spektralphotometer n	phytoplankton	Phytoplankton n
physical state	s. state of aggregation	phytotron	Phytotron n
physical statistics	physikalische Statistik f	pibal	s. pilot balloon
physical system of mechanical units	physikalisches Einheitensystem n [der Mechanik], physikalisches Maßsystem n [der Mechanik]	pi-bond, π-bond	π-Bindung f, Pi-Bindung f
		Picard circuit	Picard-Schaltung f
		Picard['s] method	s. iterative method
physical system of units	s. c.g.s. system	Picard['s] theorem	Satz m von Picard, Picardscher Satz
physical tensor component, physical component	physikalische Komponente (Tensorkomponente) f	Piche evaporimeter	Verdunstungsmesser m nach Piche, Piche-Verdunstungsmesser m
physical theory of meteors	Physik f der Meteore, Meteortheorie f	Pickering[-Fowler] series	Pickering-Serie f
physical tracer, non-specific tracer	nichtspezifischer Tracer (Indikator) m, physikalischer Tracer (Indikator)	pick-holding control, optimum (optimizing, optimalizing, extremal) control	Optimalwertregelung f, Extremalwertregelung f
		picking [out]	s. sorting [out] by hand
physical vacuum	s. free space	pickling	s. scouring ‹met.›
physical variable [star], proper (intrinsic) variable, intrinsically variable star	physischer Veränderlicher m, eigentlicher Veränderlicher	pick-off	s. sensitive element
		pick[-]up, pick up, response ‹of relay›	Ansprechen n; Anziehen n ‹Relais›
physical weathering, disintegration ‹geo.›	mechanische (physikalische) Verwitterung f ‹Geo.›	pick-up, playback (reproducing) head, pick-up (phonograph) cartridge ‹ac.›	Abtaster m, Tonabnehmerkopf m ‹Ak.›
physical yield point, physical yield strength	physikalische Streckgrenze f		
physico-biological weathering	physikalisch-biologische Verwitterung f	pick-up, pick-up reaction ‹nucl.›	„pick-up"-Reaktion f, „pick-up" n, Abstreifreaktion f, inverse Strippingreaktion f, Herausreißen n eines Nukleons aus dem Kern, Aufpickprozeß m
physico[-]chemical	physikalisch-chemisch, physikochemisch		
physico-chemical mechanics	physikalisch-chemische Mechanik f		
physicochemistry, physical chemistry	physikalische Chemie f, Physikochemie f	pick-up	s. a. material pick-up
physics of condensed matter, condensed matter physics	Physik f der kondensierten Materie	pick-up	s. a. transducer ‹meas.›
		pick-up arm	Tonarm m, Tonabnehmerarm m
physics of elementary particles	Elementarteilchenphysik f, Physik f der Elementarteilchen	pick-up cartridge	s. pick-up ‹ac.›
		pick-up coil, Rogowski coil, Rogowski loop	Rogowski-Spule f, Rogowski-Spannungsmesser m, Rogowski-Gürtel m
physics of failures, failure physics	Physik f des Versagens		
physics of heat, heat physics	Wärmephysik f	pick-up electrode	Abnahmeelektrode f, Ableitelektrode f

pick-up

pick-up electrode ‹acc.›	Strahlsonde f, „pick-up"-Elektrode f ‹Beschl.›	Pierce-type electron gun, Pierce [electron] gun	Pierce-Kanone f, Elektronenkanone f nach Pierce
pick-up plate	s. mosaic screen	piercing	s. intersection
pick-up reaction	s. pick-up ‹nucl.›	piercing	s. a. penetration
pick-up tube, cathode-ray tube for flying-spot scanner	Abtaströhre f [für Lichtpunktabtaster]	piercing point	s. point of intersection
		pie[-type] winding, interleaved (sandwich coil, disk-type) winding	Scheibenwicklung f
pick-up value ‹of relay›	Ansprechwert m ‹Relais›	piezobirefringence	s. double refraction under pressure
pico..., p ‹absolete: micromicro..., μμ›	Piko..., Pico..., p	piezocaloric coefficient	piezokalorischer Koeffizient m
P.I. control[ler]	s. proportional integral control[ler]	piezocaloric effect	piezokalorischer Effekt m
Pictet-Trouton rule	Pictet-Troutonsche Regel f	piezochemistry	Piezochemie f, Druckchemie f
pictogram	Piktogramm n	piezochrom[at]ism	Farbänderung f durch Druckeinwirkung, Piezochromie f
picture, perspective picture ‹of perspective projection›	perspektivisches Bild n, Bild ‹Perspektive›	piezocrystallization	Piezokristallisation f, Druckkristallisation f
picture definition, picture resolution	Bildauflösung f	piezoeffect	s. piezoelectric effect
		piezoelectric, piezoelectric material	piezoelektrischer Stoff m, Piezoelektrikum n
picture-dot interlace (interlacing)	s. dot interlacing	piezoelectric coefficient	piezoelektrischer Koeffizient m, Piezokoeffizient m
picture-dupe negative, dupe negative, duplicated negative	Duplikatnegativ n, Dupnegativ n	piezoelectric constant	piezoelektrische Konstante f, Piezokonstante f
picture-dupe positive, dupe positive, duplicated positive	Duplikatpositiv n, Duppositiv n	piezoelectric crystal element, piezoelectric element	piezoelektrisches Element n
picture of flow, flow pattern, flow diagram	Strömungsbild n, Stromlinienbild n, Strömungsfigur f, Strömungsdiagramm n	piezoelectric effect; piezoeffect, piezoelectricity; direct piezoelectric effect, polarization by distortion	piezoelektrischer Effekt m, Piezoeffekt m; direkter (eigentlicher) piezoelektrischer Effekt
picture plane, plane of projection, projection plane ‹of perspective projection›	Bildtafel f, Bildebene f, Projektionsebene f ‹der Perspektive›	piezoelectric element, piezoelectric crystal element	piezoelektrisches Element n
picture resolution	s. picture definition	piezoelectric filter, crystal filter; quartz filter	Filterquarz m, Quarzfilter n; Kristallfilter n, piezoelektrisches Filter n
picture screen, viewing screen ‹tv.›	Bildschirm m, Leuchtschirm m der Bildröhre ‹Fs.›	piezoelectric generator	s. piezoelectric oscillator
		piezoelectricity	Piezoelektrizität f, Druckelektrizität f
pictures in fast motion, fast-motion picture[s]	Zeitrafferfilm m, Zeitrafferaufnahme f	piezoelectricity	s. a. piezoelectric effect
		piezoelectric loudspeaker, crystal loudspeaker	piezoelektrischer Lautsprecher m, Kristalllautsprecher m
pictures in slow motion, slow-motion picture[s]	Zeitlupenfilm m, Zeitlupenaufnahme f	piezoelectric material, piezoelectric	piezoelektrischer Stoff m, Piezoelektrikum n
picture tube, kinescope, electronic picture reproducing tube	Bild[wiedergabe]röhre f, Wiedergaberöhre f, Fernseh[bild]röhre f, Kineskop n	piezoelectric matrix	piezoelektrische Matrix f
		piezoelectric microphone, crystal microphone	Kristallmikrophon n, piezoelektrisches Mikrophon n
P.I.D. control[ler]	s. proportional integral derivative control[ler]	piezoelectric modulus	piezoelektrischer Modul m, Piezomodul m
piecewise continuous, sectionally continuous	stückweis[e] stetig, abteilungsweise stetig	piezoelectric oscillator, piezoelectric generator	piezoelektrischer Schwingungserzeuger (Schwinger; Schallgeber) m
piecewise differentiable	stückweise (abteilungsweise) differenzierbar	piezoelectric probe	piezoelektrische Sonde f
piecewise smooth, sectionally smooth	stückweise glatt ‹Kurve›; stückweise (abteilungsweise) stetig differenzierbar ‹Funktion›	piezoelectric resonator; crystal (quartz-crystal) resonator, quartz resonator	piezoelektrisches Resonanzsystem n, piezoelektrischer Resonator m, Piezoresonator m, Kristallresonator m; Quarzresonator m
pie diagram	Perigramm n		
piedmont glacier, piedmont-type glacier, Alaskian-type glacier	Vorlandgletscher m, Piedmontgletscher m, Alaskatyp m	piezoelectric tensor	piezoelektrischer Tensor m
		piezoglypt, rhegmaglypt	Rhegmaglypte f
		piezoid	s. oscillating quartz
		piezoisobath	Piezoisobathe f
		piezoluminescence	Piezolumineszenz f
pi-electron, π-electron	π-Elektron n, pi-Elektron n	piezomagnetic coefficient	piezomagnetischer Koeffizient m
pier; pillar	Pfeiler m; Säule f		
Pierce circuit	s. Pierce oscillator	piezomagnetic effect; piezomagnetism	piezomagnetischer Effekt m; Piezomagnetismus m
Pierce electrode	Pierce-Elektrode f	piezomagnetic moment	piezomagnetisches Moment n
Pierce [electron] gun, Pierce-type electron gun	Pierce-Kanone f, Elektronenkanone f nach Pierce	piezomagnetic tensor	piezomagnetischer Tensor m
piercement folding, diapir fold[ing]	Quellfaltung f, Diapirfaltung f	piezomagnetism	s. piezomagnetic effect
Pierce optics	s. Pierce system	piezometer	Piezometer n
Pierce oscillator, Pierce circuit	Pierce-Schaltung f, Schaltung f nach Pierce, Pierce-Oszillator m	piezometer level	Standrohrspiegel m
		piezometer tube, static pressure tube	Drucksonde f, Piezometerrohr n
Pierce system, Pierce optics	Pierce-Fernfokussystem n, Pierce-System n, Pierce-Optik f	piezometric gradient	Piezometergefälle n

piezometric height	Piezometerdruckhöhe f, Piezometerhöhe f	pileus	Pileus m
piezometric line; pressure surface contour	Piezometerdrucklinie f, Piezometerlinie f; Grundwasserdrucklinie f, Drucklinie f	piling; lamination; stacking; stratification, layering	Schichtung f, Schichten n, Schichtbildung f, Stratifikation f
piezometric pressure	Piezometerdruck m	piling up	s. pile-up <of dislocations>
piezometric surface, pressure surface	Piezometerdruckfläche f, Piezometerfläche f; Grundwasserdruckfläche f, Druckfläche f	piling up pillar; pier	s. a. water-surface ascent Pfeiler m; Säule f
piezo-optic coefficient	piezooptischer Koeffizient m	pillar, pillar-type switchgear	Schaltsäule f
piezo-optic constant	piezooptische Konstante f	pilot	s. pilot wire <el.>
piezoresistance	Piezowiderstand m, piezoelektrischer Widerstand m	pilot balloon, pibal	Pilotballon m, Registrierballon m
piezoresistance [effect], piezoresistive effect	piezoresistiver Effekt m, Piezowiderstandseffekt m, Piezowiderstandsänderung f	pilot circuit, pilot wire circuit	Pilotkreis m, Steuerstromkreis m, Steuerkreis m
piezoresistivity	spezifischer piezoelektrischer Widerstand m, spezifischer Piezowiderstand m	pilot flame, ignition flame, igniting flame	Zündflamme f; Lockflamme f
piezotropic equation of state	piezotrope Zustandsgleichung f	pilot frequency, drive frequency	Steuerfrequenz f, Pilotfrequenz f
piezotropic modulus of elasticity	Piezotropiemodul m	pilotherm	Thermostat m mit Bimetallfühler
piezotropy	Piezotropie f	pilot ion coulometry	Pilotionencoulometrie f
pi-filter, Π-filter	Π-Filter n, Collins-Filter n, Pi-Filter n	pilot leader, pilot streamer	Pilotblitz m; Vorentladung f
pig	s. ingot	pilotless; unmanned, without crew; unattended	unbemannt; unbesetzt, nichtbesetzt
PIG discharge, Penning [gas] discharge	Penning-Entladung f		
PIG ion source	s. Penning ion source		
pigment, chemical colour (pigment), dry colour; dye-stuff	Pigment n, Körperfarbe f; Trockenfarbe f; Farbkörper m; Pigmentfarbstoff	pilot plant, pilot scale equipment	Pilotanlage f, Versuchsanlage f [im halbtechnischen Maßstab], halbtechnische (halbindustrielle) Anlage f
pigmented glass filter, coloured (stained) glass	Farbglas n		
PIG type source	s. Penning ion source	pilot pulse, starting pulse	Einschaltimpuls m, Startimpuls m; Urimpuls m
pile, [nuclear] reactor, nuclear (chain-reacting) pile <nucl.>	Reaktor m, Kernreaktor m, Pile m <Kern.>	pilot reactor, development reactor	Versuchsreaktor m, Pilotreaktor m
pile activation, reactor activation	Reaktoraktivierung f, Pileaktivierung f, Aktivierung f im Kernreaktor	pilot scale equipment pilot spark, ignition spark	s. pilot plant Zündfunke m
piled-up group [of dislocations]	Versetzungsgruppe f, Versetzungsanhäufung f	pilot streamer pilot wave	s. pilot leader Führungswelle f [nach de Broglie], de Brogliesche Führungswelle, Pilotwelle f
piled up lengthwise, piled up longitudinally; longitudinally stratified, lengthwise stratified	längsgeschichtet		
piled up transversally, transversally stratified	quergeschichtet	pilot wire, surveying wire, pilot <el.>	Pilotleitung f, Pilotdraht m, Meßdraht m <El.>
pile-emitted radiation	s. pile radiation	pilot wire circuit	s. pilot circuit
pile factor	Pilefaktor m	pi-mesic atom	s. pionic atom
pile fluctuation, pile (reactor) noise, reactor fluctuation	Reaktorrauschen n, Rauschen n des Reaktors	pi meson, π meson, pion, nuclear force meson, British meson <π+, π0, π->	π-Meson n, Pi-Meson n, Pion n <π+, π0, π->
pile neutron, nuclear pile neutron, reactor neutron	Reaktorneutron n		
pile neutron spectrum	s. pile spectrum	pi meson decay, decay of the pi-meson, pion decay	Zerfall m des Pi-Mesons, Pionzerfall m, π-Zerfall m, Pi-Zerfall m
pile noise, reactor noise, pile (reactor) fluctuation	Reaktorrauschen n, Rauschen n des Reaktors		
pile-oscillation method	Reaktoroszillatormethode f, Pileoszillatormethode f	pinacoid, terminal face pinacoidal class	Pinakoid n, Endfläche f s. holohedry of the triclinic class
pile oscillator, nuclear pile oscillator, reactivity (reactor) oscillator	Reaktoroszillator m, Pileoszillator m	pin-and-arc indicator; indicating goniometer	Winkelanzeigegerät n, Winkelindikator m; Pin and Arc n
pile radiation, pile-emitted radiation, reactor[-emitted] radiation	Reaktorstrahlung f	pinball board pinch, pinching; constriction; necking [down]; contraction of area; waist	s. Galton['s] apparatus Einschnürung f
pile spectrum, pile neutron spectrum, reactor [neutron] spectrum	Reaktorneutronenspektrum n, Energiespektrum n der Reaktorneutronen, Reaktorspektrum n	pinch; squeeze, squeezing; squashing; crimp[ing]	Quetschung f
pile-up effect, pile-up of pulses	Aufstocken n der Impulse, Impulsaufstockung f, „pile-up"-Effekt m, Aufeinandertürmen n	pinch <of plasma> pinch	Pinch m <Plasma> s. a. pinch effect <of plasma>
pile-up of dislocations	Versetzungsaufstauung f, Aufstauung f (Aufstau m) von Versetzungen	pinch clamp pinch cock; pinch clamp, snap valve	s. pinch cock Quetschhahn m, Schraubklemme f
pile-up of pulses	s. pile-up effect		

pinch discharge	s. pinch effect	pion-nucleon scattering	Pion-Nukleon-Streuung f
pinch effect, pinch[ing], selfconstricting effect, pinch [effect] discharge, pinching discharge <of plasma>	Pincheffekt m, eigenmagnetische Kompression f, Selbsteinschnürung f, Einschnüreffekt m, Pinchentladung f, Selbstabschnürung f, Abschnüreffekt m <Plasma>	pip, spike of the pulse; kick[back]	Überschwingimpuls m, Überschwingspitze f, Pip m, Zacke f
		pipe, funnel, pipe of ingot	trichterförmiger Lunker (Schwindungslunker) m
pinch effect discharge	s. pinch effect	pipe, whistle <ac.>	Pfeife f <Ak.>
pinching, pinch; constriction; necking [down]; contraction of area; waist	Einschnürung f	pipe, volcanic pipe <geo.>	Explosionsröhre f, [vulkanische] Durchschlag[s]-röhre f, Pipe f, Diatrem n
pinching [discharge]	s. pinch effect	pipe coil, winding pipe (tube), coil	Rohrschlange f, Schlangenrohr n, Schlange f
pinch-off effect	„pinch-off"-Effekt m, Abschnür[ungs]effekt m	pipe connection	Rohrverbindung f
		pipe cooler, trumpet cooler	Röhrenkühler m, Rohrkühler m; Rohrbündelkühler m
pinch-off voltage	„pinch-off"-Spannung f, Abschnür[ungs]spannung f	pipe diffusion, dislocation pipe diffusion	„pipe diffusion" f, Röhrendiffusion f, Diffusion f in Röhren [längs der Versetzungslinien]
pin-connected	gelenkig gelagert; gelenkig verbunden		
p-i-n contact	pin-Kontakt m	pipe filter, tubular filter, tubular electrical dust filter	Röhrenfilter n, Rohrfilter n
pin coupling	Stiftkopplung f		
pin[-]cushion distortion, pincushioning, positive distortion	kissenförmige Verzeichnung f, Kissenverzeichnung f, positive Verzeichnung	pipe flow, flow through pipes, tubular flow	Rohrströmung f
		pipe of ingot	s. pipe
		pipe resistance	Leitungswiderstand m
pine crystal	s. dendrite	pipet[te] holder (stand)	Pipettenständer m
Pines['] relation	Pines-Beziehung f, Beziehung f von Pines, Pinessche Beziehung	pipe under pressure	Druckleitung f
Pi[-] network, Π[-] network, Pi[-] section, Π[-] section	P-Glied n, Π-Glied n, Pi-Schaltung f, Π-Schaltung f, Pi-Netzwerk n, Π-Netzwerk n, Π-Vierpol m; Π-Grundkette f, Π-Grundschaltung f, Grund-Π-Schaltung f	piping <of ingots>, liquid shrinkage, shrinking	Lunkerung f, Lunkerbildung f, flüssiges Schwinden n
		piping	s. a. underwashing
		piping around a corner; turn[-back], deflection [around a corner]	Umlenkung f
		Pippard['s] equation	Pippardsche Gleichung f
pinging noise	s. microphonic effect <el.>	Pirani bridge	Pirani-Brücke f
pinhole, pseudo lens	Loch n <Lochkamera>	Pirani gauge, Pirani pressure gauge, Pirani resistance gauge, hot-wire gauge, hot-wire [manometer]	Pirani-Manometer n, Wärmeleitungsmanometer n nach Pirani, Piranisches Widerstandsmanometer n, Widerstandsmanometer [nach Pirani]
pinhole; pinhole porosity <met.>	Fadenlunker m, Feinlunker m; Feinporosität f <Met.>		
pinhole action, action of pinhole camera	Lochkamerawirkung f, Lochkammerwirkung f		
pinhole camera, camera obscura	Lochkamera f, Portasche Kamera f, Camera f obscura	Pi[-] section	s. Pi[-] network
		pistolgraph	s. instantaneous shot
		piston <of the pump>	Stempel m <Pumpe>
pinhole diaphragm	s. aperture diaphragm <opt.>	piston <techn.>	Kolben m <Techn.>
pinhole image; pinhole photograph	Lochkamerabild n; Lochkameraaufnahme f	piston	s. a. shorting plunger <el.>
		piston air pump	s. piston pump
		piston attenuator	variables Dämpfungsglied n, Kolbendämpfungsglied n, Kolbenattenuator m
pinhole porosity; pinhole <met.>	Fadenlunker m, Feinlunker m; Feinporosität f <Met.>		
pinion	Ritzel n	piston compressor, reciprocating [piston] compressor	Kolbenkompressor m, Kolbenverdichter m
		piston diaphragm	Kolbenmembran f
		piston flowmeter (fluid meter)	s. piston-type flowmeter
pin joint, hinge joint	gelenkiger (gelenkartiger) Knoten m, Gelenkknoten m	piston gauge <US>	s. manometric balance
pinning down	s. locking <of dislocations>	piston meter	s. piston-type flowmeter
p-i-n rectifier	pin-Gleichrichter m	piston[]phone	Pistonphon n, Kolbenmikrophon n
		piston pressure	Kolbendruck m
		piston pressure gauge	s. manometric balance
pin support, pin suspension	Pinnenaufhängung f, Pinnenlagerung f; Stiftlagerung f	piston pump, reciprocating pump, piston air pump	Kolbenpumpe f, Stiefelpumpe f; Kolbenluftpumpe f, Hubkolbenpumpe f
pin-type insulator	Schaftisolator m	piston stroke	s. stroke of piston
Piobert effect	Piobert-Effekt m	piston-swept volume, displacement [volume], volume of stroke	Hubraum m, Hubvolumen n
Piola-Kirchhoff stress tensor	Piola-Kirchhoffscher Spannungstensor m		
		piston-type flowmeter, piston-type [fluid] meter, piston flowmeter, piston [fluid] meter	Kolbenzähler m, Verdrängungszähler m
Piola['s] theorem	Piolascher Satz m		
pion	s. pi meson		
pion decay, decay of the pi-meson, pi-meson decay	Zerfall m des Pi-Mesons, Pionzerfall m, π-Zerfall m, Pi-Zerfall m	pit, recess, depression, indent[ation]	Aussparung f, Ausschnitt m, Vertiefung f, Höhlung f, Einbuchtung f
pionic atom, pi-mesic atom, π-mesic atom	Pi-Meso[n]atom n, pi-mesonisches Atom n, Pionatom n, π-Mesonatom n	pit, etch pit	Ätzgrübchen n, Ätzgrube f
		pit	s. a. cock[-]pit <geo.>
		pit	s. a. pitting

pitch; lead	Steigung f; Teilung f; Schrittweite f	pitpoint corrosion	s. pitting
pitch, lead <of the helix, screw>, screw pitch, pitch of screw	Ganghöhe f, Steigung f <Schraube>, Schraubensteigung f; Schraubengang m, Gang m <Schraube>	pitting, hydrogen blister, pit	Wasserstoffpore f, Grübchen n, Korrosionsgrübchen n
		pitting	Grübchenkorrosion f, Pitting n, Grübchenbildung f
pitch, pitch of note, pitch of the tone, tone (sound) pitch <ac.>	Tonhöhe f, Höhe f <Ton> <Ak.>	pitting, pitting corrosion, pitpoint corrosion, localized corrosion; point[ed] corrosion	Lochfraß m, Lochfraßkorrosion f, punktförmige tiefe Anfressur.g f, Punktkorrosion f, Punktfraß m, punktförmiger Korrosionsangriff m
pitch, musical pitch <ac.>	Stimmung f <Ak.>		
pitch, pitching <aero.>	Längsneigung f <Aero.>		
pitch, pitching, rocking, plunging <hydr.>	Stampfen n, Stampfbewegung f <Hydr.>	pitting factor	Pittingfaktor m
pitch angle	Steig[ungs]winkel m	Pi-type waveguide, Π-type waveguide, Π waveguide	Steghohlleiter m
pitch angle	s. a. pitching angle		
pitch chord ratio	Teilungsverhältnis n <Aero., Hydr.>	pivot	s. centre of rotation
		pivot	s. a. axis of rotation
pitch circle theodolite	Zahnkreistheodolit m	pivot	s. a. pivot journal
		pivot friction, bearing friction	Lagerreibung f
pitch error	Steigungsfehler m	pivoting <mech.>	Bohren n, Drehung f um die gemeinsame Normale <Mech.>
pitchfork, tuning[-] fork	Stimmgabel f		
pitching, pitch <aero.>	Längsneigung f <Aero.>	pivoting friction	Bohrreibung f, bohrende Reibung f
pitching, pitch, rocking, plunging <hydr.>	Stampfen n, Stampfbewegung f <Hydr.>	pivoting friction torque, moment of pivoting friction	Bohrreibungsmoment n
pitching angle, pitch angle	Längsneigungswinkel m <Aero.>; Stampfwinkel m <Hydr.>		
		pivot journal, pivot, swivel pin; trunnion	Zapfen m, Spitze f; Lagerzapfen m; Stützzapfen m, Tragzapfen m, Spurzapfen m; Drehzapfen m
pitching moment, pitch moment <of wing>, longitudinal moment <aero.>	Längsmoment n, Kippmoment n [des Tragflügels] <Aero.>		
		pivot point	s. centre of rotation
pitching moment coefficient, pitch moment coefficient, coefficient of pitching moment; [over]turning moment coefficient, tilting (tipping) moment coefficient	Kippmomentenbeiwert m <Flugzeug>; Stampfmomentenbeiwert m <Schiff>; Querneigungsmomentenbeiwert m	pivot support, journal support	Zapfenlagerung f
		pK, pK value	pK-Wert m, pK
		place; point; position; site	Ort m, Stelle f, Platz m; Position f; Standort m
		place, position <of a star>	Ort m [eines Gestirns], Position f [eines Gestirns], Sternort m
pitch interval	Tonhöhenverhältnis n	place exchange	s. interchange of sites
pitch length	Ganglänge f	place isomer, position isomer	Stellungsisomer n
pitch moment, pitching moment <of wing>, longitudinal moment <aero.>	Längsmoment n, Kippmoment n [des Tragflügels] <Aero.>	place-isomeric, position-isomeric	stellungsisomer
pitch moment coefficient	s. pitching moment coefficient	place isomerism, position (substitutional) isomerism	Stellungsisomerie f, Positionsisomerie f, Substitutionsisomerie f, Ortsisomerie f
pitch of deflection sag	Biegungspfeil m, Biegepfeil m, Durchbiegung f		
pitch of note	s. pitch <ac.>	place theory [of Helmholtz]	s. Helmholtz['] place theory
pitch of screw	s. pitch	place value	Stellenwert m
pitch of the perforation	s. perforation pitch	placing	s. introduction
		Placzek['s] function	Placzek-Funktion f
pitch of the teeth, tooth pitch	Zahnteilung f	Placzek['s] theory [of polarizability]	Placzeksche Theorie f [der Polarisierbarkeit]
pitch of the tone	s. pitch <ac.>	plage, plage area, chromospheric facula	[chromosphärische) Fackel f, Chromosphärenfackel f
pitch of the worm	Schneckensteigung f, Schneckenteilung f		
pitch of the wrench, parameter of the screw	Parameter m der Dyname, Pfeil m der Schraube	plage	s. a. flocculus
		plage area	s. plage
		plagihedral class	s. enantiomorphous hemihedry of the regular system
pitch recorder	Tonhöhenschreiber m	plagiotropic	plagiotrop, plagiogeotropisch
pitch variation	Tonhöhenschwankung f	plagiotropism	Plagiotropismus m
		plain <geo.>	Ebene f <Geo.>
pith-ball electroscope	Holundermarkkugelelektroskop n	plain carbon, homogeneous carbon, pure carbon, retort carbon	Homogenkohle f, Reinkohle f, Retortenkohle f, Reindochtkohle f
pi-theorem, Buckingham['s] pi theorem, Π-theorem, π-theorem	Pi-Theorem n, Π-Theorem n		
		plain colour, free colour, surface colour	freie (unbezogene) Farbe f, Flächenfarbe f
pitometer	s. Pitot tube	plain specimen, unnotched specimen	Vollprobestab m, Vollstab m
Pitot comb	s. Pitot rake		
Pitot pressure	Pitot-Druck m		
Pitot rake, Pitot comb	Druckmeßrechen m [aus zusammengefaßten Pitot-Rohren]	plaited filter, [pre]folded filter, pleated filter	Faltenfilter n
		plait point	s. critical solution temperature
Pitot static tube	s. Pitot tube	plait point curve	s. solubility curve
Pitot tube, pitot, impact tube; Pitot static tube; pitometer	Pitot-Rohr n, Pitotsches Rohr n, Gesamtdruck-Meßsonde f, Pitotsche Röhre f, Pitot-Sonde f	plan, design, test programme <of the first or second order>	Versuchsplan m <erster oder zweiter Ordnung>

planar 604

planar; plane; flat	eben, plan; planar; flächenhaft [ausgedehnt], Flächen-; flach, in der gleichen Ebene, in einer Ebene	Planck['s] quantum	s. Planck['s] constant
		Planck['s] radiation constant	Plancksche Strahlungskonstante f
planar diode	Planardiode f	Planck['s] radiation formula (law)	s. Planck['s] law [of radiation]
		Planck['s] thermodynamic potential	s. Planck['s] function
		plane	Ebene f
plan area	s. cross-sectional area	plane, optically flat (plane), flat <opt.>	optisch eben, eben; optisch flach, flach <Opt.>
planar epitaxial transistor (triode)	s. epiplanar transistor		
planar eyepiece	Planokular n	plane	s. a. planar
		plane angle	ebener Winkel m
planar feature <geo.>	planares Element n, Spaltbarkeit f <Geo.>	plane antenna, flat-top antenna, sheet antenna	Flächenantenne f
planar graph	planarer Graph m	plane at infinity, ideal plane	uneigentliche (unendlich[-]ferne) Ebene f, Fernebene f
planar Hall effect	planarer Hall-Effekt m		
planar interface	ebene Grenzfläche f	plane-centred	s. face-centred
		plane[-]concave, plano-concave	plankonkav
planar junction	planarer Übergang m, Planarübergang m	plane[-]convex, plano-convex	plankonvex
planar lens, planar objective	Planobjektiv n	plane co-ordinates, co-ordinates in the plane	ebene Koordinaten fpl, Koordinaten in der Ebene
planar mask	s. shadow mask <tv.>		
planar molecule	ebenes Molekül n	plane co-ordinates	Ebenenkoordinaten fpl
planar moment of inertia	planares Trägheitsmoment n, Trägheitsmoment in bezug auf eine Ebene		
		plane corrugated surface, corrugated surface (structure)	[ebene] Oberfläche f mit Einschnitten
		plane[-]cylindrical, plano-cylindrical	planzylindrisch
planar objective	s. planar lens		
planar radius of inertia, gyration modulus	planarer Trägheitsradius m	plane cylindric wave	ebene Zylinderwelle f
planar transistor, planar triode	Planartransistor m, Planartriode f	plane diffusion kernel	Diffusionskern m für ebene Quellen
		plane elasticity	ebene Elastizitätstheorie f
		plane flow, two-dimensional flow	ebene Strömung f, zweidimensionale Strömung, ebene Bewegung f
Planck['s] constant, quantum of action, elementary quantum of action, action quantum, Planck['s] quantum	Plancksche (lichtelektrische) Konstante f, [Plancksches] Wirkungsquantum n, [Plancksche] Wirkungskonstante f, [Plancksches] Wirkungsquant n, Plancksches Wirkungselement n		
		plane flow	s. a. flow along a slab
		plane frame[-work]; plane truss	ebenes Fachwerk n; ebenes Tragwerk n
		plane glass	s. optical flat
		plane grating <opt.>	Plangitter n <Opt.>
		plane grating spectrograph	Plangitterspektrograph m
Planck distribution	Planck-Verteilung f, Plancksche Verteilung f	plane ground joint	Planschliff m
Planck-Einstein function	Planck-Einstein-Funktion f, Planck-Einsteinsche Funktion f	plane horopter	Planhoropter m
		plane lattice, two-dimensional lattice	Flächengitter n, zweidimensionales Gitter n, ebenes Gitter
Planck['s] formula	s. Planck['s] law		
Planck['s] function, Planck['s] potential, Planck['s] thermodynamic potential	Plancksche Funktion f, Plancksches [thermodynamisches] Potential n, thermodynamisches Potential von Planck, thermodynamisches Plancksches Potential, Planck-Funktion f	plane mathematical pendulum, mathematical (simple) pendulum	mathematisches Pendel n, Punktkörperpendel n
		plane mirror, flat mirror	Planspiegel m, ebener Spiegel m, Flachspiegel m
		plane motion, uniplanar motion	ebene Bewegung f
Planck['s] fundamental length	Plancksche Elementarlänge f	planeness, flatness, smoothness	Ebenheit f, Glätte f
		plane of bending	s. plane of flexure
Planck['s] hypothesis	Plancksche Hypothese f	plane of curvature	s. osculating plane
Planckian colour	Plancksche Farbe f	plane of deformation	Verformungsebene f, Verzerrungsebene f, Umform[ungs]ebene f, Formänderungsebene f
Planckian locus	s. achromatic locus		
Planckian radiator	s. black body		
Planck-Kelvin['s] formulation of the second law of thermodynamics	s. second law		
		plane of denudation, denudation plane (level)	Rumpffläche f, Endrumpf m, Rumpfebene f; Primärrumpf m, Trugrumpf m
Planck's law <$E = h\nu$>	Plancksche Relation f		
Planck['s] law [of radiation], Planck['s] radiation law, Planck['s] radiation formula, Planck['s] formula	Plancksches Strahlungsgesetz (Gesetz) n, Strahlungsgesetz von Planck, Plancksche Strahlungsformel (Formel) f, Strahlungsformel von Planck, Plancksche Strahlungsgleichung (Gleichung) f, Strahlungsgleichung von Planck	plane of discontinuity	Sprungfläche f; elektrische Sprungfläche
		plane of division	Teilungsebene f
		plane of ecliptic	s. ecliptic[al] plane
		plane of flexure, plane of bending, bending line plane, flexural plane	Biegungsebene f
Planck['s] mean	Mittelwert m nach Planck, Plancksches Mittel n	plane of floatation, waterplanc, floatation plane	Schwimmebene f
Planck['s] oscillator	Planckscher Oszillator m, Oszillator von Planck		
Planck['s] potential	s. Planck['s] function	plane of flow, plane of the flow	Stromebene f, Strömungsebene f

plane of gravity, gravity plane	Schwerebene f	plane polarized oscillation, linear[ly polarized] oscillation	linear polarisierte Schwingung f, lineare (geradlinige) Schwingung
plane of ground glass; groundglass plane; image plane	[Gaußsche] Bildebene f <Opt.>; Mattscheibenebene f, Auffangebene f <Phot.>	plane radiator; surface radiator, surface emitter	Flächenstrahler m; Oberflächenstrahler m
plane of measurement, working plane	Meßebene f	plane reflector antenna	Flachreflektorantenne f
plane of mirror [reflection symmetry], mirror plane, reflection plane	Spiegelebene f	plane resection	ebenes Rückwärtseinschneiden n, ebener Rückwärtseinschnitt m, Rückwärtseinschneiden in der Ebene
plane of mirror reflection symmetry	s. plane of symmetry		
plane of motion	s. plane of the orbit	plane source	ebene Quelle f; Flächenquelle f, flache (flächenhaft ausgedehnte) Quelle
plane of optic[al] axes, optic[al] axial plane, axial plane	Achsenebene f, optische Achsenebene		
plane of oscillation, plane of vibration[s], vibration plane	Schwingungsebene f, Schwingebene f	plane[-]spherical, plano-spherical	plansphärisch
plane of paper, plane of the paper, drawing plane	Zeichenebene f, Papierebene f	plane strain	ebener Verformungszustand (Deformationszustand, Verzerrungszustand, Formänderungszustand) m, „plane strain" m
plane of principal section	s. principal section <cryst., opt.>		
plane of projection, projection (picture) plane <of perspective projection>	Bildtafel f, Bildebene f, Projektionsebene f <der Perspektive>	plane stress, biaxial stress, state of plane stress	ebener Spannungszustand m, zweiachsiger Spannungszustand
plane of reference	s. reference plane	plane surface, optically flat surface <opt.>	Planfläche f <Opt.>
plane of shear	s. shear plane	plane surface	s. a. face <of polyhedron>
plane of slip, slip plane, glide plane, shearing plane <cryst.>	Gleitebene f, Translationsebene f <Krist.>	plane symmetry	ebene Symmetrie f, Flächensymmetrie f
		plane table, plane-table	Meßtisch m
plane of stratification <geo.>	Schichtfläche f; Schichtebene f; Schicht[en]fuge f <Geo.>	plane-table map	Meßtischblatt n
plane of support, supporting plane	Stützebene f, Stützhyperebene f	plane-table photogrammetry	Meßtischphotogrammetrie f, Einschneidephotogrammetrie f
plane of symmetry, symmetry[-] plane; plane of mirror reflection symmetry <cryst.>	Symmetrieebene f	plane-table survey, stadia method	Meßtischaufnahme f
		plane-table tachymetry	Meßtischtachymetrie f
plane of the cut; plane of the section, section plane; cut plane	Schnittebene f, Schnittfläche f	planetarium, orrery	Planetarium n
		planetary	s. planetary nebula
		planetary aberration	Planetenaberration f, planetarische Aberration f
plane of the eye	Augenebene f	planetary albedo	planetarische Albedo f
plane of the flow	s. plane of flow		
plane of the meridian, meridian plane, meridional plane	Meridianebene f	planetary configuration, planet configuration, configuration of planet <astr.>	Konstellation f <Astr.>
plane of the orbit, orbit[al] plane, plane of motion	Bahnebene f	planetary electron	s. orbital electron
		planetary ellipsoid	planetarisches Ellipsoid n
plane of the paper	s. plane of paper	planetary gear, epicyclic gear, planet gear, cryptogear	Planetengetriebe n, Umlaufgetriebe n
plane of the section, section plane; plane of the cut, cut plane	Schnittebene f, Schnittfläche f		
		planetary geomagnetic index	s. planetary [magnetic] index
plane of transmission, transmission plane	Transmissionsebene f	planetary hypothesis <of atomic structure>	Planetenhypothese f <der Atomstruktur>
plane of vibration[s], plane of oscillation, vibration plane	Schwingungsebene f, Schwingebene f	planetary [magnetic] index, planetary geomagnetic index	planetarischer [geomagnetischer] Index m
plane of vision, visual plane	Visionsebene f; Blickebene f	planetary nebula, planetary	planetarischer Nebel m
plane of zero luminosity	s. alychn	planetary orbit, orbit of planet	Planetenbahn f
plane[-] parallel, parallel[-] plane	planparallel	planetary precession	Planetenpräzession f, planetar[isch]e Präzession f
		planetary system	Planetensystem n
plane-parallel atmosphere	planparallele Atmosphäre f	planetary system of winds, planetary wind system	planetarisches Windsystem n
		planetary vorticity flux	planetarischer Vorticityfluß m
plane-parallel capacitor, plate capacitor, parallel plate capacitor	Plattenkondensator m	planetary west wind drift	planetarische Westwinddrift f
plane parallel glass	s. optical flat	planetary wind belt	planetarischer Windgürtel m
plane parallelism, parallelism	Planparallelität f		
plane plasticity	ebene Plastizitätstheorie f	planetary wind system	s. planetary system of winds
plane polar co-ordinates, polar co-ordinates [in the plane]	Polarkoordinaten fpl [in der Ebene], ebene Polarkoordinaten	planet configuration	s. planetary configuration <astr.>
		planet gear	s. planetary gear
plane polarization, linear polarization	lineare (geradlinige) Polarisation f, Linearpolarisation f	planetocentric co-ordinates; planetocentric set [of co-ordinates], planetocentric system [of co-ordinates]	planetozentrische Koordinaten fpl; planetozentrisches Koordinatensystem n
plane polarized, linearly polarized	linear polarisiert, geradlinig polarisiert		
		planetogenic vortex	planetogener Wirbel m

planetographic coordinates; planetographic set [of coordinates], planetographic system [of coordinates]	planetographische Koordinaten *fpl*; planetographisches Koordinatensystem *n*	plant scale	Produktionsmaßstab *m*, Betriebsmaßstab *m*
		plaque	s. plate
		plasma accelerator	Plasmabeschleuniger *m*
		plasma annulus	Plasmaring *m*
planetoid, asteroid, minor planet, small planet	Planetoid *m*, Asteroid *m*, Kleiner Planet *m*, Zwergplanet *m*	plasma balance	Plasmagleichgewicht *n*
		plasma beam	Plasmastrahl *m*
planetology	s. astrogeology	plasma betatron	Plasmabetatron *n*
plane truss; plane frame [-work]	ebenes Fachwerk *n*; ebenes Tragwerk *n*	plasma boundary layer	s. protoplasmic surface <bio.>
plane wake	ebener Nachlauf *m*	plasma capacitor	Plasmakondensator *m*
plane wave	ebene Welle *f*, Planwelle *f*	plasma channel	s. plasma column
plane wave expansion; expansion in plane waves	Entwicklung *f* nach ebenen Wellen	plasma chromatography	Plasmachromatographie *f*
planform; outline, contour; structural shape <of steel>	Kontur *f*; Umrißlinie *f*; Begrenzungslinie *f*; Umriß *m*, Bildgrenze *f*; Profilform *f*	plasma cluster, plasmoid	Plasmoid *n*, Plasmaklumpen *m*, Plasmawolke *f*, Plasmamasse *f*, Plasmapaket *n*
planform taper, taper <of the wing>	Zuspitzung *f*, Zuspitzungsverhältnis *n* <Flügel>	plasma column, plasma cylinder, plasma channel	Plasmasäule *f*, Plasmafaden *m*, Plasmazylinder *m*, Plasmakanal *m*, Plasmaschnur *f*
planigraph	s. laminograph		
planigraphy	Körperschichtaufnahme [-verfahren *n*] *f* mittels Planigraphen, Schicht[bild]aufnahme *f* mittels Planigraphen, Planigraphie *f*	plasma confinement, plasma containment, containment of plasma, confinement of plasma, confining of plasma, plasma isolation	Einschließung (Halterung, Begrenzung, Isolation) *f* des Plasmas, Plasmaeinschließung *f*, Plasmahalterung *f*, Plasmabegrenzung *f*, Plasmaisolation *f*, „confinement" *n*, „containment" *n*, Plasma„confinement" *n*
planimeter constant	Planimeterkonstante *f*		
planimeter eyepiece, eyepiece planimeter	Planimeterokular *n*, Okularplanimeter *n*		
planimetering, planimetration; measurement of area, area (surface) measurement	Planimetrierung *f*; Flächen[aus]messung *f*		
		plasma cylinder	s. plasma column
		plasma density	Plasmadichte *f*
planimetric detail	Situationseinzelheit *f*, Einzelheit *f* der Situation	plasmadesma <*pl.*: -desmata>	Plasmodesmus *m* <*pl.*: -desmen>
planimetric survey [operations]	Situationsaufnahme *f*, Grundrißaufnahme *f*; Lageaufnahme *f*	plasma diagnostic, diagnostics of plasma	Plasmadiagnostik *f*, Diagnostik (Diagnose) *f* des Plasmas, Plasmadiagnose *f*
planimetry	Planimetrie *f*; Flächenmeßlehre *f*, Flächenmessung *f*	plasma diode	Plasmadiode *f*
		plasma electron oscillation, electron plasma oscillation	Elektronenplasmaschwingung *f*
planing	s. surfing <on the water surface>	plasma-filled waveguide, plasma[-type] waveguide	Plasmawellenleiter *m*
planing boat, skimming boat, glider, hydroplane	Gleitboot *n*, Wassergleiter *m*	plasma flow	Plasmaströmung *f*
planishing, flattening <of the bump>	Ausbeulung *f*, Beulen *n*, Austreibung *f* der Beule	plasma frequency	Plasmafrequenz *f*
		plasma frequency	s. a. Langmuir frequency
planisphere	Planiglob *m*, Planiglobium *n* <*pl.*: -bien>; Planisphäre *f*	plasmagram	Plasma[chromato]gramm *n*
		plasma gun	Plasmakanone *f*
planispiral	s. helical	plasma heating, heating of plasma	Plasmaaufheizung *f*, Aufheizung *f* des Plasmas
plankton	Plankton *n*		
planning of experiment	s. design of experiment	plasma injection, injection of plasma	Plasmaeinbringung *f*, Plasmainjektion *f*, Plasmaeinschuß *m*, Einbringung *f* (Injektion *f*, Einschuß *m*) des Plasmas
plano-achromat[e], plano-achromatic lens (objective)	Planachromat *n* (*m*)		
plano-apochromat[e], plano-apochromatic lens (objective)	Planapochromat *n* (*m*)		
		plasma injector	Plasmainjektor *m*
plano-concave, plane[-]concave	plankonkav	plasma instability, instability of plasma [column]	Plasmainstabilität *f*, Instabilität *f* der Plasmasäule
plano-concave lens	plankonkave Linse *f*, Plankonkavlinse *f*; Plankonkavglas *n*	plasma ion oscillation	Ionenplasmaschwingung *f*
plano-convex, plane[-]convex	plankonvex	plasma ion source	Plasmaionenquelle *f*
plano-convex lens	plankonvexe Linse *f*, Plankonvexlinse *f*; Plankonvexglas *n*	plasma isolation	s. plasma confinement
		plasma jet	Plasmastrahl *m*
plano-cylindrical, plane[-]cylindrical	planzylindrisch	plasmalemma	Plasmalemma *n*, protoplasmatische Membran *f*
plano-cylindrical lens	Planzylinderlinse *f*, planzylindrische Linse *f*; Planzylinderglas *n*	plasmalemma potential	Plasmalemmapotential *n*
		plasma lens	Plasmalinse *f*
plan of transposition	s. Williot diagram	plasmal reaction, Feulgen procedure (reaction)	Feulgensche Reaktion *f*
plano-spherical, plane[-]spherical	plansphärisch		
plano-spherical lens	plansphärische Linse *f*	plasma of gaseous discharge, [gas] discharge plasma	Gasentladungsplasma *n*, Entladungsplasma *n*
plan-position indicator, indicator, radarscope, scope, display, radar screen (display panel)	Radarbildschirm *m*, Radarschirm *m*, Bildschirm *m*, Schirm *m* <Radar>		
		plasma oscillation	Plasmaschwingung *f*
		plasmapause	Plasmapause *f*
		plasma physics	Plasmaphysik *f*, Physik *f* des Plasmas
plant cell	Pflanzenzelle *f*	plasma reactor	Plasmareaktor *m*, Plasmaspaltungsreaktor *m*
Planté plate	Planté-Platte *f*		
		plasma resonance	Plasmaresonanz *f*

plasma = das Plasma

plasma sheath	Plasmahülle *f*	plastic flow	*s.* yielding ‹of metal, material, solid›
plasma sound	Plasmaschall *m*	plastic-flow persistence	*s.* plastic after flow
plasma sphere	Plasmakugel *f*	plastic gel	*s.* plastigel
plasma state	Plasmazustand *m*, vierter Aggregatzustand *m*	plastic hysteresis	plastische Hysterese *f*
		plastic impact	*s.* perfectly inelastic impact ‹mech.›
plasma streaming, protoplasmic streaming	Plasmaströmung *f*, Protoplasmaströmung *f*	plasticity	Plastizität *f*, Bildsamkeit *f*
plasma swelling	Plasmaquellung *f*	plasticity agent	*s.* softener
plasma torch	Plasmabrenner *m*; Wolfram-Inert-Gas-Brenner *m*, WIG-Brenner *m*	plasticity condition	*s.* yield condition
		plasticity index	Plastizitätszahl *f*; Plastizitätsindex *m* ‹Kohle›
plasma torch	Plasmafackel *f*	plasticity modulus, module of plastic strain	Modul *m* der plastischen Formänderung
plasma torch cutting	Wolfram-Inert-Gas-schneiden *n*, WIG-Schneiden *n*, Plasmaschneiden *n*, WIG-Verfahren *n*, Wolfram-Inert-Gas-Verfahren *n*	plasticity of crystals, crystal plasticity	Kristallplastizität *f*, kristallographisch orientierte Plastizität *f*
		plasticity theory of Hencky	Henckysche Plastizitätstheorie *f*
		plasticity threshold	Plastizitätsschwelle *f*
plasmatron, plasmotron	Plasmatron *n*	plasticization, plasticizing, plastifying, plastification, softening; fluxing, fluxion	Weichmachen *n*, Plastifikation *f*, Plastifizierung *f*; Plastizierung *f*
plasma-type parametric amplifier	parametrischer Plasmaverstärker *m*		
plasma-type waveguide, plasma[-filled] waveguide	Plasmawellenleiter *m*	plasticizer ‹of caoutchouc›	Plastikator *m*, Plastiziermittel *n*, Peptisiermittel *n* ‹Gummi›
plasma wave	Plasmawelle *f*		
		plasticizer	*s. a.* softener
		plasticizing, plastication ‹of caoutchouc›	Weichmachen *n* ‹Gummi›
plasma waveguide	*s.* plasma-type waveguide		
plasma wavelength, ionospheric plasma wavelength	Plasmawellenlänge *f*	plasticizing	*s. a.* plasticization
		plasticizing agent	*s.* softener
		plastic layer	*s.* plastic range
plasmochisis	Plasmochise *f*	plastic lens	Plastiklinse *f*, plastische Linse *f*
plasmograph	Plasmagraph *m*, Plasmograph *m*		
		plastic limit	*s.* yield strength
plasmoid, plasma cluster	Plasmoid *n*, Plasmaklumpen *m*, Plasmawolke *f*, Plasmamasse *f*, Plasmapaket *n*	plastic material	*s.* plast
		plasticodynamics	Dynamik *f* plastischer Körper
		plasticostatics	Statik *f* plastischer Körper
plasmolysis form method	Plasmolyseformmethode *f*	plastic potential	plastisches Potential *n*
		plastic radiograph	*s.* X-ray stereogram
plasmolysis time method	Plasmolysezeitmethode *f*	plastic range, plastic layer, non-elastic range, inelastic range	plastischer Bereich *m*, unelastischer Bereich, Plastizitätsgebiet *n*
plasmolytic coefficient	plasmolytischer Koeffizient *m*		
plasmon ‹phys., bio.›	Plasmon *n* ‹Phys., Bio.›	plastic-rigid boundary	plastisch-starre Grenze *f*
		plastic scintillator	Kunststoffszintillator *m*, Plast[ik]szintillator *m*, plastischer Szintillator *m*
plasmon spectroscopy	Plasmonenspektroskopie *f*		
		plastic shear	*s.* slip ‹cryst.›
plasmoptysis	Plasmoptyse *f*	plastic sheet, lamina ‹*pl.*: laminae›	Plastfolie *f*
plasmorrhysis	Plasmorrhyse *f*, Plasmorhyse *f*		
		plastic sol, plastisol	plastisches Sol *n*, Plastisol *n*
plasmotron, plasmatron	Plasmatron *n*		
plast, plastic, plastic material	Plast *m*, Plastwerkstoff *m*, plastischer (bildsamer) Werkstoff *m*; plastischer Stoff *m*; Kunststoff *m*; Kunstharz *n*	plastic solid, plastic body	plastischer Festkörper (Körper) *m*
		plastic strain	*s.* plastic deformation
		plastic strain rate	*s.* rate of strain
		plastic strength	plastische Festigkeit *f*
plastic, plastic effect, illusion of depth	Plastik *f*	plastic stress	plastischer Spannungszustand *m*
		plastic stress function	plastische Spannungsfunktion *f*
plastic after flow, after[-]flow, plastic-flow persistence	plastische Nachwirkung *f*, Nachfließen *n*, Relaxation *f*	plastic stress surface	plastische Spannungsfläche *f*
		plastic viscosity	plastische Viskosität *f*
		plastic wave	plastische Welle *f*
		plastic work	plastische Arbeit *f*
plastic bending	plastische Verbiegung *f*	plastidom	Plastidom *n*
plastication, plasticizing ‹of caoutchouc›	Weichmachen *n* ‹Gummi›	plastification	*s.* plasticization
		plastifier	*s.* softener
plastic body, plastic solid	plastischer Festkörper *m*, plastischer Körper *m*	plastifying	*s.* plasticization
		plastigel, plastic gel, plastogel, Schwedoff body	plastisches Gel *n*, Plastigel *n*, Schwedoffscher Körper *m*
plastic buckling, inelastic (non-elastic) buckling	plastische Knickung *f*, unelastische Knickung		
		plastisol, plastic sol	plastisches Sol *n*, Plastisol *n*
plastic collision	*s.* perfectly inelastic impact ‹mech.›	plasto-elastic	plastisch-elastisch
plastic deformation, plastic strain, permanent deformation, permanent set	plastische Verformung (Formänderung, Deformation) *f*, bleibende Formänderung, bleibende (bildsame) Verformung	plastogel	*s.* plastigel
		plasto-inelastic	plastisch-unelastisch
		plastomer	Plastomer[e] *n*
plastic effect, plastic, illusion of depth	Plastik *f*	plastometer	Plastometer *n*, Plastizitätsmesser *m*
plastic elongation	plastische Dehnung *f*, bleibende Dehnung	plastometry	Plastizitätsmessung *f*, Plastometrie *f*

plate; slab, flat slab; plaque	Platte *f*	plate-like generator, plate-like oscillator, plate-like vibrator, flat vibrator	Plattenschwinger *m*
plate; platform; dish	Teller *m*		
plate, vane <of capacitor>	Belag *m*, Belegung *f* <Kondensator>, Kondensatorbelag *m*, Kondensatorbelegung *f*, Kondensatorplatte *f*	plate modulation	s. anode modulation
		plate orifice [meter]	s. orifice plate
		plate potential	Anodenpotential *n*
plate, tray, head; stage <chem.>	Boden *m*, Platte *f*; Stufe *f* <Chem.>	plate reaction	Anodenrückwirkung *f*
plate, photographic plate, photoplate <phot.>	Platte *f*, photographische Platte, Photoplatte *f* <Phot.>	plate rectifier, semiconductor (bimetallic, dry) rectifier	Halbleitergleichrichter *m*, Trockengleichrichter *m*, Plattengleichrichter *m*
plate analogy	Plattengleichnis *n*	plate rigidity	s. rigidity of the plate
plate anemometer	s. vane anemometer	plate-shaped conductor, flat conductor, plate conductor, conducting plate	plattenförmiger Leiter *m*, Plattenleiter *m*
plate anode, disk anode	Scheibenanode *f*, Telleranode *f*		
plate at zero incidence	längsangeströmte Platte *f*	plate spark-gap	Plattenfunkenstrecke *f*
		plate-type fuel element, fuel plate <of reactor>	plattenförmiges Brennelement *n*, Plattenelement *n*, Brennstoffplatte *f* <Reaktor>
plateau, plateau region <of the curve>	Plateau *n*, Plateaubereich *m*, Konstanzbereich *m*, horizontaler Abschnitt *m* <Kurve>		
plateau characteristic	Plateaucharakteristik *f*		
Plateau['s] experiment	Plateauscher Versuch *m*	plate-type voltmeter, Seidler voltmeter	Plattenvoltmeter *n* [nach Seidler], Seidlersches Plattenvoltmeter
Plateau figure [of equilibrium]	Plateausche Gleichgewichtsfigur (Fläche) *f*		
plateau glacier, Norwegian-type glacier	Plateaugletscher *m*, Hochlandeis *n*, norwegischer Gletschertyp *m*	plate valve	s. disk valve
		plate variometer	Anodenvariometer *n*
		plate wave	Plattenwelle *f*
		platform; plate; dish	Teller *m*
		platform <of balance>	Brücke *f* <Waage>
plateau length, length of plateau	Plateaulänge *f*		
		platform, table <geo.>	Tafel *f* <Geo.>
		platform balance (scale), weigh[ing] bridge, bridge scale	Brückenwaage *f*
plateau of the counter, Geiger plateau, voltage plateau <of the counter>	Plateau *n*, Geiger-Plateau *n*, Plateaubereich *m* <Zählrohrcharakteristik>		
		plating, cladding	Plattierung *f*
plateau region	s. plateau <of the curve>	platinization, platinum deposition (plating)	Platinierung *f*
plateau slope, relative plateau slope	Plateauanstieg *m*, Plateauneigung *f*, Plateausteigung *f*	platinum black	Platinmohr *n*, Platinschwarz *m*
plate camera	Plattenkamera *f*	platinum crucible	Platintiegel *m*
		platinum deposition	s. platinization
plate capacitor, parallel plate capacitor, plane-parallel capacitor	Plattenkondensator *m*	platinum [group] metal	Platinmetall *n*
		platinum plating	s. platinization
"plate carrée" projection	rechteckige Plattkarte *f*, quadratische Plattkarte	platinum/platinum-rhodium thermocouple, Pt-PtRh thermocouple, Le Chatelier thermocouple, standard thermocouple of platinum and platinum-rhodium	Platin-Platinrhodium-Thermoelement *n*, Platin-Platinrhodium-Element *n*, Pt-PtRh-Thermoelement *n*, Pt-PtRh-Element *n*, Le-Chatelier-Thermoelement *n*, Le-Chatelier-Element *n*
plate characteristic [curve]	Anodenstrom-Anodenspannung[s]-Kennlinie *f*, Anodenstromcharakteristik *f*, I_a-U_a-Kennlinie *f*		
plate column	Bodenkolonne *f*	platinum point, freezing point of platinum, point of freezing platinum	Platinpunkt *m*, Erstarrungspunkt *m* des Platins
plate conductor	s. plate-shaped conductor		
plate-coupled multivibrator	anodengekoppelter Multivibrator *m*, Multivibrator mit Anodenkopplung	platinum sponge, spongy platinum	Platinschwamm *m*
		plation, plation tube	Plattensteuerröhre *f*, Plation *n*
plated circuit	plattierte Schaltung *f*		
plate detector	s. anode detector	Platonic year	Platonisches Jahr *n*
plate dissipation	s. anode dissipation	platykurtosis, negative excess	Flachgipfligkeit *f*, negativer Exzeß *m*
plate efficiency, plate efficiency factor, Murphree plate efficiency <chem.>	Bodenwirkungsgrad *m*, Verstärkungsverhältnis *n*		
		platzwechsel	s. interchange of sites
		platzwechsel force, position-exchange force; exchange force	Austauschkraft *f*; Platzwechselkernkraft *f*
plate efficiency	s. a. overall plate efficiency		
plate efficiency <el.>	Anodenwirkungsgrad *m* <El.>	plausibility	s. likelihood
		play	s. gap <techn.>
plate efficiency factor	s. plate efficiency <chem.>	playback characteristic, reproducing characteristic, reproduction curve	Wiedergabecharakteristik *f*, Wiedergabekurve *f*
plate efficiency factor	s. a. overall plate efficiency		
plate equation	Plattengleichung *f*		
plate glass	Tafelglas *n*	playback head, pick-up, reproducing head, pick-up (phonograph) cartridge <ac.>	Abtaster *m*, Tonabnehmerkopf *m* <Ak.>
plate glass, mirror glass	Spiegelglas *n*		
plate-group strap, strap	Polbrücke *f*		
		play in bearing	Lagerspiel *n*; Lagerluft *f*; Achsenluft *f*; Spitzenluft *f*
plate level	Stehachsenlibelle *f*, Alhidadenlibelle *f*		
		playing of the pointer, swinging of the pointer <around the rest position>	Spielen *n* des Zeigers
plate-like crystal	plattenförmiger Kristall *m*	pleated filter	s. plaited filter

pleiade of isotopes, isotopic pleiade	Plejade f, Pleiade f, Isotopenplejade f	plug-in unit, rack assembly	Steckbaueinheit f, Steckbaustein m, Steckeinheit f; Einschub m
pleiotropy	Pleiotropie f		
Plemelj-Sokhotskii theorem	Plemel-Sochozkyscher Satz m		
pleochroic halo	pleochroitischer Hof m		
pleochroism, pleochromatism	s. polychroism	plug of the cock, cock plug, faucet <US>	Hahnküken n, Küken n, Hahnkegel m
pleomorphism	Pleomorphie f	plug resistance [box], plug rheostat, resistance box with plugs	Stöpselwiderstand m, Stöpselrheostat m, Widerstandskasten m [mit Stöpseln]
plethysm	Plethysmus m		
plethysmography	Plethysmographie f		
pleuston	Pleuston n	plug-type bridge, plug-type measuring bridge	Stöpselbrücke f, Stöpselmeßbrücke f
pliability	s. flexibility		
plication	s. folding <geo.>		
pliobar, pliobaric line	Pliobare f	plumb; plummet, bob, sounding lead	Lot n, Senklot n, Senkwaage f, Bleilot n, Senkblei n, Peillot n
PLK-method	s. Poincaré-Lighthill-Kuo method		
Plößl['s] eyepiece	Plößlsches Okular n	plumb deviation	s. plumb-line deflection
plot, graphical representation (construction), graph <of a function>	[graphische] Darstellung f, Kurvendarstellung f, Kurvenbild n <Funktion>	plumbing	s. sounding
		plumb line, perpendicular [line], normal, vertical line	Senkrechte f, Lot n, Normale f
		plumb line	s. a. vertical
plot of the equation of time, curve of the equation of time	Zeitgleichungskurve f	plumb-line deflection (deviation)	s. deflection of the plumb line
		plumb-line direction, direction of plumb line	Lotrichtung f
plotter	s. plotting machine		
plotter	s. a. characteristic recorder	plumb point, nadir [point] <of aerophotogram>	Nadirpunkt m, Bildnadir m <Luftmeßbild>
plotter	s. a. recorder		
plotting	Abtragen n <Strecke, Meßwert>; Auftragen n <Meßwert>	plumb-point triangulation, nadir point triangulation	Nadirpunkttriangulation f, Nadirtriangulation f
		plume	Rauchfahne f, Rauchsäule f
plotting, recording, record, registration, registering <of the curve>	Registrierung f; Schreiben n; Aufzeichnung f, Zeichnung f; Aufnahme f <Kurve>	plume, polar ray <of the solar corona>	Polarstrahl m <Sonnenkorona>
		plume	s. a. water column
		plummet, bob; plumb; sounding lead	Lot n, Senklot n, Senkwaage f, Bleilot n, Senkblei n, Peillot n
plotting	s. a. photogrammetrical restitution		
plotting device <photogrammetry>	Auswertegerät n, Auswertungsgerät n <Photogrammetrie>	plunge	s. dipping
		plunge	s. a. sudden fall
		plunger	Tauchkörper m
plotting equipment	s. plotting machine		
plotting from aerial photographs	s. restitution from aerial photographs		
plotting machine, plotter, plotting equipment	Bildkartiergerät n, Kartiergerät n, Kartograph m	plunger [piston]	Tauchkolben m, Tau her m, Plungerkolben m
		plunger	s. a. shorting plunger <el.>
		plunger	s. a. stub
plotting paper	s. square paper	plunger pump	Tauchkolbenpumpe f
ploughing	Furchung f, Furchenbildung f, Rillenbildung f		
plucked instrument	Zupfinstrument n	plunging; moving in, insertion; dipping; immersion <of rods>	Einfahren n; Absenken n; Hinablassen n; Einschieben n; Eintauchen n <Stäbe>
Plucker co-ordinates, line co-ordinates	[Plückersche] Linienkoordinaten fpl, Plückersche Koordinaten fpl, Geradenkoordinaten fpl		
		plunging	s. a. dipping
		plunging	s. a. pitch <hydr.>
		plural	s. multiple
		plural creation, plural formation	s. plural production
Plucker equations, equations of Plucker	Plückersche Gleichungen fpl		
plug	Pfropfen m	plural process; multiple process	Vielfachprozeß m; Mehrfachprozeß m
plug capacitance box, capacitance box with plugs	Stöpselkondensator m		
		plural production, plural creation, plural formation	Mehrfacherzeugung f, Mehrfachbildung f, plurale Erzeugung f
plug drawing, mandrel drawing	Stopfenzug m, Ziehen n über einen Stopfen, Ziehen über eine Nuß		
plug flow	plastisches Fließen n mit festem Kern	plural production of mesons, meson plural production	Mehrfacherzeugung f von Mesonen, plurale Mesonenerzeugung f
		plural scatter[ing]	Mehrfachstreuung f
		plurivalent	s. polyvalent <chem.>
plug-in	steckbar, Steck-	plus, positive pole	Pluspol m, positiver Pol m, Plus n
plug-in amplifier, amplifier plug-in, amplifier subassembly, amplifier unit	Verstärkereinschub m		
		plus material	s. screenings
		plus sight, back sight	Rückwärtsvisur f, Rückwärtsvisieren n
		plus wave	Pluswelle f
plug-in capacitor	Einsteckkondensator m	plus wire, positive wire, positive conductor	positiver Leiter m, Plusleiter m, positive Leitung f, Plusleitung f, Plusdraht m
plug-in card	Steckkarte f		
plug-in coil	Steckspule f	pluton	Pluton m, Tiefengesteinskörper m
		plutonic rock, plutonite, intrusive rock, abyssal rock	Tiefengestein n, Intrusivgestein n, plutonisches Gestein n, Plutonit m
plug-in diaphragm	s. sliding stop		
plug inductance box, inductance box with plugs	Stöpselinduktivität f		
		plutonium, $_{94}$Pu, esperium	Plutonium n, $_{94}$Pu

plutonium cycle	Plutoniumzyklus m, Plutonium-Brennstoffzyklus m	p-n junction diode, junction diode, semiconductor junction diode	Halbleiterflächendiode f, Flächendiode f, pn-Diode f, Schichtdiode f, pn-Flächendiode f
plutonium pile	s. plutonium reactor		
plutonium poisoning	Plutoniumvergiftung f	p-n junction phototransistor	pn-Phototransistor m, pn-Flächenphototransistor m, pn-Verbindungs-Phototransistor m
plutonium-producing reactor, plutonium reactor, production[-type] reactor	Produktionsreaktor m ‹zur Plutoniumgewinnung›, Plutoniumerzeugungsreaktor m		
		p-n junction photovoltaic effect	s. photovoltaic effect
plutonium reactor, plutonium pile	Plutoniumreaktor m	p-n junction rectifier, p-n rectifier	pn-Gleichrichter m
		p-n junction rectifier	s. a. barrier-layer rectifier
plutonium reactor	s. plutonium-producing reactor	p-n junction transistor, p-n type transistor	pn-Transistor m, pn-Flächentransistor m
plutonium recycle	Plutoniumrückführung f, Plutoniumrückführungsprozeß m		
plutonium reprocessing	Plutoniumrückgewinnung f	p-n-p-n diode, four-layer p-n-p-n diode	pnpn-Diode f, pnpn-Flächendiode f, pnpn-Vierschichtdiode f
pluvial period	Pluvialzeit f, Feuchtbodenzeit f; Regenzeit f, Regenperiode f		
		p-n-p-n transistor, four-layer p-n-p-n transistor	pnpn-Transistor m, pnpn-Flächentransistor m, pnpn-Vierschichttransistor m
pluviogram, ombrogram	Pluviogramm n, Ombrogramm n, Niederschlagsdiagramm n, Niederschlagskurve f		
		p,n process	s. proton-neutron reaction
pluviograph, recording pluviometer, recording rain gauge, ombrograph, recording ombrometer, hyetograph	Pluviograph m, Niederschlagsschreiber m, Regenschreiber m, registrierender (selbstschreibender) Niederschlagsmesser m, registrierender (selbstschreibender) Regenmesser m, Ombrograph m, schreibender Regenmesser, Hyetograph m	p-n-p transistor, p-n-p type transistor	pnp-Transistor m
		p,n reaction	s. proton-neutron reaction
		p-n rectifier, p-n junction rectifier	pn-Gleichrichter m
		p-n transition	s. p-n junction
		p-n type transistor, p-n junction transistor	pn-Transistor m, pn-Flächentransistor m
pluviography	s. pluviometry		
pluviometer	s. rain gauge		
pluviometer-association, totalizer	Totalisator m, Niederschlagstotalisator m, Niederschlagssammler m	Pochhammer-Barnes equation	s. Kummer['s] differential equation
		Pockels effect, longitudinal (linear) electro-optical effect	Pockels-Effekt m, elektrooptischer Längseffekt m
pluviometry, ombrometry, hyetometry; pluviography, ombrography, hyetography	Niederschlags[mengen]-messung f, Regenmessung f, Hyetometrie f, Pluviometrie f; Hyetographie f, Pluviographie f		
		pocket ‹of mass spectrometer target›	Tasche f [des Auffängers], Auffängertasche f
		pocket chamber, pocket ion[ization] chamber	Taschenionisationskammer f
p-n boundary	s. p-n junction		
pneumatic elevator	Druckluftförderer m	pocket current	Taschenstrom m
pneumatic frogsuit	Druckluftanzug m, Druckluftschutzanzug m	pocket dosimeter, pocket meter	Taschendosimeter n
pneumatic gauging ‹meas.›	pneumatische Eichung f ‹Meß.›	pocketed valve	s. disk valve
		pocket instrument, pocket meter	Taschenmeßgerät n, Taschengerät n, Tascheninstrument n
pneumatic helmet	Druckhelm m		
pneumatic loudspeaker	s. pressure-chamber loudspeaker	pocket ion[ization] chamber	s. pocket chamber
pneumatic mariograph	s. pneumatic water gauge	pocket meter	s. pocket instrument
pneumatic post, pneumatic tube[-installation], rabbit channel	Rohrpostkanal m, Rohrpost m, Bestrahlungskanal m im Reaktor	pocket meter	s. pocket dosimeter
		pocket spectroscope	Taschenspektroskop n
		pockhole	s. shrinkage cavity
pneumatic receiver	s. Golay cell	Poehler switch	Pöhler-Schalter m
pneumatic shell	Tragluftschale f		
pneumatic sizer	s. air separator	Poggendorff['s] compensating (compensation) method, potentiometer method, Poggendorff['s] [potentiometer] principle, compensation (compensating, Poggendorff['s]) method	Kompensationsverfahren n, [Poggendorffsche] Kompensationsmethode f, Kompensationsmethode von (nach) Poggendorff
pneumatic tube[-installation]	s. pneumatic post		
pneumatic water gauge, pneumatic mariograph	Druckluftpegel m		
pneumatolytic	pneumatolytisch		
pneumatosphere	Pneumatosphäre f		
pneumogram	Pneumogramm n		
pneumonics, compressed air technique	Pneumonik f	Poggendorf compensator, Poggendorff-Du Bois-Raymond potentiometer, Poggendorff potentiometer, valve potentiometer	Poggendorff-Kompensator m, Kompensationsschaltung f nach Poggendorff
pneutronic	pneutronisch, elektronisch-pneumatisch		
p-n-i-p transistor	s. intrinsic-barrier transistor		
p-n junction; p-n transition; p-n boundary	pn-Übergang m, pn-Übergangsschicht f; pn-Flächenverbindung f, pn-Verbindung f; pn-Schicht f; pn-Kontakt m; pn-Grenzschicht f, pn-Grenze f, pn-Grenzfläche f; pn-Sperrschicht f	Poggendorff['s] method	s. Poggendorff['s] compensating method
		Poggendorff potentiometer	s. Poggendorff compensator
		Poggendorff['s] potentiometer principle	s. Poggendorff['s] compensating method
		Pogson['s] equation	Pogson-Gleichung f

Pogson['s] ratio	Pogson-Verhältnis *n*
Pogson['s] scale [of stellar magnitude]	Pogsonsche Helligkeitsskala *f*, Pogson-Skala *f*
*p*OH, *p*OH factor, *p*OH value, hydroxyl-ion exponent	*p*OH-Wert *m*, *p*OH ‹nur in Verbindung mit dem Zahlenwert›, Hydroxylionenexponent *m*
Pohl commutator	Pohlsche Wippe *f*
Pohl effect	Pohl-Effekt *m*
Pohlhausen['s] method	Pohlhausen-Verfahren *n*, Pohlhausensche Methode *f*, Methode von Pohlhausen
*p*OH value	s. *p*OH, *p*OH factor, hydroxyl-ion exponent
poid	s. centroed
poikilotherm, cold-blooded animal	Wechselwarmblüter *m*, Kaltblüter *m*, Poikilotherm *m*
Poincaré['s] cycle period	Poincarésche Wiederkehrzeit *f*
Poincaré['s] equations	Poincarésche Gleichungen *fpl*
Poincaré group, inhomogeneous Lorentz group	inhomogene Lorentz-Gruppe *f*, Poincaré-Gruppe *f*
Poincaré invariant	Poincarésche Invariante *f*
Poincaré-Lighthill-Kuo method, PLK-method, approximation method of M.J. Lighthill, Lighthill['s] method	Poincaré-Lighthill-Kuosche Methode *f*, PLK-Methode *f*, Poincaré-Lighthill-Methode *f*, Lighthillsche Methode
Poincaré pressure	Poincaréscher Druck *m*
Poincaré['s] recurrence theorem, recurrence theorem [of Poincaré]	Poincaréscher Wiederkehrsatz *m*, Wiederkehrsatz [von Poincaré]
Poincaré['s] representation	Poincarésche Darstellung *f*, Poincaré-Darstellung *f*
Poincaré['s] sphere	Poincarésche Kugel *f*
Poincaré variable	Poincarésche Koordinate *f*; Poincarésches kanonisches Element *n*, kanonisches Poincarésches Element
Poinsot['s] construction	Poinsotsche (Poinsots) Konstruktion *f*, Poinsot-Konstruktion *f*
Poinsot['s] ellipsoid, ellipsoid of Poinsot, momental ellipsoid	Poinsot-Ellipsoid *n*, Poinsotsches Ellipsoid (Trägheitsellipsoid) *n*, Cauchy-Poinsotsches Trägheitsellipsoid, Trägheitsellipsoid von Poinsot, Energieellipsoid *n*
Poinsot['s] motion	Poinsot-Bewegung *f*, Poinsotsche Bewegung *f*
point, rhumb, point of the compass, wind reference number	Windstrich *m*, Windziffer *f*
point, rhumb <=11°15'>	Strich *m*, nautischer Strich <= 11°15'>
point, station ‹geo.›	Standpunkt *m* ‹Geo.›
point	s. a. place
point approximation	punktweise Näherung *f*
point at infinity, ideal point ‹math.›	uneigentlicher (unendlich[] ferner) Punkt *m*, Fernpunkt *m* ‹Math.›
point brilliance	Punkthelle *f*, Punkthelligkeit *f*
point-by-point method	s. point technique
point cathode ‹semi.›	Punktkatode *f*, Spitzenkatode *f* ‹Halb.›
point characteristic [function] ‹of Hamilton›	s. Hamilton['s] characteristic function
point charge	Punktladung *f*, punktförmige Ladung *f*
point contact, spot contact	Punktkontakt *m*, Spitzenkontakt *m*
point contact diode	Punktkontaktdiode *f*, Spitzendiode *f*, Punktdiode *f*
point contact junction	Spitzen[kontakt]übergang *m*, Punkt[kontakt]-übergang *m*
point contact photodiode, point photodiode	Punktkontakt-Photodiode *f*, Spitzenphotodiode *f*, Punktphotodiode *f*
point contact phototransistor, point phototransistor	Punktkontakt-Phototransistor *m*, Spitzenphototransistor *m*, Punktphototransistor *m*
point contact rectification	Spitzengleichrichtung *f*, Spitzenkontaktgleichrichtung *f*
point contact rectifier	Punkt[kontakt]gleichrichter *m*, Spitzen[kontakt]gleichrichter *m*, Spitzendetektor *m*
point contact tetrode, point tetrode, point-to-point tetrode	Punktkontakttetrode *f*, Spitzentetrode *f*, Punkttetrode *f*
point contact transistor, point-to-point transistor	Spitzen[kontakt]transistor *m*, Punkt[kontakt]transistor *m*, Punkt[kontakt]triode *f*, A-Transistor *m*
point corona [discharge]	Spitzenkorona[entladung] *f*
point corrosion	s. pitting
point counter	s. point counter tube ‹nucl.›
point counter of Glagolev, Glagolev['s] point counter	Pointcounter *m* nach Glagolev, Glagolevscher Pointcounter
point counter tube, point counter ‹nucl.›	Spitzenzählrohr *n*, Spitzenzähler *m* ‹Kern.›
point defect point imperfection	Punktdefekt *m*, punktförmige Störstelle *f*, Punktstörstelle *f*, Punktfehlordnung *f*, Punktfehlstelle *f*, atomare (nulldimensionale) Fehlordnung (Fehlstelle) *f*, Eigenfehlordnung *f*, thermische Fehlordnung
point density	Punktdichte *f*
point diagram	Punktdiagramm *n*
point dipole	Punktdipol *m*
point discharge, edge discharge	Spitzenentladung *f*, Punktentladung *f*
point discharge current	Spitzenstrom *m*, Spitzenentladungsstrom *m*
point disparity	punktuelle Disparation *f*, Punktdisparation *f*
pointed cathode	Spitzenkatode *f*, spitze Katode *f*, angespitzte Katode
pointed corrosion	s. pitting
pointed electrode, point electrode	Spitzenelektrode *f*
pointed jet flame	s. shooting flame
pointed lightning protector, point lightning arrester	Spitzenblitzableiter *m*
point effect of electrostatics	s. needle effect of electrostatics
point eikonal	s. eikonal
point electrode	s. pointed electrode
pointer, tongue ‹of the balance›	Zunge *f* ‹Waage›
pointer, needle ‹of measuring instrument›; indicator, index	Zeiger *m* ‹allg.; Meßgerät›
pointer deflection, needle deflection, deflection of the needle (pointer); movement of the pointer	Zeigerausschlag *m*, Zeigerauslenkung *f*

pointer galvanometer, pointer-type galvanometer	Zeigergalvanometer n	**point of condensation** **point of confluence**	s. condensation point Zusammenflußpunkt m
pointer instrument, pointer-type instrument, dial indicator	Zeigermeßgerät n, Zeigergerät n, Zeigerinstrument n; Ausschlagmeßgerät n, Ausschlaggerät n, Ausschlaginstrument n	**point of congelation,** congealing (pour, solidifying, solidification) point <of oil> **point of connection**	Fließpunkt m, Stockpunkt m <Öl> s. driving point
pointer thermometer, solid-expansion thermometer	Zeigerthermometer n	**point of contact;** point of tangency, tangency point; tacpoint **point of contraflexure**	Berührungspunkt m; Berührungsstelle f; Kontaktpunkt m s. point of inflexion
pointer-type galvanometer, pointer galvanometer	Zeigergalvanometer n	**(contrary flexure)** **point of contrary flexure**	s. point of inflexion <of the curve> <math.>
pointer-type instrument **point estimation**	s. pointer instrument Punktschätzung f	**point of detachment** **point of determination**	Ablösungspunkt m s. regular singularity
point force, concentrated force, single force **point function** **point gauge**	Einzelkraft f, Punktkraft f, konzentrierte Kraft f Punktfunktion f Stechpegel m	**point of discontinuity,** discontinuity **point of division**	Unstetigkeitspunkt m, Unstetigkeitsstelle f; Sprungstelle f, Sprungpunkt m Teilpunkt m
point grid, grid of points	Punktnetz n, Punktgitter n; Zahlengitter n	**point of emergency;** initial point, origin; starting point <e.g. of a	Anfangspunkt m, Ausgangspunkt m
point[-] group [of symmetry], point symmetry group, group <cryst.> **point hypocentre**	Punktsymmetriegruppe f, Punktgruppe f <Krist.> Punktherd m	motion> **point of freezing** **point of freezing gold,** gold point, freezing	s. solidification point Goldpunkt m, Erstarrungspunkt m des Goldes
point image; sharp image, high-definition image <opt.>	Punktabbildung f, punktförmige Abbildung f; scharfe Abbildung; scharfes Bild n <Opt.>	point of gold **point of freezing platinum,** platinum point, freezing point of platinum	Platinpunkt m, Erstarrungspunkt m des Platins
point imperfection **pointing**	s. point defect Anschneiden n, Anzielen n	**point of freezing silver** **point of growth,** growth point <math.>	s. silver point Wachstumspunkt m <Math.>
pointing <of telescope> **point interaction** **point-junction transistor**	Einstellung f <Fernrohr> Punktwechselwirkung f Spitzen-Flächen-Transistor m	**point of impact** **point of indetermination** **point of inflexion,** point of contraflexure, point of contrary flexure, point of	s. impact point s. irregular singularity Momentennullpunkt m
point lamp **point lattice** <cryst.> **point light lamp** **point lightning arrester**	s. point-source lamp Punktgitter n <Krist.> s. point-source lamp s. pointed lightning protector	zero moments **point of inflexion,** point of contrary flexure, inflexion point, flex point <of the curve> <math.>	Wendepunkt m, Inflexionspunkt m erster Ordnung; Inflexionspunkt <der Kurve> <Math.>
pointlike probe, point probe	Punktsonde f, punktförmige (punktartige) Sonde f	**point of intersection,** intersection [point], intersecting point; intercept; piercing point	Schnittpunkt m; Durchstoßpunkt m
pointlike sound source, point source [of sound] <ac.>	punktförmige Schallquelle f, Punktstrahler m <Ak.>	**point of libration** **point of measurement,** measuring point; control	s. libration point Meßstelle f, Meßort m, Meßpunkt m
pointlike source of light, point source of light	punktförmige (punktartige) Lichtquelle f, Punktlichtquelle f, Punktstrahler m	point; measuring junction <of thermocouple> **point of neutralization**	s. equivalence point
point load **point mass,** concentrated mass, particle mass **point mechanics,** mass point mechanics	s. concentrated load Punktmasse f, konzentrierte Masse f Punktmechanik f, Massenpunktmechanik f, Mechanik f des Massenpunktes	**point of neutral stability** **point of origin** **point of osculation** **point of reference**	Indifferenzpunkt m, Instabilitätspunkt m Ursprungspunkt m s. tacnode s. reference point
point method **point model** **point of accumulation**	s. point technique Punktmodell n s. accumulation point <math.>	**point of reflection,** reflection point <el.> **point of resonance,**	Stoßstelle f <El.> Resonanzstelle f, Resonanz-
point of action [of the force], point of application [of the force], origin [of the force]	Angriffspunkt m, Wirkungspunkt m <Kraft>	resonance point, resonance **point of return** **point of saturation** **point of self-intersection,**	punkt m, Resonanz f s. stagnation point s. saturation point Selbstdurchdringungspunkt
point of admission (application)	Zuführungspunkt m	self-intersection point **point of sight**	m Hauptpunkt m, Augenpunkt m <Perspektive>
point of application [of the force] **point of boiling sulphur** **point of branching,** front stagnation point, forward stagnation point <hydr.>	s. point of action [of the force] s. sulphur point vorderer Staupunkt m <Hydr.>	**point of solidification** **point of source,** source point, source **point of sublimation,** temperature of sublimation, sublimation	s. solidification point Quellpunkt m; Quellstelle f Sublimationstemperatur f, Sublimationspunkt m, Sbp.
point of clearest vision <opt.>	Blickpunkt m; Fixierpunkt m, Fixationspunkt m; Kernpunkt m, Kernstelle f <Opt.>	temperature (point) **point of support,** supporting point; fulcrum <of lever>	Stützpunkt m, Unterstützungspunkt m; Einspannstelle f
point of closure **point of coalescence** **point of cold,** cold point **point of collision,** collision point; impact point, point of impact	s. adherent point <of the set> s. rear stagnation point Kältepunkt m Stoßpunkt m; Aufschlagpunkt m, Auftreffpunkt m; Einschlagstelle f	**point of suspension,** fulcrum of suspension, suspension point **point of symmetry,** symmetry point <meteo., cryst.>	Aufhängepunkt m Symmetriepunkt m <Meteo., Krist.>
point of colour, locus [of point] <in chromaticity diagram>	Farbort m, Farbpunkt m	**point of tangency**	s. point of contact

point of the compass	s. point	point-to-point gap, point-to-point spark gap, point-to-point arrester	Spitze-Spitze-Funkenstrecke f, Spitze-Spitze-Entladungsstrecke f, Spitze-Spitze-Zündstrecke f
point of the dummy scale	Zapfenpunkt m		
point of transition	s. transition point <aero., hydr.>	point-to-point tetrode	s. point contact tetrode
point of zero moments	s. point of inflexion	point-to-point transistor	s. point contact transistor
point photodiode	s. point contact photodiode	point transformation	Punkttransformation f, Punktabbildung f <Math.>
point phototransistor, point contact phototransistor	Punktkontakt-Phototransistor m, Spitzenphototransistor m, Punktphototransistor m	point-type suspension, needle-type suspension	Spitzenlagerung f, Nadellagerung f
point-plate type of discharge	s. point-to-plane discharge	point under consideration, field point, test point, station	Aufpunkt m
point pole, magnetic point pole	Punktpol m, magnetischer Punktpol		
point probe, pointlike probe	Punktsonde f, punktförmige (punktartige) Sonde f	point vortex	Punktwirbel m
point projection [electron] microscope	s. field emission microscope	point vortex, potential vortex, free vortex	freier Wirbel m, abgehender Wirbel
point projection microscope	s. shadow projection microscope	pointwise discontinuous poise, P	punktweise unstetig Poise n, P
point projection microscopy, shadow projection microscopy, shadow microscopy	Schattenmikroskopie f, Elektronenschattenmikroskopie f	Poiseuille equation Poiseuille flow, Poiseuille pipe flow	s. Poiseuille['s] formula Poiseuille-Strömung f, Poiseuillesche Strömung f, Hagen-Poiseuille-Strömung f, Poiseuillesche Rohrströmung f
point record	s. point recording		
point recorder, chopper bar recorder, chopped bar recorder, hoop drop recorder, dot recorder, dotting recorder	Fallbügelschreiber m, Punktschreiber m	Poiseuille['s] formula, Poiseuille[-Hagen] law, Poiseuille equation, Hagen-Poiseuille law, Hagen-Poiseuille equation	Hagen-Poiseuillesches Gesetz n, Hagen-Poiseuillesche Gleichung f, Poiseuillesches Gesetz n, Poiseuillesche Gleichung, Poiseuille-Hagensches Gesetz, Poiseuille-Gesetz n, Poiseuillesche Formel f
point recording, point record	Punktaufzeichnung f, Punktregistrierung f, Punktschrieb m		
point set, set (assemblage) of points	Punktmenge f	Poiseuille pipe flow	s. Poiseuille flow
point-shapedness	Punktförmigkeit f	Poiseuille velocity profile, parabolic velocity profile	parabolisches Geschwindigkeitsprofil n
point singularity	Punktsingularität f		
point slope method, Euler['s] method <math.>	Polygonzugverfahren n <Math.>	poison, poisoning agent, toxicant, toxic agent	Gift n, Giftstoff m, toxischer Stoff m
point source, point source of sound, pointlike sound source <ac.>	punktförmige Schallquelle f, Punktstrahler m <Ak.>	poison <nucl.>	Gift n <Kern.>
point source, point source of radiation	punktförmige (punktartige) Strahlungsquelle f, punktförmige Quelle f, Punktquelle f	poisoning effect, poisonous effect	Vergiftungseffekt m
		poisoning factor	Vergiftungsfaktor m, Vergiftungskoeffizient m, Gefährdungsfaktor m
point-source lamp, point light lamp, point lamp, punctiform lamp	Punktlichtlampe f, Punktlampe f, Punktstrahllampe f	poisoning of catalyst	s. catalyst poisoning
		poisoning of cathode, cathode contamination (poisoning)	Katodenvergiftung f, Vergiftung f der Katode
point-source model	Punktquellenmodell n		
point source of light, pointlike source of light	punktförmige (punktartige) Lichtquelle f, Punktlichtquelle f, Punktstrahler m	poisoning of the nuclear reactor [by fission products], fission product poisoning, neutron poison effect, neutron poisoning	Vergiftung f des Reaktors [mit Spaltprodukten]
point source of radiation	s. point source		
point source of sound, pointlike sound source, point source <ac.>	punktförmige Schallquelle f, Punktstrahler m <Ak.>		
point-source photometry	Punktphotometrie f	poisoning overshoot	Vergiftungsüberschlag m
point spectrum, discrete spectrum <math.>	Punktspektrum n, diskretes Spektrum n <Math.>	poison of enzyme, substance poisoning an enzyme; enzyme inactivator; enzyme inhibitor	Fermentgift n, Fermenthemmstoff m, Fermentinhibitor m
point spread function	Punktverwaschungsfunktion f		
point-surface transformation	Punkt-Flächen-Transformation f	poisonous effect, poisoning effect	Vergiftungseffekt m
point symmetric	punktsymmetrisch	Poisson['s] adiabatic [line]	Poissonsche Adiabate f
point symmetry	Punktsymmetrie f	Poisson-Boltzmann equation	Poisson-Boltzmann-Gleichung f
point symmetry group, point[-] group [of symmetry], group <cryst.>	Punktsymmetriegruppe f, Punktgruppe f <Krist.>	Poisson['s] bracket[s], classical Poisson bracket[s]	Poisson-Klammer f, Poissonsche Klammer f, Poissonscher Klammerausdruck m, Poissonsches Klammersymbol n, klassische Poisson-Klammer f
point technique, point method, point-by-point method	Punktverfahren n, Punktmethode f, Punkt-für-Punkt-Methode f		
point tetrode	s. point contact tetrode	Poisson bracket[s] in quantum mechanics, quantum Poisson bracket[s]	quantenmechanische Poisson-Klammer[n fpl] f, quantentheoretische Poisson-Klammer[n]
point-to-plane arrester	s. point-to-plane spark gap		
point-to-plane discharge, point-plate type of discharge	Spitze-Platte-Entladung f		
		Poisson['s] constant	s. Poisson['s] ratio
point-to-plane gap	s. point-to-plane spark gap	Poisson['s] differential equation	s. Poisson['s] equation
point-to-plane spark gap, point-to-plane gap, point-to-plane arrester	Spitze-Platte-Funkenstrecke f, Spitzen-Platten-Funkenstrecke f, Spitze-Platte-Entladungsstrecke f, Spitze-Platte-Zündstrecke f	Poisson['s] diffraction	Poissonsche Beugung f
		Poisson distribution [law]	Poisson-Verteilung f, Poissonsche Verteilung f, Verteilung von Poisson
point-to-point arrester	s. point-to-point gap		
point-to-point discharge	Spitze-Spitze-Entladung f	Poisson effect	Poisson-Effekt m, Polsterwirkung f

Poisson['s]

Poisson['s] equation, Poisson's differential equation	Poissonsche Gleichung (Differentialgleichung, Potentialgleichung) *f*, Poisson-Gleichung *f*, Laplace-Poissonsche Gleichung (Differentialgleichung)	polar co-ordinate oscillographic tube, polar co-ordinate tube	Polarkoordinatenröhre *f*, Polarkoordinaten-Oszillographenröhre *f*
Poisson['s] equation of state	Poissonsche Zustandsgleichung *f*	polar co-ordinate oscilloscope	s. cycloscope
Poisson['s] formula	Poissonsche Formel *f*	polar co-ordinate recorder	Polarkoordinatenschreiber *m*, Polardiagrammschreiber *m*, Polarschreiber *m*
Poisson['s] integral [formula]	Poissonsches Integral *n*; Poissonsche Integralformel *f*		
Poisson-Jacobi identity	Poisson-Jacobische Identität *f*	polar co-ordinates	s. spherical co-ordinates
		polar co-ordinates [in the plane], plane polar co-ordinates	Polarkoordinaten *fpl* [in der Ebene], ebene Polarkoordinaten
Poisson['s] kinematic equations	Poissonsche kinematische Kreiselgleichungen *fpl*		
Poisson['s] law	s. Poisson['s] relation	polar co-ordinate tube	s. polar co-ordinate oscillographic tube
Poisson['s] matrix	Poisson-Matrix *f*		
Poisson['s] number	s. Poisson['s] ratio	polar corona, corona ⟨of polar aurora⟩	Polarlichtkrone *f*, Korona *f*, Polarlichtfächer *m*
Poisson [probability] paper	Poisson-Papier *n*, Poissonsches Wahrscheinlichkeitspapier *n*	polar crystal, ionic crystal	Ionenkristall *m*, polarer Kristall *m*
Poisson process	Poissonscher Prozeß *m*, Poisson-Prozeß *m*	polar curve ⟨of the airfoil⟩	Polare *f*, [Lilienthalsches] Polardiagramm *n* ⟨Tragflügel⟩
Poisson['s] ratio, Poisson['s] constant, Poisson['s] number, transverse contraction	Poissonsche Zahl (Konstante) *f*, Poisson-Zahl *f*, Poisson-Konstante *f*, Quer[kontraktions]zahl *f*, Poissonsche Querzahl (Elastizitätskonstante *f*), Poissonscher Modul *m*, Poissons Modul, Querkontraktionskoeffizient *m*	polar curve ⟨math.⟩	Polarkurve *f*, Polkurve *f* ⟨Math.⟩
		polar day, midnight Sun	Mitternachtssonne *f*, Polartag *m*
		polar decomposition	polare Zerlegung *f*
		polar diagram	Polardiagramm *n*, Darstellung *f* in Polarkoordinaten
Poisson['s] relation [between pressure and density], adiabatic equation, Poisson['s] law	Adiabatengleichung *f*, Adiabatengesetz *n*, Poissonsche Gleichung *f*, Poissonsches Gesetz *n*	polar diagram [of antenna]	s. radiation pattern
		polar diagram of luminous flux	s. luminous-flux distribution
		polar diagram of luminous intensity	s. light distribution curve
		polar displacement	s. polar motion
Poisson['s] spot, bright spot of Poisson, Arago['s] spot	Poissonscher Fleck *m*, Aragoscher Fleck	polar distance, north polar distance, co-declination, P.D., PD	Poldistanz *f*, Polabstand *m*, Nordpolabstand *m*, Polardistanz *f*
Poisson['s] sum[mation] formula	Poissonsche Summationsformel *f*, Poissonsche Summenformel *f*	polar drift	s. polar motion
		polar equation	Polargleichung *f*
Poisson['s] theorem	Satz *m* von Poisson, Poissonscher Satz, Poissonsches Theorem *n*	polar facula	polare Sonnenfackel (Fackel) *f*, Polarfackel *f*
		polar flattening of the Earth	s. flattening of the Earth
polanret microscope, polanret system	Polanretmikroskop *n*, „polanret"-Mikroskop *n*	polar form	Polarform *f*
Polanyi machine, Polanyi tensile test[ing] machine	Polanyischer Apparat *m*, Polanyischer Zugapparat *m*	polar front	Polarfront *f*
		polar group	polare Gruppe *f*
		polarimeter, polaristrobometer	Polarimeter *n*, Polaristrobometer *n*
polar, polar line ⟨math.⟩	Polare *f* ⟨Math.⟩		
polar addition, ionic (heterolytic) addition	ionische (polare, heterolytische) Addition *f*	polarimetry	Polarimetrie *f*, Polarometrie *f*, Messung *f* der Drehung der Polarisationsebene; Untersuchung *f* mit Hilfe von polarisiertem Licht
polar angle, vectorial angle	Polarwinkel *m*		
polar angle, amplitude, argument, arg ⟨of a complex number⟩	Argument *n*, arg, arc ⟨komplexe Zahl⟩		
		polar impedance chart, Smith chart, polar circle diagram, circle diagram of Smith	Smith-Diagramm *n*, Smithsches Diagramm *n*, Kreisdiagramm *n* nach Smith
polar aurora, polar lights aurora ⟨pl.: aurorae⟩	Polarlicht *n*, polare Aurora *f*		
polar axis, hour axis ⟨astr.⟩	Stundenachse *f*, Pol[ar]achse *f*, Rektaszensionsachse *f* ⟨Astr.⟩	polar indicator	s. polarity indicator
		Polaris	s. Polar Star
		polariscopy	Polariskopie *f*, Nachweis *m* der Polarisation
polar axis, polaxis ⟨math.; cryst.⟩	Polarachse *f* ⟨Math.; Krist.⟩; Nullstrahl *m* ⟨Math.⟩	polariser, polarizer	Polarisator *m*
		polaristrobometer	s. polarimeter
polar band	Polarbande *f*	polariton	Polariton *n*, kleines Polaron *n*
		polarity	Polarität *f*; Polung *f*
		polarity alternation	s. alternation of polarity
		polarity formula	s. electronic formula
polar blackout, no-echo condition	Langzeitschwund *m* in Polargegenden, Polverdunklung *f*, Polarblackout *m*	polarity indicating lamp, pole indicating lamp	Polsuchlampe *f*
polar bond	s. electrovalent bond	polarity indicator, pole tester, pole (polar, sign) indicator, pole finder	Polsucher *m*, Polprüfer *m*, Pol[aritäts]anzeiger *m*, Stromrichtungsanzeiger *m*
polar cap [of Mars]	Polkappe *f* [des Mars]		
polar circle	Polarkreis *m*		
polar circle diagram, Smith chart, circle diagram of Smith, polar impedance chart	Smith-Diagramm *n*, Smithsches Diagramm *n*, Kreisdiagramm *n* nach Smith	polarity reversal	s. alternation of polarity
		polarity reversing switch	s. pole-changing switch
		polarity test paper	s. pole finding paper
polar compound, ionic compound, heteropolar compound	Ionenverbindung *f*, ionogene (heteropolare, polare) Verbindung *f*	polarizability, electric polarizability	Polarisierbarkeit *f*, elektrische Polarisierbarkeit
polar continental air	kontinentale Polarluft *f*	polarizability catastrophe, spontaneous polarization	spontane Polarisation *f*, spontane Polarisierung *f*
polar co-ordinate oscillograph	s. cycloscope	polarizability ellipsoid	Polarisierbarkeitsellipsoid *n*

polarizability of the molecule	s. molecular polarizability	**polarization helioscope**	Polarisationshelioskop n
polarizability tensor, tensor of electric polarizability	Polarisierbarkeitstensor m, Tensor m der elektrischen Polarisierbarkeit	**polarization index**	Polarisationsindex m
		polarization interaction of molecules	Polarisationswechselwirkung f der Moleküle
polarizable electrode	polarisierbare Elektrode f	**polarization interference filter**	s. Lyot filter
polarization	Polarisation f, Polarisierung f	**polarization loss**	Polarisationsverlust m
polarization	s. a. electrolytic polarization	**polarization-magnetization [four-] tensor,** four-tensor of dielectric polarization and magnetization intensity	Polarisations-Magnetisierungs-Tensor m, Polarisations-Magnetisierungs-Vierertensor m, Vierertensor m der Polarisation und Magnetisierung
polarization	s. a. polarization vector <el.>		
polarization [brought about] by atomic and electronic movement	s. "displacement polarization"		
polarization by deformation	Deformationspolarisation f, Polarisation f bei Deformation	**polarization microscope**	s. polarizing microscope
		polarization microscopy	Polarisationsmikroskopie f
polarization by distortion	s. piezoelectric effect		
polarization by double refraction	Doppelbrechungspolarisation f, Polarisation f durch Doppelbrechung	**polarization modulation**	Polarisationsmodulation f
polarization by exchange, exchange polarization	Austauschpolarisation f	**polarization of dielectric**	s. dielectric polarization <el.>
		polarization of fluorescence, polarization of fluorescence radiation (light), polarized fluorescence	polarisierte Fluoreszenz f, Polarisation f der Fluoreszenzstrahlung, Polarisation des Fluoreszenzlichts
polarization by reflection	Reflexionspolarisation f, Polarisation f durch Reflexion		
polarization by refraction	Brechungspolarisation f, Polarisation f durch Brechung	**polarization of free space,** polarization of vacuum, vacuum polarization	Polarisation f des Vakuums, Vakuumpolarisation f
polarization by scattering	Streuungspolarisation f, Polarisation f durch Streuung	**polarization of luminescence light (radiation)**	s. polarized luminescence
polarization capacitance	Polarisationskapazität f	**polarization of vacuum**	s. polarization of free space
polarization cell	Polarisationszelle f, Polarisationselement n	**polarization operator**	Polarisationsoperator m
polarization charge, bound charge	Polarisationsladung f	**polarization-optical tensometry**	polarisationsoptische Tensometrie f (Untersuchung f von Spannungszuständen)
polarization charge density	s. density of polarization charge		
polarization condenser	Polarisationskondensor m	**polarization optics,** optics of polarized light	Polarisationsoptik f
polarization current, polarizing current <el.chem.>	[elektrolytischer] Polarisationsstrom m <El.Chem.>	**polarization ovaloid**	Polarisationsovaloid n
		polarization parameter	Polarisationsparameter m
polarization current	s. a. displacement current	**polarization photometer**	Polarisationsphotometer n
polarization curve <el.chem.>	Polarisationskurve f <El.Chem.>	**polarization photometry**	Polarisationsphotometrie f
polarization degree, degree (proportion) of polarization	Polarisationsgrad m	**polarization plateau,** ionization plateau, Fermi plateau	Fermi-Plateau n
polarization diagram, polarization function of Mie scattering	Polarisationsdiagramm n, Polarisationsfunktion f der Mie-Streuung	**polarization potential,** Hertzian vector, Hertz vector	Hertzscher Vektor m, [elektrisches] Polarisationspotential n, Hertzsches Potential n
polarization diversity	Polarisationsdiversity f; Polarisationsmehrfachempfang m, Polarisationsdiversityempfang m	**polarization potential,** polarization voltage, polarization e.m.f., polarization electromotive force <el.chem.>	Polarisationsspannung f, Polarisationspotential n, Polarisations-EMK f <El. Chem.>
polarization effect [in ionic conduction]	Polarisationseffekt m [bei Ionenleitung]		
polarization efficiency	Polarisationsausbeute f	**polarization prism,** polarizing prism	Polarisationsprisma n
polarization electromotive force	s. polarization potential <el.chem.>	**polarization pyrometer**	s. Wanner pyrometer
		polarization resistance	Polarisations[wirk]widerstand m
polarization ellipse	Polarisationsellipse f		
polarization ellipsoid, ellipsoid of polarization	Polarisationsellipsoid n	**polarization rotator**	Polarisationsdreher m
polarization energy	Polarisationsenergie f		
polarization error	s. night effect <el.>		
polarization factor, Thomson factor	Polarisationsfaktor m, Thomson-Faktor m, Thomsonscher Faktor m	**polarization rule**	Polarisationsregel f
		polarization spectacles, polarizing spectacles	Polarisationsbrille f
polarization fading	Polarisationsschwund m, Polarisationsfading n	**polarization tensor**	Polarisationstensor m
polarization field, reaction field in the dielectric structure	Polarisationsbereich m, Polarisationsfeld n	**polarization vector** <nucl.>	Polarisationsvektor m <Kern.>
		polarization vector	s. a. dielectric polarization
polarization filter, polarizing filter, polarizer	Polarisationsfilter n	**polarization voltage,** bias voltage, biasing voltage, bias <el.>	Vorspannung f <El.>
polarization foil; polaroid [filter]	Polarisationsfolie f; Polaroidfilter n, Polaroid f	**polarization voltage**	s. a. polarization potential
		polarization volume density, volume density of polarization	Polarisationsdichte f [pro Volumeneinheit], Volum[en]dichte f der Polarisation, Volum[en]polarisationsdichte f
polarization force	Polarisationskraft f		
polarization function of Mie scattering, polarization diagram	Polarisationsdiagramm n, Polarisationsfunktion f der Mie-Streuung	**polarization wave**	Polarisationswelle f

polarized 616

polarized ammeter	Strommesser *m* mit Nullstellung in der Skalenmitte, Strommesser mit beidseitigem Ausschlag
polarized atomic bond, mixed bond	gemischte Bindung *f*, polarisierte Atombindung *f*
polarized fluorescence, polarization of fluorescence, polarization of fluorescence radiation (light)	polarisierte Fluoreszenz *f*, Polarisation *f* der Fluoreszenzstrahlung, Polarisation des Fluoreszenzlichts
polarized luminescence, polarization of luminescence light (radiation)	polarisierte Lumineszenz *f*, Polarisation *f* der Lumineszenzstrahlung, Polarisation des Lumineszenzlichts
polarizer, polariser	Polarisator *m*
polarizer, polarizing filter, polarization filter	Polarisationsfilter *n*
polarizing angle	*s.* Brewster angle
polarizing apparatus	Polarisationsapparat *m*
polarizing capacity, polarizing power	Polarisationsvermögen *n*, Polarisationsfähigkeit *f*, polarisierende Wirkung *f*
polarizing combination	*s.* polarizing equipment
polarizing constant	Polarisationskonstante *f*
polarizing current, polarization current ⟨el.chem.⟩	Polarisationsstrom *m*, elektrolytischer Polarisationsstrom ⟨El.Chem.⟩
polarizing device (equipment), polarizing combination	Polarisationseinrichtung *f*
polarizing filter, polarization filter, polarizer	Polarisationsfilter *n*
polarizing-filter analyzer, filter analyzer	Filteranalysator *m*
polarizing interferometer	Polarisationsinterferometer *n*
polarizing microscope, polarization microscope	Polarisationsmikroskop *n*
polarizing optical system, polarizing optics	Polarisationsoptik *f*
polarizing potential, polarizing voltage	polarisierende Spannung *f*
polarizing power, polarizing capacity	Polarisationsvermögen *n*, Polarisationsfähigkeit *f*, polarisierende Wirkung *f*
polarizing prism, polarization prism	Polarisationsprisma *n*
polarizing pyrometer	*s.* Wanner pyrometer
polarizing spectacles, stereo-visor	Stereobetrachtungsbrille *f*, Stereobrille *f*
polarizing spectacles	*s. a.* polarization spectacles
polarizing spectrometer	Polarisationsspektrometer *n*
polarizing vertical condenser, polarizing vertical illuminator	Polarisationsopakilluminator *m*
polarizing voltage, polarizing potential	polarisierende Spannung *f*
polar lights, polar aurora, aurora ⟨*pl.*: aurorae⟩	Polarlicht *n*, polare Aurora *f*
polar line	*s.* polar
polar maritime air, maritime polar air	maritime Polarluft *f*, polare Meeresluft *f*
polar mode	polare Mode *f*, polarer Schwingungstyp *m*
polar mode oscillation	polare Schwingung *f*
polar molecule, dipole molecule	polares Molekül *n*, Dipolmolekül *n*
polar moment of inertia	polares Trägheitsmoment (Moment) *n*, Binetsches Trägheitsmoment, Trägheitsmoment in bezug auf einen Punkt, Trägheitsmoment bei Drehung
polar moment of inertia of the line, moment of inertia of the line with respect to a point	polares Linienträgheitsmoment *n*
polar moment of resistance, polar resisting moment	
polar motion, movement (shifting) of the pole, polar wandering (drift, displacement, shift), wandering of [the] pole	Polbewegung *f*, Polschwankung *f*, Polwanderung *f*, Polverschiebung *f*, Polverlagerung *f*
polar night	Polarnacht *f*
polarogram	Polarogramm *n*, polarographische Strom-Spannungs-Kurve *f*
polarographic technique	*s.* polarography
polarographic wave	polarographische Stufe *f*, polarographische Welle *f*
polarography, polarographic technique	Polarographie *f*
polaroid	*s.* polarization foil
polaroid	*s.* polaroid material
Polaroid camera	*s.* Polaroid-Land camera
polaroid filter	*s.* polarization foil
Polaroid-Land camera, one-step photographic camera, Polaroid camera, Land camera	Landsche Ein-Minuten-Kamera *f*, Polaroid-Land-Kamera *f*, Polaroid-Kamera *f*
polaroid material, polaroid	polaroides Material *n*, Polaroid *n*
polaron	Polaron *n*
polar plane	Polarebene *f*
polar potentiometer	*s.* polar type alternating-current potentiometer
polar projection	polständige (normale, polare) Projektion *f*, polständiger (normaler, polarer) Entwurf *m*
polar radius	Polradius *m*, Polhalbmesser *m*
polar radius of gyration (interia)	polarer Trägheitsradius *m*
polar ray, plume ⟨of the solar corona⟩	Polarstrahl *m* ⟨Sonnenkorona⟩
polar resisting moment, polar moment of resistance	polares Widerstandsmoment *n*
polar semi-axis	polare Halbachse *f*, Polarhalbachse *f*
polar sequence, north polar sequence	Polsequenz *f*, Nordpolarsequenz *f*, Polfolge *f*
polar shift	*s.* polar motion
polar solid angle, terminal angle	Endecke *f* ⟨Krist.⟩; Polarecke *f*, Polecke *f*
polar space, elliptic space	elliptischer Raum *m*
polar space	*s. a.* adjoint space
Polar Star, Polaris, polestar, Stella Polaris	Polarstern *m*, Nord[polar]stern *m*, Polaris *f*, α Ursae Minoris, α UMi
polar surface of light distribution	*s.* solid of light distribution
polar telescope	Polteleskop *n*, Polfernrohr *n*
polar triangle, astronomical (parallactic) triangle, triangle of position, navigational triangle	Poldreieck *n*, Polardreieck *n*, nautisches (parallaktisches, astronomisches) Dreieck *n*
polar type alternating-current potentiometer, polar type potentiometer, polar type a.c. potentiometer, polar potentiometer	Phasenschieberkompensator *m*, Wechselstromkompensator *m* mit einfacher Vergleichsspannung, phasenschiebender Wechselstromkompensator, Polarkoordinaten[-Wechselstrom]kompensator *m*, Polarkompensator *m*
polar vector	polarer (translatorischer) Vektor *m*, Schubvektor *m*, Richtungsvektor *m*
polar voltage	*s.* pole voltage
polar wandering	*s.* polar motion
polar year	Polarjahr *n*
polaxis, polar axis ⟨math.; cryst.⟩	Polarachse *f* ⟨Math.; Krist.⟩; Nullstrahl *m* ⟨Math.⟩
Pol['s] differential equation / Van der, Van der Pol['s] equation, differential equation of Van der Pol	van der Polsche Differentialgleichung *f*, van der Polsche Gleichung *f*
Poldi hardness [number]	Poldi-Härte *f*

Poldi hardness tester	Poldi-Hammer m, Poldi-Härteprüfgerät n
pole \<gen.; also of polar curve\>	Pol m \<allg.; auch des Polarkoordinatensystems\>
pole \<of the analytic function\>	Pol m, Polstelle f, außerwesentlich singuläre Stelle f \<analytische Funktion\>
pole arc, real pole arc	Polbogen m, tatsächlicher Polbogen
pole arc-to-pole pitch ratio	Polbedeckungsfaktor m
pole change, pole changing, reversing \<el.\>	Polumschaltung f \<El.\>
pole change	s. a. alternation of polarity
pole changer	s. pole-changing switch
pole changing	s. alternation of polarity
pole changing	s. a. pole change \<el.\>
pole-changing switch, pole changer, pole reverser, current reverser, polarity reversing switch, reversing switch, commutator switch	Polwechselschalter m, Polwechsler m, Umpolschalter m; Polumschalter m; Polwender m; Polwendeschalter m, Wendeschalter m, Umkehrschalter m
pole dislocation	Polversetzung f
pole effect	Poleffekt m, Polaritätseffekt m, Elektrodeneffekt m
pole face	Polfläche f
pole face	s. pole piece face
pole face	s. a. pole piece
pole face leakage	s. pole leakage
pole figure	Polfigur f
pole finder	s. polarity indicator
pole finding paper, pole paper, pole test paper, polarity test paper	Polreagenzpapier n, Polsuchpapier n, Polpapier n
pole float	s. staff float
pole gap, gap between poles	Pollücke f
pole gap	s. a. magnet gap
pole indicating lamp, polarity indicating lamp	Polsuchlampe f
pole indicator	s. polarity indicator
pole leakage, pole piece leakage, pole face leakage	Polstreuung f
poleless magnet	polloser Magnet m
pole of cold	s. cold pole
pole of ecliptic	Pol m der Ekliptik, ekliptikaler Pol, Ekliptikpol m
pole of inaccessibility	Unzugänglichkeitspol m, Pol m der Unzugänglichkeit
pole of magnetic dip	s. magnetic dip pole
pole of the axis of rotation	Pol m der Bewegung
pole of zone, zone pole	Zonenpol m
pole paper	s. pole finding paper
pole piece, pole tip, pole shoe, pole face	Polschuh m, Magnetpolschuh m, Magnetschenkel m; Polschuhrand m
pole piece face, pole face	Polschuhfläche f, Polschuh-Stirnfläche f
pole piece factor, pole shoe factor	Polschuhfaktor m
pole piece leakage, pole leakage, pole face leakage	Polstreuung f
pole piece lens, pole piece magnetic lens	Polschuhlinse f [nach E. Ruska], magnetische Polschuhlinse
pole pitch	Polteilung f
pole plate, attraction plate \<bio.\>	Polkappe f \<Bio.\>
Pol['s] equation / Van der	s. Pol['s] differential equation / Van der
pole reversal	s. alternation of polarity
pole reverser	s. pole-changing switch
pole shoe	s. pole piece
pole shoe factor, pole piece factor	Polschuhfaktor m
pole sphere	Polkugel f
pole-star	s. Polar Star
pole strength	s. magnetic pole strength
pole term	Polterm m
pole tester	s. polarity indicator
pole test paper	s. pole finding paper
pole tip	Polspitze f, Polschuhspitze f, Polhorn n
pole tip	s. a. pole piece
pole voltage, polar voltage	Polspannung f, magnetische Polspannung
poleward migration of prominence	polwärtige Wanderung f der Protuberanz
pole wheel, field rotor	Schenkelpolläufer m, Polrad n
Poley['s] method	Poleysche Methode f, Poley-Verfahren n
pole-zero configuration, location of poles and zeros	P-N-Verteilung f, P-N-Bild n, Pol-Nullstellen-Verteilung f, Pol-Nullstellen-Bild n
polhode, polhodie, moving centrode, moving curve of instantaneous centres \<mech.\>	Polhodie f, Pol[hodie]kurve f, Gangpolkurve f, Polbahn f, Poloide f, bewegte Zentrode f (Polkurve, Momentanzentrenkurve f), Zentrode \<Mech.\>
polhode (polhodie) cone	s. moving cone of instantaneous axes
poling	Polen n
poling	s. a. alternation of polarity
polished sample (section)	s. metallographic specimen
polished section, polished surface	Anschliff m
pollen analysis; panynological analysis, spore analysis	Pollenanalyse f; Sporenanalyse f
pollen diagram	Pollendiagramm n
pollen tube	Pollenschlauch m
pollination	Bestäubung f; Einstauben n; Einstäuben n; Stäuben n
pollutant, contaminant	Verschmutzer m, Verunreiniger m, Verunreinigung f
pollution, contamination	Verschmutzung f, Verunreinigung f
pollution of air (the atmosphere)	s. atmospheric pollution
poloidal field, poloidal magnetic field, poloidal part of the magnetic field	poloidales Feld n, poloidaler Teil m des magnetischen Feldes, Poloidfeld n
poloidal mode	poloidale Mode f, poloidaler Typ (Wellentyp) m
poloidal part of the magnetic field	s. poloidal field
polology, determination of the residues of poles of the scattering matrix	Pologie f, Bestimmung f der Residuen der Streumatrixpole
Pol relaxation oscillation / Van der	van der Polsche Kippschwingung f
polyad	Polyade f
polyaddition	s. addition polymerization
polyaddition product, addition product	Polyaddukt n, Polyadditionsprodukt n
Pólya['s] distribution, Pascal['s] distribution, negative binomial [series] distribution	Pascalsche Verteilung f, negative Binomialverteilung f, Pólya-Verteilung f, Pascal-Verteilung f
polyampholyte	Polyampholyt m
polychroism, pleochroism, pleochromatism, polychromatism, dispersion of polarization	Pleochroismus m, Polychroismus m
polychromatic	s. heterogeneous \<of radiation\>
polychrom[at]ic	polychrom, vielfarbig
polycondensate, polycondensation product	Polykondensat n, Polykondensationsprodukt n
polycondensation, condensation polymerization, C-polymerization	Polykondensation f
polycondensation product	s. polycondensate
polyconic projection	polykonischer Entwurf m, polykonische Projektion f
polycrystal	Vielkristall m, Polykristall m, Kristallhaufwerk n, Vielling m, Sammelkristall m, Kristallvielling m, Mehrkristall m, Haufwerk n

polycrystalline 618

polycrystalline aggregat	polykristallines Aggregat n
polycyclic	s. multinuclear
polydictiality	Polydiktyalität f
polydisperse, heterodisperse	polydispers, heterodispers
polydispersity	Polydispersität f
polydomain particle	Mehrbereichsteilchen n, Vielbereichsteilchen n
polydynamic	polydynamisch
polyelectrode	Polyelektrode f
polyelectrolyte solution	Polyelektrolytlösung f
polyelectron	Polyelektron n
polyelectronic atom, multi-electron atonm	Mehrelektronenatom n; Vielelektronenatom n
poly-electron spectrum, multi-electron spectrum, many-electron spectrum	Mehrelektronenspektrum n; Vielelektronenspektrum n
polyenergetic	s. heterogeneous
polyenergid cell	polyenergide Zelle f
polyfluorochromatism	Polyfluorochromie f
polyfunctional	polyfunktionell
polygenetic	polygen[etisch]
polygonal connection, polygon connection	Vieleckschaltung f, Polygonschaltung f
polygonal method, polygonation, polygonometry; minor control; traversing, traverse geo.>	Polygon[is]ierung f, Polygon[zug]verfahren n, Polygon[zug]methode f, Polygonometrie f <Geo.>
polygonal mirror	Spiegelpolygon n, Vieleckspiegel m
polygonal mirror	s. a. mirror wheel
polygonal soil	Polygon[al]boden m
polygonation	s. polygonal method
polygon circumscribed about a circle	Tangentenvieleck n eines Kreises, umschriebenes Vieleck n
polygon connection	s. polygonal connection
polygon growth	Polygonwachstum n
polygonization <cryst.>	Polygonisation f, Polygonisierung f <Krist.>
polygon mapping, Schwarz-Christoffel polygon mapping, Schwarz-Christoffel transformation	Polygonabbildung f, Schwarz-Christoffelsche Abbildung f (Polygonabbildung) f
polygon of forces, force polygon, load polygon	Kräfteeck n, Kräftepolygon n, Kräftevieleck n, Krafteck n, Kraftpolygon n
polygon of stresses	s. stress polygon
polygon of vectors, vector polygon	Vektorpolygon n
polygonometry <math.>	Polygonometrie f <Math.>
polygonometry	s. a .polygonal method
polyharmonic equation	polyharmonische Gleichung f, polyharmonische Differentialgleichung f
polyharmonic function	polyharmonische Funktion f
polyhedral diffusion of flame	polyedrische Diffusion f der Flamme, Vielflächendiffusion f der Flamme
polyhedral flame	polyedrische Flamme f, Vielflächenflamme f
polyhedral group	Polyedergruppe f
polyhedral projection	Polyederprojektion f, Polyederentwurf m, Polyederabbildung f, preußische Polyederprojektion
polyhedrometry	Polyedrometrie f
polyhedron	Polyeder n, Vielflach n, Vielflächner m
polyhomoeity, polyhomogeneity	Polyhomoität f, Polyhomogenität f
polyion	Polyion n
polymer, polymeric compound, polymeride	Polymer[e] n
polymer-analogue, analogous polymeric compound	Polymeranalog[e] n
polymer chain	Polymerenkette f
polymer degradation, depolymerization	Depolymerisation f
polymer-homologue, homologous polymeric compound	Polymerhomolog[e] n
polymer-homologue range	polymerhomologe Reihe f
polymeric compound, polymeride	s. polymer
polymerism	Polymerie f
polymer-isomer	Polymerisomer[e] n
polymer-isomeric	polymerisomer
polymerizate	s. polymerization product
polymerization accelerator (catalyst)	s. initiator
polymerization inhibitor	s. polymerization retarder
polymerization product, polymerizate	Polymerisat n, Polymerisationsprodukt n
polymerization regulator	Polymerisationsregler m
polymerization retarder, polymerization inhibitor	Polymerisationsinhibitor m, Inhibitor m [der Polymerisation]
polymeter	Polymeter n
polymict	polymikt
polymolecularity	Polymolekularität f
polymolecular layer, multilayer, multimolecular layer	Mehrfachschicht f, mehrfachmolekulare (multimolekulare, polymolekulare) Schicht f
polymorphic transformation	polymorphe Umwandlung f
polymorphism, polymorphy	Polymorphie f, Polymorphismus m, Heteromorphie f, physikalische Isomerie f
polymorphism of motional variance	Bewegungspolymorphie f
polymorphism under pressure	Polymorphie f unter Druck, Druckpolymorphie f
polymorphy	s. polymorphism
polynary alloy, multicomponent alloy	Mehrstofflegierung f, polynäre Legierung f
polynary system, multicomponent system	Mehrstoffsystem n, polynäres System n
polynomial, integral rational function	Polynom n, ganze rationale Funktion f
polynomial distribution	s. multinomial distribution
polynomial expansion	poiynomische Entwicklung f, Polynomialentwicklung f
polynomial function	Polynomfunktion f
polynomial in several variables, multinomial	Polynom n in mehreren Variablen
polynomial method	Polynommethode f
polynomial regression	polynomische Regression f
polynomial ring	Polynomring m
polynuclear	s. multinuclear
polynucleate	s. polynuclear
polyode [valve]	s. multielectrode tube
polyopia	Mehrfachsehen n, Polyopie f
polyphase current	Mehrphasenstrom m, mehrphasiger Wechselstrom m, Mehrphasenwechselstrom m
polysalt	Polysalz n
polyslip, multiple slip	Mehrfachgleitung f, Mehrfachgleitprozeß m
polysulfide polymer (rubber)	s. elastothiomer
polysynthetic twin, repeated twin, multiple twin <cryst.>	polysynthetischer (polysymmetrischer) Zwilling m, Wiederholungszwilling m <Krist.>
polytrope, polytropic curve, polytropic line <therm.>	Polytrope f <Therm.>
polytrope	s. a. polytropic curve <math.>

polytropic atmosphere	polytrope Atmosphäre f	pool boiling heat transfer	Wärmeübergang m beim Sieden unter freier Konvektion
polytropic change, polytropic process	polytrop[isch]e Zustandsänderung f, polytrop-reversible Zustandsänderung, polytroper Prozeß (Vorgang) m	pooled error	zusammengefaßter Fehler m
		Poole['s] formula	s. Poole['s] relation
		Poole-Frenkel effect (field-assisted association)	Poole-Frenkel-Effekt m
polytropic curve, polytropic line, polytrope <math.>	polytropische Kurve f, polytropische Linie f, Polytrope f <Math.>		
polytropic curve	s. polytrope <therm.>	pool reactor	s. swimming pool reactor
polytropic exponent, coefficient of polytropy	Polytropenexponent m, Exponent m der Polytrope, Ordnung f der Polytrope	Poole['s] relation, Poole['s] formula	Poolesche Beziehung f, Poolesche Regel f
		pooling of classes (data) <stat.>	Zusammenfassung f von Daten <Stat.>
polytropic gas ball (sphere)	polytrope Gaskugel f, Gaskugel der Polytropenklasse	poor conductor, bad conductor	schlechter Leiter m
polytropic index	Polytropenindex m, Klasse f der Polytrope		
polytropic line	s. polytrope <therm.>	poor heat conductor	schlechter Wärmeleiter m
polytropic line	s. polytropic curve <math.>	poor visibility	schlechte Sicht f
polytropic process	s. polytropic change	P operator	s. Dyson['s] chronological operator
polytropic relation, equation of the polytropic line	Polytropenbeziehung f, Polytropengleichung f, Gleichung f der Polytrope	poppet valve	Durchgangsventil n
polytypism <cryst.>	Polytypie f <Krist.>	poppet valve	s. a. disk valve
polyvalent, multivalent, quantivalent, plurivalent <chem.>	mehrwertig, mehrbindig, polyvalent, vielwertig, multivalent <Chem.>	population <of the level>, level population	Besetzung f [des Niveaus]
polywater, superwater, anomalous water	Polywasser n, Superwasser n, anomales (polymeres, überschweres) Wasser n, Derjagin-Wasser n	population, stellar population, star population <astr.>	Sternpopulation f, Population f <Astr.>
pomeranchon	s. pomeranchukon	population <stat.; gen.>; parent population, universe	Population f <Stat.; allg.>, Grundgesamtheit f, Gesamtheit f <Stat.>
Pomeranchuk effect	Pomerantschuk-Effekt m		
pomeranchukon, Pomeranchuk particle, Pomeranchuk pole, pomeranchon, vacuon	Pomerantschukon n, Pomerantschuk-Teilchen n, Pomerantschuk-Pol m, Vakuon n	population I, population I of Baade, stellar population I	Population f I [nach Baade], Feldpopulation f
		population II, population II of Baade, stellar population II	Population f II [nach Baade], Kernpopulation f
Pomeranchuk['s] theorem	Pomerantschuk-Theorem n, Pomerantschuksches Theorem n, Theorem von Pomerantschuk	population density	Besetzungsdichte f
		population excess	Überschußbesetzung f
Pomp and Siebel draw widening test, Pomp and Siebel test, Siebel and Pomp test	Tiefziehweitungsversuch m [nach Pomp und Siebel], Pomp-Siebelscher Tiefziehweitungsversuch	population inversion	Besetzungsinversion f
		population mean	s. mathematical expectation
		population I of Baade	s. population I
		population II of Baade	s. population II
pond	Weiher m	population I of the Galaxy	s. disk population
pond	s. a. gramme-weight	population II of the Galaxy	s. halo population
ponderability, heaviness, ponderosity	Schwere f	porcelain	Porzellan n
ponderable, weighable	wägbar	pore	Pore f
ponderable mass	s. heavy mass	pore	s. a. Smekal defect
ponderator	Ponderator m	pore conduction; pore conductivity	Porenleitung f; Porenleitfähigkeit f
ponderomotive action, ponderomotive effect	ponderomotorische Wirkung f		
ponderomotive equations	s. Lorentz equations of motion	pore fluid anelasticity, consolidation	Porenflüssigkeitsanelastizität f, Fließverfestigung f
ponderomotive force	ponderomotorische Kraft f	pore size distribution	Porengrößenverteilung f
ponderomotive force density	ponderomotorische Kraftdichte f		
ponderomotive four-force	ponderomotorische Viererkraft f		
		pore space; void space	Porenraum m
ponderomotive interaction of currents	ponderomotorisch-magnetische Wirkung f von Strömen	pore volume	Porenvolumen n, Porenanteil m, Porenraum m, Gesamtporenvolumen n, Hohlraumvolumen n, Porosität f, GPV, PV
ponderomotive law; equation of motion	Bewegungsgleichung f		
ponderomotive wattmeter, radiation-pressure wattmeter	Strahlungsdruck-Leistungsmesser m, Strahlungsdruck-Wattmeter n		
		porometry	Porenmessung f
		porosimeter, porosity apparatus	Porositätsmesser m
ponderosity, heaviness, ponderability	Schwere f		
pond for nuclear reactor, cooling pond, stillpot	Brennelemente-Abklingbehälter m, Abklingbehälter m für Brennelemente, Brennelemente-Lagerbehälter m, Lagerbehälter m für Brennelemente	porosity	Porosität f; Porigkeit f
		porosity	s. a. porosity factor
		porosity apparatus	s. porosimeter
		porosity factor, porosity	Porenziffer f, Porositätszahl f, Porositätsgrad m, Porositätskoeffizient m, Porosität f
ponor, catavothre	Flußschwinde f, Schlundloch n, Ponor m, Katavothre f		
Pontryagin['s] maximum principle	Pontrjaginsches Maximumprinzip n	porous; spongy, sponge	porös, porig; schwammig, schwammartig
pool, temporary waters	temporäres (periodisches) Gewässer n, Tümpel m	porous barrier	s. porous partition
		porous diaphragm, porous membrane	poröse Membran f
pool <bio.>	Pool m <Bio.>	porous diaphragm	s. a. porous partition
pool, reach <hydr.>	Haltung f <Hydr.>	porous diffusion	Porendiffusion f

porous electrode, diffusion electrode	Diffusionselektrode *f*
porous membrane, porous diaphragm	poröse Membran *f*
porous partition, porous barrier, porous wall; porous diaphragm	poröse Wand *f*, poröse Zwischenwand *f*, poröse Trennwand *f*
porous structure	Porenstruktur *f*, poröse Struktur *f*
porous wall	s. porous parition
porphyropsin	Porphyropsin *n*, Sehviolett *n*
Porro-Koppe principle, principle of Porro and Koppe; Porro['s] principle	Porro-Koppesches Prinzip *n*, Porro-Koppe-Prinzip *n*, Prinzip von Porro-Koppe; Porro-Prinzip *n*, Porrosches Prinzip
Porro-Koppe type [of] plotting machine, stereoplanigraph, stereoplanigraph	Stereoplanigraph *m*
Porro['s] principle	s. Porro-Koppe principle
Porro['s] prism [system], Porro['s] system <of the first or second kind>	Porro-Prismensystem *n*, Porro-System *n*, Porro-Prisma *n* (erster *oder* zweiter Art)
port <el.>	Tor *n* <El.>
port	s. a. orifice
portable, portative; field	tragbar; Feld-
portable, package	transportabel, ortsbeweglich <im Betrieb ortsfest, aber ab- und an anderer Stelle wieder aufbaubar>
portable calorimeter	tragbares Kalorimeter *n*, Handkalorimeter *n*
portable instrument	tragbares Meßgerät (Gerät, Instrument) *n*
portable photogrammetric chamber, portable precision chamber	Handkammer *f*, Handmeßkammer *f*
portable photometer, universal photometer	tragbares Photometer *n*, Universalphotometer *n*
portable precision chamber	s. portable photogrammetric chamber
portal, outlet, outcome	Austrittsöffnung *f*, Ausflußöffnung *f*, Ablaßöffnung *f*
portative	s. portable
port basin wave	Hafen[becken]welle *f*
Porter-Thomas distribution	Porter-Thomas-Verteilung *f*
Portevin-Le Chatelier effect	Portevin-le-Chatelier-Effekt *m*
porthole	s. orifice
portrait attachment (lens)	Porträtlinse *f*
posistor	= positive temperature coefficient thermistor
position	Stellung *f*, Stand *m*, Lage *f*
position, place <of a star>	Ort *m* [eines Gestirns], Position *f* [eines Gestirns], Sternort *m*
position, line of application	Trägergerade *f* <Vektor>
position	s. a. place
position adjustment	s. positioning
positional astronomy	Positionsastronomie *f*
positional error, positioning error	Lageeinstellungsfehler *m*
positional micrometer, position micrometer	Positions[faden]mikrometer *n*
position angle	Positionswinkel *m*
position at rest	s. position of rest
position catalogue	Positionskatalog *m*
position circle, circle of position	Positionskreis *m*
position co-ordinates	s. space co-ordinates
position correlation	Lagekorrelation *f*
position determination	s. localization
position effect <bio.>	Positionseffekt *m*, Lagewirkung *f* <Bio.>
positioner	Stellungsregler *m*, Positionier *m*
position error	s. offset <control>
position-exchange force; exchange force; platzwechsel force	Austauschkraft *f*; Platzwechselkernkraft *f*
position factor	s. Coddington position factor
position finder, location finder, locator	Ortungsgerät *n*, Ortungsinstrument *n*; Ortungsanlage *f*
position finding	s. localization
position fixing	s. localization
position function, function of the position [of the point], local function	Ortsfunktion *f*, Koordinatenfunktion *f*
position head, geometrical head, gravity head	wirkliche Höhe *f*, Höhenlage *f*
positioning, position adjustment	Lageeinstellung *f*; Positionierung *f*
positioning element	s. final control element
positioning error	s. positional error
position isomer, place isomer	Stellungsisomer *n*
position-isomeric, place-isomeric	stellungsisomer
position isomerism, place isomerism, substitutional isomerism	Stellungsisomerie *f*, Positionsisomerie *f*, Substitutionsisomerie *f*, Ortsisomerie *f*
position line, Sumner line	Positionslinie *f*, Standlinie *f*
position micrometer, positional micrometer	Positions[faden]mikrometer *n*
position of equilibrium, equilibrium position	Gleichgewichtslage *f*, Ruhelage *f*
position of extinction, extinction position	Auslöschungsstellung *f*
position of level	s. level position
position of rest, position at rest, rest position; normal position; home position; settled position; zero position	Ruhelage *f*, Ruhestellung *f*
position operator	Ortsoperator *m*, Koordinatenoperator *m*
position-sensitive, sensitive to position	ageempfindlich
position variable	s. space variable
position vector, radius vector <*pl.*: radii vectores>	Radiusvektor *m*, Ortsvektor *m*, Fahrstrahl *m*, Polstrahl *m*, Leitstrahl *m*
positivation	Positivierung *f*
positive; positive image	Positiv *n*, photographisches Positiv; Positivbild *n*
positive, electrically positive; positively charged <el.>	positiv, elektrisch positiv; positiv [auf]geladen <El.>
positive arc flame	s. positive flame
positive beta particle, β^+ particle	positives Beta-Teilchen *n*, β^+-Teilchen *n*
positive branch	s. R-branch
positive catalyst	s. accelerator <chem.>
positive clamping	Positivklemmung *f*, positive Klemmung *f*
positive column	positive Säule *f*, Glimmsäule *f*, Säule *f* der Glimmentladung, Entladungsrumpf *m*
positive conductor, positive wire, plus wire	positiver Leiter *m*, Plusleiter *m*, positive Leitung *f*, Plusleitung *f*, Plusdraht *m*
positive contact	zwang[s]läufiger Kontakt *m*
positive correlation, direct correlation	positive Korrelation *f*
positive definite	positiv[-]definit
positive density, PD	Positivschwärzung *f*, Positivdichte *f*
positive developer	Positiventwickler *m*
positive displacement pump	mechanische Pumpe *f*
positive distortion	s. pin[-]cushion distortion
positive electricity	s. vitreous electricity
positive electron, positron, anti-electron, antiparticle of electron, e$^+$	Positron *n*, positives Elektron *n*, Antielektron *n*, Antiteilchen *n* des Elektrons, e$^+$

positive element of telephoto lens	Telepositiv *n*	**positive sequence component**	Mitkomponente *f*
positive emulsion	Positivemulsion *f*	**positive sequence current [component]**	Mitstrom *m*
positive excess	positiver Überschuß *m*		
positive eyepiece, Ramsden eyepiece, Ramsden magnifier	Ramsdensches Okular *n*, positives Okular, Okular nach Ramsden, Ramsden-Okular *n*	**positive sequence field,** positive field	Mitfeld *n*
positive feedback, feedforward	Mitkopplung *f*, positive Rückkopplung *f*; Aufschaltung *f*	**positive sequence impedance**	Mitimpedanz *f*, Mitscheinwiderstand *m*, mitläufige Impedanz *f*, Impedanz des mitläufigen Feldes
positive field, positive sequence field	Mitfeld *n*		
positive flame, positive arc flame, anodic flame, Beck flame, Beck arc flame	positive (anodische) Flamme *f*, Anodenflamme *f*, Beck-Flamme *f*	**positive sequence reactance**	Mitreaktanz *f*, Mitblindwiderstand *m*, mitläufiger Blindwiderstand *m*, Blindwiderstand des mitläufigen Feldes
positive frequency part	Teil *m* mit positiven Frequenzen		
positive glow	*s.* anode glow	**positive sequence system,** positive system	Mitsystem *n*
positive-going pulse, positive pulse	positiver Impuls *m*, Plusimpuls *m*, Positivimpuls *m*	**positive sequence voltage [component]**	Mitspannung *f*, mitläufige Spannung *f*
positive-grid oscillator	*s.* retarding-field oscillator		
positive hole, hole, electron hole, electron vacancy, vacant electron site, vacancy	Defektelektron *n*, [positives] Loch *n*, [positives] Elektronenloch *n*, Mangelelektron *n*, Löcherelektron *n*, [positives] Ersatzelektron *n*, Elektronenleerstelle *f*, Elektronenfehlstelle *f*, Lückenelektron *n*	**positive skewness**	positive Schiefe *f*
		positive stability	*s.* stable equilibrium
		positive system	*s.* positive sequence system
		positive terminal, positive limb	Plusklemme *f*, positive Klemme *f*, Pluspol *m*
positive image	*s.* positive	**positive wire,** plus wire, positive conductor	positiver Leiter *m*, Plusleiter *m*, positive Leitung *f*, Plusleitung *f*, Plusdraht *m*
positive-ion oscillation, ion oscillation	Ionenschwingung *f*, Schwingung *f* der positiven Ionen		
positive ion vacancy, cation vacancy	Kationenleerstelle *f*, Kationenfehlstelle *f*, Kationenlücke *f*	**positivity wave**	Positivitätswelle *f*
		positron, positives electron, anti-electron, antiparticle of electron, e^+	Positron *n*, positives Elektron *n*, Antielektron *n*, Antiteilchen *n* des Elektrons, e^+
positive lens, convergent lens, converging lens	Sammellinse *f*, Positivlinse *f*		
positive limb, positive terminal	Plusklemme *f*, positive Klemme *f*, Pluspol *m*		
		positron camera	Positronenkamera *f*
positively charged	*s.* positive <el.>	**positron capture**	Positroneneinfang *m*, β-Einfang *m*
positive meniscus, converging meniscus; concavo-convex lens	sammelnder (positiver) Meniskus *m*; konkavkonvexe Linse *f*	**positron decay,** positron disintegration, $β^+$-decay	$β^+$-Zerfall *m*, Positronenzerfall *m*
positive mu-meson, positive muon, $µ^+$-meson	positives Myon *n*, positives Mv-Meson *n*, My-plus-Meson *n*, $µ^+$-Meson *n*	**positron-electron annihilation**	*s.* electron-positron pair annihilation
positive-negative process, positive-negative technique	Positiv-Negativ-Verfahren *n*, Positiv-Negativ-Prozeß *m*	**positron-electron collision**	Positron-Elektron-Stoß *m*
positive parity, even parity, parity $+1$	gerade Parität *f*, Parität $+1$, positive Parität *f*	**positron-electron pair,** electron-positron pair, electron pair, e^+e^- pair, twin electron <nucl.>	Positron-Elektron-Paar *n*, Elektron-Positron-Paar *n*, e^+e^--Paar *n*, Elektronenpaar *n*, Elektronenzwilling *m* <Kern.>
positive polarity, reciprocal polarity	Pluspolung *f*, positive (reziproke) Polung *f*, positive Polarität *f*		
positive pole, plus	Pluspol *m*, positiver Pol *m*, Plus *n*	**positron emission,** $β^+$ emission; positron radiation, $β^+$ radiation	Positronenemission *f*, $β^+$-Emission *f*; Positronenstrahlung *f*, $β^+$-Strahlung *f*
positive pressure, superpressure, superatmospheric pressure, overpressure	Überdruck *m*, Mehrdruck *m*		
positive pressure gauge, overpressure gauge	Überdruckmanometer *n*, Überdruckmesser *m*	**positron emitter,** positron radiator	Positronenstrahler *m*, $β^+$-Strahler *m*
positive pressure head, head of pressure above atmospheric	Überdruckhöhe *f*	**positronium,** Ps	Positronium *n*
		positronium molecule	Positroniummolekül *n*
positive pressure wave <hydr.>	primäre Druckwelle *f* <Hydr.>	**positronium triplet**	Positroniumtriplett *n*
positive process	Positivprozeß *m*, Positivverfahren *n*	**positron radiation**	*s.* positron emission
		positron radiator	*s.* positron emitter
		positron spectrum, $β^+$ spectrum	Positronenspektrum *n*, $β^+$-Spektrum *n*
positive pulse	*s.* positive-going pulse	**Posnow number**	Posnow-Zahl *f*, Posnowsche Kennzahl *f*
positive ray, canal ray	positiver Strahl *m*, Kanalstrahl *m*		
positive-ray method, canal-ray method	Kanalstrahlmethode *f*	**possible displacement**	mögliche Verrückung *f*
positive reactance	*s.* inductive reactance <el.>		
positive refraction	positive Brechung *f*		
		possible velocity, virtual velocity, velocity compatible with the constraints	virtuelle Geschwindigkeit *f*
positive rotation	*s.* dextrorotation		
positive semidefinite	positiv semidefinit		

Possio['s] 622

Possio['s] equation	Possiosche Integralgleichung *f*	**pot**, electrolytic cell (couple)	Elektrolysezelle *f*, Elektrolysiergefäß *n*, Elektrolysegefäß *n*, elektrolytische Zelle *f*
post	s. terminal pillar		
post-accelerating electrode, post-accelerator electrode, intensifier electrode, intensifier ring, second gum electrode	Nachbeschleunigungselektrode *f*	**potassium-argon dating (method)**, argon method, K-Ar method, ^{40}K-^{40}Ar method	Argonmethode *f*, Kalium-Argon-Methode *f*, Argon-Kalium-Methode *f*
postalloy diffusion	s. outdiffusion	**potassium pump**	Kaliumpumpe *f*
post[-]amplifier	Nachverstärker *m*	**potency**	s. power <math.>
post-buckling behaviour	Nachbeulverhalten *n*	**potential**	Potential *n*
postdeflection, postdeflection focusing	Nachfokussierung *f*, Nachablenkung *f*	**potential**	Potential-; potentiell
		potential, irrotational	wirbelfrei, Potential-, drehungsfrei, rotationsfrei, rotorlos
		potential	s. a. potential function
		potential	s. a. voltage <el.>
post[-]deflection acceleration, p.d.a. <in cathode-ray tube>	Nachbeschleunigung *f* <Elektronenstrahlröhre>	**potential barrier**, barrier, potential hill, potential wall; potential threshold	Potentialwall *m*, Potentialbarriere *f*, Potentialberg *m*; Potentialschwelle *f*
		potential barrier at the contact, contact potential barrier	Kontaktpotentialwall *m*
postdeflection focusing	s. postdeflection	**potential barrier model**, barrier model	Potentialwallmodell *n*
postelectron emission	Postelektronenemission *f*, abklingende Nachemission *f*	**potential-barrier penetration probability**	s. penetration probability
Postel-Mercator projection	Postel-Mercator-Projektion *f*, Postel-Mercator-Entwurf *m*, Postel-Mercatorscher Entwurf *m*	**potential box**	s. sharp cornered potential well
postemphasis, de-emphasis	Deakzentuierung *f*, Deemphasis *f*	**potential box**	s. a. square well potential
		potential circuit	s. voltage circuit
		potential cone	s. potential funnel
posterior-anterior view, PA view, PA projection anterior projection, frontal projection	Projektion *f* von hinten nach vorn	**potential correction**, dynamic error	vorübergehende Regelabweichung *f*
		potential curve; potentiel-energy curve <of the molecule>	Potentialkurve *f*; Potentialverlauf *m*
posterior chamber <of eye>	hintere Augenkammer *f*, Hinterkammer *f*	**potential density**	potentielle Dichte *f*
posterior probability	s. inverse probability	**potential determining ion**	potentialbestimmendes Ion *n*
posterior projection, AP view, AP projection, anterior-posterior view, dorsal projection	Projektion *f* von vorn nach hinten	**potential diagram**, voltage diagram, vector diagram of voltage <el.>	Spannungsdiagramm *n*, Spannungsbild *n* <El.>
posterization, posterizing	Isohelieverfahren *n*, Isohelie *f*	**potential difference**	Potentialunterschied *m*, Potentialdifferenz *f*
post-exposure, flashing	Nachbelichtung *f*	**potential difference**, diffusion potential difference, diffusion voltage <semi.>	Diffusionsspannung *f* <Halb.>
post-frontal situation	postfrontale Lage *f*	**potential difference**	s. a. voltage
post interaction	Nachumordnungswechselwirkung *f*, Wechselwirkung *f* nach Umordnung	**potential distribution [curve]**, distribution of potential	Potentialverteilung *f*, Potentialverteilungskurve *f*, Potentialverlauf *m*
post-maximum	Postmaximum *n*	**potential divider**, voltage divider, potentiometer	Spannungsteiler *m*, Potentiometer *n*
post mortem [routine]	Post-mortem-Pronramm *n*	**potential drop**, potential fall, decline in potential, drop (fall) of potential; voltage drop (loss)	Potentialabfall *m*, Potentialfall *m*; Spannungsabfall *m*, Spannungsfall *m*
post[-]multiplication, post[-]multiplying, right multiplication	Multiplikation *f* von rechts	**potential energy**	potentielle Energie *f*, Energie der Lage, Lageenergie *f*, Macht *f*, Spannungsenergie *f*, Potential *n*
		potential energy	s. a. energy content
		potential energy <of elastic body>	s. a. total strain energy
post-nova, ex-nova <pl.: ex-novae, post-novae>	Postnova *f*, Exnova *f* <pl.: Postnovae, Exnovae>	**potential-energy curve** <of the molecule>; potential curve	Potentialkurve *f*; Potentialverlauf *m*
post-nova spectrum, ex-nova spectrum	Postnovaspektrum *n*		
post-nova state, ex-nova state	Postnovazustand *m*	**potential energy of deformation**	s. total strain energy
postsynaptic	postsynaptisch	**potential energy of deformation per unit volume**	s. specific strain energy
postulate	Postulat *n*		
postulate of coherency, coherency postulate, Weyl['s] postulate	Kohärenzpostulat *n*, Weylsches Postulat *n*	**potential energy of stress**	potentielle Spannungsenergie *f*
postulate of homogeneity	Homogenitätspostulat *n*, Weltpostulat *n*	**potential energy of the deformed body**	s. total strain energy
postulate of relativity of inertia, mathematical postulate of relativity of inertia	Postulat *n* der Relativität der Trägheit, mathematisches Postulat der Relativität der Trägheit	**potential energy per unit volume**	s. specific strain energy
		potential-energy surface	Potentialfläche *f* [des Moleküls]
postulates of Einstein's theory of relativity	Relativitätspostulate *npl*	**potential equalization**, equalization (compensation) of potential[s]	Potentialausgleich *m*
postulation	Postulieren *n*		

potential equation	s. Laplace['s] differential equation	potential of nuclear forces, nuclear potential	Kernkraftpotential n, Potential n der Kernkräfte, Kernpotential n
potential fall	s. potential drop	potential of rotation, rotation potential	Rotationspotential n
potential fall region (zone), region (zone) of potential fall	Fallraum m, Fallgebiet n	potential of simple layer	Potential n der einfachen Schicht
potential field	s. irrotational field	potential of the diffusion force	s. diffusion potential
potential flow, potential motion, irrotational flow, irrotational motion	Potentialströmung f, wirbelfreie Strömung f, drehungsfreie Strömung, Potentialbewegung f, wirbelfreie Bewegung f, drehungsfreie Bewegung	potential of the intermolecular forces, intermolecular potential	Potential n der zwischenmolekularen Kräfte, zwischenmolekulares (intermolekulares) Potential, Intermolekularpotential n
potential force	s. conservative force	potential of thermal diffusion, thermal diffusion potential	Thermodiffusionspotential n
potential function, potential, harmonic function <math.>	Potentialfunktion f, Potential n, harmonische Funktion f	potential operator	Potentialoperator m
potential function of Airy, Airy['s] stress function	Airysche Spannungsfunktion f, Potentialfunktion f von Airy, Airy-Spannungsfunktion f	potentialoscope, potentialscope	Potentialoskop n
		potential pit (pot)	s. potential well
		potential probe <geo.>	Potentialsonde f, Kollektor m, Ausgleicher m, Elektrode f <Geo.>
potential function of Muskhelishvili	s. Muskhelishvili potential	potential rate of evaporation, evaporativity, evaporating capacity	Verdunstungsvermögen n
potential function of Urey-Bradley-Simanouti	s. Urey-Bradley-Simanouti['s] potential function	potential relief	Potentialgebirge n
potential funnel, potential cone	Potentialtrichter m; Spannungstrichter m	potential relief	s. a. latent electrical image
		potential rise	Potentialanstieg m
potential gradient, voltage gradient	Potentialgradient m, Gradient m des Potentials, Spannungsgradient m, Potentialgefälle n, Spannungsgefälle n, negative Feldstärke f	potential scattering	Potentialstreuung f, äußere (potentialelastische) Streuung f, Kernpotentialstreuung f
		potential scattering cross-section, cross-section for potential scattering	Potentialstreuquerschnitt m, Wirkungsquerschnitt m für (der) Potentialstreuung
potential gradient in the air, electric potential atmosphere gradient	luftelektrisches Potentialgefälle n, luftelektrischer Potentialgradient m, atmosphärisches Spannungsgefälle n, elektrische Feldstärke f in der Atmosphäre, luftelektrische Feldstärke f, Luftfeldstärke f	potential scattering length	Potentialstreulänge f
		potentialscope	s. potentialoscope
		potential series	s. electrochemical series
		potential stability	potentielle Stabilität f
		potential step	s. potential jump
		potential surface	s. equipotential surface <also el.>
potential head, elevation head, geodesic head, elevation <hydr.>	Ortshöhe f <Hydr.>	potential temperature	potentielle Temperatur f
potential hill	s. potential barrier	potential theory	Potentialtheorie f
potential hole	s. potential well	potential theory / by (in, of, using)	potentialtheoretisch
potential image	s. electric image		
potential independent of isobaric spin, neutral potential	neutrales Potential n	potential threshold	s. potential barrier
		potential transformer, voltage transformer, shunt transformer	Spannungswandler m, Spannungsumsetzer m
potential internal energy	innere potentielle Energie f	potential trough	s. potential well
potential in the air, electric potential in the air	luftelektrisches Potential n	potential variability	potentielle (kryptische) Variabilität f
potentiality, irrotationality <of vector field>	Wirbelfreiheit f, Drehungsfreiheit f <Vektorfeld>	potential vector, irrotational vector	wirbelfreier Vektor m, Potentialvektor m, wirbelfreies Vektorfeld n
potential jump, potential step	Potentialsprung m	potential vector field	Vektorpotentialfeld n
potential limiting, voltage limiting	Spannungsbegrenzung f	potential vortex, irrotational vortex	Potentialwirbel m
potential line, potential wire	Potentialleitung f	potential vortex, free vortex, point vortex	freier Wirbel m, abgehender Wirbel
		potential wall	s. potential barrier
potential line	s. a. equipotential line	potential well, potential trough, potential pot (pit), potential hole potential hole	Potentialtopf m, Potentialsenke f, Potentialtrog m, Topfpotential n; Potentialmulde f
potential loop, antinode of potential	Spannungsbauch m		
potential matrix	Potentialmatrix f	potential well depth, well depth, depth of the potential well	Tiefe f des Potentials (Potentialtopfs), Stärke f des Potentials, Potential[topf]tiefe f, Topftiefe f, Potentialstärke f, Tiefe der Mulde (Energiemulde), Walltiefe f
potential motion	s. potential flow		
potential node, node of potential	Spannungsknoten m		
potential of central forces, central potential	Zentralpotential n, zentrales Potential n, Potential der Zentralkräfte		
potential of discontinuity, discontinuity potential	Unstetigkeitspotential n	potential well model, well model	Potentialtopfmodell n
		potential-well resonance	Potentialkastenresonanz f, Potentialtopfresonanz f
potential of equilibrium, equilibrium potential	Gleichgewichtspotential n	potential well with rounded edges	Potentialtopf m, Potentialkasten m mit abgerundeten Ecken <Gauß-, Yukawa- oder Exponential-Potentialtopf>
potential of Majorana forces, Majorana potential, space-exchange potential	Majorana-Potential n, Ortsaustauschpotential n, Potential n der Majorana-Kräfte		

potential

potential wire	s. potential line
potentiometer, balance-type potentiometer, compensator <el.>	Kompensator m, kompensierendes Potentiometer n, Kompensationsapparat m, Kompensationsgerät n <El.>
potentiometer	s. a. voltage divider
potentiometer circuit	Potentiometerschaltung f, Spannungsteilerschaltung f
potentiometer method (principle)	s. Poggendorff['s] compensation method
potentiometer recorder, recording potentiometer	Kompensograph m, Kompensationsschreiber m, selbsttätiger Kompensator m als Registrierinstrument; Kompensationsbandschreiber m, Kompensationsstreifenschreiber m, Potentiometerschreiber m
potentiometer-type resistor	ohmscher Spannungsteiler m, Teilerwiderstand m; Potentiometerwiderstand m
potentiometer-type rheostat	ohmscher Steller m, Potentiometerregler m
potentiometric analysis	s. potentiometry
potentiometric pressure gauge, rheostatic pressure gauge	potentiometrisches Manometer n, rheostatisches Manometer
potentiometric titration; potentiometry; electrometric titration; pH titration; potentiometric analysis, electrometric analysis	Potentiometrie f; potentiometrische Titration f; potentiometrische Analyse f, potentiometrische Maßanalyse f
potentiostat	Potentiostat m
potentiostatic method, potentiostatic technique	potentiostatisches Verfahren n
pot experiment	Gefäßversuch m
pot-hole, crater <geo.>	Kolk m, Strudelloch n, Strudeltopf m, Strudelkessel m
Potier['s] diagram	Potier-Diagramm n
Potier['s] triangle	Potiersches Dreieck n, Potier-Dreieck n
pot magnet, pot-type magnet, pot-type electromagnet	Topfmagnet m; Kernmagnet m
pot magnet	s. a. shell-type magnet
potometer	Potometer n, Potetometer n
Potsdam standard filter	Potsdamer Normalfilter n
Potsdam system	Potsdamer Schweresystem n
potted capacitor	Becherkondensator m
potted circuit	vergossene Schaltung f
potted measuring transformer, pot-type measuring transformer	Topfmeßwandler m
Potter-Bucky [grid]	s. moving grid
potting	Vergießen n, Verguß m, Ausgießen n
potting compound	Vergußmasse f, Ausgußmasse f
pot-type capacitor	Topfkondensator m
pot-type core, cylindrical core	Topfkern m
pot-type electromagnet (magnet)	s. pot magnet
pot-type measuring transformer, potted measuring transformer	Topfmeßwandler m
Pouillet pyrheliometer	Pouillet-Pyrheliometer n
Poulsen arc	Poulsenscher Lichtbogen m, Poulsen-Bogen m
Poulsen transmitter, arc transmitter	Poulsen-Sender m, Lichtbogensender m
poultice corrosion	s. subsurface corrosion
Pound and Rebka['s] experiment	Pound-Rebkascher Versuch m, Versuch von Pound und Rebka
Pound-Cranshaw experiment	Pound-Cranshawscher Versuch m
Pound-Knight oscillator	Pound-Knight-Oszillator m
Pound-Knight spectrometer	Pound-Knight-Spektrometer n
Pourbaix diagram	Pourbaix-Diagramm n
pouring into another vessel	s. decantation <chem.>
pour point; point of congelation, congealing point, solidifying (solidification) point <of oil>	Stockpunkt m, Fließpunkt m <Öl>
powder camera, X-ray powder camera	Debye-Scherrer-Kammer f, Pulverbeugungskammer f
powder cathode	Sinterkatode f, Pulverglühkatode f
powder density	s. apparent density
powder diagram	s. Debye-Scherrer pattern
powder diffraction	Beugung f am Pulver, Pulverbeugung f
powder diffraction method, powder diffractometry	s. Debye-Scherrer method
powdered core	s. dust core
powdered-core variometer	Massekernvariometer n
powdered crystal, crystal powder	Kristallpulver n
powdered-crystal method [of X-ray diffraction]	s. Debye-Scherrer method
powdered-crystal pattern (photograph)	s. Debye-Scherrer pattern
powdering, pulverization, pulverizing	Pulverisieren n
powdering	s. a. rubbing
powder magnet	Pulvermagnet m
powder metallurgy	Pulvermetallurgie f, Metallkeramik f, Sintermetallurgie f
powder method	s. Debye-Scherrer method
powder pattern	s. Bitter figure
powder pattern (photograph)	s. Debye-Scherrer pattern
powder photography	s. Debye-Scherrer method
powdery avalanche	s. dry snow avalanche
powdery sand	Mehlsand m, mehlfeiner Sand m; Schluff[sand] m
Powell band	Powellscher Streifen m
power, capacity	Leistungsvermögen n, Kapazität f, Leistung f
power, useful energy, energy	Nutzenergie f, nutzbare Energie f
power, length strength parameter <of electronic lens>	Lichtstärke f <Elektronenlinse>
power <of optical system, telescope>	Leistung f <optisches System, Fernrohr>
power <math.>	Potenz f <Math.>
power, potency; cardinal, cardinal number; cardinality <math.>	Mächtigkeit f; Kardinalzahl f <Math.>
power <mech.>	Leistung f <Mech.>
power <stat.>	Macht f <Stat.>
power	s. a. focal power <opt.>
power	s. a. active power <el.>
power absorption	s. consumption
power amplification, power gain	Leistungsverstärkung f

power amplification coefficient, power amplification ratio, power gain	Leistungsverstärkungsfaktor m, Leistungsverstärkung f	power law of distribution	Potenzverteilung f, Potenzverteilungsgesetz n
power at the terminals, terminal power	Klemmenleistung f, Klemmleistung f	power law spectrum, power spectrum	Potenzspektrum n
power capacitor	Leistungskondensator m	power level, sound power level, acoustic power level ‹ac.›	Schalleistungspegel m
power coefficient	Leistungsbedarfszahl f	power level ‹nucl., meas.›	Leistungspegel m ‹Kern., Meß.›; Leistungshöhe f, Leistungsniveau n ‹Kern.›
power coefficient [of reactivity]	Leistungskoeffizient m [der Reaktivität]		
power conservation law	s. law of conservation of power	power level of the reactor, power of the reactor, reactor power, reactor power level	Leistung f des Reaktors, Reaktorleistung f
power consumption	s. consumption ‹el.›		
power control rod	Leistungsregelstab m, Regelstab m		
		power limiting	Leistungsbegrenzung f
		power line	Starkstromleitung f
power conversion	Leistungsumsetzung f, Leistungsumwandlung f	power-line frequency, line frequency, mains frequency, [power] supply frequency	Netzfrequenz f
power conversion	s. a. transformation of energy		
power converter	Leistungswandler m, Leistungsumsetzer m, Leistungskonverter m	power line hum, alternating-current (mains line) hum; hum; ripple	Brumm m, Brummen n; Netzbrumm m, Netzbrummen n
power current, heavy current	Starkstrom m	power loop ‹of oscillograph›	Leistungsmeßschleife f, Leistungsschleife f ‹Lichtstrahloszillograph›
power delivery	s. actual output		
power demand	s. consumption ‹el.›	power magnetron	Hochleistungsmagnetron n
power density	Leistungsdichte f	power matching	Leistungsanpassung f
		power meter	Leistungsmesser m, Leistungsmeßgerät n
		power meter	s. a. wattmeter
power density spectrum	s. power spectrum ‹el.›	power noise, power fluctuation ‹of reactor›	Leistungsrauschen n, Leistungsschwankung f ‹Reaktor›
power detector	s. anode detector		
power directive coefficient	Leistungsrichtfaktor m	power of adsorption, adsorption ability, adsorption capacity	Adsorptionsfähigkeit f
power directivity pattern, power pattern	Leistungsrichtdiagramm n	power of capacitor	Kondensatorleistung f
power divider	Leistungsteiler m	power of force	s. power ‹mech.›
powered flight, active flight, rocket flight	Antriebsflug m, Treibflug m	power of ten	s. tenth power
		power of the continuum / having (of) the, continuum infinite	von der Mächtigkeit des Kontinuums, kontinuumsmächtig
power equalizer	Echofalle f	power of the point	Potenz f [des Punktes]
power excursion	Leistungsexkursion f, plötzlicher Leistungsanstieg m; Leistungsdurchgang m	power of the pulse, pulse power	Impulsleistung f, Impulsstoßleistung f, Leistung f je Impuls
power extraction, taking (removal, extraction) of power	Leistungsentnahme f; Leistungsentzug m	power of the reactor, power level of the reactor, reactor power, reactor power level	Leistung f des Reaktors, Reaktorleistung f
power factor ‹el.›	Leistungsfaktor m, Wirkfaktor m ‹El.›	power of the test ‹stat.›	Trennschärfe f des Tests, Teststärke f, Strenge f des Tests ‹Stat.›
power-factor indicator, power-factor meter, phase meter, phasometer	Leistungsfaktormesser m, Phasenmesser m, Phasenmeßgerät n, Phasenanzeiger m, cos φ-Messer m	power operation, power regime	Leistungsbetrieb m
		power oscillation ‹of reactor›	Leistungsschwingung f ‹Reaktor›
power flow	Leistungsfluß m	power output, output power, output	Ausgangsleistung f, Output m; Leistungsabgabe f, abgegebene Leistung f
power flow per unit area	s. energy flux density ‹gen., el.›		
power fluctuation ‹el.›	Leistungsschwankung f, Leistungspendelung f, Leistungsschwebung f ‹El.›	power output	s. a. actual output
		power pack, power unit, power supply unit, mains unit, feed equipment, feed power pack	Netz[anschluß]teil m (n), Netzanschlußgerät n, Netzgerät n; Speisegerät n; Stromversorgungsgerät n
power fluctuation	s. power noise ‹of reactor›		
power fluctuation	s. a. current fluctuation		
power frequency converter, inverter, converter, frequency converter ‹el.›	Umrichter m ‹El.›; Umkehrrohr n	power pattern, power directivity pattern	Leistungsrichtdiagramm n
		power per unit area	Leistung f je Oberflächeneinheit (Flächeneinheit), Flächendichte f der Leistung; Leistungsbelag m
powerful test	trennscharfer Test m		
power function ‹math.›	Potenzfunktion f ‹Math.›	power pile	s. power reactor
power function ‹stat.›	Schärfefunktion f, Machtfunktion f, Gütefunktion f, Powerfunktion f ‹Stat.›	power plant	Energieerzeugungsanlage f
		power producer	s. power reactor
power gain, power amplification ratio, power amplification coefficient	Leistungsverstärkungsfaktor m, Leistungsverstärkung f	power production	s. energy generation
		power range	Leistungsbereich m; Ausgleichbereich m
power gain, power amplification	Leistungsverstärkung f	power reactor, power pile, power producer	Leistungsreaktor m, Energiereaktor m; Kraftwerk[s]reaktor m; Antriebsreaktor m
power gain	s. a. aerial gain		
power generation	s. energy generation		
power input	s. consumption		
power klystron, high-power klystron	Leistungsklystron n, Hochleistungsklystron n	power recorder	Leistungsschreiber m; linearer Leistungsschreiber
power law	Potenzgesetz n		
power law filter, exponential filter	Potenzfilter n		

power rectifier	Netzgleichrichter m, Hochstromgleichrichter m, Leistungsgleichrichter m
power regime, power operation	Leistungsbetrieb m
power requirement	s. consumption <el.>
power series	[beständig (überall) konvergente] Potenzreihe f
power source, source of power; source of energy, energy source	Energiequelle f; Energieträger m; Kraftquelle f
power source, source of current, current source	Stromquelle f
power spectrum, power law spectrum	Potenzspektrum n
power spectrum, power density spectrum <el.>	Leistungsspektrum n, Leistungsdichtespektrum n, Spektraldichte f [der Leistung] <El.>
power stroke, working stroke	Arbeitstakt m, Verbrennungstakt m
power supply, electric supply, current supply, supply <el.>	Stromversorgung f; Leistungseinströmung f; Hilfsenergie f <El.>
power supply, mains supply, mains electricity supply, mains connection <el.>	Netzanschluß m <El.>
power supply frequency, [power-]line frequency, mains frequency, supply frequency	Netzfrequenz f
power supply unit	s. power pack
power theorem	Leistungstheorem n
power thyratron	Hochleistungsthyratron n
power transfer factor, response to power	Leistungsübertragungsfaktor m
power triangle	Leistungsdreieck n
power unit	s. power pack
Poynting analyzer	s. Poynting polarimeter
Poynting effect	Poynting-Effekt m
Poynting polarimeter, Poynting analyzer	Poyntingsches Polarimeter n, Polarimeter von Poynting
Poynting-Robertson effect	Poynting-Robertson-Effekt m
Poynting['s] theorem	Poyntingscher Satz m, Energiesatz m der Elektrodynamik, Poyntingsches Gesetz n
Poynting-Thomson body, anelastic material, Thomson['s] body	Poynting-Thomson-Körper m, [Poynting-]Thomsonscher Körper m, anelastische Substanz f
Poynting['s] vector	s. energy flux density <gen., el.>
ppb, p.p.b.	s. part per billion
p-p interaction, proton-proton interaction	Proton-Proton-Wechselwirkung f, p-p-Wechselwirkung f
p-p junction, p-p+ junction	pp-Übergang m, pp-Schicht f, pp+-Übergang m
ppm, p.p.m.	s. part per million
PPM	s. pulse-position modulation
p-position, para-position	para-Stellung f, p-Stellung f
p-p range, proton-proton range	Proton-Proton-Reichweite f, p-p-Reichweite f
PP ray, PP wave, longitudinal wave once-reflected downwards at the Earth's outer surface	PP-Welle f, einfach reflektierte Longitudinalwelle f
p process	p-Prozeß m
P-product, Dyson['s] chronological product	P-Produkt n, Dysonsches Produkt n
PP wave	s. PP ray
practical efficiency	praktischer Wirkungsgrad m
practical electromotive series, practical potential series	praktische Spannungsreihe f
practical enthalpy	praktische Enthalpie f
practical entropy	praktische Entropie f
practical geodesy	s. surveying
practical grade	s. engineering-grade
practical potential series, practical electromotive series	praktische Spannungsreihe f
practical resolving power	praktisches Auflösungsvermögen n
practical system of units, practical units system	praktisches Einheitensystem n, praktisches Maßsystem n
practical unit	praktische Einheit f, praktische Maßeinheit f
practical units system	s. practical system of units
Prager['s] function	Pragersche Funktion f
Prager['s] [theory of] plasticity	Pragersche Plastizitätstheorie f
Prandtl['s] analogy	s. soap film analogy
Prandtl angle	Prandtlscher Winkel m
Prandtl[-] body, elastic-plastic body	Prandtlscher Körper m, elastisch-plastischer Körper, elastisch-plastische Substanz f
Prandtl['s] boundary layer	Prandtlsche Grenzschicht f
Prandtl['s] boundary layer approximation	Prandtlsche Grenzschichtnäherung f
Prandtl['s] boundary layer equations	Prandtlsche Grenzschichtgleichungen fpl, [Prandtlsche] Grenzschicht-Differentialgleichungen fpl
Prandtl['s] boundary layer theory, Prandtl['s] theory of boundary layer	Prandtlsche Grenzschichttheorie f
Prandtl-Busemann characteristic line diagram	s. characteristic diagram
Prandtl-Busemann graphical procedure	Prandtl-Busemannsches graphisches Verfahren n
Prandtl['s] correspondence rules	s. Prandtl-Glauert law
Prandtl['s] equation [for the circulation]	Prandtlsche Tragflügelgleichung (Integralgleichung, Integro-Differentialgleichung, Zirkulationsgleichung) f
Prandtl-Glauert law, Prandtl-Glauert rule, Prandtl['s] correspondence rules	Prandtl-Glauertsche Regel f, Prandtlsche Korrespondenzregeln fpl
Prandtl group	s. Prandtl-No.
Prandtl['s] jet spectrum	Prandtlsches Strahlenbild n
Prandtl['s] lifting line theory, simple lifting line theory	Prandtlsche Theorie f der tragenden Linie, Prandtlsche (einfache) Traglinientheorie f
Prandtl-Meyer expansion	s. Prandtl-Meyer flow
Prandtl-Meyer flow, Prandtl-Meyer expansion, centred expansion fan	Prandtl-Meyersche Expansion (Strömung, Eckenströmung) f, Prandtl-Meyer-Expansion f, Prandtl-Meyer-Strömung f, Prandtlcher Expansionskeil (Ausdehnungskeil) m
Prandtl-Meyer function	Prandtl-Meyersche Funktion f
Prandtl-Meyer wave	Meyer-Prandtlsche Welle f, Meyer-Prandtl-Welle f
Prandtl['s] mixing length, mixing length	[Prandtlscher] Mischungsweg m, [Prandtlsche] Mischungslänge f
Prandtl-No., Prandtl['s] number, Prandtl group, Pr	Prandtl-Zahl f, Prandtlsche Kennzahl f, Prandtlsche Zahl f, Pr
Pandtl['s] relation <for shock waves>	Prandtlsche Beziehung f <Stoßwellen>
Prandtl-Reuss body, Prandtl-Reuss material	Prandtl-Reußscher Körper m
Prandtl-Reuss equations, Reuss equations	Prandtl-Reußsche (Reußsche) Gleichungen fpl
Prandtl-Reuss material	s. Prandtl-Reuss body
Prandtl-Reuss theory, Reuss['] theory	Prandtl-Reußsche Theorie f, Reußsche Theorie f
Prandtl['s] rule	Prandtlsche Regel f

Prandtl['s] theory of boundary layer, Prandtl['s] boundary layer theory	Prandtlsche Grenzschichttheorie f	precipitate, deposit, precipitation [product] <chem.>	Niederschlag m, Präzipitat n, Fällprodukt n, Ausfällung f, Bodensatz m; Ausscheidung f <Chem.>
Prandtl['s] torsion function, torsion (warping) function	Torsionsfunktion f, Prandtlsche Torsionsfunktion f	precipitating	s. precipitation <chem.>
		precipitating agent	s. precipitant
Prandtl['s] tube	Prandtlsches Staurohr n, Prandtl-Rohr n, Prandtlsches Rohr n, Staugerät n [nach Prandtl], Staurohr n [nach Prandtl]	precipitating alloy, precipitation-hardening alloy	Ausscheidungslegierung f
		precipitating fusion, bottom fusion	niederschlagendes Schmelzen n, Niederschlagsschmelzen n
Prandtl-Vandrey['s] law	Prandtl-Vandreysches Fließgesetz n, Fließgesetz nach Prandtl-Vandrey	precipitation <in electrolysis>	Abscheidung f, Ausscheidung f <Elektrolyse>
Pratt-Hayford isostatic system, Pratt-Hayford system	Isostasie f nach Pratt [Hayford]; isostatisches System n nach Pratt[-Hayford]	precipitation; demixing; separation; segregation <of emulsion>	Entmischung f, Zerfall m <Gemisch>
		precipitation, separation <of vacancy>	Ausscheidung f <Leerstelle>
P ray, P wave, longitudinal wave <geo.>	P-Welle f, Longitudinalwelle f <Geo.>	precipitation, precipitating, deposition <chem.>	Fällung f; Ausfällung f; Präzipitieren n; Ausfallen n; Fallen n; Niederschlagen n, Niederschlag m <Chem.>
pre-absorption	Vorabsorption f		
preacceleration	Vorbeschleunigung f	precipitation, atmospheric precipitation, rainfall <meteo.>	Niederschlag m, atmosphärischer Niederschlag <Meteo.>
preaccelerator, preinjector	Vorbeschleuniger m, Vorinjektor m		
pre[-]accentuation	s. pre[-]emphasis	precipitation	s. a. precipitate <chem.>
pre-adaptation	Voradaptation f	precipitation	s. a. segregation <met.>
		precipitation analysis, volumetric precipitation analysis	Fällungsanalyse f, Fällungsmaßanalyse f, Gewichtsanalyse f
preag[e]ing, artificial ag[e]ing	Voralterung f, künstliche Alterung f, Alterungsvorbehandlung f		
		precipitation enthalpy	s. precipitation heat
pre[-]amp	s. pre[-]amplifier	precipitation fractionation	Fällungsfraktionierung f
pre[-]amplifier, pre[-]amp; head amplifier	Vorverstärker m, Anfangsstufenverstärker m; Kopfverstärker m	precipitation gauge	s. rain gauge
		precipitation hardening, age-hardening, dispersion hardening	Aushärtung f, Ausscheidungshärtung f, Altershärtung f
pre-amplifier stage	Vorverstärkerstufe f		
pre-annealing, preliminary annealing	Vorglühen n	precipitation-hardening alloy, precipitating alloy	Ausscheidungslegierung f
preassigned	s. pre[-]set	precipitation heat; precipitation enthalpy	Fällungswärme f; Fällungsenthalpie f
pre bombardment analysis	Vorbestrahlungsanalyse f		
pre-breakdown current, pre-breakdown electric current	Vordurchschlagstrom m	precipitation index	Niederschlagsfaktor m
		precipitation polymerization	Fällungspolymerisation f
preceding spot, p-spot, leading sunspot, leading spot, leader, western spot	P-Fleck m, vorangehender Fleck m	precipitation potential	Abscheidungspotential n
		precipitation product	s. precipitate
		precipitation recorder	s. rain gauge
precession; precessional motion	Präzession f; Präzessionsbewegung f	precipitation rule <of Fajans or Hahn>	Fällungsregel f <Fajans>; Fällungssatz m, Fällungsregel <Hahn>, Hahnsche Fällungsregel
precessional constant, Newcomb['s] precession constant, Newcomb['s] constant	Newcombsche Präzessionskonstante f, Newcombsche Konstante f, Präzessionskonstante		
		precipitation titration	Fällungstitration f
precessional motion	s. precession	precipitator	s. precipitant
precession camera [of Buerger]	Buergerscher Retigraph m	precise level, precise levelling instrument	Präzisionsnivellier[instrument] n, Feinnivellier n
		precise levelling, precision levelling	Präzisionsnivellement n, Feinnivellement n, Feineinwägung f
		precise levelling instrument	s. precise level
precession cone	Präzessionskegel m	precision balance	Präzisionswaage f, Feinwaage f
precession magnet, precessor	Präzessionsmagnet m, Spinpräzessionsmagnet m	precision gauge block	s. end block
precession of orbit	Präzession f der Bahn, Bahnpräzession f	precision instrument, precision measuring instrument, precision meter, high-accuracy instrument	Präzisionsmeßgerät n, Präzisions[meß]instrument n, Präzisionsgerät n, Feinmeßgerät n
precession of the equinoxes	Vorrücken n der Tagundnachtgleichen, Verlagerung, (Verschiebung, Präzession) f der Äquinoktialpunkte, allgemeine Präzession		
		precision levelling	s. precise levelling
		precision magnifier, measuring magnifier, scale magnifying glass	Feinmeßlupe f, Meßlupe f
precession time	Präzessionszeit f		
precessor, precession magnet	Präzessionsmagnet m, Spinpräzessionsmagnet m	precision measuring instrument	s. precision instrument
		precision meter	s. precision instrument
prechamber	Vorkammer f	precision micrometer eyepiece	Feinmeßokular n
precipitability, settleability	Fällbarkeit f, Ausfällbarkeit f		
precipitable water	ausfällbares Wasser n	precision mirror instrument, mirror-type precision instrument	Spiegelfeinmeßgerät n
precipitant, precipitator, precipitating agent	Fällungsmittel n, Fällmittel n, Fällungsreagens n		
		precision of image	s. image sharpness
		precision of measurement	s. accuracy of measurement
		precision screw	Feinmeßschraube f

precision theodolite	Feinmeßtheodolit m, Präzisionstheodolit m, Sekundentheodolit m	pre[-]emphasis, pre[-]accentuation, accentuation	Preemphasis f, Akzentuierung f, Vorverzerrung f
precleaning	Vorreinigung f		
precompression; supercharging	Vorverdichtung f	preevacuation pump	s. forepump
precondensation, preliminary condensation	Vorkondensation f	pre-existent, pre-existing	präexistent
		pre-expansion saturation	Sättigung f vor der Expansion
preconduction current	Vor[entladungs]strom m	preexponential [factor]	präexponentieller Faktor m; Proportionalitätsfaktor m, exponentieller Vorfaktor m ‹Exponentialgesetz›
precorrosion, preliminary corrosion	Vorkorrosion f		
precursor ‹bio.›	Vorstufe f, Precursor m ‹Bio.›		
precursor, fore-runner ‹géo.›	Vorläufer m ‹Geo.›	pre-exponential factor	s. a. frequency factor ‹in the Arrhenius equation›
precursor	s. a. delayed neutron emitter ‹nucl.›	pre-exposure, preliminary [uniform] exposure, extra exposure, prefogging	Vorbelichtung f
precursor	s. a. predecessor		
predawn enhancement	Vordämmerungsverstärkung f		
predecessor ‹math.›; precursor, progenitor ‹nucl.›	Vorgänger m	preference region	Entscheidungsbereich m
		preference relation	Präferenzbeziehung f
pre-deflection	Vorablenkung f; Vorauslenkung f	preference zone	Entscheidungszone f
predesigned	s. pre[-]set	preferential absorption	bevorzugte Absorption f, Vorzugsabsorption f
predetermination, prediction	Vorausbestimmung f, Vorausberechnung f, Vorherberechnung f	preferential direction	s. preferred orientation
		preferential recombination	Vorzugsrekombination f, bevorzugte Rekombination f
predetermination ‹bio.›	Prädetermination f ‹Bio.›	preferential solvation	s. selective solvation
predetermined	s. pre[-]set	preferred axis, privileged axis	Vorzugsachse f, bevorzugte Achse f, Hauptachse f
predetonation; preknock	vorzeitige Detonation f		
		preferred direction	s. preferred orientation
predicate ‹math.›	Attribut n, Prädikat n ‹Math.›	preferred direction of magnetization	s. easy direction of magnetization
predicate calculus, functional calculus, quantification theory, predicate logic	Prädikatenkalkül m, Funktionenkalkül m, Attributenkalkül n, Relationenkalkül n, Prädikatenlogik f, Quantorenlogik f	preferred orientation, privileged direction, preferred direction, preferential direction; high-preferred orientation, h.p.o.	bevorzugte Orientierung (Richtung) f, Vorzugsorientierung f, Vorzugsrichtung f, Hauptrichtung f
predicated variable, regressor, determining variable, explanatory (cause) variable	Regressor m; Einflußgröße f	preferred orientation / with, textured	mit Textur, texturbehaftet, vorzugsgerichtet, texturiert
predictand ‹meteo.›	Vorhersageelement n. ‹Meteo.›	preferred plane	Vorzugsebene f
predictand	s. regressand	prefield lens	Vorfeldlinse f
predicted value	s. theoretical value	prefilter, first filter	Vorfilter n
predictibility	Vorhersagbarkeit f		
predicting filter	Filter n mit Vorhalt		
		prefix, pre-pulse, prepulse ‹tv.›	Vorlaufimpuls m; Vorimpuls m; Vorläufer m; Frühimpuls m ‹Fs.›
prediction	s. predetermination		
prediction; forecast, forecasting; prognosis, prognostication	Vorhersage f, Voraussage f, Prognose f	prefix used in the metric system	Dezimalvorsatz m, Dezimalpräfix n, Vorsatz m zur Bildung eines Vielfachen oder Teiles von metrischen Einheiten
prediction, lead ‹control›	Vorhalt m ‹Regelung›		
prediction	s. a. theoretical value	prefocusing, preliminary focusing	Vorfokussierung f
prediction function	s. predictor		
prediction theory	Vorhersagetheorie f	prefocusing lens	Vorsammellinse f
predictor, prediction function	Prädiktor m, Vorhersagefunktion f	pre-focus lamp	Prefocuslampe f
predischarge	Vorentladung f	prefogging	s. pre-exposure
predischarge pulse	Vorentladungsimpuls m	prefolded filter	s. folded filter
predischarge vorticity equation; vorticity equation	Wirbelgleichung f; Vorticitygleichung f ‹Geo.›	preformed precipitate	vorgefällter Niederschlag m
		prefrontal fog	Vorfrontennebel m
predissociation	Prädissoziation f	prefrontal situation	präfrontale Lage f
predissociation limit	Prädissoziationsgrenze f, Prädissoziationsschwelle f	p-region	p-leitende Zone f, p-leitender Bereich m, p-Gebiet n, p-Zone f, p-Schicht f
predissociation time	Prädissoziationszeit f		
predominance	Überwiegen n, Übergewicht n, Vorherrschen n	preheating	Vorwärmung f; Vorerhitzung f, Vorerwärmung f; Anwärmung f, Anheizung f
predominant mode	s. dominant mode ‹of waveguide›		
Predvodytelev number	Predwodytelew-Zahl f, Predwodytelewsche Kennzahl f	preheating ‹el.›	Vorheizung f ‹El.›
		preheat[ing] time	s. warm-up time
		prehension	s. hold-back
pre-echo, leading echo	Vorecho n	prehistory, history	Vorgeschichte f

preimage, inverse image, antecedent <math.>	Urbild n, Original n <Math.>	preparation technique	Präpariertechnik f
preinjector, preaccelerator	Vorbeschleuniger m, Vorinjektor m	preparative electrophoresis	präparative Elektrophorese f
preionization	s. autoionization	preparatory treatment; pretreatment; prior processing	Vorbehandlung f; Vorbearbeitung f
pre-ionized channel	vorionisierter Kanal m		
prejudicial resistance	s. parasite drag	preplanetary cloud, protoplanetary cloud	Urwolke f
preliminary alloy	Vorlegierung f		
preliminary annealing, pre-annealing	Vorglühen n	prepolarized	vorpolarisiert
preliminary condensation, precondensation	Vorkondensation f	p representation, momentum representation	Impulsdarstellung f, p-Darstellung f
preliminary corrosion, precorrosion	Vorkorrosion f	pre-pulse, prepulse, prefix <tv.>	Vorlaufimpuls m; Vorimpuls m; Vorläufer m; Frühimpuls m <Fs.>
preliminary data, tentation data	vorläufige Werte mpl	prerelativistic	vorrelativistisch
preliminary dispersion	Grobzerlegung f, Vorzerlegung f	prerelativistic region	nichtrelativistischer Bereich
preliminary dose	Vordosis f	prerequisite	s. supposition
preliminary experiment	Vorversuch m	prerosion facet	Prärosionsfläche f
preliminary exposure	s. pre-exposure	presbyopia	Alterssichtigkeit f, Weitsichtigkeit f, Presbyopie f
preliminary focussing	s. prefocusing		
preliminary glow <opt.>	Vorglühen n <Opt.>	prescribed	s. pre[-]set
preliminary investigation, preliminary study	Voruntersuchung f	pre-selected pulse count	s. preset count
		preselection <el.>	Vorwahl f <El.>
		preselection <el.>	Vorselektion f <El.>
		presence	s. residence
		presentation time	Präsentationszeit f
preliminary mechanical magnification	mechanische Vorvergrößerung f, Vorvergrößerung [nach Menzel]	preservation; storage; holding in storage; hold-up; keeping	Lagerung f; Aufbewahrung f, Lagerhaltung f
preliminary melting, premelting	Vorschmelzen n	preservation of angles	s. isogonality <math.>
preliminary membrane	Vormembran[e] f	preserving the separation, distance-preserving	abstandstreu; zwischenstandstreu
preliminary strain	s. prestrain		
preliminary study, preliminary investigation	Voruntersuchung f		
preliminary test, preliminary trial	Vorprüfung f, Vorprobe f, Vorversuch m	pre[-]set, given, predetermined, prescribed, preassigned, predesigned, specified	vorgewählt; voreingestellt; vorgegeben
preliminary twist	Vordrall m		
preliminary uniform exposure	s. pre-exposure	pre-set, semi-fixed	veränderbar zur einmaligen Einstellung
preliminary vacuum	s. fore-vacuum	pre-set adjustment, pre-set control; presetting	Voreinstellung f; Vorwahl f; Vorwahleinstellung f
preliminary work hardening	Vorverfestigung f	pre-set capacitor	veränderbarer Kondensator m [zur einmaligen Einstellung]
preload, minor load, initial load	Vorlast f		
preload Rockwell hardness test, minor load Rockwell hardness test	Vorlast-Härteprüfung f	pre-set control	s. pre-set adjustment
		preset count, preset pulse rate, pre-selected pulse count	vorgewählte (voreingestellte) Impulszahl f, vorgewählte Anzahl f von Impulsen; Impuls[zahl]vorwahl f
premature separation	vorzeitige Trennung f		
pre-maximum	Prämaximum n	preset counting	s. preset pulse counting
premelting, preliminary melting	Vorschmelzen n	preset diaphragm	Vorwahlblende f
premise	s. supposition		
premodification <num. math.>	Vorwegänderung f <num. Math.>	preset parameter	Vorwegparameter m
pre[-]multiplication, pre[-]multiplying, left multiplication	Multiplikation f von links		
pre-nova <pl.: pre-novae>	Pränova f, Praenova f <pl.: Praenovae>	preset pulse counting, preset counting	Zählung (Messung) f mit Impulsvorwahl
		preset pulse rate	s. preset count
		preset shutter	Spannverschluß m; Spannblende f
pre-nova state	Pränovazustand m	preset time	vorgegebene Zeit[spanne] f; vorgewählte Zeit f, voreingestellte Zeit[spanne]; Zeitvorwahl f
pre[-]onset streamer	Sprühvorgänger m [der Koronaentladung], Streamer m vor der Zündung		
pre[-]oscillation	Vorschwingung f	preset time counting	Zählung f mit Zeitvorwahl, Messung f mit Zeitvorwahl
preoscillation current, starting current	Anschwingstrom m	presetting; preset adjustment, preset control	Voreinstellung f; Vorwahl f; Vorwahleinstellung f
preoscillation phenomenon	Anschwingerscheinung f	pre[-]shaping	Vorformung f
preoscillation time	Anschwingzeit f	presolar nebula, primeval nebula, solar nebula	Nebelscheibe f, Urnebel m <Ursonne>
preparation; lining-up	Herstellung f, Bereitung f, Präparation f, Vorbereitung f	pre[-]spark	Vorfunke m
		pressductor	Preßduktor m
preparation	Präparat n		
preparation, batch, charge, trial solution <chem.>	Ansatz m	pressed density	Preßdichte f
		pressed-glass base	Preßglassockel m, Preß[glas]fuß m, Preßteller m, Preßnapf m
preparation of labelled compounds, synthesis of isotopically labelled compounds	Markierungssynthese f	pressing	Pressen n; Verpressen n; Preßformung f

pressing screw, screw press, thumb-screw	Druckschraube f	pressure distribution curve [over the aerofoil section]	Profildruckverteilungskurve f
press pump, pressure pump, force pump	Druckpumpe f	pressure drag, compression resistance, pressure resistance	Druckwiderstand m
pressure	Druck m		
pressure, tension <of vapour>	Druck m, Spannung f <Dampf>	pressure drag, normal-pressure drag <aero.>	Druckwiderstand m <Aero.>
pressure	s. a. voltage <el.>	pressure drop	Druckabfall m; Druckverlust m
pressure accumulator	Druckspeicher m	pressure drop	s. a. pressure jump
pressure altimeter, barometric altimeter, height measuring barometer	barometrischer Höhenmesser m, Höhenbarometer n	pressure due to gravity, gravity pressure, pressure due to the own weight	Schweredruck m
pressure amplitude, sound pressure amplitude	Schalldruckamplitude f, Druckamplitude f	pressure due to shrinkage, contraction (shrinkage) pressure	Schrumpfdruck m
pressure angle <at pitch point>, angle of pressure	Eingriffswinkel m, Eingriffslinienwinkel m <Zahnrad>; Druckwinkel m	pressure due to the own weight, pressure due to gravity, gravity pressure	Schweredruck m
pressure area	s. surface of contact	pressure elasticity	Druckelastizität f
pressure atomization	Druckzerstäubung f	pressure energy	Druckenergie f
		pressure ensemble	„pressure ensemble" n
pressure balance	Druckwaage f	pressure equalizer	Druckausgleicher m
pressure below atmospheric	s. underpressure	pressure equation	Druckgleichung f
pressure box	s. pressure vessel		
pressure broadening	Druckverbreiterung f	pressure field	Druckfeld n
pressure build-up test	Druckanstiegsverfahren n	pressure figure	Druckfigur f
		pressure filter	Druckfilter n
pressure cell	s. pressure vessel		
pressure chamber	Druckkammer f; Druckraum m	pressure float technique	Schwebemethode f mit Druckvariation (Variation des Druckes)
		pressure flow	Druckströmung f
		pressure fluctuation	Druckschwankung f
pressure-chamber loudspeaker, pneumatic loudspeaker	Druckkammerlautsprecher m, Kompressorlautsprecher m, pneumatischer Lautsprecher m	pressure force, compressive force	Druckkraft f; Kompressionskraft f
pressure coefficient	Druckkoeffizient m, Druckbeiwert m	pressure front, shock front, shock [surface]	Stoßfront f, Stoßwellenfront f
		pressure gas	s. pressurized gas
pressure coefficient, C_p, E, Euler['s] number	Eulersche Zahl f, Eu	pressure gauge, pressure meter, pressure-measuring device, manometer, gauge	Druckmesser m, Manometer n
pressure coefficient, coefficient of increase of pressure, stress coefficient	Spannungskoeffizient m, Druckkoeffizient m	pressure-gradient microphone, velocity microphone, velocity sensitive detector of sound	Druckgradientenempfänger m, Druckgradient[en]mikrophon n, Geschwindigkeitsempfänger m, Geschwindigkeitsmikrophon n, Schnelleempfänger m, Schnellemikrophon n, geschwindigkeitsempfindlicher Schalldetektor m
pressure coefficient of clock, barometer error of clock	druckbedingter Gang m der Uhr, barometrischer Fehler m der Uhr		
pressure coefficient of reactivity	Druckkoeffizient m der Reaktivität	pressuregraph	s. pressure recorder
		pressure head	s. dynamic pressure
pressure coefficient of resistance	Druckkoeffizient m des Widerstandes	pressure head	s. static head
		pressure head coefficient, velocity head coefficient	Staudruckbeiwert m
		pressure increase	s. pressure rise
pressure curve, pressure diagram	Druckdiagramm n, Druckkurve f, Drucklinie f	pressure-induced nuclear reaction, pyconuclear reaction	druckinduzierte Kernreaktion f, pyknonukleare Reaktion f
pressure deep drawing	Fließpressen n	pressure-induced spectrum	druckinduziertes Spektrum n
pressure deficiency	s. underpressure	pressure-induced whisker	Druckwhisker m
pressure-defined chamber	Kammer f für veränderlichen Druck, druckgesteuerte (durch Druckänderung gesteuerte) Kammer		
		pressure inside	s. internal pressure
		pressure intensity, static pressure, actual pressure	statischer Druck m, ruhender Druck, Ruhedruck m
pressure-density integral	Druckfunktion f, Druckintegral n	pressure ionization, ionization by pressure	Druckionisation f
		pressure jump, pressure drop	Drucksprung m
pressure deterioration of the luminescence	Druckzerstörung f der Lumineszenz	pressure level, sound pressure level, S.P.L.	Schalldruckpegel m, Schallpegel m
pressure diagram, pressure curve	Druckdiagramm n, Druckkurve f, Drucklinie f	pressure line, pipe under pressure; high-pressure pipe line	Druckleitung f; Hochdruckleitung f
pressure differential	s. differential pressure		
pressure diffusion	Druckdiffusion f, Diffusion f infolge Druckunterschieds		
		pressure line, thrust line, line of thrust	Eingriffslinie f <Zahnrad>; Drucklinie f
pressure displacement	s. pressure shift	pressure line	s. a. thrust line

pressure load, pressure (compressive, compression) stress, compressive (compression) loading, compression — Druckbelastung f, Druckbeanspruchung f

pressure loss, loss of pressure — Druckverlust m

pressure maximum, maximum pressure — Druckmaximum n, Druckberg m; Höchstdruck m, Maximaldruck m

pressure measurement of height — s. barometric measurement of altitude

pressure-measuring device, pressure meter, pressure gauge, manometer, gauge — Druckmesser m, Manometer n

pressure microphone <el.> — Druckmikrophon n, Druckempfänger m <El.>

pressure minimum, minimum pressure — Druckminimum n, Drucktal n, Mindestdruck m

pressure of light, light pressure — Lichtdruck m <Phys.>

pressure of melting, melting pressure — Schmelzdruck m

pressure of mountain mass, pressure of rock, rock pressure — Gebirgsdruck m

pressure of one atmosphere — s. standard pressure <760 Torr>

pressure of rock — s. pression of mountain mass

pressure of sound radiation — s. acoustic radiation pressure

pressure of the column — Säulendruck m

pressure on bearing, pressure on support, bearing pressure — Auflagerdruck m, Auflagedruck m; Stützdruck m, Lagerdruck m

pressure outside, exterior pressure — äußerer Druck m, Außendruck m

pressure permeation — Druckpermeation f

pressure-plate anemometer; Wild['s] pressure plate anemometer, pendulum anemometer — Winddruckmesser m, Winddruckplatte f; Wildsche Stärketafel (Windstärketafel, Tafel) f, Windstärketafel nach Wild, Wildscher Windmesser m, Wildsches Anemometer n, Pendelanemometer n

pressure propagation, transmission of pressure, pressure transmission — Druckfortpflanzung f, Druckübertragung f

pressure pump, press pump, force pump — Druckpumpe f

pressure receptor <bio.> — Druckrezeptor m, Druckempfänger m <Bio.>

pressure recorder, pressuregraph, recording manometer, manograph — Registriermanometer n, Druckschreiber m, Manograph m, registrierendes Manometer n

pressure recovery — Druckrückgewinn m

pressure-reducing valve, reducing valve — Reduzierventil n, Druck[ver]minderungsventil n, Druckminderventil n

pressure relief, pressure relieving, decompression — Druckentlastung f

pressure resistance — s. pressure drag

pressure response — s. sound-pressure transmission factor <ac.>

pressure rise, pressure increase, increase of pressure, elevation of pressure — Druckerhöhung f, Drucksteigerung f; Druckanstieg m

pressure-sealed — s. pressure-tight

pressure sensitivity — Druckempfindlichkeit f

pressure sensitivity — s. a. sound-pressure transmission factor <ac.>

pressure shift, pressure displacement — Druckverschiebung f

pressure shock, compression shock, shock — Verdichtungsstoß m

pressure side, lower surface, high pressure surface <of the airfoil> — Flügelunterseite f, Unterseite f <des Flügels>

pressure side, delivery side <of the pump> — Druckseite f [der Pumpe]

pressure spectrum level, spectrum pressure level — Schalldruckpegel m je Hertz Bandbreite

pressure stress, compressive stress — Druckspannung f, Kompressionsspannung f

pressure stress — s. a. pressure load

pressure surface — s. piezometric surface

pressure surface contour — s. piezometric line

pressure tank — s. pressure vessel

pressure tendency — s. barometric tendency

pressure tensor — Drucktensor m

pressure test — Druckprüfung f

pressure test — s. a. proof test

pressure thermomechanical effect — s. thermomechanical effect

pressure-tight, pressure-sealed — druckdicht

pressure transducer — Druckwandler m

pressure transmission — s. transmission of pressure

pressure tube, force pipe — Druckrohr n

pressure tube, impact tube (pipe) <meas.> — Staurohr n, Staudruckrohr n, Staudruckmesser m; Staudruckfahrtmesser m <Meß.>

pressure-tube anemograph — Druckrohranemograph m; Staudruckanemograph m

pressure-tube anemometer — Druckrohranemometer m, Staudruckanemometer n, Staurohrwindmesser m

pressure tube reactor — Druckröhrenreaktor m

pressure twin, compressive twin — Kippzwilling m, Druckzwilling m, Gleitzwilling m

pressure-type cornice — Druckwächte f

pressure-type Van de Graaff accelerator — Hochdruck-Van-de-Graaff-Generator m, Drucktankgenerator m, Van-de-Graaff-Hochdruckgenerator m

pressure valve — Druckventil n

pressure vessel, high-pressure vessel, pressure tank; pressure cell, pressure box — Druckgefäß n, Druckbehälter m, Drucktank m; Hochdruckbehälter m, Hochdruckgefäß n, Hochdrucktank m

pressure viscosity — s. bulk viscosity

pressure-volume diagram of fluids, Andrews diagram — Andrews-Diagramm n

pressure-volume-temperature relation, equation of state, state equation, characteristic equation <therm.> — Zustandsgleichung f <Therm.>

pressure water — gespanntes Wasser n

pressure wave — Druckwelle f

pressurized gas, pressure gas, compressed gas — Druckgas n, Preßgas n

pressurized water reactor, PWR — Druckwasserreaktor m, druckwassergekühlter Reaktor m, PWR

pressurizer — Druckerzeuger m

pressurizer — s. a. surge tank <therm.>

Preston['s] law (rule) — Prestonsche Regel f

prestrain — Vorverformung f

prestrain, preliminary strain — Vorbeanspruchung f

prestress, prestressing, pretensioning <mech.> — Vorspannung f <Mech.>

prestressed <mech.> — vorgespannt <Mech.>

prestressed glass — Einscheibensicherheitsglas n, vorgespanntes Glas (Sicherheitsglas) n.

prestressing	s. prestress <mech.>	primary cosmic radiation [component], primary cosmic rays, primary component [of cosmic radiation]	Primärkomponente f [der kosmischen Strahlung], Primärstrahlung f, kosmische Primärstrahlung, Nukleonenstrahlung f, primäre Komponente f [der kosmischen Strahlung]
prestressing	s. a. Bauschinger effect		
pre-sub[script]	linker unterer Index m		
presumption	s. supposition		
pre-super[script]	linker oberer Index m		
presupposition	s. supposition		
presynaptic	präsynaptisch		
pretensioning	s. prestress <mech.>		
pretreatment; preparatory treatment; prior processing	Vorbehandlung f; Vorbearbeitung f	primary creep	s. transient creep
		primary dark space	s. Aston's dark space
		primary element	s. sensitive element
		primary emission	Primäremission f, Primärstrahlung f
pretrigger, pre-triggering pulse (signal)	Vortriggerimpuls m		
pre-vacuum pump	s. forepump	primary emitter, primary radiator	Primärstrahler m
prevailing wind; dominant wind	vorherrschender Wind m; herrschender Wind	primary etching	Primärätzung f, Seigerungsätzung f
Prévost filter, rotatory dispersion filter	Rotationsdispersionsfilter n [von Prévost]	primary extinction	primäre Extinktion (Löschung) f
		primary fission yield, independent fission yield	primäre Spalt[produkt]ausbeute f, Fragmentausbeute f
Prévost['s] law	Prévostsches Gesetz n, Prévostscher Satz m	primary focus	s. meridian focal line
Prévost line	Prévost-Burkhardtsche Gerade f	primary frequency, fundamental frequency, basic frequency	Grundfrequenz f, Fundamentalfrequenz f
Prévost['s] theory [of exchange], Prévost['s] theory of heat exchange	Prévostsche Theorie f		
		primary hydration, chemical hydration	primäre Hydratation f, chemische Hydratation
Prey['s] reduction	Preysche Reduktion f		
Price current meter	Price-Flügel m	primary inductance	Primärinduktanz f, induktive Primärreaktanz f, induktiver Blindwiderstand m auf der Primärseite, primärseitiger induktiver Blindwiderstand, Primärinduktion f
Prigogine['s] equation	Gleichung f von Prigogine, Prigoginesche Gleichung, Prigogine-Gleichung f		
Prigogine['s] theorem [of minimum entropy production], principle of minimum production of entropy	Prigogine-Theorem n, Satz m (Theorem n) von Prigogine, Prinzip m der minimalen Entropieproduktion		
		primary ionization	primäre Ionisation (Ionisierung) f, Primärionisation f, Primärionisierung f
primage; water content <of steam>	Wassergehalt m; Wasserhaltigkeit f	primary ionizing event, initial ionizing event	primäres Ionisationsereignis n
primary, primary (initial, original) particle, progenitor	Primärteilchen n, Primäres n	primary ion pair, initial (original) ion pair	primäres Ionenpaar n
		primary light source	s. primary source <of light>
primary, matching stimulus, instrumental stimulus	Meßvalenz f	primary material (matter)	s. ylem
		primary maximum, principal maximum	Hauptmaximum n <Lichtkurve>
primary	s. a. primary component	primary meter, [international] prototype meter, metre des archives	Urmeter n
primary	s. a. primary winding		
primary	s. a. reference stimulus		
primary aberration	s. first-order aberration		
primary acoustical radiator	primärer Schallstrahler m	primary mirror, objective mirror <of telescope>	Hauptspiegel m <Fernrohr>
		primary natural radionuclide	primäres natürliches Radionuklid n $<T_{1/2} > 10^8 a>$
primary back reaction	primäre Rückreaktion f		
primary beam	Primärstrahl m, Primärstrahlenbündel n	primary optic axis, optic binormal, optic axis, line of single normal velocity, axis of single wave velocity	Binormale f, primäre optische Achse f, Achse der [optischen] Isotropie der dielektrischen Verschiebung
primary cell	Primärelement n, Primärzelle f		
primary circuit	s. primary coolant circuit	primary particle, primary, initial (original) particle, progenitor	Primärteilchen n, Primäres n
primary cleavage; parallel (bedding) cleavage	primäre Schieferung f; Parallelschieferung f	primary photochemical process	photochemischer Primärprozeß m, photochemische Primärreaktion f
		primary photocurrent, primary photoelectric current	lichtelektrischer (photoelektrischer) Primärstrom m, primärer Photostrom m
		primary quantity	s. fundamental quantity
		primary radiation	Primärstrahlung f, primäre Strahlung f
primary colour, basic colour, fundamental colour	Urfarbe f, Grundfarbe f, Primärfarbe f	primary radiator, primary emitter	Primärstrahler m
primary component, primary <of binary star>	Hauptkomponente f, Hauptstern m <Doppelsternsystem>	primary rainbow	Hauptregenbogen m
		primary recrystallization texture	s. recrystallization texture
primary component [of cosmic radiation]	s. primary cosmic radiation	primary rock, protogeneous rock, original rock	primäres Gestein n, Primärgestein n, Grundgebirge n, kristallines Gebirge n, Kristallin n; Urgebirge n; Urgestein n
primary condensate, first condensate	Vorkondensat n		
		primary salt effect	primärer Salzeffekt m, Primärsalzeffekt m
primary coolant circuit, primary circuit <of reactor>	erster Kreislauf (Kühlkreislauf) m, Primärkreis m, Primärkreislauf m, Primärkühlkreis[lauf] m <Reaktor>	primary solid solution	s. terminal solid solution
		primary solvation	primäre (chemische) Solvatation f

primary source <of light>, primary light source, self-luminous object; self-luminous surface; self-luminous substance — Primärlichtquelle f; Selbstleuchter m, Erstleuchter m; Selbststrahler m, Eigenstrahler m, selbstleuchtendes Objekt n, selbstleuchtende Fläche f

primary source of alternating current [with zero intrinsic admittance] — Wechsel-Urstromquelle f

primary specific ionization — s. probable specific ionization

primary spectrum, first-order spectrum — Primärspektrum n, Spektrum n erster Ordnung

primary spectrum — s. a. chromatic aberration

primary standard, fundamental standard — Urnormal n, Urmaß n, Primärnormal n, Primärstandard m

primary standard [of light source], primary standard of light, luminous standard — Lichtstärkenormal n, Einheitslichtquelle f, Primärstandard m, Lichtstandard m, Primärnormal n, Lichteinheit f

primary standard X-ray ionization chamber — Faßkammer f

primary titre — Urtiter m

primary titrimetric standart substance — s. titrimetric standard substance

primary tone — s. fundamental tone

primary triangulation — Haupttriangulation f, Triangulation f erster (I.) Ordnung

primary unit — s. fundamental unit

primary valence, primary valency, main valency, principal valency, chief valence — Hauptvalenz f

primary valence bond — Hauptvalenzbindung f

primary valence chain, chain of primary valencies — Hauptvalenzkette f

primary valence force — Hauptvalenzkraft f

primary valency — s. primary valence

primary wave, P-wave — Primärwelle f, P-Welle f

primary winding, primary — Primärwicklung f, primärseitige Wicklung f

prime, prime number <math.> — Primzahl f <Math.>

prime, accent, unison <ac.> — Prime f <Ak.>

prime, accent <sign of operation in math.> — Strich m <Operationszeichen in der Math.>

primed quantity, accented quantity — gestrichene Größe f

prime focus, Newtonian focus — Newton-Fokus m, Primärfokus m

prime meridian — s. zero meridian

prime number, prime <math.> — Primzahl f <Math.>

primer — s. initial detonating agent

primeval nebula, solar nebula, presolar nebula — Nebelscheibe f, Urnebel m <Ursonne>

primeval ocean — s. primitive ocean

prime vertical — Erster Vertikal m

priming — s. bias voltage

priming explosive — s. initial detonating agent

priming grid voltage — s. grid-bias voltage

primitive, simple <of lattice> — primitiv, einfach <Gitter>

primitive — s. a. antiderivative

primitive atom — Uratom n

primitive axis — primitive Achse f

primitive cell — s. unit cell <cryst.>

primitive continent, primordial continent — Urkontinent m

primitive element, primordial element — Urelement n

primitive elementary cell — primitive Elementarzelle f

primitive idempotent [element] — primitive Idempotente f

primitive lattice — s. simple lattice

primitive material (matter) — s. ylem

primitive ocean, primordial ocean, primeval ocean — Urozean m, Urmeer n

primitive period, fundamental period — primitive Periode f

primitive period parallelogram, fundamental periodic parallelogram — Periodenparallelogramm n, Fundamentalparallelogramm n, Elementarparallelogramm n

primitive sublattice — primitives Untergitter n

primordial continent, primitive continent — Urkontinent m

primordial element, primitive element — Urelement n

primordial magma, parental magma — Urmagma n, Stammagma n, Ausgangsmagma n

primordial ocean — s. primitive ocean

primordial plasma — s. ylem

principal angle of incidence — Haupteinfallswinkel m

principal axis of index ellipsoid, principal direction of oscillation — Hauptschwingungsrichtung f, Hauptachse f des Indexellipsoids

principal axis of inertia — Hauptträgheitsachse f, Trägheitshauptachse f

principal axis of permittivity, dielectric principal axis — dielektrische Hauptachse f

principal axis of polarization, principal polarization axis — Polarisationshauptachse f

principal axis of strain — Hauptdilatationsachse f, Hauptachse f des Verformungszustandes (Formänderungszustandes, Verzerrungszustandes)

principal axis of stress, principal stress axis, stress axis — Hauptachse f des Spannungszustandes, Hauptspannungsachse f, Spannungshauptachse f

principal[-] axis transformation — Hauptachsentransformation f

principal bending moment — Hauptbiegemoment n

principal component of strain — s. principal strain

principal component of stress, principal stress — Hauptspannung f

principal conjunctive normal form — ausgezeichnete (kanonische) konjunktive Normalform f

principal co-ordinate system — Hauptachsensystem n

principal curvature — Hauptkrümmung f

principal deformation — s. principal strain

principal diagonal, leading diagonal, [main] diagonal — Hauptdiagonale f; Hauptschräge f

principal dilatation — s. principal strain

principal direction, principal direction of dilation (strain), principal strain direction — Hauptdilatationsrichtung f, Hauptrichtung f [der Verzerrung], Hauptverzerrungsrichtung f

principal direction of curvature — s. direction of principal curvature <math.>

principal direction of dilation — s. principal direction

principal direction of glide — Hauptgleitrichtung f

principal direction of oscillation, principal axis of index ellipsoid — Hauptschwingungsrichtung f, Hauptachse f des Indexellipsoids

principal direction of strain — s. principal direction

principal direction of stress, principal stress direction — Hauptspannungsrichtung f, Haupt[achsen]richtung f des Spannungszustandes

principal disjunctive normal form — ausgezeichnete disjunktive Normalform f, kanonische alternative Normalform f

principal elongation — s. principal strain

principal E plane — Hauptschwingungsebene f des [elektrischen] Feldstärkevektors

principal equation	s. fundamental equation
principal extension	s. principal strain
principal extension ratio, principal strain ratio	Hauptdehnungsverhältnis n
principal flux, useful flux	Nutzfluß m, Hauptfluß m
principal focal length	Hauptbrennweite f
principal focus	Hauptbrennpunkt m
principal function [of Hamilton], Hamilton's principal function, action integral	[Hamiltonsche] Prinzipalfunktion f, [zeitabhängige] Wirkungsfunktion f, Wirkungsintegral n, extremaler Abstand m, geodätische Distanz f, Hamiltons Hauptfunktion f
principal glide system	Hauptgleitsystem n
principal group <math.>	Frattini-Gruppe f, Hauptgruppe f, Φ-Untergruppe f <Math.>
principal horizon point, principal point of horizon	Haupthorizontalpunkt m
principal horizontal [line]	Haupthorizontale f
principal horizontal plane	Haupthorizontalebene f
principal ideal	Hauptideal n
principal ideal ring, PIR, P.I.R.	Hauptidealring m
principal inductance, useful inductance	Hauptinduktivität f, Nutzinduktivität f
principal invariant <of tensor>	Hauptinvariante f <Tensor>
principal lobe, main lobe, major [radiation] lobe, antenna major lobe	Hauptlappen m, Hauptkeule f, Hauptzipfel m, Hauptmaximum n <Richtdiagramm>
principal maximum	s. primary maximum
principal minor	Hauptminor m, Hauptunterdeterminante f; Hauptabschnittsdeterminante f
principal mode	s. dominant mode <of waveguide>
principal mode	s. principal wave
principal moment of inertia	Hauptträgheitsmoment n
principal motion <turbulence>	Hauptbewegung f <Turbulenz>
principal net of the flow, Mach net	Hauptnetz n der Strömung, Machsches Netz n
principal normal; principal normal [unit] vector; unit principal normal [vector], unit first normal [vector]; vector of principal normal	Hauptnormale f; Hauptnormalenvektor m
principal part	Hauptteil m; meromorpher Teil m <Math.>
principal permittivity	Hauptdielektrizitätskonstante f
principal plane, unit plane <opt.>	Hauptebene f <Opt.>
principal plane	s. a. principal section <cryst., opt.>
principal plane of flexure <of beam>	Hauptebene f, Hauptbiegeebene f <Balken>
principal plane of glide	Hauptgleitebene f
principal plane of incidence	Haupteinfallsebene f
principal plane of inertia	Hauptträgheitsebene f
principal plane of symmetry, principal symmetry plane	Hauptsymmetrieebene f
principal point <of aerophotogram>	Hauptpunkt m, Bildhauptpunkt m <Luftmeßbild>
principal point, Gauss point <opt.>	Hauptpunkt m <Opt.>
principal point of horizon, principal horizon point	Haupthorizontalpunkt m
principal point triangulation	Hauptpunkttriangulation f, Bildhauptpunkttriangulation f
principal polarization axis, principal axis of polarization	Polarisationshauptachse f
principal pole	Hauptpol m
principal quantum number, total (main, first) quantum number	Hauptquantenzahl f
principal radius of curvature	s. radius of principal curvature
principal ray, chief ray <opt.>	Hauptstrahl m <Opt.>
principal refractive index	Hauptbrechungsindex m
principal section; principal section plane, principal plane, plane of principal section <cryst., opt.>	Hauptschnitt m; Hauptschnittebene f <Krist., Opt.>
principal series	Hauptserie f, Prinzipalserie f
principal shear[ing] stress	Hauptschubspannung f
principal shock	Hauptstoß m; Hauptwelle f
principal solution, fundamental solution	Grundlösung f, Fundamentallösung f, Fundamentalintegral n
principal spectrum <of nova>	Hauptspektrum n <Nova>
principal strain, principal stretch[ing] (extension, dilatation, deformation, elongation, component of strain)	Hauptdehnung f, Hauptdilatation f, Hauptverlängerung f, Hauptstreckung f, Hauptverformung f
principal strain direction	s. principal direction
principal strain ratio	s. principal extension ratio
principal stress, principal component of stress	Hauptspannung f
principal stress axis, principal axis of stress, stress axis	Hauptachse f des Spannungszustandes, Hauptspannungsachse f, Spannungshauptachse f
principal stress direction	s. principal direction of stress
principal stress moment	Hauptwiderstandsmoment n
principal stress ratio	Hauptspannungsverhältnis n
principal stress trajectory	s. trajectory of principal stresses
principal stretch[ing]	s. principal strain
principal surface <opt.>	Hauptfläche f <Opt.>
principal surface tension	Hauptoberflächenspannung f
principal symmetry plane, principal plane of symmetry	Hauptsymmetrieebene f
principal tensile stress	Hauptzugspannung f
principal trajectory <of tensor field>	Haupttrajektorie f <Tensorfeld>
principal valency	s. primary valence
principal value <of analytical function>	Hauptwert m, Hauptzweig m <analytische Funktion>
principal value	s. a. eigenvalue <of a matrix>
principal value of the integral, Cauchy's principal value	Cauchyscher Hauptwert m, Hauptwert [des Integrals]
principal vanishing point	Hauptfluchtpunkt m; Hauptverschwindungspunkt m
principal vector	Hauptvektor m
principal velocity of light	Hauptlichtgeschwindigkeit f
principal vertical [line]	Hauptvertikale f
principal vertical plane	Hauptvertikalebene f
principal wave, transverse electromagnetic wave, TEM-wave, principal mode, transverse electromagnetic mode, TEM mode	TEM-Welle f, transversalelektromagnetische Welle (Mode) f, transversale elektromagnetische Welle, TEM-Mode f, Lecher-[Typ-]Welle f, L-[Typ-]Welle f, Leitungswelle f
principle of action, action principle	Wirkungsprinzip n
principle of action and reaction	s. Newton['s] third law

principle

principle of balayage	„balayage"-Prinzip n	principle of increase of entropy	s. second law
principle of Blackmann and Putter	s. Blackmann-Putter['s] principle	principle of indeterminacy	s. indeterminacy principle
principle of Carathéodory	s. principle of inaccessibility	principle of indistinguishability, indistinguishability principle	Ununterscheidbarkeitsprinzip n
principle of causality, causality (causal) principle	Kausalitätsprinzip n, Kausalprinzip n, Kausalgesetz n	principle of interchange	Austauschprinzip n
principle of charged particle coherent acceleration, charged particle principle of coherent acceleration	Prinzip n der kohärenten Beschleunigung geladener Teilchen	principle of irritability	Gesetz n der spezifischen Energien
		principle of Lagrange and d'Alembert	s. Lagrange-d'Alembert principle
principle of choice	s. axiom of choice	principle of least action, least action principle	Prinzip n der kleinsten Wirkung (Aktion), Prinzip der stationären Wirkung
principle of complementarity, complementarity principle	Komplementaritätsprinzip n		
principle of conservation of angular momentum	s. angular momentum conservation law	principle of least action	s. a. Hamilton['s] principle
		principle of least action [of Maupertuis]	s. Maupertuis['] principle
principle of conservation of areas, integral of areas, law of areas, Kepler['s] second law, Kepler['s] area law	Flächensatz m, zweites Keplersches Gesetz n	principle of least constraint, principle of the least constraint <mech.>	Gaußsches Prinzip n [des kleinsten Zwanges], Prinzip des kleinsten Zwanges, Prinzip vom kleinsten Zwang <Mech.>
principle of conservation of areas	s. a. angular momentum conservation law	principle of least curvature, Hertz['] principle	Prinzip n der geradesten Bahn, [Hertzsches] Prinzip der kleinsten Krümmung, Hertzsches Prinzip [der geradesten Bahn]; Prinzip der kürzesten Bahn
principle of conservation of density-in-phase, Liouville['s] theorem, Liouville['s] principle <stat.>	Liouvillescher Satz m, Liouville-Boltzmannscher Satz		
principle of conservation of electric charge	s. law of conservation of charge	principle of least proper time, principle of stationary proper time, Fermat['s] principle of least proper time, Fermat['s] principle in relativity	[Fermatsches] Prinzip n der stationären Eigenzeit, Prinzip der stationären Weltlinie, relativistisches Fermatsches Prinzip
principle of conservation of linear momentum	s. momentum conservation law		
principle of conservation of mass (matter)	s. law of conservation of mass		
principle of conservation of momentum	s. angular momentum conservation law	principle of least squares	s. least squares method
principle of conservation of momentum	s. momentum conservation law	principle of least time	s. Fermat['s] principle
		principle of least work, theorem of minimum potential energy, theorem of minimum energy, principle of potential energy, principle of minimum strain energy, minimum potential energy theorem, theorem of minimum potential	Prinzip n der kleinsten Formänderungsarbeit, Satz m von Menabrea, Satz vom Minimum der potentiellen Energie, Minimalprinzip n für die Verschiebungen eines elastischen Körpers
principle of conservation of parity	s. law of conservation of parity		
principle of continuity, continuity equation, equation of continuity	Kontinuitätsgleichung f		
principle of continuity of path	s. ergodic hypothesis		
principle of continuity of states	Prinzip n der Kontinuität der Zustände		
principle of correspondence	s. correspondence principle	principle of Le Chatelier [and Braun]	s. Le Chatelier['s] principle
principle of corresponding states	s. theorem of corresponding states	principle of linear momentum, momentum theorem, momentum equation, momentum law, theorem of momentum <mech., hydr.>	Impulssatz m
principle of detailed balance, principle of detailed balancing, principle of microscopic reversibility	Prinzip n des detaillierten Gleichgewichts, Prinzip vom detaillierten Gleichgewicht, Prinzip der mikroskopischen Reversibilität (Umkehrbarkeit)		
		principle of linear superposition	Prinzip n der linearen Überlagerung
principle of dissipation, Clausius-Duhem inequality	Dissipationsprinzip n, Clausius-Duhemsche Ungleichung f	principle of mass-energy equivalence	s. principle of equivalence
principle of duality, duality principle	Dualitätsprinzip n	principle of material frame indifference, material [frame-]indifference principle	Unabhängigkeit f der Materialgleichungen vom Beobachter, Prinzip n der Bezugsindifferenz
principle of economy, economy principle	Sparsamkeitsregel f [von Pauling]		
principle of entropy increase	s. second law	principle of Maupertuis	s. Maupertuis['] principle
principle of equipartition [of energy]	s. law of equipartition [of energy]	principle of maximum work, maximum work principle	Prinzip n der maximalen Arbeit
principle of equipresence, equipresence principle	Äquipräsenzprinzip n, Prinzip n der Äquipräsenz		
principle of equivalence [of mass and energy]	s. equivalence of mass and energy principle	principle of microscopic reversibility	s. principle of detailed balancing
principle of general covariance, covariance principle	Kovarianzprinzip n, Prinzip n der allgemeinen Kovarianz	principle of minimum, minimum principle	Minimumprinzip n; Minimalprinzip n <Math., Mech.>
principle of gradual construction	s. aufbauprinciple	principle of minimum dissipation of energy	Prinzip n der minimalen Energiedissipation
principle of hydrodynamic images, method of hydrodynamic images, method of images [in hydrodynamics]	Prinzip n der hydrodynamischen Bilder, Methode f der hydrodynamischen Bilder		
		principle of minimum dissipation of entropy	Prinzip n der minimalen Entropiedissipation
principle of inaccessibility, inaccessibility axiom [of Carathéodory], Carathéodory['s] axiom of inaccessibility, principle of Carathéodory, Carathéodory['s] principle	Carathéodorysches Unerreichbarkeitsaxiom n, Unerreichbarkeitsaxiom [von Carathéodory], [Carathéodorysches] Prinzip n der adiabatischen Unerreichbarkeit	principle of minimum entropy, minimum entropy principle	Prinzip n der minimalen Entropie
		principle of minimum production of entropy	s. Prigogine['s] theorem
		principle of minimum strain energy	s. principle of least work

principle

principle of minimum virtual mass	Prinzip *n* der minimalen virtuellen Masse	principle of virtual displacement (work), virtual work principle	Prinzip *n* der virtuellen Arbeit (Verrückungen, Verschiebung, Verschiebungen, Geschwindigkeiten); Fouriersche Erweiterung *f* des Prinzips der virtuellen Arbeit, Fouriersches Prinzip ‹bei einseitigen Bindungen›
principle of mobile equilibrium	Prinzip *n* des fließenden Gleichgewichts		
principle of Montigny, Montigny['s] principle	Montignysches Prinzip *n*, Prinzip von (nach) Montigny		
principle of operation	s. mode of operation ‹of apparatus›		
principle of parallel flow, parallel[-] flow principle	Gleichstromprinzip *n*	principle of Zorn	s. Zorn['s] lemma
		printed board, [printed] circuit board, printed wiring board	Leiterplatte *f*
principle of parting limits, Tammann['s] principle	Tammannsches Prinzip *n*, Tammann-Prinzip *n*		
principle of Pascal	s. Pascal['s] law	printed circuit	gedruckte Schaltung *f*
principle of phase stability, phase-focusing principle	Prinzip *n* der Phasenstabilität (selbständigen Phasenstabilisierung)		
principle of Porro and Koppe	s. Porro-Koppe principle	printed circuit (wiring) board	s. printed board
principle of potential energy	s. principle of least work	printer, print-out device; data printer	Drucker *m*, Druckwerk *n*; Datendrucker *m*, Datenausdrucker *m*, Wertedrucker *m*
principle of quasicontinuity, quasi-continuity equation	Quasikontinuitätsgleichung *f*		
		printing, printing[-] out	Ausdrucken *n*, Drucken *n*
principle of Rayleigh and Jeans, Rayleigh-Jeans['] principle	Rayleigh-Jeanssches Prinzip *n*, Prinzip von Rayleigh und Jeans	printing ‹phot.›	Kopieren *n* ‹Phot.›
principle of reciprocity, reciprocity principle	Reziprozitätsprinzip *n*	printing mask, mask, shutter mask	Maske *f*, Abdeckmaske *f*, Abdeckblende *f*, Kopiermaske *f*
principle of reflection	s. Schwarz['s] reflection principle	printing method	s. replica method
		printing[-] out, printing	Ausdrucken *n*, Drucken *n*
principle of relativity, principle of reversibility, relativity principle	Relativitätsprinzip *n*, Prinzip *n* der Relativität	printing-out, copying on printing-out paper ‹phot.›	Auskopieren *n*, Auskopierprozeß *m* ‹Phot.›
principle of reversibility	s. principle of reciprocity		
principle of reversibility [of the path of rays]	Prinzip *n* (Satz *m* von) der Umkehrbarkeit [des Strahlenganges]; Umkehrbarkeit *f* des Strahlenganges	printing reader	s. chart recorder
		printometer	Printometer *n*
principle of similarity	s. similarity principle	print-out device	s. printer
principle of solidification	s. Stevin['s] principle	print-out effect	„print-out"-Effekt *m*, Auskopiereffekt *m*
principle of special relativity	s. Einstein['s] principle of special relativity	prior interaction	Vorumordnungswechselwirkung *f*, Wechselwirkung *f* vor Umordnung
principle of stationary phase, stationary phase method	Methode *f* der stationären Phase		
		priority ‹math.›	Prioritätsordnung *f* ‹Math.›
principle of stationary proper time	s. principle of least proper time		
		priority coefficient	Vorrangkoeffizient *m*
principle of superposition, superposition principle, superimposition principle, superposition theorem, law of superposition	Superpositionsprinzip *n*, Prinzip *n* der ungestörten Superposition, Überlagerungsprinzip *n*, Superpositionssatz *m*, Unabhängigkeitsprinzip *n*	prior probability	s. a priori probability
		prior processing, pretreatment; preparatory treatment	Vorbehandlung *f*; Vorbearbeitung *f*
		prism antenna, pyramidal antenna	Reusenantenne *f*, Reusendipol *m*, Reusendipolantenne *f*
principle of the conservation of energy	s. energy conservation law		
principle of the inertia of energy	Prinzip *n* von der Trägheit der Energie	prismatic astrolabe, prismatic transit instrument	Prismenastrolabium *n* [von Danjon]
principle of the least action [of Maupertuis]	s. Maupertuis['] principle		
principle of the least constraint	s. Le Chatelier['s] principle	prismatic beta spectrometer	Prismen-Beta-Spektrometer *n*, Prismen-β-Spektrometer *n*
principle of the least constraint	s. principle of least constraint	prismatic class	s. monoclinic holohedry
principle of the lever	s. lever principle	prismatic compass	Prismenkompaß *m*; Prismenbussole *f*
principle of the maximum, maximum principle; maximum-modulus principle	Maximumprinzip *n*; Prinzip *n* vom Maximum, Satz *m* vom Maximum		
		prismatic compensator, prism compensator	Prismenkompensator *m*
principle of the parallelogram of forces, parallelogram law	Parallelogrammregel *f*, Parallelogrammgesetz *n*, Satz *m* vom Parallelogramm der Kräfte	prismatic dislocation, prismatic loop	prismatische Versetzung *f*
		prismatic dispersion	s. dispersion ‹opt.›
principle of the successive building up of atoms	s. aufbauprinciple	prismatic eyepiece, ocular prism	Okularprisma *n*
		prismatic lens	prismatisches Brillenglas *n*
principle of the unattainability of the absolute zero	s. third law	prismatic loop	s. prismatic dislocation
		prismatic punching [of single crystals]	prismatisches Stanzen *n* [von Einkristallen]
principle of transfer	Übertragungsprinzip *n*	prismatic sextant	Prismenkreis *m*
principle of uncertainty	s. uncertainty principle		
principle of using travelling waves, surf-riding principle, surfing principle ‹acc.›	Wellenreiterprinzip *n*, Verwendung *f* von fortschreitenden Wellen ‹Beschl.›	prismatic spectrograph	s. prism spectrograph
		prismatic spectrometer, prism spectrometer	Prismenspektrometer *n*
principle of vinylogy, vinylogy	Vinylogieprinzip *n*	prismatic spectroscope, prism spectroscope	Prismenspektroskop *n*

prismatic spectrum	s. prism spectrum	probability factor, steric factor	sterischer Faktor m, Wahrscheinlichkeitsfaktor m
prismatic square	s. prism square		
prismatic stereoscope, Brewster stereoscope	Prismenstereoskop n [nach Brewster], Brewstersches Prismenstereoskop, Brewsters Stereoskop n	probability field, probability space	Wahrscheinlichkeitsfeld n, Wahrscheinlichkeitsraum m
prismatic transit instrument	s. prismatic astrolabe	probability for exceeding	s. exceeding probability
prismatoid	Prismatoid n, Trapezoidalkörper m, Körperstumpf m	probability frequency function, frequency function	Häufigkeitsfunktion f, Wahrscheinlichkeitshäufigkeitsfunktion f
prismatometer, prismometer	Prismometer n, Prismatometer n	probability function	Wahrscheinlichkeitsfunktion f
prism compensator, prismatic compensator	Prismenkompensator m	probability function	s. a. probability density
prism dioptre	Prismendioptrie f, pdpt	probability integral	Wahrscheinlichkeitsintegral n
prism dispersing system, dispersing system with prism	Prismenspektralapparat m, Prismenapparat m	probability law, law of probability	Wahrscheinlichkeitsgesetz n
		probability matrix	s. stochastic matrix
prism of the first order, protoprism	Protoprisma n, Prisma n erster Art	probability measure	Wahrscheinlichkeitsmaß n
prismoid	Prismoid n	probability model	Wahrscheinlichkeitsmodell n
		probability net	Wahrscheinlichkeitsnetz n
prismoidal formula [of areas]	s. Simpson's rule	probability of attachment, probability of a collision leading to attachment	Anlagerungswahrscheinlichkeit f
prismometer, prismatometer	Prismometer n, Prismatometer n		
prism photometer	Prismenphotometer n	probability of binary collisions	Zweierstoßwahrscheinlichkeit f
prism spectrograph, prismatic spectrograph	Prismenspektrograph m	probability of collision, collision probability, collision rate	Stoßwahrscheinlichkeit f
prism spectrometer, prismatic spectrometer	Prismenspektrometer n		
prism spectroscope, prismatic spectroscope	Prismenspektroskop n	probability of collision (hit, impact) <radiobiology>	Trefferwahrscheinlichkeit f <Strahlenbiologie>
prism spectrum, dispersion spectrum, prismatic spectrum	Dispersionsspektrum n, Brechungsspektrum n, Prismenspektrum n, prismatisches Spektrum n	probability of interception	Abfangwahrscheinlichkeit f
		probability of ionization, ionization probability	Ionisationswahrscheinlichkeit f, Ionisierungswahrscheinlichkeit f
prism square, prismatic square	Prismeninstrument n; Prismenkreuz n, Doppelprisma n, Kreuzprisma n, Winkelprisma n	probability of occurrence [of event]	Eintrittswahrscheinlichkeit f, Wahrscheinlichkeit f für das Eintreten [eines Ereignisses]
prism telescope	Prismenfernrohr n	probability of presence	s. probability to find a particle at a given place
prism-type beam splitter	Prismenstrahlteiler m	probability of recombination, recombination probability, recombination rate	Rekombinationswahrscheinlichkeit f
		probability of state	Zustandswahrscheinlichkeit f, Wahrscheinlichkeit f des Zustandes
privileged axis, preferred axis	Vorzugsachse f, bevorzugte Achse f, Hauptachse f		
privileged direction	s. preferred orientation	probability of survival	Überlebenswahrscheinlichkeit f
probabilistic	wahrscheinlichkeitstheoretisch; probabilistisch	probability of tunnelling	s. penetration probability
		probability paper	Wahrscheinlichkeitspapier n
probability	Wahrscheinlichkeit f; Erwartung f	probability ratio test	s. likelihood ratio test
probability amplitude	Wahrscheinlichkeitsamplitude f	probability sampling	Wahrscheinlichkeits-Stichprobenverfahren n
probability a posteriori	s. inverse probability	probability statement	Wahrscheinlichkeitsaussage f
probability a priori	s. a priori probability		
probability calculus	s. probability theory	probability table	Wahrscheinlichkeitstabelle f
probability convergence	s. convergence in probability	probability theory, theory of probabilities (chances) probability calculus, calculus of probability (probabilities)	Wahrscheinlichkeitsrechnung f, Wahrscheinlichkeitstheorie f
probability current	Wahrscheinlichkeitsstrom m		
probability current density	Wahrscheinlichkeitsstromdichte f		
probability curve	s. error curve	probability to find a particle at a given place, probability of presence	Aufenthaltswahrscheinlichkeit f
probability density, probability density function, density function, probability function, distribution density, relative frequency function	Wahrscheinlichkeitsdichte f, Verteilungsdichte f, Dichtefunktion f, Dichte f der Wahrscheinlichkeit		
		probability unit, probit	Probit n
		probability viewpoint	Wahrscheinlichkeitsgesichtspunkt m
		probability wave	Wahrscheinlichkeitswelle f
		probable error	wahrscheinlicher Fehler m
probability density distribution [of electrons]	Wahrscheinlichkeitsdichteverteilung f [der Elektronen]	probable specific ionization, primary specific ionization	primäre spezifische Ionisation f, spezifische Primärionisation f, wahrscheinliche spezifische Ionisierung (Ionisation) f <je Längeneinheit der Spur>
probability density function	s. probability density		
probability distribution	Wahrscheinlichkeitsverteilung f		
probability distribution function	s. distribution function	probe, feeler, sound, sonde	Sonde f; Fühler m; Taster m; Spürgerät n

probe | **638**

probe; sensing head; scanning head	Tastkopf *m*
probe	*s. a.* measuring head
probe antenna	Sondenantenne *f*, Tastantenne *f*
probe electrode	*s.* sounding electrode
probe extraction, extraction by means of a probe	Sondenextraktion *f*
probe head	*s.* measuring head
probe-induced distortion (interference)	Sondenstörung *f*
probe microphone	Sondenmikrophon *n*
probe polarograph, sampling polarograph	Tastpolarograph *m*
probe tip	Sondenspitze *f*
probe[-type] voltmeter, diode probe-type voltmeter	Taströhrenvoltmeter *n*, Tastvoltmeter *n*
probing	Sondierung *f*
probing, sounding, plumbing	Lotung *f*
probit, probability unit	Probit *n*
probit analysis	Probitanalyse *f*
probit method, probit technique, probit transformation	Probittransformation *f*, Probitmethode *f*, Probit *n*
problem involving edges, diffraction problem involving edges	Kantenproblem *n*, Kantenbeugungsproblem *n*
problem of Boussinesq [and Cerruti]	*s.* Boussinesq['s] problem
problem of fixed detachment	Kielwasserablösung[sproblem *n*] *f*
problem of moments, moment problem	Momentenproblem *n*
problem of moving punch, moving punch problem	Problem *n* des bewegten Stempels, Problem der bewegten Stanzlinie
problem of n bodies, *n*-body problem	*n*-Körper-Problem *n*
problem of principal axes (axis)	Hauptachsenproblem *n*
problem of random walk, random walk problem	Irrfahrtsproblem *n*
problem of Schwarzschild, Schwarzschild['s] problem	Schwarzschildsches Problem *n*
problem of smooth detachment, prow problem	Bugwellenproblem *n*, Bugwellenablösungsproblem *n*
problem of the halfspace	*s.* Boussinesq['s] problem
problem of the plane	*s.* Boussinesq['s] problem
problem of three bodies, three-body problem	Dreikörperproblem *n*
problem of two bodies	*s.* two-body problem
Proca['s] equation[s]	Procasche Gleichung[en *f pl*] *f*
procedural bias	*s.* error of approximation
procedure; process; technique, method	Verfahren *n*; Technik *f*; Methode *f*
proceeding	*s.* run ‹of process›
process; reaction	Prozeß *m*; Vorgang *m*; Reaktion *f*
process; procedure; technique, method	Verfahren *n*; Technik *f*; Methode *f*
process annealing, intermediate annealing	Zwischenglühung *f*
process camera	Reproduktionskamera *f*
process chart	*s.* flow chart ‹num. math.›
process computer; on-line computer	Prozeßrechner *m*, Prozeßrechenanlage *f*; On-line-Rechner *m*
processing; working; handling; treatment	Verarbeitung *f*
processing, treatment, treating, working, machining ‹mech.›	Behandlung *f*; Bearbeitung *f* ‹Mech.›
processing	*s. a.* evaluation ‹of dates›
process instrumentation and control engineering	BMSR-Technik *f*; Betriebs-Meß-, -Steuer- und -Regelungstechnik *f*
process of interchange [of sites]	*s.* interchange process
process of measurement, measurement process, measuring process	Meßprozeß *m*, Meßvorgang *m*
process of vision, vision process	Sehvorgang *m*
process time	Prozeßzeit *f*, Verfahrenszeit *f*
Procopiu effect	Procopiu-Effekt *m*
producer; generator	Generator *m*; Erzeuger *m*; Sender *m*
producer	*s. a.* manufacturer
producing reactor	*s.* production reactor
product, outer product, general product ‹of tensors›	[allgemeines] Tensorprodukt *n*, direktes Produkt *n* ‹Tensoren›
product detector, ring demodulator	Produktgleichrichter *m*, Ringdemodulator *m*
product deviation	Produktabweichung *f*
production, formation, creation, generation, birth	Bildung *f*, Erzeugung *f*, Generation *f*
production, manufacturing, manufacture	Herstellung *f*, Gewinnung *f*, Fertigung *f*, Erzeugung *f*, Darstellung *f*; Produktion *f*
production; causing; effecting; inducing, induction	Verursachen *n*, Bewirken *n*, Bedingen *n*, Hervorrufen *n*; Auslösung *f*; Erzeugung *f*
production ‹of the line›	*s.* lengthening
production cross-section, creation (generation, formation) cross-section, cross-section for production (creation, generation, formation)	Wirkungsquerschnitt *m* für (der) Bildung, Wirkungsquerschnitt für (der) Erzeugung, Erzeugungs[wirkungs]querschnitt *m*, Bildungs[wirkungs]querschnitt *m*
production of cold, refrigeration	Kälteerzeugung *f*
production of entropy, entropy production, rate of entropy production	Entropieerzeugung[sdichte] *f*, Entropieproduktion[sdichte] *f*
production of heat	*s.* generation of heat
production of light, technique of light production	Lichterzeugung *f*, Leuchttechnik *f*
production of poles, creation of poles	Polerzeugung *f*
production of the line	*s.* lengthening
production operator, creation (emission) operator	Erzeugungsoperator *m*
production rate, creation rate, formation rate, birth-rate ‹nucl.›	Erzeugungsrate *f*, Erzeugungsgeschwindigkeit *f*, Bildungsrate *f* ‹Kern.›
production reactor, producing reactor, production-type reactor	Produktionsreaktor *m* ‹Reaktor zur Erzeugung von Brutstoffen oder Radionukliden›
production reactor, plutonium[-producing] reactor, production-type reactor	Produktionsreaktor *m* ‹zur Plutoniumgewinnung›, Plutoniumerzeugungsreaktor *m*
production spectrum	Erzeugungsspektrum *n*
production-type reactor	*s.* production reactor
productive evaporation	produktive Verdunstung *f*
productiveness ‹of sound generator› ‹ac.›	Ergiebigkeit *f* ‹Ak.›
productivity, output; efficiency; efficacy; performance	Leistungsfähigkeit *f*, Leistung *f*, Produktionsleistung *f*, Produktivität *f*
productivity [of neutrons], neutron productivity	Produktivität *f* [von Neutronen], Neutronenproduktivität *f*
productivity of source	Quell[en]ergiebigkeit *f*, Ergiebigkeit (Schüttung) *f* der Quelle, Quell[en]schüttung *f*
product moment, joint moment	Produktmoment *n*
product-moment correlation	Maßkorrelation *f*, Produkt-Moment-Korrelation *f* [nach Bravais und Pearson], Produktmomentkorrelation *f* [nach Bravais und Pearson]

product-moment correlation coefficient | s. Bravais correlation coefficient
product nucleus <e.g. of fission> | Produktkern m, Endkern m <z. B. der Spaltung>
product of electrolysis, electrolysate | Elektrolyseprodukt n
product of inertia, centrifugal moment | Deviationsmoment n, Zentrifugalmoment n, Trägheitsprodukt n
product of metabolism; metabolite | Stoffwechselprodukt n; Metabolit m
product particle | Produktteilchen n
product rule, quantity of stimulus rule, hyperbola rule, reciprocity rule (law) <bio.> | Reizmengengesetz n, Produktgesetz n, Hyperbelgesetz n <Bio.>
product rule | s. a. Teller-Redlich product rule
product space | Produktraum m
product transformation | Produkttransformation f
profile chart; profile curve; profile record; profilogram | Profilbild n; Profilkurve f; Profilschrieb m, Profilogramm n
profile coefficient | Profilbeiwert m
profile curve | s. profile chart
profile drag, ideal drag | Profilwiderstand m
profile flow | Profilumströmung f, Profilströmung f
profile gauge | Profillehre f
profile Goettingen | Göttinger Profil n, Profil Göttingen
profile mean line | s. skeleton line
profile nose; aerofoil profile nose, aerofoil border of attack | Profilnase f
profile of equilibrium, equilibrium profile | Gleichgewichtsprofil n, Normalprofil n; Normalgefällskurve f <Geo.>
profile of the [spectral] line | s. line profile
profile of wind [velocity], wind profile, profile of wind | Windprofil n, Windgeschwindigkeitsprofil n
profile plane | Profilebene f
profile projector, shadow outline projector, contour projector | Profilprojektor m
profile record | s. profile chart
profile scanner | Profilscanner m
profile testing meter | s. profilometer
profiling; shaping | Formgebung f; Formung f; Profilierung f
profilogram | s. profile chart
profilometer; profile testing meter; talysurf; roughometer | Rauhigkeits[tiefen]messer m; Profilmeßgerät n, Profilmesser m, Profilometer n
profundal | Profundal n
progenitor, precursor <nucl.>; predecessor <math.> | Vorgänger m
progenitor | s. a. primary particle
progeny | s. daughter
prognosis, prognostication; prediction; forecast, forecasting | Vorhersage f, Voraussage f, Prognose f
prognosis formula, prognostic formula | Prognoseformel f
prognostication | s. prognosis
prognostic formula, prognosis formula | Prognoseformel f
program <US>, programme, routine <num. math.> | Programm n
programme composition; programming | Programmierung f; Programmherstellung f, Programmfertigung f
programme[d] control | s. sequential control
programme[d] control | s. time schedule control
programme parameter | Jeweils-Parameter m, Programmparameter m
programme register, control register | Programmspeicher m
programming; programme composition | Programmierung f; Programmherstellung f, Programmfertigung f
progression <math.> | Progression f <Math.>
progression | s. series <math.>
progression of bands, band progression | Bandenserie f
progressive error | progressiver (sich fortpflanzender, fortschreitender) Fehler m
progressive freezing | normales Erstarren n, gerichtetes Erstarren
progressive load[ing], stepwise loading, loading in steps, gradually applied load | stufenweise Belastung f; stufenweise aufgebrachte Last f
progressive motion | s. translational movement
progressive nutation | progressive Nutation f
progressive phosphorescence | progressive Phosphoreszenz f
progressive precession | progressive Präzession f
progressive reducer | s. superproportional reducer
progressive series of greys, series of greys, grey series, grey scale | Graureihe f, Grauleiter f, Grauskala f, unbunte Reihe f, Grauwertskala f
progressive wave | s. advancing wave
prohibition of intercombinations, forbiddenness of combination, [inter]combination law <of spectral terms> | Interkombinationsverbot n, Interkombinationsregel f, Kombinationsverbot n
projected angle | projizierter Winkel m, Winkelprojektion f
projected scale | Projektionsskala f, Projektionsskale f, projizierte Skala (Skale) f; projektive Skala (Skale), projektive Leiter f
projected-scale instrument | Projektionsskaleninstrument n, Projektionsskalenmeßgerät n
projectile, missile | Projektil n, Geschoß n
projectile | s. a. bombarding particle
projectile blast | s. projectile report
projectile motion | Wurfbewegung f
projectile report (sound), projectile blast | Geschoßknall m
projecting, projection, reproduction; demonstration <opt.> | Projizieren n, Projektion f, Wiedergabe f; Werfen n, Wurf m <Opt.>
projecting beam (cone) | s. projecting ray
projecting lens, projection lens | Projektionslinse f; Projektiv n, Projektivlinse f <Elektronenmikroskop>
projecting ray; projecting (projection) beam; projection (projecting) cone, ray of projection | Projektionsstrahl m; Projektionskegel m
projecting schlieren method, shadow schlieren method; schlieren scanning technique | Schattenschlierenverfahren n, Schattenschlierenmethode f
projection; component <math.> | Komponente f; Bild n; Projektion f <Math.>
projection, throw, cast <mech.> | Wurf m; Werfen n <Mech.>
projection | s. a. overhang
projection | s. a. projecting <opt.>
projection adaptometer | Projektionsadaptometer n [von Novack-Wetthauer]
projection apparatus | s. projector
projection area; projection surface | Projektionsfläche f
projection beam (cone) | s. projecting ray
projection eyepiece, photo[-]eyepiece | Projektionsokular n, Projektiv n, Photookular n, mikrophotographisches Okular n
projection factor | Projektionsfaktor m

projection

projection lamp <US>, projector lamp	Lichtwurflampe f, Projektionslampe f <Typen: A, B, C, K, L, O, S, T>
projection lens, projecting lens	Projektionslinse f; Projektiv n, Projektivlinse f <Elektronenmikroskop>
projection lens, projection objective	Projektionsobjektiv n, Projektiv n
projection microscope	Projektionsmikroskop n
projection objective	s. projection lens
projection of shadow, shadow projection (casting)	Schattenwurf m, Schattenprojektion f
projection of solid angle	Raumwinkelprojektion f
projection operator, projector <qu.>	Projektionsoperator m, Projektor m, Projektion f <Qu.>
projection optical system, projection optics, optical system of (for the) projection	Projektionsoptik f, Wiedergabeoptik f, Projektionsspiegelsystem n
projection optimeter	Projektionsoptimeter n
projection picture, screen picture	Projektionsbild n
projection plane, plane of projection, picture plane <of perspective projection>	Bildtafel f, Bildebene f, Projektionsebene f <der Perspektive>
projection printing	Vergrößerungskopieren n
projection screen, screen; cinema screen	Projektionsschirm m; Bildwand f, Projektionswand f; Leinwand f, Leinwandschirm m
projection surface; projection area	Projektionsfläche f
projection X-ray microscope	Röntgenschattenmikroskop n
projection X-ray microscopy	Röntgenschattenmikroskopie f
projective co-ordinates; projective co-ordinate system, set of projective co-ordinates, projective system [of co-ordinates]	projektive Koordinaten fpl; projektives Koordinatensystem n
projective distillation	s. molecular distillation
projective field theory	projektive Feldtheorie f, fünfdimensionale Feldtheorie
projective group	projektive Gruppe f
projective mensuration, projective metric determination	projektive (Cayleysche, Cayley-Kleinsche) Maßbestimmung f
projective plane	projektive Ebene f
projective relation, projectivity, projective transformation	Projektivität f, projektive Abbildung (Transformation, Verwandtschaft) f
projective relativity	projektive (fünfdimensionale) Relativitätstheorie f
projective space	projektiver Raum m
projective system [of co-ordinates]	s. projective co-ordinates
projective transformation, projectivity, projective relation	Projektivität f, projektive Abbildung (Transformation, Verwandtschaft) f
projector, projection apparatus	Bildwerfer m, Projektor m, Projektionsgerät n, Projektionsapparat m, Bildwurfgerät n
projector; search light	Scheinwerfer m
projector	s. a. projection operator <qu.>
projector arc lamp, arc lamp of the projector	Projektionsbogenlampe f
projector lamp, projection lamp <US>	Lichtwurflampe f, Projektionslampe f <Typen: A, B, C, K, L, O, S, T>
projector lamp	Scheinwerferlampe f, Lichtwurflampe f C
prolate, oblong	verlängert, gestreckt; länglich
prolate basin <geo.>, oblong basin	Wanne f <Geo.>
prolate ellipsoid [of revolution], prolate spheroid, ovary ellipsoid	verlängertes Rotationsellipsoid n, gestrecktes Rotationsellipsoid
prolate-spherical co-ordinates	s. prolate spheroidal co-ordinates
prolate spheroid, prolate ellipsoid [of revolution], ovary ellipsoid	verlängertes Rotationsellipsoid n, gestrecktes Rotationsellipsoid
prolate spheroidal co-ordinates, prolate-spherical co-ordinates	verlängert-rotationselliptische (gestreckt-rotationselliptische) Koordinaten fpl, Koordinaten des verlängerten (gestreckten) Rotationsellipsoids
prolate top	verlängerter Kreisel m, gestreckter Kreisel
prolongation; lengthening; production [of the line], protraction of the line	Verlängerung f
prolonged development	Langzeitentwicklung f
prominence, solar prominence, solar surge	Protuberanz f, Sonnenprotuberanz f
prominence eyepiece	Protuberanzenokular n
prominence knot, knot of the prominence	Protuberanzenknoten m
prominence spectroscope	Protuberanzenspektroskop n
prominence streamer, streamer of the prominence	Protuberanzenfaden m, Faden m der Protuberanz
promoted electron	begünstigtes (angehobenes, an der Molekülbildung beteiligtes) Elektron n
promoter, promotor <chem.>	synergetischer Verstärker m, Aktivator m, Promotor m <Chem.>
promotion	Begünstigung f; Anheben n
promotion of quantum number	Zunahme f der Quantenzahl bei Molekülbildung
promotor	s. promoter
prompt, promptly born <e.g. of neutron, gamma ray>	prompt, momentan, nichtverzögert <z. B. Neutron, γ-Quant>
prompt coincidence curve, prompt curve	Promptkurve f, prompte Kurve f, Promptkoinzidenzkurve f
prompt counting rate	Promptzählrate f
prompt[-] critical	prompt[-] kritisch
prompt criticality	promptkritischer Zustand m, prompte Kritizität f
prompt curve, prompt coincidence curve	Promptkurve f, prompte Kurve f, Promptkoinzidenzkurve f
prompt fission neutron	s. prompt neutron
promptly born	s. prompt
prompt multiplication	prompte Multiplikation f
prompt neutron, prompt fission neutron	promptes Neutron (Spaltneutron) n, Promptneutron n
prompt neutron fraction	Anteil m der Promptneutronen (prompten Neutronen)
prompt-subcritical, delayed-supercritical	prompt[-]unterkritisch, verzögert[-]überkritisch

prompt-supercritical	prompt[-]überkritisch
prong <of the emulsion star>	Arm *m*, Zacken *m* <Zertrümmerungsstern>
pronged, toothed, spiked, indented	zackig, gezackt
prong hoe	s. cock[-]pit
prong-type ammeter, clip-on (hook-on) ammeter	Zangenstrommesser *m*, Anlegerstrommesser *m*, Anlegeamperemeter *n*
prong-type instrument, prong-type measuring instrument	Zangenmeßgerät *n*, Zangengerät *n*, Zangeninstrument *n*, Zangenanleger *m*
prong-type measuring transformer	Zangenstromwandler *m*, Zangenwandler *m*
prong-type wattmeter	Zangenleistungsmesser *m*, Zangenwattmeter *n*
Prony brake	Pronyscher Zaum *m*, Bremszaum *m*, Bremsdynamometer *n*
proof	s. detection
proof, demonstration <math.>	Beweis *m*
proof	s. a. testing
proof	s. a. tight
proof against water jets	spritzwassergeschützt; spritzwassersicher, spritzwasserdicht
proof by reductio ad absurdum	s. indirect proof
proofing	s. leak test
proof of existence	Existenzbeweis *m*
proof plate	s. optical test chart
0.2% proof stress, 0.2% yield strength	Zweizehnteldehngrenze *f*, Zweizehntelfließgrenze *f*, $\sigma_{0,2}$-Grenze *f*, 0,2-Dehngrenze *f*, 0,2-Grenze *f*, Nullzweidehngrenze *f*
proof test, pressure test	Abdrückversuch *m*
propagating wave, divergent (diverging) wave	auslaufende Welle *f*, fortlaufende Welle
propagation; spread <in>	Ausbreitung *f*, Fortpflanzung *f* <in>
propagation coefficient	s. propagation constant
propagation coefficient	s. wavelength constant
propagation constant, propagation factor, propagation coefficient <of the line>; transfer constant, transmission constant <of the network>	Ausbreitungskonstante *f*, Fortpflanzungskonstante *f*, Ausbreitungsfaktor *m*, Ausbreitungskoeffizient *m* <Leitung>; [komplexes] Übertragungsmaß *n*, Übertragungskonstante *f* <Vierpol>
propagation constant propagation factor	s. a. wavelength constant s. propagation constant <of the line>
propagation factor propagation function	s. a. wavelength constant s. quantum Green['s] function <qu.>
propagation kernel	Ausbreitungskern *m*
propagation of error[s], error propagation	Fehlerfortpflanzung *f*
propagation of flames, flame propagation, flame spread, spread of flames	Flammenausbreitung *f*, Flammenfortpflanzung *f*
propagation of heat, heat propagation	Wärmeausbreitung *f*, Wärmefortpflanzung *f*, Wärmefortleitung *f*
propagation of pressure	Druckausbreitung *f*, Druckfortpflanzung *f*
propagation of the nerve impulse	s. nerve conduction
propagation of the tide, tide propagation	Gezeitendehnung *f*
propagation of wave	s. wave propagation
propagation rate of the crack, rate of crack propagation	Vordringgeschwindigkeit *f* des Risses
propagation reaction	s. chain growth
propagation theorem, error propagation theorem (law), law of the propagation of errors	[Gaußsches] Fehlerfortpflanzungsgesetz *n*, Fehlerfortpflanzungsgesetz von Gauß
propagation vector	s. circular wave vector
propagation velocity, velocity of propagation (transmission), speed of propagation, spread velocity, rate of spread	Ausbreitungsgeschwindigkeit *f*, Fortpflanzungsgeschwindigkeit *f*
propagation velocity	s. a. phase velocity
propagation velocity of pulses	s. pulse propagation velocity
propagator	Propagator *m*, Feynmanscher Propagator
propane chamber, propane-filled bubble chamber	Propanblasenkammer *f*, Propankammer *f*
proparaclase, transcurrent fault, cross fault	Querverwerfung *f*
propellant, fuel, rocket fuel	Treibstoff *m*, Raketentreibstoff *m*
propellant, propellent	s. motive power
propeller, impeller, airscrew	Propeller *m*, Luftschraube *f*, Saugschraube *f*, Flügelschraube *f*
propeller blade	s. blade
propeller effect (modulation), rotor modulation	Propellermodulation *f*, Propellereffekt *m*
propeller turbine, fixed-blade turbine, turbo-prop [drive]	Propellerturbine *f*; Turboproptriebwerk *n*, Propeller-Gasturbinentriebwerk *n*, Propellerturbinentriebwerk *n*
propeller-type current meter	s. hydrometric vane <hydr.>
propeller-type flowmeter, propeller-type [fluid] meter, screw-type flowmeter, screw-type [fluid] meter, velocity [flow]meter, vaned (lobed) flowmeter	Flügelradzähler *m*; Flügelradmengenmesser *m*
propelling force	s. propelling power
propelling nozzle	s. jet nozzle
propelling power, thrust, thrust power, propelling force, repulsive (forward) thrust, push	Schub *m*, Schubkraft *f*, Vortriebskraft *f*, Vortrieb *m*
propensity	s. tendency
proper action variable	s. proper phase integral
proper angle variable	eigentliche Winkelvariable *f*
proper boundary value problem	echtes Randwertproblem *n*
proper double refringence, structure double refraction, structure birefringence	Eigendoppelbrechung *f*, Strukturdoppelbrechung *f*, Texturdoppelbrechung *f*
proper existence	Eigenexistenz *f*
proper field, eigenfield	Eigenfeld *n*
proper frame of reference	Eigenbezugssystem *n*
proper function, eigenfunction, characteristic function	Eigenfunktion *f*, Eigenlösung *f*, Eigenelement *m*, Eigenvektor *m*
proper length	Eigenlänge *f*, Ruhlänge *f*, Ruhelänge *f*
proper limit	eigentlicher Grenzwert *m*
proper Lorentz group, group of restricted homogeneous Lorentz transformations	eigentliche Lorentz-Gruppe *f*, homogene orthochrone Lorentz-Gruppe ohne Spiegelungen
properly nilpotent element, proper nilpotent element, root element	eigentlich nilpotentes Element *n*, Wurzelgröße *f*
proper mass, rest[-] mass, mass at rest	Ruhemasse *f*, Ruhmasse *f*
proper mass, self mass, intrinsic mass <qu.>	Selbstmasse *f*, Eigenmasse *f* <Qu.>
proper moment, eigenmoment	Eigenmoment *n*
proper motion, characteristic motion <of stars, of sunspots>	Eigenbewegung *f* <Sterne, Sonnenflecke>

proper motion in declination	Eigenbewegung f in Deklination	**proportional band** <control>	Proportional[itäts]bereich m, P-Bereich m <Regelung>
proper motion in right ascension	Eigenbewegung f in Rektaszension	**proportional chamber,** proportional ionization chamber	Proportionalionisationskammer f
proper nilpotent element, properly nilpotent element, root element	eigentlich nilpotentes Element n, Wurzelgröße f	**proportional compasses,** proportional dividers <US>	Reduktionszirkel m, Proportionalzirkel m
proper number	s. eigenvalue <of a matrix>	**proportional control,** proportional-action control, proportional position control, P. control, static control	P-Regelung f, Proportionalregelung f, statische Regelung f
proper orthogonal group, rotation[s] group	Drehgruppe f, Drehungsgruppe f, eigentliche orthogonale Gruppe f		
proper orthogonal mapping (transformation)	eigentlich orthogonale Abbildung f, eigentliche orthogonale Transformation f		
proper orthogonal matrix	s. rotation matrix	**proportional controller,** proportional-action controller, proportional position controller, P. controller, static controller, static regulator	Proportionalregler m, P-Regler m, statischer Regler m
proper phase	Eigenphase f		
proper phase integral, proper action variable	eigentliche Wirkungsvariable f		
proper power, self-power	Eigenleistung f		
proper radiation, self-radiation	Eigenstrahlung f		
proper rate <of clock>	Eigenganggeschwindigkeit f	**proportional counter [tube]; proportional counting system**	Proportionalzählrohr n; Proportionalzähler m <Zählrohr + Elektronik>
proper rearrangement, proper transposition	echte Umlagerung f, Umlagerung im engeren Sinn		
proper rotation	s. eigenrotation	**proportional derivative control,** derivative proportional control, P.D. control	PD-Regelung f, Proportionalregelung f mit Differentialeinfluß (Vorhalt)
proper state, characteristic state, eigenstate	Eigenzustand m		
proper symmetry	Eigensymmetrie f		
proper time	Eigenzeit f		
proper time element	Eigenzeitelement n	**proportional dividers** <US>	s. proportional compasses
proper time unit	Eigenzeiteinheit f	**proportional feedback**	starre (statische) Rückführung f
proper transformation	eigentliche Transformation f	**proportional-flow weir,** Sutro weir	Sutro-Überfall m, Überfall m nach Sutro
proper transposition, proper rearrangement	echte Umlagerung f, Umlagerung im engeren Sinn	**proportional frequency**	s. relative frequency
property of being orthotomic, orthotomy	Orthotomie f	**proportional input**	s. proportional action
property tensor	Eigenschaftstensor m	**proportional, integral, and derivative action**	Proportional-Integral-Differential-Verhalten n, PID-Verhalten n; PID-Einfluß m, Proportional-Integral-Differential-Einfluß m, PID-Einwirkung f
property to oscillate	Schwingfähigkeit f		
proper value	s. eigenvalue		
proper value problem	s. eigenvalue problem		
proper variable	s. physical variable		
proper vector, eigenvector; latent vector, characteristic vector, model column	Eigenvektor m	**proportional integral control,** proportional plus reset control, P.I. control	PI-Regelung f, Proportional-Integral-Regelung f
proper velocity; natural velocity	Eigengeschwindigkeit f		
proper volume of ion, eigenvolume of the ion, ion eigenvolume, ion proper volume	Ioneneigenvolumen n, Eigenvolumen n des Ions	**proportional integral control[ler],** proportional plus reset control[ler], P.I. control[ler]	PI-Regler m, Proportional-Integral-Regler m, Regler m mit vorübergehender Statik; Isodromregler m
prophage	Prophage f	**proportional integral derivative control[ler]**	s. derivative proportional integral controller
proportion	Proportion f, Verhältnis n, Verhältnisanteil m	**proportional intensification** <phot.>	multiplikative (proportionale) Verstärkung f <Phot.>
proportion	s. a. mixture proportion		
proportion	s. a. ratio		
proportional; directly proportional	proportional, verhältnisgleich; direkt proportional	**proportional ionization chamber,** proportional chamber	Proportionalionisationskammer f
proportional action, proportional input	Proportionalverhalten n, P-Verhalten n; Proportionaleinfluß m, P-Einfluß m, proportionale Einwirkung f	**proportionality coefficient**	s. factor of proportionality
		proportionality constant (factor)	s. factor of proportionality
		proportional[ity] limit, limit of proportionality, proportional limit	Proportionalitätsgrenze f [im Hookeschen Gesetz], elastische Proportionalitätsgrenze, Gleichmaß[dehn]grenze f
proportional-action control	s. proportional control		
proportional-action controller	s. proportional controller		
proportional amplifier	s. linear amplifier	**proportional plus reset control[ler]**	s. proportional integral control[ler]
proportional and derivative action	Proportional-Differential-Verhalten n, PD-Verhalten n; PD-Einfluß m, Proportional-Differential-Einfluß m	**proportional position control[ler]**	s. proportional control[ler]
		proportional reducer, true scale reducer	proportionaler Abschwächer m
proportional and derivative action controller, derivative proportional controller, P.D. controller	PD-Regler m, Proportionalregler m mit Differentialeinfluß, Proportionalregler mit Vorhalt	**proportional region**	Intervall n der Proportionalität, Hookescher Bereich m
		proportional region <of the counter>	Proportionalbereich m <des Zählrohrs>
proportional and integral action	Proportional-Integral-Verhalten n, PI-Verhalten n, Proportional-Integral-Einfluß m, PI-Einfluß m, proportionale und integrale Einwirkung f, PI-Einwirkung f	**proportional to time**	s. linear in time
		proportioning; dimensioning; sizing; choice of parameters; design	Dimensionierung f, Bemessung f

proportioning	s. a. dosage	protective reactance coil, current-limiting reactor	Strombegrenzungsdrossel f, Kurzschlußdrossel f
proportion of polarization, polarization degree, degree of polarization	Polarisationsgrad m	protective resistance; protective resistor	Schutzwiderstand m
proposition, assertion <math.>	Behauptung f <Math.>	protective screen (shield), shield, shielding	Abschirmung f, Schild m, Schutzschirm m, Schirm m
proposition	s. a. statement	protective solution	Schutzlösung f
propositional calculus, propositional logic, theory of propositions, sentential calculus (logic)	Aussagenlogik f, Aussagenkalkül m	protective substance	s. protective material
		protective tube housing	s. X-ray tube housing
proposition variable	Aussagenvariable f, Wahrheitswertvariable f	protective value	s. lead equivalent
		protective wall, radiation protective wall, protective barrier	Strahlenschutzwand f, Schutzwand f
propulsion	s. forward movement		
propulsive jet	s. ram jet		
prospecting, search	Erkundung f, Lagerstättensuche f, Prospektion f, Schürfung f		
prospecting geophysics	Erkundungsgeophysik f	protein coat, protein shadow	Proteinhülle f
prospective current <of the circuit>	Netzkurzschlußstrom m	protein metabolism	Eiweißstoffwechsel m
pros-position	pros-Stellung f	protein shadow	s. protein coat
		protic acid	s. proton donor
prosthetic group	prosthetische Gruppe f, Wirkgruppe f	protic base	s. proton acceptor
		protium, light hydrogen, ^{1}H	leichter Wasserstoff m, Protium n, ^{1}H
protactinide	Protaktinid n, Protactinid n		
protanomalous vision	Protanomalie f, Rotschwäche f	proto-arctic	Uraktik f
		protoatmosphere, initial atmosphere	Uratmosphäre f, Protoatmosphäre f
protanopia, red blindness	Protanopie f, Rotblindheit f		
protected, semi-enclosed <of instrument>	geschützt <Gerät>	protocol of the experiment, record of the experiment; test protocol, test record	Versuchsprotokoll n
protected group	geschützte Gruppe f		
protection <against, from>	Schutz m <gegen, vor>		
protection against lightning, lightning protection	Blitzschutz m	protogalaxy	Protogalaxis f, Urgalaxis f, Urnebel m
protection against radiations	s. radiation protection	protogeneous rock	s. primary rock
		protogenic solvent	protogenes Lösungsmittel n
protection against shock hazard, shock-hazard protection, contact protection <el.>	Berührungsschutz m	protolysis, protolytic reaction	Protolyse f, protolytische Reaktion f
		protolysis constant	Protolysekonstante f
		protolyte	Protolyt m
protection against X-radiation, X-ray protection	Röntgen[strahlen]schutz m, Schutz m gegen (vor) Röntgenstrahlung	protolytic equilibrium	protolytisches Gleichgewicht n
		protolytic reaction, protolysis	Protolyse f, protolytische Reaktion f
protection factor	Schutzfaktor m		
protection of sol	Solschutz m	protomagmatic	protomagmatisch
protection potential	s. protective potential	proton, p	Proton n, p
protection survey, health (radiation) monitoring, radiation survey	Strahlenschutzüberwachung f	proton accelerator	Protonenbeschleuniger m
		proton acceptor, emprotid, proton base, prot[on]ic base, base [according to Brønsted]	Protonenakzeptor m, Emprotid n, Proton[en]base f, Base f [im Sinne von Brønsted]
protection voltage	s. protective potential		
protective action	s. protective effect		
protective atmosphere, protective (inert) medium, inert atmosphere	Schutz[gas]atmosphäre f, Inertgasatmosphäre f; Schutzgaspolster n	proton acid	s. proton donor
		proton activity, proton radioactivity	Protonenaktivität f
protective barrier	s. protective wall	proton affinity	Protonenaffinität f
protective cap, lens cap (lid, cover, guard)	Schutzkappe f, Objektivdeckel m	proton base	s. proton acceptor
		proton beam; proton ray; H ray	Protonenstrahl m, Protonenstrahlenbündel n, Protonenbündel n; H-Strahl m
protective clothing	Schutzkleidung f, Überkleidung f		
protective coating	Schutzüberzug m	proton binding capacity	Protonenbindungsvermögen n
protective colloid	Schutzkolloid n		
protective compound	s. protective material	proton binding energy	Bindungsenergie f des Protons, Protonenbindungsenergie f
protective crust, crust	Kruste f, Schutzrinde f		
protective effect, protective action	Schutzwirkung f, Schutzeffekt m	proton bremsstrahlung	Protonenbremsstrahlung f
protective film, protective layer, cover film	Schutzschicht f	proton cloud	Protonenwolke f
		proton component	Protonenkomponente f
protective gap, spill gap	Schutzfunkenstrecke f	proton cross-section, cross-section for protons	Protonen[wirkungs]querschnitt m, Wirkungsquerschnitt m für Protonen
protective gas; inert gas	inertes Gas n, Inertgas n; Schutzgas n	proton decay	Protonenzerfall m
protective gloves	Schutzhandschuhe mpl	proton-deuteron collision	Proton-Deuteron-Stoß m, p,d-Stoß m
protective layer	s. protective film		
protective material, protective compound (substance)	Schutzstoff m		
protective medium	s. protective atmosphere	proton donor, dysprotid, proton acid, prot[on]ic acid, acid [according to Brønsted]	Protonendonator m, Dysprotid n, Proton[en]säure f, Säure f [im Sinne von Brønsted]
protective potential, protection potential (voltage)	Schutzpotential n, Schutzspannung f		

proton-electron hypothesis, proton-electron theory	Proton-Elektron-Hypothese f, Protonen-Elektronen-Hypothese f, Proton-Elektron-Theorie f, Protonen-Elektronen-Theorie f	**proton-proton force**	Proton-Proton-Kraft f
		proton-proton interaction, p-p interaction	Proton-Proton-Wechselwirkung f, p-p-Wechselwirkung f
proton-electron model	Proton-Elektron-Modell n, Protonen-Elektronen-Modell n	**proton-proton range,** p-p range	Proton-Proton-Reichweite f, p-p-Reichweite f
proton-electron theory	s. proton-electron hypothesis	**proton-proton reaction,** H-H reaction, H process	Proton-Proton-Reaktion f, H-H-Reaktion f, H-Prozeß m, Wasserstoffzyklus m, Wasserstoffprozeß m, Wasserstoffreaktion f
proton emitter, proton radiator	Protonenstrahler m		
proton evaporation	Protonenverdampfung f	**proton-proton scattering**	Proton-Proton-Streuung f, p-p-Streuung f, (p,p')-Prozeß m
proton excess	Protonenüberschuß m		
proton fission, proton-induced fission, p, f reaction	protoneninduzierte (protonenausgelöste) Spaltung f, Spaltung (Kernspaltung f) durch ein Proton, (p, f)-Prozeß m, (p, f)-Reaktion f	**proton radiator,** proton emitter	Protonenstrahler m
		proton radioactivity, proton activity	Protonenaktivität f
proton flare	Protonenfackel f, Protonenflare n	**proton radius,** electrostatic radius <of nucleus>	elektrostatischer Radius m, Protonenradius m
proton-gamma resonance, (p, γ) resonance	Proton-Gamma-Resonanz f, (p, γ)-Resonanz f	**proton ray**	s. proton beam
		proton recoil	Protonenrückstoß m
proton group	Protonengruppe f	**proton recoil counter [tube]**	Rückstoßprotonenzählrohr n, Protonenrückstoßzählrohr n
proton-induced fission	s. proton fission		
proton linac (linear) accelerator	Linearbeschleuniger m für Protonen, Protonenlinearbeschleuniger m	**proton recoil detector**	Rückstoßprotonendetektor m, Protonenrückstoßdetektor m
proton-magic	mit magischer Protonenzahl	**proton recoil scintillation counter**	Rückstoßprotonen-Szintillationszähler m, Protonenrückstoß-Szintillationszähler m
proton magnetic moment, magnetic moment of the proton	magnetisches Moment n des Protons		
proton magnetic resonance, ¹H magnetic resonance, PMR	magnetische Protonenresonanz f, proton[en]-magnetische Resonanz f, PMR	**proton resonance**	Protonenresonanz f
		proton resonance frequency	Protonenresonanzfrequenz f
		proton space charge	Protonenraumladung f
proton magnetometer, proton precession[al] magnetometer, nuclear precession magnetometer	Kernpräzessionsmagnetometer n, Proton[en]präzessionsmagnetometer n, Präzessionsmagnetometer n	**proton spectrometer**	Protonenspektrometer n
		proton spectrum	Protonen[energie]spektrum n
proton mass, mass of the proton	Protonenmasse f, Masse f des Protons	**proton spin**	Protonenspin m
		proton state	Protonzustand m
proton microscope	Protonenmikroskop n	**proton storm**	Protonensturm m
proton-neutron [exchange] force	Proton-Neutron-Kraft f, Proton-Neutron-Austauschkraft f	**proton stripping**	Protonenstripping n, Herausreißen n eines Protons <aus dem Atomkern>
proton-neutron hypothesis	s. proton-neutron theory	**proton synchrotron**	s. heavy-particle synchrotron
proton-neutron model [of the nucleus]	Proton-Neutron-Modell n [des Atomkerns], Protonen-Neutronen-Modell n [des Atomkerns]	**proton target;** hydrogen target	Wasserstofftarget n; Protonentarget n
		proton transfer reaction, hydrogen atom transfer [reaction]	Protonentransferreaktion f, Wasserstoffatom-Transferreaktion f
proton-neutron reaction, (p,n) reaction, (p,n) process	Proton-Neutron-Reaktion f, Proton-Neutron-Prozeß m, (p,n)-Reaktion f, (p,n)-Prozeß m		
		proton transition	Protonenübergang m
		proton wave	Protonenwelle f
proton-neutron theory, proton-neutron hypothesis	Protonen-Neutronen-Theorie f, Proton-Neutron-Theorie f, Protonen-Neutronen-Hypothese f, Proton-Neutron-Hypothese f	**proton wavelength**	Protonenwellenlänge f
		protophilic solvent	protophiles Lösungsmittel n
		protoplanet	Urplanet m, Protoplanet m
proton number	s. atomic charge <nucl.>	**protoplanetary cloud,** preplanetary cloud	Urwolke f
protonogram	Protonogramm n, Protonenbeugungsaufnahme f	**protoplasmic bridge**	Protoplasmabrücke f
protonosphere	Protonosphäre f	**protoplasmic colloid**	Plasmakolloid n
proton peak	Protonenlinie f, Protonenpeak m	**protoplasmic droplet**	Plasmatröpfchen n
proton precession	Protonenpräzession f, Protonpräzession f	**protoplasmic potential**	Protoplasmapotential n
proton precessional magnetometer	s. proton magnetometer	**protoplasmic streaming,** plasma streaming	Plasmaströmung f, Protoplasmaströmung f
proton precession frequency	Proton[en]präzessionsfrequenz f	**protoplasmic surface,** plasma boundary layer <bio.>	Plasmagrenzschicht f <Bio.>
proton projection operator	Protonenprojektionsoperator n		
proton-proton chain	Proton-Proton-Kette f	**protoplasm in connection with the wall**	wandständiges Protoplasma n
proton-proton cross-section	Wirkungsquerschnitt m für (der) Proton-Proton-Wechselwirkung, Proton-Proton-Wechselwirkungsquerschnitt m, Proton-Proton-Querschnitt m	**protoprism,** prism of the first order, unit prism	Protoprisma n, Prisma n erster Art
		protopyramid, pyramid of the first order, unit pyramid	Protopyramide f, Pyramide f erster Art

protosatellite	Urmond m, Protomond m	pseudocritical temperature	pseudokritische Temperatur f
protostar	Protostern m, Urstern m	pseudocritical volume	pseudokritisches Volumen n
protostellar	protostellar		
protosun	Ursonne f, Protosonne f	pseudocrystal, pseudo-crystallite	Pseudokristall m
prototropic work	prototroper Arbeitsaufwand m	pseudo-damping	Pseudodämpfung f
prototropy	Prototropie f	pseudodipolar coupling	Pseudodipolkopplung f, pseudodipolare Kopplung f
prototype	Prototyp m, Urmuster n, Urtyp m		
prototype meter, international prototype meter, mètre des archives, primary meter	Urmeter n	pseudodipolar effect (interaction)	s. pseudodipole effect
		pseudo dipole-dipole interaction	Pseudo-Dipol-Dipol-Wechselwirkung f
prototype of kilogramme	Kilogrammprototyp m	pseudodipole effect, pseudodipolar effect, pseudodipolar interaction	Pseudodipolwechselwirkung f, pseudodipolare Wechselwirkung f, Pseudodipoleffekt m
prototype of metre	Meterprototyp m		
protracted irradiation (treatment)	s. protraction [of dose]		
protraction [of dose], dose protraction, protracted treatment, protracted irradiation	Protrahierung f [der Dosis], Dosisprotrahierung f, protrahierte Bestrahlung f, Coutardsche Bestrahlung	pseudodislocation <geo.>	Pseudodislokation f, Pseudostörung f <Geo.>
		pseudo[-]effect	Scheinwirkung f; Pseudoeffekt m
		pseudoelliptic integral	pseudoelliptisches Integral n
protraction of the line	s. lengthening	pseudo-equilibrium	Pseudogleichgewicht n
protractor	s. angle protractor	pseudo-equilibrium process	Pseudogleichgewichtsprozeß m
protractor	s. contact goniometer		
protractor ocular head, eyepiece goniometer, goniometer (goniometric) eyepiece	Goniometerokular n, Winkelmeßokular n, Okulargoniometer n	pseudo-Euclidean metric	pseudoeuklidische Metrik f
		pseudo-Euclidean space	pseudoeuklidischer Raum m
protrusion	s. bulging	pseudo E-wave	Pseudo-E-Welle f
Prött['s] formula	Pröttsche Näherungsformel (Formel) f	pseudo-exact solution	pseudoexakte Lösung f
		pseudo exchange interaction	Pseudoaustauschwechselwirkung f
Prött temperature	Prött-Temperatur f, Pröttsche Temperatur f	pseudo-fading	Pseudofading n, Pseudoschwund m
protuberance	s. prominence		
proustide	s. daltonide	pseudo four-tensor, pseudo 4-tensor	Pseudovierertensor m
Prout['s] hypothesis	Proutsche Hypothese f		
provable	beweisbar	pseudo-frequency	Pseudofrequenz f
provisional mean	s. working mean	pseudofront, apparent front, false front	Scheinfront f
prow problem, problem of smooth detachment	Bugwellenproblem n, Bugwellenablösungsproblem n		
proximity	s. vicinity	pseudogel	Pseudogel n
proximity effect	Nahewirkung f, Nahwirkung f, Naheffekt m	pseudogley	Pseudogley m, gleyartiger (marmorierter) Boden m, Staunässegley m, nasser (wechselfeuchter) Waldboden m
proximity theory, Faraday's theory	Nahewirkungstheorie f, Faradaysche Nahewirkungstheorie		
PR unit, photofluorograph[ic unit], photoroentgen unit	Schirmbildgerät n, Röntgenschirmbildgerät n	pseudo g-value	Pseudo-g-Wert m
		pseudoharmonic function	pseudoharmonische Funktion f
Prym['s] function	Prymsche Funktion f		
pseudo acidity	Pseudoacidität f	pseudoharmonic oscillation, pseudoharmonic vibration, non-linear vibration, non-linear oscillation	nichtlineare Schwingung f, pseudoharmonische Schwingung
pseudoadiabat	s. moist adiabat		
pseudoadiabatic	s. moist adiabat		
pseudoadiabatic line	s. moist adiabat		
pseudo-allelism	Pseudoallelie f		
pseudoanalytic function	pseudoanalytische Funktion f	pseudo Hermitian symmetry	Pseudo-Hermite-Symmetrie f, pseudo-Hermitesche Symmetrie f
pseudo-anomaly coefficient, coefficient of pseudo-anomaly	Pseudoanomaliekoeffizient m		
		pseudo-high vacuum	Pseudohochvakuum n
pseudo-anomaly potential	Pseudoanomaliepotential n	pseudohomogeneous	pseudohomogen
pseudoantagonism	Pseudoantagonismus m	pseudo H-wave	Pseudo-H-Welle f
pseudoatom	Pseudoatom n	pseudoimage	Pseudobild n
pseudo-axisymmetric flow of the first <second> kind	pseudorotationssymmetrische Strömung f erster <zweiter> Art	pseudo instruction, pseudo-order	symbolischer Befehl m, Pseudobefehl m
pseudobalance, symbolic balance <of the bridge>	Pseudoabgleich m <Brücke>	pseudo-integral equation	Pseudointegralgleichung f
pseudo basicity	Pseudobasizität f	pseudo-isochromatic plate	pseudoisochromatische Farbtafel (Tafel) f
pseudo Brewster angle	pseudo-Brewsterscher Winkel m, Pseudo-Brewster-Winkel m	pseudoisomerism	Pseudoisomerie f
		pseudo-labile	s. moist-labile
pseudocatalysis	Pseudokatalyse f	pseudolaminar flow	pseudolaminare Strömung f
pseudocatenoid	Pseudokatenoid n		
pseudocavitation	Pseudokavitation f	pseudo lens, pinhole	Loch n <Lochkamera>
pseudo[-]cirrus	Pseudocirrus m, Pseudozirrus m	pseudo-lineal motion	pseudolineale Bewegung f
pseudocleavage, false cleavage	Pseudoschieferung f	pseudo-Maxwellian molecular force	pseudo-Maxwellsche Molekularkraft f
pseudocolloid	Pseudokolloid n	pseudo Maxwellian molecule	pseudo-Maxwellsches Molekül n
pseudocombination, dummy combination	Scheinkombination f, Scheinbehandlung f		
pseudo co-ordinate, non-holonomic co-ordinate, quasi co-ordinate	nichtholonome Koordinate f, Pseudokoordinate f, Quasikoordinate f	pseudomerism	Pseudomerie f

pseudo-monocrystal

pseudo-monocrystal, pseudo single crystal	Pseudoeinkristall m	pseudo solarization, Sabattier effect <phot.>	Sabattier-Effekt m, Sabattier-Bildumkehrung f <Phot.>
pseudomonotropy	Pseudomonotropie f	pseudo[-]solution	Pseudolösung f
pseudomorph (crystal), pseudomorphous crystal	pseudomorpher Kristall m, Afterkristall m	pseudosphere, pseudospherical surface	Pseudosphäre f, pseudosphärische Fläche f
pseudomorphism	s. pseudomorphosis	pseudospherical space	pseudosphärischer Raum m
pseudomorphie [of crystals], pseudomorphy, crystal pseudomorphism	Pseudomorphie f, Kristallpseudomorphie f	pseudospherical surface	s. pseudosphere
		pseudostable state	pseudostabiler Zustand m
pseudomorphosis, pseudomorphism	Pseudomorphose f, Kristallpseudomorphose f, Afterkristallbildung f	pseudostationary boundary layer	pseudostationäre Grenzschicht f
pseudomorphous crystal, pseudomorph [crystal]	pseudomorpher Kristall m, Afterkristall m	pseudostereoscopic effect	s. stroboscopic effect
pseudomorphy	s. pseudomorphism	pseudo[-]stress	Pseudospannung f
pseudo-order, pseudo instruction	symbolischer Befehl m, Pseudobefehl m	pseudo[-]symmetry	Pseudosymmetrie f
pseudo parallel	pseudoparallel	pseudotemperature	Pseudotemperatur f
pseudo-parallel displacement	s. parallel displacement <of vectors>	pseudotensor	Pseudotensor m
pseudoperiod	Pseudoperiode f	pseudo tensor density	Pseudotensordichte f
pseudoperiodic quantity	pseudoperiodische Größe f	pseudo-thermostatics	Pseudothermostatik f
		pseudotime	Pseudozeit f
pseudoplane flow	s. pseudoplane motion	pseudotopotaxis	Pseudotopotaxis f
pseudoplane motion; pseudoplane flow <of the first, second kind>	pseudoebene Bewegung f; pseudoebene Strömung f <erster, zweiter Art>	pseudo-turbulent flow; pseudo-turbulent motion	pseudoturbulente Bewegung f; pseudoturbulente Strömung f
pseudoplastic fluid	pseudoplastische Flüssigkeit f	pseudo[-]twin	Pseudozwilling m
pseudoplasticity	Pseudoplastizität f	pseudo-unimolecular reaction	pseudomonomolekulare Reaktion f
pseudopotential	Pseudopotential n	pseudo-unitary	pseudounitär
pseudopotential temperature	pseudopotentielle Temperatur f	pseudo[]variable [star], improper variable [star], extrinsic variable [star]	Pseudoveränderlicher m, uneigentlicher Veränderlicher m
pseudopsy, optical illusion	geometrisch-optische Wahrnehmungsverzerrung f, [geometrisch-]optische Täuschung f	pseudovector	s. axial vector
		pseudovector coupling, axial coupling, axial vector coupling	pseudovektorielle Kopplung f, Pseudovektorkopplung f, Axialvektorkopplung f, axiale Kopplung
pseudoquadrupolar effect (interaction), pseudoquadrupole effect	Pseudoquadrupolwechselwirkung f, Pseudoquadrupoleffekt m	pseudovector effect	s. pseudovectorial interaction
pseudoquadrupole	Pseudoquadrupol m	pseudovectorial field; pseudovectorial potential field	pseudovektorielles Feld n, Pseudovektorfeld n; pseudovektorielles Potentialfeld n
pseudoquadrupole effect, pseudoquadrupolar effect (interaction)	Pseudoquadrupolwechselwirkung f, Pseudoquadrupoleffekt m		
pseudoracemate	Pseudorazemat n, pseudorazemische Verbindung f	pseudovectorial interaction, pseudovector interaction, pseudovector effect, axial vector interaction, axial interaction	pseudovektorielle Wechselwirkung f, Pseudovektorwechselwirkung f, Pseudovektoreffekt m, Axialvektorwechselwirkung f, axiale Wechselwirkung
pseudorandom function	Pseudozufallsfunktion f		
pseudorandom number	Pseudozufal!szahl f		
pseudorandom sequence	Pseudozufallsfolge f		
pseudoregular precession	pseudoreguläre Präzession f		
pseudoscalar, pseudoscalar quantity	Pseudoskalar m, pseudoskalare Größe f	pseudovectorial potential <of nuclear forces>	pseudovektorielles Potential n [der Kernkräfte], Pseudovektorpotential n [der Kernkräfte]
pseudoscalar coupling	pseudoskalare Kopplung f	pseudovectorial potential field	s. pseudovectorial field
pseudoscalar coupling constant	pseudoskalare Kopplungskonstante f	pseudovector interaction	s. pseudovectorial interaction
pseudoscalar effect	s. pseudoscalar interaction	pseudovelocity of sound	Pseudoschallgeschwindigkeit f
pseudoscalar field; pseudoscalar potential field	pseudoskalares Feld n, Pseudoskalarfeld n; pseudoskalares Potentialfeld n	pseudo-wet-bulb temperature	Pseudofeuchttemperatur f
		pseudo-zero point, symbolic zero	Pseudonullpunkt m
pseudoscalar interaction, pseudoscalar effect	pseudoskalare Wechselwirkung f, Pseudoskalarwechselwirkung f, Pseudoskalareffekt m	psi-function, digamma function	Digammafunktion f, [Gaußsche] Psi-Funktion f, Gaußsche Ψ-Funktion, Ψ-Funktion
pseudoscalar meson theory, pseudoscalar theory	pseudoskalare Mesonentheorie (Mesonenfeldtheorie) f, pseudoskalare Theorie f	p-s-n rectifier	psn-Gleichrichter m
pseudoscalar potential <of nuclear forces>	pseudoskalares Potential n [der Kernkräfte]	psophometer, noise [measuring] meter <el.>	Geräusch[spannungs]messer m, Psophometer n <El.>
pseudoscalar potential field	s. pseudoscalar field	psophometer filter, psophometric filter	Psophometerfilter n, A-Filter n
pseudoscalar quantity	s. pseudoscalar	psophometric electromotive force, psophometric e.m.f.	Geräusch-EMK f, geräuschelektromotorische Kraft f
pseudoscalar theory	s. pseudoscalar meson theory		
pseudoscopic effect, pseudoscopic phenomenon	pseudoskopische Erscheinung f, pseudoskopischer Effekt m, pseudostereoskopischer Eindruck m	psophometric filter, psophometer filter	Psophometerfilter n, A-Filter n
		psophometric voltage	s. noise voltage <el.>
		p-spot	s. preceding spot
pseudoscopy	Pseudoskopie f, Tiefenverkehrung f, tiefenverkehrte Wiedergabe f	psychoacoustics, psychological acoustics	Psychoakustik f, psychologische Akustik f
pseudo single crystal	s. pseudo-monocrystal		

psychokinesis — Psychokinese f
psychological acoustics — s. psychoacoustics
psycho-physics — Psychophysik f
psychrometer, wet- and dry-bulb psychrometer (hygrometer, thermometer), evaporation psychrometer — Psychrometer n, Verdunstungsfeuchtigkeitsmesser m
psychrometer constant, psychrometric constant — Psychrometerkonstante f
psychrometer difference, psychrometric difference, depression of wet bulb, wet-bulb temperature difference, wet-bulb depression — psychrometrische Differenz (Temperaturdifferenz) f, Psychrometerdifferenz f
psychrometer equation, psychrometric formula, wet- and dry-bulb hygrometer equation — Psychrometerformel f, psychrometrische Gleichung f
psychrometric chart, psychrometric table — Psychrometertafel f, Psychrometertabelle f, psychrometrische Tafel (Tabelle) f
psychrometric constant, psychrometer constant — Psychrometerkonstante f
psychrometric difference — s. psychrometer difference
psychrometric formula — s. psychrometer equation
psychrometric table — s. psychrometric chart
P symbol of time ordering — s. Dyson['s] chronological operator
Ptolemaic system — Ptolemäisches Weltsystem (System) n
p-type, p-conducting — p-leitend, p-, p-Typ-, defektleitend
p-type conduction (conductivity), hole conduction — Defekt[elektronen]leitung f, p-[Typ-]Leitung f, Mangelleitung f, Löcherleitung f, Lückenleitung f, Leerstellenleitung f, Ersatzleitung f, Akzeptorenleitung f, Störstellenleitung f vom p-Typ
p-type conductivity — s. hole conductivity
p-type conductor — s. p-type semiconductor
p-type impurity — s. acceptor
p-type ionic conduction — Ionenmangelleitung f, Ionendefektleitung f
p-type ionic conductor — Ionenmangelleiter m, Ionendefektleiter m
p-type metallic conduction — metallische Defektelektronenleitung f
p-type semiconductor, hole semiconductor, p-type conductor — p-Halbleiter m, Defekt[halb]leiter m, p-Leiter m, p-Typ-Halbleiter m, Störstellenhalbleiter m vom p-Typ, Löcherhalbleiter m, Oxydations[halb]leiter m, Mangel[halb]leiter m, Fehlstellenhalbleiter m
puff <bio.> — Puff m <pl.: Puffs>; Balbiani-Ring m <Bio.>
puffing — s. decrepitation
puffy wind — s. choppy wind
Puiseux['] series [expansion] — Puiseux-Entwicklung f; Puiseux-Reihe f
Pulfrich effect, Pulfrich stereoeffect — Pulfrichscher Stereoeffekt m, Pulfrich-Effekt m
Pulfrich photometer, step photometer — Pulfrich-Photometer n, Stufenphotometer n
Pulfrich refractometer — Pulfrich-Refraktometer n, Refraktometer n für Chemiker
Pulfrich stereoeffect — s. Pulfrich effect
pull, pulling; traction; drawing; tug; drag — Ziehen n, Zug m, Fortziehen n; Schleppen n
pull; tension; pulling; traction — Ziehen n, Zug m, Auseinanderziehen n
pull — s. a. suction <aero.>
pull — s. a. tensile force
pull drive — Zugmittelgetriebe n
pulled crystal — gezogener Kristall m, Ziehkristall m
pulled junction, grown junction — gezogener Übergang m
puller airscrew — s. tractor airscrew
pulley; roller; wheel — Rolle f; Scheibe f; Rad n

pulley [block], pulley hoist, pulley tackle, assembly (block, compound, tackle) pulley, block and tackle, block, tackle, treble block <mech.> — Flaschenzug m, Rollenzug m, Seilrollenzug m, Klobenzug m, Kloben m <Mech.>
pull force — s. tensile force
pull-in — s. frequency pulling
pull-in effect — s. pulling effect <el.>
pulling — s. frequency pulling
pulling — s. pull
pulling capacitance — s. capacitance connected in series for pulling the resonance frequency of a crystal oscillator
pulling effect, pulling phenomenon, pull-in effect; backlash <el.> — Mitnahmeeffekt m, Mitnahmeerscheinung f, Mitzieheffekt m, Zieherscheinung f <El.>
pulling figure — Frequenzziehwert m, Belastungsverstimmung f
pulling force — s. tensile force
pulling into tune — s. frequency pulling
pulling method — s. pulling of crystals
pulling of crystals, [single-]crystal pulling, pulling technique, pulling method, growing from the melt [of crystals] — Ziehen n von Kristallen [aus der Schmelze], Kristallziehen n, Kristallziehverfahren n
pulling on whites — Nachziehen n, Fahnennachziehen n, Weißdehnung f
pulling oscillator — Mitziehoszillator m
pulling phenomenon — s. pulling effect <el.>
pulling range — s. pull-in range
pulling stress — s. stretching strain
pulling technique — s. pulling of crystals
pulling technique of Czochralski — s. Czochralski['s] method
pull-in range, pulling range; hold range, retention range; lock-in range, locking range; interception range — Mitnahmebereich m; Synchronisierbereich m, Synchronisierungsbereich m, Synchronisationsbereich m; Haltebereich m; Einspringbereich m; Fangbereich m
pull-in range [of the klystron] — Ziehbereich m [des Klystrons]
pulsar — s. pulsating radiofrequency source
pulsatance, pulsation <especially el.>; angular frequency, radian frequency — Kreisfrequenz f, Winkelfrequenz f
pulsating — s. pulsed
pulsating arc, PA — pulsierender Bogen m
pulsating bending strength — s. fatigue strength under repeated bending stress[es] in one direction
pulsating body, pulsator <hydr.> — Pulsator m, pulsierender Körper m <Hydr.>
pulsating current, pulsing (pulsed, pulse) current — pulsierender Strom m, Impulsstrom m, Impulsfolgestrom m
pulsating current, pulsating direct current — pulsierender Gleichstrom m, Schwellstrom m
pulsating fatigue strength under bending stress[es] — s. fatigue strength under repeated bending stress[es] in one direction
pulsating flow, pulsating motion — pulsierende Strömung f, pulsierende Bewegung f
pulsating load, pulsating strain, load varying between zero and maximum positive strain — Schwellbeanspruchung f, schwellende (pulsierende) Beanspruchung f, Schwellbelastung f, schwellende (pulsierende) Belastung f

pulsating magnetic field, pulsed magnet field, pulsed magnet power	Impulsmagnetfeld n, pulsierendes Magnetfeld n	pulse-code modulation, PCM, pulse-number modulation	Pulscodemodulation f, Pulskodemodulation f, Pulszahlmodulation f, Impulscodemodulation f, Impulskodemodulation f, Impulszahlmodulation f, PCM
pulsating motion	s. pulsating flow		
pulsating radio[-frequency] source, pulsar	Pulsar m, pulsierende Radioquelle f, pulsierender Radiostern m	pulse column, pulsed (pulsing)column	Pulsatorkolonne f, Impulskolonne f, Pulskolonne f
pulsating star	pulsierender Stern m; Pulsationsveränderlicher m	pulse-controlled time-of-flight spectrometer	Impulslaufzeitspektrometer n, impulsgetastetes Laufzeitspektrometer n
pulsating strain	s. pulsating load		
pulsating stress, stress varying from zero to maximum, one-way stress, zero alternating stress	schwellende Spannung f, Schwellspannung f	pulse correction, pulse regeneration	Impulsentzerrung f, Impulsverbesserung f
		pulse corrector	Impulskorrektor m
pulsating surface	pulsierende Fläche f		
pulsating voltage	s. ripple voltage	pulse counter (counting assembly), pulse counting unit, [radiation] counting assembly, [radiation] counting unit, [radiation] counter, radioactive radiation counter (counting assembly) <nucl.>	Zähler m, Zählgerät n, Impulszähler m Impulszählgerät n, Strahlungszähler m, Strahlungszählgerät n, Kernstrahlungszähler m, Kernstrahlungszählgerät n, Impulszählanlage f, Zählanlage f <Kern.>
pulsating vortex	pulsierender Wirbel m		
pulsation, pulsing; ripple	Pulsation f, Pulsieren n, Pulsung f, Pulsion f; Tröpfeln n <HF-Oszillator>		
pulsation	s. a. pulsatance		
pulsation instability	Pulsationsinstabilität f		
pulsation theory	Pulsationstheorie f		
pulsative	s. pulsed	pulse counting channel, counting channel, channel	Zählkanal m, Impulszählkanal m, Kanal m
pulsator, pulsating body <hydr.>	Pulsator m, pulsierender Körper m <Hydr.>		
		pulse counting circuit, counting circuit	Impulszählschaltung f, Zählschaltung f
pulsatory	s. pulsed		
pulsatron, pulse tube	Pulsatron n, Impulsröhre f	pulse counting technique, counting technique	Zähltechnik f, Impulszähltechnik f
pulse <bio.>	Puls m <Bio.>	pulse counting unit	s. pulse counter <nucl.>
pulse, impulse, surge <gen., el.>	Impuls m, Stoß m <allg., El.>; Anstoß n	pulse current, surge current	Stoßstrom m, Impulsstrom m, Impulsfolgestrom m
pulse, count, counter pulse, counting pulse, counting impulse, c <nucl.>	Impuls m, Zählstoß m, Zählerimpuls m, Zählimpuls m, Imp. <Kern.>	pulse current	s. a. pulsating current
		pulse current generator, impulse current generator, surge current generator	Stoßstromgenerator m, Stoßstromerzeuger m
pulse	s. a. pulsed		
pulse alternating current	Stoßwechselstrom m	pulse curve	Impulskurve f
pulse amplifier, impulse amplifier; pulse repeater	Impulsverstärker m	pulse cyclotron	s. pulsed cyclotron
		pulsed; pulse-operated; pulse; pulsating; pulsive; pulsative; pulsatory	Impuls-, Puls-, Stoß-, gepulst, pulsierend, impulsartig [betrieben], impulsbetrieben; impulsförmig
pulse amplitude, pulse height, pulse elevation	Impulshöhe f, Impulsamplitude f, Impulsgröße f; Impulshöchstwert m, Impulsscheitelwert m		
		pulsed beam	Impulsstrahl m
pulse-amplitude analyzer	s. amplitude analyzer	pulsed beam current	Impulsstrahlstrom m
pulse-amplitude discriminator	s. discriminator	polsed column, pulse column, pulsing column	Pulsatorkolonne f, Impulskolonne f, Pulskolonne f
		pulsed combustion	Pulsverbrennung f
pulse-amplitude modulation, PAM	Pulsamplitudenmodulation f, Impulsamplitudenmodulation f, PAM	pulsed current; pulsed flow <hydr.>	Impulsströmung f; Impulsstrom m <Hydr.>
		pulsed current	s. a. pulsating current
pulse-amplitude selector	s. pulse selector	pulsed cyclotron, pulse cyclotron, pulse-operated cyclotron	Impulszyklotron n, Zyklotron n mit Impulsbetrieb
pulse-amplitude spectrum, pulse height spectrum	Impulshöhenspektrum n, Impulsamplitudenspektrum n, Amplitudenspektrum n [der Impulse], Impulsspektrum n		
		pulsed discharge	s. impulsive discharge
		pulsed discharge lamp, pulsed gas-discharge lamp	Impulslampe f, Impulsentladungslampe f
pulse at break, break impulse, break pulse	Öffnungsimpuls m, Abreißimpuls m		
		pulsed discharge tube	Impulsentladungsrohr n
		pulse decay	Impulsabfall m, Flankenabfall m
pulse bandwidth, pulse spectrum bandwidth	Impulsbandbreite f, Pulsbandbreite f, Breite f des Impulsspektrums (Pulsspektrums)		
		pulse decay time	Impulsabfallzeit f, Impulsabklingzeit f
pulse base, base of the pulse	Impulsbasis f, Impulsfuß m, Basis f <Impuls>	pulse deflection; pulse sweep	Impulsauslenkung f
pulse capacitance, surge capacitance	Stoßkapazität f	pulse delay line	Impulsverzögerungsleitung f
pulse centre	Impulsmitte f	pulsed emission	s. pulsed radiation
pulse chamber, pulse (counting) ionization chamber, pulse[-type] chamber	Impulsionisationskammer f, zählende Ionisationskammer f, Zählkammer f	pulsed emission of the cathode	Impulsemission f der Katode
		pulsed excitation	Impulsanregung f
pulse clipper	s. clipper	pulsed flow; pulsed current <hydr.>	Impulsströmung f; Impulsstrom m <Hydr.>
pulse clipping, pulse stripping	Impulsbegrenzung f, Impulsbeschneidung f		
		pulsed frequency	s. pulse recurrence frequency

pulsed gas-discharge lamp, pulsed discharge lamp — Impulslampe f, Impulsentladungslampe f

pulse diagram, pulse-response diagram; pulse scheme — Impulsdiagramm n, Impulsschaubild n, Impulsplan m; Impulsschema n

pulse-differentiating stage, pulse differentiator — Impulsdifferenzierstufe f

pulse differentiation — Impulsdifferenzierung f, Impulsdifferentiierung f

pulse differentiator, pulse-differentiating stage — Impulsdifferenzierstufe f

pulse direction finding, impulse direction finding, impulse radar, pulsed (pulse) radar — Impulspeilverfahren n, Impulspeilung f, Impulsradar n

pulse discharge — s. impulsive discharge

pulse distortion — Impuls[form]verzerrung f, Imputsverformung f

pulse dividing, pulse-rate division, repetition-rate division, skip keying, count-down — Impulsteilung f, Impulsfrequenzteilung f

pulse dividing circuit — s. scaling circuit

pulsed klystron, pulse klystron — Impulsklystron n

pulsed laser, pulse-type laser — Impulslaser m, Laser m mit Impulsanregung

pulsed light source — s. pulsed source of light

pulsed magnet field, pulsed magnet power, pulsating magnetic field — Impulsmagnetfeld n, pulsierendes Magnetfeld n

pulsed magnetron — Impulsmagnetron n, Impulsmagnetfe dröhre f

pulsed maser, pulse-type maser — Impulsmaser m, Maser m mit Impulsanregung.

pulsed neutron experiment — Neutronenimpulsexperiment n

pulsed neutron source — Impulsneutronenquelle f, gepulste Neutronenquelle f

pulsed operation, pulse operation — Impulsbetrieb m

pulsed oscillation, pulse-shaped oscillation — Impulsschwingung f, impulsförmige Schwingung f

pulsed oscillograph, pulsed oscilloscope, surge oscillograph — Impulsoszillograph m, Impulsoszilloskop n

pulsed radar, pulse radar — Pulsradar n

pulsed radar — s. a. pulse direction finding

pulsed radiation, pulse radiation, pulsing radiation; pulsed emission, pulse emission, pulsing emission — Impulsstrahlung f, pulsierende Strahlung f; Impulsemission f, pulsierende Emission f

pulsed radiolysis — s. pulse radiolysis

pulsed reactor — Impulsreaktor m, Pulsreaktor m

pulsed source of light, pulsed light source — Impulslichtquelle f, pulsierende Lichtquelle f

pulse[-] duct — s. pulse jet

pulse duration; pulse length; pulse width — Impulsdauer f, Flankendauer f; Impulsbreite f; Impulslänge f; Impulszeit f

pulse-duration modulation, pulse-width modulation, pulse-length modulation, pulse-time modulation, time modulation, PWM — Pulslängenmodulation f, Pulsdauermodulation f, Pulsbreitenmodulation f, Impulsbreitenmodulation f, Impulsdauermodulation f, Impulslängenmodulation f, Zeitmodulation f, Impulszeitmodulation f, Pulszeitmodulation f, Einsatz[punkt]modulation f, PLM, PDM

pulse duration ratio — s. pulse width-repetition ratio

pulse duty factor — s. pulse width — repetition ratio

pulsed voltage — s. ripple voltage

pulse echo meter — Impulsechomesser m

pulse-echo method, pulse-sounding method — Impuls-Echo-Verfahren n; Impulsecholotung f, Impulslotung f

pulse elevation — s. pulse amplitude

pulse emission — s. pulsed radiation

pulse energy, energy of the pulse — Impulsenergie f, Impulsarbeit f

pulse excitation, impact (shock, repulse, impulse) excitation <of oscillation> — Stoßanregung f, Stoßerregung f <Schwingung>

pulse firing — Impulszündung f

pulse forming — s. pulse shaping

pulse-forming amplifier — s. shaping amplifier

pulse-frequency modulation — Pulsfrequenzmodulation f, Impulsfrequenzmodulation f, PFM

pulse front, front of the pulse, edge of the pulse — Impulsflanke f, Impulsfront f, Flanke f des Impulses

pulse function, impulse function — Stoßfunktion f, Impulsfunktion f, Nadelfunktion f

pulse generating device — s. impulse generator

pulse generation — Impulserzeugung f, Impulsbildung f

pulse generator, synchronizing pulse generator, clock generator, clock multivibrator — Taktgeber m, Impulsgeber m

pulse generator — s. a. impulse generator

pulse group — Impulsgruppe f

pulse height, pulse amplitude, pulse elevation — Impulshöhe f, Impulsamplitude f, Impulsgröße f; Impulshöchstwert m, Impulsscheitelwert m

pulse height analyzer — s. pulse-amplitude analyzer

pulse-height clipping, amplitude clipping — Impulsamplitudenbegrenzung f, Impulshöhenbegrenzung f

pulse-height discriminator — s. discriminator

pulse height selector — s. pulse selector

pulse height spectrum — s. pulse-amplitude spectrum

pulse height-to-time converter — Amplitude-Zeit-Wandler m, Amplitude-Zeit-Konverter m, Impulshöhe-Zeit-Konverter m, AZ-Wandler m

pulse interval — s. pulse separation

pulse interval analyzer, interval analyzer, time sorter — Impulsintervallanalysator m, Intervallanalysator m

pulse-interval modulation, pulse-separation modulation, pulse-spacing modulation — Pulsabstandsmodulation f, Impulsabstandsmodulation f

pulse ionization chamber, pulse[-type] chamber, counting ionization chamber — Impulsionisationskammer f, zählende Ionisationskammer f, Zählkammer f

pulse jet, pulse[-] duct, intermittend (resonant) jet — Verpuffungsstrahltriebwerk n, Verpuffungsstrahlrohr n, Pulsostrahlrohr n; Schmidt[-Argus]-Rohr n

pulse klystron — s. pulse klystron

pulse length; pulse duration; pulse width — Impulsdauer f, Flankendauer f; Impulsbreite f; Impulslänge f; Impulszeit f

pulse length modulation — s. pulse-duration modulation

pulse limiting rate — Impulsbegrenzungsmaß n

pulse line — Impulsleitung f

pulse magnetization, impulse magnetization — Stoßmagnetisierung f

pulse meter — Impulsmesser m, Impulsmeßgerät n

pulse mixer; pulse mixing circuit — Impulsmischer m; Impulsmischschaltung f

pulse mixing — Impulsmischung f

pulse mixing circuit	s. pulse mixer	pulse rate	s. a. pulse recurrence frequency
pulse mode	Impulsart f	pulse-rate divider, repetition-rate divider	Impulsteiler m, Impulsfrequenzteiler m
pulse modulation	Pulsmodulation f, Impulsmodulation f	pulse-rate division, pulse dividing, repetition-rate division, skip keying, count-down	Impulsteilung f, Impulsfrequenzteilung f
pulse modulator, impulser, pulser	Impulsmodulator m	pulse ratio	s. pulse width – repetition ratio
pulse noise, impulse noise	Impulsrauschen n	pulse recorder	Impulsschreiber m; Pulsschreiber m
pulse-number modulation, pulse-code modulation, PCM	Pulscodemodulation f, Pulskodemodulation f, Pulszahlmodulation f, Impulscodemodulation f, Impulskodemodulation f, Impulszahlmodulation f, PCM	pulse recurrence frequency, recurrence (pulse repetition) frequency, [pulse-]repetition rate, recurrence rate, pulsed frequency, pulse rate, p.r.f.	Impuls[folge]frequenz f, Impulshäufigkeit f, Impulswiederholungsfrequenz f, Wiederholungsfrequenz f, Folgefrequenz f, Impulstaktfrequenz f, Taktfrequenz f
pulse of current	s. impulse of current	pulse reflection method	Impulsreflexionsverfahren n, Inpulsrückstrahlverfahren n
pulse of particles, particle pulse	Teilchenimpuls m		
pulse of tension (voltage)	s. impulse of voltage	pulse regeneration, pulse correction	Impulsentzerrung f, Impulsverbesserung f
pulse of waves	s. wave train		
pulse onset	Impulseinsatz m	pulse repeater	s. pulse amplifier
pulse-operated	s. pulsed	pulse repetition frequency	s. pulse recurrence frequency
pulse-operated cyclotron, pulsed cyclotron, pulse cyclotron	Impulszyklotron n, Zyklotron n mit Impulsbetrieb	pulse repetition frequency range, range of pulse repetition frequency	Impulsbereich m
		pulse repetition period	s. pulse period
pulse operation	s. pulsed operation	pulse-repetition rate	s. pulse recurrence frequency
pulse oscillator, impulse oscillator	Impulsoszillator m	pulse response	s. unit[-] impulse response
pulse overexcitation	Stoßübererregung f	pulse-response diagram, pulse diagram; pulse scheme	Impulsdiagramm n, Impulsschaubild n, Impulsplan m; Impulsschema n
pulse overlap	Impulsüberlagerung f, Impulsüberlappung f, Impulsüberschneidung f	pulse restoration	Impulserneuerung f, Impulswiederherstellung f
pulse-overlap converter, pulse-overlap time converter	Impulsüberlappungskonverter m, Zeitkonverter m nach dem Impulsüberlappungsprinzip	pulse rise time	Impulsanstiegszeit f, Flankenanstiegszeit f
pulse-overlap principle	Impulsüberlappungsprinzip n	pulse scaling circuit, scaling circuit	Untersetzerschaltung f, Zählschaltung f, Impulsuntersetzerschaltung f
pulse-overlap time converter	s. pulse-overlap converter	pulse scheme	s. pulse-response diagram
pulse passage	Impulsdurchgang m	pulse selection	Impulsauswahl f; Impulsaussiebung f; Impulssiebung f
pulse period, pulse repetition period, repetition period	Impulsperiode f, Periode f des Impulses, Taktperiode f; Tastperiode f ‹bei periodischen Impulsfolgen›	pulse selector, pulse-amplitude selector, pulse height selector	Impulshöhenselektor m, Impulsamplitudenselektor m, Amplitudenselektor m, Impulsselektor m, Impulssieb n
pulse phase	s. pulse position		
pulse-phase modulation	s. pulse-position modulation	pulse sender	s. pulser
pulse-phase spectrum, phase spectrum of the pulse	Impulsphasenspektrum n, Phasenspektrum n des Impulses, Spektrum n der Impulsphasen	pulse sending, impulsing, pulsing, impulse sending	Impulsgebung f, Impulsgabe f
		pulse separation	Impulstrennung f; Impulsabtrennung f
pulse polarography	Pulspolarographie f		
pulse position, impulse position, pulse (impulse) phase	Impulslage f, Impulsphase f	pulse separation, pulse spacing, pulse-to-pulse interval, pulse interval, interpulse interval	Impulsabstand m, Impulsintervall n, Impulspause f, Impulslücke f
pulse-position modulation, displacement modulation, pulse-phase modulation, PPM	Pulslagemodulation f, Pulslagenmodulation f, Impulslagenmodulation f, Pulsphasenmodulation f, Impulsphasenmodulation f, PPM		
		pulse-separation modulation, pulse-spacing modulation, pulse-interval modulation	Pulsabstandsmodulation f, Impulsabstandsmodulation f
pulse power, power of the pulse	Impuls[stoß]leistung f, Leistung f je Impuls		
pulse propagation velocity, propagation velocity of pulses, pulse velocity, velocity of the pulse	Impulsausbreitungsgeschwindigkeit f, Impulslaufgeschwindigkeit f, Impulsgeschwindigkeit f	pulse separation stage, pulse separator	Impulstrennstufe f; Impulsabtrennstufe f
pulser, impulser, impulse sender (exciter), pulse sender	Impulsgeber m		
pulser	s. a. pulse modulator	pulse sequence	s. pulse train
pulse radar, pulsed radar	Pulsradar n	pulse series	s. pulse train
pulse radar	s. a. pulse direction finding	pulse shape	Impulsform f; Impulsfigur f
pulse radiation	s. pulsed radiation		
pulse radiolysis, pulsed radiolysis	Pulsradiolyse f, Impulsradiolyse f	pulse-shaped oscillation, pulsed oscillation	Impulsschwingung f, impulsförmige Schwingung f
pulse rate, impulsing rate; counting rate	Zählrate f, Zählgeschwindigkeit f; Impulsdichte f, Impulsrate f		
		pulse shaper	s. shaping unit

pulse shaping, pulse forming — Impulsform[geb]ung f
pulse shaping circuit (stage) — s. shaping unit
pulse slope, pulse (edge) steepness, edge slope, slope (steepness) of edge — Impulsflankensteilheit f, Flankensteilheit f, Impulssteilheit f
pulse sound, impulse ultrasound (sound), pulse ultrasound — Impulsschall m
pulse-sounding method — s. pulse-echo method
pulse spacing — s. pulse separation
pulse-spacing modulation, pulse-separation modulation, pulse-interval modulation — Pulsabstandsmodulation f, Impulsabstandsmodulation f
pulse spectrograph — Impulsspektrograph m

pulse spectrum, impulse spectrum <el.> — Impulsspektrum n <El.>
pulse spectrum bandwidth, pulse bandwidth — Impulsbandbreite f, Pulsbandbreite f, Breite f des Impulsspektrums (Pulsspektrums)
pulse spike, spike of the pulse — Impulsspitze f
pulse steepness — s. pulse slope
pulse step function — s. unit[-] impulse response
pulse strength, strength of the impulse, impulse strength — Impulsstärke f, Fläche f unter der Impulskurve
pulse stretcher — Impulsdehner m
pulse stretching — Impulsdehnung f, Impulsbasisverlängerung f; Impulsverbreiterung f, Impulsverlängerung f
pulse stripping — s. pulse clipping
pulse sweep; pulse deflection — Impulsauslenkung f
pulse synchronization, pulse timing — Impulstastung f; Impulssynchronisierung f

pulse tail, tail of the pulse — Impulsabfall m, Impulsschwanz m; Nachleuchtschleppe f
pulse test[ing], impulse test (testing) — Impulsprüfverfahren n; Impuls-Echo-Prüfung f
pulse tilt, pulse top, top [of the pulse], horizontal part of the pulse — Impulsdach n, Dach n
pulse tilt — s. a. tilt <of pulse>
pulse-time modulation — s. double modulation
pulse-time modulation — s. pulse-width modulation
pulse time ratio — s. pulse width-repetition ratio
pulse timing, pulse synchronization — Impulstastung f; Impulssynchronisierung f
pulse top — s. pulse tilt
pulse-to-pulse interval — s. pulse separation
pulse train, impulse train, train of impulses (waves), wave train, [im]pulse sequence, [im]pulse series, series of [im]pulses — Impulsfolge f, Impulsreihe f; Impulsserie f
pulse train — s. a. wave train
pulse transformer — Impulstransformator m, Impulsumspanner m, Impulsumformer m, Impulsumsetzer m, Impulsübertrager m, Impulswandler m
pulse transmission <el.> — Impulsübertragung f <El.>

pulse triggering — Impulsauslösung f, Impulsanregung f; Impulsanstoß m

pulse tube, pulsatron — Pulsatron n, Impulsröhre f

pulse-type chamber, pulse (counting) ionization chamber, pulse chamber — Impulsionisationskammer f, zählende Ionisationskammer f, Zählkammer f
pulse-type laser — s. pulsed laser

pulse-type maser — s. pulsed maser
pulse ultrasound — s. pulse sound
pulse velocity — s. pulse propagation velocity
pulse voltage — s. ripple voltage
pulse voltage generator, impulse voltage generator, surge voltage generator — Stoßspannungsgenerator m, Stoßspannungserzeuger m, Stoßspannungsanlage f
pulse wave <bio.> — Pulswelle f <Bio.>
pulse-wave velocity — Pulswellengeschwindigkeit f
pulse width; pulse duration; pulse length — Impulsdauer f, Flankendauer f; Impulsbreite f; Impulslänge f; Impulszeit f
pulse width-amplitude converter, pulse width-to-amplitude converter — Impulsbreite-Impulshöhe-Konverter m, Impulsbreiten-Impulshöhen-Wandler m
pulse-width clipping, width clipping — Impulsbreitenbegrenzung f
pulse-width control — Impulsbreitenregelung f; Impulsbreitenverfahren n
pulse-width modulation — s. pulse-duration modulation
pulse width-repetition ratio, pulse duration (time) ratio, pulse ratio, mark-to-space ratio, pulse duty factor; duty cycle — Impulskennziffer f, Impuls[leistungs]verhältnis n; Tastverhältnis n, Impulstastverhältnis n, Schaltverhältnis n, Impulsschaltverhältnis n, Impuls[breiten]verhältnis n, Impuls-Pause-Verhältnis n

pulse width-to-amplitude converter — s. pulse width-amplitude converter
pulsing, pulsation; ripple — Pulsation f, Pulsieren n, Pulsung f, Pulsion f; Tröpfeln n <HF-Oszillator>
pulsing, impulsing, impulse sending, pulse sending — Impulsgebung f, Impulsgabe f
pulsing column — s. pulsed column
pulsing current — s. pulsating current
pulsing emission (radiation) — s. pulsed radiation
pulsing voltage — s. ripple voltage
pulsive — s. pulsed
pulsometer pump — Pulsometer n, Pulsometerpumpe f
pulverization — s. powdering
pulverization — s. rubbing
pulverizer — s. atomizer
pulverizing — s. powdering
pulverulence — Pulverförmigkeit f, pulverförmiger Zustand m

pump — Pumpe f
pump, pump source, pumping source — Pumpquelle f
pumpability — Pumpfähigkeit f

pumpage, pumping action — Pumpwirkung f, Pumpen n
pumpage — s. a. pump capacity
pump assembly, pumping system, vacuum pump system — Pumpstand m, Pump[en]system n, Vakuumpump[en]system n, Pump[en]anlage f
pump capacity, exhausting power, delivery of pump, pumping capacity, pumpage — Saugleistung f, Förderleistung f, Pumpleistung f
pump current, pumping current — Pumpstrom m
pump energy, pumping energy — Pumpenergie f
pump frequency, pumping frequency — Pumpfrequenz f

pumping, pumping over, pumpover — Durchpumpen n, Umpumpen n, Pumpen n <durch Rohre>, Umwälzung f durch Pumpen; Überpumpen n
pumping <maser> — Pumpen n <Molekularverstärker>

pumping action — s. pumpage

pumping capacity	s. pump capacity	punctum remotum, far point of clear vision <opt.>	Fernpunkt m, punctum n remotum; Fernpunkt im engeren Sinne, manifester Fernpunkt <Opt.>
pumping current, pump current	Pumpstrom m	puncture	s. breakdown
pumping device, pumping unit, pump light reflector	Pumpanordnung f	puncture of the [X-ray] tube	Durchschlag m der Röntgenröhre, Röhrendurchschlag m
pumping energy, pump energy	Pumpenergie f	puncture voltage	s. breakdown voltage
pumping frequency	s. pump frequency	Pungs choke	Pungs-Drossel f
pumping intensity, pump intensity	Pumpintensität f	pupil <of the optical instrument>	Pupille f <optisches Instrument>
pumping lamp, pump lamp	Pumplampe f	pupil aberration	Pupillenaberration f
pumping lead	s. exhaust tube	pupil function	Pupillenfunktion f
pumping light	Pumplicht n	pupillary aperture	Pupillenweite f; Pupillenöffnung f
pumping out	s. evacuation		
pumping over	s. pumping	pupillary reflex	Lichtreaktion f (Lichtreflex m) der Pupille, Pupillarreflex m, Pupillenreflex m
pumping power	Pump[en]leistung f, Pumpenantriebsleistung f, Antriebsleistung f der Pumpe, der Pumpe zugeführte Energie f		
		Pupin cable	s. coil-loaded cable
		Pupin coil, loading coil	Pupin-Spule f
pumping power, pump power <of parametric amplifier>	Pumpleistung f <Reaktanzverstärker>	pupinization, loading <of a line>, coil loading	Bespulung f, Pupinisierung f
		pupinization section	s. loading coil section
		pupinized cable	s. coil-loaded cable
pumping pressure	Förderdruck m der Pumpe	pure bending, simple bending (flexure), pure flexure	reine Biegung f
pumping resistance	Pumpwiderstand m	pure beta emitter, beta emitter only	reiner Beta-Strahler m
pumping scheme	Pumpdiagramm n, Pumpschema n		
pumping source, pump source, pump	Pumpquelle f	pure carbon, homogeneous carbon, plain carbon, retort carbon	Homogenkohle f, Reinkohle f, Retortenkohle f, Reindochtkohle f
pumping speed	s. exhaustion rate		
pumping stem	s. exhaust tube		
pumping system	s. pump assembly	pure case; maximum observation	reiner Fall m <Weyl>; Maximalbeobachtung f <Dirac>
pumping transition, pump transition	Pumpübergang m		
pumping unit	s. pumping device	pure dilatational strain, uniform dilatation, dilatational strain	gleichförmige Dilatation f, reine Volumenänderung f
pumping voltage, pump voltage	Pumpspannung f		
pump intensity, pumping intensity	Pumpintensität f	pure element, monoisotopic element, anisotopic (simple) element	Reinelement n, isotopenreines (monoisotopisches, anisotopes) Element n
pump lamp, pumping lamp	Pumplampe f		
pump light reflector	s. pumping device	pure ensemble	reine Gesamtheit f
pumpover	s. pumping	pure flexure	s. pure bending
pump power, pumping power <of parametric amplifier>	Pumpleistung f <Reaktanzverstärker>	pure imaginary	s. purely imaginary
		pure kinematics	s. kinematics
		purely elastic	rein elastisch
		pureley imaginary, pure imaginary	rein imaginär
pump source, pumping source, pump	Pumpquelle f	pure material, pure substance	Reinstoff m
pump speed	s. exhaustion rate	pure metal	Reinmetall n
pump transition, pumping transition	Pumpübergang m	pureness	s. purity <gen.>
pump-turbine	s. rotodynamic pump	pure non-dilatational strain, non-dilatational strain, change of shape	[reine] Gestalt[s]änderung f, Deformation f ohne Volumenänderung
pump-type dispenser; syphon, siphon	Heber m; Saugheber m, Ansaugheber m; Stechheber m		
		pure number, dimensionless number	reine Zahl f, unbenannte Zahl, dimensionslose Zahl
pump voltage, pumping voltage	Pumpspannung f		
pump with working fluid	Treibmittelpumpe f	pure pitch	reine Stimmung f
		pure purples	s. purple boundary
punch	Ziehstempel m; Stempel m, Patrize f; Stanze f	pure rolling	reines Rollen n
		pure rotation spectrum, rotation spectrum, rotational spectrum	Rotationsspektrum n, reines Rotationsspektrum
punch card, punched card	Lochkarte f		
punched tape	Lochstreifen m; Lochband n	pure semiconductor	s. simple semiconductor
		pure shearing stress	reiner Schubspannungszustand m
punched tape storage	s. paper tape storage	pure state <qu.>	reiner Zustand m <Qu.>
punching, perforation; sprocket hole	Lochung f; Perforation f; Stanzloch n	pure strain	reine Dehnung f, reine (eigentliche) Deformation f
punching	Stanzen n		
punch-through	s. breakdown	pure stress	reiner Spannungszustand m
punch-through effect, punch-through from collector to emitter	Kollektor-Emitter-Durchbruch m, Kollektor-Emitter-Durchschlag m, „punch-through"-Effekt m		
		pure substance, pure material	Reinstoff m
		pure tone	reiner Ton m
		purification; cleansing <chem.>	Reinigung f <Chem.>
punctiform flashing, aventurization	Aventurisieren n		
punctiform lamp	s. point-source lamp	purification of water	s. water purification
punctual image	punktuelle Abbildung f	purity, chemical purity <chem.>	Reinheit f, chemische Reinheit <Chem.>
punctum proximum, near point of clear vision	Nahpunkt m, punctum n proximum; Nahpunkt im engeren Sinne, manifester Nahpunkt	purity; cleanliless; cleanness; pureness <gen.>	Sauberkeit f, Reinheit f <allg.>
		purity discrimination; saturation discrimination	Farbsättigungs-Unterscheidungsvermögen n, Farbsättigungs-Unterschiedsempfindlichkeit f
punctum proximum of convergence	Konvergenznahpunkt m, Fusionsnahpunkt m		

purity of colour, colour purity	Farbreinheit f, Reinheit f der Farbe	pycnonuclear reaction, pressure-induced nuclear reaction	druckinduzierte Kernreaktion f, pyknonukleare Reaktion f
purity of tone	Reinheit f des Tones, Tonreinheit f	pygmaean star, pygmean star, pygmy, pygmy star	Pygmäenstern m
Purkinje effect, Purkinje phenomenon, Purkinje shift	Purkinje-Phänomen n, Purkinje-Effekt m ‹korrekt: Purkyně-Phänomen›	pygmy cap	Zwergsockel m
Purkinje image, Purkinje-Sanson['s] image	Purkinje-Bildchen n, Purkinje-Sanson-Bildchen n	pygmy current meter	Kleinflügel m, Mikroflügel m
Purkinje phenomenon	s. Purkinje effect	pygmy galaxy	Pygmäengalaxis f
Purkinje-Sanson['s] image	s. Purkinje image	pygmy lamp, miniature bulb (lamp)	Zwerglampe f, Zwergglühlampe f
Purkinje-Sanson['s] image formed by the cornea	Reflexbild n der Hornhaut	pygmy resonance	Zwergresonanz f
		pygmy star	s. pygmy
		pyknometer, pycnometer, weighing (density) bottle, [specific] gravity bottle	Pyknometer n, Wägefläschchen n, Wägeflasche f, Meßflasche f, Tarierfläschchen f
Purkinje-Sanson['s] image formed by the crystalline lens	Linsenbildchen n, Spiegelbildchen n der Linse	pyod	s. thermocouple
		pyramidal antenna, prism antenna	Reusenantenne f, Reusendipol m, Reusendipolantenne f
Purkinje shift	s. Purkinje effect	pyramidal class	s. hemimorphic hemihedry of the orthorhombic system
purling	Rieseln n		
purple	Purpurfarbe f, Purpur m	pyramidal class	s. paramorphic hemihedry of the hexagonal system
purple boundary, pure purples, colour stimuli on the purples	Purpurgerade f, Purpurlinie f	pyramidal class	s. paramorphic hemihedry of the tetragonal system
purple light	Purpurlicht n	pyramidal error	Pyramidalfehler m
purple spot	Purpurfleck m	pyramidal hemimorphic class	s. tetartohedry of the hexagonal system
purple twilight	Purpurdämmerung f	pyramidal hemimorphic class	s. tetartohedry of the tetragonal system
purposive sampling	bewußte Auswahl f		
push; impact; shock; percussion; stroke; blow; shove; impulse	Schlag m, Stoß m, Anstoß m	pyramidal horn, quasi-pyramidal horn [waveguide]	Pyramidentrichter m, Pyramidenhorn n, Reusenstrahler m
push	s. a. thrust	pyramidal octahedron, triakisoctahedron, tris-octahedron	Pyramidenoktaeder n, Triakisoktaeder n, Trisoktaeder n
pushing ahead	s. pushing forward		
pushing figure	Stromverstimmung f, Stromverstimmungsmaß n	pyramidal plane	Pyramidalebene f
		pyramidal system	s. tetragonal crystal system
pushing forward, driving, drifting, pushing ahead ‹gee.›	Vortrieb m ‹Geo.›	pyramidal tetrahedron, triakistetrahedron, tris-tetrahedron	Pyramidentetraeder n, Triakistetraeder n, Tristetraeder n
pushing forward	s. a. forward movement		
pushing of frequency	s. frequency drift	pyramid of the first order, protopyramid	Protopyramide f, Pyramide f erster Art
push moraine	Staumoräne f, Stauchmoräne f	pyramid of vicinal faces	Pyramide f von Vizinalflächen
push-pull [amplifier], balanced [valve] amplifier, paraphase amplifier	Gegentaktverstärker m	pyramid of visual rays, visual ray pyramid	Sehstrahlpyramide f
push-pull arrangement	s. push-pull circuit	pyranometer with blackened surfaces	Schwarzflächenpyranometer n
push-pull cascade	s. push-pull circuit	pyranometry	Pyranometrie f, Globalstrahlungsmessung f
push-pull circuit (connection), push-pull arrangement (system, connection, stage, cascade)	Gegentaktschaltung f, Gegentaktstufe f	pyrgeometer	Pyrgeometer n
		pyrheliometer	Pyrheliometer n, Sonnenstrahlungsmesser m
push-pull demodulator	s. full-wave rectifier	pyrheliometric scale	Pyrheliometerskala f
push-pull detector	s. full-wave rectifier		
push-pull mode, push-pull wave, wave in opposition of phase, wave in the push-pull mode	Gegentaktwelle f	pyrheliometry	Aktinometrie f, Pyrheliometrie f
		pyriform, pearshaped	birnenförmig
		pyritohedral class	s. paramorphic hemihedry of the regular system
push-pull modulation, balanced modulation	Gegentaktmodulation f	pyritohedron	s. pentadodecahedron
		pyroacoustic loudspeaker	pyroakustischer Lautsprecher m
push-pull output, balanced output, symmetric output	symmetrischer Ausgang m, Gegentaktausgang m	pyrocaloric effect	pyrokalorischer Effekt m
push-pull stage (system)	s. push-pull circuit		
push-pull wave, wave in opposition of phase, [wave in the] push-pull mode	Gegentaktwelle f	pyrocarbon, pyrographite	Pyrographit m
		pyroceram[ic]	Vitrokeram n; Pyroceram n; Sitall n
push-push amplifier	s. parallel-tube amplifier		
putting into operation, commissioning, start-up, starting	Inbetriebnahme f; Inbetriebsetzung f	pyroconductivity	Heißleitfähigkeit f
		pyroelectric	Pyroelektrikum n
p-vector	s. multivector ‹math.›	pyroelectric coefficient, pyroelectric constant	pyroelektrischer Koeffizient m, pyroelektrische Konstante f
P.V. filter, panchromatic filter, panchromatic vision filter	Panfilter n, panchromatisches Filter n		
P-wave, primary wave	Primärwelle f, P-Welle f	pyroelectric current	pyroelektrischer Strom m
P wave, P ray, longitudinal wave ‹geo.›	P-Welle f, Longitudinalwelle f ‹Geo.›	pyroelectric effect	pyroelektrischer Effekt m
pycnometer	s. pyknometer	pyroelectricity	Pyroelektrizität f
pycnometric determination of density	pyknometrische Dichtemessung f		

pyrogenetic s. pyrogenic
pyrogenetic decomposition s. pyrolysis
pyrogenic, pyrogenetic pyrogen
pyrographite s. pyrocarbon
pyrohydrolysis Pyrohydrolyse f
pyrolysis; pyrogenetic decomposition Pyrolyse f; Brenzreaktion f, Brenzen n
pyrolysis [gas] chromatography Pyrolyse[gas]chromatographie f

pyromagnetism Pyromagnetismus m
pyrometallurgy Pyrometallurgie f, Trockenmetallurgie f, Schmelzflußmetallurgie f, trockenes Verfahren n <Met.>
pyrometamorphism Pyrometamorphose f; Pyrometamorphismus m
pyrometasomatism Pyrometasomatose f
pyrometer Pyrometer n; Hochtemperaturmeßgerät n, Hitzemesser m, Hitzemeßgerät n
pyrometer s. a. radiation pyrometer
pyrometer cone s. pyrometric cone
pyrometer in protection tube <US> s. pyrometric rod
pyrometer probe, thermometer probe Temperaturfühler m
pyrometer [protecting] tube s. pyrometric rod
pyrometric cone, pyrometer cone, pyroscope, fusible cone, fusion cone, melting cone, sentinel pyrometer; Seger cone; Orton cone <US> pyrometrischer Kegel m, Schmelzkegel m, Schmelzkörper m, Brennkegel m; Seger-Kegel m, SK; Orton-Kegel m
pyrometric cone equivalent, softening point of the pyrometric cone, P.C.E. Kegelfallpunkt m
pyrometric rod, sheathed pyrometer, pyrometer in protection tube <US>, pyrometer [protecting] tube, thermometer tube Pyrometerstab m, Pyrometerrohr n, Fühler m, Temperaturfühler m mit Schutzrohr
pyrometry Pyrometrie f, Hochtemperaturmessung f
pyromorphous pyromorph
pyrophoric; self-inflammable, self-igniting, self-ignitable; hypergolic selbstentzündlich, selbstentflammbar; pyrophor; selbstzündend
pyrophorus Pyrophor m, selbstzündender Stoff m

pyroreaction Pyroreaktion f
pyroscope s. pyrometric cone
pyrosol Pyrosol n
pyrosphere Pyrosphäre f
pyrotron s. mirror machine
pyrradio Pyrradio n
pyrylium salt Pyryliumsalz n

Pythagorean comma pythagoreisches Komma n
Pythagorean gamut, Pythagorean scale pythagoreische Tonleiter f; pythagoreische Stimmung f

Q

Q, Q factor, quality factor, factor of quality, factor of merit <of resonant circuit, cavity resonator, coil, capacitor>; coil constant, figure of merit Gütefaktor m Güte f, bezogene Güte, Q-Faktor m, Güte Q <Resonanzkreis, Hohlraumresonator, Spule, Kondensator>; Gütewert m, Q-Wert m <Hohlraumresonator>; Spulengüte f, Spulenkonstante f; Kreisgüte f
Q band <25.5–40 or 22–33 or 36–46 Gc/s> Q-Band n <25,5 ··· 40 oder 22 ··· 33 oder 36 ··· 46 GHz>

Q-branch, zero branch <opt.> Q-Zweig m, Nullzweig m <Opt.>
Q bridge, differential bridge [of Jaumann], Jaumann differential bridge Jaumann-Brücke f, Differentialmeßbrücke f nach Jaumann
Q-disk, A band, anisotropic band, A segment Q-Streifen m, anisotrope Querscheibe (Schicht) f <Muskel>
Q factor s. Q
Q factor modulation s. Q-switch[ing]
Q meter, Q-meter Gütemesser m, Güteschaltmesser m, Gütefaktormeßgerät n, Q-Meter n

q-number q-Zahl f
Q-number theory Theorie f der Q-Zahlen, Q-Zahlen-Theorie f
q-process q-Prozeß m
q-representation s. co-ordinate representation
Q-switch[ing] [process], quality (Q) factor modulation Gütemodulation f, Gütewertmodulation f, Q-Wert-Modulation f
quad, quadded cable Vierer m, Viererseil n

quadrangle connection Viereckschaltung f
quadrangle grid, quadrangular grid Vierecksnetz n
quadrangular prism vierseitiges Prisma n, Vierkantprisma n
quadrant Quadrant m; Viertelkreis m; Viertelebene f
quadrantal [deviation], quadrantal error, quadrantal in form Viertelkreisfehler m, Quadrantfehler m

quadrant electrometer Quadrantelektrometer n, Quadrantenelektrometer n, Quadrant[en]voltmeter n
quadrant instrument (meter), square-scale instrument (meter), square-dial instrument (meter) Quadrantinstrument n, Quadratinstrument n
quadrant system [of units] Quadrantsystem n
quadrant unit Quadranteinheit f, Q.E.
quadrate s. quadrature <astr.>
quadratically convergent Newton-Raphson process s. Newton-Raphson method
quadratically integrable, square-integrable, square-summable quadratisch integrierbar, quadratisch integrabel
quadratically integrable function, normalizable function normierbare Funktion f, quadratisch integrierbare Funktion
quadratic Doppler effect, Doppler effect of the second order Doppler-Effekt m zweiter Ordnung, quadratischer Doppler-Effekt
quadratic effect, quadratic response quadratische Wirkung f
quadratic form, quadric quantic, quadric quadratische Form f
quadratic group, Klein['s] [quadratic] group, Klein['s] four-group (4-group), four-group, 4-group, vierer group <math.> Kleinsche Vierergruppe f, Vierergruppe f [von Klein] <Math.>
quadratic intermodulation factor quadratischer Differenztonfaktor m, Differenztonfaktor erster Ordnung, quadratischer Intermodulationsfaktor m
quadratic matrix s. square matrix
quadratic mean s. root mean square
quadratic piezoelectric effect quadratischer piezoelektrischer Effekt m

quadratic prism, Newton['s] prism Newton-Prisma n
quadratic response s. quadratic effect
quadratic system s. tetragonal crystal system
quadratic yield condition s. Mises yield condition
quadrature, quartile [aspect], quadrate, tetragon <astr.> Quadratur f, Quadraturstellung f, Geviertschein m, Quadratschein m <Astr.>

quadrature <math.> — Quadratur f <Math.>
quadrature <phase>, phase quadrature, quadrature shift — 90°-Phasenverschiebung f, Phasenverschiebung f um 90°, Phasenquadratur f

quadrature / in, in phase quadrature — [um] 90° phasenverschoben
quadrature in time, time quadrature — zeitliche Verschiebung f um 90°, zeitliche 90°-Verschiebung f
quadrature shift — s. quadrature
quadric, quadratic form, quadric quantic — quadratische Form f
quadric, quadric surface, conicoid <nondegenerate case> — Quadrik f, Fläche f zweiter Ordnung; Hyperfläche f zweiter Ordnung
quadric of elongation, elongation quadric, strain quadric — Elongationsfläche f, Tensorfläche (quadratische Form) f des Elongationstensors
quadric of stress, stress quadric, surface of tension, deflection surface — Spannungsfläche f, Tensorfläche (quadratische Form) f des Spannungstensors
quadric of stretching, stretching quadric — Streckungsfläche f, Tensorfläche (quadratische Form) f des Streckungstensors
quadric of the tensor, tensor quadric — Tensorfläche f, Tensorellipsoid n, quadratische Form f des Tensors

quadric quantic — s. quadric
quadric surface — s. quadric
quadrielectron — Quadrielektron n
quadrillé paper — s. squared paper
quadripole — s. four-terminal network
quadripole amplifier — Vierpolverstärker m

quadripole attenuation — s. image attenuation factor
quadripole determinant, characteristic determinant of the four-terminal network — Vierpoldeterminante f
quadripole equations — s. characteristic relations of the two-terminal-pair network
quadripole matrix — s. characteristic matrix of the two-terminal-pair network
quadripole phase factor, image phase constant, image phase factor — Vierpolwinkelmaß n, Vierpolphasenfaktor m, Vierpolphasenkonstante f

quadripole propagation factor — s. image transfer constant
quadripole relations — s. characteristic relations of the two-terminal-pair network

quadrode — s. tetrode
quadruped, tetrapod, four nuple, 4-nuple, vierbein quadruple — Vierbein n
quadruple — Quadrupel n
quadruple bond, quadruple link[age], eight-electron bond — Vierfachbindung f, Achtelektronenbindung f
quadruple coincidence — Vierfachkoinzidenz f, Viererkoinzidenz f
quadruple link[age] — s. quadruple bond
quadruple point — Quadrupelpunkt m, Vierfachpunkt m
quadruple scattering — Vierfachstreuung f
quadruple serial photogrammetric camera — Vierfach-Reihenmeßkammer f
quadruplet — Quadruplett n
quadruplet, quadruplet lens — Vierlinser m, Quadruplet n, vierlinsiges Objektiv n
quadruplet splitting — Quadruplettaufspaltung f

quadrupolar absorption — s. quadrupole absorption
quadrupolar field, quadrupole field — Quadrupolfeld n
quadrupolarization — Quadrupolarisation f
quadrupole — Quadrupol m
quadrupole absorption, quadrupolar absorption — Quadrupolabsorption f
quadrupole antenna — Quadrupolantenne f

quadrupole broadening — Quadrupolverbreiterung f

quadrupole coupling — Quadrupolkopplung f
quadrupole coupling constant — Quadrupolkopplungskonstante f
quadrupole electric absorption — elektrische Quadrupolabsorption f
quadrupole excitation — Quadrupolanregung f

quadrupole field — s. quadrupolar field
quadrupole force — Quadrupolkraft f
quadrupole frequency, frequency of quadrupole transition — Quadrupolübergangsfrequenz f, Quadrupolfrequenz f
quadrupole hyperfine structure — Quadrupolhyperfeinstruktur f
quadrupole interaction — Quadrupolwechselwirkung f
quadrupole interaction energy, energy of quadrupole interaction — Quadrupolwechselwirkungsenergie J, Quadrupolenergie f

quadrupole lens — Quadrupollinse f

quadrupole molecule — Quadrupolmolekül n
quadrupole moment — Quadrupolmoment n

quadrupole moment tensor — Quadrupolmomenttensor m
quadrupole oscillation — s. quadrupole vibration
quadrupole potential — Quadrupolpotential n

quadrupole precession — Quadrupolpräzession f
quadrupole-quadrupole coupling — Quadrupol-Quadrupol-Kopplung f

quadrupole radiation — Quadrupolstrahlung f

quadrupole resonance — Quadrupolresonanz f
quadrupole resonance spectrometer, quadrupole spectrometer — Quadrupolresonanzspektrometer n, Quadrupolspektrometer n, Kernquadrupolresonanzspektrometer n

quadrupole source — Quadrupolquelle f
quadrupole spectrometer — s. quadrupole resonance spectrometer
quadrupole spectrum — Quadrupolspektrum n
quadrupole splitting — Quadrupolaufspaltung f

quadrupole state — Quadrupolzustand m
quadrupole transition — Quadrupolübergang m
quadrupole vibration, quadrupole oscillation — Quadrupolschwingung f

quadrupole wave — Quadrupolwelle f
quad twisting — Viererverseilung f

quake; quiver[ing]; tremor; trembling — Beben n; Zittern n
qualimeter, penetrometer, penetration meter, radiochrometer — Qualitätsmesser m, Qualimeter n, Penetrometer n, Penetrationsmesser m, Strahlungshärtemesser m <für Röntgenstrahlen>

qualitative spectral analysis — qualitative Spektralanalyse f
qualitative variability — s. alternative variability <stat.>
quality, hue <of colour> — Farbton m, Ton m [der Farbe], Qualität f <Farbe>
quality control — Qualitätskontrolle f

quality factor <of amplifier> — Gütefaktor m <Verstärker>
quality factor, QF <radiobiology> — Qualitätsfaktor m, Bewertungsfaktor m, F, QF <Strahlenbiologie>

quality factor — s. a. Q
quality factor modulation — s. Q-switch[ing]
quality of radiation, radiation quality — Strahlenqualität f, Qualität f der Strahlung, Strahlungsqualität f; Röntgenstrahlenhärte f

quality of sound, timbre of sound, tone colour (quality); tone <el.> — Klangfarbe f, Tonfarbe f, Farbe f des Klangs
quality of transmission — s. sound transmission quality

quantal phenomenon	s. quantum phenomenon	**quantizing noise,** quantization noise	Quantisierungsrauschen n
quantal response	Alternativreaktion f	**quantometer**	Quantometer n
quantameter	Quantameter n		
quantasome	Quantasom n		
quantic	s. form <math.>		
quantic	s. quantum theoretical	**quantometer**	s. a. ballistical galvanometer
quantification <math.>	Quantifizierung f <Math.>	**quantor**	s. quantifier
		quantor of existence, existential quantifier, existential operator	Partikularisator m, Existentialoperator m, Existenzquantor m
quantification theory	s. predicate calculus		
quantifier, quantor, operator	Quantifikator m, Quantor m, [prädikatenlogischer] Funktor m	**quantor of generality**	s. generality quantifier
		quantrol	Quantrol n
quantile	Quantil n	**quantum** <pl: quanta>	Quant n, Quantum n <pl.: Quanten>
quantimeter	s. dosimeter	**quantum**	s. a. photon
quantimetric point	quantimetrischer Punkt m	**quantum acoustics**	Quantenakustik f
quantitative spectral analysis	quantitative Spektralanalyse f	**quantum amplifier**	s. maser
		quantum annihilation	s. photon annihilation
quantitative variability continuous variability, fluctuating variability	kontinuierliche (fluktuierende, quantitative) Variabilität f	**quantum biology**	Quantenbiologie f
		quantum character; quantum structure; quantum property	Quanteneigenschaft f; Quantencharakter m; quantenhafte Natur (Struktur) f
quantity, physical quantity, physical magnitude	Größe f, physikalische Größe; Größenart f		
quantity	s. a. lightness <of surface colour>	**quantum chemistry**	Quantenchemie f
		quantum condition	Quantenbedingung f
quantity concept, concept of physical quantity	[physikalischer] Größenbegriff m, Begriff m der physikalischen Größe	**quantum counter**	s. photon counter
		quantum crystal	Quantenkristall m
quantity in the formula, formula quantity	Formelgröße f	**quantum defect**	Quantendefekt m
		quantum defect, Rydberg correction [term]	Rydberg-Korrektion f
quantity measured	s. measured quantity		
quantity of action, action quantity, action magnitude	Wirkungsgröße f	**quantum efficiency,** photochemical yield, photochemical quantum yield, quantum yield	Quantenausbeute f, photochemische Quantenausbeute, photochemische Ausbeute f
quantity of electricity	s. charge <el.>	**quantum efficiency** <of luminescence>, energy quantum efficiency, quantum yield [of luminescence], luminescence efficiency	Quantenausbeute f [der Lumineszenz], Lumineszenzausbeute f; Lichtausbeute f, Leuchtwirkungsgrad m
quantity of heat, amount of heat, heat quantity	Wärmemenge f, Wärme f		
quantity of illumination, exposure <quantity> <opt., phot.>	Belichtung f <Größe> <Opt., Phot.>; Exposition f <Größe> <Phot.>		
		quantum efficiency [of photoelectric effect]	s. a. photoelectric efficiency
quantity of information	s. information content		
quantity of light, luminous energy	Lichtmenge f, Lichtarbeit f	**quantum electrodynamic correction**	quantenelektrodynamische Korrektion f
quantity of magnetism	s. magnetic charge	**quantum electrodynamics**	Quantenelektrodynamik f
quantity of motion	s. momentum <mech.>	**quantum electronics**	Quantenelektronik f
quantity of radiant energy	s. radiant energy	**quantum energy,** energy content of quanta	Quantenenergie f
quantity of radiation	s. radiant exposure	**quantum field,** quantized field	gequanteltes Feld n, Quantenfeld n
quantity of radiation	s. a. radiant energy		
quantity of reflux; reflux <chem.>	Rückfluß m, Rücklauf m, Phlegma n <Chem.>	**quantum field theory,** quantum theory of wave fields, quantum theory of field[s], quantized field theory	Quantenfeldtheorie f, Quantentheorie f der Wellenfelder
quantity of sound field, sound field quantity, acoustic[al] quantity	Schallfeldgröße f, Schallgröße f		
		quantum fluctuation [of radiation]	Quantenfluktuation f [der Strahlung]
quantity of steam	Dampfgehalt m	**quantum fluid**	Quantenflüssigkeit f
quantity of stimulus, stimulation quantity	Reizmenge f	**quantum flux density**	Quantenflußdichte f, Quantenstromdichte f
quantity of stimulus rule	s. product rule		
quantity to be controlled <control>	Wirkungsgröße f; Auslösegröße f <Regelung>	**quantum frequency,** quantized frequency	Quantenfrequenz f, gequantelte Frequenz f
		quantum frequency converter	Quantenfrequenzwandler m
quantity to be measured; measurable variable, measurand	Meßgröße f, zu messende Größe f	**quantum geometrodynamics**	Quantengeometrodynamik f
quantity weighed	s. amount weighed	**quantum Green['s] function,** Green['s] function [in quantum field theory], propagation function <qu.>	quantenfeldtheoretische Greensche Funktion f, Greensche Funktion [in der Quantentheorie der Wellenfelder], Ausbreitungsfunktion f <Qu.>
quantivalent	s. polyvalent <chem.>		
quantization	Quantelung f <Phys.>; Quantisierung f <El., Phys.>		
quantization circuit, quantizing circuit	Quantisierungsschaltung f	**quantum H-theorem,** quantum mechanical H-theorem	quantenmechanisches H-Theorem n
quantization noise, quantizing noise	Quantisierungsrauschen n	**quantum jump (leap)**	s. quantum transition
quantization rule	Quantelungsregel f, Quantelungsvorschrift f, Quantisierungsregel f	**quantum level**	Quantenniveau n
		quantum limit, end radiation, maximum frequency, limiting frequency <of continuous X-rays>	kurzwellige Grenzfrequenz f, Frequenz f der kurzwelligen Grenze
quantized field, quantum field	gequanteltes Feld n, Quantenfeld n		
quantized field theory	s. quantum field theory		
quantized frequency, quantum frequency	Quantenfrequenz f, gequantelte Frequenz f	**quantum magnetometer with free precession**	Quantenmagnetometer n mit freier Präzession
quantized law	Quantengesetz n, gequanteltes Gesetz n	**quantum mechanical aspect**	quantenmechanisches Bild n, quantenmechanische Darstellung f
quantized oscillator	s. quantum oscillator		
quantizing circuit, quantization circuit	Quantisierungsschaltung f		

quantum mechanical ensemble	quantenmechanische Gesamtheit *f*	quark model	Quarkmodell *n*
quantum mechanical *H*-theorem, quantum *H*-theorem	quantenmechanisches *H*-Theorem *n*	quarter-chord point, quarter point [of chord]	Viertelpunkt *m*, Viertelspunkt *m*
quantum mechanical oscillator	s. quantum oscillator	quarter of the period, quarter period	Viertelperiode *f*
quantum mechanical resonance	quantenmechanische Resonanz *f*	quarter point [of chord]	s. quarter-chord point
quantum mechanics	Quantenmechanik *f*; quantenmechanische Theorie *f*	quarter wave, quarter wavelength	Viertelwelle *f*, Viertelwellenlänge *f*
quantum mole, einstein, E	Einstein *n*, E	quarter-wave accelerator	Viertelwellenbeschleuniger *m*
quantum noise	Quantenrauschen *n*	quarter-wave antenna, quarter-wave dipole, $\lambda/4$ antenna, $\lambda/4$ dipole	Viertelwellen[längen]antenne *f*, Viertelwellen-[längen]dipol *m*, Lambda-Viertel-Antenne *f*, Lambda-Viertel-Dipol *m*, $\lambda/4$-Antenne *f*, $\lambda/4$-Dipol *m*
quantum number	Quantenzahl *f*		
quantum number of the total angular momentum	s. inner quantum number		
quantum of acoustic wave energy	s. phonon		
quantum of action	s. Planck['s] constant	quarter-wave choke, $\lambda/4$ choke	Viertelwellen[längen]-drossel *f*, $\lambda/4$-Drossel *f*
quantum of energy, energy quantum	Energiequant *n*	quarter wave compensator	s. quarter-wave plate compensator
quantum of gravitational radiation, graviton, gravitino, gravitational quantum, gion	Graviton *n*, Gravitationsquant *n*, Gravitino *n*, Quant *n* des Gravitationsfeldes	quarter-wave dipole	s. quarter-wave antenna
		quarter-wave layer, quarter wavelength layer, $\lambda/4$ layer	Viertelwellen[längen]-schicht *f*, Lambda-Viertel-Schicht *f*, $\lambda/4$-Schicht *f*
quantum of light	s. photon	quarter wavelength, quarter wave	Viertelwelle *f*, Viertelwellenlänge *f*
quantum optics	Quantenoptik *f*		
quantum orbit; quantum path	Quantenbahn *f*	quarter wavelength layer	s. quarter-wave layer
quantum oscillator, quantized (quantum mechanical) oscillator	Quantenoszillator *m*, quantenmechanischer Oszillator *m*	quarter-wavelength line	s. quarter-wave line
		quarter-wavelength plate	s. quarter-wave plate
quantum oscillator	s. a. maser oscillator	quarter-wavelength radiator	s. quarter-wave radiator
quantum path	s. quantum orbit	quarter-wave line, quarter-wavelength line, $\lambda/4$ line	Viertelwellen[längen]-leitung *f*, Lambda-Viertel-Leitung *f*, $\lambda/4$-Leitung *f*
quantum phenomenon, quantal phenomenon	Quantenerscheinung *f*, Quantenphänomen *n*		
quantum physics	Quantenphysik *f*		
quantum Poisson bracket[s], Poisson bracket[s] in quantum mechanics	quantenmechanische Poisson-Klammer[n *fpl*] *f*, quantentheoretische Poisson-Klammer[n]	quarter-wave plate, quarter-wavelength plate, $\lambda/4$ plate, Venetian blind	Viertelwellen[längen]-plättchen *n*, $\lambda/4$-Wellenlängenplättchen *n*, $\lambda/4$-Plättchen *n*, $\lambda/4$-Blättchen *n*, Lambda-Viertel-Plättchen *n*, Lambda-Viertel-Blättchen *n*, Viertelwellenplatte *f*, Viertelwellen[längen]blättchen *n*, Viertelundulationsblättchen *n*
quantum postulate	Quantenpostulat *n*		
quantum potential	Quantenpotential *n*		
quantum property	s. quantum character		
quantum radiation	Quantenstrahlung *f*		
quantum requirement	Quantenbedarf *m*		
quantum size effect, QSE	Quanteneffekt *m* der Abmessungen		
quantum state	Quantenzustand *m*, gequantelter Energiezustand *m*	quarter-wave plate compensator, quarter wave compensator, De Sénarmont compensator (polarimeter, polariscope), elliptic (Sénarmont) compensator	elliptischer Kompensator *m*, De-Sénarmont-Kompensator *m*, Kompensator (Polarimeter *n*) nach de Sénarmont, [de] Sénarmontscher Kompensator
quantum[-] statistical	quantenstatistisch		
quantum statistics	Quantenstatistik *f*		
quantum structure	s. quantum character		
quantum theoretical, quantum	quantentheoretisch, Quanten-		
quantum theory, old quantum theory	Quantentheorie *f*, ältere Quantenmechanik *f*	quarter-wave radiator, quarter-wavelength radiator, $\lambda/4$ radiator	Viertelwellen[längen]-strahler *m*, Lambda-Viertel-Strahler *m*, $\lambda/4$-Strahler *m*
quantum theory of chemical bond	quantenmechanische Bindungstheorie *f*, Quantentheorie *f* der chemischen Bindung	quarter-wave transformer, one-quarter wave skirt	Viertelwellenumformer *m*
		quartet	Quartett *n*
		quartic [curve]	Quartik *f*, Kurve *f* vierter Ordnung
quantum theory of dispersion	Quantentheorie *f* der Dispersion, quantenmechanische Dispersionstheorie *f*	quartic equation, biquadratic equation, equation of the fourth degree	biquadratische Gleichung *f*, Gleichung vierten Grades
quantum theory of field[s]	s. quantum field theory	quartile	Quartil *n*
quantum theory of light	s. Einstein['s] hypothesis of light quanta	quartile [aspect]	s. quadrature <astr.>
quantum theory of solids	Quantentheorie *f* der Leitfähigkeit (Festkörper), Quantentheorie der Elektronenleitung [in Festkörpern]	quartz balance	Quarzwaage *f*
		quartz calibrator, crystal calibrator	Quarzeichgenerator *m*, Quarzeichoszillator *m*, Quarzeicher *m*
quantum theory of wave fields	s. quantum field theory	quartz clock, crystal-controlled clock	Quarzuhr *f*
quantum transition; quantum jump, quantum leap	Quantenübergang *m*, quantenmechanischer Übergang *m*; Quantensprung *m*	quartz-[crystal-]controlled oscillator	s. crystal-controlled oscillator
		quartz-crystal oscillator	s. oscillating quartz
		quartz-crystal oscillator	s. crystal-controlled oscillator
quantum voltage	Quantenspannung *f*	quartz-crystal resonator	s. crystal resonator
quantum weight	Quantengewicht *n*	quartz-crystal-stabilized oscillator	s. crystal-controlled oscillator
quantum yield	s. quantum efficiency		
quaquaversal structure	quaquaversale Struktur *f*	quartz-crystal subaqueous microphone	Unterwasser-Quarzmikrophon *n*
quark	Quark *n* <*pl*.: Quarks>		

quartz-fibre electrometer	Quarzfadenelektrometer n	quasi[-]chemical approximation	quasichemische Näherung f
quartz-fibre manometer	Quarzfadenmanometer n	quasi[-]chemical equation	quasichemische Gleichung f
quartz fibre type direct reading dosemeter	Quarzfadendosimeter n mit Direktablesung	quasi[-]classical approximation [of Wentzel-Kramers-Brillouin [-Jeffreys]]	s. W.K.B. approximation
quartz filter; crystal filter, piezoelectric filter	Filterquarz m, Quarzfilter n; Kristallfilter n, piezoelektrisches Filter n	quasi-closed system	quasiabgeschlossenes System n
quartz-fluorite achromat[e], quartz-fluorite lens	Quarz-Flußspat-Achromat m (n), Quarz-Fluorit-Achromat m (n), Quarz-Flußspat-Linse f	quasi-coincidence	Quasikoinzidenz f
		quasiconductor	Quasileiter m
		quasiconformal mapping, quasiconformal representation	quasikonforme Abbildung f
quartz glass lamp	s. quartz lamp	quasi constant	quasikonstant
quartz-glass pyrheliometer, silica pyrheliometer	Quarzglaspyrheliometer n	quasi continuity equation, principle of quasi-continuity	Quasikontinuitätsgleichung f
quartz-glass thermometer, quartz thermometer	Quarzthermometer n, Quarzglasthermometer n	quasi-continuous	quasistetig
		quasi-continuous laser	quasikontinuierlicher Laser m
quartz horizontal force magnetometer, quartz horizontal magnetometer, Q.H.M.	Quarz-Horizontalmagnetometer n, Quarzfaden-Horizontalintensitätsmagnetometer n, QHM	quasi-continuous spectrum, quasi-continuum	Quasikontinuum n, quasikontinuierliches Spektrum n
quartz iodine lamp <US>, tungsten iodine lamp	Jodglühlampe f, Quarz-Jodglühlampe f	quasiconventional electric circuit, quasiconventional circuit	quasikonventioneller Stromkreis m
quartz lamp, quartz mercury lamp, quartz glass lamp	Quarzlampe f, Quarz-Quecksilber[dampf]-lampe f, Quarzglaslampe f		
quartz-lens method	Quarzlinsenmethode f [von Rubens und Wood]	quasi co-ordinate, non-holonomic co-ordinate, pseudo co-ordinate	nichtholonome Koordinate f, Pseudokoordinate f, Quasikoordinate f
quartz magnetometer, quartz-thread magnetometer	Quarzfadenmagnetometer n, Quarzmagnetometer n	quasi-crystal	Quasikristall m
		quasi-crystalline	quasikristallin
quartz mercury lamp	s. quartz lamp	quasidielectric	Quasidielektrikum n
quartz mirror	Quarzspiegel m	quasi-diffusion propagation	Quasidiffusionsausbreitung f
quartz oscillator	s. quartz-controlled oscillator	quasi-elastic force	quasielastische Kraft f
quartz piezoelectric transducer, quartz pressure transducer	Quarzdruckgeber m, Quarzdruckmeßdose f	quasi-elastic oscillation	s. quasi-elastic vibration
		quasi-elastic scattering	quasielastische Streuung f
		quasi-elastic spectrum	quasielastisches Spektrum n
quartz plate	Quarzplatte f, Quarzplättchen n	quasi-elastic vibration, quasi-elastic oscillation	quasielastische Schwingung f
quartz pressure transducer	s. quartz piezoelectric transducer	quasi-emulsifier	Quasiemulgator m
		quasi-equilibrium	Quasigleichgewicht n
quartz resonator	s. piezoelectric resonator	quasi-equilibrium distribution	Quasigleichgewichtsverteilung f
quartz spectrophotometer	Quarz-Spektralphotometer n, Quarzspektrophotometer n	quasi-ergodic hypothesis	Quasi-Ergodenhypothese f
quartz spring balance, McBain-Bakr quartz spring balance	Quarzfederwaage f	quasi[-] Fermi level, imref <US>	Quasi-Fermi-Niveau n, Quasi-Fermi-Kante f
quartz-stabilized oscillator	s. crystal controlled oscillator	quasi[-] Fermi potential	Quasi-Fermi-Potential n
quartz thermometer	s. quartz-glass thermometer		
quartz-thread magnetometer, quartz magnetometer	Quarzfadenmagnetometer n, Quarzmagnetometer n	quasi-free electron	quasifreies Elektron n
		quasigeoid	Quasigeoid n
		quasi-geostrophic flow	quasigeostrophische Strömung f
quartz-thread pendulum	Quarzfadenpendel n, Quarzpendel n	quasi-geostrophic wind	quasigeostrophischer Wind m
quartz transducer	s. ultrasonic quartz transducer	quasi harmonic oscillation, quasi-harmonic vibration, vibration of systems with variable characteristics	quasiharmonische Schwingung f
quartz ultraviolet, quv, QUV	Quarzultraviolett n		
quartz wedge	Quarzkeil m		
quartz-wedge compensator, Michel-Lévy compensator	Quarzkeilkompensator m [nach Michel-Lévy], Michel-Lévy-Kompensator m	quasi-heterogeneous	quasiheterogen
		quasi-homogeneous	quasihomogen
quartz wind	Quarzwind m	quasi-homopolar approximation	quasihomöopolare Näherung f
		quasi-hydrostatic approximation (assumption)	s. hydrostatic approximation
quartz Z-magnetometer	s. Schelting magnetometer	quasi-isothermal	quasiisotherm
quasag[e], quasistellar galaxy, interloper, blue stellar object, Q.S.G., B.S.O.	Quasage f, Quasag m, quasistellare Galaxis f, Interloper m, blaues Objekt (Sternchen) n, QSG, BSO	quasilinear equation	quasilineare Gleichung f
		quasilinear plasma theory, quasilinear theory of plasma	quasilineare Theorie f [des Plasmas], quasilineare Plasmatheorie f
quasar, quasistellar radio source, quasistellar source, quasistellar object, superstar, Q.S.S.	Quasar m, quasistellare Radioquelle (Quelle) f, quasistellares Objekt n, echter Radiostern m, Superstern m, QSS	quasi-longitudinal propagation	quasilongitudinale Ausbreitung f
		quasi-Lorentz gas	Quasi-Lorentz-Gas n
		quasi-Markovian process	quasi-Markoffscher Prozeß m
quasi-adiabatic	quasiadiabatisch	quasi maximum field	Quasimaximumfeld n
quasi-atomic model	s. shell model	quasi minimum field	Quasiminimumfeld n
quasibarotropic	quasibarotrop	quasi-Minkowski case	quasi-Minkowskischer Fall m
quasi-bound state	quasigebundener Zustand m	quasimolecular model [of nucleus]	s. unified model
quasi-Cartesian system [of co-ordinates]	quasikartesisches Koordinatensystem n	quasimolecule	Quasimolekül n

quasi[-]momentum, crystal momentum	Quasiimpuls m, Kristallimpuls m	quasi T-mode quasi-transverse propagation	s. quasi transverse wave quasitransversale Ausbreitung f
quasi-monochromatic oscillation	quasimonochromatische Schwingung f	quasi transverse wave, quasi T-wave, quasi T-mode	Quasi-T-Welle f, Quasi-T-Mode f
quasi[-]neutrality	Quasineutralität f		
quasi-neutral plasma	quasineutrales Plasma n	quasiviscous creep, quasiviscous flow, constant-rate creep, steady-state creep, steady creep, kappa flow, stationary (settled, secondary) creep	stationäres Kriechen n, quasiviskoses Kriechen, quasiviskoses Fließen n, stationäres Fließen, zweites Kriechstadium n, zweiter Bereich m der Kriechkurve
quasinilpotent operator	eigenwertfreier Operator m, quasinilpotenter Operator		
quasi-normalized	quasinormiert		
quasi-ohmic contact	quasiohmscher Kontakt m		
quasi-optical propagation	quasioptische Ausbreitung f		
quasi-optical visibility	quasioptische Sicht f		
		quasi[-]wave	Quasiwelle f
		quaternary <chem.; met.>	quaternär; Vierstoff-; quartär
quasiparticle of the superconductor, normal electron	Quasiteilchen n des Supraleiters, Normalelektron n	quaternary <math.>	quaternär <Math.>
		quaternary combination band	Vierfachkombinationsbande f
quasiparticle tunnel current, single-particle tunnel current	Einteilchentunnelstrom m, Quasiteilchen-Tunnelstrom m	quaternion	Quaternion f
		quench capacitor, quenching capacitor	Löschkondensator m
quasiparticle tunnelling, single-particle tunnelling	Einteilchentunnelung f, Quasiteilchentunnelung f	quench circuit	s. quenching circuit
		quench correction	Quenchkorrektion f, Quenchkorrektur f
quasiperiodical oscillation	quasiperiodische Schwingung f	quench cracking	s. cold cracking
		quenched frequency, quench[ing] frequency	Pendelfrequenz f
quasi-periodic function	quasiperiodische Funktion f	quenched gap	s. quenched spark gap
quasi-permanent	quasipermanent	quenched spark; contact-breaking spark	Löschfunken m, Löschfunke m, Wienscher Funken m; Abreißfunken m, Abreißfunke m
quasi-plane stress	quasiebener Spannungszustand m		
quasi-probability	Quasiwahrscheinlichkeit f		
quasipyramidal horn [waveguide], pyramidal horn	Pyramidentrichter m, Pyramidenhorn n, Reusenstrahler m	quenched spark gap; quenched gap	Löschfunkenstrecke f, tönende Funkenstrecke f, Tonfunkenstrecke f
quasi[-] racemate, partial racemate	Quasirazemat n, quasirazemische Verbindung f, partielles Razemat n	quenched spark system, quenched spark transmitter	Löschfunkensender m, tönender Funkensender m
quasi random sampling	bedingte Zufallsauswahl f		
quasi range	s. partial range	quench effect <of fluorescence> <nucl.>	Quencheffekt m, Tilgungseffekt m, Löscheffekt m
quasi-rigid molecule	quasistarres Molekül n		
quasi-saturation	Quasisättigung f	quencher	s. quenching agent
quasi[-] shock wave	Quasistoßwelle f	quench frequency, quenched (quenching) frequency	Pendelfrequenz f
quasi single mode laser	Quasieinfrequenzlaser m		
		quench hardening, isothermal quenching	Abschreckhärtung f, Umwandlungshärtung f
quasi-solid	quasifest		
quasi-stable state	quasistabiler Zustand m	quenching, extinction <of discharge>	Löschung f <Entladung>
quasi-standing wave	s. quasi-stationary wave	quenching <of luminescence>	Tilgung f, Löschung f <Lumineszenz>; Quenchen n <Kern.>
quasi[-]static[al]	quasistatisch, quasistationär		
quasistatic deformation	quasistatische Deformation f	quenching, chilling <met.>	Abschrecken n <Met.>
quasistatic process; equilibrium process	quasistatischer Prozeß m; Gleichgewichtsprozeß m	quenching absorption	auslöschende Absorption f
		quenching agent, quencher	Löschzusatz m, Löschmittel n <Zählrohr>
quasistatic transition	quasistatischer Übergang m		
quasistationarity	Quasistationarität f	quenching centre	Löschzentrum n, Tilgungszentrum n
quasi-stationary current, quasi-stationary state of current	quasistationärer Strom m	quenching circuit, quench circuit	Löschschaltung f, Löschkreis m
quasi-stationary diffusion	quasistationäre Diffusion f	quenching coil	Löschdrossel f
quasi-stationary discharge	quasistationäre Entladung f		
quasi-stationary level	quasistationäres Niveau n	quenching crack, cold crack, hardening crack	Kaltriß m, Härteriß m, Riß m beim Erkalten
quasi-stationary oscillation	quasistationäre Schwingung f	quenching effect	Löscheffekt m, Löschwirkung f
quasi-stationary state, quasi-steady state	quasistationärer Zustand m	quenching frequency	s. quench frequency
quasi-stationary state of current, quasi-stationary current	quasistationärer Strom m	quenching gas	Löschgas n
		quenching of orbital angular momenta	Einfrieren n der Bahndrehimpulse (Bahnmomente), Quenching n, „quenching" n
quasi-stationary wave, quasi-standing wave	quasistationäre Welle f, quasistehende Welle		
quasi-steady flow	quasistationäre Strömung f	quenching of photoconductivity	Löschung f der Photoleitfähigkeit; Tilgung f der Photoleitfähigkeit
quasi-steady state	s. quasi-stationary state	quenching of sparks, spark quenching	Funkenlöschung f
quasistellar galaxy	s. quasag[e]		
quasistellar object (radio source, source)	s. quasar	quenching of spin	s. spin quenching
		quenching pulse	s. quench pulse
quasisymmetric top, nearly symmetric top	quasisymmetrischer Kreisel m	quenching spectrum, quench spectrum	Tilgungsspektrum n
quasi-symmetry	Quasispiegelung f	quench pulse, quenching pulse; reset pulse	Löschimpuls m
quasitensor	Quasitensor m		
quasithermodynamic theory	quasithermodynamische Theorie f		

quench

quench spectrum	s. quenching spectrum	Q_{10} value	Q_{10}-Wert m
Quetelet fringe	s. interference of diffracted light		
queue, waiting line	Warteschlange f	Q wave, Love wave, Love's wave	Love-Welle f, Lovesche Welle f, Q-Welle f
queu[e]ing problem, waiting line problem	Warteschlangenproblem n		
queu[e]ing process	Wartezeitprozeß m		
queu[e]ing theory, theory of queues, waiting line theory	Bedienungstheorie f, Massenbedienungstheorie f, Warteschlangentheorie f, Theorie f der Warteschlangen		

R

quick-access storage (store)	s. rapid-access memory	Raabe['s] ratio test, Raabe['s] test [for convergence]	Raabesches Kriterium n
quick analysis, rapid analysis	Schnellanalyse f, Schnellbestimmung f, Rapidanalyse f, Expreßanalyse f	rabbit, shuttle	Rohrpostbüchse f, Bestrahlungskapsel f
quick corrosion test, accelerated corrosion test, rapid corrosion test	Schnellkorrosionsversuch m	rabbit channel, pneumatic post, pneumatic tube[-installation]	Rohrpostkanal m, Rohrpost f, Bestrahlungskanal m im Reaktor
quick flashing light	Funkelfeuer n	Rabi['s] method, magnetic resonance method	Molekularstrahlresonanzmethode f, Rabi-Verfahren n, Rabi-Methode f, Methode f der magnetischen Resonanz, Methode von Rabi
quick-motion camera	s. time-lapse camera		
quick-motion effect (method)	s. low-speed photography		
quick start lamp, rapid start lamp	Schnellstartlampe f		
quick test	s. accelerated test		
quiescent carrier; suppressed carrier	unterdrückter Träger m	Racah coefficient, Racah function	Racah-Koeffizient m, Racahscher Dreieckskoeffizient m
quiescent current	s. resting current	Racah coupling, j-L coupling	Racah-Kopplung f, jL-Kopplung f
quiescent nucleus, resting stage nucleus <bio.>	Ruhekern m <Bio.>	Racah function	s. Racah coefficient
quiescent point	statischer Arbeitspunkt m	race-finish photography	Zielphotographie f
quiescent prominence, hedgerow prominence	ruhende Protuberanz f		
quiescent reading	Ruheausschlag m	racemate, racemoid, racemic substance; racemic compound	Razemat n, Racemat n, razemisches Gemisch n; razemische Verbindung f
quiescent value	Ruhewert m		
quiescent volcano, dormant volcano, dead volcano	untätiger Vulkan m		
quiet, calm, undisturbed	ruhig, ungestört	racemation	s. racemization
quiet, magnetically quiet, magnetically calm, calm <geo.>	magnetisch ruhig, ruhig <Geo.>	racemic compound	s. racemate
		racemic conglomerate	razemisches Konglomerat n
		racemic form (modification)	razemische (nichtdrehende) Form f, razemische Modifikation f
quiet arc, calm arc	ruhig leuchtender Bogen m, ruhiger Bogen	racemic substance	s. racemate
quiet day	ruhiger Tag m	racemization, racemation	Razemisation f, Razemisierung f, optische Inaktivierung f, Racemisation f
quietest day	ruhigster Tag m		
quiet polar light, calm polar light	ruhiges Polarlicht n, ruhige Polarlichtform f	racemization heat, heat of racemization	Razemisierungswärme f
		racemoid	s. racemate
		race[-]track	„race track" f, Rennbahn f
quiet sun, undisturbed sun	ruhige Sonne f		
quilo	s. kilogramme		
Quincke balance	Quincke-Waage f, Quinckesche Waage f	racetrack synchrotron, synchrotron with straight sections	„racetrack"-Synchrotron n, Rennbahnsynchrotron n, Synchrotron n mit geradlinigen Beschleunigungsstrecken
Quincke effect	Quincke-Effekt		
Quincke['s] method	Quinckesche Steighöhenmethode (Methode) f		
Quincke tube	Interferenzrohr n [nach Quincke], Quinckesches Interferenzrohr (Resonanzrohr n), Quincke-Rohr n	raceway	s. supply pipe
		rack	Zahnstange f
		rack-and-pinion, rack-and-pinion drive (gear, movement), rack gear[ing]	Zahntrieb m, Zahnstangenantrieb m, Zahnstangentrieb m
quinhydrone electrode (half-cell)	Chinhydronelektrode f		
quintet	Quintett n	rack assembly	s. plug-in unit
quintile	Quintil n	rack gear[ing]	s. rack-and-pinion
quintuple point	Quintupelpunkt m, Fünffachpunkt m	rack wheel	s. pawl and ratchet motion
quintuplet	Quintplett n	rad, rad unit, rd	Rad n, rad-Einheit f, rd, rad
quiver[ing]	s. quake	radan, Radan system	RADAN-System n, Radan-System n
quota sampling	Quoten-Stichprobenverfahren n	radar, radio detecting (detection) and ranging, radiolocation; radio-position finding	Radar n (m); Funkmeßverfahren n; Rückstrahlmeßverfahren n; Rückstrahlortung f; Funkortung f
quotient field, fraction field	Quotientenkörper m		
quotient group, factor[-] group, difference group	Faktorgruppe f, Restklassengruppe f, Differenzgruppe f		
		radar, radar device (apparatus, set, equipment), radiolocator; radio position finder; radar station	Funkmeßgerät n, Funkmeßanlage f, Radaranlage f, Radargerät n; Funkortungsgerät n, Radarstation f
quotient meter	s. ratio[-] meter		
quotient ring	Quotientenring m		
Q value, [nuclear] reaction energy, energy of the nuclear reaction <nucl.>	Q-Wert m, Energie [-tönung] f der Kernreaktion, Reaktionsenergie f <Kern.>	radar antenna	Radarantenne f
		radar apparatus	s. radar

radar astronomy	Radarastronomie f
radar beacon, ramark, raymark	Radarbake f
radar beam, radar ray	Radarstrahl m
radar chaff	s. windows
radar chart	Lagebild n, Lagekarte f, elektronische Lagekarte
radar coverage	Radarbedeckung f, Radarüberdeckung f
radar coverage diagram, coverage diagram	Radarbedeckungsdiagramm n, Bedeckungsdiagramm n, Überdeckungsdiagramm n
radar detection	Radarerfassung f
radar device	s. radar
radar direction finder	s. direction finder
radar display	s. radar screen picture
radar display panel	s. plan-position indicator
radar dome	s. radome
radar echo, radar response; radio echo	Radioecho n; Radarecho n
radar echo cross-section, target radar (scattering) cross-section, equivalent echoing area	Rückstrahlquerschnitt m, Radarquerschnitt m, [äquivalente] Echofläche f
radar engineering	Radartechnik f, Funkmeßtechnik f, Rückstrahlmeßtechnik f
radar equation	Radargleichung f
radar equipment	s. radar
radar height finding	Radarhöhenmessung f
radar horizon	Radarhorizont m
radar indication	s. radar screen picture
radar jamming	s. radar perturbation
radar measurement of wind	s. radar wind measurement
radar meteorology	Radarmeteorologie f
radar observation	s. radio-echo observation
radar perturbation, radar jamming	Funkmeßstörung f, Radarstörung f
radar perturbation by ropes (windows), window jamming	Verdüppelung f, Düppelung f; Düppelstörung f, Folienstörung f
radar range	Radarreichweite f
radar ray	s. radar beam
radar response	s. radio echo
radar scatterometry	[Radar-]Streuechomessung f
radarscope, radar screen	s. plan-position indicator <radar>
radar screen picture; radar display; radar indication	Radarschirmbild n, Radarbild n; Radaranzeige f
radar set	s. radar
radar sounding balloon, wind sounding balloon for radar wind measurement	Windradarballon m
radar station	s. radar
radar wind measurement, radar measurement of wind	Windpeilung f, Radarwindmessung f, Windmessung f mit Radar
radechon, radechon storage device, radechon storage tube, barrier[-] grid storage tube	Sperrgitter[speicher]röhre f, Signalspeicherröhre f mit Streuelektronen-Sperrgitter, Radechon n
rad equivalent man radial	s. rem unit radial
radial, radiate	strahlenförmig
radial; starlike, star-shaped	sternförmig
radial, sagittal, equatorial <opt.>	sagittal, äquatorial, felgenrecht, Sagittal-, Äquatoreal-, Äquatorial- <Opt.>
radial acceleration	Radialbeschleunigung f
radial-axial turbine	s. Francis turbine
radial-beam tube	Radialstrahlröhre f
radial betatron frequency, radial focusing frequency; radial oscillations frequency	Radialfrequenz f [der Betatronschwingungen]
radial betatron oscillation	radiale Betatronschwingung f
radial cross-section	Radialschnitt m; Spiegelschnitt m
radial cylinder rotating pump	s. rotary multiplate vacuum pump
radial derivative	radiale Ableitung f, Ableitung in Richtung des Radius[vektors]
radial distortion, radial image distortion	Bildradialdehnung f, Zerdehnung f
radial distribution function	radiale Verteilungsfunktion f
radial eigenfunction	radiale Eigenfunktion f, Radialeigenfunktion f
radial electron density	Radialelektronendichte f
radial expansion	Radialausdehnung f, radiale Ausdehnung f
radial extension	radiale Verlängerung f
radial extent	radiale Ausdehnung f
radial-flow turbine	Radialturbine f
radial focus	s. sagittal focus
radial focusing frequency	s. radial betatron frequency
radial grounding-system	Strahlenerde f, Strahlenerder m
radial image distortion	s. radial distortion
radially homogeneous field	radialhomogenes Feld n
radially symmetric	radialsymmetrisch
radial mode	Radialmode f, Radialschwingung f, Radialschwingungstyp m
radial motion	Radialbewegung f
radial net	Zentralsystem n, Radialsystem n
radial network, star network, tandem network	Sternnetz n, sternförmiges Netzwerk n, Sternglied n
radial nomogram, radiant nomogram	Strahlentafel f, Radiantentafel f, Strahlennomogramm n, Radiantennomogramm n
radial oscillations frequency	s. radial betatron frequency
radial-phase oscillation, [radial-]synchrotron oscillation	Synchrotronschwingung f
radial point <of aerophotogram>	Radialpunkt m <Luftmeßbild>
radial quantum number	radiale Quantenzahl f, Radialquantenzahl f
radial ridge	s. radial sector
radial-ridge cyclotron, radial-sector cyclotron, Thomas[-type] cyclotron, Thomas-shim cyclotron	Isochronzyklotron n nach Thomas, Thomas-Zyklotron n, Radialsektorzyklotron n
radial-ridge synchrotron	s. FFAG radial-ridge synchrotron
radial sector, radial ridge, straight-ridge sector	Radialsektor m
radial-sector cyclotron	s. radial-ridge cyclotron

radial-sectored field, Thomas['] field	Radialsektorfeld n, Thomas-Feld n	**radiant heat, radiating** heat, radiation heat	Strahlungswärme f, strahlende Wärme f
radial-sector synchrotron	s. FFAG radial-ridge synchrotron	**radiant heat flow rate**	Strahlungswärmestrom m
radial structure, ray structure, radiate structure	Strahlenstruktur f, strahlenförmige Struktur f, strahlenförmiger Aufbau m	**radiant heat interchange,** interchange of radiant heat	Strahlungswärmeaustausch m
radial symmetry	Radialsymmetrie f; Radiärsymmetrie f ‹Bio.›	**radiant intensity,** radiance, luminous [energy] intensity, luminous power	Strahlstärke f
radial-synchrotron oscillation	s. radial-phase oscillation	**radiant intensity**	s. a. intensity of radiation
radial triangulation	Radialtriangulation f	**radiant intensity per unit area**	s. radiance
radial triangulator	Radialtriangulator m	**radiant law,** law of radiation, radiation law, radiation formula	Strahlungsgesetz n, Strahlungsformel f
radial velocity, line-of-sight velocity ‹of star›	Radialgeschwindigkeit f ‹Himmelskörper›	**radiant nomogram,** radial nomogram	Strahlentafel f, Radiantentafel f, Strahlennomogramm n, Radiantennomogramm n
radian, radian unit, rad	Radiant m, Radian m, rad		
radiance, irradiance, radiant intensity per unit area, luminosity, radiancy	Strahldichte f, Strahlendichte f, Strahlungsdichte f	**radiant of meteor shower,** shower radiant	Stromradiant m
radiance	s. a. radiant flux	**radiant position**	Lage (Position) f des Radianten
radiance	s. a. luminosity	**radiant power**	s. radiant flux
radiance	s. a. radiant intensity	**radiant reflectance**	s. total reflection factor
radiance factor	Remissionsgrad m, Strahldichtefaktor m	**radiant sensitivity**	s. sensitivity to radiation
radiance temperature	s. radiation temperature	**radiant spectral absorptivity,** spectral absorption factor, spectral absorptance ‹US›	spektraler Absorptionsgrad m, spektrales Absorptionsvermögen n
radiance temperature	s. a. black-body temperature		
radiancy	s. radiance		
radiancy	s. a. total radiant energy	**radiant surface**	s. emitting surface
radian frequency, angular frequency; pulsatance, pulsation ‹especially el.›	Kreisfrequenz f, Winkelfrequenz f	**radiant total absorptance,** radiant total absorptivity, total absorptance, total absorptivity ‹opt.›	totaler Absorptionsgrad m, totales Absorptionsvermögen (Strahlungsabsorptionsvermögen) n ‹Opt.›
radian length	Bogenlänge f		
radian measure, circular measure	Bogenmaß n	**radiant total reflectance**	s. total reflection factor
radiant, meteor radiant ‹of meteor stream›	Radiant m, Ausstrahlungspunkt m, Radiationspunkt m ‹Meteorstrom, Meteor›	**radian unit**	s. radian
		radiate, radial	strahlenförmig
		radiated energy	s. radiant energy
radiant absorption	s. radiation absorption	**radiated field,** radiation field	Strahlungsfeld n, Strahlenfeld n
radiant centre, radiating centre, radiative centre	Strahlungszentrum n, strahlendes Zentrum n		
radiant density	Radiantendichte f	**radiate packing,** chord packing ‹chem.›	Strahlenkörper m
radiant efficiency, radiating efficiency ‹of radiation source›	Strahlungsausbeute f [der Strahlungsquelle]	**radiate structure,** ray structure, radial structure	Strahlenstruktur f, strahlenförmige Struktur f, strahlenförmiger Aufbau m
radiant emittance, emittance, radiant exitance	spezifische Ausstrahlung f, Ausstrahlung		
		radiating body	s. source of radiation
		radiating capacity	s. emissivity
		radiating centre, radiant centre, radiative centre	Strahlungszentrum n, strahlendes Zentrum n
radiant energy, quantity of radiant energy, radiated (radiating, radiation, radiative) energy, energy (quantity) of radiation, radiation	Strahlungsenergie f, Strahlungsmenge f, Strahlungsenergiemenge f, Strahlungsarbeit f	**radiating dipole,** active dipole, driven dipole	Strahlungsdipol m, strahlender Dipol m, Dipolstrahler m
		radiating efficiency, radiant efficiency ‹of radiation source›	Strahlungsausbeute f [der Strahlungsquelle]
radiant energy density, radiant energy per unit volume, energy density of radiation, radiation [energy] density	Strahlungsdichte f, Energiedichte f der Strahlung, Strahlungsenergiedichte f, Bestrahlungsdichte f, spezifische Strahlungsintensität f	**radiating element**	Strahlerelement n, Strahlungselement n
		radiating energy	s. radiant energy
		radiating heat, radiant heat, radiation heat	Strahlungswärme f, strahlende Wärme f
radiant energy flux	s. radiant flux	**radiating power**	s. emissivity
radiant energy per unit volume	s. radiant energy density	**radiating surface;** heat-absorbent surface; cooling surface	Kühlfläche f, Abkühlungsfläche f, Abkühlungsoberfläche f
radiant exitance	s. radiant emittance		
radiant exposure, energy exposure, irradiation, quantity of radiation ‹quantity›	Bestrahlung f ‹Bestrahlungsstärke × Zeit, Größe›	**radiating surface**	s. a. emitting surface
		radiating term, radiation term	Strahlungsterm m, Strahlungsglied n
		radiation	Strahlung f
radiant flux, radiant power, radiance, radiant energy flux [of radiation], radiation [energy] flux, flux of radiation (radiant energy)	Strahlungsfluß m, Strahlungsleistung f, Strahlungsenergiefluß m, Energiefluß m [der Strahlung]	**radiation,** irradiation ‹upon›	Einstrahlung f
		radiation	s. a. emission
		radiation	s. a. radiant energy
		radiation	s. a. radio-frequency ‹astr.›
		radiation absorption, absorption of radiation, radiant absorption	Strahlungsabsorption f, Strahlenabsorption f
radiant flux [surface] density, flux density [of radiation], radiosity	Strahlungsflußdichte f, Strahlungsleistungsdichte f, Strahlungsstromdichte f	**radiation accident**	Strahlungsunfall m, Strahlenunfall m
		radiation annealing	Strahlungsausheilung f, Bestrahlungserholung f, Strahlungserholung f, Strahlenausheilung f
radiant gas	strahlendes Gas n		

radiation antidamping, radiation oscillation antidamping	Strahlungsantidämpfung f, Strahlungsaufschauk[e]lung f, Strahlungsanfachung f	radiation cooling, cooling by radiation	Strahlungskühlung f
radiation attenuation, attenuation, attenuation of radiation	Schwächung f [der Strahlung], Strahlenschwächung f, Strahlungsschwächung f	radiation cooling <meteo.>	Strahlungsabkühlung f <Meteo.>
radiation background	s. natural background radiation	radiation correction, radiative correction	Strahlungskorrektion f, Strahlungskorrektionsterm m
radiation balance	Strahlungsbilanz f; Strahlungshaushalt m, Strahlenhaushalt m <Meteo.>	radiation corrosion, radiation-induced corrosion, corrosion due to radiation [effect]	Strahlungskorrosion f
radiation balance, radio balance, Callendar radio balance, radiobalance	Strahlungswaage f [nach Callendar]		
radiation balance in the atmosphere	s. radiation balance of the Earth	radiation counter, counter, counter tube, counting tube <nucl.>	Zählrohr n, Zähler m, Strahlungszählrohr n <Kern.>
radiation balance meter	Strahlungsbilanzmesser m	radiation counter (counting assembly, counting unit)	s. pulse counter <nucl.>
radiation balance of the Earth, radiation balance in the atmosphere	Strahlungshaushalt m der Atmosphäre (Erde)	radiation coupled element	s. parasitic element
radiation beam angular width, radiation beam divergence	s. beam divergence	radiation-coupled reflector	s. parasitic reflector <el.>
radiation belt	s. Allen radiation belt / Van	radiation coupling	Strahlungskopplung f
radiation biochemistry	Strahlenbiochemie f, Strahlungsbiochemie f		
radiation-biological effect, radiobiological effect, radiobiological action	strahlenbiologischer Effekt m, strahlenbiologische Wirkung f	radiation coupling resistance	Strahlungskopplungswiderstand m
		radiation cross[-]linking, radiation-induced cross linking	Strahlenvernetzung f, Strahlungsvernetzung f
radiation biology, radiobiology	Strahlenbiologie f, Strahlungsbiologie f, Radiobiologie f		
radiation blocker, chemical protector, radiation protector	Strahlenschutzstoff m, chemischer Strahlenschutz [-stoff] m, Strahlenblocker m	radiation curve, Milankovitch['s] curve	Strahlungskurve f [von Milankovitch]
radiation broadening	s. natural broadening	radiation cytology	Strahlenzytologie f, Strahlungszytologie f
radiation burn	Strahlenverbrennung f, Strahlungsverbrennung f	radiation damage	Strahlungsschaden m, Strahlenschaden m, Bestrahlungsschaden m
radiation burst	Strahlungsstoß m		
radiation burst	s. a. radio burst		
radiation calorimeter	Strahlungskalorimeter n		
radiation capture	s. radiation diffusion	radiation damage	s. a. radiation injury
radiation catalysis, radiation-induced catalysis	Strahlungskatalyse f	radiation damping, radiation oscillation damping	Strahlungsdämpfung f
radiation channel	Strahlungsmeßkanal m, Strahlungsüberwachungskanal m		
radiation characteristic (chart)	s. radiation pattern	radiation danger zone	strahlungsgefährdete Zone f
radiation-chemical equilibrium	strahlenchemisches Gleichgewicht n	radiation decomposition	s. radiolysis
		radiation density	s. radiant energy density
radiation-chemical protection	s. chemical protection against radiation	radiation density constant	s. Stefan-Boltzmann constant
radiation-chemical yield	s. G-value	radiation destruction, radiation-induced destruction	Strahlungsabbau m, Strahlenabbau m
radiation chemistry	Strahlenchemie f, Strahlungschemie f; Kernstrahlenchemie f, Kernstrahlungschemie f; Radiationschemie f, Iochemie f, Io-chemie f		
		radiation detecting instrument, radiation detector	s. detector
radiation climate	Strahlungsklima n	radiation diagram	s. radiation pattern
radiation cold	Strahlungskälte f	radiation diffusion, imprisonment of resonance radiation, [resonance] radiation trapping (capture)	Strahlungsdiffusion f, Resonanzstrahlungseinfang m
radiation condition, outgoing radiation condition; "ausstrahlungsbedingung", Sommerfeld['s] radiation condition	Ausstrahlungsbedingung f; Ausstrahlungsbedingung von Sommerfeld, Sommerfeldsche Ausstrahlungsbedingung		
		radiation disease	s. radiation sickness
		radiation divider	Strahlungsteiler m
radiation conductivity	Strahlungsleitfähigkeit f	radiation dosage, radiation dose	Bestrahlungsdosis f; Strahlungsdosis f, Strahlendosis f
radiation constant	Strahlungskonstante f	radiation dose meter	s. dosimeter
		radiation effect, action of radiation	Strahlen[ein]wirkung f, Strahlungs[ein]wirkung f, Strahlungseffekt m, Strahleneffekt m
radiation content	Strahlungsinhalt m		
radiation contrast	Strahlungskontrast m	radiation efficiency [of antenna]	Wirkungsgrad m der Sendeantenne (Antenne, Strahlung), Strahlungswirkungsgrad m, Strahlungsleistung f der Antenne
radiation control	s. radiation monitoring		
radiation conversion, conversion of radiation	Strahlungsumwandlung f, Strahlungswandlung f		
radiation converter	Strahlungswandler m, Strahlungsumformer m	radiation emissive surface	s. emitting surface

radiation-energetic parallax	strahlungsenergetische Parallaxe f	radiation-induced (radiation-initiated) polymerization	s. radiation polymerization
radiation energy	s. radiant energy	radiation initiation	Strahleninitiierung f, Strahlungsinitiierung f
radiation energy density	s. radiant energy density		
radiation energy flux	s. radiant flux	radiation injury, radiation [-induced] lesion, radiation damage <bio.>	Bestrahlungsschaden m, Strahlenaffektion f, Strahlenschaden m, Strahlenschädigung f <Bio.>
radiation entropy	Strahlungsentropie f		
radiation equilibrium	s. radiative equilibrium		
radiation excitation	Strahlungsanregung f, Strahlenanregung f, Anregung f durch [elektromagnetische] Strahlung	radiation instrument	s. measuring assembly
		radiation intensity, intensity of radiation	Strahlungsintensität f, Intensität f der Strahlung, Intensität, Strahlenintensität f
radiation-exposed, exposed; irradiated	strahlenexponiert, bestrahlt; strahlenbelastet		
		radiation interchange factor	Strahlungsaustauschfaktor m
radiation factor	Strahlungsfaktor m		
radiation field, radiated field	Strahlungsfeld n, Strahlenfeld n	radiation inversion	Strahlungsinversion f
		radiation ionization	Strahlungsionisation f
radiation field, irradiation (exposure) field	Bestrahlungsfeld n, Strahlungsfeld n	radiation law, law of radiation, radiant law, radiation formula	Strahlungsgesetz n, Strahlungsformel f
radiation field	s. a. distant field		
radiation field method, radiation field technique	Strahlungsfeldmethode f, Strahlenfeldmethode f	radiation leakage	s. leakage
		radiation length	s. cascade unit
		radiation lesion	s. radiation injury <bio.>
radiation filter	Strahlungsfilter n, Strahlenfilter n	radiationless capture, non-radiative capture	strahlungsloser (nichtstrahlender) Einfang m
radiation fluctuation, fluctuation in radiation	Strahlungsschwankung f	radiationless recombination	s. non-radiative recombination
radiation flux	s. radiant flux	radiationless transition, non-radiative transition, Auger transition	strahlungsloser Übergang m, Auger-Übergang m
radiation fluxmeter	Strahlungsflußmesser m, Flußmesser m		
radiation fog	Strahlungsnebel m	radiation loss, radiative loss	Strahlungsverlust m
radiation formula, law of radiation, radiation law, radiant law	Strahlungsgesetz n, Strahlungsformel f	radiation magnetization	Strahlungsmagnetisierung f
		radiation maze, radiation trap, maze	Abschirmungslabyrinth n, Eingangslabyrinth n, Strahlungsschleuse f, Strahlenschleuse f
radiation frost	Strahlungsfrost m		
radiation genetics	Strahlengenetik f, Strahlungsgenetik f		
		radiation measurement, radiometry	Radiometrie f, Strahlungsmessung f, Strahlenmessung f
radiation hardening, hardening of the radiation	Strahlenhärtung f, Strahlungshärtung f		
		radiation measuring assembly (instrument)	s. measuring assembly
radiation hardness	s. penetrating power	radiation measuring technique	s. technique of radiation measurement
radiation hazard, radiohazard	Strahlungsrisiko n, Strahlenrisiko n, Strahlengefährdung n, Strahlungsgefährdung f	radiation meter	s. measuring assembly
		radiation microbiology, radiomicrobiology	Strahlenmikrobiologie f, Strahlungsmikrobiologie f, Radiomikrobiologie f
radiation heat, radiant heat, radiating heat	Strahlungswärme f		
radiation heating	Strahlungsaufheizung f; Strahlungserwärmung f	radiation monitor, monitor, radiation monitoring instrument, monitoring instrument, radiation survey meter, survey meter, survey instrument <nucl.>	Strahlenüberwachungsgerät n, Strahlungsüberwachungsgerät n, Überwachungs[meß]gerät n, Überwachungsinstrument n, Kontrollgerät n, Kontrollinstrument n, Kontroll- und Überwachungsgerät n, Strahlungskontrollgerät n, Strahlenkontrollgerät n, Monitor m; Warngerät n, Strahlungswarngerät n, Strahlenwarngerät n <Kern.>
radiation height	s. effective height of the antenna		
radiation hygiene	Strahlungshygiene f, Strahlenhygiene f		
radiation impedance	s. sound radiation impedance <ac.>		
radiation indicator	Strahlungsindikator m, Strahlungsanzeiger m, Strahlenindikator m, Strahlenanzeiger m		
		radiation monitoring; radiation survey (surveillance); radiation control	Strahlungskontrolle f, Strahlenkontrolle f; Strahlungsüberwachung f, Strahlenüberwachung f; Strahlungswarnung f, Strahlenwarnung f
radiation-induced catalysis	s. radiation catalysis		
radiation-induced corrosion	s. radiation corrosion		
radiation-induced cross linking	s. radiation cross[-] linking	radiation monitoring	s. a. health monitoring
radiation-induced defect	strahlungserzeugte Fehlstelle f, strahlungsinduzierte Fehlordnung f	radiation monitoring instrument	s. radiation monitor
		radiation morbidity, radiation sickness	Strahlenkrankheit f; Strahlenkater m
radiation-induced destruction	s. radiation destruction		
radiation-induced embrittlement	strahlungsinduzierte Versprödung f, Strahlungsversprödung f, Strahlenversprödung f	radiation of energy, energy radiation	Energieabstrahlung f, Energieausstrahlung f; Energiestrahlung f
		radiation of heat	s. heat radiation
radiation-induced growth	Strahlungswachstum n, Wachstum n infolge Bestrahlung	radiation of sound, sound radiation, sound projection, acoustic radiation	Schallstrahlung f, akustische Strahlung f; Schallabstrahlung f, Schallausstrahlung f, Schallaussendung f
radiation-induced lesion	s. radiation injury <bio.>		
radiation-induced mutation	s. radiomutation	radiation oscillation antidamping	s. radiation antidamping

radiation oscillation damping s. radiation damping

radiation pattern, directive pattern, directional pattern, directional response pattern, lobe pattern, space pattern, radiation chart, radiation diagram, directional characteristic, radiation characteristic; polar diagram [of antenna], directional diagram
Richtcharakteristik f, Richtungscharakteristik f; Richtdiagramm n, Richtungsdiagramm n; Strahlungsdiagramm n; Richtkennlinie f; Richtkennfläche f, räumliche Richtungscharakteristik f; Strahlungscharakteristik f, Strahlungskennlinie f

radiation physicist, radiological physicist
Strahlungsphysiker m, Strahlenphysiker m

radiation physics
Strahlungsphysik f, Strahlenphysik f

radiation polymerization, radiation-induced (radiation-initiated) polymerization
Strahlungspolymerisation f, Strahlenpolymerisation f

radiation potential
Strahlungspotential n, Strahlenpotential n

radiation pressure
Strahlungsdruck m

radiation pressure [in acoustics], radiation pressure in sound
s. acoustic radiation pressure

radiation-pressure wattmeter, ponderomotive wattmeter
Strahlungsdruck-Leistungsmesser m, Strahlungsdruck-Wattmeter n

radiation processing, radiation treatment
Strahlenbehandlung f, Bestrahlung f

radiation-proof; ray[-]proof
strahlungssicher, strahlungsgeschützt, strahlensicher, strahlengeschützt

radiation protection, protection against radiations; radiological protection
Strahlenschutz m

radiation protective wall
s. protective wall

radiation protector
s. radiation blocker

radiation pump
Strahlungspumpe f

radiation pyrometer, optical pyrometer, heat radiation pyrometer, pyrometer
Strahlungspyrometer n, Strahlenpyrometer n, optisches Pyrometer n, Pyrometer

radiation quality, quality of radiation
Strahlenqualität f, Qualität f der Strahlung, Strahlungsqualität f; Röntgenstrahlenhärte f

radiation quantum, photon, quantum
Photon n, Strahlungsquant n, Quant n

radiation reaction, radiative reaction
Strahlungsrückwirkung f, Strahlungsreaktion f; Strahlungsbremsung f

radiation reaction force, reaction force, damping term
Strahlungsreaktionskraft f, Lorentzsche Dämpfungskraft f, Strahlungsrückwirkung f, Strahlungsbremsung f

radiation receiver (receptor), receptor [of radiation]
Strahlungsempfänger m

radiation recoil
Strahlungsrückstoß m

radiation recombination
s. radiative recombination

radiation resistance
s. characteristic acoustic impedance

radiation resistance
s. a. radioresistance

radiation resistance [of the antenna] <el.>
Strahlungswiderstand m [der Antenne] <El.>

radiation safety
Strahlungssicherheit f, Strahlensicherheit f

radiation selection
Strahlenselektion f, Strahlungsselektion f

radiation sensitivity
s. sensitivity to radiation

radiation shield, radiation shielding
Strahlungsabschirmung f, Strahlenabschirmung f, Strahlenschutz m, Strahlenschild m, Strahlungsschild m

radiation sickness, radiation disease, radiation morbidity
Strahlenkrankheit f; Strahlenkater m

radiation source
s. source of radiation

radiation stability
s. radioresistance

radiation standard, standard radiation source, standard source of radiation
Strahlungsnormallampe f, Strahlungsnormal n

radiation stop; beam limiting, limitation of the beam
Strahlbegrenzung f; Strahlenbegrenzung f; Bündelbegrenzung f

radiation stream
Strahlungsstrom m

radiation streaming, streaming; channel[l]ing effect, channel[l]ing <nucl.>
Strahlungstransport m durch Kanäle; Kanalisierungseffekt m, Kanalisierung f, Kanaleffekt m; Kanalverlust m <Kern.>

radiation sum
Strahlungssumme f

radiation surface
s. emitting surface

radiation surplus
Strahlungsüberschuß m

radiation surveillance
s. radiation monitoring

radiation survey, radiation monitoring, health monitoring, protection survey
Strahlenschutzüberwachung f

radiation survey
s. a. radiation monitoring

radiation survey meter
s. radiation monitor

radiation temperature; brightness temperature, luminance temperature, radiance temperature
Strahlungstemperatur f; Luminanztemperatur f

radiation tensor
Strahlungstensor m

radiation term, radiating term
Strahlungsterm m, Strahlungsglied n

radiation therapy, radiotherapy; therapeutic radiology
Strahlentherapie f

radiation thermocouple
Strahlungsthermoelement n

radiation thermometer
s. black-bulb thermometer

radiation tolerance
s. tolerance dose

radiation transmission
Strahlungsdurchgang m, Strahlendurchgang m

radiation transparent
s. transparent

radiation transport, radiative transfer <through>
Strahlungstransport m

radiation trap
s. radiation maze

radiation trapping
s. radiation diffusion

radiation treatment, radiation processing
Strahlenbehandlung f, Bestrahlung f

radiation tube
Strahlungsröhre f

radiation type of weather, radiation-type weather
Strahlungswetterlage f, Strahlungswetter n

radiation unit
s. cascade unit

radiation vector
s. energy flux density <el.>

radiation width
Strahlungsbreite f, Gamma-Breite f

radiation zone, far zone, distant zone, wave zone, Fraunhofer['s] zone, Fraunhofer['s] region
Wellenzone f, Fernzone f, Strahlungszone f, Fraunhofersche Zone f, Fraunhofersches Gebiet n

radiation zone
s. a. Allen radiation belt / Van

radiative capture
Strahlungseinfang m, strahlender Einfang m, (x,γ)-Prozeß m <x = n,p usw.>

radiative capture cross-section, cross-section for radiative capture
Strahlungseinfangquerschnitt m, Wirkungsquerschnitt m für Strahlungseinfang, Wirkungsquerschnitt des Strahlungseinfangs, Strahlungseinfang-Wirkungsquerschnitt m; Wirkungsquerschnitt der (für die) (n,y)-Reaktion

radiative centre, radiating centre, radiant centre — Strahlungszentrum n, strahlendes Zentrum n

radiative collision — s. inelastic collision

radiative correction, radiation correction — Strahlungskorrektion f, Strahlungskorrektionsterm m

radiative energy — s. radiant energy

radiative envelope — Gashülle f im Strahlungsgleichgewicht

radiative equilibrium, radiation equilibrium — Strahlungsgleichgewicht n; Gleichgewichtsstrahlung f

radiative frequency shift — s. Lamb-Retherford shift

radiative heat exchange (transfer, transmission) — s. heat transfer by radiation

radiative inelastic scattering — strahlende unelastische Streuung f

radiative inelastic scattering cross-section, cross-section for radiative inelastic scattering — Wirkungsquerschnitt m für strahlende unelastische Streuung, Wirkungsquerschnitt der strahlenden unelastischen Streuung

radiative layer — Strahlungszone f

radiative loss, radiation loss — Strahlungsverlust m

radiative mechanism, luminescence (luminous) mechanism — Leuchtmechanismus m [der Lumineszenz]

radiative power — s. emissivity

radiative reaction — s. radiation reaction

radiative recombination, radiation recombination — Zweierstoß[-Strahlungs]-rekombination f, strahlende Rekombination f, Strahlungsrekombination f, Rekombination im Zweierstoß

radiative temperature gradient — Temperaturgradient m bei Strahlungsgleichgewicht

radiative transfer, radiation transport <through> — Strahlungstransport m <durch>

radiative transfer [of heat] — s. heat transfer by radiation

radiative transition — strahlender Übergang m, Strahlungsübergang m, Übergang mit Gamma-Emission

radiative transition probability (rate) — Strahlungsübergangswahrscheinlichkeit f

radiator <of spectrometer> — Erzeugerplatte f, Radiator m <Spektrometer>

radiator, emitter <nucl.> — Strahler m <Kern.>

radiator for comparison, reference (comparison) radiator — Vergleichsstrahler m

radical <math., chem.>; rest <chem.> — Radikal n <Math., Chem.>; Rest m <Chem.>

radical addition, homolytic addition — radikalische (homolytische) Addition f

radical axis — Potenzlinie f, Chordale f, Radikalachse f; Potenzachse f

radical centre — Potenzpunkt m

radicaloid, inactive radical — Radikaloid n, inaktives Radikal n

radical plane — Potenzebene f

radical reaction — Radikalreaktion f <insbesondere die Reaktion: $H_2O \rightarrow H^{\bullet} + OH^{\bullet}$>

radical rearrangement, radical transposition — radikalische Umlagerung f

radical sign — Wurzelzeichen n

radical transposition — s. radical rearrangement

radicand — Radikand m

radioacoustics — Radioakustik f

radioactinium, RdAc, ^{227}Th — Radioaktinium n, Radioactinium n, RdAc, ^{227}Th

radioactivation, activation <nucl.> — Aktivierung f <Kern.>

radioactivation analysis — s. activation analysis

radioactive aerosol — radioaktiver Schwebstoff m, radioaktives Aerosol n

radioactive age — radioaktives (radiogenes) Alter n

radioactive age determination — s. radioactive dating

radioactive battery — s. atomic battery

radioactive carbon — s. radiocarbon

radioactive chain product, member of a radioactive chain — Glied n einer radioaktiven Zerfallsreihe

radioactive clock — „radioaktive" Uhr f <Zeitbestimmung auf Grund des radioaktiven Zerfalls>

radioactive colloid, radio[-]colloid — radioaktives Kolloid n, Radiokolloid n

radioactive contamination, contamination, radiocontamination — Kontamination f, radioaktive Verseuchung f, Verseuchung

radioactive dating, radioactive age determination — radioaktive Altersbestimmung f, radioaktive Zeitmessung f, absolute Altersbestimmung

radioactive decay, decay of radioactivity, activity decay — Aktivitätsabfall m, Aktivitätsabnahme f

radioactive decay — s. a. decay <nucl.>

radioactive decay constant — s. decay constant

radioactive decay law — s. radioactive disintegration law

radioactive deposit, active deposit — radioaktiver Niederschlag m; radioaktive Ablagerung f

radioactive disintegration — s. decay

radioactive disintegration — s. radioactive decay

radioactive disintegration constant — s. decay constant

radioactive disintegration law — s. law of radioactive disintegration

radioactive displacement law, displacement law of radioactive disintegration, Soddy-Fajans displacement law, displacement law [of Soddy and Fajans] — radioaktives Verschiebungsgesetz n, Verschiebungssatz m von Soddy und Fajans, radioaktive Verschiebungssätze mpl von Fajans und Soddy, radioaktiver (Soddy-Fajansscher) Verschiebungssatz, Soddy-Fajanssches Verschiebungsgesetz

radioactive dry deposit, dry deposit (fallout) — trockener Fallout m, Fallout außerhalb der Niederschläge

radioactive effluent — flüssiges oder gasförmiges radioaktives Abfallprodukt n, radioaktiver Abfall m <flüssig oder gasförmig>

radioactive emanation, [active] emanation, radioactive noble gas — Emanation f, radioaktives Edelgas n

radioactive emanation, emanation — Emanation f, Emanieren n; Ausströmen n radioaktiver Gase; Ausstrahlung f radioaktiver Gase

radioactive emanation — s. a. radon <element>

radioactive equilibrium — radioaktives Gleichgewicht n

radioactive fall-out — s. fall-out

radioactive family — s. disintegration series <nucl.>

radioactive family of actinium — s. actinium family

radioactive family of neptunium — s. neptunium family

radioactive family of radium — s. uranium series

radioactive family of thorium — s. thorium family

radioactive family of uranium	s. uranium series	radio[]balance	s. radiation balance
radioactive family of uranium-actinium	s. actinium family	radio balloon, radiosonde, radiometeorograph, radio wind flight, rawin	Radiosonde f, Funksonde f, Aerosonde f, Radiometeorograph m
radioactive family of uranium-radium	s. uranium series	radiobeacon, beacon <el.>	Funkbake f; Radiobake f; Funkfeuer n <El.>
radioactive gamma-rays	s. gamma rays	radio[-] bearing	s. bearing
radioactive half-life, half-life, period, physical half-life <nucl.>	Halbwert[s]zeit f [des radioaktiven Zerfalls], radioaktive Halbwertzeit f, physikalische Halbwertzeit <Kern.>	radiobearing	s. bearing
		radiobiochemistry	Radiobiochemie f
		radiobiological action (effect), radiationbiological effect	strahlenbiologischer Effekt m, strahlenbiologische Wirkung f
radioactive heat, radiogenic heat	radiogene Wärme f, radioaktive Wärme	radiobiological sensitive volume [of the cell], sensitive volume [of the cell], sensitive region [of the cell], target <radiobiology>	strahlenempfindlicher Bereich m [der Zelle], strahlenempfindliches Volumen n [der Zelle], empfindlicher Bereich [der Zelle], empfindliches Volumen [der Zelle], Treff[er]bereich m, Treffvolumen n <Strahlenbiologie>
radioactive indicator	s. radioactive tracer		
radioactive inspection [of materials]	s. radiographic testing of materials		
radioactive isotope of carbon	s. radiocarbon		
		radiobiology	Radiobiologie f
radioactive noble gas, [active] emanation, radioactive emanation	Emanation f, radioaktives Edelgas n	radiobiology	s. a. radiation biology
		radiobuoy	Funkboje f
radioactive nucleus, unstable nucleus, decaying nucleus	radioaktiver Kern m, instabiler Kern, zerfallender Kern	radio burst [on the Sun], radio noise burst [on the Sun], solar noise burst, radiation burst, burst, radio outburst [on the Sun], radio noise outburst [on the Sun], solar noise outburst	Strahlungsausbruch m [auf der Sonne] [im Radiofrequenzbereich], Radiostrahlungsausbruch (Radiofrequenzausbruch) m [der Sonne], Strahlungsstoß m, kurzzeitiger Strahlungsstoß, Burst m, Outburst m
radioactive preparation	radioaktives Präparat n		
radioactive purity	radioaktive Reinheit f		
radioactive radiation	radioaktive Strahlung f		
radioactive radiation counter (counting assembly)	s. pulse counting assembly <nucl.>		
radioactive radiation in the lower atmosphere	s. atmospheric radioactive radiation	radiocarbon, ¹⁴C; radioactive carbon; radioactive isotope of carbon	Radiokohlenstoff m, ¹⁴C; radioaktiver Kohlenstoff m; radioaktives Kohlenstoffisotop n, radioaktives Isotop n des Kohlenstoffs
radioactive rainout	s. rainout		
radioactive relationship	radioaktive Verwandtschaft f		
radioactive relay	Isotopenrelais n, „radioaktives" Relais n; Strahlenschranke f, Strahlungsschranke f	radiocarbon age	Kohlenstoffalter n, ¹⁴C-Alter n
		radiocarbon dating, radiocarbon method, carbon method, ¹⁴C dating	Altersbestimmung f nach dem ¹⁴C-Gehalt, ¹⁴C-Datierung f, Kohlenstoffmethode f, Radiokohlenstoffmethode f, ¹⁴C-Methode f, Radiokohlenstoffdatierung f, Radiocarbonmethode f
radioactive series	s. disintegration series		
radioactive source, radioactivity source, source <nucl.>	Quelle f, Strahlungsquelle f, Aktivitätsquelle f; radioaktives Präparat n, Präparat <Kern.>		
radioactive standard	s. radioactivity standard		
radioactive tracer, radiotracer, radioactive indicator, radioindicator, tracer <nucl.>	radioaktiver Tracer (Indikator) m, radioaktives Leitisotop n, Radiotracer m, Radioindikator m, Leitisotop, Tracer <Kern.>	radiochemical purity	radiochemische Reinheit f
		radiochemistry	Radiochemie f
		radiochromatogram, radiochromatograph	Radiochromatogramm n
		radiochromatography	Radiochromatographie f
radioactive transformation (transmutation)	s. decay <of atomic nucleus>	radio-cinematography	s. roentgen cinematography
radioactive unit	s. radioactivity unit	radiochrometer	s. qualimeter
radioactive waste	s. atomic waste	radio[-]colloid, radioactive colloid	radioaktives Kolloid n, Radiokolloid n
radioactivity	s. activity <nucl.>		
radioactivity meter, activity meter	Aktivitätsmesser m	radiocontamination	s. radioactive contamination
radioactivity of air	s. airborne radioactivity	radio crystallography, X-ray crystallography	Röntgenkristallographie f, Röntgenstrahlenkristallographie f
radioactivity source	s. radioactive source		
radioactivity standard	s. standard source		
radioactivity unit, radioactive unit	Aktivitätseinheit f, Einheit f der Aktivität (Radioaktivität), radioaktive Einheit	radio crystallography	s. a. X-ray crystallographic analysis
		radiode	Radiumkapsel f
radio[-]altimeter	Radioecholot n, Radiohöhenmesser m, Funkhöhenmesser m, Funkecholot n	radio detecting (detection) and ranging	s. radar
		radio direction	s. bearing
radio amplification by stimulated emission of radiation	s. raser	radio direction finder, radio[-]goniometer	Funkpeiler m, Radiogoniometer n, Funkpeilgerät n, Radiopeilgerät n, Goniometerpeilanlage f
radioassay	Aktivitätsbestimmung f, Aktivitätsanalyse f; Radioassay m	radio disturbance	s. radio[-]interference
		radio echo; radar echo, radar response	Radioecho n; Radarecho n
radioastronomic interferometer	s. radio interferometer <astr.>	radio echo observation; radar observation	Radioechomethode f, Radio-Echo-Methode f; Radarbeobachtung f
radio astronomy, radioastronomy	Radioastronomie f		
radio aurora	Radioaurora f		
		radioeclipse	Radiofinsternis f, Radioverfinsterung f
radioautogram, radioautograph, autoradiogram, autoradiograph <US>	Autoradiogramm n, autoradiographische Aufnahme f, Autoradiographie f	radioecology	Radioökologie f
		radioelectric effect	radioelektrischer Effekt m
		radioelectric wave	s. radio wave
radioautography, autoradiography <US>	Autoradiographie f, Radioautographie f	radio-electromotive force, radio-e.m.f.	Hochfrequenz-EMK, HF-elektromotorische Kraft f

radioelectronics s. radiofrequency unit
radio-e.m.f. s. radio-electromotive force
radio emission s. radio-frequency ‹astr.›
radioexamination s. fluoroscopy
radio fade-out, sudden ionospheric disturbance, Dellinger effect ‹US›, sudden short wave fade-out, [Dellinger] fade-out, S.I.D., S.S.W.F. [Mögel-]Dellinger-Effekt m, Kurzwellentotalschwund m, Fade-out n, Sonneneruptionseffekt m im Kurzwellenbereich, plötzliche Ionosphärenstörung f
radio[-]frequency, R.F., r.f. Funkfrequenz f, Radiofrequenz f
radio-frequency, R.F., r.f.; high frequency, H.F., h.f., HF Hochfrequenz f, HF
radio-frequency accelerator, R.F. accelerator Hochfrequenzbeschleuniger m, HF-Beschleuniger m
radio-frequency alternating-current voltage, R.F. a-c voltage Hochfrequenz-Wechselspannung f, HF-Wechselspannung f
radio-frequency band, R.F. band Hochfrequenzband n, HF-Band n
radio-frequency bandwidth, R.F. bandwidth Hochfrequenzbandbreite f, HF-Bandbreite f
radio-frequency bunching, phase grouping, bunching, phase bunching Phasenbündelung f
radio-frequency capture, radio-frequency particle capture, R.F. capture Hochfrequenzeinfang m, HF-Einfang m
radio-frequency conductivity, high-frequency (H.F., R.F.) conductivity Hochfrequenzleitfähigkeit f, HF-Leitfähigkeit f
radio frequency connection, R.F. connection Hochfrequenzanschluß m, HF-Anschluß m
radio-frequency degassing, R.F. degassing Hochfrequenzentgasung f, HF-Entgasung f
radio-frequency discharge, R.F. discharge Hochfrequenz[-Gas]entladung f, HF-Entladung f, HF-Gasentladung f
radio-frequency electronics, R.F. electronics Hochfrequenzelektronik f, HF-Elektronik f
radio-frequency energy, high-frequency energy, R.F. energy, H.F. energy Hochfrequenzenergie f, HF-Energie f
radio-frequency field strength, R.F. field strength Hochfrequenzfeldstärke f, HF-Feldstärke f
radio-frequency gas tube, R.F. gas tube Hochfrequenz[-Gas]entladungsröhre f, HF-Gasentladungsröhre f, HF-Entladungsröhre f
radio-frequency glow discharge tube, radio-frequency glow tube, R.F. glow tube Hochfrequenzröhre f, Hochfrequenzglimmröhre f, HF-Röhre f, HF-Glimmröhre f
radio-frequency heat, r.f. heat Hochfrequenzwärme f, HF-Wärme f
radio-frequency high-voltage generator, R.F. high-voltage generator Hochfrequenz-Hochspannungsgenerator m, HF-Hochspannungsgenerator m
radio-frequency leakage, R.F. leakage Hochfrequenzstreuung f, HF-Streuung f
radio-frequency linear accelerator, R.F. linac Hochfrequenz-Linearbeschleuniger m, HF-Linearbeschleuniger m
radio-frequency low-pass filter, R.F. low-pass filter Hochfrequenzsperre f, HF-Sperre f; Hochfrequenzsperrkette f, HF-Sperrkette f
radio-frequency magnetic mirror, high-frequency magnetic mirror, R.F. magnetic mirror [magnetischer] Hochfrequenzspiegel m, Hochfrequenzpfropfen m, HF-Spiegel m, HF-Pfropfen m
radio-frequency mass spectrometer s. high-frequency mass spectrometer
radio-frequency oscillation, high-frequency oscillation, R.F. oscillation, H.F. oscillation Hochfrequenzschwingung f, HF-Schwingung f
radio-frequency particle capture, radio-frequency capture, R.F. capture Hochfrequenzeinfang m, HF-Einfang m
radio-frequency permeability, high-frequency permeability, H.F. permeability, R.F. permeability Hochfrequenzpermeabilität f, HF-Permeabilität f
radio-frequency physics, radiophysics Hochfrequenzphysik f, HF-Physik f
radio-frequency pulse, R.F. pulse, wave impulse Hochfrequenzimpuls m, HF-Impuls m, Wellenstoß m, Wellenimpuls m
radio-frequency pump power, R.F. pump power Hochfrequenz-Pumpleistung f, HF-Pumpleistung f
radio-frequency radiation, radio radiation, radio emission ‹astr.› Radiofrequenzstrahlung f, Radiostrahlung f ‹Astr.›
radio-frequency radiation, R.F. radiation hochfrequente Strahlung f, Hochfrequenzstrahlung, HF-Strahlung f, Radiofrequenzstrahlung f
radio-frequency radiation of perturbed Sun gestörte Sonnenstrahlung f, Radiofrequenzstrahlung f der gestörten Sonne
radio-frequency radiation of quiet Sun ungestörte Sonnenstrahlung f, Radiofrequenzstrahlung f der ruhigen Sonne
radio-frequency range, R.F. range Funkfrequenzbereich m; Radiofrequenzbereich m; Hochfrequenzbereich m, HF-Bereich m
radio-frequency signal generator, R.F. signal generator Hochfrequenzmeßsender m, HF-Meßsender m
radio-frequency source s. radio source
radio-frequency spectrograph, R.F. spectrograph Hochfrequenzspektrograph m, HF-Spektrograph m, Radiofrequenzspektrograph m
radio-frequency spectrometer, R.F. spectrometer Hochfrequenzspektrometer n, HF-Spektrometer n, Radiofrequenzspektrometer n
radio-frequency spectroscopy, R.F. spectroscopy Hochfrequenzspektroskopie f, HF-Spektroskopie f, Radiofrequenzspektroskopie f
radio-frequency spectrum, R.F. spectrum Hochfrequenzspektrum n, HF-Spektrum n, Radiofrequenzspektrum n, Funkfrequenzspektrum n
radio-frequency susceptibility, R.F. susceptibility Hochfrequenzsuszeptibilität f, HF-Suszeptibilität f
radio-frequency time-of-flight spectrometer, time-of-flight radio-frequency spectrometer, R.F. time-of-flight spectrometer, time-of-flight R.F. spectrometer Hochfrequenz-Laufzeitspektrometer n, HF-Laufzeitspektrometer n
radio-frequency titration s. high-frequency titration
radio-frequency transconductance, R.F. transconductance Hochfrequenzsteilheit f, HF-Steilheit f
radio-frequency transparent, R.F. transparent hochfrequenzdurchlässig, HF-durchlässig
radio-frequency two-wire line s. Lecher system
radio-frequency unit, R.F. unit, electronics, radioelectronics Hochfrequenzteil m, HF-Teil m, Elektronikteil m
radio[-]galaxy, radio nebula Radiosternsystem n, Radiogalaxis f, Radiogalaxie f

radiogenic	radiogen, radioaktiven Ursprungs, durch radioaktiven Zerfall entstanden	radioisotope thermoelectric generator, RTG	s. thermoelectric battery
radiogenic heat	s. radioactive heat	radio jamming	s. radio[-]interference
radiogeodesy	Radiogeodäsie f	radiolead, $^{210}_{82}$Pb, RaD	Radioblei n, RaD, $^{10}_{82}$Pb
radio[-]goniometer, radio direction finder	Funkpeiler m, Radiogoniometer n	radio lens, lens antenna	Linsenantenne f
radiogoniometry	s. bearing	radiolocation	s. radar
radiogram, radio message	Funkspruch m	radiolocator	s. radar
radiogram	s. a. radiograph	radiological consultation report	Röntgenbefund m
radiograph, radiogram, roentgenogram, roentgenograph, X-ray picture (photograph, image), X-rayogram, exograph	Röntgenbild n, Röntgenogramm n, Röntgenaufnahme f	radiological physicist, radiation physicist	Strahlungsphysiker m, Strahlenphysiker m
		radiological physics	radiologische Physik f, physikalische Radiologie f
radiograph, X-ray apparatus (machine), roentgen apparatus (machine)	Röntgenapparat m, Röntgengerät n	radiological protection	s. radiation protection
		radiological safety officer	Strahlenschutzbeauftragter m, Verantwortlicher m für die Strahlenschutzüberwachung, Strahlenschutzobmann m, qualifizierter Sachverständiger m
radiograph	s. a. screen photograph		
radiographic contrast	Röntgenkontrast m		
radiographic detail	Röntgendetail n		
radiographic emulsion, X-ray emulsion, roentgenographic emulsion	Röntgenemulsion f		
		radiology	Radiologie f, Strahlenkunde f, Lehre f von den Strahlungen <insbesondere den radioaktiven und Röntgenstrahlungen>
radiographic film, X-ray film	radiographischer Film m, Röntgenfilm m		
radiographic materials testing	s. radiographic testing of materials		
radiographic paper; X-ray paper	Röntgenpapier n; Radiographiepapier n	radiology, medical radiology	medizinische Radiologie f, Radiologie
radiographic plate, X-ray plate	Röntgenplatte f	radiolucent, radiotransparent	röntgenstrahlendurchlässig, durchgängig für Röntgenstrahlen
radiographic source, X-ray source	Röntgenstrahlenquelle f, Röntgenstrahl[ungs]quelle f, Röntgenstrahler m, Röntgenquelle f		
		radioluminescence	Radiolumineszenz f
radiographic stereometry, X-ray stereometry	Röntgenstereometrie f	radiolysis, radiation decomposition, decomposition by radiation	Radiolyse f, Strahlendissoziation f, Strahlenzersetzung f, strahlenchemische Zersetzung f, Zersetzung infolge Strahleneinwirkung, Strahlungsdissoziation f, Strahlungszersetzung f
radiographic stereoscopy, X-ray stereoscopy	Röntgenstereoskopie f		
radiographic testing of materials, radiographic materials testing radiomateriology; radioactive inspection [of materials]	[zerstörungsfreie] Werkstoffprüfung f mittels Strahlung, radiographische Werkstoffprüfung f; Durchstrahlungsprüfung f mittels Radiographie, [zerstörungsfreie] Werkstoffprüfung mittels radioaktiver Strahlung		
		radiomagnitude	s. radiometric stellar magnitude
		radiomateriology	s. radiographic testing of materials
		radiomaximograph	Radiomaximograph m
radiography	Radiographie f		
radiography	s. a. roentgenography	radio message	s. radiogram
radiography by gamma-rays	s. gammagraphy	radiometallography	s. X-ray metallography
		radio meteor	Radiometeor n
radiohalation, radiohalo	Radiohalo m		
radiohazard	s. radiation hazard	radiometeorograph, radiosonde, radio balloon, radio wind flight, rawin	Radiosonde f, Funksonde f, Aerosonde f, Radiometeorograph m
radioheliogram	Radioheliogramm n		
radioimmunoassay	radioimmunologische Bestimmung f		
radioindicator	s. radioactive tracer <nucl.>	radiometeorology	Radiometeorologie f
radio[-]interference, radio disturbance; radio jamming	Funkstörung f, Rundfunkstörung f, Radiostörung f		
		radiometer, fluxmeter	Radiometer n; Strahlungs[fluß]messer m; Strahlenmesser m
radio[-]interferometer, radioastronomic interferometer, interferometer <astr.>	Radiointerferometer n, Interferenzsystem n, Interferenzantennensystem n, Interferometer n <Astr.>		
		radiometer	s. a. measuring assembly
		radiometer action, radiometric effect	Radiometereffekt m, Radiometerwirkung f
		radiometer gauge, radiometer-vacuummeter, radiometric gauge	Radiometer-Vakuummeter n, absolutes Vakuummeter n
radio-isophot	Radioisophote f, Isophote f der Radiofrequenzstrahlung		
radioisotope battery	s. atomic battery		
radioisotope device (gauge)	s. radioisotope instrument	radiometer vane	Radiometerflügel m
radioisotope-excited X-ray fluorescence analysis, isotope-excited X-ray fluorescence analysis	Radioisotopen-Röntgenfluoreszenzanalyse f, Röntgenfluoreszenzanalyse f mit Anregung durch Radionuklidquelle, isotopenangeregte (radionuklidangeregte) Röntgenfluoreszenzanalyse	radiometric adsorption analysis	radiometrische Adsorptionsanalyse f
		radiometric assay, radiometric determination	radiometrische Bestimmung f
		radiometric effect	s. radiometer effect
		radiometric force	Radiometerkraft f
		radiometric gauge	s. radiometer gauge
		radiometric instrument	s. measuring assembly
		radiometric magnitude	s. radiometric stellar magnitude
radioisotope generator	s. isotopic generator		
radioisotope instrument, radioisotope gauge (meter, device)	Radioisotopenmeßgerät n, Isotopenmeßgerät n		
radioisotope lamp	s. radionuclide lamp		
radioisotope meter	s. radioisotope instrument	radiometric materials testing, transmission radiometric materials testing	radiometrische Werkstoffprüfung f, Durchstrahlungsprüfung f <Nachweis durch Zählrohr, Ionisationskammer oder Szintillationszähler>
radioisotope production, isotope production	Isotopenherstellung f, Isotopenproduktion f, Herstellung f radioaktiver Isotope, Radioisotopenproduktion f		

radiometric | | | 670

radiometric stellar magnitude, radiometric magnitude, radiomagnitude	Radiohelligkeit f, radiometrische Helligkeit f <eines Gestirns>	**radio silence**	Funkstille f
		radiosity	s. radiant flux density
		radiosonde, radiometeorograph, radio balloon, radio wind flight, rawin	Radiosonde f, Funksonde f, Aerosonde f, Radiometeorograph m
		radiosorption luminescence	Radiosorptionslumineszenz f
radiometry, radiation measurement	Radiometrie f, Strahlungsmessung f, Strahlenmessung f	**radio-sounding technique**	Radiosondenverfahren n, Radiosondenmethode f
radiomicrobiology, radiation microbiology	Strahlenmikrobiologie f, Strahlungsmikrobiologie f, Radiomikrobiologie f	**radio source**, radio-frequency source, source of radio-frequency radiation, radio star	Radioquelle f, diskrete Radioquelle, Radiostern m
radiomimetic	Radiomimetikum n, Ruhekerngift n	**radio-spectrograph**, **radio spectrograph**, radio-wave spectrograph	Radiospektrograph m, Radiowellenspektrograph m, Radiostrahlungsspektrograph m
radiomutation, radiation-induced mutation, mutation due to radiation	strahlungsbedingte (strahlungsinduzierte) Mutation f, Mutation als Folge einer Strahleneinwirkung	**radio-spectrometer**, **radio spectrometer**, **radio-spectroscope**, **radio spectroscope**, radio-wave spectrometer, radio-wave spectroscope	Radio[wellen]spektrometer n, Radio[wellen]-spektroskop n, Radiostrahlungsspektrometer n, Radiostrahlungsspektroskop n
radionavigation	Funknavigation f, Funkortung f		
radio nebula, radio[-]galaxy	Radiosternsystem n, Radiogalaxis f, Radiogalaxie f		
radio noise burst [on the Sun]	s. radio burst	**radio star**	s. radio source
radio noise field intensity, perturbing field strength	Störfeldstärke f	**radio surface wave**	s. surface wave
		radiosusceptibility	s. sensitivity to radiation
		radiosynthesis	Strahlungssynthese f, Strahlensynthese f, Radiosynthese f
radio noise outburst [on the Sun]	s. radio noise burst [on the Sun]	**radio telescope**, radio-telescope	Astropeiler m, Radioteleskop n
radionuclide lamp, radioisotope lamp	Radionuklidlampe f	**radio[ ]theodolite**	Radiotheodolit m, Höhenwinkelpeiler m
radio observation	Radiobeobachtung f	**radiotherapy**, radiation therapy; therapeutic radiology	Strahlentherapie f
radio orientation	s. bearing		
radio outburst [on the Sun]	s. radio burst	**radiothermoluminescence**	Radiothermolumineszenz f
radiopacity	Strahlenundurchlässigkeit f, Strahlungsundurchlässigkeit f; Schattengebung f	**radiothorium**, RdTh, ^{228}Th	Radiothorium n, Radiothor n, RdTh, ^{228}Th
		radiotoxicity	Radiotoxizität f
		radiotracer	s. radioactive tracer
radiopaque	strahlungsundurchlässig, strahlenundurchlässig <speziell für radioaktive und Röntgenstrahlen>; schattengebend	**radio transmitter**	Sender (Kleinst-Kurzwellensender) m der Radiosonde, Radiosender m
		radiotransparent	s. radiolucent
		radio wave	Funkwelle f, Radiowelle f
		radio wave amplification by stimulated emission of radiation	s. raser
radiopaque medium, opaque medium	Kontrastmittel n, Röntgenkontrastmittel n		
		radio-wave spectrograph	s. radio-spectrograph
		radio-wave spectrometer (spectroscope)	s. radio-spectrometer
		radio wind flight, radiosonde, radiometeorograph, radio balloon, rawin	Radiosonde f, Funksonde f, Aerosonde f, Radiometeorograph m
radiophotoluminescence	Radiophotolumineszenz f		
radiophysics	Funkphysik f		
radiophysics	s. a. radio-frequency physics	**radiowindow** <of Earth's atmosphere>	Radiofenster n <der Erdatmosphäre>
radio position finder	s. radar		
radio position finding	s. radar	**radium age**	Radiumalter n, geologisches Alter n nach der Radiummethode
radio radiation	s. radio-frequency <astr.>		
radio-receiver aerial	s. receiving aerial		
radio-receiver antenna	s. receiving aerial	**radium emanation**, radon, $^{222}_{86}$Rn, $^{222}_{86}$Em <nuclide>	Radiumemanation f, Radon n, $^{222}_{86}$Rn <Nuklid>
radioresistance, radiation stability, radiation resistance, resistance to radiation	Strahlungsbeständigkeit f, Strahlenbeständigkeit f, Strahlungsfestigkeit f, Strahlenfestigkeit f, Strahlungsstabilität f, Strahlenstabilität f; Strahlungsresistenz f, Strahlenresistenz f, Widerstandsfähigkeit f gegen Bestrahlung f <Bio.>		
		radium equivalent	Radiumäquivalent n, Radium-Gammaäquivalent n, Radium-Gammagleichwert m
		radium family	s. uranium series
		radium G, $^{206}_{82}$Pb, RaG, uranium lead, radium lead	Radium n G, Uranblei n, Radiumblei n, $^{206}_{82}$Pb, RaG
		radium G method, uranium lead method, RaG method, ^{206}Pb method <of radioactive dating>	Radium-G-Methode f, Uranbleimethode f, RaG-Methode f, [^{235}U-]^{206}Pb-Methode f <der Altersbestimmung>
radio scintillation, scintillation of radio source, scintillation of radio star	Szintillieren n der Radioquelle, Radioszintillation f		
radioscope	s. fluoroscope		
radioscopy	s. fluoroscopy	**radium lead**	s. radium G
radiosensitivity	s. sensitivity to radiation	**radium needle**, radium seed	Radiumnadel f, Radiumkapillare f, Radiumseed f
radiosensitization	Strahlungssensibilisierung f, Strahlensensibilisierung f, Sensibilisierung f als Folge einer Strahlenwirkung		
		radium radioactive series	s. radium series
radio shadow	Funkschatten m	**radium seed**	s. radium needle
		radium series	s. uranium series

radium standard	Radiumstandard m, Radium-Standardpräparat n; Radiumnormal n, radioaktiver Stromstandard m	**rain and snow,** mixed rain and snow	Regen m mit Schnee, Schneeregen m, Regenschnee m, Schlack[er]schnee m, Schlack m
radius at bend	s. radius of curvature	**rain band**	Regenbande f
radius effect	Radiuseffekt m		
radius mounting [of grating]	s. Rowland mounting		
radius of action	s. reach		
radius of convergence	Konvergenzradius m	**rainbow angle**	Regenbogenwinkel m
radius of curvature, radius at bend	Krümmungsradius m, Krümmungshalbmesser m, Radius m der ersten Krümmung, Biegungsradius m	**rainbow display,** colour rainbow display	Regenbogenfarbmuster n
		rainbow expansion	Regenbogenentwicklung f
radius of gyration, radius of inertia, gyration radius	Trägheitsradius m, Trägheitsarm m, Trägheitshalbmesser m, Gyrationsradius m	**rainbow integral of Airy,** Airy['s] [rainbow] integral	Airys[ches] Regenbogenintegral n, Regenbogenintegral von Airy, Airysches Integral n
		rainbow scattering approximation, Ford-Wheeler approximation	Ford-Wheeler-Näherung f, Ford-Wheelersche Näherung f
radius of gyration of the atom	s. gyration radius of atom	**rainbow term**	Regenbogenterm m
radius of inertia	s. radius of gyration	**rainbow theory of Airy,** Airy['s] rainbow theory	Regenbogentheorie f von Airy, Airysche Theorie f des Regenbogens
radius of nuclear reaction channel, channel radius	Kanalradius m, Radius m des Reaktionskanals		
		rain climate	Regenklima n
radius of principal curvature, principal radius of curvature	Hauptkrümmungsradius m	**rain cloud**	s. nimbus
		rain clutter	Regenecho n
radius of second curvature	s. radius of torsion		
radius of the core of a section <mech.>	Kernradius m <Stab> <Mech.>	**rain day**	s. rainy day
		rain erosion; [jet] impingement attack (corrosion)	Regenerosion f; Tropfenschlagerosion f; Tropfenschlagkavitation f
radius of the ionic atmosphere	s. Debye length		
radius of the profile nose	Profilnasenradius m, Radius m der Profilnase	**rain erosion**	s. a. rainwash <geo.>
		rain factor	Regenfaktor m
radius of the universe, world radius	Weltradius m	**rainfall,** precipitation, atmospheric precipitation <meteo.>	Niederschlag m, atmosphärischer Niederschlag <Meteo.>
radius of torsion, torsion radius, radius of second curvature	Windungsradius m, Torsionsradius m, Schmiegungsradius m, Radius m der zweiten Krümmung	**rainfall**	s. a. height of precipitation
		rainfall distribution coefficient	Niederschlagsverteilungskoeffizient m, Regenverteilungskoeffizient m
radius of visibility	s. visibility		
radius of vision	s. line of vision	**rainfall frequency**	Regenhäufigkeit f
radius parameter	Radiusparameter m		
radius vector <pl.: radii vectores>, position vector	Radiusvektor m, Ortsvektor m, Fahrstrahl m, Polstrahl m, Leitstrahl m	**rainfall intensity**	s. rate of rainfall
		rainfall recorder	s. rain gauge
radlux, rlx	= 1.005 lx	**rain gauge,** pluviometer, udometer, ombrometer, hyetometer, precipitation gauge (recorder), rainfall recorder	Niederschlags[mengen]messer m, Regenmesser m, Hyetometer n, Pluviometer n, Ombrometer n, Udometer n
rad meter	Radmesser m <in Rad geeichtes Dosimeter>		
Radok['s] solution	Radoksche Lösung f		
radome, radar dome	Antennenverkleidung f, Radarhaube f, Radom n, Radardom m, Funkmeßhaube f, Radarnase f		
		rain[ ]gauge bucket	Niederschlagsmessergefäß n, Regenmessergefäß n, Meßgefäß n des Regenmessers
radon, radium emanation, $^{222}_{86}Rn$, $^{222}_{86}Em$ <nuclide>	Radiumemanation f, Radon n, $^{222}_{86}Rn$ <Nuklid>	**rain height**	s. height of precipitation
		rain-like condensation, dropwise condensation, weeping-out	Tröpfchenkondensation f, Tropfenkondensation f, Kondensation f in Tropfenform
radon, emanon, emanium, [radioactive] emanation, $_{86}Rn$, $_{86}Em$ <element>	Radon n, Emanation f, $_{86}Rn$, $_{86}Em$ <Element>		
		rain making	Regenerzeugung f
radon needle, radon seed	Radonhohlnadel f, Radonseed f	**rainout,** radioactive rainout	Fallout m mit (in) den Niederschlägen, mit den Niederschlägen ausgewaschener Fallout, [mit dem Regen] ausgewaschener Fallout
radphot, rph = 10^4 lx	Radphot n, rph = 10^4 lx		
radstilb, rsb = 1 sb	Radstilb n, rsb = 1 sb		
rad unit, rad, rd	Rad n, rad-Einheit f, rd, rad		
radwaste	s. atomic waste	**rainout activity**	mit dem Regen ausgewaschene Aktivität f, Aktivität des ausgewaschenen Fallout
Raether['s] condition, Raether['s] criterion	Raethersche Bedingung f, Raether-Bedingung f, Raether-Kriterium n		
		rain[-]proof	s. drip-proof
rafted ice, rafting ice	Schiebeeis n	**rain shadow**	Regenschatten m
ragged cloud, fractus [form]	zerrissene Wolke f, Fractusform f, Fractowolke f	**rain squall**	Regenbö f
RaG method	s. radium G method	**rainwash,** rain erosion <geo.>	Regenauswaschung f, Regenerosion f <Geo.>
rag of cloud, ribbon (wisp) of cloud, cloud rag (ribbon, wisp)	Wolkenfetzen m		
		rainy day, rain day	Regentag m
raie blanche, RB	weiße Linie f, „raie blanche" f, RB	**raised table**	gehobene Tafel f
raie ultime, sensitive (persistent, distinctive) line, letzte linie	letzte Linie f, Restlinie f, beständige Linie, Nachweislinie f	**raising** <of an index>	Heraufziehen n, Heben n <Index>
railing phenomenon, palisade phenomenon, fence phenomenon	Staketenphänomen n		

raising <to, into>; lifting <to, into>; hoisting <to>	Heben n, Hebung f	ramp [function]	Rampenfunktion f
raising and lowering <of indices>, building an isomer <math.>	Herauf- und Herunterziehen n <Indizes>	ramp voltage, sawtooth voltage	Sägezahnspannung f
raising of temperature, temperature rise, rise of (in) temperature	Temperaturerhöhung f, Temperatursteigerung f	Ramsauer effect, Ramsauer-Townsend effect	Ramsauer-Effekt m
raising of the boiling point	s. elevation of the boiling point	Ramsauer-Townsend collision cross-section, total effective cross-section for electronic collisions	Wirkungsquerschnitt m gegenüber langsamen Elektronen, Gesamtwirkungsquerschnitt m für Stöße langsamer Elektronen im Gas, Ramsauer-Stoßquerschnitt m, Ramsauer-Querschnitt m, Ramsauer-Streuquerschnitt m
raising of water level by the effect of wind	Windstau m		
raising to a power	Erhebung f (Erheben n) in eine Potenz, Potenzieren n		
Raman[-] active	Raman-aktiv, ramanaktiv		
		Ramsauer-Townsend collision [mean] free path, mean free path of low energy electrons moving through a gas	mittlere freie Weglänge f langsamer Elektronen im Gas, Ramsauer Weglänge f
Raman and Nath's formula	Raman-Nathsche Formel f		
Raman band	Raman-Bande f		
		Ramsauer-Townsend effect, Ramsauer effect	Ramsauer-Effekt m
Raman effect	Raman-Effekt m, Smekal-Raman-Effekt m, Raman-Smekal-Effekt m, Kombinationsstreuung f des Lichtes	Ramsay['s] two-field method, two-field method [of Ramsay]	Zweifeldermethode f [von Ramsay], Ramsaysche Zweifeldermethode
		Ramsay-Young['s] rule	Ramsay-Youngsche Regel f
		Ramsden circle	s. exit pupil
Raman-effect maser	s. Raman maser	Ramsden dynameter	Dynameter n nach Ramsden, Ramsdensches Dynameter
Raman[-] inactive	Raman-inaktiv, raman-inaktiv		
		Ramsden eyepiece, Ramsden magnifier, positive eyepiece	Ramsdensches (positives) Okular n, Okular nach Ramsden, Ramsden-Okular n
Raman-Laval theory	Raman-Lavalsche Theorie f		
Raman line	Raman-Linie f	Ramsey['s] degenerate phase	Ramseysche Degenerationsphase f (degenerierte Phase f)
Raman maser, Raman-effect maser	Raman-Maser m, Raman-Effekt-Maser m	Ramsey['s] hypothesis	Ramseysche Hypothese f
		random, accidental, chance	zufällig, Zufalls-, zufallsbedingt
Raman quantometer	Raman-Quantometer n	random	s. a. randomly distributed
Raman rotational spectrum, rotational Raman spectrum	Rotations-Raman-Spektrum n, Raman-Rotationsspektrum n	random action	zufällige (stochastische) Einwirkung f
		random chain model	statistisches Kettenmodell n
Raman scattered light	Ramansches Streulicht n	random coincidence, spurious (accidental, chance) coincidence	zufällige Koinzidenz f, Zufallskoinzidenz f
Raman scattering	Raman-Streuung f, unelastische Streuung f	random deviate (deviation)	Zufallsabweichung f
Raman shift	Raman-Verschiebung f	random distribution, random partition	ungeordnete (statistisch ungeordnete, zufällige, regellose) Verteilung f, Zufallsverteilung f
Raman spectrograph	Raman-Spektrograph m		
		random error, sampling (accidental) error, unbiased error	zufälliger (unregelmäßiger) Fehler m, Zufallsfehler m
		random flight	s. disordered motion
Raman spectrometer	Raman-Spektrometer n	random fluctuation, accidental fluctuation	zufällige Schwankung f, Zufallsschwankung f
		random function	Zufallsfunktion f, statistische Funktion f
		random-incidence response, random sensitivity <of microphone>	Empfindlichkeit f im diffusen Schallfeld
Raman spectroscopy	Raman-Spektroskopie f		
		randomization	s. randomizing
		randomization test, Fisher-Pitman test, permutation test	Permutationstest m, Randomisationstest m, Fisher-Pitman-Test m
Raman spectrum	Raman-Spektrum n		
		randomized block	randomisierter Block m
Raman vibrational spectrum	s. vibrational Raman spectrum		
ramark, radar beacon, raymark	Radarbake f	randomizing, randomization	Chaotisierung f; Randomisation f, zufällige Anordnung f
ramification, branching; bifurcation; furcation, forking	Verzweigung f; Verästelung f, Aufspaltung f, Aufzweigung f; Gabelung f; Gabelteilung f	randomly distributed, random	zufällig (statistisch, regellos) verteilt, zufallsverteilt
		random motion	s. disordered motion
ram jet, propulsive jet	Staustrahltriebwerk n, Staustrahlrohr n, Lorin-Rohr n, Staurohr n	random motion of the molecules	s. molecular motion
		randomness; stochasticity	Zufälligkeit f, Zufallscharakter m, zufälliger Charakter m, Stochastizität f, Regellosigkeit f
rammability; compactibility <of the material>	Verdichtbarkeit f, Verdichtungsfähigkeit f <Material>		
		random noise, noise, fluctuation noise, statistical noise <of thermionic valve>	Rauschen n, statistisches Rauschen <Elektronenröhre>
Ramo['s] theorem	Theorem n (Satz m) von Ramo, Ramoscher Satz		

random number	Zufallszahl *f*	range-finding telescope	*s.* filament rangefinder
random orientation	regellose (zufällige, nicht-bevorzugte) Orientierung *f*	range formula, transmission range formula	Reichweitenformel *f*
random partition	*s.* random distribution	range mark	Entfernungsmarke *f*
random phase approximation, RPA	RPA-Näherung *f*, Näherung *f* der zufallsverteilten Phasen	range of action <math.>	Wirkungsbereich *m* <Math.>
		range of adaptation	Adaptationsbreite *f*
random process	*s.* stochastic process	range of alternating stresses, alternating stress amplitude	Wechselbereich *m*
random pulse	Zufallsimpuls *m*, wahlloser (regelloser, zufälliger) Impuls *m*		
random pulse generator	Zufallsimpulsgenerator *m*	range of alternating tensile stress	Zugschwellbereich *m*
random sample	*s.* sample <stat.>		
random sampling (selection)	zufällige Stichprobenentnahme *f*, Zufallsauswahl *f*	range of application	*s.* limits of validity
		range of audibility	*s.* frequency range of hearing
random sensitivity, random-incidence response <of microphone>	Empfindlichkeit *f* im diffusen Schallfeld	range of audiofrequency	*s.* audio frequency range
		range of boiling	*s.* boiling range
		range of change	*s.* range of variation
random storm wave	Schlagwelle *f*	range of contrast, contrast range	Kontrastumfang *m*
		range of definition	*s.* domain <math.>
random train of pulses	Zufallsfolge *f* von Impulsen, Zufallsimpulsfolge *f*	range of dependence, domain of dependence, dependency area	Abhängigkeitsgebiet *n*, Abhängigkeitszone *f*, Abhängigkeitsbereich *m*
random variable, stochastic variable, chance variable, variate	Zufallsvariable *f*, Zufallsveränderliche *f*, Zufallsgröße *f*, zufällige Größe *f*, stochastische Variable *f*, aleatorische Größe, Variate *f*		
		range of extra-high (extremely high) frequency	*s.* extra-high frequency range
		range of hearing	*s.* frequency range of hearing
random walk, walk	Irrfahrt *f*, zufällige (stochastische) Irrfahrt, zufällige Schrittfolge *f*, Zufallsbewegung *f*	range of high frequency	*s.* high frequency range
		range of hurling	*s.* range of the projection
		range of integration, region of integration	Integrationsgebiet *n*, Integrationsbereich *m*, Integrationsgrenzen *fpl*
random walk problem, problem of random walk	Irrfahrtsproblem *n*		
Raney catalyst, skeleton catalyst, skeletal catalyst	Skelettkatalysator *m*, Legierungsskelettkatalysator *m*; Raney-Katalysator *m*	range of linearity, linear range, linear operation limits	Linearitätsbereich *m*
range, range of particle	Reichweite *f* <Teilchen>; Grenzdicke *f* <β-Teilchen>	range of low frequency	*s.* low frequency range
		range of luminance, luminance range, brightness range	Helligkeitsumfang *m*
range, interval, region <gen.>	Intervall *n*, Bereich *m*, Gebiet *n*	range of measurements	*s.* measuring range
range, range of values, range of the function, codomain, set of values <math.>	Wertevorrat *m*; Wertebereich *m*, Nachbereich *m*, Bildbereich *m*, Gegenbereich *m* <Math.>	range of medium frequencies	*s.* medium frequency range
		range of modulation, drive range, range of uniform control, control range	Aussteuerbereich *m*, Aussteuerungsbereich *m*, Aussteuerungsumfang *m*
range, variability <stat.>	Variationsbreite *f*, Spannweite *f*, Schwankungsbreite *f* <Stat.>		
		range of partial radiation	Teilstrahlungsbereich *m*
range	*s. a.* domain <math.>	range of particle	*s.* range
range	*s. a.* effective range	range of pulse repetition frequency, pulse repetition frequency range	Impulsbereich *m*
range	*s. a.* region <gen.>		
rangeability	Stellverhältnis *n*		
range determination, range finding, rangefinding, telemetry; measurement of distance	Entfernungsmessung *f*, Entfernungsbestimmung *f*	range of sensitivity, sensitive region <of counter>	empfindlicher Bereich *m*, Ansprechbereich *m* <Zählrohr>
		range of sensitivity; latitude <of an emulsion>	Empfindlichkeitsbereich *m*
range distribution, range spectrum	Reichweitenspektrum *n*, Reichweitenverteilung *f*	range of sight	*s.* visibility
		range of subject contrast	*s.* subject range
range[-] energy relation	Reichweite-Energie-Beziehung *f*, Energie-Reichweite-Beziehung *f*	range of superhigh frequency	*s.* superhigh frequency range
range extension, extension of effective part [of scale]	Bereichserweiterung *f*, Meßbereichserweiterung *f*, Erweiterung *f* des Meßbereichs	range of temperature, temperature range (interval, band)	Temperaturbereich *m*, Temperaturgebiet *n*, Temperaturintervall *n*
		range of the function	*s.* range <math.>
range-extension factor	Umrechnungsfaktor *m* der Anzeigewerte bei Bereichserweiterung	range of the instrument	*s.* range
		range of the projection, range of throw, range of hurling, throwing range, cast	Wurfweite *f*
rangefinder, optical rangefinder, ranger, [optical] telemeter, [optical] distance meter	[optischer] Entfernungsmesser *m*, Distanzmesser *m*, Telemeter *n*; Abstandsmesser *m*		
		range of the spectrum	*s.* spectral region
		range of the Yukawa potential	Reichweite *f* des Yukawa-Potentials
rangefinder groundglass	*s.* reflex-prism split image rangefinder	range of throw	*s.* range of the projection
rangefinder of the double observer type	*s.* long-baseline rangefinder	range of tide, tidal range; amplitude of tide	Gezeitenhub *m*, Tidenhub *m*, Tidenstieg *m*
rangefinder wedge	Meßkeil *m*		
		range of ultra-high frequency	*s.* ultra-high frequency range
range finding, rangefinding, ranging, range determination, telemetry; measurement of distance	Entfernungsmessung *f*, Entfernungsbestimmung *f*	range of uniform control	*s.* range of modulation
		range of validity	*s.* domain <math.>
		range of validity	*s. a.* limits of validity
		range of values	*s.* range <math.>

range of variation, range of change	Variationsbereich m, Änderungsbereich m, Schwankungsbereich m	**rapid-access memory, rapid-access storage, rapid-access store,** rapid store, fast-access storage (store, memory), fast storage (store), high-speed storage (store), quick-access storage (store)	Schnellspeicher m
range of very high frequency	s. very high frequency range		
range of very low frequency	s. very low frequency range	**rapid analysis**, quick analysis	Schnellanalyse f, Schnellbestimmung f, Rapidanalyse f, Expreßanalyse f
range of visibility (vision)	s. visibility		
ranger	s. rangefinder		
range reduction	Reichweitenverkürzung f	**rapid change of weather**; snap, break-up in the weather, sudden break in weather	Wettersturz m; Umschlagen n des Wetters, Wetterumschlag m
range spectrum, range distribution	Reichweitenspektrum n, Reichweitenverteilung f		
range straggling	Reichweitenstreuung f		
range straggling parameter	Reichweitenstreuparameter m	**rapid corrosion test**, accelerated (quick) corrosion test	Schnellkorrosionsversuch m
range switching, band switching	Umschaltung f des Meßbereichs, Bereich[s]umschaltung f	**rapid developer**	Rapidentwickler m, Schnellentwickler m
range test	Spannweitentest m	**rapid emulsion**	Rapidemulsion f
range-velocity relation [-ship]	Reichweite f in Abhängigkeit von der Geschwindigkeit, Reichweite-Geschwindigkeit[s]-Beziehung f	**rapid flow**	s. shooting flow <hydr.>
		rapidity	s. speed <of the emulsion>
		rapidity of action	s. responsiveness
		rapidity of convergence, speed of convergence	Güte f der Konvergenz, Konvergenzgeschwindigkeit f
range-viewfinder, single-window range-viewfinder, combined range-finder and viewfinder, combined view and range finder, measuring viewfinder	Meßsucher m, Universalmeßsucher m	**rapidity of diffusion**	s. diffusion rate
		rapid magnetic balance	Rapidfeldwaage f
		rapid river	reißender Strom m
ranging	s. range finding	**rapids**, rapid, shoot, chute, riffle <of river>	Stromschnelle f, Katarakt m, Gefällsstelle f <Fluß>
ranging pole	Visierstab m		
rank; grade <of matrix> <math.>	Rang m; Rangzahl f <Math.>	**rapid sequence camera**	s. high-speed camera
rank, order, degree, valence <of tensor>	Stufe f <Tensor>, Tensorstufe f	**rapid start lamp**, quick start lamp	Schnellstartlampe f
rank concordance coefficient	Rangkonkordanzkoeffizient m	**rapid store**	s. rapid-access memory
rank correlation	Rangkorrelation f	**rapid test**	s. accelerated test
rank correlation coefficient	s. coefficient of rank correlation	**rapid test**	s. a. short cut test
		rapid wind lever camera, lever wind camera	Schnellaufzugkamera f
°Rank	s. degree Rankine		
Rankine balance	Rankine-Waage f, Rankinesche Waage f	**rare earth** <compound>	Seltenerde f, Seltene Erde f, seltene Erde <Verbindung: Oxid eines Seltenerdmetalls>
Rankine body	Rankinescher Festkörper m, Rankine-Körper m		
Rankine cycle, Clausius-Rankine cycle	Rankine-[Clausius-]Prozeß m, Rankine[-Clausius]-scher Kreisprozeß m, Clausius-Rankine-Prozeß m, Clausius-Rankinescher Kreisprozeß	**rare earth**	s. a. rare-earth element
		rare-earth element, rare-earth metal, rare earth, REE	Seltenerdmetall n, Metall n der Seltenerden (Seltenen Erden), Seltenerdelement n, Element n der Seltenen Erden, Seltenes Erdmetall n, Seltene (seltene) Erde f, SEE
Rankine-Dupré['s] equation, Rankine-Dupré['s] formula	Rankine-Duprésche Gleichung f		
Rankine-Hugoniot curve, Hugoniot curve, Hugoniot	[Rankine-]Hugoniot-Kurve f, dynamische Adiabate f, Rankine-Hugoniotsche Kurve f	**rarefaction** <of gas>	Verdünnung f <Gas>
		rarefaction <of gas>	Verdünnungsgrad m <Gas>
		rarefaction	s. a. evacuation
Rankine-Hugoniot equation (law, relation[s])	Rankine-Hugoniotsche Gleichung f, Rankine-Hugoniot-Gleichung f	**rarefactional shock**	s. rarefaction shock
		rarefactional wave, rarefaction wave, wave of rarefaction, expansion wave, dilatation[al] wave <aero., hydr.>	Verdünnungswelle f, Verdünnungslinie f <Aero., Hydr.>
Rankine scale, Rankine temperature scale	Rankine-Skala f; Rankine-Skale f		
Rankine['s] theory, maximum stress theory	Theorie f der Maximalbelastung, Theorie von Rankine, Rankinesche Theorie	**rarefaction shock**, rarefactional shock, dilatational shock, shock of rarefaction	Verdünnungsstoß m
Rankine vortex	Rankinescher Wirbel m, Rankine-Wirbel m	**rarefaction wave**	s. rarefactional wave
		rarefied air	verdünnte Luft f, Verdünnungsluft f; Höhenluft f
Ranque-Hilsch vortex tube	s. Hilsch tube		
R-antisymmetric case, F-case	R-antisymmetrischer Fall m, F-Fall m	**rarefied gas dynamics**	s. superaerodynamics
		rare gas, inert gas, noble gas, helium group gas	Edelgas n
Ranvier node, node of Ranvier	Ranvierscher Schnürring (Schnürknoten) m	**rare-gas configuration**	Edelgaskonfiguration f
Rao['s] formula	Raosche Formel f		
Raoult['s] absorption coefficient, Raoult['s] coefficient of absorption	Raoultscher Absorptionskoeffizient m	**rare-gas lightning arrester**, lightning protector	Luftleerblitzableiter m
		Rasch-Hinrichsen formula, Rasch-Hinrichsen relation	Rasch-Hinrichsensche Formel (Beziehung) f
Raoult['s] law	Raoultsches Gesetz n, Raoults Gesetz		
rapid	s. rapids	**Raschig ring, Raschig tube**	Raschig-Ring m

raser, [radio] wave amplification by stimulated emission of radiation — Raser *m*
Rasmussen étalon, wedge-shaped étalon — Keiletalon *m* [nach Rasmussen]
raster — *s.* screen
raster microscope — *s. a.* scanning electron microscope
raster microscope, screen microscope — Rastermikroskop *n*
raster optics, grid optics — Rasteroptik *f*
raster scan microscope — *s.* scanning electron microscope
raster therapy — Rastertherapie *f*
ratchet — Ratsche *f*
ratcheting, ratchetting, ratchet mechanism — Verklinkung *f*
ratcheting, ratchetting <nucl.> — „ratcheting" *n* <Kern.>
ratchet mechanism — *s.* ratcheting
ratchet motion — *s.* ratchet wheel drive
ratchet oscillation — *s. a.* relaxation oscillation
ratchet time base — Sperrzeitbasis *f*
ratchetting — *s.* ratcheting
ratchet wheel, pawl wheel — Sperrad *n*
ratchet wheel drive, pawl and ratchet motion, ratchet motion, rack wheel — Zahngesperre *n*, Klinkengesperre *n*, Klinkenschaltwerk *n*, Zahnklinkenschaltwerk *n*
rate, time rate — Geschwindigkeit *f*; Häufigkeit *f*; Rate *f*
rate <of clock> — *s.* rate of clock
rate — *s. a.* ratio
rate — *s. a.* thermodynamic flux
rate — *s. a.* derivative <math.>
rate action, rate response, response to the derivative, derivative action — Vorhaltwirkung *f*, D-Einfluß *m*, D-Verhalten *n*
rate-action control, derivative-action control, derivative (rate, differential) control — Regelung *f* mit Differential[quotienten]einfluß (Differential[quotienten]aufschaltung), Regelung mit Vorhalt, Differentialregelung *f*, D-Regelung *f*, differenzierend wirkende Regelung
rate-action controller, derivative-action controller, derivative controller — Regler *m* mit Differential[quotienten]einfluß, Regler mit Vorhalt, Differentialregler *m*, D-Regler *m*, Regler mit Differential[quotienten]aufschaltung, differenzierend wirkender Regler
rate constant, specific reaction rate, specific rate <chem.> — Geschwindigkeitskonstante *f* [der Reaktion], Reaktions[geschwindigkeits]konstante *f*, spezifische Reaktionsgeschwindigkeit *f* <Chem.>
rate control — *s.* rate-action control
rate controlling step — *s.* rate-determining step
rated burden — *s.* rated power [output]
rate-determining step, rate-controlling step <in a chemical reaction> — geschwindigkeitsbestimmender Schritt *m* <der chemischen Reaktion>, limitierende Zwischenreaktion *f*
rated impedance — Nennbürde *f*
rated output — *s.* rated power [output]
rated phase angle — Fehlwinkelgrenze *f*
rated power, design power, demand power — Solleistung *f*
rated power [output], nominal power, rated output, rated burden, rating — Nennleistung *f*, Nominalleistung *f*

rated primary current — primärer Nennstrom *m*, Nennprimärstrom *m*
rated primary voltage — primäre Nennspannung *f*, Nennprimärspannung *f*
rated ratio error — Übersetzungsfehlergrenze *f*
rated short-circuit current, thermal short-time current rating <US> — thermischer Grenzstrom *m*, thermischer Kurzschlußstrom *m*
rated temperature-rise current <of an instrument> — maximal zulässiger Betriebsstrom *m* <Meßgerät>
rated temperature-rise voltage — *s.* nominal circuit voltage <of an instrument>
rated value, rating, nominal value — Nennwert *m*, Nominalwert *m*

rate equation — *s.* balance equation <el.>
rate growing — *s.* rate growth <cryst.>
rate-grown junction — stufengezogener Übergang *m*, stufengezogener pn-Übergang *m*
rate growth, rate growing <cryst.> — Stufenziehverfahren *n*, Stufenziehen *n* <Krist.>

rate gyro[scope] — Kreisel *m* mit zwei Freiheitsgraden
rate[ ]meter — *s.* counting-rate meter
rate method of cooling — Abkühlung *f* mit konstanter Geschwindigkeit
rate of adaptation — Adaptationszeit *f*
rate of advance, advancing rate — Voreilgeschwindigkeit *f*
rate of angular motion — *s.* angular speed
rate of ascent — *s.* rate of climb
rate of burn-up — *s.* rate of depletion
rate of change — *s.* time rate of change
rate of climb, climbing speed, climbing velocity, ascending velocity, rate of ascent — Steiggeschwindigkeit *f*, Aufstiegsgeschwindigkeit *f*
rate of clock — Uhrgang *m*, täglicher Gang *m* [der Uhr]; Ganggeschwindigkeit *f* <Uhr>
rate of combustion; velocity of combustion [reaction], speed of combustion, burning velocity — Verbrennungsgeschwindigkeit *f*, Brenngeschwindigkeit *f*
rate of cooling — kalorimetrische Abkühlungsgeschwindigkeit *f*
rate of crack propagation, propagation rate of the crack — Vordringgeschwindigkeit *f* des Risses
rate of cubical dilatation, rate of cubical expansion — Raumdehnungsgeschwindigkeit *f*
rate of decay, decay rate — Abklinggeschwindigkeit *f* <Schwingung; Lumineszenz>; Zerfallsgeschwindigkeit *f* <Lumineszenz>
rate of decay — *s. a.* disintegration rate <nucl.>
rate of deformation — *s.* rate of strain
rate[-]of[-]deformation tensor — *s. a.* rate-of-strain tensor
rate of depletion, rate of burn up <nucl.> — Abbrandgeschwindigkeit *f* <Kern.>
rate of descent — *s.* rate of fall
rate of descent — *s.* descent velocity
rate of diffusion — *s.* diffusion rate
rate of discharge — *s.* discharge <per unit time>
rate of discharge — *s. a.* discharge rate <of liquid>
rate of disintegration — *s.* disintegration rate <nucl.>
rate of entropy production — *s.* production of entropy
rate of evacuation — *s.* exhaustion rate <of pump>
rate of evaporation, evaporation coefficient, coefficient of evaporation — Verdunstungsgeschwindigkeit *f*, Verdunstungskennzahl *f*, Verdunstungskoeffizient *m*; Verdampfungskoeffizient *m*, Verdampfungswert *m*, Verdampfungszahl *f*

rate 676

rate of evaporation, evaporation (evaporative, vaporization) rate, rate of vaporization	Verdampfungsgeschwindigkeit *f*; Verdunstungsgeschwindigkeit *f*	**rate of star deaths,** rate of stellar extinction, stellar extinction rate	Sternsterberate *f*
rate of fall, velocity of fall, velocity (rate) of descent, falling speed	Fallgeschwindigkeit *f*	**rate of star formation,** star formation rate	Sternentstehungsrate *f*
rate of fission, fission rate	Spaltrate *f*, Spalthäufigkeit *f*, Spaltungen *fpl* pro Zeiteinheit	**rate of stellar extinction**	*s.* rate of star deaths
rate of flame propagation, speed of flame propagation, flame speed (velocity), ignition velocity (rate), combustion (burning) velocity <US>	Zündgeschwindigkeit *f*, Flammenfortpflanzungsgeschwindigkeit *f*, Flammen[ausbreitungs]geschwindigkeit *f*, Verbrennungsgeschwindigkeit *f*, Brenngeschwindigkeit *f*	**rate of strain,** rate of deformation, [plastic] strain rate, deformation rate, speed of deformation; strain velocity; stress rate	Formänderungsgeschwindigkeit *f*, Verform[ungs]geschwindigkeit *f*, Verzerrungsgeschwindigkeit *f*, Deformationsgeschwindigkeit *f*; Fließgeschwindigkeit *f*, Umform[ungs]geschwindigkeit *f*; Spannungsgeschwindigkeit *f*; Anstrengungsgeschwindigkeit *f*, Beanspruchungsgeschwindigkeit *f*
rate of flow, intensity of flow, flow rate, flow; rate of flux; throughput	Durchsatz *m*, Durchfluß *m*, Durchflußstärke *f*, Stoffstrom *m*, Mengenstrom *m*, Belastung *f*, Durchgang *m*, Durchlauf *m*	**rate of strain field**	Deformationsgeschwindigkeitsfeld *n*
rate of flow	*s. a.* flow rate	**rate of strain hardening**	*s.* rate of work hardening
rate of flow of energy across unit area	*s.* energy flux density	**rate-of-strain tensor,** rate[-] of [-]deformation tensor	Formänderungsgeschwindigkeitstensor *m*, Deformations[geschwindigkeits]tensor *m*, Verformungsgeschwindigkeitstensor *m*, Verzerrungsgeschwindigkeitstensor *m*
rate of flux	*s.* rate of flow		
rate of gain	*s.* absolute growth rate <stat.>		
rate of gas flow, gas flow rate, flow rate of the gas	Gasströmungsgeschwindigkeit *f*, Gasstrom *m*	**rate of stream flow** <hydr.>	Wasserführung *f* <Hydr.>
rate of grain boundary diffusion	Korngrenzendiffusionsgeschwindigkeit *f*	**rate of vaporization**	*s.* rate of evaporation
		rate of vertical descent	*s.* descent velocity
rate of growth, growth rate, growth velocity <cryst.; bio.>	Wachstumsgeschwindigkeit *f*, Wachstumsrate *f* <Krist.>; Wachstumsschnelligkeit *f* <Bio.>	**rate of volume flow**	*s.* volume flow
		rate of work hardening	*s.* work-hardening coefficient
		rate response	*s.* rate action
rate of growth <math.>	Wachstumsgeschwindigkeit *f* <Math.>	**rate time**	*s.* derivative-action time
rate of heat flow, thermal transmission, specific rate of heat flow, heat flow [rate], flow of heat, thermal flow (flux), heat flux, flux of heat, heat current	Wärmestrom *m*, Wärmefluß *m*	**rating,** end scale value, maximum scale value	Meßbereichsendwert *m*, Meßbereichendwert *m*
		rating, rated value, nominal value	Nennwert *m*, Nominalwert *m*
rate of heat removal	Wärmeabführungsgeschwindigkeit *f*	**rating**	*s. a.* rated power
rate of increase	*s.* absolute growth rate <stat.>	**rating**	*s. a.* valuation
		rating curve	*s.* discharge rating curve
rate of leakage	*s.* leak rate	**ratio,** rate, proportion	Verhältnis *n*, Verhältniszahl *f*
rate of mass flow	*s.* mass flow	**ratio accuracy**	Verhältnisgenauigkeit *f*
rate of motion (movement) <bio.>	Bewegungsgeschwindigkeit *f* <Bio.>	**ratio arm bridge circuit**	Verhältnisarm-Brückenschaltung *f*
rate of nucleation	*s.* nucleation rate		
rate of percolation	Sickerdurchflußstärke *f*, Sickermenge *f*	**ratio between the principal specific heats**	*s.* ratio of the specific heats
		ratio control	Verhältnisregelung *f*
rate of rainfall, rainfall intensity	Niederschlagsintensität *f*, Niederschlagsstärke *f*, Niederschlagsmenge *f* pro Zeiteinheit; Regenintensität *f*, Regenstärke *f*, Regenspende *f*, Regendichte *f*	**ratio detector**	Ratiodetektor *m*, Verhältnisgleichrichter *m*, Verhältnisdetektor *m*
		ratio error	Übersetzungsfehler *m* <in %>, prozentualer Übersetzungsfehler
		ratio estimator	Verhältnisschätzung *f*, Quotientenschätzung *f*
rate of reaction, reaction rate (velocity) <chem.>	Reaktionsgeschwindigkeit *f* <Chem.>	**ratio[-]meter; ratiometer movement;** logometer, quotient meter	[dynamometrischer] Quotientenmesser *m*, Quotientenmesser *m*; Quotientenstrommesser *m*; Drehspul-Quotientenmesser *m*, Kreuzspulinstrument *n*, T-Spulinstrument *n*, Quotientenmesser mit Drehspulsystem, Kreuzfeldinstrument *n*; Quotientenmeßwerk *n*; Kreuzspulmeßwerk *n*; Drehspul-Quotientenmeßwerk *n*; T-Spulmeßwerk *n*, T-Spul-Meßwerk *n*, T-Spul-Quotientenmeßwerk *n*
rate of recombination	*s.* recombination rate		
rate of response, speed of response <el.>	Reaktionsgeschwindigkeit *f*, Ansprechgeschwindigkeit *f* <El.>		
rate of runoff	*s.* specific flow		
rate of sedimentation, settling rate, velocity of settling	Sedimentationsgeschwindigkeit *f*, Sinkgeschwindigkeit *f* [bei der Sedimentation]		
rate of shear	*s.* shearing		
rate of shooting stars, hourly rate of meteors, number of meteors per hour, frequency of meteors	Häufigkeit *f* der Meteore, Anzahl *f* der Meteore pro Stunde		
		rational formula	*s.* structural formula
rate of speed; acceleration	Beschleunigung *f*	**rational function**	[gebrochen] rationale Funktion *f*
rate of spontaneous mutation, spontaneous frequency <of mutations>	Spontanhäufigkeit *f*, Spontanrate *f* <von Mutationen>, Spontanmutationsrate *f*		
		rational integer	*s.* integer
		rationality law	*s.* law of rational indices
rate of spread	*s.* propagation velocity	**rationalized form**	*s.* rationalized notation

rationalized m.k.s. coulomb system [of units]	MKSQ-System n, Meter-Kilogramm-Sekunde-Coulomb-System n
rationalized notation, rationalized form	rationale Schreibweise f, rationale Form f
rationalized system [of units]	rationales Einheitensystem (Maßsystem, System) n
rationalized unit	rationale Einheit f, rationale Maßeinheit f
rationalized unit	s. a. absolute unit
ratio network	Verhältnisnetzwerk n
ratio of bearing contact area, ratio of contact area, [bearing] contact area ratio, bearing contact area percentage	Traganteil m
ratio of components	s. mixture proportion
ratio of concentration	s. distribution coefficient
ratio of concentrations, concentration ratio	Konzentrationsverhältnis n
ratio of contact area	s. ratio of bearing contact area
ratio of contraction of volume, cubic contraction	kubische Kontraktion f, kubische Zusammenziehung f
ratio of reduction	s. reduction ratio
ratio of similitude	Ähnlichkeitsverhältnis n
ratio of the lens aperture, aperture ratio, relative aperture <of objective>	Öffnungsverhältnis n, relative Öffnung f, [geometrisch-optische] Lichtstärke f <Objektiv>
ratio of the specific heat at constant pressure to that at constant volume, ratio of the specific heat capacities, ratio of the specific heats, ratio between the principal specific heats, specific heat ratio, heat capacity ratio, adiabatic exponent, adiabatic index, gamma	Verhältnis n der spezifischen Wärmen, Verhältnis der spezifischen Wärmekapazitäten, Adiabatenexponent m
ratio of the windings, turns ratio, winding ratio	Windungs[zahl]verhältnis n, Windungsübersetzung f
ratio of transmission	s. transmission ratio
ratio of verniers, vernier ratio	Nonienverhältnis n
ratio of voltage division, voltage division ratio	Spannungsteilungsverhältnis n
ratio resistor	Verhältniswiderstand m
ratio test	s. Cauchy['s] ratio test
ratran, ratran system	RATRAN-System n, Ratran-System n
Raubitschek curve	Raubitschek-Kurve f
Rau['s] spectrum of freezing nuclei	Rausches Gefrierkernspektrum n
rawin, radiosonde, radiometeorograph, radio balloon, radio wind flight	Radiosonde f, Funksonde f, Aerosonde f, Radiometeorograph m
raw moment, unadjusted moment	unbereinigtes Moment (Stichprobenmoment) n
ray, half-line <math.>	Halbgerade f, Strahl m <Math.>
ray, ray[-] trajectory <opt.>	Strahl m <Opt.>
ray	s. a. lunar ray
ray aberration	Strahlaberration f
ray acoustics	Schallstrahlenmethode f, Schallstrahlenverfahren n
ray acoustics	s. a. geometric acoustics
ray analysis	Strahlanalyse f
ray cone	s. cone of light rays
ray direction, direction of ray, direction of Poynting vector	Strahlrichtung f, Richtung des Poyntingschen Vektors
ray ellipsoid, Fresnel['s] ellipsoid	Fresnelsches Ellipsoid (Ausbreitungsellipsoid) n, Strahlenellipsoid n
ray equation	Strahlengleichung f, Strahlgleichung f
ray from image point	s. image ray
ray from object point, object ray	Dingstrahl m
ray index	Strahlenindex m
rayl	Rayl n
Rayleigh ampere balance, Rayleigh balance	Stromwaage f nach Rayleigh, Rayleighsche Stromwaage, Rayleigh-Stromwaage f
Rayleigh and Jansen['s] method	s. Rayleigh-Jansen approach
Rayleigh and Jeans['] law	s. Rayleigh-Jeans['] law
Rayleigh['s] approximation	Rayleighsche Näherung f; Rayleighscher Grenzfall m <Beugung>
Rayleigh atmosphere	Rayleigh-Atmosphäre f, Luftsphäre f
Rayleigh balance	s. Rayleigh ampere balance
Rayleigh constant	Rayleigh-Konstante f, Rayleighsche Konstante f
Rayleigh criterion, Rayleigh number, Ra	Rayleigh-Zahl f, Rayleighsche Kennzahl (Zahl) f, Ra
Rayleigh['s] criterion [for (of) resolution (resolving power)]	Rayleighsches Auflösungskriterium (Kriterium) n, Rayleigh-Kriterium n, Lambda-Viertel-Kriterium n, [Rayleighsches] λ/4-Kriterium n; Rayleighsche Lambda-Viertel-Regel f, Rayleighsche λ/4-Regel f, Viertelwellenlängenregel f
Rayleigh['s] criterion of stability, Rayleigh['s] stability criterion	Rayleighsches Stabilitätskriterium n
Rayleigh cross-section, Rayleigh scattering cross-section, cross-section for Rayleigh scattering	Rayleigh-Streuquerschnitt m, Wirkungsquerschnitt m für (der) Rayleigh-Streuung
Rayleigh curve	Rayleighsche Kurve f
Rayleigh disk	Rayleigh-Scheibe f, Rayleighsche Scheibe f, Schallreaktionsrad n
Rayleigh['s] dissipation function [of hydrodynamics]	s. viscous dissipation function <hydr.>
Rayleigh distillation	Rayleigh-Destillation f, Rayleighsches Destillierverfahren n
Rayleigh distribution	Rayleighsche Verteilung f, Rayleigh-Verteilung f
Rayleigh['s] equation [of group waves]	Rayleighsche Gleichung f [für die Gruppengeschwindigkeit], Rayleigh-Gleichung f
Rayleigh flow, diabatic flow	diabatische Strömung f
Rayleigh['s] formula <for distillation>	Rayleigh-Formel f, Rayleigh-Beziehung f, Rayleighsche Formel (Beziehung) f <Destillation>
Rayleigh['s] formula <el.>	Rayleighsche Formel f <El.>
Rayleigh-Gans['] approximation	Rayleigh-Ganssche Näherung f
Rayleigh['s] integral equations	Rayleighsche Integralgleichungen fpl
Rayleigh interferometer, Rayleigh refractometer	Interferometer n nach Rayleigh-Haber-Löwe, Rayleigh-[Haber-Löwe-]Interferometer n, Grubengasinterferometer n, Rayleigh-Refraktometer n
Rayleigh-Jansen approach (method), Rayleigh and Jansen['s] method	Rayleigh-Jansensche Methode f
Rayleigh-Jeans['] equation (formula, law), Rayleigh-Jeans['] radiation formula, Jeans['] [radiation] law, Rayleigh and Jeans['] law	[Rayleigh-]Jeanssches Strahlungsgesetz n, Rayleigh-Jeanssche Strahlungsformel f, Strahlungsformel (Strahlungsgesetz) von Rayleigh und Jeans, Rayleigh-Jeanssche Formel f, Gesetz n von Rayleigh-Jeans
Rayleigh-Jeans['] principle, principle of Rayleigh and Jeans	Rayleigh-Jeanssches Prinzip n, Prinzip von Rayleigh und Jeans
Rayleigh-Jeans['] radiation formula	s. Rayleigh-Jeans['] equation
Rayleigh['s] law, Rayleigh['s] scattering formula	Rayleighsches Gesetz n, Rayleighsche Streuformel f, 1/λ4-Gesetz n von Rayleigh

Rayleigh['s]

Rayleigh['s] law <for ferromagnetics>	Rayleighsches Gesetz n, Rayleigh-Gesetz n <für Ferromagnetika>
Rayleigh limit [for spherical aberration]	Rayleigh-Grenze f, Lambda-Viertel-Grenze f, λ/4-Grenze f
Rayleigh line	Rayleigh-Linie f
Rayleigh loop	Rayleigh-Schleife f, Rayleighsche Schleife f
Rayleigh mass scattering coefficient, mass attenuation coefficient for coherent scattering	Massenschwächungskoeffizient m für kohärente Streuung, Rayleigh-Massenstreukoeffizient m
Rayleigh number	s. Rayleigh criterion
Rayleigh pression	Rayleighscher Schallstrahlungsdruck m
Rayleigh['s] principle	Rayleighsches Prinzip n, Prinzip von Rayleigh
Rayleigh['] quotient	Rayleighscher Quotient m
Rayleigh refractometer	s. Rayleigh interferometer
Rayleigh region	Rayleigh-Bereich m, Rayleighscher Bereich m
Rayleigh-Ritz['] method, Rayleigh-Ritz-Weinstein['s] method	Methode f von Rayleigh-Ritz, Rayleigh-Ritz[-Weinstein]sche Methode
Rayleigh-Ritz method	s. a. Ritz['] method
Rayleigh-Ritz principle	s. Ritz['] method
Rayleigh-Ritz-Weinstein['s] method	s. Rayleigh-Ritz['] method
Rayleigh scatter	s. Rayleigh scattering
Rayleigh scattered radiation	Rayleighsche Streustrahlung f
Rayleigh scattering <of light>, Rayleigh scatter	Rayleigh-Streuung f, Luftstreuung f, Rayleighsche Streuung f (Lichtstreuung f, diffuse Reflexion f), elastische (kohärente, klassische) Streuung
Rayleigh scattering coefficient	Rayleigh-Streukoeffizient m, Rayleighscher Streukoeffizient m, Luftstreukoeffizient m
Rayleigh scattering cross-section	s. Rayleigh cross-section
Rayleigh['s] scattering formula, Rayleigh['s] law	Rayleighsches Gesetz n, Rayleighsche Streuformel f, 1/λ⁴-Gesetz n von Rayleigh
Rayleigh scattering function	Rayleighsche Streufunktion f
Rayleigh['s] scattering ratio	Rayleighsches Streuverhältnis n
Rayleigh-Schrödinger perturbation theory	s. time-independent perturbation theory
Rayleigh['s] series	Rayleigh-Reihe f, Rayleighsche Reihe f
Rayleigh['s] stability criterion, Rayleigh['s] criterion of stability	Rayleighsches Stabilitätskriterium n
Rayleigh['s] surface	Rayleighsche Fläche f
Rayleigh['s] transformation	Rayleigh-Transformation f, Rayleighsche Transformation f
Rayleigh wave, surface wave of the Rayleigh type	Rayleigh-Welle f, Rayleighsche Welle (Oberflächenwelle) f, Oberflächenwelle Rayleighscher Art, R-Welle f
raymark, radar beacon, ramark	Radarbake f
ray of light, light ray	Lichtstrahl m
ray of projection	s. projecting ray
ray of reference	s. reference ray
ray of sound, sound ray, acoustic ray, sonic ray	Schallstrahl m
ray of the funicular polygon	Seilstrahl m
ray optics, geometrical optics	geometrische Optik f, Strahlenoptik f
ray pole <geo.>	Strahlenpol m <Geo.>
rayproof	s. radiation-proof
ray space	Strahlenraum m
ray structure, radiate structure, radial structure	Strahlenstruktur f, strahlenförmige Struktur f, strahlenförmiger Aufbau m
ray surface, ray velocity surface, wave surface	Strahlenfläche f, Wellenfläche f
ray tracing, tracing of the rays	Strahlengangsbestimmung f
ray[-] trajectory, ray <opt.>	Strahl m <Opt.>
ray[-] trajectory, path of rays, run of rays; trace of rays <US>	Strahlengang m, Strahlenverlauf m, Strahlenweg m, Strahlenbahn f
ray vector	Strahlvektor m
ray velocity, energy velocity, velocity of energy transmission	Strahlengeschwindigkeit f, Geschwindigkeit f der Energiefortpflanzung, Energie[transport]geschwindigkeit f
ray velocity surface	s. ray surface
ray velocity surface	s. a. elementary wave
Razin effect, Razin-Zytovich effect	Razin-Effekt m, Razin-Zytowitsch-Effekt m
R band <26.5 – 40 Gc/s>	R-Band n <26,5 ··· 40 GHz>
RBE dose, relative biological effectiveness dose <radiobiology>	RBW-Dosis f, biologische Äquivalenzdosis f <Strahlenbiologie>
R-branch, positive branch	R-Zweig m, positiver Zweig m
R-C ...	s. resistance-capacitance ...
R Corona Borealis-type star	R Coronae Borealis-Stern m, R Coronae-Veränderlicher m
reabsorption	Reabsorption f; Rückresorption f
reach, stretch <of the river>	Stromstrecke f, Flußstrecke f, Flußabschnitt m, Wasserstrecke f [des Flusses]
reach, pool <hydr.>	Haltung f <Hydr.>
reach; radius of action	Reichweite f; Wirkungsradius m, Aktionsradius m
reach [of sight]	s. visibility
reactance, effective reactance, reactive impedance	Blindwiderstand m, Reaktanz f
reactance amplification	s. parametric amplification
reactance amplifier, parametric amplifier, mavar <mixer amplification by variable reactance>	parametrischer Verstärker m, Reaktanzverstärker m, Mavar m
reactance-capacitance coupling, complex coupling	komplexe Kopplung f, induktiv-kapazitive Kopplung
reactance circuit	Stromkreis m mit Blindwiderstand, Reaktanzkreis m
reactance current	s. reactive current
reactance diode	Reaktanzdiode f, parametrische Diode f
reactance four-terminal network, reactance quadripole	Reaktanzvierpol m
reactance function	Reaktanzfunktion f
reactance matrix	Reaktanzmatrix f
reactance meter	Reaktanzmesser m
reactance modulator tube	s. reactance valve
reactance output	s. reactive power
reactance quadripole	s. reactance four-terminal network
reactance theorem [of Foster]	s. Foster['s] reactance theorem
reactance tube	s. reactance valve
reactance two-terminal network	Reaktanzzweipol m

reactance valve; reactance tube, reactance modulator tube — Reaktanzröhre f, Blindröhre f, Blindleistungsröhre f, Impedanzröhre f
reactance voltage, leakage (stray) voltage — Streuspannung f, Reaktanzspannung f
reactant; reacting agent, reacting substance; reagent — Reaktionsteilnehmer m, Reaktionspartner m, Reaktant m; Reagens n, Reaktionsmittel n

reaction — s. process
reaction, retroaction, reactive effect <also el.> — Rückwirkung f, Reaktion f
reaction, countereffect, counteraction <mech.> — Gegenwirkung f, Reaktion f, „reactio" f <Mech.>
reaction, reaction of constraints, reactive force, constraining (restraining, restraint) force <mech.> — Zwangskraft f, Reaktionskraft f, Führungskraft f <Mech.>
reaction — s. a. feedback <el.>
reaction accelerator — s. accelerator
reaction apparatus — s. chemical reactor
reaction capacitance, reflected capacitance — Rückwirkungskapazität f

reaction chain, reaction sequence — Reaktionskette f, Reaktionsfolge f
reaction channel, reaction species <nucl.> — Reaktionskanal m, Reaktionsweg m, Kanal m der Reaktion <Kern.>
reaction coil — s. reactor
reaction conductance; grid-anode conductance <of thermionic valve>; feedback admittance — Rückwirkungsleitwert m

reaction constant — Reaktionskonstante f

reaction co-ordinate — Reaktionskoordinate f
reaction coupling — s. feedback
reaction cross-section, nuclear reaction cross-section, cross-section for the reaction, cross-section for the nuclear reaction, cross-section for the nuclear process — Reaktionsquerschnitt m, Wirkungsquerschnitt m der (für die) Reaktion, Wirkungsquerschnitt der (für die) Kernreaktion, Wirkungsquerschnitt des Kernprozesses, Wirkungsquerschnitt für den Kernprozeß, Reaktionswirkungsquerschnitt m, Kernreaktions[wirkungs]querschnitt m
reaction dynamics — Reaktionsdynamik f

reaction energy — s. Q value <nucl.>
reaction enthalpy, enthalpy of reaction — Reaktionsenthalpie f, Reaktionswärme f bei konstantem Druck
reaction equation, reaction formula, equation of the reaction, formula of the reaction — Reaktionsgleichung f
reaction field, Onsager['s] reaction field — Reaktionsfeld n [von Onsager]
reaction field <cryst.> — Rückwirkungsfeld n <Krist.>

reaction field in the dielectric structure, polarization field — Polarisationsbereich m, Polarisationsfeld m
reaction force, radiation reaction force, damping term — Strahlungsreaktionskraft f, Lorentzsche Dämpfungskraft f, Strahlungsrückwirkung f, Strahlungsbremsung f
reaction force — s. a. restoring force <mech.>
reaction formula — s. reaction equation
reaction-free four-terminal network — rückwirkungsfreier Vierpol m, Trennvierpol m

reaction fusion — s. reaction melting
reaction gas chromatography — Reaktionsgaschromatographie f
reaction heat — s. heat effect
reaction impedance, reflected impedance — Rückwirkungswiderstand m, übertragener Scheinwiderstand m
reaction isobar, isobar of reaction, Van 't Hoff reaction isobar — Reaktionsisobare f, van't Hoffsche Reaktionsisobare, Gleichung f der Reaktionsisobaren, van't Hoffsche Gleichung f
reaction isochore, isochore of reaction, van 't Hoff [reaction] isochore — Reaktionsisochore f, van't Hoffsche Reaktionsisochore, Gleichung f der Reaktionsisochoren
reaction isotherm — s. law of mass action
reaction[-] kinetic, kinetic <chem.> — reaktionskinetisch, kinetisch <Chem.>
reaction kinetics, kinetics of reaction, chemical kinetics — Reaktionskinetik f, chemische Reaktionskinetik, chemische Kinetik f
reactionless — s. passive <chem.>
reactionlessness, inactivity, inertness <chem.> — chemische Trägheit f, Reaktionsträgheit f, Inaktivität f <Chem.>
reaction limit, limit of reaction — Reaktionsgrenze f
reaction mass — Reaktionsmasse f
reaction melting, reaction fusion — Reaktionsschmelzen n
reaction of constraints — s. reaction <mech.>
reaction of first <zero; second; n-th; higher> **order,** first-order reaction — Reaktion f erster <nullter; zweiter; n-ter; höherer> Ordnung

reaction of (n,p) type — s. (n,p) reaction
reaction of the third order, trimolecular reaction, termolecular reaction — trimolekulare Reaktion f, Reaktion dritter Ordnung
reaction order, order of reaction, order of chemical reaction — Reaktionsordnung f, Ordnung f der Reaktion
reaction overpotential; reaction polarization — Reaktionsüberspannung f; Reaktionspolarisation f

reaction paper — s. indicator paper
reaction polarization — s. reaction overpotential
reaction pressure, backpressure, back pressure, counterpressure — Gegendruck m
reaction principle — Rückstoßprinzip n

reaction proceeding directly — s. direct interaction type of reaction <nucl.>
reaction propulsion; rocket propulsion; jet propulsion — Strahlantrieb m; Düsenantrieb m; Raketenantrieb m

reaction rate, rate of reaction, reaction velocity <chem.> — Reaktionsgeschwindigkeit f <Chem.>
reactions at the supports — s. support reactions
reaction sequence, reaction chain — Reaktionskette f, Reaktionsfolge f
reaction species — s. reaction channel
reaction stage (step) — Reaktionsschritt m; Reaktionsstufe f; Reaktionsstadium n
reaction threshold, threshold of the reaction — Reaktionsschwelle f, Schwellenenergie f der Reaktion
reaction time; response time; time of the onset of the excitation <bio.> — Reaktionszeit f
reaction turbine, Parsons turbine — Überdruckturbine f, Reaktionsturbine f, Parsons-Turbine f

reaction velocity — s. reaction rate <chem.>
reaction wheel — s. Segner['s] water wheel

reaction width — Reaktionsbreite f
reaction yield, nuclear reaction yield — Ausbeute f der Kernreaktion, Reaktionsausbeute f

reaction zone — s. core <of reactor>

reactivation; reconstruction, reconstruction of plasma structure <bio.> — Reaktivierung *f*

reactive <chem.> — reaktionsfähig <Chem.>

reactive, wattless, idle <el.> — Blind-, wattlos, leistungslos <El.>

reactive admittance — s. reaction conductance

reactive coil — s. choke

reactive component, wattless (idle, imaginary) component — Blindanteil *m*, Blindkomponente *f*, Imaginärteil *m* einer komplexen elektrischen Größe, wattlose Komponente *f*, Wattloskomponente *f*

reactive current, wattless current, idle current, imaginary current, reactance current — Blindstrom *m*, wattloser Strom *m*, Wattlosstrom *m*

reactive effect — s. reaction <also el.>

reactive element — Blindelement *n*

reactive-energy meter, var-hour meter, wattless component meter — Blindverbrauchszähler *m*, Blindwattstundenzähler *m*

reactive evaporation — reaktive Aufdampfung *f*

reactive factor <el.> — Blindfaktor *m*, Blindleistungsfaktor *m* <El.>

reactive feedback, wattless feedback — Blindrückkopplung *f*, Blindstromrückkopplung *f*

reactive force — Rückwirkungskraft *f*

reactive force — s. a. reaction <mech.>

reactive impedance — s. reactance

reactive load <el.> — Blindlast *f*, Blindbelastung *f* <El.>

reactive mixture — Treibstoffgemisch *n*

reactiveness — s. reactivity <chem.>

reactive permeability — s. imaginary part of complex permeability

reactive power, wattless (idle, imaginary) power, reactive volt-amperes, blind power — Blindleistung *f*, wattlose Leistung *f*, Wattlosleistung *f*

reactive voltage, wattless (idle, imaginary) voltage, reactance power — Blindspannung *f*, wattlose Spannung *f*, Wattlosspannung *f*

reactive volt[-]ampere — s. var

reactive volt-amperes — s. reactive power

reactive wave — rückwirkende Welle *f*

reactivity, reactiveness <chem.> — Reaktionsfähigkeit *f*, Reaktionsvermögen *n*, Reaktivität *f* <Chem.>

reactivity <of reactor> — Reaktivität *f* <Reaktor>

reactivity balance — Reaktivitätsbilanz *f*

reactivity coefficient — Reaktivitätskoeffizient *m*

reactivity density, multiplication density — Reaktivitätsdichte *f*

reactivity equivalent — Reaktivitätsäquivalent *n*

reactivity excess — Reaktivitätsüberschuß *m*, überschüssige Reaktivität *f*, Überschußreaktivität *f*

reactivity fluctuation — s. reactivity noise

reactivity meter — Reaktivitätsmesser *m*

reactivity noise, reactivity fluctuation — Reaktivitätsrauschen *n*, Reaktivitätsschwankung *f*

reactivity oscillation — Reaktivitätsoszillation *f*

reactivity oscillator — s. reactor oscillator

reactivity temperature coefficient, temperature coefficient of reactivity — Temperaturkoeffizient *m* der Reaktivität, Reaktivitäts-Temperaturkoeffizient *m*

reactor, chemical reactor, reaction apparatus <chem.> — chemischer Reaktor *m*, Reaktor, Reaktionsapparat *m* <Chem.>

reactor, reactor (reaction) coil <el.> — Reaktanzspule *f*, Reaktanz *f* <El.>

reactor, nuclear reactor, pile, nuclear pile, chain-reacting pile <nucl.> — Reaktor *m*, Kernreaktor *m*, Pile *m* <Kern.>

reactor activation, pile activation — Reaktoraktivierung *f*, Pileaktivierung *f*, Aktivierung *f* im Kernreaktor

reactor behaviour — Reaktorverhalten *n*, Reaktorbetriebsverhalten *n*, Reaktorbetriebsregime *n*

reactor calculation; reactor computation — Reaktorberechnung *f*

reactor coil — s. reactor <el.>

reactor computation — s. reactor calculation

reactor coolant, coolant, cooling agent <of reactor> — Kühlmittel *n* <Reaktor>

reactor cooled and moderated by ordinary water — s. water-water reactor

reactor core — s. core <of reactor>

reactor coupling — s. choke coupling

reactor design, reactor planning — Reaktorprojektierung *f*; Reaktorplanung *f*

reactor-emitted radiation — s. reactor radiation

reactor envelope, reactor shell — Reaktormantel *m*

reactor fluctuation, pile noise, reactor noise, pile fluctuation — Reaktorrauschen *n*, Rauschen *n* des Reaktors

reactor-grade — reaktorrein

reactor lattice, core lattice — Reaktorgitter *n*

reactor neutron, nuclear pile neutron, pile neutron — Reaktorneutron *n*

reactor neutron spectrum — s. pile spectrum

reactor noise — s. [nuclear] reactor fluctuation

reactor oscillator, [nuclear] pile oscillator, reactivity oscillator — Reaktoroszillator *m*, Pileoszillator *m*

reactor period — s. period

reactor period meter — s. period meter

reactor planning — s. reactor design

reactor plant — Reaktoranlage *f*

reactor poison, nuclear poison, neutron poison — Reaktorgift *n*, Neutronengift *n*, starker Neutronenabsorber *m*

reactor power, reactor power level, power of the reactor, power level of the reactor — Leistung *f* des Reaktors, Reaktorleistung *f*

reactor purity — Reaktorreinheit *f*

reactor radiation, pile radiation, pile-emitted radiation, reactor-emitted radiation — Reaktorstrahlung *f*

reactor runaway, runaway of the reactor — Reaktordurchgang *m*, Durchgang *m* (Durchgehen *n*) des Reaktors

reactor shell, reactor envelope — Reaktormantel *m*

reactor shielding — Reaktorabschirmung *f*

reactor shut-down, shut-down of the reactor — Abschaltung (Außerbetriebsetzung, Stillsetzung) *f* des Reaktors

reactor simulator — Reaktorsimulator *m*

reactor spectrum — s. pile spectrum

reactor tank — s. reactor vessel

reactor time constant — s. period

reactor vessel, reactor tank, core tank — Reaktordruckgefäß *n*; Reaktorgefäß *n*, Reaktorbehälter *m*

read — s. read off

Read diode — Read-Diode *f*

reader lens, reading magnifier — Leseglas *n*, Ableselupe *f*

readily volatile, easily volatilized — leichtflüchtig

read-in — Einlesen *n*

reading — Ablesung *f*; Stand *m* <Meß.>

reading, readout <of storage> — Lesen *n*, Abfragen *n* <Speicher>

reading magnifier — s. reader lens

reading micrometer — Ablesemikrometer *n*

reading microscope, reading-off microscope — Ablesemikroskop *n*; Schätzmikroskop *n*, Strichmikroskop *n*

reading microscope with optical flat	Planglasmikroskop n	rear projection	Durchprojektion f
reading-off microscope	s. reading microscope	rearrangement; transposition; permutation <gen.>	Umlagerung f, Verlagerung f; Umordnung f; Umstellung f; Umsetzung f; Vertauschung f <allg.>
reading of the barometer, barometer reading, barometric height	Barometerstand m		
reading on the dry-bulb thermometer	s. dry-bulb reading	rearrangement, reorganization, transposition, transformation <chem.>	Umlagerung f, Umgruppierung f <Chem.>
reading on the wet-bulb thermometer	s. wet-bulb temperature	rearrangement, shuffling <math.>	Umordnung f <Math.>
reading telescope	Ablesefernrohr n	rearrangement collision	Umordnungsstoß m, Umlagerungsstoß m
readjustment	Nachjustierung f; Nachstellung f; Nachregulierung f, Nachregelung f		
		rearrangement reaction, transposition reaction	Umlagerungsreaktion f
		rearrangement structure	Umordnungsstruktur f
Read['s] model	Readsches Modell n	rearranging operator	Anordnungsoperator m; Umordnungsoperator m
read off, read, take readings	ablesen, eine Ablesung vornehmen	rear side of the cyclone, back side of the cyclone	Zyklonenrückseite f, Zyklonenrücken m
readout	s. reading <of storage>		
reagent	s. reactant	rear silver coating (surfacing)	s. mirror lining
real; true, veritable	real; echt, wahr, tatsächlich, wirklich, absolut	rear stagnation point, point of coalescence <hydr., aero.>	Abflußpunkt m, hinterer Staupunkt m <Hydr., Aero.>
real <math.>	reell <Math.>		
real circuit, side circuit, physical circuit (line)	Stammleitung f		
real component, active component, effective component	Wirkkomponente f, Wattkomponente f, Wirkanteil m, Wirkwert m	rear vergence, image vergence, back vergence	bildseitige Vergenz f, Bildvergenz f
		reasons of symmetry / for, for symmetry sake	aus Symmetriegründen
real component	s. a. real part	re[-]attachment of boundary layer	Wiederanlegen n der Grenzschicht
real correction	Realkorrektion f		
real crystal	s. imperfect crystal	re[-]attachment of flow, flow re-attachment	Wiederanlegen n der Strömung
real current, active current, wattful current	Wirkstrom m, Wattstrom m		
real displacement	wirkliche Verrückung f, wirkliche Verschiebung f	re[-]attachment of the jet, jet re[-]attachment	Wiederanlegen n des Strahles
real element, active element, in-phase element	Wirkelement n	Réaumur scale	Réaumur-Skala f; Réaumur-Skale f
real gas, imperfect gas	reales Gas n, Realgas n	rebounce	Prellschlag m
real height [of reflection], true height [of reflection]	tatsächliche Reflexionshöhe f	rebound, height of rebound	Rückprallhöhe f, Rücksprunghöhe f
		rebound, recoil, kickback	Rückprall m, Zurückprallen n, Rückspringen n, Zurückspringen n, Zurückschnellen n; Abprall m, Springen n, Sprung m; Zurückprellen n; Rückfederung f
real horizon	natürlicher Horizont m		
real image	reelles (auffangbares, wirkliches) Bild n		
realization function	Realisierungsfunktion f		
real lattice	Realgitter n, reales Gitter n		
real liquid	reale Flüssigkeit f, wirkliche Flüssigkeit	rebound, repercussion, kickback, recursion	Rückstoß m, Rückschlag m
real part	Realteil m	rebound elasticity, impact elasticity	Rückprallelastizität f, Rücksprungelastizität f, Sprungelastizität f, Stoßelastizität f
real part of complex permeability	Reiheninduktivitätspermeabilität f, Realteil m der komplexen Permeabilität		
		rebound hardness	Rückprallhärte f, Rücksprunghärte f
real part of the admittance, effective conductance	Wirkleitwert m, Wirkanteil m des komplexen Gesamtleitwertes, Parallelwirkleitwert m	rebound hardness test, rebound test <techn.>	Rückprallhärteprüfung f, Rücksprunghärteprüfung f, Stoßversuch m, Rückprallversuch m <Gummi> <Techn.>
real pole arc, pole arc	Polbogen m, tatsächlicher Polbogen	rebuttal, refutation	Widerlegung f, Gegenbeweis m
real power	s. active power <el.>	recalescence	Rekaleszenz f, Wärmeabgabe f beim Durchgang durch den Haltepunkt
real power	s. actual power		
real resistance	s. resistance <el.>		
real-to-random ratio	Verhältnis n der echten Impulse zu den zufälligen	recalescence curve, cooling curve	Abkühlungskurve f
real value	s. actual value <meas.>	recalescence point, critical point of recalescence, transformation point on cooling, Ar point	Haltepunkt m der Abkühlungslinie, Haltepunkt bei der Abkühlung, kritischer Punkt m bei der Abkühlung
real-valued function	reelle Funktion f		
real value indication	s. indication of absolute value		
real voltage	s. active voltage		
ream	s. stria <in glass>	recalibration, secondary calibration; restandardization; re-graduation	Nacheichung f; Umeichung f; Neueichung f
rear depth of field, backward depth of field	Hintertiefe f, rückwärtige Tiefe f		
rear diaphragm, back diaphragm	Hinterblende f		
rear lens	s. back lens		
rear lobe	s. side lobe		
rear principal point, image principal point, internal perspective centre	Bildhauptpunkt m, bildseitiger (hinterer) Hauptpunkt m		

recapture	s. retrapping	reciprocal action, mutual [inter]action; interaction	Wechselwirkung f; wechselseitige Beeinflussung f, gegenseitige Wechselwirkung, Wechselspiel n
receding	s. backstreaming		
receding motion of the nebulae	s. recession of the nebulae		
receipt	s. reception <el.>	reciprocal axes	reziproke Achsen fpl
receiver	Empfänger m, Empfangsgerät n	reciprocal base vectors, reciprocal basis, inverse basis	reziproke Basis f, Basisvektoren mpl des reziproken Gitters
receiver	Hörer m	reciprocal constringence, dispersive (dispersing) power	relative Dispersion f
receiver, receiving vessel <of the still>	Vorlage f <Chem.>		
receiver	s. a. flask	reciprocal depreciation factor	s. maintenance factor
receiver cap (earpiece)	Hör[er]muschel f, Muschel f des Hörers	reciprocal dispersive power, constringence Abbé number	Abbesche Zahl f, Abbe-Zahl f
receiver of the vacuum apparatus	Vakuumvorlage f		
receiving	s. reception <el.>	reciprocal ellipsoid	s. index ellipsoid
receiving aerial (antenna), radio-receiver aerial (antenna), wave collector	Empfangsantenne f, Rezeptor m; Empfängerantenne f	reciprocal equation	reziproke Gleichung f
		reciprocal force diagram	s. force diagram
		reciprocal four-terminal network, reciprocal network	umkehrbarer Vierpol m, übertragungssymmetrischer Vierpol
receiving vessel	s. receiver <of the still>		
recemented glacier, reconstructed glacier, romanic glacier	regenerierter Gletscher m	reciprocal lattice, dual lattice	reziprokes Gitter n, Reziprokgitter n, Dualgitter n, duales Gitter
receptacle	s. flask	reciprocal matrix	s. inverse matrix <of the matrix>
reception, receipt, receiving <el.>	Empfang m; Aufnahme f <El.>	reciprocal network	s. reciprocal four-terminal network
reception; perception <bio.>	Rezeption f; Perzeption f; Erregung f; Induktion f <Bio.>	reciprocal of amplification factor	s. penetrance
reception diagram	Empfangsdiagramm n, Empfangsantennendiagramm n	reciprocal of heat-transfer coefficient, heat-transfer resistance	Wärmeübergangswiderstand m
reception potential	s. receptor potential		
receptor <of radiation>, radiation receptor, radiation receiver	Strahlungsempfänger m	reciprocal of heat-transmission coefficient, heat-transmission resistance	Wärmedurchgangswiderstand m
receptor <bio.>	Rezeptor m <Bio.>		
receptoric	rezeptorisch	reciprocal of screen grid amplification	s. shielding factor <el.>
receptor potential, reception potential	Rezeptorpotential n, Generatorpotential n	reciprocal of the distance of punctum remotum from eye	Fernpunktsrefraktion f, Fernpunktsbrechwert m, Fernpunktsbrechkraft f
recess, pit, depression, indent[ation]	Aussparung f, Ausschnitt m, Vertiefung f, Höhlung f, Einbuchtung f		
recession, retreat, regression <geo.>	Regression f, Rückzug m, Rückgang m, Zurückgehen n, Zurückweichen n <Geo.>	reciprocal of the notch [fatigue] factor	s. reduced factor of stress concentration
		reciprocal of Young's modulus	s. coefficient of linear extension
		reciprocal paper	Reziprokpapier n
recessional moraine, retreatal moraine	Rückzugsmoräne f	reciprocal phase space	reziproker Phasenraum m
recessional period, period of recession; stage of retreat	Rückzugsperiode f, Rückzugsstadium n	reciprocal polarity, positive polarity	Pluspolung f, positive (reziproke) Polung f, positive Polarität f
		reciprocal ratio, inverse ratio	umgekehrtes Verhältnis n
recession curve, normal recession curve, recession hydrograph, draw-down curve <hydr.>	Senkungskurve f, Senkungslinie f <Hydr.>		
		reciprocal relation	Reziprozitätsbeziehung f
		reciprocal relations, Maxwell['s] relations (equations) <therm.>	Maxwellsche Beziehungen fpl, Maxwellsche Relationen fpl <Therm.>
recession curve	s. a. depletion curve <hydr.>		
recession hydrograph	s. recession curve <hydr.>	reciprocal sentence, dual sentence	dualisierte Aussage f
recession of the galaxies	s. recession of the nebulae		
recession of the nebulae, receding motion of the nebulae, recession of the galaxies, flight of the nebulae	Nebelflucht f, Fluchtbewegung f der Sternsysteme	reciprocal space <cryst.>	reziproker Raum m, dualer Raum
		reciprocal spiral, hyperbolic spiral	hyperbolische Spirale f
		reciprocal strain ellipsoid	reziprokes Verzerrungsellipsoid (Deformationsellipsoid) n
recessivity	Rezessivität f	reciprocal theorem	s. reciprocity theorem <el.>
recharge, charge exchange, umladung, recharging, reversal of charge	Umladung f, Trägerumladung f, Trägerumwandlung f; Ladungsaustausch m	reciprocal theorem in classical elasticity theory	s. Betti['s] reciprocal theorem
		reciprocal to the resistance, resistance-reciprocal	widerstandsreziprok
recharge, recharging <of secondary cell>	Nachladung f; Wiederaufladung f <Sammler>		
		reciprocal transmission matrix	s. transfer matrix
recharge term, charge exchange term	Umladungsterm m	reciprocal trihedral	reziprokes Dreibein n, adjungiertes Dreibein
recharging	s. recharge		
recharging	s. a. recharge <of secondary cell>	reciprocal vector, inverse lattice vector	reziproker Vektor m, inverser Gittervektor m
		reciprocating compressor, [reciprocating] piston compressor	Kolbenkompressor m, Kolbenverdichter m
recharging current	Wiederaufladestrom m		
		reciprocating device, inversor, reversing device <math., opt.>	Inversor m
recharging time constant	Umladungszeitkonstante f, Umladezeitkonstante f		
recipient	Rezipient m	reciprocating grid	s. moving grid

reciprocating motion, to-and-fro motion, back-and-forth motion	hin- und hergehende Bewegung f, Hin- und Herbewegung f, Hin- undherbewegung f, Hin- und Hergang m; Vor- und Rückwärtsbewegung f; Wechselbewegung f; Gegenbewegung f	recoil spectrum	Rückstoßspektrum n, Energiespektrum n der Rückstoßkerne
		recoil streamer	Rückstroßstreamer m
		recoil synthesis	Rückstoßsynthese f
		recoil track	Spur f des Rückstoßteilchens, Rückstoßteilchenspur f, Rückstoßbahn f
reciprocating piston compressor	s. reciprocating compressor	recoil vector	Rückstoßvektor m
reciprocating piston type [flow]meter	Hubkolbenzähler m	recombination	Rekombination f, Wiedervereinigung f, Wiederverbindung f
		recombination apparatus	s. recombiner
reciprocating pump, piston pump, piston air pump	Kolbenpumpe f, Stiefelpumpe f; Hubkolbenpumpe f; Kolbenluftpumpe f	recombination at walls, wall recombination	Wandrekombination f
reciprocation theorem	s. reciprocity theorem	recombination coefficient, coefficient of recombination	Rekombinationskoeffizient m, Rekombinationsbeiwert m, Wiedervereinigungskoeffizient m, Vereinigungskoeffizient m
reciprocity calibration	Reziprozitätseichung f		
reciprocity coefficient, reciprocity parameter	Reziprozitätsparameter m		
reciprocity condition	Reziprozitätsbedingung f	recombination continuum	Rekombinationskontinuum n
reciprocity failure	s. toe		
reciprocity failure	s. a. Schwarzschild effect	recombination cross-section, cross-section for recombination	Rekombinationsquerschnitt m, Wirkungsquerschnitt m für (der) Rekombination, Rekombinationswirkungsquerschnitt m
reciprocity law	s. Bunsen-Roscoe reciprocity law		
reciprocity law	s. a. product rule <bio.>		
reciprocity[-] law failure	s. Schwarzschild effect		
reciprocity parameter	s. reciprocity coefficient	recombination fraction, recombination value <bio.>	Rekombinationswert m, Rekombinationsprozentsatz m, Rekombinationszahl f <Bio.>
reciprocity principle, principle of reciprocity (reversibility)	Reziprozitätsprinzip n		
reciprocity principle	s. a. reciprocity theorem	recombination law, dissipation law, law of recombination	Wiedervereinigungsgesetz n, Rekombinationsgesetz n
reciprocity relations	s. Onsager equations		
reciprocity rule	s. product rule <bio.>	recombination light	s. recombination radiation
reciprocity theorem; reciprocation theorem <in electric field theory>; reciprocal theorem, electric[al] network reciprocity theorem, reciprocity principle	Reziprozitätssatz m <El.; Kern.; Mech.; Opt.; Rel.; Therm.>; Reziprozitätstheorem n <El., speziell der Vierpoltheorie und der drahtlosen Telegraphie; Kern.>; Reziprozitätsgesetz n <der Beugung>; Umkehrsatz m, Umkehrungssatz m <der Vierpoltheorie>	recombination probability, probability of recombination, recombination rate	Rekombinationswahrscheinlichkeit f
		recombination radiation, recombination light; free-bound radiation	Rekombinationsstrahlung f, Rekombinationsleuchten n, Wiedervereinigungsleuchten n; Frei-Gebunden-Strahlung f
		recombination rate, rate of recombination	Rekombinationsgeschwindigkeit f, Wiedervereinigungsgeschwindigkeit f; Rekombinationsrate f, Rekombinationsquote f
reciprocity theorem of Maxwell and Betti	s. Betti['s] reciprocal theorem		
recirculated air; circulating air	Umluft f	recombination rate	s. a. recombination probability
recirculation	Rückführung f; Wiedereinführung f	recombination rate on the semiconductor surface	s. surface recombination rate
recirculation coefficient	Umlaufverhältnis n, Umwälzverhältnis n	recombination resistance	Rekombinationswiderstand m
Recknagel disk	Recknagelsche Scheibe f	recombination theory	Rekombinationstheorie f
reclosing	Wiedereinschaltung f	recombination time	Rekombinationszeit f
recoil	Rückstoß m	recombination trap	Rekombinationshaftstelle f, Rekombinationstrap m, Rekombinationsfalle f
recoil	s. a. rebound		
recoil / without	s. recoilless		
recoil chemistry	s. hot-atom chemistry	recombination value	s. recombination fraction <bio.>
recoil counter	Rückstoßzählrohr n; Rückstoßzähler m		
		recombination velocity on the semiconductor surface	s. surface recombination rate
recoil electron	Rückstoßelektron n		
recoil energy	Rückstoßenergie f	recombiner [system], recombination apparatus	Rekombinationsanlage f, Rekombinationsapparat m
recoil force	Rückstoßkraft f		
recoil impulse, impulse of recoil	Rückstoßimpuls m	recommendation	s. recommended value
		recommended value, recommendation	Richtwert m; empfohlener Wert m
recoiling nucleus	s. recoil nucleus		
recoil ionization	Rückstoßionisation f, Rückstoßionisierung f		
recoil labelling	Rückstoßmarkierung f	reconcilable, homotopic	homotop
recoil length	Rückstoßlänge f, Rückstoßspurlänge f		
recoilless, without recoil	rückstoßfrei	reconstructed glacier, recemented glacier, romanic glacier	regenerierter Gletscher m
recoil mean free path, mean free path for recoil	[mittlere freie] Rückstoßweglänge f, Rückstoßlänge f, mittlere freie Weglänge f für Rückstoß	reconstruction [of plasma structure]	s. reactivation <bio.>
		re-conversion	Rückmischung f; Rückumwandlung f
recoil nucleus, recoiling nucleus	Rückstoßkern m	recooling	Rückkühlung f
recoil particle	Rückstoßteilchen n		
recoil phenomenon	Rückstoßerscheinung f		
recoil range	Rückstoßreichweite f		
recoil rays	Rückstoßstrahlung f		

re-cooling	Wiederabkühlung f	recording ultra-violet spectrometer	s. ultra-violet spectrophotometer
record	Schrieb m	recording variometer, variograph	registrierendes Variometer n, Registriervariometer n, Variograph m
record, record of sound, recording, recording of sound, sound record[ing] ‹ac.›	Tonaufnahme f, Schallaufnahme f, Aufnahme f; Schallaufzeichnung f, Tonaufzeichnung f; Schallspeicherung f, Tonspeicherung f ‹Ak.›	recording vibration meter, vibrograph, vibration recorder, vibration recording apparatus	schreibender Schwingungsmesser m, Schwingungsschreiber m, Vibrograph m
record	s. a. recording	recording visibility meter	Sichtschreiber m
recorder, recording device, recording instrument, recording meter, graph recorder, logger, graphic instrument; plotter	[selbst]registrierendes Meßgerät n, Schreiber m, Schreibgerät n, Meß[wert]schreiber m, [selbst]schreibendes Meßgerät, registrierendes Gerät (Instrument) n, Registriergerät n, Registrierinstrument n, Registrierapparat m, Selbstschreiber m; Kurvenschreiber m; Plotter m, Zeichengerät n	record of sound	s. record
		record of the experiment, test record; protocol of the experiment, test protocol	Versuchsprotokoll n
		record paper	s. recording paper
		record sheet (strip, tape), recorder strip (tape)	Registrierstreifen m, Schreibstreifen m
recorder connection	Schreiberanschluß m	recoverable strain work	s. strain work
		recoverable work	wiedergewinnbare Arbeit f
recorder strip (tape)	s. record sheet	recovering of the backward resistance [in a junction]	Wiederherstellung f des Sperrwiderstandes [des Übergangs]
recording, record, registration, registering; plotting ‹of the curve›	Registrierung f; Schreiben n; Aufzeichnung f, Zeichnung f; Aufnahme f ‹Kurve›	recovery; return; reinstatement ‹of defects›; restoration	Erholung f ‹Krist.›; Wiederherstellung f
recording, derivation ‹of bioelectrical currents›	Ableitung f ‹bioelektrischer Ströme›		
recording	s. a. record	recovery; recuperation	Rückgewinnung f; Wiedergewinnung f; Bergung f
recording altimeter	s. altigraph		
recording anemometer	s. anemograph		
recording balloon, registering balloon	Registrierballon m	recovery; regeneration ‹bio., geo., meteo., phot., el.›	Regeneration f; Regenerierung f ‹Bio., Geo., Meteo., Phot., El.›
recording camera; moving pictures camera	Registrierkamera f, Aufnahmekamera f	recovery[-] creep, recovery flow	Rückdehnung f, Kriecherholung f, Erholungskriechen n, Erholungsfließen n
recording device	s. recorder		
recording dynamometer, dynamograph	Dynamograph m, Registrierdynamometer n	recovery curve	Erholungskurve f; Ausheilungskurve f
		recovery effect	Erholungseffekt m, Erholungserscheinung f
recording electronic potentiometer	s. electronic potentiometer recorder		
recording fork	Schreibstimmgabel f	recovery factor	Rückgewinnungsfaktor m, Rückgewinnungsgrad m, Rückgewinn[ungs]ziffer f, Rückgewinn[ungs]zahl f
recording gauge	s. limnigraph		
recording infra-red spectrometer	s. infra-red spectrophotometer	recovery flow	s. recovery[-] creep
recording instrument	s. recorder	recovery of mechanical properties, mechanical recovery	mechanische Erholung f
recording manometer	s. pressure recorder		
recording maximum meter	Maxigraph m, Maximumschreiber m, Höchstleistungsschreiber m	recovery of shape	Rückformung f
		recovery power	s. regenerative power
recording meter	s. recorder	recovery rate	Erholungsgeschwindigkeit f
recording of sound	s. recording ‹ac.›	recovery temperature	Erholungstemperatur f, „recovery"-Temperatur f
recording ombrometer	s. recording pluviometer		
recording on magnetic tape	s. magnetic recording	recovery time ‹el.›	Erholungszeit f, Erholzeit f, Wiederherstellungszeit f, innere Totzeit f ‹El.›
recording oscillometer	s. vibrograph		
recording paper, record paper	Registrierpapier n		
		recovery time ‹semi.›	Sperrverzögerung f, Relaxationszeit f ‹Halb.›
recording period, recording time, period of recording	Registrierzeit f, Schreibzeit f, Schreibdauer f	recovery time constant	Erholungszeitkonstante f
		recovery voltage	wiederkehrende Spannung f, Wiederkehrspannung f
recording pluviometer	s. pluviograph		
recording potentiometer	s. potentiometer recorder	recrystallization, crystallographic reorientation	Umkristallisation f, Umkristallisierung f; Rekristallisation f
recording rain gauge	s. pluviograph		
recording spectrum analyzer	Spektrenleser m	recrystallization annealing	Rekristallisationsglühen n
recording speed, writing speed, tracing speed; writing rate	Registriergeschwindigkeit f, Schreibgeschwindigkeit f		
		recrystallization centre, recrystallization nucleus	Rekristallisationszentrum n, Rekristallisationskeim m, Rekristallisationskern m
recording spot	Schreibfleck m		
recording thermometer	s. thermograph	recrystallization in hot-worked material	Warmrekristallisation f
recording time	s. recording period		
recording torsiometer (torsion meter)	s. torsiograph	recrystallization nucleus	s. recrystallization centre
recording transmission-measuring set, level recorder ‹el.›	Pegelschreiber m ‹El.›	recrystallization temperature	Rekristallisationstemperatur f, Rekristallisationsschwelle f

recrystallization texture, primary recrystallization texture — Rekristallisationstextur *f*

recrystallization twin, annealing twin — Rekristallisationszwilling *m*

rectangular conductor, square-section[al] conductor, rectangular-section conductor, conductor of rectangular (square) section — Rechteckleiter *m*, Leiter *m* mit rechteckigem Querschnitt

rectangular co-ordinates; right-angled co-ordinates — rechtwinklige Koordinaten *fpl*; Rechteckkoordinaten *fpl*

rectangular co-ordinate system, grid <geo.> — Gitternetz *n*, Gitter *n*, Gauß-Krüger-Koordinaten *fpl*, Gauß-Krügersche Koordinaten *fpl* (Meridianstreifen *mpl*) <Geo.>

rectangular distance from equator — Hochwert *m*, rechtwinkliger Abstand *m* vom Äquator <Gauß-Krüger-System>

rectangular distance from mean meridian — Rechtswert *m*, rechtwinkliger Abstand *m* vom Mittelmeridian <Gauß-Krüger-System>

rectangular distribution — *s.* equipartition

rectangular ferrite, square-loop ferrite, rectangular loop ferrite — Rechteckferrit *m*

rectangular formula — Rechteckformel *f*

rectangular function — Rechteckfunktion *f*

rectangular hyperbola, equilateral (equiangular) hyperbola — gleichseitige Hyperbel *f*

rectangularity — *s.* perpendicularity

rectangular loop ferrite — *s.* rectangular ferrite

rectangular-notch weir, rectangular weir — Rechtecküberfall *m*, rechteckiger Überfall *m*; Rechteckwehr *n*

rectangular parallelepiped, rectangular solid, cuboid, right parallelepiped, block <math.> — Quader *m*, rechtwinkliges Parallelepiped[on] *n* <Math.>

rectangular partition — *s.* equipartition

rectangular pulse — *s.* square-wave pulse

rectangular-section conductor — *s.* rectangular conductor

rectangular sheet lines — Rechteckkarte *f*

rectangular solid — *s.* rectangular parallelepiped <math.>

rectangular symmetry — rechtwinklige Symmetrie *f*, Rechtecksymmetrie *f*

rectangular wave — *s.* square wave

rectangular weir — *s.* rectangular-notch weir

rectifiable <math.> — rektifizierbar <Math.>

rectificate — Rektifikat *n*

rectification, countercurrent distillation <chem.> — Rektifikation *f*, Gegenstromdestillation *f* <Chem.>

rectification; detection; demodulation <el.> — Gleichrichtung *f*, Gleich-Demodulation *f*; Demodulation *f*, Rückmodelung *f*, Rückumsetzung *f* <El.>

rectification <math.> — Rektifikation *f*, Rektifizierung *f* <Math.>

rectification — *s. a.* equalization

rectification — *s. a.* erection <of image> <opt.>

rectification by barrier layer — *s.* barrier-layer rectification

rectification coefficient, rectification constant <of diode> — Richtkonstante *f*

rectification coefficient — *s. a.* rectification ratio

rectification column — Rektifizierkolonne *f*, Rektifikationskolonne *f*

rectification constant — *s.* rectification coefficient

rectification effect — *s.* valve action

rectification efficiency — *s.* rectification ratio

rectification of aerial photograph — Luftbildentzerrung *f*

rectification ratio, rectification coefficient; rectification efficiency, efficiency of rectification, valve ratio — Richtverhältnis *n*; Gleichrichterfaktor *m*, Richtfaktor *m*, Gleichrichtungskoeffizient *m*; Gleichrichterwirkungsgrad *m*, Richtwirkungsgrad *m*

rectified aerial photograph — entzerrtes Luftbild *n*

rectified current — Richtstrom *m*

rectified diffusion — rektifizierte Diffusion *f*

rectified voltage — Richtspannung *f*

rectifier, rectifying column, rectifying section; upper part of the rectifying column <chem.> — Rektifiziersäule *f*, Rektifikationssäule *f*, Rektifikator *m*, Rektifizierer *m*, Rektifizierkolonne *f*, Austauschsäule *f*, Trennsäule *f*, Rektifikationsteil *m*, Rektifizierteil *m*; Verstärkungssäule *f* <Chem.>

rectifier; detector; demodulator <el.> — Gleichrichter *m*; Hochfrequenzgleichrichter *m*, HF-Gleichrichter *m*; Demodulator *m*, Hochfrequenzdemodulator *m*, HF-Demodulator *m* <El.>

rectifier, transformation apparatus, transforming camera, direct optical type of plotting machine, direct optical type plotting machine <opt.> — Entzerrungsgerät *n*; Umbildegerät *n*, Umbildungsgerät *n*, Umbildungsapparat *m* <Opt.>

rectifier — *s. a.* rectifying device <el.>

rectifier cell — *s.* photovoltaic cell

rectifier diode; detector diode — Richtdiode *f*

rectifier instrument — Gleichrichterinstrument *n*, Gleichrichter[meß]gerät *n*, Meßgleichrichter *m*, Meßgerät *n* mit Gleichrichter

rectifier load resistance, load resistance of the rectifier; directional resistance — Richtwiderstand *m*

rectifier photocell — *s.* photovoltaic cell

rectifier tube, rectifying tube, rectifier (detecting) valve, detector tube (valve), valve [tube] <el.> — Gleichrichterröhre *f*, Gleichrichterrohr *n*, Ventilröhre *f*, Ventilrohr *n*, [elektrisches] Ventil *n*, Gleichrichterventil *n* <El.>

rectifier valve, rectifying (detecting) valve, valve of the rectifier — Gleichrichterventil *n*, Ventil *n* des Gleichrichters

rectifier valve — *s. a.* rectifier tube <el.>

rectifying action, rectifying effect <of transistors> — Gleichrichtereffekt *m*, Gleichrichterwirkung *f*, Gleichrichtereffekt *m*, Gleichrichtungseffekt *m*, Richteffekt *m* <Transistoren>

rectifying column — *s.* rectifier

rectifying contact — Gleichrichterkontakt *m*

rectifying crystal, detecting crystal — Detektorkristall *m*

rectifying device, rectifier <el.> — Richtleiter *m*, Richtungsleiter *m* <El.>

rectifying effect — *s.* rectifying action

rectifying electrode, blocking (barrier, unidirectional) electrode — sperrende Elektrode *f*, Sperrelektrode *f*

rectifying four-terminal network — Richtvierpol *m*

rectifying junction, unidirectional junction, blocking junction — sperrender Übergang *m*, Gleichrichterübergang *m*

rectifying plane — rektifizierende Ebene *f*

rectifying plate, rectifying tray — Rektifizierboden *m*

rectifying point diode — Richtleiterspitzendiode *f*

rectifying section	s. rectifier <chem.>
rectifying tray	s. rectifying plate
rectifying tube	s. rectifier tube <el.>
rectifying valve, rectifier valve, detecting valve, valve of the rectifier	Gleichrichterventil n, Ventil n des Gleichrichters
rectilinear, free from distortion, orthoscopic	verzeichnungsfrei, rektolinear, orthoskopisch, tiefenrichtig
rectilinear diameter law of Cailletet and Mathias	s. Cailletet-Mathias law
rectilinear manipulator	Koordinatenmanipulator m
rectilinear motion, straight line motion, motion in a straight line	geradlinige Bewegung f
rectilinear neutral wedge, straight-line wedge	gerader Keil m, gerader Graukeil m
rectilinear scanning, zone scanning	Streifenabtastung f
rectisorption	Rektisorption f
recuperation; recovery	Rückgewinnung f; Wiedergewinnung f; Bergung f
recuperation <therm.>	Rekuperation f <Therm.>
recuperation of current, regeneration of current	Stromrückgewinnung f, Rückgewinnung (Rückführung) f der elektrischen Energie
recuperator	Rekuperator m, Wärmeaustauscher m ohne Zwischenspeicherung
recurrence	s. return
recurrence formula	s. recursion formula
recurrence frequency	s. pulse recurrence frequency
recurrence frequency [of periodic pulses]	s. repetition frequency
recurrence interval	Wiederholungsintervall n
recurrence paradox [of Zermelo], Zermelo['s] recurrence paradox, wiederkehreinwand	Zermeloscher Wiederkehreinwand m, Wiederkehreinwand [von Zermelo]
recurrence period, repetition period	Wiederholungszeit f
recurrence rate, repetition rate	Tastgeschwindigkeit f
recurrence rate	s. recurrence frequency
recurrence relation	s. recursion formula
recurrence theorem [of Poincaré], Poincaré['s] recurrence theorem	Poincaréscher Wiederkehrsatz m, Wiederkehrsatz [von Poincaré]
recurrence time	Wiederkehrzeit f
recurrent	s. recursive <math.>
recurrent event	rekurrentes Ereignis n, wiederkehrendes Ereignis
recurrent network	Vierpolkette f
recurrent nova, repeated nova, permanent nova	wiederkehrende Nova f, periodisch wiederkehrende Nova, Novula f <pl:. Novulae>
recurrent pulses, repetitive pulse, repetition pulse, periodic pulse train	Puls m, periodische Impulsreihe f, periodisch wiederkehrender Impuls m, rhythmische Impulse mpl, Impulsrhythmus m
recursion	s. rebound
recursion	s. a. return
recursion formula, recurrence formula, recurrence relation	Rekursionsformel f
recursive, recurrent <math.>	rekursiv <Math.>
recursive function	rekursive Funktion f
recurvation, recurvature, recurvity	Umbiegen n
recycling, reuse	Rückführung f; Wiedereinsetzen n; Wiederverwendung f, Wiederverwertung f

red blindness, protanopia	Protanopie f, Rotblindheit f
red content [of radiation]	Rotgehalt m [der Strahlung]
red degradation, degradation to[wards] the red	Rotabschattierung f
reddening of the skin, erythema, skin erythema	Erythem n, Hautrötung f
red dwarf, dwarf red star	roter Zwerg m
redevelopment, photographic redevelopment	Umentwicklung f, photographische Umentwicklung
re-development, second development	Nachentwicklung f
Redfield['s] theory <of relaxation>	Redfieldsche Relaxationstheorie (Theorie) f
red giant	roter Riese m
red glow	s. red heat
red-green fog	Rotgrünschleier m
red-green shadow	Rotgrünschatten m, Rot-Grün-Schatten m
red hardness	Rotgluthärte f, Rotglühhärte f, Rotwarmhärte f
red heat, red glow	Rotglut f
rediffusion <of electrons>	s. backscattering
redistillation; repeated distillation, cohobation	Redestillation f; Umdestillieren n; wiederholte (mehrfache) Destillation f
redistribution	Neuverteilung f, Umverteilung f
red lamp	Rotlampe f, Rotlichtlampe f
Redlich-Teller product rule	s. Teller-Redlich product rule
red magnitude, red stellar magnitude	Rothelligkeit f <Gestirn>
redox chain, oxidation-reduction chain	Redoxkette f
redox electrode, oxidation-reduction electrode	Redoxelektrode f
redox equilibrium, oxidation reduction-equilibrium	Redoxgleichgewicht n, Reduktions-Oxydations-Gleichgewicht n
redox exchanger	s. redox ion exchanger
redox fuel cell, oxidation-reduction fuel cell	Redox-Brennstoffelement n
redox indicator	s. oxidation-reduction indicator
redox ion exchanger, oxidation-reduction ion exchanger, redox exchanger	Redoxaustauscher m, Redox-Ionenaustauscher m
redoxite	s. redox resin
redox meter	Redoxmeter n
redoxogram	Redoxogramm n
redox potential	s. oxidation-reduction potential
redox process	s. oxidation-reduction process
redox reaction	s. oxidation-reduction reaction
redox resin, redoxite	Redoxharz n, Redoxit m
redox system, oxidation-reduction system	Redoxsystem n, Reduktions-Oxydations-System n
redox titration	s. oxidimetry
red rainbow, twilight rainbow	Dämmerungsregenbogen m, roter Regenbogen m
red response	s. red sensitivity
redresser	s. rectifier <el.>
redressment, reestablishment; unsqueezing, spreading <opt.>	Entzerrung f <Opt.>
red-sensitive plate	Rotplatte f, rotempfindliche Platte f
red sensitivity, sensitivity to red light, red response	Rotempfindlichkeit f
red separation, magenta separation	Rotauszug m, Rotfilterauszug m
red-shaded	s. degraded to the red

reductio

red shift, cosmological red-shift, Hubble['s] red-shift (effect) — Rotverschiebung f, kosmologische Rotverschiebung, Hubble-Effekt m

red-short, hot-short, hot-brittle — warmbrüchig, rotbrüchig
red shortness — s. hot shortness
red solar radiation, long-wave solar radiation — Rotstrahlung f der Sonne

red stellar magnitude, red magnitude — Rothelligkeit f ‹Gestirn›

reduced area [of sunspots], corrected area [of sunspots] — korrigierte Fleckenfläche f
reduced buckling length, free length, modified length — [reduzierte] Knicklänge f, freie Knicklänge

reduced cofactor — Kofaktor m, dividiert durch die Determinante; reduzierter Kofaktor
reduced depression [of the freezing point] — s. reduced lowering [of the freezing point]
reduced difference [of the thermodynamic function] — reduzierte Differenz f [der thermodynamischen Funktion]
reduced distribution function — reduzierte Verteilungsfunktion f
reduced elevation [of the boiling point] — s. reduced rising [of the boiling point]
reduced equation of state — reduzierte Zustandsgleichung f
reduced equilibrium constant — reduzierte Gleichgewichtskonstante f
reduced eye — reduziertes Auge n
reduced factor of stress concentration, fatigue stress concentration factor, fatigue notch (strength reduction) factor, notch [fatigue] factor; reciprocal of the notch [fatigue] factor — Kerbwirk[ungs]zahl f, Kerbeinflußzahl f, Kerbziffer f, Kerbfaktor m
reduced focal length — reduzierte Brennweite f

reduced hodograph — reduzierte Laufzeitkurve f

reduced impedance — s. normalized impedance
reduced isotopic spin — reduzierter Isospin m

reduced length [of pendulum], equivalent length of pendulum, length of the equivalent simple pendulum, length of the simple equivalent pendulum — reduzierte Pendellänge f, korrespondierende Pendellänge
reduced level width, reduced width [of neutron level], reduced neutron width — reduzierte Breite f [des Neutronenniveaus], reduzierte Niveaubreite (Neutronenbreite) f
reduced lifetime — s. comparative life
reduced lowering [of the freezing point], reduced depression [of the freezing point] — reduzierte Gefrierpunktserniedrigung f
reduced luminance — reduzierte Leuchtdichte f
reduced mass — reduzierte Masse f
reduced model — verkleinertes Modell n

reduced modulus [of elasticity], double modulus, modulus of inelastic buckling — Knickmodul m [nach Kármán], Knickzahl f, Kármánscher Knickmodul
reduced moment of inertia, fictitious moment of inertia — reduziertes Trägheitsmoment n
reduced neutron width — s. reduced width
reduced partial width — reduzierte Partialbreite f

reduced particle momentum — reduzierter Teilchenimpuls m
reduced particle velocity, reduced velocity — reduzierte (bezogene) Geschwindigkeit f
reduced partition function ratio — reduziertes Zustandssummenverhältnis n
reduced period — reduzierte Schwingungsperiode f

reduced Planck['s] formula (law) — s. reduced radiation law
reduced pressure — reduzierter Druck m

reduced print — Verkleinerungskopie f

reduced radiation law, reduced Planck['s] law, reduced Planck['s] formula — reduzierte [Plancksche] Strahlungsformel f, reduzierte Plancksche Strahlungsgleichung f, reduziertes [Plancksches] Strahlungsgesetz n

reduced range — reduzierte Reichweite f
reduced representation — reduzierte Darstellung f

reduced rising [of the boiling point], reduced elevation [of the boiling point] — reduzierte Siedepunktserhöhung f
reduced scale, small scale, reduction scale, scale of reduction; reduction ratio — Verkleinerungsmaßstab m, Verjüngungsmaßstab m, Reduktionsmaßstab m
reduced stress tensor — s. stress deviator
reduced temperature — reduzierte Temperatur f

reduced troland — reduziertes Troland n
reduced variable [of state] ‹therm.› — reduzierte Zustandsgröße f, reduzierte Variable f ‹Therm.›
reduced velocity, reduced particle velocity — reduzierte (bezogene) Geschwindigkeit f
reduced vergency — reduzierte Vergenz f ‹Vergenz, dividiert durch den Brechungsindex›
reduced volume — reduziertes Volumen n
reduced wave equation, Helmholtz['s] equation, wave equation — Helmholtzsche Gleichung f, Helmholtzsche Schwingungsgleichung f
reduced wave impedance — s. normalized impedance
reduced width [of neutron level], reduced neutron width, reduced level width — reduzierte Breite f [des Neutronenniveaus], reduzierte Niveaubreite (Neutronenbreite) f
reduced Young['s] modulus — reduzierter Elastizitätsmodul m

reducer, photographic reducer, reducing agent — Abschwächer m, photographischer Abschwächer

reducer — s. a. reducing apparatus
reducer — s. a. reducing agent
reducer — s. a. reduction gear
reducibility, reducibleness ‹chem.; math.› — Reduzierbarkeit f ‹Chem.; Math.›
reducible class, reducible crystal class — reduzible Kristallklasse f
reducibleness — s. reducibility ‹chem.; math.›
reducible representation — reduzible Darstellung f
reducing — s. reduction
reducing ability; reducing power — Reduktionsfähigkeit f; Reduktionsvermögen n

reducing agent, reductant, reductive agent, reducer — Reduktionsmittel n, Reduktor m
reducing agent — s. a. reducer
reducing apparatus, reducer; reduction printer — Verkleinerungsapparat m, Verkleinerungsgerät n, Verkleinerer m
reducing atmosphere, reducing environment — reduzierende Atmosphäre f, Reduktionsatmosphäre f

reducing attachment — Verkleinerungsaufsatz m
reducing flame — Reduktionsflamme f
reducing fusion — reduzierendes Schmelzen n, Reduktionsschmelzen n
reducing power — s. reducing ability
reducing resistor — Abschwächungswiderstand m

reducing transformer — s. step-down transformer
reducing valve, pressure-reducing valve — Reduzierventil n, Druck[ver]minderungsventil n, Druckminderventil n
reductant — s. reducing agent
reductio ad absurdum proof — s. reduction ad absurdum proof

reduction, lowering, lessening, diminishing, diminution	Herabsetzung f, Verkleinerung f, Verminderung f, Verringerung f, Abschwächung f, Schwächung f, Reduktion f, Reduzierung f	**reduction of contrast,** contrast reduction	Kontrastminderung f
reduction; simplification; idealization	Vereinfachung f; Idealisierung f	**reduction of cross-sectional area,** reduction of (in) area, percentage reduction [of cross-sectional area]	Einschnürung f, Querschnittsverminderung f, Querschnittsabnahme f, Abnahme f [des Querschnitts]
reduction <math., astr., geo.>	Reduktion f, Reduzierung f <Math., Astr., Geo.>; Zurückführung f <Math.>	**reduction of cross-section per pass**	s. reduction per pass
reduction, chemical reduction <chem.>; electronation <el.chem.>	Reduktion f, chemische Reduktion <Chem.>	**reduction of fading**	Schwundminderung f
reduction, speed reduction <mech.>	Untersetzung f <Mech.>	**reduction of gravity**	Reduktion f der Schwerewerte
reduction, photographic reduction <phot.>	photographische Verkleinerung f, Verkleinerung <Phot.>	**reduction of observations** <astr., geo.>	Reduktion f der Beobachtungsdaten <Astr., Geo.>
reduction <phot.>	Abschwächung f <Phot.>	**reduction of pressure,** lowering of pressure	Druckerniedrigung f, Druckabsenkung f, Druckminderung f, Druckreduzierung f
		reduction of the damping; deattenuation; regeneration, regenerative amplification	Dämpfungsreduktion f
reduction	s. a. concentration <by evaporation> <chem.>	**reduction of volume**	s. decrease in volume
reduction	s. a. diminution	**reduction-oxidation index,** oxidation-reduction index, oxidation-reduction value, O/R value	Redoxindex m, O/R-Wert m
reduction ad absurdum proof, reductio ad absurdum proof, proof by reduction ad absurdum, indirect proof, indirect demonstration	indirekter Beweis m, Widerspruchsbeweis m	**reduction-oxidation reaction**	s. oxidation-reduction reaction
		reduction per pass, reduction of cross-section per pass	Stichabnahme f
reduction affinity	Reduktionsaffinität f	**reduction potential,** reduction affinity per unit charge	Reduktionspotential n
reduction affinity per unit charge	s. reduction potential	**reduction printer**	s. reducing apparatus
reduction coefficient	s. reduction factor <el.; meas.; opt.>	**reduction printing [process]**	Verkleinerungskopieren n
reduction coefficient	s. a. reduction factor	**reduction ratio,** ratio of reduction <mech.>	Untersetzung f, Untersetzungsverhältnis n <Mech.>
reduction cone	Reduktionskegel m		
reduction current	Reduktionsstrom m		
reduction electric tension, reduction voltage	Reduktionsspannung f	**reduction ratio**	s. a. fineness of grinding
		reduction ratio	s. a. reduced scale
reduction equilibrium	Reduktionsgleichgewicht n	**reduction reaction**	Reduktionsreaktion f
		reduction scale	s. reduced scale
reduction factor, reduction coefficient, conversion factor (coefficient)	Umrechnungsfaktor m	**reduction to** <ecliptic; equator; horizon>	Reduktion f auf <die Ekliptik; den Äquator; den Horizont>
reduction factor, diminishing factor	Verkleinerungsfaktor m	**reduction to sea level**	Reduktion f auf den Meeresspiegel, Reduktion auf Normalnull
reduction factor <of dipole element>	Schlankheitsverhältnis n, Schlankheitsgrad m <Dipol>	**reduction to zenith,** zenith reduction	Zenitreduktion f
reduction factor, velocity factor, velocity rate, <of the line or antenna>	Verkürzungsfaktor m; Leitungsverkürzungsfaktor m; Antennenverkürzungsfaktor m	**reduction voltage**	s. reduction electric tension
		reductive agent	s. reducing agent
		reductor	s. reduction gear
		reduite	s. convergent <e.g. nth, of a continued fraction>
reduction factor <chem.>	Reduktionsfaktor m <Chem.>	**redundance, redundancy,** information redundance	Redundanz f, Informationsüberschuß m
reduction factor <el.; meas.; opt.>; reduction coefficient <meas.>; spherical reduction factor <opt.>	Reduktionsfaktor m <El.; Meß.; Opt.>	**redundant bar,** redundant member <mech.>	überzähliger Stab m
		redundant information	redundante (überschüssige) Information f, Überschußinformation f
		redundant member	s. redundant bar
		red variable [star]	roter Veränderlicher m
reduction factor <hydr.>	Reduktionsfaktor m, Reduktionsbeiwert m <Hydr.>	**Redwood-second,** Rs, RI	Redwood-Sekunde f, Redwood-Zahl f, Redwood-I-Sekunde f, Rs, RI
reduction gear[ing], reductor, reducer	Reduziergetriebe n, Reduktionsgetriebe n, Untersetzungsgetriebe n, Untersetzer m, Getriebe n	**Redwood** <No. 1 or No. 2> **viscometer**	Redwood-Viskosimeter n
reduction in area	s. reduction of cross-sectional area	**re-echo,** echo, resounding, reverberation; woolliness	Widerhall m
reduction in load	Last[ab]senkung f	**reed; tongue; tag**	Zunge f
reduction in volume	s. decrease in volume	**reed**	s. a. reed pipe
reduction of area	s. reduction of cross-sectional area	**reed comb,** set of elastic reeds	Zungenkamm m
reduction of area in tension, necking in tension	Brucheinschnürung f, Bruchquerschnittsverminderung f	**reed frequency**	Zungenfrequenz f
		reed frequency meter, reed indicator	s. reed-type frequency meter

reed pipe, tongue pipe, reed	Zungenpfeife *f*	reference line	Bezugslinie *f*
reed-type frequency meter, [tuned-]reed frequency meter, vibrating-reed frequency meter, vibrating-reed instrument, reed indicator, Frahm frequency meter	Zungenfrequenzmesser *m*, Frahm-Frequenzmesser *m*, Zungenfrequenzindikator *m*, Zungeninstrument *n*, Frahmscher Zungenfrequenzmesser	reference mark; height mark	Höhenmarke *f*, Höhenkote *f*
		reference mark; index mark	Strichmarke *f*
		reference moment [of the colour]	Eichmoment *n* [der Farbe]
reed-type musical instrument <ac.>	Zungeninstrument *n* <Ak.>	reference plane, plane of reference	Bezugsebene *f*, Referenzebene *f*
reed vibration, vibration of reed	Zungenvibration *f*, Zungenschwingung *f*	reference point, point of reference, fixed (set) point	Bezugspunkt *m*; Festpunkt *m*
re-emission	Reemission *f*		
re-emission probability (rate)	Reemissionswahrscheinlichkeit *f*		
re-enrichment	Wiederanreicherung *f*, Neuanreicherung *f*		
reentering angle, re-entrant [angle], reflex angle	einspringender Winkel *m*	reference prism, comparison prism	Vergleichsprisma *n*
		reference radiation source	s. standard source
re-entrant cavity	H-Resonator *m*	reference radiator, comparison radiator, radiator for comparison	Vergleichsstrahler *m*
re-entry <into the atmosphere>	Wiedereintritt *m* [in die Atmosphäre], Wiedereintauchen *n* [in die Atmosphäre]	reference ray, ray of reference, comparison ray	Bezugsstrahl *m*, Vergleichsstrahl *m*, Vergleichslichtstrahl *m*
re-entry angle	Wiedereintrittswinkel *m*, Wiedereintauchwinkel *m*, Eintauchwinkel *m*	reference resistance, comparison (comparative) resistance	Vergleichswiderstand *m*
re-entry path (trajectory) <into the atmosphere>	Wiedereintauchbahn *f*, Eintauchbahn *f*, Wiedereintrittsbahn *f* <Rakete in die Erdatmosphäre>	reference schliere, standard schliere, normal schliere	Normalschliere *f*
		reference solution, comparison solution	Vergleichslösung *f*
re-entry velocity	Wiedereintrittsgeschwindigkeit *f*		
re-establishing force	s. restoring force	reference source [of radiation]	s. standard source
reestablishment	s. redressment	reference spectrum; standard spectrum	Bezugsspektrum *n*; Vergleichsspektrum *n*; Standardspektrum *n*
re-examination	s. testing		
reextraction, back washing, back-wash, stripping <US>	Rückextraktion *f*, Reextraktion *f*		
reference absorber	Vergleichsabsorber *m*	reference star, comparison (standard) star	Anschlußstern *m*, Vergleichsstern *m*
reference arrow	Bezugspfeil *m*, Zählpfeil *m*	reference star, guide star	Leitstern *m*, Haltestern *m*
reference black level	Schwarzbezugswert *m*	reference stimulus, unitary stimulus, primary	Primärvalenz *f*, Eichreiz *m*, Eichlicht *n*, Bezugs-Farbvalenz *f*, Bezugsfarbe *f*, Grundfarbe *f*
reference branch	Vergleichszweig *m*		
reference capacitance, comparison capacitance	Vergleichskapazität *f*, Bezugskapazität *f*		
reference capacitor, capacitor for comparison	Vergleichskondensator *m*	reference surface	Referenzfläche *f*, Bezugsfläche *f*
		reference system	s. frame of reference
		reference system at rest, rest frame	ruhendes Bezugssystem *n*, Ruhsystem *n*, Ruhesystem *n*
reference chord, mean aerodynamic chord	Bezugssehne *f*		
		reference tone	Vergleichston *m*
reference damping	Vergleichsdämpfung *f*	reference value, fiducial value	Vergleichswert *m*, Bezugswert *m*
reference datum	s. null plane		
reference direction	Bezugsrichtung *f*	reference voltage, comparison voltage <el.>	Bezugsspannung *f*, Vergleichsspannung *f* <El.>
reference electrode, comparison electrode, reference half-cell	Bezugselektrode *f*, Normalelektrode *f*, Vergleichselektrode *f*		
		reference white, standard white	Normalweiß *n*, Bezugsweiß *n*
reference ellipsoid, comparison ellipsoid, ellipsoid of comparison	Referenzellipsoid *n*, Bezugsellipsoid *n*, Vergleichsellipsoid *n*; Referenzsphäroid *n*	referential	s. frame of reference
		refinement <of the mesh>, mesh refinement <math.>	Verfeinerung *f* [der Unterteilung] <Math.>
		refinement of grains, grain refinement, refining of grains, grain refining	Kornverfeinerung *f*, Kornfeinung *f*
reference eyepiece, comparison eyepiece, eyepiece for comparison	Vergleichsokular *n*		
		refining; displacement <chem.>	Treibprozeß *m*, Treiben *n*; Austreiben *n*; Abtreiben *n* <Chem.>
reference frame	s. frame of reference		
reference half-cell	s. reference electrode	refining of grains	s. refinement of grains
reference horizon	Vergleichshorizont *m*, Bezugshorizont *m*	reflectance	s. reflection factor
		reflectance	s. a. total reflection factor
reference inductance, comparison inductance	Vergleichsinduktivität *f*	reflectance	s. a. diffuse reflection factor
		reflectance edge	Reflexionskante *f*
reference input	s. command variable	reflectance factor	s. direct reflection factor
reference input <US>	s. set level	reflectance spectrophotometry	Reflexionsspektralphotometrie *f*
reference input element, set point adjuster, setting device	Stelleinrichtung *f*, Sollwerteinsteller *m*		
		reflectance spectroscopy	Reflexionsspektroskopie *f*, Remissionsspektroskopie *f*

reflectance spectrum	s. diffuse reflection spectrum	reflecting screen, fill-in screen	Reflexschirm m, Reflexwand f; Aufheller m, Aufhellschirm m, Aufhellblende f
reflected amplitude	reflektierte Amplitude f, Reflexionsamplitude f		
reflected capacitance	s. reaction capacitance	reflecting square, mitre square	Spiegelinstrument n; Winkelspiegel m; Spiegelscheibe f
reflected colour	s. surface colour		
reflected energy	Reflexionsenergie f	reflecting surface, catopter	Reflexionsfläche f, reflektierende Oberfläche f; Reflektorfläche f; Abstrahlfläche f
reflected fringe	s. interference fringe by reflection		
reflected glare	Reflexblendung f, Reflexionsblendung f	reflecting telescope, reflector, [reflecting-] mirror telescope, reflection telescope <astr.>	Spiegelteleskop n, Reflektor m, Spiegelfernrohr n <Astr.>
reflected halo	gespiegelter Halo m		
reflected image, mirror image, image	Spiegelbild n		
		reflection, re-radiation, re-radiation	Reflexion f, Zurückwerfung f, Rückwurf m; Rückstrahlung f, Zurückstrahlung f; Reflex m
reflected impedance	s. reaction impedance		
reflected intensity, part of reflected intensity	reflektierte Intensität f, Bruchteil (Anteil) m der reflektierten Intensität, reflektierter Intensitätsanteil m	reflection	s. a. direct reflection <opt.>
		reflection	s. a. symmetry <cryst.>
		reflection	s. a. backscattering
reflected light; direct light; incident light	reflektiertes Licht n, Reflexlicht n, Reflexionslicht n; Auflicht n; einfallendes (auffallendes) Licht n	reflection angle, angle of reflection	Reflexionswinkel m
		reflection case, Bragg case	Bragg-Fall m
		reflection characteristic; echoing characteristic	Rückstrahlcharakteristik f
reflected-light mode of microscopic viewing	s. direct-light microscopy	reflection coefficient, reflection factor, albedo <for particles, e.g. neutrons>	Albedo f, Reflexionsfaktor m, Reflexionskoeffizient m, Reflexionsvermögen n, Rückstrahl[ungs]vermögen n <für Teilchen, z. B. Neutronen>
reflected pressure	Reflexdruck m		
reflected rainbow	gespiegelter Regenbogen m		
reflected reactor	Reaktor m mit Reflektor, reflektierter Reaktor		
reflected resistance	übertragener Widerstand m, hineintransformierter Widerstand m, Rückwirkwiderstand m; übertragener Wirkwiderstand m, Realteil m des Rückwirkwiderstandes	reflection coefficient, acoustic[al] reflection factor, sound reflection factor, acoustical (sound) reflection coefficient, reflection coefficient for sound, acoustic[al] reflectivity, sound reflectivity <ac.>	Reflexionskoeffizient m, Schallreflexionsgrad m, Schallreflexionskoeffizient m, Schallreflexionsfaktor m, Schallrückwurfgrad m, Rückwurfgrad m <Ak.>
reflected tone	Reflexionston m		
reflected wave, R wave, back wave	reflektierte Welle f, R-Welle f, Reflexionswelle f, [zu]rücklaufende Welle; Spiegelwelle f		
		reflection coefficient, reflection factor <el.>	Reflexionskoeffizient m, Reflexionsfaktor m <El.>
reflected wave, indirect wave <geo.>	reflektierte Welle f, indirekte Welle <Geo.>	reflection coefficient	s. a. reflection factor <opt.>
		reflection coefficient	s. a. reflection factor <opt., normal incidence>
reflecting ability	s. albedo		
reflecting body, white body, white object	spiegelnder (weißer) Körper m, weißes Objekt n	reflection coefficient	s. a. Bond['s] albedo <opt.>
		reflection coefficient for sound	s. reflection coefficient <ac.>
reflecting coefficient	s. total reflection factor <opt.>		
reflecting delay line	Reflexionskette f	reflection-coefficient meter	s. reflectometer
reflecting dichroic mirror	s. colour selective mirror	reflection cone	Reflexionskegel m
		reflection densitometer	Reflexionsdensitometer n, Reflexionsschwärzungsmesser m
reflecting electron microscope	s. reflection electron microscope		
reflecting factor	s. total reflection factor <opt.>	reflection densitometry	Reflexionsdensitometrie f, Reflexionsschwärzungsmessung f
reflecting galvanometer, mirror galvanometer, reflective galvanometer	Spiegelgalvanometer n, Reflexgalvanometer n, Reflexionsgalvanometer n	reflection density, external (reflection) optical density	Schwärzung (optische Dichte) f bei Reflexion, Reflexionsdichte f
		reflection depth, depth of reflection	Reflexionstiefe f
reflecting goniometer, reflective goniometer	Reflexgoniometer n, Reflexionsgoniometer n, Spiegelgoniometer n, Rückstrahlungsgoniometer n; Kristallgoniometer n	reflection échelon	Reflexionsstufengitter n, Spiegelgitter n, Spiegelflächengitter n
		reflection echo; returning echo	Rückstrahlecho n
		reflection electron diffraction	Elektronenbeugung f in Reflexion, Reflexionselektronenbeugung f
reflecting grating	s. reflection grating		
reflecting interference microscope	Auflicht-Interferenzmikroskop n		
		reflection electron microscope, reflection-type electron microscope, reflection microscope, reflecting electron microscope, REM	Reflexionsmikroskop n [nach von Borries], Reflexionsübermikroskop n, Reflexionselektronenmikroskop n
reflecting mirror <of illuminating system>	Beleuchtungsspiegel m		
reflecting-mirror telescope	s. reflecting telescope <astr.>		
reflecting nephoscope, [mirror] nephoscope	Nephoskop; Wolkenspiegel m	reflection electron microscopy, reflection microscopy, electron microscopy by reflection, microscopy by reflection, REM	Reflexionselektronenmikroskopie f, Reflexionsmikroskopie f
reflecting power, reflection factor, reflectivity <opt., oblique incidence>	Reflexionsvermögen n <Opt., schiefer Einfall>		
reflecting power	s. a. reflection factor	reflection experiment	Reflexionsexperiment n
reflecting prism, totally reflecting prism, total reflection prism, reflex prism	Reflexionsprisma n, totalreflektierendes Prisma n, Totalreflexionsprisma n, Spiegelprisma n, Winkelprisma n	reflection factor, Fresnel['s] reflection factor, [Fresnel['s]] reflection coefficient<opt.>	Reflexionskoeffizient m, Fresnelscher Reflexionskoeffizient, Reflexionsfaktor m <Opt.>

reflection factor, reflecting power, reflectance, reflection coefficient <opt., normal incidence>	Reflexionsgrad m, Reflexionskoeffizient m <Opt., senkrechter Einfall>	reflection-type electron microscope	s. reflection electron microscope
reflection factor, reflecting power, reflectivity <opt., oblique incidence>	Reflexionsvermögen n <Opt., schiefer Einfall>	reflection-type radiometric [materials] testing	Reflexionsprüfung f, radiometrische Werkstoffprüfung f in Reflexion
reflection factor	s. a. reflection coefficient <for particles, e.g. neutrons>	reflection with respect to the plane	s. reflection in the plane
reflection factor	s. a. reflection coefficient <el.>	reflection X-ray microscopy	Reflexionsröntgenmikroskopie f
reflection factor	s. a. total reflection factor <opt.>	reflective galvanometer	s. reflecting galvanometer
reflection filter	Reflexionsfilter n	reflective goniometer	s. reflecting goniometer
		reflective optics	s. Schmidt['s] optical system
reflection grating, reflecting grating	Reflexionsgitter n	reflectivity <opt.>	Sättigungsreflexionsgrad m, Reflexionsgrad m <eines Körpers, dessen Schichtdicke so groß ist, daß sich eine weitere Erhöhung der Dicke auf den Wert des Reflexionsgrades nicht mehr auswirkt> <Opt.>
reflection halation, reflex halation	Reflexionslichthof m		
reflection halo	Spiegelhalo m, Spiegelungshalo m		
		reflectivity	s. a. total reflection factor <opt.>
		reflectivity, reflection factor, reflecting power <opt., oblique incidence>	Reflexionsvermögen n <Opt., schiefer Einfall>
		reflectogram; echogram	Echogramm n; Reflektogramm n
reflection hologram	Reflexionshologramm n	reflectometer, reflection-coefficient meter	Reflexionsmesser m, Reflektometer n
reflection in a point	Spiegelung f an einem Punkt	reflectometer value	Reflektometerwert m
reflection in depth	Tiefenreflexion f	reflector; mirror; tamper <of reactor>	Reflektor m
reflection in the plane, reflection with respect to the plane	Spiegelung f an der Ebene	reflector <opt.; el.>	Reflektor m, Rückstrahler m <Vorrichtung zur Veränderung der räumlichen Verteilung des Lichtstroms einer Lichtquelle durch reflektierende Flächen> <Opt.>; Rückstrahler <El.>
reflection invariance	Spiegelungsinvarianz f, Spiegelinvarianz f		
reflection-invariant	spiegelungsinvariant, spiegelinvariant		
reflectionless; non-reflecting	reflexionsfrei; nichtreflektierend		
reflection loss	Reflexionsverlust m, Lichtverlust m infolge Reflexionsminderung	reflector	s. a. reflecting telescope <astr.>
		reflector	s. a. parasitic reflector <el.>
reflection matrix	Reflexionsmatrix f	reflector antenna	Spiegelantenne f, Reflektorantenne f, Antenne f mit Spiegelreflektor
reflection method <hydr.; el.>	Spiegelungsmethode f <Hydr.; El.>		
		reflector aperture, mirror aperture	Spiegelöffnung f
reflection microscope	s. direct-light microscope	reflector arc lamp, mirror arc lamp	Spiegelbogenlampe f
reflection microscope	s. reflection electron microscope	reflector coating, mirror coating, coating of the mirror; mirror silvering	Spiegelbelag m, Belag m des Spiegels
reflection microscopy	s. reflection electron microscopy		
reflection modulation	Modulation f des Reflexionsgrades		
reflection nebula	Reflexionsnebel m	reflector heat, heat dissipated in the reflector	Reflektorwärme f
		reflector lamp	Reflektorlampe f, Strahlerlampe f
reflection of heat, heat reflection	Wärmerückstrahlung f, Wärmereflexion f	reflector microphone	Reflektormikrophon n
reflection optical density	s. reflection density	reflector-moderator, moderator-reflector	Moderator-Reflektor m, Reflektor-Moderator m
reflection order, order of reflection	Reflexionsordnung f, Ordnung f der Reflexion		
reflection paramagnetic maser amplifier	paramagnetischer Reflexionsquantenverstärker m	reflector saving[s]	Reflektorgewinn m, Reflektoreinsparung f, Reflektorersparnis f
reflection plane, mirror plane, plane of mirror [reflection symmetry]	Spiegelebene f	reflector voltage	Reflektorspannung f
reflection point, point of reflection <el.>	Stoßstelle f <El.>	reflex <bio.>	Reflex m <Bio.>
		reflex	s. a. flare <phot.>
		reflex amplifier	Reflexionsverstärker m
reflection polarizer	Reflexionspolarisator m		
reflection principle	s. Schwarz['s] reflection principle	reflex angle	s. reentering angle
reflection rainbow	s. secondary rainbow	reflex attachment, mirror-reflex attachment	Spiegelreflexaufsatz m, Spiegelreflexansatz m, Spiegelreflexvorsatz m
reflection shooting	Reflexionsseismik f, Reflexionsschießen n		
		reflex camera, mirror-reflex camera, reflex-through-the lens camera	Spiegelreflexkamera f, Reflexkamera f
reflection spectrum	Reflexionsspektrum n	reflex circuit	Reflexschaltung f
reflection target	Reflexionstarget n		
reflection telescope	s. reflecting telescope <astr.>	reflex finder	s. reflex viewfinder
		reflex focusing device, pentaprism eye-level viewfinder	Prismeneinsatz m, Prismenaufsatz m
reflection-type cavity maser, one-port cavity maser	Reflexionsmaser m, Einstrahlmaser m		
		reflex halation	s. reflection halation

reflexivity <math.>	Reflexivität f <Math.>	refraction index	s. refractive index
		refraction law, law of refraction	Brechungsgesetz n
reflex klystron	Reflex[ions]klystron n, Reflexionslaufzeitröhre f, Reflexionstriftröhre f, Spiegeltriftröhre f, Spiegelklystron n	refraction of light	Lichtbrechung f, Brechung (Refraktion) f des Lichtes
		refractionometer	s. optimeter
reflexotation	s. improper orthogonal mapping <math.>	refraction shooting	Refraktionsseismik f, Refraktionsschießen n
reflex printing [method]	Reflexkopierverfahren n, Reflexkopieren n	refraction spectrum	s. dispersion spectrum
		refraction table, table of refraction	Refraktionstabelle f, Refraktionstafel f
		refraction term	Brechungsterm m, Brechungsanteil m, Brechungsglied n
reflex prism	s. reflecting prism		
reflex-prism split image rangefinder, groundglass rangefinder, rangefinder groundglass	Entfernungsmesser m für photographische Zwecke, Meßlupe f <Phot.>	refraction wave <geo.>	gebrochene Welle f <Geo.>
		refractive coefficient	s. refractive index
		refractive dispersion; refractive dispersivity	Brechungsdispersion f; Refraktionsdispersion f
reflex reflection, retro-reflection	katadioptrische Reflexion f, Reflexreflexion f, Retroreflexion f <Lichtrückwurf in der Einfallsrichtung benachbarten Richtungen, unabhängig vom Einfallswinkel>	refractive dispersivity	s. a. dispersivity quotient
		refractive index, index of refraction, refraction index; refraction (refractive) coefficient; absolute refractive index, absolute index of refraction	Brechungsindex m, Brech[ungs]zahl f, Brechungsfaktor m, Brechungsexponent m, Brechungskoeffizient m, Brechungsvermögen m, Brechungsquotient m, Brechungsverhältnis n; absoluter Brechungsindex m; Refraktionsvermögen n
reflex reflector, retro-reflector	Reflexreflektor m, Rückstrahler m		
reflex-through-the lens camera	s. reflex camera		
reflex viewfinder, reflex finder	Spiegelreflexsucher m, Reflexsucher m	refractive index matrix	Brechungsindexmatrix f
		refractive modulus	Refraktionsmodul m
		refractive power	s. focal power <opt.>
reflux	Rückfluß m	refractivity	Refraktivität f <n-1 oder 1-n>
		refractivity	s. a. molecular refraction
reflux; phlegma; quantity of reflux <chem.>	Rückfluß m, Rücklauf m, Phlegma n <Chem.>	refractivity constant	s. refraction constant
		refractometer	Refraktometer n, Brechzahlmesser m; Augenrefraktometer n
reflux condenser	Rückflußkühler m		
reflux cooling, refluxing	Rückflußkühlung f	refractometric analysis	refraktometrische Analyse f
refluxer, reflux exchanger	s. dephlegmator	refractometry	Refraktometrie f, Brechzahlbestimmung f, Brechzahlmessung f
refluxing	s. reflux cooling		
reflux ratio, reflux-to-product ratio	Rückflußverhältnis n, Rückflußzahl f, Rücklaufverhältnis n	refractor <opt.>	Refraktor m, Lichtbrechungskörper m <Vorrichtung zur Veränderung der räumlichen Verteilung des Lichtstroms einer Lichtquelle durch lichtbrechende Medien> <Opt.>
reforming	Reformierung f		
refracted wave	gebrochene Welle f, Brechungswelle f		
refracting angle	brechender Winkel m, Prismenwinkel m		
refracting astrograph, lens astrograph	Linsenastrograph m	refractor, refracting telescope, lens telescope <astr.>	Refraktor m, Linsenfernrohr n, Linsenteleskop n <Astr.>
refracting edge	brechende Kante f	refractoriness	s. fireproofness
refracting surface	brechende Fläche f, Brechfläche f	refractoriness	s. refractory phase <bio.>
		refractory, refractory material, refractory brick	feuerfester Stoff (Werkstoff, Stein) m, feuerfeste Keramik f
refracting telescope, refractor, lens telescope <astr.>	Refraktor m, Linsenfernrohr n, Linsenteleskop n <Astr.>	refractory <bio.>	refraktär <Bio.>
refraction; refringence, refringency	Brechung f; Strahlenbrechung f, Strahlungsbrechung f; Refraktion f	refractory	s. a. fire-resistant
		refractory	s. a. high-melting
		refractory brick	s. refractory material
		refractory cathode	hochschmelzende Katode f
refraction angle, angle of refraction	Brechungswinkel m, Refraktionswinkel m	refractory electrode transition	Übergang m Glimmstrom—Lichtbogen bei hochschmelzenden Elektroden
refraction anomaly, anomaly in refraction	Refraktionsanomalie f		
refraction coefficient	s. refractive index	refractory material, refractory, refractory brick	feuerfester Stoff (Werkstoff, Stein) m, feuerfeste Keramik f
refraction constant, constant of [mean] refraction, refractivity constant	Refraktionskoeffizient m, Refraktionskonstante f		
		refractory period	Refraktärzeit f, Refraktärperiode f, Refraktärphase f
refraction equation, refraction formula	Refraktionsformel f		
refraction equivalent, equivalent refraction	Refraktionsäquivalent n	refractory phase, refractoriness <bio.>	Refraktärstadium n, Refraktärphase f, Refraktarität f <Bio.>
refraction error	Refraktionsfehler m, Brechungsfehler m <Auge>	refrangibility	Brechbarkeit f; Brechungsvermögen n, Brechungsfähigkeit f
refraction factor <el.>	Refraktionszahl f <El.>	refrigerant, refrigerating agent, refrigerating medium	Kältemittel n, Kältemedium n, Kälteübertragungsmittel h, Kälteüberträger m, Kälteträger m
refraction formula	s. refraction equation		
refraction halo	Brechungshalo m	refrigerated finger, cold finger	Kühlfinger m

refrigerated trap	s. cold trap	regenerative power, regeneration power, recovery power	Regenerationsfähigkeit f, Regenerierfähigkeit f, Regenerationsvermögen n, Regeneriervermögen n, Erholungsfähigkeit f
refrigerating agent	s. refrigerant		
refrigerating capacity	Kälteleistung f		
refrigerating effect	Kühlwirkung f	regenerative process	regenerativer Prozeß m, Regenerativprozeß m, Regenerationsprozeß m
refrigerating machine	s. refrigerator		
refrigerating medium	s. refrigerant		
refrigerating mixture, frigorific mixture, cryohydrate, freezing mixture, cryogen	Kältemischung f, Kryohydrat n	regenerative reactor	s. converter <nucl.>
		regenerative valve detector	s. regenerative [grid-current] detector
		regenerator, heat regenerator, thermal regenerator	Regenerator m, periodisch arbeitender Wärmeaustauscher m, Regenerativwärmeaustauscher m, Wärmeregenerator m, Wärmespeicher m
refrigerating plant	Kälteanlage f		
refrigerating plant	s. a. refrigerator		
refrigerating tubing	Kühlrohrsystem n		
refrigeration; cooling	Kühlung f; Abkühlung f	Regge cut	Regge-Schnitt m
		Regge family	Regge-Familie f
refrigeration, production of cold	Kälteerzeugung f	reggeization	Reggeisierung f
		reggeon	Reggeon n
refrigeration [engineering], refrigeration technology	Kältetechnik f	reggeon graph	Reggeongraph m
		Regge pole	Regge-Pol m
		Regge recurrence	Regge-Rekurrenz f, Regge-Wiederholung f
refrigeration cycle	Kältekreisprozeß m		
refrigeration laboratory, low-temperature laboratory	Kältelaboratorium n, Tieftemperaturlaboratorium n	Regge trajectory	Regge-Trajektorie f, Regge-Bahn f
refrigeration machine	s. refrigerator	reggistics	Reggeistik f
refrigeration technology	s. refrigeration engineering	regime, régime	s. mode of operation
refrigerator, refrigerating machine, refrigerating plant, refrigeration machine	Kältemaschine f; Kühlmaschine f; Refrigerator m <Kälteanlage ohne Flüssigkeitsentnahme>	regime of flight	Flugzustand m
		regime of winds	Windregime n
		regime theory	Regimetheorie f [des Massentransports]
		region; range; zone; sphere <gen.>	Gebiet n; Bereich m; Zone f; Sphäre f <allg.>
refrigerator	Kühlschrank m		
refringence, refringency	s. refraction	region, interval, range <gen.>	Intervall n, Bereich m, Gebiet n <allg.>
refueling, refuelling; reloading	Brennstoffwechsel m, Wiederbeladung f, Wiederbeschickung f, Neubeschickung f; Brennstoffumladung f	regional compensation	regionale Kompensation (Ausgleichsbewegung) f, großräumige Kompensation
refuse, rubbish	Schutt m	regional time, standard time, zone time	Zonenzeit f, Einheitszeit f
		region of alimentation	Nährgebiet n, Nährbereich m
refusion, repeated melting; remelting	Umschmelzen n	region of alimentation, river basin, basin, drainage <geo.>	Einzugsgebiet n; Stromgebiet n, Flußgebiet n <Geo.>
refutation, rebuttal	Widerlegung f, Gegenbeweis m		
		region of alimentation of the source (spring) <geo.>	Quellgebiet n <Geo.>
regelation, refreezing	Regelation f		
		region of audibility	s. audibility zone
regenerating solution	Wiederbelebungslösung f	region of barometric tendency	Tendenzgebiet n [des Luftdrucks]
regeneration, reprocessing	Wiederaufarbeitung f, Aufarbeitung f, Wiederaufbereitung f; Rückvergütung f	region of cathode fall	s. cathode fall region
		region of continuum, region of energy continuum	Kontinuumsbereich m, Kontinuumsgebiet n, Kontinuumsteil m der Energieabhängigkeit des Wirkungsquerschnitts
regeneration; recovery <bio., geo., meteo., phot., el.; cryst.>	Regeneration f; Regenerierung f <Bio., Geo., Meteo., Phot., El., Krist.>		
		region of convergence, region of fusion <opt.>	Konvergenzbereich m, Fusionsbereich m <Opt.>
regeneration <e.g. of catalyst>	Wiederbelebung f, Wiederauffrischung f <z. B. Katalysator>	region of convergence	s. a. domain of convergence
		region of correct exposure	s. straight line portion of the characteristic curve
regeneration	s. a. feedback		
regeneration	s. a. reduction of the damping	region of crystal	s. crystal domain <cryst.>
regeneration heat	nachhinkende Wärme f	region of energy continuum	s. region of continuum
regeneration of current, recuperation of current	Stromrückgewinnung f, Rückgewinnung f (Rückführung) f der elektrischen Energie	region of evaporation, evaporation zone, evaporation region	Verdampfungsteil m, Verdampferteil m, Verdampfungsgebiet n
		region of fusion	s. region of convergence
regeneration of heat, heat regeneration	Wärmerückgewinnung f, Wärmerückgewinn m, Wärmeregeneration f	region of image reversal	s. region of solarization
		region of incipient current flow	s. region of residual current
regeneration power	s. regenerative power	region of integration, range of integration	Integrationsgebiet n, Integrationsbereich m, Integrationsgrenzen fpl
regenerative amplification, retroactive amplification	Rückkopplungsverstärkung f		
		region of intrinsic conduction	s. intrinsic region
regenerative amplification	s. a. reduction of the damping	region of limited proportionality	Bereich m begrenzter Proportionalität
regenerative circuit	s. feedback loop		
regenerative converter	s. converter <nucl.>	region of liquefaction	Verflüssigungsbereich m
regenerative detector, self-interference audion	Rückkopplungsgleichrichter m	region of normal exposure	s. straight line portion of the characteristic curve
		region of origin	Ursprungsgebiet n
regenerative [grid-current] detector, self-interference audion, regenerative valve detector	Rückkopplungsaudion n	region of overexposure	s. shoulder <phot., opt.>
		region of overlap	s. overlap region
		region of partial shadow	Halbschattengebiet n, Halbschatten m
regenerative loop of the circuit	s. feedback loop		

region of potential fall, potential fall region (zone), zone of potential fall — Fallraum *m*, Fallgebiet *n*

region of precipitation — Niederschlagsgebiet *n*

region of residual current, residual current region, region of incipient current flow — Anlaufgebiet *n*, Anlaufstromgebiet *n*

region of reversal and re-reversal of solarization — Zone *f* der Solarisation und Resolarisation

region of saturated steam — *s.* saturated-steam region

region of silence — *s.* silent zone

region of single vision — *s.* Panum['s] area

region of solarization, region of image reversal, zone of solarization — Solarisationsbereich *m*, Solarisationszone *f*, Solarisationsteil *m*

region of stability, stability region, stability domain <control> — Stabilitätsbereich *m*, Stabilitätsgebiet *n* <Regelung>

region of stable orbits, stability region, stable region <acc.> — Stabilitätsbereich *m*, Bereich *m* stabiler Bahnen <Beschl.>

region of the infra-red spectrum, infra-red region, I.R. region — Infrarotgebiet *n*, Gebiet *n* des infraroten Spektrums, IR-Gebiet *n*

region of the spectrum — *s.* spectral region

region of the ultra-violet spectrum, ultra-violet region, U.V. region — Ultraviolettgebiet *n*, Gebiet *n* des ultravioletten Spektrums, UV-Gebiet *n*

region of turbulence — *s.* turbulent region

region of underexposure — *s.* toe

register; counting mechanism, counter — Zählwerk *n*, Zähler *m*; Register *n*

registering — *s.* recording

registering balloon, recording balloon — Registrierballon *m*

registering chronograph — Registrierchronograph *m*

registering siphon barometer, siphon recording barometer — Registrier-Heberbarometer *n*

register rotation, cyclic shift, rotation of register <num.math.> — zyklische Vertauschung *f*, zyklische Verschiebung *f* <num. Math.>

register ton, reg. ton — Registertonne *f*, RT

registration — *s.* recording

registrogram — Registrogramm *n*

re-graduation — *s.* recalibration

regressand, predictand — Regressand *m*

regression, retreat, recession <geo.> — Regression *f*, Rückzug *m*, Rückgang *m*, Zurückgehen *n*, Zurückweichen *n* <Geo.>

regression — *s. a.* fading <phot.>

regression <stat.> — Regression *f* <Stat.>

regression — *s. a.* regression curve

regression analysis — Regressionsanalyse *f*

regression coefficient — Regressionskoeffizient *m*

regression curve, regression — Regressionslinie *f*, Ausgleichslinie *f*, Regressionskurve *f*

regression effect, Marx effect — Marx-Effekt *m*

regression equation — Regressionsgleichung *f*

regression function — Regressionsfunktion *f*, Ausgleichsfunktion *f*

regression line, line of regression — Regressionsgerade *f*, Ausgleichsgerade *f*, Beziehungsgerade *f*, ausgleichende Gerade *f*

regression of latent image — *s.* fading <phot.>

regression period, period of regression — Regressionsperiode *f*

regression surface — Regressionsfläche *f*

regressive erosion — rückschreitende Erosion *f*, regressive Erosion

regressive wave — rückschreitende (regressive) Welle *f*

regressor, predicated variable, determining (cause, explanatory) variable <stat.> — Regressor *m*; Einflußgröße *f*

reg. ton — *s.* register ton

regula falsi, rule of false position, method of false position — Regula *f* falsi, Eingabeln *n* der Nullstelle, Sekantenverfahren *n*

regular, holomorphic <geo., math.>; regular analytic <math.> — holomorph, regulär <Geo., Math.>; regulär analytisch <Math.>

regular <math.> — regulär; regelmäßig <Math.>

regular analytic — *s.* regular <geo., math.>

regular analytic function — *s.* holomorphic function

regular astigmatism — regelmäßiger Astigmatismus *m*, Astigmatismus regularis

regular branch of the analytical function — regulärer Zweig *m* der analytischen Funktion

regular crystal[lographic] system — *s.* cubic system

regular enantiomorphy — *s.* enantiomorphous hemihedry of the regular system

regular error — *s.* systematic error

regular extinction — reguläre Auslöschung *f*

regular field theory — reguläre Feldtheorie *f*

regular flash — *s.* photoflash lamp

regular function — reguläre Funktion *f*

regular function — *s. a.* holomorphic function

regular galaxy, regular nebula — regelmäßiges (reguläres) Sternsystem *n*, regelmäßiger Nebel *m*

regular hemimorphy — *s.* hemimorphic hemihedry of the regular system

regular hexahedron, cube, hexahedron — Würfel *m*, regelmäßiges Sechsflach (Hexaeder) *n*, regelmäßiger Sechsflächner *m*, Hexaeder *n*

regular holohedry — *s.* holohedry of the regular system

regularity attenuation, [structural] return loss; echo current attenuation — Rückflußdämpfung *f*; Echodämpfung *f*

regularization — Regularisierung *f*

regularizing variable — regularisierende Variable *f*

regular lattice site — *s.* regular site

regular matrix — *s.* invertible matrix

regular multiplet, normal multiplet — regelrechtes (reguläres, normales) Multiplett *n*, Multiplett mit normaler Termordnung

regular nebula — *s.* regular galaxy

regular paramorphy — *s.* paramorphic hemihedry of the regular system

regular part — regulärer Teil *m*

regular point — regulärer Punkt *m*

regular point system, regular system of points — reguläres Punktsystem *n*

regular polygon — regelmäßiges Vieleck *n*, reguläres Polygon *n*

regular polyhedron — regelmäßiges Vielflach *n*, reguläres Polyeder *n*

regular position — Regellage *f*; Gleichlage *f*

regular position of frequencies — Frequenz[en]gleichlage *f*, Gleichlage *f* der Frequenzen

regular precession, steady precession, steady precessional motion — reguläre Präzession *f*, gleichmäßige Präzession

regular reflectance — *s.* direct reflection factor

regular reflection — *s.* direct reflection <opt.>

regular refraction — *s.* specular refraction

regular representation — reguläre Darstellung *f*

regular singularity, regular singular point, inessential singularity, point of determination <of differential equation> — außerwesentlich[e] singuläre Stelle *f*, [singuläre] Stelle *f* der Bestimmtheit, Bestimmtheitsstelle *f*, außerwesentliche (reguläre) Singularität *f*, schwach singuläre Stelle

regular site, regular lattice site — Regelgitterplatz *m*

regular system — *s.* cubic system

regular system of points — *s.* regular point system

regular tetartohedry — *s.* tetartohedry of the regular system

regular trace — reguläre Spur *f*

regular transmission — *s.* direct transmission

regular transmittance — *s.* direct transmission factor

regular variable; periodic variable	regelmäßiger Veränderlicher m; periodischer Veränderlicher; Pulsationsveränderlicher m	rejection number <stat.>	Ablehnungszahl f, Rückweisezahl f <Stat.>
		rejection of heat	s. heat removal
regular wave	reguläre Welle f, regelmäßige Welle	rejection ratio	Unterdrückungsverhältnis n
regulated condition	s. manipulated variable	rejection region, critical region; rejection zone <stat.>	kritischer Bereich m, Ablehnungsbereich m; Ablehnungszone f <Stat.>
regulated quantity	s. controlled variable		
regulated unit	s. final control element		
regulated variable	s. controlled variable		
regulated voltage, stabilized voltage	stabilisierte Spannung f	rejection zone	s. rejection region
		rejector circuit, rejection (stopper) circuit, interference suppression device	Sperrkreis m
regulating	s. fine adjustment		
regulating rod, fine control rod	Regelstab m, Feinregelstab m		
regulating screw	s. setting screw		
regulating system	s. control loop	rejuvenation	s. contraction <of tensor> <math.>
regulating transformer	s. variable ratio transformer	rel	= 10^8 A/Wb
regulation	s. adjustment <to>	relation <math.>	Relation f <Math.>
regulation	s. fine adjustment	relation; relationship; mathematical relationship	Relation f; Beziehung f; Zusammenhang m
regulator <bio.; chem.>	Regulator m <Bio.>; Reglersubstanz f <Chem.>		
regulatory	regulatorisch	relation for the jumps, jump relation	Sprungrelation f
Rehbinder effect	Rehbinder-Effekt m	relation of J. R. Mayer, equation of Robert Mayer, Mayer['s] equation	Gleichung f von J. R. Mayer, Beziehung f von Robert Mayer, Mayersche Beziehung
Reid potential	Reid-Potential n		
re[-]ignition, after count, after discharge	Nachentladung f, Nachimpuls m, Wiederzündung f; Nachzündung f; Rückzündung f	relationship <nucl.>	radioaktive Verwandtschaft f <Kern.>
		relationship	s. a. relation
		relativation	Relativierung f
		relative absorption coefficient	relativer Absorptionskoeffizient m
reignition field strength	s. reignition strength	relative abundance [of isotopes]	s. relative isotopic abundance
reignition of arc	Wiederzündung f des Bogens		
reignition strength [of field], reignition field strength	Wiederzündfeldstärke f	relative abundance [of the element]	s. abundance of the element
		relative abundance [of the isotope]	s. abundance of isotopes
		relative amount of wear	Verschleißbetragsverhältnis n, Verschleißverhältnis n, Verschleißverhältniszahl f, Verhältniszahl f des Verschleißes
reignition voltage, restriking voltage	Wiederzündspannung f		
Reiner effect	Reiner-Effekt m		
Reiner-Rivlin fluid	Reiner-Rivlinsche Flüssigkeit f		
		relative aperture <acc.>	relative Apertur f <Beschl.>
reinforcement	Armierung f, Bewehrung f	relative aperture	s. a. aperture ratio <of objective>
reinforcement; stiffening, strengthening <mech.>	Versteifung f; Verstärkung f; Absteifung f; Verstrebung f <Mech.>		
		relative articulation	s. intelligibility
reinforcer, reinforcing material <mech.>	Verstärker m, Verstärkungsmaterial n, Versteifungsmaterial n <Mech.>	relative atomic weight, atomic weight	Atomgewicht n, relative Atommasse f, Atomverhältniszahl f
		relative biological effectiveness <of the radiation>, relative biological efficiency, RBE	relative biologische Wirksamkeit f [der Strahlung], RBW-Faktor m, RBW, RBE
reinsertion of carrier, carrier reinsertion <el.>	Trägerwellenzusatz m, Trägerzusatz m <El.>		
reinstatement	s. recovery		
Reiss microphone	Reiß-Mikrophon n		
Reissner['s] membrane	Reißnersche Membran f	relative biological effectiveness dose, RBE dose <radiobiology>	RBW-Dosis f, biologische Äquivalenzdosis f <Strahlenbiologie>
Reissner-Nordström metric	Reißner-Nordström-Metrik f		
Reissner-Nordström solution	Reißner-Nordströmsche Lösung f, statische kugelsymmetrische Lösung der Einstein-Maxwellschen Feldgleichungen	relative biological efficiency	s. relative biological effectiveness
		relative content, content by per cent, percentage content	Prozentgehalt m, prozentualer Gehalt m
reiteration, repetition	Wiederholung f	relative curvature [of profile]	relative Wölbung f [des Profils]
rejection, suppression	Unterdrückung f		
		relative density, specific gravity <relative to or referred to>, sp.gr.	Dichtezahl f, relative Dichte f, bezogene Dichte, Dichteverhältnis n <zu>
rejection; blocking; interlocking, locking; cut-off; paralysis; blackout; bottoming <el.>	Sperrung f <El.>		
		relative determination, differential determination <of star position or brightness>	Anschlußbeobachtung f
rejection <stat.>	Verwerfen n, Ablehnen n, Abweisen n, Zurückweisen n, Rückweisen n <Stat.>		
		relative dielectric constant	s. relative permittivity <of the material>
rejection, throwing-away <chem.>	Verwerfen n <Chem.>	relative distortion, percentage distortion	relative Verzeichnung f, Verzeichnung <in %>
rejection band	s. stop band		
rejection circuit	s. rejector circuit	relative efficiency; relative potency	relative Wirksamkeit f; Wirksamkeitsfaktor m, Wirksamkeitsgrad m
rejection filter, suppression filter, elimination filter, exclusion filter	Sperrfilter n <El.; Opt.>; Okularsperrfilter n <Opt.>; Sperrsieb n <El.>		
		relative efficiency, efficiency ratio; thermodynamic efficiency; diagram factor <therm.>	thermodynamischer Wirkungsgrad m; Ausnutzungsfaktor m <Therm.>; relativer Nutzeffekt m <Kältetechnik>
rejection limit; rejection line <stat.>	Ablehnungsschwelle f, Ablehnungsgrenze f; Ablehnungslinie f <Stat.>		

relative electrode potential, relative electrode tension, electrode potential, electrode tension, single[-electrode] potential — [relatives] Elektrodenpotential n, [relative] Elektrodenspannung f, Einzelpotential n, Halbzellenpotential n, elektromotorische Kraft f der Halbzelle

relative error; percentage error — relativer Fehler m; prozentualer Fehler

relative escape ‹of thermal neutrons› — Anteil m der thermischen Neutronen, die den Reaktor verlassen

relative extremum, local extremum — relatives Extremum n, relativer Extremwert m, lokales Extremum, Extremum im Kleinen

relative flow — Relativströmung f

relative frame — Relativsystem n

relative frequency — relative Schwingungszahl (Frequenz) f

relative frequency, proportional frequency, frequency ‹stat.› — relative Häufigkeit f, Häufigkeit ‹Stat.›

relative frequency function — s. probability density

relative gradient — relative Steilheit f ‹z. B. der Energiekurve›

relative hardness [number], RHN — Härtegrad m RH, relative Härte f

relative hue, contrast hue — gebundene Farbe f, bezogene Farbe

relative humidity, hygrometric state, saturation ratio, percentage of moisture — relative Feuchtigkeit (Feuchte) f, prozentuale Feuchtigkeit, Feuchtigkeitsgrad m

relative index of refraction — s. relative refractive index

relative inductivity — s. permittivity ‹of the material›

relative intrinsic parity — relative innere Parität f

relative isotopic abundance, relative abundance [of isotopes], abundance ratio [of isotopes], isotopic ratio — Isotopenhäufigkeitsverhältnis n, Häufigkeitsverhältnis n [der Isotope], Isotopenverhältnis n

relative luminance factor — Relativhelligkeit f, relative Helligkeit f

relative luminosity, relative luminous efficiency — Hellempfindungsgrad m, Hellempfindlichkeitsgrad m, [relative] Hellempfindlichkeit f

relative luminosity curve — spektrale Hellempfindlichkeitskurve f

relative luminosity factor — s. relative luminous efficiency

relative luminous efficiency, relative luminosity factor, spectral luminous efficiency ‹of a monochromatic radiation of wavelength λ for photopic vision› — spektraler Hellempfindungsgrad m, spektraler Hellempfindlichkeitsgrad m, relative spektrale Hellempfindlichkeit f

relative luminous efficiency — s. a. relative luminosity

relative luminous efficiency — s. a. photometric radiation equivalent

relative luminous efficiency curve — s. relative spectral luminous distribution

relative luminous efficiency curve for photopic vision — Tageswertkurve f, Hellempfindlichkeitskurve f, Zapfenkurve f

relative luminous efficiency curve for scotopic vision — Dämmer[ungs]wertkurve f, Stäbchenkurve f, [spektrale] Dunkelempfindlichkeitskurve f

relative luminous efficiency curve for the photometric standard observer — internationale spektrale Hellempfindlichkeitskurve f, V_λ-Kurve f, V-Lambda-Kurve f

relative luminous efficiency for peripheral vision — Peripheriewert m, Wert m der spektralen Hellempfindlichkeitskurve für peripheres Sehen

relative luminous efficiency of a monochromatic radiation of wavelength λ for scotopic vision — Dämmer[ungs]wert m, [spektrale] Dämmerempfindlichkeit f, [spektrale] Dunkelempfindlichkeit f, spektraler Dunkelempfindungsgrad (Dunkelempfindlichkeitsgrad m, Dämmerempfindungsgrad, Dämmerempfindlichkeitsgrad) m, spektraler Hellempfindungsgrad m für Nachtsehen

relatively prime — relativ prim, teilerfremd

relative maximum, local maximum, maximum turning value — relatives (lokales) Maximum n, Maximum im Kleinen

relative minimum, local minimum, minimum turning value — relatives (lokales) Minimum n, Minimum im Kleinen

relative molecule mass — s. molecular weight

relative motion — Relativbewegung f, relative Bewegung f

relative orientation — relative (gegenseitige) Orientierung f

relative permeability, magnetic constant — Permeabilitätszahl f, relative [magnetische] Permeabilität f, relative Induktionskonstante f

relative permittivity, relative dielectric constant, dielectric constant ‹of the material› — relative Dielektrizitätskonstante f, Dielektrizitätszahl f, DK-Zahl f, Elektrisierungszahl f, Dielektrizität f

relative plateau slope, plateau slope — Plateauanstieg m, Plateauneigung f, Plateausteigung f

relative potency — s. relative efficiency

relative pump[ing] speed — relative Sauggeschwindigkeit f [der Pumpe]

relative pumping speed — s. exhaustion rate

relative quantity; dimensionless quantity; abstract number — bezogene Größe f, relative Größe, dimensionslose Größe, Dimensionslose f, Verhältnisgröße f, dimensionslose Variable (Größe, Zahlengröße) f; reine Zahl f, unbenannte Zahl (Größe)

relative rate of growth — relative (spezifische) Wachstumsgeschwindigkeit f

relative refractive index, relative index of refraction — Brechungsverhältnis n, relativer Brechungsindex m, Verhältnis n der Brechungsindizes zweier Medien

relative response — s. relative sensitivity

relative retardation of optical paths — s. difference of path ‹of rays›

relative sensitivity; relative response — relative Empfindlichkeit (Ansprechempfindlichkeit) f

relative specific ionization — relative spezifische Ionisation f ‹bezogen auf die spezifische Ionisation im Medium bei 15 °C und 760 Torr›

relative specific weight, relative weight — Wichtezahl f, Relativgewicht n, relatives Gewicht n

relative spectral energy distribution, relative spectral power distribution — Strahlungsfunktion f, relative spektrale Strahlungsverteilung (Energieverteilung) f

relative spectral luminous distribution, relative luminous efficiency curve — [spektrale] Augenempfindlichkeitskurve f, Kurve f der spektralen Augenempfindlichkeit, spektrale Empfindlichkeitskurve f [des Auges]

relative spectral power distribution — s. relative spectral energy distribution

relative speed of wind, relative velocity of wind — relative Windgeschwindigkeit f

relative sunspots number — s. Wolf number

relative tensor of unit weight, relative tensor of weight unity, tensor density — Tensordichte f

relative thickness of the aerofoil, thickness [chord] ratio — relative Profildicke f, relative Dicke f [des Profils]

relative trigonometric parallax	relative Parallaxe f	**relativity correction**	s. relativistic correction
relative unit	Relativeinheit f, relative Einheit f	**relativity displacement of spectral lines**	s. gravitational red-shift
relative velocity of wind	s. relative speed of wind	**relativity mechanics**	s. relativistic mechanics
relative weight	s. relative specific weight	**relativity precession**	s. Thomas precession
relativistic	relativistisch	**relativity principle,** principle of relativity	Relativitätsprinzip n, Prinzip n der Relativität
relativistic aberration ‹of beam of charged particles›	relativistische Ablenkung (Aberration) f ‹Teilchenstrahl›	**relativity theory,** theory of relativity, relativity	Relativitätstheorie f
relativistic accelerator	relativistischer Beschleuniger m	**relaxation**	Relaxation f ‹Rückkehr in den Normalzustand nach Abschaltung eines Spannungsfeldes›
relativistic advance of perihelion, relativistic motion of perihelion	relativistische Periheldrehung (Perihelbewegung) f	**relaxation,** sweep ‹el.›	Kippung f, Kippen n ‹El.›
relativistic catastrophe	relativistische Katastrophe f	**relaxation,** relaxation method ‹of Southwell› ‹math.›	Relaxationsmethode f [von Southwell], Maschenverfahren n, Relaxation f; Relaxationsmethode nach Gauß-Southwell ‹Math.›
relativistic composition of velocities, velocity addition formula in special relativity	relativistisches (Einsteinsches) Additionstheorem n der Geschwindigkeiten	**relaxation,** relaxing, relieving of stress, release from tension ‹mech.›	Erschlaffung f; Entspannung f; Relaxation f ‹Mech.›
relativistic contraction	s. Lorentz contraction		
relativistic correction; relativity correction	relativistische Korrektion f; Relativitätskorrektion f		
relativistic covariance, Lorentz covariance	relativistische Kovarianz f	**relaxation**	s. a. relaxation function
		relaxation[al] absorption	Relaxationsabsorption f
relativistic cyclotron	s. relativistic particle cyclotron	**relaxational dispersion,** relaxation dispersion	Relaxationsdispersion f
relativistic deflection of light, Einstein displacement [of light], Einstein['s] light deflection, gravitational aberration [of light], Einstein effect	relativistische Ablenkung f des Lichts, relativistische Lichtablenkung f, Lichtkrümmung f (Krümmung f von Lichtstrahlen) im Schwerefeld, Lichtablenkung (Ablenkung der Lichtstrahlen) im Schwerefeld, Gravitationsaberration f	**relaxation amplitude,** sweep amplitude	Kippamplitude f, Ablenk[ungs]weite f
		relaxation behaviour	Relaxationsverhalten n
		relaxation body	s. relaxing medium
		relaxation circuit, sweep circuit	Kippkreis m
relativistic dynamics	relativistische Dynamik f, Relativitätsdynamik f	**relaxation coefficient**	Relaxationskoeffizient m
relativistic electrodynamics	relativistische Elektrodynamik f, Relativitätselektrodynamik f	**relaxation constant**	Relaxationskonstante f
relativistic hydrodynamics	relativistische Hydrodynamik f, Relativitätshydrodynamik f	**relaxation diagram,** sweep diagram, sweep characteristic	Kippdiagramm n, Kippkennlinie f
relativistic increase, relativistic rise	relativistischer Anstieg m; relativistischer Zuwachs m	**relaxation dispersion**	s. relaxational dispersion
relativistic invariance, Lorentz invariance	Lorentz-Invarianz f	**relaxation distance**	s. relaxation length
		relaxation effect	s. relaxation phenomenon
		relaxation equation	Relaxationsgleichung f
relativistic isochronous cyclotron	s. AVF cyclotron	**relaxation freezing-in,** dynamic freezing-in	dynamisches Einfrieren n, Relaxationseinfrieren n
relativistic mass	relativistische Masse f, Impulsmasse f, Masse f der Bewegung	**relaxation frequency,** sweep frequency	Kippfrequenz f; Relaxationsfrequenz f; Sägezahnfrequenz f
relativistic mass equation	s. expression for the variation of mass with velocity		
relativistic mass increase	relativistische Massenzunahme f, relativistischer Massenzuwachs m	**relaxation function,** relaxation	Relaxationsfunktion f
relativistic mechanics, relativity mechanics	relativistische Mechanik f, Relativitätsmechanik f	**relaxation generator,** sweep generator, relaxation (sweep) oscillator, scanning generator	Kipp[schwingungs]generator m, Kippschwinger m; Kipp[schwingungs]gerät n; Kippspannungserzeuger m; Kippstromerzeuger m; Kipp[schwingungs]oszillator m
relativistic motion of perihelion	s. relativistic advance of perihelion		
relativistic neutron	relativistisches Neutron n ‹$E_{kin} > 20$ MeV›		
relativistic particle cyclotron, relativistic cyclotron	relativistisches Zyklotron n	**relaxation length,** relaxation distance ‹of radiation›	Relaxations[weg]länge f, Relaxationsstrecke f
relativistic quantum mechanics	relativistische Quantenmechanik f	**relaxation loss**	Relaxationsverlust m
		relaxation matrix	Relaxationsmatrix f
relativistic region	relativistischer Bereich m	**relaxation method** ‹math.›	Relaxationsmethode f, Korrektionsverfahren n, Korrekturverfahren n
relativistic rise	s. relativistic increase		
relativistic Schrödinger equation, Klein-Gordon equation, Fock-Klein-Gordon equation	Klein-Gordon-Gleichung f, relativistische Schrödinger-Gleichung f	**relaxation method [of Southwell]**	s. relaxation ‹math.›
		relaxation modulus	Relaxationsmodul m
relativistic thermodynamics	relativistische Thermodynamik f, Relativitätsthermodynamik f	**relaxation of deformation**	s. strain relaxation
relativistic variation of mass with velocity, variation of mass with velocity	Massenveränderlichkeit f, relativistische Massenveränderlichkeit	**relaxation of muscle,** muscular relaxation	Muskelerschlaffung f, Erschlaffung f des Muskels
relativity	Relativität f	**relaxation of strain**	s. strain relaxation
		relaxation of stress, stress relaxation	Spannungsrelaxation f
relativity	s. a. relativity theory		

relaxation oscillation, ratched oscillation	Kippschwingung *f*; Relaxationsschwingung *f*	released heat	freigesetzte Wärme *f*, erzeugte Wärme
relaxation oscillator	s. relaxation generator	release from tension	s. relaxation ‹mech.›
relaxation part	relaxierender Anteil *m*, Relaxationsanteil *m*	release into atmosphere	Auswurf *m* in die Atmosphäre
relaxation period	Kipperiode *f*; Sägezahnperiode *f*; Kippschwingungsdauer *f*	release of elastic stresses	s. elastic relaxation
relaxation phase	Erschlaffungsphase *f*	release of heat	s. heat release
relaxation phenomenon; relaxation effect	Relaxationserscheinung *f*; Kipperscheinung *f*	release of oscillations	s. excitation of oscillations
		release of radiation	s. emission
		release pulse	s. initiating pulse
		release time	s. releasing time
		release time of relay, relay release time	Relaisabfallzeit *f*, Abfallzeit *f* des Relais, Abklingzeit *f* ‹Relais›
relaxation polarization	Relaxationspolarisation *f*	releasing	s. release ‹of relay›
relaxation spectrum	Relaxationsspektrum *n*	releasing time, release time, lag of release	Auslösezeit *f*
relaxation strength	Relaxationsstärke *f*		
relaxation theory [of elasticity], theory of relaxation	Relaxationstheorie *f* [der Elastizität]	reliability; dependability [in service], use reliability, reliability of operation	Zuverlässigkeit *f*, Verläßlichkeit *f*; Betriebssicherheit *f*, Sicherheit *f* [des Betriebes]
relaxation time, natural time	Relaxationszeit *f*, Zeitkonstante *f*; Abklingzeit *f*; Einstellzeit *f*; Erholungszeit *f*		
relaxation time, time of relaxation	Kippzeit *f*	reliability, degree of reliability	Sicherheitsgrad *m*, Zuverlässigkeitsgrad *m*
		reliability engineering	Zuverlässigkeitstechnik *f* ‹Technik der Vorhersage, Kontrolle, Messung und Analyse von Versagensphänomenen›
relaxation time constant, sweep time constant	Kippzeitkonstante *f*		
relaxation time tensor	Relaxationszeittensor *m*	reliability gain	Zuverlässigkeitsgewinn *m*
		reliability of contact	Kontaktsicherheit *f*
relaxation transition	Relaxationsübergang *m*	reliability of operation	s. reliability
relaxed modulus of elasticity	s. longitudinal modulus of elasticity	relic	Relikt *n*
		relic radiation	Reliktstrahlung *f*
relaxed state of accommodation	Akkommodationsruhelage *f*	relief	Relief *n*; Betragsfläche *f*
relaxing	s. relaxation ‹mech.›		
relaxing gel, elastic sol, Lethersich body, Jeffreys body	elastisches Sol *n*, Lethersichscher (Jeffreysscher) Körper, *m*, relaxierendes Gel *n*	relief	Relief *n*, Hochbild *n*, Geländemodell *n*
		relief	s. a. relieving
		relief annealing, stress relief annealing, destrengthening annealing	Spannungsfreiglühen *n*
relaxing medium, relaxation body	relaxierendes Medium *n*, relaxierender Körper *m*, Relaxationskörper *m*		
relay amplifier	Relaisverstärker *m*	relief condenser	Reliefkondensor *m*
		relief curve	Entlastungskurve *f*
		relief effect	Reliefeffekt *m*, Reliefwirkung *f*
relay chain, relay line	Relaisstrecke *f*, Relaiskette *f*, Relaislinie *f*	relief image, matrix ‹phot.›	Reliefbild *n*, Reliefgelatinebild *n* ‹Phot.›
relay core	Relaiskern *m*		
relay group	Relaissatz *m*, Relaisgruppe *f*	relief map	Reliefkarte *f*
relay line	s. relay chain	relief telescope	Relieffernrohr *n*
relay-operated controller, indirect[-action] controller, controller with power amplification	Regler *m* mit Hilfsenergie, indirekter (indirekt wirkender, mittelbarer, mittelbar wirkender) Regler	relieving, relief; removal of the load; unloading	Entlastung *f*
		relieving of stress	s. relaxation ‹mech.›
		Rellich['s] theorem	Rellichscher Satz *m*, Satz von Rellich
relay release time	s. release time of relay	reloading	s. refueling
relay station satellite	Relaissatellit *m*	reluctance, magnetic resistance	magnetischer Widerstand *m*, Reluktanz *f*
		reluctivity	spezifischer magnetischer Widerstand *m*, reziproke Permeabilität *f*
relay-type recording instrument	s. instrument with locking device	rem	s. rem unit
relay valve	s. cold-cathode valve	remagnetization; alternating magnetization; reversal of magnetization, magnetic reversal; rotary magnetization	Ummagnetisierung *f*
relay with sequence action	Stufenrelais *n*; sequentielles Relais *n*		
release; liberation; setting free; disengagement	Freisetzung *f*; Freiwerden *n*; Auslösung *f*; Ablösung *f*; Abgabe *f*; Entbindung *f*		
		remagnetization energy (work)	s. hysteresis energy
release	Freigabe *f*	remainder, remainder term ‹math.›	Restglied *n*, Rest *m* ‹Math.›
		remaining austenite, residual austenite	Restaustenit *m*
release, drop out, releasing ‹of relay›	Abfallen *n*, Abfall *m*	remaining current	s. residual current
		remanence; after-effect, memory effect	Nachwirkung *f*, Nachwirkungseffekt *m*, Nachwirkungserscheinung *f*
release; tripping; clearing ‹el.›	Auslösung *f* ‹El.›		
		remanence, magnetic remanence; remanent (residual) magnetization, residual induction, remanent induction ‹B_r›	Remanenz *f*; remanente Magnetisierung *f*, Restmagnetisierung *f*; remanente Induktion *f*, Restinduktion *f*, Remanenzinduktion *f*, nachwirkender Teil *m* der Induktion; Remanenzwert *m*, Restmagnetismus *m*
release agent	s. abherent		
release current	Auslösestrom *m*, Auslösestromstärke *f*		
release current ‹of relay›	Abfallstrom *m* ‹Relais›		

remanence coefficient, coefficient of remanent induction, remanent induction coefficient	Nachwirkungsbeiwert m	removal of heat	s. heat removal
remanence loss, loss of remanent induction, residual loss	Nachwirkungsverlust m	removal of power, taking (extraction) of power, power extraction	Leistungsentnahme f; Leistungsentzug m
remanence point	Remanenzpunkt m	removal of the ions from the cloud chamber	Absaugen n der [störenden] Ionen aus der Nebelkammer, Ausräumen n der Ionen aus der Nebelkammer, Reinigung f der Nebelkammer von [störenden] Ionen
remanent; residual	remanent, bleibend, zurückbleibend; Rest-	removal of the load	s. relieving
remanent elongation	s. residual elongation	removal of water	s. dehydration <chem.>
remanent induction	s. remanence	removal theory	Removaltheorie f, „removal"-Theorie f, Ausscheidtheorie f
remanent induction coefficient	s. remanence coefficient	remove by transformation, eliminate by transformation	wegtransformieren
remanent magnetic field, residual [magnetic] field	remanentes Magnetfeld n, [magnetisches] Restfeld n	removing	s. removal
remanent magnetism, residual magnetism	remanenter Magnetismus m, Restmagnetismus m	removing	s. a. removal <of heat>
remanent magnetism of ships	halbflüchtiger (remanenter) Schiffsmagnetismus m	removing of dust	s. dedusting
remanent magnetization, residual magnetization	remanente Magnetisierung f	rem unit, rem; roentgen equivalent, man; rad equivalent man	Rem n, rem-Einheit f, biologisches Röntgenäquivalent n; biologisches Radäquivalent n; rem
remanent magnetization	s. a. remanence		
remanent permeability	Nachwirkungspermeabilität f	rendering astatic, astatization, astatizing	Astasierung f
remelting; refusion, repeated melting	Umschmelzen n	rendering soluble	s. conversion into a soluble form
remnants of the supernova [explosion]	s. supernova remnants	rendering visible, visualization	Sichtbarmachung f
remodulation <el.>	Ummodulation f, Modulationsübertragung f, Umsteuerung f <El.>	rendezvous, space rendezvous	Rendezvous m [im Raum], Raumrendezvous n
remote action	s. action at a distance	rendezvous-compatible orbit	s. rendezvous orbit
remote control	s. telecontrol	rendezvous maneuver	Rendezvousmanöver n
remote control	s. remote operation		
remote control engineering; remote control technique	Fernwirktechnik f	rendezvous orbit, rendezvous-compatible orbit	Rendezvousbahn f
remote handling	s. remote operation	rendezvous technique	Rendezvoustechnik f
remote handling device (equipment, tool); long-handed tool	Fernbedienungsgerät n, Fernbedienungswerkzeug n; Gerät n mit verlängertem Griff	rending	s. rupture <mech.>
		rendition of contrast, contrast rendition	Kontrastwiedergabe f
remote-indicating instrument, remote indicator	fernanzeigendes Gerät n, Gerät mit Fernanzeige, Fernanzeiger m	renewal theory	Erneuerungstheorie f
		Renner effect	Renner-Effekt m
remote instrument	s. telemeter	Renninger effect, umweganregung	Renninger-Effekt m, Umweganregung f
remote manipulation	s. remote operation	renormalizability	Renormierbarkeit f
remote manipulator	fernbedienter Greifer m, Fernmanipulator m	renormalizable theory	renormierbare Theorie f
remote measurement	s. telemetering	renormalization	Renormierung f
remote metering	s. telemetering	renormalization of charge, charge renormalization	Ladungsrenormierung f
remote operation, remote control, remote handling, remote manipulation	Fernbedienung f; Fernbetätigung f	renormalization of mass, mass renormalization	Massenrenormierung f, Renormierung f der Masse
remote radiation field	s. distant field	renormalization rule	Renormierungsregel f
remote thermometer, telethermometer, distance thermometer	Fernthermometer n	re-occupation, repopulation	Umbesetzung f
		reorganization, rearrangement, transposition, transformation <chem.>	Umlagerung f, Umgruppierung f <Chem.>
remote transfer; remote transmission; long-distance transmission	Fernübertragung f	reorientational motion of the domains	Reorientierungsbewegung f der Domänen
		reorientation energy	Reorientierungsenergie f
remous	s. swirl	reorientation of spin	s. spin flip
remous	s. a. wake	rep	s. roentgen equivalent, physical
removable singularity (singular point)	hebbare Singularität f, hebbare singuläre Stelle f		
		reparametrization	Reparametrisierung f
removal, removing, disposal	Beseitigung f, Entfernung f	repeatability	Wiederholbarkeit f
		repeatability, reproducibility	Reproduzierbarkeit f; Präzision f <Stat.>
removal, removing <of heat>	Abfuhr f, Abführung f, Abfluß m; Ableitung f; Entzug m; Entnahme f <Wärme>	repeatability coefficient	Wiederholbarkeitskoeffizient m
		repeated; multiple, manifold <math.; gen.>	mehrfach, vielfach <Math.; allg.>
removal, displacement, dislocation, shifting, shift removal	Verschiebung f, Verlagerung f <allg.> s. a. detachment <of an electron>		
		repeated dissolution, re-solution	wiederholtes Lösen n, Umlösen n; Wiederauflösung f
removal cross-section, group removal cross-section	Removalquerschnitt m, „removal"-Querschnitt m, Ausscheidquerschnitt m	repeated distillation, cohobation; redistillation	Redestillation f; Umdestillieren n; wiederholte Destillation f, mehrfache Destillation
removal of after-heat	Restwärmeabfuhr f		

repeated hardening crack, crack due to multiple hardening	Vielhärtungsriß *m*	**repetition rate**, recurrence rate	Tastgeschwindigkeit *f*
repeated load	*s.* repeated stress	**repetition rate**, check-back frequency, return question frequency	Rückfragehäufigkeit *f*
repeated-load impact test, impact endurance test	Vielschlagversuch *m*	**repetition-rate divider**, pulse-rate divider	Impulsteiler *m*, Impulsfrequenzteiler *m*
repeated-load torsional fatigue testing machine	*s.* torsion vibration testing machine	**repetition-rate division**, pulse-rate division, pulse dividing, skip keying, count-down	Impulsteilung *f*, Impulsfrequenzteilung *f*
repeated mapping	*s.* multiple mapping		
repeated melting; remelting; refusion	Umschmelzen *n*	**repetitive computer**	repetierender Rechner (Analogrechner) *m*
repeated nova, recurrent nova, permanent nova	wiederkehrende Nova *f*, periodisch wiederkehrende Nova, Novula *f* <*pl.*: Novulae>	**repetitive error**	Wiederholungsfehler *m*
		repetitive measurement	Wiederholungsmessung *f*
		repetitive pulse	*s.* recurrent pulses
repeated quenching hardenability test	Vielhärtungsversuch *m*	**Repetti discontinuity**	Repettische Diskontinuitätsfläche *f*, Repetti-Diskontinuität *f*
repeated root, multiple root	mehrfache Nullstelle *f*; mehrfache Wurzel *f*	**replaced by an isotope**, isotopically replaced (substituted), substituted by an isotope	isotopensubstituiert
repeated solidification; resolidification	Wiedererstarrung *f*, Wiederverfestigung *f*; wiederholte Erstarrung *f*		
repeated solution, multiple solution	mehrfache Lösung *f*	**replacement**, substitution	Austausch *m*, Ersatz *m*, Ersetzung *f*, Substitution *f*, Substituierung *f*
repeated stress, repeated load	Schwellbeanspruchung *f*	**replacement**, substitution <chem.>	Substitution *f* <Chem.>
		replacement, interchangeable <of a meter>	austauschbar, auswechselbar, Austausch- <Gerät>
		replacement	*s. a.* metasomatosis <geo.>
		replacement collision	Austauschstoß *m*
repeated transformation	*s.* multiple mapping		
repeated twin	*s.* polysynthetic twin <cryst.>	**replacement diagram (scheme)**, equivalent circuit (network)	Ersatz[schalt]bild *n*; Ersatzschaltung *f*; Ersatz[strom]kreis *m*
repeater; follower <el.>	Verstärker *m* <El.>	**replacement pseudomorphism**	Veränderungspseudomorphose *f*
		replacement tube; equivalent tube, equivalent valve	Ersatzröhre *f*; Austauschröhre *f*
repeater [coil], repeating coil, repeater transformer, transformer of ratio 1:1	Übertrager *m*	**replay unit**; reproducing apparatus	Wiedergabegerät *n*; Wiedergabeeinrichtung *f*
repeater compass	Tochterkompaß *m*	**replenishment of charge carriers**	*s.* carrier replenishment
		replica, surface replica	Oberflächenabdruck *m*, Abdruck *m*
repeater distance	Verstärkerfeldlänge *f*, Verstärkerabstand *m*		
repeater section	Verstärkerfeld *n*		
repeater transformer	*s.* repeater [coil]	**replica grating**	Gitterkopie *f*
repeating back	Vielfachansatz *m*	**replica method**, replica technique, surface replica method, printing method, model[l]ing	Abdruckverfahren *n*, Abdrucktechnik *f*
repeating coil	*s.* repeater [coil]		
repeating theodolite, double-centre theodolite	Repetitionstheodolit *m*, Repetiertheodolit *m*		
repellent force	*s.* repelling force	**replicated experiment (run)**, replication, parallel experiment, repetition	Parallelversuch *m*, Parallele *f*, Wiederholung *f*
repeller, ion repeller <of mass spectrometer>	Repeller *m*, Repellerplatte *f*, Ionenrepeller *m* <Massenspektrometer>		
repeller electrode	Reflektorelektrode *f*	**repolarization**	Umpolarisierung *f*; Repolarisation *f*
repelling force, force of repulsion, repulsive force, repellent force	Abstoßungskraft *f*, abstoßende Kraft *f*; Repulsivkraft *f*	**repopulation**, re-occupation	Umbesetzung *f*
		report <ac.>	Knall *m* <Ak.>
repelling force of magnet	*s.* magnetic repulsion	**reprecipitation**	Umfällung *f*
repercussion	*s.* rebound		
repetition, reiteration	Wiederholung *f*	**representation** <in terms of> <math., qu.>	Darstellung *f* <Math., Qu.>
repetition	*s.* repetition method	**representation**, mapping, map <math.>	Abbildung *f* <Math.>
repetition	*s. a.* replicated experiment		
repetition frequency [of periodic pulses], recurrence frequency [of periodic pulses], sequence repetition rate	Tastfrequenz *f*, Wiederholungsfrequenz *f* [periodischer Impulsfolgen]	**representation module (space)**, space of representation	Darstellungsmodul *m*, Darstellungsraum *m*
		representative	Repräsentant *m*; Darsteller *m* <Qu.>
		representative	repräsentativ
repetition interval	Tastintervall *n*		
		representative ensemble	repräsentative Gesamtheit *f*, repräsentatives Ensemble *n*
repetition method, method by repetition [of measurement of angles], repetition	repetitionsweise Winkelmessung *f*, Repetitionswinkelmessung *f*, Repetition *f*	**representative point**	repräsentativer Punkt *m*
repetition period, recurrence period	Wiederholungszeit *f*	**representative point**, phase point	Phasenpunkt *m*, Phasenbildpunkt *m*
repetition period	*s. a.* pulse period	**representative region**	Repräsentabilitätsbereich *m*
repetition pulse	*s.* recurrent pulses	**representative sample**	repräsentative Stichprobe *f*
repetition rate	*s.* pulse recurrence frequency	**repressor**	Repressor *m*

reprocessing, regeneration	Wiederaufarbeitung f, Aufarbeitung f, Wiederaufbereitung f; Rückvergütung f	research mass spectrometer, special purpose mass spectrometer	Massenspektrometer n für Forschungszwecke, Forschungs-Massenspektrometer n
reprocessing of irradiated fuel, fuel reprocessing	Brennstoff-Wiederaufarbeitung f, Wiederaufarbeitung f des bestrahlten Kernbrennstoffs	research of high atmosphere, altitude research	Höhenforschung f
reproducibility, repeatability	Reproduzierbarkeit f; Präzision f <Stat.>	research reactor	Forschungsreaktor m
reproducing apparatus	s. replay unit		
reproducing characteristic, playback characteristic, reproduction curve	Wiedergabecharakteristik f, Wiedergabekurve f		
reproducing head	s. pick-up <ac.>	research rocket, sounding rocket	Forschungsrakete f, Raketensonde f
reproduction	s. projecting <opt.>		
reproduction curve	s. reproducing characteristic		
reproduction equalizer	Wiedergabeentzerrer m	réseau, network [of stations] <geo.>	Stationsnetz n <Geo.>
reproduction factor	s. multiplication factor		
reproduction fidelity	s. fidelity [of reproduction]	resection	Rückwärtseinschneiden n, Rückwärtseinschnitt m
reproduction of surface features, surface reproduction	Oberflächenabbildung f	resequent river	resequenter Fluß m
		reservation, reserve, restriction	Vorbehalt m
		reserve	Reserve f
reproduction property	Reproduktionseigenschaft f, Multiplikationseigenschaft f	reserve buoyancy	Auftriebsreserve f, Hilfsauftrieb m, Hilfsschwimmkraft f
reproportionation, synproportionation	Synproportionierung f		
reptation effect	Reptationseffekt m	reserve factor, stand-by power factor	Reservefaktor m
repulse excitation, impact (shock, impulse, pulse) excitation <of oscillation>	Stoßanregung f, Stoßerregung f <Schwingung>	reserve of clock rate	Gangreserve f
		reservoir, storage reservoir, storage work	Speicher m, Wasserspeicher m; Rückhaltebecken n; Staubecken n; Stauraum m; Stausee m
repulsion	Abstoßung f; Repulsion f		
repulsion coefficient	Abstoßungskoeffizient m	reservoir	s. a. flask
		reservoir barometer	s. reservoir mercury barometer
repulsion energy	s. repulsive energy		
repulsion motor	Repulsionsmotor m	reservoir capacity	Wehrstauraum m, Speicherinhalt m, Stauvolumen n
repulsion potential	s. repulsive potential	reservoir mercury barometer, cistern barometer, reservoir (cup, bulb) barometer	Gefäßbarometer n, Gefäß-Quecksilberbarometer n
repulsion-type instrument	Repulsionsmeßgerät n, Repulsionsinstrument n, Repulsionsgerät n		
repulsive centre, centre of repulsion	abstoßendes Zentrum n, Abstoßungszentrum n	reset, resetting; set[ ]back	Rückstellung f; Rücksetzung f; Rückfall m
repulsive energy, repulsion energy	Abstoß[ungs]energie f	reset, resetting <of counter>	Löschung f, Rückstellung f <Zählwerk>
repulsive force, force of repulsion, repelling force, repellent force	Abstoßungskraft f, abstoßende Kraft f; Repulsivkraft f	reset pulse; quench pulse, quenching pulse	Löschimpuls m
repulsive force <of comet>	Repulsivkraft f <beim Kometen>	reset time, resetting time, restoring time	Rückstellzeit f
repulsive force of magnet	s. magnetic repulsion	reset time, integral action time, resetting time	Nachstellzeit f, Nachlaufzeit f, Nachgebezeit f
repulsive potential, repulsion potential	Abstoßungspotential n	resetting	s. reset
repulsive thrust	s. thrust	resetting characteristic	Rückfallkurve f
rep unit; roentgen equivalent, physical; rep	rep-Einheit f, Rep n, physikalisches Röntgenäquivalent n, rep	resetting device	Rückstellvorrichtung f, Rückstelleinrichtung f
required frequency, ideal frequency	Sollfrequenz f	resetting interval	Rückstellintervall n
required frequency	s. a. velocity rating	resetting ratio	Rückgangsverhältnis n
required position, desired position, nominal position	Sollstellung f	resetting time <of relay>	Rückfallzeit f, Rückgangszeit f, Rücklaufzeit f <Relais>
required room (volume), volume (room, space) requirement	Raumbedarf m	resetting time	s. a. reset time
		resetting to zero	s. zero adjustment
requirement	s. demand	resetting value <of relay>	Rückgangswert m, Rückfallwert m <Relais>
requirement of store locations	Speicherplatzbedarf m	reshaping of pulse	Rückformung f, Rückbildung f <Impuls>
requirements, demand	Bedarf m		
re-radiation	Wiederausstrahlung f, Wieder[ab]strahlung f	residence, presence, lingering	Verweilen n, Aufenthalt m
re[-]radiation	s. a. reflection	residence	s. a. residence time
re-radiation error	Wiederausstrahlungsfehler m	residence hclf-life	Verweilhalbwertzeit f
rerecording; dubbing, mixing <of sound>	Mischen n, Mischung f <Ton>, Tonmischung f	residence time, residence, holding time, hold-up time; detention time <e.g. in the plant>	Verweilzeit f; Aufenthaltszeit f; Durchlaufzeit f; Haltezeit f <z. B. in der Anlage>
re-reversal of solarization	negative Solarisation f		
re-run point, roll-back point	Wiederhol[ungs]punkt m		
re-run routine, roll-back routine	Wiederholungsprogramm n, Wiederholprogramm n	residence time distribution (spectrum)	Verweilzeitspektrum n, Verweilzeitverteilung f
Résal['s] theorem, theorem of Résal	Résalscher Satz m		

residual

residual; remanent	remanent, bleibend, zurückbleibend; Rest-	residual rays, reststrahlen, residual radiation	Reststrahlen *mpl*, Reststrahlbanden *fpl*, Reststrahlung *f*
residual aberration <opt.>	Restfehler *m*, Restaberration *f* <Opt.>		
residual activity	Restaktivität *f*	residual resistance <el.; hydr.>	Restwiderstand *m* <El.; Hydr.>
residual activity method, method of residual activity	Restaktivitätsmethode *f*	residual ripple	Restwelligkeit *f*
residual affinity	Restaffinität *f*	residual spectrum <math.>	Restspektrum *n*, Residualspektrum *n* <Math.>
residual air [volume]	s. residual volume <bio.>		
residual austenite, remaining (retained) austenite	Restaustenit *m*	residual strain	Restverformung *f*, Restdeformation *f*
residual block	Rumpfscholle *f*	residual stress	s. internal stress
residual bond	s. Waals bond / Van der	residual thermal radiation	Restwärmestrahlung *f*
residual central intensity	Restintensität *f* im Linienkern	residual valence	s. partial valence
residual charge	Restladung *f*, Rückstandsladung *f*	residual valency	s. partial valence
		residual variance	Restvarianz *f*
residual charge pattern [recording the image in xerography]	s. latent electric[al] image	residual voltage <el.>; discharge voltage <US> <of surge diverter> <el.>	Restspannung *f* <El.>
residual conductivity	Restleitfähigkeit *f*	residual voltage at zero field, zero-field residual voltage	Nullfeldrestspannung *f*
residual correlation	Restkorrelation *f*		
residual coupling	Restkopplung *f*		
residual crystallization	Restkristallisation *f*	residual volume, residual air volume; residual air <bio.>	Residualvolumen *n*; Residualluft *f*, Restluft *f* <Bio.>
residual current <of diode>, initial current of emission	Anlaufstrom *m*	residue	Rückstand *m*; Schlamm *m*
residual current, remaining current, capacitance current, non-faradaic current; leakage current <of electrolytic capacitor>	Reststrom *m*, nichtfaradischer Strom *m*	residue <math.>	Residuum *n* <Math.>
		residue	s. a. rest <chem.>
		residue class, residue system, coset <of ring> <math.>	Restklasse *f* <eines Rings> <Math.>
		residue[-] class field, residue field, field of residue classes	Restklassenkörper *m*
residual current law, initial current law (curve)	Anlaufstromgesetz *n*, Anlaufstromkurve *f*	residue[-] class ring, residue ring, factor ring, difference ring	Restklassenring *m*, Faktorring *m*, Differenzring *m*
residual current region, region of residual current, region of incipient flow	Anlaufgebiet *n*, Anlaufstromgebiet *n*	residue field	s. residue[-] class field
		residue heat	s. residual heat capacity
		residue of combustion, combustion residue	Verbrennungsrückstand *m*
residual depth; residual layer	Resttiefe *f*; Restschichtdicke *f*	residue of ignition	Glührückstand *m*
residual deviation	s. zero variation		
residual dislocation loop	Restversetzungsschleife *f*	residue ring	s. residue[-] class ring
		residue series	Residuenreihe *f*
residual elongation, remanent (permanent, persisting) elongation	Restdehnung *f*; bleibende Dehnung *f*	residue system	s. residue class <math.>
		residue theorem	s. Cauchy['s] residue theorem
residual error	Restfehler *m*	residue wave, term of the residue series	Residuenwelle *f*
residual field	s. remanent magnetic field		
residual-field method [of materials testing]	Stromimpulsmethode *f*	resilience	Nachgiebigkeit *f*, reziproke Steifigkeit *f*, Auslenkung / Kraft *f*; Federkraft *f*; Schnellkraft *f*
residual force	s. Waals['s] force / Van der Nachlauf *m*, Rückstandsfraktion *f* <Chem.>		
residual fraction, tail fraction, tails <chem.>		resilience	s. a. notch impact strength
		resilience per unit volume	[mittlere] spezifische Formänderungsarbeit (Formänderungsenergie) *f*, Energiedichte *f*
residual gas	Restgas *n*, Gasrest *m*		
residual gas pressure	s. residual pressure	resilient suspension	s. spring suspension
residual hardness	Resthärte *f*	resin-bond laminated fabric	s. laminate
residual head	Restgefälle *n*	resinoid	s. thermosetting resin
residual heat capacity, after-heat, residue heat <therm.>	Restwärme *f* <Therm.>	resinous electricity, negative electricity	Harzelektrizität *f*, harzelektrischer Zustand *m*, negative Elektrizität *f*
residual image	s. afterimage		
residual induction	s. remanence	resin state	Harzzustand *m*
residual interaction	Restwechselwirkung *f*	resistance, drag, frontal resistance, aerodynamic drag (resistance), resistance to air flow <aero.>	Widerstand *m* [in Richtung der Strömung], Strömungswiderstand *m*, Rücktrieb *m* <Aero.>
residual layer	s. residual depth		
residual liquid	Restschmelze *f*		
residual loss	s. remanence loss	resistance, electric[al] resistance <el.>	Widerstand *m*, elektrischer Widerstand <El.>
residual machining stress	s. internal stress		
residual magnetic field	s. remanent magnetic field	resistance, active resistance, effective alternating-current resistance, effective resistance, real resistance <el.>	[Wechselstrom-]Wirkwiderstand *m*, Gleichstromwiderstand *m*, Resistanz *f*, reeller Wechselstromwiderstand *m*, Echtwiderstand *m* <El.>
residual magnetism, remanent magnetism	remanenter Magnetismus *m*, Restmagnetismus *m*		
residual magnetization, remanent magnetization	remanente Magnetisierung *f*, Restmagnetisierung *f*		
residual magnetization	s. a. remanence		
residual pressure, residual gas pressure	Restdruck *m*	resistance, stability, resistivity <gen.>	Festigkeit *f*, Widerstandsfähigkeit *f*, Widerstand *m*, Resistenz *f*, Beständigkeit *f*; Sicherheit *f* <allg.>
residual radiation	s. residual rays		
residual range	Restreichweite *f*		
		resistance	s. a. hydraulic resistance

resistance	s. a. strength
resistance, ohmic, resistive <el.>	ohmsch, ohmisch <El.>
resistance accelerometer	Widerstandsbeschleunigungsmesser m
resistance alloy	Widerstandslegierung f
resistance amplifier, resistance-capacitance, (R-C) coupled amplifier	Widerstandsverstärker m, widerstandsgekoppelter Verstärker m, Verstärker mit RC-Kopplung, RC-Verstärker m
resistance box	Widerstandskasten m [für Meßzwecke], Widerstandssatz m
resistance box with plugs, plug resistance, plug rheostat, plug resistance box	Stöpselwiderstand m, Stöpselrheostat m, Widerstandskasten m [mit Stöpseln]
resistance branch, ohmic branch	ohmscher Zweig m, Widerstandszweig m
resistance bridge	Wirkbrücke f, Wirkwiderstandsbrücke f, Widerstandsbrücke f, Widerstandsmeßbrücke f
resistance-capacitance coupled amplifier	s. resistance amplifier
resistance-capacitance coupling, R-C coupling, resistance-capacity coupling <of thermionic valves>	Widerstandskopplung f, RC-Kopplung f, R/C-Kopplung f, Widerstands-Kondensator-Kopplung f, Widerstands-Kapazitäts-Kopplung f <Röhren>
resistance-capacitance element	s. resistance-capacitance network
resistance-capacitance high pass, R-C high pass	RC-Hochpaß m
resistance-capacitance ladder filter, R-C ladder filter	RC-Filter n, RC-Siebschaltung f
resistance-capacitance line, R-C line, Thomson line	RC-Leitung f, Thomson-Leitung f
resistance-capacitance low pass, R-C low pass	RC-Tiefpaß m
resistance-capacitance network, R-C network (section), resistance-capacitance section (element), R-C element	RC-Glied n; RC-Netzwerk n
resistance-capacitance oscillator, R-C oscillator	RC-Generator m, RC-Oszillator m
resistance-capacitance phase-angle bridge, R-C phase-angle bridge	RC-Phasenbrücke f
resistance-capacitance section	s. resistance-capacitance network
resistance-capacity coupling	s. resistance-capacitance coupling
resistance characteristic, resistive profile, resistivity profile <el.>	Widerstandskennlinie f, Widerstandsprofil n, Widerstandskurve f <El.>
resistance circuit, resistive circuit	ohmscher Kreis m
resistance coefficient <el.>	Widerstandskoeffizient m <El.>
resistance coefficient, coefficient of resistance, resistance number, friction factor, hydraulic friction factor, Darcy['s] coefficient <hydr.>	Widerstandsbeiwert m, Beiwert m des Widerstandes, Strömungswiderstandsbeiwert m, [hydraulische] Widerstandszahl f, hydraulischer Reibungskoeffizient m, Widerstandsziffer f; Rohrwiderstandsziffer f <Hydr.>
resistance collector	s. resistance commutator
resistance column	Widerstandssäule f
resistance commutator, resistance collector, resistive commutator (collector)	Widerstandsstromwender m, Widerstandskollektor m, Widerstandskommutator m
resistance controller, rheostatic controller	Widerstandsregler m; Kontroller m
resistance coupling	s. direct coupling
resistance derivative, aerodynamic derivative, partial air force	partielle Ableitung f von aerodynamischen Kräften <oder Momenten>
resistance divider	s. resistance voltage divider
resistance drag	s. parasite drag
resistance during charge, charging resistance; charging resistor	Ladewiderstand m, Aufladewiderstand m
resistance feedback	Widerstandsrückkopplung f
resistance gauge	s. resistance pressure gauge
resistance gauge	s. a. resistance strain gauge
resistance head, drag head	Widerstandshöhe f
resistance-inductance-capacitance bridge	s. universal bridge
resistance-inductance element	s. resistance-inductance network
resistance-inductance network, R-L network (section), resistance-inductance section (element), R-L element	RL-Glied n; RL-Netzwerk n
resistance-inductance phase-angle bridge, R-L phase-angle bridge	RL-Phasenbrücke f
resistance-inductance section	s. resistance-inductance network
resistance in humid state, resistance in wet state	Naßfestigkeit f
resistance instrument	Widerstandsgerät n, Widerstandsinstrument n
resistance in the cold state	s. cold resistance
resistance in the dark	s. dark resistance
resistance in wet state, resistance in humid state	Naßfestigkeit f
resistance lamp	s. barretter
resistanceless motion	widerstandsfreie Bewegung f
resistance limit	s. tensile yield strength
resistance line	Widerstandsgerade f
resistance line <mech.>	Stützlinie f <Mech.>
resistance loss	s. ohmic loss
resistance matrix <of four-terminal network>	Widerstandsmatrix f, W-Matrix f, r-Matrix f <Vierpol>
resistance net	Widerstandsnetz n
resistance noise	Widerstandsrauschen n
resistance number	s. resistance coefficient
resistance of air; aerodynamic drag (resistance), drag; air resistance, windage	Luftwiderstand m
resistance of grid circuit	s. grid resistance
resistance of materials, strength of materials	Materialfestigkeit f
resistance operator	s. impedance <el.>
resistance per unit length	Widerstandsbelag m
resistance-pressure curve	Widerstand[s]-Druck-Kurve f
resistance pressure gauge, resistance gauge	Widerstandsmanometer n
resistance pyrometer	s. resistance thermometer
resistance ratio arm	Widerstandsverhältnisarm m
resistance-reciprocal, reciprocal to the resistance	widerstandsreziprok

resistance

resistance reciprocity	Widerstandsreziprozität *f*	resistance to surge voltage, surge voltage resistance	Stoßspannungsfestigkeit *f*
resistance standard	*s.* standard resistance		
resistance star	Widerstandsstern *m*		
resistance strain gauge, resistance wire strain gauge, [wire] resistance gauge	Widerstandsdehnungsmeßstreifen *m*, Widerstandsdehnungsmesser *m*; Widerstandsklebstreifen *m*; Draht-Dehnungsmeßstreifen *m*, Drahtdehnungsmesser *m*	resistance to switching [operations]	*s.* switching resistance
		resistance to tearing	*s.* tensile strength
		resistance to torsion	*s.* torsional strength
		resistance to torsional vibration	*s.* torsional endurance strength at alternating load
resistance temperature coefficient, temperature coefficient of resistance	Temperaturkoeffizient *m* des [elektrischen] Widerstandes, linearer Temperaturkoeffizient des [elektrischen] Widerstands, Widerstands-Temperaturkoeffizient *m*, Widerstandstemperaturbeiwert *m*	resistance to twist[ing]	*s.* torsional strength
		resistance to vibration[s]	*s.* vibration resistance
		resistance to vibrations	*s.* dynamic strength
		resistance to wear	*s.* wear resistance
		resistance transducer, variable-resistance transducer, resistance transformer	Widerstandsgeber *m*, Widerstandsumformer *m*, Widerstandssender *m*; Drahtwiderstandsgeber *m*, Drahtwiderstandsumformer *m*
resistance thermometer, resistance pyrometer, thermometer resistor	Widerstandsthermometer *n*, elektrisches Thermometer *n* (Widerstandsthermometer), Widerstandspyrometer *n*	resistance transformation, impedance transformation	Widerstandswandlung *f*, Widerstandstransformation *f*; Widerstandsumformung *f*, Widerstandsumwandlung *f*, Widerstandsübersetzung *f*
resistance thermometer of phosphor-bronze, phosphor-bronze thermometer	Widerstandsthermometer *n* aus Phosphorbronze *f*, Phosphorbronzethermometer *n*		
		resistance transformer	*s.* resistance transducer
resistance thermometry	Widerstandsthermometrie *f*	resistance-type mercury barograph	Quecksilberwiderstandsbarograph *m*
resistance to abrasion	*s.* wear resistance	resistance-type pressure pick-up	Widerstandsdruckgeber *m*
resistance to air flow	*s.* resistance <aero.>		
resistance to alternating current	Wechselstromfestigkeit *f*	resistance vacuummeter	Widerstandsvakuummeter *n*, Widerstandsvakuummesser *m*
resistance to arc, arc resistance	Lichtbogenfestigkeit *f*, Lichtbogensicherheit *f*	resistance voltage divider, resistance divider	ohmscher Spannungsteiler *m*
resistance to bending [strain]	*s.* bending strength		
resistance to bending [strain]	*s. a.* resistance to flexure		
resistance to buckling, cross breaking strength, buckling strength	Knickfestigkeit *f*		
resistance to climatic changes	Klimabeständigkeit *f*	resistance wave	Widerstandswelle *f*
		resistance winding	Widerstandswicklung *f*; ohmsche Wicklung *f*
resistance to cold, cold resistance; cold hardiness <bio.>	Kältefestigkeit *f*, Kältebeständigkeit *f*; Kälteresistenz *f* <Bio.>	resistance wire	Widerstandsdraht *m*
resistance to compression	*s.* compressive strength	resistance wire strain gauge	*s.* resistance strain gauge
resistance to contraction, resistance to shrinking	Schrumpffestigkeit *f*	resistant; resistive	fest, resistent, widerstandsfähig, beständig
resistance to corrosion	*s.* corrosion resistance		
resistance to creep	*s.* limiting creep stress		
resistance to deformation, deformation resistance	Umform[ungs]widerstand *m*, Verformungswiderstand *m*; Formänderungswiderstand *m*	resistant group	resistente Gruppe *f*
		resistant to atmospheric conditions (corrosion)	*s.* weatherproof
		resistant to fire	*s.* fire-resistant
resistance to diffusion	*s.* diffusion resistance <bio.>	resistant to heat	*s.* fire-resistant
		resistant to heat	*s.* heat-proof
resistance to displacement, displacement resistance	Verschiebungswiderstand *m*	resistant to overvoltage, overvoltage-proof, self-protecting	überspannungsfest, überspannungssicher
resistance to elongation	*s.* tensile yield strength		
resistance to flexure, resistance to bending [strain[	Biegungswiderstand *m*, Biegewiderstand *m*	resistant to swelling	quellbeständig, quellfest
		resistant to tropic climate	*s.* tropicalized
resistance to flow	*s.* hydraulic resistance <hydr.>	resistant to twist[ing], torsion-resistant	torsionsfest, verdrehfest, verdrehungsfest
resistance to glow	Glimmfestigkeit *f*	resistant to weathering	*s.* weatherproof
resistance to heat	*s.* heat resistance	resisting moment (torque)	*s.* section modulus
resistance to heat cracking	Warmrißbeständigkeit *f*, Wärmerißbeständigkeit *f*	resistive, ohmic, resistance <el.>	ohmsch, ohmisch <El.>
resistance to impact	*s.* impact strength	resistive	*s. a.* resistant
resistance to liquid flow	*s.* hydraulic resistance	resistive arm [of the bridge]	Widerstandsarm *m* [der Brücke]
resistance to low temperature	Tieftemperaturbeständigkeit *f*, Tieftemperaturfestigkeit *f*	resistive circuit	*s.* resistance circuit
		resistive collector (commutator)	*s.* resistance commutator
resistance to oscillations	*s.* dynamic strength		
resistance to radiation	*s.* radioresistance	resistive component, active (ohmic) component	Wirkstromkomponente *f*, ohmsche Komponente *f*
resistance to rupture	*s.* tensile strength		
resistance to shaking	*s.* vibration resistance		
resistance to shear[ing]	*s.* shear strength	resistive coupling	*s.* resistance coupling <of circuit>
resistance to shock	*s.* impact strength		
resistance to shrinking	*s.* resistance to contraction	resistive drop	*s.* ohmic drop
resistance to sliding (slip), sliding resistance	Gleitwiderstand *m*	resistive drop in potential	*s.* ohmic drop
		resistive drop of voltage	*s.* ohmic drop
resistance to spreading	*s.* diffusion resistance	resistive element	Widerstandselement *n*
resistance to stretching	*s.* tensile yield strength		

resistive film, resistive layer	Widerstandsschicht f, Widerstandsfilm m	**resolvent**	Resolvente f
		resolvent kernel	lösender Kern m, Resolvente f <Integralgleichung>
		resolvent set	Resolventenmenge f
resistive force, friction[al] force, force of friction <mech.>	Reibungskraft f; Inhärenzkraft f <Mech.>	**resolver**	s. peptizing agent
		resolving	s. resolution <of the vector into its components>
resistive heating	s. ohmic heating	**resolving limit**	s. resolution limit
resistive instability	Instabilität f bei Anwesenheit eines Stromes, stromkonvektive Instabilität	**resolving of binary star**, detachment of binary	Auflösung f (Trennung f der Komponenten) des Doppelsterns
resistive layer	s. resistive film	**resolving power**; resolution, definition	Auflösungsvermögen n; Auflösung f
resistive load	s. active load		
resistive load reaction, active load reaction	Wirklastrückwirkung f, Wirklaststoß m		
resistive loss	Wirkverlust m, Wirkabfall m; Wirkarbeitsverlust m, Wirkleistungsverlust m	**resolving power**, chromatic resolving power <of grating>	Auflösungsvermögen n, Auflösungskraft, Trennschärfe f <Beugungsgitter>
resistive polarization	s. ohmic overpotential	**resolving power in depth**, depth resolving power; resolution in depth, depth resolution	Tiefenauflösungsvermögen n; Tiefenauflösung f
resistive profile	s. resistivity profile <el.>		
resistive transition	Widerstandsübergang m		
resistive variable	ohmsche Variable f		
resistivity, volume resistivity, specific resistance (resistivity), unit resistance	spezifischer [elektrischer] Widerstand m	**resolving power of coincidence system**, coincidence resolving power	Koinzidenzauflösungsvermögen n, Auflösungsvermögen n des Koinzidenzsystems
resistivity, resistance, stability <gen.>	Festigkeit f, Widerstandsfähigkeit f, Widerstand m, Resistenz f, Beständigkeit f; Sicherheit f <allg.>	**resolving time**, resolution time	Auflösungszeit f
		resolving time correction, dead time correction	Totzeitkorrektion f
resistivity coefficient for tension	s. tension coefficient of resistivity	**resonance**, point of resonance, resonance point	Resonanzstelle f, Resonanzpunkt m, Resonanz f
resistivity profile, resistance characteristic, resistive profile <el.>	Widerstandskennlinie f, Widerstandsprofil n, Widerstandskurve f <El.>	**resonance**, resonance state <of fundamental particles>	Resonanz f, Resonanzzustand m, Resonanzteilchen n <Elementarteilchen>
resistor	Widerstand m, Widerstandsgerät n <Bauteil>	**resonance**, mesomerism, structural resonance <chem.>	Mesomerie f, Strukturresonanz f, Resonanz f <Chem.>
resistor block	Widerstandsblock m	**resonance**	s. a. resonant vibration
resistor matrix	Widerstandsmatrix f	**resonance absorber**	Resonanzabsorber m
		resonance absorption, resonant absorption	Resonanzabsorption f
resistor-quenched counter circuit	Zählrohrlöschschaltung f mit [hohem] Außenwiderstand	**resonance absorption cross-section**, cross-section for resonance absorption	Resonanzabsorptionsquerschnitt m, Wirkungsquerschnitt m für (der) Resonanzabsorption, Resonanzabsorptions-Wirkungsquerschnitt m
resistor with high positive coefficient of temperature, cold conductor	Kaltleiter m		
resistron	Resistron n	**resonance absorption energy**	Resonanzabsorptionsenergie f
resnatron	Resnatron n, Resnotron n	**resonance absorption integral**	Resonanzintegral n der Absorption, Resonanzabsorptionsintegral n
resolidification; repeated solidification	Wiedererstarrung f, Wiederverfestigung f; wiederholte Erstarrung f		
resoluble	wiederlöslich, resolubel	**resonance absorption spectrum**	Resonanzabsorptionsspektrum n
resolution, resolving, decomposition, vector resolution <of the vector into its components>	Zerlegung f <des Vektors in seine Komponenten>, Komponentenzerlegung f	**resonance acceleration**	Resonanzbeschleunigung f
		resonance accelerator	Resonanzbeschleuniger m
		resonance activation	Resonanzaktivierung f
resolution <chromatography>	Trennschärfe f, Auflösung f, Trenngüte f, Resolution f <Chromatographie>	**resonance activation cross-section**, cross-section for resonance activation	Resonanzaktivierungsquerschnitt m, Wirkungsquerschnitt m für (der) Resonanzaktivierung, Resonanzaktivierungs-Wirkungsquerschnitt m
re-solution, repeated dissolution	wiederholtes Lösen n, Umlösen n; Wiederauflösung f		
resolution	s. a. resolving power	**resonance activation integral**	Resonanzintegral m der Aktivierung, Resonanzaktivierungsintegral n
resolution function	Auflösungsfunktion f		
resolution in depth	s. resolving power in depth	**resonance amplifier**, tuned amplifier	abgestimmter Verstärker m, selektiver Spannungsverstärker m, Resonanzverstärker m
resolution limit, limit of resolution	Auflösungsgrenze f		
resolution of force[s], decomposition of force[s]	Zerlegung f der Kraft, Kraftzerlegung f; Kräftezerlegung f	**resonance amplitude**	Resonanzamplitude f
		resonance band	s. resonance region
resolution of the edges	s. edge acuity	**resonance box**	s. resonant cavity
resolution sensitivity	Auflösungsempfindlichkeit f	**resonance bridge**	s. distortion bridge
		resonance broadening, self-broadening	Resonanzverbreiterung f, Kopplungsverbreiterung f, Selbstverbreiterung f
resolution time, resolving time	Auflösungszeit f		
resolvability, solvability, solubility <math.>	Lösbarkeit f; Auflösbarkeit f <Math.>	**resonance capacitor transformer**	kapazitiver Spannungswandler m in Resonanzschaltung
resolvability, separability, separableness <opt.; math.>	Auflösbarkeit f, Trennbarkeit f <Opt.; Math.>		
		resonance capture	Resonanzeinfang m
		resonance capture cross-section	s. resonance cross-section
resolved binary; detached binary	getrennter Doppelstern m, getrenntes System n; aufgelöster Doppelstern	**resonance capture integral**	Resonanzintegral n des Einfangs, Resonanzeinfangintegral n

resonance

resonance catastrophe	Resonanzkatastrophe *f*
resonance cavity	s. resonant cavity
resonance chamber	s. resonant cavity
resonance chamber	s. a. cavity resonator
resonance circuit, resonant (resonating) circuit	Resonanz[strom]kreis *m*
resonance condition	Resonanzbedingung *f*
resonance conductance	Resonanzleitwert *m*
resonance correction	Resonanzentzerrung *f*
resonance covibration	s. resonant vibration
resonance criterion	Resonanzkriterium *n*
resonance cross-section, resonance capture cross-section, cross-section for resonance capture	Resonanzeinfangquerschnitt *m*, Wirkungsquerschnitt *m* für Resonanzeinfang, Resonanzeinfang-Wirkungsquerschnitt *m*
resonance curve	Resonanzkurve *f*
resonance detector	Resonanzdetektor *m*
resonance doublet	Resonanzdublett *n*
resonance effect, resonance phenomenon, R. effect	Resonanzerscheinung *f*, Resonanzeffekt *m*
resonance electron	Resonanzelektron *n*
resonance energy; resonance stabilization energy	Resonanzenergie *f*
resonance energy <chem.>	Mesomerieenergie *f*, Resonanzenergie *f* <Chem.>
resonance escape	Vermeiden *n* des Resonanzeinfangs, Resonanzflucht *f*
resonance escape probability	Bremsnutzung *f*, Resonanzdurchlaßwahrscheinlichkeit *f*, Durchlaßwahrscheinlichkeit *f*, Resonanzentkommwahrscheinlichkeit *f*, Resonanzfluchtfaktor *m*, Bremsnutzfaktor *m*
resonance exchange of charge	Resonanzumladung *f*
resonance excitation	Resonanzanregung *f*
resonance fatigue testing	Resonanzschwingprüfung *f*, Resonanzschwingversuch *m*, Resonanz-Dauerschwingprüfung *f*
resonance field	Resonanzfeld *n*
resonance fission	Resonanzspaltung *f*
resonance fission integral	Resonanzintegral *n* der Spaltung, Resonanzspaltungsintegral *n*
resonance fluorescence; resonance radiation, resonant radiation	Resonanzfluoreszenz *f*; Resonanzstrahlung *f*, Resonanzleuchten *n*, Resonanzlicht *n*; Linienresonanz *f*
resonance flux	Resonanzfluß *m*, Resonanzneutronenfluß *m*
resonance foil	Resonanzsonde *f*
resonance frequency, resonant frequency	Resonanzfrequenz *f*
resonance frequency meter; resonance wave[-]meter	Resonanzwellenmesser *m*; Resonanzfrequenzmesser *m*, Phasensprungfrequenzmesser *m*
resonance heating	Resonanzaufheizung *f*
resonance hybride	Resonanzhybrid *m*
resonance indicator	Resonanzanzeiger *m*, Resonanzröhre *f*
resonance induction	Resonanzinduktion *f*
resonance in ferrimagnetic materials, ferrimagnetic resonance	ferrimagnetische Resonanz *f*
resonance instrument, resonance-type instrument	Resonanzgerät *n*, Resonanzmeßgerät *n*, Resonanzmesser *m*, Resonanzinstrument *n*
resonance integral, nuclear resonance integral	[gewöhnliches] Resonanzintegral *n*, Resonanzintegral *n* für unendliche Verdünnung
resonance interaction	Resonanzwechselwirkung *f*
resonance isolator, resonant isolator	Resonanzisolator *m*
resonance lamp, resonance valve	Resonanzlampe *f*
resonance level	Resonanzniveau *n*
resonance line <opt.>	Resonanzlinie *f* <Opt.>
resonance line	s. a. resonance peak
resonance loss	Resonanzverlust *m*
resonance magnetometer	Resonanzmagnetometer *n*
resonance method	s. valence bond theory <chem.>
resonance moment	Resonanzmoment *n*
resonance neutron	Resonanzneutron *n*
resonance overlap	Resonanzüberlagerung *f*, Überdeckung *f* der Resonanzniveaus
resonance overvoltage	Resonanzüberspannung *f*
resonance parameter	Resonanzparameter *m*
resonance passage	s. resonance penetration
resonance peak, resonance line	Resonanzpeak *m*, Resonanzspitze *f*, Resonanzmaximum *n*, Resonanzlinie *f*
resonance penetration, resonance passage	durch Resonanz ermöglichtes Eindringen *n* [in den Kern], Resonanzdurchgang *m*
resonance phenomenon, resonance effect, R. effect	Resonanzerscheinung *f*, Resonanzeffekt *m*
resonance photon	Resonanzphoton *n*
resonance point, point of resonance, resonance	Resonanzstelle *f*, Resonanzpunkt *m*, Resonanz *f*
resonance potential, first critical potential	Resonanzpotential *n*, erstes kritisches Potential *n*, Resonanzspannung *f*
resonance proton	Resonanzproton *n*
resonance quenching	Resonanzlöschung *f*
resonance radiation	s. resonance fluorescence
resonance radiation capture (trapping)	s. imprisonment of resonance radiation
resonance Raman effect	Resonanz-Raman-Effekt *m*
resonance ratio, peak value of magnification	Resonanzüberhöhung *f* der Amplitude
resonance reactor	Resonanzneutronenreaktor *m*, Resonanzreaktor *m*
resonance region; resonance band	Resonanzbereich *m*, Resonanzgebiet *n*; Resonanzband *n*
resonance relay	s. vibrating relay
resonance resistance	Resonanzwiderstand *m*
resonance scattering, nuclear resonance scattering, resonant scattering, nuclear resonant scattering, internal scattering; compound-elastic scattering, elastic scattering with formation of compound nucleus	Resonanzstreuung *f*, Kernresonanzstreuung *f*, innere Streuung *f*; compoundelastische Streuung (Resonanzstreuung), [elastische] Zwischenkernstreuung *f*, elastische Streuung über den Compoundkern, elastische Streuung über das Compoundkernstadium, elastische Streuung mit Zwischenkernbildung
resonance scattering cross-section, nuclear resonance scattering cross-section, cross-section for resonance scattering	Resonanzstreuquerschnitt *m*, Wirkungsquerschnitt *m* für (der) Resonanzstreuung
resonance scattering integral	Resonanzintegral *n* der Streuung, Resonanzstreuintegral *n*
resonance series	Resonanzserie *f*
resonance shape	Resonanzkurvenform *f*
resonance sharpness, sharpness of resonance	Resonanzschärfe *f*, Schärfe *f* der Resonanz

resonance sharpness, Resonanzschärfe f,
sharpness of resonance, Resonanzüberhöhung f,
sharpness of tuning, reziproke Dämpfung f,
magnification factor, Güte f des Schwing-
selectivity of [the] kreises <El.>
resonance <el.>

resonance sieve Resonanzsieb n

resonance spectrum Resonanz[en]spektrum n
resonance stabilization Resonanzenergie f
energy; resonance
energy
resonance state, resonance Resonanzzustand m,
<of fundamental Resonanz f <Elementar-
particles> teilchen>, Resonanz-
teilchen n
resonance structure, Resonanzstruktur f
resonant (resonating)
structure
resonance theory s. valence bond theory
<chem.>
resonance theory s. Helmholtz['] place
[of Helmholtz] theory
resonance tone, resonant Resonanzton m
tone
resonance transfer Resonanzübertragung f
[der Anregung]
resonance transfer Resonanzübertragungs-
collision stoß m
resonance transfer Resonanzübertragungs-
theory [of theorie f [der Sensibi-
sensitization] lisierung]
resonance-type s. resonance instrument
instrument
resonance valve, Resonanzlampe f
resonance lamp
resonance velocity Resonanzgeschwindigkeit f
resonance vibration s. resonant vibration
resonance voltage s. resonant voltage
resonance wave Resonanzwelle f
resonance wavelength Resonanzwellenlänge f

resonance wave[-] Resonanzwellenmesser m;
meter; resonance Resonanzfrequenz-
frequency meter messer m, Phasensprung-
frequenzmesser m

resonance width s. resonant width
resonance yield, yield of Resonanzausbeute f,
resonance radiation Resonanzfluoreszenzaus-
beute f, Resonanz-
strahlungsausbeute f
resonant absorption s. resonance absorption
resonant absorption Resonanzabsorption f nach
following Coulomb Coulomb-Anregung
excitation, RACE
resonant angular Resonanzkreisfrequenz f
frequency
resonant cavity, Resonanzhohlraum m,
resonance cavity, cavity, Resonanzkammer f,
cavity resonator, Resonanzkörper m,
resonator, resonance Resonanzkasten m,
chamber (box) resonierender Hohlraum
m, Resonator[raum] m
resonant cavity, coaxial Topfkreis m, Topf-
resonant cavity resonator m, Topf m;
Schwingkammer f,
Schwingtopf m <Mehr-
kreistriftröhre>
resonant cavity fre- s. cavity wavemeter
quency meter
resonant-cavity maser Hohlraummaser[ver-
[amplifier], cavity stärker] m, Resonator-
maser, resonator maser maser m, Resonator-
amplifier quantenverstärker m

resonant-cavity para- parametrischer Verstärker
metric amplifier, m mit Hohlraumre-
cavity-type parametric sonator
amplifier

resonant cavity tube Hohlraumresonatorröhre f
resonant cavity s. cavity wavemeter
wavemeter
resonant circuit, Resonanz[strom]kreis m
resonance (resonating)
circuit
resonant circuit with Leitungskreis m, Lecher-
distributed param- Kreis m, Resonanzkreis
eters, distributed m mit verteilten Para-
resonant circuit, Lecher metern
circuit

resonant covibration s. resonant vibration
resonant diaphragm s. resonant iris
resonant feeder abgestimmte Speiseleitung f

resonant frequency, Resonanzfrequenz f
resonance frequency
resonant iris s. resonant window
resonant isolator s. resonance isolator
resonant jet s. pulse jet
resonant length Resonanzlänge f
resonant line <el.> Resonanzleitung f <El.>

resonant mode, Resonatormode f, Resona-
resonator mode torschwingung f,
Resonatorwelle f
resonant motion Resonanzbewegung f
resonant radiation s. resonance fluorescence
resonant rise <of Aufschaukelung f
oscillation> <Schwingung>

resonant scattering s. resonance scattering
resonant shunt Resonanznebenschluß m
resonant structure s. resonance structure
resonant system Resonanzsystem n; Mit-
schwingungssystem n
resonant tone, resonance Resonanzton m
tone
resonant transformer, Resonanztransformator m,
tuned transformer abgestimmter Transformator m
resonant vibration, Resonanzschwingung f,
resonance vibration, Resonanz f; Mit-
resonance, covibration, schwingung f; Reso-
resonance (resonant) co- nanzerschütterung f;
vibration Mittönen n
resonant voltage, Resonanzspannung f
resonance voltage

resonant width s. resonance width
resonant window, Resonanzblende f
resonant iris (diaphragm)
resonate resonieren; mitschwingen
resonating circuit s. resonant circuit
resonating structure s. resonance structure
resonator s. resonant cavity
resonator s. a. cavity resonator
resonator magnetron s. magnetron
resonator maser s. resonant-cavity maser
amplifier
resonator mode s. resonant mode
resonator theory s. Helmholtz['] place
theory <of hearing>
resonon, Fermi resonance Fermi-Resonanz f,
Resonon n

resonoscope Resonoskop n
resorption Resorption f, Aufsaugen n,
Aufnahme f

resorptivity Resorptionsvermögen n;
Resorptionsfähigkeit f;
Resorbierbarkeit f
resounding s. echo
respiration Atmung f, Respiration f
respiration inhibitor Atmungsinhibitor m,
Atmungsgift n, Atem-
gift n
respiratory quotient respiratorischer Quotient m,
Atmungsquotient m, RQ
responding speed s. responsiveness <meas.>
response, actuation Ansprechen n

response Antwort f, Reaktion f;
Wirkung f

response, response curve Ganglinie f; Gangkurve f

response, pick up Ansprechen n; Anziehen n
<of relay> <Relais>

response <bio.> Reizantwort f <Bio.>
response, sensitivity Empfindlichkeitsüber-
<electro-acoustics> tragungsfaktor m
<Elektroakustik>
response s. a. response curve <el.>
response s. a. behaviour
response s. a. counter efficiency
response s. a. frequency response
response curve Wirkungskurve f

response curve, response <in the pass-band> <el.>	Durchlaßkurve f <El.>	restitution from aerial photographs, plotting from aerial photographs; interpretation of aerial photographs	Luftbildauswertung f; Luftbildinterpretation f
response curve	s. a. response		
response curve	s. a. sensitivity curve	restitution nucleus <bio.>	Restitutionskern m <Bio.>
response function	s. contrast transmission function	restitutive force	s. restoring force
response limit	s. threshold of sensitivity	rest[-] mass, proper mass, mass at rest	Ruhemasse f, Ruhmasse f
response of the counter	s. counter efficiency	rest mass density, rest density	Ruh[e]massendichte f, Ruh[e]dichte f; Kesseldichte f, Gesamtdichte f <Gasströmung>
response surface <bio.; stat.>	Wirkungsfläche f <Bio.; Stat.>		
response threshold	s. threshold of sensitivity		
response time; actuation time	Ansprechzeit f	restoration	s. recovery
		restoration coefficient	s. restitution coefficient
response time; reaction time, time of the onset of the excitation <bio.>	Reaktionszeit f	restoration constant, control constant	Rückstellungskonstante f
		restoration time	Wiederherstellungszeit f
response time	s. a. sluggishness	restoring force, reaction force, directing force, directive force, directional force, elastic constant, versorial force, re-establishing (restitutive) force, restoring force coefficient <mech.>	Richtgröße f, Direktionskraft f, Richtkraft f, Rückstellkraft f, Richtvermögen n, Steifigkeit f <Mech.>
response time to within 5%	95%-Zeit f		
response to current	Stromübertragungsfaktor m, Strömungsübertragungsfaktor m		
response to power, power transfer factor	Leistungsübertragungsfaktor m		
response to the derivative	s. rate action		
response to voltage <transducer>; voltage transformation factor	Spannungsübertragungsmaß n; Spannungsübertragungsfaktor m <elektroakustischer Wandler>	restoring force / without	richtkraftfrei, richtkraftlos
		restoring force coefficient	s. restoring force
		restoring moment	s. restoring torque
		restoring moment	s. a. righting moment
		restoring time, reset time, resetting time	Rückstellzeit f
response vector locus	s. transfer locus		
responsiveness; responsivity, speed of response, mobility resistance, responding speed, rapidity of action <meas.>	Reaktionsfähigkeit f, Ansprechgeschwindigkeit f <Meß.>	restoring torque, restoring (directing) moment <meas.>	Richtmoment n, Rückstellmoment n, Rückstellung f, Rückführ[ungs]moment n, Winkelrichtgröße f, Direktionsmoment n, Richtgröße f, Drehstarre f, Richtkraft f, Direktionskraft f, Rückdrehmoment n <Meß.>
responsiveness, responsivity	s. a. sensitivity <of instrument, organ>		
rest; residue; group <chem.>	Rest m; Gruppe f <Chem.>	rest point	Ruhepunkt m
rest	s. a. radical <math.; chem.>		
rest	s. a support	rest position, off-position <e.g. of relay>	Ruhestellung f, „Aus"-Stellung f <z. B. Relais>
rest / at, non-moving, motionless, fixed	in Ruhe, ruhend, fest, bewegungslos, unbewegt		
		rest position	s. a. position of rest
restandardization	s. recalibration	rest potential	s. resting potential
rest charge density, rest density of charge	Ruhladungsdichte f, Ruheladungsdichte f, Ruhdichte (Ruhedichte) f der Ladung	restraining <phot.>	Verzögerung f, Hemmung f, Entwicklungsverzögerung f <Phot.>
		restraining bath, retardation bath	Verzögerungsbad n
rest contact, resting (break) contact, break, normal contact; normally closed contact, normally closed interlock <US>, N.C. contact	Ruhekontakt m, Öffnungskontakt m, Öffner m	restraining condition	s. constraint <mech.>
		restraining force	s. reaction <mech.>
		restraint	s. restriction
		restraint force	s. reaction <mech.>
rest current	s. resting current	restricted Bayes['] solution	eingeschränkte Bayessche Lösung f
rest density	s. rest mass density		
rest density of charge	s. rest charge density	restricted cosmological principle	eingeschränktes kosmologisches Prinzip n
rest energy	Ruhenergie f, Ruheenergie f		
rest energy operator, operator of rest energy	Ruhenergieoperator m, Ruheenergieoperator m	restricted diffusion chromatography	s. gel chromatography
		restricted linear collision stopping power	s. linear energy transfer
rest frame, reference system at rest	ruhendes Bezugssystem n, Ruhsystem n, Ruhesystem n	restricted motion	unfreie (gebundene, eingeschränkte) Bewegung f
restimulation, reversal of tonus	Stimmungsänderung f, Umstimmung f; Verstimmung f	restricted problem, restricted three body problem	eingeschränktes Dreikörperproblem n, „problème restreint" n, restringiertes (asteroidisches) Dreikörperproblem, eingeschränktes (restringiertes) Problem n Poincarés
resting contact	s. rest contact		
resting current; closed-circuit current, rest (static, quiescent) current	Ruhestrom m		
resting potential, rest (no-signal) potential <bio.>	Ruhepotential n, Ruhespannung f, Bestandpotential n <Bio.>	restricted solubility	beschränkte Löslichkeit f
		restricted theory of relativity	s. special relativity
resting stage	Ruhestadium n	restricted three body problem	s. restricted problem
resting stage nucleus, quiescent nucleus <bio.>	Ruhekern m <Bio.>		
		restriction, limitation, restraint	Einschränkung f, Beschränkung f, Begrenzung f
rest injury potential, injury potential at rest	Verletzungsruhepotential n		
restitution apparatus	s. aerocartograph	restriction	s. a. constraint <mech.>
restitution coefficient, coefficient of restitution, restoration coefficient, impact coefficient, collision coefficient <mech.>	Wiederherstellungskoeffizient m, Restitutionskoeffizient m, Rückkehrkoeffizient m, Stoßkoeffizient m, Stoßzahl f, Kollisionszahl f, Stoßbeiwert m <Mech.>	restriction	s. a. reservation
		restriction of free rotation, restriction of internal rotation	Rotationsbehinderung f, Rotationshinderung f, Rotationshemmung f
		restrictor	s. throat <of flow>
		restriking voltage, reignition voltage	Wiederzündspannung f
		restriking voltage	s. a. transient voltage
		reststrahlen	s. residual rays

reststrahlen energy	Reststrahlenenergie f, Reststrahlenergie f	retarded echo, delayed echo	Nachecho n
reststrahlen frequency	Reststrahlenfrequenz f, Reststrahlfrequenz f	retarded elasticity	s. delayed elasticity
reststrahlen method, method of residual rays	Reststrahlenmethode f [von Rubens], Reststrahlmethode f	retarded field	retardiertes Feld n
		retarded field triode	s. retarding field tube
rest temperature, temperature at rest	Ruhetemperatur f	retarded Green function, retarded propagation function	retardierte Greensche Funktion f, retardierte Ausbreitungsfunktion f
resublimation	Umsublimieren n, Umsublimation f; Resublimation f, Bidestillation f	retarded motion	verzögerte Bewegung f
		retarded potential	retardiertes Potential n
resultant, eliminant <math.>	Resultierende f, Resultante f <Math.>	retarded propagation function	s. retarded Green function
resultant, net force, resultant force <mech.>	resultierende Kraft f, Resultierende f, Resultante f <Mech.>	retarded solution	retardierte Lösung f
		retarded time	retardierte Zeit f
		retarded wave	retardierte Welle f
resultant	s. a. convolution integral	retarder	s. inhibitor <chem.>
resultant acceleration, net acceleration	Gesamtbeschleunigung f, resultierende Beschleunigung f	retarding electrode	s. decelerating electrode
		retarding field	Bremsfeld n, Verzögerungsfeld n
resultant damping, net damping; total damping	Gesamtdämpfung f; resultierende Dämpfung f	retarding field oscillations	s. Barkhausen-Kurz oscillations
resultant force	s. resultant <mech.>	retarding-field oscillator, positive-grid oscillator, Barkhausen[-Kurz] oscillator; Barkhausen-Kurz oscillator circuit, retardation field circuit [scheme]	Bremsfeldgenerator m; Barkhausen-Kurz-Schaltung f, Bremsfeldschaltung f
resultant magnetic field, resulting (compound, net) magnetic field	resultierendes Magnetfeld n, Gesamtmagnetfeld n, zusammengesetztes Magnetfeld		
resultant moment of momentum, total angular momentum	Gesamtdrehimpuls m		
resultant motion, compound motion	resultierende Bewegung f	retarding field potential	Bremsfeldspannung f
resultant torque	s. resulting torque	retarding field tube, brake-field tube, retarded field triode	Bremsfeldröhre f, Barkhausen-Kurz-Röhre f
resultant vector, single vector, sum of the system of vectors	Einzelvektor m, resultierender Einzelvektor		
		retarding force	Bremskraft f
resultant velocity, net velocity	resultierende Geschwindigkeit f	retarding lens, stopping lens	Verzögerungslinse f
resulting aerodynamic force, total aerodynamic force	aerodynamische Resultante f, resultierende aerodynamische Kraft f	retarding moment	Verzögerungsmoment n
		retarding parachute, deceleration parachute	Bremsfallschirm m
resulting magnetic field	s. resultant magnetic field	retarding potential, stopping (retardation) potential	Bremspotential n, Bremsspannung f; Verzögerungspotential n
resulting sound	resultierender Ton m		
resulting torque, resultant torque, net torque	Gesamtdrehmoment n, resultierendes Drehmoment n		
		retarding potential method	s. Lenard['s] method of opposing field
result measured	s. result of measurement		
result of measurement, measurement (measured) result, result measured, test result; experimental result	Meßergebnis n, Meßresultat n; Versuchsergebnis n	retarding torque, braking moment, brake torque	Bremsmoment n
		retentate	Retentat n
		retention, hold-back, hold-up	Zurückhaltung f, Retention f
resymmetrization	Umsymmetrierung f	retention <quantity>	Retention f, Rückhaltegrad m <Größe>
retained austenite	s. residual austenite		
retaining dam (dike)	s. dam <hydr.>	retention analysis	Retentionsanalyse f
retardant	s. inhibitor <chem.>	retention band	Retentionsband n
retardation	Retardierung f; Retardation f <Bio.>	retention coefficient, initial body retention <bio.>	Retentionsfaktor m <Bio.>
retardation	s. a. braking <mech.>	retention factor, R_f value, R_f	R_f-Wert m, R_f, Verzögerungsfaktor m
retardation	s. a. deceleration <mech.>		
retardation	s. a. difference of path <of rays>		
retardation	s. a. time lag	retention index, Kovats index, RI	Retentionsindex m [nach Kovats], Kovats-Index m
retardation age	s. slowing-down time		
retardation angle; angle of lag, lag angle	Nacheilwinkel m, Nacheilungswinkel m; Verzögerungswinkel m	retention power	s. retentivity <bio.>
		retention range	s. hold range
		retention time	Retentionszeit f, Rückhaltezeit f
retardation bath, restraining bath	Verzögerungsbad n		
retardation coil, filter coil	Siebdrossel f, Siebspule f	retention time, maximum retention time; storage time <num. math.>	Speicherzeit f, Speicherungszeit f, Speicherdauer f <num. Math.>
retardation effect	Retardierungseffekt m		
retardation factor	Retardierungsfaktor m		
retardation field circuit [scheme]	s. retarding-field oscillator	retention volume	Retentionsvolumen n, Rückhaltevolumen n
retardation function	Retardationsfunktion f		
retardation of phase	s. phase lagging	retentiveness, true remanence	wahre Remanenz f
retardation potential	s. retarding potential		
retardation pressure	Verzögerungsdruck m		
retardation spectrum, bremsspectrum, bremsstrahlung spectrum	Bremsspektrum n, Bremsstrahlungsspektrum n, Bremskontinuum n		
		retentivity, magnetic retentivity, apparent remanence	scheinbare Remanenz f
retardation spectrum <in viscoelasticity>	Retardierungsspektrum n, Retardationsspektrum n <Viskoelastizität>		
		retentivity, retention power <bio.>	Retentionsvermögen n <Bio.>
retardation time	Retardierungszeit f, Retardationszeit f	retentivity	s. a. remanence
retarded argument	nacheilendes Argument n	retentivity of vision	s. persistence of vision
retarded control	s. threshold control		

Retgers['] law, law of Retgers	Retgerssches Gesetz *n*	**retrograde-vision Daubresse prism, retrograde-vision tetrahedral prism**	rücksichtiges Umkehrprisma *n*, Tetraeder-Umkehrprisma *n*, rücksichtiges Daubresse-Prisma *n*
reticular structure, cellular network, grid structure	Netzstruktur *f*, Netzverband *m*	**retrogression**	*s.* retrograde motion ‹astr.›
reticulation ‹of the emulsion›	Netzstruktur *f*, Netzstrukturbildung *f*, Netzbildung *f* ‹der Emulsion›, Runzelkorn *n*	**retrogression of temperature**	*s.* temperature drop
		retrogressive wave	rückschreitende (zurücklaufende) Welle *f*
reticule [of the oscilloscope]	Vorsatzskale *f*, Vorsatzskala *f* ‹Oszillograph›	**retron**	Retron *n* ‹γ-Spektrometer›
retinal image	Netzhautbild *n*	**retro-reflecting material**	Reflexstoff *m*
retinene	Retinen *n*, Sehgelb *n*, Indikatorgelb *n*	**retro-reflecting optical unit**	Rückstrahloptik *f*
retinula cell	Retinulazelle *f*	**retro-reflection**	*s.* reflex reflection
retort	Retorte *f*	**retro-reflector**, reflex reflector	Reflexreflektor *m*, Rückstrahler *m*
retort	*s. a.* flask		
retort carbon, homogeneous carbon, plain carbon, pure carbon	Homogenkohle *f*, Reinkohle *f*, Retortenkohle *f*, Reindochtkohle *f*	**retrorocket**	*s.* braking rocket
		retrosection	Rückkehrschnitt *m*
retort graphite	Retortengraphit *m*	**return; recurrence; recursion**	Umkehr *f*, Rückkehr *f*; Wiederkehr *f*; Rekursion *f*, Rekurrenz *f*
retrace ‹cathode-ray tubes; tv.; relaxation oscillations›	Rücklauf *m* ‹Elektronenstrahlröhren; Fs.; Kippschwingungen›		
		return	*s. a.* return line ‹el.›
retrace blanking	*s.* blanking	**return**	*s. a.* recovery
retrace interval (period, time), return period	Rücklaufzeit *f*	**return albedo**	Rückkehralbedo *f*
		return circuit	*s.* return line ‹el.›
retractile spring	Abreißfeder *f*, Rückzugfeder *f*	**return coefficient**	*s.* return factor
		return conductor	*s.* return line ‹el.›
		return current	*s.* reverse (inverse) current
		return earthquake, return tremor	Wiederkehrbeben *n*
retraction stress, shrinkage stress, cooling stress, stress due to shrinkage	Schrumpfspannung *f*, Schwindungsspannung *f*		
		return energy ‹el.›	Rückfluß *m* ‹El.›
retransformation; reverse transformation	Zurückverwandlung *f*, Rückverwandlung *f*	**return factor**, return coefficient	Rückflußfaktor *m*, Rückflußkoeffizient *m*
		return flow	*s.* backstreaming
retranslation, retransmission	Weiterleitung *f*, Weitergabe *f*	**return-flow channel [of wind tunnel]**	Umkehrkanal *m* [des Windtunnels]
retrapping, recapture	„retrapping" *n*, Wiedereinfangen *n*, Wiedereinfang *m*	**return-flow wind tunnel**, closed[-circuit] wind tunnel, closed tunnel, wind tunnel of closed-circuit type, wind tunnel with continuous closed circuit	Windkanal *m* mit Rückführung, geschlossener Windkanal, Rundlaufkanal *m*, Umlaufwindkanal *m*, Umlaufkanal *m*, Ringkanal *m*
retreat, recession, regression ‹geo.›	Regression *f*, Rückzug *m*, Rückgang *m*, Zurückgehen *n*, Zurückweichen *n* ‹Geo.›		
		returning echo; reflection echo	Rückstrahlecho *n*
retreat	*s. a.* shrinkage	**return line**, return circuit, return conductor, return ‹el.›	Rückleitung *f*, Rückleiter *m* ‹El.›
retreatal moraine, recessional moraine	Rückzugsmoräne *f*		
		return line	*s. a.* return pipe [line] ‹techn.›
retreatment	*s.* rework[ing]	**return line**	*s. a.* return trace
retrieval ‹of stored information›	Wiederauffindung *f* ‹gespeicherter Information›	**return loss**, regularity attenuation, structural return loss; echo current attenuation	Rückflußdämpfung *f*; Echodämpfung *f*
retrieval ‹of distorted information›	Wiederherstellung *f* ‹verzerrter Information›		
		return loss	*s. a.* balance attenuation
retroaction, reaction, reactive effect ‹also el.›	Rückwirkung *f*, Reaktion *f*	**return loss measuring set**, impedance unbalance measuring set	Fehlerdämpfungsmesser *m*, Nachbildungsmesser *m*, Nachbildmesser *m*
retroaction	*s.* feedback		
retroactive amplification, regenerative amplification	Rückkopplungsverstärkung *f*	**return of the comet**	Wiederkehr *f* des Kometen
		return period	*s.* retrace interval
retroactive tube (valve), retroactor [tube]	Rückkopplungsröhre *f*	**return pipe [line]**, return line ‹techn.›	Rücklaufleitung *f*, Rückleitung *f* ‹Techn.›
retrodiffused, backward diffused	zurückdiffundiert, rückdiffundiert		
retrodiffusion	*s.* backscattering	**return question frequency**	*s.* repetition rate
retrodirective illumination	Beleuchtung *f* mit der Lichtquelle auf der Kameraseite	**return spring**	Rückstellfeder *f*; Rückholfeder *f*
retrodirective mirror	*s.* corner cube		
retrograde	rückläufig, retrograd	**return stroke**, main stroke ‹of lightning›	Hauptentladung *f*, Rückentladung *f*, Aufwärtsblitz *m* ‹Blitz›
retrograde condensation of the second kind, isobaric retrograde condensation	retrograde Kondensation *f* zweiter Art, isobare retrograde Kondensation	**return stroke channel**, leader channel	Blitzkanal *m*, Entladungskanal *m* des Blitzes
retrograde evaporation, retrograde vaporization	retrograde Verdampfung *f*		
retrograde image	rückläufige Abbildung *f*	**return trace**, return line ‹cathode-ray tubes; tv.; relaxation oscillations›	Rücklauflinie *f*, Rücklaufspur *f* ‹Elektronenstrahlröhren; Fs.; Kippschwingungen›
retrograde motion, retrogression ‹astr.›	rückläufige (retrograde) Bewegung *f*; Rückläufigkeit *f* ‹Astr.›		
		return tremor	*s.* return earthquake
retrograde nutation	retrograde Nutation *f*	**return voltage**	*s.* inverse voltage
retrograde precession	retrograde Präzession *f*	**return wave**	wiederkehrende Welle *f*, Wiederkehrwelle *f*
retrograde rocket	*s.* braking rocket		
retrograde vaporization	*s.* retrograde evaporation		
retrograde vernier	vortragender Nonius *m*	**reunion** ‹bio.›	Reunion *f* ‹Bio.›

reuse — s. recycling
Reuss approximation — Reuß-Näherung f, Reußsche Näherung f
Reuss equations, Prandtl-Reuss equations — Prandtl-Reußsche (Reußsche) Gleichungen fpl
Reuss['] theory, Prandtl-Reuss theory — Prandtl-Reußsche Theorie f, Reußsche Theorie
reverberant sound, reverberation, lingering sound (tone) — Nachhall m, Hall m
reverberation — s. a. echo
reverberation chamber, reverberation room (enclosure), echo (diffusion, sound) room — Hallraum m, Echoraum m, Nachhallraum m
reverberation characteristic (curve), echoing characteristic — Nachhallkurve f, Nachhallcharakteristik f
reverberation enclosure — s. reverberation chamber
reverberation method — Hallraumverfahren n
reverberation period — s. reverberation time
reverberation room — s. reverberation chamber
reverberation time, reverberation period — Nachhallzeit f, Nachhalldauer f
reversal, reversion, reversing — Spiegelumkehrung f, Spiegelverkehrung f, Reversion f, Umkehr[ung] f; Seitenverkehrung f
reversal ‹of direction› — Umkehrung f der Richtung, Richtungsumkehrung f, Richtungsumkehr f, Richtungswechsel m, Wechsel m der Richtung; Umschlagen n ‹um 180°›; Umwendung f
reversal — s. a. reversal of motion
reversal — s. a. improper orthogonal mapping
reversal — s. a. reverse run
reversal development — Umkehrentwicklung f
reversal film — Umkehrfilm m
reversal of charge, charge exchange, umladung, recharging, recharge — Umladung f, Trägerumladung f, Trägerumwandlung f; Ladungsaustausch m
reversal of charge, charge reversal — Ladungsumkehr f, Ladungsumkehrung f
reversal of current — Stromumkehr[ung] f
reversal of damping, compensation of damping; partial reversal of damping, partial compensation of loss — Entdämpfung f
reversal of magnetization — s. remagnetization
reversal of motion, reversal ‹el.› — Umsteuerung f, Umkehrung f [der Drehrichtung], Umkehr f [der Drehrichtung], Drehrichtungsumkehr f, Bewegungsumkehr f, Reversierung f ‹El.›
reversal of photographic image — s. solarization
reversal of polarity — s. alternation of polarity
reversal of sign, sign reversal, change of sign — Umkehrung f des Vorzeichens, Vorzeichenwechsel m, Vorzeichenumkehr f, Vorzeichenänderung f
reversal of spectral (spectrum) line, spectral line reversal — Linienumkehr f, Umkehr (Umkehrung) f der Spektrallinie
reversal of the main geomagnetic field, main geomagnetic field reversal — Umkehr f des geomagnetischen Hauptfeldes
reversal of tonus, restimulation — Stimmungsänderung f; Umstimmung f; Verstimmung f
reversal of wind — s. sudden change of the wind
reversal plate — s. reversal type plate
reversal point — s. stagnation point
reversal process[ing] ‹phot.› — Umkehrprozeß m, Direkt-Positiv-Prozeß m ‹Phot.›

reversal reaction — s. reverse reaction
reversal spectrum — s. inversion spectrum
reversal stage — s. inverter stage
reversal threshold — s. reverse threshold
reversal transfer process — Umkehrübertragung f, Umkehrübertragungsverfahren n
reversal type plate, reversal plate — Umkehrplatte f

reverse, mirror-symmetric, specular — spiegel[bild]symmetrisch, spiegelbildlich, spiegelverkehrt, spiegelrecht
reverse ‹the telescope› — durchschlagen ‹das Fernrohr›
reverse bearing — Rückenpeilung f
reverse bend[ing] test, to-and-fro test — Hin- und Herbiegeversuch m, Umbiegeversuch m
reverse bias, reverse biasing potential, cut-off bias[ing potential] — Sperrvorspannung f, Vorspannung f in Sperrrichtung
reverse characteristic; turn-off characteristic, blocking characteristic — Sperrcharakteristik f, Sperrkennlinie f
reverse collector voltage — Kollektorsperrspannung f
reverse creep — Zurückkriechen n
reverse current, inverse (return) current; stray emission current [of thermionic valve]; back stream [of electrons] — Rückstrom m ‹El.›
reverse current, countercurrent, counter current — Gegenstrom m
reverse current; back current, cut-off current ‹semi.› — Sperrstrom m; Rückstrom m, Rückwärtsstrom m ‹Halb.›
reverse current density — Sperrstromdichte f
reverse current gain — Rückstromverstärkung f
reversed base current — Absaugstrom m
reversed bending fatigue test, alternating bending test — Wechselbiege[dauer]versuch m, Wechselbiegeprüfung f
reversed Carnot cycle — umgekehrter Carnotscher Kreisprozeß m
reversed cyclotron — umgekehrtes Zyklotron n
reversed fatigue strength — s. fatigue strength
reversed fault — s. overfault ‹geo.›
reversed fold — s. inverted fold
reversed grid current — s. reverse grid current
reverse direction, backward direction, back direction, high-resistance direction ‹semi.› — Sperrichtung f ‹Halb.›
reversed phase, opposite phase, antiphase, [phase] opposition — Gegenphase f
reversed phase technique — s. reverse-phase chromatography
reversed right to left, left-to-right reversed, inverted right to left, right-to-left (laterally) inverted, laterally transposed, side-inverted ‹of image› — seitenverkehrt, rückwendig; seitenvertauscht, gespiegelt ‹Bild›
reversed stress — umgekehrte Beanspruchung f
reversed top to bottom, top-to-bottom reversed (inverted), inverted top to bottom ‹of image› — höhenverkehrt; höhenvertauscht ‹Bild›
reversed upside-down — s. upside-down

reverse emitter current, Emitterrückstrom *m*
  inverse emitter current
reverse feedback, Gegenkopplung *f*, negative
  inverse feedback, Rückkopplung *f*
  negative feedback,
  degenerative feedback,
  countercoupling
reverse flow s. backstreaming
reverse flow theorem Reziprozitätssatz *m* der
  Tragflügeltheorie
reverse fluctuation, Rückwärtsschwankung *f*
  fluctuation in reverse
  direction
reverse frontal technique Technik *f* mit umgekehrten
  Fronten
reverse grid current, Gitterrückstrom *m*,
  reversed (inverse) grid negativer Gitterstrom *m*
  current, backlash
reverse grid voltage, Gittergegenspannung *f*
  inverse grid voltage,
  inverse grid potential,
  back-lash potential
reverse half-cycle Sperrhalbperiode *f*

reverse isotopic umgekehrte Isotopenver-
  dilution analysis dünnungsanalyse *f*
reverse osmosis, hyper- umgekehrte Osmose *f*,
  filtration Hyperfiltration *f*
reverse-phase Verteilungschromato-
  chromatography, graphie *f* (Chromato-
  reversed phase technique graphie *f*, Technik *f*) mit
  <of chromatography> Phasenumkehr[ung],
  Phasenumkehrungs-
  technik *f*, Phasenumkehr
  f, Umkehrphasen-
  chromatographie *f* <der
  Chromatographie>
reverse potential s. inverse voltage
  <el.>
reverse power Rückleistung *f*, Rücklauf-
  leistung *f*, Rückwatt *npl*
reverse printing Kontern *n*
reverser Richtungswender *m*; Um-
  kehreinrichtung *f*

reverse reaction, umgekehrte Reaktion *f*,
  reversal reaction Umkehrreaktion *f*
reverse reaction s. a. back reaction
reverse resistance s. back resistance
reverse rotation s. turn back
reverse-rotation method Rückarbeitsverfahren *n*

reverse short-circuit Rückwärts-Kurzschluß-
  current, backward strom *m*
  short-circuit current

reverse strain Zurückfließen *n*, Rück-
  wärtsverformung *f*
reverse threshold, Schwelle *f* der Umkehr-
  reversal threshold reaktion, Umkehr-
  schwelle *f*
reverse torsion s. turn back
reverse transcon- Rückwärtssteilheit *f*,
  ductance, revertive Rücksteilheit *f*
  conductance, revertive
  transconductance
reverse transfer Leerlaufkernwiderstand *m*
  impedance, backward rückwärts; Über-
  transfer impedance tragungswiderstand *m*
  rückwärts
reverse transformation; Zurückverwandlung *f*,
  retransformation Rückverwandlung *f*

reverse-vision prism Rücksichtprisma *n*
reverse voltage, inverse Sperrspannung *f*,
  voltage <semi.> Grenzspannung *f*
  <Halb.>
reverse voltage transfer Spannungsrückwirkung *f*
reversibility Reversibilität *f*, Umkehr-
  barkeit *f*
reversibility Umsteuerbarkeit *f*

reversibility coefficient Reversibilitätskoeffizient *m*

reversibility paradox Loschmidtscher Umkehr-
  [of Loschmidt], einwand *m*, Umkehr-
  Loschmidt['s] reversi- einwand von Loschmidt
  bility paradox, umkehr-
  einwand
reversible reversibel, umkehrbar

reversible adiabatic reversibel adiabatische Zu-
  change of state standsänderung *f*, Zustandsänderung ohne
  Wärmezufuhr
reversible adsorption s. physisorption
reversible boundary reversible Wandver-
  movement, reversible schiebung *f*
  displacement of the
  Bloch wall
reversible cell, reversible reversible Kette *f*, um-
  electrical cell kehrbares Element *n*,
  reversibles [galvanisches]
  Element
reversible colloid reversibles Kolloid *n*
reversible counter s. bidirectional counter
reversible displacement s. reversible boundary
  of the Bloch wall movement
reversible electrical cell s. reversible cell
reversible electrode reversible Elektrode *f*,
  umkehrbare Elektrode

reversible emulsion Umkehremulsion *f*

reversible film s. reversal film
reversible level, reversion Reversionslibelle *f*, Um-
  (reversible spirit) level kehrlibelle *f*, Wende-
  libelle *f*

reversible motor Umkehrmotor *m*, Rever-
  siermotor *m*, Wende-
  motor *m*
reversible pendulum Reversionspendel *n*,
  Umkehrpendel *n*
reversible permeability reversible (umkehrbare)
  Permeabilität *f*

reversible relative Gleichgewichts-Galvani-
  potential at zero Potential *n*, Gleich-
  current, equilibrium gewichts-Galvani-
  inner electrical potential Spannung *f*, Gleich-
  gewichts-Potential-
  differenz *f*, Einzel-
  potential *n*
reversible spirit level s. reversible level
reversible turbine Kehrturbine *f*
reversing <el.> Reversierung *f* <El.>

reversing s. a. reversal
reversing s. a. pole change <el.>
reversing bath Umkehrbad *n*

reversing circuit Umkehrschaltung *f*,
  Umkehrungsschaltung *f*;
  Wendeschaltung *f*
reversing contact Pendelunterbrecher *m*
  breaker
reversing device s. reciprocating device
  <math., opt.>
reversing layer <of the umkehrende Schicht *f*
  chromosphere> <Chromosphäre>
reversing mirror Umkehrspiegel *m*

reversing pole s. commutating interpole
reversing prism, image Reversionsprisma *n*, Dove-
  reversing prism, Dove Prisma *n*, Dovesches
  (Delaborne-Dove) prism Reflexionsprisma *n*,
  Amici-Prisma *n*, Wende-
  prisma *n*, Umkehrprisma
  n nach Dove
reversing prism s. a. image erecting prism
reversing switch s. pole-changing switch
reversing telescope s. image erecting telescope
reversing thermometer, Kippthermometer *n*, Tief-
  sea-water thermometer see[kipp]thermometer *n*,
  Tiefenthermometer *n*,
  Tiefwasserthermometer *n*,
  Umkehrthermometer *n*,
  Umkippthermometer *n*
reversion s. reversal

reversion right to left	s. lateral inversion of image	Reynolds['] slip	Reynoldssche Gleitung f
revertive conductance, revertive transconductance, reverse transconductance	Rückwärtssteilheit f, Rücksteilheit f	Reynolds stress, Reynolds turbulent shear stress, eddy stress	Reynoldssche Spannung f, Reynolds-Spannung f, turbulente Scheinschubspannung f, [turbulente] Scheinreibung f, Turbulenzreibung f
revolution, rotation	Umdrehung f		
revolution, turn	Umdrehung f, Tour f, U	Reynolds['] stress tensor	Tensor m der turbulenten Scheinreibung, Reynoldsscher Spannungstensor m
revolution <around, round>, circling <round>, circumrotation; orbiting	Umlaufen n <um einen Zentralkörper>; Umkreisen n, Kreisen n <um>; Umfliegen n <auf einer geschlossenen Bahn>	Reynolds turbulent shear stress	s. Reynolds stress
		re-zeroing	Zurückstellen n auf Null
revolution <astr.>	Umlauf m, Bahnumlauf m, Revolution f <Astr.>	R.F.	s. radio-frequency
revolution <geo.>	s. a. orogenesis	R_s factor, spreading factor	R_s-Wert m, R_s
revolutionary motion	s. orbiting	rhabdom	Rhabdom n
revolution counter (indicator)	s. speedometer		
revolution of Earth, Earth's revolution	Erdumlauf m, Erdrevolution f	rhabdomere	Rhabdomer n
revolution period	s. rotation period		
revolution solid, body of revolution (rotation), solid of revolution (rotation)	Rotationskörper m, Drehkörper m, Umdrehungskörper m	rhe $<= 1/P$	Rhe n, rhe $<= 1/P>$
		rhegmaglypt, piezoglypt	Rhegmaglypte f
		rheidity <geo.>	Rheidität f <Geo.>
revolutions per minute, number of revolutions per minute, turns per minute, rpm, r.p.m., revs per min	Umdrehungen fpl je Minute, U/min	rheochord	Rheochord n
		rheodynamics	Rheodynamik f
		rheoelectric analogy	rheoelektrische Analogie f
revolutions per unit time	s. speed	rheogoniometer [of Weissenberg and Roberts], cone-and-plate rheogoniometer	Rheogoniometer n [von Weissenberg], Rheogoniometer von Weissenberg und Roberts, Weissenbergsches Rheogoniometer
revolving crystal	s. rotating crystal		
revolving diaphragm	s. rotating diaphragm		
revolving disk monochromator	s. rotating-disk monochromator		
revolving dome	s. rotating dome	rheogram	Rheogramm n
revolving eyepiece head	s. eyepiece turret	rheograph	Rheograph m [nach Abraham]
revolving fatigue [testing] machine	s. rotary-bending fatigue testing machine	rheological equation, rheologic formula	rheologische Gleichung f
revolving field machine, rotating-field-type machine, internal (inner) pole machine	Innenpolmaschine f	rheology	Rheologie f, Fließkunde f
		rheometer	s. current meter
		rheometry	Rheometrie f
revolving mirror	s. rotating mirror		
revolving nosepiece (objective changer)	s. turret head	rheonomic	s. time-dependent <mech.>
		rheonomic constraint, constraint dependent on the time	rheonome Bedingung f, rheonome Bedingungsgleichung f, zeitabhängige Bedingung
revolving prism, rotating prism	rotierendes Prisma n		
revolving storm	s. tropical cyclone		
rework[ing], retreatment	Umarbeitung f; Nachbearbeitung f	rheonomous	s. time-dependent <mech.>
		rheopectic	rheopektisch
rewriting, transformation, conversion <of the equation> <math.>	Umformung f, Umschreibung f <der Gleichung> <Math.>	rheopexy	Rheopexie f, Fließverfestigung f, thixogene Koagulation f
reyn $<= 68.947 \times 10^3$ P>	Reyn n $<= 68,947 \cdot 10^3$ P>		
Reynolds['] analogue (analogy)	Reynoldssche Analogie f	rheospectrometer	Rheospektrometer n
		rheostat	s. variable resistor
Reynolds analogy factor	Reynoldsscher Analogiefaktor m	rheostatic controller, resistance controller	Widerstandsregler m; Kontroller m
Reynolds['] boundary layer	Reynoldssche Grenzschicht f	rheostatic pressure gauge, potentiometric pressure gauge	potentiometrisches Manometer n, rheostatisches Manometer
Reynolds['] criterion [of turbulence]	Reynoldssches Kriterium (Turbulenzkriterium) n, Turbulenzkriterium	rheostriction [effect]	s. pinch effect
		rheotaxic	rheotaktisch
Reynolds' experiment, dye experiment	Farbfadenversuch m, Reynoldsscher Farbfadenversuch	rheotaxis	Rheotaxis f
		rheotron	s. betatron
		rheotropic	rheotrop
Reynolds group	s. Reynolds-No	rheotropism	Rheotropismus m
Reynolds law of similarity, Reynolds scale law	Reynoldssches Ähnlichkeitsgesetz n	rhexis, fragmentation <bio.>	Fragmentation f, Chromosomenfragmentation f, Rhexis f <Bio.>
Reynolds-No, Reynolds number, Reynolds parameter, Reynolds group, Re, R	Reynolds-Zahl f, Reynoldssche Kennzahl f, Reynoldssche Zahl f, Re-Zahl f, Re-Wert m, Re, R		
		rhm unit, roentgen per hour at one metre, roentgen-hour-metre, rhm	Röntgen n pro Stunde in einem Meter Abstand [von der Strahlungsquelle], rhm-Einheit f, rhm
Reynolds number for boundary layer thickness	Grenzschicht-Reynolds-Zahl f, Reynolds-Zahl f für Grenzschichtdicke	rho, rho unit	rho-Einheit f, Rho n, rho
Reynolds parameter	s. Reynolds-No	rho-dominant model	rho-dominantes Modell n
Reynolds percolation number	Reynoldssche Durchsickerungszahl f	rhodopsin, visual purple	Rhodopsin n, Sehpurpur m
Reynolds['] rule	Reynoldssche Modellregel f	rhombic antenna, diamond-shaped antenna, Bruce antenna	Rhombusantenne f, Rautenantenne f, Bruce-Antenne f
Reynolds scale law, Reynolds law of similarity	Reynoldssches Ähnlichkeitsgesetz n	rhombic bisphenoid	rhombisches Bisphenoid (Tetraeder) n

rhombic | | | **714**

rhombic crystal system, rhombic system, orthorhombic crystal system, orthorhombic system	rhombisches Kristallsystem (System) n, orthorhombisches Kristallsystem (System), prismatisches Kristallsystem (System)	ribbed shell	Rippenschale f
		ribbing, finning	Berippung f; Verrippung f
rhombic dodecahedron	s. rhombododecahedron	ribbon, ribbon of stacking fault	Stapelfehlerband n
rhombic prism	Rhomboidprisma n, rhombisches Prisma n	ribbon antenna, tape antenna	Bandantenne f
rhombic sphenoid	rhombisches Sphenoid n	ribbon lightning	Bandblitz m
rhombic system	s. rhombic crystal system	ribbon loudspeaker, band loudspeaker, ribbon-type dynamic speaker	Bändchenlautsprecher m, Bandlautsprecher m
rhombdodecahedron, granatohedron, rhombic dodecahedron	Rhombendodekaeder n, Granatoeder n		
rhombohedral class	s. rhombohedral crystal class	ribbon microphone, ribbon-type velocity microphone, tape microphone	Bandmikrophon n, Bändchenmikrophon n
rhombohedral class	s. a. rhombohedral holohedry		
rhombohedral crystal class, rhombohedral class	rhomboedrische Klasse (Kristallklasse, Symmetrieklasse) f, paramorphe Hemiedrie f des rhomboedrischen Systems		
		ribbon of cloud	s. rag of cloud
		ribbon of stacking fault	s. ribbon
		ribbon-type dynamic speaker	s. ribbon loudspeaker
rhombohedral crystal system, rhombohedral system, trigonal crystal system, trigonal system	rhomboedrisches Kristallsystem (System) n, rhomboedrische Abteilung f des hexagonalen Systems, trigonales Kristallsystem (System)	ribbon-type velocity microphone	s. ribbon microphone
		ribosomal ribonucleic acid, ribosomal RNA, ribosome RNA, rRNA	ribosomale Ribonukleinsäure f, ribosomale RNS, rRNS
		ribosome	Ribosom n, Pallade-Granulum n, RNS-Protein-Granulum n, Ribonukleo-Protein-Granulum n
rhombohedral enantiomorphy	s. trigonal holoaxial class		
rhombohedral hemimorphic class, rhombohedral hemimorphy	s. hemimorphic hemihedry of the rhombohedral class		
rhombohedral holohedry, holohedry of the rhombohedral system, ditrigonal scalenohedry, rhombohedral class, hexagonal-scalenohedral [crystal] class, holohedral class of the trigonal system, dihexagonal alternating class	rhomboedrische Hemiedrie f, Holoedrie f des rhomboedrischen Systems, ditrigonal-skalenoedrische Klasse f, ditrigonal skalenoedrische Klasse	ribosome RNA	s. ribosomal ribonucleic acid
		Riccati-Bloch function	Riccati-Blochsche Funktion f
		Riccati['s] equation, differential equation of Riccati	[allgemeine] Riccatische Differentialgleichung f
		Riccati['s] equation	spezielle Riccatische Gleichung f
		Ricci calculus, absolute differential calculus, tensor calculus	Ricci-Kalkül m, absoluter Differentialkalkül m
		Ricci coefficient	Ricci-Koeffizient m
rhombohedral system	s. rhombohedral crystal system	Ricci['s] equation, Ricci['s] identity	Riccische Gleichung f, Identität f von Ricci
rhombohedral tetartohedry	s. trigonal pyramidal [crystal] class	Ricci['s] lemma	s. Ricci['s] theorem
rhombohedral tetartohedry	s. hexagonal tetartohedry of the second sort ⟨rhombohedral system⟩	Ricci['s] tensor, Einstein['s] tensor	Ricci-Tensor m, Einstein-Tensor m
		Ricci['s] theorem, Ricci['s] lemma	Satz m von Ricci, Lemma n von Ricci
rhombohedron	Rhomboeder n, Rautenflächner m	Ricco['s] law	Riccoscher Satz m
rhomboid	s. deltoid	Rice-Kellogg loudspeaker, electrodynamic loudspeaker [of Rice-Kellogg]	elektrodynamischer Lautsprecher m [nach Rice-Kellogg], Lautsprecher nach Rice-Kellogg, Rice-Kelloggscher Lautsprecher
rho-meson, rho-resonance, ϱ meson, ϱ-resonance	Rho-Meson n, ϱ-Meson n, Rho-Resonanz f, ϱ-Resonanz f		
rho unit, rho	rho-Einheit f, Rho n, rho		
rhumb, point ⟨= 11°15'⟩	Strich m, nautischer Strich, ⁓ ⟨= 11°15'⟩	Richardson and Dushman['s] equation, Richardson-Dushman['s] equation, Richardson-Dushman['s] formula, Richardson['s] equation	Richardson-Dushmansche Gleichung (Formel) f, Richardson-Gleichung f, Richardsonsche Gleichung (Formel) f, Richardsonsches Gesetz n
rhumb, point [of the compass], wind reference number	Windstrich m, Windziffer f		
rhumb line, Rhumb line, loxodrome [curve], loxodromic line (curve, spiral) ⟨on Earth⟩	Loxodrome f, Kursgleiche f, Schieflaufende f, Rhumblinie f		
		Richardson effect	s. thermionic emission
		Richardson[-Einstein-De-Haas] effect	s. a. Einstein-de Haas effect
rH value, rH	rH-Wert m, rH	Richardson['s] equation	Richardson-Gleichung f, Richardsonsche Gleichung f, Richardsonsches Gesetz n, Richardsonsche Formel f
rhythmical growth	rhythmisches Wachstum n		
rhythmical potential	rhythmisches Potential n	Richardson['s] equation	s. a. Richardson and Dushman['s] equation
rhythmic light	Taktfeuer n		
rhythmic precipitation	s. periodic precipitation	Richardson['s] law of dispersion	Richardsonsches Dispersionsgesetz n
rhythmic source; periodic source	periodisch fließende Quelle f; episodisch fließende Quelle; Hungerquelle f	Richardson['s] number, Richardson['s] similarity number, stratification parameter, Ri	Richardsonsche Zahl f, Richardson-Zahl f, Richardsonsche Ähnlichkeitszahl f, dimensionslose Schichtungsgröße f, Ri
rhythmic time signals	rhythmische Zeitzeichen npl, Koinzidenzzeitzeichen npl		
Riabouchinsky cavity	Riabouchinskyscher Hohlraum m	Richardson plot	Richardsonsche Gerade f
Riabouchinsky flow	Riabouchinskysche Strömung f	Richardson['s] similarity number	s. Richardson['s] number
		Richards['] rule	Richardssche Regel f, Richardssches Gesetz n, Gesetz von Richards
Riabouchinsky['s] model	Riabouchinskysches Modell n		
Riabouchinsky['s] solution	Riabouchinskysche Lösung f	Richartz compensator, Richartz double half-shade analyzer, Richartz halfshade analyzer	Richartz-Kompensator m, Kompensator (Halbschattenanalysator) m von Richartz
ria coast	Riasküste f, Riaküste f, Trichterbuchtenküste f		
rib, frame, timber	Spant m, Spante f	rich in contrast, contrasty, high-contrast	kontrastreich

Richter lag, diffusion after-effect, diffusion magnetic after-effect	Diffusionsnachwirkung f, Richtersche Nachwirkung f, Richter-Nachwirkung f
Richter magnitude	Richtersche Magnitude f, M_L
ricochet	Abprall m, Abprallen n, Rikoschett n
riddle; sieve, screen	Sieb n
riddlings	s. screenings
rider, jockey weight	Reiter m, Reiterchen n, Reitergewicht n, Aufsetzgewicht n
ridged waveguide	gefurchter Hohlleiter m
ridge of high pressure	Hochdruckbrücke f, Hochdruckrücken m
ridge prism, roof prism; Amici prism	Dachkantprisma n, Dachprisma n; Amici-Prisma n
Rieffler clock	Rieffler-Uhr f, RieffIersche Uhr f
Rieffler pendulum	Rieffler-Pendel n
Riegels['] factor	Riegels-Faktor m
Riegger circuit (discriminator)	Riegger-Kreis m
Riegger gauge	Riegger-Vakuummeter n
Riegler coefficient	Riegler-Faktor m
Riehl effect	Riehl-Effekt m
Rieke diagram	Rieke-Diagramm n
Riemann-Christoffel curvature tensor, Riemann-Christoffel symbol, Riemann-Christoffel tensor [of the first kind], [covariant] curvature tensor, four-index symbol	Krümmungstensor m, Riemannscher (Riemann-Christoffelscher) Krümmungstensor m, Riemann-Christoffelscher Tensor m, Vierindizessymbol n
Riemann-Christoffel three-index symbol	s. Christoffel symbol
Riemann['s] differential equation, Riemann-Papperitz equation, Papperitz['s] equation	Riemannsche (Papperitzsche) Differentialgleichung f
Riemann['s] equation	Riemannsche Gleichung f
Riemann['s] function	Riemannsche Funktion f
Riemann-Hilbert problem, coupling problem	Kopplungsproblem n, Riemann-Hilbert-Problem n
Riemannian curvature	Riemannsche Krümmung f, Riemannsches Krümmungsmaß n, Büschelinvariante f der Krümmung
Riemannian domain	Riemannsches Gebiet n, Riemannscher Raum m
Riemannian geometry	Riemannsche Geometrie f
Riemannian metric	Riemannsche Metrik f
Riemannian space	Riemannscher Raum m; Riemannsche Mannigfaltigkeit f
Riemannian surface, Riemann['s] surface	Riemannsche Fläche f
Riemann['s] integral	Riemannsches Integral n
Riemann invariant	Riemannsche Invariante f
Riemann-Lebesgue theorem	Riemann-Lebesguesches Lemma n, Riemann-Lebesguesches Fundamentallemma n, Riemann-Lebesguescher Satz m, Satz von Riemann-Lebesgue
Riemann['s] localization theorem	Riemannscher Lokalisationssatz m, Lokalisationssatz von Riemann
Riemann['s] mapping theorem, Riemann['s] theorem	Riemannscher Abbildungssatz m, Riemannscher Hauptsatz m, Riemannscher Fundamentalsatz m, Hauptsatz (Fundamentalsatz) der konformen Abbildung; Koebe-Poincarésches Grenzkreistheorem n
Riemann-Papperitz equation	s. Riemann['s] differential equation
Riemann relations	s. Cauchy-Riemann differential equations
Riemann sphere, complex sphere	Riemannsche Zahlenkugel f, Zahlenkugel
Riemann-Stieltjes integral	Riemann-Stieltjessches Integral n
Riemann sum, integral sum	Integralsumme f
Riemann['s] surface, Riemannian surface	Riemannsche Fläche f
Riemann['s] theorem	s. Riemann['s] mapping theorem
Riemann['s] theorem, Green['s] theorem for $n = 2$	Gaußsche Integralformel f im Fall $n = 2$, Greensche Integralformel, Integralformel von Green, Riemannsche Integralformel, Riemannsche Formel f, Gaußscher Integralsatz m im Fall $n = 2$
Riemann wave	Riemannsche Stoßwelle (Welle) f
Riemann zeta function, zeta function	Riemannsche Zeta-Funktion f
rieseliconoscope	s. photo-electron-stabilized photicon
Riesz-Fischer['s] theorem	s. Fischer-Riesz theorem
Riesz representation theorem [for Hilbert spaces]	s. Fischer-Riesz theorem
riffle	s. rapids <of river>
riffle	s. a. ripple mark
riffle	s. a. ripple
rifle telescope	s. sighting telescope
rift [valley]; fault-line valley	Rift n; Verwerfungstal n; Klufttal n, Spaltental n
Righi['s] formula	Righische Formel f, Formel von Righi
Righi-Leduc coefficient	Righi-Leduc-Koeffizient m
Righi-Leduc effect, Leduc effect	Righi-Leduc-Effekt m
right-angled prism, right prism <opt.>	rechtwinkliges Prisma n <Opt.>
right-angle mirror	Rechtwinkelspiegel m
right-angle mirror interferometer	Winkelspiegelinterferometer n
right-angle mirror square, crossed-mirror square	Spiegelkreuz n; Kreuzspiegel m
right ascension, R. A.	Rektaszension f, gerade Aufsteigung f, AR
right ascension circle	s. hour circle
right circular cylinder, cylinder, roller	gerader Kreiszylinder m, Walze f, Zylinder m
right[-hand] derivative, derivative on the right	rechtsseitige Ableitung f
right-handed, dextrogyric, dextrorse <techn.>	rechtsgängig, rechtsdrehend, Rechts[-]; rechtsläufig; rechtswendig <Techn.>
right-handed circular[ly polarized], clockwise circularly polarized	zirkular rechtspolarisiert, rechtszirkular [polarisiert], rechtsdrehend zirkular polarisiert, rechtspolarisiert zirkular
right-handed circular polarization	zirkulare Rechtspolarisation f, rechtszirkulare Polarisation f
right-handed co-ordinate system, right-handed system [of co-ordinates], right system [of co-ordinate axes]	Rechtssystem n, rechtshändiges Koordinatensystem n, rechtshändiges System n
right-handed cycle, clockwise process	Rechtsprozeß m
right-handed elliptic[ally polarized], clockwise elliptically polarized	elliptisch rechtspolarisiert, rechtselliptisch [polarisiert], rechtsdrehend elliptisch polarisiert, rechtspolarisiert elliptisch

right-handed elliptical polarization — elliptische Rechtspolarisation f, rechtselliptische Polarisation f

right-handed helix — s. right-twisted helix

right-handed polarization, dextropolarization — Rechtspolarisation f, rechtshändige Polarisation f

right-handed polarized, clockwise polarized — rechtspolarisiert, rechtsdrehend polarisiert, rechtshändig polarisiert

right-handed quartz — s. dextrorotatory quartz

right-handed screw[ing] — s. right-twisted helix

right-handed system [of co-ordinates] — s. right-handed co-ordinate system

right-handed twist — s. right-hand twist

right-hand helix — s. right-twisted helix

right-hand lay, right-hand[ed] twist — Rechtsdrall m

right-hand limit, limit on the right — rechtsseitiger Grenzwert m, rechtsseitiger Limes m

right-hand rule, Fleming['s] [second] rule — Dreifingerregel f der rechten Hand, Rechte-Hand-Regel f; Flemingsche Dreifingerregel f, Flemingsche Regel f; Dynamoregel f

right-hand screw — s. right-twisted helix

right-hand screw rule — s. corkscrew rule

right-hand side, right side, right member <of the equation> — rechte Seite f <Gleichung>

right-hand twist, right-handed twist, right-hand lay — Rechtsdrall m

righting moment, restoring moment <aero.> — aufrichtendes (rückdrehendes) Moment n, Aufrichtmoment n, Rückdrehmoment n, Rückführmoment n <Aero.>

right inverse — Rechtsinverses n

right-left asymmetry — Rechts-Links-Asymmetrie f

right-left ratio [of scattered particles] — Rechts-Links-Streuverhältnis n, Rechts-Links-Verhältnis n

right member — s. right-hand side

right multiplication — s. post[-]multiplication

rightness, truth, trueness; correctness <num. math.> — Richtigkeit f <num. Math.>

right parallelepiped — s. rectangular parallelepiped

right prism <math.> — gerades Prisma n <Math.>

right prism, right-angled prism <opt.> — rechtwinkliges Prisma n <Opt.>

right side, right-hand side <of the equation> — rechte Seite f <Gleichung>

right-skew distribution, distribution skew on the right — rechtsschiefe Verteilung f, linkssteile Verteilung

right system [of co-ordinate axes] — s. right-handed co-ordinate system

right-to-left inverted — s. reversed right to left

right-twisted helix, right-hand[ed] helix, dextrorse helix, right-twisted screw, right-hand[ed] screw, right-handed screwing — Rechtsschraube f

right-twisted screw — s. right-twisted helix

rigid — starr; rig

rigid arch — s. hingeless arch

rigid body; Euclidean solid, Euclid solid <rheology> — starrer Körper m

rigid-body displacement — Starrkörperverschiebung f

rigid body pendulum, physical pendulum, compound pendulum — physisches Pendel n, physikalisches Pendel, Starrkörperpendel n, zusammengesetztes Pendel

rigid boundary surface — s. sound-hard boundary

rigid dynamics — Dynamik f starrer Körper

rigid fixing, built-in mounting <of beam> — starre Einspannung f, festes Klemmlager n <Balken>

rigidity — Starrheit f, Starre f, Righeit f, elastische Widerstandsfähigkeit f

rigidity; stiffness, inflexibility — Steifigkeit f, Steifheit f, Steife f

rigidity — s. a. shape elasticity

rigidity — s. a. shear modulus

rigidity <of the spring> — s. a. spring constant

rigidity coefficient — s. stiffness coefficient

rigidity matrix — Starrheitsmatrix f

rigidity modulus — s. shear modulus

rigidity number — s. stiffness coefficient

rigidity of the plate, flexural rigidity of the plate, plate rigidity — Platten[biegungs]steifigkeit f, Biegungssteifigkeit (Biegesteifigkeit, Steifigkeit) f der Platte

rigidity parameter — Steifigkeitsparameter m

rigid joint, stiff joint — starrer (steifer) Knoten m, Steifknoten m

rigid model; Frank-Van der Merwe mechanism <cryst.> — Modell n der starren Teilchen; Frank-van-der-Merwe-Mechanismus m <Krist.>

rigid motion — starre Bewegung f

rigid-perfectly plastic — starr-idealplastisch

rigid-plastic approximation — starr-plastische Näherung f

rigid-plastic body — s. St. Venant body

rigid plastic theory — starr-plastische Theorie f

rigid point of support, fixed bearing — fester Stützpunkt m

rigid rotating frame — starres rotierendes Bezugssystem n

rigid rotation — starre Drehung f, starre Rotation f

rigid rotator — starrer Rotator m

rigid sphere gas (model) — s. hard-sphere [lattice] gas

rigorous cold, severe cold — strenge Kälte f; strenger Frost m

rigorous solution, strict solution, exact solution — strenge Lösung f, exakte Lösung

rill, rille, groove, furrow, cleft <on the Moon's surface> — Rille f <auf der Mondoberfläche>

rill erosion, concentrated wash — Rillenspülung f

rim; boundary, bound; limit, limitation; margin — Grenze f; Begrenzung f; Rand m; Berandung f

rim angle, angle of contact, contact angle, wetting angle, angle of capillarity, boundary angle — Kontaktwinkel m, Randwinkel m, Grenzwinkel m, Benetzungswinkel m

rime [ice] — Rauhfrost m, Rauheis n, Anraum m

Rimlock-base tube (valve), Rimlock tube (valve) — Rimlock-Röhre f

rim ray — s. marginal ray

rim vortex — s. tip vortex

ring — Ring m

ring, cycle, nucleus <chem.> — Ring m, Kern m, Zyklus m

ring <math.> — Ring m <Math.>

ring — s. a. torus

ring / 22°- — s. halo of 22°

ring / 46°- — s. halo of 46°

ring A, outer ring — äußerer Ring m, A-Ring m

ring antenna, ring dipole, hula-loop antenna — Ringdipol m, Ringantenne f, Ringdipolantenne f

ring armature — Ringanker m, Grammescher Ring m

ring B, inner ring — Innenring m, B-Ring m

ring balance, ring balance manometer, tilting-ring manometer — Ringwaage f, Ringwaage[n]manometer n, Kreisrohrmanometer n, Kreismikromanometer n

ring C, crape ring, crepe ring, gauze ring, dusky ring — Kreppring m, Florring m, C-Ring m

ring cleavage, ring scission (opening), cleavage of the ring, scission (opening) of the ring — Ringspaltung f, Spaltung f des Rings, Aufspaltung f der Ringstruktur, Ringöffnung f

ring closure — s. cyclization

ring-core magnetometer — Ringkernmagnetometer n

ring current; circular current; circulating current — Ringstrom m; Kreisstrom m

ring demodulator, product detector — Produktgleichrichter m, Ringdemodulator m

ring diffusion	Ringdiffusion *f*	rip current	Ripströmung *f*, Uferströmung *f* ‹Inlandsee›
ring dipole	s. ring antenna	ripening, cooking ‹of the emulsion›, maturing	Reifung *f* [der Emulsion]
ring discharge	s. toroidal discharge		
ring electron	Ringelektron *n*		
Ringer['s] solution	Ringer-Lösung *f*	ripple; riffle; corrugation	Riffelung *f*, Rippelung *f*; Riefelung *f*; Wellung *f*; Faltung *f*
ring focus	Ringfokus *m*		
ring-focus diaphragm	Ringfokusblende *f*	ripple, waviness	Welligkeit *f*
		ripple; pulsing, pulsation	Pulsation *f*, Pulsieren *n*, Pulsung *f*, Pulsion *f*; Tröpfeln *n* ‹HF-Oszillator›
ring-focus [X-ray] tube	Ringfokus[-Röntgen]röhre *f*		
ring formation, cyclization, ring closure	Zyklisierung *f*, Ringschluß *m*, Ringbildung *f*	ripple; hum; alternating-current (mains line) hum, power line hum	Brumm *m*, Brummen *n*; Netzbrumm *m*, Netzbrummen *n*
ring fracture	Ringbruch *m*, Kreisbruch *m*	ripple, capillary waves, ripples; rippling; ruffle	Kapillarwellen *fpl*, Kräuselwellen *fpl*, Rippelwellen *fpl*, Krauswellen *fpl*, Rippeln *fpl*, Riffeln *fpl*; Kräuselung *f*
ring function, toroidal function	Ringfunktion *f*, toroidale Funktion *f*, Torusfunktion *f*		
ring furnace	s. ring oven	ripple	Magnetisierungsverteilung *f*, Magnetisierungsripple *n*, Ripple *n*
ring graph	Ringgraph *m*		
ring grating	Ringgitter *n*	ripple ‹of rectifier›	Welligkeit *f* [des Gleichrichters], Oberwelligkeit *f*
ring halo, ring-shaped halo ‹opt.›	Ringhalo *m*, Hof *m*, Ring *m* ‹Opt.›	ripple cloud	Schäfchenwolke *f*, Lämmerwolke *f*
ring hybrid [junction]	Ringverzweigung *f*, Ringgabel *f*, Ringverbindung *f*	ripple contrast	Ripplekontrast *m*, Kontrastübertragung *f* des Magnetisierungsripple
ring kiln	s. ring oven		
ring laser	Ringlaser *m*, optischer Ringquantengenerator *m*	ripple crest	s. crest [of the wave]
		ripple current, surge current ‹el.›	Wellenstrom *m*, Rippelstrom *m*, Kräuselstrom *m* ‹El.›
Ringleb flow	Ringlebsche Strömung *f*		
Ringleb nozzle	Ringlebsche Düse *f*	rippled sea	s. rippling sea
ring-like eclipse, annular eclipse	ringförmige Finsternis *f*	ripple factor, ripple ratio, hum factor, hum level	Brummabstand *m*, Brummfaktor *m*, Brummspannungsverhältnis *n*
ring mirror	Ringspiegel *m*		
ring mirror [condenser], convergent ring mirror	Ringspiegelkondensor *m*, sammelnder Ringspiegel *m*, Ringspiegel, Spiegelkondensor *m*	ripple filter	Stromreiniger *m*, Stromglätter *m*, Welligkeitsfilter *n*
ring mirror lens	Ringspiegellinse *f*	ripple-filter choke, smoothing choke	Überlappungsdrossel [-spule] *f*, Glättungsdrossel *f*, Beruhigungsdrossel *f*
ring molecule	Ringmolekül *n*		
ring mountain	s. lunar crater		
ring nebula	Ringnebel *m*	ripple frequency	Pulsationsfrequenz *f*; Tröpfelfrequenz *f* ‹HF-Oszillator›
ring of matrices	s. matrix algebra		
ring of smoke	Rauchring *m*		
ring opening	s. ring cleavage	ripple mark, riffle	Rippelmarke *f*; Wellenmarke *f*, Wellenfurche *f*; Windrippeln *fpl*
ring oven, ring furnace, ring kiln	Ringofen *m*		
ring radiator	Ringstrahler *m*	ripple ratio	s. ripple factor
ring resonator	s. toroidal resonator	ripples	s. capillary waves
ring scaler	s. ring scaling circuit	ripple voltage, ripple potential	Brummspannung *f*; Welligkeitsspannung *f*
ring scaling circuit; ring scaler	rückgekoppelte Untersetzerschaltung (Zählschaltung) *f*, Ringschaltung *f*; Untersetzer *m* in Ringschaltung, Ringzähler *m*		
		ripple voltage, surge voltage, pulsating (pulsing, pulsed, pulse) voltage ‹el.›	Rippelspannung *f*, Kräuselspannung *f*, Wellenspannung *f*, pulsierende Spannung *f*, Impulsspannung *f*, Stoßspannung *f* ‹El.›
ring scission	s. ring cleavage		
ring seal	Ringdichtung *f*		
ring-shaped halo	s. ring halo ‹opt.›	rippling	s. capillary waves
ring shift	s. cyclic shift	rippling, rips, lumpy sea	Kabbelung *f*, Kabbelsee *f*, kabbelige See *f*
ring shooting	Ringschießen *n*, Ringseismik *f*		
		rippling sea, rippled sea	gekräuselte See *f*, sehr ruhige See ‹Stärke 1›
ring slot	s. annulus ‹techn.›		
ring spherometer	Ringsphärometer *n*	rips	s. rippling
ring structure	s. ring texture	rise ‹of star›	Aufgang *m* ‹Gestirn›
ring surface	s. torus	rise	s. a. increase
ring texture, ring structure	Ringfaserstruktur *f*, Ringfasertextur *f*	rise	s. a. launch
		rise	= difference of ordinates
ring to infinity	s. fringe of equal inclination	rise in temperature	s. rise of temperature
		rise of field, field raising	Feldaufbau *m*, Aufbau *m* des Feldes
ring transformer	s. toroidal-core transformer		
ring vibrator	Ringschwinger *m*	rise of luminescence [intensity]	Anklingung *f* der Lumineszenz, Aufbau *m* der Lumineszenz, Lumineszenzaufbau *m*
ring vortex	Ringwirbel *m*		
rinsing	Spülung *f*		
		rise of temperature, temperature rise, rise in temperature, raising of temperature	Temperaturerhöhung *f*, Temperatursteigerung *f*
rinsing, washing, watering ‹of photographic layers›	Wässerung *f*, Auswässerung *f* ‹photographischer Schichten›		
rinsing roller	s. eddy motion of the water particles	rise of temperature	s. a. temperature increase
		rise of the pulse [front]	Impulsanstieg *m*, Flankenanstieg *m*
rinsing water, wash water, washing water, washings	Waschwasser *n*, Spülwasser *n*		
riometer	Riometer *n*		

rise of zero	s. secular rise of zero	roaring <of wind>	Heulen n, Tosen n <Wind>
rise time, build-up time	Anlaufzeit f	roaring	s. a. drone <ac.>
		roaring flame	s. blue flame
		roaring forties	brave Westwinde mpl, heulende Vierziger mpl
rise time <of luminescence>	Anklingzeit f, Aufbauzeit f <Lumineszenz>		
		roast[ing]	Rösten n
rise time	s. build-up time <of oscillation>	Robert['s] law	Robertsches Gesetz n
		Robertson line element	Robertsonsches Linienelement n
rise time, build-up time, building-up time, time response <e.g. of pulse>	Anstiegszeit f; Aufbauzeit f <z. B. Impuls>		
		Robertson-Walker metric	Robertson-Walker-Metrik f
rise time <of nuclear reactor>	s. period	Roberts-von Hippel method	Hippel-Robertssches Meßverfahren n
rise-time distortion	s. phase distortion	Robin['s] law	Robinsches Gesetz n
rising	s. increase	Robin['s] problem, third boundary value problem <of the Laplace equation>	Robinsches Problem n
rising branch, ascending branch, rising portion <of a curve>	aufsteigender (ansteigender) Ast m		
rising of the boiling point	s. elevation of the boiling point	Robinson bridge, Wien-Robinson bridge	Robinson-Brücke f, Wien-Robinson-Brücke f
rising portion	s. rising branch		
rising prominence, ascending prominence	aufsteigende Protuberanz f	Robinson cup anemometer	Robinsonsches Schalenkreuzanemometer n, Robinsonsches Windmesser m
rising-sun magnetron	„rising-sun"-Magnetron n, Sonnenstrahlmagnetron n, Magnetron n vom Typ „rising sun"		
		Robinson-Dadson equal loudness contour, S.P.L. (sound pressure level) equal loudness contour	Robinson-Dadson-Kurve f, Kurve f gleicher Lautstärke [nach Robinson und Dadson]
risk <of the first kind or I type risk or type I risk or K-risk, of the second kind or II type risk or type II risk or β-risk, of the third kind or III type risk or type III risk>	Risiko n, Wagnis n <erster oder 1., zweiter oder 2., dritter oder 3. Art>	Robitzsch bimetallic actinometer, bimetallic actinometer, Michelson actinometer	Bimetallaktinometer n, Robitzsch-Aktinometer n, Michelson-Aktinometer n
		Robitzsch bimetallic pyranograph, bimetallic pyranograph	Bimetallpyranograph m, Robitzsch-Pyranograph m
risk function	Risikofunktion f	Robitzsch diagram, Robitzsch plot	Robitzsch-Diagramm n
risk point	Risikopunkt m		
Risley prism	Risley-Prisma n, Risleysches Prisma n	robot	Roboter m; Robotgreifer m
		robust test <stat.>	widerstandsfähiger (robuster) Test m <Stat.>
Ritchie photometer	s. Ritchie wedge photometer		
Ritchie prism	Ritchie-Prisma n	Roche distance, Roche['s] limit	Rochesche Distanz f, Rochesche Grenze f, Roche-Radius m
Ritchie wedge	Ritchie-Keil m		
Ritchie wedge photometer, Ritchie photometer	Ritchie-Photometer n	Rochelle salt, Seignette salt, sodium potassium tartrate, $KNaC_4H_4O_6$	Seignettesalz n, Rochellesalz n, Kaliumnatriumtartrat n, $KNaC_4H_4O_6$ [$4 \cdot H_2O$]
Ritter['s] method [of sections], method of sections	Rittersches Schnittverfahren (Momentenverfahren) n, Ritterscher Schnitt m		
		Roche model	Roche-Modell n, Rochesches Modell n
Ritter section	Ritterscher Schnitt m	roche moutonnée	s. bump <geo.>
Rittmann['s] hypothesis	Rittmannsche Hypothese f, Hypothese von Rittmann	Rochon [prism]	Rochon-Prisma n, Doppelprisma n nach Rochon
Ritz['] combination principle	s. combination principle	rock awash	blinde Klippe f
		rock basin, glacial basin	Gletschertopf m
Ritz['] formula	Ritzsche Serienformel f	rocket dynamics	Raketendynamik f
Ritz['] hypothesis	Ritzsche Hypothese f	rocket engine, rocket motor	Raketenmotor m, Raketentriebwerk n, Raketenantrieb m
Ritz['] method, Rayleigh-Ritz method, Rayleigh-Ritz principle	Ritzsches Verfahren n, Ritzsche Variationsmethode f, Verfahren (Methode f, Variationsmethode) von Ritz		
		rocket flight	Raketenflug m
		rocket flight, active flight, powered flight	Antriebsflug m, Treibflug m
river / up the, up-stream	stromaufwärts, stromauf, gegen die Strömung		
		rocket fuel	s. propellant
river basin, basin, region of alimentation, drainage <geo.>	Einzugsgebiet n; Stromgebiet n, Flußgebiet n <Geo.>	rocket motor	s. rocket engine
		rocket propulsion; reaction propulsion; jet propulsion	Strahlantrieb m; Düsenantrieb m; Raketenantrieb m
river bed sinuosity	Laufentwicklung f, Flußentwicklung f		
river discharge (flow, runoff), flow of the river <geo.>	Abfluß m, Abflußmenge f; Wasserführung f <Fluß> <Geo.>	rocket research, rocketry	Raketenforschung f
river pattern <cryst.>	„river pattern" n <Krist.>	rocket sounding	Raketenaufstieg m, Raketensondierung f
Rivlin-Ericksen tensor	Rivlin-Ericksenscher Tensor m	rocket stage, stage of the rocket	Stufe f der Rakete, Raketenstufe f, Raketeneinheit f
RKKY interaction	= Ruderman-Kittel-Kasuya-Yosida interaction	rocking, rocking vibration	Nickschwingung f, ebene Pendelschwingung f, Pendelschwingung f <Molekül>; Nickbewegung f
R-L element (network)	s. resistance-inductance network		
R-L phase-angle bridge, resistance-inductance phase-angle bridge	RL-Phasenbrücke f		
R-L section	s. resistance-inductance network	rocking, pitch, pitching, plunging <hydr.>	Stampfen n, Stampfbewegung f <Hydr.>
R matrix, derivative matrix	R-Matrix f, „derivative matrix" f, Hilfsmatrix f	rocking beam, beam, scale beam	Waagebalken m
r-meter	s. roentgen meter		
r.m.s.	s. root-mean-square	rocking beam oscillator	Waagebalkenoszillator m
roaming electron	s. stray electron		

rocking cell, Castner-Kellner cell	Schaukelzelle f [nach Castner und Kellner], Castner-Kellner-Zelle f	rod thermometer	Stabthermometer n
rocking curve <in X-ray reflection from single crystals>	Schwenkkurve f, „rocking"-Kurve f <Röntgenkristallreflexion>	rod-type dilatometer, rod dilatometer	Stabdehnungsmesser m
		rod-type dynamometer	s. rod dynamometer
		rod-type fuel element	s. rod-shaped fuel element
rocking mirror	Pendelspiegel m	rod-type suspension insulator	Langstabisolator m
rocking suspension	s. pendulum suspension		
rocking vibration	s. rocking		
rock magnetism	Gesteinsmagnetismus m	Roemer['s] method, Römer['s] method, method of Olaf Roemer	Methode f von Olaf (Ole, Olaus) Römer, Römers Methode
rock mechanics, mechanics of the rocks	Felsmechanik f, Gesteinsmechanik f	roentgen, roentgen unit, R-unit, R, r	Röntgen n, Röntgeneinheit f, R-Einheit f, R, r
rock movement	Gebirgsbewegung f		
rockoon	Raketenstart m vom Ballon aus	roentgen apparatus, X-ray apparatus, X-ray machine, roentgen machine, radiograph	Röntgenapparat m, Röntgengerät n
rock pressure	s. pressure of mountain mass		
rock slide	s. soil slide		
rock stream, stone stream	Schuttstrom m	roentgen cinematography, X-ray cinematography, cineradiography, radio-cinematography, X-ray movies	Röntgenkinematographie f; Bioröntgenographie f
Rockwell hardness [number], Rockwell number, RHN, R <R_A; B; C; D; E; F; G; H; K; L; M, N, P; R; S; T; V; W; X or Y>	Rockwell-Härte f, Härtewert m nach Rockwell, HR <HR A, ..., HR Y>		
		roentgen equivalent, equivalent röntgen	Röntgenäquivalent n
		roentgen equivalent, man	s. rem unit
Rockwell hardness test, Rockwell test, Rockwell method [of hardness testing]	Rockwell-Härteprüfung f, Härteprüfung f nach Rockwell, Rockwell-Verfahren n	roentgen equivalent, physical; physical roentgen equivalent; rep unit, rep	rep-Einheit f, Rep n, physikalisches Röntgenäquivalent n, rep
Rockwell hardness tester	Rockwell-Härteprüfgerät n, Rockwell-Härteprüfmaschine f	roentgen-hour-metre	s. roentgen per hour at one metre
		roentgenization	s. X-ray irradiation
Rockwell method [of hardness testing]	s. Rockwell hardness test	roentgen kymograph, kymograph	Röntgenkymograph m, Kymograph m; Kymographion n
Rockwell number	s. Rockwell hardness		
Rockwell test	s. Rockwell hardness test	roentgen machine	s. roentgen apparatus
Rocky-Point effect, flash arc	„Rocky-Point"-Effekt m	roentgenmateriology	s. X-ray test
		roentgen meter, roentgenometer, r-meter	Röntgenmeter n, Röntgenmeßgerät n, r-Meter n
		roentgen microspectrography, X-ray microspectrography	Röntgenmikrospektrographie f
rod, bar of circular section	Rundstab m; Stange f		
rod <in the reactor>	Stab m <im Reaktor>	roentgenofluorescence, X-ray fluorescence	Röntgenfluoreszenz f
rod <of the eye>	Stäbchen n <Auge>		
rod, bar; column <mech.>	Stab m <Mech.>	roentgenogram	s. radiograph
rod birefringence	s. rod double refraction	roentgenograph	s. radiograph
rod dilatometer	s. rod-type dilatometer	roentgenographic emulsion, X-ray emulsion, radiographic emulsion	Röntgenemulsion f
rod double refraction, rod birefringence	Stäbchendoppelbrechung f		
rod-drop experiment	Stabfallversuch m	roentgenography, radiography; X-ray photography	Röntgenographie f, Roentgenaufnahme f, Röntgenaufnahmeverfahren n; Röntgenphotographie f
rod dynamometer, rod-type dynamometer	Stangendynamometer n		
rod float	s. staff float		
rod gauge, end gauge	Stichmaß n	roentgenology	Röntgenologie f, Röntgenstrahlenkunde f, Röntgenkunde f, Röntgenlehre f
rod graduated on both sides	s. double-sided staff		
		roentgenoluminescence, X-ray luminescence	Röntgenlumineszenz f
rod lattice	Stabgitter n	roentgenomateriology	s. X-ray test
rod mirror	s. rod reflector	roentgenometer	s. roentgen meter
rod of inertia, inertia rod	Trägheitsstab m	roentgenometer, ionometer	Röntgenstrahlintensitätsmesser m, Ionometer n
		roentgenoscope	s. fluoroscope
rod-plate spark gap	Stab-Platte-Funkenstrecke f, Elektrodenanordnung f Stab – Platte	roentgenoscopy	s. fluoroscopy
		roentgen per hour at one metre, roentgen-hour-metre, rhm unit, rhm	Röntgen n pro Stunde in einem Meter Abstand [von der Strahlungsquelle], rhm-Einheit f, rhm
rod radiator	s. dielectric rod antenna		
rod reflector, rod mirror	Stabreflektor m		
rod resistance; rod resistor	Stabwiderstand m	roentgen photogrammetry, X-ray photogrammetry	Röntgenphotogrammetrie f
Rodrigues['] formula, Rodriguez['] formula	Rodriguessche Formel f	Roentgen (roentgen) radiation (rays)	s. X-rays
rod-shaped <bio.>	stäbchenförmig <Bio.>	roentgen spectrum, X-ray spectrum	Röntgenspektrum n
rod-shaped fuel element, rod-type fuel element <of the reactor>	stabförmiges Brennelement n, Stabelement n <Reaktor>	roentgen tube, Roentgen tube, Röntgen tube, X-ray tube	Röntgenröhre f, Röntgenlampe f
		roentgen unit, roentgen, R-unit, R, r	Röntgen n, Röntgeneinheit f, R-Einheit f, R, r
		Rogallo['s] wing	Rogallo-Flügel m
		Roget['s] spiral	Rogetsche Spirale f, Roget-Spirale f
rod-shaped tube, rod-shaped valve	Stabröhre f, Außengitterröhre f, Außensteuerröhre f		
rod-suspended current meter	Stangenflügel m, Stangenmeßflügel m	Rogowski coil, pick-up coil, Rogowski loop	Rogowski-Spule f, Rogowski-Gürtel m, Rogowski-Spannungsmesser m

Rogowski factor	Rogowski-Faktor m	rolling moment coefficient, coefficient of rolling moment; heeling moment coefficient, coefficient of heeling moment	Rollmomentenbeiwert m <Flugzeug>; Krängungsmomentenbeiwert m <Schiff>; Längsneigungsmomentenbeiwert m
Rogowski loop	s. Rogowski coil		
roll	s. a. bank <aero.>		
roll	s. a. eddy motion of the water particles		
roll	s. a. rumbling	rolling motion (movement)	s. rolling <mech.>
roll	s. a. rolling <hydr.>		
rollability, rolling property	Walzbarkeit f	rolling motion (movement)	s. rolling <hydr.>
roll-back point, re-run point	Wiederholpunkt m, Wiederholungspunkt m	rolling of eye	Augenrollen n, Rollbewegung f des Auges, Rollen n des Auges
roll-back routine, re-run routine	Wiederholungsprogramm n, Wiederholprogramm n	rolling pendulum	Rollpendel n
roll bonding	Verbindung f durch Walzen, Walzverbindung f	rolling pressure	Umformungswiderstand m beim Walzen, Walzdruck m, Walzwiderstand m
roll cloud, roller <meteo.>	Böenwalze f, Wolkenwalze f, Walze f, Wulstcumulus m, Wolkenwall m; Böenkragen m, Wolkenkragen m <Meteo.>	rolling property	s. rollability
		rolling resistance	Rollwiderstand m
		rolling screen	s. rolling grid
		rolling surface	Wälzfläche f, Wälzbahn f, Wälzebene f
rolled-up vortex sheet	sich aufrollende Wirbelfläche f		
roller; pulley; wheel	Rolle f; Scheibe f; Rad n	rolling texture, texture resulting from rolling	Walztextur f
roller	s. roll cloud <meteo.>		
roller	s. a. right circular cylinder	rolling-up <of vortex>	Aufrollen n <Wirbel>
roller	s. a. ground roll		
roller bearing <mech.>	Rollen[auf]lager n <Mech.>	rolling wear, wear by rolling [motion]	Rollverschleiß m, rollender Verschleiß m
roller dam	s. roller weir		
roller fading	Seegangschwund[effekt] m	roll wave	Rollwelle f, rollende Welle f, Roller m
roller-type bridge	s. roller-type measuring bridge	Roman balance	s. Roman steelyard
roller-type capacitor, wrapped capacitor	Wickelkondensator m	romanic glacier, reconstructed glacier, recemented glacier	regenerierter Gletscher m
roller-type measuring bridge, roller-type bridge	Walzenbrücke f, Walzenmeßbrücke f	Roman steelyard, steel[-]yard, steelyard balance, Roman balance	Laufgewichtsdynamometer n, Laufgewichtswaage f, Schnellwaage f
roller weir, roller dam, cylindrical barrage	Walzenwehr n, Trommelwehr n, zylindrisches Wehr n, Zylinderwehr n		
Rolle['s] theorem	Satz m von Rolle, Rollescher Satz (Mittelwertsatz m)	Römer['s] method, Roemer['s] method, method of Olaf Roemer	Methode f von Olaf (Ole, Olaus) Römer, Römers Methode
Rollin film	s. helium film	Ronchi grating	Ronchi-Gitter n
rolling; roll; rolling motion (movement) <hydr.>	Schlingern n, Schlingerbewegung f, Pivotieren n, Rollen n, Rollbewegung f <Hydr.>	Ronchi test	Verfahren n nach Ronchi, Ronchi-Verfahren n, Ronchi-Test m
		röntgen	s. roentgen
		Röntgen current	Röntgen-Strom m
		Röntgen effect	Röntgen-Effekt m
rolling, rolling motion (movement) <mech.>	Rollen n, Rollbewegung f, Wälzen n, wälzende Bewegung f <Mech.>	Röntgen-Eichenwald['s] experiment	Röntgen-Eichenwald-Versuch m, Röntgen-Eichenwaldscher Versuch m, Versuch von Röntgen und Eichenwald
rolling <techn.>	Walzen n, Auswalzen n <Techn.>		
		Röntgen radiation (rays)	s. X-rays
rolling	s. a. bank <aero.>	Röntgen tube	s. roentgen tube
rolling angle	Wälzwinkel m	roof photometer, Dach photometer, Trotter and Weber photometer	Dachphotometer n, Trotter-Weber-Photometer n
rolling anisotropy	Walzanisotropie f		
rolling ball test	s. hardness test using rolling balls	roof prism	s. ridge prism
		roof weir	Dachwehr n
rolling circle, moving circle, generating circle	Wälzkreis m, Rollkreis m	room	Raum m
rolling cone	Wälzkegel m	room acoustics, architectural acoustics; acoustics of buildings	Raumakustik f
rolling direction, direction of rolling	Walzrichtung f		
rolling friction	Rollreibung f, rollende Reibung f; Wälzreibung f, wälzende Reibung	room constant <ac.>	Raumkonstante f <Ak.>
		room illumination	Raumbeleuchtung f
rolling friction torque, moment of rolling friction	Rollreibungsmoment n	room index <opt.>	Raumindex m <Opt.>
rolling grid, rolling screen	Rollblende f	room noise	Raumgeräusch n, Saalgeräusch n
rolling line	Wälzgerade f		
		room requirement	s. required volume
rolling load	s. live load	room scattering	Raumstreuung f, Wandstreuung f
rolling moment	Rollmoment n		
		room temperature, normal room temperature, ordinary temperature, R.T.	Raumtemperatur f, Zimmertemperatur f

room-temperature ageing (hardening), ageing at room temperature, age hardening at room temperature, age hardening by cold work[ing] <of metals> — Kalthärtung f, Kaltverfestigung f <Metalle>

room utilization factor, utilance — Raumwirkungsgrad m

root <geo.> — Wurzel f, Deckenwurzel f <Geo.>

root deviation — s. standard deviation

root diagram, Dynkin diagram, chromosome <math.> — Dynkin-Diagramm n, Wurzeldiagramm n <Math.>

rooted tree <math.> — Wurzelbaum m <Math.>

root element, properly nilpotent element, proper nilpotent element — eigentlich nilpotentes Element n, Wurzelgröße f

root element — s. a. nilpotent element

root locus — Wurzelort m, Wurzelhodograph m

root locus analysis (method, technique), Evans['] root-locus method, Evans['] method, method of Evans — Wurzelort[s]verfahren n, Wurzelort[s]methode f, Evanssche Methode f, Evans-Methode f

root-mean-square, root-mean-square value, root-sum-square [value], r.m.s. value, r.s.s. value, r.m.s., quadratic mean — quadratischer Mittelwert m, quadratisches Mittel n, Quadratmittel m

root-mean-square current — s. current root-mean-square

root-mean-square deviation — s. standard deviation

root-mean-square distance, mean square distance — mittlerer quadratischer Abstand m, quadratisch gemittelter Abstand

root-mean-square error, standard error, least mean square error, mean error; mean square error <US> — mittlerer Fehler m, mittlerer quadratischer Fehler, quadratischer Fehler, Standardfehler m, Normalfehler m, Unsicherheitsmaß n, Quadratfehler m; mittleres Fehlerquadrat n

root-mean-square fluctuation — mittlere quadratische Schwankung f, mittlere [statistische] Schwankung

root-mean-square of the deviation — s. standard deviation <stat.>

root-mean-square sound pressure, mean square sound pressure, effective sound pressure — effektiver Schalldruck m, Effektivwert m des Schalldrucks

root-mean-square speed; root-mean-square velocity, mean square velocity; effective velocity — mittlere quadratische Geschwindigkeit f, mittlere Geschwindigkeit; Effektivgeschwindigkeit f, effektive Geschwindigkeit

root-mean-square value, [mean] effective value, mean square value, r.m.s. value <el.> — Effektivwert m, quadratischer Mittelwert m <der Wechselgröße> <El.>

root-mean-square value — s. a. root-mean-square

root-mean-square value of current — s. current root-mean-square

root-mean-square velocity — s. root-mean-square speed

root-mean-square voltage, voltage root-mean-square, voltage r.m.s., r.m.s. voltage — Effektivwert m der Spannung, Effektivspannung f, effektive Spannung f

root-mean-square voltmeter, r.m.s. voltmeter — Effektivwertmesser m, Effektivwertzeiger m, Effektiv[wert]voltmeter n

root of the notch, notch groove, groove of the notch, base of the notch — Kerbgrund m

root of unity — Einheitswurzel f

Roots blower — Roots-Gebläse n

Roots pump, Roots-type pump — Roots-Pumpe f, Millitorrpumpe f, Feinvakuumpumpe f, Wälzkolbenpumpe f

root-sum-square [value] — s. root-mean-square

root test — s. Cauchy['s] nth root test

rope friction, friction of the rope — Umschlingungsreibung f, Seilreibung f

rope pulley, rope sheave — Seilrolle f; Seilscheibe f

ropes — s. windows <radar>

rope tension — s. tension relief

ropiness — s. viscidity

Rösch colour solid — Farbkörper m nach Rösch, Röschscher Farbkörper

rose — Rosenkurve f, Rhodanee f

Rose-Gorter method — Rose-Gortersche Methode f, Rose-Gorter-Methode f

Rosenberg generator — Rosenberg-Maschine f, Rosenberg-Generator m, Rosenbergscher Querfeldgenerator m

Rosenbluth['s] formula — Rosenbluth-Formel f

Rosenbluth potential — Rosenbluth-Potential n

Rosen['s] function — Rosen-Funktion f

Rose ring — Rose-Ring m, Shimring m [nach Rose]

rosette — Rosette f

rosette curve — Rosettenkurve f

rosette orbit, rosette shaped path — Rosettenbahn f

Roshko model — Roshkosches Modell n

Rossby chart (diagram) — s. Rossby plot

Rossby number, Ro — Rossby-Zahl f, Rossbysche Kennzahl f, Rossbysche Zahl f, Ro

Rossby parameter — Rossbyscher Parameter m

Rossby plot, Rossby diagram (chart) — Rossby-Diagramm n

Rossby wave — Rossby-Welle f

Rosseland['s] mean — Mittelwert m nach Rosseland, Rosselandsches Mittel n

Rosseland mean absorption coefficient — mittlerer Absorptionskoeffizient m nach Rosseland

Rossi alpha experiment — Rossi-alpha-Experiment n

Rossi alpha probability — Rossi-alpha-Wahrscheinlichkeit f

Rossi circuit — Rossi-Schaltung f, Koinzidenzschaltung f nach Rossi

Rossi curve — s. Rossi transition curve

Rossi-Forel [intensity] scale, scale of Rossi and Forel — Rossi-Forel-Skala f, Rossi-Forelsche Skala f, Skala von Rossi und Forel

Rossini calorie, thermochemical calorie, $cal_{thermochem}$ — thermochemische Kalorie f, Rossini-Kalorie f, $cal_{thermochem}$

Rossi shower — Rossi-Schauer m

Rossi transition curve, Rossi curve — Rossi-Kurve f

Ross['] lens system, Ross['] system [of lenses] — Linsenkorrektionssystem n [nach Ross], Ross-Linsensystem n, Rosssches Linsensystem n

rot — s. rotor <math.>

rotable antenna — s. rotating antenna

rotamer — s. conformation isomer

rotameter, flowrator <US> — Schwebekörper-Durchflußmesser m, Durchflußmesser m mit Schwebekörper, Schwimmkörper-Durchflußmesser m, Schwimmer[durchfluß]messer m, Schwimmerverbrauchsmesser m; Rotamesser m, Rotameter m

rotary air pump — s. rotary pump

rotary alternating axis — s. rotation-reflection axis

rotary antenna — s. rotating antenna

rotary-beam antenna — Drehrichtstrahler m, „rotary-beam"-Antenne f

rotary-bending fatigue test	Umlaufbiegeversuch m	rotary seal	rotierende Dichtung f
rotary-bending fatigue testing machine, rotation (revolving) fatigue [testing] machine	Umlaufbiegemaschine f	rotary shutter	Rotationsverschluß m
rotary capacitor	s. rotating capacitor ‹acc.›	rotary shutter, rotating shutter; rotary (rotating) disk shutter, rotating disk-type shutter	Umlaufverschluß m; Umlaufblende f; umlaufende Blende f; Verschlußblende f; Sektorblende f
rotary compressor	Rotationskompressor m, Rotationsverdichter m, Umlaufverdichter m	rotary shutter	s. a. sector shutter
rotary condenser ‹acc.›	s. rotating capacitor	rotary slide valve vacuum pump, rotary sliding vane type compressor, rotary vane pump, mechanical backing pump	Drehschieberpumpe f, Drehschiebervakuumpumpe f, Kapselpumpe f
rotary converter, motor-converter, single-armature (synchronous) converter, genemotor ‹US›	Einankerumformer m, rotierender (umlaufender) Umformer m, Drehumformer m, Umformer		
rotary current	s. three-phase current	rotary spark gap, rotary gap, rotary discharger	Abreißfunkenstrecke f, Stoßfunkenstrecke f, umlaufende (rotierende) Funkenstrecke f, Taktfunkenstrecke f
rotary discharger	s. rotary spark gap		
rotary disk shutter	Flügelblende f		
rotary disk shutter; rotary (rotating) shutter; rotating disk (disk-type) shutter	Umlaufverschluß m; Umlaufblende f, umlaufende Blende f		
		rotary stream, counter[-]current	Neerstrom m
rotary dispersion	s. rotatory dispersion	rotary swash plate pump, swash plate pump, wobble pump	Taumelscheibenpumpe f, Wobbelpumpe f
rotary field	s. rotating field		
rotary flow	s. rotational flow	rotary vacuum filter	Vakuumdrehfilter n, rotierendes Vakuumfilter n, Rotationsvakuumfilter n
rotary force	s. torsional force		
rotary gap	s. rotary spark gap		
rotary gas pump	s. rotary pump	rotary vacuum pump	s. rotary pump
rotary inertia, rotational inertia	Rotationsträgheit f, Drehungsträgheit f; Drehwucht f	rotary-vane anemometer	s. vane anemometer
		rotary vane magnetometer	s. Gulf magnetometer
rotary inversion, rotoinversion, rotation-inversion	Drehinversion f	rotary vane pump	s. rotary slide valve vacuum pump
rotary inversion axis	s. rotation-inversion axis	rotary vibration	s. torsional vibration
rotary magnetization	s. remagnetization	rotary viscometer	s. rotational viscometer
rotary mercury pump, mercury rotating pump	Gaedesche Kapselpumpe f, Kapselpumpe, Gaede-Kapselpumpe f, rotierende Quecksilberpumpe (Quecksilber-.luftpumpe) f	rotary voltmeter	Rotationsvoltmeter n
		rotatable, swivel, swivelling	schwenkbar
		rotatable direction finder	s. rotating-reflector direction finder
rotary mirror, rotating mirror	Drehspiegel m; rotierender Spiegel m	rotating[-] anode [X-ray] tube	Drehanodenröhre f
rotary motion, rotary movement, rotational motion, motion of rotation, rotatory motion	Drehbewegung f, Rotationsbewegung f, drehende Bewegung f	rotating antenna, rotary antenna, rotable antenna	rotierende Antenne f, Drehantenne f, Rotationsantenne f; drehbare Antenne
rotary motion	s. a. orbital motion	rotating antenna direction finder	s. rotating-reflector direction finder
rotary motion of the Earth, Earth's rotation, rotation of the Earth	Erddrehung f, Erdrotation f, Erdumdrehung f, Erdumschwung m	rotating beam	umlaufender Leitstrahl m
rotary movement	s. rotary motion	rotating bending, bending with rotating bar	Umlaufbiegebeanspruchung f, Umlaufbiegung f
rotary multiplate vacuum pump, radial cylinder rotating pump, sliding vane pump	rotierende Mehrschieberpumpe f	rotating biplate	drehende Doppelplatte f, drehende Halbschattenplatte f; Halbschattenapparat m mit drehender Doppelplatte
rotary oil [air] pump, rotary oil vacuum pump	rotierende Öl[luft]pumpe f, Rotations-Ölluftpumpe f, Rotationsölpumpe f		
rotary oscillation	s. torsional vibration	rotating capacitor, rotary capacitor, rotary condenser ‹acc.›	rotierender Kondensator m ‹Beschl.›
rotary piston engine, Wankel engine	Wankel-Motor m, Kreiskolbenmotor m	rotating coil, moving coil	Rotationsspule f; Drehspule f
rotary piston pump, rotary reciprocating pump	Umlaufkolbenpumpe f; Drehkolbenpumpe f, Wälzpumpe f	rotating co-ordinate system, rotating system of co-ordinates	rotierendes Koordinatensystem n
		rotating crystal, revolving crystal	Drehkristall m
		rotating crystal diagram	Drehkristallaufnahme f
rotary polarization	s. optical activity		
rotary potentiometer	Drehpotentiometer n	rotating crystal method	s. Bragg's rotating crystal method
rotary power	Drehvermögen n		
rotary pump, rotary air pump, rotary vacuum pump; rotary gas pump	rotierende Luftpumpe (Vakuumpumpe, Pumpe) f, Rotations[vakuum]pumpe f, Rotationsluftpumpe f	rotating-cup anemometer	s. cup anemometer
		rotating cylinder viscometer	Drehzylinderviskosimeter n
		rotating diaphragm, revolving diaphragm	Revolverblende f; Blendenrevolver m
rotary pump	s. a. rotodynamic pump	rotating directional diagram	umlaufendes Richtdiagramm n
rotary reciprocating pump	s. rotary piston pump	rotating-disk column	Drehscheibenkolonne f
rotary reflection ‹cryst.›	Drehspiegelung f, Element n der zusammengesetzten Symmetrie ‹Krist.›	rotating-disk monochromator, revolving disk monochromator	Drehscheibenmonochromator m
rotary reflection	s. a. improper orthogonal mapping ‹math.›	rotating-disk phosphoroscope	Drehscheibenphosphoroskop n
rotary rheostat	Drehwiderstand m	rotating disk[-type] shutter	s. rotary shutter

rotating-disk vacuum gauge	s. Langmuir manometer
rotating dome, revolving dome	Drehkuppel f
rotating field, rotary field	rotierendes Feld n, Drehfeld n, Rotationsfeld n, umlaufendes Feld
rotating field antenna	Drehfeldantenne f
rotating field instrument	Drehfeldinstrument n, Drehfeldmeßgerät n
rotating-field oscillation	Drehfeldschwingung f
rotating-field-type machine	s. revolving field machine
rotating lobe meter	s. lobed impeller meter
rotating magnetic field, magnetic rotating field	magnetisches Drehfeld n
rotating mirror, rotary mirror, revolving mirror; rotating reflector	Drehspiegel m; rotierender Spiegel m
rotating-mirror camera	Drehspiegelkamera f, Drehspiegel-Schmierkamera f
rotating-mirror oscillograph	s. loop oscillograph
rotating-mirror photometer <with one mirror>	Spiegelapparat m [nach Brodhun]
rotating-mirror photometer <with two mirrors>	Doppelspiegelphotometer n, Doppelspiegelapparat m von (nach) Brodhun-Martens, Drehspiegelphotometer n, Photometer n mit rotierenden Spiegeln, Martens-Brodhunscher Doppelspiegelapparat
rotating mirrors method	s. Foucault's method
rotating potentiometer	Umlaufpotentiometer n
rotating prism, revolving prism	rotierendes Prisma n
rotating rack	Schwenkrahmen m
rotating radome	Rotodom n, rotierende Antennenverkleidung f
rotating reflector	s. rotating mirror
rotating-reflector direction finder, rotatable (rotating antenna) direction finder	Drehrahmenpeiler m, Peiler m mit Drehrahmen
rotating Reynolds number, rotation Reynolds number	Rotations-Reynolds-Zahl f
rotating rigid frame	rotierendes starres Bezugssystem n
rotating sector, rotating shutter, sector disk	rotierender Sektor m; rotierende Sektorscheibe f, Scheibe f <Lichtschwächung, speziell zur Bestimmung der Geschwindigkeit von Meteoren>
rotating shutter	Drehverschluß m, Revolververschluß m
rotating shutter	s. a. rotary shutter
rotating shutter	s. a. rotating sector
rotating system of co-ordinates, rotating co-ordinate system	rotierendes Koordinatensystem n
rotating tensor, rotation tensor <math.>	Versor m, Drehungsaffinor m, Drehtensor m, Drehungstensor m, Rotator m <Math.>
rotating the plane of polarization anticlockwise	s. laevogyric
rotating the plane of polarization clockwise	s. dextrogyric
rotating vector	Drehvektor m, momentaner Winkelgeschwindigkeitsvektor m <Mech.>; umlaufender Zeiger m, rotierender Vektor m <El.>
rotating viscometer gauge	s. Langmuir manometer
rotating-wave approximation	Näherung f der rotierenden Welle
rotating wheel anemograph	s. vane anemograph
rotating wheel anemometer	s. vane anemometer
rotating wheel method	s. Fizeau['s] method
rotation; circumgyration <about a free axis>	Rotation f, Drehung f; Rotieren n
rotation, revolution	Umdrehung f
rotation	s. curl <of the vector field>
rotation about a point, rotation around a point, spherical rotation	Drehung (Rotation) f um einen Punkt, sphärische Rotation
rotational absorption line	Rotationsabsorptionslinie f
rotational absorption spectrum	Rotationsabsorptionsspektrum n
rotational acceleration, acceleration due to rotation	Rotationsbeschleunigung f, Drehbeschleunigung f
rotational acceleration	s. a. angular acceleration
rotational analysis	Analyse f der Rotationsspektren, Rotationsanalyse f
rotational axis	s. axis of rotation
rotational band, rotation band	Rotationsbande f
rotational band spectrum	Rotationsbandenspektrum n
rotational-band temperature	s. rotational temperature
rotational broadening [of spectral line]	Rotationsverbreiterung f
rotational characteristic temperature	s. rotational temperature
rotational compliance, mechanical rotational compliance	Torsionsfederung f
rotational constant	Rotationskonstante f
rotational degree of freedom	Rotationsfreiheitsgrad m
rotational diffusion	Rotationsdiffusion f
rotational diffusion coefficient	Rotationsdiffusionskonstante f
rotational distortion	Drehungsverzeichnung f; Rotationsverzerrung f; Bildzerdrehung f, Zerdrehungsfehler m
rotational eigenfunction	Rotationseigenfunktion f
rotational electromotive force, rotational e.m.f.	Rotationsspannung f, Rotations-EMK f
rotational energy, rotation energy, energy of rotation; angular kinetic energy	Rotationsenergie f
rotational energy level	s. rotational level
rotational entropy	Rotationsentropie f
rotational excitation	s. rotational state excitation
rotational fault	Scharnierverwerfung f
rotational field, curl field, vortex field, field of vorticity, eddy field, circuital field, circuital vector field	Wirbelfeld n, Drehfeld n
rotational fine structure	Rotationsfeinstruktur f
rotational flattening	Rotationsabplattung f
rotational flow, vortex-type flow, vortex flow, vortical (rotary) flow; vortex motion, eddy motion, eddying whirl, whirl	Wirbelströmung f, drehungsbehaftete Strömung f, Drehströmung f, Rotationsströmung f, Kreisströmung f; Wirbelstrom m; Wirbelbewegung f
rotational freedom	Rotationsfreiheit f
rotational frequency	Rotationsfrequenz f
rotational frequency	s. a. rotational speed
rotational Hamiltonian	Rotations-Hamilton-Operator m, Rotationsanteil m des Hamilton-Operators

rotational heat [capacity]	Rotationswärme f	rotational state excitation, rotational excitation	Rotationsanregung f
rotational homogenization	Rotationshomogenisierung f	rotational structure	Rotationsstruktur f
rotational hysteresis, rotation hysteresis, rotational magnetic hysteresis	Rotationshysterese f, drehende Hysterese f, magnetische Hysteresis f bei rotierender Probe	rotational sum rule	Rotationssummenregel f
rotational impedance	s. mechanical rotational impedance	rotational-symmetric rotational symmetry	s. rotationally symmetric Rotationssymmetrie f, Drehsymmetrie f, Drehungssymmetrie f
rotational inertia	s. rotary inertia		
rotational inertia	s. a. torque	rotational temperature, rotation (rotational-band, rotational characteristic) temperature, temperature from the rotation spectrum	Rotationstemperatur f, aus dem Rotationsspektrum bestimmte Temperatur f, charakteristische Rotationstemperatur
rotational instability	Rotationsinstabilität f		
rotational invariance	Dreh[ungs]invarianz f, Rotationsinvarianz f		
rotational isomer	s. conformation isomer		
rotational-isomeric	rotationsisomer	rotational term, rotational level	Rotationsterm m
rotational isomerism; molecular dissymmetry due to hindered rotation	Rotationsisomerie f, Konformationsisomerie f, Konstellationsisomerie f; Atropisomerie f		
		rotational term diagram	s. rotational level diagram
		rotational term scheme	s. rotational level diagram
rotational isotope effect	Rotationsisotopieeffekt m	rotational therapy, rotation therapy	Rotationstherapie f, Therapie f mit Rotationsbestrahlung; Therapie mit rotierender Strahlungsquelle; Therapie mit rotierendem Behandlungstisch bei fester Strahlungsquelle
rotational level, rotational energy level	Rotationsniveau n, Rotationsenergieniveau n		
rotational level	s. a. rotational term		
rotational level diagram (scheme), rotational term diagram, rotational term scheme	Rotationstermschema n, Rotationsniveauschema n	rotational transform[ation]	Rotationstransformation f, magnetische Transformation f der Querschnittsebene, Rotationsformation f
rotational line	Rotationslinie f	rotational transition	Rotationsübergang m
rotationally symmetric, rotational-symmetric	rotationssymmetrisch, drehsymmetrisch, kreissymmetrisch	rotational variable [star]	Rotationsveränderlicher m
		rotational variation in light	Rotationslichtwechsel m
rotationally symmetric field	rotationssymmetrisches Feld n	rotational viscometer, rotation (rotary) viscometer, drag-torque viscometer	Rotationsviskosimeter n, Rotationszylinderviskosimeter n, Drehviskosimeter n
rotationally symmetric stress, axially symmetric stress [distribution]	rotationssymmetrischer Spannungszustand m		
		rotational wave	Wirbelwelle f
rotational magnetic hysteresis	s. rotational hysteresis	rotational wave	s. a. shear wave
rotational mechanical impedance	s. mechanical rotational impedance	rotational wave function	Rotationswellenfunktion f
		rotation and stretching, rotation-stretching	Drehstreckung f
rotational mechanical reactance	s. mechanical rotational reactance	rotation anemometer	Rotationsanemometer n
rotational mechanical resistance	s. mechanical rotational resistance	rotation around a point	s. rotation about a point
		rotation axis	s. axis of rotation
rotational moment, rotation moment <of molecules; of the Earth>	Rotationsmoment n <der Moleküle; der Erde>	rotation[-] axis	s. axis of symmetry <cryst.>
		rotation band, rotational band	Rotationsbande f
rotational moment	s. a. torque	rotation by magnetization	s. Einstein-de Haas effect
rotational motion	s. rotary motion		
rotational partition function	Rotationszustandssumme f, Rotationsanteil m der Zustandsfunktion (Zustandssumme)	rotation camera	Drehkristallkammer f
		rotation centre	s. centre of rotation
		rotation diagram	s. rotation pattern
rotational quantum number	s. secondary quantum number	rotation double refraction, double refraction due to rotation	Rotationsdoppelbrechung f
rotational Raman spectrum, Raman rotational spectrum	Rotations-Raman-Spektrum n, Raman-Rotationsspektrum n		
		rotation dynamometer	Rotationsdynamometer n
rotational reactance	s. mechanical rotational reactance	rotation effect	Rotationseffekt m
		rotation energy	s. rotational energy
rotational relaxation	Rotationsrelaxation f	rotation fatigue [testing] machine, rotary-bending fatigue testing machine	Umlaufbiegemaschine f
rotational resistance	s. mechanical rotational resistance		
rotational resonance interaction	Rotationsresonanzwechselwirkung f	rotation frequency	s. rotational speed
		rotation group, rotations group, proper orthogonal group	Drehgruppe f, Drehungsgruppe f, eigentliche orthogonale Gruppe f
rotational spectrum, rotation spectrum, pure rotation spectrum	Rotationsspektrum n, reines Rotationsspektrum		
		rotation hysteresis	s. rotational hysteresis
rotational speed	s. speed [of rotation]	rotation hysteresis integral	Rotationshystereseintegral n, Rotationshysteresisintegral n
rotational speed	s. angular speed		
rotational stabilization	Rotationsstabilisierung f		
rotational state	Rotationszustand m		

rotation inductor	Rotationserdinduktor m, Rotationsinduktor m	**rotation-vibration energy,** vibration-rotation energy	Rotationsschwingungsenergie f
rotation-invariant, invariant under rotation	dreh[ungs]invariant, rotationsinvariant	**rotation-vibration interaction,** vibration-rotation interaction	Rotationsschwingungswechselwirkung f
rotation-inversion	s. rotary inversion	**rotation-vibration spectrum**	s. vibration-rotation spectrum
rotation-inversion axis, rotoinversion axis, axis of rotary inversion, axis of rotation-inversion, rotary inversion axis	Drehinversionsachse f, Inversionsachse f	**rotation viscometer**	s. rotational viscometer
		rotative component of motion <cryst.>	rotativer Bestandteil m der Bewegung <Krist.>
rotation-inversion axis	s. a. rotation-reflection axis	**rotative speed**	s. speed
rotation irradiation	Rotationsbestrahlung f	**rotator** <mech.>	Rotator m <um eine freie Achse beweglicher Körper> <Mech.>
rotation magnetism	Rotationsmagnetismus m		
rotation matrix, proper orthogonal matrix	Rotationsmatrix f, Drehungsmatrix f	**rotatory dispersion,** [optical] rotary dispersion, dispersion of rotation	Rotationsdispersion f
rotation method	s. rotating crystal method		
rotation moment	s. rotational moment		
rotation of molecules	s. molecular rotation	**rotatory dispersion filter,** Prévost filter	Rotationsdispersionsfilter n [von Prévost]
rotation of polarization plane	s. rotation of the plane of polarization		
rotation of register, cyclic shift, register rotation <num.math.>	zyklische Vertauschung f, zyklische Verschiebung f <num.Math.>	**rotatory inertia**	rotatorische Trägheit f
		rotatory motion	s. rotary motion
		rotatory polarization	s. optical activity
rotation of the Earth, rotary motion of the Earth, Earth's rotation	Erddrehung f, Erdrotation f, Erdumdrehung f, Erdumschwung m	**rotatory power**	s. optical rotatory power <quantity>
		rotaversion	cis-trans-Umwandlung f
rotation of the plane of polarization, rotation of polarization plane	Polarisationsdrehung f, Drehung f der Polarisationsebene	**Rothe['s] method**	Rothe-Verfahren n, Rothesches Verfahren n
		Rothery['s] rule	Rotherysche Regel f
		Roth['s] theorem	Rothsche Beziehung f
rotation of transport	Führungsrotation f	**rotodynamic pump,** rotary pump, impeller pump; centrifugal pump; turbo-pump, turbine pump, pump-turbine	Kreiselpumpe f, Drallpumpe f, rotodynamische Pumpe f; Zentrifugalpumpe f, Schleuderpumpe f; Axialpumpe f; Turbopumpe f
rotation parallax	Rotationsparallaxe f		
rotation pattern, rotation diagram	Rotationsdiagramm n		
rotation period, period of rotation, rotation time, time of one revolution, period of revolution, revolution period	Umdrehungszeit f, Umdrehungsperiode f, Umdrehungsdauer f; Rotationsperiode f, Rotationszeit f; Umlauf[s]zeit f, Umlauf[s]periode f, Umlauf[s]dauer f		
		rotoflection axis	s. rotation-reflection axis
		rotoinversion, rotation-inversion, rotary inversion	Drehinversion f
		rotoinversion axis	s. rotation-inversion axis
		roton	Roton n, Rotationsquant n
		roton part	Rotonenanteil m
rotation photograph, X-ray rotation photograph, rotating crystal diagram	Drehkristallaufnahme f, Drehaufnahme f	**rotor** <el.>	Läufer m, Rotor m <El.>
		rotor	s. a. curl <of the vector field>
rotation potential, potential of rotation	Rotationspotential n	**rotor**	s. a. runner
		rotor modulation, propeller modulation, propeller effect	Propellermodulation f, Propellereffekt m
rotation quantum number	s. secondary quantum number		
rotation-reflection axis, rotation-inversion axis, rotoflection axis, rotoinversion axis, axis of rotary inversion, [symmetry] axis of the second sort, rotary inversion (alternating) axis, gyroide	Drehspiegelungsachse f, Drehspiegelachse f, Symmetrieachse f zweiter Art, Drehinversionsachse f, Gyroide f	**rotor ship,** Flettner ship	[Flettnersches] Rotorschiff n, Flettner-Schiff n
		rotor wheel	s. runner
		rottenness <of steel>; brittleness; breakability; fragility; friability; shortness; crackiness	Sprödigkeit f, Brüchigkeit f, Zerbrechlichkeit f
		Rouché['s] theorem	Satz m von Rouché
		rough, hydraulically rough <hydr.>	rauh, hydraulisch rauh <Hydr.>
rotation Reynolds number, rotating Reynolds number	Rotations-Reynolds-Zahl f		
rotations group	s. rotation group	**rough adjustment,** coarse adjustment, coarse setting (control)	Grobeinstellung f
rotation shell	Rotationsschale f		
rotation spectrum, rotational spectrum, pure rotation spectrum	Rotationsspektrum n, reines Rotationsspektrum	**rough-and-ready rule**	s. rough rule
		rough atomic weight, mass number, nuclear (nucleon) number, A	Massenzahl f, Nukleonenzahl f, A, M
rotation speed	s. rotational speed		
rotation speed	s. velocity of rotation	**rough calculation,** computation	Überschlagsrechnung f
rotation-stretching	s. rotation and stretching		
rotation tensor, rotating tensor <math.>	Versor m, Drehungsaffinor m, Drehtensor m, Drehungstensor m, Rotator m <Math.>		
		roughened	s. rough-surfaced
		roughening	Aufrauhung f
rotation temperature	s. rotational temperature		
rotation therapy	s. rotational therapy	**roughening** <num. math.>	Aufrauhung f, Aufrauh[ungs]erscheinung f <num. Math.>
rotation time	s. rotation period		
rotation transformation <cryst.>	Rotationsumwandlung f <Krist.>		
		roughing pump	s. forepump
		rough landing, hard landing	harte Landung f
rotation twin	Rotationszwilling m		
rotation vector	Rotationsvektor m	**rough law regime**	s. rough regime
rotation-vibration band	s. vibration-rotation band	**roughness;** rugosity; asperity	Rauheit f, Rauhigkeit f; Rauhigkeitserhebung f
rotation-vibration constant, vibration-rotation constant	Rotationsschwingungskonstante f		

roughness 726

roughness coefficient, coefficient of roughness, roughness factor, degree of roughness, rugosity coefficient	Rauhigkeitszahl f, Rauheitszahl f, Rauhigkeitsbeiwert m, Rauheitsbeiwert m, Rauhigkeitskoeffizient m, Rauheitskoeffizient m, Rauhigkeitsfaktor m, Rauheitsfaktor m, Rauhigkeitsgrad m, Rauheitsgrad m, Rauhigkeitswert m, Rauheitswert m, Rauhwert m	**Routh-Hurwicz criterion,** Routh['s] criterion [of stability], stability criterion of Routh	Routhsches Stabilitätskriterium n, Stabilitätskriterium nach Routh, Routh-Stabilitätskriterium n, Routh-Kriterium n, Routhsches Kriterium n, Kriterium von Routh
roughness element	Rauhigkeitselement n	**Routhian function**	Routhsche Funktion f, Routh-Funktion f
roughness factor	s. roughness coefficient	**Routh method,** ignoration of co-ordinates	Routhsche Methode f
roughness height, height of roughness	Rauhigkeitshöhe f	**Routh['s] rule**	Routhsche Regel f
roughness Reynolds number	Rauhigkeits-Reynolds-Zahl f, Rauhigkeitskennzahl f, für die einzelne Rauhigkeit charakteristische Reynolds-Zahl f	**routine,** computer (machine) programme	Maschinenprogramm n
		routine	s. a. programme <num. math.>
		routine analysis	Routineanalyse f
roughness spectrum	Rauheitsspektrum n, Rauhigkeitsspektrum n	**routing control**	s. routing guidance
roughometer; profilometer; profile testing meter; talysurf	Rauhigkeitstiefenmesser m, Rauhigkeitsmesser m; Profilmeßgerät n, Profilmesser m, Profilometer n	**routing guidance,** routing control	Leitwegführung f, Leitweglenkung f, Leitwegsteuerung f
		row <cryst.>	Punktreihe f <Krist.>
		Rowe osmometer	Osmometer n nach Rowe, Rowe-Osmometer n
rough regime, rough law regime, completely rough regime	vollkommen rauher Bereich m, vollkommen ausgebildete Rauhigkeitsströmung f	**row index,** line index	Zeilenindex m
		Rowland arrangement [of reflection grating]	s. Rowland mounting [of diffraction grating]
		Rowland bridge	Rowland-Brücke f
rough rule	s. rule of thumb	**Rowland circle**	Rowland-Kreis m
rough sea, angry sea, pecky sea	grobe See f, ziemlich grobe See, ziemlich hoher Wellengang m, ziemlich hohe Wellen fpl <Stärke 5>	**Rowland effect**	Rowland-Effekt m
		Rowland['s] experiment	Rowlandscher Versuch m, Versuch von Rowland
		Rowland ghosts	Rowland-Geister mpl
rough service lamp	stoßfeste Lampe f	**Rowland grating mounting, Rowland mounting [of diffraction grating],** Rowland arrangement [of reflection grating], radius mounting [of grating]	Rowlandsche Gitteraufstellung f
rough-surfaced, roughened	aufgerauht		
rough vacuum	Grobvakuum n		
roulette <math.>	Rollkurve f, Roulette f <Math.>	**Rowland wavelength system**	Rowlandsches Wellenlängensystem n
round angle	s. perigon	**row matrix,** single-row matrix, row vector, single-row vector	Zeilenmatrix f, Zeilenvektor m
round bracket, parenthesis <math.>	[runde] Klammer f <Math.>		
round-coil instrument, round-coil measuring instrument	Rundspulinstrument n	**row of dipoles**	s. dipole row
		row of dislocations, dislocation row	Versetzungsreihe f
round edgewise pattern instrument	Rundprofilinstrument n	**row of vortices,** vortex row, single row of vortices	Wirbelreihe f
round filter, circular filter	Rundfilter n	**row rank**	Zeilenrang m
		row vector	s. row matrix
rounding, rounding off, roundoff	Rundung f <Math.>	**Rozhdestvensky interferometer**	Roshdestwenski-Interferometer n
rounding down	Abrundung f, Rundung f nach unten, Abrunden n	**Rozhdestvensky['s] method,** crochet method	Hakenmethode f [von Roshdestwenski], Methode f von Roshdestwenski
		r process, fast process, fast neutron capture, capture of neutrons on a fast time scale <astr.>	r-Prozeß m, schneller Prozeß m, schneller Neutroneneinfang m <Astr.>
rounding error, round-off error	Rundungsfehler m		
		R region	R-Gebiet n
rounding off	s. rounding <math.>	**RR Lyrae star, RR Lyrae variable,** cluster[-type] variable [star], short-period Cepheid	RR Lyrae-Stern m, Haufenveränderlicher m, Antalgolstern m
rounding-off upward, rounding-up	Aufrundung f, Rundung f nach oben, Aufrunden n		
rounding rule, rule of rounding	Rundungsregel f	**R-shower**	R-Schauer m, Mesonenschauer m mit Kernverdampfung
rounding-up	s. rounding-off upward		
round-looking scan[ning]	Rundsuchbetrieb m	**R-symmetric case,** D-case	R-symmetrischer Fall m, D-Fall m
round of angles	Richtungssatz m	**rubber,** vulcanized rubber, vulcanizate	Gummi m, vulkanisierter Kautschuk m, Vulkanisat n
roundoff	s. rounding <math.>		
round-off error	s. rounding error		
round window	rundes Fenster n		
Rouse number	Rousesche Zahl f	**rubber ball,** india-rubber ball	Gummiball m
Rousseau diagram	Rousseau-Diagramm n		
route, traffic channel	Leitweg m	**rubber bulb**	Gummiball m, Gummiblase f
		rubber elasticity	s. rubberlike elasticity
Routh['s] criterion [of stability]	s. Routh-Hurwicz criterion	**rubber[-]like,** rubbery	gummiähnlich; kautschukähnlich, kautschukartig; gummielastisch
Routh['s] equations	Routhsche Gleichungen fpl, Routhsche Bewegungsgleichungen fpl	**rubber-like elasticity,** rubber elasticity	Gummielastizität f

rubber membrane model, membrane model	Gummimodell n, Gummimembranmodell n, Membranmodell n	**rule of maximum multiplicity**	Regel f der maximalen Multiplizität
rubber softness standard	Weichheitszahl f, Gummihärte f	**rule of moving around**	Umfahrungsregel f, Umlaufregel f, Umlaufungsregel f
rubber-tissue model	Gummituchmodell n, Gummimodell n, Gummihautmodell n	**rule of proportion**	s. rule of three
		rule of rounding, rounding rule	Rundungsregel f
rubbery	s. rubber[-]like	**rule of signs**, Descartes' rule of signs	Descartessche Zeichenregel f, Cartesische Zeichenregel, Harriotsche Zeichenregel
rubbing; grating; smearing; wiping	Reiben n; Wischen n		
rubbing <to powder>, grinding [to powder], grinding-down; triturating, mincing, powdering, pulverization	Zerreibung f, Zerstoßung f, Pulverisierung f	**rule of signs**	s. a. sign convention
		rule of sums, sum rule	Summenregel f, Summensatz m
		rule of three, rule of proportion, golden rule	Regeldetri f, Dreisatz m
rubbing contact	s. wiping contact		
rubbish, refuse	Schutt m		
		rule of thumb, rough rule, rough-and-ready rule, snap regula	Faustformel f, Faustregel f
rubble, clastic rock	Trümmergestein n, klastisches Sedimentgestein n		
rubble, rubble-stone	Schotter m	**rule of triads**, triad rule	Triadenregel f
rubble	s. a. boulder <geo.>	**ruler**	s. rule
rubble-stone, rubble	Schotter m	**ruling** <of gratings>, manufacture of gratings, ruling technique	Gitterteilung f, Gitterherstellung f, Gitterschneidetechnik f
Ruben cell, Ruben-Mallory cell	Ruben-Mallory-Element n, Ruben-Mallory-Zelle f, Quecksilberoxidzelle f		
Ruben-Mallory cell, Ruben cell	Ruben-Mallory-Element n, Ruben-Mallory-Zelle f, Quecksilberoxidzelle f	**ruling**	s. a. generator <of a surface>
		ruling engine, ruling machine	Gitterteilmaschine f
Rubens['] flame tube	Rubenssches Flammenrohr n	**ruling technique**	s. ruling <of gratings>
Rubens['] thermopile	Rubenssche Thermosäule f	**rumble**, vibration resonance	Schüttelresonanz f
ruby laser, ruby optical maser	Rubinlaser m	**rumble noise**	Rumpelgeräusch n
		rumbling; roll <ac.>	Rollen n; Grollen n <Ak.>
		rumbling	s. a. drone <ac.>
		Rumford [photoshadow] photometer	Schattenphotometer n nach Rumford, Rumford-Photometer n
ruby maser	Rubinmaser m	**rump electron**	Rumpfelektron n
		run, running, motion, movement	Gang m, Lauf m
ruby optical maser	s. ruby laser	**run**, proceeding <of process>	Verlauf m, Ablauf m <Prozeß>
Rudstam['s] formula	Rudstamsche Formel f	**run**, trend <geo.>	Streichen n [der Schicht], Schichtenstreichen n <Geo.>
Rudzki['s] transformation	Rudzki-Transformation f		
Rue cell / De la	De-la-Rue-Element n	**run** <num. math.>	Lauf m <num. Math.>
		run	= difference of abscissae
ruffle	s. ripple	**run**	s. a. experiment
rugged, ruggedized; shockresistant, shockproof	stoßfest	**run**	s. a. flow <of liquid>
		run	s. a. series of measurements
		runaway effect [of electrons]	„runaway"-Effekt m <der Elektronen>
ruggedization	s. hardening <of electronic tube>	**runaway electron**	„runaway"-Elektron n
ruggedness, sturdiness, solidity, stability <gen.>	Stabilität f, Festigkeit f, Dauerhaftigkeit f, Solidität f; Robustheit f <allg.>	**runaway of the reactor**	s. reactor runaway
		runaway star	s. Barnard['s] star
		run down	s. running-out
rugosity	s. roughness	**run-forward time**	Hinlaufzeit f
rugosity	s. a. unevenness		
rugosity coefficient	s. roughness coefficient	**Runge domain**	Rungesches Gebiet n
Ruhmkorff['s] [induction] coil	s. inductorium	**Runge-Kutta-Fehlberg method**	Runge-Kutta-Fehlberg-Verfahren n, Runge-Kutta-Fehlbergsches Verfahren n
rule, ruler	Lineal n, fester Maßstab m		
rule, measuring rule, comparing rule	Maßstab m, Maßstablineal n	**Runge-Kutta method**, method of Runge and Kutta	Runge-Kutta-Verfahren n, Runge-Kuttasches Verfahren n, Verfahren von Runge und Kutta, Runge-Kutta-Methode f; Runge-Kuttasche Formeln fpl
rule, jointing-rule, straightedge	Richtlatte f; Richtscheit n		
rule/8-N	s. Hume-Rothery rule		
ruled diffraction grating, ruled grating	Strichgitter n, Liniengitter n	**Runge['s] method**	s. Runge['s] scheme
		Runge['s] rule	Rungesche Regel f
ruled function	Regelfunktion f; Funktion f, die höchstens Unstetigkeiten erster Art hat	**Runge['s] scheme**, Runge['s] method	Rungesches Schema n, Rungesches Verfahren n, Runge-Verfahren n, Verfahren von Runge
ruled grating	s. ruled diffraction grating		
ruled paper	s. scale paper		
ruled surface <math.>	Regelfläche f, geradlinige Fläche f <Math.>	**Runge['s] theorem**	Approximationssatz m von Runge, Rungescher Satz m; Satz von Runge
rule of alligation, alligation	Mischungsrechnen n		
		R-unit, r-unit, roentgen, roentgen unit, R	Röntgen n, Röntgeneinheit f, R-Einheit f, R
rule of composition	s. law of composition		
rule of eight	s. octet rule	**R. unit [of Solomon]**	R-Einheit f [nach Solomon]
rule of false position, regula falsi, method of false position	Regula f falsi, Eingabeln n der Nullstelle, Sekantenverfahren n		
		runner <of water turbine>; impeller <of pump>; rotor, rotor wheel	Laufrad n, Kreiselrad n, Rotor m, Läufer m <Turbine, Pumpe>

running, streaking <of colours>	Auslaufen n; Ineinanderlaufen n; Zerfließen n <Farben>	Russell-Adams phenomenon	Russell-Adams-Phänomen n, Russell-Adams-Effekt m
running	s. a. run	Russell angle	Russell-Winkel m
running co-ordinate	laufende Koordinate f	Russell diagram	s. Hertzsprung-Russell diagram
running crack	laufender Riß m		
running current	s. operating current	Russell effect, Vogel-Colson-Russell effect	Russell-Effekt m, Vogel-Colson-Russell-Effekt m
running-down	s. running-out <mech.>		
running high	Hochgehen n	Russell mixture	Russell-Mischung f, Russell-Gemisch f
running index, variable index	Laufindex m, laufender Index m, variabler Index	Russell-Saunders coupling, L-S coupling	Russell-Saunders-Kopplung f, LS-Kopplung f, „normale" Kopplung f [der Atomelektronen]
running layer, travelling layer	laufende Schicht f		
running mean	s. moving average		
running modification	Jeweilsänderung f		
running of the colours; blending of the colours, shading[-off] of the colours	Verlaufen n der Farben		
		Russell-Vogt theorem	Eindeutigkeitssatz m des Sternaufbaus [nach Russell und Vogt]
running-out, running-down, run down <mech.>	Auslaufen n, Auslauf m; Nachlaufen n, Nachlauf m <Mech.>	rust	Rost m
		Rutgers['] equation, Rutgers['] relation	Rutgerssche Beziehung (Formel) f
running-out energy, deceleration energy	Auslaufenergie f	rutherford, rutherford unit, rd <= 27.0 µCi>	Rutherford n, Rutherford-Einheit f, rd <= 27,0 µCi>
running term <in the series formula>	Laufterm m, Laufzahl f <Serienformel>		
		Rutherford atom	Rutherfordsches Atom n
running time	Rechenzeit f	Rutherford atom model	Planetenmodell n [des Atoms] [nach Rutherford], Rutherfordsches Planetenmodell, Rutherfordsches Atommodell n, Atommodell von Rutherford, Lenard-Rutherfordsches Atommodell n
running to full speed	s. run-up		
running voltage	s. burning voltage <of discharge, arc>		
running wave	s. travelling wave		
running without load	s. idling		
run-off <of water>, flow of water, water flow	Abfluß m <Wasser>, Wasserabfluß m, Wasserfracht f		
runoff <per unit time>	s. discharge		
runoff coefficient	s. flow coefficient	Rutherford-Bohr atom model	Rutherford-Bohrsches Atommodell n
runoff groove	Spülrinne f		
		Rutherford cross-section, Rutherford scattering cross-section	Rutherford-Streuquerschnitt m, Rutherford-Querschnitt m, Wirkungsquerschnitt m für (der) Rutherford-Streuung, Rutherford-Wirkungsquerschnitt m
runoff percentage	s. flow coefficient		
runoff per day, daily runoff	Tagesabflußmenge f, Tagesabfluß m		
run of rays, path of rays, ray [-]trajectory; trace of rays <US>	Strahlengang m, Strahlenverlauf m, Strahlenweg m, Strahlenbahn f		
		Rutherford dispersion formula	s. Rutherford scattering formula
run test	Iterationstest m		
run-up, running to full speed, start-up, starting	Hochlaufen n, Hochlauf m	Rutherford['s] experiment	Versuch m von Rutherford, Rutherfordscher Streuversuch m (Versuch), Streuversuch von Rutherford
rupture, abruption; tearing, tear; bursting; splitting; rending <mech.>	Zerreißung f; Reißen n, Riß m; Sprungbildung f; Einreißen n <Mech.>		
		Rutherford formula	s. Rutherford scattering formula
rupture, cleavage (cleave, separation) fracture	Trennungsbruch m, Trennbruch m	rutherfordium	s. kurchatovium
		Rutherford prism	s. Rutherfurd prism
rupture <el.>, breaking off	Abreißen n <El.>	Rutherford scattering	Rutherford-Streuung f, Rutherfordsche Streuung f
rupture	s. a. breakdown		
rupture; rupture area	s. fracture <mech.>	Rutherford scattering cross-section	s. Rutherford cross-section
rupture device, tensile testing machine, tensile [strength testing] machine	Zugprüfmaschine f, Zerreißmaschine f	Rutherford scattering formula (law, relation), Rutherford dispersion formula, Rutherford formula	Rutherfordsche Streuformel f, Rutherford-Formel f, Rutherfordsche Formel f, Rutherfordsches Streugesetz n
rupture energy	Zerreißenergie f		
rupture line, fracture line, line of fracture	Bruchlinie f		
rupture modulus	s. modulus of rupture <mech.>	rutherford unit	s. rutherford
		Rutherfurd prism, compound prism	Rutherfurd-Prisma n, Compoundprisma n
rupture of slope, slope rupture	Gefällsbruch m, Neigungsbruch m, Neigungswechsel m	R_f value, retention factor, R_f	R_f-Wert m, R_f Verzögerungsfaktor m
rupture strength, separating strength	Trennfestigkeit f, Trennwiderstand m, Trennungsfestigkeit f		
rupture strength	s. tensile strength	R_g value, R_g, R_x value, R_x	R_g-Wert m, R_g, R_x-Wert m, R_x
rupture stress	Zerreißspannung f; Bruchspannung f		
		RV Tauri[-type] star	RV Tauri-Stern m
rupture stress	Zerreißkraft f	RW Aurigae-type star, T Tauri star, nebular variable	RW Aurigae-Stern m, T Tauri-Stern m, Nebelveränderlicher m
rupture work, stretching strain, work of rupture	Zerreißarbeit f		
		R wave	s. reflected wave
rush current	Schwellstrom m, Rushstrom m, Rush m, „rush"-Strom m	rydberg, Ry	Rydberg n, Ry
rush of current	s. impulse of current		

Rydberg constant; Rydberg wave number — Rydberg-Konstante f <R_∞>; Rydberg-Zahl f, Rydberg-Wellenzahl f, Rydberg[-Ritz]sche Wellenzahl f <massenabhängig>

Rydberg correction [term], quantum defect — Rydberg-Korrektion f

Rydberg equation (formula) — Rydberg-Formel f

Rydberg frequency — Rydberg-Frequenz f

Rydberg-Ritz combination principle — s. combination principle

Rydberg-Schuster law — Rydberg-Schustersche Regel f

Rydberg series — Rydberg-Serie f

Rydberg wave number — s. Rydberg constant

Ryle['s] method, phase-switching method — Phasenschaltverfahren n, Ryle-Verfahren n

S

Sabathé cycle — Sabathé-Prozeß m

Sabattier effect, pseudo solarization <phot.> — Sabattier-Effekt m, Sabattier-Bildumkehrung f <Phot.>

Sabattier['s] method — Sabattier-Verfahren n, Einplattenverfahren n

sabin — Sabin n, Sabine-Einheit f

Sabine['s] formula, Sabine['s] law — Sabinesche Formel f, Sabinesches Gesetz n

sabouraud-noiré, Sabouraud-Noiré unit, S-N unit — Sabouraud-Noiré n, Sabouraud-Noiré-Einheit f, SN-Einheit f

sa[c]charimeter — Saccharimeter n, Zuckerpolarimeter n

saccharometer — Saccharometer n, Zuckerwaage f

saccharometer — s. a. saccharimeter

Sachs['] average — Sachs-Mittel n

Sachs['] drawing test, wedge drawing test — Keilziehversuch m [nach Kayseler-Sachs]

Sackur-Tetrode constant, entropy constant — Sackur-Tetrode-Konstante f, [Sackur-Tetrodesche] Entropiekonstante f

sacrifice of time, time required, waste of time, loss of time — Zeitaufwand m

sacrificing, killing — Tötung f, Abtötung f

saddle, col — Sattel m

saddle, saddle-shaped filling (cap) <chem.> — Sattelkörper m <Chem.>

saddle — s. a. anticlinal fold <geo.>

saddle coil — Sattelspule f

saddle-field lens — Sattelfeldlinse f

saddle point, hyperbolic point, col <math.> — Sattelpunkt m, hyperbolischer Punkt m <Math.>

saddle point approximation, saddle-point method — s. method of steepest descents

saddle point method — s. Fowler-Darwin method

saddle-point singularity <of the differential equation> — Sattelpunkt n <Differentialgleichung>

saddle-shaped cap (filling), saddle <chem.> — Sattelkörper m <Chem.>

saddle surface — Sattelfläche f

Sadovski effect — Sadowski-Effekt m

safe distance, safety distance — Sicherheitsabstand m

safe geometry — sichere Geometrie f

safelight filter, safelight screen, darkroom safelight filter — Dunkelkammerfilter n, Schutzfilter n

safe stress — s. permissible stress

safety assembly — Schutzsystem n, Sicherheitssystem n

safety coefficient — s. safety factor

safety container — s. containment vessel

safety distance — s. safe distance

safety element, safety member — Sicherheitsorgan n

safety factor, factor of safety, margin of safety, assurance coefficient, safety coefficient, FS, fs — Sicherheitsbeiwert m, Sicherheitsfaktor m, Sicherheitskoeffizient m, Sicherheitszahl f, Sicherheitsgrad m, Sicherheit f

safety factor against yielding, safety factor with respect to plastic flow — Sicherheitsfaktor m gegen Fließen

safety factor with respect to rupture — Sicherheitsfaktor m gegen Bruch

safety glass, splinterproof glass, unsplintered glass — Sicherheitsglas n, splitterfreies Glas n

safety limit — Sicherheitsgrenze f; Ungefährlichkeitsgrenze f

safety member — s. safety element

safety regulation — Sicherheitsvorschrift f; Sicherheitsbestimmung f

safety requirements — Sicherheitsforderungen fpl, Sicherheitsanforderungen fpl

safety ring — Sicherungsring m

safety rod, cut-off rod; emergency shut-down rod, scram rod <US> — Sicherheitsstab m, Schnellschlußstab m, Notstab m

safety shut-down — s. emergency shut-down

safety valve — Sicherheitsventil n

safe voltage, low voltage — Kleinspannung f

sag, sagitta; slack; height of the vault, camber; maximum deflection; use (height) of the shell — Durchhang m, Pfeilhöhe f; Stich m, Stichhöhe f; Bogenhöhe f

sagging, dip, dipping — Durchhängen n, Durchhang m; Durchbiegung f

sagging — s. a. untensioned

sagitta — s. sag

sagittal, equatorial, radial <opt.> — sagittal, äquatorial, felgenrecht, Sagittal-, Äquatoreal-, Äquatorial- <Opt.>

sagittal beam — s. sagittal pencil [of rays]

sagittal coma, equatorial coma — Rinnenfehler m, sagittale Koma f, Sagittalkoma f, äquatoriale Koma

sagittal curvature of the image field — sagittale Bildfeldwölbung (Bildfeldkrümmung) f, äquatoriale Bildfeldwölbung (Bildfeldkrümmung)

sagittal fan, sagittal pencil [of rays], equatorial fan, equatorial pencil [of rays] — Sagittalbüschel n, Äquatorealbüschel n, Äquatorialbüschel n

sagittal focal line, equatorial focal line — sagittale Brennlinie f, äquatoriale Brennlinie

sagittal focal plane — s. sagittal plane <opt.>

sagittal focus, secondary focus, radial focus — sagittaler Brennpunkt m, Sagittalbrennpunkt m

sagittal image point, equatorial image point — sagittaler (äquatorialer) Bildpunkt m

sagittal pencil [of rays], equatorial pencil [of rays], sagittal beam, equatorial beam — Sagittal[strahlen]bündel n, Äquatoreal[strahlen]bündel n, Äquatorial[strahlen]bündel n

sagittal pencil [of rays] — s. sagittal fan

sagittal plane, sagittal focal plane <opt.> — Sagittalebene f, Äquatorealebene f, Äquatorialebene f <Opt.>

sagittal ray, equatorial ray — Sagittalstrahl m, Äquatorealstrahl m, Äquatorialstrahl m

sagittal section, equatorial section	Sagittalschnitt m, zweiter Hauptschnitt m, Äquatorealschnitt m, Äquatorialschnitt m	salt-spray [fog] test, spray test	Salzsprühversuch m, Sprühversuch m
sagitta method	Sagittamethode f	saltus	s. step
Sagnac['s] experiment	Sagnacscher Versuch m, Sagnac-Versuch m, Versuch von Sagnac, optischer Wirbelversuch m [von Sagnac]	salt-water wedge, saline-water wedge	Salzwasserkeil m
		samarium poisoning	Samariumvergiftung f
		same magnitude, but oppositely directed / of the; opposite and equal; equal of magnitude, but opposite of sign	entgegengesetzt gleich
Saha['s] equation, Saha['s] [equilibrium] formula, Saha['s] ionization formula	Saha-Gleichung f, Saha-Formel f, Eggert-Saha-Gleichung f, Eggert-Saha-Formel f		
Saha-Langmuir law	Saha-Langmuirsches Gesetz n	same polarity / having (of) the, like, having (of) the same sign	gleichnamig, gleicher Polarität, gleichen Vorzeichens
Saint Elmo['s] fire, St. Elmo['s] fire, corposant	St. Elms-Feuer n, Sankt-Elms-Feuer n, Elmsfeuer n, Saint-Elms-Feuer n, Eliasfeuer n	same sense / in (of) the, equidirectional, codirectional	gleichsinnig, gleichgerichtet
Saint-Venant	s. Venant		
Sakata model	Sakata-Modell n		
Sakata particles, elementary particles of Sakata, fundamental particles of Sakata	Sakatasche Teilchen npl, Sakata-Teilchen npl, Elementarteilchen (Fundamentalteilchen) npl von Sakata	same sign / having (of) the	s. same polarity / of the
		sample; specimen; assay; test piece, test specimen; test component, component under examination	Probe f; Probestück n, Prüfstück n; Probekörper m, Prüfkörper m; Prüfling m; Präparat n; Untersuchungsobjekt n
Sakata-Taketani equation	Sakata-Taketanische Gleichung f		
salient	s. overhang	sample, random (spot) samples <stat.>	Stichprobe f, Probe f <Stat.>
salient point, break, fraction; kink, knee <of the curve>	Knick m; Knie n; Abknicken n <Kurve>		
salification, salifying, salt formation	Salzbildung f	sample changer	Probenwechsler m
saline-water wedge	s. salt-water wedge		
Salinger's condition	Salinger-Bedingung f		
salinity; salt[i]ness; salt content; salt concentration	prozentualer Gesamtsalzgehalt m, Gesamtsalzgehalt, Salzigkeit f, Salinität f; Salzgehalt m; Salzkonzentration f	sample container [with contents] <of calorimeter>, calorimeter	Kalorimetergefäß n
		sample correlation coefficient	empi. ischer Korrelationskoeffizient m
		sampled-data system, sampling system	Tastsystem n, Impulssystem n
salinity diagram	Salzgehaltdiagramm n, Salzdiagramm n		
salinometer, halometer	Salzspindel f, Salzgehaltmesser m, Salinometer n, Salzmesser m	sample drawing	s. sampling
		sample function	Probenfunktion f
		sample function	s. a. statistic <stat.>
Salpeter-Bethe [two-nucleon] equation, Bethe-Salpeter equation, Bethe-Salpeter wave equation	Salpeter-Bethe-Zweinukleonengleichung f, Bethe-Salpeter-Gleichung f, Bethe-Salpeter-Wellengleichung f	sample mean, mean of sample, mean <stat.>	Stichprobenmittel[wert m] n, Mittelwert m der Stichprobe, empirischer Mittelwert, Mittel n <Stat.>
Salpeter process	s. triple-alpha process	sample moment	Stichprobenmoment n
saltation <through air or water>	Feststofftransport m, Beförderung f von Feststoffen <in Sprüngen durch Luft oder Wasser>	sample probability	Stichprobenwahrscheinlichkeit f
		sampler, sampling system, sampling unit	Probenehmer m, Probenahmesystem n, Probenentnahmegerät n; Probenstecher m; Probenzieher m
saltatory [nerve] conduction, saltatory transmission [of the nervous impulse], electro-saltatory transmission [of nerve impulse]	saltatorische Leitung f, saltatorische Erregungsleitung f, saltatorische Nervenleitung f		
		sample retreatment, sample treatment	Umarbeitung f der Proben; Probenchemie f
salt bath, molten-salt bath	Salzbad n	sample size, size of the sample	Umfang m der Stichprobe, Stichprobenumfang m
salt bridge	Stromschlüssel m, Haber-Luigin-Kapillare f, Salzbrücke f		
		sample space	Stichprobenraum m
salt concentration	s. salinity		
salt content	s. salinity	sample statistic	s. statistic <stat.>
salt crust	Salzkruste f	sample taken by water bottle, silt sample, suspended load sample, bottle sample	Schöpfprobe f
salt cryoscopy	Salzkryoskopie f		
salt effect	Salzeffekt m		
salt error	Salzfehler m		
salt exchange capacity	Salzaustauschvermögen n, Salzaustauschkapazität f	sample treatment	s. sample retreatment
		sample variance, empiric variance	empirische Varianz f
salt formation	s. salification	sampling, taking (drawing) of samples, sample drawing	Entnahme f von Proben, Probenahme f, Probe[n]entnahme f
saltiness	s. salinity		
salting agent	Salzagens n, Salzzuschlag m		
salting-in	Einsalzen n	sampling <stat.>	Stichprobenerhebung f, Erhebung (Entnahme) f von Stichproben, Stichprobenentnahme f; Ziehen n <Stat.>
salting-out, graining out	Aussalzung f		
salting-out agent	Aussalzer m	sampling [action]	periodische Einstellung f
salt isomerism	Salzisomerie f	sampling distribution	Stichprobenverteilung f
saltness	s. salinity		

sampling error, zufälliger Fehler *m*, un-
accidental error, random regelmäßiger Fehler,
error, unbiased error Zufallsfehler *m*
sampling error Stichprobenfehler *m*

sampling fraction, Stichprobenanteil *m*, Stich-
sampling ration probenquote *f*, Auswahl-
satz *m*
sampling moment Stichprobenmoment *n*,
empirisches Moment *n*
sampling oscilloscope Samplingoszillograph *m*,
„sampling"-Oszillo-
graph *m*, Abtast-
oszillograph *m*
sampling polarograph, Tastpolarograph *m*
probe polarograph
sampling process Samplingprozeß *m*,
„sampling"-Prozeß *m*

sampling ratio s. sampling fraction
sampling system s. sampled-data system
sampling system s. sampler
sampling theorem Abtasttheorem *n*, Proben-
satz *m*, Sampling-
theorem *n*, Kotelnikow-
Theorem *n*
sampling unit s. sampler
sampling without Ziehen *n* ohne Zurück-
replacement legen

sampling with Ziehen *n* mit Zurücklegen
replacement

sandbag model Sandsackmodell *n* [des
[of nucleus] Atomkerns], Bohrsches
Sandsackmodell
sand bath Sandbad *n*

sand devil s. dust devil
sand erosion Sandschliff *m*, Sand-
erosion *f*

sand figures s. Chladni['s] figures
sand heap analogy, sand Sandhaufengleichnis *n*
hill analogy [of Nádai] [von Nádai]
sandr Sander *m*, Sandr *m*
⟨*pl.*: Sandur⟩; Sander-
fläche *f*
sand roughness Sandrauhigkeit *f*, Sand-
kornrauhigkeit *f*
sand spout s. dust devil
sand storm s. dust storm
sandwich Schichtelement *n*, Sand-
wichelement *n*

sandwich s. a. intermediate layer
sandwich coil winding, Scheibenwicklung *f*
pie (pie-type, inter-
leaved) winding, disk-
type winding
sandwich complex s. low-spin complex
sandwich detector Schichtendetektor *m*,
Sandwichdetektor *m*

sandwiched source, Schichtenquelle *f*, Schicht-
sandwich source quelle *f*, Sandwichquelle *f*

sandwiching Schichtemulsion *f*,
Schichtenemulsion *f*,
Sandwichschicht *f*
sandwiching Zwischenlegung *f*,
Zwischenschichtung *f*,
Einlegung *f*
sandwich irradiation Sandwichbestrahlung *f*

sandwich plate Schichtplatte *f*, Schichten-
platte *f*, Sandwichplatte *f*

sandwich source s. sandwiched source
Sankey diagram Sankey-Diagramm *n*

Sanson['s] net, "onion" Sanson-Netz *n*, Sanson-
diagram sches Netz *n*
Sanson['s] projection Sansonsche Projektion *f*
sapide, saponide s. syndet
saponification number Verseifungszahl *f*
(ratio, value)

sarcolemma Sarkolemm *n*, Sarkolemma *n*
sarcomere Sarkomer *n*, Myomer *n*

Sargent curve, Sargent Sargent-Diagramm *n*,
diagram Sargent-Kurve *f*
Saros Sarosperiode *f*, Saros-
zyklus *m*, Chaldäische
Periode *f*, Saros *m*
Sarrau number Sarrau-Zahl *f*, Sarrausche
Kennzahl (Zahl) *f*
Sarrus['] rule Sarrussche Regel *f*,
Regel von Sarrus

Sartorius balance, Sedimentationswaage *f*
sedimentation balance [nach Sartorius]
Satche diagram Satche-Diagramm *n*
satellite s. non-diagram line
satellite, moon Mond *m*, Nebenplanet *m*,
⟨of a planet⟩ Satellit *m*, Trabant *m*,
natürlicher Begleiter *m*
⟨eines Planeten⟩
satellite band Satellitenbande *f*
satellite branch Satellitenzweig *m*

satellite carrier vehicle s. satellite-launching rocket
satellite depression s. secondary depression
⟨meteo.⟩
satellite experiment Satellitenversuch *m*
satellite geodesy Satellitengeodäsie *f*

satellite geoid Satellitengeoid *n*

satellite in X-ray s. non-diagram line
spectrum
satellite launcher s. carrier rocket
satellite-launching Satellitenträgerrakete *f*,
rocket, satellite vehicle, Trägerrakete *f*
satellite carrier vehicle [für Satelliten]

satellite line s. non-diagram line
satellite pulse ⟨el.⟩ Begleiter *m*, Satellitimpuls
m, Nebenimpuls *m*
⟨El.⟩
satellite rainbow s. secondary rainbow
satellite station, exzentrischer Standpunkt *m*
auxiliary point ⟨geo.⟩ ⟨Geo.⟩

satellite vehicle s. satellite-launching rocket
satellite X-ray line s. non-diagram line
satelloid Satelloid *m*

satin-etched bulb innenmattierter Kolben *m*

saturable absorber selektives sättigbares Filter *n*

saturable core Sättigungskern *m*,
Saturationskern *m*
saturable-core device Saturationskernmagneto-
(magnetometer), meter *m*, SK-Magneto-
saturable-core-type meter *n*, Saturations-
magnetometer, saturated- kernsonde *f*, SK-Sonde *f*,
core magnetometer, elektromagnetische
fluxgate, flux[-] gate, Sonde *f*; Förster-
fluxgate magnetometer, Sonde *f*
flux gate detector
saturable-core reactor, Sättigungsdrossel *f*,
saturable reactor; Sättigungskerndrossel *f*
saturating reactor,
saturating-core device

saturable-core-type s. saturable-core
magnetometer magnetometer
saturable reactor s. saturable-core reactor
saturable reactor Sättigungsdrosselspulen-
amplifier verstärker *m*
saturant Sättigungsmittel *n*
saturate s. saturated compound
saturated activity, Sättigungsaktivität *f*
saturation activity

saturated adiabatic feuchtadiabatischer Tempe-
lapse rate, moist raturgradient *m*, feucht-
adiabatic lapse rate, wet adiabatisches Tempera-
adiabatic lapse rate, satu- turgefälle *n*
ration-adiabatic lapse rate

saturated

saturated adiabatic stability, moist stability	Feuchtstabilität f, feuchtadiabatische Stabilität f	saturation effect saturation emission	Sättigungseffekt m Sättigungsemission f
saturated compound, saturate	gesättigte Verbindung f	saturation equilibrium saturation factor	Sättigungsgleichgewicht n Sättigungsfaktor m
saturated-core magnetometer	s. saturable-core magnetometer	saturation field saturation field intensity, saturation field strength	Sättigungsfeld n Sättigungsfeldstärke f
saturated diode	Sättigungsdiode f		
saturated index, dummy index, umbral index, umbral suffix <of tensor>; dummy, summation dummy	Summationsindex m	saturation humidity, maximum humidity [of air]	Sättigungsfeuchte f, maximale Luftfeuchtigkeit f
saturated liquid, orthobaric liquid, liquid at its bubble point	orthobare Flüssigkeit f	saturation index, stability index	Sättigungsindex m
		saturation induction saturation ion current	Sättigungsinduktion f Sättigungsionenstrom m
saturated steam	Sattdampf m <Wasser>		
saturated steam	s. a. wet steam	saturation limit	s. saturation point
saturated vapour	Sattdampf m, gesättigter Dampf m	saturation magnetization	Sättigungsmagnetisierung f, [magnetische] Sättigungspolarisation f
saturated-vapour density	Sättigungsdampfdichte f	saturation magnetostriction	Sättigungsmagnetostriktion f
saturated vapour pressure (tension), saturation vapour pressure, saturation pressure, saturation vapour tension, saturation tension, vapour pressure, vapour tension	Sättigungsdampfdruck m, Sättigungsdruck m, Sättigungsspannung f, Dampfdruck m, Dampfspannung f, Tension f, Sattdampfdruck m	saturation magnetostriction coefficient	Sättigungsmagnetostriktionskoeffizient m
		saturation moment saturation noise saturation of nuclear matter, nuclear saturation	Sättigungsmoment n Sättigungsrauschen n Kernsättigung f, Sättigung f der Kernmaterie
		saturation of the shell	s. closure of the shell
saturating-core device saturating reactor saturation	s. saturable-core reactor s. saturable-core reactor Sättigung f	saturation point, saturation limit, point of saturation, limit saturation	Sättigungspunkt m, Sättigungsgrenze f
saturation <of colour>	Farbsättigung f, Sättigung f, Weißlichkeit f <Farbe>	saturation potential, saturation voltage <el.>	Sättigungsspannung f, Sättigungspotential n <El.>
saturation <e.g. of the nuclear forces or of chemical bond>	Absättigung f <z. B. der Kernkräfte oder der chemischen Bindung>	saturation pressure saturation range saturation ratio	s. saturated vapour pressure s. saturation region s. relative humidity
saturation, factor loading <stat.>	Faktorladung f, Saturation f <Stat.>	saturation region; saturation range	Sättigungsgebiet n, Sättigungsbereich m
		saturation scale	Sättigungsskala f, Sättigungsreihe f
saturation activation	Sättigungsaktivierung f		
saturation activity, saturated activity	Sättigungsaktivität f	saturation temperature, temperature of saturation	Sättigungstemperatur f, Sättigungspunkt m
saturation adiabat	s. moist adiabat	saturation tension	s. saturated vapour pressure
saturation-adiabatic lapse rate	s. saturated adiabatic lapse rate	saturation thickness [layer]	Sättigungsdicke f, Sättigungsschichtdicke f
saturation backscattering	Rückstreusättigung f	saturation vapour pressure (tension)	s. saturated vapour pressure
saturation broadening	Sättigungsverbreiterung f	saturation voltage	s. saturation potential <el.>
		saturator	Sättiger m, Saturator m, Sättigungsapparat m, Saturateur m
saturation capacity	Sättigungsvermögen n, Sättigungskapazität f		
saturation characteristic	Sättigungscharakteristik f, Sättigungskennlinie f	saturnium, Sa, St Saturn['s] ring system	= protactinium Ringsystem n des Saturn
saturation collection of ions	Sammlung f von Ionen im Sättigungsbereich	Saurel['s] theorem	Saurel-Theorem n, Satz m von Saurel
saturation concentration	Sättigungskonzentration f, Sättigungsgrenze f	sausage instability, sausage-type instability	Instabilität f gegen lokale (örtliche) Einschnürung, Instabilität gegen Einschnürung, „sausage"-Instabilität f, Würstcheninstabilität f
saturation current	Sättigungsstrom m		
saturation current density	Sättigungsstromdichte f		
saturation current law	Sättigungsstromgesetz n		
saturation current of cathode, cathode saturation current	Katodensättigungsstrom m, Katodenergiebigkeit f	Saussure['s] hygrometer [/de], hair hygrometer	Haarhygrometer n
saturation curve	Sättigungskurve f, Sättigungslinie f	Sauter camera	Sauter-Kammer f
		Sauter method Sautreaux['s] [inverse] method	Sauter-Methode f Sautreauxsche inverse Methode f
saturation deficit, vapour pressure deficit, undersaturation	Sättigungsdefizit n, Sättigungsmangel m, Sättigungsfehlbetrag m, Untersättigung f, Dampfhunger m	savart, Sav Savart [plate], Savart polariscope	Savart n, Sav Savartsche Doppelplatte (Platte) f, Quarzdoppelplatte f, Savartsches Polariskop n
saturation density, density of saturated phase (vapour)	Sättigungsdichte f	saving, gain	Einsparung f; Ersparnis f, Gewinn m
		saving of time, time saving	Zeitersparnis f, Einsparung f an Zeit
saturation discrimination; purity discrimination	Farbsättigungs-Unterscheidungsvermögen n, Farbsättigungs-Unterschiedsempfindlichkeit f	sawtooth, sawtooth waveform; sawtooth pulse; sawtooth signal	Sägezahn m; Sägezahnimpuls m; Sägezahnsignal n, sägezahnförmiges Signal n

sawtooth current generator, sawtooth current oscillator	Sägezahnstromgenerator *m*	scale division	s. scale
		scale division	s. a. division <of the scale>
		scale division error	s. error of division
saw-toothed oscillator, sawtooth generator, sawtooth oscillator, sawtooth-wave generator	Sägezahngenerator *m*, Sägezahnoszillator *m*	scaled tube	Skalenrohr *n*
		scale end value	s. infinity
		scale error	Maßstabfehler *m*, Skalenfehler *m*
sawtooth oscillation	s. sawtooth wave		
sawtooth oscillator	s. sawtoothed oscillator	scale extension, scale stretching	Skalendehnung *f*
sawtooth pulse (signal)	s. sawtooth		
sawtooth voltage, ramp voltage	Sägezahnspannung *f*	scale factor, scale-up factor, scaling factor	Maßstabsfaktor *m*
sawtooth voltage generator (oscillator)	Sägezahnspannungsgenerator *m*	scale factor, scale-up factor <num. math.>	Skalenfaktor *m* <num. Math.>
sawtooth wave, sawtooth [-wave] oscillation, sawtooth waveform	Sägezahnschwingung *f*, Sägezahnwelle *f*	scale formation, scaling	Kesselsteinbildung *f*
sawtooth waveform	s. sawtooth		
sawtooth waveform	s. sawtooth wave	scale formation, scaling, formation of scale	Verzunderung *f*, Zunderbildung *f*, Zunderung *f*
sawtooth-wave generator	s. sawtooth generator		
sawtooth-wave oscillation	s. sawtooth wave	scale function	Skalenfunktion *f*
		scale graduation	s. division <of the scale>
Saxon-Woods potential	Saxon-Woods-Potential *n*	scale graduation	s. scale
		scale height	Skalenhöhe *f*, Maßstabshöhe *f*, Maßstabhöhe *f*
Sayboldt Universal Second, S.U.S., Ss	Sayboldt-Sekunde *f*, Sayboldt-Zahl *f*, Sayboldt-Universal-Sekunde *f*, Ss, S.U.S.		
		scale interval	s. scale value
Sayboldt viscometer	Sayboldt-Viskosimeter *m*	scale invariant	maßstabinvariant
Saytzeff['s] rule	Saizewsche Regel *f*, Saizew-Regel *f*, Saytzeffsche Regel, Saytzeff-Regel *f*	scale length; lineal scale length; scale span	Skalenlänge *f*
		scale magnifying glass	s. precision magnifier
S band <2.7 – 4 or 1.55 – 5.2 Gc/s>	S-Band *n* <2,7 ... 4 oder 1,55 ... 5,2 GHz>	scale mark	s. scale
		scale mean value, mean value of the scale	Skalenmittelwert *m*
S branch	S-Zweig *m*	scale micrometer	Skalenmikrometer *n*
scalar, scalar quantity, scalar tensor, scalar invariant, invariant	Skalar *m*, skalare Größe *f*, skalarer Tensor *m*, skalare Invariante *f*	scale microscope	Skalenmikroskop *n*
		scale model	maßstäbliches Modell *n*, maßstabgetreues Modell
scalar density, scalar of weight unity	skalare Dichte *f*	scale-model flow, model flow	Modellströmung *f*
scalar electric potential, electric scalar potential	skalares elektrisches Potential *n*	scale-model test[ing]; model experiment, model test[ing], model study	Modellversuch *m*, Versuch *m* am Modell
scalar field, sc field	Skalarfeld *n*, skalares Feld *n*		
scalar invariant	s. scalar	scalene, scalenous; inequilateral	ungleichseitig
scalar magnetic potential	s. magnetic scalar potential	scalenohedral class	s. hemihedry of the second sort of the tetragonal system
scalar matrix	skalare Matrix *f*, Skalarmatrix *f*		
scalar of weight unity	s. scalar density	scalenohedron	Skalenoeder *n*
scalar part <of quaternion>	Skalarteil *m*, Skalar *m* <Quaternion>	scalenous	s. scalene
		scale numbering	Skalenbezifferung *f*
scalar photon	skalares Photon *n*		
scalar potential	skalares Potential *n*, Skalarpotential *n*	scale of atomic masses	s. scale of atomic weights
		scale of atomic weights, scale of atomic masses, atomic weight scale	Nuklidmassenskala *f*, relative Atommassenskala *f*, Atomgewichtsskala *f*
scalar product, inner (dot) produkt	Skalarprodukt *n*, skalares Produkt *n*, inneres Produkt		
		scale-of-2^n circuit, dual scaling circuit; dual scaler	Dualuntersetzerschaltung *f*; Dualuntersetzer *m*
scalar quantity (tensor)	s. scalar		
scalar triple product	s. parallelepipedal product		
scalar wave part of the Hamiltonian	skalarer Wellenanteil *m* des Hamilton-Operators	scale of 10^n circuit; decimal scaler	Dezimaluntersetzer *m*, 10^nfach-Untersetzer *m*, Zehnfachuntersetzer *m*
scala tympani	scala *f* tympani, Paukentreppe *f*, Paukenhöhle *f*		
scala vestibuli	scala *f* vestibuli, Vorhoftreppe *f*, Vorhofhöhle *f*	scale of enlargement, enlargement scale, enlarging scale	Vergrößerungsmaßstab *m*
scale	Skala *f*; Skale *f* <Meßgerät>; Maßstab *m*		
scale, scale mark, graduation, scale division, scale graduation	Skalenteilung *f*, Skaleneinteilung *f*	scale of one hundred circuit	s. ampliscaler
		scale of reduction	s. reduced scale
scale, weighing scale, pan, scale pan, weighing dish, dish [of the scales]	Waagschale *f*, Waageschale *f*	scale of Rossi and Forel, Rossi-Forel [intensity] scale	Rossi-Forel-Skala *f*, Rossi-Forelsche Skala *f*, Skala von Rossi und Forel
scale	Zunder *m*; Sinter *m*; Hammerschlag *m*	scale of seismic intensity	s. modified Mercalli intensity scale [of 1931]
scale, gamut, tone scale, musical scale <ac.>	Tonleiter *f*, Tonskala *f*, Tonreihe *f* <Ak.>	scale of ten circuit	s. decade scalar
		scale of the chart, chart scale	Kartenmaßstab *m*, Maßstab *m* der Karte
scale, scaling [down] <nucl.>	Untersetzung *f*, Impulsuntersetzung *f*, Zählung *f* [mit Untersetzung] <Kern.>	scale of the compass	s. compass card
scale	s. a. scales		
scale beam	s. beam		
scale decade	s. decade scaler		

scale of turbulence, degree of turbulence	Turbulenzlänge *f*, Turbulenzgrad *m*, Größe *f* der Turbulenzballen, Durchmesser *m* der Turbulenzkörper, Turbulenzstufe *f*, Turbulenzfaktor *m*	**scalping**	Oberflächenhautentfernung *f*, Oberflächenschichtentfernung *f*, Oberflächenentfernung *f*
		scan	s. scanning
		scan base	s. time-base unit
scale-of-two	Zweifachuntersetzung *f*, binäre Untersetzung *f*	**scan frequency**	s. scanning frequency
scale-of-two circuit	Zweifachuntersetzerschaltung *f*	**scanner,** scanning device	Abtastgerät *n*, Abtastvorrichtung *f*, Abtaster *m*, Scanner *m*
scale of wind force, wind scale	Windstärkeskala *f*, Windskala *f*		
scale pan	s. scale	**scanning,** scan, scansion; exploring; sweep, sweepout; coverage	Abtastung *f*, Scanning *n*; Überstreichung *f*
scale paper	s. millimetre squared paper		
scale paper	s. a. squared paper		
scale parameter	Skalenparameter *m*		
scale-preserving mapping, scale-preserving transformation	maßstab[s]treue Abbildung *f*, streckentreue Abbildung	**scanning**	s. a. scansion <of image>
		scanning aperture	s. scanning diaphragm
		scanning beam	Abtaststrahl *m*
scale-printer	s. scaler-printer		
scaler, scaling system <nucl.>	Untersetzer *m* <Kern.>	**scanning camera**	s. scintillation camera
		scanning coils	s. deflection coils
		scanning device	s. scanner
scaler	s. a. frequency divider	**scanning diaphragm,** scanning aperture	Abtastblende *f*; Rasterblende *f*
scale range, scale span	Skalenbereich *m*, Skalenumfang *m*		
scale reading	Skalenablesung *f*	**scanning electron microscope,** scanning microscope, electronscan[ning] microscope, raster [scan] microscope, screen microscope, stereoscanning electron microscope, stereoscan [electron] microscope, SEM	Rasterelektronenmikroskop *n*, Elektronenrastermikroskop *n*, Rastermikroskop *n*, Rasterstrahl[-Elektronen]mikroskop *n*, Elektronenstrahlraster-Sekundärelektronen-emissions-Mikroskop *n*, Stereoscanmikroskop *n*, Abtastmikroskop *n*
scaler-printer	Zähl- und Druckwerk *n*; Untersetzer *m* mit angekoppeltem Schreibgerät		
scaler tube	s. counting tube		
scales, pair of scales <US also sing.>; balance	Waage *f*		
scale sextant, direct-reading sextant	Skalensextant *m*		
		scanning electron microscopy, SEM	Rasterelektronenmikroskopie *f*
scale spacing	s. scale value		
scale span	s. scale range	**scanning frequency,** scan frequency	Abtastfrequenz *f*, Tastfrequenz *f*, Rasterfrequenz *f*
scale span	s. scale length		
scale stretching	s. scale extension		
scale transformation	Maßstabstransformation *f*, Skalentransformation *f*	**scanning head;** sensing head; probe	Tastkopf *m*
		scanning microscope	s. scanning electron microscope
scale-up factor	s. scale factor <num. math.>		
		scanning oscillator	s. relaxation generator
		scanning pitch	s. line spacing
scale-up factor	s. a. scale factor	**scanning separation,** line spacing, line advance, scanning pitch	Zeilenabstand *m*
scale value, scale-value, scale interval (spacing), width of scale division, value of the scale division	Skalenwert *m*, Skw., Skalenteilwert *m*, Skalenintervall *n*, Teilstrichabstand *m*		
		scanning voltage	s. sweep voltage
		scanning yoke	s. deflection coils
scale with omitted zero, scale with suppressed zero	Skala *f* mit unterdrücktem Nullpunkt	**scan polarography**	Tastpolarographie *f*
scaling, scale formation, formation of scale	Verzunderung *f*, Zunderbildung *f*, Zunderung *f*	**scansion,** scanning, exploring; image field dissection <of image>	Bildfeldzerlegung *f*; Bildzerlegung *f*
scaling, scale formation	Kesselsteinbildung *f*	**scansion**	s. a. scanning
		scatter <el.>	Streuausbreitung *f* <El.>
scaling	Schuppenbildung *f*, Schuppung *f*, Abblättern *n*	**scatter**	s. a. scattering
		scatter	s. spread <gen., e.g. of data>
scaling	s. scale <nucl.>	**scatter diagram,** dispersion diagram, aggregate of points, collection of points, bivariate point distribution <stat.>	Punktwolke *f*, Punkthaufen *m*, Punktgruppe *f*, Streubild *n*, Streuungsdiagramm *n* <Stat.>
scaling accelerator, fixed-orbit accelerator	Festbahnbeschleuniger *m*		
scaling circuit, pulse scaling circuit	Untersetzerschaltung *f*, Zählschaltung *f*, Impulsuntersetzerschaltung *f*		
scaling circuit	s. a. scaler	**scatter echo**	Streuecho *n*, Scatterecho *n*
scaling down	s. scale <nucl.>	**scattered,** containing sprinklings, scattered here and there <geo.>	eingesprengt, dispers; zerstreut <Geo.>
scaling factor <nucl.>	Untersetzungsfaktor *m*, Untersetzung *f*, Zählfaktor *m* <Kern.>		
		scattered forward, forescattered	vorwärts[]gestreut
scaling factor	s. a. scale factor		
scaling law	Maßstabgesetz *n*	**scattered heat radiation**	Wärmestreustrahlung *f*
scaling stage, frequency-divider stage, step-down stage	Untersetzerstufe *f*, Teilerstufe *f*, Frequenzteilerstufe *f*		
		scattered here and there	s. scattered <geo.>
		scattered light method	Streulichtmethode *f*, Streulichtverfahren *n*
scaling system	s. scaler <nucl.>		
scaling unit	Untersetzereinheit *f*, Untersetzerblock *m*; Untersetzerstufe *f*	**scattered light photometer,** stray light photometer	Streulichtphotometer *n*
scall, loose rock	Lockergestein *n*, unverfestigtes Gestein *n*	**scattered radiation,** diffuse radiation, scattered rays	Streustrahlung *f*, gestreute Strahlung *f*, diffuse Strahlung
scallop, ear <met.>	Zipfel *m*, Falte *f* <Met.>		
scalloped <met.>	zipfelförmig <Met.>	**scattered radiation dose**	Streustrahlungsdosis *f*

scattered rays	s. scattered radiation	scattering matrix, transition matrix <el.>	Streumatrix f, Verteilungsmatrix f <El.>
scattered reflection	s. diffuse reflection	scattering mean free path, mean free path for scattering	[mittlere freie] Streuweglänge f, mittlere freie Weglänge f für Streuung, mittlerer Streuweg m
scattered refraction	s. diffuse refraction		
scattered showers, desultory precipitations	vereinzelte Niederschläge (Schauer) mpl		
scattered transmission	s. diffuse transmission		
scatterer, scattering material	Streukörper m, Streumaterial n, Streusubstanz f, Streuer m	scattering of light	s. scattering
		scattering of light by Coulomb field, scattering of light by light, photon-photon scattering, Delbrück scattering [of photons]	Streuung f von Licht an Licht, Photon-Photon-Streuung f, Delbrück-Streuung f [von Lichtquanten], Delbrücksche Streuung
scatter fading	Streuschwund m		
scattering, scattering of light, scatter [of light], light scatter[ing]; diffusion [of light]	Streuung f [des Lichtes], Zerstreuung f [des Lichtes], Lichtstreuung f, Lichtzerstreuung f; Diffusion f [des Lichtes]		
		scattering operator, S-operator	Streuoperator m, S-Operator m
		scattering phase	Streuphase f
scattering	s. diffuse reflection	scattering power	Streuvermögen n; Zerstreuungsvermögen n
scattering < from, by; at or through an angle; into> <of radiation>	Streuung f <an; um; in> <Strahlung>	scattering problem	Streuproblem n
		scattering resonance	Streuresonanz f
scattering	s. a. spread <gen., e.g. of data>	scattering stage	Komparatortisch m für Dispersionsmessungen
scattering amplitude	Streu[ungs]amplitude f	scattering submatrix, S-submatrix	Streuuntermatrix f, S-Untermatrix f
scattering amplitude matrix	Streuamplitudenmatrix f	scattering term	Streuterm m, Streuglied n
scattering angle, angle of scattering	Streuwinkel m	scattering transmission, scatter transmission	Streustrahlübertragung f
scattering area	Streufläche f		
scattering area coefficient (ration)	Streuflächenverhältnis n	scattering vector	Streuvektor m
		scattering volume	Streuvolumen n
scattering by haze particles, haze scattering	Dunststreuung f		
scattering chamber	Streukammer f	scatter of light	s. scattering
scattering channel	Streukanal m	scatter transmission, scattering transmission	Streustrahlübertragung f
scattering coefficient	Streukoeffizient m		
scattering coefficient [in Mie's theory], Mie scattering coefficient	Streukoeffizient m der Mie-Streuung, Miescher Streukoeffizient	scatter unsharpness	Unschärfe f infolge Streuung
		scavenger	Radikalfänger m, Scavenger m; Desoxydationsmittel n, Ladungsfänger m
scattering collision	Streustoß m		
scattering cone, cone of dispersion, cone of spread, dispersing cone	Streukegel m, Streuungskegel m	scavenging <chem.>	Scavenging n, Reinigungsfällung f <Chem.>
		scedastic equation	skedastische Gleichung f
scattering constant	Streukonstante f, Streuungskonstante f	scedasticity	Streuungsverhalten n, Skedastizität f
scattering continuum	Streukontinuum n	scedastic line	skedastische Linie f
scattering cross-section, cross-section for scattering	Streuquerschnitt m, Wirkungsquerschnitt m für Streuung, Streuungsquerschnitt m, Streuwirkungsquerschnitt m, Streuungswirkungsquerschnitt m	scedastic transformation	skedastische Transformation f, Varianzstabilisierung[stransformation] f
		s-centre, site centre	s-Zentrum n
		Schaaffs['] theory	Schaaffssche Theorie f
		Schauder's fixed point theorem	Schauderscher Fixpunktsatz m
scattering ellipse	Streuungsellipse f, Streuellipse f		
scattering error	Streufehler m	Scheimpflug['s] condition	Scheimpflug-Bedingung f
scattering experiment	Streuversuch m, Streuexperiment n	Scheimpflug principle	Scheimpflug-Prinzip n
scattering factor, atomic scattering factor	Streufaktor m, atomarer Streufaktor	Scheiner['s] experiment	Scheinerscher Versuch m
scattering factor	s. a. atom form factor	Scheiner rating, degree Scheiner	Scheiner-Grad m
scattering factor	s. a. scattering coefficient	Scheiner sensitometer	Scheiner-Sensitometer n
scattering foil	Streufolie f	Scheiner's halo, Scheiner's ring	Halo m von Scheiner
scattering fraction	Streuanteil m		
scattering frequency	Streufrequenz f	Schellbach tube	Schellbach-Rohr n
scattering function	Streufunktion f		
scattering-in	s. inscattering	Schelting magnetometer, quartz Z-magnetometer	Quarzrahmenmagnetometer n [von Schelting], Z-Quarzmagnetometer n [von Schelting], Scheltingsches Z-Quarzmagnetometer
scattering indicatrix, diffusion indicatrix, indicatrix of diffusion	Streuindikatrix f; Streudiagramm n, Streuungsdiagramm n, Strahlendiagramm n, Strahlungsdiagramm n <Miesche Theorie>		
scattering intensity, scatter intensity	Streuintensität f		
scattering interaction	Streuwechselwirkung f, Streuungswechselwirkung f	schematic [circuit] diagram, basic circuit diagram, basic diagram, circuit diagram, connection diagram, connecting diagram, cording diagram, wiring diagram, wiring layout <el.>	Stromlaufplan m, Schaltplan m <El.>
scattering in the centre-of-mass system	Streuung f im Schwerpunktsystem, S-Streuung f		
scattering in the laboratory system	Streuung f im Laborsystem, L-Streuung f		
scattering length, Fermi intercept	Streulänge f		
scattering loss	Streuverlust m, Streuungsverlust m	schematic [circuit] diagram, simplified (skeleton) diagram	Prinzipschaltbild n, Prinzipschema n, Prinzipbild n, Prinzipstromlaufbild n, Grundschaltbild n, Grundschaltung f
scattering material, scatterer	Streukörper m, Streumaterial n, Streusubstanz f, Streuer m		
		schematic eye	schematisches Auge n
		scheme of terms	s. term diagram
scattering matrix, S-matrix	Streumatrix f, S-Matrix f	Scherbius cascade	Scherbius-Kaskade f

Schering-Alberti circuit	Schering-Alberti-Schaltung f, Stromwandler-Prüfeinrichtung f von Schering-Alberti, Meßwandler-Prüfeinrichtung f nach Schering-Alberti
Schering bridge	Schering-Brücke f, Schering-Meßbrücke f
Scherrer constant	Scherrersche Konstante f
Scherzer['s] correction	Scherzersche Korrektur f
Schiebold camera	Schiebold-Kammer f
Schiebold['s] method	Schiebold-Methode f, Schieboldsche Methode f
Schiebold-Sauter goniometer	Schiebold-Sauter-Goniometer n
Schiebold-Sauter method (technique)	Schiebold-Sauter-Verfahren n, Schiebold-Sautersches Verfahren n
Schiff['s] base	Schiffsche Base f, Azomethin n
schillerization, iridescence	Schillern n
schiller layer	opaleszierende Schicht f
Schilling-type effusion bottle <US>	s. effusiometer
schism <ac.>	Schisma n <Ak.>
schistosity	s. cleavage <geo.>
schizolite, diaschistic rock	Spaltungsgestein n, diaschistes Gestein n, Schizolith m, Ganggefolge n
Schläfli['s] formula	Schläflische Formel f, Schläflische Integraldarstellung f (der Kugelfunktionen)
Schläfli['s] polynomial	Schläflisches Polynom n
Schläfli['s] integral	Schläflische Integraldarstellung f (der Zylinderfunktion)
Schläfli['s] integral	s. Bessel['s] integral
Schleiermacher['s] [hot wire] method	Schleiermachersche Methode (Hitzdrahtmethode) f
Schleiermacher['s] theory	Schleiermachersche Lehre (Theorie) f
Schlesinger['s] criterion	Schlesinger-Kriterium n
schlichtartig	schlichtartig
schlicht function, univalent function	schlichte (univalente, einwertige) Funktion f
schliere <pl.: schlieren>; streak, smear; flow layer <geo.>	Schliere f
schlieren chamber, streak camera	Schlierenkammer f
schlieren diaphragm, schlieren edge, schlieren slit	Schlierenblende f
schlieren head	Schlierenkopf m
schlieren image	s. schlieren photograph
schlieren image of Toepler, Toepler['s] schlieren image	Toeplersches Schlierenbild n, Schlierenbild nach Toepler
schlieren method, striation method, striation technique; **schlieren photography,** streak photography, smear photography, shadow fringe test, strioscopic method	Schlierenmethode f, Schlierenverfahren n, Schlierentechnik f; Schlierenaufnahmeverfahren n, Schlierenaufnahme f
schlieren method [in aerodynamics]	Schlierenmethode f [der Gasdynamik]
schlieren microscope	Schlierenmikroskop n
schlieren microscopy	Schlierenmikroskopie f
schlieren object	Schlierenobjekt n
schlieren optical system, schlieren optics	Schlierenoptik f
schlieren photograph; schlieren picture, schlieren image	Schlierenaufnahme f; Schlierenbild n
schlieren photography	s. schlieren method
schlieren picture	s. schlieren photograph
schlieren scanning technique; shadow schlieren method, projecting schlieren method	Schattenschlierenverfahren n, Schattenschlierenmethode f
schlieren slit	s. schlieren diaphragm
Schloemilch detector, electrolytic detector	elektrolytischer Detektor m, Elektrolytdetektor m, Schloemilch-Zelle f
Schloemilch['s] expansion (series)	Schlömilchsche Reihe f
Schlumberger photoclinometer	Schlumbergerscher Neigungsmesser m
Schmalcalder compass	Schmalcalder-Bussole f
Schmaltz [profile] microscope	Oberflächenprüfgerät n nach Schmaltz, Lichtschnittprüfgerät n, Lichtschnittgerät n, Lichtschnittmikroskop n nach Schmaltz, Schmaltz-Lichtschnittmikroskop n, 45°-Lichtschnittmikroskop n
Schmid['s] [law of critical shear stress], critical shear stress law of Schmid	Schmidsches Schubspannungsgesetz n, Schubspannungsgesetz von Schmid
Schmidt	s. Schmidt camera
Schmidt balance	s. Schmidt['s] field balance
Schmidt camera, Schmidt telescope, Schmidt system, Schmidt	Schmidt-Spiegel m, Schmidt-Spiegelteleskop n, Schmidt-System n
Schmidt-Cassegrain camera (system, telescope), Cassegrain type of Schmidt camera	Schmidt-Cassegrain-System n, Schmidt-Cassegrain-Spiegel m
Schmidt corrector plate, corrector plate	Schmidt-Platte f, Schmidtsche Platte f, Korrektionsplatte f [nach Schmidt], Schmidtsche Korrektionsplatte
Schmidt curve	s. Schmidt lines
Schmidt['s] field balance, Schmidt [vertical field] balance	Schmidtsche Feldwaage f, Schmidt-Waage f
Schmidt group	Schmidt-Gruppe f
Schmidt['s] hypothesis	Theorie f von O. J. Schmidt
Schmidt lens	Schmidt-Linse f
Schmidt lens, Schmidt objective	Schmidt-Objektiv n
Schmidt limits	Schmidt-Grenzen fpl
Schmidt lines, Schmidt curve	Schmidt-Linien fpl, Schmidt-Kurven fpl, Schmidtsche Linien fpl, Schmidt-Diagramm n
Schmidt magnetometer, Schmidt-type magnetometer	Schmidt-Magnetometer n, Magnetometer n vom Schmidt-Typ
Schmidt['s] model [of nuclei]	Schmidt-Modell n
Schmidt net	[flächentreues] Schmidtsches Netz n
Schmidt number, Sc	Schmidt-Zahl f, Schmidtsche Kennzahl f, Schmidtsche Zahl f, Sc
Schmidt objective	s. Schmidt lens
Schmidt['s] optical system, optical system of the Schmidt telescope, Schmidt system, Schmidt optics, reflective optics	Schmidt-Optik f, Hohlspiegeloptik f, Schmidt-System n
Schmidt optics	s. Schmidt['s] optical system
Schmidt['s] orthogonalization process	s. Gram-Schmidt orthogonalization
Schmidt prism	Schmidt-Prisma n
Schmidt['s] process	s. Gram-Schmidt orthogonalization
Schmidt['s] rule	Schmidtsche Doppelbindungsregel f
Schmidt system	s. Schmidt['s] optical system
Schmidt system	s. Schmidt camera
Schmidt telescope	s. Schmidt camera
Schmidt['s] theodolite	Theodolit m nach Adolf Schmidt, Schmidtscher Theodolit, Schmidt-Theodolit m
Schmidt['s] theory [of integral equations], theory of E. Schmidt	Schmidtsche Theorie f [der Integralgleichungen]

Schmidt['s] vertical field balance	s. Schmidt['s] field balance	**Schrödinger picture (representation)**	s. co-ordinate representation
Schmidt-typemagnetometer	s. Schmidt magnetometer	**Schrödinger representative**	Schrödinger-Darsteller m
Schmitt trigger	s. Schmitt trigger circuit	**Schrödinger['s] theory of perturbation**	s. time-independent perturbation theory
Schmitt trigger circuit, Schmitt trigger	Schmitt-Trigger m, Schmitt-Triggerschaltung f	**Schrödinger['s] wave equation**	s. Schrödinger['s] equation
		Schrödinger['s] wave function	s. wave function
Schnadt specimen	Schnadt-Probe f	**Schrot effekt, Schroteffekt, schrot noise**	s. shot effect
schneidenton, edge tone	Schneidenton m; Hiebton m	**Schubert['s] rule**	Schubertsche Regel f
Schoenflies crystallographic notation, Schoenflies notation	Schoenflies-Symbolik f, Schoenfliessche Bezeichnung[sweise] f	**schubweg,** displacement, displacement distance	Schubweg m
Schoenflies crystal symbol	Schoenflies-Symbol n	**Schuler['s] clock**	Schuler-Uhr f
Schoenflies notation	s. Schoenflies crystallographic notation	**Schuler['s] pendulum,** 84 min pendulum, 84-minute[s] pendulum	Schuler-Pendel n, 84-Minuten-Pendel n, Schuler-Kreiselpendel n
Schofield's equation	Schofieldsche Gleichung f		
Scholz counter	Scholzscher Kernzähler m, Scholz-Zähler m		
Schönrock	s. Schönrock halfshade	**Schuler period,** 84.4-minutes period, 84.4 min period	Schuler-Frequenz f, 84,4-Minuten-Periode f, 84,4-min-Periode f
Schönrock autocollimating eyepiece	Autokollimationsokular n nach Schönrock	**Schuler['s] theorem**	Schulerscher Satz m
Schönrock halfshade; Schönrock prism; Schönrock	Halbschattenapparat m nach Schönrock; Schönrock-Prisma n, Prisma n von Schönrock	**Schulz-Blaschke formula**	Schulz-Blaschkesche Formel f
		Schulze-Hardy law, Schulze-Hardy rule, Hardy-Schulze rule	Schulze-Hardysche Regel f
Schönwaldt['s] rule	Schönwaldtsche Regel f	**Schulz transition**	Schulz-Zerlegung f
schooping	s. metal spraying	**Schumann['s] condition**	Schumannsche Durchschlagsbedingung f
schoop-plating	s. metal spraying	**Schumann plate**	Schumann-Platte f
Schoop process	s. metal spraying		
Schott filter, Schott glass	Schott-Glas n, Schott-Filter n	**Schumann region**	Schumann-Gebiet n, Schumann-Bereich m, Schumann-Spektralbereich m, Schumann-Ultraviolett n
Schott['s] formula	Schottsche Formel f, Formel von Schott		
Schott glass	s. Schott filter	**Schumann-Runge band**	Schumann-Runge-Bande f, Runge-Schumann-Bande f
Schottky barrier, Schottky barrier layer	Schottkysche Randschicht f, Schottky-Barriere f		
Schottky barrier diode, hot-carrier diode	Schottky-Barriere-Diode f, Metall-Halbleiter-Diode f	**Schur function**	Schur-Funktion f, Schursche Funktion f
Schottky barrier layer	s. Schottky barrier	**Schur['s] lemma**	Schursches (Schurs) Lemma n
Schottky barrier model	Schottkysches Sperrschichtmodell n		
Schottky['s] barrier theory, Schottky['s] theory	Schottkysche Randschichttheorie f	**Schuster bridge**	Schuster-Brücke f
		Schuster method	Schustersches Verfahren n
Schottky defect (discorder); vacancy-type Schottky defect, Schottky vacancy; interstitial type Schottky defect, Schottky interstitial	Schottky-Fehlordnung f, Schottky-Defekt m, Schottkysche Fehlordnung f, Schottkysche Fehlstelle f, Schottkysche Störstelle f, Schottkysche Leerstelle f, Schottky-Leerstelle f	**Schuster-Smith coil magnetometer**	Spulenmagnetometer n von Schuster und Smith, Schuster-Smithsches Spulenmagnetometer, Schuster-Smith-Coil-magnetometer n
Schottky doping	Schottkysche Dotierung f	**Schwann's sheath**	s. neurilemma
Schottky effect	Schottky-Effekt m	**Schwarz['s] alternating method**	s. alternating method
Schottky effect	s. a. shot effect	**Schwarz-Christoffel formula,** Schwarz-Christoffel theorem	Schwarz-Christoffelsche Formel f, Schwarz-Christoffelsches Integral n, Schwarz-Christoffelscher Abbildungssatz m
Schottky['s] equation [of field emission]	Schottkysche Feldemissionsgleichung f		
Schottky['s] formula	Schottkysche Formel f		
Schottky interstitial	s. Schottky defect		
Schottky-Langmuir law	s. Langmuir-Schottky law	**Schwarz-Christoffel polygon mapping,** polygon mapping, Schwarz-Christoffel transformation	Polygonabbildung f, Schwarz-Christoffelsche Abbildung (Polygonabbildung) f
Schottky['s] model	Schottkysches Napfmodell n, Napfmodell n		
Schottky noise	s. shot effect		
Schottky['s] theory	s. Schottky['s] barrier theory	**Schwarz-Christoffel theorem**	s. Schwarz-Christoffel formula
Schottky transition	Schottky-Übergang m	**Schwarz-Christoffel transformation**	s. Schwarz-Christoffel polygon mapping
Schottky vacancy	s. Schottky defect	**Schwarz['s] constant**	Schwarzsche Konstante f
Schreiber['s] method	kombinationsweise Winkelmessung f, Schreibersches Winkelmeßverfahren n, Winkelmeßverfahren nach Schreiber, Schreibersche Methode f		
		Schwarz['s] derivative	Schwarzsche Differentialinvariante f, Schwarzsche Ableitung f
Schröder [corrector] plate	Schrödersche Platte f	**Schwarz['s] function**	Schwarz-Funktion f
Schröder-van Laar equation	Schröder-van-Laar-Gleichung f	**Schwarz-Hora effect**	Schwarz-Hora-Effekt m
Schrödinger['s] constant	Schrödinger-Konstante f	**Schwarz['s] inequality** <for integrals, series>; Cauchy-Schwarz inequality, Buniakowsky-Schwarz inequality <for integrals>	Schwarzsche Ungleichung (Ungleichheit) f, [Cauchy-]Bunjakowskische Ungleichung <für Integrale, Folgen>; Cauchysche (Lagrangesche, Lagrange-Cauchysche) Ungleichung <für Folgen>
Schrödinger-Dirac equation	Schrödinger-Dirac-Gleichung f		
Schrödinger['s] equation, Schrödinger['s] wave equation, wave equation	Schrödinger-Gleichung f, Schrödingersche Wellengleichung f, Wellengleichung f		
Schrödinger['s] field theory, field theory of Schrödinger	Schrödingers rein affine Feldtheorie f, rein affine Feldtheorie [von Schrödinger]		
		Schwarz['s] lemma	Schwarzsches Lemma n
		Schwarz principle of reflection	s. Schwarz['s] reflection principle
Schrödinger['s] function	s. wave function	**Schwarz['s] quotient**	Schwarzscher Quotient m
Schrödinger operator	Schrödinger-Operator m	**Schwarz reflection**	s. Schwarz['s] reflection principle

Schwarz['s] reflection principle, reflection principle, symmetry principle, principle of reflection, spiegelungsprinzip, Schwarz [principle of] reflection	Schwarzsches Spiegelungsprinzip n, Spiegelungsprinzip	**science of light reflection**, catoptrics, anacamptics	Katoptrik f, Lehre f von der Reflexion des Lichtes
		science of metals, physical metallurgy, metal science	Metallkunde f, Metallographie f im weiteren Sinne, Metallwissenschaft f, wissenschaftliche Metallkunde
Schwarzschild anastigmat	Schwarzschildscher Anastigmat m	**science of reflection and refraction of light**, catadioptrics	Katadioptrik f, Lehre f von der Reflexion und Brechung des Lichtes
Schwarzschild['s] angle eikonal, Schwarzschild['s] eikonal	Schwarzschildsches Winkeleikonal n	**science of the strength [of materials]**, strength of materials	Festigkeitslehre f
Schwarzschild antenna	Schwarzschild-Antenne f	**scientific kinematography**	wissenschaftliche Kinematographie f, Wissenschaftskinematographie f
Schwarzschild effect, reciprocity[-] law failure, reciprocity failure <phot.>	Schwarzschild-Effekt m, Reziprozitätsabweichung f, Ultrakurzzeiteffekt m <Phot.>	**scinticounting**	s. scintillation counting
		scintigram, scintiscan	Szintigramm n, Gammagramm n; Strichszintigramm n
Schwarzschild['s] eikonal	s. Schwarzschild['s] angle eikonal	**scintigraph**	s. scintiscanner
Schwarzschild['s] equation	Schwarzschild-Gleichung f	**scintigraphy**, scintiscanning	Szintigraphie f
Schwarzschild exponent	Schwarzschild-Exponent m	**scintillant**	s. scintillating material
		scintillating liquid	s. liquid scintillator
Schwarzschild['s] exterior solution	s. Schwarzschild['s] solution	**scintillating material**, scintillant	Szintillationssubstanz f, szintillierende Substanz f, szintillierendes Material n
Schwarzschild['s] iteration method	Schwarzschildsches Iterationsverfahren n	**scintillation**; illuminating flash; flash; flash of light, light flash	Szintillation f; Aufblitzen n, Szintillationsblitz m; Blitz m, Lichtblitz m
Schwarzschild['s] law	s. Schwarzschild['s] reciprocity law		
Schwarzschild mass	Schwarzschildsche Masse f		
Schwarzschild['s] metric	Schwarzschildsche Metrik f, Schwarzschild-Metrik f		
		scintillation, twinkling <of stars> <astr.>	Szintillieren n, Funkeln n, Zittern n, Flimmern n, Luftflimmern n, Luftunruhe f, Luftzittern n, Szintillation f <Sterne> <Astr.>
Schwarzschild-Milne equation, integral equation of Schwarzschild and Milne	Schwarzschild-Milnesche Integralgleichung f		
Schwarzschild['s] principle	Schwarzschildsches Prinzip n [der Korpuskularoptik]	**scintillation beta-ray spectrometer**, beta-ray scintillation spectrometer	Szintillations-Beta-Spektrometer n
Schwarzschild['s] problem, problem of Schwarzschild	Schwarzschildsches Problem n		
Schwarzschild['s] radius	Gravitationsradius m [einer Masse], Schwarzschild-Radius m, Schwarzschildscher Radius m	**scintillation camera**, gamma-camera, gamma[-ray] camera, scanning camera	Szintillationskamera f, Gammakamera f, Gamma-Kamera f, Anger-Kamera f
		scintillation coincidence spectrometer, coincidence scintillation spectrometer	Szintillationskoinzidenzspektrometer n, Szintillations-Koinzidenzspektrometer n, Koinzidenzszintillationsspektrometer n
Schwarzschild['s] reciprocity law, Schwarzschild['s] law	Schwarzschildsches Gesetz n, Schwarzschildsches Reziprozitätsgesetz n		
Schwarzschild singularity	Schwarzschildsche Singularität f		
Schwarzschild['s] solution; Schwarzschild['s] exterior solution	Schwarzschildsche Lösung f	**scintillation counter**, scintillation detector	Szintillationszähler m, Szintillationsdetektor m
Schwarzschild system	Zweispiegelsystem n [nach (von) Schwarzschild], Schwarzschild-System n, Schwarzschild-Typ m, aplanatisches Zweispiegelsystem [von Schwarzschild]	**scintillation counter crystal**	s. scintillation crystal
		scintillation counting, scinticounting	Szintillationszählung f, Auszählen n der Szintillationen
		scintillation crystal; scintillation counter crystal	Szintillatorkristall m, Szintillationskristall m
Schwarzschild['s] velocity ellipsoid	Schwarzschildsches Geschwindigkeitsellipsoid n	**scintillation decay time**	Szintillationsabfallzeit f, Abfallzeit f der Szintillation, Szintillationsabklingzeit f, Abklingzeit f der Szintillation
Schwarzschild['s] world	Schwarzschildsche Welt f		
		scintillation detector	s. scintillation counter
Schwedoff body, plastigel, plastic gel, plastogel	plastisches Gel n, Plastigel n, Schwedoffscher Körper m	**scintillation dosimeter**	Szintillationsdosimeter n
Schweidler oscillation	radioaktive Schwankung f	**scintillation fading**	Szintillationsschwund m
Schwinger['s] delta function	Schwingersche Deltafunktion f		
Schwinger['s] equation	Schwingersche Gleichung f	**scintillation gamma-ray spectrometer**, gamma-ray scintillation spectrometer	Szintillations-Gamma-Spektrometer n
Schwinger-Levine variational method	Schwinger-Levinesches Variationsverfahren n		
Schwinger radiation	s. synchrotron radiation	**scintillation gel**	Szintillationsgel n
Schwinger scattering	Schwinger-Streuung f, Schwingersche Streuung f	**scintillation head**	Szintillations[meß]kopf m
Schwinger['s] variation method	Schwingersches Variationsverfahren n	**scintillation of radio source (star)**, radioscintillation	Szintillieren n der Radioquelle, Radioszintillation f
sciagram	s. shadowgraph		
science of colour	Farbenlehre f	**scintillation probe**	Szintillationssonde f
science of fluid flow, fluid mechanics	Strömungsmechanik f, Strömungslehre f, Mechanik f der Flüssigkeiten und Gase	**scintillation response**	Szintillationsausbeute f, Lichtausbeute f des Szintillators
science of heat, heat technology	Wärmelehre f, Kalorik f	**scintillation rise time**	Anstiegszeit f der Szintillation, Szintillationsanstiegszeit f
science of light, physical optics, photology	physikalische Optik f, Lehre f vom Licht	**scintillation scanner**	s. scintiscanner

scintillation screen	Szintillationsschirm *m*	scour	*s. a.* underwashing
scintillation spectrometer	Szintillationsspektrometer *n*, Lichtblitzspektrometer *n*, Lichtblitz-Spektralapparat *m*, Lichtblitz-Sortierapparat *m*, Lichtblitzspektrograph *m*	scouring, pickling <met.>	Beizen *n*, Abbeizen *n* Dekapieren *n* <Met.>
		scouring	*s. a.* scoring
		scram <US>	*s.* emergency shut-down <of reactor>
		scram delay, shut down delay <of reactor>	Abschaltverzögerung *f* <Reaktor>
scintillation spectrum	Szintillationsspektrum *n*		
scintillator	Szintillator *m*	scram rod, emergency shut-down rod <US>; safety rod, cut-off rod	Sicherheitsstab *m*, Schnellschlußstab *m*, Notstab *m*
scintillator prospecting radiation meter, scintillometer	Szintillometer *n*		
scintiphotogram, photoscintigram	Photoszintigramm *n*, Photogammagramm *n*, Szintiphoto *n*	scratch	Kratzer *m*, Ritz *m*
		scratch, surface noise, needle scratch	Nadelgeräusch *n*, Nadelrauschen *n*, Kratzen *n* der Nadel
scintiscan, scintigram	Szintigramm *n*		
scintiscanner, scintillation scanner, scintigraph	Szintiscanner *m*, Szintillationsscanner *m*, Szintigraph *m*, Scanner *m*	scratch hardness, sclerometric hardness, scleroscope hardness, abrasive hardness	Ritzhärte *f*; Kratzfestigkeit *f*
scintiscanning, scintigraphy	Szintigraphie *f*		
scission <bio.>	Abspaltung *f* <Bio.>	scratching	Ritzung *f*
scission	*s. a.* splitting		
scission of the ring, ring cleavage, ring scission, cleavage of the ring; ring opening, opening of the ring	Ringspaltung *f*, Spaltung *f* des Rings; Ringöffnung *f*	screaming, screeching	Kreischen *n*; Knirschen *n*
		screen	Schirm *m*
		screen, grid, raster, mesh, pattern	Raster *m*
scissoring vibration, scissors mode	Scherenschwingung *f*		
		screen, sieve; riddle; sifter	Sieb *n*
scissors telescope, stereoscopic telescope	Scherenfernrohr *n*		
		screen <of cathode-ray tube>	Leuchtschirm *m* <Elektronenstrahlröhre>
sclerometer	Sklerometer *n*, Ritzhärteprüfer *m*	screen <hydr., aero.>	Gleichrichter *m* <Hydr., Aero.>
sclerometric hardness	*s.* scratch hardness		
scleronomic[al], scleronomous <mech.>; time-independent, independent of time	zeitunabhängig, zeitfrei; skleronom <Mech.>	screen	*s. a.* instrument screen
		screen	*s. a.* projection screen
		screenage, screening	Abschirmung *f*; Schirmung *f*
scleronomous binding, constraint independent of time, non varying constraint	skleronome Bedingung *f*, starrgesetzliche Bedingung	screenage	*s. a.* size separation by screens
		screen analysis	*s.* particle-size analysis
scleroprotein, fibrous protein	Skleroprotein *n*, Gerüsteiweiß[stoff *m*] *n*, Faserprotein *n*, Linearprotein *n*	screen capacity, screening capacity	Siebleistung *f*; Siebkennziffer *f*
		screen control, screen grid control	Schirmgittersteuerung *f*
scleroscope, Shore scleroscope	Shore-Härteprüfer *m*, Shore-Härteprüfgerät *n*; Shoresches Skleroskop *n*, Skleroskop		
		screen current	*s.* screen grid current
scleroscope hardness, Shore hardness [number], Shore scleroscope hardness	Shore-Härte *f*, Shoresche Härte *f*	screened, partially enclosed <of apparatuses>	gegen zufällige Berührung geschützt <Geräte>
		screened cage	*s.* Faraday cage
		screened grid, screen grid	Schirmgitter *n*
scleroscope hardness	*s. a.* scratch hardness	screened valve	*s.* screen grid tube
sclerosphere	Sklerosphäre *f*	screen efficiency, sieve efficiency	Siebwirkungsgrad *m*
S.C.N.A.	*s.* sudden cosmic noise absorption		
scope	*s.* plan-position indicator <radar>	screen efficiency	Schirmausbeute *f*
scope, observation telescope	Beobachtungsfernrohr *n*, Betrachtungsfernrohr *n*	screen factor, shielding factor <el.>	Schirmfaktor *m* <El.>
		screen film	Verstärkerfilm *m*
scope of direction finder	*s.* display of direction finder		
scopometry	Skopometrie *f*	screen filter	Siebfilter *n*
scorching; singing	Sengen *n*		
scorching <of contacts>	Schmoren *n*; Verschmorung *f* <Kontakte>	screen grid, screened grid	Schirmgitter *n*
		screen grid bias, screen grid potential	Schirmgittervorspannung *f*, Schirmgitterpotential *n*
score <stat.>	Note *f*, Beitrag *m* <Stat.>		
scorification	*s.* slagging	screen grid control	*s.* screen control
scoring, scouring <in wear>	Ritzung *f*, Ritzbildung *f*, Ausfressen *n* <Verschleißerscheinung>	screen grid current, screen current	Schirmgitterstrom *m*
		screen grid dissipation	Schirmgitterverlustleistung *f*, Schirmgitterbelastung *f*
scoring <stat.>	Bonitur *f* <Stat.>		
Scotch mist	*s.* drizzling fog	screen grid Heising modulation	Schirmgitter-Heising-Modulation *f*
scotophor	*s.* killer		
scotopic system	skotopisches System *n*		
scotopic vision, nocto-vision	Nachtsehen *n*, Dämmerungssehen *n*, Dunkelsehen *n*, Stäbchensehen *n*, skotopisches Sehen *n*	screen grid modulation	Schirmgittermodulation *f*, Wirkungsgradmodulation *f*
		screen grid potential	*s.* screen grid bias
Scott circuit	Scott-Schaltung *f*, Scottsche Schaltung *f*	screen grid resistance	Schirmgitterwiderstand *m*
		screen grid tension	*s.* screen grid voltage
Scott effect, Scott [thermomagnetic] torque, thermomagnetic torque	Scott-Effekt *m*, thermomagnetisches Drehmoment *n*	screen grid tube, screen grid valve, screened valve	Schirmgitterröhre *f*
Scott transformer	Scott-Transformator *m*		
		screen grid voltage, screen voltage, screen grid tension	Schirmgitterspannung *f*
scour <geo.>	Seitenerosion *f*, Wandererosion *f* <Geo.>		
scour	*s. a.* crater		

screen 740

screen image	Schirmbild n	screw eyepiece micrometer, eyepiece micrometer screw, screw micrometer eyepiece	Okularschraubenmikrometer n, Okularschraublehre f, Okularmeßschraube f
screening <stat.>	verbessernde Auswahl f <Stat.>		
screening	s. screenage		
screening	s. screening action	screw field, corkscrew field	Schraubenfeld n, schraubenförmiges Feld n
screening	s. size separation by screens		
screening action, screening, shielding action, shielding	Schirmwirkung f, Abschirm[ungs]wirkung f	screw gauge, screw micrometer, micrometer caliper	Schraubenmikrometer n, Schraublehre f, Schraubenlehre f
screening box	Abschirmgehäuse n		
screening capacity	s. screen capacity		
screening constant, screening number <nucl.>	Abschirm[ungs]konstante f, Abschirmungszahl f <Kern.>		
		screw ice	Schraubeis n
		screwing [motion]	s. screw displacement
		screw-like	s. screw
screening constant <mol.>	Abschirm[ungs]konstante f <Mol.>	screw micrometer	s. screw gauge
		screw micrometer eyepiece	s. screw eyepiece micrometer
screening doublet	Abschirmungsdublett n, Abschirmdublett n, irreguläres Dublett n	screw motion	s. screw displacement
		screw orientation	s. orientation of the screw
		screw pitch	s. pitch <of the helix, screw>
		screw pitch gauge	Gewindelehre f, Gewindeganglehre f; Gewindeschablone f
screening effect	Abschirmeffekt m, Schirmeffekt m		
screening effect	s. screening of nucleus <nucl.>		
screening factor, shield factor <el.>	Abschirmfaktor m <El.>		
screening number	s. screening constant <nucl.>	screw press, pressing screw, thumb-screw	Druckschraube f
screening of nucleus, electron screening, screening effect <nucl.>	Kernabschirmung f, Abschirmung f der Kernladung, Abschirmung des Atomkerns, atomare Abschirmung f, Abschirm[ungs]wirkung f	screw[-]sense, screw sense	s. orientation of the screw
		screw slip band	Schraubengleitband n
		screw-thread micrometer cal[l]iper	Schraubenlehrenstichmaß n; Gewindeschraublehre f
screening radius	s. Debye length	screw-type distance finder	s. screw-type range finder
screenings; riddlings; sieve residue, plus material, oversize	Siebrückstand m; Überkorn n	screw-type flowmeter	s. propeller-type flowmeter
		screw-type [fluid] meter	s. propeller-type flowmeter
		screw-type range finder, screw-type distance finder	Schraubendistanzmesser m
		scribing block	Winkelstreichmaß n, Reißmaß n, Flächenlehre f
screening sphere	Schirmeffektkugel f	scroll	s. skew surface
screen microscope	s. scanning electron microscope	scrubbing <US>, stripping; washing; washing-out	Waschen n, Wäsche f; Gaswäsche f; Turmwäsche f; Herauswaschen n; Auswaschung f
screen microscope	s. a. raster microscope		
screen photograph, radiograph, fluorogram, photofluorogram	Schirmbild n, Schirmbildaufnahme f, Schirmbildphotographie f, Röntgenschirmbild n, Röntgenschirmbildaufnahme f, Röntgenschirmbildphotographie f	scud	s. fracto[-]stratus
		scuffing, galling; seizure, seizing	adhäsiver Verschleiß m; örtliche Verschweißung f; Kommabildung f; Fressen n; Festfressen n
		scuffing	s. a. wear
		S-curve	s. sigmoid curve
screen picture, projection picture	Projektionsbild n	sea, motion of the sea, sea-way	Seegang m, See f, Wellengang m
		sea, mare <pl.: maria> <on the Moon>	Mare n <pl.: Maria>, Mondmeer n
screen process, colour screen process	Farbrasterverfahren	S.E.A.	s. sudden enhancement of atmospherics
		sea breaking on shore, on-shore breakers, surf on shore	Strandbrandung f
screen size, sieve size, size of sieve	Maschenweite f <Sieb>, Siebgröße f, Siebweite f, Siebnummer f		
screen test	s. particle-size analysis	sea breeze, sea wind, on-shore wind	Seewind m
screen voltage	s. screen grid voltage	sea cave	Brandungshöhle f; Brandungskehle f
screw, wheel, blade <of current meter or vane>	Schaufel f, Flügelschaufel f		
screw, helical, screw-like, coiled	schraubenförmig, Schrauben[linien]-; wendelförmig	sea clutter, sea echo	Seegangreflex m, Seegangsreflex m
screw axis, axis of twist <cryst.>	Schraubenachse f, Schraubungsachse f, Helikogyre f <Krist.>	sea echo, sea clutter	Seegangreflex m, Seegangsreflex m
screw axis <mech.>	Schraubenachse f, Achse f des Nullsystems <Mech.>	sea floor, ocean floor, floor of ocean; ocean core	Meeresboden m, Meeresgrund m
screw axis of order n, n-fold screw axis, n-al screw axis	n-zählige Schraubenachse f	sea forecast, marine forecast	Wellenvorhersage f, Wellenprognose f
screw direction	s. orientation of the screw	sea gauge; water gauge; tide gauge <hydr.>	Pegel m; Gezeitenpegel m <Hydr.>
screw dislocation, Burgers dislocation	Schraubenversetzung f, Querversetzung f, Burgers-Versetzung f		
		sea horizon	s. apparent horizon
screw displacement, helicoidal displacement, screw[ing] (helical, helicoidal) motion, motion along a helix, spirallinig, screwing, twist	Schraubenbewegung f, schraubenförmige Bewegung f, Schraubung f, Bewegungsschraube f	sea interferometer, cliff interferometer, cliff-top interferometer	Kliffinterferometer n
		seal	Dichtung f

seal, sealing	Zuschmelzung *f*; Siegeln *n*; Hermetisierung *f*	secant, secant line, transversal	Sekante *f*, Transversale *f*, Treffgerade *f*
seal, sealing, soldering <on, together>, soft soldering	Verlötung *f*, Lötung *f* <an, zusammen>, Weichlötung *f*	secant, sec	Sekans *m*, Sekantenfunktion *f*, sec
seal, sealing	Einschmelzung *f*, Einschmelzstelle *f*	secant compass	Sekantenbussole *f*
		secant line	s. secant
sealed-in source, sealed radioactive material (source)	s. sealed source	Secchi['s] classification, Secchi['s] spectral classification	Secchische Spektralklassifikation *f*, Secchi-Klassifikation *f*
sealed source, sealed-in (encapsulated) source, sealed radioactive source (material)	umschlossene Quelle *f*, geschlossene Quelle (Strahlungsquelle *f*, radioaktive Quelle), geschlossenes [radioaktives] Präparat *n*, gekapselte Quelle *f*	Secchi disk	Secchi-Scheibe *f*, Secchische Scheibe *f*, Sichtscheibe *f*
		Secchi['s] spectral classification	s. Secchi['s] classification
		seclusion	Seklusion *f*
sealed tube	s. sealing tube	secon	s. secondary electron conduction tube
sea level [elevation]	s. mean-sea-level		
sealing	s. seal	second, second of arc, angular second, sexagesimal second [of arc], ", sec <of angle>	Sekunde *f* [im Bogenmaß], Winkelsekunde *f*, Bogensekunde *f*, Altsekunde *f*, " <Winkelmaß>
sealing alloy	Einschmelzlegierung *f*		
sealing diaphragm	Abschlußmembran *f*		
		second, s, sec	Sekunde *f*, s
		second / per	sekundlich, pro Sekunde
sealing fluid (liquid)	s. confining liquid	second adjoint space, bidual	zweiter adjungierter Raum *m*, Bidual *m*, bidualer Raum
sealing tube, sealed (bomb, Carius) tube	Bombenrohr *n* [nach Carius], Einschmelzrohr *n*, Einschmelzröhre *f*, Einschlußrohr *n*, Schießrohr *n*		
		secondary <of binary star>, companion, secondary component	Begleiter *m* <Doppelsternsystem>
sealing veil	Schleierdichtung *f*	secondary	s. a. secondary particle
		secondary	s. a. secondary wave <geo.>
sea mile, international mile, US-nautical mile, nautical mile, intern. mile <= 1 852 m>	Seemeile *f*, internationale Seemeile, sm <= 1 852 m>	secondary axis <cryst.>; minor axis, transverse axis	kleine Achse *f*; Nebenachse *f* <Krist.>
		secondary calibration	s. recalibration
		secondary caustic, anticaustic	Antikaustik *f*, sekundäre Kaustik *f*
seaquake, submarine earthquake	Seebeben *n*	secondary cell	Sekundärelement *n*
		secondary circuit	s. secondary coolant circuit
search, prospecting <for>	Erkundung *f*, Lagerstättensuche *f*, Prospektion *f*, Schürfung *f*	secondary cleavage; secondary schistosity	sekundäre Schieferung *f*
		secondary clock	s. slave clock
		secondary collision	Sekundärstoß *m*
search coil, measuring coil	Meßspule *f*, Suchspule *f*, Prüfspule *f*		
search for comets	Kometensuche *f*, Kometenjagd *f*	secondary component	s. secondary <of binary star>
		secondary component [of cosmic radiation]	s. secondary cosmic radiation [component]
search for leaks, leak hunting, leak detection, leakage survey; checking for gas leaks	Lecksuche *f*, Aufsuchen *n* von Undichtheiten	secondary condition <math.>	Nebenbedingung *f* <Math.>
search light; projector	Scheinwerfer *m*	secondary coolant circuit, secondary circuit <of reactor>	zweiter Kühlkreislauf (Kreislauf) *m*, Sekundärkreis[lauf] *m*, Sekundärkühlkreis[lauf] *m* <Reaktor>
search tone	Suchton *m*		
sea[-]shore, beach, shore, strand	Strand *m*		
sea-shore zone, littoral, littoral zone	Litoral *n*, Uferregion *f*, Uferzone *f*, Gezeitenzone *f*, Strandbereich *m*	secondary cosmic radiation [component], secondary cosmic rays, secondary component [of cosmic radiation]	Sekundärkomponente *f* [der kosmischen Strahlung], [kosmische] Sekundärstrahlung *f*, sekundäre kosmische Strahlung *f*, sekundäre Höhenstrahlung *f*
sea smoke	Seerauch *m*		
seasonal average, seasonal mean	Jahreszeitenmittel *n*, jahreszeitliches Mittel *n*		
seasonal factor	jahreszeitlicher Faktor *m*		
seasonal mean	s. seasonal average	secondary creation	s. secondary generation
seasonal solifluction	Jahrezeitensolifluktion *f*	secondary creep	s. quasiviscous creep
season crack[ing]	Altersriß *m*, Alterungsriß *m*	secondary cyclone [depression]	s. secondary depression
seasoning <of material>, ageing, aging	Alterung *f* <natürliche, der Werkstoffe>	secondary depression, secondary cyclone depression, secondary cyclone, satellite depression, secondary low <meteo.>	Teiltief *n*, Teiltiefdruckgebiet *n*, Teildepression *f*, Sekundärdepression *f*, Sekundärzyklone *f*; Randzyklone *f*, Randtief *n*, Randwirbel *m* <Meteo.>
seat, seating, bearing area	Sitz *m*, Sitzfläche *f*		
seat <of origin>, focus, origin, hearth, centre <geo., meteo.>	Herd *m* <Geo., Meteo.>		
		secondary diagonal	Nebendiagonale *f*
seating	s. seat	secondary disturbance	s. elementary wave
seat of the valve, valve seating, valve seat	Ventilsitz *m*, Sitz *m* des Ventils	secondary drive, driven side (end), output	Abtrieb *m*
sea triangulation	Hochseetriangulation *f*	secondary effect	Sekundäreffekt *m*, Sekundärwirkung *f*, Nebenerscheinung *f*, Nebenwirkung *f*, Nebeneffekt *m*
sea-water desalination	Meerwasserentsalzung *f*		
sea-water thermometer	s. reversing thermometer		
sea wave, ocean wave	Meereswelle *f*, Meereswoge *f*	secondary electron atomic battery	s. secondary emission radioactive battery
sea-way, motion of the sea, sea	Seegang *m*, See *f*, Wellengang *m*	secondary electron conduction tube (vidicon), secon	Secon *n*, Sec-Vidikon *n*, SEC-Röhre *f*
sea wind, sea breeze, on-shore wind	Seewind *m*		
		secondary electron counter	Sekundärelektronenzähler *m*

secondary

secondary electron current, secondary emission current — Sekundärelektronenstrom m, Sekundäremissionsstrom m

secondary electron emission, secondary emission, SEE; dynatron effect — Sekundärelektronenemission f, sekundäre Elektronenemission f, Sekundäremission f, SEE; Dynatroneffekt m

secondary electron multiplication — Sekundärelektronenvervielfachung f

secondary electron nuclear battery — s. secondary emission radioactive battery

secondary electron resonance — Sekundärelektronenresonanz f

secondary electron resonance breakdown — Sekundärelektronenresonanzdurchschlag m

secondary electron spectrum — Sekundärelektronenspektrum n

secondary emission — s. secondary electron emission

secondary emission amplification — Sekundäremissionsverstärkung f

secondary emission cathode — s. dynode

secondary emission coefficient, secondary emission ratio (factor), secondary yield, yield of secondary electrons — Sekundärelektronenausbeute f, Sekundäremissionsausbeute f, Sekundäremissionsfaktor m, Sekundäremissionskoeffizient m, SE-Faktor m

secondary emission current — s. secondary electron current

secondary emission factor — s. secondary emission coefficient

secondary emission isotopic power generator — s. secondary emission radioactive battery

secondary emission multiplier — s. photomultiplier

secondary emission noise — Sekundäremissionsrauschen n

secondary emission photocell — Sekundäremissions-Photozelle f

secondary emission radioactive (radioisotope) battery, secondary emission isotopic power generator, secondary electron atomic (nuclear) battery — Sekundärelektronenbatterie f, Sekundäremissionsbatterie f, Radionuklidbatterie f mit Sekundäremission

secondary emission ratio — s. secondary emission coefficient

secondary emitter, secondary radiator — Sekundärstrahler m

secondary emitting dynode — s. dynode

secondary face <cryst.> — Nebenfläche f <Krist.>

secondary flow <of fluids> — Sekundärströmung f, sekundäre Strömung f <Flüssigkeiten>

secondary focus — s. sagittal focus

secondary front — Nebenfront f, Sekundärfront f

secondary generation, secondary production, secondary creation — Sekundärerzeugung f

secondary hydration, physical hydration — sekundäre Hydratation f, physikalische Hydratation

secondary interference — sekundäre Inferenzerscheinung f, Sekundärinterferenz f; sekundäre Abbildung f, Sekundärabbildung f

secondary ionization — Sekundärionisation f, sekundäre Ionisation f

secondary light source — s. secondary source

secondary low — s. secondary depression <meteo.>

secondary luminous standard — s. working standard

secondary maximum, submaximum, subsidiary maximum <e.g. of light curve> — Nebenmaximum n <z. B. Lichtkurve>

secondary mirror, auxiliary mirror <e.g. of telescope> — Hilfsspiegel m, Sekundärspiegel m <z. B. Fernrohr>

secondary motion, disturbance velocity, collateral motion <turbulence> — Nebenbewegung f, Schwankungsbewegung f, Querbewegung f <Turbulenz>

secondary natural radionuclide — sekundäres natürliches Radionuklid n

secondary offspring — s. secondary particle

secondary optic[al] axis, optic[al] biradial, line of single ray velocity — Strahlenachse f, sekundäre optische Achse f, Biradiale f, Achse der [optischen] Isotropie [der elektrischen Feldstärke], optische Achse <des optisch zweiachsigen Kristalls>

secondary particle, secondary, off-spring — Sekundärteilchen n, Sekundäres n

secondary photochemical reaction — photochemischer Sekundärprozeß m, photochemische Sekundärreaktion f

secondary photocurrent, secondary photoelectric current — lichtelektrischer (photoelektrischer) Sekundärstrom m, sekundärer Photostrom m

secondary production — s. secondary generation

secondary quantity, derived quantity — abgeleitete Größe[nart] f

secondary quantum number, second (azimuthal, azimuth, orbital, angular momentum, rotational, rotation) quantum number — Nebenquantenzahl f, Bahn[dreh]impulsquantenzahl f, Bahnquantenzahl f, [azimutale] Quantenzahl f, Drehimpulsquantenzahl f, Rotationsquantenzahl f

secondary radiation — Sekundärstrahlung f, sekundäre Strahlung f

secondary radiator, secondary emitter — Sekundärstrahler m

secondary rainbow, interference rainbow, satellite rainbow, reflection rainbow — Nebenregenbogen m, sekundärer Regenbogen m, Interferenz[regen]bogen m

secondary reaction — Sekundärreaktion f, sekundäre Reaktion f

secondary recrystallization texture, growth texture — Wachstumstextur f

secondary resistance — Sekundärwiderstand m

secondary resonance, subordinate resonance; spurious resonance; spurious response — Nebenresonanz f

secondary salt effect — sekundärer Salzeffekt m, Sekundärsalzeffekt m

secondary schistosity — s. secondary cleavage

secondary series, subordinate series — Nebenserie f

secondary solvation, physical solvation — sekundäre (physikalische) Solvatation f

secondary source [of light], secondary light source — Fremdleuchter m, Fremdstrahler m, Sekundärlichtquelle f, Zweitleuchter m

secondary standard — Sekundärstandard m; Sekundärnormal n

secondary standard — s. a. working standard

secondary standard lamp (light source) — s. working standard

secondary standard of light — s. working standard

secondary structure, secondary texture — Sekundärgefüge n, Sekundärkorn n

secondary valence, secondary valency, supplementary (auxiliary, partial, side) valence — Nebenvalenz f

secondary valence bond — Neben[valenz]bindung f

secondary valence force, subsidiary valence force — Nebenvalenzkraft f

secondary valency — s. secondary valence

secondary voltage — Sekundärspannung f, Zweitspannung f

secondary wave, secondary <geo.>	Secunda f, S-Welle f, Sekundärwelle f <Geo.>	second mean value theorem of the differential calculus, double law of the mean, Cauchy['s] mean value formula, generalized (extended) mean value theorem	zweiter (verallgemeinerter, erweiterter) Mittelwertsatz m der Differentialrechnung
secondary wave	s. elementary wave		
secondary winding	Sekundärwicklung f, sekundärseitige Wicklung f		
secondary X-ray radiation	s. secondary X-rays		
secondary X-rays, secondary X-ray radiation	sekundäre Röntgenstrahlung f, Sekundär[röntgen]strahlung f, sekundäre Wellenstrahlung f	second neighbour	s. next-nearest neighbour
		second of arc, second, angular second, sexagesimal second [of arc], '', sec <of angle>	Sekunde f [im Bogenmaß], Winkelsekunde f, Bogensekunde f, Altsekunde f, '' <Winkelmaß>
secondary yield	s. secondary emission coefficient	second[-] order change	s. second[-] order transition
second boundary condition	s. Neumann['s] boundary condition	second-order derivative, derivative of the second order	Ableitung f zweiter Ordnung, zweite Ableitung
second boundary [value] problem	s. Neumann['s] problem	second order glacier, glacieret	Gletscher m zweiter Ordnung
second bright segment	zweites helles Segment n	second-order Newton-Raphson process	s. Newton-Raphson method
second channel frequency	s. image frequency	second-order Raman effect	Raman-Effekt m zweiter Ordnung
second-class conductor, ionic conductor, ion conductor	Ionenleiter m, Leiter m zweiter Ordnung (Klasse), Leiter II. Ordnung	second-order tensor, double tensor, tensor of order two, tensor of second (2nd) order	Tensor m zweiter Stufe, zweistufiger Tensor
second class constraint, constraint of the second class	Zwangsbedingung f der zweiten Klasse	second[-] order transformation	s. second[-] order transition
second coefficient of viscosity	s. second viscosity coefficient	second[-] order transition, second [-] order transformation (change), transition (change) of second order, transformation of second order, lambdatransition, transition of the "lambda" type	Umwandlung f zweiter (II.) Ordnung, Umwandlung zweiter Art, Übergang m zweiter (II.) Ordnung, Übergang zweiter Art, Lambda-Umwandlung f, Lamda-Übergang m
second collision	Zweitstoß m, „second collison" f		
second control grid	Stromverteilungsgitter n, zweites Steuergitter n		
second curvature, torsion <of the curve> <math.>	Windung f, Torsion f, Schmiegung f, zweite Krümmung f <Raumkurve> <Math.>		
		second order transition temperature	s. freesing-in temperature
second development, re-development	Nachentwicklung f	second pendulum	Sekundenpendel n
		second polar moment of plane area	polares Flächenträgheitsmoment n
second equatorial system [of coordinates]	s. independent equatorial co-ordinates	second purple light	zweites Purpurlicht n, Nachpurpurlicht n, Nachpurpurdämmerung f
second filter	Sekundenfilter n		
second focal point, image focus, back focus	Bildbrennpunkt m, bildseitiger Brennpunkt m, hinterer Brennpunkt	second quantization, hyperquantization	zweite Quantelung f, Hyperquantelung f, Hyperquantisierung f, zweite Quantisierung
second focus	zweiter Brennfleck m, Reservebrennfleck m	second quantum number	s. secondary quantum number
second forbidden	s. twice forbidden	seconds-counter	s. stop[-]watch
second fundamental form	zweite Fundamentalform f	second sound	zweiter Schall m, „second sound" m, Wärmewelle f zweiter (2.) Art, Schall- und Wärmewellen fpl zweiter (2.) Art, Wärmewellenintensität f zweiter (2.) Art
second Green formula, Green['s] formula of the second kind	Greensche Formel f zweiter Art, zweite Greensche Formel		
second gun electrode	s. intensifier electrode		
second harmonic magnetic modulator	s. Förster probe		
second law, second law of thermodynamics, principle of entropy increase, principle of increase of entropy, entropy principle, law of degradation of energy; [Planck] Kelvin['s] formulation of the second law of thermodynamics, Kelvin['s] statement [of the second law of thermodynamics]	zweiter Hauptsatz m [der Thermodynamik], Entropiesatz m, Entropieprinzip n, Satz m über die Entropiezunahme, Satz von der Vermehrung der Entropie, Prinzip n der Entropievermehrung, Carnotsches Prinzip; Satz von der Unmöglichkeit eines Perpetuum mobile zweiter Art, Fassung f des zweiten Hauptsatzes von Planck, Theorem n von Thomson	second theorem of the mean [for integrals], second law of the mean [for integrals]	zweiter Mittelwertsatz m der Integralrechnung
		second Townsend discharge	sekundäre Townsend-Entladung f
		second-trace echo	Sekundärecho n
		second twilight arch, main twilight arch	zweiter Dämmerungsbogen m, Hauptdämmerungsbogen m
		second variation	zweite Variation f
		second virial coefficient	zweiter Virialkoeffizient m
		second viscosity	s. volume viscosity
		second viscosity	s. second viscosity coefficient
second law of Kirchhoff	s. Kirchhoff['s] voltage law	second viscosity coefficient, second viscosity, second coefficient of viscosity, bulk coefficient of friction, dilatational coefficient of friction	Volum[en]viskositätskoeffizient m, Volum[en]reibungskoeffizient m, Volum[en]viskosität f, zweite Viskosität f, zweiter Viskositätskoeffizient m
second law of motion	s. Newton['s] second law [of motion]		
second law of the mean [for integrals]	s. second theorem of the mean [for integrals]		
second law of thermodynamics	s. second law		
second limit theorem	zweiter Grenzwertsatz m	secretion of water, water secretion <bio.>	Wasserabgabe f, Wasserausscheidung f <Bio.>
second mean Sun, fictitious Sun moving along the equator	zweite mittlere Sonne f; [fiktive] mittlere Sonne, die sich gleichförmig im Äquator bewegt	section	Abschnitt m, Teil m, Teilabschnitt m, Sektion f, Strecke f, Teilstück n

section <of the recurrent structure>	Teilvierpol *m*
section, link, element, segment, member	Glied *n* <Techn., El.>
section	s. a. metallographic specimen
section / 45°	s. cut / 45°
sectional area	s. cross-sectional area
sectionalization, partition[ing], segmentation, subdivision	Unterteilung *f*
sectionally continuous, piecewise continuous	stückweis[e] stetig, abteilungsweise stetig
sectionally smooth, piecewise smooth	stückweise glatt <Kurve>; stückweise (abteilungsweise) stetig differenzierbar <Funktion>
sectional pump	Gliederpumpe *f*
Π-section filter	Π-Schaltung *f*, Kettenleiter *m* erster Art
sectioning technique; serial sectioning technique	Schichtentrennungsverfahren *n*, Serienschnittverfahren *n*
section modulus [of bending]; moment of resistance [of the beam section], resisting moment (torque)	Widerstandsmoment *n* [des Querschnitts] [gegen Biegung], äquatoriales (axiales) Widerstandsmoment, Biegungswiderstandsmoment *n*, Rückkehrmoment *n*
section modulus of torsion	Widerstandsmoment *n* [des Querschnitts] gegen Verdrehung (Drehung, Torsion), polares Widerstandsmoment, Drillungswiderstandsmoment *n*
section paper	s. squared paper
section plane, plane of the section; plane of the cut, cut plane	Schnittebene *f*, Schnittfläche *f*
section wave	Schnittwelle *f*
sector	Sektor *m*, Ausschnitt *m*
sector acceleration	s. surface acceleration
sectoral horn	s. multicellular horn
sectoral horn waveguide	s. multicellular horn
sectoral instrument	Sektormeßgerät *n*, Sektorinstrument *n*
sector angle	Sektorwinkel *m*
sector aperture, open sector	Hellsektor *m*
sector chamber	Sektorkammer *f*
sector disk	Sektorscheibe *f*, Sektorenscheibe *f*
sector disk	s. a. rotating sector
sector-field spectroscope	Sektorfeldspektroskop *n*
sector-focused cyclotron, sector-focusing cyclotron	sektorfokussiertes Zyklotron *n*
sector-focused isochronous cyclotron	s. AVF cyclotron
sector focusing	Sektorfokussierung *f*
sector-focusing cyclotron	s. sector-focused cyclotron
sectorial area	Sektorfläche *f*, Sektorialfläche *f*
sectorial growth [of crystals]	Sektorwachstum *n*
sectorial harmonic	sektorielle Kugelfunktion *f*
sectorial moment of inertia	Sektor[en]trägheitsmoment *n*
sectorial wave	Sektorwelle *f*
sector ionization chamber	Sektorionisationskammer *f*
sector magnetic field, magnetic sector field	magnetisches Sektorfeld *n*
sector of the circle, circular sector	Kreisausschnitt *m*, Kreissektor *m*
sector photometer	Sektorenphotometer *n*, Sektorphotometer *n*
sector shutter, rotary shutter	Sektorenverschluß *m*, Flügelverschluß *m*, Sektorverschluß *m*
sector velocity	s. surface velocity
secular aberration	säkulare Aberration *f*, Säkularaberration *f*
secular acceleration [of Moon], secular acceleration of the Moon's mean motion	säkulare Akzeleration (Beschleunigung) *f*, Säkularbeschleunigung *f* <Mond>
secular advance of the perihelion, secular motion of the perihelion	säkulares Fortschreiten *n* des Perihels, säkulare Perihelverschiebung *f*
secular constant	Säkularkonstante *f*
secular determinant, characteristic determinant (polynomial), determinantal polynomial <of matrix>	Säkulardeterminante *f*, charakteristische Determinante *f*, charakteristisches Polynom *n* <Matrix>
secular disturbance	s. secular perturbation
secular equation	s. characteristic equation
secular equilibrium, secular radioactive equilibrium	[radioaktives] Dauergleichgewicht *n*, säkulares (ständiges, dauerndes radioaktives) Gleichgewicht *n*
secular inequality	s. secular perturbation
secular magnetic variation, magnetic secular variation	magnetische Säkularvariation *f*, säkulare magnetische Variation *f*
secular motion of the perihelion, secular advance of the perihelion	säkulares Fortschreiten *n* des Perihels, säkulare Perihelverschiebung *f*
secular parallax	säkulare Parallaxe *f*, Säkularparallaxe *f*
secular perturbation, secular disturbance; secular inequality	säkulare Störung *f*; säkulare Ungleichung *f*
secular perturbation function	säkulare Störungsfunktion *f*
secular precession, centennial precession	säkulare Präzession *f*, Säkularpräzession *f*
secular radioactive equilibrium	s. secular equilibrium
secular retardation	säkulare Verzögerung *f*, Säkularverzögerung *f*
secular rise of zero, rise of zero, zero rise	Nullpunktsanstieg *m*, Nullpunktanstieg *m*, säkularer Nullpunktsanstieg, säkularer Anstieg *m* des Eispunktes
secular term	säkulares Glied *n*, säkularer Term *m*
secular variation	säkulare Variation (Änderung) *f*, Säkularvariation *f*, säkulare Schwankung *f*; säkularer Gang *m*
security digit	s. guard digit <num. math.>
sediment, deposit	Ablagerung *f*, Sediment *n*; Sinkstoff *m*
sedimentary deposition	s. settling
sedimentary remanent magnetization, SRM	sedimentäre remanente Magnetisierung *f*
sedimentary rock, stratified rock, aqueous rock	Sedimentgestein *n*, Absatzgestein *n*, Schichtgestein *n*, Sediment *n*
sedimentation; silting, siltation	Verschlammung *f*; Verschlickung *f*; Beschlämmung *f*; Aufschotterung *f*; Stauraumverlandung *f*; Verlandung *f*
sedimentation	s. a. settling
sedimentation	s. a. decantation <chem.>
sedimentation analysis, sedimentometric (sedimetric) analysis	Sedimentationsanalyse *f*, Sedimentanalyse *f*
sedimentation balance, Sartorius balance	Sedimentationswaage *f* [nach Sartorius]
sedimentation constant	Sedimentationskonstante *f*
sedimentation curve, sedimentation plot	Sedimentationskurve *f*
sedimentation diagram, sedimentation plot	Sedimentationsdiagramm *n*
sedimentation equilibrium	Sedimentationsgleichgewicht *n*

sedimentation plot	s. sedimentation curve	seepage velocity	s. percolation velocity
sedimentation plot	s. sedimentation diagram	seepage water	s. water of infiltration
sedimentation potential, Dorn effect	Sedimentationspotential n, Dorn-Effekt m, elektrophoretisches Potential n	see-saw	s. swinging
		see-saw circuit	s. grounded-cathode circuit
		see-saw equilibrium	Schaukelgleichgewicht n
sediment catcher	s. sediment sampler	see-saw motion	s. swinging
sediment discharge (load)	s. sediment runoff	Seger cone	s. pyrometric cone
		segment	Segment n, Abschnitt m
sedimentology ‹geo.›	Sedimentologie f ‹Geo.›	segment, line segment ‹math.›	Strecke f ‹Math.›
sedimentometric analysis	s. sedimentation analysis	segment, closed interval ‹math.›	abgeschlossenes Intervall n, Segment n ‹Math.›
sediment runoff, sediment discharge (load)	Schwebstofführung f, Schwebstofffracht f, Sinkstoffführung f, Geröllführung f, Schwemmstoffführung f, Geschiebeführung f	segment	s. a. link ‹techn., el.›
		segmental horn	segmentförmiger Trichter m, segmentförmiges Horn n
sediment sampler, bed load sampler, sediment catcher	Geschiebefänger m; Geschiebefangkasten m; Geschiebefangbeutel m	segmentation, partition[ing], sectionalization, subdivision	Unterteilung f
		segmentation, abscission, constriction	Abschnürung f
sedimetric analysis	s. sedimentation analysis		
Seebeck coefficient	Seebeck-Koeffizient m	segmentation ‹bio.›	Segmentation f, Metamerie f ‹Bio.›
Seebeck effect, thermoelectric effect	Seebeck-Effekt m, thermoelektrischer Effekt m	segment dam, segment weir	Segmentwehr n
		segment length	Gliederlänge f
		segment model	Segmentmodell n
seed	Hohlnadel f, Kapillare f, Seed f	segment of chain, link of chain, chain segment, chain element	Kettenglied n, Glied n der Kette
seed	s. a. seed crystal	segment of the circle, circular segment	Kreisabschnitt m, Kreissegment n
seed	s. a. seed element		
seed crystal, seed, inoculating crystal	Impfkristall m; Saatkristall m; Zuchtkeim m, Kristallzuchtkeim m	segment of the circle, circular arc, arc of the circle	Kreisbogen m, Kreisbogenabschnitt m
seeded combustion gas	Verbrennungsgas n mit leicht ionisierbaren Beimischungen	segment voltage, commutator segment voltage	Segmentspannung f, Lamellenspannung f, Stegspannung f
seed element, seed ‹of reactor›	Saatelement n ‹Reaktor›	segment weir, segment dam	Segmentwehr n
		Segner['s] water wheel, reaction wheel, wheel of recoil	Segnersches Wasserrad n, Reaktionsrad n
seeding; inoculation ‹also cryst.›	Impfen n; Impfung f		
		Segrè chart	Segrè-Diagramm n
seedy glass	blasiges Glas n	segregate	Segregat n
seeing	„seeing" n, Bildruhe f, Bilddefinition f, Bildgüte f, Bildschärfe f, Sichtbedingung f, Luftruhe f	segregation; demixing; separation; precipitation ‹of emulsion›	Entmischung f, Zerfall m ‹Gemisch›
seeing ‹astr.›; visibility ‹meteo., astr.›; conspicuity ‹with the naked eye› ‹astr.›	Sichtbarkeit f ‹Meteo., Astr.›; Sicht f ‹Meteo.›; Sichtgrad m ‹Meteo.›	segregation, phase separation ‹bio.›	Segregation f, Sonderung f, Aufspaltung f, Entmischung f ‹Bio.›
		segregation, eliquation, sweating-out, precipitation ‹met.›	Seigerung f, Entmischung f, Ausscheidung f ‹Met.›
seeing distance	s. visibility		
Seeliger['s] rule	[Seeligersche] Glimmsaumregel f	segregation	s. a. macroscopic segregation
Seeliger's paradox, gravitational paradox	Gravitationsparadoxon n, Neumann-Seeligersches Paradoxon n	segregation coefficient	Segregationskoeffizient m
		segregation constant	Seigerungskonstante f
Seemann-Bohlin camera	Seemann-Bohlinsche Beugungskammer f	Seibt bridge	Seibt-Brücke f, Kapazitätsmeßbrücke f nach Seibt
		seiche	Seiche f; Binnenwassertide f
Seemann-Bohlin diagram	Seemann-Bohlin-Diagramm n	Seidel aberration	s. first-order aberration
		Seidel['s] [angle] eikonal	Seidelsches Eikonal n, Seidelsches Winkeleikonal n
Seemann-Bohlin method	Seemann-Bohlinsche Methode f, Seemann-Bohlinsches Verfahren n, Seemann-Bohlin-Methode f	Seidel coefficient	s. Seidel sum
		Seidel-Glaser dioptrics	Seidel-Glasersche Dioptrik f
Seemann['s] method	Lochkameramethode f von Seemann, Seemannsche Methode f, Seemann-Methode f, Seemann-Verfahren n, Seemannsches Verfahren n	Seidel-Glaser eikonal	Seidel-Glasersches Eikonal n
		Seidel method	s. Gauss-Seidel method
		Seidel region	Seidelsches Gebiet n, Seidelscher Raum m
		Seidel sum, Seidel coefficient	Seidelsche Summe f, [Seidelscher] Flächenteilkoeffizient m, [Seidelscher] Linsenteilkoeffizient m
Seemann spectrograph	s. wedge spectrograph		
seeming error, apparent error	scheinbarer (plausibelster) Fehler m		
seepage, oozing, trickling through	Durchsickern n, Eindringen n	Seidel['s] theory [of aberrations]	Seidelsche Theorie f der Bildfehler, Seidelsche Bildfehlertheorie f
seepage flow, subsurface flow; base flow	Sickerströmung f; unterirdischer Abfluß m		
		Seidler voltmeter, plate-type voltmeter	Plattenvoltmeter n [nach Seidler], Seidlersches Plattenvoltmeter

Seifert [X-ray] tube	Seifert-Röhre f, Seifert-Röntgenröhre f	seismonastic movement	seismonastische Bewegung f, Seismonastie f
Seignette[-]electric	s. ferroelectric	seismonic reaction	Seismoreaktion f; seismonastische Reaktion f
Seignette electricity	s. ferroelectricity		
Seignette salt, Rochelle salt, sodium potassium tartrate, KNaC$_4$H$_4$O$_6$	Seignettesalz n, Rochellesalz n, Kaliumnatriumtartrat n, KNaC$_4$H$_4$O$_6$[·4H$_2$O]	seismonic stimulus	s. seismic stimulus
		seismophysics	Seismophysik f
seism	seismische Bewegung (Erschütterung, Erscheinung) f	seismoscope	Seismoskop n
seism	s. a. seismic surge	seismotectonic line	seismotektonische Linie f
seismic alternative wave, alternative wave	Wechselwelle f, seismische Wechselwelle	seismotectonics	Seismotektonik f
seismic conductivity	seismische Leitfähigkeit f	seizing, seizure; galling, scuffing	adhäsiver Verschleiß m; Fressen n; Festfressen n
seismic focus	s. focus of earthquake	selectance	s. discrimination
seismicity	Seismizität f, Erdbebenaktivität f	selected area, Kapteyn['s] selected area	Kapteynsches Eichfeld n, Eichfeld „selected area" n, ausgewähltes Feld n
seismic pendulum	seismisches Pendel n		
seismic prospecting, shooting	seismische Erkundung f, Schießen n	selected area diffraction	s. fine range diffraction
		selection	Auswahl f; Selektion f; Auslese f
seismic ray	Erdbebenstrahl m, seismischer Strahl m	selection, choice	Wahl f
		selection <el.>	Wahl f; Wählen n <El.>
seismic ray reflected downwards at the inner core boundary, I ray	I-Welle f, am inneren Kern gebrochene Erdbebenwelle f	selection, filtering, filtering out, filtration, elimination <el.>	Siebung f, Sieben n, Aussiebung f, Filterung f <El.>
seismic ray reflected downwards at the outer core boundary, K ray	K-Welle f, am Kern gebrochene Erdbebenwelle f	selection of frame	Wahl f des Bezugsystems
		selection rule	Auswahlregel f
seismic ray reflected upwards at the outer core boundary, c ray	c-Welle f, am Kern reflektierte Erdbebenwelle f	selective absorption, differential absorption	selektive Absorption f, Selektivabsorption f
seismic region, zone of earthquake shocks	Schüttergebiet n, seismischer Raum m, seismisches Gebiet n	selective adsorption	selektive Adsorption f
		selective amplifier, accentuator	Selektivverstärker m, selektiver Verstärker m
seismicrophone	Seismikrophon n	selective amplifier rejection [device]	s. selective rejection
seismic scale	s. modified Mercalli intensity scale	selective diffuser	selektiv streuender Körper m
		selective emitter	s. selective radiator
seismic shock	s. seismic surge	selective erosion	selektive Erosion f
seismic station	Erdbebenwarte f, Erdbebenstation f, seismische Station f	selective fading, differential fading	selektiver Schwund m, Selektivschwund m, Interferenzschwund m
seismic stimulus, seismonic stimulus	Erschütterungsreiz m, Stoßreiz m, Schüttelreiz m, seismischer Reiz m	selective filter, exclusion filter <opt.>	Selektionsfilter n, Selektivfilter n <Opt.>
		selective heat radiation	selektive Wärmestrahlung f
seismic surge; seismic shock; seism, [earthquake] shock, earth tremor <geo.>	Erdstoß m, seismischer Stoß m, Bodenstoß m, Erdbebenstoß m	selective permeability	selektive Permeabilität f
		selective photoeffect	s. selective photoelectric effect
seismic wave, earthquake wave, earth wave	Erdbebenwelle f, seismische Welle f; seismische Woge f, Dislokationswoge f	selective photoelectric effect (emission), selective photoeffect	selektiver Photoeffekt m, selektiver lichtelektrischer Effekt m
		selective radiator, selective emitter	selektiver Strahler m, Selektivstrahler m
seismic wave travelling along a surface of discontinuity	s. surface wave <geo.>	selective reaction	selektive Reaktion f, Auswahlreaktion f
seismoacoustic	seismoakustisch		
seismoelectric effect	seismoelektrischer Effekt m	selective rejection [device], selective amplifier rejection [device]	Selektojekt n
seismoelectric effect of the first kind, I effect	seismoelektrischer Effekt m erster (1.) Art, I-Effekt m		
seismoelectric effect of the second kind, E effect	seismoelektrischer Effekt m zweiter (2.) Art, E-Effekt m	selective resonance penetrability	selektive Resonanzdurchlassung f
		selective scattering of light	selektive Streuung f des Lichtes
seismogram	Seismogramm n	selective solvation, preferential solvation	selektive Solvatation f
seismograph	Seismograph m, registrierendes Seismometer n	selectivity; specifity <chem.>	Selektivität f; Spezifität f <Chem.>
seismology	Seismik f; Seismologie f, Erdbebenforschung f; Erdbebenkunde f	selectivity <el.>	Trennwirkung f, Selektion f; Trennschärfe f, Selektivität f <El.>
seismology of atmosphere, atmospheric seismology, air seismology	Luftseismik f	selectivity	s. a. discrimination
		selectivity	s. a. filter discrimination
		selectivity characteristic	s. selectivity curve
		selectivity characteristic	s. a. tuning characteristic
seismometer	Seismometer n, Erdbebenmesser m, Erdbebeninstrument n, Bebenmesser m, Erschütterungsmesser m	selectivity coefficient	Selektivitätskoeffizient m
		selectivity curve, selectivity characteristic	Selektivitätskurve f, Selektionskurve f; Durchlaßkurve f

selectivity discrimination	s. filter discrimination	**self-balancing bridge**	selbstabgleichende Meßbrücke f, Meßbrücke mit Selbstabgleich
selectivity of [the] resonance	s. resonance sharpness		
selectivity ratio, degree of selectivity	Selektionsgrad m		
selectode	s. variable mu		
selector	Selektor m; Wähler m	**self-balancing dot recorder**	s. self-balancing point recorder
selector switch	s. changeover switch	**self-balancing instrument movement**	Nullmotormeßwerk n
selector tube	Wählröhre f, Wählschaltröhre f, Selektorröhre f		
selenium barrage [photo]cell, selenium barrier cell, selenium barrier layer [photovoltaic] cell	s. selenium photovoltaic cell	**self-balancing point recorder**, self-balancing dot recorder	Nullmotorpunktschreiber m, Nullmotorpunktdrucker m
selenium [photo]cell	s. selenium photoconductive cell		
selenium [photo]cell	s. a. selenium photovoltaic cell	**self-balancing potentiometer**	s. automatic potentiometer
selenium photoconductive cell, selenium photocell, selenium cell	Selen-Widerstandszelle f, Selen-Photozelle f, [lichtelektrische] Selenzelle f	**self-balancing recorder**	Nullmotorschreiber m
selenium photovoltaic cell, selenium barrier layer [photovoltaic] cell, selenium barrier cell, selenium barrage [photo]cell, selenium [photo]cell	Selen-Sperrschichtzelle f, Selen-Sperrschichtphotozelle f, Selenphotoelement n, Selenlichtelement n, Selenelement n, Selenauge n, Selenphotozelle f, Selenzelle f	**self-ballasted mercury lamp** <US>	s. compound lamp
		self-bias	Selbstvorspannung f, automatische Gittervorspannung[serzeugung] f
selenium rectifier; selectron	Selengleichrichter m; Selenventil n	**self-blocking**	Selbsthaltung f; Selbstsperrung f
selenocentric orbit, lunar orbit	Mondumlaufbahn f, selenozentrische Umlaufbahn f	**self-broadening**	s. resonance broadening
		self-calibration	Selbstkalibrierung f, Selbsteichung f
selenographic co-ordinates	selenographische Koordinaten fpl	**self-capacitance**, inherent (natural) capacitance	Eigenkapazität f
selenography	Selenographie f, Mondbeschreibung f, Lehre f von den Oberflächenformen des Mondes	**self-catalyzed**, autocatalytic	autokatalytisch
selenophone	Selenophon n	**self-centring head**, centre head, centring head	Zentrierkopf m
seletron	s. selenium rectifier		
self-absorption, internal absorption <of ionizing radiation>	Selbstabsorption f, Eigenabsorption f, Eigenstrahlungsabsorption f <ionisierende Strahlung>	**self charge**	Selbstladung f
		self-check[ing], self-verifying, self- verification	Selbstprüfung f
self-absorption, self-reversal <of spectral lines>	Selbstumkehr[ung] f, Selbstabsorption f <Spektrallinien>, Linienabsorption f	**self-cleaning**	Selbstreinigung f, Selbstregenerierung f
		self-cloudiness; self-turbidity	Eigentrübung f
self-absorption coefficient	Selbstabsorptionskoeffizient m	**self-coagulation**	Selbstausflockung f, Selbstkoagulation f
self-absorption half-value layer (thickness)	Selbstabsorptions-Halbwertsdicke f	**self-collision**	Selbststoß m, Stoß m gleichartiger Teilchen
self-acceleration	Selbstbeschleunigung f	**self-collision time**	Selbststoßzeit f, Stoßzeit f bei Stößen gleichartiger Teilchen
self-acting control	s. direct control		
self-activated conductivity	selbstaktivierte Leitfähigkeit f		
self-activation, intrinsic activation	Eigenaktivierung f, Selbstaktivierung f	**self-computing chart**	s. alignment nomogram
		self-condensation	s. intermolecular condensation
self-actuated controller	s. self-operated controller	**self-conjugate nucleus**	s. self-mirrored nucleus
self-adhesion	s. autohesion	**self-conjugate sub-group**	s. normal divisor
self-adjoint equation	selbstadjungierte Gleichung f	**self-consistence**, self-consistency	Selbstkonsistenz f
self-adjoint matrix, Hermitian matrix	hermitesche Matrix f, selbstadjungierte Matrix, Hermite-Matrix f	**self-consistency**	s. a. consistency <math.>
		self-consistent field, SCF	selbstkonsistentes Feld n, „self-consistent field" n, „self-consistent"-Feld n
self-adjoint operator	selbstadjungierter Operator m, hypermaximaler Operator	**self-consistent-field method**	s. Hartree-Fock-Dirac self-consistent-field method
self-adjoint transformation	selbstadjungierte Transformation f	**self-consistent solution**	selbstkonsistente Lösung f, „self-consistent"-Lösung f
self-adjustment; adaptive control	Selbsteinstellung f	**self-constricting effect**, self-constriction	s. pinch effect <of plasma>
self-aligning	s. self-orientating	**self-contained instrument**	unabhängiges Meßinstrument n
self-association	Selbstassoziation f		
self-association constant	Selbstassoziationskonstante f		
self-baking electrode, Soederberg electrode, Söderberg electrode	Söderberg-Elektrode f	**self-contraction**	Selbstkontraktion f
		self-control, automatic control	Selbststeuerung f
self-balancing	selbstabgleichend; selbstausgleichend	**self-convection**	Eigenkonvektion f
		self-correcting	selbstkorrigierend
		self-correction, automatic correction	Selbstkorrektion f
		self-correlation function	s. autocorrelation function

self-corrosion	Selbskorrosion *f*	self[-]ignition, spontaneous ignition, autogeneous ignition, autoignition	Selbstentflammung *f*, Selbstentzündung *f*, Selbstzündung *f*
self-corrosion rate	Selbstkorrosionsgeschwindigkeit *f*		
self-damping	Eigendämpfung *f*		
self-decomposition, spontaneous decomposition	spontane Zersetzung *f*, Selbstzersetzung *f*	self-ignition point, spontaneous ignition temperature, S.I.T.	Selbstentzündungstemperatur *f*
		self impedance	Selbstinduktionswiderstand *m*
self-demagnetization	Selbstentmagnetisierung *f*	self-induced voltage	s. self-induction electromotive force
self-diffusing coefficient	s. self-diffusion coefficient	self[-]inductance	s. self-induction coefficient
self diffusion, self-diffusion	Selbstdiffusion *f*, Eigendiffusion *f*	self-inductance standard	s. standard inductance
		self-induction	Selbstinduktion *f*
self diffusion along grain boundaries	Korngrenzenselbstdiffusion *f*	self-induction coefficient	s. inductance
self-diffusion coefficient, self-diffusivity, coefficient of self-diffusion, self-diffusing coefficient	Selbstdiffusionskoeffizient *m*	self-induction electromotive force, self-induction e.m.f., self-induced voltage	Selbstinduktionsspannung *f*
self-diffusion current	Selbstdiffusionsstrom *m*	self-inductor	s. inductance coil
		self-inflammable, self-igniting, self-ignitable; pyrophoric; hypergolic	selbstentzündlich, selbstentflammbar; pyrophor; selbstzündend
self-diffusion velocity	Selbstdiffusionsgeschwindigkeit *f*		
self-diffusivity	s. self-diffusion coefficient	self-intensification [of oscillations], self-reinforcing [of vibration]	Selbstaufschauk[e]lung *f*
self-discharge	Selbstentladung *f*		
self-discharge current	Selbstentladestrom *m*	self-interaction	Selbstwirkung *f*
self[-]dual	selbstdual		
		self-interference audion	s. regenerative detector
		self-intersection	Selbstdurchdringung *f*
self-duplication	s. autoreduplication ⟨bio.⟩	self-intersection point, point of self-intersection	Selbstdurchdringungspunkt *m*
self-electrode	Selbstemissionselektrode *f*	self-inversion	s. self-absorption ⟨of spectral lines⟩
self-energizing	s. self-excited		
self-energy	Selbstenergie *f* ⟨Energieäquivalent der Teilchenmasse⟩	self-irradiation	Selbstbestrahlung *f*
		self-levelling instrument	Nivellier[instrument] *n* mit automatisch horizontierter Ziellinie
self-erecting folding camera	Springkamera *f*		
self-evaporation	Selbstverdampfung *f*	self-light, self-luminosity	Eigenlicht *n*
self-exchange	Selbstaustausch *m*, Eigenaustausch *m*	self-limiting chain reaction	selbstbremsende Kettenreaktion *f*
self-exchange coefficient	Eigenaustauschkoeffizient *m*	self-loading target	selbstspeisendes Target *n*
		self-locking	s. squagging
self-excitation, autoexcitation	Selbsterregung *f*, Eigenerregung *f*; Schwingungseinsatz *m*	self-luminescence of upper atmosphere	s. airglow
		self-luminosity	s. self-light
self-excitation boundary	Selbsterregungsgrenze *f*	self-luminous object (substance, surface)	s. primary source [of light]
self-excitation formula	Selbsterregungsformel *f*	self-luminous train	leuchtender Schweif *m*
		self-magnetic	eigenmagnetisch
self-excited, self-energizing	eigenerregt, selbsterregt	self-magnetism	Eigenmagnetismus *m*
self-excited constant-current generator	s. electric generator ⟨el.⟩	self-maintained discharge	s. self-sustaining discharge
self-excited direct-current generator	s. electric generator ⟨el.⟩	self-maintaining gas discharge	s. self-sustaining discharge
self-excited dynamo	selbsterregter Dynamo *m*	self mass, intrinsic mass, proper mass ⟨qu.⟩	Selbstmasse *f*, Eigenmasse *f* ⟨Qu.⟩
self-excited oscillation	s. self-excited vibration	self-mirrored nucleus; self-conjugate nucleus	Selbstspiegelkern *m*; selbstkonjugierter Kern *m*
self-excited vibration, self-excited oscillation	selbsterregte Schwingung *f*		
		self-modulation	Selbstmodulation *f*; Eigenmodulation *f*
self-exciting	selbsterregend, eigenerregend		
self-filtering, inherent filtration	Eigenfilterung *f*, Selbstfilterung *f*	self-multiplying chain reaction	selbstmultiplizierende Kettenreaktion *f*
		self-noise, internal noise	Eigenrauschen *n*
self-focusing	Selbstfokussierung *f*, Selbstkonzentrierung *f*	self-operated controller, self-actuated controller, direct controller, direct-action controller, controller without power amplification	Regler *m* ohne Hilfsenergie, direkt wirkender Regler, direkter Regler, unmittelbarer Regler, unmittelbar wirkender Regler
self-focusing lens	Selbstfokussierlinse *f*		
self force	Selbstkraft *f*		
self-frequency	s. natural frequency		
self-healing ⟨of the film⟩	Selbstheilung *f* [des Films]	self-optimization	Selbstoptimierung *f*
self-healing [of the capacitor]	Selbstheilung *f* [des Kondensators]	self-orientating, self-aligning	selbstorientierend, selbstausrichtend
self-heating, spontaneous heating	Selbsterhitzung *f*, Selbsterwärmung *f*	self-oscillating system	s. self-oscillatory system
		self-oscillation	Selbstschwingung *f*, Grenzzyklus *m*
self-holding contact	Selbsthaltekontakt *m*	self-oscillation	s. a. vibrational mode
		self-oscillator	s. free-running oscillator
self-ignitable, self-igniting	s. self-inflammable	self-oscillatory system, self-oscillating system	schwingungsfähiges (selbstschwingendes) System (Gebilde) *n*

self-oxidation	s. autoxidation
self-passivation	Selbstpassivierung f
self-polar tetrahedron	Polartetraeder n, Poltetraeder n <der Polarität>
self-polar triangle	Polardreieck n, Poldreieck n <der Polarität>
self-potential	Selbstpotential n, Eigenpotential n
self-power, proper power	Eigenleistung f
self-powered detector	„self-powered"-Detektor m, unabhängiger Detektor
self-powered maser, SP maser	selbstverstärkender Maser m, Maser mit Selbstverstärkung
self-preservation	Selbsterhaltung f
self-priming pump	selbstansaugende Pumpe f
self-protecting, overvoltage-proof, resistant to overvoltage	überspannungsfest, überspannungssicher
self-quenched counter [tube]	selbstlöschendes Zählrohr n
self-quenching, self-quenching action, internal quenching	Selbstlöschung f
self-quenching, concentration quenching <of luminescence>	Selbstauslöschung f, Konzentrationsauslöschung f <Lumineszenz>
self-quenching action, self-quenching, internal quenching	Selbstlöschung f
self-quenching oscillator, blocking oscillator, squegging oscillator, blocking generator, squegger	Sperrschwinger m, Blockingoszillator m
self-radiant exitance	spezifische Eigenausstrahlung f
self-radiation, proper radiation	Eigenstrahlung f
self reactance	Selbstreaktanz f, Selbstinduktionsreaktanz f
self-recorder	s. recorder
self-recovery	s. self-repair
self-recovery	s. a. self-regulation
self-rectifying tube	selbstgleichrichtende Röhre f
self-reducing tacheometer	selbstreduzierendes Tachymeter n, Reduktionstachymeter n
self-regulating reactor	sich selbst regulierender (stabilisierender) Reaktor m, selbstregelnder Reaktor
self-regulation, inherent regulation, self-recovery	Selbstregelung f, Selbstregulierung f; Selbstausgleich m, Ausgleich m
self-reinforcing [of vibration]	s. self-intensification
self-repair, self-recovery; self-restoring	Selbstregenerierung f, Selbstheilung f
self-reproduction	s. autoreduplication <bio.>
self-repulsion	Selbstabstoßung f
self-restoring	s. self-repair
self-reversal, self-absorption <of spectral lines>	Selbstumkehr[ung] f, Selbstabsorption f <Spektrallinien>, Linienabsorption f
self-rotation, eigenrotation, proper rotation	Eigenrotation f, Eigendrehung f
self-saturation	Selbstsättigung f
self-scattering	Selbststreuung f, Eigenstreuung f
self-screening	s. self-absorption
self-screening	s. self-shielding
self-sealing, automatic sealing, self-tightening	Selbstdichtung f
self-serve	s. self-stabilization
self-shielding	Selbstabschirmung f
self-shielding correction	Selbstabschirmungskorrektion f, Korrektion f für die Selbstabschirmung
self-similar flow, "similar" flow	ähnliche (selbstähnliche) Strömung f
self-similar solution	s. similar solution
self-similar unsteady flow	selbstähnliche (ähnliche) nichtstationäre Strömung f
self-simulating problem	gegenüber einer Gruppe von Ähnlichkeitsabbildungen aller eingehenden Variablen invariantes Problem n, selbstäquivalentes Problem, selbstähnliches Problem
self-simulating variable	selbstäquivalente Variable f, selbstähnliche Variable
self-stability [of phase]	s. phase stability
self-stabilization, self-serve	Selbststabilisierung f, Eigenstabilisierung f
self stress <mech.>	Selbstspannung f <Mech.>
self-supported foil, self-supporting foil	selbsttragende (freitragende) Folie f
selfsustained chain reaction	s. selfsustained nuclear chain reaction
self-sustained glow	selbständiges Leuchten n; selbständige Glimmentladung f
selfsustained nuclear chain reaction, selfsustained chain reaction, selfsustained reaction, sustained [nuclear] chain reaction, sustained reaction, critical [nuclear] chain reaction, critical reaction	selbständige Kernkettenreaktion (Kettenreaktion) f, sich selbst erhaltende Kernkettenreaktion (Kettenreaktion), kritische Kernkettenreaktion (Kettenreaktion), selbständig ablaufende Kettenreaktion
self-sustained oscillation	s. undamped oscillation
selfsustained reaction	s. selfsustained nuclear chain reaction
self-sustaining conduction	elbständige Leitung f
self-sustaining discharge, self-maintained discharge, self-maintaining gas discharge	elbständige Entladung (Gasentladung, Elektrizitätsleitung f in Gasen)
self-tangency	Selbstberührung f
self-thermal diffusion	Selbstthermodiffusion f
self-tightening, automatic sealing, self-sealing	Selbstdichtung f
self-trapping	Selbstanlagerung f
self-turbidity; self-cloudiness	Eigentrübung f
self-verification, self-verifying, self check[ing]	Selbstprüfung f
self-whistle	s. superheterodyne interference
Sellmeier['s] [dispersion] formula, Sellmeier['s] equation [for refractive dispersion]	Dispersionsformel f von Sellmeier, Sellmeiersche Dispersionsformel
selsyn, selsyn system, synchro; synchrotransmitter, synchrodrive	Drehmelder m, Drehfeldgeber m, Synchro m
semantics <math.>	Semantik f <Math.>
semi-angle of the cone	s. cone semi-angle
semi-annular electromagnet, semicircular electromagnet	Halbringelektromagnet m, Halbringmagnet m
semi-apex angle <of wedge>	halber Öffnungswinkel m; halber Scheitelwinkel m <Keil>
semi-apex angle [of the cone]	s. cone semi-angle
semi-apochromat[e], fluorite system, fluorite lens	Fluoritobjektiv n, Fluoritsystem n, Semiapochromat m, Halbapochromat m
semiarid <of climate>	semiarid <Klima>
semi-axis	Halbachse f
semi-beam	s. cantilever beam
semi-bright	s. semi-gloss
semicanonical equations [of motion]	halbkanonische Differentialgleichungen fpl, halbkanonische Bewegungsgleichungen fpl

semicircular beta-spectrograph	Halbkreis-Beta-Spektrograph m, Beta-Halbkreisspektrograph m
semicircular canals	Bogengänge mpl
semicircular deviation, semicircular error	Halbkreisfehler m
semicircular electromagnet, semi-annular electromagnet	Halbringelektromagnet m, Halbringmagnet m
semicircular electrometer	Halbkreiselektrometer n
semicircular error, semicircular deviation	Halbkreisfehler m
semicircular focusing	Halbkreisfokussierung f
semicircular lens, hemispherical lens	Halbkugellinse f
semicircular protractor, protractor	Transporteur m
semicircular protractor	s. a. contact goniometer
semicircular spectrometer, semicircular spectroscope	Halbkreisspektrometer n, Halbkreisspektroskop n
semicircumference; semiperimeter	halber Umfang m
semiclassical approximation	halbklassische Näherung f
semicolloid, hemicolloid, mesocolloid	Semikolloid n, Hemikolloid n, Mesokolloid n
semiconducting; semiconductive; semiconductor	halbleitend, Halbleiter-
semi-conducting bolometer	Halbleiterbolometer n
semiconducting crystal	Halbleiterkristall m
semiconducting laser, injection laser	Halbleiterlaser m, Injektionslaser m
semiconduction	Halbleitung f
semiconductive	s. semiconducting
semiconductivity	Halbleitfähigkeit f
semiconductor	Halbleiter m
semiconductor	s. semiconducting
semiconductor atomic battery, semiconductor isotopic power generator	Sperrschichtbatterie f, Halbleiter-Radionuklidbatterie f, Halbleiterisotopenbatterie f
semiconductor bridge	Halbleiterbrücke f
semiconductor cell	s. photovoltaic cell
semiconductor counter (detector), semiconductor particle counter	Halbleiterdetektor m, Halbleiterzähler m
semiconductor device	Halbleitergerät n
semiconducter diode, crystal diode	Halbleiterdiode f, Kristalldiode f
semiconductor diode [parametric] amplifier	Halbleiterdiodenverstärker m
semiconductor electronics	Halbleiterelektronik f
semiconductor integrated circuit; solid circuit; single-chip circuit; single-chip device	integrierte Festkörperschaltung f, integrierte Halbleiterschaltung f, Festkörperschaltung f
semiconductor isotopic power generator	s. semiconductor atomic battery
semiconductor junction, junction <semi.>	Flächenübergang m, Übergang m, Halbleiterübergang m, Übergangsschicht f, Schicht f, „junction" f <Halb.>
semiconductor junction diode, junction diode, p-n junction diode	Halbleiterflächendiode f, Flächendiode f, pn-Diode f, Schichtdiode f, pn-Flächendiode f
semiconductor junction transistor	s. junction transistor
semiconductor-metal barrier, metal-semiconductor barrier	Metall-Halbleiter-Sperrschicht f; Metall-Halbleiter-Randschicht f
semiconductor-metal contact, metal-semiconductor contact, contact semiconductor-metal	Halbleiter-Metall-Kontakt m, Metall-Halbleiter-Kontakt m, Kontakt Halbleiter—Metall
semiconductor-metal interface	s. metal-semiconductor interface
semiconductor-metal junction, metal-semiconductor junction	Metall-Halbleiter-Übergang m, Halbleiter-Metall-Übergang m
semiconductor particle counter	s. semiconductor counter
semiconductor photodetector	Halbleiterphotodetektor m
semiconductor photodiode, photodiode	Photodiode f, Halbleiterphotodiode f
semiconductor physics	Halbleiterphysik f
semiconductor plasma	Halbleiterplasma n
semiconductor rectifier, bimetallic (dry, plate) rectifier	Halbleitergleichrichter m, Trockengleichrichter m, Plattengleichrichter m
semiconductor regime	Halbleiterbetrieb m; Halbleiterbetriebszustand m
semiconductor resistance; semiconductor resistor	Halbleiterwiderstand m
semiconductor-semiconductor junction	Halbleiter-Halbleiter-Übergang m
semiconductor stabilitron	s. Zener diode
semiconductor strain gauge	Halbleiter-Dehnungsmeßstreifen m, Halbleiterdehnungsmesser m, Halbleiter-Dehnungsmeßgerät n, Halbleitertensometer n
semiconductor subassembly, semiconductor unit	Halbleiterbauelement n
semiconductor tetrode, transistor tetrode, tetrode transistor, crystal tetrode	Halbleitertetrode f, Transistortetrode f, Tetrodentransistor m, Schirmgittertransistor m
semiconductor thermocouple, semiconductor thermoelement	Halbleiterthermoelement n
semiconductor thermometer	Halbleiterthermometer n
semiconductor triode	s. transistor
semiconductor unit	s. semiconductor subassembly
semi-cone angle	s. cone semi-angle
semicontinuous	halbkontinuierlich; halbstetig <Math.>
semi-convergent series	s. asymptotic series
semicrystalline	halbkristallin[isch]
semicubical parabola, Neil's parabola	Neilsche (semikubische) Parabel f
semidarkness	Halbdunkel n
semi-definite	semidefinit, halbdefinit
semi-detached binary	halbgetrennter Doppelstern m, halbgetrenntes System n
semidiaphanous	halbdurchsichtig
semi-direct lighting	vorwiegend direkte Beleuchtung f, Vorwiegenddirektbeleuchtung f
semidiurnal component of magnetic variation	halbtägige Komponente f der magnetischen Variation
semi-diurnal [lunisolar] inequality, luni-solar semi-diurnal inequality	halbtägige Ungleichheit f, halbtägige lunisolare Ungleichheit
semidiurnal[-type] tides	halbtägige Gezeiten pl, Halbtagsgezeiten pl
semidiurnal wave	Halbtagswelle f
semi-empirical mass formula	s. Weizsäcker['s] formula [/ von]
semi-empirical theory	halbempirische Theorie f
semi-enclosed	berührungsgeschützt, gegen [zufällige] Berührung geschützt

semi-enclosed, protected <of instrument> — geschützt <Gerät>

semi-fixed, pre-set — veränderbar zur einmaligen Einstellung

semi-fixed resistance — halbregelbarer Widerstand m, Widerstand mit versetzbarer Abgriffschelle

semi[-]fluid, semi[-]liquid — semifluid, halbfluid, halbflüssig

semifluid friction, mixed friction — Mischreibung f, gemischte Reibung f

semifocal chord <aero.> — halbe Profilsehne f, halber Parameter m <Aero.>

semi-girder — s. cantilever beam

semi-gloss, semi-bright — halbglänzend, mattglänzend

semigraphical method — halbgraphisches (halbzeichnerisches) Verfahren n

semi[-]group, hemigroup, demigroup, associative groupoid, associative system, monoid — Halbgruppe f, assoziatives System n, assoziatives Gruppoid n, Assoziativ n, multiplikatives System n, Monoid[e] n

semi-heavy water, deuterium-protium oxide, HDO — halbschweres Wasser n, Deuterium-Protium-Oxid n, HDO

semi-holonomic — semiholonom

semi-hot laboratory — s. warm laboratory

semihumid <of climate> — semihumid, subhumid <Klima>

semi-indirect lighting — vorwiegend indirekte Beleuchtung f, Vorwiegendindirektbeleuchtung f

semi-infinite — einseitig unendlich ausgedehnt, einseitig unbegrenzt, halbunendlich [ausgedehnt], [unendlicher] Halb-

semi-infinite body — [unendlicher] Halbkörper m

semi-infinite channel — einseitig unendlicher Kanal m

semi-infinite space, half-space, infinite half-space — Halbraum m, unendlicher Halbraum

semi-infinite strip — Halbstreifen m

semi-insulator — Halbisolator m, Semiisolator m

semi-integer, semi-integral — s. half-integer

semi-interquartile range — halber Quartilabstand m

semi-invariant — Semiinvariante f

semi-invariant — s. a. cumulant <stat.>

semi-inverse method — semiinverse Methode f

semi-ionic bond — s. dative bond

semileptonic decay (disintegration) — semileptonischer Zerfall m

semi[-]liquid, semi[-]fluid — semifluid, halbfluid, halbflüssig

semi-liquid state, semi-solid state — halbflüssiger Zustand m

semilogarithmic co-ordinate paper, semilog[arithmic] paper — einfachlogarithmisches (halblogarithmisches) Papier n, Exponentialpapier n; einfachlogarithmisches (halblogarithmisches) Netz n, Exponentialnetz n

semilogarithmic plot, semilog plot — einfachlogarithmische (halblogarithmische) Darstellung f

semi-major axis — große Halbachse f

semi-major axis [of orbit], mean distance — große Halbachse f <Bahnelement>

semi-mat — halbmatt

semi-metal, half-metal, metalloid — Halbmetall n, Metall m zweiter Art

semi-micro analysis — Halbmikroanalyse f, Semimikroanalyse f, Zentigrammmethode <10 ··· 250 mg>

semi-micro-analytical (semimicro-analytical) balance — Halbmikroanalysewaage f, halbmikroanalytische Waage f

semi-microculorimeter — Halbmikrokalorimeter n

semi-micro scale — Halbmikromaßstab m, halbmikroskopischer Maßstab m

semi-minor axis — kleine Halbachse f

semimirror nuclei, conjugate nuclei — konjugierte Kerne mpl

seminival climate — seminivales Klima n

seminormal solution — 0,5 n Lösung f, n/2 Lösung

semi-opaque — s. semi-transparent

semioscillation — s. semiperiod

semiosis — Semiosis f

semiotics — Semiotik f

semipancratic — halbpankratisch

semiperimeter — s. semicircumference

semiperiod, semi-period, half-period, half-cycle, half cycle — Halbperiode f, halbe Periode f

semiperiodic eigenvalue — halbperiodischer Eigenwert m

semi[-]permeable — halbdurchlässig, semipermeabel

semipermeable diaphragm (membrane), semipermeable wall — semipermeable (halbdurchlässige) Membran f, semipermeable (halbdurchlässige) Haut f, semipermeable (halbdurchlässige) Wand f

semi-permeable mirror — s. semi-transparent mirror

semipermeable wall — s. semipermeable diaphragm

semipermeability — Semipermeabilität f, Halbdurchlässigkeit f

semi-phenomenological — halbphänomenologisch

semi-polar bond — s. dative bond

semi-polar co-ordinates — s. cylindrical co-ordinates

semi-polar double bond — s. dative bond

semi[-]quantitative — halbquantitativ

semi-range, half-width, half-range <stat.> — halbe Spannweite f, halbe Breite f <Stat.>

semi-regular variable [star], half-regular variable [star] — halbperiodischer (halbregelmäßiger) Veränderlicher m

semi-remote — halbferngesteuert, teilweise fernbedient, Halbfern-

semi-rigid — halbstarr; halbsteif

semi-self-sustained discharge — s. hot-cathode discharge

semi-self-sustained discharge — s. non-self-maintained discharge

semi-simple — halbeinfach

semi[-]solid; subsolid — semisolid, halbfest

semi-solid state, semi-liquid state — halbflüssiger Zustand m

semispan — halbe Spannweite f

semi-stall — halbüberzogener (teilüberzogener) Flug[zustand] m

semisymmetric[al] — halbsymmetrisch

semit — s. semitone <ac.>

semiterrestrial soil — semiterrestrischer Boden m

semi-tone, half-tone, middle tone, continuous tone <opt.> — Halbton m <Opt.>

semitone, half-tone, half-step, semit <ac.> — Halbton m, halber Ton m <Ak.>

semi-translucent — halbdurchscheinend

semi-transparent, partially transmitting; semi-opaque <opt.> — halbdurchlässig, teildurchlässig, teilweise durchlässig <Opt.>

semi-transparent mirror, semi-permeable mirror, two-way mirror — halbdurchlässiger Spiegel m, teildurchlässiger Spiegel

semi-transparent model [of nucleus], optical model [of particle scattering], optical model of nucleus, cloudy crystal ball [model]; complex potential model, CPM — optisches Kernmodell n, optisches Modell n [der Kernwechselwirkung], halbdurchlässiges Kernmodell

semi-tropical zone — s. subtropical zone

semi-turbulent — halbturbulent

semivalence, semivalency — s. singlet linkage

semivalence

semivalence, semivalency	s. one-electron bond	sense organ	Sinnesorgan n, Rezeptionsorgan n, Reizaufnahmeorgan n
semivertex angle [of the cone]	s. cone semi-angle	sense organelle	Sinnesorganell n
semi-wave antenna, half-wave dipole, half-wave antenna	Halbwellendipol m, Halbwellenantenne f	sensibility	s. sensitivity
		sensible element	s. sensitive element
		sensible heat	fühlbare Wärme f
Sénarmont	s. Sénarmont prism	sensible horizon	s. apparent horizon
Sénarmont compensator / [De]	s. quarter-wave plate compensator	sensing	s. sensation
Sénarmont['s] method / [De]	Sénarmontsche Kompensationsmethode (Methode) f, de-Sénarmontsche Methode, Methode von de Sénarmont	sensing antenna	Suchantenne f
		sensing element	s. sensitive element
		sensing head; scanning head; probe	Tastkopf m
		sensing head	s. a. measuring head
		sensing lever	Fühlhebel m
Sénarmont polarimeter / De, Sénarmont polariscope / De	s. quarter-wave plate compensator	sensing probe	s. measuring head
		sensitive cross-section, sensitive section <radiobiology>	strahlenempfindlicher Querschnitt m <Strahlenbiologie>
Sénarmont prism [/ De], Sénarmont, De Sénarmont prism	Sénarmont-Prisma n, Prisma n nach de Sénarmont, De-Sénarmont-Prisma n, Sénarmontsches Doppelprisma n		
		sensitive element, sensing element, sensible element, sensor, detection element, primary element; contacting unit; pick-off	empfindliches Element (Teil) n; Fühler m, Fühlglied n, Fühlerelement n; Meßfühler m
sender	s. transmitter		
sending aloft the radiosonde	Radiosondenaufstieg m		
sending antenna	s. transmitting antenna		
sending end impedance	s. input impedance	sensitive flame, sound-sensitive flame, microphonic flame	empfindliche Flamme f, schallempfindliche Flamme
sending power	s. transmitting power		
sending tube, transmitting valve, transmitting (transmitter) tube	Senderöhre f	sensitive layer	s. photolayer
		sensitive line, persistent (distinctive) line, raie ultime, letzte linie	letzte Linie f, Restlinie f, beständige Linie, Nachweislinie f
senditron, sendytron	Senditronröhre f		
Senftleben-Beenakker effect, magnetic Senftleben-Beenakker effect of viscosity	Senftleben-Beenakker-Effekt m	sensitiveness	s. sensitivity <of instrument, organ>
		sensitiveness of the level, level constant, value of level division	Parswert m, Teilwert m der Libelle, Angabe f der Libelle, Empfindlichkeit f der Libelle
Senftleben effect	Senftleben-Effekt m		
seniority	Seniorität[szahl] f	sensitive region, range of sensitivity <of counter>	empfindlicher Bereich m, Ansprechbereich m <Zählrohr>
sensation; impression	Empfindung f; Eindruck m		
sensation leval, level above threshold	Hörpegel m, Empfindungspegel m	sensitive region [of the cell]	s. radiobiological sensitive volume
sensation of brightness, sensation of luminosity	Helligkeitsempfindung f, Hellempfindung f	sensitive section, sensitive cross-section <radiobiology>	strahlenempfindlicher Querschnitt m <Strahlenbiologie>
sensation of colour, chromatic sensation, colour sensation	Farbempfindung f		
		sensitive time	Empfindlichkeitszeit f; Ansprechzeit f
sensation of depth	s. space impression		
sensation of hearing, auditory sensation	Hörempfindung f		
sensation of light, light sensation	Lichtempfindung f; Lichteindruck m	sensitive tint, tint of passage, sensitive violet	empfindliche Farbe f, „teinte sensible" f, empfindliche Färbung f, Rot n erster (I.) Ordnung
sensation of luminosity	s. sensation of brightness		
sensation time	Empfindungszeit f	sensitive to daylight	tageslichtempfindlich
sense, sense of direction, direction	Richtungssinn m, Sinn m	sensitive to infra-red [rays], infrared-sensitive, I.R. sensitive	infrarotempfindlich, IR-empfindlich
sense	s. a. sense of rotation		
sense antenna	Seitenbestimmungsantenne f		
sense cell	Sinneszelle f, Sensillus m	sensitive to light	s. photosensitive <phot.>
sense determination	Seitenbestimmung f, Seitenkennung f	sensitive to neutrons, neutron-sensitive	neutronenempfindlich, empfindlich gegen[über] Neutronen
sense of absolute pitch, absolute pitch	absolutes Gehör n	sensitive to position, position-sensitive	lageempfindlich
sense of colour	Farbsinn m, Farbensinn m	sensitive to real structure	realstrukturempfindlich
sense of direction	s. sense	sensitive to temperature	s. temperature-sensitive
sense of hearing, hearing	Gehör n		
sense of magnetization, direction of magnetization	Magnetisierungsrichtung f	sensitive to ultra-violet [rays], ultravioletsensitive, U.V. sensitive	ultraviolettempfindlich, UV-empfindlich
sense of rotation, sense; direction of rotation; direction of revolution	Dreh[ungs]sinn m, Dreh[ungs]richtung f; Umlauf[s]sinn m, Umlauf[s]richtung f; Umfahrungssinn m		
sense of sight, light sense	Lichtsinn m, Gesicht n		
sense of smell, smell [sense]	Geruchssinn m, Geruch m		
sense of taste, taste [sense]	Geschmackssinn m, Geschmack m	sensitive violet, tint of passage, sensitive tint	empfindliche Farbe f, „teinte sensible" f, empfindliche Färbung f, Rot n erster (I.) Ordnung
sense of the clock	Uhrzeigerrichtung f, Uhrzeigersinn m		
		sensitive volume <of counter>	empfindliches Volumen n, Zählvolumen n, Zählraum m <Zählrohr>
sense of touch, touch [sense]	Tastsinn m		

752

sensitive volume <of instrument>	wirksames Volumen n <Gerät>	sensitizer, sensitizing agent <in luminescence>	Sensibilisator m, Sensibilisierungsmittel n, Sensibilisierungsstoff m
sensitive volume [of the cell]	s. radiobiological sensitive volume	sensitizer, photographic sensitizer <phot.>	Sensibilisator m, Photosensibilisator m, photographischer Sensibilisator, Aktivator m <Phot.>
sensitivity, sensitiveness <of instrument, organ>; responsivity, responsiveness <of instrument>; sensibility <of organ>	Empfindlichkeit f <Gerät, Organ>; Ansprechvermögen n <Strahlungsdetektor>; Sensibilität f <Organ>; Sensitivität f <Organ>	sensitizing agent	s. sensitizer
		sensitizing dye	sensibilisierender Farbstoff m, Sensibilisierungsfarbstoff m
sensitivity, speed <of the emulsion>	Empfindlichkeit f, Lichtempfindlichkeit f <Emulsion>	sensitizing intensity, intensity of sensitization	Sensibilisierungsintensität f
		sensitogram	Sensitogramm n, Sensitometerstreifen m
sensitivity, response <electro-acoustics>	Empfindlichkeitsübertragungsfaktor m <Elektroakustik>	sensitometer	Sensitometer n
sensitivity centre	s. sensitivity speck	sensitometric tablet	s. neutral step wedge
sensitivity constant	Ansprechkonstante f	sensitometry	Sensitometrie f
		sensor	s. sensitive element
sensitivity curve, response curve	Empfindlichkeitskurve f; Lichtempfindlichkeitskurve f	sensor	s. a. transducer
		sensory	sensorisch
		sentential calculus (logic)	s. propositional calculus
		sentinel pyrometer	s. pyrometric cone
sensitivity curve of the eye	Augenempfindlichkeitskurve f	separability, separableness <math.>	Separierbarkeit f, Separabilität f <Math.>
sensitivity drift, sensitivity shift	Veränderung f der Empfindlichkeit, Empfindlichkeitsänderung f	separability, separableness <chem.>	Trennbarkeit f <Chem.>
sensitivity factor	Empfindlichkeitszahl f, Empfindlichkeitsziffer f, Empfindlichkeitsfaktor m	separability, resolvability, separableness <opt.; math.>	Auflösbarkeit f, Trennbarkeit f <Opt.; Math.>
		separable	separierbar; [ab]trennbar
sensitivity limit	s. threshold of sensitivity		
sensitivity measure <num. math.>	Empfindlichkeitsmaß n, Schrittkennzahl f <num. Math.>	separable <math.>	separabel <Math.>
		separableness	s. separability
		separable [topological] space	separabler [topologischer] Raum m
sensitivity nucleus	s. sensitivity speck	separable variables	separierbare Veränderliche (Variable) fpl
sensitivity nut, gravity bob	Empfindlichkeitseinstellschraube f, Reguliergewicht n <Waage>		
		separably degenerate	trennbar entartet
sensitivity of grain, speed of grain	Kornempfindlichkeit f <Emulsion>	separated boundary layer	abgelöste Grenzschicht f
sensitivity shift, sensitivity drift	Veränderung f der Empfindlichkeit, Empfindlichkeitsänderung f	separated-orbits cyclotron, separated orbit cyclotron	Zyklotron n mit getrennten Bahnen
sensitivity speck, sensitivity centre, sensitivity nucleus, concentration speck	Empfindlichkeitskeim m, Empfindlichkeitszentrum n, Lichtempfindlichkeitszentrum n	separated [topological] space	s. Hausdorff space
		separate excitation, independent excitation, external excitation	Fremderregung f; äußere Erregung f
sensitivity speck, speck of sensitivity, centre of ripening	Reifkeim m		
sensitivity threshold	s. threshold of sensitivity	separately heated cathode, indirectly heated cathode	indirekt geheizte Katode f
sensitivity to all colours, panchromatism	Panchromatismus m, Allfarbenempfindlichkeit f, Panchromasie f	separate nuclei theory	Theorie f der Bildung getrennter Kerne <Doppelsternentstehung>
sensitivity to blue	Blauempfindlichkeit f		
sensitivity to contact stimulus	Berührungsempfindlichkeit f	separating break	s. separation fracture
		separating calorimeter	Abscheidekalorimeter n
sensitivity to heat, heat sensitivity	Wärmeempfindlichkeit f, Wärmesensibilität f	separating capacitor	Trennkondensator m
		separating capacity	s. separative power
		separating column	s. separation column
		separating column	s. a. stripper
sensitivity to infra-red rays	s. infra-red sensitivity	separating film	s. separating layer
		separating filter	s. separation filter
sensitivity to radiation, radiation sensitivity, radiant sensitivity; radiosensitivity, radiosusceptibility	Strahlungsempfindlichkeit f, Strahlenempfindlichkeit f	separating filtration	Trennfiltration f
		separating funnel, separatory funnel	Scheidetrichter m, Schütteltrichter m, Trenntrichter m
		separating layer; separating film; abscission layer <bio.>	Trennschicht f, Trennungsschicht f
sensitivity to red light, red sensitivity, red response	Rotempfindlichkeit f	separating line, dividing (separation) line, split line	Trennlinie f, Trennungslinie f
sensitivity to ultra-violet rays	s. ultra-violet sensitivity	separating strength	s. rupture strength
		separating of the variables	s. separation <of variables>
sensitivity to under-heat[ing]	Unterheizempfindlichkeit f	separating system, focusing system	Fokussier[ungs]system n
sensitization	Sensibilisierung f, Aktivierung f	separating unit	Trenneinheit f, Trennglied n, Trennzelle f, Trenngruppe f
sensitization time	Sensibilisierungszeit f <Phys.>; Sensitivierungszeit f <Bio.>		
sensitized	s. photosensitive <phot.>	separation, spacing	<räumlicher> Abstand m, Zwischenraum m
sensitized discomposition	sensibilisierte Zersetzung f		
sensitized fluorescence	sensibilisierte Fluoreszenz f	separation, separation coefficient <in separation of isotopes>	Trennkoeffizient m, Anreicherungskoeffizient m <bei der Isotopentrennung>
sensitized luminescence	sensibilisierte Lumineszenz f		

separation, detachment <e.g. of flow, vortex, boundary layer>; shedding <of vortices>	Ablösung *f*	**separation nozzle,** nozzle separator	Trenndüse *f*, Schäldüse *f*
separation <of sizes>; parting	Scheidung *f*	**separation of air**	s. air separation
		separation of bodies adhering to each other	Enthaften *n*
separation <of variables>, separating the variables	Separierung *f* der Variablen, Separation *f* der Variablen, Trennung *f* der Variablen, Abseparieren *n*	**separation of burnt out stage**	Abtrennung *f* der ausgebrannten Stufe
		separation of fringes, separation of the interference fringes	Streifenabstand *m*, Interferenzstreifenabstand *m*, Abstand *m* zweier Interferenzstreifen
separation; partition, parting; isolation <chem.>	Abtrennung *f*; Trennung *f*, Zerlegung *f*; Abscheidung *f*; Ausscheidung *f*; Isolierung *f*; Auftrennung *f* <Chem.>	**separation of fundamental points,** fundamental interval	Fundamentalabstand *m*
		separation of isotopes	s. isotope separation
separation, splitting off <nucl.>	Abspaltung *f*, Abtrennung *f* <Kern.>	**separation of isotopes by electromagnetic method,** electromagnetic separation of isotopes; calutron separation	elektromagnetische Isotopentrennung *f*, elektromagnetische Trennmethode *f*; Calutrontrennung *f*
separation <of the elements of grating>, grating constant, groove spacing <opt.>	Gitterkonstante *f* [des Beugungsgitters] <Opt.>, optische Gitterkonstante		
separation, interval <of two events>, separation between events <rel.>	Intervall *n*, Weltintervall *n*, Abstand *m* zwischen zwei Ereignissen (Weltpunkten) <Rel.>	**separation of isotopes by thermal diffusion,** thermal diffusion method	Trennrohrverfahren *n*, Thermodiffusionsverfahren *n*, Isotopentrennung *f* durch Thermodiffusion, Clusius-Dickel-Verfahren *n*
separation	s. a. precipitation <of vacancy>		
separation	s. a. blanking <of a pulse>		
separation	s. a. demixing	**separation of masses,** mass separation	Massentrennung *f*
separation	s. a. division		
separation <of isotopes>	s. a. isotope separation	**separation of principal points**	Interstitium *n*
separation between events	s. separation <rel.>	**separation of stereophotographs**	Bildtrennung *f*
separation break	s. separation fracture		
separation bubble	Ablösungsblase *f*, Ablöseblase *f*	**separation of the division lines**	Strichabstand *m*
separation by development (displacement)	Trennung *f* durch Verdrängungschromatographie	**separation of the flow**	Stromablösung *f*, Strömungsablösung *f*
		separation of the interference fringes	s. separation of fringes
separation by recoil	Rückstoßtrennung *f*	**separation parameter,** separation characteristic	Trennparameter *m*, Separationsparameter *m*
separation cascade	s. gaseous diffusion cascade		
separation characteristic	s. separation parameter	**separation pipe**	s. thermal diffusion column
separation circuit	s. buffer circuit		
separation coefficient, separation <in separation of isotopes>	Trennkoeffizient *m*, Anreicherungskoeffizient *m* <bei der Isotopentrennung>	**separation potential,** separative work content, value	Trennpotential *n*
		separation process	s. separation method
separation column, separation tower, separating column	Trennkolonne *f*, Trennsäule *f*	**separation surface**	s. interface
		separation technique	s. separation method
separation curve	Separationskurve *f*, Trennungskurve *f*	**separation tower,** separation column, separating column	Trennkolonne *f*, Trennsäule *f*
separation cylinder	Trennwalze *f*	**separation tube**	s. thermal diffusion column
separation efficiency	Trennwirkungsgrad *m*, Trenngüte *f*; Trennwirksamkeit *f*	**separative element**	Trennelement *n*
		separative power	Trennleistung *f*
separation energy, energy necessary for separating a particle from the nucleus, work function of a nuclear particle	Abtrennarbeit *f*, Abtrennungsarbeit *f*, Trennungsarbeit *f*, Trennungsenergie *f*, Trennenergie *f*	**separative power,** separating capacity	Trennvermögen *n*; Trennkraft *f*; Trennfähigkeit *f*
		separative work	Trennarbeit *f*
		separative work content, separation potential, value	Trennpotential *n*
separation factor, isotope separation factor	Trennfaktor *m*, Isotopentrennfaktor *m*		
separation factor for a single stage	s. simple process factor	**separatography**	adsorptive Trennung *f* [farbloser Verbindungen], Separatographie *f*
separation factor of the centrifuge	Zentrifugenzahl *f*, Trennfaktor *m* bei der Zentrifugierung	**separator,** water separator, water trap; moisture separator	Wasserabscheider *m*; Feuchtigkeitsabscheider *m*; Flüssigkeitsabscheider *m*
separation filter, separating filter	Trennfilter *n*; Weichenfilter *n*		
		separator <in batteries>	Separator *m*, Scheider *m* <Akkumulator>
separation fracture, cleavage (cleave) fracture, rupture	Trennungsbruch *m*, Trennbruch *m*	**separator**	s. a. spacer
		separatory funnel	s. separating funnel
separation from the Sun	Ablösung *f* von der Sonne	**separatriss**	s. separatrix
separation function <of filter>	Abscheidefunktion *f* <Filter>	**separatrix,** separatriss <acc.>	Separatrix *f* <Beschl.>
separation line, dividing line, separating (split) line	Trennlinie *f*, Trennungslinie *f*	**septum**	Septum *n*
separation method, method of separation, separation technique; separation process	Trennverfahren *n*, Trennungsverfahren *n*, Trennmethode *f*, Trennungsmethode *f*, Trenn[ungs]prozeß *m*	**septum**	s. a. partition <chem.>
		septum	s. a. shutter <opt.>
		septuplet	Septuplett *n*
		sequence <math.; geo.; bio.>	Folge *f* <Math.>; Abfolge *f* <Geo.>; Sequenz *f* <Bio.; Geo.>

sequence	s. a. order of sequence	serial photograph, serial air-survey photograph	Reihenmeßbild n, Reihenbild n, Reihenaufnahme f
sequence control	s. sequential control		
sequence control	s. servo control		
sequence of bands, band sequence, series (set) of bands	Bandengruppe f	serial radiography, seriography	Schnellserienaufnahmetechnik f, Serienaufnahme f, Seriographie f <Röntgenbilder>
sequence of levels, sequence of terms	Termfolge f		
sequence of numbers	Zahlenfolge f	serial sectioning technique	s. sectioning technique
		series, series of lines, spectral series	Serie f [von Spektrallinien], Spektralserie f, Linienserie f, Spektrallinienserie f
sequence of phases, phase sequence	Phasenfolge f		
sequence of relaxation processes	Kippfolge f, Folge f von Kippvorgängen	series; progression <math.>	Reihe f <Math.>
sequence of terms, sequence of levels	Termfolge f	series	s. a. disintegration series
		series	s. a. series connected
sequence repetition rate	s. repetition frequency	series / in	s. series connected
sequence tending to zero, null sequence	Nullfolge f	series acceptor circuit	s. series resonant circuit
		series admittance	Reihenschlußleitwert m, Reihenleitwert m, Serienleitwert m; Längsleitwert m
sequential analysis, sequential test	Sequentialanalyse f, Sequenzanalyse f, Sequentialtest m, Folgeprüfung f	series arm	s. series element
		series arrangement	s. series connection
		series camera	s. serial photogrammetric camera
sequential control, sequence control, programme[d] control	Ablaufsteuerung f, Konditionalsteuerung f	series capacitance	Reihenschlußkapazität f, Reihenkapazität f, Serienkapazität f; Längskapazität f
sequential control	s. a. servo control		
sequential control[ler], servo control[ler], servo governor	Folgeregler m, Nachlaufregler m	series capacitor	Reihenkondensator m, Serienkondensator m, in Reihe geschalteter Kondensator m, reihengeschalteter Kondensator
sequential operator	sequentieller Operator m		
sequential processing	Reihenfolgeverarbeitung f	series capacitor	Vorschaltkondensator m, Vorkondensator m
		series characteristic	Hauptstromcharakteristik f, Reihenschlußkennlinie f
sequential subtraction	sequentielle Subtraktion f	series choke, series reactor	Seriendrossel f
sequential test	s. sequential analysis		
sequestering agent	s. chelant		
sequestration	s. chelating action	series circuit	s. current path <el.>
sérac	Gletscherfirnblock m, Firnblock m	series coil of wattmeter, wattmeter series coil	Wattmeterstromspule f
Serber force	Serber-Kraft f		
Serber potential	Serber-Potential n, Potential n der Serber-Kräfte	series conductivity	Reihenschlußleitfähigkeit f, Reihenleitfähigkeit f, Serienleitfähigkeit f; Längsleitfähigkeit f
Serber-Wilson method	Serber-Wilson-Methode f	series connected, cascade connected, tandem connected, connected in series, series, cascade, tandem, in series, in cascade <el., gen.>	hintereinandergeschaltet, in Reihe [geschaltet], reihengeschaltet, in Serie [geschaltet], Reihenschluß-, Reihen-, Serien- <El., allg.>
Serdex hygrometer	Serdex-Hygrometer n		
Ser disk	Sersche Scheibe f		
serial access computer store, serial access store	Rechenspeicher m mit Serienzugriff		
		series-connected element	s. series element
serial addition	Reihenaddition f	series connection, series arrangement, connection in series, in-series connection, cascade connection, tandem connection <el., gen.>	Reihenschaltung f, Reihenschluß m, Hintereinanderschaltung f, Serienschaltung f; Vorschaltung f <El., allg.>
serial aerial [cine] camera	s. serial photogrammetric camera		
serial aerophotogrammetric (air) survey, survey by serial photographs	Reihenbildaufnahme f, Reihenaufnahme f, Streifenaufnahme f		
		series cut-off	s. series limit
serial air-survey camera	s. serial photogrammetric camera	series decay (disintegration), chain disintegration (decay)	Kettenzerfall m, Kettenumwandlung f
serial air-survey photograph, serial photograph	Reihenmeßbild n, Reihenbild n, Reihenaufnahme f	series edge	s. series limit
		series-efficiency diode	s. efficiency diode
serial correlation	s. autocorrelation	series element, series-connected element, series section; series arm	Reihenschlußglied n, Serienglied n, Reihenglied n; Längsglied n; Längszweig m
serial correlation coefficient	Reihenkorrelationskoeffizient m, Serienkorrelationskoeffizient m		
		series equivalent resistance	Serienersatzwiderstand m
serial correlation function	s. autocorrelation function <statistics>	series excitation, serial excitation	Reihenschlußerregung f, Hauptschlußerregung f, Serienerregung f, Hauptstromerregung f
serial excitation	s. series excitation		
serial extinction	Serienauslöschung f		
serial film camera	s. serial photogrammetric camera	series expansion	s. expansion in a series
serial machine	Serienmaschine f	series exposure slide, multiplying back, dividing back	Belichtungsreihenschieber m, Multiplikator m
		series-fed vertical antenna, end-fed vertical antenna	fußpunktgespeiste Vertikalantenne f, Vertikalantenne mit Zuführung der Energie am Fußpunkt
serial photogrammetric (photogrammetry) camera, serial film camera, series camera, serial air-survey camera, serial aerial [cine] camera	Reihenmeßkammer f, Reihenbildmeßkammer f, Reihenbildaufnahmekammer f, Reihenbildkammer f, Reihenkammer f, Meßreihenbildner m, Reihenbildner m		
		series feedback	Reihen[schluß]rückkopplung f, Serienrückkopplung f

series 756

series feedback	*s. a.* series inverse feedback	series reactor, series choke	Seriendrossel *f*
series formula, series law	Serienformel *f*, Seriengesetz *n*		
series generator	*s.* series-wound generator	series reactor	Vorschaltdrossel *f*, Vordrossel *f*
series impedance	Reihen[schluß]impedanz *f*, Serienimpedanz *f*, Serienscheinwiderstand *m*; Längsimpedanz *f*		
		series representation	Reihendarstellung *f*
		series resistance; series resistor; series rheostat	Reihenschlußwiderstand *m*, Reihenwiderstand *m*, Serienwiderstand *m*; Längswiderstand *m*
series inductance, series self-inductance	Reihen[schluß]induktivität *f*, Serien[selbst]induktivität *f*, Serienselbstinduktion *f*; Längsinduktivität *f*		
series inverse feedback, series feedback	Seriengegenkopplung *f*, Reihengegen[schluß]kopplung *f*	series resistance	*s.* series resistor
		series resistor, dropping resistor; series resistance, additional resistance	Vorwiderstand *m*, Vorschaltwiderstand *m*, vorgeschalteter Widerstand *m*
series lamp	Serienlampe *f*,		
series law, series formula	Serienformel *f*, Seriengesetz *n*	series resistor	*s. a.* series resistance
		series resonance	*s.* voltage resonance
		series resonance circuit	*s.* series resonant circuit
series limit, limit of the series, series cut-off (edge)	Seriengrenze *f*	series resonance frequency	*s.* series resonant frequency
series line, diagram line	Serienlinie *f*, Diagrammlinie *f*	series resonant circuit, series resonance circuit, acceptor, [series] acceptor circuit	Reihenresonanzkreis *m*, Serienresonanzkreis *m*, Spannungsresonanzkreis *m*, Serienschwingkreis *m*, Serienschwingungskreis *m*
series machine	*s.* series-wound machine		
series magnetic flux	Reihenschlußkraftfluß *m*, Reihenkraftfluß *m*, Serienkraftfluß *m*; Längskraftfluß *m*		
		series resonant circuit, series tuned circuit	Reihenresonanzschaltung *f*, Serienresonanzschaltung *f*, Spannungsresonanzschaltung *f*
series measurement	Serienmessung *f*		
series modulation	Reihenröhrenmodulation *f*, Vorröhrenmodulation *f*		
		series resonant frequency, series resonance frequency, voltage resonance frequency	Reihenresonanzfrequenz *f*, Serienresonanzfrequenz *f*, Spannungsresonanzfrequenz *f*
series motor	*s.* series-wound motor		
series-multiple connection (transition)	*s.* series-parallel transition		
		series rheostat	*s.* series resistance
series of aerofoil sections	Profilserie *f*	series section	*s.* series element
		series self-inductance	*s.* series inductance
series of bands	*s.* sequence of bands	series spectrum	Serienspektrum *n*
series of cyclones, family of cyclones	Zyklonenfamilie *f*, Zyklonenserie *f*	series statement	Potenzreihenansatz *m*, Reihenansatz *m*
series of experiments	*s.* series of tests	series transformer, current transformer	Stromwandler *m*, Stromtransformator *m*
series of functions, function series	Funktionenreihe *f*, Funktionsreihe *f*		
series of fundamental stars, fundamental series, Küstner series ⟨astr.⟩	Fundamentalreihe *f*, Fundamentalsternreihe *f*, Küstnersche Reihe *f*	series transformer	Vorschalttransformator *m*
		series tuned circuit	*s.* series resonant circuit
series of greys	*s.* progressive series of greys	series winding, banked winding	Reihen[schluß]wicklung *f*, Hauptschlußwicklung *f*, Serienwicklung *f*, Hauptstromwicklung *f*, verschachtelte Wicklung *f*
series of impulses	*s.* pulse train		
series of lines	*s.* series		
series of measurements, run, train of measurand	Meßreihe *f*, Meßserie *f*, Meßwertreihe *f*		
series of mixed crystals	*s.* complete series of solid solutions	series-wound generator, series generator	Reihenschlußgenerator *m*, Hauptschlußgenerator *m*, Seriengenerator *m*, Hauptstromgenerator *m*, Hauptschlußdynamo *m*, Gleichstrom-Reihenschlußgenerator *m*, Gleichstrom-Hauptschlußgenerator *m*, Gleichstrom-Seriengenerator *m*
series of pulses	*s.* pulse train		
series of solid solutions	*s.* complete series of solid solutions		
series of tests, test series, set of tests; experiment series, series of experiments	Versuchsreihe *f*, Versuchsserie *f*		
series-opposed connection, series-opposing connection, series opposition, opposing connection	Gegenreihenschaltung *f*, Gegenschaltung *f*, Gegeneinanderschaltung *f*, Gegensinnreihenschaltung *f*	series-wound machine, series machine	Reihenschlußmaschine *f*, Hauptschlußmaschine *f*, Serienmaschine *f*, Hauptstrommaschine *f*, Gleichstrom-Reihenschlußmaschine *f*, Gleichstrom-Hauptschlußmaschine *f*, Gleichstrom-Serienmaschine *f*
series-parallel connection	*s.* series-parallel transition		
series-parallel matrix	Reihenparallelmatrix *f*		
		series-wound motor, series motor	Reihenschlußmotor *m*, Hauptschlußmotor *m*, Serienmotor *m*, Hauptstrommotor *m*, Gleichstrom-Reihenschlußmotor *m*, Gleichstrom-Hauptschlußmotor *m*, Gleichstrom-Serienmotor *m*
series-parallel transition, series-parallel connection, series-multiple connection (transition)	Reihenparallelschaltung *f*, Serienparallelschaltung *f*; Gruppenschaltung *f*		
series-parallel winding	Reihenparallelwicklung *f*	seriography	*s.* serial radiography
		serpentine	*s.* winding pipe
		serpentine line, sinuous line	Schlangenlinie
series reactance	Reihenschlußreaktanz *f*, Reihenreaktanz *f*, Serienreaktanz *f*, Serienblindwiderstand *m*; Längsreaktanz *f*	serrated flow	inhomogene Gleitung *f*, inhomogenes Kriechen *n*
		Serret-Frenet formulae, Frenet[-Serret] formulae, formulae of [Serret-]Frenet	Frenetsche Formeln *fpl*, Frenet-Formeln *fpl*, Serretsche Formeln

serum albumin	Serumalbumin n	set of glass plates	Glasplattensatz m
serviceable life	s. lifetime <techn.>	set of information	s. information content
service voltage	s. burning voltage <of discharge, arc>	set of instruments	Meßsatz m, Meßgerätesatz m
servicing tower, launching tower	Startturm m	set of lenses	s. convertible lens
		set of linear equations	s. system of linear equations
servo	s. servomechanism	set of measure zero, null set	Nullmenge f, Menge f vom Maß Null
servo amplifier	Servoverstärker m	set of parallel co-ordinates	s. parallel co-ordinates
		set of points, point set; assemblage of points	Punktmenge f
servo control, servo-operated control, servo-powered control, sequential (sequence) control, automatic following	Folgesteuerung f, Führungssteuerung f; Folgeregelung f, Servoregelung f; Nachlaufregelung f	set of prisms	Prismensatz m
		set of projective co-ordinates	s. projective co-ordinates
		set of simultaneous linear equations	s. system of linear equations
servo control[ler], servo governor, sequential control[ler]	Folgeregler m, Nachlaufregler m	set of space-time co-ordinates	s. space-time co-ordinates
		set of tests	s. test series
servo drive	Stell[an]trieb m	set of values	s. range <math.>
servo governor	s. servo control[ler]	setpoint, setting <of relay>	Einstellwert m <Relais>
servomechanism, servosystem, servo, follow-up system, follower control, follower, servounit	Folgeregelungssystem n, Folgeregelung f, Folge[steuerungs]system n, Folgesteuerung f, Servomechanismus m; Nachlauf[regelungs]system n; Nachlaufeinrichtung f, Nachlaufsteuerung f, Nachlaufsteuergerät n, Nachlaufwerk n, Nachlaufregler m	set point	s. command variable
		set point	s. reference point
		set point	s. set level
		set point adjuster, reference input element, setting device	Stelleinrichtung f, Sollwerteinsteller m
		set screw, setscrew	s. setting screw
		set square, square	Winkelmaß n, Zeichendreieck n, Reißdreieck n; Meßwinkel m <Gerät>
		set[-] theoretical	mengentheoretisch
servomotor, servo motor	Stellmotor m, Servomotor m, Hilfsmotor m, Steuermotor m, Regelmotor m, Verstellmotor m, Steller m, Steuertriebwerk n	set theory	s. theory of sets
		set time	Untergangszeit f
		setting, setpoint <of relay>	Einstellwert m <Relais>
		setting	s. a. adjustment <to>
		setting	s. a. set
		setting	s. a. set <of concrete>
servo-operated control, servo-powered control	s. servo control	setting device, reference input element, set point adjuster	Stelleinrichtung f, Sollwerteinsteller m
servosystem, servounit	s. servomechanism	setting free; release; liberation; disengagement	Freisetzung f; Freiwerden n; Auslösung f; Ablösung f; Abgabe f; Entbindung f
SESER	= source of electrons in a selected energy range		
sessile bubble	sitzende Blase f	setting frequency	Verstellhäufigkeit f
sessile dislocation	nichtgleitfähige (sessile) Versetzung f	setting gauge	Einstellehre f
		setting of lens	s. lens mount
sessile drop method	Methode f der sitzenden Tropfen	setting range <of relay>	Einstellbereich m <Relais>
seston	Seston n	setting screw, set screw, setscrew, regulating screw	Stellschraube f, Regulierschraube f; Klemmschraube f
set, setting; solidification solidifying, freezing	Erstarrung f, Festwerden n, Verfestigung f		
set, setting; hardening <of concrete>	Erhärtung f, Verfestigung f; Verhärtung f; Abbinden n; Anziehen n	setting-up	s. adjustment <to>
		settleability	s. precipitability
		settled creep	s. quasiviscous creep
		settled position	s. position of rest
set, setting <of the star>	Untergang m [des Gestirns], Deszendenz f [des Gestirns]	settler	Kläranlage f, Klärungsanlage f, Filteranlage f <zur Abtrennung suspendierter Teilchen aus Flüssigkeiten und Gasen>
set, aggregate, manifold, class, ensemble; assemblage <infinite> <math.>	Menge f <Math.>		
		settling, settling down, sedimentation, sedimentary deposition, deposition; settling-out	Sedimentation f, Sedimentierung f, Ablagerung f, Absetzen n, Absedimentierung f; Niedersinken n, Absinken n; Ausfallen n; Sedimentbildung f
setback, set back	s. reset		
set function	Mengenfunktion f		
set level, set point, desired value, reference input <US>	Sollwert m [der Regelgröße], Aufgabewert m, kommandierter Wert m		
		settling	s. a. decantation <chem.>
		settling down, settling-out	s. settling
set noise; amplifier noise	Verstärkerrauschen n; Verstärkergeräusch n	settling rate, rate of sedimentation	Sedimentationsgeschwindigkeit f, Sinkgeschwindigkeit f [bei der Sedimentation]
set noise; inherent noise	Eigengeräusch n		
set of bands	s. sequence of bands	set union	s. union <of sets>
set of characteristics	s. family of characteristic[s]	set[-]up	s. statement <math.>
set of curves	s. system of curves	set[-]up for calculating machine	Rechenschaltung f
set of definition	s. domain <math.>		
set of elastic reeds, reed comb	Zungenkamm m		

set value; fixed value; constant	Festwert *m*; Konstante *f*
set-value control	Festwertregelung *f*
seven-element lens	Siebenlinser *m*
seven-membered ring, seven ring	Siebenring *m*, Siebenring *m*
S-event, S event	S-Ereignis *n*
severe cold, rigorous cold	strenge Kälte *f*; strenger Frost *m*
sexagesimal minute [of arc], minute [of arc], angular minute, ', min <of angle>	Minute *f* [im Bogenmaß], Winkelminute *f*, Bogenminute *f*, Altminute *f*, ' <Winkelmaß>
sexagesimal second [of arc], second [of arc], angular second, ", sec <of angle>	Sekunde *f* [im Bogenmaß], Winkelsekunde *f*, Bogensekunde *f*, Altsekunde *f*, " <Winkelmaß>
sextant; mirror sextant	Sextant *m*, Spiegelsextant *m*
sextet rearrangement, sextet transposition	Sextettumlagerung *f*
sextic, sextic equation	Gleichung *f* sechsten Grades
sextile	Sextil *m*
sextuplet	Sextuplett *n*
sextupole	Sextupol *m*
sextupole lens	Sextupollinse *f*
Seyfert galaxy, Seyfert-type radiogalaxy	Seyfert-Galaxis *f*, Radiogalaxis *f* vom Seyfert-Typ
sferics	Sferics *m*
sferics	*s. a.* spherics
shade, open shade	Schatten *m*
shade; shading; tinge, tint	Schattierung *f*
shade	*s. a.* tint
shaded by black	*s.* having non-zero black content <of chromatic colour>
shaded by white	*s.* having non-zero white content <of chromatic colour>
shaded to[wards] the red	*s.* degraded to[wards] the red
shaded to[wards] the violet, degraded to[wards] the violet, violet-shaded	violettabschattiert
shade mark, shadow mark	Schattenmarke *f*
shade temperature, temperature in shade, temperature of air, air temperature, shadow temperature	Lufttemperatur *f*, Temperatur *f* im Schatten, Schattentemperatur *f*
shadiness	Schattigkeit *f*
shading; shade; tinge, tint	Schattierung *f*
shading	Beschattung *f*; Schattenspende *f*; Abschattung *f*, Shading *n*
shading, hill shading	Schummerung *f*
shading, degradation <of a band head>	Bandenabschattierung *f*, Abschattierung *f* <Bande>
shading, veiling, masking <of chromatic colours by a portion of white and/or black>	Verhüllung *f* [bunter Farben]
shading by black	*s.* veiling by black
shading by grey	*s.* veiling by grey
shading by white	*s.* veiling by white
shading [-off] of the colours, blending of the colours; running of the colours	Verlaufen *n* der Farben
shading of the specimens, shadowing of the specimens	Objektabschattung *f*
shading value	*s.* tint
shadow, cast shadow	Schlagschatten *m*, Schatten *m*
shadow angle, shadow sector	Schattensektor *m*, Schattenwinkel *f*; Leuchtwinkel *m*
shadow area	*s.* shadow region
shadow bands	fliegende Schatten *mpl*
shadow border, shadow boundary, boundary of shadow	Schattengrenze *f*; Eigenschattengrenze *f*, Lichtgrenze *f*; Schlagschattengrenze *f*
shadow casting	Schrägbedampfung *f*, Schrägaufdampfung *f*; Metallaufdampfung *f*, Metall[schräg]bedampfung *f*
shadow casting	*s. a.* shadow projection
shadow column	Schattenzeiger *m*, Schattenpfeil *m*, Schattenstrich *m*
shadow column instrument	Schattenzeigerinstrument *n*, Schattenzeigermeßgerät *n*
shadow cone	Begrenzungskegel *m*, Schattenkegel *m*
shadow effect, umbra effect	Schatteneffekt *m*
shadow factor	Schattenfaktor *m*
shadow fringe test	*s.* schlieren method
shadow fringe test	*s.* shadow method
shadowgraph, skiagram, sciagram	Röntgenschattenbild *n*
shadowgraph, shadow image	Schattenbild *n*
shadowing, formation of shadows	Schattenbildung *f*
shadowing of the specimens, shading of the specimens	Objektabschattung *f*
shadow mark, shade mark	Schattenmarke *f*
shadow mask, aperture mask, apertured shadow mask, planar mask <tv.>	Lochmaske *f*, Maske *f* der Farbbildröhre <Fs.>
shadow-mask tube, shadow mask tube	Maskenröhre *f*, Masken-Farbbildröhre *f*
shadow method, shadow technique, direct shadow method; shadow fringe test	Schattenverfahren *n*, Schattenmethode *f*, direktes Schattenverfahren
shadow method [in aerodynamics]	Schattenmethode *f* [der Gasdynamik]
shadow microscope	*s.* shadow projection microscope
shadow microscopy, point (shadow) projection microscopy	Schattenmikroskopie *f*, Elektronenschattenmikroskopie *f*
shadow outline projector	*s.* profile projector
shadow photograph	Schattenaufnahme *f*, Schattenphotographie *f*, Schattenbild *n*
shadow photography	Schattenphotographie *f*
shadow photometer	Schattenphotometer *n* [nach Lambert]
shadow projection, shadow casting, projection of shadow	Schattenwurf *m*, Schattenprojektion *f*
shadow projection microscope, point projection [electron] microscope, shadow microscope	Schattenmikroskop *n*, Elektronenschattenmikroskop *n*
shadow projection microscopy, point projection microscopy, shadow microscopy	Schattenmikroskopie *f*, Elektronenschattenmikroskopie *f*
shadow region; shadow area	Schattenbereich *m*, Schattengebiet *n*
shadow region	*s. a.* silent zone
shadow scattering, diffraction scattering	Schattenstreuung *f*, Diffraktionsstreuung *f*, Beugungsstreuung *f*
shadow schlieren method, projecting schlieren method; schlieren scanning technique	Schattenschlierenverfahren *n*, Schattenschlierenmethode *f*

shadow sector, shadow angle	Schattensektor m, Schattenwinkel m; Leuchtwinkel m	Shannon['s] theory	Shannonsche Theorie f, Shannon-Theorie f
shadow shield	Schattenschutz m, Schattenschild m, Partialschild m	shape, form shape, course ‹of the curve›; behaviour, character, response ‹of the quantity›	Form f, Gestalt f Verlauf m ‹Kurve oder Größe›; Gang m ‹Größe›
shadow side, shady side; night side	Nachtseite f; Schattenseite f	shape anisotropy	s. anisotropy of form
shadow synchronoscope	Schattensynchronoskop n	shape elasticity, elasticity in (of) shape, elasticity in (of) shear, elasticity of form, rigidity	Formelastizität f, Spannungselastizität f
shadow technique	s. shadow method	shape factor ‹aero.›	Formparameter m, Formfaktor m ‹Aero.›
shadow temperature	s. shade temperature		
shadow zone	s. silent zone		
shady side	s. shadow side	shape factor, form factor ‹nucl.›	Formfaktor m ‹Kern.›
Shafranov['s] [stability] diagram, stability diagram of Shafranov	Stabilitätsdiagramm n nach Schafranow, Schafranow-Diagramm n	shape factor	s. a. Coddington shape factor
shaft, spindle	Spindel f	shape factor	s. a. stress concentration factor
shaft, shank	Schaft m	shape function	Gestaltsfunktion f, Gestaltfunktion f
shaft gland	s. shaft packing		
shaft horsepower	Wellenleistung f, Wellenpferdestärke f, Wellen-PS fpl	shape function of the line, line shape function	Linienformfunktion f
shaft packing (sealing ring); simmer ring (gasket), shaft gland	Wellendichtung f; Wellendichtring m, Radialdichtring m; Simmerring m	shape number, dimensionless specific speed	dimensionslose Schnellläufigkeitszahl f
		shape of equilibrium, form of equilibrium	Gleichgewichtsfigur f, Gleichgewichtsform f
shake	s. shaking	shape of the crystal	s. habit of the crystal
shake[]down	Wechselverfestigung f	shape of the [spectral] line	s. line profile
shake-off effect	Abschüttel[ungs]effekt m, „shake-off"-Effekt m	shape of the surface, macrogeometrical shape, macroshape	Oberflächengestalt f, makrogeometrische Gestalt f, Makrogestalt f, Oberflächenform f
shake-off transition	s. shaking off transition		
shaking, agitation	Schütteln n	shape parameter	Gestaltsparameter m
shaking, shake, chatter, vibration, percussion	Erschütterung f	shape parameter ‹of boundary layer›	Grenzschichtformparameter m, Formfaktor m ‹Grenzschicht›
shaking, tottering	Wackelschwingung f, Wackeln n	shaper	s. shaping unit
shaking off transition, shake-off transition	„shaking-off"-Übergang m, Übergang m durch „Abschütteln", „Abschüttelungs"übergang m	shape relaxation	Formrelaxation f, Gestaltsrelaxation f
		shaping; profiling	Formgebung f; Formung f; Profilierung f
shaking out, extraction by shaking with solvent	Ausschütteln n		
shallow junction	flachliegender (hochliegender) Übergang m	shaping amplifier, pulse-forming amplifier, signal-shaping amplifier, signal-forming amplifier	impulsformender Verstärker m, signalformender Verstärker
shallow level, high-lying level; shallow state, high-lying state	flaches (flachliegendes) Niveau n, hochliegendes Niveau; flacher (flachliegender) Zustand m, hochliegender Zustand		
		shaping circuit	s. shaping unit
		shaping unit, shaper, pulse shaper; pulse shaping stage; shaping circuit, pulse shaping circuit	Impulsformer m; Impulsformerstufe f; Impulsformerschaltung f
shallow sea	Flachsee f; Schelfsee f, Schelfmeer n, Schelf n; Sublitoral n		
shallow shell	flache Schale f		
shallow state	s. shallow level		
shallow trap	flachliegende Haftstelle f, flachliegender Haftterm (Trap) m, hochliegende (flache) Haftstelle	Shapiro step, Shapiro wave	Shapiro-Stufe f
		sharp adjustment	s. sharp focusing
		sharp corner	scharfe Ecke f
shallow water; shoal water; fleet water, tidal shallow (flat)	Seichtwasser n, seichtes Wasser n, Flachwasser n	sharp cornered potential well, sharp cornered well, potential box	Potentialkasten m, Kastenpotential n, Potentialtopf m mit scharfen Ecken ‹Coulomb- oder Rechteckpotentialtopf›
shallow-water analogy	Flachwasseranalogie f, Seichtwasseranalogie f		
shallow-water approximation, Friedrichs['] shallow-water expansion	Flachwassernäherung f, Seichtwassernäherung f, Friedrichssche Seichtwasserentwicklung f	sharp-crested weir, thin-plate weir	Überfall m mit scharfer Kante, scharfkantiger Überfall; scharfkantiges Wehr n, Wehr mit scharfer Kante
shallow-water channel, flat channel	Flachwasserkanal m, Seichtwasserkanal m	sharp double layer	scharfe Doppelschicht f
shallow-water first-order approximation	Flachwassernäherung (Seichtwassernäherung) f erster Ordnung	sharp-edged wave	s. surge ‹el.›
		sharp-edge orifice meter plate ‹US›, thin-walled orifice plate	dünnwandige Blende f
shallow-water theory	Flachwassertheorie f, Seichtwassertheorie f, Theorie f des seichten Wassers	sharpening, strengthening ‹math.›	Verschärfung f ‹Math.›
		sharpening of minimum ‹el.›	Schärfung f, Enttrübung f ‹El.›
shallow-water tide	Seichtwassertide f		
shallow-water wave, Lagrangian wave, long wave ‹hydr.›	lange Welle f, Seichtwasserwelle f, seichte Welle ‹Hydr.›	sharpening of the crystal; tapering of the crystal	Zuspitzung f des Kristalls, Zuschärfung f des Kristalls
shank, shaft	Schaft m	sharp field, field of sharpness	Schärfenfeld n
Shannon['s] formula	Shannon[-Wiener]sche Formel f, Shannon-Wiener-Formel f, Shannon-Boltzmann-Formel f	sharp focusing, sharp setting (adjustment), focusing adjustment; focusing control ‹opt.›	Scharfeinstellung f, Scharfstellung f, Fokussierung f ‹Opt.›
Shannon['s] [sampling] theorem	Theorem n von Shannon, Shannonsches Theorem, Shannon-Theorem n	sharp-focus lens, high-definition lens	Scharfzeichner m, scharfzeichnendes Objektiv n

sharp image, high-definition image <opt.>	Punktabbildung *f*, punktförmige Abbildung *f*; scharfe Abbildung; scharfes Bild *n* <Opt.>
sharpness, keenness <of the cutting edge>	Schärfe *f* <Schneide>
sharpness	s. a. definition <opt., phot.>
sharpness limit	Schärfenfeldgrenze *f*
sharpness of resonance, resonance sharpness	Resonanzschärfe *f*, Schärfe *f* der Resonanz
sharpness of resonance (tuning)	s. a. resonance sharpness <el.>
sharpness of vision	s. visual acuity
Sharp['s] plate	Sharpsche Auffangfläche *f*, Sharpsche Platte *f*
sharp resonance	scharfe Resonanz *f*, ausgeprägte Resonanz
sharp series	zweite Nebenserie *f*, scharfe Nebenserie
sharp setting	s. sharp focusing
sharp tuning; fine tuning	Feinabstimmung *f*, Scharfabstimmung *f*, scharfe Abstimmung *f*; Feinabgleich *m*
sharp zone, zone of sharpness, definition range	Schärfenbereich *m*, Schärfentiefe[n]bereich *m*
shatter-proof, splinterproof	splitterfrei, nichtsplitternd
shaving	Schaben *n*
sheaf <math.>	Büschel *n* <Math.>
shear, shearing; shear[ing] deformation, shear[ing] strain; shear[ing] action; shear[ing] effect, shearing operation	Scherung *f*; Schub *m*; Schiebung *f*; Gleitung *f*; Scherdeformation *f*, Scherverformung *f*, Schubdeformation *f*, Schubverformung *f*, Schubformänderung *f*, Schubformgebung *f*, Schubumformung *f*; Scherwirkung *f*; Schubwirkung *f*; Abscherung *f*
shear action	s. shear
shear centre, shearing centre, flexural centre	Schubmittelpunkt *m*, Querkraftmittelpunkt *m*
shear cleft <geo.>	Scherkluft *f* <Geo.>
shear coefficient (compliance)	s. coefficient of shear
shear cone	Scherungskegel *m*
shear crack	Scherriß *m*
shear deformation	s. shear
shear diagram	s. shearing force diagram
shear distortion	s. spiral distortion
shear effect	s. shear
shear failure	s. ductile fracture
shear flow, shearing flow	scherende Strömung *f*, Scherungsströmung *f*, Scherströmung *f*, ebene Couette-Strömung *f*
shear flow turbulence	s. shear turbulence
shear force, shearing force, transverse force, bending force, lateral force <mech.>	Scherkraft *f*, Scherungskraft *f*, Querkraft *f*, Schubkraft *f* <Mech.>
shear fracture	s. ductile fracture
shear gradient	Schergefälle *n*
shearing, shearing velocity, rate of shear, shear strain rate	Scherungsgeschwindigkeit *f*, Scherverformungsgeschwindigkeit *f*
shearing	s. a. shear
shearing action	s. shear
shearing area	Scherfläche *f*
shearing centre, shear centre, flexural centre	Schubmittelpunkt *m*, Querkraftmittelpunkt *m*
shearing coefficient	s. coefficient of shear
shearing curve, curve of correction of the hysteresis loop	Scherungskurve *f*, Scherungslinie *f*, Scherungsgerade *f*
shearing deformation	s. shear
shearing effect	s. shear
shearing error	Scherungsfehler *m*
shearing field rheometer	Scherfeldrheometer *n*
shearing field strength	s. shearing strength [of field]
shearing flow	s. shear flow
shearing force	s. shear force
shearing force diagram, shear diagram, transverse force diagram; bending moment diagram	Querkraftdiagramm *n*; Biegemomentdiagramm *n*
shearing impact	Scherstoß *m*
shearing instability, Helmholtz instability	Scherungsinstabilität *f*, Scherungslabilität *f*
shearing intensity	Scherungsstärke *f*
shearing interference [type] microscope	Polarisationsmikroskop *n* mit Franconschem Interferenzokular
shearing interferometer, wavefront shearing interferometer	Überschneidungsinterferometer *n*, Shearinginterferometer *n*
shearing interferometer of Drew, Drew interferometer	Interferometer *n* nach Drew, Drew-Interferometer *n*
shearing load, shear load	Scherbelastung *f*; Schublast *f*
shearing method, correction of the hysteresis loop	Scherungsmethode *f*
shearing method	s. a. shearing technique <opt.>
shearing modulus [of elasticity]	s. shear modulus
shearing moment	Schermoment *n*
shearing operation	s. shear
shearing plane, slip plane, plane of slip, glide plane <cryst.>	Gleitebene *f*, Translationsebene *f* <Krist.>
shearing resistance	s. shear strength
shearing rigidity	Schubsteifigkeit *f*
shearing strain	s. shear strain
shearing strength	s. shear strength
shearing strength [of field], shearing field strength	Scherungsfeldstärke *f*
shearing stress	s. shear stress
shearing stress curve (line)	s. shear line
shearing technique, wavefront shearing technique, shearing method <opt.>	Verdopplungsverfahren *n*, Shearingverfahren *n* <Opt.>
shearing velocity	s. shearing
shear lag	Scherverzögerung *f*
shear layer	s. boundary layer <hydr.>
shear line, shear stress line, shearing stress line (curve), line of maximum shearing stress	Scherlinie *f*, Scherungsgrenze *f*, Schubspannungslinie *f*, Hauptschublinie *f*, Schublinie *f*, Querkraftlinie *f*
shear load	s. shearing load
shear mode; shear vibration	Scherschwingung *f*, Scherungsschwingung *f*, Scherungsmode *f*, Scherschwingungstyp *m*
shear modulus, elastic shear modulus, modulus of elasticity in shear, coefficient of elasticity in shear, shearing modulus [of elasticity], modulus of rigidity, rigidity modulus, rigidity, constant of Coulomb, modulus of torsion, torsion[al] modulus, torsional rigidity per unit length	Schubmodul *m*, zweiter Elastizitätsmodul *m*, zweite Elastizitätskonstante *f*, Elastizitätsmodul bei Schub, Schubelastizitätsmodul *m*, elastischer Schubmodul, Gleitmodul *m*, Gleitmaß *n*, Gleitzahl *f*, Scherungsmodul *m*, Schermodul *m*, Schiebungsmodul *m*, Elastizitätsmodul *m* der Torsion, Torsionsmodul *m*, Torsionskoeffizient *m*, Drillungsmodul *m*, Drillungsmaß *n*, Starrheitsmodul *m*, Starrheitskoeffizient *m*, Righeitskoeffizient *m*, Righeit *f*

shear of the magnetic field, magnetic shearing	Scherung f [des Magnetfelds], magnetische Scherung, Scherung der Magnetisierungskurve, Magnetfeldscherung f, Verscherung f des Magnetfeldes	sheath, jacket ⟨techn.⟩	Mantel m ⟨Techn.⟩
		sheathed electrode	Mantelelektrode f
		sheathed pyrometer	s. pyrometric rod
		sheath loss, cable-sheath loss	Mantelverlust m
shear of the warm front	Warmfrontscherung f	sheath model	Scheidenmodell n
shear plane, plane of shear	Scherebene f, Ebene f der Scherung	sheath of solvent molecules	s. solvation sheath
shear profile	Scherprofil n	shed ⟨= 10^{-24} b⟩	Shed n, shed ⟨= 10^{-24} barn⟩
shear resistance	s. shear strength	shedding ⟨of vortices⟩	s. separation ⟨e.g. of flow etc.⟩
shear stiffness	Scherungssteifigkeit f	Shedlovsky electrode	Shedlovsky-Elektrode f, Chlor-Silber-Elektrode f
shear strain, shearing strain, amount of shear ⟨tangent of shear angle⟩	Schubverformung f, Schiebung f ⟨Tangens der Winkeländerung⟩	sheet, nappe ⟨of the surface⟩ ⟨math.⟩	Schale f ⟨Fläche⟩, Flächenschale f, Fläche f ⟨Math.⟩
shear strain, shearing strain	Scherbeanspruchung f, Schubbeanspruchung f	sheet	= two-dimensional vein
		sheet antenna, flat-top antenna, plane antenna	Flächenantenne f
shear strain	s. a. angle of shear		
shear strain	s. a. shear	sheet boiling, film boiling	Filmverdampfung f, Filmsieden n
shear strain energy	s. strain energy due to the distortion		
shear strain rate	s. shearing	sheet discharge	s. sheet lightning
shear strain tensor	Scherungsanteil m des Deformationstensors, Scherdeformationstensor m	sheet erosion, unconcentrated wash	Flächenspülung f; Abspülung f
shear strength, shearing strength, shearing resistance, transverse strength, transverse resistance, resistance to shear[ing], shear resistance	Schubfestigkeit f, Scherfestigkeit f, Abscherfestigkeit f, Abscherungsfestigkeit f, Bruchschubspannung f; Scherwiderstand m, Schubwiderstand m	sheeting	s. sheet structure
		sheet ligthning; sheet discharge	Flächenblitz m; Flächenentladung f
		sheet lightning, summer lightning, heat lightning	Wetterleuchten n
		sheet of charge; layer of charge	Ladungsschicht f
		sheet of glass	s. optical flat
		sheet resistance [of films], film resistance	Schichtwiderstand m
shear stress, shearing stress, tangential stress	Schubspannung f, Scherspannung f, Scherungsspannung f; Schubspannungszustand m	sheet structure, sheeting	Schichtstruktur f
		shelf, continental shelf	Schelf m, Kontinentalsockel m, neritischer Bereich m
		shelf ice	Schelfeis n
		shell ⟨nucl.⟩	Schale f; Hülle f ⟨Kern.⟩
shear stress line	s. shear line	shell, thin shell (slab) ⟨in theory of elasticity⟩	Schale f, krumme Platte f ⟨Elastizitätstheorie⟩
shear surface	Scherfläche f	shell electrode	Schalenelektrode f
shear transfer	Scherungsübertragung f		
shear[-type] transformation	s. diffusionless transformation	shell electron	Schalenelektron n
shear turbulence, shear flow turbulence	Scherungsturbulenz f		
		shell model [of nucleus], nuclear shell model, Hartree-Fock model [of nucleus], quasiatomic model	Schalenmodell n [des Kerns], Kernschalenmodell n, Haxel-Jensen-Süß-Modell n; Potentialtopfmodell n [des Atomkerns]
shear vibration; shear mode	Scherschwingung f, Scherungsschwingung f; Scherungsmode f, Scherschwingungstyp m		
shear viscosity	Schubviskosität f, Scherungsviskosität f, Scherviskosität f, Scherungszähigkeit f, Scherungsreibung f, Scherreibung f	shell of comet, coma of comet	Koma f des Kometen, Kernhülle f, Hülle f des Kometenkerns
		shell of electrons	s. atomic electron shell
		shell of revolution	Umdrehungsschale f
shear viscosity coefficient	s. coefficient of viscosity	shell-source model	Schalenquellenmodell n
shear wave, S wave, equivoluminal (distortional, rotational) wave ⟨elasticity⟩	Scherungswelle f, Scherwelle f, Schubwelle f, S-Welle f ⟨Elastizität⟩	shell star, star with extended atmosphere, star with extended envelope	Hüllenstern m, Stern m mit ausgedehnter Gashülle
		shell structure of nucleus, nuclear shell structure	Schalenstruktur f des Atomkerns (Kerns), Schalenbau m des Atomkerns (Kerns), Kernschalenstruktur f
shear wave	s. a. Helmholtz['] wave		
shear wave	s. a. transverse wave ⟨geo.⟩		
sheath; coating, coat, surface coat; covering, coverage; layer ⟨gen.⟩	Überzug m, Schicht f, Überzugsschicht f; Beschichtung f; Belag m; Bedeckung f ⟨allg.⟩	shell theory, theory of shells	Schalentheorie f
		shell-type core	Schalenkern m
sheath ⟨in gaseous discharge⟩	Raumladungsschicht f, Raumladungsgebiet n, Schicht f ⟨in der Gasentladung⟩	shell-type core	Mantelkern m

shell-type magnet, encased magnet, boxed (pot) magnet — Mantelmagnet *m*
shell vacancy, vacancy in the shell, empty place in the shell — Leerstelle *f* in der Schale
shelly texture — Schalentextur *f*
shelly weathering — Schalenverwitterung *f*, schalige Verwitterung *f*
shelter — s. instrument screen
Shepart tube — s. klystron
Sheppard['s] correction — Sheppardsche Korrektion *f*
sherardizing — Sherardisierung *f*

Shercliff layer, Shercliff-Schicht *f*
Sherwood No., Sherwood number, *Sh* — Sherwood-Zahl *f*, Sherwoodsche Kennzahl *f*, Sherwoodsche Zahl *f*, *Sh*
S.H.F. — s. superhigh frequency
Shida number — Shida-Zahl *f*
shield; protective shield (screen); shielding — Abschirmung *f*, Schild *m*, Schutzschirm *m*, Schirm *m*
shield ‹geo.› — Schild *m* ‹Geo.›
shielded ‹of instrument› — abgeschirmt, gepanzert, Panzer- ‹Gerät›

shielded actinometer, Linke-Feussner actinometer, panzeractinometer — Panzeraktinometer *n* [nach Linke und Feußner], Linke-Feußner-Aktinometer *n*
shielded box — s. flask
shielded electrode — s. shield electrode
shielded galvanometer, iron-clad galvanometer — Panzergalvanometer *n*

shielded nuclide — abgeschirmtes Nuklid *n*
shielded potential — abgeschirmtes Potential *n*

shield electrode; shielded electrode — Schirmelektrode *f*
shield factor — s. screening factor ‹el.›
shielding ‹e.g. of cable› — Panzerung *f* ‹z. B. Kabel›

shielding — s. a. shield
shielding [action] — s. screening action
shielding castle — Abschirmkammer *f*
shielding factor, screen factor ‹el.› — Schirmfaktor *m* ‹El.›
shielding factor ‹of the screen grid›, reciprocal of screen grid amplification ‹el.› — Schirmgitterdurchgriff *m* ‹El.›
shielding material, shield material — Abschirmmaterial *n*, Abschirmwerkstoff *m*

shielding window — s. shield window
shield opening, channel through the shielding — Kanal *m* durch die Abschirmung

shield volcano — Schildvulkan *m*

shield window, shielding window — Schutzfenster *n*
shift, shifting, offset, misalignment — Versetzung *f*, Verschiebung *f*, Versatz *m*
shift, displacement ‹geo.› — Verschiebung *f* ‹Geo.›
shift — s. a. shifting ‹gen.›
shift angle, displacement angle — Verschiebungswinkel *m*
shift defect — Verschiebungsdefekt *m*, Verschiebungsfehler *m*
shift diagram — Verschiebungsdiagramm *n*

shifter, shift unit ‹num. math.› — Verschiebeeinrichtung *f* ‹num. Math.›

shift factor — Verschiebungsfaktor *m*, Kosinus *m* des Verschiebungswinkels, cos φ *m*

shifting, displacement, shift, removal ‹gen.› — Verschiebung *f*, Verlagerung *f* ‹allg.›
shifting — s. a. shift
shifting gauge, surface gauge, marking gauge — Höhenreißer *m*, Reißmaß *n*, Streichmaß *n*, Parallelmaß *n*, Parallelreißer *m*

shifting of Bloch wall — s. boundary movement
shifting of the pole — s. polar motion
shifting of wind [to] — s. veering of wind [to]
shifting operation — Verschiebeoperation *f*
shifting theorem [of Laplace transform] — s. time-shift theorem
shifting wind; variable wind; baffling wind — veränderlicher Wind *m*, umlaufender Wind; unbeständiger Wind; umspringender Wind

shift matrix — Verschiebematrix *f*
shift of spectral line — s. line shift
shift structure — Verwerfungsstruktur *f*

shift surface, displacement surface — Verschiebungsfläche *f*
shift unit — s. shifter
shim — Shim[stück *n*] *m* ‹Blech, Draht od. ä.›; Einlegeblech *n*

shimmer — s. gleam
shimming — Einlegen *n* dünner Bleche zur Feldkorrektion, Verwendung *f* von Shims, Feldfeinkorrektion *f*, Feldkorrektion *f* durch Shims
shimming — s. a. coarse control
shim rod — s. coarse control rod
shim[-]safety rod — Trimmabschaltstab *m*

ship hull, hull of the ship — Schiffskörper *m*, Schiffsrumpf *m*, Körper (Rumpf) *m* des Schiffes
ship magnetic field, magnetic field of the ship — Schiffsfeld *n*
ship magnetism — Schiffsmagnetismus *m*
ship oscillation, ship vibration — Schiffsschwingung *f*
shipping container — s. transfer container
ship vibration, ship oscillation
ship wave — Schiffswelle *f*, Welle *f* vom Machschen Typ, Machsche Welle

shoal[s]; bank ‹geo.› — Untiefe *f*; Bank *f*; Watt *n*; Wattenmeer *n* ‹Geo.›
shoal water — s. shallow water
shock; impact; percussion; stroke; blow; push; shove, impulse — Schlag *m*, Stoß *m*, Anstoß *m*
shock, bound, bounce, impact, knock-on, impingement, impinging — Aufschlag *m*, Aufprall *m*, Anprall *m*, Prall *m*
shock; collision; impact; encounter; impinging — Stoß *m*; Zusammenstoß *m*; Kollision *f*; Zusammenprall *m*
shock, compression shock, pressure shock — Verdichtungsstoß *m*
shock, shock front, shock surface, pressure front — Stoßfront *f*, Stoßwellenfront *f*
shock, earthquake shock ‹geo.›, earth tremor — Erdstoß *m*, Bodenstoß *m* ‹Geo.›

shock / without — s. shock-free
shock absorption ‹mech.› — Stoßdämpfung *f* ‹Mech.›

shock adiabatic line — Stoßadiabate *f*
shock angle; angle of impact — Stoßwinkel *m*
shock coefficient — s. restitution coefficient
shock condition — Stoßbedingung *f*
shock condition, condition for shock waves — Stoßwellenbedingung *f*
shock curvature, shock wave curvature — Stoßfrontkrümmung *f*
shock diffuser — Stoßdiffusor *m*, Stoßwellendiffusor *m*
shock equation — Stoßwellengleichung *f*, Stoßgleichung *f*
shock excitation, impact excitation, repulse (impulse, pulse) excitation ‹of oscillation› — Stoßanregung *f*, Stoßerregung *f* ‹Schwingung›
shock expansion — Stoßentwicklung *f*
shock-free, collisionless, without collision, without shock — stoßfrei
shock-free entry — stoßfreier Eintritt *m*

shock frequency	s. collision frequency	shoot, rapids, rapid, chute <of river>	Stromschnelle f, Katarakt m, Gefällssteile f <Fluß>
shock front, shock surface, shock, pressure front	Stoßfront f, Stoßwellenfront f	shooting	s. seismic prospecting
shock front thickness, thickness of shock layer	Stoßfronttiefe f	shooting	s. taking <phot.>
		shooting angle	Aufnahmewinkel m
		shooting flame, explosive flame, jet [of] flame, narrow (tongue, thin, pointed jet, fine pointed) flame	Stichflamme f
shock-hazard protection, contact protection, protection against shock hazard <el.>	Berührungsschutz m		
shock layer	Stoßfrontschicht f, Stoßschicht f	shooting flow, fast flow, super-critical flow, superundal flow, rapid flow <hydr.>	Schießen n [der Strömung], schießende Strömung f, schießende Bewegungsart f, reißende Strömung f <Hydr.>
Shockley barrier [layer], Shockley-type barrier layer	Shockleysche Randschicht f		
Shockley diode	s. four-layer diode	shooting for fast motion effect	s. stop-motion camera shooting
Shockley dislocation	s. Shockley['s] partial dislocation	shooting for high-speed (slow-motion) effect	s. high-speed camera shooting
Shockley['s] equation, Shockley-type barrier layer equation	Shockleysche Randschichtgleichung f	shooting star, falling star	Sternschnuppe f
Shockley['s] partial dislocation, Shockley dislocation, Shockley-type dislocation	Shockleysche (gleitfähige) unvollständige Versetzung f, Shockley-Versetzung f	shop microscope	Werkstattmeßmikroskop n
		Shoran, shoran, shortrange navigation system, short-range navigation radar	Shoran n, Shoran-Verfahren n, Shoran-System n, Kurzstrecken-Navigationsradar n
Shockley-Road type generation-recombination noise source	Generation-Rekombination-Rauschquelle f vom Shockley-Read-Typ		
Shockley-type barrier layer	s. Shockley barrier [layer]	shore	Seeufer n, Ufer n <See>
Shockley-type barrier layer equation	s. Shockley['s] equation	shore, beach, sea[-]shore, strand	Strand m
Shockley-type dislocation	s. Shockley['s] partial dislocation	shore	s. a. support <mech.>
		shore development	Umfangsentwicklung f, Uferentwicklung f
shock limitation	Stoßbegrenzung f	Shore hardness [number], Shore scleroscope hardness, scleroscope hardness	Shore-Härte f, Shoresche Härte f
shock line, line of shock	Stoßlinie f		
shock load	s. impact load		
shock Mach number	Stoß-Mach-Zahl f		
shock momentum	s. momentum of the impact		
		Shore hardness test[ing]	Shore-Härteprüfung f, Kugeldruck-Härteprüfung f nach Shore
shock normal, impact normal	Stoßnormale f		
shock of rarefaction, rarefaction shock, rarefactional shock, dilatational shock	Verdünnungsstoß m	shoreline, shore line, coastline	Küstenlinie f
		shore migration, beach migration	Küstenversetzung f, Strand-Härteprüfgerät n; [Shoresches] Skleroskop n
shock polar	Stoßpolare f		
shock polaric diagram, shock polars['] diagram	Stoßpolarendiagramm n	Shore scleroscope, scleroscope	Shore-Härteprüfer m, Shore-Härteprüfgerät n; [Shoresches] Skleroskop n
shock potential	Stoßpotential n		
shock pressure	s. impact pressure	Shore scleroscope hardness, Shore hardness [number], scleroscope hardness	Shore-Härte f, Shoresche Härte f
shockproof	s. shockresistant		
shock propagation	Stoßausbreitung f		
shock relation, shock wave relation	Stoßwellenrelation f		
shock resistance	s. impact strength	shore terrace, face terrace, abrasive platform	Abrasionsplatte f, Strandplatte f, Strandterrasse f; Uferterrasse f
shock-resistant, shockproof; rugged, ruggedized	stoßfest		
		short, short-circuit, short out	kurzschließen
shock stability	s. impact strength	short-base radiogoniometer	Kleinbasispeiler m, Kurzbasispeiler m
shock stall[ing], compressibility stall	Abreißen n hinter dem Verdichtungsstoß, Verdichtungsstoßabreißen n, Stoßabreißen n		
		short-circuit, short out, short	kurzschließen
shock strength, collision strength	Stoßstärke f; Stoßleistung f	short-circuit arc	Kurzschlußlichtbogen m
shock strength	s. a. impact strength		
shock stress	s. impact load	short-circuit conductance, free conductance	Kurzschlußleitwert m
shock surface, shock front, shock pressure front	Stoßfront f, Stoßwellenfront f		
shock therapeutics, shock therapy	Schockbehandlung f, Schocktherapie f	short-circuit current <of the current source> <el.>	Einströmung f, Urstrom m, eingeprägter Strom m, Kurzschlußstrom m <der Stromquelle> <El.>
shock transfer, impact transfer	Stoßübertragung f		
shock tube, shock-tube; shock tunnel, shock-tunnel <aero.>	Stoßwellenrohr n; Stoßrohr n <Aero.>	short-circuit current density	Kurzschlußstromdichte f
		short-circuit current gain	Kurzschluß-Stromverstärkungsfaktor m, Kurzschlußstromverstärkung f
shock wave, impact wave, blast	Stoßwelle f, Schockwelle f, Verdichtungsstoß m		
shock wave curvature, shock curvature	Stoßfrontkrümmung f	short-circuit current to earth (ground), loss current to earth (ground)	Erdschlußstrom m
shock-wave heating	Stoßheizung f, Stoßwellenheizung f		
		short circuiter	Kurzschließer m
shock wave luminescence	Verdichtungsstoßleuchten n, Stoßwellenleuchten n		
		short-circuit force	Kurzschlußkraft f
shock wave relation, shock relation	Stoßwellenrelation f		

short-circuit impedance, free impedance	Kürzschlußimpedanz f, elektrische Kurzschluß-impedanz; Kurzschluß-widerstand m	shortness; brittleness; breakability; fragility; friability; crackiness; rottenness <of steel>	Sprödigkeit f, Brüchigkeit f, Zerbrechlichkeit f
short-circuiting bridge	Kurzschlußbrücke f	short out	s. short-circuit
short-circuiting plunger	s. shorting plunger <el.>	short-path distillation, molecular distillation, projective distillation	Molekulardestillation f, Kurzwegdestillation f, Freiwegdestillation f, Hochvakuumdestillation f
short-circuit input resistance	Kurzschluß-Eingangswiderstand m		
short-circuit output admittance	Kurzschluß-Ausgangsleitwert m	short-path principle, Hittorf['s] principle	Hittorfsches Prinzip n
		short-period activity	s. short-lived activity
		short-period Cepheid	s. RR Lyrae star
		short-period comet	kurzperiodischer Komet m
short-circuit output conductance	Kurzschluß-Ausgangs-[wirk]leitwert m, Ausgangskurzschluß[wirk]-leitwert m	short-period perturbation	kurzperiodische Störung f
		short-period term, term of short period	kurzperiodischer Term m, kurzperiodisches Glied n
short-circuit ratio	Stoßkurzschlußverhältnis n, Leerlauf-Kurzschlußverhältnis n	short-period variable [star]	kurzperiodischer Veränderlicher m
short-circuit strength	Kurzschlußfestigkeit f	short-range	kurzreichweitig, [von] geringer Reichweite, Nahwirkungs-, Nahewirkungs-, nahwirkend, nahewirkend
short-circuit to earth, short to earth, contact to earth, ground leak, accidental ground	Erdschluß m		
		short-range disorder	Nahunordnung f
short-circuit transconductance	s. transconductance	short-range exchange force	nahewirkende (nahwirkende) Austauschkraft f, Austauschkraft geringer Reichweite
short-circuit transfer admittance	s. transfer admittance		
short-circuit transfer current ratio	Kurzschluß-Stromübertragungsfaktor m rückwärts	short-range fading	Nahschwund m
		short-range field <phot.>	Nahfeld n <Phot.>
short-circuit voltage	Kurzschlußspannung f	short-range focusing, near-zone focusing	Nahfeldeinstellung f
short-crested wave, short-crested wavelet	kurzkämmige Welle f, Welle mit kurzem Kamm	short-range force	Nahwirkungskraft f, Nahewirkungskraft f, nahewirkende Kraft f, kurzreichweitige Kraft
short cut test, short test, rapid test <stat.>	Kurztest m <Stat.>		
short-day plant	Kurztagpflanze f		
short-distance irradiation	Nahbestrahlung f	short-range forecast, short-term forecast (prediction)	kurzfristige Vorhersage f
short-distance receiving (reception)	Nahempfang m		
short-distance scatter[ing]	Nahstreuung f	short-range interaction	kurzreichweitige Wechselwirkung f
short-duration, short-time, short-term	Kurzzeit-, kurzzeitig	short-range navigation radar (system)	s. Shoran
shortening	s. shrinkage	short-range order	Nahordnung f
shortening	s. a. contraction		
shortening capacitor	Verkürzungskondensator m		
		short-range order[ing] parameter	Nahordnungsparameter m
		short-range order theory	Nahordnungstheorie f
shortest [most selective] confidence interval	kürzestes (engstes) Konfidenzintervall n	short-sightedness	s. myopia
		short-sighted person, myope	Kurzsichtige m, Myop m
short focal length lens, short-focus lens	Kurzfokuslinse f, kurzbrennweitige Linse f, Linse kleiner Brennweite	short-stop	s. stop bath
		short-stop bath	s. stop bath
		Shortt clock	Shortt-Uhr f
short-focus magnetic lens	magnetische Kurzlinse f, magnetische Kurzfokuslinse f	short-term, short-time, short-duration	Kurzzeit-, kurzzeitig
		short-term forecast (prediction)	s. short-range forecast
short-half-life activity	s. short-lived activity	short test	s. short cut test <stat.>
short-grained	s. fine-grain	short-time, short-duration, short-term	Kurzzeit-, kurzzeitig
shorting, shorting out	Kurzschließen n		
shorting plunger, short-circuiting (choke) plunger, plunger, non-contact (choke) piston, piston <el.>	Kurzschlußschieber m; Kurzschlußkolben m <El.>	short time behaviour	Kurzzeitverhalten n
		short-time creep strength, short-time strength	Kurzzeitfestigkeit f
shorting time	Kurzschlußzeit f	short-time creep test, short-time test	Kurzzeitversuch m, Kurzzeitstandversuch m
short irradiation	s. short-time exposure		
short lens spectrometer	Spektrometer n mit kurzen Linsen, Kurzlinsenspektrometer n	short-time current	Kurzzeitstrom m, thermische Stromfestigkeit f
		short-time exposure, short[-time] irradiation	Kurzzeitbestrahlung f, Kurzbestrahlung f
short life	Kurzlebigkeit f		
		short-time-interval measurement, short-time measurement	Kurzzeitmessung f
short-lived activity, short-period (short-half-life) activity	kurzlebige Aktivität f		
		short-time-interval meter; microchronometer	Kurzzeitmesser m
short measure, undersize	Untermaß n		
short-mouth[ed]	s. short-neck[ed]	short-time-interval technique, technique of short-time measurement	Kurzzeittechnik f, Kurzzeitmeßtechnik f
short-neck[ed], short-mouth[ed]	Kurzhals-, kurzhalsig		

short-time irradiation	s. short-time exposure	shower unit	Schauerlänge f, Schauereinheit f <Strahlungslänge × ln 2>
short-time measurement, short-time-interval measurement	Kurzzeitmessung f	show ion	s. large ion
		show-release (show-releasing) relay	s. time-delay relay
short-time operation, temporary operation, temporary service	Kurzzeitbetrieb m	Shpolsky effect	Schpolski-Effekt m
		shredding	Zerfaserung f
short time[-]scale	kurze Zeitskala f, kurze Skala f		
short-time strength, short-time creep strength	Kurzzeitfestigkeit f	shreds, emulsion shreds	Nudeln fpl <Emulsion>
		shrinkage, shrinking; contraction; shortening; retreat	Schrumpfung f; Schwindung f, Schwinden n, Schwund m
short-time test, short-time creep test	Kurzzeitversuch m, Kurzzeitstandversuch m		
short to earth	s. short-circuit to earth		
short wave	Kurzwelle f, kurze Welle f, Dekameterwelle f, KW		
		shrinkage	s. a. shrinking
short-wave band	Kurzwellenband n	shrinkage cavity	Lunker m, Schwindungslunker m, Schwindungshohlraum m
short-wavelength radiation, short-wave radiation	kurzwellige Strahlung f, Kurzwellenstrahlung f	shrinkage fault, shrinkage hole, shrink hole, pockhole, blister, sinkhole	
short wave region	s. short waves	shrinkage crack, contraction crack, casting crack	Schrumpfriß m, Schwindriß m, Schwindungsriß m
short waves, short wave region, S.W., s-w, sw, s/w	Kurzwellenbereich m, Kurzwelle f, KW		
		shrinkage factor	Schrumpfungsfaktor m, Schrumpffaktor m, Schwindungszahl f, Schwindungskoeffizient m
short-wave spectroscopy	Kurzwellenspektroskopie f		
shot current, shot noise current	Schrotstrom m		
		shrinkage fault (hole)	s. shrinkage cavity
		shrinkage of cell	Zusammenschrumpfung f der Zelle
shot effect, shot noise, schroteffekt, schrot-effect, schrot noise, Schottky effect (noise), noise effect	Schroteffekt m, Schrotrauschen n, Schottky-Effekt m, Rauscheffekt m, Schottky-Rauschen n	shrinkage of the film, film shrinkage	Filmschrumpfung f, Schrumpfung f des Films
		shrinkage of volume	s. volume shrinkage
		shrinkage porosity	Schwindungsporosität f, Sekundärlunker m
shot firing, firing	Zündung f der Sprengladung	shrinkage pressure, contraction pressure, pressure due to shrinkage	Schrumpfdruck m
shot noise	s. shot effect	shrinkage rule	Schwindmaßstab m
shot noise current	s. shot current	shrinkage stress, retraction stress, cooling stress, stress due to shrinkage	Schrumpfspannung f, Schwindungsspannung f
shot noise power	Schrotrauschleistung f		
shot-noise reduction factor <of the diode>	Schwächungsfaktor m <Diode>	shrink hole	s. shrinkage cavity
		shrinking, contraction	Kontraktion f, Zusammenziehung f
shot point	Schußpunkt m, Schußstelle f		
		shrinking, shrinkage	flüssiges Schwinden n, Lunkerbildung f, Lunkerung f
shoulder <of wedge>	Kante f <Keil>		
shoulder [of the characteristic curve], region of overexposure <phot., opt.>	Schulter f [der Schwärzungskurve], Gebiet n der Überexposition, Gebiet n maximaler Schwärzung <Phot., Opt.>	shrinking, dehydration	Entquellung f
		shrinking	s. a. shrinkage
		Shubnikov-de Haas effect, de Haas-Shubnikov effect	Schubnikow-de-Haas-Effekt m, De-Haas-Schubnikow-Effekt m
shove; impact; shock; percussion; stroke; blow; push, impulse	Schlag m, Stoß m, Anstoß m	Shubnikov group	s. magnetic space group
		shuffling, rearrangement <math.>	Umordnung f <Math.>
shove, ice push <geo.>	Eisversetzung f, Eisruck m <Geo.>	shunt, shunt circuit, bypass; branch circuit, branch <el.>	Nebenschluß m, Shunt m; Nebenweg m; Nebenschlußkreis m, Nebenschlußstromkreis m, Teilstromkreis m, Stromzweig m, Zweigstromkreis m, Stromabzweigung f <El.>
shove fault, epiparaclase, thrust <geo.>	Überschiebung f <Geo.>		
shower, cosmic-ray shower, shower of cosmic radiation, shower of particles	Schauer m [der kosmischen Strahlung], kosmischer Schauer, Teilchenschauer m		
		shunt	s. a. shunt resistance
		shunt arm; shunt section; shunt leg	Querglied n; Querzweig m
shower activity, stream activity	Stromtätigkeit f		
shower angle	Schauerwinkel m		
		shunt-arm capacitance	s. parallel capacitance
		shunt branching ratio <el.>	Verzweigungsverhältnis n <El.>
shower branch, stream branch, branch of the stream, branch of the shower <astr.>	Zweig m des Meteorstromes, Stromzweig m <Astr.>	shunt capacitance	s. parallel capacitance
		shunt capacitor	s. parallel capacitor
		shunt characteristic	Nebenschlußcharakteristik f, Nebenschlußverhalten n
shower core, core of the shower	Schauerkern m		
shower fringe	Schauerstreifen m, Schauerband n	shunt circuit, shunt path, voltage circuit, volt circuit, voltage path <el.>	Spannungspfad m, Spannungskreis m <El.>
shower meteor	Strommeteor n		
		shunt circuit	s. a. shunt <el.>
shower of cosmic radiation, shower of particles, cosmic-ray shower, shower	Schauer m [der kosmischen Strahlung], kosmischer Schauer, Teilchenschauer m	shunt connection	s. parallel connection
		shunt current; cross current, transverse current <el.>	Querstrom m, Nebenschlußstrom m, Zweigstrom m <El.>
shower radiant, radiant of meteor shower	Stromradiant m	shunt current	s. a. branch current <el.>

shunt | | | **766**

shunt generator	s. shunt-wound generator	shutting, closing, closure; stopping down <of diaphragm>	Schließen n
shunt impedance; parallel [resonant] impedance	Querimpedanz f; Nebenschlußimpedanz f, Shuntimpedanz f, Parallelimpedanz f, Parallelscheinwiderstand m	shutting movement [of guard cells]	Schließbewegung f [der Schließzellen]
		shutting pressure, closing pressure	Schließdruck m, Schließungsdruck m
shunt inductance	s. cross inductance		
shunting	Shunten n, Nebenschlußschaltung f, Nebenschaltung f, Nebenschlußbildung f, Nebenschluß m; Überbrückung f	shuttle, rabbit	Rohrpostbüchse f, Bestrahlungskapsel f
		sial	Sial n, Sal n, Granitschale f
		sialic	sialisch
shunting capacitor	s. parallel capacitor	siallitic weathering	tonige Verwitterung f, siallitische Verwitterung
shunt leg	s. shunt arm		
shunt machine, shunt-wound machine	Nebenschlußmaschine f, Gleichstrom-Nebenschlußmaschine f	sialma	Sialma n
		siccative	s. dehydrator
		sideband <el.>	Seitenband n <El.>
shunt motor	s. shunt-wound motor	sideband	s. a. additional band <spectr.>
shunt path	s. shunt circuit <el.>	sideband filter	s. vestigial[-] sideband filter
shunt reactance	Querreaktanz f	sideband interference, sideband splash, monkey chatter [interference]	Seitenbandstörung f, Seitenbandinterferenz f
		sideband spectrum	Seitenbandspektrum n
shunt resistance, shunt, bridging (parallel, leak) resistance	Nebenwiderstand m, Nebenschlußwiderstand m, Nebenschluß m, Parallelwiderstand m, Abzweigwiderstand m, Shuntwiderstand m; Überbrückungswiderstand m; Shunt m; Wehr n	sideband splash	s. sideband interference
		sideband width	Seitenbandbreite f
		side bottoms; side fraction; side-cut distillate	Seitenfraktion f
		side chain, lateral chain	Seitenkette f
shunt resistance (resistor), cross resistance; shunt (cross) resistor	Querwiderstand m	side circuit, real circuit, physical circuit, physical line	Stammleitung f
shunt section	s. shunt arm	side circuit loading coil	Stamm-Pupin-Spule f, Stammspule f
shunt transformer, voltage transformer, potential transformer	Spannungswandler m, Spannungsumsetzer m	side-curtain fader	Kulissenblende f
		side-cut distillate; side fraction; side bottoms	Seitenfraktion f
shunt-wound generator, shunt generator	Nebenschlußgenerator m, Gleichstrom-Nebenschlußgenerator m, Nebenschlußdynamo m	side draw	Seitenzug m
		side echo, side[-] lobe echo	Seitenzipfelecho n, Nebenzipfelecho n, Seitenecho n
shunt-wound machine, shunt machine	Nebenschlußmaschine f, Gleichstrom-Nebenschlußmaschine f	side fraction; side-cut distillate; side bottoms	Seitenfraktion f
		side group	Seitengruppe f
		side-inverted	s. reversed right to left
		sidelight	Seitenlicht n
shunt-wound motor, shunt motor	Nebenschlußmotor m, Gleichstrom-Nebenschlußmotor m	side lobe, minor lobe, rear lobe	Seitenzipfel m, Seitenlappen m, Nebenzipfel m, Nebenkeule f, Nebenlappen m
shut-down	Anhalten n; Abschaltung f; Abstellen n; Außerbetriebsetzung f; Schließung f; Stillsetzung f; Stillegung f	side[-] lobe attenuation	s. side[-] lobe suppression
		side[-] lobe echo, side echo	Seitenzipfelecho n, Nebenzipfelecho n, Seitenecho n
shut down delay, scram delay <of reactor>	Abschaltverzögerung f <Reaktor>	side[-] lobe radiation, fringe radiation	Zusatzstrahlung f
shut-down heat	s. after-heat <of reactor>	side[-] lobe suppression, side[-]lobe attenuation	Seitenzipfelunterdrückung f, Seitenzipfeldämpfung f, Nebenzipfeldämpfung f
shut-down of the reactor, reactor shut-down	Abschaltung (Außerbetriebsetzung, Stillsetzung) f des Reaktors		
shut-down period	s. shut-down time		
shut-down reactivity	Abschaltreaktivität f	side-on observation	Beobachtung f senkrecht zur Achsenrichtung
shut-down time, shut-down period	Abschaltzeit f		
shut-down time	s. a. down time	side pressure	s. lateral pressure
shutoff cock	s. stopcock	side reaction, by-reaction; parallel reaction	Nebenreaktion f; Parallelreaktion f
shutter; diaphragm; stop; blind; septum <opt.>	Blende f, Diaphragma n <Opt.>	sidereal clock	Sternzeituhr f
shutter, photographic shutter <phot.>	Verschluß m, photographischer Verschluß <Phot.>	sidereal day	Sterntag m, siderischer Tag m, Sternentag m
shutter <phot.>	Verschlußblende f <Phot.>	sidereal hour	Sternstunde f, siderische Stunde f, Sternenstunde f
shutter efficiency	Verschlußwirkungsgrad m	sidereal hour angle	s. hour angle
		sidereal minute	Sternminute f, siderische Minute f, Sternenminute f
shutter mask	s. printing mask	sidereal month	Sternmonat m, siderischer Monat m, Sternenmonat m
shutter speed	Verschlußgeschwindigkeit f	sidereal period	siderische Umlaufzeit f
shutter speed	Verschlußzeit f		
shutter weir	Klappenwehr n	sidereal second	Sternsekunde f, siderische Sekunde f, Sternensekunde f

sidereal time, stellar time	Sternzeit f, siderische Zeit f	**sight**	s. a. visibility
sidereal year	Sternjahr n, siderisches Jahr n, Sternenjahr n	**sight**	s. a. vision
side-reversed	s. reversed right to left	**sight axis**	s. visual axis
siderial time	s. sidereal time	**sight deficiency**	s. ametropia
siderite, iron meteorite	Eisenmeteorit m, Siderit m	**sight distance**	s. visibility
		sight graticule	s. collimating mark <opt.>
		sight-hole, sight	Visier n, optisches Visier
siderolite	Siderolith m	**sighting**	s. aiming
siderosphere, barysphere	Barysphäre f, Siderosphäre f	**sighting arm**, alidade, alhidade, sight-rule	Alhidade f
siderostat	Siderostat m	**sighting device**, sighting apparatus, sight	Zielvorrichtung f, Zieleinrichtung f, Zielgerät n; Visiereinrichtung f, Visiervorrichtung f, Absehvorrichtung f
side scattering	seitliche Streuung f, Seitenstreuung f		
side[-]slip	Abgleiten n, seitliches Ausgleiten n, seitliches Abrutschen n		
side spectrum	Seitenspektrum n	**sighting knob**	s. sighting mark
side thrust	s. lateral displacement	**sighting line**	s. line of sight
side thrust	s. lateral pressure	**sighting mark**, sighting knob, sight knob	Visiermarke f; Sichtmarke f
side[-]tone	Rückhören n	**sighting mark**	s. a. collimating mark <opt.>
side-tone attenuation, **side-tone reference equivalent**	Rückhörbezugsdämpfung f, Rückhördämpfung f	**sighting microscope**	Zielmikroskop n
		sighting telescope, rifle telescope, telescopic (optical, glass) sight, sight	Zielfernrohr n; Visierfernrohr n
side-to-side cross[-]talk; cross[-]talk, cross induction	Übersprechen n; Nebensprechen n	**sight knob**	s. sighting mark
		sight-rule, alidade, alhidade, sighting arm	Alhidade f
		sigma-algebra, countably additive algebra, σ-algebra	Sigmaalgebra f, σ-Algebra f, Sigmaring m, σ-Ring m
side-to-side unbalance	s. crosstalk coupling		
side wash	s. lateral erosion		
side wave	Seitenwelle f	**sigma-bond**, σ-bond	Sigma-Bindung f, σ-Bindung f
Siebel and Pomp test, Pomp and Siebel test, Pomp and Siebel draw widening test	Tiefziehweitungsversuch m [nach Pomp und Siebel], Pomp-Siebelscher Tiefziehweitungsversuch		
		sigma-function [of Weierstrass], Weierstrassian sigma-function	Sigmafunktion f <von Weierstraß], Weierstraßsche Sigmafunktion
Siegbahn['s] molecular drag pump	Molekularluftpumpe f vom Scheibentyp	**sigma hyperon**, Σ hyperon <Σ^+, Σ^- or Σ^0>	Sigma-Hyperon n, Σ-Hyperon n <Σ^+, Σ^- oder Σ^0>
Siegbahn-Slätis [magnetic] spectrometer, **Siegbahn-Slätis-type beta-ray spectrometer**, intermediate-focus beta-ray-spectrometer	Siegbahn-Slätis-Spektrometer n, magnetisches Beta-Spektrometer n mit Zwischenbildfokussierung [nach Siegbahn-Slätis], Zwischenbildfokus-Spektrometer n nach Siegbahn und Slätis	**sigma meson**, σ	= π^- meson
		sigma-monogenic functions [of Bers-Gelbart]	sigma-monogene Funktionen fpl [von Bers-Gelbart]
		sigma orbital	Wellenfunktion f des Sigma-Elektrons, Sigma-Orbital n
		sigma particle, σ	= π^- meson
		sigma pile	Sigma-Anordnung f, Sigma-Reaktor m <Exponentialexperiment mit Neutronenquelle>
Siegbahn [X] unit, X-unit, X, XU, XuX- <≈ 1.00202×10⁻¹³ m>	X-Einheit f, Siegbahnsche X-Einheit f, Siegb. XE, X <≈ 1,00202 · 10⁻¹³ m>		
siemens, mho <US>, S, ℧	Siemens n, S	**sigma star**	Sigma-Stern m, σ-Stern m
Siemens heat	Siemens-Wärme f	**sigmoid[-shaped] curve**, S-shaped curve, S-curve	S-Kurve f
		sign <math.>	Vorzeichen n <Math.>
sieve, screen; riddle; sifter	Sieb n		
sieve analysis	s. particle-size analysis	**sign**; symbol; character <num. math.>	Zeichen n <auch num. Math.>; Symbol n
sieve efficiency, screen efficiency	Siebwirkungsgrad m	**signal**	Signal n
		signal amplitude, signal height	Signalamplitude f, Signalgröße f, Signalhöhe f
sieve mesh	s. mesh		
sieve plate, perforated plate	Siebboden m; Siebplatte f	**signal converter storage tube**	Signalspeicherröhre f
		signal current amplifier	Signalstromverstärker m
sieve-plate column, sieve-tray column, perforated-plate column	Siebbodenkolonne f; Turbogridkolonne f	**signal field**, useful field	Nutzfeld n
		signal flow diagram (graph)	Signalflußbild n, Signalflußdiagramm n
sieve-plate irradiation	Siebbestrahlung f	**signal-forming amplifier**	s. shaping amplifier
sieve residue	s. screenings	**signal function**	Signalfunktion f
Sievers index	Sievers-Wert m	**signal generator**; test generator	Prüfsender m; Prüfoszillator m, Prüfgenerator m
Sievert chamber	Sievert-Kammer f		
Sievert unit, intensity millicurie, ImC	Sievert-Einheit f, ImC		
sieve size, size of sieve, screen size	Maschenweite f <Sieb>, Siebgröße f, Siebweite f, Siebnummer f	**signal generator**	s. a. measurement transmitter
		signal height, signal amplitude	Signalamplitude f, Signalgröße f, Signalhöhe f
sieve test	s. particle-size analysis		
sieve-tray column	s. sieve-plate column	**signal[l]ing**; indication	Signalisierung f; Meldung f
sieving	s. size separation by screens		
sieving analysis	s. particle-size analysis	**signal matrix**	Signalmatrix f
sifter	s. sieve	**signal meter**, S meter	Signalstärkemesser m
sifting	s. size separation by screens	**signal / noise ratio**, signal noise ratio	s. signal-to-noise ratio
siftings	s. undersize		
sight, sight-hole	Visier n, optisches Visier	**signal oscillator**	s. measurement transmitter
sight	s. a. sighting device	**signal plate**	s. mosaic screen
sight	s. a. sighting telescope		

signal pulse	Signalimpuls m	silent zone, dead zone, shadow zone, zone of silence, silent area, skip region, skip zone, region of silence, shadow region	Zone f des Schweigens, Schweigzone f, Schattenzone f, tote Zone, Totraum m, Totzone f, empfangslose Zone, Auslöschzone f, Leerbereich m
signal resolution	Signalauflösung f		
signal separation	Signaltrennung f		
signal shaper	Signalformer m		
		silhouette effect	Silhouetteneffekt m
		silica[-]gel, silica gel	Kieselgel n, Kieselsäuregel n; Silikagel n, Silicagel n; Trockengel n
signal-shaping amplifier	s. shaping amplifier		
signal spectrum	Signalspektrum n		
signal strength	Signalstärke f	silica microbalance	Quarzfadenmikrowaage f
signal tail	Signalschwanz m	silica pyrheliometer, quartz-glass pyrheliometer	Quarzglaspyrheliometer n
sign-altering focusing	Fokussierung f mit alternierenden Feldern		
signal-to-noise merit	s. noise factor	siliceous earth	s. kieselguhr
signal-to-noise power ratio	Signal-Rausch-Leistungsverhältnis n	silicon barrage photocell, silicon photocell	Siliziumphotoelement n, Silizium-Sperrschichtelement n
signal-to-noise ratio, signal / noise ratio, signal noise ratio, S/N ratio	Signal-Rausch-Verhältnis n, Störabstand m, Signal-Rausch-Quotient m; Störfaktor m, Signalabstand m, Störspiegelabstand m, Störpegelabstand m; Rauschabstand m, Geräuschabstand m, Rauschspannungsabstand m	silicon semiconductor detector, Si semiconductor detector	Siliziumhalbleiterdetektor m, Si-Halbleiterdetektor m
		silicothermic process; silicothermics	Silikothermie f; silikothermisches Verfahren n
		silk thread	Seidenfaden m
		sillometer, log	Log n, Logge f, Fahrtgeschwindigkeitsmesser m
		Silsbee effect	Silsbee-Effekt m
		Silsbee['s] rule	Silsbeesche Regel f
		silt	s. ooze
		silt	s. a. suspended load
signal transition	Signalübergang m	siltation	s. silting
signal velocity	Signalgeschwindigkeit f	silt charge, silt load	Schlammgehalt m, Schwebstoffgehalt m, Schwebstoffbeladung f, Schwebstoffdichte f, Schwebdichte f
signal voltage	Signalspannung f		
signal width	Signalbreite f		
sign-constant focusing	Fokussierung f mit Gleichfeldern	silting, siltation, sedimentation	Verschlammung f; Verschlickung f; Beschlämmung f; Aufschotterung f; Stauraumverlandung f; Verlandung f
sign convention; rule of signs	Vorzeichenfestsetzung f, Vorzeichenkonvention f, Vorzeichenregel f		
sign digit	Vorzeichenziffer f	silt load	s. suspended load
		silt load	s. silt charge
signed	mit Vorzeichen, vorzeichenbehaftet	silt sample, suspended load sample, bottle sample, sample taken by water bottle	Schöpfprobe f
signed-minor, cofactor, algebraic conjunct <math.>	algebraisches Komplement n, Kofaktor m, Adjunkte f, algebraische Adjungierte f <Math.>		
		silt sampler, suspended load sampler	Schwebstoffentnahmegerät n, Schwebstoffmeßgerät n, Schwebstoffschöpfer m
significance, statistical significance, statistical evidence	Signifikanz f, statistische Signifikanz f, statistische Sicherung f		
		silt transport; aerosol transport	Schwebstofftransport m, Schwebstoffverfrachtung f, Schwebstofffracht f; Aerosoltransport m
significance level	s. level of significance		
significance point	Ablehnungsschwelle f, Signifikanzgrenze f, Signifikanzpunkt m	silver chloride half-cell, silver-silver chloride electrode	Silber-Silberchlorid-Elektrode f, Silberchloridelektrode f, Silberchloridhalbzelle f
significance test	Signifikanztest m		
significant <stat.>	signifikant <Stat.>	silver-coated mirror, silvered mirror	Silberspiegel m
significant digit, [meaningful] significant figure	bedeutsame Stelle f, bedeutsame Ziffer f	silver coulometer, silver voltameter	Silbercoulometer n, Silbervoltameter n
significant digits / having n, having n significant figures, having n-figure accuracy	auf n bedeutsame Stellen genau, auf n-Stellen [nach dem Komma] genau	silver-disk actinometer	Silverdiskaktinometer n, Silberscheibenaktinometer n
significant figure	s. significant digit	silver-disk pyrheliometer, Abbot silver-disk pyrheliometer	Silverdiskpyrheliometer n [nach Abbot und Fowle], Silberscheibenpyrheliometer n
significant figures / having n	s. significant digits / having n		
sign indicator	s. polarity indicator	silvered mirror, silver-coated mirror	Silberspiegel m
sign of the zodiac, zodiacal sign	Tierkreiszeichen n, Sternzeichen n	silver point, freezing point of silver, point of freezing silver	Silberpunkt m, Erstarrungspunkt m (Erstarrungstemperatur f) des Silbers
sign of weather	Wetterzeichen n, Wetterbote m, Wetteranzeichen n		
		silver-silver chloride electrode, silver chloride half-cell	Silber-Silberchlorid-Elektrode f, Silberchloridelektrode f, Silberchloridhalbzelle f
Signorini['s] stress inequality	Signorinische Spannungsungleichung f		
sign reversal, reversal of sign, change of sign	Umkehrung f des Vorzeichens, Vorzeichenwechsel m, Vorzeichenumkehr f, Vorzeichenänderung f	silver voltameter, silver coulometer	Silbercoulometer n, Silbervoltameter n
		sima	Sima n
sign test	s. statistical sign test	simatic	simatisch
signum [function], sgn, sg	signum n, sign	simatic rock	simatisches Gestein n
Silberstein-Bateman vector	Silberstein-Bateman-Vektor m	"similar" flow	s. self-similar flow
silencing	s. noise suppression	similarity, similitude	Ähnlichkeit f
silent area	s. silent zone	similarity consideration	Ähnlichkeitsbetrachtung f
silent discharge	s. Townsend discharge		
silent point	Nullschwebungspunkt m	similarity criterion	s. similarity parameter <therm.>

similarity factor	Ähnlichkeitsfaktor m	simple harmonic oscillator, linear [harmonic] oscillator	linearer harmonischer Oszillator m
similarity law	s. similarity principle	simple integral	einfaches Integral n
similarity parameter, similarity criterion, dimensionless parameter (number, group), number, nondimensional quantity (group), characteristic, pi ‹therm.; aero., hydr.›	Ähnlichkeitskennzahl f, Ähnlichkeitszahl f, dimensionslose Kennzahl (Größe) f, Kennzahl, Kennwert m ‹Therm.; Aero., Hydr.›	simple lattice, primitive lattice	primitives Gitter n
		simple lens	Einlinser m, Einlinsenobjektiv n
		simple lifting line theory	s. Prandtl['s] lifting line theory
		simple machine	einfache Maschine f
		simple magnetic field, simple field	Einzelfeld n
similarity principle, law (principle) of similarity, similarity law (theorem)	Ähnlichkeitsgesetz n, Ähnlichkeitsprinzip n, Similaritätsprinzip n	simple ordering	s. ordering ‹math.›
		simple oscillation, simple vibration; linear oscillation	einfache Schwingung f; lineare Schwingung
similarity principle, law of similarity transformation ‹of Laplace transformation›	Ähnlichkeitssatz m ‹Laplace-Transformation›	simple oscillatory motion	s. simple harmonic motion
		simple pendulum, [plane] mathematical pendulum	mathematisches Pendel n, Punktkörperpendel n
similarity rule	Ähnlichkeitsregel f		
similarity theorem	s. similarity principle	simple process ‹of separation›	elementarer Trenneffekt m
similarity transformation	s. homothetic transformation	simple process factor, single stage separation factor, separation factor for a single stage	elementarer Trennfaktor m, Trennfaktor einer Stufe, Trennfaktor der Einzelstufe
similarity variable	Ähnlichkeitsvariable f		
similarly charged (electrified)	s. like		
similar representation, equivalent representation	ähnliche Darstellung f, äquivalente Darstellung		
similar solution, self-similar solution	ähnliche Lösung f	simple reaction, one-step reaction	einstufige Reaktion f
similar test	ähnlicher Test m	simple refraction, single refraction, unirefringence	Einfachbrechung f
similitude, similarity	Ähnlichkeit f		
similitude	s. a. homothetic transformation ‹math.›	simple representation	s. irreducible representation
		simple root, single root	einfache Wurzel f, einfache Nullstelle f
Simmance-Abady flicker photometer	Flimmerphotometer n von Simmance und Abady, Simmance-Abady-Flimmerphotometer n		
		simple semiconductor, pure semiconductor, element (elementary) semiconductor	Einfachhalbleiter m, elementarer (reiner) Halbleiter m, Elementhalbleiter m
simmer[ing]	leichtes Sieden n; Wallen n; Perlen n		
simmer gasket	s. shaft packing	simple series	einfache Reihe f
Simon['s] [melting] equation	Simonsche Gleichung (Schmelzgleichung f, Formel)	simple shear	einfache Scherung f, ebene gleichförmige Scherbewegung f
simple, primitive ‹of lattice›	primitiv, einfach ‹Gitter›	simple shearing strain	ebene Gestaltsänderung f
simple algebra	einfache Algebra f	simple shearing stress	einfacher Schubspannungszustand m
simple analytic function	s. simple function		
simple apposition ‹autoradiography›	Kontaktmethode f ‹Autoradiographie›	simple space group	einfache (symmorphe) Raumgruppe f
simple beam, simply supported beam, beam supported at both ends	frei aufliegender Träger m, einfacher (frei aufliegender) Balken m	simple symmetric glide	symmetrische ebene Formänderung f
		simple system	s. triangular web ‹mech.›
		simple tension	einfache Zugspannung f
simple bending	s. pure bending	simple torsion, torsion	einfache Torsion (Drillung, Verdrehung) f
simple closed curve, closed simple (Jordan) curve	doppelpunktfreie geschlossene Kurve f, geschlossene Jordan-Kurve f		
		simple vibration	s. simple oscillation
		simple wave [flow]	Einfachwellenströmung f
simple crystal form	einfache Form f	simplex circuit	Simplexleitung f
simple cubic lattice	kubisch primitives Gitter n		
simple curve	s. Jordan curve	simplex[-]method, simplex process	Simplexmethode f
simple cusp, cuspidal point of the first kind, cusp of the first kind	Spitze f erster Art, Umkehrpunkt m erster Art		
		simplicial partition	simpliziale Unterteilung f
simple decay curve	einfache Zerfallskurve f, Zerfallskurve für eine radioaktive Substanz	simplification; reduction; idealization	Vereinfachung f; Idealisierung f
		simplified diagram	s. schematic [circuit] diagram
simple detachment	einfache Ablösung f		
simple element	s. pure element	simplifying assumption	vereinfachende Voraussetzung (Annahme) f
simple elongation	s. linear expansion		
simple equivalent pendulum	s. equivalent pendulum	simply connected region	einfach zusammenhängender Bereich m
simple event ‹stat.›	Elementarereignis n ‹Stat.›	simply periodic function	einfach-periodische Funktion f
simple extension	einfache Dehnung f	simply[-]supported, freely supported	frei aufliegend (gelagert)
simple field, simple magnetic field	Einzelfeld n		
simple flexure	s. pure bending	simply supported beam	s. simple beam
simple function, simple analytic function, univalent [analytic] function	eindeutige [analytische] Funktion f, einblättrige Funktion	simply supported bearing (end), freely supported bearing (end)	festes Drehlager n, [festes] Zylindergelenk n
		simply supported edge	frei gelagerter Rand m
simple glide, single slipping	Einfachgleitung f	Simpson['s] model [of thunderstorm cloud]	Simpsonsches Modell n [der Gewitterwolke]
simple group	einfache Gruppe f		
simple harmonic motion (oscillation), simple oscillatory motion, linear harmonic oscillation	lineare harmonische Schwingung f	Simpson['s] pile, neutron pile	Neutronenzählrohrteleskop n, Simpsonsche Säule f

Simpson['s]

Simpson['s] rule, parabolic rule; prismoidal formula [for areas]	Keplersche Faßregel f, Faßregel; Simpsonsche Regel (Formel) f
simulation; model[l]ing; imitation	Modellierung f; Nachbildung f; Simulation f; Nachahmung f
simulator; simulant	Simulator m; Sumuliergerät n; Analog[ie]modell n
simultaneity concept [of Einstein]	Gleichzeitigkeitsbegriff m [von Einstein]
simultaneity factor	Gleichzeitigkeitsfaktor m, Gleichzeitigkeitszahl f, Gleichzeitigkeitsziffer f
simultaneous contrast	Simultankontrast m, Nebenkontrast m
simultaneous crystallization, syncrystallization	gleichzeitige Kristallisation f, Synkristallisation f
simultaneous differential equations	s. simultaneous ordinary differential equations
simultaneous [electron] diffraction method	Simultanbeugungsverfahren n
simultaneous earthquake	Relaisbeben n, Simultanbeben n
simultaneous estimation	simultane Schätzung f
simultaneous events	gleichzeitige Ereignisse npl
simultaneous glare	Simultanblendung f
simultaneous iteration	Simultaniteration f
simultaneous linear equations	s. system of simultaneous linear equations
simultaneous multi-section laminography	Simultanschichtverfahren n
simultaneous ordinary differential equations, simultaneous differential equations, system of ordinary differential equations	gewöhnliches Differentialgleichungssystem n, System n von gewöhnlichen Differentialgleichungen, gekoppelte (simultane) Differentialgleichungen fpl
simultaneous reaction	Simultanreaktion f
SIN curve, Wöhler curve, stress number curve, fatigue curve; Wöhler diagram	Wöhler-Kurve f, Ermüdungskurve f, Wöhler-Linie f; Wöhler-Schaubild n, Wöhler-Diagramm n, SN-Diagramm n
sine amplitude, sn	sinus m amplitudinis, sn
sine bcr	Sinuslineal n
sine compass	s. sine galvanometer
sine condition, Abbé['s] sine condition	Abbesche Sinusbedingung f, Sinusbedingung
sine-cosine potentiometer	Sinus-Kosinus-Potentiometer n, Sinus-Kosinus-Kompensator m
sine curve, sinusoidal curve, sinusoidal line, sinusoid; harmonic curve	Sinuskurve f, Sinuslinie f; harmonische Kurve f
sine galvanometer, sine compass	Sinusbussole f, Sinusgalvanometer n
sine generator, sine-wave oscillator	Sinusgenerator m, Sinuswellenerzeuger m
sine integral; Si; si	Integralsinus m, sinus m integralis; Si; si
sine law, sinusoidal law; sine rule <geotropism>	Sinusgesetz n
sine law, law of sines <of trigonometry or spherical trigonometry>	Sinussatz m <der ebenen oder sphärischen Trigonometrie>
sine of semi-cone angle of entrance pupil	Apertur f
sine potentiometer, sinusoidal potentiometer	Sinuspotentiometer n, Sinuskompensator m
sine rule; sine law, sinusoidal law <geotropism>	Sinusgesetz n
sine wave, sinusoidal wave, harmonic wave	Sinuswelle f, sinusförmige Welle f, harmonische Welle
sine-wave oscillator, sine generator	Sinusgenerator m, Sinuswellenerzeuger m
singeing; scorching	Sengen n
singing <el.>	Pfeifen n <El.>
singing arc	tönender Bogen (Lichtbogen) m, singender Bogen (Lichtbogen), sprechender Bogen (Lichtbogen)
singing flame	singende Flamme f
singing of the arc, arc noise, arc hum	Summen n des Lichtbogens
singing path; feedback path	Rückkopplungsweg m, Rückführungsweg m, Rückführpfad m, Rückkopplungszweig m
singing point; swinging point	Pfeifgrenze f, Pfeifpunkt m; Schwingungseinsatzpunkt m
singing spark, musical spark	tönender Funke m
singing tube	tönendes Rohr n
single acceleration	Einfachbeschleunigung f
single-action process	Einfachprozeß m, Einzelprozeß m
single-anode rectifier, single-plate rectifier	einanodige Gleichrichterröhre f, einanodiger Ventilgleichrichter m, einanodiges Gleichrichterventil n, Einanodenventil n, Einanodengleichrichter m; Einanodengefäß n, Einanoden-Stromrichtergefäß n
single-armature converter	s. rotary converter
single-beam line storage tube	s. line storage tube
single-beam oscillograph	Einstrahloszillograph m
single-beam spectrometer	Einstrahlspektrometer n
single-body problem	s. one-body problem
single bond, two-electron bond, ordinary bond, ordinary link[age]	Einfachbindung f, einfache Bindung f, Zweielektronenbindung f
single-cavity klystron, single-circuit klystron, single-circuit drift tube, floating-drift klystron (tube, tube type klystron)	Einkreistriftröhre f, Einkreisklystron n, Einkammertriftröhre f, freischwebende Triftröhre f
single-centre wave function	Einzentren-Wellenfunktion f
single-channel coincidence spectrometry	Einkanal-Koinzidenzspektrometrie f
single-channel discriminator	Einkanaldiskriminator m
single-channel multichannel two-parametric analysis	Einkanal-Vielkanal-Methode f
single-channel pulse amplitude selector unit, single-channel pulse-height analyzer	Einkanal-Impulshöhenanalysator m
single-channel single-channel two-parametric analysis	Einkanal-Einkanal-Methode f
single-channel time analyzer	Einkanal-Zeitanalysator m
single-chip circuit (device); semiconductor integrated circuit; solid circuit	integrierte Festkörperschaltung (Halbleiterschaltung) f, Festkörperschaltung
single-circuit drift tube, single-circuit klystron	s. single-cavity klystron
single-coil filament	Einfachwendel f
single-coil lamp	Einfachwendellampe f
single coincidence spectrometer	Einfachkoinzidenzspektrometer n

single colour group	Einfarbengruppe f, einfarbige Gruppe f <Schwarz- oder Weißgruppe>	single-line source	Einlinienquelle f
single-column manometer, vertical-tube manometer	Gefäßmanometer n, einschenkliges Manometer n, Manometer mit senkrechtem Meßrohr	single-line spectroscopic binary	Doppelstern m mit einem Spektrum
		single-line spectrum	Einlinienspektrum n, Spektrum n mit einer Linie
single-conductor [current] transformer	Einleiter-Stromwandler m, Einleiterwandler m	single link[age]	s. single bond
		single load	s. concentrated load
single-core flux-gate magnetometer	Einzelkernsonde f	single-loop[-type] galvanometer, loop galvanometer	Schleifengalvanometer n, Schleife f
single counter	Einzelzähler m	single-meson pole	Einmeson[en]pol m
single crystal, monocrystal	Einkristall m	single-mirror condenser, paraboloid[al] condenser	Einspiegelkondensor m, Paraboloidkondensor m
single-crystal diffractometry	Einkristalldiffraktometrie f, Beugungsuntersuchung f an Einkristallen mittels Strahlungsdetektor	single mode laser	Einfrequenzlaser m
single-crystal pulling	s. pulling of crystals		
single-crystal spectrometer	Einkristallspektrometer n, Spektrometer n mit einem Kristall	single nucleon-nucleon encounter	Einzelstoß m zweier Nukleonen, Nukleon-Nukleon-Einzelstoß m
single-cycle engine	s. one-stroke engine	single observation	Einzelbeobachtung f
single dislocation	Einzelversetzung f		
single-distance-layer graded interference filter	Verlauflinienfilter n	single observer rangefinder	Einstand-Entfernungsmesser m
single-domain particle	s. one-domain particle	single-pan balance	einschalige Waage f
single dose	Einzeldosis f; Einzeitdosis f	single particle	Einzelteilchen n
		single-particle equation, one-particle equation	Einteilchengleichung f
single-edge variablearea recording, singlesound track	Einzackenschrift f	single-particle excitation	Einzelteilchenanregung f
single-electrode potential	s. relative electrode potential	single-particle glide	Einteilchengleitung f
single electron, lone electron	Einzelelektron n	single-particle Green['s] function, one-particle Green['s] function	Greensche Einteilchenfunktion f, Einteilchen-Green-Funktion f
single-electron bond	s. one-electron bond		
single-electron eigenfunction	Einelektroneneigenfunktion f	single-particle level	Einzelteilchenniveau n, Einteilchenniveau n
single electron lens, unipotential lens, single lens, einzel lens	Einzellinse f, Dreielektrodenlinse f, elektrostatische Einzellinse	single-particle model	s. one-body model of nucleus
		single-particle operator	Einteilchenoperator m
single-electron limit <photomultiplier>	Einelektrongrenze f, Einelektronnäherung f <Photovervielfacher>	single-particle pole term	Einteilchen-Polterm m
		single-particle transition	Einzelteilchenübergang m, Einteilchenübergang m
single-electron problem	s. one-electron problem	single-particle tunnel current, quasiparticle tunnel current	Einteilchentunnelstrom m, Quasiteilchen-Tunnelstrom m
single-electron pulse	Einzelelektronimpuls m		
single-electron response function	Einelektron-Ansprechfunktion f	single-particle tunnelling, quasiparticle tunnelling	Einteilchentunnelung f, Quasiteilchentunnelung f
single-ended push-pull [cascade]	s. parallel push-pull [cascade]		
single experiment	Einzelversuch m	single-phase alternating current	einphasiger Wechselstrom m, Einphasenwechselstrom m
single exposure	einmalige Bestrahlung f, Einzeitbestrahlung f		
single-factor method	Einfaktormethode f	single-phase dosimeter	Einphasendosimeter n
single force, point force, concentrated force	Einzelkraft f, Punktkraft f, konzentrierte Kraft f	single-phase rectification, alternating-current rectification, a.c. rectification	Wechselstromgleichrichtung f
single-force hypothesis	„single-force"-Hypothese f, Einkrafthypothese f		
single-frequency	s. monochromatic	single-phase rectifier	s. single-wave rectifier
single-grid tube (valve)	s. triode	single-phase three-wire system	Einphasen-Dreileitersystem n
single-hit, single-hit phenomenon	Eintreffer[vorgang] m, Einzeltreffer m		
single-hole directional coupler	s. Bethe hole coupler	single-phonon interaction, one-phonon interaction	Einphononwechselwirkung f
single image prism	einteiliges Polarisationsprisma n	single-picture taking	s. stop-motion camera shooting
single impact ionization, ionization by single impact	Ionisierung f durch Einzelstoß, Einzelstoßionisierung f	single-pion exchange model	Einpionaustauschmodell n
		single-plate rectifier	s. single-anode rectifier
single intersection theorem, intersection theorem	Schnittpunktsatz m [von Serrin]	single polarity pulse	Unipolarimpuls m, unipolarer Impuls m
		single-pole switch	einpoliger Schalter m
single-kick multivibrator	s. univibrator	single potential	s. relative electrode potential
single leaf electrometer	Einblattelektrometer n	single-prism spectrograph	Babinet-Bunsen-Spektrograph m, Spektrograph m mit einem Prisma
single-lens; monocular	einäugig; monokular		
single lens	s. a. single electron lens		
single-lens telescope, Steinheil['s] cone	Steinheilscher Glaskonus m, Einlinsenfernrohr n	single pulse, discrete (isolated) pulse	Einzelimpuls m, diskreter Impuls m
single-level approximation, one-level approximation	Einniveau[an]näherung f	single pulse method	Ein[im]pulsverfahren n
single-level formula, one-level formula	Einniveauformel f, Einniveau-Resonanzformel f	single-quantum annihilation	Einquantenvernichtung f, Einquantenzerstrahlung f

single-quantum transition	Einquantenübergang *m*	singlet	*s. a.* singlet term
single-range instrument	Einbereich-Meßgerät *n*	single-tail[ed] test	*s.* one-sided test
		singlet boson, π_0^0 meson	Singulettboson *n*, singulettes Boson *n*, singlettes Boson, π_0^0-Meson *n*
single reflection	Einfachreflexion *f*; Einfachrückstreuung *f*	singlet distribution function	Einteilchen-Verteilungsfunktion *f*
		single-throw switch, on-off switch	Ein-Aus-Schalter *m*
single refraction, simple refraction, unirefringence	Einfachbrechung *f*	single-throw switch	*s. a.* tumbler
single region reactor	*s.* one-region reactor	singlet linkage, semivalence, semivalency	Singulettbindung *f*
single resonance level	Ein[zel]resonanzniveau *n*		
single root	*s.* simple root	singlet neutron-proton potential, singlet n-p potential	Singulett-Neutron-Proton-Potential *n*, Singulett-n-p-Potential *n*
single-row matrix, row matrix, row vector, single-row vector	Zeilenmatrix *f*, Zeilenvektor *m*		
		singlet positronium	*s.* para[-]positronium
single row of vortices, vortex row, row of vortices	Wirbelreihe *f*	singlet range	Singulettreichweite *f*
		single transfer	„single transfer" *m*
single-row vector	*s.* single-row matrix	singlet scattering	Singulettstreuung *f*
single-runner Francis turbine	*s.* Francis turbine	singlet scattering cross-section, cross-section for singlet scattering	Singulettstreuquerschnitt *m*, Wirkungsquerschnitt *m* für (der) Singulettstreuung
single scattering	Einfachstreuung *f*		
single-shot multivibrator	*s.* univibrator	singlet spectrum	Singulettspektrum *n*
single sideband, single-side band	Einseitenband *n*	singlet spin function	Singulettspinfunktion *f*, Singulett-Spinfunktion *f*
single-sideband amplitude modulation	Einseitenband-Amplitudenmodulation *f*	singlet spin state	Singulettspinzustand *m*, Singulettzustand *m* des Spins
single-side coated, one-side coated	einseitig beschichtet	singlet state	Singulettzustand *m*
single slipping, simple glide	Einfachgleitung *f*	singlet system, singlet term system	Singulettermsystem *n*, Singulettsystem *n*
single-sound track, single-edge variable-area recording	Einzackenschrift *f*	singlet term, singlet	Singuletterm *m*
single spherical optical surface separating two media, spherical optical surface separating two media	einzelne Kugelfläche *f* <brechend *oder* spiegelnd>	singlet term system, singlet system	Singulettermsystem *n*, Singulettsystem *n*
		single turn	*s.* turn
		single vacancy	Einfachleerstelle *f*
single spot	isolierter Fleck *m*, Einzelfleck *m*	single-valued function, one-valued function	eindeutige Funktion *f*
single-stage amplifier	Einstufenverstärker *m*	single-valued mapping, single-valued representation <math.>	eindeutige Abbildung *f* <Math.>
single-stage compression, single-step compression	einstufige Kompression *f*	single-valuedness	*s.* uniqueness
		single-valued representation	*s.* single-valued mapping
single-stage process	Einstufenprozeß *m*, einstufiges Verfahren *n*	single-valued representation	*s. a.* univalent representation
single-stage recycle	Einstufenrückführung *f*; Stufe *f* mit Rückführung	single vector, sum of the system of vectors, resultant vector	Einzelvektor *m*, resultierender Einzelvektor
single-stage rocket, single-step rocket	Einstufenrakete *f*, einstufige Rakete *f*, Raketeneinheit *f*		
		single vision, Panum['s] vision, binocular single vision	Panum-Sehen *n*, beidäugiges Einfachsehen *n*
single stage separation factor	*s.* simple process factor		
single-stage sliding vane pump	einstufige Vielschieberpumpe *f*	single wave, solitary wave	Einzelwelle *f*, solitäre Welle *f*
		single-wavelength	*s.* monochromatic
		single-wave rectification	*s.* half-wave rectification
single star	Einzelstern *m*	single-wave rectifier	*s.* half-wave rectifier
single-step compression, single-stage compression	einstufige Kompression *f*	single-way rectification	*s.* half-wave rectification
		single-way rectifier	*s.* half-wave rectifier
single-step iteration <for solving linear equations>	*s.* Gauss-Seidel method	single-way switch	*s.* tumbler
		single-wheel Pelton turbine	*s.* impulse turbine
single-step iteration (method)	Einzelschrittverfahren *n*, Iteration *f* in Einzelschritten	single-window range-viewfinder	*s.* range-viewfinder
		single-wire antenna	Eindrahtantenne *f*
single-step multivibrator	*s.* univibrator	singly ionized	einfach ionisiert
single-step rocket, single-stage rocket	Einstufenrakete *f*, einstufige Rakete *f*, Raketeneinheit *f*	singular <math.>	singulär <Math.>
		singular distribution, degenerate distribution	singuläre (entartete) Verteilung *f*
single-stroke [cycle] engine	*s.* one-stroke engine	singular integral, singular solution	singuläres Integral *n*, singuläre Lösung *f*
singlet	Singulett *n*, Einfachlinie *f*		
		singularity	*s.* singular point
		singularity [of weather] <meteo.>	Singularität *f* <Meteo.>
		singularity function	*s.* parametrix
		singularity problem	Singularitätsproblem *n*
		singular matrix	singuläre Matrix *f*

singular point; singularity, critical point	Singularität f; singuläre Stelle f, singulärer Punkt m, kritischer Punkt; stationärer Punkt <Differentialgleichungssystem>	**siphon; syphon,** pump-type dispenser	Heber m; Saugheber m, Ansaugheber m; Stechheber m
singular solution, singular integral	singuläres Integral n, singuläre Lösung f	**siphonage** **siphon barometer** **siphon cistern barometer**	s. siphoning s. syphon barometer Gefäßheber-Quecksilberbarometer n, Gefäßhebermanometer n
singular state <cosmology>	Singularität f <Kosmologie>	**siphoning,** siphonage, syphoning	Hebern n; Aushebern n; Abhebern n; Heberwirkung f
singular surface, discontinuity surface, surface of discontinuity <hydr., aero.>	Unstetigkeitsfläche f [im engeren Sinne], Diskontinuitätsfläche f <Hydr., Aero>		
sinistrogyric, left-handed <techn.>	linksgängig, linksdrehend, Links-; linksläufig; linkswendig <Techn.>	**siphon pump,** thermosiphon pump **siphon recorder**	Thermosiphonpumpe f, Heberpumpe f Kapillarschreiber m, Heberschreiber m
sinistrorse, on the left, left-handed <math.>	linksseitig, Links- <Math.>		
sinistrorse helix (screw)	s. left-twisted helix	**siphon recording barometer,** registering siphon barometer	Registrier-Heberbarometer n
sink <of the field>	Senke f, Senkstelle f, Verschwindungspunkt m <Feld>	**siphon weir**	Heberwehr n
sinker, weight	Senkkörper m, Sinkkörper m, Belastungskörper m, Belastungsgewicht n		
sink flow	s. flow from sinks	**siren**	Sirene f, Lochsirene f
sinkhole	s. shrinkage cavity		
sinking	Sinken n; Versinken n		
sinking, sinking[-down]; submersion	Versenkung f	**siriometer,** astron	Astron n, Siriometer n, Makron n, Metron n, Sternenweite f, Sternweite f
sinking	s. a. breakdown <geo.>		
sinking-down	s. sinking	**SI system [of units]**	s. nternational system of units
sinking point, sinking temperature, working point	Einsinkpunkt m, Einsinktemperatur f, Verarbeitungspunkt m, Verarbeitungstemperatur f	**site;** position	Position f; Standort m
sinking speed	s. descent velocity	**site,** atom site, lattice site, site in the lattice, atomic site, lattice position	Gitterplatz m, Gitterstelle f
sinking velocity, fall velocity <hydr.>	Sinkgeschwindigkeit f <Hydr.>		
sink of heat, heat sink	Wärmesenke f; Wärmeabfuhrelement n	**site** **site centre,** s-centre **site error;** distant site error, inter-site error **site group**	s. a. place s-Zentrum n Standortfehler m; Standortumgebungsfehler m Gitterplatz-Symmetriegruppe f, lokale Symmetriegruppe f
sink-source method, method of sources, source-sink method, source-and-sink method; small source theory <nucl.>	Quelle-Senken-Methode f, Quelle-Senken-Verfahren n		
		site-hopping mechanism	s. interchange mechanism of diffusion
sino-auricular node, Keith-Flack['s] node	[Keith-Flackscher] Sinusknoten m, Keith-Flackscher-Knoten m	**site in the lattice** **Sitter-Fokker effect / De**	s. site De-Sitter-Fokker-Effekt m
sintered alloy; sintered metal	Sinterlegierung f; Sintermetall n	**Sitter-Friedmann['s] model [of universe] / De**	de-Sitter-Friedmannsche Welt f
sintering, agglomeration; caking; firing <of ceramics>	Sintern n; Sinterbrennen n, Brennen n <Keramik>; Zusammenbacken n, Zusammenballung f, Zusammenfrittung f, Zusammensinterung f	**Sitter['s] model / De, Sitter['s] universe / De**	De-Sitter-Universum n, de Sitters Weltmodell n, de Sittersche Welt f
		situation **SI unit**	s. state SI-Einheit f, Einheit f des SI-Systems
sintering point; sintering temperature, temperature of sintering	Sinterpunkt m; Sintertemperatur f	**six-colour photometry**	Sechsfarbenphotometrie f
sintering point **sintering point range** **sintering temperature** **Sinton band** **sinuosity,** tortuosity **sinuous line,** serpentine line	s. a. softening point Sinterungsintervall n s. sintering point Sinton-Bande f Flußentwicklung f Schlangenlinie f	**six-colour recorder**	Sechsfarbenschreiber m
		six-component balance	Sechskomponentenwaage f <Windkanal>
sinusoid[al curve], sinusoidal line, sine curve; harmonic curve	Sinuskurve f, Sinuslinie f; harmonische Kurve f	**six-dimensional**	sechsdimensional
sinusoidal law, sine law; sine rule <geotropism>	Sinusgesetz n	**six-electron bond** **six-element lens** **six-factor formula**	s. triple bond Sechslinser m Sechsfaktorformel f
sinusoidal line, sinusoidal curve, sinusoid, sine curve; harmonic curve	Sinuskurve f, Sinuslinie f; harmonische Kurve f	**six-fold axis [of symmetry]** **six-fold axis of the second sort** **six-grid tube,** octode, eight-electrode tube, eight-element tube	s. hexad axis s. hexad axis of the second sort Oktode f, Achtpolröhre f, Sechsgitterröhre f
sinusoidal potentiometer, sine potentiometer	Sinuspotentiometer n, Sinuskompensator m		
sinusoidal transient	Wechselstromsprung m		
sinusoidal wave, sine wave, harmonic wave	Sinuswelle f, sinusförmige Welle f, harmonische Welle	**six-j symbol of Wigner** **six-membered ring,** six ring	s. Wigner coefficient Sechs[er]ring m

six-phase bridge rectifier circuit	Sechsphasenbrückenschaltung *f*	skeleton catalyst, skeletal catalyst, Raney catalyst	Skelettkatalysator *m*, Legierungsskelettkatalysator *m*, Raney-Katalysator *m*
six-phase ring circuit (connection)	Sechsphasenringschaltung *f*	skeleton crystal	s. dendrite
six-phase star circuit (connection)	Sechsphasensternschaltung *f*	skeleton diagram	s. schematic [circuit] diagram
six ring, six-membered ring	Sechs[er]ring *m*	skeleton growth, dendritic growth	Skelettwachstum *n*, dendritisches Wachstum *n*, Dendrit[en]wachstum *n*
six-terminal network	Sechspol *m*	skeleton line, squelette, mean camber line, profile mean line, mean (middle) line of the profile	Skelettlinie *f*, Profilmittellinie *f*, Profilskelettlinie *f*, Profilmitte *f*, Flügelmitte *f*
Six['s] thermometer, maximum-minimum thermometer, maximum and minimum thermometer	Maximum-Minimum-Thermometer *n*, Maximum- und Minimumthermometer *n*	skeleton of crystal	s. dendrite
		skeleton profile	Skelettprofil *n*
Sixtus-Tonks['] experiment	Sixtus-Tonks-Versuch *m*, Versuch *m* von Sixtus und Tonks	skeleton-type bridge	s. impedance bridge
		skerry coast	Schärenküste *f*
six-valve circuit	Sechsröhrenschaltung *f*	sketch, location sketch, area sketch	Kroki *n*
six-vector, 6-vector, antisymmetric tensor of rank 2 <in space time>	Sechservektor *m*, Flächentensor *m*	skew <also math.>	windschief <auch Math.>
six-wire [feeder] line	Sechsdrahtleitung *f*, Sechsdraht-Speiseleitung *f*	skew, oblique, slant <opt.>	schräg einfallend, schräg, schief <Opt.>
size, magnitude	Größe *f*	skew	s. a. oblique
size, grain size, size of grain; granulation size	Korngröße *f*	skew anisotropy	Schiefanisotropie *f*, „skew"-Anisotropie *f*
		skew curve	s. space curve
size	s. a. glue	skew distribution, asymmetrical distribution	schiefe Verteilung *f*, asymmetrische Verteilung
size	s. a. linear dimension <gen.>		
size distribution, particle size distribution	Korngrößenverteilung *f*, Körnung *f*, Kornzusammensetzung *f*, Kornverteilung *f*	skew field; division ring	Schiefkörper *m*, [nichtkommutativer] Körper *m*
		skew-Hermitian, anti-Hermitian, antihermitian	schiefhermitesch, antihermitesch
size distribution of nuclei	s. size spectrum of nuclei	skew-Hermitian kernel	schiefhermitescher Kern *m*
size effect	Einfluß *m* der Abmessungen, Dickeneffekt *m* <„easy glide">; Größeneffekt *m* <bei Tieftemperaturerscheinungen>	skew-Hermitian matrix	schiefhermitesche Matrix *f*
		skew lines	windschiefe Geraden *fpl*
		skewness <math.>	Schiefe *f*, Schiefheitsmaß *n*, Asymmetrie *f* <Math.>
		skewness factor	Schiefheitsmaß *n* von Johannsen
size factor	Größenfaktor *m*	skew product	s. vector product
size fraction, grain fraction	Kornfraktion *f*, Korngrößenfraktion *f*	skew projection, oblique projection, oblique view	zwischenständige (schiefe, gebrochene, schräge, achsige) Projektion *f*, zwischenständiger Entwurf *m*, schiefachsiger [kartographischer] Entwurf, Schiefentwurf *m*, windschiefe Perspektivität *f*, schiefe Parallelprojektion *f*, Schrägbild *n*, Schrägprojektion *f*, Schiefprojektion *f*
size of grain	s. size		
size of sieve, sieve size, screen size	Maschenweite *f* <Sieb>, Siebgröße *f*, Siebweite *f*, Siebnummer *f*		
size of the Barkhausen discontinuity	Sprunggröße *f*		
size of the sample, sample size	Umfang *m* der Stichprobe, Stichprobenumfang *m*		
size reduction, crushing, mechanical subdivision, chopping <mech.>	Brechung *f*, Grobzerkleinerung *f*, Zerkleinerung *f*, Zerstückelung *f* <Mech.>	skew ray, slant ray, oblique ray	schräger (schiefer) Strahl *m*, Schrägstrahl *m*; windschiefer Strahl
		skew [ruled] surface, scroll, warped (twisted) surface	windschiefe Fläche (Regelfläche) *f*
size separation	s. sizing	skew-symmetric[al], alternating, antisymmetric[al] <math.>	schiefsymmetrisch, alternierend, antisymmetrisch <Math.>
size separation by screens, sieving, screening, screenage; sifting	Sieben *n*; Absieben *n*; Sichten *n*		
		skew-symmetric[al] kernel, alternating kernel, antisymmetric kernel	schiefsymmetrischer (alternierender, antisymmetrischer) Kern *m*
size spectrum of nuclei; size distribution of nuclei, distribution of nuclei size	Kerngrößenspektrum *n*; Kerngrößenverteilung *f*		
		skew-symmetric[al] tensor	s. alternating tensor
sizing, classification, classifying process, size separation, grading, sorting	Klassieren *n* [nach der Korngröße], Trennung *f* nach der Korngröße	skew-symmetric[al] tensor density, alternating tensor density	alternierende (schiefsymmetrische) Tensordichte *f*
		skew symmetry, antisymmetry	Antisymmetrie *f*, Schiefsymmetrie *f*
sizing; proportioning; dimensioning; choice of parameters; design	Dimensionierung *f*, Bemessung *f*	skew T-log p diagram	s. emagram
		skiagram	s. shadowgraph
		skiascopy	Skiaskopie *f*, Schattenprobe *f*, Retinoskopie *f*
skeletal catalyst	s. skeleton catalyst		
skeletal vibration	Gerüstschwingung *f*	skiatron, dark-trace tube	Dunkelschriftröhre *f*, Skiatron *n*
skeleton	s. dendrite		

skimming boat, planing boat, glider, hydroplane	Gleitboot *n*; Wassergleiter *m*	**sky wave**, space (spatial) wave, indirect (atmospheric, downcoming) wave <el.>	Raumwelle *f* <El.>
skin <in skin effect>	Skinschicht *f*, Leitschicht *f*, Haut *f* <Skineffekt>	**slab**, flat slab; plate; plaque	Platte *f*
skin burden; skin dose	Hautdosis *f*; Hautbelastung *f*, Strahlenbelastung *f* der Haut	**slab**	*s. a.* wafer
		slab avalanche	*s.* dry snow avalanche
skin depth, penetration depth [in skin effect]	Eindringtiefe *f* [beim Skineffekt], Hauttiefe *f*, Hautdicke *f*, Skintiefe *f*, Skindicke *f*	**slab coil**, pancake coil, flat coil	Flachspule *f*
		slab geometry, infinite-slab geometry	Geometrie *f* der unendlich ausgedehnten Platte, Plattengeometrie *f*
skin dose; skin burden	Hautdosis *f*; Hautbelastung *f*, Strahlenbelastung *f* der Haut	**slack**	*s.* sag
		slack	*s. a.* untensioned
skin effect, Kelvin [skin] effect, current displacement, displacement of current	Skineffekt *m*, Hautwirkung *f*, Hauteffekt *m*, Stromverdrängung *f*, Stromverdrängungseffekt *m*, Kelvin-Effekt *m*	**slackening**; loosening	Lockerung *f*, Auflockerung *f*, Erschlaffen *n*, Nachlassen *n*
		slack flow	*s.* water-surface acsent
		slackness, looseness, flabbiness	Schlaffheit *f*
skin erythema, erythema, reddening of the skin	Erythem *n*, Hautrötung *f*	**slackness**	*s. a.* gap <techn.>
		slack tide	*s.* turn of tide
skin friction, frictional resistance, surface friction, superficial friction, wall shear stress, skin friction stress	Hautreibung *f*, Oberflächenreibung *f*, Flächenreibung *f*, Wandschubspannung *f*	**slack variable**	Schlupfvariable *f*
		slack water	*s.* turn of tide
		slack water	*s. a.* water-surface acsent
		slag <of reactor>	Schlacke *f* <stabile und langlebige Spaltprodukte im Reaktor in in geschmolzenem Uran unlöslicher Form>
skin friction coefficient	*s.* surface[-]friction coefficient		
skin friction resistance, skin resistance <aero., hydr.>	Hautreibungswiderstand *m*, Wandreibungswiderstand *m* <Aero., Hydr.>	**slagging**; scorification	Verschlackung *f*; Schlakkenbildung *f*
skin friction stress	*s.* skin friction	**slant**, oblique; skew <opt.>	schräg einfallend, schräg, schief <Opt.>
skin friction temperature	Hautreibungstemperatur *f*, Wandreibungstemperatur *f*	**slant**	*s. a.* oblique
		slant bundle, oblique bundle	schiefes Bündel *n*
skin friction term, wall shear stress term, surface friction term	Wandschubspannungsglied *n*	**slant distance**, slope distance; slant range	Schrägabstand *m*; Schrägentfernung *f*
skin resistance	Hautwiderstand *m*, Oberflächenwiderstand *m*		
skin resistance	*s. a.* impedance <el.>	**slant distance**	*s. a.* slant range <nucl.>
skin resistance	*s. a.* skin friction resistance <aero., hydr.>	**slant range**, slant distance <nucl.>	Geradeausentfernung *f*, Entfernung *f* <Kern.>
skin temperature	*s.* surface temperature	**slant range**	*s. a.* slant distance
skin time	Skinzeit *f*	**slant ray**	*s.* skew ray
		Slater constant	Slater-Konstante *f*, Slatersche Konstante *f*
skin unit [of McKee]	Hauteinheit *f* [nach McKee]	**Slater curve**	Slater-Kurve. *f*
		Slater determinant	*s.* determinantal wave function
skiodrome, skiodromic line	Skiodrome *f*, Schattenläufer *m*	**Slater function**	Slater-Funktion *f*
		Slater integral	Slater-Integral *n*
skioscopy	*s.* fluoroscopy	**Slater orbital**	Slater-Orbital *n*
skip distance, skipped distance, leap distance	Sprungentfernung *f*		
		Slater['s] rule	Slatersche Regel *f*
		Slater sum	Slater-Summe *f*
		Slater['s] theory [of ferroelectrics]	Slatersche Theorie *f* [der Ferroelektrika]
skip distance	*s. a.* silent zone	**slaty cleavage**	*s.* schistosity
skip keying, pulse-rate division, pulse dividing, repetition-rate division, count-down	Impulsteilung *f*, Impulsfrequenzteilung *f*	**slave clock**, secondary clock	Nebenuhr *f*, Sekundäruhr *f*, Tochteruhr *f*
skipped distance	*s.* skip distance	**slave instrument**	Tochtergerät *n*
skip phenomenon	Sprungerscheinung *f*	**sleeping polymer**	schlafendes Polymer *n*
skip region (zone)	*s.* silent zone	**sleeping top**	schlafender Kreisel *m*, [symmetrischer] Kreisel ohne Präzession
skleroprotein	*s.* scleroprotein		
skot, sk	Skot *n*, sk	**sleet** <US>, ice pellet, graupel	Frostgraupel *f*, Graupel *f*
skull melting	tiegelloses (tiegelfreies) Schmelzen *n*		
		sleeve dipole	Manschettendipol *m*; Mantelstrahler *m*; Hülsendipol *m*; Rohrdipol *m*
sky back radiation, sky counterradiation, [atmospheric] counterradiation	Gegenstrahlung *f*		
sky component of daylight factor	Himmelslichtanteil *m* des Tageslichtquotienten		
		slender body	schlanker Körper *m*
sky factor	Himmelslichtfaktor *m*, Himmelslichtquotient *m*	**slenderness [ratio]**, flexibility <of rod>	Schlankheitsgrad *m*, Schlankheit *f* <Stab>
		slender profile	schlankes Profil *n*
sky light, skylight	Himmelslicht *n*	**slender wing**	schlanker Tragflügel *m*
sky radiation	Himmelsstrahlung *f*	**slice**	Scheibe *f*
		slice	*s. a.* wafer
sky shine <of gamma rays>	Luftstreuung *f* <Gamma-Strahlung>	**Slichter coefficient**	Slichterscher Koeffizient *m* [der Wasserdurchlässigkeit]

slickenside — 776

slickenside ‹geo.› — Gleitspiegel m, Spiegel m; Harnisch m ‹Geo.›
slide, slider — Schieber m
slide, slide way — Gleitbahn f
slide, microscope (specimen, object) slide, specimen (object) holder, specimen-mount, object-mount; support — Objektträger m; Objekthalter m
slide ‹of slide rule› — Zunge f ‹Rechenschieber›
slide — s. a. diapositive
slide — s. a. soil slip
slide — s. a. slide valve
slide — s. a. slipping
slide-back voltmeter — vergleichendes Voltmeter n, Kompensationsvoltmeter n, Vergleichsvoltmeter n, Vergleichsspannungsmesser m
slide caliper — s. vernier caliper
slide coil, slider-type coil (inductor) — Schiebespule f
slide-coil variometer — s. sliding-coil variometer
slide contact — s. sliding contact
slide gauge — s. vernier caliper
slide line — s. slip line
slide projection — s. still projection
slide projector — s. still projector
slider, slide — Schieber m
slider — s. a. wiper ‹el.›
slide rheostat — s. slide-wire potentiometer
slider-type coil (inductor) — s. slide coil
slide rule — Rechenschieber m
slide-rule nomogram — s. nomogram with moving transparents
slide surface ‹geo.› — Gleitfläche f, Rutschfläche f ‹Geo.›
slide valve, sliding valve, slide — Schieberventil n, Schieberventil n, Schieber m; Absperrschieber m; Gleitventil n
slide valve air pump — Schieberluftpumpe f
slide valve distribution, slide valve gear — Schiebersteuerung f
slide way — s. slide
slide wire — Schleifdraht m; Gleitdraht m; Meßdraht m ‹Brückenschaltung›
slide-wire bridge — Schleifdrahtmeßbrücke f, Schleifdrahtbrücke f; Gleitdrahtbrücke f, Gleitdrahtmeßbrücke f, Meßdrahtbrücke f
slide-wire potentiometer; slide rheostat — Schleifdrahtpotentiometer n, Schleifdrahtkompensator m, Schleifdrahtspannungsteiler m; Schieberwiderstand m, Schiebewiderstand m; Schleifdrahtwiderstand m, Drahtschiebewiderstand m, Gleitdrahtwiderstand m
sliding, slipping[-down], gliding, slide — Rutschen n, Gleiten n; Abgleiten n; Abrutschen n
sliding, movable — beweglich; [gegeneinander] verschiebbar, verschieblich
sliding — s. a. slip
sliding average — s. moving average
sliding caliper — s. vernier caliper
sliding-coil transformer — s. movable-core transformer

sliding-coil variometer, slide-coil variometer — Schiebespulenvariometer n, Schiebedrossel f
sliding contact — s. wiping contact
sliding-core transformer — s. movable-core transformer
sliding diaphragm — s. sliding stop
sliding discharge — Gleitentladung f, Gleitfunkenentladung f
sliding fold, gliding fold, slip fold — Gleitfalte f
sliding fracture — s. ductile fracture
sliding frequency — s. slip frequency
sliding friction, friction of sliding — Gleitreibung f, gleitende Reibung f, Reibung der Bewegung
sliding friction torque, moment of sliding friction — Gleitreibungsmoment n
sliding gauge — s. vernier caliper
sliding lens — Schiebelinse f
sliding motion (movement) — s. slip
sliding plane — s. slip plane
sliding pressure — Gleitdruck m
sliding resistance — s. resistance to sliding
sliding rupture — s. ductile fracture
sliding-screen tube — s. variable mu
sliding-screen valve — s. variable mu
sliding stop, sliding diaphragm, Waterhouse diaphragm, plug-in diaphragm — Steckblende f, Einsteckblende f, Waterhouse-Blende f
sliding surface; gliding surface; slip surface; glider ‹hydr.› — Gleitfläche f
sliding valve — s. slide valve
sliding vane, vane — Visierscheibe f, Nivellierscheibe f
sliding vane pump — s. rotary multiplate vacuum pump
sliding vector — linienflüchtiger (gleitender) Vektor m, Stab m ‹Math.›
sliding wear, wear due to slip — Gleitverschleiß m, gleitender Verschleiß m
sliding wedge micrometer — Schiebekeilmikrometer n
sliding weight — Laufgewicht n, Läufer m
sliding weight balance — s. steel[-]yard
slight earthquake — Kleinbeben n
slightly irradiated, lightly irradiated — schwachbestrahlt
slightly soluble, sparingly soluble — schwerlöslich, weniglöslich, schlecht löslich, kaum löslich
slime, mud, sludge, slurry — Schlamm m; Mudd m; Mudde f
slime, sludge — Trübe f, Pulpe f
sling psychrometer, whirling (whirled) psychrometer, whirling hygrometer — Schleuderpsychrometer n
sling thermometer, whirling (whirled, gyrostatic, fronde) thermometer — Schleuderthermometer n
slip, slippage, slipping — Schleifen n; Schlupf m
slip ‹of magnetic field lines› — Schlupf m [der magnetischen Feldlinien]
slip, slipping, slip process, sliding, sliding motion, gliding, glide motion, translatory shift, plastic shear ‹cryst.› — Gleitung f, Gleitprozeß m, Gleitvorgang m, Gleitbewegung f, Gleiten n, Translation f, Translationsplatzwechsel m; Abgleitung f, Abgleiten n ‹Krist.›
slip, slippage ‹el.; hydr.› — Schlupf m, Schlüpfung f ‹El.; Hydr.›; Slip m ‹Hydr.›
slip — s. a. slipstream
slip avalanche — Gleitlawine f
slip band, glide band, Lüders band, stretcher strain, strain figure, flow figure — Gleitband n, Fließfigur f, Gleitfigur f, Lüdersches Band n, Lüdersscher Streifen m
slip-band spacing — Gleitbandabstand m
slip-band transition — Gleitbandübergang m

slip cleavage	Gleitschieferung f	slip ring, contact ring <el.>	Schleifring m, Kontaktring m <El.>
slip coefficient	Schlupfkoeffizient m, Schlupfzahl f, Gleitkoeffizient m	slip speed	Schlupfdrehzahl f, Schlupfgeschwindigkeit f
slip direction, glide direction, direction of slipping (slip, translation)	Gleitrichtung f, Translationsrichtung f	slipstream, slip	Propellerstrahl m, Propellerwind m, Propeller[nach]strom m
slip dislocation, glissile dislocation	gleitfähige Versetzung f	slipstream effect, slipping stream [effect], diocotron effect	Propellerstrahleffekt m, Propellerwindeffekt m, Diocotroneffekt m
slip element, element of slip (translation)	Gleitelement n, Translationselement n	slip surface, sliding (gliding) surface; glider <hydr.>	Gleitfläche f, Schubfläche f, Schiebungsfläche f
slip ellipse, glide ellipse	Gleitellipse f	slip system, glide system	Gleitsystem n
slip flow	Schlüpfströmung f, Schlupfströmung f, Gleitströmung f, „slip flow" n	slip vector, glide vector	Gleitvektor m
		slip vector	s. a. Burgers vector
slip fold	s. sliding fold	slip velocity <of fluids>, velocity of slip	Gleitgeschwindigkeit f
slip frequency, sliding frequency	Gleitfrequenz f, Schlupffrequenz f	slip zone	Gleitzone f
		slit; gap; space; slot	Spalt m; Schlitz m
slip gauge, block gauge, parallel gauge, Johansson gauge	Parallelendmaß n	slit <opt.>	Spalt m <Opt.>
		slit collimation	Spaltkollimation f
slip line, glide line, slide line, Lüders['] line, characteristic, stretcher line, Hartmann['s] line	Gleitlinie f, Gleitspur f, Hartmannsche (Lüderssche) Linie f, Charakteristik f, Verformungslinie f, Verzerrungslinie f, Fließlinie f	slit collimator, slit-type collimator	Schlitzkollimator m, Spaltkollimator m
		slit condensor [lens]	Spaltkondensor m
		slit diaphragm, slotted diaphragm	Schlitzblende f, Schlitz m, Spaltblende f
		slit illumination, illumination of the slit	Spaltbeleuchtung f; Spaltausleuchtung f
slip meter	Schlupfmesser m	slit image, image of the slit	Spaltbild n, Schlitzbild n, Spaltabbildung f
slip moment	Schlupfmoment n	slitless spectrograph	spaltloser (schlitzloser) Spektrograph m
slip motion, conservative motion <of dislocations>	konservative Bewegung f, Gleitbewegung f <Versetzung>	slitness spectroscopy	spaltlose (schlitzlose) Spektroskopie f
slip-on diaphragm, slip-on stop	Aufsteckblende f	slit source	spaltförmige Quelle f
		slit spectrograph	Spaltspektrograph m
slip-on filter	Aufsteckfilter n	slit-type collimator	s. slit collimator
		slit-width correction <in spectroradiometry>	Schlitzbreitenkorrektion f, Spaltbreitenkorrektion f <in der Spektroradiometrie>
slip-on stop	s. slip-on diaphragm		
slippage, slipping, slip	Schleifen n; Schlupf m	slob[-] ice	Trümmereis n
slippage, glide, gliding <at surfaces>	Gleiten n <auf Oberflächen>	slope; inclination, incline; tilt	Neigung f; Gefälle n; Steigung f
		slope, ascent, angular coefficient, gradient <of the curve>	Anstieg m, Richtungskoeffizient m, Steigung f, Neigung f <Kurve>
slippage, slip <el.>	Schlupf m, Schlüpfung f <El.>	slope, declivity <geo.>	Hang m; Böschung f <Geo.>
slippage along (on) the wall	Wandgleitung f	slope, descent <geo.>	Fallen n <Geo.>
		slope <hydr.>	Oberflächengefälle n <Hydr.>
slippage tensor	Gleittensor m	slope	s. a. sloping
slippage test	Verschiebungstest m; „slippage"-Test m, Slippagetest m	slope	s. a. transconductance
		slope angle	s. angle of slope
slipping, slipping down, sliding, gliding, slide	Rutschen n, Gleiten n; Abgleiten n; Abrutschen n	slope conductance	s. transconductance
		slope deflection method, deformation method	Deformationsmethode f, Formänderungsmethode f, Drehwinkelverfahren n, Formänderungsverfahren n
slipping, gliding <geo.>	Abgleitung f <Geo.>		
slipping	s. a. slip	slope distance	s. slant distance
slipping	s. slippage	sloped source	s. tilted source
slipping clutch	Rutschkupplung f, Schlupfkupplung f	slope line	s. helix
		slope of edge, pulse slope (steepness), edge steepness (slope), steepness of edge	Impulsflankensteilheit f, Flankensteilheit f, Impulssteilheit f
		slope of repose, angle of repose, angle of rest, angle of natural slope (slip), angle of friction, natural slope	Schüttwinkel m, Ruhewinkel m, Rutschwinkel m, natürlicher Böschungswinkel m
slipping-down	s. slipping		
slipping of the dislocation	s. dissociation of the dislocation		
slipping-on of the filter	Vorsetzen n des Filters	slope of the emission characteristic	s. transconductance
		slope of the terrace	Terrassenhang m
slipping stream [effect]	s. slipstream effect	slope rupture, rupture of slope	Gefällsbruch m, Neigungsbruch m, Neigungswechsel m
slip plane, plane of slip, glide plane, shearing (sliding) plane <cryst.>	Gleitebene f, Translationsebene f, Schubebene f, Schiebungsebene f <Krist.>	slope scale	Neigungsmaßstab m, Böschungsmaßstab m
		slope spring	Hangquelle f
slip-plane blocking	Gleitebenenblockierung f	slope wind	Hangwind m, Berg- und Talwind m, Berg-und-Tal-Wind m
slip process	s. slip <cryst.>		

sloping, slope — abfallend, abschüssig, schräg
sloping top — s. tilt <of pulse>
slot; gap; space; slit — Spalt m; Schlitz m

slot <el.> — Nut[e] f <El.>

slot antenna, slotted antenna, split antenna — Schlitzantenne f
slot array — Schlitzstrahlerkombination f

slot coupling — Schlitzkopplung f, Schlitzankopplung f

slot excitation [of antenna] — Schlitzanregung f [der Antenne]

slot-fed dipole — s. slotted dipol
slot magnetron — s. split anode magnetron
slot radiator — Schlitzstrahler m

slot suction — Spaltsog m
slotted antenna — s. slot antenna
slotted cylinder antenna, slotted-guide antenna, slotted waveguide antenna, leaky-pipe antenna, leaky waveguide — Schlitzrohrstrahler m, Rohrschlitzstrahler m, Rohrschlitzantenne f, Schlitzhohlleiterantenne f

slotted diaphragm — s. slit diaphragm
slotted dipol, slot-fed dipole — Schlitzdipol m

slotted guide — s. slotted waveguide
slotted-guide antenna — s. slotted cylinder antenna
slotted line — geschlitzte Leitung f

slotted shutter, focal-plane shutter — Schlitzverschluß m; Bildfensterverschluß m

slotted waveguide, slotted guide — geschlitzter Hohlleiter m, Schlitzhohlleiter m

slotted waveguide antenna — s. slotted cylinder antenna
slot-type current transformer — Querlochwandler m, Querlochstromwandler m; Querloch-Durchführungswandler m

slow approximation — langsame Näherung f
slow boundary layer — langsame Grenzschicht f
slow coincidence — langsame Koinzidenz f
slow coincidence circuit — langsame Koinzidenzschaltung f

slow combustion — s. deflagration
slow combustion — s. a. sluggish combustion
slow down — s. slowing down
slow fission, slow neutron fission — langsame Spaltung f, Spaltung durch langsame Neutronen

slow flight, slow-speed flight — Langsamflug m
slow flow — s. tranquil flow
slowing-down, slow-down, moderation <of neutrons> — Bremsung f, Abbremsung f, Moderierung f <Neutronen>
slowing-down area, moderation area — Bremsfläche f
slowing-down cross-section, cross-section for slowing down; stopping cross-section — Bremsquerschnitt m, Wirkungsquerschnitt m für (der) Bremsung, Bremswirkungsquerschnitt m

slowing-down density — Bremsdichte f
slowing-down equation — Bremsgleichung f
slowing-down flux — Bremsfluß m
slowing-down kernel — Bremskern m

slowing-down length, length of moderation, moderation length — Bremslänge f

slowing-down neutron — Bremsneutron n

slowing-down power <for alpha-rays> — Bremsvermögen n <von Materie gegenüber Alpha-Teilchen>
slowing-down power, moderating power <for neutrons> — Bremsvermögen n, Bremskraft f <Neutronen>
slowing-down radiation — s. bremsstrahlung
slowing-down spectrometer — s. slowing-down time spectrometer
slowing-down theory — Bremstheorie f
slowing-down time, fast-neutron lifetime, retardation age — Bremszeit f <Zeit, nach der die Neutronen auf thermische Geschwindigkeit abgebremst sind>

slowing-down time spectrometer, slowing-down spectrometer — Bremszeitspektrometer n, Bremszeit-Neutronenspektrometer n, „slowing-down"-Spektrometer n

slowing-down time spectrometry — Bremszeitspektrometrie f
slow ion — s. large ion
slow lens, low-power objective (lens), low-speed lens — lichtschwaches Objektiv n, schwaches Objektiv
slowly varying component — langsam variable Komponente f

slow motion, micromotion, micrometric displacement; fine focusing motion — Feinbewegung f
slow-motion camera, slow-motion equipment, slow-motion device, slow-motion pictures camera, high-speed camera, time magnifier — Zeitlupe f, Zeitlupenkamera f, Zeitdehnerkamera f, Zeitdehnergerät n, Zeitdehner m

slow-motion camera shooting — s. high-speed camera shooting
slow-motion device — s. slow-motion camera
slow-motion drive; fine focus[ing adjustment], mechanism of fine adjustment; slow-motion screw — Feintrieb m; Feinstellschraube f, Feinbewegungsschraube f
slow-motion effect — s. high-speed photography
slow-motion equipment — s. slow-motion camera
slow-motion method — s. high-speed photography
slow-motion picture[s], pictures in slow motion — Zeitlupenfilm m, Zeitlupenaufnahme f
slow-motion pictures camera — s. slow-motion camera
slow-motion record — s. high-speed camera shooting

slow-motion screw — s. show-motion drive
slow-motion shooting — s. slow-motion camera shooting

slowness — s. sluggishness
slow neutron — langsames Neutron n
slow neutron — s. a. thermal neutron
slow neutron capture — s. slow process
slow-neutron detector — Detektor m für langsame Neutronen
slow neutron fission — s. slow fission
slow nova — langsame Nova f
slow-operating relay — s. delayed relay
slow process, s process, slow neutron capture, capture of neutrons on a slow time scale <astr.> — s-Prozeß m, langsamer Prozeß m, langsamer Neutroneneinfang m <Astr.>
slow reaction; clock reaction — Zeitreaktion f, chemische Uhr f
slow reactor — langsamer Reaktor m <meist: thermischer Reaktor>

slow release — Zeitauslösung f

slow-release (slow-releasing) relay — s. time-delay relay
slow-response — s. inertial
slow-speed flight, slow flight — Langsamflug m
slow storage, low-speed storage (store) — langsamer Speicher m

slow-wave structure	s. delay line	small hardness, microhardness	Mikrohärte f
sludge, mud, slime, slurry	Schlamm m; Mudd m; Mudde f	small ion, light ion, fast ion <geo.>	Kleinion n, kleines (leichtes) Ion n, Mikroion n <Geo.>
sludge, slime	Trübe f, Pulpe f	Small Magellanic Cloud	Kleine Magellansche Wolke f
sludge, slush; snow slush	Matsch m; Schneematsch m, Schneeschlamm m	smallness	Kleinheit f
sludge activation	Schlammbelebung f	small oscillation	kleine Schwingung f
sludging of photographic solutions	Verschlammung f photographischer Lösungen	small planet	s. asteroid
		small scale	s. reduced scale
slug <in the reactor>	Brennelement n in Form eines kurzen dicken Stabes, kurzer dicker Stab	small-scale turbulence, microturbulence	kleinräumige (kleinmaßstäbliche) Turbulenz f, Kleinturbulenz f, Mikroturbulenz f, Turbulenz f im Kleinen (mikroskopischen Ausmaß)
slug flow	schleichende Rohrströmung f	small-scale turbulent flame	turbulente Flamme f im Kleinen, kleinmaßstäblich turbulente Flamme
sluggish	s. viscid	small signal	Kleinsignal n
sluggish; inertial, inertia, inert	träg[e]	small-signal current amplification; small-signal current gain	Kleinsignalstromverstärkung f
sluggish	s. a. high-melting		
sluggish combustion, slow combustion	träge (langsame, schleichende) Verbrennung f	small-signal parameter	Kleinsignalparameter m
sluggishness, slowness, response time, time constant	Trägheit f, Einstellzeit f, Einstelldauer f	small-signal theory	Kleinsignaltheorie f
		small-signal voltage amplification; small-signal voltage gain	Kleinsignalspannungsverstärkung f
sluggishness	s. viscidity		
slurry	s. sludge	small source theory	s. sink-source method
slurry	s. a. suspension	small strain	s. small deformation
slurry polymerization [process]	s. pearl polymerization	S-matrix, scattering matrix	Streumatrix f, S-Matrix f
slurry reactor, suspension reactor, suspension-type reactor	Suspensionsreaktor m, Reaktor m mit nasser Suspension, Wassersuspensionsreaktor m	smear	s. smearing-out
		smear	s. a. schliere
		smeared, blurred, indistinct, indefinite, featureless, structureless, washed-out, weakened	verwaschen, verschwommen, undeutlich, unscharf, wenig ausgeprägt
		smeared[-out]	verschmiert
		smeared[-out] density	verschmierte Dichte f
		smeared particle	verschmiertes Teilchen n
slush	s. sludge	smearing; rubbing; grating; wiping	Reiben n; Wischen n
slush [ice], frazil ice, frazil, holly ice	Eisbrei m, Eistost m, Tost m, Grundeisscholle f, Rogeis n, Sulzeis n, Siggeis n, Schwebeis n	smearing[-out], smear; blurring <gen.>	Verschmierung f; Verwaschenheit f; Verwaschung f; Unschärfe f, Verschwommenheit f; Auflockerung f; Zerfließen n <allg.>
small / in the, im Kleinen, locally <math.>	im Kleinen, lokal <Math.>		
small-angle boundary	s. small-angle grain boundary	smearing-out of boundary, diffuse edge	Randauflockerung f, Randverschmierung f
small-angle collision	Kleinwinkelstoß m	smear photography	s. schlieren method
small-angle collision	s. a. glancing collision	smear test, wipe test	Wischtest m, Wischversuch m; Wischprobe f; Reibtest m, Reibversuch m
small-angle grain boundary, small-angle tilt boundary, small-angle (low-angle) boundary, low-angle grain boundary, sub-boundary, sub-grain boundary	Kleinwinkelkorngrenze f, Feinwinkelkorngrenze f, Feinkorngrenze f	smectic phase	smektische Phase, bz-Phase f, smektische kristalline Flüssigkeit f
		smectic sheet	smektische Ebene f
		Smekal defect (flaw), pore, flaw of Smekal, loose place [of Smekal], lockerstelle	Lockerstelle f [nach Smekal], Smekalsche Lockerstelle, Lockerion n
small-angle scattering, SAS	Kleinwinkelstreuung f, Streuung f um kleine Winkel; Streuung überwiegend in Vorwärtsrichtung	Smekal['s] formula	Smekalsche Formel f
		Smekal-Raman effect	s. Raman effect
		smell	s. sense of smell
		smelling	Riechen n
small-angle tilt boundary	s. small-angle grain boundary		
small-angle X-ray scattering	s. X-ray small-angle scattering	smell sense	s. sense of smell
		smelting	Reaktionsschmelzen n
small-area transition	kleinflächiger Übergang m		
small calorie	s. calorie	smelting	s. a. melting
small crater, craterlet, crater pit	Kratergrube f	smelting-flux electrolysis	s. electrolysis in the dry way
small crystal, little crystal	Kriställchen n	S meter, signal meter	Signalstärkemesser m
small deformation, small strain	kleine Deformation f, infinitesimale Formänderung f	S_n method [of Carlson], Carlson['s] S_n method	S_n-Methode f [von Carlson], Carlsonsche S_n-Methode
smallest angular resolution [for distinct vision]	physiologischer Grenzwinkel m	Smith chart (diagram), polar circle diagram, circle diagram of Smith, polar impedance chart	Smith-Diagramm n, Smithsches Diagramm n, Kreisdiagramm n nach Smith
smallest convex polygon containing all the points of support	Stützpolygon n		
small-grained, fine-grain, fine grained, finely granular, short grained	feinkörnig, kleinkörnig; Feinkorn-	Smith diagram <mech.>	Schleifendiagramm n, Dauerfestigkeitsschaubild n nach Smith, Smith-Diagramm n <Mech.>

smith forging, hammer forging, flat-die forging, hammering; peening	Freiformschmieden n, Hämmern n	smouldering	Schwelen n
Smith-Helmholtz equation (law)	s. Lagrange['s] theorem	SMOW	s. standard mean ocean water
Smithsonian [pyrheliometric] scale	Smithsonian-Skala f	snail, cochlea <of ear>	Schnecke f, Cochlea f <Ohr>
		snail form	Schneckenform f
Smithsonian water-flow pyrheliometer, water-flow pyrheliometer	Waterflowpyrheliometer n [von Abbot und Fowle], Durchflußpyrheliometer n, Wasserstrompyrheliometer n	snap, break-up in the weather; rapid change of weather	Wettersturz m; Umschlagen n des Wetters, Wetterumschlag m
smog, <smoke and fog>	Smog m, „smog" m, Rauchnebel m, [dichter] Stadtnebel m, starker Dunst m <über Großstädten>	SNAP	= system for nuclear auxiliary power
		snap-action amplifier	s. sweep amplifier
		snap-action contact	Schnappkontakt m, Sprungkontakt m
smokatron	Smokatron n, Elektronenringbeschleuniger m	snap gauge	Rachenlehre f, Grenzrachenlehre f
smoke cloud; smoke column, cloud column	Rauchwolke f; Rauchsäule f, Rauchgassäule f	snap-off diode	s. step recovery diode
		snap regula	s. rule of thumb
smoke density meter	s. smokometer	snapshot	s. instantaneous shot
smoked glass	rußgeschwärztes (berußtes) Glas n, Rußglas n	snap valve	s. pinch cock
smoked glass	s. a. neutral glass	sneak current	s. parasite current
smoke gas, fluc[-]gas	Rauchgas n	sneak currents	s. surface leakage current
smoke train	Rauchschweif m <Meteor>	Snellen['s] "illiterate E"; Snellen letter	Snellenscher Haken m
smoke tunnel	Rauchwindkanal m	Snell['s] law [of refraction], Descartes['] law, optical law of refraction	Snelliussches Brechungsgesetz (Gesetz) n, optisches Brechungsgesetz, Brechungsgesetz (Gesetz) von Snellius, Descartes-Snelliusscher Satz m [der Brechung], Brechungsgesetz n
smokometer, smoke density meter	Rauchdichtemesser m, Rauchgasdichtemesser m		
Smoluchowski effect	Smoluchowski-Effekt m		
Smoluchowski-Einstein theory	s. fluctuation theory of light scattering		
Smoluchowski['s] equation	Smoluchowskische Integralgleichung f		
Smoluchowski['s] formula	Smoluchowskische Formel f	sniperscope	s. infra-red image converter
		Snoek effect	Snoek-Effekt m
		Snoek['s] law	Snoeksches Gesetz n
Smoluchowski['s] solution	Smoluchowskische Lösung f	snoot, limitation diaphragm, barn doors	Strahlenbegrenzungsblende f
smooth, hydraulically smooth <hydr.>	glatt, hydraulisch glatt	snowberg, iceberg covered with snow	schneebedeckter Eisberg m
smooth approximation, Symon['s] smooth approximation	„smooth approximation" f [nach Symon], Symonsche glatte Approximation f	snow climate, nival climate	nivales Klima n; vollnivales Klima
		snow core	Schneekern m
smooth as a mirror	spiegelglatt	snow cover, snow mantle (pack)	Schneedecke f
smooth curve, smoothed curve, fair[ed] curve	glatte Kurve f		
smooth detachment, smooth separation	Bugwellenablösung f	snow density	Schneedichte f
smooth flow	glatter Abfluß m	snow drift, snow wreath	Schneewehe f
		snow[-]fall	Schneefall m
smooth function	glatte Funktion f	snow[-]flake	Schneeflocke f
smoothing, tranquillization <e.g. of oscillation, flow>	Beruhigung f	Snow['s] formula	Snowsche Operationsformel f
smoothing <math., el., techn.>; flattening, graduation <math.>	Glättung f, Ausgleichung f <Math., El., Techn.>; Glättungsprozeß m <Techn.>; Ebnung f	snow[-] gauge, snow sampler	Schneeausstecher m, Schneemesser m, Schneestecher m
		snow grain	Griesel f
		snow level, snow scale (stake)	Schneepegel m, Schneelatte f, Schneekreuz n
smoothing capacitor	Glättungskondensator m, Beruhigungskondensator m	snow limit, snow[-] line, perpetual snow[]line, firn line, névé line; orographic snow[]line	Schneegrenze f, Firngrenze f; eigentliche Schneegrenze, wirkliche Schneegrenze, orographische Schneegrenze; Firnlinie f, Schneelinie f
smoothing choke	s. ripple-filter choke		
smoothing factor <el.>	Glättungsfaktor m <El.>		
smoothing resistor	Glättungswiderstand m	snow mantle	s. snow cover
smooth muscle	glatter Muskel m, längsgestreifter Muskel	snowmelt, melt-water, thawing water	Schmelzwasser n
		snow pack	s. snow cover
smoothness, flatness, planeness	Ebenheit f, Glätte f	snow pack water equivalent	s. water equivalent of snow pack
smooth object	kantenloser Körper m	snow pellet, soft hail	Reifgraupel f, Graupel f, Schneegraupel f
smooth pipe, smooth tube	Glattrohr n, glattes Rohr n	snow pressure	Schneedruck m
smooth sea, glassy sea, unrippled sea	spiegelglatte See f, vollkommen glatte See, glatte See, Meeresstille f <Stärke 0>	snow sampler	s. snow[-]gauge
		snow scale	s. snow level
		snow-shovel reflector	Trogreflektor m
smooth separation	s. smooth detachment	snow slush	s. sludge
smooth surface <math., techn., hydr.>	glatte Fläche f <Math., Techn., Hydr.>; glatte Oberfläche f <Techn., Hydr.>	snow stake	s. snow level
		snow storm; buran	Schneesturm m; Buran m, Winterburan m; Schneegestöber f
		snow water	Schneewasser n
smooth tube	s. smooth pipe	snow wreath	s. snow drift

S/N ratio	s. signal-to-noise ratio	**soft focusing**	Weichzeichnung f
S-N unit, sabouraud-noiré, Sabouraud-Noiré unit	Sabouraud-Noiré n, Sabouraud-Noiré-Einheit f, SN-Einheit f	**soft focus lens**	weichzeichnende Linse f, Weichzeichnerlinse f, „soft-focus"-Linse f, Weichzeichner m; Mollarlinse f
soak[age], soaking	s. impregnation		
soak[age], soaking	s. swelling	**soft-glass envelope**	Weichglaskolben m
soap bubble model, Bragg['s] soap bubble model, bubble model [of crystal], bubble raft	Seifenblasenmodell n, Braggsches Seifenblasenmodell	**soft hail**, snow pellet	Reifgraupel f, Graupel f, Schneegraupel f
soap film	Seifenhaut f; Seifenfilm m	**soft-iron bar**	Weicheisenstab m
soap film analog, soap film analogy [of Prandtl], Prandtl['s] analogy, membrane analogy [in torsion], analogy of membrane, membrane model [of Prandtl]	Seifenhautgleichnis n [von Prandtl], Prandtlsches Seifenhautgleichnis, Gleichnis n von Prandtl, Membrangleichnis n [von Prandtl], Prandtlsche Analogie f, Prandtl-Analogie f	**soft-iron galvanometer**, moving-iron galvanometer, electromagnetic galvanometer	Weicheisengalvanometer n, Dreheisengalvanometer n, elektromagnetisches Galvanometer n
		soft-iron instrument	s. moving iron instrument
		soft iron oscillograph, moving-iron oscillograph	Dreheisenoszillograph m, Weicheisenoszillograph m
Sobolev['s] lemma	Sobolews Lemma n, Lemma von Sobolew	**soft [magnetic] material**, magnetically soft material	weichmagnetischer (magnetisch weicher) Werkstoff m
Sochozki-Planelj formulae	Sochozki-Planeljsche Formeln fpl, Formeln von Sochozki-Planelj	**softness of lines**	Weichheit f der Linien
socket [of ground-in joint], ground-joint female part [of ground-in joint]	Schliffhülse f; Stopfenbett n	**soft picture**, non-contrasty (uncontrasty) picture	weiches Bild n, kontrastloses (flaues) Bild
Soddy-Fajans displacement law	s. radioactive displacement law	**soft radiation**; low-energy radiation	weiche Strahlung f, Weichstrahlung f; energiearme Strahlung
Söderberg electrode, self-baking electrode, Soederberg electrode	Söderberg-Elektrode f	**soft-radiation region**	Weichstrahlgebiet n
sodion	= sodium ion	**soft radiator**, nuclide emitting soft radiation, isotope emitting low-energy radiation <nucl.>	weicher Strahler m, weichstrahlendes Radionuklid n, Weichstrahler m <Kern.>
sodium-carbon reactor, sodium-graphite reactor, sodium reactor	Natrium-Graphit-Reaktor m		
sodium-cooled fast [breeder] reactor	natriumgekühlter schneller Brüter m	**soft solder**	Weichlot n
		soft soldering	s. seal
sodium lamp, sodium vapour [discharge] lamp	Natriumdampflampe f, Natriumlampe f	**soft tube**	s. soft X-ray tube
		soft water	weiches Wasser n, Weichwasser n
sodium light	Natriumlicht n	**soft X-rays**, long-wave X-rays	weiche Röntgenstrahlung f, langwellige Röntgenstrahlung, weiche Strahlen mpl, Weichstrahlung f
sodium line	Natriumlinie f		
sodium potassium tartrate	s. Rochelle salt		
sodium pump	Natriumpumpe f		
"sodium pump" mechanism	Pumpmechanismus m [der Erregung]	**soft X-ray tube**, soft tube	Weichstrahlröhre f
sodium reactor	s. sodium-graphite reactor	**sogasoid**	s. aerosol
sodium vapour [discharge] lamp	s. sodium lamp	**soil erosion**	Bodenzerstörung f, Bodenabtragung f, Bodenerosion f
Soederberg electrode, self-baking electrode, Söderberg electrode	Söderberg-Elektrode f	**soil evaporation**	Bodenverdunstung f
soft	s. low-energy <of radiation>	**soil evaporation pan, soil evaporimeter**, soil pan	Bodenverdunstungsmesser m, Bodenvaporimeter n
soft annealing, full annealing, spheroidizing	Weichglühen n	**soil horizon**	Bodenhorizont m
soft component, low-energy component	weiche Komponente f [der kosmischen Strahlung]; weiche Sekundärstrahlung f	**soil humidity**	s. soil moisture
		soil moisture, soil humidity, field moisture	Bodenfeuchtigkeit f, Bodenfeuchte f; Grundfeuchtigkeit f
softener, softening agent, plasticizer, plasticizing (plasticity) agent, plastifier	Plastifikator m, Weichmacher m, Weichmachungsmittel n	**soil moisture meter**	Bodenfeuchtemesser m
		soil moisture tension	Bodenwasserspannun.g f
softener	s. a. water softener		
softening, plasticization, plasticizing, plastifying, plastification, fluxing, fluxion	Weichmachen n, Plastifikation f, Plastifizierung f, Plastizierung f	**soil of weathering**	s. eluvial soil
		soil pan	s. soil evaporation pan
		soil physics	Bodenphysik f
		soil slip, landslip, mountain slip, landslide, rock-slide, slide, landfall <geo.>	Rutschung f, Rutsch m, Erdschlipf m, Erdrutsch m <Geo.>
softening, mollification, emollescence	Erweichung f		
softening	s. a. destrengthening		
softening agent	s. softener	**soil suction force**, suction force of the soil	Saugkraft f des Bodens, Bodensaugkraft f
softening interval	Erweichungsintervall n		
softening of the X-ray tube	Weich[er]werden n der Röntgenröhre	**soil temperature**	Bodentemperatur f; Temperatur f am Boden
softening of water	Enthärtung f des Wassers	**soil thermometer**, earth thermometer	Bodenthermometer n, Erdbodenthermometer n
softening point, sintering point	Erweichungspunkt m, Erweichungstemperatur f	**soil water**, ground water	Bodenwasser n; Grundfeuchtigkeit f
softening point of the pyrometric cone	s. pyrometric cone equivalent	**Sokolovsky yield condition**, yield condition of Sokolovsky	Sokolovskysche Fließbedingung f, Fließbedingung von Sokolovsky
soft-focus effect	Weichzeichnereffekt m		

sol

sol, colloidal suspension, soliquid, suspensoid, suspension colloid, incoherent colloidal system — Sol n, Suspensoid n, Suspensionskolloid n, Suspension f, inkohärentes kolloides System n

solar activity, solar weather — Sonnenaktivität f, Sonnentätigkeit f

solar anomalistic inequality — s. Sun['s] anomalistic inequality

solar antapex, antapex of the Sun — Antapex m der Sonne[nbewegung]

solar apex, apex of the Sun — Apex m der Sonne[nbewegung]

solar attraction — Sonnenanziehung f

solar aureole — s. solar corona

solar battery, solar cells; solar-cell matrix — Sonnenbatterie f, Solarbatterie f

solar cell — Solarelement n, Solarzelle f, Sonnenzelle f

solar-cell matrix; solar cells — s. solar battery

solar centre of activity, centre of activity — Aktivitätszentrum n

solar climate — solares Klima n, Solarklima n, Sonnenklima n

solar climatic zone, mathematical climatic zone — solare Klimazone f, mathematische Klimazone

solar compass, sun compass, dial compass — Sonnenkompaß m

solar component [of cosmic rays], solar cosmic rays — Solarkomponente f [der kosmischen Strahlung], solare kosmische Strahlung f, solare Höhenstrahlung f

solar constant [of radiation] — Solarkonstante f

solar converter — s. solar energy converter

solar corona, Sun['s] corona, corona [of the Sun] — Sonnenkorona f, Korona f [der Sonne]

solar corona, solar aureole — Sonnenkranz m, Sonnenkrone f

solar corpuscular radiation — Partikelstrahlung f der Sonne, solare Korpuskularstrahlung f

solar cosmic rays — s. solar component

solar cross — Sonnenkreuz n

solar cycle, activity cycle — Zyklus m der Sonnenaktivität, Aktivitätszyklus m, Sonnenzyklus m, Sonnenzirkel m

solar daily inequality — s. diurnal solar inequality

solar daily magnetic variation — tägliche solare magnetische Variation f, sonnentäglicher (sonnentägiger) Gang m, S-Variation f

solar day — Sonnentag m

solar depression [angle], Sun['s] depression — Sonnendepression f

solar disk, Sun['s] disk — Sonnenscheibe f

solar ebb — Sonnenebbe f

solar diurnal inequality
solar eclipse, eclipse of the Sun — s. diurnal solar inequality
Sonnenfinsternis f

solar electrodynamics — Sonnenelektrodynamik f

solar elliptical inequality — s. Sun['s] anomalistic inequality

solar energy conversion — Sonnenenergie[um]wandlung f

solar energy converter, solar converter — Sonnenenergiewandler m, Solarkonverter m

solar energy output — s. solar luminosity

solar eruption — s. solar flare

solar eyepiece; helioscope — Sonnenokular n, helioskopisches Okular n; Helioskop n, Sonnenfernrohr n

solar facula — s. solar mountain

solar flare, flare, flare <on the Sun>, solar eruption, eruption, eruption on the Sun — Sonneneruption f, Eruption f [auf der Sonne], Strahlungsausbruch m [auf der Sonne], Ausbruch m [auf der Sonne], „flare" n

solar flare effect, s.f.e., sfe — [geomagnetischer] Sonneneruptionseffekt m

solar flood [tide] — Sonnenflut f

solar furnace — Sonnenofen m

solar halo — Sonnenhalo m; Sonnenhof m, Sonnenring m, Sonnenringhalo m

solarimeter — Solarimeter n <z. B. von Moll-Gorczinsky>

solarization <bio.> — Solarisation f <Bio.>

solarization, image reversal, reversal of photographic image <phot.> — Solarisation f, Bildumkehrung f <Phot.>

solarization curve — Solarisationskurve f

solarization density, density of solarization — Solarisationsdichte f

solarization image — Solarisationsbild n

solar limb, limb of the Sun, Sun's limb — Rand m der Sonnenscheibe, Sonnenscheibenrand m, Sonnenrand m

solar luminosity, solar energy output, energy output of the Sun — Sonnenstrahlungsintensität f, Sonnenintensität f <in erg/s>

solar magnetograph — Sonnenmagnetograph m [nach Babcock]

solar magnitude, magnitude of the Sun — Sonnenhelligkeit f

solar microscope — Sonnenmikroskop n

solar mountain, facula <pl.: -lae>, solar facula; facula area <pl.: -lae -as> — Sonnenfackel f, Fackel f; Fackelgebiet n

solar nebula, primeval nebula, presolar nebula — Nebelscheibe f, Urnebel m <Ursonne>

solar neutrino unit, SNU — = 10^{-36} reactions per ^{36}Cl atom and second

solar noise, solar radio noise — Sonnenrauschen n

solar noise [out]burst — s. radio burst

solar observatory — Sonnenobservatorium n

solar parallax, Sun['s] parallax — Sonnenparallaxe f

solar particle stream, solar stream — solarer Teilchenstrom m

solar patrol, solar survey — Sonnenüberwachung f

solar periscope, Sun periscope — Sonnenperiskop n, Sonnenkammer f

solar photography, heliophotography — Sonnenphotographie f

solar physics, physics of the Sun, heliophysics — Sonnenphysik f, Physik f der Sonne

solar prominence, prominence, solar surge — Protuberanz f, Sonnenprotuberanz f

solar radiation — Sonnenstrahlung f

solar radio-frequency radiation, solar radiowaves — Radiofrequenzstrahlung f der Sonne, Radiostrahlung f der Sonne, solare Radiostrahlung

solar radio noise — s. solar noise

solar radio-waves — s. solar radio-frequency radiation

solar research — Sonnenforschung f

solar short-wave radiation — Kurzstrahlung f, kurzwellige Sonnenstrahlung f

solar spectrograph — Sonnenspektrograph m

solar spectrum — Sonnenspektrum n

solar star, G star, sun-type star	G-Stern *m*, Sonnenähnlicher *m*	solid analytic geometry, elementary geometry, solid geometry	Elementargeometrie *f*
solar stream	*s.* solar particle stream	solid angle	Raumwinkel *m*, räumlicher (körperlicher) Winkel *m*
solar surge	*s.* solar prominence	solid anode	*s.* heavy anode
solar survey, solar patrol	Sonnenüberwachung *f*	solid anode tube, heavy anode tube	Vollanodenröhre *f*
solar system	Sonnensystem *n*, Planetensystem *n*		
solar-terrestrial phenomenon	*s.* Sun-Earth relationship	solid bath	Festsubstanzbad *n*
solar terrestrial radiation	terrestrische Sonnenstrahlung *f*	solid bed	Festbett *n*
solar-terrestrial relationship	*s.* Sun-Earth relationship	solid body, solid	Festkörper *m*, fester Körper *m*
solar thermometer	*s.* black-bulb thermometer	solid body, solid <math.>	Vollkörper *m*, Körper *m* <Math.>
solar tidal wave	*s.* solar wave	solid-borne sound, sound conducted through solids, body-borne sound	Körperschall *m*
solar tide	Sonnentide *f*		
solar tides	Sonnengezeiten *pl*		
solar time	Sonnenzeit *f*	solid-borne sound insulation	Körperschalldämmung *f*
solar total radiation, total radiation	Gesamtstrahlung *f* [der Sonne]	solid carbon dioxide	*s.* dry ice
solar tower, tower telescope	Turmteleskop *n*, Sonnenturm *m*	solid catalyst, contact [mass] <chem.>	Feststoffkatalysator *m*, Kontakt *m*, Kontaktstoff *m*, Kontaktmasse *f* <Chem.>
solar wave, solar tidal wave	Sonnenwelle *f*, Sonnengezeitenwelle *f*, Sonnenflutwelle *f*	solid circuit; semiconductor integrated circuit; single-chip circuit, single-chip device	integrierte Festkörperschaltung *f*, integrierte Halbleiterschaltung *f*, Festkörperschaltung
		solid conductor; solid line	massiver Leiter *m*, Volleiter *m*; massive Leitung *f*
solar wave radiation	Wellenstrahlung *f* der Sonne		
solar weather	*s.* solar activity	solid content, solid contents	Feststoffgehalt *m*
solar wind	Sonnenwind *m*, solarer Wind *m*		
solar year	Sonnenjahr *n*, Erdjahr *n*	solid-crystalline	fest-kristallin
		solid curve, full line, solid line	ausgezogene Kurve *f*, fette Linie *f*
solation, sol formation	Übergang *m* in den Solzustand, Solbildung *f*	solid detector	*s.* solid-state detector
solation, gel-sol transformation, gel-sol change	Gel-Sol-Umwandlung *f*	solid diffusion, intersolid diffusion	Festkörperdiffusion *f*, Diffusion *f* in der festen Phase, Diffusion zwischen Festkörpern
solder	Lot *n*, Lötlegierung *f*		
solder, solder[ed] connection, soldered joint, solder joint; connection by solder; junction <semi.>	Lötstelle *f*; Lötverbindung *f*	solid echo	Solidecho *n*, Festkörperecho *n*
		solid effect	*s.* solid state effect
		solidensing	*s.* desublimation
		solid-expansion thermometer, pointer thermometer	Zeigerthermometer *n*
soldering	*s.* seal		
solder joint	*s.* solder	solid film lubrication	Feststoffschmierung *f*
sole; sole fault	*s.* underlayer <geo.>		
Soleil [biquartz], Soleil compensator, Soleil halfshade (plate), Soleil['s] rotating biplate, bi[-]quartz [of Soleil]	Soleilsche Doppelplatte *f*, Soleil-Doppelplatte *f*, Doppelquarzplatte *f*, Doppelquarz *m*, Biquarzplatte *f*, Biquarz *m*, Soleilscher Kompensator *m*, [Babinet-]Soleil-Kompensator *m*, Halbschattenapparat *m* mit Soleilscher Doppelplatte	solid friction, dry friction	trockene Reibung *f*, Festkörperreibung *f*
		solid-gas interface, gas-solid interface	Festkörper/Gas-Grenzfläche *f*, Gas/Festkörper-Grenzfläche *f*, Grenzfläche *f* Festkörper — Gas (Gas — Festkörper, fest — gasförmig, gasförmig — fest)
solenoid, cylindrical coil	Solenoid *n*, Solenoidspule *f*, Zylinderspule *f*, Drahtspule *f*	solid geometry	*s.* solid analytic geometry
		solid geometry, stereometry	Stereometrie *f*, Körpermessung *f*
solenoidal field, source-free field	quellenfreies (divergenzfreies) Feld *n*, solenoidales Feld (Vektorfeld *n*)	solidification, solidifying, freezing; set, setting	Erstarrung *f*, Festwerden *n*, Verfestigung *f*
solenoidal inductor	*s.* standard inductance		
solenoidality	Quellenfreiheit *f*, Divergenzfreiheit *f*	solidification curve, melting (fusion, melting pressure) curve; ice line	Schmelzkurve *f*
solenoidal lens	*s.* solenoid lens	solidification heat, heat of solidification, latent heat of solidification	Erstarrungswärme *f*; Erstarrungsenthalpie *f*
solenoidal spectrometer	Solenoidspektrometer *n*		
solenoidal vector	quellenfreier Vektor *m*, solenoidaler Vektor	solidification interval	Erstarrungsintervall *n*
solenoid lens, Glaser lens, solenoidal lens	Glaser-Linse *f*, Solenoidlinse *f*	solidification point, solidifying temperature, solidification temperature, solidifying (solid) point, point of solidification; freezing point (temperature), point of freezing; congealing point	Verfestigungspunkt *m*, Verfestigungstemperatur *f*; Erstarrungspunkt *m*, Erstarrungstemperatur *f*; Gefrierpunkt *m*, Gefriertemperatur *f*
sole thrust	*s.* underlayer <geo.>		
solfatara	Solfatare *f*		
sol formation	*s.* solation		
sol-forming	solbildend		
sol-gel change	*s.* sol-gel transformation		
sol-gel process	Sol-Gel-Prozeß *m*		
sol-gel transformation, sol-gel change	Sol-Gel-Umwandlung *f*	solidification point	*s. a.* point of congelation
		solidification shrinkage, contraction of soldification	Erstarrungskontraktion *f*, Erstarrungsschwinden *n*
solid, solid body	Festkörper *m*, fester Körper *m*		
solid, solid material, solid substance	Feststoff *m*	solidification temperature	*s.* solidification point
		solidified gas	verfestigtes Gas *n*
solid, solid-state	fest	solidified lava, cool lava	erstarrte Lava *f*
solid	*s. a.* solid body <math.>	solidifying	*s.* solidification
solid-amorphous	fest-amorph		

solidifying point, point of congelation, congealing point, pour point, solidification point <of oil>	Stockpunkt m, Fließpunkt m <Öl>	solid-state electronic physics	Festkörper-Elektronenphysik f
solidifying point	s. a. solidification point	solid-state laser	s. solid-state optic[al] maser
solidifying temperature	s. solidification point	solid-state maser	Festkörpermaser m
solid injection	Festkörperinjektion f	solid state nuclear track detector	s. solid state track detector
solidity	Eigenschaft f, fest zu sein; Festkörpereigenschaft f	solid-state optic[al] maser, solid-state laser	Festkörperlaser m
solidity <of blades>	Ausfüllungsgrad m, Blattdichte f		
solidity	s. a. ruggedness <gen.>		
solidity	s. a. solid state	solid state physics, physics of solids	Festkörperphysik f
solid jet	Vollstrahl m, zusammenhaltender Strahl m	solid-state radiation detector	s. solid-state detector
solid line	s. solid conductor	solid-state reaction	Festkörperreaktion f
solid line	s. a. solid curve		
solid-liquid extraction; leaching; lixiviation	Laugung f, Auslaugung f, Auswaschung f, Festflüssig-Extraktion f	solid state track detector, solid state nuclear track detector, fission track detector	Festkörperspurdetektor m
solid-liquid interface, liquid-solid interface	Festkörper/Flüssigkeit-Grenzfläche f, Flüssigkeit/Festkörper-Grenzfläche f, Grenzfläche f Festkörper—Flüssigkeit (Flüssigkeit—Festkörper, fest—flüssig, flüssig—fest)	solid substance	s. solid
		solid suspensoid	festes Suspensoid n
		solidus, solidus curve, solidus line	Soliduslinie f, Soliduskurve f
		solifluction	Solifluktion f, Bodenfließen n, Bodenfluß m, subnivale (periglaziale) Denudation f
solid lubricant	s. grease		
solid material	s. solid		
solid measure	s. measure	solion	Solion n
solid of light distribution, solid of luminous-intensity distribution, surface of intensity distribution, polar surface of light distribution	Lichtstärkeverteilungskörper m, Lichtverteilungskörper m, Lichtverteilungsfläche f	solion detector	Soliongleichrichter m
		soliquid	s. sol
		solitary	s. isolated
		solitary wave, single wave	Einzelwelle f, solitäre Welle f
		soliton	Soliton n
		Soller slits, Soller slit system	Soller-Blende f, Soller-Spaltsystem n
solid of revolution (rotation), body of revolution (rotation), revolution solid	Rotationskörper m, Drehkörper m, Umdrehungskörper m	solstice	Solstitium n <pl.: -tien>, Sonnenwende f
		solstice	s. a. solstitial point
solid opal [glass]	Massivtrübglas n, Opalmassivglas n	solstice tide	Solstitialtide f
solid-plastic	fest-plastisch		
solid point	s. solidification point	solsticial, solstitial	solstitial, Solstitial-
solid profile	Vollprofil n		
solid-propellant motor, solid-propellant rocket engine	Raketenmotor m mit Festtreibstoff, Raketentriebwerk n mit festem Treibstoff	solstitial colure	Solstitialkolur m
		solstitial line	Solstitiallinie f
		solstitial point, solstice	Solstitialpunkt m, Sonnenwendpunkt m
solid residue, filter cake	Filterkuchen m, Filterrückstand m	solubility, dissolubility, dissolvability <chem.>	Löslichkeit f, Auflösbarkeit f <Chem.>
solid residue [from evaporation], total solids	Trockenrückstand m; Abdampfrückstand m	solubility, solvability, resolvability <math.>	Lösbarkeit f; Auflösbarkeit f <Math.>
solid sol	festes Sol n	solubility coefficient, Ostwald['s] solubility coefficient	Löslichkeitskoeffizient m, Löslichkeitszahl f
solid-solid interface	Festkörper/Festkörper-Grenzfläche f, Grenzfläche f Festkörper—Festkörper, Grenzfläche fest—fest		
		solubility curve, mutual solubility curve, plait point curve, critical curve, binodal [curve], solvus [curve]	Löslichkeitslinie f, Löslichkeitskurve f, Grenzkurve f [der Löslichkeit], Sättigungsisotherme f, Binodalkurve f
		solubility curve	s. a. solubility-temperature curve
solid solution; crystalline solid solution, mixcrystal, mixed [isomorphic] crystal	feste Lösung f, Festlösung f, Lösung im festen Zustand; [echter] Mischkristall m	solubility equilibrium	s. solution equilibrium
		solubility exponent	Löslichkeitsexponent m, Löslichkeitsindex m
solid sphere; full sphere	Vollkugel f		
		solubility limit	Löslichkeitsgrenze f
solid spherical harmonic	s. spatial spherical function	solubility potential, solution potential	Lösungspotential n
solid state, solidity	fester Zustand (Aggregatzustand) m, Festkörperzustand m; fest-kristalliner Zustand	solubility pressure	s. solution pressure
		solubility product [constant]	Löslichkeitsprodukt n
solid-state, solid	fest	solubility-temperature curve, solubility versus temperature curve, solubility curve	Löslichkeits-Temperatur-Kurve f, Löslichkeits-Temperaturkurve f, Löslichkeitskurve f
solid-state atomic physics	Festkörper-Atomphysik f		
solid-state bonding	Verbindung f im festen Zustand <unter Druckanwendung>	solubilization	Solubilisation f, Solubilisierung f, Lösungsvermittlung f
solid-state detector, solid-state radiation detector, solid detector	Festkörperdetektor m, Festkörper-Strahlungsdetektor m	solubilizer; solutizer	Solubilisator m; Lösungsvermittler m
		soluble electrode	Lösungselektrode f
solid state effect, solid effect, Abragam-Jeffries effect	Festkörpereffekt m, Abragam-Jeffries-Effekt m	soluble glass, water glass	Wasserglas n

soluble in cold state	kaltlöslich
soluble in hot liquids	warmlöslich, in der Wärme löslich
soluble in water, water-soluble	wasserlöslich
soluble ribonucleic acid, soluble RNA	s. transfer ribonucleic acid
solute	Gelöstes n, [auf]gelöster Stoff m, in Lösung gegangener Stoff, gelöste Substanz f
solutide	s. true solution
solution <chem.>	Lösung f <Chem.>
solution <math.>	Lösung f; Auflösung f <Math.>
solution	s. a. medium <chem.>
solution	s. a. dissolution <chem.>
solution annealing	s. solution treatment
solution capacity, solving capacity	Lösungskapazität f
solution cavity, cave <geo.>	Karsthöhle f <Geo.>
solution concentration	s. solution strength
solution enthalpy	s. heat of solution
solution equilibrium, solubility equilibrium	Lösungsgleichgewicht n
solution heat	s. heat of solution
solution heat treatment	s. solution treatment
solution potential, solubility potential	Lösungspotential n
solution power, solvency	Lösevermögen n, Lösungsvermögen n, Solvenz f
solution pressure, solution tension, electrolytic[al] solution pressure (tension), solubility pressure	[elektrolytischer] Lösungsdruck m, Lösungstension f
solution reactor	Lösungsreaktor m, Reaktor m mit Brennstofflösung
solution sea	Karstsee m
solution spectrum, dissolution spectrum	Lösungsspektrum n
solution strength, solution concentration	Lösungskonzentration f, Lösungsgehalt m, Lösungsstärke f, Reaktionsstärke f der Lösung
solution surface <math.>	Lösungsfläche f <Math.>
solution to be tested, trial solution	Probenlösung f, Probelösung f
solution treatment, solution heat treatment, solution annealing	Lösungsglühen n
solutizer	s. solubilizer
solutrope	solutropes Gemisch n, Solutrop n
solvability	s. solubility
solvate	Solvat n, Solvatationskomplex m
solvation	Solvatation f, Solvatisierung f
solvation constant	Solvatationskonstante f
solvation energy	Solvatationsenergie f
solvation force	Solvatationskraft f
solvation number	Solvatationszahl f
solvation sheath (shell, sphere), sheath of solvent molecules	Solvathülle f
solvation water	Solvatwasser n
solvatochromism, solvatochromy	Solvatochromie f
solvency	s. solution power
solvent, solvent agent; dissolvent; developer liquid, mobile (moving) phase <chromatography>	Lösungsmittel n, Lösemittel n, Solvens n <pl.: -zien>; Laufmittel n, Fließmittel n <Chromatographie>
solvent action	s. solvent effect
solvent agent	s. solvent
solvent effect, solvent action	Lösungsmitteleinfluß m, Lösungs[mittel]effekt m
solvent extraction	Solventextraktion f, Lösungsmittelextraktion f
solvent front	s. band of moving phase
solvent-hating, lyophobic, lyophobe	lyophob, lösungsmittelabstoßend
solvent-loving, lyophilic, lyophile	lyophil, lösungsmittelanziehend
solvent phase	Lösungsmittelphase f, Solventphase f
solvent shift	Lösungsmittelverschiebung f, Solventshift m, „solvent shift" m
solving capacity, solution capacity	Lösungskapazität f
solving space	lösender Raum m
solvolysis, lyolysis	Solvolyse f, Lyolyse f
solvolyte	Solvolyseprodukt n, Solvolyt m
solvolytic equilibrium	Solvolysegleichgewicht n
solvus [curve]	s. solubility curve
Somigliana['s] dislocation	Somiglianasche Versetzung f
Sommerfeld['s] criterion	Sommerfeldsches Kriterium (Entartungskriterium) n
Sommerfeld fine structure constant	s. fine structure constant
Sommerfeld['s] fine structure formula, Sommerfeld['s] formula of fine structure	Sommerfeldsche Feinstrukturformel f
Sommerfeld['s] fine structure theory, Sommerfeld['s] theory of fine structure	Sommerfeldsche Feinstrukturtheorie f
Sommerfeld['s] formula <el.>	Formel f von Sommerfeld, Sommerfeldsche Formel <El.>
Sommerfeld['s] formula of fine structure	s. Sommerfeld['s] fine structure formula
Sommerfeld-Kossel displacement law	s. displacement law for complex spectra
Sommerfeld['s] law of dublets	Sommerfeldsches Dublettgesetz n, Dublettgesetz von Sommerfeld
Sommerfeld line	s. Sommerfeld['s] single-wire transmission line
Sommerfeld orbit	Sommerfeldsche Bahn f, Bohr-Sommerfeldsche Bahn
Sommerfeld['s] radiation condition	s. radiation condition
Sommerfeld['s] single-wire transmission line, Sommerfeld wire (line)	Sommerfeldscher Wellenleiter m
Sommerfeld['s] surface wave	s. surface wave
Sommerfeld['s] theory of fine structure, Sommerfeld['s] fine structure theory	Sommerfeldsche Feinstrukturtheorie f
Sommerfeldt plate	Sommerfeldtsche Doppelplatte f
Sommerfeld-Watson transform[ation]	s. Watson-Sommerfeld transform[ation]
Sommerfeld wave	s. surface wave <el.>
Sommerfeld wire	s. Sommerfeld['s] single-wire transmission line
sonar listening set	Wasserschallempfänger m
sonar transmitter	s. underwater sound projector
sondage	s. sounding
sonde	s. probe
sone	Sone n, sone
sonic altimeter	s. sonic depth finder
sonic analysis	s. sound analysis
sonic analyzer	s. sound analyzer
sonic bang	s. supersonic bang
sonic barrier	s. sound barrier
sonic beam, beam of sound, sound beam, acoustic beam	Schallstrahlenbündel n, Schallwellenbündel n, Schallbündel n
sonic boom	s. supersonic bang
sonic circle	sonischer Kreis m, Schallkreis m
sonic delay line	s. ultrasonic delay line

sonic depth finder, sonic echo sounder, sonic altimeter, acoustic sounder	Tonlot n, Tonecholot n, akustisches Echolot n
sonic energy, sound energy, acoustic energy	Schallenergie f
sonic field	s. sound field
sonic flow	Schallströmung f, Strömung f im Schallbereich
sonic jet	sonischer Strahl m
sonic line	sonische Linie f, Schallinie f
sonic oscillation	s. sound oscillation
sonic point	sonischer Punkt m, Schallpunkt m
sonic pressure, acoustic[al] pressure, sound pressure	Schalldruck m, Schallwechseldruck m, akustischer Druck m
sonic probe, sound probe	Schallsonde f
sonic range	s. sonic region
sonic ray, ray of sound, sound ray, acoustic ray	Schallstrahl m
sonic regime	s. sonic region
sonic region, sonic range; sonic regime	Schallbereich m
sonics	Sonik f ‹technische Anwendung von Schallschwingungen›
sonic spark chamber, acoustic spark chamber	akustische Funkenkammer f, Funkenkammer mit akustischer Lokalisierung
sonic speed	s. velocity of sound ‹ac.›
sonic thermometer	Schallthermometer n
sonic velocity	s. velocity of sound ‹ac.›
sonic wave, sound wave, acoustic[al] wave	Schallwelle f
sonigage	s. ultrasonic thickness gauge ‹for metals›
Sonine['s] expansion	Soninesche Entwicklung f
Sonine['s] polynomial	Soninesches Polynom n, Polynom von Sonine
soniscope	s. ultrasonic flaw detector
sonochemiluminescence	Sonochemilumineszenz f
sonochemistry, ultrasonic chemistry	Ultraschallchemie f
sonoluminescence	Sonolumineszenz f
sonometer, monochord	Monochord n, Sonometer n
soot colloid[al] solution	s. carbon sol
S-operator, scattering operator	Streuoperator m, S-Operator m
sorbate	Sorbat n, Sorptiv n, Sorbend m
sorbent, sorbing agent, sorptive material	Sorbens n ‹pl.: -zien›, Sorptionsmittel n
Sørensen pH scale	Sørensensche pH-Skala f
Soret band	Soret-Bande f
Soret effect, Ludwig-Soret effect	Soret-Effekt m, Soret-Phänomen n, Ludwig-Soret-Effekt m
Soret effect	s. a. thermal diffusion
Soret zone plate	Soretsche Zonenplatte f
sorption	Sorption f, Sorbieren n
sorption balance [of McBain]	Sorptionswaage f [nach McBain]
sorption capacity, T value ‹bio.›	T-Wert m, Umtauschkapazität f, Austauschkapazität f, Sorptionskapazität f ‹Bio.›
sorption capacity	s. a. cation exchange capacity
sorption complex	Sorptionskomplex m, Austauschkomplex m, Ton-Humus-Komplex m
sorption isotherm	Sorptionsisotherme f
sorption pump; getter pump, all-dry high-vacuum pump	Sorptionspumpe f; Getterpumpe f
sorption pump	s. a. getter-ion pump
sorption theory [of cell permeability]	Sorptionstheorie f ‹der Zellpermeabilität oder Erregung›, Nassonow-Troschinsche Theorie f; Paranekrosetheorie f [der Erregung]
sorption water	Sorptionswasser n
sorptive binding (linkage)	sorptive Bindung f
sorptive material	s. sorbent
sort, grade	Güteklasse f; Gütegrad m; Sorte f
sorting	s. sizing
sorting ‹e.g. of electrons›	Sortierung f, Trennung f ‹z. B. Elektronen›
sorting[-out] by hand, picking [out]	Klauben n, Handscheidung f
sort of atom, nuclide, nuclear species, atomic species	Nuklid n, Kernart f, Kernsorte f, Atomart f, Atomsorte f
sort of particle, kind of particle; type of particle	Teilchensorte f; Teilchenart f
Sothic cycle	Sothisperiode f, Hundssternperiode f
Soucy-Bayly bridge	Soucy-Bayly-Brücke f
sound, probe, feeler, sonde	Sonde f; Fühler m; Taster m; Spürgerät n
sound ‹ac.›	Schall m ‹Ak.›
sound, tone ‹ac.›	Ton m ‹Ak.›
sound ‹ac.›	Laut m ‹Ak.›
sound, musical sound, tone ‹ac.›	Klang m ‹Ak.›
sound absorber, sound absorbing material, absorbing material, acoustic[al] material, material for sound absorption	Schallschluckstoff m, schallschluckender Stoff, schallschluckendes Material n, Schallabsorptionsstoff m, schallabsorbierendes Material, Dämpfungsmaterial n
sound-absorbing, sound-absorptive	schallschluckend, schallabsorbierend
sound absorbing material	s. sound absorber
sound absorbing wall, sound damping (deadening) wall	Schallschluckwand f
sound absorption, absorption of sound, acoustic[al] absorption	Schallabsorption f, Schallschluckung f
sound absorption capacity, sound absorption power	Schallschluckvermögen n, Schallabsorptionsvermögen n
sound absorption coefficient (factor)	s. acoustic absorption factor ‹ac.›
sound absorption power	s. sound absorption capacity
sound-absorptive	s. sound-absorbing
sound absorptivity	s. acoustic absorption factor ‹ac.›
sound amplifier	Tonverstärker m; Schallverstärker m; Lautverstärker m
sound analysis, acoustic analysis, sonic analysis	Schallanalyse f; Klanganalyse f; Tonanalyse f
sound analyzer, sound wave analyzer, sonic analyzer; audio frequency analyzer	Schallanalysator m, Schallanalysegerät n, Schallwellenanalysator m; Klanganalysator m; Tonanalysator m; Tonfrequenzanalysator m
sound attenuating material	s. sound insulator ‹ac.›
sound attenuation	s. attenuation of sound
sound attenuation coefficient (factor)	s. coefficient of sound damping
sound barrier, sonic barrier	Schallmauer f; Schallgrenze f
sound beam, beam of sound, acoustic beam, sonic beam	Schallstrahlenbündel n, Schallwellenbündel n, Schallbündel n
sound board, sounding board	Resonanzboden m; Resonanzkörper m; Schallboden m, Klangboden m
sound column	Tonsäule f, Schallsäule f
sound combination, unpitched sound ‹ac.›	Klanggemisch n ‹Ak.›
sound composition, composition of sound	Klangzusammensetzung f

sound concentration, focusing of sound, sound focusing, concentration of sound	Schallbündelung f, Schallkonzentrierung f, Schallkonzentration f, Schallfokussierung f	**sound generation,** generation of sound, sound excitation, excitation of sound	Schallerzeugung f, Schallerregung f, Schallanregung f; Klangerzeugung f
sound concentrator, acoustic concentrator	Schallkonzentrator m, akustischer Konzentrator m	**sound generator,** generator of sound, acoustic generator, sound producer	Schallerzeuger m, Schallgenerator m; Schallgeber m; Schallerreger m
sound conducted through solids, solid-borne sound, body-borne sound	Körperschall m		
sound-conducting	schalleitend	**sound-hard,** acoustically hard, acoustically rigid	schallhart
sound conduction, conduction of sound	Schalleitung f	**sound-hard boundary [surface],** acoustically rigid boundary [surface], rigid boundary surface	schallharte Grenzfläche f, starre Grenzfläche
sound conductivity	Schalleitfähigkeit f	**sound hardness**	s. acoustic stiffness
		sound horn	s. sound funnel
sound conductivity	s. a. sound conduction	**sound image,** acoustic[al] image	Schallbild n, akustisches Bild n, akustische Abbildung f
sound conductor; acoustic line, sound line	Schalleiter m; Schalleitung f	**sound in air**	s. sound transmitted in air
sound-damping	s. sound-deadening	**sounding**	Schallen n; Ertönen n, Erklingen n
sound damping	s. a. attenuation of sound		
sound damping coefficient (factor)	s. coefficient of sound damping	**sounding,** sondage	Sondierung f
		sounding, probing, plumbing	Lotung f
sound damping material	s. sound insulator <ac.>		
sound damping wall	s. sound absorbing wall	**sounding balloon,** test balloon, air-sonde	Ballonsonde f, Sondenballon m, Sonde f
sound deadener	s. sound insulator <ac.>	**sounding board**	s. sound board
sound deadening, sound (acoustical) insulation, sound proofing, [sound] deafening	Schallisolierung f, Schallisolation f, Schalldämmung f	**sounding electrode,** probe electrode	Sondierelektrode f, Sondenelektrode f
		sounding lead	s. plumb
sound-deadening, sound-insulating, sound-deafening, sound-damping	schalldämmend; schalldämpfend; schallisolierend	**sounding machine**	Lotmaschine f, Patentlot n
		sounding pole	s. sounding rod
sound deadening [material]	s. sound insulator <ac.>	**sounding rocket**	s. research rocket
		sounding rod, sounding pole	Sondierstange f, Peilstange f, Peil n
sound deadening wall	s. sound absorbing wall		
sound deafener	s. sound insulator <ac.>	**sound-insulating,** sound-deadening, sound-deafening, sound-damping	schalldämmend; schalldämpfend; schallisolierend
sound-deafening	s. sound deadening		
sound deafening [material]	s. sound insulator <ac.>	**sound insulating material**	s. sound insulator <ac.>
sound dispersion, dispersion of sound, acoustic dispersion	Schalldispersion f	**sound insulation,** acoustical insulation, sound proofing (deadening, deafening), deafening, deadening	Schallisolierung f, Schallisolation f, Schalldämmung f
sound dissipation factor, dissipation factor, acoustic dissipation factor <ac.>	Schalldissipationsgrad m, Dissipationsgrad m, Verwärmgrad m <Ak.>		
sound duct, duct, wave duct <ac.>	akustischer Wellenleiter m, Wellenleiter <Ak.>	**sound insulation material**	s. sound insulator <ac.>
sound emitter	s. sound transmitter	**sound insulator,** [sound] insulating material, [sound] insulation material, [sound] isolation material, sound deadener, sound deadening [material], sound deafener, sound deafening [material], [sound] damping material, [sound] attenuating material <ac.>	Schalldämmstoff m, schalldämmender Stoff, Dämmstoff m, Dämmaterial n, schalldämmendes Material n, Schalldämpfstoff m, schalldämpfender Stoff m, schalldämpfendes Material n, Schallisolationsstoff m <Ak.>
sound emitter	s. a. acoustical radiator.		
sound-emitting fireball, detonating fireball	explodierende Feuerkugel f, Feuerkugel mit anhaltendem Donner		
sound energy, sonic (acoustic) energy	Schallenergie f		
sound energy density	Schalldichte f, Schallenergiedichte f		
sound energy flux, sound power, acoustic power	Schalleistung f, akustische Leistung f, Leistung der Schallquelle, Schallquellenleistung f		
		sound intensity, intensity of sound, specific sound-energy flux, sound energy flux density	Schallstärke f, Schalleistungsdichte f, Schallintensität f, Intensität f des Schalls; Tonstärke f, Stärke f des Tones
sound energy flux, instantaneous acoustic power [across a surface element]	momentane Schalleistung f, Schallenergiefluß m		
sound energy flux density	s. sound intensity	**sound intensity level,** intensity level, sound energy flux density level, specific sound energy flux level <ac.>	Schallpegel m, Schallstärkepegel m
sound energy flux density level	s. sound intensity level <ac.>		
sound entrainment, entrainment of sound	Schallmitführung f	**sound intensity meter,** volume meter	Tonmesser m, Tonmeßgerät n
sound excitation	s. sound generation		
sound field, sonic field	Schallfeld n	**sound interferometer,** acoustic interferometer	Schallinterferometer n
sound field quantity, quantity of sound field, acoustic[al] quantity	Schallfeldgröße f, Schallgröße f	**sound in water,** waterborne sound, sound propagating in water	Wasserschall m
		sound isolation material	s. sound insulator <ac.>
sound fixing-and-ranging, sound location, sound ranging	Schallortung f, Schallquellenortung f, Schallradar n, akustische Ortung f, Horchortung f; akustisches Meßverfahren n	**sound lens,** acoustic lens	akustische Linse f, Schallinse f
		sound level, audio level	Tonpegel m
sound focusing	s. sound concentration	**sound level indicator**	s. volume indicator
sound funnel, acoustic horn, [scund] horn <ac.>	Schalltrichter m, Trichter m <Ak.>	**sound level meter,** volume meter, vu-meter <ac.>	[objektiver] Lautstärkemesser, Schallpegelmesser m mit Bewertung, Volum[en]messer m, VU-Meter n <Ak.>

sound

sound line	s. sound conductor	sound ranging	s. sound fixing-and-ranging
sound location	s. sound fixing-and-ranging	sound ray, ray of sound, acoustic ray, sonic ray	Schallstrahl m
sound locator	Schallortungsgerät n	sound receiver; sound receptor	Schallempfänger m, Schallaufnehmer m; Tonempfänger m; Schallrezeptor m
sound mirage	Schallspiegelung f		
sound-on-film recording	s. photographic sound recording		
sound-on-wire recording, wire recording	Stahldrahtverfahren n	sound record, phonogram	Phonogramm n, Schallaufzeichnung f
		sound record[ing]	s. record [of sound] <ac.>
		sound reduction factor	s. acoustical reduction factor
		sound reflection coefficient (factor), sound reflectivity	s. reflection coefficient <ac.>
sound optics	Schalloptik f		
sound oscillation, sound vibration, sonic oscillation; acoustic oscillation, acoustic vibration	Schallschwingung f; akustische Schwingung f	sound rejection; sound suppression	Schallunterdrückung f
		sound relaxation	Schallrelaxation f
sound particle velocity	s. particle velocity	sound reproduction	Tonwiedergabe f, Schallwiedergabe f
sound path, trajectory of sound, sound trajectory	Schallbahn f, Schallweg m		
sound pattern	s. Chladni['s] figures	sound resonance, acoustical resonance	Schallresonanz f, akustische Resonanz f
sound perception, acoustic perception	Schallwahrnehmung f	sound room	s. reverberation chamber
sound permeability	s. sound transmittance	sound sensation	Schallempfindung f, Klangempfindung f
sound pitch, pitch [of the tone], pitch of note, tone pitch <ac.>	Tonhöhe f, Höhe f <Ton> <Ak.>	sound-sensitive flame, sensitive flame, microphonic flame	empfindliche Flamme f, schallempfindliche Flamme
sound power	s. sound energy flux		
sound power level, [acoustic] power level <ac.>	Schalleistungspegel m	sound shadow, acoustic shadow	Schallschatten m
		sound-soft, acoustically soft, yielding	schallweich
sound power meter, acoustic power meter	Schalleistungsmesser m	sound-soft boundary [surface], acoustically soft boundary [surface], yielding boundary [surface]	schallweiche Grenzfläche f, nachgebende Grenzfläche
sound pressure, acoustic[al] pressure, sonic pressure	Schalldruck m, Schallwechseldruck m, akustischer Druck m		
sound pressure amplitude, pressure amplitude	Schalldruckamplitude f, Druckamplitude f	sound source, source of sound, acoustic source, source of acoustic energy	Schallquelle f
sound pressure directivity factor	Schalldruckrichtfaktor m		
		sound spectrograph, acoustic[al] spectrograph	Schallspektrograph m
sound pressure increase	Druckstauung f, Schalldruckstauung f	sound spectrography, acoustic[al] spectrography	Schallspektrographie f
sound pressure level, pressure level, S.P.L.	Schalldruckpegel m, Schallpegel m	sound spectroscopy, acoustic[al] spectroscopy	Schallspektroskopie f
sound pressure level equal loudness contour	s. Robinson-Dadson equal loudness contour	sound spectrum, acoustic[al] spectrum; audible spectrum, audio spectrum	Schallspektrum n; Niederfrequenzspektrum n, NF-Spektrum n, Tonfrequenzspektrum n, Hörfrequenzspektrum n; Klangspektrum n; Tonspektrum n
sound pressure meter	Schalldruckmesser m		
sound pressure receiver, acoustic pressure receiver	Schalldruckempfänger m		
sound pressure transformation	Drucktransformation f		
		sound suppression	s. sound rejection
		sound synthesis	Klangsynthese f
		sound track	Tonspur f
sound pressure transmission factor, pressure response (sensitivity) <ac.>	Druckübertragungsmaß n, Druckempfindlichkeit f, Druckübertragungsfaktor m <Ak.>	sound trajectory, trajectory of sound, sound path	Schallbahn f, Schallweg m
		sound transducer	Schallwandler m
sound probe, sonic probe	Schallsonde f		
sound producer	s. sound generator	sound transmission	s. transmission of sound
sound projection	s. radiation of sound	sound transmission coefficient (factor)	s. acoustic transmission factor <ac.>
sound-proof	schalldicht, schallundurchlässig, schallsicher	sound transmission quality, transmission quality (performance), quality of transmission, microphone quality	Übertragungsgüte f
sound proofing	s. sound insulation		
sound propagating in water, waterborne sound, sound in water	Wasserschall m		
sound propagation time	Schallaufzeit f	sound transmittance; sound permeability	Schalldurchlässigkeit f
sound propagation velocity	s. velocity of sound <ac.>	sound transmitted in air, airborne sound, sound in air	Luftschall m
sound pulse	Schallimpuls m, Schallstoß m		
sound quantum, phonon, quantum of acoustic wave energy	Phonon n, Schallquant n	sound transmitter, sound emitter	Schallsender m
		sound transmittivity	s. acoustic transmission factor <ac.>
sound radar	Schallradar n, Schallortungsradar n	sound velocity	s. velocity of sound <ac.>
sound radiation	s. radiation of sound	sound vibration	s. sound oscillation
sound radiation impedance, radiation impedance <ac.>	Schallstrahlungsimpedanz f, Schallstrahlungswiderstand m, Strahlungswiderstand m, Strahlungsimpedanz f <Ak.>	sound volume, volume of sound <ac.>	Klangumfang m <Ak.>
		sound wave, sonic wave, acoustic[al] wave	Schallwelle f
		sound wave analyzer	s. sound analyzer
sound radiation pressure	s. acoustic radiation pressure	sound wave impedance	s. characteristic acoustic impedance
sound radiometer	s. acoustical radiometer	source, origination, origin	Ursprung m, Entstehung f, Bildung f; Herkunft f, Zustandekommen n
sound ranger	akustischer Entfernungsmesser m		

source ⟨gen.; e.g. of field⟩	Quelle *f* ⟨allg.; z. B. des Feldes⟩	source of error, source of inaccuracy	Fehlerquelle *f*
source; spring; well ⟨geo.⟩	Quelle *f* ⟨Geo.⟩	source of glare, dazzle source	Blendquelle *f*
source ⟨hydr.⟩	Quelle *f* ⟨Hydr.⟩	source of heat, heat source; heat pole	Wärmequelle *f*; Wärmepol *m*; Wärmespender *m*
source, spring ⟨geo.⟩	Schichtquelle *f* ⟨Geo.⟩	source of illumination, light source of microscope [illumination] ⟨of microscope⟩	Mikroskopierleuchte *f*, Mikroleuchte *f*
source, radioactive source, radioactivity source ⟨nucl.⟩	Quelle *f*, Strahlungsquelle *f*, Aktivitätsquelle *f*; radioaktives Präparat *n*, Präparat ⟨Kern.⟩	source of inaccuracy	s. source of error
		source of light, light source, luminous source	Lichtquelle *f*
source ⟨semi.⟩	Sourceelektrode *f*, Source *f*, Quelle *f*, s-Pol *m* ⟨Halb.⟩	source of power	s. source of energy
		source of radiation, radiation source; radiating body	Strahlungsquelle *f*, Strahlenquelle *f*; Strahlengeber *m*, Strahler *m*
source	s. a. source point		
source admittance	Quellenleitwert *m*, Quellleitwert *m*		
source-and-sink distribution, source-sink distribution	Quelle-Senken-Verteilung *f*, Belegungsfunktion *f*	source of radiofrequency radiation	s. radio source
		source of river	Flußquelle *f*, Wasserquellgebiet *n*, Ursprung *m* des Flusses
source-and-sink method, method of sources, source-sink method, sink-source method; small source theory ⟨nucl.⟩	Quelle-Senken-Methode *f*, Quelle-Senken-Verfahren *n*	source of sound, sound (acoustic) source, source of acoustic energy	Schallquelle *f*
		source of standard tone, standard tone source ⟨1 000 c/s⟩	Normaltonquelle *f* ⟨1 000 Hz⟩
source-and-sink system, source-sink system	Quelle-Senken-System *n*, Quell-Senken-System *n*	source of stimulation	Reizquelle *f*
source cask ⟨US⟩	s. source flask		
source container	s. source flask		
source core	Quellkern *m*	source particle	Quellteilchen *n*
source density, density of sources (source distribution)	Quelldichte *f*, Quellendichte *f*	source point, point of source, source	Quellpunkt *m*; Quellstelle *f*
		source production, manufacturing of sources	Quellenherstellung *f*
source distribution	Quellverteilung *f*, Quellenverteilung *f*; Quellenbelegung *f*		
source emitting according to a cosine law, cosine source, cosine surface source	Kosinusquelle *f* [von Lambert], Lambertsche Kosinusquelle *f*	source range	Quell[en]bereich *m*, Reaktorbetrieb *m* mit Hilfsquelle
source erosion, spring erosion	Quellerosion *f*		
source excitation	Sourceanregung *f*		
source field	Quellenfeld *n*	source reactor	Quellreaktor *m*, Quellenreaktor *m*
source fissure	Quellschlot *m*	source region ⟨of vector field⟩	Quellgebiet *n* ⟨Vektorfeld⟩
source flask, source cask ⟨US⟩, source container	Quellenkontainer *m*, Quellenbehälter *m*, Kontainer *m* für Strahlungsquellen	source resistance, internal resistance ⟨of source⟩	Innenwiderstand *m*, innerer Widerstand *m*; Eigenwiderstand *m* ⟨Stromquelle⟩
source flow	s. flow from sources	source resistance	s. a. source impedance
source flux	Quellfluß *m*	source-sink distribution, source-and-sink distribution	Quelle-Senken-Verteilung *f*, Belegungsfunktion *f*
source follower circuit, common drain circuit, common drain connection	Source-Folgerschaltung *f*, Drain-Basisschaltung *f*		
		source-sink method	s. source-and-sink method
		source-sink pair	Quelle-Senken-Paar *n*
source force	Quellenkraft *f*	source-sink representation	Quellen-Senken-Darstellung *f*, Quelle-Senken-Darstellung *f*
source-free field	s. solenoidal field		
source function, Green's function, Green function	Greensche Funktion *f*, Einflußfunktion *f*, Quellenfunktion *f*		
		source-sink system, source-and-sink system	Quelle-Senken-System *n*, Quell[en]-Senken-System *n*
source function ⟨astr.⟩	Ergiebigkeit *f* ⟨Quelle⟩, Quellfunktion *f*, Quellenfunktion *f* ⟨Astr.⟩	source strength, strength of source, strength	Quell[en]stärke *f*; Stärke (Ergiebigkeit) *f* der Strahlungsquelle, Präparatstärke *f*
source funnel	Quelltrichter *m*; Quelltopf *m*		
		source system, system of sources	Quellsystem *n*, Quellensystem *n*
		source term	Quell[en]term *m*, Quellenglied *n*
source hardening	Quellenhärtung *f*, Härtung *f* des Quellenspektrums	source-to-film distance	Quelle-Film-Abstand *m*
source impedance, source resistance	Quell[en]widerstand *m*, Quell[en]impedanz *f*	source-to-skin distance, SSD	Abstand *m* Strahlungsquelle—Haut, Strahlungsquelle-Haut-Abstand *m*
source interlock	Quellenverriegelung *f*		
source layer	Quellschicht *f*		
source line, line of sources	Quellinie *f*, Quellfaden *m*	source-type solution	quellenförmige Lösung *f*
		source-vortex distribution	Quelle-Wirbel-Verteilung *f*
source neutron	Quellneutron *n*		
source of alpha-particles, alpha-particle source	Alpha-Strahlungsquelle *f*, Alpha-Quelle *f*	source water, spring water	Quellwasser *n*
		sourdine, mute, muffler	Sordine *f*, Sordino *m*, Dämpfer *m*
source of current, current source, power source	Stromquelle *f*	southern dawn	s. southern lights
		southern hemisphere	südliche Hemisphäre (Halbkugel) *f*, Südhalbkugel *f*, Südhemisphäre *f*
source of energy; power source, source of power; energy source	Energiequelle *f*, Energieträger *m*; Kraftquelle *f*		

southern lights, southern dawn, aurora australis — Südlicht *n*, Aurora *f* australis

south magnetic pole — magnetischer Südpol *m*

south point [of the horizon] — Südpunkt *m*, Mittagspunkt *m*

Southwell method [of critical load] — Southwellsche Methode *f*

soxhlet, Soxhlet [extraction] apparatus — Soxhlet-Apparat *m*, Soxhlet *m*

space <math.> — Raum *m*; Raumgebiet *n*, Gebiet *n* <Math.>

space; gap; slit; slot — Spalt *m*; Schlitz *m*

space, spatial — räumlich, Raum-

space — s. a. spatial

space — s. a. gap <techn.>

space and time — s. space-time <math.>

space and time localization, localization in space and time — räumliche und zeitliche Lokalisierung *f*

space axis — Raumachse *f*

space between Fabry-Pérot interferometer plates — Luftplatte *f*, planparallele Luftplatte, Fabry-Pérotscher (Pérot-Fabryscher, Pérotscher) Luftraum *m*

space centered <US>, **space-centred,** body-centred, body-centered <US>, b.c. — raumzentriert, innenzentriert, r. z.

space charge — Raumladung *f*, elektrische Raumladung; Eigenladung *f*

space-charge accumulation — Raumladungsanhäufung *f*, Raumladungsstauung *f*

space-charge attenuation <of shot effect> — Raumladungsschwächung *f* <Schroteffekt>

space-charge attenuation factor — Raumladungsschwächungsfaktor *m*

space-charge barrier [layer] — Raumladungsgrenzschicht *f*, Raumladungs[sperr]-schicht *f*

space-charge beam spreading — Strahlverbreiterung (Bündelverbreiterung) *f* durch Eigenladung

space-charge build up — Raumladungsaufbau *m*

space-charge capacitance — Raumladungskapazität *f*

space charge capacitance — s. barrier-layer capacitance

space-charge-controlled [electron] lens — s. space-charge lens

space-charge current — Raumladungsstrom *m*, Raumladestrom *m*; Raumladungsströmung *f*

space charge density, spatial charge density, spatial density of [electric] charge, volume density of [electric] charge, density of volume charge, space charge per unit volume — Raumladungsdichte *f*, räumliche Ladungsdichte *f*

space-charge detector — Raumladungsdetektor *m*

space-charge diode — Raumladungsdiode *f*

space-charge distortion — Raumladungsverzerrung *f*

space-charge effect, influence of space charge — Raumladungseinfluß *m*, Raumladungseffekt *m*, Raumladungswirkung *f*

space-charge equivalent lens — s. space-charge lens

space-charge factor, perveance — Perveanz *f*, Raumladungskonstante *f*, Raumladungsfaktor *m*

space-charge field — Raumladungsfeld *n*

space-charge force — Raumladungskraft *f*

space-charge grid, cathode grid, control grid — Raumladegitter *n*, Raumladungsgitter *n*, Raumladungszerstreuungsgitter *n*

space-charge-grid tube — Raumladegitterröhre *f*, Raumladungsgitterröhre *f*

space charge law — s. Langmuir['s] law

space-charge layer — Raumladungsschicht *f*, Raumladeschicht *f*

space-charge lens, space-charge equivalent lens, space-charge-controlled [electron] lens — Raumladungslinse *f*

space-charge limitation [of currents] — Raumladungsbegrenzung *f*

space-charge-limited current, SCL current — raumladungsbegrenzter Strom *m*; raumladungsbegrenzte Strömung *f*

space-charge-limited operation — raumladungsbegrenzter Betrieb *m*

space-charge modulation — Raumladungsmodulation *f*

space-charge movement — Raumladungswanderung *f*

space charge per unit volume — s. space charge density

space-charge polarization — Raumladungspolarisation *f*

space-charge region <semi.> — Raumladungszone *f*, Raumladezone *f*, Raumladungsbereich *m*, Raumladebereich *m*, Raumladungsgebiet *n*, Raumladegebiet *n*, Raumladungsschicht *f*, Raumladeschicht *f* <Halb.>

space-charge relaxation time — Raumladungs-Relaxationszeit *f*

space-charge wave — Raumladungswelle *f*

space-charge wavelength — Raumladungswellenlänge *f*

space chemistry, astrochemistry, cosmochemistry, cosmic chemistry — Kosmochemie *f*, Astrochemie *f*

space coherence — Raumkohärenz *f*, räumliche Kohärenz *f*

space cone, herpolhode cone — Herpolhodiekegel *m*, Rastpolkegel *m*; Ruhekegel *m*, Festkegel *m*, raumfester Drehkegel *m*

space continuum — s. space-time <math.>

space co-ordinates, spatial co-ordinates, position co-ordinates, co-ordinates; space-fixed co-ordinates, co-ordinates fixed in space — Ortskoordinaten *fpl*, Raumkoordinaten *fpl*, Lagekoordinaten *fpl*; raumfeste Koordinaten *fpl*

space co-ordinates, co-ordinates in space — räumliche Koordinaten *fpl*, Koordinaten im Raum

space[-]craft — s. space vehicle

space curve, spatial curve; twisted curve, curve of double curvature, skew curve — Raumkurve *f*; doppeltgekrümmte Kurve *f*, Kurve doppelter Krümmung, nichtebene Kurve

space degeneration, directional (spatial) degeneration — Richtungsentartung *f*

space density — s. volume density

space dependence; local variation — Ortsabhängigkeit *f*

space devoid of matter — s. free space

space diffraction grating — s. space grating <opt.>

space distribution — s. spatial distribution

space diversity — Raumdiversity *f*; Raumdiversityempfang *m*, Raummehrfachempfang *m*

space electronics — Raumfahrtelektronik *f*

space element, element of volume, volume element, element of extension — Volum[en]element *n*, Raumelement *n*

space-energy distribution — Raum-Energie-Verteilung *f*, räumliche und Energieverteilung *f*

space erosion	Masseverlust m ‹der Meteoriten› im Weltraum	space passed through	s. distance
space-exchange force, Majorana force	Majorana-Kraft f, Ortsaustauschkraft f	space pattern	s. radiation pattern
space-exchange operator, Majorana operator	Majorana-Operator m, Ortsaustauschoperator m, Operator m der Majorana-Kräfte	space perception, perception of depth	Raumwahrnehmung f, Tiefenwahrnehmung f, Raumsehen n, Tiefensehen n
		space pilot	Raumpilot m, Pilot m des Raumschiffs
space exchange potential, Majorana potential, potential of Majorana forces	Majorana-Potential n, Ortsaustauschpotential n, Potential n der Majorana-Kräfte	space potential	Raumpotential n
		space principle	Raumausnutzungsprinzip n
space factor; fill factor, filling factor	Füllfaktor m ‹z. B. des paramagnetischen Quantenverstärkers›; Ausnutzungsfaktor m	space probe	s. cosmic rocket
		space quantization, spatial quantization, directional quantization	Richtungsquantelung f, räumliche Quantelung f, Raumquantelung f, Richtungsquantisierung f, räumliche Quantisierung f, Raumquantisierung f; Einquantelung f in die Feldrichtung
space factor ‹of antenna array›	Raumfaktor m ‹Antennensystem›		
space filling	Raumerfüllung f		
space-fixed co-ordinates	s. space co-ordinates	spacer, separator	Distanzhalter m, Abstandshalter m
space focusing	s. direction focusing ‹of the first, second order›	space radiation	s. cosmic radiation
space frame [work], space truss, truss, truss[ed] frame	räumliches Fachwerk n, räumliches Tragwerk n	space reddening, interstellar reddening	interstellare Verfärbung f
space garment	s. space suit	space reflection, space inversion, inversion of space	Raumspiegelung f, räumliche Inversion f, Rauminversion f, Inversion f des Raumes
space grating, space diffraction grating ‹opt.›	räumliches Beugungsgitter n, Raumgitter n ‹Opt.›		
space group, space-group	Raumgruppe f, Raumsymmetriegruppe f	space rendezvous, rendezvous	Rendezvous n [im Raum], Raumrendezvous n
space group extinction	Raumgruppenauslöschung f, Raumgruppenlöschung f	space requirement, required volume, volume requirement, required room, room requirement	Raumbedarf m
space gyroscope	s. free gyroscope		
space harmonic, Hartree harmonic, spatial harmonic	räumliche Harmonische f, Hartree-Harmonische f, Raumharmonische f; Oberschwingung f ‹Oberflächenleiter›	space research, cosmic research, cosmic exploration, exploration of space	Weltraumforschung f, Raumforschung f
space helmet	Raumhelm m, Helm m des Astronauten (Kosmonauten)	space resolution	s. spatial resolution
		space rocket	s. cosmic rocket
space image	s. stereogram	space rotation	Raumdrehung f
space impression, stereoscopic impression, impression (sensation) of depth	Raumeindruck m, Tiefeneindruck m	space[-]ship	s. space vehicle
		space simulation chamber, space simulator	Raumflugsimulator m, Raumsimulator m
space integral	s. volume integral	space station	Weltraumstation f, Außenstation f, Raumstation f
space inversion	s. space reflection		
space isomerism	s. stereoisomerism	space statistics	Raumstatistik f
space lattice, three-dimensional lattice	Raumgitter n, dreidimensionales Gitter n		
space lattice structure	Raumgitterstruktur f	space suit; space garment	Raumanzug m, Raumschutzanzug m; Raumkleidung f
space-like interval	raumartiges Intervall n		
space-like surface	raumartige Fläche f	space symmetry element, element of space symmetry	Raumsymmetrieelement n
space-like vector	raumartiger Vektor m	space tensor	Raumtensor m
space mark	Raummarke f	space-time, space-time continuum, space and time, Minkowski[an] universe, Minkowski world, Minkowskian four-space, Einstein-Minkowski space, World space, space of events, Minkowski[an] space, space continuum ‹math.›	Raumzeit f, Raum-Zeit f, Raum m und Zeit f, Raumzeitkontinuum n, Raum-Zeit-Kontinuum n, Raum-Zeit-Welt f, Raum-Zeit-Mannigfaltigkeit f, Minkowski-Welt f, Ereignisraum m, Minkowskischer Raum, Minkowski-Raum m ‹Math.›
space motion, motion in space, three-dimensional motion, motion in three dimensions	räumliche Bewegung f, dreidimensionale Bewegung		
space network polymer	raumvernetztes Molekül (Polymer) n Raumnetzmolekül n, räumliches Netzpolymer n		
space of events	s. space-time ‹Math.›	space-time, spatio-temporal	raumzeitlich, Raumzeit-, Raum-Zeit-
space of momentum and energy, momentum-energy space	Energie-Impuls-Raum m, Impuls-Energie-Raum m		
		space-time algebra	Raumzeitalgebra f, Raum-Zeit-Algebra f
space of representation, representation module (space)	Darstellungsmodul m, Darstellungsraum m	space-time concept[ion]	Raum-Zeit-Vorstellung f, Raum-Zeit-Konzeption f, Raum-Zeit-Konzept n; Raum-Zeit-Begriff m, Begriff m der Raum-Zeit[lichkeit]
space of states	Zustandsraum m		
space of states and energy	Energie-Zustands-Raum m		
space parity	räumliche Parität f, Raumparität f, Parität des Raumes	space-time continuum	s. space-time ‹math.›

space-time co-ordinates; system of space-time co-ordinates, set of space-time co-ordinates	Raumzeitkoordinaten *fpl*, Raum-Zeit-Koordinaten *fpl*; Raumzeit-Koordinatensystem *n*, Raum-Zeit-Koordinatensystem *n*	spallation fragment; spallation product	Spallationsbruchstück *n*; Spallationsprodukt *n*
		spallation product yield, spallation yield	Spallations[produkt]ausbeute *f*
space-time correlation, time-space correlation	zeitlich-räumliche Korrelation *f*, räumlich-zeitliche Korrelation	spalling; peeling off; leafing	Abplatzen *n*; Ausschalung *f*; [grober] Ausbruch *m*; Abblättern *n*
space-time curvature	Raumzeitkrümmung *f*, Raum-Zeit-Krümmung *f*	spalling test	Hitzebeständigkeitsversuch *m* ‹gegen Abblättern›
		spallogenic	spallogen
		span ‹of the beam›	Feld *n* ‹Balken›
space-time curve	Weg-Zeit-Kurve *f*	span, span length, length of span, unsupported length ‹mech.›	Spannweite *f*, Stützweite *f*, Stützlänge *f*, Freilänge *f*, freie Länge *f* ‹Mech.›
space-time element	Raumzeitelement *n*, Raum-Zeit-Element *n*		
space-time interval	Raumzeitintervall *n*, Raum-Zeit-Intervall *n*	span angle	s. angle of embrace
		span length	s. span ‹mech.›
space-time law, path-time law	Weg-Zeit-Gesetz *n*	span of the wing, wing span, spread of the wing	Spannweite *f* [des Flügels], Flügelspannweite *f*
space-time metric	Raumzeitmetrik *f*, Raum-Zeit-Metrik *f*, raumzeitliche Metrik *f*	spar, longeron	Holm *m*
		spar	s. a. Iceland spar
		spare set, spare unit	Reservesatz *m*
space-time point, event, world point	Ereignis *n*, Raumzeitpunkt *m*, Raum-Zeit-Punkt *m*, Weltpunkt *m*	sparging; bubbling	Durchsprudeln *n*; Druckluftmischen *n*; pneumatisches Rühren *n*; Barbotage *f*
space-time reflection	Raum-Zeit-Spiegelung *f*	sparingly soluble, slightly soluble	schwerlöslich, weniglöslich, schlecht löslich, kaum löslich
space-time resolution; space-time resolving power	raum-zeitliche Auflösung *f*; raum-zeitliches Auflösungsvermögen *n*	spark, bomb, moustaches ‹opt.›	„moustaches" *mpl*, Helle Punkte *mpl* ‹Sonne› ‹Opt.›
space-time structure	Raumzeitstruktur *f*, Raum-Zeit-Struktur *f*	spark at break	s. break spark
space-time transformation	Raum-Zeit-Transformation *f*	spark at make, closing spark	Schließungsfunke *m*, Schließfunke *m*
space trajectory	räumliche Bahn (Bahnkurve) *f*	spark chamber ‹nucl.›	Funkenkammer *f* ‹Kern.›
space transformation	Raumtransformation *f*	spark chamber spectrometer	Funkenkammerspektrometer *n*
space truss	s. space framework	spark channel	Funkenkanal *m*, Funkenbahn *f*
space variable, position variable	Ortsvariable *f*, Ortsveränderliche *f*	spark coil	s. inductorium
space vehicle, space[]-craft, space[]ship	Weltraumfahrzeug *n*, Raumfahrzeug *n*; Raumfluggerät *n*; Raumschiff *n*	spark counter	s. spark detector
		spark detector, spark counter	Funkendetektor *m*, Funkenzähler *m*, Funkenplattenzähler *m*
space velocity, spatial velocity	Raumgeschwindigkeit *f*, Geschwindigkeit *f* im Raum	spark discharge	Funkenentladung *f*
space wave, spatial (sky, indirect, atmospheric, downcoming) wave ‹el.›	Raumwelle *f* ‹El.›	spark-discharge ion source	Funken[entladungs]ionenquelle *f*
		spark-discharge plasma	s. spark plasma
space which the body falls, height of fall, height of the fall, height of drop	Fallhöhe *f*	spark discharger	s. spark gap
		sparker	s. cracking spark
		spark erosion	Funkenerosion *f*, Ausfunken *n*
space winding	unterbrochene Wendel *f*	spark formation, sparking	Funkenbildung *f*, Funken *n*
space with torsion	Raum *m* mit Torsion		
spacial	s. spatial		
spacing, separation	‹räumlicher› Abstand *m*, Zwischenraum *m*	spark gap, gap, arrester, spark discharger, air gap, discharger	Funkenstrecke *f*, Funkenentladungsstrecke *f*; Funkenbrücke *f*; Entladungsstrecke *f*; Elektrodenabstand *m*
spacing error	Winkelabweichungsfehler *m*		
spacing of layers	Schichtenabstand *m*	spark-gap discharger	s. surge diverter
spacing of the layer lines	Schichtlinienabstand *m*	spark generator	Funkenerzeuger *m*, Funkengenerator *m*
spacing plate	Abstandsplatte *f*, Distanzplatte *f*	spark-ignition engine	s. Otto engine
		sparking	s. spark formation
spacing wave, compensating wave	Pausenwelle *f*, Verstimmungswelle *f*	sparking distance, striking distance, spark length	Funkenschlagweite *f*, Schlagweite *f*, Funkenlänge *f*
spacistor	Spacistor *m*		
spallation ‹nucl.›	Spallation *f*, Kern[zer]splitterung *f*, Zersplitterung *f*, Vielfachzerlegung *f*, Absplitterung *f*, Atomzersplitterung *f* ‹Kern.›	sparking of brushes, commutator sparking	Bürstenfeuer *n*, Rundfeuer *n*
		sparking potential (voltage), minimum breakdown voltage of a gap, initial potential (voltage), spark potential (voltage) ‹el.›	Funkenpotential *n*, Funkenspannung *f*, Anfangsspannung *f*, Anfangspotential *n* ‹El.›
spallation cross-section, cross-section for spallation	Spallationsquerschnitt *m*, Wirkungsquerschnitt für (der) Spallation, Spallationswirkungsquerschnitt		

sparking voltage	s. a. breakdown voltage <el.>	spatial dispersion, volume dispersion	räumliche Dispersion f
spark lag	s. ignition lag	spatial distribution	räumliche Verteilung f, Raumverteilung f
spark length	s. sparking distance	spatial energy density	s. spatial density of energy
spark line	Funkenlinie f, Funkenspektrallinie f	spatial expansion; spatial extension	räumliche (körperliche, volumenhafte) Ausdehnung f; räumliche Erstreckung f
sparkling	s. twinkle		
spark meter, micrometric spark discharger	Funkenmikrometer n	spatial focusing	s. direction focusing <of the first, second order>
spark[-]over, flash[-]over, dart[-]over	Funkenüberschlag m, Überschlag m, Überschlagen n; Überspringen n <Funke>; Funkendurchbruch m	spatial force density	s. spatial density of force
		spatial formula, stereochemical formula, stereometric formula, stereoformula	Raumformel f, stereochemische Formel f, stereometrische Formel f
		spatial harmonic	s. space harmonic
		spatialization function	Raumorientierungsfunktion f, Orientierungsfunktion f im Raum
sparkover voltage, flashover voltage	Überschlagsspannung f		
spark photography	Funkenphotographie f	spatial mean, spatial average	räumliches Mittel n, Raumgrößenmittel n
spark plasma, sparkdischarge plasma	Funkenplasma n	spatial mesh	räumliche Masche f
spark potential	s. sparking potential	spatial pendulum	räumliches Pendel n, Raumpendel n
spark quench, spark quenching circuit	Funkenlöschkreis m	spatial quantization	s. space quantization
spark quenching, quenching of sparks	Funkenlöschung f	spatial resolution, space resolution; spatial resolving power	räumliche Auflösung f, Raumauflösung f; räumliches Auflösungsvermögen n, Raumauflösungsvermögen n
spark-quenching capacitor	Funkenlöschkondensator m		
spark quenching circuit	s. spark quench	spatial resolving power	s. spatial resolution
spark recorder	Funkenschreiber m	spatial shear wave	Raumscherungswelle f, Scherungsraumwelle f
spark resistance	Funkenfestigkeit f	spatial spherical function, solid spherical harmonic	räumliche Kugelfunktion f
		spatial variable	s. Eulerian variable
spark sender	s. spark transmitter	spatial velocity, space velocity	Raumgeschwindigkeit f, Geschwindigkeit f im Raum
sparks of the meteor	Funkenschauer m des Meteors		
spark source	Funkenquelle f	spatial wave, space wave, sky (indirect, atmospheric, down-coming) wave <el.>	Raumwelle f <El.>
spark spectrum	Funkenspektrum n		
spark test[ing]	Schleiffunkenprüfung f	spatio-temporal	s. space-time
spark transmitter, spark sender	Funkensender m	spatter, splash	Spritzer m
		speaking coil	s. voice coil <of loudspeaker>
spark transmitter with simple gap	Knallfunkensender m, Knarrfunkensender m	speaking tube, megaphone	Sprachrohr n
		Spearman['s] coefficient of rank correlation	s. coefficient of rank correlation
		Spearman['s] matrix	Spearmansche Matrix f, Spearman-Matrix f
spark voltage	s. sparking potential		
Sparrow['s] criterion	Sparrow-Kriterium n	Spearman['s] [foot] rule	Spearmansche Faustregel f
spath	s. Iceland spar	special case, particular case	Spezialfall m, spezieller Fall m, Sonderfall m
spatial, space	räumlich, Raum-		
spatial	s. three-dimensional	special experiment	besonderer Versuch m, spezieller Versuch
spatial, fixed in space	raumfest	special function [of mathematical physics]	spezielle Funktion f [der mathematischen Physik]
spatial arrangement, configuration, arrangement	Konfiguration f, Anordnung f, räumliche Anordnung		
spatial average	s. spatial mean	special linear group	s. unimodular group
spatial charge density	s. space charge density	special orthogonal group, SO(n)	spezielle orthogonale Gruppe f, SO(n)
spatial compressional wave	räumliche Verdichtungswelle f, Raumverdichtungswelle f	special perturbation	spezielle Störung f
		special perturbation theory	spezielle Störungsrechnung f
spatial co-ordinates	s. space co-ordinates		
spatial current density	s. volume current density	special-purpose, unique	unikal, Spezial-
spatial curve	s. space curve		
spatial degeneration, directional (space) degeneration	Richtungsentartung f	special purpose mass spectrometer, research mass spectrometer	Massenspektrometer n für Forschungszwecke, Forschungs-Massenspektrometer n
spatial density	s. volume density		
spatial density of charge	s. space charge density	special relativity [theory], special theory of relativity, restricted theory of relativity	spezielle Relativitätstheorie f
spatial density of current	s. volume current density		
spatial density of electric charge	s. space charge density		
spatial density of energy, spatial energy density	räumliche Energiedichte f	special unitarian group, unitary unimodular group, SU(n)	spezielle unitäre Gruppe f, SU(n)
spatial density of force, spatial force density	räumliche Kraftdichte f	species of cloud, cloud species, class of cloud	Wolkengattung f
spatial derivative	räumliche Ableitung f	species of terms	Termrasse f, Rasse f [von Termen]

specific absorption	spezifische Absorption f	specific gamma-ray constant (emission), k-factor, gamma[-ray dose-rate] constant	spezifische Gamma-Strahlungskonstante f, Dosiskonstante f [für Gamma-Strahlung]
specific acoustic impedance, unit-area acoustic impedance	spezifische Schallimpedanz f, spezifische [akustische] Impedanz f, akustischer Widerstand m je Flächeneinheit, spezifischer Widerstand <Ak.>		
		specific gas constant, gas constant per gramme	spezifische Gaskonstante f
		specific gravity, specific weight, absolute specific mass	spezifisches Gewicht n, Wichte f, Artgewicht n
specific acoustic reactance, unit-area acoustic reactance	spezifische Schallreaktanz f	specific gravity <relative to or referred to>, relative density, sp.gr.	Dichtezahl f, relative Dichte f, bezogene Dichte, Dichteverhältnis n <zu>
specific acoustic resistance, unit-area acoustic resistance	spezifische Schallresistanz f		
specific action potential, S.A.P.	spezifisches Aktionspotential n, SAP	specific gravity bottle	s. pyknometer
specific activity	spezifische Aktivität f	specific head, specific energy <hydr.>	spezifischer hydrostatischer Druck m <Hydr.>
specific adhesion	spezifische Adhäsion f	specific heat, specific heat capacity, heat capacity per unit mass, coefficient of specific heat, sp.ht.	spezifische Wärme f, spezifische Wärmekapazität f, Eigenwärme f, Artwärme f
specific admittance	spezifischer Wellenleitwert m		
specific adsorption	spezifische Adsorption f		
specific area	s. specific surface		
specifications of the test, test specifications	Prüfbedingungen fpl	specific heat at constant pressure, coefficient of specific heat at constant pressure, isopiestic specific heat	spezifische Wärme f bei konstantem Druck
specific atmospheric humidity, specific humidity	spezifische Feuchtigkeit (Feuchte) f		
specific beta-particle constant (emission)	spezifische Beta-Strahlungskonstante f	specific heat at constant volume, coefficient of specific heat at constant volume, isovolumic (isovolume, constant volume, isometric) specific heat	spezifische Wärme f bei konstantem Volumen
specific binding energy	spezifische Bindungsenergie f		
specific burn-up	spezifischer Abbrand m, Abbrandtiefe f <in MWd/t>		
		specific heat capacity	s. specific heat
		specific heat of fusion, specific heat of melting, specific melting heat; specific enthalpy of melting	spezifische Schmelzwärme f; spezifische Schmelzenthalpie f
specific charge, charge-to-mass ratio, charge-mass ratio	spezifische Ladung f, Ladung-Masse-Verhältnis n		
specific cohesion, capillary constant, Laplace['s] constant, capillary tension	Kapillarkonstante f, Kapillaritätskonstante f, Kapillarspannung f	specific heat of transformation (transition), specific transformation (transition) heat	spezifische Umwandlungswärme f
specific conductance (conductivity)	s. conductivity	specific heat per unit volume	s. heat capacity per unit volume
specific consumption, unit consumption	spezifischer Verbrauch m	specific heat ratio	s. ratio of the specific heats
specific curvature	s. Gauss curvature	specific humidity, specific atmospheric humidity	spezifische Feuchtigkeit (Feuchte) f
specific damping	s. damping exponent		
specific damping capacity, specific loss	spezifische Werkstoffdämpfung (Dämpfung) f, spezifischer Hysteresisverlust m	specific humidity of saturation, specific saturation humidity	spezifische Sättigungsfeuchte f
		specific impulse	s. specific thrust
specific density	s. density	specific inductive capacity, specific inductivity	s. permittivity <of the material>
specific discharge, flux density	Flußdichte f		
specific dispersion	spezifische Dispersion f	specific inertance	spezifische akustische Masse f
specific dispersivity	s. molecular dispersion		
specific electric susceptibility	spezifische elektrische Suszeptibilität f	specific intensity [of radiation]	s. radiant intensity
		specific internal energy	spezifische innere Energie f
specific electronic charge	s. charge-to-mass ratio of the electron		
specific elongation	s. unit elongation	specific ionization, linear specific ionization	spezifische Ionisierung f, spezifische (differentielle) Ionisation f, Ionisierungsstärke f
specific emission density	spezifische Emissionsdichte f		
specific energy	spezifische Energie f		
specific energy	s. a. specific head <hydr.>	specific ionization coefficient	differentieller Ionisationskoeffizient m
specific enthalpy	spezifische Enthalpie f		
specific enthalpy of melting	s. specific heat of fusion	specific ionization curve	Kurve f der spezifischen Ionisation <in Abhängigkeit von der kinetischen Energie, Geschwindigkeit oder Reichweite>
specific entropy	spezifische Entropie f		
specific exchange constant	spezifische Austauschkonstante f		
specific extinction coefficient, extinction coefficient for (per, at) unit density	Extinktionskonstante f, bezogen auf die Dichte; spezifische Extinktionskonstante	specific ionization loss	spezifischer Ionisationsverlust m
		specific kinetic energy, velocity energy	spezifische kinetische Energie f, Geschwindigkeitsenergie f
		specific magnetic rotatory power	s. Verdet constant
specific flow, specific modulus, discharge in litre per second per square kilometre, rate of runoff	Abflußspende f, spezifischer Abfluß m, Wasserspende f, Spende f, Wassermengenspende f	specific magnetic susceptibility, mass susceptibility, susceptibility per unit mass	spezifische magnetische Suszeptibilität f, spezifische Suszeptibilität f, Grammsuszeptibilität f, Massensuszeptibilität f
specific flow rate	spezifischer Durchsatz m	specific mass	s. density
specific force	spezifische Kraft f	specific mass effect	spezifischer Kernmasseneffekt m [der Isotopie]
specific free energy	spezifische freie Energie f		
		specific melting heat	s. specific heat of fusion

specific meson charge of nucleon	spezifische Mesonenladung f des Nukleons	specific viscosity	spezifische Viskosität f, spezifische Zähigkeit f
specific modulus	s. specific flow	specific volume	spezifisches Volumen n, Räumigkeit f
specific parameter of state, specific variable of state, specific [thermodynamic] property	spezifische Zustandsgröße f		
specific plastic	spezifische Plastik f	specific volumetric dilatation	spezifische räumliche Ausdehnung f, Dilatation f
specific potential	spezifisches Potential n		
specific potential energy of deformation	s. elastic potential <mech.>	specific weight, specific gravity, absolute specific mass	spezifisches Gewicht n, Wichte f, Artgewicht n
specific power	spezifische Leistung f		
specific power conversion	Leistungsumsatz m	specific wind pressure specified	s. specific pressure of wind s. pre[-]set
specific pressure of wind, specific wind pressure	spezifischer Winddruck m	specified achromatic light; white light	weißes Licht n
specific property	s. specific parameter of state	specifity, uniqueness <stat.>	Spezifität f <Stat.>
specific radiation impedance	spezifischer Strahlungswiderstand m	specifity	s. a. selectivity <chem.>
specific radioactivity	s. specific activity	specimen	s. sample
specific rate	s. rate constant <chem.>	specimen	s. test bar
specific rate of heat flow	s. rate of heat flow	specimen	s. object <gen., opt., bio.>
specific reaction	spezifische Reaktion f	specimen airlock, object airlock	Objektschleuse f
specific reaction rate	s. rate constant <chem.>	specimen chamber	Objektkammer f
specific refraction, specific refractivity	spezifische Refraktion f, spezifische Brechung f	specimen damage, object damage	Objektschaden m
		specimen holder, specimen mount	s. slide
specific refractive index	spezifischer Brechungsindex m	specimen plane, object plane	Dingebene f, Gegenstandsebene f, Objektebene f
specific refractivity	s. specific refraction		
specific reluctance	s. reluctivity	specimen slide	s. slide
specific resistance (resistivity)	s. resistivity	specimen stage	s. stage
		speck; spot <also el.>; patch	Fleck m
specific retention	s. water-holding capacity		
specific rotary power, specific rotation	s. optical rotatory power <quantity>	speck of dust, dust particle	Staubpartikel f, Staubteilchen n, Staubkorn n, Stäubchen n
specific saturation humidity, specific humidity of saturation	spezifische Sättigungsfeuchte f	speck of sensitivity, sensitivity speck, centre of ripening	Reifkeim m
specific sound-energy flux	s. sound intensity	specpure	s. spectroscopically pure
		spectacle glass	s. spectacle lens
specific sound energy flux level	s. sound intensity level <ac.>	spectacle lens, ophthalmic lens, lens, spectacle glass	Brillenglas n, Glas n
specific speed	spezifische Drehzahl (Umdrehungsgeschwindigkeit) f	specter of the Brocken <US>	s. Brocken bow
		spectral absorptance <US>	s. spectral absorption factor
specific speed of combustion	spezifische Verbrennungsgeschwindigkeit f	spectral absorption analysis, absorption analysis	Absorptionsspektralanalyse f, Absorptionsanalyse f
specific speed of the pump	spezifische Pumpgeschwindigkeit f		
specific strain energy, strain energy per unit volume, strain-energy function, strain-energy density, strain-energy density function, energy [per unit volume] of deformation, potential energy [of deformation] per unit volume; elastic potential [per unit volume]	spezifische Formänderungsarbeit (Verzerrungsarbeit) f, Energiedichte f der Formänderung, [auf die Volumeneinheit bezogene] Formänderungsarbeit f, [auf die Volumeneinheit bezogene] Deformationsarbeit f, Deformationsenergie pro Volumeneinheit, bezogene Formänderungsarbeit f, Verzerrungsenergiefunktion f; elastisches Potential n [der Volumeneinheit]	spectral absorption curve	Kurve f der spektralen Absorption, spektrale Absorptionskurve f
		spectral absorption factor, radiant spectral absorptivity, spectral absorptance <US>	spektraler Absorptionsgrad m, spektrales Absorptionsvermögen n
		spectral actinometer	s. spectroactinometer
		spectral analysis	s. spectrographic analysis
		spectral analysis <math.>	Spektralanalysis f <Math.>
		spectral apparatus	s. dispersing system
		spectral average	Mittelwert m über die Spektralverteilung, spektraler Mittelwert
specific strength	spezifische Stärke f, spezifische Strahlungsstärke f <γ-Quanten/cm³>; spezifische Intensität f	spectral band, band, molecular band	Spektralbande f, Bande f, Molekülbande f
		spectral band method	Spektralbandverfahren n
specific stress	spezifische Spannung f	spectral band photography	Spektralbandaufnahme f
specific surface, specific area; surface area	spezifische Oberfläche f	spectral brightness, spectral surface brightness, spectral intrinsic brilliance	spektrale Helligkeit f
specific surface energy	s. surface tension		
specific susceptibility	spezifische Suszeptibilität f		
		spectral centroid	Schwerpunkt m der spektralen Empfindlichkeit, Schwerpunktwellenlänge f, Spektralschwerpunkt m, Empfindlichkeitsschwerpunkt m, Empfindlichkeitsmaximum n
specific thermoelectromotive force, specific thermo-e.m.f.	spezifische thermoelektromotorische Kraft f, spezifische Thermo-EMK f		
specific thrust, specific impulse	spezifischer Schub m, spezifischer Impuls m		
specific transformation (transition) heat	s. specific heat of transformation	spectral characteristic	s. spectral response curve
specific variable of state	s. specific parameter of state		

spectral chart, spectrum chart	Spektralkarte f; Spektrenlehre f	spectral index	spektraler Index m, Spektralindex m
spectral class, spectral type	Spektralklasse f, Spektraltyp m	spectral integral	Spektralintegral n, Integral n bezüglich des Spektralmaßes
spectral classification	Spektralklassifikation f	spectral intensity	spektrale Intensität f, Spektralintensität f
spectral colour, spectrum colour	Spektralfarbe f	spectral intrinsic brilliance	s. spectral brightness
spectral component, spectrum component	Spektralkomponente f	spectral irradiance	spektrale Bestrahlungsstärke f
spectral composition, spectrum composition	spektrale Zusammensetzung f, Spektralzusammensetzung f		
spectral concentration, spectral density <of radiometric quantity> <opt.>	spektrale Dichte f [einer Strahlungsgröße] <Opt.>	spectrality	Spektralität f
		spectral light, spectral radiation	Spektrallicht n, Spektralstrahlung f
spectral concentration in terms of frequency	spektrale Dichte f im Frequenzmaßstab	spectral line, spectrum line, line <opt.>	Spektrallinie f, Linie f <Opt.>
spectral concentration of radiant flux, spectral [flux] density	spektrale Strahlungsflußdichte f (Dichte f des Strahlungsflusses)	spectral line broadening	s. line broadening
		spectral line contour	s. spectral line profile
		spectral line curvature, curvature of the spectral line	Spektrallinienkrümmung f, Krümmung f der Spektrallinie
spectral condenser [lens]	Spektralkondensor m	spectral line intensity	s. intensity of the spectral line
spectral condition	Spektralitätsbedingung f		
spectral coverage	s. spectral region	spectral line narrowing	s. line narrowing
spectral curve	Spektralkurve f	spectral-line photometer	Spektrallinienphotometer n, Schnellphotometer n
spectral curve of density, spectral density curve	spektrale Schwärzungskurve f		
		spectral line profile	s. line profile
		spectral line quality factor	Spektralliniengüte f
spectral decomposition <math.>	Spektraldarstellung f, Spektralzerlegung f <Math.>	spectral line reversal, reversal of spectral (spectrum) line, line reversal	Linienumkehr f, Umkehr (Umkehrung) f der Spektrallinie
spectral density <math.>	Spektraldichte f <Math.>		
spectral density	s. a. spectral concentration <opt.>	spectral line shape	s. line profile
spectral density	s. a. spectral concentration of radiant flux	spectral line widening	s. line broadening
		spectral line width	s. line width
spectral density	s. a. spectral energy distribution	spectral location	s. spectral position
		spectral luminance factor	spektraler Remissionsgrad m
spectral density curve	s. spectral curve of density		
spectral diaphragm, spectral mask	Spektralmaske f, Staffelblende f	spectral luminous efficiency	s. relative luminous efficiency
spectral dispersion	s. dispersion <opt.>	spectrally pure	s. spectroscopically pure
spectral displacement, spectral shift <math.>	Spektralverschiebung f <Math.>	spectral mask, spectral diaphragm	Spektralmaske f, Staffelblende f
spectral distribution	spektrale Verteilung f, Spektralverteilung f	spectral measure	Spektralmaß n
spectral distribution graph	s. spectral response curve	spectral mercury [vapour] lamp, mercury spectral lamp	Quecksilberspektraldampflampe f, Quecksilberspektrallampe f
spectral distribution of energy	s. spectral energy distribution <of radiation>	spectral method of colorimetry	Spektralverfahren n zur Farbmessung
spectral distribution of optical stimulation	Ausleuchtungsverteilung f, spektrale Verteilungskurve f der Ausleuchtung	spectral narrowing	s. line narrowing
		spectral norm	s. spectrum radius
		spectral plate	Spektralplatte f
spectral emissivity [of thermal radiator], monochromatic emissive power, emissive power for the wavelength λ	spektraler Emissionsgrad m, spektrales Emissionsvermögen n [eines Temperaturstrahlers]		
		spectral position, spectral location	spektrale Lage f
		spectral position	s. a. Crova wavelength
		spectral purity, spectroscopic purity, spectroquality	spektrale Reinheit f, spektroskopische Reinheit
spectral energy distribution, spectral distribution of energy, spectral density <of radiation>	spektrale Strahlungsverteilung f, spektrale Energieverteilung f [einer Strahlung], Energieverteilung im Spektrum [einer Strahlung], spektrale Dichte f [einer Strahlung]		
		spectral pyrometer	Spektralpyrometer n
		spectral radiance, spectral radiant intensity per unit area	spektrale Strahldichte f
spectral eyepiece	Spektralokular n		
spectral family	s. spectral function		
spectral filter	Spektralfilter n		
spectral flux density	s. spectral concentration of radiant flux	spectral radiant energy density	spektrale Strahlungsdichte f, reduzierte Strahlungsdichte
spectral frequency	Spektralfrequenz f		
spectral function <phys.; math.; stat.>; spectral family <math.>; [integrated] power function <stat.>	Spektralfunktion f <auch Stat.>; Spektralschar f, Zerlegung f der Einheit <Math.>		
		spectral radiant flux	s. monochromatic radiant power
spectral grate ghost	s. ghost <in grating spectra>	spectral radiant intensity, monochromatic radiant intensity	spektrale Strahlstärke f
spectral hardening, spectrum hardening	Spektrumhärtung f, Härtung f des Neutronenspektrums	spectral radiant intensity per unit area	s. spectral radiance
spectral hue	spektraler Farbton m	spectral radiant power	s. monochromatic radiant power

spectral radiation, spectral light — Spektrallicht n, Spektralstrahlung f

spectral radius — s. spectrum radius
spectral range — s. spectral region
spectral reflectance <US>, spectral reflection factor — spektraler Reflexionsgrad (Reflexionskoeffizient) m, spektrales Reflexionsvermögen n

spectral region, region (range, part) of the spectrum, spectral range (coverage) — Spektralbereich m, Spektralgebiet n, Bereich m des Spektrums, Gebiet n des Spektrums

spectral relaxation time — spektrale Relaxationszeit f

spectral resolution — s. spectral resolving power
spectral resolving power, spectral resolution <of ear> — spektrales Auflösungsvermögen n, spektrale Auflösung f <des Ohres>

spectral response — spektrales Ansprechvermögen n

spectral response — s. a. spectral sensitivity <of ear>

spectral response characteristic (curve), spectral characteristic (distribution graph); taking characteristic — spektrale Charakteristik f, spektrale Verteilungscharakteristik f, Spektralcharakteristik f

spectral sensitivity; spectrophotoelectric sensitivity — spektrale Empfindlichkeit f, Spektralempfindlichkeit f

spectral sensitivity, spectral response <of ear> — spektrale Empfindlichkeitsverteilung f [des Ohres]

spectral sensitivity characteristic — spektrale Empfindlichkeitscharakteristik (Empfindlichkeitskurve) f, Spektralempfindlichkeitskurve f

spectral sensitivity for photopic vision — spektrale Hellempfindlichkeit f

spectral sensitizer — spektraler Sensibilisator m

spectral sequence — Spektralreihe f, Spektralsequenz f, Spektralfolge f

spectral series, series [of lines] — Serie f [von Spektrallinien], Spektralserie f, Linienserie f, Spektrallinienserie f

spectral shift, spectral displacement <math.> — Spektralverschiebung f <Math.>
spectral shift — s. a. line shift
spectral surface brightness — s. spectral brightness

spectral term, term, spectroscopic term <opt.> — Spektralterm m, Term m, spektroskopischer Term <Opt.>

spectral theory — Spektraltheorie f
spectral transmission — spektrale Durchlässigkeit f
spectral transmission curve — Kurve f der spektralen Durchlässigkeit (Transmission), spektrale Durchlässigkeitskurve (Transmissionskurve) f

spectral transmission factor, spectral transmittance <US> — spektraler Durchlaßgrad (Transmissionsgrad) m, spektrale Durchlässigkeit f
spectral type — s. spectral class
spectral-type parallax — Spektraltypparallaxe f

spectre of the Brocken — s. Brocken bow
spectroactinometer, spectral actinometer — Spektralaktinometer n
spectrobologram — Spektrobolographenkurve f, Spektrobologramm n
spectrobolometer — Spektrobolometer n, Spektralbolometer n
spectrochemical analysis — s. spectrographic analysis
spectrocomparator, spectrum comparator — Spektrokomparator m
spectrofluorimeter — Spektralfluorometer n, Spektralfluorimeter n, Spektrofluorometer n, Spektrofluorimeter n

spectrogram, spectrum record[ing]; spectrum chart — Spektrogramm n, Spektralaufnahme f, Spektralaufzeichnung f

spectrographic analysis, spectrochemical (spectroscopic, spectral, spectrum) analysis, spectroscopic test, spectrology — Spektralanalyse f, chemische Spektralanalyse, spektrochemische Analyse f, spektroskopische Analyse

spectroheliogram, filtergram — Spektroheliogramm n
spectroheliokinematograph — Spektroheliokinematograph n
spectrology — s. spectrographic analysis
spectrometer — Spektrometer n; Wellenlängenspektrometer n <Opt.>

spectrometer with high resolving power, high-resolution spectrometer — hochauflösendes Spektrometer n

spectrometry — s. spectroscopy
spectrophone — Spektrophon n
spectrophotoelectric sensitivity — s. spectral sensitivity
spectrophotography — s. spectroscopic photography
spectrophotometer — Spektralphotometer n, Spektrophotometer n
spectrophotometry — Spektralphotometrie f, Spektrophotometrie, spektroskopische Photometrie f

spectropolarimeter — Spektropolarimeter n, Spektralpolarimeter n
spectropolarimetry — Spektropolarimetrie f, Spektralpolarimetrie f
spectropyrheliometry — Spektropyrheliometrie f
spectroquality — s. spectroscopic purity
spectroradiometer — Spektroradiometer n
spectroscope of direct vision, direct-vision spectroscope — Geradsichtspektroskop n, geradsichtiges Spektroskop n
spectroscopically pure, spectroscopic-grade, spectrally pure, specpure — spektral rein, spektroskopisch rein

spectroscopic analysis — s. spectrographic analysis
spectroscopic analysis using X-rays — s. X-ray spectroscopic analysis
spectroscopic apparatus — s. dispersing system
spectroscopic binary [star] — spektroskopischer Doppelstern m

spectroscopic eyepiece, ocular (eyepiece) spectroscope — Okularspektroskop n
spectroscopic-grade — s. spectroscopically pure
spectroscopic illuminator — Spektralbeleuchtungsapparat m
spectroscopic lamp, spectrum lamp — Spektrallampe f

spectroscopic parallax — spektroskopische Parallaxe f

spectroscopic photography, spectrophotography, photography of spectra — Spektralaufnahme f, Spektralphotographie f

spectroscopic purity, spectral purity, spectroquality — spektrale Reinheit f, spektroskopische Reinheit
spectroscopic splitting factor — s. Landé g-factor
spectroscopic standard air, standard air — spektroskopische Normalluft f, Normalluft f

spectroscopic term — s. spectral term <opt.>
spectroscopic test — s. spectrographic analysis
spectroscopic value of ionization potential — s. adiabatic ionization potential
spectroscopy; spectrometry — Spektroskopie f; Spektrometrie f
spectroscopy by diffraction grating — Beugungsspektroskopie f, Gitterspektroskopie f
spectroscopy by prism — Prismenspektroskopie f

spectrosensitogram — Spektrosensitogramm n
spectrosensitometer — Spektrosensitometer n
spectrotron — Spektrotron n
spectrum / 1/E — 1/E-Spektrum n
spectrum analysis — s. spectrographic analysis
spectrum analyzer — Spektralanalysator m, Spektrumanalysator m

spectrum binary — s. double-line spectroscopic binary
spectrum chart — s. spectrogram
spectrum chart — s. a. spectral chart

spectrum 798

spectrum colour, spectral colour — Spektralfarbe *f*

spectrum comparator, spectrocomparator — Spektrokomparator *m*

spectrum component — *s.* spectral component

spectrum composition — *s.* spectral composition

spectrum generator — Spektralgenerator *m*, Spektrumgenerator *m*

spectrum hardening, spectral hardening — Spektrumhärtung *f*, Härtung *f* des Neutronenspektrums

spectrum intensity line — *s.* intensity of the spectral line

spectrum kernel, kernel of the spectrum — Spektralkern *m*

spectrum lamp — *s.* spectroscopic lamp

spectrum line, spectral line, line <opt.> — Spektrallinie *f*, Linie *f* <Opt.>

spectrum locus — Spektralfarbenzug *m*, Farbort *m* der Spektralfarbe, Spektralfarbenkurve *f*

spectrum-luminosity relation — *s.* Hertzsprung-Russell diagram

spectrum matrix — Spektralmatrix *f*

spectrum model — Spektrummodell *n*

spectrum of additive coloration — additives Verfärbungsspektrum *n*

spectrum of colour [-ation], colouration spectrum — Verfärbungsspektrum *n*

spectrum of diffuse reflection, diffuse reflection spectrum — Spektrum *n* diffuser Reflexion, Remissionsspektrum *n*

spectrum of direct reflection, direct reflection spectrum — Spektrum *n* spiegelnder Reflexion

spectrum of freezing nuclei — Gefrierkernspektrum *n*

spectrum of the meteor train, meteor train spectrum — Schweifspektrum *n* des Meteors, Spektrum *n* des Meteorschweifs, Meteorschweifspektrum *n*

spectrum of the wind waves, distribution of the wind waves, wave spectrum — Windseeverteilung *f*, Windseespektrum *n*, Windwellenspektrum *n*

spectrum of turbulence, eddy (turbulence) spectrum — Turbulenzspektrum *n*, Spektrum *n* der Turbulenz

spectrum parameter — Spektrumparameter *m*

spectrum pressure level, pressure spectrum level — Schalldruckpegel *m* je Hertz Bandbreite

spectrum produced by ionized atoms, ionic spectrum — Spektrum *n* ionisierter Atome

spectrum projector — Spektrenprojektor *m*

spectrum radius, spectral radius (norm) <math.> — Spektralradius *m* <Math.>

spectrum recorder — Spektrumschreiber *m*

spectrum record[ing] — *s.* spectrogram

spectrum tensor — Spektraltensor *m*

spectrum variable — Spektrumveränderlicher *m*, Spektrumsvariabler *m*

spectrum width — Spektralbreite *f*

specular, mirror-symmetric, reverse — spiegel[bild]symmetrisch, spiegelbildlich, spiegelverkehrt, spiegelrecht

specular cast (pig) iron — *s.* spiegeleisen

specular reflection — *s.* direct reflection

specular reflectivity — *s.* direct reflection factor

specular refraction, regular refraction — gerichtete (regelmäßige) Brechung *f*

specular surface — *s.* mirror surface

specular symmetry, mirror symmetry — Spiegelsymmetrie *f*

speculum, speculum metal — Spiegelmetall *n*, Speculum *n*

speech analyzer — Sprachanalysator *m*

speech audiometer, live-voice audiometer — Sprachaudiometer *n*

speech current, voice current, telephone current — Sprechstrom *m*

speech frequency — *s.* audio[-]frequency

speech-frequency range, voice-frequency band — Sprachfrequenzbereich *m*, Sprachfrequenzband *n*, Sprechfrequenzbereich *m*, Sprechfrequenzband *n*

speech level, electrical speech level, vocal level, volume level — Sprachpegel *m*

speech modulated — sprachmoduliert

speech power, audio[-frequency] power, audio-frequency [power] output — Sprechleistung *f*

speech test, voice-ear test, volume comparison — Sprech-Hör-Versuch *m*

speech velocity — Sprechgeschwindigkeit *f*

speed, sensitivity, rapidity <of the emulsion> — Empfindlichkeit *f*, Lichtempfindlichkeit *f* <Emulsion>

speed <of rotation>, rotational speed, rotation speed, rotative speed, turn speed, number of revolutions per unit time, number of turns per unit time, revolutions per unit time, turns per unit time, rotational frequency, rotation frequency — Drehzahl *f* [je Zeiteinheit], Umdrehungszahl *f* [je Zeiteinheit], Tourenzahl *f* [je Zeiteinheit], Umlaufgeschwindigkeit *f*, Umdrehungsgeschwindigkeit *f*, Anzahl *f* der Umdrehungen (Umläufe) in der Zeiteinheit, Zahl *f* der Umdrehungen (Umläufe) in der Zeiteinheit, Umdrehungen *fpl* (Umläufe *mpl*) je Zeiteinheit, Umlauf[s]frequenz *f*

speed <gen.>; velocity — Geschwindigkeit *f* <allg.>

speed, magnitude of the velocity vector <mech.> — Geschwindigkeitsbetrag *m*, Geschwindigkeit *f* <Mech.>

speed <of camera lens> — *s. a.* f-number

speed <of pump> — *s. a.* exhaustion rate

speed counter — *s.* speedometer

speed factor, intensifying factor, intensification factor <phot.> — Verstärkungsfaktor *m* <Phot.>

speed factor — *s. a.* gain

speed faster than that of light — *s.* supervelocity of light

speed gauge (indicator) — *s.* speedometer

speedlight — *s.* electronic-flash lamp

speed lower than that of light — *s.* subvelocity of light

speed of autorotation [of the gyroscope] — Eigendrehgeschwindigkeit *f* [des Kreisels]

speed of combustion, velocity of combustion [reaction], burning velocity, rate of combustion — Verbrennungsgeschwindigkeit *f*, Brenngeschwindigkeit *f*

speed of compression, compression speed — Verdichtungsgeschwindigkeit *f*, Kompressionsgeschwindigkeit *f*; Stauchgeschwindigkeit *f*

speed of conduction of the nerve — *s.* velocity of the nerve impulse

speed of contrast perception — Kontrastwahrnehmungsgeschwindigkeit *f*; Unterschiedswahrnehmungsgeschwindigkeit *f*, Unterschiedsempfindungsgeschwindigkeit *f*

speed of convergence, rapiditiy of convergence — Güte *f* der Konvergenz, Konvergenzgeschwindigkeit *f*

speed of deformation — *s.* rate of strain

speed of diffusion — *s.* diffusion rate

speed of escape — *s.* escape speed

speed of flame propagation — *s.* rate of flame propagation

speed of grain, sensitivity of grain — Kornempfindlichkeit *f* <Emulsion>

speed of heat propagation — Wärmeausbreitungsgeschwindigkeit *f*, Wärmefortpflanzungsgeschwindigkeit *f*; Wärmefortleitungsgeschwindigkeit *f*

speed of light; velocity of light — Lichtgeschwindigkeit *f*

speed of light in empty (free) space, speed of light in vacuo (vacuum) — *s.* velocity of light in vacuum

speed of perception — Wahrnehmungsgeschwindigkeit *f*

speed of perception of form — Formempfindungsgeschwindigkeit *f*; Formwahrnehmungsgeschwindigkeit *f*

speed of propagation, propagation velocity, velocity of propagation, velocity of transmission, spread velocity — Ausbreitungsgeschwindigkeit *f*, Fortpflanzungsgeschwindigkeit *f*

speed of response, rate of response <el.> — Reaktionsgeschwindigkeit *f*, Ansprechgeschwindigkeit *f* <El.>

speed of response — s. a. responsiveness <meas.>

speed of rotation — s. velocity of rotation

speed of sensation <of light> — Empfindungsgeschwindigkeit *f*

speed of sound — s. velocity of sound <ac.>

speed of transmission — s. transmission rate

speed of travel, travelling speed — Zuggeschwindigkeit *f*

speedometer, speed counter, speed gauge, speed indicator, tachometer; velometer; revolution counter, revolution indicator — Tachometer *n*, Geschwindigkeitsmesser *m*, Drehgeschwindigkeitsmesser *m*, Drehfrequenzmesser *m*; Tachoskop *n*; Umdrehungszähler *m*, Umdrehungszahlmesser *m*, Drehzahlmesser *m*, Drehzähler *m*, Tourenzähler *m*, Tourenzahlmesser *m*, Tourenmesser *m*

speed reduction, [ratio of] reduction <mech.> — Untersetzung *f* <Mech.>

speed triangle — s. velocity diagram

speed-up; advance, advancing; leading, lead — Voreilung *f*

speedy detection, fast detection — schneller Nachweis *m*

spel[a]eology — Höhlenkunde *f*, Höhlenforschung *f*, Speläologie *f*

Spencer disk — Spencer-Scheibe *f*

Spencer-Fano method — Spencer-Fano-Methode *f*, Methode *f* von Spencer und Fano

spent <of nuclear fuel> — abgebrannt, verbraucht, ausgebrannt <Kernbrennstoff>

sperm[aceti] candle <= 1.029 cd> — Spermazeti-Kerze *f* <= 1,029 cd>, Spermazeti-Walratkerze *f*

Sperry compass — Sperry-Kompaß *m*

sphaerocrystal — s. spherocrystal
sphalerite lattice — s. zinc blende lattice
sphalerite structure, zinc blende structure — Zinkblende[n]struktur *f*, Zinkblende[n]typ *m*

sphenoid — Sphenoid *n*
sphenoid[al] — s. wedge-shaped <cryst.>
sphenoidal class — s. enantiomorphous hemihedry of the orthorhombic system

sphenoidal class — s. hemihedry of the second sort of the tetragonal system

sphenoidal hemihedry — s. trigonal holohedry
sphenoidal tetartohedry — s. tetartohedry of the second sort of the tetragonal system

sphenoidal tetartohedry — s. a. trigonal bipyramidal class

sphere <= 4π sr> — räumlicher Vollwinkel *m* <= 4π sr>

sphere, celestial sphere <astr.> — Himmelskugel *f*, Himmelssphäre *f*, Sphäre *f* <Astr.>

sphere — s. a. region <gen.>
sphere — s. a. spherical surface
sphere-gap voltmeter — Kugelvoltmeter *n*
sphere of complex numbers with exclusion of one point — punktierte Zahlenkugel *f*

sphere of curvature — s. osculating sphere
sphere of punctum proximum — Nahpunktskugel *f*

sphere of punctum remotum — Fernpunktskugel *f*

sphere of reflection, Ewald sphere — Ewaldsche Kugel *f*, Ausbreitungskugel *f*, Reflexionskugel *f*, Ewald-Kugel *f*

sphere photometer — s. photometric integrator

sphere transmission method measurement — Messung *f* nach dem Durchstrahlungsverfahren bei Kugelsymmetrie

spherical aberration, aperture aberration <opt.> — sphärische Aberration (Abweichung) *f*, Öffnungsfehler *m*, Kugelgestalt[s]fehler *m*, Abweichung <Opt.>

spherical albedo — s. Bond['s] albedo <opt.>
spherical angle — sphärischer Winkel *m*, Kugelwinkel *m*

spherical antenna, isotropic (ball) antenna — Isotropantenne *f*, Kugelantenne *f*, sphärische Antenne *f*

spherical astronomy — s. astrometry
spherical Bessel function — sphärische (halbzahlige) Zylinderfunktion *f*; sphärische (halbzahlige) Bessel-Funktion *f*, Kugel-Bessel-Funktion *f*

spherical cap, cap <math.> — Kugelhaube *f*, Kugelkalotte *f*, Kugelkappe *f*, Kalotte *f* <Math.>

spherical capacitor — Kugelkondensator *m*

spherical chamber, spherical ionization chamber — Kugel[ionisations]kammer *f*

spherical coil — Kugelspule *f*
spherical-coil variometer — s. ball variometer

spherical component cepheid, W Virginis [-type] star — W Virginis-Stern *m*

spherical co-ordinates, spherical polar co-ordinates, polar co-ordinates [in space] — Kugelkoordinaten *fpl*, räumliche (sphärische) Polarkoordinaten *fpl*, Polarkoordinaten [im Raum]

spherical correction — sphärische Korrektion *f*
spherical curvature — sphärische Krümmung *f*
spherical diffusion — sphärische Diffusion *f*
spherical excess, spheric excess — sphärischer Exzeß *m*

spherical function — s. spherical harmonic
spherical geometry; spherics <math.> — Kugelgeometrie *f*, kugelsymmetrische Geometrie *f*; sphärische Geometrie, Sphärik *f*, Geometrie auf der Kugel <Math.>

spherical gyroscope — s. spherical top
spherical Hankel function — sphärische Hankel-Funktion *f*, Kugel-Hankel-Funktion *f*

spherical harmonic, spherical function
spherical harmonic — Kugelfunktion *f*

spherical harmonic — Kugelharmonische *f*, sphärische Harmonische *f*, sphärisch-harmonische Funktion *f*

spherical harmonic of the first kind — s. Legendre function of the first kind
spherical harmonic of the first kind — s. a. Legendre polynomial
spherical harmonic of the second kind — s. Legendre function of the second kind
spherical harmonics method — Methode *f* der Kugelfunktionen, Kugelfunktionenmethode *f*, Kugelfunktionsmethode *f*

spherical image — s. spherical indicatrix
spherical indicatrix; spherical image — sphärische Indikatrix *f*; Tangentenbild *n*, Hauptnormalenbild *n*, Binormalenbild *n*, sphärisches Bild *n* <Raumkurve>

spherical ionization chamber — s. spherical chamber
spherical joint — s. spherically ground joint
spherical layer — Kugelschicht *f*
spherical lens — sphärische Linse *f*, Kugel[flächen]linse *f*

spherically ground joint, spherical joint — Kugelschliff *m*

spherically symmetric, sphero-symmetric[al], spherosymmetric[al]	kugelsymmetrisch, sphärosymmetrisch	**spherical valve**	Kugelverschluß *m*
spherical mapping, spherical (Gaussian) representation ‹of surface›	sphärische Abbildung *f*	**spherical vector wave function**	s. Mie['s] scattering function
		spherical vortex of Hill	Kugelwirbel *m* von Hill
		spherical wave	Kugelwelle *f*
spherical mirror	sphärischer Spiegel (Hohlspiegel) *m*; Kugelspiegel *m* ‹Beleuchtungsapparat›	**spherical wave front**	kugelflächige Wellenfront *f*, Kugelflächenfront *f*
		spherical wedge; spherical ungula	Kugelkeil *m*
spherical molecule	Kugelmolekül *n*, sphärisches (korpuskulares) Molekül *n*; verzweigtes Makromolekül (Fadenmolekül) *n*	**spherical zone**	Kugelzone *f*
		spheric excess	s. spherical excess
		sphericity, spherical shape, spheroidal form	Kugelgestalt *f*, Kugelform *f*, Kugelförmigkeit *f*
spherical motion	sphärische Bewegung *f*, Bewegung im sphärischen Raum	**spheric polymer**	sphärisches Polymer *n*
spherical Neumann function	sphärische Neumann-Funktion *f*, Kugel-Neumann-Funktion *f*	**spherics,** atmospheric radio noise, atmospherics, sturbs, statics, sferics	atmosphärische (luftelektrische, statische) Störungen *fpl*, Atmospherics *pl*, Spherics *pl*
spherical optical surface separating two media, single spherical optical surface separating two media	einzelne Kugelfläche *f* ‹brechend *oder* spiegelnd›	**spherics**	s. *a.* spherical geometry ‹math.›
		spherochromatism, chromatic variation of spherical aberration	Gauß-Fehler *m*, chromatische Differenz *f* der sphärischen Aberration
spherical overcorrection	sphärische Überkorrektion *f*		
		sphero[-]colloid	Sphärokolloid *n*
spherical particle, spherule	Kügelchen *n*	**sphero-conical co-ordinates**	sphärokonische Koordinaten *fpl*
spherical pendulum	Kugelpendel *n*, sphärisches Raumpendel (Pendel) *n*	**spherocrystal,** sphaerocrystal	Sphärokristall *m*
spherical point, umbilical point	Nabelpunkt *m*, Nabel *m*, Kreispunkt *m*, Umbilikalpunkt *m*	**sphero-cylindrical lens**	sphärozylindrische Linse *f*; sphärozylindrisches Brillenglas *n*
spherical polar co-ordinates	s. spherical co-ordinates	**spheroid,** ellipsoid of revolution, spheroid of revolution	Rotationsellipsoid *n*, Drehellipsoid *n*, Umdrehungsellipsoid *n*, Rotationssphäroid *n*, Sphäroid *n*
spherical radiator, isotropic radiator	Isotropstrahler *m*, isotroper Strahler *m*, Kugelstrahler *m*, Strahler *m* nullter Ordnung; atmende Kugel *f* ‹Ak.›	**spheroidal,** spheroidical	sphäroidisch, sphäroidal; rotationselliptisch
		spheroidal azimuth, geodesic azimuth	geodätisches Azimut *n*
spherical reduction factor	s. reduction factor ‹el., opt.›	**spheroidal co-ordinates**	rotationselliptische Koordinaten *fpl*, Koordinaten des Rotationsellipsoids, Sphäroidkoordinaten *fpl*
spherical representation	s. spherical mapping		
spherical resonator, Helmholtz['] resonator	Helmholtz-Resonator *m*, Helmholtzscher Resonator *m*, Kugelresonator *m*	**spheroidal core**	sphäroidaler Rumpf *m*
spherical rotation	s. rotation about a point	**spheroidal equation**	Sphäroiddifferentialgleichung *f*
spherical sector	Kugelsektor *m*, Kugelausschnitt *m*		
spherical segment	Kugelabschnitt *m*, Kugelsegment *n*	**spheroidal form**	s. sphericity
spherical shape	s. sphericity	**spheroidal function**	Sphäroidfunktion *f*, zugeordnete Mathieusche Funktion *f*
spherical shell ‹mech.›	Kugelschale *f*, kugelförmige Schale *f*		
spherical shock wave	sphärische Stoßwelle *f*	**spheroidal mirror**	Sphäroidspiegel *m*
		spheroidal protein, globular protein	Globulärprotein *n*, Sphäroprotein *n*
spherical space, antipodal space	sphärischer Raum *m*		
spherical stage, hemispherical stage ‹of microscope›	Kugeltisch *m*, Halbkugeltisch *m* ‹Mikroskop›	**spheroidal state**	Sphäroidzustand *m*
		spheroidal triangle	Sphäroiddreieck *n*
		spheroidal wave function ‹of the first, second, *or* third kind›	Sphäroidwellenfunktion *f* ‹erster, zweiter *oder* dritter Art›
spherical strain tensor	Kugeltensor *m* des Verzerrungszustandes		
spherical stress tensor	Kugeltensor *m* des Spannungszustandes	**spheroidal well**	kugelförmiger Potentialtopf *m*
spherical surface, sphere	sphärische Fläche *f*, Kugelfläche *f*; Sphäre *f*, Kugelschale *f*	**spheroidical**	s. spheroidal
		spheroidization, spheroidizing ‹of graphite›	Zusammenballung *f* [des Graphits], Sphäroidisierung *f* [des Graphits], Sphäroidisation *f* [des Graphits]
spherical surface, surface of the sphere	Kugeloberfläche *f*, Kugelfläche *f*		
spherical symmetry	Kugelsymmetrie *f*, sphärische Symmetrie *f*	**spheroidizing,** soft annealing, full annealing	Weichglühen *n*
spherical tensor	Kugeltensor *m*	**spheroid of revolution,** ellipsoid of revolution, spheroid	Rotationsellipsoid *n*, Drehellipsoid *n*, Umdrehungsellipsoid *n*, Rotationssphäroid *n*, Sphäroid *n*
spherical texture	Kugeltextur *f*		
spherical top, spherical gyroscope	Kugelkreisel *m*, sphärischer Kreisel *m*	**spherometry**	Sphärometrie *f*
		spheron	Sphäron *n*
spherical top, spherical top molecule	Kugelkreiselmolekül *n*, sphärisches Kreiselmolekül *n*, Molekül *n* vom Typ sphärischer Kreisel, Kugelkreisel *m*, sphärischer Kreisel *m*	**sphero[-]symmetric[al],** spherically symmetric	kugelsymmetrisch, sphärosymmetrisch
		spherotoric lens	s. toric lens
		spherule, spherical particle	Kügelchen *n*
		spherulite	Sphärolith *m*
spherical undercorrection	sphärische Unterkorrektion *f*	**spherulitic**	sphärolithisch
spherical ungula	s. spherical wedge	**sphingometer**	Sphingometer *n*

sphygmobolometer	Sphygmobolometer n	**spin correlation coeffi-**	Koeffizient m der Spin-
sphygmogram	Sphygmogramm n	**cient,** coefficient of spin	korrelation, Spinkorrela-
sphygmomanometer	Sphygmomanometer n	correlation	tionskoeffizient m
sphygmophone	Sphygmophon n	**spin correlation function**	Spinkorrelationsfunktion f
spicule, fine mottling, fine mottle	Spiculum n, Spikule f <pl.: Spicula, Spikulen>	**spin coupling**	s. spin-spin coupling
spiders web coil, spider-web coil	Spinngewebspule f	**spin decoupling**	s. spin uncoupling
spider-web antenna	Spinngewebantenne f	**spin-degenerate**	spinentartet
spider-web coil	s. spiders web coil	**spin density**	Spindichte f
spiegel[eisen]	Spiegeleisen n	**spin density operator**	Spindichteoperator m
spiegelungsprinzip	s. Schwarz['s] reflection principle	**spin-dependent scat-tering,** spin incoherent scattering	spin-inkohärente Streuung f, Spinstreuung f, spin-abhängige Streuung
spike, tracer <in isotope dilution analysis>	Tracer m, [markierte] Zugabe f, [markierter] Zusatz m, ,,spike'' m <Isotopenverdünnungs-analyse>	**spin detector**	Spindetektor m, Brücken-detektor m
		spin diffusion	Spindiffusion f
spike; tooth <el.>	Zacken m, Zacke f <El.>	**spin direction**	s. spin orientation
spiked, toothed, pronged, indented	zackig, gezackt	**spindle,** shaft	Spindel f
spike function	s. delta function	**spindle [apparatus],** mitotic spindle <of mitosis>	Kernspindel f, Teilungs-spindel f, Spindel f, Spindelapparat m <Mitose>
spike mode emission [operation]	Spikeemission[sbetrieb] m f		
spike of the laser, laser spike	Laserblitz m	**spindle in colloid systems**	Spindel f in Kolloidsystemen
spike of the pulse	s. pip	**spindle-like**	s. spindle-shaped
spike of the pulse	s. a. pulse spike	**spindle-operated rheostat**	Spindelwiderstand m
spiking	Spickmethode f, Spicken n		
spiking	Zackenbildung f	**spindle-shaped,** spindle-like	spindelförmig
spill	Ausufern n, Uferübertritt m, Übertreten n des Ufers	**spin doublet**	Spindublett n
spill, backscatter loss, backscattering loss	Rückstreuverlust m	**spin doubling,** spin splitting	Spinaufspaltung f
		spin echo	Spinecho f
spillage	s. leaking	**spin-echo method**	Spinechomethode f, Spin-echoverfahren n, Spin-Echo-Methode f
spill gap	s. protective gap		
spilling	Verspritzen n		
spilling	s. a. leaking	**spin-echo spectrometer**	Spinechospektrometer n
spill-over	s. overflowing	**spin effect,** effect of nuclear spin	Kernspineffekt m
spill port	Überlaufkanal m, Über-strömkanal m		
		spin eigenfunction	Spineigenfunktion f
spill shield, louvre	Raster m, Lichtraster m <lichttechnisches Bau-element>	**spin eigenstate**	Spineigenzustand m
		spin eigenvalue	Spineigenwert m
		spinel ferrite	s. ferrospinel
spillway, overflow tube	Überlaufrohr n	**spinel lattice**	Spinellgitter n
spillway [dam], overflow weir, overflow dam, spillway weir	Überfallwehr n, offenes Wehr n; Überfallstau-mauer f, Überfallwehr f	**spinel law**	Spinellgesetz n
		spinel structure	Spinellstruktur f
		spin energy	Spinenergie f
spillway weir	Entlastungswehr n; Ent-lastungsüberfall m	**spin exchange**	Spinaustausch m
		spin-exchange force, Bartlett force	Bartlett-Kraft f, Spinaus-tauschkraft f
spillway weir	s. a. spillway		
spin	Spin m	**spin-exchange inter-action**	s. spin-spin exchange inter-action
spin	s. a. spinning		
spin	s. a. spin angular momentum	**spin-exchange operator,** Bartlett operator	Bartlett-Operator m, Spin-austauschoperator m
spin alignment	Spinausrichtung f, Spin-ordnung f, Spineinstel-lung f		
		spin-exchange potential, Bartlett potential	Bartlett-Potential n, Poten-tial n der Bartlett-Kräfte, Spinaustauschpotential n
spin angle function	Spin-Bahn-Funktion f, Spinbahnfunktion f, Kugelfunktion f mit Spin, Spinwinkelfunktion f		
		spin-field coupling	Spin-Feld-Kopplung f
		spin-field interaction	Spin-Feld-Wechselwirkung f
spin angular momentum [vector], spin momentum [vector], spin vector, spin moment, intrinsic angular momentum, angular momentum due to the intrinsic rotation, eigen angular momentum	Spindrehimpuls[vektor] m, Spinvektor m, mechani-scher Eigendrehimpuls m, Eigendrehimpuls, Eigen-drall m, mechanisches Eigenmoment n, mecha-nisches Moment n, Spin-moment n	**spin flip,** flip-over of spin, flop-over of spin, reorien-tation of spin, spin reorientation, spin in-version	Umklappen n des Spins, Spinumkehr[ung] f, Umkehrung f des Spins, Umkehr f des Spins, Spinumklappung f
		spin flip operator	Spinumkehroperator m, Umkehroperator m, Umklappoperator m, Spinumklappoperator m
spin atomic orbital, spin wave function, spin orbital, SO	Spinwellenfunktion f, Spinatomorbital n, Spin-orbital n		
		spin flip scattering	Spinumkehrstreuung f, Umkehrstreuung f, Spin-umklappstreuung f, Um-klappstreuung f, Streuung f mit Umklappen des Spins, Streuung mit Änderung der Spin-orientierung
spin axis, gyroaxis, gyro-scope axis, axis of the top	Kreiselachse f		
spin contribution	Spinanteil m, Spinbeitrag m		
spin co-ordinate, spin variable	Spinkoordinate f, Spin-variable f		

spin

spin flip spectrum, spin reorientation spectrum	Spinumkehrspektrum *n*, Spinumklappspektrum *n*
spin fluctuation	Spinfluktuation *f*
spin-free complex; high-spin complex; outer-orbital complex	Normalkomplex *m*, magnetisch normaler Komplex *m*, [„normaler"] Anlagerungskomplex *m*
spin function	Spinfunktion *f*
spin gas	Spingas *n*
spin generator	Spingenerator *m*
spin Hamiltonian	Spin-Hamilton-Operator *m*
spin-harmonic coupling, cross relaxation	Kreuzrelaxation *f*, Cross-relaxation *f*
spin-heat conductivity	Spinwärmeleitfähigkeit *f*
spin incoherence	Spininkohärenz *f*
spin incoherent scattering, spin-dependent scattering	spin-inkohärente Streuung *f*, Spinstreuung *f*, spin-abhängige Streuung
spin interaction	Spinwechselwirkung *f*
spin inversion	*s.* spin flip
spin-lattice coupling	Spin-Gitter-Kopplung *f*
spin-lattice interaction	Spin-Gitter-Wechselwirkung *f*
spin-lattice relaxation, nuclear spin-lattice relaxation	Spin-Gitter-Relaxation *f*
spin-lattice relaxation time, longitudinal relaxation time, thermal relaxation time	Spin-Gitter-Relaxationszeit *f*, longitudinale Relaxationszeit *f*, thermische Relaxationszeit
spin-lattice transition probability	Spin-Gitter-Übergangswahrscheinlichkeit *f*
spinless particle, spin[-] zero particle	Spin-0-Teilchen *n*, Teilchen *n* mit dem Spin 0, Teilchen ohne Spin, spinloses Teilchen
spin level	Spinniveau *n*
spin magnetic moment	magnetisches Spinmoment *n*, Spinanteil *m* des magnetischen Moments
spin magnetic quantum number, magnetic spin quantum number	magnetische Spinquantenzahl *f*, Mangnetspinquantenzahl *f*, Spinmagnetismus *m*
spin magnetic resonance	magnetische Spinresonanz *f*
spin magnetism	Spinmagnetismus *m*
spin matrix	*s.* Pauli spin matrix
spin matrix of Dirac, Dirac [spin] matrix, gamma matrix	Diracsche Spinmatrix *f*, Dirac-Matrix *f*, Spinmatrix *f* von Dirac
spin matrix of Pauli	*s.* Pauli spin matrix
spin mode	Spinmode *f*, Spinmodus *m*
spin moment	*s.* spin angular momentum
spin momentum [vector]	*s.* spin angular momentum
spin multiplet	Spinmultiplett *n*
spinning, spin, free spinning, tail spin	Trudeln *n*, Trudelbewegung *f*, Trudelflug *m*
spinning detonation	rotierende Detonation *f*, Spin *m* der Detonation
spinning electron	rotierendes Elektron *n*, Elektron mit Eigendrehimpuls
spinning molecule	*s.* top molecule
spinning obstacle	rotierendes Hindernis *n*
spinning of the nucleon, spin of the nucleon	Spinbewegung *f* des Nukleons, Eigenrotation *f* des Nukleons
spinning top	rotierender Kreisel *m*
spinning upside down	Rückentrudeln *n*
spinning wind tunnel	*s.* free spinning tunnel
spinodal curve	Spinodale *f*
spinodal decomposition	spinodale Entmischung *f*
spinodal point	spinodaler Punkt *m*
spinode	*s.* cusp
spin of the nucleon, nucleon spin	Spin *m* des Nukleons, Nukleon[en]spin *m*
spin of the nucleon, spinning of the nucleon	Spinbewegung (Eigenrotation) *f* des Nukleons
spin operator	Spinoperator *m*
spinor	Spinor *m*
spinor analysis	Spinoranalysis *f*
spin orbital	*s.* spin wave function
spin-orbital coupling	*s.* spin-orbit coupling
spin-orbit coupling, spin-orbital coupling, orbit-spin coupling	Spin-Bahn-Kopplung *f*, Spin-Bahndrehimpuls-Kopplung *f*
spin-orbit coupling constant	Konstante *f* der Spin-Bahn-Kopplung, Spin-Bahn-Kopplungskonstante *f*
spin-orbit coupling shell model	Schalenmodell *n* mit Spin-Bahn-Kopplung
spin-orbit coupling term, spin-orbit term	Spin-Bahn-Kopplungsterm *m*, Spin-Bahn-Term *m*
spin-orbit doublet	Spin-Bahn-Dublett *n*
spin-orbit interaction	Spin-Bahn-Wechselwirkung *f*
spin-orbit potential	Spin-Bahn-Potential *n*
spin-orbit splitting	Spin-Bahn-Aufspaltung *f*
spin-orbit term	*s.* spin-orbit coupling term
spinor calculus	Spinorkalkül *m*
spinor component	Spinorkomponente *f*
spinor field, spinorial field	Spinorfeld *n*
spinor field theory	Spinorfeldtheorie *f*
spinor gravitation, spinorial gravitation	Spinorgravitation *f*
spinorial Dirac equation	spinorielle Dirac-Gleichung *f*
spinorial field	*s.* spinor field
spinorial gravitation	*s.* spinor gravitation
spinorial S-matrix, *M* function, spinor *S*-matrix	*M*-Funktion *f*, Spinor-*S*-Matrix *f*, spinorielle *S*-Matrix *f*
spinorial wave equation	*s.* spinor wave equation
spin orientation; spin direction	Spinorientierung *f*; Spinrichtung *f*
spin orientation exchange	Spinorientierungsaustausch *m*
spinor index	Spinorindex *m*
spinor of four components, four-component spinor	vierkomponentiger Spinor *m*
spinor of two components, two-component spinor, Weyl spinor	zweikomponentiger Spinor *m*, Weylscher Spinor
spinor representation	Spinordarstellung *f*, Spindarstellung *f*
spinor S-matrix	*s.* spinorial *S*-matrix
spinor space	Spinorraum *m*
spinor wave	Spinorwelle *f*
spinor wave equation, spinorial wave equation	Spinwellengleichung *f*, Spinorwellengleichung *f*
spinor wave function	Spinorwellenfunktion *f*
spin packet	Spinpaket *n*
spin-paired complex, low-spin complex, inner-orbital complex, sandwich complex	Durchdringungskomplex *m*, magnetisch anomaler Komplex *m*
spin pairing	Spinpaarung *f*
spin paramagnetism	Spinparamagnetismus *m*
spin particle, particle with spin	Teilchen *n* mit Spin, Spinteilchen *n*
spin 1 particle, particle with spin 1	Spin-1-Teilchen *n*, Teilchen *n* mit dem Spin 1

spin ½ particle, particle with spin ½	Spin-½-Teilchen n, Teilchen n mit dem Spin ½	spin [-] zero particle, spinless particle	Spin-0-Teilchen n, Teilchen n mit dem Spin 0, Teilchen ohne Spin, spinloses Teilchen
spin partition function	Spinzustandssumme f	spiral, helix, spire	Spirale f <ebene Kurve>
spin polarization tensor	Spinpolarisationstensor m	spiral, helical	Spiral-, spiralförmig, spiralig
spin quantum number	Spinquantenzahl f	spiral	s. a. helical conductor <el.>
spin quenching, quenching spin	Spinauslöschung f, „spin quenching" n	spiral arm, arm of the spiral nebula	Spiralarm m
spin Raman effect	Spin-Raman-Effekt m	spiral chromosome	spiralisiertes Chromosom n
spin relativity doublet	relativistisches Dublett n, reguläres Dublett (Spindublett n)	spiral condenser, spiral cooler	Spiralkühler m
spin relaxation	Spinrelaxation f	spiral crystal	spiralförmiger Kristall m, Spiralkristall m
spin reorientation	s. spin flip	spiral dial microscope	Spiralmikroskop n
spin reorientation spectrum	s. spin flip spectrum	spiral disk, helical disk	Spiralscheibe f
spin resonance	Spinresonanz f		
spin resonance frequency	Spinresonanzfrequenz f; ESR-Frequenz f	spiral disk, Nipkow disk, exploring disk, apertured disk	Nipkow-Scheibe f, Abtastscheibe f, Spirallochscheibe f
spin-rotation interaction	Spin-Rotations-Wechselwirkung f	spiral dislocation, helical dislocation	Spiralversetzung f, spiralförmige Versetzung f
spin saturation	Spinabsättigung f	spiral dislocation source, spiral source	Spiralversetzungsquelle f, Spiralquelle f
spin selection rule	Spinauswahlregel f	spiral distortion, anisotropic distortion, shear distortion	anisotrope Verzeichnung f, Zerdrehung f
spin sequence	Spinfolge f, Spinsequenz f		
spin space	Spinraum m, Spinkonfigurationsraum m	spiral-eight twisting, eightfold twisting	Doppelsternverseilung f, Achterverseilung f
spin-spin coupling, spin coupling	Spin-Spin-Kopplung f, Spinkopplung f; Spinverkopplung f		
spin-spin exchange interaction, spin-exchange interaction	Spin-Spin-Austauschwechselwirkung f, Spinaustauschwechselwirkung f	spiral fibre structure	Spiralfaserstruktur f, spiralförmige Faserstruktur f
spin-spin interaction	Spin-Spin-Wechselwirkung f	spiral field, helical field	Spiralfeld n
		spiral flow	Spiralströmung f
spin-spin relaxation, nuclear spin-spin relaxation	Spin-Spin-Relaxation f		
spin-spin relaxation time, transverse relaxation time	Spin-Spin-Relaxationszeit f, transversale Relaxationszeit f		
		spiral-four formation, spiral-four twisting, star quad formation, spiral quad formation	Sternverseilung f, Sternviererverseilung f
spin-spin splitting	Spin-Spin-Aufspaltung f		
spin-splitting	s. spin doubling		
spin state	Spinzustand m	spiral galaxy	s. spiral nebula
spin susceptibility, Pauli spin susceptibility	[Paulische] Spinsuszeptibilität f	spiral growth	Spiralwachstum n, spiralförmiges Wachstum n, Schraubenwachstum n
spin system	Spinsystem n		
spin [system] temperature	Spin[system]temperatur f	spiralization	Spiralisierung f
		spiral line	s. helix
		spiralling	s. screw displacement
spin tensor	Spintensor m, Spindrehimpulstensor m	spiralling orbit, spiral orbit, spiral trajectory	Spiralbahn f, spiralförmige Bahn f
spin tensor operator	Spintensoroperator m	spiral micrometer	Spiralokular n, Spiralmikrometer n
spin term	Spinterm m		
spinthariscope, geigerscope	Spinthariskop n	spiral nebula, spiral galaxy	Spiralnebel m, Spiralgalaxie f, Spiralsystem n, Spirale f <Astr.>
spin uncoupling, spin decoupling	Spinentkopplung f	spiral of Archimedes	s. Archimedean screw
spin valence	Spinvalenz f	spiral of Ekman, Ekman spiral	Spirale f von Ekman, Ekman-Spirale f, Ekmansche Spirale
spin-valence theory	s. Heitler-London theory		
spin variable, spin co-ordinate	Spinkoordinate f, Spinvariable f	spiral of Hamel, Hamel spiral	Spirale f von Hamel, Hamelsche Spirale, Hamel-Spirale f
spin vector	s. spin angular momentum		
spin vector operator	Spinvektoroperator m	spiral orbit, spiralling orbit, spiral trajectory	Spiralbahn f, spiralförmige Bahn f
		spiral-orbit spectrometer	Spiralbahnspektrometer n
spin wave	Spinwelle f	spiral plasmolysis	Schraubenplasmolyse f
spin wave approximation	Spinwellennäherung f	spiral point, focal point, focus <math.>	Strudelpunkt m <Math.>
spin wave function, spin atomic orbital, spin orbital, SO	Spinwellenfunktion f, Spinatomorbital n, Spinorbital n	spiral pump	s. Archimedean screw
		spiral quad formation	s. spiral-four formation
		spiral ridge; spiral sector	Spiralrücken m; Spiralsektor m
spin wave spectrum	Spinwellenspektrum n	spiral-ridge cyclotron, spiral-sector cyclotron	Spiralrückenzyklotron n, Spiralsektorzyklotron n
spin wave theory	Spinwellentheorie f	spiral-ridge field, spiral-sectored field	Spiralsektorfeld n, Spiralrückenfeld n
		spiral-ridge synchrotron	s. FFAG spiral-ridge synchrotron

spiral scanning	s. helical scanning	split ring; gapped ring	Schlitzring m, Spaltring m
spiral sector	s. spiral ridge		
spiral-sector cyclotron	s. spiral-ridge cyclotron		
spiral-sectored field, spiral-ridge field	Spiralsektorfeld n, Spiralrückenfeld n	split-ring mounting	Splitringmontierung f, „split-ring"-Montierung f, Sprengringmontierung f
spiral-sector synchrotron	s. FFAG spiral-ridge synchrotron		
spiral source, spiral dislocation source	Spiralversetzungsquelle f, Spiralquelle f	split source	geteilte Quelle f
spiral spring seismograph, spring seismograph	Spiralfederseismograph m, Federseismograph m		
spiral-staircase coil	s. Bitter coil	splitting, splitting up, scission	Aufspaltung f, Spaltung f, Zerspaltung f; Aufteilung f; Teilung f
spiral strain gauge	Spiralmeßstreifen m, Spiral-Dehnungsmeßstreifen m		
spiral structure <astr.>	Spiralstruktur f <Astr.>	splitting, line splitting <of the spectral line>	Linienaufspaltung f, Aufspaltung f <Spektrallinie>
spiral texture	Schraubentextur f, Spiraltextur f		
spiral trajectory, spiral orbit, spiralling orbit	Spiralbahn f, spiralförmige Bahn f	splitting, dissociation <of molecules>	Dissoziation f, Aufspaltung f, Zerlegung f <Moleküle>
spiral turn, turn of the spiral	Spiralwindung f, Windung f der Spirale	splitting; rupture, abruption; tearing; bursting; rending, tear <mech.>	Zerreißung f; Reißen n, Riß m; Sprungbildung f, Einreißen n <Mech.>
spiral vernier	Spiralnonius m	splitting	s. a. level splitting <of energy level>
spiral vortex	Spiralwirbel m	splitting factor	s. Landé g-factor
spire, helix, spiral	Spirale f <ebene Kurve>	splitting off, separation <nucl.>	Abspaltung f, Abtrennung f <Kern.>
spire	s. a. turn	splitting of the dislocation	s. dissociation of the dislocation
spirit level	s. level	splitting parameter	Aufspaltungsparameter m
spirit thermometer	s. alcohol thermometer	splitting plate	s. beam splitting plate
spiro compound	Spiran n, spirozyklische Verbindung f	splitting up	s. splitting
spirometer	Spirometer n, Anapnometer n, Pneumonometer n	split transformer, tapped transformer	Anzapftransformator m
spit [of land]	Nehrung f; Lido m; Peressyp f	split-wire-type current transformer	Anlegestromwandler m
spitting, spurting, sputter	Spratzen n	SP maser	s. self-powered maser
s plane <in Laplace transformation>	Unterbereich m, Bildbereich m, p-Ebene f <Laplace-Transformation>	spodogram	Spodogramm n, Aschenbild n
		Spoerer['s] law, law of zones, zone law	Spörersches Gesetz n, Zonengesetz n
splash, spatter	Spritzer m	spoke	Speiche f
splash ring	Schirmring m	spoking	s. stroboscopic effect
splat quenching [technique]	Klatschkühlung f	sponge, spongious, spongy; porous	porös, porig; schwammig, schwammartig
splatter	s. adjacent-channel interference	spongelike decay	Spongiose f, Graphitierung f
S.P.L. equal loudness contour	s. Robinson-Dadson equal loudness contour	spongious, spongy	s. sponge
splinter	s. nuclear fragment <nucl.>	spongy platinum, platinum sponge	Platinschwamm m
splinterable	splitternd, splitterbar	spontaneity	Spontaneität f, Spontanität f
splintering	Splitterung f, Zersplitterung f	spontaneous afterglow	spontanes Nachleuchten n, Spontanleuchten n, Momentanleuchten n, m-Leuchten n
splinter-proof, shatterproof	splitterfrei, nichtsplitternd		
splinter-proof glass, safety glass, unsplintered glass	Sicherheitsglas n, splitterfreies Glas n	spontaneous combustion	spontane Verbrennung f
		spontaneous decay	s. spontaneous transformation
splintery fracture	splittriger Bruch m	spontaneous crack propagation	spontane Rißausbreitung f
split anode magnetron, slot magnetron	Schlitzanodenmagnetron n, Schlitzmagnetron n, Magnetron n (Magnetfeldröhre f) mit geschlitzter Anode, Schlitzanoden-Magnetfeldröhre f	spontaneous decomposition, self-decomposition	spontane Zersetzung f, Selbstzersetzung f
		spontaneous discharge	Spontanentladung f
		spontaneous disintegration	s. spontaneous transmission
split antenna, slot antenna, slotted antenna	Schlitzantenne f	spontaneous emission	spontane Emission f, Spontanemission f; Ausstrahlung f
split-dose irradiation; fractionated irradiation	„split-dose"-Bestrahlung f; fraktionierte Bestrahlung f	spontaneous fission	spontane Spaltung f, spontane Kernspaltung f, Spontanspaltung f
split-field rangefinder	s. coincidence rangefinder	spontaneous frequency <of mutations>, rate of spontaneous mutation	Spontanhäufigkeit f, Spontanrate f <von Mutationen>, Spontanmutationsrate f
split image, partial image	Teilbild n		
split-image rangefinder	s. coincidence rangefinder		
split lens	Spaltlinse f		
split line, dividing (separation, separating) line	Trennlinie f, Trennungslinie f	spontaneous heating, self-heating	Selbsterhitzung f, Selbsterwärmung f
split pole	Spaltpol m		

spontaneous heat transition	s. spontaneous transition of heat	spotted, spotty, stained, mottled	fleckig
spontaneous ignition	s. self-ignition	spot test[ing], dropping test, drop test, drop method <chem.>	Tüpfelprobe f <Chem.>
spontaneous ignition temperature, self-ignition point, S.I.T.	Selbstentzündungstemperatur f	spotting box, negatoscope, negative viewer, light box	Negatoskop n, Negativschaukasten m, Negativbetrachter m
spontaneous inflammability	Selbstentzündlichkeit f, Selbstentzündbarkeit f	spotty	s. spotted
spontaneous lifetime [of the level]	spontane Lebensdauer f [des Niveaus]	spotty emission	Punktleuchten n
spontaneous magnetization, intrinsic magnetization	spontane Magnetisierung f, Spontanmagnetisierung f	spot umbra, umbra	Umbra f des Sonnenflecks
spontaneous noise	spontanes Rauschen n	spot zone	Fleckenzone f
spontaneous nuclear reaction (transformation)	s. spontaneous transformation	spout, nozzle <of waveguide>	Wellenleiteröffnung f, Austrittsöffnung f [des Wellenleiters], Wellenleiter-Austrittsöffnung f
spontaneous polarization, polarizability catastrophe	spontane Polarisation f, spontane Polarisierung f	spouting of the source	Springen n der Quelle
spontaneous radiation	spontane Strahlung f	spouting spring, fount	Springquelle f
spontaneous Raman effect (scattering)	s. linear Raman effect		
spontaneous strain	spontane Verformung (Deformation) f	spoutnik	s. artificial Earth's satellite
spontaneous transformation, spontaneous decay, spontaneous disintegration, spontaneous nuclear transformation, spontaneous nuclear reaction, natural [nuclear] transformation	spontaner Zerfall m, natürlicher radioaktiver Zerfall m, spontane Kernumwandlung f, spontane Kernreaktion f, natürliche Kernumwandlung	spray, water dust, water spray	Wasserstaub m
		spray, water spray, water veil	Wasserschleier m, Wassersprühregen m
		spray	s. a. atomizer
		spray development, spray processing	Sprühentwicklung f
spontaneous transition	spontaner Übergang m	spray discharge	s. corona
		spray discharge	s. a. brush discharge
spontaneous transition of heat, spontaneous heat transition	spontaner Wärmeübergang m	spray drying	Sprühtrocknung f, Zerstäubungstrocknung f
sporadic, sporadic meteor, non-shower meteor	sporadisches Meteor n, Feldmeteor n	sprayed water, jet water, water jets	Spritzwasser n
		spray effect	s. spraying effect
sporadic	s. a. isolated	sprayer	s. atomizer
sporadic E-layer, Es-layer, anomalous E-layer	sporadische E-Schicht f, anomale E-Schicht, E_s-Schicht f	spraying, spraying-on	Aufsprühen n; Besprühen n; Bespritzen n
		spraying <on> <of charge>	Aufsprühen n [auf], Sprühen n [auf] <Ladung>
sporadic meteor	s. sporadic	spraying	s. a. atomization
sporadosiderite	Sporadosiderit m	spraying effect, spray effect	Zerstäubungsgrad m, Zerstäubungswirkung f; Versprühungsgrad m
spore analysis	s. pollen analysis		
spot <also el.>; patch; speck	Fleck m	spraying electrode, brushing electrode	Sprühelektrode f
spot, tubular lamp, tubular line lamp, tubular light, strip lamp	Soffittenlampe f, Soffitte f, Lichtwurflampe f L	spraying-on	s. spraying
		spray nozzle, atomization jet	Zerstäuberdüse f, Zerstäubungsdüse f; Verneblungsdüse f; Sprühdüse f
spot	s. a. light spot		
spot acuity, acuity of the spot	Punktschärfe f		
spot analysis	Tüpfelanalyse f		
spot area, area of sunspot	Fleckenfläche f	spray point, corona point, discharge point; active spot [of corona discharge]	Sprühspitze f, Koronaentladungsspitze f, Sprühstelle f, Sprühpunkt m
spot contact	s. point contact		
spot corrosion	s. staining		
spot distortion, deflection aberration	Ablenkfehler m, Fleckverzerrung f	spray points	Spitzenkamm m, Sprühkamm m, Sprühstellen fpl, Spitzenkammabnehmer m
spot group, group of sunspots	Fleckengruppe f, Sonnenfleckengruppe f	spray processing	s. spray development
spot height	s. cote	spray prominence	Spritzprotuberanz f
spotlight	Punktlichtscheinwerfer m, Punktlicht n, Richtungslampe f, „spotlight" n, Spotlicht n; Linsenscheinwerfer m	spray region, exosphere, fringe region	Exosphäre f, äußere Atmosphäre f
		spray test	s. salt-spray test
		spread, spreading, stretch[ing], extension	Spreizung f
spot noise factor	spektrale Rauschzahl f	spread, spread band, spreading range, zone of dispersion	Streubereich m, Streuungsbereich m, Streuungszone f
spot on the cathode-ray tube	s. luminous spot		
spot penumbra, penumbra	Penumbra f (Hof m) des Sonnenflecks	spread; propagation <in>	Ausbreitung f, Fortpflanzung f <in>
spot prominence, sunspot prominence	Fleckenprotuberanz f	spread, straggling, statistical straggling, scattering <gen., e. g. of data>	Streuung f, statistische Streuung; Streubreite f <allg., z. B. von Daten>
spot sample	s. sample <stat.>		
spots caused by developing agent, developer stains	Entwicklerflecke mpl		
spot shape distortion	s. astigmatism	spread, stretch <a surface>	aufspannen <eine Fläche>
spot size divergence, emittance <acc.>	Emittanz f <Beschl.>		

spread	*s. a.* spreading <e.g. of a liquid film>	Springfield mounting	Springfield-Montierung *f*
spread angle	*s.* beam aperture		
spread band	*s.* spread		
spread function	Verwaschungsfunktion *f*	spring galvanometer	Federgalvanometer *n*
spread in energy, energy straggling; energy fluctuation *f*	Energiestreuung *f*; Energieschwankung *f*	spring gravimeter, spring-type gravimeter	Federgravimeter *n*
		springiness <US>	*s.* elastic recovery
spreading, spread, stretch[ing], extension	Spreizung *f*	springing back	zurückfedernd
		spring manometer	*s.* Bourdon gauge
spreading <in the form of a monomolecular layer>	Spreitung *f*	spring model	Federmodell *n*
		spring pendulum	Federpendel *n*
spreading, widening <of beam>	Strahlverbreiterung *f*, Bündelverbreiterung *f*, Verbreiterung *f* des Strahls	spring pressure	Federdruck *m*
		spring pressure gauge	*s.* Bourdon tube
		spring scales	*s.* spring balance
spreading, spread <e. g. of liquid film>	Ausbreitung *f*, Auseinanderlaufen *n*, Auseinanderfließen *n* <z. B. Flüssigkeitsschicht>	spring seismograph, spiral spring seismograph	Spiralfederseismograph *m*, Federseismograph *m*
		spring suspension, resilient suspension	federnde Aufhängung *f*, Federaufhängung *f*
spreading, redressment, reestablishment; unsqueezing <opt.>	Entzerrung *f* <Opt.>	spring tide, syzygial tide, big tide	Springflut *f*, Springtide *f*
spreading agent, wetting agent	Netzmittel *n*, Benetzungsmittel *n*, Benetzer *m*		
		spring-type gravimeter	*s.* spring gravimeter
		spring-type pressure gauge	*s.* Bourdon gauge
spreading coefficient	Ausbreitungskoeffizient *m*, Spreitungskoeffizient *m*	spring water, source water	Quellwasser *n*
		sprinkler [installation]	Sprinkleranlage *f*
spreading factor	*s.* R_s factor		
spreading force	*s.* spreading pressure	s process, slow process, slow neutron capture, capture of neutrons on a slow time scale <astr.>	s-Prozeß *m*, langsamer Prozeß *m*, langsamer Neutroneneinfang *m* <Astr.>
spreading of excitation, spread of excitation	Erregungsausbreitung *f*		
spreading of the band, band spread	Bandspreizung *f*, Spreizung *f* des Bandes		
		sprocket hole; punching, perforation	Lochung *f*; Perforation *f*, Stanzloch *n*
spreading pressure, spreading force	Spreitungsdruck *m*, Ausdehnungsdruck *m*, Ausbreitungsdruck *m*	sprocket-hole noise, sprocket hum (noise)	Perforationsgeräusch *n*
		Sprung['s] formula, Sprung['s] psychrometer formula	Sprungsche Psychrometerformel (Formel) *f*, Psychrometerformel nach Sprung
spreading range	*s.* spread		
spreading resistance	*s.* diffusion resistance <semi.>	spur, trace, diagonal sum, main diagonal sum, tr <of matrix, operator>	Spur *f*, Diagonalsumme *f*, Sp <Matrix, Operator>
spread layer chromatography	*s.* layer chromatography		
spread of excitation, spreading of excitation	Erregungsausbreitung *f*	spur <of particle track>	Ionisationszentrum *n* <in der Teilchenbahn>
spread of flames, flame propagation, propagation of flames, flame spread	Flammenausbreitung *f*, Flammenfortpflanzung *f*	spur <geo.>	Ausläufer *m* <Geo.>
		spurion	Spurion *n*
		spurious capacitance	*s.* stray capacitance
spread of the wing, wing span, span of the wing	Spannweite *f* [des Flügels], Flügelspannweite *f*	spurious coincidence, random (accidental, chance) coincidence	zufällige Koinzidenz *f*, Zufallskoinzidenz *f*
		spurious correlation	künstliche Korrelation *f*
spread velocity, propagation velocity, velocity (speed) of propagation	Ausbreitungsgeschwindigkeit *f*, Fortpflanzungsgeschwindigkeit *f*	spurious count	*s.* spurious pulse
		spurious coupling	*s.* stray coupling
		spurious electromotive force, stray electromotive force, spurious e.m.f., stray e.m.f.	Streu-EMK *f*
spring; source; well <geo.>	Quelle *f* <Geo.>		
spring, source <geo.>	Schichtquelle *f* <Geo.>	spurious emission	*s.* perturbing radiation <el.>
spring-back	*s.* elastic recovery		
spring balance, spring scales, spring dynamometer	Federwaage *f*, Federdynamometer *n*, Zugwaage *f*, Federzugmesser *m*	spurious frequency, interfering frequency	Nebenfrequenz *f*; Störfrequenz *f*
spring constant, force constant [of the spring], rigidity [of the spring], stiffness [of the spring]	Federkonstante *f*, Starre *f* [der Feder], Federstarre *f*, Federsteife *f* [der Feder], Federsteifigkeit *f*, Steifigkeit *f* [der Feder], elastische Kopplungskonstante *f*, Federeinheitskraft *f*, Einheitskraft *f*, Starrheit *f* [der Feder], Federweichheit *f*		
		spurious oscillation, parasitic oscillation; spurious wave, parasitic wave	wilde Schwingung *f*, Nebenschwingung *f*; Nebenwelle *f*, Störwelle *f*
		spurious period	Scheinperiode *f*
		spurios periodicity	Scheinperiodizität *f*
		spurious printing, magnetic printing, crosstalk	Kopiereffekt *m*
spring contact	Federkontakt *m*		
spring dynamometer	*s.* spring balance	spurious pulse, ghost pulse; spurious count	unechter Impuls *m*, falscher Impuls; unechter Zählimpuls *m*, falscher Zählimpuls, unechter Zählstoß *m*, falscher Zählstoß
spring equinox, vernal equinox, northern vernal equinox	Frühlingsäquinoktium *n*, Frühlings-Tagundnachtgleiche *f*		
spring erosion, source erosion	Quellerosion *f*		

spurious radiation, parasitic radiation, stray radiation	Nebenstrahlung *f*, Parasitärstrahlung *f*, wilde Strahlung *f*, Störstrahlung *f*	**square grid** **square-integrable,** square-summable, quadratically integrable	*s.* square mesh grid quadratisch integrierbar, quadratisch integrabel
spurious radiation	*s. a.* perturbing radiation <el.>	**square iron-core coil** **square law**	*s.* square-core coil quadratisches Gesetz *n*
spurious reactance, parasitic reactance	Störblindwiderstand *m*, Störreaktanz *f*	**square-law capacitor,** straight-line-wavelength	Nierenplattenkondensator *m*
spurious resonance, subordinate (secondary) resonance; spurious response	Nebenresonanz *f*	capacitor **square-law detector,** **square-law rectifier**	quadratischer Gleichrichter *m*, quadratischer Detektor *m*
spurious response	*s.* spurious signal		
spurious response	*s.* spurious resonance		
spurious scattering, ghost scattering	„spurious scattering" *n*, unechte Streuung *f*, falsche Streuung	**square loop antenna** **square-loop ferrite,** rectangular loop ferrite, rectangular ferrite	*s.* loop antenna Rechteckferrit *m*
spurious signal, interfering (parasitic, unwanted) signal, spurious response; ghost signal	Störsignal *n*; unechtes Signal *n*, falsches Signal	**square matrix,** square array, quadratic matrix **square measure,** measure of area	quadratische Matrix *f* Flächenmaß *n*
spurious state	„Geisterzustand" *m*	**square mesh grid,** square grid, square net	Quadratnetz *n*, quadratisches Netz *n*, Quadratliniennetz *n*
spurious wave	*s.* spurious oscillation		
spurium	Spurium *n*		
spur of the traverse, open (unclosed) traverse; offshoot of the traverse	offener Polygonzug *m*, offener Zug *m*	**squareness** **square net** **square of distance** **square of the standard deviation,** variance, dispersion, var <stat.>	*s.* perpendicularity *s.* square mesh grid Abstandsquadrat *n* Varianz *f*, Dispersion *f*, Streuungsquadrat *n*, Streuung *f*, var <Stat.>
spurting	*s.* spitting		
sputnik	*s.* artificial Earth's satellite		
sputter	*s.* spitting		
sputtering, disintegration <of cathode>	Zerstäubung *f* <Katode>	**square pulse** **square pyramid**	*s.* square-wave pulse vierseitige Pyramide *f*, quadratische Pyramide
sputtering	*s. a.* atomization		
sputter-ion pump	Ionenzerstäuberpumpe *f*	**square-root computer**	Quadratwurzelrechner *m*
		square-root law [of Kohlrausch]	*s.* Kohlrausch square-root law
squagging, squegging; self-locking, automatic interlock	Selbstsperrung *f* <durch Aufschaukeln der Überschwingungen>; Selbstunterbrechung *f*; Selbstblockierung *f*	**square-scale instrument (meter)** **square-section[al] conductor**	*s.* quadrant instrument *s.* rectangular conductor
		square-sided pulse	*s.* square-wave pulse
		square-summable	*s.* square-integrable
squall	Bö *f*, Windbö *f*	**square-topped pulse**	*s.* square-wave pulse
squall line	Böenlinie *f*, Böenfront *f*, Squall-Linie *f*	**square-topped pulse train**	*s.* square-wave pulse train
squally wind	*s.* choppy wind	**square wave;** rectangular wave	Quadratwelle *f*; Rechteckwelle *f*
squarability, squareability	Quadrierbarkeit *f*		
squarable set	quadrierbare Menge *f*	**square-wave generator,** square-wave oscillator, square-wave radiator, micropulser	Rechteck[wellen]generator *m*, Rechteckwellen-Impulsgenerator *m*, Rechteckimpulsgenerator *m*, Rechteckimpulserzeuger *m*, Rechteckspannungsgenerator *m*, Rechteckspannungserzeuger *m*, Sprunggenerator *m*
square, optical square	Winkelinstrument *n*, Rechtwinkelinstrument *n* <für 90°>; Flachwinkelinstrument *n* <für 180°>; Winkelkreuz *n*		
square, set square	Winkelmaß *n*, Zeichendreieck *n*, Reißdreieck *n*; Meßwinkel *m* <Gerät>	**square-wave oscillation**	Rechteckschwingung *f*; Mäanderschwingung *f*
squareability	*s.* squarability	**square-wave oscillator**	*s.* square-wave generator
square array, square (quadratic) matrix	quadratische Matrix *f*	**square-wave pulse,** square-topped pulse, square-sided pulse, square pulse, rectangular pulse	Rechteckimpuls *m*, Rechteckwellenimpuls *m*, rechteckiger (rechteckförmiger, rechteckwellenförmiger) Impuls *m*
square bracket	eckige Klammer *f*, scharfe Klammer		
square cascade	rechteckige Kaskade *f*, Rechteckkaskade *f*		
square contingency	quadratische Kontingenz *f*	**square-wave pulse [repetition] frequency**	Rechteckfrequenz *f*; Mäanderfrequenz *f*
square-core coil; square iron-core coil	Rechteckspule *f*		
		square-wave pulse train, square-topped pulse train	Rechteck[impuls]folge *f*, Rechteckimpulsserie *f*
		square-wave radiator	*s.* square-wave generator
		square-wave response	*s.* transient response
		square-wave voltage	Rechteckspannung *f*; Mäanderspannung *f*; Zinnenspannung *f* <Fs.>
square degree, □², (°)²	Quadratgrad *m*, □², (°)²		
squaredial instrument (meter)	*s.* quadrant instrument	**square well** **square well potential;** square well, potential box	*s.* square well potential rechteckiger Potentialtopf (Topf) *m*, RechteckPotentialtopf *m*, Potentialkasten *m*; Kastenpotential *n*, Rechteckpotential *n*, „square-well"-Potential *n*; quadratischer Potentialtopf (Topf)
squared paper; scale paper; graph paper, co-ordinate paper, plotting paper, section paper	Koordinatenpapier *n*		
squared paper, quadrillé paper	kariertes Papier *n*		
square fluctuation	Schwankungsquadrat *n*		

squariance, sum of squares	Quadratsumme f, Summe f der Abweichungsquadrate	stability criterion of Leonhard (Michailov, Michailov-Leonhard)	s. Michailov['s] criterion
squaring ⟨of pulse⟩	Rechteckformung f, Umformung f in Rechteckimpulse	stability criterion of Nyquist	s. Nyquist['s] criterion [of stability]
		stability criterion of Nyquist-Cauchy	s. Nyquist-Cauchy criterion
squaring of the cascade	Quadrierung f der Kaskade	stability criterion of Nyquist-Michailov	s. Nyquist['s] criterion [of stability]
squashing, crushing, bruising	Zerdrückung f; Zerquetschung f; Zermalmung f	stability criterion of Routh, Routh-Hurwicz criterion, Routh['s] criterion [of stability]	Routhsches Stabilitätskriterium (Kriterium) n, Stabilitätskriterium nach Routh, Routh-Stabilitätskriterium n, Routh-Kriterium n, Kriterium von Routh
squashing; squeeze, squeezing; pinch; crimp[ing]	Quetschung f		
		stability curve	s. stability line
squegger	s. squegging oscillator	stability derivative	Stabilitätsableitung f
squegging	s. squagging	stability diagram of Shafranov, Shafranov['s] stability diagram, Shafranov['s] diagram	Stabilitätsdiagramm n nach Schafranow, Schafranow-Diagramm n
squegging oscillator, squegger, blocking oscillator, selfquenching oscillator, blocking generator	Sperrschwinger m, Blockingoszillator m		
		stability domain, region of stability, stability region ⟨control⟩	Stabilitätsbereich m, Stabilitätsgebiet n ⟨Regelung⟩
squelch circuit	s. squelch unit	stability equation of Orr and Sommerfeld	s. Orr-Sommerfeld perturbation equation
squelch unit; squelch circuit	Geräuschunterdrückung[sschaltung] f, Unterdrückungsschaltung f, „squelch unit " f	stability factor	s. stability margin
		stability index	s. saturation index
squelette	s. skeleton line	stability in time, time stability	zeitliche Konstanz f, Zeitkonstanz f
squid	s. superconducting quantum interference device		
squint[ing], strabismus	Schielen n; manifestes Schielen, Strabismus m	stability layer, layer of stability	Stabilitätsschicht f
squint of antenna	Schielen n der Antenne	stability limit, limit of stability, critical stability	Stabilitätsgrenze f
squirrel cage magnetron	Käfigmagnetron n		
squirrel-cage rotor, cage rotor	Käfiganker m, Käfigläufer m, Kurzschlußläufer m mit Käfigwicklung	stability line, line of stability, curve of stability, stability curve	Stabilitätslinie f, Stabilitätskurve f
		stability map, Strutt['s] map	Stabilitätskarte f [der Hillschen Differentialgleichung], Struttsche Karte f
S ray, S wave, transverse wave ⟨geo.⟩	S-Welle f, Transversalwelle f, Scherwelle f ⟨Geo.⟩		
		stability margin, stability factor	Stabilitätsreserve f
		stability of foam	Schaumbeständigkeit f, Schaumhaltung f
S ray in the inner core, J ray	J-Welle f, S-Welle f im inneren Kern	stability of shape	Formbeständigkeit f
		stability of the orbit	s. orbital stability
SS Cygni star, SS Cygni variable, U Geminorum star, U Geminorum-type star, UG	U Geminorum-Stern m, SS Cygni-Stern m, SS Cygni-Veränderlicher m, Zwergnova f	stability parabola, metacentric parabola, parabola of stability	Auftriebsparabel f, Metazenterparabel f, Stabilitätsparabel f
		stability parameter	Stabilitätsparameter m
S-shaped curve, sigmoid [shaped] curve, S-curve	S-Kurve f	stability region, region of stable orbits, stable region ⟨acc.⟩	Stabilitätsbereich m, Bereich m stabiler Bahnen ⟨Beschl.⟩
S-shaped distribution	S-förmige Verteilung f		
SS ray, SS wave, transverse wave oncereflected downwards at the Earth's outer surface	SS-Welle f, einfach reflektierte Transversalwelle f	stability region	s. a. stability domain ⟨control⟩
		stability rule	Stabilitätsregel f
		stability tensor	Stabilitätstensor m
S-submatrix, scattering submatrix	Streuuntermatrix f, S-Untermatrix f	stability theorem of Dirichlet, Dirichlet['s] theorem [of stability]	Dirichletscher Stabilitätssatz m, Stabilitätssatz von Dirichlet
SS wave	s. SS ray		
stabilidyne	Stabilidyn[e]schaltung f	stability theorem of Liapunov, Liapunov['s] theorem [of stability]	Ljapunowscher Stabilitätssatz m, Stabilitätssatz von Ljapunow
stabilitron	s. Zener diode		
stabilitron	s. a. stabilizer tube		
stability; balance, equilibrium	Gleichgewicht n; Stabilität f	stabilivolt	s. stabilizer tube
stability, constancy, tolerance ⟨of instrument, source⟩	Konstanz f, Stabilität f ⟨Gerät, Quelle⟩	stabilization	Stabilisierung f, Stabilisation f; Gleichhaltung f, Konstanthaltung f
stability, resistance, resistivity ⟨gen.⟩	Festigkeit f, Widerstandsfähigkeit f, Widerstand m, Resistenz f, Beständigkeit f; Sicherheit f ⟨allg.⟩	stabilization energy	Stabilisierungsenergie f
		stabilization factor	Stabilisierungsfaktor m
		stabilization loss	Stabilisierungsverlust m
stability ⟨math., nucl.⟩	Stabilität f ⟨Math., Kern.⟩	stabilization of the iteration	Stehen n der Iteration
		stabilization of variance	Varianzstabilisierung f
stability	s. a. ruggedness ⟨gen.⟩	stabilization resistance	Stabilisierungswiderstand m
stability	s. a. static stability ⟨statics⟩		
stability condition [for vortex street]	Kármánsche Bedingung f ⟨Wirbelstraße⟩	stabilization voltage, stabilizing voltage	Stabilisierungsspannung f
		stabilizer	s. stabilizer ⟨chem.⟩
stability constant	Beständigkeitskonstante f, Stabilitätskonstante f	stabilized glass, non[-]browing glass	stabilisiertes Glas n
stability criterion of Hurwitz	s. Hurwitz['s] criterion	stabilized high-voltage power unit	stabilisierter Hochspannungsgenerator m
stability criterion of Küpfmüller	s. Küpfmüller['s] criterion	stabilized power supply	s. stable current source
		stabilized power supply unit	stabilisiertes Netzanschlußteil n

stabilized voltage, regulated voltage	stabilisierte Spannung f	stable nucleus	stabiler Kern m, stabiler Atomkern m
stabilized-zero, stabilized zero / with	nullpunktkonstant, nullpunktkonstant	stable orbit, equilibrium orbit; circular equilibrium orbit	stabile Bahn f, Sollbahn f; Gleichgewichtsbahn f; Sollkreis m
stabilizer, stabilizator, stabilizing agent <chem.>	Stabilisator m, Stabilisierungsmittel n <Chem.>	stable-orbit break-up, breaking-up of the equilibrium orbit	Sollkreissprengung f
stabilizer <el.>	Stabilisator m; Gleichhalter m, Konstanthalter m <El.>	stable period stable power source	s. stable reactor period s. stable current source
stabilizer	s. a. control gear <of discharge lamp>	stable reactor period, stable period	stabile Periode f, stabile Reaktorperiode f
stabilizer	s. a. stabilizing fin <aero., hydr.>	stable region	s. stability region <acc.>
stabilizer cavity	s. stabilizing cavity	stable rotation	stabile Rotation f; stabile Drehung f
stabilizer tube, voltage stabilizer (stabilizing) tube, voltage stabilizer, stabilivolt, stabilovolt, stabilitron	Stabilisatorröhre f, Spannungsstabilisatorröhre f, Stabilovoltröhre f, Stabilisierungsröhre f	stable solution <chem.>	beständige Lösung f, stabile Lösung <Chem.>
		stable solution <math.>	stabile Lösung f <Math.>
stabilizing agent	s. stabilizer <chem.>	stable source <el.>	Konstantquelle f, konstante Quelle f <El.>
stabilizing cavity, stabilizer cavity	Stabilisierungs[hohl]raum m, Stabilisator[hohl]raum m	stable state stable stratification	stabiler Zustand m stabile Schichtung f
stabilizing cell, back e.m.f. cell	Gegenzelle f	stable structure / of stable truss stable voltage source	s. structural-stable s. stable frame konstante (stabile) Spannungsquelle f, Konstantspannungsquelle f
stabilizing feedback, monitoring feedback	stabilisierende Rückführung f, Dämpfungsreflexschaltung f		
stabilizing fin, fin, stabilizer <aero., hydr.> <e.g. of rocket>	Stabilisierungsflosse f, Flosse f, Stabilisierungsfläche f <Aero., Hydr.> <z. B. Rakete>	stable wave, permanent (persistent, neutral) wave	stabile Welle f
		Stab-Werner projection	Stab-Wernerscher [kartographischer] Entwurf m, Stab-Wernersche Projektion f
stabilizing force	Stabilisierungskraft f		
stabilizing gyroscope	Stabilisierungskreisel m, Stützkreisel m	stack	Stapel m
stabilizing incandescent lamp	Stabilisierungsglühlampe f, Stabilisationsglühlampe f	stacked antenna, stagger antenna	Etagenantenne f, Mehretagenantenne f
stabilizing network	Stabilisierungsnetzwerk n	stacked cubic metre, stere, stère, st	Raummeter n, rm, Ster n, st
stabilizing potential	stabilisierendes Potential n, Stabilisierungspotential n		
stabilizing voltage	s. stabilization voltage	stacked dipoles, dipole column	Dipolspalte f
stabilotron	Stabilotron n		
stabilovolt	s. stabilizer tube		
stabistor	Stabistor m	stacking	Stapelung f
stable, constant <of instrument, source>	konstant, stabil <Gerät, Quelle>	stacking; lamination; piling; stratification; layering	Schichtung f, Schichten n, Schichtbildung f, Stratifikation f
stable <chem.>	beständig, stabil <Chem.>		
stable; inactive, non-active, non-radioactive; cold <nucl.>	stabil; inaktiv, nichtaktiv, nichtradioaktiv; kalt <Kern.>	stacking disorder stacking energy stacking fault, stacking disorder; fault	s. stacking fault s. storing energy Stapelfehler m [im engeren Sinne], Stapelfehlordnung f; Anordnungsfehler m
stable <statics>	standfest, standsicher, stabil, kippsicher, sicher gegen Umkippen <Statik>		
stable achromaticity, stable achromatism	stabile Achromasie f	stacking fault energy, energy of stacking faults	Stapelfehlerenergie f
stable axis [of rotation]	s. permanent axis of rotation	stacking fault plane	Stapelfehlerebene f
stable carrier, inactive carrier, non-active carrier	stabiler Träger m, inaktiver Träger, nichtaktiver Träger	stacking fault tetrahedron, tetrahedral stacking fault	Stapelfehlertetraeder n
stable coupling	stabile Kopplung f	stacking fault triangle, triangular stacking fault	Stapelfehlerdreieck n
stable current source, stable power source, stabilized power supply, constant current source	konstante Stromquelle f, Konstantstromquelle f, stabile Stromquelle	stacking fault width, width of the stacking faults	Stapelfehlerbreite f
		stacking operator	Stapeloperator m
stable disturbance	stabile Störung f	stacking order	Stapelordnung f; Stapelfolge f
stable emulsion	Stabilemulsion f, stabile Emulsion f	stacking sequence	Stapelfolge f
stable equilibrium, positive stability	stabiles Gleichgewicht n, sicheres Gleichgewicht	stadia stadia method, planetable survey	s. surveyor's rod Meßtischaufnahme f
stable equilibrium phase	stabile Sollphase f, stabile Gleichgewichtsphase f	stadia rod, topographic stadia rod, level rod <US>	Tachymeterlatte f
stable equilibrium position	stabile Gleichgewichtslage f		
stable frame; stable truss	stabiles Fachwerk n, kinematisch bestimmtes Fachwerk	stadia rod <US> stadiometric straightedge	s. a. levelling staff Entfernungsmeßlatte f
stable gravimeter; static gravimeter	statisches Gravimeter n, statischer Schweremesser (Schwerkraftmesser) m	Staeble-Lihotzky condition	s. condition of isoplanatism
stable isotherm	stabile Isotherme f	staff	s. surveyor's rod
stable isotope	stabiles Isotop n		

staff float, pole float, rod float, velocity rod, tube float — Stabschwimmer m, Stangenschwimmer m, Stockschwimmer m, hydrometrische Stange f, Schwimmstange f

staff gauge — s. water scale <hydr.>
staff graduated on both sides — s. double-sided staff
stage; step — Stadium n; Stufe f; Phase f

stage, state, status — Stand m, Lage f
stage, microscope stage, object stage, specimen stage, microscope table, cross table — Objekttisch m, Kreuztisch m, Mikroskoptisch m, Objektträgertisch m
stage; plate, tray, head <chem.> — Boden m, Platte f; Stufe f <Chem.>
stage, cascade <el.> — Stufe f <El.>
stage cooler — Zonenkühler m

stage-discharge relation — s. station rating curve
staged rocket — s. multistage rocket
stage noise — Tischrauschen n, Objekttischrauschen n, Kreuztischrauschen n, Rauschen n des Kreuztisches

stage of amplification, amplifier (amplifying, amplification) stage — Verstärkerstufe f, Verstärkungsstufe f
stage of multiplication, multiplier (multiplying) stage — Vervielfacherstufe f, Vervielfachungsstufe f
stage of retreat; period of recession, recessional period — Rückzugsperiode f, Rückzugsstadium n
stage of separation — Trennstufe f
stage of the rocket, rocket stage — Stufe f der Rakete, Raketenstufe f, Raketeneinheit f

stage I of work-hardening — s. easy glide region
stagger, staggering — Staffelung f; Versetzung f; Stufung f

stagger angle — Staffelwinkel m, Staffelungswinkel m
stagger antenna — s. stacked antenna
staggered, stepped — abgesetzt; abgestuft
staggered, checkered — schachbrettartig [angeordnet], schachbrettförmig, versetzt [angeordnet], gestaffelt
staggered <spectr.> — in Stellung auf Lücke, verdreht, verzahnt <Spektr.>
staggered circuits — [gegeneinander] verstimmte Kreise mpl, versetzte (gestaffelte) Kreise
staggered conformation — s. staggering
staggering, staggered conformation <spectr.> — Lückenstellung f, Stellung f auf Lücke, verdrehte Stellung, Verdrehstellung f <Spektr.>
staggering — s. a. stagger
staggering — s. a. staggering motion
staggering advantage — Versetzungsgewinn m
staggering effect — Staggeringeffekt m, „staggering"-Effekt m
staggering motion, staggering, tumbling, wob[b]le, wobbling <mech.> — Taumelbewegung f, taumelnde Bewegung f, Taumeln n; Taumelflug m, Taumelschwingung f, Torkeln n <Mech.>
staging altitude, altitude of stage separation — Stufentrennungshöhe f <Höhe, bei der sich die Raketenstufe abtrennt>
stagnant ice — Toteis n
stagnant waters — stehendes Gewässer n
stagnation <aero.> — Stauung f, Stau m; Stillstand m; Stockung f <Aero.>

stagnation band — Stagnationsstreifen m
stagnation curve, backwater curve, backwater profile — Staukurve f, Staulinie f
stagnation density <aero.> — Staudichte f <Aero.>

stagnation enthalpy — Stauenthalpie f

stagnation point, point of return, inversion point, reversal point — Umkehrpunkt m; Inversionspunkt m; Umkehrlage f

stagnation point, critical point of the flow <aero., hydr.> — Staupunkt m <Aero., Hydr.>

stagnation point flow — Staupunktströmung f

stagnation point temperature — Staupunkt[s]temperatur f
stagnation pressure — s. dynamic pressure
stagnation temperature <aero., hydr.> — Stautemperatur f

stagnopseudogley — Stagnopseudogley m
stagoscopy — Stagoskopie f, Tropfenschau f
Stahl['s] phlogiston theory — s. phlogiston theory
stain — Schmutzfleck m, Fleck m
stain — s. a. colorant
stain corrosion — s. staining
stained, spotted, mottled — fleckig
stained glass, pigmented glass filter, coloured glass — Farbglas n
staining, stain (spot) corrosion — stellenweise Korrosion f, Anfraß m, Anfressung f
staining — s. tinging
stainless steel, non-corrosive steel, corrosion-proof (corrosion-resistant) steel — nichtrostender (rostbeständiger, korrosionsbeständiger) Stahl m
staircase — s. stepped
staircase estimation method — s. up-and-down method
staircase function, step function — Treppenfunktion f, Stufenfunktion f
staircase generator, staircase waveform generator — Treppen[spannungs]generator m, Treppenwellenformgeber m, Kipptreppengenerator m
staircase method — s. up-and-down method
staircase shape, step shape — Treppenform f
staircase waveform generator — s. staircase generator
stair-rod dislocation — s. edge dislocation
staking <US>, marking-out, pegging-out <US> — Verpflockung f, Verpfählung f
stalactite — Stalaktit m, [hängender] Tropfstein m, herabhängender (nach unten wachsender) Tropfstein, [von oben wachsender] Tropfsteinzapfen m

stalagmite — Stalagmit m, [stehender] Tropfstein m, nach oben wachsender Tropfstein, [von unten wachsende] Tropfsteinsäule f, Tropfsteinkegel m
stalagmometer — s. drop counter
stalagmometer — s. a. surface tension meter
stalagnate — Stalagnat m, Tropfsteinsäule f

stall, stalling, burbling, overclimb, overzoom <aero.> — Überziehen n, Abkippen n, Abrutschen n, Durchsacken n <Aero.>
stall — s. a. stalled condition <aero.>
stall characteristics, stalling characteristics <of wing> — Abreißverhalten n <Flügel>
stalled airfoil — s. stalled wing
stalled condition, stall, stalling flight <aero.> — überzogener Flugzustand m, Sackflug m <Aero.>

stalled flow — Strömung f mit Ablösung

stalled wing, stalled airfoil — überzogener Flügel m
stalling — s. stall <aero.>
stalling characteristics — s. stall characteristics <of wing>
stalling flight — s. stalled condition <aero.>

Stammer colorimeter	Stammer-Kolorimeter n	**standard density,** normal density <20 °C, 760 Torr>	Normaldichte f, Normdichte f <20 °C, 760 Torr>
stand	s. tripod		
standard; norm	Standard m; Norm f		
standard, étalon, standard measure, standardized measure; gage, gauge	Etalon m, Eichmaß n, Normalmaß n, Normal n, Meßnormal n, Eichnormal n, Norm f	**standard depth**	Standardtiefe f
		standard developer, normal developer	Normalentwickler m, Standardentwickler m
standard, normal	Standard-, Normal-, normal	**standard deviation,** coefficient of standard variation, root-mean-square of the deviation, mean square deviation, root-mean-square deviation, root deviation <stat.>	Standardabweichung f, mittlere quadratische Abweichung f, quadratische Abweichung f, Streuung f, mittlere Schwankung f <Stat.>
standard absorber	Standardabsorber m		
standard acceleration of free fall	s. standard value of gravity		
standard acoustic signal, standard tone, test tone	Meßton m		
standard actinometer	Normalaktinometer n	**standard distribution coefficient**	s. C.I.E. distribution coefficient
standard air, spectroscopic standard air	spektroskopische Normalluft f, Normalluft	**standard distribution curve**	s. C.I.E. distribution function
		standard distribution function	s. C.I.E. distribution function
standard air	s. standard atmosphere	**standard dosimetry**	Standarddosimetrie f
standard air capacitor, standard air-spaced capacitor	Normalluftkondensator m	**standard electric potential (tension)**	s. standard electrode potential
standard aneroid [barometer]	Normalaneroid[barometer] n	**standard electrode,** normal electrode	Normalelektrode f
standard atmosphere, standard air; standard radio atmosphere	Normalatmosphäre f, Standardatmosphäre f	**standard electrode potential,** standard potential, standard electric potential, standard electric tension, normal potential	Normalpotential n, [elektrochemisches] Standardpotential n, Standard-Bezugs-EMK f, Standard-Bezugs-EMK-Wert m, Standardgleichgewichts-Galvani-Spannung f, elektromotorische Grundkraft f, Grund-Bezugsspannung f
standard atmosphere, physical atmosphere, atm <unit>	physikalische Atmosphäre (Normalatmosphäre) f, Normalatmosphäre, atm, Atm <Maßeinheit>		
standard bar, standard scale	Normalmaßstab m		
standard calomel electrode, normal calomel electrode, Ostwald['s] electrode	Normalkalomelelektrode f, Ostwald-Elektrode f	**standard electrode-potential series**	s. electrochemical series
		standard electromotive force, standard e.m.f.	Normal-EMK f, Standard-EMK f
standard candle	Normalkerze f, Standardkerze f	**standard electromotive series**	Norm[al]spannungsreihe f
standard capacitance, capacitance standard, standard of capacitance, standard capacitor; calibration capacitor	Normalkondensator m, Normalkapazität f, Kapazitätsnormal n; Eichkondensator m	**standard emitter,** standard radiator	Normalstrahler m
		standard energy of formation, standard formation energy	Standardbildungsenergie f, Standardbildungsarbeit f
standard capacitor	s. standard capacitance		
standard celestial sphere	Normalhimmelskugel f, Standardhimmelskugel f, normale Himmelskugel f	**standard equation,** normal equation	Normalgleichung f
		standard equipment	Standardausrüstung f, Normalausrüstung f
standard cell, standard voltage cell, normal cell	Normalelement n		
standard chamber	s. standard ionization chamber	**standard error**	s. root-mean-square error
		standard eye, normal eye	mittleres, normales menschliches Auge n; Normalauge n, normales Auge, Standardauge n
standard chromaticity co-ordinate	s. chromaticity co-ordinate in the C.I.E. standard colorimetric system		
		standard fluorescence	Standardfluoreszenz f
standard chronometer	Regelchronometer n	**standard focal length / of**	normalbrennweitig
standard clock	Normaluhr f		
		standard formation energy	s. standard energy of formation
standard coil	s. standard inductance	**standard formation reaction**	Standardbildungsreaktion f
standard colorimetric observer	s. standard observer		
standard colour, normal colour	Normalfarbe f	**standard free enthalpy**	freie Standardenthalpie f
standard colour stimulus [specification]	s. C.I.E. colour stimulus	**standard frequency,** normal frequency; calibration frequency	Normalfrequenz f; Eichfrequenz f; Einheitsfrequenz f
standard column of water, standard water column	Standardwassersäule f	**standard-frequency spectrum**	Normalfrequenzspektrum n
standard conditions, normal (standard) pressure and temperature, normal (standard) temperature and pressure, normal conditions, NPT, S.P.T., NTP <phys., for gases: 0 °C, 760 Torr; techn.: 20 °C, 1 at or 15 °C, 1 at; therm., el.chem., for heat of formation: 25 °C, 760 Torr; ac.: 0 °C, 760 Torr or 15 °C, 760 Torr>	Normalbedingungen fpl, Normbedingungen fpl, Normaldruck m und -temperatur f, NPT, NTP <Phys., für Gase: 0 °C, 760 Torr; Techn.: 20 °C, 1 at oder 15 °C, 1 at; Therm., El.Chem., für die Bildungswärme: 25 °C, 760 Torr; Ak.: 0 °C, 760 Torr oder 15 °C, 760 Torr>	**standard gauge,** master gauge	Kontrollehre f, Normallehre f, Urlehre f, Paßlehre f, Prüflehre f
		standard generator	s. standard-level generator
		standard geometry	Standardgeometrie f, Normalgeometrie f
		standard ground joint	Normschliff m, NS
		standard heat of formation	Standardbildungswärme f, Normalbildungswärme f; Standardbildungsenthalpie f, Normalbildungsenthalpie f

standard

standard hydrogen electrode, standard hydrogen reference electrode, hydrogen standard electrode, normal hydrogen electrode	Normal-Wasserstoffelektrode f, Standard-Wasserstoffelektrode f, Wasserstoff-Normalelektrode f
standard illuminant, colorimetric standard illuminant <A, B, or C>	Normlichtart f, Normalbeleuchtung f <A, B oder C>
standard incandescent lamp	Normalglühlampe f
standard inductance, inductance standard, standard of inductance; standard coil; solenoidal inductor; self-inductance standard	Normalinduktivität f; Induktivitätsnormal n, Normalspule f; Normalgegeninduktivität f
standard infra-red, infrared standard, I.R. standard	Infrarotstandard m, Infrarotnormal n, IR-Standard m, IR-Normal n
standard instrument	Normalgerät n, Normalinstrument n, Standardmeßgerät n, Standardgerät n, Standardinstrument n
standard instrument, standard measuring instrument, standardizing [measuring] instrument, calibration instrument (apparatus), test gauge	Eichgerät n, Eichinstrument n
standard international atmosphere	s. international standard atmosphere
standard ion dose <similar with, but not equal to "exposure">	Gleichgewicht[s]-Ionendosis f, Standard-Ionendosis f, Standardionendosis f
standard ionization chamber, standard chamber	normale Ionisationskammer f, Normalionisationskammer f, Normalkammer f, Standardkammer f
standardization	Standardisierung f, Normierung f; Normung f; Einstellung f
standardization	s. a. calibration
standardization	s. a. unification
standardized measure	s. standard
standardized signal	s. unified signal
standardizing [measuring] instrument	s. standard instrument
standard lamp, photometer lamp, [standard] photometric lamp	Normallampe f, Photometerlampe f, Photometernormal n
standard leak	Standardleck n
standard-level generator, standard generator	Normalgenerator m; Normalpegelsender m
standard lighting	Standardbeleuchtung f
standard line, calibration line; standard transmission line	Eichleitung f
standard load	Normalbelastung f
standard magnet	Magnetetalon n
standard man	Standardmensch m, „Durchschnittsmensch" m [mittleres] Standardmeerwasser n, SMOW
standard mean ocean water, SMOW	
standard measure	s. standard
standard measuring instrument	s. standard instrument
standard meridian	Normalmeridian m
standard meridian	s. a. zero meridian
standard meter	s. international prototype meter
standard molar volume	Molnormalvolumen n
standard neutron source	s. neutron standard
standard noise factor	Standardrauschzahl f
standard observer, ICI observer, [C.I.E.] standard colorimetric observer	Normalbeobachter m, CIE-Normalbeobachter m
standard of capacitance	s. standard capacitance
standard of inductance	s. standard inductance
standard of length, length standard	Längennormal n
standard orifice [plate] <hydr.>	Normblende f <Hydr.>
standard oxidation affinity per unit charge	s. standard oxidation potential
standard oxidation potential, standard oxidation affinity per unit charge	Normal-Oxydationspotential n, Standard-Oxydationspotential n
standard oxidation-reduction potential, normal oxidation-reduction potential	Normal-Redoxpotential n, Standard-Redoxpotential n
standard parameter [of state] <therm.>	Standardgröße f, Standardzustandsgröße f <Therm.>
standard period <meteo.>	Normalperiode f <Meteo.>
standard photometric lamp	s. standard lamp
standard pile	Standardpile m, Standardanordnung f
standard pitch	s. philharmonic pitch
standard plate	Normalplatte f
standard position, normal position	Normalstellung f; Normallage f
standard potential	s. standard electrode potential
standard potentiometer, master potentiometer	Normalpotentiometer n; Normalkomparator m
standard pressure, normal pressure, atmospheric pressure, pressure of one atmosphere <760 Torr>	Normaldruck m, Normdruck m, Atmosphärendruck m <760 Torr>
standard pressure and temperature	s. standard conditions
standard radiation source	s. standard source of radiation
standard radiator, standard emitter	Normalstrahler m
standard radioactive source	s. standard source
standard radio atmosphere; standard atmosphere, standard air	Normalatmosphäre f, Standardatmosphäre f
standard rating[s] <of lamps>	Hauptreihe f <Lampen>
standard recorder	s. chart recorder
standard reduction <geo.>	Standardreduktion f <isostatische Reduktion für 30 km Krustenmächtigkeit> <Geo.>
standard reduction affinity per unit charge	s. standard reduction potential
standard reduction potential, standard reduction affinity per unit charge	Normal-Reduktionspotential n, Standard-Reduktionspotential n
standard refraction	Standardrefraktion f
standard resistance; standard resistor, resistance standard	Widerstandsnormal n, Normalwiderstand m
standard rod, standard test bar	Normstab m, Normalprüfstab m
standard scale, standard bar	Normalmaßstab m
standard schliere, reference schliere, normal schliere, standard streak	Normalschliere f
standard-signal generator (oscillator)	s. measurement transmitter
standard solid	Standardfestkörper m
standard solution, test solution	Normallösung f, Testlösung f, Standardlösung f, Prüflösung f, genormte (eingestellte) Lösung f
standard solution, normal solution, 1 N solution	Normallösung f, n-Lösung f, normale Lösung f, 1 n Lösung
standard solution	s. a. titrant

standard source [of radiation], standard source of radioactivity, standard radioactive source, radioactivity (radioactivity) standard; reference source [of radiation], reference radiation source; calibration source [of radiation], calibrating source [of radiation], calibrating radiation source	Standard[strahlungs]quelle f, radioaktive Standardquelle, [radioaktives] Standardpräparat n, radioaktiver Standard m; Vergleichs[strahlungs]quelle f, radioaktive Vergleichsquelle, Musterquelle f; [radioaktive] Eichquelle f, [radioaktives] Eichpräparat n	**standard wavelength**	s. wavelength standard
		standard weight, gauge weight, gauging weight	Eichgewicht n
		standard white, reference white	Normalweiß n, Bezugsweiß n
		standard wind	Standardwind m
		stand-by power	Reserveleistung f
		stand-by power factor, reserve factor	Reservefaktor m
		stand chamber	s. stand photogrammetric chamber
standard source of radiation, radiation standard, standard radiation source	Strahlungsnormallampe f, Strahlungsnormal n	**standing sonic (sound) vibration, standing sound wave**	s. stationary sound-wave
		standing vibration	s. standing wave
standard source of radioactivity	s. standard source	**standing wave**; stationary wave; immobile wave; standing vibration, stationary vibration	stehende Welle f, Stehwelle f; stehende Schwingung f
standard spectrum	s. reference spectrum		
standard spheroid	Normalsphäroid n		
standard star	s. comparison star		
standard state, normal state, state under normal conditions	Normzustand m, Normalzustand m, Zustand m unter Normalbedingungen	**standing wave**	s. a. eddy motion of the water particles <hydr.>
		standing wave detector	s. standing wave indicator
		standing wave indicator, standing wave meter, standing wave detector	Stehwellenmesser m, Stehwellenmeßgerät n, Stehwellenverhältnismesser m, Stehwellenanzeiger m
standard steam, normal steam	Normaldampf m <gesättigter Wasserdampf von 100 °C>		
standard system	s. dependent equatorial co-ordinates		
standard temperature, normal temperature	Normtemperatur f, Normaltemperatur f	**standing[-] wave ratio**, matching equivalent	Stehwellenverhältnis n, Wellenverhältnis n, Amplitudenverhältnis n, Anpassungsmaß n
standard temperature and pressure	s. standard conditions		
standard test bar	s. standard rod	**stand photogrammetric chamber**, stand chamber	Stativmeßkammer f, Stativkammer f
standard thermocouple of platinum and platinum-rhodium	s. platinum—platinum-rhodium thermocouple		
		Stanton['s] No., Stanton['s] number, Margoulis number, Margoulis No., St, Mg	Stanton-Zahl f, Stantonsche Kennzahl (Zahl) f, Margoulis-Zahl f, Margoulissche Kennzahl, St, Mg
standard time, legal time	Normalzeit f, Nationalzeit f		
standard time, zone time, regional time	Zonenzeit f, Einheitszeit f	**Stanton['s] number of the second kind**, St'	Stanton-Zahl f zweiter Art, St'
standard time, time standard	Zeitnormal n		
standard time constant, time constant standard	Zeitkonstantennormal n	**Stanton tube**	Stanton-Rohr n
		star, fixed star <astr.>	Fixstern m, Stern m; Gestirn n <Astr.>
standard tone, standard acoustic signal, test tone	Meßton m	**star**	s. a. emulsion star <nucl.>
		star atlas	Sternatlas m, Himmelsatlas m
		star catalogue	Sternkatalog m, Sternverzeichnis n
standard tone <1,000 c/s>	Normalton m <1 000 Hz>	**star chain**	Sternkette f
		star chart	s. star map
standard tone source, source of standard tone <1,000 c/s>	Normaltonquelle f <1 000 Hz>	**star class**, star type, class of stars	Sternklasse f, Sterntyp m
standard ton of refrigeration	= 3.03861×10⁸ J	**star cloud**, cloud <astr.>	Sternwolke f, Wolke f <Astr.>
		star cluster	Sternhaufen m
standard transmission line, calibration line, standard line	Eichleitung f	**star collapse**	s. collapse of the star
		star-connected circuit	s. star connection
		star connection, star grouping, Y grouping, Y-connection; star-connected circuit	Sternschaltung f, S-Schaltung f, Y-Schaltung f
standard tristimulus value	s. tristimulus value		
standard ultra-violet	s. ultra-violet standard		
standard value	Normwert m, Normalwert m	**star correlation**	Sternkorrelation f
		star cosmogony	s. stellar cosmogony
		star count[ing]	Zählung f der Sterne, Sternzählung f
standard value of gravity, standard acceleration of free fall	Normfallbeschleunigung f, Normwert m der Fallbeschleunigung, Normalbeschleunigung f, normale Schwerebeschleunigung f [der Erde], normale Schwereintensität f [der Erde], Normalschwere f	**star-delta connection**, wye-delta connection	Stern-Dreieck-Schaltung f, Sterndreieckschaltung f
		star-delta transformation	Stern-Dreieck-Transformation f, Stern-Dreieck-Umwandlung f
		star drift	s. star-stream
standard visibility	s. meteorological optical range	**star formation**, formation of stars <astr.>	Sternentstehung f, Sternbildung f <Astr.>
standard voltage <el.>	Normspannung f, Normalspannung f <El.>		
		star formation rate, rate of star formation	Sternentstehungsrate f
standard voltage cell, standard cell, normal cell	Normalelement n	**star gap**, stellar gap	Sternleere f, Sternlücke f
standard volume	Normvolumen n, Normalvolumen n	**star group**	Sterngruppe f
		star grouping	s. star connection
standard water	Normalwasser n, Standardwasser n	**star-interconnected star connection**	Stern-Zickzack-Schaltung f
standard water column, standard column of water	Standardwassersäule f		

Stark broadening, Stark effect broadening — Stark-Effekt-Verbreiterung f, Stark-Verbreiterung f
Stark['s] constant — Stark-Konstante f
Stark effect — Stark-Effekt m
Stark effect broadening — s. Stark broadening
Stark effect splitting — s. Stark splitting
Stark effect width, Stark width — Stark-Effekt-Breite f, Stark-Breite f
Stark-Einstein['s] law — s. law of photochemical equivalence
Starke-Schröder voltmeter — Starke-Schröder-Spannungsmesser m, Starke-Schröder-Voltmeter n
Stark-Koch line — Stark-Kochsche Linie f
Stark-Lunelund effect — Stark-Lunelund-Effekt m
Stark modulation — Stark-[Effekt-]Modulation f
Stark splitting, Stark effect splitting, electrical splitting of spectral lines — Stark-Effekt-Aufspaltung f, Stark-Aufspaltung f, elektrische Aufspaltung f der Spektrallinien
Stark width — s. Stark effect width
star light, illumination from stars — Sternlicht n
star-like, star-shaped; radial — sternförmig
star-like — s. a. star-shaped ‹math.›
starlit — sternklar
star magnitude — s. stellar brightness
star map, star chart; astrographic chart, Carte du Ciel — Sternkarte f, Himmelskarte f
star mass-luminosity relation — s. mass-luminosity law
star modulator — Sternmodulator m, Doppelgegentaktmodulator m
star network, radial network, tandem network — Sternnetz n, sternförmiges Netzwerk, Sternglied n
star of the system, member of the system — Systemstern m, Mitgliedstern m ‹des Systems›
star photography — s. stellar photography
star photometer, stellar photometer; astronomical photometer, astro[photo]meter; extinction photometer — Sternphotometer n, Astrophotometer n; Photometer n mit Abschwächungsvorrichtung
star[-] point — s. neutral point
star point voltage, neutral point voltage, voltage to neutral — Sternpunktspannung f
star population, stellar population, population ‹astr.› — Sternpopulation f, Population f ‹Astr.›
star-producing particle — sternerzeugendes Teilchen n
star production ‹nucl.› — Sternerzeugung f, Sternbildung f ‹Kern.›
star production cross-section, cross-section for star production — Sternerzeugungsquerschnitt m, Wirkungsquerschnitt m für (der) Sternerzeugung, Sternerzeugungs-Wirkungsquerschnitt m
star prong — Sternarm m
star quad formation — s. spiral-four formation
starquake — Sternbeben n
starred — s. star-shaped ‹math.›
star-shaped — s. star-like
star-shaped, star-like, starred ‹math.› — sternkonvex, sternförmig, sternig ‹Math.›
star-shaped antenna — s. star-shaped dipole
star-shaped diaphragm — Sternblende f, Ausgleichsblende f
star-shaped dipole, star-shaped antenna — Spreizdipol m, Sternantenne f
star spectrum — s. stellar spectrum
star spectrum-luminosity relation — s. Hertzsprung-Russell diagram
star-star connection — Stern-Stern-Schaltung f
star[-] stream; star streaming, streaming of stars, star drift — Sternstrom m; Sternströmung f
start, start-up ‹of engine› — Anfahren n; Start m ‹Motor, Maschine›
start ‹of engine› — Anlassen n ‹Motor›
start — s. a. start point ‹chromatography›
starter ‹of discharge lamp› — Starter m ‹Gasentladungslampe›

star test — Sterntest m
star test plate — Sterntestplatte f
starting, commissioning, putting into operation, start-up — Inbetriebnahme f, Inbetriebsetzung f
starting, run-up, running to full speed, start-up — Hochlaufen n, Hochlauf m
starting — s. a. initiation
starting aid — Starthilfe f
starting anode, exciting anode, ignition anode, igniting anode — Zündanode f; Anlaßanode f
starting characteristic of thyratron, ignition characteristic of thyratron — Zündkennlinie f des Thyratrons, Zündeinsatzkennlinie (Zündeinsatzkurve) f des Thyratrons
starting current, preoscillation current — Anschwingstrom m
starting current, initial current — Anfangsstrom m; Anzugsstrom m; Anlaßstrom m
starting device, ignition device ‹of the discharge lamp› — Zündvorrichtung f, Zündeinrichtung f, Zündanlage f ‹Entladungslampe›
starting electrode, ignition electrode — Zündelektrode f
starting of oscillations — s. start of oscillation
starting of the arc by means of an ignitron electrode, ignition start — Ignitronzündung f [des Lichtbogens]
starting of the chain — s. chain initiation ‹chem.›
starting oscillation, ignition oscillation — Zündschwingung f
starting phase, initial phase — Anfangsphase f; Initialphase f ‹Bio.›
starting point ‹e.g. of a motion›; initial point, origin; point of emergency — Anfangspunkt m, Ausgangspunkt m
starting point — s. start point ‹chromatography›
starting potential — s. striking voltage ‹of discharge or tube›
starting pulse, pilot pulse — Einschaltimpuls m, Startimpuls m; Urimpuls m
starting pulse — s. a. ignition pulse
starting range [of thyratron] — Zündbereich m [des Thyratrons]
starting reaction, initiating reaction — Startreaktion f
starting resistance ‹of a tube› — Anlaufwiderstand m ‹Elektronenröhre›
starting time, start-up time; start-up period — Anlaufzeit f; Inbetriebsetzungszeit f; Anfahrzeit f; Hochfahrzeit f; Hochlaufzeit f; Startzeit f; Anfahrperiode f; Hochfahrperiode f; Startperiode f
starting torque — s. initial torque
starting voltage — Einsatzspannung f, Anlaufspannung f
starting voltage — s. a. breakdown voltage ‹of discharge›
starting vortex — s. cast-off vortex
starting with load — s. start with load
starting without load — s. start without load
start of oscillation, starting of oscillations — Anschwingen n, Schwingungseinsatz m
start point, starting point, start ‹chromatography› — Start m, Startpunkt m; Startfleck m; Startzone f; Startstrich m; Startband n; Auftragstelle f; Auftropfstelle f ‹Chromatographie›
star tracker — s. guiding telescope
star tracking — s. guiding ‹of telescope›
start-stop converter — Start-Stop-Konverter m
start-stop key — Start-Stop-Taste f
start-stop multivibrator — s. univibrator

start-stop unit	Start-Stop-Gerät n	state of full adaptation, full adaptation	vollendete Adaptation f, Adaptationszustand m
		state of inertia	s. steady state
start-up, start <of engine>	Anfahren n; Start m <Motor, Maschine>	state of ionization	s. charge state
		state of ions	s. ionic state
start-up <of reactor>, start-up procedure	Reaktorstart m, Start m [des Reaktors], Anfahren n des Reaktors; Hochfahren n des Reaktors	state of matter	s. state of aggregation
		state of order, order state	Ordnungszustand m
		state of plane stress	s. plane stress
		state of rest <aero.>	Kesselzustand m, Ruhezustand m <Aero.>
start-up	s. a. commissioning		
start-up	s. a. run-up	state of rest, period of rest <bio.>	Ruhezustand m, Ruheperiode f <Bio.>
start-up period	s. starting time		
start-up procedure	s. start-up <of reactor>		
start-up time	s. starting time	state of strain, strain, strained state <mech.>	Verzerrungszustand m, Verformungszustand m, Formänderungszustand m, Deformationszustand m, Zerrungszustand m <Mech.>
star twisting	Sternverseilung f		
start with load, starting with load	Lastanlauf m		
		state of strain [at the point]	s. strain tensor
start without load, starting without load	Leeranlauf m	state of strain [in the body]	s. strain field
		state of stress, stress, stressed state	Spannungszustand m
star type, star class, class of stars	Sternklasse f, Sterntyp m		
		state of stress [at the point]	s. stress tensor
star voltage	s. phase-to-neutral voltage		
star with expanding atmosphere	s. star with expanding envelope	state of stress [in the body]	s. stress field
		state of suspension	s. suspension
star with expanding envelope, star with expanding atmosphere, star with outward moving atmosphere, emission star	Emissionsliniensterm m, Stern m mit expandierender Gashülle, Stern mit Emissionslinien	state of the development	Entwicklungsstand m, Stand m der Entwicklung
		state of the weather	s. general weather situation
		state of turbulence, turbulent state	Turbulenzzustand m, turbulenter Zustand
star with extended atmosphere (envelope), shell star	Hüllenstern m, Stern m mit ausgedehnter Gashülle	state of weightlessness	Zustand m der Schwerelosigkeit
		state parameter	s. parameter of state
star with outward moving atmosphere	s. star with expanding envelope	state sum	s. partition function
		state under normal conditions	s. standard state
star zero point	s. neutral point <el.>		
stat, St <= 3.64×10⁻⁷ Ci>	Stat n, St <= 3,64·10⁻⁷ Ci>	state value	Zustandswert m
		state variable	s. parameter of state
statcoulomb	s. franklin	state vector, vector of state	Zustandsvektor m
state, conditions, situation	Zustand m, Lage f, Beschaffenheit f, Verhältnisse npl, Bedingungen fpl; Situation f <z. B. Geo.>		
		stathm	s. kilogram[me]
		static	s. static charge
		static[al] accuracy, static[al] precision, static[al] fidelity	statische Genauigkeit f
state, status, stage	Stand m, Lage f		
state <phys.>	Zustand m <Phys.>		
state	s. a. state of energy	statical deflection <mech.>	statische Durchsenkung (Durchbiegung) f <Mech.>
state continuity, continuity of state[s]	Zustandskontinuität f, Kontinuität f der Zustandsübergänge		
		statical fidelity	s. static[al] accuracy
		statical load	s. static load
state curve, curve of state	Zustandskurve f	statically admissible	s. statically permissible
		statically defined (determinable, determinate, determined), determinate	statisch bestimmt
state density, density of states	Zustandsdichte f		
state diagram	s. phase diagram		
state equation	s. equation of state	statically indeterminable (indeterminate), statically undetermined, undetermined, indeterminate, hyperstatic	statisch unbestimmt
state exchange, exchange of states	Zustandsaustausch m		
state formula, formula of state	Zustandsformel f		
state function, function of state	Zustandsfunktion f		
		statically permissible, statically admissible	statisch zulässig
statement, proposition, sentence; information	Aussage f; Information f		
		statically undetermined	s. statically indeterminable
statement, ansatz, set[-]up <math.>	Ansatz m <Math.>	statical moment, static moment [of force], moment of first order, linear (mass) moment	statisches Moment n, Moment erster Ordnung, lineares Moment
state of aggregation, state of matter, aggregation (physical) state	Aggregatzustand m, Formart f		
		statical precision	s. static[al] accuracy
		statical tide	s. equilibrium tide
state of being suspended	s. suspension	static amplification factor, static gain	statischer Verstärkungsfaktor m, statische Verstärkung f
state of binding, binding state	Bindungszustand m		
		static autonomy	statische Autonomie f
state of charge	s. charge state		
state of energy, energetic state, energy state, state	Energiezustand m, energetischer Zustand m, Zustand	static characteristic	statische Kennlinie (Charakteristik) f; Standkennlinie f; Kurzschlußkennlinie f
state of energy term, term, term of energy, energy [state] term; term value	Term m, Energieterm m, Energiestufe f	static charge, static electric charge, electrostatic charge, static	statische Ladung f, elektrostatische Ladung (Aufladung f)
		static coefficient of friction	s. coefficient of static friction
state of equilibrium, equilibrium state	Gleichgewichtszustand m		
		static control	s. proportional control
state of excitation, excited state <bio.>	Erregungszustand m <Bio.>	static controller	s. proportional controller

static

static converter	ruhender Stromrichter m
static current	s. resting current
static electric charge	s. static charge
static electricity	statische Elektrizität f, Influenzelektrizität f
static electrode potential	s. static potential
static eliminator	Antistatikgerät n, Gerät n zur Beseitigung elektrostatischer Aufladungen
static equilibrium	statisches Gleichgewicht n
static fidelity	s. statical accuracy
static field	statisches Feld n
static force	statische Kraft f
static forward conductance, static forward transconductance	Kurzschluß-Vorwärtssteilheit f, statische Vorwärtssteilheit f
static fracture	statischer Bruch m
static friction, friction at rest, friction of rest (repose); limiting friction, stiction	Haftreibung f, Ruh[e]reibung f, Reibung f der Ruhe, ruhende Reibung f; Haltereibung f; Grenzreibung f, maximale Reibungskraft f
static fundamental equation of the atmosphere	statische Grundgleichung f der Atmosphäre
static gain, static amplification factor	statischer Verstärkungsfaktor m, statische Verstärkung f
static galvanometer constant	s. galvanometer constant
static gravimeter; stable gravimeter	statisches Gravimeter n, statischer Schweremesser (Schwerkraftmesser) m
static head, pressure head, head	statische Höhe f, Druckhöhe f
static hysteresis curve, static hysteresis loop	statische Hystereseisschleife (Hystereseiskennlinie, magnetische Zustandskurve, Kennlinie) f
static indeterminateness, hyperstaticity	statische Unbestimmtheit f
static labelling	statische Markierung f
static level indicator (meter)	statischer Füllstandsanzeiger m
static lift, uplift, upthrust <aero.>	aerostatischer (statischer) Auftrieb m <Aero.>
static lift	s. a. hydrostatic buoyancy <hydr.>
static line width	statische Linienbreite f
static load, statical load	statische Belastung f; ruhende Belastung, Ruhebelastung f
static magnetic field, magnetostatic field	magnetostatisches Feld n, statisches Magnetfeld n
static magnetic susceptibility, static susceptibility	statische magnetische Suszeptibilität f, statische Suszeptibilität
static modulus of elasticity	statischer Elastizitätsmodul m
static moment [of force]	s. statical moment
static moment of the surface, first moment of the surface	statisches Flächenmoment n, statisches Moment n der Fläche
static multipole moment	statisches Multipolmoment n
static mutual conductance	s. transconductance
static noise	s. atmospheric radio noise
static nucleus, stationary nucleus, nucleus at rest	ruhender Kern m, stationärer Kern
static phase advancer, cosine capacitor, phase-shift capacitor, phase-shifting capacitor, capacitor phase shifter	Phasenschieberkondensator m, ruhender Phasenschieber m, Kondensator m zur Verbesserung des Leistungsfaktors, Leistungskondensator m
static plate	s. orifice plate
static potential, static electrode potential	statisches Potential n
static precision	s. statical accuracy
static pressure, actual pressure, pressure intensity	statischer Druck m, ruhender Druck, Ruhedruck m, Standdruck m
static pressure tube, piezometer tube	Drucksonde f, Piezometerrohr n
static reaction	statische Reaktion (Rückwirkung) f
static regulator	s. proportional controller
static revertive conductance, static revertive transconductance	Kurzschluß-Rückwärtssteilheit f, Kurzschluß-Rücksteilheit f, statische Rückwärtssteilheit f, statische Rücksteilheit f
static rolling friction	Haftreibung f gegen Rollen
statics	Statik f, Geometrie f der Kräfte
statics	s. a. atmospheric radio noise
static safety factor	statischer Sicherheitsfaktor m, Sicherheitsfaktor bei statischer Belastung
static shield winding	Schirmwicklung f
static slip	statische Gleitung f
static solution	statische Lösung f
static stability, stability <statics>	Standsicherheit f, Standfestigkeit f, Stabilität f, Kippsicherheit f, Sicherheit f gegen Umkippen <Statik>, statische Stabilität
static strength	statische Festigkeit f
static stress	statische Spannung f
static subroutine	statisches Unterprogramm n
static surface tension, equilibrium surface tension	Gleichgewichts-Oberflächenspannung f, statische Oberflächenspannung f
static susceptibility, static magnetic susceptibility	statische magnetische Suszeptibilität f, statische Suszeptibilität
static temperature	statische Temperatur f
static temperature coefficient	statischer Temperaturkoeffizient m
static transconductance	s. transconductance
static water	s. water-surface ascent
station, point <geo.>	Standpunkt m <Geo.>
station	s. a. point under consideration
stationarity	Stationarität f
stationary; fixed	stationär <zeitlich konstant>; unbeweglich, ortsfest, feststehend; Stand-
stationary, immobile <astr.>	stationär, stillstehend <Astr.>
stationary	s. a. steady
stationary absorption line	s. interstellar absorption line
stationary charge	ruhende Ladung f
stationary coil of the variometer, variometer stator	feste Variometerspule f
stationary conductivity, steady-state conductivity	stationäre Leitfähigkeit f
stationary creep	s. quasiviscous creep
stationary current	s. steady-state current
stationary discharge	stationäre Entladung f
stationary distribution	stationäre Verteilung f
stationary electrolysis	Standelektrolyse f, stationäre Elektrolyse f
stationary ensemble	stationäre Gesamtheit f
stationary equilibrium	stationäres Gleichgewicht n
stationary field, steady-state field	stationäres (ruhendes) Feld n, Stehfeld n
stationary field irradiation	Stehfeldbestrahlung f
stationary flow	s. steady flow
stationary gravimeter	stationäres Gravimeter n, stationärer Schweremesser m
stationary grid, grid, Lysholm grid	feststehende Streustrahlenblende (Blende) f, Streustrahlenblende nach Lysholm, Lysholm-Blende f, Festblende f, feststehender Streustrahlenraster (Raster) m

stationary line	ruhende Linie f	statistical decision theory, stochastic decision theory, theory of choice, theory of statistical decision[s]	statistische Entscheidungstheorie f, Entscheidungstheorie
stationary motion	stationäre Bewegung f		
stationary nucleus, static nucleus, nucleus at rest	ruhender Kern m, stationärer Kern		
stationary orbit	stationäre Bahn f	statistical description of turbulence, statistical theory of turbulence	Turbulenzstatistik f, statistische Theorie f der Turbulenz
stationary phase method, principle of stationary phase	Methode f der stationären Phase		
		statistical distribution; statistical distribution function	statistische Verteilung f; statistische Verteilungsfunktion f
stationary photometer	feststehendes Photometer n		
stationary point, station of planet <astr.>	Stillstand m, stationäre Bewegung f <Planet> <Astr.>		
		statistical ensemble, statistical population (universe) <stat.>	statistische Gesamtheit f, statistische Masse f, Gesamtmasse f, Kollektiv n <Stat.>
stationary point	s. a. critical point <of function>		
stationary point	s. a. cusp	statistical equilibrium	statistisches Gleichgewicht n
stationary potential	s. steady potential	statistical ergodic theorem, ergodic theorem in the mean, von Neumann['s] ergodic theorem	statistischer Ergodensatz m, Ergodensatz im Mittel, Ergodensatz von J. von Neumann, Neumannscher Ergodensatz
stationary quantum state, stationary state in quantum theory	stationärer Quantenzustand m, stationärer Zustand m in der Quantentheorie		
stationary random process, stationary stochastic process	stationärer Prozeß m, stationärer stochastischer Prozeß	statistical evidence, significance, statistical significance	Signifikanz f, statistische Signifikanz, statistische Sicherung f
		statistical fluctuation, fluctuation	statistische Schwankung f, Schwankung, Fluktuation f
stationary satellite, geostationary satellite, motionless satellite	[geo]stationärer Satellit m, Satellit in geostationärer Umlaufbahn		
		statistical fluctuation effect (phenomenon)	s. fluctuation phenomenon
stationary solution	s. steady-state solution	statistical independence, statistic independence	statistische Unabhängigkeit f
stationary sonic vibration (wave), stationary sound vibration (wave), standing sound wave, standing sound (sonic) vibration	stehende Schallwelle f; stehende Schallschwingung f		
		statistically evident, statistically significant	statistisch gesichert
		statistically independent	statistisch unabhängig
stationary state	s. steady state	statistically significant, statistically evident	statistisch gesichert
stationary state in quantum theory, stationary quantum state	stationärer Quantenzustand m, stationärer Zustand m in der Quantentheorie	statistical map	s. cartogram
		statistical matrix	s. density matrix
		statistical mechanics; statistical physics	statistische Mechanik f; statistische Physik f
stationary state of current, steady-state current, steady current, stationary current	stationärer Strom m, stationärer elektrischer Strom	statistical model of atom, statistical atomic model	statistisches Atommodell n, statistisches Modell n des Atoms
stationary stochastic process, stationary random process	stationärer Prozeß m, stationärer stochastischer Prozeß	statistical model of nucleus, Wigner model of nucleus, uniform model of nucleus	statistisches Kernmodell n [nach Wigner], statistisches Modell n [des Kerns], Wigner-Modell n, statistisches Compoundmodell n
stationary tangent	s. inflectional tangent		
stationary vibration	s. standing wave		
stationary vortex, steady vorticity motion	stationärer Wirbel m, Standwirbel m; stationäre Wirbelung (Wirbelbewegung) f		
		statistical noise, noise, random noise, fluctuation noise <of thermionic valve>	Rauschen n, statistisches Rauschen <Elektronenröhre>
stationary wave	s. standing wave		
station barometer	Stationsbarometer n	statistical nuclear decay	s. statistical nuclear disintegration
station density, density of stations	Stationsdichte f		
		statistical nuclear disintegration, statistical nuclear decay	statistische Kernumwandlung f, statistischer Kernzerfall m, statistischer Zerfall m der Atomkerne
station equation	Stationsgleichung f; Standortgleichung f; Standpunktsgleichung f		
station index	Stationsindex m, Stationskennziffer f	statistical operator	s. density matrix
		statistical parallax	[stellar]statistische Parallaxe f, Eigenbewegungsparallaxe f
station of planet, stationary point <astr.>	Stillstand m, stationäre Bewegung f <Planet> <Astr.>		
		statistical physics; statistical mechanics	statistische Mechanik f; statistische Physik f
station rating curve	s. discharge rating curve		
statism	Regelfehler m, Statismus m	statistical population	s. statistical ensemble
		statistical purity	statistische Reinheit f
statistic <stat.>	statistische Größe f, Größe f <Stat.>	statistical significance, significance, statistical evidence	Signifikanz f, statistische Signifikanz, statistische Sicherung f
statistic, sample statistic; sample function <stat.>	statistische Maßzahl f, Statistik f, Kennzahl f, Kennziffer f; Stichprobenfunktion f <Stat.>		
		statistical sign test, sign test	Vorzeichentest m, Zeichentest m
		statistical spinel structure	statistischer Spinelltyp m
statistical atomic model, statistical model of atom	statistisches Atommodell n, statistisches Modell n des Atoms		
		statistical star stream	statistischer Sternstrom m
statistical average	statistischer Mittelwert m	statistical straggling, spread, straggling, scatter[ing] <gen., e.g. of data>	Streuung f, statistische Streuung; Streubreite f <allg., z. B. von Daten>
statistical averaging	statistische Mittelbildung f		
statistical broadening	statistische Verbreiterung f		
statistical climatology	statistische Klimatologie f, Mittelwertsklimatologie f	statistical test, test <stat.>	Test m, statistischer Test <Stat.>
statistical counter (counting) time lag, counting (counter) time lag	Zählverzögerung f, statistische Zählverzögerung		
		statistical theory of turbulence, statistical description of turbulence	Turbulenzstatistik f, statistische Theorie f der Turbulenz

statistical thermodynamics, thermostatistics	statistische Thermodynamik f, statistische Theorie f der Wärme	**steady precession, steady precessional motion,** regular precession	reguläre Präzession f, gleichmäßige Präzession
statistical time lag in discharge	statistische Zeitverzögerung f der Entladung, statistische Entladungsverzögerung f	**steady radiation**	s. white radiation
		steady rain; continuous rain	Dauerregen m; Landregen m
statistical uncertainty	statistische Unsicherheit f, statistische Unschärfe f	**steady sound,** sustained sound, continuous tone	Dauerton m
statistical unit	Statistikgerät n	**steady source [of radiation]**	konstante Quelle (Strahlungsquelle) f
statistical universe	s. statistical ensemble	**steady state,** stationary state; state of inertia; final state; steady-state motion	stationärer Zustand m; eingeschwungener Zustand; Dauerzustand m; Endzustand m; Beharrungszustand m
statistical weight	s. degree of degeneracy <qu.>		
statistical weight factor <nucl.>	statistischer Gewichtsfaktor m <Kern.>		
statistic independence	s. statistical independence	**steady state,** flux equilibrium, flowing equilibrium, open system equilibrium <bio.>	Fließgleichgewicht n, Flußgleichgewicht n <Bio.>
statitron	s. electrostatic generator		
statolith, otolith	Statolith m, Hörstein m, Gehörsteinchen n, Otolith m, Otokonie f, Statokonie f		
		steady-state, steady, stationary	stationär, Gleichgewichts-; eingeschwungen
		steady-state characteristic	stationäre Kennlinie f, stationäre Charakteristik f
statolith theory	Statolithentheorie f		
statometer	Statometer n	**steady-state condition**	Stationaritätsbedingung f
stator	Ständer m; Stator m, Anker m <Synchronmaschine>; Feldmagnet m <Gleichstrommaschine>	**steady-state conductivity,** stationary conductivity	stationäre Leitfähigkeit f
		steady-state creep	s. quasiviscous creep
statoscope	Statoskop n, Feinmanometer m, Feinhöhenmesser m	**steady-state current,** steady current, stationary state of current, stationary current	stationärer Strom m, stationärer elektrischer Strom
statu nascendi / in	in statu nascendi		
status, state, stage	Stand m, Lage f	**steady-state electric field** <el.>	[elektrisches] Strömungsfeld n, Stromdichtefeld n, stationäres elektrisches Feld n (Strömungsfeld), Feld der elektrischen Stromdichte <El.>
status nascens	s. nascent state		
statute mile, mile, English statute mile, British mile, mi, st.Mi., m <= 1,609 m>	englische Meile f, Meile, angelsächsische Meile <= 1609 m>		
Staude cone	Staude-Kegel m		
Staudinger['s] formula	Staudinger-Gleichung f	**steady-state error**	bleibende Regelabweichung f
Staudinger['s] law of viscosity	Staudingersches Viskositätsgesetz n, Viskositätsgesetz von Staudinger	**steady-state field**	s. stationary field
		steady-state flow	s. steady flow
stauroscope	Stauroskop n	**steady-state magnetic field,** stationary magnetic field	stationäres Magnetfeld n, stationäres magnetisches Feld n
stauroscopic figure	stauroskopische Figur f		
stay	s. diagonal member <mech.>	**steady-state motion**	s. steady state
stay	s. a. vertical member	**steady-state operation**	stationärer Betrieb m
St.Clair generator, St.Clair sound generator, St. Clair['s] transducer	Schallgenerator m von (nach) St. Clair, St. Clairscher Schallgenerator	**steady-state oscillation,** steady-state vibration	stationäre Schwingung f
		steady-state potential	s. steady potential
		steady-state solution, stationary solution	stationäre Lösung f, Lösung für den stationären Zustand
steadiness <of the image>	Stehen n <Bild>, Bildruhe f		
steady, permanent, continuous, constant, continual	ständig, stetig, permanent, Dauer-, kontinuierlich	**steady-state transient technique**	,,steady-state transient''-Methode f
steady, steady-state, stationary	stationär, Gleichgewichts-; eingeschwungen	**steady-state value,** equilibrium value, steady value	Gleichgewichtswert m, stationärer Wert m
steady anode current	Anodenruhestrom m		
steady background	ständiger Untergrund m	**steady-state vibration,** steady-state oscillation	stationäre Schwingung f
steady climate	stetiges Klima n		
steady current	s. steady-state current		
steady current pulse	nichtabklingender Stromimpuls m	**steady value,** equilibrium value, steady-state value	Gleichgewichtswert m, stationärer Wert m
		steady vorticity motion, stationary vortex	stationärer Wirbel m, Standwirbel m; stationäre Wirbelung (Wirbelbewegung) f
steady density	stationäre Dichte f		
steady discharge	Dauerentladung f		
		steam air ejector	s. steam ejector
steady exposure	s. continuous light	**steam atmosphere,** water-vapour atmosphere, water-vapour medium, steam medium	Wasserdampfatmosphäre f
steady flow, steady-state flow, stationary flow, fully developed flow; constant flow	stationäre Strömung f, stationärer Strom m; ausgebildete Strömung		
		steam band, water vapour band	Wasserdampfbande f
steady gas flow	stationäre Gasströmung f	**steam bath,** vapour bath	Dampfbad n, Wasserdampfbad n
steady load	s. permanent load	**steam bleeding**	s. taking of steam
steady load	s. a. continuous load <el.>	**steam boiler**	s. steam generator
steady motion	ständige Bewegung f, ,,steady motion'' f	**steam calorimeter,** vaporization calorimeter	Kondensationskalorimeter n, Dampfkalorimeter n, Verdampfungskalorimeter n
steady potential, steady-state potential, stationary potential	stationäres Potential n		
		steam consumption meter	s. steam flow meter

steam content, water vapour content	Wasserdampfgehalt m	steam turbine	Dampfturbine f
steam density	Dampfdichte f, Wasserdampfdichte f	steam-water circuit	Wasser-Dampf-Kreislauf m, Dampf-Wasser-Kreislauf m
steam diagram	s. indicator diagram	steam wetness	s. moisture of steam
steam dissociation, dissociation of water vapour, water vapour dissociation	Wasserdampfspaltung f	stecometer	Stecometer n
		steel	Stahl m
		steel-prism bearing, knife-edge bearing, blade bearing	Schneidenlagerung f, Schneidenlager n
steam distillation, steam refining	Wasserdampfdestillation f, Dampfdestillation f	steel[-]yard [balance], Roman steelyard, Roman balance, sliding weight balance	Laufgewichtsdynamometer n, Laufgewichtswaage f, Schnellwaage f
steam ejector, steam air ejector, steam-jet air ejector	Wasserdampfstrahlsauger m, Dampfstrahl-Luftpumpe f, Dampfstrahl-Luftsauger m, Dampfstrahler m	Steenbeck condition	Steenbeck-Bedingung f, Steenbecksche Bedingung f, zweite Grundbedingung f des Betatrons
steam ejector	s. a. vapour pump	steep	steil
steam engine; steam power engine	Dampfmaschine f, Dampfkraftmaschine f	steep cast[ing]	s. steep throw <mech.>
		steepest[-] descent method	s. method of steepest descent
steam extinction, extinction by steam	Wasserdampfextinktion f	steepest descent method	s. Fowler-Darwin method
steam extraction	s. taking of steam	steep gradient, steep ramp	Steilrampe f
steam-filled counter [tube]	dampfgefülltes Zählrohr n, Dampfzählrohr n, Zählrohr mit Dampffüllung	steep growth, steep rise	steiler Anstieg m
		steepness of edge	s. slope of edge
steam flow meter, steam consumption meter	Dampfmengenmesser m, Dampfmesser m	steepness of gradation, gradation <phot.>	Gradation f, Steilheit f Gradationssteilheit f <Phot.>
steam generating plant	s. steam generator		
steam generation, steam production	Dampferzeugung f	steepness of wave edge, wave steepness	Wellensteilheit f, Steilheit f der Wellenflanke
		steep pulse	steiler Impuls m, steil ansteigender Impuls
steam generator; steam generating plant, steam raising plant; steam boiler	Dampferzeuger m; Dampferzeugungsanlage f; Dampfkessel m, Wasserdampfkessel m, Kessel m	steep ramp, steep gradient	Steilrampe f
		steep rise, steep growth	steiler Anstieg m
steam gradient	Wasserdampfgradient m	steep shot	s. vertical photography
		steep slope <geo.>	Steilhang m, Steilabfall m, Steilabsturz m <Geo.>
steam injector, injector, [steam] jet pump	Dampfstrahlpumpe f, Wasserdampfstrahlpumpe, Injektor m		
		steep throw, vertical throw, steep cast[ing], vertical casting <mech.>	Steilwurf m, Steilschuß m, Bogenwurf m, Bogenschuß m, steiler Wurf m, steiler Schuß m <Mech.>
steam-jet air ejector	s. steam ejector		
steam jet pump	s. steam injector		
steam line	s. steam pressure curve		
steam medium, watervapour atmosphere, water-vapour medium, steam atmosphere	Wasserdampfatmosphäre f		
		Stefan-Boltzmann['s] constant, Stefan['s] constant, Boltzmann['s] factor, "black body" constant, coefficient of total radiation, total radiation coefficient, radiation density constant	Stefan-Boltzmannsche Konstante f, Stefan-Boltzmann-Konstante f, Stefansche Konstante, Stefan-Konstante f, Strahlungskonstante f, Strahlungszahl f, Stefan-Boltzmann-Zahl f
steam moisture	s. moisture of steam		
steam parameter	Dampfparameter m		
steam point	s. boiling point of water		
steam power engine	s. steam engine		
steam pressure, water vapour pressure, steam tension	Wasserdampf[partial]druck m, Wasserdampfspannung f, Dampfspannung f		
		Stefan-Boltzmann['s] law, Boltzmann law of radiation, Stefan['s] law	Stefan-Boltzmannsches Gesetz (Strahlungsgesetz) n, T^4-Gesetz n, Stefan-Boltzmann-Gesetz n, Strahlungsgesetz von Stefan-Boltzmann
steam pressure curve, steam line	Dampfdruckkurve f		
		Stefan['s] constant	s. Stefan-Boltzmann constant
steam pressure diagram	s. indicator diagram	Stefan['s] law	s. Stefan-Boltzmann['s] law
steam production	s. steam generation	Stefan number	Stefansche Zahl f <Verhältnis der inneren Verdampfungswärme zur molaren freien Oberflächenenthalpie>
steam proofness, steam tightness	Wasserdampfdichte f		
steam pump	Wasserdampfpumpe f, Dampfpumpe f		
steam raising plant	s. steam generator		
steam rate	[spezifischer] Dampfverbrauch m	Stefan['s] relations <for diffusion>	Stefansche Beziehungen fpl <Diffusion>
		Steffensen['s] method	Steffensen-Verfahren n
steam refining, steam distillation	Wasserdampfdestillation f, Dampfdestillation f	Steichen['s] equation	Steichensche Gleichung f
		Steiner['s] theorem	s. parallel axis theorem
		Steinheil['s] cone, single-lens telescope	Steinheilscher Glaskonus m, Einlinsenfernrohr n
steam superheating, superheating of steam	Dampfüberhitzung f, Überhitzung f des Dampfes		
		Steinmetz coefficient	Steinmetz-Koeffizient m
steam table	Wasserdampftabelle f	Steinmetz curve	Steinmetz-Kurve f
		Steinmetz['] law	Steinmetz-Gesetz n, Steinmetzsches Gesetz n
steam-table calorie	s. international steam-table calorie	Steklov['s] function	Steklowsche Funktion f
		Stella Polaris	s. Polar Star
steam tension	s. steam pressure	stellar association	Sternassoziation f
steam tightness, steam proofness	Wasserdampfdichte f	stellar astronomy	Stellarastronomie f
		stellar atmosphere	Sternatmosphäre f
steam transfer, steam transport	Wasserdampftransport m, Wasserdampfverfrachtung f	stellarator	Stellarator m
		stellar body	s. fixed star

stellar

stellar brightness, stellar magnitude, star magnitude, brightness, magnitude <astr.> — Helligkeit *f*, Sternhelligkeit *f*, Größe *f*, Größenklasse *f*, Klasse *f*, Sterngröße *f*, Sternklasse *f* <Astr.>

stellar convection — Sternkonvektion *f*

stellar cosmogony, star cosmogony — Kosmogonie *f* der Sterne, Stellarkosmogonie *f*, Theorie *f* der Sternentstehung, Sternkosmogonie *f*

stellar curve of growth, curve of growth <astr.> — Sternwachstumskurve *f*, Wachstumskurve *f* <Astr.>

stellar density — Sterndichte *f*

stellar density function, density function — Dichtefunktion *f* des Sterns, Sterndichtefunktion *f* <Astr.>

stellar dynamic parallax — s. dynamical parallax

stellar dynamics — Stellardynamik *f*, Sterndynamik *f*

stellar embryo, goblet — Sternembryo *m*

stellar energy — stellare Energie *f*, Sternenergie *f*

stellar energy curve — Sternenergiekurve *f*, Energiekurve *f* des Sterns

stellar evolution, evolution of stars — Sternentwicklung *f*

stellar explosion — Sternexplosion *f*

stellar extinction rate, rate of star deaths, rate of stellar extinction — Sternsterberate *f*

stellar gap, star gap — Sternleere *f*, Sternlücke *f*

stellar guidance, celestial guidance — Astrolenkung *f*

stellar interferometer, Michelson stellar interferometer — [Michelsonsches] Sterninterferometer *n*, Michelson-Sterninterferometer *n*

stellar interior — Sterninneres *n*

stellar luminosity, luminosity [of the star] — Leuchtkraft *f* [des Gestirns]

stellar magnetic field — Magnetfeld *n* der Sterne, stellares Magnetfeld

stellar magnetism — Stellarmagnetismus *m*, Magnetismus *m* der Sterne

stellar magnitude — s. stellar brightness

stellar mass-luminosity relation — s. mass-luminosity law

stellar material, stellar matter — Sternmaterie *f*, stellare Materie *f*

stellar opacity, opacity of stellar interior — Sternopazität *f*

stellar parallax — Sternparallaxe *f*, Fixsternparallaxe *f*

stellar photography, star photography — Sternphotographie *f*, Stellarphotographie *f*

stellar photometer — s. star photometer

stellar photometry — s. astronomical photometry

stellar population, population, star population <astr.> — Sternpopulation *f*, Population *f* <Astr.>

stellar population I, population I [of Baade] — Population *f* I [nach Baade], Feldpopulation *f*

stellar population II, population II [of Baade] — Population *f* II [nach Baade], Kernpopulation *f*

stellar pyranometer — Sternpyranometer *n*

stellar space density — räumliche Dichte *f* der Sterne

stellar spectrograph, astrospectrograph — Sternspektrograph *m*, Astrospektrograph *m*

stellar spectrometry (spectroscopy) — s. astrospectroscopy

stellar spectrum, star spectrum — Sternspektrum *n*

stellar spectrum-luminosity relation — s. Hertzsprung-Russell diagram

stellar spectrum-temperature relation, effective temperature-spectral type relation — Spektrum-Temperatur-Beziehung *f*, Beziehung *f* Spektralklasse — effektive Temperatur

stellar statistics — Stellarstatistik *f*

stellar structure — Sternaufbau *m*, Sternstruktur *f*

stellar system, galactic system, galaxy, system of stars, island universe — Sternsystem *n*, Galaxis *f*, Galaxie *f* <*pl.*: Galaxien>

stellar time, sidereal time — Sternzeit *f*

stellar triangulation — Stellartriangulation *f*

St. Elm['s] fire — s. Saint Elm['s] fire

stem — „stem" *n*, Dee-Halterung *f*, Deehalterung *f*, Deehals *m*, Hals *m* des Dee

stem <of the tube> — Röhrenfuß *m*, Fuß *m* der Röhre, Stiel *m* [der Röhre]

stem correction — s. thermometric correction

stem radiation — Stielstrahlung *f*, außerfokale Strahlung *f*, extrafokale Strahlung

stenopeic spectacles — stenopäische Brille *f*, Lochbrille *f* <Sieb-, Schlitz-, Spalt- *oder* Zielbrille>

step — Stufe *f*, Sprung *m*

step; pace; stride — Schritt *m*, Stufe *f*

step, discontinuity, jump, saltus — Sprung *m*, sprungartige Änderung *f*, sprunghafte Änderung; Diskontinuität *f*

step <stacking fault> — Staffel *f*, Stufe *f* <Stapelfehler>

step <geo.> — Stufe *f* <Geo.>

step, step of relief <geo.> — Schichtstufe *f*, Landstufe *f* <Geo.>

step <math.> — Schritt *m*, Spanne *f* <Math.>

step — s. a. stage

step — s. a. stepped

step attenuator, stepped attenuator, step-type attenuator <el.> — Stufenabschwächer *m* <El.>

step-by-step, stepwise; in steps — schrittweise; stufenweise

step-by-step control — s. step control

step-by-step excitation — s. stepwise excitation

step-by-step method [of heterochromatic comparison] — s. cascade method

step-by-step switch — s. stepping switch

step cone — s. stepped pulley

step control, stepped control, incremental control, step-by-step control, stepping control — Stufenregelung *f*, stufenweise Regelung *f*, Schrittregelung *f*, Schritt-für-Schritt-Regelung *f*

step controller, step regulator, contact controller — Schrittregler *m*, schrittweiser Regler *m*

step curve, stepped curve; step-like curve, stepwise curve — Treppenkurve *f*; Stufenkurve *f*

step disturbance — Sprungstörung *f*, sprungartige Störung *f*

step-down, stepping-down <by transformer> — Hinuntertransformieren *n*, Heruntertransformieren *n*, Herabtransformieren *n*, Abspannen *n*

step-down heat transformer — untersetzender Wärmetransformator *m*, Wärmetransformator vom untersetzenden Typ

step-down ratio, step-down turns ratio <of transformer> — Untersetzung *f*, Untersetzungsverhältnis *n* <Abwärtstransformator>

step-down stage, scaling stage, frequency-divider stage — Unterserzerstufe *f*, Teilerstufe *f*, Frequenzteilerstufe *f*

step-down transformer, reducing transformer — Abwärtstransformator *m*, spannungserniedrigender (untersetzender) Transformator *m*, Transformator zur Spannungserniedrigung, Reduziertransformator *m*

step-down turns ratio, step-down ratio <of transformer> — Untersetzung *f*, Untersetzungsverhältnis *n* <Abwärtstransformator>

step filter — Stufenfilter *n*, Stufenabschwächer *m*

step function, jump function	Sprungfunktion *f*, Schrittfunktion *f*	**step rocket**	*s.* multistage rocket
step function, staircase function	Treppenfunktion *f*, Stufenfunktion *f*	**steps / in**	*s.* step-by-step
		step shape, staircase shape	Treppenform *f*
step function time response	*s.* unit[-] step response	**step size**	*s.* interval ‹in numerical integration›
step-function voltage	*s.* step voltage	**step slip band**	Stufengleitband *n*
Stephan-Boltzmann['s] law	*s.* Stefan-Boltzmann['s] law	**step switch,** stepping switch, tapping switch	Stufenschalter *m*
step in altitude, step in height	Höhenstufe *f*		
step junction	Stufenübergang *m*	**step time**	Schrittzeit *f*
step leader	*s.* stepped leader		
step length, unit duration of signal	Schrittlänge *f*, Schrittdauer *f*	**step tube,** stepping tube	Stufenröhre *f*
		step-type attenuator, stepped (step) attenuator ‹el.›	Stufenabschwächer *m* ‹El.›
step lens	*s.* stepped lens		
stepless regulation; continuous regulation, continuous variation	stufenlose Regelung *f*	**step-up,** stepping-up ‹by transformer›	Hinauftransformieren *n*, Herauftransformieren *n*, Aufspannen *n*
step-like, steplike	*s.* stepped		
step-like curve	*s.* step curve		
step method, method of scales	Methode *f* der Stufenschätzung, [Argelandersche] Stufenschätzungsmethode *f*, Stufenschätzung *f*	**step-up heat transformer**	übersetzender Wärmetransformator *m*, Wärmetransformator vom übersetzenden Typ
		step-up ratio ‹of transformer›	Übersetzung *f*, Übersetzungsverhältnis *n* ‹Aufwärtstransformator›
step of iteration, iteration step	Iterationsschritt *m*		
step of relief	*s.* step ‹geo.›	**step-up transformer**	spannungserhöhender (übersetzender) Transformator *m*, Transformator zur Spannungserhöhung, Aufwärtstransformator *m*, Hochtransformator *m*
step of the resistance	Widerstandsstufe *f*		
stepped, step-like; step, staircase	stufenförmig; treppenförmig		
stepped, staggered	abgesetzt; abgestuft	**step voltage,** step-function voltage	Treppenspannung *f*
stepped, step[-]like; jump-like; discontinuous; unsteady; sudden	sprunghaft; diskontinuierlich		
		step voltage, step potential	Schrittspannung *f*
		step wedge	*s.* neutral step wedge
stepped attenuator, step[-type] attenuator ‹el.›	Stufenabschwächer *m* ‹El.›	**stepwise**	*s.* step-by-step
		stepwise adsorption	stufenweise Adsorption *f*
		stepwise approximation	*s.* successive approximation
stepped cirque	Treppenkar *n*; Kartreppe *f*	**stepwise curve**	*s.* step curve
stepped cone pulley	*s.* stepped pulley	**stepwise distillation**	stufenweise Destillation *f*
stepped control	*s.* step control		
stepped curve	*s.* step curve	**stepwise excitation,** step-by-step excitation	stufenweise Anregung *f*
stepped leader, lightning stepped leader, step leader	Stufenleader *m*, stufenweise vordringende Vorentladung *f*, Stufenleitblitz *m*		
		stepwise ionization	Stufenionisation *f*
		stepwise loading, progressive load[ing], loading in steps, gradually applied load	stufenweise Belastung *f*; stufenweise aufgebrachte Last *f*
stepped lens, Fresnel lens, echelon lens, step lens	Fresnel-Linse *f*, Fresnelsche Linse *f*, Stufenlinse *f*		
stepped pulley, [stepped] cone pulley, step cone, step pulley	Stufenscheibe *f*		
		stepwise reaction	*s.* step reaction
		sterad	*s.* steradian
stepped pulse, step pulse	Stufenimpuls *m*	**steradian,** sr	Steradiant *m*, sr
stepped slit	Stufenspalt *m*	**stere, stère,** stacked cubic metre, st	Raummeter *n*, rm, Ster *n*, st
stepped winding	Treppenwicklung *f*, Stufenwicklung *f*		
		stereo attachment; stereo unit; stereo prism attachment	Stereovorsatz *m*; Stereoaufsatz *m*; Stereoprismenvorsatz *m*
step photometer, Pulfrich photometer	Pulfrich-Photometer *n*, Stufenphotometer *n*		
stepping control	*s.* step control	**stereoautograph**	Stereoautograph *m*, Raumautograph *m*, Autostereograph *m*
stepping-down	*s.* step-down		
stepping relay	*s.* stepping switch		
stepping switch, step-by-step switch; stepping relay	Schrittwähler *m*; Schrittschaltwerk *n*, Schrittschaltrelais *n*; Schrittschalter *m*, Schrittschaltersystem *n*	**stereoblock**	Stereoblock *m*
		stereoblock [co]polymer	Stereoblock[ko]polymer *n*
		stereoblock [co]polymerization	*s.* stereospecific polymerization
stepping switch	*s. a.* step switch	**stereo[-]camera,** stereophotographic camera, stereoscopic camera, stereophotographic apparatus	Stereokamera *f*, stereophotographische Kamera *f*, Raumbildkamera *f*; Stereoaufnahmegerät *n*
stepping tube, step tube	Stufenröhre *f*		
stepping-up	*s.* step-up ‹by transformer›		
step potential, step voltage	Schrittspannung *f*		
step potentiometer	Stufenpotentiometer *n*		
step process [in the plasma]	Stufenprozeß *m* [im Plasma]		
step pulley	*s.* stepped pulley	**stereochemical formula**	*s.* stereoformula
step pulse, stepped pulse	Stufenimpuls *m*	**stereochemical selectivity**	*s.* stereospecificity
step reaction, stepwise reaction	Stufenreaktion *f*	**stereo[-]cinematography**	Stereokinematographie *f*
step recovery diode, snap-off diode, charge-storage diode, Boff diode	Ladungsspeicherdiode *f*, „step-recovery"-Diode *f*		
		stereo[-]comparator	Stereokomparator *m*, Raumbildmeßgerät *n*, Raumbildmesser *m*
step regulator, step (contact) controller	Schrittregler *m*, schrittweiser Regler *m*		
step resistance	Stufenwiderstand *m*		
step response	*s.* unit[-] step response		

stereo-comparator   822

stereo-comparator	s. a. stereoscopic rangefinder	**stereophony** ⟨localization of complex sounds by a person with normal binaural hearing⟩	Lokalisierung f von Schallquellen durch binaurales Hören
stereocopolymer	Stereokopolymer n		
stereo electron microscope, stereoscopic electron microscope, electron stereomicroscope	Stereoelektronenmikroskop n [nach Kinder]	**stereophotogrammeter**	Stereophotogrammeter n, Raumbildmeßgerät n
stereo electron microscopy, stereoscopic electron microscopy, electron stereomicroscopy	Stereoelektronenmikroskopie f	**stereophotogrammetric camera,** photogrammetric stereocamera	Raumbildmeßkammer f, Raumbildkammer f, Stereomeßkammer f, Stereokammer f, Doppelkammer f, Zweibildkammer f, stereoskopische Bildmeßkammer f
stereofluoroscopy, stereoscopic fluoroscopy, stereoradioscopy	Stereodurchleuchtung f		
stereoformula, spatial formula, stereochemical formula, stereometric formula	Raumformel f, stereochemische Formel f, stereometrische Formel	**stereophotogrammetric instrument**	Zweibildgerät n, Zweibildinstrument n
		stereophotogrammetric restitution	stereophotogrammetrische Auswertung f, Stereoauswertung f
stereogram; stereograph, stereophotograph, stereoscopic photograph, stereoscopic picture, stereoscopic image, stereo image, stereopicture, space image	Stereogramm n; Raumbild n, Stereobild n, Stereoskopbild n, stereoskopisches Bild n; Raumaufnahme f, Stereoaufnahme f, stereoskopische Aufnahme f; Raummeßbild n, optisches Modell n	**stereophotogrammetry**	Stereophotogrammetrie f, Raumbildmessung f
		stereophotograph	s. stereogram
		stereophotographic apparatus (camera)	s. stereo camera
		stereophotographic lay-down, stereo lay-down	Raumbildplan m, Stereobildplan m
stereographic net, Wulff['s] net, net of Wulff	Wulffsches Netz n		
stereographic projection, zenithal orthomorphic projection	stereographische Projektion f, winkeltreue Azimutalprojektion f, Kugelprojektion f	**stereophotographic plotting machine**	Stereophotokartograph m
		stereophotography, stereoscopic photography	Stereophotographie f, Stereoaufnahme f, Raumbildphotographie f; Raumbildaufnahme f, Raumaufnahme f
stereographic zenithal projection	stereographische Zenitalprojektion f, stereographischer Zenitalentwurf m		
stereo image	s. stereogram	**stereophotometer,** stereoscopic photometer	Stereophotometer n
stereoisomer, stereoisomeride, stereomer, stereomeride	Stereoisomer n	**stereophotomicrography**	Stereomikrophotographie f
stereoisomerism, stereochemical isomerism, space isomerism	Stereoisomerie f, stereochemische Isomerie f, Raumisomerie f	**stereopicture**	s. stereogram
		stereoplanegraph, stereoplanigraph, Porro-Koppe type [of] plotting machine	Stereoplanigraph m
stereo lay-down	s. stereophotographic lay-down		
stereology	Stereologie f	**stereoplotter, stereoplotting machine,** stereoscopic plotter	Raumbildauswertegerät n, Stereoauswertegerät n, stereoskopisches Auswertegerät n, stereophotogrammetrisches Auswertegerät [für Meßbilder], stereophotogrammetrisches Meßbild-Auswertegerät n; Stereokartiergerät n, Zweibildkartiergerät n
stereomer, stereomeride, stereoisomer, stereoisomeride	Stereoisomer n		
stereometer	Stereometer n, Stereometergerät n		
stereometric formula	s. stereoformula		
stereometrograph	Stereometrograph n		
stereometry, solid geometry	Stereometrie f, Körpermessung f		
stereomicroscope, stereoscopic microscope	Stereomikroskop n [nach Greenough], stereoskopisches Mikroskop n, Greenough-Mikroskop n	**stereo-power,** total plastic	totale Plastik f
		stereo prism attachment; stereo attachment; stereo unit	Stereovorsatz m; Stereoaufsatz m; Stereoprismenvorsatz m
stereomicroscopy, stereoscopic microscopy	Stereomikroskopie f, stereoskopische Mikroskopie f	**stereo projection,** stereoscopic projection, 3-D projection	Stereoprojektion f, stereoskopische Projektion f, Raumbildprojektion f, 3-D-Projektion f
stereomodel [of atom]	Atomkalotte f		
stereopair	s. stereoscopic pair	**stereoradiography,** stereoscopic radiography	Stereoradiographie f
stereophonic effect, stereophonism ⟨ac.⟩	Raumtoneffekt m, Raumtonwirkung f, Raumwirkung f, Stereoeffekt m ⟨Ak.⟩		
		stereoradioscopy, stereofluoroscopy, stereoscopic fluoroscopy	Stereodurchleuchtung f
stereophonic hearing	stereophones (stereoakustisches) Hören n	**stereo rangefinder**	s. stereoscopic rangefinder
		stereoregular	s. stereospecific
stereophonic reproduction of sound, stereophonic sound reproduction, stereophonics	stereophonische Wiedergabe f, Stereowiedergabe f, Stereotonwiedergabe f, Stereophonie f	**stereoregular polymerization**	s. stereospecific polymerization
		stereo reverberation, stereophonic reverberation	Stereonachhall m
stereophonic reverberation, stereo reverberation	Stereonachhall m	**stereoscan [electron] microscope,** stereo-scanning electron microscope	s. scanning electron microscope
stereophonics	s. stereophonic reproduction of sound		
stereophonic sound, stereo sound, 3-D sound	Raumton m, 3-D-Ton m, Stereoton m; Raumklang m, 3-D-Klang m, stereophonischer Klang m	**stereoscope,** stereo viewer	Stereoskop n; Stereobetrachter m, Stereobetrachtungsgerät n
		stereoscopic camera	s. stereo camera
		stereoscopic effect, effect of perspective ⟨opt.⟩	stereoskopischer (plastischer) Effekt m, Raumeffekt m, Raumwirkung f, räumliche (plastische) Wirkung f, 3-D-Effekt m ⟨Opt.⟩
stereophonic sound reproduction	s. stereophonic reproduction of sound		
stereophonism	s. stereophonic effect ⟨ac.⟩		

stereoscopic electron microscope, stereo electron microscope, electron stereomicroscope	Stereoelektronenmikroskop n [nach Kinder]	sterically hindered	sterisch behindert
		steric factor, probability factor	sterischer Faktor m, Wahrscheinlichkeitsfaktor m
stereoscopic electron microscopy, stereo electron microscopy, electron stereomicroscopy	Stereoelektronenmikroskopie f	steric hindrance	sterische Hinderung (Behinderung) f
		sterile male technique	Sterile-Männchen-Methode f
		sterile slip	sterile Gleitung f
stereoscopic fluoroscopy, stereoradioscopy, stereofluoroscopy	Stereodurchleuchtung f	sterilization dose	Sterilisierungsdosis f
		stern	Heck n
stereoscopic image	s. stereogram		
stereoscopic impression	s. space impression	Stern double layer	Sternsche Doppelschicht f
stereoscopic microscope, stereomicroscope	Stereomikroskop n [nach Greenough], stereoskopisches Mikroskop n, Greenough-Mikroskop n	Sterneck pendulum / von Stern['s] experiment	von Sterneckscher Pendel n Sternscher Versuch m, Stern-Versuch m, Versuch von Stern
stereoscopic microscopy, stereomicroscopy	Stereomikroskopie f, stereoskopische Mikroskopie f	Stern-Gerlach effect Stern-Gerlach experiment	Stern-Gerlach-Effekt m Stern-Gerlach-Versuch m, Stern-Gerlach-Experiment n
stereoscopic pair, stereopair	Stereobildpaar n, Stereopaar n, [stereoskopisches] Bildpaar n, Zweibild n	Sternheimer effect Sternheimer['s] equation	Sternheimer-Effekt m Sternheimer-Gleichung f
stereoscopic parallax	s. binocular parallax		
stereoscopic photograph	s. stereogram	Stern-Volmer constant	Stern-Volmer-Konstante f
stereoscopic photography	s. stereophotography	Stern-Volmer equation (relation)	Stern-Volmer-Gleichung f
stereoscopic photometer, stereophotometer	Stereophotometer n	stern wave	Heckwelle f
stereoscopic picture	s. stereogram	Sterry effect	Sterry-Effekt m
stereoscopic plotter	s. stereoplotting machine	Sterry forebath, Sterry process	Sterry-Vorbad n
stereoscopic projection	s. stereo projection		
stereoscopic radiograph	s. X-ray stereogram		
stereoscopic radiography, stereodiography	Stereoradiographie f		
stereoscopic rangefinder, stereoscopic telemeter, stereo rangefinder, stereo[-]comparator, two-image rangefinder	Raumbild-Entfernungsmesser m, Stereo-Entfernungsmesser m, stereoskopischer Entfernungsmesser m, Entfernungsmesser mit beidäugiger Beobachtung, Einstand-Entfernungsmesser m mit binokularer Beobachtung, Raumbilddistanzmesser m, Zweibildentfernungsmesser m	stethoscope <aero., hydr.>	Stethoskop n, Hörrohr n <Aero., Hydr.>
		Stevenson element, Stevenson section	Stevenson-Glied n
		Stevenson screen	Stevenson-Hütte f, englische Hütte f, meteorologische Hütte [nach Stevenson], Thermometerhütte f
		Stevenson section, Stevenson element	Stevenson-Glied n
stereoscopic telescope, scissors telescope	Scherenfernrohr n	Stevin['s] paradox, hydrostatic paradox	hydrostatisches Paradoxon n, Satz m von Stevin, Stevinscher Satz
stereoscopic threshold	Minimaldisparation f		
stereoscopic vision	räumliches (stereoskopisches, körperliches) Sehen n, Raumsehen n, Tiefensehen n	Stevin['s] principle, principle of solidification	Erstarrungsprinzip n, Stevinsches Prinzip n
		Stewart number	Stewart-Zahl f, Stewartsche Kennzahl (Zahl) f
stereoselectivity	s. stereospecificity	Stewartson['s] transformation	Stewartsonsche Transformation f
stereo sound	s. stereophonic sound		
stereospecific, stereoregular	stereospezifisch, stereoregulär, stereoreguliert	sthen	= 10^3 N
		stiameter, mercury electrolytic meter	Stiazähler m, Quecksilberelektrolytzähler m, Quecksilberzähler m, Stiameter n
stereospecificity, stereoselectivity, stereochemical selectivity	Stereospezifität f, stereochemische Spezifität (Selektivität) f, Stereoselektivität f	stickiness	s. viscidity
		sticking	s. adhesion
		sticking potential [of phosphor]	Haftpotential n, „sticking"-Potential n, „sticking potential" n
stereospecific polymerization, stereoregular (tactical) polymerization, stereoblock [co]polymerization	stereospezifische Polymerisation f, stereoreguläre (stereoregulierte, taktische) Polymerisation, Stereoblock[ko]polymerisation f	sticking probability	Anlagerungswahrscheinlichkeit f, Haftwahrscheinlichkeit f, „sticking"-Wahrscheinlichkeit f; Reaktionskoeffizient m für die Adsorption [beim Aufdampfen]
stereotopography	Stereotopographie f		
stereo unit	s. stereo attachment	sticking surface; surface of adherence	Haftfläche f
stereovectograph, vectograph	Vektograph m, Stereovektograph m	Stickler coefficient	Stickler-Koeffizient m
stereovectograph[ic] film, vectograph[ic] film	Vektographenfilm m	stick slip [phenomenon]	„stick slip" n, „stick-slip"-Phänomen n, „stick-slip"-Reibung f, Reibungsschwingung f, Reibschwingung f, Stotterbewegung f, Steckschleifen n
stereovectograph[ic] layer	Vektographenschicht f		
stereo viewer, stereoscope	Stereoskop n; Stereobetrachter m, Stereobetrachtungsgerät n		
stereo viewfinder	Stereosucher m		
stereo-visor, polarizing spectacles	Stereobetrachtungsbrille f, Stereobrille f	sticky	s. viscid
		sticky limit (point)	Klebgrenze f, Klebegrenze f
steric acceleration	sterische Beschleunigung f		

stiction	s. static friction
Stieltjes integral	Stieltjessches Integral n, Stieltjes-Integral n
Stieltjes planimeter	Stieltjes-Planimeter n, Produktplanimeter n, Stieltjes-Integrator m
Stieltjes transformation	Stieltjes-Transformation f
stiff chain	steife Kette f
stiffening; reinforcement; strengthening <mech.>	Versteifung f, Verstärkung f; Absteifung f; Verstrebung f <Mech.>
stiffening plate, stiffening rib	Versteifungsrippe f, Verstärkungsrippe f
stiff joint	s. rigid joint
stiffness, rigidity; inflexibility	Steifigkeit f, Steifheit f, Steife f
stiffness	s. a. elastance <el.>
stiffness	s. a. viscidity
stiffness	s. a. spring constant
stiffness coefficient, stiffness factor, coefficient of stiffness, rigidity coefficient (number)	Steifigkeitskoeffizient m, Steifekoeffizient m, Steifigkeitszahl f, Steifigkeitsziffer f
stiffness matrix	Steifheitsmatrix f, Steifigkeitsmatrix f
stiffness modulus, modulus of stiffness	Steifigkeitsmodul m
stiffness reactance	Steifigkeitsreaktanz f
stiffness term	Rückstellglied n, Rückstellterm m, Steifigkeitsglied n, Steifigkeitsterm m
stigma, eye spot	Augenfleck m, Stigma n
stigmatic beam	s. homocentric beam
stigmatic image	stigmatische Abbildung f, stigmatisches Bild n
stigmatic mounting	stigmatische Aufstellung f
stigmatism	Stigmatismus m, Stigmatischsein n
stigmator	Stigmator m
stilb, sb <= 1 cd/cm²	Stilb n, sb <= 1 cd/cm²
stilbmeter, luminance meter, lucimeter	Leuchtdichtemesser m, Helligkeitsmesser m; Stilbmeter n
Stiles-Crawford effect, aperture effect	Apertureffekt m; Stiles-Crawford-Effekt m
still, distilling still, distillation flask (retort, still), distilling flask	Blase f, Destillierblase f, Destillationsblase f, Destillierkolben m, Destillationskolben m
still	s. a. still picture
stillage, stilling	Blasendestillation f
still bottom heel, still bottoms, heel, tailings, bottoms, leavings	Destillierrückstand m, Blasenrückstand m, Destillationsrückstand m, Bodensatz m
stilling, stillage	Blasendestillation f
stilling basin	Tosbecken n, Sturzbecken n
still picture, still	Stehbild n, Standbild n, ruhendes Bild n
stillpot	s. pond for nuclear reactor
still projection, diascopic projection, slide projection, diaprojection	Stehbildprojektion f, Standbildprojektion f, Standprojektion f, diaskopische Projektion f, Diaprojektion f
still projector, lantern-slide projector, slide projector, film-strip and slide projector	Stehbildwerfer m, Stehbildprojektor m, Stehbildgerät n, Standbildprojektor m, Standbildgerät n, Diaprojektor m
still water	s. wake space
stimulated absorption	s. induced absorption
stimulated Brillouin scattering	stimulierte Brillouin-Streuung f
stimulated echo	angeregtes Echo n, stimuliertes Echo, ,,stimulated echo" n <nach Hahn>
stimulated emission [of light], induced emission [of light], negative absorption	induzierte (erzwungene, stimulierte, angeregte) Emission f, negative Absorption (Einstrahlung) f
stimulated inverse Compton effect	stimulierter inverser Compton-Effekt m
stimulated radiation, induced radiation	stimulierte (induzierte) Strahlung f
stimulated Raman effect (scattering), induced Raman effect	stimulierter Raman-Effekt m, induzierter Raman-Effekt
stimulated transition, induced transition	induzierter (stimulierter, erzwungener) Übergang m
stimulating action	stimulierende Wirkung f, Stimulationswirkung f
stimulating agent	s. stimulation substance
stimulating current, exciting (excitation) current <bio.>	Reizstrom m, Reizstromstärke f <Bio.>
stimulation <of luminescence>	Ausleuchtung f, Austreibung f der aufgespeicherten Lichtsumme <Lumineszenz>
stimulation <bio.>	Reizung f <Bio.>
stimulation <bio.>	Stimulation f <Bio.>
stimulation	s. a. excitation
stimulation angle	Reizlagenwinkel m
stimulation effect	Stimulationseffekt m
stimulation frequency	Reizfrequenz f
stimulation impulse	Reizimpuls m
stimulation movement, induced movement <bio.>	Reizbewegung f <Bio.>
stimulation of nerve, nerve stimulation, excitation in nerves	Nervenreizung f
stimulation of photoconductivity	Ausleuchtung f der Photoleitfähigkeit
stimulation quantity, quantity of stimulus	Reizmenge f
stimulation substance, exciting agent (substance), stimulating agent	Reizmittel n, Reizstoff m, Stimulans n
stimulative plasmolysis, irritation plasmolysis	Reizplasmolyse f
stimulus, kind of stimulus	Reizart f
stimulus, colour stimulus	Farbvalenz f; Farbreiz m
stimulus, irritant <bio.>	Reiz m <Bio.>
stimulus	s. a. sound intensity
stimulus conduction, conduction of stimulus (excitation), transmission of stimulus <bio.>	Reizleitung f, Erregungsleitung f <Bio.>
stimulus energy, excitation energy <bio.>	Reizenergie f <Bio.>
stimulus intensity <bio.>	Reizstärke f, Reizintensität f <Bio.>
stimulus of light, light stimulus	Lichtreiz m
stimulus threshold	s. excitation threshold
stimulus time, excitation time <bio.>	Reizzeit f, Reizdauer f <Bio.>
stippled lens	Riffellinse f, geriffelte Linse f
Stirling['s] approximation, Stirling['s] formula	Stirlingsche Formel (Näherungsformel) f, Stirling-Formel f
Stirling cycle	Stirlingscher Kreisprozeß m, Stirling-Prozeß m
Stirling engine	Stirling-Motor m
Stirling['s] formula, Stirling['s] approximation	Stirlingsche Formel (Näherungsformel) f, Stirling-Formel f
Stirling['s] formula of integration	Stirlingsche Integrationsformel f
Stirling['s] formula of interpolation, Stirling['s] interpolation formula, Newton-Stirling interpolation formula	Stirlingsche Interpolationsformel f
Stirling['s] machine	Stirlingsche Luftmaschine f

Stirling['s] number, factorial coefficient (number)	Stirlingsche Zahl f
Stirling['s] polynomial	Stirlingsches Polynom n
Stirling['s] series	Stirlingsche Reihe f
stirrer, stirring device, stirring apparatus, agitator	Rührer m, Rührwerk n, Rührvorrichtung f
stirring ⟨in or into⟩	Rühren n; Verrühren n; Umrühren n
stirring apparatus (device)	s. stirrer
stirrup	Steigbügel m
Stöber['s] method	Stöbersche Methode f, Stöber-Methode f
Stöber plate	Stöbersche Glimmerplatte f
stochastic acceleration	stochastische Beschleunigung f
stochastic convergence	s. convergence in probability
stochastic decision theory	s. statistical decision theory
stochastic differentiation	stochastische Differentiation f
stochastic force	stochastische Kraft f
stochastic integration	stochastische Integration f
stochasticity	s. randomness
stochastic matrix, probability matrix	stochastische Matrix f
stochastic probability	s. convergence in probability
stochastic problem	stochastisches Problem n
stochastic process, random process	stochastischer Prozeß m, Zufallsprozeß m
stochastic process with independent increments	s. additive process
stochastic sequence	stochastische Folge f
stochastic variable	s. random variable
Stockbarger['s] method	Stockbarger-Methode f, Stockbargersche Methode f
stock bottle	Vorratsflasche f
stocking; accumulation, congestion, aggregation; storing, storage	Häufung f; Anhäufung f; Anreicherung f; Ansammlung f; Speicherung f; Aufspeicherung f
Stockmayer potential	Stockmayer-Potential n
Stock['s] number	Stocksche Zahl f, Stock-Zahl f
stock solution	Vorratslösung f
stock solution	Stammlösung f
Stoicheff absorption	s. induced absorption
stoichiometric amount, stoichiometric proportion	stöchiometrischer Verhältnisanteil m, stöchiometrische Menge f
stoichiometric coefficient, stoichiometric number, stoichiometric factor	stöchiometrischer Faktor m, stöchiometrischer Koeffizient m
stoichiometric composition, stoichiometry	stöchiometrischer Zusammensetzung f
stoichiometric excess	stöchiometrischer Überschuß m
stoichiometric factor, stoichiometric number, stoichiometric coefficient	stöchiometrischer Faktor m, stöchiometrischer Koeffizient m
stoichiometric impurity [centre], stoichiometric lattice defect	stöchiometrische Störstelle f, stöchiometrische Verunreinigung f
stoichiometric melt	stöchiometrische Schmelze f
stoichiometric molality	stöchiometrische Molalität f
stoichiometric number, stoichiometric coefficient, stoichiometric factor	stöchiometrischer Faktor m, stöchiometrischer Koeffizient m
stoichiometric proportion, stoichiometric amount	stöchiometrischer Verhältnisanteil m, stöchiometrische Menge f
stoichiometric ratio, stoichiometric relation-ship	stöchiometrisches Verhältnis n
stoichiometric valence	stöchiometrische Wertigkeit f
stoichiometry	Stöchiometrie f
stoichiometry, stoichiometric composition	stöchiometrische Zusammensetzung f
stokes, St, S	Stokes n, St
Stokes-Christoffel condition ⟨for shocks⟩	Stokes-Christoffelsche Bedingung f ⟨für Stoßwellen⟩
Stokes-Cunningham law	Stokes-Cunningham-Gesetz n, Stokes-Cunninghamsches Gesetz n
Stokes['] current function, Stokes['] stream function, Stokes['] potential	Stokessches Potential n
Stokes['] drift	Stokessche Geschwindigkeit f
Stokes-Einstein equation (type relation)	Stokes-Einsteinsche Gleichung f
Stokes['] equation	Stokessche Gleichung f
Stokes['] flow, Stokesian flow	Stokessche Strömung f
Stokes['] fluid, Stokesian fluid	Stokessche Flüssigkeit f
Stokes['] formula ⟨for determination of geoid undulations⟩	Stokessche Formel f [zur Bestimmung der Geoidundulationen]
Stokes['] formula	s. a. Stokes['] law
Stokes['] function	Stokes-Funktion f
Stokes['] hypothesis, Stokes['] principle	Stokessches Prinzip n, Stokessche Hypothese f
Stokesian flow, Stokes['] flow	Stokessche Strömung f
Stokesian fluid, Stokes['] fluid	Stokessche Flüssigkeit f
Stokes['] integral formula	Stokessche Integralformel f
Stokes['] law ⟨of resistance⟩, Stokes['] formula	Stokessches Gesetz (Widerstandsgesetz, Reibungsgesetz) n, Reibungsgesetz von Stokes, Stokessche Formel f, Stokesscher Reibungsansatz m, Widerstandsgesetz von Stokes
Stokes['] law [of fluorescence]	Stokessche Regel f [für die Fluoreszenz], Stokessche Fluoreszenzregel f, Stokessches Fluoreszenzgesetz n
Stokes lens	Zylinderkompensator m, Stokessche Linse f
Stokes line	Stokessche Linie f
Stokes['] number	Stokessche Zahl f, Stokes-Zahl f
Stokes operator	s. convective derivative
Stokes['] paradox, paradox of Stokes	Stokessches Paradoxon n, Paradoxon von Stokes
Stokes['] parameter	Stokesscher Parameter m
Stokes['] phenomenon	Stokessches Phänomen f
Stokes['] polarization theorem	Stokessches Polarisationstheorem n
Stokes['] potential, Stokes['] stream function, Stokes['] current function	Stokessches Potential n
Stokes['] principle, Stokes['] hypothesis	Stokessches Prinzip n, Stokessche Hypothese f
Stokes shift	Stokes-Verschiebung f
Stokes['] stream function, Stokes['] current function, Stokes['] potential	Stokessches Potential n
Stokes['] theorem, integral theorem of Stokes, Kelvin['s] transformation	Stokesscher Satz (Integralsatz) m, Integralsatz von Stokes, Stokessche Integralformel (Formel) f
Stokes transform[ation]	Stokessche Transformation f
Stokes['] vector	Stokesscher Vektor m
Stoletov['s] capacitor	Stoletow-Kondensator m
Stoletov effect, actinoelectric effect, actinoelectricity	Stoletow-Effekt m, aktinoelektrischer Effekt m
stoma ⟨pl.: stomata⟩	Spaltöffnung f, Stoma n ⟨pl.: Stomata⟩
stone, peg ⟨meas.⟩	Meßstab m, Meßstange f, Stab m ⟨Meß.⟩
Stoneley['s] wave	Stoneleysche Welle f, Stoneley-Welle f
Stoner['s] rule	Stonersche Regel f
stone stream, rock stream	Schuttstrom m

stony-iron meteorite, lithosiderite — Stein-Eisen-Meteorit *m*, Lithosiderit *m*

stony meteorite, aerolite, meteoritic stone, meteorolite — Steinmeteorit *m*, Aerolith *m*, Meteorstein *m*, Asiderit *m*

stop <of pointer> — Anschlag *m* <Zeiger>

stop; diaphragm; shutter; blind; septum <opt.> — Blende *f*, Diaphragma *n* <Opt.>

stop band, filter stop band, rejection band, filter rejection band, attenuation band, filter attenuation band; off-region, cut-off range — Sperrband *n*; Sperrbereich *m*

stop band, stopband, unstable stop band, instability stop band <acc.> — Stoppband *n* [im Diamanten], instabiler Streifen *m* <Beschl.>

stop-band effect <of filter>; blocking action, blockage effect — Sperrwirkung *f*, Sperreffekt *m*

stop bath, short-stop bath, short-stop; stop-bath solution — Unterbrecherbad *n*, Unterbrechungsbad *n*, Stoppbad *n*; Unterbrecherlösung *f*

stop-bath solution — *s*. stop bath

stop clock — *s*. stop watch

stopcock, conductor's valve, shutoff cock — Absperrhahn *m*, Hahn *m*, Sperrhahn *m*, Abschlußhahn *m*, Verschlußhahn *m*

stoplog dam, barrage with stop planks against logs — Dammbalkenwehr *n*

stop-motion camera shooting — *s*. time-lapse camera shooting

stop-motion device — *s*. time-lapse camera

stop-motion record — *s*. time lapse camera shooting

stop number, *f*-number, *f*-ratio, focal ratio; speed <of camera lens> — Blendenzahl *f*, Blendennummer *f*, Öffnungszahl *f*

stopped pipe, closed pipe — gedackte Pfeife *f*

stopper — Stopfen *m*; Stöpsel *m*

stopper circuit, rejector circuit, rejection circuit, interference suppression device — Sperrkreis *m*; Drosselkreis *m*

stopping cross-section; slowing-down cross-section; cross-section for slowing down — Bremsquerschnitt *m*, Wirkungsquerschnitt *m* für (der) Bremsung, Bremswirkungsquerschnitt *m*

stopping down <of diaphragm>; closing, shutting, closure — Schließen *n*

stopping equivalent [thickness] — Bremsäquivalent *n*, Bremsäquivalentdicke *f*

stopping lens — *s*. retarding lens

stopping potential, retarding (retardation) potential — Bremspotential *n*, Bremsspannung *f*; Verzögerungspotential *n*

stopping power — Bremsvermögen *n*

stopping power ratio — Bremsvermögensverhältnis *n*

stop-start [unit] — Stop-Start-Vorrichtung *f*, Stop-Start-Gerät *n*

stop value, *f* stop — Blendenwert *m*

stop[-]watch, stop clock, timer; seconds-counter — Stoppuhr *f*, Stopuhr *f*; Sekundenmesser *m*, Sekundenzähler *m*,

storage, storage device, storage unit, storing device, store; memory — Speicher *m*; Speicherwerk *n*; Gedächtnis *n*

storage; holding in storage; hold-up; keeping; preservation — Lagerung *f*; Aufbewahrung *f*; Lagerhaltung *f*

storage, storing <num. math.> — Speicherung *f*, Schreiben *n*, Einschreiben *n* <num. Math.>

storage — *s. a.* storing

storage blemish, blemish — Speicherfehler *m*

storage capability — Speicherfähigkeit *f*

storage capacitor — Speicherkondensator *m*

storage capacity — *s*. memory capacity

storage cave — *s*. storage tank

storage cell — *s*. storage location

storage compliance, dynamic compliance — Speicherkomplianz *f*, dynamische Nachgiebigkeit (Komplianz) *f*

storage container — *s*. storage tank

storage device — *s*. storage

storage efficiency — Speicherwirkungsgrad *m*

storage location, location, storage cell, memory cell, storage unit — Speicherzelle *f*; Speicherplatz *m*, Speicherstelle *f*

storage matrix — Speichermatrix *f*

storage mesh — Speichergitter *n*

storage modulus — Speichermodul *m*

storage of heat — *s*. heat storage

storage oscilloscope, storage-type oscilloscope — Speicheroszillograph *m*, Speicheroszilloskop *n*

storage reservoir, reservoir, storage work — Speicher *m*, Wasserspeicher *m*; Rückhaltebecken *n*; Staubecken *n*; Stauraum *m*; Stausee *m*

storage ring; accelerated particle storage ring — Speicherring *m*, Ringspeicher *m*

storage ring synchrotron — Speicherringsynchrotron *n*

storage tank; storage vessel; storage vault (container); storage cave — Lagerbehälter *m*; Lagertank *m*; Lagerungsgefäß *n*

storage time; retention time, maximum retention time <num. math.> — Speicherzeit *f*, Speicherungszeit *f*, Speicherdauer *f* <num. Math.>

storage time <semi.> — Sperrverzögerungszeit *f* <Halb.>

storage tube — *s*. electrostatic storage tube

storage-type camera tube, image-storing tube; iconoscope — Bildspeicherröhre *f*, speichernde Aufnahmeröhre *f*, Aufnahmeröhre mit Speicherung, Speicherröhre *f*; Ikonoskop *n*

storage-type oscilloscope — *s*. storage oscilloscope

storage unit — *s*. storage location

storage unit — *s. a.* storage

storage vault (vessel) — *s*. storage tank

storage work — *s*. storage reservoir

store — *s*. storage

stored energy — gespeicherte Energie *f*, gebundene Energie

stored-program[me] calculator (computer), program[me] controlled computer (calculator) — programmgesteuerter Rechner *m*, programmgesteuerte Rechenmaschine (Rechenanlage, Datenverarbeitungsanlage) *f*, Rechner mit Programmsteuerung

storing, storage; accumulation, congestion, aggregation; stocking — Häufung *f*; Anhäufung *f*, Anreicherung *f*; Ansammlung *f*; Speicherung *f*; Aufspeicherung *f*

storing — *s. a.* storage <num.math.>

storing device — *s*. storage

storing energy, stacking energy — Speicherenergie *f*

storm, tempest <gen.> — Sturm *m* <allg.>

storm <of Beaufort No. 11> — orkanartiger Sturm *m* <Stärke 11>

stormburst — *s*. type I burst

storm cloud — *s*. cumulonimbus

storm cyclone, storm depression — Sturmtief *n*

Störmer cone, Störmer region, forbidden cone — Störmerscher Kegel *m*, Störmer-Kegel *m*

Störmer current ring, Chapman-Störmer current ring — Störmerscher Stromring *m*, Chapman-Störmerscher Stromring *m*

Störmer['s] extrapolation formula	Störmersche Extrapolationsformel f	straight-line wedge, rectilinear neutral wedge	gerader Keil m, gerader Graukeil m
Störmer['s] interpolation formula	Störmersche Interpolationsformel f	straight magnet	s. bar magnet
Störmer['s] method, Adams-Störmer method	Störmersches Extrapolationsverfahren n	straight-on angle shot, horizontal shot	Horizontalaufnahme f, Waagerechtaufnahme f
Störmer['s] method	Störmersches Integrationsverfahren n	straight-ridge sector, radial sector, radial ridge	Radialsektor m
Störmer region, Störmer cone, forbidden cone	Störmerscher Kegel m, Störmer-Kegel m	straight-through amplifier	Geradeausverstärker m
Störmer['s] theory	Störmersche Theorie (Polarlichttheorie) f	straight-through reactor	Durchlaufreaktor m
Störmer unit	Störmersche Längeneinheit (Einheit) f, Störmer-Einheit f, Störmer n	straight transconductance	Geradeaussteilheit f
storm sea	s. very high seas	strain	Verspannung f
storm surge; surge	Flutwelle f	strain <bio.>	Stamm m <Bio.>
		strain; deformation; change of form <mech.>	Verformung f, Form[ver]änderung f, Deformation f, Verzerrung f [der Form], Deformierung f <Mech.>
storm track	s. track of the storm		
stormy sea	s. very high sea		
stosszahlansatz	Stoßzahlansatz m, Hypothese f des molekularen Chaos, Hypothese der molekularen Unordnung, Stoßansatz m	strain; stress; load; charge <quantity> <mech.>	Beanspruchung f <Größe> <Mech.>
		strain, compression <mech.>	Stauchung f <Mech.>
Stout['s] method	Stoutsche Methode f		
strabismus, squinting, squint	Schielen n; manifestes Schielen, Strabismus m	strain	s. a. strain field
straggling, spread, statistical straggling, scatter[ing] <gen., e.g. of data>	Streuung f, statistische Streuung; Streubreite f <allg., z. B. von Daten>	strain	s. a. strain tensor
		strain	s. a. elongation <in %>
		strain	s. a. state of strain <mech.>
		strain ageing	Reckalterung f
straggling parameter	Streuparameter m		
straight ahead approximation	„straight-ahead"-Näherung f		
straight-ahead holography	Geradeausholographie f	strain anisotropy, magnetoelastic anisotropy	Spannungsanisotropie f
straight-ahead scattering, straight-forward scattering	Geradeausstreuung f, Vorwärtsstreuung f	strain-anneal method	Streck-Anlaß-Methode f
straight amplification	Geradeausverstärkung f	strain at the point	s. strain tensor
straight angle, flat angle	gestreckter Winkel m	strain birefringence	s. stress birefringence
straight chain	s. unbranched chain	strain burst	diskontinuierliche Dehnung f
straight cock	Einweghahn m, Durchgangshahn m	strain compensator	Spannungs-Polarisationskompensator m
straight-edge rule, jointing-rule	Richtlatte f; Richtscheit n	strain component, component of strain, component of deformation	Deformationskomponente f, Formänderungskomponente f, Verzerrungskomponente f, Verformungskomponente f, Komponente f des Verzerrungstensors
straight filament	glatter (gestreckter, geradliniger) Leuchtdraht m		
straight-forward scattering	s. straight-ahead scattering	strain crack	Verformungsriß m, Deformationsriß m
straight line, line <math.>	Gerade f, gerade Linie f <Math.>		
straight-line capacitor	Kreisplatten-Drehkondensator m, Kreisplattenkondensator m	strain deviator, deviator of stretching, deformation deviator, deviator strain tensor, deviatoric [part of the] strain tensor	Deviator m der Streckung, Deviator des Dehnungstensors (Deformationstensors)
		strained crystal	verspannter Kristall m
straight-lined edge dislocation	gerade Stufenversetzung f	strained state	s. state of strain
straight-line-frequency capacitor	frequenzgerader Kondensator (Drehkondensator) m	strain ellipsoid, ellipsoid of deformation, deformation ellipsoid	Verzerrungsellipsoid n, Verformungsellipsoid n, Formänderungsellipsoid n, Deformationsellipsoid n, Strainellipsoid n
straight line motion, rectilinear motion, motion in a straight line	geradlinige Bewegung f		
		strain energy	s. total strain energy
straight-line plot of the bending stress	Geradliniendiagramm n	strain-energy density [function]	s. specific strain energy
		strain energy due to the change of volume, volumetric energy	Volum[en]änderungsenergie f, Volum[en]änderungsarbeit f, Raumänderungsenergie f, Raumänderungsarbeit f, Verdichtungsarbeit f, Kompressionsarbeit f
straight line portion of the characteristic curve, region of normal exposure, region of correct exposure	geradliniger Teil m der Schwärzungskurve, Gebiet n der normalen Exposition		
straight-line source	s. line source	strain energy due to the distortion, strain energy of distortion, distortion energy, distortional (shear) strain energy	Gestaltänderungsenergie f, Gestaltänderungsarbeit f
straight line traverse	gestreckter Polygonzug (Zug) m		
straight-line-wavelength capacitor, square-law capacitor	Nierenplattenkondensator m		
		strain energy function	Verformungsenergiefunktion f
		strain-energy function	s. a. specific strain energy

strain energy method	energetische Methode f	strain potential	Dehnungspotential n
strain energy of distortion	s. strain energy due to the distortion	strain quadric	Verzerrungsfläche f, Formänderungsfläche f, Deformationsfläche f, Dilatationsfläche f, Dehnungsfläche f
strain energy per unit mass, elastic potential per unit mass	elastisches Potential n pro Masseneinheit		
strain energy per unit volume	s. specific strain energy	strain quadric	s. a. elongation quadric
		strain rate	s. rate of strain
strain energy theory, maximum strain energy theory	Hypothese f der größten Formänderungsarbeit	strain-rate vector	Deformationsgeschwindigkeitsvektor m
		strain relaxation, relaxation of strain, relaxation of deformation	Verformungsrelaxation f, Verzerrungsrelaxation f, Formänderungsrelaxation f, Deformationsrelaxation f
strainer, colander	Seihfilter n, Seiher m, Sieb n		
strain field, state of strain [in the body], strain [in the body]	Verzerrungsfeld n, Verformungsfeld n	strain relief, stress relieving (relief)	Spannungsbeseitigung f, Beseitigung f der Spannung; Spannungsentlastung f, Entlastung f; Spannungserholung f
strain figure, slip band, glide band, Lüders band, stretcher strain, flow figure	Gleitband n, Fließfigur f, Gleitfigur f, Lüderssches Band n, Lüdersscher Streifen m	strain-slip cleavage; crenulation cleavage; crenulation	Runzelschieferung f; Runzelung f
strain-free lattice	verspannungsfreies Gitter n	strain-stress curve	s. stress-strain curve
strain function, function of strain	Verformungsfunktion f, Verzerrungsfunktion f	strain-stress relation	s. stress-strain relation
strain gauge, strip tensometer	Dehn[ungs]meßstreifen m, Dehnungsmeßgeber m, Meßstreifen m, Streifendehnungsmesser m, Dehnungsmesser m	strain tensor, deformation tensor, distortion tensor, state of strain [at the point], strain [at the point]; elongation tensor	Verzerrungstensor m, Verformungstensor m, Formänderungstensor m, Deformationstensor m, Tensor m des Verzerrungszustandes; Dehnungstensor m; Elongationstensor m
strain-gauge balance	Dehnungsstreifenwaage f	strain tensor of Green, Green['s] deformation tensor	Greenscher Deformationstensor m, Deformationstensor von Green
strain gauging	s. strain measurement		
strain hardening, work hardening, cold work effect	Verfestigung f [durch Kaltbearbeitung], Gleitverfestigung f, Kaltverfestigung f, Kalthärtung f, Druckhärtung f, Spannungsvergütung f	strain theory	Deformationstheorie f
		strain theory	s. a. Baeyer['s] strain theory
		strain velocity	Dehn[ungs]geschwindigkeit f
		strain velocity	s. a. rate of strain
strain-hardening capacity	s. work-hardening capacity	strain[-] viewer	Spannungsprüfer m, spannungsoptisches Prüfgerät n
strain-hardening coefficient	s. work-hardening coefficient	strain work, recoverable strain work, elastic work of deformation	reversible Deformationsarbeit (Verformungsarbeit) f
strain-hardening curve, work-hardening curve	Verfestigungskurve f		
strain-hardening exponent (index), work-hardening exponent (index)	Verfestigungsexponent m, Verfestigungsindex m	Strakhovitch solution	Strachowitschsche Lösung f
strain-hardening property	s. strain-hardening capacity	strand, stranded wire; litz wire, litzendraht, litzendraht wire	Litze f
strain history	Deformations-Vorgeschichte f		
straining; stretch; tensioning ‹e.g. of the spring›; cocking ‹e.g. of the shutter›	Spannen n	strand, beach, sea[-]shore, shore	Strand m
		stranded wire	s. strand
		strand[-] line, water edge, edge of water	Strandlinie f, Küstenlinie f, Streichlinie f, Uferlinie f, Wasserspiegelrand f
straining, colation ‹chem.›	Seihen n, Kolieren n ‹Chem.›		
straining; stressing; loading ‹mech.›	Beanspruchung f; Belastung f ‹Mech.›	strangeness [number]	Strangeness f, „strangeness" f, Seltsamkeit f, Fremdheitsquantenzahl f
straining frame experiment; tensile test[ing], tension test[ing]	Zugversuch m, Zugprüfung f, Zugprobe f, Zerreißversuch m, Zerreißprüfung f, Zerreißprobe f	strange particle	„strange particle" n, „seltsames" (fremdes) Teilchen n
		strangling of indices	s. contraction ‹of tensor›
strain invariant	s. invariant of strain	Stranski-Krastamanov mechanism	s. Stranski-Krastamanov model
strain matrix, deformation matrix, elongation matrix, distortion matrix	Verzerrungsmatrix f, Verformungsmatrix f, Formänderungsmatrix f, Deformationsmatrix f, Dehnungsmatrix f	Stranski-Krastamanov model; Stranski-Krastamanov mechanism ‹cryst.›	Stranski-Krastamanow-Modell n; Stranski-Krastamanow-Mechanismus m ‹Krist.›
strain measure, deformation measure, measure of strain ‹mech.›	Verzerrungsmaß n, Verformungsmaß n, Formänderungsmaß n ‹Mech.›	strap, plate-group strap	Polbrücke f
strain measurement, strain gauging, extensometry	Dehnungsmessung f	strap ‹of magnetron›	Kopplungsbügel m, Strapbügel m, Koppelring m, Strapring m
strain of eye, eyestrain	Augenermüdung f, Ermüdung f des Auges	strapped magnetron, stripped magnetron	Magnetron n mit Kopplungsbügeln, Mehrschlitzmagnetron n mit Kopplungsbügeln, „strapped"-Magnetron n
strain of volume, volume strain, bulk strain, dilatational strain	relative Volum[en]änderung f, Volum[en]dilatation f, Dilatation f		
		strapping	„strapping" n
strainometer	s. extensometer	stratameter	Stratameter n
strain parameter	s. deformation parameter	Stratford['s] method	Stratfordsche Methode f
strain point	unterer Kühlpunkt m	straticulation	s. striation

stratification; striation; lamination stack	Schichtung f	stray current	s. a parasite current
stratification; lamination; piling; stacking; layering	Schichtung f, Schichten n; Schichtbildung f, Stratifikation f	stray current stray displacement current	s. a. surface leakage current vagabundierender Verschiebungsstrom m
stratification <stat.>	Schichtung f <Stat.>	stray electromotive force, spurious electromotive force, spurious e.m.f., stray e.m.f.	Streu-EMK f
stratification	s. a. bedding <geo.>		
stratification coefficient	Schichtungskoeffizient m	stray electron, roaming electron	Streuelektron n, vagabundierendes (verirrtes) Elektron n
stratification curve	geometrische Zustandskurve f, Schichtungskurve f	stray emission current	s. reverse (inverse, return) current
		stray field	s. magnetic stray field
		stray field energy	Streufeldenergie f
stratification of atmosphere	Luftschichtung f, Schichtung f der Atmosphäre	stray flux, magnetic leakage flux, leakage flux	magnetischer Streufluß m, Streufluß
stratification of water mass	Wasserschichtung f	stray flux density, leakage flux density	Streuflußdichte f
		stray impedance, leakage impedance	Streuimpedanz f
stratification of wind	Windschichtung f	stray inductance, leakage inductance, leakage inductive	Streuinduktivität f
stratification parameter	s. Richardson number		
stratified dielectric	geschichtetes Dielektrikum n	straying	s. magnetic leakage <el.>
stratified rock, sedimentary rock, aqueous rock	Sedimentgestein n, Absatzgestein n, Schichtgestein n, Sediment n	stray light	Streulicht n; Falschlicht n
		stray light, vagabond ray	Irrstrahl m
stratified sample	geschichtete Stichprobe f	stray light error	Streulichtfehler m
stratiform cloud, layer cloud	schichtförmige (stratiforme) Wolke f, Stratiformisform f, Stratiformis m	stray light photometer, scattered light photometer	Streulichtphotometer n
stratiform structure	s. laminated structure	stray magnetic field	s. magnetic stray field
stratigraph	s. laminograph	stray neutron	Streuneutron n, vagabundierendes Neutron n
stratigraphic discordance, discordance of stratification	Schichtungsdiskordanz f, Diskordanz f, ungleichsinnige Lagerung f	stray radiation	s. spurious radiation
		stray radiation	s. perturbing radiation <el.>
stratigraphic sequence	s. order of superposition	stray voltage	s. reactance voltage
stratigraphy <geo.>	Stratigraphie f, Schichtenkunde f <Geo.>	stray wave	s. surge <el.>
stratigraphy	s. a. body section roentgenography	stray wave charge, surge charge	Wanderwellenbelastung f, Wanderwellenbeanspruchung f
stratocumulus [cloud], Sc	Stratocumulus m, Stratokumulus m, Haufenschichtwolke f, geschichtete Haufenwolke f, Sc	streak, schliere <pl.: schlieren>	Schliere f
		streak, trace <of mineral>	Strich m <Mineral>
stratopause	Stratopause f	streak camera	s. schlieren chamber
stratosphere	Stratosphäre f, isotherme Schicht f [der Atmosphäre]	streaked, striated, striped	gebändert, gestreift, streifig
		streakiness of film	Streifung (Streifigkeit) f des Films
stratospheric fallout	Fallout m aus der Stratosphäre, Stratosphärenfallout m	streaking, running <of colours>	Auslaufen n; Ineinanderlaufen n; Zerfließen n <Farben>
stratostat	Stratostat m	streak lightning	Linienblitz m, Funkenblitz m
stratovolcano, bedded volcano	Schichtvulkan m, Stratovulkan m	streak photography	s. schlieren method
stratum <pl.: strata>, bed <geo.>	Lage f, Schicht f <Geo.>	streak resolution	Strichauflösung f
stratum weight	Schichtgewicht n	streaks <tv.>	Streifen mpl <Fs.>
stratus	Schichtbewölkung f	streaks of fog	s. fog in patches
stratus, stratus cloud, St	Stratus m, tiefe Schichtwolke f, Schichtwolke, St	stream; current; flow <aero., hydr.>	Strom m, Strömung f <Aero., Hydr.>
		stream	s. a. jet <aero., hydr.>
stratus fractus, fracto[-]stratus, scud	Fractostratus m, zerrissene Schichtwolke f	stream activity, shower activity	Stromtätigkeit f
Straubel contour	Straubelscher Umriß m	stream branch, shower branch, branch of the stream, branch of the shower <astr.>	Zweig m des Meteorstromes, Stromzweig m <Astr.>
Straubel [dispersion] prism	Straubel-Prisma n, Quarzprisma n von Straubel		
Straubel['s] theorem	Straubelscher Satz m	stream chromatography; liquid chromatography	Durchflußchromatographie f; Flüssigkeitschromatographie f
Straumanis['] method	Straumanis-Methode f		
Strauss test	Strauß-Prüfung f		
		stream cross-section centre, centre of the stream cross-section	Wasserschwerpunkt m
stray	s. magnetic leakage <el.>		
stray capacitance, spurious capacitance	Streukapazität f; Störkapazität f	streamer	Streamer m, Kanal m [der Entladung], Plasmaschlauch m, Leuchtfaden m; Gleitbüschel n, Polbüschel n; Stielbüschel n
stray capacitive coupling	Wechselstromeinstreuung f		
stray coupling, spurious coupling	Streukopplung f; Störungskopplung f	streamer <of gas, smoke>	Schwaden m <Gas, Rauch>; Gasschliere f; Rauchschliere f
stray current[s], leakage (creeping) current	Irrstrom m; Fehlstrom m; Leckstrom m; Ableit[ungs]strom m; Isolationsstrom m	streamer	s. a. wind-direction indicator

streamer chamber, streamer spark chamber — Streamerkammer *f*, Streamerfunkenkammer *f*

streamer channel — Streamerkanal *m*
streamer discharge — s. streamer-type discharge
streamer of the prominence, prominence streamer — Protuberanzenfaden *m*, Faden *m* der Protuberanz
streamers — s. a. draperies
streamer spark chamber, streamer chamber — Streamerkammer *f*, Streamerfunkenkammer *f*
streamer-type breakdown, streamer-type discharge, streamer discharge — Kanalentladung *f*, Kanaldurchbruch *m*, Kanaldurchschlag *m*, Streamerentladung *f*
stream filament — Stromfaden *m*, Strömungsfaden *m*
stream[ ]flow — s. free jet
stream[ ]flow — s. a. flow of the river <geo.>
stream function, current function — Stromfunktion *f*, Strömungsfunktion *f*, Feldfunktion *f*
streaming; flow; movement; fluid flow <gen.> — Strömung *f*, Strömen *n* <allg.>
streaming, flow [around] a body, flow [past] a body, passing motion [around], streaming around, streaming round — Umströmung *f*; Umfließen *n*
streaming — s. a. radiation streaming <nucl.>
streaming around — s. streaming
streaming birefringence — s. double refraction in flow
streaming calorimeter — s. continuous-flow calorimeter
streaming factor, channel[l]ing effect factor — Kanal[effekt]faktor *m*, Kanalverlustfaktor *m*
streaming flow — s. tranquil flow
streaming mercury electrode — s. venous mercury electrode
streaming of stars; star-stream; star streaming; star drift — Sternstrom *m*; Sternströmung *f*
streaming potential, stream potential — Strömungspotential *n*, komplexes Potential *n* des Strömungsfeldes
streaming potential, stream potential <el. chem.> — Strömungspotential *n* <El. chem.>
streaming round — s. streaming
streaming term — s. stream term
stream instability; two-stream instability — Strahlinstabilität *f*
streamline, stream line, line of flow, flow line, line of equal stream function — Stromlinie *f*, Strömungslinie *f*
streamline — s. a. air streamline <meteo.>
streamline analogy — Stromlinienanalogie *f*
streamline-shaped body — s. streamlined body
stream[-]lined — stromlinienförmig
streamlined body, fish-type body, body of good streamline shape, teardrop body, streamline-shaped body — Stromlinienkörper *m*, stromlinienförmiger Körper *m*
streamlined weight, torpedo sinker, Columbus-type weight, C-type weight — fischförmiger Belastungskörper *m*, Fischgewicht *n*
streamline field — Stromlinienfeld *n*
streamline flow — s. laminar flow
streamline of discontinuity — Unstetigkeitsstromlinie *f*
streamline of gas — s. gas streamline
streamline profile — Stromlinienprofil *n*
streamline shape — Stromlinienform *f*
streamline theory of glaciers — Stromlinientheorie *f* der Gletscher

streamlining — Stromlinienverkleidung *f*
stream of charge carriers — s. carrier flow
stream potential, streaming potential — Strömungspotential *n*, komplexes Potential *n* des Strömungsfeldes
stream potential, streaming potential <el. chem.> — Strömungspotential *n* <El. chem.>
stream sheet, current sheet — Stromblatt *n*, Stromfläche *f*
stream term, streaming term — Strömungsterm *m*
stream tube, tube of flow — Stromröhre *f*, Stromlinienröhre *f*
stream[-]tube theory — Stromfadentheorie *f*

stream velocity — s. flow rate
Strehl effect — Strehl-Effekt *m*
Strehl factor — Strehlscher Lichtverdichtungsfaktor *m*
Strehl number — Strehl-Zahl *f*, Strehlsche Zahl *f*
strength, stringency <of the test> — Strenge *f* [des Tests]
strength, resistance; strength factor <mech.> — Festigkeit *f*; Festigkeitswert *m* <Mech.>
strength, limit of strength, ultimate strength <mech.> — Festigkeitsgrenze *f*, Festigkeit *f* <Mech.>
strength calculation, calculation for the [mechanical] strength — Festigkeitsberechnung *f*
strength coefficient — s. modulus of resistance
strength criterion — Festigkeitskriterium *n*
strengthening — s. sharpening <math.>
strengthening — s. a. stiffening <mech.>
strength factor — s. strength <mech.>
strength function — Stärkefunktion *f*, „strength function" *f*
strength in bending — s. bending strength
strength in compression — s. compressive strength
strength in tension — s. tensile strength
strength of adsorption, adsorption strength — Adsorptionsstärke *f*, Stärke *f* der Adsorption
strength of barrier — s. strength of potential wall
strength of bond, bond strength — Bindungsstärke *f*; Festigkeit *f* der Bindung, Bindungsfestigkeit *f*
strength of coupling — Kopplungsstärke *f*
strength of current — s. current
strength of dislocation — Versetzungsstärke *f*
strength of field — s. field strength
strength of layer of charge — Stärke *f* der Ladungsschicht <Moment / Flächeneinheit>
strength of lens — s. focal power
strength of line — s. intensity of the spectral line
strength of magnetic pole — s. magnetic pole strength
strength of materials, resistance of materials — Materialfestigkeit *f*
strength of materials, science of the strength [of materials], stress analysis — Festigkeitslehre *f*
strength of potential wall, strength of barrier — Stärke *f* des Potentialwalls (Potentialberges) <Breite × Höhe>
strength of source — s. source strength
strength of the impulse, impulse strength, pulse strength — Impulsstärke *f*, Fläche *f* unter der Impulskurve
strength of the interaction, interaction strength — Stärke *f* der Wechselwirkung, Wechselwirkungsstärke *f*
strength of the resonance — Stärke *f* des Resonanzniveaus

strength of the system of differential equations	Stärke f des Differentialgleichungssystems	stress ellipsoid	s. a. ellipsoid of elasticity
strength of the vortex, vortex strength	Stärke f des Wirbels, Wirbelstärke f	stress-energy-momentum tensor	s. energy-momentum tensor
strength of the vortex tube	Stärke f der Wirbelröhre	stress equalizing ‹mech.›	Spannungsausgleich m ‹Mech.›
		stress field, state of stress [in the body], stress [in the body]	Spannungsfeld n
strength per unit, unit strength	spezifische Festigkeit f	stress fluctuation in creep	Spannungsschwankung f beim Kriechen
stress ‹geo., bio.›	Streß m ‹Geo., Bio.›	stress-free	s. unstressed ‹mech.›
stress, tension ‹mech.›	Spannung f, mechanische Spannung, Beanspruchung f ‹Mech.›	stress freezing	Einfrieren n des Spannungszustandes
stress	s. a. state of stress		
stress	s. a. strain ‹mech.›	stress fringe pattern, photoelastic fringe pattern	spannungsoptisches Streifenbild n, Spannungsstreifenbild n
stress	s. a. stress field		
stress	s. a. stress tensor	stress function	Spannungsfunktion f
stress amplitude; amplitude of stress, stress range ‹mech.›	Spannungsamplitude f; Schwingbreite f der Spannung ‹Mech.›	stress function tensor	Spannungsfunktionstensor m
stress analysis	s. strength of materials	stress graph	s. stress-strain curve
stress at rest ‹mech.›	Ruhespannung f ‹Mech.›	stressing; straining; loading ‹mech.›	Beanspruchung f; Belastung f ‹Mech.›
stress at the point	s. stress tensor		
stress axis, principal axis of stress, principal stress axis	Hauptachse f des Spannungszustandes, Hauptspannungsachse f, Spannungshauptachse f	stress intensity; intensity of stress	Spannungsintensität f
		stress intensity factor	Spannungsintensitätsfaktor m
stress birefringence, strain birefringence	Spannungsdoppelbrechung f	stress in the bar	Stabspannung f
		stress invariant, invariant of stress	Spannungstensorinvariante f, Invariante f des Spannungszustands
stress by pressure	s. compressive stress		
stress by pull	s. tensile stress	stressless	s. unstressed ‹mech.›
stress by thrust	Schubbeanspruchung f	stressless deformation	spannungslose Deformation f
stress coefficient	s. pressure coefficient		
stress component, component of stress	Spannungskomponente f, Komponente f des räumlichen Spannungszustandes, Komponente des Spannungstensors, Komponente der Spannung	stress line, stress trajectory, line of stress, line of tension	Spannungslinie f
		stress line ‹of elasticity›; equipotential line, contour line ‹el.›	Äquipotentiallinie f, Niveaulinie f, Potentiallinie ‹El.; Elastizität›
stress-compression diagram	Spannungs-Stauchungs-Diagramm n	stress-momentum tensor	Spannungs-Impuls-Tensor m
		stress number curve	s. Wöhler curve
stress concentration, stress raising	Spannungskonzentration f	stress of rocks	Gebirgsspannung f
		stress of the first ‹second, third› kind ‹cryst.›	Spannung f erster ‹zweiter, dritter› Art ‹Krist.›
stress concentration factor [produced by the notch], concentration factor, shape factor, geometric stress concentration factor	Kerbwirk[ungs]zahl f, Kerbziffer f, Kerbfaktor m, Formzahl f, Formziffer f, Spannungskonzentrationsfaktor m	stressometer ‹mech.›	Spannungsmesser m, Spannungsmeßgerät n ‹Mech.›
		stress-optic[al], photoelastic	spannungsoptisch; photoelastisch
		stress-optic[al] coefficient, photoelastic coefficient	spannungsoptischer (photoelastischer) Koeffizient m
stress concentrator	s. stress raiser		
stress conic	Spannungskegelschnitt m	stress-optic[al] constant, photoelastic constant	spannungsoptische Konstante f, photoelastische Konstante
stress[-]corrosion; stress corrosion cracking, corrosion cracking	Spannungsrißkorrosion f, Spannungskorrosion f; Rißbildung f durch Spannungskorrosion	stress pattern, photoelastic stress pattern, photoelastic pattern	Isochromatenbild n, Spannungsmodell n
		stress phase	Spannungsphase f
		stress polygon, polygon of stresses	Spannungspolygon n, Spannungsvieleck n
stress crack	Spannungsriß m	stress power	Spannungsleistung f
stress cycle	s. cycle of load stressing	stress-probing extensometer	Setzdehnungsmesser m
stress-deformation relation	s. stress-strain relation	stress produced by impact ‹mech.›	Stoßspannung f ‹Mech.›
stress deviator, deviatoric [part of the] stress tensor, deviator stress tensor, reduced stress tensor	Spannungsdeviator m, Deviator m der Spannung, Deviator des Spannungstensors		
		stress quadric, quadric of stress, surface of tension, deflection surface	Spannungsfläche f, Tensorfläche (quadratische Form) f des Spannungstensors
stress diagram	s. stress-strain curve		
stress due to negative pressure	Unterdruckspannung f	stress raiser, stress concentrator	spannungserhöhende Unstetigkeitsstelle f, Spannungskonzentrator m
stress due to shrinkage	s. shrinkage stress		
stressed membrane	gespannte Membran f	stress range	s. amplitude of stress
stressed state	s. a. state of stress	stress rate	s. rate of strain
stress ellipse	Spannungsellipse f	stress relaxation, relaxation of stress	Spannungsrelaxation f
stress ellipsoid, Lamé['s] stress ellipsoid	Spannungsellipsoid n, Lamésches Spannungsellipsoid	stress relaxation curve	Spannungsrelaxationskurve f

stress 832

stress relief	s. strain relief	stretching force, tensile force, pull; tractive force, tractive effort, traction	Zugkraft f, Zug m
stress relief annealing	s. relief annealing		
stress relieving	s. strain relief	stretching force constant	Kraftkonstante f der Valenzschwingung
stress resultant	Spannungsresultante f, Schnittgröße f, Schnittkraft f	stretching frequency	Valenzschwingungsfrequenz f
stress space	Spannungsraum m	stretching quadric, quadric of stretching	Streckungsfläche f, Tensorfläche (quadratische Form) f des Streckungstensors
stress-strain curve, stress-strain diagram, strain-stress curve, tensile test diagram, stress graph, load-extension diagram, stress diagram	Spannungs-Dehnungs-Kurve f, Spannungs-Dehnungs-Linie f, Spannung-Dehnungs-Kurve f, Spannungs-Dehnungs-Diagramm n, Dehnungskurve f, Dehnungslinie f, Dehnungsdiagramm n, Spannungs-Verformungs-Kurve f, Spannungsdiagramm n, Kraft-Verlängerung-Schaubild n, Zugkurve f, Spannungs-Dehnungs-Schaubild n, Zerreißdiagramm n, Formänderungskurve f, Fließkurve f, Spannungsbild n, Beanspruchungs-Dehnungs-Diagramm n	stretching strain, tension strain, tensile strain, stretching stress, pulling stress	Zugbeanspruchung f, Beanspruchung f durch innere Zugkräfte, innere Zugspannung f
		stretching strain, work of rupture, rupture work	Zerreißarbeit f
		stretching strain	s. a. elongation
		stretching stress	s. tensile stress
		stretching stress	s. a. stretching strain
		stretching tensor	Streckungstensor m
		stretching tensor of Euler, Euler['s] stretching tensor	Eulerscher Streckungstensor m, Streckungstensor von Euler
		stretching vibration, valence vibration, st	Valenzschwingung f, Bindungs-Streckungs-Schwingung f, Streckungsschwingung f, Dehnungsschwingung f
stress-strain relation, stress-deformation relation, constitutive equation, strain-stress relation	Spannungs-Dehnungs-Beziehung f, Spannungs-Dehnungs-Relation f, Spannungs-Verformungs-Beziehung f, Spannungs-Formänderungs-Beziehung f, Dehnungs-Spannungs-Beziehung f, Dehnungs-Spannungs-Gleichung f	stretch modulus	s. modulus of rupture <mech.>
		stretch-out of burnup	Abbrandverlängerung f
		stria, band of secondary slip <cryst.>	Striemen m, Band n zweiter Gleitung <Krist.>
stress tensor, state of stress [at the point], stress [at the point]	Spannungstensor m	stria <pl.: striae>, thread; ream <in glass>	Fadenschliere f, Schliere f <Glasfehler>
		striae	s. glacial scratches
stress-time diagram	Spannungs-Zeit-Diagramm n	striated; streaked; striped	gebändert; gestreift; streifig
		striated appearance, striation <bio.>	Querstreifung f <Bio.>
stress trajectory, trajectory of stress	Spannungstrajektorie f	striated muscle, banded muscle	quergestreifter Muskel m
stress trajectory	s. a. stress line	striated rock[-pavements]	gekritztes Geschiebe n, Kritzgeschiebe n, gekritztes Geröll n
stress varying from zero to maximum	s. pulsating stress		
stress vector <mech.>	Spannungsvektor m <Mech.>	striated structure	s. banded structure
		striation, straticulation, banding	Bänderung f, Streifung f; Riefung f; Streifenbildung f; Striemendung f; Wachstumsstreifen mpl
stress wave, elastic wave	elastische Welle f		
stress wave analysis [technique], SWAT	Analyse f der elastischen Wellen		
stretch, spread[ing], stretching, extension	Spreizung f		
stretch, reach <of the river>	Stromstrecke f, Flußstrecke f, Flußabschnitt m, Wasserstrecke f [des Flusses]	striation; stratification; lamination stack	Schichtung f
		striation	Schlierenbildung f
		striation, striated appearance <bio.>	Querstreifung f <Bio.>
stretch; straining; tensioning <e.g. of the spring>; cocking <e.g. of the shutter>	Spannen n	striation method	s. schlieren method
		striation technique	s. schlieren method
		Stribeck curve	Stribeck-Kurve f
		Strickler coefficient	Strickler-Koeffizient m, Stricklerscher Koeffizient m
stretch, spread <a surface>	aufspannen <eine Fläche>	strict causality	strenge Kausalität f
		striction <math.>	Einengung f; Verengerung f <Math.>
stretch	s. a. elongation <in %>		
stretchability	s. ductility	striction stress, strictive stress	Striktionsspannung f
stretchable	s. ductile		
stretched, tight, taut	straff [gespannt], gespannt	striction term	Striktionsterm m
stretched spring	gespannte Feder f	strictive stress, striction stress	Striktionsspannung f
stretched tip, extended tip <of wing>	ausgezogene Spitze f <Tragflügel>		
		strict solution, rigorous solution, exact solution	strenge Lösung f, exakte Lösung
stretcher line	s. slip line		
stretcher strain	Ziehriefe f	stride; step; pace	Schritt m, Stufe f
		striding level, mason's level	Setzlibelle f, Setzwaage f; Reitlibelle f
stretcher strain	s. a. slip band		
stretch forming	Streckformen n		
stretching, spread[ing], stretch, extension	Spreizung f	stridulation	Stridulation f, Zirpen n
		strike, trend <geo.>	Streichen n <Geo.>
stretching <process>	Reckung f; Streckung f <Vorgang>		
		strike note	s. impact sound
		strike plate [of the comparator]	Meßplatte f des Komparators
stretching <e.g. of field lines> <math.>	Dehnung f, Streckung f <z. B. Feldlinien> <Math.>	striking angle	s. angle of incidence
		striking current; ignition current; firing current	Zündstrom m; Zündstromstärke f, Zündungsstromstärke f
stretching band	Valenzschwingungsbande f		

striking distance, sparking distance, spark length	Funkenschlagweite f, Schlagweite f, Funkenlänge f
striking drag reduction at the critical Reynolds number	s. "crisis" of drag
striking energy	s. impact energy
striking momentum	s. momentum of the impact
striking of the arc, breakdown of the arc	Zündung f (Durchbruch m) des Lichtbogens
striking potential	s. breakdown voltage
striking speed, striking velocity	Schlaggeschwindigkeit f
striking voltage	s. breakdown voltage
string	Saite f
string <num.math.>	Zeichenkette f, Kette f <num. Math.>
string ammeter	Saitenamperemeter n, Saitenstrommesser m
stringed instrument, string instrument	
string electrometer, fibre (filament) electrometer	Fadenelektrometer n, Saitenelektrometer n
stringency, strength <of the test>	Strenge f [des Tests]
stringer <nucl.>	Bestrahlungszug m, Zug m <zu bestrahlender Materialien> <Kern.>
stringer	s. a. longitudinal beam
stringer corrosion	„stringer"-Korrosion f, Korrosion f in Zeilen, schnurartiger Korrosionsschaden m
string galvanometer, cord galvanometer, Einthoven galvanometer	Fadengalvanometer n, [Einthovensches] Saitengalvanometer n, Bändchengalvanometer n, Saitenstrommesser m
string gravimeter	Saitengravimeter n
stringiness	s. ductility
string instrument, stringed instrument	Saiteninstrument n
string model	Saitenmodell n
string oscillograph, string oscilloscope	Saitenoszillograph m, Saitenoszilloskop n
string polygon, funicular polygon, link polygon	Seilpolygon n, Seileck n
string strainmeter, fibre strainmeter	Saitendehnungsmesser m
string tension	s. thread tension
string vibration, vibration of the string	Saitenschwingung f
strioscopic method	s. schlieren method
strip <of airphotos>	Streifen m, Flugstreifen m <auf dem Luftmeßbild>
strip attenuator, flap attenuator	Streifenabschwächer m
strip chart instrument (recorder, recording instrument)	s. chart recorder
stripcoat, strip coating	s. stripping emulsion
strip core	Streifenkern m
striped, striated, streaked	gebändert, gestreift, streifig
stripe running across; cross stripe, transverse stripe	Querstreifen m
strip focus	bandförmiger Brennfleck m, Bandfokus m
strip grating	Streifengitter n
strip lamp, tubular lamp, tubular line lamp, tubular light, spot	Soffittenlampe f, Soffitte f, Lichtwurflampe f L
strip line, strip transmission line, microstrip, microwave strip	Streifenleiter m, Streifenleitung f, Mikrostreifenleiter m
strip load	Streifenlast f, Linienlast f; Streifenbelastung f, Linienbelastung f
strip of bolometer	Bolometerstreifen m
strip of photographs	Bildstreifen m, Bildreihe f
strippable coating	s. stripping film
strippable film paint	Abziehlack m
stripped; highly ionized	hochionisiert
stripped atom	hochionisiertes Atom n, geschältes Atom, nacktes Atom, abgestreiftes Atom, „stripped atom" n
stripped emulsion	„stripped emulsion" f, abgezogene Emulsion (Emulsionsschicht) f
stripped magnetron	s. strapped magnetron
stripped neutron	„stripped neutron" n, abgestreiftes Neutron n, Strippingneutron n, Neutron der (d,p)-Reaktion
stripped output	Ausbeute f des abgereicherten Materials
stripper; stripping section; stripping (separating) column	Abstreifer m, Abscheider m; Abtriebsäule f, Strippingkolonne f
stripper <acc.>	Hochspannungselektrode f mit Umladungseinrichtung, Stripper m <Beschl.>
stripping, scrubbing <US>; washing; washing-out	Waschen n, Wäsche f; Gaswäsche f; Turmwäsche f, Herauswaschen n; Auswaschung f
stripping, peeling [off] <from>, frilling <of emulsion, coating>	Abziehen n, Ablösung f, Abstreifen n <Emulsion, Schicht>
stripping <nucl.>	Stripping n, Abstreifen n <Kern.>
stripping <nucl.>; depletion	Verarmung f; Abreicherung f <Kern.>
stripping <US>	s. a. reextraction
stripping column	s. stripper
stripping cross-section, cross-section for stripping [reaction]	Wirkungsquerschnitt m der (für die) Strippingreaktion, Stripping-[wirkungs]querschnitt m
stripping emulsion, stripping film, strippable coating, stripcoat, strip coating	Abziehfilm m, Abziehemulsion f, Strippingfilm m, Strippingemulsion f
stripping film method	Abziehfilmmethode f, „stripping-film"-Methode f, Strippingfilmmethode f
stripping off the emulsion, emulsion stripping	Schichtablösung f
stripping reaction	Strippingreaktion f
stripping section	s. stripper
strip tensometer	s. strain gauge
strip theory <acro.>	Streifentheorie f <Acro.>
strip transmission line	s. strip line
strobe	s. strobe pulse
strobe	s. a. stroboscopic disk
strobe marker	stroboskopische Marke f
strobe pulse, strobe, gating pulse, gate	Stroboskopimpuls m, Strobimpuls m, Auftastimpuls m, Torimpuls m; Markierungsfenster n
stroboglow	Stroboskop n mit Neonthyratron
stroboresonance, stroboscopic resonance	stroboskopische Resonanz f
stroboresonance galvanometer	Galvanometer n mit stroboskopischer Resonanz, Stroboresonanzgalvanometer n
stroboscope	s. flash-type stroboscope
stroboscopic dilatation of time, stroboscopic time dilatation	stroboskopische Zeitdehnung f
stroboscopic disk, stroboscopic pattern wheel, episcotister, strobe	stroboskopische Scheibe f, Stroboskopscheibe f
stroboscopic effect, pseudostereoscopic effect; spoking	stroboskopischer Effekt m, Stroboskopeffekt m; Radphänomen n, Radeffekt m; Phi-Phänomen n, φ-Phänomen n; stroboskopische Bewegung f, Bewegungstäuschung f, Scheinbewegung f

stroboscopic pattern wheel, stroboscopic disk	stroboskopische Scheibe f, Stroboskopscheibe f	strontium method	Strontiummethode f
stroboscopic principle	Stroboskopprinzip n	strontium unit, sunshine unit, s.u., pCi/g Ca	Strontiumeinheit f, Sunshine-Einheit f, S. U., pCi/g Ca
stroboscopic resonance	s. stroboresonance	strophotron	Strophotron f
stroboscopic time dilatation, stroboscopic dilatation of time	stroboskopische Zeitdehnung f	Strouhal['s] formula	Strouhalsche Formel f
stroboscopic transformation	stroboskopische Abbildung f	Strouhal number, S	Strouhal-Zahl f, Strouhalsche Kennzahl f, Strouhalsche Zahl f, S
stroke; impact; shock; percussion; blow; push; shove, impulse	Schlag m, Stoß m, Anstoß m	struck instrument	s. percussion instrument
		struck particle, bombarded particle, target particle	beschossenes Teilchen n, getroffenes Teilchen, Targetteilchen n
stroke; lift	Hub m	structon	Strukton n
stroke; stroke length; lifting height	Hubweg m; Hublänge f; Hubhöhe f	structural activator	struktureller Verstärker m
		structural aging	Gefügealterung f, Strukturalterung f
stroke ⟨of flash or lightning⟩	Blitzschlag m, Einschlag m ⟨Blitz⟩, Blitzeinschlag m	structural analysis	s. crystal-structure determination
stroke, cycle ⟨mech.⟩	Takt m ⟨Mech.⟩	structural anisotropy	Strukturanisotropie f
stroke length; stroke; lifting height	Hubweg m; Hublänge f; Hubhöhe f	structural bond	Strukturbindung f
		structural bridge, atomic bridge ⟨chem.⟩	Strukturbrücke f, Atombrücke f, Brücke f ⟨Chem.⟩
stroke of piston, piston stroke	Hub m [des Kolbens], Kolbenhub m	structural composition	s. structural constitution
stroke volume, systolic volume	Schlagvolumen n	structural constituent	Gefügebestandteil m
stroke work; lifting work, hoisting work	Hubarbeit f	structural constitution, structural composition	Gefügeaufbau m
Strombolian eruption, central eruption	Zentraleruption f, Schloteruption f	structural correlation	Strukturkorrelation f
		structural crystallography	s. crystal-structure determination
		structural defect	s. defect
Strömgren sphere, H II region, H⁺ region	H II-Gebiet n, Wasserstoff-Emissionsgebiet n	structural diagram	Strukturdiagramm n
strong-absorption model	Modell n der starken Absorption	structural diffusion	Strukturdiffusion f
		structural dipole	Strukturdipol m, struktureller Dipol m
strong acid	starke Säure f		
strong base	starke Base f	structural disarrangement (disarray, disorder)	strukturelle Unordnung f
strong breeze, strong wind ⟨of Beaufort No. 6⟩	starker Wind m ⟨Stärke 6⟩	structural dissimilarity	Strukturunähnlichkeit f
strong collision	starker Stoß m	structural effect	Struktureffekt m, Struktureinfluß m
strong convergence	s. convergence in mean ⟨of functions⟩	structural energy	Strukturenergie f
strong coupling, tight bond, tight binding ⟨nucl.⟩	starke Kopplung f, überkritische Kopplung ⟨Kern.⟩	structural entropy	Strukturentropie f
		structural equality, equality of structure	Strukturgleichheit f
strong coupling approximation, tight binding approximation	Näherung f mit starker Kopplung	structural etching	Schliffätzung f
		structural failure (fault)	s. defect
strong coupling meson theory	Mesonentheorie f mit starker Kopplung	structural formula, constitution formula, constitutional formula, graphic formula, rational formula	Strukturformel f, Konstitutionsformel f, Valenzstrichformel f
strong discontinuity	starke Unstetigkeit f		
strong earthquake, violent earthquake	Großbeben n, heftiges Beben n, schweres Erdbeben n		
strong electrolyte	starker Elektrolyt m	structural fracture, grain structure of fracture	Bruchgefüge n
strong extremum	starkes Extremum n		
strong field, high (high-intensity, high-strength, enhanced) field	starkes Feld n, Starkfeld n	structural group analysis	Strukturgruppenermittlung f
strong focusing	s. alternating-gradient focusing	structural-homogeneous	s. homogeneous structure / of
strong-focusing accelerator	s. alternating-gradient accelerator	structural imperfection	s. defect
strong-focusing synchrotron	s. alternating gradient synchrotron	structural inhomogeneity ⟨in glass⟩	strukturelle Inhomogenität f ⟨in Glas⟩
strong gale, gale ⟨of Beaufort No. 9⟩	Sturm m ⟨Stärke 9⟩	structural-inhomogeneous	s. inhomogeneous structure / of
strong interaction	starke Wechselwirkung f	structural irregularity	s. defect
strong line, intense line	starke (intensive) Linie f	structural isomer, structure isomer, structural (structure) isomeride	Strukturisomer[e] n
strongly absorbing	stark absorbierend		
strongly damped	s. aperiodic		
strong shock	starker Verdichtungsstoß m	structural-isomeric	strukturisomer
strong solution ⟨math.⟩	starke Lösung f ⟨Math.⟩	structural isomeride	s. structural isomer
strong stability	starke Stabilität f	structural isomerism, structure isomerism	Strukturisomerie f
strong topology, metric topology	starke Topologie f	structurally homogeneous	s. homogeneous structure / of
strong wind, strong breeze ⟨of Beaufort No. 6⟩	starker Wind m ⟨Stärke 6⟩	structurally inhomogeneous	s. inhomogeneous structure / of
strong wind, moderate gale ⟨of Beaufort No. 7⟩	steifer Wind m ⟨Stärke 7⟩	structurally stable	s. structural-stable
		structurally unstable	s. structural-unstable
strontium age, Rb-Sr age	geologisches Alter n nach der Strontiummethode, Strontiumalter n, Rubidium-Strontium-Alter n, ⁸⁷Sr-Alter n	structural material	Konstruktionswerkstoff m, Konstruktionsmaterial n, Konstiutionsmaterial n, Strukturmaterial n; Baustoff

structural mechanics, theory of structures	Baumechanik f, Theorie f der Baukonstruktionen	structure-insensitive, insensitive to structure, structure-independent, independent of structure	strukturunempfindlich, strukturunabhängig
structural modification	strukturelle Modifikation f, Strukturform f	structure-insensitive property, intrinsic property	strukturunempfindliche Eigenschaft f
structural order	strukturelle Ordnung f	structure isomer[ide], structural isomer, structural isomeride	Strukturisomer[e] n
structural parameter, structure parameter	Strukturparameter m, Strukturgröße f, Strukturkonstante f	structure isomerism, structural isomerism	Strukturisomerie f
structural porosity	Strukturporosität f	structureless	s. smeared
structural property, constitutive property	Struktureigenschaft f, konstitutive Eigenschaft f	structurelessness	s. amorphism
		structure of the molecule	s. molecular structure
structural radiograph, structural X-ray pattern	Röntgenstrukturaufnahme f, Röntgenstrukturdiagramm n, Röntgenstrukturbild n	structure parameter, structural parameter	Strukturparameter m, Strukturgröße f, Strukturkonstante f
		structure problem	Strukturproblem n
structural redundance	strukturelle Redundanz f		
structural relaxation	Strukturrelaxation f	structure-sensitive, structure-dependent, dependent on structure	strukturempfindlich, strukturabhängig
structural research	s. crystal-structure determination		
structural resonance, mesomerism, resonance <chem.>	Mesomerie f, Strukturresonanz f, Resonanz f <Chem.>	structure-sensitive conductivity	strukturabhängige Leitfähigkeit f
structural return loss, regularity attenuation, return loss; echo current attenuation	Rückflußdämpfung f; Echodämpfung f	structure-sensitive property, extrinsic property	strukturempfindliche Eigenschaft f
		structure theory	Strukturtheorie f
structural rigidity	Struktursteifigkeit f, Struktursteifheit f, Struktursteife f	structure type	Strukturtyp m, Kristallgittertyp m, Gittertyp m
structural shape <of steel>	s. outline	structurization	Strukturierung f
structural shrinkage	strukturelle Schrumpfung f	structurized, structured	strukturiert
structural stability	strukturelle Stabilität f, Gefügebeständigkeit f	struggle for life	Kampf m ums Dasein
structural-stable, structurally (constitutionally) stable, of stable structure	strukturstabil, strukturbeständig	strut, vertical member, vertical strut, stanchion, column	Vertikalstab m, Pfosten m
		strut	s. diagonal member
structural transformation (transition)	Gefügeumwandlung f	strut bracing, bracing, diagonal web, system of web members	Strebenfachwerk n; Strebewerk n; Ständerfachwerk n
structural-unstable, structurally (constitutionally) unstable, of unstable structure	strukturinstabil, strukturunbeständig	strut frame	Sprengwerk n
structural viscosity, pseudoplasticity	Strukturviskosität f, Strukturzähigkeit f, nicht-Newtonsches (Binghamsches) Fließen n, Pseudoplastizität f	Strutt['s] map, stability map	Stabilitätskarte f [der Hillschen Differentialgleichung], Struttsche Karte f
		Struve['s] function	Struvesche Funktion f, Struve-Funktion f
structural-viscous, non-Newtonian	strukturviskos, nicht-Newtonsch, anomal fließend	stub, matching stub, correcting stub, waveguide stub, plunger <el.>	Stichleitung f, Anpassungsstichleitung f, Blindschwanz m, Anpaßstichleitung f, Anpaßstück n, „stub" n, Stub n <El.>
structural X-ray pattern, structural radiograph	Röntgenstrukturaufnahme f, Röntgenstrukturdiagramm n, Röntgenstrukturbild n		
structure; constitution	Struktur f, Aufbau m, Bau m; Konstitution f, Beschaffenheit f		
structure, lattice <math.>	Verband m <Math.>	stub[-matched] antenna	Stichleitungsantenne f, mit Stichleitung angepaßte Antenne f
structure amplitude	Strukturamplitude f	Student['s] distribution	s. Student['s] t distribution
structure analysis	s. crystal-structure determination	studentization	Studentisierung f
structure argument	Strukturargument n	Student['s] ratio t	Größe f t in Students Test
structure birefringence	s. structure double refraction	Student['s] t distribution, Student['s] distribution, t distribution	Studentsche t-Verteilung f, t-Verteilung, Studentsche Verteilung f, Student-Verteilung f
structure-breaking effect	Strukturstörungseffekt m, Unordnungseffekt m		
structure current	Strukturstrom m	Student['s] test, t-test	Students Test m, Student-Test m, t-Test m, Studentscher t-Test
structured, structurized	strukturiert		
structure-dependent, structure-sensitive, dependent on structure	strukturempfindlich, strukturabhängig	study at the reactor	Reaktoruntersuchung f
		stuntedness	Vergeilen n, Verspillern n, Etiolement n, Verkümmern n
structure double refraction, structure birefringence, proper double refringence	Eigendoppelbrechung f, Strukturdoppelbrechung f, Texturdoppelbrechung f	sturbs	s. spherics
		sturdiness	s. ruggedness <gen.>
structured soil, textured soil	Strukturboden m	Sturges['] rule	Sturgessche Regel f
structure en échelon, échelon structure	kulissenartige Struktur f, Staffelstruktur f	Sturm['s] conoid	Sturmsches Konoid n
		Sturm['s] function, Sturmian function	Sturmsche Funktion f
structure factor	Strukturfaktor m		
structure formation, formation of structures	Strukturbildung f	Sturm-Liouville['s] boundary condition	Sturmsche Randbedingung f, Sturm-Liouvillesche Randbedingung
structure function	Strukturfunktion f		
structure-independent	s. structure-insensitive		

Sturm-Liouville['s] boundary value problem, Sturm-Liouville['s] problem — Sturm-Liouvillesches Randwertproblem n, Sturmsche (Sturm-Liouvillesche) Randwertaufgabe f

Sturm-Liouville['s] eigenvalue problem, Sturm-Liouville['s] problem — Sturm-Liouvillesches Eigenwertproblem n, Sturmsche Eigenwertaufgabe f, Sturm-Liouvillesche Eigenwertaufgabe

Sturm-Liouville['s] equation — Sturm-Liouvillesche Differentialgleichung (Gleichung) f

Sturm-Liouville['s] expansion, Sturm-Liouville['s] series — Sturm-Liouvillesche Entwicklung f, Sturm-Liouvillesche Reihe f

Sturm-Liouville operator — Sturm-Liouvillescher Operator m

Sturm-Liouville problem — s. Sturm-Liouville boundary value problem

Sturm-Liouville problem — s. Sturm-Liouville eigenvalue problem

Sturm-Liouville['s] series, Sturm-Liouville['s] expansion — Sturm-Liouvillesche Entwicklung f, Sturm-Liouvillesche Reihe f

Sturm['s] oscillation theorem — Oszillationssatz m von Sturm, Sturmscher Oszillationssatz

Sturm['s] sequence — Sturmsche Kette f

Sturm['s] spiral — Sturmsche Spirale f, Spirale von Norwich

Sturm['s] theorem — Sturmscher Satz m

Stüve diagram — Stüve-Diagramm n

StV-body — s. St.-Venant body

St. Venant body, StV-body, rigid-plastic body, Saint-Venant body — St. Venantscher Körper m, St.-Venant-Körper m, StV-Körper m, starrplastischer Körper, starrplastische Substanz f

St. Venant['s] compatibility conditions (equations), equations of compatibility of strain — St.-Venantsche Kompatibilitätsbedingungen fpl

St. Venant-Lévy-Mises relations, Saint-Venant-Lévy-Mises relations — St.-Venant-Lévy-Misessche Beziehungen fpl

St. Venant-Mises material — s. Mises ideal plastic body

St. Venant plasticity — s. perfect plasticity

St. Venant['s] principle, Saint-Venant['s] principle — St.-Venantsches Prinzip n, Prinzip von de St.-Venant, Saint-Venantsches Prinzip, Saint-Venant-Methode f, St. Venant-Methode f

St. Venant['s] theory, maximum strain theory — Theorie f der maximalen Deformation, Theorie von de St. Venant, St. Venantsche Theorie, Hypothese f der größten Dehnung [oder Gleitung]

St. Venant torsion, free torsion — freie Torsion f

St. Venant-Tresca yield condition, Tresca['s] yield condition (criterion), maximum shearing-stress yield condition (criterion), maximum shearing stress condition, hexagonal [yield] condition — Tresca-St.-Venant-Mohrsche Fließbedingung f, St. Venant-Trescasche Fließbedingung, Trescasche Fließbedingung, Fließbedingung von Tresca, hexagonale Fließbedingung

St. Venant-Wantzel formula — St. Venant-Wantzelsche Formel f

stylization, stylizing, crispening — Umrißversteilerung f

stylos, stylus ⟨US⟩ — Schreibstift m, Schreibspitze f

styloscintigraphy — Styloszintigraphie f, Strichszintigraphie f

sub — s. subtractor

subacoustic — s. infrasonic

subacoustic speed (velocity) — s. subsonic speed

subadiabatic — unteradiabatisch

subaeric — subaeril, subaerisch

sub-aggregate — s. subset

subalgebra — Teilalgebra f, Subalgebra f, Unteralgebra f

subaqueous — subaquatisch

subaqueous microphone — s. hydrophone

subaqueous sound ranging — s. hydrolocation

subaqueous spring, submerged spring, drowned spring — untermeerische (unterseeische) Quelle f, Untermeeresquelle f, Unterseequelle f

subaqueous visibility, underwater visibility — Unterwassersichtweite f

subassembly, sub-unit, subgroup ⟨el.⟩ — Untergruppe f, Baugruppe f, Baueinheit f ⟨El.⟩

subassembly — s. a. component ⟨of construction⟩

subatmospheric — bei einem Druck kleiner als dem atmosphärischen, subatmosphärisch

subatomic — subatomar

subaudio, infrasonic, subsonic, infra-acoustic — Infraschall-, infraakustisch, unter dem Hörbereich

subaudio frequency, infrasonic frequency, subsonic frequency — Infraschallfrequenz f, Unterschallfrequenz f

subaudio frequency — Unterhörfrequenz f, Untertonfrequenz f

subaudio frequency range — Untertonbereich m

sub-band — Teilband n

sub[-]band ⟨opt.⟩ — Teilbande f ⟨Opt.⟩

sub[-]band, subrange ⟨meas.⟩ — Unterbereich m ⟨Meß.⟩

sub[-]boundary, sub-grain boundary — Subkorngrenze f, Feinkorngrenze f

sub[-]boundary — s. a. small-angle grain boundary

subcadmium — subcadmisch, subkadmisch

subcapillary [interstice] — Subkapillare f

subcarrier [frequency] — Hilfsträger m, Subcarrier m, Subträger m, Sekundärträger m, Hilfsträgerfrequenz f, Unterträger m

subcentre ⟨astr.⟩ — Nebenradiant m ⟨Astr.⟩

subcentre — s. a. sub[-]latent centre

subcentre [of development] — Tiefenzentrum n [der Entwicklung]

subcircuit, branch circuit — Nebenkreis m, Nebenstromkreis m; Teilschaltung f

subclass number, cell frequency — Klassenbesetzung f

subcoat — s. sublayer

subcollection — s. subset ⟨math.⟩

subcooled boiling — unterkühltes Sieden n

subcooled boiling, surface boiling — Oberflächensieden n

subcooled boiling, local boiling — örtliches Sieden n, lokales Sieden

subcooling — s. supercooling

subcooling heat, supercooling heat, heat of subcooling (supercooling) — Unterkühlungswärme f

subcooling refrigerating effect — Unterkühlungs-Kühleffekt m, Unterkühlungs-Kühlwirkung f

subcosmic radiation, subcosmic rays — subkosmische Strahlung f

subcritical ⟨nucl.⟩ — unterkritisch, subkritisch ⟨Kern.⟩

subcritical assembly — unterkritische Anordnung f, subkritische Anordnung

subcritical damping, underdamping — unterkritische Dämpfung f, Unterdämpfung f

subcritical flow — unterkritische Strömung f

subcritical flow — s. a. tranquil flow ⟨hydr.⟩

subcritical multiplication — unterkritische Multiplikation f, subkritische Multiplikation

subcritical multiplication factor	Quell[en]verstärkung f, unterkritischer Multiplikationsfaktor m
subcritical nuclear chain reaction, convergent nuclear chain reaction	konvergente Kernkettenreaktion f, unterkritische Kernkettenreaktion
subcritical pressure	unterkritischer Druck m
subcritical state of flow	unterkritischer Strömungszustand m
subcritical velocity <hydr.>	Unterschwallgeschwindigkeit f <Hydr.>
subcritical velocity of flow	unterkritische Strömungsgeschwindigkeit f
subcrustal	subkrustal
subcutaneous, s.c. <geo., bio.>	subkutan <Geo., Bio.>
subdeterminant, minor, minor determinant	Unterdeterminante f, [komplementärer] Minor m, Subdeterminante f
subdiagonal matrix, lower triangular matrix	untere Halbmatrix f
subdichromatism	Subdichromasie f
subdivided <math.>	unterteilt <Math.>
subdividing comparator, longitudinal comparator	Longitudinalkomparator m
subdivision, partition, segmentation, sectionalization	Unterteilung f
subdivision, division <math.>	Unterteilung f <Math.>
subdivision of potential	Potentialaufteilung f
subdivision of the current, current division	Stromteilung f
subdomain	Teilbereich m
subdomain, sub-domain, partial domain, subregion <math.>	Untergebiet n, Unterbereich m, Teilgebiet n, Teilbereich m <Math.>
subduing	s. dimming <of light>
sub-dwarf [star]	Unterzwerg m
subfield	Unterkörper m
subflare, microflare	Supereruption f, Mikroeruption f
subformant	Unterformant m
subfreezing temperature	s. subzero temperature
subfrequency	s. subharmonic frequency
sub-giant [star]	Unterriese m, Untergigant m
subglacial moraine	s. ground moraine
sub[-]grain, minus material	Subkorn n
sub-grain boundary	s. small-angle grain boundary
subgrain formation	Subkornbildung f
subgroup <math.>	Untergruppe f, Teiler m der Gruppe, Subgruppe f <Math.>
subgroup	s. a. B subgroup <chem.>
subgroup	s. a. subassembly <el.>
subharmonic, subharmonic oscillation, subharmonic vibration; subharmonic tone	subharmonische Schwingung f [von der Ordnung n], Subharmonische f, [harmonische] Unterschwingung f, Unterharmonische f; Unterton m, subharmonischer Ton m
subharmonic frequency, subfrequency, submultiple frequency	subharmonische Frequenz f, Unterfrequenz f
subharmonic function	subharmonische Funktion f
subharmonic oscillation	s. subharmonic
subharmonic series	subharmonische Reihe f
subharmonic tone	s. subharmonic
subharmonic vibration	s. subharmonic
subhydric soil, underwater soil	Unterwasserboden m, subhydrischer Boden m
sub-image	s. latent image
subinterval	Teilintervall n
subintrusion	Subintrusion f
subject contrast	Objektkontrast m
subject distance	Objektabstand m
subjective brightness, luminosity, brightness, brilliance, brilliancy <US>	Helligkeit f, Eindruckshelligkeit f, Helligkeitseindruck m, subjektive Helligkeit
subjective brightness	s. a. lightness <of surface colour>
subjective combination sound	subjektiver Kombinationston m
subjective noise meter	subjektiver Lautstärkemesser m
subjective photometer, visual photometer	visuelles (subjektives) Photometer n
subjective photometry, visual photometry	visuelle Photometrie f, subjektive Photometrie
subjective probability	s. personal probability
subjective spectrophotometer, visual spectrophotometer	visuelles Spektralphotometer n, subjektives Spektralphotometer
subject range, range of subject contrast	Objektumfang m
subject range method, method of subject range	Objektumfangmethode f
sublaminar	sublaminar
sub[-]latent centre, subcentre	Subkeim m, sublatentes Zentrum n
sublation	Sublation f
sublattice	Untergitter n, Teilgitter n
sublattice <math.>	Teilverband m <Math.>
sublayer, subcoat	Unterschicht f
sublethal dose	subletale Dosis f
sublevel	Unterniveau n, Teilniveau n
sublimability	Sublimierbarkeit f
sublimate	Sublimat n
sublimating	s. sublimation
sublimation; subliming, sublimating, deposition	Sublimation f; Sublimieren n
sublimation, distillation, volatilization, vaporization	Destillation f, Destillieren n, Siedetrennung f
sublimation adiabatic	Sublimationsadiabate f
sublimation centre, sublimation nucleus	Sublimationskern m, Sublimationskeim m, Sublimationszentrum n
sublimation curve, curve of sublimation; hoar-frost line	Sublimationskurve f, Sublimationslinie f, Sublimationsdruckkurve f
sublimation enthalpy	s. [latent] heat of sublimation
sublimation heat	s. [latent] heat of sublimation
sublimation interval, sublimation limits	Sublimationsgebiet n, Sublimationsbereich m
sublimation nucleus, sublimation centre	Sublimationskern m, Sublimationskeim m, Sublimationszentrum n
sublimation point (temperature), temperature of sublimation, point of sublimation	Sublimationstemperatur f, Sublimationspunkt m, Sbp.
sublimation pressure	Sublimationsdruck m
sublimation temperature	s. sublimation point
subliminal, subthreshold	unterschwellig
subliminal stimulus	unterschwelliger Reiz m
subliming	s. sublimation
sublinear	sublinear
sublittoral	sublitoral
sub-load; partial load	Teillast f, Teilbelastung f
submanifold	Untermannigfaltigkeit f, Teilmannigfaltigkeit f
submarine earthquake, seaquake	Seebeben n
submarine microphone	s. hydrophone
submarine relief	submarines Relief n, unterseeisches Relief, untermeerisches Relief

submarine | | | | 838

submarine ridge	s. submerged ridge	subordinate resonance, secondary resonance; spurious resonance; spurious response	Nebenresonanz f
submarine slope	Meereshalde f; Seehalde f		
submarine valley	submarines Tal n, unterseeisches Tal, unterseeische Talung f	subordinate series, secondary series	Nebenserie f
submatrix, partial matrix	Untermatrix f, Teilmatrix f	subpermafrost water	Niefrostbodenwasser n
submaximum, secondary maximum, subsidiary maximum <e.g. of light curve>	Nebenmaximum n <z. B. Lichtkurve>	subphotospheric	subphotosphärisch
		subpolar	subpolar
submerged	untergetaucht	subpressure	s. underpressure
submerged area	s. overflow area	subproblem, partial problem	Teilproblem n
submerged ridge, submarine ridge	submariner (untermeerischer) Rücken m, Untermeeresrücken m, unterseeischer Rücken, Unterseerücken m	subprogram[me]	s. subroutine
		subproportional reducer	subproportionaler Abschwächer m, unterproportionaler Abschwächer
submerged spring, subaqueous spring; drowned spring	untermeerische (unterseeische) Quelle f, Untermeeresquelle f, Unterseequelle f	subrange, sub-band <meas.>	Unterbereich m <Meß.>
		subrefraction, substandard refraction	Subrefraktion f, Infrabrechung f, unternormale Brechung f
submerged weir, drowned weir; dam on bed of river, non-overflow dam	Grundwehr n [mit gewelltem Strahl]; Grundwasserwehr n; unvollkommener Überfall m	subregion; subzone	Subregion f; Subzone f, Teilzone f
		subregion	s. a. subdomain <math.>
		subresonance, partial resonance	Teilresonanz f, Unterresonanz f, Subresonanz f
submergence, submersion	Untertauchen n, Eintauchen n	subring	Unterring m, Teilring m
		subrosion, suffosion, underground leaching <geo.>	Subrosion f, Suffosion f, unterirdische Auslaugung f <Geo.>
submergence, depth of immersion (penetration), immersion depth	Eintauchtiefe f, Tauchtiefe f		
submergible taintor gate dam	Sektorwehr n	subroutine; subprogram[me]	Unterprogramm n
		subsatellite	Subsatellit m
submersion, submergence	Untertauchen n, Eintauchen n	subscript, lower index	unterer Index m
submersion	s. a. sinking[-down]	subsequence	Teilfolge f
submicroanalysis, submicrogram[me] analysis	s. submicroscopic analysis		
submicrogram[me] method (technique)	s. submicroscopic technique	subsequent adjustment, alignment of tuned circuit	Nachstimmung f
		subsequent river (stream)	subsequenter Fluß m, Nachfolgefluß m
submicron	Submikron n, Ultramikron n	subsequent treatment, additional treatment, after-treatment	Nachbehandlung f; Nachbearbeitung f
submicron realm, submicroscopic realm	submikroskopischer Bereich m, Submikronbereich m		
submicroscopic analysis, submicroanalysis, submicrogram[me] analysis	Submikroanalyse f, submikroskopische Analyse f, Nanogrammethode f <10⁻⁹ ··· 10⁻⁸ g>	subseries	Teilreihe f
		subset, sub-aggregate, subcollection, part <math.>	Untermenge f, Teilmenge f, Teil m <Math.>
submicroscopic realm, submicron realm	submikroskopischer Bereich m, Submikronbereich m	subshell <nucl.>	Unterschale f, Zwischenschale f <Kern.>
submicroscopic technique, submicro technique, submicrogram[me] method (technique)	Submikromethode f	subsidence, atmospheric subsidence	atmosphärisches Absinken n, Absinken der Luftmasse
		subsidence	s. a. depression <of land>
submicrowave	Submikrowelle f	subsidence earthquake	s. earthquake due to collapse
submillimetre wave	Submillimeterwelle f	subsidence inversion	Schrumpfungsinversion f, Absinkinversion f, Subsidenzinversion f
submineering	s. subminiature construction		
sub[-]miniature [component]	Subminiaturbauteil n	subsidiary absorption	Nebenabsorption f
subminiature construction; subminiature engineering, submineering	Subminiaturtechnik f; Subminiaturbauweise f	subsidiary glide system	Nebengleitsystem n
		subsidiary line	s. by-pass <therm., el.>
		subsidiary maximum, secondary maximum, submaximum <e.g. of light curve>	Nebenmaximum n <z. B. Lichtkurve>
subminiature tube (valve), midget tube, midget valve	Subminiaturröhre f, Gnomröhre f, Kleinröhre f		
submonoid	Submonoid n		
submonolayer	Submonoschicht f	subsidiary quantity, auxiliary quantity	Hilfsgröße f
submultiple <math.>	Bruchteil m, Submultiplum n <Math.>		
submultiple frequency	s. subharmonic frequency	subsidiary valence force	s. secondary valence force
submultiplet	Submultiplett n	subsidiary variable, auxiliary variable	Hilfsvariable f, Hilfsveränderliche f
subnival climate	subnivales Klima n	subsoil, C horizon <geo.>	Untergrund m, C-Horizont m <Geo.>
subnormal	Subnormale f		
subnormal, substandard	unternormal		
subnormal discharge	s. subnormal glow discharge		
subnormal glow discharge, subnormal discharge	subnormale Glimmentladung f, subnormale Entladung f, unternormale Entladung	subsoil coefficient	Untergrundkoeffizient m
		subsoil flow	s. seepage flow
		subsoil source, subsoil spring	Untergrundquelle f
subnuclear	subnuklear	subsoil water	s. underground water
subordinate line	Nebenlinie f	subsolar point	Subsolarpunkt m

subsolid	s. semi[-]colloid	**substitution** <math.>	Substitution f; Substituierung f; Einsetzung f; Ersetzung f <Math.>
subsolifluction	Subsolifluktion f, submarine Rutschung f	**substitution** <meas.>	Substitution f <Meß.>
subsonic	Unterschall-, subsonisch	**substitutional alloy**	Substitutionslegierung f
subsonic	s. a. subaudio	**substitutional compound**	Substitutionsverbindung f
subsonic aerodynamics, subsonics	Unterschallaerodynamik f		
subsonic edge, subsonic ridge	Unterschallkante f	**substitutional impurity**	Substitutionsstörstelle f
subsonic flow, flow at subsonic velocity	Unterschallströmung f	**substitutional isomerism**	s. position isomerism
subsonic frequency	s. subaudio frequency	**substitutional phosphor**	Substitutionsphosphor m, Substitutionsleuchtstoff m
subsonic frequency region	s. subsonic region		
subsonic jet	Unterschallstrahl m	**substitutional position**	Substitutionslage f
subsonic part [of the profile]	Unterschallteil m [des Profils]	**substitutional site**	Substitutionsplatz m
		substitutional site	s. a. vacant site <cryst.>
subsonic potential flow	Unterschall-Potentialströmung f	**substitutional solid solution, substitutional solution**	Austauschmischkristall m, Substitutionsmischkristall m
subsonic range; subsonic region	Unterschallbereich m, subsonischer Bereich m, Unterschallgebiet n, subsonisches Gebiet n	**substitution Borda weighing,** substitution weighing, weighing by substitution	Substitutionswägung f
subsonic range, subsonic regime	Unterschallbereich m, Unterschallregime n	**substitution conduction**	Substitutionsleitung f
subsonic region	s. subsonic range	**substitution conductivity**	Substitutionsleitfähigkeit f
subsonic region	s. a. infrasonic region	**substitution group** <math.>	Substitutionsgruppe f <Math.>
subsonic ridge, subsonic edge	Unterschallkante f	**substitution lattice**	Einsatzgitter n
subsonics	s. subsonic aerodynamics	**substitution method,** Borda['s] method <of weighing>	Substitutionsmethode f [nach Borda], Tariermethode f [nach Borda], Tarierverfahren n <Wägung>
subsonic speed, subacoustic speed; subsonic velocity	Unterschallgeschwindigkeit f		
subsonic velocity	s. subsonic speed	**substitution method of photometry**	Substitutionsmethode f der Photometrie
subsonic whistle	Unterschallpfeife f		
subsonic wind tunnel	Unterschallwindkanal m	**substitution of the variable**	s. change of the variable
subspace	Unterraum m, Teilraum m	**substitution product,** substitute	Substitutionsprodukt n
substance; material; matter; mass	Stoff m; Werkstoff m; Substanz f; Material n; Masse f	**substitution tensor**	s. unit tensor
substance poisoning an enzyme, poison of enzyme; enzyme inactivator; enzyme inhibitor	Fermentgift n, Fermenthemmstoff m, Fermentinhibitor m	**substitution weighing,** substitution Borda weighing	Substitutionswägung f
		substoichiometric analysis	substöchiometrische Analyse f
substance used for the filling of thermometer	s. thermometric substance	**substrate** <bio.>	Substrat n; Trägersubstanz f, Träger m; Nährsubstrat n <Bio.>
substandard	Substandard m	**substrate**	s. a. substratum <phot.>
substandard, subnormal	unternormal	**substratosphere,** tropopause, upper inversion, lower stratosphere	Tropopause f, obere Inversion f, Substratosphäre f; substratosphärische Inversion
substandard propagation	Unterreichweite f		
substandard refraction, subrefraction	Subrefraktion f, Infrabrechung f, unternormale Brechung f	**substratum,** substrate <phot.>	Unterguß m, Substratschicht f, Haftschicht f, Präparation f, Substrat n <Phot.>
substantial acceleration, material acceleration	substantielle Beschleunigung f		
		substratum <stat.>	Unterschicht f <Stat.>
substantial constant	substantielle Konstante f	**substratum**	s. a. intermediate layer
substantial co-ordinates	s. material co-ordinates	**sub[-]structure**	Unterstruktur f
substantial derivative	s. material derivative	**substructure**	s. a. mosaic structure
substantiation	Objektivierung f	**subsurface carrier density, subsurface concentration**	s. subsurface density
substantive dye, direct dye	Direktfarbstoff m, substantiver Farbstoff m, Substantivfarbstoff m, direktziehender Farbstoff	**subsurface corrosion,** poultice corrosion, undermining corrosion; underfilm corrosion	Unterwanderungserscheinung f, Unterwanderungsschaden m, Unterschichtkorrosion f
substate	Unterzustand m, Teilzustand m	**subsurface defect**	innerer Fehler m, innerer Werkstoffehler m
substituend	Substituend m		
substituent	Substituent m	**subsurface density,** subsurface carrier density, subsurface concentration	„subsurface"-Dichte f [der Ladungsträger], oberflächennahe Dichte f
substitute, substitution product, derivative	Substitutionsprodukt n		
substituted by an isotope, isotopically replaced, isotopically substituted, replaced by an isotope	isotopensubstituiert	**subsurface float,** composite float, ball and line float, depth float, double float	Tiefenschwimmer m, Tiefschwimmer m
substitute t-test, G-test	Spannweite-t-Test m, G-Test m	**subsurface flow,** underflow; undercurrent, underset current	Unterströmung f, Unterstrom m; Grundströmung f; Bodenströmung f
substituting group <chem.>	Substitutionsgruppe f <Chem.>		
substitution, replacement	Austausch m, Ersatz m, Ersetzung f, Substitution f, Substituierung f	**subsurface flow,** subsurface runoff, subsoil flow, seepage flow; base flow	Sickerströmung f; unterirdischer Abfluß m
substitution; displacement	Verdrängung f		
substitution, replacement <chem.>	Substitution f <Chem.>	**subsurface ice**	s. fossile ice
		subsurface runoff	s. subsurface flow

subsurface | **840**

subsurface water	s. underground water	subzone; subregion	Subregion f; Subzone f, Teilzone f
subsurface wave <geo.>	s. bodily seismic wave	succession	s. order of sequence
subsynchronous, undersynchronous, hyposynchronous	untersynchron, subsynchron	succession of crystallization	Kristallisationsfolge f, Sukzession f der Kristalle
subsynchronous resonance	untersynchrone Resonanz f	successive approximation, stepwise approximation, iteration; iterating	sukzessive Approximation f, schrittweise Näherung f, Iteration f; Iterieren n
subsystem	Teilsystem n		
subsystem	Systemgruppe f		
subsystem <astr.>	Untersystem n <Astr.>	successive colour contrast	s. successive contrast of colour
subtangent	Subtangente f	successive contrast	Sukzessivkontrast m, Nachkontrast m, sukzessiver Kontrast m
subterranean current, (flow, stream), underground current, underground stream, underground flow	unterirdischer Strom m, unterirdische Strömung f	successive contrast of colour, successive colour contrast	farbiger Sukzessivkontrast m, sukzessiver Farbkontrast m
subterranean water	s. underground water		
subthermal	unterthermisch	successive emission	sukzessive Emission f, sukzessive Strahlung f
subthreshold, subliminal	unterschwellig		
subthreshold dose	unterschwellige Dosis f	successive gamma-rays, cascade gamma-rays	Kaskaden-Gamma-Strahlung f, Gamma-Quantenemission f in einer Kaskade
subtotal; intermediate result	Zwischenergebnis n		
subtracter	s. subtractor	successive glare	Sukzessivblendung f
subtraction circuit	Subtraktionsschaltung f	successive integration	sukzessive Integration f
subtraction crystal (lattice)	Subtraktionskristall m, Subtraktionsgitter n	successive substitution method	Methode f der sukzessiven Substitution, sukzessive Substitution f
subtraction position	Subtraktionsstellung f	successive reaction	s. consequent reaction
subtraction sign	s. minus sign	sucker; suctorial disk; suction cup	Saugnapf m, Haftscheibe f, Gummisauger m
subtraction spectrometer	Subtraktionsspektrometer n	sucking	s. suction
subtraction spectrum, subtractive spectrum	Subtraktionsspektrum n	sucking away the boundary layer, suck off of boundary layer, boundary layer suction, suction of [laminar] boundary layer	Absaugen n der Grenzschicht, Grenzschichtabsaugung f
subtractive colouration	subtraktive Verfärbung f		
subtractive colour mixture	s. subtractive mixture		
subtractive colour process	subtraktives Verfahren n	sucking up	s. suction
subtractive colour system	subtraktives Farbensystem n	suck off of boundary layer	s. sucking away of boundary layer
subtractive mixture [of colours], subtractive colour mixture, subtractive synthesis	subtraktive Farbmischung f, multiplikative Farbmischung	suction, absorption, sucking [up], imbibition	Aufsaugen n, Aufnahme f; Einsaugung f; Absorption f
		suction <e.g. of gases, harmonics>	Absaugen n <z. B. von Gasen, Oberwellen>
subtractive reducer, cutting reducer	subtraktiver Abschwächer m		
		suction; pull <aero.>	Sog m
subtractive spectrum, subtraction spectrum	Subtraktionsspektrum n		
subtractive synthesis	s. subtractive mixture	suction; sucking; aspiration; drawing-in <of pump>	Saugen n, Ansaugen n
subtractor, subtracter, sub	Subtraktionsgerät n, Subtraktionseinheit f		
subtract pulse	Subtraktionsimpuls m, Subtrahierimpuls m	suction	s. a. underpressure
		suction anode	Sauganode f
subtrahend	Subtrahend m	suction circuit	s. absorption circuit <el.>
subtransient reactance	subtransitorische Reaktanz f, Subtransientreaktanz f, Anfangsreaktanz f	suction cup; suctorial disk; sucker	Saugnapf m, Haftscheibe f, Gummisauger m
		suction current, suction stream	Saugströmung f, Saugen n
subtropical calm belt, subtropical calms	Roßbreiten pl		
		suction filter	Saugfilter n
		suction filter, glass filter funnel	Glasfilternutsche f
		suction flask	Saugflasche f, Absaugflasche f
subtropical region; subtropical zone, subtropics, semi-tropical zone	Subtropen pl, subtropische Zone f	suction force, suction tension, suction potential, water pressure deficit	Saugkraft f, Saugspannung f, Saugpotential n
sub-unit	s. subassembly <el.>		
subvelocity of light, velocity (speed) lower than that of light	Unterlichtgeschwindigkeit f	suction force of the soil, soil suction force	Saugkraft f des Bodens, Bodensaugkraft f
		suction gauge	Saugmanometer n, Saugmesser m
subwave, evanescent wave <opt.>	Subwelle f, [optische] Oberflächenwelle f <Opt.>	suction height (lift)	s. height of lift
		suction line, suction pipeline, suction pipes, intake line	Saugleitung f, Saugrohrleitung f
subwave; partial wave; partial mode	Teilwelle f, Partialwelle f		
subzero temperature, subfreezing temperature, temperature below 0 °C	Temperatur f unter Null, Temperatur unter 0 °C, Minustemperatur f		

suction of [laminar] boundary layer	s. sucking away the boundary layer
suction pipe, suction tube	Saugrohr n, Saugröhre f
suction pipeline	s. suction line
suction pipes	s. suction line
suction potential	s. suction force
suction pressure, intake pressure	Saugdruck m; Ansaugdruck m
suction pump, aspiring pump	Saugpumpe f, Absaugpumpe f
suction pyrometer, high velocity thermocouple <US>, high velocity pyrometer <US>	Ansaugepyrometer n, Aspirationspyrometer n
suction side, inlet side	Saugseite f, Saugende n
suction side of the airfoil, upper surface of the airfoil, low pressure surface	Flügeloberseite f, Oberseite f des Tragflügels
suction stream, suction current	Saugströmung f, Saugen n
suction stroke	s. intake stroke
suction tension	s. suction force
suction tube	s. suction pipe
suction-type cornice	Sogwächter f
suctorial disk; suction cup; sucker; vacuum cup	Saugnapf m, Haftscheibe f, Gummisauger m
sudden; jump-like; stepped, step-like; discontinuous; unsteady	sprunghaft; diskontinuierlich
sudden break in weather	s. rapid change of weather
sudden change of load	s. impact load
sudden change of the wind, reversal of wind	Umspringen n des Windes; Umschlagen n des Windes; Umschwenken n des Windes
sudden cosmic noise absorption, S.C.N.A.	plötzliche Verminderung f des kosmischen Störpegels, Sonneneruptionseffekt m im kosmischen Störpegel
sudden disappearance [of a filament], S.D.F.	plötzliche Auflösung f [eines Filaments]
sudden drop	s. sudden fall
sudden enhancement of atmospherics, S.E.A.	plötzliche Erhöhung f des atmosphärischen Störpegels, Sonneneruptionseffekt m im atmosphärischen Störpegel
sudden fall, sudden drop, great fall, fall, plunge, tumbling	Sturz m
sudden fall of temperature	Temperatursturz m
sudden increase of cosmic-ray intensity, cosmic-ray jet	Höhenstrahlungseruption f, Höhenstrahlungsausbruch m, Ausbruch m der kosmischen Strahlung
sudden ionospheric disturbance	s. radio fade-out
sudden load	s. impact load
sudden phase anomaly, S.P.A.	plötzliche Phasenanomalie f, Sonneneruptionseffekt m im Langwellenbereich
sudden phase shift, phase jump	Phasensprung m
sudden push	s. jerk
sudden short wave fade-out	s. radio fade-out
Suess effect	Suess-Effekt m
sufficiency <math.>	Hinlänglichkeit f <Math.>; Suffizienz f <Stat.>
sufficient <math.>	hinreichend
sufficient estimate	erschöpfende Schätzung f
sufficient statistic	erschöpfende Größe f
suffosion	s. subrosion
sugar content, sugariness	Zuckergehalt m
sugar degree, degree of the International Sugar Scale, degree sugar, °S	Grad n der internationalen Zuckerskala, internationaler Zuckergrad m, Zuckergrad, Grad Sugar, °S
sugariness, sugar content	Zuckergehalt m
sugar refractometer	Zuckerrefraktometer n
SU(3) [group] <also: SU(2), SU(6) etc.>	SU(3)[-Gruppe] f <auch: SU(2)-, SU(6)- usw.>
Suhl effect	Suhl-Effekt m
Suhl-Nakamura interaction	Suhl-Nakamura-Wechselwirkung f
suitable for tropical climate (service)	s. tropicalized
sulphur point, boiling point of sulphur, point of boiling sulphur	Schwefelpunkt m, Siedepunkt m des Schwefels
sultriness	Schwüle f
sum, logical sum, joint, union <of sets>, sum-set	Vereinigungsmenge f, Vereinigung f, Summe f <von Mengen>
sum Compton spectrum	Compton-Summenspektrum n
sum curve, sum line, summation (summary) curve	Summenlinie f, Summenkurve f
summability	Summierbarkeit f
summarizing	s. tabulation
summary curve	s. sum curve
summated current, integrated current	Integralstrom m, Integralstromstärke f
summated voltage, integrated voltage	Integralspannung f
summational invariant, collisional invariant	Summationsinvariante f
summation band	Summationsbande f
summation by parts	s. Abel['s] identity
summation check	Summenprobe f
summation convention [of Einstein], Einstein['s] summation convention, Einstein['s] convention, dummy suffix notation, dummy suffix summation convention	Einsteinsche Summationsbezeichnung (Summation) f, Einstein-Summation f, Einsteinsche Summationskonvention f, Summationskonvention [von Einstein], Einsteinsche Summenkonvention f, Summenkonvention [von Einstein], Einsteinsche Konvention f [für die Summation], Einstein-Konvention f [für die Summation], Einsteinsche Summierungsvorschrift f, Summierungsvorschrift [von Einstein], Einsteinsche Summationsvorschrift f, Summationsvorschrift [von Einstein], Summationsübereinkunft f [von Einstein], Einsteinsche Summationsübereinkunft (Festlegung f)
summation curve	s. sum curve
summation dummy; dummy, dummy index, umbral index, umbral suffix, saturated index <of tensor>	Summationsindex m
summation formula	Summationsformel f
summation instrument, summing instrument	summierendes Meßgerät n
summation loudness, overall loudness	Gesamtlautstärke f, Summenlautstärke f
summation method, method of summation <math.>	Summationsverfahren n, Summationsmethode f, Limitierungsverfahren n, Summierungsverfahren n <Math.>
summation potential	Summationspotential n
summation tone	Summationston m, Summenton m
summative fractionation	summative Fraktionierung f

summerday	Sommertag *m*	sunlit aurora	sonnenbeschienenes Polarlicht *n*
summer half-year	Sommerhalbjahr *n*	Sun periscope, solar periscope	Sonnenperiskop *n*, Sonnenkammer *f*
summer lightning, sheet lightning, heat lightning	Wetterleuchten *n*	sun-pillar, Sun pillar	*s.* vertical pillar
summer solstice, June solstice	Sommersolstitium *n*, Sommersonnenwende *f*	sunrise colours, sunrise glow	Morgenrot *n*
summing coincidence spectrometer	*s.* sum-peak spectrometer	sunrise effect	Sonnenaufgangseffekt *m*, Einfluß *m* des Sonnenaufgangs
summing instrument	*s.* summation instrument	sunrise glow	*s.* sunrise colours
summing point	*s.* error detector <control>	Sun's altitude	Sonnenstand *m*, Sonnenhöhe *f*
summit, peak [value], crest [value] <US>, apex <gen.>	Scheitelwert *m*, Gipfelwert *m*, Scheitel *m* <allg.>	Sun's anomalistic inequality, solar anomalistic inequality, Sun's elliptical inequality, solar elliptical inequality, elliptical inequality	solare anomalistische Ungleichheit *f*, solare elliptische Ungleichheit, elliptische Ungleichheit
summit pond (pool, reach)	Scheitelhaltung *f*		
Sumner line, position line, line of position	Positionslinie *f*, Standlinie *f*	Sun's corona, solar corona, corona [of the sun]	Sonnenkorona *f*, Korona *f* [der Sonne]
sum of precipitation	Niederschlagssumme *f*	Sun's daily inequality	*s.* diurnal solar inequality
sum of products [of deviations from the mean]	Produktsumme *f*	Sun's depression, solar depression [angle]	Sonnendepression *f*
sum of relative atomic masses	Summe *f* der relativen Atommassen, Atomgewichtssumme *f*		
sum of squares, squariance	Quadratsumme *f*, Summe *f* der Abweichungsquadrate	Sun's disk, solar disk	Sonnenscheibe *f*
sum of squares between samples (treatments)	Quadratsumme *f* zwischen den Klassen, Summe *f* der Abweichungsquadrate zwischen den Gruppen	Sun's diurnal inequality	*s.* diurnal solar inequality
		sunseeker, sun follower	Sonnensucher *m*
sum of squares within samples (treatments)	Quadratsumme *f* innerhalb der Klassen, Summe *f* der Abweichungsquadrate innerhalb der Gruppen	Sun's elliptical inequality	*s.* Sun's anomalistic inequality
		sunset colours, sunset glow	Abendrot *n*
sum of temperatures, temperature sum	Temperatursumme *f*	sun shade, lens hood, lens shade, lens shield	Lichtkappe *f* [des Objektivs]; Sonnenblende *f*, Sonnenschutz *m*; Gegenlichtblende *f*
sum of the digits, total of the digits <of the number>	Quersumme *f*		
		sunshine	Sonnenschein *m*
sum of the system of vectors, single vector, resultant vector	Einzelvektor *m*, resultierender Einzelvektor	sunshine	*s. a.* sunlight
		sunshine recorder, heliograph	Heliograph *m*, Sonnenscheinautograph *m*, Sonnenscheinschreiber *m*
sum of tristimulus values	*s.* tristimulus sum		
Sumoto effect	Sumoto-Effekt *m*	sunshine unit, strontium unit, s.u., pCi/g Ca	Strontiumeinheit *f*, Sunshine-Einheit *f*, S. U., pCi/g Ca
sum over states, sum-over-states, partition function, zustandssumme, state sum <therm.>	Zustandssumme *f* [von Planck], Plancksche Zustandssumme, Verteilungsfunktion *f* <Therm.>		
		sunside	*s.* sunward side
		Sun's limp	*s.* solar limp
sum over time, time sum	Zeitsumme *f*	Sun's parallax, solar parallax	Sonnenparallaxe *f*
sump <of the column>	Sumpf *m* <Kolonne>	sun[-]spot	Sonnenfleck *m* <*pl.*: -ecke>
		sunspot activity	Sonnenfleckentätigkeit *f*, Fleckentätigkeit *f*, Sonnenfleckenaktivität *f*, Fleckenaktivität *f*
sum-peak spectrometer, [integral bias] summing coincidence spectrometer	Summenkoinzidenzspektrometer *n*	sunspot curve	Sonnenfleckenkurve *f*
Sumptner['s] principle	Sumptnersches Prinzip *n*	sunspot cycle, sunspots cycle, sunspots period, period of sunspots	Sonnenfleckenzyklus *m*, Fleckenzyklus *m*, Sonnenfleckenperiode *f*, Fleckenperiode *f*
sum rule, rule of sums	Summenregel *f* <Opt., Rel.>, Summensatz *m* <Opt.>		
sum spectrum	Summenspektrum *n*	sunspot frequency	Sonnenfleckenhäufigkeit *f*, Fleckenhäufigkeit *f*
sun-air temperature	Sonnenlufttemperatur *f*	sunspot prominence, spot prominence	Fleckenprotuberanz *f*
sunburn	Sonnenbrand *m*		
S.U.N. Committee; Committee on Symbols, Units and Nomenclature [in Physics]	Kommission *f* für Symbole, Einheiten und Nomenklatur [in der Physik]; SUN-Kommission *f*	sunspots cycle	*s.* sunspot cycle
		sunspots maximum	Sonnenfleckenmaximum *n*, Fleckenmaximum *n*
		sunspots minimum	Sonnenfleckenminimum *n*, Fleckenminimum *n*
sun compass, solar compass, dial compass	Sonnenkompaß *m*	sunspots number	Sonnenfleckenzahl *f*, Fleckenzahl *f*
		sunspot spectrum	Sonnenfleckenspektrum *n*, Fleckenspektrum *n*
sundial, sun dial, dial	Sonnenuhr *f*	sunspots period	*s.* sunspot cycle
sundial time; apparent solar time, true solar time	wahre Sonnenzeit *f*; wahre Ortszeit *f*	sun-type star, G star, solar star	G-Stern *m*, Sonnenähnlicher *m*
sun-dog, parhelion, mocksun	Nebensonne *f*	Sun['s] vertical [circle]	Sonnenvertikal *m*
Sun-Earth relationship, solar-terrestrial relationship (phenomenon), terrestrial effect of solar activity	solar-terrestrische Erscheinung *f*	sunward, directed towards the Sun	zur Sonne gerichtet, der Sonne zugewandt
		sunward side, sunside	Sonnenseite *f*, Tagseite *f*
		sup	*s.* least upper bound
sun follower, sunseeker	Sonnensucher *m*	superacceptor	Superakzeptor *m*
sunlight, sunshine	Sonnenlicht *n*	superacoustic	*s.* ultrasonic
sunlit	sonnenbeschienen, sonnenbeleuchtet, tagseitig	superadditivity	Superadditivität *f*
		superadiabatic	überadiabatisch

superaerodynamics, molecular aerodynamics, rarefied gas dynamics	Supraaerodynamik f, Superaerodynamik f, Molekularaerodynamik f, Dynamik f der stark verdünnten Gase, Nichtkontinuumsströmung f mit Höchstgeschwindigkeit	**supercooled rain droplet**	s. supercooled droplet
		supercooled state	s. supercooling
		supercooled vapour	s. supersaturated vapour
		supercooling, supercooled state ‹below equilibrium temperature of phase transition›; subcooling ‹below condensation temperature›; undercooling	Unterkühlung f
superallowed transition, favoured [forbidden] transition	übererlaubter (supererlaubter, erleichterter, begünstigter) Übergang m		
superaperiodic	überaperiodisch	**supercooling heat,** subcooling heat, heat of subcooling (supercooling)	Unterkühlungswärme f
superatmospheric pressure	s. superpressure		
superaudibility frequency	s. superaudible frequency	**supercooling pressure**	Unterkühlungsdruck m
superaudible	s. ultrasonic	**supercooling temperature,** temperature of supercooling	Unterkühlungstemperatur f
superaudible (superaudio) frequency, superaudibility frequency	Überhörfrequenz f, Übertonfrequenz f		
		super cosmic radiation (rays), super cosmic radiation	ultraharte kosmische Strahlung f, superkosmische Strahlung, kosmische Strahlung höchster Energie, Höchstenergie-Höhenstrahlung f
superaudio frequency	s. a. ultrasonic frequency		
superbang	Superknall m		
superbolide, giant bolide	Überbolid m, Riesenmeteorit m		
supercapillary [interstice]	Superkapillare f	**supercosmotron**	Superkosmotron n
		supercritical	überkritisch; superkritisch
supercavitation	Superkavitation f		
supercentrifuge	s. ultracentrifuge	**supercritical damping,** overdamping	überkritische Dämpfung f, Überdämpfung f
supercharger	Vorverdichter m		
supercharging; precompression	Vorverdichtung f		
super chopper	ultraschneller Chopper m		
		supercritical flow	überkritische Strömung f
supercirculation	Superzirkulation f		
supercluster	s. supergalaxy		
superconducting; superconductive	supraleitend; supraleitfähig	**supercritical flow**	s. a. shooting flow ‹hydr.›
		supercritical mass	überkritische Masse f
superconducting bolometer	Supraleitungsbolometer n, supraleitendes Bolometer n	**supercritical nuclear chain reaction,** divergent nuclear chain reaction	divergente Kernkettenreaktion f, überkritische Kernkettenreaktion
superconducting critical temperature	s. transition temperature ‹of superconductor›		
superconducting galvanometer	Supraleitungsgalvanometer n, supraleitendes Galvanometer n	**supercritical pressure**	überkritischer Druck m
superconducting quantum interference device, squid	„squid" n	**supercritical state of flow**	überkritischer Strömungszustand m
		supercritical velocity ‹hydr.›	Überschwallgeschwindigkeit f ‹Hydr.›
superconducting state	supraleitender Zustand m, Supraleitungszustand m	**supercritical velocity of flow**	überkritische Strömungsgeschwindigkeit f
superconducting transition, superconductive transition	Supraleitungsübergang m	**supercurrent**	Suprastrom m, Supraleitungsstrom m
superconduction, superconductivity	Supraleitung f, Supraleitfähigkeit f	**supercurrent accelerator**	Höchststrombeschleuniger m
superconduction electron	s. superelectron	**superdeterminated system** ‹mech.›	überbestimmtes System n ‹Mech.›
superconduction model, superconductivity model	Supraleitungsmodell n, Supraleitfähigkeitsmodell n	**superdiagonal matrix**	obere Halbmatrix f
superconduction phenomenon	Supraleitungserscheinung f	**superdirective antenna,** super[-]gain (pencil-beam) antenna	scharfbündelnde Antenne f, Supergainantenne f, „supergain"-Antenne f; Schmalbündelantenne f
superconductive; superconducting	supraleitend; supraleitfähig		
superconductive suspension	supraleitende Suspension f, Supraleitungssuspension f		
superconductive transition, superconducting transition	Supraleitungsübergang m		
superconductivity	Supraleitfähigkeit f	**superdirectivity**	s. supergain
		superdonor	Superdonator m
superconductivity	s. superconduction	**superefficient**	supereffizient
superconductivity model	s. superconduction model	**superelastic**	s. high-elastic[ity]
superconductor ‹of the first or second kind›	Supraleiter m, supraleitender Stoff m, Superleiter m, Überleiter m ‹1. oder 2. Art›	**superelastic collision**	s. collision of the second kind
		superelastic strain, highly elastic strain	hochelastische Verformung f
		superelectron, superconduction electron	Supraleitungselektron n, Supraelektron n
superconvergence	Superkonvergenz f		
superconvergence sum rule	Superkonvergenz-Summenregel f		
supercooled, undercooled	unterkühlt	**superelevation**	s. surmount
		superemitron	s. superorthicon
		superenergy	Superenergie f
supercooled droplet ‹of water, rain›, supercooled rain droplet	unterkühlter Tropfen m, unterkühlter Wassertropfen m, unterkühlter Regentropfen m	**superenergy accelerator,** super-high energy accelerator, super-high accelerator, ultrahigh-energy accelerator, UHE accelerator	Höchstenergiebeschleuniger m, Beschleuniger m für höchste Energien
supercooled liquid, undercooled liquid	unterkühlte Flüssigkeit f		
		supereriscope	s. image iconoscope
		superexchange	s. Kramers['] superexchange

superexchange interaction	Superaustauschwechselwirkung f, indirekte Spinaustauschwechselwirkung (Spinaustauschkopplung) f	superheating of steam, steam superheating	Dampfüberhitzung f, Überhitzung f des Dampfes
superexcitation	s. overexcitation	superheavy element	überschweres Element n, fernes Transuran n
superextended dislocation	s. paired dislocation	superheavy ion	überschweres Ion n
superfast coincidence circuit, coincidence circuit operating in the nanosecond range	Koinzidenzschaltung f im Nanosekundenbereich	superheavy nucleus	überschwerer Kern m
superficial	s. surface	superheterodyne frequency, intermediate frequency, I.F., IF, i.f., if	Zwischenfrequenz f, ZF
superficial activity coefficient	Oberflächen-Aktivitätskoeffizient m	superheterodyne interference, heterodyne interference, self-whistle, heterodyne whistle	Zwischenfrequenzpfeifen n, ZF-Pfeifen n, Überlagerungspfeifen n; Pfeifton m; Pfeifstelle f
superficial area (content)	s. area		
superficial density	s. surface density		
superficial density of the entropy	s. superficial entropy	superheterodyne reception	Superheterodyneempfang m, Superhetempfang m, Mischempfang m, Überlagerungsempfang m, Zwischenfrequenzempfang m, Zwischenempfang m, Transponierempfang m
superficial density of the internal energy, surface energy	Oberflächendichte f der inneren Energie, Oberflächenenergie f		
superficial enthalpy	Oberflächenenthalpie f		
superficial entropy, surface entropy; superficial density of the entropy	Oberflächenentropie f, Oberflächendichte f der Entropie		
		super-high accelerator	s. superenergy accelerator
superficial free energy	s. surface energy	superhigh energy, extra-high energy, very high energy	Höchstenergie f
superficial friction	s. skin friction		
superficial gravity	s. surface gravity		
superficial internal energy	innere Oberflächenenergie f, innere Energie f der Oberfläche	super-high energy accelerator	s. superenergy accelerator
		superhigh energy physics, physics of superhigh energies	Höchstenergiephysik f
superficial number density	Oberflächendichte f der Teilchen		
superficial ray, surface ray	Oberflächenstrahl m	superhigh frequency, superfrequency, S.H.F., SHF, s.h.f., shf <3,000−30,000 Mc/s>	Superhochfrequenz f, Zentimeterwellenfrequenz f, Höchstfrequenz f im Zentimeterwellenbereich, SHF <3 000 ... 30 000 MHz>
superficial reduction, surface reduction	Oberflächenabschwächung f		
superficial velocity	Oberflächengeschwindigkeit f		
superficial velocity	s. a. surface velocity		
superfluid	Supraflüssigkeit f, Superflüssigkeit f	superhigh frequency range, range of superhigh frequency, centimetric wavelength [range], S.H.F. range, S.H.F.	Zentimeterwellenbereich m, Zentimeterbereich m, Zentibereich m, SHF-Bereich m, SHF
superfluid, suprafluid	suprafluid, superfluid; supraflüssig		
superfluid density	suprafluide Dichte f		
superfluidity	Suprafluidität f, Supraflüssigkeit f <Zustand>		
superfluidity onset, onset of superfluidity	Einsetzen n der Suprafluidität	superhigh frequency wave, centimetre wave, S.H.F. wave <1−10 cm>	Zentimeterwelle f <1 ... 10 cm>
superfluid part	suprafluider Anteil m		
superfrequency	s. superhigh frequency		
supergain, superdirectivity	Supergain m, sehr hoher Gewinn m [der Antenne], Supergewinn m	superhigh pulse	übergroßer Impuls m
		superhigh vacuum	s. ultra-high vacuum
super[-]gain antenna	s. superdirective antenna	superhyperfine structure, SHFS	Superhyperfeinstruktur f, SHFS
supergalaxy, metagalaxy, hypergalaxy, supercluster	Metagalaxis f, Hypergalaxis f, Metagalaxie f, Superhaufen m, Supergalaxis f	supericonoscope	s. image iconoscope
		superimposed fluids	s. superposed fluids
		superimposing	s. superimposition
supergene	Supergen n	superimposition, superposition, superposing, superimposing, overlying	Superposition f, Überlagerung f
supergiant [star]	Überriese m, Übergigant m, Supergigant m, Superriese m		
		superimposition, superimposing, superposition	Übereinanderlagerung f, Übereinanderschichtung f, Schichtenlagerung f
superglacial moraine, surface moraine	Obermoräne f		
supergradient wind	Übergradientwind m, übergradientischer Wind m		
supergranulation	Supergranulation f	superimposition; coincidence <math.>	Deckung f <Math.>
supergroup	Übergruppe f, Obergruppe f	superimposition principle	s. principle of superposition
superharmonic function	superharmonische Funktion f	superionic [conductor]	Supraionenleiter m
superheat	Überhitzungswärme f	superior conjunction	obere Konjunktion f
superheat	s. a. superheated steam	superior function	s. original
superheat	s. a. superheating	superior geodesy	höhere Geodäsie f, Erdmessung f
super heat conduction (conductivity)	s. superthermal conduction		
super heat conductor, thermal superconductor	Suprawärmeleiter m, thermischer Supraleiter m	superior limit	s. upper limit
		superior mirage, looming	obere Luftspiegelung f, Luftspiegelung nach oben
superheated region, superheated zone	Überhitzungsgebiet n		
superheated steam; superheated vapour; superheat, overheated steam	Heißdampf m <Wasser>; überhitzter Dampf m	superior mirage on sea	Seegesicht n, Kimmung f
		superior planet, outer planet	äußerer Planet m, oberer Planet
		superior space, original space, object space <math.>	Objektbereich m, Objektraum m, Oberbereich m, Originalbereich m, Originalraum m <Math.>
superheated zone	s. superheated region		
superheating	s. degree of superheating		
superheating, overheating, overheat, superheat	Überhitzung f, Überwärmung f, Wärmestauung f, Wärmestau m	superior voltage, higher voltage	Oberspannung f

superlattice, superlattice structure, superstructure	Überstruktur f, Überstrukturbildung f, Überstrukturgitter n, Übergitter n, übergeordnetes Teilgitter n, übergeordnetes Gitter n
superlattice line; superlattice reflection	Überstrukturlinie f, Überstrukturreflex m
superlattice structure	s. superlattice
superlattice transformation	Überstrukturumwandlung f
superleak	Supraleck n, Superleck n
superlinearity	Superlinearität f
superloading	s. overload
super long-range reception	Überfernempfang m, Überreichweitenempfang m
superluminescence	Superlumineszenz f
super many-time formalism	Supermehrzeitformalismus m, Super-„many-time"-Formalismus m
supermolecule	s. molecule aggregate
supermultiplet, hypermultiplet	Supermultiplett n, Hypermultiplett n
supermultiplet theory	Supermultipletttheorie f
supernatant [liquid], supernate	überstehende Flüssigkeit f, Überstand m
supernormal	übernormal
supernova, super-nova <pl.: super-novae> <of type I or II>	Supernova f <pl.: Supernovae> <vom Typ I oder II>
supernova explosion, supernova outburst	Supernovaausbruch m
supernova remnants, remnants of the supernova [explosion]	Supernovaüberrest m, Überrest m der Supernova, Supernovarest m, Endprodukte npl der Supernova
supernucleus	s. hyperfragment
superorbital velocity	Geschwindigkeit f größer als die Kreisbahngeschwindigkeit
superorthicon; superemitron, image orthicon	Superorthikon n, Zwischenbildorthikon n, Image-Orthicon n; Superemitron n
superosculation	s. osculation
superpair	Superpaar n
superparamagnetism	Superparamagnetismus m
superperiod	Superperiode f
superplasticity	Superplastizität f
superposable	superponierbar; übereinanderlegbar, deckend; überlagerbar
superposable motions	superponierbare Bewegungen fpl
superposed circuit	Überlagerungskreis m
superposed current	Überlagerungsstrom m
superposed direct-current voltage, superposed d.c. voltage	Überlagerungsgleichspannung f, überlagerte Gleichspannung f
superposed fluids, superimposed fluids	übereinandergeschichtete Flüssigkeiten fpl, übereinander gelagerte Flüssigkeiten
superposed oscillation	überlagerte Schwingung f, Überlagerungsschwingung f
superposing	s. superposition
superposition, superimposition, superposing, superimposing, overlying	Superposition f, Überlagerung f
superposition <geo.>	Auflagerung f, Superposition f <Geo.>
superposition	s. a. superimposition
superposition approximation	Überlagerungsnäherung f, Superpositionsnäherung f
superposition eye	Superpositionsauge n
superposition principle	s. principle of superposition
superposition theorem <of Laplace transformation>	Überlagerungssatz m, Additionssatz m <Laplace-Transformation>
superposition theorem	s. a. principle of superposition
superpotential	Superpotential n, Überpotential n
superpressure, superatmospheric pressure, overpressure, positive pressure	Überdruck m, Mehrdruck m
superproportional reducer, flattening reducer, progressive reducer	superproportionaler Abschwächer m, progressiver Abschwächer m
superproton	Superproton n
superradiance	Superstrahlung f
superrefraction	Superrefraktion f, Superbrechung f, Suprarefraktion f
superregeneration, superretroaction	Pendelrückkopplung f, Superregeneration f, Überrückkopplung f
superregenerative amplifier	Pendelrückkopplungsverstärker m, Superregenerativverstärker m
superregenerative detector	Pendelrückkopplungsdetektor m; Pendelgleichrichter m, Pendelaudion n
superregenerative reception	Superregenerativempfang m
superrelativistic velocity	s. super-velocity of light
superretroaction	s. superregeneration
super Rockwell test	Super-Rockwell-Verfahren n
supersaturated solid solution	übersättigter Mischkristall m
supersaturated steam	übersättigter Dampf m
supersaturated vapour, supercooled vapour	übersättigter Dampf m, unterkühlter Dampf
supersaturation, oversaturation	Übersättigung f
supersaturation coefficient	Übersättigungszahl f, Übersättigungsverhältnis n
supersaturation energy	Übersättigungsenergie f
super Schmidt [camera]	Super-Schmidt-System n, Super-Schmidt-Spiegel m, Super-Schmidt-Kamera f
superscript, upper index	oberer Index m
superselection rule	Superauswahlregel f, Überauswahlregel f, Superselektionsregel f
supersensitivity, ultrasensitivity, extreme sensitivity	Höchstempfindlichkeit f, Superempfindlichkeit f, extreme Empfindlichkeit f
supersensitivity, oversensitivity	Überempfindlichkeit f
supersensitization	s. hypersensitization
supersensitizer, hypersensitizer	Übersensibilisator m, Supersensibilisator m, Hypersensibilisator m
supersign	Superzeichen n
supersociation	Supersoziation f
supersonic aerodynamics, supersonics	Überschallaerodynamik f
supersonic bang, sonic bang (boom), bang	Überschallknall m
supersonic cavitation	s. cavitation induced by ultrasonics
supersonic centrifuge, ultrasonic centrifuge	Ultraschallzentrifuge f
supersonic coagulation, ultrasonic (acoustic) coagulation	Ultraschallkoagulation f, Koagulation f durch Schallwellen

supersonic   846

supersonic delay line	s. ultrasonic delay line	supersonic wing	Überschallflügel m
supersonic diffuser	Überschalldiffusor m	superspeed, excess velocity	Übergeschwindigkeit f
supersonic echo sounder	s. ultrasonic echo-sounding device	superstar	s. quasar
supersonic edge, supersonic ridge	Überschallkante f	superstereoscopic effect	Überplastik f
		superstructure	s. superlattice
supersonic emitter	s. ultrasonic radiator	super surface film phenomenon [of helium], film creep [of helium]	Kriechen n dünner Flüssigkeitsschichten [von Helium]
supersonic expansion	Überschallexpansion f		
supersonic flight	Überschallflug m		
supersonic flow, supersonic stream, flow at supersonic velocity	Überschallströmung f; Überschallstrom m; Überschallumströmung f	supersynchronous, hypersynchronous	übersynchron
		super temperature	Supertemperatur f
		supertension	s. extra-high tension
supersonic flow ‹against, towards, to, on to›	Überschallanströmung f	superthermal conduction (conductivity), super heat conduction (conductivity), thermal superconduction, thermal superconductivity	Suprawärmeleitung f, thermische Supraleitung f, Suprawärmeleitfähigkeit f, thermische Supraleitfähigkeit f
supersonic flow from the source	Überschall-Quellströmung f		
supersonic fluorometer, ultrasonic fluorometer	Ultraschallfluorometer n		
supersonic frequency	Überschallfrequenz f		
supersonic generator, ultrasonic generator, ultrasound generator; vibratory unit, transducer, transformer	Ultraschallgenerator m, Ultraschallerzeuger m, Ultraschallgeber m; Ultraschallschwinger m, Schwinger m	superthreshold dose	überschwellige Dosis f
		super[-]turnstile [antenna]	Superdrehkreuzstrahler m, Mehrfach-Schmetterlingsantenne f, „superturnstile"-Antenne f
supersonic interferometer	Ultraschallinterferometer n		
supersonic isobar	Überschallisobare f	superundal flow	s. shooting flow ‹hydr.›
supersonic lens, ultrasonic lens	Ultraschallinse f	super-velocity of light, superrelativistic velocity, hypervelocity	Überlichtgeschwindigkeit f
supersonic microtome, ultrasonic microtome	Ultraschallmikrotom n		
supersonic pipe	s. supersonic whistle	supervision	s. monitoring
supersonic pocket	Überschalltasche f	supervisory relay	Überwachungsrelais n
supersonic probe, ultrasonic probe	Ultraschallsonde f, Überschallsonde f	supervoltage	s. extra-high tension
		supervoltage X-ray generator	Supervolt-Röntgengenerator m, Höchstspannungs-Röntgengenerator m
supersonic profile	Überschallprofil n		
supersonic radiator	s. ultrasonic radiator		
supersonic range, supersonic region	Überschallbereich m, Überschallgebiet n, supersonischer Bereich m, supersonisches Gebiet n	superwater	s. polywater
		supplement[al angle], supplementary angle	Supplementwinkel m
supersonic reflectoscope	Ultraschallecho-Impulsgerät n, Ultraschallimpulsreflexionsgerät n, Ultraschallreflektoskop n	supplementary apparatus, auxiliary apparatus, complementary instrument, add-on (additional, peripheral, ancillary) unit, additional equipment, accessory attachment, facility added, added facility	Zusatzgerät n; Zusatzeinrichtung f
supersonic region ‹of flow›	supersonisches Gebiet n, Überschallgebiet n ‹Strömung›		
supersonic region	s. a. supersonic range		
supersonic ridge, supersonic edge	Überschallkante f		
supersonics	Überschallehre f, Lehre f vom Überschall, Überschallakustik f	supplementary lens, attachment lens, auxiliary lens	Vorsatzlinse f, Zusatzlinse f
supersonics, theory of supersonic speed	Überschalltheorie f	supplementary prism, attachment prism	Vorsatzprisma n
supersonics, supersonic aerodynamics	Überschallaerodynamik f		
		supplementary short-circuit current, additional short-circuit current	Zusatzkurzschlußstrom m
supersonic sounding	s. ultrasonic echo sounding		
supersonic source, ultrasound source, ultrasonic source	Ultraschallquelle f	supplementary valence	s. secondary valence
		supplementary vector, cross	Ergänzungsvektor m, Ergänzung f
supersonic spectrometer	s. ultrasonic spectrometer	supply	s. power supply ‹el.›
supersonic spectrometry	s. ultrasonic spectroscopy	supply diagonal	Speisediagonale f
supersonic spectroscope	s. ultrasonic spectrometer		
supersonic spectroscopy	s. ultrasonic spectroscopy	supply frequency	s. power-line frequency
supersonic spectrum	s. ultrasonic spectrum	supply of charge carriers	s. carrier replenishment
supersonic speed, supersonic velocity	Überschallgeschwindigkeit f	supply pipe (tube), feed pipe, inlet pipe, intake pipe, lead; penstock [pipe], raceway ‹of turbine›	Zuleitungsrohr n, Zuführungsrohr n, Zuflußrohr n; Zulaufrohr n
supersonic storage	s. ultrasonic delay line		
supersonic stream	s. supersonic flow		
supersonic stroboscope, ultrasonic stroboscope	Ultraschallstroboskop n	supply voltage	Speisespannung f, Versorgungsspannung f
supersonic testing	s. ultrasonic inspection		
supersonic transmitter	s. ultrasonic radiator		
supersonic velocity	s. supersonic speed	supply voltage, line voltage, mains input, mains voltage, voltage of the main	Netzspannung f
supersonic vibration, ultrasonic vibration	Ultraschallschwingung f		
supersonic wave, ultrasound wave, ultrasonic wave	Ultraschallwelle f, Überschallwelle f	support; holder; mount, mounting support	Halterung f, Halter m
supersonic whistle, supersonic pipe	Ultraschallpfeife f	support, supporter, supporting structure, carrier ‹of the catalyst›	Katalysatorträger m, Träger m ‹Katalysator›
supersonic wind tunnel	Überschall-Windkanal m		

support, carrier <math.>	Träger m <Math.>	suppressed carrier; quiescent carrier	unterdrückter Träger m
support, bearing; rest; shore <mech.>	Auflager n; Auflagestütze f, Stütze f, Auflage f; Unterstützung f <Mech.>	suppressed frequency band, suppressed band	unterdrücktes Band n
support	s. a. film base	suppressed weir	s. contracted weir
support	s. a. slide	suppressed zero instrument, instrument with suppressed zero	Meßgerät (Gerät, Instrument) n mit unterdrücktem Nullpunkt
supported	gestützt		
supported catalyst	Trägerkatalysator m, Trägerkontakt m	suppression, rejection	Unterdrückung f
support electrolyte	s. supporting electrolyte		
supporter	s. support <of the catalyst>	suppression filter, rejection filter, elimination filter, exclusion filter	Sperrfilter n <El.; Opt.>; Okularsperrfilter n <Opt.>; Sperrsieb n <El.>; Sperrkreisfilter n <El.>
support function, function of support, supporting function	Stützfunktion f		
supporting capacity	s. carrying capacity		
supporting electrode	Trägerelektrode f	suppression of the discharge	Unterdrückung f der Entladung
supporting electrolyte, support electrolyte; background electrolyte, base electrolyte; conducting salt	Leitelektrolyt m, Trägerelektrolyt m; Leitsalz n	suppressor effect	Unterdrückungseffekt m
		suppressor grid	Bremsgitter n; Anodenschutzgitter n; Fanggitter n
supporting film; supporting foil <in electron microscopy>	Objektträgerhäutchen n, Objektträgerfilm m; Oberflächenabdruckfilm m; Objektträgerfolie f; Oberflächenabdruckfolie f <Elektronenmikroskopie>	suppressor[-grid] modulation	Bremsgittermodulation f, Bremsmodulation f, Fanggittermodulation f
		suprafluid, superfluid	suprafluid, superfluid; supraflüssig
		supraliminal	überschwellig
		supraliminal stimulus	überschwelliger Reiz m
supporting foil	Trägerfolie f	supralittoral	supralitoral
supporting foil	s. a. supporting film	supramolecular structure	übermolekulare Struktur f, Überstruktur f
supporting force, support reaction, upward force at the support, force at the support, support pressure	Stützkraft f, Stützdruck m, Auflage[r]kraft f	suprasphere	Suprasphäre f
		supremum	s. least upper bound
		surf; surge, breakers	Brandung f
supporting forces	s. support reactions	surface; bounding surface, boundary, boundary surface; periphery surface	Oberfläche f, Fläche f; Begrenzungsfläche f; Randfläche f
supporting function	s. support function		
supporting grid	Tragrost m, Stützgitter n, Traggerüst n, Unterstützungsgerüst n		
supporting-insulator type transformer	Stützerstromwandler m	surface, water table, table, free surface of water, water stage, water plane <hydr.>	freie Oberfläche f, Spiegel m, Wasserspiegel m <Hydr.>
supporting material, supporting substance <chromatography>	Träger m <Chromatographie>		
		surface, superficial; near the surface, near-surface	Oberflächen-, oberflächlich; oberflächennah
supporting material	s. a. base material		
supporting plane, plane of support	Stützebene f, Stützhyperebene f	surface acceleration, areal (sector) acceleration	Flächenbeschleunigung f
supporting plate, base plate, backing plate, base support	Trägerplatte f	surface-acting development, surface development <phot.>	Oberflächenentwicklung f <Phot.>
supporting point	s. point of support <of lever>	surface-active, surface active, capillary-active	grenzflächenaktiv, oberflächenaktiv, kapillaraktiv
supporting reactions	s. support reactions		
supporting rod	Trägerstab m	surface active agent, surfactant, interfacially active agent, detergent	grenzflächenaktiver (oberflächenaktiver, kapillaraktiver) Stoff m, Tensid n, Detergens n, Surfactant m
supporting structure, support, carrier <of the catalyst>	Katalysatorträger m, Träger m <Katalysator>		
supporting structure, support structure <mech.>	Tragkonstruktion f, Tragwerk n <Mech.>	surface activity, capillary activity	Oberflächenaktivität f, Kapillaraktivität f, Grenzflächenaktivität f
supporting substance	s. supporting material <chromatography>	surface activity <nucl.>	Oberflächenaktivität f <Kern.>
supporting surface, bearing surface <mech.>	tragende Fläche f, Tragfläche f <Mech.>	surface admittance	Oberflächenleitwert m, Oberflächenscheinleitwert m, Oberflächenadmittanz f
support material	s. base material	surface adsorption	Oberflächenadsorption f
support pressure	s. supporting force	surface air	s. near-soil atmospheric layer
support reaction	s. supporting force		
support reactions, reactions (upward forces) at the supports, supporting forces (reactions), end reactions	Auflagerreaktion f, Auflagerkräfte fpl	surface area	s. area
		surface area	s. specific surface
		surface array of dislocations, dislocation wall	Versetzungswand f
support resonance	Stützresonanz f	surface band	Oberflächenband n, Oberflächenenergieband n
support structure, supporting structure <mech.>	Tragkonstruktion f, Tragwerk n <Mech.>	surface barrier	s. barrier layer
supposition, presupposition, presumption, assumption; prerequisite; premise; condition	Voraussetzung f; Annahme f; Prämisse f; Bedingung f	surface barrier detector	Oberflächenbarrieredetektor m, Oberflächensperrschichtdetektor m, „surface-barrier"-Detektor m, Randschichtdetektor m, Barrieredetektor m
suppressed band, suppressed frequency band	unterdrücktes Band n		

surface-barrier diode	Oberflächenbarrierediode f, Oberflächensperrschichtdiode f, „surface-barrier"-Diode f, Randschichtdiode f, Barrierediode f	surface-contact rectifier, large-area-contact rectifier	Flächengleichrichter m
		surface contamination <nucl.>	Oberflächenkontamination f, Oberflächenverseuchung f <Kern.>
surface-barrier field effect transistor, MESFET	Oberflächenbarriere-Feldeffekttransistor m, MESFET	surface conversion	Oberflächenkonversion f
		surface corrosion, general (uniform) corrosion	diffuse (gleichmäßige) Korrosion f, gleichmäßiger Angriff m von der Oberfläche her
surface barrier junction	Oberflächenbarriereübergang m, Oberflächensperrschichtübergang m, „surface-barrier"-Übergang m, Oberflächengrenzschichtübergang m, Oberflächenrandschichtübergang m, Randschichtübergang m	surface coupling	Oberflächenkopplung f
		surface crack	Oberflächenriß m
		surface crystallization	Oberflächenkristallisation f
		surface curl, areal curl, Curl	Flächenrotation f, Flächenwirbel m, Flächenrotor m, Rot
surface barrier layer	s. barrier layer	surface current, surface flow; near-surface flow	Oberflächenströmung f; oberflächennahe Strömung f
surface barrier transistor	Oberflächenbarrieretransistor m, Oberflächensperrschichttransistor m, „surface-barrier"-Transistor m, Randschichttransistor m, Barrieretransistor m	surface current <el.>	Oberflächenstrom m, Flächenstrom m <El.>
		surface current density, surface density of current	Oberflächenstromdichte f, Flächenstromdichte f, Oberflächendichte f des Stroms, Flächendichte f des Stroms; spezifische Strombelastung f
surface boiling, subcooled boiling	Oberflächensieden n	surface damping	s. edge damping
		surface defect, surface failure	zweidimensionale Fehlstelle f, zweidimensionale Störstelle f, flächenhafte Störstelle, Oberflächenfehler m; Flächenstörung f
surface bolometer	Großflächenbolometer n		
surface breakdown	Oberflächenüberschlag m, Oberflächendurchbruch m		
		surface density, superficial density	Flächendichte f; Oberflächendichte f; Belegungsdichte f; Flächenbelegung f, Oberflächenbelegung f
surface charge	Oberflächenladung f, Flächenladung f; elektrische Flächenladung		
		surface density	s. a. mass per unit area
surface charge density, surface density of charge, surface density of electric charge	Oberflächenladungsdichte f, Flächenladungsdichte f, Oberflächendichte f der Ladung, Flächendichte f der Ladung, elektrische Flächendichte (Flächenladungsdichte, Verschiebungsdichte f), Dichte f der Oberflächenladungen	surface density of activity	s. activity density relative to surface
		surface density of charge	s. surface charge density
		surface density of current	s. surface current density
		surface density of electric charge	s. surface charge density
		surface depletion layer	s. depleted surface boundary layer
surface coat, coating, coat; covering, coverage; sheath layer <gen.>	Überzug m, Schicht f, Überzugsschicht f; Beschichtung f; Belag m; Bedeckung f <allg.>	surface derivative, areal derivative	Flächenableitung f
		surface development	s. surface-acting development <phot.>
surface-coated mirror, front-surface mirror, front-coated mirror; surface-silvered mirror, front-silvered mirror	Oberflächenspiegel m; oberflächenversilberter Spiegel m	surface development nucleus, surface nucleus	Oberflächenkeim m
		surface diffusion	Oberflächendiffusion f
surface colour, colour (colouration) of the body in reflected light, colour in reflected light, reflected colour	Aufsichtfarbe f		
		surface diffusion coefficient	Oberflächendiffusionskoeffizient m
		surface discharge; discharge over (on) the surface <el.>	Oberflächenentladung f <El.>
surface colour	s. a. free colour		
surface combustion	s. catalytic combustion	surface discharge, surface effluent, overland flow (runoff), sheet flow, surface flow (run[-]off) <hydr.>	[reiner] Oberflächenabfluß m, oberirdischer Abfluß m <Hydr.>
surface concentration	Flächenkonzentration f; Oberflächenkonzentration f		
surface condenser	Oberflächenkondensator m		
		surface discharge spark, creepage spark	Gleitfunke m
surface condition	Oberflächenbeschaffenheit f, Oberflächenbedingung f		
		surface dislocation	Oberflächenversetzung f
		surface dispersion	Oberflächendispersion f
		surface displacement	Oberflächenverschiebung f
surface conductance	Oberflächenwirkleitwert m, Oberflächenkonduktanz f, Oberflächenleitwert m	surface distribution	Flächenverteilung f; Oberflächenverteilung f
		surface divergence, areal divergence, Div	Flächendivergenz f, Sprungdivergenz f, Div
surface conduction	Oberflächenleitung f		
surface conductivity	Oberflächenleitfähigkeit f	surface dose, field dose	Oberflächendosis f

surface eddy, surface vortex — Flächenwirbel *m*

surface-effect ship — *s.* hovercraft

surface effluent — *s.* surface discharge <hydr.>

surface element, element of area, differential of area, areal element — Flächenelement *n*, Oberflächenelement *n*

surface emitter — *s.* plane radiator

surface emitting according to the cosine law, uniform emitting surface, Lambertian radiator — Lambertscher Strahler *m*, Lambert-Strahler *m*

surface energy, free energy of the surface [per unit area], free surface energy, surface (superficial) free energy — Oberflächenenergie *f*, freie Oberflächenenergie, Oberflächenarbeit *f*, freie Energie *f* der Oberfläche

surface energy, superficial density of the internal energy — Oberflächendichte *f* der inneren Energie, Oberflächenenergie *f*

surface energy of the nucleus, nuclear surface energy — Oberflächenenergie *f* des Kerns, Kernoberflächenenergie *f*

surface entropy — *s.* superficial entropy

surface eruption — Oberflächeneruption *f*

surface evaporation, evaporation [from the surface] — Verdunstung *f*, Evaporation *f*, unproduktive Verdunstung *f*; Ausdünstung *f*

surface excess, absorbed quantity — Oberflächenüberschuß *m*

surface expansion — Flächenausdehnung *f*, flächenhafte Ausdehnung *f*; Oberflächenausdehnung *f*

surface failure — *s.* surface defect

surface film, surface tension film — Oberflächenfilm *m*, Oberflächenhaut *f*, Oberflächenhäutchen *n*

surface finish, surface quality — Oberflächengüte *f*, Oberflächenbeschaffenheit *f*, Oberflächenqualität *f*

surface finish, surface finishing [process] — Oberflächennachbehandlung *f*; Oberflächennachbearbeitung *f*

surface finish tester — Oberflächenprüfgerät *n*

surface flood, surface flow — Schichtflut *f*, flächenhaftes Abfließen *n*

surface flow, surface current; near-surface flow — Oberflächenströmung *f*; oberflächennahe Strömung *f*

surface flow — *s. a.* surface discharge

surface force; surface traction — Oberflächenkraft *f*, Flächenkraft *f*, Berührungskraft *f*

surface free energy — *s.* surface energy

surface friction — *s.* skin friction

surface[-] friction coefficient, skin friction coefficient — Oberflächenreibungskoeffizient *m*, Hautreibungskoeffizient *m*

Reibungswiderstand *m* <Aero., Hydr.>

surface friction term, wall shear stress term, skin friction term — Wandschubspannungsglied *n*

surface gauge, shifting gauge, marking gauge — Höhenreißer *m*, Reißmaß *n*, Streichmaß *n*, Parallelmaß *n*, Parallelreißer *m*

surface generation — Oberflächenerzeugung *f*

surface gloss — Oberflächenglanz *m*

surface glow — Glimmhaut *f*

surface gradient, areal gradient, Grad — Flächengradient *m*, Sprunggradient *m*, Grad

surface gravity, surficial gravity, superficial gravity — Schwerebeschleunigung (Schwerkraft) *f* an der Oberfläche, Oberflächenschwerebeschleunigung *f*, Oberflächenschwere *f*, Oberflächenschwerkraft *f*

surface growth — [tangentiales] Flächenwachstum *n*

surface Hamiltonian — Oberflächen-Hamilton-Operator *m*, Oberflächenanteil *m* des Hamilton-Operators

surface hardening, flame hardening, torch hardening, face hardening — Brennhärtung *f*, Oberflächenhärtung *f*, Flammenhärtung *f*, Autogenhärtung *f*

surface hardening by glow discharge in nitrogen — Glimmnitrierung *f*

surface hardness — Oberflächenhärte *f*

surface harmonic, surface spherical harmonic; Laplace['s] spherical harmonic (function) — Kugelflächenfunktion *f*; Laplacesche Kugelfunktion *f*, allgemeine Kugelfunktion

surface impedance — Oberflächenimpedanz *f*, Flächenimpedanz *f*, Oberflächen[schein]widerstand *m*, Flächenwiderstand *m*; Oberflächenwellenwiderstand *m*

surface imperfection, surface irregularity — Oberflächenstörung *f*, Oberflächendefekt *m*

surface-inactive, capillary-inactive — oberflächeninaktiv, kapillarinaktiv

surface inhomogeneity — *s.* surface irregularity

surface integral, closed surface integral, integral over a closed surface — Oberflächenintegral *n*, Randintegral *n*, Hüllenintegral *n*, Flächenintegral *n* [über die geschlossene Fläche]

surface interaction, direct interaction <nucl.> — direkte Wechselwirkung *f*, Oberflächenwechselwirkung *f* <Kern.>

surface inversion, ground inversion — Bodeninversion *f*

surface ionization — Oberflächenionisierung *f*, Oberflächenionisation *f*

surface ionization coef.icient — Oberflächenionisierungskoeffizient *m*

surface ionization ion source — thermische Ionenquelle *f*

surface ionization source — Oberflächenionisierungsquelle *f*

surface irregularity; surface inhomogeneity — Oberflächenunregelmäßigkeit *f*; Oberflächenunstetigkeit *f*; Oberflächeninhomogenität *f*

surface irregularity — *s. a.* surface imperfection

surface laser — Oberflächenlaser *m*

surface layer — Oberflächenschicht *f*; oberflächennahe Schicht *f*

surface layer, peripheral layer — Randschicht *f*, periphere Schicht *f*, Mantelschicht *f*

surface leakage, leakage <el.> — Kriechstromableitung *f*, Ableitung *f* von Kriechströmen, Kriechen *n*; Oberflächenableitung *f*, Oberflächenverlust *m* <El.>

surface leakage current, leakage (creeping) current, tracking current, stray current, discharge current, sneak currents — Kriechstrom *m*, Oberflächenkriechstrom *m*

surface level — *s.* surface state

surface lifetime — Oberflächenlebensdauer *f*, oberflächliche Lebensdauer *f*

surface load — *s.* area load

surface magnetization — Oberflächenmagnetisierung *f*; flächenhaft verteilte Magnetisierung *f*

surface marking, surface waviness

surface mass — *s.* mass per unit area

surface measurement, planimetering, planimetration; measurement of area, area measurement — Planimetrierung *f*; Flächen[aus]messung *f*

surface

surface metric, areal metric	Flächenmetrik f	surface of revolution (rotation)	Rotationsfläche f, Drehfläche f, Umdrehungsfläche f
surface migration	Oberflächenwanderung f	surface of separation	s. interface
surface mobility	Oberflächenbeweglichkeit f, Beweglichkeit f an der Oberfläche	surface of subsidence	s. surface of descending glissade
surface moraine, superglacial moraine	Obermoräne f	surface of tension, stress quadric, quadric of stress, deflection surface	Spannungsfläche f, Tensorfläche (quadratische Form) f des Spannungstensors
surface noise, needle scratch, scratch	Nadelgeräusch n, Nadelrauschen n, Kratzen n der Nadel	surface of the cylinder	Zylinderoberfläche f
surface normal, normal to the surface, normal, normal of surface	Flächennormale f, Normale f der Fläche		
surface nucleus	s. surface development nucleus	surface of the Earth, Earth's surface, earth-surface, terrene	Erdoberfläche f
surface of absorption <opt., therm., cryst.>	Absorptionsfläche f <Opt., Therm., Krist.>	surface of the liquid	s. liquid level
		surface of the sea	Meeresspiegel m, Meeresoberfläche f, Meeresniveau n
surface of acuity	Schärfenfläche f	surface of the sphere	s. spherical surface
surface of adherence; sticking surface	Haftfläche f	surface of the tip, tip surface of the tooth	Zahncheitel m, Zahnrücken m
surface of ascending glissade, surface of ascent, anabatic surface	anabatische Frontfläche f, Anafrontfläche f, Aufgleitfläche f	surface oscillation of the nucleus, nuclear surface oscillation	Oberflächenschwingung f des Kerns, Kernoberflächenschwingung f
surface of centres of displacement	Auftriebsfläche f	surface phase	Oberflächenphase f
surface of centres of the surface	s. evolute [of surface]	surface phenomenon	Oberflächenerscheinung f, Oberflächenphänomen n
surface of constant curvature	Fläche f konstanter Krümmung, Fläche konstanten Krümmungsmaßes	surface photoeffect, surface photoelectric effect	Oberflächenphotoeffekt m, lichtelektrischer Oberflächeneffekt m
		surface plate	Richtplatte f
surface of constant optical path	s. equiphase surface	surface porosity	s. external porosity
surface of constant phase	s. equiphase surface	surface potential	Oberflächenpotential n, Flächenpotential n
surface of constant phase	s. wave front	surface-potential barrier, surface-potential wall	Oberflächenpotentialwall m
surface of constant phase difference	s. isochromatic surface	surface pressure, surfacing pressure	Oberflächendruck m; Laplacescher Druck m; Flächendruck m; Manteldruck m
surface of constant potential	s. equipotential surface		
surface of constant pressure	s. isobaric surface		
surface of constant slope	Böschungsfläche f	surface probe coil	Tastspule f
surface of contact, contact surface, contact interface, pressure area	Kontaktfläche f, Kontaktoberfläche f; Druckfläche f	surface quality	s. surface finish
		surface radiator	s. plane radiator
		surface ray, superficial ray	Oberflächenstrahl m
		surface reactance	Oberflächen-Blindwiderstand m, Oberflächenreaktanz f
surface of descending glissade, surface of descent, surface of subsidence, catabatic surface	katabatische Frontfläche f, Katafrontfläche f, Abgleitfläche f		
		surface reaction	Oberflächenreaktion f
surface of discontinuity, discontinuity surface, singular surface <hydr., aero.>	Unstetigkeitsfläche f [im engeren Sinne], Diskontinuitätsfläche f <Hydr., Aero.>	surface reaction	Wandreaktion f, Wandrückwirkung f
		surface recombination	Oberflächenrekombination f
surface of discontinuity, discontinuity surface <math.; phys.; met.>	Unstetigkeitsfläche f, Sprungfläche f, Diskontinuitätsfläche f <Math.; Phys.; Met.>	surface recombination rate (velocity), recombination rate (velocity) on the semiconductor surface	Oberflächenrekombinationsgeschwindigkeit f [des Halbleiters], Rekombinationsgeschwindigkeit f an der Oberfläche, Oberflächenrekombinationsrate f
surface of equal amplitude, equiamplitude surface	Fläche f gleicher Amplitude		
surface of equal density	äquidense Fläche f		
surface of equal energy, isoenergetic surface	Fläche f gleicher Energie, isoenergetische Fläche	surface reducer	Oberflächenabschwächer m
surface of equal phase	s. equiphase surface		
surface of equal pressure	s. isobaric surface	surface reduction, superficial reduction	Oberflächenabschwächung f
surface of equal specific volume, isosteric surface	Isosterenfläche f, isostere Fläche f	surface replica, replica	Oberflächenabdruck m, Abdruck m
surface of floatation fields	Umhüllungsfläche f der Schwimmflächen	surface replica method	s. replica method
surface of intensity distribution	s. solid of light distribution	surface reproduction, reproduction of surface features	Oberflächenabbildung f
surface of inversion, inversion surface	Inversionsfläche f	surface resistance <el.>	Oberflächenwiderstand m <El.>
surface of negative total curvature	s. anticlastic surface		
surface of no motion <aero., hydr.>	stromlose Fläche f <Aero., Hydr.>	surface resistivity	spezifischer Oberflächenwiderstand m, spezifischer Flächenwiderstand m
surface of positive total curvature, synclastic surface	Fläche f positiver [Gaußscher] Krümmung	surface resonance	Oberflächenresonanz f

surface rigidity	Oberflächenstarrheit *f*	surface traction	*s.* surface force
surface roll[ing]	*s.* surface standing wave	surface trap	Oberflächenhaftstelle *f*, Oberflächenhaftterm *m*
surface roughening	*s.* wrinkling ‹techn.›	surface treatment, surfacing	Oberflächenbehandlung *f*; Oberflächenbearbeitung *f*
surface roughness	Oberflächenrauheit *f*, Oberflächenrauhigkeit *f*	surface vacancy, surface vacant site	Oberflächenleerstelle *f*
surface run[-]off	*s.* surface discharge	surface velocity, areal velocity, area velocity, superficial (sector) velocity	Flächengeschwindigkeit *f*
surface scanning	Flächenscanning *n*		
surface scattering	Oberflächenstreuung *f*		
surface scratch	Oberflächenkratzer *m*	surface viscosity	Oberflächenzähigkeit *f*, Oberflächenviskosität *f*
surface seismic wave	*s.* surface wave ‹geo.›		
surface separating two media ‹opt.›	Grenzfläche *f* zweier Medien ‹Opt.›	surface visibility	Sichtweite *f* in Bodennähe, Sicht *f* in Bodennähe, Bodensicht *f*
surface shear wave	Oberflächenscherungswelle *f*, Scherungsoberflächenwelle *f*		
		surface / volume ratio	*s.* surface-to-volume ratio
surface-silvered mirror	*s.* surface-coated mirror	surface vortex, surface eddy	Flächenwirbel *m*
surface slope of the water level	Spiegelgefälle *n*, Wasserspiegelgefälle *n*	surface water	Oberflächenwasser *n*, oberirdisches Wasser *n*
		surface waters	Oberflächengewässer *n*; Oberflächenwässer *npl*
surface soil	*s.* eluvial soil		
surface source	Flächenquelle *f*, Oberflächenquelle *f*	surface wave, near-surface wave, direct wave ‹el.›	Bodenwelle *f*, direkte Welle *f* ‹El.›
surface space charge layer	Oberflächenraumladungsschicht *f*, oberflächennahe Raumladungsschicht *f*	surface wave, radio surface wave, Sommerfeld's surface wave, surface wave of the Sommerfeld type, Sommerfeld wave ‹el.›	Oberflächenwelle *f* [Sommerfeldscher Art], Sommerfeld-Welle *f*, Sommerfeldsche Oberflächenwelle ‹El.›
surface spark	Oberflächenfunke *m*		
surface spherical harmonic	*s.* surface harmonic		
surface spherical harmonic	*s. a.* Laplace['s] coefficient	surface wave, surface seismic wave; seismic wave travelling along a surface of discontinuity ‹geo.›	Oberflächenwelle *f*, seismische Oberflächenwelle (Grenzflächenwelle *f*) ‹Geo.›
surface stain	Oberflächen[an]färbung *f*		
surface standing wave, eddy motion of the water particles near the surface, surface roll[ing]	Deckwalze *f*	surface-wave guide (guiding structure)	Oberflächenwellenleiter *m*
surface state; surface level, surface term	Oberflächenzustand *m*; Oberflächenterm *m*, Oberflächenniveau *n*	surface wave of the Rayleigh type	*s.* Rayleigh wave
		surface wave of the Sommerfeld type	*s.* surface wave
surface step	Oberflächenstufe *f*	surface wave on liquids, liquid surface wave, wave on the surface of liquids	Oberflächenwelle *f* auf Flüssigkeiten, Welle *f* auf Flüssigkeitsoberflächen
surface strength ‹mech.›	Oberflächenfestigkeit *f* ‹Mech.›		
surface structure	*s.* surface texture	surface waviness, surface marking	Randschliere *f*
surface temperature; skin temperature	Oberflächentemperatur *f*; Hauttemperatur *f*	surface wind	Bodenwind *m*
		surface wrinkling	*s.* wrinkling ‹techn.›
		surface zonal harmonic of the second kind	*s.* Legendre function of the second kind
surface tension, specific surface energy; interfacial tension	Oberflächenspannung *f*, spezifische Oberflächenenergie (Oberflächenarbeit, Grenzflächenenergie) *f*	surfacing, surface treatment	Oberflächenbehandlung *f*; Oberflächenbearbeitung *f*
		surfacing	*s. a.* landing on water
		surfacing pressure	*s.* surface pressure
		surfactant	*s.* surface active agent
surface tension balance	*s.* surface tension meter	surfeit effect	Übersättigungseffekt *m*
surface tension constant, constant of surface tension ‹nucl.›	Konstante *f* der Oberflächenspannung, Oberflächenspannungskonstante *f* ‹Kern.›	surficial gravity	*s.* surface gravity
		surfing, surf riding, planing ‹on the water surface›	Wellenreiten *n*, Gleiten *n* ‹auf der Wasseroberfläche›
surface tension film, surface film	Oberflächenfilm *m*, Oberflächenhaut *f*, Oberflächenhäutchen *n*	surfing principle, principle of using travelling waves, surf-riding principle ‹acc.›	Wellenreiterprinzip *n*, Verwendung *f* von fortschreitenden Wellen ‹Beschl.›
surface tension meter, surface tension balance, tensiometer; stalagmometer	Oberflächenspannungsmesser *m*, Tensiometer *n*		
		surfon	Surfon *n*, Energiequant *n* der Oberflächenschwingungen
surface term	*s.* surface state		
surface texture, surface structure	Oberflächenstruktur *f*, Oberflächengefüge *n*	surf on shore, on-shore breakers, sea breaking on shore	Strandbrandung *f*
		surf riding	*s.* surfing
surface theory, theory of surfaces	Flächentheorie *f*	surf-riding principle	*s.* surfing principle ‹acc.›
		surf wave [breaker], roller	Brandungswelle *f*
surface thermometer	Oberflächenthermometer *n*	surge, surf	Brandung *f*
		surge; storm surge	Flutwelle *f*
surface-to-volume ratio, surface/volume ratio	Oberfläche/Volumen-Verhältnis *n*, Oberfläche:Volumen-Verhältnis *n*, Oberfläche-Volumen-Verhältnis *n*, Verhältnis *n* Oberfläche zu Volumen	surge, surge prominence; ejection of matter, mass ejection	Auswurf *m* von Materie, Ausschleudern *n* von Materie, Materieauswurf *m*, Materieausbruch *m*

surge, voltage surge, overvoltage wave, overvoltage transient, stray wave, sharp-edged wave, travelling wave [with sharp-edged front] <el.>
    Überspannungsstoß m, Überspannungs[stoß]welle f, Stoßwelle f, Sprungwelle f, Spannungs[wander]welle f, Wanderwelle f [mit steiler Front], steile Wanderwelle, Stoßüberspannung f <El.>
surge   s. a. impulse of current
surge   s. a. pulse
surge absorber   Wellenschlucker m
surge admittance   s. characteristic admittance <of transmission line>
surge admittance of free space, surge admittance of vacuum   s. characteristic admittance of free space
surge amplitude   Stoßamplitude f
surge arrester   s. surge diverter
surge capacitance, pulse capacitance   Stoßkapazität f
surge chamber, surge tank, intake chamber <hydr.>   Wasserschloß n, Ausspiegelungsbehälter m, Ausgleichsbehälter m, Ausgleichsbecken n <Hydr.>
surge characteristic   s. surge voltage characteristic
surge charge, stray wave charge   Wanderwellenbelastung f, Wanderwellenbeanspruchung f
surge current, pulse current   Stoßstrom m, Impulsstrom m, Impulsfolgestrom m
surge current   s. a. ripple current <el.>
surge current generator, [im]pulse current generator   Stoßstromgenerator m, Stoßstromerzeuger m
surge dissipator (diverter), lightning (surge) arrester, surge suppressor, overvoltage suppressor; lightning conductor (protector, rod), sparkgap discharger   Überspannungsableiter m; Überspannungsfunkenstrecke f; Blitzableiter m
surge generator   s. surge voltage test circuit
surge impedance, characteristic impedance, natural impedance <of the transmission line>   Wellenwiderstand m <Leitung>, Leitungswellenwiderstand m
surge impedance of free space, surge impedance of vacuum   s. characteristic impedance of free space
surge method   Wanderwellenmethode f
surge oscillograph, pulsed oscillograph, pulsed oscilloscope   Impulsoszillograph m, Impulsoszilloskop n
surge oscillography   Impulsoszillographie f
surge prominence   s. surge
surge protection, overvoltage protection, transient protection   Überspannungsschutz m
surge suppressor   s. surge dissipator
surge tank, expansion tank, expansion chamber, expansion vessel, compensator, pressurizer <therm.>   Ausgleichsbehälter m, Ausgleichgefäß n; Ausdehnungsgefäß n; Kompensator m, Volum[en]kompensator m <Therm.>
surge tank   s. a. surge chamber <hydr.>
surge voltage   s. ripple voltage
surge voltage characteristic, surge characteristic   Stoßkennlinie f, Stoßcharakteristik f
surge voltage generator, [im]pulse voltage generator   Stoßspannungsgenerator m, Stoßspannungserzeuger m, Stoßspannungsanlage f
surge voltage resistance, resistance to surge voltage   Stoßspannungsfestigkeit f
surge voltage test circuit, surge generator   Stoßkreis m

surging sea, heavy (angry, ugly) sea   schwere See f, starke See
surmount; superelevation   Überhöhung f
surmounting the potential barrier   s. tunnelling through the [potential] barrier
surplus conduction   s. n-type conduction
surplus electron, excess electron   Überschußelektron n
surplus gas pump, gas ballast pump   Gasballastpumpe f
surplus heat   s. excess heat
surplus neutron   Überschußneutron n, überschüssiges Neutron n
surplus proton   Überschußproton n
surrosion   Massezunahme (Gewichtszunahme) f bei der Korrosion
surround, surround of [the] comparison field <opt.>   Umfeld n, Umgebung f <beim Photometer; farbmeßtechnisch> <Opt.>
surroundings luminance   Umfeldleuchtdichte f
surroundings of the system   Umgebung f des Systems
surround of [the] comparison field   s. surround <opt.>
survey <stat.>   Erhebung f <Stat.>
survey   s. a. surveying <geo.>
survey   s. a. monitoring
survey   s. a. topographic mapping
survey by serial photographs, serial aerophotogrammetric survey, serial air survey   Reihenbildaufnahme f, Reihenaufnahme f, Streifenaufnahme f
surveying, practical geodesy   praktische Geodäsie f, Vermessungswesen n
surveying, survey <geo.>   Vermessung f; Vermessungsarbeit f <Geo.>
surveying instrument   Vermessungsgerät n, Vermessungsinstrument n
surveying tape comparator, [geodesic] tape comparator, geodesic base comparator, mural comparator   Meßbandkomparator m
surveying wire   s. pilot wire <el.>
survey instrument   s. radiation monitor <nucl.>
survey mark   s. bench mark
survey meter   s. radiation monitor <nucl.>
survey of the relief, contour survey, altimetric survey   Höhenaufnahme f
surveyor's chain   s. measuring chain <geo.>
surveyor's heliotrope, heliotrope <instrument>   Heliotrop n, Sonnenspiegel m <Instrument>
surveyor's level, levelling instrument, [geodesic] level   Nivellier n, Nivellierinstrument n
surveyor's perch (pole)   s. surveyor's staff
surveyor's rod, surveyor's staff, surveyor's perch, surveyor's pole, rod, staff stadia   Meßstab m, Meßstange f; Meßlatte f, Latte f; Meßrute f
surveyor's tape   s. tape measure
surveyor's tape comparator   Meßbandkomparator m
survival   Überleben n
survival average   mittlere Überlebenszeit f
survival curve   Überlebenskurve f
survival time   Überlebenszeit f

Surwell clinometer   Surwellscher Neigungsmesser m

susceptance	Blindleitwert *m*, Suszeptanz *f*	sustained sound, steady sound	Dauerton *m*
susceptibility, dielectric susceptibility, electric susceptibility <el.>	dielektrische Suszeptibilität *f*, elektrische Suszeptibilität, Suszeptibilität <El.>	sustained wave SU(3) symmetry <also: SU(2), SU(6) etc.> Sutherland['s] constant	s. continuous wave SU(3)-Symmetrie *f* <auch: SU(2)-, (SU(6)- usw.> Sutherland-Konstante *f*, Sutherlandsche Konstante *f*
susceptibility, susceptivity <gen.>	Suszeptibilität *f*; Empfänglichkeit *f*; Anfälligkeit *f* <allg.>	Sutherland effect	Sutherland-Effekt *m*
susceptibility	s. a. magnetic susceptibility	Sutherland['s] equation, Sutherland['s] formula	Sutherlandsche Formel (Gleichung, Relation) *f*, Sutherland-Formel *f*, Sutherland-Gleichung *f*
susceptibility meter, susceptometer	Suszeptibilitätsmesser *m*, Suszeptibilitätsmeßgerät *n*, Suszeptometer *n*	Sutherland['s] model	Sutherlandsches Modell *n*, Sutherland-Modell *n*
susceptibility per unit mass	s. specific magnetic susceptibility	Sutherland temperature	Sutherland-Temperatur *f*
susceptibility per unit volume, volume susceptibility	Volum[en]suszeptibilität *f*	Sutro weir, proportional-flow weir	Sutro-Überfall *m*, Überfall *m* nach Sutro
		Suydam['s] condition, Suydam['s] criterion	Suydam-Kriterium *n*, Suydam-Bedingung *f*
susceptibility tensor, magnetic susceptibility tensor, tensor of magnetic susceptibility	Suszeptibilitätstensor *m*, Tensor *m* der magnetischen Suszeptibilität	Suzuki effect S value	Suzuki-Effekt *m* S-Wert *m*, Menge *f* der austauschbaren Basen
susception, susception of stimulus	Reizaufnahme *f*, Suszeption *f*	Svanberg['s] theorem, Svanberg['s] vorticity	Svanbergscher Wirbelsatz *m*, Wirbelsatz von Svanberg
susceptivity	s. susceptibility <gen.>	svedberg, Svedberg unit, S	Svedberg *n*, Svedberg-Einheit *f*, S
susceptometer	s. susceptibility meter		
suspended drop, floating drop	schwebender Tropfen *m*	Svedberg['s] equation	Svedbergsche Gleichung *f*
suspended glacier, cornice glacier, cliff glacier	Hanggletscher *m*, Hängegletscher *m*, Gehängegletscher *m*	Svedberg unit Sverdrup wave	s. svedberg Sverdrupsche Welle *f*, Sverdrup-Welle *f*
suspended level, hanging level	Hängelibelle *f*	S Vulpeculae star, S Vulpeculae variable [star]	S Vulpeculae-Stern *m*, S Vulpeculae-Veränderlicher *m*
suspended load, silt load, silt; fine silt; suspended matter (sediment)	Schwebstoffe *mpl*, Sinkstoffe *mpl*; Schwemmstoffe *mpl*; Schwimmstoffe *mpl*; Flußtrübe *f*, Schweb *m*	swaging	Hämmerverdichtung *f*; Gesenkschmieden *n*
		swallow holes swamping [of spectral lines]	s. channelling <geo.> Überstrahlung *f*, Überdeckung *f*, Untergehen *n* <von Spektrallinien>
suspended load sample suspended load sampler, silt sampler	s. silt sample Schwebstoffentnahmegerät *n*, Schwebstoffmeßgerät *n*, Schwebstoffschöpfer *m*	Swan band Swan cube Swan photometer	Swan-Bande *f* s. Lummer-Brodhun cube s. Lummer-Brodhun photometer head
suspended matter (sediment)	s. suspended load	swarming	Filmregen *m*
suspended state	s. suspension		
suspended truss	s. suspension girder	swarm of electrons, electron swarm	Elektronenschwarm *m*
suspended valley	Hängetal *n*	swarm of particles, cloud of particles	Teilchenwolke *f*
suspending	Suspendieren *n*	swash[]plate, wobble plate, wobbler	Taumelscheibe *f*
suspending agent	Suspensionsmittel *n*		
suspension, slurry	Suspension *f*, Aufschlämmung *f*, Aufschwemmung *f*	swash plate pump, rotary swash plate pump, wobble pump	Taumelscheibenpumpe *f*, Wobbelpumpe *f*
suspension	Aufhängung *f*	swath of mist; fog in patches	Nebelschwaden *m*; Nebelfetzen *m*
suspension, state of suspension, suspended state, state of being suspended	Schwebezustand *m*, Schwebe *f*, Schweben *n*	S wave, S ray, transverse wave, <geo.>	S-Welle *f*, Transversalwelle *f*, Scherwelle *f* <Geo.>
suspension colloid	s. sol	S wave	s. a. shear wave
suspension girder; suspended truss	Hängeträger *m*; Hängewerk *n*	S wave S-wave swaying	s. a. transverse wave s. elementary wave s. transverse vibration
suspension in space	s. levitation	sweat cooling, transpiration cooling	Schwitzkühlung *f*, Transpirationskühlung *f*
suspension microphone	Hängemikrophon *n*		
suspension point, point (fulcrum) of suspension	Aufhängepunkt *m*	sweating-out sweep, waves, swell	s. segregation <met.> Wellengang *m*
suspension polymerization	s. pearl polymerization	sweep <aero.> sweep, relaxation <el.>	Pfeilung *f* <Aero.> Kippung *f*, Kippen *n* <El.>
suspension reactor	s. slurry reactor		
suspension tube	Suspensionsrohr *n*		
suspension-type reactor	s. slurry reactor	sweep <radar>	Spur *f* <Radar>
suspensoid	s. sol		
sustained chain reaction	s. self-sustained nuclear chain reaction	sweep <spectr.>	Sweepen *n* <Spektr.>
sustained-load tension test	Zugdauerversuch *m*, Dauerzugversuch *m*	sweep sweep	s. a. scanning s. a. time base
sustained nuclear chain reaction	s. self-sustained nuclear chain reaction	sweep amplifier, snap-action amplifier	Kippverstärker *m*, Ablenkverstärker *m*
sustained oscillation	s. undamped oscillation		
sustained reaction	s. self-sustained nuclear chain reaction		
sustained short-circuit current, permanent short-circuit current	Dauerkurzschlußstrom *m*	sweep amplitude, relaxation amplitude	Kippamplitude *f*; Ablenk[ungs]weite *f*

sweep

sweep angle, angle of sweep	Pfeilwinkel *m* ‹Flügel›
sweepback	positive Pfeil[stell]ung *f*
sweep base	s. time-base unit
sweep capacitor ‹el.›	s. deflecting capacitor
sweep characteristic	s. relaxation diagram
sweep circuit, time-base circuit; deflection circuit	Kippschaltung *f*, Zeitablenkschaltung *f*, Ablenkschaltung *f*
sweep circuit, relaxation circuit	Kippkreis *m*
sweep coil, sweeping coil, deflection coil	Ablenkspule *f*; Kippspule *f*
sweep current	s. deflecting current
sweep deflection	Kippablenkung *f*
sweep delay	Zeitablenk[ungs]verzögerung *f*
sweep diagram	s. relaxation diagram
sweep expansion, time-base expansion, time-base extension, time magnification (magnifying) ‹of oscilloscope›	Zeitdehnung *f*, Zeilendehnung *f*, Zeitbasisdehnung *f*, Zeitachsendehnung *f*, Dehnung *f* der Zeitachse, Dehnung des Zeitmaßstabes ‹Oszilloskop›
sweepforward	negative Pfeil[stell]ung *f*
sweep frequency, time-base frequency	Zeitablenkfrequenz *f*, Zeitbasisfrequenz *f*, Zeitachsenfrequenz *f*, Ablenkfrequenz *f*, Kippfrequenz *f*
sweep frequency, relaxation frequency	Kippfrequenz *f*; Relaxationsfrequenz *f*
sweep frequency generator	s. wobbler
sweep gas	Spülgas *n*; Waschgas *n*
sweep generator	s. relaxation generator
sweep generator	s. a. time base generator
sweep generator	s. a. wobbler
sweeping-away, washing-away, encroaching [upon]	Wegschwemmen *n*, Fortschwemmen *n*, Fortspülen *n*
sweeping coil	s. sweep coil
sweeping dislocation	s. moving dislocation
sweeping field	s. clearing field
sweeping trajectory	s. flat trajectory
sweeping voltage, clearing voltage, ion draw-out voltage	Reinigungsspannung *f*, Ziehspannung *f*, Ionenziehspannung *f*, Absaugspannung *f*
sweeping voltage	s. a. sweep voltage
sweep oscillator	s. relaxation generator
sweep-out	s. scanning
sweep rate	s. deflection speed
sweep signal generator	s. wobbler
sweep speed	s. deflection speed
sweep time constant, relaxation time constant	Kippzeitkonstante *f*
sweep transmitter	Durchdrehsender *m*
sweep unit	s. time-base unit
sweep voltage, sweeping voltage, scanning voltage	Ablenkspannung *f*, Ablenkungsspannung *f*; Abtastspannung *f*
sweep voltage, sweeping voltage; breakover voltage	Kippspannung *f*
sweep velocity	s. deflection speed
sweep voltage, sweeping voltage, time-base voltage	Zeitablenkspannung *f*, Ablenkspannung *f*; Zeitachsenspannung *f*
sweep width	Wobbelbereich *m*, Zeitablenkbreite *f*
Sweet-Parker model	Sweet-Parker-Modell *n*
sweet water, fresh[]water	Süßwasser *n*, süßes Wasser *n*
swell, waves, sweep	Wellengang *m*
swell; Airy['s] free wave	Schwall *m*
swell, underswell	Dünung *f*
swell	s. a. swelling
swelling	Schwellung *f*, Schwellen *n*; Anschwellen *n*
swelling; soaking, soak[age]; imbibition	Quellung *f*; Aufquellung *f*; Imbibition *f*
swelling; bulge; bulb	Wulst *m*
swelling ‹of fissile material›	Swelling *n* ‹von Spaltmaterial›
swelling ‹of water›	Schwellen *n* ‹des Wassers›
swelling	s. a. water-surface ascent
swelling agent	Quellungsmittel *n*, Quellmittel *n*
swelling capacity (degree)	s. swelling value
swelling equilibrium	Quellungsgleichgewicht *n*
swelling heat, heat of swelling, heat of imbibition	Quellungswärme *f*
swelling hysteresis	Quellungshysterese *f*
swelling isotherm, isotherm of swelling	Quellungsisotherme *f*
swelling parameter	Quellungsparameter *m*
swelling plasmoptysis	Quellungsplasmoptyse *f*
swelling pressure, imbibition pressure	Quellungsdruck *m*
swelling value; degree of swelling, swelling degree, swelling capacity	Quellungsgrad *m*; Quellwert *m*
swell water	Schwallwasser *n*
swept aerofoil (airfoil, back wing)	s. variable sweep aerofoil
swept aerofoil (airfoil, backwing)	s. swept wing
swept-lobe interferometer, phase-swept interferometer	„swept-lobe"-Interferometer *n*, Phasendrehinterferometer *n*
swept volume	s. displacement
swept wing	s. variable sweep airfoil
swept wing, swept aerofoil (airfoil, back wing)	Pfeilflügel *m*, gepfeilter Flügel *m*
swimming pool reactor, swimming-pool-type reactor, pool reactor, aquarium reactor	Schwimmbadreaktor *m*, Schwimmbeckenreaktor *m*, Swimming-Pool-Reaktor *m*, „swimming-pool"-Reaktor *m*
Swinburne circuit	Swinburne-Schaltung *f*, temperaturfreie Schaltung *f*
swing; deflection	Ablenkung *f*; Auslenkung *f*
swinging; oscillation	Schwenkung *f*
swinging, see-saw [motion]	Schaukelbewegung *f*, Schaukeln *n*
swinging ‹of the vessel›	Schwenken *n*, Umschwenken *n* ‹Gefäß›
swinging before the anchor	Schwojen *n*, Schwojbewegung *f*, Schwajen *n*
swinging choke	Schwingdrossel *f*
swinging of the pointer, playing of the pointer ‹around the rest position›	Spielen *n* des Zeigers
swinging plate anemometer	Plattenanemometer *n*, Schwingplattenanemometer *n*
swinging point	s. singing point
swing separator	s. gasschaukel
swirl, whirlpool, whirl; vortex [of fluid], eddy [of fluid], remous ‹hydr.›	Strudel *m*, Fließwirbel *m*, Längsumdrehung *f* um die Fortbewegungsachse, Wirbel *m*, Struden *m*; Wasserstrudel *m*, Wasserwirbel *m*; Sogwirbel *m*, Neer *m* ‹Hydr.›
swirling motion	s. whirling
swishing ‹ac.›; unpitched sound	Rauschen *n*, Geräusch *n* ‹Ak.›
switch, disconnecting switch; circuit breaker, interrupter ‹el.›	Schalter *m*, Trennschalter *m*, Ausschalter *m*
switch, circuit closer, contactor	Einschalter *m*

switch	s. a. changeover switch	switching sequence	Schaltfolge f
switch algebra	s. Boolean algebra		
switch arc	Schaltbogen m, Schaltlichtbogen m	switching spark	s. break spark
		switching speed	s. switching rate
switch capacitance box	Kurbelkondensator m	switching step	Schaltschritt m
switched-off interaction	ausgeschaltete Wechselwirkung f	switching surge	Schaltüberspannung f; Schaltstoß m
switch[-] gear, switchgear installation; controller ‹el.›	Schaltanlage f, Schaltapparat m	switching threshold	Schaltschwelle f
		switching time; breaking period	Schaltzeit f
switch[-] gear, switching gear (device, unit), switch unit ‹el.›	Schaltgerät n	switching time constant	Schaltzeitkonstante f
		switching transistor	s. transistor switch
switch[-] gear	s. a. switching gear ‹mech.›	switching tube, switching tube, switching valve	Schaltröhre f
switchgear installation	s. switch gear	switching unit	s. switch[-] gear ‹el.›
switch inductance box	Kurbelinduktivität f	switching valve	s. switching tube
		switching voltage	Schaltspannung f
switching; operation of switch; connection, connecting; breaking ‹el.›	Schalten n, Schaltung f ‹El.›	switching work	Schaltarbeit f
		switch-off period, cut-off time, off-period ‹semi.›	Sperrzeit f ‹Halb.›
switching	s. a. switching-over ‹el.›	switch-over	umschaltbar
switching action	s. switching process	switch resistance box	Kurbelwiderstand m
switching behaviour	Schaltverhalten n; Umschaltverhalten n		
		switch tube	s. switching tube
		switch unit	s. switch[-] gear ‹el.›
		swivel, swivelling, rotatable	schwenkbar, drehbar
switching circuit	Schaltkreis m	swivel pin	s. pivot journal
		swivel point	s. centre of rotation
switching component	s. switching element	syllabic articulation	s. logatom articulation
switching current	Schaltstrom m	sylphon bellows, bellows-and-strap arrangement, bellows	Faltenbalg m, Balg m; Balgmembran f
switching delay	s. time delay		
switching device	s. switch[-] gear ‹el.›		
switching device	s. a. switching element	sylphon cooler, corrugated tube cooler	Wellrohrkühler m
switching diode	Schaltdiode f		
switching element, switching component, switching device	Schaltelement n, Schaltglied n	Sylvester['s] determinant	Sylvestersche Determinante f
switching element, logic[al] element, logic[al] circuit module, switching member	logisches Element n, Logikelement n, Verknüpfungselement n, Verknüpfungsglied n, Schaltglied n	Sylvester['s] dialytic method	Sylvestersche Dialysemethode f
		symbiotic star	symbiotischer Stern m
		symbol	Symbol n; Formelzeichen n
switching frequency; breaking frequency; switching rate; changeover frequency	Schalthäufigkeit f; Schaltfrequenz f; Umschalthäufigkeit f	symbol; sign; character ‹num. math.›	Zeichen n ‹auch num. Math.›; Symbol n
		symbolic admittance, admittance operator	Operatoradmittanz f
switching function, function of switching; logic function ‹in information processing›	Schaltfunktion f		
		symbolic age [of neutron]	s. Fermi age
switching function	s. a. logic[al] operation	symbolic balance, pseudobalance ‹of the bridge›	Pseudoabgleich m ‹Brücke›
switching gear, switch[-] gear, control mechanism ‹mech.›	Schaltgetriebe n, Schaltwerk n, Umschaltgetriebe n ‹Mech.›		
		symbolic impedance, impedance operator	Operatorimpedanz f
switching gear	s. a. switch[-] gear ‹el.›		
switching jack	Schaltklinke f		
switching member	s. switching element	symbolic method [in alternating-current theory]	symbolische Methode f [der Wechselstromrechnung], Verfahren n der komplexen Wechselstromrechnung, komplexe Wechselstromrechnung f, komplexe Berechnung f von Wechselstromschaltungen, symbolische Rechnung f, Zeigerrechnung f
switching operation	s. switching process		
switching operation	s. a. logic[al] operation		
switching-over	s. switching ‹el.›		
switching process, switching operation, switching action	Schaltvorgang m		
switching rate, switching speed, changeover rate	Schaltgeschwindigkeit f, Umschaltgeschwindigkeit f		
switching rate	s. switching frequency		
switching ratio	Schaltverhältnis n	symbolic programmation	adressenfreie Programmierung f
		symbolic zero, pseudo-zero point	Pseudonullpunkt m
switching reliability	Schaltsicherheit f	symbolism; designation; notation; system of notation	Bezeichnung f; Bezeichnungsweise f; Schreibweise f; Symbolik f
switching resistance, resistance to switching [operations], resistance to switching transients	Schaltfestigkeit f		

symbol

symbol of the crystal edge
s. index of the crystal edge

symbol of the crystal face, index [of the crystal face] <cryst.>
Flächenindex m, Flächensymbol n, Symbol n der Kristallfläche <Krist.>

symbol of unit, symbol of units
Einheiten[kurz]zeichen n, Einheitensymbol n

symmetric, symm.; symmetrical; sym. <chem.>
symmetrisch, symm.; sym. <Chem.>

symmetric about an axis, in axial symmetry, axially symmetric, axisymmetric
axialsymmetrisch, achsensymmetrisch

symmetrical
s. symmetric

symmetrical dispersion
symmetrische Dispersion f

symmetrical fission
symmetrische Spaltung f

symmetrical four-terminal network, symmetrical quadrupole
symmetrischer Vierpol m

symmetrical group
s. symmetric group

symmetrical heterostatic circuit [of Mascart]
Nadelschaltung f [nach Mascart], symmetrisch-heterostatische Schaltung f

symmetrical Joukowski profile
Joukowski-Tropfen m

symmetrical kernel, symmetrical kernel function <math.>
symmetrischer Kern m, reell-symmetrischer Kern, symmetrische Kernfunktion f <Math.>

symmetrical multivibrator, balanced multivibrator
symmetrischer Multivibrator m

symmetrical network
symmetrisches Netzwerk n

symmetrical neutral [meson] theory
symmetrische neutrale Mesonentheorie (Theorie) f

symmetrical operator
s. Hermitian operator

symmetrical [pseudoscalar] meson theory
symmetrische pseudoskalare Mesonentheorie (Theorie) f

symmetrical quadrupole, symmetrical four-terminal network
symmetrischer Vierpol m

symmetrical scalar meson theory, symmetrical scalar theory
symmetrische skalare Mesonentheorie f, symmetrische skalare Theorie f

symmetrical tensor, symmetric tensor, tensor

symmetrical top, symmetric top
symmetrischer Kreisel m, zweiachsiger Kreisel

symmetrical top, symmetrical top molecule, symmetric top [molecule]
symmetrisches Kreiselmolekül n, Molekül n vom Typ symmetrischer Kreisel, symmetrischer Kreisel m

symmetrical waviness, earing, development of scallops
Zipfelbildung f, Faltenbildung f, Wellung f der Oberfläche

symmetric difference <of sets>
symmetrische Differenz f, Überschuß m, Boolesche Summe f <Mengen>

symmetric fold, normal fold
stehende (aufrechte) Falte f

symmetric group, symmetrical group
symmetrische Gruppe f

symmetric in time, time-symmetric
zeitsymmetrisch

symmetric output, balanced output, push-pull output
symmetrischer Ausgang m, Gegentaktausgang m

symmetric rotator
symmetrischer Rotator m

symmetric spherical harmonic
symmetrische Kugelfunktion f, Kugelfunktion mit Kristallsymmetrie

symmetric top
s. symmetrical top

symmetric tensor
s. symmetrical tensor

symmetrization; balancing <el.>
Symmetrierung f, Symmetrisierung f

symmetrized representation
symmetrisierte Darstellung f

symmetry, reflection <cryst.>
Symmetrie f, Spiegelgleichheit f; Spiegelung f <Krist.>

symmetry; balance <el.>
Symmetrie f <El.>

symmetry argument
Symmetriebetrachtung f

symmetry[-] axis
s. axis of symmetry <cryst.>

symmetry axis of order n, axis of order n, n-fold axis [of symmetry], n-al axis, n-al rotation axis
n-zählige Symmetrieachse (Achse) f, Symmetrieachse der Ordnung n, n-zählige Drehungsachse (Drehachse) f, Drehungsachse (Rotationsachse) f der Ordnung n, n-zählige Rotationsachse

symmetry axis of the second sort
s. rotation-reflection axis

symmetry[-axis] of the second sort of order n
s. n-al axis of the second sort

symmetry breakdown, symmetry breaking, breakdown of symmetry
Symmetriebrechung f

symmetry[-] centre, centre of symmetry, symmetry of inversion
Symmetriezentrum n

symmetry character
Symmetriecharakter m

symmetry class, class of symmetry
Symmetrieklasse f

symmetry coefficient
Symmetriekoeffizient m

symmetry condition
Symmetriebedingung f

symmetry co-ordinates
Symmetriekoordinaten fpl

symmetry effect
Symmetrieeffekt m

symmetry[-] element
Symmetrieelement n

symmetry factor
Symmetriefaktor m

symmetry group
Symmetriegruppe f [des Gitters], Gruppe f der Deckoperationen (Symmetrien)

symmetry line, line of symmetry
Symmetriegerade f, Symmetrale f

symmetry multiplet
Symmetriemultiplett n

symmetry number, symmetry value
Symmetriezahl f

symmetry of inversion, centre of symmetry, symmetry[-]centre
Symmetriezentrum n

symmetry of lattice
s. crystal symmetry

symmetry of order eight (8), octad symmetry, 8-al symmetry
achtzählige Symmetrie f, 8zählige Symmetrie

symmetry of order n, n-fold symmetry, n-al symmetry
n-zählige Symmetrie f, n-Zähligkeit f, Symmetrie f der Ordnung n, Zähligkeit f n

symmetry of order six (6), hexad symmetry, 6-al symmetry
sechszählige Symmetrie f, 6zählige Symmetrie

symmetry[-] operation
Deckoperation f, Decktransformation f, Deckbewegung f, Symmetrie[-operation] f

symmetry operator
Symmetrieoperator m

symmetry[-] plane, plane of symmetry; plane of mirror reflection symmetry <cryst.>
Symmetrieebene f

symmetry point, point of symmetry <meteo., cryst.>
Symmetriepunkt m <Meteo., Krist.>

symmetry principle
s. Schwarz reflection principle

symmetry principle <qu.; nucl.>
Symmetrieprinzip n <Qu.; Kern.>

symmetry properties of the lattice
s. crystal symmetry

symmetry quantum number
Symmetriequantenzahl f

symmetry relation
Symmetriebeziehung f

symmetry sake / for
s. reasons of symmetry / for

symmetry type, type of symmetry
Symmetrietyp m

symmetry value, symmetry number
Symmetriezahl f

Symon['s] smooth approximation, smooth approximation
„smooth approximation" f [nach Symon], Symonsche glatte Approximation f

sympathetic oscillation, co-oscillation, covibration
Mitschwingung f, Resonanzschwingung f

sympathetic reactions	s. coupled reactions	synchronous orbit	s. equilibrium orbit
sympiezometer	Sympiezometer n	synchronous particle, equilibrium particle, phase-stable particle, phase-stationary particle	Sollteilchen n, Synchronteilchen n
symplectic group	symplektische Gruppe f, Komplexgruppe f		
symplectic invariant	symplektische Invariante f, Komplexinvariante f	synchronous phase, charged particle equilibrium phase, equilibrium phase	Sollphase f, Synchronphase f, Gleichgewichtsphase f
symplectic mapping	s. symplectic transformation		
symplectic matrix	symplektische Matrix f		
symplectic transformation, symplectic mapping	symplektische Transformation (Abbildung) f	synchronous phase shifter [advancer]	Synchronphasenschieber m
		synchronous scanning	Synchronabtastung f
synapse	Synapse f	synchronous timer	Synchronzeitgeber m
synaptic transmission	synaptische Transmission f		
synchro	s. synchrodrive	synchronous timer, synchronous electric clock, synchronous clock, synchroclock, synchronometer	Synchronuhr f
synchrobetatron resonance	Synchrobetatronresonanz f		
synchroclock	s. synchronous timer		
synchrocyclotron [accelerator], frequency-modulated cyclotron, f[-]m cyclotron, phasotron, cyclosynchrotron	Synchrozyklotron n, frequenzmoduliertes Zyklotron n, FM-Zyklotron n, Phasotron n	synchrophasotron	s. heavy-particle synchrotron
		synchroscope	Synchroskop n
synchrodetector	s. synchronous detector	synchrotector	s. synchronous detector
synchrodrive, synchrotransmitter, synchro; selsyn, selsyn system	Drehmelder m, Drehfeldgeber m, Synchro m	synchrotransmitter	s. synchrodrive
		synchrotron [accelerator]	Synchrotron n
synchrodyne, synchrodyne receiver	Synchrodyn[e]empfänger m	synchrotron oscillation, radial-synchrotron (radial-phase) oscillation	Synchrotronschwingung f
synchrometer, mass synchrometer, cyclotron[ic] resonance mass spectrometer, cyclotron[ic] mass spectrometer	Synchrometer n, Zyklotronresonanz-Massenspektrometer n, Massensynchrometer n, Höchstfrequenz-Massenspektrometer n	synchrotron period	Synchrotronperiode f
		synchrotron radiation, acceleration radiation, cyclotron radiation, Schwinger radiation	Synchrotronstrahlung f, Zyklotronstrahlung f
synchromicrotron	Synchromikrotron n		
synchrone	Synchrone f	synchrotron reabsorption	Synchrotronreabsorption f
synchronism; synchronization, synchronizing	Synchronismus m, Gleichlauf m; Gleichlaufen n; Synchronisation f	synchrotron regime	Synchrotronbetrieb m
synchronism of phases	s. phase coincidence	synchrotron with straight sections	s. racetrack synchrotron
synchronization	s. synchronism	synclastic surface	s. surface of positive total curvature
synchronized multivibrator, master-excited (driven) multivibrator	fremdgesteuerter (fremderregter, getasteter, frequenzgesteuerter, passiver) Multivibrator m	synclinal, synclinal fold	s. syncline
		synclinal valley	Synklinaltal n, Senkungstal n, Muldental n
synchronized resonance	Synchronresonanz f	syncline, synclinal, synclinal fold, trough; synform <geo.>	Synklinale f, Synkline f, Mulde f, Einsenkung f; Trog m <Geo.>
synchronizer	s. synchronizing device		
synchronizing	s. synchronism		
synchronizing device, synchronizer	Synchronisiereinrichtung f, Synchronisier[ungs]gerät n, Synchronisierungseinrichtung f, Synchronisierungsstufe f, Synchronisiervorrichtung f, Synchronisator m, Gleichlaufeinrichtung f, Gleichlaufgerät n	synclinore, synclinorium	Synklinorium n, Verbiegungsbecken n
		syn configuration	s. syn modification
		syncriminator	Synkriminator m
		syncrystallization, simultaneous crystallization	gleichzeitige Kristallisation f, Synkristallisation f
synchronizing interval	Synchronisierlücke f		
synchronizing pulse	Synchronisierimpuls m, Synchronisierungsimpuls m, Gleichlaufimpuls m, Synchronimpuls m	syndet, synthetic detergent, saponide, sapide	Saponid n, Sapid n, Syndet n <pl.: -ts>
		syndiotactic, syndyotactic	syndiotaktisch
		syndyname	Syndyname f
synchronizing pulse generator, pulse generator, clock generator, clock multivibrator	Taktgeber m, Impulsgeber m	syndyotactic	s. syndiotactic
		synentropy	s. mutual information
		syneresis, bleeding	Synärese f, Synäresis f
synchronizing signal	Synchronisier[ungs]signal n, Gleichlaufsignal n, Gleichlaufzeichen n, Synchrosignal n, Synchronisierzeichen n	synerg[et]ic	synergetisch
		synerg[et]ic activator	s. synerg[et]ic intensifier
		synerg[et]ic curve	Synergiekurve f
synchronome	Synchronome f	synerg[et]ic intensifier, synerg[et]ic activator	synergetischer Verstärker m
synchronometer	s. synchronous timer		
synchronous clock	s. synchronous timer	synergism	Synergismus m
synchronous computer, synchronous machine <num. math.>	Synchronrechner m <num. Math.>	synergy	Synergie f
		synform	s. a. syncline <geo.>
		syn form	s. syn modification
synchronous condition	Synchronbedingung f	syngenetic	syngenetisch
		synionism, syniony	Synionie f
synchronous converter	s. rotary converter	synistor	Synistor m
synchronous demodulator (detector), synchro[de]tector	Synchrodetektor m, Synchrondetektor m, Synchrondemodulator m	synkinematic	synkinematisch
		syn modification, syn form (configuration)	syn-Form f
synchronous electric clock	s. synchronous timer	synodic[al] month, lunar month, lunation	synodischer Monat m, Mondmonat m, Lunation f
synchronous machine	s. synchronous computer <num. math.>		

synodic[al]

synodic[al] [revolution] period — synodische Umlaufzeit f, synodischer Umlauf m

synopsis, synoptic table <meteo.> — Synopse f, Synopsis f <Meteo.>

synoptic analysis, weather analysis, synoptic situation analysis — Wetteranalyse f

synoptic chart — s. synoptic map <meteo.>

synoptic code, weather code — Wetterkode m, Wettercode m, Wetterschlüssel m

synoptic constant — synoptische Konstante f

synoptic front, meteorological front — Wetterfront f

synoptic map <astr.> — synoptische Karte f, heliographische Karte <Astr.>

synoptic map, synoptic chart; weather map, weather chart, meteorological chart <meteo.> — synoptische Karte f, synoptische Wetterkarte f; Wetterkarte <Meteo.>

synoptic meteorology, synoptics — Synoptik f, synoptische Meteorologie f

synoptic phenomenon — s. meteorologic phenomenon

synoptics, synoptic meteorology — Synoptik f, synoptische Meteorologie f

synoptic situation — s. general weather situation

synoptic situation analysis — s. synoptic analysis

synoptic table, synopsis <meteo.> — Synopse f, Synopsis f <Meteo.>

synoptic wind — synoptischer Wind m

synoptic zone — Wetterzone f

synorogenesis — Synorogenese f

syn-position — syn-Stellung f

synproportionation, reproportionation — Synproportionierung f

syntactic — syntaktisch

syntactics — Syntaktik f

syntax — Syntax f

syntectonic — syntektonisch

syntexis <geo.> — Syntexis f, Syntexe f <Geo.>

synthesis; build-up <chem., nucl.> — Synthese f; Aufbau m <Chem., Kern.>

synthesis of electrical network, network synthesis, electrical network synthesis — Netzwerksynthese f

synthesis of isotopically labelled compounds, preparation of labelled compounds — Markierungssynthese f

synthesizer — Synthetisator m, Synthesegerät n, Syntheseeinrichtung f

synthetical geometry — synthetische Geometrie f

synthetic crystal — synthetischer (künstlicher) Kristall m

synthetic detergent — s. syndet

syntonic comma — syntonisches Komma n

syntonizing variometer, tuning variometer — Abstimmvariometer n

syphon, siphon; pump-type dispenser — Heber m; Saugheber m, Ansaugheber m; Stechheber m

syphonage — s. syphoning

syphon barometer, siphon barometer — Heberbarometer n; Phiolenbarometer n; Zimmerbarometer n; Manometerprobe f, Barometerprobe f, abgekürztes Barometer n

syphoning, siphoning, syphonage, siphonage — Hebern n; Aushebern n; Abhebern n; Heberwirkung f

syringe — Injektionsspritze f, Spritze f

system, network [of lines] <el.> — Netzwerk n, Netz n, Streckenkomplex m <El.>

system analysis — Systemanalyse f

systematic error, fixed error, bias; regular error <stat.> — systematischer Fehler m, erwartungsmäßige Abweichung f, Verzerrung f, Verfälschung f, Bias m; regelmäßiger Fehler <Stat.>

systematic sample — systematische Probe f

systematic sampling — s. patterned sampling

system based on three fundamental units — Dreiersystem n

system constant — Systemkonstante f

system current, line current, interlinked current — verketteter Strom m

system determinant — Systemdeterminante f

system element, network element; network parameter, system parameter — Netzwerkelement n, Netzelement n; Netzwerkparameter m, Netzparameter m

system equations, equations of the network — Netzwerkgleichungen fpl, Systemgleichungen fpl

system function, function of the network — Systemfunktion f, Netzwerkfunktion f

system function — s. a. closed-loop transfer function <control>

system having negative thermodynamical temperature — System n mit negativer absoluter Temperatur, außergewöhnliches System

systemic action — systemische Wirkung f, Systemwirkung f

systemic insecticide — s. systemic pesticide

systemic pesticide; systemic insecticide — systemisches Mittel n, innertherapeutisches Mittel; systemisches Insektizid n, Systeminsektizid n

system matrix — Systemmatrix f

system of absolute electrical units — s. Giorgi system [of units]

system of atomic units, system of natural units, system of Hartree units, atomic (natural) system of units, Hartree system [of units] — Hartreesches Maßsystem (Einheitensystem) n, atomares Einheitensystem, natürliches Einheitensystem (Maßsystem)

system of bars, framework — Fachwerk n

system of clefts, cleft system — Kluftsystem n

system of complanar forces, complanar forces — ebenes Kräftesystem n

system of couples — Kräftepaarsystem n

system of crystal symmetry, crystal system — Kristallsystem n, Syngonie f

system of curves, set of curves; family of curves, group of curves — Kurvenschar f, Schar f [von Kurven]

system of cylinders, packing of cylinders — Zylinderpackung f

system of functions — Funktionensystem n, Funktionssystem n

system of fundamental stars, fundamental system <astr.> — Fundamentalsystem n <Astr.>

system of Hartree units — s. system of atomic units

system of linear equations, [system of] simultaneous linear equations, set of [simultaneous] linear equations — lineares Gleichungssystem n

system of mass (material) points — s. system of points

system of measurement (measures), system of units, system of scales of measurements — Einheitensystem n, Maßsystem n

system of natural units — s. system of atomic units

system of notation; designation; notation; symbolism — Bezeichnung f; Bezeichnungsweise f; Schreibweise f; Symbolik f

system of numbers, number system, numeration — Zahlensystem n

system of ordinary differential equations   s. simultaneous ordinary differential equations
system of points, system of material points, system of mass points   Massenpunktsystem n
system of rays <on the Moon's surface>   Strahlensystem n <Oberflächenform des Mondes>
system of reference   s. frame of reference
system of scales of measurement, system of units, system of measures   Einheitensystem n, Maßsystem n
system of sources, source system   Quellsystem n, Quellensystem n
system of space-time co-ordinates   s. space-time co-ordinates
system of spheres, packing of spheres   Kugelpackung f
system of stars, galactic system, stellar system, galaxy, island universe   Sternsystem n, Galaxis f, Galaxie f <pl.: Galaxien>
system of surfaces, family of surfaces   Flächenschar f, Flächensystem n
system of units, system [of scales] of measurement, system of measures   Einheitensystem n, Maßsystem n
system of units used in engineering and technology   s. engineering system
system of variational equations   System n der Variationsgleichungen, Variationssystem n
system of vectors, vector system   Vektorsystem n, Kräftesystem n; Stabsumme f, Stabwert m, Stäbesumme f <Study>, Liniensumme f <Timerding>, Streckensystem n <Mohr>, Vektorensystem n, heteraptische Summe f <Budde>
system of web members   s. strut bracing
system parameter   s. system element
system theory   Systemtheorie f
system to be controlled   s. controlled system
system voltage   s. line voltage
system with four fundamental units   Vierersystem n
system without constraints, unconstrained system   System n ohne Zwang[sbedingungen]
system with zero position error, astatic system   integral wirkendes System n, System ohne P-Abweichung, astatisches System
systolic pressure   systolischer Druck m
systolic volume, stroke volume   Schlagvolumen n
systrophe   Systrophe f
syzygial period, syzygial time   Springzeit f, syzygiale Hochwasserzeit f
syzygial tide   s. spring tide
syzygial time, syzygial period   Springzeit f, syzygiale Hochwasserzeit f
syzygy   Syzygie f, Syzygium n <pl.: Syzygien>
Szilard-Chalmers detector   Szilard-Chalmers-Detektor m
Szilard-Chalmers effect   Szilard-Chalmers-Effekt m
Szilard-Chalmers process (reaction)   Szilard-Chalmers-Prozeß m, Szilard-Chalmers-Reaktion f
Szilard['s] paradox   Szilardsches Paradoxon n
Szilard['s] thought experiment   Gedankenversuch m von Szilard
Szivessy compensator (instrument, simple half-shade compensator)   Szivessy-Kompensator m

T

tabet soil, mollisol   Auftauboden m, Mollisol m

table, platform <geo.>   Tafel f <Geo.>
table, surface, water table, free surface of water, water stage, water plane <hydr.>   freie Oberfläche f, Spiegel m, Wasserspiegel m <Hydr.>
table / 2 × 2, four[-]fold table, two-by-two [contingency] table   Vierfeldertafel f, Zweimal-zwei-Tafel f, 2 × 2-Tafel f, 2 · 2-Tafel f
table of Laplace transformation (transforms)   Laplacesche Korrespondenztafel f, Laplace-Tabelle f, Laplacesche Tabelle f
table of random [sampling] numbers   Zufallszahlentabelle f, Zufallszahlentafel f, Zufallstafel f
table of refraction, refraction table   Refraktionstabelle f, Refraktionstafel f
tablet   Tablette f
tablet getter, getter tablet   Gettertablette f

tabular   tafelförmig, Tafel-

tabular   s. a. tabulated
tabular iceberg   Tafeleisberg m
tabular value, tabulated value, tabulated datum   Tabellenwert m, tabellarisierter (tabulierter) Wert m
tabulated, tabular   tabuliert, tabellarisiert, tabelliert, vertafelt, Tabellen-; tabellarisch
tabulated datum, tabulated value, tabular value   Tabellenwert m, tabellarisierter (tabulierter) Wert m
tabulated function   tabulierte Funktion f
tabulated value, tabular value, tabulated datum   Tabellenwert m, tabellarisierter (tabulierter) Wert m
tabulation; summarizing [in a table]; compilation [in a table]   Tabulierung f, Tabell[aris]ierung f, Zusammenstellung f [in einer Tabelle]; Vertafelung f; tabellarische Darstellung f

tacheometer, tachymeter   Tachymeter n
tacheometer compas, tacheometric compas   Tachymeterbussole f
tacheometer diagram, tacheometer plot   Tachymeterdiagramm n
tacheometer level, theodolite level, transit level   Nivelliertachymeter n
tacheometer plot, tacheometer diagram   Tachymeterdiagramm n
tacheometer theodolite   Tachymetertheodolit m, Kreistachymeter n, Streckenmeßtheodolit m
tacheometer traverse   Tachymeterzug m

tacheometric compas, tacheometer compas   Tachymeterbussole f
tacheometry, tachymetry   Tachymetrie f
tachistoscope   Tachistoskop n
tacho-alternator, tachodynamo, tacho-generator   Tacho[meter]generator m, Tacho[meter]dynamo m, Tachometermaschine f
tachogram   Tachogramm n
tachometer   s. speedometer
tachygenesis   Tachygenese f
tachymeter, tacheometer   Tachymeter n
tachymetering, tachymetric plotting   Tachymetrieren n, tachymetrische Aufnahme f

tachymetry, tacheometry   Tachymetrie f
tachyon, faster-than-light particle   Tachyon n
tachyseismic   tachyseismisch

tacitron   Tacitron n
tackiness   s. adhesive power
tackle [pulley]   s. pulley <mech.>
tack-sharp   gestochen scharf, haarscharf

tacnode, double cusp, point of osculation   Selbstberührungspunkt m
tacpoint   s. point of contact
tactical <chem.; bio.>   taktisch <Chem.; Bio.>
tactical polymerization   s. stereospecific polymerization

tactical 860

tactical reaction <bio.>	taktische Reaktion f <Bio.>	Tait['s] equation	Taitsche Gleichung f
tacticity	Taktizität f	Tait-Thomson theorem	Satz m von Tait und Thomson, Tait-Thomsonscher Satz
tactocatalytic	taktokatalytisch		
tactoid	Taktoid n		
tactophase	Taktophase f	take-off	s. launch
tactosol	Taktosol n	take readings, read off, read	ablesen, eine Ablesung vornehmen
tadpole model	„Kaulquappen"modell n		
Tafel constant	Tafelsche Konstante f, Konstante in der Tafelschen Gleichung		
Tafel['s] equation	Tafelsche Gleichung f	taking	Entnehmen n, Entnahme f
		taking <a shot>, exposure, photographing, shooting <phot.>	Aufnahme f, Aufnehmen n, <Phot.>, Photographieren n
Tafel line, Tafel plot	Tafel-Diagramm n		
tafoni	Tafoni mpl, Bröckellöcher npl	taking an indicator diagram, indication <mech.>	Indizierung f, Aufnahme f eines Indikatordiagramms <Mech.>
tag, label	Markierung f, Marke f		
tag; tongue; reed	Zunge f	taking characteristic	s. spectral response curve
		taking into account, taking into consideration	Berücksichtigung f
tagged	s. labelled		
tagged atom, tracer, labelled atom, indicator, marker <nucl.>	Tracer m, markiertes Atom n, Indikator m <Kern.>	taking of a bearing, interception	Anpeilung f
		taking off; measurement, measuring, metering	Messung f, Ausmessung f; Vermessung f; experimentelle Bestimmung f
tagged compound	s. tracer compound		
tagged with isotope	s. labelled	taking of power, removal (extraction) of power, power extraction	Leistungsentnahme f; Leistungsentzug m
tagged with radioactive isotope, labelled with radioactive isotope	radioaktiv markiert, markiert mit einem radioaktiven Isotop		
		taking of samples	s. sampling
tagging [with isotope]	s. labelling [with isotope] <nucl.>	taking of steam, steam bleeding (extraction)	Dampfentnahme f, Entnahme f von Dampf
tail, tailing <of the curve>	Abfall m, Schwanz m, Ausläufer m, Ende n, Schwanzteil m <Kurve>		
		taking the aim, aiming <opt.>	Visieren n, Visur f; Zielen n; Visierkunst f; Richten n <Opt.>
tail, tailing <chromatography>	Schwänze mpl, Schwanzbildung f, Schweifbildung f, Streifenbildung f, Kometbildung f	talbot $<= 10^7$ lumergs>	Talbot $n <= 10^7$ lm erg>
		Talbot['s] band	Talbotscher Streifen m, Talbotsche Linie f
tail	s. a. long wavelength tail	Talbot['s] law	Talbotsches Gesetz n
tail absorption	s. absorption confined to emission centres	talbotype	Talbotypie f
		Talcott['s] method [for latitude]	Horrebow-Talcottsche Methode f
tail area of distribution	Fläche f am Verteilungsende	Talcott pair	Talcott-Paar n
tail band	Schwanzbande f	Talmage hardness	Talmage-Härte f
tail condensation, knot within cometary tail	Schweifwolke f		
		Talmi coefficient	Talmi-Koeffizient m
tail current	Schwanzstrom m	Talmi integral	Talmi-Integral n
		Talmi-Moshinsky transformation	Talmi-Moshinsky-Transformation f
tail fraction, residual fraction, tails <chem.>	Nachlauf m, Rückstandsfraktion f <Chem.>	talus fan	s. debris cone
		talweg, thalweg	Talweg m
tailheaviness	Schwanzlastigkeit f		
tailing	s. tail	talysurf; profilometer; profile testing meter; roughometer	Rauhigkeitstiefenmesser m, Rauhigkeitsmesser m; Profilmeßgerät n, Profilmesser m, Profilometer n
tailings, still bottom heel, still bottoms, heel, bottoms, leavings	Destillierrückstand m, Blasenrückstand m, Destillationsrückstand m		
tail of absorption spectrum	s. long wavelength tail	tamaid, t	Tamaid n, t
		tame distribution	s. tempered distribution
tail of the comet, comet tail, cometary tail	Kometenschweif m, Schweif m des Kometen	Tammann['s] equation [of state]	Tammannsche Gleichung f
tail of the pulse, pulse tail	Impulsabfall m, Impulsschwanz m, Nachleuchtschleppe f	Tammann['s] parting limit	Tammann-Grenze f
tail photoconduction	Ausläuferphotoleitung f	Tammann['s] principle, principle of parting limits	Tammannsches Prinzip n, Tammann-Prinzip n
tailpiece, tail vane <of the current meter>	Steuer n [des Meßflügels], Schwimmsteuer n	Tammann temperature	Tammann-Temperatur f, Tammannsche Temperatur f
tail race	s. tail water		
tail region	Ausläufergebiet n, Ausläuferbereich m	Tamm-Dancoff approximation, Tamm-Dancoff type approximation, TDA	Tamm-Dancoff-Näherung f, Näherung f vom Tamm-Dancoff-Typ
tails	s. tail fraction <chem.>		
tail shock wave	s. tail wave	Tamm-Dancoff equation	Tamm-Dancoff-Gleichung f
tail spin, spinning, spin, free spinning	Trudeln n, Trudelbewegung f, Trudelflug m		
		Tamm-Dancoff formalism	Tamm-Dancoff-Formalismus m
tail-to-tail arrangement, tail-to-tail structure of polymer	Schwanz-Schwanz-Verknüpfung f	Tamm-Dancoff type approximation, Tamm-Dancoff approximation	Tamm-Dancoff-Näherung f, Näherung f vom Tamm-Dancoff-Typ
tail vane	s. tailpiece		
tail water, lower pool, lower pond, lower reach, after bay, tail race, underwater	untere Haltung f, Unterhaltung f, Unterwasser n, Talseite f	Tamm level	Tamm-Niveau n, Tamm-Term m, Tammscher Oberflächenterm m, Tamm-Oberflächenterm m, Tamm-Zustand m, Tammscher Oberflächenzustand m, Tamm-Oberflächenzustand m
tail wave, tail shock wave	Schwanzwelle f [bei Überschallströmung]		

Tamm operator — Tamm-Operator m, Tammscher Operator m
tamper — s. blanket
tamper — s. reflector <of reactor>
Tanberg effect — Tanberg-Effekt m
tandem — s. tandem connected
tandem [accelerator] — s. tandem electrostatic generator
tandem ascent, tandem climb — Zwillingsaufstieg m, Gespannaufstieg m
tandem connected — s. series connected <el., gen.>
tandem connection <el.>; cascade connection, connection in cascade <el., chem.>; cascade circuit <el.>; concatenation <chem.> — Kaskadenschaltung f, Schaltung f in Kaskade <El., Chem.>
tandem connection — s. a. series connection
tandem electrostatic accelerator — s. tandem electrostatic generator
tandem electrostatic generator, tandem-type generator, tandem generator, tandem electrostatic accelerator, tandem-type accelerator, tandem [accelerator], tandem Van de Graaff [accelerator] — Tandem-Van-de-Graaff-Generator m, Tandemgenerator m, Van-de-Graaff-Generator m vom Tandemtyp, Tandembeschleuniger m
tandem engine — Tandemmaschine f, Tandem-Dampfmaschine f
tandem generator — s. tandem electrostatic generator
tandem-joined, mounted in line, arranged in line — hintereinander angeordnet
tandem network, radial network, star network — Sternnetz n, sternförmiges Netzwerk n, Sternglied n
tandem potentiometer — s. dual potentiometer
tandem radiosonde, twin radiosonde — Radiosondengespann n
tandem spectrometer — Tandemspektrometer n
tandem-type accelerator (generator), tandem Van de Graaff [accelerator] — s. tandem electrostatic generator
tangency — s. contiguity
tangency point — s. point of contact
tangensoid, tangent curve (line) — Tangenskurve f, Tangenslinie f
tangent approximation — Tangensapproximation f, Tangensnäherung f
tangent Bloch wall — tangierende Bloch-Wand f
tangent condition — [Airysche] Tangentenbedingung f, Tangensbedingung f, Bedingung f für die Verzeichnungsfreiheit
tangent curve, tangensoid, tangent line — Tangenskurve f, Tangenslinie f
tangent distortion correction, tangent equalization — Tangensentzerrung f
tangent formula — s. Maclaurin['s] formula
tangent galvanometer — Tangentenbussole f
tangential, touching — tangential, Tangential-; berührend, tangierend; Tangenten-
tangential, meridian, meridional <opt.> — Meridional-, Tangential-, meridional, tangential, speichenrecht <Opt.>
tangential acceleration, tangential component of acceleration — Tangentialbeschleunigung f
tangential arc of halo — Berührungsbogen m
tangential beam — s. tangential pencil
tangential coma — s. coma
tangential component of acceleration — s. tangential acceleration
tangential co-ordinates — Tangentialkoordinaten fpl

tangential couple, tangential force — Tangentialschubkraft f, Drehschub m
tangential curvature — s. geodesic curvature
tangential curvature of the image field — meridional curvature of the image field
tangential discontinuity, discontinuity of tangential component — Tangentialsprung m, Sprung m der Tangentialkomponente
tangential displacement — Tangentialverschiebung f, Tangentialkomponente f der Verschiebung
tangential fan — s. tangential pencil
tangential field probe, tangential probe — Tangentialsonde f
tangential focal line — s. meridian focal line
tangential focal plane — s. meridian plane
tangential focus — s. meridian focal line
tangential force — Tangentialkraft f
tangential force, tangential couple — Tangentialschubkraft f, Drehschub m
tangential image point, meridian (meridional) image point — meridionaler Bildpunkt m, tangentialer Bildpunkt
tangential pencil [of rays], meridian fan, tangential fan, meridian, pencil [of rays] — Meridionalbüschel n, Tangentialbüschel n
tangential pencil [of rays], meridian pencil [of rays], meridian beam, tangential beam — Meridional[strahlen]bündel n, Tangentialstrahlenbündel n, Tangentialbündel n
tangential plane — s. tangent plane
tangential plane — s. a. meridian plane
tangential point — Tangentialpunkt m
tangential pressure — Tangentialdruck m, Umfangsdruck m
tangential probe, tangential field probe — Tangentialsonde f
tangential ray, meridian ray, meridional ray — Meridionalstrahl m, Tangentialstrahl m
tangential reaction, friction — Tangentialreaktion f
tangential section, meridian (meridional) section <opt.> — Meridionalschnitt m, Tangentialschnitt m <Opt.>
tangential speed, tangential velocity — Tangentialgeschwindigkeit f, tangentiale Geschwindigkeit f
tangential stress, circumferential stress, hoop stress — Tangentialspannung f; Ringspannung f; Tangentialbeanspruchung f
tangential stress — s. a. shear stress
tangential stress field — Tangentialspannungsfeld n
tangential vector, tangent vector — Tangentenvektor m, Tangentialvektor m
tangential velocity — s. tangential speed
tangential wind stress — Windschubspannung f
tangent law, tangent theorem — Tangentensatz m
tangent line — s. tangensoid
tangent modulus — Tangentialmodul m
tangent plane, tangential plane — Tangentialebene f, Berührungsebene f; Tangentenebene f
tangent relief — Tangensrelief n
tangent screw — Gefällschraube f, Tangentenschraube f
tangent screw tacheometer — Gefällschraubentachymeter n, Tachymeter n, mit Tangentenschraube
tangent theorem, tangent law — Tangentensatz m
tangent-trapezoidal formula — s. Maclaurin['s] formula
tangent unit vector — s. unit tangent
tangent vector, tangential vector — Tangentenvektor m, Tangentialvektor m
tangling — s. entanglement
tangling [of magnetic field lines] — Verwirrung f [von magnetischen Feldlinien]
Tang['s] table — Tangsche Tabelle f

tank circuit	Tankkreis *m*	tapping, tap <of voltage>	Spannungsabgriff *m*
Tank['s] current-distribution law, Tank['s] law	Tanksches Stromverteilungsgesetz *n*, Tanksches Gesetz *n*	tapping, branch, branching, branching-off <el.>	Abzweigung *f*, Abzweig *m*, Ableitung *f* <El.>
tank development, box development	Standentwicklung *f*; Dosenentwicklung *f*; Tankentwicklung *f*	tapping tapping tapping point tapping switch, step switch, stepping switch	*s. a.* tap <el.> *s. a.* tap <of current> Anzapfungspunkt *m* Stufenschalter *m*
Tank['s] law, Tank['s] current-distribution law	Tanksches Stromverteilungsgesetz *n*, Tanksches Gesetz *n*	tap water	Leitungswasser *n*
tank reactor	Tankreaktor *m*	Tardy['s] method tare	Tardysche Methode *f* Tara *f*
tank rectifier, metallic rectifier, metallic valve	Metallgleichrichter *m*	tare balance tare shot	*s.* pharmaceutical balance Tariergewicht *n*, Tarierschrot *n*
Tank['s] region	Tanksches Stromübernahmegebiet (Gebiet) *n*	target	Target *n*; Auffänger *m*, Treffplatte *f*, Prallplatte *f*
tank-type [electrostatic] generator, tank-type Van de Graaff generator	Tankgenerator *m*	target; object target target target current	Ziel *n* *s. a.* radiobiological sensitive volume [of the cell] *s. a.* collimating mark Targetstrom *m*
tannage, hardening <of emulsion> tannin-coated collodion plate	Härtung *f*, Gerbung *f* <Emulsion> Kollodiumtanninplatte *f*, Tanninplatte *f*	target distance, object distance	Zielweite *f*, Zielabstand *m*, Zielentfernung *f*
tantile tap, tapping <el.>	Tantil *n* Abgriff *m*; Anzapfung *f*, Anzapf *m*; Abzapfung *f* <El.>	target electrode target element target nucleus target of the superorthicon	Auffängerelektrode *f* Targetelement *n* Targetkern *m* Speicherplatte *f* des Superorthikons
tap, tapping <of current>	Stromableitung *f*, Stromabführung *f*; Stromabgriff *m*	target particle, bombarded particle, struck particle	beschossenes Teilchen *n*, getroffenes Teilchen, Targetteilchen *n*
tap, tapping <of voltage>	Spannungsabgriff *m*	target theory; hit theory	Treffertheorie *f*, Depottheorie *f*; Treffbereichstheorie *f*
tap density tape tape antenna tape comparator	Klopfdichte *f* *s.* tape measure *s.* ribbon antenna *s.* surveying tape comparator	taring taring vane tarnish tarnishing	Tarierung *f* Tarierflügel *m*, Tarierungsflügel *m* *s.* fog *s.* covered with damp / getting
tapeline tape loudspeaker tape measure, measuring tape, surveyor's tape, tapeline, tape	*s.* tape measure *s.* ribbon loudspeaker Bandmaß *n*, Meßband *n*	Tashiro indicator T association taste [sense] Tate['s] law tau, τ Tauberian theorem	Tashiro-Indikator *m* T-Assoziation *f* *s.* sense of taste Tatesches Gesetz *n* *s.* alphina particle Tauberscher Satz *m*
tape microphone taper, planform taper <of the wing>	*s.* ribbon microphone Zuspitzung *f*, Zuspitzungsverhältnis *n* <Flügel>	tau meson, τ meson, tauon <= K meson> tau meter, τ meter; ultra tau meter, ultra τ meter	τ-Meson *n*, Tauon *n*, Tau-Meson *n* Taumeter *n*, τ-Meter *n*; Ultrataumeter *n*, Ultra-τ-Meter *n*, Nachleuchtmeßgerät *n*, Nachleuchtmesser *m*
taper tape recording taper gauge	*s. a.* tapering *s.* magnetic recording Kegellehre *f*		
tapering, tapering of cross-section, taper	Querschnittsverjüngung *f*, Verjüngung *f* [des Querschnitts], Zuspitzung *f*, konische Querschnittsverminderung *f*, konische Abnahme *f* des Querschnitts; Verjüngungsmaß *n*	tauon tau phenomenon, τ phenomenon	*s.* tau meson Gelb-Benussi-Phänomen *n*, τ-Phänomen *n*, Tau-Phänomen *n*
		taut, tight, stretched tau-theta puzzle, τ-Θ puzzle tautochrone, tautochronous curve	straff [gespannt], gespannt Tau-Theta-Rätsel *n*, τ-Θ-Rätsel *n* Tautochrone *f*
tapering of the crystal; sharpening of the crystal	Zuspitzung *f* des Kristalls, Zuschärfung *f* des Kristalls	tautochronism	Tautochronismus *m*
tape store, magnetic tape store	Magnetbandspeicher *m*, Bandspeicher *m*	tautochronous curve, tautochrone tautochronous motion tautomer, tautomeride	Tautochrone *f* tautochrone Bewegung *f* Tautomer[e] *n*, tautomere Form *f*
tap grease taphrogenesis tapped coil	*s.* cock grease Taphrogenese *f* Anzapfspule *f*; angezapfte Spule *f*; Abzweigspule *f*	tautomeric change, tautomeric transition	tautomere Umwandlung *f*, tautomerer Übergang *m*
tapped resistor	Anzapfwiderstand *m*	tautomeric constant tautomeric equilibrium tautomeric transition tautomeric wave tautomeride, tautomer	Tautomeriekonstante *f* Tautomeriegleichgewicht *n* *s.* tautomeric change tautomere Welle *f* Tautomer[e] *n*, tautomere Form *f*
tapped transformer, split transformer	Anzapftransformator *m*	tautomerism, dynamic isomerism; desmotropism	Tautomerie *f*; Desmotropie *f*
		tautozonal	tautozonal
tapper	*s.* decoherer		

taut string	gespannte Saite f
taut strip	s. taut tape
taut-strip galvanometer	Spannbandgalvanometer n
taut-strip instrument	Spannbandgerät n, Spannbandmeßgerät n, Spannbandinstrument n
taut strip suspension, taut suspension	Spannbandaufhängung f, Spannbandlagerung f
taut tape, taut strip	Spannband n; Spannbügel m
taut wire suspension	Spanndrahtaufhängung f, Spanndrahtlagerung f
taxis	Taxis f
Taylor annular vorticity, Taylor vortex	Taylor-Wirbel m, Taylorscher Ringwirbel m
Taylor-Batchelor theory	Taylor-Batchelorsche Theorie f
Taylor circuit	Taylor-Schaltung f
Taylor coefficient	Taylor-Koeffizient m, Taylorscher Koeffizient m
Taylor effect	Taylor-Effekt m
Taylor['s] expansion	s. Taylor['s] series
Taylor['s] experiment	s. Taylor['s] interference experiment
Taylor['s] flow	Taylorsche Strömung f
Taylor['s] formula, Taylor['s] theorem, general[ized] (extended) mean value theorem	Taylorsche Formel f, Taylorscher Satz m
Taylor['s] formula	Taylorsche Quadraturformel f
Taylor instability	Taylor-Instabilität f, Taylorsche Instabilität f
Taylor['s] interference experiment, Taylor['s] experiment	Taylorscher Interferenzversuch m, Taylor-Versuch m, Taylorscher Versuch m
Taylor lens, Cooke lens	Cooke-Linse f, „Cooke lens" f, Taylor-Linse f
Taylor modulation	Taylor-Modulation f, Taylorsche Modulation f
Taylor number, Ta	Taylor-Zahl f, Taylorsche Kennzahl (Zahl) f, Ta
Taylor-Orowan dislocation	s. edge dislocation
Taylor['s] series; Taylor['s] expansion	Taylor-Reihe f, Taylorsche Reihe f; Taylor-Entwicklung f, Taylorsche Entwicklung f
Taylor['s] spiral	Taylorsche Spirale f, Taylor-Spirale f
Taylor strengthening, Taylor work hardening	Taylor-Verfestigung f
Taylor['s] theorem	s. Taylor['s] formula
Taylor transmitter	Taylor-Sender m, Sender m mit Taylor-Modulation
Taylor vortex, Taylor annular vorticity	Taylor-Wirbel m, Taylorscher Ringwirbel m
Taylor['s] vortex system	Taylorsches Wirbelsystem n
Taylor work hardening	s. Taylor strengthening
T-beam, tee	T-Träger m
T-bridge, tee bridge	T-Brücke f
Tchaplygin['s] condition	s. Chaplygin['s] condition
Tchebycheff['s] (Tchebyshev['s]) polynomial	s. Chebyshev['s] polynomial
Tcherenkov effect, Čerenkov (Cherenkov) effect, Vavilov-Čerenkov effect	Čerenkov-Effekt m, [Wawilow-]Tscherenkow-Effekt m
TCP theorem	s. CPT theorem
t-distribution	s. Student['s] t distribution
T² distribution	s. Hotelling['s] distribution
T-μ distribution, grand canonical distribution	große kanonische Verteilung f
TEA laser	= transversally excited atmospheric pressure laser
tear	s. tearing
teardrop body	s. streamlined body
tearing, tear, rupture, abruption; bursting; splitting; rending <mech.>	Zerreißung f; Reißen n, Riß m; Einreißen n; Sprungbildung f <Mech.>
tear of glass	Glasträne f
technical data	s. operating parameters
technical system [of units]	s. engineering system [of units]
tecnical unit, engineering unit, industrial unit	technische Einheit f, technische Maßeinheit f
technique, method; process; procedure	Verfahren n; Technik f; Methode f
technique of axial section, axial section method, method of axial sections	Achsenschnittverfahren n Schneidenmessung f
technique of Czochralski	s. Czochralski['s] method
technique of layer division, layer division technique	Schichtenteilungsmethode f, Schichtenteilungsverfahren n
technique of light production	s. production of light
technique of measurement	s. method of measurement
technique of model testing	Modellmeßverfahren n
technique of moiré fringes, moiré method, moiré technique	Moirémethode f, Isopachenverfahren n, interferometrisches Isopachenverfahren
technique of nuclear resonance absorption	s. nuclear induction technique
technique of radiation measurement, radiation measuring technique	Strahlungsmeßtechnik f, Kernstrahlungsmeßtechnik f, Strahlenmeßtechnik f
technique of rotation photograph	s. Bragg['s] rotating crystal method
technique of short-time measurement, short-time-interval technique	Kurzzeittechnik f, Kurzzeitmeßtechnik f
technological layout	s. flowsheet
technological physics, industrial physics	technische Physik f
Teclu burner	Teclu-Brenner m
tecnetron	Tecnetron n
tectogene	Tektogen n
tectogenesis, orogenesis	Tektogenese f, Orogenese f
tectonic analysis	tektonische Analyse f, Gefügeanalyse f, Strukturanalyse f <der Gesteine>
tectonic cycle, geotectonic cycle	geotektonischer Zyklus m
tectonic dislocation, tectonic fault	tektonische Störung f, tektonische Dislokation f
tectonic earthquake, dislocation earthquake	tektonisches Beben n, tektonisches Erdbeben n, Dislokationsbeben n
tectonic fault	s. tectonic dislocation
tectonic fissure	Kluftspalte f, tektonische Spalte f
tectonism	Tektonismus m
tectonophysics	Tektonophysik f
tectonosphere	Tektonosphäre f
tectorial membrane	Deckmembran f, Membrana f tectoria, Cortische Membran f
tectosphere, astenosphere	Astenosphäre f, Tektosphäre f
tedious	s. time-consuming
tee, conduit tee; three-way pipe, T-pipe, T	T-Stück n; T-Rohr n, T-Rohrstück n
tee, T-beam	T-Träger m
tee bridge, T-bridge	T-Brücke f
teinochemistry	Teinochemie f
tektite	Glasmeteorit m; Tektit m
telecentric path of rays	telezentrischer Strahlengang m
telecentric projection	telezentrische Perspektive f; telezentrische Projektion f
telecommunication; telecommunication[s] engineering; telecommunication technics; communication[s] engineering	Fernmeldewesen n; Fernmeldetechnik f; Nachrichtentechnik f

telecontrol, remote control, [long-]distance control, distant control	Fernsteuerung f	telescope level tube, zenith level	Fernrohrlibelle f
		telescope mounting	Fernrohrmontierung f
		telescopic, extensible	teleskopisch, zusammenschiebbar, ausziehbar
telefocus system	Fernfokussystem n		
telegauge	s. telemeter	telescopic alidade	Kippregel f
telegraph (telegrapher's, telegraphic) equation, equation of telegraphy	Telegraphengleichung f		
telegraph modulation	Telegraphenmodulation f	telescopic image	s. afocal image
		telescopic magnifier	Fernrohrlupe f
telegraphone	Telegraphon n		
tele-irradiation	Fernbestrahlung f	telescopic meteor	teleskopisches Meteor n, Telemeteor n
telemeasurement	s. telemetering	telescopic pipe, telescopic tube	Teleskoprohr n, Ausziehrohr n
telemeasuring	s. telemetering		
telemechanics	Telemechanik f	telescopic sight	s. sighting telescope
telemeteorometry	Telemeteorometrie f, Fernmessung f meteorologischer Daten	telescopic tube	Ausziehtubus m
		telescopic tube	s. a. telescopic pipe
telemeter, telegauge, telemetering instrument, remote instrument, apparatus for remote measurements; telemetering device, telemetering system, telemetry equipment; distant-reading instrument	Fernmeßgerät n, Ferninstrument n, Fernmesser m; Fernmeßeinrichtung f, Fernmeßanlage f	telescoping	Teleskopieren n, „telescoping" n
		teleseism, distant earthquake, earthquake of distant origin	Fernbeben n
		telespectroscope	Fernspektroskop n
		telestereoscope	Telestereoskop n
		telethermometer, [long-]distance thermometer, remote thermometer	Fernthermometer n, Telethermometer n, Temperaturfernmeßgerät n
telemeter, [optical] rangefinder, optical telemeter, [optical] distance meter	[optischer] Entfernungsmesser m, Distanzmesser m, Telemeter n; Abstandsmesser m	television image	Fernsehbild n
		television microscopy	Fernsehmikroskopie f, Mikroskopie f nach dem Fernsehprinzip
telemetering, telemeasuring, telemeasurement, remote metering (measurement, gauging), telemetry	Fernmessung f, Telemetrie f	television receiver, television set, televisor	Fernsehempfänger m, Fernsehgerät n, Fernseher m
telemetering device (instrument, system)	s. telemeter	telewattmeter	Leistungsfernmeßgerät n, Leistungsfernmesser m, Telewattmeter n
telemetry	s. telemetering		
telemetry	s. range finding		
telemetry equipment	s. telemeter	Tellegen effect	s. Luxembourg effect
teleparallelism, absolute parallelism	Fernparallelismus m, absoluter Parallelismus m	Teller-Redlich [product] rule, Redlich-Teller product rule, product rule	Produktregel f [von Teller und Redlich], Redlich-Tellersche Produktregel, Teller-Redlichsche Produktregel
telephone, telephone earphone, [telephone] receiver	Hörer m, Telephonhörer m, Fernhörer m, Telephon n		
telephone bridge, measuring bridge with telephone	Telephonmeßbrücke f, Telephonbrücke f	telluric force	tellurische Kraft f
		telluric line, terrestrial line	terrestrische (tellurische) Linie f
telephone current; voice current, speech current	Sprechstrom m	tellurometer	Tellurometer n
		telocentric	telozentrisch
telephone earphone, telephone receiver, telephone, receiver	Hörer m, Telephonhörer m, Fernhörer m, Telephon n	telomer	Telomer n <Bio.; Chem.>; Telomere n <Chem.>
		telotaxis	Telotaxis f
telephone theory [of Rutherford], frequency theory [of Rutherford], frequency theory of pitch	Telephontheorie f [des Hörens], Rutherfordsche Telephontheorie	Temkin isotherm	Temkinsche Adsorptionsisotherme f
		TEM mode	s. principal wave
		TE[-] mode	s. H[-] mode
		temper	s. tempering
telephone transmitter, transmitter unit, transmitter inset, transmitter <of telephone>	Fernsprechmikrophon n, Sprechkapsel f, Mikrophonkapsel f, Mikrophon n <Telephon>	temperament	s. equally tempered scale <ac.>
		temperate glacier	warmer Gletscher m, temperierter Gletscher
telephoning	s. telephony	temperate zone	gemäßigte Zone f, gemäßigt-warme Zone
telephonometry	Fernsprechmeßtechnik f		
telephony; telephoning, phoning	Telephonie f, Fernsprechwesen n; Fernsprechen n, Telephonieren n	temperature above freezing (zero, 0 °C)	Temperatur f über Null (0 °C), Plustemperatur f
telephoto attachment	Televorsatz m, Teleansatz m, Teleaufsatz m	temperature aloft, altitude temperature, hypsometric temperature	Höhentemperatur f
telephotography <phot.>	Fernphotographie f, Telephotographie f, Fernaufnahme[technik] f <Phot.>	temperature amplitude	Temperaturamplitude f
		temperature at rest, rest temperature	Ruhetemperatur f
		temperature at which reaction commences, threshold reaction temperature	Temperaturschwelle f der Reaktion, Anfangstemperatur f der Reaktion
telephoto lens	Teleobjektiv n, Fernobjektiv n		
telephotometry	Telephotometrie f	temperature balance	s. heat balance
teleradiography, teleroentgenography	Fernaufnahme[technik] f, Teleaufnahme[technik] f	temperature band	s. range of temperature
telescope	Fernrohr n, Teleskop n	temperature below freezing (zero, 0 °C), subzero (subfreezing) temperature	Temperatur f unter Null, Temperatur unter 0 °C, Minustemperatur f
telescope	s. a. counter telescope <nucl.>		

temperature boundary layer, thermal boundary, thermal boundary layer — Temperaturgrenzschicht f, thermische Grenzschicht f

temperature coefficient — Temperaturkoeffizient m, Temperaturbeiwert m, Temperaturfaktor m

temperature coefficient of capacitance — Temperaturkoeffizient m der Kapazität, Kapazitäts-Temperaturkoeffizient m

temperature coefficient of cell elongation, Q_{10} of cell elongation — Temperaturkoeffizient m der Zellstreckung, Q_{10} der Zellstreckung

temperature coefficient of conductivity — s. conductivity temperature coefficient

temperature coefficient of density, density temperature coefficient — Temperaturkoeffizient m der Dichte, Dichte-Temperaturkoeffizient m

temperature coefficient of reactivity, reactivity temperature coefficient — Temperaturkoeffizient m der Reaktivität, Reaktivitäts-Temperaturkoeffizient m

temperature coefficient of resistance — s. resistance temperature coefficient

temperature compensation, thermal compensation — Temperaturkompensation f

temperature compensation — s. a. heat balance

temperature compensator, temperature equalizer — Temperaturausgleicher m, Temperaturkompensator m

temperature conductivity — s. thermal diffusivity

temperature contrast, contrast of temperatures — Temperaturgegensatz m

temperature control, thermoregulation, thermocontrol, attemperation — Temperaturregelung f, Thermoregelung f

temperature-controlled — s. thermostated
temperature controller — s. thermoregulator
temperature control vessel, constant temperature vessel — Temperiergefäß n

temperature correction — Temperaturkorrektion f

temperature corresponding to the spectral distribution of energy of the radiator, distribution temperature — Verteilungstemperatur f

temperature cycle, thermal cycle — Temperaturwechsel m, Thermozyklus m, Wechsel m ‹beim Temperaturwechselversuch›

temperature cycle method, temperature development, thermal development ‹of nuclear emulsions› — Temperaturentwicklungsverfahren n, Temperaturentwicklung f ‹von Kernemulsionen›

temperature damage — Temperaturschaden m

temperature decrease — s. temperature drop
temperature delay, temperature lag — Temperaturverzögerung f

temperature development, temperature cycle method, thermal development ‹of nuclear emulsions› — Temperaturentwicklungsverfahren n, Temperaturentwicklung f ‹von Kernemulsionen›

temperature difference, difference of temperature — Temperaturdifferenz f, Temperaturunterschied m ‹in grd›

temperature diffuse scattering — s. inelastic scattering by crystals
temperature dispersion — Temperaturdispersion f
temperature displacement — s. temperature-induced shift

temperature drop, temperature fall (decrease), drop (fall) in temperature, fall of temperature, decrease in temperature; retrogression of temperature; cooling — Temperaturabnahme f, Temperatur[ab]fall m, Sinken (Fallen) n der Temperatur; Temperaturrückgang m, Zurückgehen n der Temperatur, Abkühlung f

temperature effect ‹of cosmic rays› — Temperatureffekt m ‹kosmische Strahlung›

temperature-entropy chart, temperature-entropy diagram, entropy-temperature plot, entropy [temperature] diagram, T,s diagram — Temperatur-Entropie-Diagramm n, Entropiediagramm n, Entropie-Temperatur-Diagramm n, TS-Diagramm n, T,s-Diagramm n, Wärmebild n, Wärmediagramm n

temperature equalizer, temperature compensator — Temperaturausgleicher m, Temperaturkompensator m

temperature equilibrium, thermal equilibrium — thermisches Gleichgewicht n, Wärmegleichgewicht n, Temperaturgleichgewicht n

temperature factor ‹of reflection› — Temperaturfaktor m ‹bei der Reflexion›

temperature fall — s. temperature drop
temperature field — Temperaturfeld n

temperature flash, thermal flash — Temperaturblitz m

temperature float technique — Schwebemethode f mit Variation der Temperatur, Schwebemethode mit Temperaturvariation

temperature fluctuation, temperature variation, hunting of temperature, oscillation of temperature about the mean value — Temperaturschwankung f

temperature from the rotation spectrum — s. rotational temperature
temperature from the vibration-rotation (rotational) spectrum — s. vibration temperature

temperature gradient, thermal gradient — Temperaturgradient m, Temperaturgefälle n

temperature gradient method — s. flotation method
temperature-height curve — Temperatur-Höhen-Kurve f

temperature increase, increase of (in) temperature, temperature rise, rise of (in) temperature; warming — Temperaturanstieg m, Temperaturzunahme f, Temperaturerhöhung f; Erwärmung f

temperature-independent factor ‹in theory of absolute reaction rate› — temperaturunabhängiger Faktor m ‹Theorie der absoluten Reaktionsgeschwindigkeit›

temperature in depth — Tiefentemperatur f

temperature-indicating crayon, thermometric crayon, tempilstik ‹US› — Temperaturfarbstift m, Farbstift m für Temperaturmessung, Temperaturmeßstift m

temperature indicating paint, temperature-sensitive paint, tempilstik ‹US› — Temperaturmeßfarbe f, Thermochrom n, Thermochromfarbe f, Thermofarbe f

temperature indicator — Temperaturanzeiger m, Temperaturanzeigegerät n; Temperaturindikator m

temperature-induced shift, temperature displacement, displacement by temperature effect — Temperaturverschiebung f

temperature in shade — s. shade temperature
temperature instability — Temperaturlabilität f, Temperaturinstabilität f

temperature interval — s. temperature range
temperature inversion, inversion, umkehr ‹meteo.› — Inversion f, Temperaturinversion f, Temperaturumkehr f, Sperrschicht f, Sperrzone f ‹Meteo.›

temperature jump — Temperatursprung m
temperature jump distance — Temperatursprungdistanz f; Temperatursprungentfernung f

temperature lag, temperature delay — Temperaturverzögerung f

temperature

temperature lapse [rate]	s. lapse rate	**temperature regulating device**	s. thermoregulator
temperature level, temperature value	Temperaturwert m, Temperaturniveau n	**temperature regulator**	s. thermoregulator
temperature-limited	temperaturbegrenzt	**temperature resistance**	s. temperature stability
		temperature-resistant	s. heat-proof
temperature marker	Temperaturkennkörper m, Temperaturmeßkörper m	**temperature-resistant quality**	s. temperature stability
temperature measuring device	Temperaturmeßgerät n, Temperaturmesser m	**temperature rise,** rise of (in) temperature, raising of temperature	Temperaturerhöhung f, Temperatursteigerung f
temperature minimum, minimum temperature	Tiefsttemperatur f, tiefste Temperatur f, minimale Temperatur, Temperaturminimum n	**temperature rise**	s. a. temperature increase
		temperature rise voltage	s. nominal circuit voltage <of an instrument>
temperature of air	s. shade temperature	**temperature seiche**	Temperaturseiche f
temperature of combustion, combustion temperature, flame temperature	Verbrennungstemperatur f		
		temperature-sensible	s. temperature-sensitive
		temperature-sensing element	s. temperature sensor
temperature of condensation	s. condensation temperature	**temperature-sensitive,** sensitive to temperature; temperature-sensing	temperaturempfindlich; temperatursensibel <Bio.>
temperature of equilibrium, equilibrium temperature	Gleichgewichtstemperatur f		
temperature of equilibrium between liquid oxygen and its vapour, oxygen point	Sauerstoffpunkt m	**temperature-sensitive element**	s. temperature sensor
temperature of liquefaction	s. liquefaction temperature	**temperature-sensitive paint,** temperature indicating paint, tempilstik <US>	Temperaturmeßfarbe f, Thermochrom n, Thermochromfarbe f, Thermofarbe f
temperature of melting <bio.>	T_m-Wert m, Schmelztemperatur f <Bio.>		
temperature of melting	s. a. melting point	**temperature sensor,** temperature-sensitive element, temperature-sensing element, thermometric element	Temperaturfühler m, Wärmefühler m, Fühlerelement n
temperature of saturation, saturation temperature	Sättigungstemperatur f, Sättigungspunkt m		
temperature of sintering, sintering point, sintering temperature	Sinterpunkt m, Sintertemperatur f	**temperature-solubility curve;** temperature-solubility plot, temperature-solubility pattern	Temperatur-Löslichkeits-Diagramm n, Temperatur-Löslichkeits-Kurve f
temperature of sublimation, sublimation temperature, point of sublimation, sublimation point	Sublimationstemperatur f, Sublimationspunkt m, Sbp.		
		temperature-solubility pattern	s. temperature-solubility curve
temperature of supercooling, supercooling temperature	Unterkühlungstemperatur f	**temperature-solubility plot**	s. temperature-solubility curve
		temperature source of light, thermal source of light, thermal light source	thermische Lichtquelle f
temperature of the barrier layer	s. barrier layer temperature		
temperature of the bulk	s. bulk temperature		
temperature of the surrounding air, ambient temperature, environmental temperature	Umgebungstemperatur f	**temperature stability,** independence of temperature	Temperaturunabhängigkeit f; Temperaturkonstanz f, Temperaturstabilität f
		temperature stability	s. a. thermal stability
temperature of the zero field transition	s. Ounes temperature	**temperature stabilization**	Temperaturstabilisierung f
temperature on the Kelvin scale, absolute temperature, Kelvin temperature	absolute Temperatur f, Kelvin-Temperatur f	**temperature-stabilized**	s. thermostated
		temperature state	Temperaturzustand m
		temperature stress	s. thermal stress
		temperature sum, sum of temperatures	Temperatursumme f
temperature oscillation, temperature vibration	Temperaturschwingung f	**temperature sum rule,** initial flow	Temperatursummenregel f
temperature outside	s. exterior temperature	**temperature thickness of boundary layer**	Temperaturdicke f der Grenzschicht
temperature overshoot	Temperaturüberschlag m	**temperature-time-transformation diagram,** TTT diagram	Zeit-Temperatur-Umwandlungs-Schaubild n, ZTU-Schaubild n, TTT-Diagramm n
temperature peak	Temperaturspitze f		
temperature-pressure curve	Temperatur-Druck-Kurve f		
		temperature treatment, heat treatment	Wärmebehandlung f
		temperature value, temperature level	Temperaturwert m, Temperaturniveau n
temperature profile	Temperaturprofil n	**temperature variation;** variation of temperature, heating pattern	Temperaturgang m; Temperaturverlauf m
temperature radiation; thermactinic radiation	Temperaturstrahlung f, Temperaturleuchten n; thermaktine Strahlung f	**temperature variation**	s. a. temperature fluctuation
		temperature variation chart (map), chart of temperature variations	Temperaturkarte f
temperature radiation	s. a. black-body radiation		
temperature range, range of temperature, temperature interval, temperature band	Temperaturbereich m, Temperaturgebiet n, Temperaturintervall n	**temperature velocity**	Temperaturgeschwindigkeit f
		temperature vibration, temperature oscillation	Temperaturschwingung f
temperature recorder	s. thermograph	**temperature-viscosity curve**	Temperatur-Viskositäts-Kurve f
temperature reduction	Temperaturreduktion f		

temperature-viscosity effect	Temperatur-Viskositäts-Effekt m	temporary stream	instabiler Meteorstrom m, temporärer Meteorstrom
temperature voltage <el.>	Temperaturspannung f, Temperaturäquivalent n <El.>	temporary waters, pool	temporäres (periodisches) Gewässer n, Tümpel m
temperature-volume diagram, T-v diagram	Temperatur-Volumen-Diagramm n, T, v-Diagramm n	temposcopy	Temposkopie f <Verfahren und Geräte zur Sichtbarmachung extrem schneller und langsamer Prozesse>
temperature wave	Temperaturwelle f	TEM-wave	s. principal wave
temperature zone, zone of equal temperature	Temperaturzone f; Temperaturgürtel m	tenacious	s. tough
temper brittleness	Anlaßprödigkeit f	tenaciousness, tenacity	s. toughness
temper colour, tempering (annealing) colour	Anlaßfarbe f, Anlauffarbe f	tenaciousness, tenacity ten-days average, decade average, decade mean	s. viscidity Dekadenmittel n, Zehntagemittel n
		tendency; propensity; trend	Neigung f, Tendenz f
tempered	temperiert <auch Ak.>; gemäßigt <Meteo.>; mäßig	tendency; weather outlook <meteo.>	Wetteraussichten fpl, Aussichten fpl; Tendenz f <Meteo.>
tempered distribution, tame distribution	gemäßigte Distribution f	tendency equation, equation of tendency	Tendenzgleichung f
		tendency of rotations to parallelism	Regel f vom gleichstimmigen Parallelismus der Drehachsen, Tendenz f zum gleichsinnigen Parallelismus [nach Klein und Sommerfeld], Tendenz zum homologen Parallelismus
tempered interval, equally tempered interval	gleichschwebend temperiertes Intervall n, temperiertes Intervall		
tempered scale	s. equally tempered scale <ac.>	tendency to sing, near singing	Pfeifneigung f
temper hardening	s. hardening and tempering		
tempering, temper, drawing	Anlassen n <Met.; Glas>; Anlaufen n <Glas>	tending to zero	nach Null gehend, nach Null strebend
tempering after hardening	s. hardening and tempering <met.>	tend to a limit	gegen einen Grenzwert gehen (streben)
tempering colour	s. temper colour	tenebrescence; twilight	Dämmerung f; Zwielicht n
tempering glass	Anlaufglas n		
tempest	s. storm <gen.>	ten-membered ring, ten-ring	Zehnerring m, Zehnring m
tempilstik <US>, temperature indicating paint, temperature-sensitive paint	Temperaturmeßfarbe f, Thermochrom n, Thermochromfarbe f, Thermofarbe f	tensammetric wave tensile tensile and shear strength	tensammetrische Welle f s. ductile Zugscherfestigkeit f
tempilstik <US>, temperature-indicating crayon, thermometric crayon	Temperaturfarbstift m, Farbstift m für Temperaturmessung, Temperaturmeßstift m	tensile breaking test tensile creep test[ing]	s. tensile test Zeitstandversuch m mit Zugbelastung
template <bio.>	Matrix f; Matrize f <Bio.>	tensile deformation	s. elongation
template and dispersion photometer	s. dispersion and mask photometer	tensile deformation tensile elasticity, elasticity of elongation, elasticity of extension	s. tensile strain Zugelastizität f
template ribonucleic acid, template RNA	s. messenger ribonucleic acid		
Temple['s] bound	Templesche Schranke f <für Eigenwerte>	tensile elastic limit, elastic limit for tension	Zugelastizitätsgrenze f, Elastizitätsgrenze f gegenüber Zug
Temple['s] quotient	Templescher Quotient m		
temporal coherence, time coherence, coherence in time	Zeitkohärenz f, zeitliche Kohärenz f	tensile force, stretching force, pull[ing] force, pull; tractive force (effort), traction	Zugkraft f, Zug m
temporal parallax	zeitliche Parallaxe f		
temporary current	zeitweilige Strömung f		
temporary deformation	s. temporary strain		
temporary hardness [of water]	Karbonathärte f, Carbonathärte f, temporäre (vorübergehende, schwindende) Härte f, KH <Wasser>	tensile fracture, tension fracture tensile impact strength, impact tensile strength	Dehnungsbruch m, Dehnbruch m Schlagzugfestigkeit f
temporary magnetism	vorübergehender (temporärer, flüchtiger, transi[en]ter) Magnetismus m	tensile impact test[ing] tensile load[ing], tension load	s. tension impact test[ing] Zugbelastung f, Belastung f durch äußere Zugkräfte, Beanspruchung f durch äußere Zugkräfte, äußere Zugspannung f
temporary magnetism of ships	flüchtiger (transi[en]ter) Schiffsmagnetismus m		
temporary operation, temporary service, short-time operation	Kurzzeitbetrieb m	tensile machine	s. tensile testing machine
temporary perched water, ver[k]hovodka	Werchowodka f	tensile modulus of elasticity, modulus of elasticity for (in) tension	E-Modul m für Zug, Elastizitätsmodul m für Zug, Zugelastizitätsmodul m
temporary service, temporary operation, short-time operation	Kurzzeitbetrieb m	tensile resultant	Zugresultante f
temporary snow[]line	temporäre Schneegrenze f, zeitweilige Schneegrenze	tensile rigidity, tensile stiffness	Zugsteifigkeit f
temporary storage	Zwischenspeicherung f		
		tensile strain, tensional strain, tensile straining (deformation)	Zugverformung f, Zugdehnung f
temporary storage temporary strain, temporary deformation	s. a. internal memory vorübergehende Formänderung f, vorübergehende Verformung f, vorübergehende Verzerrung f		
		tensile strain	s. a. stretching strain
		tensile strain	s. a. unit elongation
		tensile straining	s. tensile strain

tensile | **868**

tensile strength, rupture strength, breaking strength, breaking stress, strength in tension, resistance to rupture (tearing); ultimate tensile (breaking) strength, U.T.S. — Zugfestigkeit f, Zerreißfestigkeit f, Reißfestigkeit f; Zugfestigkeitsgrenze f, Zugdehngrenze f, Zerreißgrenze f

tensile strength for alternative load — Zugschwellfestigkeit f

tensile strength test — s. tensile test
tensile strength testing machine — s. tensile testing machine
tensile stress, tension stress, tensional stress, tension, yield stress in tension, normal stress, stretching stress, stress by pull — Zugspannung f, Zug m, äußere Zugspannung; Streckspannung f

tensile stress field, tension field — Zugfeld n, Zugspannungsfeld n
tensile stress-strain curve — Zugspannungs-Dehnungs-Schaubild n, Zugspannungs-Dehnungs-Diagramm n, Zug-Dehnungs-Diagramm n, Zugdiagramm n, Zerreißschaubild n, Zerreißdiagramm n, Zerreißkurve f

tensile test, tensile testing, tension test[ing], tensile strength (breaking) test; straining frame experiment — Zugversuch m, Zugprüfung f, Zugprobe f, Zerreißversuch m, Zerreißprüfung f, Zerreißprobe f; Streckbarkeitsprobe f

tensile test at elevated temperature, high-temperature creep test — Warmzugversuch m

tensile test diagram — s. stress-strain curve
tensile testing — s. tensile test
tensile testing machine, tensile [strength testing] machine, rupture device — Zugprüfmaschine f, Zerreißmaschine f

tensile yield point — s. tensile yield strength
tensile yield point at elevated temperature; yield point at elevated temperature — Warmfließgrenze f; Warmstreckgrenze f

tensile yield strength, tensile yield point, yield strength (stress) in tension, yield value, resistance limit, resistance to elongation (stretching) — Streckgrenze f

tensility — s. ductility
tensimeter — Sättigungsdruckmesser m, Dampfdruckmesser m, Dampfspannungsmesser m, Tensimeter n

tensiometer, surface tension meter, surface tension balance — Oberflächenspannungsmesser m, Tensiometer n

tensiometry — Tensiometrie f, Oberflächenspannungsmessung f

tension; pull, pulling; traction — Ziehen n, Zug m, Auseinanderziehen n
tension, pressure <of vapour> — Druck m, Spannung f <Dampf>
tension, stress <mech.> — Spannung f, mechanische Spannung <Mech.>

tension — s. a. tensile stress
tension — s. a. underpressure
tension — s. a. voltage <el.>
tensional strain, tensile strain, tensile straining (deformation) — Zugverformung f, Zugdehnung f

tensional stress — s. tensile stress
tensional wave — Zugwelle f

tension bar; tension specimen — Probestab m für den Zugversuch, Zugstab m; Zugprobe f, Zugfestigkeitskörper m, Zugkörper m, Zerreißprobe f

tension cleaving — Zugspaltung f

tension coefficient for (of) resistivity, resistivity coefficient for tension — Spannungskoeffizient m des spezifischen Widerstandes

tension-compression fatigue strength — s. fatigue strength for tension-compression
tension-compression fatigue testing machine — Zug-Druck-Maschine f, Zug-Druck-Prüfmaschine f, Zug-Druck-Schwingprüfmaschine f

tension-compression modulus of elasticity — s. Young['s] modulus
tension-compression test — Zug-Druck-Wechselversuch m, Zug-Druck-Versuch m

tension dynamometer, traction dynamometer; tractive force meter — Zugdynamometer n, Zugkraftmesser m, Zugkraftmeßgerät n, Zugmeßgerät n, Zugmesser m

tension fault <geo.> — Ausweitungsbruch m, Zerrbruch m <Geo.>

tension fault, centripetal fault <geo.> — Abschiebung f <Geo.>

tension field, tensile stress field — Zugfeld n, Zugspannungsfeld n
tension fracture — s. tensile fracture
tension-free — s. unstressed <mech.>
tension impact test[ing], tensile impact test[ing], impact tension test[ing] — Schlagzugversuch m; Schlagzerreißversuch m

tensioning <e.g. of the spring>; straining; stretch; cocking <e.g. of the shutter> — Spannen n

tension load — s. tensile load[ing]
tension member, tie rod, bar in tension, tension tie, tie — Zugstange f

tension modulus — s. modulus of rupture <mech.>

tension of the cable, tension of the string, rope tension — Seilspannung f

tension relief, tension relieving; traction relief, traction relieving — Zugentlastung f

tension specimen — s. tension bar
tension spring — Zugfeder f; Spannfeder f

tension strain — s. elongation
tension strain — s. stretching strain
tension stress — s. tensile stress
tension test[ing], tensile test[ing]; straining frame experiment — Zugversuch m, Zugprüfung f, Zugprobe f, Zerreißversuch m, Zerreißprüfung f, Zerreißprobe f

tension tie — s. tension member
tensodiffusion — Tensodiffusion f, Spannungsdiffusion f

tensoelectric — tensoelektrisch
tensoelectric semiconductor device — tensoelektrisches Halbleitergerät n

tensometer — Querdehnungsmesser m, Tensometer n

tensometric; extensometric — extensometrisch; tensometrisch
tensometry — Tensometrie f

tensor	Tensor m	tensor of permeability, permeability tensor	Permeabilitätstensor m, Durchlässigkeitstensor m, Tensor m der Durchlässigkeit
tensor ‹of the quaternion›	Tensor m, Betrag m ‹Quaternion›		
tensor	s. a. symmetrical tensor	tensor of permittivity	s. dielectric tensor
tensor algebra	Tensoralgebra f	tensor of rank n, tensor of valence n, tensor of order n	Tensor m n-ter Stufe
tensor analysis	Tensoranalysis f		
tensor antisymmetric in time, time-antisymmetric tensor	zeitantisymmetrischer Tensor m, c-Tensor m	tensor of second order	s. tensor of order two
		tensor of torsion, torsion tensor	Torsionstensor m
tensor calculus	Tensorrechnung f, Tensorkalkül m	tensor of total angular momentum	Gesamtdrehimpulstensor m
tensor calculus	s. a. Ricci calculus	tensor of valence n, tensor of rank n, tensor of order n	Tensor m n-ter Stufe
tensor condition	Tensorbedingung f		
tensor coupling	tensorielle Kopplung f, Tensorkopplung f		
tensor density, relative tensor of unit weight, relative tensor of weight unity	Tensordichte f	tensor of Weyl and Eddington, Weyl-Eddington tensor	Weyl-Eddingtonscher Tensor m
		tensor operator	Tensoroperator m
		tensor potential	Tensorpotential n
tensor derivative	tensorielle Ableitung f	tensor product ‹of vector spaces›	Tensorprodukt n, tensorielles Produkt n ‹Vektorräume›
tensor differential equation	Tensordifferentialgleichung f, Affinordifferentialgleichung f		
		tensor quadric, quadric of the tensor; tensor ellipsoid	Tensorfläche f; Tensorellipsoid n; quadratische Form f des Tensors
tensor ellipsoid	s. tensor quadric		
tensor equation	Tensorgleichung f		
tensoresistance, tensoresistive effect	tensoelektrischer Effekt m, Tensowiderstand[seffekt] m, Tensiwiderstand[seffekt] m	tensor representation	Tensordarstellung f
		tensor sheet	Tensorblatt n
		tensor space	Tensorraum m
		tensor symmetric in time, time-symmetric tensor	zeitsymmetrischer Tensor m, i-Tensor m
tensor field, tensorial field	Tensorfeld n		
tensor force, non-central force	Tensorkraft f, Nichtzentralkraft f, nichtzentrale Kraft f	tensor transformation	tensorielle Abbildung f
		tensor volume	Tensorvolumen n
		tentation (tentative) data, preliminary data	vorläufige Werte mpl
tensor function	Tensorfunktion f		
tensorial field, tensor field	Tensorfeld n	tenthmeter	s. ångström unit
		tenth-normal, decinormal, 0.1 N, N/10	zehntelnormal, dezinormal, 0,1 n, n/10
tensorial non-linearity	tensorielle Nichtlinearität f		
tensor identity of Levi-Cività	s. epsilon-tensor	tenth-normal solution, 0.1 N solution	Zehntelnormallösung f, 0,1 n Lösung f
tensor index	Tensorindex m	tenth-peak divergence (spread)	s. one-tenth-peak divergence
tensor interaction	tensorielle Wechselwirkung f, Tensorwechselwirkung f		
		tenth power, power of ten; order, order of magnitude	Größenordnung f; Zehnerpotenz f
tensor invariant	Tensorinvariante f		
		tenth-power width	Zehntelwert[s]breite f des Richtdiagramms
tensor line	Tensorlinie f		
tensor multiplication, outer multiplication of tensors	tensorielle Multiplikation f, Tensormultiplikation f	tenth-value layer, tenth-value thickness, attenuation tenth-value thickness, TVL	Zehntelwertschicht[dicke] f, Zehntelwert[s]dicke f, ZWS
tensor notation	Tensorschreibweise f		
tensor of dislocation density, dislocation density tensor	Versetzungsdichtetensor m, Tensor m der Versetzungsdichte	tephigram, $T\varphi$ gram	Tephigramm n, T,φ-gramm n
tensor of effective mass[es], effective mass tensor	Tensor m der effektiven Masse[n], Effektive-Masse-Tensor m	tepid, lukewarm	lauwarm
		tera..., T ‹10^{12}›	Tera..., T
		terella	s. terrella ‹of Birkeland›
tensor of electric polarizability, polarizability tensor	Polarisierbarkeitstensor m, Tensor m der elektrischen Polarisierbarkeit	term, term of energy, energy [state] term, state of energy term, level; term value	Term m, Energieterm m, Energiestufe f
tensor of heat conductivity, heat conductivity tensor	Wärmeleitfähigkeitstensor m, Tensor m der Wärmeleitfähigkeit		
		term ‹math.›	Glied n, Term m ‹Math.›
tensor of hyperpolarizability, hyperpolarizability tensor	Tensor m der Hyperpolarisierbarkeit, Hyperpolarisierbarkeitstensor m	term, spectral term, spectroscopic term ‹opt.›	Spektralterm m, Term m, spektroskopischer Term ‹Opt.›
tensor of inertia, moment of inertia tensor, inertial (inertia) tensor	Trägheitstensor m	term analysis, level analysis, analysis of energy levels	Termanalyse f
		term assignment	Termzuordnung f
tensor of inverse effective masses	Tensor m der reziproken effektiven Massen	term by term, by terms, in terms, termwise ‹math.›	gliedweise ‹Math.›
tensor of magnetic polarizability	Tensor m der magnetischen Polarisierbarkeit, Polarisierbarkeitstensor m		
		term-by-term differentiation, differentiation term by term	gliedweise Differentiation f
tensor of magnetic susceptibility, susceptibility tensor, magnetic susceptibility tensor	Suszeptibilitätstensor m, Tensor m der magnetischen Suszeptibilität		
		term-by-term integration, integration term by term	gliedweise Integration f
tensor of momentum density, momentum density tensor	Impulsdichtetensor m	term diagram, term scheme, scheme of terms	Termschema n
tensor of order n, tensor of rank n, tensor of valence n	Tensor m n-ter Stufe	term displacement, term shift, level shift, level displacement	Termverschiebung f, Niveauverschiebung f, Levelshift m
tensor of order two, tensor of second (2nd) order, second-order tensor, double tensor	Tensor m zweiter Stufe, zweistufiger Tensor	terminal angle, polar solid angle	Endecke f ‹Krist.›; Polarecke f, Polecke f

terminal ballistics — Endballistik *f*

terminal basin — Zungenbecken *n*

terminal block — Reihenklemme *f*

terminal capacitor — s. terminating capacitor
terminal current, current at the terminals — Klemmenstrom *m*, Klemmstrom *m*
terminal edge <cryst.> — Polkante *f* <Krist.>
terminal face — s. pinacoid
terminal impedance, load (terminating) impedance — Abschlußimpedanz *f*, Abschlußscheinwiderstand *m*; Belastungsimpedanz *f*, Lastimpedanz *f*

terminal moraine, end moraine, frontal moraine — Endmoräne *f*, Stirnmoräne *f*, Moränenwall *m*

terminal pillar; [terminal] post — Polkopf *m*, Polstutzen *m*, Bandableitung *f*, Polschuh *m* <Bleiakkumulator>; Polbolzen *m* <Stahlakkumulator>

terminal point — s. end <math.>
terminal post — s. terminal pillar
terminal potential — s. terminal voltage
terminal power, power at the terminals — Klemmenleistung *f*, Klemmleistung *f*
terminal resistance, load resistance — Abschlußwiderstand *m*, Abschluß *m*

terminal solid solution, primary solid solution — primäre feste Lösung *f*, Festlösung *f* im Reinelement

terminal speed, final speed; final velocity, terminal velocity — Endgeschwindigkeit *f*
terminal speed, limiting velocity, limiting speed <mech., hydr.> — Grenzgeschwindigkeit *f*
terminal synchrone — letzte Synchrone *f*
terminal velocity, final speed; final velocity, terminal speed — Endgeschwindigkeit *f*
terminal voltage, voltage at the terminals, terminal potential — Klemmenspannung *f*, Klemmspannung *f*
terminating, termination <el.> — Abschluß *m*
terminating capacitor, terminal capacitor — Abschlußkondensator *m*, Endkondensator *m*
terminating impedance — s. terminal impedance
termination — s. terminating <el.>
termination [of the chain], termination reaction — s. chain stopping
terminator, lunar terminator — Terminator *m*, Schattengrenze *f*
terminator <bio.> — Terminator *m* <Bio.>
terminator — s. a. chain stopper
terminus — s. end
term multiplet, multiplet of terms — Termmultiplett *n*
term of energy, term, energy state term, [state of] energy term; term value — Term *m*, Energieterm *m*, Energiestufe *f*

term of forecast — Vorhersagedauer *f*, Vorhersagezeitraum *m*

term of ground state, ground (normal, fundamental) term — Grundterm *m*, Term *m* des Grundzustandes
term of higher degree (order), higher order (degree) term — Glied *n* höherer Ordnung
term of long period, long-period term — langperiodischer Term *m*, langperiodisches Glied *n*
term of short period, short-period term — kurzperiodischer Term *m*, kurzperiodisches Glied *n*
term of the residue series, residue wave — Residuenwelle *f*
termolecular reaction, trimolecular reaction, reaction of the third order — trimolekulare Reaktion *f*, Reaktion dritter Ordnung

term order, order of terms, order of levels, level order — Termordnung *f*

term position; level position, position of level — Termlage *f*; Niveaulage *f*
term representation — Termdarstellung *f*
terms/by (in), term by term, termwise <math.> — gliedweise <Math.>
term scheme — s. term diagram
term separation, term splitting — Termaufspaltung *f*
term shift — s. level shift
term structure — s. level structure
term system — Termsystem *n*
term temperature — Termtemperatur *f*
term value — s. term
termwise — s. term by term <math.>
ternary combination band — Dreifachkombinationsbande *f*
ternary diagram, three-component diagram — ternäres Zustandsdiagramm *n*, Dreistoffdiagramm *n*

ternary fission, tripartition, triple fission — ternäre Spaltung *f*, Dreifachspaltung *f*, Dreierspaltung *f*, Dreifachteilung *f*
ternary mixture — ternäres Gemisch *n*, Dreistoffgemisch *n*
ternary system — ternäres System *n*, Dreistoffsystem *n*
terpolymer, trimer — Trimer[e] *n*

terrella, terella <of Birkeland> — Terella *f* <von Birkeland>
terrene — s. Earth surface
terrestrial deposit, terrestrial sediment — terrestrisches Sediment *n*, terrestrische Ablagerung *f*
terrestrial dust — terrestrischer Staub *m*
terrestrial effect of solar activity — s. Sun-Earth relationship
terrestrial ellipsoid — s. earth ellipsoid
terrestrial extinction — terrestrische Extinktion *f*
terrestrial eyepiece, erecting eyepiece, inverting eyepiece — terrestrisches Okular *n*, Okular mit Bildumkehr, Erdfernrohrokular *n*
terrestrial greenhouse effect — s. greenhouse effect
terrestrial horizon — s. apparent horizon
terrestrial line, telluric line — terrestrische (tellurische) Linie *f*
terrestrial magnetic field, Earth's magnetic field, geomagnetic field — Magnetfeld *n* der Erde, erdmagnetisches Feld *n*, magnetisches Erdfeld *n*, Erdmagnetfeld *n*, magnetisches Feld der Erde
terrestrial magnetic pole — s. magnetic dip pole
terrestrial magnetism, geomagnetism — Geomagnetismus *m*, Erdmagnetismus *m*
terrestrial orbit, Earth's orbit — Erdbahn *f*
terrestrial orientation — terrestrische Orientierung *f*
terrestrial photogram — s. terrestrial survey
terrestrial photogrammetry, geophotogrammetry, ground photogrammetry — Erdbildmessung *f*, terrestrische Photogrammetrie *f*, Geophotogrammetrie *f*
terrestrial planet, minor planet — erdähnlicher (terrestrischer) Planet *m*
terrestrial radiation, Earth's radiation, Earth radiation — terrestrische Strahlung *f*, Erdstrahlung *f*
terrestrial refraction — terrestrische (irdische) Refraktion *f*; terrestrische (irdische) Strahlenbrechung *f*
terrestrial satellite — s. artificial Earth's satellite
terrestrial sediment, terrestrial deposit — terrestrisches Sediment *n*, terrestrische Ablagerung *f*
terrestrial spheroid — s. earth ellipsoid
terrestrial survey, terrestrial photogram — Erdmeßbild *n*, terrestrische Aufnahme *f*, terrestrisches Bild *n*, Erdbild *n*
terrestrial telescope — terrestrisches Fernrohr *n*, Erdfernrohr *n*
terrestrial tides, earth tides, bodily tides — Gezeiten *pl* des Erdkörpers, Erdgezeiten *pl*
terrigenous deposit, terrigenous sediment — terrigenes Sediment *n*, terrigene Ablagerung *f*

tertiary, tert. <chem.> — tertiär, tert. <Chem.>
tertiary radiation — Tertiärstrahlung *f*

tertiary creep — s. accelerating flow

tertiary spectrum	tertiäres Spektrum n	testing, test; checking, check; examination; inspection; re-examination; aftertrial; control; verification; proof	Prüfung f; Nachprüfung f, Kontrolle f, Test m
tertium exclusum (non datur)	s. law of excluded middle		
tesla, T	Tesla n, T		
Tesla coil, Tesla induction coil	Tesla-Spule f	testing device	s. testing instrument
Tesla current	Tesla-Strom m	testing floor, measuring room, test room, testing room	Meßraum m, Meßzimmer n
Tesla induction coil	s. Tesla coil	testing floor	s. a. test room
Tesla interrupter	Tesla-Unterbrecher m	testing instrument, test instrument, testing device, tester; inspection instrument; checking (check) instrument	Prüfinstrument n, Prüfgerät n
Tesla luminescence	Tesla-Lumineszenz f		
Tesla rays (sparks)	Tesla-Büschel n		
Tesla transformer	Tesla-Transformator m	testing of materials, materials testing, materiology	Werkstoffprüfung f, Materialprüfung f
tessellated mirror	Facettenspiegel m		
tessellated stresses	interne mosaikartige mikroskopische Spannungsverteilung f beim unbelasteten Körper, Mosaikspannungen fpl	testing reactor	s. materials testing reactor
		testing room	s. test room
		test instrument	s. testing instrument
		test loop, measuring loop	Meßschleife f
tesseral central class	s. paramorphic hemihedry of the regular system		
tesseral coefficient	tesseraler Koeffizient m		
tesseral harmonic	tesserale Kugelfunktion f	test measurement	Prüfmessung f, Kontrollmessung f
tesseral holoaxial class	s. enantiomorphous hemihedry of the regular system	test object, object to be measured, object under measurement (test)	Meßobjekt n, Meßling m; Prüfobjekt n, Prüfling m; Testobjekt n
tesseral polar class	s. tetartohedry of the regular system	test object, optical test object, optotype, identifiable design <opt.>	Sehzeichen n, Optotype f; Testobjekt n <Opt.>
test, statistical test <stat.>	Test m, statistischer Test <Stat.>	test of convergence	s. test for convergence
		test of dispersion	Streuungstest m
test	s. a. testing	test of goodness of fit	Anpassungstest m
test	s. a. experiment		
test amplifier, measuring (measurement) amplifier, phantom repeater	Meßverstärker m	test of normality	Normalitätstest m, Normaltest m <Stat.>
		test of randomness	Zufälligkeitstest m
		test operation	Versuchsbetrieb m
test at elevated temperature	s. heat test	test oscillator	s. measurement transmitter
		test panel, test bay, test bench	Prüffeld n
test balloon, sounding balloon, air-sonde	Ballonsonde f, Sondenballon m, Sonde f		
		test paper	s. indicator paper
test bar, bar to be tested, specimen, test rod, trial rod, test beam	Probestab m	test particle	Testpartikel f, Testteilchen n, Sondenteilchen n, Probepartikel f
test barometer, gauge barometer	Eichbarometer n	test piece	s. sample
		test plate <of photometer>, photometer screen, photometer test plate	Photometerschirm m, Auffangschirm m, Meßplatte f <des Photometers>
test bay, test panel, test bench	Prüffeld n		
test bench, test stand, test rack	Prüfstand m; Meßstand m, Meßplatz m	test point	s. point under consideration
		test programme, design, plan <of the first or second order>	Versuchsplan m <erster oder zweiter Ordnung>
test beam	s. test bar		
test bench, test panel, test bay	Prüffeld n		
		test protocol, protocol of the experiment; test record, record of the experiment	Versuchsprotokoll n
test buzzer	Meßsummer m		
		test pulse	Prüfimpuls m, Testimpuls m, Prüfstoß m
test cell; oil test cell	Ölprüfgerät n, Ölprüfeinrichtung f; Gerät n für Durchschlagprüfungen an Flüssigkeiten		
		test pulse, measuring pulse	Meßimpuls m
		test rack, test stand, test bench	Prüfstand m; Meßstand m, Meßplatz m
test chart	s. optical test chart	test record	Meßschallplatte f
test circuit, check circuit; checking circuit; control circuit; circuit model	Prüfschaltung f; Testschaltung f; Prüfstromkreis m, Prüfkreis m		
		test record	s. a. test protocol
		test result	s. result of measurement
test component	s. sample	test rod	s. test bar
test diatoms	Testdiatomeen fpl	test room, testing room, check room, testing floor	Prüfraum m, Prüffeld n
test electrode, measuring electrode	Meßelektrode f		
		test room, measuring room, testing room, testing floor	Meßraum m, Meßzimmer n
tester	s. testing instrument		
test film	Testfilm m		
		test section	Meßstrecke f
test for convergence, criterion of convergence, test of convergence, convergence test	Konvergenzkriterium n	test series, series (set) of tests, experiment series, series of experiments	Versuchsreihe f, Versuchsserie f
		test set-up	s. experimental set-up
test function	Testfunktion f	test solution, standard solution	Normallösung f, Testlösung f, Standardlösung f, Prüflösung f, genormte (eingestellte) Lösung f
test gas	Testgas n, Prüfgas n		
test gauge	s. standard instrument		
test generator; signal generator	Prüfsender m; Prüfoszillator m, Prüfgenerator m		
		test specifications, specifications of the test	Prüfbedingungen fpl

test specimen s. test piece
test stand, test bench, test rack Prüfstand *m*; Meßstand *m*, Meßplatz *m*
test statistic, test variable <stat.> Testgröße *f*, Prüfzahl *f* <Stat.>

test tone, standard acoustic signal, standard tone Meßton *m*

test transmitter s. measurement transmitter
test tube Reagenzglas *n*, Probierglas *n*, Probierröhrchen *n*, Prüfglas *n*
test using progressive load; impact test using progressive load Stufenversuch *m*; Stufenschlagversuch *m*
test value s. experimental value
test-value generating device Meßwertgeber *m*, Testwertgeber *m*

test variable s. test statistic
tetartohedral class s. tetartohedry of the regular system
tetartohedral class s. tetartohedry of the second sort of the tetragonal system
tetartohedral class of the cubic system s. tetartohedry of the regular system
tetartohedral class of the hexagonal system s. tetartohedry of the hexagonal system
tetartohedral class of the tetragonal system s. tetartohedry of the tetragonal system
tetartohedral class of the trigonal system s. trigonal pyramidal [crystal] class
tetartohedral class with inversion axis of the tetragonal system s. tetartohedry of the second sort of the tetragonal system
tetartohedral class with threefold axis of the hexagonal system s. trigonal bipyramidal [crystal] class
tetartohedron Tetartoeder *n*, Viertel[s]flächner *m*, Viertel[s]flach *n*

tetartohedry Tetartoedrie *f*
tetartohedry of the hexagonal system, hexagonal tetartohedry, tetartohedral class of the hexagonal system, pyramidal hemimorphic class, hexagonal-pyramidal [crystal] class, hexagonal polar class Tetartoedrie *f* I. Art des hexagonalen Systems, hexagonal-pyramidale Klasse *f*, Hemimorphie *f* der pyramidalen Hemiedrie

tetartohedry of the regular system, regular tetartohedry, tetartohedral class of the cubic system, tetartoidal [crystal] class, pentagondodecahedral class, tesseral polar class, tetartohedral class Tetartoedrie *f* des kubischen Systems, tetartoidische Klasse *f*, tetraedrisch pentagondodekaedrische Klasse, tetraedrisch-pentagondodekaedrische Klasse

tetartohedry of the rhombohedral system s. trigonal pyramidal [crystal] class
tetartohedry of the second sort of the tetragonal system, sphenoidal tetartohedry, tetragonal tetartohedry of the second sort, tetartohedral class, bisphenoidal class, tetragonal-disphenoidal [crystal] class, tetragonal alternating class, tetartohedral class with inversion axis of the tetragonal system Tetartoedrie *f* II. Art des tetragonalen Systems, sphenoidische Tetartoedrie, bisphenoidische Klasse *f*, tetragonalbisphenoidische Klasse, tetragonal disphenoidische Klasse

tetartohedry of the tetragonal system, tetragonal tetartohedry, tetragonal polar class, tetragonal-pyramidal [crystal] class, pyramidal hemimorphic class, tetartohedral class of the tetragonal system Tetartoedrie *f* I. Art des tetragonalen Systems, tetragonal-pyramidale Klasse *f*, tetragonal pyramidale Klasse, Hemimorphie *f* der pyramidalen Hemiedrie

tetartoid, tetrahedral pentagon-dodecahedron Tetartoid *n*, tetraedrisches Pentagondodekaeder *n*
tetartoidal [crystal] class s. tetartohedry of the regular system

tetartopyramid Tetartopyramide *f*, Viertelpyramide *f*
tetartosymmetry Tetartosymmetrie *f*
tetrachoric correlation [coefficient] tetrachorischer Korrelationskoeffizient *m*; tetrachorische Korrelation *f*

tetracuspid s. astroid
tetracyclic co-ordinates tetrazyklische Koordinaten *fpl*

tetrad <math.; bio.> Tetrade *f* <Math.; Bio.>
tetrad axis, 4-al axis, axis of order 4, four-fold axis [of symmetry], 4-fold axis, tetragyre vierzählige Symmetrieachse *f*, vierzählige Drehungsachse *f*, vierzählige Achse *f*, Tetragyre *f*, 4zänlige Symmetrieachse

tetrad axis of the second sort, 4-al [symmetry] axis of the second kind, four-fold (4-fold) axis of the second sort, axis of the second sort of order 4 vierzählige Drehspiegel[ungs]achse *f*, Tetragyroide *f*

tetradentate ligand vierzähniger (tetradentaler, vierzähliger) Ligand *m*
tetragon s. quadrature <astr.>
tetragonal alternating class s. tetartohedry of the second sort of the tetragonal system
tetragonal bisphenoid tetragonales Bisphenoid *n*, tetragonales Tetraeder *n*
tetragonal crystal system, tetragonal system [of crystallization], pyramidal system, quadratic system tetragonales System (Kristallsystem) *n*, pyramidales System, quadratisches System (Kristallsystem)
tetragonal-dipyramidal [crystal] class s. paramorphic hemihedry of the tetragonal system
tetragonal-disphenoidal [crystal] class s. tetartohedry of the second sort of the tetragonal system
tetragonal enantiomorphy s. enantiomorphous hemihedry of the tetragonal system
tetragonal equatorial class s. paramorphic hemihedry of the tetragonal system
tetragonal hemihedry of the second sort s. hemihedry of the second sort of the tetragonal system
tetragonal hemimorphy s. hemimorphic hemihedry of the tetragonal system
tetragonal holoaxial class s. enantiomorphous hemihedry of the tetragonal system
tetragonal holohedry s. holohedry of the tetragonal system
tetragonal paramorphy s. paramorphic hemihedry of the tetragonal system
tetragonal polar class s. tetartohedry of the tetragonal system
tetragonal-pyramidal [crystal] class s. tetartohedry of the tetragonal system
tetragonal-scalenohedral [crystal] class s. hemihedry of the second sort of the tetragonal system
tetragonal scalenohedron tetragonales Skalenoeder *n*
tetragonal soil Tetragonalboden *m*
tetragonal system [of crystallization] s. tetragonal crystal system
tetragonal tetartohedry s. tetartohedry of the tetragonal system
tetragonal tetartohedry of the second sort s. tetartohedry of the second sort of the tetragonal system
tetragonal-trapezohedral [crystal] class s. enantiomorphous hemihedry of the tetragonal system
tetragonometry Tetragonometrie *f*
tetragontrioctahedron, tetrakisoctahedron Tetrakisoktaeder *n*
tetragyre s. tetrad axis
tetrahedral angle Tetraederwinkel *m*
tetrahedral bond Tetraederbindung *f*, tetraedrische Bindung *f*
tetrahedral class s. hemimorphic hemihedry of the regular system
tetrahedral co-ordinates Tetraederkoordinaten *fpl*
tetrahedral group Tetraedergruppe *f*, tetraedrische Gruppe *f*
tetrahedrally symmetric tetraedersymmetrisch

tetrahedral modification	Tetraederform *f*	thawing	Tauen *n*; Auftauen *n*
tetrahedral pentagon-dodecahedron, tetartoid	Tetartoid *n*, tetraedrisches Pentagondodekaeder *n*	thawing water, meltwater, snowmelt	Schmelzwasser *n*
		thawing weather	s. thaw
		thaw point	s. yield point
tetrahedral prism, Nachet prism	Nachet-Prisma *n*, Tetraederprisma *n*	thaw weather	s. thaw
		theodolite goniometer	s. two-circle goniometer
tetrahedral site, A site, A position	Tetraederplatz *m*, tetraedrischer Lückenplatz *m*, Tetraederlücke *f*, A-Lage *f*, Tetraederzentrum *n*	theodolite level, transit level, tacheometer level	Nivelliertachymeter *n*
		theodolite telescope	Theodolitenfernrohr *n*
tetrahedral stacking fault, stacking fault tetrahedron	Stapelfehlertetraeder *n*	theodolite traverse, traverse, traverse line, transit traverse <geo.>	Polygonzug *m*, Streckenzug *m*, Linienzug *m*, Theodolitzug *m* <Geo.>
tetrahedral structure	tetraedrische Struktur *f*, Tetraederstruktur *f*	theodolite with saturable core probe	Sondentheodolit *m*
tetrahedral symmetry	Tetraedersymmetrie *f*	Theodorsen['s] method	Theodorsensches Verfahren *n*
tetrahedroid [of Cayley]	Tetraedroid *n* [von Cayley]	Theorema egregium, Gauss['] equation	Gaußsche Gleichung *f*, Theorema *n* egregium
tetrahedron	Tetraeder *n*, Vierflach *n*, Vierflächner *m*	theorem of Blasius	s. Blasius['] theorem
tetrahedron equation	Tetraedergleichung *f*	theorem of Carnot, cosine formula, cosine law, law of cosine['s] <math.>	Kosinussatz *m* <Math.>
tetrahexahedron, tetrakishexahedron	Pyramidenwürfel *m*, Tetrakishexaeder *n*, Tetrahexaeder *n*		
		theorem of Castigliano	s. Castigliano['s] first theorem
tetrakisoctahedron, tetragontrioctahedron	Tetrakisoktaeder *n*	theorem of Castigliano	s. Castigliano['s] second theorem
tetrality principle	Tetralitätsprinzip *n*	theorem of Cauchy	s. Cauchy condition
tetrapod, quadruped, four nuple, vierbein	Vierbein *n*	theorem of centre of mass	s. centre of mass theorem <rel.>
tetrode, four-electrode valve (tube), four-element valve (tube), double-grid valve (tube), two-grid valve (tube), quadrode, bigrid	Tetrode *f*, Schirmgitterröhre *f*, Doppelgitterröhre *f*, Zweigitterröhre *f*, Vierelektrodenröhre *f*, Vierpolröhre *f*, Vierpolschirmröhre *f*, Vierpolraumladungsröhre *f*	theorem of conformal states	s. theorem of corresponding states
		theorem of corresponding states, law of corresponding states, principle of corresponding states, theorem of conformal states, law of correspondent states	Gesetz *n* von den übereinstimmenden Zuständen, Gesetz (Theorem *n*, Prinzip *n*) der übereinstimmenden (korrespondierenden) Zustände
tetrode transistor	s. semiconductor tetrode		
TE[-] wave	s. H[-] mode		
textural stress	Gefügespannung *f*		
texture	Textur *f*; Struktur *f*; bevorzugte Orientierung *f*, Vorzugsorientierung *f*; Maserung *f* <Holz>	theorem of equivalence, law of equivalence <opt., theory of four terminal network>	Äquivalenzsatz *m* <Opt., Vierpoltheorie>
texture / without, untextured	ohne Textur, nicht vorzugsgerichtet, nicht texturbehaftet, texturfrei	theorem of Euler, Euler's theorem [for (on) homogeneous functions]	Satz *m* von Euler, Eulerscher Satz <über homogene Funktionen>
textured, with preferred orientation	mit Textur, texturbehaftet, vorzugsgerichtet, texturiert	theorem of Lagrange and Cauchy, velocity potential theorem of Lagrange and Cauchy	Lagrange-Cauchyscher Satz *m*
textured soil, structured soil	Strukturboden *m*		
texture hardening	Texturhärtung *f*	theorem of least work	s. Castigliano['s] second theorem
texture in drawn wires, wire texture, drawing texture, texture resulting from drawing	Ziehtextur *f*, Zugtextur *f*	theorem of Meusnier, Meusnier['s] theorem	Meusnierscher Satz *m*, Satz von Meusnier
		theorem of minimum energy	s. principle of least work
texture of cast metal	s. cast texture	theorem of minimum entropy production	s. Prigogine['s] theorem
texture resulting from casting	s. cast texture	theorem of minimum potential [energy]	s. principle of least work
texture resulting from deformation, deformation texture	Verformungstextur *f*, Verzerrungstextur *f*	theorem of minimum strain energy	s. Castigliano['s] second theorem
texture resulting from drawing	s. texture in drawn wires	theorem of momentum	s. principle of linear momentum <mech., hydr.>
texture resulting from rolling, rolling texture	Walztextur *f*		
		theorem of parallel axes	s. parallel axis theorem
texturing, texturization	Texturierung *f*	theorem of principal axes	Hauptachsentheorem *n*
thalamide electrode	Thalamidelektrode *f*		
thalassic, thalassogenetic	thalassogen	theorem of reciprocity	s. Betti['s] reciprocal theorem
thalassocratic period	Thalassokratie *f*	theorem of Résal, Résal['s] theorem	Résalscher Satz *m*
thalassogenetic, thalassic	thalassogen	theorem of residues, Cauchy['s] residue theorem	Residuensatz *m*
Thalen-Tiberg magnetometer	Thalen-Tiberg-Magnetometer *n*	theorem of the mean for harmonic functions	s. Gauss mean value theorem [for potential functions]
thallium-activated scintillator, Tl-activated scintillator	thalliumaktivierter Szintillator *m*, Tl-aktivierter Szintillator, mit Thallium aktivierter Szintillator	theorem of three moments	s. equation of three moments
thallium photocell, thalofide cell	Thalliumsulfid-Photoelement *n*, Thalliumsulfidzelle *f*, Thalliumzelle *f*, Thal[l]ofid-[widerstands]zelle *f*	theorem on the isotropy of pressure	s. Pascal['s] law
		theoretical, theor.; calculated, cal.	theoretisch, theor.; berechnet, ber.
thalweg, talweg	Talweg *m*	theoretical ceiling, absolute ceiling	theoretische Gipfelhöhe (Deckenhöhe) *f*
thaw, thaw[ing] weather	Tauwetter *n*	theoretical density, true density, T.D.	theoretische Dichte *f*, Reindichte *f*, th. D.

theoretical

theoretical efficiency	theoretischer Wirkungsgrad m; Strahlwirkungsgrad m <Propeller>	theory of four-terminal networks, network theory	Vierpoltheorie f
theoretical nuclear physics	theoretische Kernphysik f	theory of functions [of a complex variable], function theory	Funktionentheorie f
theoretical plate, theoretical stage	theoretischer Boden m, theoretische Stufe f	theory of games, games theory	Spieltheorie f
theoretical plate in molecular distillation	theoretischer Boden m der Moleklardestillation	theory of gyroscope, theory of tops, gyroscopic theory	Kreiseltheorie f, Theorie f des Kreisels
theoretical stage, theoretical plate	theoretischer Boden m, theoretische Stufe f	theory of hearing	Hörtheorie f
theoretical value; calculated value; predicted value, prediction	theoretischer Wert m; Sollwert m; berechneter Wert; vorausgesagter Wert, vorherberechneter Wert	theory of heat	Wärmetheorie f
		theory of heredity	Nachwirkungstheorie f
		theory of invariants	s. invariant theory
		theory of Kelvin [and Helmholtz]	s. Kelvin contraction theory [of stars]
theory of absolute reaction rates	s. transition-state theory	theory of lattice defects (imperfections), theory of defects	Fehlordnungstheorie f
theory of action at a distance, action-at-a-distance theory	Fernwirkungstheorie f	theory of lattices	Gittertheorie f
		theory of limiting stress condition, Mohr's [strength] theory	Hypothese f des elastischen Grenzzustandes [von Mohr]
theory of adsorption isotherms of Brunauer, Emmett and Teller, BET theory, B.E.T. theory	BET-Theorie f, Brunauer-Emmett-Tellersche Theorie f	theory of linkages, mechanical kinematics	Zwang[s]lauflehre f, Getriebelehre f, Theorie f der Getriebe
theory of aeroelasticity	Aeroelastizitätslehre f	theory of locally isotropic turbulence, Kolmogoroff['s] theory [of turbulence]	Theorie f der lokal isotropen Turbulenz, Kolmogorowsche Turbulenztheorie f
theory of aggregates	s. theory of sets		
theory of Arrhenius, dissociation theory of Arrhenius-Ostwald	Arrheniussche Theorie f, Arrhenius-Ostwaldsche Dissoziationstheorie f [von Arrhenius-Ostwald]	theory of machines	Maschinentheorie f, Maschinenkunde f
theory of automatic control	s. automatic control theory	theory of maximum strain energy due to distortion, maximum distortion energy theory	Hypothese f der größten Gestaltsänderungsarbeit
theory of backwater	Theorie f des Stauproblems		
theory of Bardeen-Cooper-Schrieffer	s. Bardeen-Cooper-Schrieffer theory	theory of motion	s. kinematics
		theory of multiplets, multiplet theory	Multiplettheorie f, Theorie f der Multipletts
theory of cable, cable theory	Kabeltheorie f	theory of non-linear vibrations, non-linear mechanics	Theorie f der nichtlinearen Schwingungen, nichtlineare Mechanik f
theory of chances	s. probability theory		
theory of Chapman-Enskog	Chapman-Enskogsche Theorie f	theory of Obukhoff, Obukhoff['s] theory	Obuchowsche Theorie f, Theorie von Obuchow
theory of choice	s. statistical decision theory	theory of oscillations, theory of vibrations	Schwingungstheorie f, Schwingungslehre f
theory of circuits, theory of electric circuits	Theorie f der Stromkreise (Schaltkreise), Stromkreistheorie f, Schaltkreistheorie f	theory of perturbations	s. perturbation theory
		theory of probabilities	s. probability theory
		theory of propositions	s. propositional calculus
theory of circuits	s. a. theory of electric circuits	theory of queues	s. queueing theory
		theory of radiation	Strahlungstheorie f
theory of colours, colour theory, chromatics, chromatology	Farbenlehre f, Farblehre f	theory of relativity, relativity [theory]	Relativitätstheorie f
		theory of relativity	s. a. general theory of relativity
theory of combinations	s. combinatorial (combinatory) analysis	theory of relaxation, relaxation theory [of elasticity]	Relaxationstheorie f [der Elastizität]
theory of control systems	s. automatic control theory		
theory of cool ocean floor	Kühlbodentheorie f	theory of reliability	Zuverlässigkeitstheorie f
theory of cycles	Zyklentheorie f		
theory of defects, theory of lattice imperfections (defects)	Fehlordnungstheorie f	theory of representations	Darstellungstheorie f
		theory of Seitz, heat spike theory	Seitzsche Wärmespitzentheorie f, Wärmespitzentheorie [von Seitz]
theory of elasticity, elastomechanics	Elastizitätstheorie f, Elastomechanik f	theory of sets, set theory, theory of aggregates, mengenlehre	Mengenlehre f, Mengentheorie f
theory of electrical networks, network theory	Netzwerktheorie f		
		theory of shells, shell theory	Schalentheorie f
theory of electric circuits, theory of circuits, circuit theory	Schaltungstheorie f, Schaltungslehre f, Schalttheorie f, Schaltlehre f	theory of statistical decision[s]	s. statistical decision theory
		theory of strain energy of distortion, distortion energy theory	Gestaltänderungsenergiehypothese f
theory of electric circuits	s. a. theory of circuits		
theory of elementary divisor	Elementarteilertheorie f	theory of strength, theory of failure	Festigkeitshypothese f, Festigkeitstheorie f
theory of epicycles	Epizyklentheorie f, Epizyklenlehre f	theory of structures	s. structural mechanics
theory of errors	Fehlerrechnung f	theory of subterranean flow	Unterströmungstheorie f
theory of E. Schmidt, Schmidt['s] theory [of integral equations]	Schmidtsche Theorie f [der Integralgleichungen]	theory of supersonic speed, supersonics	Überschalltheorie f
theory of estimation	Schätztheorie f	theory of surfaces, surface theory	Flächentheorie f
theory of failure, theory of strength	Festigkeitshypothese f, Festigkeitstheorie f	theory of the double solution	Theorie f der doppelten Lösung
theory of flight, mechanics of flight, flight mechanics	Flugmechanik f	theory of the energy bands, band theory [of metals]	Bändertheorie f [der Metalle], Bandtheorie f
theory of flow	s. fluid mechanics		

thermal

theory of tops, theory of gyroscope, gyroscopic theory	Kreiseltheorie *f*, Theorie *f* des Kreisels
theory of transmission lines, line theory	Leitungstheorie *f*
theory of vacuum	Vakuumtheorie *f*
theory of valence	Valenztheorie *f*
theory of vibrations, theory of oscillations	Schwingungstheorie *f*, Schwingungslehre *f*
theory of visibility	Sichttheorie *f*
theory of yielding	Fließtheorie *f*
therapeutic dose, therapy dose	Therapiedosis *f*, therapeutische Dosis *f*
therapeutic radiology; radiation therapy, radiotherapy	Strahlentherapie *f*
therapy dose, therapeutic dose	Therapiedosis *f*, therapeutische Dosis *f*
therma	*s.* thermal spring
thermactinic radiation	*s.* temperature radiation
thermal, thermal bubble	Thermikblase *f*, Luftballen *m*
thermal	*s. a.* laminar thermal convection in the atmosphere
thermal absorptivity	*s.* heat capacity
thermal acceptor, thermium	Thermium *n*, thermischer Akzeptor *m*
thermal accumulator	*s.* heat absorber
thermal action	*s.* action of heat
thermal activation	thermische Aktivierung *f*
thermal activation cross-section, thermal neutron activation cross-section	Aktivierungsquerschnitt *m* für thermische Neutronen
thermal adhesion technique	Wärmehafttechnik *f*, Wärmehaftmethode *f*
thermal ageing, heat ageing	thermische Alterung *f*, Wärmealterung *f*
thermal agitation, thermal motion, heat motion	Wärmebewegung *f*, thermische Bewegung (Unruhe, Agitation) *f*, Temperaturbewegung *f*
thermal agitation noise	*s.* Johnson noise
thermal agitation of molecules	*s.* molecular motion
thermal agitation voltage, thermal noise voltage	Wärmerauschspannung *f*
thermal analysis, thermoanalysis, thermography	thermische Analyse *f*, Thermoanalyse *f*
thermal analysis / by, thermoanalytic[al]	thermoanalytisch
thermal arc	hermischer Bogen *m*; thermischer Lichtbogen *m*
thermal balance, heat balance	Wärmebilanz *f*
thermal barrier	*s.* heat barrier
thermal beam, thermal neutron beam	thermischer Neutronenstrahl *m*, thermisches Neutronenbündel *n*, Bündel *n* thermischer Neutronen
thermal behaviour	thermisches Verhalten *n*
thermal boundary, thermal boundary layer, temperature boundary layer	Temperaturgrenzschicht *f*, thermische Grenzschicht *f*
thermal boundary resistance	*s.* Kapitza thermal resistance
thermal branch of lattice vibrations	*s.* thermal lattice vibration
thermal breakdown <semi.; el.>; thermal dielectric breakdown <el.>; thermal punch-through <semi.>	Wärmedurchschlag *m*, thermischer Durchschlag *m* <El.; Halb.>; Wärmedurchbruch *m*, thermischer Durchbruch *m* <Halb.>; thermischer dielektrischer Durchschlag <El.>
thermal breeder [reactor], thermal-breeder reactor	thermischer Brüter *m*, thermischer Brutreaktor *m*
thermal breeding, thermal neutron breeding	thermisches Brüten *n*
thermal brine	Warmsole *f*
thermal bubble	*s.* thermal
thermal capacitance	*s.* heat capacity
thermal capacity	*s.* heat capacity
thermal capture cross-section, thermal neutron capture cross-section, cross-section for thermal neutron capture, capture cross-section for thermal neutrons	Wirkungsquerschnitt *m* für den Einfang thermischer Neutronen, Einfangquerschnitt *m* für thermische Neutronen, thermischer Neutroneneinfangquerschnitt *m*, thermischer Einfangquerschnitt
thermal coefficient of cubical expansion	*s.* thermal coefficient of volume expansion
thermal coefficient of expansion	*s.* thermal expansion coefficient
thermal coefficient of volume expansion, coefficient of volume expansion, [thermal] coefficient of cubical expansion, volume (cubic) expansion coefficient	kubischer Ausdehnungskoeffizient *m*, kubische Ausdehnungszahl *f*, räumlicher Ausdehnungskoeffizient, räumliche Ausdehnungszahl, Raumausdehnungskoeffizient *m*, Raumausdehnungszahl *f*
thermal column	thermische Säule *f*, thermische Grube *f*, Graphitsäule *f*
thermal combustion	Wärmeverbrennung *f*
thermal comparator	thermischer Komparator *m*
thermal compensation, temperature compensation	Temperaturkompensation *f*
thermal condensation	thermische Kondensation *f*
thermal conductance	Wärmeleitwert *m* <in kcal/h grd>
thermal conduction	*s.* heat conduction
thermal conductivity [coefficient], coefficient of thermal conductivity, heat conductivity, coefficient of heat conductivity, heat conductivity coefficient, *k* factor	Wärmeleitfähigkeit *f*, Wärmeleitzahl *f*, Wärmeleitungsvermögen *n*, spezifisches Wärmeleitungsvermögen, spezifische Wärmeleitfähigkeit, Wärmeleitvermögen *n*, spezifisches Wärmeleitvermögen, Wärmeleitkoeffizient *m*, thermische Leitfähigkeit *f*, innere Wärmeleitfähigkeit, Koeffizient *m* der Wärmeleitung
thermal conductivity detector, TCD	Wärmeleitfähigkeitsdetektor *m*
thermal conductor, heat conductor	Wärmeleiter *m*
thermal confinement	Wärmeeinschließung *f*, thermisches Confinement *n*
thermal contact, heat contact	thermischer Kontakt *m*, thermische Kopplung *f*, Wärmekontakt *m*, Thermokontakt *m*
thermal continentality	thermische Kontinentalität *f*
thermal contraction	Wärmeschrumpfung *f*
thermal-convection, thermoconvective	thermokonvektiv
thermal convection	*s. a.* convection of heat
thermal convection	*s. a.* laminar thermal convection in the atmosphere
thermal converter, thermo[-]converter, electrically heated thermocouple	Thermoumformer *m*
thermal creep	thermische Kriechströmung *f*, thermisches Kriechen *n*, Wärmekriechen *n*
thermal creep velocity	thermische Kriechgeschwindigkeit *f*
thermal cross	*s.* thermocross
thermal cross-section, thermal neutron cross-section, cross-section for thermal neutrons	thermischer Neutronen-[wirkungs]querschnitt *m*, Wirkungsquerschnitt *m* für thermische Neutronen, Wirkungsquerschnitt der thermischen Neutronen, thermischer Wirkungsquerschnitt (Querschnitt) *m*
thermal cycle	Wärmekreislauf *m*
thermal cycle, temperature cycle	Temperaturwechsel *m*, Thermozyklus *m*, Wechsel *m* <beim Temperaturwechselversuch>

thermal 876

thermal cycling	Temperaturwechselbeanspruchung f; Temperaturwechselversuch m, Temperaturwechselprüfung f, thermische Wechselbeanspruchung f	thermal dissipation, dissipation of heat, heat dissipation	Wärmezerstreuung f, Wärmedissipation f, Wärmeableitung f
thermal cycling stability	Temperaturwechselfestigkeit f, Temperaturwechselbeständigkeit f, Abschreckfestigkeit f	thermal dissociation, thermolysis; thermal decomposition	thermische Dissoziation f, Thermolyse f; thermische Zersetzung f
		thermal distribution	thermische Verteilung f
		thermal disturbance	thermische Störung f
		thermal drift	Wärmedrift f
		thermal effect	s. thermal action
		thermal efficiency, heat[ing] efficiency	[thermischer] Wirkungsgrad m, Wärmewirkungsgrad m, [thermischer] Nutzeffekt m
thermal decomposition	s. thermal dissociation		
thermal deformation, thermal strain	thermische Verformung (Deformation) f, Wärmeformänderung f	thermal effusion	thermische Effusion f
thermal destruction [of polymers]	thermischer Abbau m [von Polymeren]	thermal e.m.f., thermoelectromotive force, thermo-e.m.f., thermoelectric power, thermoelectric voltage, thermo[-] voltage; thermocouple electromotive force	Thermo-EMK f, thermoelektromotorische Kraft f, Thermospannung f, Thermokraft f, thermoelektrische Spannung (Kraft) f, Thermo-Urspannung f; Seebeck-EMK f
thermal detector	Wärmedetektor m		
thermal detector [of nuclear radiations], thermal-neutron detector	Detektor m für thermische Neutronen, thermischer Detektor m [für Kernstrahlungen]		
thermal detuning, thermal frequency shift	thermische Verstimmung f	thermal emission	s. thermionic emission
		thermal emission <in the r.f. range>	s. a. thermal radio-frequency radiation
thermal development, temperature cycle method, temperature development <of nuclear emulsions>	Temperaturentwicklungsverfahren n, Temperaturentwicklung f <von Kernemulsionen>	thermal emissivity	Wärmeabgabevermögen n <in kcal/s grd>
		thermal emittance	s. thermal exitance
		thermal energy	thermische Energie f
thermal diagram	Wärmediagramm n	thermal energy, heat energy, calorific energy, thermal work, heat work, heat	Wärmeenergie f, thermische Energie f, Wärmearbeit f, thermische Arbeit f, Wärme f
thermal dielectric breakdown	s. thermal breakdown		
thermal diffuse scattering	s. inelastic scattering by crystals		
thermal diffusion, thermodiffusion	Thermodiffusion f	thermal equation of state, thermal state equation	thermische Zustandsgleichung f
		thermal equator	Wärmeäquator m
thermal diffusion coefficient, [coefficient of] thermal diffusivity, coefficient of thermal diffusion, thermodiffusion coefficient	Thermodiffusionskoeffizient m	thermal equilibrium, temperature equilibrium	thermisches Gleichgewicht n, Wärmegleichgewicht n, Temperaturgleichgewicht n
		thermal equivalent, equivalent of heat	Wärmeäquivalent n
thermal diffusion column, Clusius column, Clusius-Dickel column, thermodiffusion column, thermal diffusion pipe, separation pipe, separation tube	Trennrohr n [von Clusius], Clusiussches Trennrohr, Clusius-Dickel-Trennrohr n, Thermodiffusionstrennrohr n, Thermodiffusionskolonne f	thermal equivalent of mechanical energy, thermal equivalent of work	thermisches (kalorisches) Arbeitsäquivalent n, Arbeitsäquivalent der Wärme, Arbeitswert m
		thermal etching	thermische Ätzung f, Heißätzung f, Kristallabdampfung f
		thermal excitation	thermische Anregung f
thermal diffusion effect	Thermodiffusionseffekt m, Koeffizient m des Diffusionsthermoeffekts	thermal exitance, thermal luminous exitance, thermal emittance	thermische spezifische Lichtausstrahlung (Leuchtstärke) f
thermal diffusion factor	Thermodiffusionsfaktor m	thermal expansion, thermal extension (dilation, dilatation), expansion by heat	Wärme[aus]dehnung f, thermische Ausdehnung (Dehnung) f, Wärmeschub m
thermal diffusion flow	thermischer Diffusionsstrom m, Thermodiffusionsstrom m		
thermal diffusion length	Diffusionslänge f für thermische Neutronen	thermal expansion coefficient	s. coefficient of thermal expansion
thermal diffusion method	s. separation of isotopes by thermal diffusion	thermal expansivity	s. thermal expansion coefficient
		thermal explosion	Wärmeexplosion f
thermal diffusion pipe	s. thermal diffusion column	thermal extension	s. thermal expansion
thermal diffusion plant	Thermodiffusionsanlage f	thermal farad	Wärmefarad n
		thermal fatigue	thermische Ermüdung f
thermal diffusion potential, potential of thermal diffusion	Thermodiffusionspotential n	thermal feedback	thermische Rückkopplung f
		thermal field	Wärmefeld n
		thermal fission, thermal neutron fission, thermofission	thermische Spaltung f, Spaltung durch thermische Neutronen
thermal diffusion ratio, thermodiffusion ratio	Thermodiffusionsverhältnis n		
thermal diffusivity, diffusivity [for heat], heat diffusivity, temperature (thermometric) conductivity, coefficient of thermometric conductivity	Temperaturleitfähigkeit f, Temperaturleitzahl f, Temperaturleitvermögen n	thermal fission cross-section, thermal neutron fission cross-section, fission cross-section for thermal neutrons	thermischer Spaltquerschnitt m, Spaltquerschnitt für thermische Neutronen, Wirkungsquerschnitt m für Spaltung durch thermische Neutronen
thermal diffusivity	s. a. thermal diffusion coefficient	thermal fission factor	thermischer Spaltfaktor m
thermal dilatation	s. thermal expansion		
thermal dilation	s. thermal expansion		

thermal flash, temperature flash — Temperaturblitz *m*
thermal flow — s. rate of heat flow
thermal flow — s. thermal convection
thermal fluctuation — thermische Schwankung (Fluktuation) *f*, Wärmeschwankung *f*
thermal flux, thermal neutron flux — Fluß *m* der thermischen Neutronen, thermischer Fluß, thermischer Neutronenfluß *m*
thermal flux — s. a. rate of heat flow
thermal flux vector, heat flow (flux) vector — Wärmeflußvektor *m*, Wärmestromvektor *m*
thermal focal spot, thermal focus — thermischer Brennfleck *m*
thermal frequency shift, thermal detuning — thermische Verstimmung *f*
thermal generation, thermal production — thermische Erzeugung *f*
thermal glow, thermoluminescence — Thermolumineszenz *f*
thermal glow curve, thermoluminescence curve; glow curve — Thermolumineszenzkurve *f*; Glowkurve *f*
thermal glow peak, glow peak — Glowmaximum *n*, Glow-peak *m*
thermal gradient, temperature gradient — Temperaturgradient *m*, Temperaturgefälle *n*
thermal gradient — thermische Höhenstufe *f*
thermal gradient — s. a. geothermal gradient
thermal head — Wärmegefälle *n*

thermal henry — Wärmehenry *n*
thermal history, thermal prehistory — thermische Vorgeschichte (Geschichte) *f*
thermal hum — thermisches Brumm[en] *n*
thermal hysteresis — thermische Hysteresis (Hysterese) *f*
thermal inductance — thermische Induktivität *f*
thermal inelastic scattering cross-section, cross-section for thermal inelastic scattering — unelastischer Streuquerschnitt *m* für thermische Teilchen, Wirkungsquerschnitt *m* für die unelastische Streuung thermischer Teilchen, Wirkungsquerschnitt der unelastischen Streuung von thermischen Teilchen
thermal inertia, thermal lag — thermische Trägheit *f*, Wärmeträgheit *f*, Wärmebeharrungsvermögen *n*, Wärmeverzug *m*, thermische Verzögerung *f*
thermal instrument, electrothermic instrument <US> — elektrothermisches (thermisches) Meßgerät *n*, elektrothermisches (thermisches) Instrument *n*
thermal insulation, thermal insulation of plasma — Thermoisolation *f* [des Plasmas]
thermal insulation — s. a. heat insulation <therm.>
thermal insulation of plasma — s. thermal insulation
thermal intrinsic conduction — thermische Eigenleitung *f*
thermal ionization — thermische Ionisierung *f*, thermische Ionisation *f*, Thermoionisation *f*, Temperaturionisation *f*, Temperaturionisierung *f*
thermalization — Thermalisierung *f*, Thermalisation *f*, Abbremsung auf thermische Geschwindigkeit (Energie)
thermalization power — Thermalisierungskraft *f*
thermalization time — Thermalisierungszeit *f*
thermal jump — thermischer Sprung *m*
thermal junction — s. thermocouple junction
thermal lag — s. thermal inertia
thermal laminar boundary layer — thermische laminare Grenzschicht *f*

thermal lattice vibration, thermal branch of lattice vibrations — thermische Gitterschwingung *f*, thermischer Zweig *m* der Gitterschwingungen
thermal leakage — thermischer Ausfluß (Abfluß, Verlust) *m*, Ausfluß thermischer Neutronen
thermal leakage factor — thermischer Verlustfaktor *m*
thermal leakage modulus, accomodation coefficient — Akkomodationskoeffizient *m*
thermal level — thermisches Niveau *n*, Wärmeniveau *n*
thermal light source, thermal source of light, temperature source of light
thermal load[ing], heat load[ing], thermal stress — Wärmebelastung *f*, Wärmebeanspruchung *f*
thermal luminous exitance — s. thermal exitance
thermally conducting, heat-conducting, heat conductive — wärmeleitend
thermally fissionable material — durch thermische Neutronen spaltbares Material *n*, thermisch spaltbares Material
thermally sensitive resistor — s. thermistor
thermally stable — s. heat-proof
thermally stimulated exoelectron emission, TSEE — thermisch stimulierte (angeregte) Exoelektronenemission *f*, TSEE
thermal magnetization — s. thermomagnetization
thermal Maxwell flux distribution — Maxwellsche Flußverteilung *f* im thermischen Gebiet
thermal microphone — s. hot[-]wire microphone
thermal mobility — thermische Beweglichkeit *f*, Wärmebeweglichkeit *f*
thermal molecular flow — s. Knudsen effect
thermal molecular pressure, thermomolecular pressure, molecular thermal pressure — Thermomolekulardruck *m*, thermomolekularer Druck *m*, thermischer Molekulardruck *m*
thermal motion — s. thermal agitation
thermal motion of the molecules — s. molecular motion
thermal neutron — thermisches Neutron *n*
thermal neutron activation cross-section — s. thermal activation cross-section
thermal neutron beam — s. thermal beam
thermal neutron breeding, thermal breeding — thermisches Brüten *n*
thermal neutron capture cross-section — s. thermal capture cross-section
thermal neutron cross-section — s. thermal cross-section
thermal-neutron detector, thermal detector [of nuclear radiations] — Detektor *m* für thermische Neutronen, thermischer Detektor *m* [für Kernstrahlungen]
thermal neutron fission — s. thermal fission
thermal neutron fission cross-section — s. thermal fission cross-section
thermal neutron flux, thermal flux — Fluß *m* der thermischen Neutronen, thermischer Fluß, thermischer Neutronenfluß *m*
thermal neutron lifetime — s. diffusion time
thermal neutron spectrum, thermal spectrum — thermisches Spektrum *n*, Energiespektrum *n* der thermischen Neutronen
thermal neutron yield, thermal yield — Ausbeute *f* thermischer Neutronen, thermische Neutronenausbeute *f*
thermal noise — s. Johnson noise
thermal noise generator — Wärmerauschgenerator *m*
thermal noise source — Wärmerauschquelle *f*
thermal noise voltage, thermal agitation voltage — Wärmerauschspannung *f*
thermal ohm — Wärmeohm *n*
thermal oil — Thermalöl *n*
thermal overload capacity — thermische Überlastbarkeit *f*

thermal

thermal phenomenon, heat phenomenon	Wärmeerscheinung f
thermal pile, thermal reactor	thermischer Reaktor m
thermal pinch effect	thermischer Pincheffekt m
thermal Pitot tube	thermisches Pitot-Rohr n
thermal pole <geo.>	Wärmepol m <Geo.>
thermal polymer, thermopolymer	Thermopolymerisat n
thermal potential	s. free enthalpy
thermal power	Wärmekraft f, nutzbare Wärmeenergie f
thermal power <of the reactor> <in MW or MW(th)>	Wärmeleistung f [des Reaktors], thermische Leistung f [des Reaktors], Reaktorwärmeleistung f <in MW, MW$_{th}$ oder MW(th)>
thermal power	s. a. heat output
thermal prehistory, thermal history	thermische Vorgeschichte (Geschichte) f
thermal pretreatment	thermische Vorbehandlung f
thermal production, thermal generation	thermische Erzeugung f
thermal protection	Wärmeschutz m, Wärmeabschirmung f
thermal punch-through	s. thermal breakdown
thermal quantity	thermische Größe f
thermal quenching, thermoquenching	thermische Löschung f, Temperaturlöschung f, Thermolöschung f; thermische Tilgung f, Temperaturtilgung f, Thermotilgung f
thermal radiant emittance (exitance)	thermische spezifische Ausstrahlung f
thermal radiation	s. heat radiation
thermal radiation	s. thermal radio-frequency radiation
thermal radiator	Temperaturstrahler m, Wärmestrahler m, Strahler m <Therm.>
thermal radio-frequency radiation, thermal radiation (emission) <in the r.f. range>	thermische Radiofrequenzstrahlung f (Strahlung) f, <im Radiofrequenzbereich>
thermal range, thermal region <of energy>	thermisches Gebiet (Energiegebiet) n
thermal reactor, thermal pile	thermischer Reaktor m
thermal rearrangement, thermal transposition	thermische Umlagerung f, Mehrzentrenumlagerung f
thermal regenerator	s. regenerator
thermal regime of the lake	Wärmeklima n des Sees
thermal region, thermal range <of energy>	thermisches Gebiet (Energiegebiet) n
thermal regulation	Wärmeregulierung f, Wärmeregelung f
thermal relaxation	thermische Relaxation f
thermal relaxation time	s. spin-lattice relaxation time
thermal relay, electrothermal relay, thermorelay	Thermorelais n, thermoelektrisches Relais n, Temperaturrelais f, Hitzdrahtrelais n; Temperaturbegrenzer m, Temperaturwächter m
thermal relay, thermostat <techn.>	Thermoschalter m, Temperaturschalter m, Thermostat m <Techn.>
thermal resilience, thermoresilience	Thermorückfederung f
thermal resistance	Wärmewiderstand m
thermal resistance <of transistor>, transistor thermal resistance	thermischer Widerstand m [des Transistors]
thermal resistance noise	Wärme[durchgangs]widerstandsrauschen n
thermal resistivity	spezifischer Wärmewiderstand m, spezifischer Wärmeleitungswiderstand m <reziproke Wärmeleitzahl>
thermal response	Temperaturanstiegsrate f
thermal saturated activity	thermische Sättigungsaktivität f
thermal scattering	thermische Streuung f
thermal self-diffusion current	Selbstthermodiffusionsstrom m, thermischer Selbstdiffusionsstrom m
thermal sensitive resistor	s. thermistor
thermal shield, heat shield	thermische Abschirmung f, Wärmeabschirmung f; thermischer Schild m; Hitzeschild m, Wärmeschild m; Wärmeschutz [-schirm] m
thermal shock	Thermoschock m, Wärmeschock m, Wärmestoß m
thermal shock protection, thermal shock shield	Wärmeschockschild m, Wärmeschockabschirmung f
thermal short-time current rating <US>, rated short-circuit current	thermischer Grenzstrom m, thermischer Kurzschlußstrom m
thermal source	s. thermal spring
thermal source of light, thermal light source, temperature source of light	thermische Lichtquelle f
thermal spectrum, heat radiation spectrum, heat spectrum	Wärmestrahlungsspektrum n, Wärmespektrum n
thermal spectrum, thermal neutron spectrum	thermisches Spektrum n, Energiespektrum n der thermischen Neutronen
thermal spike	„thermal spike" m, thermischer Störungsbereich m, Störungsbereich, [örtlicher] Erhitzungsbereich m
thermal spring, thermal source, therma <pl.: thermae>; warm spring, warm source; hot spring, hot source, hot spa	Therme f, Thermalquelle f; warme Quelle f; heiße Quelle
thermal stability, thermostability, heat resistance, resistance to heat, heat-resisting quality, heat proofness, heatproof quality, heat endurance, heat fastness, heat-fast quality, high-temperature resistance, high-temperature strength; temperature stability, temperature resistance, temperature-resistant quality	Wärmebeständigkeit f, Warmfestigkeit f, Wärmefestigkeit f, Wärmebeharrung f, Wärmesicherheit f, Temperaturbeständigkeit f, Temperaturfestigkeit f, thermische Stabilität f, Hitzebeständigkeit f, Hitzefestigkeit f, Hochtemperaturbeständigkeit f, Hochtemperaturfestigkeit f, Hochwarmfestigkeit f, Hochwärmebeständigkeit f, Hochwärmefestigkeit f; Wärmeformbeständigkeit f, Formbeständigkeit f in der Wärme <Plaste>; Wärmestandfestigkeit f <Plaste>
thermal state	Wärmezustand m
thermal state equation, thermal equation of state	thermische Zustandsgleichung f
thermal stimulation, thermostimulation	thermische Ausleuchtung (Stimulation) f, Temperaturausleuchtung f, Thermoausleuchtung f, Thermostimulation f
thermal stimulus	thermischer Reiz m, Wärmereiz m
thermal strain	s. thermal deformation
thermal strain	s. thermal stress
thermal stratification	Temperaturschichtung f, Temperaturstruktur f
thermal stress, temperature stress; thermal strain	Wärmespannung f, thermische Spannung f

thermal stress, heat load [-ing], load[ing] thermal	Wärmebelastung f, Wärmebeanspruchung f	thermionic converter, thermionic energy converter	thermionischer Wandler (Konverter) m, Thermionikkonverter m, Thermoemissionsumformer m, Thermoemissionsenergieumformer m, Thermoemissionsumsetzer m, Thermoemissionswandler m, glühelektrischer Generator m, Anlaufstromgenerator m
thermal superconduction	s. superthermal conduction		
thermal superconductivity	s. superthermal conduction		
thermal superconductor, super heat conductor	Suprawärmeleiter m, thermischer Supraleiter m		
thermal transition	thermischer Übergang m		
thermal transition probability	thermische Übergangswahrscheinlichkeit f		
thermal transmission	s. rate of heat flow	thermionic current, thermionic emission current	Glühelektronenstrom m, thermischer Emissionsstrom m
thermal transmission factor	s. thermal transmittance		
thermal transmittance, thermal transmission factor <quantity>	Durchlaßgrad m (Transmissionsgrad m, Durchlässigkeit f) für Wärmestrahlung, Wärmedurchlässigkeit f, Wärmetransmission f <Größe>	thermionic current	Thermionenstrom m
		thermionic detector	s. valve rectifier
		thermionic diode	Röhrendiode f
		thermionic discharge	Glühelektronenentladung f; Thermionenentladung f
thermal transmittance	s. a. heat[-] transmission coefficient	thermionic electron source	Glühelektronenquelle f
thermal transpiration	thermische Transpiration f	thermionic emission, thermal emission, Richardson effect, Edison effect, thermoelectronic emission, thermoelectronic effect	Glühemission f, thermische Elektronenemission f, thermische Emission f, glühelektrischer Effekt m, glühelektrische Elektronenemission, Richardson-Effekt m, Edison-Effekt m, Glühelektronenemission f, Glühelektronenverdampfung f, Thermoemission f; Glühkatodenemission f
thermal transposition, thermal rearrangement	thermische Umlagerung f, Mehrzentrenumlagerung f		
thermal tripping	Wärmeauslösung f		
thermal unit	s. unit of heat		
thermal utilization	thermische Nutzung f		
thermal utilization factor	Faktor m der thermischen Ausnutzung (Nutzung), thermischer Nutzfaktor m, Ausnutzungsgrad m für thermische Neutronen		
thermal value, heat equivalent [of the work done]	kalorisches Arbeitsäquivalent n, Wärmewert m [der Arbeitseinheit]	thermionic emission, thermoionic emission	Thermionenemission f, thermionische Emission f
		thermionic emission current, thermionic current	Glühelektronenstrom m, thermischer Emissionsstrom m
thermal valve	Wärmeventil n		
thermal velocity	thermische Geschwindigkeit f		
thermal vibration	Wärmeschwingung f, thermische Schwingung f, Thermoschwingung f	thermionic energy converter	s. thermionic converter
thermal wave	Wärmewelle f	thermionic generation of electricity	s. thermionic conversion
		thermionic generator	s. valve oscillator
thermal wave	Wärmestrahlungswelle f	thermionic ion source, thermionic source	Thermionenquelle f
thermal weathering, insolation weathering	Insolationsverwitterung f, Temperaturverwitterung f	thermionic rectifier	s. valve rectifier
		thermionics	= theory and application of thermionic emission
thermal wind	s. thermic wind		
thermal wind rose	thermische Windrose f	thermionic source, thermionic ion source	Thermionenquelle f
thermal work	s. thermal energy		
thermal yield	s. thermal neutron yield	thermionic transistor	Heißelektronentransistor m, Glühelektronentransistor m
thermel	s. thermocouple		
thermel	s. a. thermocouple thermometer		
thermic	s. thermal	thermionic tube, hot-cathode tube, hot-cathode valve, thermionic valve	Glühkatodenröhre f, Glühkatodenrohr n
thermic upwash	s. laminar thermal convection in the atmosphere		
		thermionic tube	s. a. cathode-ray tube
		thermionic tube	s. a. thermionic valve
thermic wind; thermal wind	thermischer Wind m	thermionic vacuum tube, vacuum tube, vacuum valve	Vakuumröhre f, Hochvakuumröhre f
thermion	Thermion n	thermionic valve, valve, electron[ic] valve, thermionic tube, electron tube, tube <el.>	Elektronenröhre f, Röhre f <El.>
thermion, thermoelectron	Glühelektron n, Thermoelektron n		
thermionic	Glühelektronen-, glühelektrisch, Thermoelektronen-	thermionic valve	s. a. cathode-ray tube
		thermionic valve	s. a. thermionic tube
thermionic, thermoionic	thermionisch, Thermionen-, thermoionisch	thermionic valve electronics, tube electronics	Röhrenelektronik f
thermionic arc	thermionischer Bogen (Lichtbogen) m	thermionic valve equation, tube equation	Röhrengleichung f, Röhrenformel f
		thermionic valve transmitter	s. vacuum-tube transmitter
thermionic [atomic] battery	thermionische Batterie (Radionuklidbatterie) f	thermionic voltmeter	s. vacuum tube voltmeter
thermionic cathode	s. hot cathode	thermionic work function	Austrittsarbeit f bei der Glühemission, Glühelektronen-Austrittsarbeit f
thermionic conduction	Glühelektronenleitung f		
thermionic constant, emission constant	Glühemissionskonstante f, Emissionskonstante f <Konstante K der Richardson-Gleichung>	thermistor, thermally sensitive resistor, thermal sensitive resistor, heat-variable resistor, N.T.C. resistor, negative temperature coefficient resistor	Thermistor m, Heißleiter m, Thernewid m, NTC-Widerstand m, thermisch negativer Widerstand m
thermionic conversion, thermionic generation of electricity	thermionische Umwandlung (Umformung, Umsetzung, Energieumwandlung, Energieumformung) f		

thermistor bridge — Thermistorbrücke *f*
thermistor resistance — Thermistorwiderstand *m*
thermistor thermometer — Heißleiterthermometer *n*
thermistor vacuummeter — Thermistorvakuummeter *n*
thermium, thermal acceptor — Thermium *n*, thermischer Akzeptor *m*
thermoacoustics — Thermoakustik *f*
thermo-adsorption — Thermoadsorption *f*
thermo-alcoholometer — Thermoalkoholometer *f*
thermo-ammeter — Thermoamperemeter *n*, Thermostrommesser *m*
thermoanalysis, thermal analysis, thermography — thermische Analyse *f*, Thermoanalyse *f*
thermoanalytic[al], by thermal analysis — thermoanalytisch
thermo-anelasticity — Thermoanelastizität *f*
thermo-anemometer — *s.* thermocouple anemometer
thermo-areometer — *s.* thermocouple areometer
thermobalance, thermogravity balance — Thermowaage *f*; Temperaturwaage *f*
thermobaric field — thermobarisches Feld *n*
thermobaric wave — thermobarische Welle *f*
thermobarometer — Thermobarometer *n*
thermobattery — *s.* thermopile
thermocapillarity — Thermokapillarität *f*
thermocell — *s.* thermocouple
thermochemical calorie, Rossini calorie, $cal_{thermochem}$ <= 4.1840 J> — thermochemische Kalorie *f*, Rossini-Kalorie *f*, $cal_{thermochem}$
thermo[-]chemistry, chemical thermodynamics — Thermochemie *f*, chemische Thermodynamik *f*
thermochromism — Thermochromie *f*
thermocline, discontinuity layer — Temperatursprungschicht *f*, [thermische] Sprungschicht *f*
thermocline, metalimnion <of lake> — Sprungschicht *f*, Metalimnion *n* <See>
thermocline gradient, gradient of the thermocline — Sprungschichtgradient *m*
thermoclinic — thermoklin
thermocolorimeter — Thermokolorimeter *n*
thermo[-]compression [bond] — Thermodruckbindung *f*, Thermokompression *f*, „thermocompression" *f*
thermocompressor — Thermokompressor *m*
thermoconductometric analysis, thermoconductometry — thermokonduktometrische Analyse *f*, Thermokonduktometrie *f*
thermocontrol — *s.* temperature control
thermocontroller — *s.* thermoregulator
thermoconvection — *s.* convection of heat
thermoconvective, thermal-convection — thermokonvektiv
thermo[-]converter, thermal converter, electrically heated thermocouple — Thermoumformer *m*
thermo[-]couple, thermoelectric couple, thermoelement couple; thermoelement, thermoelectric element, thermel, thermocell; pyod — Thermoelement *n*, thermoelektrisches Element *n*; Thermozelle *f*; Thermopaar *n*
thermocouple amplifier — Thermoelementverstärker *m*
thermocouple anemometer, thermoelectric anemometer, thermoanemometer — thermoelektrisches Anemometer *n*, thermoelektrischer Windmesser *m*, Thermo[element]anemometer *n*, Anemometer mit Thermoelement, Windmeßgerät *n* (Windgeschwindigkeitsmesser *m*) mit Thermoelement
thermocouple areometer, thermoelectric areometer, thermoareometer — Thermoaräometer *n*, thermoelektrisches Aräometer *n*
thermocouple circuit — Thermomeßkreis *m*
thermocouple electromotive force — *s.* thermal e.m.f.
thermocouple galvanometer, thermo[-]galvanometer, thermocouple-type galvanometer, hot-wire galvanometer — Thermogalvanometer *n*, Hitzdrahtgalvanometer *n*
thermocouple gauge head — Thermoelementmeßkopf *m*
thermocouple instrument, thermoelectric instrument, thermoinstrument — Thermoumformer-Meßgerät *n*, Thermoumformergerät *n*, Thermoumformerinstrument *n*, thermoelektrisches Meßgerät *n*, Thermomeßgerät *n*, Thermoinstrument *n*
thermocouple junction, thermojunction, thermal junction — Lötstelle (Kontaktstelle) *f* des Thermoelements, thermoelektrische Lötstelle
thermocouple microphone, thermoelectric microphone — thermoelektrisches Mikrophon *n*, Thermoelementmikrophon *n*
thermocouple pile — *s.* thermopile
thermocouple thermometer, thermoelectric thermometer, thermoelectric pyrometer, thermel — Temperaturmeßgerät *n* mit Berührungsthermoelement, thermoelektrisches Thermometer (Pyrometer) *n*
thermocouple-type galvanometer — *s.* thermocouple galvanometer
thermocouple vacuum gauge, thermoelectric vacuummeter, heat-conduction gauge, thermotron — thermoelektrisches Vakuummeter *n*, Thermoelement-Vakuummeter *n*, Wärmeleitungsmanometer *n*, Wärmeleitungsvakuummeter *n*, Thermotron *n*
thermocouple voltmeter, thermovoltmeter — Thermovoltmeter *n*, Thermospannungsmesser *m*
thermocouple wattmeter — *s.* thermowattmeter
thermocouple wire — Thermodraht *m*, Thermoelementdraht *m*
thermocross, thermoelectric cross, thermal cross — Thermokreuz *n*
thermocross bridge — Thermokreuzbrücke *f*
thermocurrent, thermoelectric current — Thermostrom *m*, thermoelektrischer Strom *m*
thermode — Thermode *f*
thermodepolarization [current] method — Methode *f* der Depolarisationsthermoströme
thermo detector, thermo[-]detector, thermo-electric detector — Thermodetektor *m*, thermoelektrischer Detektor *m*
thermodielectric effect, Costa de Ribeiro effect — thermodielektrischer Effekt *m*, Costa-de-Ribeiro-Effekt *m*
thermodiffusion — *s.* thermal diffusion
thermoduct — durch Temperaturinversion entstandener Troposphärenkanal *m*, Inversions-Troposphärenkanal *m*
thermodynamic[al] activity — thermodynamische Aktivität *f*
thermodynamically unstable — thermodynamisch instabil
thermodynamic constant, constant of thermodynamics — Konstante *f* der Thermodynamik, thermodynamische Konstante
thermodynamic co-ordinate, thermodynamic parameter [of state], thermodynamic property — thermodynamischer Parameter *m*, thermodynamische Koordinate *f*
thermodynamic co-ordinate — *s. a.* parameter of state
thermodynamic cycle — thermodynamischer Kreisprozeß *m*
thermodynamic degeneracy — thermodynamische Entartung *f*
thermodynamic diagram — thermodynamisches Diagramm *n*

thermoelectric

thermodynamic diagram s. a. phase diagram
thermodynamic efficiency s. relative efficiency
thermodynamic equation of state thermodynamische Zustandsgleichung f
thermodynamic equilibrium thermodynamisches Gleichgewicht n
thermodynamic excess function s. enthalpy of mixing
thermodynamic exponent thermodynamischer Exponent m
thermodynamic factor thermodynamischer Faktor m
thermodynamic flux, flux, flow, current, rate <therm.> thermodynamischer Fluß m, Fluß <Therm.>
thermodynamic freezing-in thermodynamisches Einfrieren n, Gleichgewichtseinfrieren n
thermodynamic function thermodynamische Funktion f
thermodynamic interaction constant thermodynamische Wechselwirkungskonstante f
thermodynamic isotope effect thermodynamischer Isotopieeffekt m
thermodynamic machine, heat motor, heat engine Wärmekraftmaschine f, kalorische Maschine f
thermodynamic model [of nucleus] thermodynamisches Kernmodell n, thermodynamisches Modell n [des Atomkerns]
thermodynamic parameter [of state] s. thermodynamic co-ordinate
thermodynamic perturbation theory thermodynamische Störungstheorie f
thermodynamic phase diagram s. phase diagram
thermodynamic potential thermodynamisches Potential n
thermodynamic potential s. a. free enthalpy
thermodynamic power cycle Wärmekraftprozeß m
thermodynamic pressure thermodynamischer Druck m
thermodynamic probability thermodynamische Wahrscheinlichkeit f
thermodynamic process, thermodynamic transformation thermodynamischer Prozeß m
thermodynamic property s. thermodynamic co-ordinate
thermodynamic property s. a. parameter of state
thermodynamic quantity [of state], thermodynamic variable [of state] thermodynamische Größe f, thermodynamische Zustandsgröße f
thermodynamics Thermodynamik f <im weiteren Sinne>, Wärmemechanik f, Wärmekraftlehre f, mechanische Wärmelehre f, Wärmelehre f
thermodynamic similarity thermodynamische Ähnlichkeit f
thermodynamics of reactions Reaktionsthermodynamik f
thermodynamics of the nucleus, nuclear thermodynamics Kernthermodynamik f, Thermodynamik f des Atomkerns
thermodynamic stiffness thermodynamische Steifigkeit f
thermodynamic temperature scale thermodynamische Temperaturskala f, normale Temperaturskala f, Normskala f der Temperatur
thermodynamic tension s. intensive variable
thermodynamic transformation, thermodynamic process thermodynamischer Prozeß m
thermodynamic variable [of state], thermodynamic quantity [of state] thermodynamische Größe f, thermodynamische Zustandsgröße f
thermoelastic attenuation, thermoelastic damping thermoelastische Dämpfung f

thermoelastic coefficient, thermoelasticity coefficient Thermoelastizitätskoeffizient m, thermoelastischer Koeffizient m
thermoelastic constant thermoelastische Konstante f
thermoelastic coupling thermoelastische Kopplung f
thermoelastic damping, thermoelastic attenuation thermoelastische Dämpfung f
thermoelastic dissipation thermoelastische Dissipation f
thermoelastic effect thermoelastischer Effekt m, thermoelastische Erscheinung f
thermoelastic inversion thermoelastische Inversion f
thermoelasticity Thermoelastizität f
thermoelasticity coefficient, thermoelastic coefficient Thermoelastizitätskoeffizient m, thermoelastischer Koeffizient m
thermoelastic stress thermoelastische Spannung f
thermoelectret Thermoelektret n
thermoelectric anemometer s. thermocouple anemometer
thermoelectric areometer, thermocouple areometer, thermoareometer Thermoaräometer n, thermoelektrisches Aräometer n
thermoelectric battery, thermoelectric nuclear battery, thermo-e.m.f. nuclear battery, thermo-e.m.f. [atomic] battery, isotope powered thermoelectric generator, radioisotope thermoelectric generator, RTG thermoelektrische Batterie f, thermoelektrische Radionuklidbatterie f, Thermokraftbatterie f
thermoelectric battery s. a. thermobattery
thermoelectric conversion s. thermoelectric generation of electricity
thermoelectric converter; thermoelectric generator thermoelektrischer Wandler (Konverter; Generator) m
thermoelectric couple s. thermocouple
thermoelectric cross s. thermocross
thermoelectric current, thermocurrent Thermostrom m, thermoelektrischer Strom m
thermoelectric detector s. thermo[-]detector
thermoelectric effect thermoelektrische Erscheinung f, thermoelektrischer Effekt m
thermoelectric effect, Seebeck effect Seebeck-Effekt m, thermoelektrischer Effekt m
thermoelectric electromotive series s. electrothermal series
thermoelectric element s. thermocouple
thermoelectric force s. thermal e.m.f.
thermoelectric generation of electricity; thermoelectric conversion thermoelektrische Energieerzeugung (Stromerzeugung; Energie-Direktumwandlung, Wandlung) f
thermoelectric generator s. thermoelectric converter
thermoelectric instrument s. thermocouple instrument
thermoelectricity Thermoelektrizität f, Wärmeelektrizität f
thermoelectric microphone, thermocouple microphone thermoelektrisches Mikrophon n, Thermoelementmikrophon n
thermoelectric nuclear battery s. thermoelectric battery
thermoelectric photometry thermoelektrische Photometrie f
thermoelectric pile s. thermopile
thermoelectric potential, thermojunction potential thermoelektrisches Potential n
thermoelectric potential series s. electrothermal series
thermoelectric power s. thermal e.m.f.
thermoelectric pyrometer s. thermocouple thermometer
thermoelectric scale of temperature thermoelektrische Temperaturskala f
thermoelectric series s. electrothermal series
thermoelectric thermometer s. thermocouple thermometer

thermoelectric 882

thermoelectric vacuum-meter	s. thermocouple vacuum gauge	thermoluminescence dating	Thermolumineszenz-datierung f, Altersbestimmung f aus Thermolumineszenzdaten
thermoelectric voltage	s. thermal e.m.f.		
thermoelectrode	Thermoelektrode f	thermoluminescence (thermoluminescent) dosimeter, TLD	Thermolumineszenz-dosimeter n
thermoelectrodynamics	Thermoelektrodynamik f		
thermoelectromotive force	s. thermal e.m.f.	thermoluminescence (thermoluminescent) dosimeter reader	Thermolumineszenzdosi-meter-Auswertegerät n
thermoelectromotive force plotted against the temperature	s. curve of the thermoelectromotive force versus (vs.) temperature	thermolysis	s. thermal dissociation
		thermomagnetic analysis	thermomagnetische Analyse f
thermoelectron, thermion	Glühelektron n, Thermoelektron n	thermomagnetic effect	thermomagnetischer Effekt m, thermomagnetische Erscheinung f
thermoelectronic effect (emission)	s. thermionic emission		
thermoelectrostatics	Thermoelektrostatik f	thermomagnetic hysteresis	thermomagnetische Hysteresis f
thermoelement [couple]	s. thermocouple	thermomagnetic torque	s. Scott effect
thermo-e.m.f.	s. thermal e.m.f.	thermomagnetism	Thermomagnetismus m
thermo-e.m.f. [atomic] battery, thermo-e.m.f. nuclear battery	s. thermoelectric battery	thermomagnetization, thermal magnetization	Thermomagnetisierung f
thermofission	s. thermal fission	thermomechanical curve	thermomechanische Kurve f
thermogalvanic corrosion	thermogalvanische Korrosion f	thermomechanical effect, pressure thermomechanical effect, fountain effect	thermomechanischer Druckeffekt (Effekt) m, Fontäne[n]effekt m, Fountaineffekt m, „fountain effect" m, „fountain"-Effekt m, Springbrunnenwirkung f, Springbrunneneffekt m, Sprudeleffekt m
thermo[-]galvanometer, thermocouple galvanometer, thermocouple-type galvanometer, hot-wire galvanometer	Thermogalvanometer n, Hitzdrahtgalvanometer n		
thermo gas chromatography, gas chromathermography	Thermogaschromatographie f	thermomechanics	Thermomechanik f, Thermodynamik f im engeren Sinne
thermogauge, heat-pressure gauge	Thermomanometer n	thermometamorphism	Thermometamorphose f
thermogradient coefficient	Thermogradientkoeffizient m	thermometer bulb, cistern of the thermometer	Thermometerkugel f, Thermometergefäß n
thermogradientometric analysis	Thermogradientometrie f, thermogradientometrische Analyse f	thermometer collar	Bohrung f für das Thermometer, Thermometerbohrung f
thermogram	Thermogramm n	thermometer column, thermometric column	Thermometerfaden m, Thermometersäule f
thermograph, recording thermometer, temperature recorder, thermometrograph	Thermograph m, Temperaturschreiber m, registrierendes (schreibendes) Thermometer n, Schreibthermometer n, Temperaturselbstschreiber m, Thermometrograph m	thermometer correction	s. thermometric correction
		thermometer for measuring the water temperature	Schöpfthermometer n, Wasserthermometer n
thermography ‹bio.›	Thermographie f ‹Bio.›	thermometer probe, pyrometer probe	Temperaturfühler m
thermography, thermal analysis, thermoanalysis	thermische Analyse f, Thermoanalyse f	thermometer problem	Thermometerproblem n
		thermometer resistor	s. resistance thermometer
thermogravimetric analysis, thermogravimetry	Thermogravimetrie f, thermogravimetrische Analyse f	thermometer stem	Thermometerkapillare f, Thermometerröhre f
		thermometer substance	s. thermometric substance
thermogravitational convection	thermogravitationelle Konvektion f	thermometer tube	s. pyrometric rod
thermogravity balance	s. thermobalance	thermometer with saturated vapour	s. vapour pressure thermometer
thermohydrodynamic[al]	thermohydrodynamisch	thermometrical rate of cooling	thermometrische Abkühlungsgeschwindigkeit f
thermohygrometer	Thermohygrometer n	thermometric column	s. thermometer column
thermoinduction	Thermoinduktion f	thermometric conductivity	s. thermal diffusivity
thermoinstrument	s. thermocouple instrument		
thermoionic	s. thermionic	thermometric correction, thermometer correction, stem correction; exposed-stem (exposed-thread) correction, emergent column (stem) correction; capillary stem correction	Thermometerkorrektion f, Fadenkorrektion f, Korrektion f für den herausragenden Faden
thermoisodrome	Thermoisodrome f		
thermoisogradient	Thermoisogradient m		
thermoisopleth	Thermoisoplethe f		
thermojunction, thermocouple junction, thermal junction	Lötstelle f des Thermoelements, thermoelektrische Lötstelle		
thermojunction ‹semi.›	Thermoübergang m, Thermokontakt m ‹Halb.›	thermometric crayon, temperature-indicating crayon, tempilstik ‹US›	Temperaturfarbstift m, Farbstift m für Temperaturmessung, Temperaturmeßstift m
thermojunction potential, thermoelectric potential	thermoelektrisches Potential n	thermometric element, temperature sensor, temperature-sensitive element, temperature-sensing element	Temperaturfühler m, Wärmefühler m, Fühlerelement n
thermokinetics	Thermokinetik f		
thermolabile, heat-unsteady	thermolabil		
		thermometric fluid	s. thermometric liquid
		thermometric gas	Thermometergas n
thermoluminescence, thermal glow, TL	Thermolumineszenz f	thermometric liquid, thermometric fluid	Thermometerflüssigkeit f
thermoluminescence curve, thermal glow curve; glow curve	Thermolumineszenzkurve f; Glowkurve f	thermometric paper	Thermometerpapier n
		thermometric parameter	Thermometerparameter m, thermometrischer Parameter m

thermometric substance, thermometer substance, substance used for the filling of thermometer	Thermometersubstanz f	thermoplastic material thermopolymer, thermal polymer	s. thermoplastic Thermopolymerisat n
thermometric analysis (titration)	s. thermometry	thermopositive thermoquenching	thermopositiv s. thermal quenching
thermometrograph	s. thermograph	thermoreceptor, heat receptor	Thermorezeptor m, Wärmerezeptor m
thermometry, thermometric analysis; thermometric titration, enthalpometric titration	Thermometrie f, thermometrische Analyse f, Enthalpometrie f, thermometrisch Titration f	thermoregulation thermoregulator, thermostatic regulator, thermocontroller, temperature regulating device, temperature controller, temperature regulator, attemperator	s. temperature control Temperaturregler m, Thermoregler m, Thermoregulator m
thermomicrophone	s. hot[-] wire microphone		
thermomolecular flow	s. Knudsen effect		
thermomolecular pressure, thermal molecular pressure, molecular thermal pressure	Thermomolekulardruck m, thermomolekularer Druck m, thermischer Molekulardruck m	thermorelay thermoremanence, thermoremanent magnetization, TRM	s. thermal relay Thermoremanenz f, thermoremanente Magnetisierung f, TRM
thermomotor	s. hot-air engine	thermoresilience, thermal resilience	Thermorückfederung f
thermomultiplicator	Thermomultiplikator m	thermoresonance thermos [bottle]	Thermoresonanz f s. thermos flask
thermonastic	thermonastisch	thermoscope	Thermoskop n
thermonasty	Thermonastie f	thermoset	s. thermosetting plastic
thermo[-]needles	Thermonadeln fpl, Tastthermometer n	thermosetting, hardenable at elevated temperatures, hardenable by heat treatment	warmhärtend, warmhärtbar, warmaushärtbar, wärmehärtend, wärmehärtbar
thermonegative	thermonegativ		
thermoneutral	thermoneutral	thermosetting plastic, thermoset, duromer	Duroplast m, Duromer n, duroplastisches Hochpolymer n, härtbarer Kunststoff m
thermonuclear; fusion	thermonuklear; Fusions-, Kernfusions-, Verschmelzungs-		
thermonuclear apparatus; thermonuclear plant	Kernfusionsgerät n; Kernfusionsanlage f, Fusionsanlage f; thermonukleare Anlage f	thermosetting resin, resinoid	duroplastisches Kunstharz n, härtbares Kunstharz
		thermos flask, thermos [bottle]	Thermosflasche f
thermonuclear energy	s. fusion energy	thermos flask	s. a. Dewar vacuum flask
thermonuclear explosion	thermonukleare Explosion f, Kernfusionsexplosion f	thermosiphon cooling, thermo syphon cooling <US>	Wärmeumlaufkühlung f, Umlaufkühlung f, Thermosiphonkühlung f
thermonuclear fusion	thermonukleare Kernfusion f, thermonukleare Fusion f	thermosiphon pump thermosphere, ionosphere, Heaviside layer	s. siphon pump Ionosphäre f, Thermosphäre f, Heaviside-Schicht f, Ionisationsschicht f
thermonuclear plant	s. thermonuclear apparatus		
thermonuclear process, thermonuclear reaction	thermonukleare Reaktion (Fusionsreaktion) f, thermonuklearer Prozeß m	thermostability thermostable thermostat	s. thermal stability s. thermally stable Thermostat m; Wärmeschrank m
thermonuclear reactor; nuclear fusion reactor, fusion reactor	Fusionsreaktor m, Kernfusionsreaktor m; thermonuklearer Reaktor m	thermostat thermostat thermostated, thermostatically controlled, temperature-controlled	s. a. thermal relay <techn.> s. a. thermoregulator thermostatiert, temperaturstabilisiert, temperaturgeregelt, thermisch stabilisiert, thermostabilisiert
thermonuclear transformation, thermonuclear transmutation	thermonukleare Umwandlung f		
thermonucleonics	Thermonukleonik f, Technik f und Lehre f von den thermonuklearen Reaktionen	thermostatic bath, constant-temperature bath	Temperaturbad n, Temperierbad n
thermo-optoelectric cooling	thermooptoelektrische Kühlung f	thermostatic delay relay	thermostatisches Verzögerungsrelais n
thermo-osmosis	Thermoosmose f	thermostatic regulator	s. thermoregulator
thermopause	Thermopause f	thermostatics	Thermostatik f
thermoperiodical reaction	thermoperiodische Reaktion f	thermostatistics	s. statistical thermodynamics
thermoperiodicity, thermoperiodism	Thermoperiodismus m, Thermoperiodizität f, Temperaturperiodizität f	thermostimulation thermostriction	s. thermal stimulation Thermostriktion f
thermophilic	thermophil, wärmeliebend, wärmefreundlich	thermo syphon cooling <US>, thermosiphon cooling	Wärmeumlaufkühlung f, Umlaufkühlung f, Thermosiphonkühlung f
thermophily	Thermophilie f		
thermophone	Thermophon n	thermotactic	thermotaktisch
thermophore	Thermophor m, Wärmeträger m	thermotactism, thermotaxis	Thermotaxis f
thermophoresis	Thermophorese f	thermotonus	Thermotonus m
thermophosphorescence	Thermophosphoreszenz f	thermotransport	Thermotransport m
thermo-photovoltaic	thermophotoelektrisch, thermophotovoltaisch, wärmelichtelektrisch	thermotron	s. thermocouple vacuum gauge
thermophysics	Thermophysik f	thermotropic	thermotropisch
thermopile, thermoelectric pile, thermocouple pile; thermobattery, thermoelectric battery	Thermosäule f, thermoelektrische Säule f; Thermokette f; Thermobatterie f	thermotropism thermotube thermoviscometer	Thermotropismus m Thermotube f Thermoviskosimeter n
		thermoviscous number	Thermoviskositätszahl f
		thermo[-]voltage	s. thermal e.m.f.
thermoplastic, thermoplastic material	Thermoplast m, thermoplastischer Kunststoff m, Plastomer n	thermovoltmeter thermowattmeter, thermocouple wattmeter	s. thermocouple voltmeter Thermowattmeter n, Thermoleistungsmesser m, thermischer Leistungsmesser m
thermoplasticity	Thermoplastizität f		

theta characteristic	Theta-Charakteristik f	thigmonastic	thigmonastisch, haptonastisch
theta function	s. Jacobi['s] theta function	thigmonasty	Thigmonastie f, Haptonastie f
thetagram	Thetagramm n	thigmo reaction	Thigmoreaktion f, Haptoreaktion f, haptische Reaktion f
theta meson, theta particle, Θ^0 <= K° meson>	Theta-Meson n, Theta-Teilchen n	thigmotactic	thigmotaktisch
theta-pinch, ϑ-pinch, azimuthal pinch	Theta-Pinch m, ϑ-Pinch m	thigmotaxis	Thigmotaxis f
		thigmotropic	thigmotropisch, haptotropisch
		thigmotropism	Thigmotropismus m, Haptotropismus m
theta polarization	Theta-Polarisation f	thimble [chamber], thimble ionization chamber	Fingerhutkammer f, Fingerhutionisationskammer f
theta series, ϑ series	Theta-Reihe f, ϑ-Reihe f		
theta state	Theta-Zustand m, Theta-Punkt m		
theta temperature of Flory, Flory temperature	Theta-Temperatur f [von Flory], Florysche Temperatur f, Θ-Temperatur f	thimble of micrometer, micrometer thimble	Mikrometertrommel f, Trommel f des Mikrometers; Meßtrommel f
thetatron	Thetatron n	thin	dünn[schichtig]
Thévenin['s] equivalent [generator], Thévenin['s] generator	Ersatzgenerator m (Ersatzspannungsquelle f) [nach dem Helmholtzschen Satz], Helmholtzscher Ersatzgenerator, Zweipolquelle f	thin film	s. thin layer
		thin-film integrated circuit	integrierte Dünnfilmschaltung f, Dünnfilmschaltung f
		thin-film transistor	Dünnschichttransistor m, Dünnfilmtransistor m
Thévenin-Helmholtz theorem, Thévenin['s] theorem, Helmholtz['] theorem <el.>	Helmholtzscher (Théveninscher) Satz m, Satz (Theorem) von Helmholtz (Thévenin)	thin flame	s. shooting flame
		thin fog	s. mist
		thin ground section	s. thin metal film
thickening <mech.>	Verdickung f <Mech.>	thin layer; [thin] film; pellicle; wash	dünne Schicht f; Haut f, Häutchen n; Film m
thickening	s. a. inspissation <chem.>		
thick lens	dicke (lange) Linse f	thin layer chromatography, TLC	Dünnschichtchromatographie f
thick liquid	s. viscidity		
thickly liquid	s. viscid		
thickness	Dicke f, Stärke f; Dickschichtigkeit f	thin layer electrophoresis	Dünnschichtelektrophorese f
thickness, thickness of layer <geo.>	Mächtigkeit f, Schichtmächtigkeit f, Schichthöhe f, Schichtdicke f, Schichtstärke f <Geo.>	thin lens	dünne (kurze) Linse f
		thin metal film (layer), thin polished section, thin ground section, thin section	Dünnschliff m
thickness	s. a. thickness of layer		
thickness by reflection	in Reflexion gemessene Dicke f, nach der Reflexionsmethode gemessene Dicke	thinning, dilution, desaturation <of the solution>	Verdünnung f, Konzentrationsverminderung f <Lösung>
		thinning[-down] [of cross-section]	s. contraction
thickness chord ratio	s. thickness ratio	thinning-out <geo.>	Verdrückung f der Schicht, Schichtverdrückung f, Schichtenverdrückung f; Auskeilen n <Geo.>
thickness control	s. thickness gauging		
thickness gauge, thickness meter; lateral extensometer	Dickenmesser m, Dickenmeßgerät n		
thickness gauge	s. a. thickness meter		
thickness gauging; thickness control	Dickenmessung f	thin plate	s. wafer
		thin-plate weir	s. sharp-crested weir
		thin [polished] section	s. thin metal film
		thin section	s. microsection <bio.>
thickness measurement by backscatter[ing], backscatter[ing] gauging	Rückstreudickenmessung f, Reflexionsdickenmessung f	thin shell (slab)	s. shell <in theory of elasticity>
		thin-target excitation curve	Anregungskurve f für dünnes Target
thickness meter, thickness gauge, film thickness meter (gauge), coating thickness meter (gauge)	Schichtdickenmesser m, Schichtdickenmeßgerät n	thin track	schwache (leichte, dünne) Spur f
		thin-wall[ed] counter tube	dünnwandiges Zählrohr n
thickness meter	s. a. thickness gauge	thin-walled ionization chamber	dünnwandige Ionisationskammer f
thickness of layer, layer thickness; film thickness; coating thickness; thickness <in g cm^{-2}>	Schichtdicke f, Schichtstärke f; Filmdicke f; Hautdicke f; Dicke f des Belages (Überzuges); Dicke <in g/cm²>	thin-walled orifice plate, sharp-edge orifice meter plate <US>	dünnwandige Blende f
		thin window counter [tube]	Zählrohr n mit dünnem Fenster
		thioplast	s. elastothiomer
thickness of layer	s. a. thickness <geo.>	third boundary condition, boundary condition of the third kind	Randbedingung f dritter Art, dritte Randbedingung
thickness of shock layer, shock front thickness	Stoßfronttiefe f		
thickness of the barrier layer	s. barrier width	third boundary [value] problem, boundary value problem of the third kind	drittes (gemischtes) Randwertproblem n, dritte (gemischte) Randwertaufgabe f, Randwertproblem (Randwertaufgabe) dritter Art
thickness of the cloud, cloud thickness	Wolkenmächtigkeit f, Wolkendicke f		
thickness of the lens on the optic axis	Achsendicke f, Achsenstärke f <Linse>		
thickness ratio, thickness chord ratio, relative thickness of the aerofoil	relative Profildicke f, relative Dicke f [des Profils]	third boundary value problem <of the Laplace equation>	s. Robin['s] problem
		third law of motion	s. Newton third law
thickness vibration	s. flexural vibration	third law [of thermodynamics], Nernst['s] law, Nernst['s] [heat] theorem, heat theorem, principle of the unattainability of the absolute zero	Nernstscher Wärmesatz m, Wärmesatz [von Nernst], dritter Hauptsatz m [der Thermodynamik], Nernstsches Wärmetheorem n, Wärmetheorem von Nernst
thick-target excitation curve	Anregungskurve f für [unendlich] dickes Target		
Thiele transformation	Thielesche Transformation f		
thigmic stimulus, contact stimulus, haptic stimulus	Berührungsreiz m, Kontaktreiz m, Tastreiz m, haptischer (thigmischer) Reiz m		

third-moment method	Methode f der dritten Momente
third-order distortion, distortion of third order	kubische Verzerrung f, Verzerrung dritter Ordnung
third purple light	drittes Purpurlicht n
thirteen-moment approximation, thirteen moments approximation, 13 moments approximation	Dreizehnmomentenmethode f [nach H. Grad]
thixotrometer	Thixotrometer n
thixotropic effect	thixotroper Effekt m
thixotropic fluid	thixotrope Flüssigkeit f
thixotropic state	thixotroper Zustand m
thixotropy	Thixotropie f
Thollon prism	Thollon-Prisma n, Thollonsches Prisma n
Thoma cavitation number	Thomasche Kavitationszahl f, Kavitationszahl nach Thoma
Thomas cyclotron, Thomas-type cyclotron, Thomas-shim cyclotron, radial-sector cyclotron, radial-ridge cyclotron	Isochronzyklotron n nach Thomas, Thomas-Zyklotron n, Radialsektorzyklotron n
Thomas distribution, double Poisson distribution	doppelte Poisson-Verteilung f, Thomas-Verteilung f
Thomas effect	Thomas-Effekt m
Thomas-Fermi approximation	Thomas-Fermi-Näherung f
Thomas-Fermi [differential] equation	s. Fermi-Thomas equation
Thomas-Fermi model <of the atom>	Thomas-Fermi-Modell n <des Atoms>
Thomas-Fermi model <of the nucleus>	s. Fermi-gas model
Thomas-Fermi radius	Thomas-Fermi-Radius m
Thomas['] field, radial-sectored field	Radialsektorfeld n, Thomas-Feld n
Thomas flowmeter, Thomas meter	Thomasscher Strömungsmesser (Mengenmesser) m
Thomas precession, relativity precession	Thomas-Präzession f
Thomas-Reiche-Kuhn f-sum rule	s. Kuhn-Thomas-Reiche [f-] sum rule
Thomas-shim (Thomas type) cyclotron	s. Thomas cyclotron
Thompson['s] bridge	Thompsonsche Brückenschaltung f, Thompson-Brücke f
Thompson prism	Thompsonsches Prisma n, Thompson-Prisma n
Thompson weir	Thompson-Überfall m
Thomson['s] atom model, Thomson['s] model	Atommodell n von Thomson, Thomsonsches Atommodell (Modell n), Thomson-Modell n
Thomson-Bakhmet'ev effect	Thomson-Bachmetjew-Effekt m
Thomson-Berthelot['s] principle	Thomson-Berthelotsches Prinzip n
Thomson['s] body	s. Poynting-Thomson body
Thomson circulation theorem	s. Kelvin circulation theorem
Thomson coefficient	Thomson-Koeffizient m, Thomsonscher Koeffizient m
Thomson cross-section, Thomson scattering cross-section, cross-section for Thomson scattering	Thomson-Streuquerschnitt m, Wirkungsquerschnitt m für (der) Thomson-Streuung
Thomson double bridge	s. Kelvin bridge
Thomson effect, Kelvin effect	Thomson-Effekt m, Kelvin-Effekt m
Thomson['s] experiment	Thomsonscher Versuch m, Thomson-Versuch m, Versuch von Elihu Thomson
Thomson factor, polarization factor	Polarisationsfaktor m, Thomson-Faktor m, Thomsonscher Faktor m
Thomson['s] formula <el.>	Thomsonsche Schwingungsformel (Gleichung, Formel) f, [Thomson-]Kirchhoffsche Formel <El.>
Thomson['s] formula, Thomson['s] scattering formula <nucl.>	Thomsonsche Streuformel f, Thomsonsche Formel f, Thomson-Formel f <Kern.>
Thomson-Freundlich equation	Thomson-Freundlichsche Gleichung f
Thomson['s] function	s. Kelvin['s] function
Thomson-Gibbs equation	Thomson-Gibbssche Gleichung f
Thomson heat	Thomson-Wärme f, Thomsonsche Wärme f
Thomson['s] heat current	Thomsonscher Wärmestrom m
Thomson interaction	Thomson-Wechselwirkung f, Thomsonsche Wechselwirkung f
Thomson isotherm	Thomson-Isotherme f
Thomson line, resistance-capacitance line, R-C line	RC-Leitung f, Thomson-Leitung f
Thomson meter	elektrodynamischer Zähler m, elektrodynamischer Motorzähler m
Thomson['s] model	s. Thomson['s] atom model
Thomson['s] parabola method, parabola method [of J. J. Thomson], method of parabolas	Parabelmethode f [von J. J. Thomson], Thomsonsche Parabelmethode
Thomson-Planck perpetual motion of the second kind	Thomson-Plancksches Perpetuum n mobile zweiter Art
Thomson['s] potential gradient	Thomsonscher Potentialgradient m
Thomson['s] principle	Thomsonsches Prinzip n
Thomson['s] relation <first or second>	Thomsonsche Beziehung f, Thomsonsche Gleichung f <erste bzw. zweite>
Thomson['s] rose	Thomson-Rose f
Thomson['s] rule	Thomsonsche Regel f
Thomson scattering, classical scattering	Thomson-Streuung f, Thomsonsche Streuung f, klassische Streuung
Thomson scattering coefficient	Thomsonscher Streukoeffizient m, Thomson-Streukoeffizient m
Thomson scattering cross-section	s. Thomson cross-section
Thomson['s] scattering formula	s. Thomson['s] formula <nucl.>
Thomson-Thalen magnetometer	Thomson-Thalen-Magnetometer n
Thomson['s] theorem	s. Thomson['s] circulation theorem
Thomson['s] theorem [of electrostatics]	Thomsonscher Satz m [der Elektrostatik]
Thomson['s] transformation, Kelvin['s] transformation	Kelvin-Transformation f, Thomson-Transformation f
Thomson-Wheatstone bridge	Thomson-Wheatstone-Brücke f
Thomson-Whiddington law	Thomson-Whiddingtonsches Gesetz n
Thonemann[-type] ion source, Thonemann-type source	Thonemann-Ionenquelle f, Thonemann-Quelle f
Thoraeus filter	Thoraeus-Filter n, Thoräusfilter n <Sn-Cu-Al-Filter>
thoride, thoroide	Thorid n, Thoroid n
thorium cycle	Thoriumzyklus m, Thorium-Brennstoffzyklus m, Thoriumkreislauf m
thorium D age	s. thorium lead age
thorium D method, thorium lead method <of dating>	Thorium-Blei-Methode f, Thoriumbleimethode f, Thorium-D-Methode f
thorium emanation	s. thoron
thorium family	s. thorium series
thorium lead age, thorium D age	Thorium-Blei-Alter n, Thoriumbleialter n, Thorium-D-Alter n, [232Th-] 208Pb-Alter n
thorium lead method	s. thorium D method
thorium radioactive family	s. thorium series
thorium [radioactive] series, 4n series; thorium family, thorium radioactive family, radioactive family of thorium, 4n family	Thoriumzerfallsreihe f, Thoriumreihe f, 4n-Zerfallsreihe f, Zerfallsreihe f des Thoriums; radioaktive Familie f des Thoriums, Thoriumfamilie f

thoroide	s. thoride	three-dimensional lattice	s. space lattice
thoron, thorium emanation, $^{220}_{86}$Rn, Tn	Thoron n, Thoriumemanation f, Tn, $^{220}_{86}$Rn	three-dimensional momentum	s. three-momentum
Thorpe and Rodger['s] formula, Thorpe-Rodger['s] formula	Thorpe-Rodgersche Formel f, Formel von Thorpe und Rodger	three-dimensional motion	s. space motion
thought experiment	s. imaginary experiment	three-dimensional strain	s. general state of strain
thraustics	Thraustik f, Technologie f der spröden Werkstoffe	three-dimensional stress	s. volume stress
thread; filament	Faden m	three-eights rule, Newton['s] three-eights (3/8 th) rule	Newtons Lieblingsformel f, Drei-Achtel-Regel f
thread	Gewinde n	three-electrode tube	s. triode
thread	s. a. stria ‹in glass›	three-electrode valve	s. triode
threaded core	Schraubkern m	three-electron bond	Dreielektron[en]bindung f
thread-like molecule, linear molecule, linear macromolecule	Fadenmolekül n, lineares Molekül (Makromolekül) n, Linearmolekül n	three-fold axis [of symmetry]	s. triad axis
thread pendulum	Fadenpendel n	three-force, 3-force	Dreierkraft f
thread probe	Fadensonde f	three-gang capacitor	s. triple-gang capacitor
thread-probe technique	s. wooltuft technique	three-grid ion tube, ion pentode, gas-filled pentode	Gaspentode f
thread-shaped, filiform, filamentous, filamentary	fadenförmig		
thread suspension	Fadenaufhängung f	three-grid valve, pentode, pentode tube, pentode valve, five-electrode tube	Pentode f, Fünfpolröhre f, Fünfelektrodenröhre f, Dreigitterröhre f
thread tension; string tension ‹mech.›	Fadenspannung f; Saitenspannung f ‹Mech.›		
		three-group theory	Dreigruppentheorie f
thread-type field (magnetic) balance	s. band-type magnetic balance	three-gun deflection system	Dreistrahlablenksystem n
three-ammeter method	Dreiamperemetermethode f	three-halves power law	s. Langmuir['s] law
		three-hinged arch, three-pinned arch	Dreigelenkbogen m
three-beam problem	Dreistrahlproblem n	three-index symbol	s. Christoffel symbol
three-body collision	s. triple collision	three-index symbol of the first ‹or second› kind	s. Christoffel symbol of the first ‹or second› kind
three-body decay	Zerfall m in drei Teilchen, Dreiteilchenzerfall m, Dreikörperzerfall m	three-junction diode	s. four-layer diode
		three-junction triode	s. four-layer transistor
three-body problem, problem of three bodies	Dreikörperproblem n	three-leafed rose	reguläres Dreiblatt n, Dreiblatt, Kleeblatt n
three-body recombination	Dreikörperrekombination f, Dreierrekombination f	three-level maser	Dreiniveaumaser m
three-carrier model	Dreiladungsträgermodell n		
three-cavity klystron, triple-cavity klystron	Dreikreisklystron n, Dreikammerklystron n	three-level solid-state maser	Dreiniveau-Festkörpermaser m
three-circles theorem, Hadamard['s] three-circles theorem	[Hadamardscher] Dreikreissatz m, Hadamard-Faber-Blumenthalscher Dreikreissatz	three-liquid theory	Dreiflüssigkeitstheorie f
		three-membered ring	Dreierring m, Dreiring m
		three-mirror system, three-mirror telescope	Dreispiegler m, Spiegeltriplet n, Triplet n, Dreispiegelsystem n
three-colour colorimetry, three-colour method colorimetry	Dreifarbenkolorimetrie f		
		three-mirror telescope, three-mirror system	Dreispiegler m, Spiegeltriplet n, Triplet n, Dreispiegelsystem n
three-colour method	Dreifarbenverfahren n		
three-colour method colorimetry	s. three-colour colorimetry	three-moment (three moments) equation, three-moment theorem	s. equation of three moments
three-colour photometry	Dreifarbenphotometrie f		
three-colour projection [method]	Dreifarbenprojektion f	three-momentum, 3-momentum, three-dimensional momentum	Dreierimpuls m, dreidimensionaler Impuls m
three-colour tube	s. tricolour tube		
three-component balance, balance for three-component force measurements	mechanische Dreikomponentenwaage f	three-nucleon system	Dreinukleonensystem n
		three-particle collision	s. triple collision
		three-particle Coulomb problem	Coulombsches Dreikörperproblem n
three-component diagram	s. ternary diagram	three-particle interaction	Dreiteilchenwechselwirkung f
three-component field-intensity (field-strength) meter	Dreikomponenten-Feldstärkemesser m	three-particle state	Dreiteilchenzustand m
		three-phase bridge-type rectifying circuit	Dreiphasen-Graetz-Gleichrichter m, Dreiphasen-Graetz-Schaltung f
three-component marine magnetometer	Dreikomponenten-Schiffsmagnetometer n		
three-current density	s. three-dimensional current density vector	three-phase current, rotary current	Drehstrom m, Dreiphasenstrom m
three-decision test	Dreientscheidungstest m	three-phase equilibrium	Dreiphasengleichgewicht n
		three-phase rectifier, three-phase rectifying circuit	Dreiphasengleichrichter m, Dreiphasengleichrichterschaltung f
three-digit group, trigram	Trigramm n		
three-dimensional, tridimensional; cubic[al]; volume, volumic; spatial, space; extended [in space]	dreidimensional; räumlich [ausgedehnt]; kubisch; Raum-, Volum[en]-	three-phase X-ray generator	Sechsspulengenerator m, Sechsventil-Hochspannungsgenerator m, Dreiphasengenerator m, Drehstromapparat m
three-dimensional current density vector, three-current density	Dreierstromdichte f, dreidimensionale Stromdichte f, dreidimensionaler Stromdichtevektor m	three-phonon process	Dreiphononenprozeß m
		three-photon annihilation	s. three-quantum annihilation
three-dimensional elasticity	dreidimensionale Elastizität f	three-pinned arch	s. three-hinged arch
		three-point assay	Dreipunkt[e]prüfung f
three-dimensional flow, flow in three dimensions	dreidimensionale Strömung f, räumliche Strömung	three-point circuit	Dreipunktschaltung f
		three-point Colpitts circuit	s. Colpitts oscillator
		three-point Hartley circuit	s. Hartley oscillator

three-position controller	Dreipunktregler *m*	threshold field, critical field <superconductivity>	kritisches Magnetfeld *n*, kritisches Feld *n*, kritische Feldstärke *f* <Supraleitfähigkeit>
three-pronged star, trident <nucl.>	Dreierstern *m*, dreiarmiger Stern *m*, Dreizackereignis *n*, Dreizackspur *f* <Kern.>	threshold field curve, critical field curve	magnetische Schwell[en]-wertkurve, Schwell[en]-wertkurve *f*, kritische Feldkurve *f*
three-quantum annihilation, three-photon annihilation	Dreiquantenvernichtung *f*	threshold frequency <for photoelectric effect>	Grenzfrequenz *f* des Photoeffekts (lichtelektrischen Effekts)
three-quarter-wave resonant circuit	Dreiviertelwellen[längen]-Resonanzkreis *m*	threshold frequency	*s. a.* limiting frequency
three-ray interference	Dreistrahlinterferenz *f*	threshold indicator	Schwell[en]wertindikator *m*, Indikator *m* mit Ansprechschwelle, Schwellenindikator *m*
three-sigma rule	Dreisigmaregel *f*, Drei-Sigma-Regel *f*, 3σ-Regel *f*	threshold law <of single ionization>	Schwellengesetz *n* <für Einfachionisation>
three-slit interference	Dreispaltinterferenz *f*	threshold light	Schwellenfeuer *n*
three-slot magnetron	Dreischlitzmagnetron *n*, Dreischlitzmagnetfeldröhre *f*	threshold line [of glare]	Blend[ungs]gerade *f*, Blendungsgrenze *f*, Schwellengerade *f* [der Blendung]
three-stage rocket, three-step rocket	Dreistufenrakete *f*	threshold of audibility	*s.* threshold of hearing
three-stage tandem [accelerator]	Dreistufen-Tandemgenerator *m*	threshold of cirque	Karschwelle *f*
three-step rocket, three-stage rocket	Dreistufenrakete *f*	threshold of colour, colour threshold	Farbschwelle *f*
three-term control	*s.* derivative proportional integral control	threshold of detectability	*s.* threshold of hearing
three-term controller	*s.* derivative proportional integral controller	threshold of detectability (detection), detection threshold	untere Nachweisgrenze *f*
three-terminal circuit	*s.* three-terminal network	threshold of discomfort	*s.* upper threshold of hearing
three-terminal contact; twin contacts	Doppelkontakt *m*	threshold of efficiency, efficiency threshold	Wirksamkeitsschwelle *f*, Effektivitätsschwelle *f*
three-terminal network, tri-pole; three-terminal circuit	Dreipol *m*; Dreiklemmenschaltung *f*	threshold of feeling	*s.* upper threshold of hearing
three-track reaction	Dreispurenreaktion *f*	threshold of hearing, lower (minimum) threshold of hearing, threshold of audibility (detectability)	Hörschwelle *f*, untere Hörschwelle, Reizschwelle *f* (Intensitätsschwelle) *f* des Ohres, Nullschwelle *f*
three-valued logic[al calculus], trivalent logic[al calculus]	dreiwertige Logik *f*	threshold of hue [discrimination]	Farbton-Unterschiedsschwelle *f*
three-vector, 3-vector, trivector	Dreiervektor *m*, Trivektor *m*	threshold of irritation	*s.* excitation threshold
three-voltmeter method	Dreivoltmetermethode *f*, Dreispannungsverfahren *n*	threshold of pain	*s.* upper threshold of hearing
three-way cock, three-way stop-cock, three-way tap, three-way valve	Dreiwegehahn *m*, Dreiweghahn *m*, Dreiwegventil *n*	threshold of response	*s.* threshold of sensitivity
three-way pipe, T-pipe, T; tee, conduit tee	T-Stück *n*; T-Rohr *n*, T-Rohrstück *n*	threshold of sensation <bio.>	Empfindungsschwelle *f*, Empfindungsgrenze *f*, Schwellenwert *m*, Schwelle[nhöhe] *f*, Empfindlichkeitsschwelle *f* <Bio.>
three-way stop-cock	*s.* three-way cock		
three-way switch	Dreiweg[e]schalter *m*, Dreiwegumschalter *m*	threshold of sensitivity, sensitivity threshold (limit), threshold sensitivity, limit of sensitivity, limiting (ultimate) sensitivity; threshold [of] response, response threshold (limit), limit of response; detection limit, limit of detectability; limit of sensibility	Empfindlichkeitsschwelle *f*, Empfindlichkeitsgrenze *f*, Schwellenempfindlichkeit *f*; Grenzempfindlichkeit *f* <z. B. Empfänger>; Ansprechgrenze *f*, Ansprechschwelle *f*; Nachweisgrenze *f*
three-way tap (valve)	*s.* three-way cock		
three-wire system	Dreileitersystem *n*		
threo-polymer	threo-Polymer *n*		
threshold, threshold value; liminal value <bio.>	Schwelle *f*, Schwellenwert *m*, Schwellwert *m*, Grenze *f*		
threshold	*s. a.* energy threshold		
threshold audiogram	*s.* audiogram	threshold of stimulation (stimulus)	*s.* excitation threshold
threshold condition	Schwellenbedingung *f*	threshold of the reaction, reaction threshold	Reaktionsschwelle *f*, Schwellenenergie *f* der Reaktion
threshold control, delayed control, retarded control	Schwellenwertregelung *f*, Schwellwertregelung *f*, verzögerte Regelung *f*	threshold of tickle	*s.* upper threshold of hearing
threshold current	Schwellenstrom *m*, Schwellwertstrom *m*, Schwellenwertstrom *m*, Schwellstrom *m*	threshold of visibility, threshold of vision	Sichtbarkeitsschwelle *f*
threshold detector	Schwellwertdetektor *m*, Schwellendetektor *m*	threshold potential	*s.* threshold voltage
threshold dose	Schwellendosis *f*, Schwell[en]wertdosis *f*	threshold potential	*s. a.* appearance potential
threshold effect	Schwelleneffekt *m*, Schwellenwirkung *f*	threshold probe	Schwellensonde *f*
threshold energy	*s.* energy threshold	threshold reaction	Schwellenreaktion *f*
threshold energy of normal photoelectric effect	*s.* photoelectric threshold	threshold reaction temperature, temperature at which reaction commences	Temperaturschwelle *f* der Reaktion, Anfangstemperatur *f* der Reaktion
threshold erythema dose, erythema dose	Erythemdosis *f*	threshold response	*s.* threshold of sensitivity
threshold excitation, threshold stimulation	schwellige Reizung *f*, Schwellenreiz *m*	threshold sensitivity	*s.* threshold of sensitivity
		threshold stimulation, threshold excitation	schwellige Reizung *f*, Schwellenreiz *m*
		threshold stimulus	*s.* excitation threshold
		threshold temperature	Schwellentemperatur *f*
		threshold value	*s.* threshold
threshold field	Schwellenfeld *n*	threshold velocity	Schwellengeschwindigkeit *f*

threshold voltage, threshold potential	Schwellenspannung f, Schwellwertspannung f, Schwellenwertspannung f, Spannungsschwelle f, Schwellenpotential n	thrust of arch, horizontal thrust of arch	Horizontalschub (Seitenschub) m des Bogens
		thrust performance	s. thrust horsepower
		thrust plane	s. overthrust surface
		thrust power	s. thrust horsepower
threshold wavelength [for photoelectric effect]	Grenzwellenlänge f [des Photoeffekts], Grenzwellenlänge des lichtelektrischen Effekts, langwellige (rote) Grenze f [des Photoeffekts]	thrust power	s. a. thrust
		thrust strength	Schubstärke f
		thrust surface	s. overthrust surface
		thrust-to-mass ratio, thrust-to-weight ratio, thrust loading	Schub-Masse-Verhältnis n
threshold wave number	Grenzwellenzahl f	thrust vector	Schubvektor m
throat	Vereng[er]ungsstelle f, Vereng[er]ung f, Einschnürungsstelle f, Hals m	thumb rule	s. corkscrew rule
		thumb-screw, screw press, pressing screw	Druckschraube f
throat, restrictor <of flow>	Einschnürung f, Drosselstelle f <Durchfluß>	thundercloud, cumulonimbus, storm cloud, Cb	Cumulonimbus m, Kumulonimbus m, Gewitterwolke f, getürmte Haufenwolke f, Böenwolke f, Gewitterturm m, Cb
throat, experimental section <e.g. of the wind tunnel>	Versuchsstrecke f; Versuchsstelle f; Versuchsplatz m <z. B. Windkanal>		
		thunder effect	Donnereffekt m
throat microphone, laryngophone	Kehlkopfmikrophon n	thunderhead	s. thunderstorm line
		thundersquall	Gewitterbö f
throat of the nozzle, nozzle throat	Düsenhals m, Hals m (Verengung f) der Düse, kritischer Düsenquerschnitt m	thunderstorm activity	Gewitteraktivität f, Gewittertätigkeit f
		thunderstorm cell	Gewitterzelle f
throat of the Venturi tube	Verengung f des Venturi-Rohres	thunderstorm electricity	Gewitterelektrizität f
		thunderstorm frequency, frequency of thunderstorms	Gewitterhäufigkeit f
throttle, throttle-valve	Drosselventil n, Expansionsventil n, Drosselklappe f		
		thunderstorm line, thundery front, thunderhead	Gewitterfront f, Gewitterlinie f
throttling, Joule-Thomson expansion	Drossel[entspann]ung f, Joule-Thomsonsche Ausdehnung (Expansion) f, Joule-Thomson-Expansion f		
		Thwaites['] method	Thwaitessche Methode f
		thyratron, thyratron valve, gas triode	Thyratron n, Thyratronröhre f, Stromtor n, Stromtorröhre f, Stromrichter m, Kippschwingröhre f, Kippschwingungsröhre f, Kippröhre f, Gastriode f, steuerbarer Gleichrichter m, Eingitterthyratron n
throttling calorimeter	Drosselkalorimeter n		
throttling coefficient	Drosselungskoeffizient m		
throttling experiment [of Joule and Kelvin]	s. Joule-Kelvin throttling experiment		
through corrosion, penetration corrosion, perforation	Durchlöcherung f, Penetrationskorrosion f, Perforation f		
		thyratron pre-striking current	Vorzündstrom (Vorentladungsstrom) m des Thyratrons
through-hardening	Durchhärtung f		
through-illumination	Beleuchtung f mit der Lichtquelle auf der Seite gegenüber der Kamera, Durchlichtbeleuchtung f	thyratron transistor	s. thyristor
		thyratron valve	s. thyratron
		thyristor, thyratron transistor	Thyristor m, steuerbarer Kristallgleichrichter m, steuerbares (gesteuertes) Halbleiterventil n, steuerbare Einkristallgleichrichterzelle f, Halbleiterthyratron n, Halbleiterstromtor n, Thyratrontransistor n, Vierschicht[en]triode f, Kipptriode f
throughput	s. rate of flow		
throw, projection, cast <mech.>	Wurf m; Werfen n <Mech.>		
throw	s. a. fault height <geo.>		
throw	s. a. deflection <of a pointer, a needle>		
throwing-away, rejection <chem.>	Verwerfen n <Chem.>		
throwing index <el.chem.>	Streuindex m <El. Chem.>		
throwing power <el.chem.>	Streuvermögen n, Streukraft f, Streufähigkeit f <El. Chem.>	thyristron	Thyristron n
		thyrite	Thyrit m, Thyritwiderstand m
throwing range, range of the projection, range of throw (hurling), cast	Wurfweite f	thyrode	Thyrode f
		tick	s. ticking
		ticker	Ticker m, Schnellunterbrecher m
throw-over relay, trigger-action relay	Kipprelais n, Umschlagrelais n	ticking, tick	Ticken n
		ticking frequency	Tickfrequenz f
thrust, thrust power, propelling power, propelling force, repulsive thrust, forward thrust; push	Schub m, Schubkraft f, Vortriebskraft f, Vortrieb m	tidal bore, eagre, tidal eagre	Springwelle f, Springflutwelle f
		tidal bulge	Gezeitenberg m, Flutberg m
		tidal component, constituent of tide	Gezeitenkomponente f, Gezeitenglied n, Tidenkomponente f
thrust	s. a. epiparaclase <geo.>		
thrust	s. a. dynamic lift <aero., hydr.>		
		tidal constant	Tidenkonstante f, Gezeitenkonstante f
thrust centre, centre of thrust	Schubmittelpunkt m, Schubzentrum n, Vortriebsmittelpunkt m, Vortriebszentrum n	tidal current, tide current; tide flux	Gezeitenstrom m, Tidestrom m; Gezeitenströmung f, Tideströmung f
thrust coefficient; traction coefficient	Belastungsgrad m, Schubkoeffizient m, Schubverhältnis n, Schubbeiwert m; Traktionskoeffizient m	tidal curve	Tidekurve f, Tidenkurve f
		tidal day	Tidentag m
		tidal deformation	Gezeitendeformation f
thrust fault	s. overfault	tidal eagre	s. tidal bore
thrust horsepower, thrust performance, thrust power	Schubleistung f, Vortriebsleistung f	tidal flat	s. shallow water
		tidal forces	s. tide-generating forces
thrust line, line of thrust, pressure line	Drucklinie f	tidal friction	Gezeitenreibung f
thrust loading	s. thrust-to-mass ratio		

tidal-generating forces — s. tide-generating forces
tidal impulse — s. tidal motion
tidal instability — Gezeiteninstabilität *f*

tidal limit, limit of tides — Tidegrenze *f*

tidal motion, tidal impulse — Gezeitenbewegung *f*, Tide[n]bewegung *f*

tidal potential — s. tide-generating potential
tidal power, tide energy — Gezeitenenergie *f*, Tidenenergie *f*

tidal range, range of tide; amplitude of tide — Gezeitenhub *m*, Tidenhub *m*, Tidenstieg *m*

tidal river — Tidefluß *m*, Gezeitenfluß *m*; Tidegebiet *n* [des Flusses]

tidal shallow — s. shallow water
tidal station, tide station — Gezeitenobservatorium *n*, Gezeitenbeobachtungsstation *f*

tidal wave — Gezeitenwelle *f*, Tide[n]welle *f*; Gezeitenwoge *f*, Tidewoge *f*; Flutwelle *f*

tidal wind — Gezeitenwind *m*
tide — Tide *f*
tide current — s. tidal current
tide current meter — Gezeitenstrommesser *m*

tide curve — s. tide diagram
tide diagram; tide curve — Gezeitendiagramm *n*, Gezeitenkurve *f*

tide energy — s. tidal power
tide equation, equation of tides — Gezeitengleichung *f*

tide flux — s. tidal current
tide gauge; water gauge; sea gauge ‹hydr.› — Pegel *m*; Gezeitenpegel *m* ‹Hydr.›

tide gauge — Gezeitenhubmesser *m*

tide-generating forces, tidal-generating forces, tide-producing forces, tide-raising forces, tidal forces — Gezeitenkräfte *fpl*, gezeitenerzeugende (tideerzeugende, fluterzeugende) Kräfte *fpl*, Flutkräfte *fpl*

tide-generating potential, tidal potential — Gezeitenpotential *n*, gezeitenerzeugendes (fluterzeugendes) Potential *n*, Flutpotential *n*

tide-producing forces — s. tide-generating forces
tide propagation, propagation of the tide — Gezeitendehnung *f*
tide-raising forces — s. tide-generating forces
tides, inflow and outflow, ebb and flood, ebb and flow, ebb-and-float — Gezeiten *pl*, Tiden *fpl*, Ebbe *f* und Flut *f*

tides in the atmosphere, atmospheric tides, barometric tides — Atmosphärengezeiten *pl*, Gezeiten *pl* der Atmosphäre
tide station — s. tidal station
tide table — Gezeitentafel *f*
tie ‹stat.› — Bindung *f*, Ranggleichheit *f* ‹Stat.›

Tiede['s] rule — Tiedesche Regel *f*
tied gyroscope — Kreisel *m* mit äußeren Drehmomenten
tie line — Verbindungslinie *f*, Verbindungsachse *f*

tie line, conode — Konode *f*, Konnode *f*
tie of the traverse ‹onto another› — Anschluß *m* des Polygonzuges ‹an einen anderen›

tie rod, tension member, tie, tension tie, bar in tension — Zugstange *f*

tight, proof; leakproof, leak-tight; impermeable; impenetrable; impervious [to] — dicht, undurchlässig; undurchdringlich [für], undurchdringbar [für]; leckdicht, lecksicher; impermeabel

tight, taut, stretched — straff [gespannt], gespannt
tight binding — s. strong coupling ‹nucl.›
tight binding approximation — s. strong coupling approximation
tight bond — s. strong coupling ‹nucl.›
tight contact — guter Kontakt *m*
tight coupling, close coupling, overcritical coupling, overcoupling ‹el.› — feste Kopplung *f*, überkritische Kopplung, Überkopplung *f* ‹El.›
tightness; impermeability; impenetrability; imperviousness — Dichtigkeit *f*; Undurchlässigkeit *f*; Undurchdringlichkeit *f*, Undurchdringbarkeit *f*; Impermeabilität *f*

tightness, vacuum tightness ‹vac.› — Dichtigkeit *f*, Dichtheit *f*, Lecksicherheit *f*, Hermetizität *f* ‹Vak.›

tilt; slope; inclination, incline — Neigung *f*; Gefälle *n*; Steigung *f*

tilt, obliquity — Schiefe *f*, Schräge *f*
tilt; oblique position; obliquity — Schräglage *f*, schräge Lage *f*; Schiefstellung *f*; Schrägstellung *f*; Verkippung *f*; Neigung *f*

tilt, pulse tilt, sloping top ‹of pulse› — Dachschräge *f*, Dachabfall *m*, Impulsdachschräge *f*, Schräganstieg *m*

tilt ‹of balance› — ausschlagen ‹Waage›

tilt angle, angle of tilt; inclination, angle of inclination, slope angle, angle of slope — Neigungswinkel *m*, Neigung *f*; Fallwinkel *m*; Hangneigung *f*, Böschungswinkel *m*, Gefälle *n* ‹Geo.›
tilt angle, tilting angle, angle of inclination ‹mech.› — Kippwinkel *m*, Kippungswinkel *m* ‹Mech.›

tilt boundary ‹of dislocation› — Neigungskorngrenze *f*, „tilt boundary" *f*, Kipp[korn]grenze *f* ‹Versetzung›

tilted source, sloped source — schräg angeordnete Quelle *f*, gekippte Quelle
tilting — Verkantung *f*, Kanten *n*
tilting, tipping — Kippen *n*; Umkippen *n*; Umklappen *n*
tilting — s. a. inclination ‹to›
tilting angle — s. tilt angle
tilting axis, axis of tilt — Verkantungsachse *f*
tilting coil — Kippspule *f*, Klappspule *f*

tilting level — Nivellier[instrument] *n* mit Kippschraube [und Libelle]

tilting manometer, inclined tube manometer — Schrägrohrmanometer *n*, Flüssigkeitsmanometer *n* mit geneigtem Schenkel

tilting mechanism — Kippvorrichtung *f*
tilting-mirror [Martens] gauge — s. Martens strain gauge
tilting moment — s. maximum torque
tilting moment coefficient — s. pitching moment coefficient
tilting motion — Kippbewegung *f*

tilting over, canting, overturn, upturning ‹geo.› — Überkippung *f*, Kippung *f* ‹Geo.›
tilting plate micrometer — Schwenkplattenmikrometer *n*

tilting-ring manometer, ring balance, ring balance manometer — Ringwaage *f*, Ringwaage[n]manometer *n*, Kreisrohrmanometer *n*, Kreismikromanometer *n*

tilt meter — s. clinometer
timber — s. rib
timbre of sound, quality of sound, tone colour, tone quality; tone ‹el.› — Klangfarbe *f*, Tonfarbe *f*, Farbe *f* des Klangs

time	Zeit *f*
time, hour	Uhrzeit *f*, Uhr *f*, ʰ
time, instant [of time], moment, epoch	Zeitpunkt *m*, Zeit *f*, Moment *m*, Augenblick *m*
time, measure <ac.>	Takt *m*, Zeitmaß *n* <Ak.>
time action [of relay]	Relaisanzugszeit *f*, Anzugszeit *f* des Relais
time-amplitude converter	s. time-to-amplitude converter
time analyzer	Zeitanalysator *m*
time-antisymmetric, antisymmetric in time	zeitantisymmetrisch
time-antisymmetric tensor, tensor antisymmetric in time	zeitantisymmetrischer Tensor *m*, c-Tensor *m*
time average	Zeitmittel *n*, Zeitmittelwert *m*, zeitlicher Mittelwert *m*, zeitliches Mittel *n*
time-axis plate	Zeitplatte *f*; Horizontalplatte *f* der Zeitachse, Kippplatte *f* der Zeitachse
time balance	Zeitwaage *f*
time base	Zeitachse *f*, Zeitlinie *f*, Zeitnullinie *f*, Zeitbasis *f*, Zeitmaßstab *m*, Zeitablenkung *f*
time base, time-base sweep, time sweep, sweep	Zeitablenkung *f*
time base	s. time-base unit
time-base capacitor	Zeitkreiskondensator *m*, Kippkapazität *f*
time-base circuit	s. sweep circuit
time-base expansion	s. sweep expansion
time-base extension	s. sweep expansion
time-base frequency	s. sweep frequency
time base generator, sweep generator	Zeitablenkgenerator *m*, Zeitbasisgenerator *m*
time-base sweep	s. time base
time-base unit, time base, sweep unit, sweep base, scan base	Zeitablenkgerät *n*, Zeitbasisgerät *n*
time-base velocity	s. deflection speed
time-base voltage	s. sweep voltage
time behaviour	zeitliches Verhalten *n*, Zeitverhalten *n*
time behaviour, time history, time slope, time lapse, lapse	Zeitablauf *m*, zeitlicher Ablauf *m*, zeitlicher Verlauf *m*, Zeitverlauf *m*
time belt	s. time zone
time coherence, temporal coherence, coherence in time	Zeitkohärenz *f*, zeitliche Kohärenz *f*
time component [of four-vector]	zeitliche Komponente *f*, Zeitkomponente *f* <Vierervektor>
time compression [technique]	s. low-speed photography
time compressor [camera]	s. time-lapse camera
time constant; time response; characteristic time <el.>	Zeitkonstante *f*; RC-Konstante *f*, elektrische Zeitkonstante, RC <El.>
time constant	s. a. sluggishness
time constant [of nuclear reactor]	s. time constant
time constant of rise	Anstiegszeitkonstante *f*
time constant range	s. period range <of reactor>
time constant standard, standard time constant	Zeitkonstantennormal *n*
time-consuming, tedious	zeitraubend, zeitaufwendig, langwierig
time contraction	Zeitkontraktion *f*, Zeitverkürzung *f*
time control	s. time schedule control
time conversion	Zeitkonvertierung *f*, Zeitkonversion *f*
time converter	Zeitkonverter *m*
time co-ordinate	Zeitkoordinate *f*
time correlation	zeitliche Korrelation *f*, Zeitkorrelation *f*
time decrease of permeability, disaccommodation of permeability, magnetic disaccommodation	Nachwirkung *f* der Permeabilität, zeitlicher Permeabilitätsabfall *m*, Desakkommodation *f* der Permeabilität, magnetische Desakkommodation
time delay	s. a. time lag
time delay, time lag, switching delay	Schaltverzug *m*, Schaltverzögerung *f*
time delay circuit, timing circuit	Verzögerungsschaltung *f*, Zeitverzögerungsschaltung *f*
time-delay relay, time-lag relay, delay relay, time-limit relay, time relay, slow-release (slow-releasing) relay, timing circuit	Zeitrelais *n*, Verzögerungsrelais *n*, Relais *n* mit Zeitauslösung (verzögerter Auslösung)
time-delay switch, time[-lag] switch, timing interrupter (relay)	Zeitschalter *m*, Zeitkontakteinrichtung *f*, Zeitrelais *n*
time-delay-type overcurrent relay	Überstromzeitrelais *n*
time-dependent, dependent on time, varying with time, as a function of time, non-stationary; rheonomic, rheonomous <mech.>	zeitabhängig *f*, nichtstationär; rheonom <Mech.>
time-dependent perturbation theory, time-dependent theory of perturbations, Dirac['s] theory of perturbations	zeitabhängige Störungstheorie *f*, Diracsche Störungstheorie
time derivative, derivative with respect to time	Zeitableitung *f*, zeitliche Ableitung *f*, Ableitung nach der Zeit
time determination; chronology	Zeitbestimmung *f*, Chronologie *f*
time dilatation, Einstein['s] time dilation, time dilation <rel.>	Zeitdilatation *f*, Zeitdehnung *f*, Einstein-Dilatation *f*, Einsteinsche Zeitdilatation, Einsteinsche Zeitdehnung <Rel.>
time dilation	s. time dilatation
time discriminator	Zeitdiskriminator *m*
time displacement	s. time shift
time displacement error, time shift error	Zeitversetzungsfehler *m*, Zeitverschiebungsfehler *m*
time distribution	zeitliche Verteilung *f*, Zeitverteilung *f*
time distribution, time transmission	Zeitübermittlung *f*, Zeitübertragung *f*
time distribution system	s. electrical time distribution system
time division multiplex, time multiplex	Zeitmultiplex[system] *n*, Zeitteilungsmultiplex *n*; Vierkanal-Zeit-Multiplex[system] *n*, MUX-System *n*
time-edge effect	Randveränderung[seffekt *m*] *f*
timed neutron	nach der Flugzeit ausgewähltes Neutron *n*
time factor <bio.>	Zeitfaktor *m* <Bio.>
time fluctuation; time jitter	zeitliche Schwankung *f*
time-gamma curve	Zeit-Gamma-Kurve *f*, Zeitgammakurve *f*
time gate	Zeittor *n*
time history	s. time behaviour

time-independent, independent of time; scleronomous, scleronomic[al] <mech.>	zeitunabhängig, zeitfrei; skleronom <Mech.>	**time[-]like**	zeitartig
		time-like four-vector	s. time-like vector
		time-like interval	zeitartiges Intervall n
time-independent perturbation theory, time-independent theory of perturbations, Schrödinger['s] theory of perturbations, Rayleigh-Schrödinger perturbation theory	zeitunabhängige Störungstheorie f, Schrödingersche Störungstheorie	**time-like vector, time-like four-vector**	zeitartiger Vektor m, zeitartiger Vierervektor m
		time-limit relay	s. time-delay relay
		time line	s. isochrone
		time magnification	s. sweep expansion
		time magnifier	s. slow-motion camera
		time magnifying	s. high-speed photography
time-independent wave equation, oscillation equation, equation of oscillation	Schwingungsgleichung f, zeitfreie Wellengleichung f, zeitunabhängige Schrödinger-Gleichung f	**time magnifying**	s. a. sweep expansion
		time mark, time trace	Zeitmarke f, Zeitmeßmarke f
time integral	Zeitintegral n, Integral n über die Zeit	**time marker**	s. time mark generator
		time marker pulse	Zeitmarkenimpuls m
time integral of flux	s. integrated flux <in n/cm²>	**time mark frequency**	Zeitmarkenfrequenz f
time integral of force, impulse [of force] <mech.>	Impuls m, Kraftstoß m, Kraftimpuls m, Zeitintegral n der Kraft <Mech.>	**time mark generator,** time marker, time signal injector	Zeitmarkengenerator m, Zeitmarkengeber m
		time marking, time record	Zeitmarkierung f, Zeitmarkengebung f
time interval meter [unit], intervalometer	Zeitintervallmesser m, Zeitintervallmeßgerät n, Intervallmesser m	**time mark recorder**	Zeitmarkenschreiber m
time-invariant	zeitinvariant		
time inversion	s. time reversal	**time measure,** time scale	Zeitmaß n
time inversion operation	s. time reversal operation	**time measurement,** measurement of time, timing, chronometry; time[-]keeping	Zeitmessung f, Chronometrie f; Zeitnahme f; Aufnahme f von Zeitmarken
time jitter	s. time fluctuation		
time keeper; time piece, chronometer; clock; watch	Zeitmesser m, Zeitmeßgerät n; Uhr f, Chronometer n; Zeitnehmer m		
		time measuring equipment (instrument)	s. timing system
time keeper, metronome	Metronom n	**time meter**	Zeitzähler m
time[-]keeping; measurement of time, time measurement, timing, chronometry	Zeitmessung f, Chronometrie f; Zeitnahme f; Aufnahme f von Zeitmarken	**time metering,** time reference	Zeitzählung f
		time modulation	s. pulse-duration modulation
time lag, lagging, lag, delay, time delay, retardation, hangover	zeitliche Verzögerung f, Zeitverzögerung f, Verzögerung f, Verzug m, Zeitverzug m, Nachhinken n, zeitliches Nacheilen n, Nacheilen, Nacheilung f, Nachbleiben n, Zurückbleiben n	**time multiplex**	s. time division multiplex
		time of climb, duration of ascent	Steigzeit f, Steigdauer f
		time of collision, collision time, time of impact, collision period	Stoßzeit f, Stoßdauer f
		time of conservation	Erhaltungszeit f
time lag	s. a. time delay	**time of dead tide,** time of neap tide	Nippzeit f
time lag in discharge	Entladeverzug m, Entladungsverzug m		
time lag of the ignition, ignition delay, ignition lag, firing delay, firing lag <of discharge>	Zündverzögerung f, Zündverzug m <Entladung>; Zündmomentverspätung f <Gleichrichter>	**time of decay**	s. decay time
		time of deplasmolysis	Deplasmolysezeit f
		time of detachment <bio.>	Abhebungszeit f <Bio.>
		time of energy exchange, energy exchange time	Energieaustauschzeit f
time lag of the ignition	s. a. ignition lag	**time of fall,** time the body is falling	Fallzeit f
time-lag relay	s. time-delay relay		
time-lag switch	s. time-delay switch	**time of first passage**	Zeit f des ersten Durchgangs
time lapse	s. time behaviour		
time-lapse camera, time-lapse motion camera, time-lapse equipment, stop-motion device, quick-motion camera, time compressor [camera]	Zeitraffer m, Zeitrafferkamera f	**time of flight,** flight time, transit time <nucl.>	Flugzeit f, Laufzeit f <Kern.>
		time-of-flight analysis	Laufzeitanalyse f
		time-of-flight analyzer	Laufzeitanalysator m
time-lapse camera shooting, time-lapse shooting, stop-motion camera shooting, stop-motion record, single-picture taking, shooting for fast motion effect, low-speed shooting for high-speed projection	Zeitrafferaufnahme f, Zeitraffaufnahme f	**time-of-flight arrangement (array, device, equipment)**	Laufzeitanordnung f, Flugzeitanordnung f, Laufzeitgerät n
		time-of-flight mass separator	s. time-of-flight separator
		time-of-flight mass spectrograph	Laufzeitmassenspektrograph m
time-lapse cinematography	s. low-speed photography		
time-lapse equipment (motion camera)	s. time-lapse camera	**time-of-flight neutron spectrometer**	Neutronenflugzeitspektrometer n
time lapse photography	s. low-speed photography	**time-of-flight radio-frequency spectrometer**	s. radio-frequency time-of-flight spectrometer
time-lapse shooting	s. time-lapse camera shooting		
time law	Zeitgesetz n	**time-of-flight separator [of isotopes],** time-of-flight mass separator	Laufzeitmassentrenner m, Flugzeitmassentrenner, Laufzeitisotopentrenner m, Flugzeitisotopentrenner m, elektromagnetischer Massentrenner m nach dem Laufzeitprinzip
time-light output curve	Zeit-Lichtleistungs-Kurve f, Zeitlichtleistungskurve f		

time-of-flight spectrograph, velocity spectrograph	Laufzeitspektrograph *m*, Geschwindigkeitsspektrograph *m*	**time quadrature,** quadrature in time	zeitliche Verschiebung *f* um 90°, zeitliche 90°-Verschiebung *f*
time-of-flight spectrography, velocity spectrography	Laufzeitspektrographie *f*, Geschwindigkeitsspektrographie *f*	**time quantization**	Zeitquantelung *f*, Zeitquantisierung *f*
		timer, time schedule controller, cyclelog	Zeitplanregler *m*, Programmregler *m*
		timer, timing element ‹el.›	Zeitglied *n*, Zeitelement *n* ‹El.›
time-of-flight spectrometer, velocity spectrometer, transit-time spectrometer	Laufzeitspektrometer *n*, Geschwindigkeitsspektrometer *n*, Flugzeitspektrometer *n*	**timer**	s. a. stop[-]watch
		timer	s. a. clock relay
		timer	s. a. electronic timer
time-of-flight spectrometry	s. time-of-flight spectroscopy	**time rate,** rate	Geschwindigkeit *f*, Häufigkeit *f*, Rate *f*
time-of-flight spectroscope, velocity spectroscope	Laufzeitspektroskop *n*, Geschwindigkeitsspektroskop *n*	**time rate of change,** rate of change	zeitliche Änderung *f*; Änderungsgeschwindigkeit *f*
		time reckoning, chronology	Zeitrechnung *f*, Chronologie *f*
time-of-flight spectroscopy, time-of-flight spectrometry, velocity spectroscopy, velocity spectrometry	Laufzeitspektroskopie *f*, Laufzeitspektrometrie *f*, Geschwindigkeitsspektroskopie *f*, Geschwindigkeitsspektrometrie *f*, Flugzeitspektroskopie *f*, Flugzeitspektrometrie *f*	**time record,** time marking	Zeitmarkierung *f*, Zeitmarkengebung *f*
		time record, time recording, time registering	Zeitregistrierung *f*
		time recorder	s. chronograph
		time recording	s. time record
		time recording apparatus	s. time recorder
time-of-flight velocity selector	Geschwindigkeitsselektor *m* nach der Laufzeitmethode	**time reference**	s. time metering
time of impact, collision time, time of collision, collision period	Stoßzeit *f*, Stoßdauer *f*	**time registering**	s. time record
		time relay	s. time-delay relay
		time required, sacrifice of time, waste of time, loss of time	Zeitaufwand *m*
time of measurement	Meßzeit *f*		
time of neap tide, time of dead tide	Nippzeit *f*	**time resolution,** time resolving power	Zeitauflösung *f*, zeitliches Auflösungsvermögen *n*, Zeitauflösungsvermögen *n*
time of one revolution, period, period of revolution, orbital period ‹astr.›	Umlaufszeit *f*, Umlaufzeit *f*, Umlauf[s]dauer *f*, Umlauf[s]periode *f* ‹Astr.›		
		time resolving power, time resolution	Zeitauflösung *f*, zeitliches Auflösungsvermögen *n*, Zeitauflösungsvermögen *n*
time of one revolution	s. a. rotation period		
time of operation, operating time, transit time ‹of relay›	Ansprechzeit *f* ‹Relais›	**time response**	Zeitgang *m*, Zeitcharakteristik *f*
		time response; time constant; characteristic time ‹el.›	Zeitkonstante *f*; RC-Konstante *f*, elektrische Zeitkonstante, RC ‹El.›
time of partial shutter opening, opening period ‹phot.›	Öffnungszeit *f* ‹Phot.›	**time response,** rise time, build-up time, building-up time ‹e.g. of pulse›	Anstiegszeit *f*; Aufbauzeit *f* ‹z. B. Impuls›
time of periastron passage	s. epoch of periastron		
time of perihelion passage	Perihelzeit *f*		
time of persistence	s. persistence	**time response**	s. a. unit[-] step response
time of relaxation	s. relaxation time	**time reversal,** time inversion	Zeitumkehr *f*
time of the onset of the excitation, reaction time ‹bio.›; response time	Reaktionszeit *f*		
		time[-] reversal invariance, *T* invariance, time reversibility	T-Invarianz *f*, Zeitumkehrinvarianz *f*
time of travel, travel time, travelling time, transit time ‹geo., ac.›	Laufzeit *f* ‹Geo., Ak.›		
		time reversal operation, time inversion operation	Zeitumkehroperation *f*
time of travel	s. a. transit time ‹el.›		
time-ordered product	s. chronological product	**time reversal operator,** operator of time reversal	Operator *m* der (für die) Zeitumkehr, Zeitumkehroperator *m*
time ordering operator	s. Dyson chronological operator		
time parameter	Zeitparameter *m*	**time reversibility**	s. time[-] reversal invariance
time parity	Zeitparität *f*, Parität *f* der Zeit		
		timer switch	Programmzeitschalter *m*
time-path curve	Zeit-Weg-Kurve *f*	**time saving,** saving of time	Zeitersparnis *f*, Einsparung *f* an Zeit
time-path diagram, time-traverse diagram	Zeit-Weg-Diagramm *n*, Zeit-Weg-Schaubild *n*	**time scale**	Zeitskala *f*; Zeitmaßstab *m*
time pattern control	s. time schedule control	**time scale,** time measure	Zeitmaß *n*
time-pattern control system, timing system	Zeitplansystem *n*, Zeitplanregelsystem *n*, Regelsystem *n* mit Zeitplan, System *n* mit Zeitplanregelung	**time scale factor**	Zeitmaßfaktor *m*
		time schedule	Zeitplan *m*, Zeitprogramm *n*
time[ ]piece, chronometer; clock; watch; time keeper	Zeitmesser *m*, Zeitmeßgerät *n*; Uhr *f*, Chronometer *n*; Zeitnehmer *m*	**time schedule control,** time pattern control, time control, programme control, programmed control	Zeitplanregelung *f*, Programmregelung *f*, programmierte Regelung *f*, Fahrplanregelung *f*; Zeitplansteuerung *f*, Programmsteuerung *f*
time[ ]piece, timing generator, time transmitter	Zeitgeber *m*		
time-preserving	zeitgetreu, zeittreu		
time printer	s. chronograph	**time schedule controller,** cyclelog, timer	Zeitplanregler *m*, Programmregler *m*
time-proportional, linear in time, proportional to time	zeitlinear; zeitproportional		

time selection	Zeitselektion f, Zeitschachtelung f	time zone, time belt	Zeitzone f, Zone f gleicher Zeit, Meridianstreifen m
time selection pulse	Zeitselektionsimpuls m, Zeitschachtelungsimpuls m	timing	Zeitsteuerung f, Steuerung f; Zeitregelung f, Regelung f
time sense	Zeitsinn m	timing	s. a. time measurement
time sensitometry	Zeitsensitometrie f	timing circuit	Zeitschaltung f, Zeitsteuerschaltung f, Zeitsteuerungsschaltung f, Zeitregelungsschaltung f
time sequence	s. chronology		
time series <stat.>	Zeitreihe f <Stat.>		
time service	Zeitdienst m		
time sharing [scheme], multi-access computing <num. math.>	Teilnehmer-Rechenbetrieb m, Multikonsolbetrieb m, Zeitverteilung f, "time sharing" n <num. Math.>	timing circuit	s. a. time delay circuit
		timing circuit	s. a. time-delay relay
		timing element, timer <el.>	Zeitglied n, Zeitelement n <El.>
		timing generator, time transmitter, time piece	Zeitgeber m
time shift, time displacement	Zeitversetzung f, Zeitverschiebung f, Zeittranslation f	timing impulse	s. timing pulse
		timing interrupter	s. time-delay switch
time shift error, time displacement error	Zeitversetzungsfehler m, Zeitverschiebungsfehler m	timing pulse, clock[-]pulse	Taktimpuls m
		timing pulse generator	s. electronic timer
time-shift theorem [of Laplace transform], shifting (lag) theorem [of Laplace transform]	Verschiebungssatz m [der Laplace-Transformation], Heavisidescher Verschiebungssatz	timing relay	s. time-delay switch
		timing system, timing unit, time measuring equipment, time measuring instrument	Zeitmeßanordnung f; Zeitmeßanlage f, Zeitmeßgerät n
time signal	Zeitzeichen n		
time signal injector	s. time mark generator		
time-slice axiom	Zeitschichtaxiom n		
time slicing	Zeitunterteilung f	timing system	Zeitmarkiersystem n, Zeitmarkensystem n
time slope, time behaviour, time history, time lapse, lapse	Zeitablauf m, zeitlicher Ablauf m, zeitlicher Verlauf m, Zeitverlauf m	timing system	s. a. time-pattern control system
		timing unit	Taktgerät n
time sorter, pulse interval analyzer, interval analyzer	Impulsintervallanalysator m, Intervallanalysator m	timing unit	s. a. timing system
		timing voltage	Taktspannung f
time-space correlation, space-time correlation	zeitlich-räumliche (räumlich-zeitliche) Korrelation f	tin cry	Zinngeschrei n, Zinnschrei m
		tinge	s. tint
		tinging, colouring, colouration, tinting, tintage, dyeing, staining	Anfärbung f
time spectrum	Zeitspektrum n		
time stability, stability in time	zeitliche Konstanz f, Zeitkonstanz f		
time standard, standard time	Zeitnormal n	tinging method, tinging technique	Anstrichmethode f
time strength	s. fatigue strength for limit life	tin pest, tin plague	Zinnpest f
		tint, tinge; shading; shade	Schattierung f
time sum, sum over time	Zeitsumme f		
time sweep, time base, time-base sweep, sweep	Zeitablenkung f	tint, colour shade, tinge, colour tinge (tint), shade; shading value	Farbnuance f, Farbschattierung f, Farbstufe f; Farbtönung f; Färbung f, Tönung f
		tintage, tinting	s. tinging
time switch	s. clock relay	tint of passage, sensitive tint, sensitive violet	empfindliche Farbe (Färbung) f, "teinte sensible" f, Rot n erster (I.) Ordnung
time switch	s. time-delay switch		
time-symmetric	s. symmetric in time		
time-symmetric tensor, tensor symmetric in time	zeitsymmetrischer Tensor m, i-Tensor m		
		tintometer	s. Lovibond tintometer
time-to-amplitude converter, time-to-pulse height converter, time amplitude converter, TAC	Zeit-Amplitude[n]-Konverter m, Zeit-Impulshöhe[n]-Konverter m, Zeitamplitudenwandler m	T invariance, time[-]reversal invariance, time reversibility	T-Invarianz f, Zeitumkehrinvarianz f
		tip curve, curve of magnetization tips, curve of normal magnetization	Kommutierungskurve f, Kommutierungskennlinie f, Spitzenkurve f
time-to-time converter	Zeit-Zeit-Konverter m, Zeit-Zeit-Wandler m	tip dispersion, tooth tip dispersion	Zahnkopfstreuung f
time trace, time mark	Zeitmarke f, Zeitmeßmarke f	tip eddy	s. tip vortex
		tip of the tooth, tooth tip	Zahnkopf m, Zahnkrone f
time transformer	Zeittransformator m	tipping, tilting	Kippen n; Umkippen n; Umklappen n
		tipping moment coefficient	s. tilting moment coefficient
		tip surface of the tooth, surface of the tip	Zahnscheitel m, Zahnrücken m
		tip vortex, wing-tip vortex, tip eddy, trailing vortex, marginal vortex, rim vortex, vortex rope	Randwirbel m, Wirbelzopf m
time transmission, time distribution	Zeitübermittlung f, Zeitübertragung f	Tirrill regulator	Tirrill-Regler m
time transmitter, timing generator, time piece	Zeitgeber m	Tisserand['s] criterion	Tisserands[ches] Kriterium n [für die Identität von Kometen]
time-traverse diagram, time-path diagram	Zeit-Weg-Diagramm n, Zeit-Weg-Schaubild n		
time variant, variable with time, variable in time	zeitlich veränderlich, zeitvariabel	Tissot indicatrix, indicatrix, distortion ellipse <geo.>	Tissotsche Indikatrix f, Indikatrix, Verzerrungsellipse f <Geo.>
time vector	s. vector <in alternating-current theory>	tissue culture	Gewebekultur f

tissue

tissue dose	Gewebedosis f, Gewebsdosis f
tissue equivalence, equivalence to tissue	Gewebeäquivalenz f
tissue-equivalent ionization chamber	gewebeäquivalente Ionisationskammer f
tissue-equivalent material, phantom material	gewebeäquivalentes Material n, Gewebeäquivalent n, Phantomsubstanz f
tissue-equivalent proportional counter	gewebeäquivalentes Proportionalzählrohr n
tissue half-value depth, half-value depth, HVD, $D_{1/2}$	Gewebe-Halbwerttiefe f, GHT, $D_{1/2}$
tissue tension	Gewebespannung f
titanium getter-ion pump	Titangetter-Ionenpumpe f
titer <US>	s. titre
Titius-Bode law	s. law of planetary distances
Titius-Bode series	Titius-Bodesche Reihe f
titrant, titrating solution, standard solution <chem.>	Maßlösung f, Maßflüssigkeit f, Titrierlösung f; Titrierflüssigkeit f, Titerlösung f, Titerflüssigkeit f, Meßflüssigkeit f, Meßlösung f, Reagenzlösung f, Titrans n
titratable acidity	s. titration acidity
titratable alkalinity	s. titration alkalinity
titrate, titrated substance	Titrat n, titrierte Substanz f
titrating solution	s. titrant
titration acidity, titratable acidity	Titrationsacidität f
titration alkalinity, titratable alkalinity	Titrationsalkalinität f
titration analysis	s. volumetric analysis
titration coulometer	s. titration voltameter
titration curve	Titrationskurve f
titration end[-] point, end[-] point [of titration]	Titrationsendpunkt m, Endpunkt m [der Titration]
titration level	Titrationsniveau n
titration test	s. volumetric analysis
titration voltameter, titration coulometer	Titrationscoulometer n, Titrationsvoltameter n
titre, titer <US>	Titer m, Normalfaktor m, Reaktionsstärke f der Normallösung
titrimeter	Titrimeter n, Titriermesser m
titrimetric	s. volumetric[al]
titrimetric analysis	s. volumetric analysis
titrimetric standard substance; primary titrimetric standard substance	Urtitersubstanz f; primäre Urtitersubstanz
titrimetry	s. volumetric analysis
tjaele, permafrost, perpetually frozen soil, everfrost, pergelisol	Dauerfrostboden m, ewige Gefrornis n, Gefrornis, Permafrost m, Pergelisol m, Kongelisol m, Congelisol m
T-layer effect	T-Schicht-Effekt m
TM[-] mode	s. wave of electric type
T-mode	s. transverse mode
TM[-] wave	s. wave of electric type
T[-] network, T[-] section <of the filter>	T-Glied n, T-Schaltung f, T-Netzwerk n, T-Vierpol m; T-Grundkette f, T-Grundschaltung f, Grund-T-Schaltung f
to-and-fro motion	s. reciprocating motion
to-and-fro test	s. reverse bend[ing] test
Tobolsky-Leaderman-Ferry reduction formula	Tobolsky-Leaderman-Ferrysche Reduktionsformel f
toe [of the characteristic curve], lower part of the characteristic curve, region of underexposure, reciprocity failure	Durchhang m [der Schwärzungskurve], Gebiet n der Unterexposition, Fuß m [der Schwärzungskurve]
Toepler generator	Toepler-Generator m, Toepler-Maschine f
Toepler-Holtz generator, Holtz-type generator	Toepler-Holtz-Generator m
Toepler['s] method, Toepler['s] schlieren method (technique, procedure), Toepler['s] shadow technique	Toeplersches Schlierenverfahren n, Toeplersche Schlierenmethode f
Toepler['s] method [for the determination of refractive index]	Toeplersche Methode f [zur Brechzahlbestimmung]
Toepler pump	Toepler-Pumpe f, Geißlersche Quecksilberpumpe f, Geißler-Pumpe f, Geisler-Pumpe f
Toepler['s] schlieren image, schlieren image of Toepler	Toeplersches Schlierenbild n, Schlierenbild nach Toepler
Toepler['s] schlieren method (procedure, technique), Toepler['s] shadow technique	s. Toepler method
Toeplitz['] limit theorem, Toeplitz['] theorem	Toeplitzscher Grenzwertsatz m, Toeplitzscher Satz m
Toeplitz matrix	Toeplitzsche Matrix f
Toeplitz['s] theorem	s. Toeplitz['] limit theorem
Toeplitz['] theorem [for reciprocals]	Toeplitzsches Reziprokentheorem n
tog $<=$ 4,180 cm² s °C/cal	Tog n, tog $<=$ 4180 cm² s °C/cal
toggle lever	s. bent lever
toggle switch	s. tumbler
tokamak, toroidal diffuse-pinch configuration	Tokamak m, Tokamak-Anlage f
Tolansky['s] method	Tolanskysche Methode f, Methode von Tolansky
tolerance, allowance, permissible tolerance, permissible limits, allowable limits, margin	Toleranz f, Maßtoleranz f, zulässige Abweichung f, zulässiger Fehler m, Spielraum m
tolerance	s. a. stability
tolerance analysis, dose-effect method	Dosis-Wirkungs-Verfahren n, Toleranzanalyse f
tolerance bridge, limit bridge	Toleranzmeßbrücke f, Toleranzbrücke f
tolerance concentration, permissible concentration	zulässige Konzentration f, verträgliche Konzentration, Toleranzkonzentration f
tolerance dose, permissible dose, permissible tolerance [dose], radiation tolerance	zulässige Dosis f, zulässige Strahlungsdosis f, verträgliche Dosis, verträgliche Strahlungsdosis, Toleranzdosis f
tolerance gauge	s. limit gauge
tolerance interval	s. tolerance range
tolerance limit <stat.>	Toleranzgrenze f, Duldungsgrenze f <Stat.>
tolerance limit gauge	s. limit gauge
tolerance limits	s. tolerance range
tolerance meter	Toleranzmeßgerät n, Toleranzmesser m
tolerance range, tolerance interval, tolerance limits, limits of tolerance	Toleranzbereich m, Toleranzgebiet n, Toleranzintervall n, Toleranzfeld n
Tollmien-Schlichting wave	Tollmien-Schlichting-Welle f, Tollmien-Schlichtingsche Welle f
Tolman effect	Tolman-Effekt m
Tolman['s] experiment	Tolman-Versuch m, Tolmanscher Versuch m, Versuch von Tolman, Tolmanscher Nachweis m freier Ladungsträger, Experiment n von Tolman <Brems- oder Schüttelversuch>
toluene thermometer	Toluolthermometer n
tombac [sylphon]	Tombakschlauch m
tomograph	s. laminograph
tomography	s. body section roentgenography
Tomonaga equation	Tomonaga-Gleichung f, Tomonagasche Gleichung f
Tomonaga-Schwinger['s] equation, interaction picture equation	Tomonaga-Schwinger-Gleichung f, Tomonaga-Schwingersche Gleichung f

Tomonaga-Schwinger picture	s. interaction representation	tool holder	Geräthalter m, Werkzeughalter m
tomophoto[fluoro-]graphy	Schirmbildschichtverfahren n, Tomophotographie f	tooth <el.>; spike	Zacken m, Zacke f <El.>
		toothed, spiked, pronged, indented	zackig, gezackt
Tomotika and Tamada fluid, Tomotika-Tamada fluid, idealized fluid of Tomotika and Tamada	Tomotika-Tamada-Flüssigkeit f, Tomotika-Tamadasche Flüssigkeit f, idealisierte Flüssigkeit von Tomotika und Tamada	toothed disk	Zahnscheibe f
		toothed wheel method	s. Fizeau method
		tooth flank, tooth form	Zahnflanke f
Tomotika and Tamada gas, Tomotika-Tamada gas	Tomotika-Tamada-Gas n, Tomotika-Tamadasches Gas n		
Tomotika-Tamada profile	Tomotika-Tamada-Profil n	tooth form, tooth profile, tooth shape	Zahnprofil n, Zahnform f
Toms effect	Toms-Effekt m	tooth pitch, pitch of the teeth	Zahnteilung f
ton, ton of refrigeration <= 840 cal/s, unit in refrigeration engineering = 288,000 B.t.u./day>	„ton" f, Tonne f Eis <= 840 cal/s, Einheit in der Kältetechnik>		
		tooth profile, tooth shape, tooth form	Zahnprofil n, Zahnform f
		tooth tip, tip of the tooth	Zahnkopf m, Zahnkrone f
tonality	Tonalität f		
tonality, mode <ac.>	Tonart f <Ak.>	tooth tip dispersion, tip dispersion	Zahnkopfstreuung f
tonal range	Tonumfang m	top; gyroscope, gyro	Kreisel m
tone, sound <ac.>	Ton m <Ak.>	top <of the pulse>, pulse tilt, pulse top, horizontal part of the pulse	Impulsdach n, Dach n
tone, sound, musical sound <ac.>	Klang m <Ak.>		
tone <el.>; tone colour, timbre of sound, quality of sound, tone quality	Klangfarbe f, Tonfarbe f, Farbe f des Klangs	top chord, upper chord	Obergurt m
tone frequency	s. audio[-] frequency	T operator, Wick['s] chronological operator, Wick['s] operator	Wick-Operator m, Wickscher Operator m, T-Operator m, Wickscher Zeitordnungsoperator m
tone generator	s. audio generator		
tone interval	Tonintervall n, Tonschritt m, Tonstufe f, Tonabstand m		
		topic	topisch
		top molecule, spinning molecule	Kreiselmolekül n
tone oscillator	s. audio generator		
tone pitch, pitch [of the tone], pitch of note, sound pitch <ac.>	Tonhöhe f, Höhe f <Ton> <Ak.>	topmost level, uppermost level	oberstes (höchstes) Niveau n
tone quality	s. tone <el.>	topocentre	Topozentrum n
tone scale, gamut, scale, musical scale <ac.>	Tonleiter f, Tonskala f, Tonreihe f <Ak.>	topochemical reaction	topochemische Reaktion f
		topochemistry	Topochemie f, ortsgebundene Chemie f
tone source	s. audio generator	topochronotherm	Topochronotherme f
tone space, tonraum	Tonraum m	topoclimate	Topoklima n
		top of the atmosphere, ceiling of the atmosphere	Atmosphärengipfel m, Grenze f der Erdatmosphäre, Atmosphärengrenze f
tone wheel, phonic wheel	phonisches Rad n, Tonrad n		
tongue; reed; tag	Zunge f		
		top of the atmospheric layer, peak of the atmospheric layer	Gipfel m (Maximum n) der Atmosphärenschicht
tongue, pointer <of the balance>	Zunge f <Waage>		
tongue flame	s. shooting flame	top of the cloud, cloud top, cloud dome	Wolkenkuppe f
tongue of the glacier, glacier tongue	Gletscherzunge f	top of the column	Kolonnenkopf m, Kopf m der Kolonne
tongue pipe	s. reed pipe	top of the valence band	obere Kante f des Valenzbandes, oberer Rand m des Valenzbandes, Oberkante f des Valenzbandes
tonguing <ac.>	Ansatzrohr n <Ak.>		
tonic	Tonika f, Grundton m		
tonic stimulus	tonischer Reiz m		
toning, bronzing <of photographic pictures>	Tonung f <photographischer Bilder>, photographische Tonung	top of the wave	s. crest [of the wave]
		topogenic vortex	topogener Wirbel m
		topogram	Topogramm n
		topographical criterion	s. Nyquist['s] criterion [of stability]
toning bath	Tonbad n, Tonungsbad n	topographic correction	topographische Korrektion f, Geländekorrektion f
Tonks-Dattner resonance	Tonks-Dattner-Resonanz f		
		topographic inequality, inequality; unevenness	Unebenheit f
Tonks['] equation [of state]	Tonkssche Zustandsgleichung f, Tonkssche Gleichung f		
		topographic mapping, mapping, topographic survey, survey	Kartenaufnahme f, topographische Aufnahme f, Geländeaufnahme f, Aufnahme; Kartierung f
tonne, metric ton, t, millier	Tonne f, t		
ton of refrigeration	s. ton		
tonometer	Tonometer n		
tonometry	Tonometrie f		
		topographic mapping	s. a. mapping
tonotron	Tonotron n	topographic projection, coted projection	kotierte Projektion f, topographisches Verfahren n
tonpilz	Tonpilz m	topographic reduction	topographische Reduktion f; Reduktion auf ebenes Terrain
		topographic refraction	topographische Refraktion f
tonraum, tone space	Tonraum m		
tonus <bio.>	Tonus m, Spannkraft f <Bio.>	topographic stadia rod, stadia rod, level rod <US>	Tachymeterlatte f
Tool elliptic analyzer, Tool halfshade analyzer	Halbschattenanalysator m nach Tool, Toolscher Halbschattenapparat m (Halbschattenanalysator)	topographic survey	s. topographic mapping
		topological graph	s. topologic graph
		topological group, continuous group	topologische (kontinuierliche) Gruppe f

topological

topological isomerism	topologische Isomerie f
topologically equivalent <math.>; homeomorphic <math.; opt.>	homöomorph; topologisch äquivalent <math.>; raumähnlich <opt.>
topological mapping	s. bi-continuous mapping <math.>
topological transformation	s. bi-continuous mapping <math.>
topologic graph, topological graph, graph	topologischer Graph m, Graph, Streckenkomplex m
topophototaxis	Topophototaxis f
topotactic reaction	topotaktische Reaktion f
topotaxis	Topotaxis f
topothermogram	Topothermogramm n
topotropism	s. morphotropism
top-to-bottom inverted (reversed)	s. reversed top to bottom <of image>
top view; horizontal projection	Horizontalprojektion f; Grundriß m; Draufsicht f
tor	s. millibar
torch cell	Stabelement n, Stabzelle f
torch hardening	s. surface hardening
tore	s. torus <math.>
toric lens; spherotoric lens	punktuell abbildende Linse f, Punktallinse f; Punktalglas n; torische Linse; sphärotorische Linse
toric surface, toroidal surface	torische Fläche f <tonnen- oder wulstförmig>
tornado	Tornado m, Großtrombe f
tornado hook	Trombenhaken m
tornado prominence	Tornadoprotuberanz f
toroid, doughnut, vacuum doughnut, donut <of betatron>	Ringkammer f, Ringröhre f, [ringförmige] Vakuumkammer f <Betatron>
toroid, toroidal coil, annular coil, annulus <el.>	Toroid n, Toroidspule f, Ringsolenoid n, Kreisringspule f, Ringspule f, ringförmige Spule f; Ringdrossel f <El.>
toroid <math.>	Toroid n <Math.>
toroid <math.>	Toroide f <Math.>
toroidal chamber, torus	Toroidkammer f, Toroidröhre f, Torus m
toroidal coil	s. toroid <el.>
toroidal co-ordinates	Ringkoordinaten fpl, Toruskoordinaten fpl, Thomsonsche Koordinaten fpl, Koordinaten von Thomson, annulare (toroidale) Koordinaten
toroidal-core permeability, permeability of the toroidal core	Ringkernpermeabilität f, Werkstoffpermeabilität f
toroidal-core storage, toroidal-core store, toroidal storage	Ringspeicher m, Ringkernspeicher m
toroidal-core transformer, toroidal transformer, toroidal repeating coil, ring transformer	Ringkernwandler m, Ringkernstromwandler m, Ringwandler m; Ringkernübertrager m, Ringübertrager m, Ringkerntransformator m, Ringtransformator m, Toroidtransformator m
toroidal diffuse-pinch configuration	s. tokamak
toroidal discharge, ring discharge	Toroidentladung f, Ringentladung f
toroidal field, toroidal magnetic field, toroidal part of the magnetic field	toroidales Feld n, toroidaler Teil m des magnetischen Feldes, toroidales Magnetfeld n, Toroidfeld n
toroidal function, ring function	Ringfunktion f, toroidale Funktion f, Torusfunktion f
toroidal magnetic field	s. toroidal field
toroidal mode	toroidale Mode f, toroidaler Typ m
toroidal part of the magnetic field	s. toroidal field
toroidal photocell	Ringphotozelle f
toroidal pinch [effect]	toroidaler Pinch m, Toroidpinch m
toroidal plasmoid	Toroidplasmoid n, toroidales Plasmoid n
toroidal potentiometer	Ringpotentiometer n
toroidal repeating coil	s. toroidal-core transformer
toroidal resonator, ring resonator	Ringresonator m
toroidal spectrometer	Toroidspektrometer n
toroidal storage	s. toroidal-core storage
toroidal surface, toric surface	torische Fläche f <tonnen- oder wulstförmig>
toroidal transformer	s. toroidal-core transformer
Toronto burner	Toronto-Brenner m, Welsh-Crawford-Brenner m
Toronto function	Toronto-Funktion f
torpedo sinker, torpedo-type weight, streamlined weight, Columbus-type weight, C-type weight	fischförmiger Belastungskörper m, Fischgewicht n
torque, moment of couple (rotation), exerted moment, turning moment, rotational moment, rotational inertia, torque moment	Drehmoment n, Moment n des Kräftepaares
torque	s. a. torsional moment
torque converter, fluid converter	Strömungsumwandler m
torque-error constant	Momentenverstärkungskoeffizient m
torque force	s. torsional force
torque load	s. torsional strain
torque magnetometer, torsion magnetometer	Torsionsmagnetometer n, Drehmagnetometer n
torque meter	s. torsimeter
torque moment	s. torque
torque moment	s. a. torsional moment
torque of torsion	s. torsional moment
torque resistance	s. torsional strength
torque-weight ratio <of a meter>	bezogenes Drehmoment n <Zähler>
torr; millimetre of mercury, conventional millimetre of mercury, mm of mercury, mm Hg	Torr n, torr; Millimeter n Quecksilbersäule, mm Hg, mm QS
torrential	wolkenbruchartig
torrential wash	s. mud stream
Torrey oscillation	s. transient nutation
Torricellian vacuum	s. Torricelli vacuum
Torricelli['s] experiment	Torricellischer Versuch m
Torricelli['s] formula, Torricelli['s] law [of efflux]	Torricellisches Gesetz (Theorem, Ausflußtheorem) n, Torricelli-Theorem n, Torricellische Formel (Ausflußformel) f, Satz m von Torricelli
Torricelli['s] principle	Torricellisches Prinzip n
Torricelli tube	Torricellis Rohr n
Torricelli vacuum, Torricellian vacuum, barometric chamber	Torricellische Leere f
torrid zone, tropics, tropic zone	Tropen pl, tropische Zone f, warme Zone, Tropenzone f
torsator	Torsator m
torse, developable surface	abwickelbare Fläche f, Torse f
torsimeter, torque meter, torsion torque meter, torsiometer	Torsions[moment]messer m, Torsiometer n, Drehmomentmesser m
torsiogram	Torsiogramm n
torsiograph, recording torsion meter, recording torsiometer	Torsiograph m, Torsionsschreiber m, Drehschwingungsschreiber m, Drillschwingungsschreiber m, Verdrehungsschreiber m, Verdrehschwingungsschreiber m

torsiometer	s. torsimeter	**torsional moment**, torsion[al] couple, torsion torque, torque [of torsion], twisting moment, external twisting moment, moment of torsion, twisting couple, torque moment	Torsionsmoment n, Verdreh[ungs]moment n, Drill[ungs]moment n, Drehmoment n [der Torsion], Drehungsmoment n [der Torsion]
torsion, twist[ing]	Torsion f, Drillung f, Verdrehung f, Verdrillung f, Drehung f		
torsion ‹bio›.; turn, turn of winding, single turn, spire; worm ‹of screw›	Windung f; Lage f		
		torsional oscillation	s. torsional vibration
		torsional oscillation resonance, torsional resonance	Torsionsresonanz f, Torsionsschwingungsresonanz f, Drehresonanz f
torsion, second curvature ‹of the curve› ‹math.›	Windung f, Torsion f, Schmiegung f, zweite Krümmung f ‹Raumkurve› ‹Math.›		
torsion	s. a. simple torsion	**torsional pendulum**, torsion pendulum	Torsionspendel n, Drehpendel n, Verdrehpendel n
torsional angle [of twist]	s. angle of twist	**torsional resistance**	s. torsional strength
torsional axis, axis of twist, axis of torsion	Torsionsachse f, Verdreh[ungs]achse f, Drill[ungs]achse f	**torsional resonance**	s. torsional oscillation resonance
torsional buckling	s. twist buckling	**torsional resonance frequency**	Torsionsresonanzfrequenz f
torsional couple	s. torsional moment	**torsional rigidity**, torsional stiffness	Torsionssteifigkeit f, Verdreh[ungs]steifigkeit f, Drill[ungs]steifigkeit f
torsional crystal, twister, twister crystal	Torsionskristall m, Drillungskristall m, Verdreh[ungs]kristall m		
		torsional rigidity per unit length	s. shear modulus
torsional deformation	s. torsional strain	**torsional sound vibration**	Torsionsschallschwingung f
torsional disclination	Torsionsdisklination f		
torsional eigenoscillation, torsional eigenvibration	Torsionseigenschwingung f	**torsional spring**	s. torsion spring
		torsional stiffness	s. torsional rigidity
		torsional strain, twisting strain, torque load	Torsionsbeanspruchung f, Verdreh[ungs]beanspruchung f, Verdrehungsbelastung f, Verdrehungsbelastung f
torsional elasticity	Torsionselastizität f, Verdreh[ungs]elastizität f, Drehungselastizität f		
torsional endurance limit	s. torsional strength		
torsional endurance limit at alternating load	s. torsional endurance strength at alternating load	**torsional strain**	s. a. torsional stress
		torsional strain	s. a. torsional work
		torsional strain	s. a. twisting strain
torsional endurance limit at repeated load	s. torsional endurance strength at repeated load	**torsional strength**, torsional endurance (fatigue) strength, twisting strength, torsional endurance (fatigue) limit, torsional (twisting) resistance, resistance to torsion, resistance to twist[ing], torque resistance, ultimate torsional strength	Verdrehfestigkeit f, Verdrehungsfestigkeit f, Torsionsfestigkeit f, Drehfestigkeit f, Drehungsfestigkeit f
torsional endurance strength	s. torsional strength		
torsional endurance strength at alternating load, torsional fatigue strength at alternating load, torsional endurance limit at alternating load, torsional fatigue limit at alternating load, torsional vibration resistance, resistance to torsional vibration	Verdreh[ungs]wechselfestigkeit f, Verdreh[ungs]schwingungsfestigkeit f, Torsionsschwingungsfestigkeit f, Dauerschwingfestigkeit f gegenüber Verdrehwechselbeanspruchung, Wechselfestigkeit f gegenüber Verdrehbeanspruchung (Torsionsbeanspruchung)		
		torsional stress, torsional strain, intensity of torsional stress (strain), twisting stress	Torsionsspannung f, Verdrehspannung f, Verdrehungsspannung f, Drehspannung f
		torsional stress	tordierter Spannungszustand m
		torsional susceptibility meter, torsion susceptometer	Torsionssuszeptometer n
torsional endurance strength at repeated load [in one direction], torsional fatigue strength at repeated load, torsional endurance limit at repeated load, torsional fatigue limit at repeated load	Verdreh[ungs]schwellfestigkeit f, Torsionsschwellfestigkeit f, Dauerschwellfestigkeit f gegenüber Verdrehbeanspruchung (Torsionsbeanspruchung), Schwellfestigkeit f gegenüber Verdrehbeanspruchung (Torsionsbeanspruchung)	**torsional suspension**, torsion suspension	Torsionsaufhängung f, Torsionsstabaufhängung f, Torsionsgehänge n; Torsionslagerung f
		torsional test, twist test	Verdreh[ungs]versuch m, Torsionsversuch m; Verwindeversuch m ‹Faden oder Draht›
torsional fatigue	Torsionsermüdung f, Verdreh[ungs]ermüdung f	**torsional vibration**, torsion[al] oscillation, torsion vibration, twisting vibration (oscillation); rotary vibration (oscillation)	Torsionsschwingung f, Drill[ungs]schwingung f, Verdreh[ungs]schwingung f; Dreh[ungs]schwingung f, Torsionspendelung f
torsional fatigue limit (strength)	s. torsional strength		
torsional fatigue limit (strength) at alternating load	s. torsional endurance strength at alternating load		
torsional fatigue limit (strength) at repeated load	s. torsional endurance strength at repeated load	**torsional vibration gauge**	Drehschwingungsmanometer n
		torsional vibration resistance	s. torsional endurance strength at alternating load
torsional fissure	Torsionsspalte f		
torsional flow	Torsionsfließen n	**torsional vibrator**, twisting vibrator	Drehschwinger m, Torsionsschwinger m, Drillschwinger m
torsional force, twisting force, torque force, rotary force, rotating force, rotation[al] force	Drehkraft f, Drehungskraft f, drehende Kraft f, verdrehende Kraft, Torsionskraft f, Drillungskraft f, Drillkraft f, Verdrehkraft f, Verdrehungskraft f		
		torsional wave	Torsionswelle f, Verdrehungswelle f
		torsional wave generating machine	Torsionswellenmaschine f
torsional frequency	Torsionsschwingungsfrequenz f		
torsional impact, torsion impact	Torsionsstoß m, Verdrehungsstoß m, Verdrehstoß m, Drillstoß m, Drehstoß m, Drehungsstoß m	**torsional work**, work of twisting, twisting (torsional) strain	Torsionsarbeit f, Verdreharbeit f, Verdrehungsarbeit f
		torsion angle	s. angle of twist
torsional instability	s. wriggle instability	**torsion balance**	Schneckenfederwaage f, Torsionswaage f, Drehwaage f, Verdreh[ungs]waage f
torsional mode	Torsionsschwingungstyp m, Drehschwingungstyp m, Drillschwingungstyp m		
torsional modulus	s. shear modulus	**torsion bar**	s. torsion rod

torsion

torsion constant [of the thread] — Torsionskonstante *f* [des Fadens], Verdrehungskonstante *f*

torsion couple — *s.* torsional moment

torsion curve — Torsionskurve *f*, Verdreh[ungs]kurve *f*

torsion dynamometer — Torsionsdynamometer *n*, Torsionselektrodynamometer *n*

torsion electrometer — Torsionselektrometer *n*, Torsionsfadenelektrometer *n*

torsion endurance test, torsion fatigue test, endurance torsion test, fatigue torsion test — Dauerverdrehversuch *m*, Dauertorsionsversuch *m*, Torsionsdauerversuch *m*, Verdrehdauerversuch *m*, Dauerschwingversuch *m* mit Verdrehbeanspruchung

torsion failure — Verdrehungsbruch *m*, Torsionsbruch *m*

torsion fatigue test — *s.* torsion endurance test

torsion flexure — Torsionsbiegung *f*

torsion[-] free, torsionless, twist-free — torsionsfrei, verdrehungsfrei, verdrehfrei

torsion function, Prandtl['s] torsion function, warping function — Torsionsfunktion *f*, Prandtlsche Torsionsfunktion *f*

torsion galvanometer — Torsionsgalvanometer *n*

torsion group, periodic group — periodische (ordnungsfinite) Gruppe *f*, Torsionsgruppe *f*

torsion-head instrument — Torsionsinstrument *n*, Torsionsmeßgerät *n*, Torsionskopfmeßgerät *n*, Torsionskopfinstrument *n*, Torsionsgerät *n*

torsion-head wattmeter — Torsionsleistungsmesser *m*, Torsionskopfleistungsmesser *m*, Torsionswattmeter *m*, Torsionskopfwattmeter *n*

torsion impact — *s.* torsional impact

torsion impact test, impact torsion test — Schlagverdrehversuch *m*, Schlagtorsionsversuch *m*, Schlagdrehversuch *m*

torsionless, torsion[-]free, twist-free — torsionsfrei, verdrehungsfrei, verdrehfrei

torsionless stress — torsionsfreier Spannungszustand *m*

torsion magnetometer, torque magnetometer — Torsionsmagnetometer *n*, Drehmagnetometer *n*

torsion meter, twist-measuring device, troptometer — Torsionsmesser *m*, Verdrehungsmesser *m*

torsion modulus — *s.* shear modulus

torsion movement <bio.> — Torsionsbewegung *f* <Bio.>

torsion oscillation — *s.* torsional vibration

torsion pendulum — *s.* torsional pendulum

torsion permeameter — Torsionspermeabilitätsmesser *m*, Torsionspermeameter *n*

torsion radius, radius of torsion, radius of second curvature — Windungsradius *m*, Torsionsradius *m*, Schmiegungsradius *m*, Radius *m* der zweiten Krümmung

torsion ratio — Torsionsverhältnis *n*

torsion-resistant, resistant to twist[ing] — torsionsfest, verdrehfest, verdrehungsfest

torsion rod, torsion bar — Torsionsstab *m*, Drillstab *m*, Verdrehungsstab *m*, Verdrehstab *m*, Drehstab *m*

torsion seismograph — Torsionsseismograph *m*, Drehseismograph *m* <nach Wood-Anderson>

torsion seismometer — Torsionsseismometer *n*, Drehseismometer *n*

torsion spring, torsional spring — Torsionsfeder *f*, Drehfeder *f*, Verdrehungsfeder *f*, Verdrehfeder *f*

torsion strain gauge — Torsionsdehnungsmeßstreifen *m*

torsion suspension — *s.* torsional suspension

torsion tape — Torsionsband *n*

torsion tensor, tensor of torsion — Torsionstensor *m*

torsion testing machine — Torsions[prüf]maschine *f*, Verdreh[ungs]prüfmaschine *f*, Verdrehungsmaschine *f*, Verdrehfestigkeits-Prüfmaschine *f*

torsion torque — *s.* torsional moment

torsion torque meter — *s.* torsimeter

torsion variometer, magnetic torsion balance — Torsionsvariometer *n*, magnetische Drehwaage (Torsionswaage) *f*

torsion vector — Torsionsvektor *m*

torsion vibration — *s.* torsional vibration

torsion vibration testing machine, repeated-load torsional fatigue testing machine — Verdrehschwingungs[prüf]maschine *f*, Verdrehungsschwingungsprüfmaschine *f*, Drehschwing[ungs]maschine *f*

torsion viscometer — Torsionsviskosimeter *n*

torsion wire — Torsionsfaden *m*; Torsionsdraht *m*

torson — Torson *n*

torsor, impulsor, ejector <math.> — Impulsor *m*, Ejektor *m*, Torsor *m* <Math.>

tortuosity, sinuosity — Flußentwicklung *f*

tortuosity <of porous medium>; twist per unit length, amount of torsion (twist), twist — Verwindung *f*

tortuosity <of rock> — Tortuosität *f* Tortuositätsfaktor *m* <Gestein>

torus, toroidal chamber — Toroidkammer *f*, Toroidröhre *f*, Torus *m*

torus [ring], tore, anchor ring, ring [surface] <math.> — Torus *m*, Kreiswulst *f*, Wulstfläche *f*, Wulst *f*; Ringfläche *f*, Ringwulst *f*, Ring *m*; Ringkörper *m* <Math.>

total absorptance — *s.* radiant total absorptance <opt.>

total absorption — Gesamtabsorption *f*, Totalabsorption *f*

total absorption coefficient — Gesamtabsorptionskoeffizient *m*, totaler Absorptionskoeffizient *m*

total absorptivity — *s.* radiant total absorptance <opt.>

total activity — Gesamtaktivität *f*

total adaptation — Totaladaptation *f*

total aerodynamic force, resulting aerodynamic force — aerodynamische Resultante *f*, resultierende aerodynamische Kraft *f*

total albedo — Gesamtalbedo *f*

total amplitude — *s.* peak-to-peak

total angular momentum, resultant moment of momentum — Gesamtdrehimpuls *m*

total angular momentum operator, operator of total angular momentum — Gesamtdrehimpulsoperator *m*, Operator *m* des Gesamtdrehimpulses

total angular momentum quantum number — *s.* inner quantum number

total astigmatism — Gesamtastigmatismus *m*, Totalastigmatismus *m*

total attenuation — Gesamtschwächung *f*

total beta activity, gross beta activity — Gesamt-Beta-Aktivität *f*, Brutto-Beta-Aktivität *f*

total binding energy, total nuclear binding energy — Gesamtbindungsenergie *f* des Kerns, totale Kernbindungsenergie *f*

total body exposure — *s.* whole-body exposure

total body irradiation — *s.* whole-body exposure

total break time, interrupting time <US> — Ausschaltdauer *f*, elektrische Ausschaltdauer

total brightness — *s.* total luminance

total cloudiness, total overcast — Gesamtbewölkung *f*, Gesamtbedeckung *f*

total collision cross-section, total effective collision cross-section — totaler Stoßquerschnitt *m*, Gesamtstoßquerschnitt *m*, gesamter Stoßquerschnitt *m*

total Compton mass attenuation coefficient — Massenschwächungskoeffizient *m* für den Compton-Effekt, Massenschwächungskoeffizient des Compton-Prozesses, Compton-Massenschwächungskoeffizient *m*

total conductance, combination conductance, overall conductance	Kombinationsleitwert m, Gesamtleitwert m	total-force magnetometer	Totalintensitätsmagnetometer n
total correlation, perfect correlation	totale Korrelation f, vollkommene Korrelation	total-force variometer	s. total-intensity variometer
total correlation coefficient	totaler Korrelationskoeffizient m	total formula	s. empirical formula
		total Hamiltonian	s. complete Hamiltonian
total covariant derivative	totale kovariante Ableitung f	total hardness of water	Gesamthärte f des Wassers, GH
total cross-section, bulk cross-section	totaler Wirkungsquerschnitt m, Gesamt[wirkungs]querschnitt m	total head, total energy head	Energiehöhe f, hydraulische Höhe f, gesamte Energiehöhe f
total cross-section of the winding, winding cross-section	Wicklungsquerschnitt m, Wickelquerschnitt m	total head	s. a. total pressure <aero.>
		total head pressure	s. total pressure <aero.>
		total heat	s. enthalpy <at constant pressure>
total curvature	Gesamtkrümmung f, Totalkrümmung f, curvatura f integra	total horopter	Totalhoropter m, Punkthoropter m, Vollhoropter m, totaler Horopter m
total curvature	s. a. Gauss curvature	total impulse	s. total momentum
total damping; resultant damping, net damping	Gesamtdämpfung f; resultierende Dämpfung f	total inflow	Zuflußsumme f, Gesamtzufluß m
		total intensity	Gesamtintensität f; Gesamtfeldstärke f
total deflection of plumbline	totale Lotabweichung f		
total derivative	totale Ableitung f	total intensity	s. a. total force <magn.>
total derivative	s. a. material derivative	total-intensity variometer, total-force variometer	Totalintensitätsvariometer n
total determination	= square of the multiple correlation coefficient		
total differential, exact differential, perfect differential, complete differential	vollständiges Differential n, totales Differential, exaktes Differential		
total differential equation, Pfaffian differential equation, exact [differential] equation	exakte Differentialgleichung f, totale Differentialgleichung, Pfaffsche Gleichung f	total internal conversion coefficient	totaler Konversionskoeffizient m
		total ionization	Gesamtionisation f; totale Ionisation f; Gesamtzahl f der erzeugten Ionenpaare; Gesamtladung f der Ionen eines Vorzeichens
total dispersion	totale Dispersion f		
total eclipse	totale Finsternis f, vollständige Verfinsterung f		
		total ionization, complete ionization, full ionization	vollständige Ionisation f, vollständige Ionisierung f, Vollionisation f, Vollionisierung f
total eclipse of the Sun, total solar eclipse	totale Sonnenfinsternis f		
		total isodynam	Totalisodyname f
total effective collision cross-section, total collision cross-section	totaler Stoßquerschnitt m, Gesamtstoßquerschnitt m, gesamter Stoßquerschnitt	totality, totality of eclipse	Totalität f [der Verfinsterung]
total effective cross-section for electronic collisions	s. Ramsauer-Townsend collision cross-section	totalizer, pluviometer-association	Totalisator m, Niederschlagstotalisator m, Niederschlagssammler m
total elastic potential energy	s. total strain energy		
total electrode capacitance	s. interelectrode capacitance	total kinetic energy	kinetische Gesamtenergie f
total electron binding energy	Gesamtbindungsenergie f des Elektrons, totale Elektronenbindungsenergie f	total level width, total width	Gesamtbreite f [des Niveaus], totale Niveaubreite f
		total light flux, total luminous flux	Gesamtlichtstrom m, Leistung f <Lichtquelle>
total emissivity <e.g. of a thermal radiator>	Gesamtemissionsvermögen n, Gesamtemissionsgrad m, Gesamtausstrahlung f, Emissionsgrad m <z. B. Temperaturstrahler>	total load	Gesamtbelastung f
		total loss, flop	Totalausfall m
		total luminance, total brightness	Gesamtleuchtdichte f, Gesamthelligkeit f
total energy head	s. total head	total luminous flux, total light flux	Gesamtlichtstrom m, Leistung f <Lichtquelle>
total energy of radiation	s. total radiant energy		
total error	Gesamtfehler m	totally additive	s. countably additive
total error of measurement, total measuring error	Gesamtmeßfehler m	totally disconnected <math.>; disconnected, unconnected	zusammenhangslos, punkthaft, total unzusammenhängend; total zusammenhangslos <Math.>
total extension	s. breaking elongation		
total extinction	Gesamtextinktion f		
total filter	Gesamtfilter n	totally enclosed <of instrument>	geschlossen <Gerät>
total flow, total flux <hydr.>	Gesamtfluß m <Hydr.>		
total fluctuation, total variation <also of a function>	Gesamtschwankung f	totally reflecting prism	s. reflecting prism
		totally symmetric	totalsymmetrisch
		total magnetic flux	s. total flux
total flux, total magnetic flux	Gesamtfluß m, magnetischer Gesamtfluß, Gesamtkraftfluß m, Flußverkettung f	total magnification, overall magnification	Gesamtvergrößerung f
		total mass absorption coefficient	totaler Massenabsorptionskoeffizient m
total flux, total flow <hydr.>	Gesamtfluß m <Hydr.>	total mass attenuation coefficient	totaler Massenschwächungskoeffizient m
total force, total intensity <magn.>	Totalintensität f <Magn.>		
		total mass stopping power	totales Massenbremsvermögen n, Gesamtmassenbremsvermögen n
total force <mech.>	Gesamtkraft f <Mech.>		

total

total mean square	s. total variance	total scattering coefficient	totaler Streukoeffizient m
total measuring error	s. total error of measurement		
total modulation, full modulation	Vollaussteuerung f	total scattering cross-section	totaler Streuquerschnitt m, Gesamtstreuquerschnitt m, gesamter Streuquerschnitt
total moment	resultierendes Moment n		
total momentum, total impulse, overall momentum (impulse)	Gesamtimpuls m; resultierender Impuls m	total solar eclipse, total eclipse of the Sun	totale Sonnenfinsternis f
total neutron cross-section	s. neutron total cross-section	total solids, solid residue [from evaporation]	Trockenrückstand m; Abdampfrückstand m
		total specific activity	spezifische Gesamtaktivität f
total neutron importance	Gesamteinfluß m, „gewogener" (verallgemeinerter) Neutroneninhalt m	total specific ionization	s. specific ionization
		total-step iteration (method)	Gesamtschrittverfahren n, Iteration f in Gesamtschritten
total nuclear binding energy, total binding energy	Gesamtbindungsenergie f des Kerns, totale Kernbindungsenergie f		
		total step iteration [for solving linear equations]	s. Gauss-Seidel method
total of the digits	s. sum of the digits		
total operating time <of fuse>	Abschaltzeit f, Ausschaltzeit f <Sicherung>	total strain energy, total elastic potential energy, elastic strain energy, strain energy, potential energy of deformation, potential energy of the deformed body, potential energy <of elastic body>	Deformationsenergie f, Formänderungsenergie f, [innere] Formänderungsarbeit f, Verzerrungsarbeit f, Verzerrungsenergie f, innere Energie f, Verformenergie f, Formenergie f, Verformungsenergie f, Spannungsenergie f
total orbital angular momentum, total orbital moment [of momentum]	Gesamtbahndrehimpuls m		
total ordering	s. ordering <math.>		
total overcast, total cloudiness	Gesamtbewölkung f, Gesamtbedeckung f		
total permeability	totale Permeabilität f, Gleichfeldpermeabilität	total stress, interior force	Spannkraft f
total plastic, stereo-power	totale Plastik f	total stress <mech.>	Gesamtspannung f <Mech.>
		total temperature <aero.>	Gesamttemperatur f, Kesseltemperatur f, Ruhetemperatur f <Aero.>
total pressure, total head pressure, total head, true stagnation pressure <aero.>	Gesamtdruck m, Kesseldruck m, Ruhedruck m, ruhender Druck m <statischer + dynamischer Druck> <Aero.>		
		total temperature profile	Staupunkttemperaturprofil n
		total temporal derivative	totale zeitliche Ableitung f
total probability	totale Wahrscheinlichkeit f	total term	Gesamtterm m
total quantum number	s. principal quantum number	total thermodynamic potential	s. free enthalpy
total radiant energy, total energy of radiation; radiancy <total radiant energy per sec and cm²>	Energie f der Gesamtstrahlung, Gesamtstrahlungsenergie f, gesamte Strahlungsenergie f, Gesamtstrahlung f	total tide, high tide, high water	Hochwasser n, Gezeitenhochwasser n, Tidehochwasser n
		total time of exposure per week	Arbeitsfaktor m, Beschäftigungsfaktor m
total radiation	Gesamtstrahlung f, Totalstrahlung f	total transmission factor	s. transmission factor
		total transmittance	s. transmission factor
		total turbidity factor [of Linke]	Gesamttrübungsfaktor m [nach Linke]
total radiation, solar total radiation	Gesamtstrahlung f [der Sonne]		
total radiation coefficient	s. Stefan-Boltzmann['s] constant	total variance, total mean square	Gesamtvarianz f
total radiation pyrometer	s. Féry pyrometer	total variation, total fluctuation <also of a function>	Gesamtschwankung f
total radiation standard	Gesamtstrahlungsnormal n	total width	s. total level width
		total width of grating, overall width [of grating]	Gitterbreite f, Gesamtbreite f des Beugungsgitters
total radiation temperature, bolometric radiation temperature, full radiator temperature <opt.>	Gesamtstrahlungstemperatur f		
		total zone of obscuration, band of totality, zone of totality	Totalitätszone f
		totient	Eulersche Funktion f $\varphi(n)$
total radiation type pyrometer	s. Féry pyrometer	totipotency	Totipotenz f
		totipotent	totipotent
total reflectance	s. total reflection factor <opt.>	tottering	s. shaking
		touch	s. contiguity <gen.>
total reflection	Totalreflexion f, totale Reflexion f, vollkommene Spiegelung f	touch	s. a. sense of touch
		touching, tangential	tangential, Tangential-; berührend, tangierend; Tangenten-
total reflection factor, reflection factor, total reflectance, reflectance, radiant total reflectance, radiant reflectance, reflectivity, reflecting factor, reflecting coefficient <opt.>	totaler Reflexionsgrad m, Gesamtreflexionsgrad m, Reflexionsgrad, totaler Reflexionskoeffizient m, Gesamtreflexionskoeffizient m, Reflexionskoeffizient m <Opt.>	touch organ, feeling organ	Tastsinnesorgan n, Tastorgan n, Tangorezeptor m, Fühlorgan n
		touch sense	s. sense of touch
		touch spark	s. break spark
		tough, tenacious <of materials, especially metals>	zäh, zähfest, zähhart [vergütet], widerstandsfähig, fest, biegsam <Werkstoffe, besonders Metalle>
total reflection layer	Totalreflexionslamelle f		
total reflection prism	s. reflecting prism		
total reflectivity	s. total reflection factor		
total refraction	Gesamtrefraktion f	toughness, tenaciousness, tenacity <of materials, especially metals>	Zähigkeit f, Zähfestigkeit f, Zähhärte f, Widerstandsfähigkeit f, Festigkeit f, Biegsamkeit f <Werkstoffe, besonders Metalle>
total resistance [coefficient]	Gesamtwiderstandsbeiwert m		
total run-off	Gesamtabfluß m, gesamter Abfluß m		
		toughness	s. a. impact strength

toughness	s. a. notch impact strength	trace metal, tracer metal	Spurenmetall n
Toulon bridge	Toulon-Brücke f	trace nutrient	s. tracer element <bio.>
tourmalin[e] plate, turmalin[e] plate	Turmalinplatte f	trace of impurity	s. trace impurity
tourmalin[e] tongs, turmalin[e] tongs	Turmalinzange f	trace of rays <US>; path of rays, run of rays, ray[-] trajectory	Strahlengang m, Strahlenverlauf m, Strahlenweg m, Strahlenbahn f
Touschek effect	Touschek-Effekt m	trace of the line, trace of the straight line	Spurpunkt m, Spur f der Geraden
towering, castellatus, cas <meteo.>	castellatus, zinnenförmig, türmchenförmig, zinnenartig, cas <Meteo.>	trace of the plane	s. trace of the surface
		trace of the straight line	s. trace of the line
tower telescope, solar tower	Turmteleskop n, Sonnenturm m	trace of the surface; trace of the plane	Spurlinie f; Spurgerade f
town fog	Stadtnebel m, Großstadtnebel m	trace of the surface, trace <cryst.>	Spur f [der Fläche] <Krist.>
Townsend avalanche	Townsend-Lawine f	trace of trajectory, track of trajectory, track	Bahnspur f
Townsend breakdown	Townsend-Durchbruch m, Townsend-Durchschlag m	tracer, labelled atom, tagged atom, indicator, marker <nucl.>	Tracer m, markiertes Atom n, Indikator m <Kern.>
Townsend coefficient	s. Townsend ionization coefficient	tracer	s. a. radioactive tracer <nucl.>
Townsend current	Townsend-Strom m, dunkler Vorstrom m, Vorstrom	tracer	s. a. spike <in isotope dilution analysis>
		tracer amount	s. trace
Townsend discharge, dark discharge, silent discharge	Townsend-Entladung f, Dunkelentladung f, stille Entladung f, dunkle Entladung, dunkler Vorstrom m	tracer analysis	Traceranalyse f, Indikatoranalyse f, Hevesy-Paneth-Analyse f
		tracer compound, labelled compound, tagged compound, isotopically labelled compound	Tracerverbindung f, markierte Verbindung f, Indikatorverbindung f, isotop markierte Verbindung
Townsend discharge mechanism, Townsend mechanism	Townsend-Mechanismus m, Townsendscher Entladungsmechanismus m		
Townsend energy factor (ratio)	Townsendscher Energiefaktor m	tracer concentration	s. trace concentration
Townsend['s] formula, Townsend['s] relation	Townsendsche Beziehung f	tracer detector	Spurenfinder m
Townsend ionization	Townsend-Ionisation f	tracer diffusion	Tracerdiffusion f
Townsend ionization coefficient, Townsend coefficient, ionization coefficient, ionization constant, specific ionization, total specific ionization	Townsend-Koeffizient m, [Townsendscher] Ionisierungskoeffizient m, Ionisierungskonstante f, Townsendsche Stoßzahl f, spezifische Ionisation (Ionisierung) f, differentielle Ionisation, Ionisierungsstärke f, Ionisationsstärke f; Ionisierungszahl f <Gasentladung>	tracer element	Tracerelement n, Leitelement n, Indikatorelement n
		tracer element, trace element, microelement, trace nutrient <bio.>	Spurenelement n, Mikronährstoff m, Mikroelement n, Hochleistungselement n, katalytisches Element n, Spurenstoff m <Bio.>
		tracer investigation	s. tracer study
		tracer isotope	s. isotopic tracer
		tracer metal, trace metal	Spurenmetall n
Townsend mechanism, Townsend discharge mechanism	Townsend-Mechanismus m, Townsendscher Entladungsmechanismus m	tracer method, tracer technique, method of labelled atoms, isotope method	Tracermethode f, Tracerverfahren n, Tracertechnik f, Methode f der markierten Atome, Indikatorverfahren n, Indikatormethode f, Hevesy-Paneth-Verfahren n, Leitisotopenmethode f, Isotopenmethode f
Townsend['s] relation, Townsend['s] formula	Townsendsche Beziehung f		
toxicant, toxic agent, poison	Gift n, Giftstoff m, toxischer Stoff m		
		tracer study, tracer investigation	Traceruntersuchung f, Indikatoruntersuchung f, Untersuchung f mit markierten Atomen, Leitisotopenuntersuchung f
toxicity	Toxizität f, Giftigkeit f		
toxoid	Toxoid n		
T-μ partition function, grand canonical partition function	große kanonische Verteilungsfunktion f		
TPC theorem	s. CPT theorem	tracer technique	s. tracer method
T-pipe; tee, conduit tee; three-way pipe, T	T-Stück n; T-Rohr n, T-Rohrstück n	tracht [of crystal], crystal tracht	Kristalltracht f, Tracht f [des Kristalls]
		tracing	s. tracking
Trabert['s] formula	Trabertsche Formel f	tracing	s. labelling <nucl.>
trace	Schreibspur f	tracing arm <of planimeter>	Fahrarm m, Fahrstange f <Planimeter>
trace, diagonal sum, main diagonal sum, spur, tr <of matrix, operator>	Spur f, Diagonalsumme f, Sp <Matrix, Operator>	tracing distortion	Rillenverzerrung f
trace, streak <of mineral>	Strich m <Mineral>		
trace, trace of the surface <cryst.>	Spur f [der Fläche] <Krist.>	tracing error	Rillenfehler m
trace; trace amount; tracer amount	Spur f, gewichtslose Menge f, Indikatormenge f; Tracermenge f	tracing of the rays, ray tracing	Strahlengangsbestimmung f
		tracing point <of planimeter>	Fahrstift m <Planimeter>
trace analysis	Spurenanalyse f	tracing speed, recording speed, writing speed; writing rate	Registriergeschwindigkeit f, Schreibgeschwindigkeit f
trace chemistry <US>, microchemistry <GB>	Mikrochemie f, Spurenchemie f		
		track, track of the particle, particle track <nucl.>	Spur f [des Teilchens], Teilchenspur f, Partikelspur f <Kern.>
trace concentration; tracer concentration	Spurenkonzentration f, Indikatorkonzentration f; Tracerkonzentration f < ≈ 10^{-9} mol>		
		track	s. a. track of trajectory
		track breadth	s. track width
		track chamber	s. track detector
trace element	s. tracer element <bio.>	track-chamber experiment	Spur[en]kammerexperiment n, Kammerexperiment n
trace impurity, trace of impurity	Spurenverunreinigung f, Indikatorverunreinigung f		

track-chamber photograph	Spur[en]kammeraufnahme f, Kammeraufnahme f	tractional resistance, tractive resistance	Zugwiderstand m; Fahrtwiderstand m
track clogging	Spurverunreinigung f	traction coefficient	s. thrust coefficient
track concentration	s. track density	traction dynamometer, tension dynamometer; tractive force meter	Zugdynamometer n, Zugkraftmesser m, Zugkraftmeßgerät n, Zugmeßgerät n, Zugmesser m
track delineating chamber, gas discharge track chamber, gas discharge track detector	Gasspurenkammer f, Gasspurkammer f, Gasentladungs-Spurdetektor m		
track delineating chamber, isotropic [spark] chamber	isotrope Funkenkammer f	traction relief, traction relieving; tension relief tension relieving	Zugentlastung f
track density, track concentration, concentration of the tracks ‹nucl.›	Spurdichte f, Spurendichte f ‹Kern.›	tractive action	Zugwirkung f
		tractive effort	s. tractive force
track detector, nuclear track detector, tracking detector; [nuclear] track chamber, tracking chamber	Spurdetektor m, Kernspurdetektor m, Spurendetektor; Spurkammer f, Kernspurkammer f, Spurenkammer f	tractive force, tractive effort, traction; tensile (stretching) force, pull, pull[ing] force	Zugkraft f, Zug m
		tractive force meter; tension dynamometer, traction dynamometer	Zugdynamometer n, Zugkraftmesser m, Zugkraftmeßgerät n, Zugmeßgerät n, Zugmesser m
track displacement	Spurverschiebung f		
track distortion	Spurverzerrung f	tractive force meter, tractive force transducer	Zugkraftmeßdose f, Zugkraftdose f. Zugmeßdose f, Zugkraftgeber m
track edge	Spurbegrenzung f		
track fading	Spurfading n, Fading n der Spur	tractive force recorder	Zugkraftschreiber m, Zugschreiber m
tracking; detection; tracing; proof; verification; evidence	Nachweis m, Detektion f, Detektierung f, Beobachtung f, Feststellung f, Entdeckung f; [experimenteller] Beweis m	tractive force transducer, tractive force meter	Zugkraftmeßdose f, Zugkraftdose f, Zugmeßdose f, Zugkraftgeber m
		tractive resistance, tractional resistance	Zugwiderstand m; Fahrtwiderstand m
tracking, tracing	Verfolgung f ‹Spur›		
tracking ‹in insulation›	Kriechwegbildung f	tractor, derived vector ‹math.›	derivierter Vektor m, Traktor m ‹Math.›
		tractor airscrew (propeller, screw), forward airscrew, puller airscrew	Zugschraube f
tracking, following ‹in the trajectory›	Nachlauf m ‹in der Bahn›	tractory	Traktorie f
		tractory of Huyghens, tractrix, Huyghens tractory	Traktrix f, Schleppkurve f, Traktorie f von Huyghens, Hundekurve f
tracking ‹of discharge›	Spurbildung f [bei der Entladung]		
tracking beam	Spurstrahl m	trade, trade wind	Passat m, Passatwind m
tracking chamber	s. track detector	trade inversion	Passatinversion f
tracking circuit	Nachlaufschaltung f	trade-name	Handelsname f, Handelsbezeichnung f, handelsübliche Bezeichnung f
tracking current	s. surface leakage current		
tracking detector	s. track detector	trade wind, trade	Passat m, Passatwind m
tracking noise	s. track noise	traffic channel, route	Leitweg m
tracking of path	Bahnverfolgung f		
		trailing ‹of the spiral arms›	feuerradähnliche Rotation f
tracking path; leakage path ‹el.›	Kriechweg m; Kriechstrecke f ‹El.›	trailing edge, lagging edge, back edge ‹of the pulse›, back pulse front	Rückflanke f, Hinterflanke f, Rückkante f, Hinterkante f, Schleppkante f ‹Impuls›, Impulshinterflanke f, Impulsrückflanke f
tracking radar	Verfolgungsradar n		
tracking resistance, non-tracking quality	Kriechstromfestigkeit f, Gleichstrom-Kriechstromfestigkeit f		
		trailing edge ‹aero.›	Hinterkante f; Abströmkante f ‹Aero.›
track in nuclear emulsion	s. nuclear track	trailing-edge drag, trailing-vortex drag, edge drag, induced drag, drag due to lift, drag from lift, vortex drag, additional drag, additional resistance ‹aero.›	induzierter Widerstand m, Randwiderstand m, zusätzlicher Widerstand ‹Aero.›
track length	Spurenlänge f, Spurlänge f		
track noise, tracking noise	Spurverwaschung f		
track of the nucleus	s. nuclear track		
track of the particle	s. track ‹nucl.›	trailing-edge flap	s. camber changing flap ‹of airfoil›
track of the storm, storm track	Sturmbahn f		
track of trajectory, trace of trajectory, track	Bahnspur f	trailing motion	s. creeping motion ‹bio.›
		trailing point	Abströmungspunkt m
track photograph, nuclear track photograph	Kernspuraufnahme f, Spuraufnahme f	trailing-pointer instrument	Schleppzeigergerät n, Schleppzeigerinstrument n
track placement	Spurlage f	trailing vortex, trailing vorticity	Kantenwirbel m
track population	Bahnzahl f, Spurenzahl f		
track resistant	s. non-tracking	trailing vortex	s. a. tip vortex
track-sensitive volume ‹of cloud chamber›	empfindliches Volumen n ‹Nebelkammer›	trailing-vortex drag	s. trailing-edge drag
		trailing vorticity	s. trailing vortex
track width, width of the track	Spurbreite f	trail of the meteor, meteor trail	Spur f des Meteors, Meteorspur f
track width, track breadth, width of the track ‹nucl.›	Spurbreite f, Spurenbreite f ‹Kern.›	training ‹of cathode›	Einbrennen n, Trainieren n ‹Katode›
		training reactor	Ausbildungsreaktor m, Hochschulreaktor m
traction; tension; pull, pulling	Ziehen n, Zug m, Auseinanderziehen n	train of impulses	s. pulse train
		train of measurand	s. series of measurements
traction; pull[ing]; draw-ing; tug; drag	Ziehen n, Zug m, Fortziehen n; Schleppen n	train of the meteor, meteor train	Schweif m des Meteors, Meteorschweif m
traction	s. a. tractive force		

train of waves, wave train, pulse of waves	Wellenzug *m*, Schwingungszug *m*	transconductance transconductance characteristic, mutual characteristic	*s. a.* transadmittance Steilheitskennlinie *f*, Steilheitscharakteristik *f*
train of waves	*s. a.* pulse train	transconductance constant	Steilheitskonstante *f*
train weather	Rückseitenwetter *n*	transconductance distortion, anode current distortion	Steilheitsverzerrung *f*, Anodenstromverzerrung *f*
trajection	Trajektion *f*		
trajectory, path, pathway, path line, flight path, way	Bahn *f*, Bahnkurve *f*, Bahnlinie *f*, Flugbahn *f*, Trajektorie *f*, Zugstraße *f*, Weg *m*	transconductance-to-capacitance ratio, figure of merit	S/C-Verhältnis *n*, Steilheit/Elektrodenkapazität-Verhältnis *n*
trajectory ‹math.›	Trajektorie *f* ‹Math.›	trans[-]configuration	trans-Konfiguration *f*
trajectory of air [mass], trajectory of air particle, air trajectory	Luftbahn *f*, Lufttrajektorie *f*, Trajektorie *f* der Luftteilchen	transcriber, converter unit ‹num. math.›	Übersetzer *m*, Umschreiber *m*, Umsetzer *m* ‹num. Math.›
trajectory of ejection	Ejektionsbahn *f*	transcription ‹bio.›	Transkription *f*, Umschreibung *f* ‹Bio.›
trajectory of principal extensions (strains)	Hauptdehnungslinie *f*, Hauptdehnungstrajektorie *f*	transcrystalline cleavage, transgranular cleavage	intrakristalline Spaltung *f*, transkristalline Spaltung
trajectory of principal stresses, principal stress trajectory, line of principal stresses	Hauptspannungslinie *f*, Hauptspannungstrajektorie *f*, Hauptlinie *f*, Hauptdehnungslinie *f*	transcrystalline fracture, transgranular fracture, fracture across the grains	intrakristalliner (transkristalliner) Bruch *m*, Bruch quer durch Einzelkristalle
trajectory of projection	*s.* trajectory of the body thrown	transcrystallization transcurium nuclide	*s.* columnar granulation Transcuriumnuklid *n* ‹Nuklid mit einer Ordnungszahl > 96›
trajectory of sound, sound trajectory, sound path	Schallbahn *f*, Schallweg *m*		
trajectory of stress, stress trajectory	Spannungstrajektorie *f*	transcurrent fault, cross fault, proparaclase	Querverwerfung *f*
trajectory of the body thrown, trajectory of projection	Wurfbahn *f*	trans[-]donor	trans-Donator *m*, Transdonator *m*
trajectory of the meteor, meteor path	Bahn *f* des Meteors, Meteorbahn *f*	transducer, communication (transmission, transfer) system	Übertragungssystem *n*
trajectory of the vortex, vortex trajectory, vortex path	Wirbelbahn *f*	transducer, measuring transformer, instrument transformer, transformer, converter, pick-up, sensor detector ‹meas.›	Meßgrößenumformer *m*; Meßwandler *m*, Wandler *m*, Transducer *m*, Transformator *m*, Meßumformer *m*, Meßtransformator *m*, Meßtrafo *m*; Meßgeber *m*, Geber *m*; Taster *m*; Sonde *f*; Aufnehmer *m*; Umsetzer *m*; Sender *m*; Meßwertumformer *m*, Meßwertwandler *m* ‹Meß.›
trajectory of the wind, wind trajectory, wind course, wind path	Windbahn *f*, Windweg *m*		
trajectory of water particle, water trajectory	Wasserbahn *f*		
trajectory parabola	Wurfparabel *f*		
Tralles degree	Tralles-Grad *m*		
trammel, ellipsograph, elliptic trammel	Ellipsograph *m*, Ellipsenzirkel *m*, Ovalzirkel *m*		
tranquil flow, streaming flow, slow flow, subcritical flow ‹hydr.›	ruhiges Fließen *n*, ruhige Strömung *f*, ruhiger Strom *m*, Strömen *n*, strömende Bewegungsart *f* ‹Hydr.›	transducer transducer loss	*s. a.* ultrasonic generator Wandlerverlust *m*
		transducing of experimental values, transduction of experimental values	Meßwertumformung *f*
tranquillization, smoothing ‹e.g. of oscillation, flow›	Beruhigung *f*	transduction ‹bio.› transductor	Transduktion *f* ‹Bio.› Transduktor *m*, gleichstromvormagnetisierbare Drosselspule *f*
trans-acceptor, transacceptor	trans-Akzeptor *m*, Transakzeptor *m*		
transactinide [element], transactinoide	Transaktinoid *n*, Transactinoid *n*, Transaktinid *n*, Transactinid *n*	transductor transection-type glacier, trough glacier	*s. a.* magnetic amplifier Jochgletscher *m*
trans-addition	trans-Addition *f*, Transaddition *f*	trans-effect transelectron, passing electron	Trans-Effekt *m* Transelektron *n*
transadmittance, transconductance	Durchgangsscheinleitwert *m*; Elektronenleitfähigkeit *f*	trans-elimination	trans-Eliminierung *f*, trans-Abspaltung *f*
transadmittance	*s. a.* transconductance	transfer, transference, transport, carrying[-] over	Übertragung *f*; Überführung *f*; Übergang *m*; Transfer *m*
transauroral line	Transauroralinie *f*; rote Polarlichtlinie *f*; Nebellinie *f* ‹Übergang vom höchsten metastabilen in den Grundzustand›	transfer, material pick-up, pick-up material transfer	Werkstoffübertragung *f*, Übertragung *f* von Werkstoffen
transceiver, transmitter receiver	Sende-Empfangs-Gerät *n*, Sendeempfänger *m*, Senderempfänger *m*, Tran[s]ceiver *m*	transfer ‹of relay› transfer ‹num. math.›	Umschlagen *n* ‹Relais› Überführung *f* ‹num. Math.›
transcendality, transcendence, transcendency	Transzendenz *f*	transfer ‹phot.›	Übertragung *f*, Transfer *m* ‹Phot.›
transcendental, transcendental number	transzendente Zahl *f*	transfer	*s. a.* jump
transconductance, gridplate transconductance, mutual conductance, internal conductance; static transconductance, static mutual conductance, short-circuit transconductance, transadmittance, slope [of the emission characteristic], slope conductance	Steilheit *f* [der Elektronenröhre], Röhrensteilheit *f*, Elektronenröhrensteilheit *f*, Kennliniensteilheit *f*, [der Elektronenröhre]; Kurzschlußsteilheit *f*, statische Steilheit, statische Kennliniensteilheit, statische Röhrensteilheit	transfer admittance, forward transadmittance, short-circuit transfer admittance	Übertragungsleitwert *m*, Kernleitwert *m*, Kurzschluß-Kernleitwert *m*, Kopplungsleitwert *m*
transconductance ‹of the transistor›	Steilheit *f* [des Transistors], Transistorsteilheit *f*		

transfer agent	s. carrier	transfer of the length	Längenübertragung f
transfer characteristic	Übertragungscharakteristik f, Übertragungskennlinie f	transferometer, transfer function meter	Transferometer n
transfer characteristic	Übergangscharakteristik f, Übergangskennlinie f, Ausgleichscharakteristik f	transfer orbit	s. transfer trajectory
		transfer overpotential	s. transition overpotential
transfer characteristic, control characteristic	Steuerkennlinie f, Steuercharakteristik f; Steuerstabkennlinie f <Reaktor>	transfer phenomenon <therm.>	Überführungsphänomen n <Therm.>
		transfer polarization	s. transition overpotential
transfer coefficient, transport coefficient	Transportkoeffizient m	transfer process <phot.>	Übertragungsprozeß m <Phot.>
transfer coefficient, transfer factor <el.chem.>	Durchtrittsfaktor m <El. Chem.>	transfer ratio, transfer coefficient, transfer factor <of network>	Übertragungsfaktor m, Übersetzung f, Übertragungsverhältnis n <Vierpol>
transfer coefficient	s. a. heat transfer coefficient		
transfer coefficient	s. a. propagation constant	transfer reaction <el.chem.>	Durchtrittsreaktion f <El. Chem.>
transfer coefficient	s. a. transfer ratio <of network>		
transfer collision	Umladungsstoß m, Stoß m mit Umladung	transfer reaction <nucl.>	Transferreaktion f, Transferkernreaktion f <Kern.>
transfer command	s. jump	transfer reaction	s. a. charge transfer reaction
transfer constant	s. propagation constant	transfer resistance, transmission resistance	Übertragungswiderstand m, Übertragungswirkwiderstand m
transfer container, shipping container, container	Transportbehälter m, Transportkontainer m, Kontainer m, Container m		
		transfer resistor	s. transistor
		transfer ribonucleic acid, transfer RNA, soluble ribonucleic acid, soluble RNA, tRNA, sRNA	Transfer-Ribonukleinsäure f, Überträger-Ribonukleinsäure f, lösliche Ribonukleinsäure f, Transfer-RNS f, Überträger-RNS f, lösliche RNS f, Aminosäure-Akzeptor-RNS f, tRNS, t-RNS, sRNS
transfer current ratio	Stromübertragungsfaktor m [rückwärts]		
transfer effect	Übertragungseffekt m		
transfer element; transfer section	Übertragungsglied n		
transfer ellipse	s. transfer trajectory	transfer RNA	s. transfer ribonucleic acid
transference	s. transfer	transfer section	s. transfer element
transference experiment	Überführungsexperiment n	transfer symmetry	Übertragungssymmetrie f, Kopplungssymmetrie f, Kernsymmetrie f, Umkehrbarkeit f <Vierpol>
transference number, transport number	Überführungszahl f, Hittorfsche Überführungszahl		
		transfer system, communication (transmission) system, transducer	Übertragungssystem n
transference of heat	s. heat transfer		
transfer energy, energy of transfer <therm.>	Überführungsenergie f <Therm.>	transfer technique <chromatography>	Übertragung f, Überführung f, Transfertechnik f <Chromatographie>
transfer entropy	s. entropy of transfer		
transfer equation	Übertragungsgleichung f		
transfer factor, conjugon <bio.>	Transferfaktor m, Konjugon n <Bio.>	transfer theorem for moment of inertia	s. parallel[-] axis theorem
transfer factor	s. a. propagation constant	transfer theory	s. transport theory
transfer factor	s. a. transfer ratio <of network>	transfer trajectory; transfer ellipse; transfer orbit	Übergangsbahn f; Übergangsellipse f
transfer factor	s. a. transfer coefficient <el. chem.>		
		transfer voltage ratio, transmission gain	Spannungsübertragungsfaktor m [rückwärts]
transfer function, performance operator, TF	Übertragungsfunktion f, ÜF		
transfer function meter	s. transferometer	transfiguration of network, transformation of network, network transformation	Netztransfiguration f, Netzumwandlung f
transfer function of the closed-loop system	s. closed-loop transfer function <control>		
transfer function of the open-loop system	s. open-loop transfer function	transfinite diameter	transfiniter Durchmesser m
		transfinite induction	transfinite Induktion f, [transfinite] Rekursion f
transfer impedance	Übertragungsimpedanz f, Übertragungswiderstand m, Kernwiderstand m, Kopplungswiderstand m	transfluence	Transfluenz f
		transfluxor	Transfluxor m
transfer jack, break jack, disconnect jack	Trennklinke f	transfocator	Transfokator m [von Gramatzki]
transfer locus, Nyquist plot, Nyquist locus, response vector locus	Nyquist-Diagramm n, Nyquist-Kurve f, Ortskurve f des Frequenzganges	trans-form, trans-[stereo]isomer, trans-isomeride	trans-Form f, trans-Isomer n
		transform, image function, image <math.>	Transformierte f, Unterfunktion f, Bildfunktion f, Resultatfunktion f <Math.>
transfer matrix; reciprocal transmission matrix	Übertragungsmatrix f, Betriebs-Kettenmatrix f		
transfer mechanical impedance	mechanische Übertragungsimpedanz f		
		transform	s. a. transformation <math.>
transfer medium	s. heat-transfer agent	transformability	Transformierbarkeit f
transfer of air masses, transport (journey) of air masses	Luftmassentransport m, Luftmassenverfrachtung f, Luftmassenversetzung f	transformation, rearrangement, reorganization, transposition <chem.>	Umlagerung f, Umgruppierung f <Chem.>
transfer of constant	s. jump		
transfer of heat, heat transfer, transition of heat, heat transition <from a solid to a streaming fluid in direct contact with it>	Wärmeübergang m <Wärmeaustausch zwischen einem Körper und einem ihn berührenden strömenden Stoff>	transformation <bio.>	Transformation f <Bio.>
		transformation <el.>	Transformation f; Umspannung f <El.>
transfer of heat	s. a. heat transfer	transformation, transform <math.>	Transformation f <Math.>
transfer of momentum	s. momentum transfer		
transfer of solids	s. transport of solids <geo.>		

transformation, rewriting, conversion <of the equation> <math.> — Umformung *f*, Umschreibung *f* <der Gleichung> <Math.>

transformation, transition, phase change, change <met.> — Umwandlung *f*, Übergang *m*, Phasenumwandlung *f*, Phasenübergang *m* <Met.>

transformation, nuclear transformation, transformation of nucleus, atomic transformation, nuclear transmutation, transmutation of nucleus, atomic transmutation <nucl.> — Kernumwandlung *f*, Umwandlung *f* [des Atomkerns], Atomumwandlung *f*, Transmutation *f* <Kern.>

transformation <phot.> — Umbildung *f* <Phot.>

transformation apparatus — s. rectifier

transformation by zones — Zonentransformation *f*

transformation carrying circles into circles — s. circle property

transformation chain — s. disintegration chain

transformation circle — Transformationskreis *m*

transformation constant — s. decay constant

transformation drawing apparatus, mechanical type plotting machine, mechanical type of plotting machine — Umzeichengerät *n*; Luftbildumzeichner *m*

transformation energy, energy of transformation, energy of transition, transition energy — Umwandlungsenergie *f*

transformation enthalpy — s. heat of transformation

transformation entropy, entropy of transformation, entropy of transition, transition entropy — Umwandlungsentropie *f*

transformation equation — Transformationsgleichung *f*

transformation factor [of the discharge gap] — Transformationsfaktor *m* [der Entladungsstrecke]

transformation family — s. radioactive family <nucl.>

transformation group — Transformationsgruppe *f*

transformation heat — s. heat of transformation

transformation hysteresis — Umwandlungshysteresis *f*, Umwandlungshysterese *f*

transformation interval — s. transformation range

transformation into firn (névé) — Verfirnung *f*

transformation line — Transformationsleitung *f*

transformation loop — Transformationsschleife *f*

transformation matrix, matrix of the transformation — Transformationsmatrix *f*, Koeffizientenmatrix *f* der Transformation·

transformation network — Transformationsvierpol *m*

transformation of air mass — Umwandlung *f* der Luftmasse

transformation of Clebsch, Clebsch['s] transformation — Clebsch-Transformation *f*, Clebschsche Transformation *f*

transformation of co-ordinates, co-ordinate transformation, change of co-ordinates — Koordinatentransformation *f*, Koordinatenwechsel *m*

transformation of energy, energy transformation, conversion of energy, energy conversion, power conversion — Energieumwandlung *f*, Energieumformung *f*, Energieumsetzung *f*, Energieumsatz *m*, Energietransformation *f*, Umwandlung *f* von Energie

transformation of first order — s. first order transition

transformation of heat flow, heat flow transformation — Wärmeflußtransformation *f*

transformation of network, transfiguration of network, network transformation — Netztransfiguration *f*, Netzumwandlung *f*

transformation of n-th order — s. n-th order transition

transformation of nucleus — s. nuclear transformation

transformation of second order — s. second order transition

transformation of similitude — s. homothetic transformation

transformation of variables, variable transformation, change of variables <bio., stat.> — Variablentransformation *f* <Bio., Stat.>

transformation operator — Transformationsoperator *m*

transformation period — Umwandlungsperiode *f*, Umwandlungszeit *f*

transformation period — s. a. transmutation period

transformation point, transformation temperature, transition point (temperature); critical point (temperature) <of steel> — Umwandlungspunkt *m*, Umwandlungstemperatur *f*, Transformationspunkt *m*, Transformationstemperatur *f*, Tp.

transformation point on cooling — s. recalescence point

transformation point on heating — s. decalescence point

transformation pressure — Umwandlungsdruck *m*

transformation product, transmutation product — Umwandlungsprodukt *n*

transformation property — Transformationseigenschaft *f*

transformation range, transformation interval — Transformationsintervall *n*, Transformationsbereich *m*, Umwandlungsbereich *m*; Einfriergebiet *n*, Einfrierbereich *m* <bei Polymeren>

transformation rate, transition rate — Umwandlungsgeschwindigkeit *f*

transformation ratio <of transformer> — Übersetzung *f*, Übersetzungsverhältnis *n*, Transformatorübersetzungsverhältnis *n*, Umspannungsverhältnis *n*, Transformationsverhältnis *n*, Transformationskoeffizient *m* <Transformator>

transformation series — s. disintegration series

transformations per minute — s. transmutations per minute

transformations per second — s. transmutations per second

transformation stage structure — Zwischenstufengefüge *n*, Bainit *m*

transformation superplasticity, transition superplasticity — Umwandlungs-Superplastizität *f*

transformation temperature — s. transformation point

transformation theory — Transformationstheorie *f*, [quantenmechanische] Darstellungstheorie *f*

transformation to principal axes, principal[-] axis transformation — Hauptachsentransformation *f*, Transformation *f* auf die Hauptachsen

transformer — Transformator *m*, Trafo *m*; Umspanner *m*

transformer — s. a. ultrasonic generator

transformer — s. a. transducer <meas.>

transformer bridge — Transformatorbrücke *f*

transformer container — s. transformer shell

transformer core — Transformatorkern *m*

transformer-core yoke; magnetic yoke, magnetic return path — magnetische Rückleitung *f*, magnetischer Rückschluß *m*, Rückschlußjoch *n*; Rückschlußschenkel *m*

transformer coupling — Transformator[en]kopplung *f*, Übertragerkopplung *f*, transformatorische (gegeninduktive) Kopplung *f*; Transformatorankopplung *f*

transformer equivalent circuit — Transformatorersatzschaltung *f*, Transformatorersatzschaltbild *n*

transformer feedback	Transformatorrückkopplung f, transformatorische Rückkopplung f	transient function	s. transient
transformer iron, transformer lamination, transformer sheet	Transformatorenblech n, Transformatorblech n	transient longitudinal reactance	Stoßlängsreaktanz f
		transient motion, Brownian motion, Brownian movement	Brownsche Bewegung f, Brownsche Molekularbewegung f
transformer of ratio 1:1, repeater coil, repeater	Übertrager m	transient motion	Einschwingbewegung f
transformer principle	Transformatorprinzip n	transient nutation, Torrey oscillation	Torrey-Schwingung f, Übergangsnutation f
transformer sheet	s. transformer iron	transient oscillation, build-up	Einschwingen n
transformer shell (tank), transformer container	Transformatormantel m, Transformatorgehäuse n		
transforming camera	s. rectifier	transient oscillation	gedämpfte Schwingung f eines Stromkreises nach plötzlicher Störung
transforming function	Abbildungsfunktion f		
transfusion	Transfusion f	transient period <of reactor>	vorübergehende Periode f, intermediäre Periode <Reaktor>
transfusion rate	Transfusionsgeschwindigkeit f	transient period <of oscillation>	s. a. transient time
transgranular cleavage, transcrystalline cleavage	intrakristalline Spaltung f, transkristalline Spaltung	transient phenomenon	s. transient
transgranular fracture	s. transcrystalline fracture	transient problem	Einschwingproblem n; Anlaufproblem n
transgranulation	s. columnar granulation		
transgressing sea	transgredierendes Meer n	transient process, transient <control>	Übergangsprozeß m <Regelung>
transgression	Transgression f, Meeresüberflutung f, Überflutung f durch das Meer	transient process	s. a. transient
transgression	s. a. overrun	transient protection, overvoltage protection, surge protection	Überspannungsschutz m
transgressive discordance, transgressive stratification	übergreifende Lagerung f, transgrediente Lagerung		
		transient pulse	Einschwingimpuls m
		transient pulse, make pulse	Einschaltstoß m, Einschaltstromstoß m
transgrid action	s. penetrance	transient radioactive equilibrium	s. transient equilibrium
transient, transient phenomenon	Übergangserscheinung f, Übergangsphänomen n, Transient m	transient reactance	Übergangsreaktanz f, transitorische Reaktanz f, Transientreaktanz f; Stoßreaktanz f, Stoßblindwiderstand m
transient, transient function	Transiente f, Übergangsfunktion f; Einschaltfunktion f		
transient, electrical transient, transient process	Ausgleichsvorgang m, Ausgleichsprozeß m, Übergangsprozeß m, Übergangsvorgang m; Einschwing[ungs]vorgang m, Einschwingprozeß m; Einschaltvorgang m, Einschaltprozeß m; Umschaltvorgang m, Umschaltprozeß m	transient region	s. boundary
		transient response, transient characteristic, jump characteristic, square-wave response; transient behaviour	Sprungcharakteristik f, Sprungkennlinie f; Einschwingverhalten n
transient, transient process <control>	Übergangsprozeß m <Regelung>	transient response	s. a. transient behaviour
transient	s. a. transient state	transient response	s. a. unit[-] step response
transient	s. a. transient voltage	transient shower, passing shower, local shower	Strichregen m
transient behaviour; transient response	Übergangsverhalten n; Übergangsbetrieb m	transient state, transient, transitional state	Ausgleichszustand m, Übergangszustand m, nichtstationärer (vorübergehender, flüchtiger) Zustand m, Nichtgleichgewichtszustand m; Einschwingzustand m
transient behaviour	s. a. transient response		
transient buckling	Durchschlag m		
transient characteristic	s. transient response		
transient characteristic of thyratron, E_p/E_g characteristic of thyratron	Übergangssteuerkennlinie f des Thyratrons	transient surge, voltage transient	Stoßspannungswelle f
		transient time	s. build-up time
transient creep, beta flow, primary creep, initial creep, initial flow	Übergangskriechen n, erstes Kriechstadium n, erster Bereich m der Kriechkurve	transient transverse reactance	Stoßquerreaktanz f
		transient voltage, restriking voltage	Übergangsspannung f; Einschwingspannung f; flüchtige Spannung f
transient current; making current; inrush current	Einschaltstrom m; Übergangsstrom m; Ausgleichsstrom m; flüchtiger Strom m; Anpassungsstrom m		
		transient voltage, voltage transient, transient	vorübergehende Überspannung f, momentane Überspannung
		transient voltage	s. a. instantaneous voltage
transient decay current	Nachwirkungsstrom m	transillumination, illumination in transmitted light	Durchlichtbeleuchtung f, Transillumination f; Durchleuchtung f
transient equilibrium, transient radioactive equilibrium, dynamic equilibrium, kinetic equilibrium	laufendes [radioaktives] Gleichgewicht n, [radioaktives] Laufgleichgewicht n, dynamisches [radioaktives] Gleichgewicht, [radioaktives] Übergangsgleichgewicht n		
		transimpedance	reziproke Steilheit f
		transinformation	Transinformation f, richtig übermittelte Information f, Wirkinformation f
transient flow	s. transition flow		
transient formation	Übergangskomplex m	transinformation content	Transinformationsgehalt m

trans-isomer[ide], trans-stereoisomer, trans-form	trans-Form f, trans-Isomer n	transitional state transitional structure	s. transient state Übergangsstruktur f
transistor; transistor triode	Transistor m, Halbleitertriode f, Transistortriode f, Kristalltriode f	transition between levels, interlevel transition	Niveauübergang m
transistor action	Transistoreffekt m, Transistorwirkung f	transition capacitance	s. barrier-layer capacitance
		transition colour	Übergangsfarbe f
		transition conductor	Übergangsleiter m, Übergangs-Typ-Leiter m
transistor amplifier	Transistorverstärker m, Kristallverstärker m	transition cone transition curve	Übergangskegel m Übergangskurve f, Transitionskurve f
		transition effect <radiobiology>	Transitionseffekt m, Energieverteilungseffekt m <Radiobiologie>
transistor analyzer	Transistorenanalysator m		
transistor characteristic	Transistorkennlinie f	transition element	s. transition metal
transistor circuit	Transistorschaltung f	transition energy, energy of transformation, transformation energy, energy of transition	Umwandlungsenergie f
transistored	s. transistorized		
transistor electronics	Transistorelektronik f		
		transition energy <of charged particle> <acc.>	Transitionsenergie f, kritische Energie f <geladenes Teilchen> <Beschl.>
transistor equivalent circuit	Transistorersatzschaltbild n, Transistorersatzschaltung f	transition enthalpy	s. heat of transformation
		transition entropy, entropy of transformation, transformation entropy, entropy of transition	Umwandlungsentropie f
transistor gain	Transistorverstärkung f, Transistorverstärkungsfaktor m		
transistor in coaxial packing	s. coaxial transistor		
transistorized, transistored	transistorisiert, transistorbestückt	transition flow, transient flow	Übergangsströmung f
transistorized circuit	transistorisierte Schaltung f, Transistorschaltung f	transition frequency	Übergangsfrequenz f
		transition frequency, jump frequency	Sprungfrequenz f
transistor noise	Transistorrauschen n	transition from laminar to turbulent flow	s. transition to turbulence
transistor physics	Transistorphysik f	transition half-life	Übergangshalbwertzeit f
		transition heat	s. heat of transformation
		transition index, transition number	Umschlag[s]zahl f
transistor structure as a photoelectric cell, phototransistor, photistor, phototriode	Phototransistor m, lichtempfindlicher Transistor m, Phototriode f		
		transition interval [of indicator], indicator range, indicator interval	Umschlagbereich m, Umschlagsbereich m, Umschlagsgebiet n, Umschlag[s]intervall n <Farbindikator>
transistor switch, switching transistor	Schalttransistor m, Schaltertransistor m		
		transition layer	Übergangsschicht f
		transition line	Umschlag[s]linie f
transistor tetrode	s. semiconductor tetrode		
transistor thermal resistance, thermal resistance <of transistor>	thermischer Widerstand m [des Transistors]	transition loss	Übergangsverlust m
transistor triode	s. transistor		
transit	s. drift		
transit	s. passage <of a star>	transition matrix	Übergangsmatrix f
transit	s. passing <of light, particles>	transition matrix	s. a. scattering matrix <cl.>
transit	s. transit instrument <astr.>	transition metal, transition[al] element, meta-element	Übergangsmetall n, Übergangselement n
transit across the solar disk	Vorübergang m vor der Sonne[nscheibe]		
transit angle; transit phase angle, bunching angle	Laufwinkel m, Laufzeitwinkel m	transition moment	Übergangsmoment n
		transition multipole moment	Übergangsmultipolmoment n
transit-circle, meridian circle, meridian instrument	Meridiankreis m	transition number	s. transition index
		transition of first order	s. first order transition
		transition of heat	s. transfer of heat
transit instrument, passage instrument, transit <astr.>	Durchgangsinstrument n, Passageninstrument n, Passageinstrument n <Astr.>	transition of n-th order	s. n-th order transition
		transition of second order	s. second order transition
		transition of the "lambda" type	s. second order transition
transition <bio.>	Transition f <bio.>	transition operator	Übergangsoperator m
transition, transformation, phase change, change <met.>	Umwandlung f, Übergang m, Phasenwandlung f, Phasenübergang m <Met.>	transition overpotential, transfer overpotential, transition polarization, transfer polarization	Durchtrittsüberspannung f; Durchtrittspolarisation f
transition, jump, jumping <qu.>	Übergang m, Sprung m <Qu.>	transition point; transition temperature	Übergangspunkt m; Übergangstemperatur f; Umschlag[s]temperatur f, Umschlag[s]punkt m <Schlagzähigkeit>
transition	s. a. transition to turbulence <aero., hydr.>		
transitional climate	Übergangsklima n		
transitional coupling	transitionale Kopplung f	transition point [of indicator]	Umschlag[s]punkt m <Farbindikator>
transitional element	s. transition metal		
transitional Knudsen number	Übergangs-Knudsen-Zahl f	transition point	s. transition temperature

transition point <from laminar to turbulent flow>, point of transition <aero., hydr.>	Umschlag[s]punkt m, Umschlagstelle f <Aero., Hydr.>	transition wire, trip wire, tripping wire	Stolperdraht m, Turbulenzdraht m
transition point	s. a. transformation point <of steel>	transition zone, transition region <geo.>	Übergangsgebiet n, Übergangszone f, Übergangsbereich m <Geo.>
transition polarization	s. transition overpotential	transitive group	transitive Gruppe f
transition probability <also stat.>	Übergangswahrscheinlichkeit f <auch Stat.>	transitive law	Transitivgesetz n
transition probability of Einstein	s. Einstein coefficient	transitiveness, transitivity	Transitivität f
transition range <aero., hydr.>	Umschlagsgebiet n, Umschlaggebiet n <Aero., Hydr.>	transit level, theodolite level, tacheometer level	Nivelliertachymeter n
transition rate, transformation rate	Umwandlungsgeschwindigkeit f	transitory stimulus	Übergangsreiz m
transition rate	Übergangsrate f	transit phase angle	s. transit angle
transition régime (regime) <of turbulent flow>	Übergangsbereich m <turbulente Rohrströmung>	transitron multivibrator	Transitronmultivibrator m
		transit through the central meridian	s. central-meridian passage
transition region, inversion region	Inversionszone f, Inversionsbereich m, Inversionsgebiet n	transit through the meridian	s. meridian transit
transition region, transition zone <geo.>	Übergangsgebiet n, Übergangszone f, Übergangsbereich m <Geo.>	transit time <of relay>	Umschlag[s]zeit f <Relais>
transition region [of core], F region <geo.>	Kernzwischenschicht f, Kernübergangsschicht f, Zwischenschicht (Übergangsschicht) f des Kerns, F-Schicht f, F-Schale f <Geo.>	transit time, travel time, time of travel <el.>	Laufzeit f <El.>
		transit time, time of flight, flight time <nucl.>	Flugzeit f, Laufzeit f <Kern.>
		transit time	s. a. transition time
		transit time	s. a. time of operation <of relay>
transition region [of mantle], C region <geo.>	Mantelzwischenschicht f, Zwischenschicht f [des Mantels], C-Schicht f, C-Schale f <Geo.>	transit time	s. a. travelling time <geo., ac.>
		transit time compensation, transit time correction	Laufzeitausgleich m
transition region, interface, junction region, junction transition region <semi.>	Übergangszone f, Übergangsgebiet n, Übergangsbereich m <Halb.>	transit time delay	Laufzeitverzögerung f
		transit-time difference	Laufzeitdifferenz f, Laufzeitunterschied m
transition region capacitance	s. barrier-layer capacitance	transit time distortion	s. phase distortion
transition relations	Übergangsrelationen fpl	transit time error; delay error, phase-delay error	Laufzeitfehler m
transition resistance, contact resistance <el.chem.>	Übergangswiderstand m <El.Chem.>	transit-time oscillation	Laufzeitschwingung f
transition Reynolds number	s. critical Reynolds number	transit-time oscillator, travelling-wave-tube oscillator, travelling-wave oscillator	Laufzeitoszillator m, Laufzeitgenerator m
transition-state theory, theory of absolute reaction rates, absolute reaction rate theory	Theorie f des Übergangszustandes, Theorie des aktivierten Komplexes, Theorie der absoluten Reaktionsgeschwindigkeit	transit time phenomenon, velocity-modulation effect	Laufzeiterscheinung f, Laufzeiteffekt m, Laufzeiteinfluß m
		transit-time region	Laufzeitgebiet n
transition superplasticity, transformation superplasticity	Umwandlungs-Superplastizität f	transit-time spectrometer	s. time-of-flight spectrometer
transition temperature, transition point, critical temperature, critical point <of superconductor>, superconducting transition temperature	Sprungtemperatur f, Sprungpunkt m, Übergangstemperatur f, Übergangspunkt m <Supraleiter>	transit traverse, traverse, traverse line, theodolite traverse <geo.>	Polygonzug m, Streckenzug m, Linienzug m, Theodolitzug m <Geo.>
		translation	s. translational motion
		translation <bio.>	Translation f, Übersetzung f <Bio.>
		translation <cryst.>	Schiebung f <Krist.>
transition temperature <el.>	Übergangstemperatur f <El.>	translation <math.>	Translation f <Math.>
transition temperature	s. a. transformation point	translation <math.>	Umrechnung f, Umwertung f <Math.>
transition temperature	s. a. transition point		
transition time, transit time	Übergangszeit f	translation, parallel displacement, parallel shift <mech.>	Translation f, Parallelverschiebung f, [translatorische] Verschiebung f <Mech.>
transition time	„transition time" f, Transitionszeit f, Sprungzeit f		
transition time	s. a. build-up time	translation <tv.>	Umsetzung f <Fs.>
transition to turbulence, origin of turbulence	Turbulenzentstehung f	translational acceleration	Translationsbeschleunigung f
transition to turbulence (turbulent flow), transition from laminar to turbulent flow, transition <aero., hydr.>	Umschlag m laminar-turbulent, laminar-turbulenter Umschlag, turbulenter Umschlag, Umschlag, Turbulentwerden n der Strömung <Aero., Hydr.>	translational characteristic temperature	charakteristische Temperatur f der Translation, charakteristische Translationstemperatur f
		translational degree of freedom	Translationsfreiheitsgrad m
		translational energy [of molecule]	Translationsenergie f [des Moleküls]
transition to turbulence in boundary layer	s. boundary-layer transition		
transition-type galaxy, transition-type nebula	S0-Spirale f, SB0-Spirale f	translational enthalpy	s. translational heat
		translational entropy	Translationsentropie f

translational group	s. translation group	transmission, transparency, transmittance <phot.>	Transparenz f, Durchlassung f, Durchlässigkeit f, Transmission f <Phot.>
translational heat [capacity]; translational enthalpy	Translationswärme f, Translationswärmekapazität f; Translationsenthalpie f	transmission	s. passing <of light, particles>
		transmission agent	s. transmission medium
translational motion, translational movement, motion of translation, translation movement (motion), translation, progressive (advancing) motion	Translation f, Translationsbewegung f, translatorische Bewegung f, fortschreitende Bewegung, Fortschreitung f	transmission band, transmitted frequency band, transmission region	Übertragungsbereich m, Übertragungsfrequenzband n, Übertragungsband n
		transmission band; pass[-]band, filter range; pass range; transmission range, free transmission range	Durchlässigkeitsbereich m, Durchlässigkeitsband n, Durchlaßbereich m; nutzbare Bandbreite f
translational partition function	Translationszustandssumme f, Translationsanteil m der Zustandsfunktion	transmission band <spectr.>	Transmissionsbande f <Spektr.>
translational state	Translationszustand m	transmission beam method, transmission method <nucl.>	Durchstrahlungsverfahren n, Durchstrahlungsmethode f, Transmissionsmethode f <Kern.>
translational symmetry	Translationssymmetrie f		
translational temperature	Translationstemperatur f	transmission Čerenkov counter	Transmissions-Čerenkov-Zähler m
translational vibration	Translationsschwingung f	transmission channel	s. communication channel
translational wave, wave of translation, translatory wave	Translationswelle f	transmission coefficient <for wave>	Durchlaßkoeffizient m, Durchlässigkeitskoeffizient m <für Wellen>
translation component	Translationskomponente f, translativer Bestandteil m [der Bewegung]	transmission coefficient <of antenna>	Übertragungskoeffizient m <Antenne>
translation curve	Schiebkurve f, Erzeugende f der Translationsfläche	transmission coefficient <of the atmosphere>	Transmissionsfaktor m, Transmissionskoeffizient m, Durchlässigkeitsfaktor m <Atmosphäre>
translation field	Translationsfeld n		
translation formula for variance <stat.>	Verschiebungssatz m <Stat.>	transmission coefficient, transmission factor <control>	Übertragungsfaktor m <Regelung>
translation group, translational group, group of translations	Translationsgruppe f		
translation invariant	Schiebungsinvariante f, Translationsinvariante f	transmission coefficient <qu.>	Transmissionskoeffizient m, Durchlaßkoeffizient m <Qu.>
translation[-] invariant	translationsinvariant	transmission coefficient	s. a. propagation constant
		transmission coefficient [for sound]	s. acoustic transmission factor <ac.>
translation lattice	s. Bravais lattice	transmission constant	s. propagation constant
translation motion (movement)	s. translational motion	transmission cross-section	Übertragungs[wirkungs]querschnitt m
translation of the wave	s. wave propagation	transmission cross-section <nucl.>	Transmissionsquerschnitt m, Transmissions-Wirkungsquerschnitt m, Durchlaßquerschnitt m <Kern.>
translation period	Translationsperiode f		
translation plane, Veblen-Wedderburn plane <math.>	Translationsebene f, Veblen-Wedderburn-Ebene f <Math.>	transmission curve	Dosisleistungs-Absorberdicke-Kurve f, Absorptionskurve f
translation slip	Translationsgleitung f		
translation surface	Translationsfläche f, Schiebfläche f	transmission curve <opt.>	Durchlässigkeitskurve f <Opt.>
translator	Umrechner m, Umwerter m, Zuordner m, Translator m	transmission density	s. optical density
		transmission diagram	Sendediagramm n, Sendeantennendiagramm n
translator <tv.>	Umsetzer m <Fs.>		
translatory	s. movable		
translatory flow	Translationsströmung f, translatorische Strömung f	transmission direction	s. forward direction
		transmission dynamometer	Transmissionsdynamometer n
translatory shift	s. slip		
translatory velocity, velocity of translation	Translationsgeschwindigkeit f	transmission échelon	Transmissionsstufengitter n
		transmission efficiency	Übertragungswirkungsgrad m
translatory wave	s. translational wave		
translocation (of chromosome), chromosome translocation	Chromosomenstückverlagerung f, Chromosomentranslokation f, Translokation f	transmission electron diffraction	Transmissionselektronenbeugung f, Elektronenbeugung f in Durchstrahlung
		transmission electron microscope	s. transmission-type electron microscope
translucency, diaphanousness, diaphaneity	Diaphanität f	transmission electron microscopy, transmission microscopy, microscopy by transmission, TEM	Durchstrahlungselektronenmikroskopie f
translucent, diaphanous	durchscheinend, diaphan		
translucent glass	leichttrübes Glas n		
translucent light, transmitted light, permeating light	Durchlicht n		
		transmission equivalent	s. network transmission equivalent
translucide (translucidus) cloud	durchscheinende Wolke f, Translucidusform f	transmission error	Übertragungsfehler m
transmission	Fortleitung f	transmission experiment	Transmissionsexperiment n, Durchgangsversuch m, Durchstrahlungsexperiment n
transmission <of radiation, light>	Durchlassung f, Transmission f <Strahlung, Licht>		
transmission <el.>	Übertragung f, Transmission f; Wellenleitung f; Übermittlung f; Sendung f <El.>		
transmission <el. opt.>	Durchstrahlung f <El. Opt.>		
transmission <mech.>	Transmission f; Übertragung f <Mech.>		

transmission 910

transmission factor, total transmission factor, transmittance <US>, total transmittance <US>, transmissivity	[totaler] Durchlaßgrad m, [totaler] Transmissionsgrad m, Durchlässigkeit f, Lichtdurchlässigkeit f, Lichtdurchlässigkeitsfaktor m, Durchlässigkeitsgrad m, Durchlassungsvermögen n <Opt.>; Strahlendurchlässigkeit f, Strahlungsdurchlässigkeit f
transmission factor	s. a. transmission constant
transmission factor	s. transmission coefficient <control>
transmission factor [for sound]	s. acoustic transmission factor <ac.>
transmission gain, modulation gain	Sendegewinn m [für Modulationsverfahren]
transmission gain, transfer voltage ratio	Spannungsübertragungsfaktor m [rückwärts]
transmission grating	Transmissionsgitter n, Durchlaßgitter n
transmission index	Übertragungsindex m
transmission line	Übertragungsleitung f
transmission loss	Übertragungsverlust m, Übertragungsdämpfung f
transmission matrix	Übertragungsmatrix f, Transmissionsmatrix f
transmission measuring set, TMS	Pegelbildgerät n
transmission medium, communication medium, transmission agent	Übertragungsmittel n, Übertragungsmedium n
transmission method	s. transmission beam method <nucl.>
transmission microscope	s. microscope arranged for transillumination
transmission microscope	s. a. transmission-type electron microscope
transmission microscopy	s. transmission electron microscopy
transmission modulation, transmitting modulation	Modulation f des Transmissionsgrades, Sendemodulation f
transmission of heat, heat transmission, passage of heat, heat passage <from one fluid through a solid wall to another fluid>	Wärmedurchgang m <Wärmeaustausch zwischen zwei strömenden Stoffen, die durch eine feste Wandung voneinander getrennt sind>
transmission of heat	s. a. heat transfer
transmission of light, light transmission; permeability to light; light permeability (perviousness)	Lichtdurchlässigkeit f; Lichtdurchlassung f
transmission of motion (movement)	Bewegungsübertragung f, Bewegungsfortleitung f, Bewegungsfortpflanzung f, Transmission f
transmission of pressure, pressure propagation (transmission)	Druckfortpflanzung f, Druckübertragung f
transmission of sound, sound transmission	Schallübertragung f; Tonübertragung f
transmission of sound, sound transmission	Schalldurchgang m, Schalltransmission f
transmission of stimulus	s. stimulus conduction <bio.>
transmission optical density	s. optical density
transmission performance	s. sound transmission quality
transmission plane, plane of transmission	Transmissionsebene f
transmission power	s. transmitting power
transmission pulse technique; transmission ultrasonic materials testing	Durchschallungsprüfung f; Schalldurchstrahlungsverfahren n
transmission quality	s. sound transmission quality
transmission radiometric materials testing	s. radiometric materials testing
transmission range	s. transmission band
transmission range formula, range formula	Reichweitenformel f
transmission rate, transmission speed; speed of transmission	Übertragungsgeschwindigkeit f, Signalübertragungsgeschwindigkeit f; Fortleitungsgeschwindigkeit f
transmission ratio, gear ratio, ratio of transmission	Übersetzung f, Übersetzungsverhältnis n
transmission region	s. transmission band
transmission resistance, transfer resistance	Übertragungswiderstand m, Übertragungswirkwiderstand m
transmission speed	s. transmission rate
transmission symmetry	Übertragungssymmetrie f
transmission system, communication system, transfer system, transducer	Übertragungssystem n
transmission target	Transmissionstarget n
transmission technique of X-ray crystallographic analysis	Röntgen-Durchstrahl[ungs]verfahren n, Durchstrahlungsverfahren, Durchstrahlverfahren n
transmission time <bio.>	Leitungszeit f <Bio.>
transmission-type cavity maser, two-port cavity maser, two-jet maser, two-beam maser	Transmissionshohlraummaser m, Zweistrahlmaser m
transmission-type electron microscope, transmission [electron] microscope	Durchstrahlungsmikroskop n, Durchstrahlungselektronenmikroskop n, Transmissionselektronenmikroskop n
transmission ultrasonic materials testing	s. transmission pulse technique
transmissivity, internal transmission factor of unit length (thickness), transmitting power, transmittivity	Durchsichtigkeitsmodul m; Durchsichtigkeitsgrad m, bezogen auf die Längeneinheit; Reintransmissionsmodul m; Reintransmissionsgrad m, bezogen auf die Längeneinheit; Reintransmissionsgrad für die Schichtdicke Eins
transmissivity	s. a. transmission factor
transmissometer	Transmissometer n
transmittance	s. transmission factor <US>
transmittance, transparency, transmission <phot.>	Transparenz f, Durchlassung f, Durchlässigkeit f, Transmission f <Phot.>
transmitted colour	s. colour of the body in transmitted light
transmitted frequency band, transmission band, transmission region	Übertragungsbereich m, Übertragungsfrequenzband n, Übertragungsband n
transmitted fringe	s. interference fringe by transmission
transmitted intensity, part of transmitted intensity	durchgelassene Intensität f, Bruchteil (Anteil) m der durchgelassenen Intensität, durchgelassener Intensitätsanteil m
transmitted light, translucent light, permeating light	Durchlicht n
transmitted-light bright-field condenser	Durchlicht-Hellfeldkondensor m
transmitted-light bright-field microscopy, bright-field microscopy in transmitted light	Durchlicht-Hellfeldmikroskopie f
transmitted-light condenser, condenser for transillumination	Durchlichtkondensor m
transmitted-light dark-field condenser	Durchlicht-Dunkelfeldkondensor m
transmitted-light dark-field microscopy, dark-field microscopy in transmitted light	Durchlicht-Dunkelfeldmikroskopie f
transmitted-light microscope	s. microscope arranged for transillumination
transmitted-light microscopy, microscopy in transmitted light	Durchlichtmikroskopie f
transmitted load	mittelbare Belastung f
transmitted power, transported power	übertragene Leistung f; Durchgangsleistung f

transmitted power meter	Durchgangsleistungsmesser m, Durchgangswattmeter n
transmitter, transmitting set, sender	Sender m; Hochfrequenzgenerator m, HF-Generator m
transmitter	Transmitter m, Meßgeber m mit einheitlichen Ausgangsdaten
transmitter <bio.>	Transmitter m, Neurotransmitter m <Bio.>
transmitter	s. a. telephone transmitter
transmitter aerial (antenna)	s. transmitting aerial <el.>
transmitter diaphragm; microphone diaphragm	Mikrophonmembran f
transmitter diversity	Senderdiversity n, Ablagewellenfunk m
transmitter inset	s. telephone transmitter
transmitter noise; microphone noise, microphone burning	Mikrophonrauschen n, Mikrophongeräusch n
transmitter receiver, transceiver	Sende-Empfangs-Gerät n, Sendeempfänger m, Senderempfänger m, Tran[s]ceiver m
transmitter-receiver cell, TR cell	Sperröhre f
transmitter-responder, transponder	Transponder m, TSP
transmitter tube	s. transmitting tube
transmitter unit	s. telephone transmitter
transmitting aerial (antenna), emitting (sending, transmitter) antenna, transmitter aerial <el.>	Sendeantenne f; Senderantenne f; Strahler m <El.>
transmitting direction	s. forward direction
transmitting light	s. transparent
transmitting modulation	s. transmission modulation
transmitting power, transmission power, sending power	Sendeleistung f
transmitting power	s. a. transmissivity
transmitting set	s. transmitter
transmitting tube, transmitting valve, sending tube, transmitter tube	Senderöhre f
transmitting wave	Übertragungswelle f
transmittivity	s. transmissivity
transmodulation	s. cross modulation
transmutation	s. nuclear transformation
transmutation constant	s. decay constant
transmutation of nucleus	s. nuclear transformation
transmutation period, transformation (decay) period, disintegration period (time), decay time <nucl.>	Umwandlungszeit f, Zerfallszeit f <Kern.>
transmutation probability	s. nuclear transformation probability <nucl.>
transmutation product, transformation product	Umwandlungsprodukt n
transmutation rate	s. disintegration rate <nucl.>
transmutation rate	s. nuclear transformation probability <nucl.>
transmutations per minute, transformations per minute, disintegrations per minute, tpm, dpm	Anzahl (Zahl) f der Zerfälle pro Minute, Zerfälle mpl pro Minute, Zerf./min, tpm-Zahl f, tpm-Einheit f, tpm
transmutations per second, transformations per second, disintegrations per second, tps, dps	Anzahl (Zahl) f der Zerfälle pro Sekunde, Zerfälle mpl pro Sekunde, Zerf./s, tps-Zahl f, tps-Einheit f, tps
transonic, transsonic	schallnah, transsonisch
transonic	s. a. transonic flow
transonic equation	schallnahe gasdynamische Gleichung f
transonic flow, transonic	schallnahe (transsonische) Strömung f
transonic nozzle	transsonische Düse f
transonic range (regime)	s. transonic region
transonic region, transonic range; transonic regime	schallnaher Bereich m, Transsonikbereich m, transsonischer Bereich, Schallgrenzbereich m
transonics	Aerodynamik f im Schallgrenzbereich, schallnahe Aerodynamik
transonic wind tunnel	transsonischer Windkanal m, Transsonikwindkanal m
transosonde	Transosonde f; Transozeansonde f
transparence	s. penetrance
transparence, transparency <opt.>	Durchsichtigkeit f, Transparenz f <Opt.>
transparency, transmittance, transmission <phot.>	Transparenz f, Durchlassung f, Durchlässigkeit f, Transmission f <Phot.>
transparency meter	Transparenzmesser m
transparency of the potential barrier	s. barrier factor
transparency of water	Sichttiefe f
transparent, clear, limpid <e.g. of water>	klar, durchsichtig <z. B. Wasser>
transparent <to light, electromagnetic radiation>; transmitting light, permeable to light; radiation transparent	durchsichtig, durchlässig, transparent <für Licht, elektromagnetische Strahlung>; lichtdurchlässig; strahlungsdurchlässig, strahlendurchlässig
transparent, penetrable <to particles>	durchlässig <für Teilchen>
transparent colour	Lasurfarbe f, nichtdeckende Farbe f, Nichtdeckfarbe f
transparent nucleus model	durchlässiges Kernmodell n
transparent to infra-red [rays]	s. infra-red transmitting
transparent to ultra-violet [rays]	s. ultra-violet transmitting
transparent window	Strahlenaustrittsfenster n
transpassivation	Transpassivierung f
transpassivity	Transpassivität f
transpiration	Transpiration f, produktive Verdunstung f
transpirational pull	s. transpiration pull
transpiration coefficient	Transpirationskoeffizient m
transpiration cooling, sweat cooling	Schwitzkühlung f, Transpirationskühlung f
transpiration method, dynamic[al] method <of vapour-pressure measurement>	dynamische Methode f, Siedemethode f <der Dampfdruckbestimmung>, Mitführung f im Gasstrom
transpiration pull, transpirational pull	Transpirationssog m
transpiration resistance	Transpirationswiderstand m
trans-plutonian planet	Transpluto m
transplutonium element	Transplutoniumelement n, Transplutonium n
transponder, transmitter-responder	Transponder m, TSP
transport; transportation	Transport m; Beförderung f
transport	s. a. transfer
transportable	transportabel
transportation	s. transport
transport[ation] by wind, wind transport	Windverschleppung f
transportation problem	Transportproblem n
transport coefficient, transport factor <neutron transport theory>	Transportfaktor m, Transportkoeffizient m <Neutronentransporttheorie>

transport 912

transport coefficient	s. a. transfer coefficient	**transposition**	s. a. frequency conversion <el.>
transport cross-section, neutron transport cross-section, cross-section for [neutron] transport	Transportquerschnitt m, Transportwirkungsquerschnitt m, Neutronentransport[wirkungs]querschnitt m	**transposition [by crossing]**; crossing <of wires>	Kreuzung f <Leitungen>
transported power	s. transmitted power	**transposition of pairs,** phantom transposition; interchange of sites; exchange of site, place exchange	Platzwechsel m
transport effect	s. transport phenomenon		
transport entropy	s. entropy of transfer		
transport equation	Transportgleichung f; Maxwellsche Transportgleichung	**transposition of pairs**	s. a. phantom transposition <el.>
transport equation of angular momentum	Drehimpulstransportgleichung f	**transposition of the matrix,** interchanging the rows and columns of the matrix	Transponieren n (Stürzen n, Transposition f) der Matrix, Vertauschung f von Spalten und Zeilen <Matrix>
transport factor, transport coefficient <neutron transport theory>	Transportfaktor m, Transportkoeffizient m <Neutronentransporttheorie>		
transport kernel	Transportkern m	**transposition reaction,** rearrangement reaction	Umlagerungsreaktion f
transport lag	Transportverzögerung f	**transrectifier**	s. valve rectifier
		transrector	Transrektor m, Transrector m
transport mean free path, mean free path for transport	[mittlere freie] Transportweglänge f, mittlere freie Weglänge f für Transport	**trans-situation**	s. trans-position
		transsonic	s. transonic
		trans-stereoisomer, trans-isomer, trans-isomeride, trans-form	trans-Form f, trans-Isomer n
		trans-substitution	trans-Substitution f
		trans-tactic	trans-taktisch
		transtat	s. variable ratio transformer
		Transtrojans	Transtrojaner mpl
		transuranic element, (metal), transuranium element	Transuran n
transport number, transference number	Überführungszahl f, Hittorfsche Überführungszahl	**transvection** <math.>	Transvektion f <Math.>
		transvection, contraction, inner multiplication <of tensor>	Überschiebung f [von Indizes] <Tensor>
transport number of the anion	s. anion transport number		
transport number of the cation, cation transport (transference) number	Kationenüberführungszahl f	**transversal,** secant	Sekante f, Transversale f, Treffgerade f
		transversal	s. a. transverse
transport of air masses	s. transfer of air masses	**transversal derivative,** transverse derivative	Ableitung f in Richtung der Konormalen
transport of momentum	s. transfer of momentum <mech.>	**transversality**	Transversalität f
transport of solids, transfer of solids, mass transport, mass transfer <e.g. by rivers> <geo.>	Massentransport m, Materialtransport m, Massenverlagerung f, Massenverfrachtung f, Feststofftransport m <z. B. durch Flüsse> <Geo.>	**transversality condition**	Transversalitätsbedingung f
		transversally damped wave	s. inhomogeneous wave
		transversally stratified, piled up transversally	quergeschichtet
transport of water [particles], water transport	Wassertransport m, Wasserverfrachtung f, Wasserversetzung f	**transverse aberration**	s. transverse ray aberration
		transverse acceleration, transverse componente of acceleration	Querbeschleunigung f, Transversalbeschleunigung f, transversale Beschleunigung f, transversale (azimutale) Komponente f der Beschleunigung
transport phenomenon, transport effect	Transporterscheinung f, Transportphänomen n		
transport reaction	Transportreaktion f		
transport term	Transportterm m, Transportglied n		
transport theorem	Transportsatz m	**transverse axis,** minor axis; secondary axis <cryst.>	kleine Achse f; Nebenachse f <Krist.>
transport theory, transfer theory	Transporttheorie f		
transport theory, neutron transport theory	Transporttheorie f, Neutronentransporttheorie f, kinetische Diffusionstheorie f	**transverse Bauschinger effect**	transversaler Bauschinger-Effekt m
		transverse beam, bridge beam, cross[-] beam, cross girder; cross[-]arm, cross[-]bar, cross[-] piece, traverse <mech.>	Querbalken m; Querträger m; Traverse f <Mech.>
transport vessel	Transportgefäß n		
transpose	s. transposed matrix		
transposed and conjugate matrix	s. adjoint matrix		
transposed kernel	transponierter Kern m		
transposed matrix, transpose	transponierte Matrix f, gestürzte Matrix, Transponierte f	**transverse bending,** cross bending, bending in flexure	allgemeine Biegung f, Querkraftbiegung f
		transverse Bloch wall	Bloch-Querwand f
trans-position, trans-situation, anti-position	trans-Stellung f, anti-Stellung f	**transverse chromatic aberration**	s. lateral chromatic aberration
transposition <of lines>	Verdrillung f <Fernmeldeleitung>	**transverse comparator**	Transversalkomparator m
		transverse component, cross component	Querkomponente f, Transversalkomponente f, transversale (azimutale) Komponente f
transposition, rearrangement, reorganization, transformation <chem.>	Umlagerung f, Umgruppierung f <Chem.>		
transposition <el.>	Verschränkung f <El.>		
transposition; rearrangement; permutation <gen.>	Umlagerung f, Verlagerung f; Umordnung f; Umstellung f; Umsetzung f; Vertauschung f <allg.>	**transverse component of acceleration**	s. transverse acceleration
		transverse conductance	Querleitwert m
transposition <math.>	Transposition f <Math.>		

transverse conductivity, transverse electric conductivity	Querleitfähigkeit f, transversale Leitfähigkeit f
transverse contraction, contraction <elast.>	Querkontraktion f, Querverkürzung f, Querkürzung f, Kontraktion f
transverse contraction	s. a. Poisson ratio
transverse-control cathode-ray tube, transverse-control tube	Quersteuerröhre f, Quersteuer-Elektronenstrahlröhre f
transverse crevasse	Querspalte f
transverse current, cross current, diagonal current; shunt current <el.>	Nebenschlußstrom m, Zweigstrom m; Querstrom m <El.>
transverse-current carbon microphone	Querstrommikrophon n
transverse curvature	Querkrümmung f
transverse damping	Querdämpfung f, Querfelddämpfung f; Schrägdämpfung f
transverse derivative	s. transversal derivative
transverse diffusion	Querdiffusion f, Diffusion f in Querrichtung
transverse direction, direction of conormal	Konormalenrichtung f
transverse Doppler effect	transversaler Doppler-Effekt m
transverse earthquake	Querbeben n
transverse effect	Quereffekt m, Transversaleffekt m
transverse electric conductivity	s. transverse conductivity
transverse electric mode	s. H[-] mode
transverse electric wave	s. H[-] mode
transverse electromagnetic mode	s. transverse electromagnetic wave
transverse electromagnetic wave	s. principal wave
transverse E[-] mode	s. H[-] mode
transverse E[-] wave	s. H[-] mode
transverse expanion (extension)	s. transverse strain
transverse field amplifier, transverse-field parametric amplifier, Adler tube	parametrischer Verstärker m mit Querfeld, Adler-Röhre f
transverse field instrument	Querfeldinstrument n
transverse-field parametric amplifier	s. transverse field amplifier
transverse force, cross force <mech.>	Querkraft f, seitliche Kraft f <Mech.>
transverse force	s. a. shear force
transverse force coefficient	Querkraftbeiwert m
transverse force diagram	s. shearing force diagram
transverse galvanomagnetic effect	galvanomagnetischer Transversaleffekt m
transverse geotropism	Transversalgeotropismus m, Plagiogeotropismus m, Horizontalgeotropismus m
transverse H[-] mode	s. wave of electric type
transverse horizontal shift	transversale Horizontalverschiebung f
transverse horopter, horizontal horopter	Querhoropter m, Horizontalhoropter m
transverse H[-] wave	s. wave of electric type
transverse impulse	s. transverse momentum
transverse inclination; transverse slope	Quergefälle n, Querneigung f; Querkippung f
transverse inductance	s. cross inductance
transverse Joule effect	transversaler Joule-Effekt m
transverse load, lateral load	seitliche Belastung f, Belastung in der Querrichtung, Querbelastung f
transverse magnetic field	magnetisches Querfeld n, transversales Magnetfeld n
transverse magnetic mode (wave)	s. wave of electric type
transverse magnetization, cross magnetization, perpendicular magnetization	Quermagnetisierung f, transversale Magnetisierung f
transverse magnetoresistance, transverse magnetoresistance (magnetoresistive) effect	transversale magnetische Widerstandsänderung f, transversaler W.-Thomson-Effekt m
transverse magnetostriction	transversale Magnetostriktion f, Quermagnetostriktion f
transverse magnification	s. magnification
transverse mass	transversale Masse f
transverse Mercator projection, Gauss-Krüger projection, Gauss conformal projection	Gauß-Krüger-Projektion f, Gaußsche Projektion f, querachsige Mercator-Projektion f, transversale Mercator-Projektion, Gauß-Krüger-Entwurf m
transverse metacentre, little metacentre	Breitenmetazentrum n, kleines Metazentrum n
transverse mode, T-mode, transverse wave, T-wave <el.>	Transversalwelle f, T-Welle f, Transversaltyp m, T-Typ m, T-Typ-Welle f, Transversalmode f, T-Mode f <El.>
transverse momentum, transverse impulse	Impuls m senkrecht zur Bewegungsrichtung des Teilchens, Querimpuls m
transverse motion, transverse movement	Transversalbewegung f, Querbewegung f, transversale Bewegung f
transverse Nernst-Ettingshausen coefficient	transversaler Nernst-Ettingshausen-Koeffizient m
transverse Nernst-Ettingshausen effect	transversaler (erster) Nernst-Ettingshausen-Effekt m
transverse oscillation	s. transverse vibration
transverse part of the Hamiltonian	transversaler Anteil m des Hamilton-Operators
transverse photon	transversales (transversal polarisiertes, querpolarisiertes) Photon n
transverse phototropism	Transversalphototropismus m
transverse piezoelectric effect	transversaler Piezoeffekt (piezoelektrischer Effekt) m
transverse pilling	s. transverse stratification
transverse polarity	Querpolarität f
transverse polarization, cross polarization	Querpolarisation f, transversale Polarisation f, Transversalpolarisation f
transverse pore	durchgehende Pore f
transverse pressure	s. lateral pressure
transverse projection, equatorial projection	äquatorständige (transversale, querachsige, äquatoriale) Projektion f, Transversalprojektion f, äquatorständiger (transversaler, querachsiger, äquatorialer) Entwurf m
transverse pull	Querzug m
transvers ray aberration, transverse [spherical] aberration, lateral [spherical] aberration	Queraberration f, sphärische Queraberration, Breitenabweichung f
transverse relaxation	transversale Relaxation f
transverse relaxation time	s. spin-spin relaxation time
transverse resistance <semi.>	transversaler Widerstand m, Transversalwiderstand m <Halb.>
transverse resistance	s. a. shear strength
transverse rigidity	Quersteifigkeit f, Quersteife f
transverse scale	Transversalmaßstab m, Transversalskala f, Transversalnonius m; Transversalskale f
transverse shear	Querschub m, transversale Scherung f
transverse shrinkage, cross shrinkage	Querschrumpfung f

transverse slope; transverse inclination	Quergefälle n; Querneigung f; Querkippung f	trapezohedral [crystal] class	s. a. enantiomorphous hemihedry of the tetragonal system
transverse sound velocity	s. transverse velocity <ac.>	trapezohedral [crystal] class	s. a. trigonal holoaxial class
transverse sound wave	transversale Schallwelle f	trapezohedron	Trapezoeder n
transverse spherical aberration	s. transverse ray aberration	trapezohedron	s. a. pentagonal icositetrahedron
transverse stability [of charged particle]	Querstabilität f [des Teilchens]	trapezoid	Trapez n, Paralleltrapez n
		trapezoid	s. a. trapezium
		trapezoidal distortion	s. keystone distortion
		trapezoidal function	Trapezfunktion f
transverse strain, transverse extension (expansion), lateral strain	Querdehnung f; Querverzerrung f; Querdehnungszahl f	trapezoidal generator, trapezoidal-wave generator	Trapezgenerator m, Trapezwellengenerator m
transverse stratification; transverse piling	Querschichtung f; Querrippelung f		
transverse strength	s. shear strength	trapezoidal hemihedry	trapezoidale Hemiedrie f
transverse stress, bending stress, flexural stress	Biegespannung f, Biegenormalspannung f	trapezoidal load	Trapezlast f
transverse stripe, cross stripe; stripe running across	Querstreifen m	trapezoidal oscillation	Trapezschwingung f
		trapezoidal pulse	Trapezimpuls m
transverse tension coefficient of resistivity	transversaler Spannungskoeffizient m des spezifischen Widerstandes	trapezoidal rule, trapezoid rule, trapezoid formula	Trapezregel f, Trapezformel f, Trapezmethode f, Sehnentrapezregel f, Sehnentrapezformel f
transverse tomography	Querschichtenaufnahmetechnik f, Transversaltomographie f	trapezoidal-wave generator	s. trapezoidal generator
transverse valley	Quertal n, Durchbruchstal n, Transversaltal n	trapezoidal wing	Trapezflügel m
transverse velocity, transverse sound velocity, velocity of transverse waves <ac.>	Ausbreitungsgeschwindigkeit f transversaler Schallwellen, transversale Schallgeschwindigkeit f, Transversalgeschwindigkeit f <Ak.>	trapezoid formula (rule)	s. trapezoidal rule
		trap level, trapping level, trapping term (state)	Hafterm m, Haftstellenniveau n, Haftniveau n; Trapniveau n
		trap model	Trapmodell m
		trapped electron	Haftelektron n
transverse vibration, transverse oscillation; lateral oscillation (vibration); swaying	transversale Schwingung f, Transversalschwingung f, Querschwingung f	trapped-radiation region	s. Allen radiation belt / Van
		trapping; collection; gathering; interception	Auffangen n; Fangen n; Sammlung f
transverse Villari effect	transversaler Villari-Effekt m		
transverse voltage, cross voltage, perpendicular voltage	Querspannung f	trapping, attachment, capture, addition	Anlagerung f
		trapping, capture <of electrons>	Einfang m, Einfangen n
		trapping <semi.>	Trapping n, „trapping" n, Haftung f <Halb.>
transverse wave, shear wave, S wave	Transversalwelle f, transversale Welle f, Querwelle f, Scherwelle f, S-Welle f	trapping centre, trap	Haftzentrum n, Anlagerungszentrum n, Einfangzentrum n
transverse wave, shear wave, S ray, S wave <geo.>	S-Welle f, Transversalwelle f, Scherwelle f <Geo.>	trapping cross-section, [effective] cross-section of carrier trapping, cross-section for trapping <semi.>	Haftungsquerschnitt m, Wirkungsquerschnitt m für (der) Haftung, Haftungswirkungsquerschnitt m, Haftquerschnitt m <Halb.>
transverse wave	s. a. transverse mode <el.>		
transverse wave along the string	Seilwelle f		
transverse wave once-reflected downwards at the Earth's outer surface, SS ray (wave)	SS-Welle f, einfach reflektierte Transversalwelle f	trapping effect	„trapping"-Effekt m
		trapping level	s. trap level
transverse Zeeman effect	transversaler Zeeman-Effekt m, Transversaleffekt m	trapping mode	„trapping mode" f, Einfangmode f
		trapping of air, inclusion of air	Lufteinschluß m
transversion <bio.>	Transversion f <Bio.>	trapping rate	Einfangrate f
transverter	Transverter m, Gleichrichter m	trapping region, trapping spot	Kontaktenge f
trap <semi.>	Haftstelle f, Trap m, Falle f, Fangstelle f, Anlagerungsstelle f, Hafterm m <Halb.>	trapping sphere, capture sphere	Einfangkugel f
		trapping spot	s. trapping region
trap	Falle f, Abscheider m	trapping state (therm)	s. trap level
trap, filter element <el.>	Siebglied n <El.>	trapping time	Einfangzeit f; Haftzeit f <Halb.>
trap	s. a. absorption circuit <el.>	traser	Traser m
trap	s. a. cold trap	Traube plate	Traubesche Glimmer-Doppelplatte f
trap	s. a. trapping centre		
TRAPATT	= trapped plasma avalanche triggered transit diode	Traube['s] rule	Traubesche Regel f
		traumataxis, traumatotaxis	Traumatotaxis f
trap coefficient	Haftkoeffizient m		
trap depth	Haftstellentiefe f	traumatic action	traumatische Einwirkung f
trapezium	Trapezoid n	traumatonasty	Traumatonastie f
		traumatotaxis, traumataxis	Traumatotaxis f
trapezium	s. a. trapezoid	trauma[to]tropism	Traumatotropismus m
trapezium distortion	s. keystone distortion	travel	s. path
trapezohedral [crystal] class	s. enantiomorphous hemihedry of the hexagonal system	travelling dune	Wanderdüne f

travelling field	Wanderfeld n, Lauffeld n
travelling layer, running layer	laufende Schicht f
travelling load	s. live load
travelling microscope; measuring microscope	Meßmikroskop n; Feinmeßmikroskop n
travelling screen, diaphragm [for measuring stream velocity]	Meßschirm m
travelling screen technique, diaphragm technique	Schirmverfahren n der Wassermengenmessung, Schirmmessung f
travelling speed, speed of travel	Zuggeschwindigkeit f
travelling spot	s. flying spot
travelling time, travel time, time of travel, transit time <geo., ac.>	Laufzeit f <Geo., Ak.>
travelling time difference, travelling time residual <geo.>	Laufzeitunterschied m, Laufzeitdifferenz f <Geo.>
travelling wave, running wave; advancing wave, progressive wave, wave of translation	Wanderwelle f; fortschreitende Welle f, laufende Welle, Ausbreitungswelle f
travelling wave	s. a. surge <el.>
travelling-wave accelerator, travelling-wave linear accelerator	Wanderwellenbeschleuniger m, Wanderwellen-Linearbeschleuniger m
travelling-wave amplifier	Wanderfeldverstärker m, Wanderwellenverstärker m
travelling-wave amplifier tube	Wanderfeldverstärkerröhre f
travelling-wave helix, helix waveguide, helix <acc.>	Wendel f, Helix f, Hohlleiterwendel f, Wendelhohlleiter m <Beschl.>
travelling-wave helix; delay-line helix	Wendelleiter m als Verzögerungsleitung, Verzögerungswendel f
travelling-wave helix tube	Wanderfeldwendelröhre f, Wendelröhre f
travelling-wave laser	s. travelling-wave optical maser
travelling-wave linear accelerator	s. travelling-wave accelerator
travelling-wave magnetron	Wanderfeldmagnetron n, „travelling-wave"-Magnetron n
travelling-wave maser [amplifier]	Wanderwellenmaser[verstärker] m, Wanderfeldmaser[verstärker] m
travelling-wave maser generator (oscillator)	Wanderwellenmaser[oszillator] m, Wanderfeldmaser[oszillator] m
travelling-wave optical maser, travelling-wave laser	optischer Wanderwellenmaser m, optischer Wanderfeldmaser m, Wanderwellenlaser m, Wanderfeldlaser m
travelling-wave oscillation	Wanderwellenschwingung f
travelling-wave oscillator, transit-time oscillator, travelling-wave-tube oscillator	Laufzeitoszillator m, Laufzeitgenerator m
travelling-wave paramagnetic maser amplifier	paramagnetischer Wanderwellenmaserverstärker m
travelling-wave parametric amplifier, parametric travelling-wave amplifier	parametrischer Wanderfeldverstärker m, parametrischer Wanderwellenverstärker m
travelling-wave slotted antenna	Wanderwellenschlitzantenne f
travelling-wave tube, travelling-wave-type wave tube, wave tube, TWT	Lauffeldröhre f, Wanderfeldröhre f, „travelling-wave"-Röhre f
travelling-wave tube amplifier, TWT amplifier	Wanderfeldröhrenverstärker m
travelling-wave-tube oscillator	s. travelling-wave oscillator
travelling-wave-type wave tube	s. travelling-wave tube
travelling wave with sharp-edged front	s. surge <el.>
travel of the valve, valve travel	Ventilspiel n
travel time	s. transit time <el.>
travel time <geo., ac.>	s. travelling time
traversal	s. traverse <geo.>
traverse, traverse line, transit traverse, theodolite traverse, traversal <geo.>	Polygonzug m, Streckenzug m, Linienzug m, Theodolitzug m, Zug m <Geo.>
traverse	s. a. polygonal method
traverse	s. a. transverse beam <mech.>
traversed by a current, current-carrying, carrying a current, live	stromführend; stromdurchflossen; unter Strom
traverse line	s. traverse <geo.>
traverse of levelling	Nivellementszug m; Nivellementsschleife f
traverse which closes on itself, closed traverse, closed-on-itself traverse	geschlossener Polygonzug m
traversing; intersection; intercepting; piercing	Schneiden n, Schnitt m; Durchstoßen n
traversing	s. a. passing <of light, particles>
traversing	s. a. polygonal method
trawl, trawl[-] net	Trawl n, Trawlnetz n, Schleppnetz n
tray; plate, head, stage <chem.>	Boden m, Platte f; Stufe f <Chem.>
treating	s. processing <mech.>
treatment; processing; working; handling	Verarbeitung f
treatment <of a problem>	Behandlung f <Problem>
treatment	s. a. evaluation <of data>
treatment	s. a. processing <mech.>
treatment cone	Bestrahlungskegel m
treatment of the experimental data	Versuchsauswertung f
treble block	s. pulley <mech.>
treble cut	Höhenabsenkung f
trebling	s. tripling
Treder['s] field equation	Tredersche Feldgleichung f
tree <math.>	Baum m <Math.>
tree discharge	s. brush discharge
tree function	Baumfunktion f
tree-like crystal	s. dendrite
Trefftz-Glauert method	Trefftz-Glauertsches Verfahren n
Trefftz['] integral equation	Trefftzsche Integralgleichung f
Trefftz['] method	Trefftzsches Verfahren n
Trefftz plane	Trefftzsche Ebene f, Trefftz-Ebene f
Treiman-Yang angle	Treiman-Yang-Winkel m
Treiman-Yang criterion	Treiman-Yangsches Kriterium n
trellis	s. frame <mech.>
trembling, trembling motion, vibratory motion	Zittern n, Zitterbewegung f
trembling, vibration <of image> <opt.>	Tanzen n, Zittern n, Springen n <Bild> <Opt.>
trembling	s. a. quake
trembling effect, irregular photophoresis	irreguläre (unregelmäßige) Photophorese f
trembling motion	s. trembling
trembling motion	s. a. zitterbewegung <of electron>

tremolo effect	Tremoloeffekt *m*	triangle relation <for angular momentum quantum number>	Dreiecksrelation *f*, Dreiecksregel *f* <für die Drehimpulsquantenzahl>
tremor	s. quake		
trench; trough <geo.>	Graben *m*, Grabenbruch *m* <Geo.>		
		triangular co-ordinates, trilinear co-ordinates	Dreieckskoordinaten *fpl*
trench <geo.>	Furche *f*; Rinne *f* <Geo.>	triangular distribution	Dreiecksverteilung *f*
trench in the ocean floor, trough in the ocean [floor], ultra-abyssal region, ultra-abyssal zone	Tiefseegraben *m*, Tiefseegesenke *n*, ultraabyssale Zone *f*; Tiefseerinne *f*	triangular frame	s. triangular web <mech.>
		triangular load	Dreiecksbelastung *f*
		triangular matrix, superdiagonal matrix <zeroes below diagonal>; subdiagonal matrix <zeroes above diagonal>	Dreiecksmatrix *f*, Halbmatrix *f*
		triangular-notch weir	s. V-notch weir
trend	Trend *m*	triangular pulse oscillation	Dreieck-Stoßschwingung *f*
trend	s. a. tendency	triangular stacking fault, stacking fault triangle	Stapelfehlerdreieck *n*
trend	s. a. strike <geo.>	triangular transient pulse	s. triangle pulse
trend[-]line	tektonische Linie *f*		
trennschaukel	s. gasschaukel	triangular web, triangular frame, triangulated system, simple system <mech.>	einfaches System *n*, einfaches Fachwerk *n*, Dreiecknetz *n*, Dreiecksystem *n* <Mech.>
Tresca['s] hexagon	s. Tresca['s] yield hexagon		
Tresca['s] yield condition (criterion)	s. St.Venant-Tresca yield condition		
Tresca['s] yield hexagon, Tresca['s] hexagon	Trescasches Sechseck *n*, Tresca-Sechseck *n*, Sechseck von Tresca	triangular weir	s. V-notch weir
		triangulated system	s. triangular web <mech.>
		triangulation	Triangulation *f*, Dreiecks[ver]messung *f*, Triangulierung *f*
Trevelyan rocker	Trevelyan-Schaukel *f*, Trevelyansche Schaukel *f*		
TRIAC, triode alternating-current semiconductor switch	Wechselstromthyristor *m*, bidirektionaler Wechselstromthyristor, TRIAC *m*	triangulation, triangulation grid, field triangulation	Triangulationsnetz *n*
		triangulation point, trigonometric point, triangulation station	Triangulationspunkt *m*, trigonometrischer Punkt *m*, Stationspunkt *m*, T. P.
triac	s. a. trigger triode		
triad, Döbereiner['s] triad	Triade *f* [nach Döbereiner], Döbereinersche Triade		
triad axis, 3-al axis, axis of order 3, three-fold axis [of symmetry], 3-fold axis, axis of threefold symmetry, trigonal axis, triple axis	dreizählige Symmetrieachse (Drehungsachse, Drehsymmetrieachse, Achse) *f*, Trigyre *f*, 3zählige Symmetrieachse	triangulation signal, trigonometric signal, beach	Triangulationssignal *n*
triadic structure	triadische Struktur *f*, Dreigliedrigkeit *f*	triax	Triax *f*, Triax-Anlage *f*
triad rule, rule of triads	Triadenregel *f*	tri-axial ellipsoid	dreiachsiges Ellipsoid *n*
triakisdodecahedron, trigonal dodecahedron, hemiakisoctahedron, trigondodecahedron	Triakisdodekaeder *n*, Trisdodekaeder *n*, Trigon[o]dodekaeder *n*	triaxiality	s. volume stress
		tri-axial strain	s. general state of strain
		tri-axial stress	s. volume stress
		triboabsorption	Triboabsorption *f*
triakisoctahedron, [trigonal] trisoctahedron, pyramidal octahedron	Pyramidenoktaeder *n*, Triakisoktaeder *n*, Trisoktaeder *n*	tribocatalytic reaction	tribokatalytische Reaktion *f*
		tribochemical energy relation	tribochemische Energiebeziehung *f*
triakistetrahedron, tristetrahedron, pyramidal tetrahedron	Pyramidentetraeder *n*, Triakistetraeder *n*, Tristetraeder *n*	tribochemical equilibrium	tribochemisches Gleichgewicht *n*
		tribochemical reaction	tribochemische Reaktion *f*
trial and error, trial-and-error method	„trial-and-error"-Methode *f*, Probiermethode *f*, Lernen *n* durch Versuch und Irrtum, Lernen durch den Erfolg, empirisches Bestimmungsverfahren *n*, empirische Näherung *f*	tribochemistry	Tribochemie *f*
		tribodesorption	Tribodesorption *f*
		triboelectric effect	triboelektrischer Effekt *m*, reibungselektrischer Effekt
		triboelectricity, frictional electricity, friction electricity	Reibungselektrizität *f*, Triboelektrizität *f*
trial rod	s. test bar		
trial solution, solution to be tested	Probenlösung *f*, Probelösung *f*		
		triboelectric series	reibungselektrische Spannungsreihe *f*, Spannungsreihe für Reibungselektrizität
trial solution, preparation, batch, charge <chem.>	Ansatz *m*		
triangle axiom, triangle inequality <math.>	Dreiecksungleichung *f*, Dreiecksaxiom *n*, Abstandsungleichung *f*, Dreiecksrelation *f*	triboelectrification, frictional electrification	Reibungselektrisierung *f*
		triboemission, triboluminescence emission, triboluminescent emission	Triboemission *f*
triangle connection	s. delta connection		
triangle inequality	s. triangle axiom <math.>	tribology	Tribologie *f*, Reibungslehre *f*
triangle of forces	Kräftedreieck *n*		
triangle of impedances, impedance triangle, vector diagram of impedance	Widerstandsdreieck *n*	triboluminescence	Triboluminiszenz *f*, Trennungsleuchten *n*, Reibungsluminiszenz *f*, Reibungsleuchten *n*
triangle of position	s. polar triangle		
triangle of velocities, velocity diagram, velocity vector diagram, speed triangle	Geschwindigkeitsdreieck *n*	triboluminescence emission, triboluminescent emission, triboemission	Triboemission *f*
triangle pulse; triangular transient pulse	Dreieckimpuls *m*	tribometer	Tribometer *n*, Reibungsmesser *m*, Reibungskraftmesser *m*

tribometry	Tribometrie *f*, Reibungskräftemessung *f*
tribophysics	Reibungsphysik *f*, Tribophysik *f*
triboplasma	Triboplasma *n*
tribosublimation	Tribosublimation *f*
tributary <of river>	tributär <Fluß>
tricarboxylic acid cycle	s. Krebs cycle
Trichel oscillation	Trichel-Schwingung *f*, Trichelsche Schwingung *f*
Trichel pulse	Trichel-Impuls *m*
trichotomy	Trichotomie *f*
trichroism	Trichroismus *m*
trichromatic coefficient	trichromatische Maßzahl *f*
trichromatic colorimeter	Dreifarbenmeßgerät *n*, trichromatisches Kolorimeter *n*
trichromatic system	trichromatisches Farbmaßzahlensystem (System) *n*
trichromatic unit	Farbvalenzeinheit *f*
trichromatic vision	trichromatisches Sehen *n*, Dreifarbensehen *n*
trichromatism	Trichromasie *f*, Farbennormalsichtigkeit *f*, Farbentüchtigkeit *f*
trichrome filter, yellowish and blue colour filter	Trichromfilter *n*
trick, artifice, wrinkle	Kunstgriff *m*, Kniff *m*
trickling filter	s. biological filter
trickling through, seepage, oozing	Durchsickern *n*, Eindringen *n*
trickling water, dripping water, dropping water	Tropfwasser *n*
triclinic crystal system, triclinic system, anorthic [crystal] system, asymmetric [crystal] system	triklines System *n*, triklines Kristallsystem *n*
triclinic hemihedral class, triclinic hemihedry	s. hemihedry of the triclinic system
triclinic holohedral class, triclinic holohedry	s. holohedry of the triclinic system
triclinic system	s. triclinic crystal system
tricolour kinescope	Dreifarbenkineskop *n*, Tricolorkineskop *n*, „trichrome"-Kineskop *n*, Trichromoskop *n*
tricolour tube, three-colour tube	Dreifarbenröhre *f*, Dreifarbenbildröhre *f*, Dreifarben-Elektronenstrahlröhre *f*
Tricomi['s] boundary value problem, Tricomi['s] problem	Tricomisches Randwertproblem *n*, Tricomisches Problem *n*
Tricomi['s] equation	Tricomische Differentialgleichung (Gleichung) *f*, Tricomi-Gleichung *f*
Tricomi['s] function	Tricomische Funktion *f*
Tricomi gas	Tricomi-Gas *n*
Tricomi['s] problem, Tricomi['s] boundary value problem	Tricomisches Randwertproblem *n*, Tricomisches Problem *n*
tricrystal	s. trilling
trident	s. three-pronged star
tridental ligand	dreizähniger (dreizähliger) Ligand *m*
tridimensional	s. three-dimensional
triductor	Triduktor *m*
trifilar gravimeter	Dreifadengravimeter *n*, Trifilargravimeter *n*
trigatron	Trigatron *n*, Hochdruckstromtor *n*
trigger, trigger circuit, triggering circuit, triggered circuit; trigger pair	Trigger *m*, Triggerkreis *m*, Triggerschaltung *f*; Röhrenwippe *f*, Wippe *f*
trigger action	s. triggering
trigger-action relay	s. throw-over relay
trigger circuit	s. trigger
trigger diode, diac	Triggerdiode *f*, Diac *f*
trigger discharge tube, trigger tube	Triggerröhre *f*
triggered circuit	s. trigger
triggered time base	getriggerte Zeitbasis (Zeitablenkung) *f*
trigger electrode	Triggerelektrode *f*, Auslöschelektrode *f*
triggering, trigger action	Triggerung *f*, Triggerauslösung *f*
triggering circuit	s. trigger
triggering pulse	s. trigger pulse
trigger pair	s. trigger
trigger pulse	s. initiating pulse
trigger switch	s. tumbler
trigger triode, triac	Triggertriode *f*, Triac *f*
trigger tube, trigger discharge tube	Triggerröhre *f*
trigonal axis	s. triad axis
trigonal bipyramidal [crystal] class, trigonal dipyramidal [crystal] class, trigonal equatorial [crystal] class, trigonal paramorphic hemihedry [of the hexagonal system], trigonal paramorphy, sphenoidal tetartohedry, tetartohedral class with threefold axis of the hexagonal system	trigonal[-] bipyramidale Klasse *f*, trigonal[-] bipyramidale Symmetrieklasse *f*, trigonal[-] dipyramidale Klasse, trigonal[-] dipyramidale Symmetrieklasse, pyramidale Hemiedrie *f*, trigonale Tetartoedrie *f*, Tetartoedrie II. Art des hexagonalen Systems
trigonal bond	trigonale Bindung *f*, Dreieckbindung *f*
trigonal crystal system	s. rhombohedral crystal system
trigonal dipyramidal [crystal] class	s. trigonal bipyramidal class
trigonal dodecahedron	s. triakisdodecahedron
trigonal equatorial [crystal] class	s. trigonal bipyramidal class
trigonal holoaxial class, trapezohedral [crystal] class, trigonal-trapezohedral [crystal] class, rhombohedral enantiomorphy, enantiomorphous hemihedral class of the trigonal system, enantiomorphous hemihedry of the rhombohedral system	trigonal-trapezoedrische Klasse *f*, trigonal trapezoedrische Klasse, trapezoedrische Tetartoedrie *f*, enantiomorphe Hemiedrie *f* des rhomboedrischen Systems
trigonal holohedry [of the hexagonal system], ditrigonal equatorial class, trigonotype class, sphenoidal hemihedry, ditrigonal bipyramidal [crystal] class, hemihedral class with threefold axis of the hexagonal system, ditrigonal dipyramidal [crystal] class	Hemiedrie *f* II. Art des hexagonalen Systems, ditrigonal-bipyramidale Klasse *f*, trigonale Hemiedrie, ditrigonal dipyramidale Klasse
trigonal paramorphic hemihedry [of the hexagonal system]	s. trigonal bipyramidal [crystal] class
trigonal paramorphy	s. trigonal bipyramidal [crystal] class
trigonal polar class, trigonal pyramidal [crystal] class, tetartohedral class of the trigonal system, rhombohedral tetartohedry, tetartohedry of the rhombohedral system, hexagonal ogdohedry	trigonal-pyramidale Klasse *f*, trigonal pyramidale Klasse, Tetartoedrie *f* I. Art des rhomboedrischen Systems, Ogdoedrie *f*

trigonal

trigonal system	s. rhombohedral crystal system	triode alternating-current semiconductor switch, TRIAC	Wechselstromthyristor *m*, bidirektionaler Wechselstromthyristor, TRIAC *m*
trigonal-trapezohedral [crystal] class	s. trigonal holoaxial class	triode oscillator, oscillion	Triodenoszillator *m*, Triodengenerator *m*
trigonal trisoctahedron	s. triakisoctahedron	triode-tetrode, tri-tet	Triode-Tetrode *f*
trigondodecahedron	s. triakisdodecahedron	triode tube (valve)	s. triode
trigonometrical altitude measurement	s. trigonometric levelling	triorthogonal	s. triply orthogonal
trigonometric calculation [of optical systems]	trigonometrische Durchrechnung *f*	tripack film	Dreischichtenfilm *m*
		tripartition	s. ternary fission
trigonometric function, circular function	trigonometrische Funktion *f*, Kreisfunktion *f*, Winkelfunktion *f*	trip coil	Unterbrecherspule *f*
		triple-alpha process, alpha process, Salpeter process, jamming alpha-particles together	Heliumreaktion *f*, Salpeter-Prozeß *m*, Alpha-Prozeß *m*
trigonometric levelling, trigonometric measurement of height, trigonometrical altitude measurement	trigonometrische Höhenmessung *f*, trigonometrisches Nivellement *n*	triple axis	s. triad axis
		triple bond[ing], six-electron bond, triple link[age]	Dreifachbindung *f*, Sechselektronenbindung *f*
trigonometric parallax	trigonometrische Parallaxe *f*	triple-cavity klystron, three-cavity klystron	Dreikreisklystron *n*, Dreikammerklystron *n*
trigonometric point	s. triangulation point		
trigonometric polynomial	trigonometrisches Polynom *n*, Exponentialpolynom *n*, endliche trigonometrische Summe *f*	triple coincidence counter	Dreifachkoinzidenzzähler *m*
		triple collision, three-body collision, three-particle collision	Dreierstoß *m*, Dreifachstoß *m*, Dreikörperstoß *m*, Dreiteilchenstoß *m*
trigonometric series	trigonometrische Reihe *f*, Sinus-Kosinus-Reihe *f*	triple condenser [lens]	Tripelkondensator *m*, Triplexkondensator *m*
trigonometric signal	s. triangulation signal	triple crystal	s. trilling
trigonotype class	s. trigonal holohedry	triple electron-nuclear-nuclear resonance method, electron-nuclear-nuclear triple resonance method	Elektron-Kern-Kern-Dreifachresonanzmethode *f*
trigram, three-digit group	Trigramm *n*		
trihedral, co-ordinate trihedral	Dreibein *n*, Koordinatendreibein *n*		
trihedral	s. a. trihedron	triple fission	s. ternary fission
trihedral angle	Triederwinkel *m*, dreiseitige körperliche Ecke *f*, Dreikant *n*	triple focusing mass spectrometer	dreifach fokussierendes Massenspektrometer *n*, Massenspektrometer mit Dreifachfokussierung (dreifacher Fokussierung)
trihedron, trihedral	Trieder *n*, Dreiflach *n*, Dreiflächner *m*		
trilateration, long-range triangulation	Trilateration *f*, streckenmessende Triangulation *f*	triple gamma-ray cascade	dreistufige Gamma-Kaskade *f*, sukzessive Emission *f* von drei Gamma-Quanten
trilinear co-ordinates	s. triangular co-ordinates		
trilling, triplet crystal, triple crystal, tricrystal	Drilling *m*, Drillingskristall *m*, Kristalldrilling *m*, Trikristall *m*	triple-gang capacitor, three-gang capacitor	Dreifach-Drehkondensator *m*, Dreigang-Drehkondensator *m*, Dreifachkondensator *m*
trim	s. trimming <el.>		
trim <hydr.>	Trimm *m* <Hydr.>	triple integral; volume integral	Volum[en]integral *n*, Raumintegral *n*; dreifaches Integral *n*
trimer	Trimer *n*		
		triple isomorphism, isotrimorphism	Isotrimorphie *f*
trimetric projection	trimetrische Parallelperspektive *f*; trimetrische (anisometrische) Projektion *f*	triple link[age]	s. triple bond
		triple mirror	s. corner cube
		triple of numbers, number triple	Zahlentripel *n*
trimmer, trimmer capacitor, trimming capacitor	Abgleichkondensator *m*; Trimmerkondensator *m*, Trimmer *m*, Trimmkondensator *m*; Quetschkondensator *m*, Quetschtrimmer *m*	triple point	Tripelpunkt *m* <Zustandsdiagramm>; Dreieckpunkt *m* <Stoßfront>
		triple pressure	Tripelpunktsdruck *m*
		triple product [of three vectors]	s. parallelepipedal product
trimmer potentiometer	Trimmerpotentiometer *n*	tripler	Verdreifacher *m*
trimming <aero.; hydr.>	Trimmung *f* <Aero.; Hydr.>	triple salt	Tripelsalz *n*
		triple scalar product	s. parallelepipedal product
trimming, trim <el.>	Trimmen *n* <El.>	triple scattering	Dreifachstreuung *f*
		triple split[ting]	Dreifachaufspaltung *f*
trimming capacitor	s. trimmer	triple star <astr.>	Dreifachstern *m*, dreifaches Sternsystem *n*, Tripelsystem *n* <Astr.>
trimming moment	Trimmoment *n*		
trimodal distribution	dreigipflige Verteilung *f*	triple state	Tripel[punkts]zustand *m*
trimolecular reaction, termolecular reaction, reaction of the third order	trimolekulare Reaktion *f*, Reaktion dritter Ordnung	triple-substituted, trisubstituted, triply substituted	dreifach substituiert
		triplet; triplet lens	Triplet[t] *n*, Dreilinser *m*; Dreilinsensystem *n*
trimorphic, trimorphous trimorphism	trimorph Trimorphie *f*, Trimorphismus *m*		
trimorphous, trimorphic	trimorph	triplet <spectr.>	Triplett *n* <Spektr.>
trinitrotoluene equivalent, T.N.T. equivalent	Trinitrotoluoläquivalent *n*, TNT-Äquivalent *n*, TNT-Energieäquivalent *n*	triplet crystal	s. trilling
		triplet density	Triplettdichte *f*
trinomial	trinomisch, dreigliedrig	triplet fine structure	Triplettfeinstruktur *f*
triode, three-electrode tube, three-electrode valve, triode tube, triode valve, single-grid tube, single-grid valve	Triode *f*, Dreipolröhre *f*, Dreielektrodenröhre *f*, Dreielektrodenrohr *n*, Eingitterröhre *f*, Triodenröhre *f*	triplet interaction	Triplettwechselwirkung *f*
		triplet lens	s. triplet
		triplet level	s. triplet state

triplet level	s. a. triplet term	tritanomalous vision	Tritanomalie f, Blauschwäche f, Gelbblaublindheit f
triplet neutron-proton interaction, triplet n-p interaction	Triplett-Neutron-Proton-Wechselwirkung f, Triplett-n-p-Wechselwirkung f	tritanopia	Tritanopie f
		tri-tet, triode-tetrode	Triode-Tetrode f
triplet neutron-proton potential, triplet n-p potential	Triplett-Neutron-Proton-Potential n, Triplett-n-p-Potential n	tri-tet circuit, tri-tet oscillator	Tri-Tet-Schaltung f, Tri-Tet-Oszillator m
triplet positronium	s. ortho[-]positronium	tritiated	tritiiert, tritiert, tritiummarkiert, ³H-markiert, mit Tritium markiert; tritiumgesättigt, mit Tritium gesättigt
triplet potential	Triplettpotential n		
triplet scattering	Triplettstreuung f		
triplet scattering cross-section, cross-section for triplet scattering	Triplettstreuquerschnitt m, Wirkungsquerschnitt m für (der) Triplettstreuung	tritide	Tritid n, überschweres Hydrid n
triplet spectrum	Triplettspektrum n	tritium, T, ³₁H	Tritium n, überschwerer Wasserstoff m, T, ³₁H
triplet spin state	Triplettspinzustand m, Triplettzustand m des Spins	tritium nucleus, triton, t	Triton n, Tritiumkern m, t, t
triple state, triplet level	Triplettzustand m; Triplettniveau n	tritium unit, TU	Tritiumeinheit f, T. E., TE, TU
triplet system	Triplettsystem n	trituration	s. rubbing
triplet term; triplet level	Triplettterm m	trivalent logic[al calculus]	s. three-valued logic
triple velocity correlation	dreifache Geschwindigkeitskorrelation f	trivector, three-vector, 3-vector	Dreiervektor m, Trivektor m
tripling, trebling	Verdreifachung f	trivector, 3-vector <math.>	Trivektor m, 3-Vektor m <Math.>
triply charged negative ion	dreifach geladenes Anion n	trivial solution	triviale Lösung f
triply charged positive ion	dreifach geladenes Kation n		
triply orthogonal, trirectangular, triorthogonal	dreifach-rechtwinklig, dreifach-orthogonal	Trkal flow	Trkalsche Strömung f
		TRM	s. thermoremanent magnetization
triply saturated, trisaturated	dreifachgesättigt	tRNA	s. transfer ribonucleic acid
triply substituted	s. trisubstituted	trochoid	Trochoide f, Trochoidale f
tripod, stand	Stativ n; Dreifuß m	trochoidal analyzer	Zykloidenanalysator m; Trochoidenanalysator m, Trochoidalanalysator m
tri-pole	s. three-terminal network		
tripole antenna	Tripolantenne f	trochoidal theory	Trochoidentheorie f
tripoli, kieselguhr, diatomaceous earth, diatomite, infusorial earth, siliceous earth.	Kieselgur n, Infusorienerde f, Diatomeenerde f, Tripel m, Polierschiefer m	trochoidal time-of-flight mass spectrometer	Zykloiden-Laufzeit[massen-]spektrometer n; Trochoiden-Laufzeitspektrometer n, Trochoidal-Laufzeitspektrometer n
tripping; release; clearing <el.>	Auslösung f <El.>		
		trochoidal wave	Trochoidalwelle f, trochoidale Welle f
tripping wire	s. trip wire	trochoid equation, trochoid formula, equation of the trochoid	Trochoidengleichung f, Trochoidenformel f
trip Reynolds number	s. critical Reynolds number		
trip wire, transition wire, tripping wire	Stolperdraht m, Turbulenzdraht m	trochotron	Trochotron n
triquetra	s. parallactic rule	troikatron	Troikatron n
trirectangular	s. triply orthogonal	Trojan asteroid	Trojaner m
trirhombohedral class	s. hexagonal tetartohedry of the second sort	Trojan group, Trojans	Trojaner mpl
trisaturated, triply saturated	dreifachgesättigt	troland, luxon, international photon, photon	Troland n, internationales Photon n, Photon, Luxon n
trisection	Dreiteilung f, Trisektion f		
trisectrix	Trisektrix f	Trompeter zone	Trompeter-Zone f, Trompetersche Zone f
trisoctahedron	s. triakisoctahedron		
trisonics	= subsonics, transonics, and supersonics	tropadyne circuit	Tropadyneschaltung f
tristable	tristabil	tropic air wheel	Tropikluftrad n
tristetrahedron, triakistetrahedron, pyramidal tetrahedron	Pyramidentetraeder n, Triakistetraeder n, Tristetraeder n	tropical cyclone; whirling storm; cyclone, [tropical] revolving storm <Indian Ocean>; hurricane <Atlantic and Caribbean>; typhoon <West Pacific>; willy-willy <Australia>	tropischer Wirbelsturm m, Wirbelsturm, Zyklon m; Hurrikan m; Taifun m; Willy-Willy m
tristimulus sum, sum of tristimulus values, tristimulus weight, colour [stimulus] weight, colour value sum	Farbwertsumme f, Farbreizvalenzgewicht n, Farbgewicht n, Farbreizsumme f		
		tropical day, hot day	Tropentag m, heißer Tag m
tristimulus value, value, colour value	Farbwert m, Eichreizbetrag m, Farbreizbetrag m; Farbmaßzahl f	tropical diurnal lunar inequality	tropische tägliche lunare Ungleichheit f
		tropical diurnal solar inequality	tropische tägliche solare Ungleichheit f
tristimulus value [in the C.I.E. standard colorimetric system], standard tristimulus value	Normfarbwert m, trichromatische Maßzahl f [im Normvalenzsystem], Normalfarbwert m, Normalreizbetrag m	tropical front wave	Tropikfrontwelle f
		tropicalized, tropic-proof, resistant to tropic climate, suitable for tropical service, suitable for tropical climate	klimafest, klimabeständig, tropenfest, tropenbeständig, tropengeeignet
tristimulus weight	s. tristimulus sum		
trisubstituted, triple-substituted, triply substituted	dreifach substituiert		

tropical maritime air, maritime tropical air	maritime Tropikluft f, tropische Meeresluft f	trough	Trog m
tropical month	tropischer Monat m	trough, trough of the wave, wave trough	Wellental n
tropical rain, zenithal rain	Zenitalregen m, Tropenregen m, tropischer Regen m	trough	s. a. barometric trough
		trough	s. a. syncline <geo.>
		trough	s. a. trench <geo.>
tropical year	tropisches Jahr n	trough glacier, transection-type glacier	Jochgletscher m
tropic continental air	kontinentale Tropikluft f		
		trough in the ocean [floor]	s. trench in the ocean floor
		trough line, line depression <meteo.>	Troglinie f <Meteo.>
tropic of Cancer	Wendekreis m des Krebses, nördlicher Wendekreis	trough of low pressure	s. barometric trough
		trough of the wave	s. trough
tropic of Capricorn	Wendekreis m des Steinbocks, südlicher Wendekreis	trough valley, U-shaped valley	Trogtal n, U-Tal n, trogförmiges Tal n, Trog m
tropic-proof	s. tropicalized		
tropics, tropic zone, torrid zone	Tropen pl, tropische Zone f, warme Zone, Tropenzone f	Trouton and Noble experiment	s. Trouton-Noble experiment
		Trouton['s] constant	Troutonsche Konstante f, Trouton-Konstante f
tropism, tropistic movement	Tropismus m, tropistische Krümmungsbewegung (Bewegung) f	Trouton['s] law	s. Trouton['s] rule
		Trouton-Noble experiment	Trouton-Nobelscher Versuch m
tropopause, substratosphere, upper inversion, lower stratosphere	Tropopause f, obere Inversion f, Substratosphäre f; substratosphärische Inversion	Trouton-Rankine body	Trouton-Rankine-Körper m
		Trouton['s] rule, Trouton['s] law	Troutonsche Regel f
tropopause bump	Tropopausenhöcker m	Trouton viscosity	Trouton-Viskosität f, Troutonsche Viskosität f
tropopause cyclone	Tropopausenzyklone f		
tropopause fluctuation, tropopause oscillation	Tropopausenschwankung f, Tropopausenschwingung f	true, real, veritable	echt, wahr, tatsächlich, wirklich, absolut, real
		true absorption	echte Absorption f, absolute Absorption, wahre Absorption
tropopause hill (mountain), tropopause peak	Tropopausenberg m	true acronycal rising	wahrer akronychischer Aufgang m
		true acronycal setting	wahrer akronychischer Untergang m
tropopause oscillation	s. tropopause fluctuation	true anomaly	wahre Anomalie f
tropopause peak	s. tropopause hill	true astronomical refraction	wahre astronomische Refraktion f
tropopause wave	Tropopausenwelle f		
troposphere	Troposphäre f	true bearing, true radio bearing, corrected bearing	rechtweisende Peilung f, wahre Peilung
tropospheric duct	s. atmospheric duct		
tropospheric fading	troposphärischer Schwund m		
		true cavitation	s. vaporous cavitation
tropospheric mode, mode of tropospheric propagation	troposphärischer Schwingungstyp (Wellentyp) m, troposphärische Schwingungsart (Mode) f	true charge, free charge	freie (ableitbare, wahre) Ladung f
		true coincidence, genuine coincidence	echte Koinzidenz f
		true colloid, eucolloid, natural colloid	Eukolloid n
tropospheric scatter	troposphärische Streuausbreitung f, Streuausbreitung in der Troposphäre	true conic projection	echte Kegelprojektion f, echter Kegelentwurf m, echte konische Projektion f, echter konischer Entwurf m, wahre Kegelprojektion, wahrer Kegelentwurf, wahre konische Projektion, wahrer konischer Entwurf
tropospheric scattering	troposphärische Streuung f, Troposphärenstreuung f, Streuung f in der Troposphäre		
tropospheric wave	troposphärische Welle f, Troposphärenwelle f		
tropotactic	tropotaktisch		
tropotaxis	Tropotaxis f		
troptometer, torsion meter, twist-measuring device	Torsionsmesser m, Verdrehungsmesser m	true co-ordinates, holonomic co-ordinates	holonome Koordinaten fpl, wahre Koordinaten
		true current density	wahre Stromdichte f
Trotter and Weber photometer, roof photometer, Dach photometer	Dachphotometer n, Trotter-Weber-Photometer n	true cylindrical projection	echte (wahre) Zylinderprojektion f, echter (wahrer) Zylinderentwurf m
Trotter photometer	Trotter-Photometer n	true degeneracy, true degeneration	echte Entartung f, Symmetrieentartung f
trouble	Störung f; Schaden m; Fehler m	true density	s. theoretical density
		true diameter, linear diameter <of star>	wahrer Durchmesser m, linearer Durchmesser <Gestirn>
trouble, microvariations, microscopic variations, disturbances	Unruhe f		
		true elevation of boiling point, true rising of boiling point	wahre Siedepunkt[s]erhöhung f
trouble coefficient	s. turbidity coefficient	true equilibrium	wahres Gleichgewicht n
trouble factor	s. turbidity factor	true error	wahrer Fehler m
trouble shooting	Störungsbeseitigung f	true glacier, valley glacier, valley-type glacier	Talgletscher m
trouble spot, weak spot, weak point	Schwachstelle f	true height, absolute height, height	wahre Höhe f, absolute Höhe, Höhe
troubling; turbidity; turbidness	Trübung f, optische Trübung; Trübheit f, Trübe f; Eintrübung f	true height, flying altitude (height), flight altitude (height), altitude	Flughöhe f
troubling layer, layer of troubling	Trübschicht f, Trübungsschicht f		
		true height, real height <of reflection>	tatsächliche Reflexionshöhe f
troubling particle, troubling particulate	trübendes Teilchen n, trübendes Körperchen n		

true height of ionosphere	wahre Ionosphärenhöhe f, wahre Höhe f der Ionosphäre	truncation of crystal	Abstumpfung f der Kristallkanten
true horizon, geocentric horizon, celestial horizon, geometrical horizon	wahrer Horizont m, geozentrischer Horizont	trunk circuit (junction line)	s. long distance transmission line <el.>
true horopter, empiric horopter	wahrer Horopter m, empirischer Horopter	trunk of the nucleus, core of the nucleus, nuclear core, nuclear trunk, nuclear frame	Kernrumpf m, Rumpf m des Atomkerns
true ionization potential	s. adiabatic ionization potential	trunnion	s. pivot journal
true isotherm	wahre Isotherme f	trunnion axis	Schwenkachse f
true linear [energy] absorption coefficient	wahrer linearer Absorptionskoeffizient m		
		trunnion axis, horizontal axis, horizontal trunnion axis <of theodolite>	Kippachse f, Horizontalachse f <Theodolit>
true lowering of the freezing point	wahre Gefrierpunkt[s]erniedrigung f	truss, truss[ed] frame	s. space framework
true mass [energy] absorption coefficient	wahrer Massenabsorptionskoeffizient m	truth, rightness, trueness; correctness <num. math.>	Richtigkeit f <num. Math.>
true motion	wahre Schiffsbewegung f, „true motion" f	truth function, function of formal logic	Wahrheitsfunktion f
trueness	s. rightness	truth of running error, trueness of rotation error	Rundlauffehler m
trueness of rotation error	s. truth of running error	truth value	Wahrheitswert m
true noon, apparent noon	wahrer Mittag m		
true osmotic pressure	wahrer osmotischer Druck m		
true place [of the star], true position [of the star]	wahrer Ort m [des Gestirns], wahrer Sternort m	try square, back square	Anschlagwinkel m
		Tschebyscheff['s] polynomial	s. Chebyshev['s] polynomial <of the first or second kind>
true pole, apparent pole	wahrer Pol m		
true position [of the star], true place [of the star]	wahrer Ort m [des Gestirns], wahrer Sternort m	Tscherning['s] curve	Tscherningsche Kurve f
		T-S diagram	S-T-Diagramm n
true projection	s. perspective projection		
true radiant	wahrer Radiant m	T,s diagram	s. temperature-entropy chart
true radio bearing	s. true bearing		
true range	wahre Reichweite f	T[-] section	s. T[-] network
true refraction	wahre Refraktion f	T-section filter	T-Schaltung f, Kettenleiter m zweiter Art, Sternschaltung f
true remanence	s. retentiveness		
true rising of boiling point, true elevation of boiling point	wahre Siedepunkt[s]erhöhung f	$T_2[-]$ space	s. Hausdorff space
		tsunami	Tsunami m, Tsunami-Welle f, zerstörende Seebebenwelle f, Seebebenwelle, seismische Meereswelle f
true scale reducer, proportional reducer	proportionaler Abschwächer m		
		Tswett['s] absorption method, Tswett['s] chromatography	Tswettsche Säulenchromatographie (Chromatographie) f, Säulenchromatographie nach Tswett
Truesdell number	Truesdellsche Zahl f		
true sided, laterally uninverted, correct <of image>	seitenrichtig <Bild>		
		T Tauri star, RW Aurigae-type star, nebular variable	RW Aurigae-Stern m, T Tauri-Stern m, Nebelveränderlicher m
true sidereal day, apparent sidereal day	wahrer Sterntag m		
true sidereal time, apparent sidereal time	wahre Sternzeit f	t-test	s. Student['s] test
		TTT diagram	s. temperature-time-transformation diagram
true solar day, apparent solar day	wahrer Sonnentag m	tube	s. thermionic valve
true solar radiation	wahre Sonnenstrahlung f	tube amplifier, vacuum-tube amplifier, valve amplifier	Röhrenverstärker m, Elektronenröhrenverstärker m, Vakuumröhrenverstärker m
true solar time, apparent solar time; sundial time	wahre Sonnenzeit f; wahre Ortszeit f		
true solution, molecular solution, solitude	echte Lösung f, molekulare Lösung	tube analyzer	Tubusanalysator m
		tube capacitance	s. interelectrode capacitance
true stagnation pressure	s. total pressure <aero.>	tube characteristic	s. current-voltage characteristic
true stress-strain curve, true stress-strain diagram	wahres Spannungs-Dehnungs-Schaubild n, wahre Spannungs-Dehnungs-Kurve f		
		tube chromatography	Tubechromatographie f
true Sun, apparent Sun	wahre Sonne f	tube circuit, valve circuit, vacuum-tube circuit	Röhrenschaltung f
true surface [area]	wahre Oberfläche f	tube constant	s. tube parameter
true transference number, true transport number, Nernst transport number	wahre Überführungszahl f, Nernstsche Überführungszahl	tube-controlled, valve-controlled, vacuum-tube-controlled	röhrengesteuert
		tube counter	s. counter <nucl.>
true value	s. actual value <meas.>	tube drawing, drawing of tubes	Ziehen n von Rohren, Rohrziehen n, Rohrzug m
true zenithal distance	wahre Zenitdistanz f		
trumpet cooler	s. pipe cooler	tube electrometer, vacuum tube electrometer	Röhrenelektrometer n
Trümpler's star	Trümplerscher Stern m		
truncated cone	Kegelstumpf m	tube electronics, thermionic valve electronics	Röhrenelektronik f
truncated cylinder	Zylinderstumpf m		
truncated distribution	gestutzte Verteilung f	tube entrance, entrance [of the tube]	Rohreinlauf m, Einlauf m [des Rohres]
truncated distribution function	teilintegrierte Verteilungsfunktion f	tube equation, thermionic valve equation	Röhrengleichung f, Röhrenformel f
truncated sample	gestutzte Stichprobe f		
truncated transient [voltage]	abgeschnittene Stoßspannung f	tube expander, expander	Aufweitedorn m, Rohraufweitedorn m, Streckdorn m, Aufweitestopfen m
truncation, cut <of the series, math.>	Abbrechen n <der Reihe, Math.>		
		tube extension, extension of the tube	Tubusauszug m
truncation <stat.>	Stutzung f <Stat.>	tube factor <opt.>	Tubusfaktor m, Vergrößerungsfaktor m <Opt.>
truncation error	Abbruchfehler m, Abbrechfehler m		
truncation number	„truncation number" f		

tube filter   Schlauchfilter *n*
tube float, staff float, pole float, rod float, velocity rod   Stabschwimmer *m*, Stangenschwimmer *m*, Stockschwimmer *m*, hydrometrische Stange *f*, Schwimmstange *f*
tube generator, valve oscillator, vacuum-tube oscillator, tube oscillator, valve generator, vacuum-tube generator, tube-oscillator generator, thermionic generator   Röhrenoszillator *m*, Röhrengenerator *m*
tube housing   s. X-ray tube housing
tube lens   Tubuslinse *f*, Tubussystem *n*
tube manometer   Rohrmanometer *n*, Röhrenmanometer *n*
tube noise, vacuum tube noise, valve noise, tube rustle, valve rustle   Röhrenrauschen *n*
tube of flow   s. stream tube
tube of flux, tube of force, tube of lines of force   Kraft[feld]röhre *f*, Feldröhre *f*, Feldlinienröhre *f*, Kraftflußröhre *f*
tube of [magnetic] induction, tube of magnetic lines of force   Induktionsröhre *f*
tube of microscope, microscope tube   Mikroskoptubus *m*, Tubus *m* des Mikroskops
tube of the polarizing microscope   Polarisationstubus *m*
tube of the vector field, vector tube   Vektorröhre *f*, Vektorfeldröhre *f*, Feldröhre *f*, Feldlinienröhre *f*
tube oscillator, tube-oscillator generator   s. tube generator
tube-oscillator high-voltage generator   s. vacuum-tube transmitter
tube parameter, tube constant, valve parameter (constant)   Röhrenkonstante *f*
tube photometer   Tubusphotometer *n*
tube plate   Rohrboden *m*, Rohrplatte *f*, Rohrtafel *f*
tube quality, valve quality   Röhrengüte *f*
tubercular corrosion, tuberculation, honeycomb corrosion, honeycombing   Narbenkorrosion *f*, [flache] narbenartige Korrosion *f*, narbenartige Anfressung *f*
tube rectifier   s. valve rectifier
tube rustle   s. tube noise
tube spring manometer, tube spring pressure gauge, elastic tube pressure gauge   Rohrfedermanometer *n*, Rohrfedermeßwerk *n*, Rohrfederdruckmesser *m*, Röhrenfedermanometer *n*, Röhrenfedermeßwerk *n*, Röhrenfederdruckmesser *m*, Röhrenfeder *f*, Rohrfeder *f*
tube stand   Röhrenstativ *n*
tube telescope   Tubusfernrohr *n*
tube thickness, tube wall thickness   Rohrwanddicke *f*, Rohrwandstärke *f*, Rohrdicke *f*
tube transmitter   s. vacuum-tube transmitter
tube-type camera   Tubuskamera *f*
tube-type galvanometer, valve galvanometer, vacuum-tube galvanometer   Röhrengalvanometer *n*
tube voltmeter   s. vacuum-tube voltmeter
tube wall thickness, tube thickness   Rohrwanddicke *f*, Rohrwandstärke *f*, Rohrdicke *f*
tube wind tunnel   Rohrwindkanal *m*
tubular anemometer   Tubenanemometer *n*, Rohranemometer *n*, Röhrenanemometer *n*
tubular antenna   Rohrantenne *f*, Röhrenantenne *f*
tubular capacitor   Rohrkondensator *m*, Röhrenkondensator *m*; Rollkondensator *m*, Rollenkondensator *m*
tubular conductor   s. hollow waveguide
tubular discharge lamp, high-voltage tubular discharge lamp   Hochspannungsleuchtröhre *f*, Leuchtröhre *f*; röhrenförmige Niederdruckentladungslampe (Entladungslampe) *f*
tubular electrical dust filter, pipe filter, tubular filter   Röhrenfilter *n*, Rohrfilter *n*
tubular electrodynamometer   Röhrenelektrodynamometer *n*
tubular exchanger   Röhrenwärmeaustauscher *m*, Röhrenwärmetauscher *m*, Rohrbündel-Wärmeaustauscher *m*, Rohrbündelaustauscher *m*
tubular extension   röhrenförmiger Ansatz *m*
tubular filter, pipe filter, tubular electrical dust filter   Röhrenfilter *n*, Rohrfilter *n*
tubular flow   s. pipe flow
tubular lamp, tubular line lamp, tubular light, strip lamp, spot   Soffittenlampe *f*, Soffitte *f*, Lichtwurflampe *f* L
tubular level, level tube   Röhrenlibelle *f*
tubular light (line lamp)   s. tubular lamp
tubular microphone, wave-type microphone   Rohrmikrophon *n*, Rohrrichtmikrophon *n*, Wellenleitermikrophon *n*
tubular pinch   Hohlpinch *m*
tubular resistor   Rohrwiderstand *m*; Schlauchwiderstand *m*
tubular source, hollow cylinder source   hohlzylinderförmige Quelle *f*, Hohlzylinderquelle *f*, rohrförmige Quelle
tubular trimmer   Tauchkondensator *m*

Tuchel contact   Tuchel-Kontakt *m*
Tudor plate   Tudor-Platte *f*
tug; traction; pull[ing]; drawing; drag   Ziehen *n*, Zug *m*, Fortziehen *n*; Schleppen *n*
tug   s. a. jerk
Tukey test   Tukey-Test *m*
tumbler, tumbler switch; trigger switch; toggle switch, single-throw switch, single-way switch   Kippschalter *m*, Kipphebelschalter *m*, Kellog-Schalter *m*; Hebel[um]schalter *m*; Einweg[um]schalter *m*; Tumblerschalter *m*
tumbling   s. sudden fall
tumbling   s. staggering motion
tumour dose   Tumordosis *f*, Herddosis *f*
tunable chemical laser   abstimmbarer chemischer Laser *m*
tunable dye laser   abstimmbarer Farbstofflaser *m*
tune   s. tuning
tuned amplifier, resonance amplifier   abgestimmter Verstärker *m*, selektiver Spannungsverstärker *m*, Resonanzverstärker *m*
tuned circuit   s. tuning circuit
tuned coupling   Sperrkreiskopplung *f*
tuned-reed frequency meter   s. reed-type frequency meter
tuned-reed relay   s. vibrating relay
tuned transformer, resonant transformer   Resonanztransformator *m*, abgestimmter Transformator *m*
tungsten arc lamp   Wolframbogenlampe *f*, Punktlichtlampe *f*, Wolframpunktlampe *f*
tungsten cathode   Wolframkatode *f*, Wolframreinmetallkatode *f*
tungsten emitter   s. tungsten lamp
tungsten filament bolometer   Wolframbolometer *n*
tungsten filament lamp   Wolframfadenlampe *f*, Wolframfadenglühlampe *f*, Wolframdrahtlampe *f*, Wolframdrahtglühlampe *f*; Wolframwendellampe *f*

tungsten halogen lamp	Halogenglühlampe f, Halogenlampe f
tungsten-hydrogen barretter	Wolframwasserstoffwiderstand m
tungsten iodine lamp	s. quartz iodine lamp
tungsten lamp, tungsten light source, tungsten emitter	Wolframlampe f, Wolframlichtquelle f, Wolframemitter m, Wolframstrahler m
tungsten ribbon lamp, tungsten strip lamp	Wolframbandlampe f, Bandlampe f
tuning, tune	Abstimmung f
tuning <ac.>	Stimmen n <Ak.>
tuning characteristic, tuning curve, selectivity characteristic	Abstimmcharakteristik f, Abstimmkurve f, Abstimmdiagramm n
tuning circuit; tuned circuit	Abstimmkreis m, Abstimmungs[strom]kreis m
tuning curve	s. tuning characteristic
tuning eye [tube]	s. tuning indicator
tuning-fork, tuning fork, pitchfork	Stimmgabel f
tuning-fork frequency modulator	Stimmgabelmodulator m
tuning-fork oscillator	Stimmgabelgenerator m, Stimmgabeloszillator m, Stimmgabelsummer m
tuning indicator, tuning-indicator tube, tuning eye [tube], tunoscope, magic eye, "Magic Eye" tube, magic fan	Abstimmanzeigeröhre f, magisches Auge n, magischer Fächer m, magisches Band n; Abstimmanzeige f
tuning variometer, syntonizing variometer	Abstimmvariometer n
tunnel <in the emulsion>	„Tunnel" m <Emulsionstechnik>
tunnel	s. a. wind tunnel
tunnel breakthrough	Tunneldurchbruch m
tunnel coefficient, coefficient of utilization of the tunnel	Kanalfaktor m <Aero.>
tunnel contact, Josephson contact (junction)	Josephson-Kontakt m, Tunnelkontakt m
tunnel current, tunnelling current	Tunnelstrom m
tunnel diode, Esaki diode	Tunneldiode f, Esaki-Diode f
tunnel-diode trigger	Tunneldiodentrigger m
tunnel effect; tunnelling, tunneling	Tunneleffekt m; Tunneln n
tunnel efficiency	s. tunnel coefficient
tunnel emission	Tunnelemission f
tunnel-emitter triode	s. tunnel transistor
tunnel exponential	Tunnelexponent m
tunnel furnace	Tunnelofen m
tunneling	s. tunnel effect
tunnel injection	Tunnelinjektion f
tunnel junction	Tunnelübergang m
tunnelling	s. tunnel effect
tunnelling current, tunnel current	Tunnelstrom m
tunnelling energy	Durchtunnelungsenergie f, Tunnelenergie f, Überwindungsenergie f
tunnelling probability	Durchtunnelungswahrscheinlichkeit f, Tunnelwahrscheinlichkeit f, Überwindungswahrscheinlichkeit f
tunnelling resistance	Tunneleffektwiderstand m
tunnelling through the [potential] barrier; overcoming the potential barrier, surmounting the potential barrier, getting over the potential barrier	Durchtunnelung f des Potentialwalls, Durchgang m durch den Potentialwall, Durchdringung f des Potentialwalls; Überwindung f des Potentialwalls
tunnel model	Tunnelmodell n
tunnel model	s. a. wind tunnel model
tunnel transistor, tunnel-emitter triode	Tunneltransistor m, Tunnel-Emitter-Triode f
tunnel triode	Tunneltriode f
tunoscope	s. tuning indicator
turbator	Turbator m
turbid; troubled, muddy, thick, mothery <of liquid>; dull <of glass>	trüb; getrübt
turbidimeter, turbidity meter	Lufttrübungsmesser m; Trübungsmesser m, Trübungsmeßgerät n; Schwebstoffmesser m
turbidimetric titration	turbidimetrische Titration f, Trübungstitration f
turbidimetry, measurement of turbidity	Trübungsmessung f, Extinktionsmessung f, Turbidimetrie f
turbidity; troubling; turbidness; dimness	Trübung f, optische Trübung; Trübheit f, Trübe f; Eintrübung f
turbidity, photographic turbidity <phot.>	photographische Unschärfe (Streuunschärfe) f, Streuunschärfe, Unschärfe <Phot.>
turbidity coefficient [of Ångström], Ångström['s] turbidity coefficient, Ångström['s] turbidity parameter, coefficient of turbidity, Ångström['s] coefficient of turbidity, trouble coefficient	Trübungskoeffizient m [nach Ångström], Ångströmscher Trübungskoeffizient, Ångströmsches Trübungsmaß n
turbidity current <in dissolution of salts>; convective flow	konvektive Strömung f, Konvektionsströmung f; Konvektionsstrom m
turbidity current	Trübstrom m; Suspensionsströmung f
turbidity due to atmospheric haze	Dunsttrübung f, Dunsttrübe f
turbidity due to condensation, condensation turbidity	Kondensationstrübe f, Kondensationstrübung f
turbidity factor <of Linke>, Linke['s] turbidity factor (parameter), factor of turbidity, Linke['s] factor of turbidity, trouble factor	Trübungsfaktor m [nach Linke], Linkescher Trübungsfaktor, Linkesches Trübungsmaß n
turbidity factor for short-wave radiation <of Linke>	Kurztrübungsfaktor m [nach Linke]
turbidity measure, measure of turbidity, turbidity parameter	Trübungsmaß n
turbidity meter	s. turbidimeter
turbidity of water	Wassertrübung f, Trübung f des Wassers; Gewässertrübung f
turbidity parameter	s. turbidity measure
turbidness	s. turbidity
turbine expansion engine	s. turbine liquefier
turbine interrupter	s. turbo[-]interrupter
turbine inverter	s. turbo[-]inverter
turbine liquefier, turbo-expansion engine, turbine expansion engine	Entspannungsturbine f, Turboexpansionsmaschine f, Turbinenexpansionsmaschine f, Turbinenverflüssiger m, Turbodetander m [nach Kapitza]
turbine meter	Turbinenzähler m
turbine pump	s. rotodynamic pump
turbine stirrer	Turbinenrührer m, Turbinenrührwerk n
turbo-alternator	Turboalternator m, Wechselstrom-Turbogenerator m

turbo-blower	Kreiselgebläse n, Turbogebläse n	turbulent flame	turbulente Flamme f
turbo-compressor	Kreiselverdichter m, Turbokompressor m, Turboverdichter m	turbulent flow; turbulent stream; turbulent motion, eddy motion, eddying whirl	turbulente Strömung f, Flechtströmung f, wirblige (wirbelnde) Strömung; turbulente Bewegung f, Turbulenzbewegung f, Quirlung f, Wirbelung f
turbo[-]dynamo	Turbodynamo m, Gleichstrom-Turbogenerator m	turbulent flow field, turbulent field	turbulentes Strömungsfeld n, turbulentes Feld n, Turbulenzfeld n
turbo-electric	turboelektrisch		
turbo-expansion engine	s. turbine liquefier		
turbo[-]interrupter, turbine interrupter	Turbinenunterbrecher m, Turbounterbrecher m <mit Quecksilberstrahl>	turbulent flow of heat	s. turbulent heat flow
		turbulent fluctuation	turbulente Schwankung f, Turbulenzschwankung f
turbo[-]inverter, turbine inverter	Turbowechselrichter m, Turbinenwechselrichter m <mit Quecksilberstrahl>	turbulent fluctuation, phenomenon of turbulent fluctuation	turbulente Schwankungserscheinung f
		turbulent fluctuation of density, turbulent density fluctuation	turbulente Dichteschwankung f
		turbulent flux, vortex (eddy, vorticity) flux, flux of vorticity	Wirbelfluß m, Vorticityfluß m <Geo.>
turbo-jet [drive]	Turbinenstrahltriebwerk n, Turbojettriebwerk n, Turbojet m	turbulent friction; apparent friction, virtual friction	turbulente Scheinreibung f, Turbulenzreibung f; Scheinreibung f, scheinbare Reibung f
turbomolecular drag pump	Turbomolekularpumpe f	turbulent heat conduction	s. eddy conduction [of heat]
turpo-prop [drive]	s. propeller turbine		
turbo-pump	s. rotodynamic pump		
turbosphere	Turbosphäre f	turbulent heat flow, turbulent flow of heat	turbulenter Wärmestrom m, Turbulenzwärmestrom m
turbulator	Turbulator m, Verwirbler m, Wirbler m; Wirbelplatte f		
turbulence	Turbulenz f	turbulent jet	turbulenter Strahl m, Wirbelstrahl m
turbulence	s. a. whirling	turbulent jet burner	Wirbelstrahlbrenner m
turbulence axis	s. vortex axis		
turbulence element	s. element of turbulence	turbulent law of resistance, law of resistance for turbulent flow	turbulentes Widerstandsgesetz n
turbulence factor	Turbulenzfaktor m, Turbulenzziffer f		
turbulence heating	Turbulenzaufheizung f, turbulente Aufheizung f	turbulent layer	turbulente Schicht f, Turbulenzschicht f
turbulence intensifier, turbulizer	Turbulenzverstärker m	turbulent mixing	turbulente Durchmischung f, turbulente Mischung f, Turbulenzmischung f
turbulence intensity, intensity of turbulence	Turbulenzstärke f	turbulent motion	s. turbulent flow
		turbulent Prandtl number, Pr_t	turbulente Prandtl-Zahl f, Pr_t
turbulence near the wall, wall turbulence	Wandturbulenz f	turbulent region, turbulent zone, zone of turbulence, region of turbulence	Turbulenzbereich m, Turbulenzgebiet n, Turbulenzzone f, turbulenter Bereich m, turbulentes Gebiet n, turbulente Zone f; Turbulenzstrecke f
turbulence paradox	Turbulenzparadoxon n		
turbulence spectrum	s. spectrum of turbulence		
turbulence theory	s. Weizsäcker['s] turbulence theory		
turbulency	s. turbulence	turbulent separation, eddy making	turbulente Ablösung f
turbulent boundary layer	turbulente Grenzschicht f, turbulente Reibungsschicht f		
turbulent burner	Wirbelbrenner m, Wirbelstrombrenner m	turbulent spot	Turbulenzfleck[en] m
		turbulent state, state of turbulence	Turbulenzzustand m, turbulenter Zustand
turbulent cloud	Turbulenzwolke f	turbulent stream	s. turbulent flow
turbulent combustion	turbulente Verbrennung f	turbulent thermal conductivity	s. eddy conductivity
turbulent conduction [of heat]	s. eddy conduction	turbulent thermal diffusivity	s. eddy diffusivity
turbulent conductivity	s. eddy conductivity	turbulent transfer, eddy transfer (transport)	turbulenter Transport m, Turbulenztransport m
turbulent convection, convection by turbulence	turbulente Konvektion f, Wirbelkonvektion f	turbulent transfer coefficient, eddy transfer coefficient	turbulente Austauschgröße f
turbulent core [flow]	s. vortex-core flow		
turbulent density fluctuation, turbulent fluctuation of density	turbulente Dichteschwankung f	turbulent transfer coefficient	s. a. effective turbulent diffusivity
		turbulent viscosity	s. eddy viscosity
turbulent diffusion	s. eddy diffusion	turbulent wake	turbulenter Nachlauf m
turbulent diffusion coefficient	s. eddy diffusivity	turbulent wedge	Turbulenzkeil m
turbulent diffusivity	s. eddy diffusivity	turbulent zone	s. turbulent region
turbulent energy, energy of turbulence, eddy energy, eddy kinetic energy	Turbulenzenergie f, turbulente Energie f; Wirbelungsenergie f, Wirbelungsarbeit f	turbulizer, turbulence intensifier	Turbulenzverstärker m
		turgescence	s. turgidity
		turgescence motion	s. turgor motion
turbulent energy density	turbulente Energiedichte f, Turbulenzenergiedichte f	turgid	turgeszent
turbulent energy equation	Turbulenzenergiegleichung f	turgidity, turgidness, turgor, turgescence, turgor pressure	Turgordruck m, Turgor m, Turgeszenz f, Turgeszenzdruck m
turbulent exchange	turbulenter Austausch m, Turbulenzaustausch m	turgor change	Turgorschwankung f
turbulent field	s. turbulent flow field	turgor deficit	Turgordefizit n

turgor motion, turgescence motion — Turgorbewegung *f*
turgor pressure — s. turgor
turgor state — Turgeszenzzustand *m*

Turing machine — Turing-Maschine *f*

Turkestan-type glacier — Firnkesselgletscher *m*, Turkestanischer Gletschertyp *m*

turmalin[e] plate — s. tourmalin[e] plate
turmalin[e] tongs — s. tourmalin[e] tongs
turn, turn of winding, single turn, spire; worm ‹of screw›; torsion ‹bio.› — Windung *f*; Lage *f*
turn, revolution — Umdrehung *f*, Tour *f*, U
turn, turn-back; diversion; deflection [around a corner]; piping around a corner — Umlenkung *f*
turn — s. a. turn-back
turn-and-bank indicator, turn indicator, turnmeter — Wendezeiger *m*
turn aperture — Windungsöffnung *f*
turn area — Windungsfläche *f*

turn-back, turn, turning-back, turning — Wendung *f*; Drehung *f*; Umwendung *f*
turn-back; reverse torsion; reverse rotation — Rückdrehung *f*, Rückwärtsdrehung *f*; Gegendrehung *f*; Gegenrotation *f*

turn-back — s. a. turn
turn cross-section, cross-section of single turn — Windungsquerschnitt *m*
Turner filter, Turner interference filter — Filter *n* der verhinderten Totalreflexion, Turner-Filter *n*

turn flux, flux through single turn — Windungsfluß *m*

turn indicator, turn-and-bank indicator, turnmeter — Wendezeiger *m*
turning[-back] — s. turn-back
turning moment — s. torque
turning moment coefficient — s. tilting moment coefficient
turnmeter — s. turn indicator
turn-off characteristic; reverse characteristic; blocking characteristic — Sperrcharakteristik *f*, Sperrkennlinie *f*

turn of the drum, turn of the thimble — Trommelumdrehung *f*
turn of the spiral, spiral turn — Spiralwindung *f*, Windung *f* der Spirale

turn of the thimble, turn of the drum — Trommelumdrehung *f*
turn of tide, change of tide; slack tide, slack water, slack — Flutwechsel *m*, Gezeitenwechsel *m*; Kentern *n* des Gezeitenstromes, Umkehr *f* des Gezeitenstromes, Umschlagen *n* des Gezeitenstromes, Umschlagen der Strömung, Stillstand *m* der Gezeiten; Stillwasser *n*, Stauwasser *n*

turn of winding — s. turn
turnover; complete revolution; complete turn — volle Umdrehung *f*, vollständige Umdrehung; voller Umlauf *m*, Vollumlauf *m*, ganzer Umlauf

turnover ‹bio.› — Umsatz *m*, Umsetzung *f*; Austausch *m*, Wechsel *m* ‹Bio.›
turnover — s. a. alternation of polarity
turnover frequency — s. Nyquist frequency
turnover rate — Umsatzrate *f*, Umsatzgeschwindigkeit *f*

turnover rate constant — Umsatzgeschwindigkeitskonstante *f*, Umsatzkonstante *f*
turnover time — Umsatzzeit *f*
turn-over voltage, Zener voltage — Zener-Spannung *f*
turnover voltage — s. a. knee voltage
turn speed — s. speed
turns per minute — s. revolutions per minute
turns per unit time — s. speed
turns ratio, winding ratio, ratio of the windings — Windungs[zahl]verhältnis *n*, Windungsübersetzung *f*
turnstile antenna — Drehkreuzantenne *f*, Kreuzdipol *m*, Quirlantenne *f*, „turnstile"-Antenne *f*; Drehkreuzstrahler *m*, Kreuzstrahler *m*
turn-up circle — Rückkehrkreis *m*
turret — s. turret head
turret eyepiece — Revolverokular *n*
turret head, turret, revolving nosepiece, revolving objective changer; lens turret; cine turret — Revolverkopf *m*, Revolver *m*, Objektivrevolver *m*

turret telescope — Turret-Teleskop *n* [nach Hartness]
tutton salt, complex salt — komplexes Salz *n*
tuyere, measuring nozzle — Meßdüse *f*
T value, cation exchange capacity, CEC, sorption capacity ‹bio.› — T-Wert *m*, Kationenaustauschkapazität *f*, Umtauschkapazität *f*, Austauschkapazität *f*, Sorptionskapazität *f* ‹Bio.›

T-v diagram, temperature-volume diagram — Temperatur-Volumen-Diagramm *n*, T*v*-Diagramm *n*

Twaddle degree, degree Twaddle — Twaddle-Grad *m*, Twaddel[l]-Grad *m*
T-wave — s. transverse mode ‹el.›
tweeter — Hochtonlautsprecher *m*

twelve-membered ring, twelve ring — Zwölferring *m*, Zwölfring *m*

twenty-one-centimetre line, 21 cm emission line, 21 cm line — 21-cm-Linie *f* [des Wasserstoffs], Einundzwanzig-Zentimeter-Linie *f*

twenty-seven-day recurrence effect, 27-day period — Siebenundzwanzig-Tage-Periode *f*, 27-d-Periode *f*
twice forbidden, doubly forbidden, second forbidden — zweifach verboten
twice-reflected — zweimal reflektiert, doppelt-reflektiert
twilight; tenebrescence — Dämmerung *f*; Zwielicht *n*
twilight — Dämmerlicht *n*, Dämmerungslicht *n*
twilight, dusk, owl-light gloaming — Abenddämmerung *f*
twilight airglow, twilight glow — Dämmerungsleuchten *n*
twilight arch — Dämmerungsbogen *m*
twilight brightness, twilight luminance — Dämmerungsbeleuchtung *f*, Dämmerungshelligkeit *f*
twilight effect — s. night effect
twilight glow — s. twilight airglow
twilight luminance, twilight brightness — Dämmerungsbeleuchtung *f*, Dämmerungshelligkeit *f*
twilight phenomenon — Dämmerungserscheinung *f*
twilight rainbow, red rainbow — Dämmerungsregenbogen *m*, roter Regenbogen *m*
twilight sky — Dämmerungshimmel *m*
twilight visibility [distance] — Dämmerungssichtweite *f*, Dämmerungssicht *f*

twilight zone — Zwielichtzone *f*

twin, twin crystal, twinned crystals, bicrystal, hemitrope, macle <cryst.>	Zwilling m, Kristallzwilling m, Zwillingskristall m, Doppelkristall m, Bikristall m, Zwillingsindividuum n <Krist.>	twin plane reflection	Reflexion f an der Zwillingsfläche, Zwillingsebenenreflexion f, Zwillingsflächenreflexion f
twin aggregate, twinned aggregate	Zwillingsaggregat n	twin position	Zwillingsstellung f
twin axis	s. twinning axis	twin prism	Zwillingsprisma n
twin band, Neumann band	Neumannsches Band n, Zwillingsstreifen m	twin probe, double probe, dual probe	Doppelsonde f
twin boundary	Zwillingsgrenze f	twin radiosonde, tandem radiosonde	Radiosondengespann n
		twin resistance box	[gegenläufiger] Doppelkurbelwiderstand m
twin boundary energy	Zwillingsgrenzenenergie f	twin serial camera, double serial camera, double serial cine camera [for serial shots]	Zweifachreihenkammer f, Zweifachreihenbildkammer f, Zwillingsreihenkammer f
twin calorimeter, differential calorimeter	Differentialkalorimeter n, Zwillingskalorimeter n		
twin circuit (conductor)	s. two-wire line	twin slippage	Zwillingsgleitung f
twin contact	Zwillingskontakt m		
twin contacts; three-terminal contact	Doppelkontakt m	twin striae, twin striation	Zwillingsstreifung f
twin corner, twinning corner	Zwillingsecke f	twin structure, twinned structure	Zwillingsstruktur f, Zwillingsbau m
twin crystal	s. twin <cryst.>	twin T-bridge, double T-bridge [circuit]	Doppel-T-Brücke f, Doppel-T-Meßbrücke f, T-T-Netzwerk n
twin edge, twinning edge	Zwillingskante f	twin tube	Doppelröhre f
twin electron	s. positron-electron pair	twin water-flow pyrheliometer	Zwillings-Waterflowpyrheliometer n, Zwillings-Durchflußpyrheliometer n
twin element	Zwillingselement n		
twin energy, twinning energy	Zwillingsenergie f		
twin formation	s. twinning <cryst.>	Twiss coefficient	Twiss-Koeffizient m
twin-gang capacitor	s. two-gang variable capacitor	twist, angular momentum, moment of momentum; angular momentum vector	Drehimpuls m, Impulsmoment f; Drehimpulsvektor m, Drall m, Schwung m
twin graded [interference] filter	Verlaufdoppelfilter n		
twinkle, twinkling, sparkling, glitter	Funkeln n, Blinken n, Blitzen n, Glitzern n; Glänzen n	twist, lay	Drallänge f, Schlaglänge f, Drall m
twinkling	s. scintillation <of stars> <astr.>	twist, twisting <of cable>	Verdrillung f [der Leitung], Verseilung f
twin lamella, twin lamina	Zwillingslamelle f	twist <of wing>	Verwindung f <Tragflügel>
		twist	s. a. screw displacement
		twist	s. a. twisting <of fibre or wire>
twin lens; binary lens	Zwillingslinse f; Doppellinse f, Bilinse f	twist	s. a. twisting
twin-lens reflex camera	zweiäugige Spiegelreflexkamera f	twist	s. a. twist per unit length
		twist angle	s. angle of torsion
		twist boundary	„twist boundary" f, Verdrehungskorngrenze f, Verdrillungskorngrenze f, Verdrillungsgrenze f, Dreh[korn]grenze f
twin lever	s. double lever		
twin line	s. two-wire line		
twinned	hemitrop, Zwillings-	twist buckling, torsional buckling	Drillknickung f, Drehknickung f
twinned aggregate	s. twin aggregate		
twinned crystals	s. twin <cryst.>	twisted curve, curve of double curvature; space curve, spatial curve	Raumkurve f; doppeltgekrümmte Kurve f, Kurve doppelter Krümmung, nichtebene Kurve
twinned cyclones, two-centre cyclone	Zwillingstief n		
twinned structure, twin structure	Zwillingsstruktur f, Zwillingsbau m	twisted halo	verdrehter Halo m
twinning, twin formation, hemitropism <cryst.>	Zwillingsbildung f, Zwillingsverwachsung f, Verzwillingung f <Krist.>	twisted line	verdrillte Leitung f
		twisted ring scaler, twisted ring scaling circuit, Moebius counter	„twisted-ring"-Zähler m, Möbius-Zähler m
twinning axis, twin axis	Zwillingsachse f		
twinning corner, twin corner	Zwillingsecke f	twisted surface	s. skew ruled surface
twinning direction	s. direction of twinning	twisted waveguide	verwundener Hohlleiter m
twinning dislocation	Zwillingsversetzung f	twister, twister crystal, torsional crystal	Torsionskristall m, Drillungskristall m, Verdreh[ungs]kristall m
twinning edge	s. twin edge		
twinning energy, twin energy	Zwillingsenergie f	twist form	Twistform f
twinning law	Zwillingsgesetz n	twist-free, torsionless, torsion[-] free	torsionsfrei, verdrehungsfrei, verdrehfrei
		twisting, torsion, twist	Torsion f, Drillung f, Verdrehung f, Verdrillung f, Drehung f
twinning plane	s. twin plane		
twin paradox, paradox of the space traveller	Zwillingsparadoxon n	twisting, twist <of fibre or wire>	Verdrehung f, Verwindung f <Faden oder Draht>
twin plane, twinning plane	Zwillingsebene f, Zwillingsfläche f, Zwillingsäquator m	twisting, twisting vibration <of molecule>	Torsionsschwingung f, Drillschwingung f <Molekül>
		twisting	s. a. twist <of cable>
		twisting deformation	s. twisting strain

twisting force	s. torsional force	two-body motion, Keplerian motion, Keplerian elliptic motion	Kepler-Bewegung f, Keplersche Bewegung f, Kegelschnittsbewegung f, Zweikörperbewegung f
twisting moment	s. torsional moment		
twisting oscillation	s. twisting vibration		
twisting polymorphy	Verdrillungspolymorphie f		
twisting resistance	s. twisting strength	two-body potential	Zweikörperpotential n, Zweinukleonenpotential n
twisting strain, torsional strain, twisting deformation, torsional deformation	Torsionsverzerrung f, Torsionsdeformation f, Torsionsverformung f, Verdrehverformung f, Verdrehungsverformung f		
		two-body problem problem of two bodies; Kepler problem	Zweikörperproblem n; Kepler-Problem n, Einkörperproblem n mit ruhendem zweitem Körper
twisting strain	s. a. torsional strain		
twisting strain	s. a. work of twisting	two-by-two [contingency] table, four[-]fold table, 2×2 table	Vierfeldertafel f, Zwei-mal-zwei-Tafel f, 2·2-Tafel f, 2×2-Tafel f
twisting strength	s. torsional strength		
twisting stress	s. torsional stress		
twisting vibration	s. torsional vibration		
twisting vibration	s. a. twisting ‹of molecule›	two-by-two Pauli matrix	s. Pauli spin matrix
twisting vibrator, torsional vibrator	Drehschwinger m, Torsionsschwinger m, Drillschwinger m	two-carrier theory	Zweiträgertheorie f
		two-cavity klystron, double-cavity klystron, double-resonator klystron	Zweikammerklystron n, Zweikreisklystron n
twist-measuring device, torsion meter, troptometer	Torsionsmesser m, Verdrehungsmesser m		
		two-centre cyclone, twinned cyclones	Zwillingstief n
twistor	Twistor m		
twist per unit length, amount of torsion (twist), twist; tortuosity ‹of porous medium›	Verwindung f	two-centre problem	Zweizentrenproblem n
		two-chamber filter	Zweikammerfilter n
		two-channel coincidence spectrometry	Zweikanal-Koinzidenzspektrometrie f
twist test, torsional test	Verdreh[ungs]versuch m, Torsionsversuch m; Verwindeversuch m ‹Faden oder Draht›		
		two-channel probe	Zweifingersonde f
twitch ‹of muscle›	Einzelzuckung f [des Muskels]	two-circle crystal diffractometer	Zweikreis-Kristalldiffraktometer f
twitch duration	Zuckungsdauer f	two-circle goniometer, theodolite goniometer	Zweikreisgoniometer n, Zweikreis-Reflexgoniometer n, Zweikreis-Reflexionsgoniometer n, zweikreisiges Goniometer n, Theodolitgoniometer n
twitch induced by a stimulus at break	Öffnungszuckung f		
twitch induced by a stimulus at make	Schließungszuckung f		
two-accelerator effect	Zweibeschleunigereffekt m		
two-anode rectifier, two-plate rectifier, biplate rectifier	zweianodiger Ventilgleichrichter m	two-circuit boiling water reactor	indirekter Siedewasserreaktor m, Zweikreis-Siedewasserreaktor m
two-aperture electronic lens, two-aperture lens	Zweiloch-Elektronenlinse f, Zweilochlinse f	two-circuit filter	Zweikreisfilter n
		two-circuit system, two-loop system, two-cycle system, bicyclic system	Zweikreislaufsystem n
two-armed lever	zweiarmiger Hebel m		
two aspects of the nature of light, wave and particle aspects of light	Doppelnatur f des Lichtes, Welle-Teilchen-Natur f des Lichtes	two-coil instrument	Zweispulen[meß]gerät n, Zweispuleninstrument n, Doppelspul[meß]gerät n, Doppelspulinstrument n
two-axis plotter	s. X-Y plotter	two-colour	s. dichroic
two-band filter	Doppelbandfilter n	two-colour process	Zweifarbenprozeß m
two-band model	Zweibändermodell n		
two-band picture, two-band representation	Zweibänderdarstellung f	two-colour pyrometry	Zweifarbenpyrometrie f
two-basic transistor, double-base transistor	Doppelbasistransistor m ‹Typ pnp oder npn›	two-colour separation	Zweifarbentrennung f
two-bath development	s. two-solution development	two-column matrix	zweispaltige Matrix f
two-beam interference, two-ray interference	Zweistrahlinterferenz f	two-component balance	Zweikomponentenwaage f
		two-component equation of the neutrino	s. Weyl['s] equation
two-beam maser	s. transmission-type cavity maser	two-component mixture, binary mixture	Zweistoffgemisch n, Zweikomponentengemisch n, binäres Gemisch n, binäre Mischung f
two-beam oscilloscope	s. double-beam oscillograph		
two-bed filter, two-layer filter	Zweibettfilter n, Zweischicht[en]filter n	two-component neutrino, longitudinally polarized neutrino	Zweikomponentenneutrino n, longitudinal polarisiertes Neutrino n, longitudinales Neutrino
two-bladed airscrew	zweiblättrige Schraube f, Zweiblattschraube f		
two-blade shutter, two-wing shutter	Zweiflügelblende f	two-component spinor, spinor of two components, Weyl spinor	zweikomponentiger Spinor m, Weylscher Spinor
two-body collision [process]	s. binary collision		
two-body decay, two-body disintegration	Zerfall m in zwei Teilchen, Zweiteilchenzerfall m, Zweikörperzerfall m, Zweizentrenzerfall m	two-component system, binary system	binäres System n, Zweistoffsystem n, Zweikomponentensystem n, zweikomponentiges System
two-body equation	Zweikörpergleichung f, Bewegungsgleichung f des Zweikörperproblems	two-component theory [of neutrino]	Zweikomponententheorie f [des Neutrinos]
two-body force	Zweikörperkraft f, Zweinukleonenkraft f	two-component theory of the irritability process, two-factor theory of excitation, two-factor excitation theory	Zweikomponententheorie f des Erregungsvorganges
two-body interaction	Zweikörperwechselwirkung f		

two-conductor circuit, two-wire circuit	Zweileiterschaltung f	two-field method [of Ramsay], Ramsay['s] two-field method	Zweifeldermethode f [von Ramsay], Ramsaysche Zweifeldermethode
two-cycle engine (motor), two-stroke [cycle] engine (motor)	Zweitaktmotor m, Zweitaktmaschine f, Zweitakter m	two-film theory	Zweifilmtheorie f
two-cycle system, two-loop system, two-circuit system, bicyclic system	Zweikreislaufsystem n	two-fluid barometer	Zweistoffbarometer n, Zweiflüssigkeitsbarometer n, Zweiflüssigkeitsbarometer n
two-decision problem	Zweientscheidungsproblem n, Alternativentscheidungsproblem n	two-fluid concept	s. two-fluid model
two-diaphragm condenser [lens]	Zweiblendenkondensor m [nach Berek], Zweiblenden-Hellfeldkondensor m	two-fluid manometer, two-liquid manometer, Chattock gauge	Zweistoffmanometer n, Zweiflüssigkeitenmanometer n, Zweiflüssigkeitsmanometer n, Manometer n mit zwei Flüssigkeiten, Chattock-Manometer n, Seegersches Manometer
two-dimensional classification, two-dimensional spectral classification	zweidimensionale Spektralklassifikation f	two-fluid model, two-fluid concept <of superfluidity>	Zweiflüssigkeitenmodell n [der Suprafluidität]
two-dimensional coincidence spectrometer	zweidimensionales Koinzidenzspektrometer n	two-fold axis [of symmetry]	s. diad axis
two-dimensional flow, plane flow	ebene Strömung f, zweidimensionale Strömung, ebene Bewegung f	two-fold axis of the second sort	s. diad axis of the second sort
		two-fold primitive	zweifach primitiv
		two-fold rotary axis	s. diad axis
		two-from-three circuit	Zwei-von-drei-Schaltung f
two-dimensional Fourier transformation, double Fourier transformation	zweifache Fourier-Transformation f	two-gang capacitor, two-gang variable capacitor, twin-gang capacitor	Zweigang-Drehkondensator m, Zweigangkondensator m, Zweifach-Drehkondensator m, Zweifachkondensator m
two-dimensional grating, crossed grating <opt.>	Kreuzgitter n, Flächengitter n, zweidimensionales Gitter n <Opt.>		
two-dimensional lattice, plane lattice	Flächengitter n, zweidimensionales (ebenes) Gitter n	two-grid tube (valve)	s. tetrode
		two-group constant	Zweigruppenkonstante f
two-dimensional photometry	zweidimensionale Photometrie f		
two-dimensional spectral classification, two-dimensional classification	zweidimensionale Spektralklassifikation f	two-group model	Zweigruppenmodell n
		two-hinged arch, two-pinned arch	Zweigelenkbogen m
two-dimensional time analyzer	zweidimensionaler Zeitanalysator m		
two-dimensional wave, cylindrical wave, cylinder wave	Zylinderwelle f, Kreiszylinderwelle f, zweidimensionale Welle f	two-hole coupler, two-hole directional coupler	Zweilochkoppler m, Zweiloch-Richtungskoppler m, Richtungskoppler m mit zwei Löchern
two-directional focusing	Richtungsdoppelfokussierung f, Fokussierung f in zwei Richtungen	two-ideal	s. two-sided ideal
		two-image photogrammetry	s. intersection photogrammetry
		two-image rangefinder	s. stereoscopic rangefinder
two-directional reaction	Zweiweg[e]reaktion f	two-jet maser	s. transmission-type cavity maser
two-disk phosphoroscope, phosphoroscope [of Becquerel], Becquerel phosphoroscope	Phosphoroskop n, Becquerel-Phosphoroskop n	two-layer conductor	Zweischicht[en]leiter m
two-distance-layer graded interference filter	Verlaufbandfilter n	two-layer electrode	Doppelschichtelektrode f
		two-layer filter, two-bed filter	Zweibettfilter n, Zweischicht[en]filter n
		two-layer lattice	Zweischicht[en]gitter n
two-drift hypothesis, two-stream hypothesis	Zweistromtheorie f	two-layer model of the atmosphere	Zweischichtenmodell (Doppelschichtmodell) n der Atmosphäre
two-effect evaporator, double-effect evaporator	Zweistufenverdampfer m	two-layer problem	Zweischichtenproblem n
two-electrode tube (valve)	s. diode		
two-electron bond	s. single bond	two-layer winding	Zweischicht[en]wicklung f, Zweilagenwicklung f, Zweietagenwicklung f
two-electron problem	Zweielektronenproblem n		
two-electron recombination	s. dielectronic recombination	two-level maser [amplifier]	Zweiniveaumaser[verstärker] m
two-electron shell, K-shell	K-Schale f, K-Schale f, Zweierschale f		
		two-line method; method of homologous pairs of lines	Verfahren n der homologen Linienpaare
two-electron transfer	Zweielektronentransfer m, Zweielektronenüberführung f	two-liquid manometer	s. two-fluid manometer
		two-liquid model	s. hydrodynamical model
two-element tube (valve)	s. diode	two-liquid nuclear model	s. hydrodynamical model
two-event characteristic function	vierdimensionales Eikonal n, vierdimensionale Wirkungsfunktion f	two-liquid theory	Zweiflüssigkeitentheorie f, Zweiflüssigkeitstheorie f
two eyes / by; binocular	binokular, beidäugig; zweiäugig		
two-factor excitation theory	s. two-component theory of the irritability process	two-loop system, two-circuit system, two-cycle system, bicyclic system	Zweikreislaufsystem n
two-factor model	Zweifaktormodell n		
two-factor theory of excitation	s. two-component theory of the irritability process	two-medium photogrammetry	Zweimedienphotogrammetrie f
two-fibre electrometer	s. Wulf electrometer	two-pair network	s. two-port network

two-parameter family	zweiparametrige Schar f
two-parametric gradient	s. differential parameter of the first order
two-particle collision	s. binary collision
two-particle Green['s] function	Greensche Zweiteilchenfunktion f, Zweiteilchen-Green-Funktion f
two-particle interaction	Zweiteilchen-Wechselwirkung f
two-particle interaction potential	Potential n der Paarwechselwirkung (Zweiteilchenwechselwirkung)
two-particle resonance	Zweiteilchenresonanz f
two-particle scattering amplitude	Zweiteilchen-Streuamplitude f
two-particle system	Zweiteilchensystem n
two-phase alloy	Zweiphasenlegierung f
two-phase bridge [circuit]	Zweiphasen-Brückenschaltung f
two-phase equilibrium	Zweiphasengleichgewicht n
two-phase five-wire system	Zweiphasen-Fünfleiter-System n
two-phase four-wire system	Zweiphasen-Vierleiter-System n
two-phase inverter, biphase inverter	Zweiphasenwechselrichter m
two-phase region, diphase region	Zweiphasenbereich m, Zweiphasengebiet n, heterogenes Gebiet n des Zweiphasengemisches
two-phase sampling	zweiphasige Stichprobenentnahme f, doppelte Stichprobenentnahme, zweiphasiges Stichprobenverfahren n
two-phase three-wire system	Zweiphasen-Dreileiter-System n
two-phonon process	Zweiphononenprozeß m
two-photon annihilation	s. two-quantum annihilation
two-pi counter, two-pi detector	s. two-pi pulse counting assembly
two-pinned arch, two-hinged arch	Zweigelenkbogen m
two-pi pulse counting assembly, 2π pulse counting assembly; 2π counter, two-pi counter; 2π detector, two-pi detector	2π-Zähler m, Zwei-pi-Zähler m; 2π-Detektor m, Zwei-pi-Detektor m
two-plate chamber	Zweiplattenkammer f
two-plate method	Zweiplattenverfahren n
two-plate rectifier, two-anode rectifier, biplate rectifier	zweianodiger Ventilgleichrichter m
two plates set to produce Brewster's fringes	Brewstersche Anordnung f [zur Erzeugung von Interferenzstreifen durch Vielfachreflexion]
two-point characteristic [function]	s. Hamilton's characteristic function
two-point regulator	s. two-step action control
two-pole network, two-terminal network, one-port [network]	Zweipol m
twoport	s. two-port network
two-port cavity maser	s. transmission-type cavity maser
two-port network, two-pair network, twoport	Zweiklemmenpaar n, Vierpol m
two-position action [control], two-position control	s. on-off control
two-position action control[ler], two-position control[ler]	s. two-step action control
two-position element	Zweipunktglied n, Zweistellungsglied n, Zweistellungselement n
two-position switch, on-and-off switch, two-way switch	Schalter m mit zwei Stellungen, Zweistellungsschalter m, Zweiweg[e]schalter m, Ein-Aus-Schalter m
two-position viewfinder, double finder telescope	Zweifachsucher m
two-probe method	s. two-probe technique
two-probe technique, two-probe method	Zweisondenverfahren n, Doppelsondenmethode f
two-pronged star	Zweierstern m, zweiarmiger Zertrümmerungsstern m, Zweistrahlstern m
two-quantum annihilation, two-photon annihilation	Zweiquantenvernichtung f, Zweiquantenzerstrahlung f
two-ray interference, two-beam interference	Zweistrahlinterferenz f
two-reflector system <el.>	Zweispiegelsystem n, Zweireflektorsystem n <El.>
two-region reactor, two-zone reactor	Zweizonenreaktor m, Zweigebietreaktor m
two-region technique, two-zone technique	Zweigebiet[s]verfahren n, Zweizonenverfahren n
two-rowed matrix, two-row matrix	zweizeilige Matrix f; zweireihige Matrix
two-sample problem	Zweistichprobenproblem n, Zwei-Stichproben-Problem n, Problem n der zwei Stichproben
two-sample test	Zweistichprobentest m, Zwei-Stichproben-Test m, Zweistichprobenverfahren n
two-section voltmeter	Zweikammerinstrument n, Zweikammervoltmeter n
two-segmented magnetron, two-slot magnetron, Habann magnetron, Habann tube	Zweischlitzmagnetron n, Habann-Magnetron n, Habann-Röhre f
two-segment electrometer, Dolezalek two-segment electrometer, Dolezalek electrometer, duant electrometer	Duantelektrometer n, Duantenelektrometer n, Binantelektrometer n, Binantenelektrometer n
two-sheeted <math.>	zweiblättrig <Math.>
two-sheet hyperboloid, parted hyperboloid, hyperboloid of two sheets	zweischaliges Hyperboloid n
two-sided ideal, two-ideal	zweiseitiges Ideal n
two-sided Laplace transformation, bilateral Laplace transform[ation]	zweiseitige Laplace-Transformation f, bilaterale Laplace-Transformation
two-sided level rod <US>; double-sided staff, staff graduated on both sides, rod graduated on both sides	Wendelatte f
two-sided surface, orientable surface	zweiseitige Fläche f, orientierbare Fläche
two-sided test, double-tailed test, double tail test	zweiseitiger Test m
two-site chemisorption	= chemisorption-chemidesorption
two-site sorption, adsorption-desorption	Adsorption-Desorption f
two-slit interference	Zweispaltinterferenz f
two-slot antenna, two-slot cylinder antenna	Doppelschlitzstrahler m, Zweischlitzstrahler m
two-slot magnetron	s. two-segmented magnetron
two-solution development, two-bath development	Zweibadentwicklung f, Zweischalenentwicklung f
two spin system	Zweispinsystem n

two-stacked antenna, two-stacked array	Zweietagenantenne *f*, Zweiebenenantenne *f*	two-way antenna, duplexer	Zweiwegantenne *f*, Simultanantenne *f*
two-stage amplifier	zweistufiger Verstärker *m*, Zweistufenverstärker *m*	two-way cock	Zweiwegehahn *m*, Doppelwegehahn *m*, Durchgangshahn *m*
two-stage demagnetization	zweistufige Entmagnetisierung *f*	two-way contact [with neutral position], double-throw contact, changeover contact	Wechselkontakt *m*, Umschaltkontakt *m*, Umschaltekontakt *m*, Umschalterkontakt *m*
two-stage microscope	Zweistufenmikroskop *n*	two-way inverter	Umkehrstromrichter *m*
two-stage rocket, two-step rocket	Zweistufenrakete *f*, zweistufige Rakete *f*		
two-state control	s. on-off control		
two-station rangefinder	s. long-baseline rangefinder	two-way mirror, semi-transparent mirror, semipermeable mirror	halbdurchlässiger Spiegel *m*, teildurchlässiger Spiegel
two-step action [control]	s. on-off control		
two-step action control[ler], two-position action control[ler], two-position control[ler], on-off control[ler], two-point regulator	Zweipunktregler *m*, Zweistellungsregler *m*, Schwarz-Weiß-Regler *m*	two-way switch, on-and-off switch, two-position switch	Schalter *m* mit zwei Stellungen, Zweistellungsschalter *m*, Zweiweg[e]schalter *m*, Ein-Aus-Schalter *m*
		two-way switch	s. a. double-throw switch
		two-winding-type transformer	Wickelwandler *m*, Wickelstromwandler *m*
two-step control	s. on-off control		
two-step microscopy	Zweischrittmikroskopie *f*		
two-step replica technique, double replica technique	Zwischenschichtverfahren *n*; zweistufiges Abdruckverfahren *n*; Mehrfachabdruckverfahren *n*	two-wing shutter, two-blade shutter	Zweiflügelblende *f*
		two-wipe slide, wipe, wipe slide; wipe fading	Wischblende *f*, Verdrängungsblende *f*
two-step rocket	s. two-stage rocket	two-wire bridge circuit	Zweileiter-Brückenschaltung *f*
two-stream hypothesis	s. two-drift hypothesis		
two-stream instability; stream instability	Strahlinstabilität *f*	two-wire circuit, two-conductor circuit	Zweileiterschaltung *f*
		two-wire circuit	s. a. two-wire line
two-stroke [cycle] engine (motor), two-cycle engine (motor)	Zweitaktmotor *m*, Zweitaktmaschine *f*, Zweitakter *m*	two-wire line, twin line, two-wire system, parallel-wire line, double-conductor line; two-wire circuit, two-wire loop circuit, loop circuit; double conductor, twin conductor	Zweidrahtleitung *f*, zweidrähtige Leitung *f*, Doppelleitung *f*, Doppeldrahtsystem *n*, Paralleldrahtsystem *n*, Paralleldrahtleitung *f*, Zweidrahtkreis *m*, Zweidrahtschaltung *f*, Doppelleiter *m*
two-stub transformer	Zweisäulentransformator *m*; Zweischenkeltransformator *m*, zweischenkliger Transformator *m*		
two-surface lens	Zweiflächenlinse *f*		
two-system wattmeter	Zweisystem-Leistungsmesser *m*, Zweisystem-Wattmeter *n*, zweisystemiger Leistungsmesser *m*, Leistungsmesser mit zwei Meßwerken	two-wire loop circuit	s. two-wire line
		two-wire system	s. two-wire line
		two-zone problem	Zweizonenproblem *n*
		two-zone reactor, two-region reactor	Zweizonenreaktor *m*, Zweigebietreaktor *m*
		two-zone technique, two-region technique	Zweigebiet[s]verfahren *n*, Zweizonenverfahren *n*
two-terminal capacitor	zweipoliger Kondensator *m*	two-zone theory [of magnetoresistance]	Zweizonentheorie *f* [der magnetischen Widerstandsänderung]
two-terminal impedance network	Impedanzzweipol *m*	Twyman-Green interferometer	Twyman-Green-Interferometer *n*, Twyman-Interferometer *n*, Interferometer *n* nach Twyman
two-terminal network, one-port [network], two-pole network	Zweipol *m*		
two-terminal-pair network	s. four-terminal network	Tycho['s] star	Tychonischer Stern *m*, Tychos Nova *f*
		tympanic cavity, drum cavity	Paukenhöhle *f*, cavum *n* tympani, Trommelhöhle *f*
two-thirds law [of Kolmogoroff]	Zwei-Drittel-Gesetz *n* [von Kolmogoroff]		
two-time Green['s] function, double time Green['s] function	Greensche Zweizeitfunktion *f*, Zweizeit-Green-Funktion *f*	tympanic membrane, tympanum, ear drum, drumhead	Trommelfell *n*
		Tyndall cone	Tyndall-Kegel *m*
two-transducer circuit	Zweiwandler-Meßschaltung *f*, Zweiwandlerschaltung *f*	Tyndall effect, Faraday-Tyndall effect	Tyndall-Effekt *m*, Faraday-Tyndall-Effekt *m*; Tyndall-Phänomen *n*
two-tube electronic lens, two-tube lens	Zweiröhren-Elektronenlinse *f*, Zweiröhrenlinse *f*		
		tyndallimeter, tyndallometer, Tyndall meter	Tyndallometer *n*, Streulichtmesser *m*
two-valued, double-valued <math.>	zweiwertig, zweideutig <Math.>		
two-valued logic	zweiwertige Logik *f*	tyndallimetry, tyndallometry, nephelometry in its proper sense	Tyndallometrie *f*, Streulichtmessung *f*, Trübungsmessung *f*, eigentliche Nephelometrie *f*
two-valuedness, double-valuedness <math.>	Zweiwertigkeit *f*, Zweideutigkeit *f* <Math.>		
two-wattmeter method	s. two-wattmeter technique	tyndallization	Tyndallisierung *f*
two-wattmeter technique, two-wattmeter method	Zweiwattmeterverfahren *n*, Zweileistungsmesserverfahren *n*, Zweileistungsmessermethode *f*	Tyndall light	Tyndall-Licht *n*
		Tyndall meter, tyndallometer, tyndallimeter	Tyndallometer *n*, Streulichtmesser *m*
two-wavelength microscopy	Zweiwellenlängenmikroskopie *f*	tyndallometry	s. tyndallimetry
two-wave property	s. double ripple	Tyndall-Röntgen effect	s. optico-acoustic phenomenon

type	s. version	ultimate pressure	s. final vacuum
type I burst, stormburst	Typ-I-Burst m, Sturmburst m	ultimate sensitivity	s. threshold of sensitivity
		ultimate strength	s. strength <mech.>
type I error	s. error of the first kind	ultimate strength	s. a. modulus of rupture <mech.>
type II error	s. error of the second kind		
type-homologous curve	Typhomologe f	ultimate stress	s. fracture stress
		ultimate tensile strength	s. tensile strength
		ultimate torsional strength	s. torsional strength
type of current	Stromart f	ultimate vacuum	s. final vacuum
type of equilibrium; equilibrium form	Gleichgewichtsform f, Gleichgewichtsart f	ultra-abyssal region	s. trench in the ocean floor
		ultra-abyssal zone	s. trench in the ocean floor
type of geomagnetic disturbance, (perturbation)	Störungstyp m	ultra-accelerator	Ultrabeschleuniger m
		ultra-acoustic, ultrasonic	Ultraschall-, ultraakustisch
type of interaction, mode of interaction, interaction type	Wechselwirkungstyp m, Wechselwirkungsart f, Art f der Wechselwirkung	ultra-acoustics, ultrasonics	Ultraschallehre f, Lehre f vom Ultraschall, Ultraschallakustik f
		ultra[ ]audible frequency	s. ultrasonic frequency
type of lattice	Gittertyp m	ultra[-]centrifugation, ultracentrifuging	Ultrazentrifugierung f, Trennung f mit der Ultrazentrifuge
type of light	Lichtart f		
type of particle; kind of particle, sort of particle	Teilchensorte f; Teilchenart f		
		ultracentrifuge, high-speed centrifuge, supercentrifuge	Ultrazentrifuge f
type of radiation, mode of radiation, character of radiation, nature of radiation	Strahlungsart f, Strahlenart f		
		ultrachromatography	Ultrachromatographie f
		ultracold neutron	ultrakaltes Neutron n
type of symmetry, symmetry type	Symmetrietyp m	ultracrystallite	Ultrakristallit m
		ultradyne	Ultradyneempfänger m
typhoon	s. tropical cyclone <Atlantic and Caribbean>	ultra-elliptic	ultraelliptisch
		ultrafast lens	s. ultrarapid lens
		ultrafast pinch	ultraschneller Pinch m, ultraschnelle Plasmaeinschnürung f

U

Ubbelohde-Umstätter viscogram	Ubbelohde-Umstätter-Viskogramm n, Viskogramm n von Ubbelohde-Umstätter	ultrafilter	s. ultrafine filter
		ultrafiltration, micro-filtration	Ultrafiltration f
Ubbelohde-type viscometer, Ubbelohde['s] viscometer	Ubbelohde-Viskosimeter n	ultrafine filter, membrane filter, ultrafilter	Membranfilter n, Ultrafilter n, Ultrafeinfilter n
(U — B) colour index, ultraviolet minus blue colour index	U-B-Farbenindex m	ultrafine focus	Feinstfokus m
		ultrafine grain	Ultrafeinkorn n
U.B.C.R. estimator	s. uniformly best constant risk estimator	ultrafine grain developer	Feinstkornentwickler m, Ultrafeinkornentwickler m
(U, B, V) system	U, B, V- System n		
udometer	s. rain gauge		
Uehling effect, Ühling effect	Ühling-Effekt m	ultrafine grinding, ultrafine [ground] section, ultra[-]thin section	Ultradünnschliff m
Uehling term, Ühling term	Ühlingscher Term m, Ühling-Term m		
U Geminorum star, U Geminorum-type star, SS Cygni variable, SS Cygni star, UG	U Geminorum-Stern m, SS Cygni-Stern m, SS Cygni-Veränderlicher m, Zwergnova f	ultragravity wave	Ultraschwerewelle f
		ultrahard	ultrahart
		ultraharmonic	s. upper harmonic
U.H.F.	s. ultra-high frequency	ultraharmonic [oscillation], ultraharmonic vibration	ultraharmonische Schwingung f, subharmonische Schwingung von der Ordnung 1/m
Uhlenbeck-Goudsmit hypothesis	s. Goudsmit-Uhlenbeck assumption		
Uhlig['s] apparatus	Uhligscher Apparat m		
Ühling effect, Uehling effect	Ühling-Effekt m	ultraharmonic resonance	ultraharmonische Resonanz f
Ühling term, Uehling term	Ühlingscher Term m, Ühling-Term m	ultraharmonic vibration	s. ultraharmonic oscillation
Ulam-von Neumann ergodic theorem	zufälliger Ergodensatz m, Ergodensatz von Ulam und von Neumann	ultrahigh-energy accelerator	s. superenergy accelerator
		ultra-high frequency, U.H.F., UHF, u.h.f., uhf <300 ··· 3,000 Mc/s>	Höchstfrequenz f im Dezimeterwellenbereich, Frequenz f im Dezimeterwellenbereich, Dezimeterwelle f, Ultrahochfrequenz f, UHF <300 ··· 3 000 MHz>
Ulbricht's globe photometer, Ulbricht sphere	s. photometric integrator		
Ulich['s] approximation, Ulich['s] formula	Ulichsche Näherung f, Ulichsche Näherungsgleichung f, Ulichsche Formel f <erste, zweite oder dritte>		
		ultra-high frequency, U.H.F., UHF, u.h.f., uhf <> 300 Mc/s>	Höchstfrequenz f, UHF <> 300 MHz>
U-line, unloaded line	U-Leitung f		
Uller['s] wave theory	Ullersche Wellentheorie f, Wellentheorie von Uller	ultra-high frequency band, U.H.F. band	Ultrahochfrequenzband n, UHF-Band n
ultimate analysis	s. elementary analysis		
ultimate bad carrying capacity	s. carrying capacity	ultrahigh-frequency cathode-ray tube	Höchstfrequenz-Elektronenstrahlröhre f
ultimate bending strength	s. bending strength		
ultimate breaking strength	s. tensile strength	ultra-high frequency discharge, U.H.F. discharge	Ultrahochfrequenzentladung f, UHF-Entladung f
ultimate elongation in percent	s. breaking elongation	ultra-high frequency engineering; microwave engineering	Höchstfrequenztechnik f; Mikrowellentechnik f
ultimate load carrying capacity	s. carrying capacity		
ultimate modulus	Endmodul m		

ultra-high frequency method	s. microwave method	**ultrarelativistic region**	extrem relativistisches Gebiet n, ER-Gebiet n
ultra-high frequency range, range of ultra-high frequency, decimetric wavelength [range], U.H.F. range, U.H.F.	Dezimeterwellenbereich m, Dezimeterbereich m, Dezibereich m, Ultrahochfrequenzbereich m, UHF-Bereich m, UHF	**ultra-sensitivity,** supersensitivity, extreme sensitivity	Höchstempfindlichkeit f, Superempfindlichkeit f, extreme Empfindlichkeit f
		ultra-short wave	s. very high frequency wave <1 – 10 m>
ultra-high frequency spectroscopy, microwave spectroscopy	Mikrowellenspektroskopie f, Höchstfrequenzspektroskopie f	**ultra soft,** ultrasoft	ultraweich
		ultrasonic, ultrasound	Ultraschall m, Überschall m, Supraschall m
ultra-high frequency technique	s. microwave method	**ultrasonic,** ultra-acoustic, superacoustic, superaudible	Ultraschall-, ultra-akustisch
ultra-high frequency voltmeter, U.H.F. voltmeter	Ultrahochfrequenzvoltmeter n, Dezivoltmeter n, UHF-Voltmeter n	**ultrasonic absorption coefficient**	Ultraschallabsorptionskoeffizient m
ultra-high frequency wave, decimetre wave, U.H.F. wave <100 – 10 cm>	Dezimeterwelle f <100 ··· 10 cm>	**ultrasonically induced,** ultrasonically initiated	ultraschallinitiiert
		ultrasonic attenuation	Ultraschalldämpfung f, Ultraschallabschwächung f, Ultraabschwächung f, Ultraschallschwächung f
ultra-high [ohmic] resistance	Höchstohmwiderstand m		
ultra high speed, ultraspeed	überschnell, ultraschnell, ultrarapid	**ultrasonic bubble chamber**	Ultraschall-Blasenkammer f
		ultrasonic centrifuge, supersonic centrifuge	Ultraschallzentrifuge f
ultra-high-speed radiography	s. flash radiography		
ultra-high vacuum, superhigh vacuum, very high vacuum, extra-high vacuum, U.H.V., UHV << 10^{-8} Torr>	Ultrahochvakuum n, Höchstvakuum n << 10^{-8} Torr>	**ultrasonic chemistry,** sonochemistry	Ultraschallchemie f
		ultrasonic coagulation, supersonic coagulation, acoustic coagulation	Ultraschallkoagulation f, Koagulation f durch Schallwellen
ultrahyperbolic differential equation	ultrahyperbolische Differentialgleichung f	**ultrasonic cross grating,** ultrasonic multiple grating, multiple grating	ebenes Ultraschallgitter n
ultraionization potential	Ultraionisationspotential n		
ultralinear amplifier circuit, ultralinear circuit	Ultralinearschaltung f	**ultrasonic crystal,** ultrasound emitting crystal	Ultraschallschwinger m
ultralong propagation	s. non-standard propagation	**ultrasonic current**	Ultraschallstrom m
ultra low temperature, ULT, U.L.T. <0.3 K>	Ultratieftemperatur f, ultratiefe Temperatur f <0,3 K>	**ultrasonic delay line,** supersonic delay line, sonic delay line, acoustic delay line, supersonic storage	Ultraschall-Laufzeitglied n, Ultraschall-Laufzeitkette f, Ultraschall-Verzögerungsleitung f, Ultraschall-Verzögerungsstrecke f, akustischer Verzugsspeicher m, akustische Verzögerungsleitung f, akustisches Laufzeitglied n
ultramacroion	Ultragroßion n		
ultramicroanalysis	Ultramikroanalyse f, Mikrogrammethode f <10^{-5} ··· 16^{-6} g>		
ultramicroassay	s. ultramicrodetermination		
ultramicrobalance	Ultramikrowaage f		
ultramicrocoacervation	Ultramikrokoazervation f		
ultramicroconcentration	Ultramikrokonzentration f		
		ultrasonic depolymerization, ultrasonic destruction of polymers	Ultraschallabbau m von Polymeren
ultramicrodetermination, ultramicroassay	Ultramikrobestimmung f		
ultramicro method, microgram[me] method	Ultramikroverfahren n, Mikrogrammethode f	**ultrasonic depth finder**	s. ultrasonic echo-sounding device
ultramicroscope, hypermicroscope	Ultramikroskop n, Spaltultramikroskop n [nach Siedentopf und Zsigmondy], Übermikroskop n	**ultrasonic destruction of polymers**	s. ultrasonic depolymerization
		ultrasonic detector	Ultraschalldetektor m
		ultrasonic dispersion	Ultraschalldispergierung f, Ultraschalldispersion f, Dispergierung f durch Ultraschall
ultramicroscope, electron microscope, hypermicroscope	Elektronenmikroskop n, Elektronenübermikroskop n, Übermikroskop n		
ultramicroscopic[al]	ultramikroskopisch	**ultrasonic echoes method**	s. ultrasonic echo sounding
ultramicroscopical	s. a. electron-microscopical	**ultrasonic echo sounder**	s. ultrasonic echo-sounding device
ultra[-]microscopy	Ultramikroskopie f, Übermikroskopie f	**ultrasonic echo sounding,** ultrasonic sounding, ultrasonic echoes method, supersonic sounding	Ultraschallechoverfahren n, Ultraschallechomethode f, Ultraschallotung f, Ultraschallecholotung f
ultramicrotomy	Ultramikrotomie f		
ultraphotic rays, invisible radiation	unsichtbare Strahlung f, Strahlung im unsichtbaren Spektralbereich		
ultra-pure water	s. conductance water		
ultra-rapid development	Ultrarapidentwicklung f	**ultrasonic echo-sounding device,** ultrasonic depth finder, ultrasonic echo sounder, supersonic echo sounder; active sonar	Ultraschall-Echolot n, Ultraschallot n, Ultraschall-Echolotgerät n
ultra-rapid high-pressure gauge	ultraschnelles Hochdruckmanometer n		
ultrarapid lens, ultrafast lens	ultralichtstarkes Objektiv n		
		ultrasonic emitter	s. ultrasonic radiator
		ultrasonic energy	Ultraschallenergie f
		ultrasonic excitation, ultrasound excitation; ultrasound stimulation, ultrasonic stimulation	Ultraschallanregung f, Anregung f mit Ultraschall; Ultraschallstimulierung f
ultra[-]rays	s. cosmic radiation		
ultra-red	s. infra-red		
ultrarelativistic case	extrem relativistischer Fall m, relativistischer Grenzfall m, ultrarelativistischer Fall		
		ultrasonic field	Ultraschallfeld n

ultrasonic flaw detector, ultrasonic inspection equipment, ultrasonic testing device, ultrasonic testing apparatus, soniscope, ultrasonoscope — Ultraschallprüfgerät n [zur Ermittlung von Fehlerstellen], Ultraschall-Werkstoffprüfgerät n, Ultraschallrißprüfer m, Ultraschalldefektoskop n

ultrasonic fluid whistle, liquid whistle — Flüssigkeitspfeife f

ultrasonic fluorometer, supersonic fluorometer — Ultraschallfluorometer n

ultrasonic frequency; superaudio frequency, ultraaudible frequency — Ultraschallfrequenz f, Ultraschallwellenfrequenz f; Überhörfrequenz f

ultrasonic frequency range, ultrasonic range — Ultraschallbereich m

ultrasonic generator, ultrasound generator, supersonic generator; vibratory unit, transducer, transformer — Ultraschallgenerator m, Ultraschallerzeuger m, Ultraschallgeber m; Ultraschallschwinger m, Schwinger m

ultrasonic grating — Ultraschallgitter n, Ultraschall-Beugungsgitter n

ultrasonic immersion technique — Ultraschallprüfung f nach der Tauchtechnik

ultrasonic inspection, ultrasonic testing, supersonic testing, ultrasonic method of materials testing — Ultraschallprüfung f, Werkstoffprüfung f mit Ultraschall, [zerstörungsfreies] Ultraschall-Werkstoffprüfverfahren n, Ultraschalldefektoskopie f

ultrasonic inspection equipment — s. ultrasonic flaw detector

ultrasonic irradiation — Ultraschallbestrahlung f, Ultrabeschallung f, Beschallung f

ultrasonic lens, supersonic lens — Ultraschallinse f

ultrasonic luminescence — Ultraschallumineszenz f

ultrasonic method of materials testing — s. ultrasonic inspection

ultrasonic microscope — Ultraschallmikroskop n

ultrasonic microtome, supersonic microtome

ultrasonic multiple grating — s. ultrasonic cross grating

ultrasonic output meter — Ultraschalleistungsmesser m

ultrasonic power — Ultraschalleistung f

ultrasonic pressure gauge — Ultraschallmanometer n

ultrasonic probe, supersonic probe — Ultraschallsonde f, Überschallsonde f

ultrasonic pulse-echo testing, ultrasonic pulse reflection testing — Ultraschallprüfung f nach dem Echo-Impuls-Verfahren n, Ultraschallimpulsreflexionsverfahren n

ultrasonic quartz — s. ultrasonic quartz generator

ultrasonic quartz generator; ultrasonic quartz — Ultraschallgenerator m mit Schwingquarz, Quarz-Ultraschallgenerator m, Quarz-Schallgenerator m; Ultraschallquarz m

ultrasonic quartz transducer, quartz transducer — Quarz-Ultraschallwandler m, Ultraschallwandler m mit Schwingquarz, Quarzwandler m, Quarzmeßwandler m

ultrasonic radiation — Ultraschallstrahlung f

ultrasonic radiator, supersonic radiator, ultrasonic (supersonic) emitter; ultrasonic (supersonic) transmitter — Ultraschallstrahler m; Ultraschallgeber m; Ultraschallsender m, Ultraschallsendekopf m

ultrasonic range, ultrasonic frequency range — Ultraschallbereich m

ultrasonic receiver — Ultraschallempfänger m

ultrasonic resonance testing — Ultraschallprüfung f nach dem Resonanzverfahren

ultrasonics, ultra-acoustics — Ultraschallehre f, Lehre f vom Ultraschall, Ultraschallakustik f

ultrasonic sounding — s. ultrasonic echo sounding

ultrasonic source, ultrasound source, supersonic source — Ultraschallquelle f

ultrasonic space grating — räumliches Ultraschallgitter n, Ultraschall-Raumgitter n

ultrasonic spectrometer, supersonic spectrometer, ultrasonic spectroscope, supersonic spectroscope — Ultraschallspektrometer n, Ultraschallspektroskop n

ultrasonic spectrometry — s. ultrasonic spectroscopy

ultrasonic spectroscope — s. ultrasonic spectrometer

ultrasonic spectroscopy, supersonic spectroscopy, ultrasonic spectrometry, supersonic spectrometry — Ultraschallspektroskopie f, Ultraschallspektrometrie f

ultrasonic spectrum, supersonic spectrum — Ultraschallspektrum n

ultrasonic stimulation — s. ultrasonic excitation

ultrasonic stroboscope — s. supersonic stroboscope

ultrasonic testing — s. ultrasonic inspection

ultrasonic testing apparatus — s. ultrasonic flaw detector

ultrasonic testing device — s. ultrasonic flaw detector

ultrasonic thickness gauge; sonigage <for metals> — Ultraschall-Dickenmesser m, Ultraschalldickenmeßgerät n

ultrasonic transducer — Ultraschallumformer m, Ultraschallwandler m

ultrasonic transmitter — s. ultrasonic radiator

ultrasonic velocity, ultrasound velocity — Ultraschallgeschwindigkeit f

ultrasonic vibration, supersonic vibration — Ultraschallschwingung f

ultrasonic visualization technique — Schallsichtverfahren n [nach Pohlman]

ultrasonic wave — s. ultrasound wave

ultrasonic wind — Quarzwind m

ultrasonography — Ultrasonographie f, Ultraschallaufzeichnung f

ultrasonoscope — s. ultrasonic flaw detector

ultrasonoscopy — Ultrasonoskopie f

ultrasound, ultrasonic — Ultraschall m, Überschall m, Supraschall m

ultrasound emitting crystal, ultrasonic crystal — Ultraschallschwinger m

ultrasound excitation — s. ultrasonic excitation

ultrasound generator — s. ultrasonic generator

ultrasound source, ultrasonic source, supersonic source — Ultraschallwelle f; Überschallwelle f

ultrasound stimulation — s. ultrasonic excitation

ultrasound velocity — s. ultrasonic velocity

ultrasound wave, ultrasonic wave, supersonic wave — Ultraschallwelle f; Überschallwelle f

ultraspeed, ultra high speed — überschnell, ultraschnell, ultrarapid

ultraspherical function, Gegenbauer['s] function — Gegenbauersche (metasphärische, ultrasphärische) Funktion f

ultraspherical polynomial — s. Gegenbauer['s] polynomial

ultrastability — Ultrastabilität f

ultra-subharmonic [oscillation], ultra-subharmonic vibration — ultra-subharmonische Schwingung f, subharmonische Schwingung von der Ordnung n/m

ultra-subharmonic resonance — ultra-subharmonische Resonanz f

ultra-subharmonic vibration — s. ultra-subharmonic oscillation

ultra 934

ultra tau meter — s. tau meter
ultratelescopic meteor, — Mikrometeor n, ultra-
  micrometeor   teleskopisches Meteor n

ultra[-]thin section, — Ultradünnschliff m
  ultrafine [ground] section,
  ultrafine grinding
ultra[-]thin section — Ultradünnschnitt m,
  ultradünner Schnitt m
ultravacuum — Ultravakuum n
  <10^{-6} Torr>   <10^{-6} Torr>
ultra-violet, ultraviolet, — ultraviolett, Ultraviolett-,
  U.V., UV, u.v., uv   UV-
ultra-violet — s. a. ultra-violet radiation
ultra-violet — s. a. ultra-violet range
ultra-violet absorption, — Ultraviolettabsorption f,
  U.V. absorption   UV-Absorption f

ultra-violet absorption — Ultraviolett-Absorptions-
  band, U.V. absorption   bande f, UV-Absorp-
  band   tionsbande f
ultra-violet absorption — Ultraviolett-Absorptions-
  microscopy, U.V. ab-   mikroskopie f, UV-
  sorption microscopy   Absorptionsmikroskopie f
ultra-violet absorption — s. ultra-violet absorption
  spectrometry   spectroscopy
ultra-violet absorption — Ultraviolett-Absorptions-
  spectroscopy, ultra-   spektroskopie f, Ultra-
  violet absorption spec-   violett-Absorptions-
  trometry, U.V. absorp-   spektrometrie f, UV-
  tion spectroscopy, U.V.   Absorptionsspektro-
  absorption spectrometry   skopie f, UV-Absorp-
    tionsspektrometrie f

ultra-violet absorption — Ultraviolett-Absorptions-
  spectrum, U.V.   spektrum n, UV-Ab-
  absorption spectrum   sorptionsspektrum n
ultra-violet active, — ultraviolettaktiv,
  U.V. active   UV-aktiv
ultra-violet A region — s. ultra-violet region A
ultra-violet band, — Ultraviolettbande f,
  U.V. band   UV-Bande f

ultraviolet band — Ultraviolett-Banden-
  spectrum, U.V. band   spektrum n, UV-
  spectrum   Bandenspektrum n
ultra-violet B region — s. ultra-violet region B
ultraviolet burst, U.V. — Ultravioletteruption f,
  burst   UV-Eruption f

ultra-violet catastrophe, — Ultraviolettkatastrophe f,
  ultra-violet problem,   Ultraviolettdivergenz f,
  ultra-violet divergence,   UV-Katastrophe f,
  U.V. catastrophe,   UV-Divergenz f
  U.V. problem, U.V.
  divergence
ultra-violet C region — s. ultra-violet region C
ultra-violet cutting — Ultraviolettschutzfilter n,
  filter, U.V. cutting   UV-Schutzfilter n,
  filter   Ultraviolettsperrfilter n,
    UV-Sperrfilter n
ultra-violet detector — s. ultra-violet radiation
  detector
ultra-violet dichroism, — Ultraviolettdichroismus m,
  U.V. dichroism   UV-Dichroismus m
ultra-violet divergence — s. ultra-violet
  catastrophe
ultra-violet dosimeter, — Ultraviolettdosimeter n,
  U.V. dosimeter   UV-Dosimeter n

ultra-violet dosimetry, — Ultraviolettdosimetrie f,
  U.V. dosimetry   UV-Dosimetrie f
ultra-violet effect — s. ultra-violet radiation
  effect
ultra-violet emission, — Ultraviolettemission f,
  U.V. emission   UV-Emission f

ultra-violet emulsion — s. ultraviolet-sensitive
  emulsion
ultra-violet excitation — s. ultra-violet stimulation
ultra-violet film — s. ultraviolet-sensitive film
ultra-violet filter, — Ultraviolettfilter n,
  U.V. filter   UV-Filter n

ultra-violet glass, — Ultraviolettglas n,
  U.V. glass   UV-Glas n
ultra-violet — s. ultra-violet irradiation
  illumination
ultra-violet image — s. ultra-violet photograph
ultra-violet irradiation, — Ultraviolettbestrahlung f,
  ultra-violet illumination,   UV-Bestrahlung f
  U.V. irradiation,
  U.V. illumination

ultra-violet lamp, — Ultraviolettstrahler m,
  ultra-violet source,   Ultraviolettlichtquelle f,
  ultra-violet radiator,   Ultraviolettlampe f,
  U.V. lamp, U.V. source,   UV-Strahler m, UV-
  U.V. radiator   Lichtquelle f, UV-
    Lampe f

ultra-violet layer — s. ultraviolet-sensitive layer
ultra-violet light — s. ultra-violet radiation
ultra-violet line, — Ultraviolettlinie f,
  U.V. line   UV-Linie f
ultra-violet lumines- — Ultraviolettlumineszenz f,
  cence, U.V. luminescence   UV-Lumineszenz f, Ul-
    traviolettleuchten n, UV-
    Leuchten n, u-Leuchten n
ultra-violet magnitude, — Ultravioletthelligkeit f,
  ultra-violet stellar   UV-Helligkeit f
  magnitude, U.V. magni-   <Gestirn>
  tude <of the star>
ultra-violet micro- — Ultraviolettmikroskop n,
  scope, U.V. microscope   Ultramikroskop n,
    UV-Mikroskop n

ultra-violet micros- — Ultraviolettmikroskopie f,
  copy, U.V. microscopy   Ultramikroskopie f,
    UV-Mikroskopie f

ultra-violet micro- — Ultraviolett-Mikrospektro-
  spectrograph, U.V.   graph m, UV-Mikro-
  microspectrograph   spektrograph m
ultra-violet micro- — Ultraviolett-Mikrospektro-
  spectrography,   graphie f, UV-Mikro-
  U.V. microspectrography   spektrographie f
ultra-violet microspec- — Ultraviolett-Mikrospektro-
  trometer, U.V. mi-   meter n, UV-Mikro-
  crospectrometer   spektrometer n
ultra-violet microspec- — s. ultra-violet
  trometry   microspectroscopy
ultra-violet micro- — Ultraviolett-Mikrospek-
  spectrophotometer,   tralphotometer n, UV-
  U.V. microspectro-   Mikrospektralphoto-
  photometer   meter n
ultra-violet micro- — Ultraviolett-Mikrospek-
  spectrophotometry,   tralphotometrie f, UV-
  U.V. microspectro-   Mikrospektralphoto-
  photometry   metrie f
ultra-violet microspec- — Ultraviolett-Mikrospek-
  troscope, U.V.   troskop n, UV-Mikro-
  microspectroscope   spektroskop n
ultra-violet micro- — Ultraviolett-Mikrospektro-
  spectroscopy,   skopie f, UV-Mikro-
  U.V. microspectroscopy,   spektroskopie f, Ultra-
  ultraviolet microspec-   violett-Mikrospektro-
  trometry, U.V. micro-   metrie f, UV-Mikro-
  spectrometry   spektrometrie f

ultraviolet minus blue — $U-B$-Farbenindex m
  colour index, $(U-B)$
  colour index
ultra-violet part — s. ultra-violet range
ultra-violet photocell, — Ultraviolettphotozelle f,
  ultraviolet-sensitive   UV-Photozelle f, Ultra-
  photocell, U.V. photocell   violettzelle f, UV-Zelle f

ultra-violet photoeffect, — Ultraviolettphotoeffekt m,
  ultra-violet photo-   UV-Photoeffekt m
  electric effect,
  U.V. photoeffect

ultra-violet photograph, ultra-violet image, U.V. photograph, U.V. image — Ultraviolettaufnahme f, Ultraviolettbild n, Ultraviolettphotographie f, UV-Aufnahme f, UV-Bild n, UV-Photographie f

ultra-violet photography, U.V. photography — Ultraviolettphotographie f, UV-Photographie f

ultra-violet photometer, U.V. photometer
ultra-violet photometry, U.V. photometry — Ultraviolettphotometer n, UV-Photometer n
Ultraviolettphotometrie f, UV-Photometrie f

ultra-violet photomicrography, U.V. photomicrography — Ultraviolett-Mikrophotographie f, UV-Mikrophotographie f

ultra-violet physics, U.V. physics — Ultraviolettphysik f, UV-Physik f
ultra-violet plate — s. ultraviolet-sensitive plate
ultra-violet portion — s. ultra-violet range
ultra-violet problem — s. ultra-violet catastrophe
ultra-violet radiation, ultra-violet, ultraviolet rays, ultra-violet light, U.V. radiation, U.V., UV, uv — Ultraviolettstrahlung f, ultraviolette Strahlung f, Ultraviolett n, Ultraviolettstrahlen mpl, ultraviolette Strahlen mpl, Ultraviolettlicht n, ultraviolettes Licht n, UV-Strahlung f, UV

ultra-violet radiation detector, ultra-violet detector, ultra-violet radiation measuring instrument, U.V. [radiation] detector — Ultraviolettdetektor m, Ultraviolett-Strahlungsmeßgerät n, Ultraviolett-Strahlungsmesser m, UV-Detektor m, UV-Strahlungsmeßgerät n, UV-Strahlungsmesser m

ultra-violet radiation effect, ultra-violet effect, U.V. [radiation] effect — Ultraviolettstrahlenwirkung f, Ultraviolettwirkung f, UV-Strahlenwirkung f, UV-Wirkung f
ultra-violet radiation measuring instrument — s. ultra-violet radiation detector
ultra-violet radiation receiver, ultra-violet receiver, U.V. [radiation] receiver — UV-Empfänger m, Ultraviolett[-Strahlungs]-empfänger m, UV-Strahlungsempfänger m
ultra-violet radiator — s. ultra-violet lamp
ultra-violet range, ultra-violet portion, ultra-violet part, ultra-violet region ⟨of the electromagnetic spectrum⟩, ultra-violet, U.V., U.V. range, U.V. portion — Ultraviolettbereich m, Ultraviolettgebiet n, ultravioletter Bereich m, ultraviolettes Gebiet n ⟨des elektromagnetischen Spektrums⟩, ultravioletter Spektralbereich m, ultraviolettes Spektralgebiet n, Ultraviolett n, UV, UV-Bereich m, UV-Gebiet n

ultraviolet rays — s. ultra-violet radiation
ultra-violet receiver — s. ultra-violet radiation receiver

ultra-violet region, region of the ultra-violet spectrum, U.V. region — Ultraviolettgebiet n, Gebiet n des ultravioletten Spektrums, UV-Gebiet n
ultra-violet region — s. a. ultra-violet range
ultra-violet region A, ultra-violet A region ⟨400–320 nm⟩ — UV-A-Gebiet n, Ultraviolett-A-Gebiet n ⟨400 ··· 320 nm⟩

ultra-violet region B, ultra-violet B region ⟨320–280 nm⟩ — UV-B-Gebiet n, Ultraviolett-B-Gebiet n ⟨320 ··· 280 nm⟩

ultra-violet region C, ultra-violet C region ⟨280–200 nm⟩ — UV-C-Gebiet n, Ultraviolett-C-Gebiet n ⟨280 ··· 200 nm⟩

ultra-violet rotational band, U.V. rotational band — Ultraviolett-Rotationsbande f, UV-Rotationsbande f

ultraviolet-sensitive — s. sensitive to ultra-violet

ultraviolet-sensitive emulsion, ultra-violet emulsion, U.V. sensitive emulsion, U.V. emulsion — ultraviolettempfindliche Emulsion f, Ultraviolettemulsion f, UV-empfindliche Emulsion, UV-Emulsion f
ultraviolet-sensitive film, ultra-violet film, U.V. sensitive film, U.V. film — ultraviolettempfindlicher Film m, Ultraviolettfilm m, UV-empfindlicher Film m, UV-Film m
ultraviolet-sensitive layer, ultra-violet layer, U.V. sensitive layer, U.V. layer — ultraviolettempfindliche Schicht f, Ultraviolettschicht f, UV-empfindliche Schicht, UV-Schicht f
ultraviolet-sensitive photocell — s. ultra-violet photocell
ultraviolet-sensitive plate, ultra-violet plate, U.V. sensitive plate, U.V. plate — Ultraviolettplatte f, ultraviolettempfindliche Platte f, UV-Platte f, UV-empfindliche Platte
ultra-violet sensitivity, sensitivity to ultra-violet rays, U.V. sensitivity — Ultraviolettempfindlichkeit f, UV-Empfindlichkeit f

ultra-violet sensitization, U.V. sensitization — Ultraviolettsensibilisierung f, UV-Sensibilisierung f

ultra-violet sensitizer, U.V. sensitizer — Ultraviolettsensibilisator m, UV-Sensibilisator m

ultra-violet shadow, U.V. shadow — Ultraviolettschatten m, UV-Schatten m
ultraviolet shift — Blauverschiebung f, Violettverschiebung f
ultra-violet source — s. ultra-violet lamp
ultra-violet spectrograph, U.V. spectrograph — Ultraviolettspektrograph m, UV-Spektrograph m
ultra-violet spectrography, U.V. spectrography — Ultraviolettspektrographie f, UV-Spektrographie f
ultra-violet spectrometer, U.V. spectrometer — Ultraviolettspektrometer n, UV-Spektrometer n
ultra-violet spectrometry — s. ultra-violet spectroscopy
ultra-violet spectrophotometer, recording ultraviolet spectrometer, U.V. spectrophotometer — Ultraviolett-Spektralphotometer n, registrierendes Ultraviolettspektrometer n, UV-Spektralphotometer n, registrierendes UV-Spektrometer n

ultra-violet spectroscope, U.V. spectroscope — Ultraviolettspektroskop n, UV-Spektroskop n

ultra-violet spectroscopy, U.V. spectroscopy, ultra-violet spectrometry, U.V. spectrometry — Ultraviolettspektroskopie f, UV-Spektroskopie f, Ultraviolettspektrometrie f, UV-Spektrometrie f
ultra-violet spectrum, U.V. spectrum — Ultraviolettspektrum n, UV-Spektrum n, ultraviolettes Spektrum n

ultra-violet standard, standard ultra-violet, U.V. standard — Ultraviolettstandard m, Ultraviolettnormal n, UV-Standard m, UV-Normal n

ultra-violet stellar magnitude, ultra-violet magnitude, U.V. magnitude ⟨of the star⟩ — Ultravioletthelligkeit f, UV-Helligkeit f ⟨Gestirn⟩
ultra-violet stimulation, ultra-violet excitation, U.V. stimulation, U.V. excitation — Ultraviolettstimulierung f, Ultravioletterregung f, Ultraviolettanregung f, UV-Stimulierung f, UV-Erregung f, UV-Anregung f

ultra-violet transmitting, ultra-violet transparent, transparent to ultra-violet [rays], U.V. transmitting	ultraviolettdurchlässig, UV-durchlässig	**unavailable soil moisture** <geo.>	Totwasser n, Totwasseranteil m <Geo.>
		unbalance	Abgleichfehler m
ultra-violet transparency, U.V. transparency	Ultraviolettdurchlässigkeit f, UV-Durchlässigkeit f, Durchlässigkeit f im ultravioletten Spektralbereich	**unbalance**	Unausgeglichenheit f, Unbalance f; Ungleichgewicht n; Unsymmetrie f <El.>; Verstimmung f <El.>
		unbalance, out-of-balance <mech.>	Unwucht f <Mech.>
ultra-violet transparent	s. ultra-violet transmitting	**unbalance**	s. a. control error
ultra-violet vibrational band, U.V. vibration[al] band	Ultraviolett-Schwingungsbande f, UV-Schwingungsbande f	**unbalance**	s. a. disturbance of equilibrium
		unbalance attenuation	Unsymmetriedämpfung f
ultra-white, whiter than white	Ultraweiß n	**unbalanced bridge;** out-of-balance bridge	verstimmte (unabgeglichene) Brücke f; Ausschlag[s]brücke f
umbilic[al point], spherical point	Nabelpunkt m, Nabel m, Kreispunkt m, Umbilikalpunkt m	**unbalanced cable,** unbalanced electric cable	unsymmetrisches Kabel n
umbra, complete shadow, core shadow	Kernschatten m; Vollschatten m; Hauptschatten m	**unbalanced current**	Unsymmetriestrom m, unsymmetrischer Strom m
umbra, spot umbra	Umbra f des Sonnenflecks	**unbalanced electric cable,** unbalanced cable	unsymmetrisches Kabel n
umbra	s. a. shadow cone	**unbalanced load,** asymmetrical load	unsymmetrische Belastung f, Schieflast f, Schiefbelastung f
umbra effect, shadow effect	Schatteneffekt m		
umbral index (suffix), dummy index, saturated index <of tensor>; dummy, summation dummy	Summationsindex m	**unbalance error,** error due to unbalance	Unsymmetriefehler m
		unbiased, unbiassed <stat.>	erwartungsfrei, unverzerrt, biasfrei, ohne Bias <stat.>
umbra of the Earth, Earth's shadow	Erdschatten m	**unbiased critical region** <stat.>	überall wirksamer kritischer Bereich m, unverzerrter kritischer Bereich <Stat.>
umbrella antenna, umbrella-shaped antenna	Schirmantenne f, dachförmige Antenne f	**unbiased error**	s. sampling error
		unbiased estimation	biasfreie Schätzung f
umkehr	s. temperature inversion <meteo.>	**unbiased estimator**	erwartungstreue (unverzerrte) Schätzfunktion f
umkehr effect	Umkehreffekt m	**unbiased ferrite**	nichtvormagnetisierter Ferrit m
umkehreinwand, Loschmidt['s] reversibility paradox, reversibility paradox [of Loschmidt]	Loschmidtscher Umkehreinwand m, Umkehreinwand von Loschmidt	**unbiased test**	überall wirksamer Test m, unverzerrter Test
		unbiassed	s. unbiased <stat.>
umklapp probability, flop-over probability, flip-over probability	Umklappwahrscheinlichkeit f	**unboundedness**	Unbeschränktheit f
		unbounded operator	nichtbeschränkter (unbeschränkter) Operator m
umklapp process, U-process, flop-over process	Umklappprozeß m; Spinumklappprozeß m, Spin-„flip-flop"-Prozeß m, „flip-flop"-Prozeß m	**unbound particle,** free particle	freies Teilchen n, nichtgebundenes Teilchen
		unbound state	ungebundener Zustand m
umklapp resistance	s. intrinsic resistance	**unbranched chain,** straight chain	unverzweigte Kette f
umladung, charge exchange, recharging, recharge, reversal of charge	Umladung f, Trägerumladung f, Trägerumwandlung f; Ladungsaustausch m	**unbranched chain reaction,** unbranching chain reaction	unverzweigte Kettenreaktion f
Umov effect	Umow-Effekt m	**unbranched section of the programme,** linear section of the programme	unverzweigtes Programmstück n, gerades Programmstück
umpire test	s. arbitrational analysis		
Umstätter visco[si]meter	Strukturviskosimeter n [nach Umstätter]; Freiflußviskosimeter n [nach Umstätter]	**unbranching chain reaction,** unbranched chain reaction	unverzweigte Kettenreaktion f
unaccelerated	s. accelerationless	**unbreakability, unbreakableness**	Unzerbrechlichkeit f
unaccented	s. unprimed <math.>		
unadjusted moment	s. raw moment	**unburned,** unburnt	unverbrannt
unaided eye, naked eye	unbewaffnetes Auge n, bloßes (freies) Auge	**unburned fraction, unburned part**	Unverbrannte n
unanimous, unison	einstimmig	**unburnt,** unburned	unverbrannt
unary system	s. unitary system	**unc**	s. uncinus <meteo.>
unassociated liquid	s. normal liquid	**uncanned fuel element**	entmanteltes (enthülstes, nacktes) Brennelement n
unattainability	Unerreichbarkeit f		
unattainable state	unerreichbarer Zustand m		
unattended; unmanned, without crew; pilotless	unbemannt; unbesetzt, nichtbesetzt	**uncertainty,** indeterminacy <phys.>	Unsicherheit f, Ungenauigkeit f, Unbestimmtheit f, Unschärfe f, Ungewißheit f <Phys.>
unattenuated	ungeschwächt		
unavailable energy, lost energy	verlorene Energie f	**uncertainty of direction,** direction uncertainty	Richtungsunschärfe f

uncertainty principle, indeterminacy principle, principle of uncertainty, Heisenberg['s] principle of uncertainty, principle of indeterminacy, Heisenberg['s] uncertainty principle — Unschärferelation f [Heisenbergs], Heisenbergsche Unschärferelation, Unschärfebeziehung f [Heisenbergs], Heisenbergsche Unschärfebeziehung, Ungenauigkeitsrelation f [Heisenbergs], Heisenbergsche Ungenauigkeitsrelation, Ungenauigkeitsbeziehung f [Heisenbergs], Heisenbergsche Ungenauigkeitsbeziehung, Unbestimmtheitsrelation f [Heisenbergs], Heisenbergsche Unbestimmtheitsrelation, Unbestimmtheitsbeziehung f [Heisenbergs], Heisenbergsche Unbestimmtheitsbeziehung, Unbestimmtheitsprinzip n [Heisenbergs], Heisenbergsche Unsicherheitsbeziehung f, Unsicherheitsbeziehung [Heisenbergs], Heisenbergsche Unsicherheitsrelation f, Unsicherheitsrelation [Heisenbergs], Unsicherheitsprinzip n [Heisenbergs]

uncharged — s. neutral
uncharged particle — s. neutral
uncinus, unc <meteo.> — uncinus, hakenförmig, unc <Meteo.>
unclosed traverse, open traverse; spur (offshoot) of the traverse — offener Polygonzug m, offener Zug m
uncoated particle — unbeschichtetes Teilchen n
uncollided neutron — s. virgin neutron
unconcentrated wash — s. sheet erosion
unconditional branch, unconditional jump, unconditional transfer [of control] — unbedingter Sprung m

unconditional probability — unbedingte Wahrscheinlichkeit f
unconditional transfer [of control] — s. unconditional jump
unconformity, discrepancy, disagreement, divergence, departure, ·deviation — Diskrepanz f, Nichtübereinstimmung f, Divergenz f, Abweichung f
unconnected, disconnected; [mass] totally disconnected <math.> — zusammenhangslos, punkthaft, total unzusammenhängend; total zusammenhangslos <Math.>
unconstrained point, free [mass] point — freier Massenpunkt (Punkt) m
unconstrained system, system without constraints — System n ohne Zwang[sbedingungen]
uncontrasty picture, soft picture, non-contrasty picture — weiches Bild n, kontrastloses Bild, flaues Bild
uncontrolled chain reaction, divergent chain reaction — ungesteuerte (unbeherrschte, nicht gesteuerte) Kettenreaktion f, Kettenexplosion f
uncontrolled fission, explosive fission, non-controlled fission — explosive Spaltung f, ungesteuerte Spaltung
uncountable, non-enumerable — nichtabzählbar, überabzählbar, unabzählbar
uncoupling — s. decoupling
uncoupling agent — Entkoppler m
uncrossed disparity — ungekreuzte (gleichnamige) Disparation f

undamped oscillation, self-sustained oscillation, sustained oscillation, continuous oscillation — ungedämpfte Schwingung f, kontinuierliche Schwingung

undamped wave, continuous wave, CW, cw, C.W., c.w. — ungedämpfte Welle f, kontinuierliche Welle
undation, epirogenetic motion — epirogenetische Bewegung f; Undation f

undation theory — Undationstheorie f
undecidability <math.> — Unentscheidbarkeit f <Math.>
undeformed, unstrained — unverformt, undeformiert, nichtdeformiert
undemonstrable, unprovable — unbeweisbar
underbalance — s. undercompensation
underbunching — unterkritische Ballung f
undercommutation, delayed commutation — Unterkommutierung f, verzögerte Kommutierung (Stromwendung) f
undercompensation, underbalance — Unterkompensation f, unvollständige Kompensation f

undercompounding — Unterkompoundierung f

undercooled, supercooled — unterkühlt

undercooled liquid, supercooled liquid — unterkühlte Flüssigkeit f

undercooling, supercooling, supercooled state — Unterkühlung f

undercorrection — Unterkorrektion f

undercritical coupling, loose coupling, weak coupling <el.> — lose Kopplung f, unterkritische Kopplung <El.>

undercurrent <el.> — Unterstrom m <El.>

undercurrent — s. a. subsurface flow
undercurrent relay — Unterstromrelais n

undercurrent tripping — Unterstromauslösung f

undercut[ting] — Unterschneidung f, Unterschnitt m
undercut[ting], underwashing, undermining, underscouring, scour; piping — Unterspülung f, Unterwaschung f, Unterkolkung f

underdamping — s. subcritical damping
underdense — unterdicht <Elektronendichte < 10^{12} e/cm>

underdeterminate system — unterbestimmtes System n
underdevelopment — Unterentwicklung f
underestimate, undervaluation, underestimation, underrating — Unterschätzung f
underestimated, undervalued — unterschätzt
underestimation, undervaluation, underestimate, underrating — Unterschätzung f
underexcitation — Untererregung f
underexposure — s. underexposure
underexposure; photographic underexposure, underexposure — Unterexposition f; Unterbelichtung f
underfault — s. underthrust
underfilm corrosion — s. subsurface corrosion
underflow — Grundwasserströmung f; Grundwasserstrom m

underflow — s. a. subsurface flow
underflow conductor — s. water-bearing stratum
underground burst, underground explosion — unterirdische Explosion f

underground current — s. subterranean current
underground discharge, underground effluent — unterirdischer Abfluß m
underground explosion, underground burst — unterirdische Explosion f

underground flow — s. subterranean current

underground 938

underground leaching, subrosion <geo.> — Subrosion *f*, unterirdische Auslaugung *f* <Geo.>
underground percolation, underground water flow — Grundwasserbewegung *f*
underground stream — s. subterranean current
underground water; ground water; subsurface water; underwater; subsoil water; subterranean water — Grundwasser *n*; unterirdisches Wasser *n*; Tiefenwasser *n*
underground water — s. a. internal water
underground water flow, underground percolation — Grundwasserbewegung *f*
underheat[ing] — Unterheizung *f*

underimpedance relay — Unterimpedanzrelais *n*, Unterimpedanzansprechglied *n*
underlayer, inferior layer, underlying surface; sole; sole fault (thrust) <geo.> — Liegendes *n*, Liegendschicht *f*, liegende Schicht *f*, Unterlage *f*; Liegendgestein *n*; Sohle *f* <Geo.>

underlight, underwater light — Unterlicht *n* <Gewässer>

underload, fractional load — Unterlast *f*, Teillast *f*; Unterbelastung *f*, Unterlastung *f*
underload relay — s. undervoltage relay
underlying surface — s. underlayer <geo.>
undermatching, matching for maximum current transfer — Unteranpassung *f*

undermining — s. underwashing
undermining corrosion — s. subsurface corrosion
undermining pitting — s. deposit attack
undermodulation — Untermodulation *f*

under-moon, lower paraselena — Untermond *m*

under-parhelion — s. lower parhelion
underpressure, negative pressure, vacuum gauge pressure, pressure deficiency, pressure below atmospheric, subpressure, partial vacuum, vacuum, suction, tension — Unterdruck *m*, negativer Druck *m*, Vakuum *n*, Teilvakuum *n*, relatives Vakuum

underrating — s. undervaluation
underreactance relay — Unterreaktanzrelais *n*

under[-]relaxation undersaturation, saturation deficit, vapour pressure deficit — Unterrelaxation *f* Sättigungsdefizit *n*, Sättigungsmangel *m*, Sättigungsfehlbetrag *m*, Untersättigung *f*, Dampfhunger *m*

underscouring — s. underwashing
undersea delta, underwater delta — Unterwasserdelta *n*
undersea wave — unterseeische (untermeerische) Welle *f*, Unterseewelle *f*
underset current — s. subsurface flow
undershoot, underswing — Unterschwingen *n*, Unterschwing *m*
undershooting — Untersteuerung *f*
undershot waterwheel — unterschlächtiges Wasserrad *n*, Poncelet-Rad *n*

undersize, short measure — Untermaß *n*
undersize [product], minus material, siftings — Siebdurchfall *m*, Siebdurchlauf *m*, Durchfall *m*, Unterkorn *n*; Untergröße *f*

understressing <mech.> — Unterbeanspruchung *f*, Unterbelastung *f* <Mech.>
under-sun — s. lower parhelion
underswell — s. swell
underswing, undershoot — Unterschwingen *n*, Unterschwing *m*

undersynchronous — s. subsynchronous
undertension — s. undervoltage
underthrust, underfault, faulted underfold — Unterschiebung *f*, Untervorschiebung *f*
undertone — Unterton *m*

undertow, undertow current — Sog *m*, Gegenströmung *f*, Gegenstrom *m*, Rückströmung *f*, Grundströmung *f*

undervaluation, underestimate, underestimation, underrating — Unterschätzung *f*
undervalued, underestimated — unterschätzt
undervoltage, undertension — Unterspannung *f*

undervoltage relay, underload relay — Unterspannungsrelais *n*, Minimalrelais *n*

undervoltage release, undervoltage trip — Unterspannungsauslöser *m*, Spannungsrückgangsauslöser *m*
undervoltage state — unterspannter Zustand *m*

undervoltage trip — s. undervoltage release
underwashing, undercut[ting], undermining, underscouring, scour; piping — Unterspülung *f*, Unterwaschung *f*, Unterkolkung *f*

underwater — s. lower pool
underwater — s. underground water
underwater acoustics — s. hydroacoustics
underwater bed — Unterwasserbett *n*
underwater delta, undersea delta — Unterwasserdelta *n*
underwater light, underlight — Unterlicht *n* <Gewässer>

underwater manipulator — Unterwassermanipulator *m*
underwater microphone — s. hydrophone
underwater period, underwater time — Untermeereszeit *f*
underwater photography — Unterwasserphotographie *f*

underwater photometer — Unterwasserphotometer *n*
underwater soil, subhydric soil — Unterwasserboden *m*, subhydrischer Boden *m*
underwater sound projector; sonar transmitter — Unterwasserschallsender *m*, Unterwasserschallstrahler *m*, Unterwasserschallgeber *m*, Wasserschallsender *m*

underwater spark — Unterwasserfunke[n] *m*
underwater time, underwater period — Untermeereszeit *f*
underwater visibility, subaqueous visibility — Unterwassersichtweite *f*
undesired noise, additional noise, disturbing noise — Nebengeräusch *n*, Stör[ungs]geräusch *n*, Rauschen *n*
undesired oscillation, parasitic oscillation — Störschwingung *f*

undetachable joint — unlösbare Verbindung *f*
undetectable, undetectably low — nichtnachweisbar [gering]; unterhalb der Nachweisgrenze
undeterminate — Unbestimmte *f*

undetermined — s. statically indeterminable
undetermined multiplier — s. Lagrange's multiplier

undeterminedness, indeterminateness, indeterminedness <mech.>	Unbestimmtheit f <Mech.>	unfeeling <bio.>; insensible; indifferent	unempfindlich <Bio.>
undeterminedness	s. a. indefiniteness	unfilled; unoccupied, non-occupied; unpopulated; empty; vacant	unbesetzt, nichtbesetzt; leer; vakant; frei
undeveloped shower	unentwickelter Schauer m	unfilled level, unoccupied level, empty level	unbesetztes Niveau n
undeviated light	direktes (nichtgebeugtes, ungebeugtes) Licht n	unfilled shell	s. incomplete shell
undirected flow	ungerichtete Strömung f	unfilled state, empty state	unbesetzter Zustand m
undirected radiation	s. non-directed radiation	unfocused photomultiplier	s. Venetian blind multiplier
undissolving, insoluble, indissoluble, indissolvable	unlöslich, nichtlöslich; unangreifbar	unfolding	s. deconvolution <of spectrum>
undistorted lattice	ungestörtes Gitter n, unverzerrtes Gitter	ungated period	s. blocking period
undistorted modulation	verzerrungsfreie Modulation f	ungula of the cylinder, cylindrical ungula	Zylinderhuf m
undistorted plane	ungestörte Netzebene f, ungestörte Ebene f	unhydrogen-like, hydrogen-unlike	wasserstoffunähnlich
undistorted wave	unverzerrte Welle f	uniaxial, optically uniaxial	optisch einachsig, einachsig
undisturbed, quiet	ruhig, ungestört	uniaxial negative	negativ einachsig, einachsig-negativ
undisturbed differential equation	ungestörte Differentialgleichung f	uniaxial positive	positiv einachsig, einachsig-positiv
undisturbed orbit	ungestörte Bahn f	uniaxial stress	einachsiger (geradliniger, linearer) Spannungszustand m
undisturbed sun, quiet sun	ruhige Sonne f	unicellular organism	Einzeller m
undor	Undor m		
undular	s. undulatory	unicity	s. uniqueness
undulated cloud, billow cloud	Wogenwolke f, Undulatusform f, streifenförmige Wolke f, Streifenwolke f	unicomponent system, one-component system, unitary system, unary system	Einstoffsystem n, unitäres System n, Einkomponentensystem n, unäres System
undulating	s. undulatory	unicursal curve	unikursale Kurve f
undulating current	s. undulatory flow	unidental ligand	einzähniger (unidentaler, einzähliger) Ligand m
undulating flow	s. undulatory flow		
undulating quantity, undulatory quantity	Mischgröße f	unidentified band	nichtidentifizierte Bande f
undulating terrain	Wellengelände n	unidentified flying object, flying saucer, UFO	unidentifiziertes fliegendes Objekt n, fliegende Untertasse f, UFO
undulation	s. wave motion	unidimensional	s. one-dimensional
undulation effect	s. flutter <el.>	unidirected, unidirectional, monodirectional	einseitig [gerichtet], einsinnig, in einer Richtung gerichtet; rückwirkungsfrei
undulation of the geoid	Undulation f des Geoids	unidirectional	
undulation theory of light	s. wave theory of light	unidirectional compression	einfache Kompression f
undulator	Undulator m		
undulatory, undulating, undular, waving, in waves	wellenförmig, wellenartig	unidirectional current	s. direct current <el.>
undulatory current, undulating current	Mischstrom m	unidirectional electrode	s. blocking electrode
		unidirectional junction	s. rectifying junction
undulatory current, undulatory flow, undulating flow, undulating current	Wellenströmung f, Wellenstrom m	unidirectional microphone, directional microphone	Richtmikrophon n, Mikrophon n mit Richtwirkung
undulatory quantity, undulating quantity	Mischgröße f	unidirectional movement, directed movement	geordnete Bewegung f, gerichtete Bewegung
		unidirectional point source, collimated point source	kollimierte Punktquelle f
undulatory radiation, wave radiation	Wellenstrahlung f	unidirectional receiver, directional receiver	Richtempfänger m, Richtungsempfänger m
undulatory shape	Undulationsform f		
undulatory theory of light	s. wave theory of light	unidirectional stress	gerichtete Spannung f
unduloid	Unduloid n	unidirectional tension	s. linear expansion
unechoic room	s. anechoic chamber	uni-di[-]valent electrolyte	uni-di[-]valenter Elektrolyt m
unenriched uranium, natural uranium, naturally occurring uranium	Natururan n, natürliches Uran n, nichtangereichertes Uran	unification, standardization	Vereinheitlichung f, Unifizierung f
unequal-armed	ungleicharmig	unified atomic mass	s. unfied mass unit
unequal strain, non-uniform strain	ungleichmäßige Verformung (Deformation) f	unified atomic mass constant, m_u	[vereinheitlichte] Atommassenkonstante f, m_u
unequal stress, non-uniform stress <mech.>	ungleichförmige Beanspruchung f, ungleichförmige Belastung f, ungleichmäßige Beanspruchung, ungleichmäßige Belastung <Mech.>	unified atomic mass unit	s. unified mass unit
		unified atomic millimass unit, atomic millimass unit, mu	tausendstel [atomare] Masseneinheit f, mu, tausendstel vereinheitlichte atomare Masseneinheit
U-network, U-type four-terminal network	U-Vierpol m	unified field theory, unitary field theory	einheitliche Feldtheorie f
unevenness; inequality, topographic inequality; rugosity	Unebenheit f		
unexcited degree of freedom	nichtangeregter Freiheitsgrad m	unified magnitude, m	Einheitsmagnitude f, einheitliche Magnitude f, m
unfavoured transition, [allowed] l-forbidden transition	erschwerter (nichtbegünstigter, unbegünstigter, l-verbotener) Übergang m	unified mass unit, unified atomic mass [unit], u	[vereinheitlichte] Masseneinheit f, [vereinheitlichte] atomare Masseneinheit, u

unified

unified model [of nucleus], collective model [of nucleus], collective nuclear model, quasimolecular model [of nucleus]	kollektives Modell n [des Kerns], Kollektivmodell n [des Kerns], kombiniertes Modell [des Kerns], quasimolekulares Modell [des Kerns], kollektives (kombiniertes, quasimolekulares) Kernmodell n, deformierbares Einzelteilchenmodell n
unified signal, standardized signal	Einheitssignal n, Signal n mit vereinheitlichtem Änderungsbereich
unifilar, unifilar variometer	Unifilarvariometer n
unifilar electrodynamometer [of Kohlrausch]	Unifilarelektrodynamometer n [nach Kohlrausch]
unifilar electrometer	Einfadenelektrometer n [nach Lutz]
unifilar galvanometer	Unifilargalvanometer n
unifilar magnetometer	Unifilarmagnetometer n
unifilar suspension	Einfadenaufhängung f
unifilar variometer, unifilar	Unifilarvariometer n
uniform acceleration, constant acceleration, uniform increase in speed	gleichförmige Beschleunigung f
uniformalization	s. uniformization
uniform bend[ing]	gleichförmige Biegung f
uniform-boundedness principle, Banach-Steinhaus theorem	Banach-Steinhausscher Satz m, Satz von Banach und Steinhaus
uniform colouration	homogene Verfärbung f
uniform combustion, homogeneous combustion	homogene Verbrennung f
uniform continuity	gleichmäßige Stetigkeit f
uniform convergence	gleichmäßige Konvergenz f
uniform corrosion	s. general corrosion
uniform diffuser, Lambertian surface	Lambertsche Fläche f, Lambert-Fläche f, vollkommen matte Fläche, vollkommen (gleichmäßig) streuender Körper m
uniform diffuse reflection	vollkommen diffuse (gestreute) Reflexion f
uniform diffuse transmission	vollkommen gestreute Transmission f, vollkommen diffuse Transmission, vollkommen gestreute Durchlassung f, vollkommen diffuse Durchlassung
uniform diffusion	gleichmäßige (vollkommene) Streuung f
uniform dilatation, dilatational strain, pure dilatational strain	gleichförmige Dilatation f, reine Volumenänderung f
uniform distribution	s. equipartition
uniform elongation	Gleichmaßdehnung f, gleichmäßige Dehnung f
uniform emitting surface, surface emitting according to the cosine law, Lambertian radiator	Lambertscher Strahler m, Lambert-Strahler m
uniform ensemble	uniforme Gesamtheit f
uniform flow ⟨hydr.⟩	gleichförmige (gleichmäßige) Strömung f, Gleichstrom m, homogene Strömung ⟨Hydr.⟩
uniform inclination fringe	s. fringe of equal inclination
uniform increase in speed	s. uniform acceleration
uniform integral ⟨therm.⟩	uniformes Integral n ⟨Therm.⟩
uniformity	Uniformität f; Gleichmäßigkeit f; Gleichgradigkeit f
uniformity ⟨math., mech.⟩	Gleichförmigkeit f; Gleichmäßigkeit f ⟨Math., Mech.⟩
uniformity coefficient ⟨of soil⟩	Gleichförmigkeitsgrad m ⟨Boden⟩
uniformity factor	Gleichmäßigkeitskoeffizient m, Gleichmäßigkeitsfaktor m
uniformity ratio [of illumination] ⟨opt.⟩	Gleichmäßigkeit f, Gleichmäßigkeitsgrad m [der Beleuchtung] ⟨Opt.⟩
uniformization, uniformalization	Uniformisierung f
uniformizing parameter	uniformisierender Parameter m, uniformierende Variable f
uniform light, general diffused light	gleichförmiges Licht n
uniform lighting, general diffused lighting	gleichförmige Beleuchtung f
uniform liquid	einheitliche Flüssigkeit f
uniform load, uniformly distributed load	gleichmäßig verteilte Belastung f, gleichmäßige Belastung, gleichförmig verteilte Belastung, Gleichflächenlast f
uniformly accelerated motion, uniformly variable motion	gleichförmig beschleunigte Bewegung f
uniformly best constant risk estimator, U.B.C.R. estimator	Schätzfunktion (Schätzung) f mit gleichmäßig bestem Risiko
uniformly bounded	gleichmäßig beschränkt
uniformly continuous	gleichmäßig stetig
uniformly convergent	gleichmäßig konvergent
uniformly distributed load	s. uniform load
uniformly most powerful test, uniformly the most powerful test, U.M.P. test	gleichmäßig trennschärfster Test m, gleichmäßig der mächtigste Test, U. M. P.-Test m
uniformly variable motion	s. uniformly accelerated motion
uniform magnetic field, homogeneous magnetic field	homogenes Magnetfeld n, homogenes magnetisches Feld n
uniform mix[ture], mixture, homogeneous mixture, mix	Gemisch n, Mischung f, homogenes Gemisch, homogene Mischung
uniform model of nucleus	s. Wigner model of nucleus
uniform mix[ture], mixture, homogeneous mixture, mix	gleichförmige Bewegung f
uniform motion in a straight line, uniform straight line motion, uniform velocity motion	gleichförmige geradlinige Bewegung f, gleichförmig geradlinige Bewegung
uniform point source	gleichförmige Punktquelle f
uniform random noise, white noise	weißes Rauschen n; Weißgeräusch n
uniform rotation	gleichförmige Drehung f, gleichförmige Rotation f, gleichförmige Drehbewegung f
uniform scale, numeric[al] line, line of numbers, number axis, numerical axis	Zahlengerade f, arithmetisches Kontinuum n
uniform shear	gleichförmige Scherung f
uniform sidereal time, mean sidereal time	mittlere Sternzeit f
uniform speed motion	s. uniform motion
uniform straight line motion	s. uniform motion in a straight line
uniform translation	gleichförmige Verschiebung (Translation) f
uniform velocity	gleichförmige Geschwindigkeit f
uniform velocity motion	s. uniform motion in a straight line
unijunction transistor	„unijunction"-Transistor m, pn-Flächentransistor m

unilateral constraint	einseitige (nicht umkehrbare) Bedingung f, einseitige (nicht umkehrbare) Bindung f, einseitige Zwangsbedingung f	unique	eindeutig
		unique, special-purpose	unikal, Spezial-
		unique creation	Schöpfung f
		unique existence	Existenz f und Eindeutigkeit f
unilateral surface, one-sided surface, non-orientable surface	einseitige Fläche f, nichtorientierbare Fläche	unique forbidden transition	s. unique transition
unimeter	s. volt-and-ammeter	uniqueness, unicity; single-valuedness	Eindeutigkeit f, Unität f
unimodal distribution	eingipflige Verteilung f, unimodale Verteilung	uniqueness	s. a. specifity <stat.>
		uniqueness theorem	Eindeutigkeitssatz m, Unitätssatz m
unimodular	unimodular		
unimodular group, special linear group	unimodulare Gruppe f, spezielle lineare Gruppe	unique transition, unique forbidden transition, parity favoured [forbidden] transition, favoured [forbidden] transition	unique-verbotener Übergang m
unimodular mapping, unimodular transformation	unimodulare Transformation (Abbildung) f		
unimolecular adsorption, monomolecular adsorption, molecular adsorption	monomolekulare Adsorption f, Adsorption in molekularer Schicht		
		unirefringence, simple refraction, single refraction, accent	Einfachbrechung f
unimolecular film (layer)	s. monolayer	unison, prime <ac.>	Prime f <Ak.>
uninodal seiche	einknotige Seiche f	unison, unanimous	einstimmig
uninuclear, uninucleate	einkernig		
uninverted crosstalk	s. intelligible crosstalk	unit, unit of measurement	Maßeinheit f, Einheit f
uninverted top to bottom <of image>	höhenrichtig <Bild>	unit	s. a. component <of construction>
		unit	s. a. unit element
		unit-area, unit of area, unit surface	Flächeneinheit f
union, sum, joint <of sets>, set union, [logical] sum, sum-set	Vereinigungsmenge f, Vereinigung f, Summe f <von Mengen>		
		unit area acoustic impedance	s. specific acoustic impedance
uniplanar filament, monoplane filament <US>	flächenförmiger Leuchtkörper m	unit-area acoustic reactance, specific acoustic reactance	spezifische Schallreaktanz f
uniplanar motion, plane motion	ebene Bewegung f	unit-area acoustic resistance, specific acoustic resistance	spezifische Schallresistanz f
unipolar	s. homopolar <chem., el.>	unitarian bond	s. atomic bond
unipolar anionic conduction; unipolar anionic conductivity	unipolare Anionenleitung f; unipolare Anionenleitfähigkeit f	unitarian matrix, unitary matrix	unitäre Matrix f
		unitarian transformation, unitary transformation	unitäre Transformation
unipolar anionic conductor	unipolarer Anionenleiter m		
unipolar cationic conduction; unipolar cationic conductivity	unipolare Kationenleitung f; unipolare Kationenleitfähigkeit f	unitarity	Unitarität f
		unitary bond	s. atomic bond
		unitary equivalence [of quadratic matrices]	s. unitary similarity
unipolar cationic conductor	unipolarer Kationenleiter m	unitary field theory	s. unified field theory
unipolar cell	Unipolarzelle f	unitary field theory [of Lanczos], Lanczos['] unitary field theory	unitäre Feldtheorie f [von Lanczos]
unipolar conduction, unipolar conductivity	unipolare Leitung (Leitfähigkeit) f		
unipolar conductivity	unipolare Leitfähigkeit f		
unipolar conductivity	s. unipolar conduction	unitary group	unitäre Gruppe f, Gruppe der unitären Transformationen, hyperorthogonale Gruppe
unipolar conductor	unipolarer Leiter m		
unipolar derivation	unipolare Ableitung f		
unipolar electromagnetic induction, unipolar induction	Unipolarinduktion f	unitary matrix, unitarian matrix	unitäre Matrix f
		unitary multiplet	unitäres Multiplett n
unipolar field-effect transistor	Unipolar-Feldeffekttransistor m	unitary operator	unitärer Operator m
		unitary similarity [of quadratic matrices], unitary equivalence [of quadratic matrices]	Unitärkongruenz f, Unitäräquivalenz f, Unitärähnlichkeit f <quadratischer Matrizen>
unipolar induction, unipolar electromagnetic induction	Unipolarinduktion f		
unipolar ionic conduction; unipolar ionic conductivity	unipolare Ionenleitung f; unipolare Ionenleitfähigkeit f	unitary similar matrix, conjunctive matrix by a unitary transformation	unitär[-]ähnliche Matrix f, unitär[-]kongruente Matrix, unitär-äquivalente Matrix
unipolar ionic conductor	unipolarer Ionenleiter m	unitary spin	unitärer Spin m
unipolar tube	Unipolarröhre f	unitary stimulus	s. reference stimulus
unipole antenna	Unipol m, Unipolantenne f	unitary symmetry	unitäre Symmetrie f
		unitary system, one-component system, unicomponent system, unary system	Einstoffsystem n, unitäres System n, Einkomponentensystem n, unäres System
		unitary transformation, unitarian transformation	unitäre Transformation f
		unitary unimodular group	s. special unitarian group
unipolyaddition	Unipolyaddition f	unit ball	s. unit sphere
unipolycondensation	Unipolykondensation f	unit barrier layer	spezifische (bezogene) Sperrschichtdicke f
unipotential lens, single lens, single electron lens, einzel lens	Einzellinse f, Dreielektrodenlinse f, elektrostatische Einzellinse		
		unit binormal	s. binormal

unit cell, basic cell, elementary cell, elementary lattice cell, primitive cell, unit of pattern, lattice unit <cryst.> — Elementarzelle *f*, Einheitszelle *f*, Basiszelle *f*, Elementarkörper *m*, Elementarbereich *m*, Elementarparallelepiped *n* <Krist.>

unit cell dimension, lattice parameter, lattice constant, lattice spacing <cryst.> — Gitterkonstante *f* [des Kristalls], kristallographische Gitterkonstante, Kristallgitterkonstante *f*, Gitterparameter *m*, Gitterabstand *m* <Krist.>

unit cell vector — Basisvektor *m* des Kristallgitters, Basisvektor der Einheitszelle, Grundtranslationsvektor *m*

unit charge — Einheitsladung *f*
unit charge — *s. a.* electronic charge
unit circle — Einheitskreis *m*

unit compressive strain — *s.* unit shortening
unit consumption — *s.* specific consumption
unit cube — Einheitswürfel *m*
unit deviation of prism, degree of prismatic deviation — Prismengrad *m*
unit duration of signal — *s.* step length
united atom — vereinigtes Atom *n*
united atom model, model of united atom — Modell *n* des vereinigten Atoms
United States yard — *s.* yard
unit element, identity element, identity, unity, unity element, unit; neutral element <math.> — Einheit *f*, Einheitselement *n*, Einselement *n*, Eins *f*; neutrales Element <Math.>
unit elongation, unit strain, linear strain, tensile strain, normal strain, specific elongation, elongation per unit length <in μ/m °C or μ/m> — relative Längenänderung *f*, relative Verlängerung *f*, relative Dehnung *f*, spezifische Dehnung, Dehnung <in μ/m/m grd bzw. μm/m>
unit first normal [vector] — *s.* principal normal
unit function [of Heaviside] — *s.* Heaviside['s] unit function
unit[-] function response — *s.* unit[-] step response
unit impulse function [of order one] — *s.* delta function
unit[-] impulse response, unit[-] pulse response, impulse response, pulse response, weighting function, pulse step function <control> — Stoßantwort[funktion] *f*, Impulsantwort[funktion] *f*, Einheitsimpulsantwort [-funktion] *f*, Impulsübergangsfunktion *f*, Impulsübergang *m*, Gewichtsfunktion *f*, Greensche Funktion *f* <Regelung>

unit interval <in the winding> — Spulenseitenteilung *f*, Spulenteilung *f*

unitized principle [of construction] — *s.* unit principle
unit legal ohm — *s.* international ohm
unit load <mech.> — Einheitslast *f*, Last *f* pro Flächeneinheit <Mech.>

unit mass, unit of mass — Masseneinheit *f*
unit matrix, identity matrix — Einheitsmatrix *f*
unit membrane — Elementarmembran *f*
unit normal [vector], normal unit vector — Normaleneinheitsvektor *m*
unit of area — *s.* unit area
unit of heat, heat unit, caloric unit, thermal unit — Wärmemengeneinheit *f*, Wärmeeinheit *f*
unit of information — Informationseinheit *f*, Nachrichteneinheit *f*
unit of luminous intensity — Lichtstärkeeinheit *f*, Lichteinheit *f*
unit of mass — *s.* unit mass
unit of measurement, unit; unity — Maßeinheit *f*, Einheit *f*; Eins *f*
unit of pattern — *s.* unit cell <cryst.>
unit of time; unit time — Zeiteinheit *f*
unit of volume, unit volume — Volum[en]einheit *f*; Raumeinheit *f*
unit operation — Grundverfahren *n*

unit operator — *s.* identity operator
unit plane <cryst.> — Einheitsfläche *f* <Krist.>
unit plane — *s. a.* principal plane <opt.>
unit point — Einheitspunkt *m*
unit principal normal [vector] — *s.* principal normal
unit principle [of construction] — *s.* modular principle
unit prism — *s.* protoprism
unit process — einheitlicher Prozeß *m*, Einreaktorprozeß *m*, Einheitsprozeß *m*

unit pulse function — *s.* Heaviside['s] unit function
unit[-] pulse response — *s.* unit[-] impulse response
unit pyramid — *s.* protopyramid
unit resistance — *s.* resistivity
units construction principle — *s.* modular principle
unit second normal — *s.* binormal
unit shortening, linear compression, longitudinal contraction, [unit] compressive strain, compression strain; percentage strain — Stauchung *f*, relative Verkürzung *f*
unit skin dose [of Seitz and Wintz], HED — Hauteinheitsdosis *f* [nach Seitz und Wintz], Hauterythemdosis *f*, Röntgenerythemdosis *f*, HED
unit source — Einheitsquelle *f*, Quelle *f* der Stärke Eins
unit sphere, unit ball — Einheitskugel *f*
unit step — *s.* Heaviside['s] unit function
unit step function — *s.* Heaviside['s] unit function
unit step function time response — *s.* unit[-] step response
unit[-] step response, step response, step function time response, time response, transient response, unit[-] function response, indicial response, unit step function time response — Übergangsfunktion *f*, Sprungübergangsfunktion *f*, Einheitssprung-Übergangsfunktion *f*, Einheitsübergangsfunktion *f*, Sprungübergang *m*, Sprungantwort *f*, Sprungantwortfunktion *f*

unit strain — spezifische Formänderung *f*
unit strain — *s. a.* unit elongation
unit strength, strength per unit — spezifische Festigkeit *f*
unit stress — bezogene (spezifische) Spannung *f*
unit surface — *s.* unit area
unit tangent [vector], tangent unit vector — Tangenteneinheitsvektor *m*

unit tensor, unit two (2) tensor, identity tensor, substitution tensor, Kronecker tensor, idemfactor — Einheitstensor *m*, Einheitsaffinor *m*, Kroneckerscher Tensor *m*, Identitätsdyade *f*, Idemfaktor *m*
unit time; unit of time — Zeiteinheit *f*
unit transformation — Einheitstransformation *f*
unit triangle <stereographic projection of a crystal> — Einheitsdreieck *n* <stereographische Projektion von Kristallen>
unit two tensor — *s.* unit tensor
unit vector, normalized vector, direction vector — Einheitsvektor *m*, normierter Vektor *m*, Einsvektor *m*
unit vector [in the direction of the coordinate axis] — Koordinateneinheitsvektor *m*
unit vector of the outward normal — Einheitsvektor *m* der äußeren Normale, äußerer Normalen[einheits]vektor *m*
unit volume, unit of volume — Volum[en]einheit *f*; Raumeinheit *f*
unit wavelength constant — *s.* image phase constant
unit weight — *s.* weight per unit volume
unity; unit, unit of measurement — Maßeinheit *f*, Einheit *f*; Eins *f*
unity [element] — *s.* identity element <math.>

unity operator, identity operator, unit operator	Identitätsoperator *m*, Einheitsoperator *m*
uni-uni[-]valent electrolyte	uni-uni[-]valenter Elektrolyt *m*
univalent, monovalent, ‹chem.›	monovalent, einwertig, einbindig ‹Chem.›
univalent [analytic] function	*s.* simple function
univalent function, schlicht function	schlichte (univalente, einwertige) Funktion *f*
univalent representation, single-valued representation	eindeutige Darstellung *f*
univariant, monovariant	univariant, monovariant
univariant equilibrium	*s.* monovariant equilibrium
univariate distribution, one-dimensional distribution	eindimensionale Verteilung *f*
universal actinometer	Universalaktinometer *n*
universal amplifier	Allverstärker *m*, Universalverstärker *m*
universal balance	kombinierte Feldwaage *f*, Feldwaage für *H*- und *Z*-Messungen
universal bridge, resistance-inductance-capacitance bridge	Universalmeßbrücke *f*, Universalbrücke *f*, Allzweckbrücke *f*, RLC-Meßbrücke *f*, RLC-Brücke *f*
universal characteristic ‹of turbine›	Muscheldiagramm *n*, Muschelschaubild *n*; Muschelkurve *f* ‹Turbine›
universal constant	universelle Konstante (Zahlenkonstante) *f*, Naturkonstante *f*, universelle Naturkonstante
universal covering group	universelle Überlagerungsgruppe *f*
universal covering manifold	universelle Überlagerungsmannigfaltigkeit *f*
universal covering surface	universelle Überlagerungsfläche *f*, Hauptüberlagerungsfläche *f*
universal equilibrium	universelles Gleichgewicht *n*
universal equilibrium hypothesis	*s.* Kolmogoroff similarity hypothesis
universal filter, all-pass filter, universal network, all-pass network	Allpaß *m*
universal finder, universal (multifocal) viewfinder, multi-focus (multifoc) finder, multifoc (multiple) viewfinder; zoom finder	Universalsucher *m*, Mehrfachsucher *m*, Vielfachsucher *m*
universal function	universelle Funktion *f*
universal gas constant	*s.* gas constant
universal gas constant per mole	*s.* gas constant
universal gravitation	*s.* gravitation
universal indicator paper	Universalindikatorpapier *n*; Unitest-Papier *n*
universal instrument, multi range multipurpose instrument, multi-purpose instrument, multimeter	Universal[meß]gerät *n*, Universal[meß]instrument *n*, Mehrzweck-Mehrbereich-Meßgerät *n*, Mehrzweck-Mehrbereich-Instrument *n*, Mehrzweckmeßgerät *n*, Vielzweckmeßgerät *n*, Mehrfach[meß]gerät *n*, Mehrfachinstrument *n*, Vielfach[meß]gerät *n*, Vielfachinstrument *n*
universal instrument, universal theodolite ‹in goniometry›	Universalinstrument *n*, Universal *n*, Universaltheodolit *m* ‹Winkelmeßinstrument›
universal instrument	*s. a.* alternating-current—direct-current instrument
universal intensifying screen	Universal[verstärker]folie *f*
universal interaction	universelle Wechselwirkung *f*
universal joint, cardan joint, cardan	Kardan-Gelenk *n*, Universalgelenk *n*
universal manometer, universal pressure gauge	Vielfachmanometer *n*
universal measuring microscope	Universalmeßmikroskop *n*
universal mounting	*s.* gimbal
universal network	*s.* universal filter
universal opaque illuminator	*s.* universal vertical illuminator
universal photometer, portable photometer	tragbares Photometer *n*, Universalphotometer *n*
universal pressure gauge, universal manometer	Vielfachmanometer *n*
universal quantifier	*s.* generality quantifier
universal rotatable stage	*s.* universal stage
universal seismograph	Universalseismograph *m*
universal shunt, Ayrton shunt	Mehrfachshunt *m*, Mehrfachnebenwiderstand *m*, Vielfachnebenschluß *m*
universal stage, universal rotatable stage ‹of microscope› ‹three-, four-, *or* five-axis›	Universaldrehtisch *m*, Fedorowscher Tisch *m*, Fedorow-Tisch *m* ‹Mikroskop› ‹drei-, vier- *oder* fünfachsig›
universal suspension	*s.* gimbal
universal tensile testing machine	Universalprüfmaschine *f* für Zugversuche
universal theodolite	*s.* universal instrument ‹in goniometry›
universal time, Universal time, Greenwich civil time, World Time, Weltzeit, Western-European time, U.T., UT, G.C.T., GCT, W.E.T., WET	Weltzeit *f*, Westeuropäische Zeit *f*, bürgerliche Zeit Greenwich (Grw.), Greenwicher Zeit, WZ, W. Z., WEZ
universal time second	Weltzeitsekunde *f*
universal tripod	Universalstativ *n*
universal tube, a.c.–d.c. tube	Allstromröhre *f*
universal vertical illuminator, universal opaque illuminator	Universal-Opakilluminator *m*, Universal-Auflichtilluminator *m*, Universal-Vertikalilluminator *m*
universal viewfinder	*s.* universal finder
universal weather, world-wide weather	Weltwetter *n*
universe	*s.* population ‹stat.; gen.›
universe of Einstein and De Sitter	*s.* Einstein-De Sitter model
universe time clock	Welt[zeit]uhr *f*
univibrator, gating multivibrator, start-stop multivibrator, one-shot [multivibrator], monovibrator, one-kick (single-kick, single-shot, multistable, single-step) multivibrator	Univibrator *m*, Monovibrator *m*; monostabiler Multivibrator *m*, unselbständiger Multivibrator, Start-Stop-Multivibrator *m*
unknown	Unbekannte *f*
unlike	*s.* opposite
unlimited life	unbegrenzte Lebensdauer *f*, Lebensdauer unendlich
unlimited solubility, complete solubility	unbegrenzte Löslichkeit *f*, vollständige Löslichkeit
unlimited swelling	unbeschränkte Quellung *f*
unloaded, no-load ‹el.›	unbelastet ‹El.›
unloaded, unstressed ‹mech.›	unbeansprucht, unbelastet ‹Mech.›

unloaded line	s. U-line	unsaturation	Ungesättigtheit f; Ungesättigtsein n; Nichtsättigung f, nichtgesättigter Zustand m
unloaded Q, unloaded Q factor, intrinsic Q	Güte f (Gütefaktor m) des unbelasteten Resonanzkreises		
unloading; relieving, relief, removal of the load	Entlastung f	unscattered	ungestreut
		unsealed radioactive material	offenes radioaktives Präparat n
unlocking	Entriegelung f, Öffnung f	unsealed source	offene Quelle f, offene Strahlungsquelle f
unmanned, without crew; pilotless; unattended	unbemannt; unbesetzt, nichtbesetzt	unshaded circle, open circle <in a figure>	heller Kreis m, offener Kreis <in der Abbildung>
		unsharpness, lack of definition, lack of focus, diffuseness, blur[ring] <opt.>	Unschärfe f <Opt.>
unmixability	s. immiscibility		
unmixing	s. demixing		
unmodified scattering	Streuung f ohne Energieänderung	unsharpness of the line, diffuseness of the line, line unsharpness	Linienunschärfe f, Unschärfe f der Spektrallinie
unnotched specimen, plain specimen	Vollprobestab m, Vollstab m	unsolidified, non-solidified	unverfestigt
		unsolvable	s. unresolvable
unoccupied, non-occupied; unfilled; unpopulated; empty; vacant	unbesetzt, nichtbesetzt; leer; vakant; frei	unsplintered glass, safety glass, splinter-proof glass	Sicherheitsglas n, splitterfreies Glas n
unoccupied level	s. unfilled level	unsqueezing, redressement, reestablishment; spreading <opt.>	Entzerrung f <Opt.>
unpaired electron	unpaares Elektron n, ungepaartes Elektron n, unpaariges Elektron		
		unstability, instability, imbalance; lability	Instabilität f, Unstabilität f; Labilität f
unpaired nucleon	unpaares Nukleon n, unpaariges Nukleon, ungepaartes Nukleon	unstability, instability <chem.>	Unbeständigkeit f, Instabilität f <Chem.>
unpitched sound; swishing <ac.>	Rauschen n, Geräusch n <Ak.>	unstable circuit, astable circuit	instabiler Kreis m
unpitched sound	s. a. sound combination <ac.>	unstable equilibrium, labile equilibrium, unsteady equilibrium, negative stability	labiles (instabiles, unsicheres, schwankendes) Gleichgewicht n, Umfallgleichgewicht n
unpolarizable (unpolarized) electrode, nonpolarizable electrode	unpolarisierbare Elektrode f	unstable equilibrium phase	instabile Gleichgewichtsphase f, instabile Sollphase f
unpolarized light	unpolarisiertes Licht n		
unponderable	s. imponderable	unstable equilibrium position	instabile Gleichgewichtslage f
unpopulated	s. unoccupied		
unprimed, unaccented <math.>	ungestrichen <Math.>	unstable frame, labile frame; unstable truss, labile truss	labiles Fachwerk n, kinematisch unbestimmtes Fachwerk
unprimed quantity	ungestrichene Größe f		
unpromoted	nichtbegünstigt	unstable nucleus, radioactive nucleus, decaying nucleus	radioaktiver Kern m, instabiler Kern, zerfallender Kern
unprovable, undemonstrable	unbeweisbar		
unquantized	nichtgequantelt, ungequantelt	unstable solution <math.>	instabile Lösung f, labile Lösung <Math.>
unreactive; insensitive <of instrument>	unempfindlich <Gerät>	unstable state	instabiler Zustand m <auch Kern.>; labiler (unstabiler) Zustand
unrelaxed modulus [of elasticity], instantaneous modulus [of elasticity]	momentaner Elastizitätsmodul m	unstable stop band, stop band, stopband, instability stop band <acc.>	Stoppband n [im Diamanten], instabiler Streifen m <Beschl.>
unresolvable <opt.>; unsolvable <math.>	nicht auflösbar <Opt.; Math.>; nichttrennbar, untrennbar <Opt.>; unlösbar, unauflösbar <Math.>	unstable stratification	labile Schichtung f, instabile Schichtung
		unstable structure / of	s. structural-unstable
		unstable to fission, unstable with respect to fission	instabil gegen Spaltung
unresolved <opt.>	nichtgetrennt, nichtaufgelöst, unaufgelöst <Opt.>	unstable truss; unstable frame, labile frame; labile truss	labiles Fachwerk n, kinematisch unbestimmtes Fachwerk
unrestricted dissipation of matter in the universe, dissipation of matter in the universe	[unbeschränkte] Zerstreuung f der Materie im Weltall	unstable with respect to fission, unstable to fission	instabil gegen Spaltung
unrestricted symmetric group	uneingeschränkte symmetrische Gruppe f	unsteadiness of light <emitted by a source>; flashing <opt., el.>; flicker <e.g. of flame>	Flackern n <Opt., El.>; Aufflackern n <z. B. des Bogens>
unrippled sea, smooth sea, glassy sea	spiegelglatte See f, vollkommen glatte See, glatte See, Meeresstille f <Stärke 0>		
		unsteady, non-steady, unsteady-state; nonstationary	nichtstationär, instationär
unrolling	Abrollen n		
unsatisfied bond	s. unsaturated bond	unsteady; jump-like; stepped, step-like; discontinuous; sudden	sprunghaft; diskontinuierlich
unsaturated, nonsaturated	ungesättigt <auch Chem.>; nicht gesättigt; nichtabgesättigt; nicht voll ausgebildet		
		unsteady equilibrium	s. unstable equilibrium
		unsteady flow	s. non-stationary flow
unsaturated bond, dangling bond, unsatisfied bond	ungesättigte (nicht abgesättigte, freie) Bindung f	unsteady motion	s. non-stationary flow
		unsteady-state, non-steady, unsteady; non-stationary	nichtstationär, instationär
unsaturated compound	ungesättigte Verbindung f		
unsaturated steam	ungesättigter Wasserdampf (Dampf) m	unstrained, undeformed	unverformt, undeformiert, nichtdeformiert
		unstrained	s. a. unstressed <mech.>
unsaturated vapour, unsaturated vapor <US>	ungesättigter Dampf m	unstrained state; unstressed state	unverspannter Zustand m
unsaturated vapor <US>	s. a. unsaturated vapour	unstratified, not stratified	ungeschichtet

unstressed, unloaded <mech.> — unbeansprucht, unbelastet <Mech.>
unstressed, stressless, free of stress, stress-free, free of tension, tension-free; unstrained, free from strain <mech.> — spannungsfrei, spannungslos, ungespannt; unverspannt, nicht verspannt, verspannungsfrei <Mech.>
unstressed state; unstrained state — unverspannter Zustand *m*
unsupported — freitragend, selbsttragend
unsupported length — *s.* span <mech.>
unsymmetric[al], asymmetric[al], dissymmetric [-al], nonsymmetric[al] — asymmetrisch, unsymmetrisch, nichtsymmetrisch
unsymmetrical top, asymmetric gyroscope — unsymmetrischer Kreisel *m*, dreiachsiger Kreisel, asymmetrischer Kreisel
unsymmetry — *s.* asymmetry
untensioned, slack, flabby, flaccid, loose, sagging, limp — schlaff, entspannt, ungespannt
untextured, without texture — ohne Textur, nicht vorzugsgerichtet, nicht texturbehaftet, texturfrei
untightness, leakiness — Undichtigkeit *f*, Undichtheit *f*
untuned aerial, aperiodic antenna — aperiodische Antenne *f*
untuned feeder, nonresonant feeder — unabgestimmte Speiseleitung *f*
unvarying; constant; invariable; fixed — konstant; unveränderlich, invariabel, fest
unwanted signal — *s.* spurious signal
unweighable — *s.* imponderable
unweighted mean — ungewogenes Mittel *n*
unyawed — nichtschiebend, mit dem Schiebungswinkel Null
up-and-down method, staircase estimation method, staircase method — Pendelmethode *f*, Treppenstufenmethode *f*, Auf-und-ab-Methode *f*
upcurrent, upwash, upward current, upflow, upward flow — Aufströmung *f*, Aufstrom *m*, aufsteigender Luftstrom *m*
up-down counter — *s.* bidirectional counter
updraft — *s.* anabatic wind
updraught — *s.* anabatic wind
uperization — Uperisation *f*, Ultrapasteurisation *f*, Ultrapasteurisierung *f*
upflow — *s.* upcurrent
upfold — *s.* anticlinal fold <geo.>
upgliding — Aufgleiten *n*
upheaval, uplift, upthrust <geo.> — Hebung *f*; Bodenerhebung *f*, Erhebung *f* <Geo.>
upheaval — *s. a.* lifting <geo.>
uphill diffusion — negative Diffusion *f*
uplift, upheaval, upthrust <geo.> — Hebung *f*; Bodenerhebung *f*, Erhebung *f* <Geo.>
uplift, static lift, upthrust <aero.> — aerostatischer (statischer) Auftrieb *m* <Aero.>
uplift — *s. a.* lifting <geo.>
uplifted peneplain — *s.* dislocation mountains
upper-air chart, aerological map, altitude chart — Höhenkarte *f*, aerologische Karte *f*; Höhenströmungskarte *f*
upper air climatology — Klimatologie *f* der oberen Luftschichten
upper-air sounding rocket — *s.* altitude rocket
upper annealing point, annealing point <of glass> — oberer Kühlpunkt *m*, Entspannungspunkt *m*, Entspannungstemperatur *f* <Glas>
upper atmosphere, upper atmospheric layer, high atmosphere, high-upper atmosphere, upper part of the atmosphere — obere Atmosphärenschicht *f*, obere Atmosphäre *f*, hohe Atmosphäre, hohe Schichten *fpl* der Atmosphäre, Hochatmosphäre *f*
upper atmospheric layer — *s.* upper atmosphere
upper bound — obere Schranke *f*
upper calorific value — *s.* gross calorific value
upper central series — aufsteigende Zentralfolge *f*, oberste Zentralfolge, obere Zentralreihe *f*
upper chord — *s.* top chord
upper chromosphere — höhere Chromosphäre *f*, hohe Chromosphäre
upper consolute temperature, upper plait-point, upper critical point — oberer kritischer Entmischungspunkt *m*
upper course, head waters, upper waters <of river> — Oberlauf *m* <Fluß>
upper critical point, upper plait-point, upper consolute temperature — oberer kritischer Entmischungspunkt *m*
upper culmination — obere Kulmination *f*, oberer Kulminationspunkt *m*
upper Darboux integral — Oberintegral *n*, oberes [Darbouxsches] Integral *n*
upper front, altitude front — Höhenfront *f*
upper half-plane — obere Halbebene *f*
upper harmonic, higher harmonic, ultraharmonic, overtone — höhere Harmonische *f*, Harmonische höherer Ordnung
upper hemispherical flux, upper flux — oberer halbräumlicher (hemisphärischer) Lichtstrom *m*
upper index — *s.* superscript
upper inversion — *s.* tropopause
upper ionosphere — hohe Ionosphäre *f*
upper limit, superior limit, limit superior, lim sup, lim — limes *m* superior, oberer Limes *m*, obere Häufungsgrenze *f*, obere Unbestimmtheitsgrenze *f*, oberer Hauptlimes *m*, lim sup, lim
upper limit <gen.> — Obergrenze *f* <Allg.>
upper limiting filter — *s.* low-pass filter
upper limit of audibility, upper limit of hearing — obere Hörgrenze *f*
upper limit of the atmosphere — Grenze *f* der Atmosphäre, Grenze zum Weltraum, Weltraumgrenze *f*
upper limit of the cloud — Wolkenobergrenze *f*, obere Wolkengrenze *f*
upper limit of the integral — obere Grenze *f* des Integrals, obere Integrationsgrenze *f*
upper mantle [of Earth], B region — obere Mantelschicht *f*, oberer Mantel *m*, oberer Teil *m* des Mantels, Obermantel *m*, B-Schicht *f*, B-Schale *f*
upper measure, exterior measure, outer measure — äußeres Maß *n*
uppermost layer of soil — *s.* eluvial soil
uppermost level, topmost level — oberstes (höchstes) Niveau *n*
upper partial — *s.* overtone <ac.>
upper part of the atmosphere — *s.* upper atmosphere
upper part of the rectifying column — *s.* rectifier <chem.>
upper plait-point, upper critical point, upper consolute temperature — oberer kritischer Entmischungspunkt *m*
upper pond, upper pool, upper reach, forebay, head water — Oberhaltung *f*, obere Haltung *f*, Oberwasser *n*, Oberstau *m*
upper semicontinuous function — oberhalbstetige Funktion *f*, nach oben halbstetige Funktion
upper side[-]band — oberes Seitenband *n*
upper sum — Obersumme *f*, Darbouxsche Obersumme
upper surface of the airfoil, low pressure surface, suction side of the airfoil — Flügeloberseite *f*, Oberseite *f* des Tragflügels
upper surface of the cloud — Wolkenoberseite *f*
upper tangential arc — oberer Berührungsbogen *m*
upper threshold of audibility — *s.* upper threshold of hearing
upper threshold of hearing, pain threshold of hearing, upper threshold of audibility, level of discomfort, threshold of feeling, threshold of pain, threshold of discomfort, threshold of tickle — obere Hörschwelle *f*, Schmerzschwelle *f*, Schmerzgrenze *f*
upper trade [wind] — Oberpassat *m*

upper troposphere	obere Troposphäre f	uranium intensifier	Uranverstärker m
upper waters, upper course, head waters <of river>	Oberlauf m <Fluß>	uranium lead, radium G, radium lead, ^{206}Pb, RaG	Radium n G, Uranblei n, Radiumblei n, ^{206}Pb, RaG
upper wind, high-altitude wind; aloft wind	Höhenwind m	uranium lead method [of dating]	s. radium G method
upper yield point, upper yield point stress, upper yield strength	obere Streckgrenze f, obere Fließgrenze f, Loslösespannung f	uranium radioactive family (series), uranium-radium family (radioactive series)	s. uranium series
Uppsala scale, Ångström pyrheliometric scale, Ångström scale	Ångström-Skala f, Uppsala-Skala f	uranium-radium ratio	Uran/Radium-Verhältnis n, U/Ra-Verhältnis n
U-process, umklapp process, flop-over process	Umklappprozeß m; Spinumklappprozeß m, Spin-,,flip-flop''-Prozeß m, ,,flip-flop''-Prozeß m	uranium-radium series uranium series, uranium radioactive series, $4n+2$ series, uranium-radium series, uranium-radium radioactive series, radium series, radium radioactive series; uranium family, uranium radioactive family, radioactive family of uranium, $4n+2$ family, uranium-radium family, radium family, radioactive family of [uranium-]radium	s. uranium series Uranzerfallsreihe f, Uranreihe f, $(4n+2)$-Zerfallsreihe f, Zerfallsreihe f des Urans, Uran-Radium-Zerfallsreihe f, Uran-Radium-Reihe f, Radium[zerfalls]reihe f, Zerfallsreihe des Radiums; radioaktive Familie f des Urans, Uranfamilie f, radioaktive Familie des [Uran-]Radiums, Uran-Radium-Familie f, Radiumfamilie f
upsetting, jumping up	Stauchung f; Anstauchung f		
upsetting test	s. compression test		
upside-down, inverted, reversed upside-down <of image>	kopfstehend, umgekehrt <Bild>		
upslope fog	Hangnebel m		
upslope radiation fog	Strahlungshochnebel m		
upslope wind	s. orographic upward wind		
up-stream, up the river	stromaufwärts, stromauf, gegen die Strömung	uranography, descriptive astronomy	beschreibende Astronomie f, Himmelsbeschreibung f, Uranographie f
		uranoide	Uranoid n,
		uranolith, meteorite	Meteorit m, Uranolith m
upstream apron, upstream floor	Vorboden m, Oberteil m der Wehrsohle	uranometry <sky map>	Uranometrie f <Himmelskarte>
uptake	Uptake m, Aufnahme f <radioaktiver Stoffe> in die extrazelluläre Flüssigkeit	uranometry	s. a. astrometry
		uranoscopy	Himmelsbeobachtung f, Uranoskopie f
		uranostat	Uranostat m
uptake	s. intake	Urbach[s] rule	Urbachsche Regel f
uptake factor <bio.>	Aufnahmefaktor m <Bio.>	urban climate	Stadtklima n, städtisches Klima n
uptake of water	s. water intake		
uptake rate; absorption rate	Aufnahmegeschwindigkeit f	URCA process, loss of energy due to ordinary beta decay	URCA-Prozeß m
upthrust, upheaval, uplift <geo.>	Hebung f; Bodenerhebung f, Erhebung f <Geo.>		
upthrust	s. a. lifting <geo.>	urdox [resistor], uranium dioxide resistor	Urdoxwiderstand m, Urandioxidwiderstand m
upthrust	s. a. hydrostatic buoyancy <hydr.>		
upthrust	s. a. uplift <aero.>	Urey-Bradley field	Urey-Bradley-Feld n, Urey-Bradleysches Kraftfeld f
upturning	s. tilting over <geo.>		
upward current	s. upwash		
upward current	s. a. anabatic wind	Urey-Bradley['s] potential function	s. Urey-Bradley-Simanouti['s] potential function
upward flow	s. upwash		
upward flux	s. upper hemispherical flux		
upward force at the support	s. supporting force	Urey-Bradley-Shimanouchi['s] potential function, potential function of Urey-Bradley-Shimanouchi, Urey-Bradley['s] potential function	Potentialfunktion f von Urey-Bradley[-Shimanouchi]
upward forces at the supports	s. support reactions		
upward induced transition	induzierter Übergang m nach oben		
upward wind	s. anabatic wind	Ursa Major cluster, UMa cluster	Ursa Major-Haufen m, Bärenstrom m, UMa-Haufen m
upwash, upward current, upcurrent, upflow, upward flow	Aufströmung f, Aufstrom m, aufsteigender Luftstrom m		
		Ursell-Mayer cluster expansion	Ursell-Mayersche Clusterentwicklung (Entwicklung) f
upwash	s. a. anabatic wind		
upwash due to heat rising	s. laminar thermal convection in the atmosphere	ursigram	Ursigramm n
upwind	s. anabatic wind		
uranium-actinium family	s. actinium family	use, utilization, using	Nutzung f, Ausnutzung f; Nutzbarmachung f; Verwertung f
uranium-actinium radioactive family	s. actinium family		
uranium-actinium radioactive series	s. actinium series	useful amplitude	Nutzamplitude f
uranium-actinium series	s. actinium series	useful area, effective area <opt.>	Nutzfläche f <Opt.>
uranium-carbon lattice, uranium-graphite lattice	Uran-Graphit-Gitter n, U-D$_2$O-Gitter n	useful beam	Nutzstrahlenbündel n, Nutzstrahl m
uranium dioxide resistor, urdox resistor, urdox	Urdoxwiderstand m, Urandioxidwiderstand m	useful capture	s. fission capture
		useful cone, useful radiation cone	Nutzstrahlenkegel m
uranium family	s. uranium series	useful current, actual current	Nutzstrom m
uranium-graphite lattice, uranium-carbon lattice	Uran-Graphit-Gitter n, U-D$_2$O-Gitter n	useful energy, power, energy	Nutzenergie f, nutzbare Energie f
uranium-heavy water lattice	Uran-Schwerwasser-Gitter n	useful field, signal field	Nutzfeld n
		useful field intensity, useful strength of field	Nutzfeldstärke f

useful field of view measured externally, external field <of polarizing prism>	Gesichtsfeldwinkel m, Dingwinkel m <Polarisationsprisma>	U-tube viscometer	U-Rohr-Viskosimeter n
useful flux, principal flux	Nutzfluß m, Hauptfluß m	U-type four-terminal network, U-network	U-Vierpol m
		UV, uv	s. ultra-violet
		uvaser	Uvaser m, Ultraviolettlaser m, UV-Laser m
useful gain	nützliche Verstärkung f	UV Ceti-type star, UV Ceti-type variable [star], UV Ceti variable [star], flare star	UV Ceti-Stern m, UV Ceti-Veränderlicher m, Flackerstern m, „flare star" m
useful inductance, principal inductance	Hauptinduktivität f, Nutzinduktivität f		
useful luminous flux, utilized flux	Nutzlichtstrom m		
useful magnification	förderliche (nutzbare) Vergrößerung f	u value <US>	s. over[-]all coefficient
useful output (power)	s. actual output	uviol, uviol glass	Uviolglas n
useful power	s. actual output	uviol glass, uviol	Uviolglas n
useful radiation, effective radiation	Nutzstrahlung f	uviol lamp	Uviollampe f
		Uzawa['s] method	Uzawa-Methode f
useful radiation cone, useful cone	Nutzstrahlenkegel m		
useful reliability	s. dependability		
useful resistance	Nutzwiderstand m		
useful resistance	s. a. lift <aero., hydr.>		
useful signal	Nutzsignal n		

V

useful solid angle <of mass spectrograph>	nutzbarer Raumwinkel m, „Lichtstärke" f <Massenspektrograph>	1/v absorber	1/v-Absorber m
useful strength of field, useful field intensity	Nutzfeldstärke f	vacancy	s. vacant site <cryst.>
		vacancy	s. a. positive hole
		vacancy aggregate	s. vacancy cluster
useful thermal power [of reactor]	nutzbare thermische Leistung f, nutzbare Wärmeleistung f <Reaktor>	vacancy cluster, cluster of vacancies, vacancy aggregate	Leerstellenassoziat n, Leerstellenagglomerat n, Assoziat n von Leerstellen, Leerstellencluster m
useful voltage	Nutzspannung f		
useful work, effective work, performance	Nutzarbeit f	vacancy[-] creep	Leerstellenkriechen n, Fehlstellenkriechen n
use of moving averages	s. moving average		
use of phantom circuits	Phantomausnutzung f	vacancy diffusion, hole diffusion	Leerstellendiffusion f, Lückendiffusion f
use of the shell	s. sag		
U-shaped core	U-Kern m	vacancy-interstitial recombination	Leerstelle-Zwischengitteratom-Rekombination f
U-shaped valley, trough valley	Trogtal n, U-Tal n, trogförmiges Tal n, Trog m	vacancy in the shell, shell vacancy, empty place in the shell	Leerstelle f in der Schale
using, utilization, use	Nutzung f, Ausnutzung f; Nutzbarmachung f; Verwertung f	vacancy jog	Leerstellensprung m
		vacancy migration (motion), migration of vacancies	Leerstellenwanderung f; Ausheilung f von Leerstellen
US knot, international knot, kn, int. kn.	Knoten m, kn		
US-nautical mile, international mile, sea mile, nautical mile, intern. mile <= 1,852 m>	Seemeile f, internationale Seemeile, sm <= 1 852 m>	vacancy pair	s. double vacancy
		vacancy recovery	Ausheilung f von Leerstellen
usual calorimeter	s. liquid calorimeter	vacancy theory	s. hole theory [of electron]
US yard	s. yard	vacancy-type Schottky defect	s. Schottky defect
U test	s. Wilcoxon['s] test		
utilance	s. room utilization factor		
utility theory	Utilitytheorie f, Nutzentheorie f	vacant; unoccupied; non-occupied; unfilled; unpopulated; empty	unbesetzt, nichtbesetzt; leer; vakant; frei
utilization, use, using	Nutzung f, Ausnutzung f; Nutzbarmachung f; Verwertung f	vacant atomic site	s. vacant site <cryst.>
		vacant crystal	Lückenfehlkristall m
utilization coefficient	s. utilization factor <opt.>	vacant electron site	s. positive hole
utilization factor	Nutz[ungs]faktor m, Nutzung f	vacant lattice	Lückengitter n
utilization factor <of paramagnetic>	Ausnutzungsfaktor m <Paramagnetikum>	vacant lattice position (site)	s. vacant site <cryst.>
		vacant shell	freie Schale f, unbesetzte Schale
utilization factor, utilization coefficient, efficiency, coefficient of utilization; illumination efficiency <opt.>	Ausnutzungsfaktor m, Ausnutzungsgrad m, Ausnutzungskoeffizient m, Ausnutzungsverhältnis n, Beleuchtungswirkungsgrad m; Beleuchtungsausnutzung f <Opt.>	vacant site [in the lattice], vacant (empty) lattice site, vacant atomic site, substitutional site, [lattice] vacancy, vacant lattice position, lattice hole, open position, empty site, void, empty place <cryst.>	Leerstelle f, Gitterleerstelle f, Gitter[baustein]lücke f, Gitterloch n, Leerplatz m, Loch n, Vakanz f, leerer (unbesetzter) Gitterplatz m, Zwischengitterlücke f, Lücke f <Krist.>
utilization of energy, energy utilization; energy efficiency	energetischer Wirkungsgrad m; Energieausnutzung f		
utilization of heat, heat utilization, heat efficiency	Wärmeausnutzung f, Wärmenutzung f		
utilized flux	s. useful luminous flux	vacillation [about zero]	Einspielen n [des Zeigers]; Nulleinspielung f
U tube	U-Rohr n		
U-tube	s. a. U tube manometer	vacuojunction, vacuum thermocouple, vacuum-type thermocouple; vacuum thermoconverter	Vakuumthermoelement n; Vakuumthermoumformer m, Vakuumumformer m
U-tube capillary pycnometer	U-Rohr-Kapillarpyknometer n		
U-tube draught gauge, water draught gauge	Wassersäulenzugmesser m		
U tube manometer, U-tube manometer, U-tube	U-Rohr-Manometer n, zweischenkliges Manometer n	vacuolar contraction	Vakuolenkontraktion f
		vacuolar plasmolysis	Vakuolenplasmolyse f
		vacuolar sap, cell sap	Zellsaft m

vacuometer s. vacuum gauge
vacuon, pomeranchukon, Pomeranchuk particle, Pomeranchuk pole, pomeranchon Pomerantschukon *n*, Pomerantschuk-Teilchen *n*, Pomerantschuk-Pol *m*, Vakuon *n*

vacuscope Vakuskop *n*
vacustat Vakustat *m*

vacuum s. free space
vacuum s. underpressure
vacuum adiabatic calorimeter, vacuum-type adiabatic calorimeter adiabatisches Vakuumkalorimeter *n*
vacuum annealing, annealing in vacuo Vakuumglühen *n*

vacuum apparatus Vakuumapparat *m*

vacuum arc Vakuumlichtbogen *m*, Vakuumbogen *m*

vacuum arrestor, vacuum lightning arrestor, vacuum tube lightning arrestor Luftleerspannungsableiter *m*, Vakuumspannungsableiter *m*, Luftleerblitzableiter *m*, Vakuumblitzableiter *m*

vacuum attainable by vacuum jet pump, water jet vacuum Wasserstrahlvakuum *n*

vacuum binant electrometer, vacuum duant electrometer, vacuum two-segment electrometer Vakuumduant[en]elektrometer *n* [nach Hoffmann]

vacuum breakdown, electrical breakdown in vacuum, vacuum sparking Vakuumdurchschlag *m*, Durchschlag (Durchbruch) *m* im Vakuum

vacuum calorimeter, Dewar calorimeter Vakuumkalorimeter *n*
vacuum cement Vakuumkitt *m*
vacuum chamber Vakuumkammer *f*
vacuum coat[ing], vacuum deposit[ion] Vakuumaufdampfschicht *f*, [vakuum]aufgedampfte Schicht *f*, Aufdampfschicht *f*
vacuum coating s. a. metallization by high vacuum evaporation
vacuum coating system s. vacuum metallizer
vacuum cock Vakuumhahn *m*
vacuum column, vacuum distilling column, vacuum tower Vakuumdestillierkolonne *f*, Vakuumkolonne *f*, Vakuumturm *m*
vacuum compartment s. vacuum space
vacuum connection, vacuum joint Vakuumverbindung *f*
vacuum constant Vakuumkonstante *f*
vacuum contact Vakuumkontakt *m*
vacuum control valve, vacuum regulating valve Vakuumreglerventil *n*, Vakuumregelventil *n*

vacuum cryostat Vakuumkryostat *m*
vacuum crystallization Vakuumkristallisation *f*

vacuum cup s. suctorial disk
vacuum current Vakuumstrom *m*

vacuum deposit[ion] s. vacuum coat[ing]
vacuum deposition s. a. metallization by high vacuum evaporation
vacuum desiccation; vacuum drying Vakuumtrocknung *f*

vacuum diagram, counterpressure diagram Unterdruckfigur *f*
vacuum diffusion pump s. diffusion pump
vacuum diode s. diode
vacuum distillation, vacuum topping Vakuumdestillation *f*, Unterdruckdestillation *f*

vacuum distilling column, vacuum column, vacuum tower Vakuumdestillierkolonne *f*, Vakuumkolonne *f*, Vakuumturm *m*
vacuum doughnut, doughnut, toroid, donut <of betatron> Ringkammer *f*, Ringröhre *f*, [ringförmige] Vakuumkammer *f* <Betatron>

vacuum drying; vacuum desiccation Vakuumtrocknung *f*

vacuum duant electrometer, vacuum binant electrometer, vacuum two-segment electrometer Vakuumduant[en]elektrometer *n* [nach Hoffmann]

vacuum effect, vacuum phenomenon Vakuumeffekt *m*
vacuum electrodynamics, electrodynamics in vacuo Vakuumelektrodynamik *f*
vacuum electron Vakuumelektron *n*
vacuum envelope, vacuum jacket Vakuummantel *m*
vacuum envelope Vakuumkolben *m*
vacuum equipment Vakuumanlage *f*, Vakuumapparatur *f*, vakuumtechnische Ausrüstung *f*

vacuum evaporation s. metallization by vacuum evaporation
vacuum evaporation plant s. vacuum metallizer
vacuum evaporator Vakuumverdampfer *m*

vacuum expectation value Vakuumerwartungswert *m*
vacuum extraction still Vakuumextraktionsapparat *m*

vacuum factor <of vacuum pump> Vakuumfaktor *m* <Vakuumpumpe>
vacuum factor, gas ratio <of vacuum tube> Vakuumfaktor *m* <Mehrelektrodenröhre>
vacuum factor [of ionization gauge] Vakuumfaktor *m* [des Ionisationsmanometers]
vacuum filling, vacuum impregnating Vakuumtränkung *f*, Vakuumimprägnierung *f*
vacuum filter Vakuumfilter *n*
vacuum filtration, antigravity filtration Vakuumfiltration *f*
vacuum flask, Dewar vacuum flask, Dewar flask, Dewar vessel, thermos flask Dewar-Gefäß *n*, Dewarsches Gefäß *n*, Weinholdsches Gefäß *n*, Vakuummantelgefäß *n*, Vakuumgefäß *n*

vacuum fluctuation of the eletromagnetic field s. electromagnetic vacuum fluctuation
vacuum furnace Vakuumofen *m*
vacuum gauge, vacuum[ ]meter, vacuometer Vakuummeter *n*, Vakuummeßgerät *n*, Vakuummesser *m*, Unterdruckmesser *m*

vacuum gauge pressure s. underpressure
vacuum generation, vacuum production Vakuumherstellung *f*

vacuum grating spectrograph Vakuumgitterspektrograph *m*, Gittervakuumspektrograph *m*
vacuum grease Vakuumfett *n*
vacuum head Unterdruckhöhe *f*

vacuum impregnating, vacuum filling Vakuumtränkung *f*, Vakuumimprägnierung *f*
vacuum in the proper sense s. free space
vacuum ionization gauge s. ionization gauge

vacuum jacket s. vacuum envelope
vacuum joint, vacuum connection — Vakuumverbindung f

vacuum lamp — Vakuumglühlampe f, Vakuumlampe f
vacuum layer — Vakuumschicht f
vacuum leak — Vakuumleck n, Undichtigkeit f im Vakuumsystem
vacuum lightning arrestor s. vacuum arrestor
vacuum line, vacuum manifold — Vakuumleitung f

vacuum lock — Vakuumverschluß m
vacuum lock — Vakuumschleuse f

vacuum manifold s. vacuum line
vacuum metallization s. metallization by high vacuum evaporation
vacuum metallizer, vacuum metallizing machine, vacuum evaporation plant, vacuum coating system — Vakuumbedampfungsanlage f, Vakuummetallbedampfungsanlage f, Vakuummetallbedampfer m, Vakuumverdampfungsanlage f, Vakuumaufdampfanlage f

vacuum[ ]meter s. vacuum gauge
vacuum oil — Vakuumöl n
vacuum phenomenon, vacuum effect — Vakuumeffekt m
vacuum photocell, vacuum photoemissive tube, vacuum tube, photoemissive vacuum cell, phototube, photovalve; high-vacuum photocell — Vakuumphotozelle f, Vakuumzelle f, Vakuumemissionsphotoelement n, Vakuumemissionsphotozelle f, Vakuumphotoelement n; Hochvakuumphotozelle f, Hochvakuumzelle f

vacuum physics — Vakuumphysik f
vacuum polarization, polarization of free space, polarization of vacuum — Polarisation f des Vakuums, Vakuumpolarisation f
vacuum polarization diagram — Vakuumpolarisationsdiagramm n
vacuum prism spectrograph — Vakuumprismenspektrograph m

vacuum production s. vacuum generation
vacuum pump — Vakuumpumpe f

vacuum pump system s. pump assembly
vacuum rectifier [valve] s. vacuum valve
vacuum refrigerating machine, vacuum-type refrigerating machine — Vakuumkältemaschine f
vacuum regulating valve, vacuum control valve — Vakuumreglerventil n, Vakuumregelventil n

vacuum seal[ing] — Vakuumdichtung f; Vakuumabschluß m

vacuum space, vacuum compartment, evacuated space — Unterdruckraum m, Vakuumraum m, Vakuum n, evakuierter Raum m

vacuum spark — Vakuumfunke[n] m
vacuum sparking, vacuum breakdown, electrical breakdown in vacuum — Vakuumdurchschlag m, Durchschlag (Durchbruch) m im Vakuum
vacuum spark ion source — Vakuumfunkenionenquelle f

vacuum spectrograph — Vakuumspektrograph m

vacuum spectrometer, vacuum spectroscope — Vakuumspektrometer n, Vakuumspektroskop n

vacuum spectroscopy — Vakuumspektroskopie f
vacuum state — Vakuumzustand m
vacuum system, evacuated system — Vakuumsystem n
vacuum thermoconverter (thermocouple) s. vacuojunction
vacuum thrust — Vakuumschub m
vacuum-tight — vakuumdicht, hermetisch
vacuum tightness s. tightness ⟨vac.⟩
vacuum topping s. vacuum distillation
vacuum tower, vacuum distilling column, vacuum column — Vakuumdestillierkolonne f, Vakuumkolonne f, Vakuumturm m
vacuum trap — Vakuumfalle f

vacuum trapezoid, counterpressure trapezoid — Unterdrucktrapez n
vacuum tube, thermionic vacuum tube, vacuum valve — Vakuumröhre f, Hochvakuumröhre f
vacuum tube s. a. vacuum photocell
vacuum-tube amplifier, tube amplifier, valve amplifier — Röhrenverstärker m, Elektronenröhrenverstärker m, Vakuumröhrenverstärker m
vacuum-tube circuit, valve circuit, tube circuit — Röhrenschaltung f
vacuum-tube-controlled, valve-controlled, tube-controlled — röhrengesteuert
vacuum tube electrometer, tube electrometer — Röhrenelektrometer n
vacuum tube electronics — Vakuumröhrenelektronik f, Röhrenelektronik f
vacuum-tube galvanometer, valve galvanometer, tube-type galvanometer — Röhrengalvanometer n
vacuum-tube generator s. valve oscillator
vacuum tube lightning arrestor s. vacuum arrestor
vacuum-tube measuring instrument, measuring instrument employing vacuum tubes — Röhrenmeßgerät n, Röhrengerät n
vacuum-tube micrometer — Röhrenmikrometer n
vacuum tube noise s. tube noise
vacuum-tube oscillator s. valve oscillator
vacuum-tube photometer — Röhrenphotometer n
vacuum-tube rectifier s. vacuum valve
vacuum-tube transmitter, [thermionic] valve (tube) transmitter, tube-oscillator high-voltage generator — Röhrensender m
vacuum-tube voltmeter, tube voltmeter, valve voltmeter, thermionic voltmeter, vacuum[-]valve voltmeter — Röhrenvoltmeter n, Röhrenspannungsmesser m, Röhren-Wechselspannungsmesser m

vacuum two-segment electrometer, vacuum duant electrometer, vacuum binant electrometer — Vakuumduant[en]elektrometer n [nach Hoffmann]
vacuum-type adiabatic calorimeter, vacuum adiabatic calorimeter — adiabatisches Vakuumkalorimeter n
vacuum-type refrigerating machine, vacuum refrigerating machine — Vakuumkältemaschine f
vacuum-type thermocouple s. vacuojunction
vacuum ultraviolet, vuv, VUV — Vakuumultraviolett n, Vakuum-UV n, VUV

vacuum

vacuum value of velocity	s. velocity in free space	valence force field	Valenzkraftfeld n
vacuum value of velocity of light	s. velocity of light in vacuum	valence force model	Modell n der reinen Valenzkräfte
vacuum value of wavelength, vacuum wavelength, wavelength in vacuum (vacuo, free space, empty space)	Vakuumwellenlänge f	valence isomerism	Valenzisomerie f
		valence lattice	Valenzgitter n
		valence line, bond line, line noting the valence	Valenzstrich m, Bindungsstrich m
vacuum valve, vacuum-tube rectifier, vacuum rectifier [valve]; high-vacuum rectifier	Vakuumgleichrichterröhre f; Vakuumgleichrichter m; Hochvakuumgleichrichter m; Hochvakuum-Gleichrichterröhre f	valence link[age], valence bond	Valenzbindung f
		valence number	s. valency
		valence orbit, outermost orbit, outer orbit, peripheral orbit	Valenzbahn f, kernfernste Bahn f, äußere Elektronenbahn f
vacuum valve, vacuum tube, thermionic vacuum tube	Vakuumröhre f, Hochvakuumröhre f	valence orbital	Valenzorbital n, Valenzbahnfunktion f, Valenzfunktion f
vacuum valve <mech.>	Vakuumventil n <Mech.>	valence semiconductor	Valenzhalbleiter m
vacuum[-]valve voltmeter	s. vacuum-tube voltmeter	valence shell, outermost shell, outer shell, peripheral shell	Valenzschale f, Außenschale f, äußere Schale f, äußerste Schale, äußerste Elektronenschale f, äußere Elektronenschale, kernfernste Schale
vacuum vector	Vakuumvektor m		
vacuum volatilization	Vakuumverflüchtigung f		
vacuum wavelength	s. vacuum value of wavelength	valence stage	s. valency
vacuum window	Vakuumfenster n	valence state	Valenzzustand m
vadose water	vadoses Wasser n	valence tautomerism	Valenztautomerie f
V-aerial	s. vee antenna	valence-type symmetry co-ordinates	Valenzsymmetriekoordinaten fpl
vagabond current	s. parasite current	valence vibration	s. stretching vibration
vagabond ray, stray light	Irrstrahl m	valency, valency number, valence, valence number, hydrogen valence, valence stage, atomicity	Wertigkeit f, chemische Wertigkeit, Wertigkeitsstufe f, Valenz f, Valenzzahl f, Valenzstufe f, Wasserstoffwertigkeit f, Wasserstoffvalenz f
vagabond river <geo.>	Wechselfluß m <Geo.>		
vagabond tektite	verschleppter Tektit m		
Väisälä comparator	Interferometer n von Väisälä, Väisäläsches Interferometer		
val	s. gramme-equivalent	valency bond	s. valence bond
valence, rank, order, degree <of tensor>	Stufe f <Tensor>, Tensorstufe f	valency coefficient, valency factor	Wertigkeitsfaktor m
valence	s. a. valency	valency-controlled semiconductor	valenzgesteuerter Halbleiter m
valence angle, bond angle, angle of valence	Valenzwinkel m, Bindungswinkel m	valency electron	s. valence electron
valence band, valence electron band, valence-bond band, normal band	Valenzband n, V-Band n, Valenzelektronenband n	valency factor, valency coefficient	Wertigkeitsfaktor m
		valency force, valence force	Valenzkraft f
valence band edge	Valenzbandkante f	valency number	s. valency
valence band scattering	Valenzbandstreuung f	valency rule	Valenzregel f
valence band state	Valenzbandzustand m	valency-saturated	valenzgesättigt
valence bond, valence link[age], valency bond	Valenzbindung f		
valence-bond band	s. valence band	validity, holding; applying	Gültigkeit f
valence-bond method	s. valence bond theory <chem.>		
valence bond theory, v.b. theory, resonance theory, valence-bond method, v.b. method, resonance method, Heitler-London-Slating-Pauling theory, HLSP theory	Valenzstrukturmethode f, Valenzbindungsmethode f, Strukturresonanztheorie f Resonanztheorie f, Methode f der Valenzbindung, VB-Methode f <Chem.>	valley <geo.>	Tal n; Talung f <Geo.>
		valley	s. a. minimum <of the curve>
		valley bottom, valley floor	Talboden m, Talgrund m, Talsohle f
		valley breeze, valley wind	Talwind m
		valley current	Talstrom m
valence chain, bond chain, chain of valencies	Valenzkette f, Bindungskette f	valley divide, valley watershed	Talwasserscheide f
valence crystal	s. atomic crystal	valley floor, valley bottom	Talboden m, Talgrund m, Talsohle f
valence deflection angle, deflection angle of the valences	Valenzablenkungswinkel m	valley fog	Talnebel m
		valley glacier, valley-type glacier, true glacier	Talgletscher m
valence electron <semi.>	Valenzelektron n, Elektron n im Valenzband, Valenzbandelektron n <Halb.>	valley of stability	„Stabilitätstal" n <in der Fläche der Bindungsenergie über Ordnungs- und Massenzahl>
valence electron	s. a. bonding electron <chem., nucl.>		
valence electron band, valence band, valence-bond band, normal band	Valenzband n, V-Band n, Valenzelektronenband n	valley slope	Talhang m, Talgehänge n, Talwand f, Tallehne f, Talabhang m
valence electron concentration, electron-to-atom ratio	Valenzelektronenkonzentration f, Valenzelektronendichte f	valley source	Talquelle f
		valley station	Talstation f
		valley-type glacier, valley glacier, true glacier	Talgletscher m
valence force, valency force	Valenzkraft f	valley voltage	Talspannung f
valence force constant	Valenzkraftkonstante f		
valence-force co-ordinates	Valenzkraftkoordinaten fpl	valley watershed, valley divide	Talwasserscheide f

valley wind, valley breeze	Talwind *m*	**valve head,** valve disk, valve cone	Ventilteller *m*, Ventilkegel *m*
valuation, rating <math.>	Bewertung *f* <Math.>	**valve lift,** lift of the valve, valve travel	Ventilhub *m*, Hub *m* des Ventils, Ventilerhebung *f*
value	Wert *m*	**valve lift diagram**	Hubdiagramm *n* des Ventils, Ventilhubdiagramm *n*, Ventilerhebungsdiagramm *n*
value, separative work content, separation potential <in isotope separation>	Trennpotential *n*	**valve needle**	Ventilnadel *f*
		valve noise	s. tube noise
		valve of the rectifier, rectifier (rectifying, detecting) valve	Gleichrichterventil *n*, Ventil *n* des Gleichrichters
value, magnitude, length <of vector>	Betrag *m*, Länge *f* <Vektor>	**valve opening,** opening of the valve	Ventilöffnung *f*
value	s. a. tristimulus value		
value distribution theory	Wertverteilungslehre *f*, Theorie *f* der Wertverteilung	**valve opening area,** valve area, opening area of the valve	freier Ventilquerschnitt *m*, Ventilquerschnitt, Ventilöffnungsquerschnitt *m*
value function	Wertfunktion *f*	**valve oscillator,** vacuum-tube oscillator, tube oscillator, valve generator, vacuum-tube generator, tube generator, tube-oscillator generator, thermionic generator	Röhrenoszillator *m*, Röhrengenerator *m*
value measured	s. experimental value		
value of a turn [of the micrometer screw]	Trommelwert *m* [der Mikrometerschraube]		
value of gravity	s. acceleration of gravity		
value of level division, level constant, sensitiveness of the level	Parswert *m*, Teilwert *m* der Libelle, Angabe *f* der Libelle, Empfindlichkeit *f* der Libelle		
		valve parameter	s. tube parameter
		valve potentiometer	s. Poggendorff-Du Bois-Raymond potentiometer
value of the capacitance; capacitance, electric[al] capacitance, electric capacity <el.>	Kapazitätswert *m*; Kapazität *f*, elektrische Kapazität <El.>	**valve quality,** tube quality	Röhrengüte *f*
		valve ratio	s. rectification ratio
value of the discontinuity, discontinuity value	Sprungwert *m*, Sprunggröße *f*	**valve rectifier,** thermionic rectifier, transrectifier, tube rectifier, thermionic detector	Röhrengleichrichter *m*; Ventilgleichrichter *m*
value of the scale division	s. scale value		
value per unit length <per 1 km>	Belag *m*	**valve rustle**	s. tube noise
valve <techn.>	Ventil *n* <Techn.>	**valve seat[ing],** seat of the valve	Ventilsitz *m*, Sitz *m* des Ventils
valve	s. a. thermionic valve <el.>	**valve transmitter**	s. vacuum-tube transmitter
valve	s. a. rectifier tube <el.>	**valve travel,** travel of the valve	Ventilspiel *n*
valve action, valve effect, rectification effect	Ventilwirkung *f*, Ventileffekt *m*, Gleichrichterwirkung *f*, Gleichrichtereffekt *m*		
		valve travel	s. a. valve lift
		valve tube	s. rectifier tube <el.>
valve amplifier, vacuum-tube amplifier, tube amplifier	Röhrenverstärker *m*, Elektronenröhrenverstärker *m*, Vakuumröhrenverstärker *m*	**valve voltmeter**	s. vacuum-tube voltmeter
		valving	Ventilsystem *n*
		Vandermonde['s] determinant, alternant	Vandermondesche (Cauchysche) Determinante *f*, Alternante *f*, alternierende Funktion *f*
valve area, valve opening area, opening area of the valve	[freier] Ventilquerschnitt *m*, Ventilöffnungsquerschnitt *m*		
valve body, valve box	Ventilgehäuse *n*, Ventilkörper *m*	**vane**	Flügelrad *n*
		vane <of electrometer>	Flügel *m*, flügelförmige (lemniskatenförmige, biskuitförmige) Nadel *f* <Elektrometer>
valve characteristic	s. current-voltage characteristic		
valve circuit, vacuum-tube circuit, tube circuit	Röhrenschaltung *f*	**vane** <of the wind wheel>	Windschaufel *f*, Windflügel *m*
valve cock	Ventilhahn *m*	**vane**	s. a. sliding vane
valve cone, valve head, valve disk	Ventilteller *m*, Ventilkegel *m*	**vane**	s. a. hydrometric vane <hydr.>
		vane	s. a. plate <of capacitor>
valve constant	s. tube parameter	**vane anemometer,** rotary-vane anemometer, wind-vane anemometer, wind wheel anemometer, fan wheel anemometer, rotating wheel anemometer, anemometer of wind-mill type, windmill anemometer, plate anemometer	Windradanemometer *n*, Flügelradanemometer *n*, Flügelradwindmesser *m*, Flügelrad-Windgeschwindigkeitsmesser *m*
valve-controlled, vacuum-tube-controlled, tube-controlled	röhrengesteuert		
valve-controlled	ventilgesteuert		
valve diagram	Ventildiagramm *n*		
valve disk, valve head, valve cone	Ventilteller *m*, Ventilkegel *m*		
valve dosemeter	Röhrendosimeter *n*, Röhrendosismesser *m*	**vane current meter,** vane-type current meter	Flügelradströmungsmesser *m*, Schaufelradströmungsmesser *m*, Schaufelradstrommesser *m*
valve effect, valve action, rectification effect	Ventilwirkung *f*, Ventileffekt *m*, Gleichrichterwirkung *f*, Gleichrichtereffekt *m*		
		vaned flowmeter	s. propeller-type flowmeter
valve face	Ventilsitzfläche *f*	**vane distance**	s. electrode separation
		vane grid, blade grid, grid <hydr., aero.>	Schaufelgitter *n*, Flügelgitter *n*, Gitter *n* <Hydr., Aero.>
valve gain	s. amplification factor of the valve		
		vane pump, vane-type pump	Flügelradpumpe *f*, Kapselpumpe *f*, Schaufelradpumpe *f*
valve galvanometer, tube-type galvanometer, vacuum-tube galvanometer	Röhrengalvanometer *n*		
		vane radiometer	s. Crookes['] radiometer
		vane-type current meter	s. vane current meter
valve gear	Ventilsteuerung *f*	**vane-type draught gauge**	Klappenzugmesser *m*, Flügelzugmesser *m*, Hudlerscher Zugmesser *m*
valve generator	s. valve oscillator		

vane-type pump, vane pump	Flügelradpumpe f, Kapselpumpe f, Schaufelradpumpe f	vapour sheath, vapour shroud, vaporous envelope	Dampfmantel m, Dampfhülle f, Dampfhemd n; Dunsthülle f
vane wheel	s. wind motor	vapour tension	s. saturated vapour pressure
vanishing, disappearance, dying-away	Verschwinden n, Auflösung f	vapour tension thermometer	s. vapour pressure thermometer
vanishing <math.>	Nullwerden n, Verschwinden n <Math.>	vapour trail	s. condensation trail
vanishing current method, initial onset method	Nullstrommethode f	vapour train, fog train <of meteor>	Nebelschweif m, Dampfschweif m <Meteor>
		vapour trap	Dampffalle f
vanishing line	Fluchtgerade f, Fluchtlinie f; Verschwindungsgerade f, Verschwindungslinie f	vapourus, vaporus <US>	Kondensationskurve f, Kondensationslinie f, Taulinie f, Taupunktskurve f, Taukurve f, obere Grenzkurve f, rechte Grenzkurve, Vaporus m
vanishing plane	Fluchtebene f; Verschwindungsebene f		
vanishing point	Fluchtpunkt m; Verschwindungspunkt m		
V-antenna	s. vee antenna	Vaquier balance	Vaquier-Waage f
vapor <US>	s. vapour		
vaporability, vaporizability, evaporability, evaporative capacity	Verdampfbarkeit f, Verdampfungsfähigkeit f, Verdampfungsvermögen n	var, reactive volt[-]ampere	Var n, VAR n, var, Blindwatt n, Blindvoltampere n, bW
		var	s. a. variance <stat.>
vaporization, evaporation <by ebullition>	Verdampfung f	varactor [diode], [variable-]capacitance diode, variable capacitance semiconductor junction diode, varicap, parametric diode	Varaktor m, Kapazitätsdiode f, Kapazitäts-Variations-Diode f, Varaktordiode f, Varactor m, Varikap f (m), parametrische Diode f
vaporization, distillation, volatilization, sublimation	Destillation f, Destillieren n, Siedetrennung f		
vaporization calorimeter	s. steam calorimeter		
vaporization curve; evaporation curve	Verdampfungskurve f; Verdunstungskurve f	var-hour meter, reactive-energy meter, wattless component meter	Blindverbrauchszähler m, Blindwattstundenzähler m
vaporization equilibrium, evaporation equilibrium	Verdampfungsgleichgewicht n		
vaporization heat	s. evaporation heat	variability <of star>	Helligkeitsschwankung f <Gestirn>
vaporization rate, evaporation rate, rate of evaporation, rate of vaporization, evaporative rate	Verdampfungsgeschwindigkeit f, Verdunstungsgeschwindigkeit f		
		variability <bio., stat.>	Variabilität f <Bio., Stat.>
		variability	s. a. range <stat.>
		variable	Variable f, Veränderliche f
vaporization rate	s. a. rate of evaporation	variable, variable star	Veränderlicher m, veränderlicher (variabler) Stern m
vaporous cavitation, true cavitation, genuine cavitation	echte Kavitation f, Dampfkavitation f, Dampfblasenbildung f		
		variable acceleration	Wechselbeschleunigung f, veränderliche Beschleunigung f
vaporous envelope	s. vapour sheath		
vaporus <US>, vapourus	Kondensationskurve f	variable-area recording, variable-area track	Amplitudenschrift f, Zackenschrift f
vapour, vapor <US>	Dampf m		
vapour-absorption refrigerator	s. absorption refrigerator		
vapour bath, steam bath	Dampfbad n, Wasserdampfbad n		
vapour concentration, absolute humidity	absolute Feuchtigkeit f	variable autotransformer	s. variable ratio transformer
vapour cooling	s. evaporative cooling	variable capacitance [semiconductor junction] diode	s. varactor
vapour density, density of vapour[s], gas density, density of gas	Dampfdichte f, Gasdichte f		
		variable capacitor	Drehkondensator m
vapour diagram	s. indicator diagram		
vapour lamp	s. metal vapour lamp		
vapour-liquid equilibrium	s. liquid-vapour equilibrium	variable capacitor	s. adjustable capacitor
		variable clouding	wechselhafte (wechselnde) Bewölkung f, wechselnde Bedeckung (Himmelsbedeckung) f
vapour model	Dampfmodell n		
vapour phase	Dampfphase f, Dampfform f		
vapour pressure	s. saturated vapour pressure	variable-density sound track, variable density track	Sprossenschrift f, Intensitätsschrift f, Dichteschrift f
vapour pressure deficit	s. saturation deficit		
vapour pressure equation, equation for vapour pressure	Dampfdruckgleichung f		
vapour pressure equilibrium	Dampfdruckgleichgewicht n		
vapour pressure lowering, lowering of vapour pressure	Dampfdruckerniedrigung f, Dampfdruckverminderung f		
vapour pressure thermometer, vapour tension thermometer, thermometer with saturated vapour	Dampfdruckthermometer n, Dampfspannungsthermometer n, Spannungsthermometer n, Tensionsthermometer n, Stockthermometer n, Thalpotasimeter n	variable-focus lens	s. zoom lens
		variable-gain amplifier, adjustable gain amplifier	Regelverstärker m, regelbarer Verstärker m
		variable-immersion type hydrometer	Skalenaräometer n
		variable index, running index	Laufindex m, laufender Index m, variabler Index
vapour pump; steam ejector	Dampfstrahlpumpe f, Ejektor m; Treibdampfpumpe f	variable inductance	veränderbare Induktivität (Selbstinduktion) f, veränderliche Induktivität (Selbstinduktion), variable Induktivität (Selbstinduktion), regelbare Induktivität (Selbstinduktion)
vapours	Brodem m, Wrasen m; Schwaden m		

variable inductor, variometer, [continuously] adjustable inductor, inductometer	Variometer n	**variance ratio test,** F-test	Varianzquotiententest m, F-Test m
variable inductor	Regeldrossel[spule] f, Regulierdrosselspule f	**variance within groups (treatments)**	s. within-group variance
		variant; version	Variante f
variable in time, variable with time, time variant	zeitlich veränderlich, zeitvariabel	**variant** <stat.>	Variante f <Stat.>
		variate	s. random variable
variable mu [amplifier], variable mutual conductance valve, variable-mutual tube (valve), variable mu tube (valve), vari-mu variable-transconductance tube (valve), sliding-screen valve (tube), selectode	Regelröhre f, Variabel-S-Röhre f, Variabel-μ-Röhre f, Röhre f mit variabler Steilheit, Selektode f, Exponentialröhre f	**variation,** modification <e.g. of experimental arrangement>	Modifizierung f, Abänderung f, Abwandlung f <z. B. Versuchsanordnung>
		variation; change; alteration; varying <gen.>	Änderung f; Veränderung f; Variation f; Schwankung f; Abänderung f <allg.>
		variation, variation of the function <math.>	Variation f [der Funktion], Schwankung f [der Funktion]
variable of Blasius, Blasius['] variable	Blasiussche Variable f	**variation** <perturbation of lunar motion>	Variation f <Störung der Mondbahn>
variable of integration	Integrationsvariable f		
variable of Riemann	Riemannsche Variable f	**variational calculus,** calculus of variations	Variationsrechnung f
variable of state	s. parameter of state	**variational condition**	Variationsbedingung f
variable ratio transformer, variable autotransformer, adjustable transformer, variable-voltage -(voltage-regulating, regulating) transformer, variac, transtat	Stelltransformator m, veränderbarer Transformator m, veränderlicher Transformator, verstellbarer Transformator, regelbarer Transformator, Regeltransformator m; Variac m, Variak m; Stellumspanner m, Regelumspanner m	**variational derivative,** variation derivative, Lagrangian derivative, functional derivative	Variationsableitung f, Lagrangesche (Euler-Lagrangesche, funktionale) Ableitung f, Funktionalableitung f
		variational equation	Variationsgleichung f
		variational method	Variationsmethode f, Variationsverfahren n
		variational movement	Variationsbewegung f
variable reluctance microphone	s. electromagnetic microphone	**variational orbit,** Hill['s] variational orbit	Hillsche Variationsbahn f, Variationsbahn
variable-resistance transducer	s. resistance transducer	**variational principle,** integral variational principle, integral principle <mech.; qu.>	Variationsprinzip n, Integralprinzip n, Extremalprinzip n <Mech.; Qu.>
variable resistor, adjustable resistor, rheostat	Stellwiderstand m, veränderbarer (veränderlicher) Widerstand m, Rheostat m, Regelwiderstand m, Regelungswiderstand m, Regulierwiderstand m	**variational principle of Schwarzschild**	Schwarzschildsches Wirkungsprinzip n, Schwarzschildsches Prinzip n
		variational problem	Variationsproblem n, Variationsaufgabe f
variable star, variable	Veränderlicher m, veränderlicher (variabler) Stern m	**variational solution**	Variationslösung f
		variational wave function	Variationswellenfunktion f
variable sweep aerofoil (airfoil, wing), swept wing (aerofoil, airfoil), crescent wing (aerofoil, airfoil), swept back wing	Tragflügel m mit veränderlicher Pfeilung, Flügel m mit veränderlicher Pfeilung, Sichelflügel m	**variation at constant time**	Variation f bei konstanter Zeit
		variation chart	s. declination chart
		variation coefficient, coefficient of variation	Variationskoeffizient m, Variabilitätskoeffizient m, Variationsbeiwert m
variable-transconductance tube (valve)	s. variable mu	**variation derivative**	s. variational derivative
variable transformation, transformation of variables, change of variables <bio., stat.>	Variablentransformation f <Bio., Stat.>	**variation in light**	s. light variation
		variation in the mains voltage	s. main voltage fluctuation
		variation map	s. variation chart
variable transformer	regelbarer (veränderbarer, veränderlicher) Übertrager m	**variation of altitude of the pole**	s. variation of latitude
		variation of amplitude, amplitude swing	Amplitudenhub m
variable-voltage transformer	s. variable ratio transformer		
variable wind; shifting wind; baffling wind	veränderlicher Wind m; umlaufender Wind; unbeständiger Wind; umspringender Wind	**variation of constants,** variation of parameters	Variation f der Konstanten
variable with time, variable in time, time variant	zeitlich veränderlich, zeitvariabel	**variation of latitude;** variation of altitude of the pole	Breitenschwankung f; Polhöhenschwankung f
variac	s. variable autotransformer		
variac	s. variable ratio transformer	**variation of mass with velocity,** relativistic variation of mass with velocity	Massenveränderlichkeit f, relativistische Massenveränderlichkeit
variance, dispersion, square of the standard deviation, var <stat.>	Varianz f, Dispersion f, Streuungsquadrat n, Streuung f, var <Stat.>		
variance <of thermodynamic system>	s. a. degree of freedom	**variation of parameters**	s. variation of constants
variance analysis, analysis of variance, ANOVA	Varianzanalyse f, Streuungszerlegung f, F-Verfahren n	**variation of temperature,** temperature variation; heating pattern	Temperaturgang m; Temperaturverlauf m
variance between classes (treatments)	s. interclass variance	**variation of the compass**	s. declination
variance-covariance matrix	s. covariance matrix	**variation of the function,** variation <math.>	Variation f [der Funktion] <Math.>
variance ratio, F ratio, F-statistic	Varianzquotient m, Quotient m F, F-Prüfzahl f		

variation   954

variation of water level — Spiegelbewegung f, Spiegelgang m, Wasserspiegelbewegung f, Wasserspiegelgang m, Wasserstand[s]gang m

variation principle, minimum energy principle <chem.> — Variationsprinzip n <Chem.>

variation tone — Variationston m

variation with time <geo.> — zeitliche Variation f, zeitliche Schwankung f, zeitlicher Gang m <Geo.>

variator, non-linear semiconducting dipole — Variator m

varicap — s. varactor

varicond — Varikond m, Varicond m <spannungsabhängiger Kondensator mit ferroelektrischem Dielektrikum>

varied orbit — variierte Bahn f

variegation — Variegation f; Mosaikfleckung f

variety, modification <bio.> — Abart f, Varietät f, Spielart f, var.; Rasse f <Bio.>

variety; manifold <algebraic geometry> <math.> — Mannigfaltigkeit f; Varietät f <algebraische Geometrie> <Math.>

varifocal lens, zoom lens, zooming lens, variable-focus lens — Objektiv n mit veränderlicher Brennweite, Gummilinse f, Varioptik f, Zoomlinse f; Zoomar n

Varignon['s] theorem — Varignonscher Satz m, Satz (Theorem n) von Varignon

vari-mu — s. variable mu

variocoupler — Variokoppler m

variogram — Variogramm n

variograph, recording variometer — registrierendes Variometer n, Registriervariometer n, Variograph m

variometer, [continuously] adjustable inductor, variable inductor, inductometer — Variometer n; variable Induktionsspule f

variometer <aero.> — Variometer n <Aero.>

variometer bar, bar of the variometer — Variometerstab m, Stab m des Variometers

variometer constant — Variometerkonstante f

variometer rotor, moving coil of the variometer — drehbare Variometerspule f

variometer stator, stationary coil of the variometer — feste Variometerspule f

variopter, optical slide rule — optischer Rechenstab m, Variopter m

varioscope — Varioskop n

varistor, voltage-dependent resistor, non-linear semiconducting dipole — Varistor m, VDR-Widerstand m, spannungsabhängiger Widerstand m

Varley bridge — Varley-Brücke f
Varley effect — Varley-Effekt m
varmeter — Blindleistungsmesser m, Varmeter n

varying; change; alteration; variation <gen.> — Änderung f; Veränderung f; Variation f; Schwankung f; Abänderung f <allg.>

varying load — s. live load <statics>
varying with time — s. time-dependent
vascular resistance — Gefäßwiderstand m <Blut>
vasoconstriction — Vasokonstriktion f
vasomotor centre — Vasomotorzentrum n

vault, vaulting <statics> — Wölbung f, Gewölbe n <Statik>

vault of heaven, firmament — Himmelsgewölbe n, Himmelsgestalt f, Himmelsschale f, Gestalt f des Himmels, Firmament n

Vautier mirror — Vautierscher Spiegel m, Vautier-Spiegel m

Vavilov-Čerenkov effect, Čerenkov effect, Tcherenkov effect — Čerenkov-Effekt m, [Wawilow-]Tscherenkow-Effekt m

Vavilov['s] law — Wawilowsches Gesetz n
V band <0.536−0.652 cm> — V-Band n <0,536 ··· 0,652 cm>

V-bridge — V-Brücke f
V centre — V-Zentrum n
V-characteristic, V-shaped curve, V-curve — V-Kurve f

V connection — V-Schaltung f, Aron-Schaltung f

V-curve, V-chaped curve, V-characteristic — V-Kurve f

V-depression, vee depression, notch-type depression — V-Depression f, V-förmige Senke f

1/v detector — 1/v-Detektor m

V-dipole — Spreizdipol m; Winkeldipol m; V-Dipol m

Veblen-Wedderburn plane, translation plane <math.> — Translationsebene f, Veblen-Wedderburn-Ebene f <Math.>

vectogram, vector diagram — Zeigerdiagramm n <für Wechselstrom>; Vektordiagramm n

vectograph, stereovectograph — Vektograph m, Stereovektograph m

vectograph[ic] film, stereovectograph[ic] film, vectographic film — Vektographenfilm m

vecton, vectorial particle — Vekton n, vektorielles Teilchen n

vectopluviometer — Vektopluviometer n

vector — Vektor m

vector, time vector <in alternating-current theory> — Zeiger m, Zeitzeiger m, Zeitvektor m, ebener Vektor m, Vektor [in der Gaußschen Zahlenebene], Pfeil m, Speer m <komplexe Wechselstromrechnung>

vector <of the quaternion> — Vektorteil m, Vektor m <Quaternion>

vector addition, geometric addition, vector composition — Vektoraddition f, geometrische Addition f

vector addition coefficient — s. Clebsch-Gordan

vector algebra of Gibbs, Gibbs['] vector algebra — Gibbssche Vektoralgebra f, Vektoralgebra von Gibbs

vector analyzer, vectorlyzer — Vektoranalysator m

vector analysis — Vektoranalysis f
vector boson, vectorial boson — Vektorboson n

vector[]cardiogram, vector[]electrocardiogram — Vektorelektrokardiogramm n, Vektorkardiogramm n

vector[]cardiograph, vector[]electrocardiograph — Vektorelektrokardiograph m, Vektorkardiograph m

vector[]cardiography, vector[]electrocardiography — Vektordiagraphie f, Vektorelektrokardiographie f, Vektorkardiographie f

vector chart, vector map — Vektorkarte f

vector colorimeter — Vektorkolorimeter n
vector composition — s. vector addition
vector couple, couple of vectors — Vektorpaar n; Stäbepaar n <Study>

vector coupling — Vektorkopplung f, vektorielle Kopplung f

vector coupling coefficient — Vektorkopplungskoeffizient m

vector density — Vektordichte f, vektorielle Dichte f

vector diagram, vectogram	Zeigerdiagramm n <für Wechselstrom>; Vektordiagramm n	vector model <of atom or molecule>	Vektorgerüst n, Vektormodell n <des Atoms oder Moleküls>
vector diagram	s. a. locus <control>	vector notation	Vektorschreibweise f
vector diagram of collision, collision diagram	Stoßdiagramm n, Vektordiagramm n des Stoßvorgangs	vector of force	Kraftvektor m
		vector of four-dimensional force	s. four-force
vector diagram of impedance, impedance triangle, triangle of impedances	Widerstandsdreieck n	vector of generalized acceleration, generalized acceleration vector	verallgemeinerter Beschleunigungsvektor m
vector diagram of voltage, potential diagram, voltage diagram <el.>	Spannungsdiagramm n, Spannungsbild n <El.>	vector of generalized velocity, generalized velocity vector, generalized velocity	verallgemeinerter Geschwindigkeitsvektor m
		vector of induction, induction vector	Induktionsvektor m
vector differential operator	s. del	vector of isobaric spin	s. isotopic spin vector
vector divergence	s. divergence	vector of isotopic spin	s. isotopic spin vector
vector dominance	Vektordominanz f	vector of magnetic induction	s. magnetic induction <el.>
vector dominance model, VDM	Vektordominanzmodell n	vector of magnetic polarization	s. magnetic polarization
vectored quantity	s. directed quantity	vector of magnetization	s. intensity of magnetization
vector[]electrocardiogram, vector[]cardiogram	Vektorelektrokardiogramm n, Vektorkardiogramm n	vector of oscillation, oscillation vector	Schwingungsvektor m
vector[]electrocardiograph, vector[]cardiograph	Vektorelektrokardiograph m, Vektorkardiograph m	vector of principal normal, principal normal vector; principal normal, unit first normal	Hauptnormale f; Hauptnormalenvektor m
vector[]electrocardiography, vector[]cardiography	Vektordiagraphie f, Vektorelektrokardiographie f, Vektorkardiographie f	vector of state, state vector	Zustandsvektor m
		vector operation	Vektoroperation f
vector equation	Vektorgleichung f	vector operator	Vektoroperator m
		vector polygon, polygon of vectors	Vektorpolygon n
vector field, vectorial field	Vektorfeld n	vector potential	Vektorpotential n, vektorielles Potential n; elektrodynamisches Potential
vector field derivable from a scalar potential	s. irrotational field		
vector flux, flux [of the vector], vectorial flux <through the surface>	Fluß m [des Vektors], Vektorfluß m <durch die Fläche>	vector product, cross product, skew product, outer product	Vektorprodukt n, vektorielles Produkt n, Kreuzprodukt n, äußeres Produkt
vector function	Vektorfunktion f		
vectorgraph [unit]	s. vectorscope	vector quantity, vectorial quantity	vektorielle Größe f, Vektorgröße f, Vektor m
vectorial angle, polar angle	Polarwinkel m	vector representation	s. vectorial representation
vectorial boson, vector boson	Vektorboson n	vector resolution	s. resolution
vectorial differentiation	vektorielle Differentiation f	vectorscope [unit], vectorgraph [unit]	Vektorskop n, Vektorgraph m
vectorial effect of photoemission	Vektoreffekt m der Photoemission		
vectorial field, vector field	Vektorfeld n	vector sheet	Vektorblatt n
		vectors of opposite sense	entgegengerichtete Vektoren mpl
vectorial flux, flux [of the vector], vector flux <through the surface>	Fluß m [des Vektors], Vektorfluß m <durch die Fläche>	vectors of the same sense	gleichgerichtete Vektoren mpl
vectorial Huyghens['] principle, Huyghens['] vectorial principle	vektorielles Huygenssches Prinzip n	vector space, linear vector space, linear space	Vektorraum m, Vektorgebilde n, linearer Raum m
vectorial particle, vecton	Vekton n, vektorielles Teilchen n	vector spherical harmonic	Vektorkugelfunktion f, vektorielle Kugelfunktion f, Winkel-Spin-Funktion f
vectorial quantity, vector quantity	vektorielle Größe f, Vektorgröße f, Vektor m	vector sum, vectorial sum, geometric sum	geometrische Summe f, Vektorsumme f
vectorial recorder	Vektorschreiber m, vektorieller Schreiber m	vector system	s. system of vectors
vectorial representation, vector representation	Zeigerdarstellung f, Strahldarstellung f, Vektordarstellung f	vector transformation	Zeigertransformation f
		vector tube, tube of the vector field	Vektorröhre f, Vektorfeldröhre f, Feldröhre f, Feldlinienröhre f
vectorial sum	s. geometric sum		
vectorial wave	vektorielle Welle f	vector wave equation	Vektorwellengleichung f, vektorielle Wellengleichung f
vector in colour space, colour vector	Farbvektor m	vector wave function	Vektorwellenfunktion f, vektorielle Wellenfunktion f
vector interaction	vektorielle Wechselwirkung f, Vektorwechselwirkung f	vee[d] antenna, V-type antenna, V-shaped antenna, V-antenna, V-aerial	V-Antenne f
vector line, line of vector	Vektorlinie f, Feldlinie f des Vektorfeldes		
vectorlyzer, vector analyzer	Vektoranalysator m	vee depression, V-depression, notch-type depression	V-Depression f, V-förmige Senke f
vector magnetic potential	s. magnetic vector potential	vee filament, zigzag spiral filament	Zickzackwendel f
vector magnetometer	Vektormagnetometer n		
vector map, vector chart	Vektorkarte f	Veen specimen / Van der Veen	Van-der-Veen-Probe f
vector meson	Vektormeson n, vektorielles Meson f	veering of wind [to], shifting of wind [to]; going round of the wind, veering round of the wind	Drehung f des Windes [nach], Umschwenken n des Windes [nach]; Umlaufen n des Windes
vector meson dominance model, VMD model	Vektormesonen-Dominanzmodell n		
vector meter	Vektormesser m		

veering round of the wind	s. veering of wind	velocity diagram, velocity vector diagram, velocity triangle, triangle of velocities, speed triangle	Geschwindigkeitsdreieck n
Vegard-Kaplan band	Vegard-Kaplan-Bande f		
Vegard['s] law, Vegard['s] rule	Vegardsches Gesetz n, Vegardsche Additivitätsregel (Regel) f, Vegard-Regel f	velocity dispersion, velocity straggling	Geschwindigkeitsdispersion f, Geschwindigkeitsstreuung f
vegetational period, vegetation period	Vegetationsperiode f, Vegetationszeit f	velocity-distance relation	s. Hubble['s] law
veil	Schleier m; Nebelschleier m; Rauchschleier m	velocity distribution, distribution of velocity, distribution of velocities	Geschwindigkeitsverteilung f
		velocity distribution function	Geschwindigkeitsverteilungsfunktion f
veil due to atmospheric haze	Dunstschleier m	velocity ellipse, adiabatic ellipse	Geschwindigkeitsellipse f, Adiabatenellipse f
veiled by black	s. non-zero black content / having <of chromatic colour>	velocity ellipsoid	Geschwindigkeitsellipsoid n
veiled by grey	s. non-zero black and white content / having <of chromatic colour>	velocity energy, specific kinetic energy	spezifische kinetische Energie f, Geschwindigkeitsenergie f
		velocity factor, velocity rate, reduction factor <of the line or antenna>	Verkürzungsfaktor m; Leitungsverkürzungsfaktor m; Antennenverkürzungsfaktor m
veiled by white	s. non-zero white content / having <of chromatic colour>		
veiling, masking, shading <of chromatic colours by a portion of white and / or black>	Verhüllung f [bunter Farben]	velocity field, field of velocity	Geschwindigkeitsfeld n
		velocity filter	Geschwindigkeitsfilter n
		velocity flowmeter	s. propeller-type flowmeter
veiling by black, masking by black, shading by black, black veiling, black masking, black shading	Schwarzverhüllung f, Verschwärzlichung f	velocity focusing	Geschwindigkeitsfokussierung f
		velocity gradient	Geschwindigkeitsgradient m, Geschwindigkeitsgefälle n
veiling by grey, masking by grey, shading by grey, grey veiling, grey masking, grey shading	Grauverhüllung f, Vergrauung f	velocity greater than that of light	s. super-velocity of light
		velocity head, kinetic energy head, kinetic head, dynamic head; water rise head, water-surface elevation	Geschwindigkeitshöhe f, Geschwindigkeitsgefälle n, Fließfallhöhe f; Stauhöhe f
veiling by white, masking by white, shading by white, white veiling (masking, shading)	Weißverhüllung f, Verweißlichung f		
		velocity head coefficient, pressure head coefficient	Staudruckbeiwert m
veiling effect; fogging <phot.>	Verschleierung f; Verschleierungseffekt m <Phot.>	velocity-head tachometer, hydraulic tachometer	Staudrucktachometer n
		velocity incompatible with the constraints, impossible velocity	unmögliche Geschwindigkeit f
veiling glare	Schleierblendung f, Nebelblendung f		
		velocity in free space, vacuum value of velocity	Vakuumgeschwindigkeit f, Ausbreitungsgeschwindigkeit f im Vakuum (freien Raum), Vakuumausbreitungsgeschwindigkeit f, Vakuumfortpflanzungsgeschwindigkeit f
veil of cloud, cloud veil	Wolkenschleier m; Wolkenschirm m		
vein; jet <aero., hydr.>	Strahl m <Aero., Hydr.>		
Velick-Gorin equation, Velick-Gorin formula	Velick-Gorinsche Gleichung f, Gleichung von Velick und Gorin		
velocity; speed <gen.>	Geschwindigkeit f <allg.>	velocity limit; critical velocity; cut-off velocity; limit of velocity	Grenzgeschwindigkeit f, kritische Geschwindigkeit f
velocity	s. a. velocity vector		
velocity addition formula in special relativity	s. relativistic composition of velocities	velocity-load diagram	Geschwindigkeit-Belastung-Diagramm n, Geschwindigkeits-Belastungs-Diagramm n
velocity amplitude	Geschwindigkeitsamplitude f		
velocity analyzer	Geschwindigkeitsanalysator m	velocity loop	Schnellebauch m
velocity antiresonance	Geschwindigkeitsantiresonanz f, Geschwindigkeitsgegenresonanz f	velocity lower than that of light, subvelocity of light	Unterlichtgeschwindigkeit f
velocity band	s. velocity range	velocity meter	s. propeller-type flowmeter
velocity coefficient	s. coefficient of velocity	velocity microphone	s. pressure-gradient microphone
velocity compatibility relations	Geschwindigkeits-Kompatibilitätsrelationen fpl	velocity modulation	Geschwindigkeitsmodulation f, Geschwindigkeitssteuerung f, Laufzeitmodulation f, Klystrongruppierung f
velocity compatible with the constraints, possible velocity, virtual velocity	virtuelle Geschwindigkeit f		
		velocity-modulation effect, transit time phenomenon	Laufzeiterscheinung f, Laufzeiteffekt m, Laufzeiteinfluß m
velocity component, component of velocity, component of the velocity vector	Geschwindigkeitskomponente f, Komponente f der Geschwindigkeit, Teilgeschwindigkeit f	velocity node	Schnelleknoten m
		velocity of combustion [reaction], speed of combustion, burning velocity; rate of combustion	Verbrennungsgeschwindigkeit f, Brenngeschwindigkeit f
velocity constant <el., phys.>	Geschwindigkeitskonstante f <El., Phys.>		
velocity co-ordinates	Geschwindigkeitskoordinaten fpl		
velocity correlation tensor [of turbulence], correlation tensor of turbulence	Korrelationstensor m der Turbulenz	velocity of descent	s. velocity of fall
		velocity of dislocations, dislocation velocity	Versetzungsgeschwindigkeit f
velocity coupling	Geschwindigkeitskopplung f	velocity of drying out	Austrocknungsgeschwindigkeit f
velocity curve	Geschwindigkeitskurve f	velocity of energy transmission	s. ray velocity

velocity of entry, entry velocity, entry rate — Eintauchgeschwindigkeit f, Eintrittsgeschwindigkeit f, Eindringgeschwindigkeit f ‹in die Erdatmosphäre›
velocity of escape — s. escape velocity
velocity of fall, rate of fall, velocity (rate) of descent, falling speed — Fallgeschwindigkeit f
velocity of flight — s. velocity of motion along the path
velocity of flow — s. flow rate
velocity of inlet, entrance velocity, inlet velocity, intake velocity, admission velocity — Eintrittsgeschwindigkeit f, Geschwindigkeit f am Eingang, Einströmgeschwindigkeit f
velocity of light, light velocity; speed of light, light speed — Lichtgeschwindigkeit f
velocity of light in empty (free) space, velocity of light in vacuo (vacuum), speed of light in vacuum (vacuo, free space, empty space), vacuum value of velocity of light, electromagnetic constant, electrodynamic constant — Vakuumlichtgeschwindigkeit f, elektromagnetische Konstante f, elektrodynamische Konstante
velocity of longitudinal waves, longitudinal velocity ‹ac.› — Ausbreitungsgeschwindigkeit f longitudinaler Schallwellen, Longitudinalgeschwindigkeit f ‹Ak.›
velocity of motion along the path, orbital velocity, velocity of flight — Bahngeschwindigkeit f
velocity of propagation, propagation velocity, speed of propagation, spread velocity, velocity of transmission — Ausbreitungsgeschwindigkeit f, Fortpflanzungsgeschwindigkeit f
velocity of propagation of sound — s. velocity of sound ‹ac.›
velocity of propagation of the nervous impulse — s. velocity of the nerve impulse
velocity of pure rolling — Rollgeschwindigkeit f
velocity of recession — Fluchtgeschwindigkeit f
velocity of rotation, rotational velocity, rotation speed, speed of rotation — Drehgeschwindigkeit f, Drehungsgeschwindigkeit f, Rotationsgeschwindigkeit f, Umdrehungsgeschwindigkeit f
velocity of settling — s. rate of sedimentation
velocity of slip, slip velocity ‹of fluids› — Gleitgeschwindigkeit f
velocity of small shallow-water gravity wave — s. critical velocity ‹hydr.›
velocity of sound [propagation], velocity of propagation of sound, sound [propagation] velocity, speed of sound, sonic speed, acoustic[al] velocity ‹ac.› — Schallgeschwindigkeit f, Schallwellengeschwindigkeit f, Schallausbreitungsgeschwindigkeit f, Schallfortpflanzungsgeschwindigkeit f ‹Ak.›
velocity of the moving space — s. velocity of transport ‹mech.›
velocity of the nerve impulse, velocity of propagation of the nervous impulse, speed of conduction of the nerve — Nervenleitgeschwindigkeit f, Nervenleitungsgeschwindigkeit f, Leitungsgeschwindigkeit f der Nerven
velocity of the pulse — s. pulse propagation velocity
velocity of the wave — s. phase velocity
velocity of translation, translatory velocity — Translationsgeschwindigkeit f
velocity of transmission — s. velocity of propagation
velocity of transport — Transportgeschwindigkeit f
velocity of transport, velocity of the moving space ‹mech.› — Führungsgeschwindigkeit f ‹Mech.›
velocity of transverse waves — s. transverse velocity ‹ac.›
velocity of wave front, front velocity — Frontgeschwindigkeit f
velocity operator, operator of velocity — Geschwindigkeitsoperator m, Operator m der Geschwindigkeit
velocity parallelogram — Geschwindigkeitsparallelogramm n
velocity plane — Geschwindigkeitsebene f
velocity potential — Geschwindigkeitspotential n
velocity potential of sound ‹ac.› — Potential n der Schallschnelle, Geschwindigkeitspotential n ‹Ak.›
velocity potential theorem of Lagrange and Cauchy, theorem of Lagrange and Cauchy — Lagrange-Cauchyscher Satz m
velocity profile — Geschwindigkeitsprofil n
velocity rate — s. velocity factor
velocity rating, required frequency — Sollgeschwindigkeit f
velocity resolution — Geschwindigkeitsauflösung f
velocity resonance — Geschwindigkeitsresonanz f
velocity resonance, phase resonance — Phasenresonanz f
velocity rod — s. staff float
velocity selector — Geschwindigkeitsselektor m
velocity sensitive detector of sound — s. pressure-gradient microphone
velocity space — Geschwindigkeitsraum m
velocity spectrograph — s. time-of-flight spectrograph
velocity spectrography — s. time-of-flight spectrography
velocity spectrometer — s. time-of-flight spectrometer
velocity spectrometry — s. time-of-flight spectroscopy
velocity spectroscope — s. time-of-flight spectroscope
velocity spectroscopy — s. time-of-flight spectroscopy
velocity spectrum — Geschwindigkeitsspektrum n
velocity stage, Curtis stage — Curtis-Stufe f, Geschwindigkeitsstufe f
velocity stage turbine — s. Curtis turbine
velocity straggling, velocity dispersion — Geschwindigkeitsdispersion f, Geschwindigkeitsstreuung f
velocity through the interstices, velocity through the pores — Porengeschwindigkeit f
velocity-time law — Geschwindigkeits-Zeit-Gesetz n
velocity triangle — s. velocity diagram
velocity turbine — s. Curtis turbine
velocity vector, linear velocity, velocity — Geschwindigkeitsvektor m
velocity vector diagram, velocity diagram, triangle of velocities, speed triangle — Geschwindigkeitsdreieck n
velodyne integrator, velodyne system — Velodyn[e]integrator m, Velodyn[e]system n
velometer — s. speedometer
Veltmann['s] theorem — Veltmann-Theorem n, Theorem n von Veltmann
vena contracta, contracted vein [of the liquid], contracted stream [of the liquid] — vena f contracta, verengter Flüssigkeitsstrahl m
Venetian blind — s. quarter-wave plate
Venetian blind dynode, louver-type dynode — Jalousiedynode f
Venetian blind multiplier, mesh multiplier, unfocused photomultiplier, net multiplier — Netzvervielfacher m

Veneziano model	Veneziano-Modell n
Vening-Meinesz [isostatic] reduction	[regionale] isostatische Reduktion f von Vening-Meinesz
venous mercury electrode, streaming mercury electrode	Quecksilberstrahlelektrode f
venous pulse	Venenpuls m
vent, venthole, venting hole	Ventilationsöffnung f, Ventilationsloch n; Abzugsöffnung f
vented fuel element	ventiliertes Brennelement n
venthole	s. vent
ventilated psychrometer	s. aspiration psychrometer
ventilation loss	Ventilationsverlust m
venting hole	s. vent
ventricle	Ventrikel m
ventricular fibrillation	Kammerflimmern n, Herzkammerflimmern n
Venturi, Venturi tube	Venturi-Rohr n, Venturi-Düse f
Venturi flume	Venturi-Zuflußkanal m
Venturi meter	Venturi-Messer m, Venturimeter n, Venturi-Wassermesser m, Venturi-Kanalmesser m
Venturi tube, Venturi	Venturi-Rohr n, Venturi-Düse f
Ventzke degree, °V	Ventzke-Grad n, °V
Verant lens	Verant-Linse f, Verant-Lupe f
Verdet['s] constant, magnetic rotary power, specific magnetic rotatory power	Verdetsche Konstante f, Verdet-Konstante f
vergence, divergence <geo.>	Vergenz f, Überfaltungsrichtung f <Geo.>
vergence, vergency <opt.>	Vergenz f, reziproke Schnittweite f <Opt.>
vergence of punctum proximum	Nahpunktsrefraktion f, Nahpunktsbrechwert m, Nahpunktsbrechkraft f; Nah-Scheitelbrechwert m
vergency, vergence <opt.>	Vergenz f, reziproke Schnittweite f <Opt.>
vergency of correcting lens, vertex power	Scheitelbrechwert m, Scheitelbrechkraft f
verhovodka	s. verkhovodka
verification; detection; tracing; tracking; proof; evidence	Nachweis m, Detektion f, Detektierung f, Beobachtung f, Feststellung f, Entdeckung f
verification, confirmation, corroboration <math.>	Bestätigung f, Erhärtung f, Verifizierung f <Math.>
verification	s. a. testing
veritable, true, real	echt, wahr, tatsächlich, wirklich, absolut, real
veritable wind	wahrer Wind m
verkhovodka, temporary perched water, verhovodka	Werchowodka f
vernal equinox, northern vernal equinox, spring equinox	Frühlingsäquinoktium n, Frühlings-Tagundnachtgleiche f
vernal [equinox] point, first point of Aries	Frühlingspunkt m, Widderpunkt m
Verneuil boule	Verneuil-Birne f
Verneuil method, Verneuil technique	Verneuil-Verfahren n, Verneuil-Methode f, Kristallzüchtung f aus der Schmelze nach der Methode von Verneuil
vernier, nonius	Nonius m
vernier	s. a. vernier scale
vernier acuity, contour acuity	Noniensehschärfe f, Breitenwahrnehmung f
vernier caliper, sliding (slide) caliper, caliper[s], calliper [gauge], vernier (slide, sliding) gauge, gauge, gage	Schublehre f, Schieblehre f, Schiebelehre f, Dickenmeßlehre f, Meßschieber m
vernier capacitor, vernier-control capacitor	Spreizungskondensator m, Vernierkondensator m
vernier chronotron	Vernierchronotron n

vernier-control capacitor	s. vernier capacitor
vernier converter	Noniuskonverter m, Vernierkonverter m
vernier gauge	s. vernier caliper
vernier height gauge	Höhenreißer m mit Nonius
vernier microscope, vernier reading microscope	Noniusmikroskop n
vernier principle	Noniusprinzip n
vernier ratio, ratio of verniers	Nonienverhältnis n
vernier reading	Nonienablesung f
vernier reading microscope, vernier microscope	Noniusmikroskop n
vernier scale, fine-adjustment scale, micro-adjustment dial, vernier	Feineinstellskala f, Noniusskala f; Noniusskale f; Nonienteilung f
vernier theodolite	Nonientheodolit m
versine α	$= 1 - \cos \alpha$
version; variant	Variante f
version, design, layout, display, pattern, model, type	Ausführung f, Ausführungsform f, Ausführungsweise f, Auslegung f, Bauart f, Baumuster n, Modell n, Typ m
versor	s. normalized quaternion
versorial force	s. restoring force <mech.>
vertebrae, vertebrate waveguide	Gliederhohlleiter m
vertex; apex <highest point>, corner <geometry; cryst.>	Eckpunkt m; Spitze f <Geometrie; Krist.>
vertex, convergent point <e.g. of moving star cluster> <astr.>	Vertex m <pl.: Vertices>, Fluchtpunkt m, Zielpunkt m der Bewegung <z. B. des Bewegungshaufens> <Astr.>
vertex, apex <opt.>	Scheitel m <Opt.>
vertex <rel.; in the graph>	Eckpunkt m <Rel.>; Ecke f <Graph>
vertex <of pencil>	s. a. base point
vertex	s. a. node
vertex angle	Scheitelwinkel m
vertex-diffraction law	Kantenbrechungsgesetz n
vertex function	Vertexfunktion f
vertex of the lens, lens vertex	Linsenscheitel m; Linsenpol m
vertex part <rel.>	Eckteil m <Rel.>
vertex power, vergency of correcting lens	Scheitelbrechwert m, Scheitelbrechkraft f
vertex refraction	Scheitelpunktsrefraktion f, Scheitelrefraktion f
vertex tangent	Scheiteltangente f
vertical, vertical line, plumb line	Lotlinie f, Lotrechte f, Vertikale f, Vertikallinie f, vertikale Linie f
vertical, vertical circle, altitude circle	Vertikalkreis m, Vertikal m, Höhenkreis m, Scheitelkreis m
vertical adjustment, vertical motion, height adjustment	Höhenverstellung f
vertical aerial photograph, vertical photograph, vertical shot	Vertikalaufnahme f, Vertikalluftbild n, Vertikalbild n, Hochaufnahme f
vertical aerial photography	s. vertical photography
vertical aerial survey	Luftbild-Senkrechtaufnahme f
vertical amplifier, vertical deflection amplifier, frame amplifier, Y amplifier, Y-axis amplifier	Vertikalverstärker m, Vertikalablenkverstärker m, Y-Verstärker m

vertical angle <geo.>	Vertikalwinkel *m* <Geo.>
vertical aperture, vertical relative aperture	vertikale [relative] Apertur *f*
vertical axis <of theodolite>	Stehachse *f*, Vertikalachse *f*, Umdrehungsachse *f*, Alhidadenachse *f* <Theodolit>
vertical axis <cryst.>	Vertikalachse *f* <Krist.>
vertical axis error, error of vertical axis	Stehachsenfehler *m*
vertical-axis [spin] wind tunnel	s. free spinning vertical wind tunnel
vertical balance	Vertikalwaage *f*
vertical blanking pulse	Vertikalaustastimpuls *m*
vertical camera, vertically operated camera, vertically mounted camera	Vertikalkamera *f*
vertical casting	s. vertical throw <mech.>
vertical circle, vertical, altitude circle	Vertikalkreis *m*, Vertikal *m*, Höhenkreis *m*, Scheitelkreis *m*
vertical-circle level tube	Indexlibelle *f*, Höhenkreislibelle *f*, Noniuslibelle *f*
vertical cleft	Vertikalriß *m*, Vertikalspalte *f*
vertical condenser	s. vertical illuminator
vertical conducted heat flow, geothermal flux	geothermischer Fluß *m*
vertical current	s. air-earth current
vertical deflecting electrode	s. vertical plate
vertical deflection, Y deflection; image deflection, frame deflection, vertical sweep	Vertikalablenkung *f*, Senkrechtablenkung *f*; Y-Ablenkung *f* <Oszillograph>; Bildablenkung *f* <Fs.>
vertical deflection amplifier	s. vertical amplifier
vertical deflection electrode	s. vertical plate
vertical deflection unit	Vertikalablenkgenerator *m*, Vertikalablenkgerät *n*, Vertikalablenkungsgenerator *m*
vertical deflector	s. vertical plate
vertical dispersion	s. vertical spread
vertical displacement	Vertikalverschiebung *f*
vertical distance above ground, height above ground, elevation above ground	Höhe *f* über Grund, Höhe über dem Erdboden (Boden)
vertical distance above sea level	s. height above sea level
vertical distribution, distribution in height (altitude), hypsometric distribution	Höhenverteilung *f*, hypsometrische Verteilung *f*
vertical distribution of temperature	Temperaturschnitt *m*
vertical distribution of velocities, vertical velocity distribution	Vertikalgeschwindigkeitsverteilung *f*
vertical exchange coefficient	Vertikalaustauschkoeffizient *m*, vertikaler Austauschkoeffizient *m*
vertical fault	Seigersprung *m*, Saigersprung *m*
vertical field balance, vertical magnetic [field] balance, magnetic field balance, Z balance	Feldwaage *f* zur Messung der Vertikalintensität, Z-Waage *f*, magnetische Vertikalwaage *f*, vertikale Feldwaage *f*
vertical flow, vertical motion, vertical stream	Vertikalströmung *f*, vertikale Strömung *f*
vertical force	s. perpendicular force
vertical force	s. vertical intensity <geo.>
vertical-force variometer, vertical-intensity variometer, Z-variometer	Vertikalintensitätsvariometer *n*, Z-Variometer *n*
vertical frequency	Vertikalfrequenz *f*
vertical gust, vertical gustiness	Vertikalbö *f*
vertical horopter, longitudinal horopter	Längshoropter *m*, Vertikalhoropter *m*
vertical hydrodynamic force, hydrodynamic buoyancy	hydrodynamischer Auftrieb *m*
vertical hydrostatic force	s. hydrostatic buoyancy <hydr.>
vertical illumination, episcope illumination, illumination in reflected light, incident light illumination	Auflichtbeleuchtung *f*, Vertikalbeleuchtung *f*
vertical illuminator, opaque illuminator, illuminator; vertical condenser, incident light condenser	Auflichtilluminator *m*, Vertikalilluminator *m*, Opakilluminator *m*, Illuminator *m*; Auflichtkondensor *m*, Vertikalkondensor *m*
vertical incidence, normal incidence	senkrechter Einfall *m*, normaler Einfall, Normaleinfall *m*
vertical-incidence ionospheric sounding	vertikale Ionosphärenmessung *f*, Vertikallotung *f* der Ionosphäre
vertical intensity, vertical force <geo.>	Vertikalintensität *f*, erdmagnetische Vertikalintensität *f* <Geo.>
vertical-intensity magnetometer, vertical magnetometer, Z-magnetometer	Vertikalintensitätsmagnetometer *n*, Vertikalmagnetometer *n*, Z-Magnetometer *n*
vertical intensity meter, Z intensiometer	Z-Intensiometer *n*
vertical-intensity variometer, vertical-force variometer, Z-variometer	Vertikalintensitätsvariometer *n*, Z-Variometer *n*
vertical ionization potential, electron-impact value of ionization potential	vertikale Ionisierungsspannung *f*
vertical isodynam, vertical isodynamic line	Vertikalisodyname *f*
vertical launching, vertical take-off	Senkrechtstart *m*
vertical line, perpendicular [line], normal, plumb line	Senkrechte *f*, Lot *n*, Normale *f*
vertical line	s. a. vertical
vertically mounted camera, vertically operated camera, vertical camera	Vertikalkamera *f*
vertically polarized wave	vertikal polarisierte Welle *f*, senkrecht polarisierte Welle
vertical magnetic [field] balance	s. vertical field balance
vertical magnetometer, vertical-intensity magnetometer, Z-magnetometer	Vertikalintensitätsmagnetometer *n*, Vertikalmagnetometer *n*, Z-Magnetometer *n*
vertical member, [vertical] strut, stanchion, stay	Vertikalstab *m*, Pfosten *m*
vertical method of zone melting	s. floating-zone technique
vertical motion, vertical movement; heaving [motion]	Vertikalbewegung *f*; Hebung *f*
vertical motion, vertical flow, vertical stream	Vertikalströmung *f*, vertikale Strömung *f*
vertical motion	s. a. vertical adjustment
vertical movement	s. vertical motion
vertical pattern	Vertikaldiagramm *n*, Vertikalstrahlungsdiagramm *n*, Vertikalcharakteristik *f*
vertical phase contrast illuminator, vertical phase illuminator	Vertikalphasenkontrastkondensor *m*, Vertikalphasenkontrastilluminator *m*, Vertikalphasenilluminator *m*
vertical photograph, vertical aerial photograph, vertical shot	Vertikalaufnahme *f*, Vertikalluftbild *n*, Vertikalbild *n*, Hochaufnahme *f*

vertical

vertical photography, vertical aerial photography, vertical taking, vertical shot, steep shot	Vertikalaufnahme f, Senkrechtaufnahme f, Steilaufnahme f	**vertical velocity curve** <hydr.>	Vertikalgeschwindigkeitskurve f, Vertikalgeschwindigkeitsverteilung[skurve] f, Vertikalgeschwindigkeitspolygon n <Hydr.>
vertical pillar, sun-pillar, Sun pillar	Lichtsäule f, Sonnensäule f	**vertical velocity distribution,** vertical distribution of velocities	Vertikalgeschwindigkeitsverteilung f
vertical plate, Y plate, vertical deflecting electrode, vertical deflection electrode, vertical deflector	Vertikalablenkplatte f, Y-Platte f; Meßablenkplatte f, Meßplatte f	**vertical visibility [distance]**	vertikale Sichtweite f, Vertikalsicht f
		vertical width, vertical thickness	vertikale Mächtigkeit f
vertical projection	s. vertical throw	**vertical wind tunnel**	s. free spinning vertical wind tunnel
vertical recording, hill and dale recording	[Aufzeichnung f in] Tiefenschrift f, Edisonschrift f, Edison-Schrift f	**vertometer,** focometer, focimeter	Fokometer n, Brennweitenmesser m
vertical refraction	Höhenrefraktion f	**very angry sea,** very rough sea, surging sea	sehr grobe See f, sich türmende See <Stärke 6>
vertical relative aperture, vertical aperture	vertikale [relative] Apertur f	**very compact galaxy**	sehr kompakte Galaxie f
vertical resolution	Vertikalauflösung f, Senkrechtauflösung f	**very distant earthquake**	weites Fernbeben n
		very fast nova	sehr schnelle Nova f
		very high energy, superhigh energy, extra-high energy	Höchstenergie f
vertical rhombic antenna	Vertikalrhombusantenne f	**very high frequency,** V.H.F., VHF, v.h.f., vhf <30—300 Mc/s>	Meterwellenfrequenz f, Frequenz f im Meterwellenbereich, Frequenz im UKW-Bereich, Meterwelle f, VHF <30 ··· 300 MHz>
vertical ring	Vertikalring m		
vertical row index, column index	Spaltenindex m		
vertical scanning generator, vertical sweep circuit <tv.>	Rasterkippgenerator m, Bildwechselgenerator m, Rasterwechselgenerator m; Rasterkippgerät n, Bildkippgerät n, Bildkippteil n <Fs.>	**very high frequency range,** range of very high frequency, very high frequency wavelength [range], metric wavelength [range], V.H.F. range, V.H.F.	Ultrakurzwellenbereich m, Ultrakurzwelle f, Meterwellenbereich m, Meterbereich m, UKW-Bereich m, VHF-Bereich m, UKW, VHF
vertical section	Vertikalschnitt m		
vertical seismograph	Vertikalseismograph m	**very high frequency wave,** metre wave, ultra-short wave, very short wave, V.H.F. wave <1—10 m>	Ultrakurzwelle f, Meterwelle f, UKW <1 ··· 10 m>
vertical seismometer	Vertikalseismometer n, Vertikalerschütterungsmesser m		
vertical shock <geo.>	vertikaler Stoß m, Vertikalstoß m, Senkrechtstoß m <Geo.>		
		very high frequency wavelength [range]	s. very high frequency range
vertical shot	s. vertical photograph	**very high pressure,** extra-high pressure, hyperpressure	Höchstdruck m
vertical shot	s. a. vertical photography		
vertical spin wind tunnel	s. free spinning vertical wind tunnel	**very high seas,** storm sea, stormy sea	sehr hohe (hoch[ ]gehende) See f, sehr hoher (großer) Wellengang m, sehr hohe (große) Wellen fpl <Stärke 8>
vertical spread, vertical dispersion	Höhenstreuung f, Vertikalstreuung f		
vertical stream, vertical flow, vertical motion	Vertikalströmung f, vertikale Strömung f		
vertical sweep	s. image deflection	**very high vacuum**	s. ultra-high vacuum
vertical sweep circuit	s. vertical scanning generator <tv.>	**very light breeze,** light air <of Beaufort No. 1>	leiser Zug m, leiser Wind m <Stärke 1>
vertical sweep retrace time	Vertikalrücklaufzeit f		
		very long wave, very low frequency wave	Längstwelle f <2 ··· 30 km>
vertical take-off, vertical launching	Senkrechtstart m	**very low frequency,** V.L.F., VLF, v.l.f., vlf << 30 kc/s>	Myriameterwellenfrequenz f, Frequenz f im Myriameterwellenbereich, VLF << 30 kHz>
vertical taking	s. vertical photography		
vertical temperature gradient, geometric temperature gradient	vertikaler (geometrischer) Temperaturgradient m, vertikales Temperaturgefälle n		
		very low frequency, v.l.f., VLF <10 ··· 30 kc/s>	Frequenz f im niedrigen Langwellenbereich, niedrige Langwellenfrequenz f, VLF
vertical thickness, vertical width	vertikale Mächtigkeit f		
vertical throw, vertical projection	lotrechter Wurf m, senkrechter Wurf, vertikaler Wurf	**very low frequency range,** range of very low frequency, myriametre wavelength [range], V.L.F. range, V.L.F.	Myriameterwellenbereich m, Myriameterbereich m, Myriabereich m, VLF-Bereich m, VLF
vertical throw	s. a. steep throw		
vertical transfer, vertical transport	Vertikaltransport m	**very low frequency wave,** myriametre wave, V.L.F. wave <> 10,000 m>	Myriameterwelle f, Ultralangwelle f <> 10 000 m>
vertical-tube manometer, single-column manometer	Gefäßmanometer n, einschenkliges Manometer n, Manometer mit senkrechtem Meßrohr		
vertical velocity	Vertikalgeschwindigkeit f	**very low frequency wave,** very long wave	Längstwelle f <2 ··· 30 km>
		very low nova	sehr langsame Nova f

very near infra-red [region] <0.75—2.5 μ>	nahes Infrarot n, nahes Infrarotgebiet n, nahes IR [-Gebiet] n <IR-A- und IR-B-Gebiet> <0,76 ··· 3,0 μm>	vibrating reed electrometer, vibrating capacitor electrometer, vibration electrometer	Schwing[kondensator]-elektrometer n, Vibrationselektrometer n, Elektrometer n nach le Chaine und Waghorn, „vibrating-reed"-Elektrometer n, „vibrating reed" n
very rough sea, very angry sea, surging sea	sehr grobe See f, sich türmende See <Stärke 6>	vibrating-reed frequency meter	s. reed-type frequency meter
very short wave	s. very high frequency wave	vibrating-reed instrument	s. reed-type frequency meter
very slow flow (motion), very small motion	s. creeping motion	vibrating relay, tuned-reed relay, resonance relay	Zungenresonanzrelais n, Zungenfrequenzrelais n, Resonanzrelais n, Unterbrecherrelais n, Unterbrechungsrelais n, Vibrationsrelais n
very soluble	gut löslich		
vesicular structure	Blasenstruktur f, blasige Struktur f		
vessel	s. flask		
vessel of the rain gauge, measuring vessel of the rain gauge	Regenmessergefäß n		
vestalium	= cadmium	vibrating rod, oscillating rod	schwingender Stab m
vestigial filter	s. vestigial[-] sideband filter	vibrating rotator, oscillating rotator	schwingender Rotator m
vestigial sideband	Restseitenband n	vibrating silica fibre	schwingender Quarzfaden m, Quarzfadenpendel n <als Vakuummeter>
vestigial[-] sideband filter, vestigial filter, sideband filter	Restseitenbandfilter n, Seitenbanddämpfer m		
		vibrating strain	s. oscillating load
		vibrating stress, cyclic stress, cyclical stress, vibratory stress, oscillating stress	Schwingungsspannung f, Schwingungsspannung f, schwingende Spannung f
vestigial[-] sideband modulation	Restseitenbandmodulation f, RBM		
vestigial[-]sideband transmission, asymmetric sideband transmission	Restseitenbandübertragung f, Restseitenbandverfahren n	vibrating string	schwingende Saite f
		vibrating system	s. oscillation system
		vibrating viscometer gauge	Schwingungsmanometer n
		vibration	Vibration f; Schwingung f <z. B. Platte, Stab, Saite, Zunge>
veto counter	Zählrohr n in Antikoinzidenzschaltung		
		vibration, shaking, chatter	Erschütterung f
V event, V-event	V-Ereignis n	vibration, trembling <of image> <opt.>	Tanzen n, Zittern n, Springen n <Bild> <Opt.>
V.H.F.	s. very high frequency		
viability	Lebensfähigkeit f		
vial, phial	Phiole f, Fläschchen n	vibration	s. a. zitterbewegung <of electron>
		vibration absorber	s. attenuator
Via Lactea, Milky Way	Milchstraße f	vibrational absorption spectrum	Absorptionsschwingungsspektrum n
Vianello['s] method	Vianellosches Verfahren n, Vianello-Verfahren n	vibration acceleration	Schwingbeschleunigung f, Schwingungsbeschleunigung f
vibrant	Vibrant m		
vibrating capacitor	s. vibrating condenser		
vibrating capacitor amplifier	Schwingkondensatorverstärker m	vibrational angular momentum	Schwingungsdrehimpuls m
vibrating capacitor electrometer	s. vibrating reed electrometer		
vibrating coil, vibration coil; oscillator coil; moving coil	Oszillatorspule f; Schwingspule f, Vibrationsspule f	vibrational band, vibration band	Schwingungsbande f
		vibrational-band temperature, vibrational characteristic temperature	s. vibration temperature
vibrating-coil magnetometer	Schwingspulenmagnetometer n, Vibrations-[spulen]magnetometer n		
vibrating-coil oscillator	Schwingspulenoszillator m	vibrational compacting, compacting by vibration, compaction by vibration, vibrocompaction	Vibrationsverdichtung f
vibrating condenser, vibrating capacitor, vibrating reed [dynamic] condenser	Schwingkondensator m		
vibrating contact, oscillating contact	Schwingkontakt m		
vibrating contactor	s. chopper <el.>	vibrational constant	Schwingungskonstante f
vibrating contact rectifier, vibrator inverter	Schwingkontaktgleichrichter m, Schwinggleichrichter m, Zungengleichrichter m	vibrational co-ordinate	Schwingungskoordinate f
		vibrational corrosion	Schwingungsrißkorrosion f, Schwingungskorrosion f
vibrating field, oscillating field	Schwingungsfeld n	vibrational degree of freedom	Schwingungsfreiheitsgrad m
vibrating galvanometer	s. vibration galvanometer	vibrational density, density after vibration	Rütteldichte f
vibrating load	s. oscillating load		
vibrating magnet, moving magnet	Schwingmagnet m	vibrational discharge	Schwingentladung f
vibrating mill, vibration mill	Schwingmühle f	vibrational eigenfunction	Schwingungseigenfunktion f
vibrating mirror	s. oscillating mirror	vibrational energy, vibration energy, energy of vibration, oscillation energy	Schwingungsenergie f, Vibrationsenergie f <z. B. Moleküle>; Oszillationsenergie f
vibrating potential model	Modell n des schwingenden Potentials, Schwing[ungs]potentialmodell n		
vibrating probe	Schwingsonde f	vibrational energy level	s. vibrational level
vibrating quartz [crystal]	s. oscillating quartz	vibrational enthalpy; vibrational heat [capacity]	Schwingungswärme f; Schwingungsenthalpie f
vibrating rectifier	s. chopper <el.>		
vibrating reed [dynamic] capacitor	s. vibrating capacitor	vibrational entropy	Schwingungsentropie f

vibrational

vibrational excitation	Schwingungsanregung f, Anregung f des Schwingungszustandes	vibration instrument	Vibrationsmeßgerät n, Vibrationsinstrument n, Vibrationsgerät n, Vibrationsmesser m
vibrational fine structure	Schwingungsfeinstruktur f		
vibrational frequency	s. frequency		
vibrational function	Schwingungsfunktion f		
vibrational heat [capacity]; vibrational enthalpy	Schwingungswärme f; Schwingungsenthalpie f		
vibrational instability, oscillatory instability	Schwingungsinstabilität f		
vibrational level, vibrational energy level, vibration level	Schwingungsniveau n, Schwingungsenergieniveau n	vibration insulation (isolation)	Schwingungsisolierung f, Schwingungsschutz m
		vibration isolator	Schwingungsisolator m, Schwingungsschutz m
vibrational line	Schwingungslinie f	vibration level	s. vibrational level
		vibration load	s. oscillating load
		vibration loop	s. antinodal point
		vibration measuring apparatus, vibration meter, vibrometer	Schwingungsmesser m, Schwingungsmeßgerät n, Vibrometer n, Erschütterungsmesser m
vibrational mode, mode [of wave]; natural (characteristic) vibration, natural oscillation; self-oscillation; eigentone ‹ac.›	Eigenschwingung f; Eigenschwingungstyp m, Mode f		
		vibration microscope	Vibrationsmikroskop n
vibrational part	Schwingungsanteil m	vibration mill	s. vibrating mill
vibrational partition function	Schwingungszustandssumme f, Schwingungsanteil m der Zustandsfunktion	vibration movement	Vibrationsmeßwerk n
		vibration node	s. node
		vibration of membrane	Membranschwingung f
vibrational perturbation	Schwingungsstörung f	vibration of plate	Plattenschwingung f
		vibration of reed, reed vibration	Zungenvibration f, Zungenschwingung f
vibrational quantum number	s. vibration quantum number		
vibrational Raman spectrum, Raman vibrational spectrum	Schwingungs-Raman-Spektrum n, Raman-Schwingungsspektrum n	vibration of systems with variable characteristics	s. quasi-harmonic oscillation
vibrational relaxation	Schwingungsrelaxation f	vibration of the bar, bar vibration	Stabschwingung f; Stäbeschwingung f
vibrational scattering	Gitterschwingungsstreuung f, Streuung f an Gitterschwingung[squant]en	vibration of the molecules, molecule vibration, molecular vibration	Molekülschwingung f
vibrational spectrum, vibration spectrum, oscillation spectrum	Schwingungsspektrum n	vibration of the rope, vibration of the string	Seilschwingung f
vibrational state, vibration state	Schwingungszustand m	vibration of the string, string vibration	Saitenschwingung f
vibrational structure	Schwingungsstruktur f	vibration of two degrees of freedom	Schwingung f von zwei Freiheitsgraden
		vibration patterns	s. Chladni['s] figures
		vibration period	s. period of oscillation
vibrational sum rule	Schwingungssummenregel f, Summenregel f für die Schwingungen	vibration plane, plane of vibration[s], plane of oscillation	Schwingungsebene f, Schwingebene f
vibrational temperature	s. vibration temperature		
vibrational term, vibration term	Schwingungsterm m, Schwingungsglied n	vibration quantum number, vibrational (oscillation) quantum number	Schwingungsquantenzahl f
vibrational theory of solids	Schwingungstheorie f der Festkörper		
vibrational transition	Schwingungsübergang m	vibration recorder (recording apparatus), vibrograph, recording vibration meter, vibration recording apparatus	schreibender Schwingungsmesser m, Schwingungsschreiber m, Vibrograph m
vibrational wave function	Schwingungswellenfunktion f		
vibrational weight, weight after vibration	Rüttelgewicht n	vibration resistance, resistance to vibration[s] (shaking)	Rüttelfestigkeit f; Erschütterungsfestigkeit f
vibration amplitude	s. amplitude ‹of vibration, oscillation›		
vibration antinode	s. antinodal point	vibration resistance	s. a. dynamic strength
vibration band	s. vibrational band	vibration resonance, rumble	Schüttelresonanz f
vibration coil	s. vibrating coil		
vibration due to unbalance	Unwuchtschwingung f	vibration-rotation band, rotation-vibration band	Rotationsschwingungsbande f
vibration electrometer	s. vibrating reed electrometer	vibration-rotation band spectrum	Rotationsschwingungsbandenspektrum n, Rotationsschwingungs-Bandenspektrum n
vibration energy	s. vibrational energy		
vibration excitation	s. excitation of oscillations		
vibration frequency	s. frequency		
vibration galvanometer, vibrating galvanometer	Vibrationsgalvanometer n, Nadelvibrationsgalvanometer n, Nadelschwingungsgalvanometer n, Schwingungsgalvanometer n	vibration-rotation constant, rotation-vibration constant	Rotationsschwingungskonstante f
		vibration-rotation energy, rotation-vibration energy	Rotationsschwingungsenergie f
vibration generation	s. excitation of oscillations	vibration-rotation interaction, rotation-vibration interaction	Rotationsschwingungswechselwirkung f
vibration generator	s. oscillator ‹el.›		
vibration gravimeter	Schwingungsgravimeter n		

vibration-rotation spectrum, rotation-vibration spectrum	Rotationsschwingungsspektrum n	**vicinal face[t]**, vicinal	Vizinalfläche f, Vizinalebene f
		vicinity; proximity; contiguity; neighbourhood, neighborhood <US>; closeness	Nachbarschaft f; Nähe f; Umgebung f
vibration spectrum, vibrational spectrum, oscillation spectrum	Schwingungsspektrum n	**Vickers diamond**, Vickers indenter	Vickers-Diamant m
vibration state, vibrational state	Schwingungszustand m	**Vickers [diamond] hardness, Vickers hardness number**, diamond pyramid hardness, D.P. hardness, D.P.H., V.D.H., H_D, H_V	Vickers-Härte f, Diamantpyramidenhärte f, Pyramidenhärte f, HV, H_V
vibration strain	s. oscillating load		
vibration strength	s. dynamic strength		
vibration stress	s. vibratory stress		
vibration temperature, vibrational (vibrational-band, vibrational characteristic) temperature, temperature from the vibration-rotation (vibrational) spectrum	Schwingungstemperatur f, charakteristische Schwingungstemperatur, aus dem Rotationsschwingungsspektrum bestimmte Temperatur f	**Vickers hardness test**, Vickers hardness testing, diamond pyramid hardness test	Vickers-Härteprüfung f, Härteprüfung f nach Vickers, Pyramidenhärteprüfung f
		Vickers hardness tester	s. Vickers hardness testing machine
vibration term, vibrational term	Schwingungsterm m, Schwingungsglied n	**Vickers hardness testing**	s. Vickers hardness test
vibration test	Dauerschwingversuch m, Schwingungsversuch m, Dauerversuch m	**Vickers hardness testing machine**, Vickers hardness tester, diamond pyramid hardness testing machine	Vickers-Härteprüfgerät n, Pyramidenhärteprüfgerät n
		Vickers indenter, Vickers diamond	Vickers-Diamant m
vibration test	Schüttelversuch m, Schüttelprüfung f	**victorium**	= gadolinium
		video	s. video signal
		video densitometry	Videodensitometrie f
vibration tomography	Vibrationstomographie f	**video oscillograph**, video oscilloscope	Videooszillograph m, Videooszilloskop n
vibration transducer	Schwingungswandler m	**video pulse**	s. video signal
		video signal, video; video pulse	Videosignal n; Videozeichen n, Videoimpuls m
vibrator; oscillator	Oszillator m, schwingendes Gebilde n, schwingfähiges Gebilde	**vidicon, vidicon tube, vidikon tube**	Vidikon n, Vidicon n, Vidiconröhre f, Vidiconaufnahmeröhre f
vibrator	Vibrator m; Rüttler m		
vibrator	s. a. chopper <el.>	**vierbein**, quadruped, tetrapod, four nuple	Vierbein n
vibrator inverter, vibrating contact rectifier	Schwingkontaktgleichrichter m, Schwinggleichrichter m	**Vierendeel truss**	Pfostenfachwerk n
vibratory load	s. oscillating load	**vierer group**, quadratic group, Klein['s] quadratic group, Klein['s] group, Klein['s] 4-group, Klein['s] four-group, four-group <math.>	Kleinsche Vierergruppe f, Vierergruppe [von Klein] <Math.>
vibratory motion, trembling, trembling motion	Zittern n, Zitterbewegung f		
vibratory strain	s. oscillating load		
vibratory stress, cyclic stress, cyclical stress, vibration stress, vibrating stress, oscillating stress	Schwingungsspannung f, Schwingungsspannung f, schwingende Spannung f	**Viëta['s] formulae** <relation between the roots and coefficients of an algebraic equation>	Viëtascher Wurzelsatz m, Viëtascher Lehrsatz m, Viëtescher Lehrsatz
vibratory unit	s. ultrasonic generator	**Viëta['s] theorem**	Viëtascher Satz m
vibrocompaction	s. vibrational compaction	**Vieth-Müller circle** (horopter)	s. Müller circle
vibrogel	Vibrogel n	**viewfinder** <phot.>	Sucher m <Phot.>
vibrogram, vibrorecord	Schwingungsdiagramm n, Schwingungsbild n, Vibrogramm n	**viewing distance**	s. visibility
		viewing mirror, mirror reflector	Spiegelreflektor m
vibrograph, recording vibration meter, vibration recorder, vibration recording apparatus; recording oscillometer	schreibender Schwingungsmesser m, Schwingungsschreiber m, Vibrograph m	**viewing screen**, picture screen <tv.>	Bildschirm m, Leuchtschirm m der Bildröhre <Fs.>
vibrometer	s. vibration meter	**viewing storage tube**, character display tube, character writing tube, character storage tube	Sichtspeicherröhre f, Sichtröhre f; Zeichenschreibröhre f
vibromotive force	schwingungserzeugende Kraft f		
vibronic band	Elektronenschwingungsbande f, vibronische Bande f		
vibronic model	vibronisches Modell n	**viewing unit**	s. indicator <el.>
vibronic spectrum	vibronisches Spektrum n, Elektronenschwingungsspektrum n	**viewing window**	s. observation port
		view projection	s. skew projection
		vignetter	s. vignetting mask
vibronic wave function	Elektronenschwingungs-Wellenfunktion f, vibronische Wellenfunktion f	**vignetting**, gradation; vignetting effect <phot.>	Abschattung f, Randabschattung f, Vignettierung f; Vignettierwirkung f <Phot.>
vibrorecord	s. vibrogram		
vic	s. vicinal		
vicinal, vic., 1.2.3 <chem.>	vizinal, vicinal, vic., 1,2,3- <Chem.>		
vicinal	s. vicinal face[t]	**vignetting diaphragm**	s. vignetting mask
vicinal edge	Vizinalkante f	**vignetting effect**	s. vignetting <phot.>

vignetting mask, vignetting diaphragm, vignetter	Vignettiermaske f	**virial equation of state**, general virial equation	viriale Zustandsgleichung f, Virialform f der thermischen Zustandsgleichung
Villard circuit, Villard['s] rectifier circuit	Villard-Schaltung f, Villard-Stufe f	**virial expansion**, virial series	Virialentwicklung f, Virialreihe f
Villard effect ‹phot.›	Villard-Effekt m ‹Phot.›	**virial law**	s. virial theorem
Villard['s] rectifier circuit, Villard circuit	Villard-Schaltung f, Villard-Stufe f	**virial of Clausius**	s. virial
Villari effect [of magnetostriction]	Villari-Effekt m, Villarischer Magnetostriktionseffekt m, Villari-Umkehr f	**virial representation**	Virialdarstellung f
		virial series, virial expansion	Virialentwicklung f, Virialreihe f
Villari reversal	Villari-Umkehrpunkt m, Villari-Punkt m	**virial theorem [of Clausius]**, Clausius['] virial theorem, virial law	Virialsatz m, Virialgleichung f
Vinett[-tape magnifier]	Vinettlupe f	**virtual annihilation**	virtuelle Vernichtung (Annihilation) f
Vineyard['s] theory	Vineyard-Theorie f, Vineyardsche Theorie f	**virtual cathode**	virtuelle Katode f
vinylation	Vinylierung f	**virtual chemical potential**	virtuelles chemisches Potential n
vinylogy, principle of vinylogy	Vinylogieprinzip n	**virtual colour**	virtuelle Farbe f
violation of causality, causality violation	Kausalitätsverletzung f, Verletzung f der Kausalität	**virtual creation**, virtual production	virtuelle Erzeugung f
		virtual deformation	virtuelle Verzerrung f, virtuelle Deformation f
violation of parity, non-conservation of parity, parity non-conservation (violation)	Nichterhaltung f der Parität, Paritätsverletzung f	**virtual displacement**	virtuelle Verrückung f, virtuelle Verschiebung f
violation of the selection rule, offense against the selection rule	Verletzung f der Auswahlregel	**virtual energy level**, virtual level	virtuelles Niveau n, virtuelles Energieniveau n
		virtual entropy	virtuelle Entropie f
		virtual focus	s. centre of dispersion
violent downpour, downpour, cloud burst, heavy shower	Wolkenbruch m; Platzregen m	**virtual free energy**	virtuelle freie Energie f
		virtual free enthalpy	virtuelle freie Enthalpie f
violent earthquake, strong earthquake	Großbeben n, heftiges Beben n, schweres Erdbeben n	**virtual friction**, turbulent friction; apparent friction	turbulente Scheinreibung f, Turbulentreibung f; Scheinreibung f, scheinbare Reibung f
violent reaction	heftige Reaktion f		
violent squall	heftiger Windstoß m, scharfer Windstoß, starker Windstoß	**virtual height** ‹of [ionospheric] reflection›	virtuelle Höhe f [der Ionosphärenreflexion]
violet and ultraviolet transmitting	s. diactinic	**virtual height**	s. a. apparent height
		virtual height	s. a. radiation height
violet degradation, degradation to[wards] the violet	Violettabschattierung f	**virtual image**	virtuelles (unwirkliches, scheinbares) Bild n; virtuelle Abbildung f
violet-shaded, degraded to[wards] the violet, shaded to[wards] the violet	violettabschattiert	**virtual image point**	virtueller Bildpunkt m
		virtual inertia, apparent inertia	virtuelle Trägheit f, scheinbare Trägheit
viol instrument	Streichinstrument n	**virtual level**, virtual energy level	virtuelles Niveau n, virtuelles Energieniveau n
Violle [standard], Violle unit	= 20,23 cd	**virtual mass**, induced (effective, apparent additional) mass	scheinbare Masse f, virtuelle Masse, induzierte Masse
virga, fall streak	Fallstreifen m		
virgation ‹geo.›	Virgation f ‹Geo.›	**virtual meson**	virtuelles Meson n
virgin curve of magnetization, virgin magnetization curve, initial curve of magnetization, initial magnetization curve, normal curve of magnetization, normal magnetization curve	Neukurve (Erstkurve) f [der magnetischen Induktion], Neukurve (Erstkurve) der Magnetisierung, Magnetisierungsneukurve f, jungfräuliche Magnetisierungskurve, jungfräuliche Kurve f der Magnetisierung	**virtual nucleon**, virtual nucleon pair	virtuelles Nukleonenpaar n, virtuelles Nukleon n
		virtual particle	virtuelles Teilchen n
		virtual photon field	virtuelles Photonenfeld n
		virtual production, virtual creation	virtuelle Erzeugung f
		virtual ray	virtueller Strahl m
virgin flux, virgin neutron flux	jungfräulicher Neutronenfluß m, jungfräulicher Fluß m	**virtual singlet state**	virtueller Singulettzustand m
virginium	= francium	**virtual source**, image source	Bildquelle f, virtuelle Quelle f
virgin magnetization curve	s. virgin curve of magnetization	**virtual temperature**	virtuelle Temperatur f
virgin neutron, uncollided neutron	Neutron n vor dem Stoß, jungfräuliches Neutron	**virtual transformation**	virtuelle Änderung f
virgin neutron flux, virgin flux	jungfräulicher Neutronenfluß m, jungfräulicher Fluß m	**virtual transition**	virtueller Übergang m
		virtual velocity, possible velocity, velocity compatible with the constraints	virtuelle Geschwindigkeit f
virial, virial of Clausius, energy of n-particle system	Virial n		
		virtual viscosity	s. eddy viscosity
virial coefficient	Virialkoeffizient m	**virtual work**	virtuelle Arbeit f

virtual work principle	s. principle of virtual work	viscosity number, limiting viscosity number, viscosity value	Grenzviskositätszahl f, Viskositätszahl f, Staudinger-Index m
viscid, viscous, heavy-bodied, thickly liquid; sluggish; consistent; sticky <chem.>	zähflüssig, zäh; schwerflüssig, dickflüssig, dick, dicht, konsistent; klebrig <Chem.>	viscosity pole viscosity pole height, height of the viscosity pole	Viskositätspol m Viskositätspolhöhe f
viscidity, viscosity, tenaciousness, tenacity; thick liquid; sluggishness; consistency, consistence; stickiness; stiffness; ropiness <chem.>	Zäh[flüss]igkeit f; Schwerflüssigkeit f, Dickflüssigkeit f, Dicke f, Dichtheit f, Dichte f, Konsistenz f; Klebrigkeit f; Quellungszustand m <Chem.>	viscosity pump viscosity ratio viscosity resistance, viscous resistance; viscous drag viscosity tensor	Viskositätspumpe f Viskositätsverhältnis n, Zähigkeitsverhältnis n Zähigkeitswiderstand m, Viskositätswiderstand m Viskositätstensor m, Zähigkeitstensor m
visco[-]elastic	viskoelastisch, zähelastisch	viscosity transport	Viskositätstransport m
visco[-]elasticity viscoelastic material	Viskoelastizität f s. Burgers solid	viscosity value, viscosity number, limiting viscosity number	Grenzviskositätszahl f, Viskositätszahl f, Staudinger-Index m
viscoelastic model	viskoelastisches Modell n, viskoelastisches Element n		
viscoelastic modulus viscoelastic plate equation viscoelastic solid viscoelastic wave viscoelastic wave equation	viskoelastischer Modul m viskoelastische Plattengleichung f s. Burgers solid viskoelastische Welle f viskoelastische Wellengleichung f	viscothermal equation viscothermal theory viscous, frictional <hyd., aero.> viscous viscous viscous boundary layer viscous correction	viskothermische Gleichung f viskothermische Theorie f zäh, viskos, viskös, reibungsbehaftet <Hydr., Aero.> s. a. high-melting s. a. viscid <chem.> viskose Grenzschicht f, zähe Grenzschicht Reibungskorrektion f
viscogel viscogram viscometer, viscosimeter, fluidmeter, fluidimeter	Viskogel n Viskogramm n Viskosimeter n, Viskometer n, Zähigkeitsmesser m, Viskositätsmesser m	viscous damping coefficient, friction constant <damped oscillations>	Reibungskonstante f <gedämpfte Schwingung>
viscometer gauge viscometry, viscosimetry, viscosity measurement	Reibungsmanometer n Viskosimetrie f, Zähigkeitsmessung f, Viskositätsmessung f	viscous dissipation viscous dissipation function, Rayleigh dissipation function [of hydrodynamics], dissipation function of Rayleigh <hydr.>	viskose Dissipation f [Rayleighsche] Dissipationsfunktion f, Verlustfunktion f <bei der inneren Reibung> <Hydr.>
visco[-]plastic	viskoplastisch, zäh[-]plastisch		
viscoplastic boundary layer viscoplastic deformation viscoplastic flow	viskoplastische Grenzschicht f <hydr.> s. viscoplastic strain viskoplastisches Fließen n, zäh-plastische Strömung f, plastisch-zähe Strömung	viscous dissipation of energy viscous dissipation rate viscous drag viscous flow, frictional flow, viscous motion, frictional motion	viskose Energiedissipation f viskose Dissipationsgeschwindigkeit f s. viscous resistance zähe Strömung f, viskose Strömung, reibungsbehaftete Strömung, Reibungsströmung f, zähe Bewegung f, viskose Bewegung, reibungsbehaftete Bewegung; zähes Fließen n, viskoses Fließen
visco[-]plasticity viscoplastic strain, viscoplastic deformation	Viskoplastizität f viskoplastische Verformung f, zäh-plastische Verformung, plastisch-zähe Verformung		
viscosimeter viscosimetry, viscometry, viscosity measurement	s. viscometer Viskosimetrie f, Zähigkeitsmessung f, Viskositätsmessung f		
viscosity; internal friction, damping capacity, mechanical relaxation	Viskosität f, Zähigkeit f; innere Reibung f, innere Verschiebungsfestigkeit f, Verschiebungsfestigkeit	viscous flow viscous fluid, viscous liquid	s. a. yielding (of metal, material, solid) zähe Flüssigkeit f, viskose Flüssigkeit, reibungsbehaftete Flüssigkeit
viscosity viscosity viscosity average molecular weight	s. a. coefficient of viscosity <quantity> s. a. viscidity Viskositätsmittel n des Molekulargewichts	viscous force, viscosity force viscous hysteresis, magnetic creeping	Zähigkeitskraft f, Viskositätskraft f viskose Hysteresis f, viskose Hysterese f, kriechende Hysteresis (Hysterese)
viscosity breaking, breaking of viscosity viscosity coefficient viscosity constant viscosity correction, correction for viscosity viscosity dilatancy viscosity due to the change of volume viscosity force, viscous force viscosity index	Viskositätsabnahme f, Zähigkeitsabnahme f s. coefficient of viscosity Viskositätskonstante f Viskositätskorrektion f, Zähigkeitskorrektion f s. dilatancy Volum[en]änderungszähigkeit f Zähigkeitskraft f, Viskositätskraft f Viskositätsindex m, VI, V.I.	viscous liquid, viscous fluid viscous loss viscous magnetization viscous motion viscous particle viscous resistance, viscosity resistance; viscous drag viscous shearing stress viscous slip viscous strain viscous stress, viscous shearing stress <hydr.>	zähe (viskose, reibungsbehaftete) Flüssigkeit f viskoser Verlust m viskose Magnetisierung f s. viscous flow zähes Teilchen n Zähigkeitswiderstand m, Viskositätswiderstand m s. viscous stress <hydr.> viskoses Gleiten n, zähes Gleiten viskose Formänderung f, zähe Formänderung Reibungsspannung f, Reibungsschubspannung f, Schubspannung f, viskose Spannung f <Hydr.>
viscosity integral	Viskositätsintegral n, Zähigkeitsintegral n		
viscosity limit zero	Oseenscher Grenzfall m		
viscosity measurement, viscometry, viscosimetry	Viskosimetrie f, Zähigkeitsmessung f, Viskositätsmessung f		

viscous sub-layer, laminar sublayer, laminar sub-layer	laminare Unterschicht *f*	visual double [star], visual binary	visueller Doppelstern *m*
viscous wake	viskoser Nachlauf *m*, zäher Nachlauf	visual efficiency, visual acuity of the naked eye	Sehleistung *f*, freie Sehschärfe *f*
visibility, visibility distance, visual range, range of sight (visibility, vision), reach [of sight], radius of visibility, optical range, vision range, viewing distance, optical distance, sight distance, vision distance, seeing distance, sight, visual distance, line-of-sight distance	Sichtweite *f*, Sicht *f*, Sichtreichweite *f*, Sehweite *f*	visual efficiency [of radiation]	s. luminous efficiency
		visual efficiency of visible radiation	s. luminous efficiency of visible radiation
		visual estimate, ocular estimate	visuelle Schätzung *f*, Schätzung
		visual examination	s. visual inspection
		visual field, field of vision, vision field	Gesichtsfeld *n*, Sehdingfeld *n*, Sehfeld *n*
		visual field	s. a. field of sight ⟨of instrument⟩
visibility, extremely good visibility, vista	Fernsicht *f*	visual field for a defined colour	Farbengesichtsfeld *n*
visibility ⟨meteo., astr.⟩; seeing ⟨astr.⟩; conspicuity ⟨with the naked eye⟩ ⟨astr.⟩	Sichtbarkeit *f* ⟨Meteo., Astr.⟩; Sicht *f* ⟨Meteo.⟩; Sichtgrad *m* ⟨Meteo.⟩	visual field meter, field of sight meter, kampometer	Gesichtsfeldmesser *n*, Kampimeter *n*
		visual green	Sehgrün *n*
visibility	s. a. luminous efficiency	visual impression, impression ⟨opt.⟩	Sehbild *n*, Anschauungsbild *n*, Eindruck *m* ⟨Opt.⟩
visibility at night, night visibility [distance], night visual range	Nachtsichtweite *f*, Nachtsicht *f*	visual indicator	s. indicator ⟨el.⟩
		visual inspection, visual examination	visuelle Prüfung *f*, subjektive Prüfung, Sichtprüfung *f*
visibility distance	s. visibility		
visibility distance of a point source of light	Tragweite *f*, Feuersicht *f*, Sichtweite *f* der Lichtquelle	visualization, rendering visible	Sichtbarmachung *f*
visibility estimation	Sichtschätzung *f*	visualizer	s. indicator ⟨el.⟩
visibility factor [of radiation]	s. photometric radiation equivalent	visual line	s. line of vision
		visual luminous efficiency [of radiation]	s. luminous efficiency
visibility meter	Sichtmesser *m*; Sichtweitenmesser *m*	visual luminous efficiency of visible radiation	s. luminous efficiency of visible radiation
visibility of fringes	Interferenzkontrast *m* ⟨$(I_{max} - I_{min})/(I_{max} + I_{min})$⟩	visual magnitude, visual stellar magnitude	visuelle Helligkeit *f* [eines Gestirns]
visibility of radiation	s. luminous efficiency	visual orange	Sehorange *n*
visible; conspicuous ⟨with the naked eye⟩ ⟨astr.⟩	sichtbar	visual organ	s. organ of vision
		visual part	s. visible range
visible horizon	s. apparent horizon	visual perception	Gesichtswahrnehmung *f*, optische Wahrnehmung *f*
visible part	s. visible region		
visible radiation, light, light radiation	Licht *n*, sichtbare Strahlung *f*, sichtbares Licht	visual photometer, subjective photometer	visuelles (subjektives) Photometer *n*
		visual photometry, subjective photometry	visuelle Photometrie *f*, subjektive Photometrie
visible range, visible region, visible part, visual part, visual range ⟨of the spectrum *or* radiation⟩	sichtbares Spektralgebiet *n*, sichtbarer Spektralbereich *m*, Sichtbare *n* ⟨Strahlung oder Spektrum⟩	visual plane, plane of vision	Visionsebene *f*; Blickebene *f*
		visual purple, rhodopsin	Rhodopsin *n*, Sehpurpur *m*
		visual radiation temperature	visuelle Strahlungstemperatur *f*
visible spectrum, optical spectrum, luminous spectrum, light spectrum	Lichtspektrum *n*, sichtbares Spektrum *n*, optisches Spektrum	visual range ⟨nucl.⟩	abgeschätzte (visuelle) Reichweite *f* ⟨Kern.⟩
visible speech	sichtbare Sprache *f*, „visible speech" *f*	visual range	s. a. visibility
		visual ray	Sehstrahl *m*
vis inertia, inertia, inertness	Trägheit *f*, Beharrungsvermögen *n*, Beharrung *f*	visual ray pyramid, pyramid of visual rays	Sehstrahlpyramide *f*
vision, sight	Sehen *n*	visual red	Sehrot *n*
vision distance	s. visibility		
vision field	s. visual field	visual sensation	Gesichtsempfindung *f*
vision of movements, perception of movements	Bewegungswahrnehmung *f*, Bewegungssehen *n*	visual space	Sehraum *m*, Wahrnehmungsraum *m*, Anschauungsraum *m*
vision process, process of vision	Schvorgang *m*	visual spectrophotometer, subjective spectrophotometer	visuelles Spektralphotometer *n*, subjektives Spektralphotometer
vision range	s. visibility		
Visolett[-type magnifier]	Visolettlupe *f* [nach G. Jaeckel]	visual stellar magnitude, visual magnitude	visuelle Helligkeit *f* [eines Gestirns]
visor	Visierspalt *m*, Visierspalte *f*		
vista	s. visibility	visual white	Sehweiß *n*
visual acuity, acuity of vision, sharpness of vision, keenness [of vision]	Sehschärfe *f*, Visus *m*, Schärfe *f* des Auges; Kehrwert *m* der angularen Sehschärfe	vis viva	s. kinetic energy
		vital activity	Lebenstätigkeit *f*
		vital capacity	Vitalkapazität *f*, maximales Atemhubvolumen *n*, Lebensfassungsvermögen *n*
visual acuity of the naked eye, visual efficiency	Sehleistung *f*, freie Sehschärfe *f*	vital dye, vital stain	Vitalfarbstoff *m*
visual angle	Gesichtswinkel *m*; Sehwinkel *m*		
visual axis, sight axis	Sehachse *f*, Gesichtsachse *f*	vital fluorochrome staining; vital stain[ing]	Vitalfärbung *f*; Vitalfluorochromierung *f*
visual binary, visual double [star]	visueller Doppelstern *m*	vital functions, vital process	Lebensprozeß *m*, Lebensvorgang *m*
visual cell	Sehzelle *f*		
visual colorimetry, direct colorimetry	visuelle Farbmessung *f*, subjektive Farbmessung	vital stain, vital dye	Vitalfarbstoff *m*
visual direction finder	optischer Peiler *m*, Peildiopter *m* mit Kompaß		
visual distance	s. visibility		

vital stain, vital staining; vital fluorochrome staining	Vitalfärbung f; Vitalfluorochromierung f
vitamin P, permeability factor	Permeabilitätsfaktor m, Vitamin n P, Vitamin-P-Gruppe f, Permeabilitätsvitamin n, Citrin n
viton-hour	Vitonstunde f
vitreosol	Vitreosol n
vitreous, glassy	glasig, glasartig
vitreous body, vitreous humour	Glaskörper m, Corpus vitreum n
vitreous electricity, positive electricity	positive Elektrizität f, Glaselektrizität f, glaselektrischer Zustand m
vitreous humour	s. vitreous body
vitreous state, glassy state	Glaszustand m, glasartiger Zustand m
vitrification, glass transiton, glass formation	Vitrifizierung f, Vitrifikation f, Verglasung f, Übergang m in den Glaszustand, Glasbildung f
vitrification temperature	Vitrifizierungstemperatur f
vitrification temperature	s. freezing-in temperature
vitrophyric, hyaline	glasig, hyalin, vitrophyrisch
Vlas[s]ov equation, Boltzmann-Vlasov equation	Wlassow-Gleichung f, Vlasov-Gleichung f
1/v law, Fermi['s] 1/v law	$1/v$-Gesetz n, Fermisches $1/v$-Gesetz
Vleck['s] method / Van Vleck-Weisskopf collision theory / Van, collision theory of Van Vleck and Weisskopf	van Vlecksche Methode f van Vleck-Weisskopfsche Stoßtheorie f, Stoßtheorie von van Vleck und Weisskopf
V-notch, V-shaped notch	Spitzkerbe f, V-Kerbe f, V-förmige Kerbe f
V-notch specimen	Spitzkerbprobe f
V-notch weir, triangular-notch weir, triangular weir	Dreieckwehr n, dreieckiger Überfall m, Dreiecküberfall m
vocal cord	Stimmlippe f; Stimmband n
vocal level, electrical speech level, speech level, volume level	Sprachpegel m
vocal range	Stimmumfang m
vocoder, voice coder, voice code to recreate	Vocoder m, Vokoder m
voder, voice operation demonstrator	Voder m, Sprachwirkungsvorführgerät n
Vogel-Colson-Russell effect, Russell effect	Russell-Effekt m, Vogel-Colson-Russell-Effekt m
Vogel['s] formula	Gleichung f von Vogel, Vogelsche Gleichung, Vogelsche Formel f
Vogler['s] theorem	Voglerscher Satz m
voice coder, voice code to recreate	s. vocoder
voice coil, moving coil, speaking coil ‹of loudspeaker›	Tauchspule f, Sprechspule f ‹Lautsprecher›
voice current, speech current, telephone current	Sprechstrom m
voice-ear test, speech test, volume comparison	Sprech-Hör-Versuch m
voice frequency	s. audio[-] frequency
voice-frequency band, speech-frequency range	Sprachfrequenzbereich m, Sprachfrequenzband n, Sprechfrequenzbereich m, Sprechfrequenzband n
voice operation demonstrator	s. voder
void	Leerraum m; Hohlraum m; leerer Zwischenraum m; Pore f
void	s. a. vacant site ‹cryst.›
voidage	s. void volume
void coefficient, cavity coefficient	Voidkoeffizient m, Dampfblasenkoeffizient m [der Reaktivität]; Blasenkoeffizient m, Leeranteilkoeffizient m, Leerraumkoeffizient m, Hohlraumkoeffizient m
void of air, devoid of matter	luftleer
void set	leere Menge f, Nullmenge f
void space	s. pore space
void volume, voidage	Porenvolumen n, Hohlraumvolumen n, Porenraum m
Voigt approximation	Voigt-Näherung f, Voigtsche Näherung f
Voigt-Cotton-Mouton effect, magnetic linear dichroism	Voigt-Cotton-Mouton-Effekt m
Voigt effect	Voigt-Effekt m
Voigt['s] elastic constant	Voigtsche elastische Konstante f
Voigt['s] function	Voigt-Funktion f, Voigtsche Funktion f
Voigt material (model)	s. Kelvin body
Voigt['s] notation	Voigtsche Bezeichnung f, Voigtsche Schreibweise (Darstellung) f
Voigt profile	Voigt-Profil n
Voigt-Reuss-Hill approximation	Voigt-Reuß-Hill-Näherung f, Voigt-Reuß-Hillsche Näherung f
Voigt unit	s. Kelvin body
Voith-Sinclair coupling	Voith-Sinclair-Kupplung f, VS-Kupplung f
Volarovich [zero-degree] viscometer	Wolarowitsch-Viskosimeter n; Wolarowitsch-Nullgradviskosimeter n
volatile	flüchtig
volatile, volatile substance, volatile matter	flüchtiger Stoff m, Flüchtige n
volatile fission products, fission gas	Spaltgas n, Spaltungsgas n, gasförmige Spaltprodukte npl, flüchtige Spaltprodukte
volatile matter, volatile substance, volatile	flüchtiger Stoff m, Flüchtige n
volatility	Flüchtigkeit f
volatility product	Verflüchtigungsprodukt n
volatilization	Verflüchtigung f
volatilization, distillation, vaporization, sublimation	Destillation f, Destillieren n, Siedetrennung f
volative matter	s. volatile matter
volcanic	s. eruptive rock
volcanic activity	vulkanische Tätigkeit f
volcanic ash, volcanic dust	Vulkanasche f, vulkanische Asche f, Vulkanstaub m, vulkanischer Staub m
volcanic cone	Vulkankegel m
volcanic dome	Quellkuppe f; Staukuppe f; Stoßkuppe f
volcanic dust, volcanic ash	Vulkanasche f, vulkanische Asche f, Vulkanstaub m, vulkanischer Staub m
volcanic earthquake, volcanic tremor	Ausbruchsbeben n, vulkanisches Beben n, vulkanisches Erdbeben n
volcanic embryo	Vulkanembryo m
volcanic eruption, eruption [of volcano]	Ausbruch m, Eruption f ‹Vulkan›, Vulkanausbruch m, Vulkaneruption f
volcanic exhalation, exhalation	Exhalation f; Aushauchung f; Ausdünstung f ‹Geo.›
volcanic focus, magmatic focus	Vulkanherd m, vulkanischer Herd m, Magmaherd m
volcanic igneous rock	s. eruptive rock
volcanicity	Vulkanizität f
volcanic neck	s. neck ‹geo.›
volcanic pellets	s. lapilli
volcanic pipe	s. pipe ‹geo.›
volcanic rock	s. eruptive rock

volcanic | 968

volcanic theory	Vulkantheorie *f*
volcanic tremor	*s.* volcanic earthquake
volcanogenic	vulkanogen
Volkmann['s] rule	Volkmannsche Regel *f*
volley theory [of hearing]	Salventheorie *f* [des Hörens]
Volmer['s] adsorption equation (isotherm)	*s.* Volmer['s] equation
Volmer diffusion	Volmer-Diffusion *f*
Volmer['s] equation [for adsorption], Volmer['s] adsorption equation, Volmer['s] adsorption isotherm, adsorption isotherm of Volmer, adsorption formula of Volmer, Freundlich['s] equation [for adsorption], Freundlich['s] adsorption equation, Freundlich['s] [adsorption] isotherm, adsorption isotherm of Freundlich	Adsorptionsisotherme *f* von Volmer, Adsorptionsisotherme von Freundlich, Isothermengleichung *f* von Volmer (Freundlich), Volmersche Adsorptionsgleichung *f*, Freundlichsche Adsorptionsgleichung (Adsorptionsisotherme *f*), Volmersche Gleichung *f* [für die Adsorption], Freundlichsche Gleichung [für die Adsorption]
Volmer-Heyrovsky mechanism	Volmer-Heyrovsky-Mechanismus *m*
Volmer-Tafel mechanism	Volmer-Tafel-Mechanismus *m*
Volmer-Weber mechanism; liquid-drop model, drop model <cryst.>	Tröpfchenmodell *n*; Volmer-Weber-Mechanismus *m* <Krist.>
volometer, volt-ammeter, volt-ampere[ ]meter	Scheinleistungsmesser *m*, Voltamperemeter *n*, VA-Meter *n*
volplane, gliding flight, glide	Gleitflug *m*, Segelflug *m*
volt, V, v	Volt *n*, V
Volta effect	Volta-Effekt *m*
Volta electromotive force	*s.* Volta potential difference
Volta electromotive series, voltaic electromotive series, voltaic series, Volta series	Voltasche Spannungsreihe *f*
Volta['s] experiment	Voltascher Fundamentalversuch *m*
voltage, electric[al] tension, tension, difference of potential, potential difference; potential, electric potential <el.>	Spannung *f*, elektrische Spannung, Potentialdifferenz *f*, elektrische Potentialdifferenz, Potentialunterschied *m*, elektrischer Potentialunterschied, Liniensumme *f* der elektrischen Feldstärke, Linienintegral *n* der elektrischen Feldstärke; Potential *n*, elektrisches Potential <El.>
voltage	Spannung *f* in Volt, Voltzahl *f*
voltage across bridge diagonal	Brückenspannung *f*
voltage amplification	Spannungsverstärkung *f*
voltage amplification factor, voltage gain	Spannungsverstärkungsfaktor *m*, Spannungsverstärkung *f*
voltage amplifying tube	Spannungsverstärkerröhre *f*
voltage amplitude <el.>	Spannungsamplitude *f* <El.>
voltage analog[ue]	Spannungsanalogon *n*
voltage at break, break voltage, voltage induced at break	Abreißspannung *f*, Öffnungsspannung *f*
voltage attenuation	Spannungsdämpfung *f*
voltage at the terminals, terminal voltage	Klemmenspannung *f*, Klemmspannung *f*
voltage breakdown	Spannungsdurchschlag *m*, Spannungsüberschlag *m*
voltage characteristic <el.>	Spannungscharakteristik *f*, Spannungskennlinie *f* <El.>
voltage circuit, volt circuit, shunt circuit, voltage path, shunt path, potential circuit <el.>	Spannungspfad *m*, Spannungskreis *m* <El.>
voltage collapse, collapse of the voltage	Spannungszusammenbruch *m*, Zusammenbruch *m* der Spannung
voltage component, partial voltage, voltage fraction, component of the voltage	Teilspannung *f*
voltage conversion	Spannungswandlung *f*
voltage-current characteristic	*s.* current-voltage characteristic <of photocell>
voltage curve	Spannungskurve *f*, Spannungsverlauf *m*
voltage-dependent resistor	*s.* varistor
voltage detector, voltage indicator <el.>	Spannungsprüfer *m*, Spannungsanzeiger *m* <El.>
voltage diagram, potential diagram, vector diagram of voltage <el.>	Spannungsdiagramm *n*, Spannungsbild *n* <El.>
voltage directive coefficient	Spannungsrichtfaktor *m*
voltage divider, potential divider, potentiometer	Spannungsteiler *m*, Potentiometer *n*
voltage divider chain	Spannungsteilerkette *f*
voltage-dividing factor	Spannungsteilerfaktor *m*
voltage-dividing network	Spannungsteilernetzwerk *n*
voltage division ratio, ratio of voltage division	Spannungsteilungsverhältnis *n*
voltage doubler; voltage doubler circuit, voltage doubling circuit	Spannungsverdoppler *m*; Spannungsverdopplerschaltung *f*
voltage doubling circuit [of Greinacher]	*s.* Greinacher circuit
voltage drift	Spannungsdrift *f*
voltage drop, voltage loss; potential drop, drop of potential, fall of potential, potential fall, decline in potential	Potentialabfall *m*, Potentialfall *m*; Spannungsabfall *m*, Spannungsfall *m*
voltage drop in the resistor	Spannungsabfall *m* am Widerstand, Widerstandsspannung *f*
voltage efficiency, volt efficiency	Spannungsausnutzung *f*, Spannungsausnutzungskoeffizient *m*
voltage factor	*s.* gain
voltage feed	Spannungseinkopplung *f*
voltage feedback	Spannungsrückkopplung *f*
voltage feedback amplifier	spannungsgegengekoppelter Verstärker *m*
voltage fluctuation <el.>	Spannungsschwankung *f* <El.>
voltage fraction	*s.* voltage component
voltage gain, voltage amplification factor	Spannungsverstärkungsfaktor *m*, Spannungsverstärkung *f*
voltage generator	Spannungserzeuger *m*
voltage gradient	*s.* potential gradient
voltage harmonic, harmonic of the voltage	Spannungsoberwelle *f*
voltage impulse	*s.* impulse of voltage
voltage indicator, voltage detector <el.>	Spannungsprüfer *m*, Spannungsanzeiger *m* <El.>
voltage induced at break, break voltage, voltage at break	Abreißspannung *f*, Öffnungsspannung *f*
voltage in non-active position	Ruhespannung *f*

voltage law	s. Kirchhoff['s] voltage law	voltage standard, voltage reference [value]	Spannungsnormal n
voltage limiting, potential limiting	Spannungsbegrenzung f	voltage standing wave ratio <el.>	Spannungsstehwellenverhältnis n, Spannungsverhältnis n <El.>
voltage loss	Spannungsverlust m		
voltage loss	s. a. voltage drop	voltage surge	s. surge <el.>
voltage matrix	Spannungsmatrix f	voltage surge	s. impulse of voltage
voltage maximum permissible in cold state	Kaltspannung f	voltage-time converter [unit]	Spannungs-Zeit-Konverter m, Spannungs-Zeit-Umwandlungsgerät n
voltage-multiplication-type generator	s. cascade generator	voltage-to-frequency converter, VFC, V.F.C.	Spannungs-Frequenz-Umsetzer m
voltage-multiplying circuit	Spannungsvervielfacherschaltung f	voltage to neutral	s. star point voltage
		voltage transfer, voltage transformation	Spannungsübersetzung f
voltage of electrolytic bath	Badspannung f	voltage transformation, voltage transformation ratio <quantity>	Spannungsübersetzung f <Größe>
voltage of filament battery, heater voltage, filament voltage <el.>	Heizfadenspannung f, Fadenspannung f, Heizspannung f	voltage transformation factor; response to voltage <transducer>	Spannungsübertragungsmaß n; Spannungsübertragungsfaktor m <elektroakustischer Wandler>
voltage of microphonic effect	s. microphony voltage		
voltage of the main	s. supply voltage		
voltage path	s. voltage circuit <el.>	voltage transformation ratio	s. voltage transformation <quantity>
voltage plateau, plateau of the counter, Geiger plateau <of the counter>	Plateau n, Geiger-Plateau n, Plateaubereich m <Zählrohrcharakteristik>	voltage transformer, potential transformer, shunt transformer	Spannungswandler m, Spannungsumsetzer m
voltage pole	Spannungspol m	voltage transient, transient voltage, transient	vorübergehende Überspannung f, momentane Überspannung
voltage-proof	spannungsfest	voltage transient, transient surge	Stoßspannungswelle f
		voltage transient	Spannungssprungcharakteristik f
voltage pulse	s. impulse of voltage	voltage trebling	Spannungsverdreifachung f
voltage quadrupler	Spannungsvervierfacher m	voltage triangle	Spannungsdreieck n
voltage ratio	Spannungsverhältnis n <El.>	voltage tripler	Spannungsverdreifacher m
voltage reference [value], voltage standard	Spannungsnormal n	voltage vector <el.>	Spannungszeiger m, Spannungsvektor m <El.>
voltage reflection coefficient	Spannungsreflexionskoeffizient m		
voltage regeneration	Spannungsrückgewinnung f	voltaic arc, arc, electric arc <el.>	Bogen m; Lichtbogen m, elektrischer Lichtbogen (Bogen) <El.>
voltage-regulating transformer	s. variable ratio transformer		
voltage regulator tube, VR tube	Spannungsreglerröhre f, Spannungsregelröhre f	voltaic battery, voltaic pile, voltaic column	Voltasche Säule f, Voltasche Batterie f
		voltaic cell, electrochemical cell, chemical cell, galvanic cell, current generator cell, electric cell, voltaic couple cell, chemical source of current	galvanisches Element n, Volta-Element n, elektrochemisches Element, galvanische Zelle f, elektrochemische Zelle f, galvanische Kette f, Element, chemische Stromquelle f
voltage resonance, series resonance	Reihenresonanz f, Serienresonanz f, Spannungsresonanz f		
voltage resonance frequency	s. series resonant frequency	voltaic cell	Voltasche Kette f
voltage-responsive	s. voltage-sensitive	voltaic column	s. voltaic pile
voltage r.m.s.	s. voltage root-mean-square	voltaic couple	s. voltaic cell
voltage root-mean-square, voltage r.m.s., root-mean-square voltage, r.m.s. voltage	Effektivwert m der Spannung, Effektivspannung f, effektive Spannung f	voltaic coupling, Loftin-White coupling <of thermionic valves>	galvanische Kopplung f, Loftin-White-Kopplung f <Röhren>
		voltaic electromotive series, Volta electromotive series, voltaic series, Volta series	Voltasche Spannungsreihe f
voltage saturation	Spannungssättigung f		
voltage-sensitive, voltage-responsive	spannungsempfindlich	voltaic pile, voltaic battery, voltaic column; Volta['s] pile	Voltasche Säule f, Voltasche Batterie f; Volta-Element n
		voltaic potential	s. Volta potential difference
voltage source	Spannungsquelle f	voltaic series	s. voltaic electromotive series
voltage source equivalent circuit	Spannungsquellenersatzschaltung f	voltaism	s. galvanism
		Volta['s] law	Voltasches Spannungsgesetz n, Voltasches Gesetz n
voltage stability	Spannungskonstanz f, Spannungsstabilität f, Stabilität f der Spannung	Volta luminescence	Volta-Lumineszenz f
		voltameter, coulometer, coulombmeter	Coulometer n, Voltameter n, Coulombmeter n
voltage stabilization	Spannungsstabilisierung f, Spannungsstabilisation f, Spannungsgleichhaltung f, Spannungskonstanthaltung f	voltametric	voltametrisch
		voltametric titration, voltametry	Voltametrie f, voltametrische Titration f
voltage stabilizer [tube], voltage stabilizing tube, stabilizer tube, stabilivolt, stabilovolt, stabilitron	Stabilisatorröhre f, Spannungsstabilisatorröhre f, Stabilovoltröhre f, Stabilisierungsröhre f	volt-ammeter, volt-ampere[ ]meter, volometer	Scheinleistungsmesser m, Voltamperemeter n, VA-Meter n
		volt-ammeter	s. a. volt-and-ammeter
		voltammetric	voltammetrisch

voltammetric titration, voltammetry	Voltammetrie *f*, voltammetrische Titration *f*	volume advantage factor	Volum[en]vorteilfaktor *m*, Volum[en]flußfaktor *m*
voltammetry at controlled current	*s.* voltammetric titration	volume anelasticity	Volum[en]anelastizität *f*
voltammetry at controlled potential	*s.* amperometry	volume at the absolute zero of temperature	*s.* zero-point volume
volt[-]ampere, VA	Voltampere *n*, VA	volume capacity	*s.* capacity
volt-ampere characteristic	*s.* current-voltage characteristic	volume change by shear, dilatancy, Kelvin effect, viscous dilatancy	Dilatanz *f*, Volum[en]änderung *f* durch Scherung, Kelvin-Effekt *m*
volt-ampere-hour[ ] meter, apparent-energy meter	Scheinverbrauchszähler *m*, Voltamperestundenzähler *m*	volume charge, volumetric charge	Volum[en]ladung *f*
volt-ampere[ ]meter	*s.* voltammeter		
volt-ampere-ohmmeter	*s.* volt-ohm-ammeter	volume collision[al] frequency	Volumenstoßhäufigkeit *f*
volt-and-ammeter, volt-ammeter, unimeter	Strom- und Spannungsmesser *m*, Stromspannungsmesser *m*, Strom-Spannungs-Messer *m*, Strom-Spannungs-Meßgerät *n*, Spannungs- und Strommesser *m*, Spannungs-Strom-Messer *m*, Spannungsstrommesser *m*, Volt- und Amperemeter *n*, Volt-Ampere-Messer *m*, Volt-Ampere-Meter *n*	volume comparison, voice-ear test, speech test	Sprech-Hör-Versuch *m*
		volume compressibility	*s.* compressibility
		volume compressibility	*s.* cubic compressibility
		volume compression, volume contraction ‹ac.›	Volumenpressung *f*, Dynamikpressung *f*, Dynamikverminderung *f* ‹Ak.›
		volume compression ‹mech.›	Volum[en]kompression *f* ‹Mech.›
		volume compressor	*s.* compressor ‹el.›
Volta['s] pile	*s.* voltaic pile	volume concentration, concentration by volume, volumetric concentration; bulk concentration	Konzentration *f* in Volum[en]prozent, Volum[en]konzentration *f*
Volta potential	*s.* Volta potential difference		
Volta potential difference, Volta electromotive force; Volta potential, outer electrical potential, voltaic potential	Volta-Spannung *f*, Voltasche Kontaktspannung *f*, Voltasche Kontaktpotentialdifferenz *f*; Volta-Potential *n*, äußeres elektrisches Potential *n*		
		volume conduction	Volum[en]leitung *f*
Volta series	*s.* Volta electromotive series	volume conservation	*s.* constancy of volume
		volume constancy	*s.* constancy of volume
volt circuit, voltage circuit, shunt circuit, voltage path, shunt path, potential circuit ‹el.›	Spannungspfad *m*, Spannungskreis *m* ‹El.›	volume content, content by volume	Gehalt *m* in Volumeneinheiten, Volum[en]gehalt *m*
		volume contraction, volumetric contraction, contraction in volume, cubic[al] contraction	Volum[en]kontraktion *f*, räumliche Zusammenziehung (Kontraktion) *f*, kubische Kontraktion (Zusammenziehung) *f*
volt effective, effective volt	Volt *n* effektive Spannung, Volt effektiv		
volt efficiency	*s.* voltage efficiency	volume contraction	*s.* volume compression ‹ac.›
Volterra['s] dislocation	Volterra-Versetzung *f*, Volterrasche Versetzung *f*	volume contraction	*s. a.* volume shrinkage
		volume coulometer, volume voltameter, volumetric voltameter	Volum[en]voltameter *n*, Volum[en]coulometer *n*
Volterra['s] distortion	Volterrasche Distorsion *f*		
Volterra['s] equation	Volterrasche Gleichung *f*	volume crystallization, bulk crystallization	Volum[en]kristallisation *f*
Volterra['s] integral equation ‹of the first or second kind›	Volterrasche Integralgleichung *f* ‹erster *oder* zweiter Art›	volume current, bulk current ‹el.›	Volum[en]strom *m* ‹El.›
Volterra['s] kernel	Volterrascher Kern *m*	volume current density, spatial current density, volume (spatial) density of current	räumliche Stromdichte *f*, Volum[en]stromdichte *f*, Stromdichte *f* pro Volumeneinheit
volt-line, weber, volt-second, Wb, Vs	Weber *n*, Voltsekunde *f*, Wb, Vs		
voltmeter ‹el.›	Spannungsmesser *m*, Voltmeter *n* ‹El.›	volume-defined chamber	Kammer *f* mit veränderlichem Volumen, durch Volum[en]änderung gesteuerte Kammer
volt-ohm-ammeter, volt-ampere-ohmmeter, avometer	Spannungs-Strom-Widerstandsmesser *m*, Strom-Spannungs-Widerstandsmesser *m*, Ampere-Volt-Ohm-Meter *n*, Volt-Ampere-Ohm-Meter *n*, Ampere-Volt-Ohm-Messer *m*, Avometer *n*		
		volume density, volumetric density, spatial density, space density, density by volume; bulk density	räumliche Dichte *f*, Raumdichte *f*, Volum[en]dichte *f*
volt-ohm[ ]meter	Voltohmmeter *n*, Volt-Ohm-Meter *n*, Volt-Ohm-Messer *m*, Spannungs- und Widerstandsmesser *m*, Widerstands- und Spannungsmesser *m*	volume density of charge	*s.* space charge density
		volume density of current	*s.* volume current density
		volume density of electric charge	*s.* space charge density
		volume density of ionization	*s.* ionization volume density
volt peak-to-peak, peak-to-peak volt	Volt *n* Scheitelspannung, Volt Spitze-Spitze	volume density of magnetization	Magnetisierungsdichte *f* [pro Volumeneinheit]
		volume density of polarization	*s.* polarization volume density
volt-second, weber, volt-line, Wb, Vs	Weber *n*, Voltsekunde *f*, Wb, Vs	volume diffusion	Volum[en]diffusion *f*
volume; capacity; cubical contents	Volumen *n* ‹*pl.*: Volumina›; Rauminhalt *m*, Raum *m*, Kubikinhalt *m*, körperlicher Inhalt *m*, Inhalt ‹räumlich›	volume diffusion coefficient, coefficient of volume diffusion	Volum[en]diffusionskoeffizient *m*
		volume dilatometer	Volum[en]dilatometer *n*
volume ‹ac.›	Schallvolumen *n* ‹Ak.›	volume diminution	*s.* volumetric reduction
volume	*s. a.* hypervolume	volume dispersion, spatial dispersion	räumliche Dispersion *f*
volume	*s. a.* loudness level ‹ac.›		
volume	*s. a.* three-dimensional	volume displaced, displaced volume, volume forced away, displacement ‹quantity›	verdrängtes Volumen *n*, eingetauchtes Volumen, Verdrängung *f* ‹Größe›
volume absorption, bulk absorption	Volum[en]absorption *f*		
		volume displacement	Volumenverschiebung *f*; Volumenverdrängung *f*

volume dose	Volum[en]dosis f, Raumdosis f	volume level, electrical speech level, speech level, vocal level	Sprachpegel m
volume effect, isotope volume effect, isotopic volume effect, effects due to isotopic change of volume	Kernvolumeneffekt m [der Isotopie], volum[en]abhängiger Isotopieeffekt m, volum[en]abhängiger Isotopieverschiebungseffekt m, volum[en]abhängige Isotopieverschiebung f, Volum[en]isotopieeffekt m	volume lifetime, bulk lifetime	Volum[en]lebensdauer f
		volume magnetostriction, bulk magnetostriction	Volum[en]magnetostriktion f, Magnetostriktion f des Volumens
		volume meter	s. sound intensity meter <ac.>
volume elasticity	s. bulk modulus [of elasticity] <quantity> <therm.>	volume meter	s. sound level meter <ac.>
		volume microdilatometer	Volum[en]mikrodilatometer n
volume elasticity	s. compressibility <property> <therm.>		
volume element, element of volume, space element, element of extension	Volum[en]element n, Raumelement n	volume moisture, bulk moisture	Volum[en]feuchtigkeit f
		volumenometer, volumometer <for solids>	Volumenometer n, Volumometer n, Stereometer n, Volumenmesser m <für Festkörper>
volume element	s. a. hypervolume element		
volume energy	Volum[en]energie f	volume of absolute zero	s. zero-point volume
		volume of computation, amount of calculation, computing expenditure	Rechenaufwand m
volume excitation	Volum[en]anregung f		
volume expander, expander <el.>	Dynamikdehner m <El.>	volume of displaced liquid	verdrängtes Flüssigkeitsvolumen n
		volume of information	s. information content
volume expansion <ac.>	Volumendehnung f, Dynamikdehnung f <Ak.>	volume of mixing	Mischungsvolumen n
		volume of sound, sound volume <ac.>	Klangumfang m <Ak.>
volume expansion	s. a. cubic[al] expansion <therm.>	volume of stroke	s. a. loudness level <ac.>
volume expansion coefficient	s. thermal coefficient of volume expansion	volume of stroke, displacement, displacement volume, piston-swept volume	Hubraum m; Hubvolumen n
volume flow, volume flow rate, volume flux, flux, rate of volume flow <volume per unit time>	Durchfluß m [in Volumeneinheiten], Durchflußvolumen n [je Zeiteinheit], Volum[en]durchfluß m, Volum[en]flußdichte f, Volum[en]fluß m, Volum[en]strom m, Volum[en]durchsatz m <Volumen/Zeiteinheit>		
		volume of water, water volume	Wasservolumen n, Wasserinhalt m
		volume per cent	s. volume percentage
		volume percentage, per cent by volume, volume per cent, % vol., vol. %, v/v	Volum[en]prozent n, Vol.-%, Vol. %
volume fluorescence, bulk fluorescence	Volum[en]fluoreszenz f	volume photoeffect (photoelectric effect, photoemission, photoemissive effect), bulk photoemissive effect	Volum[en]photoeffekt m, lichtelektrischer Volumeneffekt m, Volum[en]photoemission f
volume flux	s. volume flow		
volume force, volumetric force, body force	Volum[en]kraft f		
volume force	Massenkraft f	volume photovoltaic effect, bulk photovoltaic effect	Volum[en]sperrschichtphotoeffekt m
volume forced away	s. displaced volume <quantity>	volume polarization	Volum[en]polarisation f
volume fraction, volume ratio	Volum[en]bruch m, Volum[en]fraktion f, Volum[en]gehalt m, Volum[en]anteil m		
		volume porosity	Volum[en]porosität f
		volume potential, bulk potential	Volum[en]potential n
volume-generated carrier	volum[en]erzeugter Träger m	volume radiator, bulk radiator	Volum[en]strahler m
volume heat capacity	s. heat capacity per unit volume	volume range	Lautstärkebereich m; Lautstärkeumfang m, Lautstärkeverhältnis n
volume increase, increase of volume; bulking	Volum[en]zunahme f, Volum[en]vergrößerung f	volume range, dynamic range	Dynamik f, Schalldruckumfang m, Aussteuer[ungs]bereich m
volume indicator, loudness level indicator, sound level indicator	Lautstärkeanzeiger m, Volumzeiger m, Volumenzeiger m, Volumanzeiger m, Volumenanzeiger m, Aussteuerungsanzeiger m	volume range characteristic	Dynamiklinie f, Dynamikverlauf m
		volume ratio; volume relation; dilatation number	Volum[en]verhältnis n
volume inertial force	Volumenträgheitskraft f	volume ratio	s. a. volume fraction
volume integral; space integral; triple integral	Volum[en]integral n, Raumintegral n; dreifaches Integral n	volume recombination	Volum[en]rekombination f
volume ionization; Branley-Lenard effect	Volum[en]ionisation f, Volum[en]ionisierung f, Raumionisation f, Raumionisierung f; Branley-Lenard-Effekt m, Lenard-Effekt m, lichtelektrische Raumwirkung f	volume recombination rate	Volum[en]rekombinationsgeschwindigkeit f, Volum[en]rekombinationsrate f, Volum[en]rekombinationshäufigkeit f
		volume relation; volume ratio; dilatation number	Volum[en]verhältnis n
volume ionization coefficient	Volum[en]ionisierungskoeffizient m Volum[en]ionisationskoeffizient m, Raumionisationskoeffizient m	volume requirement	s. required volume
		volume resistance	Durchgangswiderstand m; Volum[en]widerstand m, Raumwiderstand m
volume ionization density	räumliche Ionisationsdichte (Ionendichte) f, Volumenionisationskonzentration f	volume resistivity	spezifischer Volumenwiderstand m
		volume resistivity	s. a. resistivity

volume resonance, bulk resonance	Volum[en]resonanz f	volume velocity [across a surface element], acoustic[al] volume velocity <ac.>	Schallfluß m, Schallenergiefluß m, Volum[en]schnelle f <Ak.>
volume shrinkage, shrinkage of volume, volume contraction	Volum[en]schwindung f, Volum[en]schrumpfung f, Raumschwindung f	volume viscosity	s. bulk viscosity
volume source	Raumquelle f, räumlich ausgedehnte Quelle f, Volum[en]quelle f	volume voltameter, volumetric voltameter, volume coulometer	Volum[en]voltameter n, Volum[en]coulometer n
volume strain, bulk strain, strain of volume, dilatational strain	relative Volum[en]änderung f, Volum[en]dilatation f, Dilatation f	volume weight	s. weight per unit volume
		volume work, volumetric work, dilatational work	Volum[en]arbeit f
volume strain	s. a. general state of strain	volumic	s. volume
volume stress, tri-axial stress, three-dimensional stress, general state of stress, cubic[al] stress, triaxiality	dreidimensionaler Spannungszustand m, dreiachsiger Spannungszustand, räumlicher Spannungszustand, allgemeiner Spannungszustand	volumometer, volumenometer <for solids>	Volumenometer n, Volumometer n, Stereometer n, Volumenmesser m <für Festkörper>
		vortex <pl.: vortices, vortexes>; eddy <large-scale>; whirl	Wirbel m; Wirbelgebilde n
		vortex	s. a. vortex tube
		vortex	s. a. vortex point <of differential equation>
volume susceptibility, susceptibility per unit volume	Volum[en]suszeptibilität f	vortex	s. a. centre <of differential equation>
		vortex	s. a. swirl <hydr.>
		vortex	s. a. vortical
volumeter <for fluids>	Volumeter n, Aräometer n mit Volumeneinteilung <für Flüssigkeiten und Gase>	vortex axis, axis of the vortex, turbulence axis; axis of the centre of vortex	Wirbelachse f; Wirbelkernachse f
		vortex beam, vortex jet	Wirbelstrahl m
volumetric[al], titrimetric	maßanalytisch, volumetrisch, titrimetrisch	vortex centre	s. vortex core
		vortex chamber, eddy chamber	Wirbelkammer f
volumetric analysis, measure analysis, titrimetric analysis, titration analysis (test), titrimetry	Maßanalyse f, Volumetrie f, volumetrische Analyse f, Titrimetrie f, titrimetrische Analyse	vortex core, core of the vortex, vortex centre, vortex nucleus	Wirbelkern m, Wirbelzentrum n
		vortex-core flow, turbulent core [flow]	Wirbelkernströmung f, turbulente Kernströmung f
volumetric assay	s. volumetric determination		
volumetric capacity	s. capacity		
volumetric charge, volume charge	Volum[en]ladung f	vortex currents	s. eddy currents
		vortex distribution, vorticity distribution	Wirbelbelegung f, Wirbelverteilung f
volumetric concentration	s. volume concentration		
volumetric contraction	s. volume contraction	vortex drag	s. trailing-edge drag
volumetric density	s. volume density	vortex element, element of vortex, elementary vortex	Wirbelelement n, Elementarwirbel m
volumetric determination, volumetric assay	maßanalytische Bestimmung f		
		vortex field	s. rotational field
		vortex filament	Wirbelfaden m
volumetric dilatation	s. cubic[al] dilatation <elasticity>		
volumetric efficiency	volumetrischer Wirkungsgrad m; Völligkeitsgrad m; Füllungsgrad m	vortex flow	s. rotational flow
		vortex flux, turbulent flux, eddy flux, vorticity flux, flux of vorticity	Wirbelfluß m; Vorticityfluß m <Geo.>
volumetric energy	s. strain energy due to the change of volume		
volumetric expansion	s. cubic[al] expansion <therm.>	vortex flux density, vorticity flux density	Wirbelflußdichte f
volumetric fluorescence analysis (titration), fluorescence titration	Fluoreszenztitration f, Fluoreszenzmaßanalyse f; fluorimetrische Endpunktbestimmung f	vortex formation	s. formation of vortices
		vortex frequency	Wirbelfrequenz f
		vortex generation	s. formation of vortices
		vortex hypothesis	s. Weizsäcker['s] turbulence theory
volumetric force, volume force, body force	Volum[en]kraft f		
volumetric heat capacity	s. heat capacity per unit volume	vortex in the wake, wake vortex	Totwasserwirbel m
		vortex invariant; eddy invariant	Wirbelinvariante f
volumetric manometry, manometry	Manometrie f, volumetrische Manometrie f; Manometermessung f, manometrische Messung f	vortex jet, vortex beam	Wirbelstrahl m
		vortex jet turbine	Wirbelstrahlturbine f
volumetric modulus of elasticity	s. bulk modulus		
		vortex-like	s. vortical
volumetric precipitation analysis	s. precipitation analysis	vortex line, line vortex	Wirbellinie f
volumetric reduction	s. decrease in volume		
volumetric refrigerating capacity	volumetrische Kälteleistung f	vortex line, vortex locus, locus of the vortices <opt.>	Scheitelkurve f <Opt.>
volumetric specific heat	s. heat capacity per unit volume	vortex line element	Wirbellinienelement n
volumetric voltameter, volume voltameter, volume coulometer	Volum[en]voltameter n, Volum[en]coulometer n	vortex locus	s. vortex line <opt.>
		vortex motion	s. rotational flow
volumetric weight	s. weight per unit volume	vortex nucleus	s. vortex core
volumetric work, volume work, dilatational work	Volum[en]arbeit f	vortex of fluid	s. swirl <hydr.>
		vortex pair	Wirbelpaar n
volume unit, vu <ac.>	Volum[en]einheit f, vu <Ak.>		
volume utilization factor	Volum[en]ausnutzungsziffer f	vortex path, trajectory of the vortex, vortex trajectory	Wirbelbahn f

vortex path	s. a. vortex street	vorticity	s. a. vorticity moment
vortex point	Wirbelpunkt m	vorticity	s. a. vorticity vector
		vorticity advection	Vorticityadvektion f, Wirbeladvektion f
vortex point, centre <of differential equation>	Wirbelpunkt m <Differentialgleichung>	vorticity average theorem	Wirbelmittelwertsatz m
vortex power flow (flux)	Wirbelleistungsfluß m	vorticity branch of spectrum	Wirbelzweig m des Spektrums
vortex pump	s. vortex vacuum pump	vorticity component	Wirbelkomponente f
vortex region, vortex zone, eddy	Wirbelbereich m, Wirbelgebiet n, Wirbelzone f; Wirbelstrecke f	vorticity curve	Wirbelstärkekurve f, Wirbelgrößenkurve f
		vorticity density, density of vorticity	Wirbeldichte f
		vorticity diffusion	s. eddy diffusion
		vorticity distribution, vortex distribution	Wirbelbelegung f, Wirbelverteilung f
vortex resistance; form drag, form resistance	Formwiderstand m	vorticity effect	Wirbeleinfluß m
		vorticity equation; predischarge vorticity equation	Wirbelgleichung f; Vorticitygleichung f <Geo.>
vortex ring, collar vortex	Wirbelring m		
vortex ring flow	Wirbelringströmung f	vorticity flux, vortex flux, flux of vorticity	Wirbelfluß m; Vorticityfluß m <Geo.>
vortex rope	s. wing-tip vortex		
vortex row, [single] row of vortices	Wirbelreihe f	vorticity flux conservation law	s. law of conservation of eddy flux
vortex sheet, vorticity sheet	Wirbelschicht f, Wirbelband n, Wirbelblatt n	vorticity flux density, vortex flux density	Wirbelflußdichte f
		vorticity formula	Wirbelformel f
vortex sink, vortex sump, eddy sink, eddy sump	Wirbelsenke f	vorticity measure, vorticity number	Wirbelmaß n
		vorticity moment, vorticity	Wirbelstärke f [des Wirbelfadens], Wirbelmoment n [des Wirbelfadens], Wirbelintensität f, Wirbelgröße f, Wirbelwert m, Vorticitymoment n
vortex source, eddy source	Wirbelquelle f		
vortex space, eddy space	Wirbelraum m		
		vorticity number	s. vorticity measure
		vorticity sheet	s. vortex sheet
vortex speed; vortex velocity	Wirbelgeschwindigkeit f	vorticity spectrum	Wirbelstärkenspektrum n
vortex street	Wirbelstraße f	vorticity surface, vortex surface	Wirbelfläche f
vortex street	s. a. Kármán['s] vortex path	vorticity tensor	Wirbeltensor m, Drehgeschwindigkeitstensor m
vortex strength, strength of the vortex	Stärke f des Wirbels, Wirbelstärke f	vorticity theorem, vortex theorem	Wirbelsatz m
vortex strip, vortex veil	Wirbelstreifen m, Wirbelschleier m		
vortex sump	s. vortex sink	vorticity transfer	Wirbeltransport m, Wirbelübertragung f, Vorticitytransport m
vortex surface, vorticity surface	Wirbelfläche f		
vortex theorem, vorticity theorem	Wirbelsatz m	vorticity transfer equation	Wirbeltransportgleichung f
vortex theory [of airscrew], vortex theory of propeller	„vortex theory" f des Propellers, „vortex"-Theorie f des Propellers, Wirbeltheorie f des Propellers	vorticity transfer theory [of G. I. Taylor], vorticity transport theory	Wirbeltransporttheorie f
vortex thermometer	Vortexthermometer n	vorticity vector, vorticity	Wirbelvektor m, „vorticity" f, Vorticity f, Wirbligkeit f, Wirbeligkeit f, Wirbelstärke f; Drehungsgeschwindigkeit f des Flüssigkeitsteilchens
vortex trail	s. vortex street		
vortex trajectory, trajectory of the vortex, vortex path	Wirbelbahn f		
vortex tube, vortex	Wirbelröhre f		
vortex tube, Hilsch tube, Hilsch['s] vortex tube	Hilschsches Wirbelrohr n, Wirbelrohr, Hilschsche Wirbelröhre f, Hilsch-Rohr n	V-particle	V-Teilchen n, V-Meson n
		V reflector, corner reflector, angled reflector <el.>	Winkelreflektor m, Winkelspiegel m <El.>
vortex-type flow	s. rotational flow		
vortex vacuum pump, vortex pump	Wirbelpumpe f	Vries effect / De	De-Vries-Effekt m
		VR tube	s. voltage regulator tube
vortex veil, vortex strip	Wirbelstreifen m, Wirbelschleier m	V-shaped antenna	s. vee antenna
		V-shaped curve, V-curve, V-characteristic	V-Kurve f
vortex velocity; vortex speed	Wirbelgeschwindigkeit f		
vortex wake	wirbliger Nachlauf m	V-shaped notch, V-notch	Spitzkerbe f, V-Kerbe f, V-förmige Kerbe f
vortex whistle	Wirbelpfeife f	V-shaped track	V-förmige Spur f, V-Spur f
vortex zone	s. vortex region	V-shaped valley	Kerbtal n, V-Tal n, V-förmiges Tal n
vortical, vortex; eddying, eddy; whirling; vortex-like	Wirbel-; wirblig, wirbelig, wirbelnd; wirbelförmig, wirbelartig; wirbelbehaftet	V-type antenna, vee antenna	V-Antenne f
		vug[g], geode <geo.>	Geod n, Sekretion f, Lösungshohlraum m, Geode f <Geo.>
vortical flow	s. rotational flow		
vortical perturbation	Wirbelstörung f	vulcanizate, rubber, vulcanized rubber	Gummi m, vulkanisierter Kautschuk m, Vulkanisat n
vortical structure	Wirbelstruktur f		
vorticity <gen.>	Wirbeligkeit f, Wirbligkeit f <allg.>		

vulcanization

vulcanization, cure, curing	Vulkanisation f
vulcanized caoutchouc	Weichgummi m, Weichkautschuk m, vulkanisierter Kautschuk m
vulcanized rubber	s. vulcanizate
vulgar logarithm	s. Brigg['s] logarithm
vu-meter	s. sound level meter <ac.>
V value, degree of saturation <geo.>	Sättigungsgrad m, V-Wert m <Geo.>

W

Waals adsorption / Van der	s. physisorption
Waals attraction / Van der	Van-der-Waals-Anziehung f, Van-der-Waals-Attraktion f, van der Waalssche Anziehung f, Van-der-Waals-Molekularattraktion f
Waals binding / Van der	s. Waals bond / Van der
Waals bond / Van der, Van der Waals binding, residual bond	Van-der-Waals-Bindung f, van der Waalssche Bindung f, VdW-Bindung f, Edelgasbindung f
Waals constant / Van der	van der Waalssche Konstante f, Van-der-Waals-Konstante f
Waals crystal / Van der	Van-der-Waals-Kristall m, van der Waalsscher Kristall m, VdW-Kristall m
Waals dispersion force / Van der	van der Waalssche Dispersionskraft f, Van-der-Waals-Dispersionskraft f, VdW-Dispersionskraft f
Waals energy / Van der	van der Waalssche Energie f, Van-der-Waals-Energie f, VdW-Energie f
Waals['] equation [of state] / Van der	van der Waalssche Zustandsgleichung (Gleichung) f, Van-der-Waals-Gleichung f, Zustandsgleichung nach van der Waals
Waals['] force / Van der, residual force	Van-der-Waals-Kraft f, van der Waalssche Kraft f, VdW-Kraft f; Nebenvalenzkraft f
Waals gas / Van der	Van-der-Waals-Gas n, van der Waalssches Gas n, VdW-Gas n
Waals interaction / Van der	Van-der-Waals-Wechselwirkung f, van der Waalssche Wechselwirkung f, VdW-Wechselwirkung f
Waals['] interaction energy / Van der	s. Waals potential / Van der
Waals isotherm / Van der	van der Waalssche Isotherme f, Van-der-Waals-Isotherme f
Waals loop / Van der	Van-der-Waals-Schleife f
Waals molecule / Van der	Van-der-Waals-Molekül n, van der Waalssches Molekül n, VdW-Molekül n
Waals['] potential / Van der; Van der Waals['] interaction energy	van der Waalssche Wechselwirkungsenergie f, Van-der-Waals-Wechselwirkungsenergie f, VdW-Wechselwirkungsenergie f; Van-der-Waals-Potential n, van der Waalssches Potential n, VdW-Potential n
Waals radius / Van der	Van-der-Waals-Radius m, van der Waalsscher Radius m, VdW-Radius m
Waals $1/R^6$ law / Van der	van der Waalssches $1/R^6$-Gesetz n, $1/R^6$-Gesetz von van der Waals
Waals theory [of liquids] / Van der	van der Waalssche Theorie f [der Flüssigkeiten]
wab[b]le	s. staggering <mech.>
wab[b]le	s. a. wobbulation
wading rod	stehende Stange f, Grundstange f
Wadsley defect	Wadsley-Defekt m, Wadsley-Fehlordnung f
Wadsworth grating mounting, Wadsworth mounting [of diffraction grating]	Wadsworthsche Gitteraufstellung f
Wadsworth prism	Wadsworth-Spiegelprisma n, Wadsworth-Prisma n, Fuchs-Wadsworth-Prisma f
Waele-Bingham['s] law / De	de Waele-Binghamsches Gesetz n
Waerden['s] [X] test / Van der, X test	Van-der-Waerden-Test m, [van-der-Waerdenscher] X-Test
wafer; slab; slice; thin plate	Plättchen n, Blättchen n; dünne Platte f; dünnes Plättchen; dünnes Blättchen
wagging, wagging vibration	Wedelschwingung f, Schaukelschwingung f, Kippschwingung f, „wagging vibration" f
wagging frequency	Wedelschwingungsfrequenz f, Schaukelschwingungsfrequenz f, Kippschwingungsfrequenz f
wagging vibration	s. wagging
Wagner bridge, Wagner double bridge	Wagner-Brücke f, Wagner-Doppelbrücke f
Wagner earth, Wagner ground [connection]	Wagner-Brückenzweig m, Wagner-Hilfszweig m, Wagner-Erde f, Wagner-Erdung f, Wagnersche Hilfsbrücke f
Wagner effect	Wagner-Effekt m
Wagner ground [connection]	s. Wagner earth
Wagner half-section	Wagner-Halbglied n
Wagner interrupter, magnetic interrupter, hammer interrupter, electromagnetic interrupter	Wagnerscher Hammer m, magnetischer Hammer, Neefscher Hammer, Hammerunterbrecher m, elektromagnetischer Unterbrecher m, Selbstunterbrecher m
Wagner-Wertheimer winding	Wagner-Wertheimer-Wicklung f
Waidner-Burgers standard	Waidner-Burgers-Normal n
waist	s. constriction
waist-level, in the height of the breast	in Brusthöhe
waiting line, queue	Warteschlange f
waiting line problem, queuing problem, queueing problem	Warteschlangenproblem n
waiting line theory, queuing theory, queueing theory, theory of queues	Bedienungstheorie f, Massenbedienungstheorie f, Warteschlangentheorie f, Theorie f der Warteschlangen
waiting time <num. math.>	Wartezeit f <num. Math.>
Waitzmann hardness [number]	Kugelschubhärte f [nach Waitzmann], Schubhärte f [nach Waitzmann], Waitzmann-Härte f
wake, remous <aero., hydr.>	Nachlauf m, Strömungsschatten m, Nachstrom m, Wirbelschleppe f <Aero., Hydr.>; Totwasser n <Hydr.>; Kielwasser n, Kielwasserströmung f, Kielwasserwirbel m <bei Schiffen> <Hydr.>; Mitstrom m
wake <of the meteor>	Schweifansatz m, Nachlauf m <Meteor>
wake boundary	Totwassergrenze f
wake of boundary layer [behind the aerofoil]	Nachlauf m der Grenzschicht
wake parameter	Nachlaufparameter m
wake pressure	Nachlaufdruck m

wake region	Nachlaufgebiet n	wall temperature	Wandtemperatur f
wake space, dead water, still water	Totwassergebiet n, Totwasserbereich m, Totwasser n, Totraum m, totes Wasser n	wall tension	Wandspannung f
		wall thickness	Wanddicke f, Dicke f der Wandung, Wandstärke f
wake vortex, vortex in the wake	Totwasserwirbel m	wall thickness gauge	Wanddickenmesser m
wake wave	Nachlaufwelle f; Kielwasserwelle f; Totwasserwelle f	wall turbulence, turbulence near the wall	Wandturbulenz f
		wall weathering, weathering of the walls	Wandverwitterung f
Wald distribution	Waldsche Verteilung f	Walpole comparator	Walpole-Komparator m
Walden['s] empirical equation, Walden['s] rule	Waldensche Regel f, Waldens Regel, Waldensche Gleichung f	Walsh function	Walsh-Funktion f
		Walsh test	Walsh-Test m
Walden['s] inversion	Waldensche Umkehrung f, Inversion f ⟨Chem.⟩	Waltenhofen['s] pendulum	Waltenhofensches Pendel n
Walden product	Waldensches Produkt n	Walters liquid	Walters-Flüssigkeit f
Walden['s] rule, Walden['s] empirical equation	Waldensche Regel f, Waldens Regel, Waldensche Gleichung f	Walther['s] equation	Walther-Gleichung f [für die Viskositäts-Temperatur-Abhängigkeit]
Waldmann['s] rule	Waldmannsche Regel f	wandering dislocation	s. moving dislocation
W*-algebra	s. Neumann['s] algebra / von	wandering of [the] pole	s. polar motion
walk	s. random walk	Wang['s] function	Wang-Funktion f, Wangsche Funktion f
Walker oscillation, magnetostatic oscillation	magnetostatische Schwingung f, Walker-Schwingung f	waning Moon	abnehmender Mond m
		Wankel engine, rotary piston engine	Wankel-Motor m, Kreiskolbenmotor m
Walkinshaw['s] frequency equation	Walkinshawsche Frequenzgleichung f	Wanner pyrometer, polarizing pyrometer, polarization pyrometer	Wanner-Pyrometer n, Polarisationspyrometer n
Walkinshaw resonance	Walkinshaw-Resonanz f		
wall	Wand f; Wandung f	Wannier['s] effective wave equation	Wanniersche effektive Wellengleichung f
wall / 180°	180°-Wand f	Wannier exciton	Wannier-Exciton n
wall absorption	Wandabsorption f	Wannier function	Wannier-Funktion f
wall action, action of the walls, influence of the walls, wall influence	Wandeinfluß m, Wandwirkung f	Wannier['s] theorem	Wannier-Theorem n
		wan sky, murky sky	trüber Himmel m
		warble	s. wobbulation
wall boundary layer	Wandgrenzschicht f	warble [tone], wobble [tone]	Wobbelton m, Heulton m, Wechselton m
wall catalysis	Wandkatalyse f	Warburg['s] apparatus	Warburg-Apparat m
		Warburg['s] law	Warburgsches Gesetz n
wall charge density	Wandladungsdichte f	Warburg['s] theory of narcosis	Narkosetheorie f von Warburg, Warburgsche Theorie f der Narkose
wall coating, wall lining (covering)	Wandbelag m		
wall condition	Wandbedingung f	Ward['s] identity	Wardsche Identität f, Ward-Identität f
wall covering	s. wall coating	Ward Leonard group	Leonard-Satz m
wall current	Wandstrom m		
wall displacement	s. boundary movement		
walled plain	Wallebene f	Waring['s] formula	Waringsche Formel f
wall effect	Wandeffekt m; Wandphänomen n	Warluzel indicator tube, Warluzel tube	Warluzel-Anzeigeröhre f
wall energy, domain boundary energy	Wandenergie f, Bloch-Wand-Energie f	warm, low-level, low-activity ⟨nucl.⟩	niedrigaktiv, geringaktiv, „low-level"-, schwachaktiv, warm ⟨Kern.⟩
wall friction	Wandreibung f	warm advection	Warmluftadvektion f, Warmadvektion f
wall friction loss, loss due to wall friction	Wandreibungsverlust m		
wall influence	s. wall action	warm air; warm air mass	Warmluft f, warme Luft; Warmluftmasse f
Wallis['] formula, Wallis['] product	Wallissche Formel f		
wall jet	Wandstrahl m	warm air wedge, wedge of warm air	Warmluftkeil m
wall lining	s. wall coating	warm air wheel, wheel of circulating warm air	Warmluftrad n
wall loss	Wandverlust m, Wandungsverlust m		
wall of the containing vessel	Gefäßwand f	warm and muggy, muggy	feuchtwarm
wall of the counter [tube], counter wall	Zählrohrwand[ung] f	warm-blooded	s. homeothermal
		warm current, warm stream	warme Strömung f
wall pressure	Wanddruck m, Zellwanddruck m	warm front	Warmfront f, Aufgleitfront f
wall reaction	Wandreaktion f	warm front line, line of warm front	Warmfrontlinie f
wall recombination, recombination at walls	Wandrekombination f	warm front occlusion, occlusion of warm front	Warmfrontokklusion f
wall reflection	Wandreflexion f	warm front precipitations	Warmfrontniederschläge mpl
wall roughness	Wandrauhigkeit f		
wall shear stress	s. skin friction	warming; heating, heat; growing warm	Aufheizung f; Ausheizung f; Erhitzung f; Erwärmung f
wall shear stress term, surface friction term, skin friction term	Wandschubspannungsglied n		
		warming	s. a. temperature increase

warm | 976

warm laboratory, semi-hot laboratory	warmes Laboratorium n, semiheißes Laboratorium <10 mCi ··· 1Ci>	wash water, washing water, washing[s], rinsing water	Waschwasser n, Spülwasser n
		wastage	Wastage n, örtlich begrenzte Abtragung f
		waste, wastes; waste product	Abfall m, Abgang m, Müll m; Abprodukt n, Abfallprodukt n
		waste disposal, waste withdrawal; waste storage	Abfallbeseitigung f; Abfallagerung f
warm source (spring)	s. thermal spring		
warm stream, warm current	warme Strömung f		
warmth; heat; hotness <gen.; geo.>	Wärme f <allg.; Geo.>	wasteful resistance, loss resistance, dissipation-loss resistance	Verlustwiderstand m
warm tongue	Warmluftzunge f, Wärmezunge f		
warm-up time, heating time, heating period, preheating time, preheat time	Anheizzeit f, Anwärmzeit f; Vorwärmzeit f, Vorheizzeit f	wasteful resistance	s. a. parasite drag
		waste heat	Abwärme f
		waste of time, time required, sacrifice of time, loss of time	Zeitaufwand m
		waste pipe	s. down pipe
warning device, monitor	Warngerät n	waste product, wastes	s. waste
		waste storage	s. waste disposal
		waste treatment	Abfallkonzentrierung f, Abfallbehandlung f
warning notice	Warnmeldung f		
warning of tempest	Unwetterwarnung f	waste withdrawal	s. waste disposal
warp	s. drift soil	watch; time piece, chronometer; clock; time keeper	Zeitmesser m, Zeitmeßgerät n; Uhr f, Chronometer n; Zeitnehmer m
warp[age]	s. warping		
warped cross-section	verwölbter Querschnitt m		
warped surface	s. shew [ruled] surface	water-absorbing capacity (power), water-absorption capacity, water-absorptive capacity	Wasseraufnahmevermögen n, Wasseraufnahmefähigkeit f, Wasseraufnahme f
warping, warping in torsion	nichtebene Torsion f, Werfung f		
warping, warpage; buckling; bending; distortion	Verziehen n, Verzug m; Werfung f, Verwerfung f; Verwölbung f; Verbiegung f; Verkrümmung f	water absorption, water intake, water uptake, intake of water, uptake of water, absorption of water	Wasseraufnahme f; Wasserschluckung f
warping	s. a. bending	water-adsorption capacity	s. water-adsorbing capacity
warping force	Verzugskraft f		
warping function	s. torsion function	water-absorption capacity [of the soil]	Wasserkapazität f [des Bodens]
warping in torsion, warping	nichtebene Torsion f, Werfung f	water-absorptive capacity	s. water-absorption capacity
Warren-Averbach analysis	Warren-Averbach-Analyse f	water after standing	abgestandenes Wasser n
wash	[glatter] Abfluß m der Strömung, Strömungsabfluß m, Abstrom m, abgehender Strom m	water-air interface	Wasser-Luft-Trenn[ungs]fläche f, Wasser/Luft-Grenzfläche f
wash	s. a. thin layer	water balance, water budget, water relations	Wasserhaushalt m, Wasserbilanz f
wash bottle	s. washing bottle		
washed-out	s. smeared	water balance	s. a. level
wash flask	s. washing bottle	water beam pump	s. water jet pump
washing; scrubbing <US>, stripping; washing-out	Waschen n, Wäsche f; Gaswäsche f; Turmwäsche f; Herauswaschen n; Auswaschung f	water-bearing horizon, water-bearing nappe	Wasserhorizont m, wasserführender Horizont m, Wasserstockwerk n
washing, watering, rinsing <of photographic layers>	Wässerung f, Auswässerung f <photographischer Schichten>	water-bearing stratum; ground water-reservoir, aquifer, underflow conductor	wasserführende Schicht f, Grundwasserleiter m, Aquifer m
washing	s. a. wash water		
washing agent	waschaktive Substanz f, WAS; Waschmittel n		
washing-away, sweeping-away, encroaching [upon]	Wegschwemmen n, Fortschwemmen n, Fortspülen n	water-binding capacity	s. water-holding capacity
		water blast [pump]	s. water jet pump
		waterborne sound, sound propagating in water, sound in water	Wasserschall m
washing bottle (flask), wash bottle, gas-washing bottle, gas bottle, wash flask	Waschflasche f, Gaswaschflasche f; Spritzflasche f	water bottle	Schöpfgerät n, Schöpfgefäß n, Schöpfer m, Wasserschöpfer m, Wasserentnahmegerät n; Schöpfflasche f
washing liquid (liquor), wash liquid, wash liquor	Waschflüssigkeit f	water breaking-in; invasion of water; water burst	Wasserdurchbruch m, Wassereinbruch m
washing-out	s. washing	water budget, water balance, water relations	Wasserhaushalt m, Wasserbilanz f
washing power	Waschkraft f, Waschwirkung f	water burst; invasion of water; water breaking-in	Wasserdurchbruch m, Wassereinbruch m
washing rate	Auswässerungsgrad m	water calorie	Wasserkalorie f
washing-round, circumcirculation, lopping-round	Umspülung f	water calorimeter	s. liquid calorimeter
		water-cement ratio	s. water-to-cement ratio
washings	s. wash water	water chamber	Wasserstube f
wash liquid (liquor)	s. washing liquid	water channel, water tunnel	Wasserkanal m, Wassertunnel m
wash liquor	s. wash liquid		
wash of the waves, beating, dashing of the waves	Wellenschlag m	water circulation, circulation of water; water cycle	Wasserzirkulation f, Wasserumlauf m, Wasserkreislauf m

water clock, clepsydra	Wasseruhr f, Klepsydra f
water cloud	Wasserwolke f
water coat; water film	Wasserfilm m; Wasserhaut f; Wasserhülle f
water colour	Wasserfarbe f
water column, column of water, head of water, plume	Wassersäule f, WS
water column pressure, hydraulic head	Wassersäulendruck m
water content; primage <of steam>	Wassergehalt m; Wasserhaltigkeit f
water content of snow	s. water equivalent of snow
water-cooled valve	wassergekühlte Röhre f, Wasserkühlröhre f
watercourse	Wasserlauf m
water cover	Wasserdecke f
water current velocity, current velocity	Strömungsgeschwindigkeit f des Wassers, Wasserströmungsgeschwindigkeit f, Wassergeschwindigkeit f
water cushion	Wasserkissen n, Wasserpolster n
water cycle	s. water circulation
water deficit	Wasserdefizit n
water demineralization (demineralizing)	s. water softening
water-deposited soil	s. drift soil
water depth gauge	s. water gauge <hydr.>
water desalination, desalination of water	Wasserentsalzung f
water displacement, displacement <hydr.>	Wasserverdrängung f, Deplacement n, eingetauchtes Volumen n <Hydr.>
water draught gauge, U-tube draught gauge	Wassersäulenzugmesser m
water dust, water spray, spray	Wasserstaub m
water edge, strand[-] line, edge of water	Strandlinie f, Küstenlinie f, Streichlinie f, Uferlinie f, Wasserspiegelrand m
water ejector	s. water-jet ejector
water ejector	s. a. water jet pump
water equivalent	Wasseräquivalent n
water equivalent, water value <of calorimeter>	Wasserwert m [des Kalorimeters]
water equivalent of snow cover (pack), snow pack water equivalent, water content of snow	Wasserwert m der Schneedecke, Wasserwert des Schnees, Schneewasserwert m, Wassergehalt der Schneedecke, spezifische Schneetiefe f
water exchange, exchange of water	Wasserwechsel m; Wasserumsetzung f, Wasserumsatz m; Wasserumtausch m, Wasseraustausch m
water filament, filament of water	Wasserfaden m
water film; water coat	Wasserfilm m; Wasserhäutchen n; Wasserhülle f
water filter	Wasserfilter n
water flow, run-off [of water], flow of water	Abfluß m <Wasser>, Wasserabfluß m, Wasserfracht f
water-flow calorimeter, Junkers-type gas calorimeter, Junkers['] calorimeter	Kalorimeter n mit Wasserdurchfluß, Junkerssches Kalorimeter n, Junkers-Kalorimeter n, Gaskalorimeter n [nach Junkers]
water flowmeter	s. water meter
water-flow pyrheliometer	s. Smithsonian water-flow pyrheliometer
water gauge, w.g.	Wasserstand[s]messer m, Wasserstand[s]meßgerät n, Wasserstand[s]meßorgan n
water gauge, w.g.	Wasserdruckmesser m, Wassermanometer n
water gauge, water depth gauge; sea gauge; tide gauge <hydr.>	Pegel m; Gezeitenpegel m <Hydr.>
water-gauge cock, water-gauge tap	Wassermeßhahn m, Wasserstand[s]hahn m
water-gauge glass, gauge glass, water glass	Standglas n, Wasserstand[s]glas n, Wasserstand[s]rohr n
water-gauge tap, water-gauge cock	Wassermeßhahn m, Wasserstand[s]hahn m
water glass, soluble glass	Wasserglas n
water glass	s. a. water-gauge glass
water hammer	Wasserschlag m, Widderstoß m, Wasserstoß m, hydraulischer Stoß m; Flüssigkeitsschlag m
water hardener, hardener, water hardening material	Wasserhärter m, Wasserhärtungsmittel n
water hardening	Wasserhärtung f
water hardening material, water hardener, hardener	Wasserhärter m, Wasserhärtungsmittel n
water hardness, hardness of water	Wasserhärte f
water-hating, hydrophobic, hydrophobous	hydrophob, wasserfeindlich
water head	Wassergefälle n
water-head ascent	s. water-surface ascent
water hemisphere [of Earth]	Wasserhalbkugel f [der Erde]
water-holding capacity, moisture-holding capacity, water-binding capacity, water-retaining capacity, specific retention, moisture capacity	Wasserhaltefähigkeit f, Wasserhaltevermögen n, Wasserhaltungsfähigkeit f, Wasserhaltungsvermögen n, Wasserbindungsvermögen n, Wasserrückhaltungsvermögen n, Wasserkapazität f, WK
water-holding capacity of snow	Wasserrückhaltevermögen n des Schnees
Waterhouse diaphragm	s. sliding stop
water immersion	Wasserimmersion f
water inflow; inflow, influx	Zufluß m; Zuflußmenge f, Zustrom m, Einströmung f
watering, washing, rinsing <of photographic layers>	Wässerung f, Auswässerung f <photographischer Schichten>
water injection pump	s. water-jet injector
water-in-oil emulsion, W/O emulsion	Wasser-in-Öl-Emulsion f, Wasser-Öl-Emulsion f, WO-Emulsion f, W/Ö
water intake, water uptake, water absorption, intake of water, uptake of water, absorption of water	Wasseraufnahme f; Wasserschluckung f
water intake; water sampling	Wasserentnahme f; Wasserentzug m; Wasserprobenahme f
water jacket	Wassermantel m
water jet air pump	s. water jet pump
water-jet ejector, water ejector	Wasserstrahlejektor m, Wasserstrahler m, Wasserstrahlanlage f, Wasserstrahlapparat m s. a. water jet pump
water jet ejector	
water-jet injector, water injection pump	s. a. water jet pump Wasserstrahlpumpe f
water jet pump, water jet vacuum pump, water jet air pump, water beam pump, water blast [pump], water jet ejector, water ejector	Wasserstrahlpumpe f, Wasserstrahlluftpumpe f, Wasserstrahlvakuumpumpe f, Wasserstrahlejektor m
water jets, sprayed water, jet water	Spritzwasser n
water-jet-type lightning arrester	Wasserstrahlerder m

water 978

water jet vacuum, vacuum attainable by vacuum jet pump — Wasserstrahlvakuum *n*
water jet vacuum pump *s.* water jet pump
water jump, hydraulic jump — Wassersprung *m*, hydraulischer Sprung *m*, Wasserschwall *m*, Wechselsprung *m*
water landing, landing on water, alighting [on water], surfacing — Landung *f* auf dem Wasser, Wasserlandung *f*, Wasserung *f*
water level — Kanalwaage *f*, Schlauchwaage *f*
water level, water level line — Wasserspiegellinie *f*
water level *s. a.* water line
water level *s. a.* level
water level *s. a.* water stage
water level curve, curve of water level variation — Wasserstand[s]ganglinie *f*, Wasserstand[s]kurve *f*, Wasserspiegelganglinie *f*, Spiegelgangkurve *f*, Spiegelganglinie *f*
water level duration curve — Wasserstand[s]dauerlinie *f*
water level fluctuation — Spiegelschwankung *f*, Wasserspiegelschwankung *f*, Wasserstand[s]schwankung *f*, Wasserschwankung *f*, Niveauschwankung *f*
water level gauge, water level indicator — Wasserstand[s]anzeiger *m*, Wasserstand[s]zeiger *m*, Flüssigkeitspegel *m*, Wasserpegel *m*
water-level gauge *s. a.* water scale <hydr.>
water level indicator *s.* water level gauge
water level line *s.* water level
water-level recorder *s.* limnigraph
water-level recorder *s. a.* mareograph
water-level scale *s.* water scale <hydr.>
water line, water level — Wasserlinie *f*

water-line centre, centre of water-line section — Wasserlinienschwerpunkt *m*
water-line section, floatation area, waterplane area — Schwimmfeld *n*, Schwimmfläche *f*, Wasserlinienfläche *f*
water logging <nucl.> — Wasserdurchtritt *m*, Wassereintritt *m* <Kern.>
water-loving, hydrophilic, hydrophilous — hydrophil, wasserfreundlich, wasserliebend, wasseranziehend
water mark — Wassermarke *f*, Wasserstand[s]marke *f*, Spiegelpfahl *m*
water-mark post, water post — Wasserpegel *m*, Pegel *m*, Peil *m*
water mass, body of water — Wasserkörper *m*, Wassermasse *f*
water-measuring vane *s.* hydrometric vane <hydr.>
water meniscus — Wassermeniskus *m*, Wasserkuppe *f*, Wasserkuppel *f*
water meter; water flowmeter — Wasseruhr *f*, Wasserzähler *m*, Wasserdurchflußmesser *m*, Wasserverbrauchsmesser *m*, Wassermengenmesser *m*, Wassermesser *m*
water mill — Wassermühle *f*
water monitor — Wasserüberwachungsgerät *n*, Wasserüberwachungsanlage *f*, Wassermonitor *m*
water monitoring, water survey — Wasserüberwachung *f*
water of constitution, constitution[al] water — Konstitutionswasser *n*
water of crystallization, crystal water, water of hydration — Kristallwasser *n*
water of hydration, hydration water, hydrate water — Hydratwasser *n*, Hydratationswasser *n*, Schwarmwasser *n*, Porenwinkelwasser *n*

water of hydration *s. a.* water of crystallization
water of imbibition — Quellungswasser *n*, Quellwasser *n*
water of infiltration, percolating water, seepage water — Sickerwasser *n*, Senkwasser *n*, Sinkwasser *n*

water permeability, permeability to water, permeability for water, perviousness to water — Wasserdurchlässigkeit *f*; Wasserpermeabilität *f* <Bio.>
water phantom — Wasserphantom *n*
water[ ]plane, plane of floatation, floatation plane — Schwimmebene *f*
water plane *s. a.* water stage
water plane *s. a.* surface <hydr.>
water[ ]plane area, floatation area, waterline section — Schwimmfeld *n*, Schwimmfläche *f*, Wasserlinienfläche *f*
water pocket <geo.> — Wasserloch *n* <Geo.>
water post, water-mark post — Wasserpegel *m*, Pegel *m*, Peil *m*
water potential — Wasserpotential *n*
water power, hydraulic power — Wasserkraft *f*, kinetische Energie *f* des Wassers, Wasserenergie *f*, hydraulische Kraft *f*

water pressure — Wasserdruck *m*, Wasserpressung *f*
water pressure deficit *s.* suction force
water pressure engine — Wassersäulenmaschine *f*, Wassersäulenmotor *m*
water pressure line, line of hydrostatic pressure — Wasserdruckfigur *f*, Wasserdrucklinie *f*
water-pressure test *s.* hydraulic test
water proofness, water tightness — Wasserdichtheit *f*, Wasserdichtigkeit *f*, Wasserundurchlässigkeit *f*
water purification, purification of water, water treatment — Wasseraufbereitung *f*; Wasserreinigung *f*
water ram *s.* hydraulic ram
water ratio, percentage of water — Wasserprozentgehalt *m*, prozentualer Wassergehalt *m*
water recirculation *s.* water reflux
water reflector — Wasserreflektor *m*, Wasserstreumantel *m*
water reflux, water return, water recirculation — Wasserrückfluß *m*, Wasserrückstrom *m*, Wasserrücklauf *m*

water relations, water balance, water budget — Wasserhaushalt *m*, Wasserbilanz *f*
water repellency *s.* hydrophoby
water repellent — wasserabstoßend, wasserabweisend
water resistance — Wasserwiderstand *m*, Strömungswiderstand *m* des Wassers
water-retaining capacity *s.* water-holding capacity
water return *s.* water reflux
water ring [air] pump — Wasserringpumpe *f*, Wasserringluftpumpe *f*; Flüssigkeitsringpumpe *f*
water rise head *s.* velocity head
waters — Gewässer *n*; Wässer *npl*
water sampling; water intake — Wasserentnahme *f*; Wasserentzug *m*; Wasserprobenahme *f*
water-saturated — wassergesättigt, wassersatt
water scale, water-level scale (gauge), staff gauge, gauge, gage <hydr.> — Lattenpegel *m*; Pegellatte *f*, Wassermeßlatte *f*, Wasserstock *m* <Hydr.>
water screw, hydraulic screw — Wasserschraube *f*, Wasserschnecke *f*
water seal *s.* liquid seal
water secretion *s.* secretion of water <bio.>
water separator *s.* separator
water[-]shed, watershed divide, divide <US>, line of separation between waters <geo.> — Wasserscheide *f*, Scheide *f*, Scheitelung *f*; Wasserscheidelinie *f*; Kammwasserscheide *f* <Geo.>

water shield; water shielding	Wasserabschirmung f; Wasserschirm m, Wasserschutzwand f	**water trap** **water-treating equipment**	s. separator Wasseraufbereitungsanlage f
water sky **water slurry,** water suspension	Wasserhimmel m wäßrige Suspension f, wäßrige Aufschlämmung f	**water treatment** **water[-] tube boiler**	s. water purification Wasserrohrkessel m, Siederohrkessel m
water softener, softener	Wasserenthärter m, Wasserenthärtungsmittel n, Enthärter m	**water tunnel,** water channel **water tunnel,** cavitation tunnel **water tunnel experiment** **water uptake** **water value** **water vane**	Wasserkanal m, Wassertunnel m Kavitationsprüfstand m Wasserkanalversuch m s. water intake s. water equivalent Wasserfahne f
water softening, water demineralizing, water demineralization, demineralization of water **water-soluble,** soluble in water **water splash,** water stain **water[-]spout**	Wasserenthärtung f wasserlöslich Wasserspritzer m Wasserhose f	**water-vapour atmosphere,** watervapour medium; steam atmosphere, steam medium **water vapour band,** steam band **water vapour content,** steam content	Wasserdampfatmosphäre f Wasserdampfbande f Wasserdampfgehalt m
water spray, spray, water veil **water spray,** water dust, spray	Wasserschleier m, Wassersprühregen m Wasserstaub m	**water vapour dissociation,** dissociation of water vapour, steam dissociation **water-vapour medium** **water vapour pressure,** steam pressure, steam tension	Wasserdampfspaltung f s. water-vapour atmosphere Wasserdampfdruck m, Wasserdampfpartialdruck m, Wasserdampfspannung f, Dampfspannung f
water stage, water level, water plane **water stage** **water stain,** water splash **water-stain mark**	Wasserstand m, Höhe f des Wasserspiegels, Wasser[spiegel]höhe f, Wasserpegel m, Wasserniveau n, W s. a. surface <hydr.> Wasserspritzer m Wasserfleck m	**water veil,** water spray, spray **water volume,** volume of water	Wasserschleier m, Wassersprühregen m Wasservolumen n, Wasserinhalt m
water-stir pyrheliometer **water streak** **water surface** **water-surface ascent,** water-head ascent, ascent; damming; swelling, swell, piling up; static water, slack [water], slack flow, afflux	Waterstirpyrheliometer n, Wasserrührpyrheliometer n; Rührwasserpyrheliometer n Wasserstreifen m Wasseroberfläche f; Wasserfläche f Stau m, hydraulischer Stau, Spiegelstau m, Wasserstau m, Aufstau m; Wasserstauung f, Stauung f, Aufstauung f	**water-water reactor,** reactor cooled and moderated by ordinary water, VVR, WWR **water wave** **water wheel** **water yield,** yield of water, discharge of water **Watkins['] factor**	Wasser-Wasser-Reaktor m, WWR <wassergekühlt und moderiert, meist: Druckwasserreaktor, selten: Siedewasserreaktor> Wasserwelle f Wasserrad n Wasserabgabe f; Wasserergiebigkeit f Watkinsscher Entwicklungsfaktor m, Watkins-Faktor m, arithmetischer Entwicklungskoeffizient m
water surface elevation **water survey,** water monitoring	s. velocity head Wasserüberwachung f	**Watson-Crick model** **Watson['s] lemma** **Watson-Sommerfeld transform[ation],** Sommerfeld-Watson transform[ation] **Watson transform[ation]**	Watson-Crick-Modell n Watsonsches Lemma n Watson-Sommerfeld-Transformation f, Sommerfeld-Watson-Transformation f Watsonsche Transformation f, Watson-Transformation f
water suspension, water slurry **water table** **water table contour,** contour [line] of water table, ground-water contour [line] **water test** **water tightness,** water proofness	wäßrige Suspension f, wäßrige Aufschlämmung f s. surface Grundwasserhöhenkurve f, Grundwasserhöhengleiche f, Grundwasserisohypse f s. hydraulic test Wasserdichtheit f, Wasserdichtigkeit f, Wasserundurchlässigkeit f	**watt,** W, w **wattage** **wattage** **Watt['s] equation**	Watt n, W Wattzahl f, Leistung f in Watt s. a. active power <el.> Wattsche Gleichung f
water-to-cement ratio, water-cement ratio	Wasser/Zement-Verhältnis n, Wasser-Zement-Faktor m, Wasser-Zement-Wert m, Wasserfaktor m, Wasser-Zement-Kennzahl f	**wattful current,** active current, real current **watt-hour meter,** active-energy meter, energy meter **Watt indicator** **Watt['s] law [for latent heat of vapour]**	Wirkstrom m, Wattstrom m Wattstundenzähler m, Wirkverbrauchszähler m, WV-Zähler m Wattscher Indikator m Wattsches Gesetz n [für die latente Wärme von Dampf]
water trajectory, trajectory of water particle **water transport,** transport of water [particles]	Wasserbahn f Wassertransport m, Wasserverfrachtung f, Wasserversetzung f	**wattless,** reactive, idle, imaginary <el.> **wattless component** **wattless component meter,** reactive-energy meter, var-hour meter	Blind-, wattlos, leistungslos <El.> s. reactive component Blindverbrauchszähler m, Blindwattstundenzähler m

wattless

wattless current, reactive current, idle current, imaginary current — Blindstrom *m*, wattloser Strom *m*, Wattlosstrom *m*

wattless feedback, reactive feedback — Blindrückkopplung *f*, Blindstromrückkopplung *f*

wattless power — s. reactive power

wattless voltage, reactive voltage, idle voltage, imaginary voltage — Blindspannung *f*, wattlose Spannung *f*, Wattlosspannung *f*

wattmeter, power meter <el.> — Wattmeter *n*, Leistungsmesser *m*, Wattmesser *m* <El.>

wattmeter constant — Wattmeterkonstante *f*

wattmeter loop — Wattmeterschwinger *m*

wattmeter parallel coil, parallel coil of wattmeter — Wattmeterspannungsspule *f*

wattmeter series coil, series coil of wattmeter — Wattmeterstromspule *f*

Watt regulator — Wattscher Regulator *m*

watt[-]second — s. joule

Watt spectrum — Wattsches Spektrum *n*

wave — Welle *f*

wave, body of the wave — Wellenkörper *m*

wave — s. a. billow

wave aberration — Wellenaberration *f*

wave acoustics, physical acoustics — Wellenakustik *f*

wave admittance, characteristic [wave] admittance <of waveguide> — Wellenleitwert *m*, charakteristischer Wellenleitwert <Wellenleiter>

wave along the line (wire) — s. axial line wave

wave analyzer — Wellenanalysator *m*

wave and particle aspects of light, two aspects of the nature of light — Doppelnatur *f* des Lichtes, Welle-Teilchen-Natur *f* des Lichtes

wave antenna; Beverage antenna — Beverage-Antenne *f*, Langdrahtantenne *f*; Wellenantenne *f*

wave antinode — s. antinodal point

wave at interface — s. boundary wave

wave band, wave range, wavelength range — Wellenbereich *m*, Wellenband *n*, Wellenlängenbereich *m*

wave base, base of the wave — Wellenbasis *f*, Wellenfuß *m*

wave beam — Wellenbündel *n*

wave cancellation, wave quenching — Wellenauslöschung *f*, Wellenlöschung *f*

wave category — Wellenkategorie *f*

wave centre, centre of the wave, origin of the wave — Wellenzentrum *n*

wave character, wave nature — Wellennatur *f*, Wellencharakter *m*

wave class — Wellenklasse *f*

wave clutter; wave reflection — Wellenreflexion *f*, Wellenrückwurf *m*

wave collector — s. receiving aerial

wave component, wave part — Wellenanteil *m*, Wellenkomponente *f*

wave contour, wave[] form, wave shape, wave profile — Wellenform *f*, Wellenkontur *f*, Wellenprofil *n*

wave-corpuscle duality — s. wave-particle duality

wave crest — s. crest [of the wave]

wave curve, wave line — Wellenlinie *f*

wave cyclone, wave depression — Wellenzyklone *f*

wave damping <hydr.> — Wellenbesänftigung *f*, Wellenberuhigung *f*, Wellendämpfung *f* <Hydr.>

wave deformation — s. waveform distortion

wave depression, wave cyclone — Wellenzyklone *f*

wave director — s. parasitic director <el.>

wave distortion — s. waveform distortion

wave disturbance, wave perturbation — Wellenstörung *f*, wellenförmige Störung *f*

wave[-] drag, wave resistance <aero., hydr.> — Wellenwiderstand *m* <Aero., Hydr.>

wave-drag coefficient <aero.> — Wellenwiderstandsbeiwert *m* <Aero.>

wave duct, duct, sound duct <ac.> — akustischer Wellenleiter *m*, Wellenleiter <Ak.>

wave duct in the atmosphere — s. atmospheric duct

wave dynamics — Wellendynamik *f*

wave dynamometer, wave-type dynamometer — Wellendynamometer *n*

wave energy flux — Wellenenergiefluß *m*

wave equation, Schröding-er['s] equation, Schröding-er['s] wave equation — Schrödinger-Gleichung *f*, Schrödingersche Wellengleichung *f*, Wellengleichung

wave equation — Wellengleichung *f*, Wellendifferentialgleichung *f*; Ausbreitungsgleichung *f*

wave equation — s. a. Helmholtz['] equation

wave excitation — Wellenanfachung *f*, Wellenanregung *f*

wave-exciting device; wave generator; wave producer — Wellenerreger *m*; Wellenerzeuger *m*

wave field — Wellenfeld *n*

wave filter — Wellenfilter *n*, Wellensieb *n*, elektrisches Filter *n*

wave[]form, wave shape, wave contour, wave profile — Wellenform *f*, Wellenkontur *f*, Wellenprofil *n*

waveform analyzer — Wellenformanalysator *m*

wave formation — s. wave generation

waveform distortion, wave distortion, wave deformation — Wellenformverzerrung *f*, Formverzerrung *f*

wave front, wave[-] front, surface of constant phase, surface of constant optical path, wave surface; wave head — Wellenfront *f*, Wellenfläche *f*; Wellenkopf *m*, Wellenstirn *f*

wavefront shearing interferometer — s. shearing interferometer

wavefront shearing technique — s. shearing technique <opt.>

wavefront velocity — Frontgeschwindigkeit *f*, Wellenfrontgeschwindigkeit *f*; Wellenkopfgeschwindigkeit *f*

wave function, Schröding-er['s] wave function, Schrödinger['s] function — Wellenfunktion *f*, Schrödingersche Wellenfunktion, Schrödinger-Funktion *f*, Schrödingersche Zustandsfunktion *f*

wave-generating — wellenerzeugend, wellenbildend; wellenschlagend

wave-generating machine — s. wave[-making] machine

wave generation, generation of waves; wave formation, formation of waves — Wellenerzeugung *f*; Wellenbildung *f*, Wellenentstehung *f*

wave generator — s. wave-exciting device

wave group — s. wave packet

wave[]guide — Wellenleiter *m*; Rohrleiter *m*; HF-Wellenleiter *m*, Hochfrequenzwellenleiter *m*

waveguide — s. a. hollow waveguide

waveguide accelerator — Wellenleiterbeschleuniger *m*

waveguide antenna — Hohlleiterantenne *f*, Hohlrohrantenne *f*

waveguide attenuation — Wellenleiterdämpfung *f*; Hohlleiterdämpfung *f*

waveguide attenuator — Hohlleiterdämpfungsglied *n*

waveguide bridge — Wellenleiterbrücke *f*, Wellenbrücke *f*

waveguide cable — Hohlleiterkabel *n*

waveguide circulator — s. circulator

waveguide effect — Wellenleitereffekt *m*

waveguide elbow, elbow of the waveguide	Wellenleiterknie n, Wellenleiterknickstelle f, Knie n des Wellenleiters, Knickstelle f des Wellenleiters; Hohlleiterknie n; Hohlleiterknickstelle f	wavelength constant, wave parameter, circular wave number, wave number, propagation factor, propagation constant, propagation coefficient $<2\pi/\lambda>$	Kreiswellenzahl f, Wellenzahl f, Wellendichte f, Betrag m des Ausbreitungsvektors, Ausbreitungsgröße f, Ausbreitungskonstante f, Fortpflanzungskonstante f, Fortpflanzungsmaß n, Phasenkonstante f $<2\pi/\lambda>$
waveguide feed	Hohlleiterspeisung f	wavelength constant	s. a. image phase constant
		wavelength constant	s. a. phase constant <el.>
waveguide filter	Wellenleitungsfilter n, Hohlleiterfilter n	wavelength cut-off, wavelength limit, wavelength threshold	Wellenlängengrenze f
waveguide impedance bridge	Hohlleiter-Impedanzmeßbrücke f, Hohlleiter-Impedanzbrücke f	wavelength in empty (free) space, wavelength in vacuo (vacuum)	s. vacuum value of wavelength
waveguide joint, waveguide junction, junction [of waveguide], joint [of waveguide]	Wellenleiterverbindung f, Wellenleiter[verbindungs]übergang m, Wellenleiter[an]kopplung f, Übergang m [zwischen Wellenleitern], Verbindung f [von Wellenleitern], Kopplung f [von Wellenleitern], Ankopplung f [von Wellenleitern], Hohlleiterübergang m, Hohlleiterverbindung f, Hohlleiter[an]kopplung f	wavelength limit, wavelength threshold, wavelength cut-off	Wellenlängengrenze f
		wavelength meter	s. wavemeter
		wavelength of the de Broglie wave[s]	s. Broglie wavelength / de
		wavelength range	s. wave range
		wavelength scale	Wellenlängenskale f, Wellenlängenskala f
		wavelength shifter, colour shifter	Wellenlängenschieber m
waveguide lens	Wellenleiterlinse f, Hohlleiterlinse f	wavelength standard, standard wavelength	Wellenlängennormal n
waveguide line	Wellenleitung f, Wellenleiter m		
waveguide line	s. a. hollow waveguide	wavelength switch	s. wave-range switch
waveguide linear accelerator	Wellenleiter-Linearbeschleuniger m	wavelength threshold, wavelength limit, wavelength cut-off	Wellenlängengrenze f
waveguide low-pass [filter]	Siebkasten m	wave-like, wavelike	wellenähnlich, wellenartig
waveguide mode, mode in guide	Hohlleiterwellentyp m, Hohlrohrwellentyp m, Rohrwellentyp m, Hohlleiterschwingungstyp m, Hohlrohrschwingungstyp m, Rohrschwingungstyp m	wave line, wave curve	Wellenlinie f
		wave loop	s. antinodal point
		wave[-making] machine, wave-generating machine	Wellenmaschine f
waveguide output	Wellenleiterauskopplung f	wave matrix	Wellenmatrix f
		wave-mechanical	wellenmechanisch
waveguide prism	Wellenleiterprisma n	wave-mechanical perturbation theory	wellenmechanische Störungsrechnung f
waveguide radiator	Rohrstrahler m, dielektrischer Rohrstrahler		
waveguide slotted line	s. measuring waveguide		
waveguide stub	s. stub	wave-mechanical resonance [of molecules]	wellenmechanische Resonanz f [der Moleküle]
waveguide subsection	Wellenleiterabschnitt m		
waveguide synchrotron	Wellenleitersynchrotron n	wave-mechanical theory of radiation	wellenmechanische Strahlungstheorie f
waveguide transformer	Hohlleitertransformator m; Wellenleitertransformator m; Wellenleiterübertrager m	wave mechanics	Wellenmechanik f, Undulationsmechanik f, Quantenmechanik f in der Ortsdarstellung
waveguide transmission line	s. hollow waveguide	wavemeter, wavelength meter; cymometer; ondometer; frequency meter, frequency indicator	Wellenmesser m, Wellenlängenmesser m; Frequenzmesser m, f-Messer m, Frequenzanzeiger m
waveguide Y circulator, gyrator, Y circulator	Gyrator m, Y-Zirkulator m, Y-Richtungsgabel f		
wave head	s. wave front	wave mode	s. mode of vibration
wave height, height of the wave	Wellenhöhe f	wave mode conversion, mode conversion, mode transformation, wave mode transformation	Wellentypumwandlung f, Wellentypumformung f, Wellentyptransformation f, Wellenformumwandlung f
wave image	s. wave representation		
wave impact	Wellenstoß m		
wave impedance	s. characteristic impedance		
wave impedance of free space	Feldwellenwiderstand m des freien Raumes	wave-mode filter	s. mode filter
wave impulse	s. radio-frequency pulse	wave mode transformation	s. wave mode conversion
wave in depth, depth wave	Tiefenwelle f	wave motion; undulation	Wellenbewegung f; wellenförmige Bewegung f; Undulation f
wave indicator, cymoscope	Wellenanzeiger m, Wellenindikator m		
wave in opposition of phase	s. push-pull wave	wave nature, wave character	Wellennatur f, Wellencharakter m
wave intensity, intensity of wave	Intensität f der Welle	wave node	s. node
wave-interference error	Welleninterferenzfehler m	wave normal	Wellennormale f, Wellenflächennormale f, Wellenfrontnormale f
wave in the push-pull mode	s. push-pull wave		
wave in the waveguide	s. guided wave	wave-normal ellipsoid	s. index ellipsoid
wave[]length, wavelength	Wellenlänge f	wave-normal surface, normal surface, wave velocity surface	Normalenfläche f, Wellennormalenfläche f, Wellenfläche f, Wellengeschwindigkeitsfläche f
wavelength comparator	Wellenlängenkomparator m		

wave normal velocity	Wellennormalengeschwindigkeit f, Normalengeschwindigkeit f	wave reflection; wave clutter	Wellenreflexion f, Wellenrückwurf m
wave number $\langle 1/\lambda \rangle$	Wellenzahl f $\langle 1/\lambda \rangle$	wave representation, wave image, wave picture, wave point of view	Wellenbild n, Wellenaspekt m, Wellenstandpunkt m
wave number	s. a. wavelength constant		
wave number vector, wave vector	Wellenzahlvektor m, Wellenvektor m		
wave number vector	s. a. circular wave vector	wave resistance, wave[-] drag <aero.>	Wellenwiderstand m <Aero.>
wave of action, action wave	Wirkungswelle f	waves, swell, sweep	Wellengang m
wave of division	Teilungswelle f	waves / in	s. waving
wave of electric type	s. $E[$-$]$ mode	wave science, wave theory	Wellenlehre f, Wellentheorie f
wave of magnetic type	s. $H[$-$]$ mode	wave shape, wave[ ]form, wave contour, wave profile	Wellenform f, Wellenkontur f, Wellenprofil n
wave of plastic strain	plastische Dehnungswelle f		
wave of rarefaction	s. rarefactional wave <aero., hydr.>	wave shaping circuit	Wellenformschaltung f
wave of the first order, billow, first-order wave, wave	Woge f, Welle f erster Ordnung	wave solution	Wellenlösung f
		wave spectrum, distribution of the wind waves, spectrum of the wind waves	Windseeverteilung f, Windseespektrum n, Windwellenspektrum n
wave of the parallel mode	Gleichtaktwelle f		
wave of translation, translational wave	Translationswelle f	wave steepness, steepness of wave edge	Wellensteilheit f, Steilheit f der Wellenflanke
wave of translation	s. a. advancing wave	wave surface, ray surface, ray velocity surface	Strahlenfläche f, Wellenfläche f
wave on the surface of liquids, liquid surface wave, surface wave on liquids	Oberflächenwelle f auf Flüssigkeiten, Welle f auf Flüssigkeitsoberflächen		
		wave surface	s. a. wave front
		wave tail	Wellenschwanz m
wave operator, Gordon['s] wave operator	Wellenoperator m, Gordonscher Wellenoperator	wave tank	Wellenwanne f, Wellentank m
		wave theory, wave science	Wellenlehre f, Wellentheorie f
wave optics, physical optics	Wellenoptik f, physikalische Optik f	wave theory of light, undulation (undulatory) theory of light, Huyghens['] undulation theory	Wellentheorie f des Lichtes [von Huygens], Undulationstheorie f, Lichttheorie f von Huygens
wave packet, wave group	Wellenpaket n, [nichtharmonische] Wellengruppe f		
wave parabola	Wellenparabel f		
wave parameter <of the line>	Wellenparameter m [der Leitung]	wave theory of matter	Wellentheorie f der Materie
wave parameter	s. wavelength constant	wave tilt	Wellenfrontwinkel m
wave parameter	s. phase constant <el.>	wave train, train of waves, pulse of waves, pulse train	Wellenzug m, Schwingungszug m
wave-parameter theory	Wellenparametertheorie f	wave train	s. a. pulse train
wave part, wave component	Wellenanteil m, Wellenkomponente f	wave trajectory, wave path	Wellenbahn f
		wave trap	s. absorption circuit <el.>
wave-particle duality, wave-particle parallelism, wave-corpuscle duality	Dualismus m Welle – Teilchen, Dualismus Welle – Korpuskel, Welle-Teilchen-Dualismus m	wave trough, trough [of the wave]	Wellental n
		wave tube, travelling-wave tube, travelling-wave-type wave tube	Lauffeldröhre f, Wanderfeldröhre f, „travelling-wave"-Röhre f
wave path, wave trajectory	Wellenbahn f	wave-type dynamometer, wave dynamometer	Wellendynamometer n
wave perturbation, wave disturbance	Wellenstörung f, wellenförmige Störung f	wave-type microphone	s. tubular microphone
wave phase velocity	s. phase velocity	wave vector, wave number vector	Wellenzahlvektor m, Wellenvektor m
wave phenomenon	Wellenerscheinung f, Wellenphänomen n	wave vector	s. a. circular wave vector
wave picture, wave point of view	s. wave representation	wave-vector space, k-space	k-Raum m, Wellenzahlvektorraum m, Wellenvektorraum m, Wellenzahlraum m
wave potential	s. Wiechert potential		
wave pressure	Wellendruck m		
wave producer	s. wave-exciting device	wave velocity	s. phase velocity
wave profile	s. wave[ ]form	wave velocity surface, normal surface, wave-normal surface	Normalenfläche f, Wellennormalenfläche f, Wellenfläche f, Wellengeschwindigkeitsfläche f
wave propagation, propagation of wave; translation of the wave	Wellenausbreitung f, Wellenfortpflanzung f, Ausbreitung f (Fortpflanzung f; Fortschreiten n) der Welle, Wellenfortschritt m		
		wave-wound coil	Wellenspule f
wave propagation velocity	s. phase velocity	wave zone	s. radiation zone
		waviness, ripple	Welligkeit f
wave property	Welleneigenschaft f	waviness in glass, internal waviness of glass	Schlieren fpl im Glas, Glasschlieren fpl
wave quenching, wave cancellation	Wellenauslöschung f, Wellenlöschung f	waving, undulatory, undulating, undular, in waves	wellenförmig, wellenartig
wave radiation, undulatory radiation	Wellenstrahlung f		
		wax block [photometer], Joly block photometer, Joly block screen	Joly-Photometer n, Jolysches Photometer n
wave radius	Wellenradius m		
wave range, wave band, wavelength range	Wellenbereich m, Wellenband n, Wellenlängenbereich m	waxed paper	Wachspapier n, Wachsschichtregistrierpapier n
wave-range switch, wavelength switch	Wellenbereichsumschalter m, Wellenbereichsschalter m, Wellenschalter m	waxed paper recorder	Wachsschreiber m, Wachspapierschreiber m
		waxing moon	zunehmender Mond m
wave ray	Wellenstrahl m	wax phantom	Wachsphantom n
wave recorder	Seegangschreiber m, Seegangsschreiber m	way, trajectory, path, pathway, path line, flight path	Bahn f, Bahnkurve f, Bahnlinie f, Flugbahn f, Trajektorie f

Wayne-Kerr universal bridge — Wayne-Kerrsche Universalmeßbrücke f, Wayne-Kerr-Universalbrücke f
way of hail squall — Hagelstraße f
Way-Wigner formula — Way-Wigner-Formel f, Formel f von Way und Wigner
Wb — s. weber
W band <≈ 0,5 cm> — W-Band n <≈ 0,5 cm>
W-boson, intermediate vector boson — W-Boson n, schweres Boson
weak absorption — schwache Absorption f
weak acid — schwache Säure f
weak base — schwache Base f
weak concentration — s. low concentration
weak convergence — s. convergence in probability
weak coupling, loose coupling, undercritical coupling <el.> — lose Kopplung f, unterkritische Kopplung <El.>
weak coupling, normal coupling <nucl.> — schwache Kopplung f, normale Kopplung <Kern.>
weak current, feeble current, low-voltage low current, low current — Schwachstrom m; niedriger Strom m, geringer Strom, schwacher Strom
weak discontinuity — schwache Unstetigkeit f
weak electrolyte — schwacher Elektrolyt m
weakened — s. smeared
weakening (of cross-section) — s. contraction <mech.>
weak extremum — schwaches Extremum n
weak focusing, constant-gradient focusing, CG focusing — schwache Fokussierung f
weak interaction — schwache Wechselwirkung f, schwache Kraft f, atonische Wechselwirkung
weak lens — schwache Linse f
weak limit — schwacher Limes m
weak line — schwache Linie f
weakly acid — schwachsauer
weak magnetic field, low magnetic field — schwaches Magnetfeld n
weak point, trouble spot, weak spot — Schwachstelle f
weak shock — schwacher Verdichtungsstoß m
weak shock wave, weak wave — schwache Stoßwelle (Welle) f
weak solution <chem.> — schwache Lösung f <Chem.>
weak spot, trouble spot, weak point — Schwachstelle f
weak topology — schwache (minimale) Topologie f
weak wave, weak shock wave — schwache Stoßwelle (Welle) f
wear, wear and tear, wearing, scuffing — Verschleiß m; Abtragung f; Abnutzung f
wearability, wearing capacity — Verschleißfähigkeit f, Verschleißbarkeit f, Abnutzbarkeit f; Verschleißkraft f
wearability, degree of wear — Verschleißgrad m, Grad m des Verschleißes, Abnutzungsgrad m
wear and tear — s. wear
wear by fatigue, fatigue wear — Ermüdungsverschleiß m
wear by impacts, impact wear, brinelling — Stoßverschleiß m
wear by rolling [motion], rolling wear — Rollverschleiß m, rollender Verschleiß m
wear due to slip — s. sliding wear
wearing — s. wear
wearing-away — s. weathering
wearing capacity, wearability — Verschleißfähigkeit f, Verschleißbarkeit f, Abnutzbarkeit f; Verschleißkraft f
wearing detail, wearing element, wearing part — Verschleißteil n (m)

wearing layer — Verschleißschicht f
wearing-off, wearing-out <of bearing> — Auslaufen n <Lager>
wearing part, wearing element, wearing detail
wearing rate — Verschleißgeschwindigkeit f
wear resistance, resistance to wear, resistance to abrasion — Verschleißfestigkeit f, Verschleißbeständigkeit f; Verschleißwiderstand m
weather; atmospheric conditions, meteorologic conditions, weather conditions — Wetter n; Witterung f, Wetterbedingungen fpl, Wetterverhältnisse npl, Witterungsverhältnisse npl
weather analysis, synoptic analysis, synoptic situation analysis — Wetteranalyse f
weather broadcast — s. weather report
weather chart — s. synoptic map <meteo.>
weather[]cock — s. wind vane
weather code, synoptic code — Wetterkode m, Wettercode m, Wetterschlüssel m
weather conditions — s. weather
weathered layer, decomposed layer — Verwitterungsschicht f
weather element — s. meteorological element
weather-eye satellite — s. weather satellite
weather factor — s. meteorological element
weather[]flag — s. wind vane
weather forecast, weather prognosis — Wettervorhersage f, Wetterprognose f
weather-induced — wetterbedingt
weather information — s. weather report
weathering, wearing-away, alteration, disintegration, decomposition, decay <geo.> — Verwitterung f <Geo.>
weathering by dissolution [of salts] — Lösungsverwitterung f
weathering by oxidation, oxidative weathering — Oxydationsverwitterung f
weathering due to salt crystallization — Salzsprengung f, Salzverwitterung f
weathering factors, active constituents of the atmosphere — Atmosphärilien pl
weathering of the walls, wall weathering — Wandverwitterung f
weather key day — Schlüsseltag m
weather limit, meteorological limit, meteorological divide — Wetterscheide f
weather map — s. synoptic map <meteo.>
weather maxim — Wetterregel f, Wetterspruch m
weather message — s. weather report
weathermometer — Verwitterungsmesser m
weather of ionosphere, ionospheric weather — Ionosphärenwetter n
weather outlook; tendency <meteo.> — Wetteraussichten fpl, Aussichten fpl; Tendenz f <Meteo.>
weather phenomenon — s. meteorologic phenomenon
weather prognosis, weather forecast — Wettervorhersage f, Wetterprognose f
weather[-]proof, weather-tight, weather-resistant, resistant to weathering, resistant to atmospheric conditions (corrosion) — wetterfest, wetterbeständig, witterungsbeständig

weather[-]proof	verwitterungsbeständig	wedge constant	Keilkonstante f, Steilheit f des Keils
weather radar	Wetterradar n; Regenradar n	wedge densitometer	Keilschwärzungsmesser m, Keildensitometer n
		wedge dislocation	Keilversetzung f
		wedge drawing test, Sachs' drawing test	Keilziehversuch m [nach Kayseler-Sachs]
weather reconnaissance	Wettererkundung f	wedge exposure meter, grey-wedge exposure meter	Keilbelichtungsmesser m
weather report; weather information, weather message; weather broadcast	Wetterbericht m; Wettermeldung f, Wetternachricht f	wedge filter	Keilfilter n
		wedge interferometer	s. wedge <opt.>
weather-resistant	s. weather[-]proof	wedge-like	s. wedge-shaped
weather satellite, weather-eye satellite, meteorological satellite	Wettersatellit m, Wetterbeobachtungssatellit m	wedge micrometer	Keilmikrometer n
		wedge of cold air, cold air wedge	Kaltluftkeil m
weather ship, meteorological ship	Wetterbeobachtungsschiff n, Wetterschiff n	wedge of high pressure	Hochdruckkeil m
		wedge of warm air, warm air wedge	Warmluftkeil m
weather-side flow	Luvströmung f	wedge photometer	Keilphotometer n <Astr.>; Graukeilphotometer n
weather-side vortex, windward eddy (vortex)	Luvwirbel m	wedge plate, wedge-shaped plate	Keilplatte f
weather-side wave, windward wave	Luvwelle f	wedge product	s. outer product
weather-side wave equation	Luvwellengleichung f	wedge rangefinder, wedge telemeter	Keilentfernungsmesser m
weather symbol	Wettersymbol n, Wetterzeichen n	wedge sensitometer	Keilsensitometer n
weather-tight	s. weather[-]proof	wedge-shaped, wedge-like	keilförmig, Keil-
weather[]vane	s. wind vane	wedge-shaped, sphenoid[al] <cryst.>	keilförmig, sphenoid[al], sphenoidisch <Krist.>
weave, interline flicker	Zwischenzeilenflimmern n, Zwischenlinienflimmern n, Zeilenflimmern n	wedge-shaped étalon, Rasmussen étalon	Keiletalon m [nach Rasmussen]
weber, volt-line, volt-second, Wb, Vs	Weber n, Voltsekunde f, Wb, Vs	wedge-shaped layer of air, lame étalon, Fabry-Pérot étalon, air wedge	Lame-étalon f, „lame étalon" f, Luftkeil m, keilförmige Luftschicht f, [keilförmige] Luftplatte f, Fabry-Pérot-Etalon m
Weber['s] Bessel function of the second kind	s. Neumann['s] function		
Weber['s] differential equation	s. differential equation of the parabolic cylinder function	wedge-shaped multilayer dielectric interference filter	s. graded interference filter
Weber-Fechner['s] law	Weber-Fechnersches Gesetz n, Weber-Fechnersches Grundgesetz n, Empfindungsgesetz n, psychophysisches Grundgesetz	wedge-shaped plate, wedge plate	Keilplatte f
		wedge-shaped shutter, wedge shutter, wedge-type shutter	Keilblende f; Keilverschluß m
Weber['s] function	s. Neumann['s] function	wedge slit	Keilspalt m, keilförmiger Spalt m
Weber['s] law	Webersches Gesetz n		
Weber['s] law of similarity, Weber['s] similarity law	Webersches Ähnlichkeitsgesetz n	wedge spectrogram	Keilspektrogramm n
Weber['s] number, Weber similarity number, W	Webersche Zahl f, Weber-Zahl f, Webersche Kennzahl f, Webersche Ähnlichkeitszahl f, W	wedge spectrograph, Seemann spectrograph, edge spectrograph	Graukeilspektrograph m, Keilspektrograph m, [Seemannscher] Schneidenspektrograph m, Seemann-Spektrograph m
Weber['s] photometer, Weber['s] tube photometer	Tubusphotometer n [von Weber], Weber-Photometer n, Webersches Photometer n, Webersches Flächenphotometer n, Flächenphotometer [nach Weber]	wedge telemeter	s. wedge rangefinder
		wedge-type shutter, wedge shutter, wedge-shaped shutter	Keilblende f; Keilverschluß m
		wedging, fastening with wedges, keying	Verkeilen n
Weber['s] rule	Webersche Regel f	wedging; invasion; irruption <meteo.>; intrusion	Einbruch m; Durchbruch m <Meteo.>
Weber['s] similarity law, Weber['s] law of similarity	Webersches Ähnlichkeitsgesetz n	weekly dose	Wochendosis f, wöchentliche Dosis f
Weber similarity number, Weber['s] number, W	Webersche Zahl f, Weber-Zahl f, Webersche Kennzahl f, Webersche Ähnlichkeitszahl f, W	weekly thermogram	Wochenthermogramm n
Weber['s] transform[ation]	Webersche Transformation f	weeping-out	s. dropwise condensation
Weber['s] tube photometer	s. Weber['s] photometer	Wegener['s] theory of continental drift	s. continental drift theory
web member	s. diagonal member	Wehnelt cathode, Wehnelt electrode	Wehnelt-Katode f, Wehnelt-Elektrode f
web network	s. lattice <mech.>	Wehnelt control grid, Wehnelt cylinder	s. modulator
Weddle['s] rule [for numerical quadrature]	Weddlesche Regel f	Wehnelt electrode, Wehnelt cathode	Wehnelt-Katode f, Wehnelt-Elektrode f
wedge, optical wedge, wedge interferometer <opt.>	Keil m, optischer Keil <Opt.>	Wehnelt grid	s. modulator
wedge, neutral wedge, grey wedge	Graukeil m, Neutralkeil m, Keil m	Wehnelt interrupter, electrolytic interrupter	elektrolytischer Unterbrecher m, Wehnelt-Unterbrecher m
		Wehnelt modulator	s. modulator
wedge compensator	Drehkeilpaar n, Herschelsches Doppelprisma n, Herschel-Prisma n, Keilkompensator m, Diasporameter n	Weibull distribution	Weibull-Verteilung f
		Weierstrass['] approximation theorem	Weierstraßscher Approximationssatz m

Weierstrass['] comparison test, Weierstrass M-test [for uniform convergence], Weierstrass['] test for convergence — Weierstraßsches Vergleichskriterium *n*

Weierstrass['] condition — Weierstraßsche Bedingung *f*

Weierstrass-Erdmann corner condition, Weierstrass-Erdmann vertex condition — Weierstraß-Erdmannsche Eckenbedingung *f*

Weierstrass function, Weierstrassian Weierstrassian 𝔈-function — s. Weierstrassian elliptical function s. Weierstrassian function 𝔈

Weierstrassian elliptical function, Weierstrass function, Weierstrassian — Weierstraßsche p-Funktion *f*, Weierstraßsche elliptische Funktion *f*, p-Funktion *f*

Weierstrassian function 𝔈, Weierstrassian 𝔈-function, 𝔈-function of Weierstrass — Weierstraßsche 𝔈-Funktion *f*, Exzeßfunktion *f*

Weierstrassian sigma-function, sigma-function [of Weierstrass] — Sigmafunktion *f* [von Weierstraß], Weierstraßsche Sigmafunktion

Weierstrass M-test [for uniform convergence] — s. Weierstrass['] comparison test

Weierstrass['] preparation theorem — Weierstraßscher Vorbereitungssatz *m*

Weierstrass['] quotient test — Weierstraßsches Quotientenkriterium *n*

Weierstrass['] test for convergence — s. Weierstrass['] comparison test

Weierstrass['] theorem — Weierstraßscher Näherungssatz *m*, Satz *m* von Caserati-Weierstraß

Weierstrass['] zeta function, zeta function [of Weierstrass], ζ function — Weierstraßsche Zeta-Funktion *f*, Zeta-Funktion [von Weierstraß], ζ-Funktion *f*

Weigert effect <phot.> — Weigert-Effekt *m*, Doppelbrechung *f* durch Belichtung <Phot.>

weighable, ponderable — wägbar
weigh bridge — s. weighing bridge
weighed amount — s. amount weighed
weighed quantity — s. amount weighed
weighing — Wägung *f*, Wägen *n*

weighing bottle — s. pyknometer
weighing bridge, weigh bridge, bridge scale, platform scale (balance) — Brückenwaage *f*
weighing by substitution — s. substitution Borda weighing
weighing dish — s. scale
weighing error — Wägefehler *m*, Wägungsfehler *m*
weighing glass — Wägeglas *n*, Wägegläschen *n*

weighing[-]machine, weighing table — Tafelwaage *f*, Roberval-Waage *f*
weighing scale, scale, pan, scale pan, weighing dish, dish [of the scales] — Waagschale *f*, Waageschale *f*
weighing table, weighing[-]machine — Tafelwaage *f*, Roberval-Waage *f*
weight, balancing weight — Gewichtsstück *n*, Massenstück *n*, Gewicht *n*

weight <for Lie group> — Gewicht *n* <für Liesche Gruppen>
weight <mech.> — Gewicht *n* <Mech.>
weight, weighting function, weight function — Gewichtsfunktion *f*, Gewicht *n*, Belegungsfunktion *f*, Einflußfunktion *f* <Opt.>

weight — s. a. degree of degeneracy
weight — s. a. sinker
weight after vibration, vibrational weight — Rüttelgewicht *n*
weight areometer, weight hydrometer, constant displacement hydrometer — Gewichtsaräometer *n*
weight average molecular weight — Gewichtsmittel *n* des Molekulargewichts

weight barometer, gravity barometer — Waagenbarometer *n*
weight by volume — s. weight per unit volume
weight concentration — s. mass concentration

weight content, mass content, content by mass, content by weight — Gehalt *m* in Masseeinheiten, Masse[n]gehalt *m*, Gewichtsgehalt *m*
weight coulometer, weight voltameter, mass coulometer (voltameter) — Massencoulometer *n*, Massenvoltameter *n*, Gewichtscoulometer *n*, Gewichtsvoltameter *n*
weight diagram — Gewichtsdiagramm *n*
weighted arithmetic average, weighted average, weighted mean — gewogenes Mittel *n*, allgemeines arithmetisches Mittel, gewogener Mittelwert *m*, Gewichtsmittel *n*, gewichtetes Mittel
weight factor, weighting factor, weighting coefficient — Gewichtsfaktor *m*, Gewicht *n*, Wichtungsfaktor *m*; Wägungsfaktor *m* <Stat.>
weight flow (rate) — s. mass flow <mass per unit time>
weight fraction, mass fraction, mass ratio, weight ratio — Massenbruch *m*, Masseanteil *m*, Massefraktion *f*, Gewichtsanteil *m*, Gewichtsfraktion *f*, Gewichtsprozentsatz *m*
weight function, loss function <stat.> — Verlustfunktion *f* <Stat.>
weight function — s. a. weighting function
weight hydrometer — s. weight areometer
weight hygrometer — Gewichtshygrometer *n*
weighting — Wichtung *f*
weighting coefficient, weighting factor — s. weight factor
weighting function, weight function, weight — Gewichtsfunktion *f*, Gewicht *n*, Belegungsfunktion *f*, Belegung *f*; Einflußfunktion *f* <Opt.>
weighting function [of system] — s. a. unit[-] impulse response
weightless, imponderable, agravic — schwerelos
weightless, imponderable, unponderable, unweighable — unwägbar [gering], Spuren-; gewichtslos
weightlessness — s. absence of gravity
weight matrix — Gewichtsmatrix *f*
weight-median aerodynamic diameter — gewichtsmedianer aerodynamischer Durchmesser *m*, Gewichts-MAD *m*
weight number — Gewichtszahl *f*
weight of structure — Strukturgewicht *n*
weight of the observation — Gewicht *n* der Beobachtung
weight of the tensor — Gewicht *n* des Tensors
weight per cent, mass per cent, mass %, wt.% — Masseprozent *n*, Gewichtsprozent *n*, Masse-%, Masse%, Gew.-%, Gew.%
weight per cents — s. percentage by mass
weight per unit length — s. mass per unit length
weight per unit volume, weight by volume, unit (volumetric, volume, bulk) weight — Rohdichte *f*, Raumgewicht *n* [ohne Wasser]
weight pressure — Gewichtsdruck *m* <Glied ρz in der Bernoullischen Gleichung>
weight ratio — s. weight fraction
weight thermometer — Überlaufthermometer *n*
weight-to-thrust ratio, mass-to-thrust ratio — Masse-Schub-Verhältnis *n*

weight voltameter — s. weight coulometer
Weimarn equation / Von — von Weimarnsche Gleichung *f*
Weingarten['s] theorem <first *or* second> — Weingartenscher Satz *m*, Satz von Weingarten <erster *oder* zweiter>
Weinland effect <phot.> — Weinland-Effekt *m* <Phot.>

Weinstein bound <for eigenvalues> — Weinsteinsche Schranke *f*
Weinstein['s] theorem — [Krylow-Bogoljubow-] Weinsteinscher Einschließungssatz *m*

weir — Wehr *n*, Wasserwehr *n*; Überfall *m*, Wasserüberfall *m*

weir, measuring weir, measurement weir, notched weir — Meßüberfall *m*, Meßwehr *n*, Wehr *n*

weir	s. dam	weld, joint	Klebstelle f
weir crest, crest of the weir, crest of the dam, dam crest	Wehrkrone f, Dammkrone f, Sperrmauerkrone f, Bekrönung f	weld decay [phenomenon]	Schweißversprödung f; Korrosion f der Schweißnaht
weir equation, formula of discharge over weir	Überfallgleichung f, Wehrformel f	welded joint	Schweißverbindung f
weir height, height of weir	Wehrhöhe f, Dammhöhe f, Höhe f der Dammkrone	welding together, fusion welding	Verschweißen n <z. B. beim Verschleiß>
weir with free fall	s. free weir	Welker effect, magnetic barrier layer effect	Welker-Effekt m
weir with lifting gates, dam with lifting gates	Schützenwehr n	well; source; spring <geo.>	Quelle f <Geo.>
Weiss constant	s. paramagnetic Curie point [of temperature]		
Weiss['] domain	s. ferromagnetic domain <magn.>	well conducting	gut leitend
Weissenberg camera, Weissenberg goniometer, Weissenberg photogoniometer	Weissenberg-Goniometer n, Weissenberg-Böhm-Goniometer n, Röntgengoniometer n nach Weissenberg[-Böhm], Weissenberg-Kammer f, Weissenberg-Kamera f	well counter	s. well-type counter
		well-defined beam, well-focused beam	scharf[fokussiert]er Strahl m
		well depth	s. potential well depth
		well-focused beam, well-defined beam	scharf[fokussiert]er Strahl m
		well logging	s. borehole logging
Weissenberg effect	Weissenberg-Effekt m	well model, potential well model	Potentialtopfmodell n
Weissenberg goniometer	s. Weissenberg camera		
Weissenberg['s] method	Weissenberg-Böhm-Verfahren n, Weissenberg-[Böhm-]-Methode f, Weissenbergsche Methode f, Weissenbergsches Verfahren n	well-ordered aggregate, well ordered-set, normally ordered aggregate	wohlgeordnete Menge f, vollständig geordnete Menge, geordnete Menge, Wohlordnung f
		well ordering, well-ordering relation	Wohlordnung f
Weissenberg pattern	s. Weissenberg photograph	well-ordering principle	s. well ordering statement
Weissenberg photogoniometer	s. Weissenberg camera	well-ordering relation	s. well[-]ordering
Weissenberg photograph, Weissenberg pattern	Weissenberg-Aufnahme f, Weissenberg-Diagramm n	well ordering statement, well-ordering theorem, well-ordering principle, Zermelo['s] theorem	Wohlordnungssatz m [von Zermelo], Zermeloscher Wohlordnungssatz, Satz m von Zermelo
Weiss field	s. Weiss internal field		
Weiss field constant	s. molecular field coefficient	well-posed problem	korrekt gestelltes Problem n, sachgemäßes Problem
Weissfloch['s] transformer theorem	Übertragertheorem n von Weissfloch, Weissflochsches Übertragertheorem	well-type counter [tube], well counter	Zählrohr n mit Probenkanal, Bohrlochzähler m
Weiss['] formula	Weisssche Beziehung f, Weissscher Ansatz m		
Weiss-Forrer method, method of Weiss and Forrer	Methode f von Weiß und Forrer, Weiß-Forrersche Methode	well-type crystal	Bohrlochkristall m
Weiss index	Weißscher Index m		
		Welsbach burner	Auer-Brenner m
Weiss internal field, Weiss molecular field, molecular field	molekulares [Weisssches] Feld n, inneres [Weisssches] Feld n, inneres Molekularfeld n [nach Weiss], Molekularfeld von Weiss, [Weisssches] Molekularfeld, Weisssches Molekülfeld (Feld, Magnetfeld n)	Welsbach [gas] light	s. gas light
		Welsbach mantle, gas mantle, incandescent mantle, mantle	Auer-Glühkörper m, Auer-Strumpf m, Glühkörper m, Glühstrumpf m, Gasglühstrumpf m
		Welton-Smets criterion	Welton-Smets-Kriterium n
Weisskopf-Ewing formula	Weisskopf-Ewing-Formel f	Weltzeit	s. Universal time
Weisskopf radius of collision	Weisskopfscher Stoßradius m	Wendt diagram, Wendt plot	Wendtsches Diagramm n, Wendt-Diagramm n
Weisskopf unit	Weisskopf-Einheit f	Wenham prism	Wenham-Prisma n
Weiss magneton	Weisssches Magneton n	Wentzel-Kramers-Brillouin[-Jeffreys] approximation (method)	s. W.K.B. approximation
Weiss molecular field	s. Weiss internal field		
Weiss temperature, characteristic temperature [of Weiss]	Weiss-Temperatur f, Weisssche Temperatur f, charakteristische Temperatur [von Weiss]		
		Werner band	Werner-Bande f
Weiss['] theory [of ferromagnetism], domain theory	Weisssche Theorie f [des Ferromagnetismus], Domänentheorie f	Werner complex, co-ordination entity; complex compound, complex, co-ordination compound	Komplexverbindung f, Komplex m, Koordinationsverbindung f
Weiss zone law	s. zone law	Wernicke [dispersion] prism	Wernicke-Prisma n
Weizsäcker['s] formula [/ von], semi-empirical mass formula	Weizsäckersche Formel f [für die Kernbindungsenergie], Weizsäcker-Gleichung f, Weizsäckersche Gleichung f, halbempirische Massenformel f von Weizsäcker, von Weizsäckersche Formel	Wertheim['s] equation	Wertheimsche Gleichung f
		Wessely keratometer, keratometer	Scheitelabstandsmesser m; Wesselysches Keratometer n, Keratometer [nach Wessely]
		Westcott cross-section	s. effective thermal cross-section
Weizsäcker['s] turbulence theory, turbulence theory, vortex hypothesis	Turbulenztheorie f von Weizsäcker[s], Wirbelhypothese f nach Weizsäcker, Weizsäckersche Wirbelhypothese	west-east flow, west-east stream	West-Ost-Strömung f
		west-east velocity	West-Ost-Geschwindigkeit f
		western amplitude, occasive amplitude	Abendweite f
Weizsäcker-Williams method	Weizsäcker-Williamssches Verfahren n, Verfahren von Weizsäcker und Williams	Western-European time	s. Universal time
		western spot	s. preceding spot
weld	Schweißstelle f, Schweißung f	western synoptic situation	Westwetterlage f, Westlage f, Westwetter n

western twilight arch	westlicher Dämmerungsbogen m	wet technique, wet process, wet method	nasses Verfahren n, nasser Weg m, Naßverfahren n
Weston cell	s. Weston normal standard cell	wetted perimeter	benetzter Umfang m, Bettumfang m, Umfang des benetzten Flußquerschnitts
Weston centrifuge	Weston-Zentrifuge f		
Weston normal standard cell, Weston cell, normal standard cell, cadmium standard cell, cadmium cell	Weston-Element n, Weston-Normalelement n, Weston-Normalzelle f, Kadmiumnormalelement n, Cadmiumnormalelement n	Wetthauer bench	Wetthauer-Bank f
		Wetthauer test	Verfahren n der streifenden Abbildung, Wetthauer-Verfahren n; Wetthauersche Spiegelprüfmethode f
Weston scale, Weston speed rating	Weston-Skala f	wetting	s. humidification
		wetting agent, spreading agent	Netzmittel n, Benetzungsmittel n, Benetzer m
West-point, west point, W	Westpunkt m, W		
westward drift	Westtrift f, Westwärtstrift f, Westdrift f, Westwärtsdrift f, Westwärtsverschiebung f, Westwärtswanderung f	wetting angle	s. angle of contact
		wetting heat, heat of wetting	Benetzungswärme f
		Weyl['s] conformal curvature tensor	s. Weyl['s] tensor
west wind belt, belt of west winds	Westwindgürtel m, Westwindzone f, Westwindband n	Weyl['s] conform tensor	s. Weyl['s] tensor
		Weyl['s] co-ordinates	Weylsche Koordinaten fp l
west wind drift	Westwinddrift f, Westwindtrift f	Weyl-Eddington tensor, tensor of Weyl and Eddington	Weyl-Eddingtonscher Tensor m
wet; wetness; humidity	Nässe f		
wet adiabat[ic]	s. moist adiabat	Weyl['s] equation, two-component equation of the neutrino	Weylsche Gleichung f, Zweikomponentengleichung f des Neutrinos
wet adiabatic lapse rate	s. saturated adiabatic lapse rate		
wet- and dry-bulb hygrometer	s. psychrometer	Weyl['s] postulate, coherency postulate, postulate of coherency	Kohärenzpostulat n, Weylsches Postulat n
wet- and dry-bulb hygrometer equation, psychrometer equation, psychrometric formula	Psychrometerformel f, psychrometrische Gleichung f	Weyl['s] solution	Weylsche Lösung f, statische zylinder symmetrische Lösung der Einsteinschen Gravitationsgleichungen
wet- and dry-bulb psychrometer (thermometer)	s. psychrometer		
wet-bulb depression	s. wet-bulb temperature difference	Weyl space	Weylscher Raum m
		Weyl spinor	s. two-component spinor
wet-bulb potential temperature; pseudo wet-bulb potential temperature	potentielle Temperatur f des feuchten Thermometers	Weyl['s] tensor, Weyl['s] conform tensor, conform tensor, Weyl['s] conformal curvature tensor, conformal curvature tensor	Weylscher Tensor m, Konformkrümmungstensor m
wet-bulb reading (temperature), reading on the wet-bulb thermometer, humid temperature, ice-bulb temperature	Feuchttemperatur f, Naßtemperatur f, Temperatur f des feuchten Thermometers	Weyl['s] uniform field theory	Weylsche einheitliche Feldtheorie f
		Whatman paper	Whatman-Papier n
wet-bulb temperature difference, wet-bulb depression, psychrometer difference, psychrometric difference, depression of wet-bulb	psychrometrische Differenz (Temperaturdifferenz) f, Psychrometerdifferenz f	Wheatstone['s] bridge, comparison bridge; Wheatstone bridge circuit	Wheatstonesche Brücke (Schleifdrahtbrücke) f, Wheatstone-Brücke f, Wheatstonesche Meßbrücke f, W-Brücke f, Wheatstonesche Brückenschaltung f, Widerstandsbrücke f
wet-bulb thermometer	befeuchtetes Thermometer n, benetztes Thermometer, Naßthermometer n		
		Wheatstone bridge circuit	s. Wheatstone['s] bridge
wet cell, hydroelectric cell	nasses Element n, Naßelement n, hydroelektrisches Element	Wheatstone photometer	Wheatstone-Photometer n, Wheatstonesches Photometer n
		Wheatstone stereoscope	Wheatstonesches Stereoskop n
wet collodion plate, collodion wet plate	nasse Kollodiumplatte f, Kollodiumnaßplatte f, Naßkollodiumplatte f, Naßplatte f	Wheatstone['s] theorem	Satz m von Wheatstone, Wheatstonescher Satz
		wheel; pulley; roller	Rolle f; Scheibe f; Rad n
wet electrolytic capacitor	Flüssigkeits[elektrolyt]kondensator m, Naßelektrolytkondensator m	wheel, blade, screw <of current meter or vane>	Schaufel f, Flügelschaufel f
		wheel barometer, dial barometer	Zeigerbarometer n
wet fog	nasser (nässender) Nebel m	Wheeler-Feynman quantum theory	Wheeler-Feynmansche Quantentheorie f
wet labile, moist-labile, pseudo-labile	feuchtlabil, pseudolabil	Wheeler['s] formula	Wheelersche Formel f
wet method, wet process, wet technique	nasses Verfahren n, nasser Weg m, Naßverfahren n		
wet method paste	s. magnetic paste	wheel magnetron, multisphere magnetron	Radmagnetron n
wetness; wet; humidity	Nässe f		
wet process, wet technique, wet method	nasses Verfahren n, nasser Weg m, Naßverfahren n	wheel of circulating warm air, warm air wheel	Warmluftrad n
		wheel of recoil	s. Segner['s] water wheel
wet-stable, moist-stable	feuchtstabil	Whewell fringe	s. interference of diffracted light
wet steam	Naßdampf m <Wasser>		
wet steam	s. a. saturated steam	Whiddington['s] law	Whiddingtonsches Gesetz n
wettability	Netzfähigkeit f; Netzbarkeit f, Benetzbarkeit f		
		while-you-wait photography	s. one-step photographic process

whirl; vortex <pl.: vortices, vortexes>; eddy <large-scale>	Wirbel m; Wirbelgebilde n	white horse, white[]cap	Schaumwelle f, schaumgekrönte Welle f; Schaumkrone f
whirl	s. a. whirlwind <meteo.>	white lamp, lamp producing white light	Weißlichtlampe f, Weißlampe f
whirl	s. a. swirl	white light; specified achromatic light	weißes Licht n, Glühlicht n
whirl	s. a. vortex motion		
whirled psychrometer	s. whirling psychrometer		
whirled thermometer	s. sling thermometer	white masking	s. veiling by white
whirling, eddying, turbulence, swirling motion, eddy	Wirbelung f, Verwirblung f; Durchwirbelung f	whiteness	Weißheit f, Weiße f
		white noise, uniform random noise	weißes Rauschen n; Weißgeräusch n
whirling; vortical, vortex; eddying, eddy; vortex-like	Wirbel-; wirblig, wirbelig, wirbelnd; wirbelförmig, wirbelartig; wirbelbehaftet	white object, reflecting body, white body	spiegelnder Körper m, weißer Körper, weißes Objekt n
whirling currents	s. eddy currents	white of higher order, high-order white	Weiß m höherer Ordnung
whirling hygrometer, whirling psychrometer, sling psychrometer, whirled psychrometer	Schleuderpsychrometer n	white peak	
		white point, location of white	Farbort m des Weiß, Weißpunkt m
		white quantum noise	weißes Quantenrauschen n
whirling squall	Wirbelbö f	white radiation, heterogeneous (continuous, steady) radiation	weiße Strahlung f, kontinuierliche Strahlung
whirling storm	s. tropical cyclone		
whirling thermometer	s. sling thermometer		
whirling up	s. wind pick-up	white rainbow, fog bow	Nebelbogen m, weißer Regenbogen m
whirling wind	s. whirlwind		
whirlpool	s. swirl		
whirlwind, whirling wind, whirl <meteo.>	Trombe f, Kleintrombe f, Luftwirbel m, Wirbelwind m, Wirbel m <Meteo.>	white reflection	weiße Reflexion f
		whiter than white, ultra-white	Ultraweiß n
whirlwind over land, wind-spout	Windhose f, Trombe f über Land, Wettersäule f	white shaded	s. non-zero white content/ having <of chromatic colour>
		white shading	s. veiling by white
whisker, crystal whisker, crystal needle; needle-shaped crystal	Whisker m <pl.: Whisker oder Whiskers>, Haarkristall m, Fadenkristall m, Einfadenkristall m, Nadelkristall m, Kristallnadel f	White Spots <of Saturn>	Weiße Flecke mpl <des Saturn>
		white-to-black amplitude range	Schwarz-Weiß-Amplitudenbereich m
		white veiling	s. veiling by white
whisker wire, Wollaston wire, capillary wire	Haardraht m; Wollaston-Draht m	Whittaker['s] confluent hypergeometric function	s. Whittaker['s] function
		Whittaker['s] differential equation	Whittakersche Differentialgleichung f
whispering	Flüstern n	Whittaker['s] function, Whittaker['s] confluent hypergeometric function, Coulomb wave function	Whittaker-Funktion f, Whittakersche Funktion f, Coulomb-Wellenfunktion f
whispering gallery	Flüstergalerie f, Flüstergewölbe n		
whispering mode	Totalreflexionsmode f, Flüstermode f, flüsternder Schwingungstyp m		
		Whittaker potential	Whittaker-Potential n, Whittakersches Potential n
whispering wind	Wisperwind m	whole-body counter, whole-body spectrometer (radiation meter), human-body counter (radiation meter, spectrometer)	Ganzkörperzähler m, Ganzkörperspektrometer n, „human-body counter" m, Ganzkörper-Aktivitätszähler m
whistle, pipe <ac.>	Pfeife f <Ak.>		
whistle	s. a. whistling <ac.>		
whistler, whistler-type noise, whistling atmospheric	Whistler m, atmosphärische Pfeifstörung f		
whistling, whistle <ac.>	Pfeifen n; Pfiff m <Ak.>	whole body dose; body burden	Körperdosis f, Ganzkörperdosis f, Vollbestrahlungsdosis f; Körperbelastung f
whistling atmospheric	s. whistler		
white body, reflecting body, white object	spiegelnder Körper m, weißer Körper, weißes Objekt n	whole-body exposure, whole-body irradiation, total body exposure, total body irradiation <externally>	Ganzkörperbestrahlung f, Vollbestrahlung f, Totalbestrahlung f <äußerlich>
white[]cap, white horse	Schaumwelle f, schaumgekrönte Welle f; Schaumkrone f		
white content	Weißgehalt m; Weißanteil m <Ostwald>	whole-body radiation meter, whole-body spectrometer	s. whole-body counter
white content meter	Weißgehaltmesser m	whole gale, gale <of Beaufort No. 10>	schwerer Sturm m <Stärke 10>
		whole half-width	s. line width
		wholeness, integrity	Ganzheit f
white dwarf, white-dwarf star	weißer Zwerg m, weißer Zwergstern m, Liliputaner m	wholesomeness	Zuträglichkeit f
white frost, hoar frost, hoar-frost; hoar frost deposit	Rauhreif m	whole tone	Ganzton m, ganzer Ton m
		Wichmann compass, Wichmann sight compass	Stockbussole f [von Wichmann]
whiteglow	s. white heat		
white halo, colourless halo	weißer Halo m, farbloser Halo	Wick['s] chronological operator, Wick['s] operator, T operator	Wick-Operator m, Wickscher Operator m, T-Operator m, Wickscher Zeitordnungsoperator m
Whitehead['s] theory of gravitation	Whiteheadsche Gravitationstheorie f		
white heart, white[-] heart iron, white[-] heart malleable cast iron	weißer Temperguß m, Weißguß m, europäischer Temperguß	Wick['s] chronological product, chronological product, time-ordered product	chronologisches Produkt n, Wicksches Produkt, zeitgeordnetes Produkt, T-Produkt n
white heat, incalescence, incandescence, glowing heat, white glow, glow heat	Weißglut f, Weißglühen n, Weißglühhitze f, Weißgluthitze f, Inkaleszenz f <1 300 °C und mehr>	Wick['s] method, Chandrasekhar['s] method, Wick-Chandrasekhar method, method of discrete ordinates	Wicksche Methode f, Verfahren n von Chandrasekhar, Methode der diskreten Ordinaten
white hole	weißes Loch n		

Wick['s] operator	s. Wick['s] chronological operator
Wick['s] theorem	Wickscher Satz m
wide-angle [aerial] camera; wide-angle lens camera	Weitwinkelkammer f <Photogrammetrie>; Weitwinkelkamera f
wide-angle cathode	Weitwinkelkatode f
wide-angle converter	Weitwinkelvorsatzlinse f
wide-angled antenna, wide-angle antenna	Weitwinkelantenne f
wide-angle eyepiece	Weitwinkelokular n [von Erfle], Okular n weit
wide-angle lens, wide-angle objective	Weitwinkelobjektiv n, Weitwinkel m
wide-angle lens camera	s. wide-angle [aerial] camera
wide angle lighting fitting	Breitstrahler m, breitstrahlende Leuchte f
wide-angle magnifier	Weitwinkellupe f
wide-angle objective	s. wide-angle lens
wide-angle observation, wide-angle viewing	Weitwinkelbeobachtung f
wide-angle scattering, large-angle scattering	Weitwinkelstreuung f, Streuung f um große Winkel, Großwinkelstreuung f
wide-angle viewing, wide-angle observation	Weitwinkelbeobachtung f
wide-aperture	s. high-power
wide-band amplifier tube	Breitbandverstärkerröhre f
wide deflection angle tube	Weitwinkelablenkröhre f
wide-gap chamber, wide-gap spark chamber	Funkenkammer f mit großem Elektrodenabstand
wide-mouthed flask, wide-necked flask	Weithalskolben m
widening; expansion	Weitung f, Ausweitung f; Aufweitung f
widening; broadening	Verbreiterung f
widening, spreading <of the beam>	Strahlverbreiterung f, Bündelverbreiterung f, Verbreiterung f des Strahls
widening, broadening, expansion, enlargement <mech.>	Erweiterung f <Mech.>
widening coil, enlarging coil	Expansionsspule f
widening of pores	Porenerweiterung f
widening of the spectral line	s. line broadening
wide-range radiation dosimeter	Weitbereichdosimeter n
Wideröe['s] condition, Wideröe['s] flux condition, condition of Wideröe	1:2-Bedingung f [des Betatrons], Wideröe-Bedingung f, Wideröescher Satz m, erste Grundbedingung f des Betatrons, Wideröesche Bahnbedingung f
Widmanstätten pattern, Widmanstätten structure	Widmanstättensches Gefüge n, Widmanstättensche Figuren fpl
width at water level	Wasserspiegelbreite f, Spiegelbreite f
width clipping, pulse-width clipping	Impulsbreitenbegrenzung f
width for capture, capture width	Einfangbreite f
width of air gap, air-gap width, gap width, length of air gap, gap length	Polschuhabstand m, Luftspaltlänge f, Luftspaltbreite f
width of bearing zone, bearing zone width	Peilbreite f
width of cloud, cloud width	Wolkenbreite f
width of scale division	s. scale value
width of the barrier layer	s. barrier width
width of the dislocation	Versetzungsbreite f
width of the forbidden gap, forbidden gap width, gap width, energy gap width	Breite f der verbotenen Zone, Breite der Energielücke, Breite des verbotenen Energiebandes
width of the potential barrier, barrier width	Potentialbreite f, Breite f des Potentialwalls
width of the potential barrier	s. a. jump distance
width of the resonance, resonant width, resonance width	Resonanzbreite f
width of the spectral line	s. line width
width of the stacking faults, stacking fault width	Stapelfehlerbreite f
width of the track, track width	Spurbreite f
width of the track, track width (breadth) <nucl.>	Spurbreite f, Spurenbreite f <Kern.>
Wiechert bridge	Wiechert-Brücke f
Wiechert-Gutenberg discontinuity	Wiechert-Gutenbergsche Diskontinuität[sfläche] f
Wiechert-Herglotz['] method	Wiechert-Herglotzsches Verfahren n, Wiechert-Herglotz-Verfahren n
Wiechert-Liénard potential	s. Wiechert potential
Wiechert['s] pendulum	Wiechert-Pendel n, Wiechertsches Pendel n, astatisch invertiertes Pendel von Wiechert, Wiechertsches astatisch invertiertes Pendel
Wiechert potential, Wiechert-Liénard potential, Liénard-Wiechert potential, wave potential	Liénard-Wiechert-Potential n, Liénard-Wiechertsches Potential n, Potential von Liénard-Wiechert, Wiechert-Liénardsches Potential, Wiechert-Liénard-Potential n, Wellenpotential n [der räumlichen Belegung], retardiertes Potential [der bewegten Punktladung]
Wiedemann double-quartz wedge	Wiedemannscher Doppelkeil m
Wiedemann effect	Wiedemann-Effekt m
Wiedemann-Franz law, Wiedemann-Franz rule	Wiedemann-Franzsches Gesetz n, Wiedemann-Franzsche Regel f, Wiedemann-Franzsche Relation f
Wiedemann-Franz-Lorenz law, Lorenz law	Wiedemann-Franz-Lorenzsches Gesetz n
Wiedemann-Franz ratio	Wiedemann-Franzsches Verhältnis n
Wiedemann-Franz rule	s. Wiedemann-Franz law
Wiedemann['s] law	Wiedemannsches Gesetz n
Wiedemann phosphor	Wiedemann-Phosphor m
wiederkehreinwand, Zermelo['s] recurrence paradox, recurrence paradox [of Zermelo]	Zermeloscher Wiederkehreinwand m, Wiederkehreinwand [von Zermelo]
Wien['s] bridge; Wien['s] bridge circuit	Wien-Brücke f, Wiensche Brückenschaltung f, Wien-Brücken-Schaltung f, Wien-Wagner-Brücke f
Wien bridge oscillator	Wien-Brücken-Oszillator m, Wien-Brücken-Generator m
Wien['s] constant	Wiensche Konstante f, Wien-Konstante f
Wien['s] curve	Wiensche Kurve f [der Leitfähigkeitserhöhung]
Wien-Debye effect	Wien-Debye-Effekt m
Wien['s] displacement law, displacement law of Wien	Wiensches Verschiebungsgesetz n, Verschiebungsgesetz [von W. Wien]
Wien['s] effect, normal Wien effect	Wien-Effekt m, normaler Wien-Effekt m, Feldstärkeeffekt m [von Wien]
Wiener['s] approach, Wiener['s] approximation	Wienersche Näherung f
Wiener['s] body	Wienerscher Mischkörper m, Mischkörper dominierender Ergodensatz
Wiener['s] ergodic theorem	m, Ergodensatz von Wiener, Wienerscher Ergodensatz

Wiener filter	Wiener-Filter n
Wiener-Hopf equation, Wiener-Hopf integral equation	Wiener-Hopfsche Integralgleichung f
Wiener-Hopf method	Wiener-Hopf-Verfahren n, Wiener-Hopfsche Methode f
Wiener['s] integral	Wienersches Integral n, Wienersches Funktionalintegral n
Wiener['s] interference	Wienersche Interferenz f
Wiener-Khintchine theorem	Wiener-Khintchinesche Beziehungen fpl, Wiener-Chintschinsche Beziehungen, Satz m von Wiener-Khintchine, Satz von Wiener-Chintschin
Wiener['s] measure	Wienersches Maß n
Wiener-Paley criterion	Wiener-Paley-Kriterium n
Wiener['s] process, Brownian process <math.>	Wienerscher Prozeß m, Wiener-Prozeß m <Math.>
Wiener spectrum	Wiener-Spektrum n
Wiener['s] theorem	Wienersches Theorem n
Wien['s] experiment	Wienscher Versuch m, Versuch von Wien
Wien filter, wienfilter	Wiensches Filter n
Wien['s] function	Wiensche Funktion f
Wien['s] law, Wien['s] law of radiation, Wien['s] radiation law	Wiensche Strahlungsformel f, Wiensches Strahlungsgesetz n, Strahlungsformel von Wien, Strahlungsgesetz von Wien, Wiensche Gleichung f, Wiensches Gesetz n
Wien['s] law, Wien['s] thermodynamic law	thermodynamisches Gesetz n von Wien, Wiensches Gesetz
Wien['s] law of radiation	s. Wien['s] law
Wien['s] method <for investigation of canal rays>	Durchströmungsmethode f [von Wien], Wiensche Durchströmungsmethode
Wien network	Wien-Netzwerk n, Wiensches Netzwerk n ·
Wien-Niven bridge	Wien-Niven-Brücke f
Wien['s] paradox, light-valve paradox of Wien	Lichtventilparadoxon n von Wien, Wiensches Lichtventilparadoxon, Wiensches Paradoxon n
Wien['s] radiation law	s. Wien['s] law [of radiation]
Wien['s] region	Wienscher Bereich m, Wien-Bereich m
Wien-Robinson bridge, Robinson bridge	Robinson-Brücke f, Wien-Robinson-Brücke f
Wien-Robinson oscillator	Wien-Robinson-Oszillator m, Wien-Robinson-Generator m
Wien-Schiele effect	s. dissociation field effect
Wien['s] thermodynamic law, Wien['s] law	thermodynamisches Gesetz n von Wien, Wiensches Gesetz
Wien velocity filter	Wiensches Geschwindigkeitsfilter n
Wigand visibility meter	Wigandscher Sichtmesser m
wiggles <in nuclear induction>	„wiggles" pl, Modulationseinflüsse mpl <Kerninduktion>
Wightman['s] function	Wightman-Funktion f, Wightmansche Funktion f
Wightman['s] reconstruction theorem, Wightman['s] theorem	Rekonstruktionstheorem n von Wightman, Wightmansches Rekonstruktionstheorem
Wigner['s] approximation	Wigner-Näherung f, Wignersche Näherung f
Wigner coefficient, six-j symbol of Wigner	Wigner-Koeffizient m
Wigner-Critchfield interaction	Wigner-Critchfield-Wechselwirkung f
Wigner-Eckart theorem	Wigner-Eckart-Theorem n, Theorem n von Wigner und Eckart
Wigner effect; discomposition effect, knocking-out effect	Wigner-Effekt m, Atomumlagerung f durch Kernstoß
Wigner energy	Wigner-Energie f
Wigner['s] expansion	Wignersche Entwicklung f, Wigner-Entwicklung f
Wigner force, ordinary force	Wigner-Kraft f, Wignersche Kraft f
Wigner function, generalized spherical harmonic	Wigner-Funktion f, Wignersche Funktion f, verallgemeinerte Kugelfunktion f
Wigner gap	Wigner-Raum m, Wigner-Fuge f
Wigner growth	Wigner-Effekt-Wachstum n, Wigner-[Effekt-]Ausdehnung f, Wachstum n durch Wigner-Effekt
Wigner kernel	Wigner-Kern m, Wigner-Bremskern m
Wigner-Kirkwood rule for one-electron jump	f-Summensatz m von Wigner-Kirkwood
Wigner limit	Wigner-Limes m
Wigner model of nucleus, uniform model of nucleus, statistical model of nucleus	statistisches Kernmodell n [nach Wigner], statistisches Modell n [des Kerns], Wigner-Modell n, statistisches Compoundkernmodell n
Wigner nuclei, Wigner nuclides	Wigner-Kerne mpl
Wigner potential	Wigner-Potential n, Wignersches Potential n, Potential der Wigner-Kräfte
Wigner-Racah theorem	Wigner-Racah-Theorem n, Theorem n von Wigner und Racah
Wigner release	Freisetzung f der Wigner-Energie, Wigner-Energie-Freisetzung f
Wigner['s] rule	Wignersche Regel f
Wigner-Seitz atomic sphere, Wigner-Seitz sphere	Wigner-Seitzsche Atomkugel f, Wigner-Seitzsche Kugel f, Wigner-Seitz-Kugel f
Wigner-Seitz cell, Wigner-Seitz polyhedron	Wigner-Seitz-Zelle f, Wigner-Seitzsche Zelle f, Wigner-Seitz-Polyeder n, Wigner-Seitzsches Polyeder n
Wigner-Seitz method, cellular method	Zellenmethode f, Polyedermethode f, Wigner-Seitz-Methode f
Wigner-Seitz polyhedron	s. Wigner-Seitz cell
Wigner-Seitz sphere, Wigner-Seitz atomic sphere	Wigner-Seitzsche Atomkugel f, Wigner-Seitzsche Kugel f, Wigner-Seitz-Kugel f
Wigner supermultiplet	Wignersches Supermultiplett n
Wigner['s] theorem	Wigner-Theorem n, Wignersches Theorem n
Wigner['s] theory [of magnetic moment]	Wignersche Theorie f [des magnetischen Moments]
Wigner-Witmer correlation rules	Wigner-Witmersche Korrelationsregeln fpl
Wilcoxon['s] test, Mann-Whitney test, U test	Wilcoxon-Test m, Wilcoxonscher Test m, Mann-Whitney-Test m, U-Test
Wilde bridge	Wilde-Brücke f
Wild evaporimeter	Wildscher Verdunstungsmesser m
Wild photometer	Wild-Photometer n, Wildsches Photometer n
Wild polarimeter, Wild saccharimeter	Wildsches Saccharimeter n, Wildsches Polarimeter n
Wild['s] pressure plate anemometer	s. pressure-plate anemometer
Wild saccharimeter, Wild polarimeter	Wildsches Saccharimeter n, Wildsches Polarimeter n
Wild screen	Wildsche Hütte f
Wilhelmy plate (slide)	Wilhelmy-Platte f, Wilhelmysche Platte f
Wilhelmy slide method	Methode f von Wilhelmy

Wilip seismograph	Wilip-Seismograph m	wind-direction indicator, wind indicator, streamer	Windrichtungs[an]zeiger m, Windanzeiger m, Windzeiger m
Wilkinson['s] theory [of photonuclear effect]	Wilkinsonsche Theorie f [des Kernphotoeffekts]	wind direction recorder	Windrichtungsschreiber m
Wilks criterion (test)	Wilks-Test m		
Williamson amplifier	Williamson-Verstärker m		
Williamson['s] equation, Williamson['s] relation	Williamsonsche Gleichung f, Gleichung von Williamson	wind divide	Windscheide f
		wind drift, windage	Windabtrift f; Winddrift f; Windversetzung f
Williams striation	Williams-Bänderung f, Williams-Streifung f	wind drift; wind drift current, wind current	Driftstrom m, Drift f, Trift f; Driftströmung f, Triftströmung f
Williot diagram, Williot-Mohr diagram, plan of transposition, displacement diagram	Williotscher Verschiebungsplan m, Williot-Verschiebungsplan m, Verschiebungsplan [nach Williot], Williotscher Plan m, Williot-Plan m	wind-driven electric, wind-electric	windelektrisch
		wind-driven electric generator, wind-mill generator, wind-electric generator	Windgenerator m, Windkraftgenerator m, Windstromerzeuger m
willy-willy	s. tropical cyclone	wind-driven generating equipment, wind-driven plant, wind electric set	Windkraftanlage f
Wilson['s] [cloud] chamber	s. Wilson['s] expansion chamber		
Wilson effect	Wilson-Effekt m		
Wilson electrometer	Wilson-Elektrometer n, Wilsonsches Elektrometer n	wind-electric, wind-driven electric	windelektrisch
Wilson['s] expansion chamber, expansion cloud chamber, Wilson['s] cloud chamber, Wilson['s] chamber	Expansionsnebelkammer f, Wilsonsche Nebelkammer f, Nebelkammer	wind-electric generator, wind-driven electric generator, wind-mill generator	Windgenerator m, Windkraftgenerator m, Windstromerzeuger m
		wind-electric set	s. wind-driven generating equipment
Wilson line	Wilson-Kurve f, Wilsonsche Kurve f	wind energy, energy of wind	Windenergie f
Wilson['s] model [of the thunderstorm cloud]	Wilsonsches Modell n [der Gewitterwolke]	wind engine	s. wind motor
		wind equation	Windgleichung f
Wilson['s] phenomenon	Wilson-Phänomen n, Schülen-Phänomen n	wind erosion	s. deflation
		wind factor	Windfaktor m
Wilson['s] rule	Wilsonsche Regel f	wind field	Windfeld n
Wilson['s] theorem	Wilson-Theorem n	wind force, wind intensity, wind strength, intensity (force) of wind	Windstärke f
wilting point; coefficient of permanent wilting	[permanenter] Welkepunkt m, Dauerwelkepunkt m, PWP; Bodenfeuchtigkeit f am Welkepunkt		
		wind force; wind power	Windkraft f
Wilzbach method, Wilzbach technique	Wilzbach-Verfahren n	wind frequency	Windhäufigkeit f, Windfrequenz f
windage, air friction	Luftreibung f	wind gauge, anemometer	Anemometer n, Windgeschwindigkeitsmesser m, Windmeßgerät n, Windmesser m
windage	s. a. aerodynamic drag		
windage	s. a. wind drift		
wind aloft chart	Höhenwindkarte f		
wind arrow	Windpfeil m	wind-generated flow, wind-generated stream; wind current	Windströmung f, winderzeugte Strömung f, windbedingte Strömung; Windstrom m
wind avalanche	Windlawine f		
wind belt	Windgürtel m, Windzone f		
wind-borne	windverschleppt, windtransportiert	wind gradient, gradient of wind	Windgradient m, Windgefälle n
wind-borne sediment, eolian deposit, wind-laid deposit	äolisches Sediment n, Windsediment n, Windablagerung f	wind indicator	s. wind-direction indicator
		winding	Wicklung f; Aufwicklung f; Bewicklung f; Windung f
wind canal	s. wind tunnel	winding capacitance	Wicklungskapazität f, Wickelkapazität f, Eigenkapazität f der Wicklung
wind-carved pebble, wind kanter; facet stone, facet rock	Windkanter m, Kantengeschiebe n, Kantengeröll n; Facettengeschiebe n, Facettengeröll n		
		winding cross-section, total cross-section of the winding	Wicklungsquerschnitt m, Wickelquerschnitt m
wind catching area; wind surface	Windfläche f, Windangriffsfläche f, Angriffsfläche f des Windes		
		winding factor	Spulenwicklungsfaktor m, Wicklungsfüllfaktor m, Wickelfaktor m; Wicklungsfaktor m
wind channel	s. wind tunnel		
wind chart	Windkarte f	winding pipe, winding tube, pipe coil, coil, serpentine	Rohrschlange f, Schlangenrohr n, Schlange f
wind component indicator	Wetterspinne f		
		winding pitch	Wickelschritt m, Wicklungsschritt m
wind cone, wind sleeve, conical streamer, wind sock <US>	Windkegel m, Windsack m, Windrüssel m, Windbeutel m	winding ratio, turns ratio, ratio of the windings	Windungsverhältnis n, Windungszahlverhältnis n, Windungsübersetzung f
wind course, trajectory of the wind, wind trajectory, wind path	Windbahn f, Windweg m		
		winding space	Wickelraum m
wind crack	Windriß m	winding tube	s. winding pipe
		wind instrument	Blasinstrument n
wind-cracked, windshaken	windrissig	wind intensity	s. wind force
wind current; wind-generated flow, wind-generated stream	Windströmung f, winderzeugte Strömung f, windbedingte Strömung; Windstrom m	wind kanter, wind-carved pebble; facet stone, facet rock	Windkanter m, Kantengeschiebe n, Kantengeröll n; Facettengeschiebe n, Facettengeröll n
wind current, wind drift, wind drift current	Driftstrom m, Drift f, Trift f; Driftströmung f, Triftströmung f	wind laid-deposit, eolian deposit, wind-borne sediment	äolisches Sediment n, Windsediment n, Windablagerung f

wind

wind load, wind loading; wind pressure	Winddruck *m*; Windlast *f*, Windbelastung *f*; Windangriff *m*	wind-shaken, wind-cracked	windrissig
wind measurement, anemometry, wind-velocity measurement	Anemometrie *f*, Windgeschwindigkeitsmessung *f*, Windmessung *f*	wind shear	Windscherung *f*
		wind shift, change of the wind	Windrehung *f*; Änderung *f* der Windrichtung, Windrichtungsänderung *f*, Windänderung *f*
wind measuring apparatus, wind measuring device	Windmeßgerät *n*, Windmesser *m*, Windmeßvorrichtung *f*	wind sleeve (sock)	*s.* wind cone
wind[-]mill	Windmühle *f*	wind sounding balloon for radar wind measurement, radar sounding balloon	Windradarballon *m*
windmill anemometer	*s.* vane anemometer		
windmill generator, wind-driven electric generator, wind-electric generator	Windgenerator *m*, Windkraftgenerator *m*, Windstromerzeuger *m*	wind speed, wind velocity	Windgeschwindigkeit *f*
		wind-spout, whirlwind over land	Windhose *f*, Trombe *f* über Land, Wettersäule *f*
windmilling ‹aero.›	Antrieb *m* durch den Fahrtwind, Fahrtwindantrieb *m* ‹Aero.›	wind strength	*s.* wind force
		wind stress	Windspannung *f*, Spannung *f* infolge Windbelastung
windmill motor	*s.* wind motor	wind surface; wind catching area	Windfläche *f*, Windangriffsfläche *f*, Angriffsfläche *f* des Windes
wind moment	Windmoment *n*		
wind motor, windmill motor, wind [power] engine; wind turbine, wind wheel, air wing, vane wheel	Windmotor *m*, Windkraftmaschine *f*, Windmaschine *f*; Windrad *n*, Windturbine *f*		
		wind trajectory	*s.* wind course
		wind transport, transportation by wind, transport by wind	Windverschleppung *f*
		wind tree	Windbaum *m*
wind of Beaufort force, Beaufort number	Beaufort-Zahl *f*, Beaufort-Windstärke *f*, Beaufort-Stärke *f*, Windstärke *f* nach Beaufort	wind tunnel, aerodynamic tunnel, tunnel, wind channel, wind canal	Windkanal *m*, Windtunnel *m*
		wind tunnel balance, aerodynamic balance	Windkanalwaage *f*, aerodynamische Waage *f*
Windom antenna	Windom-Antenne *f*	wind tunnel bell, wind tunnel funnel	Windkanaldüse *f*
window ‹counter›	Fenster *n* ‹Zählrohr›	wind tunnel contraction, contracting nozzle	Kontraktionsdüse *f* [des Windkanals]
window ‹geo.›	[geologisches] Fenster *n*, tektonisches Fenster		
window ‹opt.›	Luke *f* ‹Opt.›	wind tunnel experiment, wind tunnel test	Windkanalversuch *m*
window	*s. a.* windows		
window amplifier	Fensterverstärker *m*, Kanalverstärker *m*	wind tunnel funnel, wind tunnel bell	Windkanaldüse *f*
window in Earth's atmosphere, atmospheric window	Fenster *n* der Atmosphäre	wind tunnel model, tunnel model	Windkanalmodell *n*
window jamming	*s.* radar perturbation by ropes	wind tunnel of closed-circuit type	*s.* return-flow wind tunnel
windowless Geiger-Müller counter	fensterloses Geiger-Müller-Zählrohr *n*	wind tunnel test, wind tunnel experiment	Windkanalversuch *m*
windows, window; ropes, flashers ‹radar›, radar chaff	Düppel *pl*, Düppelstreifen *mpl*, streifenförmige Metallfolien *fpl*, Radarstörstreifen *mpl*	wind tunnel with continuous closed circuit	*s.* return-flow wind tunnel
		wind tunnel with open working section	*s.* open[-] jet wind tunnel ‹aero.›
wind path	*s.* wind course	wind turbine	*s.* wind motor
wind pick-up, whirling up	Wiederaufwirbelung *f*, Aufwirbelung *f*	wind vane, weather[]vane, weather[]flag, weather[]cock	Windfahne *f*, Wetterfahne *f*; Wetterhahn *m*
wind power	Windleistung *f*	wind vane anemometer	*s.* vane anemometer
wind power; wind force	Windkraft *f*	wind vector	Windvektor *m*
		wind velocity, wind speed	Windgeschwindigkeit *f*
		wind velocity indicator	*s.* anemometer
wind power engine	*s.* wind motor	wind velocity measurement, anemometry, wind measurement	Anemometrie *f*, Windgeschwindigkeitsmessung *f*, Windmessung *f*
wind pressure; wind load, wind loading	Winddruck *m*; Windlast *f*, Windbelastung *f*; Windangriff *m*		
wind pressure field	Winddruckfeld *n*	wind velocity recorder	*s.* anemograph
wind pressure formula	Winddruckgleichung *f*, Winddruckformel *f*	windward eddy (vortex)	*s.* weather-side vortex
		windward wave	*s.* weather-side wave
wind profile, profile of wind, profile of wind velocity	Windprofil *n*, Windgeschwindigkeitsprofil *n*	wind wave	Windsee *f*; Windwelle *f*, Windseewelle *f*
		wind wheel	*s.* wind turbine
wind radar	Windradar *n*; Windradaranlage *f*	wind wheel anemometer	*s.* vane anemometer
		windy	windig
		wine-bottle potential	Weinflaschenpotential *n*
wind reference number, rhumb, point [of the compass]	Windstrich *m*, Windziffer *f*	wing ‹of line› ‹spectr.›	Linienflügel *m* ‹Spektr.›
		wing at zero lift, zero-incidence wing	nichtangestellter Flügel *m*
wind resistance	Windwiderstand *m*	wing chord	*s.* chord
wind ripple	Windfurche *f*, Windrippe *]f*, Windmarke *f*	wing of small aspect ratio, low-aspect-ratio wing	Tragflügel (Flügel) *m* kleiner Streckung
wind rose	*s.* compass card	wing profile, airfoil section (profile)	Tragflügelprofil *n*, Flügelprofil *n*, Profil *n* des Tragflügels
wind scale, scale of wind force	Windstärkeskala *f*, Windskala *f*		
wind shadow	Windschatten *m*	wing span, span of the wing, spread of the wing	Spannweite *f* [des Flügels], Flügelspannweite *f*

wing-tip vortex, tip vortex, tip eddy, trailing vortex, vortex rope	Randwirbel *m*, Wirbelzopf *m*
Winkelmann's biprism	Biprisma *n* von Winkelmann
Winkel['s] projection	Winkelscher Entwurf *m*, Winkelsche Projektion *f*
Winkler generator	Winkler-Generator *m*
Winslow effect	Winslow-Effekt *m*
winter solstice, December solstice	Wintersolstitium *n*, Wintersonnenwende *f*
winter solstice point	Wintersolstitialpunkt *m*, Winterpunkt *m*
wipe, two wipe slide, wipe slide; wipe fading	Wischblende *f*, Verdrängungsblende *f*
wipe contact	s. wiping contact
wipe fading	s. wipe
wipe pulse	Wischimpuls *m*
wiper, wiper arm; slider, sliding cursor, cursor slide[r]; cursor <el.>	Schleifer *m*; Schieber *m*; Läufer *m* <El.>
wiper	s. a. contact brush
wiper arm	s. wiper *m*
wipe resistance	Wischfestigkeit *f*, Wischbeständigkeit *f*
wipe slide	s. wipe
wipe test, smear test	Wischtest *m*, Wischversuch *m*; Wischprobe *f*; Reibtest *m*, Reibversuch *m*
wiping; rubbing; grating; smearing	Reiben *n*; Wischen *n*
wiping contact, wipe contact, rubbing contact, sliding contact, slide contact	Gleitkontakt *m*, verschiebbarer Kontakt *m*; Schleifkontakt *m*, Schleifer *m*; Schiebekontakt *m*; Reibkontakt *m*
wire	s. a. line <el.>
wire aerial, wire antenna	Drahtantenne *f*
wire chamber, wire spark chamber	Drahtelektroden-Funkenkammer *f*, Funkenkammer *f* mit Drahtelektroden
wire drawing, drawing of wires	Ziehen *n* von Draht, Drahtziehen *n*
wire gauze, wire grating, grating, wire grid <el.>	Drahtnetz *n*, Netz *n*, Drahtgitter *n* <El.>
wire grating <opt.>	Drahtgitter *n* <Opt.>
wire grid, wire grating, grating, wire gauze <el.>	Drahtnetz *n*, Netz *n*, Drahtgitter *n* <El.>
wire recording	s. sound-on-wire recording
wire resistance	s. wire-wound resistor
wire resistance gauge	s. resistance strain gauge
wire resistor	s. wire-wound resistor
wire spark chamber	s. wire chamber
wire store, magnetic wire store	Magnetdrahtspeicher *m*, Drahtspeicher *m*
wire texture, texture in drawn wires, drawing texture, texture resulting from drawing	Ziehtextur *f*
wire-wound heavy-duty resistor	Hochlastdrahtwiderstand *m*
wire-wound potentiometer, wound potentiometer	Drahtpotentiometer *n*
wire-wound resistor, wire resistor; wire resistance	Drahtwiderstand *m*
wiring	s. circuit wiring
wiring	s. line <el.>
wiring capacitance	Schaltkapazität *f*, Schaltungskapazität *f*; Verdrahtungskapazität *f*
wiring diagram, circuit diagram, wiring scheme <el.>	Schaltbild *n*, Schaltschema *n*; Schaltskizze *f*; Verdrahtungsplan *m*, Verdrahtungsschaltbild *n* <El.>
wiring diagram (layout)	s. a. schematic circuit diagram <el.>
wiring scheme	s. wiring diagram <el.>
Wishart distribution	Wishartsche Verteilung *f*
wisp of cloud, rag of cloud, ribbon of cloud, cloud rag, cloud ribbon, cloud wisp	Wolkenfetzen *m*
wisp of precipitation	streifenförmiger Niederschlag *m*, Niederschlagsstreifen *m*
withdrawal, extraction <e.g. of rods>	Ausfahren *n*, Herausziehen *n*; Anheben *n*
within-class variance, within-group variance, intraclass variance, variance between groups (treatments)	Varianz *f* innerhalb der Gruppen, Varianz innerhalb der Klassen, Varianz in den Gruppen, Varianz in den Klassen, Binnenvarianz *f*, Innerklassenvarianz *f*
Witka circuit	Witka-Schaltung *f*, Zimmermann-Schaltung *f*
witness mark	s. bench mark
Witoszyński-Szymański flow (mouvement)	Witoszyński-Szymańskische Strömung *f*
Wittich['s] method **WKB (W.K.B.) approximation, WKBJ (W.K.B.J.) approximation, WKBJ (W.K.B.J.) method, WKB (W.K.B.) method, WKB-type (W.K.B.-type) approximation,** Wentzel-Kramers-Brillouin approximation, Wentzel-Kramers-Brillouin-Jeffreys approximation, quasi[-] classical approximation [of Wentzel-Kramers-Brillouin [-Jeffreys]]	Wittichsches Verfahren *n* WKB-Näherung *f*, WKB-Methode *f*, Wentzel-Kramers-Brillouin[-Jeffreys]-Näherung *f*, Wentzel-Kramers-Brillouin Jeffreys]-Methode *f*, quasiklassische Näherung *f* [von Wentzel-Kramers-Brillouin[-Jeffreys]], Phasenintegralmethode *f*
Wobbe number, W	Wobbe-Zahl *f*, W
wobble	s. warble tone
wobble	s. wobbulation
wobble	s. staggering <mech.>
wobble amplitude	Wobbelhub *m*
wobble circuit	Wobbelschaltung *f*
wobble factor	Wobbelfaktor *m*
wobble frequency; wobbling frequency	Wobbelfrequenz *f*, Taumelfrequenz *f*
wobble modulation	s. wobbulation
wobble period	Wobbelperiode *f*
wobble plate, swash[]plate, wobbler	Taumelscheibe *f*
wobble pump, rotary swash plate pump, swash plate pump	Taumelscheibenpumpe *f*, Wobbelpumpe *f*
wobbler, wobbulator, sweep [frequency] generator; sweep signal generator; frequency-swept oscillator; master sweep generator	Wobbler *m*, Wobbelsender *m*; Wobbelfrequenzgenerator *m*, Wobbelgenerator *m*, Heultongenerator *m*, Heulsummer *m*; Wobbelmeßsender *m*
wobbler, swash[]plate, wobble plate	Taumelscheibe *f*
wobble tone	s. warble tone
wobbling	s. wobbulation
wobbling	s. staggering <mech.>
wobbling frequency; wobble frequency	Wobbelfrequenz *f*, Taumelfrequenz *f*
wobbling pulse	Wobbelimpuls *m*
wobbling voltage	Wobbelspannung *f*
wobbulation, wobbling, wobble modulation, frequency sweep, wobble, warble	Wobbelung *f*, Wobblung *f*, Wobbelauftastung *f*, Frequenzdurchlauf *m*, Frequenzverwerfung *f*
wobbulator	s. wobbler
wobbuloscope	Wobbeloszillograph *m*, Wobbeloszilloskop *n*

W/O emulsion	s. water-in-oil emulsion
Wöhler curve; Wöhler diagram; SIN curve, stress number curve, fatigue curve	Wöhler-Kurve f, Ermüdungskurve f, Wöhler-Linie f; Wöhler-Schaubild n, Wöhler-Diagramm n, SN-Diagramm n
Wöhler['s] method	Wöhler-Verfahren n, Einstufen-Dauerschwingversuch m
Wolf bottle, Wolff bottle, Woulfe bottle	Woulfesche Flasche f, Wulfsche Flasche
Wolfenstein [triple scattering] parameter	Wolfensteinscher Dreifachstreuparameter m
Wolff bottle, Wolf bottle, Woulfe bottle	Woulfesche Flasche f, Wulfsche Flasche
Wolf['s] method [for determining absorption and distance of dark cosmic clouds]	Wolfsches Verfahren n, Wolfsche Methode f
Wolf number, Wolf['s] sunspot number, Zürich number, relative sunspots number	Fleckenrelativzahl f, Sonnenflecken-Relativzahl f, Wolfsche Zahl f, Wolfsche Relativzahl (Sonnenfleckenzahl) f
Wolf-Rayet star	Wolf-Rayet-Stern m, W-Stern m
Wolf['s] sunspot number, Wolf number, Zürich number, relative sunspots number	Fleckenrelativzahl f, Sonnenflecken-Relativzahl f, Wolfsche Zahl f, Wolfsche Sonnenfleckenzahl f
Wollaston, Wollaston['s] prism	Wollaston-Prisma n; Polarisationsprisma n von Wollaston, Wollaston-Doppelprisma n, Wollaston-Platte f; Viereckprisma n (vierseitiges Reflexionsprisma) n nach Wollaston
Wollaston wire, whisker wire, capillary wire	Haardraht m; Wollaston-Draht m
Wolter['s] method, marking of minimum beam	Minimumstrahlkennzeichnung f, Woltersche Methode f der Minimumstrahlkennzeichnung, Methode von Wolter
Woltmann['s] sailwheel	Woltmann-Flügel m, Woltmann-Zähler m, Woltmann-Wassermesser m
Wood['s] bridge	Wood-Brücke f, Woodsche Brücke f, Woodsche Brückenschaltung f
Wood['s] discharge tube	Woodsches Entladungsrohr n
Wood effect	Wood-Effekt m
Wood filter, black filter	Schwarzfilter n, Schwarzglas n, Schwarz-Uviol-Glas n, Woodsches Filter n
Wood['s] lamp	s. black-light lamp
wood-polymer composite, WPC	Polymerholz n, Holz-Polymer-Verbindung f, Holz-Polymer-Kombination f, Polymer-Holz-Verbindung f, Plast-Holz-Kombination f, Plast-Holz-Werkstoff m; Plastlagenholz n
Wood['s] resonance series	Resonanzserie f von Wood, Woodsche Resonanzserie, Wood-Serie f
woody fracture, fibrous fracture	Faserbruch m, Schieferbruch m, Holzfaserbruch m
wooliness; echo, re-echo, resounding, reverberation	Widerhall m
wooltuft technique; thread-probe technique	Fadensondenmethode f, Wollfadenmethode f
word <num. math.>	Wort n, Zahlengruppe f <num. Math.>
word group, free group	freie Gruppe f, Wortgruppe f
word length, capacity <num. math.>	Wortlänge f <num. Math.>
word problem, identity problem	Identitätsproblem n, Wortproblem n
word time	Wortlaufzeit f, Wortzeit f

work, energy	Arbeit f
workability, working properties, formability	Umformbarkeit f, Verformbarkeit f, Formbarkeit f
work against resistance	Widerstandsarbeit f
work diagram	s. indicator diagram
work done <by>	geleistete Arbeit f
work done by external forces, exterior work, external work	äußere Arbeit f, Arbeit äußerer Kräfte
work done by friction	s. work of friction
work done by the internal forces	innere Arbeit f, Arbeit der inneren Kräfte
work function, work of emission (escape), electronic work function	Austrittsarbeit f, Ablösearbeit f
work function	s. a. free energy
work function of a nuclear particle	s. separation energy
work hardening	s. strain hardening
work-hardening capacity, work-hardening property, strain-hardening capacity (property)	Verfestigungsfähigkeit f, Kalthärtbarkeit f
work-hardening coefficient, strain-hardening coefficient, rate of work (strain) hardening	Verfestigungskoeffizient m, Verfestigungsanstieg m, Verfestigungskennwert m
work-hardening curve, strain-hardening curve	Verfestigungskurve f
work-hardening exponent	s. strain-hardening exponent
work-hardening hypothesis	Verfestigungshypothese f
work-hardening index	s. strain-hardening exponent
work-hardening property	s. work-hardening capacity
work-hardening stress	Verfestigungsspannung f
working; processing; handling; treatment	Verarbeitung f
working	s. a. processing <mech.>
working blade	Zugflügel m
working characteristic	s. operating characteristic
working current	s. operating current
working curve	s. dynamic characteristic
working cycle, cycle <therm.>	Kreisprozeß m, geschlossener Prozeß m <Therm.>
working distance	Arbeitsabstand m, Abstand m für gefahrloses Arbeiten; freier Arbeitsabstand, freier Objektabstand m, freier Dingabstand m <Mikroskop>
working energy	Arbeitsvermögen n; Leistungsfähigkeit f
working fluid, working liquid <of diffusion pump>	Treibmittel n, Treibflüssigkeit f <Diffusionspumpe>
working hours	Arbeitszeit f
working hypothesis	Arbeitshypothese f
working interval, working range	Verarbeitungsbereich m, Verarbeitungsintervall n
working liquid, working fluid <of diffusion pump>	Treibmittel n, Treibflüssigkeit f <Diffusionspumpe>
working mean, provisional mean	Arbeitsmittel n
working medium	Arbeitsstoff m
working plane, plane of measurement	Meßebene f
working point, sinking point, sinking temperature	Einsinkpunkt m, Einsinktemperatur f, Verarbeitungspunkt m, Verarbeitungstemperatur f
working point, operating point	Arbeitspunkt m
working properties	s. workability
working range, working interval	Verarbeitungsbereich m, Verarbeitungsintervall n

working standard [lamp], working standard of light; secondary standard lamp, secondary luminous standard, secondary standard [of light], secondary standard light source	Anschlußlampe f, Sekundärnormallampe f, Sekundärstandardlampe f; Standardlampe f
working storage	s. internal memory
working stress	s. permissible stress
working stroke, power stroke	Arbeitstakt m, Verbrennungstakt m
working temperature; operating temperature, final temperature of operation	Betriebstemperatur f; Arbeitstemperatur f
working temperature	Umformungstemperatur f, Umformtemperatur f, Verformungstemperatur f
working voltage	s. burning voltage <of discharge, arc>
working volume <of the air pump>	Schöpfraum m, Schöpfvolumen n, Pumpraum m <Luftpumpe>
work necessary to separate two bodies adherent to one another	Arbeit f zum Enthaften zweier Körper, Abreißarbeit f
work of adhesion, energy of adhesion	Adhäsionsarbeit f, Haftarbeit f
work of cohesion, cohesive energy, cohesional work	Kohäsionsenergie f
work of compression, compression work	Verdichtungsarbeit f, Kompressionsarbeit f
work of deformation	[äußere] Formänderungsarbeit f, Umformarbeit f, Verformungsarbeit f, Deformationsarbeit f, Verzerrungsarbeit f, Arbeit f der umformenden Kräfte, Arbeit der äußeren Kräfte bei der Umformung; Lastsenkungsarbeit f
work of displacement, displacement work	Verdrängungsarbeit f
work of emission (escape)	s. work function
work of evaporation	Verdampfungsarbeit f
work of friction, frictional work, work done by friction	Reibungsarbeit f
work of magnetization	s. energy of magnetization
work of nucleation	Keimbildungsarbeit f, Kernbildungsarbeit f
work of reaction	Reaktionsarbeit f
work of rupture, stretching strain, rupture work	Zerreißarbeit f
work of twisting, torsional work, twisting strain, torsional strain	Torsionsarbeit f, Verdreharbeit f, Verdrehungsarbeit f
work softening	Verformungsentfestigung f, Entfestigung f durch Kaltverformung
work-softening	s. a. destrengthening
world acceleration vector	Weltbeschleunigungsvektor m
world curve, world line	Weltlinie f
world day	Welttag m
world force	s. gravitation
world force density	s. four-density of force
world invariant, Lorentz invariant	Lorentz-Invariante f
world-invariant, Lorentz-invariant, lorentz invariant	Lorentz-invariant, lorentzinvariant, relativistisch invariant, weltinvariant
world-invariant conservation law, world-invariant law of conservation	Lorentz-invarianter Erhaltungssatz m
world line, world curve	Weltlinie f
world picture, world system	Weltbild n, Weltsystem n
world point, event, space-time point	Ereignis n, Raumzeitpunkt m, Raum-Zeit-Punkt m, Weltpunkt m
world radius, radius of the universe	Weltradius m
world space	s. space-time <math.>
world system, world picture	Weltbild n, Weltsystem n
world tensor	Welttensor m
world tensor	s. a. four-tensor
world thunderstorm activity	Weltgewittertätigkeit f
World Time	s. Universal time
world vector	Weltvektor m
world vector	s. a. four-vector
world-wide weather, universal weather	Weltwetter n
worm, endless screw	Schnecke f, endlose Schraube f
worm <of screw>; turn, turn of winding, single turn, spire; torsion <bio.>	Windung f; Lage f
worm gear	Schneckengetriebe n, Schnecke; Wurmgetriebe n
worm's eye view	Froschperspektive f
worm wheel	Schneckenrad n
Wortmann['s] method	Tellurmethode f [nach Wortmann], Wortmannsche Methode f
Wosthoff pump	Wosthoff-Pumpe f
Woulfe bottle, Wolff bottle, Wolf bottle	Woulfesche Flasche f, Wulfsche Flasche
wound potentiometer, wire-wound potentiometer	Drahtpotentiometer n
wow, wowing, wow-wows, frequency wow <el.>	Jaulen n <El.>
wrapped capacitor, roller-type capacitor	Wickelkondensator m
wrapping, covering	Umhüllung f, Umwicklung f
wrapping angle	s. angle of embrace
wrap[ping] test	Wickelversuch m, Wickelprobe f
Wratten filter	Wratten-Filter n
wrench <math.>	Schraube f, Vektorschraube f, Dyname f <Math.>
wrench, wrench of forces <mech.>	Dyname f, Kraftschraube f, Winder m; Bewegungsschraube f <Mech.>
wriggle instability, torsional instability	Torsionsinstabilität f, Torsionsunbeständigkeit f, Verdrehungsinstabilität f, Verdrehinstabilität f, Drehungsinstabilität f
Wright biquartz, Wright compensator	Wrightscher Kompensator (Kombinationskeil) m, Quarz-Kombinationskeil m von (nach) Wright
Wright compensator, Wright biquartz	Wrightscher Kompensator (Kombinationskeil) m, Quarz-Kombinationskeil m von (nach) Wright
Wright['s] criterion	Wrightsches Kriterium n
Wright eyepiece	Wrightsches Okular n, Wrightsches Mikroskopokular n, Okular nach Wright, Wright-Okular n
wringing	Ansprengen n
wrinkle	Runzel f, Falte f
wrinkle, trick, artifice	Kunstgriff m, Kniff m
wrinkling, making deep furrows	Zerfurchung f
wrinkling <geo.>	Fältelung f, Kleinfaltung f <Geo.>
wrinkling, surface wrinkling (roughening) <techn.>	Runzelbildung f; Faltung f; Aufrauhung f, Oberflächenaufrauhung f, <Techn.>
wrinkling zone	Fältelungszone f, Zerquetschungszone f
write beam, write ray	Schreibstrahl m

writing <in a storage tube>	Schreiben n <Speicherröhre>	xenon extra-high pressure arc, extra-high pressure xenon arc	Xenon-Höchstdruckbogen m
writing rate; writing speed, recording speed, tracing speed	Registriergeschwindigkeit f, Schreibgeschwindigkeit f	xenon-filled bubble chamber, xenon bubble chamber, xenon chamber	Xenonblasenkammer f
Wronskian, Wronski['s] determinant	Wronskische Determinante f, Wronski-Determinante f	xenon poisoning [of reactor]	Xenonvergiftung f [des Reaktors]
Wu['s] experiment	Wu-Experiment n, Versuch m von Wu, Wuscher Versuch	xenon poisoning predictor	Xenonvergiftungsrechner m
Wulf electrometer, bifilar electrometer, two-fibre electrometer	Bifilarelektrometer n, Wulf-Elektrometer n, Wulfsches Elektrometer n, Zweifadenelektrometer n, Zweifadenvoltmeter n		
Wulff['s] construction, construction by Wulff	Wulffsche Konstruktion f	xerochasy	Xerochasie f
Wulff['s] net, net of Wulff, stereographic net	Wulffsches Netz n	xerogel	Xerogel n
Wulff pressure	Wulffscher Kristallflächendruck m, Wulffscher Druck m, Wulff-Druck m	xerographic development, dry development	Betonerung f, elektrophotographische (xerographische) Entwicklung f, Trockenentwicklung f
Wulff['s] surface	Wulffsche Fläche f	xerophile, xerophilic, xerophilous	xerophil
Wulff['s] theorem	Wulffsches Theorem n	xerophilous nature (property), xerophily	Xerophilie f
Wüllner['s] law	Wüllnersches Gesetz n	xerophily, xerophilous nature, xerophilous property	Xerophilie f
Wunderlich valve	Wunderlich-Röhre f		
W Ursae Majoris[-type] star	W Ursae Majoris-Stern m	xeroradiography	Xeroradiographie f; Röntgenxerographie f
		X-gamma coincidence, X_γ coincidence	Röntgen[strahl]-Gamma-Koinzidenz f, Röntgen-γ-Koinzidenz f
wurtzite structure, wurtzite-type structure	Wurtzitstruktur f, Wurtzittyp m	X-gamma dosemeter, X-ray gamma-ray dosemeter	Röntgen-Gamma-Dosimeter n, Röntgen-γ-Dosimeter n
W Virginis[-type] star, spherical component cepheid	W Virginis-Stern m	Xi-hyperon, Ξ hyperon, cascade particle, cascade hyperon, c particle <Ξ^+, Ξ^-, Ξ^0>	Ξ-Hyperon n, Xi-Hyperon n, Kaskadenhyperon n, Kaskadenteilchen n <Ξ^+, Ξ^-, Ξ^0>
wye-delta connection	s. star-delta connection	X-irradiation, X-ray irradiation	Röntgenbestrahlung f, Röntgenisation f
Wyman['s] resonance method	Wymansche Resonanzmethode f, Resonanzmethode f von Wyman		
		X plate	s. horizontal plate
		X-quadripole	s. lattice-type section
		X-radiation	s. X-rays
		X-ray	Röntgenstrahl m
X		X-ray absorptiometry (absorption analysis)	s. absorption spectrochemical analysis using X-rays
X-amplifier	s. horizontal amplifier	X-ray absorption band	Röntgenabsorptionsbande f, Röntgenabsorptionskontinuum n
X[-] antenna, double V[-] antenna	Spreizdipol m, X-Antenne f, Doppel-V-Antenne f	X-ray absorption coefficient	Absorptionskoeffizient m der Röntgenstrahlung, Röntgenabsorptionskoeffizient m
xanthopsy	Xanthopsie f, Gelbsehen n		
X-axis amplifier	s. horizontal amplifier	X-ray absorption cross-section	Röntgenabsorptionsquerschnitt m, Röntgenstrahlen-Absorptionsquerschnitt m, Absorptionsquerschnitt m für (der) Röntgenstrahlung
X band <8.5–12.5 or 5.2–11 Gc/s>	X-Band n <8,5 ··· 12,5 oder 5,2 ··· 11 GHz>		
		X-ray absorption edge, X-ray absorption limit	Röntgenabsorptionskante f
X contact, X synchronization [contact]	X-Kontakt m		
X cut, X-cut, normal cut, Curie cut	X-Schnitt m	X-ray absorption index	Röntgenabsorptionsindex m, Absorptionsindex m der Röntgenstrahlung
X-cut crystal, X-shaped crystal	X-Schnitt-Kristall m, X-geschnittener Kristall m	X-ray absorption jump	Röntgenabsorptionssprung m, Absorptionssprung m der Röntgenstrahlung
X deflection	s. horizontal deflection		
xenocryst[al]	Xenokristall m	X-ray absorption limit, X-ray absorption edge	Röntgenabsorptionskante f
xenology	Xenologie f		
xenomorphic	s. allotriomorphic		
xenon bubble chamber, xenon chamber, xenon-filled bubble chamber	Xenonblasenkammer f	X-ray absorption spectrochemical analysis	s. absorption spectrochemical analysis using X-rays
xenon build-up [after shutdown]	Xenon-Vergiftungszunahme f [nach dem Abschalten des Reaktors], Zunahme f der Xenonvergiftung [nach dem Abschalten des Reaktors]	X-ray absorption spectrum	Röntgenabsorptionsspektrum n, Absorptionsröntgenspektrum n
		X-ray analysis	Röntgenstrahl[en]analyse f, Röntgenanalyse f
xenon chamber	s. xenon bubble chamber	X-ray analysis	s. a. X-ray crystal[lographic] analysis
xenon effect	Xenoneffekt m, Xenon-Vergiftungseffekt m		

X-ray analysis	s. X-ray spectroscopic analysis	X-ray diffraction analysis [of crystals]	s. X-ray crystallographic analysis
X-ray apparatus, X-ray machine, roentgen apparatus, roentgen machine, radiograph	Röntgenapparat m, Röntgengerät n	X-ray diffraction camera, X-ray camera	Röntgenkamera f, Röntgenbeugungskamera f
X-ray astronomy	Röntgenastronomie f, Röntgenstrahlenastronomie f	X-ray diffraction instrument	s. X-ray diffractometer
X-ray background	Röntgenuntergrund m	X-ray diffraction microscopy	Röntgenbeugungsmikroskopie f
X-ray beam	Röntgenstrahlenbündel n, Röntgenbündel n	X-ray diffraction pattern (photograph, picture)	s. X-ray pattern
X-ray/beta-ray yield ratio	Röntgen/Beta-Ausbeuteverhältnis n	X-ray diffractometer, X-ray diffraction instrument	Röntgendiffraktometer n, Röntgenbeugungsgerät n
X-ray burn	Röntgenverbrennung f		
X-ray calorimetry	Röntgenkalorimetrie f	X-ray dispersion	Zerlegung f der Röntgenstrahlung f, Dispersion f der Röntgenstrahlen, Röntgenstrahlenzerlegung f, Röntgenstrahlendispersion f, Röntgenzerlegung f, Röntgendispersion f
X-ray camera, camera for X-rays	Röntgenkamera f		
X-ray camera	s. a. X-ray diffraction camera	X-ray dosemeter	Röntgendosimeter n, Röntgen[en]dosimeter n, Röntgendosismesser m
X-ray capture	Röntgeneinfang m		
X-ray cascade tube, cascade [X-ray] tube	Kaskadenröhre f, Kaskadenröntgenröhre f, Röntgenkaskadenröhre f	X-ray element	Röntgenelement n
X-ray cinematography	s. roentgen cinematography	X-ray emission analysis	s. emission spectrochemical analysis using X-rays
X-ray coverage, X-ray field	Röntgenstrahlenfeld n	X-ray emission band	Röntgenemissionsbande f, Röntgenemissionskontinuum n
X-ray critical [absorption] wavelength	kritische Wellenlänge f für Röntgenstrahlen	X-ray emission spectrochemical analysis	s. emission spectrochemical analysis using X-rays
X-ray crystal density; X-ray density	Röntgenstrahlen-Kristalldichte f; Röntgendichte f	X-ray emission spectrum	Röntgenemissionsspektrum n, Emissionsröntgenspektrum n
X-ray crystal density method, XRCD method	Röntgenstrahlen-Kristalldichtemethode f, XRCD-Methode f	X-ray emulsion, radiographic emulsion, roentgenographic emulsion	Röntgenemulsion f
X-ray crystal[lographic] analysis, X-ray crystallography, crystal analysis, radio crystallography, X-ray diffraction analysis [of crystals], X-ray analysis, X-ray structure investigation	Röntgen[-Kristall]strukturanalyse f, Röntgen[-Kristall]strukturuntersuchung f, Kristallstrukturanalyse f mit Röntgenstrahlung, Röntgenanalyse f der Kristalle, Röngenstrahl[en]analyse f (der Kristalle), Röntgenfeinstrukturanalyse f, Röntgenfeinstrukturuntersuchung f Röntgenfeinstrukturbestimmung f, röntgenographische Feinstrukturanalyse (Feinstrukturuntersuchung, Untersuchung) f, röntgenometrische Feinstrukturanalyse (Feinstrukturuntersuchung, Untersuchung), Kristallbestimmung f durch Röntgenstrahlbeugung, Röntgenstrahl[en]beugung f, Röntgenbeugungsanalyse f (der Kristalle], Röntgenbeugung f, Röntgenanalyse f	X-ray equipment, X-ray installation, X-ray unit, X-ray outfit	Röntgenanlage f; Röntgeneinrichtung f
		X-ray escape	Röntgenescape m
		X-ray examination	s. X-ray test
		X-ray examination	s. a. X-ray investigation
		X-ray field, X-ray coverage	Röntgenstrahlenfeld n
		X-ray film	s. radiographic film
		X-ray filter	Röntgenfilter n, Röntgenstrahlenfilter n
		X-ray fine structure	s. X-ray structure
		X-ray flash	Röntgenblitz m
		X-ray flash tube, flash X-ray tube	Röntgenblitzröhre f
		X-ray fluorescence, roentgenofluorescence	Röntgenfluoreszenz f
		X-ray fluorescence analysis, X-ray fluorescence spectroscopy, XRFA	Röntgenfluoreszenzanalyse f, Röntgenstrahlfluoreszenzanalyse f, Röntgenstrahl-Fluoreszenz-Spektralanalyse f, Röntgenfluoreszenz-Spektralanalyse f, Röntgenfluoreszenzspektroskopie f
		X-ray fluorescence radiation	s. characteristic X-rays
		X-ray fluorescence spectrometer	Röntgenfluoreszenzspektrometer n
X-ray crystallography, radio crystallography	Röntgenkristallographie f, Röntgenstrahlenkristallographie f	X-ray fluorescence spectroscopy	s. X-ray fluorescence analysis
X-ray crystallography	s. a. X-ray crystallographic analysis	X-ray gamma-ray dosemeter, X-gamma dosemeter	Röntgen-Gamma-Dosimeter n, Röntgen-γ-Dosimeter n
X-ray density	s. X-ray crystal density		
X-ray diagram	s. X-ray pattern		
X-ray diascope	Röntgendiaskop n	X-ray generator	Röntgengenerator m
X-ray diffraction	Beugung f von Röntgenstrahlen, Röntgenbeugung f, Röntgenstrahl[en]beugung f, Röntgendiffraktion f		

X-ray

X-ray goniometer, goniometer [for single-crystal X-ray diffraction]	Röntgengoniometer n, Goniometer n	X-ray microradiography	Röntgen-Mikroradiographie f
X-ray goniometer with [Geiger-Müller] counter	Zählrohrgoniometer n, Röntgengoniometer n mit [Geiger-Müller-] Zählrohr	X-ray microscope	Röntgenmikroskop n, Röntgenstrahlenmikroskop n
		X-ray microscopy	Röntgenmikroskopie f
X-ray goniometry, goniometer technique	Röntgengoniometerverfahren n, Röntgengoniometrie f	X-ray microspectrography, roentgen microspectrography	Röntgenmikrospektrographie f
X-ray image	s. radiograph	X-ray monochromator	Röntgenstrahlenmonochromator m, Monochromator m für Röntgenstrahlen
X-ray image amplification	s. X-ray image intensifying		
X-ray image amplifier, X-ray image amplifier tube	s. X-ray image converter	X-ray movies	s. roentgen cinematography
		X-rayogram	s. X-ray pattern
X-ray image conversion	s. X-ray image intensifying	X-rayogram	s. radiograph
X-ray image converter, X-ray image intensifier, X-ray image intensifier tube, X-ray image amplifier, X-ray image amplifier tube	Röntgenbildwandler m, Röntgenbildverstärker m, Röntgenbildverstärkerröhre f	X-ray optics	Röntgenoptik f
		X-ray oscillation photograph, oscillation photograph	Schwenkkristallaufnahme f, Schwenkaufnahme f
		X-ray outfit	s. X-ray equipment
		X-ray paper; radiographic paper	Röntgenpapier n; Radiographiepapier n
X-ray image intensifying, X-ray image amplification, X-ray image conversion	Röntgenbildverstärkung f, Röntgenbildumwandlung f	X-ray pattern, X-ray diffraction pattern (photograph, picture), X-rayogram, X-ray diagram, crystallogram	Röntgendiagramm n, Röntgenbeugungsbild n, Röntgenbeugungsaufnahme f, Röntgenstrahlendiagramm n, Kristallogramm n
X-raying	s. fluoroscopy		
X-ray inspection	s. X-ray test	X-ray photoelectron spectroscopy	s. ESCA
X-ray installation	s. X-ray equipment	X-ray photogrammetry, roentgen photogrammetry	Röntgenphotogrammetrie f
X-ray intensification	Röntgenstrahlenverstärkung f, Röntgenverstärkung f		
		X-ray photograph	s. radiograph
		X-ray photography	s. roentgenography
X-ray intensifying screen	Röntgenverstärkerfolie f	X-ray photometer	Röntgenphotometer n, Röntgenlichtmesser m
X-ray intensity	Röntgenstrahl[en]intensität f, Röntgenintensität f	X-ray photon	s. X-ray quantum
		X-ray physics, physics of X-radiation	Röntgenphysik f, Physik f der Röntgenstrahlen
X-ray intensity meter	Röntgenintensitätsmesser m	X-ray picture	s. radiograph
		X-ray plate, radiographic plate	Röntgenplatte f
		X-ray powder camera, powder camera	Debye-Scherrer-Kammer f, Pulverbeugungskammer f
X-ray interference	Röntgenstrahlinterferenz f, Röntgeninterferenz f, Röntgenstrahleninterferenz f, Reflex m		
		X-ray powdered-crystal photograph	s. Debye-Scherrer pattern
X-ray interference in crystal lattice	Raumgitterinterferenz f, Kristallgitterinterferenz f, Röntgenstrahlinterferenz f im Kristallgitter	X-ray protection, protection against X-radiation	Röntgenschutz m, Röntgenstrahlenschutz m, Schutz m gegen (vor) Röntgenstrahlung
X-ray interference in liquids	Flüssigkeitsinterferenz f, Röntgenstrahlinterferenz f in Flüssigkeiten	X-ray protective glass	Röntgenschutzglas n, Röntgenstrahlenschutzglas n
X-ray interference line	Röntgeninterferenzlinie f		
X-ray investigation, X-ray study, X-ray examination	Röntgenuntersuchung f, Untersuchung f mit Röntgenstrahlen	X-ray pulse	Röntgenimpuls m
X-ray irradiation, X-irradiation, roentgenization	Röntgenbestrahlung f, Röntgenisation f	X-ray quantum, X-ray photon	Röntgenquant n, Röntgenstrahl[ungs]quant n, Röntgen[strahl]photon n
X-ray lamp	Röntgenlampe f	X-ray radiation	s. X-rays
X-ray lens	Röntgenlinse f	X-ray radiographic examination	s. X-ray test
X-ray level; X-ray term	Röntgenniveau n; Röntgenterm m	X-ray rotation photograph, rotation photograph	Drehkristallaufnahme f, Drehaufnahme f
X-ray line	Röntgenlinie f, Röntgenspektrallinie f		
X-ray line spectrum	s. characteristic X-ray spectrum	X-rays, X rays, X-ray radiation, X-radiation, Röntgen rays roentgen (Roentgen) rays, Röntgen (Roentgen, roentgen) radiation	Röntgenstrahlung f, Röntgenstrahlen mpl; Röntgenlicht n
X-ray low angle scattering	s. X-ray small-angle scattering		
X-ray luminescence, roentgenoluminescence	Röntgenlumineszenz f		
X-ray machine	s. X-ray apparatus	X-ray scanning analysis	s. body section roentgenography
X-ray materials testing	s. X-ray test		
X-ray materiology	s. X-ray test	X-ray scattering	Röntgenstreuung f, Röntgenstrahl[en]streuung f, Streuung f von Röntgenstrahlen
X-ray metallography, radiometallography	Röntgenmetallkunde f; Röntgenmetallographie f; Radiometallographie f; Durchleuchtung (Durchstrahlung) f von Metallen <mit radioaktiver oder Röntgenstrahlung>		
		X-ray screen	Röntgenschirm m, Röntgenleuchtschirm m, Röntgen-Durchstrahlungsschirm m
X-ray micrograph	Röntgenmikroaufnahme f		

X-ray series	Röntgenserie f
X-ray small-angle scattering, X-ray low angle scattering, low-angle (small-angle) X-ray scattering	Röntgenkleinwinkelstreuung f, Röntgen-Kleinwinkelstreuung f, RKS
X-ray source, radiographic source	Röntgenstrahlenquelle f, Röntgenstrahl[ungs]quelle f, Röntgenstrahler m, Röntgenquelle f
X-ray source	s. a. X-ray star <astr.>
X-ray spectrochemical analysis	s. X-ray spectroscopic analysis
X-ray spectrogram	Röntgenspektrogramm n, Röntgenstrahl[en]spektrogramm n
X-ray spectrograph	Röntgenspektrograph m, Röntgenstrahl[en]spektrograph m
X-ray spectrography	Röntgenspektrographie f, Röntgenstrahl[en]spektrographie f, Spektrographie f der Röntgenstrahlung
X-ray spectrometer, X-ray spectroscope	Röntgenspektrometer n, Röntgenstrahl[en]spektrometer n, Röntgenspektroskop n, Röntgenstrahl[en]spektroskop n
X-ray spectroscopic analysis, X-ray spectrochemical analysis, spectroscopic analysis using X-rays, X-ray analysis	Röntgenspektralanalyse f, angewandte Röntgenspektroskopie f
X-ray spectroscopy	Röntgenspektroskopie f, Röntgenstrahl[en]spektroskopie f, Spektroskopie f der Röntgenstrahlung
X-ray spectrum, roentgen spectrum	Röntgenspektrum n
X-ray star; X-ray source <astr.>	Röntgenstern m; Röntgenquelle f <Astr.>
X-ray stereogram, X-ray stereophotograph, stereoscopic radiograph, plastic radiograph	Röntgenstereogramm n, Stereoröntgenaufnahme f, Röntgenstereoaufnahme f, Röntgenstereobild n, plastisches Röntgenbild n
X-ray stereogrammetry	Röntgenstereogrammetrie f
X-ray stereometry, radiographic stereometry	Röntgenstereometrie f
X-ray stereophotograph	s. X-ray stereogram
X-ray stereophotography	Röntgenstereoaufnahme f, Röntgenstereophotographie f
X-ray stereoscopy, radiographic stereoscopy	Röntgenstereoskopie f
X-ray structure, X-ray fine structure	Röntgen[fein]struktur f, Röntgenstrahlenfeinstruktur f
X-ray structure investigation	s. X-ray crystal[lographic] analysis
X-ray study	s. X-ray investigation
X-ray telescope	Röntgenteleskop n, Röntgenstrahlenteleskop n
X-ray term	s. X-ray level
X-ray test, X-ray materials testing, X-ray inspection, X-ray [radiographic] examination, X-ray materiology, roentgenomateriology, roentgenmateriology, radiography	Röntgenprüfung f, röntgenographische Prüfung f, Röntgenwerkstoffprüfung f, Röntgendefektoskopie f, Werkstoffprüfung f mit Röntgenstrahlen, zerstörungsfreie Werkstoffprüfung mit Röntgenstrahlen
X-ray tube, Röntgen tube, Roentgen tube	Röntgenröhre f
X-ray tube housing, protective tube housing, tube housing; fully protective tube housing	Röhrenschutzgehäuse n, Schutzgehäuse n der Röntgenröhre, Röntgenröhrenschutzgehäuse n, Schutzhaube f [der Röntgenröhre]: Vollschutzgehäuse n, Vollschutzröhrengehäuse n, Vollschutzhaube f <gegen Hochspannung>
X-ray unit	s. X-ray equipment
X-ray wave	Röntgenwelle f
X-ray wavelength	Röntgenwellenlänge f
X-ray yield	Röntgenstrahlenausbeute f, Röntgenstrahl[ungs]ausbeute f, Röntgenausbeute f
X-shaped crystal, X-cut crystal	X-Schnitt-Kristall m, X-geschnittener Kristall m
X-shaped twin	s. X twin
X synchronization [contact], X contact	X-Kontakt m
X test	s. Waerden['s] [X] test / Van der
X twin, X-shaped twin	X-Zwilling m
X-unit, Siegbahn [X] unit, X, XU, Xu <≈ 1.00202×10⁻¹³ m>	X-Einheit f, Siegbahnsche X-Einheit, Siegbahn-Einheit f, X, Siegb. XE <≈ 1,00202·10⁻¹³ m>
X wave, extraordinary wave	außerordentliche Welle f
xylometry	Xylometrie f
xy plane, xy-plane	x,y-Ebene f, xy-Ebene f, (x,y)-Ebene f, x-y-Ebene f
X-Y plotter, two-axis plotter, graph plotter	Zweiachsenschreiber m, zweiachsiger Schreiber m, X-Y-Schreiber m

Y

Yafet-Kittel angle	Yafet-Kittel-Winkel m
Yafet-Kittel configuration	Yafet-Kittel-Dreieckskonfiguration f
Yagi aerial [array], Yagi antenna, Yagi-Uda array	Yagi-Antenne f, Wellenkanal m
Yamanouchi symbol	Yamanouchi-Symbol n
Y amplifier	s. vertical amplifier
Yang-Lee-Ruelle theory	Yang-Lee-Ruellesche Theorie f
Yang-Mills field	Yang-Mills-Feld n
Yang['s] theorem [on angular distribution]	Yang-Theorem n
Y[-] antenna, Y-type antenna	Y-Antenne f
yard; imperial standard yard, imperial yard, yard UK, yd. UK <= 0.914 399 21 m (legal definition), = 0.91439841 m (scientific definition), ≈ 0.9144 m (for industrial uses)>; US yard, United States yard, yard US, yd. US <= 0.91440182 m (legal definition), ≈ 0.9144 m (for industrial uses)>	Yard n

Yarkovsky effect	Yarkovsky-Effekt *m*
Yates['] adjustment, Yates['] correction	Yates-Korrektion *f*, Yates-Korrektur *f*
yaw, yawing	Gieren *n*
yaw [angle]	s. yawing angle <aero.>
yaw axis, axis of yaw	Gierachse *f*
yawed wing	schiebender Flügel *m*
yawing	s. yaw
yawing angle, yaw angle, yaw <aero.>	Scherungswinkel *m* <Aero.>
yawing moment	s. yaw moment <aero.>
yawing moment coefficient, coefficient of yawing moment	Giermomentenbeiwert *m*, Kursmomentenbeiwert *m*, Schermomentenbeiwert *m*, Seitenmomentenbeiwert *m*, Wendemomentenbeiwert *m*
yaw[-] meter	Gierungsmesser *m*, Winkelsonde *f*
yaw moment, yawing moment <aero.>	Giermoment *n*, Wendemoment *n*, Kursmoment *n*, Schermoment *n* <Aero.>
yawn	s. gap <techn.>
Y-axis amplifier	s. vertical amplifier
Y/B ratio, yellow-blue ratio	Gelb/Blau-Verhältnis *n*
Y circulator, gyrator, waveguide Y circulator	Gyrator *m*, Y-Zirkulator *m*, Y-Richtungsgabel *f*
Y coefficient [of four-terminal network], admittance coefficient, admittance matrix coefficient	Y-Koeffizient *m* [des Vierpols]
Y-connection, star connection, star grouping, Y grouping; star-connected circuit	Sternschaltung *f*, S-Schaltung *f*
Y cut, Y-cut, parallel cut	Y-Schnitt *m*
Y-cut crystal, Y-shaped crystal	Y-Schnitt-Kristall *m*, Y-geschnittener Kristall *m*
Y deflection	s. vertical deflection
yd. UK	s. imperial standard yard
yd. US	s. US yard
year, a, yr, yr., y	Jahr *n*, a
yearly average (mean), annual average, annual mean	Jahresmittel *n*, Jahresmittelwert *m*, Jahresdurchschnitt *m*, Jahresdurchschnittswert *m*
yearly variation <of meteoric activity>	jährliche Variation *f* <Meteortätigkeit>
yellow-blue ratio, Y/B ratio	Gelb/Blau-Verhältnis *n*
yellow cloud filter, cloud filter	Wolkenfilter *n*
yellow colour index	Gelbindex *m*
yellow filter	Gelbfilter *n*, Gelbscheibe *f*
yellow flame <US>, luminous flame	leuchtende Flamme *f*, Leuchtflamme *f*
yellow fog	Gelbschleier *m*
yellow giant [star]	gelber Riese *f*
yellow glow	s. yellow heat
yellow-green filter	Gelbgrünfilter *n*
yellow heat, yellow glow	Gelbglut *f* <1000 °C>
yellowing	Vergilbung *f*
yellowish and blue colour filter, trichrome filter	Trichromfilter *n*
yellow spot, macula lutea	gelber Fleck *m*, Macula lutea
Yerkes classification, Yerkes system [of spectral classification]	Yerkes-Klassifikation *f*
Yerkes refractor	Yerkes-Refraktor *m*
Yerkes system, MKK system, Morgan-Keenan-Kellman system	MKK-System *n*, System *n* von Morgan-Keenan-Kellman
Yerkes system [of spectral classification], Yerkes classification	Yerkes-Klassifikation *f*
Y grouping, star connection, star grouping, Y-connection; star-connected circuit	Sternschaltung *f*, S-Schaltung *f*
yield	Ausbeute *f*, Ergiebigkeit *f*; Ertrag *m*
yield	s. a. yielding <of metal, material, solid>
yield	s. a. yield properties
yield behaviour	s. yield properties
yield condition, yield criterion, criterion for yield, criterion of yielding, condition of plasticity, plasticity condition, flow condition (criterion)	Fließbedingung *f*, Plastizitätsbedingung *f*
yield condition of Sokolovsky, Sokolovsky yield condition	Sokolovskysche Fließbedingung *f*, Fließbedingung von Sokolovsky
yield criterion	s. yield condition
yield criterion of von Mises	s. Mises yield condition
yield curve	Ausbeutekurve *f*
yield function	Fließfunktion *f*
yielding, yield, plastic flow, viscous flow, flow <of metal, material, solid>	Fließen *n*, Fluß *m*, plastisches Fließen
yielding, sound-soft, acoustically soft	schallweich
yielding	s. a. yield properties
yielding boundary [surface], sound-soft boundary [surface], acoustically soft boundary [surface]	schallweiche Grenzfläche *f*, nachgebende Grenzfläche
yielding support	s. elastic support
yield limit	s. yield strength
yield load; limit load; collapse load	Traglast *f*
yield locus	Fließspannungsort *m*
yield-mass curve	Ausbeute-Masse-Kurve *f*, Ausbeute-Massenzahl-Kurve *f*
yield-mass distribution	Ausbeute-Masse-Verteilung *f*
yield of current	s. current yield
yield of resonance radiation, resonance yield	Resonanzausbeute *f*, Resonanzfluoreszenzausbeute *f*, Resonanzstrahlungsausbeute *f*
yield of secondary electrons, secondary emission coefficient, secondary emission ratio, secondary yield	Sekundärelektronenausbeute *f*, Sekundäremissionsausbeute *f*, Sekundäremissionsfaktor *m*, Sekundäremissionskoeffizient *m*, SE-Faktor *m*
yield of water, water yield, discharge of water	Wasserabgabe *f*; Wasserergiebigkeit *f*
yield per day, diurnal yield	Tagesausbeute *f*
yield per ion pair	s. M/N ratio
yield per unit time	Zeitausbeute *f*, Ausbeute *f* pro Zeiteinheit
yield phenomenon	s. yield point phenomenon
yield point, yield temperature; flow[ing] point; thaw-point	Fließpunkt *m*, Fließtemperatur *f*
yield point, yield strength, yield limit, yield stress, plastic limit	Fließgrenze *f*, Plastizitätsgrenze *f*, Fließfestigkeit *f*
yield point at elevated temperature; tensile yield point at elevated temperature	Warmfließgrenze *f*; Warmstreckgrenze *f*

yield point in compression	s. yield stress in compression	Yokota glass	Yokota-Glas n, Silberphosphatglas n
yield point phenomenon, yield phenomenon	Streckgrenzenüberhöhung f, Streckgrenzeneffekt m, Streckgrenzenerscheinung f, Fließpunkterscheinung f, Fließgrenzenerscheinung f	Yokota glass dosimeter	Yokota-Glasdosimeter n
		Youkowski	s. Joukowski
		Young-Bouguer correction	Young-Bouguersche Korrektion f
yield point strain, yield strain	Fließbereich m, Fließdehnung f	Young['s] construction, Young['s] method	Youngsche Konstruktion f, Youngsches Verfahren n, Youngsche Methode f
yield point-to-tensile strength ratio	Streckgrenzenverhältnis n, Streckgrenze / Zugfestigkeit -Verhältnis n	Young['s] double slit, Young interferometer	Youngscher Doppelspalt m, Zweispaltinterferometer n, Doppelspaltinterferometer n
yield polyhedron	Fließpolyeder n	Young['s] equation	Youngsche Gleichung f
yield probability, yield rate	Ausbeutewahrscheinlichkeit f	Young['s] experiment, Young['s] interference experiment	Youngscher Interferenzversuch m, Youngscher Doppelspaltversuch m, Interferenzversuch von Young
yield properties, flow properties, yield, yielding, flow, yield behaviour, flow behaviour	Fließverhalten n, Fließeigenschaften f pl		
		Young-Helmholtz theory	Dreifarbentheorie f [von Young und Helmholtz], Young-Helmholtzsche Dreifarbentheorie
yield rate, yield probability	Ausbeutewahrscheinlichkeit f		
yield ratio	Ausbeuteverhältnis n	Young integral	Youngsches Integral n
yield strain	s. yield point strain	Young['s] interference experiment, Young['s] experiment	Youngscher Interferenzversuch m, Youngscher Doppelspaltversuch m, Interferenzversuch von Young
yield strength, yield point, yield limit, yield stress, plastic limit, yield value, flowing strength, flow limit	Fließgrenze f, Fließgrenzspannung f, Plastizitätsgrenze f, Fließfestigkeit f, Formänderungsfestigkeit f, Umformungsfestigkeit f, Verformungsfestigkeit f, Dehngrenze f		
		Young['s] interference principle, Young['s] principle	Youngsches Interferenzprinzip n, Youngsches Prinzip n
		Young interferometer, Young['s] double slit	Youngscher Doppelspalt m, Zweispaltinterferometer n, Doppelspaltinterferometer n
yield strength 0.2% yield strength, 0.2% proof stress	s. a. yield value Zweizehnteldehngrenze f, Zweizehntelfließgrenze f, $\sigma_{0,2}$-Grenze f, 0,2-Dehngrenze f, 0,2-Grenze f, Nullzwei-Dehngrenze f		
		Young-Korteweg formula	Young-Kortewegsche Gleichung f
		Young['s] method, Young['s] construction	Youngsche Konstruktion f, Youngsches Verfahren n, Youngsche Methode f
yield strength for completely reversed stress	Wechselfließgrenze f, Dauerschwingfließgrenze f bei Wechselbeanspruchung	Young['s] modulus [of elasticity], tension-compression modulus of elasticity, modulus of elasticity, elastic modulus, modulus of elongation (expansion, extension)	[linearer] Elastizitätsmodul m, E-Modul m, Youngscher Elastizitätsmodul (Modul m), Elastizitätsmaß n, Dehnungsmaß n, Dehnungsmodul m, elastische Konstante f
yield strength in tension	s. yield value		
yield stress, flow stress	Fließspannung f		
yield stress	s. a. yield strength	Young['s] operator	Youngscher Operator m
yield stress in compression, compressive yield strength (point), yield point in compression	Quetschgrenze f	Young['s] principle, Young['s] interference principle	Youngsches Interferenzprinzip n, Youngsches Prinzip n
		Young prism	Young-Prisma n, Young-Thollon-Prisma n
yield stress in tension	s. tensile stress	Young scheme, Young['s] tableau	Youngsches Schema n, Youngsches Tableau n, Young-Schema n, Young-Tableau n, Youngscher Rahmen m
yield stress in tension	s. yield value		
yield surface, limiting surface of yield, limiting surface of rupture	Fließspannungsfläche f		
yield temperature	s. yield point	Young spectrograph	Young-Spektrograph m, Youngscher Spektrograph m
yield value, tensile yield strength, tensile yield point, yield strength in tension, yield stress in tension	Streckgrenze f		
		young star	junger Stern m
		Young['s] tableau	s. Young scheme
yield value	s. a. yield strength	Y plate	s. vertical plate
ylem, primordial plasma, primitive material (matter)	Urplasma n, Ylem n, Urstoff m, Urmaterie f	yrneh	= reciprocal henry <1/H>
		Y-shaped crystal, Y-cut crystal	Y-Schnitt-Kristall m, Y-geschnittener Kristall m
Y matrix, admittance matrix <of waveguide>	Wellenleitwertmatrix f, Y-Matrix f <Wellenleiter>	yttrium ferrite, yttrium iron garnet, YIG	Yttrium-Eisen-Granat m, Yttriumeisengranat m, Yttriumferrit m
Yoffé effect, Yoffe effect, Joffé (Joffe) effect	Joffé-Effekt m, Joffé-Effekt m		
		Y-type antenna	s. Y[-] antenna
Yoffe['s] magnetic bottle	Joffe-Flasche f, magnetische Spiegelmaschine f nach Joffe, magnetische Flasche f nach Joffe	Yukawa charge	Yukawa-Ladung f
		Yukawa field	Yukawa-Feld n
		Yukawa force	Yukawa-Kraft f
		Yukawa interaction	Yukawa-Wechselwirkung f
Yoffe['s] solution	Yoffesche Lösung f	Yukawa interaction constant	Yukawa-Wechselwirkungskonstante f, Konstante f der Yukawa-Wechselwirkung
yoke <of magnet>	Joch n <Magnet>		
yoke lens	Jochlinse f		
yoke method, yoke technique	Jochmethode f, Jochverfahren n, Magnetjochverfahren n	Yukawa kernel	s. diffusion kernel
		Yukawa meson	s. nuclear pi-meson
		Yukawa['s] meson theory	s. Yukawa['s] theory
yoke suspension	s. bar suspension	Yukawa particle	s. nuclear pi-meson
yoke technique	s. yoke method	Yukawa potential	Yukawa-Potential n
yoke-type mounting, English mounting, cradle-type mount	englische Rahmenmontierung f, englische Montierung f	Yukawa potential function	Yukawa-Potentialfunktion f

Yukawa['s] solution — Yukawasche Lösung f, Yukawa-Lösung f
Yukawa['s] theory [of nuclear field], Yukawa['s] theory of nuclear forces, Yukawa['s] meson theory — Yukawa-Theorie f der Kernkräfte, Yukawa-Theorie des Kernfeldes, Yukawa-Mesonentheorie f, Mesonentheorie f der Kernkräfte von Yukawa
Yukawa well — Yukawa-Potentialtopf m, Yukawa-Potentialmulde f
yukon — s. nuclear pi-meson
Y-voltage, star voltage; phase-to-neutral voltage, phase belt voltage — Phasenspannung f, Sternspannung f, Strangspannung f
Yvon['s] integral equation — Yvonsche Integralgleichung f
Yvon['s] method, dual spherical harmonics method — Methode f von Yvon, Yvonsche Methode
Yvon photometer — Yvon-Photometer n, Yvonsches Photometer n

Z

Zachariasen['s] theory — Zachariasensche Theorie f
Zaitzeff [testing] machine — Zaitzeff-Maschine f
Zanstra['s] method [for temperature determination of the central stars in planetary nebulae] — Zanstra-Verfahren n, Zanstrasche Methode f, Methode von Zanstra
zapon foil — Zaponfolie f
Zaremba-Fromm-De Witt liquid — Zaremba-Fromm-de-Witt-Flüssigkeit f
Z balance — s. vertical field balance
Z[-] band, Z[-]disk <bio.> — Z-Linie f, Z-Streifen m, Zwischenstreifen m, Zwischenschicht f <Bio.>
Z[-] centre — Z-Zentrum n
Z-cut — Z-Schnitt m
Z-cut crystal, Z-shaped crystal — Z-Schnitt-Kristall m, Z-geschnittener Kristall m
Z[-] disk, Z[-] band <bio.> — Z-Linie f, Z-Streifen m, Zwischenstreifen m, Zwischenschicht f <Bio.>
Zeeman component — Zeeman-Komponente f
Zeeman displacement, Zeeman shift — Zeeman-Verschiebung f
Zeeman effect — Zeeman-Effekt m, magnetische Aufspaltung f der Spektrallinien
Zeeman modulation — Zeeman-Modulation f
Zeeman pattern; Zeeman structure — Aufspaltungsbild n beim Zeeman-Effekt, Zeeman-Aufspaltungsbild n; Zeeman-Struktur f
Zeeman shift — s. Zeeman displacement
Zeeman splitting; Lorentz splitting — Zeeman-Aufspaltung f; Lorentz-Aufspaltung f
Zeeman structure — s. Zeeman pattern
Zeeman transition — Zeeman-Übergang m
Zeeman triplet; Lorentz triplet — Zeeman-Triplett n; Lorentz-Triplett n, Lorentzsches Triplett n
Zehender chamber — Zehender-Kammer f
Zehender['s] method — Zehender-Verfahren n
Zener breakdown, field breakdown — Zener-Durchbruch m, Zener-Durchschlag m, Felddurchbruch m, Felddurchschlag m
Zener breakdown voltage — Zener-Durchbruchspannung f, Zener-Durchschlagspannung f, Felddurchbruchspannung f
Zener characteristic — Zener-Kennlinie f, Zener-Charakteristik f
Zener current — Zener-Strom m
Zener diode; Zener diode stabilizer semiconductor stabilitron, stabilitron — Zener-Diode f; Halbleiterstabilitron n, Stabilitron n, Zener-Dioden-Stabilisator m
Zener effect, Zener emission, internal field emission — Zener-Effekt m, innere Feldemission f, Zener-Emission f
Zener emission — s. Zener effect
Zener-Hilbert model — Zener-Hilbert-Modell n
Zener knee — Zener-Knick m
Zener relaxation, order relaxation — Ordnungsrelaxation f, Zener-Relaxation f
Zener['s] theory [of activation entropy] — Zenersche Theorie f [der Aktivierungsentropie]
Zener voltage, turn-over voltage — Zener-Spannung f
zenith — Zenit m, Scheitelpunkt m
zenithal distance, zenith distance, coaltitude — Zenitdistanz f, Zenitabstand m
zenithal eyepiece, zenith eyepiece, zenith ocular — Zenitokular n
zenithal light — Zenithimmelslicht n, Zenitlicht n
zenithal lune, zenith lune — Zenitzweieck n
zenithal magnitude [of the star], zenithal stellar magnitude — Zenithelligkeit f [des Gestirns]
zenithal orthomorphic projection, stereographic projection — stereographische Projektion f, winkeltreue Azimutalprojektion f, Kugelprojektion f
zenithal prism, zenith prism — Zenitprisma n, Steilsichtprisma n
zenithal projection — s. azimuthal projection
zenithal rain, tropical rain — Zenitalregen m, Tropenregen m, tropischer Regen m
zenithal refraction — Zenitrefraktion f
zenithal stellar magnitude, zenith magnitude [of the star] — Zenithelligkeit f [des Gestirns]
zenith angle effect — Zenitwinkeleffekt m, Zenitwinkelabhängigkeit f der Intensität
zenith attraction — Zenitanziehung f
zenith distance, zenithal distance, coaltitude — Zenitdistanz f, Zenitabstand m
zenith eyepiece, zenithal eyepiece, zenith ocular — Zenitokular n
zenith level, telescope level tube — Fernrohrlibelle f
zenith lune, zenithal lune — Zenitzweieck n
zenith ocular, zenith eyepiece, zenithal eyepiece — Zenitokular n
zenith photograph — Zenitaufnahme f
zenith point — Zenitpunkt m
zenith position — Zenitstand m
zenith prism, zenithal prism — Zenitprisma n, Steilsichtprisma n
zenith reduction, reduction to zenith — Zenitreduktion f
zenith taking — Zenitaufnahme f
zenith telescope, zenith tube — Zenitteleskop n, Zenitfernrohr n, Zenitrohr n

Zenker layer	Zenkersche Schicht f
Zenker prism	Zenker-Prisma n
Zenneck wave	Zenneck-Welle f
zeolite	Zeolith m
Zepp antenna, Zeppelin antenna	Zeppelinantenne f
Zermelo['s] recurrence paradox, recurrence paradox [of Zermelo], wiederkehreinwand	Zermeloscher Wiederkehreinwand m, Poincaré-Zermeloscher Wiederkehreinwand, Wiederkehreinwand [von Zermelo]
Zermelo['s] theorem	s. well ordering theorem
Zernike['s] formula	Zernikesche Formel f
Zernike['s] orthogonal polynomial, circle polynomial	Zernikesches Orthogonalpolynom n
Zernike['s] phase contrast method, Zernike['s] phase contrast test; phase-contrast test due to F. Zernike	Phasenkontrastverfahren n nach F. Zernike, Zernikesches Phasenkontrastverfahren
Zernike-Prins equation, Zernike-Prins formula	Zernike-Prinssche Gleichung f
zero, zero point	Nullpunkt m, Null f
zero, null <of function, curve>	Nullstelle f <Funktion, Kurve>
zero <math.>	Null f <Math.>
zero, zero element, null element <math.>	Nullelement n, Null f <Math.>
zero-access storage (store), immediate-access storage (store), instantaneous store (storage)	zugriff[s]zeitfreier Speicher m
zero-access storage (store)	s. a. rapid-access store
zero adjust control; zero-adjusting device; zero control	Nullstelleinrichtung f, Nullpunkt-Einstellvorrichtung f, Nullsteller m
zero adjustment, zero point adjustment; zero setting, zero point setting; zeroing, resetting to zero	Nullpunkteinstellung f, Nulleinstellung f; Nullstellung f
zero alternating stress, pulsating stress, stress varying from zero to maximum, one-way stress	schwellende Spannung f, Schwellspannung f
zero anode	Löschröhre f, Nullpunktanode f, Nullpotentialanode f, Nullanode f
zero balance, zero balancing, null balancing	Nullabgleich m
zero balance	s. a. adjustment <el.>
zero balancing, null balancing, zero balance	Nullabgleich m
zero band <in the electron spectrum>	Nullbande f <im Elektronenspektrum>
zero beat, zero beating	Schwebungsnull f; Nullschwebung f
zero beat frequency	Nullschwebungsfrequenz f, Schwebungsfrequenz f Null
zero beating, zero beat	Schwebungsnull f; Nullschwebung f
zero-beat reception, homodyne reception	Homodyneempfang m
zero branch, Q-branch <opt.>	Q-Zweig m, Nullzweig m <Opt.>
zero carrier	Nullamplitude f
zero centre meter, central zero instrument, centre-zero instrument	Gerät n mit zentralem Nullpunkt, Instrument n mit zentralem Nullpunkt
zero charge / of, neutral, electrically neutral; uncharged, without charge <el.>	neutral, elektrisch neutral; ungeladen, ladungsfrei, ohne Ladung <El.>
zero control	s. zero adjust control
zero correction	s. zero-point correction
zero current	Nullstrom m
zero-degree calorie, 0 °C calorie, cal$_{0°}$	Nullgradkalorie f, 0-°C-Kalorie f, cal$_0$ °C, cal$_0$
zero depression, depression of zero	Nullpunktsdepression f, Nullpunktdepression f
zero-dimensional	nulldimensional
zero divisor, zero factor, divisor of zero	Nullteiler m
zero drift, zero variation, zero offset	Nullpunktdrift f, Nulldrift f, Nullpunktsdrift f, Nullabweichung f, Nullpunkt[s]abweichung f, Nullpunkt[s]wanderung f, Nullpunkt[s]verschiebung f, Nullpunkt[s]verlagerung f, Nullversatz m
zero element	s. zero <math.>
zero-energy reactor, zero-power reactor	Nulleistungsreaktor m, Nullenergiereaktor m, Nullexperiment n, Nullreaktor m
Zero Energy Thermonuclear Assembly, ZETA, Zeta	Zeta-Anlage f, ZETA-Anlage f, ZETA n, Zeta n
zero epoch mean longitude, mean longitude at zero epoch	mittlere Länge f zur Epoche Null
zero error	s. zero variation
zero factor	s. zero divisor
zero-field; fieldless, field-free	feldfrei
zero-field level crossing [technique]	s. Hanle effect
zero-field residual voltage, residual voltage at zero field	Nullfeldrestspannung f
zero-frequency component, direct-current component, d.c. component, direct component	Gleichstromkomponente f; Gleichstromanteil m; Gleichstromwert m, Gleichstromgröße f; Gleichwert m
zero gap	s. origin of the band <opt.>
zero gravity	s. absence of gravity
zero-incidence wing, wing at zero lift	nichtangestellter Flügel m
zeroing	s. zero adjustment
zero isolychn	s. alychn
zero isotherm	Nullisotherme f
zero jitter	s. zero-point vibration
zero layer <aero., hydr.>	Nullschicht f <Aero., Hydr.>
zero layer line <rotating-crystal method>	nullte Schichtlinie f, Äquatorlinie f, Äquator m <Drehkristallverfahren>
zero lift	Nullauftrieb m
zero lift angle, no-lift angle	Nullauftriebswinkel m, Nullanstellwinkel m
zero lift direction	Nullauftriebsrichtung f
zero lift line, no-lift line, axis of zero lift	Nullauftriebslinie f, Nullinie f des Profils, erste Achse f des Profils, Nullauftriebsachse f
zero lift moment	Nullauftriebsmoment n
zero line, zero mark	Nullmarke f; Nullstrich m
zero line [gap]	s. origin of the band <opt.>
zero-line mirror	Nullspiegel m
zero line system	Kantensystem n, Bandkantensystem n
zerology	Nullstellenanalyse f

zero-loss line, dissipationless line, no-loss line, loss-free line, lossless line	verlustlose Leitung f, verlustfreie Leitung	zero-radius approximation	Nullradiusnäherung f, Näherung f mit dem Radius Null
zero mark, zero line	Nullmarke f; Nullstrich m	zero reading	Nullablesung f
zero-mass, massless	masselos, mit der Masse 0	zero reset[ting]	Nullrückstellung f, Rückstellung f auf Null
zero matrix, null matrix	Nullmatrix f	zero rest mass	Ruhemasse f 0, verschwindende Ruhemasse
zero meridian, prime (first, standard, initial, Greenwich) meridian, meridian of Greenwich	Nullmeridian m, Anfangsmeridian m, Meridian m von Greenwich, Greenwicher Meridian	zero rise	s. secular rise of zero
		zero scattering	Streuung f ohne effektive Ablenkung
		zero sequence component	Nullkomponente f
zero method	s. null method	zero sequence current	Nullstrom m
zero-moment method	Nullmoment[en]methode f		
zero offset	s. zero drift	zero sequence impedance	Nullimpedanz f, Nullscheinwiderstand m
zero-order approximation, zeroth approximation	nullte Näherung f, Näherung nullter Ordnung		
zero passage, passage of zero [point]	Nulldurchgang m	zero sequence reactance	Nullreaktanz f, Nullblindwiderstand m
zero phase angle	Nullphasenwinkel m		
zero-phase modulation, Armstrong modulation	Nullphasenwinkelmodulation f, Armstrong-Modulation f	zero sequence system <el.>	Nullsystem n <El.>
zero-phonon transition	phononenfreier Übergang m, Nullphononenübergang m	zero sequence system vector	Nullsystemvektor m
zero point, zero	Nullpunkt m, Null f	zero sequence voltage	Nullspannung f
zero point adjustment	s. zero adjustment	zero setting	s. zero adjustment
zero-point correction, zero correction	Nullpunkt[s]korrektion f, Nullpunktkorrektur f	zero shift	Nullpunktverschiebung f, Nullpunktsverschiebung f
zero-point electromagnetic field fluctuation	s. electromagnetic vacuum fluctuation	zero stability, zero point stability	Nullpunkt[s]konstanz f, Nullkonstanz f, Nullpunktstabilität f, Nullpunktsicherheit f
zero-point energy, zero-temperature energy, energy at the absolute zero of temperature, energy of absolute zero	Nullpunktsenergie f, Nullpunktenergie f		
		zero sum game	Nullsummenspiel n
		zero suppression	Nullpunktunterdrückung f, Nullpunktsunterdrückung f, Nullunterdrückung f
zero-point entropy, zero-temperature entropy, entropy at the absolute zero of temperature, entropy of absolute zero	Nullpunktsentropie f, Nullpunktentropie f		
		zero-system, null system <math.>	Nullsystem n, Nullkorrelation f <Math.>
		zero-temperature energy	s. zero-point energy
zero-point field	Nullpunkt[s]feld n, Nullfeld n	zero-temperature entropy	s. zero-point entropy
zero-point fluctuation	Nullpunktschwankung f, Nullpunktsschwankung f	zero-temperature volume	s. zero-point volume
zero-point lattice vibration	Nullpunkt[s]gitterschwingung f	zeroth approximation	s. zero-order approximation
zero-point motion	s. zero-point vibration	zeroth law of thermodynamics	s. law of thermal equilibrium
zero point of the star	s. neutral point <el.>	zero-time exchange	Nullzeitaustausch m
zero-point potential	Nullpunkt[s]potential n		
zero-point pressure	Nullpunktdruck m, Nullpunktdruck m	zero variation, zero error, residual deviation, origin distortion	Nullpunkt[s]fehler m, Nullfehler m, Nullpunkt[s]abweichung f, Nullabweichung f, Nullausschlag m; Restabweichung f; Restablenkung f, Restdeviation f
zero-point resistance	Nullpunktwiderstand m, Videowiderstand m		
zero-point resistance <semi.>	Nullpunktwiderstand m <Halb.>		
zero point setting	s. zero adjustment		
zero-point sound	Nullpunkt[s]schall m	zero variation	s. a. zero drift
zero-point stability	s. zero stability	zero vector, null vector <also rel.>	Nullvektor m <auch Rel.>
zero-point vibration, zero-point motion, zero jitter	Nullpunkt[s]schwingung f, Nullpunktsbewegung f, Nullpunkt[s]unruhe f	zero velocity curve	Hillsche Grenzkurve f, Nullgeschwindigkeitskurve f
zero-point volume, zero-temperature volume, volume at the absolute zero of temperature, volume of absolute zero	Nullpunktsvolumen n, Nullpunktvolumen n	zero velocity surface	Hillsche Grenzfläche f, Nullgeschwindigkeitsfläche f
		zero visibility	s. non-visibility
zero position	Nullage f, Nullstellung f	zero voltmeter	Nullspannungsmesser m, Nullvoltmeter n
zero position	s. a. position of rest		
zero-power lens	Nullinse f	zero-zero transition, 0-0 transition	Null-Null-Übergang m, 0-0-Übergang m
zero-power range <nucl.>	Leerlaufbereich m <Kern.>	ZETA, Zeta, Zero Energy Thermonuclear Assembly	Zeta-Anlage f, ZETA-Anlage f, ZETA n, Zeta n
zero-power reactor, zero-energy reactor	Nulleistungsreaktor m, Nullenergiereaktor m, Nullexperiment n, Nullreaktor m	zeta function <of Weierstrass>, Weierstrass['] zeta function, ζ function	Weierstraßsche Zeta-Funktion f, Zeta-Funktion [von Weierstraß], ζ-Funktion f

zeta function	s. a. Liemann zeta function	zodiacal sign, sign of the zodiac	Tierkreiszeichen n, Sternzeichen n
zeta function of Jacobi, Jacobi['s] zeta function, zn	Zeta-Funktion f von Jacobi, Jacobische Zeta-Funktion f, zn	Zöllner pendulum	Zöllnersches Pendel n
Zeta Geminorum[-type] star	Zeta Geminorum-Stern m, Zeta Geminorum-Veränderlicher m	Zöllner phenomenon, anorthoscopic illusion	Zöllnersche Erscheinung f, Spaltbildversuch m, anorthoskopische Täuschung f
		Zöllner suspension	Zöllnersche Aufhängung f, Zöllner-Aufhängung f
zeta meson, ζ meson	Zeta-Meson n, ζ-Meson n	zonal aberration, zone aberration, zone of uncorrected field of lens <opt.>	Zonenfehler m, Zwischenfehler m, Zone f <Opt.>
zeta[-] potential	s. electrokinetic potential		
Zeuner['s] diagram	Zeuner-Diagramm n		
Zeuner['s] formula	Zeunersche Formel f		
Zeuner pendulum	Zeunersches Dreischneidenpendel n	zonal arrangement	s. zonal structure
		zonal astrograph	Zonenastrograph m
Ziegler catalyst, Ziegler contact	Ziegler-Katalysator m, Ziegler-Kontakt m	zonal catalog[ue] [of stars], zone star catalog[ue], zone catalog[ue] [of stars]	Zonenkatalog m, Zonensternkatalog m
zigzag antenna	Zickzackantenne f, Sägezahnantenne f		
zigzag band-pass filter	Zickzackbandpaß m	zonal circulation	Zonalzirkulation f, zonale Zirkulation f
		zonal corrosion	Zonenkorrosion f
zigzag circuit, zigzag connection	Zickzackschaltung f	zonal current, zonal flow	zonaler Strom m, Zonalströmung f
zigzag crest	Zickzackschwelle f	zonal distribution	zonale Verteilung f, zonare Verteilung
zigzag crevice	Zickzackspaltung f	zonal extinction	zonale Auslöschung f
zigzag dislocation	Zickzackversetzung f	zonal flow, zonal current	zonaler Strom m, Zonalströmung f
zigzag folding	Zickzackfaltung f	zonal harmonic	s. Legendre polynomial
		zonal harmonic function	s. Legendre polynomial
		zonality, zoning	Zonalität f, Gürtelung f, Zonenbau m
zigzag lightning	Zickzackblitz m	zonal luminous flux, zone luminous flux	Zonenlichtstrom m
zigzag reflection	Zickzackreflexion f, Zickzackspiegelung f	zonal-meridional circulation	zonal-meridionale Zirkulation f
zigzag spiral filament, vee filament	Zickzackwendel f	zonal multipole field	zonales Multipolfeld n
		zonal quadrupole	zonaler Quadrupol m
		zonal solid angle	Zonenraumwinkel m
		zonal spherical harmonic	s. Legendre polynomial
zinc blende lattice, sphalerite lattice	Zinkblende[n]gitter n, ZnS-Gitter n	zonal structure, zonal arrangement	Zonarbau m, Zonarstruktur f; Zonenstruktur f, Zonenbau m, Zonalstruktur f, Zonalbau m
zinc blende structure, sphalerite structure	Zinkblende[n]struktur f, Zinkblende[n]typ m		
zinc-iron cell	Zink-Eisen-Element n	zonal texture, cone texture	Kegelfasertextur f, Zonentextur f
zinc sulphide phosphor	Zinksulfidphosphor m, ZnS-Phosphor m	zonation, zoning	Zoneneinteilung f, Zonengliederung f
zinc sulphide screen	Zinksulfidschirm m		
		zone, zone of crystal, crystallographic zone, crystal zone	Zone f <Krist.>, kristallographische Zone, Zonenverband m
Zinn[-type] arc	Zinn-Bogen m		
Z intensiometer, vertical intensity meter	Z-Intensiometer n	zone	s. a. region <gen.>
		zone aberration	s. zonal aberration <opt.>
Zintl border	Zintl-Grenze f	zone antenna	Zonenantenne f
Zintl line	Zintl-Linie f	zone axis, crystallographic zone axis	Zonenachse f, Zonenlinie f, Zonengerade f
Zintl phase	Zintlsche Phase f, Zintl-Phase f	zone boundary	Zonengrenze f
Zintl['s] rule	Zintlsche Regel f		
Ziolkovsky['s] formula	s. fundamental equation of rocket motion	zone boundary, Brillouin zone boundary	Begrenzung f der Brillouinschen Zone
Ziolkovsky number	s. mass ratio <rocket>	zone catalog[ue] [of stars], zone star catalog[ue], zonal catalog[ue] [of stars]	Zonenkatalog m, Zonensternkatalog m
zirconium arc lamp, zirconium lamp	Zirkonium-Punktlampe f, Zirkonium-Bogenlampe f, Zirkoniumlampe f, Zirkonlampe f		
		zone cooling, directional cooling	Zonenabkühlung f <stufenweise Abkühlung von einem Ende der Probe zum anderen>
zitterbewegung, trembling motion, vibration <of electron>	Zitterbewegung f [des Elektrons]		
		zone electrophoresis	Zonenelektrophorese f
		zone floating [method], zone floating technique	s. floating-zone melting
		zone heating	Zonenaufheizung f
Z-magnetometer, vertical-intensity magnetometer, vertical magnetometer	Vertikalintensitätsmagnetometer n, Vertikalmagnetometer n, Z-Magnetometer n		
		zone index	Zonenindex m
		zone law	s. Spoerer['s] law
		zone law, zone law of Weiss, Weiss zone law	Zonengesetz n, Zonenverbandsgesetz n
Z matrix, impedance matrix <of waveguide>	Wellenwiderstandsmatrix f, Z-Matrix f <Wellenleiter>	zone lens	s. zone plate
		zone levelling	Zonennivellierung f
Zodiac, zodiacal belt	Zodiakus m, Tierkreis m	zone luminous flux, zonal luminous flux	Zonenlichtstrom m
zodiacal band	Zodiakalband n	zone melting [technique], zone melt technique, zone refining [technique], zone purification [method]	Zonenschmelzverfahren n, Zonenschmelzen n, Zonenreinigungsverfahren n, Zonenreinigung f
zodiacal belt	s. Zodiac		
zodiacal constellation	Sternbild n des Tierkreises		
zodiacal light	Zodiakallicht n, Tierkreislicht n		

zone of ablation [of the glacier]	Ablationsgebiet f, Zehrgebiet n ‹Gletscher›	zoning, zonality	Zonalität f, Gürtelung f, Zonenbau m
zone of abnormal audibility, abnormal audibility zone	Zone f der anormalen Hörbarkeit	zonography	Zonographie f
		zoom finder	s. universal finder
zone of absence, zone of avoidance	„zone of avoidance" f, nebelfreie Zone f	zooming lens, zoom lens, varifocal lens, variable-focus lens	Objektiv n mit veränderlicher Brennweite, Gummilinse f, Varioptik f, Zoomlinse f; Zoomar n
zone of advance	Voreilzone f		
zone of avoidance, zone of absence	„zone of avoidance" f, nebelfreie Zone f	zooplankton	Zooplankton n
		Zorawski['s] theorem ‹on relative motion›	Zorawskischer Satz m ‹über die Relativbewegung›
zone of cathode fall, cathode fall region, cathode fall zone, region of cathode fall	Katodenfallraum m, Katodenfallgebiet n		
		Zorn['s] lemma, Zorn['s] [maximal] principle, Zorn['s] theorem, principle of Zorn	Zornsches Lemma n
zone of confusion ‹ac.›	Verwirrungszone f, Verwirrungsgebiet n ‹Ak.›		
zone of crush	s. crush zone	z-pinch	z-Pinch m
zone of crustal weakness	Schwächezone f der Erdkruste, Schwächungszone f der Erdkruste	Z-shaped crystal	s. Z-cut crystal
		Zsigmondy osmometer	Osmometer n nach Zsigmondy, Zsigmondy-Osmometer n
zone of crystal	s. zone		
zone of detachment ‹geo.›	Abscherungszone f ‹Geo.›	Zunker coefficient	Zunker-Koeffizient m
		Zürich classification	Züricher Klassifikation f
zone of dispersion	s. spread	Zürich number, Wolf number, Wolf['s] sunspot number, relative sunspots number	Fleckenrelativzahl f, Sonnenflecken-Relativzahl f, Wolfsche Zahl f, Wolfsche Relativzahl (Sonnenfleckenzahl) f
zone of earthquake shocks	s. seismic region		
zone of equal temperature, temperature zone	Temperaturzone f; Temperaturgürtel m		
zone of equatorial calmness, doldrum[s]	Mallung f, Doldrum n, Kalmengürtel m, Windstillengürtel m, Zone f der äquatorialen Windstillen	zustandssumme, partition function, sum over states, sum-over-states ‹therm.›	Zustandssumme f [von Planck], Plancksche Zustandssumme f, Verteilungsfunktion f ‹Therm.›
zone of faculae	Fackelzone f	Z-variometer, vertical-intensity variometer, vertical-force variometer	Vertikalintensitätsvariometer n, Z-Variometer n
zone of fracture	s. crush zone		
zone of glissade	Schleifzone f	zwitterion, amphoteric ion, hybrid ion, dipolar ion, dual ion, amphion, inner salt	Zwitterion n, amphoteres Ion n
zone of high pressure, high-pressure zone	Hochdruckgürtel m, Hochdruckzone f, Hochdruckring m		
		zygomorphous	dorsiventral, monosymmetrisch, zygomorph
zone of inflammation, ignition zone, inflammation zone	Zündzone f; Zündnest n		
zone of potential fall, potential fall region (zone), region of potential fall	Fallraum m, Fallgebiet n		
zone of sharpness, sharp zone, definition range	Schärfenbereich m, Schärfentiefe[n]bereich m		
zone of short-range fading	Nahschwundzone f		
zone of silence	s. silent zone		
zone of solarization, region of solarization, region of image reversal	Solarisationsbereich m, Solarisationszone f, Solarisationsteil m		
zone of totality, band of totality, total zone of obscuration	Totalitätszone f		
zone of turbulence	s. turbulent region		
zone of uncorrected field of lens, zonal aberration, zone aberration	Zonenfehler m, Zwischenfehler m, Zone f ‹Opt.›		
zone of unsharpness	Unschärfezone f		
zone of weakness	Schwächezone f		
zone plate ‹ac.›	Zonenplatte f ‹Ak.›		
zone plate, zone lens ‹opt.›	Zonenplatte f [nach Soret], Soretsche Zonenplatte, Zonenlinse f ‹Opt.›		
zone pole, pole of zone	Zonenpol m		
zone purification [method]	s. zone melting		
zone refining [technique]	s. zone melting		
zone scanning	s. rectilinear scanning		
zone star catalog[ue], zone catalog[ue] [of stars], zonal catalog[ue] [of stars]	Zonenkatalog m, Zonensternkatalog m		
zone theory of colour vision	Zonentheorie f des Farbensehens		
zone time, standard time, regional time	Zonenzeit f, Einheitszeit f		
zonic depth finder	s. echo-sounding device		
zoning, zonation	Zoneneinteilung f, Zonengliederung f		

Notes

Notes